Your word
is a lamp
to my feet
and a light
for my path.

PSALM 119:105

PRESENTED TO

BY

ON THE OCCASION OF

DATE

Spiritual Renewal Bible

New International Version

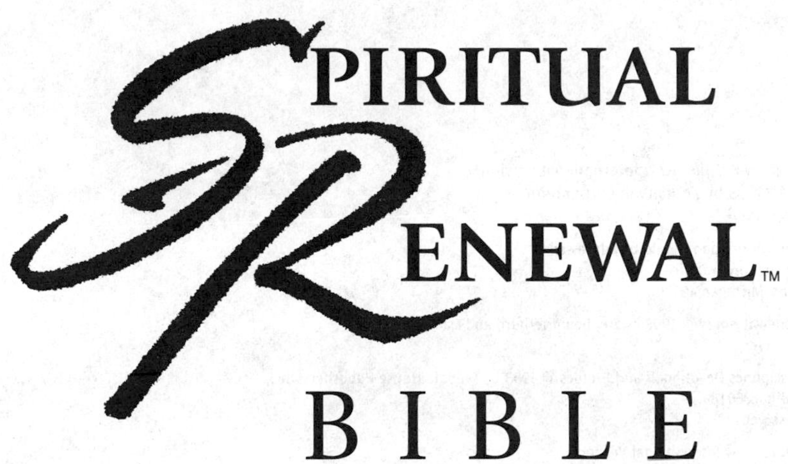

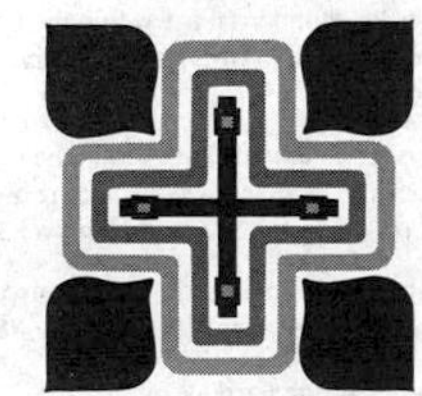

New International Version
Zondervan Publishing House
Grand Rapids, Michigan

Requests for information should be addressed to
The Zondervan Corporation
Grand Rapids, Michigan 49530

Library of Congress Catalog Card Number 97-062115
Published by Zondervan Publishing House
Grand Rapids, Michigan 49530, U.S.A.
http://www.zondervan.com

Printed in the United States of America

98 99 00 01 02 03 9 8 7 6 5 4 3 2 1

RRD-C

You will be pleased to know that a portion of the purchase price of your new NIV Bible has been provided to International Bible Society to help spread the gospel of Jesus Christ around the world!

Contents

The Old Testament

The New Testament

ALPHABETICAL LIST OF THE BOOKS OF THE BIBLE

The books of the New Testament are in *italic.*

CONTRIBUTORS

Executive Editors
Stephen F. Arterburn
David A. Stoop

General Editor
Connie Neal

Managing Editor
Gary L. Knapp

Associate Editors
Sarah M. Hupp
David P. Barrett
Mark R. Norton

Editorial Staff
Derrick Blanchette
Meg Diehl
Diane Eble
Betsy Elliott
Lela Gilbert
Dietrich Gruen
Donna Huisjen
Lucille Leonard
Phyllis LePeau
Daryl Lucas
Judith Morse
Kathy Stinnette Olson
Susan Taylor
Ramona Tucker
Sally van der Graaff
Esther Waldrop
Karen Walker
Wightman Weese

Interior Graphic Design
Sharon Wright

Cover Design
Timothy R. Botts

Writers
Donald E. Anderson
Shelley M. Chapin
R. Tony Cothren
Shelly O. Cunningham
Barry C. Davis
Harold Dollar
Joseph M. Espinoza
Thomas J. Finley
William J. Gaultiere
Ronald N. Glass
Daniel M. Hahn
Eric Hoey
Mark W. Hoffman
John C. Hutchison
Tommy A. Jarrett
Stephen M. Johnson
G. Ted Martinez
Kathy McReynolds
V. Eric Nachtrieb
Connie Neal
Stephen L. Newman
T. Ken Oberholtzer
Scott B. Rae
Richard O. Rigsby
Jane E. Rodgers
Walter B. Russell
Richard F. Travis

USER'S GUIDE

Everyone needs spiritual renewal. We see this whenever we take time to examine our own lives or the lives of those around us. Ever since Adam and Eve's first sin, everyone has experienced a life that falls short of God's original desire for his people. But there is good news: God has promised to redeem us and transform us when we seek him. In order to experience this spiritual renewal the Bible shows us that we must submit ourselves to God's plan and process. This plan requires that we daily seek God's will for our lives instead of demanding to go our own way. We must allow God to do for us what we cannot do for ourselves, while also taking the steps necessary to draw closer to our Creator and Redeemer. We must also let God heal our wounded souls so we can help others in the process of healing. All of us need to take part in this process; it is an inherent part of being human. This process can be understood as a series of insights, or keys, to spiritual renewal:

1. Surrender: Seek God and Surrender to Him We must come to the end of ourselves and allow God's plans for us to replace our plans. We find the peace of God when we are willing to do whatever it takes to grow toward him. We must allow God to help us grow as he speaks through others. "Humble yourselves, therefore, under God's mighty hand, that he may lift you up in due time" (1 Peter 5:6).

2. Acceptance: See the Truth We must come to accept the full reality of our situation. We must look honestly at our defects, weaknesses and areas of sin so that we will no longer be ruled by the problems that lie in our blind spots. This process begins when we document areas of our lives where we are weak and need spiritual maturity. "O LORD, you have searched me and you know me" (Psalm 139:1).

3. Confession: Speak the Truth We must break the barriers of silence that have been formed from our pride. We must humbly begin to open up about the reality of our lives and the nature of our sins and weaknesses. We strengthen our relationship with God as we develop authentic relationships with others. "Therefore confess your sins to each other and pray for each other so that you may be healed" (James 5:16).

4. Responsibility: Accept Responsibility We must refuse to blame others for our problems and take responsibility to make the needed changes. We must obey God's Word and repent from those things that prevent us from growing spiritually. We can then begin to mature in our walk with Christ, leaving behind our old habits of irresponsibility. "For each one should carry his own load" (Galatians 6:5).

5. Forgiveness: Grieve, Forgive and Let Go We must move beyond what was and what might have been and accept what is and what will be. We must grieve over our losses and let go of [illegible]d opportunities. We must accept Christ's forgiveness for our sins and seek forgiveness from [illegible] we make restitution for the hurt and pain we have caused them. We must also forgive [illegible] have hurt us, not excusing or condoning their actions, but freeing ourselves from bit[illegible]sentment that could destroy us. "If you forgive men when they sin against you, your [illegible] will also forgive you" (Matthew 6:14).

6. Transformation: Transform Your Life As we grow, we are released from our self-obsession and freed to reach out to others. We begin to transform our pain into a purpose, our past misery into a mission and new ministry. "Praise be to the God and Father of our Lord Jesus Christ, the Father of compassion and the God of all comfort, who comforts us in all our troubles, so that we can comfort those in any trouble with the comfort we ourselves have received from God" (2 Corinthians 1:3–4).

7. Preservation: Preserve Spiritual Gains We must protect the spiritual gains we have made and persevere through life's inevitable struggles. We must find people we can be accountable to and grow in the spiritual disciplines that strengthen our relationship with God. "For this very reason, make every effort to add to your faith goodness; and to goodness, knowledge" (2 Peter 1:5).

These keys form the basis of the notes and other helps found in the *Spiritual Renewal Bible.*

FEATURES

Each feature of this Bible leads readers to the powerful resources for spiritual renewal found in the Holy Scriptures:

Bible Book Introductions	Each book of the Bible is preceded by a brief summary of the book's contents and insights about how its wisdom can lead to spiritual renewal. These summaries include "The Big Picture," "Spiritual Renewal Themes," "Essential Facts" and an outline of the book.
Text Notes	Throughout the Bible text, brief study notes highlight spiritual renewal lessons found within a specific verse or passage.
Character Profiles	Page-length articles assess how certain Bible people experienced spiritual renewal through the various problems and challenges they encountered in their walk with God. These articles include a biographical summary, a list of strengths and weaknesses, lessons from the person's life and a key verse.
Spiritual Keys Devotional Reading Plan	A series of devotionals highlights each of the seven keys to spiritual renewal throughout Scripture and relates each one to life today. These devotionals, arranged in two reading cycles (Old Testament and New Testament), begin with the first key, "Seek God and Surrender to Him," and continue through the seventh key, "Preserve Spiritual Gains." In both the Old Testament and the New Testament, the reader is led through seven different devotionals for each key, with each key directing the reader to the next devotional in the reading plan.

Spiritual Disciplines Devotionals	These page-length articles draw lessons from Scripture regarding the spiritual disciplines of the faith (prayer, fasting, Bible study, service, etc.) and illuminate how these disciplines can help us experience spiritual renewal today. Several devotionals examine each discipline, and each devotional directs the reader to the next devotional within that discipline.
Spiritual Disciplines Profiles	Ten page-length articles describe how certain Biblical characters employed the various spiritual disciplines. Each discipline is highlighted within the article, and the reader is directed to the first devotional that corresponds to that discipline.

We suggest that you begin your study by using the Spiritual Keys Devotional Reading Plan. The first of these keys is located at Genesis 18. Or you may choose to begin your study by turning to the first Spiritual Disciplines Devotional, located at Genesis 2.

𝒫REFACE TO THE NIV

THE NEW INTERNATIONAL VERSION is a completely new translation of the Holy Bible made by over a hundred scholars working directly from the best available Hebrew, Aramaic and Greek texts. It had its beginning in 1965 when, after several years of exploratory study by committees from the Christian Reformed Church and the National Association of Evangelicals, a group of scholars met at Palos Heights, Illinois, and concurred in the need for a new translation of the Bible in contemporary English. This group, though not made up of official church representatives, was transdenominational. Its conclusion was endorsed by a large number of leaders from many denominations who met in Chicago in 1966.

Responsibility for the new version was delegated by the Palos Heights group to a self-governing body of fifteen, the Committee on Bible Translation, composed for the most part of biblical scholars from colleges, universities and seminaries. In 1967 the New York Bible Society (now the International Bible Society) generously undertook the financial sponsorship of the project—a sponsorship that made it possible to enlist the help of many distinguished scholars. The fact that participants from the United States, Great Britain, Canada, Australia and New Zealand worked together gave the project its international scope. That they were from many denominations—including Anglican, Assemblies of God, Baptist, Brethren, Christian Reformed, Church of Christ, Evangelical Free, Lutheran, Mennonite, Methodist, Nazarene, Presbyterian, Wesleyan and other churches—helped to safeguard the translation from sectarian bias.

How it was made helps to give the New International Version its distinctiveness. The translation of each book was assigned to a team of scholars. Next, one of the Intermediate Editorial Committees revised the initial translation, with constant reference to the Hebrew, Aramaic or Greek. Their work then went to one of the General Editorial Committees, which checked it in detail and made another thorough revision. This revision in turn was carefully reviewed by the Committee on Bible Translation, which made further changes and then released the final version for publication. In this way the entire Bible underwent three revisions, during each of which the translation was examined for its faithfulness to the original languages and for its English style.

All this involved many thousands of hours of research and discussion regarding the meaning of the texts and the precise way of putting them into English. It may well be that no other translation has been made by a more thorough process of review and revision from committee to committee than this one.

From the beginning of the project, the Committee on Bible Translation held to certain goals for the New International Version: that it would be an accurate translation and one that would have clarity and literary quality and so prove suitable for public and private reading, teaching, preaching, memorizing and liturgical use. The Committee also sought to preserve some measure of continuity with the long tradition of translating the Scriptures into English.

In working toward these goals, the translators were united in their commitment to the authority and infallibility of the Bible as God's Word in written form. They believe that it contains the divine answer to the deepest needs of humanity, that it sheds unique light on our path in a dark world, and that it sets forth the way to our eternal well-being.

The first concern of the translators has been the accuracy of the translation and its fidelity to the thought of the biblical writers. They have weighed the significance of the lexical and grammatical details of the Hebrew, Aramaic and Greek texts. At the same time, they have striven for more than a word-for-word translation. Because thought patterns and syntax differ from language to language, faithful communication of the meaning of the writers of the Bible demands frequent modifications in sentence structure and constant regard for the contextual meanings of words.

A sensitive feeling for style does not always accompany scholarship. Accordingly the Committee on Bible Translation submitted the developing version to a number of stylistic consultants. Two of them read every book of both Old and New Testaments twice—once before and once after the last major revision—and made invaluable suggestions. Samples of the translation were tested for clarity and ease of reading by various kinds of people—young and old, highly educated and less well educated, ministers and laymen.

Concern for clear and natural English—that the New International Version should be idiomatic but not idiosyn-

...tic, contemporary but not dated—motivated the translators and consultants. At the same time, they tried to reflect the differing styles of the biblical writers. In view of the international use of English, the translators sought to avoid obvious Americanisms on the one hand and obvious Anglicisms on the other. A British edition reflects the comparatively few differences of significant idiom and of spelling.

As for the traditional pronouns "thou," "thee" and "thine" in reference to the Deity, the translators judged that to use these archaisms (along with the old verb forms such as "doest," "wouldest" and "hadst") would violate accuracy in translation. Neither Hebrew, Aramaic nor Greek uses special pronouns for the persons of the Godhead. A present-day translation is not enhanced by forms that in the time of the King James Version were used in everyday speech, whether referring to God or man.

For the Old Testament the standard Hebrew text, the Masoretic Text as published in the latest editions of *Biblia Hebraica,* was used throughout. The Dead Sea Scrolls contain material bearing on an earlier stage of the Hebrew text. They were consulted, as were the Samaritan Pentateuch and the ancient scribal traditions relating to textual changes. Sometimes a variant Hebrew reading in the margin of the Masoretic Text was followed instead of the text itself. Such instances, being variants within the Masoretic tradition, are not specified by footnotes. In rare cases, words in the consonantal text were divided differently from the way they appear in the Masoretic Text. Footnotes indicate this. The translators also consulted the more important early versions—the Septuagint; Aquila, Symmachus and Theodotion; the Vulgate; the Syriac Peshitta; the Targums; and for the Psalms the *Juxta Hebraica* of Jerome. Readings from these versions were occasionally followed where the Masoretic Text seemed doubtful and where accepted principles of textual criticism showed that one or more of these textual witnesses appeared to provide the correct reading. Such instances are footnoted. Sometimes vowel letters and vowel signs did not, in the judgment of the translators, represent the correct vowels for the original consonantal text. Accordingly some words were read with a different set of vowels. These instances are usually not indicated by footnotes.

The Greek text used in translating the New Testament was an eclectic one. No other piece of ancient literature has such an abundance of manuscript witnesses as does the New Testament. Where existing manuscripts differ, the translators made their choice of readings according to accepted principles of New Testament textual criticism. Footnotes call attention to places where there was uncertainty about what the original text was. The best current printed texts of the Greek New Testament were used.

There is a sense in which the work of translation is never wholly finished. This applies to all great literature and uniquely so to the Bible. In 1973 the New Testament in the New International Version was published. Since then, suggestions for corrections and revisions have been received from various sources. The Committee on Bible Translation carefully considered the suggestions and adopted a number of them. These were incorporated in the first printing of the entire Bible in 1978. Additional revisions were made by the Committee on Bible Translation in 1983 and appear in printings after that date.

As in other ancient documents, the precise meaning of the biblical texts is sometimes uncertain. This is more often the case with the Hebrew and Aramaic texts than with the Greek text. Although archaeological and linguistic discoveries in this century aid in understanding difficult passages, some uncertainties remain. The more significant of these have been called to the reader's attention in the footnotes.

In regard to the divine name *YHWH,* commonly referred to as the *Tetragrammaton,* the translators adopted the device used in most English versions of rendering that name as "LORD" in capital letters to distinguish it from *Adonai,* another Hebrew word rendered "Lord," for which small letters are used. Wherever the two names stand together in the Old Testament as a compound name of God, they are rendered "Sovereign LORD."

Because for most readers today the phrases "the LORD of hosts" and "God of hosts" have little meaning, this version renders them "the LORD Almighty" and "God Almighty." These renderings convey the sense of the Hebrew, namely, "he who is sovereign over all the 'hosts' (powers) in heaven and on earth, especially over the 'hosts' (armies) of Israel." For readers unacquainted with Hebrew this does not make clear the distinction between *Sabaoth* ("hosts" or "Almighty") and *Shaddai* (which can also be translated "Almighty"), but the latter occurs infrequently and is always footnoted. When *Adonai* and *YHWH Sabaoth* occur together, they are rendered "the Lord, the LORD Almighty."

As for other proper nouns, the familiar spellings of the King James Version are generally retained. Names traditionally spelled with "ch," except where it is final, are usually spelled in this translation with "k" or "c," since the biblical languages do not have the sound that "ch" frequently indicates in English—for example, in *chant.* For well-known names such as Zechariah, however, the traditional spelling has been retained. Variation in the spelling of names in the original languages has usually not been indicated. Where a person or place has two or more different names in the Hebrew, Aramaic or Greek texts, the more familiar one has generally been used, with footnotes where needed.

To achieve clarity the translators sometimes supplied words not in the original texts but required by the context. If there was uncertainty about such material, it is enclosed in brackets. Also for the sake of clarity or style, nouns, including some proper nouns, are sometimes substituted for pronouns, and vice versa. And though the Hebrew

writers often shifted back and forth between first, second and third personal pronouns without change of antecedent, this translation often makes them uniform, in accordance with English style and without the use of footnotes.

Poetical passages are printed as poetry, that is, with indentation of lines with separate stanzas. These are generally designed to reflect the structure of Hebrew poetry. This poetry is normally characterized by parallelism in balanced lines. Most of the poetry in the Bible is in the Old Testament, and scholars differ regarding the scansion of Hebrew lines. The translators determined the stanza divisions for the most part by analysis of the subject matter. The stanzas therefore serve as poetic paragraphs.

As an aid to the reader, italicized sectional headings are inserted in most of the books. They are not to be regarded as part of the NIV text, are not for oral reading, and are not intended to dictate the interpretation of the sections they head.

The footnotes in this version are of several kinds, most of which need no explanation. Those giving alternative translations begin with "Or" and generally introduce the alternative with the last word preceding it in the text, except when it is a single-word alternative; in poetry quoted in a footnote a slant mark indicates a line division. Footnotes introduced by "Or" do not have uniform significance. In some cases two possible translations were considered to have about equal validity. In other cases, though the translators were convinced that the translation in the text was correct, they judged that another interpretation was possible and of sufficient importance to be represented in a footnote.

In the New Testament, footnotes that refer to uncertainty regarding the original text are introduced by "Some manuscripts" or similar expressions. In the Old Testament, evidence for the reading chosen is given first and evidence for the alternative is added after a semicolon (for example: Septuagint; Hebrew *father*). In such notes the term "Hebrew" refers to the Masoretic Text.

It should be noted that minerals, flora and fauna, architectural details, articles of clothing and jewelry, musical instruments and other articles cannot always be identified with precision. Also measures of capacity in the biblical period are particularly uncertain (see the table of weights and measures following the text).

Like all translations of the Bible, made as they are by imperfect man, this one undoubtedly falls short of its goals. Yet we are grateful to God for the extent to which he has enabled us to realize these goals and for the strength he has given us and our colleagues to complete our task. We offer this version of the Bible to him in whose name and for whose glory it has been made. We pray that it will lead many into a better understanding of the Holy Scriptures and a fuller knowledge of Jesus Christ the incarnate Word, of whom the Scriptures so faithfully testify.

The Committee on Bible Translation

June 1978
(Revised August 1983)

Names of the translators and editors may be secured
from the International Bible Society,
translation sponsors of the New International Version,
1820 Jet Stream Drive, Colorado Springs, Colorado
80921-3696 U.S.A.

THE OLD TESTAMENT

GENESIS

The Big Picture

The book of Genesis is a book of beginnings. It records how the world began and how God created it to be good. It tells us about the first people and how God made them to be excellent. But then it tells us about the beginning of sin—about the first time people decided to reject God's revealed will for them. It records the first days of shame and the beginnings of our separation from God, from each other and from the world God gave us.

In this book we will see how people with perfect health, living in a perfect environment, rebelled against God. We will view the consequences of their rebellion. And we will see intimate glimpses of individuals dominated by hatred, drunkenness, lust, unhealthy family relationships, money, cheating, irresponsibility, dishonesty, jealousy, violence and other vices.

But the book of Genesis doesn't leave us in despair. It tells us of another beginning. It records how God chose a man named Abraham to father a special nation and through this nation provided the solution for our separation from God. Genesis tells the story of how God began his work of healing broken humanity—a healing expressed in the laws he would give his people and culminating in the coming of Jesus, the promised Messiah.

The book of Genesis reminds us where all our problems began. It spells out the fatal consequences of rejecting God's will. But it also begins the story of God's unstoppable love for the human race. Through this book we will discover that the only way to achieve spiritual renewal is to surrender our lives to God's righteous rule.

A. GOD SETS THE STAGE (1:1–11:32)

1. Formation of the Universe (1:1–2:25)
   a. God creates matter, energy and the natural order (1:1–2:3)
   b. God prepares pristine surroundings for the first family (2:4-25)
2. Fall of the Human Race (3:1-24)
   a. Commission of sin (3:1-7)
   b. Curse on sin (3:8-24)
3. Failure of Society (4:1–9:29)
   a. Failure of humankind (4:1–6:22)
   b. Flood of judgment (7:1–9:29)
4. Folly of Rebellion (10:1–11:32)
   a. Dispersal of the people (10:1-32)
   b. Disobedience of the people (11:1-32)

B. GOD CHOOSES THE PLAYERS (12:1–50:26)

1. Abraham (12:1–25:18)
2. Isaac (25:19–28:9)
3. Jacob (28:10–37:1)
4. Joseph (37:2–50:26)

Spiritual Renewal Themes

A GOOD CREATION

Everything about God's creation was described as being good except the fact that Adam was alone. In fact, Adam's isolation was the only thing in the first two chapters of Genesis that God considered to be problematic. Once God had created a partner for man, he was then pleased with everything in his creation. Because God was pleased with what he had created, he stayed involved, even after Adam and Eve disobeyed him. In fact, ever since the fall, God has been seeking to make things right again. Our sinfulness always leads us away from God and distorts the

Essential Facts

PURPOSE:
To tell us about the beginning of things, including human opportunities and sinfulness, and to demonstrate that God's solutions are the only ones that work.

AUTHOR:
Moses.

AUDIENCE:
The people of Israel.

DATE WRITTEN:
Chapters 1–11 deal with the undatable past; the events of chapters 12–50 are dated between approximately 2000 and 1800 B.C. The book was probably written shortly after 1445 B.C.

SETTING:
Mesopotamia, then Canaan, finally Egypt.

KEY VERSE:
"Abram believed the LORD, and he credited it to him as righteousness" (15:6).

KEY EVENTS:
Creation, the fall, the flood, the tower of Babel, the establishment of a covenant with Abraham and his descendants, the Israelites' move to Egypt.

KEY PEOPLE:
Abraham, Isaac, Jacob, Joseph.

way God created us to be. But our spiritual renewal always involves growth toward God's original ideal for the human race. As we are transformed by God, we take part in God's re-creation of our fallen world.

A RUINED WORLD

Adam and Eve's disobedience affected all of God's creation. The idyllic world of the garden was gone forever. Life became a struggle. Our futile attempts to avoid the realities of a ruined world have led us into spiritual blindness and all of its destructive consequences. Spiritual renewal begins when we squarely face the broken realities of our world—its daily struggles and hardships—and enter the spiritual arena to fight for and regain what has been lost to sin.

PROMISES OF REDEMPTION

The book of Genesis presents us with a series of "new beginnings" that come out of the ruin of our sinfulness. When Adam and Eve fell into sin, God promised hope and healing for us when he told the serpent that the offspring of the woman would crush his head. When people continued to disobey, God sent the flood as a judgment for their sinfulness. After the flood, God again gave the people hope and symbolized that promise with a rainbow. Then the human race rejected God again, building a huge tower as a monument to their greatness. In response, God confused their languages, further fragmenting society. Then God chose a man named Abram and promised to bless all nations of the world through his offspring. Every time that human sin brought ruin, God promised victory and redemption.

HOPE FOR RECONCILIATION

As people began to experience the terrible consequences of their disobedience, God didn't leave them all alone to figure out a plan for redemption. He didn't leave a long list of principles or rules to follow to repair their damaged relationships. Instead, God worked with people on a personal level to renew them spiritually. As we enter into spiritual renewal, we find it to be relational. Spiritual renewal requires us to seek reconciliation with God and with people close to us. In Genesis, God models this pattern for us time and again. He chose certain individuals and worked patiently in their lives, reconciling them to himself and to the people around them.

The Beginning

1 In the beginning God created the heavens and the earth. 2Now the earth was[a]
formless and empty, darkness was over the
surface of the deep, and the Spirit of God
was hovering over the waters.
3And God said, "Let there be light," and there
was light. 4God saw that the light was
good, and he separated the light from the
darkness. 5God called the light "day," and
the darkness he called "night." And there
was evening, and there was morning—the
first day.
6And God said, "Let there be an expanse between the waters to separate water from
water." 7So God made the expanse and separated the water under the expanse from
the water above it. And it was so. 8God
called the expanse "sky." And there was
evening, and there was morning—the second day.
9And God said, "Let the water under the sky
be gathered to one place, and let dry
ground appear." And it was so. 10God called
the dry ground "land," and the gathered
waters he called "seas." And God saw that
it was good.
11Then God said, "Let the land produce
vegetation: seed-bearing plants and trees
on the land that bear fruit with seed in it,
according to their various kinds." And it
was so. 12The land produced vegetation:
plants bearing seed according to their
kinds and trees bearing fruit with seed in it
according to their kinds. And God saw that
it was good. 13And there was evening, and
there was morning—the third day.
14And God said, "Let there be lights in the expanse of the sky to separate the day from
the night, and let them serve as signs to
mark seasons and days and years, 15and let
them be lights in the expanse of the sky
to give light on the earth." And it was so.
16God made two great lights—the greater
light to govern the day and the lesser light
to govern the night. He also made the
stars. 17God set them in the expanse of the
sky to give light on the earth, 18to govern
the day and the night, and to separate light
from darkness. And God saw that it was
good. 19And there was evening, and there
was morning—the fourth day.
20And God said, "Let the water teem with living
creatures, and let birds fly above the earth
across the expanse of the sky." 21So God
created the great creatures of the sea and
every living and moving thing with which
the water teems, according to their kinds,
and every winged bird according to its
kind. And God saw that it was good. 22God
blessed them and said, "Be fruitful and
increase in number and fill the water in the
seas, and let the birds increase on the
earth." 23And there was evening, and there
was morning—the fifth day.
24And God said, "Let the land produce living
creatures according to their kinds: livestock, creatures that move along the
ground, and wild animals, each according
to its kind." And it was so. 25God made the
wild animals according to their kinds, the
livestock according to their kinds, and all
the creatures that move along the ground
according to their kinds. And God saw that
it was good.
26Then God said, "Let us make man in
our image, in our likeness, and let them

[a]2 Or possibly *became*

1:1 The Hebrew name for God that is used here, *Elohim*, demonstrates the enormity of God's power to transform lives. This name for God is written in the plural form, signifying his strength and might. It also hints that God is himself in some sense plural—a community unto himself (see also 1:26; 3:22; 11:7). But though the name usage is plural, it is treated grammatically as singular, revealing God's unified and personal nature. He is omnipotent in power but personal in his touch. He is able and willing to provide the help we need.

1:1 As the source of all things, God is always able to meet our needs. The Hebrew verb here translated "created" describes an act that only God can do; and this verb describes three things that science cannot explain: the creation of something from nothing (1:1), the creation of living things from inanimate matter (1:21–22), and the creation of human beings (1:27). A God who can create people and the world we live in can certainly empower our spiritual renewal.

1:2 This verse describes the earth before it was shaped by God's creative hand. The earth was shapeless, chaotic and dark. These three characteristics warned of nothing but trouble. But then we are told that "the Spirit of God was hovering over the waters." This fourth characteristic of the earth is a source of hope and promises new life. The presence of the Holy Spirit was a necessary element in the events of all six days of creation. In the same way, the Holy Spirit's presence in our lives is necessary before any spiritual renewal can take place.

1:3 God said, "Let there be light." The word *let* in this verse is used to introduce one of God's purposes for his creation—the need for light in the world. "Let" is used repeatedly in this chapter to introduce the various things that God intended for his creation (see 1:6, 9, 11, 14–15, 20, 24, 26). He had a purpose and a plan for everything. He also has a plan for each of us. His plan is designed to bring about the best for his creation. We need only to seek God and surrender our lives to his design and plan.

1:4 God was pleased with his creation. He declared that it was good. God stopped now and then to confirm what he had designed and created (1:4–5, 9–10, 11–12, 18, 21–22, 25, 31). Many of our problems result from the misuse of God's good creation. Our spiritual renewal may involve discovering the good things that we have misused and learning how to enjoy them in the way God intended.

1:24 The phrase "And it was so" (also in 1:9, 11, 15) shows us that God's creative activity was executed in complete conformity to the specifications he had originally intended. God accomplishes his will with certainty and precision. It should reassure us to know that God's good desires for *us* can be accomplished with the same certainty.

1:26–27 People were created in the image of God. One characteristic of God's image that all scholars agree we as

rule over the fish of the sea and the birds
of the air, over the livestock, over all the
earth,[a] and over all the creatures that
move along the ground."

27So God created man in his own image,
in the image of God he created him;
male and female he created them.

28God blessed them and said to them,
"Be fruitful and increase in number; fill
the earth and subdue it. Rule over the fish
of the sea and the birds of the air and over
every living creature that moves on the
ground."
29Then God said, "I give you every seed-
bearing plant on the face of the whole
earth and every tree that has fruit with seed
in it. They will be yours for food. 30And to
all the beasts of the earth and all the birds
of the air and all the creatures that move
on the ground—everything that has the
breath of life in it—I give every green plant
for food." And it was so.
31God saw all that he had made, and it
was very good. And there was evening, and
there was morning—the sixth day.

2 Thus the heavens and the earth were
completed in all their vast array.
2By the seventh day God had finished the
work he had been doing; so on the seventh
day he rested[b] from all his work. 3And
God blessed the seventh day and made it
holy, because on it he rested from all the
work of creating that he had done.

Adam and Eve

4This is the account of the heavens and the
earth when they were created.

When the LORD God made the earth and the
heavens— 5and no shrub of the field had yet
appeared on the earth[c] and no plant of the
field had yet sprung up, for the LORD God had
not sent rain on the earth[c] and there was no
man to work the ground, 6but streams[d] came
up from the earth and watered the whole surface of the ground— 7the LORD God formed
the man[e] from the dust of the ground and
breathed into his nostrils the breath of life, and
the man became a living being.
8Now the LORD God had planted a garden in
the east, in Eden; and there he put the man he
had formed. 9And the LORD God made all kinds
of trees grow out of the ground—trees that were
pleasing to the eye and good for food. In the
middle of the garden were the tree of life and
the tree of the knowledge of good and evil.
10A river watering the garden flowed from
Eden; from there it was separated into four
headwaters. 11The name of the first is the Pi-
shon; it winds through the entire land of Havilah, where there is gold. 12(The gold of that land
is good; aromatic resin[f] and onyx are also
there.) 13The name of the second river is the
Gihon; it winds through the entire land of
Cush.[g] 14The name of the third river is the
Tigris; it runs along the east side of Asshur. And
the fourth river is the Euphrates.
15The LORD God took the man and put him
in the Garden of Eden to work it and take care
of it. 16And the LORD God commanded the
man, "You are free to eat from any tree in the
garden; 17but you must not eat from the tree of
the knowledge of good and evil, for when you
eat of it you will surely die."
18The LORD God said, "It is not good for the
man to be alone. I will make a helper suitable
for him."
19Now the LORD God had formed out of the
ground all the beasts of the field and all the
birds of the air. He brought them to the man to
see what he would name them; and whatever
the man called each living creature, that was its
name. 20So the man gave names to all the livestock, the birds of the air and all the beasts of
the field.

[a]26 Hebrew; Syriac *all the wild animals* [b]2 Or *ceased;* also in verse 3 [c]5 Or *land;* also in verse 6 [d]6 Or *mist* [e]7 The Hebrew for *man (adam)* sounds like and may be related to the Hebrew for *ground (adamah)*; it is also the name *Adam* (see Gen. 2:20). [f]12 Or *good; pearls* [g]13 Possibly southeast Mesopotamia

---

humans bear is the ability to make moral decisions. People have the power to reason and make choices. We are accountable to God and to others for the choices we make. To continue growing in our spiritual lives we must take responsibility for this aspect of God's nature that is operative in each one of us.

2:2–3 This is the first mention of Sabbath rest—one day of rest in seven. By his example God encourages us to designate a portion of our lives to rest and spiritual rejuvenation. Without proper rest, it is very difficult to deal with the other matters in our lives and maintain the balance necessary for spiritual renewal and growth.

2:4 A new Hebrew name for God is introduced here: "The LORD God" (*Yahweh*). This is the personal name for God; it is his relationship name. It describes the God who chose Abram and established a covenant with him. It describes the God who chose to relate to the Israelites and make them his people. It is the name that reminds us that God also wants to have a relationship with us.

2:8–14 God provided a perfect environment for the first people. We often blame our outward circumstances for our difficulties. It is important to note here that in spite of their ideal surroundings, our first parents fell—they failed. Although the environment we live in can certainly add to our problems, our surroundings are never entirely at fault. We need to take responsibility for our own mistakes and failures.

2:16–17 God forbade Adam and Eve to eat from a single tree. Why did he do this? Why didn't God create a world where people couldn't sin? Why didn't he make people to always be obedient? The answer lies in the very nature of God. God is love. He desires to have a loving relationship with his creatures. He loves us and wants us to love him in return. But a true loving response is only possible when we have the choice to do otherwise. God wants us to obey because we love him, not because we have no other choice.

Spiritual Friendship

But Isn't God Enough?

Genesis 2:18 Our spiritual journey is not a solo quest. It is intimately tied to our relationships with others. One of the common misconceptions of the spiritual life is that if we are "really spiritual" we won't need anybody else. We sometimes think that it's all right for our spiritual life to be just "God and me." From the very beginning, however, God created us for fellowship with others. In the midst of God's joy and satisfaction with his creation, he saw one aspect that wasn't good: Adam was alone. So God created a companion to help Adam. While this passage in Genesis refers specifically to a marriage relationship, it also illustrates that we are all made complete through the companionship of others. God calls us to travel our spiritual journey together.

This God-intended companionship is what we might call *spiritual friendship.* Spiritual friendship is an intentional relationship, founded in Jesus Christ, between two people who nurture each other's spiritual lives. The friendship doesn't exclude casual conversation, but its primary purpose is to focus on the deeper issues of life. What can spiritual friendship do for us?

- Spiritual friendship can heighten our awareness of God's working in our lives. We can often sense God's grace more clearly through the words and actions of another.
- Spiritual friendship is a means of accountability, of evaluating our progress in areas in which God has called us to grow and mature. We are more likely to follow through on commitments when someone else knows about them. We practice accountability in such areas as health, diet, exercise and job supervision. How much more should we do this with our spiritual lives?
- Spiritual friendship is also a means of encouragement and relief when we experience grief or discouragement. We are often harder on ourselves than anyone else would be. Others, especially close friends in Christ, can speak the words of grace and refreshment that can lift our spirits and help us to keep going.

Putting It Into Practice

Do you have a spiritual friendship? Do you have close friends who nourish your life in Christ? What steps can you take to deepen such a friendship? Consider committing yourself to exploring and practicing the spiritual disciplines outlined in this Bible.

If you don't have a close spiritual friend, review your present relationships. Make a list of people who are trustworthy and encourage your spiritual vitality. Spend some time praying and ask God to lead you to a "spiritual friend." When you have selected someone, schedule an unhurried time to talk with them. Explain this concept and how you would like to practice it with him or her. Ask that person to pray about becoming your spiritual friend before making a commitment to you.

For more on spiritual friendship, turn to 1 Samuel 23.

But for Adam[a] no suitable helper was
found. 21So the LORD God caused the man to
fall into a deep sleep; and while he was sleeping, he took one of the man's ribs[b] and closed
up the place with flesh. 22Then the LORD God
made a woman from the rib[c] he had taken out
of the man, and he brought her to the man.
23The man said,

"This is now bone of my bones
  and flesh of my flesh;
she shall be called 'woman,[d]'
  for she was taken out of man."

24For this reason a man will leave his father and
mother and be united to his wife, and they will
become one flesh.
25The man and his wife were both naked,
and they felt no shame.

The Fall of Man

3 Now the serpent was more crafty than any
of the wild animals the LORD God had
made. He said to the woman, "Did God really
say, 'You must not eat from any tree in the
garden'?"
2The woman said to the serpent, "We may
eat fruit from the trees in the garden, 3but God
did say, 'You must not eat fruit from the tree
that is in the middle of the garden, and you
must not touch it, or you will die.' "
4"You will not surely die," the serpent said to
the woman. 5"For God knows that when you
eat of it your eyes will be opened, and you will
be like God, knowing good and evil."
6When the woman saw that the fruit of the
tree was good for food and pleasing to the eye,
and also desirable for gaining wisdom, she took
some and ate it. She also gave some to her husband, who was with her, and he ate it. 7Then
the eyes of both of them were opened, and they
realized they were naked; so they sewed fig
leaves together and made coverings for themselves.
8Then the man and his wife heard the sound
of the LORD God as he was walking in the garden in the cool of the day, and they hid from
the LORD God among the trees of the garden.
9But the LORD God called to the man, "Where
are you?"
10He answered, "I heard you in the garden,
and I was afraid because I was naked; so I hid."
11And he said, "Who told you that you were
naked? Have you eaten from the tree that I commanded you not to eat from?"
12The man said, "The woman you put here
with me—she gave me some fruit from the tree,
and I ate it."
13Then the LORD God said to the woman,
"What is this you have done?"
The woman said, "The serpent deceived me,
and I ate."
14So the LORD God said to the serpent, "Because you have done this,

"Cursed are you above all the livestock
  and all the wild animals!
You will crawl on your belly
  and you will eat dust
  all the days of your life.
15And I will put enmity
  between you and the woman,
  and between your offspring[e] and hers;
he will crush[f] your head,
  and you will strike his heel."

16To the woman he said,

"I will greatly increase your pains in
    childbearing;

[a]20 Or *the man* [b]21 Or *took part of the man's side* [c]22 Or *part* [d]23 The Hebrew for *woman* sounds like the Hebrew for *man.* [e]15 Or *seed* [f]15 Or *strike*

3:1–3 Eve wasn't very clear about the details of God's command. God had told Adam not to *eat* fruit from a certain tree (2:17). Yet in her conversation with the serpent, Eve claimed that God had said they were not even to *touch* the tree. Eve made God's requirements more difficult than God had intended! Her confusion about what God had said made her even more vulnerable to the serpent's wiles. In our spiritual renewal, we also need a proper understanding of God's truth in order to stand against Satan's temptations.

3:1–5 The account here pictures for us the process of temptation. The serpent offered as a very attractive option something that had been forbidden by God. The serpent also caused Eve to doubt God and the truth of his Word. During their debate, Eve offered some halfhearted opposition, but her growing doubt in God weakened her resolve. In the end she gave in. Satan strengthened his temptation by weakening Eve's faith in God. Staying close to God and preserving our faith in him will weaken the power of temptation in our life.

3:7 Adam and Eve's disobedience made them aware of their nakedness and brought them shame and embarrassment. They did their best to cover themselves for they didn't like what they saw when they looked at themselves. When we sin, we try to hide ourselves from God. We don't like what we see, so we cover it up with lies and half-truths. But our intimacy with God and others is destroyed when we hide from our sin. We need to be honest with ourselves and seek forgiveness in order to continue in our spiritual growth.

3:10 Adam admitted that he was hiding from God. One of the terrible consequences of our sin is the isolation that results. We want to hide from other people; we want to hide from God. But we must bring our sin out into the open. This will begin the restoration of the relationships with God and others and will help us preserve our spiritual gains.

3:12–13 When Adam was questioned, he blamed the woman for his problem. He also blamed God by reminding him that God was the one who gave Adam the woman in the first place. Eve blamed the serpent for the problem. Passing the blame is a standard human response to guilt. Our spiritual growth requires that we honestly examine our lives and accept responsibility for everything we have done or failed to do.

3:15 God promised that the offspring of the woman would defeat Satan. God promised that he would take charge of the redemption of their lives and overcome the enemy. This is good news—the first mention of the gospel of grace that would eventually be fulfilled by the coming of Jesus the Messiah.

Adam & Eve

It was an ideal situation: a man and his wife living in harmony in a lush, beautiful garden that God had created for their pleasure. They enjoyed perfect relationships with God and with each other. But when Adam and Eve gave in to temptation, they overstepped their God-given boundaries and plunged the human race into sin. Harmony was broken. Shame and guilt invaded their lives and created an invisible barrier between them and God. The consequences of their disobedience and lack of self-control are still felt today.

Adam and Eve knew that they had challenged God's plan—a plan that was created with their best interests in mind. The consequences of their sin followed immediately, making them afraid of the God who loved them so much. They hid from his presence. They were ashamed of their nakedness and set out to cover themselves. The personal relationship between the man and his wife began to show cracks and strains too. They made accusations, shifted blame. Neither of them wanted to be held accountable. They refused to admit that they were wrong. As a result, their relationship was damaged. Their sin separated them from God and from each other.

But the story doesn't end there. Adam and Eve stayed together in spite of the shame and guilt they felt. Though their lives were marred by sin and scarred by wounds inflicted on one another, they accepted the reality that life had to go on. They began to build a new life together. By the grace of God, they persevered through life's trials.

STRENGTHS AND ACCOMPLISHMENTS:

They were the parents of the entire human race.

They were committed to each other in spite of the trials they faced.

Their story provides us with the first illustration of God's grace.

WEAKNESSES AND MISTAKES:

They were disobedient to the plan that God had revealed to them.

They were not willing to take responsibility for their sin.

They made excuses rather than admit the truth.

They brought sin into the world and passed it on to their descendants.

LESSONS FROM THEIR LIVES:

A good marriage requires love and commitment even through the tough times.

Relationships that accept God's grace and forgiveness persevere through life's difficulties.

Complacency is a breeding ground for temptation—be on guard against Satan's schemes.

The mistakes of parents are often passed on to their descendants.

KEY VERSE:

"Then God said, 'Let us make man in our image, in our likeness, and let them rule over the fish of the sea and the birds of the air, over the livestock, over all the earth, and over all the creatures that move along the ground'" (1:26).

The story of Adam and Eve is found in the opening chapters of Genesis. Adam and/or Eve are also mentioned in 1 Chronicles 1:1; Romans 5:12–19; 1 Corinthians 15:22, 45–49; 2 Corinthians 11:3 and 1 Timothy 2:13–14.

with pain you will give birth to children.
Your desire will be for your husband,
and he will rule over you."

[17]To Adam he said, "Because you listened to
your wife and ate from the tree about which I
commanded you, 'You must not eat of it,'

"Cursed is the ground because of you;
through painful toil you will eat of it
all the days of your life.
[18]It will produce thorns and thistles for you,
and you will eat the plants of the field.
[19]By the sweat of your brow
you will eat your food
until you return to the ground,
since from it you were taken;
for dust you are
and to dust you will return."

[20]Adam[a] named his wife Eve,[b] because she
would become the mother of all the living.
[21]The LORD God made garments of skin for
Adam and his wife and clothed them. [22]And the
LORD God said, "The man has now become like
one of us, knowing good and evil. He must not
be allowed to reach out his hand and take also
from the tree of life and eat, and live forever."
[23]So the LORD God banished him from the Garden of Eden to work the ground from which he
had been taken. [24]After he drove the man out,
he placed on the east side[c] of the Garden of
Eden cherubim and a flaming sword flashing
back and forth to guard the way to the tree of
life.

Cain and Abel

4 Adam[a] lay with his wife Eve, and she became pregnant and gave birth to Cain.[d]
She said, "With the help of the LORD I have
brought forth[e] a man." [2]Later she gave birth to
his brother Abel.
Now Abel kept flocks, and Cain worked the
soil. [3]In the course of time Cain brought some
of the fruits of the soil as an offering to the
LORD. [4]But Abel brought fat portions from some
of the firstborn of his flock. The LORD looked
with favor on Abel and his offering, [5]but on
Cain and his offering he did not look with favor. So Cain was very angry, and his face was
downcast.
[6]Then the LORD said to Cain, "Why are you
angry? Why is your face downcast? [7]If you do
what is right, will you not be accepted? But if
you do not do what is right, sin is crouching at
your door; it desires to have you, but you must
master it."
[8]Now Cain said to his brother Abel, "Let's go
out to the field."[f] And while they were in the
field, Cain attacked his brother Abel and killed
him.
[9]Then the LORD said to Cain, "Where is your
brother Abel?"
"I don't know," he replied. "Am I my brother's keeper?"
[10]The LORD said, "What have you done? Listen! Your brother's blood cries out to me from
the ground. [11]Now you are under a curse and
driven from the ground, which opened its
mouth to receive your brother's blood from
your hand. [12]When you work the ground, it will
no longer yield its crops for you. You will be a
restless wanderer on the earth."
[13]Cain said to the LORD, "My punishment is
more than I can bear. [14]Today you are driving
me from the land, and I will be hidden from
your presence; I will be a restless wanderer on
the earth, and whoever finds me will kill me."
[15]But the LORD said to him, "Not so[g]; if

[a]20,1 Or *The man* [b]20 *Eve* probably means *living.* [c]24 Or *placed in front* [d]1 *Cain* sounds like the Hebrew for *brought forth* or *acquired.* [e]1 Or *have acquired* [f]8 Samaritan Pentateuch, Septuagint, Vulgate and Syriac; Masoretic Text does not have *"Let's go out to the field."* [g]15 Septuagint, Vulgate and Syriac; Hebrew *Very well*

3:18–19 After the fall, the earth responded differently to its human masters. In the beginning, the earth was their constant ally, yielding its fruits easily to their hands. After the fall, the earth brought forth thorns and thistles. Work became an arduous task, frustrating and unfulfilling.
3:20 There was no reason for Adam and Eve to expect to live on after their failure. God had clearly stated that the consequences of their sin would be death (see 2:17). Yet Adam displayed his faith in God's grace by naming his wife Eve, which sounds like the Hebrew word that means "to give life." Adam's faith in God gave him hope for the future, even when his past gave him little reason to hope.
3:21 The first death occurred on the day of Adam's sin—the death of an animal to provide a covering for Adam and Eve's nakedness. God's immediate provision for sin was the slaying of an innocent substitute to provide skins to clothe the guilty couple. The clothing they wore must have served as a reminder of the sight of the dying animal, engraving in their minds a picture of the terrible consequences of their sin. As we recognize the suffering we may have caused others, we also are reminded of the consequences of rejecting God's plan for our lives.
4:4 Abel slew an innocent substitute as his offering, and God accepted his offering. Our relationship with God hinges on accepting God's gracious forgiveness and allowing the innocent sacrifice of his Son to stand in our place. Note also that Abel's sacrifice of one of his lambs was the second death mentioned in the Bible.
4:6–8 When God rejected Cain's offering, Cain reacted first with disappointment, then with anger. God did not reject Cain for his strong feelings but offered him an opportunity for a new start. Cain refused this second chance and went out instead to kill his brother. We need to be careful when we face obstacles in life. We need to carefully weigh the strong feelings we encounter before acting on them. If we don't, we may be passing up an excellent opportunity for a fresh start. God is not put off by our strong feelings. Our spiritual renewal is based on God's grace, which always offers us an opportunity to begin again.
4:15 The mark on Cain was not, as some have taught, a badge of guilt. It was a sign that God gave Cain for his protection. Even after Cain's great failure, God desired to protect him from harm. Many of us look back and marvel at how God protected us before we began seeking him. He wants us to be restored and often protects us in the midst of evil so that we are not destroyed. Even after our greatest failures, our gracious God desires only our healing and restoration.

CAIN & ABEL

How often parents of two children have been heard to exclaim, "There have *never* been two children who were more different!" Adam and Eve could well have been the originators of that comment. Cain apparently felt he was in direct competition with Abel. This led to a rivalry that was never resolved, and resulted in a major tragedy.

Cain became a farmer and Abel became a shepherd. However, their offerings, not their occupations, revealed the true nature of their character. Abel did things God's way, following his requirements. He is called "righteous" in Matthew 23:35, and Hebrews 11:4 says that by faith Abel made an offering that was acceptable to God. Cain, on the other hand, did things his own way. Cain brought an offering of produce from his gardens. While harvest offerings would later be acceptable acts of worship, apparently Cain's motives and attitudes were unacceptable to God. Abel brought the fatty cuts of meat from his best lambs and offered them to God in an acceptable way—with a pure heart.

Abel's altar was not beautiful; the senses were assaulted by the bloody carcass lying across it. But the blood was a part of God's plan (Hebrews 12:24). Cain's offering had the potential for being beautiful. Picture fresh produce, just out of the garden—fruits, vegetables, flowers, grain—probably artistically arranged. When God accepted Abel's offering and rejected Cain's, Cain became angry. But God did not reject Cain because of his anger. Even at that point, God reasoned with him. He offered Cain another opportunity to respond in the right way, but still Cain refused. Jealous of Abel, whose offering had been accepted, and enraged because God had rejected his offering, Cain murdered his brother.

Cain tried to hide his terrible deed, but God was not fooled. God confronted Cain with the murder and assigned him the consequence of a lifelong exile. Cain spent the rest of his life as an alien, wandering in lands far from his family. Yet even in exile God protected him; God placed his mark upon Cain to keep him from being killed.

STRENGTHS AND ACCOMPLISHMENTS:

Abel was obedient to God.

Abel is the first hero mentioned in the "Gallery of Faith" in Hebrews 11.

Both sons developed skills and worked hard in the occupations they chose.

WEAKNESSES AND MISTAKES:

Cain insisted on doing things his own way.

When rejected, Cain reacted with anger.

Cain allowed his anger to lead him to commit the first murder.

LESSONS FROM THEIR LIVES:

Our righteousness comes by faith, which results in obedience to God's commands.

Anger is not inherently sinful; it is how we choose to deal with it and express it that pleases or displeases God.

Though we may try to hide our sins for a time, God's justice will prevail.

KEY VERSE:

"By faith Abel offered God a better sacrifice than Cain did. By faith he was commended as a righteous man, when God spoke well of his offerings. And by faith he still speaks, even though he is dead" (Hebrews 11:4).

The account of Cain and Abel is given in Genesis 4. Cain and/or Abel are also mentioned in Matthew 23:35; Luke 11:51; Hebrews 11:4 and 12:24; 1 John 3:12 and Jude 11.

anyone kills Cain, he will suffer vengeance sev-
en times over." Then the LORD put a mark on
Cain so that no one who found him would kill
him. 16So Cain went out from the LORD's presence and lived in the land of Nod,[a] east of
Eden.

17Cain lay with his wife, and she became
pregnant and gave birth to Enoch. Cain was
then building a city, and he named it after his
son Enoch. 18To Enoch was born Irad, and Irad
was the father of Mehujael, and Mehujael was
the father of Methushael, and Methushael was
the father of Lamech.

19Lamech married two women, one named
Adah and the other Zillah. 20Adah gave birth to
Jabal; he was the father of those who live in
tents and raise livestock. 21His brother's name
was Jubal; he was the father of all who play the
harp and flute. 22Zillah also had a son, Tubal-
Cain, who forged all kinds of tools out of[b]
bronze and iron. Tubal-Cain's sister was Naamah.

23Lamech said to his wives,

"Adah and Zillah, listen to me;
  wives of Lamech, hear my words.
I have killed[c] a man for wounding me,
  a young man for injuring me.
24If Cain is avenged seven times,
  then Lamech seventy-seven times."

25Adam lay with his wife again, and she gave
birth to a son and named him Seth,[d] saying,
"God has granted me another child in place of
Abel, since Cain killed him." 26Seth also had a
son, and he named him Enosh.

At that time men began to call on[e] the
name of the LORD.

From Adam to Noah

5 This is the written account of Adam's line.

When God created man, he made him in the
likeness of God. 2He created them male and
female and blessed them. And when they were
created, he called them "man.[f]"

3When Adam had lived 130 years, he had a
son in his own likeness, in his own image; and
he named him Seth. 4After Seth was born,
Adam lived 800 years and had other sons and
daughters. 5Altogether, Adam lived 930 years,
and then he died.

6When Seth had lived 105 years, he became
the father[g] of Enosh. 7And after he became the
father of Enosh, Seth lived 807 years and had
other sons and daughters. 8Altogether, Seth
lived 912 years, and then he died.

9When Enosh had lived 90 years, he became
the father of Kenan. 10And after he became the
father of Kenan, Enosh lived 815 years and had
other sons and daughters. 11Altogether, Enosh
lived 905 years, and then he died.

12When Kenan had lived 70 years, he became
the father of Mahalalel. 13And after he became
the father of Mahalalel, Kenan lived 840 years
and had other sons and daughters. 14Altogether,
Kenan lived 910 years, and then he died.

15When Mahalalel had lived 65 years, he became the father of Jared. 16And after he became
the father of Jared, Mahalalel lived 830 years
and had other sons and daughters. 17Altogether,
Mahalalel lived 895 years, and then he died.

18When Jared had lived 162 years, he became
the father of Enoch. 19And after he became the
father of Enoch, Jared lived 800 years and had
other sons and daughters. 20Altogether, Jared
lived 962 years, and then he died.

21When Enoch had lived 65 years, he became
the father of Methuselah. 22And after he became
the father of Methuselah, Enoch walked with
God 300 years and had other sons and daughters. 23Altogether, Enoch lived 365 years.
24Enoch walked with God; then he was no
more, because God took him away.

25When Methuselah had lived 187 years, he
became the father of Lamech. 26And after he
became the father of Lamech, Methuselah lived
782 years and had other sons and daughters.
27Altogether, Methuselah lived 969 years, and
then he died.

28When Lamech had lived 182 years, he had
a son. 29He named him Noah[h] and said, "He
will comfort us in the labor and painful toil of
our hands caused by the ground the LORD has
cursed." 30After Noah was born, Lamech lived
595 years and had other sons and daughters.
31Altogether, Lamech lived 777 years, and then
he died.

[a]16 *Nod* means *wandering* (see verses 12 and 14). [b]22 Or *who instructed all who work in* [c]23 Or *I will kill* [d]25 *Seth* probably means *granted.* [e]26 Or *to proclaim* [f]2 Hebrew *adam* [g]6 *Father* may mean *ancestor*; also in verses 7-26. [h]29 *Noah* sounds like the Hebrew for *comfort.*

4:19–24 Some people insist that the human race is developing and becoming better and better. When we compare Lamech with his ancestor Cain, it is obvious that the trend progressed in the opposite direction. Without God's help, we only get worse. It is only by following God's plan and receiving his grace that we can hope to escape the natural slide toward pain and destruction.

5:1–32 This chapter has often been called the obituary column. Its recurring refrain is "and then he died." Although Adam's physical death did not occur on the day he sinned, death did eventually come. Adam had reestablished his relationship with God, but the physical consequences of his sin could not be avoided forever. We may hope that after reestablishing our relationship with God our troubles will be over. But a relationship with God rarely frees us from the consequences of past sin. The consequences will catch up with us sooner or later. Yet if we suffer for past mistakes, we can know that God will be with us each step of the way.

5:21–24 Little is said about the spiritual state of the patriarchs of the human race. The account of Enoch's life provides us with a bright spot in this otherwise dismal chapter. Enoch "walked with God." His life should give us hope. He wasn't trapped by the mistakes or apathy of his peers and ancestors. Instead, Enoch constantly walked with God.

32After Noah was 500 years old, he became the father of Shem, Ham and Japheth.

The Flood

6 When men began to increase in number on the earth and daughters were born to them, 2the sons of God saw that the daughters of men were beautiful, and they married any of them they chose. 3Then the LORD said, "My Spirit will not contend with[a] man forever, for he is mortal[b]; his days will be a hundred and twenty years."

4The Nephilim were on the earth in those days—and also afterward—when the sons of God went to the daughters of men and had children by them. They were the heroes of old, men of renown.

5The LORD saw how great man's wickedness on the earth had become, and that every inclination of the thoughts of his heart was only evil all the time. 6The LORD was grieved that he had made man on the earth, and his heart was filled with pain. 7So the LORD said, "I will wipe mankind, whom I have created, from the face of the earth—men and animals, and creatures that move along the ground, and birds of the air—for I am grieved that I have made them." 8But Noah found favor in the eyes of the LORD.

9This is the account of Noah.

Noah was a righteous man, blameless among the people of his time, and he walked with God. 10Noah had three sons: Shem, Ham and Japheth.

11Now the earth was corrupt in God's sight and was full of violence. 12God saw how corrupt the earth had become, for all the people on earth had corrupted their ways. 13So God said to Noah, "I am going to put an end to all people, for the earth is filled with violence because of them. I am surely going to destroy both them and the earth. 14So make yourself an ark of cypress[c] wood; make rooms in it and coat it with pitch inside and out. 15This is how you are to build it: The ark is to be 450 feet long, 75 feet wide and 45 feet high.[d] 16Make a roof for it and finish[e] the ark to within 18 inches[f] of the top. Put a door in the side of the ark and make lower, middle and upper decks. 17I am going to bring floodwaters on the earth to destroy all life under the heavens, every creature that has the breath of life in it. Everything on earth will perish. 18But I will establish my covenant with you, and you will enter the ark—you and your sons and your wife and your sons' wives with you. 19You are to bring into the ark two of all living creatures, male and female, to keep them alive with you. 20Two of every kind of bird, of every kind of animal and of every kind of creature that moves along the ground will come to you to be kept alive. 21You are to take every kind of food that is to be eaten and store it away as food for you and for them."

22Noah did everything just as God commanded him.

7 The LORD then said to Noah, "Go into the ark, you and your whole family, because I have found you righteous in this generation. 2Take with you seven[g] of every kind of clean animal, a male and its mate, and two of every kind of unclean animal, a male and its mate, 3and also seven of every kind of bird, male and female, to keep their various kinds alive throughout the earth. 4Seven days from now I will send rain on the earth for forty days and forty nights, and I will wipe from the face of the earth every living creature I have made."

5And Noah did all that the LORD commanded him.

6Noah was six hundred years old when the floodwaters came on the earth. 7And Noah and his sons and his wife and his sons' wives entered the ark to escape the waters of the flood. 8Pairs of clean and unclean animals, of birds and of all creatures that move along the ground, 9male and female, came to Noah and entered the ark, as God had commanded Noah. 10And after the seven days the floodwaters came on the earth.

11In the six hundredth year of Noah's life, on the seventeenth day of the second month—on that day all the springs of the great deep burst forth, and the floodgates of the heavens were opened. 12And rain fell on the earth forty days and forty nights.

[a]3 Or *My spirit will not remain in* [b]3 Or *corrupt* [c]14 The meaning of the Hebrew for this word is uncertain. [d]15 Hebrew *300 cubits long, 50 cubits wide and 30 cubits high* (about 140 meters long, 23 meters wide and 13.5 meters high) [e]16 Or *Make an opening for light by finishing* [f]16 Hebrew *a cubit* (about 0.5 meter) [g]2 Or *seven pairs;* also in verse 3

6:5–6 The human race refused to live according to God's plan. Things were getting worse in the world, not better. This broke God's heart because of the great love he had for his creation. It should encourage us to know that God doesn't punish us simply out of anger. He loves us very much and desires that we should follow him.

6:7 God promises to judge his fallen and sinful creatures. Though God is patient with us and gives us many chances to change our ways, we cannot act with impunity. God is righteous; he will judge sin.

6:8–10 God did not destroy the righteous with the wicked. These verses are another statement of God's grace. God extended grace to Noah and his family. Noah knew Enoch's secret. He lived his life in constant fellowship with God. He broke the mold set by his ancestors and neighbors by drawing close to God. As a result, Noah lived through the flood and became the second father of the human race.

6:22 One has to wonder whether God's instructions made any sense to Noah. God told him to build a gigantic boat far from the nearest body of navigable water. But Noah was obedient even though God's instructions were hard to understand. This is one of the secrets of success in life. We may not understand how everything works, but we must always be faithful to do what God tells us to do. When we walk by faith as Noah did, God will watch over us.

Noah & Sons

Most parents are concerned about how to raise godly children in a corrupt society. Noah is a good model of a godly parent. He was the only righteous man left in a generation of corrupt individuals. He courageously led his family by example in a world that looked upon Noah as being "out of touch." Society mocked him for his belief in and obedience to God.

The principles of obedience, faithfulness and patience were taught to Noah's sons and their wives. When judgment came upon the world, Noah, his wife, his sons and their wives were spared. After the flood, the Bible tells us that Noah became drunk on the wine of his vineyard. Two of his sons (Shem and Japheth) responded to the situation in a godly manner; one (Ham) did not. Noah's drunkenness and Ham's indiscretion resulted in the suffering of some of Ham's descendants.

As we look at Noah's life, we are reminded that our children learn from our example and become like the adults around them. They often receive great blessings from the good things we do, but they can also suffer from our mistakes. All of us, like Noah, have made mistakes. But we can overcome them through repentance and obedience to God's Word.

STRENGTHS AND ACCOMPLISHMENTS:

Noah was the only follower of God left in his generation.

Noah was the second father of the human race.

Noah taught his sons patience, faithfulness and obedience to God.

WEAKNESSES AND MISTAKES:

Noah embarrassed himself by getting drunk and becoming indecent.

Ham acted in an ungodly manner, resulting in a curse upon some of his descendants.

LESSONS FROM THEIR LIVES:

God is faithful to those who trust and obey him.

Obedience to God is a lifelong commitment.

Good parents teach their children by example.

KEY VERSE:

"Noah did everything just as God commanded him" (6:22).

The story of Noah and his sons is told in Genesis 5:29—10:32. Noah is also referred to in 1 Chronicles 1:4; Isaiah 54:9; Ezekiel 14:14, 20; Matthew 24:37–38; Luke 3:36; 17:26–27; Hebrews 11:7; 1 Peter 3:20 and 2 Peter 2:5.

13On that very day Noah and his sons, Shem,
Ham and Japheth, together with his wife and
the wives of his three sons, entered the ark.
14They had with them every wild animal according to its kind, all livestock according to
their kinds, every creature that moves along the
ground according to its kind and every bird
according to its kind, everything with wings.
15Pairs of all creatures that have the breath of
life in them came to Noah and entered the ark.
16The animals going in were male and female
of every living thing, as God had commanded
Noah. Then the LORD shut him in.

17For forty days the flood kept coming on the
earth, and as the waters increased they lifted the
ark high above the earth. 18The waters rose and
increased greatly on the earth, and the ark float-
ed on the surface of the water. 19They rose greatly on the earth, and all the high mountains
under the entire heavens were covered. 20The
waters rose and covered the mountains to a
depth of more than twenty feet.[a,b] 21Every
living thing that moved on the earth perished—
birds, livestock, wild animals, all the creatures
that swarm over the earth, and all mankind.
22Everything on dry land that had the breath of
life in its nostrils died. 23Every living thing on
the face of the earth was wiped out; men and
animals and the creatures that move along the
ground and the birds of the air were wiped from
the earth. Only Noah was left, and those with
him in the ark.

24The waters flooded the earth for a hundred
and fifty days.

8 But God remembered Noah and all the
wild animals and the livestock that were
with him in the ark, and he sent a wind over the
earth, and the waters receded. 2Now the springs
of the deep and the floodgates of the heavens
had been closed, and the rain had stopped falling from the sky. 3The water receded steadily
from the earth. At the end of the hundred and
fifty days the water had gone down, 4and on the
seventeenth day of the seventh month the ark
came to rest on the mountains of Ararat. 5The
waters continued to recede until the tenth
month, and on the first day of the tenth month
the tops of the mountains became visible.

6After forty days Noah opened the window
he had made in the ark 7and sent out a raven,
and it kept flying back and forth until the water
had dried up from the earth. 8Then he sent out
a dove to see if the water had receded from the
surface of the ground. 9But the dove could find
no place to set its feet because there was water
over all the surface of the earth; so it returned
to Noah in the ark. He reached out his hand
and took the dove and brought it back to himself in the ark. 10He waited seven more days and
again sent out the dove from the ark. 11When
the dove returned to him in the evening, there
in its beak was a freshly plucked olive leaf!
Then Noah knew that the water had receded
from the earth. 12He waited seven more days
and sent the dove out again, but this time it did
not return to him.

13By the first day of the first month of Noah's
six hundred and first year, the water had dried
up from the earth. Noah then removed the covering from the ark and saw that the surface of
the ground was dry. 14By the twenty-seventh
day of the second month the earth was completely dry.

15Then God said to Noah, 16"Come out of
the ark, you and your wife and your sons and
their wives. 17Bring out every kind of living
creature that is with you—the birds, the animals, and all the creatures that move along the
ground—so they can multiply on the earth and
be fruitful and increase in number upon it."

18So Noah came out, together with his sons
and his wife and his sons' wives. 19All the animals and all the creatures that move along the
ground and all the birds—everything that moves
on the earth—came out of the ark, one kind after
another.

20Then Noah built an altar to the LORD and,
taking some of all the clean animals and clean
birds, he sacrificed burnt offerings on it. 21The
LORD smelled the pleasing aroma and said in
his heart: "Never again will I curse the ground
because of man, even though[c] every inclination of his heart is evil from childhood. And
never again will I destroy all living creatures, as
I have done.

22"As long as the earth endures,
seedtime and harvest,
cold and heat,
summer and winter,
day and night
will never cease."

God's Covenant With Noah

9 Then God blessed Noah and his sons, saying to them, "Be fruitful and increase in
number and fill the earth. 2The fear and dread
of you will fall upon all the beasts of the earth
and all the birds of the air, upon every creature

[a]20 Hebrew *fifteen cubits* (about 6.9 meters) [b]20 Or *rose more than twenty feet, and the mountains were covered*
[c]21 Or *man, for*

8:1 Noah had listened to God and obeyed all his requests. Now the ark was floating over the earth on top of the flood waters—not an ideal situation. But God didn't forget about Noah. It is comforting to know that when we obey God, he will not forget us. He will stand by us until his plans for us are complete.

9:1–17 Noah and his family were the only people left after the flood. The comforts of civilization had been washed away. They had to start all over again. God gave Noah his special blessing and instituted a plan that, if followed, would result in a healthy society. God has given us his Word, which contains the ultimate blueprint for healthy living. And just as God gave the human race a new start with Noah, he can give each of us a new start too.

that moves along the ground, and upon all the fish of the sea; they are given into your hands. 3Everything that lives and moves will be food for you. Just as I gave you the green plants, I now give you everything.

4"But you must not eat meat that has its lifeblood still in it. 5And for your lifeblood I will surely demand an accounting. I will demand an accounting from every animal. And from each man, too, I will demand an accounting for the life of his fellow man.

6"Whoever sheds the blood of man,
by man shall his blood be shed;
for in the image of God
has God made man.

7As for you, be fruitful and increase in number; multiply on the earth and increase upon it."

8Then God said to Noah and to his sons with him: 9"I now establish my covenant with you and with your descendants after you 10and with every living creature that was with you—the birds, the livestock and all the wild animals, all those that came out of the ark with you—every living creature on earth. 11I establish my covenant with you: Never again will all life be cut off by the waters of a flood; never again will there be a flood to destroy the earth."

12And God said, "This is the sign of the covenant I am making between me and you and every living creature with you, a covenant for all generations to come: 13I have set my rainbow in the clouds, and it will be the sign of the covenant between me and the earth. 14Whenever I bring clouds over the earth and the rainbow appears in the clouds, 15I will remember my covenant between me and you and all living creatures of every kind. Never again will the waters become a flood to destroy all life. 16Whenever the rainbow appears in the clouds, I will see it and remember the everlasting covenant between God and all living creatures of every kind on the earth."

17So God said to Noah, "This is the sign of the covenant I have established between me and all life on the earth."

The Sons of Noah

18The sons of Noah who came out of the ark were Shem, Ham and Japheth. (Ham was the father of Canaan.) 19These were the three sons of Noah, and from them came the people who were scattered over the earth.

20Noah, a man of the soil, proceeded[a] to plant a vineyard. 21When he drank some of its wine, he became drunk and lay uncovered inside his tent. 22Ham, the father of Canaan, saw his father's nakedness and told his two brothers outside. 23But Shem and Japheth took a garment and laid it across their shoulders; then they walked in backward and covered their father's nakedness. Their faces were turned the other way so that they would not see their father's nakedness.

24When Noah awoke from his wine and found out what his youngest son had done to him, 25he said,

"Cursed be Canaan!
The lowest of slaves
will he be to his brothers."

26He also said,

"Blessed be the LORD, the God of Shem!
May Canaan be the slave of Shem.[b]
27May God extend the territory of Japheth[c];
may Japheth live in the tents of Shem,
and may Canaan be his[d] slave."

28After the flood Noah lived 350 years. 29Altogether, Noah lived 950 years, and then he died.

The Table of Nations

10 This is the account of Shem, Ham and Japheth, Noah's sons, who themselves had sons after the flood.

The Japhethites

2The sons[e] of Japheth:
Gomer, Magog, Madai, Javan, Tubal, Meshech and Tiras.
3The sons of Gomer:
Ashkenaz, Riphath and Togarmah.
4The sons of Javan:
Elishah, Tarshish, the Kittim and the Rodanim.[f] 5(From these the mari-

[a]20 Or *soil, was the first* [b]26 Or *be his slave*
[c]27 *Japheth* sounds like the Hebrew for *extend.*
[d]27 Or *their* [e]2 *Sons* may mean *descendants* or *successors* or *nations;* also in verses 3, 4, 6, 7, 20-23, 29 and 31. [f]4 Some manuscripts of the Masoretic Text and Samaritan Pentateuch (see also Septuagint and 1 Chron. 1:7); most manuscripts of the Masoretic Text *Dodanim*

9:9–13 God assigned Noah the monumental task of rebuilding human society on earth. But God didn't just hand Noah the task and walk away. As we see in this passage, God gave Noah hope and set a rainbow in the sky as a seal of his promise. As we rebuild our lives in keeping with God's design, we can be sure that God will support us with his presence and promises. We should keep an eye out for the "rainbows" along the way, signs that remind us of God's loving presence and care.

9:20–21 With all the talk of Noah's righteousness and his fellowship with God, it is surprising to read that, by his choice, Noah fell prey to the excesses of alcohol. The account of Noah's drunkenness and shame comes as a shock to the reader, but it is a reminder that even in ideal conditions it is easy for us to slip and fall. We can never relax and feel as if we have achieved spiritual success, for that is when we become most vulnerable to sin.

10:1–32 This chapter is often called the Table of Nations. It is refreshing to realize that the God we worship is not a local deity. He is sovereign over all ethnic and language groups, nations and political entities. The God who holds kings and empires in his hands surely has the power to hold us too.

time peoples spread out into their territories by their clans within their nations, each with its own language.)

The Hamites

6The sons of Ham:
Cush, Mizraim,[a] Put and Canaan.
7The sons of Cush:
Seba, Havilah, Sabtah, Raamah and
Sabteca.
The sons of Raamah:
Sheba and Dedan.

8Cush was the father[b] of Nimrod, who grew
to be a mighty warrior on the earth. 9He was a
mighty hunter before the LORD; that is why it is
said, "Like Nimrod, a mighty hunter before the
LORD." 10The first centers of his kingdom were
Babylon, Erech, Akkad and Calneh, in[c] Shinar.[d] 11From that land he went to Assyria,
where he built Nineveh, Rehoboth Ir,[e] Calah
12and Resen, which is between Nineveh and
Calah; that is the great city.

13Mizraim was the father of
the Ludites, Anamites, Lehabites,
Naphtuhites, 14Pathrusites, Casluhites
(from whom the Philistines came) and
Caphtorites.
15Canaan was the father of
Sidon his firstborn,[f] and of the Hittites, 16Jebusites, Amorites, Girgashites, 17Hivites, Arkites, Sinites, 18Ar-
vadites, Zemarites and Hamathites.

Later the Canaanite clans scattered 19and the
borders of Canaan reached from Sidon toward
Gerar as far as Gaza, and then toward Sodom,
Gomorrah, Admah and Zeboiim, as far as La-
sha.

20These are the sons of Ham by their clans
and languages, in their territories and nations.

The Semites

21Sons were also born to Shem, whose older
brother was[g] Japheth; Shem was the ancestor
of all the sons of Eber.

22The sons of Shem:
Elam, Asshur, Arphaxad, Lud and
Aram.
23The sons of Aram:
Uz, Hul, Gether and Meshech.[h]
24Arphaxad was the father of[i] Shelah,
and Shelah the father of Eber.
25Two sons were born to Eber:
One was named Peleg,[j] because in
his time the earth was divided; his
brother was named Joktan.
26Joktan was the father of
Almodad, Sheleph, Hazarmaveth, Jerah, 27Hadoram, Uzal, Diklah, 28Obal,
Abimael, Sheba, 29Ophir, Havilah and
Jobab. All these were sons of Joktan.

30The region where they lived stretched from
Mesha toward Sephar, in the eastern hill country.

31These are the sons of Shem by their clans
and languages, in their territories and nations.

32These are the clans of Noah's sons, according to their lines of descent, within their nations. From these the nations spread out over
the earth after the flood.

The Tower of Babel

11 Now the whole world had one language and a common speech. 2As men
moved eastward,[k] they found a plain in Shinar[d] and settled there.
3They said to each other, "Come, let's make
bricks and bake them thoroughly." They used
brick instead of stone, and tar for mortar. 4Then
they said, "Come, let us build ourselves a city,
with a tower that reaches to the heavens, so that
we may make a name for ourselves and not be
scattered over the face of the whole earth."
5But the LORD came down to see the city and
the tower that the men were building. 6The
LORD said, "If as one people speaking the same
language they have begun to do this, then nothing they plan to do will be impossible for them.
7Come, let us go down and confuse their language so they will not understand each other."
8So the LORD scattered them from there over
all the earth, and they stopped building the city.
9That is why it was called Babel[l]—because
there the LORD confused the language of the

[a]6 That is, Egypt; also in verse 13 [b]8 *Father* may mean *ancestor* or *predecessor* or *founder*; also in verses 13, 15, 24 and 26. [c]10 Or *Erech and Akkad—all of them in* [d]10,2 That is, Babylonia [e]11 Or *Nineveh with its city squares* [f]15 *Or of the Sidonians, the foremost* [g]21 Or *Shem, the older brother of* [h]23 See Septuagint and 1 Chron. 1:17; Hebrew *Mash* [i]24 Hebrew; Septuagint *father of Cainan, and Cainan was the father of* [j]25 *Peleg* means *division.* [k]2 Or *from the east*; or *in the east* [l]9 That is, Babylon; *Babel* sounds like the Hebrew for *confused.*

11:3–4 Whatever else the tower of Babel might have represented, it was a mighty monument to human pride. It was a symbol of man's rebellion against the revealed will of God. This type of pride is always destructive to humanity and obstructs God's plan of redemption.

11:5–9 The tower of Babel incident records the progression of broken communication that began back in the Garden of Eden. After sin entered the world, Adam and Eve began to hide the truth. They tried to blame each other and God for their mistakes, resulting in separation from God and barriers between themselves. The sinful pride of the people of Babel caused another great rift in human communication. Numerous languages now divided people into various groups, making cooperation difficult, if not impossible. But God is in the business of restoring broken communication. He chose the nation of Israel and spoke to them, giving them his laws. His Son was born through this nation so he could speak to us and walk among us. And when the Holy Spirit came, the diversity of language was no longer a barrier to communication (Acts 2:5–11). Following God's plan enhances our communication with him and the people around us.

whole world. From there the LORD scattered
them over the face of the whole earth.

From Shem to Abram

10This is the account of Shem.

Two years after the flood, when Shem was
100 years old, he became the father[a] of Arphaxad. 11And after he became the father of
Arphaxad, Shem lived 500 years and had other
sons and daughters.
12When Arphaxad had lived 35 years, he became the father of Shelah. 13And after he became the father of Shelah, Arphaxad lived 403
years and had other sons and daughters.[b]
14When Shelah had lived 30 years, he became the father of Eber. 15And after he became
the father of Eber, Shelah lived 403 years and
had other sons and daughters.
16When Eber had lived 34 years, he became
the father of Peleg. 17And after he became the
father of Peleg, Eber lived 430 years and had
other sons and daughters.
18When Peleg had lived 30 years, he became
the father of Reu. 19And after he became the
father of Reu, Peleg lived 209 years and had
other sons and daughters.
20When Reu had lived 32 years, he became
the father of Serug. 21And after he became the
father of Serug, Reu lived 207 years and had
other sons and daughters.
22When Serug had lived 30 years, he became
the father of Nahor. 23And after he became the
father of Nahor, Serug lived 200 years and had
other sons and daughters.
24When Nahor had lived 29 years, he became
the father of Terah. 25And after he became the
father of Terah, Nahor lived 119 years and had
other sons and daughters.
26After Terah had lived 70 years, he became
the father of Abram, Nahor and Haran.

27This is the account of Terah.

Terah became the father of Abram, Nahor
and Haran. And Haran became the father of
Lot. 28While his father Terah was still alive, Haran died in Ur of the Chaldeans, in the land of
his birth. 29Abram and Nahor both married.
The name of Abram's wife was Sarai, and the
name of Nahor's wife was Milcah; she was the
daughter of Haran, the father of both Milcah
and Iscah. 30Now Sarai was barren; she had no
children.
31Terah took his son Abram, his grandson
Lot son of Haran, and his daughter-in-law Sarai, the wife of his son Abram, and together they
set out from Ur of the Chaldeans to go to Canaan. But when they came to Haran, they settled there.
32Terah lived 205 years, and he died in Haran.

The Call of Abram

12 The LORD had said to Abram, "Leave
your country, your people and your father's household and go to the land I will show
you.

2"I will make you into a great nation
 and I will bless you;
I will make your name great,
 and you will be a blessing.
3I will bless those who bless you,
 and whoever curses you I will curse;
and all peoples on earth
 will be blessed through you."

4So Abram left, as the LORD had told him;
and Lot went with him. Abram was seventy-five
years old when he set out from Haran. 5He took
his wife Sarai, his nephew Lot, all the possessions they had accumulated and the people
they had acquired in Haran, and they set out for
the land of Canaan, and they arrived there.
6Abram traveled through the land as far as
the site of the great tree of Moreh at Shechem.
At that time the Canaanites were in the land.
7The LORD appeared to Abram and said, "To
your offspring[c] I will give this land." So he built
an altar there to the LORD, who had appeared to
him.
8From there he went on toward the hills east
of Bethel and pitched his tent, with Bethel on
the west and Ai on the east. There he built an
altar to the LORD and called on the name of the
LORD. 9Then Abram set out and continued toward the Negev.

[a] *10 Father* may mean *ancestor*; also in verses 11-25.
[b] *12,13* Hebrew; Septuagint (see also Luke 3:35, 36 and note at Gen. 10:24) *35 years, he became the father of Cainan. 13And after he became the father of Cainan, Arphaxad lived 430 years and had other sons and daughters, and then he died. When Cainan had lived 130 years, he became the father of Shelah. And after he became the father of Shelah, Cainan lived 330 years and had other sons and daughters*
[c] *7* Or *seed*

12:1 A relationship with God is a two-way street. He is there to help us, but he also expects us to follow his plan. When God called Abram to leave his country and his people and go to a land that God would show him, God promised to guide him. But Abram had to walk by faith. God has promised to be with us as we seek his help, but he may also ask something of us. As with Abram, God may call us away from the familiar things of this world that drag us down. If we want to progress, we will need to follow his plan.

12:2–3 God promised Abram many things: He would make Abram into a great nation; he would bless him and make him famous; he would make Abram a blessing to others. Think about it. After receiving God's blessing, Abram would be a blessing to others, sharing God's blessing with them. Following Abram's example, we should take the blessings we have received through our spiritual renewal and share them with others.

12:4 This verse indicates the beginning of Abram's radical obedience to God. Having discovered God's will, Abram willingly did what God required of him. Our spiritual renewal begins when we learn to seek God's will and follow it without reservation.

ABRAHAM & SARAH

Many give lip service to walking by faith, but Abraham and Sarah modeled it. They were imperfect-but-willing instruments used by God to accomplish his perfect plan.

God promised Abram a land and a nation of descendants, including one through whom all the peoples of the world would be blessed. This promise, or covenant, defied human logic: Abram was seventy-five; Sarai was ten years younger and infertile. Their hopes of children had long vanished. Yet Abram believed God's promises.

During their pilgrimage, the pair often strayed from God's perfect will. They succumbed to fear and dishonesty in their dealings with Pharaoh and Abimelech. They second-guessed God, attempting at one point to fulfill God's promise for a line of descendants by using Sarai's servant Hagar as a surrogate wife and mother. This union only resulted in domestic strife and jealousy, straining familial relationships. Abram behaved irresponsibly, and Sarai acted with deliberate cruelty. Years later, a wiser Abraham would heed God's instructions for caring for Hagar and her son.

Abram and Sarai's failures neither diminished God's love for them nor altered his commitment to his promises. Despite everything, the couple's mutual affection and respect survived. God changed their names to reflect the changes that his promises were making in their lives. Sarah's faith grew, and over twenty years after God's promises had first been given, she bore a son and named him Isaac. Sarah enjoyed her son for many years. After her death, she was tenderly mourned by both husband and son.

Worship and obedience characterized Abraham's life. He was even willing to surrender his son Isaac as a sacrifice when God tested his faith. Ultimately, God provided a ram as a burnt offering to take Isaac's place on the altar. Yet Abraham's example should inspire us to obey God in all we do, trusting that he will provide all that we need.

STRENGTHS AND ACCOMPLISHMENTS:

Both are heralded in Scripture as examples of faithful obedience.

Abraham's physical descendants comprise the Jewish nation, including Jesus the Messiah.

Abraham's spiritual descendants include all who have trusted Jesus for salvation.

WEAKNESSES AND MISTAKES:

They often second-guessed God's plans and foolishly attempted to assist him in fulfilling them.

When fearful, Abraham protected himself at the expense of Sarah's safety and integrity.

Both acted intolerably toward Hagar and her son.

LESSONS FROM THEIR LIVES:

A fresh start is possible at any stage of life.

The fulfillment of God's promises does not depend on our performance but on his grace.

It is dangerous to move ahead without first seeking God's direction.

Even when we stray, God can redirect our course and redeem our lives.

KEY VERSES:

"The LORD did for Sarah what he had promised. Sarah became pregnant and bore a son to Abraham in his old age, at the very time God had promised him" (21:1–2).

The story of Abraham and Sarah is found in Genesis 11—25. Among the many other references to Abraham are Romans 4:1–24; 9:7–9; Galatians 3:6–9, 14, 18; Hebrews 6:13–15; 7:1–2, 4–10; 11:8–12, 17–19; James 2:21–23 and 1 Peter 3:6. Sarah is mentioned in Romans 4:19; 9:9; Hebrews 11:11 and 1 Peter 3:6.

am in Egypt

10Now there was a famine in the land, and Abram went down to Egypt to live there for a while because the famine was severe. 11As he was about to enter Egypt, he said to his wife Sarai, "I know what a beautiful woman you are. 12When the Egyptians see you, they will say, 'This is his wife.' Then they will kill me but will let you live. 13Say you are my sister, so that I will be treated well for your sake and my life will be spared because of you."

14When Abram came to Egypt, the Egyptians saw that she was a very beautiful woman. 15And when Pharaoh's officials saw her, they praised her to Pharaoh, and she was taken into his palace. 16He treated Abram well for her sake, and Abram acquired sheep and cattle, male and female donkeys, menservants and maidservants, and camels.

17But the LORD inflicted serious diseases on Pharaoh and his household because of Abram's wife Sarai. 18So Pharaoh summoned Abram. "What have you done to me?" he said. "Why didn't you tell me she was your wife? 19Why did you say, 'She is my sister,' so that I took her to be my wife? Now then, here is your wife. Take her and go!" 20Then Pharaoh gave orders about Abram to his men, and they sent him on his way, with his wife and everything he had.

Abram and Lot Separate

13 So Abram went up from Egypt to the Negev, with his wife and everything he had, and Lot went with him. 2Abram had become very wealthy in livestock and in silver and gold.

3From the Negev he went from place to place until he came to Bethel, to the place between Bethel and Ai where his tent had been earlier 4and where he had first built an altar. There Abram called on the name of the LORD.

5Now Lot, who was moving about with Abram, also had flocks and herds and tents. 6But the land could not support them while they stayed together, for their possessions were so great that they were not able to stay together. 7And quarreling arose between Abram's herdsmen and the herdsmen of Lot. The Canaanites and Perizzites were also living in the land at that time.

8So Abram said to Lot, "Let's not have any quarreling between you and me, or between your herdsmen and mine, for we are brothers. 9Is not the whole land before you? Let's part company. If you go to the left, I'll go to the right; if you go to the right, I'll go to the left."

10Lot looked up and saw that the whole plain of the Jordan was well watered, like the garden of the LORD, like the land of Egypt, toward Zoar. (This was before the LORD destroyed Sodom and Gomorrah.) 11So Lot chose for himself the whole plain of the Jordan and set out toward the east. The two men parted company: 12Abram lived in the land of Canaan, while Lot lived among the cities of the plain and pitched his tents near Sodom. 13Now the men of Sodom were wicked and were sinning greatly against the LORD.

14The LORD said to Abram after Lot had parted from him, "Lift up your eyes from where you are and look north and south, east and west. 15All the land that you see I will give to you and your offspring[a] forever. 16I will make your offspring like the dust of the earth, so that if anyone could count the dust, then your offspring could be counted. 17Go, walk through the length and breadth of the land, for I am giving it to you."

18So Abram moved his tents and went to live near the great trees of Mamre at Hebron, where he built an altar to the LORD.

[a] 15 Or *seed*; also in verse 16

12:10 Abram arrived at his final destination only to find the promised land ravaged by famine. It probably wasn't what he had expected or hoped for, but it was the place that God had intended for him and his descendants to live. In our lives there will be times when things are difficult. We may need to do things that are not comfortable or easy. But we need to follow God—even when his plan leads us down paths we had neither expected or hoped for.

12:11–13 Abram's lie showed his lack of faith in God. He didn't believe that God would protect him. So Abram took things into his own hands, lying to protect what was important to him. We may feel that a lie is justified in such instances, but all lies reap long-term consequences. It is best to trust God to protect us and tell the truth. The God of truth will stand with us as we dare to speak the truth.

12:11–20 As Abram and Sarai approached Egypt, Abram began to fear that the Egyptians would kill him to take his beautiful wife. So Abram and Sarai spun a lie to protect their relationship. They spread a story that they were brother and sister. This was a half-truth—they were half siblings. But a half-truth is a whole lie. Like most lies, this one backfired, almost destroying Abram and Sarai's marriage. Total honesty is an essential key to spiritual renewal. We must be careful and avoid doing what Abram and Sarai did, even though they lied with the best of intentions. Dishonesty never pays—never try to rationalize it.

13:5–11 A conflict developed between the families of Abram and Lot over pasture land for their flocks. To strengthen the strained family relationship, Abram offered Lot first choice of the land. Abram realized that people were more important than possessions, so he sacrificed his right to the best land in order to maintain harmony between the families. We need to learn this important lesson: Our relationships are more important than the things we own.

13:11–13 One bad choice often leads to another. The choices Lot made here and in the following chapters led him to his ultimate downfall. Here, Lot selfishly chose the best land and the easy lifestyle that would accompany it. In 13:12–13, Lot chose to move closer to the wicked city of Sodom. In 19:1–18, Lot chose to become an important man in this wicked place. In 19:30–38, Lot's fall reached its final depths and resulted in incestuous relations with his daughters. We need to remember Lot and think ahead, reflecting on the probable consequences of our present decisions.

Abram Rescues Lot

14 At this time Amraphel king of Shinar,[a]
Arioch king of Ellasar, Kedorlaomer
king of Elam and Tidal king of Goiim 2went to
war against Bera king of Sodom, Birsha king of
Gomorrah, Shinab king of Admah, Shemeber
king of Zeboiim, and the king of Bela (that is,
Zoar). 3All these latter kings joined forces in the
Valley of Siddim (the Salt Sea[b]). 4For twelve
years they had been subject to Kedorlaomer,
but in the thirteenth year they rebelled.
5In the fourteenth year, Kedorlaomer and the
kings allied with him went out and defeated the
Rephaites in Ashteroth Karnaim, the Zuzites in
Ham, the Emites in Shaveh Kiriathaim 6and the
Horites in the hill country of Seir, as far as El
Paran near the desert. 7Then they turned back
and went to En Mishpat (that is, Kadesh), and
they conquered the whole territory of the Amalekites, as well as the Amorites who were living
in Hazazon Tamar.
8Then the king of Sodom, the king of Gomorrah, the king of Admah, the king of Zeboiim and the king of Bela (that is, Zoar) marched
out and drew up their battle lines in the Valley
of Siddim 9against Kedorlaomer king of Elam,
Tidal king of Goiim, Amraphel king of Shinar
and Arioch king of Ellasar—four kings against
five. 10Now the Valley of Siddim was full of tar
pits, and when the kings of Sodom and Gomorrah fled, some of the men fell into them and the
rest fled to the hills. 11The four kings seized all
the goods of Sodom and Gomorrah and all
their food; then they went away. 12They also
carried off Abram's nephew Lot and his possessions, since he was living in Sodom.
13One who had escaped came and reported
this to Abram the Hebrew. Now Abram was
living near the great trees of Mamre the Amorite, a brother[c] of Eshcol and Aner, all of
whom were allied with Abram. 14When Abram
heard that his relative had been taken captive,
he called out the 318 trained men born in his
household and went in pursuit as far as Dan.
15During the night Abram divided his men to
attack them and he routed them, pursuing them
as far as Hobah, north of Damascus. 16He recovered all the goods and brought back his relative
Lot and his possessions, together with the wom-
en and the other people.
17After Abram returned from defeating Kedorlaomer and the kings allied with him, the
king of Sodom came out to meet him in the
Valley of Shaveh (that is, the King's Valley).
18Then Melchizedek king of Salem[d]
brought out bread and wine. He was priest of
God Most High, 19and he blessed Abram, saying,

"Blessed be Abram by God Most High,
Creator[e] of heaven and earth.
20And blessed be[f] God Most High,
who delivered your enemies into your
hand."

Then Abram gave him a tenth of everything.
21The king of Sodom said to Abram, "Give
me the people and keep the goods for yourself."
22But Abram said to the king of Sodom, "I
have raised my hand to the LORD, God Most
High, Creator of heaven and earth, and have
taken an oath 23that I will accept nothing belonging to you, not even a thread or the thong
of a sandal, so that you will never be able to say,
'I made Abram rich.' 24I will accept nothing but
what my men have eaten and the share that
belongs to the men who went with me—to Aner,
Eshcol and Mamre. Let them have their share."

God's Covenant With Abram

15 After this, the word of the LORD came to
Abram in a vision:

"Do not be afraid, Abram.
I am your shield,[g]
your very great reward.[h]"

2But Abram said, "O Sovereign LORD, what
can you give me since I remain childless and the
one who will inherit[i] my estate is Eliezer of
Damascus?" 3And Abram said, "You have given
me no children; so a servant in my household
will be my heir."
4Then the word of the LORD came to him:
"This man will not be your heir, but a son
coming from your own body will be your heir."
5He took him outside and said, "Look up at the
heavens and count the stars—if indeed you can
count them." Then he said to him, "So shall
your offspring be."
6Abram believed the LORD, and he credited it
to him as righteousness.

[a] *1* That is, Babylonia; also in verse 9 [b] *3* That is, the Dead Sea [c] *13* Or *a relative;* or *an ally* [d] *18* That is, Jerusalem [e] *19* Or *Possessor;* also in verse 22 [f] *20* Or *And praise be to* [g] *1* Or *sovereign* [h] *1* Or *shield; / your reward will be very great* [i] *2* The meaning of the Hebrew for this phrase is uncertain.

14:14–16 A number of important character traits emerge as we examine Abram's prompt military action. He proved himself to be a man of courage, always ready to act when the situation demanded it. He was willing to give up certain luxuries in order to follow God's plan. These are all important traits for us to emulate as we seek to maintain our spiritual gains.

15:4–5 God's promise of numerous children must have stretched Abram's faith to the limit. God's plan for Abram seemed an impossibility—thousands of descendants from an old man and a barren woman. But God's promise did actually come about. God's plans for us may be beyond belief—even impossible. But with God, nothing is impossible!

15:6 This is one of the most important verses in the Old Testament. Abram believed God, and God considered him righteous. In other words, it was Abram's faith, not his works, that made him righteous before God. To continue growing spiritually, we need to trust God more and trust our own works less. We don't have the power to overcome sin alone, but God will help us through the toughest temptations if we trust him. God will count us righteous

7He also said to him, "I am the LORD, who brought you out of Ur of the Chaldeans to give you this land to take possession of it."

8But Abram said, "O Sovereign LORD, how can I know that I will gain possession of it?"

9So the LORD said to him, "Bring me a heifer, a goat and a ram, each three years old, along with a dove and a young pigeon."

10Abram brought all these to him, cut them in two and arranged the halves opposite each other; the birds, however, he did not cut in half. 11Then birds of prey came down on the carcasses, but Abram drove them away.

12As the sun was setting, Abram fell into a deep sleep, and a thick and dreadful darkness came over him. 13Then the LORD said to him, "Know for certain that your descendants will be strangers in a country not their own, and they will be enslaved and mistreated four hundred years. 14But I will punish the nation they serve as slaves, and afterward they will come out with great possessions. 15You, however, will go to your fathers in peace and be buried at a good old age. 16In the fourth generation your descendants will come back here, for the sin of the Amorites has not yet reached its full measure."

17When the sun had set and darkness had fallen, a smoking firepot with a blazing torch appeared and passed between the pieces. 18On that day the LORD made a covenant with Abram and said, "To your descendants I give this land, from the river[a] of Egypt to the great river, the Euphrates— 19the land of the Kenites, Kenizzites, Kadmonites, 20Hittites, Perizzites, Rephaites, 21Amorites, Canaanites, Girgashites and Jebusites."

Hagar and Ishmael

16 Now Sarai, Abram's wife, had borne him no children. But she had an Egyptian maidservant named Hagar; 2so she said to Abram, "The LORD has kept me from having children. Go, sleep with my maidservant; perhaps I can build a family through her."

Abram agreed to what Sarai said. 3So after Abram had been living in Canaan ten years, Sarai his wife took her Egyptian maidservant Hagar and gave her to her husband to be his wife. 4He slept with Hagar, and she conceived.

When she knew she was pregnant, she began to despise her mistress. 5Then Sarai said to Abram, "You are responsible for the wrong I am suffering. I put my servant in your arms, and now that she knows she is pregnant, she despises me. May the LORD judge between you and me."

6"Your servant is in your hands," Abram said. "Do with her whatever you think best." Then Sarai mistreated Hagar; so she fled from her.

7The angel of the LORD found Hagar near a spring in the desert; it was the spring that is beside the road to Shur. 8And he said, "Hagar, servant of Sarai, where have you come from, and where are you going?"

"I'm running away from my mistress Sarai," she answered.

9Then the angel of the LORD told her, "Go back to your mistress and submit to her." 10The angel added, "I will so increase your descendants that they will be too numerous to count."

11The angel of the LORD also said to her:

"You are now with child
  and you will have a son.
You shall name him Ishmael,[b]
  for the LORD has heard of your misery.
12He will be a wild donkey of a man;
  his hand will be against everyone
  and everyone's hand against him,
and he will live in hostility
  toward[c] all his brothers."

13She gave this name to the LORD who spoke to her: "You are the God who sees me," for she said, "I have now seen[d] the One who sees me." 14That is why the well was called Beer Lahai Roi[e]; it is still there, between Kadesh and Bered.

15So Hagar bore Abram a son, and Abram gave the name Ishmael to the son she had borne. 16Abram was eighty-six years old when Hagar bore him Ishmael.

The Covenant of Circumcision

17 When Abram was ninety-nine years old, the LORD appeared to him and said, "I am God Almighty[f]; walk before me and be blameless. 2I will confirm my covenant between me and you and will greatly increase your numbers."

3Abram fell facedown, and God said to him, 4"As for me, this is my covenant with you: You

[a]18 Or *Wadi* [b]11 *Ishmael* means *God hears.* [c]12 Or *live to the east / of* [d]13 Or *seen the back of* [e]14 *Beer Lahai Roi* means *well of the Living One who sees me.* [f]1 Hebrew *El-Shaddai*

---

because of our trust in him, not because of our attempts to be perfect.

16:1–4 God's promise of a child had been given about two years earlier, but nothing had happened yet. Sometimes the hardest part of surrendering to God is the waiting. Here Abram and Sarai show us what not to do when things don't progress as quickly as we had hoped. Rather than waiting for God, they took matters into their own hands. They chose a servant girl, Hagar, to be a surrogate mother for Abram's son. This "solution" resulted in a complicated family relationship that has served as a source of conflict to this day. Abram's descendants through Hagar are the Arab nations. Their conflict with the Jews, Abram's descendants through Sarai, keeps the Middle East in constant turmoil.

16:7–13 When Hagar was helpless to help herself, when she recognized her desperate need, the angel of the Lord came and ministered to her. Often God waits and does not enter our situations to help us until we recognize that our situation is desperate and in need of outside help. When we see the truth, admit our need and cry out to God, he is ready to step in.

Hagar & Ishmael

Hagar's life is often overshadowed by two prominent people—Abraham and Sarah. Her story is woven into the fabric of great events that make up Abraham's life. Yet God chose this "insignificant" woman to bear a son who would become the father of the Arab nations.

When Hagar became pregnant, she looked down on her mistress, Sarah, who had been unable to bear children. Hagar's attitude caused a great deal of strife in Abraham's family and resulted in much suffering for Hagar. The pain and alienation she suffered because of her baby could have put considerable strain on her mother-child relationship, but Hagar showed no regrets about having a son. She joyfully received him and accepted him despite the complicated and emotionally charged circumstances surrounding his birth.

Hagar and her son Ishmael had much in common. They were both rejected by Abraham's household. Together they experienced the torture of the hot, barren desert after Sarah demanded that Abraham send them away. They became nameless outcasts, discarded by those who had once valued them. Under such circumstances it must have been difficult to see themselves in the same light and with the same value that God placed on them.

Yet this mother and her son persevered through these trials because of their faith in the God who had appeared to them in the wilderness. Hagar and Ishmael knew that they were of great worth in God's sight, and they rebuilt their identity upon his promises. To this day their story illustrates God's deep concern for all who have been discarded and rejected. Their story also shows us that God's assessment of our lives is often far above what other people may think about us.

STRENGTHS AND ACCOMPLISHMENTS:

Hagar was willing to humbly return to Sarah even though she had been badly mistreated.

Hagar was loyal to her son even though he was the source of many of her trials.

WEAKNESSES AND MISTAKES:

When Hagar became pregnant, she scorned Sarah, prompting much of the strife that followed.

Hagar momentarily abandoned her son under a tree at the time of his greatest need.

LESSONS FROM THEIR LIVES:

A loving mother-son relationship is a precious gift from God.

God is deeply concerned about those who have been abused and rejected.

God is able to restore a sense of self-worth even in the most trying times.

KEY VERSES:

"Go back to your mistress and submit to her . . . I will so increase your descendants that they will be too numerous to count . . . You are now with child and you will have a son. You shall name him Ishmael, for the LORD has heard of your misery" (16:9–11).

The story of Hagar and Ishmael is told in Genesis 16—21. The apostle Paul briefly discusses them in Galatians 4:21–31.

will be the father of many nations. 5No longer
will you be called Abram[a]; your name will be
Abraham,[b] for I have made you a father of
many nations. 6I will make you very fruitful; I
will make nations of you, and kings will come
from you. 7I will establish my covenant as an
everlasting covenant between me and you and
your descendants after you for the generations
to come, to be your God and the God of your
descendants after you. 8The whole land of Canaan, where you are now an alien, I will give
as an everlasting possession to you and your
descendants after you; and I will be their God."

9Then God said to Abraham, "As for you,
you must keep my covenant, you and your
descendants after you for the generations to
come. 10This is my covenant with you and your
descendants after you, the covenant you are to
keep: Every male among you shall be circumcised. 11You are to undergo circumcision, and it
will be the sign of the covenant between me and
you. 12For the generations to come every male
among you who is eight days old must be circumcised, including those born in your household or bought with money from a foreigner—
those who are not your offspring. 13Whether
born in your household or bought with your
money, they must be circumcised. My covenant
in your flesh is to be an everlasting covenant.
14Any uncircumcised male, who has not been
circumcised in the flesh, will be cut off from his
people; he has broken my covenant."

15God also said to Abraham, "As for Sarai
your wife, you are no longer to call her Sarai;
her name will be Sarah. 16I will bless her and
will surely give you a son by her. I will bless her
so that she will be the mother of nations; kings
of peoples will come from her."

17Abraham fell facedown; he laughed and
said to himself, "Will a son be born to a man
a hundred years old? Will Sarah bear a child at
the age of ninety?" 18And Abraham said to God,
"If only Ishmael might live under your blessing!"

19Then God said, "Yes, but your wife Sarah
will bear you a son, and you will call him
Isaac.[c] I will establish my covenant with him
as an everlasting covenant for his descendants
after him. 20And as for Ishmael, I have heard
you: I will surely bless him; I will make him
fruitful and will greatly increase his numbers.
He will be the father of twelve rulers, and I will
make him into a great nation. 21But my covenant I will establish with Isaac, whom Sarah
will bear to you by this time next year." 22When
he had finished speaking with Abraham, God
went up from him.

23On that very day Abraham took his son
Ishmael and all those born in his household
or bought with his money, every male in his
household, and circumcised them, as God told
him. 24Abraham was ninety-nine years old
when he was circumcised, 25and his son Ishmael was thirteen; 26Abraham and his son Ishmael
were both circumcised on that same day. 27And
every male in Abraham's household, including
those born in his household or bought from a
foreigner, was circumcised with him.

The Three Visitors

18 The LORD appeared to Abraham near
the great trees of Mamre while he was
sitting at the entrance to his tent in the heat of
the day. 2Abraham looked up and saw three
men standing nearby. When he saw them, he
hurried from the entrance of his tent to meet
them and bowed low to the ground.

3He said, "If I have found favor in your eyes,
my lord,[d] do not pass your servant by. 4Let a
little water be brought, and then you may all
wash your feet and rest under this tree. 5Let me
get you something to eat, so you can be refreshed and then go on your way—now that you
have come to your servant."

"Very well," they answered, "do as you say."

6So Abraham hurried into the tent to Sarah.
"Quick," he said, "get three seahs[e] of fine flour
and knead it and bake some bread."

7Then he ran to the herd and selected a
choice, tender calf and gave it to a servant, who
hurried to prepare it. 8He then brought some
curds and milk and the calf that had been prepared, and set these before them. While they
ate, he stood near them under a tree.

9"Where is your wife Sarah?" they asked him.

"There, in the tent," he said.

10Then the LORD[f] said, "I will surely return
to you about this time next year, and Sarah your
wife will have a son."

[a]5 *Abram* means *exalted father.* [b]5 *Abraham* means *father of many.* [c]19 *Isaac* means *he laughs.* [d]3 Or *O Lord* [e]6 That is, probably about 20 quarts (about 22 liters) [f]10 Hebrew *Then he*

17:5–6 Since Abram was childless, his name (meaning, "exalted father") must have been a source of embarrassment to him. Here his name is changed to Abraham, which means "father of many." Abraham's name, in a real sense, became his promise from God, a continual reminder and source of hope that God would come through for him in the end.

17:9–10, 24–27 Many of our significant relationships are symbolized by an outward sign. For example, many married people wear rings as a sign of their marriage commitment. Circumcision was a sign of the agreement, or covenant, between God and Abraham. It was a mark by which Abraham's descendants were set apart as God's special people. Inner changes need to be accompanied by outer signs too; beliefs need to be proven by actions. As changes begin to take place inside us as we are spiritually renewed, we need to express these changes outwardly in our actions and lifestyle.

18:1–6 Hebrews 13:2 urges the practice of hospitality since some have "entertained angels without knowing it." Abraham's treatment of the three strangers here may have been the background for this verse in Hebrews. Surely Abraham's is an example to be followed. As we progress spiritually, one of our goals should be to help others discover the new way of life that we have found. What better way than to be hospitable toward others?

Exploring God's Mercy, Learning God's Heart

Genesis 18:1 – 33 Among the many spiritual disciplines, prayer can be one of the most frustrating as well as one of the most rewarding. We know we need to pray, but few of us pray consistently with the depth that prayer deserves. Often we don't feel like praying, and our thoughts wander. Some of us aren't even convinced that God wants to listen to us.

Genesis 18 presents an encounter between God and Abraham that gives us many insights into prayer. Some see God and Abraham's exchange much like marketplace bargaining. But this passage deserves another look. It is more of a dialogue between loving friends who are tackling a mutual concern than a negotiation between opposing parties.

First, this passage shows us that *the Lord comes to us* (18:1 – 15). Even as the angel of the Lord came to Abraham, God has taken the initiative to meet us, to have fellowship with us. This process shows us that prayer centers not on our requests but on our relationship with God. Through Jesus Christ, God has come in the flesh and fulfilled his promises to us (see 2 Corinthians 1:19 – 22). We do not have to coax or cajole God to pay attention to us.

The encounter in Genesis 18 also shows us that *the Lord regards us as "friends."* The Lord's kind and thoughtful interactions with Abraham reveal that he values us and enjoys speaking and listening to us. In Isaiah 41:8 God called Abraham "my friend." In John 15:15 Jesus said, "I have called you friends." God reveals his heart to us through his Word, and our friendship with him is experienced and deepened through prayer.

This passage also reveals that *the Lord wants to show us his ways.* The Lord wanted Abraham and his descendants to sense God's justice and compassion for humanity, so God carefully investigated the complaint against Sodom and listened to Abraham's requests for mercy.

Note that Genesis 18 contains the themes of both redemption and judgment. God's redemption is shown in the three men's promise that Sarah would have a child. However, when "the men got up to leave, they looked down toward Sodom" with the intention of executing judgment on the city (18:16). In this way, a promise was given before judgment was rendered so that Abraham would see God's mercy as well as his justice. Like Abraham, we must look for both facets of God's character.

Do you see God as a loving friend or as someone with whom to negotiate? Do you trust him to fulfill his promises or expect him to reject your requests? What is your attitude toward disasters? Abraham viewed bad news as a call to intercessory prayer. Too often we wring our hands in worry when we should fold them in prayerful faith and compassionate intercession.

Putting It Into Practice

Take time to reflect on your view of God. Is there a person or situation that you desperately long to see changed? One that is worrying you because it seems so depressing or hopeless or possibly too good to happen? Bring this situation to God — not as a negotiation but as a dialogue between two special friends who both want what is best. Give God a chance to come to you as a friend and show you his way.

For more on prayer, turn to Exodus 17.

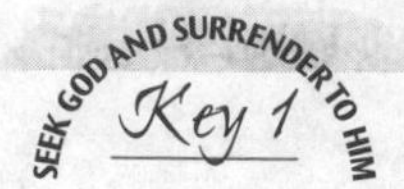

Following the Road to Life

Genesis 18:20–33 Surrendering to God places us on the narrow road that leads to life. The broad road, which leads to destruction (Matthew 7:13–14), is populated by people who have, in essence, surrendered to their own desires and will. This was the case of the inhabitants of Sodom. The sinful people who lived there had not given their lives to God and were destined for destruction. On the other hand, Abraham had chosen to follow God, even though he didn't know where God was leading him. As a result, he was blessed with provision, protection, and blessing from God. We see the how these two paths lead to very different destinations as we study the Lord's encounter with Abraham regarding Sodom's impending destruction.

The Lord revealed to Abraham that he intended to destroy the people of Sodom for their wickedness. But Abraham's nephew Lot lived among these people, and he was concerned for his welfare. So Abraham approached God, asking, "Will you sweep away the righteous with the wicked? What if there are fifty righteous people in the city? Will you really sweep it away and not spare the place for the sake of the fifty righteous people in it? Far be it from you to do such a thing" (18:23–25). After a sort of "bargaining" episode, the Lord eventually rewarded Abraham's persistent concern by agreeing to spare the city for the sake of ten innocent people (18:32). God still destroyed the city, however, because of its wickedness, but he did save Lot and his family. Yet even Lot's wife hesitated to surrender to God's leading, so she did not share in her family's dramatic rescue.

Surrendering our lives to God leads us to a relationship with him that offers safety and allows us to reach out on behalf of others. But, as we will see throughout our Scriptural readings, those who choose to map their own course and pursue their own desires inevitably encounter grave dangers. Those who refuse to surrender to God remove themselves from his gracious protection and intervention.

Turn to Deuteronomy 30.

Now Sarah was listening at the entrance to
the tent, which was behind him. 11Abraham
and Sarah were already old and well advanced
in years, and Sarah was past the age of childbearing. 12So Sarah laughed to herself as she
thought, "After I am worn out and my master[a]
is old, will I now have this pleasure?"
13Then the LORD said to Abraham, "Why did
Sarah laugh and say, 'Will I really have a child,
now that I am old?' 14Is anything too hard for
the LORD? I will return to you at the appointed
time next year and Sarah will have a son."
15Sarah was afraid, so she lied and said, "I
did not laugh."
But he said, "Yes, you did laugh."

Abraham Pleads for Sodom

16When the men got up to leave, they looked
down toward Sodom, and Abraham walked
along with them to see them on their way.
17Then the LORD said, "Shall I hide from Abraham what I am about to do? 18Abraham will
surely become a great and powerful nation, and
all nations on earth will be blessed through
him. 19For I have chosen him, so that he will
direct his children and his household after him
to keep the way of the LORD by doing what is
right and just, so that the LORD will bring about
for Abraham what he has promised him."
20Then the LORD said, "The outcry against
Sodom and Gomorrah is so great and their sin
so grievous 21that I will go down and see if what
they have done is as bad as the outcry that has
reached me. If not, I will know."
22The men turned away and went toward
Sodom, but Abraham remained standing before
the LORD.[b] 23Then Abraham approached him
and said: "Will you sweep away the righteous
with the wicked? 24What if there are fifty righteous people in the city? Will you really sweep
it away and not spare[c] the place for the sake of
the fifty righteous people in it? 25Far be it from
you to do such a thing—to kill the righteous
with the wicked, treating the righteous and the

[a]12 Or *husband* [b]22 Masoretic Text; an ancient Hebrew scribal tradition *but the LORD remained standing before Abraham* [c]24 Or *forgive;* also in verse 26

18:17–19 Many people wonder why God chose one man and his family out of all others. These verses show us that God had an important purpose for choosing this one family. God picked Abraham so he could teach his descendants God's ways. Through Abraham's ancestral line would come Jesus the Messiah, a source of blessing for all the nations of the earth. God never planned to bless only one family. God chose one family to bring blessings and a means of redemption to all of us.

18:22–32 Often, we are urged to pray for others who have problems and difficulties. In these verses, we see Abraham as he entreated God on behalf of Lot and his family. He was deeply concerned for their welfare and interceded for them as he spoke with God. We also must reach out and help others who are in need. Prayer is a powerful means of doing this.

wicked alike. Far be it from you! Will not the
Judge[a] of all the earth do right?"
26The LORD said, "If I find fifty righteous
people in the city of Sodom, I will spare the
whole place for their sake."
27Then Abraham spoke up again: "Now that
I have been so bold as to speak to the Lord,
though I am nothing but dust and ashes, 28what
if the number of the righteous is five less than
fifty? Will you destroy the whole city because of
five people?"
"If I find forty-five there," he said, "I will not
destroy it."
29Once again he spoke to him, "What if only
forty are found there?"
He said, "For the sake of forty, I will not
do it."
30Then he said, "May the Lord not be angry,
but let me speak. What if only thirty can be
found there?"
He answered, "I will not do it if I find thirty
there."
31Abraham said, "Now that I have been so
bold as to speak to the Lord, what if only twenty
can be found there?"
He said, "For the sake of twenty, I will not
destroy it."
32Then he said, "May the Lord not be angry,
but let me speak just once more. What if only
ten can be found there?"
He answered, "For the sake of ten, I will not
destroy it."
33When the LORD had finished speaking with
Abraham, he left, and Abraham returned home.

Sodom and Gomorrah Destroyed

19 The two angels arrived at Sodom in the
evening, and Lot was sitting in the gateway of the city. When he saw them, he got up
to meet them and bowed down with his face to
the ground. 2"My lords," he said, "please turn
aside to your servant's house. You can wash
your feet and spend the night and then go on
your way early in the morning."
"No," they answered, "we will spend the
night in the square."
3But he insisted so strongly that they did go
with him and entered his house. He prepared a
meal for them, baking bread without yeast, and
they ate. 4Before they had gone to bed, all the
men from every part of the city of Sodom—both
young and old—surrounded the house. 5They
called to Lot, "Where are the men who came to
you tonight? Bring them out to us so that we
can have sex with them."
6Lot went outside to meet them and shut the
door behind him 7and said, "No, my friends.
Don't do this wicked thing. 8Look, I have two
daughters who have never slept with a man. Let
me bring them out to you, and you can do what
you like with them. But don't do anything to
these men, for they have come under the protection of my roof."
9"Get out of our way," they replied. And they
said, "This fellow came here as an alien, and
now he wants to play the judge! We'll treat you
worse than them." They kept bringing pressure
on Lot and moved forward to break down the
door.
10But the men inside reached out and pulled
Lot back into the house and shut the door.
11Then they struck the men who were at the
door of the house, young and old, with blindness so that they could not find the door.
12The two men said to Lot, "Do you have
anyone else here—sons-in-law, sons or daughters, or anyone else in the city who belongs to
you? Get them out of here, 13because we are
going to destroy this place. The outcry to the
LORD against its people is so great that he has
sent us to destroy it."
14So Lot went out and spoke to his sons-in-
law, who were pledged to marry[b] his daughters. He said, "Hurry and get out of this place,
because the LORD is about to destroy the city!"
But his sons-in-law thought he was joking.
15With the coming of dawn, the angels urged
Lot, saying, "Hurry! Take your wife and your
two daughters who are here, or you will be
swept away when the city is punished."
16When he hesitated, the men grasped his
hand and the hands of his wife and of his two
daughters and led them safely out of the city,
for the LORD was merciful to them. 17As soon as
they had brought them out, one of them said,
"Flee for your lives! Don't look back, and don't
stop anywhere in the plain! Flee to the mountains or you will be swept away!"
18But Lot said to them, "No, my lords,[c]
please! 19Your[d] servant has found favor in
your[d] eyes, and you[d] have shown great kindness to me in sparing my life. But I can't flee to
the mountains; this disaster will overtake me,
and I'll die. 20Look, here is a town near enough
to run to, and it is small. Let me flee to it—it is

[a]25 Or *Ruler* [b]14 Or *were married to* [c]18 Or *No, Lord*; or *No, my lord* [d]19 The Hebrew is singular.

19:16 Despite Lot's awareness of the impending doom of Sodom, he and his family continued to linger there. The angels had to physically force them to leave. Sometimes, even when we know what course of action is required, we need a push to get us moving. At other times, we may be needed to pull others out of situations that are dangerous for them. Let us thank God for the "angels" he has provided to help all of us in times of crisis.

19:17–26 As we seek to escape our sinful ways and the consequences of them, there is no looking back, no lingering. Doing so only results in our destruction. Lot's wife failed to follow the instructions the angels had given her family. They were to run from Sodom, never looking back. Lot's wife did look back, and it spelled her destruction. As we leave the destructive situations in our lives, it will be tempting to look back. But this final episode in the life of Lot's wife demonstrates the fatal consequences of that backward look. We need to run away from sin without looking back.

Lot & Family

Many people in this world live for wealth, comfort and ease, and they want to get them as quickly as possible! To make this happen, people often sacrifice the really important things in life. This was true of Abraham's nephew Lot. Looking for the easy road to wealth and comfort, he made decisions that eventually destroyed everything he had lived for.

Lot was his own worst enemy. He tended to think only of himself. Lot demonstrated this when he chose the rich pasture land of the valleys, leaving Abraham with the rugged hill country. Embracing the comforts of the valley's cities and the physical prosperity they offered, Lot grew blind to the legacy he was leaving his descendants. When the men of Sodom demanded that Lot send his angelic guests out to take part in their sexual practices, Lot offered his daughters to the men of Sodom instead. By desiring to be accepted by the sinful people of his adopted homeland, Lot failed to treat his daughters with the respect and protection they deserved.

The result of Lot's selfishness and greed was the ultimate loss of his fortune and the ruin of his family. Lot sacrificed his family and his character to the gods of comfort and wealth. He witnessed his wife's death as a result of her disobedience to God, a disobedience he himself had modeled for her. His daughters followed Lot's example, too. They used drunkenness, seduction and incest—the quickest and easiest means available—to overcome their lonely and childless states.

Our society places great value on wealth, comfort and success, calling us to join the mad rush to attain them. This pervasive focus in our society makes it difficult for us to view this attitude as harmful or as sinful. But indeed it is. Materialism's destructive effects upon people in our world are widespread. We must learn to put God first. If we follow Lot's example and put wealth first in our lives, we will ultimately lose the things that are really important—our families and our relationship with God.

STRENGTHS AND ACCOMPLISHMENTS:

Lot was successful at generating wealth.

The apostle Peter referred to him as a just and righteous man.

WEAKNESSES AND MISTAKES:

Lot often chose the easiest course of action, usually at the expense of doing what was right.

When faced with making decisions, Lot often thought only of himself.

Lot's daughters used sinful means to fulfill their desires instead of seeking God's provision.

LESSONS FROM THEIR LIVES:

If we live for comfort and wealth, they will come between us and our families.

We must take care of our responsibilities to God and people if we want our lives to be successful.

Mistakes made by parents often lead to similar mistakes made by their children.

When we put our desires for wealth and comfort before obedience to God, the results will be destructive.

KEY VERSES:

"The angels urged Lot, saying 'Hurry! Take your wife and your two daughters who are here, or you will be swept away when the city is punished.' When he hesitated, the men grasped his hand . . . and led them safely out of the city, for the Lord was merciful to them" (19:15–16).

The story of Lot and his family is told in Genesis 13—14 and 19. Lot is also mentioned in Deuteronomy 2:9; Luke 17:28–32 and 2 Peter 2:7–8.

very small, isn't it? Then my life will be spared."
21He said to him, "Very well, I will grant this
request too; I will not overthrow the town you
speak of. 22But flee there quickly, because I cannot do anything until you reach it." (That is why
the town was called Zoar.[a])
23By the time Lot reached Zoar, the sun had
risen over the land. 24Then the LORD rained
down burning sulfur on Sodom and Gomorrah—from the LORD out of the heavens. 25Thus
he overthrew those cities and the entire plain,
including all those living in the cities—and also
the vegetation in the land. 26But Lot's wife
looked back, and she became a pillar of salt.
27Early the next morning Abraham got up
and returned to the place where he had stood
before the LORD. 28He looked down toward
Sodom and Gomorrah, toward all the land of
the plain, and he saw dense smoke rising from
the land, like smoke from a furnace.
29So when God destroyed the cities of the
plain, he remembered Abraham, and he
brought Lot out of the catastrophe that overthrew the cities where Lot had lived.

Lot and His Daughters

30Lot and his two daughters left Zoar and
settled in the mountains, for he was afraid to
stay in Zoar. He and his two daughters lived in
a cave. 31One day the older daughter said to the
younger, "Our father is old, and there is no
man around here to lie with us, as is the custom
all over the earth. 32Let's get our father to drink
wine and then lie with him and preserve our
family line through our father."
33That night they got their father to drink
wine, and the older daughter went in and lay
with him. He was not aware of it when she lay
down or when she got up.
34The next day the older daughter said to the
younger, "Last night I lay with my father. Let's
get him to drink wine again tonight, and you go
in and lie with him so we can preserve our
family line through our father." 35So they got
their father to drink wine that night also, and
the younger daughter went and lay with him.
Again he was not aware of it when she lay down
or when she got up.
36So both of Lot's daughters became pregnant by their father. 37The older daughter had a
son, and she named him Moab[b]; he is the
father of the Moabites of today. 38The younger
daughter also had a son, and she named him
Ben-Ammi[c]; he is the father of the Ammonites
of today.

Abraham and Abimelech

20 Now Abraham moved on from there
into the region of the Negev and lived
between Kadesh and Shur. For a while he stayed
in Gerar, 2and there Abraham said of his wife
Sarah, "She is my sister." Then Abimelech king
of Gerar sent for Sarah and took her.
3But God came to Abimelech in a dream one
night and said to him, "You are as good as dead
because of the woman you have taken; she is a
married woman."
4Now Abimelech had not gone near her, so
he said, "Lord, will you destroy an innocent
nation? 5Did he not say to me, 'She is my sister,'
and didn't she also say, 'He is my brother'? I
have done this with a clear conscience and clean
hands."
6Then God said to him in the dream, "Yes,
I know you did this with a clear conscience, and
so I have kept you from sinning against me.
That is why I did not let you touch her. 7Now
return the man's wife, for he is a prophet, and
he will pray for you and you will live. But if you
do not return her, you may be sure that you and
all yours will die."
8Early the next morning Abimelech summoned all his officials, and when he told them
all that had happened, they were very much
afraid. 9Then Abimelech called Abraham in and
said, "What have you done to us? How have I
wronged you that you have brought such great
guilt upon me and my kingdom? You have
done things to me that should not be done."
10And Abimelech asked Abraham, "What was
your reason for doing this?"
11Abraham replied, "I said to myself, 'There
is surely no fear of God in this place, and they
will kill me because of my wife.' 12Besides, she
really is my sister, the daughter of my father
though not of my mother; and she became my
wife. 13And when God had me wander from my
father's household, I said to her, 'This is how
you can show your love to me: Everywhere we
go, say of me, "He is my brother." ' "
14Then Abimelech brought sheep and cattle
and male and female slaves and gave them to
Abraham, and he returned Sarah his wife to

[a]22 *Zoar* means *small*. [b]37 *Moab* sounds like the Hebrew for *from father*. [c]38 *Ben-Ammi* means *son of my people*.

19:30–38 The incest in Lot's family was a direct consequence of Lot's irresponsible decisions in the past. He had spent his years in a wicked city and had failed to find suitable husbands for his daughters. Their desire for children led to their deceit and incest. But though Lot failed in so many ways, many centuries later the apostle Peter used him as a clear example of one whose righteousness came by grace through faith (2 Peter 2:7–8). Lot was an extremely flawed person, but God is an extremely gracious God. There is hope available for each of us, no matter how sordid our past.

20:1–18 Why is it so difficult to learn life's most important lessons? To protect himself, Abraham lied, telling Abimelech that his wife, Sarah, was his sister. Sadly, Abraham had made this mistake before (12:10–20). Abraham had fallen into a pattern of using lies and deceit to protect himself, a practice that only caused pain to everyone involved. His deceit also displayed how weak Abraham's faith in God was when confronted with difficult situations. The truth is crucial to building healthy relationships. If we stand by the truth, we can trust God to stand by us when things get tough.

him. 15And Abimelech said, "My land is before you; live wherever you like."

16To Sarah he said, "I am giving your brother a thousand shekels[a] of silver. This is to cover the offense against you before all who are with you; you are completely vindicated."

17Then Abraham prayed to God, and God healed Abimelech, his wife and his slave girls so they could have children again, 18for the LORD had closed up every womb in Abimelech's household because of Abraham's wife Sarah.

The Birth of Isaac

21 Now the LORD was gracious to Sarah as he had said, and the LORD did for Sarah what he had promised. 2Sarah became pregnant and bore a son to Abraham in his old age, at the very time God had promised him. 3Abraham gave the name Isaac[b] to the son Sarah bore him. 4When his son Isaac was eight days old, Abraham circumcised him, as God commanded him. 5Abraham was a hundred years old when his son Isaac was born to him.

6Sarah said, "God has brought me laughter, and everyone who hears about this will laugh with me." 7And she added, "Who would have said to Abraham that Sarah would nurse children? Yet I have borne him a son in his old age."

Hagar and Ishmael Sent Away

8The child grew and was weaned, and on the day Isaac was weaned Abraham held a great feast. 9But Sarah saw that the son whom Hagar the Egyptian had borne to Abraham was mocking, 10and she said to Abraham, "Get rid of that slave woman and her son, for that slave woman's son will never share in the inheritance with my son Isaac."

11The matter distressed Abraham greatly because it concerned his son. 12But God said to him, "Do not be so distressed about the boy and your maidservant. Listen to whatever Sarah tells you, because it is through Isaac that your offspring[c] will be reckoned. 13I will make the son of the maidservant into a nation also, because he is your offspring."

14Early the next morning Abraham took some food and a skin of water and gave them to Hagar. He set them on her shoulders and then sent her off with the boy. She went on her way and wandered in the desert of Beersheba.

15When the water in the skin was gone, she put the boy under one of the bushes. 16Then she went off and sat down nearby, about a bowshot away, for she thought, "I cannot watch the boy die." And as she sat there nearby, she[d] began to sob.

17God heard the boy crying, and the angel of God called to Hagar from heaven and said to her, "What is the matter, Hagar? Do not be afraid; God has heard the boy crying as he lies there. 18Lift the boy up and take him by the hand, for I will make him into a great nation."

19Then God opened her eyes and she saw a well of water. So she went and filled the skin with water and gave the boy a drink.

20God was with the boy as he grew up. He lived in the desert and became an archer. 21While he was living in the Desert of Paran, his mother got a wife for him from Egypt.

The Treaty at Beersheba

22At that time Abimelech and Phicol the commander of his forces said to Abraham, "God is with you in everything you do. 23Now swear to me here before God that you will not deal falsely with me or my children or my descendants. Show to me and the country where you are living as an alien the same kindness I have shown to you."

24Abraham said, "I swear it."

25Then Abraham complained to Abimelech about a well of water that Abimelech's servants had seized. 26But Abimelech said, "I don't know who has done this. You did not tell me, and I heard about it only today."

27So Abraham brought sheep and cattle and gave them to Abimelech, and the two men made a treaty. 28Abraham set apart seven ewe lambs from the flock, 29and Abimelech asked Abraham, "What is the meaning of these seven ewe lambs you have set apart by themselves?"

30He replied, "Accept these seven lambs from my hand as a witness that I dug this well."

31So that place was called Beersheba,[e] because the two men swore an oath there.

32After the treaty had been made at Beersheba, Abimelech and Phicol the commander of his forces returned to the land of the Philistines. 33Abraham planted a tamarisk tree in Beersheba, and there he called upon the name of the LORD, the Eternal God. 34And Abraham stayed in the land of the Philistines for a long time.

Abraham Tested

22 Some time later God tested Abraham. He said to him, "Abraham!"

[a]16 That is, about 25 pounds (about 11.5 kilograms)
[b]3 *Isaac* means *he laughs.*
[c]12 Or *seed*
[d]16 Hebrew; Septuagint *the child*
[e]31 *Beersheba* can mean *well of seven* or *well of the oath.*

21:1–2 God keeps his word. When we claim his promises, we know that our sovereign God is able to fulfill them. Under normal circumstances there was no way that Sarah could have become a mother. But God gave her a child anyway. We may find ourselves in situations that seem just as impossible, our spiritual renewal just as unattainable; but with God, it can be a reality. With God, anything is possible.

22:1–2 God's request that Abraham sacrifice his son was a great test of faith, perhaps the greatest such test in history. Abraham's lifelong dreams converged in his beloved son Isaac. Wouldn't God's promise of numerous descendants be fulfilled through this child? Yet Abraham believed that God had his best in mind—and Abraham was right! He believed that no matter what God required of him, his obedience to God's plan was most important.

"Here I am," he replied.
2Then God said, "Take your son, your only
son, Isaac, whom you love, and go to the region
of Moriah. Sacrifice him there as a burnt offering on one of the mountains I will tell you
about."
3Early the next morning Abraham got up and
saddled his donkey. He took with him two of
his servants and his son Isaac. When he had cut
enough wood for the burnt offering, he set out
for the place God had told him about. 4On the
third day Abraham looked up and saw the place
in the distance. 5He said to his servants, "Stay
here with the donkey while I and the boy go
over there. We will worship and then we will
come back to you."
6Abraham took the wood for the burnt offering and placed it on his son Isaac, and he himself carried the fire and the knife. As the two of
them went on together, 7Isaac spoke up and
said to his father Abraham, "Father?"
"Yes, my son?" Abraham replied.
"The fire and wood are here," Isaac said, "but
where is the lamb for the burnt offering?"
8Abraham answered, "God himself will provide the lamb for the burnt offering, my son."
And the two of them went on together.
9When they reached the place God had told
him about, Abraham built an altar there and
arranged the wood on it. He bound his son
Isaac and laid him on the altar, on top of the
wood. 10Then he reached out his hand and took
the knife to slay his son. 11But the angel of the
LORD called out to him from heaven, "Abraham! Abraham!"
"Here I am," he replied.
12"Do not lay a hand on the boy," he said.
"Do not do anything to him. Now I know that
you fear God, because you have not withheld
from me your son, your only son."
13Abraham looked up and there in a thicket
he saw a ram[a] caught by its horns. He went
over and took the ram and sacrificed it as a
burnt offering instead of his son. 14So Abraham
called that place The LORD Will Provide. And to
this day it is said, "On the mountain of the
LORD it will be provided."
15The angel of the LORD called to Abraham
from heaven a second time 16and said, "I swear
by myself, declares the LORD, that because you
have done this and have not withheld your son,
your only son, 17I will surely bless you and
make your descendants as numerous as the
stars in the sky and as the sand on the seashore.
Your descendants will take possession of the
cities of their enemies, 18and through your offspring[b] all nations on earth will be blessed,
because you have obeyed me."
19Then Abraham returned to his servants,
and they set off together for Beersheba. And
Abraham stayed in Beersheba.

Nahor's Sons

20Some time later Abraham was told, "Milcah is also a mother; she has borne sons to your
brother Nahor: 21Uz the firstborn, Buz his
brother, Kemuel (the father of Aram), 22Kesed,
Hazo, Pildash, Jidlaph and Bethuel." 23Bethuel
became the father of Rebekah. Milcah bore
these eight sons to Abraham's brother Nahor.
24His concubine, whose name was Reumah,
also had sons: Tebah, Gaham, Tahash and Maacah.

The Death of Sarah

23 Sarah lived to be a hundred and
twenty-seven years old. 2She died at
Kiriath Arba (that is, Hebron) in the land of
Canaan, and Abraham went to mourn for Sarah
and to weep over her.
3Then Abraham rose from beside his dead
wife and spoke to the Hittites.[c] He said, 4"I
am an alien and a stranger among you. Sell me
some property for a burial site here so I can bury
my dead."
5The Hittites replied to Abraham, 6"Sir, listen to us. You are a mighty prince among us.
Bury your dead in the choicest of our tombs.
None of us will refuse you his tomb for burying
your dead."
7Then Abraham rose and bowed down before the people of the land, the Hittites. 8He
said to them, "If you are willing to let me bury

[a]13 Many manuscripts of the Masoretic Text, Samaritan Pentateuch, Septuagint and Syriac; most manuscripts of the Masoretic Text *a ram behind* ⌊*him*⌋
[b]18 Or *seed*
[c]3 Or *the sons of Heth*; also in verses 5, 7, 10, 16, 18 and 20

Abraham trusted that God would still make his promises come true, even without Isaac. Our faith in God's plan for us may be similarly tested. Are we ready to follow through with obedience?

22:8–13 Abraham was about to sacrifice his son Isaac. Much to the relief of father and son, however, God provided a substitute. We do not know what Abraham had in mind when he told his son that God would provide a lamb, but we do know that God has provided a sacrifice for us—not simply a ram caught in a thicket—but his only Son. Anyone who believes in him will have the means for discovering a new life now, and throughout eternity as well.

22:16–18 The love Abraham must have felt for this long awaited son! How his heart must have ached at the thought of killing him! At the end of the story we see that God spared Isaac by providing a ram as his substitute. God has provided a substitute for all of us—Jesus Christ. God did not spare himself the pain of seeing his Son suffer and die. He suffered so that we might be kept from suffering and be redeemed from sin and its destructive effects.

23:1–2 In this chapter we see Abraham mourning for his wife Sarah. His grief was genuine. He wanted to make proper preparations for paying his last respects. Grief comes into each of our lives, and proper channels for its expression must be found. If we fail to grieve properly over our personal losses by releasing our sorrows to God, it will be easy to fall away from God as we try to hide our pain. But if we express our pain constructively, it will be less likely to undermine our relationship with God and inhibit our spiritual growth.

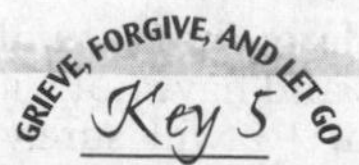

Relinquishing Our Losses

Genesis 23:1–4; 35:19–21 Whether it involves a loved one, a relationship, a dream or something of material value, we tend to carry our losses with us. Part of spiritual renewal involves releasing to God our losses and the circumstances surrounding them.

Abraham and his grandson Jacob both lost loved ones as they traveled to the promised land. When Sarah died, Abraham wept for her and then buried her there in Canaan (23:1–4, 19). A generation later, Jacob received a new name, Israel, and the promise of a great heritage in the promised land. Yet on his way there, he, too, lost his beloved wife. Rachel died while giving birth to their son Benjamin. "Over her tomb Jacob set up a pillar, and . . . Israel moved on again" (35:20–21).

As we make our journey through this life, inevitably we will experience losses. When we do, we need to respond as Abraham and Israel did: acknowledge our losses, grieve openly over them, forgive if necessary and then give our pain a proper burial. We may even build a monument to remind us of what we have loved and lost, but at some point we must relinquish our losses to God. Then we can press on to accomplish what God has called us to do in this life.

Turn to Nehemiah 8.

my dead, then listen to me and intercede with
Ephron son of Zohar on my behalf 9so he will
sell me the cave of Machpelah, which belongs
to him and is at the end of his field. Ask him to
sell it to me for the full price as a burial site
among you."
10Ephron the Hittite was sitting among his
people and he replied to Abraham in the hearing of all the Hittites who had come to the gate
of his city. 11"No, my lord," he said. "Listen to
me; I give[a] you the field, and I give[a] you the
cave that is in it. I give[a] it to you in the presence of my people. Bury your dead."
12Again Abraham bowed down before the
people of the land 13and he said to Ephron in
their hearing, "Listen to me, if you will. I will
pay the price of the field. Accept it from me so
I can bury my dead there."
14Ephron answered Abraham, 15"Listen to
me, my lord; the land is worth four hundred
shekels[b] of silver, but what is that between me
and you? Bury your dead."
16Abraham agreed to Ephron's terms and
weighed out for him the price he had named in
the hearing of the Hittites: four hundred shekels
of silver, according to the weight current among
the merchants.
17So Ephron's field in Machpelah near Mamre—both the field and the cave in it, and all the
trees within the borders of the field—was deeded 18to Abraham as his property in the presence
of all the Hittites who had come to the gate of
the city. 19Afterward Abraham buried his wife
Sarah in the cave in the field of Machpelah near
Mamre (which is at Hebron) in the land of
Canaan. 20So the field and the cave in it were
deeded to Abraham by the Hittites as a burial
site.

Isaac and Rebekah

24 Abraham was now old and well advanced in years, and the LORD had
blessed him in every way. 2He said to the
chief[c] servant in his household, the one in
charge of all that he had, "Put your hand under
my thigh. 3I want you to swear by the LORD, the
God of heaven and the God of earth, that you
will not get a wife for my son from the daughters of the Canaanites, among whom I am living, 4but will go to my country and my own
relatives and get a wife for my son Isaac."
5The servant asked him, "What if the woman
is unwilling to come back with me to this land?
Shall I then take your son back to the country
you came from?"
6"Make sure that you do not take my son
back there," Abraham said. 7"The LORD, the God
of heaven, who brought me out of my father's
household and my native land and who spoke
to me and promised me on oath, saying, 'To
your offspring[d] I will give this land'—he will

[a] 11 Or *sell* [b] 15 That is, about 10 pounds (about 4.5 kilograms) [c] 2 Or *oldest* [d] 7 Or *seed*

Isaac & Rebekah

Deception is harmful to any relationship but especially to a relationship between a husband and wife. Isaac and Rebekah started out with a marriage built on mutual love and respect. As their marriage progressed, however, deception crept in on both sides, and as a result the family was torn apart by strife.

As Abraham had lied to Abimelech about Sarah, so Isaac tried to protect himself by lying to Abimelech, claiming that Rebekah was not his wife. He feared that Abimelech would kill him in order to take his wife. Deception based on the idea that "the end justifies the means" may sometimes seem like a necessary evil within some families. But in reality, it often begins a string of hurtful lies between marriage partners and other family members.

Isaac and Rebekah were blessed with twin sons, Esau and Jacob. Isaac favored Esau, while Rebekah preferred Jacob. This playing of favorites split the family and set the stage for further conflict and deception. When the time came for Isaac to give Esau his blessing, Jacob took part in Rebekah's plan to deceive her husband and grab the blessing for her favorite son. Deception had become a natural practice in their family relationships.

This story of deception in marriage is sad but hardly uncommon. What started out as a loving marriage based on honesty and a desire to serve God soon became an adversarial relationship filled with deception and distance. It is important to notice, however, that God remained faithful to his promises to Isaac and Rebekah despite their failures.

STRENGTHS AND ACCOMPLISHMENTS:

They had a caring and loving marriage—until their sons were born.

They were the recipients of God's promises to Abraham.

WEAKNESSES AND MISTAKES:

Isaac and Rebekah sometimes allowed the end to justify the means.

When facing difficult situations, Isaac and Rebekah sometimes lied to avoid conflict.

They alienated each other by playing favorites with their sons.

LESSONS FROM THEIR LIVES:

God keeps his promises and remains faithful even when we are faithless.

God's promises and plans are bigger than we are.

Playing favorites in a family is harmful.

Deception is destructive in marriage and in other significant relationships.

KEY VERSE:

"Isaac brought her into the tent of his mother Sarah, and he married Rebekah. So she became his wife, and he loved her; and Isaac was comforted after his mother's death" (24:67).

Isaac and Rebekah's story is told in Genesis 24—28. Both are mentioned in Romans 9:10. Isaac is also referred to in Romans 9:7; Hebrews 11:17–20 and James 2:21.

send his angel before you so that you can get a
wife for my son from there. 8If the woman is
unwilling to come back with you, then you will
be released from this oath of mine. Only do not
take my son back there." 9So the servant put his
hand under the thigh of his master Abraham
and swore an oath to him concerning this
matter.
10Then the servant took ten of his master's
camels and left, taking with him all kinds of
good things from his master. He set out for
Aram Naharaim[a] and made his way to the
town of Nahor. 11He had the camels kneel
down near the well outside the town; it was
toward evening, the time the women go out to
draw water.
12Then he prayed, "O LORD, God of my master Abraham, give me success today, and show
kindness to my master Abraham. 13See, I am
standing beside this spring, and the daughters
of the townspeople are coming out to draw water. 14May it be that when I say to a girl, 'Please
let down your jar that I may have a drink,' and
she says, 'Drink, and I'll water your camels
too'—let her be the one you have chosen for
your servant Isaac. By this I will know that you
have shown kindness to my master."
15Before he had finished praying, Rebekah
came out with her jar on her shoulder. She was
the daughter of Bethuel son of Milcah, who was
the wife of Abraham's brother Nahor. 16The girl
was very beautiful, a virgin; no man had ever
lain with her. She went down to the spring,
filled her jar and came up again.
17The servant hurried to meet her and said,
"Please give me a little water from your jar."
18"Drink, my lord," she said, and quickly lowered the jar to her hands and gave him a drink.
19After she had given him a drink, she said,
"I'll draw water for your camels too, until they
have finished drinking." 20So she quickly emptied her jar into the trough, ran back to the well
to draw more water, and drew enough for all
his camels. 21Without saying a word, the man
watched her closely to learn whether or not the
LORD had made his journey successful.
22When the camels had finished drinking,
the man took out a gold nose ring weighing
a beka[b] and two gold bracelets weighing ten
shekels.[c] 23Then he asked, "Whose daughter
are you? Please tell me, is there room in your
father's house for us to spend the night?"
24She answered him, "I am the daughter of
Bethuel, the son that Milcah bore to Nahor."
25And she added, "We have plenty of straw and
fodder, as well as room for you to spend the
night."
26Then the man bowed down and worshiped
the LORD, 27saying, "Praise be to the LORD, the
God of my master Abraham, who has not abandoned his kindness and faithfulness to my master. As for me, the LORD has led me on the
journey to the house of my master's relatives."
28The girl ran and told her mother's household about these things. 29Now Rebekah had a
brother named Laban, and he hurried out to the
man at the spring. 30As soon as he had seen the
nose ring, and the bracelets on his sister's arms,
and had heard Rebekah tell what the man
said to her, he went out to the man and found
him standing by the camels near the spring.
31"Come, you who are blessed by the LORD," he
said. "Why are you standing out here? I have
prepared the house and a place for the camels."
32So the man went to the house, and the
camels were unloaded. Straw and fodder were
brought for the camels, and water for him and
his men to wash their feet. 33Then food was set
before him, but he said, "I will not eat until I
have told you what I have to say."
"Then tell us," ⌞Laban⌟ said.
34So he said, "I am Abraham's servant. 35The
LORD has blessed my master abundantly, and
he has become wealthy. He has given him
sheep and cattle, silver and gold, menservants
and maidservants, and camels and donkeys.
36My master's wife Sarah has borne him a son
in her[d] old age, and he has given him everything he owns. 37And my master made me
swear an oath, and said, 'You must not get a
wife for my son from the daughters of the Canaanites, in whose land I live, 38but go to my
father's family and to my own clan, and get a
wife for my son.'
39"Then I asked my master, 'What if the
woman will not come back with me?'
40"He replied, 'The LORD, before whom I
have walked, will send his angel with you and
make your journey a success, so that you can get
a wife for my son from my own clan and from
my father's family. 41Then, when you go to my
clan, you will be released from my oath even if
they refuse to give her to you—you will be released from my oath.'
42"When I came to the spring today, I said,
'O LORD, God of my master Abraham, if you
will, please grant success to the journey on
which I have come. 43See, I am standing beside
this spring; if a maiden comes out to draw water
and I say to her, "Please let me drink a little
water from your jar," 44and if she says to me,
"Drink, and I'll draw water for your camels too,"
let her be the one the LORD has chosen for my
master's son.'
45"Before I finished praying in my heart, Rebekah came out, with her jar on her shoulder.
She went down to the spring and drew water,
and I said to her, 'Please give me a drink.'
46"She quickly lowered her jar from her
shoulder and said, 'Drink, and I'll water your
camels too.' So I drank, and she watered the
camels also.

[a]*10* That is, Northwest Mesopotamia [b]*22* That is, about 1/5 ounce (about 5.5 grams) [c]*22* That is, about 4 ounces (about 110 grams) [d]*36* Or *his*

47"I asked her, 'Whose daughter are you?'

"She said, 'The daughter of Bethuel son of Nahor, whom Milcah bore to him.'

"Then I put the ring in her nose and the bracelets on her arms, 48and I bowed down and worshiped the LORD. I praised the LORD, the God of my master Abraham, who had led me on the right road to get the granddaughter of my master's brother for his son. 49Now if you will show kindness and faithfulness to my master, tell me; and if not, tell me, so I may know which way to turn."

50Laban and Bethuel answered, "This is from the LORD; we can say nothing to you one way or the other. 51Here is Rebekah; take her and go, and let her become the wife of your master's son, as the LORD has directed."

52When Abraham's servant heard what they said, he bowed down to the ground before the LORD. 53Then the servant brought out gold and silver jewelry and articles of clothing and gave them to Rebekah; he also gave costly gifts to her brother and to her mother. 54Then he and the men who were with him ate and drank and spent the night there.

When they got up the next morning, he said, "Send me on my way to my master."

55But her brother and her mother replied, "Let the girl remain with us ten days or so; then you[a] may go."

56But he said to them, "Do not detain me, now that the LORD has granted success to my journey. Send me on my way so I may go to my master."

57Then they said, "Let's call the girl and ask her about it." 58So they called Rebekah and asked her, "Will you go with this man?"

"I will go," she said.

59So they sent their sister Rebekah on her way, along with her nurse and Abraham's servant and his men. 60And they blessed Rebekah and said to her,

"Our sister, may you increase
  to thousands upon thousands;
may your offspring possess
  the gates of their enemies."

61Then Rebekah and her maids got ready and mounted their camels and went back with the man. So the servant took Rebekah and left.

62Now Isaac had come from Beer Lahai Roi, for he was living in the Negev. 63He went out to the field one evening to meditate,[b] and as he looked up, he saw camels approaching. 64Rebekah also looked up and saw Isaac. She got down from her camel 65and asked the servant, "Who is that man in the field coming to meet us?"

"He is my master," the servant answered. So she took her veil and covered herself.

66Then the servant told Isaac all he had done. 67Isaac brought her into the tent of his mother Sarah, and he married Rebekah. So she became his wife, and he loved her; and Isaac was comforted after his mother's death.

The Death of Abraham

25 Abraham took[c] another wife, whose name was Keturah. 2She bore him Zimran, Jokshan, Medan, Midian, Ishbak and Shuah. 3Jokshan was the father of Sheba and Dedan; the descendants of Dedan were the Asshurites, the Letushites and the Leummites. 4The sons of Midian were Ephah, Epher, Hanoch, Abida and Eldaah. All these were descendants of Keturah.

5Abraham left everything he owned to Isaac. 6But while he was still living, he gave gifts to the sons of his concubines and sent them away from his son Isaac to the land of the east.

7Altogether, Abraham lived a hundred and seventy-five years. 8Then Abraham breathed his last and died at a good old age, an old man and full of years; and he was gathered to his people. 9His sons Isaac and Ishmael buried him in the cave of Machpelah near Mamre, in the field of Ephron son of Zohar the Hittite, 10the field Abraham had bought from the Hittites.[d] There Abraham was buried with his wife Sarah. 11After Abraham's death, God blessed his son Isaac, who then lived near Beer Lahai Roi.

Ishmael's Sons

12This is the account of Abraham's son Ishmael, whom Sarah's maidservant, Hagar the Egyptian, bore to Abraham.

13These are the names of the sons of Ishmael, listed in the order of their birth: Nebaioth the firstborn of Ishmael, Kedar, Adbeel, Mibsam, 14Mishma, Dumah, Massa, 15Hadad, Tema, Jetur, Naphish and Kedemah. 16These were the sons of Ishmael, and these are the names of the twelve tribal rulers according to their settlements and camps. 17Altogether, Ishmael lived a hundred and thirty-seven years. He breathed his last and died, and he was gathered to his people. 18His descendants settled in the area from Havilah to Shur, near the border of Egypt, as you go toward Asshur. And they lived in hostility toward[e] all their brothers.

Jacob and Esau

19This is the account of Abraham's son Isaac.

[a]55 Or *she* [b]63 The meaning of the Hebrew for this word is uncertain. [c]1 Or *had taken* [d]10 Or *the sons of Heth* [e]18 Or *lived to the east of*

24:67 When we lose someone close to us, it is important that we take some time for rebuilding. It is encouraging to note that, after losing a major family relationship, Isaac found comfort in a new one. When people are taken away from us through death or other devastating circumstances, we can ask God to provide others who will give us the support we need to live a healthy and productive life.

Abraham became the father of Isaac, 20and Isaac was forty years old when he married Rebekah daughter of Bethuel the Aramean from Paddan Aram[a] and sister of Laban the Aramean.

21Isaac prayed to the LORD on behalf of his wife, because she was barren. The LORD answered his prayer, and his wife Rebekah became pregnant. 22The babies jostled each other within her, and she said, "Why is this happening to me?" So she went to inquire of the LORD.

23The LORD said to her,

"Two nations are in your womb,
and two peoples from within you will be separated;
one people will be stronger than the other,
and the older will serve the younger."

24When the time came for her to give birth, there were twin boys in her womb. 25The first to come out was red, and his whole body was like a hairy garment; so they named him Esau.[b] 26After this, his brother came out, with his hand grasping Esau's heel; so he was named Jacob.[c] Isaac was sixty years old when Rebekah gave birth to them.

27The boys grew up, and Esau became a skillful hunter, a man of the open country, while Jacob was a quiet man, staying among the tents. 28Isaac, who had a taste for wild game, loved Esau, but Rebekah loved Jacob.

29Once when Jacob was cooking some stew, Esau came in from the open country, famished. 30He said to Jacob, "Quick, let me have some of that red stew! I'm famished!" (That is why he was also called Edom.[d])

31Jacob replied, "First sell me your birthright."

32"Look, I am about to die," Esau said. "What good is the birthright to me?"

33But Jacob said, "Swear to me first." So he swore an oath to him, selling his birthright to Jacob.

34Then Jacob gave Esau some bread and some lentil stew. He ate and drank, and then got up and left.

So Esau despised his birthright.

Isaac and Abimelech

26 Now there was a famine in the land—besides the earlier famine of Abraham's time—and Isaac went to Abimelech king of the Philistines in Gerar. 2The LORD appeared to Isaac and said, "Do not go down to Egypt; live in the land where I tell you to live. 3Stay in this land for a while, and I will be with you and will bless you. For to you and your descendants I will give all these lands and will confirm the oath I swore to your father Abraham. 4I will make your descendants as numerous as the stars in the sky and will give them all these lands, and through your offspring[e] all nations on earth will be blessed, 5because Abraham obeyed me and kept my requirements, my commands, my decrees and my laws." 6So Isaac stayed in Gerar.

7When the men of that place asked him about his wife, he said, "She is my sister," because he was afraid to say, "She is my wife." He thought, "The men of this place might kill me on account of Rebekah, because she is beautiful."

8When Isaac had been there a long time, Abimelech king of the Philistines looked down from a window and saw Isaac caressing his wife Rebekah. 9So Abimelech summoned Isaac and said, "She is really your wife! Why did you say, 'She is my sister'?"

Isaac answered him, "Because I thought I might lose my life on account of her."

10Then Abimelech said, "What is this you have done to us? One of the men might well have slept with your wife, and you would have brought guilt upon us."

11So Abimelech gave orders to all the people: "Anyone who molests this man or his wife shall surely be put to death."

12Isaac planted crops in that land and the same year reaped a hundredfold, because the LORD blessed him. 13The man became rich, and his wealth continued to grow until he became very wealthy. 14He had so many flocks and

[a]20 That is, Northwest Mesopotamia [b]25 *Esau* may mean *hairy;* he was also called Edom, which means *red.* [c]26 *Jacob* means *he grasps the heel* (figuratively, *he deceives*). [d]30 *Edom* means *red.* [e]4 Or *seed*

25:23 This prenatal prophecy concerning Jacob and Esau portends conflict between the brothers beyond a normal sibling rivalry! Unfortunately, the subsequent family history amply bears this out. Sibling rivalry is often very destructive to family relationships and can easily get out of control. Siblings often separate for life, carrying with them years of hard feelings that taint their relationships with others. Reconciliation with those we have hurt is one of the goals of spiritual renewal. Let us take steps toward restoring our important relationships with our siblings and those outside our family as well.

25:34 Esau traded his rights as a firstborn son for a bowl of stew to fill his empty stomach. He was indifferent to the things in life that were really important. His primary concern was his physical satisfaction, with no thought at all for his future. Esau was impatient. He hadn't learned how to wait well. This lesson is important for all of us. We need to view things from a long-term perspective. If we can picture the positive results of life as God intended it, we will be able to give up the momentary pleasures of sin that threaten to keep us from following God's plan.

26:6–11 Children learn from their parents. Unfortunately, they are not necessarily selective about what they learn. They don't always learn the good things and ignore the bad. These verses demonstrate what Isaac learned from his father Abraham. Doubtless, he had heard how Abraham had passed Sarah off as his sister to protect himself (12:10–20; 20:1–18). It is amazing how the sinful patterns of our parents are often repeated in our own lives, generation after generation! Isaac would have been wise to tell the truth and trust God to protect him. Our trust in God is one weapon we can use to fight against destructive family patterns.

herds and servants that the Philistines envied
him. 15So all the wells that his father's servants
had dug in the time of his father Abraham, the
Philistines stopped up, filling them with earth.
16Then Abimelech said to Isaac, "Move away
from us; you have become too powerful for us."
17So Isaac moved away from there and encamped in the Valley of Gerar and settled there.
18Isaac reopened the wells that had been dug in
the time of his father Abraham, which the Philistines had stopped up after Abraham died,
and he gave them the same names his father
had given them.
19Isaac's servants dug in the valley and discovered a well of fresh water there. 20But the
herdsmen of Gerar quarreled with Isaac's herdsmen and said, "The water is ours!" So he named
the well Esek,[a] because they disputed with
him. 21Then they dug another well, but they
quarreled over that one also; so he named it
Sitnah.[b] 22He moved on from there and dug
another well, and no one quarreled over it. He
named it Rehoboth,[c] saying, "Now the LORD
has given us room and we will flourish in the
land."
23From there he went up to Beersheba. 24That
night the LORD appeared to him and said, "I am
the God of your father Abraham. Do not be
afraid, for I am with you; I will bless you and
will increase the number of your descendants
for the sake of my servant Abraham."
25Isaac built an altar there and called on the
name of the LORD. There he pitched his tent,
and there his servants dug a well.
26Meanwhile, Abimelech had come to him
from Gerar, with Ahuzzath his personal adviser
and Phicol the commander of his forces. 27Isaac
asked them, "Why have you come to me, since
you were hostile to me and sent me away?"
28They answered, "We saw clearly that the
LORD was with you; so we said, 'There ought to
be a sworn agreement between us'—between us
and you. Let us make a treaty with you 29that
you will do us no harm, just as we did not
molest you but always treated you well and sent
you away in peace. And now you are blessed by
the LORD."
30Isaac then made a feast for them, and they
ate and drank. 31Early the next morning the
men swore an oath to each other. Then Isaac
sent them on their way, and they left him in
peace.
32That day Isaac's servants came and told
him about the well they had dug. They said,
"We've found water!" 33He called it Shibah,[d]
and to this day the name of the town has been
Beersheba.[e]
34When Esau was forty years old, he married
Judith daughter of Beeri the Hittite, and also
Basemath daughter of Elon the Hittite. 35They
were a source of grief to Isaac and Rebekah.

Jacob Gets Isaac's Blessing

27 When Isaac was old and his eyes were
so weak that he could no longer see, he
called for Esau his older son and said to him,
"My son."
"Here I am," he answered.
2Isaac said, "I am now an old man and don't
know the day of my death. 3Now then, get your
weapons—your quiver and bow—and go out to
the open country to hunt some wild game for
me. 4Prepare me the kind of tasty food I like
and bring it to me to eat, so that I may give you
my blessing before I die."
5Now Rebekah was listening as Isaac spoke
to his son Esau. When Esau left for the open
country to hunt game and bring it back, 6Rebek-
ah said to her son Jacob, "Look, I overheard
your father say to your brother Esau, 7'Bring me
some game and prepare me some tasty food to
eat, so that I may give you my blessing in the
presence of the LORD before I die.' 8Now, my
son, listen carefully and do what I tell you: 9Go
out to the flock and bring me two choice young
goats, so I can prepare some tasty food for your
father, just the way he likes it. 10Then take it to
your father to eat, so that he may give you his
blessing before he dies."
11Jacob said to Rebekah his mother, "But my
brother Esau is a hairy man, and I'm a man with
smooth skin. 12What if my father touches me?
I would appear to be tricking him and would
bring down a curse on myself rather than a
blessing."
13His mother said to him, "My son, let the
curse fall on me. Just do what I say; go and get
them for me."
14So he went and got them and brought
them to his mother, and she prepared some
tasty food, just the way his father liked it.
15Then Rebekah took the best clothes of Esau
her older son, which she had in the house, and
put them on her younger son Jacob. 16She also

[a]20 *Esek* means *dispute.* [b]21 *Sitnah* means *opposition.* [c]22 *Rehoboth* means *room.* [d]33 *Shibah* can mean *oath* or *seven.* [e]33 *Beersheba* can mean *well of the oath* or *well of seven.*

26:23–24 Isaac was afraid, and he had good reason to be. He was surrounded by hostile neighbors who greatly outnumbered his household. He didn't have a place to call his own, except the burial site of his parents. Isaac lived in Gerar "by permission," as it were. So God came to Isaac with this soothing message: "Do not be afraid." We may feel as if we don't belong anywhere. We may have forfeited our place in society. It may seem as though there are enemies all around us. But even when things are at their worst, we need to be aware that God is with us, whispering, "Do not be afraid."

27:1–29 It is heartbreaking to watch Rebekah and Jacob conspire to deceive Isaac. Notice the great lengths to which they went to fool the old man. They already knew that Jacob was the heir to God's promises through Abraham (see 25:23, 29–34), but through their deceit they tried to make God's plan happen. That never works without causing pain or adding trouble somewhere else. God is in charge of the timetable of our lives. We need to stick with the truth and move at his pace.

Esau & Jacob

Sibling rivalry is a natural, though sometimes difficult, aspect of family relationships. Brothers, especially those close in age, often don't get along well either as children or young adults. But the twins Esau and Jacob took this natural conflict to a dangerous level of intensity.

The rivalry between the twins was predicted by God even before the boys were born. The situation was only worsened by the parents' playing favorites with their sons. Isaac clearly preferred Esau, while Rebekah favored Jacob. Relationships in this family went from bad to worse when Esau sold Jacob his birthright for the momentary gratification of his hungry stomach.

One event finally shattered the already fragile relationship between these brothers. Jacob deceived his nearly blind father into giving him the blessing that was intended for Esau, the firstborn. Jacob's elaborate scheme, masterminded by his mother, so enraged Esau that he vowed to kill his brother after his father's death. Jacob fled for his life, a victim of his own lack of honesty. He settled with his uncle Laban and soon married Laban's two daughters Leah and Rachel.

While living with Laban's family, Jacob became the object of his uncle's own deceitful practices and learned some painful lessons about the importance of love and honesty that he had never learned at home. God had been working in Jacob's life, drawing Jacob progressively closer to himself. After years of separation and considerable emotional and spiritual growth in both men's lives, Jacob willingly faced his past. With a sure knowledge of God's presence, he set out on the long journey home. And, despite his fears, Jacob found forgiveness and reconciliation in the waiting embrace of his brother.

STRENGTHS AND ACCOMPLISHMENTS:

Jacob and Esau were willing to let go of past failures and redirect their lives toward a better future.

Esau was able to forgive despite feeling significant disappointment and anger.

Jacob matured to the point where he could be honest and humbly seek forgiveness.

WEAKNESSES AND MISTAKES:

Jacob and Esau were each intent on having his own way with little thought of how it might affect others.

Esau surrendered to his appetites, showing disrespect for his God-given birthright and suffered great losses as a result.

Jacob was often dishonest and deceitful in his dealings.

LESSONS FROM THEIR LIVES:

Parents should never play favorites with their children.

Forgiveness can occur even when deep hurts have been suffered.

Habitually deceitful people can still face the past, see the truth, accept responsibility for their sins and restore their relationships.

KEY VERSE:

"But Esau ran to meet Jacob and embraced him; he threw his arms around his neck and kissed him. And they wept" (33:4).

The story of Esau and Jacob is told in Genesis 25—33. Both are also mentioned in Malachi 1:2–3; Romans 9:10–13, and Hebrews 11:20–21. Esau is referred to in Hebrews 12:16–17, while Jacob is mentioned in Hosea 12:2–5; Matthew 1:2; 22:32; Acts 3:13 and Hebrews 11:9.

covered his hands and the smooth part of his
neck with the goatskins. 17Then she handed to
her son Jacob the tasty food and the bread she
had made.
18He went to his father and said, "My father."
"Yes, my son," he answered. "Who is it?"
19Jacob said to his father, "I am Esau your
firstborn. I have done as you told me. Please sit
up and eat some of my game so that you may
give me your blessing."
20Isaac asked his son, "How did you find it
so quickly, my son?"
"The LORD your God gave me success," he
replied.
21Then Isaac said to Jacob, "Come near so I
can touch you, my son, to know whether you
really are my son Esau or not."
22Jacob went close to his father Isaac, who
touched him and said, "The voice is the voice
of Jacob, but the hands are the hands of Esau."
23He did not recognize him, for his hands were
hairy like those of his brother Esau; so he
blessed him. 24"Are you really my son Esau?" he
asked.
"I am," he replied.
25Then he said, "My son, bring me some of
your game to eat, so that I may give you my
blessing."
Jacob brought it to him and he ate; and he
brought some wine and he drank. 26Then his
father Isaac said to him, "Come here, my son,
and kiss me."
27So he went to him and kissed him. When
Isaac caught the smell of his clothes, he blessed
him and said,

"Ah, the smell of my son
    is like the smell of a field
    that the LORD has blessed.
28May God give you of heaven's dew
    and of earth's richness—
    an abundance of grain and new wine.
29May nations serve you
    and peoples bow down to you.
Be lord over your brothers,
    and may the sons of your mother bow
        down to you.
May those who curse you be cursed
    and those who bless you be blessed."

30After Isaac finished blessing him and Jacob
had scarcely left his father's presence, his brother Esau came in from hunting. 31He too prepared some tasty food and brought it to his
father. Then he said to him, "My father, sit up
and eat some of my game, so that you may give
me your blessing."
32His father Isaac asked him, "Who are you?"
"I am your son," he answered, "your firstborn, Esau."
33Isaac trembled violently and said, "Who
was it, then, that hunted game and brought it to
me? I ate it just before you came and I blessed
him—and indeed he will be blessed!"
34When Esau heard his father's words, he
burst out with a loud and bitter cry and said to
his father, "Bless me—me too, my father!"
35But he said, "Your brother came deceitfully
and took your blessing."
36Esau said, "Isn't he rightly named Jacob[a]?
He has deceived me these two times: He took
my birthright, and now he's taken my blessing!"
Then he asked, "Haven't you reserved any
blessing for me?"
37Isaac answered Esau, "I have made him
lord over you and have made all his relatives his
servants, and I have sustained him with grain
and new wine. So what can I possibly do for
you, my son?"
38Esau said to his father, "Do you have only
one blessing, my father? Bless me too, my father!" Then Esau wept aloud.
39His father Isaac answered him,

"Your dwelling will be
    away from the earth's richness,
    away from the dew of heaven above.
40You will live by the sword
    and you will serve your brother.
But when you grow restless,
    you will throw his yoke
    from off your neck."

Jacob Flees to Laban

41Esau held a grudge against Jacob because of
the blessing his father had given him. He said
to himself, "The days of mourning for my father are near; then I will kill my brother Jacob."
42When Rebekah was told what her older son
Esau had said, she sent for her younger son
Jacob and said to him, "Your brother Esau is
consoling himself with the thought of killing
you. 43Now then, my son, do what I say: Flee at
once to my brother Laban in Haran. 44Stay with

[a] 36 *Jacob* means *he grasps the heel* (figuratively, *he deceives*).

27:33 At this point Isaac realized he had blessed Jacob instead of Esau, but he could not take his blessing back. Jacob would receive the inheritance and blessing of the firstborn son. It had been God's plan that Jacob should be the recipient of God's promises to Abraham, so Isaac finally acquiesced to God's will. There are often times when God vetoes our plans. He often delivers us from making bad choices and protects us from the terrible consequences. We may not understand everything God is doing, but we must continually surrender our will to God if we are to grow spiritually and be renewed in our walk with him.

27:34–40 Esau demonstrated tearful remorse, but according to Hebrews 12:16–17, it was too late. As a young man he had sold his future for a bowl of stew, for immediate satisfaction, for something to dull the pain he felt inside. Now he had to suffer the consequences. Some of us may have done something similar, compromising the good future God intended for the fleeting pleasures of sin. But even though time has been lost, there is hope for those of us who are willing to confess our sins, accept responsibility for our actions, let go of what has been lost, and ask God to redeem our lives.

him for a while until your brother's fury sub-
sides. 45When your brother is no longer angry
with you and forgets what you did to him, I'll
send word for you to come back from there.
Why should I lose both of you in one day?"
46Then Rebekah said to Isaac, "I'm disgusted
with living because of these Hittite women. If
Jacob takes a wife from among the women of
this land, from Hittite women like these, my life
will not be worth living."

28 So Isaac called for Jacob and blessed[a]
him and commanded him: "Do not
marry a Canaanite woman. 2Go at once to Paddan Aram,[b] to the house of your mother's father Bethuel. Take a wife for yourself there,
from among the daughters of Laban, your
mother's brother. 3May God Almighty[c] bless
you and make you fruitful and increase your
numbers until you become a community of
peoples. 4May he give you and your descendants the blessing given to Abraham, so that
you may take possession of the land where you
now live as an alien, the land God gave to Abraham." 5Then Isaac sent Jacob on his way, and he
went to Paddan Aram, to Laban son of Bethuel
the Aramean, the brother of Rebekah, who was
the mother of Jacob and Esau.
6Now Esau learned that Isaac had blessed
Jacob and had sent him to Paddan Aram to take
a wife from there, and that when he blessed him
he commanded him, "Do not marry a Canaanite woman," 7and that Jacob had obeyed his father and mother and had gone to Paddan Aram.
8Esau then realized how displeasing the Canaanite women were to his father Isaac; 9so he
went to Ishmael and married Mahalath, the sister of Nebaioth and daughter of Ishmael son of
Abraham, in addition to the wives he already
had.

Jacob's Dream at Bethel

10Jacob left Beersheba and set out for Haran.
11When he reached a certain place, he stopped
for the night because the sun had set. Taking
one of the stones there, he put it under his head
and lay down to sleep. 12He had a dream in
which he saw a stairway[d] resting on the earth,
with its top reaching to heaven, and the angels
of God were ascending and descending on it.
13There above it[e] stood the LORD, and he said:
"I am the LORD, the God of your father Abraham and the God of Isaac. I will give you and
your descendants the land on which you are
lying. 14Your descendants will be like the dust
of the earth, and you will spread out to the west
and to the east, to the north and to the south.
All peoples on earth will be blessed through
you and your offspring. 15I am with you and
will watch over you wherever you go, and I will
bring you back to this land. I will not leave you
until I have done what I have promised you."
16When Jacob awoke from his sleep, he
thought, "Surely the LORD is in this place, and
I was not aware of it." 17He was afraid and said,
"How awesome is this place! This is none other
than the house of God; this is the gate of
heaven."
18Early the next morning Jacob took the
stone he had placed under his head and set it up
as a pillar and poured oil on top of it. 19He
called that place Bethel,[f] though the city used
to be called Luz.
20Then Jacob made a vow, saying, "If God
will be with me and will watch over me on this
journey I am taking and will give me food to eat
and clothes to wear 21so that I return safely to
my father's house, then the LORD[g] will be my
God 22and[h] this stone that I have set up as a
pillar will be God's house, and of all that you
give me I will give you a tenth."

Jacob Arrives in Paddan Aram

29 Then Jacob continued on his journey
and came to the land of the eastern
peoples. 2There he saw a well in the field, with
three flocks of sheep lying near it because the
flocks were watered from that well. The stone
over the mouth of the well was large. 3When all
the flocks were gathered there, the shepherds
would roll the stone away from the well's
mouth and water the sheep. Then they would
return the stone to its place over the mouth of
the well.
4Jacob asked the shepherds, "My brothers,
where are you from?"
"We're from Haran," they replied.
5He said to them, "Do you know Laban, Nahor's grandson?"
"Yes, we know him," they answered.
6Then Jacob asked them, "Is he well?"
"Yes, he is," they said, "and here comes his
daughter Rachel with the sheep."
7"Look," he said, "the sun is still high; it is
not time for the flocks to be gathered. Water the
sheep and take them back to pasture."
8"We can't," they replied, "until all the flocks
are gathered and the stone has been rolled away
from the mouth of the well. Then we will water
the sheep."
9While he was still talking with them, Rachel
came with her father's sheep, for she was a shep-
herdess. 10When Jacob saw Rachel daughter of
Laban, his mother's brother, and Laban's sheep,

[a] 1 Or *greeted* [b] 2 That is, Northwest Mesopotamia; also in verses 5, 6 and 7 [c] 3 Hebrew *El-Shaddai* [d] 12 Or *ladder* [e] 13 Or *There beside him* [f] 19 *Bethel* means *house of God.* [g] 20,21 Or *Since God . . . father's house, the LORD* [h] 21,22 Or *house, and the LORD will be my God, 22then*

28:20–22 Jacob's vow to God may have been just another of his schemes—something like a "foxhole" prayer. But God still honored his prayer and blessed Jacob. God's dealings with Jacob should give us some idea of how gracious God really is. Jacob wasn't exemplary or wise; he didn't know the God of his fathers as well as he should have. Yet God still was willing to work with him and bless him.

he went over and rolled the stone away from
the mouth of the well and watered his uncle's
sheep. 11Then Jacob kissed Rachel and began to
weep aloud. 12He had told Rachel that he was
a relative of her father and a son of Rebekah. So
she ran and told her father.
13As soon as Laban heard the news about
Jacob, his sister's son, he hurried to meet him.
He embraced him and kissed him and brought
him to his home, and there Jacob told him all
these things. 14Then Laban said to him, "You
are my own flesh and blood."

Jacob Marries Leah and Rachel

After Jacob had stayed with him for a whole
month, 15Laban said to him, "Just because you
are a relative of mine, should you work for
me for nothing? Tell me what your wages
should be."
16Now Laban had two daughters; the name
of the older was Leah, and the name of the
younger was Rachel. 17Leah had weak[a] eyes,
but Rachel was lovely in form, and beautiful.
18Jacob was in love with Rachel and said, "I'll
work for you seven years in return for your
younger daughter Rachel."
19Laban said, "It's better that I give her to
you than to some other man. Stay here with me."
20So Jacob served seven years to get Rachel, but
they seemed like only a few days to him because
of his love for her.
21Then Jacob said to Laban, "Give me my
wife. My time is completed, and I want to lie
with her."
22So Laban brought together all the people of
the place and gave a feast. 23But when evening
came, he took his daughter Leah and gave her
to Jacob, and Jacob lay with her. 24And Laban
gave his servant girl Zilpah to his daughter as
her maidservant.
25When morning came, there was Leah! So
Jacob said to Laban, "What is this you have
done to me? I served you for Rachel, didn't I?
Why have you deceived me?"
26Laban replied, "It is not our custom here to
give the younger daughter in marriage before
the older one. 27Finish this daughter's bridal
week; then we will give you the younger one
also, in return for another seven years of work."
28And Jacob did so. He finished the week
with Leah, and then Laban gave him his daughter Rachel to be his wife. 29Laban gave his servant girl Bilhah to his daughter Rachel as her
maidservant. 30Jacob lay with Rachel also, and
he loved Rachel more than Leah. And he
worked for Laban another seven years.

Jacob's Children

31When the LORD saw that Leah was not
loved, he opened her womb, but Rachel was
barren. 32Leah became pregnant and gave birth
to a son. She named him Reuben,[b] for she
said, "It is because the LORD has seen my misery. Surely my husband will love me now."
33She conceived again, and when she gave
birth to a son she said, "Because the LORD heard
that I am not loved, he gave me this one too." So
she named him Simeon.[c]
34Again she conceived, and when she gave
birth to a son she said, "Now at last my husband will become attached to me, because I
have borne him three sons." So he was named
Levi.[d]
35She conceived again, and when she gave
birth to a son she said, "This time I will praise
the LORD." So she named him Judah.[e] Then she
stopped having children.

30 When Rachel saw that she was not bearing Jacob any children, she became jealous of her sister. So she said to Jacob, "Give me
children, or I'll die!"
2Jacob became angry with her and said,
"Am I in the place of God, who has kept you
from having children?"
3Then she said, "Here is Bilhah, my maidservant. Sleep with her so that she can bear children for me and that through her I too can
build a family."
4So she gave him her servant Bilhah as a wife.
Jacob slept with her, 5and she became pregnant
and bore him a son. 6Then Rachel said, "God
has vindicated me; he has listened to my plea
and given me a son." Because of this she named
him Dan.[f]
7Rachel's servant Bilhah conceived again and
bore Jacob a second son. 8Then Rachel said, "I
have had a great struggle with my sister, and I
have won." So she named him Naphtali.[g]
9When Leah saw that she had stopped having
children, she took her maidservant Zilpah and
gave her to Jacob as a wife. 10Leah's servant
Zilpah bore Jacob a son. 11Then Leah said,
"What good fortune!"[h] So she named him
Gad.[i]
12Leah's servant Zilpah bore Jacob a second
son. 13Then Leah said, "How happy I am! The
women will call me happy." So she named him
Asher.[j]
14During wheat harvest, Reuben went out
into the fields and found some mandrake
plants, which he brought to his mother Leah.

[a]17 Or *delicate* [b]32 *Reuben* sounds like the Hebrew for *he has seen my misery;* the name means *see, a son.* [c]33 *Simeon* probably means *one who hears.* [d]34 *Levi* sounds like and may be derived from the Hebrew for *attached.* [e]35 *Judah* sounds like and may be derived from the Hebrew for *praise.* [f]6 *Dan* here means *he has vindicated.* [g]8 *Naphtali* means *my struggle.* [h]11 Or *"A troop is coming!"* [i]11 *Gad* can mean *good fortune* or *a troop.* [j]13 *Asher* means *happy.*

29:25 Jacob's response to Laban's trickery reveals an interesting principle: Nobody resents being cheated more than a cheater. If there is a characteristic in others that we find particularly annoying, we would be wise to examine ourselves. That characteristic is probably one of our own (see Matthew 7:1–5).

Rachel said to Leah, "Please give me some of your son's mandrakes."

15But she said to her, "Wasn't it enough that you took away my husband? Will you take my son's mandrakes too?"

"Very well," Rachel said, "he can sleep with you tonight in return for your son's mandrakes."

16So when Jacob came in from the fields that evening, Leah went out to meet him. "You must sleep with me," she said. "I have hired you with my son's mandrakes." So he slept with her that night.

17God listened to Leah, and she became pregnant and bore Jacob a fifth son. 18Then Leah said, "God has rewarded me for giving my maidservant to my husband." So she named him Issachar.[a]

19Leah conceived again and bore Jacob a sixth son. 20Then Leah said, "God has presented me with a precious gift. This time my husband will treat me with honor, because I have borne him six sons." So she named him Zebulun.[b]

21Some time later she gave birth to a daughter and named her Dinah.

22Then God remembered Rachel; he listened to her and opened her womb. 23She became pregnant and gave birth to a son and said, "God has taken away my disgrace." 24She named him Joseph,[c] and said, "May the LORD add to me another son."

Jacob's Flocks Increase

25After Rachel gave birth to Joseph, Jacob said to Laban, "Send me on my way so I can go back to my own homeland. 26Give me my wives and children, for whom I have served you, and I will be on my way. You know how much work I've done for you."

27But Laban said to him, "If I have found favor in your eyes, please stay. I have learned by divination that[d] the LORD has blessed me because of you." 28He added, "Name your wages, and I will pay them."

29Jacob said to him, "You know how I have worked for you and how your livestock has fared under my care. 30The little you had before I came has increased greatly, and the LORD has blessed you wherever I have been. But now, when may I do something for my own household?"

31"What shall I give you?" he asked.

"Don't give me anything," Jacob replied. "But if you will do this one thing for me, I will go on tending your flocks and watching over them: 32Let me go through all your flocks today and remove from them every speckled or spotted sheep, every dark-colored lamb and every spotted or speckled goat. They will be my wages. 33And my honesty will testify for me in the future, whenever you check on the wages you have paid me. Any goat in my possession that is not speckled or spotted, or any lamb that is not dark-colored, will be considered stolen."

34"Agreed," said Laban. "Let it be as you have said." 35That same day he removed all the male goats that were streaked or spotted, and all the speckled or spotted female goats (all that had white on them) and all the dark-colored lambs, and he placed them in the care of his sons. 36Then he put a three-day journey between himself and Jacob, while Jacob continued to tend the rest of Laban's flocks.

37Jacob, however, took fresh-cut branches from poplar, almond and plane trees and made white stripes on them by peeling the bark and exposing the white inner wood of the branches. 38Then he placed the peeled branches in all the watering troughs, so that they would be directly in front of the flocks when they came to drink. When the flocks were in heat and came to drink, 39they mated in front of the branches. And they bore young that were streaked or speckled or spotted. 40Jacob set apart the young of the flock by themselves, but made the rest face the streaked and dark-colored animals that belonged to Laban. Thus he made separate flocks for himself and did not put them with Laban's animals. 41Whenever the stronger females were in heat, Jacob would place the branches in the troughs in front of the animals so they would mate near the branches, 42but if the animals were weak, he would not place them there. So the weak animals went to Laban and the strong ones to Jacob. 43In this way the man grew exceedingly prosperous and came to own large flocks, and maidservants and menservants, and camels and donkeys.

Jacob Flees From Laban

31 Jacob heard that Laban's sons were saying, "Jacob has taken everything our father owned and has gained all this wealth from what belonged to our father." 2And Jacob noticed that Laban's attitude toward him was not what it had been.

3Then the LORD said to Jacob, "Go back to the land of your fathers and to your relatives, and I will be with you."

4So Jacob sent word to Rachel and Leah to

[a] 18 *Issachar* sounds like the Hebrew for *reward.*
[b] 20 *Zebulun* probably means *honor.* [c] 24 *Joseph* means *may he add.* [d] 27 Or possibly *have become rich and*

30:25–43 God blessed Jacob in spite of his trickery and deceit. Often God works that way with us, too. He blesses us when we don't really deserve it. None of us really deserves God's love; all of us have failed in many ways. But God still reaches out to help us when we look to him in faith.

31:3 Moving can be a time of major crisis. It is interesting to note that during all the major changes of Jacob's life, God always reestablished contact with him. As Jacob faced this crisis with Laban's family, God revealed to Jacob the next step in his divine plan. His instructions for Jacob's next step came just as they were needed. God is always there to help us during our crisis moments too. We must only stop and listen to what he has to say.

come out to the fields where his flocks were. [5]He said to them, "I see that your father's attitude toward me is not what it was before, but the God of my father has been with me. [6]You know that I've worked for your father with all my strength, [7]yet your father has cheated me by changing my wages ten times. However, God has not allowed him to harm me. [8]If he said, 'The speckled ones will be your wages,' then all the flocks gave birth to speckled young; and if he said, 'The streaked ones will be your wages,' then all the flocks bore streaked young. [9]So God has taken away your father's livestock and has given them to me.

[10]"In breeding season I once had a dream in which I looked up and saw that the male goats mating with the flock were streaked, speckled or spotted. [11]The angel of God said to me in the dream, 'Jacob.' I answered, 'Here I am.' [12]And he said, 'Look up and see that all the male goats mating with the flock are streaked, speckled or spotted, for I have seen all that Laban has been doing to you. [13]I am the God of Bethel, where you anointed a pillar and where you made a vow to me. Now leave this land at once and go back to your native land.' "

[14]Then Rachel and Leah replied, "Do we still have any share in the inheritance of our father's estate? [15]Does he not regard us as foreigners? Not only has he sold us, but he has used up what was paid for us. [16]Surely all the wealth that God took away from our father belongs to us and our children. So do whatever God has told you."

[17]Then Jacob put his children and his wives on camels, [18]and he drove all his livestock ahead of him, along with all the goods he had accumulated in Paddan Aram,[a] to go to his father Isaac in the land of Canaan.

[19]When Laban had gone to shear his sheep, Rachel stole her father's household gods. [20]Moreover, Jacob deceived Laban the Aramean by not telling him he was running away. [21]So he fled with all he had, and crossing the River,[b] he headed for the hill country of Gilead.

Laban Pursues Jacob

[22]On the third day Laban was told that Jacob had fled. [23]Taking his relatives with him, he pursued Jacob for seven days and caught up with him in the hill country of Gilead. [24]Then God came to Laban the Aramean in a dream at night and said to him, "Be careful not to say anything to Jacob, either good or bad."

[25]Jacob had pitched his tent in the hill country of Gilead when Laban overtook him, and Laban and his relatives camped there too. [26]Then Laban said to Jacob, "What have you done? You've deceived me, and you've carried off my daughters like captives in war. [27]Why did you run off secretly and deceive me? Why didn't you tell me, so I could send you away with joy and singing to the music of tambourines and harps? [28]You didn't even let me kiss my grandchildren and my daughters good-by. You have done a foolish thing. [29]I have the power to harm you; but last night the God of your father said to me, 'Be careful not to say anything to Jacob, either good or bad.' [30]Now you have gone off because you longed to return to your father's house. But why did you steal my gods?"

[31]Jacob answered Laban, "I was afraid, because I thought you would take your daughters away from me by force. [32]But if you find anyone who has your gods, he shall not live. In the presence of our relatives, see for yourself whether there is anything of yours here with me; and if so, take it." Now Jacob did not know that Rachel had stolen the gods.

[33]So Laban went into Jacob's tent and into Leah's tent and into the tent of the two maidservants, but he found nothing. After he came out of Leah's tent, he entered Rachel's tent. [34]Now Rachel had taken the household gods and put them inside her camel's saddle and was sitting on them. Laban searched through everything in the tent but found nothing.

[35]Rachel said to her father, "Don't be angry, my lord, that I cannot stand up in your presence; I'm having my period." So he searched but could not find the household gods.

[36]Jacob was angry and took Laban to task. "What is my crime?" he asked Laban. "What sin have I committed that you hunt me down? [37]Now that you have searched through all my goods, what have you found that belongs to your household? Put it here in front of your relatives and mine, and let them judge between the two of us.

[38]"I have been with you for twenty years now. Your sheep and goats have not miscarried, nor have I eaten rams from your flocks. [39]I did not bring you animals torn by wild beasts; I bore the loss myself. And you demanded payment from me for whatever was stolen by day or night. [40]This was my situation: The heat consumed me in the daytime and the cold at night, and sleep fled from my eyes. [41]It was like this

[a] *18* That is, Northwest Mesopotamia [b] *21* That is, the Euphrates

---

31:14–15 Leah and Rachel left their father's home willingly. This is not surprising. We have enough evidence to know that Laban's family was not operating in accordance with God's will. At this point, Jacob's family needed to move on if they were to become the family God intended them to be. Sometimes our home and early family life can be sources of pain and confusion. In such cases, it is important for us to surrender the pain and confusion of the past to God in order to build a new life in keeping with his design for the family.

31:17–20 Even though God was very active in Jacob's life, Jacob's old patterns still persisted, and he deceived Laban. The transformation of Jacob's deceitful nature was an ongoing process. Jacob's habits and tendencies certainly didn't go away overnight; neither will ours. We need to be aware of our weaknesses and continually look to God for his help.

SEE THE TRUTH

Key 2

Recognizing Areas of Weakness

Genesis 31:45–55 We all have weaknesses. It is helpful to honestly acknowledge these faults. When we recognize our flaws, we can set up boundaries to give us support in these areas of weakness. We may need to clearly communicate to others the boundary lines we have defined, and then help hold each other accountable to them. Once the boundaries have been established, honesty is needed to maintain them.

Jacob and his father-in-law Laban had some conflicts. As they worked them out, Jacob and Laban entered into an agreement by drawing a clearly defined boundary line and setting up a monument to remind them of their commitment: "May the Lord keep watch between you and me when we are away from each other . . . This heap is a witness, and this pillar is a witness, that I will not go past this heap to your side to harm you" (Genesis 31:49, 52). Then Jacob vowed before God to respect the boundary line.

Recognizing our areas of weakness allows us to take precautions to help make sure we don't give in to our weaknesses. When we see places in our lives where we need to set limits, we can ask God to help us. We can also ask others to help hold us accountable in these areas. Ultimately, however, we must remember that we are personally responsible to God for our own honesty in maintaining the boundary lines we have defined.

Turn to 1 Samuel 17.

for the twenty years I was in your household.
I worked for you fourteen years for your two
daughters and six years for your flocks, and you
changed my wages ten times. 42If the God of my
father, the God of Abraham and the Fear of
Isaac, had not been with me, you would surely
have sent me away empty-handed. But God has
seen my hardship and the toil of my hands, and
last night he rebuked you."

43Laban answered Jacob, "The women are
my daughters, the children are my children, and
the flocks are my flocks. All you see is mine. Yet
what can I do today about these daughters of
mine, or about the children they have borne?
44Come now, let's make a covenant, you and I,
and let it serve as a witness between us."

45So Jacob took a stone and set it up as a
pillar. 46He said to his relatives, "Gather some
stones." So they took stones and piled them in a
heap, and they ate there by the heap. 47Laban
called it Jegar Sahadutha,[a] and Jacob called it
Galeed.[b]

48Laban said, "This heap is a witness between you and me today." That is why it was
called Galeed. 49It was also called Mizpah,[c]
because he said, "May the LORD keep watch
between you and me when we are away from
each other. 50If you mistreat my daughters or if
you take any wives besides my daughters, even
though no one is with us, remember that God
is a witness between you and me."

51Laban also said to Jacob, "Here is this
heap, and here is this pillar I have set up between you and me. 52This heap is a witness, and
this pillar is a witness, that I will not go past this
heap to your side to harm you and that you will
not go past this heap and pillar to my side to
harm me. 53May the God of Abraham and the
God of Nahor, the God of their father, judge
between us."

So Jacob took an oath in the name of the Fear
of his father Isaac. 54He offered a sacrifice there
in the hill country and invited his relatives to a
meal. After they had eaten, they spent the night
there.

55Early the next morning Laban kissed his
grandchildren and his daughters and blessed
them. Then he left and returned home.

Jacob Prepares to Meet Esau

32 Jacob also went on his way, and the
angels of God met him. 2When Jacob
saw them, he said, "This is the camp of God!" So
he named that place Mahanaim.[d]

[a]47 The Aramaic *Jegar Sahadutha* means *witness heap.*
[b]47 The Hebrew *Galeed* means *witness heap.*
[c]49 *Mizpah* means *watchtower.* [d]2 *Mahanaim* means *two camps.*

31:49 This verse is often quoted as a sweet benediction, but in actuality it is a very negative wish that almost becomes a threat. It is as if Laban were saying, "I can't watch you anymore, so when you're out of my sight, I pray that God will keep his eye on you, you rascal!"

3Jacob sent messengers ahead of him to his brother Esau in the land of Seir, the country of Edom. 4He instructed them: "This is what you are to say to my master Esau: 'Your servant Jacob says, I have been staying with Laban and have remained there till now. 5I have cattle and donkeys, sheep and goats, menservants and maidservants. Now I am sending this message to my lord, that I may find favor in your eyes.' "

6When the messengers returned to Jacob, they said, "We went to your brother Esau, and now he is coming to meet you, and four hundred men are with him."

7In great fear and distress Jacob divided the people who were with him into two groups,[a] and the flocks and herds and camels as well. 8He thought, "If Esau comes and attacks one group,[b] the group[b] that is left may escape."

9Then Jacob prayed, "O God of my father Abraham, God of my father Isaac, O LORD, who said to me, 'Go back to your country and your relatives, and I will make you prosper,' 10I am unworthy of all the kindness and faithfulness you have shown your servant. I had only my staff when I crossed this Jordan, but now I have become two groups. 11Save me, I pray, from the hand of my brother Esau, for I am afraid he will come and attack me, and also the mothers with their children. 12But you have said, 'I will surely make you prosper and will make your descendants like the sand of the sea, which cannot be counted.' "

13He spent the night there, and from what he had with him he selected a gift for his brother Esau: 14two hundred female goats and twenty male goats, two hundred ewes and twenty rams, 15thirty female camels with their young, forty cows and ten bulls, and twenty female donkeys and ten male donkeys. 16He put them in the care of his servants, each herd by itself, and said to his servants, "Go ahead of me, and keep some space between the herds."

17He instructed the one in the lead: "When my brother Esau meets you and asks, 'To whom do you belong, and where are you going, and who owns all these animals in front of you?' 18then you are to say, 'They belong to your servant Jacob. They are a gift sent to my lord Esau, and he is coming behind us.' "

19He also instructed the second, the third and all the others who followed the herds: "You are to say the same thing to Esau when you meet him. 20And be sure to say, 'Your servant Jacob is coming behind us.' " For he thought, "I will pacify him with these gifts I am sending on ahead; later, when I see him, perhaps he will receive me." 21So Jacob's gifts went on ahead of him, but he himself spent the night in the camp.

Jacob Wrestles With God

22That night Jacob got up and took his two wives, his two maidservants and his eleven sons and crossed the ford of the Jabbok. 23After he had sent them across the stream, he sent over all his possessions. 24So Jacob was left alone, and a man wrestled with him till daybreak. 25When the man saw that he could not overpower him, he touched the socket of Jacob's hip so that his hip was wrenched as he wrestled with the man. 26Then the man said, "Let me go, for it is daybreak."

But Jacob replied, "I will not let you go unless you bless me."

27The man asked him, "What is your name?"

"Jacob," he answered.

28Then the man said, "Your name will no longer be Jacob, but Israel,[c] because you have struggled with God and with men and have overcome."

29Jacob said, "Please tell me your name."

But he replied, "Why do you ask my name?" Then he blessed him there.

30So Jacob called the place Peniel,[d] saying, "It is because I saw God face to face, and yet my life was spared."

31The sun rose above him as he passed Peniel,[e] and he was limping because of his hip. 32Therefore to this day the Israelites do not eat the tendon attached to the socket of the hip, because the socket of Jacob's hip was touched near the tendon.

Jacob Meets Esau

33 Jacob looked up and there was Esau, coming with his four hundred men; so he divided the children among Leah, Rachel and the two maidservants. 2He put the maidservants and their children in front, Leah and her children next, and Rachel and Joseph in the rear. 3He himself went on ahead and bowed down to the ground seven times as he approached his brother.

4But Esau ran to meet Jacob and embraced

[a]7 Or *camps;* also in verse 10 [b]8 Or *camp* [c]28 *Israel* means *he struggles with God.* [d]30 *Peniel* means *face of God.* [e]31 Hebrew *Penuel,* a variant of *Peniel*

32:3 Twenty years prior to these events Jacob had run away from Esau, afraid for his life. Jacob had no way of knowing whether his brother had released his old resentments and allowed his old wounds to heal. Since Jacob did not know the state of his brother's heart, Jacob made elaborate preparations for reestablishing contact. Jacob's example in this chapter gives helpful hints to those of us seeking reconciliation with people we have hurt in the past.

33:4 Although Esau did seem genuinely delighted to see his long-lost brother, this happy reunion certainly didn't signal the end of the brothers' feud. Conflict between their families continued throughout Old Testament times. The book of Obadiah records the joy that Esau's descendants, the Edomites, expressed over the Israelites' defeat. Obadiah, an Israelite, also joyfully announced the doom of Edom. In the New Testament, the hated family of Herod traced its lineage back to Esau. Some conflicts are not easily resolved, but when left unresolved, these conflicts can become a burden to generations far into the future.

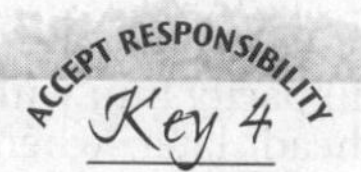

Facing Up to Our Wrongs

Genesis 33:1–11 Refusing to take responsibility for the harm we cause others only leads to further damage. As years pass, lack of communication, unrelenting anger, and hateful emotional exchanges can all create tremendous anxiety. The threatening atmosphere created by this tension often tempts us to focus on wrongs done to us, rather than on the wrongs we have committed. Then we persist in blaming others because it seems to defend us—at least temporarily—against the painful truth of our sinful behavior. When we have harmed someone in the past, we must take responsibility for the wrongs we have committed.

This was the case for Jacob upon returning to see Esau. Jacob had come to accept that he had wronged Esau in stealing his birthright. In the process of taking responsibility for his past behavior, he began to move from awareness to action (see also the devotionals for Key 5: "Grieve, Forgive, and Let Go," which instruct us to right the wrongs we have done). Prior to their reunion, Jacob and Esau's relationship was ruled by fear. But once Jacob took responsibility for his past, things began to change. When Jacob eventually faced his brother, the two were able to express love for each other even though they both remembered the pain of their past.

Accepting responsibility for our wrongdoing can be a frightening thing, because it requires that we face our weaknesses and stop blaming others for our problems. But we can take courage and instruction to do so through Jacob's example and seek God's help in restoring our relationships.

Turn to Leviticus 16.

him; he threw his arms around his neck and
kissed him. And they wept. 5Then Esau looked
up and saw the women and children. "Who are
these with you?" he asked.

Jacob answered, "They are the children God
has graciously given your servant."

6Then the maidservants and their children
approached and bowed down. 7Next, Leah and
her children came and bowed down. Last of all
came Joseph and Rachel, and they too bowed
down.

8Esau asked, "What do you mean by all these
droves I met?"

"To find favor in your eyes, my lord," he said.

9But Esau said, "I already have plenty, my
brother. Keep what you have for yourself."

10"No, please!" said Jacob. "If I have found
favor in your eyes, accept this gift from me. For
to see your face is like seeing the face of God,
now that you have received me favorably.
11Please accept the present that was brought to
you, for God has been gracious to me and I have
all I need." And because Jacob insisted, Esau accepted it.

12Then Esau said, "Let us be on our way; I'll
accompany you."

13But Jacob said to him, "My lord knows that
the children are tender and that I must care for
the ewes and cows that are nursing their young.
If they are driven hard just one day, all the
animals will die. 14So let my lord go on ahead
of his servant, while I move along slowly at
the pace of the droves before me and that
of the children, until I come to my lord in
Seir."

15Esau said, "Then let me leave some of my
men with you."

"But why do that?" Jacob asked. "Just let me
find favor in the eyes of my lord."

16So that day Esau started on his way back to
Seir. 17Jacob, however, went to Succoth, where
he built a place for himself and made shelters
for his livestock. That is why the place is called
Succoth.[a]

18After Jacob came from Paddan Aram,[b] he
arrived safely at the[c] city of Shechem in Canaan and camped within sight of the city. 19For
a hundred pieces of silver,[d] he bought from
the sons of Hamor, the father of Shechem, the
plot of ground where he pitched his tent.
20There he set up an altar and called it El Elohe
Israel.[e]

Dinah and the Shechemites

34 Now Dinah, the daughter Leah had
borne to Jacob, went out to visit the

[a]17 *Succoth* means *shelters.* [b]18 That is, Northwest Mesopotamia [c]18 Or *arrived at Shalem, a* [d]19 Hebrew *hundred kesitahs;* a kesitah was a unit of money of unknown weight and value. [e]20 *El Elohe Israel* can mean *God, the God of Israel* or *mighty is the God of Israel.*

women of the land. 2When Shechem son of Hamor the Hivite, the ruler of that area, saw her, he took her and violated her. 3His heart was drawn to Dinah daughter of Jacob, and he loved the girl and spoke tenderly to her. 4And Shechem said to his father Hamor, "Get me this girl as my wife."

5When Jacob heard that his daughter Dinah had been defiled, his sons were in the fields with his livestock; so he kept quiet about it until they came home.

6Then Shechem's father Hamor went out to talk with Jacob. 7Now Jacob's sons had come in from the fields as soon as they heard what had happened. They were filled with grief and fury, because Shechem had done a disgraceful thing in[a] Israel by lying with Jacob's daughter—a thing that should not be done.

8But Hamor said to them, "My son Shechem has his heart set on your daughter. Please give her to him as his wife. 9Intermarry with us; give us your daughters and take our daughters for yourselves. 10You can settle among us; the land is open to you. Live in it, trade[b] in it, and acquire property in it."

11Then Shechem said to Dinah's father and brothers, "Let me find favor in your eyes, and I will give you whatever you ask. 12Make the price for the bride and the gift I am to bring as great as you like, and I'll pay whatever you ask me. Only give me the girl as my wife."

13Because their sister Dinah had been defiled, Jacob's sons replied deceitfully as they spoke to Shechem and his father Hamor. 14They said to them, "We can't do such a thing; we can't give our sister to a man who is not circumcised. That would be a disgrace to us. 15We will give our consent to you on one condition only: that you become like us by circumcising all your males. 16Then we will give you our daughters and take your daughters for ourselves. We'll settle among you and become one people with you. 17But if you will not agree to be circumcised, we'll take our sister[c] and go."

18Their proposal seemed good to Hamor and his son Shechem. 19The young man, who was the most honored of all his father's household, lost no time in doing what they said, because he was delighted with Jacob's daughter. 20So Hamor and his son Shechem went to the gate of their city to speak to their fellow townsmen. 21"These men are friendly toward us," they said. "Let them live in our land and trade in it; the land has plenty of room for them. We can marry their daughters and they can marry ours. 22But the men will consent to live with us as one people only on the condition that our males be circumcised, as they themselves are. 23Won't their livestock, their property and all their other animals become ours? So let us give our consent to them, and they will settle among us."

24All the men who went out of the city gate agreed with Hamor and his son Shechem, and every male in the city was circumcised.

25Three days later, while all of them were still in pain, two of Jacob's sons, Simeon and Levi, Dinah's brothers, took their swords and attacked the unsuspecting city, killing every male. 26They put Hamor and his son Shechem to the sword and took Dinah from Shechem's house and left. 27The sons of Jacob came upon the dead bodies and looted the city where[d] their sister had been defiled. 28They seized their flocks and herds and donkeys and everything else of theirs in the city and out in the fields. 29They carried off all their wealth and all their women and children, taking as plunder everything in the houses.

30Then Jacob said to Simeon and Levi, "You have brought trouble on me by making me a stench to the Canaanites and Perizzites, the people living in this land. We are few in number, and if they join forces against me and attack me, I and my household will be destroyed."

31But they replied, "Should he have treated our sister like a prostitute?"

Jacob Returns to Bethel

35 Then God said to Jacob, "Go up to Bethel and settle there, and build an altar there to God, who appeared to you when you were fleeing from your brother Esau."

2So Jacob said to his household and to all who were with him, "Get rid of the foreign gods you have with you, and purify yourselves and change your clothes. 3Then come, let us go up to Bethel, where I will build an altar to God, who answered me in the day of my distress and who has been with me wherever I have gone." 4So they gave Jacob all the foreign gods they had and the rings in their ears, and Jacob buried them under the oak at Shechem. 5Then they set out, and the terror of God fell upon the towns all around them so that no one pursued them.

6Jacob and all the people with him came to Luz (that is, Bethel) in the land of Canaan. 7There he built an altar, and he called the place

[a]7 Or *against* [b]10 Or *move about freely;* also in verse 21 [c]17 Hebrew *daughter* [d]27 Or *because*

34:2 The act of rape is always hideous in itself, and its consequences are just as heartbreaking. In this occurrence, rape led to deception and ultimately to murder. Sinful patterns and the acts that flow out of them feed cycles of deepening destruction and hurt. Someone has to choose to break the cycle and begin the process of spiritual renewal and healing.

34:20–31 Vengeance belongs to God. When a person usurps God's role and initiates revenge on his or her own—no matter how just the cause may be—there can be serious consequences. Because of their deception and slaughter of the Hivites, Jacob and his family became extremely unpopular with their neighbors. This situation put them in grave danger since they were only a small clan at this point in time. Revenge is counterproductive. It only breaks down the reconciliation process that is necessary for spiritual growth and healthy relationships.

Jacob & Sons

While not the first deeply troubled family in the Bible, Jacob's descendants were certainly among the most controversial. Jacob's lack of discretion, honesty, patience and unconditional love had a definite, negative impact on his children.

Jacob had never been his father's favorite, and tragically he played favorites with his own sons. Joseph was obviously preferred; Benjamin ran a close second. The rest were far back in the pack and understandably jealous.

The deceptions that Jacob had used on his father and brother many years earlier were mirrored in the lies his sons told about the fate of Joseph. As the massacre at Shechem brutally illustrated, openness and honesty didn't characterize Jacob's sons' relationships with outsiders either. Jacob's silence at Dinah's rape may have even spurred Simeon and Levi to seek vengeance on their own. Certainly their father did not hold them accountable for their behavior until it was much too late.

Jacob's polygamy also influenced his sons. Reuben once slept with his father's concubine, Bilhah. Why not? He had been a party to his mother and Rachel's rivalry for Jacob's favors and had grown up watching Jacob's marriage expand to include two servant concubines. Yet Reuben was not the only one to sin sexually. Judah also succumbed to temptation with his disguised daughter-in-law Tamar.

Jacob and his sons did mature significantly over the years. When famine forced them to visit Egypt, they were no longer a selfish, jealous, deceitful band. Instead, the brothers were genuinely concerned for their aging father, protective of young Benjamin and remorseful when confronted with the truth of what they had done to Joseph. With their past reconciled, Jacob's sons could begin an exciting new life in Egypt with the brother they had given up as dead. They would become the forefathers of Israel's twelve tribes. And Judah would head the royal line, with its most famous descendant the King of kings, Jesus Christ.

STRENGTHS AND ACCOMPLISHMENTS:

In later years the brothers honestly cared about their father.

They were the forefathers of the twelve tribes of Israel.

They eventually learned the value of loyalty and honesty.

WEAKNESSES AND MISTAKES:

Jacob modeled favoritism, impatience and sexual indiscretion for his sons.

Motivated by unbridled passion and intense jealousy, the boys found it difficult to establish boundaries for their behavior.

Honesty was a learned response, acquired rather late in life for Jacob and several of his sons.

LESSONS FROM THEIR LIVES:

The sins of the parents are often reflected in their children.

Parental favoritism has devastating consequences.

God can take the evil done to us and use it to accomplish great good.

KEY VERSE:

"Now hurry back to my father and say to him, 'This is what your son Joseph says: God has made me lord of all Egypt. Come down to me; don't delay' " (45:9).

The story of Jacob and his sons is found in Genesis 34—50. Jacob is also mentioned in Hosea 12:3–5; Matthew 1:2; 22:32; Acts 3:13; 7:46; Romans 9:10–13 and Hebrews 11:9, 20–21.

El Bethel,[a] because it was there that God revealed himself to him when he was fleeing from
his brother.
8Now Deborah, Rebekah's nurse, died and
was buried under the oak below Bethel. So it
was named Allon Bacuth.[b]
9After Jacob returned from Paddan Aram,[c]
God appeared to him again and blessed him.
10God said to him, "Your name is Jacob,[d] but
you will no longer be called Jacob; your name
will be Israel.[e]" So he named him Israel.
11And God said to him, "I am God Almighty[f]; be fruitful and increase in number. A
nation and a community of nations will come
from you, and kings will come from your body.
12The land I gave to Abraham and Isaac I also
give to you, and I will give this land to your
descendants after you." 13Then God went up
from him at the place where he had talked with
him.
14Jacob set up a stone pillar at the place
where God had talked with him, and he poured
out a drink offering on it; he also poured oil
on it. 15Jacob called the place where God had
talked with him Bethel.[g]

The Deaths of Rachel and Isaac

16Then they moved on from Bethel. While
they were still some distance from Ephrath, Rachel began to give birth and had great difficulty.
17And as she was having great difficulty in childbirth, the midwife said to her, "Don't be afraid,
for you have another son." 18As she breathed her
last—for she was dying—she named her son Ben-
Oni.[h] But his father named him Benjamin.[i]
19So Rachel died and was buried on the way
to Ephrath (that is, Bethlehem). 20Over her
tomb Jacob set up a pillar, and to this day that
pillar marks Rachel's tomb.
21Israel moved on again and pitched his tent
beyond Migdal Eder. 22While Israel was living
in that region, Reuben went in and slept with
his father's concubine Bilhah, and Israel heard
of it.

Jacob had twelve sons:
23The sons of Leah:
Reuben the firstborn of Jacob,
Simeon, Levi, Judah, Issachar and Zebulun.
24The sons of Rachel:
Joseph and Benjamin.
25The sons of Rachel's maidservant Bilhah:
Dan and Naphtali.
26The sons of Leah's maidservant Zilpah:
Gad and Asher.
These were the sons of Jacob, who were born
to him in Paddan Aram.

27Jacob came home to his father Isaac in
Mamre, near Kiriath Arba (that is, Hebron),
where Abraham and Isaac had stayed. 28Isaac
lived a hundred and eighty years. 29Then he
breathed his last and died and was gathered to
his people, old and full of years. And his sons
Esau and Jacob buried him.

Esau's Descendants

36 This is the account of Esau (that is,
Edom).

2Esau took his wives from the women
of Canaan: Adah daughter of Elon the Hittite, and Oholibamah daughter of Anah
and granddaughter of Zibeon the Hivite—
3also Basemath daughter of Ishmael and
sister of Nebaioth.
4Adah bore Eliphaz to Esau, Basemath
bore Reuel, 5and Oholibamah bore Jeush,
Jalam and Korah. These were the sons of
Esau, who were born to him in Canaan.
6Esau took his wives and sons and
daughters and all the members of his
household, as well as his livestock and all
his other animals and all the goods he had
acquired in Canaan, and moved to a land
some distance from his brother Jacob.
7Their possessions were too great for them
to remain together; the land where they
were staying could not support them both
because of their livestock. 8So Esau (that
is, Edom) settled in the hill country of
Seir.

9This is the account of Esau the father of the
Edomites in the hill country of Seir.

10These are the names of Esau's sons:
Eliphaz, the son of Esau's wife Adah,
and Reuel, the son of Esau's wife Basemath.

[a]7 *El Bethel* means *God of Bethel.* [b]8 *Allon Bacuth* means *oak of weeping.* [c]9 That is, Northwest Mesopotamia; also in verse 26 [d]10 *Jacob* means *he grasps the heel* (figuratively, *he deceives*). [e]10 *Israel* means *he struggles with God.* [f]11 Hebrew *El-Shaddai* [g]15 *Bethel* means *house of God.* [h]18 *Ben-Oni* means *son of my trouble.* [i]18 *Benjamin* means *son of my right hand.*

35:22 The families in the book of Genesis were prone to every kind of human weakness and sin. Deceit and lying were common. Communication between family members was poor. The occurrence of incest was high. Here, Reuben even slept with one of his father's wives. This kind of sexual sin reaps a bitter harvest. Reuben's blessing and inheritance as the firstborn son were forfeited because of this single act of sexual gratification (49:4). Reuben needed to keep God's long-range plan in focus. If he had thought about what he stood to lose, he might have been able to withstand temptation.

36:6–8 Esau and his family could not live in the same area as Jacob and his family. Their families were too large and the land area was too small for them to be able to live together in harmony. For some families, no amount of room is enough for them to live agreeably together. The reconciliation of these brothers was begun, but it seems never to have been completed. We need to expect reconciliation to take time. It needs to be worked out over a period of time, in the everyday situations of life.

11The sons of Eliphaz:
Teman, Omar, Zepho, Gatam and Kenaz.
12Esau's son Eliphaz also had a concubine named Timna, who bore him Amalek. These were grandsons of Esau's wife Adah.
13The sons of Reuel:
Nahath, Zerah, Shammah and Mizzah. These were grandsons of Esau's wife Basemath.
14The sons of Esau's wife Oholibamah daughter of Anah and granddaughter of Zibeon, whom she bore to Esau:
Jeush, Jalam and Korah.

15These were the chiefs among Esau's descendants:
The sons of Eliphaz the firstborn of Esau:
Chiefs Teman, Omar, Zepho, Kenaz,
16Korah,[a] Gatam and Amalek. These were the chiefs descended from Eliphaz in Edom; they were grandsons of Adah.
17The sons of Esau's son Reuel:
Chiefs Nahath, Zerah, Shammah and Mizzah. These were the chiefs descended from Reuel in Edom; they were grandsons of Esau's wife Basemath.
18The sons of Esau's wife Oholibamah:
Chiefs Jeush, Jalam and Korah. These were the chiefs descended from Esau's wife Oholibamah daughter of Anah.
19These were the sons of Esau (that is, Edom), and these were their chiefs.

20These were the sons of Seir the Horite, who were living in the region:
Lotan, Shobal, Zibeon, Anah,
21Dishon, Ezer and Dishan. These sons of Seir in Edom were Horite chiefs.
22The sons of Lotan:
Hori and Homam.[b] Timna was Lotan's sister.
23The sons of Shobal:
Alvan, Manahath, Ebal, Shepho and Onam.
24The sons of Zibeon:
Aiah and Anah. This is the Anah who discovered the hot springs[c] in the desert while he was grazing the donkeys of his father Zibeon.
25The children of Anah:
Dishon and Oholibamah daughter of Anah.
26The sons of Dishon[d]:
Hemdan, Eshban, Ithran and Keran.
27The sons of Ezer:
Bilhan, Zaavan and Akan.
28The sons of Dishan:
Uz and Aran.
29These were the Horite chiefs:
Lotan, Shobal, Zibeon, Anah,
30Dishon, Ezer and Dishan. These were the Horite chiefs, according to their divisions, in the land of Seir.

The Rulers of Edom

31These were the kings who reigned in Edom before any Israelite king reigned[e]:
32Bela son of Beor became king of Edom. His city was named Dinhabah.
33When Bela died, Jobab son of Zerah from Bozrah succeeded him as king.
34When Jobab died, Husham from the land of the Temanites succeeded him as king.
35When Husham died, Hadad son of Bedad, who defeated Midian in the country of Moab, succeeded him as king. His city was named Avith.
36When Hadad died, Samlah from Masrekah succeeded him as king.
37When Samlah died, Shaul from Rehoboth on the river[f] succeeded him as king.
38When Shaul died, Baal-Hanan son of Acbor succeeded him as king.
39When Baal-Hanan son of Acbor died, Hadad[g] succeeded him as king. His city was named Pau, and his wife's name was Mehetabel daughter of Matred, the daughter of Me-Zahab.

40These were the chiefs descended from Esau, by name, according to their clans and regions:
Timna, Alvah, Jetheth,
41Oholibamah, Elah, Pinon,
42Kenaz, Teman, Mibzar,
43Magdiel and Iram. These were the chiefs of Edom, according to their settlements in the land they occupied.
This was Esau the father of the Edomites.

Joseph's Dreams

37 Jacob lived in the land where his father had stayed, the land of Canaan.
2This is the account of Jacob.
Joseph, a young man of seventeen, was tending the flocks with his brothers, the sons of

[a]16 Masoretic Text; Samaritan Pentateuch (see also Gen. 36:11 and 1 Chron. 1:36) does not have *Korah.*
[b]22 Hebrew *Hemam,* a variant of *Homam* (see 1 Chron. 1:39)
[c]24 Vulgate; Syriac *discovered water;* the meaning of the Hebrew for this word is uncertain.
[d]26 Hebrew *Dishan,* a variant of *Dishon*
[e]31 Or *before an Israelite king reigned over them*
[f]37 Possibly the Euphrates
[g]39 Many manuscripts of the Masoretic Text, Samaritan Pentateuch and Syriac (see also 1 Chron. 1:50); most manuscripts of the Masoretic Text *Hadar*

37:2 As a boy Joseph was irritatingly overconfident. He was also a tattletale. Joseph's arrogant behavior as a youth, along with his father's favoritism, planted seeds of hatred in his brothers' hearts. Consequently, Joseph suffered years of slavery in Egypt. Though Joseph was certainly more worthy of praise than his brothers in his adult years, he can hardly be given perfect marks as a youngster.

Bilhah and the sons of Zilpah, his father's wives, and he brought their father a bad report about them.

3Now Israel loved Joseph more than any of his other sons, because he had been born to him in his old age; and he made a richly ornamented[a] robe for him. 4When his brothers saw that their father loved him more than any of them, they hated him and could not speak a kind word to him.

5Joseph had a dream, and when he told it to his brothers, they hated him all the more. 6He said to them, "Listen to this dream I had: 7We were binding sheaves of grain out in the field when suddenly my sheaf rose and stood upright, while your sheaves gathered around mine and bowed down to it."

8His brothers said to him, "Do you intend to reign over us? Will you actually rule us?" And they hated him all the more because of his dream and what he had said.

9Then he had another dream, and he told it to his brothers. "Listen," he said, "I had another dream, and this time the sun and moon and eleven stars were bowing down to me."

10When he told his father as well as his brothers, his father rebuked him and said, "What is this dream you had? Will your mother and I and your brothers actually come and bow down to the ground before you?" 11His brothers were jealous of him, but his father kept the matter in mind.

Joseph Sold by His Brothers

12Now his brothers had gone to graze their father's flocks near Shechem, 13and Israel said to Joseph, "As you know, your brothers are grazing the flocks near Shechem. Come, I am going to send you to them."

"Very well," he replied.

14So he said to him, "Go and see if all is well with your brothers and with the flocks, and bring word back to me." Then he sent him off from the Valley of Hebron.

When Joseph arrived at Shechem, 15a man found him wandering around in the fields and asked him, "What are you looking for?"

16He replied, "I'm looking for my brothers. Can you tell me where they are grazing their flocks?"

17"They have moved on from here," the man answered. "I heard them say, 'Let's go to Dothan.' "

So Joseph went after his brothers and found them near Dothan. 18But they saw him in the distance, and before he reached them, they plotted to kill him.

19"Here comes that dreamer!" they said to each other. 20"Come now, let's kill him and throw him into one of these cisterns and say that a ferocious animal devoured him. Then we'll see what comes of his dreams."

21When Reuben heard this, he tried to rescue him from their hands. "Let's not take his life," he said. 22"Don't shed any blood. Throw him into this cistern here in the desert, but don't lay a hand on him." Reuben said this to rescue him from them and take him back to his father.

23So when Joseph came to his brothers, they stripped him of his robe—the richly ornamented robe he was wearing— 24and they took him and threw him into the cistern. Now the cistern was empty; there was no water in it.

25As they sat down to eat their meal, they looked up and saw a caravan of Ishmaelites coming from Gilead. Their camels were loaded with spices, balm and myrrh, and they were on their way to take them down to Egypt.

26Judah said to his brothers, "What will we gain if we kill our brother and cover up his blood? 27Come, let's sell him to the Ishmaelites and not lay our hands on him; after all, he is our brother, our own flesh and blood." His brothers agreed.

28So when the Midianite merchants came by, his brothers pulled Joseph up out of the cistern and sold him for twenty shekels[b] of silver to the Ishmaelites, who took him to Egypt.

29When Reuben returned to the cistern and saw that Joseph was not there, he tore his clothes. 30He went back to his brothers and said, "The boy isn't there! Where can I turn now?"

31Then they got Joseph's robe, slaughtered a goat and dipped the robe in the blood. 32They took the ornamented robe back to their father and said, "We found this. Examine it to see whether it is your son's robe."

33He recognized it and said, "It is my son's robe! Some ferocious animal has devoured him. Joseph has surely been torn to pieces."

34Then Jacob tore his clothes, put on sackcloth and mourned for his son many days. 35All

[a]3 The meaning of the Hebrew for *richly ornamented* is uncertain; also in verses 23 and 32. [b]28 That is, about 8 ounces (about 0.2 kilogram)

37:3 The Biblical account does not hide the fact that Joseph was Jacob's favorite son. Joseph had no choice but to accept the blessings of this distinction, along with its accompanying obstacles. The pattern of parental favoritism did not originate with the life of Joseph. Favoritism had played its part in the lives of his father Jacob and his grandfather Isaac as well. It is never healthy for parents to play favorites among their children. Favoritism is a pattern that causes untold suffering for many successive generations.

37:19–20 The terrible impact of jealousy is portrayed in this passage. The brothers were at the point of planning Joseph's murder and almost followed through on their plan, but cooler heads prevailed. The brothers ended up selling Joseph into slavery and then lied to their father, Jacob. What tragic, cumulative effects the patterns of deceit and favoritism can have on a family!

37:31–35 Jacob had always manipulated people and circumstances to serve his own purposes. He was a schemer and a trickster. Yet here the trickster was being tricked himself—by his sons. Jacob's destructive family pattern was passed on to the next generation.

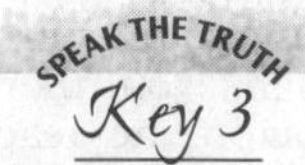

Confessing Instead of Condemning

Genesis 38:1–30 Admitting the truth about our failures and sins can be extremely difficult. We may even try making a big issue of the wrongs of others instead of doing the harder work of confessing our own faults.

According to ancient Jewish law, a widow was entitled to marry the surviving brother of her husband in order to produce children. Tamar had been married successively to two brothers who had died without giving her children. Her father-in-law Judah promised to give her his youngest son also, but he never did. This left Tamar alone and destitute. In an effort to protect herself, she disguised herself as a prostitute and became pregnant by Judah himself. She also kept his identification seal, which he had given her as a pledge for payment (38:1–23).

When Judah heard that Tamar was pregnant and unmarried, he demanded her execution. “As she was being brought out, she sent a message to her father-in-law. ‘I am pregnant by the man who owns these,’ she said. And she added, ‘See if you recognize whose seal and cord and staff these are.’ Judah recognized them and said, ‘She is more righteous than I, since I wouldn’t give her to my son Shelah’ ” (38:25–26).

It isn’t easy to be honest about our shortcomings, for “the heart is deceitful above all things and beyond cure” (Jeremiah 17:9). But once we have become aware of our own failings, it is essential that we openly confess them and begin the process of overcoming them.

Turn to Judges 16.

his sons and daughters came to comfort him,
but he refused to be comforted. “No,” he said,
“in mourning will I go down to the grave[a] to
my son.” So his father wept for him.
36Meanwhile, the Midianites[b] sold Joseph
in Egypt to Potiphar, one of Pharaoh’s officials,
the captain of the guard.

Judah and Tamar

38 At that time, Judah left his brothers and
went down to stay with a man of Adullam named Hirah. 2There Judah met the daughter of a Canaanite man named Shua. He married her and lay with her; 3she became pregnant
and gave birth to a son, who was named Er.
4She conceived again and gave birth to a son
and named him Onan. 5She gave birth to still
another son and named him Shelah. It was at
Kezib that she gave birth to him.
6Judah got a wife for Er, his firstborn, and her
name was Tamar. 7But Er, Judah’s firstborn, was
wicked in the LORD’s sight; so the LORD put him
to death.
8Then Judah said to Onan, “Lie with your
brother’s wife and fulfill your duty to her as a
brother-in-law to produce offspring for your
brother.” 9But Onan knew that the offspring
would not be his; so whenever he lay with his
brother’s wife, he spilled his semen on the
ground to keep from producing offspring for
his brother. 10What he did was wicked in the
LORD’s sight; so he put him to death also.
11Judah then said to his daughter-in-law Tamar, “Live as a widow in your father’s house
until my son Shelah grows up.” For he thought,

[a]35 Hebrew *Sheol* [b]36 Samaritan Pentateuch, Septuagint, Vulgate and Syriac (see also verse 28); Masoretic Text *Medanites*

38:1–5 Judah moved from his family home, married a Canaanite girl, and settled down among the Canaanites. Some of Judah’s unsavory activities in this chapter seem out of sync with what we might expect of one of Israel’s patriarchs. Yet some of Judah’s behavior was probably influenced by the people he lived with. The Canaanites were known for their immoral lifestyle. For us to grow spiritually, we need to spend time with people who will encourage us to live in a way that agrees with God’s will for our lives and give up the relationships that lead us into destructive activities.

38:1–30 Judah’s sensational sin of propositioning a prostitute often blinds readers to his primary failure. According to the laws of Judah’s time, if a husband died before fathering a son, his family was responsible for providing the widow with a husband. Judah fulfilled this responsibility the first time, but when his second son died soon after marrying Tamar, Judah was understandably shaken. He delayed giving her his third son, possibly hoping he would never be called upon to carry out his duty. Judah’s attitude didn’t solve the problem but only led to the sordid events that followed. It is easy for us to act like Judah and ignore our problems, refuse to see the truth or refuse to accept responsibility for our lives. We often blame our problems on something or someone else. But a key to solving any problem is admitting that we have the problem in the first place. Only then can we take responsible action to solve it.

JUDAH & TAMAR

Judah was the fourth son of Leah, Jacob's first wife. Among the patriarch's twelve sons, Judah evidently occupied a position of prominence. Early on in the Biblical narrative, Judah persuaded his brothers to let Joseph live. When they went to Egypt later for food, Judah spoke and acted on his brothers' behalf. Eventually, the royal line would come through the descendants of Judah.

As the story of Judah unfolds, we note that he left his childhood home and moved some distance away from his brothers. He settled in a Canaanite community and married a Canaanite girl. Judah's wife gave birth to three sons: Er, Onan and Shelah. Tamar, a woman of Canaanite descent, was chosen by Judah to be the wife of his oldest son Er. Er was evil in God's sight, so God punished him with death. Onan, as Tamar's brother-in-law, was expected to have sexual relations with Tamar and give her a son who could carry on Er's name and receive his inheritance. But Onan refused to fulfill his responsibility, so the Lord put him to death as well.

Now it was left to young Shelah to raise up offspring for both Er and Onan. But Judah was afraid that his last son would also die. So he told Tamar to return to her father's house until Shelah was older. Judah's intent seemed clear: Shelah would eventually fulfill his duty as a brother-in-law and have a son with Tamar. Time passed and Shelah grew old enough to father children, but Judah did not require him to fulfill his duty to Tamar. So Tamar took matters into her own hands. By assuming the guise of a prostitute, Tamar tricked Judah himself into getting her pregnant.

When Judah heard that Tamar was pregnant, he demanded her punishment. But Tamar was shrewd. She showed Judah the items he had given as a pledge, thus proving that he was the father of the child. Judah acknowledged that he was in the wrong. Tamar later gave birth to two sons, one of whom is named in the kingly lineage of David and Jesus the Messiah.

STRENGTHS AND ACCOMPLISHMENTS:

After being confronted, Judah admitted his failures and took responsibility for them.

WEAKNESSES AND MISTAKES:

Judah lost close contact with the patriarchal family by moving away, thus weakening his resolve to do right.

Judah failed to fulfill his paternal responsibilities toward Tamar.

Judah let fear dictate his actions, indicating his lack of faith.

Tamar failed to confront Judah directly, resorting to indirect manipulation.

LESSONS FROM THEIR LIVES:

A shallow walk with God can lead to trouble in family relationships.

Commitments made to others, whether stated or implied, must be kept.

God's grace can bring future blessings from our biggest mistakes.

KEY VERSE:

"Judah . . . said, '[Tamar] is more righteous than I, since I wouldn't give her to my son Shelah.' And he did not sleep with her again" (38:26).

The story of Judah and Tamar is told in Genesis 38. Judah is mentioned in Genesis 29—50 and throughout the Old Testament as one of the fathers of the twelve tribes of Israel. Judah and Tamar are both mentioned in Jesus' family tree in Matthew 1:3.

"He may die too, just like his brothers." So Tamar went to live in her father's house.
12 After a long time Judah's wife, the daughter
of Shua, died. When Judah had recovered from
his grief, he went up to Timnah, to the men who
were shearing his sheep, and his friend Hirah
the Adullamite went with him.
13 When Tamar was told, "Your father-in-law
is on his way to Timnah to shear his sheep,"
14 she took off her widow's clothes, covered herself with a veil to disguise herself, and then sat
down at the entrance to Enaim, which is on the
road to Timnah. For she saw that, though Shelah had now grown up, she had not been given
to him as his wife.
15 When Judah saw her, he thought she was a
prostitute, for she had covered her face. 16 Not
realizing that she was his daughter-in-law, he
went over to her by the roadside and said,
"Come now, let me sleep with you."

"And what will you give me to sleep with you?" she asked.

17 "I'll send you a young goat from my flock,"
he said.

"Will you give me something as a pledge until you send it?" she asked.

18 He said, "What pledge should I give you?"
"Your seal and its cord, and the staff in your
hand," she answered. So he gave them to her and
slept with her, and she became pregnant by
him. 19 After she left, she took off her veil and
put on her widow's clothes again.
20 Meanwhile Judah sent the young goat by
his friend the Adullamite in order to get his
pledge back from the woman, but he did not
find her. 21 He asked the men who lived there,
"Where is the shrine prostitute who was beside
the road at Enaim?"

"There hasn't been any shrine prostitute here," they said.

22 So he went back to Judah and said, "I
didn't find her. Besides, the men who lived
there said, 'There hasn't been any shrine prostitute here.' "
23 Then Judah said, "Let her keep what she
has, or we will become a laughingstock. After
all, I did send her this young goat, but you
didn't find her."
24 About three months later Judah was told,
"Your daughter-in-law Tamar is guilty of prostitution, and as a result she is now pregnant."

Judah said, "Bring her out and have her burned to death!"

25 As she was being brought out, she sent a
message to her father-in-law. "I am pregnant
by the man who owns these," she said. And she
added, "See if you recognize whose seal and
cord and staff these are."
26 Judah recognized them and said, "She is
more righteous than I, since I wouldn't give her
to my son Shelah." And he did not sleep with her
again.
27 When the time came for her to give birth,
there were twin boys in her womb. 28 As she was
giving birth, one of them put out his hand; so
the midwife took a scarlet thread and tied it on
his wrist and said, "This one came out first."
29 But when he drew back his hand, his brother
came out, and she said, "So this is how you
have broken out!" And he was named Perez.[a]
30 Then his brother, who had the scarlet thread
on his wrist, came out and he was given the
name Zerah.[b]

Joseph and Potiphar's Wife

39 Now Joseph had been taken down to
Egypt. Potiphar, an Egyptian who was
one of Pharaoh's officials, the captain of the
guard, bought him from the Ishmaelites who
had taken him there.
2 The LORD was with Joseph and he prospered, and he lived in the house of his Egyptian
master. 3 When his master saw that the LORD was
with him and that the LORD gave him success in
everything he did, 4 Joseph found favor in his
eyes and became his attendant. Potiphar put
him in charge of his household, and he entrusted to his care everything he owned. 5 From the
time he put him in charge of his household and
of all that he owned, the LORD blessed the
household of the Egyptian because of Joseph.
The blessing of the LORD was on everything Potiphar had, both in the house and in the field.
6 So he left in Joseph's care everything he had;
with Joseph in charge, he did not concern himself with anything except the food he ate.
Now Joseph was well-built and handsome,
7 and after a while his master's wife took notice
of Joseph and said, "Come to bed with me!"
8 But he refused. "With me in charge," he told

[a] 29 *Perez* means *breaking out.* [b] 30 *Zerah* can mean *scarlet* or *brightness.*

38:12–26 When Judah failed to deal with Tamar in a responsible way, Tamar decided to take action. Though what Tamar did was not exemplary, she wisely confronted Judah in a way that caught his attention without alienating him. Very often direct confrontation with people who have wronged us will only deepen our conflict. In such cases a less direct means of communication may prove helpful.

39:2 God blessed Joseph even in the worst of circumstances. Though God granted Joseph success in his position as a slave in a foreign land, it should not be inferred that God will also make us successful. Our chief goal should not be success but rather following Joseph's example of being faithful to God's plan, no matter what the consequences.

39:7–18 Joseph withstood the temptation of Potiphar's wife even though he was far from home. The temptation probably continued day after day, a constant, wearing temptation. How did he stand up to it? Two things seem to have helped: Joseph's respect for his master and, even more important, Joseph's respect for God. As we draw closer to God, we will begin to sense his presence in our lives. Doing something that runs counter to his plan will cause us pain. Walking close to God will provide us with added protection against the temptations we face.

her, "my master does not concern himself with
anything in the house; everything he owns he
has entrusted to my care. 9No one is greater in
this house than I am. My master has withheld
nothing from me except you, because you are
his wife. How then could I do such a wicked
thing and sin against God?" 10And though she
spoke to Joseph day after day, he refused to go
to bed with her or even be with her.

11One day he went into the house to attend
to his duties, and none of the household servants was inside. 12She caught him by his cloak
and said, "Come to bed with me!" But he left his
cloak in her hand and ran out of the house.

13When she saw that he had left his cloak in
her hand and had run out of the house, 14she
called her household servants. "Look," she said
to them, "this Hebrew has been brought to us
to make sport of us! He came in here to sleep
with me, but I screamed. 15When he heard me
scream for help, he left his cloak beside me and
ran out of the house."

16She kept his cloak beside her until his master came home. 17Then she told him this story:
"That Hebrew slave you brought us came to
me to make sport of me. 18But as soon as I
screamed for help, he left his cloak beside me
and ran out of the house."

19When his master heard the story his wife
told him, saying, "This is how your slave treated me," he burned with anger. 20Joseph's master
took him and put him in prison, the place
where the king's prisoners were confined.

But while Joseph was there in the prison,
21the LORD was with him; he showed him kindness and granted him favor in the eyes of the
prison warden. 22So the warden put Joseph in
charge of all those held in the prison, and he
was made responsible for all that was done
there. 23The warden paid no attention to anything under Joseph's care, because the LORD was
with Joseph and gave him success in whatever
he did.

The Cupbearer and the Baker

40 Some time later, the cupbearer and the
baker of the king of Egypt offended
their master, the king of Egypt. 2Pharaoh was
angry with his two officials, the chief cupbearer
and the chief baker, 3and put them in custody
in the house of the captain of the guard, in the
same prison where Joseph was confined. 4The
captain of the guard assigned them to Joseph,
and he attended them.

After they had been in custody for some
time, 5each of the two men—the cupbearer and
the baker of the king of Egypt, who were being
held in prison—had a dream the same night,
and each dream had a meaning of its own.

6When Joseph came to them the next morning, he saw that they were dejected. 7So he
asked Pharaoh's officials who were in custody
with him in his master's house, "Why are your
faces so sad today?"

8"We both had dreams," they answered, "but
there is no one to interpret them."

Then Joseph said to them, "Do not interpretations belong to God? Tell me your dreams."

9So the chief cupbearer told Joseph his
dream. He said to him, "In my dream I saw a
vine in front of me, 10and on the vine were three
branches. As soon as it budded, it blossomed,
and its clusters ripened into grapes. 11Pharaoh's
cup was in my hand, and I took the grapes,
squeezed them into Pharaoh's cup and put the
cup in his hand."

12"This is what it means," Joseph said to him.
"The three branches are three days. 13Within
three days Pharaoh will lift up your head and
restore you to your position, and you will put
Pharaoh's cup in his hand, just as you used to
do when you were his cupbearer. 14But when all
goes well with you, remember me and show me
kindness; mention me to Pharaoh and get me
out of this prison. 15For I was forcibly carried off
from the land of the Hebrews, and even here I
have done nothing to deserve being put in a
dungeon."

16When the chief baker saw that Joseph had
given a favorable interpretation, he said to Joseph, "I too had a dream: On my head were
three baskets of bread.[a] 17In the top basket
were all kinds of baked goods for Pharaoh, but
the birds were eating them out of the basket on
my head."

18"This is what it means," Joseph said. "The
three baskets are three days. 19Within three days
Pharaoh will lift off your head and hang you on
a tree.[b] And the birds will eat away your flesh."

[a] 16 Or *three wicker baskets* [b] 19 Or *and impale you on a pole*

39:19–20 Good guys often appear to finish last; the innocent seem to suffer. Here it looks as if Joseph's faithfulness to God was rewarded with years in prison. This may have discouraged Joseph, but it didn't stop him. Though in prison, Joseph continued living according to God's plan. Finally, after a number of setbacks, Joseph was rewarded. We may need to look past our present, difficult circumstances to see that God has a purpose in our suffering. It may be an important part of our preparation for future work God has for us.

39:19–23 Joseph was successful in everything he did, even in the responsibilities he held in prison. Through all his trials, Joseph remained faithful to God. It would have been easy for him to forget God's promises and just give up. When we forget God's promises, we may start to blame others and give up on our situation. But like Joseph we need to stop blaming and keep working, doing our best in the situations in which God has placed us.

40:1–8 Joseph gained the respect and trust of his jailer and his fellow prisoners. Quite possibly most of the prisoners in Joseph's day were sullen characters, intent on their own self-preservation. That Joseph would earn their respect is extremely significant. His attitude and faith in God was evident to those around him. Joseph recognized that he could do nothing to change his situation, so he sought God and surrendered to him in the midst of his trying circumstances.

[20]Now the third day was Pharaoh's birthday, and he gave a feast for all his officials. He lifted up the heads of the chief cupbearer and the chief baker in the presence of his officials: [21]He restored the chief cupbearer to his position, so that he once again put the cup into Pharaoh's hand, [22]but he hanged[a] the chief baker, just as Joseph had said to them in his interpretation.

[23]The chief cupbearer, however, did not remember Joseph; he forgot him.

Pharaoh's Dreams

41 When two full years had passed, Pharaoh had a dream: He was standing by the Nile, [2]when out of the river there came up seven cows, sleek and fat, and they grazed among the reeds. [3]After them, seven other cows, ugly and gaunt, came up out of the Nile and stood beside those on the riverbank. [4]And the cows that were ugly and gaunt ate up the seven sleek, fat cows. Then Pharaoh woke up.

[5]He fell asleep again and had a second dream: Seven heads of grain, healthy and good, were growing on a single stalk. [6]After them, seven other heads of grain sprouted—thin and scorched by the east wind. [7]The thin heads of grain swallowed up the seven healthy, full heads. Then Pharaoh woke up; it had been a dream.

[8]In the morning his mind was troubled, so he sent for all the magicians and wise men of Egypt. Pharaoh told them his dreams, but no one could interpret them for him.

[9]Then the chief cupbearer said to Pharaoh, "Today I am reminded of my shortcomings. [10]Pharaoh was once angry with his servants, and he imprisoned me and the chief baker in the house of the captain of the guard. [11]Each of us had a dream the same night, and each dream had a meaning of its own. [12]Now a young Hebrew was there with us, a servant of the captain of the guard. We told him our dreams, and he interpreted them for us, giving each man the interpretation of his dream. [13]And things turned out exactly as he interpreted them to us: I was restored to my position, and the other man was hanged.[a]"

[14]So Pharaoh sent for Joseph, and he was quickly brought from the dungeon. When he had shaved and changed his clothes, he came before Pharaoh.

[15]Pharaoh said to Joseph, "I had a dream, and no one can interpret it. But I have heard it said of you that when you hear a dream you can interpret it."

[16]"I cannot do it," Joseph replied to Pharaoh, "but God will give Pharaoh the answer he desires."

[17]Then Pharaoh said to Joseph, "In my dream I was standing on the bank of the Nile, [18]when out of the river there came up seven cows, fat and sleek, and they grazed among the reeds. [19]After them, seven other cows came up—scrawny and very ugly and lean. I had never seen such ugly cows in all the land of Egypt. [20]The lean, ugly cows ate up the seven fat cows that came up first. [21]But even after they ate them, no one could tell that they had done so; they looked just as ugly as before. Then I woke up.

[22]"In my dreams I also saw seven heads of grain, full and good, growing on a single stalk. [23]After them, seven other heads sprouted—withered and thin and scorched by the east wind. [24]The thin heads of grain swallowed up the seven good heads. I told this to the magicians, but none could explain it to me."

[25]Then Joseph said to Pharaoh, "The dreams of Pharaoh are one and the same. God has revealed to Pharaoh what he is about to do. [26]The seven good cows are seven years, and the seven good heads of grain are seven years; it is one and the same dream. [27]The seven lean, ugly cows that came up afterward are seven years, and so are the seven worthless heads of grain scorched by the east wind: They are seven years of famine.

[28]"It is just as I said to Pharaoh: God has shown Pharaoh what he is about to do. [29]Seven years of great abundance are coming throughout the land of Egypt, [30]but seven years of famine will follow them. Then all the abundance in Egypt will be forgotten, and the famine will ravage the land. [31]The abundance in the land will not be remembered, because the famine that follows it will be so severe. [32]The reason the dream was given to Pharaoh in two forms is that the matter has been firmly decided by God, and God will do it soon.

[33]"And now let Pharaoh look for a discerning and wise man and put him in charge of the land of Egypt. [34]Let Pharaoh appoint commissioners over the land to take a fifth of the harvest of Egypt during the seven years of abundance. [35]They should collect all the food of these good years that are coming and store up the grain under the authority of Pharaoh, to be

[a]22,13 Or *impaled*

40:23 After prophesying the cup-bearer's release, Joseph must have felt disappointed when he was forgotten. But Joseph refused to give in to despair. He didn't poison his life by complaining and assigning blame. He didn't give up and grow bitter. Instead, Joseph continued to live a life of faithfulness to God, trusting God to fulfill his plans.

41:14 At last Joseph was given the opportunity for freedom. God's perfect time had come. We may get discouraged by our slow progress, but we need to faithfully follow God as best we can. Someday we may find we are truly free of the things that now bind us. When we experience such deliverance, we can rejoice. Until then we must depend on God day by day to help us say "No!" to things that would detour us from God's will. And even when we find ourselves in these situations, we can still rejoice, knowing that through it all we are building a deeper relationship with God.

kept in the cities for food. 36This food should be held in reserve for the country, to be used during the seven years of famine that will come upon Egypt, so that the country may not be ruined by the famine."

37The plan seemed good to Pharaoh and to all his officials. 38So Pharaoh asked them, "Can we find anyone like this man, one in whom is the spirit of God[a]?"

39Then Pharaoh said to Joseph, "Since God has made all this known to you, there is no one so discerning and wise as you. 40You shall be in charge of my palace, and all my people are to submit to your orders. Only with respect to the throne will I be greater than you."

Joseph in Charge of Egypt

41So Pharaoh said to Joseph, "I hereby put you in charge of the whole land of Egypt." 42Then Pharaoh took his signet ring from his finger and put it on Joseph's finger. He dressed him in robes of fine linen and put a gold chain around his neck. 43He had him ride in a chariot as his second-in-command,[b] and men shouted before him, "Make way[c]!" Thus he put him in charge of the whole land of Egypt.

44Then Pharaoh said to Joseph, "I am Pharaoh, but without your word no one will lift hand or foot in all Egypt." 45Pharaoh gave Joseph the name Zaphenath-Paneah and gave him Asenath daughter of Potiphera, priest of On,[d] to be his wife. And Joseph went throughout the land of Egypt.

46Joseph was thirty years old when he entered the service of Pharaoh king of Egypt. And Joseph went out from Pharaoh's presence and traveled throughout Egypt. 47During the seven years of abundance the land produced plentifully. 48Joseph collected all the food produced in those seven years of abundance in Egypt and stored it in the cities. In each city he put the food grown in the fields surrounding it. 49Joseph stored up huge quantities of grain, like the sand of the sea; it was so much that he stopped keeping records because it was beyond measure.

50Before the years of famine came, two sons were born to Joseph by Asenath daughter of Potiphera, priest of On. 51Joseph named his firstborn Manasseh[e] and said, "It is because God has made me forget all my trouble and all my father's household." 52The second son he named Ephraim[f] and said, "It is because God has made me fruitful in the land of my suffering."

53The seven years of abundance in Egypt came to an end, 54and the seven years of famine began, just as Joseph had said. There was famine in all the other lands, but in the whole land of Egypt there was food. 55When all Egypt began to feel the famine, the people cried to Pharaoh for food. Then Pharaoh told all the Egyptians, "Go to Joseph and do what he tells you."

56When the famine had spread over the whole country, Joseph opened the storehouses and sold grain to the Egyptians, for the famine was severe throughout Egypt. 57And all the countries came to Egypt to buy grain from Joseph, because the famine was severe in all the world.

Joseph's Brothers Go to Egypt

42 When Jacob learned that there was grain in Egypt, he said to his sons, "Why do you just keep looking at each other?" 2He continued, "I have heard that there is grain in Egypt. Go down there and buy some for us, so that we may live and not die."

3Then ten of Joseph's brothers went down to buy grain from Egypt. 4But Jacob did not send Benjamin, Joseph's brother, with the others, because he was afraid that harm might come to him. 5So Israel's sons were among those who went to buy grain, for the famine was in the land of Canaan also.

6Now Joseph was the governor of the land, the one who sold grain to all its people. So when Joseph's brothers arrived, they bowed down to him with their faces to the ground. 7As soon as Joseph saw his brothers, he recognized them, but he pretended to be a stranger and spoke harshly to them. "Where do you come from?" he asked.

"From the land of Canaan," they replied, "to buy food."

8Although Joseph recognized his brothers, they did not recognize him. 9Then he remembered his dreams about them and said to them, "You are spies! You have come to see where our land is unprotected."

10"No, my lord," they answered. "Your ser-

[a]38 Or *of the gods* [b]43 Or *in the chariot of his second-in-command*; or *in his second chariot* [c]43 Or *Bow down* [d]45 That is, Heliopolis; also in verse 50
[e]51 *Manasseh* sounds like and may be derived from the Hebrew for *forget.* [f]52 *Ephraim* sounds like the Hebrew for *twice fruitful.*

41:38–40 The primary quality about Joseph that Pharaoh noticed was Joseph's dependence on God. Pharaoh ignored the fact that Joseph had a questionable past, colored by rumors and a long prison term. Pharaoh could see that God's Spirit was in Joseph, making him a very wise young man. This more than made up for any questions Pharaoh might have had about Joseph's past. So Pharaoh promoted Joseph to be the prime minister of Egypt! We may believe that our past has destroyed any hope of a prosperous future. But when we give ourselves to God, asking for his help, no past is too terrible or too dark for him to overcome.

42:7–20 When Joseph recognized his brothers, he took some time to test them. He wanted to discover something about their attitudes before he revealed himself to them. One key to achieving spiritual renewal is to work toward reconciliation with the important people in our lives. We need wisdom from God to do this in a way that will bring healing both to ourselves and to the people close to us. Joseph didn't instantly jump back into a relationship with his brothers. He took the time he needed to do it in a wise way.

vants have come to buy food. 11We are all the
sons of one man. Your servants are honest men,
not spies."
12"No!" he said to them. "You have come to
see where our land is unprotected."
13But they replied, "Your servants were
twelve brothers, the sons of one man, who lives
in the land of Canaan. The youngest is now
with our father, and one is no more."
14Joseph said to them, "It is just as I told you:
You are spies! 15And this is how you will be
tested: As surely as Pharaoh lives, you will not
leave this place unless your youngest brother
comes here. 16Send one of your number to get
your brother; the rest of you will be kept in
prison, so that your words may be tested to see
if you are telling the truth. If you are not, then
as surely as Pharaoh lives, you are spies!" 17And
he put them all in custody for three days.
18On the third day, Joseph said to them, "Do
this and you will live, for I fear God: 19If you are
honest men, let one of your brothers stay here
in prison, while the rest of you go and take grain
back for your starving households. 20But you
must bring your youngest brother to me, so that
your words may be verified and that you may
not die." This they proceeded to do.
21They said to one another, "Surely we are
being punished because of our brother. We saw
how distressed he was when he pleaded with us
for his life, but we would not listen; that's why
this distress has come upon us."
22Reuben replied, "Didn't I tell you not to
sin against the boy? But you wouldn't listen!
Now we must give an accounting for his blood."
23They did not realize that Joseph could understand them, since he was using an interpreter.
24He turned away from them and began to
weep, but then turned back and spoke to them
again. He had Simeon taken from them and
bound before their eyes.
25Joseph gave orders to fill their bags with
grain, to put each man's silver back in his sack,
and to give them provisions for their journey.
After this was done for them, 26they loaded
their grain on their donkeys and left.
27At the place where they stopped for the
night one of them opened his sack to get feed
for his donkey, and he saw his silver in the
mouth of his sack. 28"My silver has been returned," he said to his brothers. "Here it is in my
sack."
Their hearts sank and they turned to each
other trembling and said, "What is this that
God has done to us?"
29When they came to their father Jacob in the
land of Canaan, they told him all that had happened to them. They said, 30"The man who is
lord over the land spoke harshly to us and treated us as though we were spying on the land.
31But we said to him, 'We are honest men; we
are not spies. 32We were twelve brothers, sons of
one father. One is no more, and the youngest is
now with our father in Canaan.'
33"Then the man who is lord over the land
said to us, 'This is how I will know whether you
are honest men: Leave one of your brothers here
with me, and take food for your starving households and go. 34But bring your youngest brother
to me so I will know that you are not spies but
honest men. Then I will give your brother back
to you, and you can trade[a] in the land.' "
35As they were emptying their sacks, there in
each man's sack was his pouch of silver! When
they and their father saw the money pouches,
they were frightened. 36Their father Jacob said
to them, "You have deprived me of my children. Joseph is no more and Simeon is no
more, and now you want to take Benjamin.
Everything is against me!"
37Then Reuben said to his father, "You may
put both of my sons to death if I do not bring
him back to you. Entrust him to my care, and
I will bring him back."
38But Jacob said, "My son will not go down
there with you; his brother is dead and he is the
only one left. If harm comes to him on the
journey you are taking, you will bring my gray
head down to the grave[b] in sorrow."

The Second Journey to Egypt

43 Now the famine was still severe in the
land. 2So when they had eaten all the
grain they had brought from Egypt, their father
said to them, "Go back and buy us a little more
food."
3But Judah said to him, "The man warned us
solemnly, 'You will not see my face again unless your brother is with you.' 4If you will send
our brother along with us, we will go down and
buy food for you. 5But if you will not send him,
we will not go down, because the man said to
us, 'You will not see my face again unless your
brother is with you.' "
6Israel asked, "Why did you bring this trou-

[a]34 Or *move about freely* [b]38 Hebrew *Sheol*

42:21–22 After many years Joseph's brothers were still haunted by their guilty consciences. They had sold their brother into Egypt with no plans of ever seeing him again, no hope of reconciliation or forgiveness. We may wonder how many times during those years Reuben said, "I told you so." It is clear that this period had been one of misery for the brothers. A vital key to spiritual growth is seeking reconciliation with those we have wronged. Only when we are reconciled can we experience the healing we need to live a healthy and peaceful life.

42:36 How bitter with grief Jacob had become! He had harbored years of resentment and sadness. His relationship with his sons was built on dishonesty. Walls of lies had been built up, layer upon layer. This deceit separated Jacob from close fellowship with his family. He was alone in his grief, trapped by the fear that he might lose yet another son. Yet though Jacob was alone in his pain, he was not helpless. God had a plan for his redemption and would soon set him free from his years of bitterness and grief.

ble on me by telling the man you had another
brother?"
7They replied, "The man questioned us
closely about ourselves and our family. 'Is your
father still living?' he asked us. 'Do you have
another brother?' We simply answered his questions. How were we to know he would say,
'Bring your brother down here'?"
8Then Judah said to Israel his father, "Send
the boy along with me and we will go at once,
so that we and you and our children may live
and not die. 9I myself will guarantee his safety;
you can hold me personally responsible for
him. If I do not bring him back to you and set
him here before you, I will bear the blame before you all my life. 10As it is, if we had not
delayed, we could have gone and returned
twice."
11Then their father Israel said to them, "If it
must be, then do this: Put some of the best
products of the land in your bags and take them
down to the man as a gift—a little balm and a
little honey, some spices and myrrh, some pis-
tachio nuts and almonds. 12Take double the
amount of silver with you, for you must return
the silver that was put back into the mouths of
your sacks. Perhaps it was a mistake. 13Take
your brother also and go back to the man at
once. 14And may God Almighty[a] grant you
mercy before the man so that he will let your
other brother and Benjamin come back with
you. As for me, if I am bereaved, I am bereaved."
15So the men took the gifts and double the
amount of silver, and Benjamin also. They hurried down to Egypt and presented themselves
to Joseph. 16When Joseph saw Benjamin with
them, he said to the steward of his house, "Take
these men to my house, slaughter an animal
and prepare dinner; they are to eat with me at
noon."
17The man did as Joseph told him and took
the men to Joseph's house. 18Now the men were
frightened when they were taken to his house.
They thought, "We were brought here because
of the silver that was put back into our sacks the
first time. He wants to attack us and overpower
us and seize us as slaves and take our donkeys."
19So they went up to Joseph's steward and
spoke to him at the entrance to the house.
20"Please, sir," they said, "we came down here
the first time to buy food. 21But at the place
where we stopped for the night we opened our
sacks and each of us found his silver—the exact
weight—in the mouth of his sack. So we have
brought it back with us. 22We have also brought
additional silver with us to buy food. We don't
know who put our silver in our sacks."
23"It's all right," he said. "Don't be afraid.
Your God, the God of your father, has given you
treasure in your sacks; I received your silver."
Then he brought Simeon out to them.
24The steward took the men into Joseph's
house, gave them water to wash their feet and
provided fodder for their donkeys. 25They prepared their gifts for Joseph's arrival at noon,
because they had heard that they were to eat
there.
26When Joseph came home, they presented
to him the gifts they had brought into the
house, and they bowed down before him to the
ground. 27He asked them how they were, and
then he said, "How is your aged father you told
me about? Is he still living?"
28They replied, "Your servant our father is
still alive and well." And they bowed low to pay
him honor.
29As he looked about and saw his brother
Benjamin, his own mother's son, he asked, "Is
this your youngest brother, the one you told me
about?" And he said, "God be gracious to you,
my son." 30Deeply moved at the sight of his
brother, Joseph hurried out and looked for a
place to weep. He went into his private room
and wept there.
31After he had washed his face, he came out
and, controlling himself, said, "Serve the food."
32They served him by himself, the brothers
by themselves, and the Egyptians who ate with
him by themselves, because Egyptians could
not eat with Hebrews, for that is detestable to
Egyptians. 33The men had been seated before
him in the order of their ages, from the firstborn
to the youngest; and they looked at each other
in astonishment. 34When portions were served
to them from Joseph's table, Benjamin's portion was five times as much as anyone else's. So
they feasted and drank freely with him.

A Silver Cup in a Sack

44 Now Joseph gave these instructions to
the steward of his house: "Fill the
men's sacks with as much food as they can carry, and put each man's silver in the mouth of his
sack. 2Then put my cup, the silver one, in the
mouth of the youngest one's sack, along with
the silver for his grain." And he did as Joseph
said.
3As morning dawned, the men were sent on
their way with their donkeys. 4They had not
gone far from the city when Joseph said to his
steward, "Go after those men at once, and
when you catch up with them, say to them,
'Why have you repaid good with evil? 5Isn't this
the cup my master drinks from and also uses for
divination? This is a wicked thing you have
done.' "
6When he caught up with them, he repeated
these words to them. 7But they said to him,
"Why does my lord say such things? Far be it
from your servants to do anything like that!
8We even brought back to you from the land of
Canaan the silver we found inside the mouths
of our sacks. So why would we steal silver or
gold from your master's house? 9If any of your
servants is found to have it, he will die; and the
rest of us will become my lord's slaves."

[a]14 Hebrew *El-Shaddai*

10"Very well, then," he said, "let it be as you say. Whoever is found to have it will become my slave; the rest of you will be free from blame."

11Each of them quickly lowered his sack to the ground and opened it. 12Then the steward proceeded to search, beginning with the oldest and ending with the youngest. And the cup was found in Benjamin's sack. 13At this, they tore their clothes. Then they all loaded their donkeys and returned to the city.

14Joseph was still in the house when Judah and his brothers came in, and they threw themselves to the ground before him. 15Joseph said to them, "What is this you have done? Don't you know that a man like me can find things out by divination?"

16"What can we say to my lord?" Judah replied. "What can we say? How can we prove our innocence? God has uncovered your servants' guilt. We are now my lord's slaves—we ourselves and the one who was found to have the cup."

17But Joseph said, "Far be it from me to do such a thing! Only the man who was found to have the cup will become my slave. The rest of you, go back to your father in peace."

18Then Judah went up to him and said: "Please, my lord, let your servant speak a word to my lord. Do not be angry with your servant, though you are equal to Pharaoh himself. 19My lord asked his servants, 'Do you have a father or a brother?' 20And we answered, 'We have an aged father, and there is a young son born to him in his old age. His brother is dead, and he is the only one of his mother's sons left, and his father loves him.'

21"Then you said to your servants, 'Bring him down to me so I can see him for myself.' 22And we said to my lord, 'The boy cannot leave his father; if he leaves him, his father will die.' 23But you told your servants, 'Unless your youngest brother comes down with you, you will not see my face again.' 24When we went back to your servant my father, we told him what my lord had said.

25"Then our father said, 'Go back and buy a little more food.' 26But we said, 'We cannot go down. Only if our youngest brother is with us will we go. We cannot see the man's face unless our youngest brother is with us.'

27"Your servant my father said to us, 'You know that my wife bore me two sons. 28One of them went away from me, and I said, "He has surely been torn to pieces." And I have not seen him since. 29If you take this one from me too and harm comes to him, you will bring my gray head down to the grave[a] in misery.'

30"So now, if the boy is not with us when I go back to your servant my father and if my father, whose life is closely bound up with the boy's life, 31sees that the boy isn't there, he will die. Your servants will bring the gray head of our father down to the grave in sorrow. 32Your servant guaranteed the boy's safety to my father. I said, 'If I do not bring him back to you, I will bear the blame before you, my father, all my life!'

33"Now then, please let your servant remain here as my lord's slave in place of the boy, and let the boy return with his brothers. 34How can I go back to my father if the boy is not with me? No! Do not let me see the misery that would come upon my father."

Joseph Makes Himself Known

45 Then Joseph could no longer control himself before all his attendants, and he cried out, "Have everyone leave my presence!" So there was no one with Joseph when he made himself known to his brothers. 2And he wept so loudly that the Egyptians heard him, and Pharaoh's household heard about it.

3Joseph said to his brothers, "I am Joseph! Is my father still living?" But his brothers were not able to answer him, because they were terrified at his presence.

4Then Joseph said to his brothers, "Come close to me." When they had done so, he said, "I am your brother Joseph, the one you sold into Egypt! 5And now, do not be distressed and do not be angry with yourselves for selling me here, because it was to save lives that God sent me ahead of you. 6For two years now there has been famine in the land, and for the next five years there will not be plowing and reaping. 7But God sent me ahead of you to preserve for

[a]29 Hebrew *Sheol*; also in verse 31

44:18–34 Judah stepped forward to plead for Benjamin's freedom, fearing what his enslavement would do to Jacob, their father. Many years earlier, the brothers had chosen to sell Joseph into slavery because of personal hatred. This had caused their father deep pain. Now, Judah was willing to put himself on the line for his grieving father. Judah and his brothers had learned a great deal over the years from their past mistakes. They proved to Joseph that they were ready for reconciliation with their long-lost brother.
45:1–3 Joseph finally revealed his identity to his brothers. For him it was a beautiful reunion because he had experienced healing by walking with God. But for his older brothers, hidden guilt had burdened them for a long time. They were terrified when they recognized Joseph. It is frightening to expose long-hidden guilt to the light, yet that exposure is the only road to reconciliation and peace.
45:4–7 Joseph told his brothers not to be angry with themselves for the mistakes they had made in the past. It was now time to rejoice in the present! This was true forgiveness. Joseph was able to see how God had used their sin to save thousands of lives, including their own. God often turns our sins into opportunities for great success. When we begin to glimpse God's hand working in our lives, we will be better able to forgive the people who have wronged us in the past. And if we can see how God has turned around the lives of people we have wronged, we will begin to understand how much God wants our guilt to be removed and our relationships to be reconciled.

Joseph & Brothers

Overconfidence is usually viewed as a negative personality trait. The youthful boasting that Joseph displayed was no exception to this rule. Joseph's claims that his brothers would someday bow down to him, coupled with his father's favoritism, led to jealousy and broken family relationships. In the end, Joseph's brothers cut him off from his family altogether by selling him into slavery.

Through years of difficulties and suffering, Joseph's overconfidence was shaped by God into a mature self-assurance. When faced with personal struggles, Joseph's self-assurance, based on his personal knowledge of God, enabled him to ask, "What shall I do now?" instead of "Why me, God?"

Joseph's self-assurance let him tackle and succeed at jobs that most other people would have avoided. His high standards of personal integrity resulted from his relationship with God. Throughout his life these standards would take Joseph from the bottom of the social ladder to the upper echelons of power. Because of this, Joseph was in a position to save the young nation of Israel during a time of terrible famine.

Joseph's life shows us two sides of the coin of self-confidence. Overconfidence without God's perspective will invariably lead us down the pathway to personal problems and mistakes. On the other hand, self-assurance based on a strong faith in God will enable us to overcome the obstacles we face in life.

STRENGTHS AND ACCOMPLISHMENTS:

Joseph was elevated from slavery to the position of ruler of Egypt.

He had high standards of personal integrity.

He was a man of great spiritual sensitivity.

He enabled a nation to prepare for a seven-year famine.

WEAKNESSES AND MISTAKES:

As a young man, Joseph's overconfidence severely damaged his family relationships.

LESSONS FROM HIS LIFE:

Our responses to our circumstances are more important than the circumstances themselves.

God can mold our weaknesses into strengths.

God can cause good to come out of the evil intentions of others.

KEY VERSE:

"Then Pharaoh said to Joseph, 'Since God has made all this known to you, there is no one so discerning and wise as you'" (41:39).

Joseph's story is told in Genesis 37—50. Joseph is also mentioned in Acts 7:9–18 and Hebrews 11:22.

you a remnant on earth and to save your lives by a great deliverance.[a]

8“So then, it was not you who sent me here, but God. He made me father to Pharaoh, lord of his entire household and ruler of all Egypt. 9Now hurry back to my father and say to him, ‘This is what your son Joseph says: God has made me lord of all Egypt. Come down to me; don’t delay. 10You shall live in the region of Goshen and be near me—you, your children and grandchildren, your flocks and herds, and all you have. 11I will provide for you there, because five years of famine are still to come. Otherwise you and your household and all who belong to you will become destitute.’

12“You can see for yourselves, and so can my brother Benjamin, that it is really I who am speaking to you. 13Tell my father about all the honor accorded me in Egypt and about everything you have seen. And bring my father down here quickly.”

14Then he threw his arms around his brother Benjamin and wept, and Benjamin embraced him, weeping. 15And he kissed all his brothers and wept over them. Afterward his brothers talked with him.

16When the news reached Pharaoh’s palace that Joseph’s brothers had come, Pharaoh and all his officials were pleased. 17Pharaoh said to Joseph, “Tell your brothers, ‘Do this: Load your animals and return to the land of Canaan, 18and bring your father and your families back to me. I will give you the best of the land of Egypt and you can enjoy the fat of the land.’

19“You are also directed to tell them, ‘Do this: Take some carts from Egypt for your children and your wives, and get your father and come. 20Never mind about your belongings, because the best of all Egypt will be yours.’ ”

21So the sons of Israel did this. Joseph gave them carts, as Pharaoh had commanded, and he also gave them provisions for their journey. 22To each of them he gave new clothing, but to Benjamin he gave three hundred shekels[b] of silver and five sets of clothes. 23And this is what he sent to his father: ten donkeys loaded with the best things of Egypt, and ten female donkeys loaded with grain and bread and other provisions for his journey. 24Then he sent his brothers away, and as they were leaving he said to them, “Don’t quarrel on the way!”

25So they went up out of Egypt and came to their father Jacob in the land of Canaan. 26They told him, “Joseph is still alive! In fact, he is ruler of all Egypt.” Jacob was stunned; he did not believe them. 27But when they told him everything Joseph had said to them, and when he saw the carts Joseph had sent to carry him back, the spirit of their father Jacob revived. 28And Israel said, “I’m convinced! My son Joseph is still alive. I will go and see him before I die.”

Jacob Goes to Egypt

46 So Israel set out with all that was his, and when he reached Beersheba, he offered sacrifices to the God of his father Isaac.

2And God spoke to Israel in a vision at night and said, “Jacob! Jacob!”

“Here I am,” he replied.

3“I am God, the God of your father,” he said. “Do not be afraid to go down to Egypt, for I will make you into a great nation there. 4I will go down to Egypt with you, and I will surely bring you back again. And Joseph’s own hand will close your eyes.”

5Then Jacob left Beersheba, and Israel’s sons took their father Jacob and their children and their wives in the carts that Pharaoh had sent to transport him. 6They also took with them their livestock and the possessions they had acquired in Canaan, and Jacob and all his offspring went to Egypt. 7He took with him to Egypt his sons and grandsons and his daughters and granddaughters—all his offspring.

8These are the names of the sons of Israel (Jacob and his descendants) who went to Egypt:

Reuben the firstborn of Jacob.
9The sons of Reuben:
Hanoch, Pallu, Hezron and Carmi.
10The sons of Simeon:
Jemuel, Jamin, Ohad, Jakin, Zohar and Shaul the son of a Canaanite woman.
11The sons of Levi:
Gershon, Kohath and Merari.
12The sons of Judah:
Er, Onan, Shelah, Perez and Zerah (but Er and Onan had died in the land of Canaan).
The sons of Perez:
Hezron and Hamul.
13The sons of Issachar:
Tola, Puah,[c] Jashub[d] and Shimron.
14The sons of Zebulun:
Sered, Elon and Jahleel.

15These were the sons Leah bore to Jacob in

[a]7 Or *save you as a great band of survivors* [b]22 That is, about 7 1/2 pounds (about 3.5 kilograms)
[c]13 Samaritan Pentateuch and Syriac (see also 1 Chron. 7:1); Masoretic Text *Puvah* [d]13 Samaritan Pentateuch and some Septuagint manuscripts (see also Num. 26:24 and 1 Chron. 7:1); Masoretic Text *Iob*

45:24 Joseph knew his brothers so well; he knew they were inclined to argue. Even though Joseph’s brothers had matured a great deal since he had last seen them, they still had a long way to go. Deeply ingrained attitudes and habits are hard to eliminate. It takes time. Joseph’s words here show that he had a sense of humor. But they also reveal that he accepted his brothers as they were, arguments and all.

46:1–4 Some may think it was wrong for the Hebrews to leave the promised land, but God’s promise to Jacob shows that God approved of this family reunion in Egypt. God brought Jacob and his family to Egypt for their preservation and growth. When our life is subject to God’s authority, where and when we go are up to God. And God will often use surprising means to work his will.

Paddan Aram,[a] besides his daughter Dinah.
These sons and daughters of his were thirty-
three in all.

16 The sons of Gad:
Zephon,[b] Haggi, Shuni, Ezbon, Eri,
Arodi and Areli.
17 The sons of Asher:
Imnah, Ishvah, Ishvi and Beriah.
Their sister was Serah.
The sons of Beriah:
Heber and Malkiel.
18 These were the children born to Jacob by
Zilpah, whom Laban had given to his daughter
Leah—sixteen in all.

19 The sons of Jacob's wife Rachel:
Joseph and Benjamin. 20 In Egypt, Manasseh and Ephraim were born to Joseph by Asenath daughter of Potiphera, priest of On.[c]
21 The sons of Benjamin:
Bela, Beker, Ashbel, Gera, Naaman,
Ehi, Rosh, Muppim, Huppim and Ard.
22 These were the sons of Rachel who were
born to Jacob—fourteen in all.

23 The son of Dan:
Hushim.
24 The sons of Naphtali:
Jahziel, Guni, Jezer and Shillem.
25 These were the sons born to Jacob by Bilhah, whom Laban had given to his daughter
Rachel—seven in all.

26 All those who went to Egypt with Jacob—
those who were his direct descendants, not
counting his sons' wives—numbered sixty-six
persons. 27 With the two sons[d] who had been
born to Joseph in Egypt, the members of Jacob's
family, which went to Egypt, were seventy[e] in
all.

28 Now Jacob sent Judah ahead of him to Joseph to get directions to Goshen. When they
arrived in the region of Goshen, 29 Joseph had
his chariot made ready and went to Goshen to
meet his father Israel. As soon as Joseph appeared before him, he threw his arms around
his father[f] and wept for a long time.
30 Israel said to Joseph, "Now I am ready to
die, since I have seen for myself that you are still
alive."
31 Then Joseph said to his brothers and to his
father's household, "I will go up and speak to
Pharaoh and will say to him, 'My brothers and
my father's household, who were living in the
land of Canaan, have come to me. 32 The men
are shepherds; they tend livestock, and they
have brought along their flocks and herds and
everything they own.' 33 When Pharaoh calls
you in and asks, 'What is your occupation?'
34 you should answer, 'Your servants have tended livestock from our boyhood on, just as our
fathers did.' Then you will be allowed to settle
in the region of Goshen, for all shepherds are
detestable to the Egyptians."

47 Joseph went and told Pharaoh, "My father and brothers, with their flocks and
herds and everything they own, have come
from the land of Canaan and are now in Goshen." 2 He chose five of his brothers and presented them before Pharaoh.
3 Pharaoh asked the brothers, "What is your
occupation?"
"Your servants are shepherds," they replied to
Pharaoh, "just as our fathers were." 4 They also
said to him, "We have come to live here awhile,
because the famine is severe in Canaan and
your servants' flocks have no pasture. So now,
please let your servants settle in Goshen."
5 Pharaoh said to Joseph, "Your father and
your brothers have come to you, 6 and the land
of Egypt is before you; settle your father and
your brothers in the best part of the land. Let
them live in Goshen. And if you know of any
among them with special ability, put them in
charge of my own livestock."
7 Then Joseph brought his father Jacob in and
presented him before Pharaoh. After Jacob
blessed[g] Pharaoh, 8 Pharaoh asked him, "How
old are you?"
9 And Jacob said to Pharaoh, "The years of
my pilgrimage are a hundred and thirty. My
years have been few and difficult, and they do
not equal the years of the pilgrimage of my
fathers." 10 Then Jacob blessed[h] Pharaoh and
went out from his presence.
11 So Joseph settled his father and his brothers in Egypt and gave them property in the best
part of the land, the district of Rameses, as Pharaoh directed. 12 Joseph also provided his father
and his brothers and all his father's household
with food, according to the number of their
children.

Joseph and the Famine

13 There was no food, however, in the whole
region because the famine was severe; both
Egypt and Canaan wasted away because of the
famine. 14 Joseph collected all the money that
was to be found in Egypt and Canaan in pay-

[a]15 That is, Northwest Mesopotamia [b]16 Samaritan Pentateuch and Septuagint (see also Num. 26:15); Masoretic Text *Ziphion* [c]20 That is, Heliopolis [d]27 Hebrew; Septuagint *the nine children* [e]27 Hebrew (see also Exodus 1:5 and footnote); Septuagint (see also Acts 7:14) *seventy-five* [f]29 Hebrew *around him* [g]7 Or *greeted* [h]10 Or *said farewell to*

46:29 While our culture may urge people to hide their feelings, Jacob and Joseph embraced and wept a long while, openly expressing their emotions for all to see. Their example shows us that God approves of the outward expression of emotion. He tells us to grieve and mourn, releasing all the pain that wells up within us. An honest display of feelings can draw us closer to others. To hide our feelings, however, is a form of dishonesty. We need to learn to show our feelings appropriately, in wise and loving ways, whether in times of extreme sorrow or joy.

ment for the grain they were buying, and he brought it to Pharaoh's palace. 15When the money of the people of Egypt and Canaan was gone, all Egypt came to Joseph and said, "Give us food. Why should we die before your eyes? Our money is used up."

16"Then bring your livestock," said Joseph. "I will sell you food in exchange for your livestock, since your money is gone." 17So they brought their livestock to Joseph, and he gave them food in exchange for their horses, their sheep and goats, their cattle and donkeys. And he brought them through that year with food in exchange for all their livestock.

18When that year was over, they came to him the following year and said, "We cannot hide from our lord the fact that since our money is gone and our livestock belongs to you, there is nothing left for our lord except our bodies and our land. 19Why should we perish before your eyes—we and our land as well? Buy us and our land in exchange for food, and we with our land will be in bondage to Pharaoh. Give us seed so that we may live and not die, and that the land may not become desolate."

20So Joseph bought all the land in Egypt for Pharaoh. The Egyptians, one and all, sold their fields, because the famine was too severe for them. The land became Pharaoh's, 21and Joseph reduced the people to servitude,[a] from one end of Egypt to the other. 22However, he did not buy the land of the priests, because they received a regular allotment from Pharaoh and had food enough from the allotment Pharaoh gave them. That is why they did not sell their land.

23Joseph said to the people, "Now that I have bought you and your land today for Pharaoh, here is seed for you so you can plant the ground. 24But when the crop comes in, give a fifth of it to Pharaoh. The other four-fifths you may keep as seed for the fields and as food for yourselves and your households and your children."

25"You have saved our lives," they said. "May we find favor in the eyes of our lord; we will be in bondage to Pharaoh."

26So Joseph established it as a law concerning land in Egypt—still in force today—that a fifth of the produce belongs to Pharaoh. It was only the land of the priests that did not become Pharaoh's.

27Now the Israelites settled in Egypt in the region of Goshen. They acquired property there and were fruitful and increased greatly in number.

28Jacob lived in Egypt seventeen years, and the years of his life were a hundred and forty-seven. 29When the time drew near for Israel to die, he called for his son Joseph and said to him, "If I have found favor in your eyes, put your hand under my thigh and promise that you will show me kindness and faithfulness. Do not bury me in Egypt, 30but when I rest with my fathers, carry me out of Egypt and bury me where they are buried."

"I will do as you say," he said.

31"Swear to me," he said. Then Joseph swore to him, and Israel worshiped as he leaned on the top of his staff.[b]

Manasseh and Ephraim

48 Some time later Joseph was told, "Your father is ill." So he took his two sons Manasseh and Ephraim along with him. 2When Jacob was told, "Your son Joseph has come to you," Israel rallied his strength and sat up on the bed.

3Jacob said to Joseph, "God Almighty[c] appeared to me at Luz in the land of Canaan, and there he blessed me 4and said to me, 'I am going to make you fruitful and will increase your numbers. I will make you a community of peoples, and I will give this land as an everlasting possession to your descendants after you.'

5"Now then, your two sons born to you in Egypt before I came to you here will be reckoned as mine; Ephraim and Manasseh will be mine, just as Reuben and Simeon are mine. 6Any children born to you after them will be yours; in the territory they inherit they will be reckoned under the names of their brothers. 7As I was returning from Paddan,[d] to my sorrow Rachel died in the land of Canaan while we were still on the way, a little distance from Ephrath. So I buried her there beside the road to Ephrath" (that is, Bethlehem).

8When Israel saw the sons of Joseph, he asked, "Who are these?"

9"They are the sons God has given me here," Joseph said to his father.

Then Israel said, "Bring them to me so I may bless them."

10Now Israel's eyes were failing because of old age, and he could hardly see. So Joseph brought his sons close to him, and his father kissed them and embraced them.

11Israel said to Joseph, "I never expected to see your face again, and now God has allowed me to see your children too."

12Then Joseph removed them from Israel's

[a]21 Samaritan Pentateuch and Septuagint (see also Vulgate); Masoretic Text *and he moved the people into the cities* [b]31 Or *Israel bowed down at the head of his bed* [c]3 Hebrew *El-Shaddai* [d]7 That is, Northwest Mesopotamia

---

48:1–9 Before blessing his grandsons, Ephraim and Manasseh, Jacob recalled the blessings that God had bestowed upon him. We know that the sins and failures of parents are often passed on to succeeding generations. But blessings are passed on as well. Abraham had established a relationship with God that he modeled before Isaac. Isaac then passed the relationship on to Jacob, and Jacob passed it along to the succeeding generation. Let us establish the kind of relationship with God that will endure through the generations that follow. That way we will be able to bless our children with the blessings God has given us.

knees and bowed down with his face to the ground. 13And Joseph took both of them, Ephraim on his right toward Israel's left hand and Manasseh on his left toward Israel's right hand, and brought them close to him. 14But Israel reached out his right hand and put it on Ephraim's head, though he was the younger, and crossing his arms, he put his left hand on Manasseh's head, even though Manasseh was the firstborn.

15Then he blessed Joseph and said,

"May the God before whom my fathers
 Abraham and Isaac walked,
the God who has been my shepherd
 all my life to this day,
16the Angel who has delivered me from all harm
 —may he bless these boys.
May they be called by my name
 and the names of my fathers Abraham and Isaac,
and may they increase greatly
 upon the earth."

17When Joseph saw his father placing his right hand on Ephraim's head he was displeased; so he took hold of his father's hand to move it from Ephraim's head to Manasseh's head. 18Joseph said to him, "No, my father, this one is the firstborn; put your right hand on his head."

19But his father refused and said, "I know, my son, I know. He too will become a people, and he too will become great. Nevertheless, his younger brother will be greater than he, and his descendants will become a group of nations." 20He blessed them that day and said,

"In your[a] name will Israel pronounce this blessing:
 'May God make you like Ephraim and Manasseh.' "

So he put Ephraim ahead of Manasseh.

21Then Israel said to Joseph, "I am about to die, but God will be with you[b] and take you[b] back to the land of your[b] fathers. 22And to you, as one who is over your brothers, I give the ridge of land[c] I took from the Amorites with my sword and my bow."

Jacob Blesses His Sons

49 Then Jacob called for his sons and said: "Gather around so I can tell you what will happen to you in days to come.

2"Assemble and listen, sons of Jacob;
 listen to your father Israel.

3"Reuben, you are my firstborn,
 my might, the first sign of my strength,
 excelling in honor, excelling in power.
4Turbulent as the waters, you will no longer excel,
 for you went up onto your father's bed,
 onto my couch and defiled it.

5"Simeon and Levi are brothers—
 their swords[d] are weapons of violence.
6Let me not enter their council,
 let me not join their assembly,
for they have killed men in their anger
 and hamstrung oxen as they pleased.
7Cursed be their anger, so fierce,
 and their fury, so cruel!
I will scatter them in Jacob
 and disperse them in Israel.

8"Judah,[e] your brothers will praise you;
 your hand will be on the neck of your enemies;
 your father's sons will bow down to you.
9You are a lion's cub, O Judah;
 you return from the prey, my son.
Like a lion he crouches and lies down,
 like a lioness—who dares to rouse him?
10The scepter will not depart from Judah,
 nor the ruler's staff from between his feet,
until he comes to whom it belongs[f]
 and the obedience of the nations is his.
11He will tether his donkey to a vine,
 his colt to the choicest branch;
he will wash his garments in wine,
 his robes in the blood of grapes.
12His eyes will be darker than wine,
 his teeth whiter than milk.[g]

13"Zebulun will live by the seashore
 and become a haven for ships;
 his border will extend toward Sidon.

14"Issachar is a rawboned[h] donkey
 lying down between two saddlebags.[i]

[a]20 The Hebrew is singular. [b]21 The Hebrew is plural. [c]22 Or *And to you I give one portion more than to your brothers—the portion* [d]5 The meaning of the Hebrew for this word is uncertain. [e]8 *Judah* sounds like and may be derived from the Hebrew for *praise.* [f]10 Or *until Shiloh comes;* or *until he comes to whom tribute belongs* [g]12 Or *will be dull from wine, / his teeth white from milk* [h]14 Or *strong* [i]14 Or *campfires*

49:5–7 Simeon and Levi were characterized by violent tempers, and the history of these brothers in Genesis corroborates Jacob's assessment. After their sister Dinah was raped, they took revenge by deceiving and slaughtering all the men of the Hivite city (34:1–31). This tendency toward violence needed to be curbed. Many years later, however, when God called out for people to stand on his side, the Levites stood forth and vigorously defended God's cause (see Exodus 32:25–29). As a result, they were chosen as God's priests in Israel. Let us look to God to transform our weaknesses into strengths, just as he did with the descendants of Levi.

49:13–27 The remarks by Jacob concerning each of his sons seem very harsh, but the information he shared, including a confession of his own failure as a father, should have given helpful direction to each of them. We have a lot to learn from our parents, but often they aren't honest with us because we aren't really ready to listen. We need to learn to speak honestly and to listen with respect.

15When he sees how good is his resting place
and how pleasant is his land,
he will bend his shoulder to the burden
and submit to forced labor.

16"Dan[a] will provide justice for his people
as one of the tribes of Israel.
17Dan will be a serpent by the roadside,
a viper along the path,
that bites the horse's heels
so that its rider tumbles backward.

18"I look for your deliverance, O LORD.

19"Gad[b] will be attacked by a band of
raiders,
but he will attack them at their heels.

20"Asher's food will be rich;
he will provide delicacies fit for a
king.

21"Naphtali is a doe set free
that bears beautiful fawns.[c]

22"Joseph is a fruitful vine,
a fruitful vine near a spring,
whose branches climb over a wall.[d]
23With bitterness archers attacked him;
they shot at him with hostility.
24But his bow remained steady,
his strong arms stayed[e] limber,
because of the hand of the Mighty One of
Jacob,
because of the Shepherd, the Rock of
Israel,
25because of your father's God, who helps
you,
because of the Almighty,[f] who blesses
you
with blessings of the heavens above,
blessings of the deep that lies below,
blessings of the breast and womb.
26Your father's blessings are greater
than the blessings of the ancient
mountains,
than[g] the bounty of the age-old hills.
Let all these rest on the head of Joseph,
on the brow of the prince among[h] his
brothers.

27"Benjamin is a ravenous wolf;
in the morning he devours the prey,
in the evening he divides the plunder."

28All these are the twelve tribes of Israel, and
this is what their father said to them when he
blessed them, giving each the blessing appropriate to him.

The Death of Jacob

29Then he gave them these instructions: "I
am about to be gathered to my people. Bury
me with my fathers in the cave in the field
of Ephron the Hittite, 30the cave in the field
of Machpelah, near Mamre in Canaan, which
Abraham bought as a burial place from Ephron
the Hittite, along with the field. 31There Abraham and his wife Sarah were buried, there Isaac
and his wife Rebekah were buried, and there I
buried Leah. 32The field and the cave in it were
bought from the Hittites.[i]"

33When Jacob had finished giving instructions to his sons, he drew his feet up into the
bed, breathed his last and was gathered to his
people.

50 Joseph threw himself upon his father
and wept over him and kissed him.
2Then Joseph directed the physicians in his service to embalm his father Israel. So the physicians embalmed him, 3taking a full forty days,
for that was the time required for embalming.
And the Egyptians mourned for him seventy
days.

4When the days of mourning had passed,
Joseph said to Pharaoh's court, "If I have found
favor in your eyes, speak to Pharaoh for me. Tell
him, 5'My father made me swear an oath and
said, "I am about to die; bury me in the tomb
I dug for myself in the land of Canaan." Now let
me go up and bury my father; then I will return.' "

6Pharaoh said, "Go up and bury your father,
as he made you swear to do."

7So Joseph went up to bury his father. All
Pharaoh's officials accompanied him—the dignitaries of his court and all the dignitaries of
Egypt— 8besides all the members of Joseph's
household and his brothers and those belonging to his father's household. Only their children and their flocks and herds were left in
Goshen. 9Chariots and horsemen[j] also went
up with him. It was a very large company.

10When they reached the threshing floor of
Atad, near the Jordan, they lamented loudly
and bitterly; and there Joseph observed a seven-
day period of mourning for his father. 11When
the Canaanites who lived there saw the mourning at the threshing floor of Atad, they said,
"The Egyptians are holding a solemn ceremony
of mourning." That is why that place near the
Jordan is called Abel Mizraim.[k]

12So Jacob's sons did as he had commanded
them: 13They carried him to the land of Canaan
and buried him in the cave in the field of Machpelah, near Mamre, which Abraham had
bought as a burial place from Ephron the Hittite, along with the field. 14After burying his
father, Joseph returned to Egypt, together with

[a]16 *Dan* here means *he provides justice.* [b]19 *Gad* can mean *attack* and *band of raiders.* [c]21 Or *free; / he utters beautiful words* [d]22 Or *Joseph is a wild colt, / a wild colt near a spring, / a wild donkey on a terraced hill* [e]23,24 Or *archers will attack . . . will shoot . . . will remain . . . will stay* [f]25 Hebrew *Shaddai* [g]26 Or *of my progenitors, / as great as* [h]26 Or *the one separated from* [i]32 Or *the sons of Heth* [j]9 Or *charioteers* [k]11 *Abel Mizraim* means *mourning of the Egyptians.*

his brothers and all the others who had gone
with him to bury his father.

Joseph Reassures His Brothers

15When Joseph's brothers saw that their father was dead, they said, "What if Joseph holds
a grudge against us and pays us back for all the
wrongs we did to him?" 16So they sent word to
Joseph, saying, "Your father left these instructions before he died: 17'This is what you are to
say to Joseph: I ask you to forgive your brothers
the sins and the wrongs they committed in
treating you so badly.' Now please forgive the
sins of the servants of the God of your father."
When their message came to him, Joseph wept.
18His brothers then came and threw themselves down before him. "We are your slaves,"
they said.
19But Joseph said to them, "Don't be afraid.
Am I in the place of God? 20You intended to
harm me, but God intended it for good to accomplish what is now being done, the saving of
many lives. 21So then, don't be afraid. I will
provide for you and your children." And he reassured them and spoke kindly to them.

The Death of Joseph

22Joseph stayed in Egypt, along with all his
father's family. He lived a hundred and ten
years 23and saw the third generation of Ephraim's children. Also the children of Makir son
of Manasseh were placed at birth on Joseph's
knees.[a]
24Then Joseph said to his brothers, "I am
about to die. But God will surely come to your
aid and take you up out of this land to the land
he promised on oath to Abraham, Isaac and
Jacob." 25And Joseph made the sons of Israel
swear an oath and said, "God will surely come
to your aid, and then you must carry my bones
up from this place."
26So Joseph died at the age of a hundred and
ten. And after they embalmed him, he was
placed in a coffin in Egypt.

[a]23 That is, were counted as his

50:15–21 When Jacob died, Joseph's brothers feared that he would take revenge for their past differences. They thought Joseph had spared them only for the sake of their father. Here they discovered that Joseph's forgiveness was complete, with no ulterior motives. Joseph had granted his brothers complete forgiveness, but his brothers couldn't believe it and thus had not yet received it. They had needlessly lived in fear of a punishment that would never come. God hands us forgiveness that is just as complete. We need to believe it and then receive it. Only then can we experience the freedom that God offers.

50:15–21 A clear message echoes across these words: Man proposes, but God disposes. Joseph's brothers intended evil in their actions toward Joseph, but God turned those actions into good. It is wonderful that God can redeem our lives, transforming our sins and weaknesses into the means for accomplishing his gracious purposes.

Exodus

The Big Picture

- ***A. THE EXODUS: PAINFUL PATHWAY TO FREEDOM (1:1–18:27)***
  1. Need: Going From Bad to Worse (1:1–2:25)
  2. Provision: God Restores a Fallen Leader (3:1–4:31)
  3. Intervention: Tough Love, Escalating Consequences (5:1–12:36)
  4. Freedom: The Thrill of Victory, the Agony of Defeat (12:37–18:27)
- ***B. THE LAW: ESTABLISHING ACCOUNTABILITY AND BOUNDARIES (19:1–40:38)***
  1. Covenant: Faithful Relationship Between God and People (19:1–24:18)
  2. Closeness: Understanding and Drawing Near to God (25:1–31:18)
  3. Covenant Renewal: Breaking Covenant and Being Restored (32:1–35:3)
  4. Construction: Choosing to Glorify God (35:4–40:38)

Exit . . . Leave . . . Escape—these words tell us what the exodus was all about. At the end of Genesis, the sons of Jacob (Israel) went to Egypt to avoid famine and enjoyed favored status there. But as time passed, their comfortable dream turned into a nightmare. A new pharaoh enslaved the Israelites, forcing them to do backbreaking tasks in his building projects. Hopelessly enslaved, the Israelites turned their faces heavenward and begged for help.

The exodus from Egypt was God's answer to their cries. He acted by calling Moses—an ordinary man—to lead his people out of bondage to a new life. Moses had already made an exodus from Egypt, fleeing for his life after murdering an Egyptian. God came to Moses in the wilderness near Mount Sinai and called him to deliver God's people.

Moses was not exactly an eager leader—he initially balked at God's call. But God used Moses greatly despite his reluctance and weaknesses. God used Moses to work amazing miracles in Egypt that brought about Israel's deliverance. Moses spoke with God face-to-face and received God's instructions for healthy, responsible living within the community of Israel. Moses was living proof that God can use anyone who is available to him.

The exodus is also part of a much bigger deliverance story. It began with Abraham, whom God chose to father a nation that would carry God's healing touch to our world. God preserved this nation during slavery in Egypt and led them through the wilderness to the promised land. Centuries later, one of this nation's descendants, Jesus the Messiah, gave his life to deliver the human race from sin's destructive grip. Through him, each of us can add a chapter to this story.

Spiritual Renewal Themes

DELIVERANCE STARTS WITH SLAVERY

We can never really leave problems behind if we deny that they exist. Our spiritual blindness to them will only keep us from finding real solutions for these problems. If we are to be delivered from slavery, we need to begin by recognizing that we are slaves. As the book of Exodus begins, the Israelites have begun to realize that they are helplessly enslaved to the Egyptians. Over the years, the remembrance of the glorious days of

Joseph's leadership has faded and disappeared. For decades people probably denied the truth of their situation, choosing instead to remember "good old days." But now there could be no denial of the truth: the people of Israel were slaves. Their willingness to see the truth was the doorway to their deliverance. We also need to acknowledge our slavery to sin in order to start the process of freedom and spiritual renewal.

GOD HEARS THE HELPLESS

The Israelite slaves in Egypt may have felt that God was deaf to their cries for help. But the book of Exodus shows us that God listens to the heart-cries of the helpless. After their deliverance from Egypt, the Israelites were instructed to remind their children about God's faithfulness in hearing their cries for help (see Deuteronomy 6:20–25). These reminders would encourage them during the tough situations they would soon face. This knowledge should also bring us encouragement today, for God still hears the cries of the helpless.

GOD USES BROKEN PEOPLE

God responded to the cries of his people by choosing someone to lead them. He chose a man who had great skills and training but who also had great weaknesses. For forty years Moses was a fugitive and a shepherd, hiding because he had murdered an Egyptian. He was reticent to follow God's calling in his life. Pleading an inability to speak well, Moses resisted God's call until God became angry and appointed Moses' brother, Aaron, to act as his spokesman to the people. God allows us to glimpse all sides of Moses—the good and the bad—to show us that he can do great things through imperfect people whenever we seek God, surrender to him and follow his plan for our lives.

GOD'S PLAN

The story of Moses and the deliverance of the Israelites from Egypt continues God's plan for spiritual renewal that began in Genesis. God used his relationship with a chosen individual, Moses, to accomplish his will. He also gave Moses and the Israelites instructions for living healthy and holy lives as they traveled through the wilderness of Sinai. God's plan for spiritual renewal releases us from the bondage of our sinful tendencies—our personal slavery. He teaches us how to live and is personally involved in each phase of our transformation.

Essential Facts

PURPOSE:
To trace the deliverance of an enslaved people and their growth as a nation related to God.

AUTHOR:
Moses.

AUDIENCE:
The people of Israel.

DATE WRITTEN:
Sometime between 1445 and 1410 B.C., probably shortly after the writing of Genesis.

SETTING:
Egypt, then the wilderness of Sinai.

KEY VERSES:
"The LORD said, 'I have indeed seen the misery of my people in Egypt. I have heard them crying out because of their slave drivers . . . Now, go. I am sending you to Pharaoh to bring my people the Israelites out of Egypt' " (3:7, 10).

KEY PLACES:
Egypt, Midian, the Red Sea, the wilderness of Sinai.

KEY PEOPLE AND RELATIONSHIPS:
Moses and Pharaoh, Aaron and Miriam, Zipporah and Jethro, Joshua.

The Israelites Oppressed

1 These are the names of the sons of Israel who went to Egypt with Jacob, each with his family: 2Reuben, Simeon, Levi and Judah; 3Issachar, Zebulun and Benjamin; 4Dan and Naphtali; Gad and Asher. 5The descendants of Jacob numbered seventy[a] in all; Joseph was already in Egypt.

6Now Joseph and all his brothers and all that generation died, 7but the Israelites were fruitful and multiplied greatly and became exceedingly numerous, so that the land was filled with them.

8Then a new king, who did not know about Joseph, came to power in Egypt. 9"Look," he said to his people, "the Israelites have become much too numerous for us. 10Come, we must deal shrewdly with them or they will become even more numerous and, if war breaks out, will join our enemies, fight against us and leave the country."

11So they put slave masters over them to oppress them with forced labor, and they built Pithom and Rameses as store cities for Pharaoh. 12But the more they were oppressed, the more they multiplied and spread; so the Egyptians came to dread the Israelites 13and worked them ruthlessly. 14They made their lives bitter with hard labor in brick and mortar and with all kinds of work in the fields; in all their hard labor the Egyptians used them ruthlessly.

15The king of Egypt said to the Hebrew midwives, whose names were Shiphrah and Puah, 16"When you help the Hebrew women in childbirth and observe them on the delivery stool, if it is a boy, kill him; but if it is a girl, let her live." 17The midwives, however, feared God and did not do what the king of Egypt had told them to do; they let the boys live. 18Then the king of Egypt summoned the midwives and asked them, "Why have you done this? Why have you let the boys live?"

19The midwives answered Pharaoh, "Hebrew women are not like Egyptian women; they are vigorous and give birth before the midwives arrive."

20So God was kind to the midwives and the people increased and became even more numerous. 21And because the midwives feared God, he gave them families of their own.

22Then Pharaoh gave this order to all his people: "Every boy that is born[b] you must throw into the Nile, but let every girl live."

The Birth of Moses

2 Now a man of the house of Levi married a Levite woman, 2and she became pregnant and gave birth to a son. When she saw that he was a fine child, she hid him for three months. 3But when she could hide him no longer, she got a papyrus basket for him and coated it with tar and pitch. Then she placed the child in it and put it among the reeds along the bank of the Nile. 4His sister stood at a distance to see what would happen to him.

5Then Pharaoh's daughter went down to the Nile to bathe, and her attendants were walking along the river bank. She saw the basket among the reeds and sent her slave girl to get it. 6She opened it and saw the baby. He was crying, and she felt sorry for him. "This is one of the Hebrew babies," she said.

7Then his sister asked Pharaoh's daughter, "Shall I go and get one of the Hebrew women to nurse the baby for you?"

8"Yes, go," she answered. And the girl went and got the baby's mother. 9Pharaoh's daughter said to her, "Take this baby and nurse him for me, and I will pay you." So the woman took the baby and nursed him. 10When the child grew older, she took him to Pharaoh's daughter and he became her son. She named him Moses,[c] saying, "I drew him out of the water."

Moses Flees to Midian

11One day, after Moses had grown up, he went out to where his own people were and

[a]5 Masoretic Text (see also Gen. 46:27); Dead Sea Scrolls and Septuagint (see also Acts 7:14 and note at Gen. 46:27) *seventy-five* [b]22 Masoretic Text; Samaritan Pentateuch, Septuagint and Targums *born to the Hebrews* [c]10 *Moses* sounds like the Hebrew for *draw out.*

1:8–12 The Israelites had not yet come to the point of admitting their helplessness. Even though they were being oppressed with increasing severity, they continued to rise to the occasion. This did not please their Egyptian persecutors. The Egyptians feared that Israel would rise up against them, and in the event of war, might join Egypt's enemies or even leave the country (1:9–10). It was not until the Israelites asked God for help that he responded with deliverance.

1:18–21 The Hebrew midwives had to overcome their fears of the Egyptian king. It must have been terrifying to face such a cruel and powerful person, not knowing how he would respond. Their wisdom not only allowed Israel to continue growing (1:20), but the midwives were also blessed by God with families of their own. The midwives did not receive a reward from the king, but God's reward for their faith was blessing enough.

1:22—2:8 Moses' mother had a problem: She knew that she couldn't hide her beloved baby from the Egyptians indefinitely. So she displayed remarkable wisdom and faith by literally obeying Pharaoh's command to put her son into the Nile River (1:22; 2:3). Yet she did it in a way that preserved his life, trusting God to look after him. We don't know whether Moses' mother knew that Pharaoh's daughter might find the baby. But after doing all she could for her son, Moses' mother was willing to leave him in God's hands.

2:8–10 God graciously allowed Moses to be raised by his real mother. Not only did that allow for his normal, healthy development, but it also gave Moses a true understanding of who he was—a Hebrew. Apparently the further education he received in the Egyptian royal court never altered Moses' sense of identity with his people. As he grew to manhood, his desire to promote their freedom figured prominently.

2:11–14 Moses undoubtedly thought that he was helping his fellow Hebrew when he killed this Egyptian taskmaster. However, covering up his violent deed did not help

watched them at their hard labor. He saw an Egyptian beating a Hebrew, one of his own people. 12 Glancing this way and that and seeing no one, he killed the Egyptian and hid him in the sand. 13 The next day he went out and saw two Hebrews fighting. He asked the one in the wrong, "Why are you hitting your fellow Hebrew?"

14 The man said, "Who made you ruler and judge over us? Are you thinking of killing me as you killed the Egyptian?" Then Moses was afraid and thought, "What I did must have become known."

15 When Pharaoh heard of this, he tried to kill Moses, but Moses fled from Pharaoh and went to live in Midian, where he sat down by a well. 16 Now a priest of Midian had seven daughters, and they came to draw water and fill the troughs to water their father's flock. 17 Some shepherds came along and drove them away, but Moses got up and came to their rescue and watered their flock.

18 When the girls returned to Reuel their father, he asked them, "Why have you returned so early today?"

19 They answered, "An Egyptian rescued us from the shepherds. He even drew water for us and watered the flock."

20 "And where is he?" he asked his daughters. "Why did you leave him? Invite him to have something to eat."

21 Moses agreed to stay with the man, who gave his daughter Zipporah to Moses in marriage. 22 Zipporah gave birth to a son, and Moses named him Gershom,[a] saying, "I have become an alien in a foreign land."

23 During that long period, the king of Egypt died. The Israelites groaned in their slavery and cried out, and their cry for help because of their slavery went up to God. 24 God heard their groaning and he remembered his covenant with Abraham, with Isaac and with Jacob. 25 So God looked on the Israelites and was concerned about them.

Moses and the Burning Bush

3 Now Moses was tending the flock of Jethro his father-in-law, the priest of Midian, and he led the flock to the far side of the desert and came to Horeb, the mountain of God. 2 There the angel of the LORD appeared to him in flames of fire from within a bush. Moses saw that though the bush was on fire it did not burn up. 3 So Moses thought, "I will go over and see this strange sight—why the bush does not burn up."

4 When the LORD saw that he had gone over to look, God called to him from within the bush, "Moses! Moses!"

And Moses said, "Here I am."

5 "Do not come any closer," God said. "Take off your sandals, for the place where you are standing is holy ground." 6 Then he said, "I am the God of your father, the God of Abraham, the God of Isaac and the God of Jacob." At this, Moses hid his face, because he was afraid to look at God.

7 The LORD said, "I have indeed seen the misery of my people in Egypt. I have heard them crying out because of their slave drivers, and I am concerned about their suffering. 8 So I have come down to rescue them from the hand of the Egyptians and to bring them up out of that land into a good and spacious land, a land flowing with milk and honey—the home of the Canaanites, Hittites, Amorites, Perizzites, Hivites and Jebusites. 9 And now the cry of the Israelites has reached me, and I have seen the way the Egyptians are oppressing them. 10 So now, go. I am sending you to Pharaoh to bring my people the Israelites out of Egypt."

11 But Moses said to God, "Who am I, that I should go to Pharaoh and bring the Israelites out of Egypt?"

12 And God said, "I will be with you. And this will be the sign to you that it is I who have sent you: When you have brought the people out of Egypt, you[b] will worship God on this mountain."

13 Moses said to God, "Suppose I go to the Israelites and say to them, 'The God of your fathers has sent me to you,' and they ask me, 'What is his name?' Then what shall I tell them?"

14 God said to Moses, "I AM WHO I AM.[c] This is what you are to say to the Israelites: 'I AM has sent me to you.' "

15 God also said to Moses, "Say to the Israelites, 'The LORD,[d] the God of your fathers—the God of Abraham, the God of Isaac and the God

[a] 22 *Gershom* sounds like the Hebrew for *an alien there.*
[b] 12 The Hebrew is plural.
[c] 14 Or *I WILL BE WHAT I WILL BE*
[d] 15 The Hebrew for *LORD* sounds like and may be derived from the Hebrew for *I AM* in verse 14.

---

the situation. He couldn't bury his sin in the sand, or in the past, to keep it from being known and rising to haunt him. He needed to responsibly and honestly face what he had done. When we hide our sins, they have a way of coming back to trouble us. It is best to face our errors right away so we can put them to rest, once and for all.

2:23–25 When Israel finally accepted the reality of their desperate situation, they confessed their need, sought God and begged him to deliver them from their slavery. But God's deliverance didn't come right away. The Israelites had to wait patiently for God to change their dismal situation. We need to recognize we need God's help too. When we ask him to help us, we must recognize that we are also giving up control. We need to be willing to let God do things his way and according to his timing.

3:10–11 Moses felt totally unqualified to fill the role God was commanding him to assume. He was well educated; he knew the ways of the royal court of Egypt; he also possessed great leadership ability, which he would demonstrate over the next forty years. These qualities made him the best man for the job. But Moses was unable to see or accept this reality. He didn't have an accurate sense of who he was. Perhaps Moses only saw himself as a fugitive murderer, worthy of no task greater than shepherding his father-in-law's livestock. Often our past sins blind us to our present gifts. We need to see ourselves as God sees us and then respond accordingly.

Solitude

Hearing God's Voice in Wilderness Places

Exodus 3:1–4 Sometimes the only way we can truly give ourselves to others is by getting away from people for a while. Those who are always available to others soon have nothing to give of themselves. But time spent in solitude can effectively prepare us to serve God and others.

Moses longed to help the oppressed people of Israel. But when he tried to settle an injustice by killing an Egyptian, his own people turned against him, and Moses fled for his life into the wilderness (Exodus 2:11–15). It took many years of solitude in the desert before Moses finally encountered God's presence and achieved his heart's desire to help the Israelites by following God's call.

Moses' response to God at the burning bush shows us that much had happened in Moses' spiritual life during his years in the wilderness. We may be too hard on Moses if we judge him for his "string of excuses" to God. What we view as excuses might actually have been thoughtful responses borne out of his solitude and reflection.

As Moses approached the burning bush, we see that solitude had given him time and space to search his own heart. Moses may have realized that he had attempted to bring justice to the Israelites through his own power—and had failed miserably. In his dialogue with God, Moses revealed a new level of honesty with himself and with God when he admitted, "Who am I, that I should go to Pharaoh?" (3:11). Moses apparently realized the inadequacy of his own abilities. This Moses had come a long way from the brash, young fireball who took matters into his own hands years earlier. Now he was not only on the far side of the desert, he was on the far side of confidence. But God gave him the assurance that he needed to carry out God's call for his life.

Solitude had also given Moses time and space to reflect on the nature of people. As a younger man, he had misunderstood his people and misjudged their responses to his actions. It is quite possible that Moses expected his people to rejoice over his punishment of the Egyptian oppressor and to lend support to that type of leadership. His years of reflection in the wilderness, however, had given him a clearer insight into human nature.

Third, solitude helped prepare Moses to meet God. One of the primary purposes of our spiritual experiences is to free us from the distractions and demands of others while putting us in a place where we can be attentive to God. At the burning bush, Moses asked to know more about God, and God revealed his name and much more to him. Through this exercise, Moses gained a deeper understanding of the Lord as he witnessed God's power (3:2; 4:1–11), faithfulness (3:6) and compassion (3:7).

Putting It Into Practice

Review the three lessons that Moses learned in the wilderness. Consider setting aside your own time of solitude to help you deepen your walk with God. Use this time to explore your heart, to reflect on other people or to ponder the character of God. Record your reflections in a journal or in a letter to God.

For more on solitude, turn to 1 Kings 19.

of Jacob—has sent me to you.' This is my name forever, the name by which I am to be remembered from generation to generation.

16 "Go, assemble the elders of Israel and say to them, 'The LORD, the God of your fathers—the God of Abraham, Isaac and Jacob—appeared to me and said: I have watched over you and have seen what has been done to you in Egypt. 17 And I have promised to bring you up out of your misery in Egypt into the land of the Canaanites, Hittites, Amorites, Perizzites, Hivites and Jebusites—a land flowing with milk and honey.'

18 "The elders of Israel will listen to you. Then you and the elders are to go to the king of Egypt and say to him, 'The LORD, the God of the Hebrews, has met with us. Let us take a three-day journey into the desert to offer sacrifices to the LORD our God.' 19 But I know that the king of Egypt will not let you go unless a mighty hand compels him. 20 So I will stretch out my hand and strike the Egyptians with all the wonders that I will perform among them. After that, he will let you go.

21 "And I will make the Egyptians favorably disposed toward this people, so that when you leave you will not go empty-handed. 22 Every woman is to ask her neighbor and any woman living in her house for articles of silver and gold and for clothing, which you will put on your sons and daughters. And so you will plunder the Egyptians."

Signs for Moses

4 Moses answered, "What if they do not believe me or listen to me and say, 'The LORD did not appear to you'?"

2 Then the LORD said to him, "What is that in your hand?"

"A staff," he replied.

3 The LORD said, "Throw it on the ground."

Moses threw it on the ground and it became a snake, and he ran from it. 4 Then the LORD said to him, "Reach out your hand and take it by the tail." So Moses reached out and took hold of the snake and it turned back into a staff in his hand.

5 "This," said the LORD, "is so that they may believe that the LORD, the God of their fathers—the God of Abraham, the God of Isaac and the God of Jacob—has appeared to you."

6 Then the LORD said, "Put your hand inside your cloak." So Moses put his hand into his cloak, and when he took it out, it was leprous,[a] like snow.

7 "Now put it back into your cloak," he said. So Moses put his hand back into his cloak, and when he took it out, it was restored, like the rest of his flesh.

8 Then the LORD said, "If they do not believe you or pay attention to the first miraculous sign, they may believe the second. 9 But if they do not believe these two signs or listen to you, take some water from the Nile and pour it on the dry ground. The water you take from the river will become blood on the ground."

10 Moses said to the LORD, "O Lord, I have never been eloquent, neither in the past nor since you have spoken to your servant. I am slow of speech and tongue."

11 The LORD said to him, "Who gave man his mouth? Who makes him deaf or mute? Who gives him sight or makes him blind? Is it not I, the LORD? 12 Now go; I will help you speak and will teach you what to say."

13 But Moses said, "O Lord, please send someone else to do it."

14 Then the LORD's anger burned against Moses and he said, "What about your brother, Aaron the Levite? I know he can speak well. He is already on his way to meet you, and his heart will be glad when he sees you. 15 You shall speak to him and put words in his mouth; I will help both of you speak and will teach you what to do. 16 He will speak to the people for you, and it will be as if he were your mouth and as if you were God to him. 17 But take this staff in your hand so you can perform miraculous signs with it."

[a]6 The Hebrew word was used for various diseases affecting the skin—not necessarily leprosy.

3:16–22 God called Moses to speak to the elders of Israel regarding the new life awaiting them in the promised land (Genesis 15:18–21). Along with the hope of entering such wonderful new territory, however, was the reality of dealing with the king of Egypt. The promise was wonderful, but the difficulty of the process could not be underestimated. The process of receiving God's promises can be difficult, but no matter what the pain, it will be worth it if we reach the promise of freedom and blessing.

4:1–9 Here we see the series of miracles that God gave to Moses and the Israelites to bolster their faith in Moses' message and mission. God does not normally use such wondrous signs to strengthen our faith, but he has performed one miracle that should give us all the encouragement we need. He raised Jesus Christ from the dead, showing that he is no slave to the destruction of sin and death (1 Corinthians 15:1–6). This miracle should give all of us faith in God's promises and hope in the Good News he offers.

4:10–12 Moses may have had a speech impediment, but that wasn't a legitimate excuse for not following God's plan. Moses didn't have an accurate perception of who he could become with God's help. While Moses was engaging in a kind of self-examination, he was doing so with a negative, fearful attitude. He was not yet willing to be changed by God. Our weaknesses should never be an excuse to avoid spiritual renewal. With God's help, anything is possible. We need to realize that God can capitalize on our strengths, helping us reach our full potential.

4:13–17 Moses tried desperately to escape God's call for his life. He didn't want to go back to Egypt as God's spokesman. Apparently he was afraid to face the huge responsibility that this entailed. But God held Moses accountable to his divine plan. He told Moses exactly how the mission in Egypt would be accomplished, despite Moses' presumed handicap. God has a special plan for each one of us. If we follow him, he will bring it to pass no matter what our weaknesses.

Moses Returns to Egypt

18Then Moses went back to Jethro his father-in-law and said to him, "Let me go back to my own people in Egypt to see if any of them are still alive."

Jethro said, "Go, and I wish you well."

19Now the LORD had said to Moses in Midian, "Go back to Egypt, for all the men who wanted to kill you are dead." 20So Moses took his wife and sons, put them on a donkey and started back to Egypt. And he took the staff of God in his hand.

21The LORD said to Moses, "When you return to Egypt, see that you perform before Pharaoh all the wonders I have given you the power to do. But I will harden his heart so that he will not let the people go. 22Then say to Pharaoh, 'This is what the LORD says: Israel is my firstborn son, 23and I told you, "Let my son go, so he may worship me." But you refused to let him go; so I will kill your firstborn son.' "

24At a lodging place on the way, the LORD met ⌞Moses⌟[a] and was about to kill him. 25But Zipporah took a flint knife, cut off her son's foreskin and touched ⌞Moses'⌟ feet with it.[b] "Surely you are a bridegroom of blood to me," she said. 26So the LORD let him alone. (At that time she said "bridegroom of blood," referring to circumcision.)

27The LORD said to Aaron, "Go into the desert to meet Moses." So he met Moses at the mountain of God and kissed him. 28Then Moses told Aaron everything the LORD had sent him to say, and also about all the miraculous signs he had commanded him to perform.

29Moses and Aaron brought together all the elders of the Israelites, 30and Aaron told them everything the LORD had said to Moses. He also performed the signs before the people, 31and they believed. And when they heard that the LORD was concerned about them and had seen their misery, they bowed down and worshiped.

Bricks Without Straw

5 Afterward Moses and Aaron went to Pharaoh and said, "This is what the LORD, the God of Israel, says: 'Let my people go, so that they may hold a festival to me in the desert.' "

2Pharaoh said, "Who is the LORD, that I should obey him and let Israel go? I do not know the LORD and I will not let Israel go."

3Then they said, "The God of the Hebrews has met with us. Now let us take a three-day journey into the desert to offer sacrifices to the LORD our God, or he may strike us with plagues or with the sword."

4But the king of Egypt said, "Moses and Aaron, why are you taking the people away from their labor? Get back to your work!" 5Then Pharaoh said, "Look, the people of the land are now numerous, and you are stopping them from working."

6That same day Pharaoh gave this order to the slave drivers and foremen in charge of the people: 7"You are no longer to supply the people with straw for making bricks; let them go and gather their own straw. 8But require them to make the same number of bricks as before; don't reduce the quota. They are lazy; that is why they are crying out, 'Let us go and sacrifice to our God.' 9Make the work harder for the men so that they keep working and pay no attention to lies."

10Then the slave drivers and the foremen went out and said to the people, "This is what Pharaoh says: 'I will not give you any more straw. 11Go and get your own straw wherever you can find it, but your work will not be reduced at all.' " 12So the people scattered all over Egypt to gather stubble to use for straw. 13The slave drivers kept pressing them, saying, "Complete the work required of you for each day, just as when you had straw." 14The Israelite foremen appointed by Pharaoh's slave drivers were beaten and were asked, "Why didn't you meet your quota of bricks yesterday or today, as before?"

15Then the Israelite foremen went and appealed to Pharaoh: "Why have you treated your servants this way? 16Your servants are given no straw, yet we are told, 'Make bricks!' Your ser-

[a]24 Or ⌞*Moses' son*⌟; Hebrew *him* [b]25 Or *and drew near* ⌞*Moses'*⌟ *feet*

4:29—5:3 Moses and Aaron approached the elders of Israel with God's message. This alone took a great deal of courage, but by taking the chance, they were able to encourage the elders to seek freedom from the Egyptians. In an even greater step of courage, Moses and Aaron confronted Pharaoh directly, demanding that things be set straight. God's word to Moses and Aaron gave them courage to act on behalf of others. Their courage also sparked courage in others, which in turn helped them take the next step. Our own spiritual renewal, if properly shared, can inspire others to move forward as well. Their growth will ultimately strengthen us to move ahead even further.

5:3–9 Pharaoh refused to seek God and surrender to him. He refused to see the truth. He had no respect for the law of God or the people of God. Pharaoh also failed to respond properly when he was honestly confronted about the way he was treating the Israelites. When Moses sought freedom for God's people, Pharaoh became upset. Instead of examining himself, Pharaoh accused the Israelites of being lazy and demanded even more from them. We can learn from Pharaoh's bad example. When we are confronted with our sin, we must honestly assess our spiritual state and ask God to change us. Becoming hard-hearted and choosing to blame others will only make things worse.

5:10–21 The Israelite foremen needed to understand how difficult the process of achieving their freedom would be. They were deeply discouraged by Pharaoh's additional demands because they possessed unrealistic hopes of an immediate and painless deliverance. They also became disillusioned about the leadership abilities of Moses and Aaron. The Israelite foremen needed wisdom to see their troubles from a long-term perspective. These were only the first steps on the road to freedom—a road which proved long and difficult. There are few, if any, immediate and painless paths to freedom. When we realize this, we will find the difficulties we face less discouraging.

vants are being beaten, but the fault is with your own people."

[17]Pharaoh said, "Lazy, that's what you are—lazy! That is why you keep saying, 'Let us go and sacrifice to the LORD.' [18]Now get to work. You will not be given any straw, yet you must produce your full quota of bricks."

[19]The Israelite foremen realized they were in trouble when they were told, "You are not to reduce the number of bricks required of you for each day." [20]When they left Pharaoh, they found Moses and Aaron waiting to meet them, [21]and they said, "May the LORD look upon you and judge you! You have made us a stench to Pharaoh and his officials and have put a sword in their hand to kill us."

God Promises Deliverance

[22]Moses returned to the LORD and said, "O Lord, why have you brought trouble upon this people? Is this why you sent me? [23]Ever since I went to Pharaoh to speak in your name, he has brought trouble upon this people, and you have not rescued your people at all."

6 Then the LORD said to Moses, "Now you will see what I will do to Pharaoh: Because of my mighty hand he will let them go; because of my mighty hand he will drive them out of his country."

[2]God also said to Moses, "I am the LORD. [3]I appeared to Abraham, to Isaac and to Jacob as God Almighty,[a] but by my name the LORD[b] I did not make myself known to them.[c] [4]I also established my covenant with them to give them the land of Canaan, where they lived as aliens. [5]Moreover, I have heard the groaning of the Israelites, whom the Egyptians are enslaving, and I have remembered my covenant.

[6]"Therefore, say to the Israelites: 'I am the LORD, and I will bring you out from under the yoke of the Egyptians. I will free you from being slaves to them, and I will redeem you with an outstretched arm and with mighty acts of judgment. [7]I will take you as my own people, and I will be your God. Then you will know that I am the LORD your God, who brought you out from under the yoke of the Egyptians. [8]And I will bring you to the land I swore with uplifted hand to give to Abraham, to Isaac and to Jacob. I will give it to you as a possession. I am the LORD.' "

[9]Moses reported this to the Israelites, but they did not listen to him because of their discouragement and cruel bondage.

[10]Then the LORD said to Moses, [11]"Go, tell Pharaoh king of Egypt to let the Israelites go out of his country."

[12]But Moses said to the LORD, "If the Israelites will not listen to me, why would Pharaoh listen to me, since I speak with faltering lips[d]?"

Family Record of Moses and Aaron

[13]Now the LORD spoke to Moses and Aaron about the Israelites and Pharaoh king of Egypt, and he commanded them to bring the Israelites out of Egypt.

[14]These were the heads of their families[e]:

The sons of Reuben the firstborn son of Israel were Hanoch and Pallu, Hezron and Carmi. These were the clans of Reuben.

[15]The sons of Simeon were Jemuel, Jamin, Ohad, Jakin, Zohar and Shaul the son of a Canaanite woman. These were the clans of Simeon.

[16]These were the names of the sons of Levi according to their records: Gershon, Kohath and Merari. Levi lived 137 years.

[17]The sons of Gershon, by clans, were Libni and Shimei.

[18]The sons of Kohath were Amram, Izhar, Hebron and Uzziel. Kohath lived 133 years.

[19]The sons of Merari were Mahli and Mushi.

These were the clans of Levi according to their records.

[20]Amram married his father's sister Jochebed, who bore him Aaron and Moses. Amram lived 137 years.

[21]The sons of Izhar were Korah, Nepheg and Zicri.

[22]The sons of Uzziel were Mishael, Elzaphan and Sithri.

[23]Aaron married Elisheba, daughter of Amminadab and sister of Nahshon, and she bore him Nadab and Abihu, Eleazar and Ithamar.

[24]The sons of Korah were Assir, Elkanah

[a]3 Hebrew *El-Shaddai* [b]3 See note at Exodus 3:15. [c]3 Or *Almighty, and by my name the LORD did I not let myself be known to them?* [d]12 Hebrew *I am uncircumcised of lips;* also in verse 30 [e]14 The Hebrew for *families* here and in verse 25 refers to units larger than clans.

5:22–23 Moses prayed to God with perplexed honesty. He faced a real problem. In following God's plan for freeing Israel, the people encountered increased suffering. Moses, however, did not yet realize that God was preparing to force Pharaoh to let Israel go. God had not failed the test of trustworthiness. Freedom is often a lengthy process. We need to recognize this as we seek spiritual growth, for then we will be less likely to be discouraged by the obstacles we face along the way.

6:8–13 When we fail to realize how difficult the process toward freedom can be, it is all too easy to become discouraged and give up. After suffering a number of setbacks, the Israelites were ready to give up. At such times, patience and perseverance are absolutely essential. We also need to remember that difficulties and failures are often the back door to ultimate victory.

6:14–27 To a great extent, Moses and Aaron were the product of their family heritage, sketched briefly in the genealogy included here (6:14–25). Now they faced difficult opposition to their goal of freeing the Israelites. But out of their past came signs of hope. God had promised Abraham and his descendants a land of their own, free from oppression. God's promises from the past gave Moses and Aaron the encouragement they needed to continue their quest for freedom. God's promises can do the same for us today.

and Abiasaph. These were the Korahite clans.

25Eleazar son of Aaron married one of the daughters of Putiel, and she bore him Phinehas.

These were the heads of the Levite families, clan by clan.

26It was this same Aaron and Moses to whom the LORD said, "Bring the Israelites out of Egypt by their divisions." 27They were the ones who spoke to Pharaoh king of Egypt about bringing the Israelites out of Egypt. It was the same Moses and Aaron.

Aaron to Speak for Moses

28Now when the LORD spoke to Moses in Egypt, 29he said to him, "I am the LORD. Tell Pharaoh king of Egypt everything I tell you."

30But Moses said to the LORD, "Since I speak with faltering lips, why would Pharaoh listen to me?"

7 Then the LORD said to Moses, "See, I have made you like God to Pharaoh, and your brother Aaron will be your prophet. 2You are to say everything I command you, and your brother Aaron is to tell Pharaoh to let the Israelites go out of his country. 3But I will harden Pharaoh's heart, and though I multiply my miraculous signs and wonders in Egypt, 4he will not listen to you. Then I will lay my hand on Egypt and with mighty acts of judgment I will bring out my divisions, my people the Israelites. 5And the Egyptians will know that I am the LORD when I stretch out my hand against Egypt and bring the Israelites out of it."

6Moses and Aaron did just as the LORD commanded them. 7Moses was eighty years old and Aaron eighty-three when they spoke to Pharaoh.

Aaron's Staff Becomes a Snake

8The LORD said to Moses and Aaron, 9"When Pharaoh says to you, 'Perform a miracle,' then say to Aaron, 'Take your staff and throw it down before Pharaoh,' and it will become a snake."

10So Moses and Aaron went to Pharaoh and did just as the LORD commanded. Aaron threw his staff down in front of Pharaoh and his officials, and it became a snake. 11Pharaoh then summoned wise men and sorcerers, and the Egyptian magicians also did the same things by their secret arts: 12Each one threw down his staff and it became a snake. But Aaron's staff swallowed up their staffs. 13Yet Pharaoh's heart became hard and he would not listen to them, just as the LORD had said.

The Plague of Blood

14Then the LORD said to Moses, "Pharaoh's heart is unyielding; he refuses to let the people go. 15Go to Pharaoh in the morning as he goes out to the water. Wait on the bank of the Nile to meet him, and take in your hand the staff that was changed into a snake. 16Then say to him, 'The LORD, the God of the Hebrews, has sent me to say to you: Let my people go, so that they may worship me in the desert. But until now you have not listened. 17This is what the LORD says: By this you will know that I am the LORD: With the staff that is in my hand I will strike the water of the Nile, and it will be changed into blood. 18The fish in the Nile will die, and the river will stink; the Egyptians will not be able to drink its water.' "

19The LORD said to Moses, "Tell Aaron, 'Take your staff and stretch out your hand over the waters of Egypt—over the streams and canals, over the ponds and all the reservoirs'—and they will turn to blood. Blood will be everywhere in Egypt, even in the wooden buckets and stone jars."

20Moses and Aaron did just as the LORD had commanded. He raised his staff in the presence of Pharaoh and his officials and struck the water of the Nile, and all the water was changed into blood. 21The fish in the Nile died, and the river smelled so bad that the Egyptians could not drink its water. Blood was everywhere in Egypt.

6:28–30 God insisted that Moses respond in faith, despite his fears and his perceived speech problem (6:30; see 4:10; 6:12). In the process of the exodus, God repeatedly challenged Moses' personal insecurities and his negative, self-defeating attitudes by reminding Moses of God's name and his miraculous power. Faith in a trustworthy God was the solution to Moses' problem. Trusting God with our problems and insecurities and releasing them to him is a vital key to our own spiritual growth.

7:1–5 Nowhere is the stubbornness of Pharaoh's heart sketched more vividly. Moses and Aaron were fully involved in the process of confronting this unyielding persecutor. And at this point, their task of freeing the people must have seemed impossible. But God had assured them that their goal of freedom would be reached by his sovereign power. We may be internally or externally battling with a powerful, unreasonable enemy. But when God desires something to happen, it will happen, regardless of the opposition.

7:7 Notice that Aaron is the older son, but God called Moses to be the primary leader. God's choice went against the grain of cultural expectation. The firstborn was always considered the first in line for a position of power or influence. But God often chose unlikely people to accomplish his plans. Consider also Isaac, Jacob, Judah, Joseph, Gideon and David. None of them was a firstborn son, but all were given a significant part to play in God's plan. God often does things that surprise us; he uses unlikely people. No matter what our past or position, each of us has a special place in God's plan.

7:14—8:19 The first cycle of three plagues—blood (7:14–24), frogs (8:1–15) and gnats (8:16–19)—as intense as it was, did not turn Pharaoh from his cruel behavior. He still continued in his stubbornness. At the height of the frog plague, he nearly relented, asking Moses and Aaron to pray to God on his behalf (8:8–13). However, when the plagues stopped momentarily, he hardened his heart again (8:15). We must be careful to persevere to the end, not getting overconfident when things start to go well. We must realize our constant need for God, or we are doomed to failure in the long-term process toward freedom.

Moses

A flaw in an old coin will sometimes enhance its value; a flaw in a gem will often cause its value to decrease. The flaws in Moses' life followed both of these principles. In light of his many faults, the fact that Moses became a great leader is truly remarkable.

Moses often reacted impulsively to the situations around him without listening to God first. He killed an Egyptian supervisor to protect a Hebrew slave; he jumped in to referee a fight between two Hebrews; in order to protect a few shepherd girls, he chased away a group of rough shepherds. Moses also took on more work than God intended, once working from dawn till dusk just solving the people's disputes. He had to learn to set personal boundaries and share his leadership role with the people under him.

But weaknesses are just one side of Moses' coin; the other side of his life is stamped with strengths. Moses' struggles with self-doubt and personal fears became opportunities for God to reveal his power. God turned a fugitive shepherd into a great national leader. God called Moses into his very presence!

God also turned Moses' impulsive tendencies into opportunities for good. When Moses impusively killed an Egyptian to protect a Hebrew slave, Moses had to flee to the wilderness on his own personal exodus from Egypt. Through this experience, God prepared Moses to lead the nation of Israel out of Egypt. Moses' skill in responding correctly to crises undoubtedly strengthened him as the leader of this great traveling nation of Israel. He was decisive in dealing with conflicts; he knew how to get things done. God also used Moses' sacrificial leadership to help guide the Israelites for many years and turned Moses' failure to set personal boundaries into a beneficial strength for the nation.

Moses persevered through many mountaintop experiences—periods of faith and commitment to God—that resulted in extraordinary spiritual growth. However, Moses also exhibited times when his lack of patience and faith caused him severe problems. Moses is acclaimed by Scripture and by God himself as one of the greatest people who ever lived. Despite Moses' emotional ups and downs and periods of self-doubt, God was able to use him to do great things. This should give all of us hope that we can be used in amazing ways by God too.

STRENGTHS AND ACCOMPLISHMENTS:

He was self-giving and humble—one of the greatest leaders in the entire Old Testament.

He was a man of great faith and courage as he followed God.

He was willing to accept wise counsel from God and others.

WEAKNESSES AND MISTAKES:

He often acted impulsively without looking to God for guidance.

At times he became almost frozen with self-doubt.

He displayed a lack of adequate personal boundaries, resulting in exhaustion by overwork.

LESSONS FROM HIS LIFE:

We must handle the ups and downs of life with faith in God and commitment to his plan.

We don't have to be perfect to be greatly used by God; we can still be "in process."

We need to preserve our spiritual gains by keeping a balance between work and rest. This will help us avoid overwork, exhaustion, depression and burnout.

KEY VERSE:

"By faith [Moses] left Egypt, not fearing the king's anger; he persevered because he saw him who is invisible" (Hebrews 11:27).

Moses' story spans the books of Exodus, Leviticus, Numbers and Deuteronomy. The name Moses, often associated with the law, is found throughout the rest of the Bible. Moses is also referred to at some length in Acts 7:20–40, 44 and Hebrews 11:23–29.

22But the Egyptian magicians did the same things by their secret arts, and Pharaoh's heart became hard; he would not listen to Moses and Aaron, just as the LORD had said. 23Instead, he turned and went into his palace, and did not take even this to heart. 24And all the Egyptians dug along the Nile to get drinking water, because they could not drink the water of the river.

The Plague of Frogs

25Seven days passed after the LORD struck the
8 Nile. 1Then the LORD said to Moses, "Go to Pharaoh and say to him, 'This is what the LORD says: Let my people go, so that they may worship me. 2If you refuse to let them go, I will plague your whole country with frogs. 3The Nile will teem with frogs. They will come up into your palace and your bedroom and onto your bed, into the houses of your officials and on your people, and into your ovens and kneading troughs. 4The frogs will go up on you and your people and all your officials.' "

5Then the LORD said to Moses, "Tell Aaron, 'Stretch out your hand with your staff over the streams and canals and ponds, and make frogs come up on the land of Egypt.' "

6So Aaron stretched out his hand over the waters of Egypt, and the frogs came up and covered the land. 7But the magicians did the same things by their secret arts; they also made frogs come up on the land of Egypt.

8Pharaoh summoned Moses and Aaron and said, "Pray to the LORD to take the frogs away from me and my people, and I will let your people go to offer sacrifices to the LORD."

9Moses said to Pharaoh, "I leave to you the honor of setting the time for me to pray for you and your officials and your people that you and your houses may be rid of the frogs, except for those that remain in the Nile."

10"Tomorrow," Pharaoh said.

Moses replied, "It will be as you say, so that you may know there is no one like the LORD our God. 11The frogs will leave you and your houses, your officials and your people; they will remain only in the Nile."

12After Moses and Aaron left Pharaoh, Moses cried out to the LORD about the frogs he had brought on Pharaoh. 13And the LORD did what Moses asked. The frogs died in the houses, in the courtyards and in the fields. 14They were piled into heaps, and the land reeked of them. 15But when Pharaoh saw that there was relief, he hardened his heart and would not listen to Moses and Aaron, just as the LORD had said.

The Plague of Gnats

16Then the LORD said to Moses, "Tell Aaron, 'Stretch out your staff and strike the dust of the ground,' and throughout the land of Egypt the dust will become gnats." 17They did this, and when Aaron stretched out his hand with the staff and struck the dust of the ground, gnats came upon men and animals. All the dust throughout the land of Egypt became gnats. 18But when the magicians tried to produce gnats by their secret arts, they could not. And the gnats were on men and animals.

19The magicians said to Pharaoh, "This is the finger of God." But Pharaoh's heart was hard and he would not listen, just as the LORD had said.

The Plague of Flies

20Then the LORD said to Moses, "Get up early in the morning and confront Pharaoh as he goes to the water and say to him, 'This is what the LORD says: Let my people go, so that they may worship me. 21If you do not let my people go, I will send swarms of flies on you and your officials, on your people and into your houses. The houses of the Egyptians will be full of flies, and even the ground where they are.

22" 'But on that day I will deal differently with the land of Goshen, where my people live; no swarms of flies will be there, so that you will know that I, the LORD, am in this land. 23I will make a distinction[a] between my people and your people. This miraculous sign will occur tomorrow.' "

24And the LORD did this. Dense swarms of flies poured into Pharaoh's palace and into the houses of his officials, and throughout Egypt the land was ruined by the flies.

25Then Pharaoh summoned Moses and Aaron and said, "Go, sacrifice to your God here in the land."

26But Moses said, "That would not be right. The sacrifices we offer the LORD our God would be detestable to the Egyptians. And if we offer sacrifices that are detestable in their eyes, will they not stone us? 27We must take a three-day journey into the desert to offer sacrifices to the LORD our God, as he commands us."

28Pharaoh said, "I will let you go to offer sacrifices to the LORD your God in the desert, but you must not go very far. Now pray for me."

29Moses answered, "As soon as I leave you, I will pray to the LORD, and tomorrow the flies will leave Pharaoh and his officials and his people. Only be sure that Pharaoh does not act

[a]23 Septuagint and Vulgate; Hebrew *will put a deliverance*

8:20—9:12 The second cycle of three plagues—flies (8:20–32), death of Egyptian livestock (9:1–7) and boils (9:8–12)—was similarly resisted by Pharaoh. However, during the detestable onslaught of flies, Pharaoh tried to bargain with Moses and God. He agreed to allow Israel to offer sacrifices to God, first in Egypt and then a short distance away in the wilderness. But he made this concession on the condition that Moses would pray to God on his behalf to stop the plague (8:25–28). Moses did pray, but Pharaoh went back on his word, hardening his heart (8:29–32). Pharaoh failed on two counts. First, he tried to bargain with God to get what he wanted. God is more than willing to give us what is best for us, but we must accept his terms, not ours. Also, Pharaoh failed to keep his word with God. This failure could only lead to continued disaster.

deceitfully again by not letting the people go to
offer sacrifices to the LORD."
30Then Moses left Pharaoh and prayed to the
LORD, 31and the LORD did what Moses asked:
The flies left Pharaoh and his officials and his
people; not a fly remained. 32But this time also
Pharaoh hardened his heart and would not let
the people go.

The Plague on Livestock

9 Then the LORD said to Moses, "Go to Pharaoh and say to him, 'This is what the LORD,
the God of the Hebrews, says: "Let my people
go, so that they may worship me." 2If you refuse
to let them go and continue to hold them back,
3the hand of the LORD will bring a terrible
plague on your livestock in the field—on your
horses and donkeys and camels and on your
cattle and sheep and goats. 4But the LORD will
make a distinction between the livestock of Israel and that of Egypt, so that no animal belonging to the Israelites will die.' "
5The LORD set a time and said, "Tomorrow
the LORD will do this in the land." 6And the next
day the LORD did it: All the livestock of the
Egyptians died, but not one animal belonging
to the Israelites died. 7Pharaoh sent men to investigate and found that not even one of the
animals of the Israelites had died. Yet his heart
was unyielding and he would not let the people go.

The Plague of Boils

8Then the LORD said to Moses and Aaron,
"Take handfuls of soot from a furnace and have
Moses toss it into the air in the presence of
Pharaoh. 9It will become fine dust over the
whole land of Egypt, and festering boils will
break out on men and animals throughout the
land."
10So they took soot from a furnace and stood
before Pharaoh. Moses tossed it into the air,
and festering boils broke out on men and animals. 11The magicians could not stand before
Moses because of the boils that were on them
and on all the Egyptians. 12But the LORD hardened Pharaoh's heart and he would not listen to
Moses and Aaron, just as the LORD had said to
Moses.

The Plague of Hail

13Then the LORD said to Moses, "Get up early
in the morning, confront Pharaoh and say to
him, 'This is what the LORD, the God of the
Hebrews, says: Let my people go, so that they
may worship me, 14or this time I will send the
full force of my plagues against you and against
your officials and your people, so you may
know that there is no one like me in all the
earth. 15For by now I could have stretched out
my hand and struck you and your people with
a plague that would have wiped you off the
earth. 16But I have raised you up[a] for this very
purpose, that I might show you my power and
that my name might be proclaimed in all the
earth. 17You still set yourself against my people
and will not let them go. 18Therefore, at this
time tomorrow I will send the worst hailstorm
that has ever fallen on Egypt, from the day it
was founded till now. 19Give an order now to
bring your livestock and everything you have in
the field to a place of shelter, because the hail
will fall on every man and animal that has not
been brought in and is still out in the field, and
they will die.' "
20Those officials of Pharaoh who feared the
word of the LORD hurried to bring their slaves
and their livestock inside. 21But those who ignored the word of the LORD left their slaves and
livestock in the field.
22Then the LORD said to Moses, "Stretch out
your hand toward the sky so that hail will fall
all over Egypt—on men and animals and on
everything growing in the fields of Egypt."
23When Moses stretched out his staff toward the
sky, the LORD sent thunder and hail, and lightning flashed down to the ground. So the LORD
rained hail on the land of Egypt; 24hail fell
and lightning flashed back and forth. It was
the worst storm in all the land of Egypt since it
had become a nation. 25Throughout Egypt hail
struck everything in the fields—both men and
animals; it beat down everything growing in the
fields and stripped every tree. 26The only place
it did not hail was the land of Goshen, where
the Israelites were.
27Then Pharaoh summoned Moses and Aaron. "This time I have sinned," he said to them.
"The LORD is in the right, and I and my people
are in the wrong. 28Pray to the LORD, for we
have had enough thunder and hail. I will let
you go; you don't have to stay any longer."
29Moses replied, "When I have gone out of
the city, I will spread out my hands in prayer to
the LORD. The thunder will stop and there will
be no more hail, so you may know that the
earth is the LORD's. 30But I know that you and
your officials still do not fear the LORD God."
31(The flax and barley were destroyed, since
the barley had headed and the flax was in
bloom. 32The wheat and spelt, however, were
not destroyed, because they ripen later.)

[a]16 Or *have spared you*

9:13–35 During the devastating plague of hail, Pharaoh went so far as to admit that he and his people had sinned and that God was righteous (9:27–28). But after Moses prayed to God and the plagues had halted, Pharaoh and the Egyptian officials again hardened their hearts. Pharaoh still was not willing to face the reality of God's sovereign power, even though he had been clearly convicted of his rebellion. We may recognize that our circumstances are too much for us and begin seeking God. But then we may revert to self-sufficiency as we see improvement. When we begin to make progress, we must remember to continually seek God and surrender to him. If we fail to depend wholeheartedly on God's power, we will be sure to fail once again.

33Then Moses left Pharaoh and went out of the city. He spread out his hands toward the LORD; the thunder and hail stopped, and the rain no longer poured down on the land. 34When Pharaoh saw that the rain and hail and thunder had stopped, he sinned again: He and his officials hardened their hearts. 35So Pharaoh's heart was hard and he would not let the Israelites go, just as the LORD had said through Moses.

The Plague of Locusts

10 Then the LORD said to Moses, "Go to Pharaoh, for I have hardened his heart and the hearts of his officials so that I may perform these miraculous signs of mine among them 2that you may tell your children and grandchildren how I dealt harshly with the Egyptians and how I performed my signs among them, and that you may know that I am the LORD."

3So Moses and Aaron went to Pharaoh and said to him, "This is what the LORD, the God of the Hebrews, says: 'How long will you refuse to humble yourself before me? Let my people go, so that they may worship me. 4If you refuse to let them go, I will bring locusts into your country tomorrow. 5They will cover the face of the ground so that it cannot be seen. They will devour what little you have left after the hail, including every tree that is growing in your fields. 6They will fill your houses and those of all your officials and all the Egyptians—something neither your fathers nor your forefathers have ever seen from the day they settled in this land till now.' " Then Moses turned and left Pharaoh.

7Pharaoh's officials said to him, "How long will this man be a snare to us? Let the people go, so that they may worship the LORD their God. Do you not yet realize that Egypt is ruined?"

8Then Moses and Aaron were brought back to Pharaoh. "Go, worship the LORD your God," he said. "But just who will be going?"

9Moses answered, "We will go with our young and old, with our sons and daughters, and with our flocks and herds, because we are to celebrate a festival to the LORD."

10Pharaoh said, "The LORD be with you—if I let you go, along with your women and children! Clearly you are bent on evil.[a] 11No! Have only the men go; and worship the LORD, since that's what you have been asking for." Then Moses and Aaron were driven out of Pharaoh's presence.

12And the LORD said to Moses, "Stretch out your hand over Egypt so that locusts will swarm over the land and devour everything growing in the fields, everything left by the hail."

13So Moses stretched out his staff over Egypt, and the LORD made an east wind blow across the land all that day and all that night. By morning the wind had brought the locusts; 14they invaded all Egypt and settled down in every area of the country in great numbers. Never before had there been such a plague of locusts, nor will there ever be again. 15They covered all the ground until it was black. They devoured all that was left after the hail—everything growing in the fields and the fruit on the trees. Nothing green remained on tree or plant in all the land of Egypt.

16Pharaoh quickly summoned Moses and Aaron and said, "I have sinned against the LORD your God and against you. 17Now forgive my sin once more and pray to the LORD your God to take this deadly plague away from me."

18Moses then left Pharaoh and prayed to the LORD. 19And the LORD changed the wind to a very strong west wind, which caught up the locusts and carried them into the Red Sea.[b] Not a locust was left anywhere in Egypt. 20But the LORD hardened Pharaoh's heart, and he would not let the Israelites go.

The Plague of Darkness

21Then the LORD said to Moses, "Stretch out your hand toward the sky so that darkness will spread over Egypt—darkness that can be felt." 22So Moses stretched out his hand toward the sky, and total darkness covered all Egypt for three days. 23No one could see anyone else or leave his place for three days. Yet all the Israelites had light in the places where they lived.

24Then Pharaoh summoned Moses and said, "Go, worship the LORD. Even your women and children may go with you; only leave your flocks and herds behind."

[a]10 Or *Be careful, trouble is in store for you!*
[b]19 Hebrew *Yam Suph*; that is, Sea of Reeds

10:1–20 During the plague of locusts, Pharaoh again attempted to bargain with God. He first consented to let only the men go out from Egypt to worship God (10:10–11), retaining the women and children as hostages. But the severity of the locust plague caused him to admit his sin and to ask Moses to intercede before God (10:12–19). In the end, however, Pharaoh's heart was again hardened (10:20), and he still refused to let the Israelites leave. His continued stubbornness led him further and further away from obedience to God's will.

10:2 God's power over the Egyptians was to be celebrated by each successive generation of Israelites. The faith and spirit of God's people who experienced the exodus would bolster the faith of their descendants, giving them the courage to conquer enemies in the future. God's powerful acts for his people can also give us hope as we face problems too big for us. Remember, the victories we win with God's help can influence and strengthen our descendants far into the future.

10:21–29 After three days of darkness, Pharaoh agreed to let all the Israelites leave Egypt to worship God, but he refused to let them take their livestock (10:24). While this was a further concession on Pharaoh's part, it still was far from wholehearted repentance. Further perseverance by Moses only incited Pharaoh to escalate the confrontation with dangerous threats (10:24–28). Our spiritual renewal is dependent upon truthfully admitting the reality of our problems and areas of sin in our lives. If we cannot honestly admit the problems we face, we can hardly ask God to help us with them.

25But Moses said, "You must allow us to have sacrifices and burnt offerings to present to the LORD our God. 26Our livestock too must go with us; not a hoof is to be left behind. We have to use some of them in worshiping the LORD our God, and until we get there we will not know what we are to use to worship the LORD."

27But the LORD hardened Pharaoh's heart, and he was not willing to let them go. 28Pharaoh said to Moses, "Get out of my sight! Make sure you do not appear before me again! The day you see my face you will die."

29"Just as you say," Moses replied, "I will never appear before you again."

The Plague on the Firstborn

11 Now the LORD had said to Moses, "I will bring one more plague on Pharaoh and on Egypt. After that, he will let you go from here, and when he does, he will drive you out completely. 2Tell the people that men and women alike are to ask their neighbors for articles of silver and gold." 3(The LORD made the Egyptians favorably disposed toward the people, and Moses himself was highly regarded in Egypt by Pharaoh's officials and by the people.)

4So Moses said, "This is what the LORD says: 'About midnight I will go throughout Egypt. 5Every firstborn son in Egypt will die, from the firstborn son of Pharaoh, who sits on the throne, to the firstborn son of the slave girl, who is at her hand mill, and all the firstborn of the cattle as well. 6There will be loud wailing throughout Egypt—worse than there has ever been or ever will be again. 7But among the Israelites not a dog will bark at any man or animal.' Then you will know that the LORD makes a distinction between Egypt and Israel. 8All these officials of yours will come to me, bowing down before me and saying, 'Go, you and all the people who follow you!' After that I will leave." Then Moses, hot with anger, left Pharaoh.

9The LORD had said to Moses, "Pharaoh will refuse to listen to you—so that my wonders may be multiplied in Egypt." 10Moses and Aaron performed all these wonders before Pharaoh, but the LORD hardened Pharaoh's heart, and he would not let the Israelites go out of his country.

The Passover

12 The LORD said to Moses and Aaron in Egypt, 2"This month is to be for you the first month, the first month of your year. 3Tell the whole community of Israel that on the tenth day of this month each man is to take a lamb[a] for his family, one for each household. 4If any household is too small for a whole lamb, they must share one with their nearest neighbor, having taken into account the number of people there are. You are to determine the amount of lamb needed in accordance with what each person will eat. 5The animals you choose must be year-old males without defect, and you may take them from the sheep or the goats. 6Take care of them until the fourteenth day of the month, when all the people of the community of Israel must slaughter them at twilight. 7Then they are to take some of the blood and put it on the sides and tops of the doorframes of the houses where they eat the lambs. 8That same night they are to eat the meat roasted over the fire, along with bitter herbs, and bread made without yeast. 9Do not eat the meat raw or cooked in water, but roast it over the fire—head, legs and inner parts. 10Do not leave any of it till morning; if some is left till morning, you must burn it. 11This is how you are to eat it: with your cloak tucked into your belt, your sandals on your feet and your staff in your hand. Eat it in haste; it is the LORD's Passover.

12"On that same night I will pass through Egypt and strike down every firstborn—both men and animals—and I will bring judgment on all the gods of Egypt. I am the LORD. 13The blood will be a sign for you on the houses

[a]3 The Hebrew word can mean *lamb* or *kid*; also in verse 4.

11:1–3 While Pharaoh obviously hated and feared Moses and the Israelites, the majority of Egypt's leaders and populace did not share his feelings. God had caused the Egyptians to look favorably on the Israelites (11:2–3). If Moses had assumed that everyone was against him just because of Pharaoh's hatred, he would not have had a realistic view of the situation. We also may encounter people who will respond negatively to our spiritual renewal, but there will be some who will regard our progress toward renewal quite favorably; some will even cheer us on!

11:4–8 Moses warned Pharaoh of the final plague—the death of the firstborn. This plague would touch people from all levels of Egyptian society and their livestock as well. While Pharaoh's firstborn son was heir to the Egyptian throne, the firstborn son in every ancient Egyptian home filled an important role. It was this plague that finally caused Pharaoh to surrender to God—at least temporarily. It took the severe loss of his firstborn son to get the attention of his hard heart. Let us learn from Pharaoh's mistake to seek God and surrender to him while there is still hope. Continued resistance to God will only lead to suffering.

12:1–2 The event of Israel's exodus from Egypt marked a turning point for Israel. God's people were leaving their lives of slavery and gaining new lives of responsibility and freedom. It is possible to build a new life that is so markedly different that we can declare a new phase or season of life. At this point in their history the Israelites were declaring such a turning point, a new boundary line. We may find it helpful to declare such boundary lines in our lives. These boundary lines can provide us with a new sense of identity, setting us apart from our past sins and failures and reinforcing the process of spiritual renewal.

12:3–13 Here we see that those who trusted God's promise and put the sacrificial blood over their doors were spared the loss of their firstborn sons. Similarly, we who have faith in the sacrifice of Jesus Christ, the ultimate Passover lamb (1 Corinthians 5:7), are spared from eternal death (John 3:16). We also become brand-new people in Christ (2 Corinthians 5:17). God will initiate and maintain the necessary spiritual and emotional development in our lives if we are willing to trust him to do it.

where you are; and when I see the blood, I will pass over you. No destructive plague will touch you when I strike Egypt.

[14]"This is a day you are to commemorate; for the generations to come you shall celebrate it as a festival to the LORD—a lasting ordinance. [15]For seven days you are to eat bread made without yeast. On the first day remove the yeast from your houses, for whoever eats anything with yeast in it from the first day through the seventh must be cut off from Israel. [16]On the first day hold a sacred assembly, and another one on the seventh day. Do no work at all on these days, except to prepare food for everyone to eat—that is all you may do.

[17]"Celebrate the Feast of Unleavened Bread, because it was on this very day that I brought your divisions out of Egypt. Celebrate this day as a lasting ordinance for the generations to come. [18]In the first month you are to eat bread made without yeast, from the evening of the fourteenth day until the evening of the twenty-first day. [19]For seven days no yeast is to be found in your houses. And whoever eats anything with yeast in it must be cut off from the community of Israel, whether he is an alien or native-born. [20]Eat nothing made with yeast. Wherever you live, you must eat unleavened bread."

[21]Then Moses summoned all the elders of Israel and said to them, "Go at once and select the animals for your families and slaughter the Passover lamb. [22]Take a bunch of hyssop, dip it into the blood in the basin and put some of the blood on the top and on both sides of the doorframe. Not one of you shall go out the door of his house until morning. [23]When the LORD goes through the land to strike down the Egyptians, he will see the blood on the top and sides of the doorframe and will pass over that doorway, and he will not permit the destroyer to enter your houses and strike you down.

[24]"Obey these instructions as a lasting ordinance for you and your descendants. [25]When you enter the land that the LORD will give you as he promised, observe this ceremony. [26]And when your children ask you, 'What does this ceremony mean to you?' [27]then tell them, 'It is the Passover sacrifice to the LORD, who passed over the houses of the Israelites in Egypt and spared our homes when he struck down the Egyptians.' " Then the people bowed down and worshiped. [28]The Israelites did just what the LORD commanded Moses and Aaron.

[29]At midnight the LORD struck down all the firstborn in Egypt, from the firstborn of Pharaoh, who sat on the throne, to the firstborn of the prisoner, who was in the dungeon, and the firstborn of all the livestock as well. [30]Pharaoh and all his officials and all the Egyptians got up during the night, and there was loud wailing in Egypt, for there was not a house without someone dead.

The Exodus

[31]During the night Pharaoh summoned Moses and Aaron and said, "Up! Leave my people, you and the Israelites! Go, worship the LORD as you have requested. [32]Take your flocks and herds, as you have said, and go. And also bless me."

[33]The Egyptians urged the people to hurry and leave the country. "For otherwise," they said, "we will all die!" [34]So the people took their dough before the yeast was added, and carried it on their shoulders in kneading troughs wrapped in clothing. [35]The Israelites did as Moses instructed and asked the Egyptians for articles of silver and gold and for clothing. [36]The LORD had made the Egyptians favorably disposed toward the people, and they gave them what they asked for; so they plundered the Egyptians.

[37]The Israelites journeyed from Rameses to Succoth. There were about six hundred thousand men on foot, besides women and children. [38]Many other people went up with them, as well as large droves of livestock, both flocks and herds. [39]With the dough they had brought from Egypt, they baked cakes of unleavened bread. The dough was without yeast because they had been driven out of Egypt and did not have time to prepare food for themselves.

[40]Now the length of time the Israelite people lived in Egypt[a] was 430 years. [41]At the end of

[a]40 Masoretic Text; Samaritan Pentateuch and Septuagint *Egypt and Canaan*

12:14–16 The Passover was to become an occasion of celebration for future generations of Israel. It would be a time to remember their deliverance from slavery. Part of building a new life involves replacing old, unhealthy thoughts and actions with new, healthy ones. This may include taking on new traditions that celebrate our freedom from past problems. These traditions should emphasize the positive differences between our old existence and the healthy freedom we now experience in our renewed spiritual life.

12:24–27 Children are usually curious about why their parents believe and act as they do. They are quick to pick up on half-hearted or hypocritical actions. But they are also quick to learn when positive lessons and values are modeled and taught. The Israelites were supposed to teach their children important lessons about the past, recalling God's great victories for their ancestors. This would help provide the groundwork for their children's faith in God, enabling them to step forward into life with a healthy belief in him. We should remember that much of the present and future grows out of the past. Let us capitalize on the good things in the past to strengthen our prospects for the future.

12:28–51 After this final plague, the Israelites were not just *allowed* to leave; they were *commanded* to get out! Feeling the pain and shock of his son's death, Pharaoh didn't attach any conditions to the Israelites' exodus. He only asked for Moses' blessing (12:32). God had worked out the timing and all the details necessary for the exodus to take place. Similarly, the all-knowing and all-powerful God lays out the path to freedom for all those committed to him.

the 430 years, to the very day, all the LORD's divisions left Egypt. [42]Because the LORD kept vigil that night to bring them out of Egypt, on this night all the Israelites are to keep vigil to honor the LORD for the generations to come.

Passover Restrictions

[43]The LORD said to Moses and Aaron, "These are the regulations for the Passover:

"No foreigner is to eat of it. [44]Any slave you have bought may eat of it after you have circumcised him, [45]but a temporary resident and a hired worker may not eat of it.

[46]"It must be eaten inside one house; take none of the meat outside the house. Do not break any of the bones. [47]The whole community of Israel must celebrate it.

[48]"An alien living among you who wants to celebrate the LORD's Passover must have all the males in his household circumcised; then he may take part like one born in the land. No uncircumcised male may eat of it. [49]The same law applies to the native-born and to the alien living among you."

[50]All the Israelites did just what the LORD had commanded Moses and Aaron. [51]And on that very day the LORD brought the Israelites out of Egypt by their divisions.

Consecration of the Firstborn

13 The LORD said to Moses, [2]"Consecrate to me every firstborn male. The first offspring of every womb among the Israelites belongs to me, whether man or animal."

[3]Then Moses said to the people, "Commemorate this day, the day you came out of Egypt, out of the land of slavery, because the LORD brought you out of it with a mighty hand. Eat nothing containing yeast. [4]Today, in the month of Abib, you are leaving. [5]When the LORD brings you into the land of the Canaanites, Hittites, Amorites, Hivites and Jebusites—the land he swore to your forefathers to give you, a land flowing with milk and honey—you are to observe this ceremony in this month: [6]For seven days eat bread made without yeast and on the seventh day hold a festival to the LORD. [7]Eat unleavened bread during those seven days; nothing with yeast in it is to be seen among you, nor shall any yeast be seen anywhere within your borders. [8]On that day tell your son, 'I do this because of what the LORD did for me when I came out of Egypt.' [9]This observance will be for you like a sign on your hand and a reminder on your forehead that the law of the LORD is to be on your lips. For the LORD brought you out of Egypt with his mighty hand. [10]You must keep this ordinance at the appointed time year after year.

[11]"After the LORD brings you into the land of the Canaanites and gives it to you, as he promised on oath to you and your forefathers, [12]you are to give over to the LORD the first offspring of every womb. All the firstborn males of your livestock belong to the LORD. [13]Redeem with a lamb every firstborn donkey, but if you do not redeem it, break its neck. Redeem every firstborn among your sons.

[14]"In days to come, when your son asks you, 'What does this mean?' say to him, 'With a mighty hand the LORD brought us out of Egypt, out of the land of slavery. [15]When Pharaoh stubbornly refused to let us go, the LORD killed every firstborn in Egypt, both man and animal. This is why I sacrifice to the LORD the first male offspring of every womb and redeem each of my firstborn sons.' [16]And it will be like a sign on your hand and a symbol on your forehead that the LORD brought us out of Egypt with his mighty hand."

Crossing the Sea

[17]When Pharaoh let the people go, God did not lead them on the road through the Philistine country, though that was shorter. For God said, "If they face war, they might change their minds and return to Egypt." [18]So God led the people around by the desert road toward the Red Sea.[a] The Israelites went up out of Egypt armed for battle.

[19]Moses took the bones of Joseph with him because Joseph had made the sons of Israel swear an oath. He had said, "God will surely

[a]18 Hebrew *Yam Suph*; that is, Sea of Reeds

13:1–2, 11–16 The consecration of the firstborn sons of Israel points to the important position of the firstborn in family dynamics (see 22:29–30). Since God had spared the lives of the firstborn of Israel during the Passover, in a very real sense they all belonged to him. As a result, the Israelites were required to sacrifice a lamb to buy their firstborn sons back from God. All of our children should be viewed as being "on loan" from God. The public dedication of our children to God is a helpful tradition which can remind us of this fact.

13:17–18 Swinging southeast to the Red Sea was not the fastest route from Egypt to the promised land, but it was the route that God chose for the Israelites to follow. The shortest route between two points is not always the best; God's will often calls us to take the scenic routes. Scenic routes, though longer and sometimes harder, are often God's means for accomplishing his will. In the Israelites' case, they were given the opportunity to see God overcome a huge obstacle—the Red Sea. This gave the Israelites additional fuel for their faith, building their courage for the journey ahead. It also helped them avoid dangers in the land of the Philistines that they were not yet prepared to face.

13:19 Joseph's bones made the journey back to the promised land. Many years earlier, Joseph had made his descendants promise that they would bring his body back to the promised land with them (Genesis 50:24–26). Joseph believed God's promise to Abraham that someday Canaan would belong to his descendants. Joseph was a godly example to his descendants even four hundred years after his death. In our families, the good things should be remembered and treasured too, even as the bad ones must be faced, dealt with and used to teach us how to redirect our course.

come to your aid, and then you must carry my
bones up with you from this place."[a]
20After leaving Succoth they camped at
Etham on the edge of the desert. 21By day the
LORD went ahead of them in a pillar of cloud to
guide them on their way and by night in a pillar
of fire to give them light, so that they could
travel by day or night. 22Neither the pillar of
cloud by day nor the pillar of fire by night left
its place in front of the people.

14 Then the LORD said to Moses, 2"Tell the
Israelites to turn back and encamp near
Pi Hahiroth, between Migdol and the sea. They
are to encamp by the sea, directly opposite Baal
Zephon. 3Pharaoh will think, 'The Israelites are
wandering around the land in confusion,
hemmed in by the desert.' 4And I will harden
Pharaoh's heart, and he will pursue them. But I
will gain glory for myself through Pharaoh and
all his army, and the Egyptians will know that
I am the LORD." So the Israelites did this.
5When the king of Egypt was told that the
people had fled, Pharaoh and his officials
changed their minds about them and said,
"What have we done? We have let the Israelites
go and have lost their services!" 6So he had his
chariot made ready and took his army with
him. 7He took six hundred of the best chariots,
along with all the other chariots of Egypt, with
officers over all of them. 8The LORD hardened
the heart of Pharaoh king of Egypt, so that he
pursued the Israelites, who were marching out
boldly. 9The Egyptians—all Pharaoh's horses
and chariots, horsemen[b] and troops—pursued
the Israelites and overtook them as they
camped by the sea near Pi Hahiroth, opposite
Baal Zephon.
10As Pharaoh approached, the Israelites
looked up, and there were the Egyptians,
marching after them. They were terrified and
cried out to the LORD. 11They said to Moses,
"Was it because there were no graves in Egypt
that you brought us to the desert to die? What
have you done to us by bringing us out of
Egypt? 12Didn't we say to you in Egypt, 'Leave
us alone; let us serve the Egyptians'? It would
have been better for us to serve the Egyptians
than to die in the desert!"
13Moses answered the people, "Do not be
afraid. Stand firm and you will see the deliverance the LORD will bring you today. The Egyptians you see today you will never see again.
14The LORD will fight for you; you need only to
be still."
15Then the LORD said to Moses, "Why are
you crying out to me? Tell the Israelites to move
on. 16Raise your staff and stretch out your hand
over the sea to divide the water so that the Israelites can go through the sea on dry ground. 17I
will harden the hearts of the Egyptians so that
they will go in after them. And I will gain glory
through Pharaoh and all his army, through his
chariots and his horsemen. 18The Egyptians will
know that I am the LORD when I gain glory
through Pharaoh, his chariots and his horsemen."
19Then the angel of God, who had been traveling in front of Israel's army, withdrew and
went behind them. The pillar of cloud also
moved from in front and stood behind them,
20coming between the armies of Egypt and Israel. Throughout the night the cloud brought
darkness to the one side and light to the other
side; so neither went near the other all night
long.
21Then Moses stretched out his hand over the
sea, and all that night the LORD drove the sea
back with a strong east wind and turned it into
dry land. The waters were divided, 22and the
Israelites went through the sea on dry ground,
with a wall of water on their right and on their
left.
23The Egyptians pursued them, and all Pharaoh's horses and chariots and horsemen followed them into the sea. 24During the last
watch of the night the LORD looked down from
the pillar of fire and cloud at the Egyptian army
and threw it into confusion. 25He made the
wheels of their chariots come off[c] so that they
had difficulty driving. And the Egyptians said,
"Let's get away from the Israelites! The LORD is
fighting for them against Egypt."

[a] *19* See Gen. 50:25. [b] *9* Or *charioteers;* also in verses 17, 18, 23, 26 and 28 [c] *25* Or *He jammed the wheels of their chariots* (see Samaritan Pentateuch, Septuagint and Syriac)

13:21–22 God guided his people out of slavery into a new life of freedom and responsibility through his visible presence in the pillar of cloud and the pillar of fire. He led them to reclaim the promises he had given to their ancestor Abraham centuries earlier. When we are committed to God, we can also count on his leading. He has sent his Holy Spirit to lead us (John 16:7–15) and has promised to never leave or forsake us (Hebrews 13:5).

14:1–9 The Israelites were between a rock and a hard place—the Red Sea on one side and the Egyptian army on the other. Though the Israelites had already seen God do great miracles in Egypt (7:1—12:51), it must have been hard for them to wait and see how God would save them from this ominous situation. Our situations may seem just as hopeless, but nothing is a hopeless dead end for God. He will always provide a door leading to the next step in his plan.

14:10–12 In their fear, the Israelites cried out to God for help. Though their terrified complaints show that their faith in God was limited, at least they recognized their need for God in this situation and looked to him for help. As a result, their discouragement and fear were soon turned into amazement and rejoicing (14:21—15:21).

14:13–31 God opened up a dry path through the Red Sea so that the people could cross to the other side. Yet even with this miracle the Israelites had to respond to God in faith. They still had to walk between the massive walls of water that could have come crashing down at any moment. This walk through the sea required commitment to God and surely resulted in the growth of the Israelites' faith. The miracles that God works in our lives also require that we respond in faith, stepping out to receive all the blessings he has for us.

26Then the LORD said to Moses, "Stretch out
your hand over the sea so that the waters may
flow back over the Egyptians and their chariots
and horsemen." 27Moses stretched out his hand
over the sea, and at daybreak the sea went back
to its place. The Egyptians were fleeing toward[a] it, and the LORD swept them into the
sea. 28The water flowed back and covered the
chariots and horsemen—the entire army of
Pharaoh that had followed the Israelites into
the sea. Not one of them survived.
29But the Israelites went through the sea on
dry ground, with a wall of water on their right
and on their left. 30That day the LORD saved
Israel from the hands of the Egyptians, and Israel saw the Egyptians lying dead on the shore.
31And when the Israelites saw the great power
the LORD displayed against the Egyptians, the
people feared the LORD and put their trust in
him and in Moses his servant.

The Song of Moses and Miriam

15 Then Moses and the Israelites sang this
song to the LORD:

"I will sing to the LORD,
  for he is highly exalted.
The horse and its rider
  he has hurled into the sea.
2The LORD is my strength and my song;
  he has become my salvation.
He is my God, and I will praise him,
  my father's God, and I will exalt him.
3The LORD is a warrior;
  the LORD is his name.
4Pharaoh's chariots and his army
  he has hurled into the sea.
The best of Pharaoh's officers
  are drowned in the Red Sea.[b]
5The deep waters have covered them;
  they sank to the depths like a stone.

6"Your right hand, O LORD,
  was majestic in power.
Your right hand, O LORD,
  shattered the enemy.
7In the greatness of your majesty
  you threw down those who opposed
    you.
You unleashed your burning anger;
  it consumed them like stubble.
8By the blast of your nostrils
  the waters piled up.
The surging waters stood firm like a wall;
  the deep waters congealed in the heart of
    the sea.

9"The enemy boasted,
  'I will pursue, I will overtake them.
I will divide the spoils;
  I will gorge myself on them.
I will draw my sword
  and my hand will destroy them.'
10But you blew with your breath,
  and the sea covered them.
They sank like lead
  in the mighty waters.

11"Who among the gods is like you, O LORD?
  Who is like you—
    majestic in holiness,
    awesome in glory,
    working wonders?
12You stretched out your right hand
  and the earth swallowed them.

13"In your unfailing love you will lead
  the people you have redeemed.
In your strength you will guide them
  to your holy dwelling.
14The nations will hear and tremble;
  anguish will grip the people of Philistia.
15The chiefs of Edom will be terrified,
  the leaders of Moab will be seized with
    trembling,
the people[c] of Canaan will melt away;
16 terror and dread will fall upon them.
By the power of your arm
  they will be as still as a stone—
until your people pass by, O LORD,
  until the people you bought[d] pass by.
17You will bring them in and plant them
  on the mountain of your inheritance—
the place, O LORD, you made for your
    dwelling,
  the sanctuary, O Lord, your hands
    established.
18The LORD will reign
  for ever and ever."

19When Pharaoh's horses, chariots and
horsemen[e] went into the sea, the LORD
brought the waters of the sea back over them,
but the Israelites walked through the sea on dry
ground. 20Then Miriam the prophetess, Aaron's
sister, took a tambourine in her hand, and all
the women followed her, with tambourines and
dancing. 21Miriam sang to them:

"Sing to the LORD,
  for he is highly exalted.
The horse and its rider
  he has hurled into the sea."

The Waters of Marah and Elim

22Then Moses led Israel from the Red Sea and
they went into the Desert of Shur. For three days

[a]27 Or *from* [b]4 Hebrew *Yam Suph;* that is, Sea of Reeds; also in verse 22 [c]15 Or *rulers* [d]16 Or *created* [e]19 Or *charioteers*

15:1–21 Israel's escape through the Red Sea depended on a mighty miracle from God and an act of faith by the Israelites. Often the road to victory is not easy, but it is still worth it. There will be something to rejoice about in the end if we depend on God to help us through. When we have gained the victory, we need to stand up, sing and rejoice, remembering God's miracles on our behalf.
15:22–27 Those of us beginning the process of spiritual renewal often have short memories. We quickly forget the important victories that have brought us to our present

they traveled in the desert without finding water. [23]When they came to Marah, they could not drink its water because it was bitter. (That is why the place is called Marah.[a]) [24]So the people grumbled against Moses, saying, "What are we to drink?"

[25]Then Moses cried out to the LORD, and the LORD showed him a piece of wood. He threw it into the water, and the water became sweet.

There the LORD made a decree and a law for them, and there he tested them. [26]He said, "If you listen carefully to the voice of the LORD your God and do what is right in his eyes, if you pay attention to his commands and keep all his decrees, I will not bring on you any of the diseases I brought on the Egyptians, for I am the LORD, who heals you."

[27]Then they came to Elim, where there were twelve springs and seventy palm trees, and they camped there near the water.

Manna and Quail

16 The whole Israelite community set out from Elim and came to the Desert of Sin, which is between Elim and Sinai, on the fifteenth day of the second month after they had come out of Egypt. [2]In the desert the whole community grumbled against Moses and Aaron. [3]The Israelites said to them, "If only we had died by the LORD's hand in Egypt! There we sat around pots of meat and ate all the food we wanted, but you have brought us out into this desert to starve this entire assembly to death."

[4]Then the LORD said to Moses, "I will rain down bread from heaven for you. The people are to go out each day and gather enough for that day. In this way I will test them and see whether they will follow my instructions. [5]On the sixth day they are to prepare what they bring in, and that is to be twice as much as they gather on the other days."

[6]So Moses and Aaron said to all the Israelites, "In the evening you will know that it was the LORD who brought you out of Egypt, [7]and in the morning you will see the glory of the LORD, because he has heard your grumbling against him. Who are we, that you should grumble against us?" [8]Moses also said, "You will know that it was the LORD when he gives you meat to eat in the evening and all the bread you want in the morning, because he has heard your grumbling against him. Who are we? You are not grumbling against us, but against the LORD."

[9]Then Moses told Aaron, "Say to the entire Israelite community, 'Come before the LORD, for he has heard your grumbling.' "

[10]While Aaron was speaking to the whole Israelite community, they looked toward the desert, and there was the glory of the LORD appearing in the cloud.

[11]The LORD said to Moses, [12]"I have heard the grumbling of the Israelites. Tell them, 'At twilight you will eat meat, and in the morning you will be filled with bread. Then you will know that I am the LORD your God.' "

[13]That evening quail came and covered the camp, and in the morning there was a layer of dew around the camp. [14]When the dew was gone, thin flakes like frost on the ground appeared on the desert floor. [15]When the Israelites saw it, they said to each other, "What is it?" For they did not know what it was.

Moses said to them, "It is the bread the LORD has given you to eat. [16]This is what the LORD has commanded: 'Each one is to gather as much as he needs. Take an omer[b] for each person you have in your tent.' "

[17]The Israelites did as they were told; some gathered much, some little. [18]And when they measured it by the omer, he who gathered much did not have too much, and he who gathered little did not have too little. Each one gathered as much as he needed.

[19]Then Moses said to them, "No one is to keep any of it until morning."

[20]However, some of them paid no attention to Moses; they kept part of it until morning, but it was full of maggots and began to smell. So Moses was angry with them.

[21]Each morning everyone gathered as much as he needed, and when the sun grew hot, it melted away. [22]On the sixth day, they gathered twice as much—two omers[c] for each person—and the leaders of the community came and reported this to Moses. [23]He said to them, "This is what the LORD commanded: 'Tomorrow is to be a day of rest, a holy Sabbath to the LORD. So bake what you want to bake and boil what you want to boil. Save whatever is left and keep it until morning.' "

[24]So they saved it until morning, as Moses commanded, and it did not stink or get maggots in it. [25]"Eat it today," Moses said, "because today is a Sabbath to the LORD. You will not find any of it on the ground today. [26]Six days you are

[a]*23 Marah* means *bitter.* [b]*16* That is, probably about 2 quarts (about 2 liters); also in verses 18, 32, 33 and 36 [c]*22* That is, probably about 4 quarts (about 4.5 liters)

---

state of freedom. We also may fall back into reacting to crises as we did in the past, before we learned to seek God. Despite God's recent victories on the Israelites' behalf, and only a few days after the miracle at the Red Sea, the Israelites became desperate when their water supply ran out. They were unwilling, or unable, to remember God's past faithfulness and exercise trust in God. Even so, God came through with an immediate, abundant provision for their need (see Ephesians 3:20).

16:1–36 Next to our need for water (15:22–27), our need for food is the most critical. Again the Israelites failed to believe that God would meet their needs. They lacked faith in God's power and still didn't understand their privileges as God's people. But God faithfully provided for them anyway, and their faith was further strengthened. This example of God's gracious provision should encourage us to seek help during the wilderness periods of our own lives.

to gather it, but on the seventh day, the Sabbath, there will not be any."

27Nevertheless, some of the people went out on the seventh day to gather it, but they found none. 28Then the LORD said to Moses, "How long will you[a] refuse to keep my commands and my instructions? 29Bear in mind that the LORD has given you the Sabbath; that is why on the sixth day he gives you bread for two days. Everyone is to stay where he is on the seventh day; no one is to go out." 30So the people rested on the seventh day.

31The people of Israel called the bread manna.[b] It was white like coriander seed and tasted like wafers made with honey. 32Moses said, "This is what the LORD has commanded: 'Take an omer of manna and keep it for the generations to come, so they can see the bread I gave you to eat in the desert when I brought you out of Egypt.' "

33So Moses said to Aaron, "Take a jar and put an omer of manna in it. Then place it before the LORD to be kept for the generations to come."

34As the LORD commanded Moses, Aaron put the manna in front of the Testimony, that it might be kept. 35The Israelites ate manna forty years, until they came to a land that was settled; they ate manna until they reached the border of Canaan.

36(An omer is one tenth of an ephah.)

Water From the Rock

17 The whole Israelite community set out from the Desert of Sin, traveling from place to place as the LORD commanded. They camped at Rephidim, but there was no water for the people to drink. 2So they quarreled with Moses and said, "Give us water to drink."

Moses replied, "Why do you quarrel with me? Why do you put the LORD to the test?"

3But the people were thirsty for water there, and they grumbled against Moses. They said, "Why did you bring us up out of Egypt to make us and our children and livestock die of thirst?"

4Then Moses cried out to the LORD, "What am I to do with these people? They are almost ready to stone me."

5The LORD answered Moses, "Walk on ahead of the people. Take with you some of the elders of Israel and take in your hand the staff with which you struck the Nile, and go. 6I will stand there before you by the rock at Horeb. Strike the rock, and water will come out of it for the people to drink." So Moses did this in the sight of the elders of Israel. 7And he called the place Massah[c] and Meribah[d] because the Israelites quarreled and because they tested the LORD saying, "Is the LORD among us or not?"

The Amalekites Defeated

8The Amalekites came and attacked the Israelites at Rephidim. 9Moses said to Joshua, "Choose some of our men and go out to fight the Amalekites. Tomorrow I will stand on top of the hill with the staff of God in my hands."

10So Joshua fought the Amalekites as Moses had ordered, and Moses, Aaron and Hur went to the top of the hill. 11As long as Moses held up his hands, the Israelites were winning, but whenever he lowered his hands, the Amalekites were winning. 12When Moses' hands grew tired, they took a stone and put it under him and he sat on it. Aaron and Hur held his hands up—one on one side, one on the other—so that his hands remained steady till sunset. 13So Joshua overcame the Amalekite army with the sword.

14Then the LORD said to Moses, "Write this on a scroll as something to be remembered and make sure that Joshua hears it, because I will completely blot out the memory of Amalek from under heaven."

15Moses built an altar and called it The LORD is my Banner. 16He said, "For hands were lifted up to the throne of the LORD. The[e] LORD will be at war against the Amalekites from generation to generation."

Jethro Visits Moses

18 Now Jethro, the priest of Midian and father-in-law of Moses, heard of everything God had done for Moses and for his people Israel, and how the LORD had brought Israel out of Egypt.

2After Moses had sent away his wife Zipporah, his father-in-law Jethro received her 3and her two sons. One son was named Gershom,[f] for Moses said, "I have become an alien in a foreign land"; 4and the other was named Eliezer,[g] for he said, "My father's God was my

[a]28 The Hebrew is plural. [b]31 *Manna* means *What is it?* (see verse 15). [c]7 *Massah* means *testing.* [d]7 *Meribah* means *quarreling.* [e]16 Or *"Because a hand was against the throne of the LORD, the* [f]3 *Gershom* sounds like the Hebrew for *an alien there.* [g]4 *Eliezer* means *my God is helper.*

17:1–7 As we undergo the process of spiritual renewal, we may be hindered repeatedly by the same old mistakes—weaknesses that haunt us time and again. The Israelites displayed this same tendency. They had already rebelled against Moses' leadership because of a short-term lack of water (see 15:22–27). Now they were grumbling again about the same problem. To make this place a monument to the people's lack of faith, Moses named it *Massah* (meaning "testing") and *Meribah* (meaning "quarreling"). These names would remind the people of their past mistakes and encourage them to be wiser the next time. We also need to be reminded of our past mistakes from time to time in order to avoid them in the future.

17:8–16 The people had tested God, wondering whether he was with them (17:7). In response, God overwhelmed the Amalekite forces in battle by employing an instructive visual aid. Moses stood upon a hill in full view of the people and the battlefield. When his hands were raised, the Israelite army prevailed. When his hands fell, the Israelites were pushed back. The raised hands did not speak of the power of Moses but rather bespoke the power of God. By observing this, the Israelites learned that their freedom was dependent on their faith in God, not on their own strength.

Joining Together With Others in Prayer

Exodus 17:12 Prayer is sometimes a solitary activity—one individual conversing with God. But there are also times when we need to join with others in prayer. In this passage, even Moses, with all his spiritual depth and power, needed Aaron and Hur to help him as he called upon the Lord to deliver Israel. Aaron was Moses' right-hand man, the high priest of the Israelites. Hur, however, is not as well known. He may have been the grandfather of Bezalel, one of the chief craftsmen of the tabernacle (Exodus 31:2; 1 Chronicles 2:19–20). Regardless of his identity, it is clear that his assistance was vital to Moses' intercession for Israel.

In this fascinating account, the outcome of the battle is directly linked to prayer. Upraised hands were a common posture for requesting God's special help (Psalm 63:4; 1 Timothy 2:8). When Moses' hands and staff were lifted in prayer, the Israelites gained the advantage. When Moses grew tired and lowered his arms, Israel started losing. Neither the skill of the warriors nor the status and reputation of the supplicants affected Israel's success. The power of God made the difference.

In all of life, the battle is the Lord's (see 1 Samuel 17:47; Ephesians 6:10–18). We enter into this battle through prayer. These prayers become prayers of supplication and petition when we pray for our own needs and prayers of intercession when we pray for others.

The point of this passage, however, is not simply the importance of prayer but the significance of joining together with others in prayer. There are times for solitary prayer (see Matthew 6:6) but also times to pray with others. Jesus called us to join together in prayer in Matthew 18:19–20. Though the Lord is always with us, his presence is manifested in special ways when we pray with other believers. Prayer with others often fosters additional encouragement, assurance and insight into God's character. It also provides us with testimonies of God's faithfulness and keeps us accountable and faithful in our own spiritual walk. We especially need to join in prayer with others when:

- The spiritual conflict is intense. The Amalekites were fierce warriors who pressed Joshua and the Israelites to the limits. They threatened to crush the fledgling nation of Israel. Intense battles require extensive prayer support.
- God's answers take time in coming. The battle with the Amalekites lasted the entire day. Sometimes the hardest thing about prayer is waiting for a response. The presence of others encourages us to persevere as we wait for God's answer.
- We sense we have reached our limits. Moses' spiritual and physical stamina were insufficient for the challenge. Our weakness provides one of the most important links to spiritual power: the community of faith. Our need draws us together.

Putting It Into Practice

Who holds up your hands? Whom can you call anytime, day or night, for prayer and support? If you don't have such a person, begin praying now for God to provide one. It may be an old friend you can call on the phone, a person in your own church or even a person from a different congregation.

This passage encourages us to support our spiritual leaders in prayer. How could God use you to encourage your pastor or your children's teachers? Consider committing yourself to upholding them in regular prayer.

For more on prayer, turn to Matthew 6.

helper; he saved me from the sword of Pharaoh."

5Jethro, Moses' father-in-law, together with Moses' sons and wife, came to him in the desert, where he was camped near the mountain of God. 6Jethro had sent word to him, "I, your father-in-law Jethro, am coming to you with your wife and her two sons."

7So Moses went out to meet his father-in-law and bowed down and kissed him. They greeted each other and then went into the tent. 8Moses told his father-in-law about everything the LORD had done to Pharaoh and the Egyptians for Israel's sake and about all the hardships they had met along the way and how the LORD had saved them.

9Jethro was delighted to hear about all the good things the LORD had done for Israel in rescuing them from the hand of the Egyptians. 10He said, "Praise be to the LORD, who rescued you from the hand of the Egyptians and of Pharaoh, and who rescued the people from the hand of the Egyptians. 11Now I know that the LORD is greater than all other gods, for he did this to those who had treated Israel arrogantly." 12Then Jethro, Moses' father-in-law, brought a burnt offering and other sacrifices to God, and Aaron came with all the elders of Israel to eat bread with Moses' father-in-law in the presence of God.

13The next day Moses took his seat to serve as judge for the people, and they stood around him from morning till evening. 14When his father-in-law saw all that Moses was doing for the people, he said, "What is this you are doing for the people? Why do you alone sit as judge, while all these people stand around you from morning till evening?"

15Moses answered him, "Because the people come to me to seek God's will. 16Whenever they have a dispute, it is brought to me, and I decide between the parties and inform them of God's decrees and laws."

17Moses' father-in-law replied, "What you are doing is not good. 18You and these people who come to you will only wear yourselves out. The work is too heavy for you; you cannot handle it alone. 19Listen now to me and I will give you some advice, and may God be with you. You must be the people's representative before God and bring their disputes to him. 20Teach them the decrees and laws, and show them the way to live and the duties they are to perform. 21But select capable men from all the people—men who fear God, trustworthy men who hate dishonest gain—and appoint them as officials over thousands, hundreds, fifties and tens. 22Have them serve as judges for the people at all times, but have them bring every difficult case to you; the simple cases they can decide themselves. That will make your load lighter, because they will share it with you. 23If you do this and God so commands, you will be able to stand the strain, and all these people will go home satisfied."

24Moses listened to his father-in-law and did everything he said. 25He chose capable men from all Israel and made them leaders of the people, officials over thousands, hundreds, fifties and tens. 26They served as judges for the people at all times. The difficult cases they brought to Moses, but the simple ones they decided themselves.

27Then Moses sent his father-in-law on his way, and Jethro returned to his own country.

At Mount Sinai

19 In the third month after the Israelites left Egypt—on the very day—they came to the Desert of Sinai. 2After they set out from Rephidim, they entered the Desert of Sinai, and Israel camped there in the desert in front of the mountain.

3Then Moses went up to God, and the LORD called to him from the mountain and said, "This is what you are to say to the house of Jacob and what you are to tell the people of Israel: 4'You yourselves have seen what I did to Egypt, and how I carried you on eagles' wings and brought you to myself. 5Now if you obey me fully and keep my covenant, then out of all nations you will be my treasured possession. Although the whole earth is mine, 6you[a] will be for me a kingdom of priests and a holy nation.' These are the words you are to speak to the Israelites."

7So Moses went back and summoned the elders of the people and set before them all the words the LORD had commanded him to speak. 8The people all responded together, "We will do everything the LORD has said." So Moses brought their answer back to the LORD.

9The LORD said to Moses, "I am going to come to you in a dense cloud, so that the people will hear me speaking with you and will always

[a]5,6 Or *possession, for the whole earth is mine.* 6*You*

18:13–26 Moses had a difficult time accepting his limitations and living a balanced life. Jethro gave Moses some wise and creative advice, helping him protect himself from the extensive demands of the people. But even this good advice did not completely solve this problem for Moses. His tendency to assume that God expected him to do everything shows up later on in a slightly different way (Numbers 11:10–17). Moses appeared to be near exhaustion, just as Jethro had predicted (18:17–18). We need to accept our limitations and set appropriate boundaries in our own lives, maximizing the use of the time and energy we have while also protecting ourselves from exhaustion.

19:2–6 Israel's new sense of identity and ability was to be founded upon a relationship with God. The Israelites had suffered under Egyptian bondage. Their sense of identity had been defined by that terrible experience. God had graciously delivered them and brought them to himself. Now the Lord called the people of Israel to be a kingdom of priests and his holy nation (19:6). They were no longer a nation of slaves. As we progress spiritually, we also need to see ourselves as people loved and blessed by God, not as slaves to sins, passions and unwholesome desires.

put their trust in you." Then Moses told the LORD
what the people had said.
10 And the LORD said to Moses, "Go to the
people and consecrate them today and tomorrow. Have them wash their clothes 11 and be
ready by the third day, because on that day the
LORD will come down on Mount Sinai in the
sight of all the people. 12 Put limits for the people around the mountain and tell them, 'Be
careful that you do not go up the mountain
or touch the foot of it. Whoever touches the
mountain shall surely be put to death. 13 He
shall surely be stoned or shot with arrows; not
a hand is to be laid on him. Whether man or
animal, he shall not be permitted to live.' Only
when the ram's horn sounds a long blast may
they go up to the mountain."
14 After Moses had gone down the mountain
to the people, he consecrated them, and they
washed their clothes. 15 Then he said to the people, "Prepare yourselves for the third day. Abstain from sexual relations."
16 On the morning of the third day there was
thunder and lightning, with a thick cloud over
the mountain, and a very loud trumpet blast.
Everyone in the camp trembled. 17 Then Moses
led the people out of the camp to meet with
God, and they stood at the foot of the mountain. 18 Mount Sinai was covered with smoke,
because the LORD descended on it in fire. The
smoke billowed up from it like smoke from a
furnace, the whole mountain[a] trembled violently, 19 and the sound of the trumpet grew
louder and louder. Then Moses spoke and the
voice of God answered him.[b]
20 The LORD descended to the top of Mount
Sinai and called Moses to the top of the mountain. So Moses went up 21 and the LORD said to
him, "Go down and warn the people so they do
not force their way through to see the LORD and
many of them perish. 22 Even the priests, who
approach the LORD, must consecrate themselves, or the LORD will break out against them."
23 Moses said to the LORD, "The people cannot come up Mount Sinai, because you yourself
warned us, 'Put limits around the mountain
and set it apart as holy.' "
24 The LORD replied, "Go down and bring
Aaron up with you. But the priests and the people must not force their way through to come
up to the LORD, or he will break out against
them."
25 So Moses went down to the people and
told them.

The Ten Commandments

20 And God spoke all these words:
2 "I am the LORD your God, who
brought you out of Egypt, out of the
land of slavery.
3 "You shall have no other gods before[c] me.
4 "You shall not make for yourself an idol
in the form of anything in heaven
above or on the earth beneath or in
the waters below. 5 You shall not
bow down to them or worship
them; for I, the LORD your God, am
a jealous God, punishing the children for the sin of the fathers to the
third and fourth generation of those
who hate me, 6 but showing love to
a thousand ⌞generations⌟ of those
who love me and keep my commandments.
7 "You shall not misuse the name of the
LORD your God, for the LORD will
not hold anyone guiltless who misuses his name.
8 "Remember the Sabbath day by keeping
it holy. 9 Six days you shall labor and
do all your work, 10 but the seventh
day is a Sabbath to the LORD your
God. On it you shall not do any
work, neither you, nor your son or
daughter, nor your manservant or
maidservant, nor your animals, nor
the alien within your gates. 11 For in
six days the LORD made the heavens
and the earth, the sea, and all that is
in them, but he rested on the seventh day. Therefore the LORD
blessed the Sabbath day and made
it holy.
12 "Honor your father and your mother, so

[a] 18 Most Hebrew manuscripts; a few Hebrew manuscripts and Septuagint *all the people* [b] 19 Or *and God answered him with thunder* [c] 3 Or *besides*

19:12–23 God set limits or boundaries beyond which the people of Israel, or even their livestock, were not to step. There was mortal danger for those who overstepped God's boundaries. The unauthorized approach into God's holy presence meant certain death. We also must learn to respect the limits placed upon us by God's Word. We only invite painful consequences when we ignore them.
20:1–11 The first four of the Ten Commandments provided the Israelites with a few foundational principles to govern their relationship with God. They were not to worship any other gods (20:3), make idols of any kind (20:4–6), misuse God's name (20:7) or violate God's Sabbath (20:8–11). Each of these principles represents boundaries that God had set to define his relationship with his people. Jesus later summed up this vertical relationship as the greatest commandment: "Love the Lord your God with all your heart and with all your soul and with all your mind" (Matthew 22:37–38). Loving God includes living out a consistent faith and commitment to him.
20:12–17 The final six of the Ten Commandments define principles for healthy human relationships. The command to honor our parents is stated positively (20:12; see Ephesians 6:1–3). The other five are negative: Do not murder, do not commit adultery, do not steal, do not lie and do not covet anything belonging to your neighbor (20:13–17). Jesus summed up these principles like this: "Love your neighbor as yourself" (Matthew 22:39). This great commandment assumes that we have cultivated a healthy self-respect and will follow it up with loving actions that respect the boundaries of others.

The Ten Commandments: A Gracious Moral Inventory

Exodus 20:1 – 17 Many people today are suffering from the improper use of freedom. While the number of moral and ethical decisions we face seems to be multiplying, the standards that should be used for making these decisions are being stripped away in the name of enlightened freedom. The moral standards established in Scripture are being rejected out of hand as antiquated, narrow and uninformed. In their place society has set up vague ideals of behavior that cannot adequately govern humanity. Our society has become like a person trying to scale a sheer, granite cliff face in bare feet with only a ball of twine to support oneself.

The Bible teaches us that the right things are the smart things. The Ten Commandments were not given merely to restrict our lives and stifle our fun. They are meant to be guardrails that keep us from paths that lead to destruction and death. Those who violate the commandments learn the devastating cost of ignoring God's wise, gracious counsel.

One of the major steps in most recovery programs is a "ruthless, moral inventory" in which people take an honest look at the painful consequences of their past behavior. By God's grace, however, this process ends not in despair but results in restitution, reconciliation and a renewal of dignity and self-respect. It may seem ruthless at the beginning, but such an honest look brings healing at the end.

The Ten Commandments give us God's criteria for taking a moral inventory of our lives. Though prohibiting certain behaviors, these commandments also exhort us to practice behaviors that will bring us life and joy. For instance, the commandment that forbids idolatry tacitly promotes the worship of the true and living God, who is far greater than any created image. The commandment that forbids murder promotes a sacred regard for all people, a necessity for a healthy community. The commandment that forbids us to covet promotes contentment and joy in God's provision, giving us confidence and security in times of need. God's commands show us the path to life and joy. They show us God's truth that sets us free.

Putting It Into Practice

Examine your spiritual life by reviewing each of the commandments. Reflect on the different ways each commandment applies to you, especially regarding the specific attitudes and behaviors each commandment promotes and prohibits. Which of the commandments causes you the least concern? Which causes you the most concern? How can you use the Ten Commandments as a regular part of your daily prayers of confession?

For more on repentance and confession, turn to Nehemiah 9.

that you may live long in the land
the LORD your God is giving you.
13"You shall not murder.
14"You shall not commit adultery.
15"You shall not steal.
16"You shall not give false testimony
against your neighbor.
17"You shall not covet your neighbor's
house. You shall not covet your
neighbor's wife, or his manservant
or maidservant, his ox or donkey,
or anything that belongs to your
neighbor."

18When the people saw the thunder and
lightning and heard the trumpet and saw the
mountain in smoke, they trembled with fear.
They stayed at a distance 19and said to Moses,
"Speak to us yourself and we will listen. But do
not have God speak to us or we will die."
20Moses said to the people, "Do not be
afraid. God has come to test you, so that the fear
of God will be with you to keep you from sinning."
21The people remained at a distance, while
Moses approached the thick darkness where
God was.

Idols and Altars

22Then the LORD said to Moses, "Tell the
Israelites this: 'You have seen for yourselves
that I have spoken to you from heaven: 23Do
not make any gods to be alongside me; do not
make for yourselves gods of silver or gods of
gold.
24" 'Make an altar of earth for me and sacrifice on it your burnt offerings and fellowship
offerings,[a] your sheep and goats and your cattle. Wherever I cause my name to be honored,
I will come to you and bless you. 25If you make
an altar of stones for me, do not build it with
dressed stones, for you will defile it if you use
a tool on it. 26And do not go up to my altar on
steps, lest your nakedness be exposed on it.'

21 "These are the laws you are to set before them:

Hebrew Servants

2"If you buy a Hebrew servant, he is to serve
you for six years. But in the seventh year, he
shall go free, without paying anything. 3If he
comes alone, he is to go free alone; but if he has
a wife when he comes, she is to go with him. 4If
his master gives him a wife and she bears him
sons or daughters, the woman and her children
shall belong to her master, and only the man
shall go free.
5"But if the servant declares, 'I love my master and my wife and children and do not want
to go free,' 6then his master must take him before the judges.[b] He shall take him to the door
or the doorpost and pierce his ear with an awl.
Then he will be his servant for life.
7"If a man sells his daughter as a servant, she
is not to go free as menservants do. 8If she does
not please the master who has selected her for
himself,[c] he must let her be redeemed. He has
no right to sell her to foreigners, because he has
broken faith with her. 9If he selects her for his
son, he must grant her the rights of a daughter.
10If he marries another woman, he must not
deprive the first one of her food, clothing and
marital rights. 11If he does not provide her with
these three things, she is to go free, without any
payment of money.

Personal Injuries

12"Anyone who strikes a man and kills him
shall surely be put to death. 13However, if he
does not do it intentionally, but God lets it
happen, he is to flee to a place I will designate.
14But if a man schemes and kills another man
deliberately, take him away from my altar and
put him to death.

[a]24 Traditionally *peace offerings* [b]6 Or *before God*
[c]8 Or *master so that he does not choose her*

20:18–20 The people of Israel shook with fear before God's holy presence. Fear is an emotion that can be either healthy or unhealthy. When we are afraid of danger or the consequences of inappropriate actions, fear is a helpful guide. But when fear is constant or overwhelming and not connected to reality, it is unhealthy. The fear of God can be defined as thoughtful reverence for God; it is certainly a healthy emotion, based on the reality of God's holiness. Fear of God should result in a vibrant faith and motivate us to act according to God's plan for our lives.

21:2–11 God showed concern for people in bondage and granted them a means for gaining their freedom. But complications could arise from severing this master/slave relationship. Some masters were adversely affected by the freeing of a slave and tried to stop the process. Freed slaves needed to learn some difficult lessons about living responsibly without a master to direct their behavior. These same complications may face us as we enter a season of spiritual renewal. Some people may stand against our spiritual renewal because they benefit somehow from our bondage. And we also need to learn to live responsibly and unselfishly as we begin our lives of spiritual freedom.

21:5–6 God offered each slave the option of becoming a slave for life. This idea of becoming a bond servant (slave) for life by personal choice was used in the New Testament to illustrate the commitment we should have to Jesus Christ (see Philippians 1:1). Essentially we are all slaves to something—our passions, material things, alcohol, drugs, the expectations of others or any number of things. These masters are not kind. Only God truly loves his servants and is worthy of our voluntary, lifelong devotion and service. Being a servant for a loving and gracious master like God is a wonderful thing.

21:12–27 These laws deal with the consequences of inappropriate behavior, emphasizing compensation for wrong behavior. Clearly, God holds us accountable for our actions. These laws reveal God's instructions for maintaining an orderly, healthy society without overstepping proper boundaries. They safeguard human relationships and personal identities while also recognizing the worth of life and property.

THE SPIRITUAL DISCIPLINES

Worship

Take a Rest

Exodus 20:8–11 Few of the spiritual disciplines we will discuss are clearly commanded in Scripture. Most are practiced because of the example, common sense and testimony of God's people. The Bible exhorts us to pray. It is assumed that we will fast. It makes sense to take time for solitude. But observing a Sabbath rest *is* commanded. It is not merely a suggestion. The Sabbath is to serve as a worshipful reminder of the Lord's covenant with us and as a means to our well-being.

The Sabbath is a time to rest as well as a time to remember. Many communities used to reinforce a Sabbath rest through "blue laws" which curbed Sunday activities. Today, since most of our communities no longer have such laws, we must make intentional decisions to change the pace of our lives.

Physical fatigue often drains our spiritual vitality, so rest becomes a central element in our spiritual renewal. Rest is intimately tied to effective worship. When we are tired, we are more easily discouraged and more vulnerable to temptation. Stress can crowd peace and a healthy perspective from our minds. We become unreceptive and unresponsive to God. A lack of rest may bring few observable consequences at first, but the deficit accumulates over time and can result in major problems.

Worship is a primary means for the rest and refreshment of our souls. We *need* to worship. Worship is not something God needs because he has an ego problem. Worship is the means by which we meet with the living Lord. Worship releases us from the grasp of this world. In worship, we become available to God. Through that availability God blesses us with his presence, his purposes and his power in our daily lives.

Worship sets the pace for our lives. Worship recalibrates our guidance systems, freeing us from the stresses of worldly pressures and values, the weight of our "stuff" and activities of this life. Rest relieves the pressure, much like unstringing a bow. Maintaining weekly rest must become a discipline.

Putting It Into Practice

When was the last time you gave yourself a block of time in which you scheduled absolutely nothing? Take a moment to reflect on your weekly day of rest. Consider eliminating all unnecessary activities so that you have a solid block of time to truly rest on this day. There are numerous ways to rest: taking a nap, taking a leisurely walk, sitting alone, listening to music. How do you rest? Your primary purpose for this time should be a refreshment of your soul that reminds you of God's covenant with you. Not soul exercise, but soul relaxation. No demands, no distractions, no burdens.

For more on worship, turn to Exodus 31.

15 "Anyone who attacks[a] his father or his mother must be put to death.

16 "Anyone who kidnaps another and either sells him or still has him when he is caught must be put to death.

17 "Anyone who curses his father or mother must be put to death.

18 "If men quarrel and one hits the other with a stone or with his fist[b] and he does not die but is confined to bed, 19 the one who struck the blow will not be held responsible if the other gets up and walks around outside with his staff; however, he must pay the injured man for the loss of his time and see that he is completely healed.

20 "If a man beats his male or female slave with a rod and the slave dies as a direct result, he must be punished, 21 but he is not to be punished if the slave gets up after a day or two, since the slave is his property.

22 "If men who are fighting hit a pregnant woman and she gives birth prematurely[c] but there is no serious injury, the offender must be fined whatever the woman's husband demands and the court allows. 23 But if there is serious injury, you are to take life for life, 24 eye for eye, tooth for tooth, hand for hand, foot for foot, 25 burn for burn, wound for wound, bruise for bruise.

26 "If a man hits a manservant or maidservant in the eye and destroys it, he must let the servant go free to compensate for the eye. 27 And if he knocks out the tooth of a manservant or maidservant, he must let the servant go free to compensate for the tooth.

28 "If a bull gores a man or a woman to death, the bull must be stoned to death, and its meat must not be eaten. But the owner of the bull will not be held responsible. 29 If, however, the bull has had the habit of goring and the owner has been warned but has not kept it penned up and it kills a man or woman, the bull must be stoned and the owner also must be put to death. 30 However, if payment is demanded of him, he may redeem his life by paying whatever is demanded. 31 This law also applies if the bull gores a son or daughter. 32 If the bull gores a male or female slave, the owner must pay thirty shekels[d] of silver to the master of the slave, and the bull must be stoned.

33 "If a man uncovers a pit or digs one and fails to cover it and an ox or a donkey falls into it, 34 the owner of the pit must pay for the loss; he must pay its owner, and the dead animal will be his.

35 "If a man's bull injures the bull of another and it dies, they are to sell the live one and divide both the money and the dead animal equally. 36 However, if it was known that the bull had the habit of goring, yet the owner did not keep it penned up, the owner must pay, animal for animal, and the dead animal will be his.

Protection of Property

22 "If a man steals an ox or a sheep and slaughters it or sells it, he must pay back five head of cattle for the ox and four sheep for the sheep.

2 "If a thief is caught breaking in and is struck so that he dies, the defender is not guilty of bloodshed; 3 but if it happens[e] after sunrise, he is guilty of bloodshed.

"A thief must certainly make restitution, but if he has nothing, he must be sold to pay for his theft.

4 "If the stolen animal is found alive in his possession—whether ox or donkey or sheep—he must pay back double.

5 "If a man grazes his livestock in a field or vineyard and lets them stray and they graze in another man's field, he must make restitution from the best of his own field or vineyard.

6 "If a fire breaks out and spreads into thornbushes so that it burns shocks of grain or standing grain or the whole field, the one who started the fire must make restitution.

7 "If a man gives his neighbor silver or goods for safekeeping and they are stolen from the neighbor's house, the thief, if he is caught, must pay back double. 8 But if the thief is not found, the owner of the house must appear before the judges[f] to determine whether he has laid his hands on the other man's property. 9 In all cases of illegal possession of an ox, a donkey, a sheep, a garment, or any other lost property about which somebody says, 'This is mine,' both parties are to bring their cases before the judges.

[a] 15 Or *kills* [b] 18 Or *with a tool* [c] 22 Or *she has a miscarriage* [d] 32 That is, about 12 ounces (about 0.3 kilogram) [e] 3 Or *if he strikes him* [f] 8 Or *before God*; also in verse 9

21:28–36 The Israelites were required to control their animals so they couldn't damage the property of others. Even if the owners were not directly involved in an incident, they were still held accountable for the actions of their livestock or members of their household. This kind of mature accountability serves as a viable basis for a just and responsible society.

21:32 Thirty pieces of silver was likely the standard or average price for a slave in the ancient Near East. Yet thirty pieces of silver could not compare to the true value of a human life created in God's image (Genesis 1:26–27). Oppressed people are often bound by a poor self-image. It would have been of interest to all slaves at this ancient time to learn that the Son of God would someday be betrayed for thirty pieces of silver (Matthew 26:15). God's Son submitted to such humiliation so that he could heal us from our sinful past, breaking the bonds of our sin. He came to set us free, buying us back with his very life.

22:1–15 These regulations concerning restitution for property losses are related to the issues of personal boundaries and accountability. Personal boundaries and property should always be respected, and restitution should be made when such boundaries are violated or property is destroyed. Accountability for actions that violate others is an important part of God's plan for society.

The one whom the judges declare[a] guilty must pay back double to his neighbor.

10"If a man gives a donkey, an ox, a sheep or any other animal to his neighbor for safekeeping and it dies or is injured or is taken away while no one is looking, 11the issue between them will be settled by the taking of an oath before the LORD that the neighbor did not lay hands on the other person's property. The owner is to accept this, and no restitution is required. 12But if the animal was stolen from the neighbor, he must make restitution to the owner. 13If it was torn to pieces by a wild animal, he shall bring in the remains as evidence and he will not be required to pay for the torn animal.

14"If a man borrows an animal from his neighbor and it is injured or dies while the owner is not present, he must make restitution. 15But if the owner is with the animal, the borrower will not have to pay. If the animal was hired, the money paid for the hire covers the loss.

Social Responsibility

16"If a man seduces a virgin who is not pledged to be married and sleeps with her, he must pay the bride-price, and she shall be his wife. 17If her father absolutely refuses to give her to him, he must still pay the bride-price for virgins.

18"Do not allow a sorceress to live.

19"Anyone who has sexual relations with an animal must be put to death.

20"Whoever sacrifices to any god other than the LORD must be destroyed.[b]

21"Do not mistreat an alien or oppress him, for you were aliens in Egypt.

22"Do not take advantage of a widow or an orphan. 23If you do and they cry out to me, I will certainly hear their cry. 24My anger will be aroused, and I will kill you with the sword; your wives will become widows and your children fatherless.

25"If you lend money to one of my people among you who is needy, do not be like a moneylender; charge him no interest.[c] 26If you take your neighbor's cloak as a pledge, return it to him by sunset, 27because his cloak is the only covering he has for his body. What else will he sleep in? When he cries out to me, I will hear, for I am compassionate.

28"Do not blaspheme God[d] or curse the ruler of your people.

29"Do not hold back offerings from your granaries or your vats.[e]

"You must give me the firstborn of your sons. 30Do the same with your cattle and your sheep. Let them stay with their mothers for seven days, but give them to me on the eighth day.

31"You are to be my holy people. So do not eat the meat of an animal torn by wild beasts; throw it to the dogs.

Laws of Justice and Mercy

23 "Do not spread false reports. Do not help a wicked man by being a malicious witness.

2"Do not follow the crowd in doing wrong. When you give testimony in a lawsuit, do not pervert justice by siding with the crowd, 3and do not show favoritism to a poor man in his lawsuit.

4"If you come across your enemy's ox or donkey wandering off, be sure to take it back to him. 5If you see the donkey of someone who hates you fallen down under its load, do not leave it there; be sure you help him with it.

6"Do not deny justice to your poor people in their lawsuits. 7Have nothing to do with a false charge and do not put an innocent or honest person to death, for I will not acquit the guilty.

8"Do not accept a bribe, for a bribe blinds those who see and twists the words of the righteous.

9"Do not oppress an alien; you yourselves know how it feels to be aliens, because you were aliens in Egypt.

Sabbath Laws

10"For six years you are to sow your fields and harvest the crops, 11but during the seventh year let the land lie unplowed and unused. Then the poor among your people may get food from it, and the wild animals may eat what they leave. Do the same with your vineyard and your olive grove.

12"Six days do your work, but on the seventh day do not work, so that your ox and your don-

[a]9 Or *whom God declares* [b]20 The Hebrew term refers to the irrevocable giving over of things or persons to the LORD, often by totally destroying them. [c]25 Or *excessive interest* [d]28 Or *Do not revile the judges* [e]29 The meaning of the Hebrew for this phrase is uncertain.

22:16–28 There are certain kinds of behavior that are abominable to God and brutally inhumane. God has set clear boundaries in such cases and demands our accountability to them. The apostle Paul suggests that such behavior, which is totally devoid of faith and commitment to God, is not only self-destructive but also erodes the very fabric of society (Romans 1:18–32).

23:1–8 This section is an expansion of 20:16 which prohibits false testimony. The truth eventually comes out, so honesty is not only the right policy but also the smart one (see 1 Timothy 5:24–25). Even though someone seems to be getting away with lies for a time, that person must still answer to God (23:7). In the end, people will be held accountable.

23:10–19 God gave instructions concerning Sabbath regulations (20:8–11) and annual festivals for several reasons. First, these events were a time for worship, faith and renewed commitment to God. Second, they were object lessons that pictured important spiritual truths for God's people. Third, they were times for rest and protected God's people from overwork and imbalance. These events were designed to strengthen the people's health—spiritually, emotionally, physically. We also need regular times of worship, reflection and rest.

key may rest and the slave born in your household, and the alien as well, may be refreshed.
13“Be careful to do everything I have said to
you. Do not invoke the names of other gods; do
not let them be heard on your lips.

The Three Annual Festivals

14“Three times a year you are to celebrate a
festival to me.
15“Celebrate the Feast of Unleavened Bread;
for seven days eat bread made without yeast, as
I commanded you. Do this at the appointed
time in the month of Abib, for in that month
you came out of Egypt.
“No one is to appear before me empty-
handed.
16“Celebrate the Feast of Harvest with the
firstfruits of the crops you sow in your field.
“Celebrate the Feast of Ingathering at the
end of the year, when you gather in your crops
from the field.
17“Three times a year all the men are to appear before the Sovereign LORD.
18“Do not offer the blood of a sacrifice to me
along with anything containing yeast.
“The fat of my festival offerings must not be
kept until morning.
19“Bring the best of the firstfruits of your soil
to the house of the LORD your God.
“Do not cook a young goat in its mother's
milk.

God's Angel to Prepare the Way

20“See, I am sending an angel ahead of you
to guard you along the way and to bring you to
the place I have prepared. 21Pay attention to
him and listen to what he says. Do not rebel
against him; he will not forgive your rebellion,
since my Name is in him. 22If you listen carefully to what he says and do all that I say, I will be
an enemy to your enemies and will oppose
those who oppose you. 23My angel will go
ahead of you and bring you into the land of the
Amorites, Hittites, Perizzites, Canaanites, Hivites and Jebusites, and I will wipe them out.
24Do not bow down before their gods or worship them or follow their practices. You must
demolish them and break their sacred stones to
pieces. 25Worship the LORD your God, and his
blessing will be on your food and water. I will
take away sickness from among you, 26and
none will miscarry or be barren in your land. I
will give you a full life span.
27“I will send my terror ahead of you and
throw into confusion every nation you encounter. I will make all your enemies turn their backs
and run. 28I will send the hornet ahead of you
to drive the Hivites, Canaanites and Hittites out
of your way. 29But I will not drive them out in
a single year, because the land would become
desolate and the wild animals too numerous for
you. 30Little by little I will drive them out before
you, until you have increased enough to take
possession of the land.
31“I will establish your borders from the Red
Sea[a] to the Sea of the Philistines,[b] and from
the desert to the River.[c] I will hand over to you
the people who live in the land and you will
drive them out before you. 32Do not make a
covenant with them or with their gods. 33Do
not let them live in your land, or they will cause
you to sin against me, because the worship of
their gods will certainly be a snare to you.”

The Covenant Confirmed

24 Then he said to Moses, “Come up to
the LORD, you and Aaron, Nadab and
Abihu, and seventy of the elders of Israel. You
are to worship at a distance, 2but Moses alone
is to approach the LORD; the others must not
come near. And the people may not come up
with him.”
3When Moses went and told the people all
the LORD's words and laws, they responded with
one voice, “Everything the LORD has said we
will do.” 4Moses then wrote down everything the
LORD had said.
He got up early the next morning and built
an altar at the foot of the mountain and set up
twelve stone pillars representing the twelve
tribes of Israel. 5Then he sent young Israelite
men, and they offered burnt offerings and sacrificed young bulls as fellowship offerings[d] to
the LORD. 6Moses took half of the blood and put
it in bowls, and the other half he sprinkled on

[a]31 Hebrew *Yam Suph;* that is, Sea of Reeds [b]31 That is, the Mediterranean [c]31 That is, the Euphrates [d]5 Traditionally *peace offerings*

23:20–26 As the Israelites journeyed toward the promised land, God promised them the protection of his angel and gave them his instructions for wise living. As we enter a new way of life, God does the same for us. He leads us and cares for us in many ways. He gives us his Word to instruct us in living according to his plan. And if we do what God says and look to him for help, we will experience the fulfillment of his promises.

23:32–33 The temptations of life within the promised land serve as a vivid illustration of how easily proper standards and boundaries can be tragically forgotten. The Israelites were warned not to compromise their values and goals after they had made a good, clean start. They were warned not to make treaties with the people of the land. They were to push them out, replacing them with communities of their own. It is easy for us to make a good start in our spiritual renewal but then compromise too, allowing certain “little” practices to go unchecked. In the end, these things will spell disaster, eroding the new lives we have started to build.

24:1–8 Although Israel's response to God's covenant was the same as before (19:8), they were now “counting the cost” of their commitment to God as they made sacrifices to him. The animals' slaughter reminded the people of the high cost of their redemption. God allowed these animals to die as payment for the people's infractions of the law. What a clear reminder these sacrifices were of God's gracious forgiveness. As we contemplate Jesus' suffering and death on the cross, we should also recognize the high cost of our redemption, realizing that we are the ones who should have been on that cross.

the altar. 7 Then he took the Book of the Covenant and read it to the people. They responded, "We will do everything the LORD has said; we will obey."

8 Moses then took the blood, sprinkled it on the people and said, "This is the blood of the covenant that the LORD has made with you in accordance with all these words."

9 Moses and Aaron, Nadab and Abihu, and the seventy elders of Israel went up 10 and saw the God of Israel. Under his feet was something like a pavement made of sapphire,[a] clear as the sky itself. 11 But God did not raise his hand against these leaders of the Israelites; they saw God, and they ate and drank.

12 The LORD said to Moses, "Come up to me on the mountain and stay here, and I will give you the tablets of stone, with the law and commands I have written for their instruction."

13 Then Moses set out with Joshua his aide, and Moses went up on the mountain of God. 14 He said to the elders, "Wait here for us until we come back to you. Aaron and Hur are with you, and anyone involved in a dispute can go to them."

15 When Moses went up on the mountain, the cloud covered it, 16 and the glory of the LORD settled on Mount Sinai. For six days the cloud covered the mountain, and on the seventh day the LORD called to Moses from within the cloud. 17 To the Israelites the glory of the LORD looked like a consuming fire on top of the mountain. 18 Then Moses entered the cloud as he went on up the mountain. And he stayed on the mountain forty days and forty nights.

Offerings for the Tabernacle

25 The LORD said to Moses, 2 "Tell the Israelites to bring me an offering. You are to receive the offering for me from each man whose heart prompts him to give. 3 These are the offerings you are to receive from them: gold, silver and bronze; 4 blue, purple and scarlet yarn and fine linen; goat hair; 5 ram skins dyed red and hides of sea cows[b]; acacia wood; 6 olive oil for the light; spices for the anointing oil and for the fragrant incense; 7 and onyx stones and other gems to be mounted on the ephod and breastpiece.

8 "Then have them make a sanctuary for me, and I will dwell among them. 9 Make this tabernacle and all its furnishings exactly like the pattern I will show you.

The Ark

10 "Have them make a chest of acacia wood—two and a half cubits long, a cubit and a half wide, and a cubit and a half high.[c] 11 Overlay it with pure gold, both inside and out, and make a gold molding around it. 12 Cast four gold rings for it and fasten them to its four feet, with two rings on one side and two rings on the other. 13 Then make poles of acacia wood and overlay them with gold. 14 Insert the poles into the rings on the sides of the chest to carry it. 15 The poles are to remain in the rings of this ark; they are not to be removed. 16 Then put in the ark the Testimony, which I will give you.

17 "Make an atonement cover[d] of pure gold—two and a half cubits long and a cubit and a half wide.[e] 18 And make two cherubim out of hammered gold at the ends of the cover. 19 Make one cherub on one end and the second cherub on the other; make the cherubim of one piece with the cover, at the two ends. 20 The cherubim are to have their wings spread upward, overshadowing the cover with them. The cherubim are to face each other, looking toward the cover. 21 Place the cover on top of the ark and put in the ark the Testimony, which I will give you. 22 There, above the cover between the two cherubim that are over the ark of the Testimony, I will meet with you and give you all my commands for the Israelites.

The Table

23 "Make a table of acacia wood—two cubits long, a cubit wide and a cubit and a half high.[f] 24 Overlay it with pure gold and make a gold molding around it. 25 Also make around it a rim a handbreadth[g] wide and put a gold molding on the rim. 26 Make four gold rings for the table and fasten them to the four corners, where the four legs are. 27 The rings are to be close to the

[a] *10* Or *lapis lazuli* [b] *5* That is, dugongs [c] *10* That is, about 3 3/4 feet (about 1.1 meters) long and 2 1/4 feet (about 0.7 meter) wide and high [d] *17* Traditionally *a mercy seat* [e] *17* That is, about 3 3/4 feet (about 1.1 meters) long and 2 1/4 feet (about 0.7 meter) wide [f] *23* That is, about 3 feet (about 0.9 meter) long and 1 1/2 feet (about 0.5 meter) wide and 2 1/4 feet (about 0.7 meter) high [g] *25* That is, about 3 inches (about 8 centimeters)

24:9–11 One of the best ways for us to see ourselves as we actually are is to gain a clear view of God and his glorious person. People who tend to glorify themselves will quickly change their ways if they glimpse God's awesome glory. On the other hand, those who devalue themselves need to understand that they are made in God's image (Genesis 1:26–27). If we are Christians, we are destined to be in God's glorious presence forever (Revelation 21—22). One glimpse of God in his glory will remove our pride as well as our self-deprecation and will allow us to see the truth about ourselves.

25:8–9 When Adam and Eve sinned in the garden, they created a terrible rift in the relationship between God and the human race. But God has spent the centuries since then reaching out to us, longing to heal the relationship. God is in the business of restoration. God's declaration that he would dwell among the Israelites in a tabernacle was one step toward the restoration process. The details of the pattern he laid out for the tabernacle and the offerings also showed that God clearly set boundaries for his relationship with the people. Later, when Jesus Christ came to earth as a man, God's presence with the human race took on an even more personal and intimate relationship (John 1:14).

rim to hold the poles used in carrying the table.
28Make the poles of acacia wood, overlay them
with gold and carry the table with them. 29And
make its plates and dishes of pure gold, as well
as its pitchers and bowls for the pouring out of
offerings. 30Put the bread of the Presence on
this table to be before me at all times.

The Lampstand

31"Make a lampstand of pure gold and hammer it out, base and shaft; its flowerlike cups,
buds and blossoms shall be of one piece with it.
32Six branches are to extend from the sides of
the lampstand—three on one side and three on
the other. 33Three cups shaped like almond
flowers with buds and blossoms are to be on
one branch, three on the next branch, and the
same for all six branches extending from the
lampstand. 34And on the lampstand there are to
be four cups shaped like almond flowers with
buds and blossoms. 35One bud shall be under
the first pair of branches extending from the
lampstand, a second bud under the second pair,
and a third bud under the third pair—six
branches in all. 36The buds and branches shall
all be of one piece with the lampstand, hammered out of pure gold.

37"Then make its seven lamps and set them
up on it so that they light the space in front of
it. 38Its wick trimmers and trays are to be of pure
gold. 39A talent[a] of pure gold is to be used for
the lampstand and all these accessories. 40See
that you make them according to the pattern
shown you on the mountain.

The Tabernacle

26 "Make the tabernacle with ten curtains
of finely twisted linen and blue, purple
and scarlet yarn, with cherubim worked into
them by a skilled craftsman. 2All the curtains
are to be the same size—twenty-eight cubits
long and four cubits wide.[b] 3Join five of the
curtains together, and do the same with the
other five. 4Make loops of blue material along
the edge of the end curtain in one set, and do
the same with the end curtain in the other set.
5Make fifty loops on one curtain and fifty loops
on the end curtain of the other set, with the
loops opposite each other. 6Then make fifty
gold clasps and use them to fasten the curtains
together so that the tabernacle is a unit.

7"Make curtains of goat hair for the tent over
the tabernacle—eleven altogether. 8All eleven
curtains are to be the same size—thirty cubits
long and four cubits wide.[c] 9Join five of the
curtains together into one set and the other six
into another set. Fold the sixth curtain double
at the front of the tent. 10Make fifty loops along
the edge of the end curtain in one set and also
along the edge of the end curtain in the other
set. 11Then make fifty bronze clasps and put
them in the loops to fasten the tent together as
a unit. 12As for the additional length of the tent
curtains, the half curtain that is left over is to
hang down at the rear of the tabernacle. 13The
tent curtains will be a cubit[d] longer on both
sides; what is left will hang over the sides of the
tabernacle so as to cover it. 14Make for the tent
a covering of ram skins dyed red, and over that
a covering of hides of sea cows.[e]

15"Make upright frames of acacia wood for
the tabernacle. 16Each frame is to be ten cubits
long and a cubit and a half wide,[f] 17with two
projections set parallel to each other. Make all
the frames of the tabernacle in this way. 18Make
twenty frames for the south side of the tabernacle 19and make forty silver bases to go under
them—two bases for each frame, one under
each projection. 20For the other side, the north
side of the tabernacle, make twenty frames
21and forty silver bases—two under each frame.
22Make six frames for the far end, that is, the
west end of the tabernacle, 23and make two
frames for the corners at the far end. 24At these
two corners they must be double from the bottom all the way to the top, and fitted into a
single ring; both shall be like that. 25So there
will be eight frames and sixteen silver bases—
two under each frame.

26"Also make crossbars of acacia wood: five
for the frames on one side of the tabernacle,
27five for those on the other side, and five for
the frames on the west, at the far end of the
tabernacle. 28The center crossbar is to extend
from end to end at the middle of the frames.
29Overlay the frames with gold and make gold
rings to hold the crossbars. Also overlay the
crossbars with gold.

30"Set up the tabernacle according to the
plan shown you on the mountain.

31"Make a curtain of blue, purple and scarlet
yarn and finely twisted linen, with cherubim
worked into it by a skilled craftsman. 32Hang it
with gold hooks on four posts of acacia wood
overlaid with gold and standing on four silver
bases. 33Hang the curtain from the clasps and
place the ark of the Testimony behind the curtain. The curtain will separate the Holy Place
from the Most Holy Place. 34Put the atonement
cover on the ark of the Testimony in the Most
Holy Place. 35Place the table outside the curtain
on the north side of the tabernacle and put the
lampstand opposite it on the south side.

36"For the entrance to the tent make a curtain of blue, purple and scarlet yarn and finely
twisted linen—the work of an embroiderer.
37Make gold hooks for this curtain and five
posts of acacia wood overlaid with gold. And
cast five bronze bases for them.

[a]39 That is, about 75 pounds (about 34 kilograms)
[b]2 That is, about 42 feet (about 12.5 meters) long and 6 feet (about 1.8 meters) wide
[c]8 That is, about 45 feet (about 13.5 meters) long and 6 feet (about 1.8 meters) wide
[d]13 That is, about 1 1/2 feet (about 0.5 meter)
[e]14 That is, dugongs
[f]16 That is, about 15 feet (about 4.5 meters) long and 2 1/4 feet (about 0.7 meter) wide

The Altar of Burnt Offering

27 "Build an altar of acacia wood, three
cubits[a] high; it is to be square, five
cubits long and five cubits wide.[b] [2]Make a
horn at each of the four corners, so that the
horns and the altar are of one piece, and overlay
the altar with bronze. [3]Make all its utensils of
bronze—its pots to remove the ashes, and its
shovels, sprinkling bowls, meat forks and firepans. [4]Make a grating for it, a bronze network,
and make a bronze ring at each of the four
corners of the network. [5]Put it under the ledge
of the altar so that it is halfway up the altar.
[6]Make poles of acacia wood for the altar and
overlay them with bronze. [7]The poles are to be
inserted into the rings so they will be on two
sides of the altar when it is carried. [8]Make the
altar hollow, out of boards. It is to be made just
as you were shown on the mountain.

The Courtyard

[9]"Make a courtyard for the tabernacle. The
south side shall be a hundred cubits[c] long and
is to have curtains of finely twisted linen, [10]with
twenty posts and twenty bronze bases and with
silver hooks and bands on the posts. [11]The
north side shall also be a hundred cubits long
and is to have curtains, with twenty posts and
twenty bronze bases and with silver hooks and
bands on the posts.

[12]"The west end of the courtyard shall be
fifty cubits[d] wide and have curtains, with ten
posts and ten bases. [13]On the east end, toward
the sunrise, the courtyard shall also be fifty cubits wide. [14]Curtains fifteen cubits[e] long are to
be on one side of the entrance, with three posts
and three bases, [15]and curtains fifteen cubits
long are to be on the other side, with three posts
and three bases.

[16]"For the entrance to the courtyard, provide
a curtain twenty cubits[f] long, of blue, purple
and scarlet yarn and finely twisted linen—the
work of an embroiderer—with four posts and
four bases. [17]All the posts around the courtyard
are to have silver bands and hooks, and bronze
bases. [18]The courtyard shall be a hundred cubits
long and fifty cubits wide,[g] with curtains of
finely twisted linen five cubits[h] high, and with
bronze bases. [19]All the other articles used in the
service of the tabernacle, whatever their function, including all the tent pegs for it and those
for the courtyard, are to be of bronze.

Oil for the Lampstand

[20]"Command the Israelites to bring you clear
oil of pressed olives for the light so that the
lamps may be kept burning. [21]In the Tent of
Meeting, outside the curtain that is in front of
the Testimony, Aaron and his sons are to keep
the lamps burning before the LORD from evening till morning. This is to be a lasting ordinance among the Israelites for the generations
to come.

The Priestly Garments

28 "Have Aaron your brother brought to
you from among the Israelites, along
with his sons Nadab and Abihu, Eleazar and
Ithamar, so they may serve me as priests. [2]Make
sacred garments for your brother Aaron, to give
him dignity and honor. [3]Tell all the skilled men
to whom I have given wisdom in such matters
that they are to make garments for Aaron, for
his consecration, so he may serve me as priest.
[4]These are the garments they are to make: a
breastpiece, an ephod, a robe, a woven tunic, a
turban and a sash. They are to make these sacred garments for your brother Aaron and his
sons, so they may serve me as priests. [5]Have
them use gold, and blue, purple and scarlet
yarn, and fine linen.

The Ephod

[6]"Make the ephod of gold, and of blue, purple and scarlet yarn, and of finely twisted linen—
the work of a skilled craftsman. [7]It is to have
two shoulder pieces attached to two of its corners, so it can be fastened. [8]Its skillfully woven
waistband is to be like it—of one piece with the
ephod and made with gold, and with blue, purple and scarlet yarn, and with finely twisted
linen.

[9]"Take two onyx stones and engrave on
them the names of the sons of Israel [10]in the
order of their birth—six names on one stone and
the remaining six on the other. [11]Engrave the
names of the sons of Israel on the two stones
the way a gem cutter engraves a seal. Then
mount the stones in gold filigree settings [12]and
fasten them on the shoulder pieces of the ephod
as memorial stones for the sons of Israel. Aaron
is to bear the names on his shoulders as a memorial before the LORD. [13]Make gold filigree
settings [14]and two braided chains of pure gold,
like a rope, and attach the chains to the settings.

[a]*1* That is, about 4 1/2 feet (about 1.3 meters)
[b]*1* That is, about 7 1/2 feet (about 2.3 meters) long and wide
[c]*9* That is, about 150 feet (about 46 meters); also in verse 11
[d]*12* That is, about 75 feet (about 23 meters); also in verse 13
[e]*14* That is, about 22 1/2 feet (about 6.9 meters); also in verse 15
[f]*16* That is, about 30 feet (about 9 meters)
[g]*18* That is, about 150 feet (about 46 meters) long and 75 feet (about 23 meters) wide
[h]*18* That is, about 7 1/2 feet (about 2.3 meters)

27:20–21 God's command to keep the lamps burning throughout the hours of darkness indicates that God is a God of light (see 1 John 1:5). Under cover of darkness, it is difficult to judge reality; it is easier to hide the truth. To live in the light instead of the darkness means that God wants his people to be transparent in their faith and integrity. He wants them to be obedient to his plan for living. Living in the light of God's presence means living as Christ does (1 John 1:7).

The Breastpiece

15"Fashion a breastpiece for making decisions—the work of a skilled craftsman. Make it like the ephod: of gold, and of blue, purple and scarlet yarn, and of finely twisted linen. 16It is to be square—a span[a] long and a span wide—and folded double. 17Then mount four rows of precious stones on it. In the first row there shall be a ruby, a topaz and a beryl; 18in the second row a turquoise, a sapphire[b] and an emerald; 19in the third row a jacinth, an agate and an amethyst; 20in the fourth row a chrysolite, an onyx and a jasper.[c] Mount them in gold filigree settings. 21There are to be twelve stones, one for each of the names of the sons of Israel, each engraved like a seal with the name of one of the twelve tribes.

22"For the breastpiece make braided chains of pure gold, like a rope. 23Make two gold rings for it and fasten them to two corners of the breastpiece. 24Fasten the two gold chains to the rings at the corners of the breastpiece, 25and the other ends of the chains to the two settings, attaching them to the shoulder pieces of the ephod at the front. 26Make two gold rings and attach them to the other two corners of the breastpiece on the inside edge next to the ephod. 27Make two more gold rings and attach them to the bottom of the shoulder pieces on the front of the ephod, close to the seam just above the waistband of the ephod. 28The rings of the breastpiece are to be tied to the rings of the ephod with blue cord, connecting it to the waistband, so that the breastpiece will not swing out from the ephod.

29"Whenever Aaron enters the Holy Place, he will bear the names of the sons of Israel over his heart on the breastpiece of decision as a continuing memorial before the LORD. 30Also put the Urim and the Thummim in the breastpiece, so they may be over Aaron's heart whenever he enters the presence of the LORD. Thus Aaron will always bear the means of making decisions for the Israelites over his heart before the LORD.

Other Priestly Garments

31"Make the robe of the ephod entirely of blue cloth, 32with an opening for the head in its center. There shall be a woven edge like a collar[d] around this opening, so that it will not tear. 33Make pomegranates of blue, purple and scarlet yarn around the hem of the robe, with gold bells between them. 34The gold bells and the pomegranates are to alternate around the hem of the robe. 35Aaron must wear it when he ministers. The sound of the bells will be heard when he enters the Holy Place before the LORD and when he comes out, so that he will not die.

36"Make a plate of pure gold and engrave on it as on a seal: HOLY TO THE LORD. 37Fasten a blue cord to it to attach it to the turban; it is to be on the front of the turban. 38It will be on Aaron's forehead, and he will bear the guilt involved in the sacred gifts the Israelites consecrate, whatever their gifts may be. It will be on Aaron's forehead continually so that they will be acceptable to the LORD.

39"Weave the tunic of fine linen and make the turban of fine linen. The sash is to be the work of an embroiderer. 40Make tunics, sashes and headbands for Aaron's sons, to give them dignity and honor. 41After you put these clothes on your brother Aaron and his sons, anoint and ordain them. Consecrate them so they may serve me as priests.

42"Make linen undergarments as a covering for the body, reaching from the waist to the thigh. 43Aaron and his sons must wear them whenever they enter the Tent of Meeting or approach the altar to minister in the Holy Place, so that they will not incur guilt and die.

"This is to be a lasting ordinance for Aaron and his descendants.

Consecration of the Priests

29 "This is what you are to do to consecrate them, so they may serve me as priests: Take a young bull and two rams without defect. 2And from fine wheat flour, without yeast, make bread, and cakes mixed with oil, and wafers spread with oil. 3Put them in a basket and present them in it—along with the bull and the two rams. 4Then bring Aaron and his sons to the entrance to the Tent of Meeting and wash them with water. 5Take the garments and dress Aaron with the tunic, the robe of the ephod, the ephod itself and the breastpiece. Fasten the ephod on him by its skillfully woven waistband. 6Put the turban on his head and attach the sacred diadem to the turban. 7Take the anointing oil and anoint him by pouring it on his head. 8Bring his sons and dress them in tunics 9and put headbands on them. Then tie sashes on Aaron and his sons.[e] The priesthood

[a]16 That is, about 9 inches (about 22 centimeters)
[b]18 Or *lapis lazuli*
[c]20 The precise identification of some of these precious stones is uncertain.
[d]32 The meaning of the Hebrew for this word is uncertain.
[e]9 Hebrew; Septuagint *on them*

28:29–32 The priest's breastplate was inscribed with the names of Israel's tribes. These inscriptions illustrated that he represented the nation and was spiritually responsible for the people. The Urim and Thummim were a means of determining the will of God in key decisions. Similarly, those in positions of responsibility must seriously and consistently seek God's will as they make decisions, or be held accountable for acting otherwise.

29:1–46 This chapter constantly reiterates the need for consecration in a number of ways. To consecrate means "to set apart," whether it be a person or an object. It is only when there is proper consecration that the closest relationship between our holy God and sinful people is possible. In the New Testament, those who have faith in Christ are called *saints.* This means that they are "set apart"; they are "holy ones." As Christians, all of us have been set apart by God and are called to live holy lives.

is theirs by a lasting ordinance. In this way you shall ordain Aaron and his sons.

10"Bring the bull to the front of the Tent of Meeting, and Aaron and his sons shall lay their hands on its head. 11Slaughter it in the LORD's presence at the entrance to the Tent of Meeting. 12Take some of the bull's blood and put it on the horns of the altar with your finger, and pour out the rest of it at the base of the altar. 13Then take all the fat around the inner parts, the covering of the liver, and both kidneys with the fat on them, and burn them on the altar. 14But burn the bull's flesh and its hide and its offal outside the camp. It is a sin offering.

15"Take one of the rams, and Aaron and his sons shall lay their hands on its head. 16Slaughter it and take the blood and sprinkle it against the altar on all sides. 17Cut the ram into pieces and wash the inner parts and the legs, putting them with the head and the other pieces. 18Then burn the entire ram on the altar. It is a burnt offering to the LORD, a pleasing aroma, an offering made to the LORD by fire.

19"Take the other ram, and Aaron and his sons shall lay their hands on its head. 20Slaughter it, take some of its blood and put it on the lobes of the right ears of Aaron and his sons, on the thumbs of their right hands, and on the big toes of their right feet. Then sprinkle blood against the altar on all sides. 21And take some of the blood on the altar and some of the anointing oil and sprinkle it on Aaron and his garments and on his sons and their garments. Then he and his sons and their garments will be consecrated.

22"Take from this ram the fat, the fat tail, the fat around the inner parts, the covering of the liver, both kidneys with the fat on them, and the right thigh. (This is the ram for the ordination.) 23From the basket of bread made without yeast, which is before the LORD, take a loaf, and a cake made with oil, and a wafer. 24Put all these in the hands of Aaron and his sons and wave them before the LORD as a wave offering. 25Then take them from their hands and burn them on the altar along with the burnt offering for a pleasing aroma to the LORD, an offering made to the LORD by fire. 26After you take the breast of the ram for Aaron's ordination, wave it before the LORD as a wave offering, and it will be your share.

27"Consecrate those parts of the ordination ram that belong to Aaron and his sons: the breast that was waved and the thigh that was presented. 28This is always to be the regular share from the Israelites for Aaron and his sons. It is the contribution the Israelites are to make to the LORD from their fellowship offerings.[a]

29"Aaron's sacred garments will belong to his descendants so that they can be anointed and ordained in them. 30The son who succeeds him as priest and comes to the Tent of Meeting to minister in the Holy Place is to wear them seven days.

31"Take the ram for the ordination and cook the meat in a sacred place. 32At the entrance to the Tent of Meeting, Aaron and his sons are to eat the meat of the ram and the bread that is in the basket. 33They are to eat these offerings by which atonement was made for their ordination and consecration. But no one else may eat them, because they are sacred. 34And if any of the meat of the ordination ram or any bread is left over till morning, burn it up. It must not be eaten, because it is sacred.

35"Do for Aaron and his sons everything I have commanded you, taking seven days to ordain them. 36Sacrifice a bull each day as a sin offering to make atonement. Purify the altar by making atonement for it, and anoint it to consecrate it. 37For seven days make atonement for the altar and consecrate it. Then the altar will be most holy, and whatever touches it will be holy.

38"This is what you are to offer on the altar regularly each day: two lambs a year old. 39Offer one in the morning and the other at twilight. 40With the first lamb offer a tenth of an ephah[b] of fine flour mixed with a quarter of a hin[c] of oil from pressed olives, and a quarter of a hin of wine as a drink offering. 41Sacrifice the other lamb at twilight with the same grain offering and its drink offering as in the morning—a pleasing aroma, an offering made to the LORD by fire.

42"For the generations to come this burnt offering is to be made regularly at the entrance to the Tent of Meeting before the LORD. There I will meet you and speak to you; 43there also I will meet with the Israelites, and the place will be consecrated by my glory.

44"So I will consecrate the Tent of Meeting and the altar and will consecrate Aaron and his sons to serve me as priests. 45Then I will dwell among the Israelites and be their God. 46They will know that I am the LORD their God, who brought them out of Egypt so that I might dwell among them. I am the LORD their God.

The Altar of Incense

30 "Make an altar of acacia wood for burning incense. 2It is to be square, a cubit long and a cubit wide, and two cubits high[d]—its horns of one piece with it. 3Overlay the top and all the sides and the horns with pure gold, and make a gold molding around it.

[a]28 Traditionally *peace offerings* [b]40 That is, probably about 2 quarts (about 2 liters) [c]40 That is, probably about 1 quart (about 1 liter) [d]2 That is, about 1 1/2 feet (about 0.5 meter) long and wide and about 3 feet (about 0.9 meter) high

30:1–10 As graphic and compelling as the sacrificial system was, it still could provide only temporary atonement and forgiveness. While these sacrifices and offerings served as beautiful pictures of the final sacrifice of Christ (John 1:29), they could not provide permanent forgiveness. Only by the grace of God is such forgiveness possible.

4 Make two gold rings for the altar below the
molding—two on opposite sides—to hold the
poles used to carry it. 5 Make the poles of acacia
wood and overlay them with gold. 6 Put the altar
in front of the curtain that is before the ark of
the Testimony—before the atonement cover that
is over the Testimony—where I will meet with
you.

7 "Aaron must burn fragrant incense on the
altar every morning when he tends the lamps.
8 He must burn incense again when he lights the
lamps at twilight so incense will burn regularly
before the LORD for the generations to come.
9 Do not offer on this altar any other incense or
any burnt offering or grain offering, and do not
pour a drink offering on it. 10 Once a year Aaron
shall make atonement on its horns. This annual
atonement must be made with the blood of
the atoning sin offering for the generations to
come. It is most holy to the LORD."

Atonement Money

11 Then the LORD said to Moses, 12 "When you
take a census of the Israelites to count them,
each one must pay the LORD a ransom for his
life at the time he is counted. Then no plague
will come on them when you number them.
13 Each one who crosses over to those already
counted is to give a half shekel,[a] according to
the sanctuary shekel, which weighs twenty gerahs. This half shekel is an offering to the LORD.
14 All who cross over, those twenty years old or
more, are to give an offering to the LORD. 15 The
rich are not to give more than a half shekel and
the poor are not to give less when you make the
offering to the LORD to atone for your lives.
16 Receive the atonement money from the Israelites and use it for the service of the Tent of
Meeting. It will be a memorial for the Israelites
before the LORD, making atonement for your
lives."

Basin for Washing

17 Then the LORD said to Moses, 18 "Make a
bronze basin, with its bronze stand, for washing. Place it between the Tent of Meeting and
the altar, and put water in it. 19 Aaron and his
sons are to wash their hands and feet with water
from it. 20 Whenever they enter the Tent of Meeting, they shall wash with water so that they will
not die. Also, when they approach the altar to
minister by presenting an offering made to the
LORD by fire, 21 they shall wash their hands and
feet so that they will not die. This is to be a
lasting ordinance for Aaron and his descendants for the generations to come."

Anointing Oil

22 Then the LORD said to Moses, 23 "Take the
following fine spices: 500 shekels[b] of liquid
myrrh, half as much (that is, 250 shekels) of
fragrant cinnamon, 250 shekels of fragrant
cane, 24 500 shekels of cassia—all according to
the sanctuary shekel—and a hin[c] of olive oil.
25 Make these into a sacred anointing oil, a fragrant blend, the work of a perfumer. It will be
the sacred anointing oil. 26 Then use it to anoint
the Tent of Meeting, the ark of the Testimony,
27 the table and all its articles, the lampstand
and its accessories, the altar of incense, 28 the
altar of burnt offering and all its utensils, and
the basin with its stand. 29 You shall consecrate
them so they will be most holy, and whatever
touches them will be holy.

30 "Anoint Aaron and his sons and consecrate
them so they may serve me as priests. 31 Say to
the Israelites, 'This is to be my sacred anointing
oil for the generations to come. 32 Do not pour
it on men's bodies and do not make any oil
with the same formula. It is sacred, and you are
to consider it sacred. 33 Whoever makes perfume
like it and whoever puts it on anyone other than
a priest must be cut off from his people.' "

Incense

34 Then the LORD said to Moses, "Take fragrant spices—gum resin, onycha and galba-
num—and pure frankincense, all in equal
amounts, 35 and make a fragrant blend of incense, the work of a perfumer. It is to be salted
and pure and sacred. 36 Grind some of it to powder and place it in front of the Testimony in the
Tent of Meeting, where I will meet with you. It
shall be most holy to you. 37 Do not make any
incense with this formula for yourselves; consider it holy to the LORD. 38 Whoever makes any
like it to enjoy its fragrance must be cut off from
his people."

Bezalel and Oholiab

31 Then the LORD said to Moses, 2 "See, I
have chosen Bezalel son of Uri, the son
of Hur, of the tribe of Judah, 3 and I have filled
him with the Spirit of God, with skill, ability
and knowledge in all kinds of crafts— 4 to make
artistic designs for work in gold, silver and
bronze, 5 to cut and set stones, to work in wood,
and to engage in all kinds of craftsmanship.
6 Moreover, I have appointed Oholiab son of
Ahisamach, of the tribe of Dan, to help him.
Also I have given skill to all the craftsmen to
make everything I have commanded you: 7 the
Tent of Meeting, the ark of the Testimony with
the atonement cover on it, and all the other
furnishings of the tent— 8 the table and its articles, the pure gold lampstand and all its accessories, the altar of incense, 9 the altar of burnt
offering and all its utensils, the basin with its
stand— 10 and also the woven garments, both
the sacred garments for Aaron the priest and the
garments for his sons when they serve as priests,
11 and the anointing oil and fragrant incense for
the Holy Place. They are to make them just as
I commanded you."

[a] *13* That is, about 1/5 ounce (about 6 grams); also in verse 15 [b] *23* That is, about 12 1/2 pounds (about 6 kilograms) [c] *24* That is, probably about 4 quarts (about 4 liters)

The Sabbath

12Then the LORD said to Moses, 13"Say to the
Israelites, 'You must observe my Sabbaths. This
will be a sign between me and you for the generations to come, so you may know that I am
the LORD, who makes you holy.[a]
14" 'Observe the Sabbath, because it is holy
to you. Anyone who desecrates it must be put to
death; whoever does any work on that day must
be cut off from his people. 15For six days, work
is to be done, but the seventh day is a Sabbath
of rest, holy to the LORD. Whoever does any
work on the Sabbath day must be put to death.
16The Israelites are to observe the Sabbath, celebrating it for the generations to come as a lasting covenant. 17It will be a sign between me and
the Israelites forever, for in six days the LORD
made the heavens and the earth, and on the
seventh day he abstained from work and
rested.' "
18When the LORD finished speaking to Moses
on Mount Sinai, he gave him the two tablets of
the Testimony, the tablets of stone inscribed by
the finger of God.

The Golden Calf

32 When the people saw that Moses was so
long in coming down from the mountain, they gathered around Aaron and said,
"Come, make us gods[b] who will go before us.
As for this fellow Moses who brought us up out
of Egypt, we don't know what has happened to
him."
2Aaron answered them, "Take off the gold
earrings that your wives, your sons and your
daughters are wearing, and bring them to me."
3So all the people took off their earrings and
brought them to Aaron. 4He took what they
handed him and made it into an idol cast in the
shape of a calf, fashioning it with a tool. Then

[a]13 Or *who sanctifies you;* or *who sets you apart as holy*
[b]1 Or *a god;* also in verses 23 and 31

31:12–17 Keeping the weekly Sabbath was to become a regular rhythm in the lives of the Israelites. This day was set apart for God as a day of special worship and for the people as a day of rest. In modern society, the weekend is often considered a time to get away from our work. But we often fail to set aside a day for God as he intended. As we look forward to Sunday, let us look for ways to make that day holy unto God as well as spiritually refreshing for us.

32:1–20 Israel shattered the second commandment by making the golden calf. God had clearly said, "You shall not make for yourself an idol in the form of anything in heaven above or on the earth beneath or in the waters below" (20:4). Weak-kneed Aaron tried to put a good face on this blasphemy, but to no avail. The people's behavior represented a wholesale turning from their previously professed commitment to God. This incident contains a warning to those who believe they have progressed so far spiritually that they are immune to failure. No matter how far we have come, we are all prone to the danger of a downfall, especially if we are consumed with pride (see 1 John 5:21).

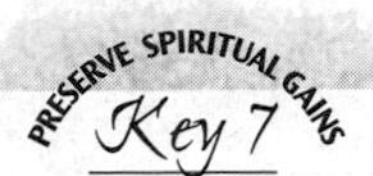

A Day of Rest

Exodus 31:12–13 Seeking to preserve our spiritual gains requires a balanced life. We need to get enough rest, and that includes taking one day of rest each week. If we allow ourselves to get overtired, we will be less able to cope with the demands of life. It will be harder for us to maintain our spiritual gains too.

The Bible recognizes the importance of rest for all of creation: for people, for farmland and for animals. Even God himself rested on the seventh day of creation (Genesis 2:2–3). God considered weekly rest important enough to include as one of the Ten Commandments. God declared:

> Six days you shall labor and do all your work, but the seventh day is a Sabbath to the LORD your God. On it you shall not do any work, neither you, nor your son or daughter, nor your manservant or maidservant, nor your animals, nor the alien within your gates. For in six days the LORD made the heavens and the earth, the sea, and all that is in them, but he rested on the seventh day. Therefore the LORD blessed the Sabbath day and made it holy (20:9–11).

The Lord further instructed the Israelites, "You must observe my Sabbaths. This will be a sign between me and you for the generations to come, so you may know that I am the LORD, who makes you holy" (31:13).

God wants us to have the rest we need in order for us to live a balanced life. A weekly Sabbath will help remind us that we follow the Lord. As we take time to relax from our regular duties and reflect on God's promises, we will also have time to remember that it is God who sustains us.

Turn to Ruth 2.

Time to Remember

Exodus 31:12–17 Remembering is vital to spiritual renewal. Spiritual amnesia can leave us lost and powerless. Remembering, however, can awaken faith, hope and love. When the psalmist was discouraged, he took time to remember what God had done (Psalm 42:4–5). Israel's festivals of worship helped the people recall the great acts of God in history. Today, in addition to being a remembrance of God's work in history, the Sabbath becomes a regular reminder for us of God's work in our own "holy history." These memories of the past fuel our faith for the present.

Many believers have placed additional remembrances into the heart of their worship experience by observing the "Christian year." The Christian year is shaped by the major events of Christ's life. The Western practice of the Christian year (which varies in several ways from the Eastern Orthodox traditions) begins with Advent, a time to prepare for the coming of Christ. It is fitting during the season of Advent not only to look back to Christ's first coming but also to look forward to his second coming. Immediately following Advent are the celebrations of Christmas and Epiphany. Epiphany commemorates the visit of the wise men to the infant Jesus, the revelation of the light to the Gentiles. It is a time to remember that God still reaches out to those who have not yet heard.

The next season of the Christian year is Lent. This forty-day period (which does not count Sundays, since even during Lent every Sunday is a "little Easter") commemorates Jesus' time in the wilderness. It is a time when we should give serious attention to the condition of our spiritual lives, to reordering our priorities and to withstanding temptations. Lent traditionally begins with Ash Wednesday and concludes with Holy Week.

Holy Week begins with the remembrance of Palm Sunday and includes Maundy Thursday, Good Friday and Easter. The dilemma that believers face during this week is how to respond appropriately to the intensity of each day. The four Gospels devote nearly one-third of their writings to this week alone! Obviously, believers cannot hope to relive all that occurred in such a short time. Still, our worship moves through the paradoxical praise of Palm Sunday, the tension of the intimacy and betrayal of Maundy Thursday as the Lord gave his disciples the Last Supper, the agony of Good Friday and the ecstasy of Easter.

The season of Eastertide culminates in Pentecost and Ascension Sundays. This is the time to reflect on the resurrection appearances of Jesus. It also reminds us of the dawning of the new era that comes with the ascension of Christ to the right hand of God and the descending of the Holy Spirit to indwell believers.

The rest of the Christian year, from approximately June through November, is commonly called the season of Kingdomtide. These weeks are devoted to the spreading of the kingdom of God in our hearts and in the world. Our worship focuses on topics such as the growth of the church, recorded in the book of Acts, as well as a full range of Biblical themes.

Putting It Into Practice

Draw a time line of your spiritual life—your own "holy history"—in your journal. When has God worked most powerfully in your life? When has God seemed closest? Farthest away? When was your exodus from the kingdom of sin and your entrance to the promised land of salvation? If you were to celebrate five or six spiritual festivals, when would they be? What would you call them?

Select one of your spiritual milestones and recount the event in as much detail as you can remember. You may find that the memory will become more vivid as you write. It may also bring a number of other memories to mind. Plan to do this with other "holy moments" over the coming weeks. This will greatly enrich your sense of God's presence, not only in the big events of the past, but in your everyday life as well.

For more on worship, turn to Mark 2.

they said, "These are your gods,[a] O Israel, who brought you up out of Egypt."

5When Aaron saw this, he built an altar in front of the calf and announced, "Tomorrow there will be a festival to the LORD." 6So the next day the people rose early and sacrificed burnt offerings and presented fellowship offerings.[b] Afterward they sat down to eat and drink and got up to indulge in revelry.

7Then the LORD said to Moses, "Go down, because your people, whom you brought up out of Egypt, have become corrupt. 8They have been quick to turn away from what I commanded them and have made themselves an idol cast in the shape of a calf. They have bowed down to it and sacrificed to it and have said, 'These are your gods, O Israel, who brought you up out of Egypt.'

9"I have seen these people," the LORD said to Moses, "and they are a stiff-necked people. 10Now leave me alone so that my anger may burn against them and that I may destroy them. Then I will make you into a great nation."

11But Moses sought the favor of the LORD his God. "O LORD," he said, "why should your anger burn against your people, whom you brought out of Egypt with great power and a mighty hand? 12Why should the Egyptians say, 'It was with evil intent that he brought them out, to kill them in the mountains and to wipe them off the face of the earth'? Turn from your fierce anger; relent and do not bring disaster on your people. 13Remember your servants Abraham, Isaac and Israel, to whom you swore by your own self: 'I will make your descendants as numerous as the stars in the sky and I will give your descendants all this land I promised them, and it will be their inheritance forever.' " 14Then the LORD relented and did not bring on his people the disaster he had threatened.

15Moses turned and went down the mountain with the two tablets of the Testimony in his hands. They were inscribed on both sides, front and back. 16The tablets were the work of God; the writing was the writing of God, engraved on the tablets.

17When Joshua heard the noise of the people shouting, he said to Moses, "There is the sound of war in the camp."

18Moses replied:

"It is not the sound of victory,
it is not the sound of defeat;
it is the sound of singing that I hear."

19When Moses approached the camp and saw the calf and the dancing, his anger burned and he threw the tablets out of his hands, breaking them to pieces at the foot of the mountain. 20And he took the calf they had made and burned it in the fire; then he ground it to powder, scattered it on the water and made the Israelites drink it.

21He said to Aaron, "What did these people do to you, that you led them into such great sin?"

22"Do not be angry, my lord," Aaron answered. "You know how prone these people are to evil. 23They said to me, 'Make us gods who will go before us. As for this fellow Moses who brought us up out of Egypt, we don't know what has happened to him.' 24So I told them, 'Whoever has any gold jewelry, take it off.' Then they gave me the gold, and I threw it into the fire, and out came this calf!"

25Moses saw that the people were running wild and that Aaron had let them get out of control and so become a laughingstock to their enemies. 26So he stood at the entrance to the camp and said, "Whoever is for the LORD, come to me." And all the Levites rallied to him.

27Then he said to them, "This is what the LORD, the God of Israel, says: 'Each man strap a sword to his side. Go back and forth through the camp from one end to the other, each killing his brother and friend and neighbor.' " 28The Levites did as Moses commanded, and that day about three thousand of the people died. 29Then Moses said, "You have been set apart to the LORD today, for you were against your own sons and brothers, and he has blessed you this day."

30The next day Moses said to the people, "You have committed a great sin. But now I will go up to the LORD; perhaps I can make atonement for your sin."

31So Moses went back to the LORD and said, "Oh, what a great sin these people have committed! They have made themselves gods of gold. 32But now, please forgive their sin—but if not, then blot me out of the book you have written."

33The LORD replied to Moses, "Whoever has

[a]4 Or *This is your god*; also in verse 8 [b]6 Traditionally *peace offerings*

32:21–29 Aaron revealed himself to be a "people pleaser." He gave in to the idolatrous desires of the Israelites in order to avoid confronting them with the sin in their lives. He also displayed a lack of honesty and an unwillingness to take responsibility for his own actions. To avoid his accountability to God and Moses he made a farfetched excuse for his behavior (32:22–24). The consequences of Aaron's failure were terrible, reaching far beyond his personal reprimand. Let us learn from Aaron's mistakes. We must defend and live out God's plan, even when it is unpopular with the crowd. If we don't, the consequences for us and the people around us could be terrible.

32:30–35 In the wake of Israel's horrible idolatry, Moses took on the role of a loving father toward them. In seeking atonement and forgiveness for the people's sins, Moses asked God to hold back the terrible consequences; he even suggested that God allow Moses to take the punishment for the people upon himself. It is difficult for many in authority to see that those under their charge must learn responsibility by facing the full consequences of their sin. Though God forgives repentant sinners, God will still punish disobedience. Both are promises of God, and God keeps his promises.

sinned against me I will blot out of my book.
34Now go, lead the people to the place I spoke
of, and my angel will go before you. However,
when the time comes for me to punish, I will
punish them for their sin."

35And the LORD struck the people with a
plague because of what they did with the calf
Aaron had made.

33 Then the LORD said to Moses, "Leave
this place, you and the people you
brought up out of Egypt, and go up to the land
I promised on oath to Abraham, Isaac and Jacob, saying, 'I will give it to your descendants.'
2I will send an angel before you and drive out
the Canaanites, Amorites, Hittites, Perizzites,
Hivites and Jebusites. 3Go up to the land flowing with milk and honey. But I will not go with
you, because you are a stiff-necked people and
I might destroy you on the way."

4When the people heard these distressing
words, they began to mourn and no one put on
any ornaments. 5For the LORD had said to Moses, "Tell the Israelites, 'You are a stiff-necked
people. If I were to go with you even for a moment, I might destroy you. Now take off your
ornaments and I will decide what to do with
you.' " 6So the Israelites stripped off their ornaments at Mount Horeb.

The Tent of Meeting

7Now Moses used to take a tent and pitch it
outside the camp some distance away, calling it
the "tent of meeting." Anyone inquiring of the
LORD would go to the tent of meeting outside
the camp. 8And whenever Moses went out to
the tent, all the people rose and stood at the
entrances to their tents, watching Moses until
he entered the tent. 9As Moses went into the
tent, the pillar of cloud would come down and
stay at the entrance, while the LORD spoke with
Moses. 10Whenever the people saw the pillar of
cloud standing at the entrance to the tent, they
all stood and worshiped, each at the entrance to
his tent. 11The LORD would speak to Moses face
to face, as a man speaks with his friend. Then
Moses would return to the camp, but his young
aide Joshua son of Nun did not leave the tent.

Moses and the Glory of the LORD

12Moses said to the LORD, "You have been
telling me, 'Lead these people,' but you have
not let me know whom you will send with me.
You have said, 'I know you by name and you
have found favor with me.' 13If you are pleased
with me, teach me your ways so I may know
you and continue to find favor with you. Remember that this nation is your people."

14The LORD replied, "My Presence will go
with you, and I will give you rest."

15Then Moses said to him, "If your Presence
does not go with us, do not send us up from
here. 16How will anyone know that you are
pleased with me and with your people unless
you go with us? What else will distinguish me
and your people from all the other people on
the face of the earth?"

17And the LORD said to Moses, "I will do the
very thing you have asked, because I am pleased
with you and I know you by name."

18Then Moses said, "Now show me your
glory."

19And the LORD said, "I will cause all my
goodness to pass in front of you, and I will
proclaim my name, the LORD, in your presence.
I will have mercy on whom I will have mercy,
and I will have compassion on whom I will
have compassion. 20But," he said, "you cannot
see my face, for no one may see me and live."

21Then the LORD said, "There is a place near
me where you may stand on a rock. 22When my
glory passes by, I will put you in a cleft in the
rock and cover you with my hand until I have
passed by. 23Then I will remove my hand and
you will see my back; but my face must not be
seen."

The New Stone Tablets

34 The LORD said to Moses, "Chisel out
two stone tablets like the first ones, and
I will write on them the words that were on the
first tablets, which you broke. 2Be ready in the
morning, and then come up on Mount Sinai.
Present yourself to me there on top of the
mountain. 3No one is to come with you or be
seen anywhere on the mountain; not even the
flocks and herds may graze in front of the
mountain."

4So Moses chiseled out two stone tablets like
the first ones and went up Mount Sinai early
in the morning, as the LORD had commanded

33:1–6 God's statement reassured Israel that he would stand by his covenant commitments. He would give them the promised land and protect them through the time of its settlement. However, God became so angry with Israel due to their stubborn disobedience that he was forced to back away so as not to destroy them. After this, the people underwent a heart-wrenching self-examination, saw the truth, confessed their sins and truly repented before God. Even when we have failed miserably, we can be assured that God's promises of forgiveness will stand. All we need to do is confess our sins openly to God and seek his forgiveness and help to find a new way of life.

33:12–23 Moses was growing spiritually in a remarkable way, and when he asked to experience more of God's presence and see his glory, Moses was not seeking to glorify himself. It is important for all of us to have a clear vision of God. As we see him more clearly, we can better understand who we are with all our strengths and limitations. All of us should seek to know God better and to experience his presence in our lives.

34:1–4 In spite of the horrible sin that the people of Israel had committed in building and worshiping the golden calf (see 32:1–35), God willingly gave them another chance to commit themselves to him and obey his covenant. When Moses came down from Mount Sinai the first time, he smashed the tablets inscribed with the Ten Commandments (32:19). God displayed his great, undeserved grace (34:6) by rewriting the tablets for his people. Our sins can never be so great that God's forgiveness becomes impossible.

him; and he carried the two stone tablets in his hands. 5Then the LORD came down in the cloud and stood there with him and proclaimed his name, the LORD. 6And he passed in front of Moses, proclaiming, "The LORD, the LORD, the compassionate and gracious God, slow to anger, abounding in love and faithfulness, 7maintaining love to thousands, and forgiving wickedness, rebellion and sin. Yet he does not leave the guilty unpunished; he punishes the children and their children for the sin of the fathers to the third and fourth generation."

8Moses bowed to the ground at once and worshiped. 9"O Lord, if I have found favor in your eyes," he said, "then let the Lord go with us. Although this is a stiff-necked people, forgive our wickedness and our sin, and take us as your inheritance."

10Then the LORD said: "I am making a covenant with you. Before all your people I will do wonders never before done in any nation in all the world. The people you live among will see how awesome is the work that I, the LORD, will do for you. 11Obey what I command you today. I will drive out before you the Amorites, Canaanites, Hittites, Perizzites, Hivites and Jebusites. 12Be careful not to make a treaty with those who live in the land where you are going, or they will be a snare among you. 13Break down their altars, smash their sacred stones and cut down their Asherah poles.[a] 14Do not worship any other god, for the LORD, whose name is Jealous, is a jealous God.

15"Be careful not to make a treaty with those who live in the land; for when they prostitute themselves to their gods and sacrifice to them, they will invite you and you will eat their sacrifices. 16And when you choose some of their daughters as wives for your sons and those daughters prostitute themselves to their gods, they will lead your sons to do the same.

17"Do not make cast idols.

18"Celebrate the Feast of Unleavened Bread. For seven days eat bread made without yeast, as I commanded you. Do this at the appointed time in the month of Abib, for in that month you came out of Egypt.

19"The first offspring of every womb belongs to me, including all the firstborn males of your livestock, whether from herd or flock. 20Redeem the firstborn donkey with a lamb, but if you do not redeem it, break its neck. Redeem all your firstborn sons.

"No one is to appear before me empty-handed.

21"Six days you shall labor, but on the seventh day you shall rest; even during the plowing season and harvest you must rest.

22"Celebrate the Feast of Weeks with the firstfruits of the wheat harvest, and the Feast of Ingathering at the turn of the year.[b] 23Three times a year all your men are to appear before the Sovereign LORD, the God of Israel. 24I will drive out nations before you and enlarge your territory, and no one will covet your land when you go up three times each year to appear before the LORD your God.

25"Do not offer the blood of a sacrifice to me along with anything containing yeast, and do not let any of the sacrifice from the Passover Feast remain until morning.

26"Bring the best of the firstfruits of your soil to the house of the LORD your God.

"Do not cook a young goat in its mother's milk."

27Then the LORD said to Moses, "Write down these words, for in accordance with these words I have made a covenant with you and with Israel." 28Moses was there with the LORD forty days and forty nights without eating bread or drinking water. And he wrote on the tablets the words of the covenant—the Ten Commandments.

The Radiant Face of Moses

29When Moses came down from Mount Sinai with the two tablets of the Testimony in his hands, he was not aware that his face was radiant because he had spoken with the LORD. 30When Aaron and all the Israelites saw Moses, his face was radiant, and they were afraid to come near him. 31But Moses called to them; so Aaron and all the leaders of the community came back to him, and he spoke to them. 32Afterward all the Israelites came near him, and he gave them all the commands the LORD had given him on Mount Sinai.

33When Moses finished speaking to them, he put a veil over his face. 34But whenever he entered the LORD's presence to speak with him, he removed the veil until he came out. And when he came out and told the Israelites what he had been commanded, 35they saw that his face was radiant. Then Moses would put the veil back over his face until he went in to speak with the LORD.

[a]*13* That is, symbols of the goddess Asherah [b]*22* That is, in the fall

34:5–7 God announced the meaning of his name to Moses, explaining who he was. In ancient cultures, the meaning of a person's name was perceived to be a window into their character, not just a surface title. As we seek God and surrender to him, it is important that we get to know God's character. His name tells us that he is compassionate, gracious, patient, loving, trustworthy, forgiving and just.

34:29–35 Moses' experience in God's presence was a transforming one. God's holy presence was so radiant that it caused Moses' face to glow. Yet the physical glow on his face was only a partial result of drawing so close to God. Moses' experience also gave him the faith he needed to continue leading the Israelites through the wilderness. Drawing close to God should also provide us with the strength we need to make it through our wilderness experiences.

Sabbath Regulations

35 Moses assembled the whole Israelite community and said to them, "These are the things the LORD has commanded you to do: 2For six days, work is to be done, but the seventh day shall be your holy day, a Sabbath of rest to the LORD. Whoever does any work on it must be put to death. 3Do not light a fire in any of your dwellings on the Sabbath day."

Materials for the Tabernacle

4Moses said to the whole Israelite community, "This is what the LORD has commanded: 5From what you have, take an offering for the LORD. Everyone who is willing is to bring to the LORD an offering of gold, silver and bronze; 6blue, purple and scarlet yarn and fine linen; goat hair; 7ram skins dyed red and hides of sea cows[a]; acacia wood; 8olive oil for the light; spices for the anointing oil and for the fragrant incense; 9and onyx stones and other gems to be mounted on the ephod and breastpiece.

10"All who are skilled among you are to come and make everything the LORD has commanded: 11the tabernacle with its tent and its covering, clasps, frames, crossbars, posts and bases; 12the ark with its poles and the atonement cover and the curtain that shields it; 13the table with its poles and all its articles and the bread of the Presence; 14the lampstand that is for light with its accessories, lamps and oil for the light; 15the altar of incense with its poles, the anointing oil and the fragrant incense; the curtain for the doorway at the entrance to the tabernacle; 16the altar of burnt offering with its bronze grating, its poles and all its utensils; the bronze basin with its stand; 17the curtains of the courtyard with its posts and bases, and the curtain for the entrance to the courtyard; 18the tent pegs for the tabernacle and for the courtyard, and their ropes; 19the woven garments worn for ministering in the sanctuary—both the sacred garments for Aaron the priest and the garments for his sons when they serve as priests."

20Then the whole Israelite community withdrew from Moses' presence, 21and everyone who was willing and whose heart moved him came and brought an offering to the LORD for the work on the Tent of Meeting, for all its service, and for the sacred garments. 22All who were willing, men and women alike, came and brought gold jewelry of all kinds: brooches, earrings, rings and ornaments. They all presented their gold as a wave offering to the LORD. 23Everyone who had blue, purple or scarlet yarn or fine linen, or goat hair, ram skins dyed red or hides of sea cows brought them. 24Those presenting an offering of silver or bronze brought it as an offering to the LORD, and everyone who had acacia wood for any part of the work brought it. 25Every skilled woman spun with her hands and brought what she had spun—blue, purple or scarlet yarn or fine linen. 26And all the women who were willing and had the skill spun the goat hair. 27The leaders brought onyx stones and other gems to be mounted on the ephod and breastpiece. 28They also brought spices and olive oil for the light and for the anointing oil and for the fragrant incense. 29All the Israelite men and women who were willing brought to the LORD freewill offerings for all the work the LORD through Moses had commanded them to do.

Bezalel and Oholiab

30Then Moses said to the Israelites, "See, the LORD has chosen Bezalel son of Uri, the son of Hur, of the tribe of Judah, 31and he has filled him with the Spirit of God, with skill, ability and knowledge in all kinds of crafts— 32to make artistic designs for work in gold, silver and bronze, 33to cut and set stones, to work in wood and to engage in all kinds of artistic craftsmanship. 34And he has given both him and Oholiab son of Ahisamach, of the tribe of Dan, the ability to teach others. 35He has filled them with skill to do all kinds of work as craftsmen, designers, embroiderers in blue, purple and scarlet yarn and fine linen, and weavers—all of them

36 master craftsmen and designers. 1So Bezalel, Oholiab and every skilled person to whom the LORD has given skill and ability to know how to carry out all the work of constructing the sanctuary are to do the work just as the LORD has commanded."

2Then Moses summoned Bezalel and Oholiab and every skilled person to whom the LORD had given ability and who was willing to come and do the work. 3They received from Moses all the offerings the Israelites had brought to carry out the work of constructing the sanctuary. And the people continued to bring freewill offerings morning after morning. 4So all the skilled craftsmen who were doing all the work on the sanctuary left their work 5and said to Moses, "The people are bringing more than enough for doing the work the LORD commanded to be done."

6Then Moses gave an order and they sent this

[a] 7 That is, dugongs; also in verse 23

35:4–9, 29 This freewill offering was given by the Israelites to show their commitment to God. Many of the sacrifices and offerings in the Law of Moses were mandatory. They were required, almost like paying taxes. The freewill offering was voluntary and was used in this case to build and finance the tabernacle. The people who had given joyfully served God and each other selflessly.

35:30—36:3 People who are greatly gifted need to have a clear sense of their identity. Often such people can be described as either boastful or self-deprecating. Neither is a healthy or accurate self-assessment, and neither is pleasing to God. There should be no sense of superiority or inferiority among God's people since every member plays a unique and important role (1 Corinthians 12:12–27).

word throughout the camp: "No man or woman is to make anything else as an offering for the sanctuary." And so the people were restrained from bringing more, 7because what they already had was more than enough to do all the work.

The Tabernacle

8All the skilled men among the workmen made the tabernacle with ten curtains of finely twisted linen and blue, purple and scarlet yarn, with cherubim worked into them by a skilled craftsman. 9All the curtains were the same size—twenty-eight cubits long and four cubits wide.[a] 10They joined five of the curtains together and did the same with the other five. 11Then they made loops of blue material along the edge of the end curtain in one set, and the same was done with the end curtain in the other set. 12They also made fifty loops on one curtain and fifty loops on the end curtain of the other set, with the loops opposite each other. 13Then they made fifty gold clasps and used them to fasten the two sets of curtains together so that the tabernacle was a unit.

14They made curtains of goat hair for the tent over the tabernacle—eleven altogether. 15All eleven curtains were the same size—thirty cubits long and four cubits wide.[b] 16They joined five of the curtains into one set and the other six into another set. 17Then they made fifty loops along the edge of the end curtain in one set and also along the edge of the end curtain in the other set. 18They made fifty bronze clasps to fasten the tent together as a unit. 19Then they made for the tent a covering of ram skins dyed red, and over that a covering of hides of sea cows.[c]

20They made upright frames of acacia wood for the tabernacle. 21Each frame was ten cubits long and a cubit and a half wide,[d] 22with two projections set parallel to each other. They made all the frames of the tabernacle in this way. 23They made twenty frames for the south side of the tabernacle 24and made forty silver bases to go under them—two bases for each frame, one under each projection. 25For the other side, the north side of the tabernacle, they made twenty frames 26and forty silver bases—two under each frame. 27They made six frames for the far end, that is, the west end of the tabernacle, 28and two frames were made for the corners of the tabernacle at the far end. 29At these two corners the frames were double from the bottom all the way to the top and fitted into a single ring; both were made alike. 30So there were eight frames and sixteen silver bases—two under each frame.

31They also made crossbars of acacia wood: five for the frames on one side of the tabernacle, 32five for those on the other side, and five for the frames on the west, at the far end of the tabernacle. 33They made the center crossbar so that it extended from end to end at the middle of the frames. 34They overlaid the frames with gold and made gold rings to hold the crossbars. They also overlaid the crossbars with gold.

35They made the curtain of blue, purple and scarlet yarn and finely twisted linen, with cherubim worked into it by a skilled craftsman. 36They made four posts of acacia wood for it and overlaid them with gold. They made gold hooks for them and cast their four silver bases. 37For the entrance to the tent they made a curtain of blue, purple and scarlet yarn and finely twisted linen—the work of an embroiderer; 38and they made five posts with hooks for them. They overlaid the tops of the posts and their bands with gold and made their five bases of bronze.

The Ark

37 Bezalel made the ark of acacia wood—two and a half cubits long, a cubit and a half wide, and a cubit and a half high.[e] 2He overlaid it with pure gold, both inside and out, and made a gold molding around it. 3He cast four gold rings for it and fastened them to its four feet, with two rings on one side and two rings on the other. 4Then he made poles of acacia wood and overlaid them with gold. 5And he inserted the poles into the rings on the sides of the ark to carry it.

6He made the atonement cover of pure gold—two and a half cubits long and a cubit and a half wide.[f] 7Then he made two cherubim out of hammered gold at the ends of the cover. 8He made one cherub on one end and the second cherub on the other; at the two ends he made them of one piece with the cover. 9The cherubim had their wings spread upward, overshadowing the cover with them. The cherubim faced each other, looking toward the cover.

The Table

10They[g] made the table of acacia wood—two

[a] 9 That is, about 42 feet (about 12.5 meters) long and 6 feet (about 1.8 meters) wide [b] 15 That is, about 45 feet (about 13.5 meters) long and 6 feet (about 1.8 meters) wide [c] 19 That is, dugongs [d] 21 That is, about 15 feet (about 4.5 meters) long and 2 1/4 feet (about 0.7 meter) wide [e] 1 That is, about 3 3/4 feet (about 1.1 meters) long and 2 1/4 feet (about 0.7 meter) wide and high [f] 6 That is, about 3 3/4 feet (about 1.1 meters) long and 2 1/4 feet (about 0.7 meter) wide [g] 10 Or *He*; also in verses 11-29

37:1–9 It is quite common for supremely gifted people to perform beneath their potential because they fear failure. High expectations are difficult for anyone to cope with, yet the craftsman Bezalel did not allow the high expectations laid upon him to hinder his work. Because God had filled him with his Spirit and had given him unusual skills, he willingly used his gifts to glorify God, not only by building the tabernacle but also by teaching others and sharing his skills (36:30–34). Bezalel's life is a good example for us to live by today.

cubits long, a cubit wide, and a cubit and a half
high.[a] 11Then they overlaid it with pure gold
and made a gold molding around it. 12They also
made around it a rim a handbreadth[b] wide
and put a gold molding on the rim. 13They cast
four gold rings for the table and fastened them
to the four corners, where the four legs were.
14The rings were put close to the rim to hold the
poles used in carrying the table. 15The poles for
carrying the table were made of acacia wood
and were overlaid with gold. 16And they made
from pure gold the articles for the table—its
plates and dishes and bowls and its pitchers for
the pouring out of drink offerings.

The Lampstand

17They made the lampstand of pure gold and
hammered it out, base and shaft; its flowerlike
cups, buds and blossoms were of one piece with
it. 18Six branches extended from the sides of the
lampstand—three on one side and three on the
other. 19Three cups shaped like almond flowers
with buds and blossoms were on one branch,
three on the next branch and the same for all six
branches extending from the lampstand. 20And
on the lampstand were four cups shaped like
almond flowers with buds and blossoms. 21One
bud was under the first pair of branches extending from the lampstand, a second bud under
the second pair, and a third bud under the third
pair—six branches in all. 22The buds and the
branches were all of one piece with the lampstand, hammered out of pure gold.

23They made its seven lamps, as well as its
wick trimmers and trays, of pure gold. 24They
made the lampstand and all its accessories from
one talent[c] of pure gold.

The Altar of Incense

25They made the altar of incense out of acacia
wood. It was square, a cubit long and a cubit
wide, and two cubits high[d]—its horns of one
piece with it. 26They overlaid the top and all the
sides and the horns with pure gold, and made
a gold molding around it. 27They made two
gold rings below the molding—two on opposite
sides—to hold the poles used to carry it. 28They
made the poles of acacia wood and overlaid
them with gold.

29They also made the sacred anointing oil
and the pure, fragrant incense—the work of a
perfumer.

The Altar of Burnt Offering

38 They[e] built the altar of burnt offering
of acacia wood, three cubits[f] high; it
was square, five cubits long and five cubits
wide.[g] 2They made a horn at each of the four
corners, so that the horns and the altar were
of one piece, and they overlaid the altar with
bronze. 3They made all its utensils of bronze—
its pots, shovels, sprinkling bowls, meat forks
and firepans. 4They made a grating for the altar,
a bronze network, to be under its ledge, halfway
up the altar. 5They cast bronze rings to hold the
poles for the four corners of the bronze grating.
6They made the poles of acacia wood and overlaid them with bronze. 7They inserted the poles
into the rings so they would be on the sides of
the altar for carrying it. They made it hollow,
out of boards.

Basin for Washing

8They made the bronze basin and its bronze
stand from the mirrors of the women who
served at the entrance to the Tent of Meeting.

The Courtyard

9Next they made the courtyard. The south
side was a hundred cubits[h] long and had curtains of finely twisted linen, 10with twenty posts
and twenty bronze bases, and with silver hooks
and bands on the posts. 11The north side was
also a hundred cubits long and had twenty
posts and twenty bronze bases, with silver
hooks and bands on the posts.

12The west end was fifty cubits[i] wide and
had curtains, with ten posts and ten bases, with
silver hooks and bands on the posts. 13The east
end, toward the sunrise, was also fifty cubits
wide. 14Curtains fifteen cubits[j] long were on
one side of the entrance, with three posts and
three bases, 15and curtains fifteen cubits long
were on the other side of the entrance to the
courtyard, with three posts and three bases.
16All the curtains around the courtyard were of
finely twisted linen. 17The bases for the posts
were bronze. The hooks and bands on the posts
were silver, and their tops were overlaid with
silver; so all the posts of the courtyard had silver
bands.

18The curtain for the entrance to the courtyard was of blue, purple and scarlet yarn and
finely twisted linen—the work of an embroiderer. It was twenty cubits[k] long and, like the
curtains of the courtyard, five cubits[l] high,
19with four posts and four bronze bases. Their
hooks and bands were silver, and their tops
were overlaid with silver. 20All the tent pegs of
the tabernacle and of the surrounding courtyard
were bronze.

[a] *10* That is, about 3 feet (about 0.9 meter) long, 1 1/2 feet (about 0.5 meter) wide, and 2 1/4 feet (about 0.7 meter) high [b] *12* That is, about 3 inches (about 8 centimeters) [c] *24* That is, about 75 pounds (about 34 kilograms) [d] *25* That is, about 1 1/2 feet (about 0.5 meter) long and wide, and about 3 feet (about 0.9 meter) high [e] *1* Or *He*; also in verses 2-9
[f] *1* That is, about 4 1/2 feet (about 1.3 meters)
[g] *1* That is, about 7 1/2 feet (about 2.3 meters) long and wide [h] *9* That is, about 150 feet (about 46 meters)
[i] *12* That is, about 75 feet (about 23 meters)
[j] *14* That is, about 22 1/2 feet (about 6.9 meters)
[k] *18* That is, about 30 feet (about 9 meters) [l] *18* That is, about 7 1/2 feet (about 2.3 meters)

The Materials Used

21These are the amounts of the materials used for the tabernacle, the tabernacle of the Testimony, which were recorded at Moses' command by the Levites under the direction of Ithamar son of Aaron, the priest. 22(Bezalel son of Uri, the son of Hur, of the tribe of Judah, made everything the LORD commanded Moses; 23with him was Oholiab son of Ahisamach, of the tribe of Dan—a craftsman and designer, and an embroiderer in blue, purple and scarlet yarn and fine linen.) 24The total amount of the gold from the wave offering used for all the work on the sanctuary was 29 talents and 730 shekels,[a] according to the sanctuary shekel.

25The silver obtained from those of the community who were counted in the census was 100 talents and 1,775 shekels,[b] according to the sanctuary shekel— 26one beka per person, that is, half a shekel,[c] according to the sanctuary shekel, from everyone who had crossed over to those counted, twenty years old or more, a total of 603,550 men. 27The 100 talents[d] of silver were used to cast the bases for the sanctuary and for the curtain—100 bases from the 100 talents, one talent for each base. 28They used the 1,775 shekels[e] to make the hooks for the posts, to overlay the tops of the posts, and to make their bands.

29The bronze from the wave offering was 70 talents and 2,400 shekels.[f] 30They used it to make the bases for the entrance to the Tent of Meeting, the bronze altar with its bronze grating and all its utensils, 31the bases for the surrounding courtyard and those for its entrance and all the tent pegs for the tabernacle and those for the surrounding courtyard.

The Priestly Garments

39 From the blue, purple and scarlet yarn they made woven garments for ministering in the sanctuary. They also made sacred garments for Aaron, as the LORD commanded Moses.

The Ephod

2They[g] made the ephod of gold, and of blue, purple and scarlet yarn, and of finely twisted linen. 3They hammered out thin sheets of gold and cut strands to be worked into the blue, purple and scarlet yarn and fine linen—the work of a skilled craftsman. 4They made shoulder pieces for the ephod, which were attached to two of its corners, so it could be fastened. 5Its skillfully woven waistband was like it—of one piece with the ephod and made with gold, and with blue, purple and scarlet yarn, and with finely twisted linen, as the LORD commanded Moses.

6They mounted the onyx stones in gold filigree settings and engraved them like a seal with the names of the sons of Israel. 7Then they fastened them on the shoulder pieces of the ephod as memorial stones for the sons of Israel, as the LORD commanded Moses.

The Breastpiece

8They fashioned the breastpiece—the work of a skilled craftsman. They made it like the ephod: of gold, and of blue, purple and scarlet yarn, and of finely twisted linen. 9It was square—a span[h] long and a span wide—and folded double. 10Then they mounted four rows of precious stones on it. In the first row there was a ruby, a topaz and a beryl; 11in the second row a turquoise, a sapphire[i] and an emerald; 12in the third row a jacinth, an agate and an amethyst; 13in the fourth row a chrysolite, an onyx and a jasper.[j] They were mounted in gold filigree settings. 14There were twelve stones, one for each of the names of the sons of Israel, each engraved like a seal with the name of one of the twelve tribes.

15For the breastpiece they made braided chains of pure gold, like a rope. 16They made two gold filigree settings and two gold rings, and fastened the rings to two of the corners of the breastpiece. 17They fastened the two gold chains to the rings at the corners of the breastpiece, 18and the other ends of the chains to the two settings, attaching them to the shoulder pieces of the ephod at the front. 19They made two gold rings and attached them to the other two corners of the breastpiece on the inside edge next to the ephod. 20Then they made two more gold rings and attached them to the bottom of the shoulder pieces on the front of the ephod, close to the seam just above the waistband of the ephod. 21They tied the rings of the

[a] 24 The weight of the gold was a little over one ton (about 1 metric ton). [b] 25 The weight of the silver was a little over 3 3/4 tons (about 3.4 metric tons). [c] 26 That is, about 1/5 ounce (about 5.5 grams) [d] 27 That is, about 3 3/4 tons (about 3.4 metric tons) [e] 28 That is, about 45 pounds (about 20 kilograms) [f] 29 The weight of the bronze was about 2 1/2 tons (about 2.4 metric tons). [g] 2 Or *He;* also in verses 7, 8 and 22 [h] 9 That is, about 9 inches (about 22 centimeters) [i] 11 Or *lapis lazuli* [j] 13 The precise identification of some of these precious stones is uncertain.

38:21–31 The dollar value of the gold, silver, bronze and other materials used to build the tabernacle would be mind boggling. But the value of the materials used does not reflect empty extravagance or excess. The expense only illustrates how precious and invaluable the presence of God really is. The people's faith had surpassed the point of hanging on to material things. They were beginning to learn to trust God and shared the wealth he had given them.

39:1–31 The priestly garments were ornate and detailed, in accordance with God's instructions to Moses. The intricate details point to the fact that the priest was to be holy—set apart for God (39:30). The death of Christ made it possible for all believers to be priests (1 Peter 2:9), for we are to be holy and pure, committed to God in everything we do. Like the priestly garments, our actions should externally reflect what we are on the inside because of the work of Christ—holy and set apart.

breastpiece to the rings of the ephod with blue cord, connecting it to the waistband so that the breastpiece would not swing out from the ephod—as the LORD commanded Moses.

Other Priestly Garments

22They made the robe of the ephod entirely of blue cloth—the work of a weaver— 23with an opening in the center of the robe like the opening of a collar,[a] and a band around this opening, so that it would not tear. 24They made pomegranates of blue, purple and scarlet yarn and finely twisted linen around the hem of the robe. 25And they made bells of pure gold and attached them around the hem between the pomegranates. 26The bells and pomegranates alternated around the hem of the robe to be worn for ministering, as the LORD commanded Moses.

27For Aaron and his sons, they made tunics of fine linen—the work of a weaver— 28and the turban of fine linen, the linen headbands and the undergarments of finely twisted linen. 29The sash was of finely twisted linen and blue, purple and scarlet yarn—the work of an embroiderer—as the LORD commanded Moses.

30They made the plate, the sacred diadem, out of pure gold and engraved on it, like an inscription on a seal: HOLY TO THE LORD. 31Then they fastened a blue cord to it to attach it to the turban, as the LORD commanded Moses.

Moses Inspects the Tabernacle

32So all the work on the tabernacle, the Tent of Meeting, was completed. The Israelites did everything just as the LORD commanded Moses. 33Then they brought the tabernacle to Moses: the tent and all its furnishings, its clasps, frames, crossbars, posts and bases; 34the covering of ram skins dyed red, the covering of hides of sea cows[b] and the shielding curtain; 35the ark of the Testimony with its poles and the atonement cover; 36the table with all its articles and the bread of the Presence; 37the pure gold lampstand with its row of lamps and all its accessories, and the oil for the light; 38the gold altar, the anointing oil, the fragrant incense, and the curtain for the entrance to the tent; 39the bronze altar with its bronze grating, its poles and all its utensils; the basin with its stand; 40the curtains of the courtyard with its posts and bases, and the curtain for the entrance to the courtyard; the ropes and tent pegs for the courtyard; all the furnishings for the tabernacle, the Tent of Meeting; 41and the woven garments worn for ministering in the sanctuary, both the sacred garments for Aaron the priest and the garments for his sons when serving as priests.

42The Israelites had done all the work just as the LORD had commanded Moses. 43Moses inspected the work and saw that they had done it just as the LORD had commanded. So Moses blessed them.

Setting Up the Tabernacle

40 Then the LORD said to Moses: 2"Set up the tabernacle, the Tent of Meeting, on the first day of the first month. 3Place the ark of the Testimony in it and shield the ark with the curtain. 4Bring in the table and set out what belongs on it. Then bring in the lampstand and set up its lamps. 5Place the gold altar of incense in front of the ark of the Testimony and put the curtain at the entrance to the tabernacle.

6"Place the altar of burnt offering in front of the entrance to the tabernacle, the Tent of Meeting; 7place the basin between the Tent of Meeting and the altar and put water in it. 8Set up the courtyard around it and put the curtain at the entrance to the courtyard.

9"Take the anointing oil and anoint the tabernacle and everything in it; consecrate it and all its furnishings, and it will be holy. 10Then anoint the altar of burnt offering and all its utensils; consecrate the altar, and it will be most holy. 11Anoint the basin and its stand and consecrate them.

12"Bring Aaron and his sons to the entrance to the Tent of Meeting and wash them with water. 13Then dress Aaron in the sacred garments, anoint him and consecrate him so he may serve me as priest. 14Bring his sons and dress them in tunics. 15Anoint them just as you anointed their father, so they may serve me as priests. Their anointing will be to a priesthood that will continue for all generations to come." 16Moses did everything just as the LORD commanded him.

17So the tabernacle was set up on the first day of the first month in the second year. 18When Moses set up the tabernacle, he put the bases in place, erected the frames, inserted the crossbars and set up the posts. 19Then he spread the tent over the tabernacle and put the covering over the tent, as the LORD commanded him.

[a]*23* The meaning of the Hebrew for this word is uncertain. [b]*34* That is, dugongs

39:33–43 The tabernacle was completed, following all of God's instructions (39:32, 42–43). It had required a great deal of tedious work, but all of it had been done God's way. Here was the melding of faith, commitment to God and perseverance. Israel's success at building the tabernacle depended on following God's specific instructions. Our spiritual renewal and sustained spiritual growth must be built in the same way.

40:1–33 Setting up the tabernacle meant a new life of worship for the Israelites. Undoubtedly, as with any large task, it took a great deal of time and patience to finish the job. The Israelites had to persevere. But because they did, their victory celebration and worship were all the more joyous. Our spiritual renewal won't take place overnight. We must learn to persevere and be accountable to others as we preserve our spiritual gains. In the end, the joyous freedom we experience will be worth it.

20He took the Testimony and placed it in the ark, attached the poles to the ark and put the atonement cover over it. 21Then he brought the ark into the tabernacle and hung the shielding curtain and shielded the ark of the Testimony, as the LORD commanded him.

22Moses placed the table in the Tent of Meeting on the north side of the tabernacle outside the curtain 23and set out the bread on it before the LORD, as the LORD commanded him.

24He placed the lampstand in the Tent of Meeting opposite the table on the south side of the tabernacle 25and set up the lamps before the LORD, as the LORD commanded him.

26Moses placed the gold altar in the Tent of Meeting in front of the curtain 27and burned fragrant incense on it, as the LORD commanded him. 28Then he put up the curtain at the entrance to the tabernacle.

29He set the altar of burnt offering near the entrance to the tabernacle, the Tent of Meeting, and offered on it burnt offerings and grain offerings, as the LORD commanded him.

30He placed the basin between the Tent of Meeting and the altar and put water in it for washing, 31and Moses and Aaron and his sons used it to wash their hands and feet. 32They washed whenever they entered the Tent of Meeting or approached the altar, as the LORD commanded Moses.

33Then Moses set up the courtyard around the tabernacle and altar and put up the curtain at the entrance to the courtyard. And so Moses finished the work.

The Glory of the LORD

34Then the cloud covered the Tent of Meeting, and the glory of the LORD filled the tabernacle. 35Moses could not enter the Tent of Meeting because the cloud had settled upon it, and the glory of the LORD filled the tabernacle.

36In all the travels of the Israelites, whenever the cloud lifted from above the tabernacle, they would set out; 37but if the cloud did not lift, they did not set out—until the day it lifted. 38So the cloud of the LORD was over the tabernacle by day, and fire was in the cloud by night, in the sight of all the house of Israel during all their travels.

40:34–38 Israel could count on God's guidance and presence in the tabernacle all the way to the promised land. This new aspect of their relationship to God provided the Israelites with the consistent challenge of self-examination and spiritual growth. Believers today follow Christ by faith, yet we still face those same challenges of self-examination and growth. God's guiding presence in our lives provides us with the strength and direction we need to progress in our spiritual renewal.

LEVITICUS

The Big Picture

A. *A PROPER PERSPECTIVE THROUGH A TRUE UNDERSTANDING OF GOD (1:1–16:34)*

1. Worship Through the Offerings (1:1–7:38)
   a. Contentment found through gratitude to God (1:1–3:17)
   b. Contentment found through complete cleansing by God (4:1–5:13)
   c. Restitution for wrongs committed against others (5:14–6:7)
   d. Other instructions for the offerings (6:8–7:38)
2. The Roles of Leaders and People in the Offerings (8:1–15:33)
3. The Completeness of God's Forgiveness–Day of Atonement (16:1-34)

B. *A PROPER PERSPECTIVE THROUGH OBEDIENCE AND ACCOUNTABILITY TO GOD (17:1–27:34)*

Rules . . . regulations . . . strange sacrifices—the book of Leviticus is full of them. What relevance could these foreign laws possibly have for us? What could the God who requires such things be like? As we look closely at the lengthy list of rules and regulations in Leviticus, we can find some comforting truths about our God and how he relates to us.

The book of Leviticus portrays a God who is awesome and holy; he is pure, clean, sinless, perfect. The numerous regulations given to the Israelites confirm these truths. The people of Israel needed to humbly obey God if they wanted to live in close fellowship with him. Though God is holy, he reaches out to broken, sinful people. He provided a way—one of laws and sacrifices—for the Israelites to be forgiven for their sins.

It has been said that "a picture is worth a thousand words." Leviticus is filled with powerful pictures—images that show us both God's gracious character and the terrible consequences of sin. Could there be a more striking reminder of the consequences of sin and God's grace than the realization that God allowed a suffering, sacrificial animal to take our place?

The laws and sacrifices in Leviticus help us understand God's character. He is holy and pure, but also gracious and forgiving. The laws and sacrifices also foreshadow God's later provision of the perfect sacrifice—Jesus Christ. God calls us to obedience, but he also knows that we are not perfect. God provides the means for our spiritual renewal and cleansing through the sacrificial death of his Son. Ongoing spiritual growth comes as we regularly recognize the truth, speak the truth by confessing sin, worship God and thank him for his forgiveness.

Spiritual Renewal Themes

GOD'S HOLY CHARACTER

When we focus on God's gracious character, it is easy to forget that he is also holy and awesome. He is far above us in his majesty and power, in his actions and thoughts. The book of Leviticus reminds us of God's holiness and power. We should be comforted by the fact that there is nothing he cannot do, and we should remember that God's holy separateness will never stop him from relating closely to his people. Though high above us, he is still intimately concerned with each one of us and our spiritual renewal.

GOD'S LOVING CHARACTER

The sacrifices so graphically detailed in Leviticus are an extension of God's love toward each of us. Throughout the book we encounter stories about the sinfulness of human individuals contrasted against the holiness of God's character. Something was needed to bridge the gap between God's holiness and our sinfulness so that we could relate to God. God graciously provided the system of sacrifices to bridge that gap, thus revealing his love for all people. His love was ultimately expressed when he sent his Son as the supreme sacrifice to pay for our sins, making it possible for us to draw near to our holy God.

OUR NEED FOR GRACE

When we see the power and majesty of God revealed in Leviticus, we are confronted with our inability to do anything about our problem of sin. Just as the Israelites were slaves in Egypt, we are slaves to our human tendency toward sin and its destructive consequences. We need help. We need grace. So God, in his mercy, set up a system of sacrifices that provided a means for our debt of sin to be paid. And God took this provision one step further. He gave his only Son to die for us as the complete and eternal payment for our past sins, present willfulness and future transgressions.

Essential Facts

PURPOSE:
To show that God desires to have personal fellowship with those who turn to him. Only through worship and personal obedience to God can we fully experience the freedom he offers.

AUTHOR:
Moses.

AUDIENCE:
The people of Israel.

DATE WRITTEN:
Shortly after the events the book records, between 1445 and 1407 B.C.

SETTING:
Camped at Mount Sinai, the people of Israel are given God's special instructions.

KEY VERSE:
"I am the LORD who brought you up out of Egypt to be your God; therefore be holy, because I am holy" (11:45).

KEY PLACE:
Mount Sinai.

KEY PEOPLE:
Moses and Aaron.

The Burnt Offering

1 The LORD called to Moses and spoke to him from the Tent of Meeting. He said, 2"Speak to the Israelites and say to them: 'When any of you brings an offering to the LORD, bring as your offering an animal from either the herd or the flock.

3" 'If the offering is a burnt offering from the herd, he is to offer a male without defect. He must present it at the entrance to the Tent of Meeting so that it[a] will be acceptable to the LORD. 4He is to lay his hand on the head of the burnt offering, and it will be accepted on his behalf to make atonement for him. 5He is to slaughter the young bull before the LORD, and then Aaron's sons the priests shall bring the blood and sprinkle it against the altar on all sides at the entrance to the Tent of Meeting. 6He is to skin the burnt offering and cut it into pieces. 7The sons of Aaron the priest are to put fire on the altar and arrange wood on the fire. 8Then Aaron's sons the priests shall arrange the pieces, including the head and the fat, on the burning wood that is on the altar. 9He is to wash the inner parts and the legs with water, and the priest is to burn all of it on the altar. It is a burnt offering, an offering made by fire, an aroma pleasing to the LORD.

10" 'If the offering is a burnt offering from the flock, from either the sheep or the goats, he is to offer a male without defect. 11He is to slaughter it at the north side of the altar before the LORD, and Aaron's sons the priests shall sprinkle its blood against the altar on all sides. 12He is to cut it into pieces, and the priest shall arrange them, including the head and the fat, on the burning wood that is on the altar. 13He is to wash the inner parts and the legs with water, and the priest is to bring all of it and burn it on the altar. It is a burnt offering, an offering made by fire, an aroma pleasing to the LORD.

14" 'If the offering to the LORD is a burnt offering of birds, he is to offer a dove or a young pigeon. 15The priest shall bring it to the altar, wring off the head and burn it on the altar; its blood shall be drained out on the side of the altar. 16He is to remove the crop with its contents[b] and throw it to the east side of the altar, where the ashes are. 17He shall tear it open by the wings, not severing it completely, and then the priest shall burn it on the wood that is on the fire on the altar. It is a burnt offering, an offering made by fire, an aroma pleasing to the LORD.

The Grain Offering

2 " 'When someone brings a grain offering to the LORD, his offering is to be of fine flour. He is to pour oil on it, put incense on it 2and take it to Aaron's sons the priests. The priest shall take a handful of the fine flour and oil, together with all the incense, and burn this as a memorial portion on the altar, an offering made by fire, an aroma pleasing to the LORD. 3The rest of the grain offering belongs to Aaron and his sons; it is a most holy part of the offerings made to the LORD by fire.

4" 'If you bring a grain offering baked in an oven, it is to consist of fine flour: cakes made without yeast and mixed with oil, or[c] wafers made without yeast and spread with oil. 5If your grain offering is prepared on a griddle, it is to be made of fine flour mixed with oil, and without yeast. 6Crumble it and pour oil on it; it is a grain

[a]3 Or *he* [b]16 Or *crop and the feathers;* the meaning of the Hebrew for this word is uncertain. [c]4 Or *and*

1:1 The first words of this book, "The LORD called," reveal a God who seeks out and initiates relationships with people. The same Hebrew word is used in Genesis 3:9 when "the LORD God called" to Adam and Eve after their disobedience and offered them a way of redemption from their sin. Through God's instructions in Exodus and Leviticus, God provided Israel with more elaborate object lessons to remind them of how much he had done for them. God is still calling to us today, offering forgiveness, hope and restored fellowship with him.

1:2–3 The offerings in Leviticus 1—3 were voluntary acts of worship for the Israelites. Each offering emphasized a different aspect of their commitment to God: complete surrender and devotion to God, recognition of God's goodness and provision, thanksgiving and fellowship with him. Our worship of God is also voluntary. By allowing God supreme reign in our lives, we can receive the same blessings of God's help and hope that were available to the people of Israel.

1:3–13 The first object lesson given to God's people in Leviticus was the burnt offering. By identifying with the offering, the person bringing the offering committed their life to God in a fresh way. In Romans 12:1–2 Paul similarly speaks of presenting our bodies as living sacrifices to God. Surrendering our lives to God in this way is a key to spiritual renewal. When we seek God and surrender to him, he will change us through his power.

1:10–14 Not every Israelite was financially able to bring a large animal to sacrifice to God. God allowed worshipers to bring smaller offerings (sheep, goat, dove or pigeon), as they were able. Joseph and Mary, the parents of Jesus, were evidently quite poor because they brought a smaller offering (see Luke 2:24). We may feel we have very little to offer to God, but he doesn't compare the size of our offerings with others. He simply asks that our worship and commitment to him reflect what he has given to us.

2:1, 4, 14 The grain offering was to consist of *fine* flour or the *first* of the grain harvest. Just as an animal without defect was required for the other offerings, so the best of one's produce was to be offered. By this, God was reminding his people that he was worthy of more than just their leftovers; he deserved the best they could offer. God wanted their undivided devotion. We cannot entrust ourselves to God halfheartedly and expect spiritual renewal to occur. We need to surrender ourselves wholeheartedly to God as we demonstrate our devotion to him.

2:1–16 The grain offering (sometimes called the cereal or meal offering) is the only offering described in Leviticus that does not involve a blood sacrifice. This offering was made up of the most common of daily foods. It symbolized that the person offering the grain had surrendered their life to God in recognition of all that God had provided. The process of spiritual renewal may involve a commitment that involves not only giving ourselves to God (the burnt offering) but also giving him the things of everyday life (the grain offering).

offering. 7If your grain offering is cooked in a pan, it is to be made of fine flour and oil. 8Bring the grain offering made of these things to the LORD; present it to the priest, who shall take it to the altar. 9He shall take out the memorial portion from the grain offering and burn it on the altar as an offering made by fire, an aroma pleasing to the LORD. 10The rest of the grain offering belongs to Aaron and his sons; it is a most holy part of the offerings made to the LORD by fire.

11" 'Every grain offering you bring to the LORD must be made without yeast, for you are not to burn any yeast or honey in an offering made to the LORD by fire. 12You may bring them to the LORD as an offering of the firstfruits, but they are not to be offered on the altar as a pleasing aroma. 13Season all your grain offerings with salt. Do not leave the salt of the covenant of your God out of your grain offerings; add salt to all your offerings.

14" 'If you bring a grain offering of firstfruits to the LORD, offer crushed heads of new grain roasted in the fire. 15Put oil and incense on it; it is a grain offering. 16The priest shall burn the memorial portion of the crushed grain and the oil, together with all the incense, as an offering made to the LORD by fire.

The Fellowship Offering

3 " 'If someone's offering is a fellowship offering,[a] and he offers an animal from the herd, whether male or female, he is to present before the LORD an animal without defect. 2He is to lay his hand on the head of his offering and slaughter it at the entrance to the Tent of Meeting. Then Aaron's sons the priests shall sprinkle the blood against the altar on all sides. 3From the fellowship offering he is to bring a sacrifice made to the LORD by fire: all the fat that covers the inner parts or is connected to them, 4both kidneys with the fat on them near the loins, and the covering of the liver, which he will remove with the kidneys. 5Then Aaron's sons are to burn it on the altar on top of the burnt offering that is on the burning wood, as an offering made by fire, an aroma pleasing to the LORD.

6" 'If he offers an animal from the flock as a fellowship offering to the LORD, he is to offer a male or female without defect. 7If he offers a lamb, he is to present it before the LORD. 8He is to lay his hand on the head of his offering and slaughter it in front of the Tent of Meeting. Then Aaron's sons shall sprinkle its blood against the altar on all sides. 9From the fellowship offering he is to bring a sacrifice made to the LORD by fire: its fat, the entire fat tail cut off close to the backbone, all the fat that covers the inner parts or is connected to them, 10both kidneys with the fat on them near the loins, and the covering of the liver, which he will remove with the kidneys. 11The priest shall burn them on the altar as food, an offering made to the LORD by fire.

12" 'If his offering is a goat, he is to present it before the LORD. 13He is to lay his hand on its head and slaughter it in front of the Tent of Meeting. Then Aaron's sons shall sprinkle its blood against the altar on all sides. 14From what he offers he is to make this offering to the LORD by fire: all the fat that covers the inner parts or is connected to them, 15both kidneys with the fat on them near the loins, and the covering of the liver, which he will remove with the kidneys. 16The priest shall burn them on the altar as food, an offering made by fire, a pleasing aroma. All the fat is the LORD's.

17" 'This is a lasting ordinance for the generations to come, wherever you live: You must not eat any fat or any blood.' "

The Sin Offering

4 The LORD said to Moses, 2"Say to the Israelites: 'When anyone sins unintentionally

[a]1 Traditionally *peace offering;* also in verses 3, 6 and 9

3:1–17 The peace offering (sometimes called the fellowship offering or the offering of thanksgiving) was brought to God as an expression of thanks for his blessings, healing or help in difficult times. The Hebrew word for peace (*shalom*) is a rich term that includes the ideas of physical health, emotional well-being, spiritual wholeness and material prosperity. The person bringing the peace offering was expressing faith and thanks for God's provision, praising him for a restoration of completeness and harmony with both God and other people. How can we thank God for the peace he has brought into our lives?

3:3–5 In ancient times, the fat portions of the animal were considered the very best parts. As with the other offerings, God asked that the choice parts be reserved for him. This is a clear reminder that we need to bring our best to God, completely committing our life to him no matter what the cost.

4:1–2 The sin offering was not a voluntary act of worship but a required response for sin. God takes sin very seriously and holds us accountable for dealing with it. Confession of sin is not just a voluntary activity; it is demanded by God and is a vital key to our continued spiritual growth.

4:1—5:13 The sin offering brought atonement and provided forgiveness for an individual's sin against God. In contrast, the guilt offering (5:14—6:7) brought atonement for acts committed against others. As we seek spiritual renewal, it is clear that we must start by seeking God. We must begin by seeing the truth that all sin is committed against God who created and loves those we may have wronged. We need to echo David's prayer, "Against you, you only, have I sinned and done what is evil in your sight" (Psalm 51:4). The consequences of our sins, however, may fall upon us or the people around us. Ultimately we must seek restoration with the people we have wronged and make any necessary restitution.

4:2 The meaning of the word for *sin* here is "to miss the mark." Romans 3:23 states "all have sinned and fall short of the glory of God." The Old and New Testament words for *sin* both emphasize the fact that sin keeps us from experiencing the fullness of life that God wants us to enjoy. All of us have sinned in some way. Through Jesus Christ, God has provided a means for our healing and restoration as we repent and receive God's forgiveness.

4:2–3, 13, 22, 27 The sin offering was not just for blatant, deliberate sins. It was primarily designed to

and does what is forbidden in any of the LORD's commands—

3" 'If the anointed priest sins, bringing guilt on the people, he must bring to the LORD a young bull without defect as a sin offering for the sin he has committed. 4He is to present the bull at the entrance to the Tent of Meeting before the LORD. He is to lay his hand on its head and slaughter it before the LORD. 5Then the anointed priest shall take some of the bull's blood and carry it into the Tent of Meeting. 6He is to dip his finger into the blood and sprinkle some of it seven times before the LORD, in front of the curtain of the sanctuary. 7The priest shall then put some of the blood on the horns of the altar of fragrant incense that is before the LORD in the Tent of Meeting. The rest of the bull's blood he shall pour out at the base of the altar of burnt offering at the entrance to the Tent of Meeting. 8He shall remove all the fat from the bull of the sin offering—the fat that covers the inner parts or is connected to them, 9both kidneys with the fat on them near the loins, and the covering of the liver, which he will remove with the kidneys— 10just as the fat is removed from the ox[a] sacrificed as a fellowship offering.[b] Then the priest shall burn them on the altar of burnt offering. 11But the hide of the bull and all its flesh, as well as the head and legs, the inner parts and offal— 12that is, all the rest of the bull—he must take outside the camp to a place ceremonially clean, where the ashes are thrown, and burn it in a wood fire on the ash heap.

13" 'If the whole Israelite community sins unintentionally and does what is forbidden in any of the LORD's commands, even though the community is unaware of the matter, they are guilty. 14When they become aware of the sin they committed, the assembly must bring a young bull as a sin offering and present it before the Tent of Meeting. 15The elders of the community are to lay their hands on the bull's head before the LORD, and the bull shall be slaughtered before the LORD. 16Then the anointed priest is to take some of the bull's blood into the Tent of Meeting. 17He shall dip his finger into the blood and sprinkle it before the LORD seven times in front of the curtain. 18He is to put some of the blood on the horns of the altar that is before the LORD in the Tent of Meeting. The rest of the blood he shall pour out at the base of the altar of burnt offering at the entrance to the Tent of Meeting. 19He shall remove all the fat from it and burn it on the altar, 20and do with this bull just as he did with the bull for the sin offering. In this way the priest will make atonement for them, and they will be forgiven. 21Then he shall take the bull outside the camp and burn it as he burned the first bull. This is the sin offering for the community.

22" 'When a leader sins unintentionally and does what is forbidden in any of the commands of the LORD his God, he is guilty. 23When he is made aware of the sin he committed, he must bring as his offering a male goat without defect. 24He is to lay his hand on the goat's head and slaughter it at the place where the burnt offering is slaughtered before the LORD. It is a sin offering. 25Then the priest shall take some of the blood of the sin offering with his finger and put it on the horns of the altar of burnt offering and pour out the rest of the blood at the base of the altar. 26He shall burn all the fat on the altar as he burned the fat of the fellowship offering. In this way the priest will make atonement for the man's sin, and he will be forgiven.

27" 'If a member of the community sins unintentionally and does what is forbidden in any of the LORD's commands, he is guilty. 28When he is made aware of the sin he committed, he must bring as his offering for the sin he committed a female goat without defect. 29He is to lay his hand on the head of the sin offering and slaughter it at the place of the burnt offering. 30Then the priest is to take some of the blood with his finger and put it on the horns of the altar of burnt offering and pour out the rest of the blood at the base of the altar. 31He shall remove all the fat, just as the fat is removed from the fellowship offering, and the priest shall burn it on the altar as an aroma pleasing to the LORD. In this way the priest will make atonement for him, and he will be forgiven.

32" 'If he brings a lamb as his sin offering, he is to bring a female without defect. 33He is to lay his hand on its head and slaughter it for a sin offering at the place where the burnt offering is slaughtered. 34Then the priest shall take some of the blood of the sin offering with his finger and put it on the horns of the altar of burnt offering and pour out the rest of the blood at the base of the altar. 35He shall remove all the fat, just as the fat is removed from the lamb of the fellowship offering, and the priest shall burn it on the altar on top of the offerings made

[a]10 The Hebrew word can include both male and female.
[b]10 Traditionally *peace offering;* also in verses 26, 31 and 35

deal with unintentional sins. All sins have great consequences—even the sins we aren't aware of. We sometimes sin unknowingly in ways that our parents have also sinned. Family sins often pass down the line. We need to prayerfully examine ourselves before God on a regular basis, asking him to show us our unintentional sins and repent of *all* sin in our lives—with no excuses. We can be thankful that God understands our human inclination toward sin and graciously provides ways for us to deal with it.

4:3 The sin offering was to be offered for the priests as much as for the rest of the Israelite people. Even Israel's high priest was not exempt from sin and its consequences. But the writer of Hebrews tells us that we have a sinless high priest, Jesus, who is able to sympathize with our weaknesses. We are to boldly approach God in prayer, that we may "receive mercy and find grace to help us in our time of need" (Hebrews 4:16).

to the LORD by fire. In this way the priest will make atonement for him for the sin he has committed, and he will be forgiven.

5 " 'If a person sins because he does not speak up when he hears a public charge to testify regarding something he has seen or learned about, he will be held responsible.

2 " 'Or if a person touches anything ceremonially unclean—whether the carcasses of unclean wild animals or of unclean livestock or of unclean creatures that move along the ground—even though he is unaware of it, he has become unclean and is guilty.

3 " 'Or if he touches human uncleanness—anything that would make him unclean—even though he is unaware of it, when he learns of it he will be guilty.

4 " 'Or if a person thoughtlessly takes an oath to do anything, whether good or evil—in any matter one might carelessly swear about—even though he is unaware of it, in any case when he learns of it he will be guilty.

5 " 'When anyone is guilty in any of these ways, he must confess in what way he has sinned 6 and, as a penalty for the sin he has committed, he must bring to the LORD a female lamb or goat from the flock as a sin offering; and the priest shall make atonement for him for his sin.

7 " 'If he cannot afford a lamb, he is to bring two doves or two young pigeons to the LORD as a penalty for his sin—one for a sin offering and the other for a burnt offering. 8 He is to bring them to the priest, who shall first offer the one for the sin offering. He is to wring its head from its neck, not severing it completely, 9 and is to sprinkle some of the blood of the sin offering against the side of the altar; the rest of the blood must be drained out at the base of the altar. It is a sin offering. 10 The priest shall then offer the other as a burnt offering in the prescribed way and make atonement for him for the sin he has committed, and he will be forgiven.

11 " 'If, however, he cannot afford two doves or two young pigeons, he is to bring as an offering for his sin a tenth of an ephah[a] of fine flour for a sin offering. He must not put oil or incense on it, because it is a sin offering. 12 He is to bring it to the priest, who shall take a handful of it as a memorial portion and burn it on the altar on top of the offerings made to the LORD by fire. It is a sin offering. 13 In this way the priest will make atonement for him for any of these sins he has committed, and he will be forgiven. The rest of the offering will belong to the priest, as in the case of the grain offering.' "

The Guilt Offering

14 The LORD said to Moses: 15 "When a person commits a violation and sins unintentionally in regard to any of the LORD's holy things, he is to bring to the LORD as a penalty a ram from the flock, one without defect and of the proper value in silver, according to the sanctuary shekel.[b] It is a guilt offering. 16 He must make restitution for what he has failed to do in regard to the holy things, add a fifth of the value to that and give it all to the priest, who will make atonement for him with the ram as a guilt offering, and he will be forgiven.

17 "If a person sins and does what is forbidden in any of the LORD's commands, even though he does not know it, he is guilty and will be held responsible. 18 He is to bring to the priest as a guilt offering a ram from the flock, one without defect and of the proper value. In this way the priest will make atonement for him for the wrong he has committed unintentionally, and he will be forgiven. 19 It is a guilt offering; he has been guilty of[c] wrongdoing against the LORD."

6 The LORD said to Moses: 2 "If anyone sins and is unfaithful to the LORD by deceiving his neighbor about something entrusted to him or left in his care or stolen, or if he cheats him, 3 or if he finds lost property and lies about it, or if he swears falsely, or if he commits any such sin that people may do— 4 when he thus sins and becomes guilty, he must return what he has stolen or taken by extortion, or what was entrusted to him, or the lost property he found, 5 or whatever it was he swore falsely about. He must make restitution in full, add a fifth of the value to it and give it all to the owner on the day he presents his guilt offering. 6 And as a penalty he must bring to the priest, that is, to the LORD, his guilt offering, a ram from the flock, one without defect and of the proper value. 7 In this way the priest will make atonement for him before the LORD, and he will be forgiven for any of these things he did that made him guilty."

The Burnt Offering

8 The LORD said to Moses: 9 "Give Aaron and his sons this command: 'These are the regulations for the burnt offering: The burnt offering is to remain on the altar hearth throughout the night, till morning, and the fire must be kept burning on the altar. 10 The priest shall then put on his linen clothes, with linen undergarments next to his body, and shall remove the ashes of the burnt offering that the fire has consumed on

[a] *11* That is, probably about 2 quarts (about 2 liters)
[b] *15* That is, about 2/5 ounce (about 11.5 grams)
[c] *19* Or *has made full expiation for his*

5:14—6:7 The guilt offering was a special kind of sin offering. It was offered by a wrongdoer to receive forgiveness from God and to make restitution for the pain or loss suffered by someone else. This offering held the wrongdoer accountable for sinful actions and paved the way for reconciliation with the wronged party. We, too, must consider the effects of our sins on others. We must seek reconciliation with God by asking for his forgiveness and then, if possible, make restitution with the people we have wronged.

the altar and place them beside the altar. 11Then
he is to take off these clothes and put on others,
and carry the ashes outside the camp to a place
that is ceremonially clean. 12The fire on the altar
must be kept burning; it must not go out. Every
morning the priest is to add firewood and arrange the burnt offering on the fire and burn the
fat of the fellowship offerings[a] on it. 13The fire
must be kept burning on the altar continuously;
it must not go out.

The Grain Offering

14" 'These are the regulations for the grain
offering: Aaron's sons are to bring it before the
LORD, in front of the altar. 15The priest is to take
a handful of fine flour and oil, together with all
the incense on the grain offering, and burn the
memorial portion on the altar as an aroma
pleasing to the LORD. 16Aaron and his sons shall
eat the rest of it, but it is to be eaten without
yeast in a holy place; they are to eat it in the
courtyard of the Tent of Meeting. 17It must not
be baked with yeast; I have given it as their
share of the offerings made to me by fire. Like
the sin offering and the guilt offering, it is most
holy. 18Any male descendant of Aaron may eat
it. It is his regular share of the offerings made to
the LORD by fire for the generations to come.
Whatever touches them will become holy.[b] ' "

19The LORD also said to Moses, 20"This is the
offering Aaron and his sons are to bring to the
LORD on the day he[c] is anointed: a tenth of an
ephah[d] of fine flour as a regular grain offering,
half of it in the morning and half in the evening. 21Prepare it with oil on a griddle; bring
it well-mixed and present the grain offering
broken[e] in pieces as an aroma pleasing to
the LORD. 22The son who is to succeed him as
anointed priest shall prepare it. It is the LORD's
regular share and is to be burned completely.
23Every grain offering of a priest shall be burned
completely; it must not be eaten."

The Sin Offering

24The LORD said to Moses, 25"Say to Aaron
and his sons: 'These are the regulations for the
sin offering: The sin offering is to be slaughtered
before the LORD in the place the burnt offering
is slaughtered; it is most holy. 26The priest who
offers it shall eat it; it is to be eaten in a holy
place, in the courtyard of the Tent of Meeting.
27Whatever touches any of the flesh will become holy, and if any of the blood is spattered
on a garment, you must wash it in a holy place.
28The clay pot the meat is cooked in must be
broken; but if it is cooked in a bronze pot, the
pot is to be scoured and rinsed with water.
29Any male in a priest's family may eat it; it is
most holy. 30But any sin offering whose blood
is brought into the Tent of Meeting to make
atonement in the Holy Place must not be eaten;
it must be burned.

The Guilt Offering

7 " 'These are the regulations for the guilt
offering, which is most holy: 2The guilt offering is to be slaughtered in the place where the
burnt offering is slaughtered, and its blood is to
be sprinkled against the altar on all sides. 3All
its fat shall be offered: the fat tail and the fat
that covers the inner parts, 4both kidneys with
the fat on them near the loins, and the covering
of the liver, which is to be removed with the
kidneys. 5The priest shall burn them on the altar as an offering made to the LORD by fire. It is
a guilt offering. 6Any male in a priest's family
may eat it, but it must be eaten in a holy place;
it is most holy.

7" 'The same law applies to both the sin offering and the guilt offering: They belong to the
priest who makes atonement with them. 8The
priest who offers a burnt offering for anyone
may keep its hide for himself. 9Every grain offering baked in an oven or cooked in a pan or on
a griddle belongs to the priest who offers it,
10and every grain offering, whether mixed with
oil or dry, belongs equally to all the sons of
Aaron.

The Fellowship Offering

11" 'These are the regulations for the fellowship offering[f] a person may present to the
LORD:

12" 'If he offers it as an expression of thankfulness, then along with this thank offering he
is to offer cakes of bread made without yeast
and mixed with oil, wafers made without yeast
and spread with oil, and cakes of fine flour well-
kneaded and mixed with oil. 13Along with his
fellowship offering of thanksgiving he is to
present an offering with cakes of bread made
with yeast. 14He is to bring one of each kind as
an offering, a contribution to the LORD; it belongs to the priest who sprinkles the blood of
the fellowship offerings. 15The meat of his fellowship offering of thanksgiving must be eaten
on the day it is offered; he must leave none of
it till morning.

16" 'If, however, his offering is the result of
a vow or is a freewill offering, the sacrifice shall
be eaten on the day he offers it, but anything

[a] 12 Traditionally *peace offerings* [b] 18 Or *Whoever touches them must be holy*; similarly in verse 27 [c] 20 Or *each* [d] 20 That is, probably about 2 quarts (about 2 liters) [e] 21 The meaning of the Hebrew for this word is uncertain. [f] 11 Traditionally *peace offering*; also in verses 13-37

7:12–13 The most common type of peace offering was the thanksgiving offering. It involved the presentation of various kinds of unleavened and leavened cakes, some of which were sacrificed and some eaten in a communal meal. The Israelite believer learned from this the importance of a public expression of thanks to God. God wants us, too, to praise him openly before others. This public expression of gratitude to God will not only enhance our spiritual renewal but can also be a step toward helping others in their spiritual growth.

left over may be eaten on the next day. [17]Any meat of the sacrifice left over till the third day must be burned up. [18]If any meat of the fellowship offering is eaten on the third day, it will not be accepted. It will not be credited to the one who offered it, for it is impure; the person who eats any of it will be held responsible.

[19]" 'Meat that touches anything ceremonially unclean must not be eaten; it must be burned up. As for other meat, anyone ceremonially clean may eat it. [20]But if anyone who is unclean eats any meat of the fellowship offering belonging to the LORD, that person must be cut off from his people. [21]If anyone touches something unclean—whether human uncleanness or an unclean animal or any unclean, detestable thing—and then eats any of the meat of the fellowship offering belonging to the LORD, that person must be cut off from his people.' "

Eating Fat and Blood Forbidden

[22]The LORD said to Moses, [23]"Say to the Israelites: 'Do not eat any of the fat of cattle, sheep or goats. [24]The fat of an animal found dead or torn by wild animals may be used for any other purpose, but you must not eat it. [25]Anyone who eats the fat of an animal from which an offering by fire may be[a] made to the LORD must be cut off from his people. [26]And wherever you live, you must not eat the blood of any bird or animal. [27]If anyone eats blood, that person must be cut off from his people.' "

The Priests' Share

[28]The LORD said to Moses, [29]"Say to the Israelites: 'Anyone who brings a fellowship offering to the LORD is to bring part of it as his sacrifice to the LORD. [30]With his own hands he is to bring the offering made to the LORD by fire; he is to bring the fat, together with the breast, and wave the breast before the LORD as a wave offering. [31]The priest shall burn the fat on the altar, but the breast belongs to Aaron and his sons. [32]You are to give the right thigh of your fellowship offerings to the priest as a contribution. [33]The son of Aaron who offers the blood and the fat of the fellowship offering shall have the right thigh as his share. [34]From the fellowship offerings of the Israelites, I have taken the breast that is waved and the thigh that is presented and have given them to Aaron the priest and his sons as their regular share from the Israelites.' "

[35]This is the portion of the offerings made to the LORD by fire that were allotted to Aaron and his sons on the day they were presented to serve the LORD as priests. [36]On the day they were anointed, the LORD commanded that the Israelites give this to them as their regular share for the generations to come.

[37]These, then, are the regulations for the burnt offering, the grain offering, the sin offering, the guilt offering, the ordination offering and the fellowship offering, [38]which the LORD gave Moses on Mount Sinai on the day he commanded the Israelites to bring their offerings to the LORD, in the Desert of Sinai.

The Ordination of Aaron and His Sons

8 The LORD said to Moses, [2]"Bring Aaron and his sons, their garments, the anointing oil, the bull for the sin offering, the two rams and the basket containing bread made without yeast, [3]and gather the entire assembly at the entrance to the Tent of Meeting." [4]Moses did as the LORD commanded him, and the assembly gathered at the entrance to the Tent of Meeting.

[5]Moses said to the assembly, "This is what the LORD has commanded to be done." [6]Then Moses brought Aaron and his sons forward and washed them with water. [7]He put the tunic on Aaron, tied the sash around him, clothed him with the robe and put the ephod on him. He also tied the ephod to him by its skillfully woven waistband; so it was fastened on him. [8]He placed the breastpiece on him and put the Urim and Thummim in the breastpiece. [9]Then he placed the turban on Aaron's head and set the gold plate, the sacred diadem, on the front of it, as the LORD commanded Moses.

[10]Then Moses took the anointing oil and anointed the tabernacle and everything in it, and so consecrated them. [11]He sprinkled some of the oil on the altar seven times, anointing the altar and all its utensils and the basin with its stand, to consecrate them. [12]He poured some of the anointing oil on Aaron's head and anointed him to consecrate him. [13]Then he brought Aaron's sons forward, put tunics on them, tied sashes around them and put headbands on them, as the LORD commanded Moses.

[14]He then presented the bull for the sin offering, and Aaron and his sons laid their hands on its head. [15]Moses slaughtered the bull and took some of the blood, and with his finger he put it on all the horns of the altar to purify the altar. He poured out the rest of the blood at the base of the altar. So he consecrated it to make atonement for it. [16]Moses also took all the fat around the inner parts, the covering of the liver, and both kidneys and their fat, and burned it on the altar. [17]But the bull with its hide and its flesh

[a]25 Or *fire is*

8:1–4 God instituted the priesthood because he desired to have fellowship with his people. The priests of Israel entered into God's holy presence with the people's requests and served as mediators between God and the people. But the mediation of the priesthood was also a stern reminder that God is an awesome and holy God who cannot be approached lightly. Since we as believers are called a "holy priesthood" (1 Peter 2:5), we may come boldly before God, offering him our life as a spiritual sacrifice. But we must be careful to approach him as a holy God and not take our sin lightly.

and its offal he burned up outside the camp, as the LORD commanded Moses.

18He then presented the ram for the burnt offering, and Aaron and his sons laid their hands on its head. 19Then Moses slaughtered the ram and sprinkled the blood against the altar on all sides. 20He cut the ram into pieces and burned the head, the pieces and the fat. 21He washed the inner parts and the legs with water and burned the whole ram on the altar as a burnt offering, a pleasing aroma, an offering made to the LORD by fire, as the LORD commanded Moses.

22He then presented the other ram, the ram for the ordination, and Aaron and his sons laid their hands on its head. 23Moses slaughtered the ram and took some of its blood and put it on the lobe of Aaron's right ear, on the thumb of his right hand and on the big toe of his right foot. 24Moses also brought Aaron's sons forward and put some of the blood on the lobes of their right ears, on the thumbs of their right hands and on the big toes of their right feet. Then he sprinkled blood against the altar on all sides. 25He took the fat, the fat tail, all the fat around the inner parts, the covering of the liver, both kidneys and their fat and the right thigh. 26Then from the basket of bread made without yeast, which was before the LORD, he took a cake of bread, and one made with oil, and a wafer; he put these on the fat portions and on the right thigh. 27He put all these in the hands of Aaron and his sons and waved them before the LORD as a wave offering. 28Then Moses took them from their hands and burned them on the altar on top of the burnt offering as an ordination offering, a pleasing aroma, an offering made to the LORD by fire. 29He also took the breast—Moses' share of the ordination ram—and waved it before the LORD as a wave offering, as the LORD commanded Moses.

30Then Moses took some of the anointing oil and some of the blood from the altar and sprinkled them on Aaron and his garments and on his sons and their garments. So he consecrated Aaron and his garments and his sons and their garments.

31Moses then said to Aaron and his sons, "Cook the meat at the entrance to the Tent of Meeting and eat it there with the bread from the basket of ordination offerings, as I commanded, saying,[a] 'Aaron and his sons are to eat it.' 32Then burn up the rest of the meat and the bread. 33Do not leave the entrance to the Tent of Meeting for seven days, until the days of your ordination are completed, for your ordination will last seven days. 34What has been done today was commanded by the LORD to make atonement for you. 35You must stay at the entrance to the Tent of Meeting day and night for seven days and do what the LORD requires, so you will not die; for that is what I have been commanded." 36So Aaron and his sons did everything the LORD commanded through Moses.

The Priests Begin Their Ministry

9 On the eighth day Moses summoned Aaron and his sons and the elders of Israel. 2He said to Aaron, "Take a bull calf for your sin offering and a ram for your burnt offering, both without defect, and present them before the LORD. 3Then say to the Israelites: 'Take a male goat for a sin offering, a calf and a lamb—both a year old and without defect—for a burnt offering, 4and an ox[b] and a ram for a fellowship offering[c] to sacrifice before the LORD, together with a grain offering mixed with oil. For today the LORD will appear to you.' "

5They took the things Moses commanded to the front of the Tent of Meeting, and the entire assembly came near and stood before the LORD. 6Then Moses said, "This is what the LORD has commanded you to do, so that the glory of the LORD may appear to you."

7Moses said to Aaron, "Come to the altar and sacrifice your sin offering and your burnt offering and make atonement for yourself and the people; sacrifice the offering that is for the people and make atonement for them, as the LORD has commanded."

8So Aaron came to the altar and slaughtered the calf as a sin offering for himself. 9His sons brought the blood to him, and he dipped his finger into the blood and put it on the horns of the altar; the rest of the blood he poured out at

[a]31 Or *I was commanded:* [b]4 The Hebrew word can include both male and female; also in verses 18 and 19. [c]4 Traditionally *peace offering;* also in verses 18 and 22

8:30–36 The priests were sprinkled with blood from the sacrifices. This symbolized their cleansing and reconciliation to God through the sacrificial death of the animal offering. The high price for their sin—the death of a living animal—would have been an acute reminder of the importance of their obedience. The apostle Peter described believers as those cleansed by Christ's blood (1 Peter 1:2). Because of the high price paid for our sins—the sacrificial death of Christ on the cross—we ought to live a life of obedience to God's Word.

9:7 Because Aaron was the high priest, he offered sacrifices to make atonement for his sins and those of the people. But Jesus Christ, our high priest, does more than offer sacrifices for us; he actually became our sin offering. He made all animal sacrifices obsolete by offering himself on the cross as the perfect sacrifice. By giving himself sacrificially for others, he set a clear example for us to give ourselves to others as well.

9:8–24 This account of Aaron's sacrifices reflects the actual order in which the various sacrifices were offered by an individual. The sin offering was first, showing the priority of confession and cleansing from sin before God. The following burnt or grain offering represented the worshiper's obedience in submitting their life to God. The peace offering then expressed gratitude for a continuing walk with God. Similarly, one key to our spiritual renewal must be the recognition that we need God's help. As we seek God, surrender our lives to him and trust Jesus Christ as our perfect sacrifice, we will experience ongoing fellowship with God, accountability for sin and spiritual renewal. Our spiritual growth will continue as we utilize these keys to sustain the gains we have made.

the base of the altar. 10On the altar he burned the fat, the kidneys and the covering of the liver from the sin offering, as the LORD commanded Moses; 11the flesh and the hide he burned up outside the camp.

12Then he slaughtered the burnt offering. His sons handed him the blood, and he sprinkled it against the altar on all sides. 13They handed him the burnt offering piece by piece, including the head, and he burned them on the altar. 14He washed the inner parts and the legs and burned them on top of the burnt offering on the altar.

15Aaron then brought the offering that was for the people. He took the goat for the people's sin offering and slaughtered it and offered it for a sin offering as he did with the first one.

16He brought the burnt offering and offered it in the prescribed way. 17He also brought the grain offering, took a handful of it and burned it on the altar in addition to the morning's burnt offering.

18He slaughtered the ox and the ram as the fellowship offering for the people. His sons handed him the blood, and he sprinkled it against the altar on all sides. 19But the fat portions of the ox and the ram—the fat tail, the layer of fat, the kidneys and the covering of the liver— 20these they laid on the breasts, and then Aaron burned the fat on the altar. 21Aaron waved the breasts and the right thigh before the LORD as a wave offering, as Moses commanded.

22Then Aaron lifted his hands toward the people and blessed them. And having sacrificed the sin offering, the burnt offering and the fellowship offering, he stepped down.

23Moses and Aaron then went into the Tent of Meeting. When they came out, they blessed the people; and the glory of the LORD appeared to all the people. 24Fire came out from the presence of the LORD and consumed the burnt offering and the fat portions on the altar. And when all the people saw it, they shouted for joy and fell facedown.

The Death of Nadab and Abihu

10 Aaron's sons Nadab and Abihu took their censers, put fire in them and added incense; and they offered unauthorized fire before the LORD, contrary to his command. 2So fire came out from the presence of the LORD and consumed them, and they died before the LORD. 3Moses then said to Aaron, "This is what the LORD spoke of when he said:

" 'Among those who approach me
  I will show myself holy;
in the sight of all the people
  I will be honored.' "

Aaron remained silent.

4Moses summoned Mishael and Elzaphan, sons of Aaron's uncle Uzziel, and said to them, "Come here; carry your cousins outside the camp, away from the front of the sanctuary." 5So they came and carried them, still in their tunics, outside the camp, as Moses ordered.

6Then Moses said to Aaron and his sons Eleazar and Ithamar, "Do not let your hair become unkempt,[a] and do not tear your clothes, or you will die and the LORD will be angry with the whole community. But your relatives, all the house of Israel, may mourn for those the LORD has destroyed by fire. 7Do not leave the entrance to the Tent of Meeting or you will die, because the LORD's anointing oil is on you." So they did as Moses said.

8Then the LORD said to Aaron, 9"You and your sons are not to drink wine or other fermented drink whenever you go into the Tent of Meeting, or you will die. This is a lasting ordinance for the generations to come. 10You must distinguish between the holy and the common, between the unclean and the clean, 11and you must teach the Israelites all the decrees the LORD has given them through Moses."

12Moses said to Aaron and his remaining sons, Eleazar and Ithamar, "Take the grain offering left over from the offerings made to the LORD by fire and eat it prepared without yeast beside the altar, for it is most holy. 13Eat it in a holy place, because it is your share and your sons' share of the offerings made to the LORD by fire; for so I have been commanded. 14But you and your sons and your daughters may eat the breast that was waved and the thigh that was presented. Eat them in a ceremonially clean place; they have been given to you and your children as your share of the Israelites' fellowship offerings.[b] 15The thigh that was presented and the breast that was waved must be brought with the fat portions of the offerings made by

[a]6 Or *Do not uncover your heads* [b]14 Traditionally *peace offerings*

10:1–3 The sin and resulting swift judgment of Aaron's two eldest sons indicates the greater responsibility of those who occupy positions of leadership and authority. Although the specifics of their sin are not explained in Scripture, it is likely that their wrong actions proceeded from wrong attitudes. Perhaps they believed that as leaders they were exempt from the moral law. While God's grace and long-suffering may often spare us from immediate judgment, we should be aware that we are still accountable to him. When we are irresponsible and disobedient to God's plan, the consequences will be grave.

10:8–9 This passage about the use of wine or other intoxicating beverages illustrates the importance of self-control on the part of the priests. Because of the importance of their work and example, God required certain boundaries and evidences of self-control. Alcohol would affect the priests' abilities to carry out the task God had called them to do. This illustrates our need for self-control and boundaries as we seek to carry an effective and positive testimony of God's love to others.

10:8–11 First, Aaron was told how to act (10:8–10); then he was told what to teach (10:11). This illustrates an important principle: Actions speak louder than words. God calls us to live in a way that will, by example, reinforce what we teach others. If we fail to live by what we teach, we might as well remain silent.

fire, to be waved before the LORD as a wave offering. This will be the regular share for you and your children, as the LORD has commanded."

16When Moses inquired about the goat of the sin offering and found that it had been burned up, he was angry with Eleazar and Ithamar, Aaron's remaining sons, and asked, 17"Why didn't you eat the sin offering in the sanctuary area? It is most holy; it was given to you to take away the guilt of the community by making atonement for them before the LORD. 18Since its blood was not taken into the Holy Place, you should have eaten the goat in the sanctuary area, as I commanded."

19Aaron replied to Moses, "Today they sacrificed their sin offering and their burnt offering before the LORD, but such things as this have happened to me. Would the LORD have been pleased if I had eaten the sin offering today?" 20When Moses heard this, he was satisfied.

Clean and Unclean Food

11 The LORD said to Moses and Aaron, 2"Say to the Israelites: 'Of all the animals that live on land, these are the ones you may eat: 3You may eat any animal that has a split hoof completely divided and that chews the cud.

4" 'There are some that only chew the cud or only have a split hoof, but you must not eat them. The camel, though it chews the cud, does not have a split hoof; it is ceremonially unclean for you. 5The coney,[a] though it chews the cud, does not have a split hoof; it is unclean for you. 6The rabbit, though it chews the cud, does not have a split hoof; it is unclean for you. 7And the pig, though it has a split hoof completely divided, does not chew the cud; it is unclean for you. 8You must not eat their meat or touch their carcasses; they are unclean for you.

9" 'Of all the creatures living in the water of the seas and the streams, you may eat any that have fins and scales. 10But all creatures in the seas or streams that do not have fins and scales—whether among all the swarming things or among all the other living creatures in the water—you are to detest. 11And since you are to detest them, you must not eat their meat and you must detest their carcasses. 12Anything living in the water that does not have fins and scales is to be detestable to you.

13" 'These are the birds you are to detest and not eat because they are detestable: the eagle, the vulture, the black vulture, 14the red kite, any kind of black kite, 15any kind of raven, 16the horned owl, the screech owl, the gull, any kind of hawk, 17the little owl, the cormorant, the great owl, 18the white owl, the desert owl, the osprey, 19the stork, any kind of heron, the hoopoe and the bat.[b]

20" 'All flying insects that walk on all fours are to be detestable to you. 21There are, however, some winged creatures that walk on all fours that you may eat: those that have jointed legs for hopping on the ground. 22Of these you may eat any kind of locust, katydid, cricket or grasshopper. 23But all other winged creatures that have four legs you are to detest.

24" 'You will make yourselves unclean by these; whoever touches their carcasses will be unclean till evening. 25Whoever picks up one of their carcasses must wash his clothes, and he will be unclean till evening.

26" 'Every animal that has a split hoof not completely divided or that does not chew the cud is unclean for you; whoever touches ⌊the carcass of⌋ any of them will be unclean. 27Of all the animals that walk on all fours, those that walk on their paws are unclean for you; whoever touches their carcasses will be unclean till evening. 28Anyone who picks up their carcasses must wash his clothes, and he will be unclean till evening. They are unclean for you.

29" 'Of the animals that move about on the ground, these are unclean for you: the weasel, the rat, any kind of great lizard, 30the gecko, the monitor lizard, the wall lizard, the skink and the chameleon. 31Of all those that move along the ground, these are unclean for you. Whoever touches them when they are dead will be unclean till evening. 32When one of them dies and falls on something, that article, whatever its use, will be unclean, whether it is made of wood, cloth, hide or sackcloth. Put it in water; it will be unclean till evening, and then it will be clean. 33If one of them falls into a clay pot, everything in it will be unclean, and you must break the pot. 34Any food that could be eaten but has water on it from such a pot is unclean, and any liquid that could be drunk from it is unclean. 35Anything that one of their carcasses falls on becomes unclean; an oven or cooking pot must be broken up. They are unclean, and you are to regard them as unclean. 36A spring, however, or a cistern for collecting water remains clean, but anyone who touches one of these carcasses is unclean. 37If a carcass falls on any seeds that are to be planted, they remain clean. 38But if water has been put on the seed and a carcass falls on it, it is unclean for you.

39" 'If an animal that you are allowed to eat dies, anyone who touches the carcass will be

[a] 5 That is, the hyrax or rock badger [b] 19 The precise identification of some of the birds, insects and animals in this chapter is uncertain.

11:1–47 The elaborate dietary laws in this section illustrate the fact that God's relationship with his people extends even to the practical areas of everyday living. While we may not be bound today by the specifics of these dietary standards, we know that God is just as interested in the details of our lives. If our eating or drinking leads to excess, abuse or poor health, God holds us accountable to deal with the problem. Personal holiness relates even to the mundane areas of life.

unclean till evening. 40Anyone who eats some of the carcass must wash his clothes, and he will be unclean till evening. Anyone who picks up the carcass must wash his clothes, and he will be unclean till evening.

41" 'Every creature that moves about on the ground is detestable; it is not to be eaten. 42You are not to eat any creature that moves about on the ground, whether it moves on its belly or walks on all fours or on many feet; it is detestable. 43Do not defile yourselves by any of these creatures. Do not make yourselves unclean by means of them or be made unclean by them. 44I am the LORD your God; consecrate yourselves and be holy, because I am holy. Do not make yourselves unclean by any creature that moves about on the ground. 45I am the LORD who brought you up out of Egypt to be your God; therefore be holy, because I am holy.

46" 'These are the regulations concerning animals, birds, every living thing that moves in the water and every creature that moves about on the ground. 47You must distinguish between the unclean and the clean, between living creatures that may be eaten and those that may not be eaten.' "

Purification After Childbirth

12 The LORD said to Moses, 2"Say to the Israelites: 'A woman who becomes pregnant and gives birth to a son will be ceremonially unclean for seven days, just as she is unclean during her monthly period. 3On the eighth day the boy is to be circumcised. 4Then the woman must wait thirty-three days to be purified from her bleeding. She must not touch anything sacred or go to the sanctuary until the days of her purification are over. 5If she gives birth to a daughter, for two weeks the woman will be unclean, as during her period. Then she must wait sixty-six days to be purified from her bleeding.

6" 'When the days of her purification for a son or daughter are over, she is to bring to the priest at the entrance to the Tent of Meeting a year-old lamb for a burnt offering and a young pigeon or a dove for a sin offering. 7He shall offer them before the LORD to make atonement for her, and then she will be ceremonially clean from her flow of blood.

" 'These are the regulations for the woman who gives birth to a boy or a girl. 8If she cannot afford a lamb, she is to bring two doves or two young pigeons, one for a burnt offering and the other for a sin offering. In this way the priest will make atonement for her, and she will be clean.' "

Regulations About Infectious Skin Diseases

13 The LORD said to Moses and Aaron, 2"When anyone has a swelling or a rash or a bright spot on his skin that may become an infectious skin disease,[a] he must be brought to Aaron the priest or to one of his sons[b] who is a priest. 3The priest is to examine the sore on his skin, and if the hair in the sore has turned white and the sore appears to be more than skin deep,[c] it is an infectious skin disease. When the priest examines him, he shall pronounce him ceremonially unclean. 4If the spot on his skin is white but does not appear to be more than skin deep and the hair in it has not turned white, the priest is to put the infected person in isolation for seven days. 5On the seventh day the priest is to examine him, and if he sees that the sore is unchanged and has not spread in the skin, he is to keep him in isolation another seven days. 6On the seventh day the priest is to examine him again, and if the sore has faded and has not spread in the skin, the priest shall pronounce him clean; it is only a rash. The man must wash his clothes, and he will be clean. 7But if the rash does spread in his skin after he has shown himself to the priest to be pronounced clean, he must appear before the priest again. 8The priest is to examine him, and if the rash has spread in the skin, he shall pronounce him unclean; it is an infectious disease.

9"When anyone has an infectious skin disease, he must be brought to the priest. 10The priest is to examine him, and if there is a white swelling in the skin that has turned the hair

[a]2 Traditionally *leprosy;* the Hebrew word was used for various diseases affecting the skin—not necessarily leprosy; also elsewhere in this chapter. [b]2 Or *descendants*
[c]3 Or *be lower than the rest of the skin;* also elsewhere in this chapter

---

11:44 What does it mean to be holy? It doesn't mean just to have a pious attitude toward God. The Hebrew word literally means "to be set apart," both unto God and from sin. This chapter emphasizes the aspect of being set apart unto God. These dietary laws and other guidelines for daily living gave the Israelites a unique identity as God's people. God also calls us to lives of holiness, lives that clearly reflect God's standards.

11:44–45 God forbade the Israelites to touch crawling creatures. God may have given this law for logical reasons, such as a concern for his people's health. It seems, however, that many of these laws were given for theological reasons as well, so the Israelites might be different from the surrounding nations—set apart or "holy" unto God. While God may sometimes show us a logical reason for doing what he says, this should not be our primary motivation for obedience. We are to obey him because he calls us to be different—set apart or "holy"—just as he is holy. We can trust that his plan will lead us to discover his best for us, whether what he asks seems logical to us or not.

13:1—15:33 These detailed health regulations excluded many Israelites from the larger society. They were banned from fellowship with others for being "ceremonially unclean." Lepers and prostitutes were automatically labeled "unclean" according to the law, and were thus ostracized. This fact should help us appreciate even more the compassionate heart of Jesus Christ. He healed lepers and the woman who had been slowly bleeding for years; he talked with prostitutes and other outcasts. He cared most about the needy, the unclean. He considered it his work to show them the way to forgiveness and healing.

white and if there is raw flesh in the swelling, 11it is a chronic skin disease and the priest shall pronounce him unclean. He is not to put him in isolation, because he is already unclean.

12"If the disease breaks out all over his skin and, so far as the priest can see, it covers all the skin of the infected person from head to foot, 13the priest is to examine him, and if the disease has covered his whole body, he shall pronounce that person clean. Since it has all turned white, he is clean. 14But whenever raw flesh appears on him, he will be unclean. 15When the priest sees the raw flesh, he shall pronounce him unclean. The raw flesh is unclean; he has an infectious disease. 16Should the raw flesh change and turn white, he must go to the priest. 17The priest is to examine him, and if the sores have turned white, the priest shall pronounce the infected person clean; then he will be clean.

18"When someone has a boil on his skin and it heals, 19and in the place where the boil was, a white swelling or reddish-white spot appears, he must present himself to the priest. 20The priest is to examine it, and if it appears to be more than skin deep and the hair in it has turned white, the priest shall pronounce him unclean. It is an infectious skin disease that has broken out where the boil was. 21But if, when the priest examines it, there is no white hair in it and it is not more than skin deep and has faded, then the priest is to put him in isolation for seven days. 22If it is spreading in the skin, the priest shall pronounce him unclean; it is infectious. 23But if the spot is unchanged and has not spread, it is only a scar from the boil, and the priest shall pronounce him clean.

24"When someone has a burn on his skin and a reddish-white or white spot appears in the raw flesh of the burn, 25the priest is to examine the spot, and if the hair in it has turned white, and it appears to be more than skin deep, it is an infectious disease that has broken out in the burn. The priest shall pronounce him unclean; it is an infectious skin disease. 26But if the priest examines it and there is no white hair in the spot and if it is not more than skin deep and has faded, then the priest is to put him in isolation for seven days. 27On the seventh day the priest is to examine him, and if it is spreading in the skin, the priest shall pronounce him unclean; it is an infectious skin disease. 28If, however, the spot is unchanged and has not spread in the skin but has faded, it is a swelling from the burn, and the priest shall pronounce him clean; it is only a scar from the burn.

29"If a man or woman has a sore on the head or on the chin, 30the priest is to examine the sore, and if it appears to be more than skin deep and the hair in it is yellow and thin, the priest shall pronounce that person unclean; it is an itch, an infectious disease of the head or chin. 31But if, when the priest examines this kind of sore, it does not seem to be more than skin deep and there is no black hair in it, then the priest is to put the infected person in isolation for seven days. 32On the seventh day the priest is to examine the sore, and if the itch has not spread and there is no yellow hair in it and it does not appear to be more than skin deep, 33he must be shaved except for the diseased area, and the priest is to keep him in isolation another seven days. 34On the seventh day the priest is to examine the itch, and if it has not spread in the skin and appears to be no more than skin deep, the priest shall pronounce him clean. He must wash his clothes, and he will be clean. 35But if the itch does spread in the skin after he is pronounced clean, 36the priest is to examine him, and if the itch has spread in the skin, the priest does not need to look for yellow hair; the person is unclean. 37If, however, in his judgment it is unchanged and black hair has grown in it, the itch is healed. He is clean, and the priest shall pronounce him clean.

38"When a man or woman has white spots on the skin, 39the priest is to examine them, and if the spots are dull white, it is a harmless rash that has broken out on the skin; that person is clean.

40"When a man has lost his hair and is bald, he is clean. 41If he has lost his hair from the front of his scalp and has a bald forehead, he is clean. 42But if he has a reddish-white sore on his bald head or forehead, it is an infectious disease breaking out on his head or forehead. 43The priest is to examine him, and if the swollen sore on his head or forehead is reddish-white like an infectious skin disease, 44the man is diseased and is unclean. The priest shall pronounce him unclean because of the sore on his head.

45"The person with such an infectious disease must wear torn clothes, let his hair be unkempt,[a] cover the lower part of his face and cry out, 'Unclean! Unclean!' 46As long as he has the infection he remains unclean. He must live alone; he must live outside the camp.

Regulations About Mildew

47"If any clothing is contaminated with mildew—any woolen or linen clothing, 48any woven or knitted material of linen or wool, any leather or anything made of leather— 49and if the contamination in the clothing, or leather, or woven or knitted material, or any leather article, is greenish or reddish, it is a spreading mildew and must be shown to the priest. 50The priest is to examine the mildew and isolate the affected article for seven days. 51On the seventh day he is to examine it, and if the mildew has spread in the clothing, or the woven or knitted material, or the leather, whatever its use, it is a destructive mildew; the article is unclean. 52He must burn up the clothing, or the woven or knitted material of wool or linen, or any leather article that

[a]45 Or *clothes, uncover his head*

has the contamination in it, because the mildew
is destructive; the article must be burned up.
53 "But if, when the priest examines it, the
mildew has not spread in the clothing, or the
woven or knitted material, or the leather article,
54 he shall order that the contaminated article be
washed. Then he is to isolate it for another sev-
en days. 55 After the affected article has been
washed, the priest is to examine it, and if the
mildew has not changed its appearance, even
though it has not spread, it is unclean. Burn it
with fire, whether the mildew has affected one
side or the other. 56 If, when the priest examines
it, the mildew has faded after the article has
been washed, he is to tear the contaminated
part out of the clothing, or the leather, or the
woven or knitted material. 57 But if it reappears
in the clothing, or in the woven or knitted material, or in the leather article, it is spreading,
and whatever has the mildew must be burned
with fire. 58 The clothing, or the woven or knitted material, or any leather article that has been
washed and is rid of the mildew, must be
washed again, and it will be clean."
59 These are the regulations concerning contamination by mildew in woolen or linen clothing, woven or knitted material, or any leather
article, for pronouncing them clean or unclean.

Cleansing From Infectious Skin Diseases

14 The LORD said to Moses, 2 "These are
the regulations for the diseased person
at the time of his ceremonial cleansing, when
he is brought to the priest: 3 The priest is to go
outside the camp and examine him. If the person has been healed of his infectious skin disease,[a] 4 the priest shall order that two live clean
birds and some cedar wood, scarlet yarn and
hyssop be brought for the one to be cleansed.
5 Then the priest shall order that one of the birds
be killed over fresh water in a clay pot. 6 He is
then to take the live bird and dip it, together
with the cedar wood, the scarlet yarn and the
hyssop, into the blood of the bird that was
killed over the fresh water. 7 Seven times he shall
sprinkle the one to be cleansed of the infectious
disease and pronounce him clean. Then he is to
release the live bird in the open fields.
8 "The person to be cleansed must wash his
clothes, shave off all his hair and bathe with
water; then he will be ceremonially clean. After
this he may come into the camp, but he must
stay outside his tent for seven days. 9 On the
seventh day he must shave off all his hair; he
must shave his head, his beard, his eyebrows
and the rest of his hair. He must wash his
clothes and bathe himself with water, and he
will be clean.
10 "On the eighth day he must bring two
male lambs and one ewe lamb a year old, each
without defect, along with three-tenths of an
ephah[b] of fine flour mixed with oil for a grain
offering, and one log[c] of oil. 11 The priest who
pronounces him clean shall present both the
one to be cleansed and his offerings before the
LORD at the entrance to the Tent of Meeting.
12 "Then the priest is to take one of the male
lambs and offer it as a guilt offering, along with
the log of oil; he shall wave them before the
LORD as a wave offering. 13 He is to slaughter the
lamb in the holy place where the sin offering
and the burnt offering are slaughtered. Like the
sin offering, the guilt offering belongs to the
priest; it is most holy. 14 The priest is to take
some of the blood of the guilt offering and put
it on the lobe of the right ear of the one to be
cleansed, on the thumb of his right hand and
on the big toe of his right foot. 15 The priest shall
then take some of the log of oil, pour it in the
palm of his own left hand, 16 dip his right forefinger into the oil in his palm, and with his
finger sprinkle some of it before the LORD seven
times. 17 The priest is to put some of the oil
remaining in his palm on the lobe of the right
ear of the one to be cleansed, on the thumb of
his right hand and on the big toe of his right
foot, on top of the blood of the guilt offering.
18 The rest of the oil in his palm the priest shall
put on the head of the one to be cleansed and
make atonement for him before the LORD.
19 "Then the priest is to sacrifice the sin offering and make atonement for the one to be
cleansed from his uncleanness. After that, the
priest shall slaughter the burnt offering 20 and
offer it on the altar, together with the grain offering, and make atonement for him, and he
will be clean.
21 "If, however, he is poor and cannot afford
these, he must take one male lamb as a guilt
offering to be waved to make atonement for
him, together with a tenth of an ephah[d] of fine
flour mixed with oil for a grain offering, a log
of oil, 22 and two doves or two young pigeons,
which he can afford, one for a sin offering and
the other for a burnt offering.
23 "On the eighth day he must bring them for
his cleansing to the priest at the entrance to the
Tent of Meeting, before the LORD. 24 The priest is
to take the lamb for the guilt offering, together
with the log of oil, and wave them before the
LORD as a wave offering. 25 He shall slaughter the
lamb for the guilt offering and take some of its
blood and put it on the lobe of the right ear of
the one to be cleansed, on the thumb of his
right hand and on the big toe of his right foot.
26 The priest is to pour some of the oil into the
palm of his own left hand, 27 and with his right
forefinger sprinkle some of the oil from his
palm seven times before the LORD. 28 Some of
the oil in his palm he is to put on the same
places he put the blood of the guilt offering—

[a] *3* Traditionally *leprosy;* the Hebrew word was used for various diseases affecting the skin—not necessarily leprosy; also elsewhere in this chapter.
[b] *10* That is, probably about 6 quarts (about 6.5 liters)
[c] *10* That is, probably about 2/3 pint (about 0.3 liter); also in verses 12, 15, 21 and 24
[d] *21* That is, probably about 2 quarts (about 2 liters)

on the lobe of the right ear of the one to be cleansed, on the thumb of his right hand and on the big toe of his right foot. 29The rest of the oil in his palm the priest shall put on the head of the one to be cleansed, to make atonement for him before the LORD. 30Then he shall sacrifice the doves or the young pigeons, which the person can afford, 31one[a] as a sin offering and the other as a burnt offering, together with the grain offering. In this way the priest will make atonement before the LORD on behalf of the one to be cleansed."

32These are the regulations for anyone who has an infectious skin disease and who cannot afford the regular offerings for his cleansing.

Cleansing From Mildew

33The LORD said to Moses and Aaron, 34"When you enter the land of Canaan, which I am giving you as your possession, and I put a spreading mildew in a house in that land, 35the owner of the house must go and tell the priest, 'I have seen something that looks like mildew in my house.' 36The priest is to order the house to be emptied before he goes in to examine the mildew, so that nothing in the house will be pronounced unclean. After this the priest is to go in and inspect the house. 37He is to examine the mildew on the walls, and if it has greenish or reddish depressions that appear to be deeper than the surface of the wall, 38the priest shall go out the doorway of the house and close it up for seven days. 39On the seventh day the priest shall return to inspect the house. If the mildew has spread on the walls, 40he is to order that the contaminated stones be torn out and thrown into an unclean place outside the town. 41He must have all the inside walls of the house scraped and the material that is scraped off dumped into an unclean place outside the town. 42Then they are to take other stones to replace these and take new clay and plaster the house.

43"If the mildew reappears in the house after the stones have been torn out and the house scraped and plastered, 44the priest is to go and examine it and, if the mildew has spread in the house, it is a destructive mildew; the house is unclean. 45It must be torn down—its stones, timbers and all the plaster—and taken out of the town to an unclean place.

46"Anyone who goes into the house while it is closed up will be unclean till evening. 47Anyone who sleeps or eats in the house must wash his clothes.

48"But if the priest comes to examine it and the mildew has not spread after the house has been plastered, he shall pronounce the house clean, because the mildew is gone. 49To purify the house he is to take two birds and some cedar wood, scarlet yarn and hyssop. 50He shall kill one of the birds over fresh water in a clay pot. 51Then he is to take the cedar wood, the hyssop, the scarlet yarn and the live bird, dip them into the blood of the dead bird and the fresh water, and sprinkle the house seven times. 52He shall purify the house with the bird's blood, the fresh water, the live bird, the cedar wood, the hyssop and the scarlet yarn. 53Then he is to release the live bird in the open fields outside the town. In this way he will make atonement for the house, and it will be clean."

54These are the regulations for any infectious skin disease, for an itch, 55for mildew in clothing or in a house, 56and for a swelling, a rash or a bright spot, 57to determine when something is clean or unclean.

These are the regulations for infectious skin diseases and mildew.

Discharges Causing Uncleanness

15 The LORD said to Moses and Aaron, 2"Speak to the Israelites and say to them: 'When any man has a bodily discharge, the discharge is unclean. 3Whether it continues flowing from his body or is blocked, it will make him unclean. This is how his discharge will bring about uncleanness:

4" 'Any bed the man with a discharge lies on will be unclean, and anything he sits on will be unclean. 5Anyone who touches his bed must wash his clothes and bathe with water, and he will be unclean till evening. 6Whoever sits on anything that the man with a discharge sat on must wash his clothes and bathe with water, and he will be unclean till evening.

7" 'Whoever touches the man who has a discharge must wash his clothes and bathe with water, and he will be unclean till evening.

8" 'If the man with the discharge spits on someone who is clean, that person must wash his clothes and bathe with water, and he will be unclean till evening.

9" 'Everything the man sits on when riding will be unclean, 10and whoever touches any of the things that were under him will be unclean till evening; whoever picks up those things must wash his clothes and bathe with water, and he will be unclean till evening.

11" 'Anyone the man with a discharge touches without rinsing his hands with water must wash his clothes and bathe with water, and he will be unclean till evening.

12" 'A clay pot that the man touches must be broken, and any wooden article is to be rinsed with water.

13" 'When a man is cleansed from his discharge, he is to count off seven days for his ceremonial cleansing; he must wash his clothes and bathe himself with fresh water, and he will be clean. 14On the eighth day he must take two doves or two young pigeons and come before the LORD to the entrance to the Tent of Meeting and give them to the priest. 15The priest is to sacrifice them, the one for a sin offering and the

[a]31 Septuagint and Syriac; Hebrew *31such as the person can afford, one*

other for a burnt offering. In this way he will make atonement before the LORD for the man because of his discharge.

[16]" 'When a man has an emission of semen, he must bathe his whole body with water, and he will be unclean till evening. [17]Any clothing or leather that has semen on it must be washed with water, and it will be unclean till evening. [18]When a man lies with a woman and there is an emission of semen, both must bathe with water, and they will be unclean till evening.

[19]" 'When a woman has her regular flow of blood, the impurity of her monthly period will last seven days, and anyone who touches her will be unclean till evening.

[20]" 'Anything she lies on during her period will be unclean, and anything she sits on will be unclean. [21]Whoever touches her bed must wash his clothes and bathe with water, and he will be unclean till evening. [22]Whoever touches anything she sits on must wash his clothes and bathe with water, and he will be unclean till evening. [23]Whether it is the bed or anything she was sitting on, when anyone touches it, he will be unclean till evening.

[24]" 'If a man lies with her and her monthly flow touches him, he will be unclean for seven days; any bed he lies on will be unclean.

[25]" 'When a woman has a discharge of blood for many days at a time other than her monthly period or has a discharge that continues beyond her period, she will be unclean as long as she has the discharge, just as in the days of her period. [26]Any bed she lies on while her discharge continues will be unclean, as is her bed during her monthly period, and anything she sits on will be unclean, as during her period. [27]Whoever touches them will be unclean; he must wash his clothes and bathe with water, and he will be unclean till evening.

[28]" 'When she is cleansed from her discharge, she must count off seven days, and after that she will be ceremonially clean. [29]On the eighth day she must take two doves or two young pigeons and bring them to the priest at the entrance to the Tent of Meeting. [30]The priest is to sacrifice one for a sin offering and the other for a burnt offering. In this way he will make atonement for her before the LORD for the uncleanness of her discharge.

[31]" 'You must keep the Israelites separate from things that make them unclean, so they will not die in their uncleanness for defiling my dwelling place,[a] which is among them.' "

[32]These are the regulations for a man with a discharge, for anyone made unclean by an emission of semen, [33]for a woman in her monthly period, for a man or a woman with a discharge, and for a man who lies with a woman who is ceremonially unclean.

The Day of Atonement

16 The LORD spoke to Moses after the death of the two sons of Aaron who died when they approached the LORD. [2]The LORD said to Moses: "Tell your brother Aaron not to come whenever he chooses into the Most Holy Place behind the curtain in front of the atonement cover on the ark, or else he will die, because I appear in the cloud over the atonement cover.

[3]"This is how Aaron is to enter the sanctuary area: with a young bull for a sin offering and a ram for a burnt offering. [4]He is to put on the sacred linen tunic, with linen undergarments next to his body; he is to tie the linen sash around him and put on the linen turban. These are sacred garments; so he must bathe himself with water before he puts them on. [5]From the Israelite community he is to take two male goats for a sin offering and a ram for a burnt offering.

[6]"Aaron is to offer the bull for his own sin offering to make atonement for himself and his household. [7]Then he is to take the two goats and present them before the LORD at the entrance to the Tent of Meeting. [8]He is to cast lots for the two goats—one lot for the LORD and the other for the scapegoat.[b] [9]Aaron shall bring the goat whose lot falls to the LORD and sacrifice it for a sin offering. [10]But the goat chosen by lot as the scapegoat shall be presented alive before the LORD to be used for making atonement by sending it into the desert as a scapegoat.

[a]31 Or *my tabernacle* [b]8 That is, the goat of removal; Hebrew *azazel*; also in verses 10 and 26

16:1–22 The Day of Atonement is a thematic pivot point for the book of Leviticus. For the Israelites who participated in the ceremony with hearts of faith, this solemn day provided assurance that their past sins had been completely dealt with. Today, through the sacrificial work of Christ, we also can find assurance of forgiveness and a right standing before God. We can leave our past sins behind and build a new life based on God's plan.

16:7–22 Two goats were set apart for the atonement ceremony. The first goat was associated with the people's sin and was sacrificed to God as a sin offering. The second goat, also associated with the sins of the people, was led into the wilderness and then released. This "scapegoat" took the sins of the people and carried them away. This pictures the truth of Psalm 103:12 that says God removes our sins "as far as the east is from the west." Jesus Christ, who has taken all our sins upon himself, is our ultimate scapegoat. One of the most important keys to our spiritual renewal is learning that God himself has taken away our sins. This fact should help us let go of our sins and receive God's forgiveness.

16:10 The word *atonement* comes from a word that means "to cover"; it appears here and in many other places in Leviticus. The covering of sin meant reconciliation between the Israelites and God. For this reason, the word could be understood as *at-one-ment.* God intends this for our lives as well. He wants us to find forgiveness for our sins and to be reconciled to him. God is in the business of restoring broken relationships. By means of forgiveness, he provides a way for the restoration of relationships that are broken by sin.

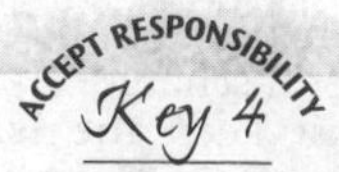

Blaming Others for Our Sin

Leviticus 16:20–22 Because we do not like to admit that we are sinful, we sometimes try to place the blame for our problems on other people. We make them the "scapegoats" for our failures and try to give them the responsibility for things we've done wrong ourselves. But blaming others merely blocks the process of our spiritual renewal and keeps us from overcoming our faults.

In the Old Testament, the Israelites were instructed to select a live, male goat, which would carry away their sins. The priest was to place his hands on this goat and confess over it all the sins of the people. Then he was to send the goat into the desert, led by a man appointed for the task. In this way, the goat carried all the sins of the people into the wilderness (16:21–22). The term "scapegoat" originated from this practice.

The "scapegoat" concept holds another important meaning for us as Christians. Although we need to take the responsibility for our sins and failures, Jesus has made it possible for us to be free from the spiritual debts our sin and failures accrue. Jesus voluntarily took our sins upon himself and carried them away, so that once we have confessed our sins and repented, the burden of our past is removed. In this way we are justified—that is, we are cleansed and made whole again, *just as if* we had never sinned.

Turn to Judges 5.

11 "Aaron shall bring the bull for his own sin offering to make atonement for himself and his household, and he is to slaughter the bull for his own sin offering. 12 He is to take a censer full of burning coals from the altar before the LORD and two handfuls of finely ground fragrant incense and take them behind the curtain. 13 He is to put the incense on the fire before the LORD, and the smoke of the incense will conceal the atonement cover above the Testimony, so that he will not die. 14 He is to take some of the bull's blood and with his finger sprinkle it on the front of the atonement cover; then he shall sprinkle some of it with his finger seven times before the atonement cover.

15 "He shall then slaughter the goat for the sin offering for the people and take its blood behind the curtain and do with it as he did with the bull's blood: He shall sprinkle it on the atonement cover and in front of it. 16 In this way he will make atonement for the Most Holy Place because of the uncleanness and rebellion of the Israelites, whatever their sins have been. He is to do the same for the Tent of Meeting, which is among them in the midst of their uncleanness. 17 No one is to be in the Tent of Meeting from the time Aaron goes in to make atonement in the Most Holy Place until he comes out, having made atonement for himself, his household and the whole community of Israel.

18 "Then he shall come out to the altar that is before the LORD and make atonement for it. He shall take some of the bull's blood and some of the goat's blood and put it on all the horns of the altar. 19 He shall sprinkle some of the blood on it with his finger seven times to cleanse it and to consecrate it from the uncleanness of the Israelites.

20 "When Aaron has finished making atonement for the Most Holy Place, the Tent of Meeting and the altar, he shall bring forward the live goat. 21 He is to lay both hands on the head of the live goat and confess over it all the wickedness and rebellion of the Israelites—all their sins—and put them on the goat's head. He shall send the goat away into the desert in the care of a man appointed for the task. 22 The goat will

---

16:15–19 The goat for the people's sin offering was slaughtered, and its blood was sprinkled on the lid of the ark of the covenant, also called the atonement cover. This yearly sacrifice atoned for the sins of the people. It had to be offered every year. Hebrews 10:1–4 makes it clear that these sacrifices were not a permanent solution to the problem of sin; they were only a temporary measure. Yet Jesus Christ has now provided a perfect and permanent sacrifice for our sins. Through faith in Christ, we can be assured of complete forgiveness—permanently!

16:22 The innocent scapegoat was sent away, carrying with it the guilt of the entire Israelite nation. People often look for a scapegoat rather than face the truth about themselves or accept responsibility for their sin. Creating a scapegoat frees people from their feelings of failure and gives them someone else to blame. For those of us who have been the scapegoat for another, it should encourage us to know that God has sent his Son to be the scapegoat

carry on itself all their sins to a solitary place; and the man shall release it in the desert.

23 "Then Aaron is to go into the Tent of Meeting and take off the linen garments he put on before he entered the Most Holy Place, and he is to leave them there. 24 He shall bathe himself with water in a holy place and put on his regular garments. Then he shall come out and sacrifice the burnt offering for himself and the burnt offering for the people, to make atonement for himself and for the people. 25 He shall also burn the fat of the sin offering on the altar.

26 "The man who releases the goat as a scapegoat must wash his clothes and bathe himself with water; afterward he may come into the camp. 27 The bull and the goat for the sin offerings, whose blood was brought into the Most Holy Place to make atonement, must be taken outside the camp; their hides, flesh and offal are to be burned up. 28 The man who burns them must wash his clothes and bathe himself with water; afterward he may come into the camp.

29 "This is to be a lasting ordinance for you: On the tenth day of the seventh month you must deny yourselves[a] and not do any work—whether native-born or an alien living among you— 30 because on this day atonement will be made for you, to cleanse you. Then, before the LORD, you will be clean from all your sins. 31 It is a sabbath of rest, and you must deny yourselves; it is a lasting ordinance. 32 The priest who is anointed and ordained to succeed his father as high priest is to make atonement. He is to put on the sacred linen garments 33 and make atonement for the Most Holy Place, for the Tent of Meeting and the altar, and for the priests and all the people of the community.

34 "This is to be a lasting ordinance for you: Atonement is to be made once a year for all the sins of the Israelites."

And it was done, as the LORD commanded Moses.

Eating Blood Forbidden

17 The LORD said to Moses, 2 "Speak to Aaron and his sons and to all the Israelites and say to them: 'This is what the LORD has commanded: 3 Any Israelite who sacrifices an ox,[b] a lamb or a goat in the camp or outside of it 4 instead of bringing it to the entrance to the Tent of Meeting to present it as an offering to the LORD in front of the tabernacle of the LORD—that man shall be considered guilty of bloodshed; he has shed blood and must be cut off from his people. 5 This is so the Israelites will bring to the LORD the sacrifices they are now making in the open fields. They must bring them to the priest, that is, to the LORD, at the entrance to the Tent of Meeting and sacrifice them as fellowship offerings.[c] 6 The priest is to sprinkle the blood against the altar of the LORD at the entrance to the Tent of Meeting and burn the fat as an aroma pleasing to the LORD. 7 They must no longer offer any of their sacrifices to the goat idols[d] to whom they prostitute themselves. This is to be a lasting ordinance for them and for the generations to come.'

8 "Say to them: 'Any Israelite or any alien living among them who offers a burnt offering or sacrifice 9 and does not bring it to the entrance to the Tent of Meeting to sacrifice it to the LORD—that man must be cut off from his people.

10 " 'Any Israelite or any alien living among them who eats any blood—I will set my face against that person who eats blood and will cut him off from his people. 11 For the life of a creature is in the blood, and I have given it to you to make atonement for yourselves on the altar; it is the blood that makes atonement for one's life. 12 Therefore I say to the Israelites, "None of you may eat blood, nor may an alien living among you eat blood."

13 " 'Any Israelite or any alien living among you who hunts any animal or bird that may be eaten must drain out the blood and cover it with earth, 14 because the life of every creature is its blood. That is why I have said to the Israelites, "You must not eat the blood of any creature, because the life of every creature is its blood; anyone who eats it must be cut off."

15 " 'Anyone, whether native-born or alien, who eats anything found dead or torn by wild animals must wash his clothes and bathe with water, and he will be ceremonially unclean till evening; then he will be clean. 16 But if he does not wash his clothes and bathe himself, he will be held responsible.' "

Unlawful Sexual Relations

18 The LORD said to Moses, 2 "Speak to the Israelites and say to them: 'I am the LORD your God. 3 You must not do as they do in Egypt, where you used to live, and you must not do as they do in the land of Canaan, where I am bringing you. Do not follow their practices. 4 You must obey my laws and be careful to fol-

[a]29 Or *must fast*; also in verse 31 [b]3 The Hebrew word can include both male and female. [c]5 Traditionally *peace offerings* [d]7 Or *demons*

---

for us. Though innocent, Jesus carried away the sin of the entire human race. We need not shoulder our burden of sin any longer. We can hand it over to him. For those of us who tend to make others into our scapegoats and blame them for our problems, we need to make sure we accept responsibility for our own sin instead of finding someone else to blame.

18:1–5 This passage sets the tone for the rest of Leviticus, affirming the fact that God's relationship with his people was intended to affect the practical areas of their moral and spiritual lives. When we commit our lives to God through a relationship with Jesus Christ, we give God the opportunity to transform us. Spiritual growth can only come about, however, when we hand over all our decisions, moral and spiritual, to his wise direction.

18:4–5 In this passage, we see the refrain "I am the LORD your God." This phrase appears more often in Leviticus than in any other book of the Bible. When God asked the

low my decrees. I am the LORD your God. 5 Keep my decrees and laws, for the man who obeys them will live by them. I am the LORD.

6 " 'No one is to approach any close relative to have sexual relations. I am the LORD.

7 " 'Do not dishonor your father by having sexual relations with your mother. She is your mother; do not have relations with her.

8 " 'Do not have sexual relations with your father's wife; that would dishonor your father.

9 " 'Do not have sexual relations with your sister, either your father's daughter or your mother's daughter, whether she was born in the same home or elsewhere.

10 " 'Do not have sexual relations with your son's daughter or your daughter's daughter; that would dishonor you.

11 " 'Do not have sexual relations with the daughter of your father's wife, born to your father; she is your sister.

12 " 'Do not have sexual relations with your father's sister; she is your father's close relative.

13 " 'Do not have sexual relations with your mother's sister, because she is your mother's close relative.

14 " 'Do not dishonor your father's brother by approaching his wife to have sexual relations; she is your aunt.

15 " 'Do not have sexual relations with your daughter-in-law. She is your son's wife; do not have relations with her.

16 " 'Do not have sexual relations with your brother's wife; that would dishonor your brother.

17 " 'Do not have sexual relations with both a woman and her daughter. Do not have sexual relations with either her son's daughter or her daughter's daughter; they are her close relatives. That is wickedness.

18 " 'Do not take your wife's sister as a rival wife and have sexual relations with her while your wife is living.

19 " 'Do not approach a woman to have sexual relations during the uncleanness of her monthly period.

20 " 'Do not have sexual relations with your neighbor's wife and defile yourself with her.

21 " 'Do not give any of your children to be sacrificed[a] to Molech, for you must not profane the name of your God. I am the LORD.

22 " 'Do not lie with a man as one lies with a woman; that is detestable.

23 " 'Do not have sexual relations with an animal and defile yourself with it. A woman must not present herself to an animal to have sexual relations with it; that is a perversion.

24 " 'Do not defile yourselves in any of these ways, because this is how the nations that I am going to drive out before you became defiled. 25 Even the land was defiled; so I punished it for its sin, and the land vomited out its inhabitants. 26 But you must keep my decrees and my laws. The native-born and the aliens living among you must not do any of these detestable things, 27 for all these things were done by the people who lived in the land before you, and the land became defiled. 28 And if you defile the land, it will vomit you out as it vomited out the nations that were before you.

29 " 'Everyone who does any of these detestable things—such persons must be cut off from their people. 30 Keep my requirements and do not follow any of the detestable customs that were practiced before you came and do not defile yourselves with them. I am the LORD your God.' "

Various Laws

19 The LORD said to Moses, 2 "Speak to the entire assembly of Israel and say to them: 'Be holy because I, the LORD your God, am holy.

[a] 21 Or *to be passed through ⌊the fire⌋*

Israelites to live holy lives, he knew it would be difficult. So he continually reminded them of his identity as the Lord their God—a God worthy of their respect and fear, a God who had revealed himself with terrifying power at Mount Sinai, a God who wanted them to live according to his plan. It should encourage us, too, to know that this fearsome, powerful, holy God sent his only Son to help us to live in obedience to him.

18:4–5 God promises life to all those who live according to his plan. The Hebrew word for "life" does not just mean "existence." It refers to finding contentment and enjoyment in life—living life to its fullest. While the personal, moral standards in this section of Leviticus are quite restrictive, God's plan offers freedom beyond our wildest dreams. It is the path of sin that is truly restrictive. When we obey God's standards, we are free to discover life as God intended it to be. His plan leads to peace and contentment.

18:6–18 God instituted marriage as a foundational human relationship and forbade anything that might destroy it—incest included. Some societies in history have endorsed incestuous relationships and have suffered tragic consequences such as physical and mental abnormalities. These consequences have eventually led to the society's decline. God's purpose in setting boundaries for both personal and family life has always been to protect us from destruction. He desires to build families that promote healing and wholeness among their members.

18:20 Fidelity in marriage is central to God's plan for society and family; it is one of the Ten Commandments (Exodus 20:14). Since the bond of marriage is a foundational building block of society, adultery is a blatant violation of a community's trust. Healthy relationships require self-control and the acceptance of self-imposed boundaries, but God didn't intend to deprive us of anything in marriage. God wants the marriage relationship to bring us joy and fulfillment.

18:24–30 Incest (18:6–18), adultery (18:20), child sacrifice (18:21), homosexuality (18:22) and bestiality (18:23) were all practiced by godless societies in the ancient Near East. God said that following these practices would lead to the deterioration and destruction of society. It is only through a relationship with God, by the power of the Holy Spirit, that people are able to be morally pure and overcome the destructive effects of sin. God's standards are given for our good.

19:1–2 God's call to holiness is repeated (see 11:44). God's holiness is the model and motivation for God's peo-

3 “ ‘Each of you must respect his mother and
father, and you must observe my Sabbaths. I am
the LORD your God.
4 “ ‘Do not turn to idols or make gods of cast
metal for yourselves. I am the LORD your God.
5 “ ‘When you sacrifice a fellowship offering[a] to the LORD, sacrifice it in such a way that
it will be accepted on your behalf. 6 It shall be
eaten on the day you sacrifice it or on the next
day; anything left over until the third day must
be burned up. 7 If any of it is eaten on the third
day, it is impure and will not be accepted.
8 Whoever eats it will be held responsible because he has desecrated what is holy to the
LORD; that person must be cut off from his people.
9 “ ‘When you reap the harvest of your land,
do not reap to the very edges of your field or
gather the gleanings of your harvest. 10 Do not
go over your vineyard a second time or pick up
the grapes that have fallen. Leave them for the
poor and the alien. I am the LORD your God.
11 “ ‘Do not steal.
“ ‘Do not lie.
“ ‘Do not deceive one another.
12 “ ‘Do not swear falsely by my name and so
profane the name of your God. I am the LORD.
13 “ ‘Do not defraud your neighbor or rob
him.
“ ‘Do not hold back the wages of a hired
man overnight.
14 “ ‘Do not curse the deaf or put a stumbling
block in front of the blind, but fear your God.
I am the LORD.
15 “ ‘Do not pervert justice; do not show partiality to the poor or favoritism to the great, but
judge your neighbor fairly.
16 “ ‘Do not go about spreading slander
among your people.
“ ‘Do not do anything that endangers your
neighbor's life. I am the LORD.
17 “ ‘Do not hate your brother in your heart.
Rebuke your neighbor frankly so you will not
share in his guilt.
18 “ ‘Do not seek revenge or bear a grudge
against one of your people, but love your neighbor as yourself. I am the LORD.
19 “ ‘Keep my decrees.
“ ‘Do not mate different kinds of animals.
“ ‘Do not plant your field with two kinds of
seed.
“ ‘Do not wear clothing woven of two kinds
of material.
20 “ ‘If a man sleeps with a woman who is a
slave girl promised to another man but who has
not been ransomed or given her freedom, there
must be due punishment. Yet they are not to be
put to death, because she had not been freed.
21 The man, however, must bring a ram to the
entrance to the Tent of Meeting for a guilt offering to the LORD. 22 With the ram of the guilt
offering the priest is to make atonement for him
before the LORD for the sin he has committed,
and his sin will be forgiven.
23 “ ‘When you enter the land and plant any
kind of fruit tree, regard its fruit as forbidden.[b]
For three years you are to consider it forbidden[b]; it must not be eaten. 24 In the fourth year
all its fruit will be holy, an offering of praise to
the LORD. 25 But in the fifth year you may eat its
fruit. In this way your harvest will be increased.
I am the LORD your God.
26 “ ‘Do not eat any meat with the blood still
in it.
“ ‘Do not practice divination or sorcery.
27 “ ‘Do not cut the hair at the sides of your
head or clip off the edges of your beard.
28 “ ‘Do not cut your bodies for the dead or
put tattoo marks on yourselves. I am the LORD.
29 “ ‘Do not degrade your daughter by making her a prostitute, or the land will turn to
prostitution and be filled with wickedness.
30 “ ‘Observe my Sabbaths and have reverence for my sanctuary. I am the LORD.
31 “ ‘Do not turn to mediums or seek out
spiritists, for you will be defiled by them. I am
the LORD your God.

[a]5 Traditionally *peace offering* [b]23 Hebrew *uncircumcised*

---

ple to lead holy lives. God knows our weaknesses and our failures, yet he places before us the goal of his righteousness. It is only with Christ's help that we can reach this goal. Through his death we are cleansed from our sins, and through his life (given to us by the Holy Spirit) we have the power to live a morally pure and holy life.

19:1–4 Holiness begins at home, and respect for parents is given a prominent place here as it was in the Ten Commandments (Exodus 20:12). Strained family relationships can become one of the greatest barriers to the life of fulfillment and contentment that God desires for us. If God places a priority on respect within family relationships, we should do the same.

19:9–10 The laws given here and illustrated in the story of Ruth show that God is concerned about poor people. There was a sense of community among the Israelites that went beyond the immediate family. The Israelites were called to consider poor or underprivileged people as their brothers or sisters. With so many needs among God's people today—physical, emotional, spiritual—we should be quick to respond. Only in an atmosphere of acceptance and love can the needs of others be discerned and truly met.

19:11–13, 35–37 God's plan for spiritual renewal demands honesty in both word and deed. Dishonesty and misrepresentation lead to suspicion, mistrust and hatred, ultimately destroying personal relationships. Human relationships can only grow and thrive if we are willing to tell the truth, the only real basis for trust between people. When there is honesty in our relationships, we can confidently look to others in times of need.

19:18, 33–34 As we compare verses 18, 33, and 34 we see that the call to love one's neighbor was extended not only to fellow Israelites but to foreigners as well. Jesus quoted this commandment as the second great commandment of the law (Matthew 22:39; Mark 12:31; Luke 10:27). It should be easier for us to have compassion on others if we remember that God had compassion on us and freed us from our slavery to sin.

32" 'Rise in the presence of the aged, show respect for the elderly and revere your God. I am the LORD.

33" 'When an alien lives with you in your land, do not mistreat him. 34The alien living with you must be treated as one of your native-born. Love him as yourself, for you were aliens in Egypt. I am the LORD your God.

35" 'Do not use dishonest standards when measuring length, weight or quantity. 36Use honest scales and honest weights, an honest ephah[a] and an honest hin.[b] I am the LORD your God, who brought you out of Egypt.

37" 'Keep all my decrees and all my laws and follow them. I am the LORD.' "

Punishments for Sin

20 The LORD said to Moses, 2"Say to the Israelites: 'Any Israelite or any alien living in Israel who gives[c] any of his children to Molech must be put to death. The people of the community are to stone him. 3I will set my face against that man and I will cut him off from his people; for by giving his children to Molech, he has defiled my sanctuary and profaned my holy name. 4If the people of the community close their eyes when that man gives one of his children to Molech and they fail to put him to death, 5I will set my face against that man and his family and will cut off from their people both him and all who follow him in prostituting themselves to Molech.

6" 'I will set my face against the person who turns to mediums and spiritists to prostitute himself by following them, and I will cut him off from his people.

7" 'Consecrate yourselves and be holy, because I am the LORD your God. 8Keep my decrees and follow them. I am the LORD, who makes you holy.[d]

9" 'If anyone curses his father or mother, he must be put to death. He has cursed his father or his mother, and his blood will be on his own head.

10" 'If a man commits adultery with another man's wife—with the wife of his neighbor—both the adulterer and the adulteress must be put to death.

11" 'If a man sleeps with his father's wife, he has dishonored his father. Both the man and the woman must be put to death; their blood will be on their own heads.

12" 'If a man sleeps with his daughter-in-law, both of them must be put to death. What they have done is a perversion; their blood will be on their own heads.

13" 'If a man lies with a man as one lies with a woman, both of them have done what is detestable. They must be put to death; their blood will be on their own heads.

14" 'If a man marries both a woman and her mother, it is wicked. Both he and they must be burned in the fire, so that no wickedness will be among you.

15" 'If a man has sexual relations with an animal, he must be put to death, and you must kill the animal.

16" 'If a woman approaches an animal to have sexual relations with it, kill both the woman and the animal. They must be put to death; their blood will be on their own heads.

17" 'If a man marries his sister, the daughter of either his father or his mother, and they have sexual relations, it is a disgrace. They must be cut off before the eyes of their people. He has dishonored his sister and will be held responsible.

18" 'If a man lies with a woman during her monthly period and has sexual relations with her, he has exposed the source of her flow, and she has also uncovered it. Both of them must be cut off from their people.

19" 'Do not have sexual relations with the sister of either your mother or your father, for that would dishonor a close relative; both of you would be held responsible.

20" 'If a man sleeps with his aunt, he has dishonored his uncle. They will be held responsible; they will die childless.

21" 'If a man marries his brother's wife, it is an act of impurity; he has dishonored his brother. They will be childless.

22" 'Keep all my decrees and laws and follow them, so that the land where I am bringing you to live may not vomit you out. 23You must not live according to the customs of the nations I am going to drive out before you. Because they did all these things, I abhorred them. 24But I said to you, "You will possess their land; I will give it to you as an inheritance, a land flowing with milk and honey." I am the LORD your God, who has set you apart from the nations.

25" 'You must therefore make a distinction between clean and unclean animals and between unclean and clean birds. Do not defile yourselves by any animal or bird or anything that moves along the ground—those which I have set apart as unclean for you. 26You are to be holy to me[e] because I, the LORD, am holy, and I have set you apart from the nations to be my own.

[a]36 An ephah was a dry measure. [b]36 A hin was a liquid measure. [c]2 Or *sacrifices;* also in verses 3 and 4 [d]8 Or *who sanctifies you;* or *who sets you apart as holy* [e]26 Or *be my holy ones*

20:1–5 The earlier prohibition against worshiping Molech (18:21) is given again here in even stronger language. Most of the Israelites probably doubted they could ever participate in this type of pagan worship, which included sacrificing children to this god. Yet Israel's history records that several centuries later, King Manasseh sacrificed some of his sons to this god and no one even objected (2 Chronicles 33:6). Our lives can also be greatly tainted by the behavior of the people around us. Given enough time, their values may become ours. With God's help, we need to stand by our commitment to the moral boundaries he has set up.

27" 'A man or woman who is a medium or spiritist among you must be put to death. You are to stone them; their blood will be on their own heads.' "

Rules for Priests

21 The LORD said to Moses, "Speak to the priests, the sons of Aaron, and say to them: 'A priest must not make himself ceremonially unclean for any of his people who die, 2except for a close relative, such as his mother or father, his son or daughter, his brother, 3or an unmarried sister who is dependent on him since she has no husband—for her he may make himself unclean. 4He must not make himself unclean for people related to him by marriage,[a] and so defile himself.

5" 'Priests must not shave their heads or shave off the edges of their beards or cut their bodies. 6They must be holy to their God and must not profane the name of their God. Because they present the offerings made to the LORD by fire, the food of their God, they are to be holy.

7" 'They must not marry women defiled by prostitution or divorced from their husbands, because priests are holy to their God. 8Regard them as holy, because they offer up the food of your God. Consider them holy, because I the LORD am holy—I who make you holy.[b]

9" 'If a priest's daughter defiles herself by becoming a prostitute, she disgraces her father; she must be burned in the fire.

10" 'The high priest, the one among his brothers who has had the anointing oil poured on his head and who has been ordained to wear the priestly garments, must not let his hair become unkempt[c] or tear his clothes. 11He must not enter a place where there is a dead body. He must not make himself unclean, even for his father or mother, 12nor leave the sanctuary of his God or desecrate it, because he has been dedicated by the anointing oil of his God. I am the LORD.

13" 'The woman he marries must be a virgin. 14He must not marry a widow, a divorced woman, or a woman defiled by prostitution, but only a virgin from his own people, 15so he will not defile his offspring among his people. I am the LORD, who makes him holy.[d]' "

16The LORD said to Moses, 17"Say to Aaron: 'For the generations to come none of your descendants who has a defect may come near to offer the food of his God. 18No man who has any defect may come near: no man who is blind or lame, disfigured or deformed; 19no man with a crippled foot or hand, 20or who is hunchbacked or dwarfed, or who has any eye defect, or who has festering or running sores or damaged testicles. 21No descendant of Aaron the priest who has any defect is to come near to present the offerings made to the LORD by fire. He has a defect; he must not come near to offer the food of his God. 22He may eat the most holy food of his God, as well as the holy food; 23yet because of his defect, he must not go near the curtain or approach the altar, and so desecrate my sanctuary. I am the LORD, who makes them holy.[e]' "

24So Moses told this to Aaron and his sons and to all the Israelites.

22 The LORD said to Moses, 2"Tell Aaron and his sons to treat with respect the sacred offerings the Israelites consecrate to me, so they will not profane my holy name. I am the LORD.

3"Say to them: 'For the generations to come, if any of your descendants is ceremonially unclean and yet comes near the sacred offerings that the Israelites consecrate to the LORD, that person must be cut off from my presence. I am the LORD.

4" 'If a descendant of Aaron has an infectious skin disease[f] or a bodily discharge, he may not eat the sacred offerings until he is cleansed. He will also be unclean if he touches something defiled by a corpse or by anyone who has an emission of semen, 5or if he touches any crawling thing that makes him unclean, or any person who makes him unclean, whatever the uncleanness may be. 6The one who touches any such thing will be unclean till evening. He must not eat any of the sacred offerings unless he has bathed himself with water. 7When the sun goes down, he will be clean, and after that he may eat the sacred offerings, for they are his food. 8He must not eat anything found dead or torn by wild animals, and so become unclean through it. I am the LORD.

9" 'The priests are to keep my requirements so that they do not become guilty and die for treating them with contempt. I am the LORD, who makes them holy.[g]

10" 'No one outside a priest's family may eat the sacred offering, nor may the guest of a priest or his hired worker eat it. 11But if a priest buys a slave with money, or if a slave is born in his household, that slave may eat his food. 12If a priest's daughter marries anyone other than a priest, she may not eat any of the sacred contributions. 13But if a priest's daughter becomes a widow or is divorced, yet has no children, and

[a]4 Or *unclean as a leader among his people* [b]8 Or *who sanctify you;* or *who set you apart as holy* [c]10 Or *not uncover his head* [d]15 Or *who sanctifies him;* or *who sets him apart as holy* [e]23 Or *who sanctifies them;* or *who sets them apart as holy* [f]4 Traditionally *leprosy;* the Hebrew word was used for various diseases affecting the skin—not necessarily leprosy. [g]9 Or *who sanctifies them;* or *who sets them apart as holy;* also in verse 16

21:7–8 The priest's personal life, including his marriage, was to be holy, reflecting his commitment to God. As believers, each one of us is a part of Christ, and our body is the home of the Holy Spirit (1 Corinthians 6:15–20). Being holy includes setting healthy boundaries that will lead to purity in sexual relationships.

she returns to live in her father's house as in her
youth, she may eat of her father's food. No unauthorized person, however, may eat any of it.
14" 'If anyone eats a sacred offering by mistake, he must make restitution to the priest for
the offering and add a fifth of the value to it.
15The priests must not desecrate the sacred offerings the Israelites present to the LORD 16by
allowing them to eat the sacred offerings and so
bring upon them guilt requiring payment. I am
the LORD, who makes them holy.' "

Unacceptable Sacrifices

17The LORD said to Moses, 18"Speak to Aaron
and his sons and to all the Israelites and say to
them: 'If any of you—either an Israelite or an
alien living in Israel—presents a gift for a burnt
offering to the LORD, either to fulfill a vow or as
a freewill offering, 19you must present a male
without defect from the cattle, sheep or goats in
order that it may be accepted on your behalf.
20Do not bring anything with a defect, because
it will not be accepted on your behalf. 21When
anyone brings from the herd or flock a fellowship offering[a] to the LORD to fulfill a special
vow or as a freewill offering, it must be without
defect or blemish to be acceptable. 22Do not
offer to the LORD the blind, the injured or the
maimed, or anything with warts or festering or
running sores. Do not place any of these on the
altar as an offering made to the LORD by fire.
23You may, however, present as a freewill offering an ox[b] or a sheep that is deformed or stunt-
ed, but it will not be accepted in fulfillment of
a vow. 24You must not offer to the LORD an
animal whose testicles are bruised, crushed,
torn or cut. You must not do this in your own
land, 25and you must not accept such animals
from the hand of a foreigner and offer them as
the food of your God. They will not be accepted
on your behalf, because they are deformed and
have defects.' "
26The LORD said to Moses, 27"When a calf, a
lamb or a goat is born, it is to remain with its
mother for seven days. From the eighth day on,
it will be acceptable as an offering made to the
LORD by fire. 28Do not slaughter a cow or a
sheep and its young on the same day.
29"When you sacrifice a thank offering to the
LORD, sacrifice it in such a way that it will be
accepted on your behalf. 30It must be eaten that
same day; leave none of it till morning. I am the
LORD.
31"Keep my commands and follow them. I
am the LORD. 32Do not profane my holy name.
I must be acknowledged as holy by the Israelites. I am the LORD, who makes[c] you holy[d]
33and who brought you out of Egypt to be your
God. I am the LORD."

23 The LORD said to Moses, 2"Speak to the
Israelites and say to them: 'These are
my appointed feasts, the appointed feasts of the
LORD, which you are to proclaim as sacred assemblies.

The Sabbath

3" 'There are six days when you may work,
but the seventh day is a Sabbath of rest, a day
of sacred assembly. You are not to do any work;
wherever you live, it is a Sabbath to the LORD.

The Passover and Unleavened Bread

4" 'These are the LORD's appointed feasts, the
sacred assemblies you are to proclaim at their
appointed times: 5The LORD's Passover begins
at twilight on the fourteenth day of the first
month. 6On the fifteenth day of that month the
LORD's Feast of Unleavened Bread begins; for
seven days you must eat bread made without
yeast. 7On the first day hold a sacred assembly
and do no regular work. 8For seven days present
an offering made to the LORD by fire. And on
the seventh day hold a sacred assembly and do
no regular work.' "

Firstfruits

9The LORD said to Moses, 10"Speak to the
Israelites and say to them: 'When you enter the
land I am going to give you and you reap its
harvest, bring to the priest a sheaf of the first
grain you harvest. 11He is to wave the sheaf
before the LORD so it will be accepted on your
behalf; the priest is to wave it on the day after
the Sabbath. 12On the day you wave the sheaf,
you must sacrifice as a burnt offering to the
LORD a lamb a year old without defect, 13togeth-
er with its grain offering of two-tenths of an
ephah[e] of fine flour mixed with oil—an offering made to the LORD by fire, a pleasing aroma—
and its drink offering of a quarter of a hin[f] of
wine. 14You must not eat any bread, or roasted
or new grain, until the very day you bring this
offering to your God. This is to be a lasting

[a] *21* Traditionally *peace offering* [b] *23* The Hebrew word can include both male and female. [c] *32* Or *made*
[d] *32* Or *who sanctifies you; or who sets you apart as holy*
[e] *13* That is, probably about 4 quarts (about 4.5 liters); also in verse 17 [f] *13* That is, probably about 1 quart (about 1 liter)

22:31–33 God calls us to remember his deliverance in the past in order to find strength to live for him in the present. He has graciously made it possible for us to be free from the power of our past sins. He has rescued us from Satan's kingdom and delivered us from our slavery to sin. He wants us to remember all he has done in the past so that we can find courage to face the challenges ahead.

23:4–8 The yearly festivals of Passover and the Feast of Unleavened Bread reminded the Israelites how God had delivered them from Egyptian bondage. In order for us to experience a true relationship with God, we must first acknowledge that Christ is our Passover lamb. John the Baptist introduced him as "the Lamb of God, who takes away the sin of the world" (John 1:29). Seeing and acknowledging who Christ truly is allows us to worship God in spirit and in truth.

ordinance for the generations to come, wherever you live.

Feast of Weeks

[15]" 'From the day after the Sabbath, the day you brought the sheaf of the wave offering, count off seven full weeks. [16]Count off fifty days up to the day after the seventh Sabbath, and then present an offering of new grain to the LORD. [17]From wherever you live, bring two loaves made of two-tenths of an ephah of fine flour, baked with yeast, as a wave offering of firstfruits to the LORD. [18]Present with this bread seven male lambs, each a year old and without defect, one young bull and two rams. They will be a burnt offering to the LORD, together with their grain offerings and drink offerings—an offering made by fire, an aroma pleasing to the LORD. [19]Then sacrifice one male goat for a sin offering and two lambs, each a year old, for a fellowship offering.[a] [20]The priest is to wave the two lambs before the LORD as a wave offering, together with the bread of the firstfruits. They are a sacred offering to the LORD for the priest. [21]On that same day you are to proclaim a sacred assembly and do no regular work. This is to be a lasting ordinance for the generations to come, wherever you live.

[22]" 'When you reap the harvest of your land, do not reap to the very edges of your field or gather the gleanings of your harvest. Leave them for the poor and the alien. I am the LORD your God.' "

Feast of Trumpets

[23]The LORD said to Moses, [24]"Say to the Israelites: 'On the first day of the seventh month you are to have a day of rest, a sacred assembly commemorated with trumpet blasts. [25]Do no regular work, but present an offering made to the LORD by fire.' "

Day of Atonement

[26]The LORD said to Moses, [27]"The tenth day of this seventh month is the Day of Atonement. Hold a sacred assembly and deny yourselves,[b] and present an offering made to the LORD by fire. [28]Do no work on that day, because it is the Day of Atonement, when atonement is made for you before the LORD your God. [29]Anyone who does not deny himself on that day must be cut off from his people. [30]I will destroy from among his people anyone who does any work on that day. [31]You shall do no work at all. This is to be a lasting ordinance for the generations to come, wherever you live. [32]It is a sabbath of rest for you, and you must deny yourselves. From the evening of the ninth day of the month until the following evening you are to observe your sabbath."

Feast of Tabernacles

[33]The LORD said to Moses, [34]"Say to the Israelites: 'On the fifteenth day of the seventh month the LORD's Feast of Tabernacles begins, and it lasts for seven days. [35]The first day is a sacred assembly; do no regular work. [36]For seven days present offerings made to the LORD by fire, and on the eighth day hold a sacred assembly and present an offering made to the LORD by fire. It is the closing assembly; do no regular work.

[37](" 'These are the LORD's appointed feasts, which you are to proclaim as sacred assemblies for bringing offerings made to the LORD by fire—the burnt offerings and grain offerings, sacrifices and drink offerings required for each day. [38]These offerings are in addition to those for the LORD's Sabbaths and[c] in addition to your gifts and whatever you have vowed and all the freewill offerings you give to the LORD.)

[39]" 'So beginning with the fifteenth day of the seventh month, after you have gathered the crops of the land, celebrate the festival to the LORD for seven days; the first day is a day of rest, and the eighth day also is a day of rest. [40]On the first day you are to take choice fruit from the trees, and palm fronds, leafy branches and poplars, and rejoice before the LORD your God for seven days. [41]Celebrate this as a festival to the LORD for seven days each year. This is to be a lasting ordinance for the generations to come; celebrate it in the seventh month. [42]Live in booths for seven days: All native-born Israelites are to live in booths [43]so your descendants will know that I had the Israelites live in booths when I brought them out of Egypt. I am the LORD your God.' "

[44]So Moses announced to the Israelites the appointed feasts of the LORD.

Oil and Bread Set Before the LORD

24 The LORD said to Moses, [2]"Command the Israelites to bring you clear oil of pressed olives for the light so that the lamps may be kept burning continually. [3]Outside the curtain of the Testimony in the Tent of Meeting, Aaron is to tend the lamps before the LORD from evening till morning, continually. This is to be a lasting ordinance for the generations to

[a]19 Traditionally *peace offering* [b]27 Or *and fast*; also in verses 29 and 32 [c]38 Or *These feasts are in addition to the LORD's Sabbaths, and these offerings are*

23:33–43 The Festival of Tabernacles, like Israel's other yearly feasts, was to remind the people of a crucial event in their history. Required for all Israelite males, this festival celebrated God's protective care of his people during their forty-year sojourn in the wilderness. It pictured the tremendous grace of God in leading his people out of slavery in Egypt to victory in Canaan. This same God is faithful to us when we leave a former life of sin; he extends his grace to us in similar fashion. We may not have a formal week of feasting to remember those times, but we should make it a point to reflect and praise God for our spiritual growth.

come. 4The lamps on the pure gold lampstand before the LORD must be tended continually.

5"Take fine flour and bake twelve loaves of bread, using two-tenths of an ephah[a] for each loaf. 6Set them in two rows, six in each row, on the table of pure gold before the LORD. 7Along each row put some pure incense as a memorial portion to represent the bread and to be an offering made to the LORD by fire. 8This bread is to be set out before the LORD regularly, Sabbath after Sabbath, on behalf of the Israelites, as a lasting covenant. 9It belongs to Aaron and his sons, who are to eat it in a holy place, because it is a most holy part of their regular share of the offerings made to the LORD by fire."

A Blasphemer Stoned

10Now the son of an Israelite mother and an Egyptian father went out among the Israelites, and a fight broke out in the camp between him and an Israelite. 11The son of the Israelite woman blasphemed the Name with a curse; so they brought him to Moses. (His mother's name was Shelomith, the daughter of Dibri the Danite.) 12They put him in custody until the will of the LORD should be made clear to them.

13Then the LORD said to Moses: 14"Take the blasphemer outside the camp. All those who heard him are to lay their hands on his head, and the entire assembly is to stone him. 15Say to the Israelites: 'If anyone curses his God, he will be held responsible; 16anyone who blasphemes the name of the LORD must be put to death. The entire assembly must stone him. Whether an alien or native-born, when he blasphemes the Name, he must be put to death.

17" 'If anyone takes the life of a human being, he must be put to death. 18Anyone who takes the life of someone's animal must make restitution—life for life. 19If anyone injures his neighbor, whatever he has done must be done to him: 20fracture for fracture, eye for eye, tooth for tooth. As he has injured the other, so he is to be injured. 21Whoever kills an animal must make restitution, but whoever kills a man must be put to death. 22You are to have the same law for the alien and the native-born. I am the LORD your God.' "

23Then Moses spoke to the Israelites, and they took the blasphemer outside the camp and stoned him. The Israelites did as the LORD commanded Moses.

The Sabbath Year

25 The LORD said to Moses on Mount Sinai, 2"Speak to the Israelites and say to them: 'When you enter the land I am going to give you, the land itself must observe a sabbath to the LORD. 3For six years sow your fields, and for six years prune your vineyards and gather their crops. 4But in the seventh year the land is to have a sabbath of rest, a sabbath to the LORD. Do not sow your fields or prune your vineyards. 5Do not reap what grows of itself or harvest the grapes of your untended vines. The land is to have a year of rest. 6Whatever the land yields during the sabbath year will be food for you—for yourself, your manservant and maidservant, and the hired worker and temporary resident who live among you, 7as well as for your livestock and the wild animals in your land. Whatever the land produces may be eaten.

The Year of Jubilee

8" 'Count off seven sabbaths of years—seven times seven years—so that the seven sabbaths of years amount to a period of forty-nine years. 9Then have the trumpet sounded everywhere on the tenth day of the seventh month; on the Day of Atonement sound the trumpet throughout your land. 10Consecrate the fiftieth year and proclaim liberty throughout the land to all its inhabitants. It shall be a jubilee for you; each one of you is to return to his family property and each to his own clan. 11The fiftieth year shall be a jubilee for you; do not sow and do not reap what grows of itself or harvest the untended vines. 12For it is a jubilee and is to be holy for you; eat only what is taken directly from the fields.

13" 'In this Year of Jubilee everyone is to return to his own property.

14" 'If you sell land to one of your countrymen or buy any from him, do not take advantage of each other. 15You are to buy from your countryman on the basis of the number of years since the Jubilee. And he is to sell to you on the basis of the number of years left for harvesting crops. 16When the years are many, you are to increase the price, and when the years are few, you are to decrease the price, because what he is really selling you is the number of crops. 17Do

[a]5 That is, probably about 4 quarts (about 4.5 liters)

25:1–7 The sabbatical year, like the weekly Sabbath day, was instituted by God as a special period of rest for the Israelites. Every seventh year was a time of rest for the land, animals and people. Their rest from work was in itself an act of faith, proving that they believed God would provide for the coming year. This time of rest also gave the Israelites time to remember that God was the true provider: Everything they owned ultimately came from his generous hand. When we realize this truth, we will be better able to commit ourselves into God's hands. He is more than able to provide for our needs and help us.

25:8–55 The Year of Jubilee took place every fifty years. At this time all the lands and possessions that had passed from one family to another during the previous forty-nine years were returned to their original owners. This reminded the Israelites that God was really the owner of all their possessions. They were only the managers. This would have helped to curb their tendency toward materialism. It would also provide families that had lost everything during the previous fifty years a chance to regain what they had lost. True contentment in life comes only when we see our material possessions as gifts from the hand of God. Jesus taught that we should give God first place in our lives and live as he wants us to; then God will provide everything we need to live in this world (Matthew 6:33).

not take advantage of each other, but fear your God. I am the LORD your God.

[18]" 'Follow my decrees and be careful to obey my laws, and you will live safely in the land. [19]Then the land will yield its fruit, and you will eat your fill and live there in safety. [20]You may ask, "What will we eat in the seventh year if we do not plant or harvest our crops?" [21]I will send you such a blessing in the sixth year that the land will yield enough for three years. [22]While you plant during the eighth year, you will eat from the old crop and will continue to eat from it until the harvest of the ninth year comes in.

[23]" 'The land must not be sold permanently, because the land is mine and you are but aliens and my tenants. [24]Throughout the country that you hold as a possession, you must provide for the redemption of the land.

[25]" 'If one of your countrymen becomes poor and sells some of his property, his nearest relative is to come and redeem what his countryman has sold. [26]If, however, a man has no one to redeem it for him but he himself prospers and acquires sufficient means to redeem it, [27]he is to determine the value for the years since he sold it and refund the balance to the man to whom he sold it; he can then go back to his own property. [28]But if he does not acquire the means to repay him, what he sold will remain in the possession of the buyer until the Year of Jubilee. It will be returned in the Jubilee, and he can then go back to his property.

[29]" 'If a man sells a house in a walled city, he retains the right of redemption a full year after its sale. During that time he may redeem it. [30]If it is not redeemed before a full year has passed, the house in the walled city shall belong permanently to the buyer and his descendants. It is not to be returned in the Jubilee. [31]But houses in villages without walls around them are to be considered as open country. They can be redeemed, and they are to be returned in the Jubilee.

[32]" 'The Levites always have the right to redeem their houses in the Levitical towns, which they possess. [33]So the property of the Levites is redeemable—that is, a house sold in any town they hold—and is to be returned in the Jubilee, because the houses in the towns of the Levites are their property among the Israelites. [34]But the pastureland belonging to their towns must not be sold; it is their permanent possession.

[35]" 'If one of your countrymen becomes poor and is unable to support himself among you, help him as you would an alien or a temporary resident, so he can continue to live among you. [36]Do not take interest of any kind[a] from him, but fear your God, so that your countryman may continue to live among you. [37]You must not lend him money at interest or sell him food at a profit. [38]I am the LORD your God, who brought you out of Egypt to give you the land of Canaan and to be your God.

[39]" 'If one of your countrymen becomes poor among you and sells himself to you, do not make him work as a slave. [40]He is to be treated as a hired worker or a temporary resident among you; he is to work for you until the Year of Jubilee. [41]Then he and his children are to be released, and he will go back to his own clan and to the property of his forefathers. [42]Because the Israelites are my servants, whom I brought out of Egypt, they must not be sold as slaves. [43]Do not rule over them ruthlessly, but fear your God.

[44]" 'Your male and female slaves are to come from the nations around you; from them you may buy slaves. [45]You may also buy some of the temporary residents living among you and members of their clans born in your country, and they will become your property. [46]You can will them to your children as inherited property and can make them slaves for life, but you must not rule over your fellow Israelites ruthlessly.

[47]" 'If an alien or a temporary resident among you becomes rich and one of your countrymen becomes poor and sells himself to the alien living among you or to a member of the alien's clan, [48]he retains the right of redemption after he has sold himself. One of his relatives may redeem him: [49]An uncle or a cousin or any blood relative in his clan may redeem him. Or if he prospers, he may redeem himself. [50]He and his buyer are to count the time from the year he sold himself up to the Year of Jubilee. The price for his release is to be based on the rate paid to a hired man for that number of years. [51]If many years remain, he must pay for his redemption a larger share of the price paid for him. [52]If only a few years remain until the Year of Jubilee, he is to compute that and pay for his redemption accordingly. [53]He is to be treated as a man hired from year to year; you must see to it that his owner does not rule over him ruthlessly.

[54]" 'Even if he is not redeemed in any of these ways, he and his children are to be released in the Year of Jubilee, [55]for the Israelites belong to me as servants. They are my servants, whom I brought out of Egypt. I am the LORD your God.

Reward for Obedience

26 " 'Do not make idols or set up an image or a sacred stone for yourselves, and

[a]36 Or *take excessive interest*; similarly in verse 37

25:35–38 God's call to love our neighbors was extended here to those who had fallen into poverty. The fellowship of God's people was always intended to be redemptive; those in need were to be cared for by those with plenty. This was true not only for physical needs but for emotional and spiritual needs as well. In a similar way, our spiritual renewal is most effectively completed with the support and encouragement of God's family.

do not place a carved stone in your land to bow
down before it. I am the LORD your God.
2" 'Observe my Sabbaths and have reverence
for my sanctuary. I am the LORD.
3" 'If you follow my decrees and are careful
to obey my commands, 4I will send you rain in
its season, and the ground will yield its crops
and the trees of the field their fruit. 5Your
threshing will continue until grape harvest and
the grape harvest will continue until planting,
and you will eat all the food you want and live
in safety in your land.
6" 'I will grant peace in the land, and you
will lie down and no one will make you afraid.
I will remove savage beasts from the land, and
the sword will not pass through your country.
7You will pursue your enemies, and they will
fall by the sword before you. 8Five of you will
chase a hundred, and a hundred of you
will chase ten thousand, and your enemies will
fall by the sword before you.
9" 'I will look on you with favor and make
you fruitful and increase your numbers, and I
will keep my covenant with you. 10You will still
be eating last year's harvest when you will have
to move it out to make room for the new. 11I
will put my dwelling place[a] among you, and I
will not abhor you. 12I will walk among you
and be your God, and you will be my people.
13I am the LORD your God, who brought you
out of Egypt so that you would no longer be
slaves to the Egyptians; I broke the bars of your
yoke and enabled you to walk with heads held
high.

Punishment for Disobedience

14" 'But if you will not listen to me and carry
out all these commands, 15and if you reject my
decrees and abhor my laws and fail to carry out
all my commands and so violate my covenant,
16then I will do this to you: I will bring upon
you sudden terror, wasting diseases and fever
that will destroy your sight and drain away your
life. You will plant seed in vain, because your
enemies will eat it. 17I will set my face against
you so that you will be defeated by your enemies; those who hate you will rule over you,
and you will flee even when no one is pursuing
you.
18" 'If after all this you will not listen to
me, I will punish you for your sins seven times
over. 19I will break down your stubborn pride
and make the sky above you like iron and
the ground beneath you like bronze. 20Your
strength will be spent in vain, because your soil
will not yield its crops, nor will the trees of the
land yield their fruit.
21" 'If you remain hostile toward me and
refuse to listen to me, I will multiply your afflictions seven times over, as your sins deserve. 22I
will send wild animals against you, and they
will rob you of your children, destroy your cattle and make you so few in number that your
roads will be deserted.
23" 'If in spite of these things you do not
accept my correction but continue to be hostile
toward me, 24I myself will be hostile toward
you and will afflict you for your sins seven times
over. 25And I will bring the sword upon you to
avenge the breaking of the covenant. When you
withdraw into your cities, I will send a plague
among you, and you will be given into enemy
hands. 26When I cut off your supply of bread,
ten women will be able to bake your bread in
one oven, and they will dole out the bread by
weight. You will eat, but you will not be satisfied.
27" 'If in spite of this you still do not listen
to me but continue to be hostile toward me,
28then in my anger I will be hostile toward you,
and I myself will punish you for your sins seven
times over. 29You will eat the flesh of your sons
and the flesh of your daughters. 30I will destroy
your high places, cut down your incense altars
and pile your dead bodies on the lifeless forms
of your idols, and I will abhor you. 31I will turn
your cities into ruins and lay waste your sanctuaries, and I will take no delight in the pleasing
aroma of your offerings. 32I will lay waste the
land, so that your enemies who live there will
be appalled. 33I will scatter you among the nations and will draw out my sword and pursue
you. Your land will be laid waste, and your
cities will lie in ruins. 34Then the land will enjoy
its sabbath years all the time that it lies desolate
and you are in the country of your enemies;
then the land will rest and enjoy its sabbaths.
35All the time that it lies desolate, the land will
have the rest it did not have during the sabbaths
you lived in it.
36" 'As for those of you who are left, I will
make their hearts so fearful in the lands of their

[a] 11 Or *my tabernacle*

26:11–13 God's promised rewards for Israel's obedience culminate in this powerful affirmation of his love for his people. Again, the exodus is used as a reminder for the Israelites that God took them from bondage and humiliation and lifted them up to become a people of dignity. As we learn to obey him, God offers us the same hope. His deliverance can provide us with a new life of moral and spiritual dignity. God assures us of this by providing Christ's personal presence for each Christian's life (Matthew 28:20).

26:14–39 God warns his people about the consequences of disobedience to God's laws. After reading this, some might believe that God is harsh and unloving, delighting in punishing those who refuse to do things his way. But this list of warnings about sin's consequences actually reveals God's love for his people. God doesn't want us to suffer; he doesn't want to punish us. But God also understands the destructive consequences of sin. He knows that certain activities will cause suffering for us and those around us. He warns us away from them, giving us a plan to follow that will lead to holy and joyful living. God's plan, though viewed by some as restrictive, is actually the path to a life of true fulfillment.

enemies that the sound of a windblown leaf will put them to flight. They will run as though fleeing from the sword, and they will fall, even though no one is pursuing them. 37They will stumble over one another as though fleeing from the sword, even though no one is pursuing them. So you will not be able to stand before your enemies. 38You will perish among the nations; the land of your enemies will devour you. 39Those of you who are left will waste away in the lands of their enemies because of their sins; also because of their fathers' sins they will waste away.

40" 'But if they will confess their sins and the sins of their fathers—their treachery against me and their hostility toward me, 41which made me hostile toward them so that I sent them into the land of their enemies—then when their uncircumcised hearts are humbled and they pay for their sin, 42I will remember my covenant with Jacob and my covenant with Isaac and my covenant with Abraham, and I will remember the land. 43For the land will be deserted by them and will enjoy its sabbaths while it lies desolate without them. They will pay for their sins because they rejected my laws and abhorred my decrees. 44Yet in spite of this, when they are in the land of their enemies, I will not reject them or abhor them so as to destroy them completely, breaking my covenant with them. I am the LORD their God. 45But for their sake I will remember the covenant with their ancestors whom I brought out of Egypt in the sight of the nations to be their God. I am the LORD.' "

46These are the decrees, the laws and the regulations that the LORD established on Mount Sinai between himself and the Israelites through Moses.

Redeeming What Is the LORD's

27 The LORD said to Moses, 2"Speak to the Israelites and say to them: 'If anyone makes a special vow to dedicate persons to the LORD by giving equivalent values, 3set the value of a male between the ages of twenty and sixty at fifty shekels[a] of silver, according to the sanctuary shekel[b]; 4and if it is a female, set her value at thirty shekels.[c] 5If it is a person between the ages of five and twenty, set the value of a male at twenty shekels[d] and of a female at ten shekels.[e] 6If it is a person between one month and five years, set the value of a male at five shekels[f] of silver and that of a female at three shekels[g] of silver. 7If it is a person sixty years old or more, set the value of a male at fifteen shekels[h] and of a female at ten shekels. 8If anyone making the vow is too poor to pay the specified amount, he is to present the person to the priest, who will set the value for him according to what the man making the vow can afford.

9" 'If what he vowed is an animal that is acceptable as an offering to the LORD, such an animal given to the LORD becomes holy. 10He must not exchange it or substitute a good one for a bad one, or a bad one for a good one; if he should substitute one animal for another, both it and the substitute become holy. 11If what he vowed is a ceremonially unclean animal—one that is not acceptable as an offering to the LORD—the animal must be presented to the priest, 12who will judge its quality as good or bad. Whatever value the priest then sets, that is what it will be. 13If the owner wishes to redeem the animal, he must add a fifth to its value.

14" 'If a man dedicates his house as something holy to the LORD, the priest will judge its quality as good or bad. Whatever value the priest then sets, so it will remain. 15If the man who dedicates his house redeems it, he must add a fifth to its value, and the house will again become his.

16" 'If a man dedicates to the LORD part of his family land, its value is to be set according to the amount of seed required for it—fifty shekels of silver to a homer[i] of barley seed. 17If he dedicates his field during the Year of Jubilee, the value that has been set remains. 18But if he dedicates his field after the Jubilee, the priest will determine the value according to the number of years that remain until the next Year of Jubilee, and its set value will be reduced. 19If the man who dedicates the field wishes to redeem it, he must add a fifth to its value, and the field will again become his. 20If, however, he does not redeem the field, or if he has sold it to someone else, it can never be redeemed. 21When the field is released in the Jubilee, it will become holy, like a field devoted to the LORD; it will become the property of the priests.[j]

22" 'If a man dedicates to the LORD a field he has bought, which is not part of his family land, 23the priest will determine its value up to the Year of Jubilee, and the man must pay its value on that day as something holy to the LORD. 24In the Year of Jubilee the field will revert to the person from whom he bought it, the one whose land it was. 25Every value is to be set according to the sanctuary shekel, twenty gerahs to the shekel.

[a] 3 That is, about 1 1/4 pounds (about 0.6 kilogram); also in verse 16 [b] 3 That is, about 2/5 ounce (about 11.5 grams); also in verse 25 [c] 4 That is, about 12 ounces (about 0.3 kilogram) [d] 5 That is, about 8 ounces (about 0.2 kilogram) [e] 5 That is, about 4 ounces (about 110 grams); also in verse 7 [f] 6 That is, about 2 ounces (about 55 grams) [g] 6 That is, about 1 1/4 ounces (about 35 grams) [h] 7 That is, about 6 ounces (about 170 grams) [i] 16 That is, probably about 6 bushels (about 220 liters) [j] 21 Or *priest*

26:40–42 Even after a harsh warning for those disobedient to his laws (26:14–39), God shows great love for his people in this promise of restoration. God delights in restoring those who repent. The Parable of the Lost Son also tells of a loving father who delights in finding his lost son (Luke 15). Though we may have wandered away from him, God still waits with open arms for us to return.

26" 'No one, however, may dedicate the firstborn of an animal, since the firstborn already
belongs to the LORD; whether an ox[a] or a
sheep, it is the LORD's. 27If it is one of the unclean animals, he may buy it back at its set
value, adding a fifth of the value to it. If he does
not redeem it, it is to be sold at its set value.
28" 'But nothing that a man owns and de-
votes[b] to the LORD—whether man or animal or
family land—may be sold or redeemed; everything so devoted is most holy to the LORD.
29" 'No person devoted to destruction[c]
may be ransomed; he must be put to death.
30" 'A tithe of everything from the land,
whether grain from the soil or fruit from the
trees, belongs to the LORD; it is holy to the LORD.
31If a man redeems any of his tithe, he must add
a fifth of the value to it. 32The entire tithe of the
herd and flock—every tenth animal that passes
under the shepherd's rod—will be holy to the
LORD. 33He must not pick out the good from the
bad or make any substitution. If he does make
a substitution, both the animal and its substitute become holy and cannot be redeemed.' "

34These are the commands the LORD gave
Moses on Mount Sinai for the Israelites.

[a]26 The Hebrew word can include both male and female.
[b]28 The Hebrew term refers to the irrevocable giving over of things or persons to the LORD.
[c]29 The Hebrew term refers to the irrevocable giving over of things or persons to the LORD, often by totally destroying them.

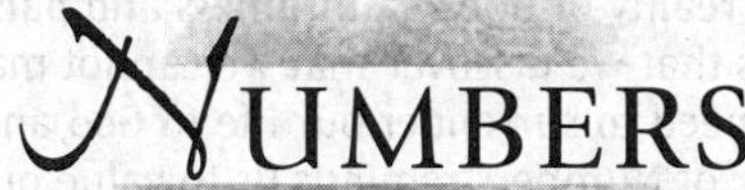

Numbers

The Big Picture

This book has long been known as Numbers because it begins and ends with a census of Israel. However, the Hebrew name for the book, "In the Wilderness," better describes what the book is about. While in the wilderness, God's people experienced not only God's kindness and patience but also his holiness and discipline. They learned that their new freedom from Egyptian bondage included the responsibility to serve and obey God.

After their exodus from Egypt, the Israelites moved quickly through the wilderness to the edge of the promised land. But when they saw the strength of the people living there, the Israelites became afraid and refused to conquer the land. Because they refused to act upon God's promises, the Israelites were sent back into the wilderness to wander for almost forty years! The book of Numbers ends with the Israelites again poised at the border of the promised land. Forty years of wilderness lessons had taught them that God's power was available to all who would trust and obey him.

The Israelites' experiences illustrate the importance of a practical faith in God. Their encounters show us the blessed fruits of obedience and the disastrous consequences of sin. Through the example of the Israelites we glimpse God's love manifested through his gracious forgiveness, wise discipline and his call to accountability.

It is usually in our own wilderness experiences that we discover the true meaning of life, faith and a personal relationship with God. God graciously offers us deliverance and cleansing, but our newfound freedom carries with it personal responsibility as well. We need to act on God's promises and follow the plan he sets out for us. When we do, he will lead us through our wilderness experiences; he will not allow us to wander forever.

A. PREPARATIONS IN SINAI FOR A LIFE OF FAITH IN THE PROMISED LAND (1:1–10:10)

1. Taking the Census (1:1–4:49)
2. Cleansing the Camp (5:1–7:89)
3. Dedicating the Priests (8:1-26)
4. Celebrating the Passover (9:1–10:10)

B. BARRIERS TO A LIFE OF FAITH IN THE WILDERNESS WANDERINGS (10:11–21:35)

1. From Sinai to Kadesh (10:11–14:45)
2. Wilderness Wanderings Near Kadesh (15:1–19:22)
3. From Kadesh to Moab (20:1–21:35)

C. PREPARATIONS IN MOAB FOR A LIFE OF FAITH IN THE PROMISED LAND (22:1–36:13)

1. God's Sovereignty Over Balaam and Balak (22:1–25:18)
2. A Final Census (26:1-65)
3. Preparations to Enter Canaan (27:1–36:13)

Spiritual Renewal Themes

EXPERIENCING THE WILDERNESS

All of us wish that our spiritual renewal would proceed from a dramatic escape from slavery to an immediate entrance into the promised land, leaving out the wilderness experiences in between. But growth and transformation in our spiritual lives

Essential Facts

PURPOSE:
To demonstrate historically that God's great mercy and forgiveness toward his people are consistent with the firm, loving discipline he shows when they disobey.

AUTHOR:
Moses.

AUDIENCE:
The people of Israel.

DATE WRITTEN:
During and shortly after Israel's wilderness experience, between 1445 and 1406 B.C.

SETTING:
Beginning with a census at the Sinai encampment, Numbers follows the people of Israel during thirty-eight years of wilderness wandering near Kadesh Barnea to the plains of Moab, just east of the promised land.

KEY VERSES:
"Now may the Lord's strength be displayed, just as you have declared: 'The LORD is slow to anger, abounding in love and forgiving sin and rebellion. Yet he does not leave the guilty unpunished; he punishes the children for the sin of the fathers to the third and fourth generation' " (14:17-18).

KEY PLACES:
Mount Sinai, Kadesh Barnea, Moab.

KEY PEOPLE:
Moses, Aaron, Caleb, Joshua.

occur within those wilderness times. While in the wilderness we come to terms with who we really are. We discover our faith anew and the reality of God's faithfulness and patience. It's in the wilderness that we discover that we cannot make it on our own, that we need to surrender our life to God and depend on him. The book of Numbers reminds us to value our own wilderness experiences as we progress in our spiritual growth.

THE IMPORTANCE OF FAITH

Faith is the opposite of self-sufficiency. The Israelites were confronted daily with the fact that if they were left to their own abilities, they would die in the wilderness. They were forced to live day by day, acting on faith that God would provide whatever they needed. The Israelites needed a practical faith—one that looked to God for safety, food and health. When we enter the wilderness experiences of our own spiritual journey, we need the same practical faith that will allow us to live day by day, trusting God to provide our needs.

PERSONAL ACCOUNTABILITY

The Israelites wandered for almost forty years in the wilderness because they believed the report of the ten faithless spies instead of trusting God's promises to deliver them from their enemies. Each wilderness step they took could have reminded them that their actions and lack of faith brought about their predicament. Most of the Israelites, however, chose to blame God and Moses for their wilderness wanderings. They refused to admit the truth that they were wandering because of the choices they had made. Many of us are in our present circumstances because of choices we have made too. We need to take personal responsibility for our lives and our choices if we desire to progress in our relationships with God and with others.

The Census

1 The LORD spoke to Moses in the Tent of
Meeting in the Desert of Sinai on the first
day of the second month of the second year
after the Israelites came out of Egypt. He said:
2"Take a census of the whole Israelite community by their clans and families, listing every
man by name, one by one. 3You and Aaron are
to number by their divisions all the men in
Israel twenty years old or more who are able to
serve in the army. 4One man from each tribe,
each the head of his family, is to help you.
5These are the names of the men who are to
assist you:

from Reuben, Elizur son of Shedeur;
6from Simeon, Shelumiel son of Zurishaddai;
7from Judah, Nahshon son of Amminadab;
8from Issachar, Nethanel son of Zuar;
9from Zebulun, Eliab son of Helon;
10from the sons of Joseph:
from Ephraim, Elishama son of Ammihud;
from Manasseh, Gamaliel son of Pedahzur;
11from Benjamin, Abidan son of Gideoni;
12from Dan, Ahiezer son of Ammishaddai;
13from Asher, Pagiel son of Ocran;
14from Gad, Eliasaph son of Deuel;
15from Naphtali, Ahira son of Enan."

16These were the men appointed from the
community, the leaders of their ancestral tribes.
They were the heads of the clans of Israel.
17Moses and Aaron took these men whose
names had been given, 18and they called the
whole community together on the first day of
the second month. The people indicated their
ancestry by their clans and families, and the
men twenty years old or more were listed by
name, one by one, 19as the LORD commanded
Moses. And so he counted them in the Desert of
Sinai:

20From the descendants of Reuben the firstborn
son of Israel:
All the men twenty years old or more
who were able to serve in the army
were listed by name, one by one, according to the records of their clans
and families. 21The number from the
tribe of Reuben was 46,500.

22From the descendants of Simeon:
All the men twenty years old or more
who were able to serve in the army
were counted and listed by name, one
by one, according to the records of
their clans and families. 23The number
from the tribe of Simeon was 59,300.

24From the descendants of Gad:
All the men twenty years old or more
who were able to serve in the army
were listed by name, according to the
records of their clans and families.
25The number from the tribe of Gad
was 45,650.

26From the descendants of Judah:
All the men twenty years old or more
who were able to serve in the army
were listed by name, according to the
records of their clans and families.
27The number from the tribe of Judah
was 74,600.

28From the descendants of Issachar:
All the men twenty years old or more
who were able to serve in the army
were listed by name, according to the
records of their clans and families.
29The number from the tribe of Issachar was 54,400.

30From the descendants of Zebulun:
All the men twenty years old or more
who were able to serve in the army
were listed by name, according to the
records of their clans and families.
31The number from the tribe of Zebulun was 57,400.

32From the sons of Joseph:
From the descendants of Ephraim:
All the men twenty years old or more
who were able to serve in the army
were listed by name, according to the
records of their clans and families.
33The number from the tribe of Ephraim was 40,500.
34From the descendants of Manasseh:

1:1 The opening expression "the LORD spoke to Moses in the Tent of Meeting" indicates God's personal interest in the lives of his people. He communicated clearly with his people, giving them instructions for right living. He was interested in the way they worshiped (Leviticus) as well as in the events of their daily lives (Numbers). He was interested in delivering and directing his people. This should remind us of his commitment to us today.

1:1 The Tent of Meeting provided a place for the people to worship and illustrated God's presence among them. God's permanent presence in our lives today can be found through a personal relationship with Jesus Christ. The apostle John recorded the ultimate fulfillment of the Old Testament Tent of Meeting: "The Word became flesh and made his dwelling [literally, "tabernacled"] among us" (John 1:14). Through the Holy Spirit, we have a tangible means of "meeting with God" each day now that Christ has returned to his Father. God's tangible presence provides the help we need to grow spiritually.

1:2–46 Taking a census of the Israelites prior to their journey to the promised land not only had organizational and military significance (1:3) but also served an important psychological purpose. As each individual identified his tribal and family background (1:18), it was a powerful reminder to the Israelites of their unity and common family heritage. This sense of unity would become essential as they faced the enemies and challenges ahead. Similarly, the assurance of support and unity within the family of Christ is a critical need for those who face wilderness periods in their lives today (Philippians 2:1–2).

All the men twenty years old or more who were able to serve in the army were listed by name, according to the records of their clans and families. 35The number from the tribe of Manasseh was 32,200.

36From the descendants of Benjamin:
All the men twenty years old or more who were able to serve in the army were listed by name, according to the records of their clans and families. 37The number from the tribe of Benjamin was 35,400.

38From the descendants of Dan:
All the men twenty years old or more who were able to serve in the army were listed by name, according to the records of their clans and families. 39The number from the tribe of Dan was 62,700.

40From the descendants of Asher:
All the men twenty years old or more who were able to serve in the army were listed by name, according to the records of their clans and families. 41The number from the tribe of Asher was 41,500.

42From the descendants of Naphtali:
All the men twenty years old or more who were able to serve in the army were listed by name, according to the records of their clans and families. 43The number from the tribe of Naphtali was 53,400.

44These were the men counted by Moses and Aaron and the twelve leaders of Israel, each one representing his family. 45All the Israelites twenty years old or more who were able to serve in Israel's army were counted according to their families. 46The total number was 603,550.

47The families of the tribe of Levi, however, were not counted along with the others. 48The LORD had said to Moses: 49"You must not count the tribe of Levi or include them in the census of the other Israelites. 50Instead, appoint the Levites to be in charge of the tabernacle of the Testimony—over all its furnishings and everything belonging to it. They are to carry the tabernacle and all its furnishings; they are to take care of it and encamp around it. 51Whenever the tabernacle is to move, the Levites are to take it down, and whenever the tabernacle is to be set up, the Levites shall do it. Anyone else who goes near it shall be put to death. 52The Israelites are to set up their tents by divisions, each man in his own camp under his own standard. 53The Levites, however, are to set up their tents around the tabernacle of the Testimony so that wrath will not fall on the Israelite community. The Levites are to be responsible for the care of the tabernacle of the Testimony."

54The Israelites did all this just as the LORD commanded Moses.

The Arrangement of the Tribal Camps

2 The LORD said to Moses and Aaron: 2"The Israelites are to camp around the Tent of Meeting some distance from it, each man under his standard with the banners of his family."

3On the east, toward the sunrise, the divisions of the camp of Judah are to encamp under their standard. The leader of the people of Judah is Nahshon son of Amminadab. 4His division numbers 74,600.

5The tribe of Issachar will camp next to them. The leader of the people of Issachar is Nethanel son of Zuar. 6His division numbers 54,400.

7The tribe of Zebulun will be next. The leader of the people of Zebulun is Eliab son of Helon. 8His division numbers 57,400.

9All the men assigned to the camp of Judah, according to their divisions, number 186,400. They will set out first.

10On the south will be the divisions of the camp of Reuben under their standard. The leader of the people of Reuben is Elizur son of Shedeur. 11His division numbers 46,500.

12The tribe of Simeon will camp next to them. The leader of the people of Simeon is Shelumiel son of Zurishaddai. 13His division numbers 59,300.

14The tribe of Gad will be next. The leader of the people of Gad is Eliasaph son of Deuel.[a] 15His division numbers 45,650.

16All the men assigned to the camp of Reuben, according to their divisions, number 151,450. They will set out second.

17Then the Tent of Meeting and the camp of the Levites will set out in the middle of the camps. They will set out in the same order as they encamp, each in his own place under his standard.

18On the west will be the divisions of the camp of Ephraim under their standard. The leader of the people of Ephraim

[a] 14 Many manuscripts of the Masoretic Text, Samaritan Pentateuch and Vulgate (see also Num. 1:14); most manuscripts of the Masoretic Text *Reuel*

2:1–34 As they traveled and camped, the Israelites were to arrange themselves by tribe around the Tent of Meeting. God wanted the Israelites to keep him in constant focus, making him the center of all their thoughts and actions. Many of us try to face the challenges of life alone but find the battle overwhelming. It is only through the power of God, as we keep him constantly before us, that true victory and renewal can be realized.

is Elishama son of Ammihud. 19His division numbers 40,500.
20The tribe of Manasseh will be next to
them. The leader of the people of Manasseh is Gamaliel son of Pedahzur. 21His division numbers 32,200.
22The tribe of Benjamin will be next.
The leader of the people of Benjamin is
Abidan son of Gideoni. 23His division
numbers 35,400.
24All the men assigned to the camp of
Ephraim, according to their divisions,
number 108,100. They will set out third.

25On the north will be the divisions of
the camp of Dan, under their standard.
The leader of the people of Dan is Ahiezer
son of Ammishaddai. 26His division numbers 62,700.
27The tribe of Asher will camp next to
them. The leader of the people of Asher is
Pagiel son of Ocran. 28His division numbers 41,500.
29The tribe of Naphtali will be next. The
leader of the people of Naphtali is Ahira
son of Enan. 30His division numbers
53,400.
31All the men assigned to the camp of
Dan number 157,600. They will set out
last, under their standards.

32These are the Israelites, counted according to their families. All those in
the camps, by their divisions, number
603,550. 33The Levites, however, were not
counted along with the other Israelites, as
the LORD commanded Moses.

34So the Israelites did everything the LORD
commanded Moses; that is the way they encamped under their standards, and that is the
way they set out, each with his clan and family.

The Levites

3 This is the account of the family of Aaron
and Moses at the time the LORD talked with
Moses on Mount Sinai.
2The names of the sons of Aaron were Nadab
the firstborn and Abihu, Eleazar and Ithamar.
3Those were the names of Aaron's sons, the
anointed priests, who were ordained to serve as
priests. 4Nadab and Abihu, however, fell dead
before the LORD when they made an offering
with unauthorized fire before him in the Desert
of Sinai. They had no sons; so only Eleazar and
Ithamar served as priests during the lifetime of
their father Aaron.
5The LORD said to Moses, 6"Bring the tribe of
Levi and present them to Aaron the priest to
assist him. 7They are to perform duties for him
and for the whole community at the Tent of
Meeting by doing the work of the tabernacle.
8They are to take care of all the furnishings of
the Tent of Meeting, fulfilling the obligations of
the Israelites by doing the work of the tabernacle. 9Give the Levites to Aaron and his sons; they
are the Israelites who are to be given wholly to
him.[a] 10Appoint Aaron and his sons to serve as
priests; anyone else who approaches the sanctuary must be put to death."
11The LORD also said to Moses, 12"I have tak-
en the Levites from among the Israelites in place
of the first male offspring of every Israelite
woman. The Levites are mine, 13for all the firstborn are mine. When I struck down all the firstborn in Egypt, I set apart for myself every
firstborn in Israel, whether man or animal.
They are to be mine. I am the LORD."
14The LORD said to Moses in the Desert of
Sinai, 15"Count the Levites by their families and
clans. Count every male a month old or more."
16So Moses counted them, as he was commanded by the word of the LORD.
17These were the names of the sons of Levi:
Gershon, Kohath and Merari.
18These were the names of the Gershonite
clans:
Libni and Shimei.
19The Kohathite clans:
Amram, Izhar, Hebron and Uzziel.
20The Merarite clans:
Mahli and Mushi.
These were the Levite clans, according to
their families.

21To Gershon belonged the clans of the Lib-
nites and Shimeites; these were the Gershonite
clans. 22The number of all the males a month
old or more who were counted was 7,500.
23The Gershonite clans were to camp on the
west, behind the tabernacle. 24The leader of the
families of the Gershonites was Eliasaph son of
Lael. 25At the Tent of Meeting the Gershonites
were responsible for the care of the tabernacle
and tent, its coverings, the curtain at the entrance to the Tent of Meeting, 26the curtains of
the courtyard, the curtain at the entrance to the
courtyard surrounding the tabernacle and altar,
and the ropes—and everything related to their
use.

27To Kohath belonged the clans of the Amramites, Izharites, Hebronites and Uzzielites;
these were the Kohathite clans. 28The number
of all the males a month old or more was

[a]9 Most manuscripts of the Masoretic Text; some manuscripts of the Masoretic Text, Samaritan Pentateuch and Septuagint (see also Num. 8:16) *to me*

3:1—4:49 The detailed organization of the Levites and priests in these chapters illustrates the principle that God's calling is accompanied by responsibility and accountability. Out of Israel, God sovereignly chose one tribe (Levi), and out of that tribe he chose specific families who were to lead in Israel's worship. With great privilege comes great responsibility. When God places us in a position of influence, we must not take it lightly. We need to recognize our responsibility to obey God and our accountability before him.

8,600.[a] The Kohathites were responsible for the care of the sanctuary. 29The Kohathite clans were to camp on the south side of the tabernacle. 30The leader of the families of the Kohathite clans was Elizaphan son of Uzziel. 31They were responsible for the care of the ark, the table, the lampstand, the altars, the articles of the sanctuary used in ministering, the curtain, and everything related to their use. 32The chief leader of the Levites was Eleazar son of Aaron, the priest. He was appointed over those who were responsible for the care of the sanctuary.

33To Merari belonged the clans of the Mahlites and the Mushites; these were the Merarite clans. 34The number of all the males a month old or more who were counted was 6,200. 35The leader of the families of the Merarite clans was Zuriel son of Abihail; they were to camp on the north side of the tabernacle. 36The Merarites were appointed to take care of the frames of the tabernacle, its crossbars, posts, bases, all its equipment, and everything related to their use, 37as well as the posts of the surrounding courtyard with their bases, tent pegs and ropes.

38Moses and Aaron and his sons were to camp to the east of the tabernacle, toward the sunrise, in front of the Tent of Meeting. They were responsible for the care of the sanctuary on behalf of the Israelites. Anyone else who approached the sanctuary was to be put to death.

39The total number of Levites counted at the LORD's command by Moses and Aaron according to their clans, including every male a month old or more, was 22,000.

40The LORD said to Moses, "Count all the firstborn Israelite males who are a month old or more and make a list of their names. 41Take the Levites for me in place of all the firstborn of the Israelites, and the livestock of the Levites in place of all the firstborn of the livestock of the Israelites. I am the LORD."

42So Moses counted all the firstborn of the Israelites, as the LORD commanded him. 43The total number of firstborn males a month old or more, listed by name, was 22,273.

44The LORD also said to Moses, 45"Take the Levites in place of all the firstborn of Israel, and the livestock of the Levites in place of their livestock. The Levites are to be mine. I am the LORD. 46To redeem the 273 firstborn Israelites who exceed the number of the Levites, 47collect five shekels[b] for each one, according to the sanctuary shekel, which weighs twenty gerahs. 48Give the money for the redemption of the additional Israelites to Aaron and his sons."

49So Moses collected the redemption money from those who exceeded the number redeemed by the Levites. 50From the firstborn of the Israelites he collected silver weighing 1,365 shekels,[c] according to the sanctuary shekel. 51Moses gave the redemption money to Aaron and his sons, as he was commanded by the word of the LORD.

The Kohathites

4 The LORD said to Moses and Aaron: 2"Take a census of the Kohathite branch of the Levites by their clans and families. 3Count all the men from thirty to fifty years of age who come to serve in the work in the Tent of Meeting.

4"This is the work of the Kohathites in the Tent of Meeting: the care of the most holy things. 5When the camp is to move, Aaron and his sons are to go in and take down the shielding curtain and cover the ark of the Testimony with it. 6Then they are to cover this with hides of sea cows,[d] spread a cloth of solid blue over that and put the poles in place.

7"Over the table of the Presence they are to spread a blue cloth and put on it the plates, dishes and bowls, and the jars for drink offerings; the bread that is continually there is to remain on it. 8Over these they are to spread a scarlet cloth, cover that with hides of sea cows and put its poles in place.

9"They are to take a blue cloth and cover the lampstand that is for light, together with its lamps, its wick trimmers and trays, and all its jars for the oil used to supply it. 10Then they are to wrap it and all its accessories in a covering of hides of sea cows and put it on a carrying frame.

11"Over the gold altar they are to spread a blue cloth and cover that with hides of sea cows and put its poles in place.

12"They are to take all the articles used for ministering in the sanctuary, wrap them in a blue cloth, cover that with hides of sea cows and put them on a carrying frame.

13"They are to remove the ashes from the bronze altar and spread a purple cloth over it. 14Then they are to place on it all the utensils used for ministering at the altar, including the firepans, meat forks, shovels and sprinkling bowls. Over it they are to spread a covering of hides of sea cows and put its poles in place.

15"After Aaron and his sons have finished

[a] 28 Hebrew; some Septuagint manuscripts *8,300*
[b] 47 That is, about 2 ounces (about 55 grams)
[c] 50 That is, about 35 pounds (about 15.5 kilograms)
[d] 6 That is, dugongs; also in verses 8, 10, 11, 12, 14 and 25

4:1–49 The efficient operation of the Israelite camp (especially the moving process) required detailed organization and cooperation. When each person cooperated and did his unique task, good results were achieved. The ministry of the church today, especially in meeting some of the greatest human needs, requires a cooperative effort by people using their unique spiritual gifts to help others (1 Corinthians 12:24–27). Only then will we be able to reach those in need and provide the necessary environment for spiritual renewal and growth.

covering the holy furnishings and all the holy articles, and when the camp is ready to move, the Kohathites are to come to do the carrying. But they must not touch the holy things or they will die. The Kohathites are to carry those things that are in the Tent of Meeting.

16"Eleazar son of Aaron, the priest, is to have charge of the oil for the light, the fragrant incense, the regular grain offering and the anointing oil. He is to be in charge of the entire tabernacle and everything in it, including its holy furnishings and articles."

17The LORD said to Moses and Aaron, 18"See that the Kohathite tribal clans are not cut off from the Levites. 19So that they may live and not die when they come near the most holy things, do this for them: Aaron and his sons are to go into the sanctuary and assign to each man his work and what he is to carry. 20But the Kohathites must not go in to look at the holy things, even for a moment, or they will die."

The Gershonites

21The LORD said to Moses, 22"Take a census also of the Gershonites by their families and clans. 23Count all the men from thirty to fifty years of age who come to serve in the work at the Tent of Meeting.

24"This is the service of the Gershonite clans as they work and carry burdens: 25They are to carry the curtains of the tabernacle, the Tent of Meeting, its covering and the outer covering of hides of sea cows, the curtains for the entrance to the Tent of Meeting, 26the curtains of the courtyard surrounding the tabernacle and altar, the curtain for the entrance, the ropes and all the equipment used in its service. The Gershonites are to do all that needs to be done with these things. 27All their service, whether carrying or doing other work, is to be done under the direction of Aaron and his sons. You shall assign to them as their responsibility all they are to carry. 28This is the service of the Gershonite clans at the Tent of Meeting. Their duties are to be under the direction of Ithamar son of Aaron, the priest.

The Merarites

29"Count the Merarites by their clans and families. 30Count all the men from thirty to fifty years of age who come to serve in the work at the Tent of Meeting. 31This is their duty as they perform service at the Tent of Meeting: to carry the frames of the tabernacle, its crossbars, posts and bases, 32as well as the posts of the surrounding courtyard with their bases, tent pegs, ropes, all their equipment and everything related to their use. Assign to each man the specific things he is to carry. 33This is the service of the Merarite clans as they work at the Tent of Meeting under the direction of Ithamar son of Aaron, the priest."

The Numbering of the Levite Clans

34Moses, Aaron and the leaders of the community counted the Kohathites by their clans and families. 35All the men from thirty to fifty years of age who came to serve in the work in the Tent of Meeting, 36counted by clans, were 2,750. 37This was the total of all those in the Kohathite clans who served in the Tent of Meeting. Moses and Aaron counted them according to the LORD's command through Moses.

38The Gershonites were counted by their clans and families. 39All the men from thirty to fifty years of age who came to serve in the work at the Tent of Meeting, 40counted by their clans and families, were 2,630. 41This was the total of those in the Gershonite clans who served at the Tent of Meeting. Moses and Aaron counted them according to the LORD's command.

42The Merarites were counted by their clans and families. 43All the men from thirty to fifty years of age who came to serve in the work at the Tent of Meeting, 44counted by their clans, were 3,200. 45This was the total of those in the Merarite clans. Moses and Aaron counted them according to the LORD's command through Moses.

46So Moses, Aaron and the leaders of Israel counted all the Levites by their clans and families. 47All the men from thirty to fifty years of age who came to do the work of serving and carrying the Tent of Meeting 48numbered 8,580. 49At the LORD's command through Moses, each was assigned his work and told what to carry.

Thus they were counted, as the LORD commanded Moses.

The Purity of the Camp

5 The LORD said to Moses, 2"Command the Israelites to send away from the camp anyone who has an infectious skin disease[a] or a discharge of any kind, or who is ceremonially unclean because of a dead body. 3Send away male and female alike; send them outside the camp so they will not defile their camp, where I dwell among them." 4The Israelites did this; they sent them outside the camp. They did just as the LORD had instructed Moses.

Restitution for Wrongs

5The LORD said to Moses, 6"Say to the Israelites: 'When a man or woman wrongs another in any way[b] and so is unfaithful to the LORD, that

[a]2 Traditionally *leprosy*; the Hebrew word was used for various diseases affecting the skin—not necessarily leprosy.
[b]6 Or *woman commits any wrong common to mankind*

5:5–7 This command for dealing with sin emphasizes the same principles as the sin and guilt offerings of Leviticus 4—5. God has provided clear instructions for those who have wronged others. These include admitting our wrongdoing and providing restitution wherever possible. If we follow God's instructions, we will make significant progress in our spiritual growth and in our relationships with others.

person is guilty 7and must confess the sin he has
committed. He must make full restitution for
his wrong, add one fifth to it and give it all to
the person he has wronged. 8But if that person
has no close relative to whom restitution can be
made for the wrong, the restitution belongs to
the LORD and must be given to the priest, along
with the ram with which atonement is made for
him. 9All the sacred contributions the Israelites
bring to a priest will belong to him. 10Each
man's sacred gifts are his own, but what he gives
to the priest will belong to the priest.' "

The Test for an Unfaithful Wife

11Then the LORD said to Moses, 12"Speak to
the Israelites and say to them: 'If a man's wife
goes astray and is unfaithful to him 13by sleeping with another man, and this is hidden from
her husband and her impurity is undetected
(since there is no witness against her and she
has not been caught in the act), 14and if feelings
of jealousy come over her husband and he suspects his wife and she is impure—or if he is
jealous and suspects her even though she is not
impure— 15then he is to take his wife to the
priest. He must also take an offering of a tenth
of an ephah[a] of barley flour on her behalf. He
must not pour oil on it or put incense on it,
because it is a grain offering for jealousy, a reminder offering to draw attention to guilt.
16" 'The priest shall bring her and have her
stand before the LORD. 17Then he shall take
some holy water in a clay jar and put some dust
from the tabernacle floor into the water. 18After
the priest has had the woman stand before the
LORD, he shall loosen her hair and place in her
hands the reminder offering, the grain offering
for jealousy, while he himself holds the bitter
water that brings a curse. 19Then the priest shall
put the woman under oath and say to her, "If
no other man has slept with you and you have
not gone astray and become impure while married to your husband, may this bitter water that
brings a curse not harm you. 20But if you have
gone astray while married to your husband and
you have defiled yourself by sleeping with a
man other than your husband"— 21here the
priest is to put the woman under this curse of
the oath—"may the LORD cause your people to
curse and denounce you when he causes your
thigh to waste away and your abdomen to
swell.[b] 22May this water that brings a curse
enter your body so that your abdomen swells
and your thigh wastes away.[c]"
" 'Then the woman is to say, "Amen. So
be it."
23" 'The priest is to write these curses on a
scroll and then wash them off into the bitter
water. 24He shall have the woman drink the
bitter water that brings a curse, and this water
will enter her and cause bitter suffering. 25The
priest is to take from her hands the grain offering for jealousy, wave it before the LORD and
bring it to the altar. 26The priest is then to take
a handful of the grain offering as a memorial
offering and burn it on the altar; after that, he
is to have the woman drink the water. 27If she
has defiled herself and been unfaithful to her
husband, then when she is made to drink the
water that brings a curse, it will go into her and
cause bitter suffering; her abdomen will swell
and her thigh waste away,[d] and she will become accursed among her people. 28If, however, the woman has not defiled herself and is free
from impurity, she will be cleared of guilt and
will be able to have children.
29" 'This, then, is the law of jealousy when
a woman goes astray and defiles herself while
married to her husband, 30or when feelings of
jealousy come over a man because he suspects
his wife. The priest is to have her stand before
the LORD and is to apply this entire law to her.
31The husband will be innocent of any wrongdoing, but the woman will bear the consequences of her sin.' "

The Nazirite

6 The LORD said to Moses, 2"Speak to the
Israelites and say to them: 'If a man or
woman wants to make a special vow, a vow of
separation to the LORD as a Nazirite, 3he must
abstain from wine and other fermented drink
and must not drink vinegar made from wine or
from other fermented drink. He must not drink
grape juice or eat grapes or raisins. 4As long as
he is a Nazirite, he must not eat anything that

[a] 15 That is, probably about 2 quarts (about 2 liters)
[b] 21 Or *causes you to have a miscarrying womb and barrenness*
[c] 22 Or *body and cause you to be barren and have a miscarrying womb*
[d] 27 Or *suffering; she will have barrenness and a miscarrying womb*

5:11–15 The seriousness of adultery is underscored in this passage. Marriage was intended to illustrate God's covenant relationship with his people. The ritual described in 5:16–31 was used to demonstrate guilt and was not simply a magic spell. God will forgive all sins, even adultery, as was shown by Christ's words to the adulterous woman. But his charge to her, "Go now and leave your life of sin" (John 8:11), emphasizes the fact that forgiveness carries with it a responsibility to live by God's standards. God's priorities for his people have always emphasized pure relationships, especially in marriage.

6:1–21 Here the Nazirite vow is explained. This was a special commitment, or promise, made to God through which a person could prove personal devotion to God and demonstrate seriousness in following him. Vows, in general, were voluntary, including the Nazirite vow mentioned here. God's endorsement of this voluntary practice emphasizes how much he delights in obedience that flows from the heart, as opposed to more legalistic compliance to a set of rules.

6:3–4 The name *Nazirite* comes from a Hebrew word meaning "to separate." One aspect of this vow was separation from various activities and attitudes, symbolizing a person's willingness to set personal standards during the time of the vow. In the same way, self-discipline and self-examination both play key roles in our relationship with God as we continue growing spiritually.

comes from the grapevine, not even the seeds or skins.

5" 'During the entire period of his vow of separation no razor may be used on his head. He must be holy until the period of his separation to the LORD is over; he must let the hair of his head grow long. 6Throughout the period of his separation to the LORD he must not go near a dead body. 7Even if his own father or mother or brother or sister dies, he must not make himself ceremonially unclean on account of them, because the symbol of his separation to God is on his head. 8Throughout the period of his separation he is consecrated to the LORD.

9" 'If someone dies suddenly in his presence, thus defiling the hair he has dedicated, he must shave his head on the day of his cleansing—the seventh day. 10Then on the eighth day he must bring two doves or two young pigeons to the priest at the entrance to the Tent of Meeting. 11The priest is to offer one as a sin offering and the other as a burnt offering to make atonement for him because he sinned by being in the presence of the dead body. That same day he is to consecrate his head. 12He must dedicate himself to the LORD for the period of his separation and must bring a year-old male lamb as a guilt offering. The previous days do not count, because he became defiled during his separation.

13" 'Now this is the law for the Nazirite when the period of his separation is over. He is to be brought to the entrance to the Tent of Meeting. 14There he is to present his offerings to the LORD: a year-old male lamb without defect for a burnt offering, a year-old ewe lamb without defect for a sin offering, a ram without defect for a fellowship offering,[a] 15together with their grain offerings and drink offerings, and a basket of bread made without yeast—cakes made of fine flour mixed with oil, and wafers spread with oil.

16" 'The priest is to present them before the LORD and make the sin offering and the burnt offering. 17He is to present the basket of unleavened bread and is to sacrifice the ram as a fellowship offering to the LORD, together with its grain offering and drink offering.

18" 'Then at the entrance to the Tent of Meeting, the Nazirite must shave off the hair that he dedicated. He is to take the hair and put it in the fire that is under the sacrifice of the fellowship offering.

19" 'After the Nazirite has shaved off the hair of his dedication, the priest is to place in his hands a boiled shoulder of the ram, and a cake and a wafer from the basket, both made without yeast. 20The priest shall then wave them before the LORD as a wave offering; they are holy and belong to the priest, together with the breast that was waved and the thigh that was presented. After that, the Nazirite may drink wine.

21" 'This is the law of the Nazirite who vows his offering to the LORD in accordance with his separation, in addition to whatever else he can afford. He must fulfill the vow he has made, according to the law of the Nazirite.' "

The Priestly Blessing

22The LORD said to Moses, 23"Tell Aaron and his sons, 'This is how you are to bless the Israelites. Say to them:

24" ' "The LORD bless you
and keep you;
25the LORD make his face shine upon you
and be gracious to you;
26the LORD turn his face toward you
and give you peace." '

27"So they will put my name on the Israelites, and I will bless them."

Offerings at the Dedication of the Tabernacle

7 When Moses finished setting up the tabernacle, he anointed it and consecrated it and all its furnishings. He also anointed and consecrated the altar and all its utensils. 2Then the leaders of Israel, the heads of families who were the tribal leaders in charge of those who were counted, made offerings. 3They brought as their gifts before the LORD six covered carts and twelve oxen—an ox from each leader and a cart from every two. These they presented before the tabernacle.

4The LORD said to Moses, 5"Accept these from them, that they may be used in the work

[a]14 Traditionally *peace offering;* also in verses 17 and 18

6:5–8 An important aspect of the Nazirite vow was the separation *unto* God, dedicating one's life for his use. Romans 12:1 commands us to present our bodies as living sacrifices to God. The Nazirite vow provided opportunities to do this on special occasions, but we are to give ourselves to God regularly. Even in the most hopeless human situations, God gives hope. We receive this hope through Jesus Christ, who will save us and transform our lives.

6:24–26 The simple words of this blessing reflect God's desire for all his people. He is the source of all blessings, grace and peace in life; only through a relationship with God can we hope to experience the fullness of life described here. The blessing seems to build to its final word—*peace.* The beautiful Hebrew word *shalom* used here means much more than an absence of conflict. It implies a complete sense of well-being, health and contentment. God offers this *shalom* to anyone who is willing to follow him, especially to those whose lives have been bruised and broken.

7:1–88 The way we use our possessions is an important part of our accountability to God. This passage shows how God's ministry among his people often depends upon the personal gifts of individuals and families. An attitude of sacrifice and generosity is needed among us if we hope to meet the needs of others. This sacrifice may involve giving physical gifts, as did each of the tribal leaders. Sometimes it involves giving of our time, as did the Levites. Yet the nature and amount of our offering is to be voluntary and from the heart.

at the Tent of Meeting. Give them to the Levites
as each man's work requires."
6So Moses took the carts and oxen and gave
them to the Levites. 7He gave two carts and four
oxen to the Gershonites, as their work required,
8and he gave four carts and eight oxen to the
Merarites, as their work required. They were all
under the direction of Ithamar son of Aaron,
the priest. 9But Moses did not give any to the
Kohathites, because they were to carry on their
shoulders the holy things, for which they were
responsible.
10When the altar was anointed, the leaders
brought their offerings for its dedication and
presented them before the altar. 11For the LORD
had said to Moses, "Each day one leader is to
bring his offering for the dedication of the altar."

12The one who brought his offering on the first
day was Nahshon son of Amminadab of the
tribe of Judah.
13His offering was one silver plate weighing a hundred and thirty shekels,[a] and
one silver sprinkling bowl weighing seventy shekels,[b] both according to the
sanctuary shekel, each filled with fine
flour mixed with oil as a grain offering;
14one gold dish weighing ten shekels,[c]
filled with incense; 15one young bull, one
ram and one male lamb a year old, for a
burnt offering; 16one male goat for a sin
offering; 17and two oxen, five rams, five
male goats and five male lambs a year old,
to be sacrificed as a fellowship offering.[d]
This was the offering of Nahshon son of
Amminadab.

18On the second day Nethanel son of Zuar, the
leader of Issachar, brought his offering.
19The offering he brought was one silver
plate weighing a hundred and thirty shekels, and one silver sprinkling bowl weighing seventy shekels, both according to the
sanctuary shekel, each filled with fine
flour mixed with oil as a grain offering;
20one gold dish weighing ten shekels,
filled with incense; 21one young bull, one
ram and one male lamb a year old, for a
burnt offering; 22one male goat for a sin
offering; 23and two oxen, five rams, five
male goats and five male lambs a year old,
to be sacrificed as a fellowship offering.
This was the offering of Nethanel son of
Zuar.

24On the third day, Eliab son of Helon, the
leader of the people of Zebulun, brought his
offering.
25His offering was one silver plate weighing a hundred and thirty shekels, and one
silver sprinkling bowl weighing seventy
shekels, both according to the sanctuary
shekel, each filled with fine flour mixed
with oil as a grain offering; 26one gold dish
weighing ten shekels, filled with incense;
27one young bull, one ram and one male
lamb a year old, for a burnt offering; 28one
male goat for a sin offering; 29and two
oxen, five rams, five male goats and five
male lambs a year old, to be sacrificed as
a fellowship offering. This was the offering
of Eliab son of Helon.

30On the fourth day Elizur son of Shedeur, the
leader of the people of Reuben, brought his
offering.
31His offering was one silver plate weighing a hundred and thirty shekels, and one
silver sprinkling bowl weighing seventy
shekels, both according to the sanctuary
shekel, each filled with fine flour mixed
with oil as a grain offering; 32one gold dish
weighing ten shekels, filled with incense;
33one young bull, one ram and one male
lamb a year old, for a burnt offering; 34one
male goat for a sin offering; 35and two
oxen, five rams, five male goats and five
male lambs a year old, to be sacrificed as
a fellowship offering. This was the offering
of Elizur son of Shedeur.

36On the fifth day Shelumiel son of Zurishaddai, the leader of the people of Simeon, brought
his offering.
37His offering was one silver plate weighing a hundred and thirty shekels, and one
silver sprinkling bowl weighing seventy
shekels, both according to the sanctuary
shekel, each filled with fine flour mixed
with oil as a grain offering; 38one gold dish
weighing ten shekels, filled with incense;
39one young bull, one ram and one male
lamb a year old, for a burnt offering; 40one
male goat for a sin offering; 41and two
oxen, five rams, five male goats and five
male lambs a year old, to be sacrificed as
a fellowship offering. This was the offering
of Shelumiel son of Zurishaddai.

42On the sixth day Eliasaph son of Deuel, the
leader of the people of Gad, brought his offering.
43His offering was one silver plate weighing a hundred and thirty shekels, and one
silver sprinkling bowl weighing seventy
shekels, both according to the sanctuary
shekel, each filled with fine flour mixed
with oil as a grain offering; 44one gold dish
weighing ten shekels, filled with incense;
45one young bull, one ram and one male
lamb a year old, for a burnt offering; 46one
male goat for a sin offering; 47and two
oxen, five rams, five male goats and five
male lambs a year old, to be sacrificed as

[a] *13* That is, about 3 1/4 pounds (about 1.5 kilograms); also elsewhere in this chapter [b] *13* That is, about 1 3/4 pounds (about 0.8 kilogram); also elsewhere in this chapter [c] *14* That is, about 4 ounces (about 110 grams); also elsewhere in this chapter
[d] *17* Traditionally *peace offering*; also elsewhere in this chapter

a fellowship offering. This was the offering
of Eliasaph son of Deuel.

48On the seventh day Elishama son of Ammihud, the leader of the people of Ephraim,
brought his offering.
49His offering was one silver plate weighing a hundred and thirty shekels, and one
silver sprinkling bowl weighing seventy
shekels, both according to the sanctuary
shekel, each filled with fine flour mixed
with oil as a grain offering; 50one gold dish
weighing ten shekels, filled with incense;
51one young bull, one ram and one male
lamb a year old, for a burnt offering; 52one
male goat for a sin offering; 53and two
oxen, five rams, five male goats and five
male lambs a year old, to be sacrificed as
a fellowship offering. This was the offering
of Elishama son of Ammihud.

54On the eighth day Gamaliel son of Pedahzur,
the leader of the people of Manasseh, brought
his offering.
55His offering was one silver plate weighing a hundred and thirty shekels, and one
silver sprinkling bowl weighing seventy
shekels, both according to the sanctuary
shekel, each filled with fine flour mixed
with oil as a grain offering; 56one gold dish
weighing ten shekels, filled with incense;
57one young bull, one ram and one male
lamb a year old, for a burnt offering; 58one
male goat for a sin offering; 59and two
oxen, five rams, five male goats and five
male lambs a year old, to be sacrificed as
a fellowship offering. This was the offering
of Gamaliel son of Pedahzur.

60On the ninth day Abidan son of Gideoni, the
leader of the people of Benjamin, brought his
offering.
61His offering was one silver plate weighing a hundred and thirty shekels, and one
silver sprinkling bowl weighing seventy
shekels, both according to the sanctuary
shekel, each filled with fine flour mixed
with oil as a grain offering; 62one gold dish
weighing ten shekels, filled with incense;
63one young bull, one ram and one male
lamb a year old, for a burnt offering; 64one
male goat for a sin offering; 65and two
oxen, five rams, five male goats and five
male lambs a year old, to be sacrificed as
a fellowship offering. This was the offering
of Abidan son of Gideoni.

66On the tenth day Ahiezer son of Ammishaddai, the leader of the people of Dan, brought his
offering.
67His offering was one silver plate weighing a hundred and thirty shekels, and one
silver sprinkling bowl weighing seventy
shekels, both according to the sanctuary
shekel, each filled with fine flour mixed
with oil as a grain offering; 68one gold dish
weighing ten shekels, filled with incense;
69one young bull, one ram and one male
lamb a year old, for a burnt offering; 70one
male goat for a sin offering; 71and two
oxen, five rams, five male goats and five
male lambs a year old, to be sacrificed as
a fellowship offering. This was the offering
of Ahiezer son of Ammishaddai.

72On the eleventh day Pagiel son of Ocran, the
leader of the people of Asher, brought his offering.
73His offering was one silver plate weighing a hundred and thirty shekels, and one
silver sprinkling bowl weighing seventy
shekels, both according to the sanctuary
shekel, each filled with fine flour mixed
with oil as a grain offering; 74one gold dish
weighing ten shekels, filled with incense;
75one young bull, one ram and one male
lamb a year old, for a burnt offering; 76one
male goat for a sin offering; 77and two
oxen, five rams, five male goats and five
male lambs a year old, to be sacrificed as
a fellowship offering. This was the offering
of Pagiel son of Ocran.

78On the twelfth day Ahira son of Enan, the
leader of the people of Naphtali, brought his
offering.
79His offering was one silver plate weighing a hundred and thirty shekels, and one
silver sprinkling bowl weighing seventy
shekels, both according to the sanctuary
shekel, each filled with fine flour mixed
with oil as a grain offering; 80one gold dish
weighing ten shekels, filled with incense;
81one young bull, one ram and one male
lamb a year old, for a burnt offering; 82one
male goat for a sin offering; 83and two
oxen, five rams, five male goats and five
male lambs a year old, to be sacrificed as
a fellowship offering. This was the offering
of Ahira son of Enan.

84These were the offerings of the Israelite
leaders for the dedication of the altar when it
was anointed: twelve silver plates, twelve silver
sprinkling bowls and twelve gold dishes. 85Each
silver plate weighed a hundred and thirty shekels, and each sprinkling bowl seventy shekels.
Altogether, the silver dishes weighed two thousand four hundred shekels,[a] according to the
sanctuary shekel. 86The twelve gold dishes filled
with incense weighed ten shekels each, according to the sanctuary shekel. Altogether, the gold
dishes weighed a hundred and twenty shekels.[b] 87The total number of animals for the
burnt offering came to twelve young bulls,
twelve rams and twelve male lambs a year old,
together with their grain offering. Twelve male
goats were used for the sin offering. 88The total
number of animals for the sacrifice of the fel-

[a]85 That is, about 60 pounds (about 28 kilograms)
[b]86 That is, about 3 pounds (about 1.4 kilograms)

lowship offering came to twenty-four oxen, sixty rams, sixty male goats and sixty male lambs a year old. These were the offerings for the dedication of the altar after it was anointed.

89When Moses entered the Tent of Meeting to speak with the LORD, he heard the voice speaking to him from between the two cherubim above the atonement cover on the ark of the Testimony. And he spoke with him.

Setting Up the Lamps

8 The LORD said to Moses, 2"Speak to Aaron and say to him, 'When you set up the seven lamps, they are to light the area in front of the lampstand.' "

3Aaron did so; he set up the lamps so that they faced forward on the lampstand, just as the LORD commanded Moses. 4This is how the lampstand was made: It was made of hammered gold—from its base to its blossoms. The lampstand was made exactly like the pattern the LORD had shown Moses.

The Setting Apart of the Levites

5The LORD said to Moses: 6"Take the Levites from among the other Israelites and make them ceremonially clean. 7To purify them, do this: Sprinkle the water of cleansing on them; then have them shave their whole bodies and wash their clothes, and so purify themselves. 8Have them take a young bull with its grain offering of fine flour mixed with oil; then you are to take a second young bull for a sin offering. 9Bring the Levites to the front of the Tent of Meeting and assemble the whole Israelite community. 10You are to bring the Levites before the LORD, and the Israelites are to lay their hands on them. 11Aaron is to present the Levites before the LORD as a wave offering from the Israelites, so that they may be ready to do the work of the LORD.

12"After the Levites lay their hands on the heads of the bulls, use the one for a sin offering to the LORD and the other for a burnt offering, to make atonement for the Levites. 13Have the Levites stand in front of Aaron and his sons and then present them as a wave offering to the LORD. 14In this way you are to set the Levites apart from the other Israelites, and the Levites will be mine.

15"After you have purified the Levites and presented them as a wave offering, they are to come to do their work at the Tent of Meeting. 16They are the Israelites who are to be given wholly to me. I have taken them as my own in place of the firstborn, the first male offspring from every Israelite woman. 17Every firstborn male in Israel, whether man or animal, is mine. When I struck down all the firstborn in Egypt, I set them apart for myself. 18And I have taken the Levites in place of all the firstborn sons in Israel. 19Of all the Israelites, I have given the Levites as gifts to Aaron and his sons to do the work at the Tent of Meeting on behalf of the Israelites and to make atonement for them so that no plague will strike the Israelites when they go near the sanctuary."

20Moses, Aaron and the whole Israelite community did with the Levites just as the LORD commanded Moses. 21The Levites purified themselves and washed their clothes. Then Aaron presented them as a wave offering before the LORD and made atonement for them to purify them. 22After that, the Levites came to do their work at the Tent of Meeting under the supervision of Aaron and his sons. They did with the Levites just as the LORD commanded Moses.

23The LORD said to Moses, 24"This applies to the Levites: Men twenty-five years old or more shall come to take part in the work at the Tent of Meeting, 25but at the age of fifty, they must retire from their regular service and work no longer. 26They may assist their brothers in performing their duties at the Tent of Meeting, but they themselves must not do the work. This, then, is how you are to assign the responsibilities of the Levites."

The Passover

9 The LORD spoke to Moses in the Desert of Sinai in the first month of the second year

---

8:5–8, 12 This section focuses on the Levitical priests, noting several important aspects of their preparation for service. They were to be cleansed prior to service. The sin offering made on their behalf showed that even they, Israel's spiritual leaders, needed to be cleansed of sin. Only our great high priest, Jesus Christ, serves in the priestly role without sin. And even though he is sinless, he can fully sympathize with our weaknesses so that we need not fear approaching him in any time of need (Hebrews 4:14–16).

8:9–11, 13–16 The Levitical priests not only offered sacrifices and offerings to God—they were to consider themselves "living sacrifices." Their lives were to be given completely over to God. The New Testament also teaches that we are to consider ourselves holy priests, giving our lives as "living sacrifices, holy and pleasing to God" (Romans 12:1; see 1 Peter 2:5). A life founded on commitment to God contains the essential ingredients of a life filled with contentment and purpose.

8:15, 21 The priest's ultimate purpose was to serve God through his responsibilities in the Tent of Meeting. Here we see that priests were sanctified (set apart) and accountable to God for active service. This accountability is an essential part of our salvation as well. We will be held accountable to God for the way we use our time, talents and treasures as we serve him.

9:1–14 The Passover was to be an annual feast for all the Israelites—a celebration of their deliverance from bondage in Egypt (Exodus 12:1–51). A problem arose, however, for those who were ceremonially unclean at the time of Passover. According to the strict standards of the law, they were not allowed to join in the celebration even though it was required of them. Moses brought this problem to God, who graciously instituted a second date of celebration for those who couldn't participate at the regular time. God wants all of us to participate in a relationship with him too. Our failures and sins should not keep us from coming to God. He has provided a means for us to come, no matter how "unclean" we may be. Our Passover lamb, Jesus Christ, has taken away all "the sin of the world" (John 1:29).

after they came out of Egypt. He said, 2"Have the Israelites celebrate the Passover at the appointed time. 3Celebrate it at the appointed time, at twilight on the fourteenth day of this month, in accordance with all its rules and regulations."

4So Moses told the Israelites to celebrate the Passover, 5and they did so in the Desert of Sinai at twilight on the fourteenth day of the first month. The Israelites did everything just as the LORD commanded Moses.

6But some of them could not celebrate the Passover on that day because they were ceremonially unclean on account of a dead body. So they came to Moses and Aaron that same day 7and said to Moses, "We have become unclean because of a dead body, but why should we be kept from presenting the LORD's offering with the other Israelites at the appointed time?"

8Moses answered them, "Wait until I find out what the LORD commands concerning you."

9Then the LORD said to Moses, 10"Tell the Israelites: 'When any of you or your descendants are unclean because of a dead body or are away on a journey, they may still celebrate the LORD's Passover. 11They are to celebrate it on the fourteenth day of the second month at twilight. They are to eat the lamb, together with unleavened bread and bitter herbs. 12They must not leave any of it till morning or break any of its bones. When they celebrate the Passover, they must follow all the regulations. 13But if a man who is ceremonially clean and not on a journey fails to celebrate the Passover, that person must be cut off from his people because he did not present the LORD's offering at the appointed time. That man will bear the consequences of his sin.

14" 'An alien living among you who wants to celebrate the LORD's Passover must do so in accordance with its rules and regulations. You must have the same regulations for the alien and the native-born.' "

The Cloud Above the Tabernacle

15On the day the tabernacle, the Tent of the Testimony, was set up, the cloud covered it. From evening till morning the cloud above the tabernacle looked like fire. 16That is how it continued to be; the cloud covered it, and at night it looked like fire. 17Whenever the cloud lifted from above the Tent, the Israelites set out; wherever the cloud settled, the Israelites encamped. 18At the LORD's command the Israelites set out, and at his command they encamped. As long as the cloud stayed over the tabernacle, they remained in camp. 19When the cloud remained over the tabernacle a long time, the Israelites obeyed the LORD's order and did not set out. 20Sometimes the cloud was over the tabernacle only a few days; at the LORD's command they would encamp, and then at his command they would set out. 21Sometimes the cloud stayed only from evening till morning, and when it lifted in the morning, they set out. Whether by day or by night, whenever the cloud lifted, they set out. 22Whether the cloud stayed over the tabernacle for two days or a month or a year, the Israelites would remain in camp and not set out; but when it lifted, they would set out. 23At the LORD's command they encamped, and at the LORD's command they set out. They obeyed the LORD's order, in accordance with his command through Moses.

The Silver Trumpets

10 The LORD said to Moses: 2"Make two trumpets of hammered silver, and use them for calling the community together and for having the camps set out. 3When both are sounded, the whole community is to assemble before you at the entrance to the Tent of Meeting. 4If only one is sounded, the leaders—the heads of the clans of Israel—are to assemble before you. 5When a trumpet blast is sounded, the tribes camping on the east are to set out. 6At the sounding of a second blast, the camps on the south are to set out. The blast will be the signal for setting out. 7To gather the assembly, blow the trumpets, but not with the same signal.

8"The sons of Aaron, the priests, are to blow the trumpets. This is to be a lasting ordinance for you and the generations to come. 9When you go into battle in your own land against an enemy who is oppressing you, sound a blast on the trumpets. Then you will be remembered by the LORD your God and rescued from your enemies. 10Also at your times of rejoicing—your appointed feasts and New Moon festivals—you are to sound the trumpets over your burnt offerings and fellowship offerings,[a] and they will be a memorial for you before your God. I am the LORD your God."

The Israelites Leave Sinai

11On the twentieth day of the second month of the second year, the cloud lifted from above

[a] 10 Traditionally *peace offerings*

9:15–23 As the cloud moved, so did the Israelites. They had to stay alert, watching each day for God's guidance. It was essential for the people to trust God rather than to depend upon their own plans. This object lesson of obedience should be the description of our day-by-day walk with God—to trust in him completely and not in ourselves (Proverbs 3:5–6).

10:11–36 This section begins the account of Israel's journey through the wilderness on the way to the promised land. They were entering new territory on their way to building a new life, but the immediate results were not encouraging. As they set out for the promised land, they were not willing to trust God to lead and protect them. Their weak faith showed up in their impatience with God, resulting in thirty-eight years of wilderness wandering. Often, building a new life involves entering uncharted territory. It takes great patience to let God guide us each step of the way. Let us learn from the mistakes of the

the tabernacle of the Testimony. 12Then the Israelites set out from the Desert of Sinai and traveled from place to place until the cloud came to rest in the Desert of Paran. 13They set out, this first time, at the LORD's command through Moses.

14The divisions of the camp of Judah went first, under their standard. Nahshon son of Amminadab was in command. 15Nethanel son of Zuar was over the division of the tribe of Issachar, 16and Eliab son of Helon was over the division of the tribe of Zebulun. 17Then the tabernacle was taken down, and the Gershonites and Merarites, who carried it, set out.

18The divisions of the camp of Reuben went next, under their standard. Elizur son of Shedeur was in command. 19Shelumiel son of Zurishaddai was over the division of the tribe of Simeon, 20and Eliasaph son of Deuel was over the division of the tribe of Gad. 21Then the Kohathites set out, carrying the holy things. The tabernacle was to be set up before they arrived.

22The divisions of the camp of Ephraim went next, under their standard. Elishama son of Ammihud was in command. 23Gamaliel son of Pedahzur was over the division of the tribe of Manasseh, 24and Abidan son of Gideoni was over the division of the tribe of Benjamin.

25Finally, as the rear guard for all the units, the divisions of the camp of Dan set out, under their standard. Ahiezer son of Ammishaddai was in command. 26Pagiel son of Ocran was over the division of the tribe of Asher, 27and Ahira son of Enan was over the division of the tribe of Naphtali. 28This was the order of march for the Israelite divisions as they set out.

29Now Moses said to Hobab son of Reuel the Midianite, Moses' father-in-law, "We are setting out for the place about which the LORD said, 'I will give it to you.' Come with us and we will treat you well, for the LORD has promised good things to Israel."

30He answered, "No, I will not go; I am going back to my own land and my own people."

31But Moses said, "Please do not leave us. You know where we should camp in the desert, and you can be our eyes. 32If you come with us, we will share with you whatever good things the LORD gives us."

33So they set out from the mountain of the LORD and traveled for three days. The ark of the covenant of the LORD went before them during those three days to find them a place to rest. 34The cloud of the LORD was over them by day when they set out from the camp.

35Whenever the ark set out, Moses said,

"Rise up, O LORD!
May your enemies be scattered;
may your foes flee before you."

36Whenever it came to rest, he said,

"Return, O LORD,
to the countless thousands of Israel."

Fire From the LORD

11 Now the people complained about their hardships in the hearing of the LORD, and when he heard them his anger was aroused. Then fire from the LORD burned among them and consumed some of the outskirts of the camp. 2When the people cried out to Moses, he prayed to the LORD and the fire died down. 3So that place was called Taberah,[a] because fire from the LORD had burned among them.

Quail From the LORD

4The rabble with them began to crave other food, and again the Israelites started wailing

[a]3 *Taberah* means *burning.*

Israelites (1 Corinthians 10; Hebrews 3—4).

10:35–36 Even though the presence of God was with Israel, evidenced by the cloud and the ark of the covenant (10:33–34), Moses continually prayed for the well-being of his people. He was their intercessor and knew the importance of the ministry of prayer. Praying for others is always important, for it is how we grasp the awesome power of God to change their lives.

11:1–3 Instead of trusting God to take care of them, the people started to complain. This first complaint against God was just one of many during their wilderness travels. God reacted quickly and harshly to their murmuring because their complaining indicated their ingratitude, impatience, and lack of faith. The difficult process of going from Egyptian bondage to God's promised home in Canaan could only be accomplished if the people patiently trusted God to get them through. The same is true for us.

11:4–5 We are told here that a group of Egyptians traveling with Israel began complaining. Notice that the complaints were then spread by the Israelites. This illustrates the importance of supportive company as we pursue spiritual growth and obedience to God's plan. One of Satan's strategies to undermine our faith can often be the negative attitudes and comments of those around us. We need to be careful about choosing our companions and should seek out people who build us up and strengthen us in our pursuit of spiritual renewal.

11:4–6 When things got tough in the wilderness, the people wanted to go back to their life of bondage in Egypt. The people seemed to think that a life of slavery in Egypt was better than a life of struggle in the wilderness. The Israelites had stopped seeing with the eyes of faith. They had lost sight of their goal and God's guiding presence. Our spiritual journey can be likened to Israel's experience in the wilderness. As things get tough, it is easy to longingly look back at our old life. We need to keep our eyes on God and his promises for us. When we do, we will discover the new and better life God has planned for us.

11:4–6 God had supplied the Israelites with a miraculous food source—manna from heaven. But the people revealed their discontent by complaining to God. They were blind to the fact that supplying an entire nation of people in a desert with ample provisions was an awesome miracle. We often fail to see our greatest blessings too. We may find ourselves complaining about our circumstances in life. We need to stop complaining and examine all the wonderful blessings we have. With the positive attitudes of faith and thanksgiving to God, our great provider, we can continue growing spiritually.

and said, "If only we had meat to eat! 5We remember the fish we ate in Egypt at no cost—also the cucumbers, melons, leeks, onions and garlic. 6But now we have lost our appetite; we never see anything but this manna!"

7The manna was like coriander seed and looked like resin. 8The people went around gathering it, and then ground it in a handmill or crushed it in a mortar. They cooked it in a pot or made it into cakes. And it tasted like something made with olive oil. 9When the dew settled on the camp at night, the manna also came down.

10Moses heard the people of every family wailing, each at the entrance to his tent. The LORD became exceedingly angry, and Moses was troubled. 11He asked the LORD, "Why have you brought this trouble on your servant? What have I done to displease you that you put the burden of all these people on me? 12Did I conceive all these people? Did I give them birth? Why do you tell me to carry them in my arms, as a nurse carries an infant, to the land you promised on oath to their forefathers? 13Where can I get meat for all these people? They keep wailing to me, 'Give us meat to eat!' 14I cannot carry all these people by myself; the burden is too heavy for me. 15If this is how you are going to treat me, put me to death right now—if I have found favor in your eyes—and do not let me face my own ruin."

16The LORD said to Moses: "Bring me seventy of Israel's elders who are known to you as leaders and officials among the people. Have them come to the Tent of Meeting, that they may stand there with you. 17I will come down and speak with you there, and I will take of the Spirit that is on you and put the Spirit on them. They will help you carry the burden of the people so that you will not have to carry it alone.

18"Tell the people: 'Consecrate yourselves in preparation for tomorrow, when you will eat meat. The LORD heard you when you wailed, "If only we had meat to eat! We were better off in Egypt!" Now the LORD will give you meat, and you will eat it. 19You will not eat it for just one day, or two days, or five, ten or twenty days, 20but for a whole month—until it comes out of your nostrils and you loathe it—because you have rejected the LORD, who is among you, and have wailed before him, saying, "Why did we ever leave Egypt?"' "

21But Moses said, "Here I am among six hundred thousand men on foot, and you say, 'I will give them meat to eat for a whole month!' 22Would they have enough if flocks and herds were slaughtered for them? Would they have enough if all the fish in the sea were caught for them?"

23The LORD answered Moses, "Is the LORD's arm too short? You will now see whether or not what I say will come true for you."

24So Moses went out and told the people what the LORD had said. He brought together seventy of their elders and had them stand around the Tent. 25Then the LORD came down in the cloud and spoke with him, and he took of the Spirit that was on him and put the Spirit on the seventy elders. When the Spirit rested on them, they prophesied, but they did not do so again.[a]

26However, two men, whose names were Eldad and Medad, had remained in the camp. They were listed among the elders, but did not go out to the Tent. Yet the Spirit also rested on them, and they prophesied in the camp. 27A young man ran and told Moses, "Eldad and Medad are prophesying in the camp."

28Joshua son of Nun, who had been Moses' aide since youth, spoke up and said, "Moses, my lord, stop them!"

29But Moses replied, "Are you jealous for my sake? I wish that all the LORD's people were prophets and that the LORD would put his Spirit on them!" 30Then Moses and the elders of Israel returned to the camp.

31Now a wind went out from the LORD and drove quail in from the sea. It brought them[b] down all around the camp to about three feet[c] above the ground, as far as a day's walk in any direction. 32All that day and night and all the next day the people went out and gathered quail. No one gathered less than ten homers.[d] Then they spread them out all around the camp. 33But while the meat was still between their teeth and before it could be consumed, the anger of the LORD burned against the people, and he struck them with a severe plague. 34Therefore the place was named Kibroth Hattaavah,[e] because there they buried the people who had craved other food.

35From Kibroth Hattaavah the people traveled to Hazeroth and stayed there.

Miriam and Aaron Oppose Moses

12 Miriam and Aaron began to talk against Moses because of his Cushite wife, for he had married a Cushite. 2"Has the LORD spoken only through Moses?" they asked. "Hasn't he also spoken through us?" And the LORD heard this.

3(Now Moses was a very humble man, more

[a]25 Or *prophesied and continued to do so* [b]31 Or *They flew* [c]31 Hebrew *two cubits* (about 1 meter) [d]32 That is, probably about 60 bushels (about 2.2 kiloliters) [e]34 *Kibroth Hattaavah* means *graves of craving.*

11:10–15 When Moses complained angrily to God about his unpleasant circumstances, God didn't rebuke him. God's response toward Moses stands in stark contrast to the severe judgment brought upon the Israelites for their complaints. God evidently saw that Moses' motives were pure and his faith genuine; thus, God responded to Moses' honest, though complaining, cry for help. God is never afraid of the anger we may feel about the situations we face. He desires honesty in our prayers.

12:3–4 This parenthetical statement about Moses' humility

Aaron & Miriam

The pecking order in most families is usually established by order of birth from the oldest to youngest. The family of Aaron, Miriam and Moses probably started out this way too. Yet with time it became clear that God had special plans for Moses. At the time of Moses' birth, his sister Miriam was given a special part in preserving him from Pharaoh's decree demanding the death of all the Hebrew baby boys. Miriam probably continued to watch Moses from a distance while he grew up in Pharaoh's palace as the adopted son of Pharaoh's daughter. Still later, Miriam most likely watched God raise up Moses to lead the Israelites out of their slavery in Egypt. Brother Aaron was also called to play a special role in the life of Moses. At one point Aaron was assigned to be his brother's spokesman. Later, God called Aaron to be Israel's high priest.

Yet Moses' older siblings were jealous that God had chosen Moses and raised him to a level above them. At a number of points during Moses' life Miriam and Aaron criticized him openly. This displeased God greatly, for it undermined the leadership of the man he had chosen to lead his people. Aaron and Miriam had been given important roles in the nation of Israel, yet their jealousy of Moses made them blind to the importance of their own gifts. God judged Miriam's criticism of Moses suddenly and harshly—with leprosy. People with this disease were not only doomed to a long and painful death but to banishment from society. It was only because of the intercessory prayer of Moses that Miriam was later healed by God.

We must be careful not to confuse constructive criticism with sibling jealousy. Sibling jealousy left unaddressed can lead to the destruction of the family and, in some cases, a much greater community. But when these problems are brought before God, he can restore even these relationships, just as he did for Aaron, Miriam and Moses.

STRENGTHS AND ACCOMPLISHMENTS:

Both were gifted to help the Israelites.

Aaron was called by God to be Israel's first high priest.

Miriam was an able leader and prophet.

WEAKNESSES AND MISTAKES:

Both were jealous of Moses' authority.

Miriam openly criticized Moses' leadership.

Both complained about Moses' marriage.

Aaron allowed himself to be manipulated by the people.

LESSONS FROM THEIR LIVES:

Order of birth doesn't necessarily define a person's level of success.

God chooses his leaders according to his own set of criteria, not ours.

The motives behind criticism, not just the criticism itself, need to be dealt with.

God gives us all special gifts, and he uses them to fulfill his plans.

Jealousy of others can easily blind us to our own special gifts.

KEY VERSES:

"Miriam and Aaron began to talk against Moses because of his Cushite wife, for he had married a Cushite. 'Has the LORD spoken only through Moses?' they asked. 'Hasn't he also spoken through us?' And the LORD heard this" (12:1–2).

The story of Aaron and Miriam is told throughout the book of Exodus. Aaron is also referred to in Leviticus, Numbers, Deuteronomy and Hebrews 7:11. Miriam is mentioned in Numbers 12:1–15; 20:1 and Deuteronomy 24:9. Both are mentioned in 1 Chronicles 6:3 and Micah 6:4.

humble than anyone else on the face of the
earth.)
4At once the LORD said to Moses, Aaron and
Miriam, "Come out to the Tent of Meeting, all
three of you." So the three of them came out.
5Then the LORD came down in a pillar of cloud;
he stood at the entrance to the Tent and summoned Aaron and Miriam. When both of them
stepped forward, 6he said, "Listen to my words:

"When a prophet of the LORD is among
you,
I reveal myself to him in visions,
I speak to him in dreams.
7But this is not true of my servant Moses;
he is faithful in all my house.
8With him I speak face to face,
clearly and not in riddles;
he sees the form of the LORD.
Why then were you not afraid
to speak against my servant Moses?"

9The anger of the LORD burned against them,
and he left them.
10When the cloud lifted from above the Tent,
there stood Miriam—leprous,[a] like snow. Aaron turned toward her and saw that she had
leprosy; 11and he said to Moses, "Please, my
lord, do not hold against us the sin we have so
foolishly committed. 12Do not let her be like
a stillborn infant coming from its mother's
womb with its flesh half eaten away."
13So Moses cried out to the LORD, "O God,
please heal her!"
14The LORD replied to Moses, "If her father
had spit in her face, would she not have been in
disgrace for seven days? Confine her outside
the camp for seven days; after that she can be
brought back." 15So Miriam was confined outside the camp for seven days, and the people
did not move on till she was brought back.
16After that, the people left Hazeroth and encamped in the Desert of Paran.

Exploring Canaan

13 The LORD said to Moses, 2"Send some
men to explore the land of Canaan,
which I am giving to the Israelites. From each
ancestral tribe send one of its leaders."
3So at the LORD's command Moses sent them
out from the Desert of Paran. All of them were
leaders of the Israelites. 4These are their names:

from the tribe of Reuben, Shammua son
of Zaccur;
5from the tribe of Simeon, Shaphat son of
Hori;
6from the tribe of Judah, Caleb son of Jephunneh;
7from the tribe of Issachar, Igal son of Joseph;
8from the tribe of Ephraim, Hoshea son of
Nun;
9from the tribe of Benjamin, Palti son of
Raphu;
10from the tribe of Zebulun, Gaddiel son
of Sodi;
11from the tribe of Manasseh (a tribe of
Joseph), Gaddi son of Susi;
12from the tribe of Dan, Ammiel son
of Gemalli;
13from the tribe of Asher, Sethur son of
Michael;
14from the tribe of Naphtali, Nahbi son
of Vophsi;
15from the tribe of Gad, Geuel son of Maki.

16These are the names of the men Moses sent to
explore the land. (Moses gave Hoshea son of
Nun the name Joshua.)
17When Moses sent them to explore Canaan,
he said, "Go up through the Negev and on into
the hill country. 18See what the land is like and
whether the people who live there are strong or
weak, few or many. 19What kind of land do they
live in? Is it good or bad? What kind of towns
do they live in? Are they unwalled or fortified?
20How is the soil? Is it fertile or poor? Are there
trees on it or not? Do your best to bring back
some of the fruit of the land." (It was the season
for the first ripe grapes.)
21So they went up and explored the land
from the Desert of Zin as far as Rehob, toward
Lebo[b] Hamath. 22They went up through the
Negev and came to Hebron, where Ahiman,
Sheshai and Talmai, the descendants of Anak,
lived. (Hebron had been built seven years before Zoan in Egypt.) 23When they reached the
Valley of Eshcol,[c] they cut off a branch bearing
a single cluster of grapes. Two of them carried
it on a pole between them, along with some
pomegranates and figs. 24That place was called
the Valley of Eshcol because of the cluster of
grapes the Israelites cut off there. 25At the end

[a] *10* The Hebrew word was used for various diseases affecting the skin—not necessarily leprosy. [b] *21* Or *toward the entrance to* [c] *23* *Eshcol* means *cluster;* also in verse 24.

---

is one of the most revealing evaluations of his character found in Scripture. Moses is described as the most humble man in the world. This is essentially the same quality commended by the third beatitude: "Blessed are the meek, for they will inherit the earth" (Matthew 5:5). Evidence of Moses' humility is found in his great patience and perseverance while leading Israel through the wilderness. Our own humility is extremely important as we surrender our lives to God.

13:25–29 The spy mission was undoubtedly planned to encourage Israel. They would see for themselves the richness of the land God had promised them. The spies' report began with a glorious description of the promised land. But the mood abruptly changed as they began to focus on the obstacles that stood between them and their new life there. They failed to recognize God's power to overcome powerful enemies, no matter how great. Because of their lack of faith, they had to wander for nearly forty more years in the wilderness. We all must keep our eyes off the obstacles of life and keep our eyes on God, whose power is sufficient for any difficulties we might face.

CALEB

Many of us seek the acceptance of others when we make decisions. We try not to admit it, but a careful examination of past decisions will probably show that we are like so many others—as we pursue the approval of others, we often side with the majority viewpoint. Unfortunately, the majority viewpoint of our world seldom gives God and his Word much consideration.

Caleb was an individual who saw things from God's perspective and stood against the majority opinion. Ten of the twelve spies who had entered Canaan, a clear majority, believed that the promised land couldn't be conquered. They came back with stories of impregnable, walled cities defended by terrible giants. They told the people that the task was hopeless, letting their fears and the majority opinion decide the course of action. But Caleb and Joshua, differed from the majority, embracing a godly, minority opinion. Caleb agreed that Canaan was well fortified and the task formidable. But he also believed that even the greatest of enemies was no match for the mighty God of Israel. Caleb spoke out, calling the people to believe in God's promises. Caleb knew that with God's help they could conquer all the obstacles and difficulties that the majority had reported.

Sadly, the people of Israel didn't listen to Caleb. They followed the majority opinion and refused to take the land God had promised them. As a direct result, the entire nation of Israel was left to wander in the wilderness for nearly forty years. Of all the adult Israelites who left Egypt, only Caleb and Joshua would enter the promised land.

It is so easy for us to focus on the obstacles in our own lives—all those things that make change seem impossible. We can learn from Caleb, who believed God's word despite the obstacles before him. When the situation appeared hopeless, Caleb knew that victory could come by seeking God and surrendering to the one who had promised his people the victory. Caleb learned to live for God's approval, not the approval of others. He realized what we also need to learn—self-worth should not be found in the approval of other people but only in the loving eyes of God.

STRENGTHS AND ACCOMPLISHMENTS:

He was one of the twelve hand-picked spies sent into Canaan.

He was able to express his faith in God even in the face of opposition.

Despite overwhelming opposition, he remained faithful to God and his promises.

He remained faithful to Joshua and Moses throughout the wilderness wanderings.

He based his self-worth on God's opinion, not on the opinions of others.

LESSONS FROM HIS LIFE:

Right and wrong can never be based solely on the majority opinion.

Boldness in a God-centered life is appropriate.

A meaningful faith has both words and actions behind it.

Our self-worth should not be based upon our acceptance by the majority.

KEY VERSE:

"But because my servant Caleb has a different spirit and follows me wholeheartedly, I will bring him into the land he went to, and his descendants will inherit it" (14:24).

Caleb's story is told in Numbers 13—14 and Joshua 14—15. He is also mentioned in Judges 1:12–21 and 1 Chronicles 4:15.

of forty days they returned from exploring the land.

Report on the Exploration

26They came back to Moses and Aaron and the whole Israelite community at Kadesh in the Desert of Paran. There they reported to them and to the whole assembly and showed them the fruit of the land. 27They gave Moses this account: "We went into the land to which you sent us, and it does flow with milk and honey! Here is its fruit. 28But the people who live there are powerful, and the cities are fortified and very large. We even saw descendants of Anak there. 29The Amalekites live in the Negev; the Hittites, Jebusites and Amorites live in the hill country; and the Canaanites live near the sea and along the Jordan."

30Then Caleb silenced the people before Moses and said, "We should go up and take possession of the land, for we can certainly do it."

31But the men who had gone up with him said, "We can't attack those people; they are stronger than we are." 32And they spread among the Israelites a bad report about the land they had explored. They said, "The land we explored devours those living in it. All the people we saw there are of great size. 33We saw the Nephilim there (the descendants of Anak come from the Nephilim). We seemed like grasshoppers in our own eyes, and we looked the same to them."

The People Rebel

14 That night all the people of the community raised their voices and wept aloud. 2All the Israelites grumbled against Moses and Aaron, and the whole assembly said to them, "If only we had died in Egypt! Or in this desert! 3Why is the LORD bringing us to this land only to let us fall by the sword? Our wives and children will be taken as plunder. Wouldn't it be better for us to go back to Egypt?" 4And they said to each other, "We should choose a leader and go back to Egypt."

5Then Moses and Aaron fell facedown in front of the whole Israelite assembly gathered there. 6Joshua son of Nun and Caleb son of Jephunneh, who were among those who had explored the land, tore their clothes 7and said to the entire Israelite assembly, "The land we passed through and explored is exceedingly good. 8If the LORD is pleased with us, he will lead us into that land, a land flowing with milk and honey, and will give it to us. 9Only do not rebel against the LORD. And do not be afraid of the people of the land, because we will swallow them up. Their protection is gone, but the LORD is with us. Do not be afraid of them."

10But the whole assembly talked about stoning them. Then the glory of the LORD appeared at the Tent of Meeting to all the Israelites. 11The LORD said to Moses, "How long will these people treat me with contempt? How long will they refuse to believe in me, in spite of all the miraculous signs I have performed among them? 12I will strike them down with a plague and destroy them, but I will make you into a nation greater and stronger than they."

13Moses said to the LORD, "Then the Egyptians will hear about it! By your power you brought these people up from among them. 14And they will tell the inhabitants of this land about it. They have already heard that you, O LORD, are with these people and that you, O LORD, have been seen face to face, that your cloud stays over them, and that you go before them in a pillar of cloud by day and a pillar of fire by night. 15If you put these people to death all at one time, the nations who have heard this report about you will say, 16'The LORD was not able to bring these people into the land he promised them on oath; so he slaughtered them in the desert.'

17"Now may the Lord's strength be displayed, just as you have declared: 18'The LORD is slow to anger, abounding in love and forgiving sin and rebellion. Yet he does not leave the guilty unpunished; he punishes the children for the sin of the fathers to the third and fourth generation.' 19In accordance with your great love, forgive the sin of these people, just as you have pardoned them from the time they left Egypt until now."

20The LORD replied, "I have forgiven them, as you asked. 21Nevertheless, as surely as I live and as surely as the glory of the LORD fills the whole earth, 22not one of the men who saw my glory and the miraculous signs I performed in Egypt and in the desert but who disobeyed me and tested me ten times— 23not one of them will

---

13:30 The minority report of Caleb, and later Joshua (14:6–9), emphasized God's power to overcome even the greatest of problems. Their faith enabled them to see obstacles not as problems but as opportunities for God to prove himself. The basis for their faith was God's promise to save his people from their enemies (10:9). When we have an active faith in God, our view of life and its challenges will emphasize the positive rather than the negative.

13:33 In this verse, the words of the ten spies reveal their perception of themselves: "We seemed like grasshoppers in our own eyes, and we looked the same to them." The Israelites failed to perceive themselves as God saw them. They were his chosen people, backed by the promises of the Creator of the universe. God had promised to give them the land of Canaan. As we face life's greatest challenges, we must see ourselves as God sees us, not as we think we appear alongside our obstacles. We need to realize that God loves us and has promised to help us overcome the adversity and sin in our lives.

14:5–11 The strong faith of four men is contrasted in these verses with the faithlessness of the entire nation. Moses and Aaron fell down before God (probably in intercessory prayer for the people). Joshua and Caleb reaffirmed their belief in God's ability to miraculously overcome the obstacles of Canaan. The entire nation, however, refused to listen and discussed stoning them. These four men wanted to follow God's plan. The majority forced them to do otherwise. The result of their faithlessness was a prolonged wilderness experience.

ever see the land I promised on oath to their forefathers. No one who has treated me with contempt will ever see it. 24But because my servant Caleb has a different spirit and follows me wholeheartedly, I will bring him into the land he went to, and his descendants will inherit it. 25Since the Amalekites and Canaanites are living in the valleys, turn back tomorrow and set out toward the desert along the route to the Red Sea.[a]"

26The LORD said to Moses and Aaron: 27"How long will this wicked community grumble against me? I have heard the complaints of these grumbling Israelites. 28So tell them, 'As surely as I live, declares the LORD, I will do to you the very things I heard you say: 29In this desert your bodies will fall—every one of you twenty years old or more who was counted in the census and who has grumbled against me. 30Not one of you will enter the land I swore with uplifted hand to make your home, except Caleb son of Jephunneh and Joshua son of Nun. 31As for your children that you said would be taken as plunder, I will bring them in to enjoy the land you have rejected. 32But you—your bodies will fall in this desert. 33Your children will be shepherds here for forty years, suffering for your unfaithfulness, until the last of your bodies lies in the desert. 34For forty years—one year for each of the forty days you explored the land—you will suffer for your sins and know what it is like to have me against you.' 35I, the LORD, have spoken, and I will surely do these things to this whole wicked community, which has banded together against me. They will meet their end in this desert; here they will die."

36So the men Moses had sent to explore the land, who returned and made the whole community grumble against him by spreading a bad report about it— 37these men responsible for spreading the bad report about the land were struck down and died of a plague before the LORD. 38Of the men who went to explore the land, only Joshua son of Nun and Caleb son of Jephunneh survived.

39When Moses reported this to all the Israelites, they mourned bitterly. 40Early the next morning they went up toward the high hill country. "We have sinned," they said. "We will go up to the place the LORD promised."

41But Moses said, "Why are you disobeying the LORD's command? This will not succeed! 42Do not go up, because the LORD is not with you. You will be defeated by your enemies, 43for the Amalekites and Canaanites will face you there. Because you have turned away from the LORD, he will not be with you and you will fall by the sword."

44Nevertheless, in their presumption they went up toward the high hill country, though neither Moses nor the ark of the LORD's covenant moved from the camp. 45Then the Amalekites and Canaanites who lived in that hill country came down and attacked them and beat them down all the way to Hormah.

Supplementary Offerings

15 The LORD said to Moses, 2"Speak to the Israelites and say to them: 'After you enter the land I am giving you as a home 3and you present to the LORD offerings made by fire, from the herd or the flock, as an aroma pleasing to the LORD—whether burnt offerings or sacrifices, for special vows or freewill offerings or festival offerings— 4then the one who brings his offering shall present to the LORD a grain offering of a tenth of an ephah[b] of fine flour mixed with a quarter of a hin[c] of oil. 5With each lamb for the burnt offering or the sacrifice, prepare a quarter of a hin of wine as a drink offering.

6" 'With a ram prepare a grain offering of two-tenths of an ephah[d] of fine flour mixed with a third of a hin[e] of oil, 7and a third of a hin of wine as a drink offering. Offer it as an aroma pleasing to the LORD.

8" 'When you prepare a young bull as a burnt offering or sacrifice, for a special vow or a fellowship offering[f] to the LORD, 9bring with the bull a grain offering of three-tenths of an ephah[g] of fine flour mixed with half a hin[h] of oil. 10Also bring half a hin of wine as a drink offering. It will be an offering made by fire, an

[a]25 Hebrew *Yam Suph*; that is, Sea of Reeds [b]4 That is, probably about 2 quarts (about 2 liters) [c]4 That is, probably about 1 quart (about 1 liter); also in verse 5
[d]6 That is, probably about 4 quarts (about 4.5 liters)
[e]6 That is, probably about 1 1/4 quarts (about 1.2 liters); also in verse 7 [f]8 Traditionally *peace offering*
[g]9 That is, probably about 6 quarts (about 6.5 liters)
[h]9 That is, probably about 2 quarts (about 2 liters); also in verse 10

14:24 In contrast to the unbelief of the other Israelites, Caleb trusted God and obeyed him fully. The positive consequence of his faith was his entrance into the promised land, though he had to wait nearly forty years to arrive there. All the other adults except Joshua died as they wandered on their forty-year wilderness trek. If we try to walk in our own strength, going our own way, we also will wander in the wilderness, never experiencing the full blessing God desires for us. But if we step out, trusting God to lead us, we will discover a new life. Even though Caleb and Joshua had to wander in the wilderness with the unbelieving Israelites, through perseverance and faith in God they finally entered the promised land.

14:34–45 After Moses announced God's judgment, the Israelites showed superficial attitudes of repentance. They tried to conquer parts of Canaan in their own strength, but their mission was unsuccessful. As we seek to overcome past areas of sin and weakness, we need to do it God's way, with God's timing and with God's help. The obstacles we face are too great to be tackled alone, but with God's help, nothing is impossible.

15:1–36 This restatement of many of the Levitical laws was intended to instruct the new generation about their accountability to God. They would be allowed to enter the promised land and enjoy God's blessings. But they needed to realize that in their new life there, they would be accountable to God. Privilege brings with it responsibility, and God was affirming this principle with a new generation of Israelites.

aroma pleasing to the LORD. [11]Each bull or ram,
each lamb or young goat, is to be prepared in
this manner. [12]Do this for each one, for as many
as you prepare.

[13]" 'Everyone who is native-born must do
these things in this way when he brings an offering made by fire as an aroma pleasing to the
LORD. [14]For the generations to come, whenever
an alien or anyone else living among you
presents an offering made by fire as an aroma
pleasing to the LORD, he must do exactly as you
do. [15]The community is to have the same rules
for you and for the alien living among you; this
is a lasting ordinance for the generations to
come. You and the alien shall be the same before the LORD: [16]The same laws and regulations
will apply both to you and to the alien living
among you.' "

[17]The LORD said to Moses, [18]"Speak to the Israelites and say to them: 'When you enter the
land to which I am taking you [19]and you eat the
food of the land, present a portion as an offering to the LORD. [20]Present a cake from the first
of your ground meal and present it as an offering from the threshing floor. [21]Throughout the
generations to come you are to give this offering
to the LORD from the first of your ground meal.

Offerings for Unintentional Sins

[22]" 'Now if you unintentionally fail to keep
any of these commands the LORD gave Moses—
[23]any of the LORD's commands to you through
him, from the day the LORD gave them and
continuing through the generations to come—
[24]and if this is done unintentionally without
the community being aware of it, then the
whole community is to offer a young bull for
a burnt offering as an aroma pleasing to the
LORD, along with its prescribed grain offering
and drink offering, and a male goat for a sin
offering. [25]The priest is to make atonement for
the whole Israelite community, and they will be
forgiven, for it was not intentional and they
have brought to the LORD for their wrong an
offering made by fire and a sin offering. [26]The
whole Israelite community and the aliens living among them will be forgiven, because all
the people were involved in the unintentional
wrong.

[27]" 'But if just one person sins unintentionally, he must bring a year-old female goat for a
sin offering. [28]The priest is to make atonement
before the LORD for the one who erred by sinning unintentionally, and when atonement has
been made for him, he will be forgiven. [29]One
and the same law applies to everyone who sins
unintentionally, whether he is a native-born Israelite or an alien.

[30]" 'But anyone who sins defiantly, whether
native-born or alien, blasphemes the LORD, and
that person must be cut off from his people.
[31]Because he has despised the LORD's word and
broken his commands, that person must surely
be cut off; his guilt remains on him.' "

The Sabbath-Breaker Put to Death

[32]While the Israelites were in the desert, a
man was found gathering wood on the Sabbath
day. [33]Those who found him gathering wood
brought him to Moses and Aaron and the whole
assembly, [34]and they kept him in custody, because it was not clear what should be done to
him. [35]Then the LORD said to Moses, "The man
must die. The whole assembly must stone him
outside the camp." [36]So the assembly took him
outside the camp and stoned him to death, as
the LORD commanded Moses.

Tassels on Garments

[37]The LORD said to Moses, [38]"Speak to the
Israelites and say to them: 'Throughout the generations to come you are to make tassels on the
corners of your garments, with a blue cord on
each tassel. [39]You will have these tassels to look
at and so you will remember all the commands
of the LORD, that you may obey them and not
prostitute yourselves by going after the lusts of
your own hearts and eyes. [40]Then you will remember to obey all my commands and will be
consecrated to your God. [41]I am the LORD your
God, who brought you out of Egypt to be your
God. I am the LORD your God.' "

Korah, Dathan and Abiram

16 Korah son of Izhar, the son of Kohath,
the son of Levi, and certain Reubenites—Dathan and Abiram, sons of Eliab, and On
son of Peleth—became insolent[a] [2]and rose up
against Moses. With them were 250 Israelite
men, well-known community leaders who had
been appointed members of the council. [3]They
came as a group to oppose Moses and Aaron
and said to them, "You have gone too far! The
whole community is holy, every one of them,

[a]1 Or *Peleth—took ⌊men⌋*

15:37–41 The Israelites were required to wear tassels on the corners of their clothing. This would remind them constantly of their covenant relationship of obedience to God. The tassels would be visual reminders that their commitment to obey God was important in every aspect of life. Although the New Testament does not command such a ritual for us today, the principle behind it is helpful. As we commit our lives to God, we need to realize that obedience is important in all areas of our lives too.

16:1—17:13 The three stories in this section illustrate the priority of Aaron's priesthood in God's leadership of Israel. God made it clear that Aaron was his chosen spiritual leader. Proper worship of God could come only through this high priesthood. The writer of Hebrews shows us that Jesus Christ is a high priest superior in every way to Aaron (Hebrews 4:14—10:39). As Aaron's budding rod demonstrated that he was chosen by God, so Christ's resurrection proved that he was the only mediator between God and the human race (1 Timothy 2:5). For us today, cleansing from sin and a proper approach to God can come only through a relationship with Christ (John 14:6). He makes it possible for us to be reconciled to God.

and the LORD is with them. Why then do you set
yourselves above the LORD's assembly?"
4When Moses heard this, he fell facedown.
5Then he said to Korah and all his followers:
"In the morning the LORD will show who belongs to him and who is holy, and he will have
that person come near him. The man he
chooses he will cause to come near him. 6You,
Korah, and all your followers are to do this:
Take censers 7and tomorrow put fire and incense in them before the LORD. The man the
LORD chooses will be the one who is holy. You
Levites have gone too far!"
8Moses also said to Korah, "Now listen, you
Levites! 9Isn't it enough for you that the God of
Israel has separated you from the rest of the
Israelite community and brought you near himself to do the work at the LORD's tabernacle and
to stand before the community and minister to
them? 10He has brought you and all your fellow
Levites near himself, but now you are trying to
get the priesthood too. 11It is against the LORD
that you and all your followers have banded
together. Who is Aaron that you should grumble against him?"
12Then Moses summoned Dathan and Abiram, the sons of Eliab. But they said, "We will
not come! 13Isn't it enough that you have
brought us up out of a land flowing with milk
and honey to kill us in the desert? And now you
also want to lord it over us? 14Moreover, you
haven't brought us into a land flowing with
milk and honey or given us an inheritance of
fields and vineyards. Will you gouge out the
eyes of[a] these men? No, we will not come!"
15Then Moses became very angry and said to
the LORD, "Do not accept their offering. I have
not taken so much as a donkey from them, nor
have I wronged any of them."
16Moses said to Korah, "You and all your
followers are to appear before the LORD tomorrow—you and they and Aaron. 17Each man is to
take his censer and put incense in it—250 censers in all—and present it before the LORD. You
and Aaron are to present your censers also." 18So
each man took his censer, put fire and incense
in it, and stood with Moses and Aaron at the
entrance to the Tent of Meeting. 19When Korah
had gathered all his followers in opposition to
them at the entrance to the Tent of Meeting, the
glory of the LORD appeared to the entire assembly. 20The LORD said to Moses and Aaron,
21"Separate yourselves from this assembly so I
can put an end to them at once."
22But Moses and Aaron fell facedown and
cried out, "O God, God of the spirits of all
mankind, will you be angry with the entire assembly when only one man sins?"
23Then the LORD said to Moses, 24"Say to the
assembly, 'Move away from the tents of Korah,
Dathan and Abiram.'"
25Moses got up and went to Dathan and Abiram, and the elders of Israel followed him. 26He
warned the assembly, "Move back from the
tents of these wicked men! Do not touch anything belonging to them, or you will be swept
away because of all their sins." 27So they moved
away from the tents of Korah, Dathan and Abiram. Dathan and Abiram had come out and
were standing with their wives, children and
little ones at the entrances to their tents.
28Then Moses said, "This is how you will
know that the LORD has sent me to do all these
things and that it was not my idea: 29If these
men die a natural death and experience only
what usually happens to men, then the LORD
has not sent me. 30But if the LORD brings about
something totally new, and the earth opens its
mouth and swallows them, with everything that
belongs to them, and they go down alive into
the grave,[b] then you will know that these men
have treated the LORD with contempt."
31As soon as he finished saying all this, the
ground under them split apart 32and the earth
opened its mouth and swallowed them, with
their households and all Korah's men and all
their possessions. 33They went down alive into
the grave, with everything they owned; the earth
closed over them, and they perished and were
gone from the community. 34At their cries, all
the Israelites around them fled, shouting, "The
earth is going to swallow us too!"
35And fire came out from the LORD and consumed the 250 men who were offering the incense.
36The LORD said to Moses, 37"Tell Eleazar
son of Aaron, the priest, to take the censers out
of the smoldering remains and scatter the coals
some distance away, for the censers are holy—
38the censers of the men who sinned at the cost
of their lives. Hammer the censers into sheets to
overlay the altar, for they were presented before
the LORD and have become holy. Let them be a
sign to the Israelites."
39So Eleazar the priest collected the bronze
censers brought by those who had been burned
up, and he had them hammered out to overlay
the altar, 40as the LORD directed him through
Moses. This was to remind the Israelites that no
one except a descendant of Aaron should come
to burn incense before the LORD, or he would
become like Korah and his followers.
41The next day the whole Israelite community grumbled against Moses and Aaron. "You
have killed the LORD's people," they said.
42But when the assembly gathered in opposition to Moses and Aaron and turned toward the
Tent of Meeting, suddenly the cloud covered it
and the glory of the LORD appeared. 43Then Moses and Aaron went to the front of the Tent of
Meeting, 44and the LORD said to Moses, 45"Get
away from this assembly so I can put an end to
them at once." And they fell facedown.
46Then Moses said to Aaron, "Take your censer and put incense in it, along with fire from

[a] 14 Or *you make slaves of*; or *you deceive* [b] 30 Hebrew *Sheol*; also in verse 33

the altar, and hurry to the assembly to make
atonement for them. Wrath has come out from
the LORD; the plague has started." 47So Aaron
did as Moses said, and ran into the midst of
the assembly. The plague had already started
among the people, but Aaron offered the incense and made atonement for them. 48He
stood between the living and the dead, and the
plague stopped. 49But 14,700 people died from
the plague, in addition to those who had died
because of Korah. 50Then Aaron returned to
Moses at the entrance to the Tent of Meeting, for
the plague had stopped.

The Budding of Aaron's Staff

17 The LORD said to Moses, 2"Speak to the
Israelites and get twelve staffs from
them, one from the leader of each of their ancestral tribes. Write the name of each man on
his staff. 3On the staff of Levi write Aaron's
name, for there must be one staff for the head
of each ancestral tribe. 4Place them in the Tent
of Meeting in front of the Testimony, where I
meet with you. 5The staff belonging to the man
I choose will sprout, and I will rid myself of this
constant grumbling against you by the Israelites."

6So Moses spoke to the Israelites, and their
leaders gave him twelve staffs, one for the leader
of each of their ancestral tribes, and Aaron's
staff was among them. 7Moses placed the staffs
before the LORD in the Tent of the Testimony.

8The next day Moses entered the Tent of the
Testimony and saw that Aaron's staff, which
represented the house of Levi, had not only
sprouted but had budded, blossomed and produced almonds. 9Then Moses brought out all
the staffs from the LORD's presence to all the
Israelites. They looked at them, and each man
took his own staff.

10The LORD said to Moses, "Put back Aaron's
staff in front of the Testimony, to be kept as a
sign to the rebellious. This will put an end to
their grumbling against me, so that they will
not die." 11Moses did just as the LORD commanded him.

12The Israelites said to Moses, "We will die!
We are lost, we are all lost! 13Anyone who even
comes near the tabernacle of the LORD will die.
Are we all going to die?"

Duties of Priests and Levites

18 The LORD said to Aaron, "You, your
sons and your father's family are to bear
the responsibility for offenses against the sanctuary, and you and your sons alone are to bear
the responsibility for offenses against the priesthood. 2Bring your fellow Levites from your ancestral tribe to join you and assist you when you
and your sons minister before the Tent of the
Testimony. 3They are to be responsible to you
and are to perform all the duties of the Tent, but
they must not go near the furnishings of the
sanctuary or the altar, or both they and you will
die. 4They are to join you and be responsible for
the care of the Tent of Meeting—all the work at
the Tent—and no one else may come near where
you are.

5"You are to be responsible for the care of
the sanctuary and the altar, so that wrath will
not fall on the Israelites again. 6I myself have
selected your fellow Levites from among the
Israelites as a gift to you, dedicated to the LORD
to do the work at the Tent of Meeting. 7But only
you and your sons may serve as priests in connection with everything at the altar and inside
the curtain. I am giving you the service of the
priesthood as a gift. Anyone else who comes
near the sanctuary must be put to death."

Offerings for Priests and Levites

8Then the LORD said to Aaron, "I myself have
put you in charge of the offerings presented to
me; all the holy offerings the Israelites give me
I give to you and your sons as your portion and
regular share. 9You are to have the part of the
most holy offerings that is kept from the fire.
From all the gifts they bring me as most holy
offerings, whether grain or sin or guilt offerings,
that part belongs to you and your sons. 10Eat it
as something most holy; every male shall eat it.
You must regard it as holy.

11"This also is yours: whatever is set aside
from the gifts of all the wave offerings of the
Israelites. I give this to you and your sons and
daughters as your regular share. Everyone in
your household who is ceremonially clean may
eat it.

12"I give you all the finest olive oil and all
the finest new wine and grain they give the
LORD as the firstfruits of their harvest. 13All the
land's firstfruits that they bring to the LORD will
be yours. Everyone in your household who is
ceremonially clean may eat it.

14"Everything in Israel that is devoted[a] to
the LORD is yours. 15The first offspring of every
womb, both man and animal, that is offered to
the LORD is yours. But you must redeem every
firstborn son and every firstborn male of unclean animals. 16When they are a month old,
you must redeem them at the redemption price
set at five shekels[b] of silver, according to the
sanctuary shekel, which weighs twenty gerahs.

17"But you must not redeem the firstborn of
an ox, a sheep or a goat; they are holy. Sprinkle
their blood on the altar and burn their fat as an
offering made by fire, an aroma pleasing to the
LORD. 18Their meat is to be yours, just as the
breast of the wave offering and the right thigh
are yours. 19Whatever is set aside from the holy
offerings the Israelites present to the LORD I give
to you and your sons and daughters as your

[a]14 The Hebrew term refers to the irrevocable giving over of things or persons to the LORD. [b]16 That is, about 2 ounces (about 55 grams)

regular share. It is an everlasting covenant of salt before the LORD for both you and your offspring."

20The LORD said to Aaron, "You will have no inheritance in their land, nor will you have any share among them; I am your share and your inheritance among the Israelites.

21"I give to the Levites all the tithes in Israel as their inheritance in return for the work they do while serving at the Tent of Meeting. 22From now on the Israelites must not go near the Tent of Meeting, or they will bear the consequences of their sin and will die. 23It is the Levites who are to do the work at the Tent of Meeting and bear the responsibility for offenses against it. This is a lasting ordinance for the generations to come. They will receive no inheritance among the Israelites. 24Instead, I give to the Levites as their inheritance the tithes that the Israelites present as an offering to the LORD. That is why I said concerning them: 'They will have no inheritance among the Israelites.' "

25The LORD said to Moses, 26"Speak to the Levites and say to them: 'When you receive from the Israelites the tithe I give you as your inheritance, you must present a tenth of that tithe as the LORD's offering. 27Your offering will be reckoned to you as grain from the threshing floor or juice from the winepress. 28In this way you also will present an offering to the LORD from all the tithes you receive from the Israelites. From these tithes you must give the LORD's portion to Aaron the priest. 29You must present as the LORD's portion the best and holiest part of everything given to you.'

30"Say to the Levites: 'When you present the best part, it will be reckoned to you as the product of the threshing floor or the winepress. 31You and your households may eat the rest of it anywhere, for it is your wages for your work at the Tent of Meeting. 32By presenting the best part of it you will not be guilty in this matter; then you will not defile the holy offerings of the Israelites, and you will not die.' "

The Water of Cleansing

19 The LORD said to Moses and Aaron: 2"This is a requirement of the law that the LORD has commanded: Tell the Israelites to bring you a red heifer without defect or blemish and that has never been under a yoke. 3Give it to Eleazar the priest; it is to be taken outside the camp and slaughtered in his presence. 4Then Eleazar the priest is to take some of its blood on his finger and sprinkle it seven times toward the front of the Tent of Meeting. 5While he watches, the heifer is to be burned—its hide, flesh, blood and offal. 6The priest is to take some cedar wood, hyssop and scarlet wool and throw them onto the burning heifer. 7After that, the priest must wash his clothes and bathe himself with water. He may then come into the camp, but he will be ceremonially unclean till evening. 8The man who burns it must also wash his clothes and bathe with water, and he too will be unclean till evening.

9"A man who is clean shall gather up the ashes of the heifer and put them in a ceremonially clean place outside the camp. They shall be kept by the Israelite community for use in the water of cleansing; it is for purification from sin. 10The man who gathers up the ashes of the heifer must also wash his clothes, and he too will be unclean till evening. This will be a lasting ordinance both for the Israelites and for the aliens living among them.

11"Whoever touches the dead body of anyone will be unclean for seven days. 12He must purify himself with the water on the third day and on the seventh day; then he will be clean. But if he does not purify himself on the third and seventh days, he will not be clean. 13Whoever touches the dead body of anyone and fails to purify himself defiles the LORD's tabernacle. That person must be cut off from Israel. Because the water of cleansing has not been sprinkled on him, he is unclean; his uncleanness remains on him.

14"This is the law that applies when a person dies in a tent: Anyone who enters the tent and anyone who is in it will be unclean for seven days, 15and every open container without a lid fastened on it will be unclean.

16"Anyone out in the open who touches someone who has been killed with a sword or someone who has died a natural death, or anyone who touches a human bone or a grave, will be unclean for seven days.

17"For the unclean person, put some ashes from the burned purification offering into a jar and pour fresh water over them. 18Then a man who is ceremonially clean is to take some hyssop, dip it in the water and sprinkle the tent and all the furnishings and the people who were there. He must also sprinkle anyone who has touched a human bone or a grave or someone who has been killed or someone who has died a natural death. 19The man who is clean is to sprinkle the unclean person on the third and seventh days, and on the seventh day he is to purify him. The person being cleansed must wash his clothes and bathe with water, and that evening he will be clean. 20But if a person who is unclean does not purify himself, he must be cut off from the community, because he has defiled the sanctuary of the LORD. The water of cleansing has not been sprinkled on him, and he is unclean. 21This is a lasting ordinance for them.

"The man who sprinkles the water of cleansing must also wash his clothes, and anyone who touches the water of cleansing will be unclean till evening. 22Anything that an unclean person touches becomes unclean, and anyone who touches it becomes unclean till evening."

Water From the Rock

20 In the first month the whole Israelite
community arrived at the Desert of Zin,
and they stayed at Kadesh. There Miriam died
and was buried.
2Now there was no water for the community,
and the people gathered in opposition to Moses
and Aaron. 3They quarreled with Moses and
said, "If only we had died when our brothers
fell dead before the LORD! 4Why did you bring
the LORD's community into this desert, that we
and our livestock should die here? 5Why did
you bring us up out of Egypt to this terrible
place? It has no grain or figs, grapevines or
pomegranates. And there is no water to drink!"
6Moses and Aaron went from the assembly to
the entrance to the Tent of Meeting and fell
facedown, and the glory of the LORD appeared
to them. 7The LORD said to Moses, 8"Take the
staff, and you and your brother Aaron gather
the assembly together. Speak to that rock before
their eyes and it will pour out its water. You will
bring water out of the rock for the community
so they and their livestock can drink."
9So Moses took the staff from the LORD's
presence, just as he commanded him. 10He and
Aaron gathered the assembly together in front
of the rock and Moses said to them, "Listen,
you rebels, must we bring you water out of this
rock?" 11Then Moses raised his arm and struck
the rock twice with his staff. Water gushed out,
and the community and their livestock drank.
12But the LORD said to Moses and Aaron,
"Because you did not trust in me enough to
honor me as holy in the sight of the Israelites,
you will not bring this community into the land
I give them."
13These were the waters of Meribah,[a] where
the Israelites quarreled with the LORD and
where he showed himself holy among them.

Edom Denies Israel Passage

14Moses sent messengers from Kadesh to the
king of Edom, saying:

"This is what your brother Israel says:
You know about all the hardships that
have come upon us. 15Our forefathers
went down into Egypt, and we lived there
many years. The Egyptians mistreated us
and our fathers, 16but when we cried out
to the LORD, he heard our cry and sent an
angel and brought us out of Egypt.

"Now we are here at Kadesh, a town on
the edge of your territory. 17Please let us
pass through your country. We will not go
through any field or vineyard, or drink
water from any well. We will travel along
the king's highway and not turn to the
right or to the left until we have passed
through your territory."

18But Edom answered:

"You may not pass through here; if you
try, we will march out and attack you with
the sword."

19The Israelites replied:

"We will go along the main road, and
if we or our livestock drink any of your
water, we will pay for it. We only want to
pass through on foot—nothing else."

20Again they answered:

"You may not pass through."

Then Edom came out against them with a
large and powerful army. 21Since Edom refused
to let them go through their territory, Israel
turned away from them.

The Death of Aaron

22The whole Israelite community set out
from Kadesh and came to Mount Hor. 23At
Mount Hor, near the border of Edom, the LORD
said to Moses and Aaron, 24"Aaron will be gathered to his people. He will not enter the land I
give the Israelites, because both of you rebelled
against my command at the waters of Meribah.
25Get Aaron and his son Eleazar and take them
up Mount Hor. 26Remove Aaron's garments and
put them on his son Eleazar, for Aaron will be
gathered to his people; he will die there."
27Moses did as the LORD commanded: They
went up Mount Hor in the sight of the whole
community. 28Moses removed Aaron's garments and put them on his son Eleazar. And
Aaron died there on top of the mountain. Then
Moses and Eleazar came down from the mountain, 29and when the whole community learned
that Aaron had died, the entire house of Israel
mourned for him thirty days.

[a]13 *Meribah* means *quarreling.*

20:2–13 After a water shortage, the Israelites started their murmuring again. The focus of this incident, however, was upon the failure of Moses and Aaron. Moses was severely judged by God for not following God's instructions specifically and for using his own method to produce water. Aaron was also judged because he evidently had a part in it. While the judgment seems severe, it illustrates the importance of obedience to God's Word, especially when we are in a leadership position. Moses and Aaron, by disobeying God's specific instructions, exhibited attitudes of personal rebellion against God. Commitment to God's plan cannot be a part-way proposition. Despite Moses' great success in the past, this failure kept him out of the promised land.

20:23–29 Aaron, Israel's first high priest, died and was mourned by the people (20:29), but this wasn't the last of Israel's priestly funerals. In contrasting the ministry of Jesus Christ with the ministry of other human priests the writer of Hebrews says, "There have been many of those priests, since death prevented them from continuing in office, but because Jesus lives forever, he has a permanent priesthood" (Hebrews 7:23–24). Our great high priest will always be available to provide us direct access to God.

Arad Destroyed

21 When the Canaanite king of Arad, who
lived in the Negev, heard that Israel was
coming along the road to Atharim, he attacked
the Israelites and captured some of them. 2Then
Israel made this vow to the LORD: "If you will
deliver these people into our hands, we will
totally destroy[a] their cities." 3The LORD listened
to Israel's plea and gave the Canaanites over
to them. They completely destroyed them and
their towns; so the place was named Hormah.[b]

The Bronze Snake

4They traveled from Mount Hor along the
route to the Red Sea,[c] to go around Edom. But
the people grew impatient on the way; 5they
spoke against God and against Moses, and said,
"Why have you brought us up out of Egypt to
die in the desert? There is no bread! There is no
water! And we detest this miserable food!"
6Then the LORD sent venomous snakes
among them; they bit the people and many
Israelites died. 7The people came to Moses and
said, "We sinned when we spoke against the
LORD and against you. Pray that the LORD will
take the snakes away from us." So Moses prayed
for the people.
8The LORD said to Moses, "Make a snake and
put it up on a pole; anyone who is bitten can
look at it and live." 9So Moses made a bronze
snake and put it up on a pole. Then when anyone was bitten by a snake and looked at the
bronze snake, he lived.

The Journey to Moab

10The Israelites moved on and camped at
Oboth. 11Then they set out from Oboth and
camped in Iye Abarim, in the desert that faces
Moab toward the sunrise. 12From there they
moved on and camped in the Zered Valley.
13They set out from there and camped alongside the Arnon, which is in the desert extending
into Amorite territory. The Arnon is the border
of Moab, between Moab and the Amorites.
14That is why the Book of the Wars of the LORD
says:

"... Waheb in Suphah[d] and the ravines,
the Arnon 15and[e] the slopes of the
ravines
that lead to the site of Ar
and lie along the border of Moab."

16From there they continued on to Beer, the
well where the LORD said to Moses, "Gather the
people together and I will give them water."
17Then Israel sang this song:

"Spring up, O well!
Sing about it,
18about the well that the princes dug,
that the nobles of the people sank—
the nobles with scepters and staffs."

Then they went from the desert to Mattanah,
19from Mattanah to Nahaliel, from Nahaliel to
Bamoth, 20and from Bamoth to the valley in
Moab where the top of Pisgah overlooks the
wasteland.

Defeat of Sihon and Og

21Israel sent messengers to say to Sihon king
of the Amorites:

22"Let us pass through your country.
We will not turn aside into any field or
vineyard, or drink water from any well.
We will travel along the king's highway
until we have passed through your territory."

23But Sihon would not let Israel pass through
his territory. He mustered his entire army and
marched out into the desert against Israel.
When he reached Jahaz, he fought with Israel.
24Israel, however, put him to the sword and
took over his land from the Arnon to the Jabbok, but only as far as the Ammonites, because
their border was fortified. 25Israel captured all

[a]2 The Hebrew term refers to the irrevocable giving over of things or persons to the LORD, often by totally destroying them; also in verse 3. [b]3 *Hormah* means *destruction.* [c]4 Hebrew *Yam Suph;* that is, Sea of Reeds [d]14 The meaning of the Hebrew for this phrase is uncertain. [e]14,15 Or *"I have been given from Suphah and the ravines / of the Arnon* [15]*to*

21:1–3 Victory! This first great success was the result of complete obedience to God's will. This victory, along with others to follow, began an important era in Israel's history. The people were able to see the truth of Joshua and Caleb's advice—faith and obedience to God would bring victory over any enemy or obstacle. God delights in proving himself in the lives of those who trust in his power to overcome life's obstacles. Our lack of power over our problems can be covered by God's unlimited power to act on our behalf.

21:4–9 This incident was referred to by the apostle John in the New Testament as an illustration of what Christ did on our behalf: "Just as Moses lifted up the snake in the desert, so the Son of Man must be lifted up" (John 3:14). Evident in both passages is God's saving grace, providing salvation and healing for anyone who responds in faith. In this instance, healing did not come to everyone in Israel but only to those who by faith looked at the bronze serpent on the pole. The apostle John explains that personal forgiveness and victory over sin can come only to those who look to Christ on the cross. God provides the powerful means of redemption from sin and failure; we need to receive it in faith.

21:7 Notice here that Moses resumed his role as Israel's leader and mediator even after he was judged for his sin at Meribah. His failure probably brought him personal pain and disappointment, for he would lead the entire nation of Israelites to the promised land but would never enter it himself. In spite of this, Moses showed no bitter feelings toward God, nor did he neglect his responsibilities. His restoration after this personal failure and his continued faithful service are evidence of Moses' great faith and dependence upon God. Our mistakes don't necessarily disqualify us from future success; they provide opportunities for learning, growth and dependence on God.

the cities of the Amorites and occupied them,
including Heshbon and all its surrounding settlements. 26Heshbon was the city of Sihon king
of the Amorites, who had fought against the
former king of Moab and had taken from him
all his land as far as the Arnon.
27That is why the poets say:

"Come to Heshbon and let it be rebuilt;
let Sihon's city be restored.

28"Fire went out from Heshbon,
a blaze from the city of Sihon.
It consumed Ar of Moab,
the citizens of Arnon's heights.
29Woe to you, O Moab!
You are destroyed, O people of
Chemosh!
He has given up his sons as fugitives
and his daughters as captives
to Sihon king of the Amorites.

30"But we have overthrown them;
Heshbon is destroyed all the way to
Dibon.
We have demolished them as far as
Nophah,
which extends to Medeba."

31So Israel settled in the land of the Amorites.
32After Moses had sent spies to Jazer, the Israelites captured its surrounding settlements and
drove out the Amorites who were there. 33Then
they turned and went up along the road toward
Bashan, and Og king of Bashan and his whole
army marched out to meet them in battle at
Edrei.
34The LORD said to Moses, "Do not be afraid
of him, for I have handed him over to you, with
his whole army and his land. Do to him what
you did to Sihon king of the Amorites, who
reigned in Heshbon."
35So they struck him down, together with his
sons and his whole army, leaving them no survivors. And they took possession of his land.

Balak Summons Balaam

22 Then the Israelites traveled to the plains
of Moab and camped along the Jordan
across from Jericho.[a]
2Now Balak son of Zippor saw all that Israel
had done to the Amorites, 3and Moab was terrified because there were so many people. Indeed, Moab was filled with dread because of the
Israelites.
4The Moabites said to the elders of Midian,
"This horde is going to lick up everything
around us, as an ox licks up the grass of the
field."
So Balak son of Zippor, who was king of
Moab at that time, 5sent messengers to summon Balaam son of Beor, who was at Pethor,
near the River,[b] in his native land. Balak said:

"A people has come out of Egypt; they
cover the face of the land and have settled
next to me. 6Now come and put a curse on
these people, because they are too powerful for me. Perhaps then I will be able to
defeat them and drive them out of the
country. For I know that those you bless
are blessed, and those you curse are
cursed."

7The elders of Moab and Midian left, taking
with them the fee for divination. When they
came to Balaam, they told him what Balak had
said.
8"Spend the night here," Balaam said to them,
"and I will bring you back the answer the LORD
gives me." So the Moabite princes stayed with
him.
9God came to Balaam and asked, "Who are
these men with you?"
10Balaam said to God, "Balak son of Zippor,
king of Moab, sent me this message: 11'A people
that has come out of Egypt covers the face of the
land. Now come and put a curse on them for
me. Perhaps then I will be able to fight them
and drive them away.' "
12But God said to Balaam, "Do not go with
them. You must not put a curse on those people, because they are blessed."
13The next morning Balaam got up and said
to Balak's princes, "Go back to your own country, for the LORD has refused to let me go with
you."
14So the Moabite princes returned to Balak
and said, "Balaam refused to come with us."
15Then Balak sent other princes, more numerous and more distinguished than the first.
16They came to Balaam and said:

"This is what Balak son of Zippor says:
Do not let anything keep you from coming to me, 17because I will reward you
handsomely and do whatever you say.
Come and put a curse on these people
for me."

18But Balaam answered them, "Even if Balak
gave me his palace filled with silver and gold, I
could not do anything great or small to go beyond the command of the LORD my God.
19Now stay here tonight as the others did, and
I will find out what else the LORD will tell me."
20That night God came to Balaam and said,

[a] 1 Hebrew *Jordan of Jericho*; possibly an ancient name for the Jordan River [b] 5 That is, the Euphrates

22:1–20 Balaam was a Mesopotamian *baru* (priest, diviner) who was hired by Balak, king of Moab, to place a curse upon Israel. King Balak wanted to prevent the Israelites from conquering Moab and other surrounding lands. Balaam openly admitted that he had no power to go beyond the will of God. He could not place a curse upon the people whom God desired to bless. This should help us realize that when it seems everyone is against us, we can be sure that God is able to provide us with the wisdom we need to survive the toughest of situations (James 1:2–5).

"Since these men have come to summon you, go with them, but do only what I tell you."

Balaam's Donkey

21 Balaam got up in the morning, saddled his donkey and went with the princes of Moab. 22 But God was very angry when he went, and the angel of the LORD stood in the road to oppose him. Balaam was riding on his donkey, and his two servants were with him. 23 When the donkey saw the angel of the LORD standing in the road with a drawn sword in his hand, she turned off the road into a field. Balaam beat her to get her back on the road.

24 Then the angel of the LORD stood in a narrow path between two vineyards, with walls on both sides. 25 When the donkey saw the angel of the LORD, she pressed close to the wall, crushing Balaam's foot against it. So he beat her again.

26 Then the angel of the LORD moved on ahead and stood in a narrow place where there was no room to turn, either to the right or to the left. 27 When the donkey saw the angel of the LORD, she lay down under Balaam, and he was angry and beat her with his staff. 28 Then the LORD opened the donkey's mouth, and she said to Balaam, "What have I done to you to make you beat me these three times?"

29 Balaam answered the donkey, "You have made a fool of me! If I had a sword in my hand, I would kill you right now."

30 The donkey said to Balaam, "Am I not your own donkey, which you have always ridden, to this day? Have I been in the habit of doing this to you?"

"No," he said.

31 Then the LORD opened Balaam's eyes, and he saw the angel of the LORD standing in the road with his sword drawn. So he bowed low and fell facedown.

32 The angel of the LORD asked him, "Why have you beaten your donkey these three times? I have come here to oppose you because your path is a reckless one before me.[a] 33 The donkey saw me and turned away from me these three times. If she had not turned away, I would certainly have killed you by now, but I would have spared her."

34 Balaam said to the angel of the LORD, "I have sinned. I did not realize you were standing in the road to oppose me. Now if you are displeased, I will go back."

35 The angel of the LORD said to Balaam, "Go with the men, but speak only what I tell you." So Balaam went with the princes of Balak.

36 When Balak heard that Balaam was coming, he went out to meet him at the Moabite town on the Arnon border, at the edge of his territory. 37 Balak said to Balaam, "Did I not send you an urgent summons? Why didn't you come to me? Am I really not able to reward you?"

38 "Well, I have come to you now," Balaam replied. "But can I say just anything? I must speak only what God puts in my mouth."

39 Then Balaam went with Balak to Kiriath Huzoth. 40 Balak sacrificed cattle and sheep, and gave some to Balaam and the princes who were with him. 41 The next morning Balak took Balaam up to Bamoth Baal, and from there he saw part of the people.

Balaam's First Oracle

23 Balaam said, "Build me seven altars here, and prepare seven bulls and seven rams for me." 2 Balak did as Balaam said, and the two of them offered a bull and a ram on each altar.

3 Then Balaam said to Balak, "Stay here beside your offering while I go aside. Perhaps the LORD will come to meet with me. Whatever he reveals to me I will tell you." Then he went off to a barren height.

4 God met with him, and Balaam said, "I have prepared seven altars, and on each altar I have offered a bull and a ram."

5 The LORD put a message in Balaam's mouth and said, "Go back to Balak and give him this message."

6 So he went back to him and found him standing beside his offering, with all the princes of Moab. 7 Then Balaam uttered his oracle:

"Balak brought me from Aram,
the king of Moab from the eastern mountains.
'Come,' he said, 'curse Jacob for me;
come, denounce Israel.'
8 How can I curse
those whom God has not cursed?
How can I denounce
those whom the LORD has not denounced?
9 From the rocky peaks I see them,
from the heights I view them.
I see a people who live apart
and do not consider themselves one of the nations.
10 Who can count the dust of Jacob
or number the fourth part of Israel?
Let me die the death of the righteous,
and may my end be like theirs!"

11 Balak said to Balaam, "What have you

[a] 32 The meaning of the Hebrew for this clause is uncertain.

22:21–35 The humorous story about Balaam and his donkey illustrates Balaam's spiritual blindness with respect to the true God. As a pagan diviner, Balaam often relied upon signs from animals and nature to determine the future. In this situation, however, he had less spiritual perception than his donkey and was prevented from carrying out the diabolical plot against Israel. From Balaam we learn that the greatest of human wisdom can often lead to spiritual blindness. True wisdom to face life's situations comes only from the sovereign, all-knowing God.

done to me? I brought you to curse my enemies,
but you have done nothing but bless them!"
12He answered, "Must I not speak what the
LORD puts in my mouth?"

Balaam's Second Oracle

13Then Balak said to him, "Come with me to
another place where you can see them; you will
see only a part but not all of them. And from
there, curse them for me." 14So he took him to
the field of Zophim on the top of Pisgah, and
there he built seven altars and offered a bull and
a ram on each altar.
15Balaam said to Balak, "Stay here beside
your offering while I meet with him over there."
16The LORD met with Balaam and put a message in his mouth and said, "Go back to Balak
and give him this message."
17So he went to him and found him standing
beside his offering, with the princes of Moab.
Balak asked him, "What did the LORD say?"
18Then he uttered his oracle:

"Arise, Balak, and listen;
hear me, son of Zippor.
19God is not a man, that he should lie,
nor a son of man, that he should change
his mind.
Does he speak and then not act?
Does he promise and not fulfill?
20I have received a command to bless;
he has blessed, and I cannot change it.

21"No misfortune is seen in Jacob,
no misery observed in Israel.[a]
The LORD their God is with them;
the shout of the King is among them.
22God brought them out of Egypt;
they have the strength of a wild ox.
23There is no sorcery against Jacob,
no divination against Israel.
It will now be said of Jacob
and of Israel, 'See what God has done!'
24The people rise like a lioness;
they rouse themselves like a lion
that does not rest till he devours his prey
and drinks the blood of his victims."

25Then Balak said to Balaam, "Neither curse
them at all nor bless them at all!"
26Balaam answered, "Did I not tell you I
must do whatever the LORD says?"

Balaam's Third Oracle

27Then Balak said to Balaam, "Come, let me
take you to another place. Perhaps it will please
God to let you curse them for me from there."
28And Balak took Balaam to the top of Peor,
overlooking the wasteland.
29Balaam said, "Build me seven altars here,
and prepare seven bulls and seven rams for me."
30Balak did as Balaam had said, and offered a
bull and a ram on each altar.

24 Now when Balaam saw that it pleased
the LORD to bless Israel, he did not resort to sorcery as at other times, but turned his
face toward the desert. 2When Balaam looked
out and saw Israel encamped tribe by tribe, the
Spirit of God came upon him 3and he uttered
his oracle:

"The oracle of Balaam son of Beor,
the oracle of one whose eye sees clearly,
4the oracle of one who hears the words of
God,
who sees a vision from the Almighty,[b]
who falls prostrate, and whose eyes are
opened:

5"How beautiful are your tents, O Jacob,
your dwelling places, O Israel!

6"Like valleys they spread out,
like gardens beside a river,
like aloes planted by the LORD,
like cedars beside the waters.
7Water will flow from their buckets;
their seed will have abundant water.

"Their king will be greater than Agag;
their kingdom will be exalted.

8"God brought them out of Egypt;
they have the strength of a wild ox.
They devour hostile nations
and break their bones in pieces;
with their arrows they pierce them.
9Like a lion they crouch and lie down,
like a lioness—who dares to rouse them?

"May those who bless you be blessed
and those who curse you be cursed!"

10Then Balak's anger burned against Balaam.
He struck his hands together and said to him, "I
summoned you to curse my enemies, but you
have blessed them these three times. 11Now
leave at once and go home! I said I would reward you handsomely, but the LORD has kept
you from being rewarded."
12Balaam answered Balak, "Did I not tell the
messengers you sent me, 13'Even if Balak gave
me his palace filled with silver and gold, I could
not do anything of my own accord, good or
bad, to go beyond the command of the LORD—
and I must say only what the LORD says'? 14Now
I am going back to my people, but come, let me

[a]21 Or *He has not looked on Jacob's offenses / or on the wrongs found in Israel.* [b]4 Hebrew *Shaddai*; also in verse 16

23:18–24 Through the words of Balaam's second oracle, God affirmed not only his sovereignty but also his truthful character: "God is not a man, that he should lie, nor a son of man, that he should change his mind" (23:19). The future of Israel was secure because a sovereign God had chosen them for his glory and promised to bless them. The New Testament tells us that we were also chosen by God before the world was even made and that he has blessed us "with every spiritual blessing in Christ" (Ephesians 1:3). Worldly wisdom, as illustrated by Balaam, cannot compare with the wisdom of God.

warn you of what this people will do to your
people in days to come."

Balaam's Fourth Oracle

15Then he uttered his oracle:

"The oracle of Balaam son of Beor,
 the oracle of one whose eye sees clearly,
16the oracle of one who hears the words of
  God,
 who has knowledge from the Most High,
who sees a vision from the Almighty,
 who falls prostrate, and whose eyes are
  opened:
17"I see him, but not now;
 I behold him, but not near.
A star will come out of Jacob;
 a scepter will rise out of Israel.
He will crush the foreheads of Moab,
 the skulls[a] of[b] all the sons of Sheth.[c]
18Edom will be conquered;
 Seir, his enemy, will be conquered,
 but Israel will grow strong.
19A ruler will come out of Jacob
 and destroy the survivors of the city."

Balaam's Final Oracles

20Then Balaam saw Amalek and uttered his
oracle:

"Amalek was first among the nations,
 but he will come to ruin at last."

21Then he saw the Kenites and uttered his
oracle:

"Your dwelling place is secure,
 your nest is set in a rock;
22yet you Kenites will be destroyed
 when Asshur takes you captive."

23Then he uttered his oracle:

"Ah, who can live when God does this?[d]
24 Ships will come from the shores of
  Kittim;
they will subdue Asshur and Eber,
 but they too will come to ruin."

25Then Balaam got up and returned home
and Balak went his own way.

Moab Seduces Israel

25 While Israel was staying in Shittim, the
men began to indulge in sexual immorality with Moabite women, 2who invited them
to the sacrifices to their gods. The people ate
and bowed down before these gods. 3So Israel
joined in worshiping the Baal of Peor. And the
LORD's anger burned against them.

4The LORD said to Moses, "Take all the leaders of these people, kill them and expose them
in broad daylight before the LORD, so that the
LORD's fierce anger may turn away from Israel."

5So Moses said to Israel's judges, "Each of
you must put to death those of your men who
have joined in worshiping the Baal of Peor."

6Then an Israelite man brought to his family
a Midianite woman right before the eyes of Moses and the whole assembly of Israel while they
were weeping at the entrance to the Tent of
Meeting. 7When Phinehas son of Eleazar, the
son of Aaron, the priest, saw this, he left the
assembly, took a spear in his hand 8and followed the Israelite into the tent. He drove the
spear through both of them—through the Israelite and into the woman's body. Then the plague
against the Israelites was stopped; 9but those
who died in the plague numbered 24,000.

10The LORD said to Moses, 11"Phinehas son
of Eleazar, the son of Aaron, the priest, has
turned my anger away from the Israelites; for he
was as zealous as I am for my honor among
them, so that in my zeal I did not put an end to
them. 12Therefore tell him I am making my covenant of peace with him. 13He and his descendants will have a covenant of a lasting priesthood, because he was zealous for the honor of
his God and made atonement for the Israelites."

14The name of the Israelite who was killed
with the Midianite woman was Zimri son of
Salu, the leader of a Simeonite family. 15And the
name of the Midianite woman who was put to
death was Cozbi daughter of Zur, a tribal chief
of a Midianite family.

16The LORD said to Moses, 17"Treat the Midianites as enemies and kill them, 18because they
treated you as enemies when they deceived you
in the affair of Peor and their sister Cozbi, the
daughter of a Midianite leader, the woman who
was killed when the plague came as a result of
Peor."

The Second Census

26 After the plague the LORD said to Moses
and Eleazar son of Aaron, the priest,
2"Take a census of the whole Israelite community by families—all those twenty years old or
more who are able to serve in the army of Israel."

[a]17 Samaritan Pentateuch (see also Jer. 48:45); the meaning of the word in the Masoretic Text is uncertain. [b]17 Or possibly *Moab, / batter* [c]17 Or *all the noisy boasters* [d]23 Masoretic Text; with a different word division of the Hebrew *A people will gather from the north.*

25:1–18 After God's victory over the false gods of Balaam, the Israelites were quickly seduced into Canaanite worship. Through this story we can see how clever and diverse Satan's strategies are. When unsuccessful in his attack from the outside (22:1—24:25), Satan succeeded in bringing decay from within. Israelite participation in immoral Canaanite worship resulted in the judgment and death of 24,000 of God's people. Our personal morality is of great importance to God.

26:1–65 The census in Numbers 1 was taken primarily for organizational purposes. This later census was intended to prepare Israel for the conquest of the promised land and the later division of property. The decrease in numbers from the census taken forty years earlier was primarily due to the judgments suffered by the Israelites in the wilderness.

[3]So on the plains of Moab by the Jordan across
from Jericho,[a] Moses and Eleazar the priest
spoke with them and said, [4]"Take a census of
the men twenty years old or more, as the LORD
commanded Moses."

These were the Israelites who came out of Egypt:

[5]The descendants of Reuben, the firstborn son of Israel, were:
through Hanoch, the Hanochite clan;
through Pallu, the Palluite clan;
[6]through Hezron, the Hezronite clan;
through Carmi, the Carmite clan.
[7]These were the clans of Reuben; those numbered were 43,730.

[8]The son of Pallu was Eliab, [9]and the sons of
Eliab were Nemuel, Dathan and Abiram. The
same Dathan and Abiram were the community
officials who rebelled against Moses and Aaron
and were among Korah's followers when they
rebelled against the LORD. [10]The earth opened
its mouth and swallowed them along with Korah, whose followers died when the fire devoured the 250 men. And they served as a warning sign. [11]The line of Korah, however, did not
die out.

[12]The descendants of Simeon by their clans were:
through Nemuel, the Nemuelite clan;
through Jamin, the Jaminite clan;
through Jakin, the Jakinite clan;
[13]through Zerah, the Zerahite clan;
through Shaul, the Shaulite clan.
[14]These were the clans of Simeon; there were 22,200 men.

[15]The descendants of Gad by their clans were:
through Zephon, the Zephonite clan;
through Haggi, the Haggite clan;
through Shuni, the Shunite clan;
[16]through Ozni, the Oznite clan;
through Eri, the Erite clan;
[17]through Arodi,[b] the Arodite clan;
through Areli, the Arelite clan.
[18]These were the clans of Gad; those numbered were 40,500.

[19]Er and Onan were sons of Judah, but they died in Canaan.
[20]The descendants of Judah by their clans were:
through Shelah, the Shelanite clan;
through Perez, the Perezite clan;
through Zerah, the Zerahite clan.
[21]The descendants of Perez were:
through Hezron, the Hezronite clan;
through Hamul, the Hamulite clan.
[22]These were the clans of Judah; those numbered were 76,500.

[23]The descendants of Issachar by their clans were:
through Tola, the Tolaite clan;
through Puah, the Puite[c] clan;
[24]through Jashub, the Jashubite clan;
through Shimron, the Shimronite clan.
[25]These were the clans of Issachar; those numbered were 64,300.

[26]The descendants of Zebulun by their clans were:
through Sered, the Seredite clan;
through Elon, the Elonite clan;
through Jahleel, the Jahleelite clan.
[27]These were the clans of Zebulun; those numbered were 60,500.

[28]The descendants of Joseph by their clans through Manasseh and Ephraim were:

[29]The descendants of Manasseh:
through Makir, the Makirite clan (Makir was the father of Gilead);
through Gilead, the Gileadite clan.
[30]These were the descendants of Gilead:
through Iezer, the Iezerite clan;
through Helek, the Helekite clan;
[31]through Asriel, the Asrielite clan;
through Shechem, the Shechemite clan;
[32]through Shemida, the Shemidaite clan;
through Hepher, the Hepherite clan.
[33](Zelophehad son of Hepher had no sons; he had only daughters, whose names were Mahlah, Noah, Hoglah, Milcah and Tirzah.)
[34]These were the clans of Manasseh; those numbered were 52,700.

[35]These were the descendants of Ephraim by their clans:
through Shuthelah, the Shuthelahite clan;
through Beker, the Bekerite clan;
through Tahan, the Tahanite clan.
[36]These were the descendants of Shuthelah:
through Eran, the Eranite clan.
[37]These were the clans of Ephraim; those numbered were 32,500.
These were the descendants of Joseph by their clans.

[38]The descendants of Benjamin by their clans were:
through Bela, the Belaite clan;
through Ashbel, the Ashbelite clan;
through Ahiram, the Ahiramite clan;
[39]through Shupham,[d] the Shuphamite clan;
through Hupham, the Huphamite clan.
[40]The descendants of Bela through Ard and Naaman were:

[a]3 Hebrew *Jordan of Jericho*; possibly an ancient name for the Jordan River; also in verse 63 [b]17 Samaritan Pentateuch and Syriac (see also Gen. 46:16); Masoretic Text *Arod* [c]23 Samaritan Pentateuch, Septuagint, Vulgate and Syriac (see also 1 Chron. 7:1); Masoretic Text *through Puvah, the Punite* [d]39 A few manuscripts of the Masoretic Text, Samaritan Pentateuch, Vulgate and Syriac (see also Septuagint); most manuscripts of the Masoretic Text *Shephupham*

through Ard,[a] the Ardite clan;
through Naaman, the Naamite clan.
41These were the clans of Benjamin; those numbered were 45,600.

42These were the descendants of Dan by their
clans:
through Shuham, the Shuhamite clan.
These were the clans of Dan: 43All of them were
Shuhamite clans; and those numbered were
64,400.

44The descendants of Asher by their clans were:
through Imnah, the Imnite clan;
through Ishvi, the Ishvite clan;
through Beriah, the Beriite clan;
45and through the descendants of Beriah:
through Heber, the Heberite clan;
through Malkiel, the Malkielite clan.
46(Asher had a daughter named Serah.)
47These were the clans of Asher; those numbered were 53,400.

48The descendants of Naphtali by their clans
were:
through Jahzeel, the Jahzeelite clan;
through Guni, the Gunite clan;
49through Jezer, the Jezerite clan;
through Shillem, the Shillemite clan.
50These were the clans of Naphtali; those numbered were 45,400.

51The total number of the men of Israel was
601,730.

52The LORD said to Moses, 53"The land is to
be allotted to them as an inheritance based on
the number of names. 54To a larger group give
a larger inheritance, and to a smaller group a
smaller one; each is to receive its inheritance
according to the number of those listed. 55Be
sure that the land is distributed by lot. What
each group inherits will be according to the
names for its ancestral tribe. 56Each inheritance
is to be distributed by lot among the larger and
smaller groups."

57These were the Levites who were counted by
their clans:
through Gershon, the Gershonite clan;
through Kohath, the Kohathite clan;
through Merari, the Merarite clan.
58These also were Levite clans:
the Libnite clan,
the Hebronite clan,
the Mahlite clan,
the Mushite clan,
the Korahite clan.
(Kohath was the forefather of Amram;
59the name of Amram's wife was Jochebed, a descendant of Levi, who was born
to the Levites[b] in Egypt. To Amram she
bore Aaron, Moses and their sister Miriam.
60Aaron was the father of Nadab and Abihu, Eleazar and Ithamar. 61But Nadab and
Abihu died when they made an offering
before the LORD with unauthorized fire.)

62All the male Levites a month old or more
numbered 23,000. They were not counted
along with the other Israelites because they received no inheritance among them.

63These are the ones counted by Moses and
Eleazar the priest when they counted the Israelites on the plains of Moab by the Jordan across
from Jericho. 64Not one of them was among
those counted by Moses and Aaron the priest
when they counted the Israelites in the Desert of
Sinai. 65For the LORD had told those Israelites
they would surely die in the desert, and not one
of them was left except Caleb son of Jephunneh
and Joshua son of Nun.

Zelophehad's Daughters

27 The daughters of Zelophehad son of
Hepher, the son of Gilead, the son of
Makir, the son of Manasseh, belonged to the
clans of Manasseh son of Joseph. The names of
the daughters were Mahlah, Noah, Hoglah, Milcah and Tirzah. They approached 2the entrance
to the Tent of Meeting and stood before Moses,
Eleazar the priest, the leaders and the whole
assembly, and said, 3"Our father died in the
desert. He was not among Korah's followers,
who banded together against the LORD, but he
died for his own sin and left no sons. 4Why
should our father's name disappear from his
clan because he had no son? Give us property
among our father's relatives."

5So Moses brought their case before the LORD
6and the LORD said to him, 7"What Zelophehad's daughters are saying is right. You must
certainly give them property as an inheritance
among their father's relatives and turn their father's inheritance over to them.

8"Say to the Israelites, 'If a man dies and
leaves no son, turn his inheritance over to his
daughter. 9If he has no daughter, give his inheritance to his brothers. 10If he has no brothers,
give his inheritance to his father's brothers. 11If
his father had no brothers, give his inheritance
to the nearest relative in his clan, that he may
possess it. This is to be a legal requirement for
the Israelites, as the LORD commanded Moses.' "

Joshua to Succeed Moses

12Then the LORD said to Moses, "Go up this

[a]40 Samaritan Pentateuch and Vulgate (see also Septuagint); Masoretic Text does not have *through Ard.*
[b]59 Or *Jochebed, a daughter of Levi, who was born to Levi*

27:12–23 The torch of Israel's leadership was passed from Moses to Joshua. Moses was able to view the land of Canaan (27:12–14) but was not allowed to enter it because of his earlier failure. Rather than being self-centered and overcome with disappointment, Moses showed that his greatest concern was still for his people. The attitude reflected in his words reveal his godly character: "Appoint a man over this community to go out and

mountain in the Abarim range and see the land
I have given the Israelites. 13After you have seen
it, you too will be gathered to your people, as
your brother Aaron was, 14for when the community rebelled at the waters in the Desert of
Zin, both of you disobeyed my command to
honor me as holy before their eyes." (These were
the waters of Meribah Kadesh, in the Desert of
Zin.)

15Moses said to the LORD, 16"May the LORD,
the God of the spirits of all mankind, appoint
a man over this community 17to go out and
come in before them, one who will lead them
out and bring them in, so the LORD's people will
not be like sheep without a shepherd."

18So the LORD said to Moses, "Take Joshua
son of Nun, a man in whom is the spirit,[a] and
lay your hand on him. 19Have him stand before
Eleazar the priest and the entire assembly and
commission him in their presence. 20Give him
some of your authority so the whole Israelite
community will obey him. 21He is to stand before Eleazar the priest, who will obtain decisions for him by inquiring of the Urim before
the LORD. At his command he and the entire
community of the Israelites will go out, and at
his command they will come in."

22Moses did as the LORD commanded him.
He took Joshua and had him stand before Eleazar the priest and the whole assembly. 23Then
he laid his hands on him and commissioned
him, as the LORD instructed through Moses.

Daily Offerings

28 The LORD said to Moses, 2"Give this
command to the Israelites and say to
them: 'See that you present to me at the appointed time the food for my offerings made by
fire, as an aroma pleasing to me.' 3Say to them:
'This is the offering made by fire that you are to
present to the LORD: two lambs a year old without defect, as a regular burnt offering each day.
4Prepare one lamb in the morning and the other at twilight, 5together with a grain offering of
a tenth of an ephah[b] of fine flour mixed with
a quarter of a hin[c] of oil from pressed olives.
6This is the regular burnt offering instituted at
Mount Sinai as a pleasing aroma, an offering
made to the LORD by fire. 7The accompanying
drink offering is to be a quarter of a hin of
fermented drink with each lamb. Pour out the
drink offering to the LORD at the sanctuary.
8Prepare the second lamb at twilight, along
with the same kind of grain offering and drink
offering that you prepare in the morning. This
is an offering made by fire, an aroma pleasing
to the LORD.

Sabbath Offerings

9" 'On the Sabbath day, make an offering of
two lambs a year old without defect, together
with its drink offering and a grain offering of
two-tenths of an ephah[d] of fine flour mixed
with oil. 10This is the burnt offering for every
Sabbath, in addition to the regular burnt offering and its drink offering.

Monthly Offerings

11" 'On the first of every month, present to
the LORD a burnt offering of two young bulls,
one ram and seven male lambs a year old, all
without defect. 12With each bull there is to be a
grain offering of three-tenths of an ephah[e] of
fine flour mixed with oil; with the ram, a grain
offering of two-tenths of an ephah of fine flour
mixed with oil; 13and with each lamb, a grain
offering of a tenth of an ephah of fine flour
mixed with oil. This is for a burnt offering, a
pleasing aroma, an offering made to the LORD
by fire. 14With each bull there is to be a drink
offering of half a hin[f] of wine; with the ram,
a third of a hin[g]; and with each lamb, a quarter
of a hin. This is the monthly burnt offering to
be made at each new moon during the year.
15Besides the regular burnt offering with its
drink offering, one male goat is to be presented
to the LORD as a sin offering.

The Passover

16" 'On the fourteenth day of the first month
the LORD's Passover is to be held. 17On the fifteenth day of this month there is to be a festival;
for seven days eat bread made without yeast.
18On the first day hold a sacred assembly and
do no regular work. 19Present to the LORD an
offering made by fire, a burnt offering of two
young bulls, one ram and seven male lambs a

[a] 18 Or *Spirit* [b] 5 That is, probably about 2 quarts (about 2 liters); also in verses 13, 21 and 29 [c] 5 That is, probably about 1 quart (about 1 liter); also in verses 7 and 14 [d] 9 That is, probably about 4 quarts (about 4.5 liters); also in verses 12, 20 and 28 [e] 12 That is, probably about 6 quarts (about 6.5 liters); also in verses 20 and 28 [f] 14 That is, probably about 2 quarts (about 2 liters) [g] 14 That is, probably about 1 1/4 quarts (about 1.2 liters)

---

come in before them, one who will lead them out and bring them in, so the LORD's people will not be like sheep without a shepherd" (27:16–17). Moses was content with God's plan for his own life. We, like Moses, must learn to be content with God's plan for us. Even when his plan brings us temporary disappointments along the way, God always desires what is best for us.

28:1–2 Just as the offerings were to be brought regularly, so our fellowship with God should be a regular occurrence, a continual reality for believers. God desires more than ritual in our worship; he invites us to have a day-by-day relationship with him.

28:1–8 Only through continual fellowship with God could God's people expect to have victory as they entered the promised land. This is probably the reason for repeating the instructions and significance of the burnt offering for the new generation of Israelites. By bringing the offering, the people committed their lives to God in a new way. Similarly, the apostle Paul calls us to present our bodies as living sacrifices to God (Romans 12:1–2). This is an essential step for our spiritual growth. As we place our lives in God's hands, he will change us through his power.

year old, all without defect. 20With each bull prepare a grain offering of three-tenths of an ephah of fine flour mixed with oil; with the ram, two-tenths; 21and with each of the seven lambs, one-tenth. 22Include one male goat as a sin offering to make atonement for you. 23Prepare these in addition to the regular morning burnt offering. 24In this way prepare the food for the offering made by fire every day for seven days as an aroma pleasing to the LORD; it is to be prepared in addition to the regular burnt offering and its drink offering. 25On the seventh day hold a sacred assembly and do no regular work.

Feast of Weeks

26" 'On the day of firstfruits, when you present to the LORD an offering of new grain during the Feast of Weeks, hold a sacred assembly and do no regular work. 27Present a burnt offering of two young bulls, one ram and seven male lambs a year old as an aroma pleasing to the LORD. 28With each bull there is to be a grain offering of three-tenths of an ephah of fine flour mixed with oil; with the ram, two-tenths; 29and with each of the seven lambs, one-tenth. 30Include one male goat to make atonement for you. 31Prepare these together with their drink offerings, in addition to the regular burnt offering and its grain offering. Be sure the animals are without defect.

Feast of Trumpets

29 " 'On the first day of the seventh month hold a sacred assembly and do no regular work. It is a day for you to sound the trumpets. 2As an aroma pleasing to the LORD, prepare a burnt offering of one young bull, one ram and seven male lambs a year old, all without defect. 3With the bull prepare a grain offering of three-tenths of an ephah[a] of fine flour mixed with oil; with the ram, two-tenths[b]; 4and with each of the seven lambs, one-tenth.[c] 5Include one male goat as a sin offering to make atonement for you. 6These are in addition to the monthly and daily burnt offerings with their grain offerings and drink offerings as specified. They are offerings made to the LORD by fire—a pleasing aroma.

Day of Atonement

7" 'On the tenth day of this seventh month hold a sacred assembly. You must deny yourselves[d] and do no work. 8Present as an aroma pleasing to the LORD a burnt offering of one young bull, one ram and seven male lambs a year old, all without defect. 9With the bull prepare a grain offering of three-tenths of an ephah of fine flour mixed with oil; with the ram, two-tenths; 10and with each of the seven lambs, one-tenth. 11Include one male goat as a sin offering, in addition to the sin offering for atonement and the regular burnt offering with its grain offering, and their drink offerings.

Feast of Tabernacles

12" 'On the fifteenth day of the seventh month, hold a sacred assembly and do no regular work. Celebrate a festival to the LORD for seven days. 13Present an offering made by fire as an aroma pleasing to the LORD, a burnt offering of thirteen young bulls, two rams and fourteen male lambs a year old, all without defect. 14With each of the thirteen bulls prepare a grain offering of three-tenths of an ephah of fine flour mixed with oil; with each of the two rams, two-tenths; 15and with each of the fourteen lambs, one-tenth. 16Include one male goat as a sin offering, in addition to the regular burnt offering with its grain offering and drink offering.

17" 'On the second day prepare twelve young bulls, two rams and fourteen male lambs a year old, all without defect. 18With the bulls, rams and lambs, prepare their grain offerings and drink offerings according to the number specified. 19Include one male goat as a sin offering, in addition to the regular burnt offering with its grain offering, and their drink offerings.

20" 'On the third day prepare eleven bulls, two rams and fourteen male lambs a year old, all without defect. 21With the bulls, rams and lambs, prepare their grain offerings and drink offerings according to the number specified. 22Include one male goat as a sin offering, in addition to the regular burnt offering with its grain offering and drink offering.

23" 'On the fourth day prepare ten bulls, two rams and fourteen male lambs a year old, all without defect. 24With the bulls, rams and lambs, prepare their grain offerings and drink offerings according to the number specified. 25Include one male goat as a sin offering, in addition to the regular burnt offering with its grain offering and drink offering.

26" 'On the fifth day prepare nine bulls, two rams and fourteen male lambs a year old, all without defect. 27With the bulls, rams and lambs, prepare their grain offerings and drink offerings according to the number specified. 28Include one male goat as a sin offering, in addition to the regular burnt offering with its grain offering and drink offering.

29" 'On the sixth day prepare eight bulls, two rams and fourteen male lambs a year old, all without defect. 30With the bulls, rams and lambs, prepare their grain offerings and drink offerings according to the number specified. 31Include one male goat as a sin offering, in addition to the regular burnt offering with its grain offering and drink offering.

32" 'On the seventh day prepare seven bulls, two rams and fourteen male lambs a year old,

[a]3 That is, probably about 6 quarts (about 6.5 liters); also in verses 9 and 14 [b]3 That is, probably about 4 quarts (about 4.5 liters); also in verses 9 and 14 [c]4 That is, probably about 2 quarts (about 2 liters); also in verses 10 and 15 [d]7 Or *must fast*

all without defect. 33With the bulls, rams and
lambs, prepare their grain offerings and drink
offerings according to the number specified.
34Include one male goat as a sin offering, in
addition to the regular burnt offering with its
grain offering and drink offering.

35" 'On the eighth day hold an assembly and
do no regular work. 36Present an offering made
by fire as an aroma pleasing to the LORD, a
burnt offering of one bull, one ram and seven
male lambs a year old, all without defect.
37With the bull, the ram and the lambs, prepare
their grain offerings and drink offerings according to the number specified. 38Include one male
goat as a sin offering, in addition to the regular
burnt offering with its grain offering and drink
offering.

39" 'In addition to what you vow and your
freewill offerings, prepare these for the LORD
at your appointed feasts: your burnt offerings,
grain offerings, drink offerings and fellowship
offerings.[a]' "

40Moses told the Israelites all that the LORD
commanded him.

Vows

30 Moses said to the heads of the tribes of
Israel: "This is what the LORD commands: 2When a man makes a vow to the LORD
or takes an oath to obligate himself by a pledge,
he must not break his word but must do everything he said.

3"When a young woman still living in her
father's house makes a vow to the LORD or obligates herself by a pledge 4and her father hears
about her vow or pledge but says nothing to
her, then all her vows and every pledge by
which she obligated herself will stand. 5But if
her father forbids her when he hears about it,
none of her vows or the pledges by which she
obligated herself will stand; the LORD will release her because her father has forbidden her.

6"If she marries after she makes a vow or
after her lips utter a rash promise by which she
obligates herself 7and her husband hears about
it but says nothing to her, then her vows or the
pledges by which she obligated herself will
stand. 8But if her husband forbids her when he
hears about it, he nullifies the vow that obligates her or the rash promise by which she obligates herself, and the LORD will release her.

9"Any vow or obligation taken by a widow
or divorced woman will be binding on her.

10"If a woman living with her husband
makes a vow or obligates herself by a pledge
under oath 11and her husband hears about it
but says nothing to her and does not forbid her,
then all her vows or the pledges by which she
obligated herself will stand. 12But if her husband nullifies them when he hears about them,
then none of the vows or pledges that came
from her lips will stand. Her husband has nulli-
fied them, and the LORD will release her. 13Her
husband may confirm or nullify any vow she
makes or any sworn pledge to deny herself.
14But if her husband says nothing to her about
it from day to day, then he confirms all her
vows or the pledges binding on her. He confirms them by saying nothing to her when he
hears about them. 15If, however, he nullifies
them some time after he hears about them, then
he is responsible for her guilt."

16These are the regulations the LORD gave
Moses concerning relationships between a man
and his wife, and between a father and his
young daughter still living in his house.

Vengeance on the Midianites

31 The LORD said to Moses, 2"Take vengeance on the Midianites for the Israelites. After that, you will be gathered to your
people."

3So Moses said to the people, "Arm some of
your men to go to war against the Midianites
and to carry out the LORD's vengeance on them.
4Send into battle a thousand men from each of
the tribes of Israel." 5So twelve thousand men
armed for battle, a thousand from each tribe,
were supplied from the clans of Israel. 6Moses
sent them into battle, a thousand from each
tribe, along with Phinehas son of Eleazar, the
priest, who took with him articles from the
sanctuary and the trumpets for signaling.

7They fought against Midian, as the LORD
commanded Moses, and killed every man.
8Among their victims were Evi, Rekem, Zur, Hur
and Reba—the five kings of Midian. They also
killed Balaam son of Beor with the sword. 9The
Israelites captured the Midianite women and
children and took all the Midianite herds, flocks
and goods as plunder. 10They burned all the
towns where the Midianites had settled, as well
as all their camps. 11They took all the plunder
and spoils, including the people and animals,
12and brought the captives, spoils and plunder
to Moses and Eleazar the priest and the Israelite
assembly at their camp on the plains of Moab,
by the Jordan across from Jericho.[b]

13Moses, Eleazar the priest and all the leaders
of the community went to meet them outside
the camp. 14Moses was angry with the officers of
the army—the commanders of thousands and
commanders of hundreds—who returned from
the battle.

15"Have you allowed all the women to live?"
he asked them. 16"They were the ones who followed Balaam's advice and were the means of
turning the Israelites away from the LORD in
what happened at Peor, so that a plague struck
the LORD's people. 17Now kill all the boys. And
kill every woman who has slept with a man,
18but save for yourselves every girl who has never slept with a man.

19"All of you who have killed anyone or
touched anyone who was killed must stay out-

[a]39 Traditionally *peace offerings* [b]12 Hebrew *Jordan of Jericho;* possibly an ancient name for the Jordan River

side the camp seven days. On the third and seventh days you must purify yourselves and your captives. 20 Purify every garment as well as everything made of leather, goat hair or wood."

21 Then Eleazar the priest said to the soldiers who had gone into battle, "This is the requirement of the law that the LORD gave Moses: 22 Gold, silver, bronze, iron, tin, lead 23 and anything else that can withstand fire must be put through the fire, and then it will be clean. But it must also be purified with the water of cleansing. And whatever cannot withstand fire must be put through that water. 24 On the seventh day wash your clothes and you will be clean. Then you may come into the camp."

Dividing the Spoils

25 The LORD said to Moses, 26 "You and Eleazar the priest and the family heads of the community are to count all the people and animals that were captured. 27 Divide the spoils between the soldiers who took part in the battle and the rest of the community. 28 From the soldiers who fought in the battle, set apart as tribute for the LORD one out of every five hundred, whether persons, cattle, donkeys, sheep or goats. 29 Take this tribute from their half share and give it to Eleazar the priest as the LORD's part. 30 From the Israelites' half, select one out of every fifty, whether persons, cattle, donkeys, sheep, goats or other animals. Give them to the Levites, who are responsible for the care of the LORD's tabernacle." 31 So Moses and Eleazar the priest did as the LORD commanded Moses.

32 The plunder remaining from the spoils that the soldiers took was 675,000 sheep, 33 72,000 cattle, 34 61,000 donkeys 35 and 32,000 women who had never slept with a man.

36 The half share of those who fought in the battle was:

337,500 sheep, 37 of which the tribute for the LORD was 675;
38 36,000 cattle, of which the tribute for the LORD was 72;
39 30,500 donkeys, of which the tribute for the LORD was 61;
40 16,000 people, of which the tribute for the LORD was 32.

41 Moses gave the tribute to Eleazar the priest as the LORD's part, as the LORD commanded Moses.

42 The half belonging to the Israelites, which Moses set apart from that of the fighting men— 43 the community's half—was 337,500 sheep, 44 36,000 cattle, 45 30,500 donkeys 46 and 16,000 people. 47 From the Israelites' half, Moses selected one out of every fifty persons and animals, as the LORD commanded him, and gave them to the Levites, who were responsible for the care of the LORD's tabernacle.

48 Then the officers who were over the units of the army—the commanders of thousands and commanders of hundreds—went to Moses 49 and said to him, "Your servants have counted the soldiers under our command, and not one is missing. 50 So we have brought as an offering to the LORD the gold articles each of us acquired—armlets, bracelets, signet rings, earrings and necklaces—to make atonement for ourselves before the LORD."

51 Moses and Eleazar the priest accepted from them the gold—all the crafted articles. 52 All the gold from the commanders of thousands and commanders of hundreds that Moses and Eleazar presented as a gift to the LORD weighed 16,750 shekels.[a] 53 Each soldier had taken plunder for himself. 54 Moses and Eleazar the priest accepted the gold from the commanders of thousands and commanders of hundreds and brought it into the Tent of Meeting as a memorial for the Israelites before the LORD.

The Transjordan Tribes

32 The Reubenites and Gadites, who had very large herds and flocks, saw that the lands of Jazer and Gilead were suitable for livestock. 2 So they came to Moses and Eleazar the priest and to the leaders of the community, and said, 3 "Ataroth, Dibon, Jazer, Nimrah, Heshbon, Elealeh, Sebam, Nebo and Beon— 4 the land the LORD subdued before the people of Israel—are suitable for livestock, and your servants have livestock. 5 If we have found favor in your eyes," they said, "let this land be given to your servants as our possession. Do not make us cross the Jordan."

6 Moses said to the Gadites and Reubenites, "Shall your countrymen go to war while you sit here? 7 Why do you discourage the Israelites from going over into the land the LORD has given them? 8 This is what your fathers did when I sent them from Kadesh Barnea to look over the land. 9 After they went up to the Valley of Eshcol and viewed the land, they discouraged the Israelites from entering the land the LORD had given them. 10 The LORD's anger was aroused that day and he swore this oath: 11 'Because they have not followed me wholeheartedly, not one of the men twenty years old or more who came up out of Egypt will see the land I promised on oath to Abraham, Isaac and Jacob— 12 not one except Caleb son of Jephunneh the Kenizzite and Joshua son of Nun, for they followed the LORD wholeheartedly.' 13 The LORD's anger burned against Israel and he made them wander in the desert forty years, until the whole generation of those who had done evil in his sight was gone.

14 "And here you are, a brood of sinners, standing in the place of your fathers and making the LORD even more angry with Israel. 15 If you turn away from following him, he will again leave all this people in the desert, and you will be the cause of their destruction."

16 Then they came up to him and said, "We

[a] 52 That is, about 420 pounds (about 190 kilograms)

would like to build pens here for our livestock and cities for our women and children. 17But we are ready to arm ourselves and go ahead of the Israelites until we have brought them to their place. Meanwhile our women and children will live in fortified cities, for protection from the inhabitants of the land. 18We will not return to our homes until every Israelite has received his inheritance. 19We will not receive any inheritance with them on the other side of the Jordan, because our inheritance has come to us on the east side of the Jordan."

20Then Moses said to them, "If you will do this—if you will arm yourselves before the LORD for battle, 21and if all of you will go armed over the Jordan before the LORD until he has driven his enemies out before him— 22then when the land is subdued before the LORD, you may return and be free from your obligation to the LORD and to Israel. And this land will be your possession before the LORD.

23"But if you fail to do this, you will be sinning against the LORD; and you may be sure that your sin will find you out. 24Build cities for your women and children, and pens for your flocks, but do what you have promised."

25The Gadites and Reubenites said to Moses, "We your servants will do as our lord commands. 26Our children and wives, our flocks and herds will remain here in the cities of Gilead. 27But your servants, every man armed for battle, will cross over to fight before the LORD, just as our lord says."

28Then Moses gave orders about them to Eleazar the priest and Joshua son of Nun and to the family heads of the Israelite tribes. 29He said to them, "If the Gadites and Reubenites, every man armed for battle, cross over the Jordan with you before the LORD, then when the land is subdued before you, give them the land of Gilead as their possession. 30But if they do not cross over with you armed, they must accept their possession with you in Canaan."

31The Gadites and Reubenites answered, "Your servants will do what the LORD has said. 32We will cross over before the LORD into Canaan armed, but the property we inherit will be on this side of the Jordan."

33Then Moses gave to the Gadites, the Reubenites and the half-tribe of Manasseh son of Joseph the kingdom of Sihon king of the Amorites and the kingdom of Og king of Bashan—the whole land with its cities and the territory around them.

34The Gadites built up Dibon, Ataroth, Aroer, 35Atroth Shophan, Jazer, Jogbehah, 36Beth Nimrah and Beth Haran as fortified cities, and built pens for their flocks. 37And the Reubenites rebuilt Heshbon, Elealeh and Kiriathaim, 38as well as Nebo and Baal Meon (these names were changed) and Sibmah. They gave names to the cities they rebuilt.

39The descendants of Makir son of Manasseh went to Gilead, captured it and drove out the Amorites who were there. 40So Moses gave Gilead to the Makirites, the descendants of Manasseh, and they settled there. 41Jair, a descendant of Manasseh, captured their settlements and called them Havvoth Jair.[a] 42And Nobah captured Kenath and its surrounding settlements and called it Nobah after himself.

Stages in Israel's Journey

33 Here are the stages in the journey of the Israelites when they came out of Egypt by divisions under the leadership of Moses and Aaron. 2At the LORD's command Moses recorded the stages in their journey. This is their journey by stages:

3The Israelites set out from Rameses on the fifteenth day of the first month, the day after the Passover. They marched out boldly in full view of all the Egyptians, 4who were burying all their firstborn, whom the LORD had struck down among them; for the LORD had brought judgment on their gods.

5The Israelites left Rameses and camped at Succoth.

6They left Succoth and camped at Etham, on the edge of the desert.

7They left Etham, turned back to Pi Hahiroth, to the east of Baal Zephon, and camped near Migdol.

8They left Pi Hahiroth[b] and passed through the sea into the desert, and when they had traveled for three days in the Desert of Etham, they camped at Marah.

9They left Marah and went to Elim, where there were twelve springs and seventy palm trees, and they camped there.

10They left Elim and camped by the Red Sea.[c]

11They left the Red Sea and camped in the Desert of Sin.

12They left the Desert of Sin and camped at Dophkah.

13They left Dophkah and camped at Alush.

14They left Alush and camped at Rephi-

[a]41 Or *them the settlements of Jair* [b]8 Many manuscripts of the Masoretic Text, Samaritan Pentateuch and Vulgate; most manuscripts of the Masoretic Text *left from before Hahiroth* [c]10 Hebrew *Yam Suph*; that is, Sea of Reeds; also in verse 11

33:1–49 Moses sketched out Israel's wilderness itinerary to remind the new generation that God had graciously provided for them since their exodus from Egyptian bondage. It was important to reaffirm these truths in order to spiritually prepare the people for the challenge of conquering the promised land. This procedure of reviewing God's past acts of faithfulness was often used by Israel's leaders to prepare the people for future challenges. Similarly, praising God for past victories and blessings (answered prayer, a helping hand, spiritual progress) is an excellent way for us to prepare for future challenges.

dim, where there was no water for the people to drink.

15 They left Rephidim and camped in the Desert of Sinai.

16 They left the Desert of Sinai and camped at Kibroth Hattaavah.

17 They left Kibroth Hattaavah and camped at Hazeroth.

18 They left Hazeroth and camped at Rithmah.

19 They left Rithmah and camped at Rimmon Perez.

20 They left Rimmon Perez and camped at Libnah.

21 They left Libnah and camped at Rissah.

22 They left Rissah and camped at Kehelathah.

23 They left Kehelathah and camped at Mount Shepher.

24 They left Mount Shepher and camped at Haradah.

25 They left Haradah and camped at Makheloth.

26 They left Makheloth and camped at Tahath.

27 They left Tahath and camped at Terah.

28 They left Terah and camped at Mithcah.

29 They left Mithcah and camped at Hashmonah.

30 They left Hashmonah and camped at Moseroth.

31 They left Moseroth and camped at Bene Jaakan.

32 They left Bene Jaakan and camped at Hor Haggidgad.

33 They left Hor Haggidgad and camped at Jotbathah.

34 They left Jotbathah and camped at Abronah.

35 They left Abronah and camped at Ezion Geber.

36 They left Ezion Geber and camped at Kadesh, in the Desert of Zin.

37 They left Kadesh and camped at
Mount Hor, on the border of Edom. 38 At
the LORD's command Aaron the priest
went up Mount Hor, where he died on the
first day of the fifth month of the fortieth
year after the Israelites came out of Egypt.
39 Aaron was a hundred and twenty-three
years old when he died on Mount Hor.

40 The Canaanite king of Arad, who lived in the Negev of Canaan, heard that the Israelites were coming.

41 They left Mount Hor and camped at Zalmonah.

42 They left Zalmonah and camped at Punon.

43 They left Punon and camped at Oboth.

44 They left Oboth and camped at Iye Abarim, on the border of Moab.

45 They left Iyim[a] and camped at Dibon Gad.

46 They left Dibon Gad and camped at Almon Diblathaim.

47 They left Almon Diblathaim and camped in the mountains of Abarim, near Nebo.

48 They left the mountains of Abarim
and camped on the plains of Moab by the
Jordan across from Jericho.[b] 49 There on
the plains of Moab they camped along the
Jordan from Beth Jeshimoth to Abel
Shittim.

50 On the plains of Moab by the Jordan across
from Jericho the LORD said to Moses, 51 "Speak
to the Israelites and say to them: 'When you
cross the Jordan into Canaan, 52 drive out all the
inhabitants of the land before you. Destroy all
their carved images and their cast idols, and
demolish all their high places. 53 Take possession of the land and settle in it, for I have given
you the land to possess. 54 Distribute the land by
lot, according to your clans. To a larger group
give a larger inheritance, and to a smaller group
a smaller one. Whatever falls to them by lot will
be theirs. Distribute it according to your ancestral tribes.

55 " 'But if you do not drive out the inhabitants of the land, those you allow to remain will
become barbs in your eyes and thorns in your
sides. They will give you trouble in the land
where you will live. 56 And then I will do to you
what I plan to do to them.' "

Boundaries of Canaan

34 The LORD said to Moses, 2 "Command
the Israelites and say to them: 'When
you enter Canaan, the land that will be allotted

[a] 45 That is, Iye Abarim [b] 48 Hebrew *Jordan of Jericho*; possibly an ancient name for the Jordan River; also in verse 50

33:50–53 God gave the Israelites specific instructions about what they were to do in order to conquer Canaan. Yet he also affirmed that he had already given them the land. Obedience was the key to attaining God's promised blessing. When we face adversaries and obstacles we must seek God's help and guidance. God also promises us victory and blessing when we carry out what he has called us to do.

33:55–56 God sternly warned his people to completely cleanse the promised land of the ungodly people living there. Yet the Israelites failed to completely push out their Canaanite neighbors and, as a result, became like them. We all are susceptible to being led astray by others. If we don't use wisdom in choosing our companions, we may find ourselves falling back into our old way of life.

34:1–29 The boundaries given here were based upon faith in God. The Israelites had to trust that God would help them conquer the promised land. This great chapter of anticipation recalls God's promise to Abraham: "The whole land of Canaan, where you are now an alien, I will

to you as an inheritance will have these boundaries:

3" 'Your southern side will include some of the
Desert of Zin along the border of Edom. On
the east, your southern boundary will start from
the end of the Salt Sea,[a] 4cross south of Scorpion[b] Pass, continue on to Zin and go south of
Kadesh Barnea. Then it will go to Hazar Addar
and over to Azmon, 5where it will turn, join the
Wadi of Egypt and end at the Sea.[c]

6" 'Your western boundary will be the coast
of the Great Sea. This will be your boundary on
the west.

7" 'For your northern boundary, run a line
from the Great Sea to Mount Hor 8and from
Mount Hor to Lebo[d] Hamath. Then the
boundary will go to Zedad, 9continue to Ziph-
ron and end at Hazar Enan. This will be your
boundary on the north.

10" 'For your eastern boundary, run a line
from Hazar Enan to Shepham. 11The boundary
will go down from Shepham to Riblah on the
east side of Ain and continue along the slopes
east of the Sea of Kinnereth.[e] 12Then the
boundary will go down along the Jordan and
end at the Salt Sea.

" 'This will be your land, with its boundaries
on every side.' "

13Moses commanded the Israelites: "Assign
this land by lot as an inheritance. The LORD has
ordered that it be given to the nine and a half
tribes, 14because the families of the tribe of Reuben, the tribe of Gad and the half-tribe of Manasseh have received their inheritance. 15These
two and a half tribes have received their inheritance on the east side of the Jordan of Jericho,[f]
toward the sunrise."

16The LORD said to Moses, 17"These are the
names of the men who are to assign the land for
you as an inheritance: Eleazar the priest and
Joshua son of Nun. 18And appoint one leader
from each tribe to help assign the land. 19These
are their names:

Caleb son of Jephunneh,
from the tribe of Judah;
20Shemuel son of Ammihud,
from the tribe of Simeon;
21Elidad son of Kislon,
from the tribe of Benjamin;
22Bukki son of Jogli,
the leader from the tribe of Dan;
23Hanniel son of Ephod,
the leader from the tribe of Manasseh
son of Joseph;
24Kemuel son of Shiphtan,
the leader from the tribe of Ephraim
son of Joseph;
25Elizaphan son of Parnach,
the leader from the tribe of Zebulun;
26Paltiel son of Azzan,
the leader from the tribe of Issachar;
27Ahihud son of Shelomi,
the leader from the tribe of Asher;
28Pedahel son of Ammihud,
the leader from the tribe of Naphtali."

29These are the men the LORD commanded to
assign the inheritance to the Israelites in the
land of Canaan.

Towns for the Levites

35 On the plains of Moab by the Jordan
across from Jericho,[g] the LORD said to
Moses, 2"Command the Israelites to give the
Levites towns to live in from the inheritance the
Israelites will possess. And give them pasturelands around the towns. 3Then they will have
towns to live in and pasturelands for their cattle, flocks and all their other livestock.

4"The pasturelands around the towns that
you give the Levites will extend out fifteen hundred feet[h] from the town wall. 5Outside the
town, measure three thousand feet[i] on the
east side, three thousand on the south side,
three thousand on the west and three thousand
on the north, with the town in the center. They
will have this area as pastureland for the towns.

Cities of Refuge

6"Six of the towns you give the Levites will be
cities of refuge, to which a person who has
killed someone may flee. In addition, give them
forty-two other towns. 7In all you must give the
Levites forty-eight towns, together with their
pasturelands. 8The towns you give the Levites
from the land the Israelites possess are to be
given in proportion to the inheritance of each
tribe: Take many towns from a tribe that has
many, but few from one that has few."

9Then the LORD said to Moses: 10"Speak to
the Israelites and say to them: 'When you cross
the Jordan into Canaan, 11select some towns to
be your cities of refuge, to which a person who

[a]3 That is, the Dead Sea; also in verse 12 [b]4 Hebrew *Akrabbim* [c]5 That is, the Mediterranean; also in verses 6 and 7 [d]8 Or *to the entrance to* [e]11 That is, Galilee [f]15 *Jordan of Jericho* was possibly an ancient name for the Jordan River. [g]1 Hebrew *Jordan of Jericho*; possibly an ancient name for the Jordan River [h]4 Hebrew *a thousand cubits* (about 450 meters) [i]5 Hebrew *two thousand cubits* (about 900 meters)

---

give as an everlasting possession to you and your descendants after you; and I will be their God" (Genesis 17:8). Those who were obedient to God would see the fulfillment of this promise that had been made hundreds of years earlier. God fulfills his promises, even though it sometimes takes longer than we expect. We must learn to trust him, following his plan with patience and humility.

35:9–34 The cities of refuge were provided by God as places where a person who had caused an accidental death could get a fair hearing. According to the law, murderers were subject to the death penalty. Even those guilty of involuntary manslaughter could be avenged by a near relative. The cities of refuge provided a place of safety for those who had accidentally killed someone. This system demanded the strict, moral accountability of every Israelite, but it also provided a way of escape for those who had sinned unintentionally. God is just, yet he is also gracious.

has killed someone accidentally may flee.
12They will be places of refuge from the avenger,
so that a person accused of murder may not
die before he stands trial before the assembly.
13These six towns you give will be your cities of
refuge. 14Give three on this side of the Jordan
and three in Canaan as cities of refuge. 15These
six towns will be a place of refuge for Israelites,
aliens and any other people living among them,
so that anyone who has killed another accidentally can flee there.

16" 'If a man strikes someone with an iron
object so that he dies, he is a murderer; the
murderer shall be put to death. 17Or if anyone
has a stone in his hand that could kill, and he
strikes someone so that he dies, he is a murderer; the murderer shall be put to death. 18Or if
anyone has a wooden object in his hand that
could kill, and he hits someone so that he dies,
he is a murderer; the murderer shall be put to
death. 19The avenger of blood shall put the
murderer to death; when he meets him, he shall
put him to death. 20If anyone with malice aforethought shoves another or throws something at
him intentionally so that he dies 21or if in hostility he hits him with his fist so that he dies,
that person shall be put to death; he is a murderer. The avenger of blood shall put the murderer to death when he meets him.

22" 'But if without hostility someone suddenly shoves another or throws something at
him unintentionally 23or, without seeing him,
drops a stone on him that could kill him, and
he dies, then since he was not his enemy and he
did not intend to harm him, 24the assembly
must judge between him and the avenger of
blood according to these regulations. 25The assembly must protect the one accused of murder
from the avenger of blood and send him back
to the city of refuge to which he fled. He must
stay there until the death of the high priest, who
was anointed with the holy oil.

26" 'But if the accused ever goes outside the
limits of the city of refuge to which he has fled
27and the avenger of blood finds him outside
the city, the avenger of blood may kill the accused without being guilty of murder. 28The accused must stay in his city of refuge until the
death of the high priest; only after the death of
the high priest may he return to his own property.

29" 'These are to be legal requirements for
you throughout the generations to come, wherever you live.

30" 'Anyone who kills a person is to be put
to death as a murderer only on the testimony of
witnesses. But no one is to be put to death on
the testimony of only one witness.

31" 'Do not accept a ransom for the life of a
murderer, who deserves to die. He must surely
be put to death.

32" 'Do not accept a ransom for anyone who
has fled to a city of refuge and so allow him to
go back and live on his own land before the
death of the high priest.

33" 'Do not pollute the land where you are.
Bloodshed pollutes the land, and atonement
cannot be made for the land on which blood
has been shed, except by the blood of the one
who shed it. 34Do not defile the land where you
live and where I dwell, for I, the LORD, dwell
among the Israelites.' "

Inheritance of Zelophehad's Daughters

36 The family heads of the clan of Gilead
son of Makir, the son of Manasseh, who
were from the clans of the descendants of Joseph, came and spoke before Moses and the
leaders, the heads of the Israelite families. 2They
said, "When the LORD commanded my lord to
give the land as an inheritance to the Israelites
by lot, he ordered you to give the inheritance of
our brother Zelophehad to his daughters. 3Now
suppose they marry men from other Israelite
tribes; then their inheritance will be taken from
our ancestral inheritance and added to that of
the tribe they marry into. And so part of the
inheritance allotted to us will be taken away.
4When the Year of Jubilee for the Israelites
comes, their inheritance will be added to that of
the tribe into which they marry, and their property will be taken from the tribal inheritance of
our forefathers."

5Then at the LORD's command Moses gave
this order to the Israelites: "What the tribe of
the descendants of Joseph is saying is right.
6This is what the LORD commands for Zelophehad's daughters: They may marry anyone they
please as long as they marry within the tribal
clan of their father. 7No inheritance in Israel is
to pass from tribe to tribe, for every Israelite
shall keep the tribal land inherited from his
forefathers. 8Every daughter who inherits land
in any Israelite tribe must marry someone in her
father's tribal clan, so that every Israelite will
possess the inheritance of his fathers. 9No inheritance may pass from tribe to tribe, for each
Israelite tribe is to keep the land it inherits."

10So Zelophehad's daughters did as the LORD
commanded Moses. 11Zelophehad's daughters—Mahlah, Tirzah, Hoglah, Milcah and
Noah—married their cousins on their father's
side. 12They married within the clans of the
descendants of Manasseh son of Joseph, and
their inheritance remained in their father's clan
and tribe.

13These are the commands and regulations
the LORD gave through Moses to the Israelites
on the plains of Moab by the Jordan across
from Jericho.[a]

[a]13 Hebrew *Jordan of Jericho;* possibly an ancient name for the Jordan River

Deuteronomy

The Big Picture

What would we do after failing repeatedly for almost forty years? How would we lay out a new pattern for living? In Deuteronomy, the Israelites were about to enter the promised land. They had been at this point before—almost forty years earlier. But the Israelites had failed to believe God's promise to give them the land of Canaan, and God had allowed them to wander in the wilderness for almost forty years.

The Israelites were rebuilding and renewing their lives. They were trying to make sense of their wilderness wanderings. They were looking for ways to overcome the fear that had caused them to fail forty years before. They needed to clearly understand God's expectations and promises. They needed assurance that God was still with them and would direct their course. In the book of Deuteronomy, Moses set forth God's law and promises, giving the Israelites the direction and assurance that they needed.

Moses began by urging the people to learn from their history. He reminded them not only of their past failures but also of God's mighty acts on their behalf. He encouraged them to use their past experiences—good and bad—to set their faith on fire. Moses also directed the people to think about their present circumstances. He reviewed God's laws, giving them detailed instructions on how to respond to the challenges of life. Finally, Moses called the people to look toward the future. What were the promised results of obeying God? What were the promised consequences of disobeying him?

Renewing our spiritual life is serious business. Deuteronomy gives that subject its full attention by providing us with some essential guidelines for God's plan of victory. God shows us how we can gain direction from the past, guidance for the present and hope for the future. Deuteronomy is a handbook for renewal.

A. LOOKING TOWARD THE PAST: LESSONS FROM HISTORY (1:1–4:43)

1. Commencing a Life of Defeat (1:1-46)
2. Continuing a Life of Defeat (2:1-37)
3. Concluding a Life of Defeat (3:1–4:43)

B. LOOKING AT THE PRESENT: LESSONS FROM THE LAW (4:44–26:19)

1. The Decalogue and Its Explanation (4:44–11:32)
2. The Directions for Israel (12:1–26:19)
   - a. Ceremonial laws (12:1–16:17)
   - b. Civil laws (16:18–20:20)
   - c. Cultural laws (21:1–26:19)

C. LOOKING TOWARD THE PROMISE: LESSONS FROM PROPHECY (27:1–34:12)

1. Reward or Rejection (27:1–28:68)
2. Removal or Repentance (29:1–30:20)
3. Reminders and Remembrances (31:1–34:12)

Spiritual Renewal Themes

LEARNING FROM THE PAST

For almost forty years the Israelites had lived out the consequences of their weak faith and disobedience. Instead of hiding their past mistakes, Moses brought them out into the open. The past holds many lessons for us. Our spiritual renewal demands

Essential Facts

PURPOSE:
To assist God's people as they live in the present, by reviewing what God has done in the past and considering what God has promised to do in the future.

AUTHOR:
Moses.

AUDIENCE:
The people of Israel.

DATE WRITTEN:
Just before Israel's entrance into the promised land, about 1406 or 1405 B.C.

SETTING:
The plains of Moab.

KEY VERSE:
"He brought us out from there to bring us in and give us the land that he promised on oath to our forefathers" (6:23).

KEY EVENTS:
Three sermons by Moses.

KEY PERSON:
Moses.

that we learn from past failures and also remember God's mighty acts on our behalf. Remembering that God will walk with us wherever we go will provide strength for the present and hope for the future.

A PLAN FOR THE PRESENT

As we look at our past, we sometimes fear that we will continue to repeat our past mistakes. Moses made it clear that we can learn from the past in order to live successfully in the present. He reviewed the laws that God had given the Israelites to help them relate to each other in godly and responsible ways. These clear guidelines can help us learn how to live responsibly as well. God does not leave us without direction—his Word provides clear instructions that we can follow every day.

HOPE FOR THE FUTURE

In many ways our future is based on what we have learned from our past and on how we live in the present. Our success or failure in the future may well depend upon whether or not we choose to follow God's plan for spiritual renewal and wholeness now. But our future is also based on God's faithfulness to us. He is a God who loves us, forgives us and redeems us from our slavery to sin. As we live each day, we can be assured that God's love and grace are a present reality, providing hope for our future.

REBUILDING AND RENEWAL

How exciting to be able to start over again! The air must have been filled with excitement as the Israelites listened to Moses, anticipating their entrance into the promised land. There is hope! There is forgiveness! We can begin again! What an encouragement to us when we have sinned. And God's grace in that process is limitless. The Israelites had sinned repeatedly and miserably for forty years, but God had now brought them to the edge of the promised land. They had another chance to begin again.

The Command to Leave Horeb

1 These are the words Moses spoke to all Israel in the desert east of the Jordan—that is, in the Arabah—opposite Suph, between Paran and Tophel, Laban, Hazeroth and Dizahab. 2(It takes eleven days to go from Horeb to Kadesh Barnea by the Mount Seir road.)

3In the fortieth year, on the first day of the eleventh month, Moses proclaimed to the Israelites all that the LORD had commanded him concerning them. 4This was after he had defeated Sihon king of the Amorites, who reigned in Heshbon, and at Edrei had defeated Og king of Bashan, who reigned in Ashtaroth.

5East of the Jordan in the territory of Moab, Moses began to expound this law, saying:

6The LORD our God said to us at Horeb, "You have stayed long enough at this mountain. 7Break camp and advance into the hill country of the Amorites; go to all the neighboring peoples in the Arabah, in the mountains, in the western foothills, in the Negev and along the coast, to the land of the Canaanites and to Lebanon, as far as the great river, the Euphrates. 8See, I have given you this land. Go in and take possession of the land that the LORD swore he would give to your fathers—to Abraham, Isaac and Jacob—and to their descendants after them."

The Appointment of Leaders

9At that time I said to you, "You are too heavy a burden for me to carry alone. 10The LORD your God has increased your numbers so that today you are as many as the stars in the sky. 11May the LORD, the God of your fathers, increase you a thousand times and bless you as he has promised! 12But how can I bear your problems and your burdens and your disputes all by myself? 13Choose some wise, understanding and respected men from each of your tribes, and I will set them over you."

14You answered me, "What you propose to do is good."

15So I took the leading men of your tribes, wise and respected men, and appointed them to have authority over you—as commanders of thousands, of hundreds, of fifties and of tens and as tribal officials. 16And I charged your judges at that time: Hear the disputes between your brothers and judge fairly, whether the case is between brother Israelites or between one of them and an alien. 17Do not show partiality in judging; hear both small and great alike. Do not be afraid of any man, for judgment belongs to God. Bring me any case too hard for you, and I will hear it. 18And at that time I told you everything you were to do.

Spies Sent Out

19Then, as the LORD our God commanded us, we set out from Horeb and went toward the hill country of the Amorites through all that vast and dreadful desert that you have seen, and so we reached Kadesh Barnea. 20Then I said to you, "You have reached the hill country of the Amorites, which the LORD our God is giving us. 21See, the LORD your God has given you the land. Go up and take possession of it as the LORD, the God of your fathers, told you. Do not be afraid; do not be discouraged."

22Then all of you came to me and said, "Let us send men ahead to spy out the land for us and bring back a report about the route we are to take and the towns we will come to."

23The idea seemed good to me; so I selected twelve of you, one man from each tribe. 24They left and went up into the hill country, and came to the Valley of Eshcol and explored it. 25Taking with them some of the fruit of the land, they brought it down to us and reported, "It is a good land that the LORD our God is giving us."

Rebellion Against the LORD

26But you were unwilling to go up; you rebelled against the command of the LORD your God. 27You grumbled in your tents and said, "The LORD hates us; so he brought us out of Egypt to deliver us into the hands of the Amorites to destroy us. 28Where can we go? Our brothers have made us lose heart. They say, 'The people are stronger and taller than we are; the cities are large, with walls up to the sky. We even saw the Anakites there.' "

1:1–5 Deuteronomy is a book of hope; it is all about making a fresh start. The Israelites' failures in the wilderness were now behind them. Opportunities for rebuilding their lives and their nation lay ahead. Israel stood once again on the threshold of the promised land. It had taken them almost forty years to accomplish an eleven-day journey because of their willful disobedience and lack of faith. Moses took time in this passage to give them principles for living within the Israelite community and for maintaining their relationship with God.

1:1–5 As the Israelites were about to enter the promised land, they took time to get back to the basics, to read God's laws once again. The name *Deuteronomy* actually means "second law" or "repetition of the law." It was necessary for Moses to share God's instructions with the new generation of Israelites because they faced new living conditions and the accompanying temptations of the promised land. We also need to take time to regularly review God's instructions for living as we face our own temptations and difficulties and move through the process of spiritual renewal.

1:6 God told the Israelites, "You have stayed long enough at this mountain." In every life there are moments when it is essential to move on. There come times when action is necessary. When we stay too long at one place, we can stagnate. If we seek to grow in our spiritual lives, we must be careful to advance according to God's schedule—neither lagging behind nor running ahead.

1:19–21 The expression "Do not be afraid" and its variations are the most common commands in Scripture. We are afraid of so many things. In challenging his people to a new course of action, God insisted that they cast away their fears. God asked his people to trust him. When we learn to turn our focus away from our circumstances and toward God and his power, our helplessness and fears will soon melt away.

29Then I said to you, "Do not be terrified; do not be afraid of them. 30The LORD your God, who is going before you, will fight for you, as he did for you in Egypt, before your very eyes, 31and in the desert. There you saw how the LORD your God carried you, as a father carries his son, all the way you went until you reached this place."

32In spite of this, you did not trust in the LORD your God, 33who went ahead of you on your journey, in fire by night and in a cloud by day, to search out places for you to camp and to show you the way you should go.

34When the LORD heard what you said, he was angry and solemnly swore: 35"Not a man of this evil generation shall see the good land I swore to give your forefathers, 36except Caleb son of Jephunneh. He will see it, and I will give him and his descendants the land he set his feet on, because he followed the LORD wholeheartedly."

37Because of you the LORD became angry with me also and said, "You shall not enter it, either. 38But your assistant, Joshua son of Nun, will enter it. Encourage him, because he will lead Israel to inherit it. 39And the little ones that you said would be taken captive, your children who do not yet know good from bad—they will enter the land. I will give it to them and they will take possession of it. 40But as for you, turn around and set out toward the desert along the route to the Red Sea.[a]"

41Then you replied, "We have sinned against the LORD. We will go up and fight, as the LORD our God commanded us." So every one of you put on his weapons, thinking it easy to go up into the hill country.

42But the LORD said to me, "Tell them, 'Do not go up and fight, because I will not be with you. You will be defeated by your enemies.'"

43So I told you, but you would not listen. You rebelled against the LORD's command and in your arrogance you marched up into the hill country. 44The Amorites who lived in those hills came out against you; they chased you like a swarm of bees and beat you down from Seir all the way to Hormah. 45You came back and wept before the LORD, but he paid no attention to your weeping and turned a deaf ear to you. 46And so you stayed in Kadesh many days—all the time you spent there.

Wanderings in the Desert

2 Then we turned back and set out toward the desert along the route to the Red Sea,[a] as the LORD had directed me. For a long time we made our way around the hill country of Seir.

2Then the LORD said to me, 3"You have made your way around this hill country long enough; now turn north. 4Give the people these orders: 'You are about to pass through the territory of your brothers the descendants of Esau, who live in Seir. They will be afraid of you, but be very careful. 5Do not provoke them to war, for I will not give you any of their land, not even enough to put your foot on. I have given Esau the hill country of Seir as his own. 6You are to pay them in silver for the food you eat and the water you drink.'"

7The LORD your God has blessed you in all the work of your hands. He has watched over your journey through this vast desert. These forty years the LORD your God has been with you, and you have not lacked anything.

8So we went on past our brothers the descendants of Esau, who live in Seir. We turned from the Arabah road, which comes up from Elath and Ezion Geber, and traveled along the desert road of Moab.

9Then the LORD said to me, "Do not harass the Moabites or provoke them to war, for I will not give you any part of their land. I have given Ar to the descendants of Lot as a possession."

10(The Emites used to live there—a people strong and numerous, and as tall as the Anakites. 11Like the Anakites, they too were considered Rephaites, but the Moabites called them Emites. 12Horites used to live in Seir, but the descendants of Esau drove them out. They destroyed the Horites from before them and settled in their place, just as Israel did in the land the LORD gave them as their possession.)

13And the LORD said, "Now get up and cross the Zered Valley." So we crossed the valley.

14Thirty-eight years passed from the time we left Kadesh Barnea until we crossed the Zered Valley. By then, that entire generation of fight-

[a]40,1 Hebrew *Yam Suph;* that is, Sea of Reeds

1:32 Moses reminded the Israelites that their refusal to believe what God had promised them resulted in their wandering in the wilderness for forty years. God had the power to deliver them and promised to do so, but the Israelites refused to believe God's promise and take advantage of his power. There is no better formula for failure. When we refuse to trust God, no human plan or program will be successful for long. Believing that God will do what he promised is essential for lasting success.

2:7 God was not rejecting his people when he consigned them to forty years of wilderness wanderings. He was lovingly guiding them in a way that would bring them some much-needed discipline. It is comforting to remember that even when we fail, God continues to shower his loving care upon us. He may allow us to go through a time of discipline, but he never leaves us during the hard times. Often he allows them for our own good. Although the Israelites had rejected his plans, God protected Israel in the wilderness. Even when the terrible consequences of sin are bearing down on us, God is there.

2:14–17 Timing is often an essential element in God's plan. Sometimes we need to see the truth about our desperate situation before we can begin to grow spiritually. The Israelites experienced what seemed to be total defeat in the wilderness, but learned through those experiences how to trust God's plan and do things his way. We need to learn from Israel's mistakes to give up our plans for our lives before we experience the disastrous consequences of our willfulness. We would be wise to accept God's plans and follow them carefully.

ing men had perished from the camp, as the LORD had sworn to them. 15The LORD's hand was against them until he had completely eliminated them from the camp.

16Now when the last of these fighting men among the people had died, 17the LORD said to me, 18"Today you are to pass by the region of Moab at Ar. 19When you come to the Ammonites, do not harass them or provoke them to war, for I will not give you possession of any land belonging to the Ammonites. I have given it as a possession to the descendants of Lot."

20(That too was considered a land of the Rephaites, who used to live there; but the Ammonites called them Zamzummites. 21They were a people strong and numerous, and as tall as the Anakites. The LORD destroyed them from before the Ammonites, who drove them out and settled in their place. 22The LORD had done the same for the descendants of Esau, who lived in Seir, when he destroyed the Horites from before them. They drove them out and have lived in their place to this day. 23And as for the Avvites who lived in villages as far as Gaza, the Caphtorites coming out from Caphtor[a] destroyed them and settled in their place.)

Defeat of Sihon King of Heshbon

24"Set out now and cross the Arnon Gorge. See, I have given into your hand Sihon the Amorite, king of Heshbon, and his country. Begin to take possession of it and engage him in battle. 25This very day I will begin to put the terror and fear of you on all the nations under heaven. They will hear reports of you and will tremble and be in anguish because of you."

26From the desert of Kedemoth I sent messengers to Sihon king of Heshbon offering peace and saying, 27"Let us pass through your country. We will stay on the main road; we will not turn aside to the right or to the left. 28Sell us food to eat and water to drink for their price in silver. Only let us pass through on foot— 29as the descendants of Esau, who live in Seir, and the Moabites, who live in Ar, did for us—until we cross the Jordan into the land the LORD our God is giving us." 30But Sihon king of Heshbon refused to let us pass through. For the LORD your God had made his spirit stubborn and his heart obstinate in order to give him into your hands, as he has now done.

31The LORD said to me, "See, I have begun to deliver Sihon and his country over to you. Now begin to conquer and possess his land."

32When Sihon and all his army came out to meet us in battle at Jahaz, 33the LORD our God delivered him over to us and we struck him down, together with his sons and his whole army. 34At that time we took all his towns and completely destroyed[b] them—men, women and children. We left no survivors. 35But the livestock and the plunder from the towns we had captured we carried off for ourselves. 36From Aroer on the rim of the Arnon Gorge, and from the town in the gorge, even as far as Gilead, not one town was too strong for us. The LORD our God gave us all of them. 37But in accordance with the command of the LORD our God, you did not encroach on any of the land of the Ammonites, neither the land along the course of the Jabbok nor that around the towns in the hills.

Defeat of Og King of Bashan

3 Next we turned and went up along the road toward Bashan, and Og king of Bashan with his whole army marched out to meet us in battle at Edrei. 2The LORD said to me, "Do not be afraid of him, for I have handed him over to you with his whole army and his land. Do to him what you did to Sihon king of the Amorites, who reigned in Heshbon."

3So the LORD our God also gave into our hands Og king of Bashan and all his army. We struck them down, leaving no survivors. 4At that time we took all his cities. There was not one of the sixty cities that we did not take from them—the whole region of Argob, Og's kingdom in Bashan. 5All these cities were fortified with high walls and with gates and bars, and there were also a great many unwalled villages. 6We completely destroyed[b] them, as we had done with Sihon king of Heshbon, destroying[b] every city—men, women and children. 7But all the livestock and the plunder from their cities we carried off for ourselves.

8So at that time we took from these two kings of the Amorites the territory east of the Jordan, from the Arnon Gorge as far as Mount Hermon. 9(Hermon is called Sirion by the Sidonians; the Amorites call it Senir.) 10We took all the towns on the plateau, and all Gilead, and all Bashan as far as Salecah and Edrei, towns of Og's kingdom in Bashan. 11(Only Og king of Bashan was left of the remnant of the Rephaites. His bed[c] was made of iron and was more than thirteen feet long and six feet wide.[d] It is still in Rabbah of the Ammonites.)

Division of the Land

12Of the land that we took over at that time,

[a] 23 That is, Crete [b] 34,6 The Hebrew term refers to the irrevocable giving over of things or persons to the LORD, often by totally destroying them. [c] 11 Or *sarcophagus* [d] 11 Hebrew *nine cubits long and four cubits wide* (about 4 meters long and 1.8 meters wide)

3:1–2 Our recognition of our lack of power provides wonderful opportunities for God to prove his power. Israel's military resources were pitifully limited, but God's strength gave them victory over the nation of Bashan. Our human resources are limited too. Once we accept this reality, we can seek God to give us his resources. God's resources, not ours, will be sufficient for all our needs.

3:12–20 Three of the Israelite tribes—Reuben, Gad and half of Manasseh—wanted land on the east side of the Jordan River, just outside the promised land. God allowed them this request but required that they follow through on their promises to fight for the conquest of Canaan. The

I gave the Reubenites and the Gadites the territory north of Aroer by the Arnon Gorge, including half the hill country of Gilead, together with its towns. 13The rest of Gilead and also all of Bashan, the kingdom of Og, I gave to the half tribe of Manasseh. (The whole region of Argob in Bashan used to be known as a land of the Rephaites. 14Jair, a descendant of Manasseh, took the whole region of Argob as far as the border of the Geshurites and the Maacathites; it was named after him, so that to this day Bashan is called Havvoth Jair.[a]) 15And I gave Gilead to Makir. 16But to the Reubenites and the Gadites I gave the territory extending from Gilead down to the Arnon Gorge (the middle of the gorge being the border) and out to the Jabbok River, which is the border of the Ammonites. 17Its western border was the Jordan in the Arabah, from Kinnereth to the Sea of the Arabah (the Salt Sea[b]), below the slopes of Pisgah.

18I commanded you at that time: "The LORD your God has given you this land to take possession of it. But all your able-bodied men, armed for battle, must cross over ahead of your brother Israelites. 19However, your wives, your children and your livestock (I know you have much livestock) may stay in the towns I have given you, 20until the LORD gives rest to your brothers as he has to you, and they too have taken over the land that the LORD your God is giving them, across the Jordan. After that, each of you may go back to the possession I have given you."

Moses Forbidden to Cross the Jordan

21At that time I commanded Joshua: "You have seen with your own eyes all that the LORD your God has done to these two kings. The LORD will do the same to all the kingdoms over there where you are going. 22Do not be afraid of them; the LORD your God himself will fight for you."

23At that time I pleaded with the LORD: 24"O Sovereign LORD, you have begun to show to your servant your greatness and your strong hand. For what god is there in heaven or on earth who can do the deeds and mighty works you do? 25Let me go over and see the good land beyond the Jordan—that fine hill country and Lebanon."

26But because of you the LORD was angry with me and would not listen to me. "That is enough," the LORD said. "Do not speak to me anymore about this matter. 27Go up to the top of Pisgah and look west and north and south and east. Look at the land with your own eyes, since you are not going to cross this Jordan. 28But commission Joshua, and encourage and strengthen him, for he will lead this people across and will cause them to inherit the land that you will see." 29So we stayed in the valley near Beth Peor.

Obedience Commanded

4 Hear now, O Israel, the decrees and laws I am about to teach you. Follow them so that you may live and may go in and take possession of the land that the LORD, the God of your fathers, is giving you. 2Do not add to what I command you and do not subtract from it, but keep the commands of the LORD your God that I give you.

3You saw with your own eyes what the LORD did at Baal Peor. The LORD your God destroyed from among you everyone who followed the Baal of Peor, 4but all of you who held fast to the LORD your God are still alive today.

5See, I have taught you decrees and laws as the LORD my God commanded me, so that you may follow them in the land you are entering to take possession of it. 6Observe them carefully, for this will show your wisdom and understanding to the nations, who will hear about all these decrees and say, "Surely this great nation is a wise and understanding people." 7What other nation is so great as to have their gods near them the way the LORD our God is near us whenever we pray to him? 8And what other nation is so great as to have such righteous decrees and laws as this body of laws I am setting before you today?

9Only be careful, and watch yourselves closely so that you do not forget the things your eyes

[a]14 Or *called the settlements of Jair* [b]17 That is, the Dead Sea

---

other tribes had counted on their support, and their failure to help in the conquest could have created deep divisions within God's chosen nation. We also must take responsibility for our promises and decisions. This is important to remember as we seek to build, reconcile and maintain our relationships with others.

3:23–29 Even Moses was not exempt from God's requirements. As great as Moses was, God's commands still applied to him. We must never presume to be a "special case." We must not rationalize and excuse ourselves from God's plan for holy living. Rather, we should seek out and then joyfully accept God's plan for us. His plans are always best.

4:2 These requirements were offered for Israel's guidance; they were a gracious provision of God's love. And God's directions are not to be tampered with. It is tempting to add to God's provisions or take away from them. But if we are to have victory in our spiritual renewal, we must accept God's way as it is—not as we might wish it to be. God, through his Word and loving presence in our lives, will provide us with all we need for lives of fulfillment and contentment.

4:9 No matter how secure we may feel in our righteousness, if we are unwary, we can easily fall. In this and the following verses we see warning exclamations, such as "be careful" and "watch yourselves closely." Israel was charged to remember what God had done for them. Remembering the victories and failures of the past helps guard against sin in the present. God was also concerned that godly attitudes and wisdom would be passed on to each successive generation, so the Israelites were instructed to share their history and experiences with their children. We also are responsible to pass on to our children the wisdom we have learned. If they choose to listen, they can avoid some of the mistakes we have made.

have seen or let them slip from your heart as
long as you live. Teach them to your children
and to their children after them. [10]Remember
the day you stood before the LORD your God at
Horeb, when he said to me, "Assemble the people before me to hear my words so that they
may learn to revere me as long as they live in the
land and may teach them to their children."
[11]You came near and stood at the foot of the
mountain while it blazed with fire to the very
heavens, with black clouds and deep darkness.
[12]Then the LORD spoke to you out of the fire.
You heard the sound of words but saw no form;
there was only a voice. [13]He declared to you his
covenant, the Ten Commandments, which he
commanded you to follow and then wrote
them on two stone tablets. [14]And the LORD directed me at that time to teach you the decrees
and laws you are to follow in the land that you
are crossing the Jordan to possess.

Idolatry Forbidden

[15]You saw no form of any kind the day the
LORD spoke to you at Horeb out of the fire.
Therefore watch yourselves very carefully, [16]so
that you do not become corrupt and make for
yourselves an idol, an image of any shape,
whether formed like a man or a woman, [17]or
like any animal on earth or any bird that flies in
the air, [18]or like any creature that moves along
the ground or any fish in the waters below.
[19]And when you look up to the sky and see the
sun, the moon and the stars—all the heavenly
array—do not be enticed into bowing down to
them and worshiping things the LORD your God
has apportioned to all the nations under heav-
en. [20]But as for you, the LORD took you and
brought you out of the iron-smelting furnace,
out of Egypt, to be the people of his inheritance,
as you now are.

[21]The LORD was angry with me because of
you, and he solemnly swore that I would not
cross the Jordan and enter the good land the
LORD your God is giving you as your inheritance. [22]I will die in this land; I will not cross
the Jordan; but you are about to cross over and
take possession of that good land. [23]Be careful
not to forget the covenant of the LORD your God
that he made with you; do not make for yourselves an idol in the form of anything the LORD
your God has forbidden. [24]For the LORD your
God is a consuming fire, a jealous God.

[25]After you have had children and grandchildren and have lived in the land a long time—if
you then become corrupt and make any kind of
idol, doing evil in the eyes of the LORD your
God and provoking him to anger, [26]I call heav-
en and earth as witnesses against you this day
that you will quickly perish from the land that
you are crossing the Jordan to possess. You will
not live there long but will certainly be destroyed. [27]The LORD will scatter you among the
peoples, and only a few of you will survive
among the nations to which the LORD will drive
you. [28]There you will worship man-made gods
of wood and stone, which cannot see or hear or
eat or smell. [29]But if from there you seek the
LORD your God, you will find him if you look
for him with all your heart and with all your
soul. [30]When you are in distress and all these
things have happened to you, then in later days
you will return to the LORD your God and obey
him. [31]For the LORD your God is a merciful
God; he will not abandon or destroy you or
forget the covenant with your forefathers,
which he confirmed to them by oath.

The LORD Is God

[32]Ask now about the former days, long before your time, from the day God created man
on the earth; ask from one end of the heavens
to the other. Has anything so great as this ever
happened, or has anything like it ever been
heard of? [33]Has any other people heard the
voice of God[a] speaking out of fire, as you have,
and lived? [34]Has any god ever tried to take for

[a]33 *Or of a god*

4:15–19 God warned the Israelites numerous times about the dangers of idolatry. Most of us aren't tempted to worship a carved figure or statue, but in our busy world many other matters clamor for our attention and affection. It is sometimes difficult to remember that we owe our primary allegiance to God. He requires absolute devotion from his people; he will not take second place in our lives. Spiritual renewal begins when we put God in his rightful place—first.

4:20 God delivered Israel for a specific purpose. He forged Israel into a nation to be his chosen possession. Through this special nation God brought salvation to the whole world. We are God's children. Why did God save us? He delivered us from sin for a purpose. And that purpose may be to bring the message of his saving grace into the lives of many who suffer from problems similar to our own.

4:23–24 All relationships come with responsibilities, including our relationship with God. Here we are reminded that we cannot remake God as we would like him to be; we must relate to him as he is. The one, true God demands that we give him our full devotion. As with any relationship, we need to be faithful to God if we wish our relationship to remain strong. Deuteronomy urged the Israelites to follow through on their responsibilities to God. The consequences for ignoring responsibilities in any relationship are great, yet failing in our relationship with God will result in problems that impact eternity.

4:29–31 In this passage God reaffirms his compassion for victims of painful circumstances, promising to come through for his people, even when they have sinned. God asks for their repentance and obedience to follow his instructions for holy living. Our relationship with God is assured because it is based upon God's compassion for us, even when we don't deserve it. God is faithful; he has provided a means for our relationship to be reconciled—the work of Jesus Christ.

4:34–40 What a glorious review of God's work on Israel's behalf! Israel's many failures aren't even mentioned in this amazing story of how God led his people from slavery in Egypt to the promised land. God's plans for them succeeded despite Israel's tendency to rebel against God and his plans. Since we all have a tendency to rebel, Israel's history should be a source of encouragement for us. God

himself one nation out of another nation, by testings, by miraculous signs and wonders, by war, by a mighty hand and an outstretched arm, or by great and awesome deeds, like all the things the LORD your God did for you in Egypt before your very eyes?

35You were shown these things so that you might know that the LORD is God; besides him there is no other. 36From heaven he made you hear his voice to discipline you. On earth he showed you his great fire, and you heard his words from out of the fire. 37Because he loved your forefathers and chose their descendants after them, he brought you out of Egypt by his Presence and his great strength, 38to drive out before you nations greater and stronger than you and to bring you into their land to give it to you for your inheritance, as it is today.

39Acknowledge and take to heart this day that the LORD is God in heaven above and on the earth below. There is no other. 40Keep his decrees and commands, which I am giving you today, so that it may go well with you and your children after you and that you may live long in the land the LORD your God gives you for all time.

Cities of Refuge

41Then Moses set aside three cities east of the Jordan, 42to which anyone who had killed a person could flee if he had unintentionally killed his neighbor without malice aforethought. He could flee into one of these cities and save his life. 43The cities were these: Bezer in the desert plateau, for the Reubenites; Ramoth in Gilead, for the Gadites; and Golan in Bashan, for the Manassites.

Introduction to the Law

44This is the law Moses set before the Israelites. 45These are the stipulations, decrees and laws Moses gave them when they came out of Egypt 46and were in the valley near Beth Peor east of the Jordan, in the land of Sihon king of the Amorites, who reigned in Heshbon and was defeated by Moses and the Israelites as they came out of Egypt. 47They took possession of his land and the land of Og king of Bashan, the two Amorite kings east of the Jordan. 48This land extended from Aroer on the rim of the Arnon Gorge to Mount Siyon[a] (that is, Hermon), 49and included all the Arabah east of the Jordan, as far as the Sea of the Arabah,[b] below the slopes of Pisgah.

The Ten Commandments

5 Moses summoned all Israel and said:

Hear, O Israel, the decrees and laws I declare in your hearing today. Learn them and be sure to follow them. 2The LORD our God made a covenant with us at Horeb. 3It was not with our fathers that the LORD made this covenant, but with us, with all of us who are alive here today. 4The LORD spoke to you face to face out of the fire on the mountain. 5(At that time I stood between the LORD and you to declare to you the word of the LORD, because you were afraid of the fire and did not go up the mountain.) And he said:

6"I am the LORD your God, who
brought you out of Egypt, out of the
land of slavery.
7"You shall have no other gods before[c] me.
8"You shall not make for yourself an idol
in the form of anything in heaven
above or on the earth beneath or in
the waters below. 9You shall not
bow down to them or worship

[a]48 Hebrew; Syriac (see also Deut. 3:9) *Sirion*
[b]49 That is, the Dead Sea [c]7 Or *besides*

---

continues to work with us, disciplining us when it is needed, comforting us when we are discouraged. As we trust him, our own history will become a glorious account of our journey from slavery to freedom—all the failures and mistakes graciously covered by the acts of God's goodness.

5:1 Moses reminded the people of the importance of obedience. God's laws gave the Israelites clear guidance as to God's standard of excellence. These guidelines supplied a pattern for right living in virtually every area of life. None of us is fully able to live up to God's standards on our own (see Romans 3:23). Because of this, God has extended his grace to us, accepting us on the basis of Jesus Christ's redeeming work. God's grace makes it possible for our spiritual renewal; God's presence provides the help we need to live our lives according to his standards.

5:5–6 Moses introduced the Ten Commandments by directing Israel's attention to the person of God, reminding the people that he was "the LORD" (*Yahweh*). This name is God's personal covenant name, reminding us of his relationship with Abraham, Isaac, Jacob, Moses and the nation of Israel. God desires a personal relationship with us; he wants to relate to us one-on-one. This passage says, "I am the LORD your God." He is our God. Our personal relationship with God and our love for him should motivate our obedience to his laws.

5:6–21 After reminding his people that he had redeemed them from slavery in Egypt, God gave the Israelites the Ten Commandments. These laws not only stated how God expected his redeemed people to act, but also contained a godly pattern of living for all people. God's laws are not so much a collection of rules as they are a "job description," a set of ideal goals that we are called to pursue throughout our lives. But these laws can only be followed as we walk in the power of the Holy Spirit. With discipline and God's gracious help, we will find that these commandments will become a natural part of our lives.

5:7–8 We are commanded to put God first, but it is easy to let our priorities get out of balance. The important things are easily forgotten; the urgent things claim our attention, affection and resources. If we are to renew our lives according to God's specifications, we need to stay clear of anything that might come between us and God. God has to be our highest priority. Anything that comes before God in our priorities becomes a false god.

5:9–10 God is jealous of our affections. When we fail to give God first place in our lives, negative consequences always result, affecting not only us but successive generations as well. God created us to live according to his plan. By following his plan, we can have hope for our future

them; for I, the LORD your God, am
a jealous God, punishing the children for the sin of the fathers to the third and fourth generation of those who hate me,
[10]but showing love to
a thousand ⌞generations⌟ of those who love me and keep my commandments.
[11]"You shall not misuse the name of the LORD your God, for the LORD will not hold anyone guiltless who misuses his name.
[12]"Observe the Sabbath day by keeping it holy, as the LORD your God has
commanded you. [13]Six days you
shall labor and do all your work,
[14]but the seventh day is a Sabbath
to the LORD your God. On it you shall not do any work, neither you, nor your son or daughter, nor your manservant or maidservant, nor your ox, your donkey or any of your animals, nor the alien within your gates, so that your manservant and maidservant may rest, as you do.
[15]Remember that you were slaves in
Egypt and that the LORD your God brought you out of there with a mighty hand and an outstretched arm. Therefore the LORD your God has commanded you to observe the Sabbath day.
[16]"Honor your father and your mother, as the LORD your God has commanded you, so that you may live long and that it may go well with you in the land the LORD your God is giving you.
[17]"You shall not murder.
[18]"You shall not commit adultery.
[19]"You shall not steal.
[20]"You shall not give false testimony against your neighbor.
[21]"You shall not covet your neighbor's wife. You shall not set your desire on your neighbor's house or land, his manservant or maidservant, his ox or donkey, or anything that belongs to your neighbor."

[22]These are the commandments the LORD proclaimed in a loud voice to your whole assembly there on the mountain from out of the fire, the cloud and the deep darkness; and he added nothing more. Then he wrote them on two stone tablets and gave them to me.
[23]When you heard the voice out of the darkness, while the mountain was ablaze with fire, all the leading men of your tribes and your
elders came to me. [24]And you said, "The LORD
our God has shown us his glory and his majesty, and we have heard his voice from the fire. Today we have seen that a man can live even if
God speaks with him. [25]But now, why should
we die? This great fire will consume us, and we will die if we hear the voice of the LORD our God
any longer. [26]For what mortal man has ever
heard the voice of the living God speaking out
of fire, as we have, and survived? [27]Go near and
listen to all that the LORD our God says. Then tell us whatever the LORD our God tells you. We will listen and obey."
[28]The LORD heard you when you spoke to me and the LORD said to me, "I have heard what this people said to you. Everything they said
was good. [29]Oh, that their hearts would be in-

---

and the future of successive generations. We need to start by putting God first.

5:11 This commandment prohibits the use of God's name in any way that would bring his name dishonor. This is often understood to refer to using God's name in an exclamation of anger or disgust. Yet this commandment refers as much to our conduct as to our speech. As people who represent the name of God, we are responsible to act in ways that will bring him glory, not shame. Thus, when our actions and attitudes bring dishonor to God, we have broken this commandment. We need to live with complete honesty in both word and deed, always bringing honor to God's name rather than dishonor.

5:12–15 We are commanded to observe the Sabbath day of rest for several reasons. God created our bodies and knows what is best for us. He knows that we need one day a week as a day of rest set apart for the Lord. When we don't give our bodies the rest they need, we can experience physical, emotional and spiritual exhaustion. Even more important, God calls us to set apart this day of rest as a sign that he has established a covenant with us.

5:16 We are commanded to honor our parents. While there are some instances when it is proper to question our parents' demands or actions, such as when a parent directly contradicts God's commands in the Bible, we ought to respect and obey our parents and show love to them. God has placed them over us and has given them the task of bringing us to maturity.

5:18 We are commanded to remain faithful in marriage. In order to stay strong, a healthy marriage relationship requires fidelity on the part of both partners. Sexual sin eventually brings destructive consequences. Many problems with venereal disease and AIDS could be avoided if only this commandment were obeyed with consistency. Whenever one or both marriage partners is unfaithful, the whole family suffers. But God can still bring restoration if the unfaithful marriage partners confess their sin and accept responsibility for their actions and the ways their sin has caused suffering in their family. They must make restitution wherever possible and ask God to redeem their marriage.

5:19 We are commanded not to steal. Healthy interpersonal relationships require that people respect each other. Such respect includes the recognition and protection of the personal property belonging to others. Stealing anything from anyone is completely forbidden by this commandment.

5:20 Honesty must be a characteristic of everyone seeking spiritual renewal. Right living before God demands that we are honest *with* others and *about* others. Being honest in our relationships is a necessary requirement for reconciliation with the people we have wronged, as well as with those who have wronged us.

5:21 This commandment is different from the others because it forbids not only certain actions but certain attitudes as well. We must carefully guard our thoughts. Notice that when this commandment is broken, it usually leads to breaking others too.

clined to fear me and keep all my commands
always, so that it might go well with them and
their children forever!
30"Go, tell them to return to their tents. 31But
you stay here with me so that I may give you all
the commands, decrees and laws you are to
teach them to follow in the land I am giving
them to possess."
32So be careful to do what the LORD your God
has commanded you; do not turn aside to the
right or to the left. 33Walk in all the way that the
LORD your God has commanded you, so that
you may live and prosper and prolong your
days in the land that you will possess.

Love the LORD Your God

6 These are the commands, decrees and laws
the LORD your God directed me to teach
you to observe in the land that you are crossing
the Jordan to possess, 2so that you, your children and their children after them may fear the
LORD your God as long as you live by keeping
all his decrees and commands that I give you,
and so that you may enjoy long life. 3Hear,
O Israel, and be careful to obey so that it may
go well with you and that you may increase
greatly in a land flowing with milk and honey,
just as the LORD, the God of your fathers, promised you.
4Hear, O Israel: The LORD our God, the LORD
is one.[a] 5Love the LORD your God with all your
heart and with all your soul and with all your
strength. 6These commandments that I give you
today are to be upon your hearts. 7Impress
them on your children. Talk about them when
you sit at home and when you walk along the
road, when you lie down and when you get up.
8Tie them as symbols on your hands and bind
them on your foreheads. 9Write them on the
doorframes of your houses and on your gates.
10When the LORD your God brings you into
the land he swore to your fathers, to Abraham,
Isaac and Jacob, to give you—a land with large,
flourishing cities you did not build, 11houses
filled with all kinds of good things you did not
provide, wells you did not dig, and vineyards
and olive groves you did not plant—then when
you eat and are satisfied, 12be careful that you
do not forget the LORD, who brought you out of
Egypt, out of the land of slavery.
13Fear the LORD your God, serve him only
and take your oaths in his name. 14Do not follow other gods, the gods of the peoples around
you; 15for the LORD your God, who is among
you, is a jealous God and his anger will burn
against you, and he will destroy you from the
face of the land. 16Do not test the LORD your
God as you did at Massah. 17Be sure to keep the
commands of the LORD your God and the stipulations and decrees he has given you. 18Do what
is right and good in the LORD's sight, so that it
may go well with you and you may go in and
take over the good land that the LORD promised
on oath to your forefathers, 19thrusting out all
your enemies before you, as the LORD said.
20In the future, when your son asks you,
"What is the meaning of the stipulations, decrees and laws the LORD our God has commanded you?" 21tell him: "We were slaves of
Pharaoh in Egypt, but the LORD brought us out
of Egypt with a mighty hand. 22Before our eyes
the LORD sent miraculous signs and wonders—
great and terrible—upon Egypt and Pharaoh and
his whole household. 23But he brought us out
from there to bring us in and give us the land

[a]4 Or *The LORD our God is one LORD;* or *The LORD is our God, the LORD is one;* or *The LORD is our God, the LORD alone*

6:5 The Israelites were told to love God with all their heart, soul and might. Jesus labeled this the most important commandment in the Bible. If we love God, we will naturally do everything else God wants us to do. The nature of the love commanded here, however, is often misunderstood. In the Bible, love is not primarily an emotion. Love is a decision that shows itself in appropriate action. Thus, loving God entails the decision to follow God's ways, looking to him constantly for help and forgiveness.

6:6 God's laws need more than our cursory attention. Thinking about God's plan for our lives once in a while isn't enough. We are to think about God's laws constantly, every day. We need frequent reminders if we are to grow in our spiritual maturity. God's plan must be reviewed regularly if we are to discover and enjoy the freedom he promises.

6:7 We should strive to keep God's Word foremost in our thoughts when we get up in the morning, when we go to bed, when we are at home or even when we are traveling. In other words, we should make God's Word a matter of primary concern. We know that spiritual growth is an all-day, each day process. Following God's prescriptions for holy living will help us as we progress spiritually, day by day.

6:7 Both blessings and curses can be passed down from generation to generation. Here we are reminded to pass on the blessings of God's Word. To do this we must make God's Word an integral part of our daily lives. We need to live his Word, not just speak it. We need to teach his wisdom, not just with our words, but with our lifestyle as well.

6:10–13 The Israelites were ending forty difficult years of wilderness wandering. They were starting the task of beginning new lives and building a new nation. Often, when things start going well in our lives, it is easy to forget the help God has given us in the past. Moses specifically warned the Israelites to give God the respect and obedience he deserves. As we begin to make spiritual progress, it is sometimes easy to forget that it is only by God's grace that we have come this far. We need to realize that without God's help, we would quickly fall back into old habits of sin. Continued respect for and obedience to God are necessary to preserve our spiritual gains.

6:18 God laid out a plan for right living within the Israelite community. Just as God loved the Israelites, he loves us too and has designed his laws for our well-being. He desires our best. This should encourage us as we seek to follow his plan, as difficult as it may be at times. We can know for certain that when God's instructions seem too difficult for us, he is right there to help us along (see Matthew 28:20).

6:23 Moses reminded the people that God's purpose was to bring them from bondage into a new life of freedom. God brought them out of bondage so that he could bring them into something much better. We have all suffered under the bondage of sin, but we can be assured that

that he promised on oath to our forefathers. 24The LORD commanded us to obey all these decrees and to fear the LORD our God, so that we might always prosper and be kept alive, as is the case today. 25And if we are careful to obey all this law before the LORD our God, as he has commanded us, that will be our righteousness."

Driving Out the Nations

7 When the LORD your God brings you into the land you are entering to possess and drives out before you many nations—the Hittites, Girgashites, Amorites, Canaanites, Perizzites, Hivites and Jebusites, seven nations larger and stronger than you— 2and when the LORD your God has delivered them over to you and you have defeated them, then you must destroy them totally.[a] Make no treaty with them, and show them no mercy. 3Do not intermarry with them. Do not give your daughters to their sons or take their daughters for your sons, 4for they will turn your sons away from following me to serve other gods, and the LORD's anger will burn against you and will quickly destroy you. 5This is what you are to do to them: Break down their altars, smash their sacred stones, cut down their Asherah poles[b] and burn their idols in the fire. 6For you are a people holy to the LORD your God. The LORD your God has chosen you out of all the peoples on the face of the earth to be his people, his treasured possession.

7The LORD did not set his affection on you and choose you because you were more numerous than other peoples, for you were the fewest of all peoples. 8But it was because the LORD loved you and kept the oath he swore to your forefathers that he brought you out with a mighty hand and redeemed you from the land of slavery, from the power of Pharaoh king of Egypt. 9Know therefore that the LORD your God is God; he is the faithful God, keeping his covenant of love to a thousand generations of those who love him and keep his commands. 10But

those who hate him he will repay to their
face by destruction;
he will not be slow to repay to their face
those who hate him.

11Therefore, take care to follow the commands, decrees and laws I give you today.

12If you pay attention to these laws and are careful to follow them, then the LORD your God will keep his covenant of love with you, as he swore to your forefathers. 13He will love you and bless you and increase your numbers. He will bless the fruit of your womb, the crops of your land—your grain, new wine and oil—the calves of your herds and the lambs of your flocks in the land that he swore to your forefathers to give you. 14You will be blessed more than any other people; none of your men or women will be childless, nor any of your livestock without young. 15The LORD will keep you free from every disease. He will not inflict on you the horrible diseases you knew in Egypt, but he will inflict them on all who hate you. 16You must destroy all the peoples the LORD your God gives over to you. Do not look on them with pity and do not serve their gods, for that will be a snare to you.

17You may say to yourselves, "These nations are stronger than we are. How can we drive them out?" 18But do not be afraid of them; remember well what the LORD your God did to Pharaoh and to all Egypt. 19You saw with your own eyes the great trials, the miraculous signs and wonders, the mighty hand and outstretched arm, with which the LORD your God brought you out. The LORD your God will do the same to all the peoples you now fear. 20Moreover, the LORD your God will send the hornet among them until even the survivors who hide from you have perished. 21Do not be terrified by them, for the LORD your God, who is among you, is a great and awesome God. 22The LORD your God will drive out those nations before you, little by little. You will not be

[a]2 The Hebrew term refers to the irrevocable giving over of things or persons to the LORD, often by totally destroying them; also in verse 26. [b]5 That is, symbols of the goddess Asherah; here and elsewhere in Deuteronomy

---

when God leads us out of our slavery he has a much better life in store for us. As we are freed from sin's shackles, God will give us new things to live for—good and godly things. This passage reminds us that God's people are delivered for a purpose, and our spiritual renewal is part of that purpose.

7:6 The people whom God chooses have a responsibility to live holy lives. This means two things: (1) that believers are set apart *from* the world's ways of living, and (2) that believers are set apart *for* God's purposes.

7:7–8 Why did God choose to treat the Israelites in a special way? Was it because they deserved it? No! In some respects they deserved God's favor less than other people did. God treated them kindly because he is a gracious God. God wants all of us to be free from bondage, whether we are "good enough" or not. If there are any chains of sin binding us, God's loving hands are ready to break those chains and set us on the road toward freedom.

7:9 This passage reminds us of God's unfailing love. He is a delivering and faithful God. He always keeps his promises. Notice, however, that he also asks something of us. A major step toward spiritual renewal is to take God at his word and believe, love and obey him.

7:21 The Israelites were about to enter the promised land and probably feared the powerful enemies they would encounter. But God made it clear that he was sufficient to see them through this task, no matter how daunting it might be. As we grow spiritually, we also face great obstacles to our progress. We need to trust God's sufficiency and strength to conquer these enemies. God is capable of overcoming any obstacles we might face.

7:22 The conquest of the promised land would take place a little at a time; throwing enemies out of the land had to be followed by immediate rebuilding. God would give his people new territory only when they were ready to move in and take advantage of their conquest. We need to recognize that spiritual growth is also a long-term process. We should look for steady progress. God gives us

allowed to eliminate them all at once, or the wild animals will multiply around you. 23But the LORD your God will deliver them over to you, throwing them into great confusion until they are destroyed. 24He will give their kings into your hand, and you will wipe out their names from under heaven. No one will be able to stand up against you; you will destroy them. 25The images of their gods you are to burn in the fire. Do not covet the silver and gold on them, and do not take it for yourselves, or you will be ensnared by it, for it is detestable to the LORD your God. 26Do not bring a detestable thing into your house or you, like it, will be set apart for destruction. Utterly abhor and detest it, for it is set apart for destruction.

Do Not Forget the LORD

8 Be careful to follow every command I am giving you today, so that you may live and increase and may enter and possess the land that the LORD promised on oath to your forefathers. 2Remember how the LORD your God led you all the way in the desert these forty years, to humble you and to test you in order to know what was in your heart, whether or not you would keep his commands. 3He humbled you, causing you to hunger and then feeding you with manna, which neither you nor your fathers had known, to teach you that man does not live on bread alone but on every word that comes from the mouth of the LORD. 4Your clothes did not wear out and your feet did not swell during these forty years. 5Know then in your heart that as a man disciplines his son, so the LORD your God disciplines you.

6Observe the commands of the LORD your God, walking in his ways and revering him. 7For the LORD your God is bringing you into a good land—a land with streams and pools of water, with springs flowing in the valleys and hills; 8a land with wheat and barley, vines and fig trees, pomegranates, olive oil and honey; 9a land where bread will not be scarce and you will lack nothing; a land where the rocks are iron and you can dig copper out of the hills.

10When you have eaten and are satisfied, praise the LORD your God for the good land he has given you. 11Be careful that you do not forget the LORD your God, failing to observe his commands, his laws and his decrees that I am giving you this day. 12Otherwise, when you eat and are satisfied, when you build fine houses and settle down, 13and when your herds and flocks grow large and your silver and gold increase and all you have is multiplied, 14then your heart will become proud and you will forget the LORD your God, who brought you out of Egypt, out of the land of slavery. 15He led you through the vast and dreadful desert, that thirsty and waterless land, with its venomous snakes and scorpions. He brought you water out of hard rock. 16He gave you manna to eat in the desert, something your fathers had never known, to humble and to test you so that in the end it might go well with you. 17You may say to yourself, "My power and the strength of my hands have produced this wealth for me." 18But remember the LORD your God, for it is he who gives you the ability to produce wealth, and so confirms his covenant, which he swore to your forefathers, as it is today.

19If you ever forget the LORD your God and follow other gods and worship and bow down to them, I testify against you today that you will surely be destroyed. 20Like the nations the LORD destroyed before you, so you will be destroyed for not obeying the LORD your God.

Not Because of Israel's Righteousness

9 Hear, O Israel. You are now about to cross the Jordan to go in and dispossess nations greater and stronger than you, with large cities that have walls up to the sky. 2The people are strong and tall—Anakites! You know about them and have heard it said: "Who can stand up against the Anakites?" 3But be assured today that the LORD your God is the one who goes across ahead of you like a devouring fire. He will destroy them; he will subdue them before you. And you will drive them out and annihilate them quickly, as the LORD has promised you.

4After the LORD your God has driven them out before you, do not say to yourself, "The LORD has brought me here to take possession of this land because of my righteousness." No, it is on account of the wickedness of these nations that the LORD is going to drive them out before you. 5It is not because of your righteousness or your integrity that you are going in to take possession of their land; but on account of the wickedness of these nations, the LORD your God will drive them out before you, to accomplish

---

victories as we are ready to take advantage of them and build on them. We need to trust God to move us forward according to his timing.

8:2 God often uses the hard times in life to teach us important lessons. He had a twofold purpose in Israel's forty years of wandering: The trials were brought upon Israel to humble them and to test them. God wanted the Israelites to learn who they really were in relationship with him and to demonstrate what was really in their hearts. Sometimes God tests us in similar ways, pushing us to examine ourselves. We need to take advantage of the difficult times, using them as stepping-stones toward spiritual renewal.

8:16–18 As we begin to experience spiritual growth, we need to remember to give credit where credit is due. We must be careful to give God the glory. We must not selfishly claim what belongs to God alone. This attitude only leads us to a proud self-sufficiency that invariably results in a fall.

9:3 This verse reminds us of the truth found in Romans 8:31: "If God is for us, who can be against us?" God went ahead of his people to guide them and prepare the way for them. He destroyed Israel's enemies. We, too, can be confident that God will go before us and give us victory.

Stewardship

A Way to Remind Yourself

Deuteronomy 8:17–18 Prosperity can easily lead to spiritual amnesia. When we're in desperate straits, we think we'll never forget the experience. Yet when things are going well, our times of need are the farthest thing from our minds. So it was with the Israelites. In the wilderness, they were living from manna to mouth because of God's daily provision. When they entered the promised land, however, they entered a time of prosperity that would sorely tempt them to forget their daily dependence on God.

The Israelites' wilderness trek taught them that neither their strength nor their abilities made them truly wealthy. Whether by daily bread or abundant provisions, the Lord sustained his people. Yet God's daily provision is not an end in itself; it is a message of his faithfulness. Every blessing is evidence that God fulfills his covenant with his people.

In the same way today, money can either numb us spiritually or awaken us to the goodness of God. It can be an anesthetic that leads to spiritual lethargy or a stimulant that results in spiritual renewal. If we allow ourselves to become numb to God through comfort and materialism, we will pay a price (Deuteronomy 8:19–20). But if our blessings awaken thanksgiving and a growing sense of dependence on God, we will experience increasing joy in his service.

Putting It Into Practice

Do you consider your money a reminder of God's provision? Can you recall a time when you were living "manna to mouth"? How did it affect your spiritual life? Use your journal to record your memories and observations.

Read all of Deuteronomy 8, noting the promises of God's provision. Record all the specific occasions you can remember when God provided for you in a special way.

For more on stewardship, turn to Luke 12.

what he swore to your fathers, to Abraham, Isaac and Jacob. [6]Understand, then, that it is not because of your righteousness that the LORD your God is giving you this good land to possess, for you are a stiff-necked people.

The Golden Calf

[7]Remember this and never forget how you provoked the LORD your God to anger in the desert. From the day you left Egypt until you arrived here, you have been rebellious against the LORD. [8]At Horeb you aroused the LORD's wrath so that he was angry enough to destroy you. [9]When I went up on the mountain to receive the tablets of stone, the tablets of the covenant that the LORD had made with you, I stayed on the mountain forty days and forty nights; I ate no bread and drank no water. [10]The LORD gave me two stone tablets inscribed by the finger of God. On them were all the commandments the LORD proclaimed to you on the mountain out of the fire, on the day of the assembly.

[11]At the end of the forty days and forty nights, the LORD gave me the two stone tablets, the tablets of the covenant. [12]Then the LORD told me, "Go down from here at once, because your people whom you brought out of Egypt have become corrupt. They have turned away quickly from what I commanded them and have made a cast idol for themselves."

[13]And the LORD said to me, "I have seen this people, and they are a stiff-necked people indeed! [14]Let me alone, so that I may destroy them and blot out their name from under heaven. And I will make you into a nation stronger and more numerous than they."

[15]So I turned and went down from the mountain while it was ablaze with fire. And the two tablets of the covenant were in my hands.[a] [16]When I looked, I saw that you had sinned against the LORD your God; you had made for yourselves an idol cast in the shape of a calf. You had turned aside quickly from the way that the LORD had commanded you. [17]So I took the two tablets and threw them out of my hands, breaking them to pieces before your eyes.

[18]Then once again I fell prostrate before the LORD for forty days and forty nights; I ate no bread and drank no water, because of all the sin you had committed, doing what was evil in the LORD's sight and so provoking him to anger. [19]I feared the anger and wrath of the LORD, for he was angry enough with you to destroy you. But again the LORD listened to me. [20]And the LORD was angry enough with Aaron to destroy him, but at that time I prayed for Aaron too. [21]Also I took that sinful thing of yours, the calf you had made, and burned it in the fire. Then I crushed it and ground it to powder as fine as dust and threw the dust into a stream that flowed down the mountain.

[22]You also made the LORD angry at Taberah, at Massah and at Kibroth Hattaavah.

[23]And when the LORD sent you out from Kadesh Barnea, he said, "Go up and take possession of the land I have given you." But you rebelled against the command of the LORD your God. You did not trust him or obey him. [24]You have been rebellious against the LORD ever since I have known you.

[25]I lay prostrate before the LORD those forty days and forty nights because the LORD had said he would destroy you. [26]I prayed to the LORD and said, "O Sovereign LORD, do not destroy your people, your own inheritance that you redeemed by your great power and brought out of Egypt with a mighty hand. [27]Remember your servants Abraham, Isaac and Jacob. Overlook the stubbornness of this people, their wickedness and their sin. [28]Otherwise, the country from which you brought us will say, 'Because the LORD was not able to take them into the land he had promised them, and because he hated them, he brought them out to put them to death in the desert.' [29]But they are your people, your inheritance that you brought out by your great power and your outstretched arm."

Tablets Like the First Ones

10 At that time the LORD said to me, "Chisel out two stone tablets like the first ones and come up to me on the mountain. Also make a wooden chest.[b] [2]I will write on the tablets the words that were on the first tablets, which you broke. Then you are to put them in the chest."

[3]So I made the ark out of acacia wood and chiseled out two stone tablets like the first ones, and I went up on the mountain with the two tablets in my hands. [4]The LORD wrote on these tablets what he had written before, the Ten Commandments he had proclaimed to you on the mountain, out of the fire, on the day of the assembly. And the LORD gave them to me. [5]Then I came back down the mountain and put the tablets in the ark I had made, as the LORD commanded me, and they are there now.

[6](The Israelites traveled from the wells of the Jaakanites to Moserah. There Aaron died and was buried, and Eleazar his son succeeded him

[a]15 Or *And I had the two tablets of the covenant with me, one in each hand* [b]1 That is, an ark

---

9:18–29 Moses prayed to God, interceding for his people. In the process of spiritual renewal we may experience times of failure. The intercession of God's people is vital to our spiritual growth and maturity. We need to build relationships of support that will result in this kind of intercession on our behalf.

10:1 Because of the people's rebellion, the first stone tablets containing the law had been completely destroyed. How encouraging to see that God instructed Moses to bring new tablets so he could rewrite his instructions to the people. God still reaches out to us, no matter how great our sin. God always gives repentant people a chance to start again. But remember: This characteristic of God should be appreciated, not presumed upon.

as priest. 7From there they traveled to Gudgodah and on to Jotbathah, a land with streams of water. 8At that time the LORD set apart the tribe of Levi to carry the ark of the covenant of the LORD, to stand before the LORD to minister and to pronounce blessings in his name, as they still do today. 9That is why the Levites have no share or inheritance among their brothers; the LORD is their inheritance, as the LORD your God told them.)

10Now I had stayed on the mountain forty days and nights, as I did the first time, and the LORD listened to me at this time also. It was not his will to destroy you. 11"Go," the LORD said to me, "and lead the people on their way, so that they may enter and possess the land that I swore to their fathers to give them."

Fear the LORD

12And now, O Israel, what does the LORD your God ask of you but to fear the LORD your God, to walk in all his ways, to love him, to serve the LORD your God with all your heart and with all your soul, 13and to observe the LORD's commands and decrees that I am giving you today for your own good?

14To the LORD your God belong the heavens, even the highest heavens, the earth and everything in it. 15Yet the LORD set his affection on your forefathers and loved them, and he chose you, their descendants, above all the nations, as it is today. 16Circumcise your hearts, therefore, and do not be stiff-necked any longer. 17For the LORD your God is God of gods and Lord of lords, the great God, mighty and awesome, who shows no partiality and accepts no bribes. 18He defends the cause of the fatherless and the widow, and loves the alien, giving him food and clothing. 19And you are to love those who are aliens, for you yourselves were aliens in Egypt. 20Fear the LORD your God and serve him. Hold fast to him and take your oaths in his name. 21He is your praise; he is your God, who performed for you those great and awesome wonders you saw with your own eyes. 22Your forefathers who went down into Egypt were seventy in all, and now the LORD your God has made you as numerous as the stars in the sky.

Love and Obey the LORD

11 Love the LORD your God and keep his requirements, his decrees, his laws and his commands always. 2Remember today that your children were not the ones who saw and experienced the discipline of the LORD your God: his majesty, his mighty hand, his outstretched arm; 3the signs he performed and the things he did in the heart of Egypt, both to Pharaoh king of Egypt and to his whole country; 4what he did to the Egyptian army, to its horses and chariots, how he overwhelmed them with the waters of the Red Sea[a] as they were pursuing you, and how the LORD brought lasting ruin on them. 5It was not your children who saw what he did for you in the desert until you arrived at this place, 6and what he did to Dathan and Abiram, sons of Eliab the Reubenite, when the earth opened its mouth right in the middle of all Israel and swallowed them up with their households, their tents and every living thing that belonged to them. 7But it was your own eyes that saw all these great things the LORD has done.

8Observe therefore all the commands I am giving you today, so that you may have the strength to go in and take over the land that you are crossing the Jordan to possess, 9and so that you may live long in the land that the LORD swore to your forefathers to give to them and their descendants, a land flowing with milk and honey. 10The land you are entering to take over is not like the land of Egypt, from which you have come, where you planted your seed and irrigated it by foot as in a vegetable garden. 11But the land you are crossing the Jordan to take possession of is a land of mountains and valleys that drinks rain from heaven. 12It is a land the LORD your God cares for; the eyes of the LORD your God are continually on it from the beginning of the year to its end.

13So if you faithfully obey the commands I am giving you today—to love the LORD your God and to serve him with all your heart and with all your soul— 14then I will send rain on your land in its season, both autumn and spring rains, so that you may gather in your grain, new wine and oil. 15I will provide grass in the fields for your cattle, and you will eat and be satisfied.

16Be careful, or you will be enticed to turn away and worship other gods and bow down to them. 17Then the LORD's anger will burn against you, and he will shut the heavens so that it will not rain and the ground will yield no produce,

[a]4 Hebrew *Yam Suph*; that is, Sea of Reeds

10:12–13 God's pattern for holy living begins with a proper relationship to him. Growing out of that relationship, which is defined by obedience, is a proper lifestyle. Obedience to God's laws brings ultimate good for the person who obeys.

10:16 Circumstances can easily harden our hearts; it's natural for us to respond to difficulties with stubbornness and rebellion. But God desires to communicate with us. We must keep our hearts soft and our ears open to God. We need to listen to him and then follow through on what he says.

11:1 Love for God is a major motivating force in our obedience to the civil, ceremonial and moral obligations he requests of us. Our obedience to God's instructions should be a result of our love relationship with him, a natural response to the love he has shown to us.

11:16–17 God's wrath is not a thing to be taken lightly. If we nurture sinful thoughts and practices, we should expect God's anger. We must honestly examine our lives to determine those areas that are out of line with God's revealed moral will. God's help and his grace are more than sufficient to help us overcome our sinful thoughts and deeds.

and you will soon perish from the good land
the LORD is giving you. 18Fix these words of
mine in your hearts and minds; tie them as
symbols on your hands and bind them on your
foreheads. 19Teach them to your children, talking about them when you sit at home and when
you walk along the road, when you lie down
and when you get up. 20Write them on the
doorframes of your houses and on your gates,
21so that your days and the days of your children may be many in the land that the LORD
swore to give your forefathers, as many as the
days that the heavens are above the earth.

22If you carefully observe all these commands I am giving you to follow—to love the
LORD your God, to walk in all his ways and to
hold fast to him— 23then the LORD will drive out
all these nations before you, and you will dispossess nations larger and stronger than you.
24Every place where you set your foot will be
yours: Your territory will extend from the desert
to Lebanon, and from the Euphrates River to
the western sea.[a] 25No man will be able to
stand against you. The LORD your God, as he
promised you, will put the terror and fear of
you on the whole land, wherever you go.

26See, I am setting before you today a blessing and a curse— 27the blessing if you obey the
commands of the LORD your God that I am
giving you today; 28the curse if you disobey the
commands of the LORD your God and turn from
the way that I command you today by following
other gods, which you have not known. 29When
the LORD your God has brought you into the
land you are entering to possess, you are to
proclaim on Mount Gerizim the blessings, and
on Mount Ebal the curses. 30As you know, these
mountains are across the Jordan, west of the
road,[b] toward the setting sun, near the great
trees of Moreh, in the territory of those Canaanites living in the Arabah in the vicinity of Gilgal.
31You are about to cross the Jordan to enter and
take possession of the land the LORD your God
is giving you. When you have taken it over and
are living there, 32be sure that you obey all the
decrees and laws I am setting before you today.

The One Place of Worship

12 These are the decrees and laws you
must be careful to follow in the land
that the LORD, the God of your fathers, has giv-
en you to possess—as long as you live in the
land. 2Destroy completely all the places on the
high mountains and on the hills and under every spreading tree where the nations you are
dispossessing worship their gods. 3Break down
their altars, smash their sacred stones and burn
their Asherah poles in the fire; cut down the
idols of their gods and wipe out their names
from those places.

4You must not worship the LORD your God in
their way. 5But you are to seek the place the
LORD your God will choose from among all
your tribes to put his Name there for his dwelling. To that place you must go; 6there bring
your burnt offerings and sacrifices, your tithes
and special gifts, what you have vowed to give
and your freewill offerings, and the firstborn of
your herds and flocks. 7There, in the presence of
the LORD your God, you and your families shall
eat and shall rejoice in everything you have put
your hand to, because the LORD your God has
blessed you.

8You are not to do as we do here today, everyone as he sees fit, 9since you have not yet
reached the resting place and the inheritance
the LORD your God is giving you. 10But you will
cross the Jordan and settle in the land the LORD
your God is giving you as an inheritance, and he
will give you rest from all your enemies around
you so that you will live in safety. 11Then to the
place the LORD your God will choose as a dwelling for his Name—there you are to bring everything I command you: your burnt offerings and
sacrifices, your tithes and special gifts, and all
the choice possessions you have vowed to the
LORD. 12And there rejoice before the LORD your
God, you, your sons and daughters, your menservants and maidservants, and the Levites from
your towns, who have no allotment or inheritance of their own. 13Be careful not to sacrifice
your burnt offerings anywhere you please. 14Of-
fer them only at the place the LORD will choose
in one of your tribes, and there observe everything I command you.

15Nevertheless, you may slaughter your animals in any of your towns and eat as much of
the meat as you want, as if it were gazelle or
deer, according to the blessing the LORD your
God gives you. Both the ceremonially unclean
and the clean may eat it. 16But you must not eat
the blood; pour it out on the ground like water.
17You must not eat in your own towns the tithe
of your grain and new wine and oil, or the
firstborn of your herds and flocks, or whatever
you have vowed to give, or your freewill offerings or special gifts. 18Instead, you are to eat
them in the presence of the LORD your God at
the place the LORD your God will choose—you,
your sons and daughters, your menservants and
maidservants, and the Levites from your
towns—and you are to rejoice before the LORD
your God in everything you put your hand to.
19Be careful not to neglect the Levites as long as
you live in your land.

[a]24 That is, the Mediterranean [b]30 Or *Jordan, westward*

12:4–5 A place of worship was essential to the well-being of God's Old Testament people. The tabernacle and the Jerusalem temple of later times provided that place of worship. It is important for God's people to be able to worship him. The encouragement that can be found by meeting with other believers to worship God will help us preserve spiritual gains.

20When the LORD your God has enlarged
your territory as he promised you, and you
crave meat and say, "I would like some meat,"
then you may eat as much of it as you want. 21If
the place where the LORD your God chooses to
put his Name is too far away from you, you may
slaughter animals from the herds and flocks the
LORD has given you, as I have commanded you,
and in your own towns you may eat as much of
them as you want. 22Eat them as you would
gazelle or deer. Both the ceremonially unclean
and the clean may eat. 23But be sure you do not
eat the blood, because the blood is the life, and
you must not eat the life with the meat. 24You
must not eat the blood; pour it out on the
ground like water. 25Do not eat it, so that it may
go well with you and your children after you,
because you will be doing what is right in the
eyes of the LORD.

26But take your consecrated things and whatever you have vowed to give, and go to the place
the LORD will choose. 27Present your burnt offerings on the altar of the LORD your God, both
the meat and the blood. The blood of your sacrifices must be poured beside the altar of the
LORD your God, but you may eat the meat. 28Be
careful to obey all these regulations I am giving
you, so that it may always go well with you and
your children after you, because you will be
doing what is good and right in the eyes of the
LORD your God.

29The LORD your God will cut off before you
the nations you are about to invade and dispossess. But when you have driven them out and
settled in their land, 30and after they have been
destroyed before you, be careful not to be ensnared by inquiring about their gods, saying,
"How do these nations serve their gods? We
will do the same." 31You must not worship the
LORD your God in their way, because in worshiping their gods, they do all kinds of detestable things the LORD hates. They even burn their
sons and daughters in the fire as sacrifices to
their gods.

32See that you do all I command you; do not
add to it or take away from it.

Worshiping Other Gods

13 If a prophet, or one who foretells by
dreams, appears among you and announces to you a miraculous sign or wonder,
2and if the sign or wonder of which he has
spoken takes place, and he says, "Let us follow
other gods" (gods you have not known) "and let
us worship them," 3you must not listen to the
words of that prophet or dreamer. The LORD
your God is testing you to find out whether you
love him with all your heart and with all your
soul. 4It is the LORD your God you must follow,
and him you must revere. Keep his commands
and obey him; serve him and hold fast to him.
5That prophet or dreamer must be put to death,
because he preached rebellion against the LORD
your God, who brought you out of Egypt and
redeemed you from the land of slavery; he has
tried to turn you from the way the LORD your
God commanded you to follow. You must
purge the evil from among you.

6If your very own brother, or your son or
daughter, or the wife you love, or your closest
friend secretly entices you, saying, "Let us go
and worship other gods" (gods that neither you
nor your fathers have known, 7gods of the peoples around you, whether near or far, from one
end of the land to the other), 8do not yield to
him or listen to him. Show him no pity. Do not
spare him or shield him. 9You must certainly
put him to death. Your hand must be the first
in putting him to death, and then the hands of
all the people. 10Stone him to death, because he
tried to turn you away from the LORD your God,
who brought you out of Egypt, out of the land
of slavery. 11Then all Israel will hear and be
afraid, and no one among you will do such an
evil thing again.

12If you hear it said about one of the towns
the LORD your God is giving you to live in 13that
wicked men have arisen among you and have
led the people of their town astray, saying, "Let
us go and worship other gods" (gods you have
not known), 14then you must inquire, probe
and investigate it thoroughly. And if it is true
and it has been proved that this detestable thing
has been done among you, 15you must certainly
put to the sword all who live in that town.
Destroy it completely,[a] both its people and its
livestock. 16Gather all the plunder of the town
into the middle of the public square and completely burn the town and all its plunder as a
whole burnt offering to the LORD your God. It
is to remain a ruin forever, never to be rebuilt.
17None of those condemned things[a] shall be
found in your hands, so that the LORD will turn
from his fierce anger; he will show you mercy,
have compassion on you, and increase your
numbers, as he promised on oath to your forefathers, 18because you obey the LORD your God,
keeping all his commands that I am giving you
today and doing what is right in his eyes.

[a] *15,17* The Hebrew term refers to the irrevocable giving over of things or persons to the LORD, often by totally destroying them.

12:32 When all else fails, follow the directions. Often we attempt to accomplish God's work in our own way and in our own strength. Yet it is possible to do the right thing in the wrong way. We are to follow God's directions, all of God's directions and nothing but God's directions. Do it God's way. That is the divine prescription for physical, emotional and spiritual health.

13:1–5 This warning about false prophets is as important today as it was in ancient times. We may know individuals who have great influence but whose teachings do not measure up to the truth of God's Word. As we seek spiritual growth, we need to measure the teachings we choose to live by against God's truth revealed in the Bible.

Clean and Unclean Food

14 You are the children of the LORD your God. Do not cut yourselves or shave the front of your heads for the dead, 2for you are a people holy to the LORD your God. Out of all the peoples on the face of the earth, the LORD has chosen you to be his treasured possession.

3Do not eat any detestable thing. 4These are the animals you may eat: the ox, the sheep, the goat, 5the deer, the gazelle, the roe deer, the wild goat, the ibex, the antelope and the mountain sheep.[a] 6You may eat any animal that has a split hoof divided in two and that chews the cud. 7However, of those that chew the cud or that have a split hoof completely divided you may not eat the camel, the rabbit or the coney.[b] Although they chew the cud, they do not have a split hoof; they are ceremonially unclean for you. 8The pig is also unclean; although it has a split hoof, it does not chew the cud. You are not to eat their meat or touch their carcasses.

9Of all the creatures living in the water, you may eat any that has fins and scales. 10But anything that does not have fins and scales you may not eat; for you it is unclean.

11You may eat any clean bird. 12But these you may not eat: the eagle, the vulture, the black vulture, 13the red kite, the black kite, any kind of falcon, 14any kind of raven, 15the horned owl, the screech owl, the gull, any kind of hawk, 16the little owl, the great owl, the white owl, 17the desert owl, the osprey, the cormorant, 18the stork, any kind of heron, the hoopoe and the bat.

19All flying insects that swarm are unclean to you; do not eat them. 20But any winged creature that is clean you may eat.

21Do not eat anything you find already dead. You may give it to an alien living in any of your towns, and he may eat it, or you may sell it to a foreigner. But you are a people holy to the LORD your God.

Do not cook a young goat in its mother's milk.

Tithes

22Be sure to set aside a tenth of all that your fields produce each year. 23Eat the tithe of your grain, new wine and oil, and the firstborn of your herds and flocks in the presence of the LORD your God at the place he will choose as a dwelling for his Name, so that you may learn to revere the LORD your God always. 24But if that place is too distant and you have been blessed by the LORD your God and cannot carry your tithe (because the place where the LORD will choose to put his Name is so far away), 25then exchange your tithe for silver, and take the silver with you and go to the place the LORD your God will choose. 26Use the silver to buy whatever you like: cattle, sheep, wine or other fermented drink, or anything you wish. Then you and your household shall eat there in the presence of the LORD your God and rejoice. 27And do not neglect the Levites living in your towns, for they have no allotment or inheritance of their own.

28At the end of every three years, bring all the tithes of that year's produce and store it in your towns, 29so that the Levites (who have no allotment or inheritance of their own) and the aliens, the fatherless and the widows who live in your towns may come and eat and be satisfied, and so that the LORD your God may bless you in all the work of your hands.

The Year for Canceling Debts

15 At the end of every seven years you must cancel debts. 2This is how it is to be done: Every creditor shall cancel the loan he has made to his fellow Israelite. He shall not require payment from his fellow Israelite or brother, because the LORD's time for canceling debts has been proclaimed. 3You may require payment from a foreigner, but you must cancel any debt your brother owes you. 4However, there should be no poor among you, for in the land the LORD your God is giving you to possess as your inheritance, he will richly bless you, 5if only you fully obey the LORD your God and are careful to follow all these commands I am giving you today. 6For the LORD your God will bless you as he has promised, and you will lend to many nations but will borrow from none. You will rule over many nations but none will rule over you.

7If there is a poor man among your brothers in any of the towns of the land that the LORD your God is giving you, do not be hardhearted or tightfisted toward your poor brother. 8Rather be openhanded and freely lend him whatever he needs. 9Be careful not to harbor this wicked thought: "The seventh year, the year for canceling debts, is near," so that you do not show ill will toward your needy brother and give him nothing. He may then appeal to the LORD against you, and you will be found guilty of sin. 10Give generously to him and do so without a grudging heart; then because of this the LORD your God will bless you in all your work and in everything you put your hand to. 11There will always be poor people in the land. Therefore I command you to be openhanded toward your brothers and toward the poor and needy in your land.

Freeing Servants

12If a fellow Hebrew, a man or a woman, sells

[a]5 The precise identification of some of the birds and animals in this chapter is uncertain. [b]7 That is, the hyrax or rock badger

14:1–2 Everything in our lives belongs to God. And because God is holy, our lives should be characterized by holiness in all things. We need to stand out from the world; we need to be different. We need to reflect on our lives, seeking to align them with his commands.

himself to you and serves you six years, in the
seventh year you must let him go free. 13And
when you release him, do not send him away
empty-handed. 14Supply him liberally from
your flock, your threshing floor and your winepress. Give to him as the LORD your God has
blessed you. 15Remember that you were slaves
in Egypt and the LORD your God redeemed you.
That is why I give you this command today.

16But if your servant says to you, "I do not
want to leave you," because he loves you and
your family and is well off with you, 17then take
an awl and push it through his ear lobe into the
door, and he will become your servant for life.
Do the same for your maidservant.

18Do not consider it a hardship to set your
servant free, because his service to you these six
years has been worth twice as much as that of
a hired hand. And the LORD your God will bless
you in everything you do.

The Firstborn Animals

19Set apart for the LORD your God every firstborn male of your herds and flocks. Do not put
the firstborn of your oxen to work, and do not
shear the firstborn of your sheep. 20Each year
you and your family are to eat them in the
presence of the LORD your God at the place he
will choose. 21If an animal has a defect, is lame
or blind, or has any serious flaw, you must not
sacrifice it to the LORD your God. 22You are to
eat it in your own towns. Both the ceremonially
unclean and the clean may eat it, as if it were
gazelle or deer. 23But you must not eat the
blood; pour it out on the ground like water.

Passover

16 Observe the month of Abib and celebrate the Passover of the LORD your
God, because in the month of Abib he brought
you out of Egypt by night. 2Sacrifice as the Passover to the LORD your God an animal from your
flock or herd at the place the LORD will choose
as a dwelling for his Name. 3Do not eat it with
bread made with yeast, but for seven days eat
unleavened bread, the bread of affliction, because you left Egypt in haste—so that all the days
of your life you may remember the time of your
departure from Egypt. 4Let no yeast be found in
your possession in all your land for seven days.
Do not let any of the meat you sacrifice on the
evening of the first day remain until morning.

5You must not sacrifice the Passover in any
town the LORD your God gives you 6except in
the place he will choose as a dwelling for his
Name. There you must sacrifice the Passover in
the evening, when the sun goes down, on the
anniversary[a] of your departure from Egypt.
7Roast it and eat it at the place the LORD your
God will choose. Then in the morning return to
your tents. 8For six days eat unleavened bread
and on the seventh day hold an assembly to the
LORD your God and do no work.

Feast of Weeks

9Count off seven weeks from the time you
begin to put the sickle to the standing grain.
10Then celebrate the Feast of Weeks to the LORD
your God by giving a freewill offering in proportion to the blessings the LORD your God has
given you. 11And rejoice before the LORD your
God at the place he will choose as a dwelling for
his Name—you, your sons and daughters, your
menservants and maidservants, the Levites in
your towns, and the aliens, the fatherless and
the widows living among you. 12Remember that
you were slaves in Egypt, and follow carefully
these decrees.

Feast of Tabernacles

13Celebrate the Feast of Tabernacles for seven
days after you have gathered the produce of
your threshing floor and your winepress. 14Be
joyful at your Feast—you, your sons and daughters, your menservants and maidservants, and
the Levites, the aliens, the fatherless and the
widows who live in your towns. 15For seven
days celebrate the Feast to the LORD your God
at the place the LORD will choose. For the LORD
your God will bless you in all your harvest and

[a]6 Or *down, at the time of day*

15:16–18 At first glance, these verses don't seem pertinent to us. But on closer inspection we can see ourselves as a servant, relating to God, our Master. As new believers, our obedience to God is often given simply out of necessity because it is required. But as we mature in our walk with God, our obedience grows out of our love and devotion for him. We soon come to realize that everything that God requires of us is for our own good. Perhaps we need to consider the vow of the perpetual slave—the bondservant of the New Testament (Romans 6:15–23).

15:19 The Israelites were to give the first of any profit they received to God. We, too, must give God the first of our resources, including our time and money. This kind of giving shows that we are aware that God is the source of all that we have and that everything belongs to him.

16:1–8 When God delivered the Israelites from Egypt, he brought them out with signs and wonders. The final plague resulted in the death of all of Egypt's firstborn sons. But God spared the firstborn sons of the Israelites by "passing over" the homes of those who had placed blood over their doors. From then on God required that the Israelites offer a sacrifice in place of all their firstborn sons. This offering would be a constant reminder of how God had spared their children. We should also remember that we have graciously been "passed over" for punishment. God gave the sacrifice of his firstborn Son, Jesus Christ, so we could be free of sin and its terrible consequences.

16:9–12 The Feast of Weeks, or Pentecost, was a season of great joy among God's people. It came near the beginning of the harvest season and was a time of commemoration and rejoicing, celebrating the gifts that God had given. It was also a time of fellowship, feasting and sharing God's gifts with those in need. God ordained festivals so his people would remember his deeds and be encouraged together. We also need the fellowship of God's people to assist us as we seek spiritual renewal. We need to join with others for mutual encouragement and celebration of what God has done for us.

in all the work of your hands, and your joy will be complete.

16Three times a year all your men must appear before the LORD your God at the place he will choose: at the Feast of Unleavened Bread, the Feast of Weeks and the Feast of Tabernacles. No man should appear before the LORD emptyhanded: 17Each of you must bring a gift in proportion to the way the LORD your God has blessed you.

Judges

18Appoint judges and officials for each of your tribes in every town the LORD your God is giving you, and they shall judge the people fairly. 19Do not pervert justice or show partiality. Do not accept a bribe, for a bribe blinds the eyes of the wise and twists the words of the righteous. 20Follow justice and justice alone, so that you may live and possess the land the LORD your God is giving you.

Worshiping Other Gods

21Do not set up any wooden Asherah pole[a] beside the altar you build to the LORD your God, 22and do not erect a sacred stone, for these the LORD your God hates.

17 Do not sacrifice to the LORD your God an ox or a sheep that has any defect or flaw in it, for that would be detestable to him.

2If a man or woman living among you in one of the towns the LORD gives you is found doing evil in the eyes of the LORD your God in violation of his covenant, 3and contrary to my command has worshiped other gods, bowing down to them or to the sun or the moon or the stars of the sky, 4and this has been brought to your attention, then you must investigate it thoroughly. If it is true and it has been proved that this detestable thing has been done in Israel, 5take the man or woman who has done this evil deed to your city gate and stone that person to death. 6On the testimony of two or three witnesses a man shall be put to death, but no one shall be put to death on the testimony of only one witness. 7The hands of the witnesses must be the first in putting him to death, and then the hands of all the people. You must purge the evil from among you.

Law Courts

8If cases come before your courts that are too difficult for you to judge—whether bloodshed, lawsuits or assaults—take them to the place the LORD your God will choose. 9Go to the priests, who are Levites, and to the judge who is in office at that time. Inquire of them and they will give you the verdict. 10You must act according to the decisions they give you at the place the LORD will choose. Be careful to do everything they direct you to do. 11Act according to the law they teach you and the decisions they give you. Do not turn aside from what they tell you, to the right or to the left. 12The man who shows contempt for the judge or for the priest who stands ministering there to the LORD your God must be put to death. You must purge the evil from Israel. 13All the people will hear and be afraid, and will not be contemptuous again.

The King

14When you enter the land the LORD your God is giving you and have taken possession of it and settled in it, and you say, "Let us set a king over us like all the nations around us," 15be sure to appoint over you the king the LORD your God chooses. He must be from among your own brothers. Do not place a foreigner over you, one who is not a brother Israelite. 16The king, moreover, must not acquire great numbers of horses for himself or make the people return to Egypt to get more of them, for the LORD has told you, "You are not to go back that way again." 17He must not take many wives, or his heart will be led astray. He must not accumulate large amounts of silver and gold.

18When he takes the throne of his kingdom, he is to write for himself on a scroll a copy of this law, taken from that of the priests, who are Levites. 19It is to be with him, and he is to read it all the days of his life so that he may learn to revere the LORD his God and follow carefully all the words of this law and these decrees 20and not consider himself better than his brothers and turn from the law to the right or to the left. Then he and his descendants will reign a long time over his kingdom in Israel.

Offerings for Priests and Levites

18 The priests, who are Levites—indeed the whole tribe of Levi—are to have no allotment or inheritance with Israel. They shall live on the offerings made to the LORD by fire, for that is their inheritance. 2They shall have no inheritance among their brothers; the LORD is their inheritance, as he promised them.

3This is the share due the priests from the people who sacrifice a bull or a sheep: the shoulder, the jowls and the inner parts. 4You are to give them the firstfruits of your grain, new wine and oil, and the first wool from the shearing of your sheep, 5for the LORD your God has chosen them and their descendants out of all your tribes to stand and minister in the LORD's name always.

[a]21 Or *Do not plant any tree dedicated to Asherah*

17:8–13 Though submission to authority is a concept that is largely lost in our culture, it is consistent with Biblical teaching. God is our supreme authority. All of us are to be submissive to God. The Bible mentions other authority structures that will support strong relationships and an orderly community. Wives and husbands are to be submissive to each other; children to parents; employees to employers; church members to elders, etc.

THE SPIRITUAL DISCIPLINES

Bible Study and Meditation

Handwriting on the Heart

Deuteronomy 17:18 One of the most fascinating requirements for Israel's king was that of making a personal copy of the law. Can you imagine a head of state of any modern nation spending time in office making handwritten copies of legislation? We would expect many other important governmental activities to take precedence over the chore of copying the law.

In Israel, however, no responsibility was more important than allowing God's Word to permeate the king's mind and heart. His commitment to God and obedience to God's law were essential to his effectiveness as a leader.

In a technological age which requires instant communication to keep up with fast-paced business, we have grown accustomed to skimming, speed-reading and glancing over summaries. We rarely take time to allow written words to sink deep into our hearts. Often we bring these fast-paced habits to our Bible study as well, missing much of what God wants to say to us. Something happens when we slow down long enough to copy God's Word, literally word for word, onto a page or journal. We discover features about familiar stories that we've never noticed before. Phrases we've taken for granted suddenly stir questions or break open with new meaning. Images we've skimmed over in the past beckon us to reflect upon them. Truths we've avoided can no longer be neglected.

The act of copying the law brought specific benefits to the king and the people he served. He learned to fear and obey the Lord and received instruction on how to live humbly as God's servant. As he copied the law, the king was repeatedly reminded of the blessings of following God and the dreadful consequences of turning away. When the king copied the law, the greatest blessing of all came to those who came after him, for the king could then pass on to them the legacy of God's grace.

For more on Bible study and meditation, turn to Psalm 1.

Putting It Into Practice

Spend a period of time copying sections of the Bible by hand. Choose one of the shorter epistles or several favorite chapters of the Bible. What do you notice as you copy? As you make your copy, keep another page handy to note insights, questions and ideas so you can give them further thought later.

6If a Levite moves from one of your towns
anywhere in Israel where he is living, and comes
in all earnestness to the place the LORD will
choose, 7he may minister in the name of the
LORD his God like all his fellow Levites who
serve there in the presence of the LORD. 8He is
to share equally in their benefits, even though
he has received money from the sale of family
possessions.

Detestable Practices

9When you enter the land the LORD your God
is giving you, do not learn to imitate the detestable ways of the nations there. 10Let no one be
found among you who sacrifices his son or
daughter in[a] the fire, who practices divination
or sorcery, interprets omens, engages in witchcraft, 11or casts spells, or who is a medium or
spiritist or who consults the dead. 12Anyone
who does these things is detestable to the LORD,
and because of these detestable practices the
LORD your God will drive out those nations before you. 13You must be blameless before the
LORD your God.

The Prophet

14The nations you will dispossess listen to
those who practice sorcery or divination. But as
for you, the LORD your God has not permitted
you to do so. 15The LORD your God will raise up
for you a prophet like me from among your
own brothers. You must listen to him. 16For this
is what you asked of the LORD your God at
Horeb on the day of the assembly when you
said, "Let us not hear the voice of the LORD our
God nor see this great fire anymore, or we will
die."

17The LORD said to me: "What they say is
good. 18I will raise up for them a prophet like
you from among their brothers; I will put my
words in his mouth, and he will tell them everything I command him. 19If anyone does not
listen to my words that the prophet speaks in
my name, I myself will call him to account.
20But a prophet who presumes to speak in my
name anything I have not commanded him to
say, or a prophet who speaks in the name of
other gods, must be put to death."

21You may say to yourselves, "How can we
know when a message has not been spoken by
the LORD?" 22If what a prophet proclaims in the
name of the LORD does not take place or come
true, that is a message the LORD has not spoken.
That prophet has spoken presumptuously. Do
not be afraid of him.

Cities of Refuge

19 When the LORD your God has destroyed
the nations whose land he is giving
you, and when you have driven them out and
settled in their towns and houses, 2then set
aside for yourselves three cities centrally located
in the land the LORD your God is giving you to
possess. 3Build roads to them and divide into
three parts the land the LORD your God is giving
you as an inheritance, so that anyone who kills
a man may flee there.

4This is the rule concerning the man who
kills another and flees there to save his life—one
who kills his neighbor unintentionally, without
malice aforethought. 5For instance, a man may
go into the forest with his neighbor to cut
wood, and as he swings his ax to fell a tree, the
head may fly off and hit his neighbor and kill
him. That man may flee to one of these cities
and save his life. 6Otherwise, the avenger of
blood might pursue him in a rage, overtake him
if the distance is too great, and kill him even
though he is not deserving of death, since he
did it to his neighbor without malice aforethought. 7This is why I command you to set
aside for yourselves three cities.

8If the LORD your God enlarges your territory,
as he promised on oath to your forefathers, and
gives you the whole land he promised them,
9because you carefully follow all these laws I
command you today—to love the LORD your
God and to walk always in his ways—then you
are to set aside three more cities. 10Do this so
that innocent blood will not be shed in your
land, which the LORD your God is giving you as
your inheritance, and so that you will not be
guilty of bloodshed.

11But if a man hates his neighbor and lies in
wait for him, assaults and kills him, and then
flees to one of these cities, 12the elders of his
town shall send for him, bring him back from
the city, and hand him over to the avenger of
blood to die. 13Show him no pity. You must
purge from Israel the guilt of shedding innocent
blood, so that it may go well with you.

14Do not move your neighbor's boundary
stone set up by your predecessors in the inheritance you receive in the land the LORD your God
is giving you to possess.

Witnesses

15One witness is not enough to convict a
man accused of any crime or offense he may

[a]10 Or *who makes his son or daughter pass through*

18:9–12 Beware of the occult. Many people think they can dabble in the occult without doing any harm, least of all to themselves. The Bible, however, condemns these activities in no uncertain terms. Mark this well: Meaningful spiritual or emotional growth is impossible for anyone who is taking part in occult activities.

19:14 This verse forbids the moving of landmarks, specifically addressing the issue of real estate rights. Physical landmarks are also important kinds of personal boundaries. As we relate to others, we need to be sure that we respect the legitimate boundaries they set up, whether physical or emotional. As we reflect honestly on our lives, looking to confess our wrongs, we should pay close attention to boundaries and the ways in which we may have trespassed wrongly in other people's lives.

have committed. A matter must be established
by the testimony of two or three witnesses.
16If a malicious witness takes the stand to
accuse a man of a crime, 17the two men involved in the dispute must stand in the presence
of the LORD before the priests and the judges
who are in office at the time. 18The judges must
make a thorough investigation, and if the witness proves to be a liar, giving false testimony
against his brother, 19then do to him as he intended to do to his brother. You must purge the
evil from among you. 20The rest of the people
will hear of this and be afraid, and never again
will such an evil thing be done among you.
21Show no pity: life for life, eye for eye, tooth
for tooth, hand for hand, foot for foot.

Going to War

20 When you go to war against your enemies and see horses and chariots and
an army greater than yours, do not be afraid of
them, because the LORD your God, who brought
you up out of Egypt, will be with you. 2When
you are about to go into battle, the priest shall
come forward and address the army. 3He shall
say: "Hear, O Israel, today you are going into
battle against your enemies. Do not be fainthearted or afraid; do not be terrified or give way
to panic before them. 4For the LORD your God
is the one who goes with you to fight for you
against your enemies to give you victory."
5The officers shall say to the army: "Has anyone built a new house and not dedicated it? Let
him go home, or he may die in battle and someone else may dedicate it. 6Has anyone planted
a vineyard and not begun to enjoy it? Let him
go home, or he may die in battle and someone
else enjoy it. 7Has anyone become pledged to a
woman and not married her? Let him go home,
or he may die in battle and someone else marry
her." 8Then the officers shall add, "Is any man
afraid or fainthearted? Let him go home so that
his brothers will not become disheartened too."
9When the officers have finished speaking to
the army, they shall appoint commanders
over it.
10When you march up to attack a city, make
its people an offer of peace. 11If they accept and
open their gates, all the people in it shall be
subject to forced labor and shall work for you.
12If they refuse to make peace and they engage
you in battle, lay siege to that city. 13When the
LORD your God delivers it into your hand, put
to the sword all the men in it. 14As for the wom-
en, the children, the livestock and everything
else in the city, you may take these as plunder
for yourselves. And you may use the plunder
the LORD your God gives you from your enemies. 15This is how you are to treat all the cities
that are at a distance from you and do not belong to the nations nearby.
16However, in the cities of the nations the
LORD your God is giving you as an inheritance,
do not leave alive anything that breathes.
17Completely destroy[a] them—the Hittites, Amorites, Canaanites, Perizzites, Hivites and Jebusites—as the LORD your God has commanded
you. 18Otherwise, they will teach you to follow
all the detestable things they do in worshiping
their gods, and you will sin against the LORD
your God.
19When you lay siege to a city for a long time,
fighting against it to capture it, do not destroy
its trees by putting an ax to them, because you
can eat their fruit. Do not cut them down. Are
the trees of the field people, that you should
besiege them?[b] 20However, you may cut down
trees that you know are not fruit trees and use
them to build siege works until the city at war
with you falls.

Atonement for an Unsolved Murder

21 If a man is found slain, lying in a field
in the land the LORD your God is giving
you to possess, and it is not known who killed
him, 2your elders and judges shall go out and
measure the distance from the body to the
neighboring towns. 3Then the elders of the
town nearest the body shall take a heifer that
has never been worked and has never worn a
yoke 4and lead her down to a valley that has not
been plowed or planted and where there is a
flowing stream. There in the valley they are to
break the heifer's neck. 5The priests, the sons of
Levi, shall step forward, for the LORD your God
has chosen them to minister and to pronounce
blessings in the name of the LORD and to decide
all cases of dispute and assault. 6Then all the
elders of the town nearest the body shall wash
their hands over the heifer whose neck was broken in the valley, 7and they shall declare: "Our
hands did not shed this blood, nor did our
eyes see it done. 8Accept this atonement for
your people Israel, whom you have redeemed,
O LORD, and do not hold your people guilty of
the blood of an innocent man." And the blood-

[a]17 The Hebrew term refers to the irrevocable giving over of things or persons to the LORD, often by totally destroying them. [b]19 Or *down to use in the siege, for the fruit trees are for the benefit of man.*

19:21 This is the famous *lex talionis*: "Life for life, eye for eye, tooth for tooth." It is the simplest form of the law of retribution. Given this kind of context, the task of restoring relationship with God and others would be virtually impossible. According to this form of law, all the wrongs we have ever committed would have to be committed against us in order to make amends for our guilt. But God has provided his Son to take the punishment on our behalf. Our spiritual renewal and restoration of relationships can only take place in the environment of grace that has been created by the redeeming work of Jesus Christ.

20:1 The great and encouraging imperative "do not be afraid" appears often in the Bible. It occurs dozens of times in Deuteronomy. In the context of Israel's enemies it seems particularly significant. Even when we face seemingly impossible odds, we should not fear. God is able to accomplish his will for us against all odds.

shed will be atoned for. [9]So you will purge from yourselves the guilt of shedding innocent blood, since you have done what is right in the eyes of the LORD.

Marrying a Captive Woman

[10]When you go to war against your enemies and the LORD your God delivers them into your hands and you take captives, [11]if you notice among the captives a beautiful woman and are attracted to her, you may take her as your wife. [12]Bring her into your home and have her shave her head, trim her nails [13]and put aside the clothes she was wearing when captured. After she has lived in your house and mourned her father and mother for a full month, then you may go to her and be her husband and she shall be your wife. [14]If you are not pleased with her, let her go wherever she wishes. You must not sell her or treat her as a slave, since you have dishonored her.

The Right of the Firstborn

[15]If a man has two wives, and he loves one but not the other, and both bear him sons but the firstborn is the son of the wife he does not love, [16]when he wills his property to his sons, he must not give the rights of the firstborn to the son of the wife he loves in preference to his actual firstborn, the son of the wife he does not love. [17]He must acknowledge the son of his unloved wife as the firstborn by giving him a double share of all he has. That son is the first sign of his father's strength. The right of the firstborn belongs to him.

A Rebellious Son

[18]If a man has a stubborn and rebellious son who does not obey his father and mother and will not listen to them when they discipline him, [19]his father and mother shall take hold of him and bring him to the elders at the gate of his town. [20]They shall say to the elders, "This son of ours is stubborn and rebellious. He will not obey us. He is a profligate and a drunkard." [21]Then all the men of his town shall stone him to death. You must purge the evil from among you. All Israel will hear of it and be afraid.

Various Laws

[22]If a man guilty of a capital offense is put to death and his body is hung on a tree, [23]you must not leave his body on the tree overnight. Be sure to bury him that same day, because anyone who is hung on a tree is under God's curse. You must not desecrate the land the LORD your God is giving you as an inheritance.

22 If you see your brother's ox or sheep straying, do not ignore it but be sure to take it back to him. [2]If the brother does not live near you or if you do not know who he is, take it home with you and keep it until he comes looking for it. Then give it back to him. [3]Do the same if you find your brother's donkey or his cloak or anything he loses. Do not ignore it.

[4]If you see your brother's donkey or his ox fallen on the road, do not ignore it. Help him get it to its feet.

[5]A woman must not wear men's clothing, nor a man wear women's clothing, for the LORD your God detests anyone who does this.

[6]If you come across a bird's nest beside the road, either in a tree or on the ground, and the mother is sitting on the young or on the eggs, do not take the mother with the young. [7]You may take the young, but be sure to let the mother go, so that it may go well with you and you may have a long life.

[8]When you build a new house, make a parapet around your roof so that you may not bring the guilt of bloodshed on your house if someone falls from the roof.

[9]Do not plant two kinds of seed in your vineyard; if you do, not only the crops you plant but also the fruit of the vineyard will be defiled.[a]

[10]Do not plow with an ox and a donkey yoked together.

[11]Do not wear clothes of wool and linen woven together.

[12]Make tassels on the four corners of the cloak you wear.

Marriage Violations

[13]If a man takes a wife and, after lying with her, dislikes her [14]and slanders her and gives her a bad name, saying, "I married this woman, but when I approached her, I did not find proof of her virginity," [15]then the girl's father and mother shall bring proof that she was a virgin to the town elders at the gate. [16]The girl's father will say to the elders, "I gave my daughter in marriage to this man, but he dislikes her. [17]Now he has slandered her and said, 'I did not find your daughter to be a virgin.' But here is the proof of my daughter's virginity." Then her parents shall

[a] 9 Or *be forfeited to the sanctuary*

21:18–21 Rebellious children are heartbreaking to their parents. Even when parents do the best they can to raise godly children, some children refuse to adhere to God's standards of conduct. In such cases, the Old Testament law commanded drastic measures. This law reveals how much God desires children's respect for and obedience to their parents. The proper authority structures in our families need to be established early so that such radical measures are not necessary.

22:5 One of the ugliest results of sin in our times is the confusion of gender roles. The Bible is unequivocal on this point: Don't reverse gender roles. Men, rejoice in your maleness. Women, celebrate your femaleness. Be the gender God intended you to be—in your appearance, in your clothing and in your thinking. Outside of these parameters, meaningful spiritual growth is impossible.

22:13–30 God spells out all of these regulations to demonstrate that the marriage relationship is of great and holy importance. God's pattern for marriage is clear. Marital fidelity is essential for establishing strong families whose members are characterized by maturity and wholeness.

display the cloth before the elders of the town,
18and the elders shall take the man and punish
him. 19They shall fine him a hundred shekels of
silver[a] and give them to the girl's father, because this man has given an Israelite virgin a
bad name. She shall continue to be his wife; he
must not divorce her as long as he lives.

20If, however, the charge is true and no proof
of the girl's virginity can be found, 21she shall be
brought to the door of her father's house and
there the men of her town shall stone her to
death. She has done a disgraceful thing in Israel
by being promiscuous while still in her father's
house. You must purge the evil from among
you.

22If a man is found sleeping with another
man's wife, both the man who slept with her
and the woman must die. You must purge the
evil from Israel.

23If a man happens to meet in a town a virgin
pledged to be married and he sleeps with her,
24you shall take both of them to the gate of that
town and stone them to death—the girl because
she was in a town and did not scream for help,
and the man because he violated another man's
wife. You must purge the evil from among you.

25But if out in the country a man happens to
meet a girl pledged to be married and rapes her,
only the man who has done this shall die. 26Do
nothing to the girl; she has committed no sin
deserving death. This case is like that of someone who attacks and murders his neighbor,
27for the man found the girl out in the country,
and though the betrothed girl screamed, there
was no one to rescue her.

28If a man happens to meet a virgin who is
not pledged to be married and rapes her and
they are discovered, 29he shall pay the girl's father fifty shekels of silver.[b] He must marry the
girl, for he has violated her. He can never divorce her as long as he lives.

30A man is not to marry his father's wife; he
must not dishonor his father's bed.

Exclusion From the Assembly

23 No one who has been emasculated by
crushing or cutting may enter the assembly of the LORD.

2No one born of a forbidden marriage[c] nor
any of his descendants may enter the assembly
of the LORD, even down to the tenth generation.

3No Ammonite or Moabite or any of his
descendants may enter the assembly of the
LORD, even down to the tenth generation. 4For
they did not come to meet you with bread and
water on your way when you came out of Egypt,
and they hired Balaam son of Beor from Pethor
in Aram Naharaim[d] to pronounce a curse on
you. 5However, the LORD your God would not
listen to Balaam but turned the curse into a
blessing for you, because the LORD your God
loves you. 6Do not seek a treaty of friendship
with them as long as you live.

7Do not abhor an Edomite, for he is your
brother. Do not abhor an Egyptian, because you
lived as an alien in his country. 8The third generation of children born to them may enter the
assembly of the LORD.

Uncleanness in the Camp

9When you are encamped against your enemies, keep away from everything impure. 10If
one of your men is unclean because of a noctur-
nal emission, he is to go outside the camp and
stay there. 11But as evening approaches he is to
wash himself, and at sunset he may return to
the camp.

12Designate a place outside the camp where
you can go to relieve yourself. 13As part of your
equipment have something to dig with, and
when you relieve yourself, dig a hole and cover
up your excrement. 14For the LORD your God
moves about in your camp to protect you and
to deliver your enemies to you. Your camp must
be holy, so that he will not see among you
anything indecent and turn away from you.

Miscellaneous Laws

15If a slave has taken refuge with you, do not
hand him over to his master. 16Let him live
among you wherever he likes and in whatever
town he chooses. Do not oppress him.

17No Israelite man or woman is to become
a shrine prostitute. 18You must not bring the
earnings of a female prostitute or of a male
prostitute[e] into the house of the LORD your
God to pay any vow, because the LORD your
God detests them both.

19Do not charge your brother interest,
whether on money or food or anything else that
may earn interest. 20You may charge a foreigner
interest, but not a brother Israelite, so that the
LORD your God may bless you in everything you
put your hand to in the land you are entering to
possess.

21If you make a vow to the LORD your God,
do not be slow to pay it, for the LORD your God
will certainly demand it of you and you will be
guilty of sin. 22But if you refrain from making a
vow, you will not be guilty. 23Whatever your

[a] 19 That is, about 2 1/2 pounds (about 1 kilogram)
[b] 29 That is, about 1 1/4 pounds (about 0.6 kilogram)
[c] 2 Or *one of illegitimate birth*
[d] 4 That is, Northwest Mesopotamia
[e] 18 Hebrew *of a dog*

23:17–18 In these verses, prostitution is singled out for special condemnation. The bounds of marriage are the only valid context for sexual activity. In our society, sex outside of marriage has become an accepted practice. Sexual purity is now considered something to be embarrassed about. Healthy marriages must be founded upon trust and based upon sexual purity. If we have sinned in this area, God offers forgiveness and hope for restoration, though the consequences of our sin may never truly be overcome.

23:21–23 Being trustworthy is an absolute necessity for building healthy relationships. All enduring relationships are built on trust. When we make promises, we must learn to keep them—even if it means great inconvenience to us.

lips utter you must be sure to do, because you made your vow freely to the LORD your God with your own mouth.

24If you enter your neighbor's vineyard, you may eat all the grapes you want, but do not put any in your basket. 25If you enter your neighbor's grainfield, you may pick kernels with your hands, but you must not put a sickle to his standing grain.

24 If a man marries a woman who becomes displeasing to him because he finds something indecent about her, and he writes her a certificate of divorce, gives it to her and sends her from his house, 2and if after she leaves his house she becomes the wife of another man, 3and her second husband dislikes her and writes her a certificate of divorce, gives it to her and sends her from his house, or if he dies, 4then her first husband, who divorced her, is not allowed to marry her again after she has been defiled. That would be detestable in the eyes of the LORD. Do not bring sin upon the land the LORD your God is giving you as an inheritance.

5If a man has recently married, he must not be sent to war or have any other duty laid on him. For one year he is to be free to stay at home and bring happiness to the wife he has married.

6Do not take a pair of millstones—not even the upper one—as security for a debt, because that would be taking a man's livelihood as security.

7If a man is caught kidnapping one of his brother Israelites and treats him as a slave or sells him, the kidnapper must die. You must purge the evil from among you.

8In cases of leprous[a] diseases be very careful to do exactly as the priests, who are Levites, instruct you. You must follow carefully what I have commanded them. 9Remember what the LORD your God did to Miriam along the way after you came out of Egypt.

10When you make a loan of any kind to your neighbor, do not go into his house to get what he is offering as a pledge. 11Stay outside and let the man to whom you are making the loan bring the pledge out to you. 12If the man is poor, do not go to sleep with his pledge in your possession. 13Return his cloak to him by sunset so that he may sleep in it. Then he will thank you, and it will be regarded as a righteous act in the sight of the LORD your God.

14Do not take advantage of a hired man who is poor and needy, whether he is a brother Israelite or an alien living in one of your towns. 15Pay him his wages each day before sunset, because he is poor and is counting on it. Otherwise he may cry to the LORD against you, and you will be guilty of sin.

16Fathers shall not be put to death for their children, nor children put to death for their fathers; each is to die for his own sin.

17Do not deprive the alien or the fatherless of justice, or take the cloak of the widow as a pledge. 18Remember that you were slaves in Egypt and the LORD your God redeemed you from there. That is why I command you to do this.

19When you are harvesting in your field and you overlook a sheaf, do not go back to get it. Leave it for the alien, the fatherless and the widow, so that the LORD your God may bless you in all the work of your hands. 20When you beat the olives from your trees, do not go over the branches a second time. Leave what remains for the alien, the fatherless and the widow. 21When you harvest the grapes in your vineyard, do not go over the vines again. Leave what remains for the alien, the fatherless and the widow. 22Remember that you were slaves in Egypt. That is why I command you to do this.

25 When men have a dispute, they are to take it to court and the judges will decide the case, acquitting the innocent and condemning the guilty. 2If the guilty man deserves to be beaten, the judge shall make him lie down and have him flogged in his presence with the number of lashes his crime deserves, 3but he must not give him more than forty lashes. If he is flogged more than that, your brother will be degraded in your eyes.

4Do not muzzle an ox while it is treading out the grain.

5If brothers are living together and one of them dies without a son, his widow must not marry outside the family. Her husband's brother shall take her and marry her and fulfill the duty of a brother-in-law to her. 6The first son she bears shall carry on the name of the dead brother so that his name will not be blotted out from Israel.

7However, if a man does not want to marry his brother's wife, she shall go to the elders at the town gate and say, "My husband's brother refuses to carry on his brother's name in Israel. He will not fulfill the duty of a brother-in-law to me." 8Then the elders of his town shall summon him and talk to him. If he persists in saying, "I do not want to marry her," 9his brother's widow shall go up to him in the presence of the elders, take off one of his sandals, spit in his face and say, "This is what is done to the man who will not build up his brother's family line." 10That man's line shall be known in Israel as The Family of the Unsandaled.

11If two men are fighting and the wife of one

[a] 8 The Hebrew word was used for various diseases affecting the skin—not necessarily leprosy.

24:1–4 Some might view this regulation as proof that God supports divorce. On the contrary, God hates divorce (see Malachi 2:16). Regulations like this were given to put controls on this unsatisfactory solution for disunity in marriage. We may have experienced the pain of divorce. Even though God hates divorce, he loves us and his grace is sufficient for our needs.

of them comes to rescue her husband from his assailant, and she reaches out and seizes him by his private parts, 12you shall cut off her hand. Show her no pity.

13Do not have two differing weights in your bag—one heavy, one light. 14Do not have two differing measures in your house—one large, one small. 15You must have accurate and honest weights and measures, so that you may live long in the land the LORD your God is giving you. 16For the LORD your God detests anyone who does these things, anyone who deals dishonestly.

17Remember what the Amalekites did to you along the way when you came out of Egypt. 18When you were weary and worn out, they met you on your journey and cut off all who were lagging behind; they had no fear of God. 19When the LORD your God gives you rest from all the enemies around you in the land he is giving you to possess as an inheritance, you shall blot out the memory of Amalek from under heaven. Do not forget!

Firstfruits and Tithes

26 When you have entered the land the LORD your God is giving you as an inheritance and have taken possession of it and settled in it, 2take some of the firstfruits of all that you produce from the soil of the land the LORD your God is giving you and put them in a basket. Then go to the place the LORD your God will choose as a dwelling for his Name 3and say to the priest in office at the time, "I declare today to the LORD your God that I have come to the land the LORD swore to our forefathers to give us." 4The priest shall take the basket from your hands and set it down in front of the altar of the LORD your God. 5Then you shall declare before the LORD your God: "My father was a wandering Aramean, and he went down into Egypt with a few people and lived there and became a great nation, powerful and numerous. 6But the Egyptians mistreated us and made us suffer, putting us to hard labor. 7Then we cried out to the LORD, the God of our fathers, and the LORD heard our voice and saw our misery, toil and oppression. 8So the LORD brought us out of Egypt with a mighty hand and an outstretched arm, with great terror and with miraculous signs and wonders. 9He brought us to this place and gave us this land, a land flowing with milk and honey; 10and now I bring the firstfruits of the soil that you, O LORD, have given me." Place the basket before the LORD your God and bow down before him. 11And you and the Levites and the aliens among you shall rejoice in all the good things the LORD your God has given to you and your household.

12When you have finished setting aside a tenth of all your produce in the third year, the year of the tithe, you shall give it to the Levite, the alien, the fatherless and the widow, so that they may eat in your towns and be satisfied. 13Then say to the LORD your God: "I have removed from my house the sacred portion and have given it to the Levite, the alien, the fatherless and the widow, according to all you commanded. I have not turned aside from your commands nor have I forgotten any of them. 14I have not eaten any of the sacred portion while I was in mourning, nor have I removed any of it while I was unclean, nor have I offered any of it to the dead. I have obeyed the LORD my God; I have done everything you commanded me. 15Look down from heaven, your holy dwelling place, and bless your people Israel and the land you have given us as you promised on oath to our forefathers, a land flowing with milk and honey."

Follow the LORD's Commands

16The LORD your God commands you this day to follow these decrees and laws; carefully observe them with all your heart and with all your soul. 17You have declared this day that the LORD is your God and that you will walk in his ways, that you will keep his decrees, commands and laws, and that you will obey him. 18And the LORD has declared this day that you are his people, his treasured possession as he promised, and that you are to keep all his commands. 19He has declared that he will set you in praise, fame and honor high above all the nations he has made and that you will be a people holy to the LORD your God, as he promised.

The Altar on Mount Ebal

27 Moses and the elders of Israel commanded the people: "Keep all these commands that I give you today. 2When you have crossed the Jordan into the land the LORD your God is giving you, set up some large stones and coat them with plaster. 3Write on them all the words of this law when you have crossed over to enter the land the LORD your God is giving you, a land flowing with milk and honey, just as the LORD, the God of your fathers, promised you. 4And when you have crossed the Jordan, set up these stones on Mount Ebal, as I command you today, and coat them with plaster. 5Build there an altar to the LORD your God, an altar of stones. Do not use any iron tool upon them. 6Build the altar of the LORD your God with fieldstones and offer burnt offerings on it to the LORD your God. 7Sacrifice fellowship offerings[a] there, eating them and rejoicing in the presence of the LORD your God. 8And you shall write very clearly all the words of this law on these stones you have set up."

Curses From Mount Ebal

9Then Moses and the priests, who are Levites, said to all Israel, "Be silent, O Israel, and listen! You have now become the people of the LORD your God. 10Obey the LORD your God and fol-

[a]7 Traditionally *peace offerings*

low his commands and decrees that I give you today."

[11]On the same day Moses commanded the people:

[12]When you have crossed the Jordan, these tribes shall stand on Mount Gerizim to bless the people: Simeon, Levi, Judah, Issachar, Joseph and Benjamin. [13]And these tribes shall stand on Mount Ebal to pronounce curses: Reuben, Gad, Asher, Zebulun, Dan and Naphtali.

[14]The Levites shall recite to all the people of Israel in a loud voice:

[15]"Cursed is the man who carves an image or casts an idol—a thing detestable to the LORD, the work of the craftsman's hands—and sets it up in secret."

Then all the people shall say, "Amen!"

[16]"Cursed is the man who dishonors his father or his mother."

Then all the people shall say, "Amen!"

[17]"Cursed is the man who moves his neighbor's boundary stone."

Then all the people shall say, "Amen!"

[18]"Cursed is the man who leads the blind astray on the road."

Then all the people shall say, "Amen!"

[19]"Cursed is the man who withholds justice from the alien, the fatherless or the widow."

Then all the people shall say, "Amen!"

[20]"Cursed is the man who sleeps with his father's wife, for he dishonors his father's bed."

Then all the people shall say, "Amen!"

[21]"Cursed is the man who has sexual relations with any animal."

Then all the people shall say, "Amen!"

[22]"Cursed is the man who sleeps with his sister, the daughter of his father or the daughter of his mother."

Then all the people shall say, "Amen!"

[23]"Cursed is the man who sleeps with his mother-in-law."

Then all the people shall say, "Amen!"

[24]"Cursed is the man who kills his neighbor secretly."

Then all the people shall say, "Amen!"

[25]"Cursed is the man who accepts a bribe to kill an innocent person."

Then all the people shall say, "Amen!"

[26]"Cursed is the man who does not uphold the words of this law by carrying them out."

Then all the people shall say, "Amen!"

Blessings for Obedience

28 If you fully obey the LORD your God and carefully follow all his commands I give you today, the LORD your God will set you high above all the nations on earth. [2]All these blessings will come upon you and accompany you if you obey the LORD your God:

[3]You will be blessed in the city and blessed in the country.

[4]The fruit of your womb will be blessed, and the crops of your land and the young of your livestock—the calves of your herds and the lambs of your flocks.

[5]Your basket and your kneading trough will be blessed.

[6]You will be blessed when you come in and blessed when you go out.

[7]The LORD will grant that the enemies who rise up against you will be defeated before you. They will come at you from one direction but flee from you in seven.

[8]The LORD will send a blessing on your barns and on everything you put your hand to. The LORD your God will bless you in the land he is giving you.

[9]The LORD will establish you as his holy people, as he promised you on oath, if you keep the commands of the LORD your God and walk in his ways. [10]Then all the peoples on earth will see that you are called by the name of the LORD, and they will fear you. [11]The LORD will grant you abundant prosperity—in the fruit of your womb, the young of your livestock and the crops of your ground—in the land he swore to your forefathers to give you.

[12]The LORD will open the heavens, the storehouse of his bounty, to send rain on your land in season and to bless all the work of your hands. You will lend to many nations but will borrow from none. [13]The LORD will make you the head, not the tail. If you pay attention to the commands of the LORD your God that I give you this day and carefully follow them, you will always be at the top, never at the bottom. [14]Do not turn aside from any of the commands I give you today, to the right or to the left, following other gods and serving them.

Curses for Disobedience

[15]However, if you do not obey the LORD your God and do not carefully follow all his commands and decrees I am giving you today, all

---

27:15–26 Ultimately, sin never goes unpunished. God considers disobedience so important that he spells out its consequences. Like a loving father, he warns us of the end results of choosing a sinful course of action. But even passages like this remind us that God only wants our best. He wants us to obey because disobedience can only bring us suffering. This should encourage us to follow God's pattern for holy living.

28:1–6 These verses reveal the one essential requirement for God's blessings—obedience. We are to obey God and his commandments, to seek to know his will and then do it. We will find God's will laid out for us in his Word, the Bible, and we should also ask the Holy Spirit to show us areas where we are disobeying God's Word.

28:15–68 Obedience results in God's blessing; disobedience brings God's curse. We need to discover what God's requirements are and then follow God's plan in humble obedience. This passage outlines many of the negative consequences for disobeying God's plan. We would be wise to take this warning to heart.

these curses will come upon you and overtake you:

16You will be cursed in the city and cursed in the country.
17Your basket and your kneading trough will be cursed.
18The fruit of your womb will be cursed, and the crops of your land, and the calves of your herds and the lambs of your flocks.
19You will be cursed when you come in and cursed when you go out.

20The LORD will send on you curses, confusion and rebuke in everything you put your hand to, until you are destroyed and come to sudden ruin because of the evil you have done in forsaking him.[a] 21The LORD will plague you with diseases until he has destroyed you from the land you are entering to possess. 22The LORD will strike you with wasting disease, with fever and inflammation, with scorching heat and drought, with blight and mildew, which will plague you until you perish. 23The sky over your head will be bronze, the ground beneath you iron. 24The LORD will turn the rain of your country into dust and powder; it will come down from the skies until you are destroyed.

25The LORD will cause you to be defeated before your enemies. You will come at them from one direction but flee from them in seven, and you will become a thing of horror to all the kingdoms on earth. 26Your carcasses will be food for all the birds of the air and the beasts of the earth, and there will be no one to frighten them away. 27The LORD will afflict you with the boils of Egypt and with tumors, festering sores and the itch, from which you cannot be cured. 28The LORD will afflict you with madness, blindness and confusion of mind. 29At midday you will grope about like a blind man in the dark. You will be unsuccessful in everything you do; day after day you will be oppressed and robbed, with no one to rescue you.

30You will be pledged to be married to a woman, but another will take her and ravish her. You will build a house, but you will not live in it. You will plant a vineyard, but you will not even begin to enjoy its fruit. 31Your ox will be slaughtered before your eyes, but you will eat none of it. Your donkey will be forcibly taken from you and will not be returned. Your sheep will be given to your enemies, and no one will rescue them. 32Your sons and daughters will be given to another nation, and you will wear out your eyes watching for them day after day, powerless to lift a hand. 33A people that you do not know will eat what your land and labor produce, and you will have nothing but cruel oppression all your days. 34The sights you see will drive you mad. 35The LORD will afflict your knees and legs with painful boils that cannot be cured, spreading from the soles of your feet to the top of your head.

36The LORD will drive you and the king you set over you to a nation unknown to you or your fathers. There you will worship other gods, gods of wood and stone. 37You will become a thing of horror and an object of scorn and ridicule to all the nations where the LORD will drive you.

38You will sow much seed in the field but you will harvest little, because locusts will devour it. 39You will plant vineyards and cultivate them but you will not drink the wine or gather the grapes, because worms will eat them. 40You will have olive trees throughout your country but you will not use the oil, because the olives will drop off. 41You will have sons and daughters but you will not keep them, because they will go into captivity. 42Swarms of locusts will take over all your trees and the crops of your land.

43The alien who lives among you will rise above you higher and higher, but you will sink lower and lower. 44He will lend to you, but you will not lend to him. He will be the head, but you will be the tail.

45All these curses will come upon you. They will pursue you and overtake you until you are destroyed, because you did not obey the LORD your God and observe the commands and decrees he gave you. 46They will be a sign and a wonder to you and your descendants forever. 47Because you did not serve the LORD your God joyfully and gladly in the time of prosperity, 48therefore in hunger and thirst, in nakedness and dire poverty, you will serve the enemies the LORD sends against you. He will put an iron yoke on your neck until he has destroyed you.

49The LORD will bring a nation against you from far away, from the ends of the earth, like an eagle swooping down, a nation whose language you will not understand, 50a fierce-looking nation without respect for the old or pity for the young. 51They will devour the young of your livestock and the crops of your land until you are destroyed. They will leave you no grain, new wine or oil, nor any calves of your herds or lambs of your flocks until you are ruined. 52They will lay siege to all the cities throughout your land until the high fortified walls in which you trust fall down. They will besiege all the cities throughout the land the LORD your God is giving you.

53Because of the suffering that your enemy will inflict on you during the siege, you will eat the fruit of the womb, the flesh of the sons and daughters the LORD your God has given you. 54Even the most gentle and sensitive man among you will have no compassion on his own brother or the wife he loves or his surviving children, 55and he will not give to one of them any of the flesh of his children that he is eating. It will be all he has left because of the suffering your enemy will inflict on you during

[a]20 Hebrew *me*

the siege of all your cities. [56]The most gentle and sensitive woman among you—so sensitive and gentle that she would not venture to touch the ground with the sole of her foot—will begrudge the husband she loves and her own son or daughter [57]the afterbirth from her womb and the children she bears. For she intends to eat them secretly during the siege and in the distress that your enemy will inflict on you in your cities.

[58]If you do not carefully follow all the words of this law, which are written in this book, and do not revere this glorious and awesome name—the LORD your God— [59]the LORD will send fearful plagues on you and your descendants, harsh and prolonged disasters, and severe and lingering illnesses. [60]He will bring upon you all the diseases of Egypt that you dreaded, and they will cling to you. [61]The LORD will also bring on you every kind of sickness and disaster not recorded in this Book of the Law, until you are destroyed. [62]You who were as numerous as the stars in the sky will be left but few in number, because you did not obey the LORD your God. [63]Just as it pleased the LORD to make you prosper and increase in number, so it will please him to ruin and destroy you. You will be uprooted from the land you are entering to possess.

[64]Then the LORD will scatter you among all nations, from one end of the earth to the other. There you will worship other gods—gods of wood and stone, which neither you nor your fathers have known. [65]Among those nations you will find no repose, no resting place for the sole of your foot. There the LORD will give you an anxious mind, eyes weary with longing, and a despairing heart. [66]You will live in constant suspense, filled with dread both night and day, never sure of your life. [67]In the morning you will say, "If only it were evening!" and in the evening, "If only it were morning!"—because of the terror that will fill your hearts and the sights that your eyes will see. [68]The LORD will send you back in ships to Egypt on a journey I said you should never make again. There you will offer yourselves for sale to your enemies as male and female slaves, but no one will buy you.

Renewal of the Covenant

29 These are the terms of the covenant the LORD commanded Moses to make with the Israelites in Moab, in addition to the covenant he had made with them at Horeb.

[2]Moses summoned all the Israelites and said to them:

Your eyes have seen all that the LORD did in Egypt to Pharaoh, to all his officials and to all his land. [3]With your own eyes you saw those great trials, those miraculous signs and great wonders. [4]But to this day the LORD has not given you a mind that understands or eyes that see or ears that hear. [5]During the forty years that I led you through the desert, your clothes did not wear out, nor did the sandals on your feet. [6]You ate no bread and drank no wine or other fermented drink. I did this so that you might know that I am the LORD your God.

[7]When you reached this place, Sihon king of Heshbon and Og king of Bashan came out to fight against us, but we defeated them. [8]We took their land and gave it as an inheritance to the Reubenites, the Gadites and the half-tribe of Manasseh.

[9]Carefully follow the terms of this covenant, so that you may prosper in everything you do. [10]All of you are standing today in the presence of the LORD your God—your leaders and chief men, your elders and officials, and all the other men of Israel, [11]together with your children and your wives, and the aliens living in your camps who chop your wood and carry your water. [12]You are standing here in order to enter into a covenant with the LORD your God, a covenant the LORD is making with you this day and sealing with an oath, [13]to confirm you this day as his people, that he may be your God as he promised you and as he swore to your fathers, Abraham, Isaac and Jacob. [14]I am making this covenant, with its oath, not only with you [15]who are standing here with us today in the presence of the LORD our God but also with those who are not here today.

[16]You yourselves know how we lived in Egypt and how we passed through the countries on the way here. [17]You saw among them their detestable images and idols of wood and stone, of silver and gold. [18]Make sure there is no man or woman, clan or tribe among you today whose heart turns away from the LORD our God to go and worship the gods of those nations; make sure there is no root among you that produces such bitter poison.

[19]When such a person hears the words of this oath, he invokes a blessing on himself and therefore thinks, "I will be safe, even though I persist in going my own way." This will bring disaster on the watered land as well as the dry.[a] [20]The LORD will never be willing to forgive him; his wrath and zeal will burn against that man. All the curses written in this book will fall upon him, and the LORD will blot out his name from under heaven. [21]The LORD will single him out from all the tribes of Israel for disaster, according to all the curses of the covenant written in this Book of the Law.

[22]Your children who follow you in later gen-

[a]19 Or *way, in order to add drunkenness to thirst."*

28:66–67 These verses graphically depict a life devoid of satisfaction, dreading both the night and the day. When it is dark, a disobedient person wishes for light. When it is light, the dark is preferable. This is one of the inevitable consequences of disobeying God's plan. There is no lasting satisfaction outside of a real relationship with God and obedience to his will. Seeking God's will and following it without reservation are essential for healthy living.

erations and foreigners who come from distant lands will see the calamities that have fallen on the land and the diseases with which the LORD has afflicted it. [23]The whole land will be a burning waste of salt and sulfur—nothing planted, nothing sprouting, no vegetation growing on it. It will be like the destruction of Sodom and Gomorrah, Admah and Zeboiim, which the LORD overthrew in fierce anger. [24]All the nations will ask: "Why has the LORD done this to this land? Why this fierce, burning anger?"

[25]And the answer will be: "It is because this people abandoned the covenant of the LORD, the God of their fathers, the covenant he made with them when he brought them out of Egypt. [26]They went off and worshiped other gods and bowed down to them, gods they did not know, gods he had not given them. [27]Therefore the LORD's anger burned against this land, so that he brought on it all the curses written in this book. [28]In furious anger and in great wrath the LORD uprooted them from their land and thrust them into another land, as it is now."

[29]The secret things belong to the LORD our God, but the things revealed belong to us and to our children forever, that we may follow all the words of this law.

Prosperity After Turning to the LORD

30 When all these blessings and curses I have set before you come upon you and you take them to heart wherever the LORD your God disperses you among the nations, [2]and when you and your children return to the LORD your God and obey him with all your heart and with all your soul according to everything I command you today, [3]then the LORD your God will restore your fortunes[a] and have compassion on you and gather you again from all the nations where he scattered you. [4]Even if you have been banished to the most distant land under the heavens, from there the LORD your God will gather you and bring you back. [5]He will bring you to the land that belonged to your fathers, and you will take possession of it. He will make you more prosperous and numerous than your fathers. [6]The LORD your God will circumcise your hearts and the hearts of your descendants, so that you may love him with all your heart and with all your soul, and live. [7]The LORD your God will put all these curses on your enemies who hate and persecute you. [8]You will again obey the LORD and follow all his commands I am giving you today. [9]Then the LORD your God will make you most prosperous in all the work of your hands and in the fruit of your womb, the young of your livestock and the crops of your land. The LORD will again delight in you and make you prosperous, just as he delighted in your fathers, [10]if you obey the LORD your God and keep his commands and decrees that are written in this Book of the Law and turn to the LORD your God with all your heart and with all your soul.

The Offer of Life or Death

[11]Now what I am commanding you today is not too difficult for you or beyond your reach. [12]It is not up in heaven, so that you have to ask, "Who will ascend into heaven to get it and proclaim it to us so we may obey it?" [13]Nor is it beyond the sea, so that you have to ask, "Who will cross the sea to get it and proclaim it to us so we may obey it?" [14]No, the word is very near you; it is in your mouth and in your heart so you may obey it.

[15]See, I set before you today life and prosperity, death and destruction. [16]For I command you today to love the LORD your God, to walk in his ways, and to keep his commands, decrees and laws; then you will live and increase, and the LORD your God will bless you in the land you are entering to possess.

[17]But if your heart turns away and you are not obedient, and if you are drawn away to bow down to other gods and worship them, [18]I declare to you this day that you will certainly be destroyed. You will not live long in the land you are crossing the Jordan to enter and possess.

[19]This day I call heaven and earth as witnesses against you that I have set before you life and death, blessings and curses. Now choose life, so that you and your children may live [20]and that you may love the LORD your God,

[a]3 Or *will bring you back from captivity*

29:29 Only God knows the secret things—the unknown future, the number of hairs on our head, the time of his return to earth. But God makes it clear that we are responsible for what we do know. We are required to be aware of his instructions. As we seek out God's will in Scripture and follow it with his gracious help, we will grow in spiritual maturity.

30:1 The Israelites were commanded to meditate on God's will for them. Both blessings and curses came from God's hand as a response to their obedience or disobedience. We should do the same. If we don't, we are only hiding from the truth.

30:2–3 God offered this gracious message to his people who were living in defeat: repent and be restored. Even though they had strayed from God, all they needed to do was to return and obey. Our wholehearted repentance brings God's wholehearted forgiveness. With God, it is never too late to make a new start.

30:15 In these verses, God lays out a clear choice for his people. On one hand there is life and prosperity. On the other is death and adversity. Choosing God and his way leads to godly living and spiritual renewal. Choosing against God leads to destruction and death. The clear consequences should make the choice easy.

30:19 God urged his people to choose life. We are reminded here of the claim of Jesus Christ: "I am the way and the truth and the life. No one comes to the Father except through me" (John 14:6). When we seek God and his gracious forgiveness through Jesus Christ we receive life too. Notice that the Israelites' decision was also important for their children. Let's make sure we choose life and encourage our children to choose this abundant life as well.

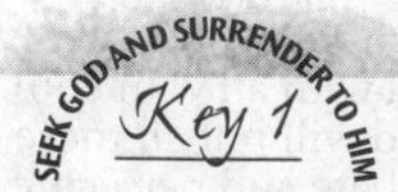

Now Choose Life!

Deuteronomy 30:15–20 Everyone has a life-or-death decision to make—the decision to follow Christ or to reject him. When we seek God and surrender to him, we choose a life of obedience to a loving and powerful, sovereign God. But if we run from God and refuse to surrender our lives to him, we choose the death of a sinful life separated from God.

God spoke to the Israelites through Moses, saying, "I set before you today life and prosperity, death and destruction. For I command you today to love the LORD your God, to walk in his ways, and to keep his commands, decrees and laws; then you will live and increase, and the LORD your God will bless you in the land you are entering to possess . . . I have set before you life and death, blessings and curses. Now choose life, so that you and your children may live" (30:15–16, 19).

Just as the Israelites were told to obey God and reap the blessings of their obedience, so we can choose life! We do this by seeking God, surrendering to him and obeying the plan God has set out for us. Our obedience will bring spiritual renewal to us and untold blessings to our children for generations to come.

Turn to 1 Samuel 13.

listen to his voice, and hold fast to him. For the LORD is your life, and he will give you many years in the land he swore to give to your fathers, Abraham, Isaac and Jacob.

Joshua to Succeed Moses

31 Then Moses went out and spoke these
words to all Israel: [2]"I am now a hundred and twenty years old and I am no longer
able to lead you. The LORD has said to me, 'You
shall not cross the Jordan.' [3]The LORD your God
himself will cross over ahead of you. He will
destroy these nations before you, and you will
take possession of their land. Joshua also
will cross over ahead of you, as the LORD said.
[4]And the LORD will do to them what he did to
Sihon and Og, the kings of the Amorites, whom
he destroyed along with their land. [5]The LORD
will deliver them to you, and you must do to
them all that I have commanded you. [6]Be
strong and courageous. Do not be afraid or terrified because of them, for the LORD your God
goes with you; he will never leave you nor forsake you."
[7]Then Moses summoned Joshua and said to
him in the presence of all Israel, "Be strong and
courageous, for you must go with this people
into the land that the LORD swore to their forefathers to give them, and you must divide it
among them as their inheritance. [8]The LORD
himself goes before you and will be with you;
he will never leave you nor forsake you. Do not
be afraid; do not be discouraged."

The Reading of the Law

[9]So Moses wrote down this law and gave it to
the priests, the sons of Levi, who carried the ark
of the covenant of the LORD, and to all the elders of Israel. [10]Then Moses commanded them:
"At the end of every seven years, in the year for
canceling debts, during the Feast of Tabernacles,
[11]when all Israel comes to appear before the
LORD your God at the place he will choose, you
shall read this law before them in their hearing.
[12]Assemble the people—men, women and children, and the aliens living in your towns—so
they can listen and learn to fear the LORD your
God and follow carefully all the words of this
law. [13]Their children, who do not know this
law, must hear it and learn to fear the LORD your
God as long as you live in the land you are
crossing the Jordan to possess."

31:3 The Israelites were on the verge of entering the promised land. They needed a fresh reminder of God's strength and a promise of victory. Some may have been putting their confidence in Joshua. Others may have been depending on the strength of their armies. But no matter how strong we or our leaders might be, victory comes from God alone. Some enemies are too great for us to conquer on our own. Our personal resources will never be adequate apart from God's help. We must learn to trust God alone, for he is greater than any of the enemies we might face.

Israel's Rebellion Predicted

14The LORD said to Moses, "Now the day
of your death is near. Call Joshua and present
yourselves at the Tent of Meeting, where I will
commission him." So Moses and Joshua came
and presented themselves at the Tent of Meeting.
15Then the LORD appeared at the Tent in a
pillar of cloud, and the cloud stood over the
entrance to the Tent. 16And the LORD said to
Moses: "You are going to rest with your fathers,
and these people will soon prostitute themselves to the foreign gods of the land they are
entering. They will forsake me and break the
covenant I made with them. 17On that day I will
become angry with them and forsake them; I
will hide my face from them, and they will be
destroyed. Many disasters and difficulties will
come upon them, and on that day they will ask,
'Have not these disasters come upon us because
our God is not with us?' 18And I will certainly
hide my face on that day because of all their
wickedness in turning to other gods.
19"Now write down for yourselves this song
and teach it to the Israelites and have them sing
it, so that it may be a witness for me against
them. 20When I have brought them into the
land flowing with milk and honey, the land I
promised on oath to their forefathers, and
when they eat their fill and thrive, they will turn
to other gods and worship them, rejecting me
and breaking my covenant. 21And when many
disasters and difficulties come upon them, this
song will testify against them, because it will
not be forgotten by their descendants. I know
what they are disposed to do, even before I
bring them into the land I promised them on
oath." 22So Moses wrote down this song that day
and taught it to the Israelites.
23The LORD gave this command to Joshua
son of Nun: "Be strong and courageous, for you
will bring the Israelites into the land I promised
them on oath, and I myself will be with you."
24After Moses finished writing in a book the
words of this law from beginning to end, 25he
gave this command to the Levites who carried
the ark of the covenant of the LORD: 26"Take
this Book of the Law and place it beside the ark
of the covenant of the LORD your God. There it
will remain as a witness against you. 27For I
know how rebellious and stiff-necked you are.
If you have been rebellious against the LORD
while I am still alive and with you, how much
more will you rebel after I die! 28Assemble before me all the elders of your tribes and all your
officials, so that I can speak these words in their
hearing and call heaven and earth to testify
against them. 29For I know that after my death
you are sure to become utterly corrupt and to
turn from the way I have commanded you. In
days to come, disaster will fall upon you because you will do evil in the sight of the LORD
and provoke him to anger by what your hands
have made."

The Song of Moses

30And Moses recited the words of this song
from beginning to end in the hearing of the
whole assembly of Israel:

32 Listen, O heavens, and I will speak;
hear, O earth, the words of my
mouth.
2Let my teaching fall like rain
and my words descend like dew,
like showers on new grass,
like abundant rain on tender plants.

3I will proclaim the name of the LORD.
Oh, praise the greatness of our God!
4He is the Rock, his works are perfect,
and all his ways are just.
A faithful God who does no wrong,
upright and just is he.

5They have acted corruptly toward him;
to their shame they are no longer his
children,
but a warped and crooked generation.[a]
6Is this the way you repay the LORD,
O foolish and unwise people?
Is he not your Father, your Creator,[b]
who made you and formed you?

7Remember the days of old;
consider the generations long past.
Ask your father and he will tell you,
your elders, and they will explain to you.
8When the Most High gave the nations their
inheritance,
when he divided all mankind,
he set up boundaries for the peoples
according to the number of the sons of
Israel.[c]
9For the LORD's portion is his people,
Jacob his allotted inheritance.

10In a desert land he found him,
in a barren and howling waste.
He shielded him and cared for him;

[a]5 Or *Corrupt are they and not his children, / a generation warped and twisted to their shame* [b]6 Or *Father, who bought you* [c]8 Masoretic Text; Dead Sea Scrolls (see also Septuagint) *sons of God*

31:23 This verse contains an important message for spiritual renewal. In spite of difficulties, we are told, "Be strong and courageous." The basis for this strength and courage is the marvelous promise "I myself will be with you." As we face difficult tasks, we can find strength and courage in this message. Our God is a God who specializes in overcoming giant challenges (see 1 Samuel 17).

32:3–4 An important part of spiritual growth is learning to worship God; an important part of worship is praise. In these verses Moses takes the time to praise God for who he is—great, glorious, strong, perfect, just, faithful and holy. We also need to take the time to rejoice in God and praise him for his greatness. He is the Rock, our foundation for a stable life. We need to recognize God's ability to help and then ask him to do his mighty work on our behalf.

he guarded him as the apple of his eye,
11like an eagle that stirs up its nest
and hovers over its young,
that spreads its wings to catch them
and carries them on its pinions.
12The LORD alone led him;
no foreign god was with him.

13He made him ride on the heights of the land
and fed him with the fruit of the fields.
He nourished him with honey from the rock,
and with oil from the flinty crag,
14with curds and milk from herd and flock
and with fattened lambs and goats,
with choice rams of Bashan
and the finest kernels of wheat.
You drank the foaming blood of the grape.

15Jeshurun[a] grew fat and kicked;
filled with food, he became heavy and sleek.
He abandoned the God who made him
and rejected the Rock his Savior.
16They made him jealous with their foreign gods
and angered him with their detestable idols.
17They sacrificed to demons, which are not God—
gods they had not known,
gods that recently appeared,
gods your fathers did not fear.
18You deserted the Rock, who fathered you;
you forgot the God who gave you birth.

19The LORD saw this and rejected them
because he was angered by his sons and daughters.
20"I will hide my face from them," he said,
"and see what their end will be;
for they are a perverse generation,
children who are unfaithful.
21They made me jealous by what is no god
and angered me with their worthless idols.
I will make them envious by those who are not a people;
I will make them angry by a nation that has no understanding.
22For a fire has been kindled by my wrath,
one that burns to the realm of death[b] below.
It will devour the earth and its harvests
and set afire the foundations of the mountains.

23"I will heap calamities upon them
and spend my arrows against them.
24I will send wasting famine against them,
consuming pestilence and deadly plague;
I will send against them the fangs of wild beasts,
the venom of vipers that glide in the dust.
25In the street the sword will make them childless;
in their homes terror will reign.
Young men and young women will perish,
infants and gray-haired men.
26I said I would scatter them
and blot out their memory from mankind,
27but I dreaded the taunt of the enemy,
lest the adversary misunderstand
and say, 'Our hand has triumphed;
the LORD has not done all this.' "

28They are a nation without sense,
there is no discernment in them.
29If only they were wise and would understand this
and discern what their end will be!
30How could one man chase a thousand,
or two put ten thousand to flight,
unless their Rock had sold them,
unless the LORD had given them up?
31For their rock is not like our Rock,
as even our enemies concede.
32Their vine comes from the vine of Sodom
and from the fields of Gomorrah.
Their grapes are filled with poison,
and their clusters with bitterness.
33Their wine is the venom of serpents,
the deadly poison of cobras.

34"Have I not kept this in reserve
and sealed it in my vaults?
35It is mine to avenge; I will repay.
In due time their foot will slip;
their day of disaster is near
and their doom rushes upon them."

36The LORD will judge his people
and have compassion on his servants
when he sees their strength is gone
and no one is left, slave or free.
37He will say: "Now where are their gods,
the rock they took refuge in,
38the gods who ate the fat of their sacrifices
and drank the wine of their drink offerings?
Let them rise up to help you!
Let them give you shelter!

39"See now that I myself am He!
There is no god besides me.
I put to death and I bring to life,
I have wounded and I will heal,
and no one can deliver out of my hand.
40I lift my hand to heaven and declare:

a 15 *Jeshurun* means *the upright one,* that is, Israel.
b 22 Hebrew *to Sheol*

32:11–13 As we seek spiritual growth, we need to be assured of God's protection and guidance. These verses from Moses' song should offer the certainty we need. As we seek him, God will guide us toward a life filled with joy and freedom.

As surely as I live forever,
41when I sharpen my flashing sword
and my hand grasps it in judgment,
I will take vengeance on my adversaries
and repay those who hate me.
42I will make my arrows drunk with blood,
while my sword devours flesh:
the blood of the slain and the captives,
the heads of the enemy leaders."

43Rejoice, O nations, with his people,[a,b]
for he will avenge the blood of his servants;
he will take vengeance on his enemies
and make atonement for his land and people.

44Moses came with Joshua[c] son of Nun and
spoke all the words of this song in the hearing
of the people. 45When Moses finished reciting
all these words to all Israel, 46he said to them,
"Take to heart all the words I have solemnly declared to you this day, so that you may command your children to obey carefully all the
words of this law. 47They are not just idle words for you—they are your life. By them you will live long in the land you are crossing the Jordan to possess."

Moses to Die on Mount Nebo

48On that same day the LORD told Moses,
49"Go up into the Abarim Range to Mount Nebo in Moab, across from Jericho, and view Canaan, the land I am giving the Israelites as
their own possession. 50There on the mountain that you have climbed you will die and be gathered to your people, just as your brother Aaron died on Mount Hor and was gathered to his
people. 51This is because both of you broke faith with me in the presence of the Israelites at the waters of Meribah Kadesh in the Desert of Zin and because you did not uphold my holiness among the Israelites.
52Therefore, you will see the land only from a distance; you will not enter the land I am giving to the people of Israel."

Moses Blesses the Tribes

33 This is the blessing that Moses the man of God pronounced on the Israelites before his death. 2He said:

"The LORD came from Sinai
and dawned over them from Seir;
he shone forth from Mount Paran.
He came with[d] myriads of holy ones
from the south, from his mountain slopes.[e]
3Surely it is you who love the people;
all the holy ones are in your hand.
At your feet they all bow down,
and from you receive instruction,
4the law that Moses gave us,
the possession of the assembly of Jacob.
5He was king over Jeshurun[f]
when the leaders of the people assembled,
along with the tribes of Israel.

6"Let Reuben live and not die,
nor[g] his men be few."

7And this he said about Judah:
"Hear, O LORD, the cry of Judah;
bring him to his people.
With his own hands he defends his cause.
Oh, be his help against his foes!"

8About Levi he said:
"Your Thummim and Urim belong
to the man you favored.
You tested him at Massah;
you contended with him at the waters of Meribah.
9He said of his father and mother,
'I have no regard for them.'
He did not recognize his brothers
or acknowledge his own children,
but he watched over your word
and guarded your covenant.
10He teaches your precepts to Jacob
and your law to Israel.
He offers incense before you
and whole burnt offerings on your altar.
11Bless all his skills, O LORD,
and be pleased with the work of his hands.
Smite the loins of those who rise up against him;
strike his foes till they rise no more."

12About Benjamin he said:
"Let the beloved of the LORD rest secure in him,
for he shields him all day long,
and the one the LORD loves rests between his shoulders."

13About Joseph he said:
"May the LORD bless his land
with the precious dew from heaven above
and with the deep waters that lie below;
14with the best the sun brings forth
and the finest the moon can yield;
15with the choicest gifts of the ancient mountains
and the fruitfulness of the everlasting hills;
16with the best gifts of the earth and its fullness
and the favor of him who dwelt in the burning bush.

a43 Or *Make his people rejoice, O nations*
b43 Masoretic Text; Dead Sea Scrolls (see also Septuagint) *people, / and let all the angels worship him /*
c44 Hebrew *Hoshea,* a variant of *Joshua*
d2 Or *from*
e2 The meaning of the Hebrew for this phrase is uncertain.
f5 *Jeshurun* means *the upright one,* that is, Israel; also in verse 26.
g6 Or *but let*

Let all these rest on the head of Joseph,
on the brow of the prince among[a] his brothers.
17In majesty he is like a firstborn bull;
his horns are the horns of a wild ox.
With them he will gore the nations,
even those at the ends of the earth.
Such are the ten thousands of Ephraim;
such are the thousands of Manasseh."

18About Zebulun he said:

"Rejoice, Zebulun, in your going out,
and you, Issachar, in your tents.
19They will summon peoples to the mountain
and there offer sacrifices of righteousness;
they will feast on the abundance of the seas,
on the treasures hidden in the sand."

20About Gad he said:

"Blessed is he who enlarges Gad's domain!
Gad lives there like a lion,
tearing at arm or head.
21He chose the best land for himself;
the leader's portion was kept for him.
When the heads of the people assembled,
he carried out the LORD's righteous will,
and his judgments concerning Israel."

22About Dan he said:

"Dan is a lion's cub,
springing out of Bashan."

23About Naphtali he said:

"Naphtali is abounding with the favor of the LORD
and is full of his blessing;
he will inherit southward to the lake."

24About Asher he said:

"Most blessed of sons is Asher;
let him be favored by his brothers,
and let him bathe his feet in oil.
25The bolts of your gates will be iron and bronze,
and your strength will equal your days.
26"There is no one like the God of Jeshurun,
who rides on the heavens to help you
and on the clouds in his majesty.
27The eternal God is your refuge,
and underneath are the everlasting arms.
He will drive out your enemy before you,
saying, 'Destroy him!'
28So Israel will live in safety alone;
Jacob's spring is secure
in a land of grain and new wine,
where the heavens drop dew.
29Blessed are you, O Israel!
Who is like you,
a people saved by the LORD?
He is your shield and helper
and your glorious sword.
Your enemies will cower before you,
and you will trample down their high places.[b]"

The Death of Moses

34 Then Moses climbed Mount Nebo from
the plains of Moab to the top of Pisgah,
across from Jericho. There the LORD showed
him the whole land—from Gilead to Dan, 2all of
Naphtali, the territory of Ephraim and Manasseh, all the land of Judah as far as the western
sea,[c] 3the Negev and the whole region from
the Valley of Jericho, the City of Palms, as far as
Zoar. 4Then the LORD said to him, "This is the
land I promised on oath to Abraham, Isaac and
Jacob when I said, 'I will give it to your descendants.' I have let you see it with your eyes, but
you will not cross over into it."
5And Moses the servant of the LORD died
there in Moab, as the LORD had said. 6He buried
him[d] in Moab, in the valley opposite Beth
Peor, but to this day no one knows where his
grave is. 7Moses was a hundred and twenty
years old when he died, yet his eyes were not
weak nor his strength gone. 8The Israelites
grieved for Moses in the plains of Moab thirty
days, until the time of weeping and mourning
was over.
9Now Joshua son of Nun was filled with the
spirit[e] of wisdom because Moses had laid his
hands on him. So the Israelites listened to him
and did what the LORD had commanded Moses.
10Since then, no prophet has risen in Israel
like Moses, whom the LORD knew face to face,
11who did all those miraculous signs and wonders the LORD sent him to do in Egypt—to Pharaoh and to all his officials and to his whole
land. 12For no one has ever shown the mighty
power or performed the awesome deeds that
Moses did in the sight of all Israel.

[a]16 Or *of the one separated from their bodies* [b]29 Or *will tread upon their bodies* [c]2 That is, the Mediterranean [d]6 Or *He was buried* [e]9 Or *Spirit*

33:29 This verse is another promise of God's saving help. He fought for his people and defended them against their enemies. He assured them of ultimate victory. When our life is in disarray, we must remember that God has genuine concern for our welfare. As we seek God and surrender to him, we can be sure that he is on our side.

JOSHUA

The Big Picture

God miraculously used Moses to lead the people of Israel from bondage in Egypt to the threshold of the promised land. But instead of conquering Canaan, the Israelites wandered in the wilderness for almost forty years. The book of Joshua records how God brought the next generation of Israelites to the borders of Canaan under Joshua's leadership.

Joshua was ideal for the job of leading Israel: He was a gifted leader and had served as Moses' assistant for many years. The primary reason for his success, however, was not his personal ability or leadership skills. Joshua was able to successfully lead the Israelites because of his trust in God and his obedience to God's instructions. Joshua constantly turned the attention of his people to the God who took care of them, who fought for them, who gave them the land. He recognized and declared that Israel's victories belonged to God alone.

The new generation of Israelites seemed to have learned valuable lessons from their parents' lack of trust and tendency toward disobedience. Instead of resisting God's plan for conquest, they agreed to do everything that Joshua commanded. As a result, this new generation witnessed miraculous victories in the face of seemingly impossible odds. As the Israelites continued to believe and obey him, God did incredible things on their behalf. God proved conclusively that he was worthy of their trust.

It is hard for some of us to believe that God has a good plan for our future or that he is able to bring it about. Such doubts are not grounded in the truth. God does care about us, and he is able to lead us to amazing victories over the most powerful enemies. Remembering these truths should help us walk by faith as we follow God's plan for spiritual renewal. As we do so, God will lead us to the good future he plans for us.

A. *SECURING THE FRUITS OF VICTORY (1:1–12:24)*

1. Inspiring the People (1:1–5:15)
2. Implementing the Plan (6:1–11:23)
3. Identifying the Progress (12:1-24)

B. *SHARING THE FRUITS OF VICTORY (13:1–24:33)*

1. Ensuring Fair Compensation (13:1–19:51)
2. Ensuring Full Cooperation (20:1–22:34)
3. Ensuring Faithful Continuance (23:1–24:33)

Spiritual Renewal Themes

SPIRITUAL RENEWAL IS ONGOING

How wonderful it would be to be completely perfect—to have arrived! That is sometimes one of our fantasies and certainly one that the Israelites must have had. The first generation had not made it into the promised land. But this second generation followed God's plan and conquered the land. What could possi-

Essential Facts

PURPOSE:
To reveal the importance of trusting and obeying God in the difficult process of achieving both physical and spiritual goals.

AUTHOR:
The book is anonymous, though tradition attributes much of it to Joshua.

AUDIENCE:
The people of Israel.

DATE WRITTEN:
Probably sometime between 1375 and 1300 B.C., soon after the recorded events.

SETTING:
Initially in the wilderness east of the Jordan River, but primarily in the promised land.

KEY VERSES:
"Be strong and courageous, because you will lead these people to inherit the land I swore to their forefathers to give them. Be strong and very courageous. Be careful to obey all the law my servant Moses gave you; do not turn from it to the right or to the left, that you may be successful wherever you go" (1:6-7).

KEY PLACES:
Jordan River, Gilead, Jericho, Ai, Shiloh, Shechem.

KEY PEOPLE:
Joshua, Rahab, Caleb.

bly go wrong now? They may have felt, "We're in the promised land at last—finally we can relax!" But the exact opposite was true. Though they had arrived at their destination, their work had just begun! The same is true for us. When we think we have arrived, we must be careful to maintain our spiritual gains. We need to recognize that spiritual renewal and transformation is a lifelong process.

THE CONFLICT WITH EVIL

God commanded his people to completely conquer Canaan and its people. He wanted to purify the land from evil people and practices. The Israelites were the people of God's promise. They were supposed to judge evil and be a blessing to all nations. But to accomplish this, they had to guard against the evil around them. Evil still surrounds us today. Though Christ is continually conforming us to his image, we must recognize that we will not be completely perfect until we enter eternity. We must be ever watchful for the old patterns of sin in our lives.

THE IMPORTANCE OF COMMUNICATION

Communication is vital for maintaining relationships that are characterized by stability and peace. The eastern tribes had built a large monument in Canaan before crossing the Jordan River. This act was misunderstood by the western tribes, who perceived it to be an act of rebellion against God. War between the tribes seemed inevitable, but a fight was averted because of a simple conversation between the two groups. Once understanding was established, the reason for battle no longer existed. We often misinterpret the actions and words of others. Open and honest communication is a prerequisite for overcoming confusion and establishing peace.

The LORD Commands Joshua

1 After the death of Moses the servant of the LORD, the LORD said to Joshua son of Nun, Moses' aide: 2"Moses my servant is dead. Now then, you and all these people, get ready to cross the Jordan River into the land I am about to give to them—to the Israelites. 3I will give you every place where you set your foot, as I promised Moses. 4Your territory will extend from the desert to Lebanon, and from the great river, the Euphrates—all the Hittite country—to the Great Sea[a] on the west. 5No one will be able to stand up against you all the days of your life. As I was with Moses, so I will be with you; I will never leave you nor forsake you.

6"Be strong and courageous, because you will lead these people to inherit the land I swore to their forefathers to give them. 7Be strong and very courageous. Be careful to obey all the law my servant Moses gave you; do not turn from it to the right or to the left, that you may be successful wherever you go. 8Do not let this Book of the Law depart from your mouth; meditate on it day and night, so that you may be careful to do everything written in it. Then you will be prosperous and successful. 9Have I not commanded you? Be strong and courageous. Do not be terrified; do not be discouraged, for the LORD your God will be with you wherever you go."

10So Joshua ordered the officers of the people: 11"Go through the camp and tell the people, 'Get your supplies ready. Three days from now you will cross the Jordan here to go in and take possession of the land the LORD your God is giving you for your own.' "

12But to the Reubenites, the Gadites and the half-tribe of Manasseh, Joshua said, 13"Remember the command that Moses the servant of the LORD gave you: 'The LORD your God is giving you rest and has granted you this land.' 14Your wives, your children and your livestock may stay in the land that Moses gave you east of the Jordan, but all your fighting men, fully armed, must cross over ahead of your brothers. You are to help your brothers 15until the LORD gives them rest, as he has done for you, and until they too have taken possession of the land that the LORD your God is giving them. After that, you may go back and occupy your own land, which Moses the servant of the LORD gave you east of the Jordan toward the sunrise."

16Then they answered Joshua, "Whatever you have commanded us we will do, and wherever you send us we will go. 17Just as we fully obeyed Moses, so we will obey you. Only may the LORD your God be with you as he was with Moses. 18Whoever rebels against your word and does not obey your words, whatever you may command them, will be put to death. Only be strong and courageous!"

Rahab and the Spies

2 Then Joshua son of Nun secretly sent two spies from Shittim. "Go, look over the land," he said, "especially Jericho." So they went and entered the house of a prostitute[b] named Rahab and stayed there.

2The king of Jericho was told, "Look! Some of the Israelites have come here tonight to spy out the land." 3So the king of Jericho sent this message to Rahab: "Bring out the men who came to you and entered your house, because they have come to spy out the whole land."

4But the woman had taken the two men and hidden them. She said, "Yes, the men came to me, but I did not know where they had come from. 5At dusk, when it was time to close the city gate, the men left. I don't know which way they went. Go after them quickly. You may catch up with them." 6(But she had taken them up to the roof and hidden them under the stalks of flax she had laid out on the roof.) 7So the men set out in pursuit of the spies on the road that leads to the fords of the Jordan, and as soon as the pursuers had gone out, the gate was shut.

8Before the spies lay down for the night, she went up on the roof 9and said to them, "I know

[a] 4 That is, the Mediterranean [b] 1 Or possibly *an innkeeper*

1:1–9 Joshua may have been devastated by the death of Moses, a close friend, mentor and father figure, but he was immediately thrust into a leadership role for which he undoubtedly felt unworthy and unprepared. How could Joshua ever fill the shoes of the man who had talked to God face to face (see Exodus 33:11)? Joshua dared not show fear before the people, or they might have lost confidence in his ability to lead them to victory. He needed to demonstrate a bold obedience to God's commands in order to ensure success. Joshua was able to do this because he was willing to seek God and surrender to him.

1:10–15 In his new role as commander in chief of Israel's armies, Joshua commanded his subordinates to prepare their people for the new and difficult venture that lay before them. He then reminded the Reubenites, Gadites and the half-tribe of Manasseh of their promise to Moses to fight side by side with their fellow Israelites until all the land had been conquered (see Numbers 32:1–32). Joshua was understandably concerned about whether they would stand with the main body of the people or defect from them, discouraging the rest of the people of Israel. We need to continue to guard ourselves against discouragement as well, so that our spiritual growth will not be stifled.

2:1–7 Joshua wisely determined to discover the strength of his enemies, the people of the city of Jericho, before setting out to encounter them in battle (see Luke 14:31–32). Rahab, a prostitute and citizen of Jericho, also made a wise decision when she took a stand for the God of Israel by assisting and protecting the spies sent to Jericho by Joshua. Rahab displayed courage when she turned away from the security and praise of the world she knew and risked following the true God, of whom she knew little. It always takes courage to make changes in our lives, especially when those changes take us into the unknown.

2:8–14 Rahab willingly surrendered to the God of Israel. She and her people saw no way of escape from the certain doom that was coming. Instead of making a futile attempt to escape, Rahab sought mercy from the only available source of help. We, too, must recognize that we

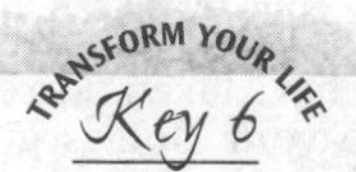

Faith to Enter the Promised Land

Joshua 1:1–9 Detours and delays, often the results of our fears and unfaithfulness, frequently hinder us in our journey toward spiritual growth. Yet God has promised to bring a joyous outcome to our difficult journey—to lead us from the dry, arid wildernesses of our lives into a fruitful promised land. So why do we allow our doubts and insecurities to slow our spiritual progress?

God led the nation of Israel out of bondage in Egypt, through the wilderness, to the edge of the promised land. But as they stood on the border, looking into the fruitful and prosperous land of Canaan, the Israelites lacked the faith and courage to go in and conquer the land. As a result, they wandered for forty years in the wilderness, and only their descendants (with the exception of Joshua and Caleb) were allowed to enter the promised land. Just before they entered the land, the Lord told them, "Be strong and courageous. Do not be terrified; do not be discouraged, for the LORD your God will be with you wherever you go" (1:9).

Like the Israelites, we have received promises of blessings from the Lord. The Lord revealed his desires for his people when he asserted, "I know the plans I have for you . . . plans to prosper you and not to harm you, plans to give you hope and a future" (Jeremiah 29:11). We need to be courageous. We need to believe the promises God has given us. No matter how long we have been lost in the wilderness and no matter how hopeless the future may yet seem, God can transform our years of wandering into a purposeful journey and lead us into the land he has promised us.

Turn to Judges 7.

that the LORD has given this land to you and
that a great fear of you has fallen on us, so that
all who live in this country are melting in fear
because of you. 10We have heard how the LORD
dried up the water of the Red Sea[a] for you
when you came out of Egypt, and what you did
to Sihon and Og, the two kings of the Amorites
east of the Jordan, whom you completely destroyed.[b] 11When we heard of it, our hearts
melted and everyone's courage failed because of
you, for the LORD your God is God in heaven
above and on the earth below. 12Now then,
please swear to me by the LORD that you will
show kindness to my family, because I have
shown kindness to you. Give me a sure sign
13that you will spare the lives of my father and
mother, my brothers and sisters, and all who
belong to them, and that you will save us from
death."

14"Our lives for your lives!" the men assured
her. "If you don't tell what we are doing, we
will treat you kindly and faithfully when the
LORD gives us the land."

15So she let them down by a rope through the
window, for the house she lived in was part of
the city wall. 16Now she had said to them, "Go
to the hills so the pursuers will not find you.
Hide yourselves there three days until they return, and then go on your way."

17The men said to her, "This oath you made
us swear will not be binding on us 18unless,
when we enter the land, you have tied this scarlet cord in the window through which you let us
down, and unless you have brought your father
and mother, your brothers and all your family
into your house. 19If anyone goes outside your
house into the street, his blood will be on his
own head; we will not be responsible. As for
anyone who is in the house with you, his blood
will be on our head if a hand is laid on him.
20But if you tell what we are doing, we will be
released from the oath you made us swear."

21"Agreed," she replied. "Let it be as you say."
So she sent them away and they departed. And
she tied the scarlet cord in the window.

22When they left, they went into the hills and
stayed there three days, until the pursuers had
searched all along the road and returned with-

[a]10 Hebrew *Yam Suph;* that is, Sea of Reeds
[b]10 The Hebrew term refers to the irrevocable giving over of things or persons to the LORD, often by totally destroying them.

---

cannot escape God's impending judgment for our sin. Our only hope is to seek mercy from God, granted through his Son, Jesus Christ.

2:15–21 Rahab completed her task of helping the spies by providing them with a rope, a window hidden from sight and a plan (hide three days in the hills until it is safe) for their safe return to their people. The spies, in turn, established the ground rules of responsibility for Rahab and her family. They outlined the specific requirements of the relationship, the rewards for success and the punishments for failure. Rahab shows us that God can use each one of us, no matter how terrible our past or how unworthy we may feel.

Rahab & Family

It is amazing that a pagan prostitute would demonstrate even rudimentary trust in God, but because Rahab believed, Joshua found an unlikely ally waiting within the city walls of Jericho. As the trumpets blared and the people thunderously marched, Rahab gathered her family members about her in anticipation of rescue. A single scarlet cord tied to her window warned the conquerors to spare the people within. Thanks to her surprising faith, Rahab's family was plucked from the ruins.

Given her line of work, Rahab probably wasn't accustomed to setting limits on her behavior. It's possible that she wasn't even aware that her profession was a sin in God's eyes. Yet Rahab's faith, like her job, was likely born of necessity. She was practical, and it made sense to believe in this powerful Hebrew God. She watched as fear paralyzed her people, and she recognized her need for something stronger than herself in this situation—her deep-seated need for God. Jericho's fall was inevitable. The God who parted seas could surely topple walls. Rahab's ability to see reality prompted her faith.

Aiding Joshua's men was a risky business, yet Rahab acted with courage and daring. She proved herself faithful by concealing the spies and giving them vital information. Rahab's strategy of deceiving the king might be questionable, although nowhere in Scripture is she criticized for her methods. Instead, Rahab is extolled as an example of righteousness and faith.

Following the rescue, God gave Rahab what she probably felt was no longer possible in Jericho: the opportunity to break with the past, redirect her course and build a new life. Rahab and her relatives found a home among the Israelites. But there was more. Rahab married Salmon and was blessed with a son, Boaz. Boaz would become the great-grandfather of King David, from whose line Jesus would descend. Rahab's transformation proves once again that God is in the business of turning lives around. Rahab shines as a stellar example of a second chance, a forgiven past and a redeemed life. Though our spiritual renewal may not be as dramatic as Rahab's, God is able to pick up our broken pieces and bring about fresh beginnings for us.

STRENGTHS AND ACCOMPLISHMENTS:

Rahab's faith in God was made visible by her actions.

Rahab had a deep love and concern for her family.

Rahab saw the truth and acknowledged the hopeless reality of her situation.

She sought help from the right source: God and his people.

WEAKNESSES AND MISTAKES:

Rahab's initial trust in God seems to have been motivated by pragmatism and fear rather than by loving gratitude.

LESSONS FROM HER LIFE:

God is alive and available to facilitate fresh starts when we cooperate with his plans.

Nothing is impossible with God.

A proper view of God should convince us of his power and worth.

KEY VERSE:

"By faith the prostitute Rahab, because she welcomed the spies, was not killed with those who were disobedient" (Hebrews 11:31).

Rahab's story is told in Joshua 2:1–21; 6:17–25. She is also mentioned in Matthew 1:5; Hebrews 11:31 and James 2:25.

out finding them. 23Then the two men started
back. They went down out of the hills, forded
the river and came to Joshua son of Nun and
told him everything that had happened to
them. 24They said to Joshua, "The LORD has
surely given the whole land into our hands; all
the people are melting in fear because of us."

Crossing the Jordan

3 Early in the morning Joshua and all the
Israelites set out from Shittim and went to
the Jordan, where they camped before crossing
over. 2After three days the officers went
throughout the camp, 3giving orders to the people: "When you see the ark of the covenant of
the LORD your God, and the priests, who are
Levites, carrying it, you are to move out from
your positions and follow it. 4Then you will
know which way to go, since you have never
been this way before. But keep a distance of
about a thousand yards[a] between you and the
ark; do not go near it."

5Joshua told the people, "Consecrate yourselves, for tomorrow the LORD will do amazing
things among you."

6Joshua said to the priests, "Take up the ark
of the covenant and pass on ahead of the
people." So they took it up and went ahead of
them.

7And the LORD said to Joshua, "Today I will
begin to exalt you in the eyes of all Israel, so
they may know that I am with you as I was with
Moses. 8Tell the priests who carry the ark of the
covenant: 'When you reach the edge of the Jordan's waters, go and stand in the river.' "

9Joshua said to the Israelites, "Come here
and listen to the words of the LORD your God.
10This is how you will know that the living God
is among you and that he will certainly drive
out before you the Canaanites, Hittites, Hivites,
Perizzites, Girgashites, Amorites and Jebusites.
11See, the ark of the covenant of the Lord of all
the earth will go into the Jordan ahead of you.
12Now then, choose twelve men from the tribes
of Israel, one from each tribe. 13And as soon as
the priests who carry the ark of the LORD—the
Lord of all the earth—set foot in the Jordan, its
waters flowing downstream will be cut off and
stand up in a heap."

14So when the people broke camp to cross
the Jordan, the priests carrying the ark of the
covenant went ahead of them. 15Now the Jordan is at flood stage all during harvest. Yet as
soon as the priests who carried the ark reached
the Jordan and their feet touched the water's
edge, 16the water from upstream stopped flowing. It piled up in a heap a great distance away,
at a town called Adam in the vicinity of Zarethan, while the water flowing down to the Sea
of the Arabah (the Salt Sea [b]) was completely
cut off. So the people crossed over opposite
Jericho. 17The priests who carried the ark of the
covenant of the LORD stood firm on dry ground
in the middle of the Jordan, while all Israel
passed by until the whole nation had completed the crossing on dry ground.

4 When the whole nation had finished crossing the Jordan, the LORD said to Joshua,
2"Choose twelve men from among the people,
one from each tribe, 3and tell them to take up
twelve stones from the middle of the Jordan
from right where the priests stood and to carry
them over with you and put them down at the
place where you stay tonight."

4So Joshua called together the twelve men he
had appointed from the Israelites, one from
each tribe, 5and said to them, "Go over before
the ark of the LORD your God into the middle
of the Jordan. Each of you is to take up a stone
on his shoulder, according to the number of the
tribes of the Israelites, 6to serve as a sign among
you. In the future, when your children ask you,
'What do these stones mean?' 7tell them that
the flow of the Jordan was cut off before the ark
of the covenant of the LORD. When it crossed
the Jordan, the waters of the Jordan were cut off.
These stones are to be a memorial to the people
of Israel forever."

[a]4 Hebrew *about two thousand cubits* (about 900 meters)
[b]16 That is, the Dead Sea

3:1–6 These were anxious times for Joshua and the people. The Israelites set out on their trek to the promised land but then had to delay their entrance into the land for three full days while their leaders gave them instructions. Those instructions dealt with both the physical and spiritual realms. The people were commanded to remain approximately a half-mile behind the ark of the covenant when the priests carried it, and they were to dedicate themselves to God. In these ways the Israelites would understand that they were not to try to run ahead of God but were to receive their direction from him and that they were supposed to commit themselves to obeying him. No doubt it was as difficult then as it is now to follow God's plan rather than rebel and go our own way.

3:7–14 God promised to drive out the enemies of Israel if the Israelites were obedient to him. Furthermore, in order for the people to see the power of God at work, the priests, acting by faith, had to carry the ark of the covenant and step into the Jordan River. Would God allow Joshua to look foolish, or would God act in the way he had promised? The Jordan River was at flood stage and hence extremely dangerous, if not impossible, to cross without God's help. But Joshua did not doubt God; he instructed the priests to stand in the river. Often God places us at a point where we must either stand for him or show that we don't really trust him. If we trust in God, we can be sure that he will never disappoint us.

4:1–7 The priests faithfully remained standing in the riverbed until the entire nation of Israel had crossed into the promised land. Joshua, at the command of God, then sent twelve men back to the place where the priests were standing. Those men were to collect one stone per tribe to set up as a memorial that would remind them and their descendants of what God had done on their behalf as they moved into the promised land. If the people ever became discouraged when they faced powerful enemies in the future, the stones would serve as a visible reminder of God's greatness. As God grants us maturity in our spiritual journey, we should establish monuments, reminders of his presence with us.

8So the Israelites did as Joshua commanded
them. They took twelve stones from the middle
of the Jordan, according to the number of the
tribes of the Israelites, as the LORD had told
Joshua; and they carried them over with them
to their camp, where they put them down.
9Joshua set up the twelve stones that had
been[a] in the middle of the Jordan at the spot
where the priests who carried the ark of the
covenant had stood. And they are there to this
day.

10Now the priests who carried the ark remained standing in the middle of the Jordan
until everything the LORD had commanded
Joshua was done by the people, just as Moses
had directed Joshua. The people hurried over,
11and as soon as all of them had crossed, the ark
of the LORD and the priests came to the other
side while the people watched. 12The men of
Reuben, Gad and the half-tribe of Manasseh
crossed over, armed, in front of the Israelites, as
Moses had directed them. 13About forty thousand armed for battle crossed over before the
LORD to the plains of Jericho for war.

14That day the LORD exalted Joshua in the
sight of all Israel; and they revered him all the
days of his life, just as they had revered Moses.

15Then the LORD said to Joshua, 16"Command the priests carrying the ark of the Testimony to come up out of the Jordan."

17So Joshua commanded the priests, "Come
up out of the Jordan."

18And the priests came up out of the river
carrying the ark of the covenant of the LORD. No
sooner had they set their feet on the dry ground
than the waters of the Jordan returned to their
place and ran at flood stage as before.

19On the tenth day of the first month the
people went up from the Jordan and camped at
Gilgal on the eastern border of Jericho. 20And
Joshua set up at Gilgal the twelve stones they
had taken out of the Jordan. 21He said to the
Israelites, "In the future when your descendants
ask their fathers, 'What do these stones mean?'
22tell them, 'Israel crossed the Jordan on dry
ground.' 23For the LORD your God dried up the
Jordan before you until you had crossed over.
The LORD your God did to the Jordan just what
he had done to the Red Sea[b] when he dried it
up before us until we had crossed over. 24He did
this so that all the peoples of the earth might
know that the hand of the LORD is powerful and
so that you might always fear the LORD your
God."

Circumcision at Gilgal

5 Now when all the Amorite kings west of
the Jordan and all the Canaanite kings
along the coast heard how the LORD had dried
up the Jordan before the Israelites until we
had crossed over, their hearts melted and
they no longer had the courage to face the Israelites.

2At that time the LORD said to Joshua, "Make
flint knives and circumcise the Israelites again."
3So Joshua made flint knives and circumcised
the Israelites at Gibeath Haaraloth.[c]

4Now this is why he did so: All those who
came out of Egypt—all the men of military age—
died in the desert on the way after leaving
Egypt. 5All the people that came out had been
circumcised, but all the people born in the
desert during the journey from Egypt had not.
6The Israelites had moved about in the desert
forty years until all the men who were of military age when they left Egypt had died, since
they had not obeyed the LORD. For the LORD
had sworn to them that they would not see the
land that he had solemnly promised their fathers to give us, a land flowing with milk and
honey. 7So he raised up their sons in their place,
and these were the ones Joshua circumcised.
They were still uncircumcised because they had
not been circumcised on the way. 8And after the
whole nation had been circumcised, they remained where they were in camp until they
were healed.

9Then the LORD said to Joshua, "Today I
have rolled away the reproach of Egypt from

[a]9 Or *Joshua also set up twelve stones* [b]23 Hebrew *Yam Suph;* that is, Sea of Reeds [c]3 *Gibeath Haaraloth* means *hill of foreskins.*

4:8–14 Joshua took a direct interest in remembering the greatness of God and honoring the faith of the priests by personally erecting a permanent memorial in the middle of the river. After Joshua crossed the river, God raised him to a new status in the eyes of the people—he was honored in the same way that his predecessor Moses had been. Sometimes it helps to commemorate events in which God provided a way when everything appeared hopeless. Then we can remember our own monuments to God's faithfulness whenever we encounter times of doubt.

4:15–24 Israel's leaders set up a monument to God at Gilgal with the stones from the Jordan River. Joshua explained that this would serve as a reminder of the miracle God had performed—the drying up of the flooded Jordan River. This miracle was reminiscent of God's deliverance of the Israelites forty years earlier when the people crossed the Red Sea on dry ground (see Exodus 14). We must remember that God is all-powerful and cares for us. Knowing that God has rescued us in the past can help us trust in his ability to save us today.

5:1–9 Although the Amorites admitted they were helpless before the God of Israel, they did not turn to him for help. The people of Israel, however, took steps to ensure that their own relationship with God was as it should be. In an act of obedience, the Israelites circumcised all the males among them, thereby removing the shame of their uncircumcision. Fortunately, we do not have to go through a physical cutting to be rid of our shame, but we do have to go through the painful process of acknowledging our sin and asking God to remove the shame from us. This process can be so painful that we may be tempted to hide our shame rather than ask God to remove it. We must learn that obedience, while sometimes painful, is the only route to a strong relationship with God.

you." So the place has been called Gilgal[a] to this day.

10On the evening of the fourteenth day of the month, while camped at Gilgal on the plains of Jericho, the Israelites celebrated the Passover. 11The day after the Passover, that very day, they ate some of the produce of the land: unleavened bread and roasted grain. 12The manna stopped the day after[b] they ate this food from the land; there was no longer any manna for the Israelites, but that year they ate of the produce of Canaan.

The Fall of Jericho

13Now when Joshua was near Jericho, he looked up and saw a man standing in front of him with a drawn sword in his hand. Joshua went up to him and asked, "Are you for us or for our enemies?"

14"Neither," he replied, "but as commander of the army of the LORD I have now come." Then Joshua fell facedown to the ground in reverence, and asked him, "What message does my Lord[c] have for his servant?"

15The commander of the LORD's army replied, "Take off your sandals, for the place where you are standing is holy." And Joshua did so.

6 Now Jericho was tightly shut up because of the Israelites. No one went out and no one came in.

2Then the LORD said to Joshua, "See, I have delivered Jericho into your hands, along with its king and its fighting men. 3March around the city once with all the armed men. Do this for six days. 4Have seven priests carry trumpets of rams' horns in front of the ark. On the seventh day, march around the city seven times, with the priests blowing the trumpets. 5When you hear them sound a long blast on the trumpets, have all the people give a loud shout; then the wall of the city will collapse and the people will go up, every man straight in."

6So Joshua son of Nun called the priests and said to them, "Take up the ark of the covenant of the LORD and have seven priests carry trumpets in front of it." 7And he ordered the people, "Advance! March around the city, with the armed guard going ahead of the ark of the LORD."

8When Joshua had spoken to the people, the seven priests carrying the seven trumpets before the LORD went forward, blowing their trumpets, and the ark of the LORD's covenant followed them. 9The armed guard marched ahead of the priests who blew the trumpets, and the rear guard followed the ark. All this time the trumpets were sounding. 10But Joshua had commanded the people, "Do not give a war cry, do not raise your voices, do not say a word until the day I tell you to shout. Then shout!" 11So he had the ark of the LORD carried around the city, circling it once. Then the people returned to camp and spent the night there.

12Joshua got up early the next morning and the priests took up the ark of the LORD. 13The seven priests carrying the seven trumpets went forward, marching before the ark of the LORD and blowing the trumpets. The armed men went ahead of them and the rear guard followed the ark of the LORD, while the trumpets kept sounding. 14So on the second day they marched around the city once and returned to the camp. They did this for six days.

15On the seventh day, they got up at daybreak and marched around the city seven times in the same manner, except that on that day they circled the city seven times. 16The seventh time around, when the priests sounded the

[a] 9 *Gilgal* sounds like the Hebrew for *roll.* [b] 12 Or *the day* [c] 14 Or *lord*

5:10–12 The celebration of the Passover—a remembrance of God's deliverance of his people from Egypt forty years earlier—undoubtedly bolstered the Israelites' faith as they faced the many battles ahead. God's miraculous provision of manna also stopped at this time. Now that the Israelites owned productive land, they no longer needed food from heaven. This change was a reminder that God would provide his people with what they needed in various ways, depending on their circumstances. They needed to trust him to act on their behalf in various ways in the future. God works with us in different ways at varying stages of our spiritual development too. When life isn't easy, it is never a sign of abandonment by God. Rather, God often allows struggles in our lives so that we will grow in wisdom and faith.

5:13–15 Note two important considerations regarding the identity of the commander of the LORD's army: (1) He allowed Joshua to bow down in reverence before him, and (2) the place where the commander stood was considered to be holy ground (see Exodus 3:1–6). This commander was more than a human being and more than a mere angel; he was none other than God himself. When he recognized who the stranger was, Joshua quickly deferred all claims of leadership to him. Like Joshua, we need to relinquish control of our lives to God. It is never too late to acknowledge God's lordship over us and to ask him to lead us in life's battles.

6:1–14 Israel was ready to attack, but God told them to wait. God required his people to do something that visibly appeared to be very foolish. They were commanded to march around the city, day after day. The Israelites obeyed God and persisted in their faith, not fully understanding how God would destroy the walls of Jericho merely by their obedient marching. When we face barriers to our spiritual growth, God can make those barriers come tumbling down, allowing us to be victorious. But we need to do things his way, even if we don't always understand why.

6:15–21 Once more Israel had to wait. The seventh day, on the verge of initiating the attack, the people of Israel were required to march seven times around the city. They were also prohibited from enjoying the spoils of victory that were to be dedicated to God—they were not to steal from God. Finally, Israel was given the go-ahead. In obedience to God, they pressed the attack and secured the victory, destroying their enemies completely. Learning to wait on God is part of growing toward maturity in our faith. God calls us to trust him, especially when we want to move ahead without delay.

trumpet blast, Joshua commanded the people, "Shout! For the LORD has given you the city! 17The city and all that is in it are to be devoted[a] to the LORD. Only Rahab the prostitute[b] and all who are with her in her house shall be spared, because she hid the spies we sent. 18But keep away from the devoted things, so that you will not bring about your own destruction by taking any of them. Otherwise you will make the camp of Israel liable to destruction and bring trouble on it. 19All the silver and gold and the articles of bronze and iron are sacred to the LORD and must go into his treasury."

20When the trumpets sounded, the people shouted, and at the sound of the trumpet, when the people gave a loud shout, the wall collapsed; so every man charged straight in, and they took the city. 21They devoted the city to the LORD and destroyed with the sword every living thing in it—men and women, young and old, cattle, sheep and donkeys.

22Joshua said to the two men who had spied out the land, "Go into the prostitute's house and bring her out and all who belong to her, in accordance with your oath to her." 23So the young men who had done the spying went in and brought out Rahab, her father and mother and brothers and all who belonged to her. They brought out her entire family and put them in a place outside the camp of Israel.

24Then they burned the whole city and everything in it, but they put the silver and gold and the articles of bronze and iron into the treasury of the LORD's house. 25But Joshua spared Rahab the prostitute, with her family and all who belonged to her, because she hid the men Joshua had sent as spies to Jericho—and she lives among the Israelites to this day.

26At that time Joshua pronounced this solemn oath: "Cursed before the LORD is the man who undertakes to rebuild this city, Jericho:

"At the cost of his firstborn son
will he lay its foundations;
at the cost of his youngest
will he set up its gates."

27So the LORD was with Joshua, and his fame spread throughout the land.

Achan's Sin

7 But the Israelites acted unfaithfully in regard to the devoted things[c]; Achan son of Carmi, the son of Zimri,[d] the son of Zerah, of the tribe of Judah, took some of them. So the LORD's anger burned against Israel.

2Now Joshua sent men from Jericho to Ai, which is near Beth Aven to the east of Bethel, and told them, "Go up and spy out the region." So the men went up and spied out Ai.

3When they returned to Joshua, they said, "Not all the people will have to go up against Ai. Send two or three thousand men to take it and do not weary all the people, for only a few men are there." 4So about three thousand men went up; but they were routed by the men of Ai, 5who killed about thirty-six of them. They chased the Israelites from the city gate as far as the stone quarries[e] and struck them down on the slopes. At this the hearts of the people melted and became like water.

6Then Joshua tore his clothes and fell facedown to the ground before the ark of the LORD, remaining there till evening. The elders of Israel did the same, and sprinkled dust on their heads. 7And Joshua said, "Ah, Sovereign LORD, why did you ever bring this people across the Jordan to deliver us into the hands of the Amorites to destroy us? If only we had been content to stay on the other side of the Jordan! 8O Lord, what can I say, now that Israel has been routed by its enemies? 9The Canaanites and the other people of the country will hear about this and they will surround us and wipe out our name from the earth. What then will you do for your own great name?"

10The LORD said to Joshua, "Stand up! What are you doing down on your face? 11Israel has sinned; they have violated my covenant, which I commanded them to keep. They have taken some of the devoted things; they have stolen,

[a]17 The Hebrew term refers to the irrevocable giving over of things or persons to the LORD, often by totally destroying them; also in verses 18 and 21. [b]17 Or possibly *innkeeper*; also in verses 22 and 25 [c]1 The Hebrew term refers to the irrevocable giving over of things or persons to the LORD, often by totally destroying them; also in verses 11, 12, 13 and 15. [d]1 See Septuagint and 1 Chron. 2:6; Hebrew *Zabdi*; also in verses 17 and 18. [e]5 Or *as far as Shebarim*

6:22–25 Joshua remembered the promise his spies had made to Rahab the prostitute. He commanded his men to fulfill that promise and provide safe passage for her and her family. After the destruction of Jericho, Rahab and her relatives began a new life with Israel because they had served God by protecting the spies. God's provision for Rahab should be significant to each of us. God honored her faith and obedience in spite of Rahab's sinful lifestyle as a prostitute. Rahab's choices are bold reminders that we should come to God as we are—sinful and disobedient—rather than try to fix ourselves first.

7:1–9 The Israelites became overconfident because of their victory over Jericho and proceeded to attack the small city of Ai without first consulting God. Their small army was soundly defeated because God was angry with Israel for the sin of Achan. The nation of Israel became utterly demoralized. Even Joshua became discouraged and complained to God, blaming him for their loss. We must be careful not to take back control of our life once we have turned it over to God. We must submit our whole life to his control—and leave it there.

7:10–12 God displays his anger with Joshua in this passage, chastising him for complaining and for not calling his people into accountability for their sin. The people needed to realize that victory was impossible for all those who disobeyed God. We also must realize that our sins affect others. Our choices and our lifestyles affect our families and friends. But rather than hide in shame, God wants us to confess our mistakes to him and to each other so that we will be able to overcome the sin in our lives.

they have lied, they have put them with their own possessions. 12That is why the Israelites cannot stand against their enemies; they turn their backs and run because they have been made liable to destruction. I will not be with you anymore unless you destroy whatever among you is devoted to destruction.

13"Go, consecrate the people. Tell them, 'Consecrate yourselves in preparation for tomorrow; for this is what the LORD, the God of Israel, says: That which is devoted is among you, O Israel. You cannot stand against your enemies until you remove it.

14" 'In the morning, present yourselves tribe by tribe. The tribe that the LORD takes shall come forward clan by clan; the clan that the LORD takes shall come forward family by family; and the family that the LORD takes shall come forward man by man. 15He who is caught with the devoted things shall be destroyed by fire, along with all that belongs to him. He has violated the covenant of the LORD and has done a disgraceful thing in Israel!' "

16Early the next morning Joshua had Israel come forward by tribes, and Judah was taken. 17The clans of Judah came forward, and he took the Zerahites. He had the clan of the Zerahites come forward by families, and Zimri was taken. 18Joshua had his family come forward man by man, and Achan son of Carmi, the son of Zimri, the son of Zerah, of the tribe of Judah, was taken.

19Then Joshua said to Achan, "My son, give glory to the LORD,[a] the God of Israel, and give him the praise.[b] Tell me what you have done; do not hide it from me."

20Achan replied, "It is true! I have sinned against the LORD, the God of Israel. This is what I have done: 21When I saw in the plunder a beautiful robe from Babylonia,[c] two hundred shekels[d] of silver and a wedge of gold weighing fifty shekels,[e] I coveted them and took them. They are hidden in the ground inside my tent, with the silver underneath."

22So Joshua sent messengers, and they ran to the tent, and there it was, hidden in his tent, with the silver underneath. 23They took the things from the tent, brought them to Joshua and all the Israelites and spread them out before the LORD.

24Then Joshua, together with all Israel, took Achan son of Zerah, the silver, the robe, the gold wedge, his sons and daughters, his cattle, donkeys and sheep, his tent and all that he had, to the Valley of Achor. 25Joshua said, "Why have you brought this trouble on us? The LORD will bring trouble on you today."

Then all Israel stoned him, and after they had stoned the rest, they burned them. 26Over Achan they heaped up a large pile of rocks, which remains to this day. Then the LORD turned from his fierce anger. Therefore that place has been called the Valley of Achor[f] ever since.

Ai Destroyed

8 Then the LORD said to Joshua, "Do not be afraid; do not be discouraged. Take the whole army with you, and go up and attack Ai. For I have delivered into your hands the king of Ai, his people, his city and his land. 2You shall do to Ai and its king as you did to Jericho and its king, except that you may carry off their plunder and livestock for yourselves. Set an ambush behind the city."

3So Joshua and the whole army moved out to attack Ai. He chose thirty thousand of his best fighting men and sent them out at night 4with these orders: "Listen carefully. You are to set an ambush behind the city. Don't go very far from it. All of you be on the alert. 5I and all those with me will advance on the city, and when the men come out against us, as they did before, we will flee from them. 6They will pursue us until we have lured them away from the city, for they will say, 'They are running away from us as they did before.' So when we flee from them, 7you are to rise up from ambush and take the city. The LORD your God will give it into your hand. 8When you have taken the city, set it on fire. Do what the LORD has commanded. See to it; you have my orders."

9Then Joshua sent them off, and they went to the place of ambush and lay in wait between Bethel and Ai, to the west of Ai—but Joshua spent that night with the people.

10Early the next morning Joshua mustered

[a]19 A solemn charge to tell the truth [b]19 Or *and confess to him* [c]21 Hebrew *Shinar* [d]21 That is, about 5 pounds (about 2.3 kilograms)
[e]21 That is, about 1 1/4 pounds (about 0.6 kilogram)
[f]26 *Achor* means *trouble.*

7:20–26 Once Achan was identified as the guilty party, he confessed his sin, but his confession came too late. Had he confessed earlier, the outcome might have been different. After Achan and his family were stoned to death, Israel erected another monument of stones (see 4:9, 20). This monument, however, was not to commemorate God's great power of deliverance but to serve as a reminder that the sin of one person can negatively affect the well-being of many people. If we are to learn from our mistakes, we must remember not only the mistake and its result but also what tempted us to turn away from God in the first place.

8:1–9 Once again God provided Joshua with detailed plans to follow. Joshua then used his God-given reasoning to assess the situation and develop a detailed strategy for defeating his enemies. For such a plan to be successful, the soldiers had to exercise discipline and self-control, attacking only when the enemy was most vulnerable. By using God's methods, Joshua and his people demonstrated that they had learned from their defeat and had grown spiritually. God's plans often require our discipline and self-control too. These character traits are attained through work and struggle.

8:10–23 The Israelites executed God's plan exactly as he gave it to them. Joshua relied on God in the midst of the battle, and God gave the Israelites victory. When our desires, urges and impulses lead us away from God, it may help to remember that Joshua's faith in God did not cre-

his men, and he and the leaders of Israel marched before them to Ai. [11]The entire force that was with him marched up and approached the city and arrived in front of it. They set up camp north of Ai, with the valley between them and the city. [12]Joshua had taken about five thousand men and set them in ambush between Bethel and Ai, to the west of the city. [13]They had the soldiers take up their positions—all those in the camp to the north of the city and the ambush to the west of it. That night Joshua went into the valley.

[14]When the king of Ai saw this, he and all the men of the city hurried out early in the morning to meet Israel in battle at a certain place overlooking the Arabah. But he did not know that an ambush had been set against him behind the city. [15]Joshua and all Israel let themselves be driven back before them, and they fled toward the desert. [16]All the men of Ai were called to pursue them, and they pursued Joshua and were lured away from the city. [17]Not a man remained in Ai or Bethel who did not go after Israel. They left the city open and went in pursuit of Israel.

[18]Then the LORD said to Joshua, "Hold out toward Ai the javelin that is in your hand, for into your hand I will deliver the city." So Joshua held out his javelin toward Ai. [19]As soon as he did this, the men in the ambush rose quickly from their position and rushed forward. They entered the city and captured it and quickly set it on fire.

[20]The men of Ai looked back and saw the smoke of the city rising against the sky, but they had no chance to escape in any direction, for the Israelites who had been fleeing toward the desert had turned back against their pursuers. [21]For when Joshua and all Israel saw that the ambush had taken the city and that smoke was going up from the city, they turned around and attacked the men of Ai. [22]The men of the ambush also came out of the city against them, so that they were caught in the middle, with Israelites on both sides. Israel cut them down, leaving them neither survivors nor fugitives. [23]But they took the king of Ai alive and brought him to Joshua.

[24]When Israel had finished killing all the men of Ai in the fields and in the desert where they had chased them, and when every one of them had been put to the sword, all the Israelites returned to Ai and killed those who were in it. [25]Twelve thousand men and women fell that day—all the people of Ai. [26]For Joshua did not draw back the hand that held out his javelin until he had destroyed[a] all who lived in Ai. [27]But Israel did carry off for themselves the livestock and plunder of this city, as the LORD had instructed Joshua.

[28]So Joshua burned Ai and made it a permanent heap of ruins, a desolate place to this day. [29]He hung the king of Ai on a tree and left him there until evening. At sunset, Joshua ordered them to take his body from the tree and throw it down at the entrance of the city gate. And they raised a large pile of rocks over it, which remains to this day.

The Covenant Renewed at Mount Ebal

[30]Then Joshua built on Mount Ebal an altar to the LORD, the God of Israel, [31]as Moses the servant of the LORD had commanded the Israelites. He built it according to what is written in the Book of the Law of Moses—an altar of uncut stones, on which no iron tool had been used. On it they offered to the LORD burnt offerings and sacrificed fellowship offerings.[b] [32]There, in the presence of the Israelites, Joshua copied on stones the law of Moses, which he had written. [33]All Israel, aliens and citizens alike, with their elders, officials and judges, were standing on both sides of the ark of the covenant of the LORD, facing those who carried it—the priests, who were Levites. Half of the people stood in front of Mount Gerizim and half of them in front of Mount Ebal, as Moses the servant of the LORD had formerly commanded when he gave instructions to bless the people of Israel.

[34]Afterward, Joshua read all the words of the law—the blessings and the curses—just as it is written in the Book of the Law. [35]There was not a word of all that Moses had commanded that Joshua did not read to the whole assembly of Israel, including the women and children, and the aliens who lived among them.

The Gibeonite Deception

9 Now when all the kings west of the Jordan heard about these things—those in the hill

[a]26 The Hebrew term refers to the irrevocable giving over of things or persons to the LORD, often by totally destroying them. [b]31 Traditionally *peace offerings*

---

ate a life free from battles. The battles were to be fought and won through continued reliance on God. Like Joshua, we need to persevere with God's strength and resist the tendency to run from our own personal battles.

8:24–35 After the Israelites' great victory, the people built a monument to God and erected an altar to him at Mount Ebal. Joshua read the words of the law—the blessings and curses—to the people to remind them of how God expected them to act in the promised land. Today, just as in Joshua's day, God's Word provides us with the guidance we need in setting limits on our own behavior—limits that are neither too lax nor too rigid, but balanced by godly principles.

9:1–15 Frightened by the defeats of Jericho and Ai by Israel, the kings of the southern coastal regions formed a coalition to attack Israel. The Gibeonites, however, took a different tactic. Recognizing their helplessness before Israel, they wisely, but deceptively, sought peace. By establishing a peace treaty, the Gibeonites avoided becoming Israel's next victims. The Israelites failed to investigate the Gibeonites' claims thoroughly or seek God's guidance in the matter. As a result, the Israelites entered into a covenant that was a violation of God's command (see Exodus 23:31–33). We must always examine the agreements we make and the relationships we form. We must ask whether God would approve of them at this particular time. A

country, in the western foothills, and along the entire coast of the Great Sea[a] as far as Lebanon (the kings of the Hittites, Amorites, Canaanites, Perizzites, Hivites and Jebusites)— [2]they came together to make war against Joshua and Israel.

[3]However, when the people of Gibeon heard what Joshua had done to Jericho and Ai, [4]they resorted to a ruse: They went as a delegation whose donkeys were loaded[b] with worn-out sacks and old wineskins, cracked and mended. [5]The men put worn and patched sandals on their feet and wore old clothes. All the bread of their food supply was dry and moldy. [6]Then they went to Joshua in the camp at Gilgal and said to him and the men of Israel, "We have come from a distant country; make a treaty with us."

[7]The men of Israel said to the Hivites, "But perhaps you live near us. How then can we make a treaty with you?"

[8]"We are your servants," they said to Joshua.

But Joshua asked, "Who are you and where do you come from?"

[9]They answered: "Your servants have come from a very distant country because of the fame of the LORD your God. For we have heard reports of him: all that he did in Egypt, [10]and all that he did to the two kings of the Amorites east of the Jordan—Sihon king of Heshbon, and Og king of Bashan, who reigned in Ashtaroth. [11]And our elders and all those living in our country said to us, 'Take provisions for your journey; go and meet them and say to them, "We are your servants; make a treaty with us."' [12]This bread of ours was warm when we packed it at home on the day we left to come to you. But now see how dry and moldy it is. [13]And these wineskins that we filled were new, but see how cracked they are. And our clothes and sandals are worn out by the very long journey."

[14]The men of Israel sampled their provisions but did not inquire of the LORD. [15]Then Joshua made a treaty of peace with them to let them live, and the leaders of the assembly ratified it by oath.

[16]Three days after they made the treaty with the Gibeonites, the Israelites heard that they were neighbors, living near them. [17]So the Israelites set out and on the third day came to their cities: Gibeon, Kephirah, Beeroth and Kiriath Jearim. [18]But the Israelites did not attack them, because the leaders of the assembly had sworn an oath to them by the LORD, the God of Israel.

The whole assembly grumbled against the leaders, [19]but all the leaders answered, "We have given them our oath by the LORD, the God of Israel, and we cannot touch them now. [20]This is what we will do to them: We will let them live, so that wrath will not fall on us for breaking the oath we swore to them." [21]They continued, "Let them live, but let them be woodcutters and water carriers for the entire community." So the leaders' promise to them was kept.

[22]Then Joshua summoned the Gibeonites and said, "Why did you deceive us by saying, 'We live a long way from you,' while actually you live near us? [23]You are now under a curse: You will never cease to serve as woodcutters and water carriers for the house of my God."

[24]They answered Joshua, "Your servants were clearly told how the LORD your God had commanded his servant Moses to give you the whole land and to wipe out all its inhabitants from before you. So we feared for our lives because of you, and that is why we did this. [25]We are now in your hands. Do to us whatever seems good and right to you."

[26]So Joshua saved them from the Israelites, and they did not kill them. [27]That day he made the Gibeonites woodcutters and water carriers for the community and for the altar of the LORD at the place the LORD would choose. And that is what they are to this day.

The Sun Stands Still

10 Now Adoni-Zedek king of Jerusalem heard that Joshua had taken Ai and totally destroyed[c] it, doing to Ai and its king as he had done to Jericho and its king, and that the people of Gibeon had made a treaty of peace with Israel and were living near them. [2]He and his people were very much alarmed at this, because Gibeon was an important city, like one of the royal cities; it was larger than Ai, and all its

[a] 1 That is, the Mediterranean [b] 4 Most Hebrew manuscripts; some Hebrew manuscripts, Vulgate and Syriac (see also Septuagint) *They prepared provisions and loaded their donkeys* [c] 1 The Hebrew term refers to the irrevocable giving over of things or persons to the LORD, often by totally destroying them; also in verses 28, 35, 37, 39 and 40.

---

seemingly right relationship at the wrong time will always produce ungodly results.

9:16–27 The leaders of Israel recognized their mistake and honored God by adhering to the conditions of the treaty. Likewise, the Gibeonites, who had confessed their deception, willingly accepted the consequences of their actions and exchanged their freedom for their lives, becoming servants of Israel. We are all aware that the results of some decisions last a lifetime. Surrendering to God involves giving up our attempts to save our own lives. We need to remember that our decision to live according to God's will offers us more freedom than the apparent freedom of going our own way.

10:1–11 The troubles associated with the undesirable treaty with Gibeon were compounded—Israel now had to fight on behalf of the Gibeonites. Israel accepted its obligation, and God promised Israel victory over all five kings. Although Joshua achieved success, his real victory came from God. God killed more of the enemy with hailstones than the entire Israelite army did with their weapons. If we examine our accomplishments, we will find that while we were working so hard, God was preparing a way that allowed us to do more than we could ever have done alone. We would be foolish to believe that all we are and have are due to our own efforts and abilities. Acknowledging God's hand in our past accomplishments allows us a firmer grasp on God's hand in the face of future challenges.

men were good fighters. 3So Adoni-Zedek king of Jerusalem appealed to Hoham king of Hebron, Piram king of Jarmuth, Japhia king of Lachish and Debir king of Eglon. 4"Come up and help me attack Gibeon," he said, "because it has made peace with Joshua and the Israelites."

5Then the five kings of the Amorites—the kings of Jerusalem, Hebron, Jarmuth, Lachish and Eglon—joined forces. They moved up with all their troops and took up positions against Gibeon and attacked it.

6The Gibeonites then sent word to Joshua in the camp at Gilgal: "Do not abandon your servants. Come up to us quickly and save us! Help us, because all the Amorite kings from the hill country have joined forces against us."

7So Joshua marched up from Gilgal with his entire army, including all the best fighting men. 8The LORD said to Joshua, "Do not be afraid of them; I have given them into your hand. Not one of them will be able to withstand you."

9After an all-night march from Gilgal, Joshua took them by surprise. 10The LORD threw them into confusion before Israel, who defeated them in a great victory at Gibeon. Israel pursued them along the road going up to Beth Horon and cut them down all the way to Azekah and Makkedah. 11As they fled before Israel on the road down from Beth Horon to Azekah, the LORD hurled large hailstones down on them from the sky, and more of them died from the hailstones than were killed by the swords of the Israelites.

12On the day the LORD gave the Amorites over to Israel, Joshua said to the LORD in the presence of Israel:

"O sun, stand still over Gibeon,
O moon, over the Valley of Aijalon."
13So the sun stood still,
and the moon stopped,
till the nation avenged itself on[a] its enemies,

as it is written in the Book of Jashar.

The sun stopped in the middle of the sky and delayed going down about a full day. 14There has never been a day like it before or since, a day when the LORD listened to a man. Surely the LORD was fighting for Israel!

15Then Joshua returned with all Israel to the camp at Gilgal.

Five Amorite Kings Killed

16Now the five kings had fled and hidden in the cave at Makkedah. 17When Joshua was told that the five kings had been found hiding in the cave at Makkedah, 18he said, "Roll large rocks up to the mouth of the cave, and post some men there to guard it. 19But don't stop! Pursue your enemies, attack them from the rear and don't let them reach their cities, for the LORD your God has given them into your hand."

20So Joshua and the Israelites destroyed them completely—almost to a man—but the few who were left reached their fortified cities. 21The whole army then returned safely to Joshua in the camp at Makkedah, and no one uttered a word against the Israelites.

22Joshua said, "Open the mouth of the cave and bring those five kings out to me." 23So they brought the five kings out of the cave—the kings of Jerusalem, Hebron, Jarmuth, Lachish and Eglon. 24When they had brought these kings to Joshua, he summoned all the men of Israel and said to the army commanders who had come with him, "Come here and put your feet on the necks of these kings." So they came forward and placed their feet on their necks.

25Joshua said to them, "Do not be afraid; do not be discouraged. Be strong and courageous. This is what the LORD will do to all the enemies you are going to fight." 26Then Joshua struck and killed the kings and hung them on five trees, and they were left hanging on the trees until evening.

27At sunset Joshua gave the order and they took them down from the trees and threw them into the cave where they had been hiding. At the mouth of the cave they placed large rocks, which are there to this day.

28That day Joshua took Makkedah. He put the city and its king to the sword and totally destroyed everyone in it. He left no survivors. And he did to the king of Makkedah as he had done to the king of Jericho.

Southern Cities Conquered

29Then Joshua and all Israel with him moved on from Makkedah to Libnah and attacked it. 30The LORD also gave that city and its king into Israel's hand. The city and everyone in it Joshua

[a] 13 Or *nation triumphed over*

10:12–15 Joshua's faith was rewarded by God's action. Joshua prayed that God would supernaturally provide additional daylight hours to enable Israel to win complete victory over the Amorite nation. God responded to Joshua's prayer by causing the sun and the moon to keep their respective positions in the sky until God himself claimed victory for Israel. For centuries, unbelievers have tried to explain away this miraculous example of God's divine intervention in the lives of his people. Unbelievers search for an intellectual explanation for these events rather than attributing them to God's power. We also sometimes tend to explain away the times when God miraculously intervenes in our lives. God does not call us to be ignorant, but we must be careful that we do not allow intellect to rob us of faith.

10:29–43 Joshua led God's people from city to city and from victory to victory. With each day came new success, as enemy after enemy was defeated in accordance with the commands of God. In these verses we see that no enemy will ever be too strong for God. If God could handle these great armies, he will certainly be able to handle our personal problems. Often we do not experience victory over our struggles because we stop our journey with God and go into battle alone, under our own power. We should always look to God and eagerly receive all the victories he has planned for us. He will work in our lives as we daily submit to his plan.

put to the sword. He left no survivors there. And
he did to its king as he had done to the king of
Jericho.
31Then Joshua and all Israel with him moved
on from Libnah to Lachish; he took up positions against it and attacked it. 32The LORD
handed Lachish over to Israel, and Joshua took
it on the second day. The city and everyone in
it he put to the sword, just as he had done to
Libnah. 33Meanwhile, Horam king of Gezer had
come up to help Lachish, but Joshua defeated
him and his army—until no survivors were left.
34Then Joshua and all Israel with him moved
on from Lachish to Eglon; they took up positions against it and attacked it. 35They captured
it that same day and put it to the sword and
totally destroyed everyone in it, just as they had
done to Lachish.
36Then Joshua and all Israel with him went
up from Eglon to Hebron and attacked it.
37They took the city and put it to the sword,
together with its king, its villages and everyone
in it. They left no survivors. Just as at Eglon, they
totally destroyed it and everyone in it.
38Then Joshua and all Israel with him turned
around and attacked Debir. 39They took the
city, its king and its villages, and put them to the
sword. Everyone in it they totally destroyed.
They left no survivors. They did to Debir and its
king as they had done to Libnah and its king
and to Hebron.
40So Joshua subdued the whole region, including the hill country, the Negev, the western
foothills and the mountain slopes, together
with all their kings. He left no survivors. He
totally destroyed all who breathed, just as the
LORD, the God of Israel, had commanded.
41Joshua subdued them from Kadesh Barnea to
Gaza and from the whole region of Goshen to
Gibeon. 42All these kings and their lands Joshua
conquered in one campaign, because the LORD,
the God of Israel, fought for Israel.
43Then Joshua returned with all Israel to the
camp at Gilgal.

Northern Kings Defeated

11 When Jabin king of Hazor heard of this,
he sent word to Jobab king of Madon,
to the kings of Shimron and Acshaph, 2and to
the northern kings who were in the mountains,
in the Arabah south of Kinnereth, in the western foothills and in Naphoth Dor[a] on the
west; 3to the Canaanites in the east and west; to
the Amorites, Hittites, Perizzites and Jebusites
in the hill country; and to the Hivites below
Hermon in the region of Mizpah. 4They came
out with all their troops and a large number of
horses and chariots—a huge army, as numerous
as the sand on the seashore. 5All these kings
joined forces and made camp together at the
Waters of Merom, to fight against Israel.
6The LORD said to Joshua, "Do not be afraid
of them, because by this time tomorrow I will
hand all of them over to Israel, slain. You are to
hamstring their horses and burn their chariots."
7So Joshua and his whole army came against
them suddenly at the Waters of Merom and
attacked them, 8and the LORD gave them into
the hand of Israel. They defeated them and pursued them all the way to Greater Sidon, to Misrephoth Maim, and to the Valley of Mizpah on
the east, until no survivors were left. 9Joshua
did to them as the LORD had directed: He hamstrung their horses and burned their chariots.
10At that time Joshua turned back and captured Hazor and put its king to the sword. (Hazor had been the head of all these kingdoms.)
11Everyone in it they put to the sword. They
totally destroyed[b] them, not sparing anything
that breathed, and he burned up Hazor itself.
12Joshua took all these royal cities and their
kings and put them to the sword. He totally
destroyed them, as Moses the servant of the
LORD had commanded. 13Yet Israel did not
burn any of the cities built on their mounds—
except Hazor, which Joshua burned. 14The Israelites carried off for themselves all the plunder
and livestock of these cities, but all the people they put to the sword until they completely destroyed them, not sparing anyone that
breathed. 15As the LORD commanded his servant Moses, so Moses commanded Joshua, and
Joshua did it; he left nothing undone of all that
the LORD commanded Moses.
16So Joshua took this entire land: the hill
country, all the Negev, the whole region of Goshen, the western foothills, the Arabah and the
mountains of Israel with their foothills, 17from
Mount Halak, which rises toward Seir, to Baal
Gad in the Valley of Lebanon below Mount

[a]2 Or *in the heights of Dor* [b]11 The Hebrew term refers to the irrevocable giving over of things or persons to the LORD, often by totally destroying them; also in verses 12, 20 and 21.

11:1–9 The situation looked hopeless for Joshua and Israel. Yet God reminded Joshua that he should act boldly because God himself would accomplish what seemed impossible. Joshua and his troops obeyed God and courageously attacked when the enemy least expected it. As promised, God gave Israel the victory. When the situations we face seem hopeless, we can look back to the example of Joshua and his people. God prevailed even when the prospects for victory were bleak. God has not changed. His power to take what we have and do great things with it continues and far exceeds whatever we could do or imagine.

11:16–23 Overtaking new territories in the promised land was not easy. There were constant battles that pitted the people of Israel against enemies entrenched in the land. Some of these enemies were the Anakites, the giants who had frightened the spies Moses sent into the land (see Numbers 13:25—14:25). With God's power, however, Israel conquered its worst fears. Whatever we fear the most today is easily handled by God's power. It often takes us a long time to realize what is so obvious: God has the power to turn defeat into victory, producing maximum results from minimal faith and obedience.

Hermon. He captured all their kings and struck
them down, putting them to death. 18Joshua
waged war against all these kings for a long
time. 19Except for the Hivites living in Gibeon,
not one city made a treaty of peace with the
Israelites, who took them all in battle. 20For
it was the LORD himself who hardened their
hearts to wage war against Israel, so that he
might destroy them totally, exterminating them
without mercy, as the LORD had commanded
Moses.

21At that time Joshua went and destroyed the
Anakites from the hill country: from Hebron,
Debir and Anab, from all the hill country of
Judah, and from all the hill country of Israel.
Joshua totally destroyed them and their towns.
22No Anakites were left in Israelite territory;
only in Gaza, Gath and Ashdod did any survive.
23So Joshua took the entire land, just as the
LORD had directed Moses, and he gave it as an
inheritance to Israel according to their tribal
divisions.

Then the land had rest from war.

List of Defeated Kings

12 These are the kings of the land whom
the Israelites had defeated and whose
territory they took over east of the Jordan, from
the Arnon Gorge to Mount Hermon, including
all the eastern side of the Arabah:

2Sihon king of the Amorites,
who reigned in Heshbon. He ruled from
Aroer on the rim of the Arnon Gorge—
from the middle of the gorge—to the Jabbok River, which is the border of the Ammonites. This included half of Gilead. 3He
also ruled over the eastern Arabah from
the Sea of Kinnereth[a] to the Sea of the
Arabah (the Salt Sea[b]), to Beth Jeshimoth, and then southward below the
slopes of Pisgah.

4And the territory of Og king of Bashan,
one of the last of the Rephaites, who
reigned in Ashtaroth and Edrei. 5He ruled
over Mount Hermon, Salecah, all of Bashan to the border of the people of Geshur
and Maacah, and half of Gilead to the border of Sihon king of Heshbon.

6Moses, the servant of the LORD, and the Israelites conquered them. And Moses the servant
of the LORD gave their land to the Reubenites,
the Gadites and the half-tribe of Manasseh to
be their possession.

7These are the kings of the land that Joshua
and the Israelites conquered on the west side of
the Jordan, from Baal Gad in the Valley of Lebanon to Mount Halak, which rises toward Seir
(their lands Joshua gave as an inheritance to the
tribes of Israel according to their tribal divisions— 8the hill country, the western foothills,
the Arabah, the mountain slopes, the desert and
the Negev—the lands of the Hittites, Amorites,
Canaanites, Perizzites, Hivites and Jebusites):

9the king of Jericho one
the king of Ai (near Bethel) one
10the king of Jerusalem one
the king of Hebron one
11the king of Jarmuth one
the king of Lachish one
12the king of Eglon one
the king of Gezer one
13the king of Debir one
the king of Geder one
14the king of Hormah one
the king of Arad one
15the king of Libnah one
the king of Adullam one
16the king of Makkedah one
the king of Bethel one
17the king of Tappuah one
the king of Hepher one
18the king of Aphek one
the king of Lasharon one
19the king of Madon one
the king of Hazor one
20the king of Shimron Meron one
the king of Acshaph one
21the king of Taanach one
the king of Megiddo one
22the king of Kedesh one
the king of Jokneam in Carmel one
23the king of Dor (in Naphoth
Dor[c]) one
the king of Goyim in Gilgal one
24the king of Tirzah one
thirty-one kings in all.

Land Still to Be Taken

13 When Joshua was old and well advanced in years, the LORD said to him,
"You are very old, and there are still very large
areas of land to be taken over.

2"This is the land that remains: all the
regions of the Philistines and Geshurites:
3from the Shihor River on the east of Egypt
to the territory of Ekron on the north, all

[a]3 That is, Galilee [b]3 That is, the Dead Sea
[c]23 Or *in the heights of Dor*

12:1–24 The Israelites constantly recounted God's great works in the past. In this instance, not only did the people recall Joshua's victories, but also those of their previous leader, Moses. These recollections of past victories served both as reminders of the great works God had done as well as springboards for trusting God to act on Israel's behalf in future times of difficulty. We, too, can become living reminders of the great things that can be realized through God's strength.

13:1 Despite Joshua's advanced age, God placed additional challenges before him. Retirement from obeying God's will is not an option. We are called to follow God's will throughout our lives until God's time for us to rest and stop fighting "the good fight" finally arrives (2 Timothy 4:7).

of it counted as Canaanite (the territory of the five Philistine rulers in Gaza, Ashdod, Ashkelon, Gath and Ekron—that of the Avvites); 4from the south, all the land of the Canaanites, from Arah of the Sidonians as far as Aphek, the region of the Amorites, 5the area of the Gebalites[a]; and all Lebanon to the east, from Baal Gad below Mount Hermon to Lebo[b] Hamath.

6"As for all the inhabitants of the mountain regions from Lebanon to Misrephoth Maim, that is, all the Sidonians, I myself will drive them out before the Israelites. Be sure to allocate this land to Israel for an inheritance, as I have instructed you, 7and divide it as an inheritance among the nine tribes and half of the tribe of Manasseh."

Division of the Land East of the Jordan

8The other half of Manasseh,[c] the Reubenites and the Gadites had received the inheritance that Moses had given them east of the Jordan, as he, the servant of the LORD, had assigned it to them.

9It extended from Aroer on the rim of the Arnon Gorge, and from the town in the middle of the gorge, and included the whole plateau of Medeba as far as Dibon, 10and all the towns of Sihon king of the Amorites, who ruled in Heshbon, out to the border of the Ammonites. 11It also included Gilead, the territory of the people of Geshur and Maacah, all of Mount Hermon and all Bashan as far as Salecah— 12that is, the whole kingdom of Og in Bashan, who had reigned in Ashtaroth and Edrei and had survived as one of the last of the Rephaites. Moses had defeated them and taken over their land. 13But the Israelites did not drive out the people of Geshur and Maacah, so they continue to live among the Israelites to this day.

14But to the tribe of Levi he gave no inheritance, since the offerings made by fire to the LORD, the God of Israel, are their inheritance, as he promised them.

15This is what Moses had given to the tribe of Reuben, clan by clan:

16The territory from Aroer on the rim of the Arnon Gorge, and from the town in the middle of the gorge, and the whole plateau past Medeba 17to Heshbon and all its towns on the plateau, including Dibon, Bamoth Baal, Beth Baal Meon, 18Jahaz, Kedemoth, Mephaath, 19Kiriathaim, Sibmah, Zereth Shahar on the hill in the valley, 20Beth Peor, the slopes of Pisgah, and Beth Jeshimoth 21—all the towns on the plateau and the entire realm of Sihon king of the Amorites, who ruled at Heshbon. Moses had defeated him and the Midianite chiefs, Evi, Rekem, Zur, Hur and Reba—princes allied with Sihon—who lived in that country. 22In addition to those slain in battle, the Israelites had put to the sword Balaam son of Beor, who practiced divination. 23The boundary of the Reubenites was the bank of the Jordan. These towns and their villages were the inheritance of the Reubenites, clan by clan.

24This is what Moses had given to the tribe of Gad, clan by clan:

25The territory of Jazer, all the towns of Gilead and half the Ammonite country as far as Aroer, near Rabbah; 26and from Heshbon to Ramath Mizpah and Betonim, and from Mahanaim to the territory of Debir; 27and in the valley, Beth Haram, Beth Nimrah, Succoth and Zaphon with the rest of the realm of Sihon king of Heshbon (the east side of the Jordan, the territory up to the end of the Sea of Kinnereth[d]). 28These towns and their villages were the inheritance of the Gadites, clan by clan.

29This is what Moses had given to the half-tribe of Manasseh, that is, to half the family of the descendants of Manasseh, clan by clan:

30The territory extending from Mahanaim and including all of Bashan, the entire realm of Og king of Bashan—all the settlements of Jair in Bashan, sixty towns, 31half of Gilead, and Ashtaroth and Edrei (the royal cities of Og in Bashan). This was for the descendants of Makir son of Manas-

[a]5 That is, the area of Byblos [b]5 Or *to the entrance to* [c]8 Hebrew *With it* (that is, with the other half of Manasseh) [d]27 That is, Galilee

---

13:8–13 These verses recite a list of the cities, moving from south to north on the east side of the Jordan River, that were the inheritances promised by Moses to Reuben, Gad and the half-tribe of Manasseh. In the midst of this list, however, a lack of faithfulness is noted: Israel had failed to trust God sufficiently to drive out the Geshurites and the Maacahites. Even though we are tempted to blame God when things don't turn out the way we've planned, we should look first to find where our faith has failed rather than where we think God has failed.

13:15–33 A detailed listing of the territories granted to the tribes of Reuben, Gad and the half-tribe of Manasseh is offered here so that everyone could see that God gave the tribes east of the Jordan an inheritance equal to that of the tribes living in the promised land. Even though the Jordan River physically separated these eastern tribes from their fellow Israelites, they were not to be separated from them spiritually. In discouraging times, we often see only our problems. It can be helpful to make a detailed list of what God has provided for us. As we recognize our many gifts from God, it becomes more difficult to be disheartened by our troubles. The God who provided the blessings of yesterday is still there for us today.

seh—for half of the sons of Makir, clan by clan.

32 This is the inheritance Moses had given when he was in the plains of Moab across the Jordan east of Jericho. 33 But to the tribe of Levi, Moses had given no inheritance; the LORD, the God of Israel, is their inheritance, as he promised them.

Division of the Land West of the Jordan

14 Now these are the areas the Israelites received as an inheritance in the land of Canaan, which Eleazar the priest, Joshua son of Nun and the heads of the tribal clans of Israel allotted to them. 2 Their inheritances were assigned by lot to the nine-and-a-half tribes, as the LORD had commanded through Moses. 3 Moses had granted the two-and-a-half tribes their inheritance east of the Jordan but had not granted the Levites an inheritance among the rest, 4 for the sons of Joseph had become two tribes—Manasseh and Ephraim. The Levites received no share of the land but only towns to live in, with pasturelands for their flocks and herds. 5 So the Israelites divided the land, just as the LORD had commanded Moses.

Hebron Given to Caleb

6 Now the men of Judah approached Joshua at Gilgal, and Caleb son of Jephunneh the Kenizzite said to him, "You know what the LORD said to Moses the man of God at Kadesh Barnea about you and me. 7 I was forty years old when Moses the servant of the LORD sent me from Kadesh Barnea to explore the land. And I brought him back a report according to my convictions, 8 but my brothers who went up with me made the hearts of the people melt with fear. I, however, followed the LORD my God wholeheartedly. 9 So on that day Moses swore to me, 'The land on which your feet have walked will be your inheritance and that of your children forever, because you have followed the LORD my God wholeheartedly.'[a]

10 "Now then, just as the LORD promised, he has kept me alive for forty-five years since the time he said this to Moses, while Israel moved about in the desert. So here I am today, eighty-five years old! 11 I am still as strong today as the day Moses sent me out; I'm just as vigorous to go out to battle now as I was then. 12 Now give me this hill country that the LORD promised me that day. You yourself heard then that the Anakites were there and their cities were large and fortified, but, the LORD helping me, I will drive them out just as he said."

13 Then Joshua blessed Caleb son of Jephunneh and gave him Hebron as his inheritance. 14 So Hebron has belonged to Caleb son of Jephunneh the Kenizzite ever since, because he followed the LORD, the God of Israel, wholeheartedly. 15 (Hebron used to be called Kiriath Arba after Arba, who was the greatest man among the Anakites.)

Then the land had rest from war.

Allotment for Judah

15 The allotment for the tribe of Judah, clan by clan, extended down to the territory of Edom, to the Desert of Zin in the extreme south.

2 Their southern boundary started from the bay at the southern end of the Salt Sea,[b] 3 crossed south of Scorpion[c] Pass, continued on to Zin and went over to the south of Kadesh Barnea. Then it ran past Hezron up to Addar and curved around to Karka. 4 It then passed along to Azmon and joined the Wadi of Egypt, ending at the sea. This is their[d] southern boundary.

5 The eastern boundary is the Salt Sea as far as the mouth of the Jordan.

The northern boundary started from the bay of the sea at the mouth of the Jordan, 6 went up to Beth Hoglah and continued north of Beth Arabah to the Stone of Bohan son of Reuben. 7 The boundary then went up to Debir from the Valley of Achor and turned north to Gilgal, which faces the Pass of Adummim south of the gorge. It continued along to the waters of En Shemesh and came out at En Rogel. 8 Then it ran up the Valley of Ben Hinnom along the southern slope of the Jebusite city (that is, Jerusalem). From there it climbed to the top of the hill west of the Hinnom Valley at the northern end of the Valley of Rephaim. 9 From the hilltop the boundary headed toward the spring of the waters of Nephtoah, came out at the towns of Mount Ephron and went down toward Baalah (that is, Kiriath Jearim).

[a] 9 Deut. 1:36 [b] 2 That is, the Dead Sea; also in verse 5 [c] 3 Hebrew *Akrabbim* [d] 4 Hebrew *your*

14:1–5 The leaders of Israel did not forget God's command given by Moses but were obedient to it, resulting in the total and proper apportionment of the promised land. As it was for the Levites who settled on the east side of the Jordan, so it was also for those Levites who served God in the promised land—they received no specific territory for an inheritance—God himself was their inheritance. God, however, did not leave the Levites homeless to roam the countryside but gave them cities and pasturelands to manage. What a great reminder to us as we compare ourselves with others. When we focus on what we have or don't have, we often forget that our greatest inheritance is God.

14:6–15 Advanced physical age did not deter Caleb from seeking the inheritance promised to him by God as a reward for his faith when he served under Moses as a spy in the promised land (see Numbers 14:24). Age alone does not make a person feel or act old. In fact, Caleb willingly sought to enter into battle against some of the more powerful armies that inhabited the land. Because he fully trusted God, Caleb secured his promised inheritance. In our own lives, we need to realize that if God wants to grant us victory over any problem we encounter, that victory is already secured.

[10]Then it curved westward from Baalah to Mount Seir, ran along the northern slope of Mount Jearim (that is, Kesalon), continued down to Beth Shemesh and crossed to Timnah. [11]It went to the northern slope of Ekron, turned toward Shikkeron, passed along to Mount Baalah and reached Jabneel. The boundary ended at the sea.

[12]The western boundary is the coastline of the Great Sea.[a]

These are the boundaries around the people of Judah by their clans.

[13]In accordance with the LORD's command to him, Joshua gave to Caleb son of Jephunneh a portion in Judah—Kiriath Arba, that is, Hebron. (Arba was the forefather of Anak.) [14]From Hebron Caleb drove out the three Anakites—Sheshai, Ahiman and Talmai—descendants of Anak. [15]From there he marched against the people living in Debir (formerly called Kiriath Sepher). [16]And Caleb said, "I will give my daughter Acsah in marriage to the man who attacks and captures Kiriath Sepher." [17]Othniel son of Kenaz, Caleb's brother, took it; so Caleb gave his daughter Acsah to him in marriage.

[18]One day when she came to Othniel, she urged him[b] to ask her father for a field. When she got off her donkey, Caleb asked her, "What can I do for you?"

[19]She replied, "Do me a special favor. Since you have given me land in the Negev, give me also springs of water." So Caleb gave her the upper and lower springs.

[20]This is the inheritance of the tribe of Judah, clan by clan:

[21]The southernmost towns of the tribe of Judah in the Negev toward the boundary of Edom were:

Kabzeel, Eder, Jagur, [22]Kinah, Dimonah, Adadah, [23]Kedesh, Hazor, Ithnan, [24]Ziph, Telem, Bealoth, [25]Hazor Hadattah, Kerioth Hezron (that is, Hazor), [26]Amam, Shema, Moladah, [27]Hazar Gaddah, Heshmon, Beth Pelet, [28]Hazar Shual, Beersheba, Biziothiah, [29]Baalah, Iim, Ezem, [30]Eltolad, Kesil, Hormah, [31]Ziklag, Madmannah, Sansannah, [32]Lebaoth, Shilhim, Ain and Rimmon—a total of twenty-nine towns and their villages.

[33]In the western foothills:

Eshtaol, Zorah, Ashnah, [34]Zanoah, En Gannim, Tappuah, Enam, [35]Jarmuth, Adullam, Socoh, Azekah, [36]Shaaraim, Adithaim and Gederah (or Gederothaim)[c]—fourteen towns and their villages.

[37]Zenan, Hadashah, Migdal Gad, [38]Dilean, Mizpah, Joktheel, [39]Lachish, Bozkath, Eglon, [40]Cabbon, Lahmas, Kitlish, [41]Gederoth, Beth Dagon, Naamah and Makkedah—sixteen towns and their villages.

[42]Libnah, Ether, Ashan, [43]Iphtah, Ashnah, Nezib, [44]Keilah, Aczib and Mareshah—nine towns and their villages.

[45]Ekron, with its surrounding settlements and villages; [46]west of Ekron, all that were in the vicinity of Ashdod, together with their villages; [47]Ashdod, its surrounding settlements and villages; and Gaza, its settlements and villages, as far as the Wadi of Egypt and the coastline of the Great Sea.

[48]In the hill country:

Shamir, Jattir, Socoh, [49]Dannah, Kiriath Sannah (that is, Debir), [50]Anab, Eshtemoh, Anim, [51]Goshen, Holon and Giloh—eleven towns and their villages.

[52]Arab, Dumah, Eshan, [53]Janim, Beth Tappuah, Aphekah, [54]Humtah, Kiriath Arba (that is, Hebron) and Zior—nine towns and their villages.

[55]Maon, Carmel, Ziph, Juttah, [56]Jezreel, Jokdeam, Zanoah, [57]Kain, Gibeah and Timnah—ten towns and their villages.

[58]Halhul, Beth Zur, Gedor, [59]Maarath, Beth Anoth and Eltekon—six towns and their villages.

[60]Kiriath Baal (that is, Kiriath Jearim) and Rabbah—two towns and their villages.

[61]In the desert:

Beth Arabah, Middin, Secacah, [62]Nibshan, the City of Salt and En Gedi—six towns and their villages.

[63]Judah could not dislodge the Jebusites, who were living in Jerusalem; to this day the Jebusites live there with the people of Judah.

Allotment for Ephraim and Manasseh

16 The allotment for Joseph began at the Jordan of Jericho,[d] east of the

[a] *12* That is, the Mediterranean; also in verse 47
[b] *18* Hebrew and some Septuagint manuscripts; other Septuagint manuscripts (see also note at Judges 1:14) *Othniel, he urged her*
[c] *36* Or *Gederah and Gederothaim*
[d] *1* *Jordan of Jericho* was possibly an ancient name for the Jordan River.

15:20–63 Of all the tribes who received an inheritance, the greatest amount of recorded information is noted about the tribe of Judah. The importance of Judah as the chosen son from whom future kings of Israel would arise and through whose lineage the Messiah would be born may account for this phenomenon (see Genesis 49:10). Merely being part of the tribe of Judah, however, did not guarantee faith or success. Despite God's promise of victory to those who obeyed him fully (see Deuteronomy 28:1–7), some of the tribe of Judah apparently lacked sufficient faith in God to oust the inhabitants of Jerusalem. We should consider what areas of our lives, thoughts or actions are enemies of God's will. As we honestly identify these, confess them to God and begin to deal with them, God can give us the power to drive them out so that we can receive our full inheritance.

16:1–10 A godly person's descendants often reap numerous benefits from that godly person's life. Because Joseph had been used by God to deliver his father, Jacob, and his family from a destructive famine, Jacob honored Joseph

waters of Jericho, and went up from there
through the desert into the hill country of
Bethel. 2It went on from Bethel (that is,
Luz),[a] crossed over to the territory of the
Arkites in Ataroth, 3descended westward
to the territory of the Japhletites as far as
the region of Lower Beth Horon and on to
Gezer, ending at the sea.
4So Manasseh and Ephraim, the descendants of
Joseph, received their inheritance.

5This was the territory of Ephraim, clan by clan:
The boundary of their inheritance went
from Ataroth Addar in the east to Upper
Beth Horon 6and continued to the sea.
From Micmethath on the north it curved
eastward to Taanath Shiloh, passing by it
to Janoah on the east. 7Then it went down
from Janoah to Ataroth and Naarah,
touched Jericho and came out at the Jordan. 8From Tappuah the border went west
to the Kanah Ravine and ended at the sea.
This was the inheritance of the tribe of the
Ephraimites, clan by clan. 9It also included all the towns and their villages that
were set aside for the Ephraimites within
the inheritance of the Manassites.
10They did not dislodge the Canaanites living in
Gezer; to this day the Canaanites live among
the people of Ephraim but are required to do
forced labor.

17 This was the allotment for the tribe of
Manasseh as Joseph's firstborn, that is,
for Makir, Manasseh's firstborn. Makir was the
ancestor of the Gileadites, who had received
Gilead and Bashan because the Makirites were
great soldiers. 2So this allotment was for the rest
of the people of Manasseh—the clans of Abiezer,
Helek, Asriel, Shechem, Hepher and Shemida.
These are the other male descendants of Manasseh son of Joseph by their clans.
3Now Zelophehad son of Hepher, the son of
Gilead, the son of Makir, the son of Manasseh,
had no sons but only daughters, whose names
were Mahlah, Noah, Hoglah, Milcah and Tirzah. 4They went to Eleazar the priest, Joshua
son of Nun, and the leaders and said, "The
LORD commanded Moses to give us an inheritance among our brothers." So Joshua gave them
an inheritance along with the brothers of their
father, according to the LORD's command. 5Ma-
nasseh's share consisted of ten tracts of land
besides Gilead and Bashan east of the Jordan,
6because the daughters of the tribe of Manasseh
received an inheritance among the sons. The
land of Gilead belonged to the rest of the
descendants of Manasseh.
7The territory of Manasseh extended
from Asher to Micmethath east of Shechem. The boundary ran southward
from there to include the people living
at En Tappuah. 8(Manasseh had the land
of Tappuah, but Tappuah itself, on the
boundary of Manasseh, belonged to the
Ephraimites.) 9Then the boundary continued south to the Kanah Ravine. There
were towns belonging to Ephraim lying
among the towns of Manasseh, but the
boundary of Manasseh was the northern
side of the ravine and ended at the sea.
10On the south the land belonged to
Ephraim, on the north to Manasseh. The
territory of Manasseh reached the sea and
bordered Asher on the north and Issachar
on the east.
11Within Issachar and Asher, Manasseh
also had Beth Shan, Ibleam and the people of Dor, Endor, Taanach and Megiddo,
together with their surrounding settlements (the third in the list is Naphoth[b]).
12Yet the Manassites were not able to occupy
these towns, for the Canaanites were determined to live in that region. 13However, when
the Israelites grew stronger, they subjected the
Canaanites to forced labor but did not drive
them out completely.
14The people of Joseph said to Joshua, "Why
have you given us only one allotment and one
portion for an inheritance? We are a numerous
people and the LORD has blessed us abundantly."
15"If you are so numerous," Joshua answered,
"and if the hill country of Ephraim is too small
for you, go up into the forest and clear land for
yourselves there in the land of the Perizzites
and Rephaites."

[a]2 Septuagint; Hebrew *Bethel to Luz* [b]11 That is, Naphoth Dor

---

by "adopting" Joseph's two Egyptian sons (Ephraim and Manasseh) and making them equal in status to Jacob's own sons (see Genesis 48:1–5). Thus, of the twelve sons of Jacob, Joseph's line was considered two tribes for the purpose of receiving an inheritance. Our faith and the life we develop around our faith will affect generations to come too. There is no greater inheritance to leave to future generations than that of a life of faith lived in prayerful submission to God.

17:1–6 The daughters of Zelophehad demonstrated true faith in God, believing that God would fulfill his promise of an inheritance for them. They based their confidence on an earlier ruling by God through Moses that gave them their father's inheritance because Zelophehad had no sons to receive it (see Numbers 27:1–7). The faith of Zelophehad's daughters was rewarded with land. God rewards our faith. The reward may not always come in the form of land or possessions, but God's rewards will come in forms that far exceed the temporal values of material goods.

17:14–18 Because they did not trust God enough to drive out all of their enemies and secure all of their inherited land (see 16:10; 17:12–13), the tribes of Ephraim and Manasseh complained that they did not have enough land for all their people. They also complained that the enemies living in the land were too strong for them to defeat. Joshua generously granted them their request for additional land but at the same time challenged them to drive out the Canaanites. The erosion of God's best always occurs when our will interferes with his. We come to believe that we know so much and often recklessly destroy what God has provided. We must seek God, his will and his power or spend a lifetime compensating for mistakes made outside of his will.

16The people of Joseph replied, "The hill country is not enough for us, and all the Canaanites who live in the plain have iron chariots, both those in Beth Shan and its settlements and those in the Valley of Jezreel."

17But Joshua said to the house of Joseph—to Ephraim and Manasseh—"You are numerous and very powerful. You will have not only one allotment 18but the forested hill country as well. Clear it, and its farthest limits will be yours; though the Canaanites have iron chariots and though they are strong, you can drive them out."

Division of the Rest of the Land

18 The whole assembly of the Israelites gathered at Shiloh and set up the Tent of Meeting there. The country was brought under their control, 2but there were still seven Israelite tribes who had not yet received their inheritance.

3So Joshua said to the Israelites: "How long will you wait before you begin to take possession of the land that the LORD, the God of your fathers, has given you? 4Appoint three men from each tribe. I will send them out to make a survey of the land and to write a description of it, according to the inheritance of each. Then they will return to me. 5You are to divide the land into seven parts. Judah is to remain in its territory on the south and the house of Joseph in its territory on the north. 6After you have written descriptions of the seven parts of the land, bring them here to me and I will cast lots for you in the presence of the LORD our God. 7The Levites, however, do not get a portion among you, because the priestly service of the LORD is their inheritance. And Gad, Reuben and the half-tribe of Manasseh have already received their inheritance on the east side of the Jordan. Moses the servant of the LORD gave it to them."

8As the men started on their way to map out the land, Joshua instructed them, "Go and make a survey of the land and write a description of it. Then return to me, and I will cast lots for you here at Shiloh in the presence of the LORD." 9So the men left and went through the land. They wrote its description on a scroll, town by town, in seven parts, and returned to Joshua in the camp at Shiloh. 10Joshua then cast lots for them in Shiloh in the presence of the LORD, and there he distributed the land to the Israelites according to their tribal divisions.

Allotment for Benjamin

11The lot came up for the tribe of Benjamin, clan by clan. Their allotted territory lay between the tribes of Judah and Joseph:

12On the north side their boundary began at the Jordan, passed the northern slope of Jericho and headed west into the hill country, coming out at the desert of Beth Aven. 13From there it crossed to the south slope of Luz (that is, Bethel) and went down to Ataroth Addar on the hill south of Lower Beth Horon.

14From the hill facing Beth Horon on the south the boundary turned south along the western side and came out at Kiriath Baal (that is, Kiriath Jearim), a town of the people of Judah. This was the western side.

15The southern side began at the outskirts of Kiriath Jearim on the west, and the boundary came out at the spring of the waters of Nephtoah. 16The boundary went down to the foot of the hill facing the Valley of Ben Hinnom, north of the Valley of Rephaim. It continued down the Hinnom Valley along the southern slope of the Jebusite city and so to En Rogel. 17It then curved north, went to En Shemesh, continued to Geliloth, which faces the Pass of Adummim, and ran down to the Stone of Bohan son of Reuben. 18It continued to the northern slope of Beth Arabah[a] and on down into the Arabah. 19It then went to the northern slope of Beth Hoglah and came out at the northern bay of the Salt Sea,[b] at the mouth of the Jordan in the south. This was the southern boundary.

20The Jordan formed the boundary on the eastern side.

These were the boundaries that marked out the inheritance of the clans of Benjamin on all sides.

21The tribe of Benjamin, clan by clan, had the following cities:

Jericho, Beth Hoglah, Emek Keziz, 22Beth Arabah, Zemaraim, Bethel, 23Avvim, Parah, Ophrah, 24Kephar Ammoni, Ophni and Geba—twelve towns and their villages.

25Gibeon, Ramah, Beeroth, 26Mizpah, Kephirah, Mozah, 27Rekem, Irpeel, Taralah, 28Zelah, Haeleph, the Jebusite city (that is, Jerusalem), Gibeah and Kiriath—fourteen towns and their villages.

This was the inheritance of Benjamin for its clans.

[a] 18 Septuagint; Hebrew *slope facing the Arabah*
[b] 19 That is, the Dead Sea

18:1–10 Despite a general rest from war, the various tribes of Israel had not yet claimed their inheritance. Joshua chided them for their failure to lay hold of that which God had apportioned to them. Joshua then gave practical guidance as to how the remaining tribes should divide up the land. The tribes who had not aggressively claimed their inheritance finally took action and followed Joshua's advice. Sometimes we need to be spurred to action by others. Maybe we don't have the courage to act, or perhaps we don't realize that we need to. But we should listen to the advice of wise leaders, recognizing that they can often see our situation more objectively than we can.

Allotment for Simeon

19 The second lot came out for the tribe of Simeon, clan by clan. Their inheritance lay within the territory of Judah. 2It included:

Beersheba (or Sheba),[a] Moladah, 3Hazar Shual, Balah, Ezem, 4Eltolad, Bethul, Hormah, 5Ziklag, Beth Marcaboth, Hazar Susah, 6Beth Lebaoth and Sharuhen—thirteen towns and their villages;

7Ain, Rimmon, Ether and Ashan—four towns and their villages— 8and all the villages around these towns as far as Baalath Beer (Ramah in the Negev).

This was the inheritance of the tribe of the Simeonites, clan by clan. 9The inheritance of the Simeonites was taken from the share of Judah, because Judah's portion was more than they needed. So the Simeonites received their inheritance within the territory of Judah.

Allotment for Zebulun

10The third lot came up for Zebulun, clan by clan:

The boundary of their inheritance went as far as Sarid. 11Going west it ran to Maralah, touched Dabbesheth, and extended to the ravine near Jokneam. 12It turned east from Sarid toward the sunrise to the territory of Kisloth Tabor and went on to Daberath and up to Japhia. 13Then it continued eastward to Gath Hepher and Eth Kazin; it came out at Rimmon and turned toward Neah. 14There the boundary went around on the north to Hannathon and ended at the Valley of Iphtah El. 15Included were Kattath, Nahalal, Shimron, Idalah and Bethlehem. There were twelve towns and their villages.

16These towns and their villages were the inheritance of Zebulun, clan by clan.

Allotment for Issachar

17The fourth lot came out for Issachar, clan by clan. 18Their territory included:

Jezreel, Kesulloth, Shunem, 19Hapharaim, Shion, Anaharath, 20Rabbith, Kishion, Ebez, 21Remeth, En Gannim, En Haddah and Beth Pazzez. 22The boundary touched Tabor, Shahazumah and Beth Shemesh, and ended at the Jordan. There were sixteen towns and their villages.

23These towns and their villages were the inheritance of the tribe of Issachar, clan by clan.

Allotment for Asher

24The fifth lot came out for the tribe of Asher, clan by clan. 25Their territory included:

Helkath, Hali, Beten, Acshaph, 26Allammelech, Amad and Mishal. On the west the boundary touched Carmel and Shihor Libnath. 27It then turned east toward Beth Dagon, touched Zebulun and the Valley of Iphtah El, and went north to Beth Emek and Neiel, passing Cabul on the left. 28It went to Abdon,[b] Rehob, Hammon and Kanah, as far as Greater Sidon. 29The boundary then turned back toward Ramah and went to the fortified city of Tyre, turned toward Hosah and came out at the sea in the region of Aczib, 30Ummah, Aphek and Rehob. There were twenty-two towns and their villages.

31These towns and their villages were the inheritance of the tribe of Asher, clan by clan.

Allotment for Naphtali

32The sixth lot came out for Naphtali, clan by clan:

33Their boundary went from Heleph and the large tree in Zaanannim, passing Adami Nekeb and Jabneel to Lakkum and ending at the Jordan. 34The boundary ran west through Aznoth Tabor and came out at Hukkok. It touched Zebulun on the south, Asher on the west and the Jordan[c] on the east. 35The fortified cities were Ziddim, Zer, Hammath, Rakkath, Kinnereth, 36Adamah, Ramah, Hazor, 37Kedesh, Edrei, En Hazor, 38Iron, Migdal El, Horem, Beth Anath and Beth Shemesh. There were nineteen towns and their villages.

39These towns and their villages were the inheritance of the tribe of Naphtali, clan by clan.

Allotment for Dan

40The seventh lot came out for the tribe of Dan, clan by clan. 41The territory of their inheritance included:

[a]2 Or *Beersheba, Sheba*; 1 Chron. 4:28 does not have *Sheba.* [b]28 Some Hebrew manuscripts (see also Joshua 21:30); most Hebrew manuscripts *Ebron* [c]34 Septuagint; Hebrew *west, and Judah, the Jordan,*

19:1–16 Judah had received more land than it required (see 15:1–62). The inheritance of the tribe of Simeon was carved out of the southern sector of the boundaries of Judah and formed the southern border of the promised land. Although several cities were transferred from Judah to Simeon's control, none of those cities was taken away from Caleb and his family. By contrast, Zebulun's inheritance was in the northern section of the promised land, a region that one day would be the site of the Messiah's hometown (i.e., Nazareth; see Matthew 2:23). There might have been a temptation to compare each tribe's inheritance rather than to see each allotment as ordained by God. True faith frees us to accept God's provision as perfectly planned for us, whether it seems great or small.

19:24–39 Neither Asher nor Naphtali was successful in driving out their enemies (see Judges 1:31–33). Failing to clear the land of all the nations dwelling in the promised land proved costly for the Israelite people. Rather than converting to God those whom they failed to destroy, the Israelites were drawn away from God to serve the idols of those heathen nations. Those nations, in turn, would be like thorns in Israel's side (see Deuteronomy 31:16–20; Judges 2:1–3, 11–15). It is essential that we, too, drive out the negative influences in our lives so that we and our descendants will be better able to follow God.

Zorah, Eshtaol, Ir Shemesh, 42 Shaalabbin, Aijalon, Ithlah, 43 Elon, Timnah, Ekron, 44 Eltekeh, Gibbethon, Baalath, 45 Jehud, Bene Berak, Gath Rimmon, 46 Me Jarkon and Rakkon, with the area facing Joppa.

47 (But the Danites had difficulty taking possession of their territory, so they went up and attacked Leshem, took it, put it to the sword and occupied it. They settled in Leshem and named it Dan after their forefather.)

48 These towns and their villages were the inheritance of the tribe of Dan, clan by clan.

Allotment for Joshua

49 When they had finished dividing the land into its allotted portions, the Israelites gave Joshua son of Nun an inheritance among them, 50 as the LORD had commanded. They gave him the town he asked for—Timnath Serah[a] in the hill country of Ephraim. And he built up the town and settled there.

51 These are the territories that Eleazar the priest, Joshua son of Nun and the heads of the tribal clans of Israel assigned by lot at Shiloh in the presence of the LORD at the entrance to the Tent of Meeting. And so they finished dividing the land.

Cities of Refuge

20 Then the LORD said to Joshua: 2 "Tell the Israelites to designate the cities of refuge, as I instructed you through Moses, 3 so that anyone who kills a person accidentally and unintentionally may flee there and find protection from the avenger of blood.

4 "When he flees to one of these cities, he is to stand in the entrance of the city gate and state his case before the elders of that city. Then they are to admit him into their city and give him a place to live with them. 5 If the avenger of blood pursues him, they must not surrender the one accused, because he killed his neighbor unintentionally and without malice aforethought. 6 He is to stay in that city until he has stood trial before the assembly and until the death of the high priest who is serving at that time. Then he may go back to his own home in the town from which he fled."

7 So they set apart Kedesh in Galilee in the hill country of Naphtali, Shechem in the hill country of Ephraim, and Kiriath Arba (that is, Hebron) in the hill country of Judah. 8 On the east side of the Jordan of Jericho[b] they designated Bezer in the desert on the plateau in the tribe of Reuben, Ramoth in Gilead in the tribe of Gad, and Golan in Bashan in the tribe of Manasseh. 9 Any of the Israelites or any alien living among them who killed someone accidentally could flee to these designated cities and not be killed by the avenger of blood prior to standing trial before the assembly.

Towns for the Levites

21 Now the family heads of the Levites approached Eleazar the priest, Joshua son of Nun, and the heads of the other tribal families of Israel 2 at Shiloh in Canaan and said to them, "The LORD commanded through Moses that you give us towns to live in, with pasturelands for our livestock." 3 So, as the LORD had commanded, the Israelites gave the Levites the following towns and pasturelands out of their own inheritance:

4 The first lot came out for the Kohathites, clan by clan. The Levites who were descendants of Aaron the priest were allotted thirteen towns from the tribes of Judah, Simeon and Benjamin. 5 The rest of Kohath's descendants were allotted ten towns from the clans of the tribes of Ephraim, Dan and half of Manasseh.

6 The descendants of Gershon were allotted thirteen towns from the clans of the tribes of Issachar, Asher, Naphtali and the half-tribe of Manasseh in Bashan.

7 The descendants of Merari, clan by clan, received twelve towns from the tribes of Reuben, Gad and Zebulun.

8 So the Israelites allotted to the Levites these towns and their pasturelands, as the LORD had commanded through Moses.

9 From the tribes of Judah and Simeon they allotted the following towns by name 10 (these towns were assigned to the descendants of Aaron who were from the Kohathite clans of the Levites, because the first lot fell to them):

11 They gave them Kiriath Arba (that is, Hebron), with its surrounding pastureland, in the hill country of Judah. (Arba was the forefather of Anak.) 12 But the fields and villages around the city they had given to Caleb son of Jephunneh as his possession.

13 So to the descendants of Aaron the priest they gave Hebron (a city of refuge for one accused of murder), Libnah, 14 Jat-

[a]50 Also known as *Timnath Heres* (see Judges 2:9)
[b]8 *Jordan of Jericho* was possibly an ancient name for the Jordan River.

19:49–50 Joshua was permitted to select a city for his inheritance. He could have chosen any city in the promised land, but he chose to live within the territory of Ephraim, the tribe from which he had come (see Numbers 13:8, 16). Joshua remembered his roots and honored them with this decision. We often lose our way when we forget where we've come from. Although our family heritage is not perfect, we can celebrate what is good about it and honor God in doing so.

21:1–8 The Levites waited patiently for the other tribes to receive their inheritance. Then they reminded Eleazar and Joshua of God's command that, as their inheritance, the Levites were to receive from the tribes of Israel towns in which to live (see Numbers 35:1–8). Israel, in obedience to God's command, fulfilled its responsibility to God and to the tribe of Levi. Acting responsibly toward others brings honor to us, others and God too.

tir, Eshtemoa, 15Holon, Debir, 16Ain, Juttah and Beth Shemesh, together with their
pasturelands—nine towns from these two
tribes.
17And from the tribe of Benjamin they
gave them Gibeon, Geba, 18Anathoth and
Almon, together with their pasturelands—
four towns.
19All the towns for the priests, the descendants
of Aaron, were thirteen, together with their pasturelands.

20The rest of the Kohathite clans of the Levites
were allotted towns from the tribe of Ephraim:
21In the hill country of Ephraim they
were given Shechem (a city of refuge for
one accused of murder) and Gezer, 22Kib-
zaim and Beth Horon, together with their
pasturelands—four towns.
23Also from the tribe of Dan they received Eltekeh, Gibbethon, 24Aijalon and
Gath Rimmon, together with their pasturelands—four towns.
25From half the tribe of Manasseh they
received Taanach and Gath Rimmon, together with their pasturelands—two towns.
26All these ten towns and their pasturelands
were given to the rest of the Kohathite clans.

27The Levite clans of the Gershonites were
given:
from the half-tribe of Manasseh,
Golan in Bashan (a city of refuge for one
accused of murder) and Be Eshtarah, together with their pasturelands—two towns;
28from the tribe of Issachar,
Kishion, Daberath, 29Jarmuth and En
Gannim, together with their pasturelands—four towns;
30from the tribe of Asher,
Mishal, Abdon, 31Helkath and Rehob, together with their pasturelands—four
towns;
32from the tribe of Naphtali,
Kedesh in Galilee (a city of refuge for one
accused of murder), Hammoth Dor and
Kartan, together with their pasturelands—
three towns.
33All the towns of the Gershonite clans were
thirteen, together with their pasturelands.

34The Merarite clans (the rest of the Levites)
were given:
from the tribe of Zebulun,
Jokneam, Kartah, 35Dimnah and Nahalal,
together with their pasturelands—four
towns;
36from the tribe of Reuben,
Bezer, Jahaz, 37Kedemoth and Mephaath,
together with their pasturelands—four
towns;
38from the tribe of Gad,
Ramoth in Gilead (a city of refuge for one
accused of murder), Mahanaim, 39Hesh-
bon and Jazer, together with their pasturelands—four towns in all.
40All the towns allotted to the Merarite clans,
who were the rest of the Levites, were twelve.
41The towns of the Levites in the territory
held by the Israelites were forty-eight in all,
together with their pasturelands. 42Each of these
towns had pasturelands surrounding it; this was
true for all these towns.

43So the LORD gave Israel all the land he had
sworn to give their forefathers, and they took
possession of it and settled there. 44The LORD
gave them rest on every side, just as he had
sworn to their forefathers. Not one of their enemies withstood them; the LORD handed all their
enemies over to them. 45Not one of all the
LORD's good promises to the house of Israel
failed; every one was fulfilled.

Eastern Tribes Return Home

22 Then Joshua summoned the Reubenites, the Gadites and the half-tribe of
Manasseh 2and said to them, "You have done
all that Moses the servant of the LORD commanded, and you have obeyed me in everything
I commanded. 3For a long time now—to this
very day—you have not deserted your brothers
but have carried out the mission the LORD your
God gave you. 4Now that the LORD your God
has given your brothers rest as he promised,
return to your homes in the land that Moses the
servant of the LORD gave you on the other side
of the Jordan. 5But be very careful to keep the
commandment and the law that Moses the servant of the LORD gave you: to love the LORD
your God, to walk in all his ways, to obey his
commands, to hold fast to him and to serve
him with all your heart and all your soul."
6Then Joshua blessed them and sent them
away, and they went to their homes. 7(To the
half-tribe of Manasseh Moses had given land in
Bashan, and to the other half of the tribe Joshua
gave land on the west side of the Jordan with
their brothers.) When Joshua sent them home,

21:43–45 God accomplished for the people of Israel all that he said he would do. The Israelites had marched into the land and taken it as their possession. God gave them rest from their enemies. Whenever the people served God faithfully and were obedient to his commands, God conquered their enemies. Israel's problems arose only when they sinned against God or failed to act in faith. Today, we face the same challenge to remain faithful. The Israelites are examples of our need to continually seek God and surrender to him.

22:1–9 Joshua declared that the tribes east of the Jordan had faithfully fulfilled their responsibilities. They had delayed enjoying their own rewards so that their brothers could receive what God had promised to them. Joshua reminded them that they should always love and obey God. Although there was much sorrow at leaving their kinsmen west of the Jordan, there undoubtedly was also much joy for the Reubenites, Gadites and the half-tribe of Manasseh. They were finally going home to their families. As they crossed the Jordan River, the eastern tribes set up a monument to remind them of their kinship with the western tribes and of their shared loyalty to God.

he blessed them, [8]saying, "Return to your
homes with your great wealth—with large herds
of livestock, with silver, gold, bronze and iron,
and a great quantity of clothing—and divide
with your brothers the plunder from your enemies."

[9]So the Reubenites, the Gadites and the half-
tribe of Manasseh left the Israelites at Shiloh in
Canaan to return to Gilead, their own land,
which they had acquired in accordance with the
command of the LORD through Moses.

[10]When they came to Geliloth near the Jordan in the land of Canaan, the Reubenites, the
Gadites and the half-tribe of Manasseh built an
imposing altar there by the Jordan. [11]And when
the Israelites heard that they had built the altar
on the border of Canaan at Geliloth near the
Jordan on the Israelite side, [12]the whole assembly of Israel gathered at Shiloh to go to war
against them.

[13]So the Israelites sent Phinehas son of Eleazar, the priest, to the land of Gilead—to Reuben,
Gad and the half-tribe of Manasseh. [14]With
him they sent ten of the chief men, one for each
of the tribes of Israel, each the head of a family
division among the Israelite clans.

[15]When they went to Gilead—to Reuben, Gad
and the half-tribe of Manasseh—they said to
them: [16]"The whole assembly of the LORD says:
'How could you break faith with the God of
Israel like this? How could you turn away from
the LORD and build yourselves an altar in rebellion against him now? [17]Was not the sin of Peor
enough for us? Up to this very day we have not
cleansed ourselves from that sin, even though
a plague fell on the community of the LORD!
[18]And are you now turning away from the
LORD?

" 'If you rebel against the LORD today, tomorrow he will be angry with the whole community of Israel. [19]If the land you possess is
defiled, come over to the LORD's land, where the
LORD's tabernacle stands, and share the land
with us. But do not rebel against the LORD or
against us by building an altar for yourselves,
other than the altar of the LORD our God.
[20]When Achan son of Zerah acted unfaithfully
regarding the devoted things,[a] did not wrath
come upon the whole community of Israel? He
was not the only one who died for his sin.' "

[21]Then Reuben, Gad and the half-tribe of
Manasseh replied to the heads of the clans of
Israel: [22]"The Mighty One, God, the LORD! The
Mighty One, God, the LORD! He knows! And let
Israel know! If this has been in rebellion or
disobedience to the LORD, do not spare us this
day. [23]If we have built our own altar to turn
away from the LORD and to offer burnt offerings
and grain offerings, or to sacrifice fellowship
offerings[b] on it, may the LORD himself call us
to account.

[24]"No! We did it for fear that some day your
descendants might say to ours, 'What do you
have to do with the LORD, the God of Israel?
[25]The LORD has made the Jordan a boundary
between us and you—you Reubenites and Gadites! You have no share in the LORD.' So your
descendants might cause ours to stop fearing
the LORD.

[26]"That is why we said, 'Let us get ready and
build an altar—but not for burnt offerings or
sacrifices.' [27]On the contrary, it is to be a witness
between us and you and the generations that
follow, that we will worship the LORD at his
sanctuary with our burnt offerings, sacrifices
and fellowship offerings. Then in the future
your descendants will not be able to say to ours,
'You have no share in the LORD.'

[28]"And we said, 'If they ever say this to us, or
to our descendants, we will answer: Look at the
replica of the LORD's altar, which our fathers
built, not for burnt offerings and sacrifices, but
as a witness between us and you.'

[29]"Far be it from us to rebel against the LORD
and turn away from him today by building an
altar for burnt offerings, grain offerings and sacrifices, other than the altar of the LORD our God
that stands before his tabernacle."

[30]When Phinehas the priest and the leaders
of the community—the heads of the clans of the

[a]20 The Hebrew term refers to the irrevocable giving over of things or persons to the LORD, often by totally destroying them. [b]23 Traditionally *peace offerings*; also in verse 27

22:10–20 Outraged that the tribes east of the Jordan had apparently turned away from God and set up another altar of worship, the tribes living in the promised land prepared to go to war against their kinsmen. Before war broke out, however, wisdom prevailed. A delegation was sent by the western tribes to urge the trans-Jordan tribes to return to God. The delegation boldly confronted their brothers, reminding them of the consequences of past rebellions against God (see 7:1–26; Numbers 25:1–9) and offering to let these tribes live with them in the promised land. Though it is often difficult and painful, at times we must confront others so that all of us can maintain our faith (see James 5:16–20). Spiritual growth is not an individual process; others must be involved—both to encourage and to confront.

22:21–29 The Reubenites, the Gadites, and the half-tribe of Manasseh responded to their western brothers' concern in amazement. They explained their actions in order to reestablish their relationship with the rest of Israel. They explained that their actions had been taken to ensure that future generations on both sides of the Jordan would know that the tribes east of the Jordan also worshiped the one true God of Israel. In this case, confrontation was effective. Even though confrontation does not always bring the desired response, it is an important part of our spiritual growth process.

22:30–34 As the leaders of the delegation of Israel listened carefully to the words of their brothers, the western leaders changed their attitude toward the tribes of Reuben, Gad and the half-tribe of Manasseh from anger to reconciliation and joy. The leaders then praised God for the faithfulness of their eastern brothers and declared peace, thus averting a potential civil war. The east-bank altar thereafter was referred to as "A Witness Between Us that the LORD is God," reminding all the people that the Lord was their God. The objective of confrontation should

Israelites—heard what Reuben, Gad and Manasseh had to say, they were pleased. 31And Phinehas son of Eleazar, the priest, said to Reuben,
Gad and Manasseh, "Today we know that the
LORD is with us, because you have not acted
unfaithfully toward the LORD in this matter.
Now you have rescued the Israelites from the
LORD's hand."
32Then Phinehas son of Eleazar, the priest,
and the leaders returned to Canaan from their
meeting with the Reubenites and Gadites in Gilead and reported to the Israelites. 33They were
glad to hear the report and praised God. And
they talked no more about going to war against
them to devastate the country where the Reubenites and the Gadites lived.
34And the Reubenites and the Gadites gave
the altar this name: A Witness Between Us that
the LORD is God.

Joshua's Farewell to the Leaders

23 After a long time had passed and the
LORD had given Israel rest from all their
enemies around them, Joshua, by then old and
well advanced in years, 2summoned all Israel—
their elders, leaders, judges and officials—and
said to them: "I am old and well advanced in
years. 3You yourselves have seen everything the
LORD your God has done to all these nations for
your sake; it was the LORD your God who fought
for you. 4Remember how I have allotted as an
inheritance for your tribes all the land of the
nations that remain—the nations I conquered—
between the Jordan and the Great Sea[a] in the
west. 5The LORD your God himself will drive
them out of your way. He will push them out
before you, and you will take possession of
their land, as the LORD your God promised you.
6"Be very strong; be careful to obey all that
is written in the Book of the Law of Moses,
without turning aside to the right or to the left.
7Do not associate with these nations that remain among you; do not invoke the names of
their gods or swear by them. You must not serve
them or bow down to them. 8But you are to
hold fast to the LORD your God, as you have
until now.
9"The LORD has driven out before you great
and powerful nations; to this day no one has
been able to withstand you. 10One of you routs
a thousand, because the LORD your God fights
for you, just as he promised. 11So be very careful
to love the LORD your God.
12"But if you turn away and ally yourselves
with the survivors of these nations that remain
among you and if you intermarry with them
and associate with them, 13then you may be
sure that the LORD your God will no longer
drive out these nations before you. Instead, they
will become snares and traps for you, whips on
your backs and thorns in your eyes, until you
perish from this good land, which the LORD
your God has given you.
14"Now I am about to go the way of all the
earth. You know with all your heart and soul
that not one of all the good promises the LORD
your God gave you has failed. Every promise
has been fulfilled; not one has failed. 15But just
as every good promise of the LORD your God
has come true, so the LORD will bring on you all
the evil he has threatened, until he has destroyed you from this good land he has given
you. 16If you violate the covenant of the LORD
your God, which he commanded you, and go
and serve other gods and bow down to them,
the LORD's anger will burn against you, and you
will quickly perish from the good land he has
given you."

The Covenant Renewed at Shechem

24 Then Joshua assembled all the tribes of
Israel at Shechem. He summoned the
elders, leaders, judges and officials of Israel, and
they presented themselves before God.
2Joshua said to all the people, "This is what
the LORD, the God of Israel, says: 'Long ago
your forefathers, including Terah the father of

[a]4 That is, the Mediterranean

---

always be loving reconciliation, even though that may not always be the outcome.

23:1–7 Joshua reminded the Israelites that God had given them all their victories, that all of the promised land had been apportioned as God had said it would be and that God would continue to defeat Israel's enemies and grant his people peace in the land. The Israelites were never supposed to forsake God or turn to the idols of the nations living within Canaan. The Israelites' walk with God was supposed to be ongoing, just like our own spiritual renewal.

23:8–13 Joshua challenged the Israelites to maintain a strong faith in God, remembering that God had accomplished a great work in defeating the powerful nations of Canaan on Israel's behalf. God gives more than enough courage and strength to succeed against all odds. In return, his people are to love and trust him fully, recognizing that if they turn away from the one true God to worship other gods, God will no longer fight on their side. Failure is always preceded by faithless acts. Each one of us will be tempted to turn our life over to a god that appears to grant immediate fulfillment. But God provides a way out of this temptation: We must seek the only true God and surrender our lives to him.

23:14–16 Joshua spoke of reality: God had not failed Israel in the past. He did everything he said he would do, and all of Israel knew that fact. Joshua issued a warning to the people. Just as God had promised to bless the Israelites because of their acts of obedience, God would also judge them harshly if they broke their covenant with him and worshiped other gods. In fact, if the Israelites were disobedient to God, he would not hesitate even to drive them from the promised land, the land he had fought to give them. In a loving relationship, others will hold us accountable for our actions because they want what is best for us, not because they want to upset us.

24:1–13 Speaking on behalf of God, Joshua declared that God alone had accomplished everything of lasting value that had been done for Israel. Joshua's story is not unique. Each of us is a testimony either to what God can do when we are faithful or to the tragedy that occurs when we are not.

JOSHUA

We all have experienced the frustration of knowing the truth but having no one believe us. Few of us, however, have had to live with the consequences of this for almost forty years.

Joshua was one of the twelve Israelites chosen to spy out the land of Canaan. Tremendous responsibility came with this job. Their report on what they saw would help an entire nation of people make a decision about entering the promised land. When the twelve spies gave their report, ten said it would be impossible to conquer the land. Their understanding of God was limited and distorted by their weak faith. Joshua and Caleb agreed that the task would be difficult, but they urged the people to trust God to help them conquer the land. They viewed God as loving, powerful, and able to lead them safely into the promised land.

Yet the people rebelled against God and sided with the majority report. They failed to see the truth because they were looking to their own strength, not God's. Because of their fear, the Israelites ran from the responsibility of surrendering their lives to God. They refused to recognize his right to rule over them. The result of their irresponsibility was tragic because that whole, unbelieving generation—with the exception of Joshua and Caleb—died in the desert.

Several important principles are illustrated by Joshua's life. First, what we think about God has a powerful effect on what we do. Also, ever since Adam's fall, human beings have had to endure pain whenever they decline to accept responsibility. Often our decision to either accept or run away from responsibility determines the type of pain we will experience and the effect it will have on us. Joshua experienced significant pain despite putting God first in his life. But Joshua's pain did not bring about his destruction. Rather, God used Joshua's pain to develop him into one of the most effective leaders in all of history.

Many of us think that we can escape pain by avoiding responsibility and its demands. What we fail to realize is that we often experience a much deeper pain when we run away from responsibility than when we accept it.

STRENGTHS AND ACCOMPLISHMENTS:

Joshua was a wise and gifted military strategist.

When faced with life's challenges, Joshua sought God's direction.

He was not afraid to go against popular opinion.

Joshua led the Israelites into the promised land.

He believed God's promises despite opposition.

LESSONS FROM HIS LIFE:

Despite opposition, it is always best to follow God.

Those we choose as mentors have a profound effect on us.

Solid preparation and encouragement are keys to training a leader.

KEY VERSE:

"But if serving the LORD seems undesirable to you, then choose for yourselves this day whom you will serve, whether the gods your forefathers served beyond the River, or the gods of the Amorites, in whose land you are living. But as for me and my household, we will serve the LORD" (24:15).

Joshua's story is told in Exodus 17; 24:13; 32:17; Numbers 11:28; 13—14; 26:65; 27; 32; 34:17; Deuteronomy 1:38; 3; 31; 32:44; 34:9; and the book of Joshua. He is also mentioned in Judges 1:1; 2; 1 Kings 16:34; 1 Chronicles 7:27; Nehemiah 8:17; Acts 7:45 and Hebrews 4:8.

Abraham and Nahor, lived beyond the River[a] and worshiped other gods. 3But I took your father Abraham from the land beyond the River and led him throughout Canaan and gave him many descendants. I gave him Isaac, 4and to Isaac I gave Jacob and Esau. I assigned the hill country of Seir to Esau, but Jacob and his sons went down to Egypt.

5" 'Then I sent Moses and Aaron, and I afflicted the Egyptians by what I did there, and I brought you out. 6When I brought your fathers out of Egypt, you came to the sea, and the Egyptians pursued them with chariots and horsemen[b] as far as the Red Sea.[c] 7But they cried to the LORD for help, and he put darkness between you and the Egyptians; he brought the sea over them and covered them. You saw with your own eyes what I did to the Egyptians. Then you lived in the desert for a long time.

8" 'I brought you to the land of the Amorites who lived east of the Jordan. They fought against you, but I gave them into your hands. I destroyed them from before you, and you took possession of their land. 9When Balak son of Zippor, the king of Moab, prepared to fight against Israel, he sent for Balaam son of Beor to put a curse on you. 10But I would not listen to Balaam, so he blessed you again and again, and I delivered you out of his hand.

11" 'Then you crossed the Jordan and came to Jericho. The citizens of Jericho fought against you, as did also the Amorites, Perizzites, Canaanites, Hittites, Girgashites, Hivites and Jebusites, but I gave them into your hands. 12I sent the hornet ahead of you, which drove them out before you—also the two Amorite kings. You did not do it with your own sword and bow. 13So I gave you a land on which you did not toil and cities you did not build; and you live in them and eat from vineyards and olive groves that you did not plant.'

14"Now fear the LORD and serve him with all faithfulness. Throw away the gods your forefathers worshiped beyond the River and in Egypt, and serve the LORD. 15But if serving the LORD seems undesirable to you, then choose for yourselves this day whom you will serve, whether the gods your forefathers served beyond the River, or the gods of the Amorites, in whose land you are living. But as for me and my household, we will serve the LORD."

16Then the people answered, "Far be it from us to forsake the LORD to serve other gods! 17It was the LORD our God himself who brought us and our fathers up out of Egypt, from that land of slavery, and performed those great signs before our eyes. He protected us on our entire journey and among all the nations through which we traveled. 18And the LORD drove out before us all the nations, including the Amorites, who lived in the land. We too will serve the LORD, because he is our God."

19Joshua said to the people, "You are not able to serve the LORD. He is a holy God; he is a jealous God. He will not forgive your rebellion and your sins. 20If you forsake the LORD and serve foreign gods, he will turn and bring disaster on you and make an end of you, after he has been good to you."

21But the people said to Joshua, "No! We will serve the LORD."

22Then Joshua said, "You are witnesses against yourselves that you have chosen to serve the LORD."

"Yes, we are witnesses," they replied.

23"Now then," said Joshua, "throw away the foreign gods that are among you and yield your hearts to the LORD, the God of Israel."

24And the people said to Joshua, "We will serve the LORD our God and obey him."

25On that day Joshua made a covenant for the people, and there at Shechem he drew up for them decrees and laws. 26And Joshua recorded these things in the Book of the Law of God. Then he took a large stone and set it up there under the oak near the holy place of the LORD.

27"See!" he said to all the people. "This stone will be a witness against us. It has heard all the words the LORD has said to us. It will be a witness against you if you are untrue to your God."

Buried in the Promised Land

28Then Joshua sent the people away, each to his own inheritance.

29After these things, Joshua son of Nun, the

[a]2 That is, the Euphrates; also in verses 3, 14 and 15
[b]6 Or *charioteers* [c]6 Hebrew *Yam Suph*; that is, Sea of Reeds

---

24:14–18 Joshua concluded his message by challenging the people to serve the true God and reject the foreign gods their ancestors foolishly served. He mockingly suggested that if the people were so unwise as reject the God of Israel as the only true God, then the people should choose to serve either the gods of the Euphrates or the gods of those heathen nations living in the promised land. Joshua and his family, however, would serve the God of Israel. The people responded positively to Joshua's challenge and declared their undying commitment to the one true God. Each day we make decisions about whom we will serve—God or this world. May we respond as the Israelites did and declare the Lord as our one true God.

24:19–28 Joshua knew that God is holy. He also was aware of the sinful tendencies of the Israelites. So Joshua urged the people once more to proclaim their commitment to follow God. Their words would be an eternal witness to their decision. To cement that commitment, Joshua, who had been a rock of faith before God throughout his life, recognized the importance of leaving one more permanent stone memorial as a reminder to the greatness and faithfulness of God. A record of our decision to follow God, noting specific times or circumstances that we surrendered our lives to him, can be helpful to us in times of trouble. Such a record can remind us that we were serious in our decision and that we are responsible for our actions.

24:29–33 Several great men of Israel had died—Moses, prior to Israel's entry into the promised land, and now, after the completion of the initial phase of Israel's conquest, Joshua and Eleazar the priest. The Israelites responded to these losses by serving God. They demonstrated their com-

servant of the LORD, died at the age of a
hundred and ten. 30And they buried him in the
land of his inheritance, at Timnath Serah[a] in
the hill country of Ephraim, north of Mount
Gaash.
31Israel served the LORD throughout the lifetime of Joshua and of the elders who outlived
him and who had experienced everything the
LORD had done for Israel.
32And Joseph's bones, which the Israelites
had brought up from Egypt, were buried at Shechem in the tract of land that Jacob bought for
a hundred pieces of silver[b] from the sons of
Hamor, the father of Shechem. This became the
inheritance of Joseph's descendants.
33And Eleazar son of Aaron died and was
buried at Gibeah, which had been allotted to
his son Phinehas in the hill country of Ephraim.

[a]30 Also known as *Timnath Heres* (see Judges 2:9)
[b]32 Hebrew *hundred kesitahs;* a kesitah was a unit of money of unknown weight and value.

---

mitment to God by burying Joseph's bones in the promised land both as a testimony to Joseph's faith and to God's faithfulness to his people (see Genesis 50:25; Exodus 13:19; Hebrews 11:22). We might ask ourselves this question: Would someone burying our bones do so as a testimony to our faith—or our faithlessness? If it is faithlessness, we can change our testimony by turning to God today. If our testimony is faith, we must persevere.

JUDGES

The Big Picture

The conquest of the promised land under Joshua had been a miraculous success. It wasn't long, however, before the people forgot what had made it all possible—their faith in God and obedience to his commands. The people became trapped in a four-step spiritual cycle: (1) They fell into sin, (2) they were enslaved by an oppressor, (3) they cried out to God for help, and (4) God sent a leader (or judge) to deliver them. At the end of each painful cycle there was a temporary period of faithfulness and stability. But soon most of the people slipped back into the same vicious cycle of sin and idolatry.

The book of Judges shows what happens to a society when its citizens do whatever they choose (17:6). The people of Israel refused to learn from their past mistakes. They closed their eyes to the needs of others and refused to follow the commands of God. As a result, the Israelites became trapped by their individual delusions and brought suffering on themselves and the people around them. They refused to follow the path to freedom by obeying God's plan for righteous and holy living.

Let us learn from Israel's mistakes. Notice that Israel's failures often came after great victories. Success sometimes sets us up for a fall. We must humbly consider our activities and relationships, keeping our eyes on God and obeying his will for us. Doing things our way leads to enslavement and suffering; following God's plan is the only path to freedom. Yet when we do fail and go our own way, we can be sure that God is listening to our cries for help and will deliver his repentant children again.

A. PROLOGUE: A PATTERN OF INCOMPLETE SURRENDER TO GOD (1:1–3:6)

1. Not Fully Dealing With the Issues (1:1–2:5)
2. Making the Same Mistake Over and Over (2:6–3:6)

B. CASE HISTORIES: THE UPS AND DOWNS OF INCOMPLETE SURRENDER TO GOD (3:7–16:31)

1. Rescued by Othniel, Ehud and Shamgar (3:7-31)
2. Rescued by Deborah and Barak (4:1–5:31)
3. Rescued by Gideon (6:1–8:35)
4. Rescued from Abimelech (9:1-57)
5. Rescued by Tola, Jair, Jephthah, Ibzan, Elon and Abdon (10:1–12:15)
6. Rescued by Samson (13:1–16:31)

C. EPILOGUE: CLASSIC EXAMPLES OF GOING OUR OWN WAY IN SPIRITUAL BLINDNESS (17:1–21:25)

1. "Doing Our Own Thing" Religiously (17:1–18:31)
2. "Doing Our Own Thing" Morally (19:1–21:25)

Spiritual Renewal Themes

THE DANGER OF PRIDE

It is so easy to think we have "arrived" and know all we need to about spiritual living. The Israelites had arrived in the promised land, their physical destination. What did they have to worry about now? After all, they were God's chosen people. Yet the Israelites still had to learn that "a man's pride brings him low, but a man of lowly spirit gains honor" (Proverbs 29:23). In the book of Judges the Israelites discovered repeatedly that overconfidence and pride lead to a fall. What was true for the Israelites is still true today. Spiritual renewal is an ongoing process that requires us to be vigilant in self-examination. To be sustained spiritually we must depend on God day by day.

Essential Facts

PURPOSE:
To see how tragic incomplete commitment to God can be, how sinful patterns tend to continue from one generation to the next and how God readily lifts us up when we repent and look to him for help.

AUTHOR:
Tradition attributes it to Samuel, though it could have been one of his contemporaries.

AUDIENCE:
The people of Israel.

DATE WRITTEN:
Probably between 1050 and 1000 B.C.

SETTING:
Various parts of the promised land of Israel.

KEY VERSE:
"In those days Israel had no king; everyone did as he saw fit" (17:6).

KEY PLACES:
Israel, Aram, Moab, Midian, Ammon, Philistia.

KEY PEOPLE AND RELATIONSHIPS:
Othniel, Ehud, Deborah and Barak, Gideon, Abimelech, Jephthah, Samson and Delilah.

THE CYCLE OF FAILURE

Why do intelligent people repeatedly fall into the same tragic traps and mistakes? Again and again God delivered the Israelites from their troubles. For short periods of time the people gratefully guarded their faith and were consistent in their worship. But ultimately their overconfidence set them up for another fall. The frequent repetition of this cycle makes it seem as if such a pattern was inevitable. It wasn't. Yet this pattern was perpetuated because the people did not realize that spiritual renewal is a lifelong process, continually based on God's help.

SUFFERING THE CONSEQUENCES

God did not protect his people from the painful consequences of their actions. He allowed them to suffer the consequences so they could learn some valuable lessons. Facing the consequences of our actions can be a healthy part of our spiritual growth. Whenever the Israelites finally came to the end of themselves and admitted their helplessness, God moved in and delivered them. If they had continually depended on God, they would have been able to break the cycle permanently. We never outgrow our need to depend on God. We are not equipped to handle the chaos in our lives alone. We must continually seek God and surrender our lives to him or suffer the consequences.

GOD USES FLAWED PEOPLE

A number of the heroes in the book of Judges are most notable because of their flaws. Barak refused to fight for God without the help of the prophetess Deborah. Gideon needed to see God prove himself through signs before he would act in faith. Samson's flaws are legendary, but God still used him to fight the enemies of Israel. We do not need to be flawless in order to call upon God, receive help or be used by God for his glory. We simply need to see and admit our need. We cannot earn God's blessings; we must simply receive his gift of grace.

Israel Fights the Remaining Canaanites

1 After the death of Joshua, the Israelites asked the LORD, "Who will be the first to go up and fight for us against the Canaanites?"

[2]The LORD answered, "Judah is to go; I have given the land into their hands."

[3]Then the men of Judah said to the Simeonites their brothers, "Come up with us into the territory allotted to us, to fight against the Canaanites. We in turn will go with you into yours." So the Simeonites went with them.

[4]When Judah attacked, the LORD gave the Canaanites and Perizzites into their hands and they struck down ten thousand men at Bezek. [5]It was there that they found Adoni-Bezek and fought against him, putting to rout the Canaanites and Perizzites. [6]Adoni-Bezek fled, but they chased him and caught him, and cut off his thumbs and big toes.

[7]Then Adoni-Bezek said, "Seventy kings with their thumbs and big toes cut off have picked up scraps under my table. Now God has paid me back for what I did to them." They brought him to Jerusalem, and he died there.

[8]The men of Judah attacked Jerusalem also and took it. They put the city to the sword and set it on fire.

[9]After that, the men of Judah went down to fight against the Canaanites living in the hill country, the Negev and the western foothills. [10]They advanced against the Canaanites living in Hebron (formerly called Kiriath Arba) and defeated Sheshai, Ahiman and Talmai.

[11]From there they advanced against the people living in Debir (formerly called Kiriath Sepher). [12]And Caleb said, "I will give my daughter Acsah in marriage to the man who attacks and captures Kiriath Sepher." [13]Othniel son of Kenaz, Caleb's younger brother, took it; so Caleb gave his daughter Acsah to him in marriage.

[14]One day when she came to Othniel, she urged him[a] to ask her father for a field. When she got off her donkey, Caleb asked her, "What can I do for you?"

[15]She replied, "Do me a special favor. Since you have given me land in the Negev, give me also springs of water." Then Caleb gave her the upper and lower springs.

[16]The descendants of Moses' father-in-law, the Kenite, went up from the City of Palms[b] with the men of Judah to live among the people of the Desert of Judah in the Negev near Arad.

[17]Then the men of Judah went with the Simeonites their brothers and attacked the Canaanites living in Zephath, and they totally destroyed[c] the city. Therefore it was called Hormah.[d] [18]The men of Judah also took[e] Gaza, Ashkelon and Ekron—each city with its territory.

[19]The LORD was with the men of Judah. They took possession of the hill country, but they were unable to drive the people from the plains, because they had iron chariots. [20]As Moses had promised, Hebron was given to Caleb, who drove from it the three sons of Anak. [21]The Benjamites, however, failed to dislodge the Jebusites, who were living in Jerusalem; to this day the Jebusites live there with the Benjamites.

[22]Now the house of Joseph attacked Bethel, and the LORD was with them. [23]When they sent men to spy out Bethel (formerly called Luz), [24]the spies saw a man coming out of the city and they said to him, "Show us how to get into the city and we will see that you are treated well." [25]So he showed them, and they put the city to the sword but spared the man and his whole family. [26]He then went to the land of the Hittites, where he built a city and called it Luz, which is its name to this day.

[27]But Manasseh did not drive out the people of Beth Shan or Taanach or Dor or Ibleam or Megiddo and their surrounding settlements, for the Canaanites were determined to live in that land. [28]When Israel became strong, they pressed the Canaanites into forced labor but never drove them out completely. [29]Nor did Ephraim drive out the Canaanites living in Gezer, but the Canaanites continued to live there among them. [30]Neither did Zebulun drive out the Canaanites living in Kitron or Nahalol, who remained among them; but they did subject them to forced labor. [31]Nor did Asher drive out those living in Acco or Sidon or Ahlab or Aczib or Helbah or Aphek or Rehob, [32]and because of this the people of Asher lived among the Canaanite inhabitants of the land. [33]Neither did Naphtali drive out those living in Beth Shemesh or Beth Anath; but the Naphtalites too lived among the Canaanite inhabitants of the land, and those living in Beth Shemesh and Beth Anath became forced laborers for them. [34]The Amorites confined the Danites to the hill country, not allowing them to come down into the

[a]14 Hebrew; Septuagint and Vulgate *Othniel, he urged her*
[b]16 That is, Jericho
[c]17 The Hebrew term refers to the irrevocable giving over of things or persons to the LORD, often by totally destroying them.
[d]17 *Hormah* means *destruction.*
[e]18 Hebrew; Septuagint *Judah did not take*

1:1 The book of Judges gives us an idea of the courage it takes to enter new territory. Even though much of the promised land (see Genesis 15:18–21) had already been conquered under Joshua, it was necessary for the Israelites to address the present reality of the enemies still living there. Only when the conquest was completed could Israel focus on building a new life in their new land. In the same way, it is important that we conquer and control what has mastered us in the past before we try to build a new life.

1:19–36 The last half of this chapter shows how incomplete Israel's conquest of the promised land really was. God had promised to be with the Israelites and guide them in this difficult process. As the Israelites displayed courage and faith in God, he brought them numerous victories. But faltering courage and lack of perseverance stopped God's people short of their goal. We also must place our faith in God and persevere to preserve our spiritual gains.

plain. 35And the Amorites were determined also to hold out in Mount Heres, Aijalon and Shaalbim, but when the power of the house of Joseph increased, they too were pressed into forced labor. 36The boundary of the Amorites was from Scorpion[a] Pass to Sela and beyond.

The Angel of the LORD at Bokim

2 The angel of the LORD went up from Gilgal to Bokim and said, "I brought you up out of Egypt and led you into the land that I swore to give to your forefathers. I said, 'I will never break my covenant with you, 2and you shall not make a covenant with the people of this land, but you shall break down their altars.' Yet you have disobeyed me. Why have you done this? 3Now therefore I tell you that I will not drive them out before you; they will be ⌊thorns⌋ in your sides and their gods will be a snare to you."

4When the angel of the LORD had spoken these things to all the Israelites, the people wept aloud, 5and they called that place Bokim.[b] There they offered sacrifices to the LORD.

Disobedience and Defeat

6After Joshua had dismissed the Israelites, they went to take possession of the land, each to his own inheritance. 7The people served the LORD throughout the lifetime of Joshua and of the elders who outlived him and who had seen all the great things the LORD had done for Israel.

8Joshua son of Nun, the servant of the LORD, died at the age of a hundred and ten. 9And they buried him in the land of his inheritance, at Timnath Heres[c] in the hill country of Ephraim, north of Mount Gaash.

10After that whole generation had been gathered to their fathers, another generation grew up, who knew neither the LORD nor what he had done for Israel. 11Then the Israelites did evil in the eyes of the LORD and served the Baals. 12They forsook the LORD, the God of their fathers, who had brought them out of Egypt. They followed and worshiped various gods of the peoples around them. They provoked the LORD to anger 13because they forsook him and served Baal and the Ashtoreths. 14In his anger against Israel the LORD handed them over to raiders who plundered them. He sold them to their enemies all around, whom they were no longer able to resist. 15Whenever Israel went out to fight, the hand of the LORD was against them to defeat them, just as he had sworn to them. They were in great distress.

16Then the LORD raised up judges,[d] who saved them out of the hands of these raiders. 17Yet they would not listen to their judges but prostituted themselves to other gods and worshiped them. Unlike their fathers, they quickly turned from the way in which their fathers had walked, the way of obedience to the LORD's commands. 18Whenever the LORD raised up a judge for them, he was with the judge and saved them out of the hands of their enemies as long as the judge lived; for the LORD had compassion on them as they groaned under those who oppressed and afflicted them. 19But when the judge died, the people returned to ways even more corrupt than those of their fathers, following other gods and serving and worshiping them. They refused to give up their evil practices and stubborn ways.

20Therefore the LORD was very angry with Israel and said, "Because this nation has violated the covenant that I laid down for their forefathers and has not listened to me, 21I will no longer drive out before them any of the nations Joshua left when he died. 22I will use them to test Israel and see whether they will keep the way of the LORD and walk in it as their forefathers did." 23The LORD had allowed those nations to remain; he did not drive them out at once by giving them into the hands of Joshua.

3 These are the nations the LORD left to test all those Israelites who had not experienced any of the wars in Canaan 2(he did this only to teach warfare to the descendants of the Israelites who had not had previous battle experience): 3the five rulers of the Philistines, all the Canaanites, the Sidonians, and the Hivites living in the Lebanon mountains from Mount Baal Hermon to Lebo[e] Hamath. 4They were left to test the Israelites to see whether they would obey the LORD's commands, which he had given their forefathers through Moses.

5The Israelites lived among the Canaanites, Hittites, Amorites, Perizzites, Hivites and Jebusites. 6They took their daughters in marriage and gave their own daughters to their sons, and served their gods.

[a]36 Hebrew *Akrabbim* [b]5 *Bokim* means *weepers.*
[c]9 Also known as *Timnath Serah* (see Joshua 19:50 and 24:30) [d]16 Or *leaders;* similarly in verses 17-19
[e]3 Or *to the entrance to*

2:1–5 The angel of the LORD stated that the fundamental reason for Israel's half-completed conquest of the promised land was because of their half-hearted commitment to God. They had allowed the altars of the various Canaanite peoples to remain. Those religious and moral temptations became repeated points of failure for God's people. To Israel's credit, they repented, attempting to set things right with God. No matter what we have done, we can turn to God. God will forgive us, but we must seek that forgiveness.

2:11–19 This passage highlights the cycle of short-term renewal that echoes throughout the book of Judges. Because of their prolonged denial of sin, various enemies repeatedly oppressed the Israelites. In their misery, they finally admitted their need for God and cried out to him. God provided judges to free the Israelites from their oppressors. Tragically, it was only a matter of time before Israel made the same mistakes again. We also must rely on God. He will support us and sustain us with his gracious power. When we fall, God is waiting to hear our cries for help. He will respond with the help we need.

Othniel

7The Israelites did evil in the eyes of the LORD; they forgot the LORD their God and served the Baals and the Asherahs. 8The anger of the LORD burned against Israel so that he sold them into the hands of Cushan-Rishathaim king of Aram Naharaim,[a] to whom the Israelites were subject for eight years. 9But when they cried out to the LORD, he raised up for them a deliverer, Othniel son of Kenaz, Caleb's younger brother, who saved them. 10The Spirit of the LORD came upon him, so that he became Israel's judge[b] and went to war. The LORD gave Cushan-Rishathaim king of Aram into the hands of Othniel, who overpowered him. 11So the land had peace for forty years, until Othniel son of Kenaz died.

Ehud

12Once again the Israelites did evil in the eyes of the LORD, and because they did this evil the LORD gave Eglon king of Moab power over Israel. 13Getting the Ammonites and Amalekites to join him, Eglon came and attacked Israel, and they took possession of the City of Palms.[c] 14The Israelites were subject to Eglon king of Moab for eighteen years.

15Again the Israelites cried out to the LORD, and he gave them a deliverer—Ehud, a left-handed man, the son of Gera the Benjamite. The Israelites sent him with tribute to Eglon king of Moab. 16Now Ehud had made a double-edged sword about a foot and a half[d] long, which he strapped to his right thigh under his clothing. 17He presented the tribute to Eglon king of Moab, who was a very fat man. 18After Ehud had presented the tribute, he sent on their way the men who had carried it. 19At the idols[e] near Gilgal he himself turned back and said, "I have a secret message for you, O king."

The king said, "Quiet!" And all his attendants left him.

20Ehud then approached him while he was sitting alone in the upper room of his summer palace[f] and said, "I have a message from God for you." As the king rose from his seat, 21Ehud reached with his left hand, drew the sword from his right thigh and plunged it into the king's belly. 22Even the handle sank in after the blade, which came out his back. Ehud did not pull the sword out, and the fat closed in over it. 23Then Ehud went out to the porch[g]; he shut the doors of the upper room behind him and locked them.

24After he had gone, the servants came and found the doors of the upper room locked. They said, "He must be relieving himself in the inner room of the house." 25They waited to the point of embarrassment, but when he did not open the doors of the room, they took a key and unlocked them. There they saw their lord fallen to the floor, dead.

26While they waited, Ehud got away. He passed by the idols and escaped to Seirah. 27When he arrived there, he blew a trumpet in the hill country of Ephraim, and the Israelites went down with him from the hills, with him leading them.

28"Follow me," he ordered, "for the LORD has given Moab, your enemy, into your hands." So they followed him down and, taking possession of the fords of the Jordan that led to Moab, they allowed no one to cross over. 29At that time they struck down about ten thousand Moabites, all vigorous and strong; not a man escaped. 30That day Moab was made subject to Israel, and the land had peace for eighty years.

Shamgar

31After Ehud came Shamgar son of Anath, who struck down six hundred Philistines with an oxgoad. He too saved Israel.

Deborah

4 After Ehud died, the Israelites once again did evil in the eyes of the LORD. 2So the LORD sold them into the hands of Jabin, a king of Canaan, who reigned in Hazor. The commander of his army was Sisera, who lived in Harosheth Haggoyim. 3Because he had nine hundred iron chariots and had cruelly oppressed the Israelites for twenty years, they cried to the LORD for help.

4Deborah, a prophetess, the wife of Lappidoth, was leading[h] Israel at that time. 5She

[a] 8 That is, Northwest Mesopotamia [b] 10 Or *leader* [c] 13 That is, Jericho [d] 16 Hebrew *a cubit* (about 0.5 meter) [e] 19 Or *the stone quarries*; also in verse 26 [f] 20 The meaning of the Hebrew for this phrase is uncertain. [g] 23 The meaning of the Hebrew for this word is uncertain. [h] 4 Traditionally *judging*

3:7–10 Notice that the rescue of Israel by Othniel was governed by the power of the Holy Spirit. As believers, we have the Holy Spirit living in us and guiding us (see 1 Corinthians 6:19; Galatians 5:18). The Holy Spirit is always there to give us direction, encouragement and power to face our problems.

3:12–30 It was Ehud's distinctiveness as a left-handed warrior that made his assassination of the Moabite king, Eglon, possible. Since Ehud reached for his weapon with his left hand, the king did not suspect anything. People often view their unique characteristics as liabilities rather than as assets. God has made us the way we are for a purpose. We should not complain about our differences; we should use our unique abilities to help others and to serve God. God isn't running an assembly line; he custom-builds all his people (see 1 Corinthians 12).

4:4–9 Deborah had served as a prophet of God in Israel. Here she was called on to take part in a military campaign to overthrow their Canaanite oppressors. Though this was new ground for her, Deborah didn't hesitate for a minute. She trusted that God would care for and direct her. Barak, however, put more trust in Deborah than in God. Because of Barak's lack of faith, God accomplished his task through another person. We all have the potential to assist others struggling with situations that have plagued us in the past. But if we don't demonstrate the courage to step out and allow God to use us, God may have to find someone else to help.

Deborah & Barak

In a lawless, enemy-occupied country, a mother in Israel became a mother to Israel. Chosen by God, Deborah gained national prominence as a prophet and judge during one of her country's blackest hours. Considering Israel's male-dominated culture, it was remarkable that a woman would be selected for such a task, but Deborah was a remarkable woman. She never hesitated to assume leadership, nor was she reluctant to risk her life later in a military campaign. She is seen as full of faith, courage and confidence in God's power and promises. Deborah surrendered her life to God, making herself available to him and trusting him for the outcome.

Under God's direction, Deborah called Barak of Kedesh to assemble ten thousand men at Mount Tabor in order to draw the enemy into battle. Barak was reluctant. This reluctance may have been prompted by insecurity, self-doubt, lack of faith, fear, concern over the reliability of Deborah's message or even simple pragmatism in the face of terrible odds. Nonetheless, Barak did eventually step out in faith, leading his outmanned and outclassed troops against a formidable foe. But the battle was God's. A Kenite woman, Jael, wrapped up the loose ends of the victory by killing Sisera in his sleep.

Barak's reticence reaped a repercussion: He was denied the honor of personally deposing the enemy leader. Still, no mention of Barak's lapse is made in the epic song found in chapter 5. Barak, despite his timidity, is also numbered among the heroes of faith listed in Hebrews 11. It was Barak's final obedience, not his initial hesitance, that God found significant. And it is the same way with us. God always commends our commitment while forgiving and forgetting our failure. He graciously did this with Barak and continues to do so with all those who trust him.

STRENGTHS AND ACCOMPLISHMENTS:

Deborah's confidence in God gave her courage in difficult situations.

Deborah proved to be a willing risk taker for God.

Despite initial reluctance, Barak demonstrated obedience to God.

WEAKNESSES AND MISTAKES:

Barak hesitated before obeying God.

LESSONS FROM THEIR LIVES:

Deborah's prominence demonstrates the value God places on women.

Lack of faith and obedience leads to oppression.

God is often willing to commend obedience and trust in spite of initial reluctance or disobedience.

A society's well-being depends on its faithfulness to God.

KEY VERSE:

"When the princes in Israel take the lead, when the people willingly offer themselves—praise the Lord!" (5:2).

The story of Deborah and Barak is told in Judges 4—5. Barak is also mentioned in 1 Samuel 12:11 and Hebrews 11:32.

held court under the Palm of Deborah between
Ramah and Bethel in the hill country of Ephraim, and the Israelites came to her to have their
disputes decided. 6She sent for Barak son of
Abinoam from Kedesh in Naphtali and said to
him, "The LORD, the God of Israel, commands
you: 'Go, take with you ten thousand men of
Naphtali and Zebulun and lead the way to
Mount Tabor. 7I will lure Sisera, the commander of Jabin's army, with his chariots and his
troops to the Kishon River and give him into
your hands.' "

8Barak said to her, "If you go with me, I will
go; but if you don't go with me, I won't go."

9"Very well," Deborah said, "I will go with
you. But because of the way you are going about
this,[a] the honor will not be yours, for the LORD
will hand Sisera over to a woman." So Deborah
went with Barak to Kedesh, 10where he summoned Zebulun and Naphtali. Ten thousand
men followed him, and Deborah also went
with him.

11Now Heber the Kenite had left the other
Kenites, the descendants of Hobab, Moses'
brother-in-law,[b] and pitched his tent by the
great tree in Zaanannim near Kedesh.

12When they told Sisera that Barak son of
Abinoam had gone up to Mount Tabor, 13Sisera
gathered together his nine hundred iron chariots and all the men with him, from Harosheth
Haggoyim to the Kishon River.

14Then Deborah said to Barak, "Go! This is
the day the LORD has given Sisera into your
hands. Has not the LORD gone ahead of you?" So
Barak went down Mount Tabor, followed by ten
thousand men. 15At Barak's advance, the LORD
routed Sisera and all his chariots and army by
the sword, and Sisera abandoned his chariot
and fled on foot. 16But Barak pursued the chariots and army as far as Harosheth Haggoyim. All
the troops of Sisera fell by the sword; not a man
was left.

17Sisera, however, fled on foot to the tent of
Jael, the wife of Heber the Kenite, because there
were friendly relations between Jabin king of
Hazor and the clan of Heber the Kenite.

18Jael went out to meet Sisera and said to
him, "Come, my lord, come right in. Don't be
afraid." So he entered her tent, and she put a
covering over him.

19"I'm thirsty," he said. "Please give me some
water." She opened a skin of milk, gave him a
drink, and covered him up.

20"Stand in the doorway of the tent," he told
her. "If someone comes by and asks you, 'Is
anyone here?' say 'No.' "

21But Jael, Heber's wife, picked up a tent peg
and a hammer and went quietly to him while
he lay fast asleep, exhausted. She drove the peg
through his temple into the ground, and he
died.

22Barak came by in pursuit of Sisera, and Jael
went out to meet him. "Come," she said, "I will
show you the man you're looking for." So he
went in with her, and there lay Sisera with the
tent peg through his temple—dead.

23On that day God subdued Jabin, the Canaanite king, before the Israelites. 24And the
hand of the Israelites grew stronger and stronger
against Jabin, the Canaanite king, until they destroyed him.

The Song of Deborah

5 On that day Deborah and Barak son of
Abinoam sang this song:

2"When the princes in Israel take the lead,
when the people willingly offer
themselves—
praise the LORD!

3"Hear this, you kings! Listen, you rulers!
I will sing to[c] the LORD, I will sing;
I will make music to[d] the LORD, the
God of Israel.

4"O LORD, when you went out from Seir,
when you marched from the land of
Edom,
the earth shook, the heavens poured,
the clouds poured down water.
5The mountains quaked before the LORD,
the One of Sinai,
before the LORD, the God of Israel.

6"In the days of Shamgar son of Anath,
in the days of Jael, the roads were
abandoned;
travelers took to winding paths.
7Village life[e] in Israel ceased,
ceased until I,[f] Deborah, arose,
arose a mother in Israel.
8When they chose new gods,
war came to the city gates,
and not a shield or spear was seen
among forty thousand in Israel.
9My heart is with Israel's princes,
with the willing volunteers among the
people.
Praise the LORD!

10"You who ride on white donkeys,
sitting on your saddle blankets,
and you who walk along the road,

[a]9 Or *But on the expedition you are undertaking* [b]11 Or *father-in-law* [c]3 Or *of* [d]3 Or / *with song I will praise* [e]7 Or *Warriors* [f]7 Or *you*

5:7, 12, 15 In this song of victory, the role of Deborah is emphasized. Women in ancient Israel rarely rose to positions of leadership. But Deborah's courage and faith in God made her an ideal prophet. She was called to lead the forces of Israel against the oppressive Canaanites. What tremendous faith it must have taken for Deborah to assume this unlikely position! Victory can come even when God puts us in positions in which we might feel uncomfortable. We must trust God's promises to us. "Is anything too hard for the LORD?" (Genesis 18:14).

Being Responsible to Do What We Can Do

Judges 5:1–12 There are times when others fail to fulfill their responsibilities or roles they should play. When this happens, we may suffer from their lack of discipline. Our lives may become chaotic. We may feel frustrated and angry. But our feelings should not keep us from doing our part, from accepting our responsibility to do what we can do to change the situation, to do what is right, to follow God's plan.

The time of the judges was a time of confusion for Israel. The people did what was right in their own eyes instead of obeying God's law. Tyrants oppressed them. One of the worst oppressors was a Canaanite named Sisera who "cruelly oppressed the Israelites for twenty years" (4:3). At this time God chose Deborah to be a judge. Her job was to settle disputes between the people. One day Deborah summoned a man named Barak and told him that God would use him to defeat the army of Sisera. Barak said, "If you go with me, I will go; but if you don't go with me, I won't go" (4:8). Barak lacked the faith to take on the responsibilities God had given him. So Deborah agreed to go along, but she added, "Because of the way you are going about this, the honor will not be yours, for the LORD will hand Sisera over to a woman" (4:9). In the end, Sisera did die at the hands of a woman. In the victory song, Deborah was honored. They sang, "Village life in Israel ceased, ceased until I, Deborah, arose, arose a mother in Israel" (5:7).

Like Deborah, when others don't fulfill their rightful duties and roles, we still must find a way to do what is right. We cannot blame others for our own behavior and lack of spiritual growth.

Turn to 1 Samuel 25.

consider 11the voice of the singers[a] at the
watering places.
They recite the righteous acts of the
LORD,
the righteous acts of his warriors[b] in
Israel.

"Then the people of the LORD
went down to the city gates.
12'Wake up, wake up, Deborah!
Wake up, wake up, break out in song!
Arise, O Barak!
Take captive your captives, O son of
Abinoam.'

13"Then the men who were left
came down to the nobles;
the people of the LORD
came to me with the mighty.
14Some came from Ephraim, whose roots
were in Amalek;
Benjamin was with the people who
followed you.
From Makir captains came down,
from Zebulun those who bear a
commander's staff.
15The princes of Issachar were with Deborah;
yes, Issachar was with Barak,
rushing after him into the valley.
In the districts of Reuben
there was much searching of heart.
16Why did you stay among the campfires[c]
to hear the whistling for the flocks?
In the districts of Reuben
there was much searching of heart.
17Gilead stayed beyond the Jordan.
And Dan, why did he linger by the
ships?
Asher remained on the coast
and stayed in his coves.
18The people of Zebulun risked their very
lives;
so did Naphtali on the heights of the
field.

19"Kings came, they fought;
the kings of Canaan fought
at Taanach by the waters of Megiddo,
but they carried off no silver, no
plunder.
20From the heavens the stars fought,
from their courses they fought against
Sisera.
21The river Kishon swept them away,
the age-old river, the river Kishon.
March on, my soul; be strong!
22Then thundered the horses' hoofs—
galloping, galloping go his mighty steeds.
23'Curse Meroz,' said the angel of the LORD.
'Curse its people bitterly,
because they did not come to help the
LORD,
to help the LORD against the mighty.'

[a]11 Or *archers;* the meaning of the Hebrew for this word is uncertain. [b]11 Or *villagers* [c]16 Or *saddlebags*

24 "Most blessed of women be Jael,
the wife of Heber the Kenite,
most blessed of tent-dwelling women.
25 He asked for water, and she gave him milk;
in a bowl fit for nobles she brought him
curdled milk.
26 Her hand reached for the tent peg,
her right hand for the workman's
hammer.
She struck Sisera, she crushed his head,
she shattered and pierced his temple.
27 At her feet he sank,
he fell; there he lay.
At her feet he sank, he fell;
where he sank, there he fell—dead.

28 "Through the window peered Sisera's
mother;
behind the lattice she cried out,
'Why is his chariot so long in coming?
Why is the clatter of his chariots
delayed?'
29 The wisest of her ladies answer her;
indeed, she keeps saying to herself,
30 'Are they not finding and dividing the
spoils:
a girl or two for each man,
colorful garments as plunder for Sisera,
colorful garments embroidered,
highly embroidered garments for my
neck—
all this as plunder?'

31 "So may all your enemies perish, O LORD!
But may they who love you be like the
sun
when it rises in its strength."

Then the land had peace forty years.

Gideon

6 Again the Israelites did evil in the eyes of
the LORD, and for seven years he gave them
into the hands of the Midianites. 2 Because the
power of Midian was so oppressive, the Israelites prepared shelters for themselves in mountain clefts, caves and strongholds. 3 Whenever
the Israelites planted their crops, the Midianites, Amalekites and other eastern peoples invaded the country. 4 They camped on the land
and ruined the crops all the way to Gaza and
did not spare a living thing for Israel, neither
sheep nor cattle nor donkeys. 5 They came up
with their livestock and their tents like swarms
of locusts. It was impossible to count the men
and their camels; they invaded the land to ravage it. 6 Midian so impoverished the Israelites
that they cried out to the LORD for help.
7 When the Israelites cried to the LORD because of Midian, 8 he sent them a prophet, who
said, "This is what the LORD, the God of Israel,
says: I brought you up out of Egypt, out of the
land of slavery. 9 I snatched you from the power
of Egypt and from the hand of all your oppressors. I drove them from before you and gave
you their land. 10 I said to you, 'I am the LORD
your God; do not worship the gods of the Amorites, in whose land you live.' But you have not
listened to me."
11 The angel of the LORD came and sat down
under the oak in Ophrah that belonged to Joash
the Abiezrite, where his son Gideon was threshing wheat in a winepress to keep it from the
Midianites. 12 When the angel of the LORD appeared to Gideon, he said, "The LORD is with
you, mighty warrior."
13 "But sir," Gideon replied, "if the LORD is
with us, why has all this happened to us? Where
are all his wonders that our fathers told us
about when they said, 'Did not the LORD bring
us up out of Egypt?' But now the LORD has
abandoned us and put us into the hand of Midian."
14 The LORD turned to him and said, "Go in
the strength you have and save Israel out of
Midian's hand. Am I not sending you?"
15 "But Lord,[a]" Gideon asked, "how can I
save Israel? My clan is the weakest in Manasseh,
and I am the least in my family."
16 The LORD answered, "I will be with you,
and you will strike down all the Midianites together."
17 Gideon replied, "If now I have found favor
in your eyes, give me a sign that it is really you
talking to me. 18 Please do not go away until I
come back and bring my offering and set it
before you."
And the LORD said, "I will wait until you
return."
19 Gideon went in, prepared a young goat,
and from an ephah[b] of flour he made bread
without yeast. Putting the meat in a basket and

[a] 15 Or *sir* [b] 19 That is, probably about 3/5 bushel (about 22 liters)

6:11–15 Gideon responded to the message of the angel with little faith or hope. He was so used to the oppression of the Midianites that he had little confidence that things could ever be any different. Not only did Gideon view himself as weak and insignificant, he also viewed God as being unfaithful to his covenant people. This is the typical response of someone trying to cope with terrible circumstances without full reliance on God. If we rely only on ourselves under such conditions, we will be worn down by continual pain and will lose hope of ever breaking free. However, facing terrible circumstances honestly can be a good starting point. Once Gideon admitted that his situation was terrible, he discovered that God was able to deliver him.

6:15–16 Gideon's response and his fear and hesitation later may have been related to feelings of inadequacy. His family was poor, and he was the least in his family. God offered Gideon his power as the means of overcoming Gideon's sense of personal inadequacy. When we seek God, he may call us to attempt great tasks—tasks that we feel inadequate to accomplish. As we confess our inadequacy, God will make us more than adequate through his power. God says that he will be with us to help us carry out whatever tasks he has assigned us. All we need to do is trust him.

its broth in a pot, he brought them out and offered them to him under the oak.

20The angel of God said to him, "Take the meat and the unleavened bread, place them on this rock, and pour out the broth." And Gideon did so. 21With the tip of the staff that was in his hand, the angel of the LORD touched the meat and the unleavened bread. Fire flared from the rock, consuming the meat and the bread. And the angel of the LORD disappeared. 22When Gideon realized that it was the angel of the LORD, he exclaimed, "Ah, Sovereign LORD! I have seen the angel of the LORD face to face!"

23But the LORD said to him, "Peace! Do not be afraid. You are not going to die."

24So Gideon built an altar to the LORD there and called it The LORD is Peace. To this day it stands in Ophrah of the Abiezrites.

25That same night the LORD said to him, "Take the second bull from your father's herd, the one seven years old.[a] Tear down your father's altar to Baal and cut down the Asherah pole[b] beside it. 26Then build a proper kind of[c] altar to the LORD your God on the top of this height. Using the wood of the Asherah pole that you cut down, offer the second[d] bull as a burnt offering."

27So Gideon took ten of his servants and did as the LORD told him. But because he was afraid of his family and the men of the town, he did it at night rather than in the daytime.

28In the morning when the men of the town got up, there was Baal's altar, demolished, with the Asherah pole beside it cut down and the second bull sacrificed on the newly built altar!

29They asked each other, "Who did this?"

When they carefully investigated, they were told, "Gideon son of Joash did it."

30The men of the town demanded of Joash, "Bring out your son. He must die, because he has broken down Baal's altar and cut down the Asherah pole beside it."

31But Joash replied to the hostile crowd around him, "Are you going to plead Baal's cause? Are you trying to save him? Whoever fights for him shall be put to death by morning! If Baal really is a god, he can defend himself when someone breaks down his altar." 32So that day they called Gideon "Jerub-Baal,[e]" saying, "Let Baal contend with him," because he broke down Baal's altar.

33Now all the Midianites, Amalekites and other eastern peoples joined forces and crossed over the Jordan and camped in the Valley of Jezreel. 34Then the Spirit of the LORD came upon Gideon, and he blew a trumpet, summoning the Abiezrites to follow him. 35He sent messengers throughout Manasseh, calling them to arms, and also into Asher, Zebulun and Naphtali, so that they too went up to meet them.

36Gideon said to God, "If you will save Israel by my hand as you have promised— 37look, I will place a wool fleece on the threshing floor. If there is dew only on the fleece and all the ground is dry, then I will know that you will save Israel by my hand, as you said." 38And that is what happened. Gideon rose early the next day; he squeezed the fleece and wrung out the dew—a bowlful of water.

39Then Gideon said to God, "Do not be angry with me. Let me make just one more request. Allow me one more test with the fleece. This time make the fleece dry and the ground covered with dew." 40That night God did so. Only the fleece was dry; all the ground was covered with dew.

Gideon Defeats the Midianites

7 Early in the morning, Jerub-Baal (that is, Gideon) and all his men camped at the spring of Harod. The camp of Midian was north of them in the valley near the hill of Moreh. 2The LORD said to Gideon, "You have too many men for me to deliver Midian into their hands. In order that Israel may not boast against me that her own strength has saved her, 3announce now to the people, 'Anyone who trembles with fear may turn back and leave Mount Gilead.' " So twenty-two thousand men left, while ten thousand remained.

4But the LORD said to Gideon, "There are still too many men. Take them down to the water,

[a]25 Or *Take a full-grown, mature bull from your father's herd*
[b]25 That is, a symbol of the goddess Asherah; here and elsewhere in Judges
[c]26 Or *build with layers of stone an*
[d]26 Or *full-grown;* also in verse 28
[e]32 *Jerub-Baal* means *let Baal contend.*

6:22–40 Gideon's responses to God alternated between faith and fear. It took courage to tear down the altar to the false god Baal and build the altars to God. A faithful Gideon blew the trumpet of assembly for those who would fight for God. Yet Gideon's fears limited him to destroying the place of idol worship in the middle of the night and questioning God's leadership (as seen in the fleece incident). Similarly, many of us will use excuses to avoid facing what we fear. Fear can be healthy; it can warn us of dangers and prompt us to be careful. But it should not stop us from doing what we know is right.

7:1–7 The enemy already outnumbered Gideon's forces, but God limited their numbers even more. In the end, only three hundred men went out to fight the Midianites. From a human standpoint, this put Israel at an impossible disadvantage. But God had limited the number of warriors for a reason: God wanted to show Israel that his power was sufficient no matter what the odds. Undoubtedly Gideon became nervous as his army began to dwindle before his eyes. But instead of walking out on God, Gideon proceeded with a stronger commitment to God's plan. Much can be accomplished with few resources if we have a strong commitment to God's will. When we surrender our lives to God each day, he can do more with us than with thousands of uncommitted soldiers.

7:4–7 By streamlining the fighting force from ten thousand to three hundred God demonstrated to Gideon that he wanted men who would face the reality of their present circumstances and keep watch for the enemy at all times. Facing the present reality is a key to successful spiritual growth. If we are constantly in touch with reality, we will not fall victim to sneak attacks—we will expect

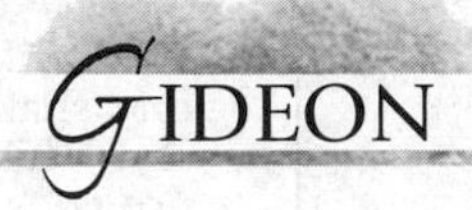

GIDEON

In times of trouble we often search for the thunder and lightning of God's voice and direction. We mistakenly think that God will provide us with the solutions we seek in a spectacular way. The truth of the matter is that God often reveals his answers quietly, in our hearts.

Gideon struggled in his commitment to God. Day in and day out he sought food and shelter for his family in a land constantly raided by hostile invaders. Gideon was under extreme pressure to remain resourceful in the face of his enemies. And his deliverance came in an unexpected way.

God called Gideon to deliver the Israelites from the rule of their oppressors. Like many of us, Gideon felt inadequate in the face of a great task. He obeyed, but his doubts made him drag his feet with reluctance. He waited time and again for confirmations of what God had clearly told him to do.

Many of us feel weak and think we are failures. We question God's interest in our lives or our situations. Just as Gideon already possessed the talents, resourcefulness and quickness that God needed, often we already have within us what God needs to overcome our obstacles. Even when our faith wavers, God will empower us if we will only act.

STRENGTHS AND ACCOMPLISHMENTS:

Gideon acted on his growing convictions, even when his faith wavered.

Even when times were difficult, Gideon was a responsible individual.

WEAKNESSES AND MISTAKES:

Because of his perceived personal limitations, Gideon was afraid to trust God.

Gideon failed to influence his family to follow after God's ways.

Gideon used Midianite gold to make a symbol that was later used for ungodly worship.

LESSONS FROM HIS LIFE:

God gives us more responsibility as we are faithful.

God uses each of us despite our personal limitations.

Even in the wake of great victory, we are still capable of making mistakes.

KEY VERSE:

"The Lord answered, 'I will be with you, and you will strike down all the Midianites together'" (6:16).

Gideon's story is told in Judges 6—8. Gideon is also mentioned in Hebrews 11:32.

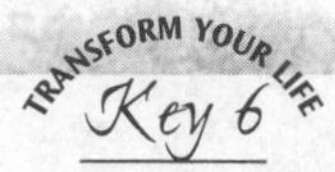

From Weakness to Strength

Judges 7:8–25 Regardless of our humble beginnings, God can lead us to a glorious future if we willingly allow him to transform us according to his perfect plan. We will need both faith and courage to allow God to make the most of our weaknesses, to reconstruct our weakness into strength, to turn our misery into a mission.

When we first meet Gideon, he is discouraged; he's a young man with little self-respect. His clan was the weakest in his whole tribe, and he was the least in his family (6:15). We see him threshing wheat in a winepress, hiding the little food he had from his Midianite oppressors. An angel appeared and called to him, "The LORD is with you, mighty warrior" (6:12). Gideon didn't look or feel like a mighty hero, but God knew his potential. By the end of the story, Gideon had become the deliverer of his people (chapters 6—8). Gideon's first step toward success was to see himself as God saw him—as a "mighty warrior." Then he was able to glimpse hope in the possibility of freedom.

No matter how weak or unworthy we may think we are, God is able to transform us into "mighty warriors" of faith. Just as Gideon was changed by trusting God to make him into a powerful man of God, we too can be changed by allowing God's strength to empower us in our areas of weakness.

Turn to 1 Chronicles 28.

and I will sift them for you there. If I say, 'This one shall go with you,' he shall go; but if I say, 'This one shall not go with you,' he shall not go."
5So Gideon took the men down to the water. There the LORD told him, "Separate those who lap the water with their tongues like a dog from
those who kneel down to drink." 6Three hundred men lapped with their hands to their mouths. All the rest got down on their knees to drink.
7The LORD said to Gideon, "With the three hundred men that lapped I will save you and give the Midianites into your hands. Let all the
other men go, each to his own place." 8So Gideon sent the rest of the Israelites to their tents but kept the three hundred, who took over the provisions and trumpets of the others.
Now the camp of Midian lay below him in
the valley. 9During that night the LORD said to Gideon, "Get up, go down against the camp, because I am going to give it into your hands.
10If you are afraid to attack, go down to the
camp with your servant Purah 11and listen to what they are saying. Afterward, you will be encouraged to attack the camp." So he and Purah his servant went down to the outposts of the
camp. 12The Midianites, the Amalekites and all the other eastern peoples had settled in the valley, thick as locusts. Their camels could no more be counted than the sand on the seashore.
13Gideon arrived just as a man was telling a friend his dream. "I had a dream," he was saying. "A round loaf of barley bread came tumbling into the Midianite camp. It struck the tent with such force that the tent overturned and collapsed."
14His friend responded, "This can be nothing other than the sword of Gideon son of Joash, the Israelite. God has given the Midianites and the whole camp into his hands."
15When Gideon heard the dream and its interpretation, he worshiped God. He returned to the camp of Israel and called out, "Get up! The LORD has given the Midianite camp into your
hands." 16Dividing the three hundred men into three companies, he placed trumpets and empty jars in the hands of all of them, with torches inside.
17"Watch me," he told them. "Follow my lead. When I get to the edge of the camp, do
exactly as I do. 18When I and all who are with me blow our trumpets, then from all around the camp blow yours and shout, 'For the LORD and for Gideon.' "
19Gideon and the hundred men with him

---

struggles with temptation. We can combat our problems only when we are alert.

7:8–25 This miraculous victory reminds us that the God we serve has the power to confuse and destroy all the opposing forces that come against us. We don't always have to directly confront those who oppose our spiritual growth. Our part is to follow God's instructions. God will win the battle.

reached the edge of the camp at the beginning
of the middle watch, just after they had changed
the guard. They blew their trumpets and broke
the jars that were in their hands. 20The three
companies blew the trumpets and smashed the
jars. Grasping the torches in their left hands and
holding in their right hands the trumpets they
were to blow, they shouted, "A sword for the
LORD and for Gideon!" 21While each man held
his position around the camp, all the Midianites ran, crying out as they fled.

22When the three hundred trumpets sounded, the LORD caused the men throughout the
camp to turn on each other with their swords.
The army fled to Beth Shittah toward Zererah as
far as the border of Abel Meholah near Tabbath.
23Israelites from Naphtali, Asher and all Manasseh were called out, and they pursued the Midianites. 24Gideon sent messengers throughout
the hill country of Ephraim, saying, "Come
down against the Midianites and seize the waters of the Jordan ahead of them as far as Beth
Barah."

So all the men of Ephraim were called out
and they took the waters of the Jordan as far as
Beth Barah. 25They also captured two of the
Midianite leaders, Oreb and Zeeb. They killed
Oreb at the rock of Oreb, and Zeeb at the winepress of Zeeb. They pursued the Midianites and
brought the heads of Oreb and Zeeb to Gideon,
who was by the Jordan.

Zebah and Zalmunna

8 Now the Ephraimites asked Gideon, "Why
have you treated us like this? Why didn't
you call us when you went to fight Midian?" And
they criticized him sharply.

2But he answered them, "What have I accomplished compared to you? Aren't the gleanings of Ephraim's grapes better than the full
grape harvest of Abiezer? 3God gave Oreb and
Zeeb, the Midianite leaders, into your hands.
What was I able to do compared to you?" At this,
their resentment against him subsided.

4Gideon and his three hundred men, ex-
hausted yet keeping up the pursuit, came to the
Jordan and crossed it. 5He said to the men of
Succoth, "Give my troops some bread; they are
worn out, and I am still pursuing Zebah and
Zalmunna, the kings of Midian."

6But the officials of Succoth said, "Do you
already have the hands of Zebah and Zalmunna
in your possession? Why should we give bread
to your troops?"

7Then Gideon replied, "Just for that, when
the LORD has given Zebah and Zalmunna into
my hand, I will tear your flesh with desert
thorns and briers."

8From there he went up to Peniel[a] and
made the same request of them, but they answered as the men of Succoth had. 9So he said
to the men of Peniel, "When I return in triumph, I will tear down this tower."

10Now Zebah and Zalmunna were in Karkor
with a force of about fifteen thousand men, all
that were left of the armies of the eastern peoples; a hundred and twenty thousand swordsmen had fallen. 11Gideon went up by the route
of the nomads east of Nobah and Jogbehah and
fell upon the unsuspecting army. 12Zebah and
Zalmunna, the two kings of Midian, fled, but he
pursued them and captured them, routing their
entire army.

13Gideon son of Joash then returned from
the battle by the Pass of Heres. 14He caught a
young man of Succoth and questioned him,
and the young man wrote down for him the
names of the seventy-seven officials of Succoth,
the elders of the town. 15Then Gideon came and
said to the men of Succoth, "Here are Zebah
and Zalmunna, about whom you taunted me
by saying, 'Do you already have the hands of
Zebah and Zalmunna in your possession? Why
should we give bread to your exhausted men?' "
16He took the elders of the town and taught the
men of Succoth a lesson by punishing them
with desert thorns and briers. 17He also pulled
down the tower of Peniel and killed the men of
the town.

18Then he asked Zebah and Zalmunna,
"What kind of men did you kill at Tabor?"

"Men like you," they answered, "each one
with the bearing of a prince."

19Gideon replied, "Those were my brothers,
the sons of my own mother. As surely as the
LORD lives, if you had spared their lives, I would
not kill you." 20Turning to Jether, his oldest son,
he said, "Kill them!" But Jether did not draw his
sword, because he was only a boy and was
afraid.

21Zebah and Zalmunna said, "Come, do it
yourself. 'As is the man, so is his strength.' " So
Gideon stepped forward and killed them, and
took the ornaments off their camels' necks.

Gideon's Ephod

22The Israelites said to Gideon, "Rule over

[a]8 Hebrew *Penuel,* a variant of *Peniel;* also in verses 9 and 17

7:24—8:3 In contrast to the anger of Ephraim's leaders, Gideon displayed great self-control and wisdom. He was willing to go to great lengths to set things straight. Self-control and wisdom are important elements of the spiritual renewal process.

8:4–21 This pursuit and execution of the Midianite kings is a striking example of perseverance on the part of Gideon. In clear contrast to the tribes of Israel who failed to finish the job of driving out the Canaanites, Gideon continued pursuing the enemy until the Midianite forces were completely defeated. He changed an oppressive situation completely, opening the doorway to a new life of freedom for Israel. We should follow Gideon's example of faithfulness, making certain to finish what God has called us to do.

8:22–35 After Gideon's death, the Israelites again turned from the true God and worshiped idols. The ephod Gideon made to commemorate the defeat of the Midianites

us—you, your son and your grandson—because you have saved us out of the hand of Midian."

23But Gideon told them, "I will not rule over you, nor will my son rule over you. The LORD will rule over you." 24And he said, "I do have one request, that each of you give me an earring from your share of the plunder." (It was the custom of the Ishmaelites to wear gold earrings.)

25They answered, "We'll be glad to give them." So they spread out a garment, and each man threw a ring from his plunder onto it. 26The weight of the gold rings he asked for came to seventeen hundred shekels,[a] not counting the ornaments, the pendants and the purple garments worn by the kings of Midian or the chains that were on their camels' necks. 27Gideon made the gold into an ephod, which he placed in Ophrah, his town. All Israel prostituted themselves by worshiping it there, and it became a snare to Gideon and his family.

Gideon's Death

28Thus Midian was subdued before the Israelites and did not raise its head again. During Gideon's lifetime, the land enjoyed peace forty years.

29Jerub-Baal son of Joash went back home to live. 30He had seventy sons of his own, for he had many wives. 31His concubine, who lived in Shechem, also bore him a son, whom he named Abimelech. 32Gideon son of Joash died at a good old age and was buried in the tomb of his father Joash in Ophrah of the Abiezrites.

33No sooner had Gideon died than the Israelites again prostituted themselves to the Baals. They set up Baal-Berith as their god and 34did not remember the LORD their God, who had rescued them from the hands of all their enemies on every side. 35They also failed to show kindness to the family of Jerub-Baal (that is, Gideon) for all the good things he had done for them.

Abimelech

9 Abimelech son of Jerub-Baal went to his mother's brothers in Shechem and said to them and to all his mother's clan, 2"Ask all the citizens of Shechem, 'Which is better for you: to have all seventy of Jerub-Baal's sons rule over you, or just one man?' Remember, I am your flesh and blood."

3When the brothers repeated all this to the citizens of Shechem, they were inclined to follow Abimelech, for they said, "He is our brother." 4They gave him seventy shekels[b] of silver from the temple of Baal-Berith, and Abimelech used it to hire reckless adventurers, who became his followers. 5He went to his father's home in Ophrah and on one stone murdered his seventy brothers, the sons of Jerub-Baal. But Jotham, the youngest son of Jerub-Baal, escaped by hiding. 6Then all the citizens of Shechem and Beth Millo gathered beside the great tree at the pillar in Shechem to crown Abimelech king.

7When Jotham was told about this, he climbed up on the top of Mount Gerizim and shouted to them, "Listen to me, citizens of Shechem, so that God may listen to you. 8One day the trees went out to anoint a king for themselves. They said to the olive tree, 'Be our king.'

9"But the olive tree answered, 'Should I give up my oil, by which both gods and men are honored, to hold sway over the trees?'

10"Next, the trees said to the fig tree, 'Come and be our king.'

11"But the fig tree replied, 'Should I give up my fruit, so good and sweet, to hold sway over the trees?'

12"Then the trees said to the vine, 'Come and be our king.'

13"But the vine answered, 'Should I give up my wine, which cheers both gods and men, to hold sway over the trees?'

14"Finally all the trees said to the thornbush, 'Come and be our king.'

15"The thornbush said to the trees, 'If you really want to anoint me king over you, come and take refuge in my shade; but if not, then let fire come out of the thornbush and consume the cedars of Lebanon!'

16"Now if you have acted honorably and in good faith when you made Abimelech king, and if you have been fair to Jerub-Baal and his family, and if you have treated him as he deserves— 17and to think that my father fought for you, risked his life to rescue you from the hand of Midian 18(but today you have revolted against my father's family, murdered his seventy sons on a single stone, and made Abimelech, the son of his slave girl, king over the citizens of Shechem because he is your brother)— 19if then you have acted honorably and in good faith toward Jerub-Baal and his family today, may

[a] *26* That is, about 43 pounds (about 19.5 kilograms)
[b] *4* That is, about 1 3/4 pounds (about 0.8 kilogram)

---

was soon worshiped by the people. Later, the Israelites resumed the worship of Baal and Baal-Berith. The people did not recognize this recurring cycle of disobedience and oppression. Unlike Israel, we should learn from our past. When tempted to return to sinful habits, we need to remember the consequences of those behaviors and strive to grow spiritually.

9:1–57 Abimelech, Gideon's son by a concubine, proved to be the virtual opposite of his father. Gideon rightly refused kingship over Israel. On the other hand, Abimelech not only demanded it, but he attempted to kill anyone who stood in his way. And Abimelech died as violently as he lived. None of the faith, patience and honesty that characterized the older, wiser Gideon is seen in his son Abimelech. Perhaps this lack indicates some serious deficiencies in Abimelech's childhood relationship with his father. It is not enough to be a strong leader outside the home; we must be a strong influence on our own families. If children lack a godly parental example, they may grow up to flout God's principles as Abimelech did.

Abimelech be your joy, and may you be his, too! 20But if you have not, let fire come out from Abimelech and consume you, citizens of Shechem and Beth Millo, and let fire come out from you, citizens of Shechem and Beth Millo, and consume Abimelech!"

21Then Jotham fled, escaping to Beer, and he lived there because he was afraid of his brother Abimelech.

22After Abimelech had governed Israel three years, 23God sent an evil spirit between Abimelech and the citizens of Shechem, who acted treacherously against Abimelech. 24God did this in order that the crime against Jerub-Baal's seventy sons, the shedding of their blood, might be avenged on their brother Abimelech and on the citizens of Shechem, who had helped him murder his brothers. 25In opposition to him these citizens of Shechem set men on the hilltops to ambush and rob everyone who passed by, and this was reported to Abimelech.

26Now Gaal son of Ebed moved with his brothers into Shechem, and its citizens put their confidence in him. 27After they had gone out into the fields and gathered the grapes and trodden them, they held a festival in the temple of their god. While they were eating and drinking, they cursed Abimelech. 28Then Gaal son of Ebed said, "Who is Abimelech, and who is Shechem, that we should be subject to him? Isn't he Jerub-Baal's son, and isn't Zebul his deputy? Serve the men of Hamor, Shechem's father! Why should we serve Abimelech? 29If only this people were under my command! Then I would get rid of him. I would say to Abimelech, 'Call out your whole army!' "[a]

30When Zebul the governor of the city heard what Gaal son of Ebed said, he was very angry. 31Under cover he sent messengers to Abimelech, saying, "Gaal son of Ebed and his brothers have come to Shechem and are stirring up the city against you. 32Now then, during the night you and your men should come and lie in wait in the fields. 33In the morning at sunrise, advance against the city. When Gaal and his men come out against you, do whatever your hand finds to do."

34So Abimelech and all his troops set out by night and took up concealed positions near Shechem in four companies. 35Now Gaal son of Ebed had gone out and was standing at the entrance to the city gate just as Abimelech and his soldiers came out from their hiding place.

36When Gaal saw them, he said to Zebul, "Look, people are coming down from the tops of the mountains!"

Zebul replied, "You mistake the shadows of the mountains for men."

37But Gaal spoke up again: "Look, people are coming down from the center of the land, and a company is coming from the direction of the soothsayers' tree."

38Then Zebul said to him, "Where is your big talk now, you who said, 'Who is Abimelech that we should be subject to him?' Aren't these the men you ridiculed? Go out and fight them!"

39So Gaal led out[b] the citizens of Shechem and fought Abimelech. 40Abimelech chased him, and many fell wounded in the flight—all the way to the entrance to the gate. 41Abimelech stayed in Arumah, and Zebul drove Gaal and his brothers out of Shechem.

42The next day the people of Shechem went out to the fields, and this was reported to Abimelech. 43So he took his men, divided them into three companies and set an ambush in the fields. When he saw the people coming out of the city, he rose to attack them. 44Abimelech and the companies with him rushed forward to a position at the entrance to the city gate. Then two companies rushed upon those in the fields and struck them down. 45All that day Abimelech pressed his attack against the city until he had captured it and killed its people. Then he destroyed the city and scattered salt over it.

46On hearing this, the citizens in the tower of Shechem went into the stronghold of the temple of El-Berith. 47When Abimelech heard that they had assembled there, 48he and all his men went up Mount Zalmon. He took an ax and cut off some branches, which he lifted to his shoulders. He ordered the men with him, "Quick! Do what you have seen me do!" 49So all the men cut branches and followed Abimelech. They piled them against the stronghold and set it on fire over the people inside. So all the people in the tower of Shechem, about a thousand men and women, also died.

50Next Abimelech went to Thebez and besieged it and captured it. 51Inside the city, however, was a strong tower, to which all the men and women—all the people of the city—fled. They locked themselves in and climbed up on the tower roof. 52Abimelech went to the tower and stormed it. But as he approached the entrance to the tower to set it on fire, 53a woman dropped an upper millstone on his head and cracked his skull.

54Hurriedly he called to his armor-bearer, "Draw your sword and kill me, so that they can't say, 'A woman killed him.' " So his servant ran him through, and he died. 55When the Israelites saw that Abimelech was dead, they went home.

56Thus God repaid the wickedness that Abimelech had done to his father by murdering his seventy brothers. 57God also made the men of Shechem pay for all their wickedness. The curse of Jotham son of Jerub-Baal came on them.

[a]29 Septuagint; Hebrew *him." Then he said to Abimelech, "Call out your whole army!"* [b]39 Or *Gaal went out in the sight of*

Tola

10 After the time of Abimelech a man of Issachar, Tola son of Puah, the son of Dodo, rose to save Israel. He lived in Shamir, in the hill country of Ephraim. 2He led[a] Israel twenty-three years; then he died, and was buried in Shamir.

Jair

3He was followed by Jair of Gilead, who led Israel twenty-two years. 4He had thirty sons, who rode thirty donkeys. They controlled thirty towns in Gilead, which to this day are called Havvoth Jair.[b] 5When Jair died, he was buried in Kamon.

Jephthah

6Again the Israelites did evil in the eyes of the LORD. They served the Baals and the Ashtoreths, and the gods of Aram, the gods of Sidon, the gods of Moab, the gods of the Ammonites and the gods of the Philistines. And because the Israelites forsook the LORD and no longer served him, 7he became angry with them. He sold them into the hands of the Philistines and the Ammonites, 8who that year shattered and crushed them. For eighteen years they oppressed all the Israelites on the east side of the Jordan in Gilead, the land of the Amorites. 9The Ammonites also crossed the Jordan to fight against Judah, Benjamin and the house of Ephraim; and Israel was in great distress. 10Then the Israelites cried out to the LORD, "We have sinned against you, forsaking our God and serving the Baals."

11The LORD replied, "When the Egyptians, the Amorites, the Ammonites, the Philistines, 12the Sidonians, the Amalekites and the Maonites[c] oppressed you and you cried to me for help, did I not save you from their hands? 13But you have forsaken me and served other gods, so I will no longer save you. 14Go and cry out to the gods you have chosen. Let them save you when you are in trouble!"

15But the Israelites said to the LORD, "We have sinned. Do with us whatever you think best, but please rescue us now." 16Then they got rid of the foreign gods among them and served the LORD. And he could bear Israel's misery no longer.

17When the Ammonites were called to arms and camped in Gilead, the Israelites assembled and camped at Mizpah. 18The leaders of the people of Gilead said to each other, "Whoever will launch the attack against the Ammonites will be the head of all those living in Gilead."

11 Jephthah the Gileadite was a mighty warrior. His father was Gilead; his mother was a prostitute. 2Gilead's wife also bore him sons, and when they were grown up, they drove Jephthah away. "You are not going to get any inheritance in our family," they said, "because you are the son of another woman." 3So Jephthah fled from his brothers and settled in the land of Tob, where a group of adventurers gathered around him and followed him.

4Some time later, when the Ammonites made war on Israel, 5the elders of Gilead went to get Jephthah from the land of Tob. 6"Come," they said, "be our commander, so we can fight the Ammonites."

7Jephthah said to them, "Didn't you hate me and drive me from my father's house? Why do you come to me now, when you're in trouble?"

8The elders of Gilead said to him, "Nevertheless, we are turning to you now; come with us to fight the Ammonites, and you will be our head over all who live in Gilead."

9Jephthah answered, "Suppose you take me back to fight the Ammonites and the LORD gives them to me—will I really be your head?"

10The elders of Gilead replied, "The LORD is our witness; we will certainly do as you say." 11So Jephthah went with the elders of Gilead, and the people made him head and commander over them. And he repeated all his words before the LORD in Mizpah.

12Then Jephthah sent messengers to the Ammonite king with the question: "What do you have against us that you have attacked our country?"

13The king of the Ammonites answered Jephthah's messengers, "When Israel came up out of Egypt, they took away my land from the Arnon

[a]2 Traditionally *judged*; also in verse 3 [b]4 Or *called the settlements of Jair* [c]12 Hebrew; some Septuagint manuscripts *Midianites*

10:1–18 After suffering under Abimelech's leadership (see chapter 9), Israel experienced forty-five stable years under the leadership of Tola and Jair. But Israel's spiritual restoration was by no means complete. After Jair died, the Israelites were so spiritually blind and proud that it took them eighteen years to turn to God for help. If we are honest with God and ourselves, we will not have to suffer long before we realize the consequences of our sins. They should be obvious to us when we start straying from God's will. If we keep our eyes open, we will be able to take immediate steps to redirect our course onto the right path.

11:1–11 Ridicule can be very hurtful, especially if we are ridiculed for things that are beyond our control. Jephthah apparently possessed considerable courage and natural leadership ability, but he was rejected by his half brothers because his mother was a prostitute. Like Jephthah, others may have taunted us because of our family background or for other problems beyond our control. We need to forgive those people, release the pain and grudges and move on in our lives so that we can put those events behind us. Then we can proceed to the tasks to which God has called us.

11:12–28 Jephthah displayed great self-control by patiently confronting the Ammonite king about his attacks against Israel. Since most oppressive people are power hungry, it was unlikely that Jephthah would be able to persuade the Ammonites to stop their unprovoked attacks. Though Jephthah argued his case well, it was totally disregarded. We are called to try to make peace and speak the truth. It is not our responsibility, however, if others do not listen to us. We can only share the truth.

to the Jabbok, all the way to the Jordan. Now
give it back peaceably."
14Jephthah sent back messengers to the Ammonite king, 15saying:

> "This is what Jephthah says: Israel did not
> take the land of Moab or the land of the
> Ammonites. 16But when they came up out
> of Egypt, Israel went through the desert to
> the Red Sea[a] and on to Kadesh. 17Then
> Israel sent messengers to the king of
> Edom, saying, 'Give us permission to go
> through your country,' but the king of
> Edom would not listen. They sent also to
> the king of Moab, and he refused. So Israel
> stayed at Kadesh.
>
> 18"Next they traveled through the
> desert, skirted the lands of Edom and
> Moab, passed along the eastern side of the
> country of Moab, and camped on the oth-
> er side of the Arnon. They did not enter
> the territory of Moab, for the Arnon was
> its border.
>
> 19"Then Israel sent messengers to Si-
> hon king of the Amorites, who ruled in
> Heshbon, and said to him, 'Let us pass
> through your country to our own place.'
> 20Sihon, however, did not trust Israel[b] to
> pass through his territory. He mustered
> all his men and encamped at Jahaz and
> fought with Israel.
>
> 21"Then the LORD, the God of Israel,
> gave Sihon and all his men into Israel's
> hands, and they defeated them. Israel took
> over all the land of the Amorites who lived
> in that country, 22capturing all of it from
> the Arnon to the Jabbok and from the
> desert to the Jordan.
>
> 23"Now since the LORD, the God of Is-
> rael, has driven the Amorites out before
> his people Israel, what right have you to
> take it over? 24Will you not take what your
> god Chemosh gives you? Likewise, what-
> ever the LORD our God has given us, we
> will possess. 25Are you better than Balak
> son of Zippor, king of Moab? Did he ever
> quarrel with Israel or fight with them?
> 26For three hundred years Israel occupied
> Heshbon, Aroer, the surrounding settle-
> ments and all the towns along the Arnon.
> Why didn't you retake them during that
> time? 27I have not wronged you, but you
> are doing me wrong by waging war against
> me. Let the LORD, the Judge,[c] decide the
> dispute this day between the Israelites and
> the Ammonites."

28The king of Ammon, however, paid no attention to the message Jephthah sent him.
29Then the Spirit of the LORD came upon
Jephthah. He crossed Gilead and Manasseh,
passed through Mizpah of Gilead, and from
there he advanced against the Ammonites.
30And Jephthah made a vow to the LORD: "If
you give the Ammonites into my hands, 31what-
ever comes out of the door of my house to meet
me when I return in triumph from the Ammonites will be the LORD's, and I will sacrifice it as
a burnt offering."
32Then Jephthah went over to fight the Ammonites, and the LORD gave them into his
hands. 33He devastated twenty towns from Aroer to the vicinity of Minnith, as far as Abel Kera-
mim. Thus Israel subdued Ammon.
34When Jephthah returned to his home in
Mizpah, who should come out to meet him but
his daughter, dancing to the sound of tambourines! She was an only child. Except for her he
had neither son nor daughter. 35When he saw
her, he tore his clothes and cried, "Oh! My
daughter! You have made me miserable and
wretched, because I have made a vow to the
LORD that I cannot break."
36"My father," she replied, "you have given
your word to the LORD. Do to me just as you
promised, now that the LORD has avenged you
of your enemies, the Ammonites. 37But grant
me this one request," she said. "Give me two
months to roam the hills and weep with my
friends, because I will never marry."
38"You may go," he said. And he let her go for
two months. She and the girls went into the
hills and wept because she would never marry.
39After the two months, she returned to her father and he did to her as he had vowed. And she
was a virgin.
From this comes the Israelite custom 40that
each year the young women of Israel go out for
four days to commemorate the daughter of
Jephthah the Gileadite.

Jephthah and Ephraim

12 The men of Ephraim called out their
forces, crossed over to Zaphon and said
to Jephthah, "Why did you go to fight the Ammonites without calling us to go with you?
We're going to burn down your house over your
head."
2Jephthah answered, "I and my people were
engaged in a great struggle with the Ammonites,
and although I called, you didn't save me out of
their hands. 3When I saw that you wouldn't
help, I took my life in my hands and crossed
over to fight the Ammonites, and the LORD gave
me the victory over them. Now why have you
come up today to fight me?"

[a]16 Hebrew *Yam Suph;* that is, Sea of Reeds [b]20 Or *however, would not make an agreement for Israel* [c]27 Or *Ruler*

12:1–7 This tragic incident is in many ways a replay of Gideon's confrontation with the angry Ephraimites in 8:1–3. The outcome, however, is very different because of the way Jephthah mishandled the situation. Instead of the humble self-control and patience shown by Gideon, Jephthah responded in angry pride. As a result, Gilead and Ephraim were unable to enjoy a relationship like the one Gideon forged, and war erupted between the two tribes.

4Jephthah then called together the men of Gilead and fought against Ephraim. The Gileadites struck them down because the Ephraimites had said, "You Gileadites are renegades from Ephraim and Manasseh." 5The Gileadites captured the fords of the Jordan leading to Ephraim, and whenever a survivor of Ephraim said, "Let me cross over," the men of Gilead asked him, "Are you an Ephraimite?" If he replied, "No," 6they said, "All right, say 'Shibboleth.' " If he said, "Sibboleth," because he could not pronounce the word correctly, they seized him and killed him at the fords of the Jordan. Forty-two thousand Ephraimites were killed at that time.

7Jephthah led[a] Israel six years. Then Jephthah the Gileadite died, and was buried in a town in Gilead.

Ibzan, Elon and Abdon

8After him, Ibzan of Bethlehem led Israel. 9He had thirty sons and thirty daughters. He gave his daughters away in marriage to those outside his clan, and for his sons he brought in thirty young women as wives from outside his clan. Ibzan led Israel seven years. 10Then Ibzan died, and was buried in Bethlehem.

11After him, Elon the Zebulunite led Israel ten years. 12Then Elon died, and was buried in Aijalon in the land of Zebulun.

13After him, Abdon son of Hillel, from Pirathon, led Israel. 14He had forty sons and thirty grandsons, who rode on seventy donkeys. He led Israel eight years. 15Then Abdon son of Hillel died, and was buried at Pirathon in Ephraim, in the hill country of the Amalekites.

The Birth of Samson

13 Again the Israelites did evil in the eyes of the LORD, so the LORD delivered them into the hands of the Philistines for forty years.

2A certain man of Zorah, named Manoah, from the clan of the Danites, had a wife who was sterile and remained childless. 3The angel of the LORD appeared to her and said, "You are sterile and childless, but you are going to conceive and have a son. 4Now see to it that you drink no wine or other fermented drink and that you do not eat anything unclean, 5because you will conceive and give birth to a son. No razor may be used on his head, because the boy is to be a Nazirite, set apart to God from birth, and he will begin the deliverance of Israel from the hands of the Philistines."

6Then the woman went to her husband and told him, "A man of God came to me. He looked like an angel of God, very awesome. I didn't ask him where he came from, and he didn't tell me his name. 7But he said to me, 'You will conceive and give birth to a son. Now then, drink no wine or other fermented drink and do not eat anything unclean, because the boy will be a Nazirite of God from birth until the day of his death.' "

8Then Manoah prayed to the LORD: "O Lord, I beg you, let the man of God you sent to us come again to teach us how to bring up the boy who is to be born."

9God heard Manoah, and the angel of God came again to the woman while she was out in the field; but her husband Manoah was not with her. 10The woman hurried to tell her husband, "He's here! The man who appeared to me the other day!"

11Manoah got up and followed his wife. When he came to the man, he said, "Are you the one who talked to my wife?"

"I am," he said.

12So Manoah asked him, "When your words are fulfilled, what is to be the rule for the boy's life and work?"

13The angel of the LORD answered, "Your wife must do all that I have told her. 14She must not eat anything that comes from the grapevine, nor drink any wine or other fermented drink nor eat anything unclean. She must do everything I have commanded her."

15Manoah said to the angel of the LORD, "We would like you to stay until we prepare a young goat for you."

16The angel of the LORD replied, "Even though you detain me, I will not eat any of your food. But if you prepare a burnt offering, offer it to the LORD." (Manoah did not realize that it was the angel of the LORD.)

17Then Manoah inquired of the angel of the

[a]7 Traditionally *judged*; also in verses 8-14

12:8–15 The brief mention of the leadership of Ibzan, Elon and Abdon might be taken to mean that they were less significant judges. However, each of the three actually ruled longer than Jephthah: Ibzan, seven years; Elon, ten years; Abdon, eight years. Apparently the events during their terms of leadership were not as tumultuous as during Jephthah's rule. But whether or not we are well-known, "making the headlines" should not be our basis for our self-worth or sense of accomplishment.

13:1–14 The instructions given by the angel to Manoah and his wife are similar to those given to Zechariah and Elizabeth, parents of John the Baptist (see Luke 1:5–15). Both sets of parents were commanded to raise their children to accomplish special tasks for God. Even their actions before their sons were born were very significant. All parents should be aware of how closely related their own actions and outlooks are to the sense of identity each child will have as an adult.

13:15–23 This interaction between Samson's parents and the angel demonstrates their balanced sense of who they were before God. Manoah and his wife had been called for the high purpose of raising a child uniquely gifted to serve God. They also had been allowed to live even though they had looked upon God. Their offering of sacrifices indicated their proper sense of faith, humility and thankfulness before God. We, too, may be called upon to do special things for God or his people. We should remember that we are serving God and that he is allowing us to do these things. Knowing this should temper any pride and arrogance we may be tempted to feel in such situations.

LORD, "What is your name, so that we may honor you when your word comes true?"

18He replied, "Why do you ask my name? It is beyond understanding.[a]" 19Then Manoah took a young goat, together with the grain offering, and sacrificed it on a rock to the LORD. And the LORD did an amazing thing while Manoah and his wife watched: 20As the flame blazed up from the altar toward heaven, the angel of the LORD ascended in the flame. Seeing this, Manoah and his wife fell with their faces to the ground. 21When the angel of the LORD did not show himself again to Manoah and his wife, Manoah realized that it was the angel of the LORD.

22"We are doomed to die!" he said to his wife. "We have seen God!"

23But his wife answered, "If the LORD had meant to kill us, he would not have accepted a burnt offering and grain offering from our hands, nor shown us all these things or now told us this."

24The woman gave birth to a boy and named him Samson. He grew and the LORD blessed him, 25and the Spirit of the LORD began to stir him while he was in Mahaneh Dan, between Zorah and Eshtaol.

Samson's Marriage

14 Samson went down to Timnah and saw there a young Philistine woman. 2When he returned, he said to his father and mother, "I have seen a Philistine woman in Timnah; now get her for me as my wife."

3His father and mother replied, "Isn't there an acceptable woman among your relatives or among all our people? Must you go to the uncircumcised Philistines to get a wife?"

But Samson said to his father, "Get her for me. She's the right one for me." 4(His parents did not know that this was from the LORD, who was seeking an occasion to confront the Philistines; for at that time they were ruling over Israel.) 5Samson went down to Timnah together with his father and mother. As they approached the vineyards of Timnah, suddenly a young lion came roaring toward him. 6The Spirit of the LORD came upon him in power so that he tore the lion apart with his bare hands as he might have torn a young goat. But he told neither his father nor his mother what he had done. 7Then he went down and talked with the woman, and he liked her.

8Some time later, when he went back to marry her, he turned aside to look at the lion's carcass. In it was a swarm of bees and some honey, 9which he scooped out with his hands and ate as he went along. When he rejoined his parents, he gave them some, and they too ate it. But he did not tell them that he had taken the honey from the lion's carcass.

10Now his father went down to see the woman. And Samson made a feast there, as was customary for bridegrooms. 11When he appeared, he was given thirty companions.

12"Let me tell you a riddle," Samson said to them. "If you can give me the answer within the seven days of the feast, I will give you thirty linen garments and thirty sets of clothes. 13If you can't tell me the answer, you must give me thirty linen garments and thirty sets of clothes."

"Tell us your riddle," they said. "Let's hear it."

14He replied,

"Out of the eater, something to eat;
out of the strong, something sweet."

For three days they could not give the answer.

15On the fourth[b] day, they said to Samson's wife, "Coax your husband into explaining the riddle for us, or we will burn you and your father's household to death. Did you invite us here to rob us?"

16Then Samson's wife threw herself on him, sobbing, "You hate me! You don't really love me. You've given my people a riddle, but you haven't told me the answer."

"I haven't even explained it to my father or mother," he replied, "so why should I explain it to you?" 17She cried the whole seven days of the feast. So on the seventh day he finally told her,

[a] 18 Or *is wonderful* [b] 15 Some Septuagint manuscripts and Syriac; Hebrew *seventh*

13:24—14:4 Samson was living proof that those who grow up in a godly home still need personal dependence on God. Even the Spirit of God in Samson's life did not protect him completely from his biggest blind spot: pagan women. Samson did not understand his unhealthy attraction to be a point of weakness. Samson's problem with pagan women is symbolic of many who struggle with similar problems today. God will provide an abundant life if we are willing to give up or avoid potential stumbling blocks that can interfere with our spiritual growth. With honest eyes focused on God, we can confess these stumbling blocks to God and ask him to remove them.

14:5–9 Even at an early point in his life, Samson was insensitive to the vows that defined his relationship with God. Samson's Nazirite vow forbade his contact with anything dead (see Numbers 6), but Samson killed a lion and then later went back and touched the carcass. It was indeed the Spirit of the Lord that strengthened him, but Samson abused this blessing when he failed to surrender his life to the one who gave him his supernatural strength. There is very little evidence of commitment to God at this point in Samson's life. Raised as a "special child," Samson was self-centered. This sinful self-obsession was the ruin of Samson, and it is the ruin of many people today too.

14:10–20 During the pre-wedding feast, Samson foolishly made a bet that his guests could not solve his riddle. After being manipulated by his wife-to-be and losing the wager, Samson slaughtered other Philistines to get the garments he needed for payment. His volatile and dangerous personality was clearly evidenced by his actions. Samson possessed the inner maturity of a boy stuffed inside the body of an incredibly strong adult. Many of us aspire to be like people with great physical beauty only to find that often these beautiful people are shallow of character. We must never forget how much God values who we are on the inside. God looks at people's hearts, not their appearances (see 1 Samuel 16:7).

because she continued to press him. She in turn
explained the riddle to her people.
[18]Before sunset on the seventh day the men
of the town said to him,

"What is sweeter than honey?
  What is stronger than a lion?"

Samson said to them,

"If you had not plowed with my heifer,
  you would not have solved my riddle."

[19]Then the Spirit of the LORD came upon him
in power. He went down to Ashkelon, struck
down thirty of their men, stripped them of their
belongings and gave their clothes to those who
had explained the riddle. Burning with anger,
he went up to his father's house. [20]And Samson's wife was given to the friend who had attended him at his wedding.

Samson's Vengeance on the Philistines

15 Later on, at the time of wheat harvest,
Samson took a young goat and went to
visit his wife. He said, "I'm going to my wife's
room." But her father would not let him go in.
[2]"I was so sure you thoroughly hated her," he
said, "that I gave her to your friend. Isn't her
younger sister more attractive? Take her instead."
[3]Samson said to them, "This time I have a
right to get even with the Philistines; I will really
harm them." [4]So he went out and caught three
hundred foxes and tied them tail to tail in pairs.
He then fastened a torch to every pair of tails,
[5]lit the torches and let the foxes loose in the
standing grain of the Philistines. He burned up
the shocks and standing grain, together with the
vineyards and olive groves.
[6]When the Philistines asked, "Who did this?"
they were told, "Samson, the Timnite's son-in-
law, because his wife was given to his friend."
So the Philistines went up and burned her
and her father to death. [7]Samson said to them,
"Since you've acted like this, I won't stop until
I get my revenge on you." [8]He attacked them
viciously and slaughtered many of them. Then
he went down and stayed in a cave in the rock
of Etam.
[9]The Philistines went up and camped in Judah, spreading out near Lehi. [10]The men of Judah asked, "Why have you come to fight us?"
"We have come to take Samson prisoner,"
they answered, "to do to him as he did to us."
[11]Then three thousand men from Judah went
down to the cave in the rock of Etam and said
to Samson, "Don't you realize that the Philistines are rulers over us? What have you done
to us?"
He answered, "I merely did to them what
they did to me."
[12]They said to him, "We've come to tie you
up and hand you over to the Philistines."
Samson said, "Swear to me that you won't
kill me yourselves."
[13]"Agreed," they answered. "We will only tie
you up and hand you over to them. We will not
kill you." So they bound him with two new ropes
and led him up from the rock. [14]As he approached Lehi, the Philistines came toward him
shouting. The Spirit of the LORD came upon
him in power. The ropes on his arms became
like charred flax, and the bindings dropped
from his hands. [15]Finding a fresh jawbone of a
donkey, he grabbed it and struck down a thousand men.
[16]Then Samson said,

"With a donkey's jawbone
  I have made donkeys of them.[a]
With a donkey's jawbone
  I have killed a thousand men."

[17]When he finished speaking, he threw away
the jawbone; and the place was called Ramath
Lehi.[b]
[18]Because he was very thirsty, he cried out to
the LORD, "You have given your servant this
great victory. Must I now die of thirst and fall
into the hands of the uncircumcised?" [19]Then
God opened up the hollow place in Lehi, and
water came out of it. When Samson drank, his
strength returned and he revived. So the spring
was called En Hakkore,[c] and it is still there in
Lehi.

[a]16 Or *made a heap or two;* the Hebrew for *donkey* sounds like the Hebrew for *heap.* [b]17 *Ramath Lehi* means *jawbone hill.* [c]19 *En Hakkore* means *caller's spring.*

14:19—15:8 Angry revenge dominated more and more of Samson's personality and actions. Because of what the Philistines had done to him, he destroyed much of their wheat and other crops. He then turned his rage on the Philistines themselves, killing many of them. If we are plagued with anger and our rage gets out of control, we must see this as an area of great concern. We must acknowledge our anger to God and prayerfully consider what we need to release to God. Those who are controlled by rage may potentially destroy themselves, as Samson did, as well as hurt the people they love. God calls us to take our anger and pain and release them to him, forgiving those who hurt us. Revenge never really repays those who have hurt us. In fact, revenge only causes the one who was hurt to be hurt again.

15:1–17 Samson was the most contradictory of Israel's judges. Called to be a Nazirite, he violently killed and destroyed, flaunting his previous "separation" before God (see Numbers 6). Samson justified his extreme actions almost totally by his angry vengeance. He also lived a solitary, lonely existence for periods of time. Samson was far from ideal. Yet God used him to begin the conquest of the Philistines—a task that would be finished much later by King David.

15:18–20 Samson was emotionally drained after his victory over the Philistines. He complained to God, perhaps exaggerating his situation, "Must I now die of thirst?" After major victories in our lives, we may feel emotionally spent or physically pained. But we must not stop and feel sorry for ourselves. This will only lead to failure. We should rely on God's power to strengthen us and meet our needs. Then we can face the next battle in our process of spiritual growth.

20 Samson led[a] Israel for twenty years in the
days of the Philistines.

Samson and Delilah

16 One day Samson went to Gaza, where
he saw a prostitute. He went in to spend
the night with her. 2 The people of Gaza were
told, "Samson is here!" So they surrounded the
place and lay in wait for him all night at the city
gate. They made no move during the night, saying, "At dawn we'll kill him."
3 But Samson lay there only until the middle
of the night. Then he got up and took hold of
the doors of the city gate, together with the two
posts, and tore them loose, bar and all. He lifted
them to his shoulders and carried them to the
top of the hill that faces Hebron.
4 Some time later, he fell in love with a woman in the Valley of Sorek whose name was Delilah. 5 The rulers of the Philistines went to her
and said, "See if you can lure him into showing
you the secret of his great strength and how we
can overpower him so we may tie him up and
subdue him. Each one of us will give you eleven
hundred shekels[b] of silver."
6 So Delilah said to Samson, "Tell me the
secret of your great strength and how you can be
tied up and subdued."
7 Samson answered her, "If anyone ties me
with seven fresh thongs[c] that have not been
dried, I'll become as weak as any other man."
8 Then the rulers of the Philistines brought
her seven fresh thongs that had not been dried,
and she tied him with them. 9 With men hidden
in the room, she called to him, "Samson, the
Philistines are upon you!" But he snapped the
thongs as easily as a piece of string snaps when
it comes close to a flame. So the secret of his
strength was not discovered.
10 Then Delilah said to Samson, "You have

[a] 20 Traditionally *judged* [b] 5 That is, about 28 pounds (about 13 kilograms) [c] 7 Or *bowstrings;* also in verses 8 and 9

16:1–3 Samson's flaw in regard to pagan women reasserts itself here. Though Samson was known as a judge in Israel—a position of great respect and responsibility—he exposed himself to shame and danger by visiting the prostitute in Gaza. Again his strength and courage rescued him. But, as we shall see, Samson's belief that he could handle his weakness was flawed. Unless we recognize our areas of weakness and confess them to God, our weaknesses will continue to reemerge throughout our lives. We may get by for a while, but eventually we will fall prey to temptation if we do not confess our sins and accept responsibility for our actions.

16:4–17 The love affair between Samson and Delilah is one of the most pathetic examples of lust and manipulation in the Bible. It should have been obvious to Samson that Delilah was working with the Philistines to destroy him. But to procure the physical pleasures he craved, Samson toyed with Delilah and stayed in a situation he should have run from. Samson blindly believed he was indestructible, leaving himself open to humiliation and suffering. Recognizing our weaknesses and avoiding situations in which we are vulnerable are vital steps to spiritual growth.

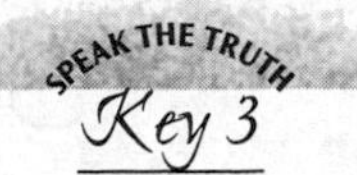

Choosing Trustworthy Friends

Judges 16:1–31 Once we have committed ourselves to confessing our faults and weaknesses to others, it is extremely important for us to keep company with trustworthy people—godly people we can entrust with our confidences. Otherwise, we will find it impossible to speak the truth and we may even find ourselves lying because we can't trust our friends.

Samson was one of Israel's judges. As a child, Samson had been dedicated to God, and God had gifted him with supernatural strength. But Samson possessed a lifelong weakness—his desire for women. Samson was especially blinded to the dangers he faced in his relationship with Delilah. Samson's enemies paid Delilah to discover the secret of his strength. Three times she begged him to let her in on his secret, and each time she tried to use this information to hand him over to his enemies. All three times, Samson lied to her and was able to escape, but each time he got closer to telling her the truth. In the end, Samson revealed his secret, was taken captive, and died a slave in enemy hands (chapters 14—16).

Samson's real problem can be found in his pursuit of unholy passions, which caused him to be drawn into the web of his treacherous enemies. His disobedience to God caused him to gradually inch his way toward destruction and a violent death.

We can protect ourselves from falling into the same trap by obeying God and developing relationships with those who love us and are devoted to God's truth. Trustworthy confidants can be relied upon to hear us speak both about our strengths and our weaknesses.

Turn to Psalm 42.

SAMSON & DELILAH

The New Testament describes Samson as a man of faith. It mentions neither his failures nor his great strength. Though he possessed great physical strength, Samson was a moral weakling, following his own selfish desires and ignoring God. Samson spent most of his life pursuing his own goals, but in the end he finally saw the truth, confessed his weakness apart from God and cried out to God for help.

It seems that after three episodes of betrayal, Samson would have learned not to trust Delilah. But like many of us, Samson thought that responding to selfish manipulation would be an expression of love. Samson chose to please Delilah in order to get what he wanted from her rather than to obey God and deliver his people. Delilah chose to use her relationship with Samson for her own gain. Most of us have experienced the pain of being used, and some of us have undoubtedly used others for our own advantage. Many of us have also known the searing agony of being betrayed.

It will accomplish nothing to look at Samson and think about what he did *not* accomplish. Likewise, it does little good for us to become depressed over what might have been. Samson shows us that as long as we have life, we still have hope. It is never too late to surrender our lives to God and allow him to redeem us and restore what we have lost. Despite his failures, Samson is listed as a champion of faith in Hebrews 11. And despite our failures, we can also be champions of faith as God continues to transform our lives.

STRENGTHS AND ACCOMPLISHMENTS:

Samson was called by God before his birth.

He is listed as a champion of faith (Hebrews 11).

Samson believed God.

He began to free his people from the Philistines.

WEAKNESSES AND MISTAKES:

Samson misused the gift of strength God had given him.

He was motivated by revenge rather than by righteousness.

Samson allowed lust to cloud his thinking.

Delilah valued riches over good relationships.

She betrayed Samson and lied to him.

LESSONS FROM THEIR LIVES:

There is great danger in placing our trust in our God-given abilities rather than in God himself.

There is a price to be paid for sin.

We must be careful to do what is right, not just what we want to do.

God can use us in spite of our failures.

KEY VERSE:

"Then Samson prayed to the LORD, 'O Sovereign LORD, remember me. O God, please strengthen me just once more, and let me with one blow get revenge on the Philistines for my two eyes'" (16:28).

The story of Samson is found in Judges 13—16, and his relationship with Delilah is described in Judges 16. Samson is also mentioned in Hebrews 11:32.

made a fool of me; you lied to me. Come now, tell me how you can be tied."

11 He said, "If anyone ties me securely with new ropes that have never been used, I'll become as weak as any other man."

12 So Delilah took new ropes and tied him with them. Then, with men hidden in the room, she called to him, "Samson, the Philistines are upon you!" But he snapped the ropes off his arms as if they were threads.

13 Delilah then said to Samson, "Until now, you have been making a fool of me and lying to me. Tell me how you can be tied."

He replied, "If you weave the seven braids of my head into the fabric ⌊on the loom⌋ and tighten it with the pin, I'll become as weak as any other man." So while he was sleeping, Delilah took the seven braids of his head, wove them into the fabric 14 and[a] tightened it with the pin.

Again she called to him, "Samson, the Philistines are upon you!" He awoke from his sleep and pulled up the pin and the loom, with the fabric.

15 Then she said to him, "How can you say, 'I love you,' when you won't confide in me? This is the third time you have made a fool of me and haven't told me the secret of your great strength." 16 With such nagging she prodded him day after day until he was tired to death.

17 So he told her everything. "No razor has ever been used on my head," he said, "because I have been a Nazirite set apart to God since birth. If my head were shaved, my strength would leave me, and I would become as weak as any other man."

18 When Delilah saw that he had told her everything, she sent word to the rulers of the Philistines, "Come back once more; he has told me everything." So the rulers of the Philistines returned with the silver in their hands. 19 Having put him to sleep on her lap, she called a man to shave off the seven braids of his hair, and so began to subdue him.[b] And his strength left him.

20 Then she called, "Samson, the Philistines are upon you!"

He awoke from his sleep and thought, "I'll go out as before and shake myself free." But he did not know that the LORD had left him.

21 Then the Philistines seized him, gouged out his eyes and took him down to Gaza. Binding him with bronze shackles, they set him to grinding in the prison. 22 But the hair on his head began to grow again after it had been shaved.

The Death of Samson

23 Now the rulers of the Philistines assembled to offer a great sacrifice to Dagon their god and to celebrate, saying, "Our god has delivered Samson, our enemy, into our hands."

24 When the people saw him, they praised their god, saying,

"Our god has delivered our enemy
  into our hands,
the one who laid waste our land
  and multiplied our slain."

25 While they were in high spirits, they shouted, "Bring out Samson to entertain us." So they called Samson out of the prison, and he performed for them.

When they stood him among the pillars, 26 Samson said to the servant who held his hand, "Put me where I can feel the pillars that support the temple, so that I may lean against them." 27 Now the temple was crowded with men and women; all the rulers of the Philistines were there, and on the roof were about three thousand men and women watching Samson perform. 28 Then Samson prayed to the LORD, "O Sovereign LORD, remember me. O God, please strengthen me just once more, and let me with one blow get revenge on the Philistines for my two eyes." 29 Then Samson reached toward the two central pillars on which the temple stood. Bracing himself against them, his right hand on the one and his left hand on the other, 30 Samson said, "Let me die with the Philistines!" Then he pushed with all his might, and down came the temple on the rulers and all the people in it. Thus he killed many more when he died than while he lived.

31 Then his brothers and his father's whole family went down to get him. They brought him back and buried him between Zorah and Eshtaol in the tomb of Manoah his father. He had led[c] Israel twenty years.

[a] *13,14* Some Septuagint manuscripts; Hebrew *"I can⌋ if you weave the seven braids of my head into the fabric ⌊on the loom⌋." 14So she* [b] *19* Hebrew; some Septuagint manuscripts *and he began to weaken* [c] *31* Traditionally *judged*

16:18–21 For years, Samson had steered around the potential disasters caused by his extreme behavior and anger. But Delilah used her knowledge about Samson to destroy him. Instead of seeing the truth about his life while there was still time to redirect his course, Samson had to be blinded by his enemy in order to see his true spiritual condition. Now he could no longer redirect his course; he had become a tortured slave of the Philistines. Samson had deserted God by his actions, and God's strength had left him. We should pray that we see our true spiritual condition—our weaknesses and sins—while there is still time to change direction.

16:22–31 Samson's lack of physical sight allowed him to gain personal and spiritual insight. Yet that was not the end of Samson's story. In this prayer, Samson finally surrendered to God. Notice that Samson accomplished more in his God-appointed death than in his entire self-centered life. Despite Samson's serious flaws, he was remembered as a man of faith (see Hebrews 11:32). We can only imagine how Samson could have altered history had he sought God and surrendered to him sooner. We need to make certain that we are not missing opportunities to serve God throughout our lives.

Micah's Idols

17 Now a man named Micah from the hill country of Ephraim 2said to his mother, "The eleven hundred shekels[a] of silver that were taken from you and about which I heard you utter a curse—I have that silver with me; I took it."

Then his mother said, "The LORD bless you, my son!"

3When he returned the eleven hundred shekels of silver to his mother, she said, "I solemnly consecrate my silver to the LORD for my son to make a carved image and a cast idol. I will give it back to you."

4So he returned the silver to his mother, and she took two hundred shekels[b] of silver and gave them to a silversmith, who made them into the image and the idol. And they were put in Micah's house.

5Now this man Micah had a shrine, and he made an ephod and some idols and installed one of his sons as his priest. 6In those days Israel had no king; everyone did as he saw fit.

7A young Levite from Bethlehem in Judah, who had been living within the clan of Judah, 8left that town in search of some other place to stay. On his way[c] he came to Micah's house in the hill country of Ephraim.

9Micah asked him, "Where are you from?"

"I'm a Levite from Bethlehem in Judah," he said, "and I'm looking for a place to stay."

10Then Micah said to him, "Live with me and be my father and priest, and I'll give you ten shekels[d] of silver a year, your clothes and your food." 11So the Levite agreed to live with him, and the young man was to him like one of his sons. 12Then Micah installed the Levite, and the young man became his priest and lived in his house. 13And Micah said, "Now I know that the LORD will be good to me, since this Levite has become my priest."

Danites Settle in Laish

18 In those days Israel had no king. And in those days the tribe of the Danites was seeking a place of their own where they might settle, because they had not yet come into an inheritance among the tribes of Israel. 2So the Danites sent five warriors from Zorah and Eshtaol to spy out the land and explore it. These men represented all their clans. They told them, "Go, explore the land."

The men entered the hill country of Ephraim and came to the house of Micah, where they spent the night. 3When they were near Micah's house, they recognized the voice of the young Levite; so they turned in there and asked him, "Who brought you here? What are you doing in this place? Why are you here?"

4He told them what Micah had done for him, and said, "He has hired me and I am his priest."

5Then they said to him, "Please inquire of God to learn whether our journey will be successful."

6The priest answered them, "Go in peace. Your journey has the LORD's approval."

7So the five men left and came to Laish, where they saw that the people were living in safety, like the Sidonians, unsuspecting and secure. And since their land lacked nothing, they

[a]2 That is, about 28 pounds (about 13 kilograms)
[b]4 That is, about 5 pounds (about 2.3 kilograms)
[c]8 Or *To carry on his profession*
[d]10 That is, about 4 ounces (about 110 grams)

17:1–6 The maxim that summarizes all of the events of chapters 17—21 is highlighted in 17:6: "In those days Israel had no king; everyone did as he saw fit." This statement rightly characterizes the do-it-yourself idolatry of Micah. Without a king or a well-defined enforcement of God's laws, there were no limits or boundaries placed upon the people. In this case, the making of idols and the creation of a private priesthood made a mockery of the true worship of God (see Exodus 20:4). When we ignore God's commands for our lives, we mock God. Showing God proper respect entails following God's will for our lives. By doing this, we will avoid self-destructive actions like those of the Israelites.

17:7–13 The depth of self-deception and religious denial in Israel during this time is clearly seen here. Not only did the priest from Bethlehem not rebuke Micah for his open idolatry, but the priest actually accepted Micah's job offer! This arrangement countered God's clearly revealed will on the matter of worship in Israel. But Micah believed it would bring him great blessing anyway. Either Micah was ignorant of God's laws, or he chose to ignore them. God shows us in the Bible all that we need to know about right living. We are responsible to learn it and then follow through on it.

18:1–2 The tribe of Dan was looking for the easy way out. The Danites had been unable to evict the Amorites from the land allotted to them under Joshua (see 1:34). They gave up persevering toward that God-given goal. Instead, the Danites sent scouts in search of an easier area to conquer that offered them significant advantages. There is no indication that the tribe ever considered the reasons for their previous defeat or sought to learn from them. Instead, they looked for another, easier solution, which led them even further away from the God who could have given them victory.

18:2–6 The Danites were initially surprised and then intrigued by Micah's arrangement of hiring a personal priest. Their first questions seem to indicate that they knew this arrangement was not right. But the Danites liked the idea of having a personal hotline to God, especially after being told that their present mission would be successful. Sadly, it appears that Micah's priest spoke only for himself, not for God. When confronted by something that is wrong or inappropriate, we must not compromise, even if there are perceptible benefits.

18:7–20 When the city of Laish appeared to offer a promising solution to their problem, the Danites concluded that Micah's priest had spoken for God. Thus, when they came to Micah's house again, they stole his idols and hired his priest. Obviously, this priest felt no sense of accountability to God. After making the wrong decision to become Micah's priest, the young man possessed no reluctance in becoming the priest for a whole tribe. We all recognize that the direction of our first step often affects the direction of the following steps. In order to continue following God's will, we should make sure that each step we take is in keeping with God's plan.

were prosperous.[a] Also, they lived a long way from the Sidonians and had no relationship with anyone else.[b]

8When they returned to Zorah and Eshtaol, their brothers asked them, "How did you find things?"

9They answered, "Come on, let's attack them! We have seen that the land is very good. Aren't you going to do something? Don't hesitate to go there and take it over. 10When you get there, you will find an unsuspecting people and a spacious land that God has put into your hands, a land that lacks nothing whatever."

11Then six hundred men from the clan of the Danites, armed for battle, set out from Zorah and Eshtaol. 12On their way they set up camp near Kiriath Jearim in Judah. This is why the place west of Kiriath Jearim is called Mahaneh Dan[c] to this day. 13From there they went on to the hill country of Ephraim and came to Micah's house.

14Then the five men who had spied out the land of Laish said to their brothers, "Do you know that one of these houses has an ephod, other household gods, a carved image and a cast idol? Now you know what to do." 15So they turned in there and went to the house of the young Levite at Micah's place and greeted him. 16The six hundred Danites, armed for battle, stood at the entrance to the gate. 17The five men who had spied out the land went inside and took the carved image, the ephod, the other household gods and the cast idol while the priest and the six hundred armed men stood at the entrance to the gate.

18When these men went into Micah's house and took the carved image, the ephod, the other household gods and the cast idol, the priest said to them, "What are you doing?"

19They answered him, "Be quiet! Don't say a word. Come with us, and be our father and priest. Isn't it better that you serve a tribe and clan in Israel as priest rather than just one man's household?" 20Then the priest was glad. He took the ephod, the other household gods and the carved image and went along with the people. 21Putting their little children, their livestock and their possessions in front of them, they turned away and left.

22When they had gone some distance from Micah's house, the men who lived near Micah were called together and overtook the Danites. 23As they shouted after them, the Danites turned and said to Micah, "What's the matter with you that you called out your men to fight?"

24He replied, "You took the gods I made, and my priest, and went away. What else do I have? How can you ask, 'What's the matter with you?'"

25The Danites answered, "Don't argue with us, or some hot-tempered men will attack you, and you and your family will lose your lives." 26So the Danites went their way, and Micah, seeing that they were too strong for him, turned around and went back home.

27Then they took what Micah had made, and his priest, and went on to Laish, against a peaceful and unsuspecting people. They attacked them with the sword and burned down their city. 28There was no one to rescue them because they lived a long way from Sidon and had no relationship with anyone else. The city was in a valley near Beth Rehob.

The Danites rebuilt the city and settled there. 29They named it Dan after their forefather Dan, who was born to Israel—though the city used to be called Laish. 30There the Danites set up for themselves the idols, and Jonathan son of Gershom, the son of Moses,[d] and his sons were priests for the tribe of Dan until the time of the captivity of the land. 31They continued to use the idols Micah had made, all the time the house of God was in Shiloh.

A Levite and His Concubine

19 In those days Israel had no king. Now a Levite who lived in a remote area in the hill country of Ephraim took a concubine from Bethlehem in Judah. 2But she was unfaithful to him. She left him and went back to her father's house in Bethlehem, Judah. After she had been there four months, 3her husband went to her to persuade her to return. He had with him his servant and two donkeys. She took him into her father's house, and when her father saw him, he gladly welcomed him. 4His father-in-law, the girl's father, prevailed upon him to stay; so he remained with him three days, eating and drinking, and sleeping there.

5On the fourth day they got up early and he prepared to leave, but the girl's father said to his son-in-law, "Refresh yourself with something to eat; then you can go." 6So the two of them sat down to eat and drink together. Afterward the girl's father said, "Please stay tonight and enjoy yourself." 7And when the man got up to go, his father-in-law persuaded him, so he stayed there that night. 8On the morning of the fifth day,

[a]7 The meaning of the Hebrew for this clause is uncertain. [b]7 Hebrew; some Septuagint manuscripts *with the Arameans* [c]12 *Mahaneh Dan* means *Dan's camp.* [d]30 An ancient Hebrew scribal tradition, some Septuagint manuscripts and Vulgate; Masoretic Text *Manasseh*

18:22–31 This episode is a classic example of an angry confrontation between two parties who both desperately need to change. Micah, the original idolater, asserted that he had been wronged because his idols and personal priest had been taken. The aggressive Danites responded with threats and intimidation. They set up an elaborate long-term worship system as a rival to true worship in Israel. Micah's original mistake had now grown and ensnared an entire tribe of Israel. We should be aware that the small mistakes in our own lives often spread into the lives of others around us.

when he rose to go, the girl's father said, "Refresh yourself. Wait till afternoon!" So the two of them ate together.

9Then when the man, with his concubine and his servant, got up to leave, his father-in-law, the girl's father, said, "Now look, it's almost evening. Spend the night here; the day is nearly over. Stay and enjoy yourself. Early tomorrow morning you can get up and be on your way home." 10But, unwilling to stay another night, the man left and went toward Jebus (that is, Jerusalem), with his two saddled donkeys and his concubine.

11When they were near Jebus and the day was almost gone, the servant said to his master, "Come, let's stop at this city of the Jebusites and spend the night."

12His master replied, "No. We won't go into an alien city, whose people are not Israelites. We will go on to Gibeah." 13He added, "Come, let's try to reach Gibeah or Ramah and spend the night in one of those places." 14So they went on, and the sun set as they neared Gibeah in Benjamin. 15There they stopped to spend the night. They went and sat in the city square, but no one took them into his home for the night.

16That evening an old man from the hill country of Ephraim, who was living in Gibeah (the men of the place were Benjamites), came in from his work in the fields. 17When he looked and saw the traveler in the city square, the old man asked, "Where are you going? Where did you come from?"

18He answered, "We are on our way from Bethlehem in Judah to a remote area in the hill country of Ephraim where I live. I have been to Bethlehem in Judah and now I am going to the house of the LORD. No one has taken me into his house. 19We have both straw and fodder for our donkeys and bread and wine for ourselves your servants—me, your maidservant, and the young man with us. We don't need anything."

20"You are welcome at my house," the old man said. "Let me supply whatever you need. Only don't spend the night in the square." 21So he took him into his house and fed his donkeys. After they had washed their feet, they had something to eat and drink.

22While they were enjoying themselves, some of the wicked men of the city surrounded the house. Pounding on the door, they shouted to the old man who owned the house, "Bring out the man who came to your house so we can have sex with him."

23The owner of the house went outside and said to them, "No, my friends, don't be so vile. Since this man is my guest, don't do this disgraceful thing. 24Look, here is my virgin daughter, and his concubine. I will bring them out to you now, and you can use them and do to them whatever you wish. But to this man, don't do such a disgraceful thing."

25But the men would not listen to him. So the man took his concubine and sent her outside to them, and they raped her and abused her throughout the night, and at dawn they let her go. 26At daybreak the woman went back to the house where her master was staying, fell down at the door and lay there until daylight.

27When her master got up in the morning and opened the door of the house and stepped out to continue on his way, there lay his concubine, fallen in the doorway of the house, with her hands on the threshold. 28He said to her, "Get up; let's go." But there was no answer. Then the man put her on his donkey and set out for home.

29When he reached home, he took a knife and cut up his concubine, limb by limb, into twelve parts and sent them into all the areas of Israel. 30Everyone who saw it said, "Such a thing has never been seen or done, not since the day the Israelites came up out of Egypt. Think about it! Consider it! Tell us what to do!"

Israelites Fight the Benjamites

20 Then all the Israelites from Dan to Beersheba and from the land of Gilead came out as one man and assembled before the LORD in Mizpah. 2The leaders of all the people of the tribes of Israel took their places in the assembly of the people of God, four hundred thousand soldiers armed with swords. 3(The Benjamites heard that the Israelites had gone up to Mizpah.) Then the Israelites said, "Tell us how this awful thing happened."

4So the Levite, the husband of the murdered woman, said, "I and my concubine came to Gibeah in Benjamin to spend the night. 5During the night the men of Gibeah came after me and surrounded the house, intending to kill me. They raped my concubine, and she died. 6I took my concubine, cut her into pieces and sent one piece to each region of Israel's inheritance, because they committed this lewd and disgraceful act in Israel. 7Now, all you Israelites, speak up and give your verdict."

8All the people rose as one man, saying,

19:11–30 This tragic episode represents the moral low point of the book of Judges. This incident is even more despicable because the uncaring Levite gave up his concubine to save his own skin. We ourselves might have sacrificed the health and stability of others so that we could do whatever we wanted to do. If so, unlike the Levite in these verses, we should accept responsibility for the consequences, recognize that we are accountable and seek the help we need for restoration and forgiveness.

20:8–25 The tribe of Benjamin foolishly denied the sins of Gibeah and self-righteously set out to defend its honor. Unwilling to admit that there was sin in their midst, the Benjamites were almost destroyed. If the Benjamites had been willing to discipline Gibeah, the rest of the tribe could have remained strong. But their pride kept them from seeing the truth and confessing it. This story powerfully illustrates the painful consequences that spiritual blindness brings. When we refuse to see the truth about ourselves or those we love, we are only hiding our problems, denying our need for help until it is too late. We

"None of us will go home. No, not one of us will return to his house. 9But now this is what we'll do to Gibeah: We'll go up against it as the lot directs. 10We'll take ten men out of every hundred from all the tribes of Israel, and a hundred from a thousand, and a thousand from ten thousand, to get provisions for the army. Then, when the army arrives at Gibeah[a] in Benjamin, it can give them what they deserve for all this vileness done in Israel." 11So all the men of Israel got together and united as one man against the city.

12The tribes of Israel sent men throughout the tribe of Benjamin, saying, "What about this awful crime that was committed among you? 13Now surrender those wicked men of Gibeah so that we may put them to death and purge the evil from Israel."

But the Benjamites would not listen to their fellow Israelites. 14From their towns they came together at Gibeah to fight against the Israelites. 15At once the Benjamites mobilized twenty-six thousand swordsmen from their towns, in addition to seven hundred chosen men from those living in Gibeah. 16Among all these soldiers there were seven hundred chosen men who were left-handed, each of whom could sling a stone at a hair and not miss.

17Israel, apart from Benjamin, mustered four hundred thousand swordsmen, all of them fighting men.

18The Israelites went up to Bethel[b] and inquired of God. They said, "Who of us shall go first to fight against the Benjamites?"

The LORD replied, "Judah shall go first."

19The next morning the Israelites got up and pitched camp near Gibeah. 20The men of Israel went out to fight the Benjamites and took up battle positions against them at Gibeah. 21The Benjamites came out of Gibeah and cut down twenty-two thousand Israelites on the battlefield that day. 22But the men of Israel encouraged one another and again took up their positions where they had stationed themselves the first day. 23The Israelites went up and wept before the LORD until evening, and they inquired of the LORD. They said, "Shall we go up again to battle against the Benjamites, our brothers?"

The LORD answered, "Go up against them."

24Then the Israelites drew near to Benjamin the second day. 25This time, when the Benjamites came out from Gibeah to oppose them, they cut down another eighteen thousand Israelites, all of them armed with swords.

26Then the Israelites, all the people, went up to Bethel, and there they sat weeping before the LORD. They fasted that day until evening and presented burnt offerings and fellowship offerings[c] to the LORD. 27And the Israelites inquired of the LORD. (In those days the ark of the covenant of God was there, 28with Phinehas son of Eleazar, the son of Aaron, ministering before it.) They asked, "Shall we go up again to battle with Benjamin our brother, or not?"

The LORD responded, "Go, for tomorrow I will give them into your hands."

29Then Israel set an ambush around Gibeah. 30They went up against the Benjamites on the third day and took up positions against Gibeah as they had done before. 31The Benjamites came out to meet them and were drawn away from the city. They began to inflict casualties on the Israelites as before, so that about thirty men fell in the open field and on the roads—the one leading to Bethel and the other to Gibeah.

32While the Benjamites were saying, "We are defeating them as before," the Israelites were saying, "Let's retreat and draw them away from the city to the roads."

33All the men of Israel moved from their places and took up positions at Baal Tamar, and the Israelite ambush charged out of its place on the west[d] of Gibeah.[e] 34Then ten thousand of Israel's finest men made a frontal attack on Gibeah. The fighting was so heavy that the Benjamites did not realize how near disaster was. 35The LORD defeated Benjamin before Israel, and on that day the Israelites struck down 25,100 Benjamites, all armed with swords. 36Then the Benjamites saw that they were beaten.

Now the men of Israel had given way before Benjamin, because they relied on the ambush they had set near Gibeah. 37The men who had been in ambush made a sudden dash into Gibeah, spread out and put the whole city to the sword. 38The men of Israel had arranged with the ambush that they should send up a great cloud of smoke from the city, 39and then the men of Israel would turn in the battle.

The Benjamites had begun to inflict casualties on the men of Israel (about thirty), and they said, "We are defeating them as in the first battle." 40But when the column of smoke began to rise from the city, the Benjamites turned and saw the smoke of the whole city going up into the sky. 41Then the men of Israel turned on them, and the men of Benjamin were terrified, because they realized that disaster had come

[a] *10* One Hebrew manuscript; most Hebrew manuscripts *Geba,* a variant of *Gibeah* [b] *18* Or *to the house of God;* also in verse 26 [c] *26* Traditionally *peace offerings*
[d] *33* Some Septuagint manuscripts and Vulgate; the meaning of the Hebrew for this word is uncertain.
[e] *33* Hebrew *Geba,* a variant of *Gibeah*

need to look honestly at the sin in our lives and in the lives of those we love. We must humbly admit our sin, seek to make things right and remember that our loved ones are susceptible to sin too.

20:26–41 Israel was willing to examine themselves and commit themselves to God and his guidance. This led to a painful yet decisive victory. God allowed the Benjamites' pride to draw them into an ambush in which they lost almost all their troops (see 20:14–15). When others confront us about our wrong behaviors or blind spots, we should acknowledge the problem and face reality before our denial of the situation destroys us and others.

upon them. [42]So they fled before the Israelites in the direction of the desert, but they could not escape the battle. And the men of Israel who came out of the towns cut them down there. [43]They surrounded the Benjamites, chased them and easily[a] overran them in the vicinity of Gibeah on the east. [44]Eighteen thousand Benjamites fell, all of them valiant fighters. [45]As they turned and fled toward the desert to the rock of Rimmon, the Israelites cut down five thousand men along the roads. They kept pressing after the Benjamites as far as Gidom and struck down two thousand more.

[46]On that day twenty-five thousand Benjamite swordsmen fell, all of them valiant fighters. [47]But six hundred men turned and fled into the desert to the rock of Rimmon, where they stayed four months. [48]The men of Israel went back to Benjamin and put all the towns to the sword, including the animals and everything else they found. All the towns they came across they set on fire.

Wives for the Benjamites

21 The men of Israel had taken an oath at Mizpah: "Not one of us will give his daughter in marriage to a Benjamite."

[2]The people went to Bethel,[b] where they sat before God until evening, raising their voices and weeping bitterly. [3]"O LORD, the God of Israel," they cried, "why has this happened to Israel? Why should one tribe be missing from Israel today?"

[4]Early the next day the people built an altar and presented burnt offerings and fellowship offerings.[c]

[5]Then the Israelites asked, "Who from all the tribes of Israel has failed to assemble before the LORD?" For they had taken a solemn oath that anyone who failed to assemble before the LORD at Mizpah should certainly be put to death.

[6]Now the Israelites grieved for their brothers, the Benjamites. "Today one tribe is cut off from Israel," they said. [7]"How can we provide wives for those who are left, since we have taken an oath by the LORD not to give them any of our daughters in marriage?" [8]Then they asked, "Which one of the tribes of Israel failed to assemble before the LORD at Mizpah?" They discovered that no one from Jabesh Gilead had come to the camp for the assembly. [9]For when they counted the people, they found that none of the people of Jabesh Gilead were there.

[10]So the assembly sent twelve thousand fighting men with instructions to go to Jabesh Gilead and put to the sword those living there, including the women and children. [11]"This is what you are to do," they said. "Kill every male and every woman who is not a virgin." [12]They found among the people living in Jabesh Gilead four hundred young women who had never slept with a man, and they took them to the camp at Shiloh in Canaan.

[13]Then the whole assembly sent an offer of peace to the Benjamites at the rock of Rimmon. [14]So the Benjamites returned at that time and were given the women of Jabesh Gilead who had been spared. But there were not enough for all of them.

[15]The people grieved for Benjamin, because the LORD had made a gap in the tribes of Israel. [16]And the elders of the assembly said, "With the women of Benjamin destroyed, how shall we provide wives for the men who are left? [17]The Benjamite survivors must have heirs," they said, "so that a tribe of Israel will not be wiped out. [18]We can't give them our daughters as wives, since we Israelites have taken this oath: 'Cursed be anyone who gives a wife to a Benjamite.' [19]But look, there is the annual festival of the LORD in Shiloh, to the north of Bethel, and east of the road that goes from Bethel to Shechem, and to the south of Lebonah."

[20]So they instructed the Benjamites, saying, "Go and hide in the vineyards [21]and watch. When the girls of Shiloh come out to join in the dancing, then rush from the vineyards and each of you seize a wife from the girls of Shiloh and go to the land of Benjamin. [22]When their fathers or brothers complain to us, we will say to them, 'Do us a kindness by helping them, because we did not get wives for them during the war, and you are innocent, since you did not give your daughters to them.' "

[23]So that is what the Benjamites did. While the girls were dancing, each man caught one and carried her off to be his wife. Then they returned to their inheritance and rebuilt the towns and settled in them.

[24]At that time the Israelites left that place and went home to their tribes and clans, each to his own inheritance.

[25]In those days Israel had no king; everyone did as he saw fit.

[a]43 The meaning of the Hebrew for this word is uncertain. [b]2 Or *to the house of God* [c]4 Traditionally *peace offerings*

21:1–12 In the heat of anger or emotions, many people make rash or unrealistic vows. In this passage, Israel was forced to keep their vows because they had made them publicly before God. The Israelites had not learned from Jephthah's tragic mistake of making a thoughtless vow (see 11:30–31, 34–39). What a great lack of wisdom and self-control! Promises are meant to be kept. We should not make a promise that we will regret or refuse to carry out later.

21:10–24 Often those who are unwilling to face reality will do whatever it takes to survive without facing their root problems. There was no hint of repentance or commitment to God on the part of the Benjamites here. Their concern was mere survival. In feeling sorry for the remnant of Benjamin, the rest of Israel used very questionable ways of making things right. While it is a very commendable thing to help others, aid should not be given improperly or strictly out of a sense of guilt.

RUTH

The Big Picture

- A. *THE BOTTOM DROPS OUT IN NAOMI'S LIFE (1:1-5)*
- B. *THE BEGINNING OF A NEW LIFE (1:6-22)*
- C. *THE SEEN PROCESS AND THE UNSEEN PROVISION (2:1-23)*
- D. *THE FASHION OF REALITY IN AN OLD-FASHIONED LOVE STORY (3:1-18)*
- E. *THE JOY OF FULFILLED RELATIONSHIPS (4:1-17)*
- F. *THE LONG-TERM CONSEQUENCES OF SHORT-TERM CHOICES (4:18-22)*

During the time of the judges, Naomi and her family moved to the neighboring country of Moab to escape a severe famine in Israel. Naomi's husband died there, and her sons married Moabite women. In time, both of her sons also died, leaving Naomi destitute and alone, far from her relatives in Israel. One daughter-in-law, Orpah, returned to her own family; the other daughter-in-law, Ruth, stayed with Naomi to comfort her in her grief.

Grief is hard work; it is painful. People who are grieving need others to grieve with them and comfort them. Ruth's faithfulness to her mother-in-law during this time is striking. She gave up the security of her family in Moab to face a future of probable loneliness and poverty in a foreign land. But Ruth's faithfulness yielded the fruits of God's blessing; Naomi experienced God's comfort and love through her.

Together Ruth and Naomi trusted God to help them, and God provided for them in his own time. The circumstances through which their desperate needs were met reveal God's unseen hand at work. God led Naomi and Ruth back to Israel where Ruth met Boaz, her future husband. In the end, not only did Ruth find security and love, but the sadness of Naomi's heart was replaced with joy.

We have all experienced some kind of loss. There are times when we may feel as if the future is hopeless even after we have given everything over to God. As we grieve, we may feel abandoned and bitter toward God and the people around us. But we can take comfort in the fact that God is still with us—even when our emotions scream the opposite message—and be reassured that he is working on our behalf behind the scenes.

Spiritual Renewal Themes

FACING OUR LOSSES

During the grief process, we face the agonizing reality of our losses. This takes time and a great deal of emotional energy. Because grieving is so hard, we often try to shut out the pain. We want to ignore what has happened, keep a stiff upper lip, smile at all costs. However, avoiding the difficult process of grief does not produce growth and healing. Naomi felt embittered

Essential Facts

PURPOSE:
To show that people who seek God and surrender to him can make an extraordinary impact and find peace in their lives.

AUTHOR:
Tradition names Samuel as the author, but it could have been a writer during the reign of David or Solomon.

AUDIENCE:
The people of Israel.

DATE WRITTEN:
Sometime between 1020 and 930 B.C.

SETTING:
During the period of the judges.

KEY VERSE:
"But Ruth replied, 'Don't urge me to leave you or to turn back from you. Where you go I will go, and where you stay I will stay. Your people will be my people and your God my God' " (1:16).

KEY PLACES:
Bethlehem, Moab.

KEY PEOPLE AND RELATIONSHIPS:
Naomi and Ruth, Ruth and Boaz, Naomi and Obed.

and abandoned by God, but she faced her loss honestly and allowed herself to grieve. This was an important step toward her healing.

COMFORT IN GRIEF

The bottom fell out of the lives of Ruth and Naomi. The easy way out for Ruth would have been to go back to the security of her own family and leave Naomi alone in her poverty. But Ruth trusted the God of Israel and chose to stay with her mother-in-law. Naomi and Ruth received great comfort from each other. Those who are grieving need those who will mourn with them and help them carry their grief. During painful times, God will often use other people to bring us comfort.

GOD'S PLAN

This story relates an important link in God's plan for the redemption of our broken world. God used the faithfulness and integrity of Ruth, Naomi and Boaz to bring about their own healing and also to bring a child, Obed, into the world. This baby would become the grandfather of King David and the ancestor of Jesus the Messiah. Through Jesus we all can find restoration from the destructive forces of sin. The faithfulness of Ruth, Naomi and Boaz made possible the spiritual restoration and renewal of the human race.

DIFFICULT TIMES

It is easy to think that if circumstances were just a little better our spiritual growth would proceed more smoothly. But the test of anyone's spiritual strength is how well they persevere when times are bad. The book of Ruth tells us about a family that suffered extreme losses. Naomi's husband died, then both of her sons. One daughter-in-law returned to her childhood family, but the other daughter-in-law persevered in this seemingly hopeless situation. Ruth refused to let difficult times determine the outcome of her future. Her perseverance in difficulty is an example for all who face painful situations.

Naomi and Ruth

1 In the days when the judges ruled,[a] there
was a famine in the land, and a man from
Bethlehem in Judah, together with his wife and
two sons, went to live for a while in the country
of Moab. 2The man's name was Elimelech, his
wife's name Naomi, and the names of his two
sons were Mahlon and Kilion. They were Eph-
rathites from Bethlehem, Judah. And they went
to Moab and lived there.
3Now Elimelech, Naomi's husband, died,
and she was left with her two sons. 4They married Moabite women, one named Orpah and
the other Ruth. After they had lived there about
ten years, 5both Mahlon and Kilion also died,
and Naomi was left without her two sons and
her husband.
6When she heard in Moab that the LORD had
come to the aid of his people by providing food
for them, Naomi and her daughters-in-law prepared to return home from there. 7With her two
daughters-in-law she left the place where she
had been living and set out on the road that
would take them back to the land of Judah.
8Then Naomi said to her two daughters-in-
law, "Go back, each of you, to your mother's
home. May the LORD show kindness to you, as
you have shown to your dead and to me. 9May
the LORD grant that each of you will find rest in
the home of another husband."
Then she kissed them and they wept aloud
10and said to her, "We will go back with you to
your people."
11But Naomi said, "Return home, my daughters. Why would you come with me? Am I going to have any more sons, who could become
your husbands? 12Return home, my daughters;
I am too old to have another husband. Even if
I thought there was still hope for me—even if I
had a husband tonight and then gave birth to
sons— 13would you wait until they grew up?
Would you remain unmarried for them? No,
my daughters. It is more bitter for me than for
you, because the LORD's hand has gone out
against me!"
14At this they wept again. Then Orpah kissed
her mother-in-law good-by, but Ruth clung to
her.
15"Look," said Naomi, "your sister-in-law is
going back to her people and her gods. Go back
with her."
16But Ruth replied, "Don't urge me to leave
you or to turn back from you. Where you go I
will go, and where you stay I will stay. Your
people will be my people and your God my
God. 17Where you die I will die, and there I will
be buried. May the LORD deal with me, be it ever
so severely, if anything but death separates you
and me." 18When Naomi realized that Ruth was
determined to go with her, she stopped urging
her.
19So the two women went on until they came
to Bethlehem. When they arrived in Bethlehem,
the whole town was stirred because of them,
and the women exclaimed, "Can this be Naomi?"
20"Don't call me Naomi,[b]" she told them.
"Call me Mara,[c] because the Almighty[d] has
made my life very bitter. 21I went away full, but
the LORD has brought me back empty. Why call
me Naomi? The LORD has afflicted[e] me; the
Almighty has brought misfortune upon me."
22So Naomi returned from Moab accompanied by Ruth the Moabitess, her daughter-in-
law, arriving in Bethlehem as the barley harvest
was beginning.

Ruth Meets Boaz

2 Now Naomi had a relative on her husband's side, from the clan of Elimelech, a
man of standing, whose name was Boaz.
2And Ruth the Moabitess said to Naomi,
"Let me go to the fields and pick up the leftover
grain behind anyone in whose eyes I find favor."
Naomi said to her, "Go ahead, my daughter."
3So she went out and began to glean in the

[a] *1* Traditionally *judged* [b] *20* *Naomi* means *pleasant*; also in verse 21. [c] *20* *Mara* means *bitter*.
[d] *20* Hebrew *Shaddai*; also in verse 21 [e] *21* Or *has testified against*

1:6–22 True spiritual renewal often grows out of painful beginnings. In choosing to leave Moab, Naomi was turning back toward Israel, seeking help from the God of her fathers. Because Naomi accepted the reality of her situation she advised her daughters-in-law to return to their families. Naomi knew that she would be unable to support them in the years ahead. But she also knew that in sending them away she was dismissing her last vestige of support and security. As bleak as the situation was, Naomi was willing to summon the courage to build a new life. Too often our desire for short-term security prevents us from stepping out in faith. We cling to the people and things that help us feel secure. This, however, can keep us from seeking God and surrendering to him. As a result, we often miss God's best for us.

1:16–18 Ruth's desire to remain close to Naomi was actually a step of faith. Naomi possessed no financial security, no family members nearby for support or protection. By staying with Naomi, Ruth was cutting herself off from her own family, land and culture. She was essentially committing her life into God's hands. After making this commitment to Naomi, Ruth supported her, doing everything she could to provide food and help for her mother-in-law. Committing ourselves to spiritual renewal is not an easy road. We must realize this before we begin, or we will be tempted to give up when things get tough. Remembering Ruth's example and sticking to our commitments will always yield great rewards in the long run.

2:1–3, 18–23 We must never forget that God is in charge of our lives. God guided Ruth into Boaz's field, though at the time Ruth was unaware of it. Naomi recognized the fact of God's guidance later on. Throughout this story God was working behind the scenes, whether or not the people involved recognized it. God often works the same way with us. He leads us to meet people and make decisions that affect our lives. It is only later that we sometimes see how God has been leading us each step of the way. Knowing that God works in this way should encourage us as we face the challenges and unknowns in our lives.

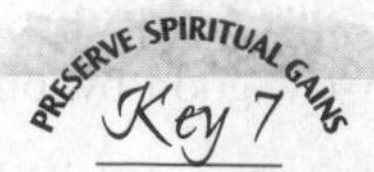

Persevering Until We Find Love

Ruth 2:4–18 "Please love me!" Isn't this the whispered cry of our hearts? We all long for the security that love brings. But finding such love can be very difficult. Yet we need to be in community with loving, faithful Christians in order to preserve our spiritual gains.

Ruth was a young woman who had loved and lost. But Ruth persevered until she found love again. Ruth's beloved husband died, and she was left unprotected for a time. So Ruth followed her mother-in-law Naomi to a foreign land and gathered leftover grain from the harvested fields just to stay alive. Though Ruth was not aware of it, the man who owned those fields was a relative who could, if he chose to, marry Ruth and fulfill her desire for love and protection. Naomi told Ruth to go to the threshing floor where this man, Boaz, was sleeping and curl up at his feet. In Naomi's culture, this act displayed the individual's request to be taken care of. Boaz was quite happy to find Ruth there. Later he married her, providing the love and provision Ruth had lost and longed for.

In Christ, we will also find all the love and security we truly need, for he cares for us very much. We can be sure that when we "curl up" at the feet of Jesus, he will be glad to find us there. He will provide for us, protect us and love us. Yet we also need to develop healthy love relationships with people in God's family. No matter how we may have loved and lost, God wants us to persevere and say, "Please love me." It may be scary, but it's worth the risk.

Turn to 2 Samuel 15.

fields behind the harvesters. As it turned out,
she found herself working in a field belonging
to Boaz, who was from the clan of Elimelech.
4Just then Boaz arrived from Bethlehem and
greeted the harvesters, "The LORD be with
you!"
"The LORD bless you!" they called back.
5Boaz asked the foreman of his harvesters,
"Whose young woman is that?"
6The foreman replied, "She is the Moabitess
who came back from Moab with Naomi. 7She
said, 'Please let me glean and gather among the
sheaves behind the harvesters.' She went into
the field and has worked steadily from morning
till now, except for a short rest in the shelter."
8So Boaz said to Ruth, "My daughter, listen
to me. Don't go and glean in another field and
don't go away from here. Stay here with my
servant girls. 9Watch the field where the men are
harvesting, and follow along after the girls. I
have told the men not to touch you. And whenever you are thirsty, go and get a drink from the
water jars the men have filled."
10At this, she bowed down with her face to
the ground. She exclaimed, "Why have I found
such favor in your eyes that you notice me—a
foreigner?"
11Boaz replied, "I've been told all about
what you have done for your mother-in-law
since the death of your husband—how you left
your father and mother and your homeland
and came to live with a people you did not
know before. 12May the LORD repay you for
what you have done. May you be richly rewarded by the LORD, the God of Israel, under whose
wings you have come to take refuge."
13"May I continue to find favor in your eyes,
my lord," she said. "You have given me comfort
and have spoken kindly to your servant—
though I do not have the standing of one of
your servant girls."
14At mealtime Boaz said to her, "Come over
here. Have some bread and dip it in the wine
vinegar."
When she sat down with the harvesters, he
offered her some roasted grain. She ate all she
wanted and had some left over. 15As she got up
to glean, Boaz gave orders to his men, "Even if
she gathers among the sheaves, don't embarrass
her. 16Rather, pull out some stalks for her from
the bundles and leave them for her to pick up,
and don't rebuke her."
17So Ruth gleaned in the field until evening.

2:4–17 This passage beautifully demonstrates God's guidance in the ordinary decisions of life. Naomi and Ruth needed food, so Ruth went searching for it. As she stepped out in faith, persevering in her commitment to Naomi, God provided what she needed—a place to gather grain in an atmosphere of safety and respect (see Philippians 4:19). God led her to the fields of Boaz, a man of outstanding character—honest and willing to help others without demanding anything in return. When we experience such fortunate "coincidences" and helpful new relationships in life, we need to take the time to thank God for his provision in each of these areas.

Then she threshed the barley she had gathered,
and it amounted to about an ephah.[a] 18She
carried it back to town, and her mother-in-law
saw how much she had gathered. Ruth also
brought out and gave her what she had left over
after she had eaten enough.

19Her mother-in-law asked her, "Where did
you glean today? Where did you work? Blessed
be the man who took notice of you!"

Then Ruth told her mother-in-law about the
one at whose place she had been working. "The
name of the man I worked with today is Boaz,"
she said.

20"The LORD bless him!" Naomi said to her
daughter-in-law. "He has not stopped showing
his kindness to the living and the dead." She
added, "That man is our close relative; he is one
of our kinsman-redeemers."

21Then Ruth the Moabitess said, "He even
said to me, 'Stay with my workers until they
finish harvesting all my grain.' "

22Naomi said to Ruth her daughter-in-law,
"It will be good for you, my daughter, to go
with his girls, because in someone else's field
you might be harmed."

23So Ruth stayed close to the servant girls of
Boaz to glean until the barley and wheat harvests were finished. And she lived with her
mother-in-law.

Ruth and Boaz at the Threshing Floor

3 One day Naomi her mother-in-law said to
her, "My daughter, should I not try to find
a home[b] for you, where you will be well provided for? 2Is not Boaz, with whose servant girls
you have been, a kinsman of ours? Tonight he
will be winnowing barley on the threshing
floor. 3Wash and perfume yourself, and put on
your best clothes. Then go down to the threshing floor, but don't let him know you are there
until he has finished eating and drinking.
4When he lies down, note the place where he
is lying. Then go and uncover his feet and lie
down. He will tell you what to do."

5"I will do whatever you say," Ruth answered.
6So she went down to the threshing floor and
did everything her mother-in-law told her
to do.

7When Boaz had finished eating and drinking and was in good spirits, he went over to lie
down at the far end of the grain pile. Ruth approached quietly, uncovered his feet and lay
down. 8In the middle of the night something
startled the man, and he turned and discovered
a woman lying at his feet.

9"Who are you?" he asked.

"I am your servant Ruth," she said. "Spread
the corner of your garment over me, since you
are a kinsman-redeemer."

10"The LORD bless you, my daughter," he replied. "This kindness is greater than that which
you showed earlier: You have not run after the
younger men, whether rich or poor. 11And now,
my daughter, don't be afraid. I will do for you
all you ask. All my fellow townsmen know that
you are a woman of noble character. 12Al-
though it is true that I am near of kin, there is
a kinsman-redeemer nearer than I. 13Stay here
for the night, and in the morning if he wants to
redeem, good; let him redeem. But if he is not
willing, as surely as the LORD lives I will do it.
Lie here until morning."

14So she lay at his feet until morning, but got
up before anyone could be recognized; and he
said, "Don't let it be known that a woman came
to the threshing floor."

15He also said, "Bring me the shawl you are
wearing and hold it out." When she did so, he
poured into it six measures of barley and put it
on her. Then he[c] went back to town.

16When Ruth came to her mother-in-law,
Naomi asked, "How did it go, my daughter?"

Then she told her everything Boaz had done
for her 17and added, "He gave me these six
measures of barley, saying, 'Don't go back to
your mother-in-law empty-handed.' "

18Then Naomi said, "Wait, my daughter, until you find out what happens. For the man will
not rest until the matter is settled today."

[a]*17* That is, probably about 3/5 bushel (about 22 liters)
[b]*1* Hebrew *find rest* (see Ruth 1:9) [c]*15* Most Hebrew manuscripts; many Hebrew manuscripts, Vulgate and Syriac *she*

3:1–7 Naomi's plan to find a husband for her daughter-in-law may seem a little strange to us. Her plan, however, was based upon a Biblical provision for the protection of widows (see Deuteronomy 25:5–10). God had assigned the responsibility of caring for a widow to the dead husband's brothers or near relatives. Since Boaz was a near relative to Ruth's dead husband, he was responsible to God for helping her. Ruth trusted Naomi's advice and followed God's plan for rebuilding her life as she took this next courageous step of faith and obedience. God provides direction for us in his Word, but this doesn't mean that the fulfillment of his will for our lives is automatic. With faith and obedience we need to use the keys God gives us to bring about his will in our lives.

3:6–14 This passage is one of the great Biblical examples of how truth, clear personal boundaries and self-respect can protect people who are faced with temptation. Both Ruth and Boaz, though in a delicate and compromising situation, chose to do what was right. They refused to yield to the temptation of the moment and considered the long-term consequences of sexual activity outside the bounds of marriage. Notice how Boaz showed an unselfish concern for Ruth's safety (3:13) and her reputation (3:14).

3:15–18 Earlier Boaz had provided abundantly for the short-term needs of Ruth and Naomi. Now that the harvest was over Boaz gave them additional provisions. Naomi saw in Boaz's generous gifts his willingness to be responsible for Ruth (and Naomi) according to the stipulations of God's law (see Deuteronomy 25:5–10). God provided for Naomi and Ruth through these wise laws and by sending a man who was willing to obey them. God also has given his Word to us for guidance. We need to follow through on God's plan if we hope to help others grow spiritually and preserve our own spiritual gains.

Ruth, Naomi & Boaz

What could be more emotionally devastating than to experience widowhood, the death of two children and poverty all at one time? Any one of these difficult situations would be enough to overwhelm most of us. And the combined effect of these losses might cause us to break beneath the load of grief.

Naomi and her daughter-in-law Ruth clung to each other under their mountain of despair. Faced with a seemingly hopeless situation, Ruth chose to stay with Naomi even though Naomi had nothing to offer her. Ruth also committed herself to Naomi's God. God helped Ruth through that difficult period of uncertainty and eventually granted her the blessing of marriage to Boaz.

As Naomi grieved, she released the anger she had been holding inside. Although her true feelings were not pleasant, she honestly expressed her bitterness, anger and depression. Naomi felt that God had dealt her bitter blows and had abandoned her. She felt hopeless and initially could not share Ruth's faith. But after Ruth's God-given success gleaning in Boaz's field, Naomi's outlook changed dramatically. She was able to see that God was indeed at work rebuilding their lives. The marriage of Ruth and Boaz proved to be a time of joyful fulfillment for Naomi. Once again Naomi had not only a son but also a grandson!

Boaz was wonderfully gentle and wise. Though strong and successful, Boaz was sensitive and concerned about the needs of those around him. He was immediately interested in Ruth and Naomi's situation while still carefully preserving Ruth's dignity. Perhaps a widower himself, and likely some years older than Ruth, Boaz also displayed admirable self-control and respect for Ruth.

God led Naomi and Ruth to a new life filled with promise for the future. The son of Ruth and Boaz would become the grandfather of King David and the ancestor of Jesus the Messiah. Ruth, Naomi and Boaz could never have known that their simple acts of faith would lead to the blessing of millions! God may have significant plans for us too. All we need to do is trust God and obey his will for us.

STRENGTHS AND ACCOMPLISHMENTS:

Naomi and Ruth's relationship was centered on God.

Ruth and Naomi were committed to each other.

Ruth's actions were characterized by faith, loyalty and boldness.

Boaz was sensitive, generous and full of integrity.

LESSONS FROM THEIR LIVES:

Trust is the necessary foundation for a healthy relationship.

Grief helps us release our pain and honestly express the depth of our losses. Grieving and mourning are vital to spiritual renewal.

Those who are grieving need people to support them.

God is intimately involved in our grief.

KEY VERSE:

"Don't urge me to leave you or to turn back from you. Where you go I will go, and where you stay I will stay. Your people will be my people and your God my God" (1:16).

The story of Ruth, Naomi and Boaz is told in the book of Ruth. Boaz and Ruth are also mentioned in Matthew 1:5, and Boaz is referred to in 1 Chronicles 2:11-12 and Luke 3:32.

THE SPIRITUAL DISCIPLINES

In the Life of Ruth

The story of Ruth cannot be told without speaking of Naomi as well. It is a story of two lives woven together by grief and grace into a spiritual friendship that would help bring about the lineage of Israel's greatest king and ultimately the Messiah.

Ruth and Naomi's friendship was born in crisis. A famine in Israel forced Elimelech and his wife, Naomi, to flee with their sons to the neighboring country of Moab. Moab was one of the nations that had oppressed Israel at the time of the exodus. While in Moab, the two sons married Moabite women, one of whom was Ruth. However, all of the men in the family soon died, and Naomi decided to return to Israel. She encouraged her daughters-in-law to return to their childhood families, but Ruth insisted on remaining with Naomi. Ruth's pledge of commitment to Naomi stands forever as one of the most moving expressions of love and faithfulness ever spoken (Ruth 1:16–17). Ruth's love for Naomi was reflected in her love for Naomi's God and was nurtured by the two spiritual disciplines she practiced.

SERVICE. Ruth's newfound faith and her love for Naomi were cultivated by her discipline of service. Ruth served Naomi by gladly gleaning the fields for food—a difficult and often dangerous task. As Ruth served, God guided her to a field where her work would be richly blessed. The compassion of Boaz reminds us of God's compassion as well, for the Lord blesses our work and watches over us as we serve him. (To learn more about service, turn to Mark 10.)

SPIRITUAL FRIENDSHIP. In her relationship with Naomi, Ruth also practiced the discipline of spiritual friendship. This discipline produced several good things in their lives that helped Ruth and Naomi draw closer to God. Ruth's friendship provided her with a valuable role model in Naomi, who drew her closer to God. Ruth's profession of faith in Naomi's God and her faithfulness thereafter were almost certainly influenced by the conduct of Naomi's family as they modeled genuine belief in trying times.

Ruth and Naomi's friendship also sustained both of them as they recuperated from the wounds of life. Naomi didn't hesitate to announce her deep grief by saying, "Call me Mara," which means bitter (1:20). But Naomi's bitterness was greatly softened by Ruth's care.

Finally, Ruth and Naomi's friendship opened the way to a new future. Boaz was deeply impressed by Ruth's love and faith, evidenced by her friendship with Naomi. Boaz paid Ruth special attention because he could glimpse her heart's attitudes in her behavior toward others. Eventually the two were married and became ancestors to King David and Jesus Christ. (To learn more about spiritual friendship, turn to Genesis 2.)

Lessons for Life

The second great commandment is that we love our neighbor as we love ourselves (see Matthew 22:38–39). What we often fail to realize is that loving our neighbors is a *means* to loving ourselves as well as an expression of our love for the Lord. By blessing others, we receive blessing. And through such love, God's love is made visible to our world. Service and spiritual friendship are two key disciplines that can help us express this love to those around us while we learn more about God and his love too.

Boaz Marries Ruth

4 Meanwhile Boaz went up to the town gate and sat there. When the kinsman-redeemer he had mentioned came along, Boaz said, "Come over here, my friend, and sit down." So he went over and sat down.

2Boaz took ten of the elders of the town and said, "Sit here," and they did so. 3Then he said to the kinsman-redeemer, "Naomi, who has come back from Moab, is selling the piece of land that belonged to our brother Elimelech. 4I thought I should bring the matter to your attention and suggest that you buy it in the presence of these seated here and in the presence of the elders of my people. If you will redeem it, do so. But if you[a] will not, tell me, so I will know. For no one has the right to do it except you, and I am next in line."

"I will redeem it," he said.

5Then Boaz said, "On the day you buy the land from Naomi and from Ruth the Moabitess, you acquire[b] the dead man's widow, in order to maintain the name of the dead with his property."

6At this, the kinsman-redeemer said, "Then I cannot redeem it because I might endanger my own estate. You redeem it yourself. I cannot do it."

7(Now in earlier times in Israel, for the redemption and transfer of property to become final, one party took off his sandal and gave it to the other. This was the method of legalizing transactions in Israel.)

8So the kinsman-redeemer said to Boaz, "Buy it yourself." And he removed his sandal.

9Then Boaz announced to the elders and all the people, "Today you are witnesses that I have bought from Naomi all the property of Elimelech, Kilion and Mahlon. 10I have also acquired Ruth the Moabitess, Mahlon's widow, as my wife, in order to maintain the name of the dead with his property, so that his name will not disappear from among his family or from the town records. Today you are witnesses!"

11Then the elders and all those at the gate said, "We are witnesses. May the LORD make the woman who is coming into your home like Rachel and Leah, who together built up the house of Israel. May you have standing in Ephrathah and be famous in Bethlehem. 12Through the offspring the LORD gives you by this young woman, may your family be like that of Perez, whom Tamar bore to Judah."

The Genealogy of David

13So Boaz took Ruth and she became his wife. Then he went to her, and the LORD enabled her to conceive, and she gave birth to a son. 14The women said to Naomi: "Praise be to the LORD, who this day has not left you without a kinsman-redeemer. May he become famous throughout Israel! 15He will renew your life and sustain you in your old age. For your daughter-in-law, who loves you and who is better to you than seven sons, has given him birth."

16Then Naomi took the child, laid him in her lap and cared for him. 17The women living there said, "Naomi has a son." And they named him Obed. He was the father of Jesse, the father of David.

18This, then, is the family line of Perez:

Perez was the father of Hezron,
19Hezron the father of Ram,
Ram the father of Amminadab,
20Amminadab the father of Nahshon,
Nahshon the father of Salmon,[c]
21Salmon the father of Boaz,
Boaz the father of Obed,
22Obed the father of Jesse,
and Jesse the father of David.

[a]4 Many Hebrew manuscripts, Septuagint, Vulgate and Syriac; most Hebrew manuscripts *he* [b]5 Hebrew; Vulgate and Syriac *Naomi, you acquire Ruth the Moabitess,* [c]20 A few Hebrew manuscripts, some Septuagint manuscripts and Vulgate (see also verse 21 and Septuagint of 1 Chron. 2:11); most Hebrew manuscripts *Salma*

4:1–10 As Boaz negotiated with the kinsman-redeemer, it became clear that he was a wise and shrewd man. He did not lie or manipulate the circumstances, though he clearly sought a specific outcome. Boaz wisely anticipated the greedy response of Naomi's closer kinsman. This other man wanted Ruth's dead husband's inheritance but had no desire to care for Ruth or father her children. When faced with the facts, this man saw that the economic advantages of taking Ruth's case were limited, and taking such action could even possibly be detrimental. He did not want to be held accountable to God's law or for the economic loss it might entail. We must be careful not to seek only the *advantages* in our relationships; we must also accept the *responsibilities*. Like Boaz, we need to seek what is best for the people close to us.

4:11–17 The story of Ruth and Naomi begins with loneliness and destitution, but it ends happily. Naomi, who had lost her family (see 1:4–5), had a family once again. Ruth, who had lost her husband and all hope of a prosperous future (see 1:8–9), was given a husband, a son and a hope for the future. Notice that Ruth's sacrificial lifestyle brought a new life not only to herself and Naomi but also to all of us. Boaz and Ruth's son was named Obed; he became the ancestor of Jesus Christ, our redeemer from sin and provider of new life.

4:18–22 Hidden in this family tree is the powerful evidence that God uses fallible people to bring about his will. Perez was mentioned as the first of David's ancestors. He was the illegitimate son of Judah and his daughter-in-law Tamar (see Genesis 38:1–30). Boaz was the son of Salmon, whose wife was Rahab, the prostitute of Jericho (see Joshua 2:1–24; Matthew 1:5). Ruth was a foreigner from Moab, not even one of God's chosen people. God used all of these imperfect people to bring about the birth of Israel's greatest king, David, and the world's only Savior, Jesus Christ. Knowing this truth should give us hope. No matter how sordid or painful our past, God can use us significantly if we are willing to put ourselves in his hands and follow his plans for our lives.

1 SAMUEL

The Big Picture

The book of 1 Samuel begins with the birth of the prophet Samuel and ends with the death of King Saul. It contains a catalog of lives for us to explore and learn from—some exemplary, others not. Samuel was born in the time of the judges, when "everyone did as he saw fit" (Judges 17:6). The people of Israel were spiritually far away from God. Eli was the high priest, but the flaws in his leadership showed in the serious problems within his own family. Since Israel lacked strong spiritual leadership God chose Samuel and prepared him to lead the Israelites back to God.

Near the end of Samuel's ministry the people demanded a king. They wanted to be like the surrounding nations. God was not pleased with Israel's demand, but he chose Saul and allowed him to lead the Israelites anyway. Though a man of great potential, Saul was self-centered and disobedient; he never achieved what God had intended for him.

While Saul was still king, Samuel anointed David to succeed Saul. David became a national hero when he killed Goliath, and he won many other great battles with God's help. But when Saul realized that David was next in line for the throne, Saul was consumed by bitterness and tried to kill him. In the end, faced with defeat in battle, Saul took his own life.

This book exhibits portraits of some people who moved toward God and his good plan for them and others who moved away from God and toward disaster. Jealousy, bitterness and disobedience destroyed the life of King Saul. But forgiveness, trust and obedience brought David great success. The book of 1 Samuel clearly shows that the only way to true success is by following God's plan with trust and obedience.

A. FINISHING WITH THE OLD—SAMUEL, THE LAST JUDGE (1:1–12:25)

1. God's Man Arrives on the Scene (1:1–3:21)
2. The Problems Continue–War With the Philistines (4:1–7:17)
3. A King Requested, Chosen and Anointed (8:1–11:15)
4. Samuel's Retirement (12:1-25)

B. STARTING WITH THE NEW—SAUL, THE FIRST KING (13:1–31:13)

1. The Sudden Failure of Saul as Leader (13:1–15:35)
2. A New Leader Appears–David (16:1–17:58)
3. Saul's Obsession With David (18:1–30:31)
4. The Death of Saul (31:1-13)

Spiritual Renewal Themes

DEPENDENCE ON GOD

Of the three prominent men in the books of Samuel (Samuel, Saul and David), only two truly depended on God. When God chose Saul as the first king, Saul clearly possessed the potential for greatness. Saul started out well, but his faith in God never matured. Instead of obeying God and trusting him for success, Saul acted out of self-sufficiency, and his life ended up as a tragic failure. When we experience success in life, or when

Essential Facts

PURPOSE:
To track Israel's transition from the period of the judges to the era of kingly rule.

AUTHOR:
Unknown, but probably most of it was written by Samuel. Nathan and Gad may have also been contributors.

AUDIENCE:
The people of Israel.

DATE WRITTEN:
The book was probably started during Samuel's lifetime and finished around 930 B.C.

SETTING:
The action takes place in Israel, between 1120 and 971 B.C.

KEY VERSE:
"Does the LORD delight in burnt offerings and sacrifices as much as in obeying the voice of the LORD? To obey is better than sacrifice, and to heed is better than the fat of rams" (15:22).

KEY PLACES:
Shiloh, Gibeah, Ramah, Bethlehem, Gath, Adullam, Hebron, the wilderness of Judah, Ziklag, Endor, Beth Shan.

KEY PEOPLE AND RELATIONSHIPS:
Samuel with Eli, with Saul and then with David.

someone threatens our success, we need to keep our eyes on God. He is the giver of all success and is the only one who can help us continue in it.

STRENGTH IN WEAKNESS

No matter how weak we may be, God is able to work through us to do mighty things. When young David killed the giant Goliath in God's name, his weakness became a funnel for God's power. Jonathan and his bodyguard virtually destroyed a vast Philistine army with God's help—a task impossible from a human perspective! There is only one way to begin our spiritual renewal: We must see the truth of our need for God's power. Then God can intervene in our lives and supply us with all the power we need to follow his will.

NECESSITY OF OBEDIENCE

Over and over again in the Bible we are confronted by the importance of obedience to God's will. In God's eyes, "To obey is better than sacrifice" (15:22). In Saul's case, his lack of obedience led to his downfall. On the other hand, David was a man after God's own heart. He trusted and obeyed God. Even when he could have killed Saul, he refused to do so because Saul was God's anointed king. Though David failed and sinned, he repented and turned back to God. Be encouraged. No one can live a flawless life, but we do need to trust God and do our best to obey him.

CONSEQUENCES OF DISOBEDIENCE

When Eli, Samuel, Saul and David disobeyed God, they all faced tragic consequences. Their sin affected not only them but also their families. Saul was given many opportunities to get his life back on track, but his self-centered heart kept him from turning to God for forgiveness and healing. Saul's lack of faith and obedience resulted in a bitter life and a tragic death.

The Birth of Samuel

1 There was a certain man from Ramathaim,
a Zuphite[a] from the hill country of Ephraim, whose name was Elkanah son of Jeroham,
the son of Elihu, the son of Tohu, the son of
Zuph, an Ephraimite. 2He had two wives; one
was called Hannah and the other Peninnah.
Peninnah had children, but Hannah had none.
3Year after year this man went up from his
town to worship and sacrifice to the LORD Almighty at Shiloh, where Hophni and Phinehas,
the two sons of Eli, were priests of the LORD.
4Whenever the day came for Elkanah to sacrifice, he would give portions of the meat to his
wife Peninnah and to all her sons and daughters. 5But to Hannah he gave a double portion
because he loved her, and the LORD had closed
her womb. 6And because the LORD had closed
her womb, her rival kept provoking her in order
to irritate her. 7This went on year after year.
Whenever Hannah went up to the house of the
LORD, her rival provoked her till she wept and
would not eat. 8Elkanah her husband would say
to her, "Hannah, why are you weeping? Why
don't you eat? Why are you downhearted?
Don't I mean more to you than ten sons?"
9Once when they had finished eating and
drinking in Shiloh, Hannah stood up. Now Eli
the priest was sitting on a chair by the doorpost
of the LORD's temple.[b] 10In bitterness of soul
Hannah wept much and prayed to the LORD.
11And she made a vow, saying, "O LORD Almighty, if you will only look upon your servant's misery and remember me, and not forget
your servant but give her a son, then I will give
him to the LORD for all the days of his life, and
no razor will ever be used on his head."
12As she kept on praying to the LORD, Eli
observed her mouth. 13Hannah was praying in
her heart, and her lips were moving but her
voice was not heard. Eli thought she was drunk
14and said to her, "How long will you keep on
getting drunk? Get rid of your wine."
15"Not so, my lord," Hannah replied, "I am
a woman who is deeply troubled. I have not
been drinking wine or beer; I was pouring out
my soul to the LORD. 16Do not take your servant
for a wicked woman; I have been praying here
out of my great anguish and grief."
17Eli answered, "Go in peace, and may the
God of Israel grant you what you have asked of
him."
18She said, "May your servant find favor in
your eyes." Then she went her way and ate something, and her face was no longer downcast.
19Early the next morning they arose and worshiped before the LORD and then went back to
their home at Ramah. Elkanah lay with Hannah
his wife, and the LORD remembered her. 20So in
the course of time Hannah conceived and gave
birth to a son. She named him Samuel,[c] saying, "Because I asked the LORD for him."

Hannah Dedicates Samuel

21When the man Elkanah went up with all
his family to offer the annual sacrifice to the
LORD and to fulfill his vow, 22Hannah did not
go. She said to her husband, "After the boy is
weaned, I will take him and present him before
the LORD, and he will live there always."
23"Do what seems best to you," Elkanah her
husband told her. "Stay here until you have
weaned him; only may the LORD make good
his[d] word." So the woman stayed at home and
nursed her son until she had weaned him.
24After he was weaned, she took the boy with

[a] 1 Or *from Ramathaim Zuphim* [b] 9 That is, tabernacle
[c] 20 *Samuel* sounds like the Hebrew for *heard of God.*
[d] 23 Masoretic Text; Dead Sea Scrolls, Septuagint and Syriac *your*

1:1–8 In ancient times, much of a woman's self-worth centered on her ability to bear children. Hannah's childless state brought her a great deal of pain. To make matters worse, Elkanah's second wife, Peninnah, ridiculed Hannah because of her infertility. Hannah had probably tried everything humanly possible to become pregnant. She was at the end of her rope, helpless to change her situation and unable to see that a fulfilling life could be found without children. Her husband Elkanah reminded Hannah of his unconditional love for her (1:8), but Hannah was unable to accept his comfort. Hannah needed to seek God with a whole heart and surrender herself and her situation to him.

1:9–11 In these verses we read Hannah's beautiful prayer uttered through her tears. She had carried her shame and grief for years. Now she released them to God. In faith Hannah sought God and surrendered to him. She not only committed her infertility to God, but she also vowed to surrender to God's service the son he would give her (1:11). Whatever grief and sorrows we carry should be released to God. As we commit ourselves and our inabilities to God, he can begin a process of spiritual renewal that can have far-reaching influence for God's kingdom. Like Hannah, we all need to release our grief to God and release control of our lives to him as well.

1:12–18 Hannah's prayer was misunderstood by Eli the priest, who assumed she was drunk. In reality, Hannah was seeking God and surrendering her infertility to him. Our attempts toward spiritual growth can also be misinterpreted, and the insensitive responses we experience can be disheartening. To her credit, Hannah persevered despite the criticism she experienced. Eli soon recognized Hannah's integrity and encouraged her in her prayer (1:17). No matter what discouragement we may face, we must persevere. God will support us, even if the people around us do not.

1:19–20 Samuel's birth shows us that God is a listening God. He solved Hannah's crisis by giving her a son. The baby's name, Samuel, sounds like the Hebrew word "heard of God." The child's name would have been a constant reminder that God heard Hannah's cries and answered them. We can be confident that when we petition God according to his will, he hears us too (see 1 John 5:14). And no problem is ever too big for him to solve (see Jeremiah 32:27).

1:24–28 The time came for Hannah to fulfill her vow to God. The process of giving up her little son certainly must have been painful. But Hannah recognized her accountability to God and unselfishly fulfilled her promise by releasing her much-loved son into God's service. Hannah's choice reflected her gratitude and her confidence in the God who had given Samuel to her in the first place. After

her, young as he was, along with a three-year-
old bull,[a] an ephah[b] of flour and a skin of
wine, and brought him to the house of the LORD
at Shiloh. 25When they had slaughtered the
bull, they brought the boy to Eli, 26and she said
to him, "As surely as you live, my lord, I am the
woman who stood here beside you praying to
the LORD. 27I prayed for this child, and the LORD
has granted me what I asked of him. 28So now
I give him to the LORD. For his whole life he will
be given over to the LORD." And he worshiped
the LORD there.

Hannah's Prayer

2 Then Hannah prayed and said:

"My heart rejoices in the LORD;
in the LORD my horn[c] is lifted high.
My mouth boasts over my enemies,
for I delight in your deliverance.

2"There is no one holy[d] like the LORD;
there is no one besides you;
there is no Rock like our God.

3"Do not keep talking so proudly
or let your mouth speak such arrogance,
for the LORD is a God who knows,
and by him deeds are weighed.

4"The bows of the warriors are broken,
but those who stumbled are armed with strength.
5Those who were full hire themselves out for food,
but those who were hungry hunger no more.
She who was barren has borne seven children,
but she who has had many sons pines away.

6"The LORD brings death and makes alive;
he brings down to the grave[e] and raises up.
7The LORD sends poverty and wealth;
he humbles and he exalts.
8He raises the poor from the dust
and lifts the needy from the ash heap;
he seats them with princes
and has them inherit a throne of honor.

"For the foundations of the earth are the LORD's;
upon them he has set the world.
9He will guard the feet of his saints,
but the wicked will be silenced in darkness.

"It is not by strength that one prevails;
10 those who oppose the LORD will be shattered.
He will thunder against them from heaven;
the LORD will judge the ends of the earth.

"He will give strength to his king
and exalt the horn of his anointed."

11Then Elkanah went home to Ramah, but
the boy ministered before the LORD under Eli
the priest.

Eli's Wicked Sons

12Eli's sons were wicked men; they had no
regard for the LORD. 13Now it was the practice of
the priests with the people that whenever anyone offered a sacrifice and while the meat was
being boiled, the servant of the priest would
come with a three-pronged fork in his hand.
14He would plunge it into the pan or kettle or
caldron or pot, and the priest would take for
himself whatever the fork brought up. This is
how they treated all the Israelites who came to
Shiloh. 15But even before the fat was burned,
the servant of the priest would come and say to
the man who was sacrificing, "Give the priest

[a]24 Dead Sea Scrolls, Septuagint and Syriac; Masoretic Text *with three bulls* [b]24 That is, probably about 3/5 bushel (about 22 liters) [c]1 *Horn* here symbolizes strength; also in verse 10. [d]2 Or *no Holy One* [e]6 Hebrew *Sheol*

Hannah gave Samuel to God's service, God blessed her with additional children. When we make commitments to God and others, we need to follow through on them. When we do, no matter how hard it may be, God will help us and bless our efforts.

2:1–3 Note the words in Hannah's prayer of rejoicing: "My heart rejoices in the LORD" (2:1). Hannah praised the one responsible for her deliverance—God himself. He had delivered her from the trauma of infertility by giving her a son. After Hannah gave Samuel into God's service, he blessed her with other children. This certainly would have lightened the burden of seeing her firstborn son only infrequently. Hannah's obedience was difficult, even painful, but it brought about good for Hannah, Samuel and ultimately all of Israel. Our obedience to God, as painful as it might be at times, will ultimately bring us joy and blessings to the people close to us.

2:4–10 Hannah continued her prayer of praise, thanking God for blessing her. She said, "Those who stumbled are armed with strength" (2:4). God provided not only Hannah's deliverance from infertility but also the strength she needed. He gave Hannah the strength to persevere in the process, to seek freedom, to adopt new attitudes, to fulfill responsibilities, to set things straight, to build a new life. Such honest praise of God's power will naturally burst forth as we surrender our lives to God and see him intervene on our behalf. As we surrender ourselves to him, grieving and letting go of our hurts and cares, the Father moves immediately to answer our prayers and do his good work in us.

2:12–17 Eli's wicked sons sinned by treating God's offerings with contempt. They failed to realize that the sacrifices were God's provision for the people's sin. They stole what they wanted from the offerings as if these ceremonies had been instituted for their own personal pleasure rather than for healing and purification. God has provided for our redemption by giving his Son as the ultimate sacrifice on our behalf. If we treat Christ with contempt, we are guilty of doing the same thing that Eli's sons did (see Hebrews 10:26–29). Let us show proper respect for the compassion, love and power that God has shown to us through Christ! Let us wholeheartedly embrace his provision for our healing.

THE SPIRITUAL DISCIPLINES

In the Life of Hannah

Pain and heartache can be powerful catalysts for spiritual growth. Nowhere is this more evident than in the story of Hannah. Hannah's childlessness was a continual source of sadness, especially because of the cruel taunting of her husband's second wife, Peninnah. Hannah's pain was particularly difficult to bear during the holy days when the entire family gathered at Shiloh for sacrifices and worship. Surrounded by relatives but having no child of her own to hold, Hannah was poignantly reminded of her loneliness.

Though she was in pain, Hannah did not turn away from God. That which could have broken her down instead broke her heart open. Hannah turned to God in prayer, for she knew that he was sovereign and able to grant her children if he chose to. She knew that God had granted children to other faithful couples who seemed unable to conceive, including Abraham and Sarah, Isaac and Rebekah and Jacob and Rachel.

Through all her experiences, Hannah's faithfulness was bolstered by three spiritual disciplines—prayer, worship and stewardship. These disciplines sustained and challenged Hannah during this difficult time.

PRAYER. Hannah fervently prayed to the Lord for a child and believed that he was able to grant her request. She found comfort in God and acted in faith when Eli assured her that God had heard her prayers (1:17–18). Hannah began living in joyful anticipation of God's answer. Hannah's discipline of prayer challenges us to pray fervently and encourages us to remain faithful even when we must wait for God's answer. (To learn more about prayer, turn to Genesis 18.)

WORSHIP. Hannah was a woman of profound worship. Her words of praise in 1 Samuel 2 richly blend theology with artistic insight. Her pain was transformed on the altar of worship and became the lens through which she glimpsed the awesome providence of God. Worship caused her to hold on to hope. (To learn more about worship, turn to Exodus 20.)

STEWARDSHIP. Hannah's deep desires for a child were kept in proper perspective by her discipline of stewardship. Hannah recognized that everything (and everyone) is a gift from God. She demonstrated her understanding of this principle by her willingness to give Samuel to God's service at the tabernacle. Some discount the significance of Hannah's decision to give Samuel to God's service, asserting that her heart's desire was more to *bear* a child than to raise one. Such an assertion is appalling. To give up her only child—giving to God the daily joy of a toddler's laugh, the comfort of a nighttime snuggle, the wonder of curious little hands maturing into competent manly hands—this was truly a sacrifice, as any loving parent can surely imagine! By giving her child to God's service, Hannah did not pray merely for God to do something *for* her, but to do something *through* her for God's glory. She wanted to give God a servant. Hannah challenges every parent to ask: Do I view my children as God's possession? Do I want them to serve God? (To learn more about stewardship, turn to Deuteronomy 8.)

Lessons for Life

Prayer, worship and stewardship—these three disciplines were not only lifelines for Hannah; they are lifelines for all of God's people. Through these disciplines, Hannah glorified God and grew in her faith. Though Samuel was raised at the tabernacle in Shiloh, he shared his mother's heart. Like Hannah, Samuel became steadfast in trials, earnest in prayer and committed to God's service rather than his own satisfaction. Hannah's life shows us that God can use anyone dedicated to these disciplines to shape not only one life but the lives of all they touch.

some meat to roast; he won't accept boiled meat from you, but only raw."

16If the man said to him, "Let the fat be burned up first, and then take whatever you want," the servant would then answer, "No, hand it over now; if you don't, I'll take it by force."

17This sin of the young men was very great in the LORD's sight, for they[a] were treating the LORD's offering with contempt.

18But Samuel was ministering before the LORD—a boy wearing a linen ephod. 19Each year his mother made him a little robe and took it to him when she went up with her husband to offer the annual sacrifice. 20Eli would bless Elkanah and his wife, saying, "May the LORD give you children by this woman to take the place of the one she prayed for and gave to the LORD." Then they would go home. 21And the LORD was gracious to Hannah; she conceived and gave birth to three sons and two daughters. Meanwhile, the boy Samuel grew up in the presence of the LORD.

22Now Eli, who was very old, heard about everything his sons were doing to all Israel and how they slept with the women who served at the entrance to the Tent of Meeting. 23So he said to them, "Why do you do such things? I hear from all the people about these wicked deeds of yours. 24No, my sons; it is not a good report that I hear spreading among the LORD's people. 25If a man sins against another man, God[b] may mediate for him; but if a man sins against the LORD, who will intercede for him?" His sons, however, did not listen to their father's rebuke, for it was the LORD's will to put them to death.

26And the boy Samuel continued to grow in stature and in favor with the LORD and with men.

Prophecy Against the House of Eli

27Now a man of God came to Eli and said to him, "This is what the LORD says: 'Did I not clearly reveal myself to your father's house when they were in Egypt under Pharaoh? 28I chose your father out of all the tribes of Israel to be my priest, to go up to my altar, to burn incense, and to wear an ephod in my presence. I also gave your father's house all the offerings made with fire by the Israelites. 29Why do you[c] scorn my sacrifice and offering that I prescribed for my dwelling? Why do you honor your sons more than me by fattening yourselves on the choice parts of every offering made by my people Israel?'

30"Therefore the LORD, the God of Israel, declares: 'I promised that your house and your father's house would minister before me forever.' But now the LORD declares: 'Far be it from me! Those who honor me I will honor, but those who despise me will be disdained. 31The time is coming when I will cut short your strength and the strength of your father's house, so that there will not be an old man in your family line 32and you will see distress in my dwelling. Although good will be done to Israel, in your family line there will never be an old man. 33Every one of you that I do not cut off from my altar will be spared only to blind your eyes with tears and to grieve your heart, and all your descendants will die in the prime of life.

34" 'And what happens to your two sons, Hophni and Phinehas, will be a sign to you—they will both die on the same day. 35I will raise up for myself a faithful priest, who will do according to what is in my heart and mind. I will firmly establish his house, and he will minister before my anointed one always. 36Then everyone left in your family line will come and bow down before him for a piece of silver and a crust of bread and plead, "Appoint me to some priestly office so I can have food to eat." ' "

The LORD Calls Samuel

3 The boy Samuel ministered before the LORD under Eli. In those days the word of the LORD was rare; there were not many visions.

2One night Eli, whose eyes were becoming so weak that he could barely see, was lying down in his usual place. 3The lamp of God had not yet gone out, and Samuel was lying down in the temple[d] of the LORD, where the ark of God was. 4Then the LORD called Samuel.

Samuel answered, "Here I am." 5And he ran to Eli and said, "Here I am; you called me."

But Eli said, "I did not call; go back and lie down." So he went and lay down.

6Again the LORD called, "Samuel!" And Samuel got up and went to Eli and said, "Here I am; you called me."

"My son," Eli said, "I did not call; go back and lie down."

[a]17 Or *men* [b]25 Or *the judges* [c]29 The Hebrew is plural. [d]3 That is, tabernacle

2:20–21 This passage tells us that Hannah was blessed with additional children. God is in the business of blessing his people beyond their requests and expectations (see Ephesians 3:20).

2:23–34 Eli confronted his sons about their blatant sin. He hoped they would make significant changes in their lives. Unfortunately, Eli's sons didn't listen to their father. The young men refused to set boundaries on their behavior, and they displayed no desire to change. Their choice to go their own way brought dire consequences—their own deaths (2:25, 34; see 1 Corinthians 11:30–32). Eli, too, made a choice: he opted to ignore his sons' continued disobedience. Eli failed in his responsibility to God and was eventually judged for it. He was told that his descendants would bring him grief; they would die in the prime of life. What a bitter harvest we reap when we refuse to turn from sin.

3:1–10 Learning to listen to God's voice is an important part of our spiritual growth (see Isaiah 30:21). God spoke directly to young Samuel, but he also speaks to us through his Word (see James 1:22–23). We need to take the time to understand God's truth in the Bible and find the wisdom and direction we need to progress spiritually.

7Now Samuel did not yet know the LORD: The word of the LORD had not yet been revealed to him.

8The LORD called Samuel a third time, and Samuel got up and went to Eli and said, "Here I am; you called me."

Then Eli realized that the LORD was calling the boy. 9So Eli told Samuel, "Go and lie down, and if he calls you, say, 'Speak, LORD, for your servant is listening.' " So Samuel went and lay down in his place.

10The LORD came and stood there, calling as at the other times, "Samuel! Samuel!"

Then Samuel said, "Speak, for your servant is listening."

11And the LORD said to Samuel: "See, I am about to do something in Israel that will make the ears of everyone who hears of it tingle. 12At that time I will carry out against Eli everything I spoke against his family—from beginning to end. 13For I told him that I would judge his family forever because of the sin he knew about; his sons made themselves contemptible,[a] and he failed to restrain them. 14Therefore, I swore to the house of Eli, 'The guilt of Eli's house will never be atoned for by sacrifice or offering.' "

15Samuel lay down until morning and then opened the doors of the house of the LORD. He was afraid to tell Eli the vision, 16but Eli called him and said, "Samuel, my son."

Samuel answered, "Here I am."

17"What was it he said to you?" Eli asked. "Do not hide it from me. May God deal with you, be it ever so severely, if you hide from me anything he told you." 18So Samuel told him everything, hiding nothing from him. Then Eli said, "He is the LORD; let him do what is good in his eyes."

19The LORD was with Samuel as he grew up, and he let none of his words fall to the ground. 20And all Israel from Dan to Beersheba recognized that Samuel was attested as a prophet of the LORD. 21The LORD continued to appear at Shiloh, and there he revealed himself to Samuel through his word.

4

And Samuel's word came to all Israel.

The Philistines Capture the Ark

Now the Israelites went out to fight against the Philistines. The Israelites camped at Ebenezer, and the Philistines at Aphek. 2The Philistines deployed their forces to meet Israel, and as the battle spread, Israel was defeated by the Philistines, who killed about four thousand of them on the battlefield. 3When the soldiers returned to camp, the elders of Israel asked, "Why did the LORD bring defeat upon us today before the Philistines? Let us bring the ark of the LORD's covenant from Shiloh, so that it[b] may go with us and save us from the hand of our enemies."

4So the people sent men to Shiloh, and they brought back the ark of the covenant of the LORD Almighty, who is enthroned between the cherubim. And Eli's two sons, Hophni and Phinehas, were there with the ark of the covenant of God.

5When the ark of the LORD's covenant came into the camp, all Israel raised such a great shout that the ground shook. 6Hearing the uproar, the Philistines asked, "What's all this shouting in the Hebrew camp?"

When they learned that the ark of the LORD had come into the camp, 7the Philistines were afraid. "A god has come into the camp," they said. "We're in trouble! Nothing like this has happened before. 8Woe to us! Who will deliver us from the hand of these mighty gods? They are the gods who struck the Egyptians with all kinds of plagues in the desert. 9Be strong, Philistines! Be men, or you will be subject to the Hebrews, as they have been to you. Be men, and fight!"

10So the Philistines fought, and the Israelites were defeated and every man fled to his tent. The slaughter was very great; Israel lost thirty thousand foot soldiers. 11The ark of God was captured, and Eli's two sons, Hophni and Phinehas, died.

Death of Eli

12That same day a Benjamite ran from the battle line and went to Shiloh, his clothes torn and dust on his head. 13When he arrived, there was Eli sitting on his chair by the side of the road, watching, because his heart feared for the ark of God. When the man entered the town and told what had happened, the whole town sent up a cry.

14Eli heard the outcry and asked, "What is the meaning of this uproar?"

The man hurried over to Eli, 15who was ninety-eight years old and whose eyes were set so that he could not see. 16He told Eli, "I have

[a]13 Masoretic Text; an ancient Hebrew scribal tradition and Septuagint *sons blasphemed God* [b]3 Or *he*

3:16–18 Samuel's honesty is obvious as he told Eli everything, even the devastating truths about the priest's own family and the suffering they would endure. Samuel confronted Eli with his failure, stating clearly the truth God had given him. Such forthrightness must be part of any spiritual-growth plan. As we discover the truth about ourselves and others through the knowledge of God's Word, we may need to speak that truth as God directs, confronting others in love for their encouragement and spiritual growth. This confrontation will never be easy, but it is an important part of any loving relationship.

4:16–22 Eli, his family and the entire nation of Israel, suffered the terrible consequences of disobedience. Eli and his sons died. Foreigners captured the ark of the Lord's covenant, the symbol of God's glorious presence with Israel. Eli's dying daughter-in-law, responding to the nation's great despair, used her last breath to name her baby Ichabod. This name means "no glory" (4:21–22), for the glory of God had departed from Israel. In the hour of her death she acknowledged the truth of her situation, but it was too late for her and her family. Life is not easy; even the best life involves surrender, loss, pain and difficulty. Yet

just come from the battle line; I fled from it this
very day."
Eli asked, "What happened, my son?"
[17]The man who brought the news replied,
"Israel fled before the Philistines, and the army
has suffered heavy losses. Also your two sons,
Hophni and Phinehas, are dead, and the ark of
God has been captured."
[18]When he mentioned the ark of God, Eli fell
backward off his chair by the side of the gate.
His neck was broken and he died, for he was an
old man and heavy. He had led[a] Israel forty
years.
[19]His daughter-in-law, the wife of Phinehas,
was pregnant and near the time of delivery.
When she heard the news that the ark of God
had been captured and that her father-in-law
and her husband were dead, she went into labor
and gave birth, but was overcome by her labor
pains. [20]As she was dying, the women attending
her said, "Don't despair; you have given birth
to a son." But she did not respond or pay any
attention.
[21]She named the boy Ichabod,[b] saying,
"The glory has departed from Israel"—because of
the capture of the ark of God and the deaths of
her father-in-law and her husband. [22]She said,
"The glory has departed from Israel, for the ark
of God has been captured."

The Ark in Ashdod and Ekron

5 After the Philistines had captured the ark of
God, they took it from Ebenezer to Ashdod. [2]Then they carried the ark into Dagon's
temple and set it beside Dagon. [3]When the people of Ashdod rose early the next day, there was
Dagon, fallen on his face on the ground before
the ark of the LORD! They took Dagon and put
him back in his place. [4]But the following morning when they rose, there was Dagon, fallen on
his face on the ground before the ark of the
LORD! His head and hands had been broken off
and were lying on the threshold; only his body
remained. [5]That is why to this day neither the
priests of Dagon nor any others who enter Dagon's temple at Ashdod step on the threshold.
[6]The LORD's hand was heavy upon the people
of Ashdod and its vicinity; he brought devastation upon them and afflicted them with tumors.[c] [7]When the men of Ashdod saw what
was happening, they said, "The ark of the god
of Israel must not stay here with us, because his
hand is heavy upon us and upon Dagon our
god." [8]So they called together all the rulers of the
Philistines and asked them, "What shall we do
with the ark of the god of Israel?"
They answered, "Have the ark of the god of
Israel moved to Gath." So they moved the ark of
the God of Israel.
[9]But after they had moved it, the LORD's hand
was against that city, throwing it into a great
panic. He afflicted the people of the city, both
young and old, with an outbreak of tumors.[d]
[10]So they sent the ark of God to Ekron.
As the ark of God was entering Ekron, the
people of Ekron cried out, "They have brought
the ark of the god of Israel around to us to kill
us and our people." [11]So they called together all
the rulers of the Philistines and said, "Send the
ark of the god of Israel away; let it go back to its
own place, or it[e] will kill us and our people."
For death had filled the city with panic; God's
hand was very heavy upon it. [12]Those who did
not die were afflicted with tumors, and the outcry of the city went up to heaven.

The Ark Returned to Israel

6 When the ark of the LORD had been in Philistine territory seven months, [2]the Philistines called for the priests and the diviners and
said, "What shall we do with the ark of the
LORD? Tell us how we should send it back to its
place."
[3]They answered, "If you return the ark of the
god of Israel, do not send it away empty, but by
all means send a guilt offering to him. Then you
will be healed, and you will know why his hand
has not been lifted from you."
[4]The Philistines asked, "What guilt offering
should we send to him?"
They replied, "Five gold tumors and five
gold rats, according to the number of the Philistine rulers, because the same plague has struck
both you and your rulers. [5]Make models of the
tumors and of the rats that are destroying the
country, and pay honor to Israel's god. Perhaps
he will lift his hand from you and your gods
and your land. [6]Why do you harden your hearts
as the Egyptians and Pharaoh did? When he[f]
treated them harshly, did they not send the Israelites out so they could go on their way?
[7]"Now then, get a new cart ready, with two

[a]18 Traditionally *judged* [b]21 *Ichabod* means *no glory.*
[c]6 Hebrew; Septuagint and Vulgate *tumors. And rats appeared in their land, and death and destruction were throughout the city* [d]9 Or *with tumors in the groin* (see Septuagint) [e]11 Or *he* [f]6 That is, God

---

the solitary death of this young woman and the shattering of Eli's family should remind us of the importance of persevering in seeking God and surrendering our lives to him.

5:1–4 The fate of the Philistine idol Dagon illustrated that Israel's God was greater than all other gods were (see Jeremiah 32:27; 33:2–3; 1 John 4:4). God is stronger than any of the false idols we might serve too. If we seek God and surrender fully to him, all false gods we once served will fall facedown before him, setting us free to love the only God worthy of our affection.

5:6–12 The physical suffering of the Philistines was a direct consequence of their disrespect toward God (5:6, 9, 12). The parallels to today are unmistakable. By setting up false gods in our own lives, we also show disrespect to the true God. We violate God's laws by living selfishly and hurting the people close to us. Often, many who violate God's standards experience physical repercussions. It is precisely this suffering that should prompt us to seek God's help.

cows that have calved and have never been yoked. Hitch the cows to the cart, but take their calves away and pen them up. [8]Take the ark of the LORD and put it on the cart, and in a chest beside it put the gold objects you are sending back to him as a guilt offering. Send it on its way, [9]but keep watching it. If it goes up to its own territory, toward Beth Shemesh, then the LORD has brought this great disaster on us. But if it does not, then we will know that it was not his hand that struck us and that it happened to us by chance."

[10]So they did this. They took two such cows and hitched them to the cart and penned up their calves. [11]They placed the ark of the LORD on the cart and along with it the chest containing the gold rats and the models of the tumors. [12]Then the cows went straight up toward Beth Shemesh, keeping on the road and lowing all the way; they did not turn to the right or to the left. The rulers of the Philistines followed them as far as the border of Beth Shemesh.

[13]Now the people of Beth Shemesh were harvesting their wheat in the valley, and when they looked up and saw the ark, they rejoiced at the sight. [14]The cart came to the field of Joshua of Beth Shemesh, and there it stopped beside a large rock. The people chopped up the wood of the cart and sacrificed the cows as a burnt offering to the LORD. [15]The Levites took down the ark of the LORD, together with the chest containing the gold objects, and placed them on the large rock. On that day the people of Beth Shemesh offered burnt offerings and made sacrifices to the LORD. [16]The five rulers of the Philistines saw all this and then returned that same day to Ekron.

[17]These are the gold tumors the Philistines sent as a guilt offering to the LORD—one each for Ashdod, Gaza, Ashkelon, Gath and Ekron. [18]And the number of the gold rats was according to the number of Philistine towns belonging to the five rulers—the fortified towns with their country villages. The large rock, on which[a] they set the ark of the LORD, is a witness to this day in the field of Joshua of Beth Shemesh.

[19]But God struck down some of the men of Beth Shemesh, putting seventy[b] of them to death because they had looked into the ark of the LORD. The people mourned because of the heavy blow the LORD had dealt them, [20]and the men of Beth Shemesh asked, "Who can stand in the presence of the LORD, this holy God? To whom will the ark go up from here?"

[21]Then they sent messengers to the people of Kiriath Jearim, saying, "The Philistines have returned the ark of the LORD. Come down and

7 take it up to your place." [1]So the men of Kiriath Jearim came and took up the ark of the LORD. They took it to Abinadab's house on the hill and consecrated Eleazar his son to guard the ark of the LORD.

Samuel Subdues the Philistines at Mizpah

[2]It was a long time, twenty years in all, that the ark remained at Kiriath Jearim, and all the people of Israel mourned and sought after the LORD. [3]And Samuel said to the whole house of Israel, "If you are returning to the LORD with all your hearts, then rid yourselves of the foreign gods and the Ashtoreths and commit yourselves to the LORD and serve him only, and he will deliver you out of the hand of the Philistines." [4]So the Israelites put away their Baals and Ashtoreths, and served the LORD only.

[5]Then Samuel said, "Assemble all Israel at Mizpah and I will intercede with the LORD for you." [6]When they had assembled at Mizpah, they drew water and poured it out before the LORD. On that day they fasted and there they confessed, "We have sinned against the LORD." And Samuel was leader[c] of Israel at Mizpah.

[7]When the Philistines heard that Israel had assembled at Mizpah, the rulers of the Philistines came up to attack them. And when the

[a]18 A few Hebrew manuscripts (see also Septuagint); most Hebrew manuscripts *villages as far as Greater Abel, where* [b]19 A few Hebrew manuscripts; most Hebrew manuscripts and Septuagint *50,070* [c]6 Traditionally *judge*

6:19 This seems a harsh judgment, but it carries with it a reminder of the high cost of disobedience. The Israelites in this passage were held accountable to the instructions God had given them regarding the treatment of the ark. Either they were ignorant of these instructions or they had chosen to ignore them. God has given us instructions in his Word for living healthy lives. When we fail to follow God's plan, whether because of ignorance or choice, the consequences will be devastating. Neglecting God's instructions on this occasion proved fatal for this group of Israelites. The same consequence may await us if we fail to hear and heed God's Word.

7:3–4 Samuel's exhortation to the Israelites gives us a clear picture of spiritual renewal. He tells them (1) to get rid of their foreign gods and idols, (2) to determine to obey God and (3) to worship God alone. Our spiritual renewal begins the same way. We must rid ourselves of the idols in our lives—those things that control us and command our loyalty—with a deep self-examination, an honest assessment of motives and priorities and an admission of our sins and disobedience. Our devotion to God cannot be hidden. We must openly confess and surrender ourselves to God, recognizing our accountability to him. We may need to grieve, forgive, let go of the past and make restitution for any wrongdoing. Only then will God transform us, redirect our course and make way for a better future. Samuel promised the Israelites that their obedience would result in God's deliverance from the Philistines. We, too, can rest assured that God will give us a fresh start in life as we use the keys to spiritual renewal that he has given us.

7:7–11 The people of Israel were helpless as they faced the attacking Philistines. They didn't know what to do, so they turned to Samuel for help. Samuel did the only thing possible: he asked God for help. God answered by giving Israel an overwhelming victory over the Philistines. In our own process of spiritual renewal we realize that we need God's help, so we turn to him. We can be sure that God will accomplish his will for us if we admit our sin and surrender our lives to him.

SAMUEL

Hannah had wept before God for a son, promising to give him back to God. After Samuel was born and weaned, Hannah kept her promise. Samuel learned the various duties of the priesthood from Eli, Israel's high priest. During his life, Samuel would serve as a priest, a prophet and Israel's last judge. He was a godly man who transformed the office of judge from that of a military leader to a highly respected leader, second only to a king.

But Samuel was human and had his blind spots. When the people asked to be like the other countries and have a king rule over them, Samuel took this request as a rejection of his own leadership. What Samuel didn't hear was the complaint of the people that his sons, whom he had appointed to be judges in his place, "accepted bribes and perverted justice" (8:3). The people hadn't rejected Samuel; they had rejected God's leadership and the leadership of Samuel's sons.

Perhaps Samuel was deaf to the complaints about his sons because he was blind to their corrupt ways. We often develop blind spots with regard to someone we love and want to protect. If Samuel had heard the people's complaints with openness, he may have seen the truth before it was too late. He could have corrected the problem and held his sons accountable for their actions before God. When we sense the rejection of others, it should be a signal for us to evaluate carefully what is being said or why we are feeling rejected. Despite his family situation, however, Samuel was one of the great men of faith. God was able to use him as one of the great leaders in Israel's history.

STRENGTHS AND ACCOMPLISHMENTS:

Samuel was sensitive to God's voice.

He was the last and greatest judge in Israel.

He commanded great respect from the people of Israel.

WEAKNESSES AND MISTAKES:

He failed to take steps to deal with his sons' wrong behavior.

LESSONS FROM HIS LIFE:

The feeling of rejection can blind us to God's truth.

Who we are with God is more important than what we accomplish in life.

KEY VERSES:

"The Lord was with Samuel as he grew up, and he let none of his words fall to the ground. And all Israel from Dan to Beersheba recognized that Samuel was attested as a prophet of the Lord" (3:19–20).

Samuel's story is found in 1 Samuel 1:1—25:1; 28:1–25. He is also mentioned in 1 Chronicles 9:22; 11:3; 26:28; 29:29; 2 Chronicles 35:18; Psalm 99:6; Jeremiah 15:1; Acts 3:24; 13:20 and Hebrews 11:32.

Israelites heard of it, they were afraid because of the Philistines. 8They said to Samuel, "Do not stop crying out to the LORD our God for us, that he may rescue us from the hand of the Philistines." 9Then Samuel took a suckling lamb and offered it up as a whole burnt offering to the LORD. He cried out to the LORD on Israel's behalf, and the LORD answered him.

10While Samuel was sacrificing the burnt offering, the Philistines drew near to engage Israel in battle. But that day the LORD thundered with loud thunder against the Philistines and threw them into such a panic that they were routed before the Israelites. 11The men of Israel rushed out of Mizpah and pursued the Philistines, slaughtering them along the way to a point below Beth Car.

12Then Samuel took a stone and set it up between Mizpah and Shen. He named it Ebenezer,[a] saying, "Thus far has the LORD helped us." 13So the Philistines were subdued and did not invade Israelite territory again.

Throughout Samuel's lifetime, the hand of the LORD was against the Philistines. 14The towns from Ekron to Gath that the Philistines had captured from Israel were restored to her, and Israel delivered the neighboring territory from the power of the Philistines. And there was peace between Israel and the Amorites.

15Samuel continued as judge over Israel all the days of his life. 16From year to year he went on a circuit from Bethel to Gilgal to Mizpah, judging Israel in all those places. 17But he always went back to Ramah, where his home was, and there he also judged Israel. And he built an altar there to the LORD.

Israel Asks for a King

8 When Samuel grew old, he appointed his sons as judges for Israel. 2The name of his firstborn was Joel and the name of his second was Abijah, and they served at Beersheba. 3But his sons did not walk in his ways. They turned aside after dishonest gain and accepted bribes and perverted justice.

4So all the elders of Israel gathered together and came to Samuel at Ramah. 5They said to him, "You are old, and your sons do not walk in your ways; now appoint a king to lead[b] us, such as all the other nations have."

6But when they said, "Give us a king to lead us," this displeased Samuel; so he prayed to the LORD. 7And the LORD told him: "Listen to all that the people are saying to you; it is not you they have rejected, but they have rejected me as their king. 8As they have done from the day I brought them up out of Egypt until this day, forsaking me and serving other gods, so they are doing to you. 9Now listen to them; but warn them solemnly and let them know what the king who will reign over them will do."

10Samuel told all the words of the LORD to the people who were asking him for a king. 11He said, "This is what the king who will reign over you will do: He will take your sons and make them serve with his chariots and horses, and they will run in front of his chariots. 12Some he will assign to be commanders of thousands and commanders of fifties, and others to plow his ground and reap his harvest, and still others to make weapons of war and equipment for his chariots. 13He will take your daughters to be perfumers and cooks and bakers. 14He will take the best of your fields and vineyards and olive groves and give them to his attendants. 15He will take a tenth of your grain and of your vintage and give it to his officials and attendants. 16Your menservants and maidservants and the best of your cattle[c] and donkeys he will take for his own use. 17He will take a tenth of your flocks, and you yourselves will become his slaves. 18When that day comes, you will cry out for relief from the king you have chosen, and the LORD will not answer you in that day."

19But the people refused to listen to Samuel. "No!" they said. "We want a king over us. 20Then we will be like all the other nations,

[a]12 *Ebenezer* means *stone of help.* [b]5 Traditionally *judge;* also in verses 6 and 20 [c]16 Septuagint; Hebrew *young men*

7:12 Ebenezer means "stone of help." The fact that Samuel set up this stone should remind us of two principles. First, God's help in the past is a promise of help in the future. God offers much more than a onetime antidote. He is our continual remedy and source of strength in our spiritual growth. Also, the fact that God's help is available on a daily basis should encourage us to look to him every day. The secret to progressive spiritual growth is to recognize its ongoing nature, day by day, moment by moment. If we depend upon God daily, we will find the strength and grace to endure and to preserve our spiritual gains.

8:3–5 Not unlike the sons of Eli, Samuel's sons also failed to set boundaries on their behavior. They were greedy for money, taking bribes and perverting justice (8:3). Though they were held accountable to God for their actions, their disobedience also embarrassed their father and prompted a national outcry for governmental change (8:5). Because of their failure in leadership, the people rejected God's rule through his judges and demanded to have what all the surrounding nations had—a king. One wonders what might have happened if Samuel's sons had acted more responsibly. It is clear by this passage, however, that God will not allow sin to continue unpunished, especially among those he has put in positions of leadership.

8:18–20 The Israelites refused to listen to Samuel's God-given advice and soon were saddled with a less-than-satisfactory ruler, Saul. Wanting to be like the other nations, the Israelites had clamored for a king. They soon found out that what they desired wasn't necessarily what they needed. The example of the Israelites parallels our own spiritual renewal in several ways. We undermine our spiritual growth whenever we reject wise counsel (see Psalm 106:15). If we yield to the constant pressure to be like everybody else, we will find it difficult to gain freedom and experience God's will for our lives. And God may allow us to have our own way in a situation so he can show us the ultimate folly of it.

with a king to lead us and to go out before us and fight our battles."

21 When Samuel heard all that the people said, he repeated it before the LORD. 22 The LORD answered, "Listen to them and give them a king."

Then Samuel said to the men of Israel, "Everyone go back to his town."

Samuel Anoints Saul

9 There was a Benjamite, a man of standing, whose name was Kish son of Abiel, the son of Zeror, the son of Becorath, the son of Aphiah of Benjamin. 2 He had a son named Saul, an impressive young man without equal among the Israelites—a head taller than any of the others.

3 Now the donkeys belonging to Saul's father Kish were lost, and Kish said to his son Saul, "Take one of the servants with you and go and look for the donkeys." 4 So he passed through the hill country of Ephraim and through the area around Shalisha, but they did not find them. They went on into the district of Shaalim, but the donkeys were not there. Then he passed through the territory of Benjamin, but they did not find them.

5 When they reached the district of Zuph, Saul said to the servant who was with him, "Come, let's go back, or my father will stop thinking about the donkeys and start worrying about us."

6 But the servant replied, "Look, in this town there is a man of God; he is highly respected, and everything he says comes true. Let's go there now. Perhaps he will tell us what way to take."

7 Saul said to his servant, "If we go, what can we give the man? The food in our sacks is gone. We have no gift to take to the man of God. What do we have?"

8 The servant answered him again. "Look," he said, "I have a quarter of a shekel[a] of silver. I will give it to the man of God so that he will tell us what way to take." 9 (Formerly in Israel, if a man went to inquire of God, he would say, "Come, let us go to the seer," because the prophet of today used to be called a seer.)

10 "Good," Saul said to his servant. "Come, let's go." So they set out for the town where the man of God was.

11 As they were going up the hill to the town, they met some girls coming out to draw water, and they asked them, "Is the seer here?"

12 "He is," they answered. "He's ahead of you. Hurry now; he has just come to our town today, for the people have a sacrifice at the high place. 13 As soon as you enter the town, you will find him before he goes up to the high place to eat. The people will not begin eating until he comes, because he must bless the sacrifice; afterward, those who are invited will eat. Go up now; you should find him about this time."

14 They went up to the town, and as they were entering it, there was Samuel, coming toward them on his way up to the high place.

15 Now the day before Saul came, the LORD had revealed this to Samuel: 16 "About this time tomorrow I will send you a man from the land of Benjamin. Anoint him leader over my people Israel; he will deliver my people from the hand of the Philistines. I have looked upon my people, for their cry has reached me."

17 When Samuel caught sight of Saul, the LORD said to him, "This is the man I spoke to you about; he will govern my people."

18 Saul approached Samuel in the gateway and asked, "Would you please tell me where the seer's house is?"

19 "I am the seer," Samuel replied. "Go up ahead of me to the high place, for today you are to eat with me, and in the morning I will let you go and will tell you all that is in your heart. 20 As for the donkeys you lost three days ago, do not worry about them; they have been found. And to whom is all the desire of Israel turned, if not to you and all your father's family?"

21 Saul answered, "But am I not a Benjamite, from the smallest tribe of Israel, and is not my clan the least of all the clans of the tribe of Benjamin? Why do you say such a thing to me?"

22 Then Samuel brought Saul and his servant into the hall and seated them at the head of those who were invited—about thirty in number. 23 Samuel said to the cook, "Bring the piece of meat I gave you, the one I told you to lay aside."

24 So the cook took up the leg with what was on it and set it in front of Saul. Samuel said, "Here is what has been kept for you. Eat, because it was set aside for you for this occasion, from the time I said, 'I have invited guests.'" And Saul dined with Samuel that day.

25 After they came down from the high place to the town, Samuel talked with Saul on the roof of his house. 26 They rose about daybreak and Samuel called to Saul on the roof, "Get ready, and I will send you on your way." When Saul got ready, he and Samuel went outside together. 27 As they were going down to the edge

[a] 8 That is, about 1/10 ounce (about 3 grams)

9:2 Saul was a man of impressive physical attributes, but in his case, his "gifts" were detrimental rather than helpful. Sometimes people gifted with beauty, intelligence, size or strength fall into the trap of self-sufficiency. They begin to think they can go it alone. This attitude only stands in the way of achieving God's success. Our pride and notions of personal potential may prevent us from ever becoming humble enough to admit that we need God. Saul looked good on paper, but he allowed his "strengths" to stand in the way of his only means of success—God's help. We must be careful to avoid Saul's pitfall.

9:14–17 Samuel approached at the very moment Saul entered the town. How perfect God's timing is in the events of our own lives too. He often leads us to meet people or experience events that direct our course his way. As we see this to be true, we should take the time to thank God for his direction (see Psalms 37:23–24; 138:8; Proverbs 3:5–6; Isaiah 48:17).

of the town, Samuel said to Saul, "Tell the servant to go on ahead of us"—and the servant did so—"but you stay here awhile, so that I may give you a message from God."

10 Then Samuel took a flask of oil and poured it on Saul's head and kissed him, saying, "Has not the LORD anointed you leader over his inheritance?[a] 2When you leave me today, you will meet two men near Rachel's tomb, at Zelzah on the border of Benjamin. They will say to you, 'The donkeys you set out to look for have been found. And now your father has stopped thinking about them and is worried about you. He is asking, "What shall I do about my son?" '

3"Then you will go on from there until you reach the great tree of Tabor. Three men going up to God at Bethel will meet you there. One will be carrying three young goats, another three loaves of bread, and another a skin of wine. 4They will greet you and offer you two loaves of bread, which you will accept from them.

5"After that you will go to Gibeah of God, where there is a Philistine outpost. As you approach the town, you will meet a procession of prophets coming down from the high place with lyres, tambourines, flutes and harps being played before them, and they will be prophesying. 6The Spirit of the LORD will come upon you in power, and you will prophesy with them; and you will be changed into a different person. 7Once these signs are fulfilled, do whatever your hand finds to do, for God is with you.

8"Go down ahead of me to Gilgal. I will surely come down to you to sacrifice burnt offerings and fellowship offerings,[b] but you must wait seven days until I come to you and tell you what you are to do."

Saul Made King

9As Saul turned to leave Samuel, God changed Saul's heart, and all these signs were fulfilled that day. 10When they arrived at Gibeah, a procession of prophets met him; the Spirit of God came upon him in power, and he joined in their prophesying. 11When all those who had formerly known him saw him prophesying with the prophets, they asked each other, "What is this that has happened to the son of Kish? Is Saul also among the prophets?"

12A man who lived there answered, "And who is their father?" So it became a saying: "Is Saul also among the prophets?" 13After Saul stopped prophesying, he went to the high place.

14Now Saul's uncle asked him and his servant, "Where have you been?"

"Looking for the donkeys," he said. "But when we saw they were not to be found, we went to Samuel."

15Saul's uncle said, "Tell me what Samuel said to you."

16Saul replied, "He assured us that the donkeys had been found." But he did not tell his uncle what Samuel had said about the kingship.

17Samuel summoned the people of Israel to the LORD at Mizpah 18and said to them, "This is what the LORD, the God of Israel, says: 'I brought Israel up out of Egypt, and I delivered you from the power of Egypt and all the kingdoms that oppressed you.' 19But you have now rejected your God, who saves you out of all your calamities and distresses. And you have said, 'No, set a king over us.' So now present yourselves before the LORD by your tribes and clans."

20When Samuel brought all the tribes of Israel near, the tribe of Benjamin was chosen. 21Then he brought forward the tribe of Benjamin, clan by clan, and Matri's clan was chosen. Finally Saul son of Kish was chosen. But when they looked for him, he was not to be found. 22So they inquired further of the LORD, "Has the man come here yet?"

And the LORD said, "Yes, he has hidden himself among the baggage."

23They ran and brought him out, and as he stood among the people he was a head taller than any of the others. 24Samuel said to all the people, "Do you see the man the LORD has chosen? There is no one like him among all the people."

Then the people shouted, "Long live the king!"

25Samuel explained to the people the regulations of the kingship. He wrote them down on a scroll and deposited it before the LORD. Then Samuel dismissed the people, each to his own home.

26Saul also went to his home in Gibeah, accompanied by valiant men whose hearts God had touched. 27But some troublemakers said,

[a]1 Hebrew; Septuagint and Vulgate *over his people Israel? You will reign over the LORD's people and save them from the power of their enemies round about. And this will be a sign to you that the LORD has anointed you leader over his inheritance:*
[b]8 Traditionally *peace offerings*

10:1 As Samuel anointed Saul to be king over Israel, he buried his personal dreams. Samuel was the last of the judges; his sons would never share this honor. Despite this disappointment, Samuel found the courage to follow God's will instead of his own. He was willing to change and assist in the process of helping Saul become king over Israel. Assisting others on their way to spiritual renewal sometimes means we must give up some personal dreams of our own. If we are following God's will, helping others will be the surest way to discover a new life for ourselves.

10:26 The phrase "whose hearts God had touched" shows us a key to spiritual growth. God touched Saul's life as well as a number of individuals who would support Saul in his new life. These words echo a verse in the New Testament: "Jesus came and touched them. 'Get up,' he said. 'Don't be afraid' " (Matthew 17:7). The touch of God's hand enables us to deal with the past, persist in the present and find direction for the future. Starting anew means we must first come to God for the salvation he offers in Jesus Christ and then depend on him for sustenance and strength (see John 3:16; 15:4–7).

"How can this fellow save us?" They despised him and brought him no gifts. But Saul kept silent.

Saul Rescues the City of Jabesh

11 Nahash the Ammonite went up and besieged Jabesh Gilead. And all the men of Jabesh said to him, "Make a treaty with us, and we will be subject to you."

2But Nahash the Ammonite replied, "I will make a treaty with you only on the condition that I gouge out the right eye of every one of you and so bring disgrace on all Israel."

3The elders of Jabesh said to him, "Give us seven days so we can send messengers throughout Israel; if no one comes to rescue us, we will surrender to you."

4When the messengers came to Gibeah of Saul and reported these terms to the people, they all wept aloud. 5Just then Saul was returning from the fields, behind his oxen, and he asked, "What is wrong with the people? Why are they weeping?" Then they repeated to him what the men of Jabesh had said.

6When Saul heard their words, the Spirit of God came upon him in power, and he burned with anger. 7He took a pair of oxen, cut them into pieces, and sent the pieces by messengers throughout Israel, proclaiming, "This is what will be done to the oxen of anyone who does not follow Saul and Samuel." Then the terror of the LORD fell on the people, and they turned out as one man. 8When Saul mustered them at Bezek, the men of Israel numbered three hundred thousand and the men of Judah thirty thousand.

9They told the messengers who had come, "Say to the men of Jabesh Gilead, 'By the time the sun is hot tomorrow, you will be delivered.' " When the messengers went and reported this to the men of Jabesh, they were elated. 10They said to the Ammonites, "Tomorrow we will surrender to you, and you can do to us whatever seems good to you."

11The next day Saul separated his men into three divisions; during the last watch of the night they broke into the camp of the Ammonites and slaughtered them until the heat of the day. Those who survived were scattered, so that no two of them were left together.

Saul Confirmed as King

12The people then said to Samuel, "Who was it that asked, 'Shall Saul reign over us?' Bring these men to us and we will put them to death."

13But Saul said, "No one shall be put to death today, for this day the LORD has rescued Israel."

14Then Samuel said to the people, "Come, let us go to Gilgal and there reaffirm the kingship." 15So all the people went to Gilgal and confirmed Saul as king in the presence of the LORD. There they sacrificed fellowship offerings[a] before the LORD, and Saul and all the Israelites held a great celebration.

Samuel's Farewell Speech

12 Samuel said to all Israel, "I have listened to everything you said to me and have set a king over you. 2Now you have a king as your leader. As for me, I am old and gray, and my sons are here with you. I have been your leader from my youth until this day. 3Here I stand. Testify against me in the presence of the LORD and his anointed. Whose ox have I taken? Whose donkey have I taken? Whom have I cheated? Whom have I oppressed? From whose hand have I accepted a bribe to make me shut my eyes? If I have done any of these, I will make it right."

4"You have not cheated or oppressed us," they replied. "You have not taken anything from anyone's hand."

5Samuel said to them, "The LORD is witness against you, and also his anointed is witness this day, that you have not found anything in my hand."

"He is witness," they said.

6Then Samuel said to the people, "It is the LORD who appointed Moses and Aaron and brought your forefathers up out of Egypt. 7Now then, stand here, because I am going to confront you with evidence before the LORD as to all the righteous acts performed by the LORD for you and your fathers.

8"After Jacob entered Egypt, they cried to the LORD for help, and the LORD sent Moses and Aaron, who brought your forefathers out of Egypt and settled them in this place.

9"But they forgot the LORD their God; so he sold them into the hand of Sisera, the com-

[a]15 Traditionally *peace offerings*

11:13–15 Saul proclaimed, "This day the LORD has rescued Israel" (11:13). Following their victory over the Ammonites, Saul, Samuel and the people confirmed Saul's kingship at Gilgal (11:14–15). It is often a good idea for us to go public with our commitments also so that we will feel responsible for them and will be held accountable by others to fulfill them. Platform speeches aren't usually necessary. Confiding in a few trusted friends who will follow through and confront us when we slip up is all we need.

12:8–11 Samuel reviewed Israel's history and described the cycle of sin, crisis and deliverance that was evident throughout the book of Judges. The Israelites sinned, and the consequences of their sins led them to enslavement. Unable to shake their oppressors, the people cried out to God, admitting their sins of disobedience. By accepting reality, they finally saw their need for God and cried out, confessing their sins to the only one who could help them—God himself. God provided a delivering judge to lead the people out of bondage. Whenever we recognize our need for God, we possess the potential for spiritual renewal. All we need to do is cry out to God, confess our sins, and he will help us break free from the sins that hold us captive.

SAUL

Saul's story is a tragic one. Though a man with great potential for leadership, Saul failed miserably. He allowed his fearfulness, disobedience and self-sufficiency to come between him and God's plan for his life.

At the beginning of his career Saul was a shy and reluctant leader. He was hiding among the baggage when Samuel called the people together to publicly anoint him as king. Saul's humble, restrained style worked well in the early days of his rule, but ultimately Saul came to a point where he had to decide to either follow or fight against God's authority in his life. Unfortunately, Saul made the wrong choice and chose to follow his own path.

During his reign, Saul enjoyed his greatest successes when he obeyed God; his greatest failures resulted from acting on his own. Yet even Saul's weaknesses could have been turned to good by God if Saul had only confessed them and left everything in God's hands.

Just like Saul, we are faced with the choice of either surrendering our lives and wills to God or continuing to fight his plan for us. As with Saul, our choice will set the course of our life.

STRENGTHS AND ACCOMPLISHMENTS:

Saul's family and troops were always loyal to him.

When he was obeying God, Saul's leadership and courage were great.

Saul had a striking, charismatic appearance.

WEAKNESSES AND MISTAKES:

Saul was a people pleaser, surrendering to outside pressure rather than to God.

He became jealous of David, God's chosen successor to the throne.

Saul disobeyed God in several crucial situations.

LESSONS FROM HIS LIFE:

God desires heartfelt obedience rather than empty, religious displays.

Though costly, obedience to God is always best.

KEY VERSE:

"Rebellion is like the sin of divination, and arrogance like the evil of idolatry. Because you have rejected the word of the LORD, he has rejected you as king" (15:23).

Saul's story is told in 1 Samuel 9—31. He is also mentioned in 2 Samuel 1—6; 9; 12:7; 21; 1 Chronicles 8—13; 15:29; 26:28 and Acts 13:21–22.

mander of the army of Hazor, and into the
hands of the Philistines and the king of Moab,
who fought against them. 10They cried out to
the LORD and said, 'We have sinned; we have
forsaken the LORD and served the Baals and the
Ashtoreths. But now deliver us from the hands
of our enemies, and we will serve you.' 11Then
the LORD sent Jerub-Baal,[a] Barak,[b] Jephthah
and Samuel,[c] and he delivered you from the
hands of your enemies on every side, so that
you lived securely.
12"But when you saw that Nahash king of
the Ammonites was moving against you, you
said to me, 'No, we want a king to rule over
us'—even though the LORD your God was your
king. 13Now here is the king you have chosen,
the one you asked for; see, the LORD has set a
king over you. 14If you fear the LORD and serve
and obey him and do not rebel against his commands, and if both you and the king who reigns
over you follow the LORD your God—good!
15But if you do not obey the LORD, and if you
rebel against his commands, his hand will be
against you, as it was against your fathers.
16"Now then, stand still and see this great
thing the LORD is about to do before your eyes!
17Is it not wheat harvest now? I will call upon
the LORD to send thunder and rain. And you
will realize what an evil thing you did in the
eyes of the LORD when you asked for a king."
18Then Samuel called upon the LORD, and
that same day the LORD sent thunder and rain.
So all the people stood in awe of the LORD and
of Samuel.
19The people all said to Samuel, "Pray to the
LORD your God for your servants so that we will
not die, for we have added to all our other sins
the evil of asking for a king."
20"Do not be afraid," Samuel replied. "You
have done all this evil; yet do not turn away
from the LORD, but serve the LORD with all your
heart. 21Do not turn away after useless idols.
They can do you no good, nor can they rescue
you, because they are useless. 22For the sake of
his great name the LORD will not reject his people, because the LORD was pleased to make you
his own. 23As for me, far be it from me that I
should sin against the LORD by failing to pray
for you. And I will teach you the way that is
good and right. 24But be sure to fear the LORD
and serve him faithfully with all your heart;
consider what great things he has done for you.
25Yet if you persist in doing evil, both you and
your king will be swept away."

Samuel Rebukes Saul

13 Saul was ⌊thirty⌋[d] years old when he
became king, and he reigned over Israel
⌊forty-⌋[e] two years.
2Saul[f] chose three thousand men from Israel; two thousand were with him at Micmash
and in the hill country of Bethel, and a thousand were with Jonathan at Gibeah in Benjamin. The rest of the men he sent back to their
homes.
3Jonathan attacked the Philistine outpost at
Geba, and the Philistines heard about it. Then
Saul had the trumpet blown throughout the
land and said, "Let the Hebrews hear!" 4So all
Israel heard the news: "Saul has attacked the
Philistine outpost, and now Israel has become
a stench to the Philistines." And the people were
summoned to join Saul at Gilgal.
5The Philistines assembled to fight Israel,
with three thousand[g] chariots, six thousand
charioteers, and soldiers as numerous as the
sand on the seashore. They went up and
camped at Micmash, east of Beth Aven. 6When
the men of Israel saw that their situation was
critical and that their army was hard pressed,
they hid in caves and thickets, among the rocks,
and in pits and cisterns. 7Some Hebrews even
crossed the Jordan to the land of Gad and Gilead.
Saul remained at Gilgal, and all the troops
with him were quaking with fear. 8He waited
seven days, the time set by Samuel; but Samuel

[a]*11* Also called *Gideon* [b]*11* Some Septuagint manuscripts and Syriac; Hebrew *Bedan* [c]*11* Hebrew; some Septuagint manuscripts and Syriac *Samson*
[d]*1* A few late manuscripts of the Septuagint; Hebrew does not have *thirty.* [e]*1* See the round number in Acts 13:21; Hebrew does not have *forty-.* [f]*1,2* Or *and when he had reigned over Israel two years, 2he* [g]*5* Some Septuagint manuscripts and Syriac; Hebrew *thirty thousand*

12:14–15 Life is filled with choices. The Bible is filled with clear direction on how to make decisions in keeping with God's plan. A wise decision always takes into account whether or not we are showing proper respect for God, worshiping and serving him as we should and obeying his commands (12:14). A poor decision fails to keep God's desires and requirements in focus (12:15). Following God's plan means we will reap positive long-term consequences, even though things may look difficult at first. But disobedience to God's revealed instructions will always lead us into bondage.

12:20 Samuel exhorted the Israelites to persevere in their obedience to God and not to be afraid. He acknowledged their past failure and didn't downplay their past sin; in fact, Samuel reminded them of it. But Samuel also called them to escape the mire of guilt associated with their past failure. He emphasized the positive, saying, "Do not turn away from the LORD, but serve the LORD with all your heart." We must recognize the sin in our past, but also look ahead to a positive future. As the spiritual renewal process continues, it is vital to remember that a new life is not built overnight.

12:23–25 Samuel identified his failure to pray for the people as a sin against God. This shows the depth of Samuel's sense of accountability to God and his feelings of responsibility for the people. Samuel's spiritual maturity manifested itself in his desire to help others: "I will teach you the way that is good and right" (12:23). Indeed, Samuel went on to outline how the people might gain freedom: "Fear the Lord and serve him faithfully with all your heart; consider what great things he has done for you" (12:24). Samuel concluded his words with a warning to the people of the dire consequences of refusing to obey God (12:25). We would all do well to heed Samuel's words.

13:8–14 When we take our eyes off God and look only at the circumstances around us, we often act with impa-

did not come to Gilgal, and Saul's men began
to scatter. 9So he said, "Bring me the burnt
offering and the fellowship offerings.[a]" And
Saul offered up the burnt offering. 10Just as he
finished making the offering, Samuel arrived,
and Saul went out to greet him.

11"What have you done?" asked Samuel.

Saul replied, "When I saw that the men were scattering, and that you did not come at the set time, and that the Philistines were assembling at Micmash, 12I thought, 'Now the Philistines
will come down against me at Gilgal, and I have not sought the LORD's favor.' So I felt compelled to offer the burnt offering."

13"You acted foolishly," Samuel said. "You have not kept the command the LORD your God gave you; if you had, he would have established your kingdom over Israel for all time. 14But now
your kingdom will not endure; the LORD has sought out a man after his own heart and appointed him leader of his people, because you have not kept the LORD's command."

15Then Samuel left Gilgal[b] and went up to
Gibeah in Benjamin, and Saul counted the men who were with him. They numbered about six hundred.

Israel Without Weapons

16Saul and his son Jonathan and the men
with them were staying in Gibeah[c] in Benjamin, while the Philistines camped at Micmash.
17Raiding parties went out from the Philistine
camp in three detachments. One turned toward
Ophrah in the vicinity of Shual, 18another to-
ward Beth Horon, and the third toward the borderland overlooking the Valley of Zeboim facing the desert.

19Not a blacksmith could be found in the
whole land of Israel, because the Philistines had said, "Otherwise the Hebrews will make swords or spears!" 20So all Israel went down to the Philistines to have their plowshares, mattocks, axes and sickles[d] sharpened. 21The price was two
thirds of a shekel[e] for sharpening plowshares and mattocks, and a third of a shekel[f] for

[a]9 Traditionally *peace offerings* [b]15 Hebrew; Septuagint *Gilgal and went his way; the rest of the people went after Saul to meet the army, and they went out of Gilgal* [c]16 Two Hebrew manuscripts; most Hebrew manuscripts *Geba,* a variant of *Gibeah* [d]20 Septuagint; Hebrew *plowshares* [e]21 Hebrew *pim;* that is, about 1/4 ounce (about 8 grams) [f]21 That is, about 1/8 ounce (about 4 grams)

tience or indiscretion. Confronted by the seemingly insurmountable threat of the Philistine army and afraid that his men were about to desert him, Saul acted irresponsibly by personally offering a burnt sacrifice rather than waiting for the arrival of a priest. Saul failed to trust God's timing and thereby disobeyed one of God's commands. The consequences for taking things into his own hands were great: His descendants would be denied the right to rule in Israel. Being patient when things seem to be running behind schedule is difficult for us too. We need to trust God's timing even when his plan seems to be moving along too slowly. God's way is always the best way.

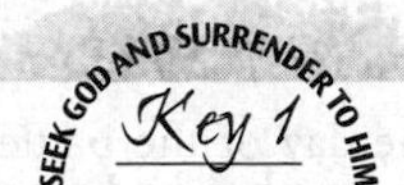

To Whom Will You Surrender?

1 Samuel 13:1–14 Pressure has become a regular part of life today. It seems as though everyone wants something from us or expects us to do something. As a result, we are often forced to choose between surrendering to the pressure of others and doing the will of God. Spiritual renewal and growth take place when we choose to obey God instead of surrendering ourselves to anyone else's expectations.

At Saul's coronation, the prophet Samuel exhorted him to obey God (12:14). But Saul allowed his men to pressure him to disobey God's commands. Israel was at war. In the midst of battle it was customary to have a priest offer sacrifices. Samuel had promised Saul that he would come at an appointed time to do this. Saul waited for a while but began to feel pressured because his troops were leaving him. He knew that it was against God's law for him to offer the sacrifices because he was not a priest. But Saul decided he couldn't take the pressure any longer, so he offered the sacrifices himself.

Just as Saul finished his sacrifice, Samuel arrived. "'You acted foolishly,' Samuel exclaimed. 'You have not kept the command the LORD your God gave you; if you had, he would have established your kingdom over Israel for all time. But now your kingdom will not endure; the LORD has sought out a man after his own heart'" (13:13–14). If Saul had not yielded to the pressure of those around him, he would have kept his kingdom.

Surrendering to God means that we resist surrendering to those who pressure us to disobey his commands. When we surrender to ungodly pressure, we pay dire consequences. When we surrender to God, we benefit, and so do generations to come.

Turn to 2 Kings 5.

sharpening forks and axes and for repointing goads.

22So on the day of the battle not a soldier with Saul and Jonathan had a sword or spear in his hand; only Saul and his son Jonathan had them.

Jonathan Attacks the Philistines

23Now a detachment of Philistines had gone out to the pass at Micmash.

14 1One day Jonathan son of Saul said to the young man bearing his armor, "Come, let's go over to the Philistine outpost on the other side." But he did not tell his father.

2Saul was staying on the outskirts of Gibeah under a pomegranate tree in Migron. With him were about six hundred men, 3among whom was Ahijah, who was wearing an ephod. He was a son of Ichabod's brother Ahitub son of Phinehas, the son of Eli, the LORD's priest in Shiloh. No one was aware that Jonathan had left.

4On each side of the pass that Jonathan intended to cross to reach the Philistine outpost was a cliff; one was called Bozez, and the other Seneh. 5One cliff stood to the north toward Micmash, the other to the south toward Geba.

6Jonathan said to his young armor-bearer, "Come, let's go over to the outpost of those uncircumcised fellows. Perhaps the LORD will act in our behalf. Nothing can hinder the LORD from saving, whether by many or by few."

7"Do all that you have in mind," his armor-bearer said. "Go ahead; I am with you heart and soul."

8Jonathan said, "Come, then; we will cross over toward the men and let them see us. 9If they say to us, 'Wait there until we come to you,' we will stay where we are and not go up to them. 10But if they say, 'Come up to us,' we will climb up, because that will be our sign that the LORD has given them into our hands."

11So both of them showed themselves to the Philistine outpost. "Look!" said the Philistines. "The Hebrews are crawling out of the holes they were hiding in." 12The men of the outpost shouted to Jonathan and his armor-bearer, "Come up to us and we'll teach you a lesson."

So Jonathan said to his armor-bearer, "Climb up after me; the LORD has given them into the hand of Israel."

13Jonathan climbed up, using his hands and feet, with his armor-bearer right behind him. The Philistines fell before Jonathan, and his armor-bearer followed and killed behind him. 14In that first attack Jonathan and his armor-bearer killed some twenty men in an area of about half an acre.[a]

Israel Routs the Philistines

15Then panic struck the whole army—those in the camp and field, and those in the outposts and raiding parties—and the ground shook. It was a panic sent by God.[b]

16Saul's lookouts at Gibeah in Benjamin saw the army melting away in all directions. 17Then Saul said to the men who were with him, "Muster the forces and see who has left us." When they did, it was Jonathan and his armor-bearer who were not there.

18Saul said to Ahijah, "Bring the ark of God." (At that time it was with the Israelites.)[c] 19While Saul was talking to the priest, the tumult in the Philistine camp increased more and more. So Saul said to the priest, "Withdraw your hand."

20Then Saul and all his men assembled and went to the battle. They found the Philistines in total confusion, striking each other with their swords. 21Those Hebrews who had previously been with the Philistines and had gone up with them to their camp went over to the Israelites who were with Saul and Jonathan. 22When all the Israelites who had hidden in the hill country of Ephraim heard that the Philistines were on the run, they joined the battle in hot pursuit. 23So the LORD rescued Israel that day, and the battle moved on beyond Beth Aven.

Jonathan Eats Honey

24Now the men of Israel were in distress that day, because Saul had bound the people under an oath, saying, "Cursed be any man who eats

[a] 14 Hebrew *half a yoke;* a "yoke" was the land plowed by a yoke of oxen in one day. [b] 15 Or *a terrible panic* [c] 18 Hebrew; Septuagint *"Bring the ephod." (At that time he wore the ephod before the Israelites.)*

14:6–14 God is famous for providing victory to those who trust him, even in seemingly impossible situations. Jonathan's confidence in God prompted him to step out in faith and tackle incredible odds. His faith and courage were rewarded with an amazing victory (14:13). Many of us never trust God enough to discover what he can do or the joy that such trust brings. Notice that Jonathan did not take his step of faith alone but was accompanied by a bodyguard. Similarly, spiritual renewal and growth is not something we accomplish by ourselves. We need support—friends like Jonathan's companion who will exclaim, "I am with you heart and soul" (14:7).

14:19–20 Saul's indecision as he heard the noise of battle in the Philistine camp caused confusion among his own troops. Saul wanted a clear message from God about what to do, but he found that he had no alternative but to attack, building upon Jonathan's victory (see 14:13–15). Saul's course of action should have been obvious. His insincere hesitation shows us that there is a time to pray and a time to act. We must avoid trying to act "spiritual" when it is time to take action.

14:24–25 Saul says here, "Before I have full revenge on my enemies." His comment gives us a clue that Saul was on a downhill slide spiritually. Earlier he had declared, "Today the LORD has rescued Israel!" (11:13). But here he has changed his tune; no longer did he see God as the vital entity in the process of victory. The battle had become Saul's; the enemies were no longer God's enemies but Saul's opponents. Thus the victory would belong to Saul and not to God. When we begin to take credit for our spiritual progress, we have already begun to regress toward failure. We must always remember that the enemies we face are too big for us unless we seek victory with the help of God.

food before evening comes, before I have avenged myself on my enemies!" So none of the troops tasted food.

25The entire army[a] entered the woods, and there was honey on the ground. 26When they went into the woods, they saw the honey oozing out, yet no one put his hand to his mouth, because they feared the oath. 27But Jonathan had not heard that his father had bound the people with the oath, so he reached out the end of the staff that was in his hand and dipped it into the honeycomb. He raised his hand to his mouth, and his eyes brightened.[b] 28Then one of the soldiers told him, "Your father bound the army under a strict oath, saying, 'Cursed be any man who eats food today!' That is why the men are faint."

29Jonathan said, "My father has made trouble for the country. See how my eyes brightened[c] when I tasted a little of this honey. 30How much better it would have been if the men had eaten today some of the plunder they took from their enemies. Would not the slaughter of the Philistines have been even greater?"

31That day, after the Israelites had struck down the Philistines from Micmash to Aijalon, they were exhausted. 32They pounced on the plunder and, taking sheep, cattle and calves, they butchered them on the ground and ate them, together with the blood. 33Then someone said to Saul, "Look, the men are sinning against the LORD by eating meat that has blood in it."

"You have broken faith," he said. "Roll a large stone over here at once." 34Then he said, "Go out among the men and tell them, 'Each of you bring me your cattle and sheep, and slaughter them here and eat them. Do not sin against the LORD by eating meat with blood still in it.' "

So everyone brought his ox that night and slaughtered it there. 35Then Saul built an altar to the LORD; it was the first time he had done this.

36Saul said, "Let us go down after the Philistines by night and plunder them till dawn, and let us not leave one of them alive."

"Do whatever seems best to you," they replied.

But the priest said, "Let us inquire of God here."

37So Saul asked God, "Shall I go down after the Philistines? Will you give them into Israel's hand?" But God did not answer him that day.

38Saul therefore said, "Come here, all you who are leaders of the army, and let us find out what sin has been committed today. 39As surely as the LORD who rescues Israel lives, even if it lies with my son Jonathan, he must die." But not one of the men said a word.

40Saul then said to all the Israelites, "You stand over there; I and Jonathan my son will stand over here."

"Do what seems best to you," the men replied.

41Then Saul prayed to the LORD, the God of Israel, "Give me the right answer."[d] And Jonathan and Saul were taken by lot, and the men were cleared. 42Saul said, "Cast the lot between me and Jonathan my son." And Jonathan was taken.

43Then Saul said to Jonathan, "Tell me what you have done."

So Jonathan told him, "I merely tasted a little honey with the end of my staff. And now must I die?"

44Saul said, "May God deal with me, be it ever so severely, if you do not die, Jonathan."

45But the men said to Saul, "Should Jonathan die—he who has brought about this great deliverance in Israel? Never! As surely as the LORD lives, not a hair of his head will fall to the ground, for he did this today with God's help." So the men rescued Jonathan, and he was not put to death.

46Then Saul stopped pursuing the Philistines, and they withdrew to their own land.

47After Saul had assumed rule over Israel, he fought against their enemies on every side: Moab, the Ammonites, Edom, the kings[e] of Zobah, and the Philistines. Wherever he turned, he inflicted punishment on them.[f] 48He fought valiantly and defeated the Amalekites, delivering Israel from the hands of those who had plundered them.

Saul's Family

49Saul's sons were Jonathan, Ishvi and Malki-Shua. The name of his older daughter was Merab, and that of the younger was Michal. 50His wife's name was Ahinoam daughter of Ahimaaz. The name of the commander of Saul's army was Abner son of Ner, and Ner was Saul's uncle. 51Saul's father Kish and Abner's father Ner were sons of Abiel.

52All the days of Saul there was bitter war with the Philistines, and whenever Saul saw a mighty or brave man, he took him into his service.

The LORD Rejects Saul as King

15 Samuel said to Saul, "I am the one the LORD sent to anoint you king over his people Israel; so listen now to the message from the LORD. 2This is what the LORD Almighty says: 'I will punish the Amalekites for what they did to Israel when they waylaid them as they came up from Egypt. 3Now go, attack the Amalekites and totally destroy[g] everything that belongs to

[a]25 Or *Now all the people of the land* [b]27 Or *his strength was renewed* [c]29 Or *my strength was renewed* [d]41 Hebrew; Septuagint *"Why have you not answered your servant today? If the fault is in me or my son Jonathan, respond with Urim, but if the men of Israel are at fault, respond with Thummim."* [e]47 Masoretic Text; Dead Sea Scrolls and Septuagint *king* [f]47 Hebrew; Septuagint *he was victorious* [g]3 The Hebrew term refers to the irrevocable giving over of things or persons to the LORD, often by totally destroying them; also in verses 8, 9, 15, 18, 20 and 21.

them. Do not spare them; put to death men and women, children and infants, cattle and sheep, camels and donkeys.' "

4So Saul summoned the men and mustered them at Telaim—two hundred thousand foot soldiers and ten thousand men from Judah. 5Saul went to the city of Amalek and set an ambush in the ravine. 6Then he said to the Kenites, "Go away, leave the Amalekites so that I do not destroy you along with them; for you showed kindness to all the Israelites when they came up out of Egypt." So the Kenites moved away from the Amalekites.

7Then Saul attacked the Amalekites all the way from Havilah to Shur, to the east of Egypt. 8He took Agag king of the Amalekites alive, and all his people he totally destroyed with the sword. 9But Saul and the army spared Agag and the best of the sheep and cattle, the fat calves[a] and lambs—everything that was good. These they were unwilling to destroy completely, but everything that was despised and weak they totally destroyed.

10Then the word of the LORD came to Samuel: 11"I am grieved that I have made Saul king, because he has turned away from me and has not carried out my instructions." Samuel was troubled, and he cried out to the LORD all that night.

12Early in the morning Samuel got up and went to meet Saul, but he was told, "Saul has gone to Carmel. There he has set up a monument in his own honor and has turned and gone on down to Gilgal."

13When Samuel reached him, Saul said, "The LORD bless you! I have carried out the LORD's instructions."

14But Samuel said, "What then is this bleating of sheep in my ears? What is this lowing of cattle that I hear?"

15Saul answered, "The soldiers brought them from the Amalekites; they spared the best of the sheep and cattle to sacrifice to the LORD your God, but we totally destroyed the rest."

16"Stop!" Samuel said to Saul. "Let me tell you what the LORD said to me last night."

"Tell me," Saul replied.

17Samuel said, "Although you were once small in your own eyes, did you not become the head of the tribes of Israel? The LORD anointed you king over Israel. 18And he sent you on a mission, saying, 'Go and completely destroy those wicked people, the Amalekites; make war on them until you have wiped them out.' 19Why did you not obey the LORD? Why did you pounce on the plunder and do evil in the eyes of the LORD?"

20"But I did obey the LORD," Saul said. "I went on the mission the LORD assigned me. I completely destroyed the Amalekites and brought back Agag their king. 21The soldiers took sheep and cattle from the plunder, the best of what was devoted to God, in order to sacrifice them to the LORD your God at Gilgal."

22But Samuel replied:

"Does the LORD delight in burnt offerings
and sacrifices
as much as in obeying the voice of the
LORD?
To obey is better than sacrifice,
and to heed is better than the fat of
rams.
23For rebellion is like the sin of divination,
and arrogance like the evil of idolatry.
Because you have rejected the word of the
LORD,
he has rejected you as king."

24Then Saul said to Samuel, "I have sinned. I violated the LORD's command and your instructions. I was afraid of the people and so I gave in to them. 25Now I beg you, forgive my sin and come back with me, so that I may worship the LORD."

26But Samuel said to him, "I will not go back with you. You have rejected the word of the LORD, and the LORD has rejected you as king over Israel!"

27As Samuel turned to leave, Saul caught hold of the hem of his robe, and it tore. 28Samuel said to him, "The LORD has torn the kingdom of Israel from you today and has given it

[a]9 Or *the grown bulls*; the meaning of the Hebrew for this phrase is uncertain.

15:10–15 God was grieved that Saul had followed his own inclinations rather than God's clear instructions. God's principles for holy living call us to obey his instructions, to make a clean break with the past, to refuse to compromise. Saul exhibited none of these qualities. He chose to spare King Agag and the finest animals instead of destroying everything as God had commanded (see 15:8–9). Saul even built a monument in his own honor rather than glorifying God for the miraculous victory (15:12). When confronted by Samuel, Saul tried to justify his actions (15:15). Making excuses has never paved the way to a better life. Until we accept responsibility for our actions there is no hope for true spiritual renewal.

15:16–21 Samuel confronted Saul, but instead of admitting his failure to obey God's instructions, Saul continued rationalizing his disobedience. He sought to excuse himself by his intention to bring sacrifices to God. Rationalization and refusal to admit our failures are two of the biggest enemies to spiritual growth. God places a premium on honesty. God does not want our pious prayers and religious activities unless a humble and obedient heart accompanies them. Hiding the sin in our lives with pious words and deeds is no substitute for confessing our sins and asking God to cleanse us.

15:22–30 Samuel's words pierced Saul's callous exterior like surgical steel (15:22–23). As we seek to grow spiritually, nothing can take the place of obedience to God. Everything in God's economy hinges on an obedient heart, and this was the arena in which Saul had failed so miserably. He tried to cover his sins with religious activities, promising to offer sacrifices to God. But God was more interested in Saul's confession and obedience than in his sacrifice. Saul's obvious regret spurred him to grasp vainly at Samuel's robe (15:27). But reality proved painful; God's rejection of Saul was real. At this point, complete restoration for Saul had become virtually impossible (15:28–29).

to one of your neighbors—to one better than you. 29He who is the Glory of Israel does not lie or change his mind; for he is not a man, that he should change his mind."

30Saul replied, "I have sinned. But please honor me before the elders of my people and before Israel; come back with me, so that I may worship the LORD your God." 31So Samuel went back with Saul, and Saul worshiped the LORD.

32Then Samuel said, "Bring me Agag king of the Amalekites."

Agag came to him confidently,[a] thinking, "Surely the bitterness of death is past."

33But Samuel said,

"As your sword has made women childless,
so will your mother be childless among women."

And Samuel put Agag to death before the LORD at Gilgal.

34Then Samuel left for Ramah, but Saul went up to his home in Gibeah of Saul. 35Until the day Samuel died, he did not go to see Saul again, though Samuel mourned for him. And the LORD was grieved that he had made Saul king over Israel.

Samuel Anoints David

16 The LORD said to Samuel, "How long will you mourn for Saul, since I have rejected him as king over Israel? Fill your horn with oil and be on your way; I am sending you to Jesse of Bethlehem. I have chosen one of his sons to be king."

2But Samuel said, "How can I go? Saul will hear about it and kill me."

The LORD said, "Take a heifer with you and say, 'I have come to sacrifice to the LORD.' 3Invite Jesse to the sacrifice, and I will show you what to do. You are to anoint for me the one I indicate."

4Samuel did what the LORD said. When he arrived at Bethlehem, the elders of the town trembled when they met him. They asked, "Do you come in peace?"

5Samuel replied, "Yes, in peace; I have come to sacrifice to the LORD. Consecrate yourselves and come to the sacrifice with me." Then he consecrated Jesse and his sons and invited them to the sacrifice.

6When they arrived, Samuel saw Eliab and thought, "Surely the LORD's anointed stands here before the LORD."

7But the LORD said to Samuel, "Do not consider his appearance or his height, for I have rejected him. The LORD does not look at the things man looks at. Man looks at the outward appearance, but the LORD looks at the heart."

8Then Jesse called Abinadab and had him pass in front of Samuel. But Samuel said, "The LORD has not chosen this one either." 9Jesse then had Shammah pass by, but Samuel said, "Nor has the LORD chosen this one." 10Jesse had seven of his sons pass before Samuel, but Samuel said to him, "The LORD has not chosen these." 11So he asked Jesse, "Are these all the sons you have?"

"There is still the youngest," Jesse answered, "but he is tending the sheep."

Samuel said, "Send for him; we will not sit down[b] until he arrives."

12So he sent and had him brought in. He was ruddy, with a fine appearance and handsome features.

Then the LORD said, "Rise and anoint him; he is the one."

13So Samuel took the horn of oil and anointed him in the presence of his brothers, and from that day on the Spirit of the LORD came upon David in power. Samuel then went to Ramah.

David in Saul's Service

14Now the Spirit of the LORD had departed from Saul, and an evil[c] spirit from the LORD tormented him.

15Saul's attendants said to him, "See, an evil spirit from God is tormenting you. 16Let our lord command his servants here to search for someone who can play the harp. He will play when the evil spirit from God comes upon you, and you will feel better."

17So Saul said to his attendants, "Find someone who plays well and bring him to me."

18One of the servants answered, "I have seen a son of Jesse of Bethlehem who knows how to play the harp. He is a brave man and a warrior. He speaks well and is a fine-looking man. And the LORD is with him."

[a]32 Or *him trembling, yet* [b]11 Some Septuagint manuscripts; Hebrew *not gather around* [c]14 Or *injurious;* also in verses 15, 16 and 23

15:32–33 Saul was not willing to obey God completely. Against God's express orders, Saul spared King Agag. Samuel's execution of Agag reminds us that surrender to God demands a distinct break with the past and complete obedience to God's Word. The past must be put to death if we hope to live renewed lives.

16:1 Samuel was paralyzed with despair over Saul's failure, but God intervened and pointed Samuel in a new direction. Saul had failed as king, but God already had another man in mind for the job. When the past quarrels with the present, there can be no future. We all need to learn from our past. But we must also stop living in the past and move on to God's new assignments and goals. Spiritual renewal involves letting go of the past so that we can take hold of what is in the present and redirect our course toward a new life for the future.

16:6–13 God's choice of Saul's successor undoubtedly surprised Samuel. In this passage God reveals how he judges the value of individuals—not by physical gifts of strength or beauty but by the attitude of their heart (16:7). It is not what we see on the outside that is important; it is who a person is on the inside. Most of us are not models of physical perfection, so it might come as a relief that God does not judge us in this way. Saul had failed, despite his external attractiveness. Anyone who hopes to succeed in God's kingdom must be concerned with humility and obedience, not outward attractiveness.

19Then Saul sent messengers to Jesse and said, "Send me your son David, who is with the sheep." 20So Jesse took a donkey loaded with bread, a skin of wine and a young goat and sent them with his son David to Saul.

21David came to Saul and entered his service. Saul liked him very much, and David became one of his armor-bearers. 22Then Saul sent word to Jesse, saying, "Allow David to remain in my service, for I am pleased with him."

23Whenever the spirit from God came upon Saul, David would take his harp and play. Then relief would come to Saul; he would feel better, and the evil spirit would leave him.

David and Goliath

17 Now the Philistines gathered their forces for war and assembled at Socoh in Judah. They pitched camp at Ephes Dammim, between Socoh and Azekah. 2Saul and the Israelites assembled and camped in the Valley of Elah and drew up their battle line to meet the Philistines. 3The Philistines occupied one hill and the Israelites another, with the valley between them.

4A champion named Goliath, who was from Gath, came out of the Philistine camp. He was over nine feet[a] tall. 5He had a bronze helmet on his head and wore a coat of scale armor of bronze weighing five thousand shekels[b]; 6on his legs he wore bronze greaves, and a bronze javelin was slung on his back. 7His spear shaft was like a weaver's rod, and its iron point weighed six hundred shekels.[c] His shield bearer went ahead of him.

8Goliath stood and shouted to the ranks of Israel, "Why do you come out and line up for battle? Am I not a Philistine, and are you not the servants of Saul? Choose a man and have him come down to me. 9If he is able to fight and kill me, we will become your subjects; but if I overcome him and kill him, you will become our subjects and serve us." 10Then the Philistine said, "This day I defy the ranks of Israel! Give me a man and let us fight each other." 11On hearing the Philistine's words, Saul and all the Israelites were dismayed and terrified.

12Now David was the son of an Ephrathite named Jesse, who was from Bethlehem in Judah. Jesse had eight sons, and in Saul's time he was old and well advanced in years. 13Jesse's three oldest sons had followed Saul to the war: The firstborn was Eliab; the second, Abinadab; and the third, Shammah. 14David was the youngest. The three oldest followed Saul, 15but David went back and forth from Saul to tend his father's sheep at Bethlehem.

16For forty days the Philistine came forward every morning and evening and took his stand.

17Now Jesse said to his son David, "Take this ephah[d] of roasted grain and these ten loaves of bread for your brothers and hurry to their camp. 18Take along these ten cheeses to the commander of their unit.[e] See how your brothers are and bring back some assurance[f] from them. 19They are with Saul and all the men of Israel in the Valley of Elah, fighting against the Philistines."

20Early in the morning David left the flock with a shepherd, loaded up and set out, as Jesse had directed. He reached the camp as the army was going out to its battle positions, shouting the war cry. 21Israel and the Philistines were drawing up their lines facing each other. 22David left his things with the keeper of supplies, ran to the battle lines and greeted his brothers. 23As he was talking with them, Goliath, the Philistine champion from Gath, stepped out from his lines and shouted his usual defiance, and David heard it. 24When the Israelites saw the man, they all ran from him in great fear.

25Now the Israelites had been saying, "Do you see how this man keeps coming out? He comes out to defy Israel. The king will give great wealth to the man who kills him. He will also give him his daughter in marriage and will exempt his father's family from taxes in Israel."

26David asked the men standing near him, "What will be done for the man who kills this Philistine and removes this disgrace from Israel? Who is this uncircumcised Philistine that he should defy the armies of the living God?"

27They repeated to him what they had been saying and told him, "This is what will be done for the man who kills him."

28When Eliab, David's oldest brother, heard him speaking with the men, he burned with anger at him and asked, "Why have you come down here? And with whom did you leave those few sheep in the desert? I know how conceited you are and how wicked your heart is; you came down only to watch the battle."

29"Now what have I done?" said David. "Can't I even speak?" 30He then turned away to someone else and brought up the same matter, and the men answered him as before. 31What David said was overheard and reported to Saul, and Saul sent for him.

32David said to Saul, "Let no one lose heart

[a] *4* Hebrew *was six cubits and a span* (about 3 meters)
[b] *5* That is, about 125 pounds (about 57 kilograms)
[c] *7* That is, about 15 pounds (about 7 kilograms)
[d] *17* That is, probably about 3/5 bushel (about 22 liters)
[e] *18* Hebrew *thousand* [f] *18* Or *some token*; or *some pledge of spoils*

17:32–37 David was confident that God would deliver him from Goliath's wrath, no matter how improbable it may have seemed. David was a young shepherd boy, armed with a sling and some stones. Goliath was a giant of a man, armed with a great sword and spear. In human terms, David didn't stand a chance; with God on his side, David couldn't lose. God is able to provide victory to all who are willing to trust him. When we face giants in our lives, when we meet problems that are too big for us to handle, when the odds are stacked against us, we can't lose if God is on our side.

17:32–37 David's courage was partly due to his acknowl-

on account of this Philistine; your servant will
go and fight him."
33Saul replied, "You are not able to go out
against this Philistine and fight him; you are
only a boy, and he has been a fighting man
from his youth."
34But David said to Saul, "Your servant has
been keeping his father's sheep. When a lion or
a bear came and carried off a sheep from the
flock, 35I went after it, struck it and rescued the
sheep from its mouth. When it turned on me,
I seized it by its hair, struck it and killed it.
36Your servant has killed both the lion and the
bear; this uncircumcised Philistine will be like
one of them, because he has defied the armies
of the living God. 37The LORD who delivered me
from the paw of the lion and the paw of the
bear will deliver me from the hand of this Philistine."

Saul said to David, "Go, and the LORD be with you."

38Then Saul dressed David in his own tunic.
He put a coat of armor on him and a bronze
helmet on his head. 39David fastened on his
sword over the tunic and tried walking around,
because he was not used to them.

"I cannot go in these," he said to Saul, "because I am not used to them." So he took them
off. 40Then he took his staff in his hand, chose
five smooth stones from the stream, put them
in the pouch of his shepherd's bag and, with his
sling in his hand, approached the Philistine.
41Meanwhile, the Philistine, with his shield
bearer in front of him, kept coming closer to
David. 42He looked David over and saw that he
was only a boy, ruddy and handsome, and he
despised him. 43He said to David, "Am I a dog,
that you come at me with sticks?" And the Philistine cursed David by his gods. 44"Come here,"
he said, "and I'll give your flesh to the birds of
the air and the beasts of the field!"
45David said to the Philistine, "You come
against me with sword and spear and javelin,
but I come against you in the name of the LORD
Almighty, the God of the armies of Israel,
whom you have defied. 46This day the LORD will
hand you over to me, and I'll strike you down
and cut off your head. Today I will give the
carcasses of the Philistine army to the birds of
the air and the beasts of the earth, and the
whole world will know that there is a God in
Israel. 47All those gathered here will know that

edgment of God's help in previous, smaller battles with lions and bears. David had learned to trust God in these smaller battles, giving him the faith he needed to confront the giant, Goliath. Sometimes we overlook our smaller victories, forgetting about the help that God provided during such times. We should remember these victories, no matter how small, and let them strengthen us for the battles still ahead.

17:45–47 As David squared off against Goliath, he knew that in human terms he didn't stand a chance. He courageously recognized that the battle belonged to God. Like David, we face many battles where we lack the power to win. But with God, the victory is certain.

Seeing Our Limitations and God's Power

1 Samuel 17:20–47 Seeing the truth about ourselves must include seeing our limitations and the power of God that is available to us.

When he was a very young man, David's father sent David to check on his brothers in the Israelite army. When he arrived, David found that the Israelites were running away from Goliath, a giant Philistine soldier. So David went to King Saul and asked permission to challenge Goliath in battle. Saul consented, and David went out to face the giant. When Goliath challenged David and the Israelite army, David replied, "You come against me with sword and spear and javelin, but I come against you in the name of the LORD Almighty, the God of the armies of Israel, whom you have defied. This day the LORD will hand you over to me, and I'll strike you down" (17:45–46).

The Israelite soldiers saw part of the truth—their limitations—so they ran in fear of Goliath. David knew his own limitations, but he also knew the power of his God. This gave him the courage he needed to take action. Whenever we seek to do God's will we need to see the whole truth. We can't do it alone, yet because of God's power helping us, we can accomplish whatever he has called us to do. Clearly seeing both of these truths will help us overcome anything that threatens to keep us from accomplishing God's will.

Turn to 2 Samuel 22.

it is not by sword or spear that the LORD saves;
for the battle is the LORD's, and he will give all
of you into our hands."
48As the Philistine moved closer to attack
him, David ran quickly toward the battle line to
meet him. 49Reaching into his bag and taking
out a stone, he slung it and struck the Philistine
on the forehead. The stone sank into his forehead, and he fell facedown on the ground.
50So David triumphed over the Philistine
with a sling and a stone; without a sword in his
hand he struck down the Philistine and killed
him.
51David ran and stood over him. He took
hold of the Philistine's sword and drew it from
the scabbard. After he killed him, he cut off his
head with the sword.
When the Philistines saw that their hero was
dead, they turned and ran. 52Then the men of
Israel and Judah surged forward with a shout
and pursued the Philistines to the entrance of
Gath[a] and to the gates of Ekron. Their dead
were strewn along the Shaaraim road to Gath
and Ekron. 53When the Israelites returned from
chasing the Philistines, they plundered their
camp. 54David took the Philistine's head and
brought it to Jerusalem, and he put the Philistine's weapons in his own tent.
55As Saul watched David going out to meet
the Philistine, he said to Abner, commander
of the army, "Abner, whose son is that young
man?"
Abner replied, "As surely as you live, O king,
I don't know."
56The king said, "Find out whose son this
young man is."
57As soon as David returned from killing the
Philistine, Abner took him and brought him
before Saul, with David still holding the Philistine's head.
58"Whose son are you, young man?" Saul
asked him.
David said, "I am the son of your servant
Jesse of Bethlehem."

Saul's Jealousy of David

18 After David had finished talking with
Saul, Jonathan became one in spirit
with David, and he loved him as himself. 2From
that day Saul kept David with him and did not
let him return to his father's house. 3And Jonathan made a covenant with David because he
loved him as himself. 4Jonathan took off the
robe he was wearing and gave it to David, along
with his tunic, and even his sword, his bow and
his belt.
5Whatever Saul sent him to do, David did it
so successfully[b] that Saul gave him a high rank
in the army. This pleased all the people, and
Saul's officers as well.
6When the men were returning home after
David had killed the Philistine, the women
came out from all the towns of Israel to meet
King Saul with singing and dancing, with joyful
songs and with tambourines and lutes. 7As they
danced, they sang:

"Saul has slain his thousands,
and David his tens of thousands."

8Saul was very angry; this refrain galled him.
"They have credited David with tens of thousands," he thought, "but me with only thousands. What more can he get but the kingdom?"
9And from that time on Saul kept a jealous eye
on David.
10The next day an evil[c] spirit from God
came forcefully upon Saul. He was prophesying
in his house, while David was playing the harp,
as he usually did. Saul had a spear in his hand
11and he hurled it, saying to himself, "I'll pin
David to the wall." But David eluded him twice.
12Saul was afraid of David, because the LORD
was with David but had left Saul. 13So he sent
David away from him and gave him command
over a thousand men, and David led the troops
in their campaigns. 14In everything he did he
had great success,[d] because the LORD was with
him. 15When Saul saw how successful[e] he was,
he was afraid of him. 16But all Israel and Judah
loved David, because he led them in their campaigns.
17Saul said to David, "Here is my older
daughter Merab. I will give her to you in marriage; only serve me bravely and fight the battles
of the LORD." For Saul said to himself, "I will not
raise a hand against him. Let the Philistines do
that!"
18But David said to Saul, "Who am I, and
what is my family or my father's clan in Israel,
that I should become the king's son-in-law?"
19So[f] when the time came for Merab, Saul's
daughter, to be given to David, she was given in
marriage to Adriel of Meholah.
20Now Saul's daughter Michal was in love
with David, and when they told Saul about it,
he was pleased. 21"I will give her to him," he
thought, "so that she may be a snare to him and
so that the hand of the Philistines may be
against him." So Saul said to David, "Now you
have a second opportunity to become my son-
in-law."
22Then Saul ordered his attendants: "Speak
to David privately and say, 'Look, the king is
pleased with you, and his attendants all like
you; now become his son-in-law.' "
23They repeated these words to David. But

[a]52 Some Septuagint manuscripts; Hebrew *a valley*
[b]5 Or *wisely* [c]10 Or *injurious* [d]14 Or *he was very wise* [e]15 Or *wise* [f]19 Or *However,*

18:1–4 God graciously provided David with a close friend in the person of Jonathan. This friendship helped David survive Saul's various attempts on his life. God created us to be close to people and to need their companionship and help. The importance of a significant friend to whom one can be accountable cannot be overestimated.

David said, "Do you think it is a small matter to become the king's son-in-law? I'm only a poor man and little known."

24When Saul's servants told him what David had said, 25Saul replied, "Say to David, 'The king wants no other price for the bride than a hundred Philistine foreskins, to take revenge on his enemies.' " Saul's plan was to have David fall by the hands of the Philistines.

26When the attendants told David these things, he was pleased to become the king's son-in-law. So before the allotted time elapsed, 27David and his men went out and killed two hundred Philistines. He brought their foreskins and presented the full number to the king so that he might become the king's son-in-law. Then Saul gave him his daughter Michal in marriage.

28When Saul realized that the LORD was with David and that his daughter Michal loved David, 29Saul became still more afraid of him, and he remained his enemy the rest of his days.

30The Philistine commanders continued to go out to battle, and as often as they did, David met with more success[a] than the rest of Saul's officers, and his name became well known.

Saul Tries to Kill David

19 Saul told his son Jonathan and all the attendants to kill David. But Jonathan was very fond of David 2and warned him, "My father Saul is looking for a chance to kill you. Be on your guard tomorrow morning; go into hiding and stay there. 3I will go out and stand with my father in the field where you are. I'll speak to him about you and will tell you what I find out."

4Jonathan spoke well of David to Saul his father and said to him, "Let not the king do wrong to his servant David; he has not wronged you, and what he has done has benefited you greatly. 5He took his life in his hands when he killed the Philistine. The LORD won a great victory for all Israel, and you saw it and were glad. Why then would you do wrong to an innocent man like David by killing him for no reason?"

6Saul listened to Jonathan and took this oath: "As surely as the LORD lives, David will not be put to death."

7So Jonathan called David and told him the whole conversation. He brought him to Saul, and David was with Saul as before.

8Once more war broke out, and David went out and fought the Philistines. He struck them with such force that they fled before him.

9But an evil[b] spirit from the LORD came upon Saul as he was sitting in his house with his spear in his hand. While David was playing the harp, 10Saul tried to pin him to the wall with his spear, but David eluded him as Saul drove the spear into the wall. That night David made good his escape.

11Saul sent men to David's house to watch it and to kill him in the morning. But Michal, David's wife, warned him, "If you don't run for your life tonight, tomorrow you'll be killed." 12So Michal let David down through a window, and he fled and escaped. 13Then Michal took an idol[c] and laid it on the bed, covering it with a garment and putting some goats' hair at the head.

14When Saul sent the men to capture David, Michal said, "He is ill."

15Then Saul sent the men back to see David and told them, "Bring him up to me in his bed so that I may kill him." 16But when the men entered, there was the idol in the bed, and at the head was some goats' hair.

17Saul said to Michal, "Why did you deceive me like this and send my enemy away so that he escaped?"

Michal told him, "He said to me, 'Let me get away. Why should I kill you?' "

18When David had fled and made his escape, he went to Samuel at Ramah and told him all that Saul had done to him. Then he and Samuel went to Naioth and stayed there. 19Word came to Saul: "David is in Naioth at Ramah"; 20so he sent men to capture him. But when they saw a group of prophets prophesying, with Samuel standing there as their leader, the Spirit of God came upon Saul's men and they also prophesied. 21Saul was told about it, and he sent more men, and they prophesied too. Saul sent men a third time, and they also prophesied. 22Finally, he himself left for Ramah and went to the great cistern at Secu. And he asked, "Where are Samuel and David?"

"Over in Naioth at Ramah," they said.

23So Saul went to Naioth at Ramah. But the Spirit of God came even upon him, and he walked along prophesying until he came to Naioth. 24He stripped off his robes and also prophesied in Samuel's presence. He lay that way all that day and night. This is why people say, "Is Saul also among the prophets?"

[a]30 Or *David acted more wisely* [b]9 Or *injurious*
[c]13 Hebrew *teraphim;* also in verse 16

19:1–2 Since David was a threat to Saul's dynasty, Jonathan could also have felt threatened by David. Yet Jonathan displayed no such insecurity. Instead, Jonathan made himself available to help his friend, warning David of Saul's intentions and assisting in his escape. True friends are never swayed by self-interest; they are willing to help even if they must make personal sacrifices to do so. A good friend will be there to help in a crisis.

19:18 In dire straits, David fled to his mentor, Samuel. Samuel was one of the great spiritual leaders of Israel. David's decision to go to Samuel for help reveals his wisdom and his desire to rely on God. Where we go when we are in trouble often reveals the kind of people we are too. It is important that we find people who will help us stay on track and persuade us to depend on God for help.

David and Jonathan

20 Then David fled from Naioth at Ramah and went to Jonathan and asked, "What have I done? What is my crime? How have I wronged your father, that he is trying to take my life?"

2"Never!" Jonathan replied. "You are not going to die! Look, my father doesn't do anything, great or small, without confiding in me. Why would he hide this from me? It's not so!"

3But David took an oath and said, "Your father knows very well that I have found favor in your eyes, and he has said to himself, 'Jonathan must not know this or he will be grieved.' Yet as surely as the LORD lives and as you live, there is only a step between me and death."

4Jonathan said to David, "Whatever you want me to do, I'll do for you."

5So David said, "Look, tomorrow is the New Moon festival, and I am supposed to dine with the king; but let me go and hide in the field until the evening of the day after tomorrow. 6If your father misses me at all, tell him, 'David earnestly asked my permission to hurry to Bethlehem, his hometown, because an annual sacrifice is being made there for his whole clan.' 7If he says, 'Very well,' then your servant is safe. But if he loses his temper, you can be sure that he is determined to harm me. 8As for you, show kindness to your servant, for you have brought him into a covenant with you before the LORD. If I am guilty, then kill me yourself! Why hand me over to your father?"

9"Never!" Jonathan said. "If I had the least inkling that my father was determined to harm you, wouldn't I tell you?"

10David asked, "Who will tell me if your father answers you harshly?"

11"Come," Jonathan said, "let's go out into the field." So they went there together.

12Then Jonathan said to David: "By the LORD, the God of Israel, I will surely sound out my father by this time the day after tomorrow! If he is favorably disposed toward you, will I not send you word and let you know? 13But if my father is inclined to harm you, may the LORD deal with me, be it ever so severely, if I do not let you know and send you away safely. May the LORD be with you as he has been with my father. 14But show me unfailing kindness like that of the LORD as long as I live, so that I may not be killed, 15and do not ever cut off your kindness from my family—not even when the LORD has cut off every one of David's enemies from the face of the earth."

16So Jonathan made a covenant with the house of David, saying, "May the LORD call David's enemies to account." 17And Jonathan had David reaffirm his oath out of love for him, because he loved him as he loved himself.

18Then Jonathan said to David: "Tomorrow is the New Moon festival. You will be missed, because your seat will be empty. 19The day after tomorrow, toward evening, go to the place where you hid when this trouble began, and wait by the stone Ezel. 20I will shoot three arrows to the side of it, as though I were shooting at a target. 21Then I will send a boy and say, 'Go, find the arrows.' If I say to him, 'Look, the arrows are on this side of you; bring them here,' then come, because, as surely as the LORD lives, you are safe; there is no danger. 22But if I say to the boy, 'Look, the arrows are beyond you,' then you must go, because the LORD has sent you away. 23And about the matter you and I discussed—remember, the LORD is witness between you and me forever."

24So David hid in the field, and when the New Moon festival came, the king sat down to eat. 25He sat in his customary place by the wall, opposite Jonathan,[a] and Abner sat next to Saul, but David's place was empty. 26Saul said nothing that day, for he thought, "Something must have happened to David to make him ceremonially unclean—surely he is unclean." 27But the next day, the second day of the month, David's place was empty again. Then Saul said to his son Jonathan, "Why hasn't the son of Jesse come to the meal, either yesterday or today?"

28Jonathan answered, "David earnestly asked me for permission to go to Bethlehem. 29He said, 'Let me go, because our family is observing a sacrifice in the town and my brother has ordered me to be there. If I have found favor in your eyes, let me get away to see my brothers.' That is why he has not come to the king's table."

30Saul's anger flared up at Jonathan and he said to him, "You son of a perverse and rebellious woman! Don't I know that you have sided with the son of Jesse to your own shame and to the shame of the mother who bore you? 31As long as the son of Jesse lives on this earth, neither you nor your kingdom will be established. Now send and bring him to me, for he must die!"

32"Why should he be put to death? What has he done?" Jonathan asked his father. 33But Saul hurled his spear at him to kill him. Then Jonathan knew that his father intended to kill David.

34Jonathan got up from the table in fierce anger; on that second day of the month he did not eat, because he was grieved at his father's shameful treatment of David.

[a]25 Septuagint; Hebrew *wall. Jonathan arose*

20:4 David was exceedingly blessed to have a friend like Jonathan. After hearing of David's difficulties, Jonathan wanted to know how he could help. Reliable and resourceful, Jonathan was ready to support David through this crisis. Jonathan's willing response should challenge all of us to similar responses when our loved ones experience crisis. We should be available to help others just as Jonathan helped David.

David & Jonathan

It is amazing that David and Jonathan formed such a close friendship, for there were vast differences between the two. The oldest son of King Saul, Jonathan was heir apparent to the throne of Israel. He was an experienced soldier, distinguished for his courage in battle. He was probably fifteen years older than David.

David, on the other hand, was the youngest son of Jesse, a shepherd boy from the town of Bethlehem. When Jonathan first met him, David was probably a teenager. Though David demonstrated the bold heart of a warrior when he defeated Goliath, he was primarily known as a talented musician in King Saul's court.

There seem to be two basic ingredients that shaped this unlikely relationship: a common faith and an uncommon love. Both Jonathan and David shared a deep commitment to God, and they loved each other unconditionally.

Yet their friendship was put to the test. David was anointed by Samuel the prophet to succeed Saul as king. As a result Saul repeatedly tried to kill David. This placed Jonathan at odds with his father. He risked himself to protect and encourage David, the one who would take his place as Israel's future king. No wonder David grieved so deeply at Jonathan's death! It is a gift to have a friend who loves unconditionally. Building these relationships is invaluable for solid spiritual growth.

STRENGTHS AND ACCOMPLISHMENTS:

David and Jonathan were men of faith and courage.

They loved each other unconditionally.

They demonstrated great perseverance in their friendship.

Jonathan was one of the great encouragers in the Bible.

LESSONS FROM THEIR LIVES:

Mutual commitment to God and unconditional love are vital ingredients in relationships.

Difficulties can test and strengthen relationships.

Encouragement vitalizes any relationship.

KEY VERSE:

"Saul's son Jonathan went to David at Horesh and helped him find strength in God" (23:16).

The story of David and Jonathan is told in 1 Samuel 18—31. It is remembered by David in 2 Samuel 1 and 9.

35In the morning Jonathan went out to the field for his meeting with David. He had a small boy with him, 36and he said to the boy, "Run and find the arrows I shoot." As the boy ran, he shot an arrow beyond him. 37When the boy came to the place where Jonathan's arrow had fallen, Jonathan called out after him, "Isn't the arrow beyond you?" 38Then he shouted, "Hurry! Go quickly! Don't stop!" The boy picked up the arrow and returned to his master. 39(The boy knew nothing of all this; only Jonathan and David knew.) 40Then Jonathan gave his weapons to the boy and said, "Go, carry them back to town."

41After the boy had gone, David got up from the south side ⌊of the stone⌋ and bowed down before Jonathan three times, with his face to the ground. Then they kissed each other and wept together—but David wept the most.

42Jonathan said to David, "Go in peace, for we have sworn friendship with each other in the name of the LORD, saying, 'The LORD is witness between you and me, and between your descendants and my descendants forever.' " Then David left, and Jonathan went back to the town.

David at Nob

21 David went to Nob, to Ahimelech the priest. Ahimelech trembled when he met him, and asked, "Why are you alone? Why is no one with you?"

2David answered Ahimelech the priest, "The king charged me with a certain matter and said to me, 'No one is to know anything about your mission and your instructions.' As for my men, I have told them to meet me at a certain place. 3Now then, what do you have on hand? Give me five loaves of bread, or whatever you can find."

4But the priest answered David, "I don't have any ordinary bread on hand; however, there is some consecrated bread here—provided the men have kept themselves from women."

5David replied, "Indeed women have been kept from us, as usual whenever[a] I set out. The men's things[b] are holy even on missions that are not holy. How much more so today!" 6So the priest gave him the consecrated bread, since there was no bread there except the bread of the Presence that had been removed from before the LORD and replaced by hot bread on the day it was taken away.

7Now one of Saul's servants was there that day, detained before the LORD; he was Doeg the Edomite, Saul's head shepherd.

8David asked Ahimelech, "Don't you have a spear or a sword here? I haven't brought my sword or any other weapon, because the king's business was urgent."

9The priest replied, "The sword of Goliath the Philistine, whom you killed in the Valley of Elah, is here; it is wrapped in a cloth behind the ephod. If you want it, take it; there is no sword here but that one."

David said, "There is none like it; give it to me."

David at Gath

10That day David fled from Saul and went to Achish king of Gath. 11But the servants of Achish said to him, "Isn't this David, the king of the land? Isn't he the one they sing about in their dances:

" 'Saul has slain his thousands,
and David his tens of thousands'?"

12David took these words to heart and was very much afraid of Achish king of Gath. 13So he pretended to be insane in their presence; and while he was in their hands he acted like a madman, making marks on the doors of the gate and letting saliva run down his beard.

14Achish said to his servants, "Look at the man! He is insane! Why bring him to me? 15Am I so short of madmen that you have to bring this fellow here to carry on like this in front of me? Must this man come into my house?"

David at Adullam and Mizpah

22 David left Gath and escaped to the cave of Adullam. When his brothers and his father's household heard about it, they went down to him there. 2All those who were in distress or in debt or discontented gathered around him, and he became their leader. About four hundred men were with him.

3From there David went to Mizpah in Moab and said to the king of Moab, "Would you let my father and mother come and stay with you until I learn what God will do for me?" 4So he left them with the king of Moab, and they stayed with him as long as David was in the stronghold.

5But the prophet Gad said to David, "Do not stay in the stronghold. Go into the land of Judah." So David left and went to the forest of Hereth.

Saul Kills the Priests of Nob

6Now Saul heard that David and his men had been discovered. And Saul, spear in hand, was

[a]5 Or *from us in the past few days since* [b]5 Or *bodies*

21:1–2 The book of Proverbs tells us: "There are six things the LORD hates, seven that are detestable to him: haughty eyes, a lying tongue, hands that shed innocent blood, a heart that devises wicked schemes, feet that are quick to rush into evil, a false witness who pours out lies and a man who stirs up dissension among brothers" (Proverbs 6:16–19). In his encounter with Ahimelech, David revealed that he, too, was vulnerable to sin. David lied, and this single lie led to others (see 21:9–15). This seemingly small falsehood, even though spoken for a good cause, proved costly—eighty-five innocent priests lost their lives (see 22:18–20). God values honesty. Minor indiscretions can have devastating effects on the lives of others, especially the people closest to us (see Ephesians 4:25).

seated under the tamarisk tree on the hill at Gibeah, with all his officials standing around him. 7Saul said to them, "Listen, men of Benjamin! Will the son of Jesse give all of you fields and vineyards? Will he make all of you commanders of thousands and commanders of hundreds? 8Is that why you have all conspired against me? No one tells me when my son makes a covenant with the son of Jesse. None of you is concerned about me or tells me that my son has incited my servant to lie in wait for me, as he does today."

9But Doeg the Edomite, who was standing with Saul's officials, said, "I saw the son of Jesse come to Ahimelech son of Ahitub at Nob. 10Ahimelech inquired of the LORD for him; he also gave him provisions and the sword of Goliath the Philistine."

11Then the king sent for the priest Ahimelech son of Ahitub and his father's whole family, who were the priests at Nob, and they all came to the king. 12Saul said, "Listen now, son of Ahitub."

"Yes, my lord," he answered.

13Saul said to him, "Why have you conspired against me, you and the son of Jesse, giving him bread and a sword and inquiring of God for him, so that he has rebelled against me and lies in wait for me, as he does today?"

14Ahimelech answered the king, "Who of all your servants is as loyal as David, the king's son-in-law, captain of your bodyguard and highly respected in your household? 15Was that day the first time I inquired of God for him? Of course not! Let not the king accuse your servant or any of his father's family, for your servant knows nothing at all about this whole affair."

16But the king said, "You will surely die, Ahimelech, you and your father's whole family."

17Then the king ordered the guards at his side: "Turn and kill the priests of the LORD, because they too have sided with David. They knew he was fleeing, yet they did not tell me."

But the king's officials were not willing to raise a hand to strike the priests of the LORD.

18The king then ordered Doeg, "You turn and strike down the priests." So Doeg the Edomite turned and struck them down. That day he killed eighty-five men who wore the linen ephod. 19He also put to the sword Nob, the town of the priests, with its men and women, its children and infants, and its cattle, donkeys and sheep.

20But Abiathar, a son of Ahimelech son of Ahitub, escaped and fled to join David. 21He told David that Saul had killed the priests of the LORD. 22Then David said to Abiathar: "That day, when Doeg the Edomite was there, I knew he would be sure to tell Saul. I am responsible for the death of your father's whole family. 23Stay with me; don't be afraid; the man who is seeking your life is seeking mine also. You will be safe with me."

David Saves Keilah

23 When David was told, "Look, the Philistines are fighting against Keilah and are looting the threshing floors," 2he inquired of the LORD, saying, "Shall I go and attack these Philistines?"

The LORD answered him, "Go, attack the Philistines and save Keilah."

3But David's men said to him, "Here in Judah we are afraid. How much more, then, if we go to Keilah against the Philistine forces!"

4Once again David inquired of the LORD, and the LORD answered him, "Go down to Keilah, for I am going to give the Philistines into your hand." 5So David and his men went to Keilah, fought the Philistines and carried off their livestock. He inflicted heavy losses on the Philistines and saved the people of Keilah. 6(Now Abiathar son of Ahimelech had brought the ephod down with him when he fled to David at Keilah.)

Saul Pursues David

7Saul was told that David had gone to Keilah, and he said, "God has handed him over to me, for David has imprisoned himself by entering a town with gates and bars." 8And Saul called up all his forces for battle, to go down to Keilah to besiege David and his men.

9When David learned that Saul was plotting against him, he said to Abiathar the priest, "Bring the ephod." 10David said, "O LORD, God of Israel, your servant has heard definitely that Saul plans to come to Keilah and destroy the town on account of me. 11Will the citizens of Keilah surrender me to him? Will Saul come down, as your servant has heard? O LORD, God of Israel, tell your servant."

And the LORD said, "He will."

12Again David asked, "Will the citizens of Keilah surrender me and my men to Saul?"

22:16–18 The priests in this passage were the innocent victims of Saul's mental illness, David's lie and Doeg's desire to be accepted. David's seemingly inconsequential lie was the catalyst for the sins of others. David's lie provided Saul with the opportunity to act without restraint. This small lie granted Doeg the chance to muster some attention. Sometimes the lies we tell combine with the failures of others to bring great suffering to innocent people. In such times, telling the truth will often put a stop to the sins of other people rather than perpetuating or compounding them. Honesty is always the best policy.

23:1–9 David repeatedly looked to God for direction in his life and had grown accustomed to trusting God for direction during times of crisis. When God commanded David to lead his men against the Philistines at Keilah, David's men were afraid to act on that command. David went to God a second time, and God affirmed his first command. He also added a reassuring message: "I am going to give the Philistines into your hand" (23:4). Like David and his men, we may respond with fear to God's direction. But we can be sure that when God tells us to do something, he will stand by us each step of the way and help us gain the victory.

And the LORD said, "They will."

13So David and his men, about six hundred in number, left Keilah and kept moving from place to place. When Saul was told that David had escaped from Keilah, he did not go there.

14David stayed in the desert strongholds and in the hills of the Desert of Ziph. Day after day Saul searched for him, but God did not give David into his hands.

15While David was at Horesh in the Desert of Ziph, he learned that Saul had come out to take his life. 16And Saul's son Jonathan went to David at Horesh and helped him find strength in God. 17"Don't be afraid," he said. "My father Saul will not lay a hand on you. You will be king over Israel, and I will be second to you. Even my father Saul knows this." 18The two of them made a covenant before the LORD. Then Jonathan went home, but David remained at Horesh.

19The Ziphites went up to Saul at Gibeah and said, "Is not David hiding among us in the strongholds at Horesh, on the hill of Hakilah, south of Jeshimon? 20Now, O king, come down whenever it pleases you to do so, and we will be responsible for handing him over to the king."

21Saul replied, "The LORD bless you for your concern for me. 22Go and make further preparation. Find out where David usually goes and who has seen him there. They tell me he is very crafty. 23Find out about all the hiding places he uses and come back to me with definite information.[a] Then I will go with you; if he is in the area, I will track him down among all the clans of Judah."

24So they set out and went to Ziph ahead of Saul. Now David and his men were in the Desert of Maon, in the Arabah south of Jeshimon. 25Saul and his men began the search, and when David was told about it, he went down to the rock and stayed in the Desert of Maon. When Saul heard this, he went into the Desert of Maon in pursuit of David.

26Saul was going along one side of the mountain, and David and his men were on the other side, hurrying to get away from Saul. As Saul and his forces were closing in on David and his men to capture them, 27a messenger came to Saul, saying, "Come quickly! The Philistines are raiding the land." 28Then Saul broke off his pursuit of David and went to meet the Philistines. That is why they call this place Sela Hammahlekoth.[b] 29And David went up from there and lived in the strongholds of En Gedi.

David Spares Saul's Life

24 After Saul returned from pursuing the Philistines, he was told, "David is in the Desert of En Gedi." 2So Saul took three thousand chosen men from all Israel and set out to look for David and his men near the Crags of the Wild Goats.

3He came to the sheep pens along the way; a cave was there, and Saul went in to relieve himself. David and his men were far back in the cave. 4The men said, "This is the day the LORD spoke of when he said[c] to you, 'I will give your enemy into your hands for you to deal with as you wish.' " Then David crept up unnoticed and cut off a corner of Saul's robe.

5Afterward, David was conscience-stricken for having cut off a corner of his robe. 6He said to his men, "The LORD forbid that I should do such a thing to my master, the LORD's anointed, or lift my hand against him; for he is the anointed of the LORD." 7With these words David rebuked his men and did not allow them to attack Saul. And Saul left the cave and went his way.

8Then David went out of the cave and called out to Saul, "My lord the king!" When Saul looked behind him, David bowed down and prostrated himself with his face to the ground. 9He said to Saul, "Why do you listen when men say, 'David is bent on harming you'? 10This day you have seen with your own eyes how the LORD delivered you into my hands in the cave. Some urged me to kill you, but I spared you; I said, 'I will not lift my hand against my master, because he is the LORD's anointed.' 11See, my father, look at this piece of your robe in my hand! I cut off the corner of your robe but did not kill you. Now understand and recognize that I am not guilty of wrongdoing or rebellion. I have not wronged you, but you are hunting me down to take my life. 12May the LORD judge between you and me. And may the LORD avenge the wrongs you have done to me, but my hand

[a]23 Or *me at Nacon* [b]28 *Sela Hammahlekoth* means *rock of parting.* [c]4 Or *"Today the LORD is saying*

23:14–15 The wonderful phrase "but God did not give David into his hands" must not be overlooked. Saul pursued David, but God protected, provided for and preserved David's life. During the difficult years of running from Saul, David might have felt alone and abandoned by God. But here we see that God was working to protect David throughout that time. When things look bad for us, God is with us too, protecting us in ways we may never know. God is indeed worthy of our confidence and trust.

23:16–18 Once Jonathan had located David, he encouraged him to find his strength in God. Jonathan was aware of the fearsome difficulties that David faced, but he also knew that God was equal to the task. We often face problems too big for us to handle alone, but God is bigger than the worst of our problems. When others face troubling times, we can always do what Jonathan did for David; we can remind them that God is with them and that he is greater than any problem they might face.

24:4–6 David refused to follow his men's advice to kill Saul. Even the small act of cutting off a piece of Saul's robe troubled David's conscience. Despite all that had happened, David's respect for the king and his position remained intact. David wisely restrained himself despite the temptation of the situation and Saul's obvious vulnerability. David's intelligent response suggests two principles vital to spiritual growth: (1) We need to be careful to assess the advice we are given by the people around us. (2) Our conscience must be in tune with God's desires for a situation, even if it is not what may be the easy way out.

THE SPIRITUAL DISCIPLINES

Spiritual Friendship

Friends for Life

1 Samuel 23:14–18 David and Jonathan were friends for life. This is not simply a description of the duration of their relationship, but an explanation of the quality of it as well. They were channels of life to one another. A spiritual friend listens without judging, gets under your load to share its weight, keeps your confidences, recalls for you both how you have made it through other tough times and reminds you that God is ultimately in control. Such was the friendship of David and Jonathan.

Three elements of their friendship fueled David's and Jonathan's spiritual lives. First, they were vulnerable with each other in times of need. David was initially a favorite of Saul's court. But then he was anointed king and suddenly became an outcast with little hope that God's promise of kingship could ever be fulfilled. Jonathan found himself in a labyrinth of difficult decisions. He had no idea how far his father would actually go in his vendetta against David. Yet how was he to live as the child of the king—the heir apparent—caught in the maze of conflicting loyalties? How could he betray his father by supporting David? Yet how could he go against his closest friend? Both David and Jonathan found their way through these dilemmas because of the gift of spiritual friendship—a friendship between those who could have been chief rivals! They shared their concerns with each other and encouraged each other to trust in the Lord and his promises.

A second vital element of David and Jonathan's friendship was their willingness to take risks for one another. In chapter 20, Jonathan risked his father's rage in order to discover Saul's plans against David. Then Jonathan warned David of the impending danger. In a similar manner, David refused to kill Saul when he had the chance. Though he stated that his refusal to kill Saul was because Saul was God's anointed (24:10), David's choice to spare Saul may have also been reinforced by his commitment to Jonathan. David chose to live with the risk of being caught by Saul rather than kill his best friend's father.

Third, David and Jonathan counted each other better than themselves. There are few more graphic pictures of this than Jonathan's surrender of his robe, his armor and his position to David (18:1–4). "You will be king over Israel, and I will be second to you," Jonathan tells David (23:17). His statement reminds us of Paul's words, "Do nothing out of selfish ambition or vain conceit, but in humility consider others better than yourselves" (Philippians 2:3).

David and Jonathan's friendship outlasted death. After Jonathan and Saul were killed in battle, David continued to honor Jonathan by caring for Jonathan's son Mephibosheth (2 Samuel 9:1–13).

Our spiritual health is greatly enhanced by maintaining at least one relationship that approaches this level of love and spiritual care. It is a costly commitment. The only thing more costly is *not* having such a friend.

Putting It Into Practice

David and Jonathan made a covenant to undergird and support their friendship (1 Samuel 18:1–3). We aren't given the specifics of the covenant, but it certainly included their commitment to God and to each other—no matter what. Think for a moment how you would establish a covenant of spiritual friendship. What would you commit to and why? Do you know anyone with whom you could make this covenant? Consider taking steps to initiate this sort of friendship with that person.

For more on spiritual friendship, turn to Matthew 18.

will not touch you. 13As the old saying goes, 'From evildoers come evil deeds,' so my hand will not touch you.

14"Against whom has the king of Israel come out? Whom are you pursuing? A dead dog? A flea? 15May the LORD be our judge and decide between us. May he consider my cause and uphold it; may he vindicate me by delivering me from your hand."

16When David finished saying this, Saul asked, "Is that your voice, David my son?" And he wept aloud. 17"You are more righteous than I," he said. "You have treated me well, but I have treated you badly. 18You have just now told me of the good you did to me; the LORD delivered me into your hands, but you did not kill me. 19When a man finds his enemy, does he let him get away unharmed? May the LORD reward you well for the way you treated me today. 20I know that you will surely be king and that the kingdom of Israel will be established in your hands. 21Now swear to me by the LORD that you will not cut off my descendants or wipe out my name from my father's family."

22So David gave his oath to Saul. Then Saul returned home, but David and his men went up to the stronghold.

David, Nabal and Abigail

25 Now Samuel died, and all Israel assembled and mourned for him; and they buried him at his home in Ramah.

Then David moved down into the Desert of Maon.[a] 2A certain man in Maon, who had property there at Carmel, was very wealthy. He had a thousand goats and three thousand sheep, which he was shearing in Carmel. 3His name was Nabal and his wife's name was Abigail. She was an intelligent and beautiful woman, but her husband, a Calebite, was surly and mean in his dealings.

4While David was in the desert, he heard that Nabal was shearing sheep. 5So he sent ten young men and said to them, "Go up to Nabal at Carmel and greet him in my name. 6Say to him: 'Long life to you! Good health to you and your household! And good health to all that is yours!

7" 'Now I hear that it is sheep-shearing time. When your shepherds were with us, we did not mistreat them, and the whole time they were at Carmel nothing of theirs was missing. 8Ask your own servants and they will tell you. Therefore be favorable toward my young men, since we come at a festive time. Please give your servants and your son David whatever you can find for them.' "

9When David's men arrived, they gave Nabal this message in David's name. Then they waited.

10Nabal answered David's servants, "Who is this David? Who is this son of Jesse? Many servants are breaking away from their masters these days. 11Why should I take my bread and water, and the meat I have slaughtered for my shearers, and give it to men coming from who knows where?"

12David's men turned around and went back. When they arrived, they reported every word. 13David said to his men, "Put on your swords!" So they put on their swords, and David put on his. About four hundred men went up with David, while two hundred stayed with the supplies.

14One of the servants told Nabal's wife Abigail: "David sent messengers from the desert to give our master his greetings, but he hurled insults at them. 15Yet these men were very good to us. They did not mistreat us, and the whole time we were out in the fields near them nothing was missing. 16Night and day they were a wall around us all the time we were herding our sheep near them. 17Now think it over and see what you can do, because disaster is hanging over our master and his whole household. He is such a wicked man that no one can talk to him."

18Abigail lost no time. She took two hundred loaves of bread, two skins of wine, five dressed sheep, five seahs[b] of roasted grain, a hundred cakes of raisins and two hundred cakes of pressed figs, and loaded them on donkeys. 19Then she told her servants, "Go on ahead; I'll follow you." But she did not tell her husband Nabal.

20As she came riding her donkey into a mountain ravine, there were David and his men descending toward her, and she met them. 21David had just said, "It's been useless—all my watching over this fellow's property in the desert so that nothing of his was missing. He has paid me back evil for good. 22May God deal with David,[c] be it ever so severely, if by morning I leave alive one male of all who belong to him!"

23When Abigail saw David, she quickly got off her donkey and bowed down before David with her face to the ground. 24She fell at his feet and said: "My lord, let the blame be on me alone. Please let your servant speak to you; hear what your servant has to say. 25May my lord pay no attention to that wicked man Nabal. He is

[a] 1 Some Septuagint manuscripts; Hebrew *Paran*
[b] 18 That is, probably about a bushel (about 37 liters)
[c] 22 Some Septuagint manuscripts; Hebrew *with David's enemies*

25:12–13 Though sometimes David appears to be a model of self-restraint, we see here that he was capable of giving in to impatience. In reacting to Nabal's offensive behavior, David failed to consult with God before taking action. David made a hasty decision while he was still angry and upset. Such impulsiveness frequently results in mistakes with long-term consequences. God provided Abigail's intervention to prevent David from acting unwisely (see 25:32). When we are angry and tempted to act impulsively, we would be wise to calm down and listen to what God is saying to us.

just like his name—his name is Fool, and folly
goes with him. But as for me, your servant, I did
not see the men my master sent.
26"Now since the LORD has kept you, my
master, from bloodshed and from avenging
yourself with your own hands, as surely as the
LORD lives and as you live, may your enemies
and all who intend to harm my master be like
Nabal. 27And let this gift, which your servant
has brought to my master, be given to the men
who follow you. 28Please forgive your servant's
offense, for the LORD will certainly make a lasting dynasty for my master, because he fights the
LORD's battles. Let no wrongdoing be found in
you as long as you live. 29Even though someone
is pursuing you to take your life, the life of my
master will be bound securely in the bundle of
the living by the LORD your God. But the lives
of your enemies he will hurl away as from the
pocket of a sling. 30When the LORD has done for
my master every good thing he promised concerning him and has appointed him leader over
Israel, 31my master will not have on his conscience the staggering burden of needless
bloodshed or of having avenged himself. And
when the LORD has brought my master success,
remember your servant."
32David said to Abigail, "Praise be to the
LORD, the God of Israel, who has sent you today
to meet me. 33May you be blessed for your good
judgment and for keeping me from bloodshed
this day and from avenging myself with my
own hands. 34Otherwise, as surely as the LORD,
the God of Israel, lives, who has kept me from
harming you, if you had not come quickly to
meet me, not one male belonging to Nabal
would have been left alive by daybreak."
35Then David accepted from her hand what
she had brought him and said, "Go home in
peace. I have heard your words and granted
your request."
36When Abigail went to Nabal, he was in the
house holding a banquet like that of a king. He
was in high spirits and very drunk. So she told
him nothing until daybreak. 37Then in the
morning, when Nabal was sober, his wife told
him all these things, and his heart failed him
and he became like a stone. 38About ten days
later, the LORD struck Nabal and he died.

25:36–38 The name *Nabal* means "fool," and in this passage Nabal demonstrated how appropriate his name was. His self-centered outlook kept him from fulfilling an act of common courtesy that was expected in ancient Israel. David and his band had protected Nabal and his herds from foreign marauders. It was expected that he would in return support David with some supplies. But Nabal lived for himself, satisfying his own appetites with little regard for others. His selfish bravado nearly resulted in the deaths of many innocent employees. It was only the intervention of his wife Abigail that prevented a disaster. Most of us have a little bit of Nabal inside us; we are a little foolish at times, making decisions that are destructive to us and to the people around us. As we reflect honestly on our spiritual lives, we must confess our foolish thoughts to God and ask him to give us his wisdom.

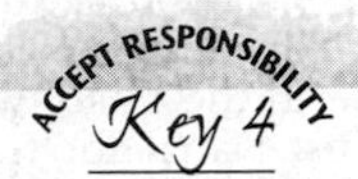

Making the Best of a Bad Situation

1 Samuel 25:18–39 There may be times when those close to us make wrong choices or act irresponsibly, creating a bad situation that threatens our welfare or spiritual growth. We are not responsible for their actions or the bad situation they create. However, we should protect ourselves and try to make the best of a bad situation.

Abigail is a good example of someone who took responsibility to make the best of a bad situation. Her husband Nabal (meaning "fool") was "surly and mean in his dealings" (25:3). Before David became king, Nabal insulted his troops to the point that David and his men were on their way to kill him and anyone who got in their way. However, with some fast thinking and fast talking, Abigail protected her family. She convinced David not to take vengeance into his own hands. A few weeks later Nabal was dead of natural (or perhaps supernatural) causes, and Abigail became David's wife.

We cannot always change other people; that is not our responsibility. But even when we can't change them, we can still make good choices in the midst of bad situations. We are not responsible for changing the character flaws of the people who affect our lives. Yet we should try to protect ourselves, as best we can, from the effects of their irresponsible behavior.

Turn to 2 Samuel 9.

39When David heard that Nabal was dead, he
said, "Praise be to the LORD, who has upheld
my cause against Nabal for treating me with
contempt. He has kept his servant from doing
wrong and has brought Nabal's wrongdoing
down on his own head."

Then David sent word to Abigail, asking her
to become his wife. 40His servants went to Carmel and said to Abigail, "David has sent us to
you to take you to become his wife."

41She bowed down with her face to the
ground and said, "Here is your maidservant,
ready to serve you and wash the feet of my
master's servants." 42Abigail quickly got on a
donkey and, attended by her five maids, went
with David's messengers and became his wife.
43David had also married Ahinoam of Jezreel,
and they both were his wives. 44But Saul had
given his daughter Michal, David's wife, to Paltiel[a] son of Laish, who was from Gallim.

David Again Spares Saul's Life

26 The Ziphites went to Saul at Gibeah
and said, "Is not David hiding on the
hill of Hakilah, which faces Jeshimon?"

2So Saul went down to the Desert of Ziph,
with his three thousand chosen men of Israel,
to search there for David. 3Saul made his camp
beside the road on the hill of Hakilah facing
Jeshimon, but David stayed in the desert. When
he saw that Saul had followed him there, 4he
sent out scouts and learned that Saul had definitely arrived.[b]

5Then David set out and went to the place
where Saul had camped. He saw where Saul and
Abner son of Ner, the commander of the army,
had lain down. Saul was lying inside the camp,
with the army encamped around him.

6David then asked Ahimelech the Hittite and
Abishai son of Zeruiah, Joab's brother, "Who
will go down into the camp with me to Saul?"

"I'll go with you," said Abishai.

7So David and Abishai went to the army by
night, and there was Saul, lying asleep inside
the camp with his spear stuck in the ground
near his head. Abner and the soldiers were lying
around him.

8Abishai said to David, "Today God has delivered your enemy into your hands. Now let
me pin him to the ground with one thrust of my
spear; I won't strike him twice."

9But David said to Abishai, "Don't destroy
him! Who can lay a hand on the LORD's anointed and be guiltless? 10As surely as the LORD
lives," he said, "the LORD himself will strike him;
either his time will come and he will die, or he
will go into battle and perish. 11But the LORD
forbid that I should lay a hand on the LORD's
anointed. Now get the spear and water jug that
are near his head, and let's go."

12So David took the spear and water jug near
Saul's head, and they left. No one saw or knew
about it, nor did anyone wake up. They were all
sleeping, because the LORD had put them into a
deep sleep.

13Then David crossed over to the other side
and stood on top of the hill some distance
away; there was a wide space between them.
14He called out to the army and to Abner son
of Ner, "Aren't you going to answer me, Abner?"

Abner replied, "Who are you who calls to the
king?"

15David said, "You're a man, aren't you? And
who is like you in Israel? Why didn't you guard
your lord the king? Someone came to destroy
your lord the king. 16What you have done is not
good. As surely as the LORD lives, you and your
men deserve to die, because you did not guard
your master, the LORD's anointed. Look around
you. Where are the king's spear and water jug
that were near his head?"

17Saul recognized David's voice and said, "Is
that your voice, David my son?"

David replied, "Yes it is, my lord the king."
18And he added, "Why is my lord pursuing his
servant? What have I done, and what wrong am
I guilty of? 19Now let my lord the king listen to
his servant's words. If the LORD has incited you
against me, then may he accept an offering. If,
however, men have done it, may they be cursed
before the LORD! They have now driven me
from my share in the LORD's inheritance and
have said, 'Go, serve other gods.' 20Now do not
let my blood fall to the ground far from the
presence of the LORD. The king of Israel has
come out to look for a flea—as one hunts a
partridge in the mountains."

21Then Saul said, "I have sinned. Come
back, David my son. Because you considered
my life precious today, I will not try to harm
you again. Surely I have acted like a fool and
have erred greatly."

22"Here is the king's spear," David answered.
"Let one of your young men come over and get
it. 23The LORD rewards every man for his righteousness and faithfulness. The LORD delivered
you into my hands today, but I would not lay

[a]44 Hebrew *Palti*, a variant of *Paltiel* [b]4 Or *had come to Nacon*

26:8–11 Even the advice of loyal friends can sometimes get us into trouble. Abishai recommended the murder of Saul, but David was unwilling to accept the consequences of assassinating God's chosen king (26:9–11). David wisely placed limits on the behavior of his men and left Saul alone. David recognized that Saul's judgment belonged in God's hands, and he wisely left it there. As we seek reconciliation with other people, we may need to give up our judgment of others and turn that job back to God. This relinquishment is an important step in the process of forgiveness and reconciliation.

26:17–21 Saul's words here are too little and too late. These words should have been uttered long before: "I have sinned . . . I have acted like a fool and have erred greatly" (26:21). Such honest admissions reflect the basis for repentance, forgiveness and reconciliation—keys to our ongoing spiritual renewal.

a hand on the LORD's anointed. 24As surely as I valued your life today, so may the LORD value my life and deliver me from all trouble."

25Then Saul said to David, "May you be blessed, my son David; you will do great things and surely triumph."

So David went on his way, and Saul returned home.

David Among the Philistines

27 But David thought to himself, "One of these days I will be destroyed by the hand of Saul. The best thing I can do is to escape to the land of the Philistines. Then Saul will give up searching for me anywhere in Israel, and I will slip out of his hand."

2So David and the six hundred men with him left and went over to Achish son of Maoch king of Gath. 3David and his men settled in Gath with Achish. Each man had his family with him, and David had his two wives: Ahinoam of Jezreel and Abigail of Carmel, the widow of Nabal. 4When Saul was told that David had fled to Gath, he no longer searched for him.

5Then David said to Achish, "If I have found favor in your eyes, let a place be assigned to me in one of the country towns, that I may live there. Why should your servant live in the royal city with you?"

6So on that day Achish gave him Ziklag, and it has belonged to the kings of Judah ever since. 7David lived in Philistine territory a year and four months.

8Now David and his men went up and raided the Geshurites, the Girzites and the Amalekites. (From ancient times these peoples had lived in the land extending to Shur and Egypt.) 9Whenever David attacked an area, he did not leave a man or woman alive, but took sheep and cattle, donkeys and camels, and clothes. Then he returned to Achish.

10When Achish asked, "Where did you go raiding today?" David would say, "Against the Negev of Judah" or "Against the Negev of Jerahmeel" or "Against the Negev of the Kenites." 11He did not leave a man or woman alive to be brought to Gath, for he thought, "They might inform on us and say, 'This is what David did.' " And such was his practice as long as he lived in Philistine territory. 12Achish trusted David and said to himself, "He has become so odious to his people, the Israelites, that he will be my servant forever."

Saul and the Witch of Endor

28 In those days the Philistines gathered their forces to fight against Israel. Achish said to David, "You must understand that you and your men will accompany me in the army."

2David said, "Then you will see for yourself what your servant can do."

Achish replied, "Very well, I will make you my bodyguard for life."

3Now Samuel was dead, and all Israel had mourned for him and buried him in his own town of Ramah. Saul had expelled the mediums and spiritists from the land.

4The Philistines assembled and came and set up camp at Shunem, while Saul gathered all the Israelites and set up camp at Gilboa. 5When Saul saw the Philistine army, he was afraid; terror filled his heart. 6He inquired of the LORD, but the LORD did not answer him by dreams or Urim or prophets. 7Saul then said to his attendants, "Find me a woman who is a medium, so I may go and inquire of her."

"There is one in Endor," they said.

8So Saul disguised himself, putting on other clothes, and at night he and two men went to the woman. "Consult a spirit for me," he said, "and bring up for me the one I name."

9But the woman said to him, "Surely you know what Saul has done. He has cut off the mediums and spiritists from the land. Why have you set a trap for my life to bring about my death?"

10Saul swore to her by the LORD, "As surely as the LORD lives, you will not be punished for this."

11Then the woman asked, "Whom shall I bring up for you?"

"Bring up Samuel," he said.

12When the woman saw Samuel, she cried out at the top of her voice and said to Saul, "Why have you deceived me? You are Saul!"

13The king said to her, "Don't be afraid. What do you see?"

27:1 David's fearful thoughts were not consistent with God's promises. David knew that God had a special plan for his life that included becoming king over Israel. Yet after years of running for his life, David seems to have become discouraged. Motivated by fear, he moved to the land of the Philistines and ended up in some compromising situations (see 28:1–2; 29:1–7). David should have persevered in his trust. God had protected him up to that point. He was perfectly capable of continuing his protection. We, too, may grow discouraged at times, but we must persevere and trust in all of God's promises.

28:1–2 Compromising our convictions often presents us with hard choices. David had left Israel to hide among the Philistines. Now he was reaping the consequences. Asked to join the Philistines in a battle against his own people, David had to deal with a difficult decision that he might never have had to face if he had only sought God's direction in the first place. When we make decisions without God and his Word in mind, we may end up in situations that could lead to our downfall. We need to keep God at the center of our decisions and carefully consider the consequences of our actions.

28:7–8 Saul's final act of rebellion involved witchcraft, which the Bible unequivocally condemns. In his desperation, Saul sought the guidance of spirits of the dead. Instead of finding help there, however, Saul's destruction was only confirmed. The world of Satan worship and occult practices will always bring trouble for those who practice them.

The woman said, "I see a spirit[a] coming up
out of the ground."
14"What does he look like?" he asked.
"An old man wearing a robe is coming up,"
she said.
Then Saul knew it was Samuel, and he
bowed down and prostrated himself with his
face to the ground.
15Samuel said to Saul, "Why have you disturbed me by bringing me up?"
"I am in great distress," Saul said. "The Philistines are fighting against me, and God has
turned away from me. He no longer answers
me, either by prophets or by dreams. So I have
called on you to tell me what to do."
16Samuel said, "Why do you consult me,
now that the LORD has turned away from you
and become your enemy? 17The LORD has done
what he predicted through me. The LORD has
torn the kingdom out of your hands and given
it to one of your neighbors—to David. 18Because
you did not obey the LORD or carry out his fierce
wrath against the Amalekites, the LORD has
done this to you today. 19The LORD will hand
over both Israel and you to the Philistines, and
tomorrow you and your sons will be with me.
The LORD will also hand over the army of Israel
to the Philistines."
20Immediately Saul fell full length on the
ground, filled with fear because of Samuel's
words. His strength was gone, for he had eaten
nothing all that day and night.
21When the woman came to Saul and saw
that he was greatly shaken, she said, "Look,
your maidservant has obeyed you. I took my
life in my hands and did what you told me to
do. 22Now please listen to your servant and let
me give you some food so you may eat and
have the strength to go on your way."
23He refused and said, "I will not eat."
But his men joined the woman in urging
him, and he listened to them. He got up from
the ground and sat on the couch.
24The woman had a fattened calf at the
house, which she butchered at once. She took
some flour, kneaded it and baked bread without yeast. 25Then she set it before Saul and his
men, and they ate. That same night they got up
and left.

Achish Sends David Back to Ziklag

29 The Philistines gathered all their forces
at Aphek, and Israel camped by the
spring in Jezreel. 2As the Philistine rulers
marched with their units of hundreds and thousands, David and his men were marching at the
rear with Achish. 3The commanders of the Philistines asked, "What about these Hebrews?"
Achish replied, "Is this not David, who was
an officer of Saul king of Israel? He has already
been with me for over a year, and from the day
he left Saul until now, I have found no fault in
him."
4But the Philistine commanders were angry
with him and said, "Send the man back, that he
may return to the place you assigned him. He
must not go with us into battle, or he will turn
against us during the fighting. How better could
he regain his master's favor than by taking the
heads of our own men? 5Isn't this the David
they sang about in their dances:

"'Saul has slain his thousands,
and David his tens of thousands'?"

6So Achish called David and said to him, "As
surely as the LORD lives, you have been reliable,
and I would be pleased to have you serve with
me in the army. From the day you came to me
until now, I have found no fault in you, but the
rulers don't approve of you. 7Turn back and go
in peace; do nothing to displease the Philistine
rulers."
8"But what have I done?" asked David.
"What have you found against your servant
from the day I came to you until now? Why
can't I go and fight against the enemies of my
lord the king?"
9Achish answered, "I know that you have
been as pleasing in my eyes as an angel of God;
nevertheless, the Philistine commanders have
said, 'He must not go up with us into battle.'
10Now get up early, along with your master's
servants who have come with you, and leave in
the morning as soon as it is light."
11So David and his men got up early in the
morning to go back to the land of the Philistines, and the Philistines went up to Jezreel.

David Destroys the Amalekites

30 David and his men reached Ziklag on
the third day. Now the Amalekites had
raided the Negev and Ziklag. They had attacked
Ziklag and burned it, 2and had taken captive the
women and all who were in it, both young and
old. They killed none of them, but carried them
off as they went on their way.
3When David and his men came to Ziklag,
they found it destroyed by fire and their wives

[a] 13 Or *see spirits;* or *see gods*

29:1–10 David's move to Philistia was a compromising one. His safety there depended on his relationship with King Achish, who asked David to fight against his own people, the Israelites. In this passage Achish released David from his service. God delivered David from the consequences of his earlier, impulsive decision. God's love is great! He often provides us with a way to escape difficult circumstances, even those of our own making (see 1 Corinthians 10:13). But remember this: When God provides the way for us to escape a compromising situation, it is our responsibility to take it.

30:1–6 During David's time away from Ziklag, marauders had come and destroyed the city and kidnapped the families of David and his men. In this crisis, David shows us where to go for direction and hope: "But David found strength in the LORD his God" (30:6). David knew where to go in a crisis. Surrendering our lives to God, no matter how dire our circumstances, is always the right choice.

and sons and daughters taken captive. 4So David and his men wept aloud until they had no strength left to weep. 5David's two wives had been captured—Ahinoam of Jezreel and Abigail, the widow of Nabal of Carmel. 6David was greatly distressed because the men were talking of stoning him; each one was bitter in spirit because of his sons and daughters. But David found strength in the LORD his God.

7Then David said to Abiathar the priest, the son of Ahimelech, "Bring me the ephod." Abiathar brought it to him, 8and David inquired of the LORD, "Shall I pursue this raiding party? Will I overtake them?"

"Pursue them," he answered. "You will certainly overtake them and succeed in the rescue."

9David and the six hundred men with him came to the Besor Ravine, where some stayed behind, 10for two hundred men were too exhausted to cross the ravine. But David and four hundred men continued the pursuit.

11They found an Egyptian in a field and brought him to David. They gave him water to drink and food to eat— 12part of a cake of pressed figs and two cakes of raisins. He ate and was revived, for he had not eaten any food or drunk any water for three days and three nights.

13David asked him, "To whom do you belong, and where do you come from?"

He said, "I am an Egyptian, the slave of an Amalekite. My master abandoned me when I became ill three days ago. 14We raided the Negev of the Kerethites and the territory belonging to Judah and the Negev of Caleb. And we burned Ziklag."

15David asked him, "Can you lead me down to this raiding party?"

He answered, "Swear to me before God that you will not kill me or hand me over to my master, and I will take you down to them."

16He led David down, and there they were, scattered over the countryside, eating, drinking and reveling because of the great amount of plunder they had taken from the land of the Philistines and from Judah. 17David fought them from dusk until the evening of the next day, and none of them got away, except four hundred young men who rode off on camels and fled. 18David recovered everything the Amalekites had taken, including his two wives. 19Nothing was missing: young or old, boy or girl, plunder or anything else they had taken. David brought everything back. 20He took all the flocks and herds, and his men drove them ahead of the other livestock, saying, "This is David's plunder."

21Then David came to the two hundred men who had been too exhausted to follow him and who were left behind at the Besor Ravine. They came out to meet David and the people with him. As David and his men approached, he greeted them. 22But all the evil men and troublemakers among David's followers said, "Because they did not go out with us, we will not share with them the plunder we recovered. However, each man may take his wife and children and go."

23David replied, "No, my brothers, you must not do that with what the LORD has given us. He has protected us and handed over to us the forces that came against us. 24Who will listen to what you say? The share of the man who stayed with the supplies is to be the same as that of him who went down to the battle. All will share alike." 25David made this a statute and ordinance for Israel from that day to this.

26When David arrived in Ziklag, he sent some of the plunder to the elders of Judah, who were his friends, saying, "Here is a present for you from the plunder of the LORD's enemies."

27He sent it to those who were in Bethel, Ramoth Negev and Jattir; 28to those in Aroer, Siphmoth, Eshtemoa 29and Racal; to those in the towns of the Jerahmeelites and the Kenites; 30to those in Hormah, Bor Ashan, Athach 31and Hebron; and to those in all the other places where David and his men had roamed.

Saul Takes His Life

31 Now the Philistines fought against Israel; the Israelites fled before them, and many fell slain on Mount Gilboa. 2The Philistines pressed hard after Saul and his sons, and they killed his sons Jonathan, Abinadab and Malki-Shua. 3The fighting grew fierce around Saul, and when the archers overtook him, they wounded him critically.

4Saul said to his armor-bearer, "Draw your sword and run me through, or these uncircumcised fellows will come and run me through and abuse me."

But his armor-bearer was terrified and would not do it; so Saul took his own sword and fell on it. 5When the armor-bearer saw that Saul was dead, he too fell on his sword and died with him. 6So Saul and his three sons and his armor-bearer and all his men died together that same day.

7When the Israelites along the valley and those across the Jordan saw that the Israelite army had fled and that Saul and his sons had died, they abandoned their towns and fled. And the Philistines came and occupied them.

8The next day, when the Philistines came to strip the dead, they found Saul and his three sons fallen on Mount Gilboa. 9They cut off his head and stripped off his armor, and they sent

---

31:3–4 Suicide was the tragic end for this man who never learned to repent. Saul's life didn't have to end this way. If Saul had admitted his sins, accepted responsibility for his disobedience to God and asked God to change him, he could have come to a noble end. One key to Saul's downfall is that he was never fully accountable to God or to others. He relied only on himself. As a result, Saul's life stands as a monument to squandered potential. Saul's tragic end should give us ample reason to embrace God's plan for spiritual renewal.

messengers throughout the land of the Philistines to proclaim the news in the temple of their
idols and among their people. 10They put his
armor in the temple of the Ashtoreths and fastened his body to the wall of Beth Shan.
11When the people of Jabesh Gilead heard of
what the Philistines had done to Saul, 12all their
valiant men journeyed through the night to
Beth Shan. They took down the bodies of Saul
and his sons from the wall of Beth Shan and
went to Jabesh, where they burned them.
13Then they took their bones and buried them
under a tamarisk tree at Jabesh, and they fasted
seven days.

2 SAMUEL

The Big Picture

The book of 2 Samuel tells the story of King David, one of the most notable people in the Bible. In the opening verses of the book, David received word that both Jonathan and Saul had been killed in battle. The Israelite army had fled in defeat, and thousands of the soldiers were dead or wounded on the battlefield. Samuel, a prophet and David's mentor, was no longer around to give him comfort or advice. David had lost most of the people he had depended on. Yet in the wake of such losses, life for David was just beginning.

In spite of his grief, David brilliantly managed the kingdom's affairs after Saul's death. David demonstrated patience and kindness toward the northern tribes during the reign of Ishbosheth. He wisely established the capital in Jerusalem, a neutral city. He brought the ark of God back to Jerusalem. And his victories over the Philistines led to further consolidation of the kingdom.

Unfortunately, David did not do as well at managing the affairs of his family or his heart. Despite his political success, he made some terrible personal mistakes. He fell into adultery and murder, which later resulted in incest and rebellion within his own family. And these sins all led to the near destruction of David's family and the kingdom he had so skillfully built.

Yet God did not allow David's mistakes to completely destroy the nation of Israel. God sent the prophet Nathan to confront David with his sins and hold him accountable for them. In this way Nathan helped David accept responsibility for his actions and redirect his course to follow God's plan. David was humble and willing to accept God's word of correction. He was willing to learn from his mistakes. For the rest of his life David continued to look to God for strength and help.

A. DAVID'S TRIUMPHS (1:1–10:19)

1. Reigning in Hebron Over Judah (1:1–4:12)
2. Reigning in Jerusalem Over All Israel (5:1–10:19)

B. DAVID'S TROUBLES (11:1–12:31)

1. David's Sexual Sin (11:1-27)
2. Nathan's Intervention by Confrontation (12:1-31)

C. THE CONSEQUENCES OF DAVID'S SINS (13:1–20:26)

1. The Serious Problems in David's Family (13:1–18:33)
2. The Problems in David's Kingdom (19:1–20:26)

D. CONCLUSION (21:1–24:25)

1. Famine and War (21:1-22)
2. David's Song (22:1-51)
3. David's Tribute (23:1-39)
4. David's Final Failure and Restoration (24:1-25)

Spiritual Renewal Themes

SPIRITUAL RENEWAL FOLLOWS FAILURE

There is life after failure; David's biography proves that fact. His list of sins included murder, adultery and the neglect of his family (see 1 Timothy 5:8). If anyone should have been written off in God's plan, it was David. But David's important place in history proves that God uses fallible people to work out his will. God's grace is more than adequate for even the greatest of our sins and failures.

Essential Facts

PURPOSE:
To record the history of King David, who, despite his personal failings, was a man who sought God.

AUTHOR:
Unknown, though it includes writings from the prophets Nathan and Gad.

AUDIENCE:
The people of Israel.

DATE WRITTEN:
Sometime after David's death, around 930 B.C.

SETTING:
The land of Israel.

KEY VERSES:
"King David went in and sat before the LORD, and he said, 'Who am I, O Sovereign LORD, and what is my family, that you have brought me this far? And as if this were not enough in your sight, O Sovereign LORD, you have also spoken about the future of the house of your servant'" (7:18-19).

KEY PLACES:
Hebron, Jerusalem, Bahurim, Mahanaim.

KEY PEOPLE AND RELATIONSHIPS:
David with Joab, Abner, Michal, Bathsheba, Nathan, Amnon, Absalom, Mephibosheth.

JUSTICE WITH MERCY

As a leader, David was just, and his justice was tempered with mercy. David demonstrated this when he refused to strike back at Saul even while being chased by him. He revealed it when he punished the murderers of Abner and Ish-bosheth even though Abner and Ish-bosheth had been David's own enemies. David never rejoiced in wrongdoing—even when it brought him personal advantage. When David himself sinned, he accepted God's judgment as right and just. David's attitudes and actions were grounded in his relationship with a just and merciful God. God had been fair with him, so David was fair with his people. God had been merciful toward him, so David dispensed mercy freely to others.

ACCEPTING REALITY

When Nathan confronted David about his sin, David saw the truth, confessed his sin and accepted responsibility for his actions. When reminded of the consequences of his sin, David repented with heartfelt sorrow. The secret to David's spiritual growth was his dependence on God and his ability to accept the truth about his sin. Our spiritual renewal also starts with our willingness to accept the reality of our sinfulness. We need to acknowledge God's reign and our great need for him.

THE SERIOUSNESS OF SIN

David did not get away with his sin; his sin brought about serious consequences. The baby born to David and Bathsheba died soon after its birth. Within David's own family, incest was followed by murder. David's favorite son, Absalom, rebelled against his father and was killed by David's own men. David had experienced the joy of God's blessing. But he also endured the depths of sorrow that resulted from his sins.

David Hears of Saul's Death

1 After the death of Saul, David returned
from defeating the Amalekites and stayed
in Ziklag two days. 2On the third day a man
arrived from Saul's camp, with his clothes torn
and with dust on his head. When he came to
David, he fell to the ground to pay him honor.
3"Where have you come from?" David asked
him.

He answered, "I have escaped from the Israelite camp."

4"What happened?" David asked. "Tell me."
He said, "The men fled from the battle.
Many of them fell and died. And Saul and his
son Jonathan are dead."
5Then David said to the young man who
brought him the report, "How do you know
that Saul and his son Jonathan are dead?"
6"I happened to be on Mount Gilboa," the
young man said, "and there was Saul, leaning
on his spear, with the chariots and riders almost
upon him. 7When he turned around and saw
me, he called out to me, and I said, 'What can
I do?'
8"He asked me, 'Who are you?'

" 'An Amalekite,' I answered.

9"Then he said to me, 'Stand over me and
kill me! I am in the throes of death, but I'm still
alive.'
10"So I stood over him and killed him, because I knew that after he had fallen he could
not survive. And I took the crown that was on
his head and the band on his arm and have
brought them here to my lord."
11Then David and all the men with him took
hold of their clothes and tore them. 12They
mourned and wept and fasted till evening for
Saul and his son Jonathan, and for the army of
the LORD and the house of Israel, because they
had fallen by the sword.
13David said to the young man who brought
him the report, "Where are you from?"

"I am the son of an alien, an Amalekite," he answered.

14David asked him, "Why were you not
afraid to lift your hand to destroy the LORD's
anointed?"
15Then David called one of his men and said,
"Go, strike him down!" So he struck him down,
and he died. 16For David had said to him,
"Your blood be on your own head. Your own
mouth testified against you when you said, 'I
killed the LORD's anointed.' "

David's Lament for Saul and Jonathan

17David took up this lament concerning Saul
and his son Jonathan, 18and ordered that the
men of Judah be taught this lament of the bow
(it is written in the Book of Jashar):

19"Your glory, O Israel, lies slain on your heights.
How the mighty have fallen!
20"Tell it not in Gath,
proclaim it not in the streets of Ashkelon,
lest the daughters of the Philistines be glad,
lest the daughters of the uncircumcised rejoice.

21"O mountains of Gilboa,
may you have neither dew nor rain,
nor fields that yield offerings ⌞of grain⌟.
For there the shield of the mighty was defiled,
the shield of Saul—no longer rubbed with oil.
22From the blood of the slain,
from the flesh of the mighty,
the bow of Jonathan did not turn back,
the sword of Saul did not return unsatisfied.

23"Saul and Jonathan—
in life they were loved and gracious,
and in death they were not parted.
They were swifter than eagles,
they were stronger than lions.

24"O daughters of Israel,
weep for Saul,
who clothed you in scarlet and finery,
who adorned your garments with ornaments of gold.

25"How the mighty have fallen in battle!
Jonathan lies slain on your heights.
26I grieve for you, Jonathan my brother;
you were very dear to me.
Your love for me was wonderful,
more wonderful than that of women.

27"How the mighty have fallen!
The weapons of war have perished!"

David Anointed King Over Judah

2 In the course of time, David inquired of the
LORD. "Shall I go up to one of the towns of
Judah?" he asked.

1:8–10 The record of Saul's suicide in 1 Samuel 31:4 raises a question about the truth of the Amalekite's claims. More than likely, the man was lying in hopes of receiving a reward from David. He did receive a reward of sorts—death. Deceit is a harbinger of disaster; honesty is always the best policy.

1:11–27 David and his men's honest outpouring of grief over the deaths of Saul, Jonathan and the other men of Israel was no sign of weakness. Instead, it indicated the love, respect and sorrow they felt for their fellow Israelites. God desires sincere expressions of emotion, and releasing them can be very healthy for us. We don't need to be afraid of expressing our emotions.

2:1–11 We often make our greatest mistakes in situations in which we are eager to act. After years as a fugitive, David must have burned with excitement at the thought of finally assuming Israel's throne. Yet he waited to take charge of the northern Israelite tribes at a later time. He listened to God's instructions and became the king of only one tribe—Judah. We would be wise to learn from David's patience and trust God's timing and plan.

The LORD said, "Go up."
David asked, "Where shall I go?"
"To Hebron," the LORD answered.

2So David went up there with his two wives, Ahinoam of Jezreel and Abigail, the widow of Nabal of Carmel. 3David also took the men who were with him, each with his family, and they settled in Hebron and its towns. 4Then the men of Judah came to Hebron and there they anointed David king over the house of Judah.

When David was told that it was the men of Jabesh Gilead who had buried Saul, 5he sent messengers to the men of Jabesh Gilead to say to them, "The LORD bless you for showing this kindness to Saul your master by burying him. 6May the LORD now show you kindness and faithfulness, and I too will show you the same favor because you have done this. 7Now then, be strong and brave, for Saul your master is dead, and the house of Judah has anointed me king over them."

War Between the Houses of David and Saul

8Meanwhile, Abner son of Ner, the commander of Saul's army, had taken Ish-Bosheth son of Saul and brought him over to Mahanaim. 9He made him king over Gilead, Ashuri[a] and Jezreel, and also over Ephraim, Benjamin and all Israel.

10Ish-Bosheth son of Saul was forty years old when he became king over Israel, and he reigned two years. The house of Judah, however, followed David. 11The length of time David was king in Hebron over the house of Judah was seven years and six months.

12Abner son of Ner, together with the men of Ish-Bosheth son of Saul, left Mahanaim and went to Gibeon. 13Joab son of Zeruiah and David's men went out and met them at the pool of Gibeon. One group sat down on one side of the pool and one group on the other side.

14Then Abner said to Joab, "Let's have some of the young men get up and fight hand to hand in front of us."

"All right, let them do it," Joab said.

15So they stood up and were counted off—twelve men for Benjamin and Ish-Bosheth son of Saul, and twelve for David. 16Then each man grabbed his opponent by the head and thrust his dagger into his opponent's side, and they fell down together. So that place in Gibeon was called Helkath Hazzurim.[b]

17The battle that day was very fierce, and Abner and the men of Israel were defeated by David's men.

18The three sons of Zeruiah were there: Joab, Abishai and Asahel. Now Asahel was as fleet-footed as a wild gazelle. 19He chased Abner, turning neither to the right nor to the left as he pursued him. 20Abner looked behind him and asked, "Is that you, Asahel?"

"It is," he answered.

21Then Abner said to him, "Turn aside to the right or to the left; take on one of the young men and strip him of his weapons." But Asahel would not stop chasing him.

22Again Abner warned Asahel, "Stop chasing me! Why should I strike you down? How could I look your brother Joab in the face?"

23But Asahel refused to give up the pursuit; so Abner thrust the butt of his spear into Asahel's stomach, and the spear came out through his back. He fell there and died on the spot. And every man stopped when he came to the place where Asahel had fallen and died.

24But Joab and Abishai pursued Abner, and as the sun was setting, they came to the hill of Ammah, near Giah on the way to the wasteland of Gibeon. 25Then the men of Benjamin rallied behind Abner. They formed themselves into a group and took their stand on top of a hill.

26Abner called out to Joab, "Must the sword devour forever? Don't you realize that this will end in bitterness? How long before you order your men to stop pursuing their brothers?"

27Joab answered, "As surely as God lives, if you had not spoken, the men would have continued the pursuit of their brothers until morning.[c]"

28So Joab blew the trumpet, and all the men came to a halt; they no longer pursued Israel, nor did they fight anymore.

29All that night Abner and his men marched through the Arabah. They crossed the Jordan, continued through the whole Bithron[d] and came to Mahanaim.

30Then Joab returned from pursuing Abner and assembled all his men. Besides Asahel, nineteen of David's men were found missing. 31But David's men had killed three hundred and sixty Benjamites who were with Abner. 32They took Asahel and buried him in his father's tomb at Bethlehem. Then Joab and his men marched all night and arrived at Hebron by daybreak.

3 The war between the house of Saul and the house of David lasted a long time. David grew stronger and stronger, while the house of Saul grew weaker and weaker.

2Sons were born to David in Hebron:

[a]9 Or *Asher* [b]16 *Helkath Hazzurim* means *field of daggers* or *field of hostilities.* [c]27 Or *spoken this morning, the men would not have taken up the pursuit of their brothers;* or *spoken, the men would have given up the pursuit of their brothers by morning* [d]29 Or *morning;* or *ravine;* the meaning of the Hebrew for this word is uncertain.

2:30–31 What a tragic picture! Hundreds died in a needless conflict between related tribes. This tragedy was the fruit of a divided nation and Joab's unwise leadership. Often our families suffer in the same way. If past conflicts are not dealt with properly or family leaders make decisions in the heat of passion, suffering and pain are the sure result. This should be a warning for us to seek restoration early, before the consequences bring destruction that cannot be repaired.

His firstborn was Amnon the son of
Ahinoam of Jezreel;
3his second, Kileab the son of Abigail
the widow of Nabal of Carmel;
the third, Absalom the son of Maacah
daughter of Talmai king of Geshur;
4the fourth, Adonijah the son of Haggith;
the fifth, Shephatiah the son of Abital;
5and the sixth, Ithream the son of David's wife Eglah.
These were born to David in Hebron.

Abner Goes Over to David

6During the war between the house of Saul
and the house of David, Abner had been
strengthening his own position in the house of
Saul. 7Now Saul had had a concubine named
Rizpah daughter of Aiah. And Ish-Bosheth said
to Abner, "Why did you sleep with my father's
concubine?"
8Abner was very angry because of what Ish-
Bosheth said and he answered, "Am I a dog's
head—on Judah's side? This very day I am loyal
to the house of your father Saul and to his family and friends. I haven't handed you over to
David. Yet now you accuse me of an offense
involving this woman! 9May God deal with Abner, be it ever so severely, if I do not do for
David what the LORD promised him on oath
10and transfer the kingdom from the house of
Saul and establish David's throne over Israel
and Judah from Dan to Beersheba." 11Ish-
Bosheth did not dare to say another word to
Abner, because he was afraid of him.
12Then Abner sent messengers on his behalf
to say to David, "Whose land is it? Make an
agreement with me, and I will help you bring all
Israel over to you."
13"Good," said David. "I will make an agreement with you. But I demand one thing of you:
Do not come into my presence unless you bring
Michal daughter of Saul when you come to see
me." 14Then David sent messengers to Ish-
Bosheth son of Saul, demanding, "Give me my
wife Michal, whom I betrothed to myself for the
price of a hundred Philistine foreskins."
15So Ish-Bosheth gave orders and had her
taken away from her husband Paltiel son of
Laish. 16Her husband, however, went with her,
weeping behind her all the way to Bahurim.
Then Abner said to him, "Go back home!" So he
went back.
17Abner conferred with the elders of Israel
and said, "For some time you have wanted to
make David your king. 18Now do it! For the
LORD promised David, 'By my servant David I
will rescue my people Israel from the hand of
the Philistines and from the hand of all their
enemies.' "
19Abner also spoke to the Benjamites in person. Then he went to Hebron to tell David everything that Israel and the whole house of Benjamin wanted to do. 20When Abner, who had
twenty men with him, came to David at Hebron, David prepared a feast for him and his
men. 21Then Abner said to David, "Let me go
at once and assemble all Israel for my lord the
king, so that they may make a compact with
you, and that you may rule over all that your
heart desires." So David sent Abner away, and he
went in peace.

Joab Murders Abner

22Just then David's men and Joab returned
from a raid and brought with them a great deal
of plunder. But Abner was no longer with David
in Hebron, because David had sent him away,
and he had gone in peace. 23When Joab and all
the soldiers with him arrived, he was told that
Abner son of Ner had come to the king and that
the king had sent him away and that he had
gone in peace.
24So Joab went to the king and said, "What
have you done? Look, Abner came to you. Why
did you let him go? Now he is gone! 25You
know Abner son of Ner; he came to deceive you
and observe your movements and find out everything you are doing."
26Joab then left David and sent messengers
after Abner, and they brought him back from
the well of Sirah. But David did not know it.
27Now when Abner returned to Hebron, Joab
took him aside into the gateway, as though to
speak with him privately. And there, to avenge
the blood of his brother Asahel, Joab stabbed
him in the stomach, and he died.
28Later, when David heard about this, he
said, "I and my kingdom are forever innocent
before the LORD concerning the blood of Abner
son of Ner. 29May his blood fall upon the head
of Joab and upon all his father's house! May
Joab's house never be without someone who
has a running sore or leprosy[a] or who leans on
a crutch or who falls by the sword or who lacks
food."

[a]*29* The Hebrew word was used for various diseases affecting the skin—not necessarily leprosy.

3:17–18 Abner displayed the courage to take an unpopular stand and make an important change in his life. He advised the elders of the northern tribes to take the necessary steps to make David their king. Abner understood that good intentions are worthless unless they are translated into actions. Spiritual renewal involves not only desiring change but also actively taking steps to pursue it. Abner's exhortation, "Now do it!" (3:18) is a clarion call to anyone who wants to progress spiritually.

3:27 Joab harbored a deep bitterness toward Abner and sought revenge rather than a new start in life. It would have been better for Joab to let go of painful past events rather than choosing to avenge the death of his brother. Joab's rash act of vengeance against Abner brought a curse upon his family and embarrassment and grief to the king. Our spiritual renewal requires that we let go of our past, no matter how painful it may be. We must learn to forgive the people who have wronged us. Forgiveness, though difficult, is the only sure way to completely let go of a painful past.

30(Joab and his brother Abishai murdered
Abner because he had killed their brother Asahel in the battle at Gibeon.)
31Then David said to Joab and all the people
with him, "Tear your clothes and put on sackcloth and walk in mourning in front of Abner."
King David himself walked behind the bier.
32They buried Abner in Hebron, and the king
wept aloud at Abner's tomb. All the people
wept also.
33The king sang this lament for Abner:

"Should Abner have died as the lawless
  die?
34 Your hands were not bound,
  your feet were not fettered.
You fell as one falls before wicked men."

And all the people wept over him again.
35Then they all came and urged David to eat
something while it was still day; but David took
an oath, saying, "May God deal with me, be it
ever so severely, if I taste bread or anything else
before the sun sets!"
36All the people took note and were pleased;
indeed, everything the king did pleased them.
37So on that day all the people and all Israel
knew that the king had no part in the murder of
Abner son of Ner.
38Then the king said to his men, "Do you
not realize that a prince and a great man has
fallen in Israel this day? 39And today, though I
am the anointed king, I am weak, and these
sons of Zeruiah are too strong for me. May the
LORD repay the evildoer according to his evil
deeds!"

Ish-Bosheth Murdered

4 When Ish-Bosheth son of Saul heard that
Abner had died in Hebron, he lost courage,
and all Israel became alarmed. 2Now Saul's son
had two men who were leaders of raiding
bands. One was named Baanah and the other
Recab; they were sons of Rimmon the Beerothite from the tribe of Benjamin—Beeroth is considered part of Benjamin, 3because the people
of Beeroth fled to Gittaim and have lived there
as aliens to this day.
4(Jonathan son of Saul had a son who was
lame in both feet. He was five years old when
the news about Saul and Jonathan came from
Jezreel. His nurse picked him up and fled, but
as she hurried to leave, he fell and became crippled. His name was Mephibosheth.)
5Now Recab and Baanah, the sons of Rimmon the Beerothite, set out for the house of
Ish-Bosheth, and they arrived there in the heat
of the day while he was taking his noonday rest.
6They went into the inner part of the house as
if to get some wheat, and they stabbed him in
the stomach. Then Recab and his brother Baanah slipped away.
7They had gone into the house while he was
lying on the bed in his bedroom. After they
stabbed and killed him, they cut off his head.
Taking it with them, they traveled all night by
way of the Arabah. 8They brought the head of
Ish-Bosheth to David at Hebron and said to the
king, "Here is the head of Ish-Bosheth son of
Saul, your enemy, who tried to take your life.
This day the LORD has avenged my lord the king
against Saul and his offspring."
9David answered Recab and his brother Baanah, the sons of Rimmon the Beerothite, "As
surely as the LORD lives, who has delivered me
out of all trouble, 10when a man told me, 'Saul
is dead,' and thought he was bringing good
news, I seized him and put him to death in
Ziklag. That was the reward I gave him for his
news! 11How much more—when wicked men
have killed an innocent man in his own house
and on his own bed—should I not now demand
his blood from your hand and rid the earth of
you!"
12So David gave an order to his men, and
they killed them. They cut off their hands and
feet and hung the bodies by the pool in Hebron. But they took the head of Ish-Bosheth
and buried it in Abner's tomb at Hebron.

David Becomes King Over Israel

5 All the tribes of Israel came to David at
Hebron and said, "We are your own flesh
and blood. 2In the past, while Saul was king
over us, you were the one who led Israel on
their military campaigns. And the LORD said to
you, 'You will shepherd my people Israel, and
you will become their ruler.' "
3When all the elders of Israel had come to
King David at Hebron, the king made a compact with them at Hebron before the LORD, and
they anointed David king over Israel.
4David was thirty years old when he became
king, and he reigned forty years. 5In Hebron he
reigned over Judah seven years and six months,
and in Jerusalem he reigned over all Israel and
Judah thirty-three years.

4:9 David acknowledged God as the source of his deliverance. If we cannot give God the credit for our victories, it may indicate that we never really surrendered our lives to him in the first place. We need to give credit where credit is due. Praising God for our victories is a good way to show how much we depend on him and appreciate his help.

5:3–5 David was anointed to be the king of Israel years before his ascension to the throne. David's coronation is a reminder that God will fulfill his promises regardless of the passage of time. God's promises to David were not fulfilled right away. David waited many years as a fugitive, without a home or country, for God to fulfill his promises. During that time, God supplied David with the help he needed to survive. Spiritual renewal and transformation are not accomplished instantly; they take strength and perseverance. They take a lifetime. But God supplies his strength and protection as we seek him and surrender our lives to him.

David Conquers Jerusalem

6The king and his men marched to Jerusalem
to attack the Jebusites, who lived there. The Jebusites said to David, "You will not get in here;
even the blind and the lame can ward you off."
They thought, "David cannot get in here." 7Nev-
ertheless, David captured the fortress of Zion,
the City of David.

8On that day, David said, "Anyone who conquers the Jebusites will have to use the water
shaft[a] to reach those 'lame and blind' who are
David's enemies.[b]" That is why they say, "The
'blind and lame' will not enter the palace."

9David then took up residence in the fortress
and called it the City of David. He built up the
area around it, from the supporting terraces[c]
inward. 10And he became more and more powerful, because the LORD God Almighty was with
him.

11Now Hiram king of Tyre sent messengers to
David, along with cedar logs and carpenters and
stonemasons, and they built a palace for David.
12And David knew that the LORD had established him as king over Israel and had exalted
his kingdom for the sake of his people Israel.

13After he left Hebron, David took more concubines and wives in Jerusalem, and more sons
and daughters were born to him. 14These are
the names of the children born to him there:
Shammua, Shobab, Nathan, Solomon, 15Ibhar,
Elishua, Nepheg, Japhia, 16Elishama, Eliada and
Eliphelet.

David Defeats the Philistines

17When the Philistines heard that David had
been anointed king over Israel, they went up in
full force to search for him, but David heard
about it and went down to the stronghold.
18Now the Philistines had come and spread out
in the Valley of Rephaim; 19so David inquired
of the LORD, "Shall I go and attack the Philistines? Will you hand them over to me?"

The LORD answered him, "Go, for I will surely hand the Philistines over to you."

20So David went to Baal Perazim, and there
he defeated them. He said, "As waters break
out, the LORD has broken out against my enemies before me." So that place was called Baal
Perazim.[d] 21The Philistines abandoned their
idols there, and David and his men carried
them off.

22Once more the Philistines came up and
spread out in the Valley of Rephaim; 23so David
inquired of the LORD, and he answered, "Do
not go straight up, but circle around behind
them and attack them in front of the balsam
trees. 24As soon as you hear the sound of marching in the tops of the balsam trees, move quickly, because that will mean the LORD has gone
out in front of you to strike the Philistine army."
25So David did as the LORD commanded him,
and he struck down the Philistines all the way
from Gibeon[e] to Gezer.

The Ark Brought to Jerusalem

6 David again brought together out of Israel
chosen men, thirty thousand in all. 2He
and all his men set out from Baalah of Judah[f]
to bring up from there the ark of God, which is
called by the Name,[g] the name of the LORD
Almighty, who is enthroned between the cherubim that are on the ark. 3They set the ark of God
on a new cart and brought it from the house of
Abinadab, which was on the hill. Uzzah and
Ahio, sons of Abinadab, were guiding the new
cart 4with the ark of God on it,[h] and Ahio was
walking in front of it. 5David and the whole
house of Israel were celebrating with all their
might before the LORD, with songs[i] and with
harps, lyres, tambourines, sistrums and cymbals.

6When they came to the threshing floor of
Nacon, Uzzah reached out and took hold of the
ark of God, because the oxen stumbled. 7The
LORD's anger burned against Uzzah because of
his irreverent act; therefore God struck him
down and he died there beside the ark of God.

8Then David was angry because the LORD's
wrath had broken out against Uzzah, and to
this day that place is called Perez Uzzah.[j]

9David was afraid of the LORD that day and

[a]8 Or *use scaling hooks* [b]8 Or *are hated by David* [c]9 Or *the Millo* [d]20 *Baal Perazim* means *the lord who breaks out.* [e]25 Septuagint (see also 1 Chron. 14:16); Hebrew *Geba* [f]2 That is, Kiriath Jearim; Hebrew *Baale Judah,* a variant of *Baalah of Judah* [g]2 Hebrew; Septuagint and Vulgate do not have *the Name.* [h]3,4 Dead Sea Scrolls and some Septuagint manuscripts; Masoretic Text *cart 4and they brought it with the ark of God from the house of Abinadab, which was on the hill* [i]5 See Dead Sea Scrolls, Septuagint and 1 Chronicles 13:8; Masoretic Text *celebrating before the LORD with all kinds of instruments made of pine.* [j]8 *Perez Uzzah* means *outbreak against Uzzah.*

5:6–8 The arrogant Jebusites thought their city was invincible: They said, "You will not get in here; even the blind and the lame can ward you off" (5:6). As we progress spiritually, it is sometimes easy to assume that we are immune to dramatic reversals. When they happen, we are as shocked as the Jebusites were. We would be wise to be humble and keep our guard up against a possible fall.
5:13 At the height of David's political career, he began to build his harem. This was customary for kings in the ancient Near East, but David's decision to be like other kings carried a price tag with it. In later years, conflicts between David's many children almost destroyed both king and kingdom. Sometimes God's plan will lead us away from the norms of the society around us. If so, we can either follow God's ideal or suffer the consequences.
6:1–8 David desired to bring the ark of God, the symbol of God's presence, to Jerusalem. But he failed to follow God's specific instructions for transporting it. Apparently David had not followed God's directive to read God's law every day (see Deuteronomy 17:18–19). God's Word was available to him, but David reaped serious consequences for failing to honor God by not following his instructions. The Bible is our primary source for discovering God's will. We are responsible for knowing what God desires of us; such knowledge will enable us to act accordingly.

said, "How can the ark of the LORD ever come to me?" 10He was not willing to take the ark of the LORD to be with him in the City of David. Instead, he took it aside to the house of Obed-Edom the Gittite. 11The ark of the LORD remained in the house of Obed-Edom the Gittite for three months, and the LORD blessed him and his entire household.

12Now King David was told, "The LORD has blessed the household of Obed-Edom and everything he has, because of the ark of God." So David went down and brought up the ark of God from the house of Obed-Edom to the City of David with rejoicing. 13When those who were carrying the ark of the LORD had taken six steps, he sacrificed a bull and a fattened calf. 14David, wearing a linen ephod, danced before the LORD with all his might, 15while he and the entire house of Israel brought up the ark of the LORD with shouts and the sound of trumpets.

16As the ark of the LORD was entering the City of David, Michal daughter of Saul watched from a window. And when she saw King David leaping and dancing before the LORD, she despised him in her heart.

17They brought the ark of the LORD and set it in its place inside the tent that David had pitched for it, and David sacrificed burnt offerings and fellowship offerings[a] before the LORD. 18After he had finished sacrificing the burnt offerings and fellowship offerings, he blessed the people in the name of the LORD Almighty. 19Then he gave a loaf of bread, a cake of dates and a cake of raisins to each person in the whole crowd of Israelites, both men and women. And all the people went to their homes.

20When David returned home to bless his household, Michal daughter of Saul came out to meet him and said, "How the king of Israel has distinguished himself today, disrobing in the sight of the slave girls of his servants as any vulgar fellow would!"

21David said to Michal, "It was before the LORD, who chose me rather than your father or anyone from his house when he appointed me ruler over the LORD's people Israel—I will celebrate before the LORD. 22I will become even more undignified than this, and I will be humiliated in my own eyes. But by these slave girls you spoke of, I will be held in honor."

23And Michal daughter of Saul had no children to the day of her death.

God's Promise to David

7 After the king was settled in his palace and the LORD had given him rest from all his enemies around him, 2he said to Nathan the prophet, "Here I am, living in a palace of cedar, while the ark of God remains in a tent."

3Nathan replied to the king, "Whatever you have in mind, go ahead and do it, for the LORD is with you."

4That night the word of the LORD came to Nathan, saying:

> 5"Go and tell my servant David, 'This is what the LORD says: Are you the one to build me a house to dwell in? 6I have not dwelt in a house from the day I brought the Israelites up out of Egypt to this day. I have been moving from place to place with a tent as my dwelling. 7Wherever I have moved with all the Israelites, did I ever say to any of their rulers whom I commanded to shepherd my people Israel, "Why have you not built me a house of cedar?" '
>
> 8"Now then, tell my servant David, 'This is what the LORD Almighty says: I took you from the pasture and from following the flock to be ruler over my people Israel. 9I have been with you wherever you have gone, and I have cut off all your enemies from before you. Now I will make your name great, like the names of the greatest men of the earth. 10And I will provide a place for my people Israel and will plant them so that they can have a home of their own and no longer be disturbed. Wicked people will not oppress them anymore, as they did at the beginning 11and have done ever since the time

[a]17 Traditionally *peace offerings;* also in verse 18

6:12–15 In his initial attempt at retrieving the ark, David had failed miserably. So David finally turned to the Scriptures to see what God had to say on the matter. When David set everything straight and followed God's instructions for moving the ark, he and the Israelites discovered that the formerly terrifying task of moving the ark became an activity punctuated with joy. When we do things God's way, we will discover that even troubling situations can become occasions for joy.

6:16–23 Michal's anger was probably fueled by far more than her embarrassment at David's conduct. Over the years, Michal had been a pawn on the chessboard of David's life. After Michal had been married to David for a short time, her father, King Saul, gave her to another man to annoy David. In later negotiations David won her back, but by then Michal found herself to be just one wife among many. Michal's anger at the injustice of her situation affected her ability to enjoy the present. The same thing can happen to us. We need to recognize our pain, confess it, accept responsibility for our actions regardless of the pain and then release the whole situation to God. When we release our pain and whatever we are holding against others, God can release us from the grip of our past.

7:9–13 God may have refused David's request to build the temple, but as we see here, God had an even better plan (see Proverbs 3:5–6). God's plan established the Davidic covenant, including with it the promise of an eternal kingdom and a descendant of David upon its throne forever. David had to delay his desire to build a temple and exercise patience and faith. There may be times when we have to wait patiently for God's will to become a reality in our lives too. But God has a special plan for each of us, and when his plan unfolds it will be better than what we ever hoped for.

I appointed leaders[a] over my people Israel. I will also give you rest from all your
enemies.
" 'The LORD declares to you that the
LORD himself will establish a house for
you: 12When your days are over and you
rest with your fathers, I will raise up your
offspring to succeed you, who will come
from your own body, and I will establish
his kingdom. 13He is the one who will
build a house for my Name, and I will
establish the throne of his kingdom forever. 14I will be his father, and he will be my
son. When he does wrong, I will punish
him with the rod of men, with floggings
inflicted by men. 15But my love will never
be taken away from him, as I took it away
from Saul, whom I removed from before
you. 16Your house and your kingdom will
endure forever before me[b]; your throne
will be established forever.' "

17Nathan reported to David all the words of
this entire revelation.

David's Prayer

18Then King David went in and sat before the
LORD, and he said:

"Who am I, O Sovereign LORD, and
what is my family, that you have brought
me this far? 19And as if this were not
enough in your sight, O Sovereign LORD,
you have also spoken about the future of
the house of your servant. Is this your usual way of dealing with man, O Sovereign
LORD?

20"What more can David say to you?
For you know your servant, O Sovereign
LORD. 21For the sake of your word and
according to your will, you have done this
great thing and made it known to your
servant.

22"How great you are, O Sovereign
LORD! There is no one like you, and there
is no God but you, as we have heard with
our own ears. 23And who is like your people Israel—the one nation on earth that
God went out to redeem as a people for
himself, and to make a name for himself,
and to perform great and awesome wonders by driving out nations and their gods
from before your people, whom you redeemed from Egypt?[c] 24You have established your people Israel as your very own
forever, and you, O LORD, have become
their God.

25"And now, LORD God, keep forever
the promise you have made concerning
your servant and his house. Do as you
promised, 26so that your name will be
great forever. Then men will say, 'The
LORD Almighty is God over Israel!' And
the house of your servant David will be
established before you.

27"O LORD Almighty, God of Israel,
you have revealed this to your servant, saying, 'I will build a house for you.' So your
servant has found courage to offer you this
prayer. 28O Sovereign LORD, you are God!
Your words are trustworthy, and you have
promised these good things to your servant. 29Now be pleased to bless the house
of your servant, that it may continue forever in your sight; for you, O Sovereign
LORD, have spoken, and with your blessing the house of your servant will be
blessed forever."

David's Victories

8 In the course of time, David defeated the
Philistines and subdued them, and he took
Metheg Ammah from the control of the Philis-
tines.

2David also defeated the Moabites. He made
them lie down on the ground and measured
them off with a length of cord. Every two
lengths of them were put to death, and the third
length was allowed to live. So the Moabites became subject to David and brought tribute.

3Moreover, David fought Hadadezer son of
Rehob, king of Zobah, when he went to restore
his control along the Euphrates River. 4David
captured a thousand of his chariots, seven thousand charioteers[d] and twenty thousand foot
soldiers. He hamstrung all but a hundred of the
chariot horses.

5When the Arameans of Damascus came to
help Hadadezer king of Zobah, David struck
down twenty-two thousand of them. 6He put
garrisons in the Aramean kingdom of Damascus, and the Arameans became subject to him
and brought tribute. The LORD gave David victory wherever he went.

7David took the gold shields that belonged
to the officers of Hadadezer and brought them

[a] 11 Traditionally *judges* [b] 16 Some Hebrew manuscripts and Septuagint; most Hebrew manuscripts *you* [c] 23 See Septuagint and 1 Chron. 17:21; Hebrew *wonders for your land and before your people, whom you redeemed from Egypt, from the nations and their gods.* [d] 4 Septuagint (see also Dead Sea Scrolls and 1 Chron. 18:4); Masoretic Text *captured seventeen hundred of his charioteers*

7:18–29 In this beautiful prayer, David called God "Sovereign LORD" seven times. David realized that God was his master; following God's will was of utmost importance. We cannot see the truth without recognizing God's authority in our lives and allowing him to direct our plans. But by submitting to God's will and looking to him for help we will discover the power we need to overcome our difficulties.

7:27–29 David took the time to review God's promises to him. God's Word is filled with promises for us, and God delights in our claiming those promises before him in prayer. This can be especially helpful for us in the midst of a crisis. *God* does not need to be reminded of his promises, but *our* memory can usually stand some refreshing.

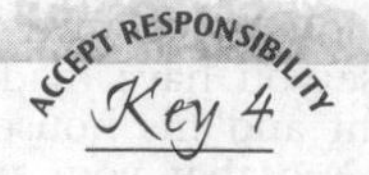

Keeping Our Promises

2 Samuel 9:1–9 How many of us are still living in the shadow of promises that we have not kept? Taking responsibility for our lives sometimes means coming to terms with promises we have not kept, because breaking promises is wrong and hurtful to those around us.

King David had made some promises to his friend Jonathan. One day David asked, "Is there anyone still left of the house of Saul to whom I can show kindness for Jonathan's sake?" (9:1). Jonathan's only living son, Mephibosheth, had lived a long time with the pain of David's unkept promise. Mephibosheth's grandfather, King Saul, had mistreated David before David became king. Perhaps Mephibosheth was afraid that David would mistreat him on account of his grandfather. Perhaps he had begun to take the guilt of his grandfather's sins upon himself. Generations of fear and guilt had been laid upon him—until David remembered and fulfilled his promise to show kindness to Saul's family.

There are probably people in our lives who have been affected by promises we have failed to keep. We must take the responsibility for not keeping our word and stop making excuses for ourselves. Then we need to be careful not to promise things we will later be unwilling or unable to accomplish.

Turn to Psalm 119.

to Jerusalem. 8From Tebah[a] and Berothai,
towns that belonged to Hadadezer, King David
took a great quantity of bronze.
9When Tou[b] king of Hamath heard that David had defeated the entire army of Hadadezer,
10he sent his son Joram[c] to King David to greet
him and congratulate him on his victory in battle over Hadadezer, who had been at war with
Tou. Joram brought with him articles of silver
and gold and bronze.
11King David dedicated these articles to the
LORD, as he had done with the silver and gold
from all the nations he had subdued: 12Edom[d]
and Moab, the Ammonites and the Philistines,
and Amalek. He also dedicated the plunder taken from Hadadezer son of Rehob, king of Zobah.
13And David became famous after he returned from striking down eighteen thousand
Edomites[e] in the Valley of Salt.
14He put garrisons throughout Edom, and all
the Edomites became subject to David. The
LORD gave David victory wherever he went.

David's Officials

15David reigned over all Israel, doing what
was just and right for all his people. 16Joab son
of Zeruiah was over the army; Jehoshaphat son
of Ahilud was recorder; 17Zadok son of Ahitub
and Ahimelech son of Abiathar were priests;
Seraiah was secretary; 18Benaiah son of Jehoiada was over the Kerethites and Pelethites; and
David's sons were royal advisers.[f]

David and Mephibosheth

9 David asked, "Is there anyone still left of
the house of Saul to whom I can show
kindness for Jonathan's sake?"
2Now there was a servant of Saul's household
named Ziba. They called him to appear before
David, and the king said to him, "Are you Ziba?"
"Your servant," he replied.
3The king asked, "Is there no one still left of
the house of Saul to whom I can show God's
kindness?"
Ziba answered the king, "There is still a son
of Jonathan; he is crippled in both feet."
4"Where is he?" the king asked.

[a]8 See some Septuagint manuscripts (see also 1 Chron. 18:8); Hebrew *Betah.* [b]9 Hebrew *Toi,* a variant of *Tou;* also in verse 10 [c]10 A variant of *Hadoram* [d]12 Some Hebrew manuscripts, Septuagint and Syriac (see also 1 Chron. 18:11); most Hebrew manuscripts *Aram* [e]13 A few Hebrew manuscripts, Septuagint and Syriac (see also 1 Chron. 18:12); most Hebrew manuscripts *Aram* (that is, Arameans) [f]18 Or *were priests*

9:1–7 David had promised to treat Saul's family well because of his friendship with Jonathan. Though many years had passed since the promise was given, David kept it. He honored the memory of Jonathan by offering Mephibosheth a place in his household. David stood by his word and did what he could to settle a painful conflict from his past. Being responsible for our promises and dealing with past conflicts are important to our spiritual growth.

Ziba answered, "He is at the house of Makir son of Ammiel in Lo Debar."

5So King David had him brought from Lo Debar, from the house of Makir son of Ammiel.

6When Mephibosheth son of Jonathan, the son of Saul, came to David, he bowed down to pay him honor.

David said, "Mephibosheth!"

"Your servant," he replied.

7"Don't be afraid," David said to him, "for I will surely show you kindness for the sake of your father Jonathan. I will restore to you all the land that belonged to your grandfather Saul, and you will always eat at my table."

8Mephibosheth bowed down and said, "What is your servant, that you should notice a dead dog like me?"

9Then the king summoned Ziba, Saul's servant, and said to him, "I have given your master's grandson everything that belonged to Saul and his family. 10You and your sons and your servants are to farm the land for him and bring in the crops, so that your master's grandson may be provided for. And Mephibosheth, grandson of your master, will always eat at my table." (Now Ziba had fifteen sons and twenty servants.)

11Then Ziba said to the king, "Your servant will do whatever my lord the king commands his servant to do." So Mephibosheth ate at David's[a] table like one of the king's sons.

12Mephibosheth had a young son named Mica, and all the members of Ziba's household were servants of Mephibosheth. 13And Mephibosheth lived in Jerusalem, because he always ate at the king's table, and he was crippled in both feet.

David Defeats the Ammonites

10 In the course of time, the king of the Ammonites died, and his son Hanun succeeded him as king. 2David thought, "I will show kindness to Hanun son of Nahash, just as his father showed kindness to me." So David sent a delegation to express his sympathy to Hanun concerning his father.

When David's men came to the land of the Ammonites, 3the Ammonite nobles said to Hanun their lord, "Do you think David is honoring your father by sending men to you to express sympathy? Hasn't David sent them to you to explore the city and spy it out and overthrow it?" 4So Hanun seized David's men, shaved off half of each man's beard, cut off their garments in the middle at the buttocks, and sent them away.

5When David was told about this, he sent messengers to meet the men, for they were greatly humiliated. The king said, "Stay at Jericho till your beards have grown, and then come back."

6When the Ammonites realized that they had become a stench in David's nostrils, they hired twenty thousand Aramean foot soldiers from Beth Rehob and Zobah, as well as the king of Maacah with a thousand men, and also twelve thousand men from Tob.

7On hearing this, David sent Joab out with the entire army of fighting men. 8The Ammonites came out and drew up in battle formation at the entrance to their city gate, while the Arameans of Zobah and Rehob and the men of Tob and Maacah were by themselves in the open country.

9Joab saw that there were battle lines in front of him and behind him; so he selected some of the best troops in Israel and deployed them against the Arameans. 10He put the rest of the men under the command of Abishai his brother and deployed them against the Ammonites. 11Joab said, "If the Arameans are too strong for me, then you are to come to my rescue; but if the Ammonites are too strong for you, then I will come to rescue you. 12Be strong and let us fight bravely for our people and the cities of our God. The LORD will do what is good in his sight."

13Then Joab and the troops with him advanced to fight the Arameans, and they fled before him. 14When the Ammonites saw that the Arameans were fleeing, they fled before Abishai and went inside the city. So Joab returned from fighting the Ammonites and came to Jerusalem.

15After the Arameans saw that they had been routed by Israel, they regrouped. 16Hadadezer had Arameans brought from beyond the River[b]; they went to Helam, with Shobach the commander of Hadadezer's army leading them.

17When David was told of this, he gathered all Israel, crossed the Jordan and went to Helam. The Arameans formed their battle lines to meet David and fought against him. 18But they fled before Israel, and David killed seven hundred of their charioteers and forty thousand of their foot soldiers.[c] He also struck down Sho-

[a] *11* Septuagint; Hebrew *my* [b] *16* That is, the Euphrates
[c] *18* Some Septuagint manuscripts (see also 1 Chron. 19:18); Hebrew *horsemen*

10:1–5 Hanun was needlessly suspicious of the motives of David's men. As a result, he treated them shamefully and brought unnecessary bloodshed upon his people. Hanun's suspicions led him to distrust others and negated David's attempts to forge a productive relationship. Allowing our fears to shape our conclusions can often lead to unnecessary conflict and a disruption of possible positive relationships. Much time, effort and energy are wasted when we respond with suspicion and fear to the friendly overtures of other people.

10:11–12 Joab gave wise counsel to Abishai before going to battle. He devised a simple attack strategy and then recognized God's role in the process. As we struggle with our adversaries, these principles can prove helpful. We need a plan to follow; God's Word is filled with valuable insights. We also need to recognize that no matter how good our plan, we still need God's help if we are going to succeed. God wants us to have victory, and "the LORD will do what is good in his sight" (10:12).

bach the commander of their army, and he died there. 19When all the kings who were vassals of Hadadezer saw that they had been defeated by Israel, they made peace with the Israelites and became subject to them.

So the Arameans were afraid to help the Ammonites anymore.

David and Bathsheba

11 In the spring, at the time when kings go off to war, David sent Joab out with the king's men and the whole Israelite army. They destroyed the Ammonites and besieged Rabbah. But David remained in Jerusalem.

2One evening David got up from his bed and walked around on the roof of the palace. From the roof he saw a woman bathing. The woman was very beautiful, 3and David sent someone to find out about her. The man said, "Isn't this Bathsheba, the daughter of Eliam and the wife of Uriah the Hittite?" 4Then David sent messengers to get her. She came to him, and he slept with her. (She had purified herself from her uncleanness.) Then[a] she went back home. 5The woman conceived and sent word to David, saying, "I am pregnant."

6So David sent this word to Joab: "Send me Uriah the Hittite." And Joab sent him to David. 7When Uriah came to him, David asked him how Joab was, how the soldiers were and how the war was going. 8Then David said to Uriah, "Go down to your house and wash your feet." So Uriah left the palace, and a gift from the king was sent after him. 9But Uriah slept at the entrance to the palace with all his master's servants and did not go down to his house.

10When David was told, "Uriah did not go home," he asked him, "Haven't you just come from a distance? Why didn't you go home?"

11Uriah said to David, "The ark and Israel and Judah are staying in tents, and my master Joab and my lord's men are camped in the open fields. How could I go to my house to eat and drink and lie with my wife? As surely as you live, I will not do such a thing!"

12Then David said to him, "Stay here one more day, and tomorrow I will send you back." So Uriah remained in Jerusalem that day and the next. 13At David's invitation, he ate and drank with him, and David made him drunk. But in the evening Uriah went out to sleep on his mat among his master's servants; he did not go home.

14In the morning David wrote a letter to Joab and sent it with Uriah. 15In it he wrote, "Put Uriah in the front line where the fighting is fiercest. Then withdraw from him so he will be struck down and die."

16So while Joab had the city under siege, he put Uriah at a place where he knew the strongest defenders were. 17When the men of the city came out and fought against Joab, some of the men in David's army fell; moreover, Uriah the Hittite died.

18Joab sent David a full account of the battle. 19He instructed the messenger: "When you have finished giving the king this account of the battle, 20the king's anger may flare up, and he may ask you, 'Why did you get so close to the city to fight? Didn't you know they would shoot arrows from the wall? 21Who killed Abimelech son of Jerub-Besheth[b]? Didn't a woman throw an upper millstone on him from the wall, so that he died in Thebez? Why did you get so close to the wall?' If he asks you this, then say to him, 'Also, your servant Uriah the Hittite is dead.' "

22The messenger set out, and when he arrived he told David everything Joab had sent him to say. 23The messenger said to David, "The men overpowered us and came out against us in the open, but we drove them back to the entrance to the city gate. 24Then the archers shot arrows at your servants from the wall, and some of the king's men died. Moreover, your servant Uriah the Hittite is dead."

25David told the messenger, "Say this to Joab: 'Don't let this upset you; the sword devours one as well as another. Press the attack against the city and destroy it.' Say this to encourage Joab."

26When Uriah's wife heard that her husband was dead, she mourned for him. 27After the time of mourning was over, David had her brought to his house, and she became his wife and bore him a son. But the thing David had done displeased the LORD.

Nathan Rebukes David

12 The LORD sent Nathan to David. When he came to him, he said, "There were two men in a certain town, one rich and the other poor. 2The rich man had a very large

[a]4 Or *with her. When she purified herself from her uncleanness,* [b]21 Also known as *Jerub-Baal* (that is, Gideon)

11:1–5 David chose to stay home and rest instead of leading his men into battle. That was his first mistake. Then, on a sleepless night, the king watched Bathsheba bathing on a nearby rooftop. David didn't have to watch her; he chose to do so. After indulging his visual lust, David gratified his sexual desire. He fell into the sin of adultery. It is our idle times in life that frequently get us into trouble. Staying busy with healthy activities can help protect us from temptation. We must diligently guard what we watch or think about. Failure in our thought life will usually lead to a fall.

11:14–17 Since Uriah refused to sleep with his wife and thereby unknowingly cover up Bathsheba's adulterous pregnancy, David engineered Uriah's death. One hidden sin almost always leads to another. Only when we confess our sins, bringing them out into the open, can we be free of this destructive cycle. Confession is an important key to breaking free from our past failures. It means admitting our wrongs to God, ourselves and often other people as well.

12:1–7 God chose his prophet Nathan to confront David with his sin. Notice how Nathan used a story to broach

David, Michal & Bathsheba

David failed in many of his relationships. He tended to avoid relational conflict and therefore did not deal with some important issues in his life. David's first wife, Michal, was the daughter of King Saul. Theirs was a fairy tale marriage. The king's daughter married the great war hero, who also happened to be a talented musician. Early in their relationship everything appeared to be fine, but over time their relationship developed difficulties. Michal was separated from David for a number of years when Saul gave her to another man to spite David. Years later David won Michal back but brought her into a house filled with other wives. Their relationship was never truly reestablished after Michal's return; they apparently held onto their pain, bitterness and anger. The outcome might have been different if they had confessed these problems to God and released them.

Michal despised David for dancing before the ark as he celebrated its return to Jerusalem (6:16). It seems that her bitterness and frustration over the years of separation and neglect had built to the boiling point. Unfortunately, there is no indication that Michal and David ever tried to heal their damaged marriage relationship. They seem to have settled instead into a destructive silence.

David complicated his life further by his infatuation and adultery with Bathsheba (11:1–27). This sin led to a tangled web of deceit, Uriah's murder and a rushed marriage to the pregnant Bathsheba. This string of self-induced tragedies hung a cloud of shame over David for the rest of his life. David's own children would repeat his mistakes, bringing further suffering to the royal family and the nation.

With all his mistakes, why was David considered more righteous than his predecessor Saul? The answer is based on heart attitudes. David's heart was open before God, and he was willing to accept God's correction in his life. After each failure, he was willing to see the truth, confess it and accept responsibility for his sins and the consequences that came as a result. This allowed David to grieve, forgive and let go. Because David responded in this way, God forgave him and redeemed his life, bringing about spiritual renewal time and again. All of us have made mistakes like David did. And we have much to learn from him about repenting from the bad choices we have made.

STRENGTHS AND ACCOMPLISHMENTS:

In the beginning, David and Michal had a strong marriage.

David kept an open relationship with God.

David was always willing to admit his sins and accept God's correction.

WEAKNESSES AND MISTAKES:

David and Michal did not communicate effectively.

David avoided family conflict and the resolution of problems.

At times, David did not hold himself accountable to others, which led him into sin.

By refusing to see the truth regarding his sin of adultery, David was driven deeper into sin.

LESSONS FROM THEIR LIVES:

Marriage can be destroyed by a refusal to let go of those things we hold against each other.

Communication must be a high priority in any relationship.

One mistake left uncorrected often leads to others.

No matter how great our sin, God is willing to forgive us if we repent.

KEY VERSES:

"As the deer pants for streams of water, so my soul pants for you, O God. My soul thirsts for God, for the living God" (Psalm 42:1–2).

David and Michal's story is told in 1 Samuel 18—19; 25:44; 2 Samuel 3; 6 and 1 Chronicles 15:29. David and Bathsheba's story is told in 2 Samuel 11—12; 1 Kings 1—2 and 1 Chronicles 3:5.

number of sheep and cattle, 3but the poor man had nothing except one little ewe lamb he had bought. He raised it, and it grew up with him and his children. It shared his food, drank from his cup and even slept in his arms. It was like a daughter to him.

4"Now a traveler came to the rich man, but the rich man refrained from taking one of his own sheep or cattle to prepare a meal for the traveler who had come to him. Instead, he took the ewe lamb that belonged to the poor man and prepared it for the one who had come to him."

5David burned with anger against the man and said to Nathan, "As surely as the LORD lives, the man who did this deserves to die! 6He must pay for that lamb four times over, because he did such a thing and had no pity."

7Then Nathan said to David, "You are the man! This is what the LORD, the God of Israel, says: 'I anointed you king over Israel, and I delivered you from the hand of Saul. 8I gave your master's house to you, and your master's wives into your arms. I gave you the house of Israel and Judah. And if all this had been too little, I would have given you even more. 9Why did you despise the word of the LORD by doing what is evil in his eyes? You struck down Uriah the Hittite with the sword and took his wife to be your own. You killed him with the sword of the Ammonites. 10Now, therefore, the sword will never depart from your house, because you despised me and took the wife of Uriah the Hittite to be your own.'

11"This is what the LORD says: 'Out of your own household I am going to bring calamity upon you. Before your very eyes I will take your wives and give them to one who is close to you, and he will lie with your wives in broad daylight. 12You did it in secret, but I will do this thing in broad daylight before all Israel.' "

13Then David said to Nathan, "I have sinned against the LORD."

Nathan replied, "The LORD has taken away your sin. You are not going to die. 14But because by doing this you have made the enemies of the LORD show utter contempt,[a] the son born to you will die."

15After Nathan had gone home, the LORD struck the child that Uriah's wife had borne to David, and he became ill. 16David pleaded with God for the child. He fasted and went into his house and spent the nights lying on the ground. 17The elders of his household stood beside him to get him up from the ground, but he refused, and he would not eat any food with them.

18On the seventh day the child died. David's servants were afraid to tell him that the child was dead, for they thought, "While the child was still living, we spoke to David but he would not listen to us. How can we tell him the child is dead? He may do something desperate."

19David noticed that his servants were whispering among themselves and he realized the child was dead. "Is the child dead?" he asked.

"Yes," they replied, "he is dead."

20Then David got up from the ground. After he had washed, put on lotions and changed his clothes, he went into the house of the LORD and worshiped. Then he went to his own house, and at his request they served him food, and he ate.

21His servants asked him, "Why are you acting this way? While the child was alive, you fasted and wept, but now that the child is dead, you get up and eat!"

22He answered, "While the child was still alive, I fasted and wept. I thought, 'Who knows? The LORD may be gracious to me and let the child live.' 23But now that he is dead, why should I fast? Can I bring him back again? I will go to him, but he will not return to me."

24Then David comforted his wife Bathsheba, and he went to her and lay with her. She gave birth to a son, and they named him Solomon. The LORD loved him; 25and because the LORD loved him, he sent word through Nathan the prophet to name him Jedidiah.[b]

26Meanwhile Joab fought against Rabbah of the Ammonites and captured the royal citadel. 27Joab then sent messengers to David, saying, "I have fought against Rabbah and taken its water supply. 28Now muster the rest of the troops and besiege the city and capture it. Otherwise I will take the city, and it will be named after me."

29So David mustered the entire army and

[a] 14 Masoretic Text; an ancient Hebrew scribal tradition *this you have shown utter contempt for the LORD*
[b] 25 *Jedidiah* means *loved by the LORD.*

---

the topic with David. When David became emotionally involved in the story, Nathan turned to direct confrontation: "You are the man!" (12:7). Nathan hoped that this piercing declaration would help David realize the serious nature of his sin and bring him to repentance. Nathan's wise intervention should serve as a model for us. He confronted David with the terrible reality of his acts, but he did it in such a way that David would listen. Part of our spiritual growth calls us to participate in the spiritual growth of others. There may even be times that God will use us to help someone else see the truth of their spiritual condition.

12:9–13 David's admission here, "I have sinned against the LORD," was the right response to his wrongdoing (12:13). Spurred on by Nathan's appeal, David's admission of guilt was an acknowledgment of his accountability before God. He saw the truth, confessed his sin, accepted responsibility for his actions, grieved before the Lord and pleaded with God to cleanse his heart and set him on the right course (see Psalm 51). Notice, however, that despite David's humble confession, he would still have to face terrible consequences (12:10–12). Our confession only starts the process toward a new life; we still must face the consequences of our past actions. We can be sure that as we build for a productive future, God will help us with the difficulties arising from our past.

12:29–31 After the death of Bathsheba's child, David returned to action. By leading the attack upon Rabbah, he returned to his proper role as commander-in-chief, a role he should have been filling at the time he sinned with Bathsheba (see 11:1). To David's credit, even though he had sinned, he made a dramatic turnaround. He went

went to Rabbah, and attacked and captured it.
30He took the crown from the head of their
king[a]—its weight was a talent[b] of gold, and it
was set with precious stones—and it was placed
on David's head. He took a great quantity of
plunder from the city 31and brought out the
people who were there, consigning them to labor with saws and with iron picks and axes, and
he made them work at brickmaking.[c] He did
this to all the Ammonite towns. Then David
and his entire army returned to Jerusalem.

Amnon and Tamar

13 In the course of time, Amnon son of
David fell in love with Tamar, the beautiful sister of Absalom son of David.
2Amnon became frustrated to the point of
illness on account of his sister Tamar, for she
was a virgin, and it seemed impossible for him
to do anything to her.
3Now Amnon had a friend named Jonadab
son of Shimeah, David's brother. Jonadab was
a very shrewd man. 4He asked Amnon, "Why
do you, the king's son, look so haggard morning after morning? Won't you tell me?"
Amnon said to him, "I'm in love with Tamar, my brother Absalom's sister."
5"Go to bed and pretend to be ill," Jonadab
said. "When your father comes to see you, say
to him, 'I would like my sister Tamar to come
and give me something to eat. Let her prepare
the food in my sight so I may watch her and
then eat it from her hand.' "
6So Amnon lay down and pretended to be ill.
When the king came to see him, Amnon said to
him, "I would like my sister Tamar to come and
make some special bread in my sight, so I may
eat from her hand."
7David sent word to Tamar at the palace:
"Go to the house of your brother Amnon and
prepare some food for him." 8So Tamar went to
the house of her brother Amnon, who was lying
down. She took some dough, kneaded it, made
the bread in his sight and baked it. 9Then she
took the pan and served him the bread, but he
refused to eat.
"Send everyone out of here," Amnon said. So
everyone left him. 10Then Amnon said to Tamar, "Bring the food here into my bedroom so
I may eat from your hand." And Tamar took the
bread she had prepared and brought it to her
brother Amnon in his bedroom. 11But when she
took it to him to eat, he grabbed her and said,
"Come to bed with me, my sister."
12"Don't, my brother!" she said to him.
"Don't force me. Such a thing should not be
done in Israel! Don't do this wicked thing.
13What about me? Where could I get rid of my
disgrace? And what about you? You would be
like one of the wicked fools in Israel. Please
speak to the king; he will not keep me from
being married to you." 14But he refused to listen
to her, and since he was stronger than she, he
raped her.
15Then Amnon hated her with intense hatred. In fact, he hated her more than he had
loved her. Amnon said to her, "Get up and get
out!"
16"No!" she said to him. "Sending me away
would be a greater wrong than what you have
already done to me."
But he refused to listen to her. 17He called his
personal servant and said, "Get this woman out
of here and bolt the door after her." 18So his
servant put her out and bolted the door after
her. She was wearing a richly ornamented[d]
robe, for this was the kind of garment the virgin
daughters of the king wore. 19Tamar put ashes
on her head and tore the ornamented[e] robe
she was wearing. She put her hand on her head
and went away, weeping aloud as she went.
20Her brother Absalom said to her, "Has that
Amnon, your brother, been with you? Be quiet

[a]30 Or *of Milcom* (that is, Molech) [b]30 That is, about 75 pounds (about 34 kilograms) [c]31 The meaning of the Hebrew for this clause is uncertain. [d]18 The meaning of the Hebrew for this phrase is uncertain. [e]19 The meaning of the Hebrew for this word is uncertain.

---

back to doing the things he should have been doing all along. We would be wise to follow David's example.

13:1–2 The consequences of our sins often remain long after the sins have been forgiven. David had pursued Bathsheba with no thought to the consequences. Amnon pursued an incestuous relationship with his half sister Tamar. Amnon's act was an indirect consequence of David's earlier failure. Amnon became obsessed with his quest to seduce the girl, and he satisfied his lusts, much as his father had done before him. Children learn by watching what we do. Our actions for good or bad can have consequences affecting generations far into the future.

13:13 As is true with all things God gives to us for pleasure, there is a right context for sexual gratification. God's Word gives us guidelines for healthy sexual relationships. God calls us to a life of discipline and self-control. Lasting sexual satisfaction can only be found in the context of a committed marriage. Tamar was aware of this truth as she tried to escape her attacker by appealing to his reason. Amnon, however, was too obsessed by his lust to stop and listen to her.

13:14–16 Amnon's selfish lust brought some terrible consequences. Tamar's future was destroyed. Her hopes for a good marriage were dashed. Amnon had to live with his guilt, and he soon discovered the bitter taste of sexual activity driven by selfish desire. His self-centered "love" turned to hate within minutes. Ultimately, Amnon would be murdered for his selfish sexual desire (see 13:29). When we give in to lust of any kind we too may experience these contradictory feelings, alternately embracing and despising the object of our lust. Love is willing to wait; lust will not. Whenever we recognize the grip of lust beginning to take hold, we need to confess it to God immediately.

13:20 Tamar probably never married; she was left a desolate woman. Her situation should remind us of the price others pay when we are driven by lust instead of love. Sometimes we try to deny the pain we may have caused others. True spiritual renewal can take place only when we honestly consider how we have hurt others, admit the wrongs we have committed and seek to restore our relationships and the lives of those we have wronged.

Amnon & Tamar

People can be destroyed emotionally by rape, incest or other kinds of sexual violation. Breaking God's laws concerning sexual behavior always causes devastation to people's lives. One tragic example of emotional devastation noted in the Bible is the scandal between Amnon and Tamar.

Amnon was David's oldest son. Tamar was Amnon's half sister. Amnon's sin began in his mind. His thoughts were full of sexual desire for his half sister. Amnon nurtured this fantasy until he finally shared it with his cousin Jonadab, who suggested a way to make Amnon's fantasy a reality. Amnon chose to follow Jonadab's advice. Blinding himself to the consequences that were sure to follow, Amnon satisfied his own desires and raped Tamar.

Tamar felt violated, abandoned, full of shame. Amnon's fleeting pleasure very likely cost Tamar the honorable future expected for a king's daughter. When Absalom, Tamar's full brother, was informed about what had happened, he was filled with rage. Absalom plotted against Amnon and finally killed him. Amnon's sin carried some severe consequences: Jonadab lost his integrity; Tamar lost her purity; Amnon lost his life; David lost a son.

David's family was out of control. David failed to confront Amnon about his sin, perhaps because of his own sexual promiscuity with Bathsheba. Tamar's family responded to her crisis with silence, deception, rage and denial. No one dared to speak the truth or vent their feelings against each other in healthy ways. Amnon's sin delivered terrible consequences to his family and those around him. David's failure to deal directly with that sin and hold Amnon accountable only compounded the devastation.

STRENGTHS AND ACCOMPLISHMENTS:

Though deeply hurt, Tamar displayed strength of character.

WEAKNESSES AND MISTAKES:

Amnon allowed temptation and lust to overwhelm him until he committed a horrible act against his half sister.

Amnon acted on some very unwise counsel.

Amnon failed to take responsibility for his actions.

LESSONS FROM THEIR LIVES:

All our moral choices have long-term, even eternal, consequences.

We must carefully consider from whom we seek advice.

If we don't deal with sin immediately, its consequences will be compounded.

The mistakes of parents are often repeated by their children.

KEY VERSE:

" 'Don't, my brother!' she said to him. 'Don't force me. Such a thing should not be done in Israel! Don't do this wicked thing' " (13:12).

The story of Amnon and Tamar is told in 2 Samuel 13. Amnon is also mentioned in 2 Samuel 3:2. Both are mentioned in David's family tree in 1 Chronicles 3.

now, my sister; he is your brother. Don't take this thing to heart." And Tamar lived in her brother Absalom's house, a desolate woman.

21When King David heard all this, he was furious. 22Absalom never said a word to Amnon, either good or bad; he hated Amnon because he had disgraced his sister Tamar.

Absalom Kills Amnon

23Two years later, when Absalom's sheepshearers were at Baal Hazor near the border of Ephraim, he invited all the king's sons to come there. 24Absalom went to the king and said, "Your servant has had shearers come. Will the king and his officials please join me?"

25"No, my son," the king replied. "All of us should not go; we would only be a burden to you." Although Absalom urged him, he still refused to go, but gave him his blessing.

26Then Absalom said, "If not, please let my brother Amnon come with us."

The king asked him, "Why should he go with you?" 27But Absalom urged him, so he sent with him Amnon and the rest of the king's sons.

28Absalom ordered his men, "Listen! When Amnon is in high spirits from drinking wine and I say to you, 'Strike Amnon down,' then kill him. Don't be afraid. Have not I given you this order? Be strong and brave." 29So Absalom's men did to Amnon what Absalom had ordered. Then all the king's sons got up, mounted their mules and fled.

30While they were on their way, the report came to David: "Absalom has struck down all the king's sons; not one of them is left." 31The king stood up, tore his clothes and lay down on the ground; and all his servants stood by with their clothes torn.

32But Jonadab son of Shimeah, David's brother, said, "My lord should not think that they killed all the princes; only Amnon is dead. This has been Absalom's expressed intention ever since the day Amnon raped his sister Tamar. 33My lord the king should not be concerned about the report that all the king's sons are dead. Only Amnon is dead."

34Meanwhile, Absalom had fled.

Now the man standing watch looked up and saw many people on the road west of him, coming down the side of the hill. The watchman went and told the king, "I see men in the direction of Horonaim, on the side of the hill."[a]

35Jonadab said to the king, "See, the king's sons are here; it has happened just as your servant said."

36As he finished speaking, the king's sons came in, wailing loudly. The king, too, and all his servants wept very bitterly.

37Absalom fled and went to Talmai son of Ammihud, the king of Geshur. But King David mourned for his son every day.

38After Absalom fled and went to Geshur, he stayed there three years. 39And the spirit of the king[b] longed to go to Absalom, for he was consoled concerning Amnon's death.

Absalom Returns to Jerusalem

14 Joab son of Zeruiah knew that the king's heart longed for Absalom. 2So Joab sent someone to Tekoa and had a wise woman brought from there. He said to her, "Pretend you are in mourning. Dress in mourning clothes, and don't use any cosmetic lotions. Act like a woman who has spent many days grieving for the dead. 3Then go to the king and speak these words to him." And Joab put the words in her mouth.

4When the woman from Tekoa went[c] to the king, she fell with her face to the ground to pay him honor, and she said, "Help me, O king!"

5The king asked her, "What is troubling you?"

She said, "I am indeed a widow; my husband is dead. 6I your servant had two sons. They got into a fight with each other in the field, and no one was there to separate them. One struck the other and killed him. 7Now the whole clan has risen up against your servant; they say, 'Hand over the one who struck his brother down, so that we may put him to death for the life of his brother whom he killed; then we will

[a]34 Septuagint; Hebrew does not have this sentence.
[b]39 Dead Sea Scrolls and some Septuagint manuscripts; Masoretic Text *But ⌊the spirit of⌋ David the king*
[c]4 Many Hebrew manuscripts, Septuagint, Vulgate and Syriac; most Hebrew manuscripts *spoke*

13:21–24 David was enraged when he first heard of Amnon's sin, but he never did anything about it. Perhaps he felt uncomfortable confronting Amnon since he had also failed in this area. David's failure to confront Amnon allowed the problem to fester. Eventually the issue exploded when Absalom murdered Amnon to avenge his sister's rape (see 13:29). When someone close to us acts irresponsibly, it may be easier to let our initial rage or concern subside rather than institute a confrontation. Selective avoidance is sometimes easier than confrontation, but as David's family situation attests, the consequences can be devastating.

13:37–39 David let two years pass and did nothing about Amnon's sin. David's failure to confront his son, hold him accountable and restore family unity planted the seeds of vengeance and murder. David also allowed three years to go by without communicating with Absalom, who had avenged his sister's rape by killing his brother Amnon. The resulting broken relationship flowered into a kingdom torn by rebellion. Forgiveness and the restoration of relationships are two primary concerns we should pursue in spiritual renewal. David's disregard for these principles brought painful consequences upon his family and his kingdom.

14:1–20 Joab, with the help of a woman from Tekoa, intervened in the conflict between David and Absalom. The wise woman gently opened David's eyes to the situation and urged him to restore his relationship with Absalom. David humbly listened and took steps to bring Absalom home from exile. When we avoid or ignore a festering problem in our lives, God may use other people to confront us with the real issues. When God provides wise counsel, we would be wise to listen humbly and then act accordingly.

get rid of the heir as well.' They would put out the only burning coal I have left, leaving my husband neither name nor descendant on the face of the earth."

8 The king said to the woman, "Go home, and I will issue an order in your behalf."

9 But the woman from Tekoa said to him, "My lord the king, let the blame rest on me and on my father's family, and let the king and his throne be without guilt."

10 The king replied, "If anyone says anything to you, bring him to me, and he will not bother you again."

11 She said, "Then let the king invoke the LORD his God to prevent the avenger of blood from adding to the destruction, so that my son will not be destroyed."

"As surely as the LORD lives," he said, "not one hair of your son's head will fall to the ground."

12 Then the woman said, "Let your servant speak a word to my lord the king."

"Speak," he replied.

13 The woman said, "Why then have you devised a thing like this against the people of God? When the king says this, does he not convict himself, for the king has not brought back his banished son? 14 Like water spilled on the ground, which cannot be recovered, so we must die. But God does not take away life; instead, he devises ways so that a banished person may not remain estranged from him.

15 "And now I have come to say this to my lord the king because the people have made me afraid. Your servant thought, 'I will speak to the king; perhaps he will do what his servant asks. 16 Perhaps the king will agree to deliver his servant from the hand of the man who is trying to cut off both me and my son from the inheritance God gave us.'

17 "And now your servant says, 'May the word of my lord the king bring me rest, for my lord the king is like an angel of God in discerning good and evil. May the LORD your God be with you.' "

18 Then the king said to the woman, "Do not keep from me the answer to what I am going to ask you."

"Let my lord the king speak," the woman said.

19 The king asked, "Isn't the hand of Joab with you in all this?"

The woman answered, "As surely as you live, my lord the king, no one can turn to the right or to the left from anything my lord the king says. Yes, it was your servant Joab who instructed me to do this and who put all these words into the mouth of your servant. 20 Your servant Joab did this to change the present situation. My lord has wisdom like that of an angel of God—he knows everything that happens in the land."

21 The king said to Joab, "Very well, I will do it. Go, bring back the young man Absalom."

22 Joab fell with his face to the ground to pay him honor, and he blessed the king. Joab said, "Today your servant knows that he has found favor in your eyes, my lord the king, because the king has granted his servant's request."

23 Then Joab went to Geshur and brought Absalom back to Jerusalem. 24 But the king said, "He must go to his own house; he must not see my face." So Absalom went to his own house and did not see the face of the king.

25 In all Israel there was not a man so highly praised for his handsome appearance as Absalom. From the top of his head to the sole of his foot there was no blemish in him. 26 Whenever he cut the hair of his head—he used to cut his hair from time to time when it became too heavy for him—he would weigh it, and its weight was two hundred shekels[a] by the royal standard.

27 Three sons and a daughter were born to Absalom. The daughter's name was Tamar, and she became a beautiful woman.

28 Absalom lived two years in Jerusalem without seeing the king's face. 29 Then Absalom sent for Joab in order to send him to the king, but Joab refused to come to him. So he sent a second time, but he refused to come. 30 Then he said to his servants, "Look, Joab's field is next to mine, and he has barley there. Go and set it on fire." So Absalom's servants set the field on fire.

31 Then Joab did go to Absalom's house and he said to him, "Why have your servants set my field on fire?"

32 Absalom said to Joab, "Look, I sent word to you and said, 'Come here so I can send you to the king to ask, "Why have I come from Geshur? It would be better for me if I were still there!" ' Now then, I want to see the king's face, and if I am guilty of anything, let him put me to death."

33 So Joab went to the king and told him this. Then the king summoned Absalom, and he came in and bowed down with his face to the ground before the king. And the king kissed Absalom.

[a] *26* That is, about 5 pounds (about 2.3 kilograms)

14:28–33 Absalom had been in limbo for five years. He had been exiled for three years to Geshur. Then he spent two more years in Jerusalem without ever speaking to his father. Absalom finally decided that he had waited long enough! Reunion with David, when it did come, was far too stilted and formal for genuine reconciliation. No tears were shed; no brokenness was in evidence; no effort was made to set things straight. The relationship between father and son was not restored. It seems that David granted Absalom only partial forgiveness. This led to further bondage and bitterness and was probably worse than no forgiveness at all. True forgiveness and reconciliation are an essential part of spiritual renewal.

Absalom's Conspiracy

15 In the course of time, Absalom provided himself with a chariot and horses
and with fifty men to run ahead of him. 2He
would get up early and stand by the side of the
road leading to the city gate. Whenever anyone
came with a complaint to be placed before the
king for a decision, Absalom would call out to
him, "What town are you from?" He would answer, "Your servant is from one of the tribes
of Israel." 3Then Absalom would say to him,
"Look, your claims are valid and proper, but
there is no representative of the king to hear
you." 4And Absalom would add, "If only I were
appointed judge in the land! Then everyone
who has a complaint or case could come to me
and I would see that he gets justice."
5Also, whenever anyone approached him to
bow down before him, Absalom would reach
out his hand, take hold of him and kiss him.
6Absalom behaved in this way toward all the
Israelites who came to the king asking for justice, and so he stole the hearts of the men of
Israel.
7At the end of four[a] years, Absalom said to
the king, "Let me go to Hebron and fulfill a
vow I made to the LORD. 8While your servant
was living at Geshur in Aram, I made this vow:
'If the LORD takes me back to Jerusalem, I will
worship the LORD in Hebron.[b]' "
9The king said to him, "Go in peace." So he
went to Hebron.
10Then Absalom sent secret messengers
throughout the tribes of Israel to say, "As soon
as you hear the sound of the trumpets, then say,
'Absalom is king in Hebron.' " 11Two hundred
men from Jerusalem had accompanied Absalom. They had been invited as guests and went
quite innocently, knowing nothing about the
matter. 12While Absalom was offering sacrifices,
he also sent for Ahithophel the Gilonite, David's counselor, to come from Giloh, his hometown. And so the conspiracy gained strength,
and Absalom's following kept on increasing.

David Flees

13A messenger came and told David, "The
hearts of the men of Israel are with Absalom."
14Then David said to all his officials who
were with him in Jerusalem, "Come! We must
flee, or none of us will escape from Absalom.

[a]7 Some Septuagint manuscripts, Syriac and Josephus; Hebrew *forty* [b]8 Some Septuagint manuscripts; Hebrew does not have *in Hebron.*

15:7–10 For Absalom, it had been nine years since he had murdered Amnon, six years since his return to Jerusalem and four years since his awkward reunion with his father David. Absalom seems to have given up hope of ever being truly reconciled with his father. Using religion as a cover, Absalom proceeded to lead an open rebellion against David. We are called to seek reconciliation with the people we have wronged. We must be careful not to delay, for if we wait too long, we may suffer as David did.

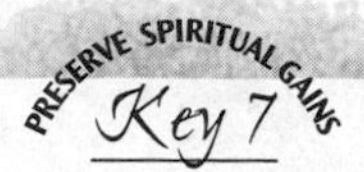

Never Too Spiritual to Stay Close to God

2 Samuel 15:1–26 There are times when we feel as though we're on top of the world and our struggle with sin is licked for good. In such times, it is tempting to relax and neglect our relationship with God. But if life surprises us with an unexpected problem, we come to our senses. We must constantly recognize that we are never so spiritually advanced that we can afford to neglect our relationship with the Lord.

King David had reached the pinnacle of political success. He had killed giants, won battles, captured the hearts of his people and overcome enemies on every side. Yet while David was in this comfortable position, life surprised him with a rebellion engineered by his own son. As David and his men were fleeing Jerusalem, he said to Zadok the priest, " 'Take the ark of God back into the city. If I find favor in the LORD's eyes, he will bring me back and let me see it and his dwelling place again. But if he says, "I am not pleased with you," then I am ready; let him do to me whatever seems good to him' " (15:25–26).

It may have been that David, in the midst of his successes, had fallen out of the habit of relying on God day by day, but he quickly placed his life back in God's hands in the midst of the rebellion. And God protected David and returned him to the throne in Jerusalem. When life hits us with unexpected threats, we should remember that our lives need to be in God's hands continually too.

Turn to 2 Chronicles 32.

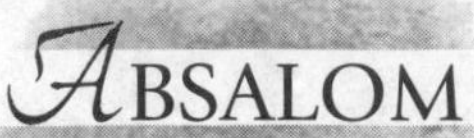

Absalom

Without true forgiveness, bitterness will inevitably tear our relationships apart. No relationship or family will hold together for long if the people involved are unable to grant forgiveness in both word and deed. Incomplete forgiveness might secure a semblance of peace within a family, but when forgiveness is not evidenced by the way we live, true reconciliation will never happen. Absalom, the third son of King David, suffered much and caused much suffering because true forgiveness was not a part of his life.

Early in his life Absalom discovered that his sister Tamar had been raped by his half brother Amnon. Absalom harbored hatred toward Amnon for a period of two years until he was able to kill him. Absalom then fled to the protection of his grandfather Talmai, king of Geshur, in order to avoid the wrath of his father. After three years of separation, David relented and permitted his son Absalom's return to Jerusalem. It wasn't until two years later that David finally spoke with Absalom. Apparently little was said between them, and David continued to ignore his son.

Although there was much weeping at the reunion of David and Absalom, the scars of isolation ran deep. Absalom was never able to regain the love he had once had for his father. Their relationship was severed. In fact, Absalom spent the rest of his life scheming against his father, and his life ended during a rebellion he led against King David. Absalom is an example of the wasted years and broken hearts that can result when we fail to speak the truth, accept responsibility for our sins, express our emotions honestly, hold each other accountable and truly forgive each other.

WEAKNESSES AND MISTAKES:

It seems that Absalom never once turned to God for guidance.

Absalom took the law into his own hands.

Absalom harbored hatred against those who opposed him, refusing to release the grudges he held and refusing to forgive.

LESSONS FROM HIS LIFE:

Incomplete forgiveness destroys relationships.

Words of forgiveness must be proven by action.

Delaying forgiveness may render reconciliation almost impossible.

The sins of parents are often repeated by their children.

KEY VERSE:

"Absalom never said a word to Amnon, either good or bad; he hated Amnon because he had disgraced his sister Tamar" (13:22).

Absalom's story is told in 2 Samuel 13—20. He is also mentioned in 2 Samuel 3:3; 1 Kings 1—2 and 1 Chronicles 3:2.

We must leave immediately, or he will move
quickly to overtake us and bring ruin upon us
and put the city to the sword."
15The king's officials answered him, "Your
servants are ready to do whatever our lord the
king chooses."
16The king set out, with his entire household
following him; but he left ten concubines to
take care of the palace. 17So the king set out,
with all the people following him, and they
halted at a place some distance away. 18All his
men marched past him, along with all the Kerethites and Pelethites; and all the six hundred
Gittites who had accompanied him from Gath
marched before the king.
19The king said to Ittai the Gittite, "Why
should you come along with us? Go back and
stay with King Absalom. You are a foreigner, an
exile from your homeland. 20You came only
yesterday. And today shall I make you wander
about with us, when I do not know where I am
going? Go back, and take your countrymen.
May kindness and faithfulness be with you."
21But Ittai replied to the king, "As surely as
the LORD lives, and as my lord the king lives,
wherever my lord the king may be, whether it
means life or death, there will your servant be."
22David said to Ittai, "Go ahead, march on."
So Ittai the Gittite marched on with all his men
and the families that were with him.
23The whole countryside wept aloud as all
the people passed by. The king also crossed the
Kidron Valley, and all the people moved on
toward the desert.
24Zadok was there, too, and all the Levites
who were with him were carrying the ark of the
covenant of God. They set down the ark of God,
and Abiathar offered sacrifices[a] until all the
people had finished leaving the city.
25Then the king said to Zadok, "Take the ark
of God back into the city. If I find favor in the
LORD's eyes, he will bring me back and let me
see it and his dwelling place again. 26But if he
says, 'I am not pleased with you,' then I am
ready; let him do to me whatever seems good to
him."
27The king also said to Zadok the priest,
"Aren't you a seer? Go back to the city in peace,
with your son Ahimaaz and Jonathan son of
Abiathar. You and Abiathar take your two sons
with you. 28I will wait at the fords in the desert
until word comes from you to inform me." 29So
Zadok and Abiathar took the ark of God back to
Jerusalem and stayed there.
30But David continued up the Mount of Olives, weeping as he went; his head was covered
and he was barefoot. All the people with him
covered their heads too and were weeping as
they went up. 31Now David had been told,
"Ahithophel is among the conspirators with
Absalom." So David prayed, "O LORD, turn
Ahithophel's counsel into foolishness."
32When David arrived at the summit, where
people used to worship God, Hushai the Arkite
was there to meet him, his robe torn and dust
on his head. 33David said to him, "If you go
with me, you will be a burden to me. 34But if
you return to the city and say to Absalom, 'I will
be your servant, O king; I was your father's servant in the past, but now I will be your servant,'
then you can help me by frustrating Ahithophel's advice. 35Won't the priests Zadok and
Abiathar be there with you? Tell them anything
you hear in the king's palace. 36Their two sons,
Ahimaaz son of Zadok and Jonathan son of
Abiathar, are there with them. Send them to me
with anything you hear."
37So David's friend Hushai arrived at Jerusalem as Absalom was entering the city.

David and Ziba

16 When David had gone a short distance
beyond the summit, there was Ziba, the
steward of Mephibosheth, waiting to meet him.
He had a string of donkeys saddled and loaded
with two hundred loaves of bread, a hundred
cakes of raisins, a hundred cakes of figs and a
skin of wine.
2The king asked Ziba, "Why have you
brought these?"
Ziba answered, "The donkeys are for the
king's household to ride on, the bread and fruit
are for the men to eat, and the wine is to refresh
those who become exhausted in the desert."
3The king then asked, "Where is your master's grandson?"
Ziba said to him, "He is staying in Jerusalem,
because he thinks, 'Today the house of Israel
will give me back my grandfather's kingdom.' "
4Then the king said to Ziba, "All that belonged to Mephibosheth is now yours."
"I humbly bow," Ziba said. "May I find favor
in your eyes, my lord the king."

Shimei Curses David

5As King David approached Bahurim, a man

[a]24 Or *Abiathar went up*

15:19–22 As we face difficulties in life, faithful friends can be our greatest asset. Ittai had commanded a foreign contingent of David's army for many years. As a foreigner, he could have returned to Jerusalem and declared his allegiance to Absalom. But instead, despite a probable tragic outcome, Ittai stood alongside his friend David. We need to seek out and cultivate true friends who will come alongside us, even when it would be to their advantage to leave. Sometimes the crucible of affliction helps us to glimpse who our real friends are and strengthens relationships that were not previously close, as in the case of David and Ittai.

16:5–12 What did David get for thirty years of successful, sacrificial leadership? Nothing but stones and curses. Notice that David refused to seek revenge against Shimei. Well aware of his own failures and beyond the point of denial, David was willing to accept Shimei's criticism. David put himself in God's hands, trusting that God would do what was right—whether it meant judgment or deliverance. As we experience failures, we need to follow Da-

from the same clan as Saul's family came out from there. His name was Shimei son of Gera, and he cursed as he came out. 6He pelted David and all the king's officials with stones, though all the troops and the special guard were on David's right and left. 7As he cursed, Shimei said, "Get out, get out, you man of blood, you scoundrel! 8The LORD has repaid you for all the blood you shed in the household of Saul, in whose place you have reigned. The LORD has handed the kingdom over to your son Absalom. You have come to ruin because you are a man of blood!"

9Then Abishai son of Zeruiah said to the king, "Why should this dead dog curse my lord the king? Let me go over and cut off his head."

10But the king said, "What do you and I have in common, you sons of Zeruiah? If he is cursing because the LORD said to him, 'Curse David,' who can ask, 'Why do you do this?' "

11David then said to Abishai and all his officials, "My son, who is of my own flesh, is trying to take my life. How much more, then, this Benjamite! Leave him alone; let him curse, for the LORD has told him to. 12It may be that the LORD will see my distress and repay me with good for the cursing I am receiving today."

13So David and his men continued along the road while Shimei was going along the hillside opposite him, cursing as he went and throwing stones at him and showering him with dirt. 14The king and all the people with him arrived at their destination exhausted. And there he refreshed himself.

The Advice of Hushai and Ahithophel

15Meanwhile, Absalom and all the men of Israel came to Jerusalem, and Ahithophel was with him. 16Then Hushai the Arkite, David's friend, went to Absalom and said to him, "Long live the king! Long live the king!"

17Absalom asked Hushai, "Is this the love you show your friend? Why didn't you go with your friend?"

18Hushai said to Absalom, "No, the one chosen by the LORD, by these people, and by all the men of Israel—his I will be, and I will remain with him. 19Furthermore, whom should I serve? Should I not serve the son? Just as I served your father, so I will serve you."

20Absalom said to Ahithophel, "Give us your advice. What should we do?"

21Ahithophel answered, "Lie with your father's concubines whom he left to take care of the palace. Then all Israel will hear that you have made yourself a stench in your father's nostrils, and the hands of everyone with you will be strengthened." 22So they pitched a tent for Absalom on the roof, and he lay with his father's concubines in the sight of all Israel.

23Now in those days the advice Ahithophel gave was like that of one who inquires of God. That was how both David and Absalom regarded all of Ahithophel's advice.

17 Ahithophel said to Absalom, "I would[a] choose twelve thousand men and set out tonight in pursuit of David. 2I would[b] attack him while he is weary and weak. I would[b] strike him with terror, and then all the people with him will flee. I would[b] strike down only the king 3and bring all the people back to you. The death of the man you seek will mean the return of all; all the people will be unharmed." 4This plan seemed good to Absalom and to all the elders of Israel.

5But Absalom said, "Summon also Hushai the Arkite, so we can hear what he has to say." 6When Hushai came to him, Absalom said, "Ahithophel has given this advice. Should we do what he says? If not, give us your opinion."

7Hushai replied to Absalom, "The advice Ahithophel has given is not good this time. 8You know your father and his men; they are fighters, and as fierce as a wild bear robbed of her cubs. Besides, your father is an experienced fighter; he will not spend the night with the troops. 9Even now, he is hidden in a cave or some other place. If he should attack your troops first,[c] whoever hears about it will say, 'There has been a slaughter among the troops who follow Absalom.' 10Then even the bravest soldier, whose heart is like the heart of a lion, will melt with fear, for all Israel knows that your father is a fighter and that those with him are brave.

11"So I advise you: Let all Israel, from Dan to Beersheba—as numerous as the sand on the seashore—be gathered to you, with you yourself leading them into battle. 12Then we will attack him wherever he may be found, and we will fall on him as dew settles on the ground. Neither he nor any of his men will be left alive. 13If he withdraws into a city, then all Israel will bring ropes to that city, and we will drag it down to the valley until not even a piece of it can be found."

14Absalom and all the men of Israel said, "The advice of Hushai the Arkite is better than that of Ahithophel." For the LORD had determined to frustrate the good advice of Ahithophel in order to bring disaster on Absalom.

15Hushai told Zadok and Abiathar, the priests, "Ahithophel has advised Absalom and the elders of Israel to do such and such, but I

[a] 1 Or *Let me* [b] 2 Or *will* [c] 9 Or *When some of the men fall at the first attack*

---

vid's example and put ourselves in God's hands; he will always do what is best for us.

17:14 No matter how strong our enemies may seem, they can never thwart God's plan (see Job 42:2). God used Hushai to lead Absalom toward disaster. God was working behind the scenes to protect David and give him a chance to recover his kingdom. As we continue following God's will day by day, God will accomplish his purposes for us. We can trust that he will work behind the scenes on our behalf, supporting us in ways we'll never know.

have advised them to do so and so. 16Now send
a message immediately and tell David, 'Do not
spend the night at the fords in the desert; cross
over without fail, or the king and all the people
with him will be swallowed up.' "
17Jonathan and Ahimaaz were staying at En
Rogel. A servant girl was to go and inform them,
and they were to go and tell King David, for
they could not risk being seen entering the city.
18But a young man saw them and told Absalom.
So the two of them left quickly and went to the
house of a man in Bahurim. He had a well in his
courtyard, and they climbed down into it. 19His
wife took a covering and spread it out over the
opening of the well and scattered grain over it.
No one knew anything about it.
20When Absalom's men came to the woman
at the house, they asked, "Where are Ahimaaz
and Jonathan?"

The woman answered them, "They crossed
over the brook."[a] The men searched but found
no one, so they returned to Jerusalem.
21After the men had gone, the two climbed
out of the well and went to inform King David.
They said to him, "Set out and cross the river at
once; Ahithophel has advised such and such
against you." 22So David and all the people with
him set out and crossed the Jordan. By daybreak, no one was left who had not crossed the
Jordan.
23When Ahithophel saw that his advice had
not been followed, he saddled his donkey and
set out for his house in his hometown. He put
his house in order and then hanged himself. So
he died and was buried in his father's tomb.
24David went to Mahanaim, and Absalom
crossed the Jordan with all the men of Israel.
25Absalom had appointed Amasa over the army
in place of Joab. Amasa was the son of a man
named Jether,[b] an Israelite[c] who had married
Abigail,[d] the daughter of Nahash and sister of
Zeruiah the mother of Joab. 26The Israelites and
Absalom camped in the land of Gilead.
27When David came to Mahanaim, Shobi
son of Nahash from Rabbah of the Ammonites,
and Makir son of Ammiel from Lo Debar, and
Barzillai the Gileadite from Rogelim 28brought
bedding and bowls and articles of pottery. They
also brought wheat and barley, flour and roasted grain, beans and lentils,[e] 29honey and
curds, sheep, and cheese from cows' milk for
David and his people to eat. For they said, "The
people have become hungry and tired and
thirsty in the desert."

Absalom's Death

18 David mustered the men who were
with him and appointed over them
commanders of thousands and commanders of
hundreds. 2David sent the troops out—a third
under the command of Joab, a third under
Joab's brother Abishai son of Zeruiah, and a
third under Ittai the Gittite. The king told the
troops, "I myself will surely march out with
you."
3But the men said, "You must not go out; if
we are forced to flee, they won't care about us.
Even if half of us die, they won't care; but you
are worth ten thousand of us.[f] It would be
better now for you to give us support from the
city."
4The king answered, "I will do whatever
seems best to you."

So the king stood beside the gate while all
the men marched out in units of hundreds and
of thousands. 5The king commanded Joab,
Abishai and Ittai, "Be gentle with the young
man Absalom for my sake." And all the troops
heard the king giving orders concerning Absalom to each of the commanders.
6The army marched into the field to fight
Israel, and the battle took place in the forest of
Ephraim. 7There the army of Israel was defeated
by David's men, and the casualties that day
were great—twenty thousand men. 8The battle
spread out over the whole countryside, and the
forest claimed more lives that day than the
sword.
9Now Absalom happened to meet David's
men. He was riding his mule, and as the mule
went under the thick branches of a large oak,
Absalom's head got caught in the tree. He was
left hanging in midair, while the mule he was
riding kept on going.
10When one of the men saw this, he told
Joab, "I just saw Absalom hanging in an oak
tree."
11Joab said to the man who had told him
this, "What! You saw him? Why didn't you
strike him to the ground right there? Then I
would have had to give you ten shekels[g] of
silver and a warrior's belt."
12But the man replied, "Even if a thousand
shekels[h] were weighed out into my hands, I
would not lift my hand against the king's son.
In our hearing the king commanded you and
Abishai and Ittai, 'Protect the young man Absalom for my sake.[i]' 13And if I had put my life
in jeopardy[j]—and nothing is hidden from the
king—you would have kept your distance
from me."
14Joab said, "I'm not going to wait like this
for you." So he took three javelins in his hand
and plunged them into Absalom's heart while

[a]20 Or *"They passed by the sheep pen toward the water."*
[b]25 Hebrew *Ithra,* a variant of *Jether* [c]25 Hebrew and some Septuagint manuscripts; other Septuagint manuscripts (see also 1 Chron. 2:17) *Ishmaelite* or *Jezreelite*
[d]25 Hebrew *Abigal,* a variant of *Abigail* [e]28 Most Septuagint manuscripts and Syriac; Hebrew *lentils, and roasted grain* [f]3 Two Hebrew manuscripts, some Septuagint manuscripts and Vulgate; most Hebrew manuscripts *care; for now there are ten thousand like us*
[g]11 That is, about 4 ounces (about 115 grams)
[h]12 That is, about 25 pounds (about 11 kilograms)
[i]12 A few Hebrew manuscripts, Septuagint, Vulgate and Syriac; most Hebrew manuscripts may be translated *Absalom, whoever you may be.* [j]13 Or *Otherwise, if I had acted treacherously toward him*

Absalom was still alive in the oak tree. 15And
ten of Joab's armor-bearers surrounded Absalom, struck him and killed him.
16Then Joab sounded the trumpet, and the
troops stopped pursuing Israel, for Joab halted
them. 17They took Absalom, threw him into a
big pit in the forest and piled up a large heap of
rocks over him. Meanwhile, all the Israelites
fled to their homes.
18During his lifetime Absalom had taken a
pillar and erected it in the King's Valley as a
monument to himself, for he thought, "I have
no son to carry on the memory of my name." He
named the pillar after himself, and it is called
Absalom's Monument to this day.

David Mourns

19Now Ahimaaz son of Zadok said, "Let me
run and take the news to the king that the LORD
has delivered him from the hand of his enemies."
20"You are not the one to take the news today," Joab told him. "You may take the news
another time, but you must not do so today,
because the king's son is dead."
21Then Joab said to a Cushite, "Go, tell the
king what you have seen." The Cushite bowed
down before Joab and ran off.
22Ahimaaz son of Zadok again said to Joab,
"Come what may, please let me run behind the
Cushite."
But Joab replied, "My son, why do you want
to go? You don't have any news that will bring
you a reward."
23He said, "Come what may, I want to run."
So Joab said, "Run!" Then Ahimaaz ran by
way of the plain[a] and outran the Cushite.
24While David was sitting between the inner
and outer gates, the watchman went up to the
roof of the gateway by the wall. As he looked
out, he saw a man running alone. 25The watchman called out to the king and reported it.
The king said, "If he is alone, he must have
good news." And the man came closer and
closer.
26Then the watchman saw another man running, and he called down to the gatekeeper,
"Look, another man running alone!"
The king said, "He must be bringing good
news, too."
27The watchman said, "It seems to me that
the first one runs like Ahimaaz son of Zadok."
"He's a good man," the king said. "He comes
with good news."
28Then Ahimaaz called out to the king, "All
is well!" He bowed down before the king with
his face to the ground and said, "Praise be to
the LORD your God! He has delivered up the
men who lifted their hands against my lord the
king."
29The king asked, "Is the young man Absalom safe?"
Ahimaaz answered, "I saw great confusion
just as Joab was about to send the king's servant
and me, your servant, but I don't know what it
was."
30The king said, "Stand aside and wait here."
So he stepped aside and stood there.
31Then the Cushite arrived and said, "My
lord the king, hear the good news! The LORD
has delivered you today from all who rose up
against you."
32The king asked the Cushite, "Is the young
man Absalom safe?"
The Cushite replied, "May the enemies of
my lord the king and all who rise up to harm
you be like that young man."
33The king was shaken. He went up to the
room over the gateway and wept. As he went, he
said: "O my son Absalom! My son, my son
Absalom! If only I had died instead of you—O
Absalom, my son, my son!"
19 Joab was told, "The king is weeping
and mourning for Absalom." 2And for
the whole army the victory that day was turned
into mourning, because on that day the troops
heard it said, "The king is grieving for his son."
3The men stole into the city that day as men
steal in who are ashamed when they flee from
battle. 4The king covered his face and cried
aloud, "O my son Absalom! O Absalom, my
son, my son!"
5Then Joab went into the house to the king
and said, "Today you have humiliated all your
men, who have just saved your life and the lives
of your sons and daughters and the lives of your
wives and concubines. 6You love those who
hate you and hate those who love you. You
have made it clear today that the commanders
and their men mean nothing to you. I see that
you would be pleased if Absalom were alive
today and all of us were dead. 7Now go out and

[a] *23* That is, the plain of the Jordan

18:15 Absalom died tragically: a rebel and the victim of a broken relationship with his father. He was the product of an unreconciled past. If painful emotions or events haunt us from our past, we also may end up fighting unnecessary battles and end up in an early grave. As with Absalom, we may not be entirely to blame for our broken relationships. Yet we are still responsible to deal with the issues and seek reconciliation. If we don't, we will probably destroy ourselves and bring down all the people close to us as well.

18:32–33 This passage shows us the importance of reconciliation if we want to build a peaceful future. David probably could have avoided this great sorrow had he been willing to forgive, set things straight and restore his relationship with Absalom. David had failed to seek reconciliation; now it was too late. He would never have Absalom back; he could never make things right with him. The consequences of David's sin lasted long after the act itself.

19:5–7 David had failed to thank his men for remaining loyal to him throughout the civil war. They deserved grateful congratulations, and Joab was courageous enough to confront David about his improper behavior. David was mourning the loss of his son, who had also been his enemy. Joab's intervention probably saved David's still shaky kingdom. The criticism of a friend is sometimes the right medicine to prompt us to proper action (see Proverbs 27:6).

encourage your men. I swear by the LORD that if you don't go out, not a man will be left with you by nightfall. This will be worse for you than all the calamities that have come upon you from your youth till now."

[8]So the king got up and took his seat in the gateway. When the men were told, "The king is sitting in the gateway," they all came before him.

David Returns to Jerusalem

Meanwhile, the Israelites had fled to their homes. [9]Throughout the tribes of Israel, the people were all arguing with each other, saying, "The king delivered us from the hand of our enemies; he is the one who rescued us from the hand of the Philistines. But now he has fled the country because of Absalom; [10]and Absalom, whom we anointed to rule over us, has died in battle. So why do you say nothing about bringing the king back?"

[11]King David sent this message to Zadok and Abiathar, the priests: "Ask the elders of Judah, 'Why should you be the last to bring the king back to his palace, since what is being said throughout Israel has reached the king at his quarters? [12]You are my brothers, my own flesh and blood. So why should you be the last to bring back the king?' [13]And say to Amasa, 'Are you not my own flesh and blood? May God deal with me, be it ever so severely, if from now on you are not the commander of my army in place of Joab.' "

[14]He won over the hearts of all the men of Judah as though they were one man. They sent word to the king, "Return, you and all your men." [15]Then the king returned and went as far as the Jordan.

Now the men of Judah had come to Gilgal to go out and meet the king and bring him across the Jordan. [16]Shimei son of Gera, the Benjamite from Bahurim, hurried down with the men of Judah to meet King David. [17]With him were a thousand Benjamites, along with Ziba, the steward of Saul's household, and his fifteen sons and twenty servants. They rushed to the Jordan, where the king was. [18]They crossed at the ford to take the king's household over and to do whatever he wished.

When Shimei son of Gera crossed the Jordan, he fell prostrate before the king [19]and said to him, "May my lord not hold me guilty. Do not remember how your servant did wrong on the day my lord the king left Jerusalem. May the king put it out of his mind. [20]For I your servant know that I have sinned, but today I have come here as the first of the whole house of Joseph to come down and meet my lord the king."

[21]Then Abishai son of Zeruiah said, "Shouldn't Shimei be put to death for this? He cursed the LORD's anointed."

[22]David replied, "What do you and I have in common, you sons of Zeruiah? This day you have become my adversaries! Should anyone be put to death in Israel today? Do I not know that today I am king over Israel?" [23]So the king said to Shimei, "You shall not die." And the king promised him on oath.

[24]Mephibosheth, Saul's grandson, also went down to meet the king. He had not taken care of his feet or trimmed his mustache or washed his clothes from the day the king left until the day he returned safely. [25]When he came from Jerusalem to meet the king, the king asked him, "Why didn't you go with me, Mephibosheth?"

[26]He said, "My lord the king, since I your servant am lame, I said, 'I will have my donkey saddled and will ride on it, so I can go with the king.' But Ziba my servant betrayed me. [27]And he has slandered your servant to my lord the king. My lord the king is like an angel of God; so do whatever pleases you. [28]All my grandfather's descendants deserved nothing but death from my lord the king, but you gave your servant a place among those who eat at your table. So what right do I have to make any more appeals to the king?"

[29]The king said to him, "Why say more? I order you and Ziba to divide the fields."

[30]Mephibosheth said to the king, "Let him take everything, now that my lord the king has arrived home safely."

[31]Barzillai the Gileadite also came down from Rogelim to cross the Jordan with the king and to send him on his way from there. [32]Now Barzillai was a very old man, eighty years of age. He had provided for the king during his stay in Mahanaim, for he was a very wealthy man. [33]The king said to Barzillai, "Cross over with me and stay with me in Jerusalem, and I will provide for you."

[34]But Barzillai answered the king, "How many more years will I live, that I should go up to Jerusalem with the king? [35]I am now eighty years old. Can I tell the difference between what is good and what is not? Can your servant taste what he eats and drinks? Can I still hear the voices of men and women singers? Why should your servant be an added burden to my lord the king? [36]Your servant will cross over the Jordan with the king for a short distance, but why should the king reward me in this way? [37]Let your servant return, that I may die in my own town near the tomb of my father and mother. But here is your servant Kimham. Let him cross over with my lord the king. Do for him whatever pleases you."

[38]The king said, "Kimham shall cross over

19:18–20 Shimei, trying to reconcile his relationship with King David, asked David to forgive and forget the stones and insults he had hurled during Absalom's rebellion. Shimei wanted to be freed from the burden of his past mistakes so he could build a solid future. God offers us this kind of forgiveness when we come to his Son, Jesus. Through him our sins are forgiven and forgotten; we are presented with the opportunity to start over again with a clean slate.

with me, and I will do for him whatever pleases
you. And anything you desire from me I will do
for you."

39So all the people crossed the Jordan, and
then the king crossed over. The king kissed Barzillai and gave him his blessing, and Barzillai
returned to his home.

40When the king crossed over to Gilgal, Kimham crossed with him. All the troops of Judah
and half the troops of Israel had taken the king
over.

41Soon all the men of Israel were coming
to the king and saying to him, "Why did our
brothers, the men of Judah, steal the king away
and bring him and his household across the
Jordan, together with all his men?"

42All the men of Judah answered the men of
Israel, "We did this because the king is closely
related to us. Why are you angry about it? Have
we eaten any of the king's provisions? Have we
taken anything for ourselves?"

43Then the men of Israel answered the men
of Judah, "We have ten shares in the king; and
besides, we have a greater claim on David than
you have. So why do you treat us with contempt? Were we not the first to speak of bringing back our king?"

But the men of Judah responded even more
harshly than the men of Israel.

Sheba Rebels Against David

20 Now a troublemaker named Sheba son
of Bicri, a Benjamite, happened to be
there. He sounded the trumpet and shouted,

"We have no share in David,
no part in Jesse's son!
Every man to his tent, O Israel!"

2So all the men of Israel deserted David to
follow Sheba son of Bicri. But the men of Judah
stayed by their king all the way from the Jordan
to Jerusalem.

3When David returned to his palace in Jerusalem, he took the ten concubines he had left to
take care of the palace and put them in a house
under guard. He provided for them, but did not
lie with them. They were kept in confinement
till the day of their death, living as widows.

4Then the king said to Amasa, "Summon the
men of Judah to come to me within three days,
and be here yourself." 5But when Amasa went to
summon Judah, he took longer than the time
the king had set for him.

6David said to Abishai, "Now Sheba son of
Bicri will do us more harm than Absalom did.
Take your master's men and pursue him, or he
will find fortified cities and escape from us." 7So
Joab's men and the Kerethites and Pelethites
and all the mighty warriors went out under the
command of Abishai. They marched out from
Jerusalem to pursue Sheba son of Bicri.

8While they were at the great rock in Gibeon,
Amasa came to meet them. Joab was wearing
his military tunic, and strapped over it at his
waist was a belt with a dagger in its sheath. As
he stepped forward, it dropped out of its sheath.

9Joab said to Amasa, "How are you, my
brother?" Then Joab took Amasa by the beard
with his right hand to kiss him. 10Amasa was
not on his guard against the dagger in Joab's
hand, and Joab plunged it into his belly, and his
intestines spilled out on the ground. Without
being stabbed again, Amasa died. Then Joab
and his brother Abishai pursued Sheba son of
Bicri.

11One of Joab's men stood beside Amasa and
said, "Whoever favors Joab, and whoever is for
David, let him follow Joab!" 12Amasa lay wallowing in his blood in the middle of the road,
and the man saw that all the troops came to a
halt there. When he realized that everyone who
came up to Amasa stopped, he dragged him
from the road into a field and threw a garment
over him. 13After Amasa had been removed
from the road, all the men went on with Joab
to pursue Sheba son of Bicri.

14Sheba passed through all the tribes of Israel
to Abel Beth Maacah[a] and through the entire
region of the Berites, who gathered together and
followed him. 15All the troops with Joab came
and besieged Sheba in Abel Beth Maacah. They
built a siege ramp up to the city, and it stood
against the outer fortifications. While they were
battering the wall to bring it down, 16a wise
woman called from the city, "Listen! Listen!
Tell Joab to come here so I can speak to him."
17He went toward her, and she asked, "Are you
Joab?"

"I am," he answered.

She said, "Listen to what your servant has to
say."

"I'm listening," he said.

18She continued, "Long ago they used to say,
'Get your answer at Abel,' and that settled it.
19We are the peaceful and faithful in Israel. You
are trying to destroy a city that is a mother in
Israel. Why do you want to swallow up the
LORD's inheritance?"

20"Far be it from me!" Joab replied, "Far be
it from me to swallow up or destroy! 21That is
not the case. A man named Sheba son of Bicri,
from the hill country of Ephraim, has lifted up
his hand against the king, against David. Hand
over this one man, and I'll withdraw from the
city."

The woman said to Joab, "His head will be
thrown to you from the wall."

22Then the woman went to all the people
with her wise advice, and they cut off the head
of Sheba son of Bicri and threw it to Joab. So he
sounded the trumpet, and his men dispersed
from the city, each returning to his home. And
Joab went back to the king in Jerusalem.

23Joab was over Israel's entire army; Benaiah
son of Jehoiada was over the Kerethites and

[a]14 Or *Abel, even Beth Maacah;* also in verse 15

Pelethites; 24 Adoniram[a] was in charge of forced labor; Jehoshaphat son of Ahilud was recorder; 25 Sheva was secretary; Zadok and Abiathar were priests; 26 and Ira the Jairite was David's priest.

The Gibeonites Avenged

21 During the reign of David, there was a famine for three successive years; so David sought the face of the LORD. The LORD said, "It is on account of Saul and his blood-stained house; it is because he put the Gibeonites to death."

2 The king summoned the Gibeonites and spoke to them. (Now the Gibeonites were not a part of Israel but were survivors of the Amorites; the Israelites had sworn to ⌊spare⌋ them, but Saul in his zeal for Israel and Judah had tried to annihilate them.) 3 David asked the Gibeonites, "What shall I do for you? How shall I make amends so that you will bless the LORD's inheritance?"

4 The Gibeonites answered him, "We have no right to demand silver or gold from Saul or his family, nor do we have the right to put anyone in Israel to death."

"What do you want me to do for you?" David asked.

5 They answered the king, "As for the man who destroyed us and plotted against us so that we have been decimated and have no place anywhere in Israel, 6 let seven of his male descendants be given to us to be killed and exposed before the LORD at Gibeah of Saul—the LORD's chosen one."

So the king said, "I will give them to you."

7 The king spared Mephibosheth son of Jonathan, the son of Saul, because of the oath before the LORD between David and Jonathan son of Saul. 8 But the king took Armoni and Mephibosheth, the two sons of Aiah's daughter Rizpah, whom she had borne to Saul, together with the five sons of Saul's daughter Merab,[b] whom she had borne to Adriel son of Barzillai the Meholathite. 9 He handed them over to the Gibeonites, who killed and exposed them on a hill before the LORD. All seven of them fell together; they were put to death during the first days of the harvest, just as the barley harvest was beginning.

10 Rizpah daughter of Aiah took sackcloth and spread it out for herself on a rock. From the beginning of the harvest till the rain poured down from the heavens on the bodies, she did not let the birds of the air touch them by day or the wild animals by night. 11 When David was told what Aiah's daughter Rizpah, Saul's concubine, had done, 12 he went and took the bones of Saul and his son Jonathan from the citizens of Jabesh Gilead. (They had taken them secretly from the public square at Beth Shan, where the Philistines had hung them after they struck Saul down on Gilboa.) 13 David brought the bones of Saul and his son Jonathan from there, and the bones of those who had been killed and exposed were gathered up.

14 They buried the bones of Saul and his son Jonathan in the tomb of Saul's father Kish, at Zela in Benjamin, and did everything the king commanded. After that, God answered prayer in behalf of the land.

Wars Against the Philistines

15 Once again there was a battle between the Philistines and Israel. David went down with his men to fight against the Philistines, and he became exhausted. 16 And Ishbi-Benob, one of the descendants of Rapha, whose bronze spearhead weighed three hundred shekels[c] and who was armed with a new ⌊sword⌋, said he would kill David. 17 But Abishai son of Zeruiah came to David's rescue; he struck the Philistine down and killed him. Then David's men swore to him, saying, "Never again will you go out with us to battle, so that the lamp of Israel will not be extinguished."

18 In the course of time, there was another battle with the Philistines, at Gob. At that time Sibbecai the Hushathite killed Saph, one of the descendants of Rapha.

19 In another battle with the Philistines at Gob, Elhanan son of Jaare-Oregim[d] the Bethlehemite killed Goliath[e] the Gittite, who had a spear with a shaft like a weaver's rod.

20 In still another battle, which took place at Gath, there was a huge man with six fingers on each hand and six toes on each foot—twenty-four in all. He also was descended from Rapha. 21 When he taunted Israel, Jonathan son of Shimeah, David's brother, killed him.

[a] *24* Some Septuagint manuscripts (see also 1 Kings 4:6 and 5:14); Hebrew *Adoram* [b] *8* Two Hebrew manuscripts, some Septuagint manuscripts and Syriac (see also 1 Samuel 18:19); most Hebrew and Septuagint manuscripts *Michal* [c] *16* That is, about 7 1/2 pounds (about 3.5 kilograms) [d] *19* Or *son of Jair the weaver* [e] *19* Hebrew and Septuagint; 1 Chron. 20:5 *son of Jair killed Lahmi the brother of Goliath*

21:1–14 The land of Israel suffered a drought because King Saul had broken a treaty with the Gibeonites. The consequences of Saul's sin lingered on, long after he had committed it. Sometimes we let things that serve as barriers to God's blessings remain hidden in our lives. We need to invite God to shine his light into the hidden areas of our lives; then God can help us remove these barriers. When the Israelites followed these principles, God answered their prayers for the land.

21:16–17 Accepting our limitations is a critical mark of maturity. David acknowledged his diminishing physical strength and agreed to stay away from battle. Sometimes our pride will not allow us to admit our limitations. As a result, we try to do things we are not capable of doing. We might think we are strong enough to resist temptation, but such an attitude of pride and self-sufficiency will only lead to a fall. We would be wise to follow David's example and admit there are certain things we cannot and should not try to do.

SEE THE TRUTH

Key 2

Seeing Our Place of Refuge

2 Samuel 22:1–33 When life seems to be coming at us fast and furiously, it may be hard to see the truth about ourselves. In order to see clearly, we must take a moment to pause and reflect. As often as possible, we need to entrust our daily battles to God, and take a thoughtful look at the big picture of our lives.

King David experienced many battles throughout his life, yet he almost always seemed to remain strong in the midst of them. How did he do it? His song in 2 Samuel gives us a clue: "The LORD is my rock, my fortress and my deliverer; my God is my rock, in whom I take refuge, my shield and the horn of my salvation. He is my stronghold, my refuge and my savior" (22:2–3). Though enemies often surrounded David on all sides, he knew that he could find refuge in the Lord, who was more than able to protect him.

When we are overwhelmed, in distress or when it's hard to see clearly, we should retreat to God. He's always there, ready to shield and protect us whenever we call on him. Once we are hidden in God, we can see what is true, what is important and what he would have us do next.

Turn to 1 Kings 19.

22These four were descendants of Rapha in
Gath, and they fell at the hands of David and
his men.

David's Song of Praise

22 David sang to the LORD the words of
this song when the LORD delivered him
from the hand of all his enemies and from the
hand of Saul. 2He said:

"The LORD is my rock, my fortress and my
deliverer;
3 my God is my rock, in whom I take
refuge,
my shield and the horn[a] of my
salvation.
He is my stronghold, my refuge and my
savior—
from violent men you save me.
4I call to the LORD, who is worthy of praise,
and I am saved from my enemies.

5"The waves of death swirled about me;
the torrents of destruction overwhelmed
me.
6The cords of the grave[b] coiled around me;
the snares of death confronted me.
7In my distress I called to the LORD;
I called out to my God.
From his temple he heard my voice;
my cry came to his ears.

8"The earth trembled and quaked,
the foundations of the heavens[c] shook;
they trembled because he was angry.
9Smoke rose from his nostrils;
consuming fire came from his mouth,
burning coals blazed out of it.
10He parted the heavens and came down;
dark clouds were under his feet.
11He mounted the cherubim and flew;
he soared[d] on the wings of the wind.
12He made darkness his canopy around him—
the dark[e] rain clouds of the sky.
13Out of the brightness of his presence
bolts of lightning blazed forth.
14The LORD thundered from heaven;
the voice of the Most High resounded.
15He shot arrows and scattered ⌞the enemies⌟,
bolts of lightning and routed them.
16The valleys of the sea were exposed
and the foundations of the earth laid
bare

[a] 3 *Horn* here symbolizes strength. [b] 6 Hebrew *Sheol*
[c] 8 Hebrew; Vulgate and Syriac (see also Psalm 18:7) *mountains* [d] 11 Many Hebrew manuscripts (see also Psalm 18:10); most Hebrew manuscripts *appeared*
[e] 12 Septuagint and Vulgate (see also Psalm 18:11); Hebrew *massed*

22:1 Near the close of his life, David still had a song in his heart because he had surrendered himself to God's sovereignty. This chapter records lyrics that also appear in Psalm 18. David's song is a celebration of his deliverance. It is this sort of unabashed, authentic praise that puts the devil to flight.

at the rebuke of the LORD,
at the blast of breath from his nostrils.

17 "He reached down from on high and took hold of me;
he drew me out of deep waters.
18 He rescued me from my powerful enemy,
from my foes, who were too strong for me.
19 They confronted me in the day of my disaster,
but the LORD was my support.
20 He brought me out into a spacious place;
he rescued me because he delighted in me.

21 "The LORD has dealt with me according to my righteousness;
according to the cleanness of my hands he has rewarded me.
22 For I have kept the ways of the LORD;
I have not done evil by turning from my God.
23 All his laws are before me;
I have not turned away from his decrees.
24 I have been blameless before him
and have kept myself from sin.
25 The LORD has rewarded me according to my righteousness,
according to my cleanness[a] in his sight.

26 "To the faithful you show yourself faithful,
to the blameless you show yourself blameless,
27 to the pure you show yourself pure,
but to the crooked you show yourself shrewd.
28 You save the humble,
but your eyes are on the haughty to bring them low.
29 You are my lamp, O LORD;
the LORD turns my darkness into light.
30 With your help I can advance against a troop[b];
with my God I can scale a wall.

31 "As for God, his way is perfect;
the word of the LORD is flawless.
He is a shield
for all who take refuge in him.
32 For who is God besides the LORD?
And who is the Rock except our God?
33 It is God who arms me with strength[c]
and makes my way perfect.
34 He makes my feet like the feet of a deer;
he enables me to stand on the heights.
35 He trains my hands for battle;
my arms can bend a bow of bronze.
36 You give me your shield of victory;
you stoop down to make me great.
37 You broaden the path beneath me,
so that my ankles do not turn.

38 "I pursued my enemies and crushed them;
I did not turn back till they were destroyed.
39 I crushed them completely, and they could not rise;
they fell beneath my feet.
40 You armed me with strength for battle;
you made my adversaries bow at my feet.
41 You made my enemies turn their backs in flight,
and I destroyed my foes.
42 They cried for help, but there was no one to save them—
to the LORD, but he did not answer.
43 I beat them as fine as the dust of the earth;
I pounded and trampled them like mud in the streets.

44 "You have delivered me from the attacks of my people;
you have preserved me as the head of nations.
People I did not know are subject to me,
45 and foreigners come cringing to me;
as soon as they hear me, they obey me.
46 They all lose heart;
they come trembling[d] from their strongholds.

47 "The LORD lives! Praise be to my Rock!
Exalted be God, the Rock, my Savior!
48 He is the God who avenges me,
who puts the nations under me,
49 who sets me free from my enemies.
You exalted me above my foes;
from violent men you rescued me.
50 Therefore I will praise you, O LORD, among the nations;
I will sing praises to your name.
51 He gives his king great victories;
he shows unfailing kindness to his anointed,
to David and his descendants forever."

The Last Words of David

23 These are the last words of David:

"The oracle of David son of Jesse,
the oracle of the man exalted by the Most High,

[a] 25 Hebrew; Septuagint and Vulgate (see also Psalm 18:24) *to the cleanness of my hands* [b] 30 Or *can run through a barricade* [c] 33 Dead Sea Scrolls, some Septuagint manuscripts, Vulgate and Syriac (see also Psalm 18:32); Masoretic Text *who is my strong refuge* [d] 46 Some Septuagint manuscripts and Vulgate (see also Psalm 18:45); Masoretic Text *they arm themselves.*

22:17–18 David was able to recognize God's hand in his life. He knew that God had reached down, taken hold of him and drawn him out of deep waters. Even at the end of his life, David recognized his vulnerability and God's sovereignty. This attitude of humility allows us to seek God and surrender to him; it is a character quality we can never afford to outgrow.

the man anointed by the God of Jacob,
Israel's singer of songs[a]:

2"The Spirit of the LORD spoke through me;
his word was on my tongue.
3The God of Israel spoke,
the Rock of Israel said to me:
'When one rules over men in righteousness,
when he rules in the fear of God,
4he is like the light of morning at sunrise
on a cloudless morning,
like the brightness after rain
that brings the grass from the earth.'

5"Is not my house right with God?
Has he not made with me an everlasting
covenant,
arranged and secured in every part?
Will he not bring to fruition my salvation
and grant me my every desire?
6But evil men are all to be cast aside like
thorns,
which are not gathered with the hand.
7Whoever touches thorns
uses a tool of iron or the shaft of a
spear;
they are burned up where they lie."

David's Mighty Men

8These are the names of David's mighty men:
Josheb-Basshebeth,[b] a Tahkemonite,[c] was
chief of the Three; he raised his spear against
eight hundred men, whom he killed[d] in one
encounter.

9Next to him was Eleazar son of Dodai the
Ahohite. As one of the three mighty men, he
was with David when they taunted the Philistines gathered ⌊at Pas Dammim⌋[e] for battle.
Then the men of Israel retreated, 10but he stood
his ground and struck down the Philistines till
his hand grew tired and froze to the sword. The
LORD brought about a great victory that day. The
troops returned to Eleazar, but only to strip the
dead.

11Next to him was Shammah son of Agee the
Hararite. When the Philistines banded together
at a place where there was a field full of lentils,
Israel's troops fled from them. 12But Shammah
took his stand in the middle of the field. He
defended it and struck the Philistines down,
and the LORD brought about a great victory.

13During harvest time, three of the thirty
chief men came down to David at the cave of
Adullam, while a band of Philistines was encamped in the Valley of Rephaim. 14At that time
David was in the stronghold, and the Philistine
garrison was at Bethlehem. 15David longed for
water and said, "Oh, that someone would get
me a drink of water from the well near the gate
of Bethlehem!" 16So the three mighty men broke
through the Philistine lines, drew water from
the well near the gate of Bethlehem and carried
it back to David. But he refused to drink it;
instead, he poured it out before the LORD.
17"Far be it from me, O LORD, to do this!" he
said. "Is it not the blood of men who went at
the risk of their lives?" And David would not
drink it.

Such were the exploits of the three mighty
men.

18Abishai the brother of Joab son of Zeruiah
was chief of the Three.[f] He raised his spear
against three hundred men, whom he killed,
and so he became as famous as the Three. 19Was
he not held in greater honor than the Three? He
became their commander, even though he was
not included among them.

20Benaiah son of Jehoiada was a valiant fighter from Kabzeel, who performed great exploits.
He struck down two of Moab's best men. He
also went down into a pit on a snowy day and
killed a lion. 21And he struck down a huge Egyptian. Although the Egyptian had a spear in his
hand, Benaiah went against him with a club. He
snatched the spear from the Egyptian's hand
and killed him with his own spear. 22Such were
the exploits of Benaiah son of Jehoiada; he
too was as famous as the three mighty men.
23He was held in greater honor than any of
the Thirty, but he was not included among
the Three. And David put him in charge of his
bodyguard.

24Among the Thirty were:
Asahel the brother of Joab,
Elhanan son of Dodo from Bethlehem,
25Shammah the Harodite,
Elika the Harodite,
26Helez the Paltite,
Ira son of Ikkesh from Tekoa,
27Abiezer from Anathoth,
Mebunnai[g] the Hushathite,
28Zalmon the Ahohite,
Maharai the Netophathite,

[a]1 Or *Israel's beloved singer* [b]8 Hebrew; some Septuagint manuscripts suggest *Ish-Bosheth,* that is, *Esh-Baal* (see also 1 Chron. 11:11 *Jashobeam*).
[c]8 Probably a variant of *Hacmonite* (see 1 Chron. 11:11)
[d]8 Some Septuagint manuscripts (see also 1 Chron. 11:11); Hebrew and other Septuagint manuscripts *Three; it was Adino the Eznite who killed eight hundred men*
[e]9 See 1 Chron. 11:13; Hebrew *gathered there.*
[f]18 Most Hebrew manuscripts (see also 1 Chron. 11:20); two Hebrew manuscripts and Syriac *Thirty*
[g]27 Hebrew; some Septuagint manuscripts (see also 1 Chron. 11:29) *Sibbecai*

23:5 In spite of all of David's ups and downs God had stood by him. Early in David's life, God had promised that David would father a dynasty that would rule forever. There must have been times when David wondered if that promise would ever happen. He had watched his kingdom crumble and his sons tear each other apart, but David knew in his heart that God could fulfill his promises. Though near the end of his life, David's faith was still strong. God promises hope and forgiveness for us too. We can be sure, no matter how bad things may seem at times, that God is faithful to his promises.

29 Heled[a] son of Baanah the Netophathite,
Ithai son of Ribai from Gibeah in Benjamin,
30 Benaiah the Pirathonite,
Hiddai[b] from the ravines of Gaash,
31 Abi-Albon the Arbathite,
Azmaveth the Barhumite,
32 Eliahba the Shaalbonite,
the sons of Jashen,
Jonathan 33 son of[c] Shammah the Hararite,
Ahiam son of Sharar[d] the Hararite,
34 Eliphelet son of Ahasbai the Maacathite,
Eliam son of Ahithophel the Gilonite,
35 Hezro the Carmelite,
Paarai the Arbite,
36 Igal son of Nathan from Zobah,
the son of Hagri,[e]
37 Zelek the Ammonite,
Naharai the Beerothite, the armor-bearer of Joab son of Zeruiah,
38 Ira the Ithrite,
Gareb the Ithrite
39 and Uriah the Hittite.

There were thirty-seven in all.

David Counts the Fighting Men

24 Again the anger of the LORD burned
against Israel, and he incited David
against them, saying, "Go and take a census of
Israel and Judah."
2 So the king said to Joab and the army commanders[f] with him, "Go throughout the
tribes of Israel from Dan to Beersheba and enroll the fighting men, so that I may know how
many there are."
3 But Joab replied to the king, "May the LORD
your God multiply the troops a hundred times
over, and may the eyes of my lord the king see
it. But why does my lord the king want to do
such a thing?"
4 The king's word, however, overruled Joab
and the army commanders; so they left the presence of the king to enroll the fighting men of
Israel.
5 After crossing the Jordan, they camped near
Aroer, south of the town in the gorge, and then
went through Gad and on to Jazer. 6 They went
to Gilead and the region of Tahtim Hodshi, and
on to Dan Jaan and around toward Sidon.
7 Then they went toward the fortress of Tyre and
all the towns of the Hivites and Canaanites.
Finally, they went on to Beersheba in the Negev
of Judah.
8 After they had gone through the entire land,
they came back to Jerusalem at the end of nine
months and twenty days.
9 Joab reported the number of the fighting
men to the king: In Israel there were eight hundred thousand able-bodied men who could
handle a sword, and in Judah five hundred
thousand.
10 David was conscience-stricken after he had
counted the fighting men, and he said to the
LORD, "I have sinned greatly in what I have
done. Now, O LORD, I beg you, take away the
guilt of your servant. I have done a very foolish
thing."
11 Before David got up the next morning, the
word of the LORD had come to Gad the prophet,
David's seer: 12 "Go and tell David, 'This is what
the LORD says: I am giving you three options.
Choose one of them for me to carry out against
you.' "
13 So Gad went to David and said to him,
"Shall there come upon you three[g] years of
famine in your land? Or three months of fleeing
from your enemies while they pursue you? Or
three days of plague in your land? Now then,
think it over and decide how I should answer
the one who sent me."
14 David said to Gad, "I am in deep distress.
Let us fall into the hands of the LORD, for his
mercy is great; but do not let me fall into the
hands of men."
15 So the LORD sent a plague on Israel from
that morning until the end of the time designated, and seventy thousand of the people from
Dan to Beersheba died. 16 When the angel
stretched out his hand to destroy Jerusalem, the
LORD was grieved because of the calamity and
said to the angel who was afflicting the people,
"Enough! Withdraw your hand." The angel of
the LORD was then at the threshing floor of
Araunah the Jebusite.
17 When David saw the angel who was striking down the people, he said to the LORD, "I am
the one who has sinned and done wrong. These
are but sheep. What have they done? Let your
hand fall upon me and my family."

[a] *29* Some Hebrew manuscripts and Vulgate (see also 1 Chron. 11:30); most Hebrew manuscripts *Heleb*
[b] *30* Hebrew; some Septuagint manuscripts (see also 1 Chron. 11:32) *Hurai*
[c] *33* Some Septuagint manuscripts (see also 1 Chron. 11:34); Hebrew does not have *son of.*
[d] *33* Hebrew; some Septuagint manuscripts (see also 1 Chron. 11:35) *Sacar*
[e] *36* Some Septuagint manuscripts (see also 1 Chron. 11:38); Hebrew *Haggadi*
[f] *2* Septuagint (see also verse 4 and 1 Chron. 21:2); Hebrew *Joab the army commander*
[g] *13* Septuagint (see also 1 Chron. 21:12); Hebrew *seven*

24:10 David sinned, but notice how sensitive his conscience was. He quickly admitted his failure. Even near the end of his life, David was obviously less than perfect. Yet he was greatly used and deeply loved by God. This reality should encourage all of us, for none of us is perfect! God never requires perfection; he looks for a humble willingness to accept correction. God's grace is extended to everyone who comes to him with a repentant heart and without pretense.

24:15–25 David's sin brought tremendous suffering upon innocent bystanders. Yet David responded properly and brought restitution, restoring his fellowship with God. We should be aware that the consequences of our sins and disobedience will touch the people around us, especially if we are in positions of leadership.

David Builds an Altar

[18]On that day Gad went to David and said to him, "Go up and build an altar to the LORD on the threshing floor of Araunah the Jebusite." [19]So David went up, as the LORD had commanded through Gad. [20]When Araunah looked and saw the king and his men coming toward him, he went out and bowed down before the king with his face to the ground.

[21]Araunah said, "Why has my lord the king come to his servant?"

"To buy your threshing floor," David answered, "so I can build an altar to the LORD, that the plague on the people may be stopped."

[22]Araunah said to David, "Let my lord the king take whatever pleases him and offer it up. Here are oxen for the burnt offering, and here are threshing sledges and ox yokes for the wood. [23]O king, Araunah gives all this to the king." Araunah also said to him, "May the LORD your God accept you."

[24]But the king replied to Araunah, "No, I insist on paying you for it. I will not sacrifice to the LORD my God burnt offerings that cost me nothing."

So David bought the threshing floor and the oxen and paid fifty shekels[a] of silver for them. [25]David built an altar to the LORD there and sacrificed burnt offerings and fellowship offerings.[b] Then the LORD answered prayer in behalf of the land, and the plague on Israel was stopped.

[a]*24* That is, about 1 1/4 pounds (about 0.6 kilogram)
[b]*25* Traditionally *peace offerings*

1 Kings

The Big Picture

The book of 1 Kings was originally part of a larger book that also included 2 Kings. It recorded Israel's history from the last days of King David to the demise of both the northern and southern kingdoms. At the opening of 1 Kings, the Israelites were obedient to God and following his plan. Israel was still one nation under Solomon's rule. Solomon led the nation to a position of world prominence, and his wisdom became legendary. Kings and queens from foreign lands traveled great distances just to meet him.

But Solomon's success and the nation's prominence led them to a feeling of self-sufficiency and pride. They turned their backs on the God who had blessed them so richly and fell into a downward spiral that led to a divided kingdom ruled by sinful, corrupt kings. The people wandered from God and began to worship idols, ignoring the laws that God had given them.

Yet throughout this period of prideful rebellion, God continued to reach out to his people. Righteous kings like Asa and godly prophets like Elijah called the people to seek God and surrender to him. Some people responded positively; others did not. Elijah's confrontation with Ahab and Jezebel was a dramatic example of how God called disobedient kings to account for their actions. Elijah, though a flawed human being, won many great victories for God by faith.

This book is filled with examples of people who trusted God and received his help. It is also filled with the accounts of people who disobeyed God and suffered the consequences of their rebellion. Yet even when the people disobeyed, God never gave up on them. He did everything he could to draw his people into a healthy, vibrant relationship with himself.

A. THE UNITED KINGDOM: PRIDE PRECEDES THE FALL (1:1–11:43)

1. Fulfillment: Going From Good to Great (1:1–2:46)
2. Greed: Serving Self Before God (3:1–8:66)
3. Spiritual Blindness: Running Away From Reality (9:1–11:43)

B. THE DIVIDED KINGDOM: A NATION SELF-DESTRUCTS (12:1–22:53)

1. Rebellion: A Failure to Let Go (12:1–14:31)
2. Indecision: An Attitude of Apathy (15:1–16:34)
3. Spiritual Renewal: God's Intervention (17:1–19:21)
4. Refusal: God's Warning Ignored (20:1–22:53)

Spiritual Renewal Themes

THE DANGERS OF SUCCESS

Solomon achieved everything he could have desired—wealth, success, prestige and power. But his experience illustrates that success can lead to failure if we are not careful, especially when we claim sole responsibility for our achievements. When we think we have it made, we are probably on our way to a fall. Solomon, in his success, became proud and stubborn before God. He refused to hear the warnings God gave him and later suffered the consequences (see 11:9–11).

Essential Facts

PURPOSE:
To record the history of Solomon and the early kings of the divided kingdom and to illustrate the blessings of obeying God and the negative consequences of disobeying him.

AUTHOR:
Unknown, but possibly Jeremiah, Ezra or Ezekiel.

AUDIENCE:
The people of Israel in Babylonian exile.

DATE WRITTEN:
Sometime between 560 and 538 B.C.

SETTING:
The united kingdom of Israel under Solomon; then the kingdoms of Israel and Judah.

KEY VERSES:
"As for you, if you walk before me in integrity of heart and uprightness, as David your father did, and do all I command and observe my decrees and laws, I will establish your royal throne over Israel forever, as I promised David your father when I said, 'You shall never fail to have a man on the throne of Israel' " (9:4-5).

KEY PEOPLE:
David, Solomon, Rehoboam, Jeroboam, Elijah, Ahab, Jezebel.

SERIOUS PROBLEMS ACROSS GENERATIONS

David's weakness with women became a weakness in his son Solomon. Solomon did not limit his sexual behavior according to God's commands. As serious problems carry over into the next generation, they are often intensified and become more destructive. In David's case, his sin with Bathsheba led to painful consequences within his family. In Solomon's case, his lust resulted in multiple, foreign wives who then led him into idolatry. His idolatry affected the whole nation of Israel by leading the people away from God.

THE IMPORTANCE OF ACCOUNTABILITY

We need to be accountable to someone who will be honest with us. Such a person will confront us and help us see our sin. When Solomon stopped listening to God, no one could get his attention. The same was true of the kings who followed him—they were accountable to no one. They were too proud to listen to God's message to them from the prophets. The results of their pride were sin and failure, which led to sin among their people. We would be wise to humble ourselves, continually reflect on our spiritual condition, remain accountable to others, and be open to wise counsel.

Adonijah Sets Himself Up as King

1 When King David was old and well advanced in years, he could not keep warm
even when they put covers over him. 2So his
servants said to him, "Let us look for a young
virgin to attend the king and take care of him.
She can lie beside him so that our lord the king
may keep warm."
3Then they searched throughout Israel for a
beautiful girl and found Abishag, a Shunammite, and brought her to the king. 4The girl was
very beautiful; she took care of the king and
waited on him, but the king had no intimate
relations with her.
5Now Adonijah, whose mother was Haggith,
put himself forward and said, "I will be king." So
he got chariots and horses[a] ready, with fifty
men to run ahead of him. 6(His father had never interfered with him by asking, "Why do you
behave as you do?" He was also very handsome
and was born next after Absalom.)
7Adonijah conferred with Joab son of Zeruiah and with Abiathar the priest, and they gave
him their support. 8But Zadok the priest, Benaiah son of Jehoiada, Nathan the prophet, Shimei and Rei[b] and David's special guard did not
join Adonijah.
9Adonijah then sacrificed sheep, cattle and
fattened calves at the Stone of Zoheleth near En
Rogel. He invited all his brothers, the king's
sons, and all the men of Judah who were royal
officials, 10but he did not invite Nathan the
prophet or Benaiah or the special guard or his
brother Solomon.
11Then Nathan asked Bathsheba, Solomon's
mother, "Have you not heard that Adonijah,
the son of Haggith, has become king without
our lord David's knowing it? 12Now then, let
me advise you how you can save your own life
and the life of your son Solomon. 13Go in to
King David and say to him, 'My lord the king,
did you not swear to me your servant: "Surely
Solomon your son shall be king after me, and
he will sit on my throne"? Why then has Adonijah become king?' 14While you are still there
talking to the king, I will come in and confirm
what you have said."
15So Bathsheba went to see the aged king in
his room, where Abishag the Shunammite was
attending him. 16Bathsheba bowed low and
knelt before the king.
"What is it you want?" the king asked.
17She said to him, "My lord, you yourself
swore to me your servant by the LORD your God:
'Solomon your son shall be king after me, and
he will sit on my throne.' 18But now Adonijah
has become king, and you, my lord the king, do
not know about it. 19He has sacrificed great
numbers of cattle, fattened calves, and sheep,
and has invited all the king's sons, Abiathar the
priest and Joab the commander of the army, but
he has not invited Solomon your servant. 20My
lord the king, the eyes of all Israel are on you,
to learn from you who will sit on the throne
of my lord the king after him. 21Otherwise, as
soon as my lord the king is laid to rest with his
fathers, I and my son Solomon will be treated
as criminals."
22While she was still speaking with the king,
Nathan the prophet arrived. 23And they told the
king, "Nathan the prophet is here." So he went
before the king and bowed with his face to the
ground.
24Nathan said, "Have you, my lord the king,
declared that Adonijah shall be king after you,
and that he will sit on your throne? 25Today he
has gone down and sacrificed great numbers of
cattle, fattened calves, and sheep. He has invited
all the king's sons, the commanders of the army
and Abiathar the priest. Right now they are eating and drinking with him and saying, 'Long
live King Adonijah!' 26But me your servant, and
Zadok the priest, and Benaiah son of Jehoiada,
and your servant Solomon he did not invite.
27Is this something my lord the king has done
without letting his servants know who should
sit on the throne of my lord the king after him?"

David Makes Solomon King

28Then King David said, "Call in Bathsheba."
So she came into the king's presence and stood
before him.
29The king then took an oath: "As surely as
the LORD lives, who has delivered me out of
every trouble, 30I will surely carry out today
what I swore to you by the LORD, the God of
Israel: Solomon your son shall be king after me,
and he will sit on my throne in my place."
31Then Bathsheba bowed low with her face
to the ground and, kneeling before the king,
said, "May my lord King David live forever!"
32King David said, "Call in Zadok the priest,
Nathan the prophet and Benaiah son of Jehoiada." When they came before the king, 33he said
to them: "Take your lord's servants with you

[a]5 Or *charioteers* [b]8 Or *and his friends*

1:5–6 The conflict between Adonijah and Solomon resulted because of one of King David's earlier mistakes. David had never disciplined his son Adonijah. David's failure as a father led to conflict among his sons on a number of occasions. Notice also that Solomon was the son of David and Bathsheba, whose relationship had begun with adultery, deceit and murder. Despite the painful start to their relationship, Bathsheba became David's favorite wife, and he promised her son Solomon the throne. Yet God used David's many failures to work his divine will for Israel. Solomon became the wisest and most powerful of all of Israel's kings. We have all made mistakes, and yet we can trust God to take our lives as they are—the bad and the good—and make something remarkable out of them.

1:28–40 Nathan the prophet and Zadok the priest anointed Solomon as king under the orders of King David. David realized that he was going to die soon. He took care of his responsibility to secure the throne for Solomon. Unwisely, many of us put off the task of providing for our family's future. Planning for our death is not being morbid; it is part of responsible living.

and set Solomon my son on my own mule and take him down to Gihon. 34There have Zadok the priest and Nathan the prophet anoint him king over Israel. Blow the trumpet and shout, 'Long live King Solomon!' 35Then you are to go up with him, and he is to come and sit on my throne and reign in my place. I have appointed him ruler over Israel and Judah."

36Benaiah son of Jehoiada answered the king, "Amen! May the LORD, the God of my lord the king, so declare it. 37As the LORD was with my lord the king, so may he be with Solomon to make his throne even greater than the throne of my lord King David!"

38So Zadok the priest, Nathan the prophet, Benaiah son of Jehoiada, the Kerethites and the Pelethites went down and put Solomon on King David's mule and escorted him to Gihon. 39Zadok the priest took the horn of oil from the sacred tent and anointed Solomon. Then they sounded the trumpet and all the people shouted, "Long live King Solomon!" 40And all the people went up after him, playing flutes and rejoicing greatly, so that the ground shook with the sound.

41Adonijah and all the guests who were with him heard it as they were finishing their feast. On hearing the sound of the trumpet, Joab asked, "What's the meaning of all the noise in the city?"

42Even as he was speaking, Jonathan son of Abiathar the priest arrived. Adonijah said, "Come in. A worthy man like you must be bringing good news."

43"Not at all!" Jonathan answered. "Our lord King David has made Solomon king. 44The king has sent with him Zadok the priest, Nathan the prophet, Benaiah son of Jehoiada, the Kerethites and the Pelethites, and they have put him on the king's mule, 45and Zadok the priest and Nathan the prophet have anointed him king at Gihon. From there they have gone up cheering, and the city resounds with it. That's the noise you hear. 46Moreover, Solomon has taken his seat on the royal throne. 47Also, the royal officials have come to congratulate our lord King David, saying, 'May your God make Solomon's name more famous than yours and his throne greater than yours!' And the king bowed in worship on his bed 48and said, 'Praise be to the LORD, the God of Israel, who has allowed my eyes to see a successor on my throne today.' "

49At this, all Adonijah's guests rose in alarm and dispersed. 50But Adonijah, in fear of Solomon, went and took hold of the horns of the altar. 51Then Solomon was told, "Adonijah is afraid of King Solomon and is clinging to the horns of the altar. He says, 'Let King Solomon swear to me today that he will not put his servant to death with the sword.' "

52Solomon replied, "If he shows himself to be a worthy man, not a hair of his head will fall to the ground; but if evil is found in him, he will die." 53Then King Solomon sent men, and they brought him down from the altar. And Adonijah came and bowed down to King Solomon, and Solomon said, "Go to your home."

David's Charge to Solomon

2 When the time drew near for David to die, he gave a charge to Solomon his son.

2"I am about to go the way of all the earth," he said. "So be strong, show yourself a man, 3and observe what the LORD your God requires: Walk in his ways, and keep his decrees and commands, his laws and requirements, as written in the Law of Moses, so that you may prosper in all you do and wherever you go, 4and that the LORD may keep his promise to me: 'If your descendants watch how they live, and if they walk faithfully before me with all their heart and soul, you will never fail to have a man on the throne of Israel.'

5"Now you yourself know what Joab son of Zeruiah did to me—what he did to the two commanders of Israel's armies, Abner son of Ner and Amasa son of Jether. He killed them, shedding their blood in peacetime as if in battle, and with that blood stained the belt around his waist and the sandals on his feet. 6Deal with him according to your wisdom, but do not let his gray head go down to the grave[a] in peace.

7"But show kindness to the sons of Barzillai of Gilead and let them be among those who eat at your table. They stood by me when I fled from your brother Absalom.

8"And remember, you have with you Shimei son of Gera, the Benjamite from Bahurim, who called down bitter curses on me the day I went to Mahanaim. When he came down to meet me at the Jordan, I swore to him by the LORD: 'I will not put you to death by the sword.' 9But now, do not consider him innocent. You are a man of wisdom; you will know what to do to him. Bring his gray head down to the grave in blood."

10Then David rested with his fathers and was buried in the City of David. 11He had reigned forty years over Israel—seven years in Hebron

[a]6 Hebrew *Sheol*; also in verse 9

1:41–53 Adonijah, David's oldest living son, expected to take Israel's throne and, for a span of a few hours, apparently held the kingship. When Solomon finally gained control, he would have been expected to kill his rival. But Solomon showed great mercy and forgiveness to Adonijah. When we are attacked at a personal level, we may want to seek revenge. Granting forgiveness requires a greater strength of character. We need to let go of our desire for revenge, releasing to God the wrongs that others have committed against us. We impede spiritual growth when we hold on to our anger and refuse to forgive.

2:1–12 David instructed his son Solomon how to rule and whom to trust. David advised his son to keep his eyes on God. Solomon learned who his allies and enemies were. Godly parents need to sit down and talk with their children just as David did with Solomon. This will help children learn respect for authority and equip them to face the challenges ahead.

and thirty-three in Jerusalem. 12So Solomon sat on the throne of his father David, and his rule was firmly established.

Solomon's Throne Established

13Now Adonijah, the son of Haggith, went to Bathsheba, Solomon's mother. Bathsheba asked him, "Do you come peacefully?"

He answered, "Yes, peacefully." 14Then he added, "I have something to say to you."

"You may say it," she replied.

15"As you know," he said, "the kingdom was mine. All Israel looked to me as their king. But things changed, and the kingdom has gone to my brother; for it has come to him from the LORD. 16Now I have one request to make of you. Do not refuse me."

"You may make it," she said.

17So he continued, "Please ask King Solomon—he will not refuse you—to give me Abishag the Shunammite as my wife."

18"Very well," Bathsheba replied, "I will speak to the king for you."

19When Bathsheba went to King Solomon to speak to him for Adonijah, the king stood up to meet her, bowed down to her and sat down on his throne. He had a throne brought for the king's mother, and she sat down at his right hand.

20"I have one small request to make of you," she said. "Do not refuse me."

The king replied, "Make it, my mother; I will not refuse you."

21So she said, "Let Abishag the Shunammite be given in marriage to your brother Adonijah."

22King Solomon answered his mother, "Why do you request Abishag the Shunammite for Adonijah? You might as well request the kingdom for him—after all, he is my older brother—yes, for him and for Abiathar the priest and Joab son of Zeruiah!"

23Then King Solomon swore by the LORD: "May God deal with me, be it ever so severely, if Adonijah does not pay with his life for this request! 24And now, as surely as the LORD lives—he who has established me securely on the throne of my father David and has founded a dynasty for me as he promised—Adonijah shall be put to death today!" 25So King Solomon gave orders to Benaiah son of Jehoiada, and he struck down Adonijah and he died.

26To Abiathar the priest the king said, "Go back to your fields in Anathoth. You deserve to die, but I will not put you to death now, because you carried the ark of the Sovereign LORD before my father David and shared all my father's hardships." 27So Solomon removed Abiathar from the priesthood of the LORD, fulfilling the word the LORD had spoken at Shiloh about the house of Eli.

28When the news reached Joab, who had conspired with Adonijah though not with Absalom, he fled to the tent of the LORD and took hold of the horns of the altar. 29King Solomon was told that Joab had fled to the tent of the LORD and was beside the altar. Then Solomon ordered Benaiah son of Jehoiada, "Go, strike him down!"

30So Benaiah entered the tent of the LORD and said to Joab, "The king says, 'Come out!' "

But he answered, "No, I will die here."

Benaiah reported to the king, "This is how Joab answered me."

31Then the king commanded Benaiah, "Do as he says. Strike him down and bury him, and so clear me and my father's house of the guilt of the innocent blood that Joab shed. 32The LORD will repay him for the blood he shed, because without the knowledge of my father David he attacked two men and killed them with the sword. Both of them—Abner son of Ner, commander of Israel's army, and Amasa son of Jether, commander of Judah's army—were better men and more upright than he. 33May the guilt of their blood rest on the head of Joab and his descendants forever. But on David and his descendants, his house and his throne, may there be the LORD's peace forever."

34So Benaiah son of Jehoiada went up and struck down Joab and killed him, and he was buried on his own land[a] in the desert. 35The king put Benaiah son of Jehoiada over the army in Joab's position and replaced Abiathar with Zadok the priest.

36Then the king sent for Shimei and said to him, "Build yourself a house in Jerusalem and live there, but do not go anywhere else. 37The day you leave and cross the Kidron Valley, you can be sure you will die; your blood will be on your own head."

38Shimei answered the king, "What you say is good. Your servant will do as my lord the king has said." And Shimei stayed in Jerusalem for a long time.

39But three years later, two of Shimei's slaves ran off to Achish son of Maacah, king of Gath, and Shimei was told, "Your slaves are in Gath." 40At this, he saddled his donkey and went to Achish at Gath in search of his slaves. So Shimei went away and brought the slaves back from Gath.

41When Solomon was told that Shimei had gone from Jerusalem to Gath and had returned, 42the king summoned Shimei and said to him, "Did I not make you swear by the LORD and

[a]34 Or *buried in his tomb*

2:13–25 Adonijah again plotted to take the throne by asking that Solomon allow him to marry David's nurse, Abishag. In ancient times, sleeping with one of the king's wives was tantamount to making a claim to the throne. Bathsheba was apparently unaware of Adonijah's plot and took him at his word. Solomon understood the true nature of Adonijah's request and ordered that he be executed, fulfilling his earlier promise (see 1:52–53). Solomon showed strength by living up to his previous promise. We need to live up to any promises we make too.

warn you, 'On the day you leave to go anywhere else, you can be sure you will die'? At that time you said to me, 'What you say is good. I will obey.' 43Why then did you not keep your oath to the LORD and obey the command I gave you?"

44The king also said to Shimei, "You know in your heart all the wrong you did to my father David. Now the LORD will repay you for your wrongdoing. 45But King Solomon will be blessed, and David's throne will remain secure before the LORD forever."

46Then the king gave the order to Benaiah son of Jehoiada, and he went out and struck Shimei down and killed him.

The kingdom was now firmly established in Solomon's hands.

Solomon Asks for Wisdom

3 Solomon made an alliance with Pharaoh king of Egypt and married his daughter. He brought her to the City of David until he finished building his palace and the temple of the LORD, and the wall around Jerusalem. 2The people, however, were still sacrificing at the high places, because a temple had not yet been built for the Name of the LORD. 3Solomon showed his love for the LORD by walking according to the statutes of his father David, except that he offered sacrifices and burned incense on the high places.

4The king went to Gibeon to offer sacrifices, for that was the most important high place, and Solomon offered a thousand burnt offerings on that altar. 5At Gibeon the LORD appeared to Solomon during the night in a dream, and God said, "Ask for whatever you want me to give you."

6Solomon answered, "You have shown great kindness to your servant, my father David, because he was faithful to you and righteous and upright in heart. You have continued this great kindness to him and have given him a son to sit on his throne this very day.

7"Now, O LORD my God, you have made your servant king in place of my father David. But I am only a little child and do not know how to carry out my duties. 8Your servant is here among the people you have chosen, a great people, too numerous to count or number. 9So give your servant a discerning heart to govern your people and to distinguish between right and wrong. For who is able to govern this great people of yours?"

10The Lord was pleased that Solomon had asked for this. 11So God said to him, "Since you have asked for this and not for long life or wealth for yourself, nor have asked for the death of your enemies but for discernment in administering justice, 12I will do what you have asked. I will give you a wise and discerning heart, so that there will never have been anyone like you, nor will there ever be. 13Moreover, I will give you what you have not asked for—both riches and honor—so that in your lifetime you will have no equal among kings. 14And if you walk in my ways and obey my statutes and commands as David your father did, I will give you a long life." 15Then Solomon awoke—and he realized it had been a dream.

He returned to Jerusalem, stood before the ark of the Lord's covenant and sacrificed burnt offerings and fellowship offerings.[a] Then he gave a feast for all his court.

A Wise Ruling

16Now two prostitutes came to the king and stood before him. 17One of them said, "My lord, this woman and I live in the same house. I had a baby while she was there with me. 18The third day after my child was born, this woman also had a baby. We were alone; there was no one in the house but the two of us.

19"During the night this woman's son died because she lay on him. 20So she got up in the middle of the night and took my son from my side while I your servant was asleep. She put him by her breast and put her dead son by my breast. 21The next morning, I got up to nurse my son—and he was dead! But when I looked at him closely in the morning light, I saw that it wasn't the son I had borne."

22The other woman said, "No! The living one is my son; the dead one is yours."

But the first one insisted, "No! The dead one is yours; the living one is mine." And so they argued before the king.

23The king said, "This one says, 'My son is alive and your son is dead,' while that one says, 'No! Your son is dead and mine is alive.' "

24Then the king said, "Bring me a sword." So they brought a sword for the king. 25He then gave an order: "Cut the living child in two and give half to one and half to the other."

26The woman whose son was alive was filled with compassion for her son and said to the king, "Please, my lord, give her the living baby! Don't kill him!"

[a]15 Traditionally *peace offerings*

3:3–15 God appeared to Solomon in a dream and told him he could have anything he wanted. Solomon asked for wisdom and discernment so he could rule God's people well. God was pleased with Solomon's request and granted him his wish, adding to it wealth and honor. Solomon put his concern for his people before his own desires. His selfless attitude brought him blessings beyond belief. Often the road to personal blessing is a life lived selflessly for others.

3:16–28 Solomon was in a difficult situation. Two women claimed to be the mother of the same child. Obviously one of the women was lying, but which one? This was a major test of Solomon's wisdom. Solomon handled the situation discerningly, and the child was returned to his real mother. Solomon had been given the special gift of wisdom to maintain peace in his kingdom. We all have gifts to offer others, and we need to use these gifts to the best of our ability.

But the other said, "Neither I nor you shall
have him. Cut him in two!"
27 Then the king gave his ruling: "Give the
living baby to the first woman. Do not kill him;
she is his mother."
28 When all Israel heard the verdict the king
had given, they held the king in awe, because
they saw that he had wisdom from God to administer justice.

Solomon's Officials and Governors

4 So King Solomon ruled over all Israel.
2 And these were his chief officials:

Azariah son of Zadok—the priest;
3 Elihoreph and Ahijah, sons of Shisha—secretaries;
Jehoshaphat son of Ahilud—recorder;
4 Benaiah son of Jehoiada—commander in chief;
Zadok and Abiathar—priests;
5 Azariah son of Nathan—in charge of the district officers;
Zabud son of Nathan—a priest and personal adviser to the king;
6 Ahishar—in charge of the palace;
Adoniram son of Abda—in charge of forced labor.

7 Solomon also had twelve district governors
over all Israel, who supplied provisions for the
king and the royal household. Each one had to
provide supplies for one month in the year.
8 These are their names:

Ben-Hur—in the hill country of Ephraim;
9 Ben-Deker—in Makaz, Shaalbim, Beth Shemesh and Elon Bethhanan;
10 Ben-Hesed—in Arubboth (Socoh and all the land of Hepher were his);
11 Ben-Abinadab—in Naphoth Dor[a] (he was married to Taphath daughter of Solomon);
12 Baana son of Ahilud—in Taanach and Megiddo, and in all of Beth Shan next to Zarethan below Jezreel, from Beth Shan to Abel Meholah across to Jokmeam;
13 Ben-Geber—in Ramoth Gilead (the settlements of Jair son of Manasseh in Gilead were his, as well as the district of Argob in Bashan and its sixty large walled cities with bronze gate bars);
14 Ahinadab son of Iddo—in Mahanaim;
15 Ahimaaz—in Naphtali (he had married Basemath daughter of Solomon);
16 Baana son of Hushai—in Asher and in Aloth;
17 Jehoshaphat son of Paruah—in Issachar;
18 Shimei son of Ela—in Benjamin;
19 Geber son of Uri—in Gilead (the country of Sihon king of the Amorites and the country of Og king of Bashan). He was the only governor over the district.

Solomon's Daily Provisions

20 The people of Judah and Israel were as numerous as the sand on the seashore; they ate,
they drank and they were happy. 21 And Solomon ruled over all the kingdoms from the River[b] to the land of the Philistines, as far as the
border of Egypt. These countries brought tribute
and were Solomon's subjects all his life.
22 Solomon's daily provisions were thirty
cors[c] of fine flour and sixty cors[d] of meal,
23 ten head of stall-fed cattle, twenty of pasture-
fed cattle and a hundred sheep and goats, as
well as deer, gazelles, roebucks and choice fowl.
24 For he ruled over all the kingdoms west of the
River, from Tiphsah to Gaza, and had peace on
all sides. 25 During Solomon's lifetime Judah
and Israel, from Dan to Beersheba, lived in safety, each man under his own vine and fig tree.
26 Solomon had four[e] thousand stalls for
chariot horses, and twelve thousand horses.[f]
27 The district officers, each in his month,
supplied provisions for King Solomon and all
who came to the king's table. They saw to it that
nothing was lacking. 28 They also brought to the
proper place their quotas of barley and straw for
the chariot horses and the other horses.

Solomon's Wisdom

29 God gave Solomon wisdom and very great
insight, and a breadth of understanding as mea-
sureless as the sand on the seashore. 30 Solomon's wisdom was greater than the wisdom of
all the men of the East, and greater than all the
wisdom of Egypt. 31 He was wiser than any other
man, including Ethan the Ezrahite—wiser than
Heman, Calcol and Darda, the sons of Mahol.
And his fame spread to all the surrounding nations. 32 He spoke three thousand proverbs and
his songs numbered a thousand and five. 33 He
described plant life, from the cedar of Lebanon
to the hyssop that grows out of walls. He also
taught about animals and birds, reptiles and
fish. 34 Men of all nations came to listen to Solomon's wisdom, sent by all the kings of the
world, who had heard of his wisdom.

[a] *11* Or *in the heights of Dor* [b] *21* That is, the Euphrates; also in verse 24 [c] *22* That is, probably about 185 bushels (about 6.6 kiloliters) [d] *22* That is, probably about 375 bushels (about 13.2 kiloliters) [e] *26* Some Septuagint manuscripts (see also 2 Chron. 9:25); Hebrew *forty* [f] *26* Or *charioteers*

4:29–34 Sharing with others what we know is one of the greatest gifts we can offer. Solomon had been granted wisdom by God (see 3:11–12). Instead of feeling pride at this point in his life, however, Solomon chose to share his wealth of knowledge with others. People came from other countries to listen and learn from the wisdom that God had given Solomon. All of us have been given a special kind of knowledge that comes from our daily experiences. We can offer our experiences and victories to others, helping them in their spiritual journeys.

Americans have traditionally valued a strong work ethic. Most of us believe that the harder we work, the greater our chance for success. But if left unchecked, this positive work ethic can cause us to overwork—devoting all of our time to working without maintaining the balance that helps us preserve spiritual gains. We may even sacrifice healthy family relationships, friendships and our walk with God in order to achieve more and advance in our profession.

After the reign of King David, Solomon became king of Israel. He faced several revolts early in his reign, but soon consolidated his power base and took firm control over the kingdom. In a dream God promised to give Solomon anything he desired, and Solomon chose wisdom so he could rule God's people wisely. God was pleased with Solomon's selfless choice. He gave this young king honor, wealth and a long life in addition to the wisdom he had requested.

But from this point on, Solomon's life became imbalanced. He started off well by building the temple. Then Solomon built his own palace and fortified his country against intruders. All of these projects were rendered on an enormous scale, even by today's standards. In order to accomplish these tasks, Solomon sacrificed important relationships with his people, his family and his God. He taxed his people heavily and required them to work hard on his many building projects. He failed to teach his son Rehoboam wisdom in ruling the people. Solomon also stopped listening to God and even disobeyed him by marrying numerous pagan women and worshiping their gods.

In our busyness with work and achievements, it is easy to forget the source of our strength and success. We must remember that God and our families are the top priorities in life. Whenever anything else is placed above these, we are headed for trouble.

STRENGTHS AND ACCOMPLISHMENTS:

Solomon was the wisest man who ever lived.

He passed on his wisdom by writing numerous proverbs and psalms.

He built God's temple in Jerusalem.

He completed many difficult long-term projects.

WEAKNESSES AND MISTAKES:

Solomon compromised his relationship with God by marrying pagan women.

He worshiped the gods of his pagan wives.

He placed loyalty to his work above his loyalty to God.

He drained the people of their resources in order to achieve his personal goals.

LESSONS FROM HIS LIFE:

If we reject God's plan, we are headed for trouble, no matter how much practical wisdom we have.

Obedience to God is the beginning of personal success.

We must seek to pass on to others the relationship we have with God.

KEY VERSE:

"Was it not because of marriages like these that Solomon king of Israel sinned? Among the many nations there was no king like him. He was loved by his God, and God made him king over all Israel, but even he was led into sin by foreign women" (Nehemiah 13:26).

Solomon's story is told in 2 Samuel 12:24; 1 Kings 1—11; 2 Kings 21:7; 23:13; 24:13; 1 Chronicles 28—2 Chronicles 13. He is also mentioned in Nehemiah 13:26; Proverbs 1:1; 10:1; 25:1; Song of Songs 3; 8; Matthew 1:7; 6:29; Luke 11:31; 12:27 and Acts 7:47.

Preparations for Building the Temple

5 When Hiram king of Tyre heard that Solomon had been anointed king to succeed his father David, he sent his envoys to Solomon, because he had always been on friendly terms with David. 2Solomon sent back this message to Hiram:

3"You know that because of the wars waged against my father David from all sides, he could not build a temple for the Name of the LORD his God until the LORD put his enemies under his feet. 4But now the LORD my God has given me rest on every side, and there is no adversary or disaster. 5I intend, therefore, to build a temple for the Name of the LORD my God, as the LORD told my father David, when he said, 'Your son whom I will put on the throne in your place will build the temple for my Name.'

6"So give orders that cedars of Lebanon be cut for me. My men will work with yours, and I will pay you for your men whatever wages you set. You know that we have no one so skilled in felling timber as the Sidonians."

7When Hiram heard Solomon's message, he was greatly pleased and said, "Praise be to the LORD today, for he has given David a wise son to rule over this great nation."

8So Hiram sent word to Solomon:

"I have received the message you sent me and will do all you want in providing the cedar and pine logs. 9My men will haul them down from Lebanon to the sea, and I will float them in rafts by sea to the place you specify. There I will separate them and you can take them away. And you are to grant my wish by providing food for my royal household."

10In this way Hiram kept Solomon supplied with all the cedar and pine logs he wanted, 11and Solomon gave Hiram twenty thousand cors[a] of wheat as food for his household, in addition to twenty thousand baths[b,c] of pressed olive oil. Solomon continued to do this for Hiram year after year. 12The LORD gave Solomon wisdom, just as he had promised him. There were peaceful relations between Hiram and Solomon, and the two of them made a treaty.

13King Solomon conscripted laborers from all Israel—thirty thousand men. 14He sent them off to Lebanon in shifts of ten thousand a month, so that they spent one month in Lebanon and two months at home. Adoniram was in charge of the forced labor. 15Solomon had seventy thousand carriers and eighty thousand stonecutters in the hills, 16as well as thirty-three hundred[d] foremen who supervised the project and directed the workmen. 17At the king's command they removed from the quarry large blocks of quality stone to provide a foundation of dressed stone for the temple. 18The craftsmen of Solomon and Hiram and the men of Gebal[e] cut and prepared the timber and stone for the building of the temple.

Solomon Builds the Temple

6 In the four hundred and eightieth[f] year after the Israelites had come out of Egypt, in the fourth year of Solomon's reign over Israel, in the month of Ziv, the second month, he began to build the temple of the LORD.

2The temple that King Solomon built for the LORD was sixty cubits long, twenty wide and thirty high.[g] 3The portico at the front of the main hall of the temple extended the width of the temple, that is twenty cubits,[h] and projected ten cubits[i] from the front of the temple. 4He made narrow clerestory windows in the temple. 5Against the walls of the main hall and inner sanctuary he built a structure around the building, in which there were side rooms. 6The lowest floor was five cubits[j] wide, the middle floor six cubits[k] and the third floor seven.[l] He made offset ledges around the outside of the temple so that nothing would be inserted into the temple walls.

7In building the temple, only blocks dressed at the quarry were used, and no hammer, chisel or any other iron tool was heard at the temple site while it was being built.

[a]11 That is, probably about 125,000 bushels (about 4,400 kiloliters) [b]11 Septuagint (see also 2 Chron. 2:10); Hebrew *twenty cors* [c]11 That is, about 115,000 gallons (about 440 kiloliters) [d]16 Hebrew; some Septuagint manuscripts (see also 2 Chron. 2:2, 18) *thirty-six hundred* [e]18 That is, Byblos [f]1 Hebrew; Septuagint *four hundred and fortieth* [g]2 That is, about 90 feet (about 27 meters) long and 30 feet (about 9 meters) wide and 45 feet (about 13.5 meters) high [h]3 That is, about 30 feet (about 9 meters) [i]3 That is, about 15 feet (about 4.5 meters) [j]6 That is, about 7 1/2 feet (about 2.3 meters); also in verses 10 and 24 [k]6 That is, about 9 feet (about 2.7 meters) [l]6 That is, about 10 1/2 feet (about 3.1 meters)

5:1–12 King David had established a sound relationship with Hiram of Tyre. Solomon continued that relationship and enjoyed its numerous benefits. Solomon's great building projects could never have been achieved alone. Hiram was able to provide some of the expertise and many of the materials that Solomon needed. God may have chosen people to encourage us and provide us with resources we need for our spiritual growth. We need to let God use these people in our lives by making ourselves accountable to them and by receiving their encouragement.

5:13–14 It is necessary to set priorities in life. Solomon recognized this when he set up shifts for his workers of one month at work in Lebanon and two months at home (5:14). This schedule showed that Solomon placed great importance on the family unit. Whenever we set up schedules at work, home and church, we need to examine the impact they will have on our families. Too often we strive for material things and lose what are much more precious—wonderful memories and warm family relationships.

8The entrance to the lowest[a] floor was on the south side of the temple; a stairway led up to the middle level and from there to the third. 9So he built the temple and completed it, roofing it with beams and cedar planks. 10And he built the side rooms all along the temple. The height of each was five cubits, and they were attached to the temple by beams of cedar.

11The word of the LORD came to Solomon: 12"As for this temple you are building, if you follow my decrees, carry out my regulations and keep all my commands and obey them, I will fulfill through you the promise I gave to David your father. 13And I will live among the Israelites and will not abandon my people Israel."

14So Solomon built the temple and completed it. 15He lined its interior walls with cedar boards, paneling them from the floor of the temple to the ceiling, and covered the floor of the temple with planks of pine. 16He partitioned off twenty cubits[b] at the rear of the temple with cedar boards from floor to ceiling to form within the temple an inner sanctuary, the Most Holy Place. 17The main hall in front of this room was forty cubits[c] long. 18The inside of the temple was cedar, carved with gourds and open flowers. Everything was cedar; no stone was to be seen.

19He prepared the inner sanctuary within the temple to set the ark of the covenant of the LORD there. 20The inner sanctuary was twenty cubits long, twenty wide and twenty high.[d] He overlaid the inside with pure gold, and he also overlaid the altar of cedar. 21Solomon covered the inside of the temple with pure gold, and he extended gold chains across the front of the inner sanctuary, which was overlaid with gold. 22So he overlaid the whole interior with gold. He also overlaid with gold the altar that belonged to the inner sanctuary.

23In the inner sanctuary he made a pair of cherubim of olive wood, each ten cubits[e] high. 24One wing of the first cherub was five cubits long, and the other wing five cubits—ten cubits from wing tip to wing tip. 25The second cherub also measured ten cubits, for the two cherubim were identical in size and shape. 26The height of each cherub was ten cubits. 27He placed the cherubim inside the innermost room of the temple, with their wings spread out. The wing of one cherub touched one wall, while the wing of the other touched the other wall, and their wings touched each other in the middle of the room. 28He overlaid the cherubim with gold.

29On the walls all around the temple, in both the inner and outer rooms, he carved cherubim, palm trees and open flowers. 30He also covered the floors of both the inner and outer rooms of the temple with gold.

31For the entrance of the inner sanctuary he made doors of olive wood with five-sided jambs. 32And on the two olive wood doors he carved cherubim, palm trees and open flowers, and overlaid the cherubim and palm trees with beaten gold. 33In the same way he made four-sided jambs of olive wood for the entrance to the main hall. 34He also made two pine doors, each having two leaves that turned in sockets. 35He carved cherubim, palm trees and open flowers on them and overlaid them with gold hammered evenly over the carvings.

36And he built the inner courtyard of three courses of dressed stone and one course of trimmed cedar beams.

37The foundation of the temple of the LORD was laid in the fourth year, in the month of Ziv. 38In the eleventh year in the month of Bul, the eighth month, the temple was finished in all its details according to its specifications. He had spent seven years building it.

Solomon Builds His Palace

7 It took Solomon thirteen years, however, to complete the construction of his palace. 2He built the Palace of the Forest of Lebanon a hundred cubits long, fifty wide and thirty high,[f] with four rows of cedar columns supporting trimmed cedar beams. 3It was roofed with cedar above the beams that rested on the columns—forty-five beams, fifteen to a row. 4Its windows were placed high in sets of three, facing each other. 5All the doorways had rectangular frames; they were in the front part in sets of three, facing each other.[g]

6He made a colonnade fifty cubits long and thirty wide.[h] In front of it was a portico, and in front of that were pillars and an overhanging roof.

7He built the throne hall, the Hall of Justice, where he was to judge, and he covered it with cedar from floor to ceiling.[i] 8And the palace in which he was to live, set farther back, was similar in design. Solomon also made a palace like this hall for Pharaoh's daughter, whom he had married.

9All these structures, from the outside to the great courtyard and from foundation to eaves, were made of blocks of high-grade stone cut to size and trimmed with a saw on their inner and outer faces. 10The foundations were laid with large stones of good quality, some measuring ten cubits[e] and some eight.[j] 11Above were high-grade stones, cut to size, and cedar beams. 12The great courtyard was surrounded by a wall of three courses of dressed stone and one course of trimmed cedar beams, as was the inner courtyard of the temple of the LORD with its portico.

[a] 8 Septuagint; Hebrew *middle* [b] 16 That is, about 30 feet (about 9 meters) [c] 17 That is, about 60 feet (about 18 meters) [d] 20 That is, about 30 feet (about 9 meters) long, wide and high [e] 23,10 That is, about 15 feet (about 4.5 meters) [f] 2 That is, about 150 feet (about 46 meters) long, 75 feet (about 23 meters) wide and 45 feet (about 13.5 meters) high [g] 5 The meaning of the Hebrew for this verse is uncertain. [h] 6 That is, about 75 feet (about 23 meters) long and 45 feet (about 13.5 meters) wide [i] 7 Vulgate and Syriac; Hebrew *floor* [j] 10 That is, about 12 feet (about 3.6 meters)

The Temple's Furnishings

13King Solomon sent to Tyre and brought Huram,[a] 14whose mother was a widow from the tribe of Naphtali and whose father was a man of Tyre and a craftsman in bronze. Huram was highly skilled and experienced in all kinds of bronze work. He came to King Solomon and did all the work assigned to him.

15He cast two bronze pillars, each eighteen cubits high and twelve cubits around,[b] by line. 16He also made two capitals of cast bronze to set on the tops of the pillars; each capital was five cubits[c] high. 17A network of interwoven chains festooned the capitals on top of the pillars, seven for each capital. 18He made pomegranates in two rows[d] encircling each network to decorate the capitals on top of the pillars.[e] He did the same for each capital. 19The capitals on top of the pillars in the portico were in the shape of lilies, four cubits[f] high. 20On the capitals of both pillars, above the bowl-shaped part next to the network, were the two hundred pomegranates in rows all around. 21He erected the pillars at the portico of the temple. The pillar to the south he named Jakin[g] and the one to the north Boaz.[h] 22The capitals on top were in the shape of lilies. And so the work on the pillars was completed.

23He made the Sea of cast metal, circular in shape, measuring ten cubits[i] from rim to rim and five cubits high. It took a line of thirty cubits[j] to measure around it. 24Below the rim, gourds encircled it—ten to a cubit. The gourds were cast in two rows in one piece with the Sea.

25The Sea stood on twelve bulls, three facing north, three facing west, three facing south and three facing east. The Sea rested on top of them, and their hindquarters were toward the center. 26It was a handbreadth[k] in thickness, and its rim was like the rim of a cup, like a lily blossom. It held two thousand baths.[l]

27He also made ten movable stands of bronze; each was four cubits long, four wide and three high.[m] 28This is how the stands were made: They had side panels attached to uprights. 29On the panels between the uprights were lions, bulls and cherubim—and on the uprights as well. Above and below the lions and bulls were wreaths of hammered work. 30Each stand had four bronze wheels with bronze axles, and each had a basin resting on four supports, cast with wreaths on each side. 31On the inside of the stand there was an opening that had a circular frame one cubit[n] deep. This opening was round, and with its basework it measured a cubit and a half.[o] Around its opening there was engraving. The panels of the stands were square, not round. 32The four wheels were under the panels, and the axles of the wheels were attached to the stand. The diameter of each wheel was a cubit and a half. 33The wheels were made like chariot wheels; the axles, rims, spokes and hubs were all of cast metal.

34Each stand had four handles, one on each corner, projecting from the stand. 35At the top of the stand there was a circular band half a cubit[p] deep. The supports and panels were attached to the top of the stand. 36He engraved cherubim, lions and palm trees on the surfaces of the supports and on the panels, in every available space, with wreaths all around. 37This is the way he made the ten stands. They were all cast in the same molds and were identical in size and shape.

38He then made ten bronze basins, each holding forty baths[q] and measuring four cubits across, one basin to go on each of the ten stands. 39He placed five of the stands on the south side of the temple and five on the north. He placed the Sea on the south side, at the southeast corner of the temple. 40He also made the basins and shovels and sprinkling bowls.

So Huram finished all the work he had undertaken for King Solomon in the temple of the LORD:

41the two pillars;
the two bowl-shaped capitals on top of the pillars;
the two sets of network decorating the two bowl-shaped capitals on top of the pillars;
42the four hundred pomegranates for the two sets of network (two rows of pomegranates for each network, decorating the bowl-shaped capitals on top of the pillars);
43the ten stands with their ten basins;
44the Sea and the twelve bulls under it;
45the pots, shovels and sprinkling bowls.

All these objects that Huram made for King Solomon for the temple of the LORD were of burnished bronze. 46The king had them cast in clay molds in the plain of the Jordan between Succoth and Zarethan. 47Solomon left all these things unweighed, because there were so many; the weight of the bronze was not determined.

[a]13 Hebrew *Hiram,* a variant of *Huram*; also in verses 40 and 45 [b]15 That is, about 27 feet (about 8.1 meters) high and 18 feet (about 5.4 meters) around [c]16 That is, about 7 1/2 feet (about 2.3 meters); also in verse 23 [d]18 Two Hebrew manuscripts and Septuagint; most Hebrew manuscripts *made the pillars, and there were two rows* [e]18 Many Hebrew manuscripts and Syriac; most Hebrew manuscripts *pomegranates* [f]19 That is, about 6 feet (about 1.8 meters); also in verse 38 [g]21 *Jakin* probably means *he establishes.* [h]21 *Boaz* probably means *in him is strength.* [i]23 That is, about 15 feet (about 4.5 meters) [j]23 That is, about 45 feet (about 13.5 meters) [k]26 That is, about 3 inches (about 8 centimeters) [l]26 That is, probably about 11,500 gallons (about 44 kiloliters); the Septuagint does not have this sentence. [m]27 That is, about 6 feet (about 1.8 meters) long and wide and about 4 1/2 feet (about 1.3 meters) high [n]31 That is, about 1 1/2 feet (about 0.5 meter) [o]31 That is, about 2 1/4 feet (about 0.7 meter); also in verse 32 [p]35 That is, about 3/4 foot (about 0.2 meter) [q]38 That is, about 230 gallons (about 880 liters)

48Solomon also made all the furnishings that
were in the LORD's temple:

the golden altar;
the golden table on which was the bread
of the Presence;
49the lampstands of pure gold (five on the
right and five on the left, in front of the
inner sanctuary);
the gold floral work and lamps and tongs;
50the pure gold basins, wick trimmers,
sprinkling bowls, dishes and censers;
and the gold sockets for the doors of the
innermost room, the Most Holy Place,
and also for the doors of the main hall
of the temple.

51When all the work King Solomon had done
for the temple of the LORD was finished, he
brought in the things his father David had dedicated—the silver and gold and the furnishings—
and he placed them in the treasuries of the
LORD's temple.

The Ark Brought to the Temple

8 Then King Solomon summoned into his
presence at Jerusalem the elders of Israel,
all the heads of the tribes and the chiefs of the
Israelite families, to bring up the ark of the
LORD's covenant from Zion, the City of David.
2All the men of Israel came together to King
Solomon at the time of the festival in the
month of Ethanim, the seventh month.

3When all the elders of Israel had arrived, the
priests took up the ark, 4and they brought up
the ark of the LORD and the Tent of Meeting and
all the sacred furnishings in it. The priests and
Levites carried them up, 5and King Solomon
and the entire assembly of Israel that had gathered about him were before the ark, sacrificing
so many sheep and cattle that they could not be
recorded or counted.

6The priests then brought the ark of the
LORD's covenant to its place in the inner sanctuary of the temple, the Most Holy Place, and put
it beneath the wings of the cherubim. 7The
cherubim spread their wings over the place of
the ark and overshadowed the ark and its carrying poles. 8These poles were so long that their
ends could be seen from the Holy Place in front
of the inner sanctuary, but not from outside the
Holy Place; and they are still there today. 9There
was nothing in the ark except the two stone
tablets that Moses had placed in it at Horeb,
where the LORD made a covenant with the Israelites after they came out of Egypt.

10When the priests withdrew from the Holy
Place, the cloud filled the temple of the LORD.
11And the priests could not perform their service because of the cloud, for the glory of the
LORD filled his temple.

12Then Solomon said, "The LORD has said
that he would dwell in a dark cloud; 13I have
indeed built a magnificent temple for you, a
place for you to dwell forever."

14While the whole assembly of Israel was
standing there, the king turned around and
blessed them. 15Then he said:

"Praise be to the LORD, the God of Israel, who with his own hand has fulfilled
what he promised with his own mouth to
my father David. For he said, 16'Since the
day I brought my people Israel out of
Egypt, I have not chosen a city in any tribe
of Israel to have a temple built for my
Name to be there, but I have chosen David
to rule my people Israel.'

17"My father David had it in his heart
to build a temple for the Name of the
LORD, the God of Israel. 18But the LORD
said to my father David, 'Because it was in
your heart to build a temple for my Name,
you did well to have this in your heart.
19Nevertheless, you are not the one to
build the temple, but your son, who is
your own flesh and blood—he is the one
who will build the temple for my Name.'

20"The LORD has kept the promise he
made: I have succeeded David my father
and now I sit on the throne of Israel, just
as the LORD promised, and I have built the
temple for the Name of the LORD, the God
of Israel. 21I have provided a place there
for the ark, in which is the covenant of the
LORD that he made with our fathers when
he brought them out of Egypt."

Solomon's Prayer of Dedication

22Then Solomon stood before the altar of the
LORD in front of the whole assembly of Israel,
spread out his hands toward heaven 23and said:

"O LORD, God of Israel, there is no
God like you in heaven above or on earth
below—you who keep your covenant of
love with your servants who continue
wholeheartedly in your way. 24You have
kept your promise to your servant David
my father; with your mouth you have
promised and with your hand you have
fulfilled it—as it is today.

25"Now LORD, God of Israel, keep for
your servant David my father the promises
you made to him when you said, 'You
shall never fail to have a man to sit before
me on the throne of Israel, if only your
sons are careful in all they do to walk before me as you have done.' 26And now,
O God of Israel, let your word that you
promised your servant David my father
come true.

27"But will God really dwell on earth?
The heavens, even the highest heaven,
cannot contain you. How much less this
temple I have built! 28Yet give attention to
your servant's prayer and his plea for mercy, O LORD my God. Hear the cry and the
prayer that your servant is praying in your
presence this day. 29May your eyes be

open toward this temple night and day,
this place of which you said, 'My Name
shall be there,' so that you will hear the
prayer your servant prays toward this
place. 30Hear the supplication of your servant and of your people Israel when they
pray toward this place. Hear from heaven,
your dwelling place, and when you hear,
forgive.
31"When a man wrongs his neighbor
and is required to take an oath and he
comes and swears the oath before your
altar in this temple, 32then hear from
heaven and act. Judge between your servants, condemning the guilty and bringing down on his own head what he has
done. Declare the innocent not guilty, and
so establish his innocence.
33"When your people Israel have been
defeated by an enemy because they have
sinned against you, and when they turn
back to you and confess your name, praying and making supplication to you in this
temple, 34then hear from heaven and forgive the sin of your people Israel and bring
them back to the land you gave to their
fathers.
35"When the heavens are shut up and
there is no rain because your people have
sinned against you, and when they pray
toward this place and confess your name
and turn from their sin because you have
afflicted them, 36then hear from heaven
and forgive the sin of your servants, your
people Israel. Teach them the right way to
live, and send rain on the land you gave
your people for an inheritance.
37"When famine or plague comes to
the land, or blight or mildew, locusts or
grasshoppers, or when an enemy besieges
them in any of their cities, whatever disaster or disease may come, 38and when a
prayer or plea is made by any of your people Israel—each one aware of the afflictions of his own heart, and spreading out
his hands toward this temple— 39then hear
from heaven, your dwelling place. Forgive
and act; deal with each man according to
all he does, since you know his heart (for
you alone know the hearts of all men),
40so that they will fear you all the time
they live in the land you gave our fathers.
41"As for the foreigner who does not
belong to your people Israel but has come
from a distant land because of your
name— 42for men will hear of your great
name and your mighty hand and your
outstretched arm—when he comes and
prays toward this temple, 43then hear
from heaven, your dwelling place, and do
whatever the foreigner asks of you, so that
all the peoples of the earth may know
your name and fear you, as do your own
people Israel, and may know that this
house I have built bears your Name.
44"When your people go to war against
their enemies, wherever you send them,
and when they pray to the LORD toward
the city you have chosen and the temple
I have built for your Name, 45then hear
from heaven their prayer and their plea,
and uphold their cause.
46"When they sin against you—for there
is no one who does not sin—and you become angry with them and give them over
to the enemy, who takes them captive to
his own land, far away or near; 47and if
they have a change of heart in the land
where they are held captive, and repent
and plead with you in the land of their
conquerors and say, 'We have sinned, we
have done wrong, we have acted wickedly'; 48and if they turn back to you with all
their heart and soul in the land of their
enemies who took them captive, and pray
to you toward the land you gave their fathers, toward the city you have chosen and
the temple I have built for your Name;
49then from heaven, your dwelling place,
hear their prayer and their plea, and
uphold their cause. 50And forgive your
people, who have sinned against you; forgive all the offenses they have committed
against you, and cause their conquerors
to show them mercy; 51for they are your
people and your inheritance, whom you
brought out of Egypt, out of that iron-
smelting furnace.
52"May your eyes be open to your servant's plea and to the plea of your people
Israel, and may you listen to them whenever they cry out to you. 53For you singled
them out from all the nations of the world
to be your own inheritance, just as you
declared through your servant Moses
when you, O Sovereign LORD, brought
our fathers out of Egypt."

54When Solomon had finished all these
prayers and supplications to the LORD, he rose
from before the altar of the LORD, where he had
been kneeling with his hands spread out toward
heaven. 55He stood and blessed the whole assembly of Israel in a loud voice, saying:

56"Praise be to the LORD, who has given
rest to his people Israel just as he prom-

8:46–53 Intercessory prayer is an important part of our relationship with God. Solomon understood this, and he prayed for himself and the people. He asked God to have mercy on them before they had even made any mistakes (8:46–50). Intercessory prayer is important for us too. When we feel overwhelmed in our journey, we can find strength from the prayers of others. We should ask at least one person to pray for us regarding specific concerns. That person can also hold us accountable for our actions.

8:56–60 Solomon's prayer provides us with a good example to follow as we come before God. It can be divided

ised. Not one word has failed of all the good promises he gave through his servant Moses. 57May the LORD our God be with us as he was with our fathers; may he never leave us nor forsake us. 58May he turn our hearts to him, to walk in all his ways and to keep the commands, decrees and regulations he gave our fathers. 59And may these words of mine, which I have prayed before the LORD, be near to the LORD our God day and night, that he may uphold the cause of his servant and the cause of his people Israel according to each day's need, 60so that all the peoples of the earth may know that the LORD is God and that there is no other. 61But your hearts must be fully committed to the LORD our God, to live by his decrees and obey his commands, as at this time."

The Dedication of the Temple

62Then the king and all Israel with him offered sacrifices before the LORD. 63Solomon offered a sacrifice of fellowship offerings[a] to the LORD: twenty-two thousand cattle and a hundred and twenty thousand sheep and goats. So the king and all the Israelites dedicated the temple of the LORD.

64On that same day the king consecrated the middle part of the courtyard in front of the temple of the LORD, and there he offered burnt offerings, grain offerings and the fat of the fellowship offerings, because the bronze altar before the LORD was too small to hold the burnt offerings, the grain offerings and the fat of the fellowship offerings.

65So Solomon observed the festival at that time, and all Israel with him—a vast assembly, people from Lebo[b] Hamath to the Wadi of Egypt. They celebrated it before the LORD our God for seven days and seven days more, fourteen days in all. 66On the following day he sent the people away. They blessed the king and then went home, joyful and glad in heart for all the good things the LORD had done for his servant David and his people Israel.

The LORD Appears to Solomon

9 When Solomon had finished building the temple of the LORD and the royal palace, and had achieved all he had desired to do, 2the LORD appeared to him a second time, as he had appeared to him at Gibeon. 3The LORD said to him:

"I have heard the prayer and plea you have made before me; I have consecrated this temple, which you have built, by putting my Name there forever. My eyes and my heart will always be there.

4"As for you, if you walk before me in integrity of heart and uprightness, as David your father did, and do all I command and observe my decrees and laws, 5I will establish your royal throne over Israel forever, as I promised David your father when I said, 'You shall never fail to have a man on the throne of Israel.'

6"But if you[c] or your sons turn away from me and do not observe the commands and decrees I have given you[c] and go off to serve other gods and worship them, 7then I will cut off Israel from the land I have given them and will reject this temple I have consecrated for my Name. Israel will then become a byword and an object of ridicule among all peoples. 8And though this temple is now imposing, all who pass by will be appalled and will scoff and say, 'Why has the LORD done such a thing to this land and to this temple?' 9People will answer, 'Because they have forsaken the LORD their God, who brought their fathers out of Egypt, and have embraced other gods, worshiping and serving them—that is why the LORD brought all this disaster on them.' "

Solomon's Other Activities

10At the end of twenty years, during which Solomon built these two buildings—the temple of the LORD and the royal palace— 11King Solomon gave twenty towns in Galilee to Hiram king of Tyre, because Hiram had supplied him with all the cedar and pine and gold he wanted. 12But when Hiram went from Tyre to see the towns that Solomon had given him, he was not pleased with them. 13"What kind of towns are

[a] 63 Traditionally *peace offerings;* also in verse 64
[b] 65 Or *from the entrance to*
[c] 6 The Hebrew is plural.

---

into six steps: (1) he began by praising God (8:56); (2) he requested God's presence (8:57); (3) he asked for help to do God's will (8:58); (4) he prayed for the desire to obey God (8:58); (5) he asked God to remember his prayer (8:59); and (6) he prayed that all people would come to know God (8:60).

9:1–9 God promised to extend to Solomon and his descendants the promises he had given to David. But along with those promises came added responsibilities: God would not bless his people unless they chose to serve him and live according to his plan. If Israel worshiped other gods, they would lose their position of blessing (9:6–7). Through the Bible, the Holy Spirit and godly friends, we are often given warning signs before we commit sins. Unfortunately, like Solomon and Israel, we often ignore the warnings and then must suffer the consequences.

9:10–28 Upon completing the temple and the palace (9:10), Solomon did not take time out for God and family. He also failed to give his labor force a chance to rest. Instead, Solomon went on a building spree, constructing the fortresses of Hazor, Megiddo and Gezer. He extended the fortified walls of Jerusalem to protect the temple and his palace (9:15). Solomon sacrificed his relationships with God, his family and his people to fulfill his compulsion to build. Solomon's son Rehoboam suffered many adverse consequences because of Solomon's driving personality. Eventually the people rebelled against Rehoboam because he promised to maintain the heavy burdens of labor and taxes initiated by his father (see 12:1–11).

these you have given me, my brother?" he asked.
And he called them the Land of Cabul,[a] a
name they have to this day. 14Now Hiram had
sent to the king 120 talents[b] of gold.
15Here is the account of the forced labor King
Solomon conscripted to build the LORD's temple, his own palace, the supporting terraces,[c]
the wall of Jerusalem, and Hazor, Megiddo and
Gezer. 16(Pharaoh king of Egypt had attacked
and captured Gezer. He had set it on fire. He
killed its Canaanite inhabitants and then gave it
as a wedding gift to his daughter, Solomon's
wife. 17And Solomon rebuilt Gezer.) He built
up Lower Beth Horon, 18Baalath, and Tadmor[d]
in the desert, within his land, 19as well as all his
store cities and the towns for his chariots and
for his horses[e]—whatever he desired to build
in Jerusalem, in Lebanon and throughout all
the territory he ruled.
20All the people left from the Amorites, Hittites, Perizzites, Hivites and Jebusites (these
peoples were not Israelites), 21that is, their
descendants remaining in the land, whom the
Israelites could not exterminate[f]—these Solomon conscripted for his slave labor force, as it
is to this day. 22But Solomon did not make
slaves of any of the Israelites; they were his
fighting men, his government officials, his officers, his captains, and the commanders of his
chariots and charioteers. 23They were also the
chief officials in charge of Solomon's projects—
550 officials supervising the men who did the
work.
24After Pharaoh's daughter had come up
from the City of David to the palace Solomon
had built for her, he constructed the supporting
terraces.
25Three times a year Solomon sacrificed
burnt offerings and fellowship offerings[g] on
the altar he had built for the LORD, burning
incense before the LORD along with them, and
so fulfilled the temple obligations.
26King Solomon also built ships at Ezion Geber, which is near Elath in Edom, on the shore
of the Red Sea.[h] 27And Hiram sent his men—
sailors who knew the sea—to serve in the fleet
with Solomon's men. 28They sailed to Ophir
and brought back 420 talents[i] of gold, which
they delivered to King Solomon.

The Queen of Sheba Visits Solomon

10 When the queen of Sheba heard about
the fame of Solomon and his relation
to the name of the LORD, she came to test him
with hard questions. 2Arriving at Jerusalem with
a very great caravan—with camels carrying
spices, large quantities of gold, and precious
stones—she came to Solomon and talked with
him about all that she had on her mind. 3Solo-
mon answered all her questions; nothing was
too hard for the king to explain to her. 4When
the queen of Sheba saw all the wisdom of Solomon and the palace he had built, 5the food on
his table, the seating of his officials, the attending servants in their robes, his cupbearers, and
the burnt offerings he made at[j] the temple of
the LORD, she was overwhelmed.
6She said to the king, "The report I heard in
my own country about your achievements and
your wisdom is true. 7But I did not believe these
things until I came and saw with my own eyes.
Indeed, not even half was told me; in wisdom
and wealth you have far exceeded the report I
heard. 8How happy your men must be! How
happy your officials, who continually stand before you and hear your wisdom! 9Praise be to
the LORD your God, who has delighted in you
and placed you on the throne of Israel. Because
of the LORD's eternal love for Israel, he has
made you king, to maintain justice and righteousness."
10And she gave the king 120 talents[b] of
gold, large quantities of spices, and precious
stones. Never again were so many spices
brought in as those the queen of Sheba gave to
King Solomon.
11(Hiram's ships brought gold from Ophir;
and from there they brought great cargoes of
almugwood[k] and precious stones. 12The king
used the almugwood to make supports for the
temple of the LORD and for the royal palace, and
to make harps and lyres for the musicians. So
much almugwood has never been imported or
seen since that day.)
13King Solomon gave the queen of Sheba all
she desired and asked for, besides what he had
given her out of his royal bounty. Then she left
and returned with her retinue to her own country.

Solomon's Splendor

14The weight of the gold that Solomon received yearly was 666 talents,[l] 15not including
the revenues from merchants and traders and
from all the Arabian kings and the governors of
the land.
16King Solomon made two hundred large
shields of hammered gold; six hundred bekas[m]
of gold went into each shield. 17He also made
three hundred small shields of hammered gold,
with three minas[n] of gold in each shield. The
king put them in the Palace of the Forest of
Lebanon.
18Then the king made a great throne inlaid
with ivory and overlaid with fine gold. 19The
throne had six steps, and its back had a rounded

[a]13 *Cabul* sounds like the Hebrew for *good-for-nothing.*
[b]14,10 That is, about 4 1/2 tons (about 4 metric tons)
[c]15 Or *the Millo*; also in verse 24 [d]18 The Hebrew may also be read *Tamar.* [e]19 Or *charioteers*
[f]21 The Hebrew term refers to the irrevocable giving over of things or persons to the LORD, often by totally destroying them. [g]25 Traditionally *peace offerings*
[h]26 Hebrew *Yam Suph*; that is, Sea of Reeds [i]28 That is, about 16 tons (about 14.5 metric tons) [j]5 Or *the ascent by which he went up to* [k]11 Probably a variant of *algumwood*; also in verse 12 [l]14 That is, about 25 tons (about 23 metric tons) [m]16 That is, about 7 1/2 pounds (about 3.5 kilograms) [n]17 That is, about 3 3/4 pounds (about 1.7 kilograms)

top. On both sides of the seat were armrests, with a lion standing beside each of them. 20Twelve lions stood on the six steps, one at either end of each step. Nothing like it had ever been made for any other kingdom. 21All King Solomon's goblets were gold, and all the household articles in the Palace of the Forest of Lebanon were pure gold. Nothing was made of silver, because silver was considered of little value in Solomon's days. 22The king had a fleet of trading ships[a] at sea along with the ships of Hiram. Once every three years it returned, carrying gold, silver and ivory, and apes and baboons.

23King Solomon was greater in riches and wisdom than all the other kings of the earth. 24The whole world sought audience with Solomon to hear the wisdom God had put in his heart. 25Year after year, everyone who came brought a gift—articles of silver and gold, robes, weapons and spices, and horses and mules.

26Solomon accumulated chariots and horses; he had fourteen hundred chariots and twelve thousand horses,[b] which he kept in the chariot cities and also with him in Jerusalem. 27The king made silver as common in Jerusalem as stones, and cedar as plentiful as sycamore-fig trees in the foothills. 28Solomon's horses were imported from Egypt[c] and from Kue[d]—the royal merchants purchased them from Kue. 29They imported a chariot from Egypt for six hundred shekels[e] of silver, and a horse for a hundred and fifty.[f] They also exported them to all the kings of the Hittites and of the Arameans.

Solomon's Wives

11 King Solomon, however, loved many foreign women besides Pharaoh's daughter—Moabites, Ammonites, Edomites, Sidonians and Hittites. 2They were from nations about which the LORD had told the Israelites, "You must not intermarry with them, because they will surely turn your hearts after their gods." Nevertheless, Solomon held fast to them in love. 3He had seven hundred wives of royal birth and three hundred concubines, and his wives led him astray. 4As Solomon grew old, his wives turned his heart after other gods, and his heart was not fully devoted to the LORD his God, as the heart of David his father had been. 5He followed Ashtoreth the goddess of the Sidonians, and Molech[g] the detestable god of the Ammonites. 6So Solomon did evil in the eyes of the LORD; he did not follow the LORD completely, as David his father had done.

7On a hill east of Jerusalem, Solomon built a high place for Chemosh the detestable god of Moab, and for Molech the detestable god of the Ammonites. 8He did the same for all his foreign wives, who burned incense and offered sacrifices to their gods.

9The LORD became angry with Solomon because his heart had turned away from the LORD, the God of Israel, who had appeared to him twice. 10Although he had forbidden Solomon to follow other gods, Solomon did not keep the LORD's command. 11So the LORD said to Solomon, "Since this is your attitude and you have not kept my covenant and my decrees, which I commanded you, I will most certainly tear the kingdom away from you and give it to one of your subordinates. 12Nevertheless, for the sake of David your father, I will not do it during your lifetime. I will tear it out of the hand of your son. 13Yet I will not tear the whole kingdom from him, but will give him one tribe for the sake of David my servant and for the sake of Jerusalem, which I have chosen."

Solomon's Adversaries

14Then the LORD raised up against Solomon an adversary, Hadad the Edomite, from the royal line of Edom. 15Earlier when David was fighting with Edom, Joab the commander of the army, who had gone up to bury the dead, had struck down all the men in Edom. 16Joab and all the Israelites stayed there for six months, until they had destroyed all the men in Edom. 17But Hadad, still only a boy, fled to Egypt with some

[a] 22 Hebrew *of ships of Tarshish* [b] 26 Or *charioteers* [c] 28 Or possibly *Muzur,* a region in Cilicia; also in verse 29 [d] 28 Probably *Cilicia* [e] 29 That is, about 15 pounds (about 7 kilograms) [f] 29 That is, about 3 3/4 pounds (about 1.7 kilograms) [g] 5 Hebrew *Milcom;* also in verse 33

10:23 In the Old Testament, a person's wealth was often viewed as a reward of their relationship with God. This was the case throughout the earlier part of Solomon's life. As Solomon grew older, however, his wealth caused him to trust in himself rather than in God. We also have a tendency to let our material wealth and pride lead us away from God. We must remember that everything we have, even life itself, is a gift from God. As we progress spiritually, we must remember to give God the credit he deserves. If we begin to think we accomplish anything alone, we are headed for trouble.

11:1–13 Solomon broke God's commands by marrying women from Moab, Edom and other nations (11:1; see Exodus 23:32–33; Deuteronomy 17:17). God had prohibited marriage with the people of Canaan because he knew that they would lead the Israelites astray into the worship of other gods. Not only did Solomon begin to worship other gods, but he even built altars to them (11:7–8). God became angry and punished Solomon for his disobedience (11:9–13). It is tempting to go about things in our own way without listening to what God has to say about any given matter. When we do this, however, we shouldn't be surprised when we run into problems. God calls attention to our mistakes, hoping we will see the truth, surrender to him and accept his offer to rescue us.

11:14–25 For years, God allowed Solomon to rule in peace. He put down the threat of hostile neighbors so Solomon could build his temple (see 1 Chronicles 28:2–3). But as Solomon turned his back on God, he was confronted with foreign enemies, such as Hadad (11:14) and Rezon (11:23). The problems we face are often consequences of choices we have already made. Before blaming others for our situation, we should examine our past. We may find that we are the ones responsible for our own trouble.

Edomite officials who had served his father. 18They set out from Midian and went to Paran. Then taking men from Paran with them, they went to Egypt, to Pharaoh king of Egypt, who gave Hadad a house and land and provided him with food.

19Pharaoh was so pleased with Hadad that he gave him a sister of his own wife, Queen Tahpenes, in marriage. 20The sister of Tahpenes bore him a son named Genubath, whom Tahpenes brought up in the royal palace. There Genubath lived with Pharaoh's own children.

21While he was in Egypt, Hadad heard that David rested with his fathers and that Joab the commander of the army was also dead. Then Hadad said to Pharaoh, "Let me go, that I may return to my own country."

22"What have you lacked here that you want to go back to your own country?" Pharaoh asked.

"Nothing," Hadad replied, "but do let me go!"

23And God raised up against Solomon another adversary, Rezon son of Eliada, who had fled from his master, Hadadezer king of Zobah. 24He gathered men around him and became the leader of a band of rebels when David destroyed the forces[a] ⌊of Zobah⌋; the rebels went to Damascus, where they settled and took control. 25Rezon was Israel's adversary as long as Solomon lived, adding to the trouble caused by Hadad. So Rezon ruled in Aram and was hostile toward Israel.

Jeroboam Rebels Against Solomon

26Also, Jeroboam son of Nebat rebelled against the king. He was one of Solomon's officials, an Ephraimite from Zeredah, and his mother was a widow named Zeruah.

27Here is the account of how he rebelled against the king: Solomon had built the supporting terraces[b] and had filled in the gap in the wall of the city of David his father. 28Now Jeroboam was a man of standing, and when Solomon saw how well the young man did his work, he put him in charge of the whole labor force of the house of Joseph.

29About that time Jeroboam was going out of Jerusalem, and Ahijah the prophet of Shiloh met him on the way, wearing a new cloak. The two of them were alone out in the country, 30and Ahijah took hold of the new cloak he was wearing and tore it into twelve pieces. 31Then he said to Jeroboam, "Take ten pieces for yourself, for this is what the LORD, the God of Israel, says: 'See, I am going to tear the kingdom out of Solomon's hand and give you ten tribes. 32But for the sake of my servant David and the city of Jerusalem, which I have chosen out of all the tribes of Israel, he will have one tribe. 33I will do this because they have[c] forsaken me and worshiped Ashtoreth the goddess of the Sidonians, Chemosh the god of the Moabites, and Molech the god of the Ammonites, and have not walked in my ways, nor done what is right in my eyes, nor kept my statutes and laws as David, Solomon's father, did.

34" 'But I will not take the whole kingdom out of Solomon's hand; I have made him ruler all the days of his life for the sake of David my servant, whom I chose and who observed my commands and statutes. 35I will take the kingdom from his son's hands and give you ten tribes. 36I will give one tribe to his son so that David my servant may always have a lamp before me in Jerusalem, the city where I chose to put my Name. 37However, as for you, I will take you, and you will rule over all that your heart desires; you will be king over Israel. 38If you do whatever I command you and walk in my ways and do what is right in my eyes by keeping my statutes and commands, as David my servant did, I will be with you. I will build you a dynasty as enduring as the one I built for David and will give Israel to you. 39I will humble David's descendants because of this, but not forever.' "

40Solomon tried to kill Jeroboam, but Jeroboam fled to Egypt, to Shishak the king, and stayed there until Solomon's death.

Solomon's Death

41As for the other events of Solomon's reign—all he did and the wisdom he displayed—are they not written in the book of the annals of Solomon? 42Solomon reigned in Jerusalem over all Israel forty years. 43Then he rested with his fathers and was buried in the city of David his father. And Rehoboam his son succeeded him as king.

Israel Rebels Against Rehoboam

12 Rehoboam went to Shechem, for all the Israelites had gone there to make him king. 2When Jeroboam son of Nebat heard this (he was still in Egypt, where he had fled from

[a]24 Hebrew *destroyed them* [b]27 Or *the Millo*
[c]33 Hebrew; Septuagint, Vulgate and Syriac *because he has*

11:26–40 The most tragic consequence of Solomon's sins was realized after his death—Israel was divided. God raised up Jeroboam as the first king of the northern kingdom of Israel. Solomon attempted to kill Jeroboam in order to prevent God's will from happening (11:40). Solomon's decisions at this point were obviously being driven by a false self-perception. He had begun to believe that his actions could rewrite the will of God. How often do we fall prey to the sin of thinking we can outmaneuver God? No matter how rich, popular or important we might become, we will never be able to change what God has said will happen.

11:41—12:1 Solomon's life ended (11:43), and his son Rehoboam inherited the throne (12:1). Before he died, David had given his son Solomon advice on how to run the kingdom (see 2:1–12). But Solomon failed to do this with his son. Rehoboam was left to rule without his father's counsel. Godly parents must never underestimate the value of helping children learn new responsibilities. Parents have valuable contributions to make—contributions that can save children the pain of learning the hard lessons on their own.

King Solomon), he returned from[a] Egypt. 3So they sent for Jeroboam, and he and the whole assembly of Israel went to Rehoboam and said to him: 4"Your father put a heavy yoke on us, but now lighten the harsh labor and the heavy yoke he put on us, and we will serve you."

5Rehoboam answered, "Go away for three days and then come back to me." So the people went away.

6Then King Rehoboam consulted the elders who had served his father Solomon during his lifetime. "How would you advise me to answer these people?" he asked.

7They replied, "If today you will be a servant to these people and serve them and give them a favorable answer, they will always be your servants."

8But Rehoboam rejected the advice the elders gave him and consulted the young men who had grown up with him and were serving him. 9He asked them, "What is your advice? How should we answer these people who say to me, 'Lighten the yoke your father put on us'?"

10The young men who had grown up with him replied, "Tell these people who have said to you, 'Your father put a heavy yoke on us, but make our yoke lighter'—tell them, 'My little finger is thicker than my father's waist. 11My father laid on you a heavy yoke; I will make it even heavier. My father scourged you with whips; I will scourge you with scorpions.' "

12Three days later Jeroboam and all the people returned to Rehoboam, as the king had said, "Come back to me in three days." 13The king answered the people harshly. Rejecting the advice given him by the elders, 14he followed the advice of the young men and said, "My father made your yoke heavy; I will make it even heavier. My father scourged you with whips; I will scourge you with scorpions." 15So the king did not listen to the people, for this turn of events was from the LORD, to fulfill the word the LORD had spoken to Jeroboam son of Nebat through Ahijah the Shilonite.

16When all Israel saw that the king refused to listen to them, they answered the king:

"What share do we have in David,
    what part in Jesse's son?
To your tents, O Israel!
    Look after your own house, O David!"

So the Israelites went home. 17But as for the Israelites who were living in the towns of Judah, Rehoboam still ruled over them.

18King Rehoboam sent out Adoniram,[b] who was in charge of forced labor, but all Israel stoned him to death. King Rehoboam, however, managed to get into his chariot and escape to Jerusalem. 19So Israel has been in rebellion against the house of David to this day.

20When all the Israelites heard that Jeroboam had returned, they sent and called him to the assembly and made him king over all Israel. Only the tribe of Judah remained loyal to the house of David.

21When Rehoboam arrived in Jerusalem, he mustered the whole house of Judah and the tribe of Benjamin—a hundred and eighty thousand fighting men—to make war against the house of Israel and to regain the kingdom for Rehoboam son of Solomon.

22But this word of God came to Shemaiah the man of God: 23"Say to Rehoboam son of Solomon king of Judah, to the whole house of Judah and Benjamin, and to the rest of the people, 24'This is what the LORD says: Do not go up to fight against your brothers, the Israelites. Go home, every one of you, for this is my doing.' " So they obeyed the word of the LORD and went home again, as the LORD had ordered.

Golden Calves at Bethel and Dan

25Then Jeroboam fortified Shechem in the hill country of Ephraim and lived there. From there he went out and built up Peniel.[c]

26Jeroboam thought to himself, "The kingdom will now likely revert to the house of David. 27If these people go up to offer sacrifices at the temple of the LORD in Jerusalem, they will again give their allegiance to their lord, Rehoboam king of Judah. They will kill me and return to King Rehoboam."

28After seeking advice, the king made two golden calves. He said to the people, "It is too much for you to go up to Jerusalem. Here are your gods, O Israel, who brought you up out of Egypt." 29One he set up in Bethel, and the other in Dan. 30And this thing became a sin; the people went even as far as Dan to worship the one there.

31Jeroboam built shrines on high places and appointed priests from all sorts of people, even though they were not Levites. 32He instituted a festival on the fifteenth day of the eighth

[a]2 Or *he remained in* [b]18 Some Septuagint manuscripts and Syriac (see also 1 Kings 4:6 and 5:14); Hebrew *Adoram* [c]25 Hebrew *Penuel,* a variant of *Peniel*

12:6–14 Rehoboam was wise to ask for counsel (12:6). He made a mistake, however, in not properly evaluating the advice he was given. Counsel should always be measured against the principles set forth in the Bible. If Rehoboam had done this, he would have seen that the advice of his peers was unwise (12:9–11). We need to carefully weigh the counsel we receive, asking God for the wisdom to know what is right to do.

12:15–33 Jeroboam and Rehoboam, the kings who reigned after Solomon, both made foolish, self-serving decisions. Rehoboam followed his selfish inclinations, which led to the division of the kingdom (12:15). Jeroboam was so afraid of losing his kingdom (even though God had appointed him king) that he broke God's laws. He made idols for the people so they wouldn't go to Jerusalem to worship. The selfish attitudes of these two men led entire kingdoms into sin. Our decisions always touch the lives of others too. We should base our decisions on God's truth and on how they will affect others.

month, like the festival held in Judah, and offered sacrifices on the altar. This he did in Bethel, sacrificing to the calves he had made. And at
Bethel he also installed priests at the high places
he had made. 33On the fifteenth day of the
eighth month, a month of his own choosing, he
offered sacrifices on the altar he had built
at Bethel. So he instituted the festival for the
Israelites and went up to the altar to make offerings.

The Man of God From Judah

13 By the word of the LORD a man of God
came from Judah to Bethel, as Jeroboam was standing by the altar to make an offering. 2He cried out against the altar by the word
of the LORD: "O altar, altar! This is what the
LORD says: 'A son named Josiah will be born to
the house of David. On you he will sacrifice the
priests of the high places who now make offerings here, and human bones will be burned on
you.' " 3That same day the man of God gave a
sign: "This is the sign the LORD has declared:
The altar will be split apart and the ashes on it
will be poured out."
4When King Jeroboam heard what the man
of God cried out against the altar at Bethel, he
stretched out his hand from the altar and said,
"Seize him!" But the hand he stretched out
toward the man shriveled up, so that he could
not pull it back. 5Also, the altar was split apart
and its ashes poured out according to the sign
given by the man of God by the word of the
LORD.
6Then the king said to the man of God, "Intercede with the LORD your God and pray for me
that my hand may be restored." So the man
of God interceded with the LORD, and the
king's hand was restored and became as it was
before.
7The king said to the man of God, "Come
home with me and have something to eat, and
I will give you a gift."
8But the man of God answered the king,
"Even if you were to give me half your possessions, I would not go with you, nor would I eat
bread or drink water here. 9For I was commanded by the word of the LORD: 'You must not eat
bread or drink water or return by the way you
came.' " 10So he took another road and did not
return by the way he had come to Bethel.
11Now there was a certain old prophet living
in Bethel, whose sons came and told him all
that the man of God had done there that day.
They also told their father what he had said to
the king. 12Their father asked them, "Which
way did he go?" And his sons showed him which
road the man of God from Judah had taken.
13So he said to his sons, "Saddle the donkey for
me." And when they had saddled the donkey for
him, he mounted it 14and rode after the man of
God. He found him sitting under an oak tree
and asked, "Are you the man of God who came
from Judah?"
"I am," he replied.
15So the prophet said to him, "Come home
with me and eat."
16The man of God said, "I cannot turn back
and go with you, nor can I eat bread or drink
water with you in this place. 17I have been told
by the word of the LORD: 'You must not eat
bread or drink water there or return by the way
you came.' "
18The old prophet answered, "I too am a
prophet, as you are. And an angel said to me by
the word of the LORD: 'Bring him back with you
to your house so that he may eat bread and
drink water.' " (But he was lying to him.) 19So
the man of God returned with him and ate and
drank in his house.
20While they were sitting at the table, the
word of the LORD came to the old prophet who
had brought him back. 21He cried out to the
man of God who had come from Judah, "This
is what the LORD says: 'You have defied the
word of the LORD and have not kept the command the LORD your God gave you. 22You came
back and ate bread and drank water in the place
where he told you not to eat or drink. Therefore
your body will not be buried in the tomb of
your fathers.' "
23When the man of God had finished eating
and drinking, the prophet who had brought
him back saddled his donkey for him. 24As he
went on his way, a lion met him on the road
and killed him, and his body was thrown down
on the road, with both the donkey and the lion
standing beside it. 25Some people who passed
by saw the body thrown down there, with the
lion standing beside the body, and they went
and reported it in the city where the old prophet
lived.
26When the prophet who had brought him
back from his journey heard of it, he said, "It
is the man of God who defied the word of the
LORD. The LORD has given him over to the lion,
which has mauled him and killed him, as the
word of the LORD had warned him."
27The prophet said to his sons, "Saddle the
donkey for me," and they did so. 28Then he went
out and found the body thrown down on the
road, with the donkey and the lion standing
beside it. The lion had neither eaten the body
nor mauled the donkey. 29So the prophet
picked up the body of the man of God, laid it
on the donkey, and brought it back to his own
city to mourn for him and bury him. 30Then
he laid the body in his own tomb, and they
mourned over him and said, "Oh, my brother!"
31After burying him, he said to his sons,
"When I die, bury me in the grave where
the man of God is buried; lay my bones beside
his bones. 32For the message he declared by
the word of the LORD against the altar in Bethel
and against all the shrines on the high places
in the towns of Samaria will certainly come
true."

33Even after this, Jeroboam did not change his evil ways, but once more appointed priests for the high places from all sorts of people. Anyone who wanted to become a priest he consecrated for the high places. 34This was the sin of the house of Jeroboam that led to its downfall and to its destruction from the face of the earth.

Ahijah's Prophecy Against Jeroboam

14 At that time Abijah son of Jeroboam became ill, 2and Jeroboam said to his wife, "Go, disguise yourself, so you won't be recognized as the wife of Jeroboam. Then go to Shiloh. Ahijah the prophet is there—the one who told me I would be king over this people. 3Take ten loaves of bread with you, some cakes and a jar of honey, and go to him. He will tell you what will happen to the boy." 4So Jeroboam's wife did what he said and went to Ahijah's house in Shiloh.

Now Ahijah could not see; his sight was gone because of his age. 5But the LORD had told Ahijah, "Jeroboam's wife is coming to ask you about her son, for he is ill, and you are to give her such and such an answer. When she arrives, she will pretend to be someone else."

6So when Ahijah heard the sound of her footsteps at the door, he said, "Come in, wife of Jeroboam. Why this pretense? I have been sent to you with bad news. 7Go, tell Jeroboam that this is what the LORD, the God of Israel, says: 'I raised you up from among the people and made you a leader over my people Israel. 8I tore the kingdom away from the house of David and gave it to you, but you have not been like my servant David, who kept my commands and followed me with all his heart, doing only what was right in my eyes. 9You have done more evil than all who lived before you. You have made for yourself other gods, idols made of metal; you have provoked me to anger and thrust me behind your back.

10" 'Because of this, I am going to bring disaster on the house of Jeroboam. I will cut off from Jeroboam every last male in Israel—slave or free. I will burn up the house of Jeroboam as one burns dung, until it is all gone. 11Dogs will eat those belonging to Jeroboam who die in the city, and the birds of the air will feed on those who die in the country. The LORD has spoken!'

12"As for you, go back home. When you set foot in your city, the boy will die. 13All Israel will mourn for him and bury him. He is the only one belonging to Jeroboam who will be buried, because he is the only one in the house of Jeroboam in whom the LORD, the God of Israel, has found anything good.

14"The LORD will raise up for himself a king over Israel who will cut off the family of Jeroboam. This is the day! What? Yes, even now.[a] 15And the LORD will strike Israel, so that it will be like a reed swaying in the water. He will uproot Israel from this good land that he gave to their forefathers and scatter them beyond the River,[b] because they provoked the LORD to anger by making Asherah poles.[c] 16And he will give Israel up because of the sins Jeroboam has committed and has caused Israel to commit."

17Then Jeroboam's wife got up and left and went to Tirzah. As soon as she stepped over the threshold of the house, the boy died. 18They buried him, and all Israel mourned for him, as the LORD had said through his servant the prophet Ahijah.

19The other events of Jeroboam's reign, his wars and how he ruled, are written in the book of the annals of the kings of Israel. 20He reigned for twenty-two years and then rested with his fathers. And Nadab his son succeeded him as king.

Rehoboam King of Judah

21Rehoboam son of Solomon was king in Judah. He was forty-one years old when he became king, and he reigned seventeen years in Jerusalem, the city the LORD had chosen out of all the tribes of Israel in which to put his Name. His mother's name was Naamah; she was an Ammonite.

22Judah did evil in the eyes of the LORD. By the sins they committed they stirred up his jeal-

[a] *14* The meaning of the Hebrew for this sentence is uncertain. [b] *15* That is, the Euphrates [c] *15* That is, symbols of the goddess Asherah; here and elsewhere in 1 Kings

---

13:33–34 Persistence in doing well is admirable. Persistence in doing wrong displays arrogance and is sure to result in great harm. Jeroboam's apostasy demonstrates just how harmful persistence can be when a person is doing the wrong thing. After he was warned about God's coming wrath (see 13:1–32), Jeroboam violated God's commands about the priesthood by appointing unqualified people as priests (see Numbers 3:10). Without accountability in relationships, all of us can start down the wrong track. We would be wise to find a trustworthy friend who will hold us accountable to the truth in God's Word.

14:1–11 Deceit was a regular practice during Jeroboam's reign over Israel. As his son was lying on his deathbed, Jeroboam asked his wife to deceive the prophet Ahijah by disguising herself. The result of their combined sin was the destruction of their family. By consciously or unconsciously calling upon another to join us in sin, we cause them to join us in the consequences of our sin as well. Jeroboam's wife would have been wise to confront Jeroboam about his sinful ways. Instead, she joined him and bore the consequences of his sin with him. Confrontation, though difficult, can often help people see that their intended actions are outside of God's will. If we dissuade others from sin, we help them avoid destructive consequences. However, if we join them in their sin, we help them cause even greater suffering.

14:22—15:3 Children learn from their parents. Rehoboam learned from Solomon that idol worship was all right. When Rehoboam became king, idol worship flourished. When Rehoboam's son Abijam became king, he followed in the footsteps of his father and "committed all the sins his father had done before him" (15:3). We may not realize how deeply our sins affect others, but here we can see that Solomon's worship of idols led to the disobedience of

ous anger more than their fathers had done. 23They also set up for themselves high places, sacred stones and Asherah poles on every high hill and under every spreading tree. 24There were even male shrine prostitutes in the land; the people engaged in all the detestable practices of the nations the LORD had driven out before the Israelites.

25In the fifth year of King Rehoboam, Shishak king of Egypt attacked Jerusalem. 26He carried off the treasures of the temple of the LORD and the treasures of the royal palace. He took everything, including all the gold shields Solomon had made. 27So King Rehoboam made bronze shields to replace them and assigned these to the commanders of the guard on duty at the entrance to the royal palace. 28Whenever the king went to the LORD's temple, the guards bore the shields, and afterward they returned them to the guardroom.

29As for the other events of Rehoboam's reign, and all he did, are they not written in the book of the annals of the kings of Judah? 30There was continual warfare between Rehoboam and Jeroboam. 31And Rehoboam rested with his fathers and was buried with them in the City of David. His mother's name was Naamah; she was an Ammonite. And Abijah[a] his son succeeded him as king.

Abijah King of Judah

15 In the eighteenth year of the reign of Jeroboam son of Nebat, Abijah[b] became king of Judah, 2and he reigned in Jerusalem three years. His mother's name was Maacah daughter of Abishalom.[c]

3He committed all the sins his father had done before him; his heart was not fully devoted to the LORD his God, as the heart of David his forefather had been. 4Nevertheless, for David's sake the LORD his God gave him a lamp in Jerusalem by raising up a son to succeed him and by making Jerusalem strong. 5For David had done what was right in the eyes of the LORD and had not failed to keep any of the LORD's commands all the days of his life—except in the case of Uriah the Hittite.

6There was war between Rehoboam[d] and Jeroboam throughout ⌊Abijah's⌋ lifetime. 7As for the other events of Abijah's reign, and all he did, are they not written in the book of the annals of the kings of Judah? There was war between Abijah and Jeroboam. 8And Abijah rested with his fathers and was buried in the City of David. And Asa his son succeeded him as king.

Asa King of Judah

9In the twentieth year of Jeroboam king of Israel, Asa became king of Judah, 10and he reigned in Jerusalem forty-one years. His grandmother's name was Maacah daughter of Abishalom.

11Asa did what was right in the eyes of the LORD, as his father David had done. 12He expelled the male shrine prostitutes from the land and got rid of all the idols his fathers had made. 13He even deposed his grandmother Maacah from her position as queen mother, because she had made a repulsive Asherah pole. Asa cut the pole down and burned it in the Kidron Valley. 14Although he did not remove the high places, Asa's heart was fully committed to the LORD all his life. 15He brought into the temple of the LORD the silver and gold and the articles that he and his father had dedicated.

16There was war between Asa and Baasha king of Israel throughout their reigns. 17Baasha king of Israel went up against Judah and fortified Ramah to prevent anyone from leaving or entering the territory of Asa king of Judah.

18Asa then took all the silver and gold that was left in the treasuries of the LORD's temple and of his own palace. He entrusted it to his officials and sent them to Ben-Hadad son of Tabrimmon, the son of Hezion, the king of Aram, who was ruling in Damascus. 19"Let there be a treaty between me and you," he said, "as there was between my father and your father. See, I am sending you a gift of silver and gold. Now break your treaty with Baasha king of Israel so he will withdraw from me."

20Ben-Hadad agreed with King Asa and sent the commanders of his forces against the towns of Israel. He conquered Ijon, Dan, Abel Beth Maacah and all Kinnereth in addition to Naphtali. 21When Baasha heard this, he stopped building Ramah and withdrew to Tirzah. 22Then King Asa issued an order to all Judah—no one was exempt—and they carried away from Ramah the stones and timber Baasha had been using there. With them King Asa built up Geba in Benjamin, and also Mizpah.

23As for all the other events of Asa's reign, all his achievements, all he did and the cities he built, are they not written in the book of the annals of the kings of Judah? In his old age, however, his feet became diseased. 24Then Asa rested with his fathers and was buried with them in the city of his father David.

[a]*31* Some Hebrew manuscripts and Septuagint (see also 2 Chron. 12:16); most Hebrew manuscripts *Abijam*
[b]*1* Some Hebrew manuscripts and Septuagint (see also 2 Chron. 12:16); most Hebrew manuscripts *Abijam*; also in verses 7 and 8 [c]*2* A variant of *Absalom*; also in verse 10 [d]*6* Most Hebrew manuscripts; some Hebrew manuscripts and Syriac *Abijam* (that is, Abijah)

his son and grandson. What are the children around us learning from our behavior and attitudes?

15:9–13 Courage is necessary to confront generations of corruption and sinful behavior in any family. Asa showed courage by confronting the sins of his forefathers and by deciding to serve God. Asa destroyed idols and deposed his grandmother from her position as queen mother. The early years of Asa's reign leave us with a wonderful example of ways to foster spiritual renewal.

And Jehoshaphat his son succeeded him as king.

Nadab King of Israel

25Nadab son of Jeroboam became king of Israel in the second year of Asa king of Judah, and he reigned over Israel two years. 26He did evil in the eyes of the LORD, walking in the ways of his father and in his sin, which he had caused Israel to commit.

27Baasha son of Ahijah of the house of Issachar plotted against him, and he struck him down at Gibbethon, a Philistine town, while Nadab and all Israel were besieging it. 28Baasha killed Nadab in the third year of Asa king of Judah and succeeded him as king.

29As soon as he began to reign, he killed Jeroboam's whole family. He did not leave Jeroboam anyone that breathed, but destroyed them all, according to the word of the LORD given through his servant Ahijah the Shilonite— 30because of the sins Jeroboam had committed and had caused Israel to commit, and because he provoked the LORD, the God of Israel, to anger.

31As for the other events of Nadab's reign, and all he did, are they not written in the book of the annals of the kings of Israel? 32There was war between Asa and Baasha king of Israel throughout their reigns.

Baasha King of Israel

33In the third year of Asa king of Judah, Baasha son of Ahijah became king of all Israel in Tirzah, and he reigned twenty-four years. 34He did evil in the eyes of the LORD, walking in the ways of Jeroboam and in his sin, which he had caused Israel to commit.

16 Then the word of the LORD came to Jehu son of Hanani against Baasha: 2"I lifted you up from the dust and made you leader of my people Israel, but you walked in the ways of Jeroboam and caused my people Israel to sin and to provoke me to anger by their sins. 3So I am about to consume Baasha and his house, and I will make your house like that of Jeroboam son of Nebat. 4Dogs will eat those belonging to Baasha who die in the city, and the birds of the air will feed on those who die in the country."

5As for the other events of Baasha's reign, what he did and his achievements, are they not written in the book of the annals of the kings of Israel? 6Baasha rested with his fathers and was buried in Tirzah. And Elah his son succeeded him as king.

7Moreover, the word of the LORD came through the prophet Jehu son of Hanani to Baasha and his house, because of all the evil he had done in the eyes of the LORD, provoking him to anger by the things he did, and becoming like the house of Jeroboam—and also because he destroyed it.

Elah King of Israel

8In the twenty-sixth year of Asa king of Judah, Elah son of Baasha became king of Israel, and he reigned in Tirzah two years.

9Zimri, one of his officials, who had command of half his chariots, plotted against him. Elah was in Tirzah at the time, getting drunk in the home of Arza, the man in charge of the palace at Tirzah. 10Zimri came in, struck him down and killed him in the twenty-seventh year of Asa king of Judah. Then he succeeded him as king.

11As soon as he began to reign and was seated on the throne, he killed off Baasha's whole family. He did not spare a single male, whether relative or friend. 12So Zimri destroyed the whole family of Baasha, in accordance with the word of the LORD spoken against Baasha through the prophet Jehu— 13because of all the sins Baasha and his son Elah had committed and had caused Israel to commit, so that they provoked the LORD, the God of Israel, to anger by their worthless idols.

14As for the other events of Elah's reign, and all he did, are they not written in the book of the annals of the kings of Israel?

Zimri King of Israel

15In the twenty-seventh year of Asa king of Judah, Zimri reigned in Tirzah seven days. The army was encamped near Gibbethon, a Philistine town. 16When the Israelites in the camp heard that Zimri had plotted against the king and murdered him, they proclaimed Omri, the commander of the army, king over Israel that very day there in the camp. 17Then Omri and all the Israelites with him withdrew from Gibbe-

15:25–31 Nadab continued to lead Israel into sin just as his father, Jeroboam, had done before him. Leadership must be taken seriously, because leaders are responsible for their followers. Because of Jeroboam's irresponsible leadership, God destroyed him and his descendants (15:30–31). Leadership and responsibility go hand in hand. If we desire to grow spiritually, we need to take responsibility for our actions. Then we can make the appropriate changes in our lives.

15:32–34 Baasha was blind to the truth. He ruled in Israel during Asa's reign in Judah (15:32–33). Baasha was probably aware of Asa's reforms and God's resultant blessings. He had also seen the sin of his forefathers and the trouble it had caused. But apparently Baasha was blind to the facts, for he repeated the sins of his fathers (15:34). We need to search our lives for spiritual blindness that keeps us from seeing the truth about ourselves. We should ask God to show us the problems that we are unable to see. If we cannot see the problems in our lives, we will never be able to deal with them.

16:15–20 Zimri held the shortest reign (seven days) of all the kings of Israel. Omri led the army of Israel against Zimri at Tirzah. Realizing that his end was near, Zimri chose to commit suicide. Though Zimri was an evil king like those before him, at the end he still had time to call upon God to save him. But rather than submit to God or face the judgment of his own people, Zimri took his own life. When it looks as if there is no way out of our problems, we need not take drastic measures. We should always start by turning to God for help.

thon and laid siege to Tirzah. 18When Zimri saw that the city was taken, he went into the citadel of the royal palace and set the palace on fire around him. So he died, 19because of the sins he had committed, doing evil in the eyes of the LORD and walking in the ways of Jeroboam and in the sin he had committed and had caused Israel to commit.

20As for the other events of Zimri's reign, and the rebellion he carried out, are they not written in the book of the annals of the kings of Israel?

Omri King of Israel

21Then the people of Israel were split into two factions; half supported Tibni son of Ginath for king, and the other half supported Omri. 22But Omri's followers proved stronger than those of Tibni son of Ginath. So Tibni died and Omri became king.

23In the thirty-first year of Asa king of Judah, Omri became king of Israel, and he reigned twelve years, six of them in Tirzah. 24He bought the hill of Samaria from Shemer for two talents[a] of silver and built a city on the hill, calling it Samaria, after Shemer, the name of the former owner of the hill.

25But Omri did evil in the eyes of the LORD and sinned more than all those before him. 26He walked in all the ways of Jeroboam son of Nebat and in his sin, which he had caused Israel to commit, so that they provoked the LORD, the God of Israel, to anger by their worthless idols.

27As for the other events of Omri's reign, what he did and the things he achieved, are they not written in the book of the annals of the kings of Israel? 28Omri rested with his fathers and was buried in Samaria. And Ahab his son succeeded him as king.

Ahab Becomes King of Israel

29In the thirty-eighth year of Asa king of Judah, Ahab son of Omri became king of Israel, and he reigned in Samaria over Israel twenty-two years. 30Ahab son of Omri did more evil in the eyes of the LORD than any of those before him. 31He not only considered it trivial to commit the sins of Jeroboam son of Nebat, but he also married Jezebel daughter of Ethbaal king of the Sidonians, and began to serve Baal and worship him. 32He set up an altar for Baal in the temple of Baal that he built in Samaria. 33Ahab also made an Asherah pole and did more to provoke the LORD, the God of Israel, to anger than did all the kings of Israel before him.

34In Ahab's time, Hiel of Bethel rebuilt Jericho. He laid its foundations at the cost of his firstborn son Abiram, and he set up its gates at the cost of his youngest son Segub, in accordance with the word of the LORD spoken by Joshua son of Nun.

Elijah Fed by Ravens

17 Now Elijah the Tishbite, from Tishbe[b] in Gilead, said to Ahab, "As the LORD, the God of Israel, lives, whom I serve, there will be neither dew nor rain in the next few years except at my word."

2Then the word of the LORD came to Elijah: 3"Leave here, turn eastward and hide in the Kerith Ravine, east of the Jordan. 4You will drink from the brook, and I have ordered the ravens to feed you there."

5So he did what the LORD had told him. He went to the Kerith Ravine, east of the Jordan, and stayed there. 6The ravens brought him bread and meat in the morning and bread and meat in the evening, and he drank from the brook.

The Widow at Zarephath

7Some time later the brook dried up because there had been no rain in the land. 8Then the word of the LORD came to him: 9"Go at once to Zarephath of Sidon and stay there. I have commanded a widow in that place to supply you with food." 10So he went to Zarephath. When he came to the town gate, a widow was there gathering sticks. He called to her and asked, "Would you bring me a little water in a jar so I may have a drink?" 11As she was going to get it, he called, "And bring me, please, a piece of bread."

12"As surely as the LORD your God lives," she replied, "I don't have any bread—only a handful of flour in a jar and a little oil in a jug. I am gathering a few sticks to take home and make a meal for myself and my son, that we may eat it—and die."

13Elijah said to her, "Don't be afraid. Go home and do as you have said. But first make a small cake of bread for me from what you have and bring it to me, and then make something for yourself and your son. 14For this is what the LORD, the God of Israel, says: 'The jar of flour will not be used up and the jug of oil will not run dry until the day the LORD gives rain on the land.' "

15She went away and did as Elijah had told

[a] *24* That is, about 150 pounds (about 70 kilograms)
[b] *1* Or *Tishbite, of the settlers*

16:29–31 We tend to fall progressively deeper into trouble unless we ask God to turn things around. God uses the stories of the kings of Israel to illustrate this principle for us. Ahab continued the downward spiral of the Israelite kings by being more wicked than any king before him. Ahab and his forefathers serve as reminders that problems left unresolved will continue, and even worsen, unless they are confronted and resolved.

17:8–16 The widow of Zarephath demonstrated her great faith in God's ability to provide for her needs. She and her son faced starvation, but she shared the last of her food with Elijah. Believing that God would provide for her, she gave up her last resource for survival and thereby found her deliverance. God provided for her need. When we are at the end of our rope, all we need to do is call out to God. He will take care of us and deliver us if we are only willing to trust him.

THE SPIRITUAL DISCIPLINES

In the Life of Elijah

From the mountaintops of spectacular experiences with God to the deepest valleys of depression and despair, Elijah's practice of the spiritual disciplines helped sustain him in his faith. Often we are intimidated by the impressive lives and experiences of the prophets—especially those of Elijah's caliber. Yet James 5:17 reminds us that "Elijah was a man just like us." We find hope in this verse that we can also be used to accomplish great things for God if we will only submit to him.

We first meet Elijah as he confronts King Ahab and then goes into the wilderness at God's command. This time in the wilderness prepared Elijah for one of the most dramatic spiritual confrontations in the Bible—the contest on Mount Carmel between Elijah and the 450 prophets of Baal.

Elijah's time in the wilderness forced him to practice three, classic, spiritual disciplines that freed him from dependence on the world and encouraged him instead to depend on God.

SOLITUDE. When God called Elijah to leave his life in Samaria and go to the wilderness near Kerith Ravine, God was calling Elijah into solitude. This solitude served at least two purposes. From a practical standpoint, solitude protected Elijah from King Ahab. On a spiritual level, however, this time of solitude provided an opportunity for Elijah to deepen his faith. At this point, Elijah was not aware that his spiritual life would soon be tested to the limits. But his time in the wilderness would prepare him for the challenge. (To learn more about solitude, turn to Exodus 3.)

SILENCE. Elijah's wilderness experience also presented him with a time of silence, allowing him to listen more clearly to God's voice. (To learn more about silence, turn to Psalm 39.)

FASTING. Elijah's third spiritual discipline in the wilderness was a form of fasting. Strictly speaking, Elijah did not abstain from food. But his food was controlled by God's special provision. Periodically, God would send ravens to Elijah, carrying food that he could eat. In this way, Elijah learned to trust God to provide for his daily needs. (To learn more about fasting, turn to 2 Chronicles 20.)

Lessons for Life

Wilderness experiences often play an important role in our spiritual formation, too. In the wilderness we are detached from the routines and resources of our usual lives. Through these experiences we can learn to free ourselves from our dependence on the world and tap into God's power and resources to find strength. Often these times of solitude, silence and fasting can initiate spiritual renewal within us. Like Elijah, withdrawing from our normal routines removes us from distraction and leads us into deeper fellowship with God. Silence makes it possible for us to listen both to our souls and to God. And fasting teaches us to depend on God to provide for us.

Following God's incredible victory and judgment against Baal worship, Elijah plunged into the depths of fear and despair. He fled into the wilderness once again to escape the wicked Jezebel. During this time, the Lord strengthened him with food and rest. Fasting was not appropriate in this case, for Elijah needed to be physically rejuvenated. This reminds us that the spiritual disciplines are what we might call "soul specific"—certain disciplines that apply best in certain situations.

her. So there was food every day for Elijah and for the woman and her family. 16For the jar of flour was not used up and the jug of oil did not run dry, in keeping with the word of the LORD spoken by Elijah.

17Some time later the son of the woman who owned the house became ill. He grew worse and worse, and finally stopped breathing. 18She said to Elijah, "What do you have against me, man of God? Did you come to remind me of my sin and kill my son?"

19"Give me your son," Elijah replied. He took him from her arms, carried him to the upper room where he was staying, and laid him on his bed. 20Then he cried out to the LORD, "O LORD my God, have you brought tragedy also upon this widow I am staying with, by causing her son to die?" 21Then he stretched himself out on the boy three times and cried to the LORD, "O LORD my God, let this boy's life return to him!"

22The LORD heard Elijah's cry, and the boy's life returned to him, and he lived. 23Elijah picked up the child and carried him down from the room into the house. He gave him to his mother and said, "Look, your son is alive!"

24Then the woman said to Elijah, "Now I know that you are a man of God and that the word of the LORD from your mouth is the truth."

Elijah and Obadiah

18 After a long time, in the third year, the word of the LORD came to Elijah: "Go and present yourself to Ahab, and I will send rain on the land." 2So Elijah went to present himself to Ahab.

Now the famine was severe in Samaria, 3and Ahab had summoned Obadiah, who was in charge of his palace. (Obadiah was a devout believer in the LORD. 4While Jezebel was killing off the LORD's prophets, Obadiah had taken a hundred prophets and hidden them in two caves, fifty in each, and had supplied them with food and water.) 5Ahab had said to Obadiah, "Go through the land to all the springs and valleys. Maybe we can find some grass to keep the horses and mules alive so we will not have to kill any of our animals." 6So they divided the land they were to cover, Ahab going in one direction and Obadiah in another.

7As Obadiah was walking along, Elijah met him. Obadiah recognized him, bowed down to the ground, and said, "Is it really you, my lord Elijah?"

8"Yes," he replied. "Go tell your master, 'Elijah is here.' "

9"What have I done wrong," asked Obadiah, "that you are handing your servant over to Ahab to be put to death? 10As surely as the LORD your God lives, there is not a nation or kingdom where my master has not sent someone to look for you. And whenever a nation or kingdom claimed you were not there, he made them swear they could not find you. 11But now you tell me to go to my master and say, 'Elijah is here.' 12I don't know where the Spirit of the LORD may carry you when I leave you. If I go and tell Ahab and he doesn't find you, he will kill me. Yet I your servant have worshiped the LORD since my youth. 13Haven't you heard, my lord, what I did while Jezebel was killing the prophets of the LORD? I hid a hundred of the LORD's prophets in two caves, fifty in each, and supplied them with food and water. 14And now you tell me to go to my master and say, 'Elijah is here.' He will kill me!"

15Elijah said, "As the LORD Almighty lives, whom I serve, I will surely present myself to Ahab today."

Elijah on Mount Carmel

16So Obadiah went to meet Ahab and told him, and Ahab went to meet Elijah. 17When he saw Elijah, he said to him, "Is that you, you troubler of Israel?"

18"I have not made trouble for Israel," Elijah replied. "But you and your father's family have. You have abandoned the LORD's commands and have followed the Baals. 19Now summon the people from all over Israel to meet me on Mount Carmel. And bring the four hundred and fifty prophets of Baal and the four hundred prophets of Asherah, who eat at Jezebel's table."

20So Ahab sent word throughout all Israel and assembled the prophets on Mount Carmel. 21Elijah went before the people and said, "How long will you waver between two opinions? If the LORD is God, follow him; but if Baal is God, follow him."

But the people said nothing.

22Then Elijah said to them, "I am the only one of the LORD's prophets left, but Baal has four hundred and fifty prophets. 23Get two bulls for us. Let them choose one for themselves, and let them cut it into pieces and put it on the wood but not set fire to it. I will prepare the other bull and put it on the wood but not set fire to it. 24Then you call on the name of your god, and I will call on the name of the LORD. The god who answers by fire—he is God."

Then all the people said, "What you say is good."

25Elijah said to the prophets of Baal, "Choose one of the bulls and prepare it first, since there are so many of you. Call on the name of your god, but do not light the fire." 26So

---

18:22–39 "The odds are against us" is a phrase commonly used in our society. Few enjoy being the underdog. The underdog in this passage was Elijah, who was greatly outnumbered by the prophets of Baal. Elijah trusted God to be with him in one of the greatest spiritual contests of all time. When God is on our side, we are always a majority. No problem will ever be able to stop our progress if we turn everything over to God. "If God is for us, who can be against us?" (Romans 8:31).

they took the bull given them and prepared it.

Then they called on the name of Baal from morning till noon. "O Baal, answer us!" they shouted. But there was no response; no one answered. And they danced around the altar they had made.

27At noon Elijah began to taunt them. "Shout louder!" he said. "Surely he is a god! Perhaps he is deep in thought, or busy, or traveling. Maybe he is sleeping and must be awakened." 28So they shouted louder and slashed themselves with swords and spears, as was their custom, until their blood flowed. 29Midday passed, and they continued their frantic prophesying until the time for the evening sacrifice. But there was no response, no one answered, no one paid attention.

30Then Elijah said to all the people, "Come here to me." They came to him, and he repaired the altar of the LORD, which was in ruins. 31Elijah took twelve stones, one for each of the tribes descended from Jacob, to whom the word of the LORD had come, saying, "Your name shall be Israel." 32With the stones he built an altar in the name of the LORD, and he dug a trench around it large enough to hold two seahs[a] of seed. 33He arranged the wood, cut the bull into pieces and laid it on the wood. Then he said to them, "Fill four large jars with water and pour it on the offering and on the wood."

34"Do it again," he said, and they did it again.

"Do it a third time," he ordered, and they did it the third time. 35The water ran down around the altar and even filled the trench.

36At the time of sacrifice, the prophet Elijah stepped forward and prayed: "O LORD, God of Abraham, Isaac and Israel, let it be known today that you are God in Israel and that I am your servant and have done all these things at your command. 37Answer me, O LORD, answer me, so these people will know that you, O LORD, are God, and that you are turning their hearts back again."

38Then the fire of the LORD fell and burned up the sacrifice, the wood, the stones and the soil, and also licked up the water in the trench.

39When all the people saw this, they fell prostrate and cried, "The LORD—he is God! The LORD—he is God!"

40Then Elijah commanded them, "Seize the prophets of Baal. Don't let anyone get away!" They seized them, and Elijah had them brought down to the Kishon Valley and slaughtered there.

41And Elijah said to Ahab, "Go, eat and drink, for there is the sound of a heavy rain." 42So Ahab went off to eat and drink, but Elijah climbed to the top of Carmel, bent down to the ground and put his face between his knees.

43"Go and look toward the sea," he told his servant. And he went up and looked.

"There is nothing there," he said.

Seven times Elijah said, "Go back."

44The seventh time the servant reported, "A cloud as small as a man's hand is rising from the sea."

So Elijah said, "Go and tell Ahab, 'Hitch up your chariot and go down before the rain stops you.'"

45Meanwhile, the sky grew black with clouds, the wind rose, a heavy rain came on and Ahab rode off to Jezreel. 46The power of the LORD came upon Elijah and, tucking his cloak into his belt, he ran ahead of Ahab all the way to Jezreel.

Elijah Flees to Horeb

19 Now Ahab told Jezebel everything Elijah had done and how he had killed all the prophets with the sword. 2So Jezebel sent a messenger to Elijah to say, "May the gods deal with me, be it ever so severely, if by this time tomorrow I do not make your life like that of one of them."

3Elijah was afraid[b] and ran for his life. When he came to Beersheba in Judah, he left his servant there, 4while he himself went a day's journey into the desert. He came to a broom tree, sat down under it and prayed that he might die. "I have had enough, LORD," he said. "Take my life; I am no better than my ancestors." 5Then he lay down under the tree and fell asleep.

All at once an angel touched him and said, "Get up and eat." 6He looked around, and there by his head was a cake of bread baked over hot coals, and a jar of water. He ate and drank and then lay down again.

7The angel of the LORD came back a second time and touched him and said, "Get up and eat, for the journey is too much for you." 8So he got up and ate and drank. Strengthened by that food, he traveled forty days and forty nights until he reached Horeb, the mountain of God. 9There he went into a cave and spent the night.

The LORD Appears to Elijah

And the word of the LORD came to him: "What are you doing here, Elijah?"

[a]32 That is, probably about 13 quarts (about 15 liters)
[b]3 Or *Elijah saw*

19:1–4 After our greatest victories, we are often the most vulnerable to a fall. Elijah had just won an amazing victory for God, but suddenly he was so discouraged he wanted to die. We often do the same thing. As we depend on God's power, we may quickly progress spiritually. But then some kind of opposition suddenly comes our way, or we are overcome by temptation. Let us learn from Elijah. We should consider our victories as warning signs, times when we should renew our dependence upon God. This will help us experience one success after another.

19:5–18 Self-doubt is a trait we all share. Elijah doubted himself when he was on the run from Jezebel. God dealt with Elijah in a loving, patient manner by reassuring him that he was not alone. Reassurance and rest are solid prescriptions for someone afflicted with self-doubt. A community of support to help us through the difficult times can also be helpful.

10He replied, "I have been very zealous for
the LORD God Almighty. The Israelites have rejected your covenant, broken down your altars,
and put your prophets to death with the sword.
I am the only one left, and now they are trying
to kill me too."
11The LORD said, "Go out and stand on the
mountain in the presence of the LORD, for the
LORD is about to pass by."
Then a great and powerful wind tore the
mountains apart and shattered the rocks before
the LORD, but the LORD was not in the wind.
After the wind there was an earthquake, but the
LORD was not in the earthquake. 12After the
earthquake came a fire, but the LORD was not in
the fire. And after the fire came a gentle whisper.
13When Elijah heard it, he pulled his cloak over
his face and went out and stood at the mouth
of the cave.
Then a voice said to him, "What are you
doing here, Elijah?"
14He replied, "I have been very zealous for
the LORD God Almighty. The Israelites have rejected your covenant, broken down your altars,
and put your prophets to death with the sword.
I am the only one left, and now they are trying
to kill me too."
15The LORD said to him, "Go back the way
you came, and go to the Desert of Damascus.
When you get there, anoint Hazael king over
Aram. 16Also, anoint Jehu son of Nimshi king
over Israel, and anoint Elisha son of Shaphat
from Abel Meholah to succeed you as prophet.
17Jehu will put to death any who escape the
sword of Hazael, and Elisha will put to death
any who escape the sword of Jehu. 18Yet I reserve seven thousand in Israel—all whose knees
have not bowed down to Baal and all whose
mouths have not kissed him."

The Call of Elisha

19So Elijah went from there and found Elisha
son of Shaphat. He was plowing with twelve
yoke of oxen, and he himself was driving the
twelfth pair. Elijah went up to him and threw
his cloak around him. 20Elisha then left his
oxen and ran after Elijah. "Let me kiss my father and mother good-by," he said, "and then I
will come with you."
"Go back," Elijah replied. "What have I done
to you?"
21So Elisha left him and went back. He took
his yoke of oxen and slaughtered them. He
burned the plowing equipment to cook the
meat and gave it to the people, and they ate.
Then he set out to follow Elijah and became his
attendant.

Ben-Hadad Attacks Samaria

20 Now Ben-Hadad king of Aram mustered his entire army. Accompanied by
thirty-two kings with their horses and chariots,
he went up and besieged Samaria and attacked
it. 2He sent messengers into the city to Ahab

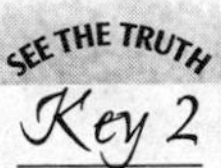

Seeing That We Are Only Human

1 Kings 19:1–21 Some of us may not like seeing the truth that we are only human. We may think of ourselves as superhuman—until we discover a flaw. Then many of us come crashing down and see ourselves as completely worthless. But seeing the whole truth about ourselves means accepting our humanity and realizing our great potential in Christ.

The prophet Elijah is one of the great heroes of the Bible. If anyone had reason to feel superhuman, it was he. His prayers brought a lengthy drought upon Israel—and then brought fire down from heaven, humiliating Queen Jezebel and her priests of Baal. But even Elijah could have a bad day. Let's consider his reaction after being threatened by Jezebel:

> I have had enough, LORD . . . Take my life; I am no better than my ancestors . . . I have been very zealous for the LORD God Almighty. The Israelites have rejected your covenant, broken down your altars, and put your prophets to death with the sword. I am the only one left, and now they are trying to kill me too (19:4, 10).

If we are able to do superhuman feats, it is because God gives us the power to do so. Even those who are used powerfully by God must always realize that they are only human. If we fail to see the truth of our humanity, we may find ourselves at great risk during the times when life reminds us of that fact.

Turn to Psalm 8.

THE SPIRITUAL DISCIPLINES

Solitude

Finding a Place of Renewal

1 Kings 19:1 – 18 The wilderness is not only a place of trial and temptation; it can also be a place of renewal and restoration. Elijah's confrontation with the prophets of Baal on Mount Carmel left him spiritually drained, and Jezebel's threat sent him running for his life. In the midst of Elijah's anxiety, however, God provided for his spiritual renewal by sending him into the wilderness. There Elijah found several blessings in his solitude.

During Elijah's solitude, God provided him with food and rest. This restored Elijah's physical strength, refreshing his spirit in the process. In the same way, God often uses solitude to give us nourishment, both in body and soul. When we find a quiet place away from the crowds and busy schedules, we recover our physical energy and experience much needed renewal.

God also used Elijah's solitude to help him encounter the Lord in a fresh way. Elijah had seen God in the wind and fire. God's power was incredible. But now Elijah needed a gentler sign of God's presence. When we withdraw from our routines, we also break from our routine view of God. We learn things we have been too busy to see before.

In his solitude, Elijah received assurance and direction from God for his next step. As Elijah fled to Sinai, he believed that all hope was lost. He felt that he was the only faithful prophet remaining in Israel. But God dismantled those incorrect assumptions and revealed reasons for hope. Like Ezekiel in the valley of dry bones (Ezekiel 37), Elijah found the wilderness to be a place of vision and hope. When we take a step back from our worrisome lifestyles for a moment, God often gives us a new perspective on life, increased hope and new direction.

Putting It Into Practice

Do you need refreshment, a new view of God or a new direction? Consider taking time away for at least three or four hours. Go to a place where you will be undisturbed and undistracted. You may want to use a room at church or a hidden corner of a library — a place that gives you the freedom to respond spontaneously to God. You may want to select some Scripture in advance to provide direction for your solitude. Record your experience in your journal and thank God for the refreshment and insights he grants you.

For more on solitude, turn to Mark 1.

king of Israel, saying, "This is what Ben-Hadad says: 3'Your silver and gold are mine, and the best of your wives and children are mine.' "

4The king of Israel answered, "Just as you say, my lord the king. I and all I have are yours."

5The messengers came again and said, "This is what Ben-Hadad says: 'I sent to demand your silver and gold, your wives and your children. 6But about this time tomorrow I am going to send my officials to search your palace and the houses of your officials. They will seize everything you value and carry it away.' "

7The king of Israel summoned all the elders of the land and said to them, "See how this man is looking for trouble! When he sent for my wives and my children, my silver and my gold, I did not refuse him."

8The elders and the people all answered, "Don't listen to him or agree to his demands."

9So he replied to Ben-Hadad's messengers, "Tell my lord the king, 'Your servant will do all you demanded the first time, but this demand I cannot meet.' " They left and took the answer back to Ben-Hadad.

10Then Ben-Hadad sent another message to Ahab: "May the gods deal with me, be it ever so severely, if enough dust remains in Samaria to give each of my men a handful."

11The king of Israel answered, "Tell him: 'One who puts on his armor should not boast like one who takes it off.' "

12Ben-Hadad heard this message while he and the kings were drinking in their tents,[a] and he ordered his men: "Prepare to attack." So they prepared to attack the city.

Ahab Defeats Ben-Hadad

13Meanwhile a prophet came to Ahab king of Israel and announced, "This is what the LORD says: 'Do you see this vast army? I will give it into your hand today, and then you will know that I am the LORD.' "

14"But who will do this?" asked Ahab.

The prophet replied, "This is what the LORD says: 'The young officers of the provincial commanders will do it.' "

"And who will start the battle?" he asked.

The prophet answered, "You will."

15So Ahab summoned the young officers of the provincial commanders, 232 men. Then he assembled the rest of the Israelites, 7,000 in all. 16They set out at noon while Ben-Hadad and the 32 kings allied with him were in their tents getting drunk. 17The young officers of the provincial commanders went out first.

Now Ben-Hadad had dispatched scouts, who reported, "Men are advancing from Samaria."

18He said, "If they have come out for peace, take them alive; if they have come out for war, take them alive."

19The young officers of the provincial commanders marched out of the city with the army behind them 20and each one struck down his opponent. At that, the Arameans fled, with the Israelites in pursuit. But Ben-Hadad king of Aram escaped on horseback with some of his horsemen. 21The king of Israel advanced and overpowered the horses and chariots and inflicted heavy losses on the Arameans.

22Afterward, the prophet came to the king of Israel and said, "Strengthen your position and see what must be done, because next spring the king of Aram will attack you again."

23Meanwhile, the officials of the king of Aram advised him, "Their gods are gods of the hills. That is why they were too strong for us. But if we fight them on the plains, surely we will be stronger than they. 24Do this: Remove all the kings from their commands and replace them with other officers. 25You must also raise an army like the one you lost—horse for horse and chariot for chariot—so we can fight Israel on the plains. Then surely we will be stronger than they." He agreed with them and acted accordingly.

26The next spring Ben-Hadad mustered the Arameans and went up to Aphek to fight against Israel. 27When the Israelites were also mustered and given provisions, they marched out to meet them. The Israelites camped opposite them like two small flocks of goats, while the Arameans covered the countryside.

28The man of God came up and told the king of Israel, "This is what the LORD says: 'Because the Arameans think the LORD is a god of the hills and not a god of the valleys, I will deliver this vast army into your hands, and you will know that I am the LORD.' "

29For seven days they camped opposite each other, and on the seventh day the battle was joined. The Israelites inflicted a hundred thousand casualties on the Aramean foot soldiers in one day. 30The rest of them escaped to the city of Aphek, where the wall collapsed on twenty-seven thousand of them. And Ben-Hadad fled to the city and hid in an inner room.

31His officials said to him, "Look, we have heard that the kings of the house of Israel are merciful. Let us go to the king of Israel with sackcloth around our waists and ropes around our heads. Perhaps he will spare your life."

32Wearing sackcloth around their waists and ropes around their heads, they went to the king of Israel and said, "Your servant Ben-Hadad says: 'Please let me live.' "

[a]12 Or *in Succoth*; also in verse 16

20:10–21 Ben-Hadad, who was drinking when he received Ahab's refusal to surrender, was soundly surprised by Ahab's attack in the middle of the day. He and the other kings of his coalition were drunk, their judgment impaired. While Ben-Hadad survived, his men did not. Our spiritual growth can be endangered whenever our judgment is impaired. We should beware of using any substance that prevents our thinking clearly.

The king answered, "Is he still alive? He is my brother."

33 The men took this as a good sign and were quick to pick up his word. "Yes, your brother Ben-Hadad!" they said.

"Go and get him," the king said. When Ben-Hadad came out, Ahab had him come up into his chariot.

34 "I will return the cities my father took from your father," Ben-Hadad offered. "You may set up your own market areas in Damascus, as my father did in Samaria."

⌞Ahab said,⌟ "On the basis of a treaty I will set you free." So he made a treaty with him, and let him go.

A Prophet Condemns Ahab

35 By the word of the LORD one of the sons of the prophets said to his companion, "Strike me with your weapon," but the man refused.

36 So the prophet said, "Because you have not obeyed the LORD, as soon as you leave me a lion will kill you." And after the man went away, a lion found him and killed him.

37 The prophet found another man and said, "Strike me, please." So the man struck him and wounded him. 38 Then the prophet went and stood by the road waiting for the king. He disguised himself with his headband down over his eyes. 39 As the king passed by, the prophet called out to him, "Your servant went into the thick of the battle, and someone came to me with a captive and said, 'Guard this man. If he is missing, it will be your life for his life, or you must pay a talent[a] of silver.' 40 While your servant was busy here and there, the man disappeared."

"That is your sentence," the king of Israel said. "You have pronounced it yourself."

41 Then the prophet quickly removed the headband from his eyes, and the king of Israel recognized him as one of the prophets. 42 He said to the king, "This is what the LORD says: 'You have set free a man I had determined should die.[b] Therefore it is your life for his life, your people for his people.' " 43 Sullen and angry, the king of Israel went to his palace in Samaria.

Naboth's Vineyard

21 Some time later there was an incident involving a vineyard belonging to Naboth the Jezreelite. The vineyard was in Jezreel, close to the palace of Ahab king of Samaria. 2 Ahab said to Naboth, "Let me have your vineyard to use for a vegetable garden, since it is close to my palace. In exchange I will give you a better vineyard or, if you prefer, I will pay you whatever it is worth."

3 But Naboth replied, "The LORD forbid that I should give you the inheritance of my fathers."

4 So Ahab went home, sullen and angry because Naboth the Jezreelite had said, "I will not give you the inheritance of my fathers." He lay on his bed sulking and refused to eat.

5 His wife Jezebel came in and asked him, "Why are you so sullen? Why won't you eat?"

6 He answered her, "Because I said to Naboth the Jezreelite, 'Sell me your vineyard; or if you prefer, I will give you another vineyard in its place.' But he said, 'I will not give you my vineyard.' "

7 Jezebel his wife said, "Is this how you act as king over Israel? Get up and eat! Cheer up. I'll get you the vineyard of Naboth the Jezreelite."

8 So she wrote letters in Ahab's name, placed his seal on them, and sent them to the elders and nobles who lived in Naboth's city with him. 9 In those letters she wrote:

> "Proclaim a day of fasting and seat Naboth in a prominent place among the people. 10 But seat two scoundrels opposite him and have them testify that he has cursed both God and the king. Then take him out and stone him to death."

11 So the elders and nobles who lived in Naboth's city did as Jezebel directed in the letters she had written to them. 12 They proclaimed a fast and seated Naboth in a prominent place among the people. 13 Then two scoundrels came and sat opposite him and brought charges against Naboth before the people, saying, "Naboth has cursed both God and the king." So they took him outside the city and stoned him to death. 14 Then they sent word to Jezebel: "Naboth has been stoned and is dead."

15 As soon as Jezebel heard that Naboth had been stoned to death, she said to Ahab, "Get up

[a] 39 That is, about 75 pounds (about 34 kilograms)
[b] 42 The Hebrew term refers to the irrevocable giving over of things or persons to the LORD, often by totally destroying them.

20:35–43 When we reject God's will in favor of our own, we are headed toward trouble. Ahab was commanded to execute Ben-Hadad, but he allowed him to live. Ahab viewed Ben-Hadad as a possible ally against Assyria. The eventual result of Ahab's disobedience was death. If God calls us to remove certain things from our lives, we must act immediately. Allowing them to remain will lead to our eventual destruction. We must learn to obey God's Word in every detail. Only then will we be able to live holy lives.

21:1–6 Ahab tried to force Naboth to sell him his vineyard, but Naboth refused his request. Even though Ahab was the king of Israel, he could not force Naboth to sell the land unless Naboth wanted to. Ahab had to abide by God's laws. Though Ahab had been worshiping idols, he still recognized God's authority. If we are in positions of authority, we must remember that we will have to answer to God for our actions. Are we following his commands?

21:7–14 Jezebel's materialism and greed drove her to the point of plotting the death of an innocent man. An obsession, such as greed, can severely taint our sense of right and wrong. If we are driven by such passions, we are in danger of committing a multitude of other sins. When we reflect honestly on our lives, we should seriously consider anything that drives us to step outside of God's will. These urges and obsessions need to be confessed and surrendered to God. Then God can help us follow his plan for us and set us free from a life enslaved to sinful passions.

Ahab & Jezebel

Bad role models can sometimes be as valuable to us as good ones. The behavior of a bad role model provides clear guidance on how we should *not* act. The consequences a bad role model suffers also provide a warning for anyone who might desire to imitate them. We can usually observe the actions of people who refuse to obey God and redirect our own course to do the opposite.

Ahab and Jezebel were classic examples of bad role models. Ahab was an exceedingly evil and oppressive king, and Jezebel taught him things about evil he never would have dreamed of alone. Ahab and Jezebel had been offered opportunities to understand and pursue the ways of God. The prophet Elijah was constantly confronting them about their sin. Again and again, Elijah intervened in their wicked dealings; again and again Ahab and Jezebel rebutted his efforts.

However, one of Elijah's confrontations made a difference in Ahab's life. After Jezebel's wicked scheme allowed Ahab the possession of Naboth's vineyard, Elijah predicted the violent death of Ahab. At that point, Ahab greatly humbled himself. He seemed to have glimpsed the truth and exhibited a desire to redirect his course. However, there is no further record of positive spiritual progress before Ahab's death in battle.

Jezebel, on the other hand, never made even the slightest move toward God and his ways. Whenever she was defeated by Elijah, Jezebel merely redoubled her efforts to maintain her idolatry and to get her own way. No wonder her name has become a byword for evil among God's people.

Like most people involved in wickedness, Ahab and Jezebel surrounded themselves with people of like mind. They avoided God's messengers and punished people who held them accountable. Whenever we are involved in destructive behavior, we often prefer to cloak ourselves in the darkness of sin and sinful friends. But spiritual renewal requires that we break with our sinfulness. We must listen to God and the people who love us and allow them to hold us accountable for our actions.

WEAKNESSES AND MISTAKES:

Ahab was the most evil king of Israel.

Ahab married Jezebel, a pagan woman.

Ahab allowed Jezebel to practice and promote idol worship in Israel.

Jezebel attempted to stamp out the worship of the true God.

LESSONS FROM THEIR LIVES:

Human ability, wealth, power and tenacity will lead to destruction if we refuse to surrender to God and follow his plan for us.

Commitment to just "any god" will not bring true spiritual renewal; we must surrender our lives to the true God through faith in Jesus Christ.

KEY VERSE:

"There was never a man like Ahab, who sold himself to do evil in the eyes of the Lord, urged on by Jezebel his wife" (21:25).

Ahab and Jezebel's story is told in 1 Kings 16—22. Jezebel's story concludes in 2 Kings 9. Ahab is also mentioned in 2 Chronicles 18; 21—22, and Micah 6:16.

and take possession of the vineyard of Naboth the Jezreelite that he refused to sell you. He is no longer alive, but dead." [16]When Ahab heard that Naboth was dead, he got up and went down to take possession of Naboth's vineyard.

[17]Then the word of the LORD came to Elijah the Tishbite: [18]"Go down to meet Ahab king of Israel, who rules in Samaria. He is now in Naboth's vineyard, where he has gone to take possession of it. [19]Say to him, 'This is what the LORD says: Have you not murdered a man and seized his property?' Then say to him, 'This is what the LORD says: In the place where dogs licked up Naboth's blood, dogs will lick up your blood—yes, yours!' "

[20]Ahab said to Elijah, "So you have found me, my enemy!"

"I have found you," he answered, "because you have sold yourself to do evil in the eyes of the LORD. [21]'I am going to bring disaster on you. I will consume your descendants and cut off from Ahab every last male in Israel—slave or free. [22]I will make your house like that of Jeroboam son of Nebat and that of Baasha son of Ahijah, because you have provoked me to anger and have caused Israel to sin.'

[23]"And also concerning Jezebel the LORD says: 'Dogs will devour Jezebel by the wall of[a] Jezreel.'

[24]"Dogs will eat those belonging to Ahab who die in the city, and the birds of the air will feed on those who die in the country."

[25](There was never a man like Ahab, who sold himself to do evil in the eyes of the LORD, urged on by Jezebel his wife. [26]He behaved in the vilest manner by going after idols, like the Amorites the LORD drove out before Israel.)

[27]When Ahab heard these words, he tore his clothes, put on sackcloth and fasted. He lay in sackcloth and went around meekly.

[28]Then the word of the LORD came to Elijah the Tishbite: [29]"Have you noticed how Ahab has humbled himself before me? Because he has humbled himself, I will not bring this disaster in his day, but I will bring it on his house in the days of his son."

Micaiah Prophesies Against Ahab

22 For three years there was no war between Aram and Israel. [2]But in the third year Jehoshaphat king of Judah went down to see the king of Israel. [3]The king of Israel had said to his officials, "Don't you know that Ramoth Gilead belongs to us and yet we are doing nothing to retake it from the king of Aram?"

[4]So he asked Jehoshaphat, "Will you go with me to fight against Ramoth Gilead?"

Jehoshaphat replied to the king of Israel, "I am as you are, my people as your people, my horses as your horses." [5]But Jehoshaphat also said to the king of Israel, "First seek the counsel of the LORD."

[6]So the king of Israel brought together the prophets—about four hundred men—and asked them, "Shall I go to war against Ramoth Gilead, or shall I refrain?"

"Go," they answered, "for the Lord will give it into the king's hand."

[7]But Jehoshaphat asked, "Is there not a prophet of the LORD here whom we can inquire of?"

[8]The king of Israel answered Jehoshaphat, "There is still one man through whom we can inquire of the LORD, but I hate him because he never prophesies anything good about me, but always bad. He is Micaiah son of Imlah."

"The king should not say that," Jehoshaphat replied.

[9]So the king of Israel called one of his officials and said, "Bring Micaiah son of Imlah at once."

[10]Dressed in their royal robes, the king of Israel and Jehoshaphat king of Judah were sitting on their thrones at the threshing floor by the entrance of the gate of Samaria, with all the prophets prophesying before them. [11]Now Zedekiah son of Kenaanah had made iron horns and he declared, "This is what the LORD says: 'With these you will gore the Arameans until they are destroyed.' "

[12]All the other prophets were prophesying the same thing. "Attack Ramoth Gilead and be victorious," they said, "for the LORD will give it into the king's hand."

[13]The messenger who had gone to summon Micaiah said to him, "Look, as one man the other prophets are predicting success for the king. Let your word agree with theirs, and speak favorably."

[14]But Micaiah said, "As surely as the LORD lives, I can tell him only what the LORD tells me."

[15]When he arrived, the king asked him, "Micaiah, shall we go to war against Ramoth Gilead, or shall I refrain?"

"Attack and be victorious," he answered, "for the LORD will give it into the king's hand."

[16]The king said to him, "How many times must I make you swear to tell me nothing but the truth in the name of the LORD?"

[17]Then Micaiah answered, "I saw all Israel scattered on the hills like sheep without a shepherd, and the LORD said, 'These people have no master. Let each one go home in peace.' "

[18]The king of Israel said to Jehoshaphat, "Didn't I tell you that he never prophesies anything good about me, but only bad?"

[19]Micaiah continued, "Therefore hear the word of the LORD: I saw the LORD sitting on his throne with all the host of heaven standing around him on his right and on his left. [20]And the LORD said, 'Who will entice Ahab into attacking Ramoth Gilead and going to his death there?'

"One suggested this, and another that. [21]Fi-

[a]*23* Most Hebrew manuscripts; a few Hebrew manuscripts, Vulgate and Syriac (see also 2 Kings 9:26) *the plot of ground at*

nally, a spirit came forward, stood before the
LORD and said, 'I will entice him.'
22" 'By what means?' the LORD asked.
" 'I will go out and be a lying spirit in the
mouths of all his prophets,' he said.
" 'You will succeed in enticing him,' said the
LORD. 'Go and do it.'
23"So now the LORD has put a lying spirit in
the mouths of all these prophets of yours. The
LORD has decreed disaster for you."
24Then Zedekiah son of Kenaanah went up
and slapped Micaiah in the face. "Which way
did the spirit from[a] the LORD go when he went
from me to speak to you?" he asked.
25Micaiah replied, "You will find out on the
day you go to hide in an inner room."
26The king of Israel then ordered, "Take Micaiah and send him back to Amon the ruler of
the city and to Joash the king's son 27and say,
'This is what the king says: Put this fellow in
prison and give him nothing but bread and water until I return safely.' "
28Micaiah declared, "If you ever return safely, the LORD has not spoken through me." Then
he added, "Mark my words, all you people!"

Ahab Killed at Ramoth Gilead

29So the king of Israel and Jehoshaphat king
of Judah went up to Ramoth Gilead. 30The king
of Israel said to Jehoshaphat, "I will enter the
battle in disguise, but you wear your royal
robes." So the king of Israel disguised himself
and went into battle.
31Now the king of Aram had ordered his
thirty-two chariot commanders, "Do not fight
with anyone, small or great, except the king of
Israel." 32When the chariot commanders saw Jehoshaphat, they thought, "Surely this is the
king of Israel." So they turned to attack him, but
when Jehoshaphat cried out, 33the chariot commanders saw that he was not the king of Israel
and stopped pursuing him.
34But someone drew his bow at random and
hit the king of Israel between the sections of his
armor. The king told his chariot driver, "Wheel
around and get me out of the fighting. I've been
wounded." 35All day long the battle raged, and
the king was propped up in his chariot facing
the Arameans. The blood from his wound ran
onto the floor of the chariot, and that evening
he died. 36As the sun was setting, a cry spread
through the army: "Every man to his town; everyone to his land!"
37So the king died and was brought to Samaria, and they buried him there. 38They washed
the chariot at a pool in Samaria (where the
prostitutes bathed),[b] and the dogs licked up
his blood, as the word of the LORD had declared.
39As for the other events of Ahab's reign, including all he did, the palace he built and inlaid
with ivory, and the cities he fortified, are they
not written in the book of the annals of the
kings of Israel? 40Ahab rested with his fathers.
And Ahaziah his son succeeded him as king.

Jehoshaphat King of Judah

41Jehoshaphat son of Asa became king of Judah in the fourth year of Ahab king of Israel.
42Jehoshaphat was thirty-five years old when
he became king, and he reigned in Jerusalem
twenty-five years. His mother's name was Azubah daughter of Shilhi. 43In everything he
walked in the ways of his father Asa and did not
stray from them; he did what was right in the
eyes of the LORD. The high places, however,
were not removed, and the people continued to
offer sacrifices and burn incense there. 44Je-
hoshaphat was also at peace with the king of
Israel.
45As for the other events of Jehoshaphat's
reign, the things he achieved and his military
exploits, are they not written in the book of the
annals of the kings of Judah? 46He rid the land
of the rest of the male shrine prostitutes who
remained there even after the reign of his father
Asa. 47There was then no king in Edom; a deputy ruled.
48Now Jehoshaphat built a fleet of trading
ships[c] to go to Ophir for gold, but they never
set sail—they were wrecked at Ezion Geber. 49At
that time Ahaziah son of Ahab said to Jehoshaphat, "Let my men sail with your men," but
Jehoshaphat refused.
50Then Jehoshaphat rested with his fathers
and was buried with them in the city of David
his father. And Jehoram his son succeeded him.

Ahaziah King of Israel

51Ahaziah son of Ahab became king of Israel
in Samaria in the seventeenth year of Jehoshaphat king of Judah, and he reigned over Israel
two years. 52He did evil in the eyes of the LORD,
because he walked in the ways of his father and
mother and in the ways of Jeroboam son of
Nebat, who caused Israel to sin. 53He served and
worshiped Baal and provoked the LORD, the
God of Israel, to anger, just as his father had
done.

[a]24 Or *Spirit of* [b]38 Or *Samaria and cleaned the weapons* [c]48 Hebrew *of ships of Tarshish*

22:30–40 Whatever God says will happen, will happen. Ahab disguised himself in battle so he wouldn't be killed, but a stray arrow shot him. Notice that the complete prophecy in 21:21–24 came true here, three years after Elijah spoke it. Justice is served by God in his time, not ours. People may seem to get away with sin for a while, but eventually their deeds will catch up with them.

22:41–43 Jehoshaphat was a good king who built his kingdom on the positive steps of his father, Asa. Successful parenting involves modeling godly standards of conduct for growing children. As children watch their godly parents progress spiritually, they will learn about God's power and the blessings that result from trust and obedience.

2 KINGS

The Big Picture

A. ISRAEL'S EXILE TO ASSYRIA: FROM SPIRITUAL BLINDNESS TO UTTER DEFEAT (1:1–17:41)

1. Confrontation by Elijah and Elisha (1:1–13:25)
2. Israel's Sin and Spiritual Blindness Lead to Defeat (14:1–17:41)

B. JUDAH'S EXILE TO BABYLON: REPEATED TRAGEDY FOR GOD'S PEOPLE (18:1–25:30)

1. Fathers and Sons: Choices for Spiritual Renewal or Oppression (18:1–23:30)
2. The Last Stages of Spiritual Blindness and Defeat (23:31–25:30)

The book of 2 Kings was originally part of a larger book that also included 1 Kings. This larger work recorded Israel's history from the end of David's reign to the demise of both its northern and southern kingdoms. The book of 2 Kings opens with the nation of Israel already divided into the northern and southern kingdoms of Israel and Judah. The book records a succession of kings, many of them ungodly, and the inevitable movement of both kingdoms toward destruction and exile—the northern kingdom to Assyria and the southern kingdom to Babylon.

The progression of events in 2 Kings could easily be likened to the deepening darkness from twilight to nightfall. God's people suffered from a progressive darkening of their spiritual nature—an unbelief that led to their spiritual blindness. Along the way, God sent prophets like Elijah, Elisha and Isaiah and kings like Hezekiah and Josiah who awakened the people to their sin and urged them to follow God's way. But eventually the influence of many godless kings brought destruction and captivity to both kingdoms.

The writer of Kings wanted to make sure that the exiled Israelites learned from the mistakes of their ancestors. Their forefathers had disobeyed God despite his repeated attempts to get their attention through his prophets and a few godly kings. By narrating past events, the author illustrated how disobedience ultimately brought about destruction.

The consequences of Israel's chronic sin were tragic and seemingly irreparable. The temple was destroyed; David's royal line no longer ruled in Jerusalem; the people were exiled from their homeland. Despite the gloomy ending of this book, however, the story of God's people continues with rebuilding and restoration. There is always hope for the future.

Spiritual Renewal Themes

THE POWER OF SPIRITUAL BLINDNESS

Few things are as frustrating as dealing with people who are spiritually blind. No matter how well we may argue our point—no matter how convincing our evidence—it is virtually impossible to penetrate their defenses. Of the thirty-nine kings who ruled Israel and Judah after the death of Solomon, only eight of them responded positively to the truth of God. The others, in

spite of all the evidence presented by the prophets, continued in their spiritual blindness and refused to admit the sin in their lives. As a result, the eight good kings spent most of their time counteracting the evil influence of their predecessors.

A MODEL OF INTERVENTION

As we reflect on God's patience with Israel, it is important that we don't mistake his patience for indifference. God confronted these evil kings through his miracles, his prophets and his Word (see 22:8–13). God was active, confronting the sins of Israel and Judah, seeking to lovingly intervene with the truth. We need to see that God still confronts his people with the truth today and calls them to follow his ways.

FACING A PAINFUL REALITY

Sometimes confrontation doesn't work. That was the case with both Israel and Judah. Their spiritual blindness persisted to the bitter end. Even when the northern kingdom was conquered and its people exiled, the people of the southern kingdom failed to change their sinful ways. This refusal to face reality can be dangerous, profoundly affecting people's lives. If we want to avoid the pain and destruction that will surely come as consequences of our sins, we would be wise to heed the confrontations of God and his messengers.

GOD'S CARE FOR US

The fact that God cares for his people is proven over and over in Israel's history and is emphasized in the book of Kings as God actively sought numerous times to stop Israel's slide toward destruction. He confronted wicked kings and punished their persistent sin. But they failed to respond with remorse and repentance to God's acts of discipline. God also gives us many chances to heed his messages and respond to his discipline. Sometimes we may be tempted to mistake God's patience for indifference, but we can be sure that God is never indifferent toward his people. He ultimately holds us accountable for our actions.

Essential Facts

PURPOSE:
To record the final years of the northern and southern kingdoms and to demonstrate that prolonged spiritual blindness and disobedience to God's plan are destructive.

AUTHOR:
Unknown, but possibly Jeremiah or another writer from the period of Babylonian exile (sixth century B.C.).

AUDIENCE:
The people of Israel in Babylonian exile.

DATE WRITTEN:
Sometime between 560 and 538 B.C.

SETTING:
The divided kingdoms of Israel and Judah, with concluding scenes in Babylonian exile.

KEY VERSE:
"But they would not listen and were as stiff-necked as their fathers, who did not trust in the LORD their God" (17:14).

KEY PEOPLE AND RELATIONSHIPS:
Elijah with Elisha; Hezekiah, Sennacherib, Isaiah, Manasseh, Josiah and Nebuchadnezzar.

The LORD's Judgment on Ahaziah

1 After Ahab's death, Moab rebelled against Israel. 2Now Ahaziah had fallen through the lattice of his upper room in Samaria and injured himself. So he sent messengers, saying to them, "Go and consult Baal-Zebub, the god of Ekron, to see if I will recover from this injury."

3But the angel of the LORD said to Elijah the Tishbite, "Go up and meet the messengers of the king of Samaria and ask them, 'Is it because there is no God in Israel that you are going off to consult Baal-Zebub, the god of Ekron?' 4Therefore this is what the LORD says: 'You will not leave the bed you are lying on. You will certainly die!' " So Elijah went.

5When the messengers returned to the king, he asked them, "Why have you come back?"

6"A man came to meet us," they replied. "And he said to us, 'Go back to the king who sent you and tell him, "This is what the LORD says: Is it because there is no God in Israel that you are sending men to consult Baal-Zebub, the god of Ekron? Therefore you will not leave the bed you are lying on. You will certainly die!" ' "

7The king asked them, "What kind of man was it who came to meet you and told you this?"

8They replied, "He was a man with a garment of hair and with a leather belt around his waist."

The king said, "That was Elijah the Tishbite."

9Then he sent to Elijah a captain with his company of fifty men. The captain went up to Elijah, who was sitting on the top of a hill, and said to him, "Man of God, the king says, 'Come down!' "

10Elijah answered the captain, "If I am a man of God, may fire come down from heaven and consume you and your fifty men!" Then fire fell from heaven and consumed the captain and his men.

11At this the king sent to Elijah another captain with his fifty men. The captain said to him, "Man of God, this is what the king says, 'Come down at once!' "

12"If I am a man of God," Elijah replied, "may fire come down from heaven and consume you and your fifty men!" Then the fire of God fell from heaven and consumed him and his fifty men.

13So the king sent a third captain with his fifty men. This third captain went up and fell on his knees before Elijah. "Man of God," he begged, "please have respect for my life and the lives of these fifty men, your servants! 14See, fire has fallen from heaven and consumed the first two captains and all their men. But now have respect for my life!"

15The angel of the LORD said to Elijah, "Go down with him; do not be afraid of him." So Elijah got up and went down with him to the king.

16He told the king, "This is what the LORD says: Is it because there is no God in Israel for you to consult that you have sent messengers to consult Baal-Zebub, the god of Ekron? Because you have done this, you will never leave the bed you are lying on. You will certainly die!" 17So he died, according to the word of the LORD that Elijah had spoken.

Because Ahaziah had no son, Joram[a] succeeded him as king in the second year of Jehoram son of Jehoshaphat king of Judah. 18As for all the other events of Ahaziah's reign, and what he did, are they not written in the book of the annals of the kings of Israel?

Elijah Taken Up to Heaven

2 When the LORD was about to take Elijah up to heaven in a whirlwind, Elijah and Elisha were on their way from Gilgal. 2Elijah said to Elisha, "Stay here; the LORD has sent me to Bethel."

But Elisha said, "As surely as the LORD lives and as you live, I will not leave you." So they went down to Bethel.

3The company of the prophets at Bethel came out to Elisha and asked, "Do you know that the LORD is going to take your master from you today?"

"Yes, I know," Elisha replied, "but do not speak of it."

4Then Elijah said to him, "Stay here, Elisha; the LORD has sent me to Jericho."

And he replied, "As surely as the LORD lives and as you live, I will not leave you." So they went to Jericho.

5The company of the prophets at Jericho went up to Elisha and asked him, "Do you know that the LORD is going to take your master from you today?"

[a]17 Hebrew *Jehoram,* a variant of *Joram*

1:2–5 Ahaziah sought guidance from the wrong spiritual source, and God made his error clear to him in no uncertain terms. Not all spiritual guidance is from God. There have been false prophets in every generation (the new age movement is one such group today) who are willing to share their guidance with those who know better but still seek spiritual renewal by means of "alternative resources." God is not pleased with this. He is the only valid source of help, and the Bible is our standard of truth.

1:5–18 Ahaziah sought to silence Elijah and persisted in trying to capture the prophet even after his first two military detachments had been destroyed by God. Ahaziah's resistance to the truth is amazing. As his spiritual blindness deepened, Ahaziah failed to see the devastation he brought on innocent lives. Often we also fail to notice the toll that our resistance to the truth takes on the people around us. Admitting our sins will help us and will also stop us from hurting the people close to us.

2:1–7 Mature believers can suffer from spiritual blindness too. It was difficult for Elisha to face the truth about Elijah's departure. Elijah had tried repeatedly to prepare him for this hard inevitability, but Elisha did not want to let go. Elisha did not want to deal with the loss that was looming on the horizon. Because we are vulnerable to spiritual blindness as well, we should be attentive to the insights of those who help us face the truth.

ELIJAH & ELISHA

Most of us know people whom we admire greatly. If we are fortunate, one or more of these people may be close enough to serve as a mentor for us in some way. Elisha had a relationship of this kind with Elijah. Elisha was the student; Elijah was the teacher. Both possessed keen hearts for God though their ministries were different.

Elijah's ministry was primarily a confrontational one—he had to rebuke and prophesy against King Ahab. Elijah prophesied a three-year drought; he destroyed the priests of Baal who were employed by Ahab; he prophesied Ahab's death after Ahab killed Naboth in order to own his vineyard. Elijah also served people—he miraculously provided food for a widow and later raised her son from the dead.

Elisha witnessed many of the events in Elijah's life and learned much about God's power from these events. Elisha learned that God would soon be taking Elijah to heaven, so he determined to stay with Elijah for as long as possible. Elisha was present when Elijah was taken to heaven in a whirlwind. Elisha became Elijah's rightful successor, receiving a double portion of Elijah's spirit.

Elisha's ministry was primarily a ministry of comfort, not confrontation. He purified poisoned water, provided drinking water for King Jehoram, provided oil for a widow, cured a poisonous stew, multiplied food to feed a hundred people, cured a leper, prophesied the birth of a son to a woman from Shunem and later raised that son from the dead.

Even though Elijah had dealt primarily with kings, Elisha did not get angry at God for directing his ministry to the common people. Elisha accepted his mission and followed God in all he did. We can learn from Elisha and accept our calling without envy or jealousy about the greatness or importance our mentors have achieved. All work is important to God. We need to do everything we can to bring honor to him, even in the insignificant tasks and places.

STRENGTHS AND ACCOMPLISHMENTS:

Both men were bold in serving God in the face of formidable enemies.

Elisha determined to secure God's blessing on his life and ministry.

WEAKNESSES AND MISTAKES:

Elijah let victory leave him isolated and vulnerable to despair.

Elijah became fearful when threatened by powerful enemies instead of turning to God.

LESSONS FROM THEIR LIVES:

We are to serve God with total commitment and without fear of the consequences.

God is able to defeat all our enemies.

We are often vulnerable to failure after our greatest victories.

KEY VERSE:

"Elijah said to Elisha, 'Tell me, what can I do for you before I am taken from you?' 'Let me inherit a double portion of your spirit,' Elisha replied" (2:9).

Elijah's and Elisha's stories are told in 1 Kings 17—19; 21; 2 Kings 1—10; 13; and 2 Chronicles 21. Elijah is mentioned in Malachi 4:5; Matthew 11:14; 17:1–5; 27:47–49; Mark 6:15; 8:28; 9; 15:35–36; Luke 1:17; 4:25–26; 9; John 1:21, 24–25; Romans 11:2–3; and James 5:17–18. Elisha is mentioned in Luke 4:27.

"Yes, I know," he replied, "but do not speak of it."

6Then Elijah said to him, "Stay here; the LORD has sent me to the Jordan."

And he replied, "As surely as the LORD lives and as you live, I will not leave you." So the two of them walked on.

7Fifty men of the company of the prophets went and stood at a distance, facing the place where Elijah and Elisha had stopped at the Jordan. 8Elijah took his cloak, rolled it up and struck the water with it. The water divided to the right and to the left, and the two of them crossed over on dry ground.

9When they had crossed, Elijah said to Elisha, "Tell me, what can I do for you before I am taken from you?"

"Let me inherit a double portion of your spirit," Elisha replied.

10"You have asked a difficult thing," Elijah said, "yet if you see me when I am taken from you, it will be yours—otherwise not."

11As they were walking along and talking together, suddenly a chariot of fire and horses of fire appeared and separated the two of them, and Elijah went up to heaven in a whirlwind. 12Elisha saw this and cried out, "My father! My father! The chariots and horsemen of Israel!" And Elisha saw him no more. Then he took hold of his own clothes and tore them apart.

13He picked up the cloak that had fallen from Elijah and went back and stood on the bank of the Jordan. 14Then he took the cloak that had fallen from him and struck the water with it. "Where now is the LORD, the God of Elijah?" he asked. When he struck the water, it divided to the right and to the left, and he crossed over.

15The company of the prophets from Jericho, who were watching, said, "The spirit of Elijah is resting on Elisha." And they went to meet him and bowed to the ground before him. 16"Look," they said, "we your servants have fifty able men. Let them go and look for your master. Perhaps the Spirit of the LORD has picked him up and set him down on some mountain or in some valley."

"No," Elisha replied, "do not send them."

17But they persisted until he was too ashamed to refuse. So he said, "Send them." And they sent fifty men, who searched for three days but did not find him. 18When they returned to Elisha, who was staying in Jericho, he said to them, "Didn't I tell you not to go?"

Healing of the Water

19The men of the city said to Elisha, "Look, our lord, this town is well situated, as you can see, but the water is bad and the land is unproductive."

20"Bring me a new bowl," he said, "and put salt in it." So they brought it to him.

21Then he went out to the spring and threw the salt into it, saying, "This is what the LORD says: 'I have healed this water. Never again will it cause death or make the land unproductive.' " 22And the water has remained wholesome to this day, according to the word Elisha had spoken.

Elisha Is Jeered

23From there Elisha went up to Bethel. As he was walking along the road, some youths came out of the town and jeered at him. "Go on up, you baldhead!" they said. "Go on up, you baldhead!" 24He turned around, looked at them and called down a curse on them in the name of the LORD. Then two bears came out of the woods and mauled forty-two of the youths. 25And he went on to Mount Carmel and from there returned to Samaria.

Moab Revolts

3 Joram[a] son of Ahab became king of Israel in Samaria in the eighteenth year of Jehoshaphat king of Judah, and he reigned twelve years. 2He did evil in the eyes of the LORD, but not as his father and mother had done. He got rid of the sacred stone of Baal that his father had made. 3Nevertheless he clung to the sins of Jeroboam son of Nebat, which he had caused Israel to commit; he did not turn away from them.

4Now Mesha king of Moab raised sheep, and he had to supply the king of Israel with a hundred thousand lambs and with the wool of a hundred thousand rams. 5But after Ahab died, the king of Moab rebelled against the king of Israel. 6So at that time King Joram set out from Samaria and mobilized all Israel. 7He also sent

[a]1 Hebrew *Jehoram,* a variant of *Joram;* also in verse 6

2:13–15 We all know that an ungodly hero can leave a distorted impact on us. But we should also realize that a godly mentor can make a significant impact for the better. In this passage, Elisha took over Elijah's ministry. Elisha was acknowledged as possessing the same spirit as Elijah. Elisha lived his life with the same faith and commitment as his mentor. We need to seek out godly examples who will teach us to obey God. By following a godly example we will discover the pathway toward spiritual maturity.

3:1–3 Joram tore down the idolatrous pillar, but that did not constitute his full surrender to God. Merely beginning the process of spiritual renewal is not enough by itself. Whatever motivated Joram to destroy the pillar was not heartfelt enough to bring about a complete break from idolatry. He had come to the point of spiritual renewal but had not surrendered fully to the true God by forsaking all others.

3:5–14 When we show the slightest inclination to seek God, God will respond in some way, perhaps directing us to someone who can encourage us in our spiritual growth and lead us closer to God. Joram's foray into the wilderness of Edom brought him and his thirsty troops to a point of desperate need. In their predicament, they consulted Elisha the prophet for insight. He challenged Joram's idolatry and urged the desperate king to be aware of the godly influence of King Jehoshaphat of Judah. We should not ignore the righteous people God has placed in our lives. They are there to encourage us and help us grow spiritually.

this message to Jehoshaphat king of Judah: "The king of Moab has rebelled against me. Will you go with me to fight against Moab?"

"I will go with you," he replied. "I am as you are, my people as your people, my horses as your horses."

8"By what route shall we attack?" he asked.

"Through the Desert of Edom," he answered.

9So the king of Israel set out with the king of Judah and the king of Edom. After a roundabout march of seven days, the army had no more water for themselves or for the animals with them.

10"What!" exclaimed the king of Israel. "Has the LORD called us three kings together only to hand us over to Moab?"

11But Jehoshaphat asked, "Is there no prophet of the LORD here, that we may inquire of the LORD through him?"

An officer of the king of Israel answered, "Elisha son of Shaphat is here. He used to pour water on the hands of Elijah.[a]"

12Jehoshaphat said, "The word of the LORD is with him." So the king of Israel and Jehoshaphat and the king of Edom went down to him.

13Elisha said to the king of Israel, "What do we have to do with each other? Go to the prophets of your father and the prophets of your mother."

"No," the king of Israel answered, "because it was the LORD who called us three kings together to hand us over to Moab."

14Elisha said, "As surely as the LORD Almighty lives, whom I serve, if I did not have respect for the presence of Jehoshaphat king of Judah, I would not look at you or even notice you. 15But now bring me a harpist."

While the harpist was playing, the hand of the LORD came upon Elisha 16and he said, "This is what the LORD says: Make this valley full of ditches. 17For this is what the LORD says: You will see neither wind nor rain, yet this valley will be filled with water, and you, your cattle and your other animals will drink. 18This is an easy thing in the eyes of the LORD; he will also hand Moab over to you. 19You will overthrow every fortified city and every major town. You will cut down every good tree, stop up all the springs, and ruin every good field with stones."

20The next morning, about the time for offering the sacrifice, there it was—water flowing from the direction of Edom! And the land was filled with water.

21Now all the Moabites had heard that the kings had come to fight against them; so every man, young and old, who could bear arms was called up and stationed on the border. 22When they got up early in the morning, the sun was shining on the water. To the Moabites across the way, the water looked red—like blood. 23"That's blood!" they said. "Those kings must have fought and slaughtered each other. Now to the plunder, Moab!"

24But when the Moabites came to the camp of Israel, the Israelites rose up and fought them until they fled. And the Israelites invaded the land and slaughtered the Moabites. 25They destroyed the towns, and each man threw a stone on every good field until it was covered. They stopped up all the springs and cut down every good tree. Only Kir Hareseth was left with its stones in place, but men armed with slings surrounded it and attacked it as well.

26When the king of Moab saw that the battle had gone against him, he took with him seven hundred swordsmen to break through to the king of Edom, but they failed. 27Then he took his firstborn son, who was to succeed him as king, and offered him as a sacrifice on the city wall. The fury against Israel was great; they withdrew and returned to their own land.

The Widow's Oil

4 The wife of a man from the company of the prophets cried out to Elisha, "Your servant my husband is dead, and you know that he revered the LORD. But now his creditor is coming to take my two boys as his slaves."

2Elisha replied to her, "How can I help you? Tell me, what do you have in your house?"

"Your servant has nothing there at all," she said, "except a little oil."

3Elisha said, "Go around and ask all your neighbors for empty jars. Don't ask for just a few. 4Then go inside and shut the door behind you and your sons. Pour oil into all the jars, and as each is filled, put it to one side."

5She left him and afterward shut the door behind her and her sons. They brought the jars to her and she kept pouring. 6When all the jars were full, she said to her son, "Bring me another one."

But he replied, "There is not a jar left." Then the oil stopped flowing.

7She went and told the man of God, and he said, "Go, sell the oil and pay your debts. You and your sons can live on what is left."

The Shunammite's Son Restored to Life

8One day Elisha went to Shunem. And a

[a] *11* That is, he was Elijah's personal servant.

3:16–20 God had a battle plan for Joram. Joram needed only to admit he desired help; God was there to ensure the victory. God always has a plan to rescue us; he provides the resources and guidance we need. We need to surrender to him and obediently follow his battle plan.

4:1–7 People willing to pursue God can count on the fact that God is the God of limitless resources who can provide incredibly for us when we are in need. As was true with the widow and her sons, God sometimes waits to act until the last minute in order to stretch our faith. Then, when he does provide for us, our faith in God's power is strengthened for the battles ahead.

4:8–37 In these verses, God used Elisha to perform two amazing miracles. First, Elisha promised that a woman unable to bear children would have a child. Then, after the child died, God used Elisha to bring him back to life. The

well-to-do woman was there, who urged him
to stay for a meal. So whenever he came by, he
stopped there to eat. 9She said to her husband,
"I know that this man who often comes our
way is a holy man of God. 10Let's make a small
room on the roof and put in it a bed and a table,
a chair and a lamp for him. Then he can stay
there whenever he comes to us."

11One day when Elisha came, he went up to
his room and lay down there. 12He said to his
servant Gehazi, "Call the Shunammite." So he
called her, and she stood before him. 13Elisha
said to him, "Tell her, 'You have gone to all this
trouble for us. Now what can be done for you?
Can we speak on your behalf to the king or the
commander of the army?' "

She replied, "I have a home among my own
people."

14"What can be done for her?" Elisha asked.

Gehazi said, "Well, she has no son and her
husband is old."

15Then Elisha said, "Call her." So he called
her, and she stood in the doorway. 16"About
this time next year," Elisha said, "you will hold
a son in your arms."

"No, my lord," she objected. "Don't mislead
your servant, O man of God!"

17But the woman became pregnant, and the
next year about that same time she gave birth to
a son, just as Elisha had told her.

18The child grew, and one day he went out to
his father, who was with the reapers. 19"My
head! My head!" he said to his father.

His father told a servant, "Carry him to his
mother." 20After the servant had lifted him up
and carried him to his mother, the boy sat on
her lap until noon, and then he died. 21She
went up and laid him on the bed of the man of
God, then shut the door and went out.

22She called her husband and said, "Please
send me one of the servants and a donkey so I
can go to the man of God quickly and return."

23"Why go to him today?" he asked. "It's not
the New Moon or the Sabbath."

"It's all right," she said.

24She saddled the donkey and said to her
servant, "Lead on; don't slow down for me unless I tell you." 25So she set out and came to the
man of God at Mount Carmel.

When he saw her in the distance, the man of
God said to his servant Gehazi, "Look! There's
the Shunammite! 26Run to meet her and ask
her, 'Are you all right? Is your husband all right?
Is your child all right?' "

"Everything is all right," she said.

27When she reached the man of God at the
mountain, she took hold of his feet. Gehazi
came over to push her away, but the man of
God said, "Leave her alone! She is in bitter
distress, but the LORD has hidden it from me
and has not told me why."

28"Did I ask you for a son, my lord?" she said.
"Didn't I tell you, 'Don't raise my hopes'?"

29Elisha said to Gehazi, "Tuck your cloak
into your belt, take my staff in your hand and
run. If you meet anyone, do not greet him, and
if anyone greets you, do not answer. Lay my
staff on the boy's face."

30But the child's mother said, "As surely as
the LORD lives and as you live, I will not leave
you." So he got up and followed her.

31Gehazi went on ahead and laid the staff on
the boy's face, but there was no sound or response. So Gehazi went back to meet Elisha and
told him, "The boy has not awakened."

32When Elisha reached the house, there was
the boy lying dead on his couch. 33He went in,
shut the door on the two of them and prayed to
the LORD. 34Then he got on the bed and lay
upon the boy, mouth to mouth, eyes to eyes,
hands to hands. As he stretched himself out
upon him, the boy's body grew warm. 35Elisha
turned away and walked back and forth in the
room and then got on the bed and stretched out
upon him once more. The boy sneezed seven
times and opened his eyes.

36Elisha summoned Gehazi and said, "Call
the Shunammite." And he did. When she came,
he said, "Take your son." 37She came in, fell at
his feet and bowed to the ground. Then she
took her son and went out.

Death in the Pot

38Elisha returned to Gilgal and there was a
famine in that region. While the company of
the prophets was meeting with him, he said to
his servant, "Put on the large pot and cook
some stew for these men."

39One of them went out into the fields to
gather herbs and found a wild vine. He gathered
some of its gourds and filled the fold of his
cloak. When he returned, he cut them up into
the pot of stew, though no one knew what they
were. 40The stew was poured out for the men,
but as they began to eat it, they cried out, "O
man of God, there is death in the pot!" And they
could not eat it.

41Elisha said, "Get some flour." He put it into
the pot and said, "Serve it to the people to eat."
And there was nothing harmful in the pot.

Feeding of a Hundred

42A man came from Baal Shalishah, bringing
the man of God twenty loaves of barley bread
baked from the first ripe grain, along with some
heads of new grain. "Give it to the people to
eat," Elisha said.

God who performed these impossible miracles is also able to provide the power we need to follow his plan. Notice that God often uses people like Elisha to bring about new or renewed life. We should be aware of this, accepting God's gifts through the people he has chosen to help us along the way. We must remember, too, that God may also want to use us to touch the lives of others in need.

43 "How can I set this before a hundred men?"
his servant asked.
But Elisha answered, "Give it to the people
to eat. For this is what the LORD says: 'They will
eat and have some left over.' " 44 Then he set it
before them, and they ate and had some left
over, according to the word of the LORD.

Naaman Healed of Leprosy

5 Now Naaman was commander of the army
of the king of Aram. He was a great man in
the sight of his master and highly regarded, because through him the LORD had given victory
to Aram. He was a valiant soldier, but he had
leprosy.[a]
2 Now bands from Aram had gone out and
had taken captive a young girl from Israel, and
she served Naaman's wife. 3 She said to her mistress, "If only my master would see the prophet
who is in Samaria! He would cure him of his
leprosy."
4 Naaman went to his master and told him
what the girl from Israel had said. 5 "By all
means, go," the king of Aram replied. "I will
send a letter to the king of Israel." So Naaman
left, taking with him ten talents[b] of silver, six
thousand shekels[c] of gold and ten sets of
clothing. 6 The letter that he took to the king of
Israel read: "With this letter I am sending my
servant Naaman to you so that you may cure
him of his leprosy."
7 As soon as the king of Israel read the letter,
he tore his robes and said, "Am I God? Can I
kill and bring back to life? Why does this fellow
send someone to me to be cured of his leprosy?
See how he is trying to pick a quarrel with me!"
8 When Elisha the man of God heard that the
king of Israel had torn his robes, he sent him
this message: "Why have you torn your robes?
Have the man come to me and he will know
that there is a prophet in Israel." 9 So Naaman

[a] 1 The Hebrew word was used for various diseases affecting the skin—not necessarily leprosy; also in verses 3, 6, 7, 11 and 27. [b] 5 That is, about 750 pounds (about 340 kilograms) [c] 5 That is, about 150 pounds (about 70 kilograms)

5:1–8 People who are hurting deeply enough will try almost anything to find relief. For Naaman, a Syrian general, looking for help from a prophet in Israel was a desperate long shot. Naaman was willing to sacrifice prestige and wealth to find healing for his terrible disease. In the end, Naaman was healed of his leprosy, but not because he offered a reward. The real issue was not how much his deliverance cost; it was more important that Naaman sought help from the only one who is really able to deliver us—the one true God.

5:9–15 Strong-willed people, especially leaders who are accustomed to getting their own way, often have a hard time humbling themselves. What Elisha asked Naaman to do was simple, but it was not dignified. Elisha didn't do things the way Naaman thought they should be done. Fortunately, Naaman was not so stubborn that he was unwilling to listen to the advice of his servants. By following Elisha's instructions, Naaman surrendered to God and received the healing God wanted to give him all along.

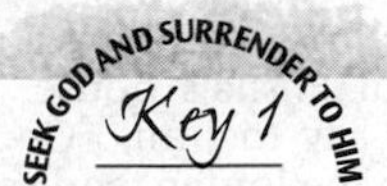

A Humble Beginning

2 Kings 5:1–15 How we handle situations that are beyond our control illustrates whether we are operating with pride and self-sufficiency or with humility and dependence on God. If we are willing to humbly depend on God and recognize our inability to handle things in our own strength, we will see the power of God bring great changes in our lives.

The experiences of a man named Naaman illustrate this truth. He was a powerful military and political figure, a man of wealth, position and power. He also had leprosy, an incurable disease that would slowly destroy his body. Lepers were outcasts from their families and society. Ultimately, they faced a slow, painful and disgraceful death.

Naaman heard that there was a prophet in Israel who could help him. He found the prophet who told him that in order to be healed Naaman needed to dip himself seven times in the Jordan River. Naaman went away outraged, having expected that his power and money would buy him an instant and easy cure. In the end, after listening to some wise advice from his servants, Naaman acknowledged that this situation was beyond his control. Humility was the key that allowed Naaman's surrender to God. Following God's instructions Naaman received the healing that only God could give him.

Humility should not be confused with humiliation. God does not allow us to face circumstances beyond our control in order to humiliate us. He intends these situations to be a means of drawing us to himself, leading us to healing and spiritual renewal.

Turn to Job 19.

went with his horses and chariots and stopped
at the door of Elisha's house. 10Elisha sent a
messenger to say to him, "Go, wash yourself
seven times in the Jordan, and your flesh will be
restored and you will be cleansed."
11But Naaman went away angry and said, "I
thought that he would surely come out to me
and stand and call on the name of the LORD his
God, wave his hand over the spot and cure me
of my leprosy. 12Are not Abana and Pharpar, the
rivers of Damascus, better than any of the waters of Israel? Couldn't I wash in them and be
cleansed?" So he turned and went off in a rage.
13Naaman's servants went to him and said,
"My father, if the prophet had told you to do
some great thing, would you not have done
it? How much more, then, when he tells you,
'Wash and be cleansed'!" 14So he went down
and dipped himself in the Jordan seven times,
as the man of God had told him, and his flesh
was restored and became clean like that of a
young boy.
15Then Naaman and all his attendants went
back to the man of God. He stood before him
and said, "Now I know that there is no God in
all the world except in Israel. Please accept now
a gift from your servant."
16The prophet answered, "As surely as the
LORD lives, whom I serve, I will not accept a
thing." And even though Naaman urged him, he
refused.
17"If you will not," said Naaman, "please let
me, your servant, be given as much earth as a
pair of mules can carry, for your servant will
never again make burnt offerings and sacrifices
to any other god but the LORD. 18But may the
LORD forgive your servant for this one thing:
When my master enters the temple of Rimmon
to bow down and he is leaning on my arm and
I bow there also—when I bow down in the temple of Rimmon, may the LORD forgive your servant for this."
19"Go in peace," Elisha said.
After Naaman had traveled some distance,
20Gehazi, the servant of Elisha the man of God,
said to himself, "My master was too easy on
Naaman, this Aramean, by not accepting from
him what he brought. As surely as the LORD
lives, I will run after him and get something
from him."
21So Gehazi hurried after Naaman. When
Naaman saw him running toward him, he got
down from the chariot to meet him. "Is everything all right?" he asked.
22"Everything is all right," Gehazi answered.
"My master sent me to say, 'Two young men
from the company of the prophets have just
come to me from the hill country of Ephraim.
Please give them a talent[a] of silver and two sets
of clothing.' "
23"By all means, take two talents," said Naaman. He urged Gehazi to accept them, and then
tied up the two talents of silver in two bags,
with two sets of clothing. He gave them to two
of his servants, and they carried them ahead of
Gehazi. 24When Gehazi came to the hill, he
took the things from the servants and put them
away in the house. He sent the men away and
they left. 25Then he went in and stood before
his master Elisha.
"Where have you been, Gehazi?" Elisha
asked.
"Your servant didn't go anywhere," Gehazi
answered.
26But Elisha said to him, "Was not my spirit
with you when the man got down from his
chariot to meet you? Is this the time to take
money, or to accept clothes, olive groves, vineyards, flocks, herds, or menservants and maidservants? 27Naaman's leprosy will cling to you
and to your descendants forever." Then Gehazi
went from Elisha's presence and he was leprous,
as white as snow.

An Axhead Floats

6 The company of the prophets said to Elisha, "Look, the place where we meet with
you is too small for us. 2Let us go to the Jordan,
where each of us can get a pole; and let us build
a place there for us to live."
And he said, "Go."
3Then one of them said, "Won't you please
come with your servants?"
"I will," Elisha replied. 4And he went with
them.
They went to the Jordan and began to cut
down trees. 5As one of them was cutting down
a tree, the iron axhead fell into the water. "Oh,
my lord," he cried out, "it was borrowed!"
6The man of God asked, "Where did it fall?"
When he showed him the place, Elisha cut a
stick and threw it there, and made the iron float.
7"Lift it out," he said. Then the man reached out
his hand and took it.

[a]22 That is, about 75 pounds (about 34 kilograms)

5:20–27 The shameful example of Gehazi and the resulting consequences he faced should serve as a warning to us. Those of us who are empowered by God and gifted to do his will need to be aware that there are those who would try to take advantage of us. Some people may try to get us to use the gifts God has given us for their own selfish gain. When we see others who are gifted by God, we must make sure that we never try to take advantage of their God-given gifts for our own selfish purposes. God is never pleased with this kind of exploitation.

6:1–7 By helping the prophet retrieve the borrowed ax head, God revealed his concern for the day-to-day needs of his people. He also revealed how interested he is in the maintenance of relationships. In ancient times, an ax head was extremely valuable. Losing such an item could have resulted in conflict between the borrower and lender. God's miracle helped the young prophets not only with their building project but also with the maintenance of their relationships.

Elisha Traps Blinded Arameans

8Now the king of Aram was at war with Israel. After conferring with his officers, he said, "I will set up my camp in such and such a place."

9The man of God sent word to the king of Israel: "Beware of passing that place, because the Arameans are going down there." 10So the king of Israel checked on the place indicated by the man of God. Time and again Elisha warned the king, so that he was on his guard in such places.

11This enraged the king of Aram. He summoned his officers and demanded of them, "Will you not tell me which of us is on the side of the king of Israel?"

12"None of us, my lord the king," said one of his officers, "but Elisha, the prophet who is in Israel, tells the king of Israel the very words you speak in your bedroom."

13"Go, find out where he is," the king ordered, "so I can send men and capture him." The report came back: "He is in Dothan." 14Then he sent horses and chariots and a strong force there. They went by night and surrounded the city.

15When the servant of the man of God got up and went out early the next morning, an army with horses and chariots had surrounded the city. "Oh, my lord, what shall we do?" the servant asked.

16"Don't be afraid," the prophet answered. "Those who are with us are more than those who are with them."

17And Elisha prayed, "O LORD, open his eyes so he may see." Then the LORD opened the servant's eyes, and he looked and saw the hills full of horses and chariots of fire all around Elisha.

18As the enemy came down toward him, Elisha prayed to the LORD, "Strike these people with blindness." So he struck them with blindness, as Elisha had asked.

19Elisha told them, "This is not the road and this is not the city. Follow me, and I will lead you to the man you are looking for." And he led them to Samaria.

20After they entered the city, Elisha said, "LORD, open the eyes of these men so they can see." Then the LORD opened their eyes and they looked, and there they were, inside Samaria.

21When the king of Israel saw them, he asked Elisha, "Shall I kill them, my father? Shall I kill them?"

22"Do not kill them," he answered. "Would you kill men you have captured with your own sword or bow? Set food and water before them so that they may eat and drink and then go back to their master." 23So he prepared a great feast for them, and after they had finished eating and drinking, he sent them away, and they returned to their master. So the bands from Aram stopped raiding Israel's territory.

Famine in Besieged Samaria

24Some time later, Ben-Hadad king of Aram mobilized his entire army and marched up and laid siege to Samaria. 25There was a great famine in the city; the siege lasted so long that a donkey's head sold for eighty shekels[a] of silver, and a quarter of a cab[b] of seed pods[c] for five shekels.[d]

26As the king of Israel was passing by on the wall, a woman cried to him, "Help me, my lord the king!"

27The king replied, "If the LORD does not help you, where can I get help for you? From the threshing floor? From the winepress?" 28Then he asked her, "What's the matter?"

She answered, "This woman said to me, 'Give up your son so we may eat him today, and tomorrow we'll eat my son.' 29So we cooked my son and ate him. The next day I said to her, 'Give up your son so we may eat him,' but she had hidden him."

30When the king heard the woman's words, he tore his robes. As he went along the wall, the people looked, and there, underneath, he had sackcloth on his body. 31He said, "May God deal with me, be it ever so severely, if the head of Elisha son of Shaphat remains on his shoulders today!"

32Now Elisha was sitting in his house, and the elders were sitting with him. The king sent a messenger ahead, but before he arrived, Elisha said to the elders, "Don't you see how this murderer is sending someone to cut off my head? Look, when the messenger comes, shut the door and hold it shut against him. Is not the sound of his master's footsteps behind him?"

33While he was still talking to them, the messenger came down to him. And ⌊the king⌋ said, "This disaster is from the LORD. Why should I wait for the LORD any longer?"

7 Elisha said, "Hear the word of the LORD. This is what the LORD says: About this time

[a]25 That is, about 2 pounds (about 1 kilogram)
[b]25 That is, probably about 1/2 pint (about 0.3 liter)
[c]25 Or *of dove's dung* [d]25 That is, about 2 ounces (about 55 grams)

6:14–20 The awesome Syrian army terrified Elisha's servant because he couldn't see the help available to him. He was totally unaware of the great army of heavenly soldiers on his side. At times, we may be tempted to give up; our spiritual enemies may seem too powerful to be overcome. But as we begin to see with the eyes of faith, we will discover the awesome power available to us. God's power is far greater than any powerful enemy we might face. If we trust God for help and ask him for the ability to see his truth in the spiritual realm, we will find his power more than sufficient for our needs.

7:1–20 Many who stand on the brink of a spiritual breakthrough never experience progress because, as much as they desire God's victory in their situation, they believe it will be impossible. The officer assisting the king tragically missed his opportunity for victory and freedom because of his unbelief. The obstacles we face are never too great for God to overcome. By looking to God for help and placing our lives in his hands, we can enjoy blessings beyond our wildest dreams!

tomorrow, a seah[a] of flour will sell for a shekel[b] and two seahs[c] of barley for a shekel at the gate of Samaria."

2The officer on whose arm the king was leaning said to the man of God, "Look, even if the LORD should open the floodgates of the heavens, could this happen?"

"You will see it with your own eyes," answered Elisha, "but you will not eat any of it!"

The Siege Lifted

3Now there were four men with leprosy[d] at the entrance of the city gate. They said to each other, "Why stay here until we die? 4If we say, 'We'll go into the city'—the famine is there, and we will die. And if we stay here, we will die. So let's go over to the camp of the Arameans and surrender. If they spare us, we live; if they kill us, then we die."

5At dusk they got up and went to the camp of the Arameans. When they reached the edge of the camp, not a man was there, 6for the Lord had caused the Arameans to hear the sound of chariots and horses and a great army, so that they said to one another, "Look, the king of Israel has hired the Hittite and Egyptian kings to attack us!" 7So they got up and fled in the dusk and abandoned their tents and their horses and donkeys. They left the camp as it was and ran for their lives.

8The men who had leprosy reached the edge of the camp and entered one of the tents. They ate and drank, and carried away silver, gold and clothes, and went off and hid them. They returned and entered another tent and took some things from it and hid them also.

9Then they said to each other, "We're not doing right. This is a day of good news and we are keeping it to ourselves. If we wait until daylight, punishment will overtake us. Let's go at once and report this to the royal palace."

10So they went and called out to the city gatekeepers and told them, "We went into the Aramean camp and not a man was there—not a sound of anyone—only tethered horses and donkeys, and the tents left just as they were." 11The gatekeepers shouted the news, and it was reported within the palace.

12The king got up in the night and said to his officers, "I will tell you what the Arameans have done to us. They know we are starving; so they have left the camp to hide in the countryside, thinking, 'They will surely come out, and then we will take them alive and get into the city.' "

13One of his officers answered, "Have some men take five of the horses that are left in the city. Their plight will be like that of all the Israelites left here—yes, they will only be like all these Israelites who are doomed. So let us send them to find out what happened."

14So they selected two chariots with their horses, and the king sent them after the Aramean army. He commanded the drivers, "Go and find out what has happened." 15They followed them as far as the Jordan, and they found the whole road strewn with the clothing and equipment the Arameans had thrown away in their headlong flight. So the messengers returned and reported to the king. 16Then the people went out and plundered the camp of the Arameans. So a seah of flour sold for a shekel, and two seahs of barley sold for a shekel, as the LORD had said.

17Now the king had put the officer on whose arm he leaned in charge of the gate, and the people trampled him in the gateway, and he died, just as the man of God had foretold when the king came down to his house. 18It happened as the man of God had said to the king: "About this time tomorrow, a seah of flour will sell for a shekel and two seahs of barley for a shekel at the gate of Samaria."

19The officer had said to the man of God, "Look, even if the LORD should open the floodgates of the heavens, could this happen?" The man of God had replied, "You will see it with your own eyes, but you will not eat any of it!" 20And that is exactly what happened to him, for the people trampled him in the gateway, and he died.

The Shunammite's Land Restored

8 Now Elisha had said to the woman whose son he had restored to life, "Go away with your family and stay for a while wherever you can, because the LORD has decreed a famine in the land that will last seven years." 2The woman proceeded to do as the man of God said. She and her family went away and stayed in the land of the Philistines seven years.

3At the end of the seven years she came back from the land of the Philistines and went to the king to beg for her house and land. 4The king was talking to Gehazi, the servant of the man of God, and had said, "Tell me about all the great things Elisha has done." 5Just as Gehazi was telling the king how Elisha had restored the dead to life, the woman whose son Elisha had brought back to life came to beg the king for her house and land.

Gehazi said, "This is the woman, my lord the king, and this is her son whom Elisha restored to life." 6The king asked the woman about it, and she told him.

Then he assigned an official to her case and said to him, "Give back everything that belonged to her, including all the income from

a1 That is, probably about 7 quarts (about 7.3 liters); also in verses 16 and 18 *b1* That is, about 2/5 ounce (about 11 grams); also in verses 16 and 18 *c1* That is, probably about 13 quarts (about 15 liters); also in verses 16 and 18 *d3* The Hebrew word is used for various diseases affecting the skin—not necessarily leprosy; also in verse 8.

her land from the day she left the country until now."

Hazael Murders Ben-Hadad

7Elisha went to Damascus, and Ben-Hadad king of Aram was ill. When the king was told, "The man of God has come all the way up here," 8he said to Hazael, "Take a gift with you and go to meet the man of God. Consult the LORD through him; ask him, 'Will I recover from this illness?' "

9Hazael went to meet Elisha, taking with him as a gift forty camel-loads of all the finest wares of Damascus. He went in and stood before him, and said, "Your son Ben-Hadad king of Aram has sent me to ask, 'Will I recover from this illness?' "

10Elisha answered, "Go and say to him, 'You will certainly recover'; but[a] the LORD has revealed to me that he will in fact die." 11He stared at him with a fixed gaze until Hazael felt ashamed. Then the man of God began to weep.

12"Why is my lord weeping?" asked Hazael.

"Because I know the harm you will do to the Israelites," he answered. "You will set fire to their fortified places, kill their young men with the sword, dash their little children to the ground, and rip open their pregnant women."

13Hazael said, "How could your servant, a mere dog, accomplish such a feat?"

"The LORD has shown me that you will become king of Aram," answered Elisha.

14Then Hazael left Elisha and returned to his master. When Ben-Hadad asked, "What did Elisha say to you?" Hazael replied, "He told me that you would certainly recover." 15But the next day he took a thick cloth, soaked it in water and spread it over the king's face, so that he died. Then Hazael succeeded him as king.

Jehoram King of Judah

16In the fifth year of Joram son of Ahab king of Israel, when Jehoshaphat was king of Judah, Jehoram son of Jehoshaphat began his reign as king of Judah. 17He was thirty-two years old when he became king, and he reigned in Jerusalem eight years. 18He walked in the ways of the kings of Israel, as the house of Ahab had done, for he married a daughter of Ahab. He did evil in the eyes of the LORD. 19Nevertheless, for the sake of his servant David, the LORD was not willing to destroy Judah. He had promised to maintain a lamp for David and his descendants forever.

20In the time of Jehoram, Edom rebelled against Judah and set up its own king. 21So Jehoram[b] went to Zair with all his chariots. The Edomites surrounded him and his chariot commanders, but he rose up and broke through by night; his army, however, fled back home. 22To this day Edom has been in rebellion against Judah. Libnah revolted at the same time.

23As for the other events of Jehoram's reign, and all he did, are they not written in the book of the annals of the kings of Judah? 24Jehoram rested with his fathers and was buried with them in the City of David. And Ahaziah his son succeeded him as king.

Ahaziah King of Judah

25In the twelfth year of Joram son of Ahab king of Israel, Ahaziah son of Jehoram king of Judah began to reign. 26Ahaziah was twenty-two years old when he became king, and he reigned in Jerusalem one year. His mother's name was Athaliah, a granddaughter of Omri king of Israel. 27He walked in the ways of the house of Ahab and did evil in the eyes of the LORD, as the house of Ahab had done, for he was related by marriage to Ahab's family.

28Ahaziah went with Joram son of Ahab to war against Hazael king of Aram at Ramoth Gilead. The Arameans wounded Joram; 29so King Joram returned to Jezreel to recover from the wounds the Arameans had inflicted on him at Ramoth[c] in his battle with Hazael king of Aram.

Then Ahaziah son of Jehoram king of Judah went down to Jezreel to see Joram son of Ahab, because he had been wounded.

Jehu Anointed King of Israel

9 The prophet Elisha summoned a man from the company of the prophets and said to him, "Tuck your cloak into your belt, take this flask of oil with you and go to Ramoth Gilead. 2When you get there, look for Jehu son of Jehoshaphat, the son of Nimshi. Go to him, get

[a] *10* The Hebrew may also be read *Go and say, 'You will certainly not recover,' for.* [b] *21* Hebrew *Joram,* a variant of *Jehoram;* also in verses 23 and 24 [c] *29* Hebrew *Ramah,* a variant of *Ramoth*

8:7–15 Spiritual renewal in the fullest sense cannot proceed when people refuse to handle things honestly. Elisha knew that King Ben-Hadad could have recovered if he had been allowed to do so. However, Hazael would not let this happen because of his own desire to dominate and control. Likewise, some of us are hindered from spiritual growth because we allow ungodly people to dominate our lives. We need to surround ourselves with people who will support our spiritual growth.

8:16–22 During King Jehoram's relatively brief rule over Judah, we see the actions and fruits of his sinful leadership. Despite God's great patience with him, Jehoram continued to follow in the evil ways of his father-in-law Ahab (8:18–19). When Jehoram found himself in dire straits, his army abandoned him. He was left alone to cope with his loss of Edom. If we resist God and oppress others, we can expect to be deserted by the people closest to us. We would be wise to learn from the sad consequences that resulted from Jehoram's wicked behavior.

9:1—10:36 The judgment that befell King Ahab's family should remind us that God punishes sin (see 1 Kings 21:19–29). No one will ever get away with it forever. God delays his judgment to give people more time to repent (see 2 Peter 3:9), but his patience will run out. After giving sinners plenty of opportunities to repent, God always acts decisively to punish those whose sinful behavior has hurt others.

him away from his companions and take him
into an inner room. 3Then take the flask and
pour the oil on his head and declare, 'This is
what the LORD says: I anoint you king over Israel.' Then open the door and run; don't delay!"
4So the young man, the prophet, went to
Ramoth Gilead. 5When he arrived, he found the
army officers sitting together. "I have a message
for you, commander," he said.

"For which of us?" asked Jehu.

"For you, commander," he replied.

6Jehu got up and went into the house. Then
the prophet poured the oil on Jehu's head and
declared, "This is what the LORD, the God of
Israel, says: 'I anoint you king over the LORD's
people Israel. 7You are to destroy the house of
Ahab your master, and I will avenge the blood
of my servants the prophets and the blood of all
the LORD's servants shed by Jezebel. 8The whole
house of Ahab will perish. I will cut off from
Ahab every last male in Israel—slave or free. 9I
will make the house of Ahab like the house of
Jeroboam son of Nebat and like the house of
Baasha son of Ahijah. 10As for Jezebel, dogs will
devour her on the plot of ground at Jezreel, and
no one will bury her.' " Then he opened the door
and ran.

11When Jehu went out to his fellow officers,
one of them asked him, "Is everything all right?
Why did this madman come to you?"

"You know the man and the sort of things he
says," Jehu replied.

12"That's not true!" they said. "Tell us."

Jehu said, "Here is what he told me: 'This is
what the LORD says: I anoint you king over Israel.' "

13They hurried and took their cloaks and
spread them under him on the bare steps. Then
they blew the trumpet and shouted, "Jehu is
king!"

Jehu Kills Joram and Ahaziah

14So Jehu son of Jehoshaphat, the son of
Nimshi, conspired against Joram. (Now Joram
and all Israel had been defending Ramoth Gilead against Hazael king of Aram, 15but King Joram[a] had returned to Jezreel to recover from
the wounds the Arameans had inflicted on him
in the battle with Hazael king of Aram.) Jehu
said, "If this is the way you feel, don't let anyone slip out of the city to go and tell the news
in Jezreel." 16Then he got into his chariot and
rode to Jezreel, because Joram was resting there
and Ahaziah king of Judah had gone down to
see him.

17When the lookout standing on the tower in
Jezreel saw Jehu's troops approaching, he called
out, "I see some troops coming."

"Get a horseman," Joram ordered. "Send him
to meet them and ask, 'Do you come in peace?' "

18The horseman rode off to meet Jehu and
said, "This is what the king says: 'Do you come
in peace?' "

"What do you have to do with peace?" Jehu
replied. "Fall in behind me."

The lookout reported, "The messenger has
reached them, but he isn't coming back."

19So the king sent out a second horseman.
When he came to them he said, "This is what
the king says: 'Do you come in peace?' "

Jehu replied, "What do you have to do with
peace? Fall in behind me."

20The lookout reported, "He has reached
them, but he isn't coming back either. The driving is like that of Jehu son of Nimshi—he drives
like a madman."

21"Hitch up my chariot," Joram ordered. And
when it was hitched up, Joram king of Israel
and Ahaziah king of Judah rode out, each in his
own chariot, to meet Jehu. They met him at the
plot of ground that had belonged to Naboth the
Jezreelite. 22When Joram saw Jehu he asked,
"Have you come in peace, Jehu?"

"How can there be peace," Jehu replied, "as
long as all the idolatry and witchcraft of your
mother Jezebel abound?"

23Joram turned about and fled, calling out to
Ahaziah, "Treachery, Ahaziah!"

24Then Jehu drew his bow and shot Joram
between the shoulders. The arrow pierced his
heart and he slumped down in his chariot.
25Jehu said to Bidkar, his chariot officer, "Pick
him up and throw him on the field that belonged to Naboth the Jezreelite. Remember
how you and I were riding together in chariots
behind Ahab his father when the LORD made
this prophecy about him: 26'Yesterday I saw the
blood of Naboth and the blood of his sons,
declares the LORD, and I will surely make you
pay for it on this plot of ground, declares the
LORD.'[b] Now then, pick him up and throw him
on that plot, in accordance with the word of the
LORD."

27When Ahaziah king of Judah saw what had
happened, he fled up the road to Beth Hag-
gan.[c] Jehu chased him, shouting, "Kill him
too!" They wounded him in his chariot on the
way up to Gur near Ibleam, but he escaped to
Megiddo and died there. 28His servants took
him by chariot to Jerusalem and buried him
with his fathers in his tomb in the City of David. 29(In the eleventh year of Joram son of
Ahab, Ahaziah had become king of Judah.)

Jezebel Killed

30Then Jehu went to Jezreel. When Jezebel
heard about it, she painted her eyes, arranged
her hair and looked out of a window. 31As Jehu
entered the gate, she asked, "Have you come in
peace, Zimri, you murderer of your master?"[d]

32He looked up at the window and called
out, "Who is on my side? Who?" Two or three
eunuchs looked down at him. 33"Throw her

[a] *15* Hebrew *Jehoram,* a variant of *Joram;* also in verses 17 and 21-24 [b] *26* See 1 Kings 21:19. [c] *27* Or *fled by way of the garden house* [d] *31* Or *"Did Zimri have peace, who murdered his master?"*

down!" Jehu said. So they threw her down, and
some of her blood spattered the wall and the
horses as they trampled her underfoot.
34Jehu went in and ate and drank. "Take care
of that cursed woman," he said, "and bury her,
for she was a king's daughter." 35But when they
went out to bury her, they found nothing except
her skull, her feet and her hands. 36They went
back and told Jehu, who said, "This is the word
of the LORD that he spoke through his servant
Elijah the Tishbite: On the plot of ground at
Jezreel dogs will devour Jezebel's flesh.[a] 37Jeze-
bel's body will be like refuse on the ground in
the plot at Jezreel, so that no one will be able
to say, 'This is Jezebel.' "

Ahab's Family Killed

10 Now there were in Samaria seventy
sons of the house of Ahab. So Jehu
wrote letters and sent them to Samaria: to the
officials of Jezreel,[b] to the elders and to the
guardians of Ahab's children. He said, 2"As
soon as this letter reaches you, since your master's sons are with you and you have chariots
and horses, a fortified city and weapons,
3choose the best and most worthy of your master's sons and set him on his father's throne.
Then fight for your master's house."
4But they were terrified and said, "If two
kings could not resist him, how can we?"
5So the palace administrator, the city governor, the elders and the guardians sent this message to Jehu: "We are your servants and we will
do anything you say. We will not appoint anyone as king; you do whatever you think best."
6Then Jehu wrote them a second letter, saying, "If you are on my side and will obey me,
take the heads of your master's sons and come
to me in Jezreel by this time tomorrow."
Now the royal princes, seventy of them, were
with the leading men of the city, who were rear-
ing them. 7When the letter arrived, these men
took the princes and slaughtered all seventy of
them. They put their heads in baskets and sent
them to Jehu in Jezreel. 8When the messenger
arrived, he told Jehu, "They have brought the
heads of the princes."
Then Jehu ordered, "Put them in two piles at
the entrance of the city gate until morning."
9The next morning Jehu went out. He stood
before all the people and said, "You are innocent. It was I who conspired against my master
and killed him, but who killed all these?
10Know then, that not a word the LORD has
spoken against the house of Ahab will fail. The
LORD has done what he promised through his
servant Elijah." 11So Jehu killed everyone in Jezreel who remained of the house of Ahab, as well
as all his chief men, his close friends and his
priests, leaving him no survivor.
12Jehu then set out and went toward Samaria.
At Beth Eked of the Shepherds, 13he met some
relatives of Ahaziah king of Judah and asked,
"Who are you?"
They said, "We are relatives of Ahaziah, and
we have come down to greet the families of the
king and of the queen mother."
14"Take them alive!" he ordered. So they took
them alive and slaughtered them by the well of
Beth Eked—forty-two men. He left no survivor.
15After he left there, he came upon Jehonadab son of Recab, who was on his way to meet
him. Jehu greeted him and said, "Are you in
accord with me, as I am with you?"
"I am," Jehonadab answered.
"If so," said Jehu, "give me your hand." So he
did, and Jehu helped him up into the chariot.
16Jehu said, "Come with me and see my zeal for
the LORD." Then he had him ride along in his
chariot.
17When Jehu came to Samaria, he killed all
who were left there of Ahab's family; he destroyed them, according to the word of the
LORD spoken to Elijah.

Ministers of Baal Killed

18Then Jehu brought all the people together
and said to them, "Ahab served Baal a little;
Jehu will serve him much. 19Now summon all
the prophets of Baal, all his ministers and all his
priests. See that no one is missing, because I am
going to hold a great sacrifice for Baal. Anyone
who fails to come will no longer live." But Jehu
was acting deceptively in order to destroy the
ministers of Baal.
20Jehu said, "Call an assembly in honor of
Baal." So they proclaimed it. 21Then he sent
word throughout Israel, and all the ministers of
Baal came; not one stayed away. They crowded
into the temple of Baal until it was full from
one end to the other. 22And Jehu said to the
keeper of the wardrobe, "Bring robes for all the

[a]36 See 1 Kings 21:23. [b]1 Hebrew; some Septuagint manuscripts and Vulgate *of the city*

10:1–11 As gory as this event was, it appears to have been motivated by a commitment to God's will. Elijah prophesied earlier about the destruction of Ahab's family (10:9–10; see 1 Kings 21:19–29). Although later events show that Jehu was not altogether pure in his motives, he seems to have been acting responsibly and with accountability toward both God and his people (10:9–10). He overstepped God's boundaries in his killing spree, however (see Hosea 1:4–5). Sometimes our own zeal can sweep us up in the emotion of the situation and cause us to go beyond what is necessary. Even our zeal to follow God's plan should not cause us to overstep what God has called us to do. We are accountable to him.

10:17–29 In this crowning victory over Ahab's legacy of Baal worship, we see two troubling defects in Jehu's personality and actions. First, Jehu was not honest about why he wanted the Baal worshipers to gather; he manipulated them with a lie (10:18–25). Jehu also rid only the northern kingdom of Baal worship and not all the false worship (10:26–29). Spiritual renewal and growth can proceed only with honesty and wholehearted commitment to God. Telling only part of the truth or changing only part of our lives leads only to partial spiritual growth.

ministers of Baal." So he brought out robes for them.

23Then Jehu and Jehonadab son of Recab went into the temple of Baal. Jehu said to the ministers of Baal, "Look around and see that no servants of the LORD are here with you—only ministers of Baal." 24So they went in to make sacrifices and burnt offerings. Now Jehu had posted eighty men outside with this warning: "If one of you lets any of the men I am placing in your hands escape, it will be your life for his life."

25As soon as Jehu had finished making the burnt offering, he ordered the guards and officers: "Go in and kill them; let no one escape." So they cut them down with the sword. The guards and officers threw the bodies out and then entered the inner shrine of the temple of Baal. 26They brought the sacred stone out of the temple of Baal and burned it. 27They demolished the sacred stone of Baal and tore down the temple of Baal, and people have used it for a latrine to this day.

28So Jehu destroyed Baal worship in Israel. 29However, he did not turn away from the sins of Jeroboam son of Nebat, which he had caused Israel to commit—the worship of the golden calves at Bethel and Dan.

30The LORD said to Jehu, "Because you have done well in accomplishing what is right in my eyes and have done to the house of Ahab all I had in mind to do, your descendants will sit on the throne of Israel to the fourth generation." 31Yet Jehu was not careful to keep the law of the LORD, the God of Israel, with all his heart. He did not turn away from the sins of Jeroboam, which he had caused Israel to commit.

32In those days the LORD began to reduce the size of Israel. Hazael overpowered the Israelites throughout their territory 33east of the Jordan in all the land of Gilead (the region of Gad, Reuben and Manasseh), from Aroer by the Arnon Gorge through Gilead to Bashan.

34As for the other events of Jehu's reign, all he did, and all his achievements, are they not written in the book of the annals of the kings of Israel?

35Jehu rested with his fathers and was buried in Samaria. And Jehoahaz his son succeeded him as king. 36The time that Jehu reigned over Israel in Samaria was twenty-eight years.

Athaliah and Joash

11 When Athaliah the mother of Ahaziah saw that her son was dead, she proceeded to destroy the whole royal family. 2But Jehosheba, the daughter of King Jehoram[a] and sister of Ahaziah, took Joash son of Ahaziah and stole him away from among the royal princes, who were about to be murdered. She put him and his nurse in a bedroom to hide him from Athaliah; so he was not killed. 3He remained hidden with his nurse at the temple of the LORD for six years while Athaliah ruled the land.

4In the seventh year Jehoiada sent for the commanders of units of a hundred, the Carites and the guards and had them brought to him at the temple of the LORD. He made a covenant with them and put them under oath at the temple of the LORD. Then he showed them the king's son. 5He commanded them, saying, "This is what you are to do: You who are in the three companies that are going on duty on the Sabbath—a third of you guarding the royal palace, 6a third at the Sur Gate, and a third at the gate behind the guard, who take turns guarding the temple— 7and you who are in the other two companies that normally go off Sabbath duty are all to guard the temple for the king. 8Station yourselves around the king, each man with his weapon in his hand. Anyone who approaches your ranks[b] must be put to death. Stay close to the king wherever he goes."

9The commanders of units of a hundred did just as Jehoiada the priest ordered. Each one took his men—those who were going on duty on the Sabbath and those who were going off duty—and came to Jehoiada the priest. 10Then he gave the commanders the spears and shields that had belonged to King David and that were in the temple of the LORD. 11The guards, each with his weapon in his hand, stationed themselves around the king—near the altar and the

[a]2 Hebrew *Joram,* a variant of *Jehoram* [b]8 Or *approaches the precincts*

10:30–33 It is entirely possible to please God in one part of our life and to displease him greatly in another. Jehu honored God by destroying Ahab's family, and he was blessed for it. However, his divided spiritual allegiance prevented the full restoration of the northern kingdom (10:31). Because there was no clean break from the sinful worship patterns established long before by King Jeroboam, Israel moved closer to judgment (10:31–33). We, too, need to turn our entire lives over to God's control. The areas we refuse to commit to the Lord will only lead to our future downfall.

11:1–3 Spiritual renewal can be difficult, even terrifying, if we live with someone who is evil. Such a person may attempt to do whatever it takes to intimidate us and undermine our spiritual growth. The flaw in Athaliah's reign was her failure to believe God's promises to David and his descendants (see 2 Samuel 7:12–16). The survival of young Joash was not only God's will; it was also a manifestation of God's ongoing care of his chosen people (see chapter 12). We must trust in God's care for us, even when we live in close proximity to someone who is evil.

11:4–21 Jehoiada's faith was the catalyst for Judah's move toward God. The process of anointing Joash and proclaiming him the rightful ruler was undergirded by Jehoiada's courage. He desired to restore Judah to a right relationship with God. Under Jehoiada's leadership, the people and king made a commitment to worship God, follow his commands and destroy all the altars to false gods. All the people were responsible for the nation's restoration. Everyone was held accountable. Courage to change our situation and personal accountability to others are necessary parts of preserving our spiritual gains.

temple, from the south side to the north side of the temple.

12Jehoiada brought out the king's son and put the crown on him; he presented him with a copy of the covenant and proclaimed him king. They anointed him, and the people clapped their hands and shouted, "Long live the king!"

13When Athaliah heard the noise made by the guards and the people, she went to the people at the temple of the LORD. 14She looked and there was the king, standing by the pillar, as the custom was. The officers and the trumpeters were beside the king, and all the people of the land were rejoicing and blowing trumpets. Then Athaliah tore her robes and called out, "Treason! Treason!"

15Jehoiada the priest ordered the commanders of units of a hundred, who were in charge of the troops: "Bring her out between the ranks[a] and put to the sword anyone who follows her." For the priest had said, "She must not be put to death in the temple of the LORD." 16So they seized her as she reached the place where the horses enter the palace grounds, and there she was put to death.

17Jehoiada then made a covenant between the LORD and the king and people that they would be the LORD's people. He also made a covenant between the king and the people. 18All the people of the land went to the temple of Baal and tore it down. They smashed the altars and idols to pieces and killed Mattan the priest of Baal in front of the altars.

Then Jehoiada the priest posted guards at the temple of the LORD. 19He took with him the commanders of hundreds, the Carites, the guards and all the people of the land, and together they brought the king down from the temple of the LORD and went into the palace, entering by way of the gate of the guards. The king then took his place on the royal throne, 20and all the people of the land rejoiced. And the city was quiet, because Athaliah had been slain with the sword at the palace.

21Joash[b] was seven years old when he began to reign.

Joash Repairs the Temple

12 In the seventh year of Jehu, Joash[c] became king, and he reigned in Jerusalem forty years. His mother's name was Zibiah; she was from Beersheba. 2Joash did what was right in the eyes of the LORD all the years Jehoiada the priest instructed him. 3The high places, however, were not removed; the people continued to offer sacrifices and burn incense there.

4Joash said to the priests, "Collect all the money that is brought as sacred offerings to the temple of the LORD—the money collected in the census, the money received from personal vows and the money brought voluntarily to the temple. 5Let every priest receive the money from one of the treasurers, and let it be used to repair whatever damage is found in the temple."

6But by the twenty-third year of King Joash the priests still had not repaired the temple. 7Therefore King Joash summoned Jehoiada the priest and the other priests and asked them, "Why aren't you repairing the damage done to the temple? Take no more money from your treasurers, but hand it over for repairing the temple." 8The priests agreed that they would not collect any more money from the people and that they would not repair the temple themselves.

9Jehoiada the priest took a chest and bored a hole in its lid. He placed it beside the altar, on the right side as one enters the temple of the LORD. The priests who guarded the entrance put into the chest all the money that was brought to the temple of the LORD. 10Whenever they saw that there was a large amount of money in the chest, the royal secretary and the high priest came, counted the money that had been brought into the temple of the LORD and put it into bags. 11When the amount had been determined, they gave the money to the men appointed to supervise the work on the temple. With it they paid those who worked on the temple of the LORD—the carpenters and builders, 12the masons and stonecutters. They purchased timber and dressed stone for the repair of the temple of the LORD, and met all the other expenses of restoring the temple.

13The money brought into the temple was not spent for making silver basins, wick trimmers, sprinkling bowls, trumpets or any other articles of gold or silver for the temple of the LORD; 14it was paid to the workmen, who used it to repair the temple. 15They did not require an accounting from those to whom they gave the money to pay the workers, because they acted with complete honesty. 16The money from the guilt offerings and sin offerings was not brought

[a]15 Or *out from the precincts* [b]21 Hebrew *Jehoash,* a variant of *Joash* [c]1 Hebrew *Jehoash,* a variant of *Joash;* also in verses 2, 4, 6, 7 and 18

12:1–3 The forty-year reign of King Joash of Judah was a time of personal and national restoration. Yet, though Joash was a model of faith, he never completely destroyed the shrines on the hills and other places of idol worship. Spiritual renewal and transformation is a lifelong process; we must not stop when we start to feel better. We need to ask God to give us the strength and patience to continue in our journey, and then persevere as God fulfills his will for our lives.

12:4–16 Repairing the temple was an important part of Judah's spiritual restoration. Yet raising the money to rebuild proved difficult. The priests and people were not willing to make the sacrifices necessary to get the job done. So Joash set up a system in which the priests were accountable for the money they received (see 12:7). With this system of accountability, the people of Judah were able to accomplish the renovation process. This should remind us that accountability and planning are important for successful renewal. Without them, we will probably take the path of least resistance and make little progress.

into the temple of the LORD; it belonged to the priests.

17About this time Hazael king of Aram went up and attacked Gath and captured it. Then he turned to attack Jerusalem. 18But Joash king of Judah took all the sacred objects dedicated by his fathers—Jehoshaphat, Jehoram and Ahaziah, the kings of Judah—and the gifts he himself had dedicated and all the gold found in the treasuries of the temple of the LORD and of the royal palace, and he sent them to Hazael king of Aram, who then withdrew from Jerusalem.

19As for the other events of the reign of Joash, and all he did, are they not written in the book of the annals of the kings of Judah? 20His officials conspired against him and assassinated him at Beth Millo, on the road down to Silla. 21The officials who murdered him were Jozabad son of Shimeath and Jehozabad son of Shomer. He died and was buried with his fathers in the City of David. And Amaziah his son succeeded him as king.

Jehoahaz King of Israel

13 In the twenty-third year of Joash son of Ahaziah king of Judah, Jehoahaz son of Jehu became king of Israel in Samaria, and he reigned seventeen years. 2He did evil in the eyes of the LORD by following the sins of Jeroboam son of Nebat, which he had caused Israel to commit, and he did not turn away from them. 3So the LORD's anger burned against Israel, and for a long time he kept them under the power of Hazael king of Aram and Ben-Hadad his son.

4Then Jehoahaz sought the LORD's favor, and the LORD listened to him, for he saw how severely the king of Aram was oppressing Israel. 5The LORD provided a deliverer for Israel, and they escaped from the power of Aram. So the Israelites lived in their own homes as they had before. 6But they did not turn away from the sins of the house of Jeroboam, which he had caused Israel to commit; they continued in them. Also, the Asherah pole[a] remained standing in Samaria.

7Nothing had been left of the army of Jehoahaz except fifty horsemen, ten chariots and ten thousand foot soldiers, for the king of Aram had destroyed the rest and made them like the dust at threshing time.

8As for the other events of the reign of Jehoahaz, all he did and his achievements, are they not written in the book of the annals of the kings of Israel? 9Jehoahaz rested with his fathers and was buried in Samaria. And Jehoash[b] his son succeeded him as king.

Jehoash King of Israel

10In the thirty-seventh year of Joash king of Judah, Jehoash son of Jehoahaz became king of Israel in Samaria, and he reigned sixteen years. 11He did evil in the eyes of the LORD and did not turn away from any of the sins of Jeroboam son of Nebat, which he had caused Israel to commit; he continued in them.

12As for the other events of the reign of Jehoash, all he did and his achievements, including his war against Amaziah king of Judah, are they not written in the book of the annals of the kings of Israel? 13Jehoash rested with his fathers, and Jeroboam succeeded him on the throne. Jehoash was buried in Samaria with the kings of Israel.

14Now Elisha was suffering from the illness from which he died. Jehoash king of Israel went down to see him and wept over him. "My father! My father!" he cried. "The chariots and horsemen of Israel!"

15Elisha said, "Get a bow and some arrows," and he did so. 16"Take the bow in your hands," he said to the king of Israel. When he had taken it, Elisha put his hands on the king's hands.

17"Open the east window," he said, and he opened it. "Shoot!" Elisha said, and he shot. "The LORD's arrow of victory, the arrow of victory over Aram!" Elisha declared. "You will completely destroy the Arameans at Aphek."

18Then he said, "Take the arrows," and the king took them. Elisha told him, "Strike the ground." He struck it three times and stopped. 19The man of God was angry with him and said,

[a] 6 That is, a symbol of the goddess Asherah; here and elsewhere in 2 Kings [b] 9 Hebrew *Joash,* a variant of *Jehoash;* also in verses 12-14 and 25

12:17–18 Joash made great strides toward leading Judah into spiritual restoration. But his faith wavered easily whenever he encountered a difficult situation. Under threat of Syrian attack, Joash gave away the temple treasury to pay off King Hazael of Syria. Joash failed to turn to God, who was capable of delivering his people from the Syrians. Instead, Joash sought his own human solution. The consequences of his choices were great national losses and a continuation of faithless living. Even after great success, we are susceptible to giving in to fear and spiritual blindness. We need to trust God to defeat the problems that threaten to overwhelm us.

13:1–7 The experience of King Jehoahaz of Israel is a solemn case study of what can happen when spiritual growth is approached halfheartedly. Jehoahaz apparently was humbled by his consistent defeats at the hands of the Syrians. He sought God when he saw his desperate situation. However, after God graciously granted a measure of relief and freedom, Jehoahaz fell back into his old sinful patterns. The consequences of his actions led to the near collapse of his rule. It is relatively easy to seek God and put our lives in his hands when we are in a desperate situation. However, true spiritual renewal and growth take place when we place our lives in God's hands even when things are going well.

13:9–19 King Jehoash of Israel was another individual who started to redirect his life toward God but didn't go far enough. Though he "did evil in the eyes of the LORD," Jehoash of Israel was greatly touched emotionally when the prophet Elisha was about to die (13:11, 14). He expressed his great respect and grief for Elisha. Elisha urged Jehoash to follow his instructions, which would lead him to victory. Jehoash only followed the instructions halfheartedly and was thus limited in his progress. Anything less than complete commitment to God will result in incomplete spiritual renewal and transformation.

"You should have struck the ground five or six times; then you would have defeated Aram and completely destroyed it. But now you will defeat it only three times."

20Elisha died and was buried.

Now Moabite raiders used to enter the country every spring. 21Once while some Israelites were burying a man, suddenly they saw a band of raiders; so they threw the man's body into Elisha's tomb. When the body touched Elisha's bones, the man came to life and stood up on his feet.

22Hazael king of Aram oppressed Israel throughout the reign of Jehoahaz. 23But the LORD was gracious to them and had compassion and showed concern for them because of his covenant with Abraham, Isaac and Jacob. To this day he has been unwilling to destroy them or banish them from his presence.

24Hazael king of Aram died, and Ben-Hadad his son succeeded him as king. 25Then Jehoash son of Jehoahaz recaptured from Ben-Hadad son of Hazael the towns he had taken in battle from his father Jehoahaz. Three times Jehoash defeated him, and so he recovered the Israelite towns.

Amaziah King of Judah

14 In the second year of Jehoash[a] son of Jehoahaz king of Israel, Amaziah son of Joash king of Judah began to reign. 2He was twenty-five years old when he became king, and he reigned in Jerusalem twenty-nine years. His mother's name was Jehoaddin; she was from Jerusalem. 3He did what was right in the eyes of the LORD, but not as his father David had done. In everything he followed the example of his father Joash. 4The high places, however, were not removed; the people continued to offer sacrifices and burn incense there.

5After the kingdom was firmly in his grasp, he executed the officials who had murdered his father the king. 6Yet he did not put the sons of the assassins to death, in accordance with what is written in the Book of the Law of Moses where the LORD commanded: "Fathers shall not be put to death for their children, nor children put to death for their fathers; each is to die for his own sins."[b]

7He was the one who defeated ten thousand Edomites in the Valley of Salt and captured Sela in battle, calling it Joktheel, the name it has to this day.

8Then Amaziah sent messengers to Jehoash son of Jehoahaz, the son of Jehu, king of Israel, with the challenge: "Come, meet me face to face."

9But Jehoash king of Israel replied to Amaziah king of Judah: "A thistle in Lebanon sent a message to a cedar in Lebanon, 'Give your daughter to my son in marriage.' Then a wild beast in Lebanon came along and trampled the thistle underfoot. 10You have indeed defeated Edom and now you are arrogant. Glory in your victory, but stay at home! Why ask for trouble and cause your own downfall and that of Judah also?"

11Amaziah, however, would not listen, so Jehoash king of Israel attacked. He and Amaziah king of Judah faced each other at Beth Shemesh in Judah. 12Judah was routed by Israel, and every man fled to his home. 13Jehoash king of Israel captured Amaziah king of Judah, the son of Joash, the son of Ahaziah, at Beth Shemesh. Then Jehoash went to Jerusalem and broke down the wall of Jerusalem from the Ephraim Gate to the Corner Gate—a section about six hundred feet long.[c] 14He took all the gold and silver and all the articles found in the temple of the LORD and in the treasuries of the royal palace. He also took hostages and returned to Samaria.

15As for the other events of the reign of Jehoash, what he did and his achievements, including his war against Amaziah king of Judah, are they not written in the book of the annals of the kings of Israel? 16Jehoash rested with his fathers and was buried in Samaria with the kings of Israel. And Jeroboam his son succeeded him as king.

17Amaziah son of Joash king of Judah lived for fifteen years after the death of Jehoash son of Jehoahaz king of Israel. 18As for the other events of Amaziah's reign, are they not written in the book of the annals of the kings of Judah?

[a] 1 Hebrew *Joash,* a variant of *Jehoash;* also in verses 13, 23 and 27 [b] 6 Deut. 24:16 [c] 13 Hebrew *four hundred cubits* (about 180 meters)

13:20–23 God's patience with Israel was tied to the covenant he had made with Abraham and his successors (13:22–23). Except for God's great covenant loyalty, the northern kingdom would have been destroyed long before its fall to Assyria in 722 B.C. God offers us a covenant through Jesus Christ, through whom we are forgiven and empowered to become God's children. God will care for anyone who believes in his Son's name. Jesus Christ is the source of all true spiritual renewal.

14:1–7 Amaziah of Judah demonstrated that a parent's behavior often significantly impacts the behavior of his children. Amaziah "followed the example of his father Joash" (14:3). Joash's various strengths and weaknesses were evidenced in the behavior of his son Amaziah. Notable in both kings was their blindness to the shrines of false worship (14:4). Perhaps it is best to say that Amaziah's commitment to God was defined by Joash's commitment. Likewise, we need to remember that children are watching us and may well follow our example. Learning to trust God and obey his plan for godly living is more than just a personal victory. It is an opportunity to leave a godly legacy for generations to come.

14:8–14 This tragic incident illustrates the dangers of overconfidence. After having defeated the Edomites, King Amaziah of Judah picked a fight with Israel—a fight that ended in disaster. It is easy to become overconfident in our own abilities after winning a major victory. We feel invincible! But we must proceed with caution because we may be letting our emotions blind us to reality. We need to continually recognize our need for God's helping hand and remain accountable to those who will help us if we become overconfident in our own abilities.

19They conspired against him in Jerusalem, and he fled to Lachish, but they sent men after him to Lachish and killed him there. 20He was brought back by horse and was buried in Jerusalem with his fathers, in the City of David.

21Then all the people of Judah took Azariah,[a] who was sixteen years old, and made him king in place of his father Amaziah. 22He was the one who rebuilt Elath and restored it to Judah after Amaziah rested with his fathers.

Jeroboam II King of Israel

23In the fifteenth year of Amaziah son of Joash king of Judah, Jeroboam son of Jehoash king of Israel became king in Samaria, and he reigned forty-one years. 24He did evil in the eyes of the LORD and did not turn away from any of the sins of Jeroboam son of Nebat, which he had caused Israel to commit. 25He was the one who restored the boundaries of Israel from Lebo[b] Hamath to the Sea of the Arabah,[c] in accordance with the word of the LORD, the God of Israel, spoken through his servant Jonah son of Amittai, the prophet from Gath Hepher.

26The LORD had seen how bitterly everyone in Israel, whether slave or free, was suffering; there was no one to help them. 27And since the LORD had not said he would blot out the name of Israel from under heaven, he saved them by the hand of Jeroboam son of Jehoash.

28As for the other events of Jeroboam's reign, all he did, and his military achievements, including how he recovered for Israel both Damascus and Hamath, which had belonged to Yaudi,[d] are they not written in the book of the annals of the kings of Israel? 29Jeroboam rested with his fathers, the kings of Israel. And Zechariah his son succeeded him as king.

Azariah King of Judah

15 In the twenty-seventh year of Jeroboam king of Israel, Azariah son of Amaziah king of Judah began to reign. 2He was sixteen years old when he became king, and he reigned in Jerusalem fifty-two years. His mother's name was Jecoliah; she was from Jerusalem. 3He did what was right in the eyes of the LORD, just as his father Amaziah had done. 4The high places, however, were not removed; the people continued to offer sacrifices and burn incense there.

5The LORD afflicted the king with leprosy[e] until the day he died, and he lived in a separate house.[f] Jotham the king's son had charge of the palace and governed the people of the land.

6As for the other events of Azariah's reign, and all he did, are they not written in the book of the annals of the kings of Judah? 7Azariah rested with his fathers and was buried near them in the City of David. And Jotham his son succeeded him as king.

Zechariah King of Israel

8In the thirty-eighth year of Azariah king of Judah, Zechariah son of Jeroboam became king of Israel in Samaria, and he reigned six months. 9He did evil in the eyes of the LORD, as his fathers had done. He did not turn away from the sins of Jeroboam son of Nebat, which he had caused Israel to commit.

10Shallum son of Jabesh conspired against Zechariah. He attacked him in front of the people,[g] assassinated him and succeeded him as king. 11The other events of Zechariah's reign are written in the book of the annals of the kings of Israel. 12So the word of the LORD spoken to Jehu was fulfilled: "Your descendants will sit on the throne of Israel to the fourth generation."[h]

Shallum King of Israel

13Shallum son of Jabesh became king in the thirty-ninth year of Uzziah king of Judah, and he reigned in Samaria one month. 14Then Menahem son of Gadi went from Tirzah up to Samaria. He attacked Shallum son of Jabesh in Samaria, assassinated him and succeeded him as king.

15The other events of Shallum's reign, and the conspiracy he led, are written in the book of the annals of the kings of Israel.

16At that time Menahem, starting out from Tirzah, attacked Tiphsah and everyone in the city and its vicinity, because they refused to open their gates. He sacked Tiphsah and ripped open all the pregnant women.

Menahem King of Israel

17In the thirty-ninth year of Azariah king of Judah, Menahem son of Gadi became king of Israel, and he reigned in Samaria ten years. 18He did evil in the eyes of the LORD. During his entire reign he did not turn away from the sins

a21 Also called *Uzziah* b25 Or *from the entrance to* c25 That is, the Dead Sea d28 Or *Judah* e5 The Hebrew word was used for various diseases affecting the skin—not necessarily leprosy. f5 Or *in a house where he was relieved of responsibility* g10 Hebrew; some Septuagint manuscripts *in Ibleam* h12 2 Kings 10:30

15:1–7 King Uzziah of Judah followed in the footsteps of his father, Amaziah (see 14:1–20), and his grandfather, Joash (see 12:1–21). Like them, he displayed a basic faith and commitment toward God (15:3). But also like them, he tolerated false worship at the pagan hilltop shrines (15:4). As a result, even though Uzziah's reign was fifty-two years long, it was a sad and solitary reign. God judged Uzziah's halfhearted devotion by giving him leprosy (15:5). Partial commitment never brings complete results. Only full devotion to God will bring lasting change.

15:8–12 The long, evil reign of Jeroboam II of the northern kingdom (see 14:23–29) could not guarantee stability or power for his equally evil son, Zechariah (15:9). God allowed Zechariah to reign for only six months before he was assassinated (15:10). God kept the word of judgment he had made against Jehu (15:12; see 10:30); this was the end of his evil line of descendants. Jehu's failure had led to the failure of his descendants. Unless we seek God now and surrender to him, the results may be disastrous for our own descendants.

of Jeroboam son of Nebat, which he had caused Israel to commit.

19 Then Pul[a] king of Assyria invaded the land, and Menahem gave him a thousand talents[b] of silver to gain his support and strengthen his own hold on the kingdom. 20 Menahem exacted this money from Israel. Every wealthy man had to contribute fifty shekels[c] of silver to be given to the king of Assyria. So the king of Assyria withdrew and stayed in the land no longer.

21 As for the other events of Menahem's reign, and all he did, are they not written in the book of the annals of the kings of Israel? 22 Menahem rested with his fathers. And Pekahiah his son succeeded him as king.

Pekahiah King of Israel

23 In the fiftieth year of Azariah king of Judah, Pekahiah son of Menahem became king of Israel in Samaria, and he reigned two years. 24 Pekahiah did evil in the eyes of the LORD. He did not turn away from the sins of Jeroboam son of Nebat, which he had caused Israel to commit. 25 One of his chief officers, Pekah son of Remaliah, conspired against him. Taking fifty men of Gilead with him, he assassinated Pekahiah, along with Argob and Arieh, in the citadel of the royal palace at Samaria. So Pekah killed Pekahiah and succeeded him as king.

26 The other events of Pekahiah's reign, and all he did, are written in the book of the annals of the kings of Israel.

Pekah King of Israel

27 In the fifty-second year of Azariah king of Judah, Pekah son of Remaliah became king of Israel in Samaria, and he reigned twenty years. 28 He did evil in the eyes of the LORD. He did not turn away from the sins of Jeroboam son of Nebat, which he had caused Israel to commit.

29 In the time of Pekah king of Israel, Tiglath-Pileser king of Assyria came and took Ijon, Abel Beth Maacah, Janoah, Kedesh and Hazor. He took Gilead and Galilee, including all the land of Naphtali, and deported the people to Assyria. 30 Then Hoshea son of Elah conspired against Pekah son of Remaliah. He attacked and assassinated him, and then succeeded him as king in the twentieth year of Jotham son of Uzziah.

31 As for the other events of Pekah's reign, and all he did, are they not written in the book of the annals of the kings of Israel?

Jotham King of Judah

32 In the second year of Pekah son of Remaliah king of Israel, Jotham son of Uzziah king of Judah began to reign. 33 He was twenty-five years old when he became king, and he reigned in Jerusalem sixteen years. His mother's name was Jerusha daughter of Zadok. 34 He did what was right in the eyes of the LORD, just as his father Uzziah had done. 35 The high places, however, were not removed; the people continued to offer sacrifices and burn incense there. Jotham rebuilt the Upper Gate of the temple of the LORD.

36 As for the other events of Jotham's reign, and what he did, are they not written in the book of the annals of the kings of Judah? 37 (In those days the LORD began to send Rezin king of Aram and Pekah son of Remaliah against Judah.) 38 Jotham rested with his fathers and was buried with them in the City of David, the city of his father. And Ahaz his son succeeded him as king.

Ahaz King of Judah

16 In the seventeenth year of Pekah son of Remaliah, Ahaz son of Jotham king of Judah began to reign. 2 Ahaz was twenty years old when he became king, and he reigned in Jerusalem sixteen years. Unlike David his father, he did not do what was right in the eyes of the LORD his God. 3 He walked in the ways of the kings of Israel and even sacrificed his son in[d] the fire, following the detestable ways of the nations the LORD had driven out before the Israelites. 4 He offered sacrifices and burned incense at the high places, on the hilltops and under every spreading tree.

5 Then Rezin king of Aram and Pekah son of

[a] 19 Also called *Tiglath-Pileser* [b] 19 That is, about 37 tons (about 34 metric tons) [c] 20 That is, about 1 1/4 pounds (about 0.6 kilogram) [d] 3 Or *even made his son pass through*

15:32–38 King Jotham of Judah, first as co-regent with his father, Uzziah (see 15:3–5), and then in his own right (15:32–33), exemplified a limited faith and commitment to God, as had his predecessors. Jotham gave attention to God's temple, but the ongoing presence of the hill shrines and false worship in Judah prompted God's judgment (15:34–35). God allowed both Syria and Israel to attack Judah in order to make Jotham see the truth (15:37). God often allows trials in our lives to help us see the truth we may have been trying to avoid.

16:1–4 It was only a matter of time before the halfhearted attempts of Judah's kings at spiritual renewal caused great damage. Ahaz completely denied his need for God and disobeyed God's laws, even sacrificing his own son to pagan gods (16:2–4). Halfhearted relationships with God over the course of many generations had a cumulative impact on the later generations. Children can quickly see through the hypocrisy of halfhearted devotion. This may cause them to reject everything we stand for—especially the good things.

16:5–9 King Ahaz paid tribute to the king of Assyria, placing his trust in the human resources at his disposal. In seeking human solutions to the conflict, however, Ahaz failed to look to God for help. The peace that Ahaz established in Judah was dependent on the payment of money. When Ahaz's son Hezekiah refused to pay tribute money to Assyria, Assyria attacked (see 18:7, 13). God protected Hezekiah and his kingdom. If Ahaz had turned to God for help, the peace he sought would have been built upon the unchanging power and presence of God. As we face difficult problems, we also need to look to God for help and not assume that we can overcome our obstacles merely by human effort.

Remaliah king of Israel marched up to fight against Jerusalem and besieged Ahaz, but they could not overpower him. 6At that time, Rezin king of Aram recovered Elath for Aram by driving out the men of Judah. Edomites then moved into Elath and have lived there to this day.

7Ahaz sent messengers to say to Tiglath-Pileser king of Assyria, "I am your servant and vassal. Come up and save me out of the hand of the king of Aram and of the king of Israel, who are attacking me." 8And Ahaz took the silver and gold found in the temple of the LORD and in the treasuries of the royal palace and sent it as a gift to the king of Assyria. 9The king of Assyria complied by attacking Damascus and capturing it. He deported its inhabitants to Kir and put Rezin to death.

10Then King Ahaz went to Damascus to meet Tiglath-Pileser king of Assyria. He saw an altar in Damascus and sent to Uriah the priest a sketch of the altar, with detailed plans for its construction. 11So Uriah the priest built an altar in accordance with all the plans that King Ahaz had sent from Damascus and finished it before King Ahaz returned. 12When the king came back from Damascus and saw the altar, he approached it and presented offerings[a] on it. 13He offered up his burnt offering and grain offering, poured out his drink offering, and sprinkled the blood of his fellowship offerings[b] on the altar. 14The bronze altar that stood before the LORD he brought from the front of the temple—from between the new altar and the temple of the LORD—and put it on the north side of the new altar.

15King Ahaz then gave these orders to Uriah the priest: "On the large new altar, offer the morning burnt offering and the evening grain offering, the king's burnt offering and his grain offering, and the burnt offering of all the people of the land, and their grain offering and their drink offering. Sprinkle on the altar all the blood of the burnt offerings and sacrifices. But I will use the bronze altar for seeking guidance." 16And Uriah the priest did just as King Ahaz had ordered.

17King Ahaz took away the side panels and removed the basins from the movable stands. He removed the Sea from the bronze bulls that supported it and set it on a stone base. 18He took away the Sabbath canopy[c] that had been built at the temple and removed the royal entryway outside the temple of the LORD, in deference to the king of Assyria.

19As for the other events of the reign of Ahaz, and what he did, are they not written in the book of the annals of the kings of Judah? 20Ahaz rested with his fathers and was buried with them in the City of David. And Hezekiah his son succeeded him as king.

Hoshea Last King of Israel

17 In the twelfth year of Ahaz king of Judah, Hoshea son of Elah became king of Israel in Samaria, and he reigned nine years. 2He did evil in the eyes of the LORD, but not like the kings of Israel who preceded him.

3Shalmaneser king of Assyria came up to attack Hoshea, who had been Shalmaneser's vassal and had paid him tribute. 4But the king of Assyria discovered that Hoshea was a traitor, for he had sent envoys to So[d] king of Egypt, and he no longer paid tribute to the king of Assyria, as he had done year by year. Therefore Shalmaneser seized him and put him in prison. 5The king of Assyria invaded the entire land, marched against Samaria and laid siege to it for three years. 6In the ninth year of Hoshea, the king of Assyria captured Samaria and deported the Israelites to Assyria. He settled them in Halah, in Gozan on the Habor River and in the towns of the Medes.

Israel Exiled Because of Sin

7All this took place because the Israelites had sinned against the LORD their God, who had brought them up out of Egypt from under the power of Pharaoh king of Egypt. They worshiped other gods 8and followed the practices of the nations the LORD had driven out before them, as well as the practices that the kings of Israel had introduced. 9The Israelites secretly did things against the LORD their God that were not right. From watchtower to fortified city they built themselves high places in all their towns. 10They set up sacred stones and Asherah poles on every high hill and under every spreading tree. 11At every high place they burned incense, as the nations whom the LORD had driven out before them had done. They did wicked things that provoked the LORD to anger. 12They worshiped idols, though the LORD had said, "You shall not do this."[e] 13The LORD warned Israel and Judah through all his prophets and seers: "Turn from your evil ways. Observe my commands and decrees, in accordance with the entire Law that I commanded your fathers to obey and that I delivered to you through my servants the prophets."

[a]12 Or *and went up* [b]13 Traditionally *peace offerings*
[c]18 Or *the dais of his throne* (see Septuagint) [d]4 Or *to Sais, to the; So* is possibly an abbreviation for *Osorkon.*
[e]12 Exodus 20:4, 5

17:1–23 This chapter records the progressive degeneration of the northern kingdom of Israel. The reign of Hoshea was the straw that broke the camel's back. He led Israel through its final climactic period of sinful resistance to God, which ended in Assyrian exile (17:1–7). But then notice that the nation of Judah is criticized for making the same mistakes, following the same evil path toward judgment and exile (17:18–23). The southern kingdom of Judah should have looked at the consequences of Israel's disobedience and then pursued God. Have we ever criticized others for their sinful behavior and taken notes on the consequences of their actions? If we have, we should be careful to redirect our course in the opposite direction. We must be careful to avoid Judah's terrible mistake.

14But they would not listen and were as stiff-
necked as their fathers, who did not trust in the
LORD their God. 15They rejected his decrees and
the covenant he had made with their fathers
and the warnings he had given them. They followed worthless idols and themselves became
worthless. They imitated the nations around
them although the LORD had ordered them,
"Do not do as they do," and they did the things
the LORD had forbidden them to do.
16They forsook all the commands of the
LORD their God and made for themselves two
idols cast in the shape of calves, and an Asherah
pole. They bowed down to all the starry hosts,
and they worshiped Baal. 17They sacrificed their
sons and daughters in[a] the fire. They practiced
divination and sorcery and sold themselves to
do evil in the eyes of the LORD, provoking him
to anger.
18So the LORD was very angry with Israel and
removed them from his presence. Only the tribe
of Judah was left, 19and even Judah did not keep
the commands of the LORD their God. They followed the practices Israel had introduced.
20Therefore the LORD rejected all the people of
Israel; he afflicted them and gave them into the
hands of plunderers, until he thrust them from
his presence.
21When he tore Israel away from the house of
David, they made Jeroboam son of Nebat their
king. Jeroboam enticed Israel away from following the LORD and caused them to commit a
great sin. 22The Israelites persisted in all the sins
of Jeroboam and did not turn away from them
23until the LORD removed them from his presence, as he had warned through all his servants
the prophets. So the people of Israel were taken
from their homeland into exile in Assyria, and
they are still there.

Samaria Resettled

24The king of Assyria brought people from
Babylon, Cuthah, Avva, Hamath and Sepharvaim and settled them in the towns of Samaria to
replace the Israelites. They took over Samaria
and lived in its towns. 25When they first lived
there, they did not worship the LORD; so he sent
lions among them and they killed some of the
people. 26It was reported to the king of Assyria:
"The people you deported and resettled in the
towns of Samaria do not know what the god of
that country requires. He has sent lions among
them, which are killing them off, because the
people do not know what he requires."
27Then the king of Assyria gave this order:
"Have one of the priests you took captive from
Samaria go back to live there and teach the people what the god of the land requires." 28So one
of the priests who had been exiled from Samaria came to live in Bethel and taught them how
to worship the LORD.
29Nevertheless, each national group made its
own gods in the several towns where they settled, and set them up in the shrines the people
of Samaria had made at the high places. 30The
men from Babylon made Succoth Benoth, the
men from Cuthah made Nergal, and the men
from Hamath made Ashima; 31the Avvites made
Nibhaz and Tartak, and the Sepharvites burned
their children in the fire as sacrifices to Adram-
melech and Anammelech, the gods of Sepharvaim. 32They worshiped the LORD, but they also
appointed all sorts of their own people to offici-
ate for them as priests in the shrines at the high
places. 33They worshiped the LORD, but they
also served their own gods in accordance with
the customs of the nations from which they had
been brought.
34To this day they persist in their former
practices. They neither worship the LORD nor
adhere to the decrees and ordinances, the laws
and commands that the LORD gave the descendants of Jacob, whom he named Israel. 35When
the LORD made a covenant with the Israelites,
he commanded them: "Do not worship any
other gods or bow down to them, serve them or
sacrifice to them. 36But the LORD, who brought
you up out of Egypt with mighty power and
outstretched arm, is the one you must worship.
To him you shall bow down and to him offer
sacrifices. 37You must always be careful to keep
the decrees and ordinances, the laws and commands he wrote for you. Do not worship other
gods. 38Do not forget the covenant I have made
with you, and do not worship other gods.
39Rather, worship the LORD your God; it is he
who will deliver you from the hand of all your
enemies."
40They would not listen, however, but persisted in their former practices. 41Even while
these people were worshiping the LORD, they
were serving their idols. To this day their children and grandchildren continue to do as their
fathers did.

Hezekiah King of Judah

18 In the third year of Hoshea son of Elah
king of Israel, Hezekiah son of Ahaz
king of Judah began to reign. 2He was twenty-
five years old when he became king, and he
reigned in Jerusalem twenty-nine years. His
mother's name was Abijah[b] daughter of Zechariah. 3He did what was right in the eyes of the
LORD, just as his father David had done. 4He

[a] 17 Or *They made their sons and daughters pass through*
[b] 2 Hebrew *Abi,* a variant of *Abijah*

18:1–8 King Hezekiah made a radical break from the evil ways of his father, Ahaz. Hezekiah's stated faith and commitment gave him the courage to stand against Judah's sinful past and take significant steps to rebuild his kingdom in God's way (18:5). His honesty in assessing the spiritual state of his kingdom and his willingness to break from sinful ways made him one of Judah's greatest kings (18:6–7). We also must honestly admit our failures and ask God to help us rebuild our lives in keeping with his commands.

Hezekiah

Hezekiah inherited a kingdom that his father had led into social, economic and spiritual decline. Upon his ascension to the throne, Hezekiah courageously implemented sweeping reforms. He abolished idolatry throughout the land and followed God's instructions to the letter—with two exceptions.

First, Hezekiah took credit for the blessings that God had given to him and the nation of Israel. Hezekiah proudly displayed the wealth of his kingdom to the Babylonians, who would eventually conquer the kingdom of Judah. Hezekiah forgot that the wealth of the kingdom was not really his; it all belonged to God.

Second, Hezekiah failed in his task as a father. He spent little time teaching his son Manasseh God's ways. When Manasseh became king, he reversed all the righteous reforms of his father. The idol worship instituted during Manasseh's reign initiated one of the greatest spiritual declines in Israel's history. The prophet Jeremiah pinned Judah's ultimate demise on Manasseh's wickedness, labeling him as the most evil king of Judah (Jeremiah 15:4).

Hezekiah's failures are easy ones to repeat. We can look at our possessions, our status and our spiritual standing and believe that we have achieved it all, forgetting that God is the one who gives us success. We can get caught up in our work, our activities, even the things we do for God, and forget to prepare the next generation to follow in the path of righteousness. What we have learned in the past and are learning in the present must be communicated to the leaders of the future. Jesus illustrated the importance of this by spending most of his time with his disciples—his hope for the future. We need to follow Jesus' positive example, not Hezekiah's negative failures.

STRENGTHS AND ACCOMPLISHMENTS:

Hezekiah instituted sweeping spiritual and political reforms.

He had a powerful prayer life.

He maintained a consistent personal relationship with God.

WEAKNESSES AND MISTAKES:

Hezekiah failed to train his son and protect the reforms he had instituted.

He showed Judah's wealth to Babylonian messengers and took credit for it.

LESSONS FROM HIS LIFE:

Our spiritual concerns must include members of our family.

When we surrender our lives to God, amazing results will occur.

KEY VERSE:

"Have you not heard? Long ago I ordained it. In days of old I planned it; now I have brought it to pass" (19:25).

Hezekiah's story is told in 2 Kings 16:20—20:21; 2 Chronicles 28:27—32; and Isaiah 36—39. He is mentioned in 1 Chronicles 3:13–14; 4:41; Proverbs 25:1; Isaiah 1:1; Jeremiah 15:4; 26:18–19; Hosea 1:1; Micah 1:1; Zephaniah 1:1 and Matthew 1:9–10.

removed the high places, smashed the sacred
stones and cut down the Asherah poles. He
broke into pieces the bronze snake Moses had
made, for up to that time the Israelites had been
burning incense to it. (It was called[a] Nehushtan.[b])
5 Hezekiah trusted in the LORD, the God of
Israel. There was no one like him among all the
kings of Judah, either before him or after him.
6 He held fast to the LORD and did not cease to
follow him; he kept the commands the LORD
had given Moses. 7 And the LORD was with him;
he was successful in whatever he undertook. He
rebelled against the king of Assyria and did not
serve him. 8 From watchtower to fortified city,
he defeated the Philistines, as far as Gaza and its
territory.
9 In King Hezekiah's fourth year, which was
the seventh year of Hoshea son of Elah king of
Israel, Shalmaneser king of Assyria marched
against Samaria and laid siege to it. 10 At the end
of three years the Assyrians took it. So Samaria
was captured in Hezekiah's sixth year, which
was the ninth year of Hoshea king of Israel.
11 The king of Assyria deported Israel to Assyria
and settled them in Halah, in Gozan on the
Habor River and in towns of the Medes. 12 This
happened because they had not obeyed the
LORD their God, but had violated his covenant—
all that Moses the servant of the LORD commanded. They neither listened to the commands nor carried them out.
13 In the fourteenth year of King Hezekiah's
reign, Sennacherib king of Assyria attacked all
the fortified cities of Judah and captured them.
14 So Hezekiah king of Judah sent this message
to the king of Assyria at Lachish: "I have done
wrong. Withdraw from me, and I will pay whatever you demand of me." The king of Assyria
exacted from Hezekiah king of Judah three hundred talents[c] of silver and thirty talents[d] of
gold. 15 So Hezekiah gave him all the silver that
was found in the temple of the LORD and in the
treasuries of the royal palace.
16 At this time Hezekiah king of Judah
stripped off the gold with which he had covered
the doors and doorposts of the temple of the
LORD, and gave it to the king of Assyria.

Sennacherib Threatens Jerusalem

17 The king of Assyria sent his supreme commander, his chief officer and his field commander with a large army, from Lachish to King
Hezekiah at Jerusalem. They came up to Jerusalem and stopped at the aqueduct of the Upper
Pool, on the road to the Washerman's Field.
18 They called for the king; and Eliakim son of
Hilkiah the palace administrator, Shebna the
secretary, and Joah son of Asaph the recorder
went out to them.
19 The field commander said to them, "Tell
Hezekiah:

"'This is what the great king, the king
of Assyria, says: On what are you basing
this confidence of yours? 20 You say you
have strategy and military strength—but
you speak only empty words. On whom
are you depending, that you rebel against
me? 21 Look now, you are depending on
Egypt, that splintered reed of a staff, which
pierces a man's hand and wounds him if
he leans on it! Such is Pharaoh king of
Egypt to all who depend on him. 22 And if
you say to me, "We are depending on the
LORD our God"—isn't he the one whose
high places and altars Hezekiah removed,
saying to Judah and Jerusalem, "You must
worship before this altar in Jerusalem"?
23 "'Come now, make a bargain with
my master, the king of Assyria: I will give
you two thousand horses—if you can put
riders on them! 24 How can you repulse
one officer of the least of my master's officials, even though you are depending on
Egypt for chariots and horsemen[e]? 25 Furthermore, have I come to attack and destroy this place without word from the
LORD? The LORD himself told me to march
against this country and destroy it.'"

26 Then Eliakim son of Hilkiah, and Shebna
and Joah said to the field commander, "Please
speak to your servants in Aramaic, since we understand it. Don't speak to us in Hebrew in the
hearing of the people on the wall."
27 But the commander replied, "Was it only
to your master and you that my master sent me
to say these things, and not to the men sitting
on the wall—who, like you, will have to eat their
own filth and drink their own urine?"

[a]4 Or *He called it* [b]4 *Nehushtan* sounds like the Hebrew for *bronze* and *snake* and *unclean thing.*
[c]14 That is, about 11 tons (about 10 metric tons)
[d]14 That is, about 1 ton (about 1 metric ton) [e]24 Or *charioteers*

18:9–16 Although Hezekiah was one of the best of Judah's kings, he responded exactly as his father had to the threat of the Assyrian invasion. Hezekiah trusted God with the smaller things, but at the threat of invasion, he looked for help elsewhere. Rather than trusting the God who gave him his kingdom, Hezekiah trusted the very enemy who was attacking him. Whenever we choose to trust in the things that are ruining our lives rather than in the God who created us, we put ourselves at great risk. Whether we are facing troubles great or small, we would do well to surrender our lives fully to God, for God can be trusted with both the small and the large problems we face.

18:17—19:1 King Hezekiah of Judah paid off his Assyrian invaders, but it was only a matter of time before the enemy would come back for more. The Assyrian spokesman knew that Hezekiah had failed to trust God in the earlier crisis. He used that point to intimidate the people of Judah into surrendering. It was a terrible situation to face, but it did lead Hezekiah to surrender—surrender to God. Even if our situation looks hopeless, it is never too late to seek God and surrender to him.

28Then the commander stood and called out in Hebrew: "Hear the word of the great king, the king of Assyria! 29This is what the king says: Do not let Hezekiah deceive you. He cannot deliver you from my hand. 30Do not let Hezekiah persuade you to trust in the LORD when he says, 'The LORD will surely deliver us; this city will not be given into the hand of the king of Assyria.'

31"Do not listen to Hezekiah. This is what the king of Assyria says: Make peace with me and come out to me. Then every one of you will eat from his own vine and fig tree and drink water from his own cistern, 32until I come and take you to a land like your own, a land of grain and new wine, a land of bread and vineyards, a land of olive trees and honey. Choose life and not death!

"Do not listen to Hezekiah, for he is misleading you when he says, 'The LORD will deliver us.' 33Has the god of any nation ever delivered his land from the hand of the king of Assyria? 34Where are the gods of Hamath and Arpad? Where are the gods of Sepharvaim, Hena and Ivvah? Have they rescued Samaria from my hand? 35Who of all the gods of these countries has been able to save his land from me? How then can the LORD deliver Jerusalem from my hand?"

36But the people remained silent and said nothing in reply, because the king had commanded, "Do not answer him."

37Then Eliakim son of Hilkiah the palace administrator, Shebna the secretary and Joah son of Asaph the recorder went to Hezekiah, with their clothes torn, and told him what the field commander had said.

Jerusalem's Deliverance Foretold

19 When King Hezekiah heard this, he tore his clothes and put on sackcloth and went into the temple of the LORD. 2He sent Eliakim the palace administrator, Shebna the secretary and the leading priests, all wearing sackcloth, to the prophet Isaiah son of Amoz. 3They told him, "This is what Hezekiah says: This day is a day of distress and rebuke and disgrace, as when children come to the point of birth and there is no strength to deliver them. 4It may be that the LORD your God will hear all the words of the field commander, whom his master, the king of Assyria, has sent to ridicule the living God, and that he will rebuke him for the words the LORD your God has heard. Therefore pray for the remnant that still survives."

5When King Hezekiah's officials came to Isaiah, 6Isaiah said to them, "Tell your master, 'This is what the LORD says: Do not be afraid of what you have heard—those words with which the underlings of the king of Assyria have blasphemed me. 7Listen! I am going to put such a spirit in him that when he hears a certain report, he will return to his own country, and there I will have him cut down with the sword.' "

8When the field commander heard that the king of Assyria had left Lachish, he withdrew and found the king fighting against Libnah.

9Now Sennacherib received a report that Tirhakah, the Cushite[a] king ⌞of Egypt⌟, was marching out to fight against him. So he again sent messengers to Hezekiah with this word: 10"Say to Hezekiah king of Judah: Do not let the god you depend on deceive you when he says, 'Jerusalem will not be handed over to the king of Assyria.' 11Surely you have heard what the kings of Assyria have done to all the countries, destroying them completely. And will you be delivered? 12Did the gods of the nations that were destroyed by my forefathers deliver them: the gods of Gozan, Haran, Rezeph and the people of Eden who were in Tel Assar? 13Where is the king of Hamath, the king of Arpad, the king of the city of Sepharvaim, or of Hena or Ivvah?"

Hezekiah's Prayer

14Hezekiah received the letter from the messengers and read it. Then he went up to the temple of the LORD and spread it out before the LORD. 15And Hezekiah prayed to the LORD: "O LORD, God of Israel, enthroned between the cherubim, you alone are God over all the kingdoms of the earth. You have made heaven and earth. 16Give ear, O LORD, and hear; open your eyes, O LORD, and see; listen to the words Sennacherib has sent to insult the living God.

17"It is true, O LORD, that the Assyrian kings have laid waste these nations and their lands. 18They have thrown their gods into the fire and destroyed them, for they were not gods but only wood and stone, fashioned by men's hands. 19Now, O LORD our God, deliver us from his hand, so that all kingdoms on earth may know that you alone, O LORD, are God."

Isaiah Prophesies Sennacherib's Fall

20Then Isaiah son of Amoz sent a message to Hezekiah: "This is what the LORD, the God of Israel, says: I have heard your prayer concerning Sennacherib king of Assyria. 21This is the word that the LORD has spoken against him:

" 'The Virgin Daughter of Zion
    despises you and mocks you.
The Daughter of Jerusalem

[a]9 That is, from the upper Nile region

19:2–36 As Hezekiah faced this seemingly impossible situation, he humbly turned to God for help. God answered Hezekiah's desperate plea and delivered his people from a formidable enemy. In this case, God didn't roar in with blaring trumpets or a terrifying earthquake. The enemy army was quietly lured from its siege of Jerusalem. We may wish for an immediate, miraculous deliverance from our problems, but it may not happen that way. God often uses quiet resources—the steady support of a friend, the encouragement of a support group, the quiet leading of the Holy Spirit—to strengthen us in our spiritual growth.

tosses her head as you flee.
22Who is it you have insulted and
blasphemed?
Against whom have you raised your
voice
and lifted your eyes in pride?
Against the Holy One of Israel!
23By your messengers
you have heaped insults on the Lord.
And you have said,
"With my many chariots
I have ascended the heights of the
mountains,
the utmost heights of Lebanon.
I have cut down its tallest cedars,
the choicest of its pines.
I have reached its remotest parts,
the finest of its forests.
24I have dug wells in foreign lands
and drunk the water there.
With the soles of my feet
I have dried up all the streams of Egypt."

25" 'Have you not heard?
Long ago I ordained it.
In days of old I planned it;
now I have brought it to pass,
that you have turned fortified cities
into piles of stone.
26Their people, drained of power,
are dismayed and put to shame.
They are like plants in the field,
like tender green shoots,
like grass sprouting on the roof,
scorched before it grows up.

27" 'But I know where you stay
and when you come and go
and how you rage against me.
28Because you rage against me
and your insolence has reached my ears,
I will put my hook in your nose
and my bit in your mouth,
and I will make you return
by the way you came.'

29"This will be the sign for you, O Hezekiah:

"This year you will eat what grows by
itself,
and the second year what springs from
that.
But in the third year sow and reap,
plant vineyards and eat their fruit.
30Once more a remnant of the house of
Judah
will take root below and bear fruit
above.
31For out of Jerusalem will come a remnant,
and out of Mount Zion a band of
survivors.
The zeal of the LORD Almighty will accomplish
this.

32"Therefore this is what the LORD says concerning the king of Assyria:

"He will not enter this city
or shoot an arrow here.
He will not come before it with shield
or build a siege ramp against it.
33By the way that he came he will return;
he will not enter this city,
declares the LORD.
34I will defend this city and save it,
for my sake and for the sake of David
my servant."

35That night the angel of the LORD went out
and put to death a hundred and eighty-five
thousand men in the Assyrian camp. When the
people got up the next morning—there were all
the dead bodies! 36So Sennacherib king of Assyria broke camp and withdrew. He returned to
Nineveh and stayed there.
37One day, while he was worshiping in the
temple of his god Nisroch, his sons Adramme-
lech and Sharezer cut him down with the
sword, and they escaped to the land of Ararat.
And Esarhaddon his son succeeded him as king.

Hezekiah's Illness

20 In those days Hezekiah became ill and
was at the point of death. The prophet
Isaiah son of Amoz went to him and said, "This
is what the LORD says: Put your house in order,
because you are going to die; you will not recover."
2Hezekiah turned his face to the wall and
prayed to the LORD, 3"Remember, O LORD,
how I have walked before you faithfully and
with wholehearted devotion and have done
what is good in your eyes." And Hezekiah wept
bitterly.
4Before Isaiah had left the middle court, the
word of the LORD came to him: 5"Go back and
tell Hezekiah, the leader of my people, 'This is
what the LORD, the God of your father David,
says: I have heard your prayer and seen your
tears; I will heal you. On the third day from
now you will go up to the temple of the LORD.
6I will add fifteen years to your life. And I will
deliver you and this city from the hand of the
king of Assyria. I will defend this city for my
sake and for the sake of my servant David.' "
7Then Isaiah said, "Prepare a poultice of figs."
They did so and applied it to the boil, and he
recovered.
8Hezekiah had asked Isaiah, "What will be
the sign that the LORD will heal me and that I
will go up to the temple of the LORD on the
third day from now?"

20:1–11 Hezekiah seems to have been greatly troubled by doubt. Hezekiah pleaded with God to spare his life and recounted his previous consistent faith and commitment to God. God did grant Hezekiah another fifteen years of life and also performed a great miracle as proof that he would fulfill Hezekiah's request. Although God may not make the sun go backward for us, we should never doubt that God can rescue us when we honestly cry out to him.

9Isaiah answered, "This is the LORD's sign to you that the LORD will do what he has promised: Shall the shadow go forward ten steps, or shall it go back ten steps?"

10"It is a simple matter for the shadow to go forward ten steps," said Hezekiah. "Rather, have it go back ten steps."

11Then the prophet Isaiah called upon the LORD, and the LORD made the shadow go back the ten steps it had gone down on the stairway of Ahaz.

Envoys From Babylon

12At that time Merodach-Baladan son of Baladan king of Babylon sent Hezekiah letters and a gift, because he had heard of Hezekiah's illness. 13Hezekiah received the messengers and showed them all that was in his storehouses—the silver, the gold, the spices and the fine oil—his armory and everything found among his treasures. There was nothing in his palace or in all his kingdom that Hezekiah did not show them.

14Then Isaiah the prophet went to King Hezekiah and asked, "What did those men say, and where did they come from?"

"From a distant land," Hezekiah replied. "They came from Babylon."

15The prophet asked, "What did they see in your palace?"

"They saw everything in my palace," Hezekiah said. "There is nothing among my treasures that I did not show them."

16Then Isaiah said to Hezekiah, "Hear the word of the LORD: 17The time will surely come when everything in your palace, and all that your fathers have stored up until this day, will be carried off to Babylon. Nothing will be left, says the LORD. 18And some of your descendants, your own flesh and blood, that will be born to you, will be taken away, and they will become eunuchs in the palace of the king of Babylon."

19"The word of the LORD you have spoken is good," Hezekiah replied. For he thought, "Will there not be peace and security in my lifetime?"

20As for the other events of Hezekiah's reign, all his achievements and how he made the pool and the tunnel by which he brought water into the city, are they not written in the book of the annals of the kings of Judah? 21Hezekiah rested with his fathers. And Manasseh his son succeeded him as king.

Manasseh King of Judah

21 Manasseh was twelve years old when he became king, and he reigned in Jerusalem fifty-five years. His mother's name was Hephzibah. 2He did evil in the eyes of the LORD, following the detestable practices of the nations the LORD had driven out before the Israelites. 3He rebuilt the high places his father Hezekiah had destroyed; he also erected altars to Baal and made an Asherah pole, as Ahab king of Israel had done. He bowed down to all the starry hosts and worshiped them. 4He built altars in the temple of the LORD, of which the LORD had said, "In Jerusalem I will put my Name." 5In both courts of the temple of the LORD, he built altars to all the starry hosts. 6He sacrificed his own son in[a] the fire, practiced sorcery and divination, and consulted mediums and spiritists. He did much evil in the eyes of the LORD, provoking him to anger.

7He took the carved Asherah pole he had made and put it in the temple, of which the LORD had said to David and to his son Solomon, "In this temple and in Jerusalem, which I have chosen out of all the tribes of Israel, I will put my Name forever. 8I will not again make the feet of the Israelites wander from the land I gave their forefathers, if only they will be careful to do everything I commanded them and will keep the whole Law that my servant Moses gave them." 9But the people did not listen. Manasseh led them astray, so that they did more evil than the nations the LORD had destroyed before the Israelites.

10The LORD said through his servants the prophets: 11"Manasseh king of Judah has committed these detestable sins. He has done more evil than the Amorites who preceded him and has led Judah into sin with his idols. 12Therefore this is what the LORD, the God of Israel, says: I am going to bring such disaster on Jerusalem and Judah that the ears of everyone who hears of it will tingle. 13I will stretch out over Jerusalem the measuring line used against Samaria and the plumb line used against the house of Ahab. I will wipe out Jerusalem as one wipes a dish, wiping it and turning it upside down. 14I will forsake the remnant of my inheritance and hand them over to their enemies. They will be looted and plundered by all their foes, 15because they have done evil in my eyes and have provoked me to anger from the day

[a]6 Or *He made his own son pass through*

20:12–21 Hezekiah made a major mistake. When the delegation from the rising nation of Babylon came to Jerusalem, Hezekiah put on the most impressive show possible. To make matters worse, he took the credit for all his wealth instead of giving the glory to God (20:15). The unconsidered consequences of Hezekiah's prideful actions came to painful fruition during the Babylonian exile (see 23:36—25:30). God desires humility from us. We must always remember that he is the true source of our success.

21:1–17 Manasseh reversed all the positive steps for Judah's national restoration that had been instituted by Hezekiah. His evil and oppressive reign further incited the Lord to punish Judah. Judah would follow the northern kingdom of Israel into exile just as it had followed them into sin. By the end of Manasseh's fifty-five-year reign, the possibility of a meaningful spiritual restoration in Judah seemed very slim. Because those who submit to authority figures will often suffer the consequences of their leaders' mistakes, leaders must be all the more careful about following God's ways.

their forefathers came out of Egypt until this day."

16Moreover, Manasseh also shed so much innocent blood that he filled Jerusalem from end to end—besides the sin that he had caused Judah to commit, so that they did evil in the eyes of the LORD.

17As for the other events of Manasseh's reign, and all he did, including the sin he committed, are they not written in the book of the annals of the kings of Judah? 18Manasseh rested with his fathers and was buried in his palace garden, the garden of Uzza. And Amon his son succeeded him as king.

Amon King of Judah

19Amon was twenty-two years old when he became king, and he reigned in Jerusalem two years. His mother's name was Meshullemeth daughter of Haruz; she was from Jotbah. 20He did evil in the eyes of the LORD, as his father Manasseh had done. 21He walked in all the ways of his father; he worshiped the idols his father had worshiped, and bowed down to them. 22He forsook the LORD, the God of his fathers, and did not walk in the way of the LORD.

23Amon's officials conspired against him and assassinated the king in his palace. 24Then the people of the land killed all who had plotted against King Amon, and they made Josiah his son king in his place.

25As for the other events of Amon's reign, and what he did, are they not written in the book of the annals of the kings of Judah? 26He was buried in his grave in the garden of Uzza. And Josiah his son succeeded him as king.

The Book of the Law Found

22 Josiah was eight years old when he became king, and he reigned in Jerusalem thirty-one years. His mother's name was Jedidah daughter of Adaiah; she was from Bozkath. 2He did what was right in the eyes of the LORD and walked in all the ways of his father David, not turning aside to the right or to the left.

3In the eighteenth year of his reign, King Josiah sent the secretary, Shaphan son of Azaliah, the son of Meshullam, to the temple of the LORD. He said: 4"Go up to Hilkiah the high priest and have him get ready the money that has been brought into the temple of the LORD, which the doorkeepers have collected from the people. 5Have them entrust it to the men appointed to supervise the work on the temple. And have these men pay the workers who repair the temple of the LORD— 6the carpenters, the builders and the masons. Also have them purchase timber and dressed stone to repair the temple. 7But they need not account for the money entrusted to them, because they are acting faithfully."

8Hilkiah the high priest said to Shaphan the secretary, "I have found the Book of the Law in the temple of the LORD." He gave it to Shaphan, who read it. 9Then Shaphan the secretary went to the king and reported to him: "Your officials have paid out the money that was in the temple of the LORD and have entrusted it to the workers and supervisors at the temple." 10Then Shaphan the secretary informed the king, "Hilkiah the priest has given me a book." And Shaphan read from it in the presence of the king.

11When the king heard the words of the Book of the Law, he tore his robes. 12He gave these orders to Hilkiah the priest, Ahikam son of Shaphan, Acbor son of Micaiah, Shaphan the secretary and Asaiah the king's attendant: 13"Go and inquire of the LORD for me and for the people and for all Judah about what is written in this book that has been found. Great is the LORD's anger that burns against us because our fathers have not obeyed the words of this book; they have not acted in accordance with all that is written there concerning us."

14Hilkiah the priest, Ahikam, Acbor, Shaphan and Asaiah went to speak to the prophetess Huldah, who was the wife of Shallum son of Tikvah, the son of Harhas, keeper of the wardrobe. She lived in Jerusalem, in the Second District.

15She said to them, "This is what the LORD, the God of Israel, says: Tell the man who sent you to me, 16'This is what the LORD says: I am going to bring disaster on this place and its people, according to everything written in the book the king of Judah has read. 17Because they have forsaken me and burned incense to other gods and provoked me to anger by all the idols their hands have made,[a] my anger will burn against this place and will not be quenched.' 18Tell the king of Judah, who sent you to inquire of the LORD, 'This is what the LORD, the God of Israel, says concerning the words you heard: 19Because your heart was responsive and you humbled yourself before the LORD when you heard what I have spoken against this place and its people, that they would become accursed and laid waste, and because you tore your robes and wept in my presence, I have heard you, declares the LORD. 20Therefore I will gather you to your fathers, and you will be buried in peace. Your eyes will not see all the disaster I am going to bring on this place.' "

So they took her answer back to the king.

[a]17 Or *by everything they have done*

21:19–26 King Amon of Judah was similar to his father, Manasseh in many ways. God had let Manasseh's oppression of the people continue for many years, but he did not do the same for Amon. God was anxious for his people in Judah to be restored from their unbelief and idolatry. Josiah, Amon's young son, would be the initiator and primary instrument for this revival among God's people (see 22:1—23:30).

Josiah Renews the Covenant

23 Then the king called together all the
elders of Judah and Jerusalem. 2He
went up to the temple of the LORD with the men
of Judah, the people of Jerusalem, the priests
and the prophets—all the people from the least
to the greatest. He read in their hearing all the
words of the Book of the Covenant, which had
been found in the temple of the LORD. 3The
king stood by the pillar and renewed the covenant in the presence of the LORD—to follow the
LORD and keep his commands, regulations and
decrees with all his heart and all his soul, thus
confirming the words of the covenant written in
this book. Then all the people pledged themselves to the covenant.

4The king ordered Hilkiah the high priest,
the priests next in rank and the doorkeepers to
remove from the temple of the LORD all the
articles made for Baal and Asherah and all the
starry hosts. He burned them outside Jerusalem
in the fields of the Kidron Valley and took the
ashes to Bethel. 5He did away with the pagan
priests appointed by the kings of Judah to burn
incense on the high places of the towns of Judah and on those around Jerusalem—those who
burned incense to Baal, to the sun and moon,
to the constellations and to all the starry hosts.
6He took the Asherah pole from the temple of
the LORD to the Kidron Valley outside Jerusalem
and burned it there. He ground it to powder
and scattered the dust over the graves of the
common people. 7He also tore down the quarters of the male shrine prostitutes, which were
in the temple of the LORD and where women
did weaving for Asherah.

8Josiah brought all the priests from the towns
of Judah and desecrated the high places, from
Geba to Beersheba, where the priests had
burned incense. He broke down the shrines[a]
at the gates—at the entrance to the Gate of Joshua, the city governor, which is on the left of the
city gate. 9Although the priests of the high
places did not serve at the altar of the LORD in
Jerusalem, they ate unleavened bread with their
fellow priests.

10He desecrated Topheth, which was in the
Valley of Ben Hinnom, so no one could use it
to sacrifice his son or daughter in[b] the fire to
Molech. 11He removed from the entrance to the
temple of the LORD the horses that the kings of
Judah had dedicated to the sun. They were in
the court near the room of an official named
Nathan-Melech. Josiah then burned the chariots dedicated to the sun.

12He pulled down the altars the kings of Judah had erected on the roof near the upper
room of Ahaz, and the altars Manasseh had
built in the two courts of the temple of the
LORD. He removed them from there, smashed
them to pieces and threw the rubble into the
Kidron Valley. 13The king also desecrated the
high places that were east of Jerusalem on
the south of the Hill of Corruption—the ones
Solomon king of Israel had built for Ashtoreth
the vile goddess of the Sidonians, for Chemosh
the vile god of Moab, and for Molech[c] the
detestable god of the people of Ammon. 14Josi-
ah smashed the sacred stones and cut down the
Asherah poles and covered the sites with human bones.

15Even the altar at Bethel, the high place
made by Jeroboam son of Nebat, who had
caused Israel to sin—even that altar and high
place he demolished. He burned the high place
and ground it to powder, and burned the Asherah pole also. 16Then Josiah looked around,
and when he saw the tombs that were there on
the hillside, he had the bones removed from
them and burned on the altar to defile it, in
accordance with the word of the LORD proclaimed by the man of God who foretold these
things.

17The king asked, "What is that tombstone I
see?"

The men of the city said, "It marks the tomb
of the man of God who came from Judah and
pronounced against the altar of Bethel the very
things you have done to it."

18"Leave it alone," he said. "Don't let anyone
disturb his bones." So they spared his bones and
those of the prophet who had come from Samaria.

19Just as he had done at Bethel, Josiah removed and defiled all the shrines at the high
places that the kings of Israel had built in the
towns of Samaria that had provoked the LORD
to anger. 20Josiah slaughtered all the priests of
those high places on the altars and burned human bones on them. Then he went back to
Jerusalem.

21The king gave this order to all the people:
"Celebrate the Passover to the LORD your God,
as it is written in this Book of the Covenant."
22Not since the days of the judges who led Israel, nor throughout the days of the kings of Israel
and the kings of Judah, had any such Passover
been observed. 23But in the eighteenth year of
King Josiah, this Passover was celebrated to the
LORD in Jerusalem.

24Furthermore, Josiah got rid of the mediums
and spiritists, the household gods, the idols and
all the other detestable things seen in Judah and
Jerusalem. This he did to fulfill the requirements of the law written in the book that Hilkiah the priest had discovered in the temple of the

[a] 8 Or *high places* [b] 10 Or *to make his son or daughter pass through* [c] 13 Hebrew *Milcom*

23:1–20 The revival under Josiah wasn't halfhearted. Unlike the moderate but incomplete restoration achieved by many of Judah's earlier kings, Josiah concluded that there could be no middle ground. Josiah destroyed all aspects of long-standing idol worship. He also reinstituted proper worship of the true God. As we seek spiritual renewal, we also must strive to completely purge sinful practices from our lives.

JOSIAH

The sinful patterns of parents are often duplicated in successive generations. Even those who do not want to be like their parents exhibit amazingly similar behaviors and personalities. But it is possible for us to break out of this ongoing spiral of sinful habits through God's power and our personal choices.

Josiah was a young king who chose to stand against a virtual tidal wave of disobedience fostered by his grandfather Manasseh and his father, Amon. Breaking out of this downward spiral was difficult since Josiah had received little instruction in God's ways to guide his actions. God's laws had been lost for years. But when Hilkiah, the high priest, discovered the Book of the Law in the temple, young Josiah immediately initiated spiritual renewal for himself and his people.

Josiah grew up in a time when idolatry and other forms of sinful behavior were an established norm. Josiah had to seek God on his own to discover God's standards for life and spiritual growth. Only then was Josiah able to embark on his own spiritual renewal and intervene in the sinful affairs of his nation. In time, Josiah was able to break the cycle of sin that had held Israel captive. Josiah possessed a faith and commitment to God as well as the courage to pursue both personal and national renewal.

In making his difficult choices, Josiah sought to break from the sins of the past and build a new life for himself and the people of Judah. Making a break from long-standing evil practices enabled the kingdom of Judah to proceed with positive reforms and a closer relationship with God, including one of the most joyful Passover celebrations that Israel had ever known. Josiah was not a perfect man, but he was a true champion of spiritual renewal. His stand for God's way redirected the course of his nation and made a significant impact on the lives of his people.

STRENGTHS AND ACCOMPLISHMENTS:

Josiah undertook the long and painful process of personal and national renewal.

He did away with idolatry and led the people to renew their commitment to God.

His heart was open to God's will, and Josiah was obedient to God's commands.

WEAKNESSES AND MISTAKES:

Josiah fought an unnecessary battle against King Neco of Egypt, which resulted in his own early death.

LESSONS FROM HIS LIFE:

We are never too young to pursue spiritual renewal or to help others around us.

One person of faith and courage can have a profound influence on those around them.

KEY VERSE:

"Neither before nor after Josiah was there a king like him who turned to the LORD as he did—with all his heart and with all his soul and with all his strength, in accordance with all the Law of Moses" (23:25).

Josiah's story is told in 2 Kings 21:24—23:30 and 2 Chronicles 33:25—35:27. He is also mentioned in Jeremiah 1:2–3; 3:6; 22:11–18; Zephaniah 1:1; and Matthew 1:10–11.

LORD. 25 Neither before nor after Josiah was
there a king like him who turned to the LORD as
he did—with all his heart and with all his soul
and with all his strength, in accordance with all
the Law of Moses.
26 Nevertheless, the LORD did not turn away
from the heat of his fierce anger, which burned
against Judah because of all that Manasseh had
done to provoke him to anger. 27 So the LORD
said, "I will remove Judah also from my presence as I removed Israel, and I will reject Jerusalem, the city I chose, and this temple, about
which I said, 'There shall my Name be.'[a]"
28 As for the other events of Josiah's reign, and
all he did, are they not written in the book of
the annals of the kings of Judah?
29 While Josiah was king, Pharaoh Neco king
of Egypt went up to the Euphrates River to help
the king of Assyria. King Josiah marched out
to meet him in battle, but Neco faced him
and killed him at Megiddo. 30 Josiah's servants
brought his body in a chariot from Megiddo to
Jerusalem and buried him in his own tomb.
And the people of the land took Jehoahaz son
of Josiah and anointed him and made him king
in place of his father.

Jehoahaz King of Judah

31 Jehoahaz was twenty-three years old when
he became king, and he reigned in Jerusalem
three months. His mother's name was Hamutal
daughter of Jeremiah; she was from Libnah.
32 He did evil in the eyes of the LORD, just as his
fathers had done. 33 Pharaoh Neco put him in
chains at Riblah in the land of Hamath[b] so
that he might not reign in Jerusalem, and he
imposed on Judah a levy of a hundred talents[c]
of silver and a talent[d] of gold. 34 Pharaoh Neco
made Eliakim son of Josiah king in place of his
father Josiah and changed Eliakim's name to
Jehoiakim. But he took Jehoahaz and carried
him off to Egypt, and there he died. 35 Jehoiakim
paid Pharaoh Neco the silver and gold he demanded. In order to do so, he taxed the land
and exacted the silver and gold from the people
of the land according to their assessments.

Jehoiakim King of Judah

36 Jehoiakim was twenty-five years old when
he became king, and he reigned in Jerusalem
eleven years. His mother's name was Zebidah
daughter of Pedaiah; she was from Rumah.
37 And he did evil in the eyes of the LORD, just
as his fathers had done.

24 During Jehoiakim's reign, Nebuchadnezzar king of Babylon invaded the
land, and Jehoiakim became his vassal for three
years. But then he changed his mind and rebelled against Nebuchadnezzar. 2 The LORD sent
Babylonian,[e] Aramean, Moabite and Ammonite raiders against him. He sent them to destroy
Judah, in accordance with the word of the LORD
proclaimed by his servants the prophets. 3 Surely these things happened to Judah according to
the LORD's command, in order to remove them
from his presence because of the sins of Manasseh and all he had done, 4 including the shedding of innocent blood. For he had filled Jerusalem with innocent blood, and the LORD was not
willing to forgive.
5 As for the other events of Jehoiakim's reign,
and all he did, are they not written in the book
of the annals of the kings of Judah? 6 Jehoiakim
rested with his fathers. And Jehoiachin his son
succeeded him as king.
7 The king of Egypt did not march out from
his own country again, because the king of Babylon had taken all his territory, from the Wadi
of Egypt to the Euphrates River.

Jehoiachin King of Judah

8 Jehoiachin was eighteen years old when he
became king, and he reigned in Jerusalem three
months. His mother's name was Nehushta
daughter of Elnathan; she was from Jerusalem.
9 He did evil in the eyes of the LORD, just as his
father had done.
10 At that time the officers of Nebuchadnezzar
king of Babylon advanced on Jerusalem and
laid siege to it, 11 and Nebuchadnezzar himself
came up to the city while his officers were besieging it. 12 Jehoiachin king of Judah, his mother, his attendants, his nobles and his officials all
surrendered to him.
In the eighth year of the reign of the king of
Babylon, he took Jehoiachin prisoner. 13 As the
LORD had declared, Nebuchadnezzar removed
all the treasures from the temple of the LORD
and from the royal palace, and took away all the
gold articles that Solomon king of Israel had
made for the temple of the LORD. 14 He carried
into exile all Jerusalem: all the officers and
fighting men, and all the craftsmen and artisans—a total of ten thousand. Only the poorest
people of the land were left.
15 Nebuchadnezzar took Jehoiachin captive
to Babylon. He also took from Jerusalem to
Babylon the king's mother, his wives, his officials and the leading men of the land. 16 The
king of Babylon also deported to Babylon the

[a] 27 1 Kings 8:29
[b] 33 Hebrew; Septuagint (see also 2 Chron. 36:3) *Neco at Riblah in Hamath removed him*
[c] 33 That is, about 3 3/4 tons (about 3.4 metric tons)
[d] 33 That is, about 75 pounds (about 34 kilograms)
[e] 2 Or *Chaldean*

23:36—24:4 The reign of King Jehoiakim of Judah was an eleven-year military and political nightmare. Rather than admitting his hopeless situation and turning to God, Jehoiakim tried to maneuver his own way out of each successive crisis. As disaster after disaster befell Jehoiakim, his spiritual blindness only deepened. He continued to trust in his own power and sank deeper into despair. There is no need for any of us to continue in the nightmare of sin. We must be willing to see the truth and face the reality of our situation. Then, when we turn to God for aid, he will help us to break out of our downward spiral.

entire force of seven thousand fighting men, strong and fit for war, and a thousand craftsmen and artisans. 17He made Mattaniah, Jehoiachin's uncle, king in his place and changed his name to Zedekiah.

Zedekiah King of Judah

18Zedekiah was twenty-one years old when he became king, and he reigned in Jerusalem eleven years. His mother's name was Hamutal daughter of Jeremiah; she was from Libnah. 19He did evil in the eyes of the LORD, just as Jehoiakim had done. 20It was because of the LORD's anger that all this happened to Jerusalem and Judah, and in the end he thrust them from his presence.

The Fall of Jerusalem

Now Zedekiah rebelled against the king of Babylon.

25 So in the ninth year of Zedekiah's reign, on the tenth day of the tenth month, Nebuchadnezzar king of Babylon marched against Jerusalem with his whole army. He encamped outside the city and built siege works all around it. 2The city was kept under siege until the eleventh year of King Zedekiah. 3By the ninth day of the ⌞fourth⌟[a] month the famine in the city had become so severe that there was no food for the people to eat. 4Then the city wall was broken through, and the whole army fled at night through the gate between the two walls near the king's garden, though the Babylonians[b] were surrounding the city. They fled toward the Arabah,[c] 5but the Babylonian[d] army pursued the king and overtook him in the plains of Jericho. All his soldiers were separated from him and scattered, 6and he was captured. He was taken to the king of Babylon at Riblah, where sentence was pronounced on him. 7They killed the sons of Zedekiah before his eyes. Then they put out his eyes, bound him with bronze shackles and took him to Babylon.

8On the seventh day of the fifth month, in the nineteenth year of Nebuchadnezzar king of Babylon, Nebuzaradan commander of the imperial guard, an official of the king of Babylon, came to Jerusalem. 9He set fire to the temple of the LORD, the royal palace and all the houses of Jerusalem. Every important building he burned down. 10The whole Babylonian army, under the commander of the imperial guard, broke down the walls around Jerusalem. 11Nebuzaradan the commander of the guard carried into exile the people who remained in the city, along with the rest of the populace and those who had gone over to the king of Babylon. 12But the commander left behind some of the poorest people of the land to work the vineyards and fields.

13The Babylonians broke up the bronze pillars, the movable stands and the bronze Sea that were at the temple of the LORD and they carried the bronze to Babylon. 14They also took away the pots, shovels, wick trimmers, dishes and all the bronze articles used in the temple service. 15The commander of the imperial guard took away the censers and sprinkling bowls—all that were made of pure gold or silver.

16The bronze from the two pillars, the Sea and the movable stands, which Solomon had made for the temple of the LORD, was more than could be weighed. 17Each pillar was twenty-seven feet[e] high. The bronze capital on top of one pillar was four and a half feet[f] high and was decorated with a network and pomegranates of bronze all around. The other pillar, with its network, was similar.

18The commander of the guard took as prisoners Seraiah the chief priest, Zephaniah the priest next in rank and the three doorkeepers. 19Of those still in the city, he took the officer in charge of the fighting men and five royal advisers. He also took the secretary who was chief officer in charge of conscripting the people of the land and sixty of his men who were found in the city. 20Nebuzaradan the commander took them all and brought them to the king of Babylon at Riblah. 21There at Riblah, in the land of Hamath, the king had them executed.

So Judah went into captivity, away from her land.

22Nebuchadnezzar king of Babylon appointed Gedaliah son of Ahikam, the son of Shaphan, to be over the people he had left behind in Judah. 23When all the army officers and their men heard that the king of Babylon had appointed Gedaliah as governor, they came to Gedaliah at Mizpah—Ishmael son of Nethaniah, Johanan son of Kareah, Seraiah son of Tanhumeth the Netophathite, Jaazaniah the son of the Maacathite, and their men. 24Gedaliah took an oath to reassure them and their men. "Do not be afraid of the Babylonian officials," he said. "Settle down in the land and serve the king of Babylon, and it will go well with you."

[a]3 See Jer. 52:6. [b]4 Or *Chaldeans;* also in verses 13, 25 and 26 [c]4 Or *the Jordan Valley* [d]5 Or *Chaldean;* also in verses 10 and 24 [e]17 Hebrew *eighteen cubits* (about 8.1 meters) [f]17 Hebrew *three cubits* (about 1.3 meters)

25:8–26 Like it or not, Judah finally had to face the truth. King Nebuchadnezzar ordered Jerusalem, the once proud capital of Judah, to be destroyed. He plundered the city and temple, carrying all its valuables off to Babylon. Realistically, the restoration of Judah was now humanly impossible. God's people needed a full-scale resurrection. Sometimes God has to allow us to come to a situation that is humanly impossible to bear. At that point we may become open to the possibility of the new life offered by Jesus Christ: "If anyone is in Christ, he is a new creation; the old has gone, the new has come!" (2 Corinthians 5:17). New life and restoration are possible no matter how impossible our situation. When we seek God's forgiveness and receive Jesus Christ into our lives, he will take away our sins and give us a new start; that is true spiritual renewal.

[25]In the seventh month, however, Ishmael son of Nethaniah, the son of Elishama, who was of royal blood, came with ten men and assassinated Gedaliah and also the men of Judah and the Babylonians who were with him at Mizpah. [26]At this, all the people from the least to the greatest, together with the army officers, fled to Egypt for fear of the Babylonians.

Jehoiachin Released

[27]In the thirty-seventh year of the exile of Jehoiachin king of Judah, in the year Evil-Merodach[a] became king of Babylon, he released Jehoiachin from prison on the twenty-seventh day of the twelfth month. [28]He spoke kindly to him and gave him a seat of honor higher than those of the other kings who were with him in Babylon. [29]So Jehoiachin put aside his prison clothes and for the rest of his life ate regularly at the king's table. [30]Day by day the king gave Jehoiachin a regular allowance as long as he lived.

[a]27 Also called *Amel-Marduk*

25:27–30 The kindness shown to captive King Jehoiachin by Evil-Merodach ends the tragic conclusion of Kings with a glimmer of hope. With the Babylonian exile and the destruction of Jerusalem the rule of the Davidic kings ended. Many of the exiled people lost all hope that God would still be with them. They might even have thought that God's promises to his people through Abraham and David were no longer valid. However, when they heard that Jehoiachin, one of David's descendants, was being treated well in exile, hope must have stirred in their heavy hearts. The story of the rebuilding after the exile shows us that God's promises were still valid. God planned for their restoration. Through this broken nation the King of kings, Jesus the Messiah, would be born. No matter how terrible a situation we face, there is hope for the future. Our sin has been paid for by the work of God's Son; God is still in the business of restoration.

1 CHRONICLES

The Big Picture

The book of 1 Chronicles was originally part of a larger book that also included 2 Chronicles. This larger work recorded Israel's history, starting with a genealogy of Adam's descendants and ending with the nation of Israel in Babylonian captivity. This condensed history of Israel was written to give a new generation of Israelites hope as they began to rebuild their homeland after the exile.

The primary focus of 1 Chronicles is the reign of King David, an example for the people to follow. The writer glosses quickly over David's faults, focusing primarily on the positive aspects of his reign.

The first nine chapters of 1 Chronicles record the ancestry of Israel from the dawn of history to the time of Israel's return from Babylon. The genealogical list emphasizes the royal line of David, which remained unbroken even through the terrible years of exile. This would have encouraged the new generation of Israelites as they sought to rebuild their broken nation. While in exile, many had begun to think that God had abandoned them. The survival of David's descendants would have reassured them of God's care and provided them hope for the future.

The second half of 1 Chronicles records the events of David's reign, emphasizing his role in leading the people's worship of God. Though David was never allowed to build God's temple, God promised to build a royal "house" for him, pledging that David's descendants would reign forever. This promise was the basis for Israel's hope upon their return from exile. They saw that David's descendants were still among them. Clearly, despite Israel's past disobedience, God had not abandoned them. God would restore his chosen people.

A. ANTICIPATING DAVID'S REIGN (1:1–9:44)

B. THE REIGN OF DAVID (10:1–29:30)

1. The Passing of Saul (10:1-14)
2. The Accession of David (11:1–12:40)
3. David and the Ark of God (13:1–17:27)
4. The Accounts of David's Wars (18:1–20:8)
5. The Census Taken by David (21:1-30)
6. The Arrangements for the Temple (22:1–29:30)

Spiritual Renewal Themes

THE POWER OF GRACE

David's life story is filled with examples of God's grace. David was no stranger to sin. In the books of Samuel he committed adultery and murder. In 1 Chronicles David proved to be impulsive. Though his intentions were good, David failed to listen to God's plan for bringing the ark to Jerusalem. His hasty decision led to the death of Uzzah. The main theme of this book, however, is not David's failure but his ability to learn from his fail-

Essential Facts

PURPOSE:
To record the history of David's reign and to encourage and admonish the people of Israel as they sought to rebuild their homeland after the Babylonian exile.

AUTHOR:
Unknown, but ancient tradition suggests that Ezra was the author.

AUDIENCE:
The people of Israel after their return from exile in Babylon.

DATE WRITTEN:
Approximately 430 B.C.

SETTING:
The period of David's reign over Israel during the eleventh century B.C.

KEY VERSE:
"And David knew that the LORD had established him as king over Israel and that his kingdom had been highly exalted for the sake of his people Israel" (14:2).

KEY PEOPLE:
David, Solomon.

ures. David had a soft heart that accepted God's correction and understood God's loving forgiveness. It was his openness to God's grace that set David apart from the other kings of Israel. David knew the pain of sin's separation and the joy of God's forgiveness.

THE IMPORTANCE OF WORSHIP
David knew how to worship. His heart was an open book before God, and David's worship of God was central to his being. He praised God corporately as well as privately. David's example should inspire us to make worship an essential part of our relationship with God. As we praise and thank God for who he is, we will find ourselves changed and spiritually renewed.

BEYOND PERSONAL SPIRITUAL RENEWAL
David was able to see beyond himself to the needs of others. Though he would never live long enough to enjoy much of what he had arranged for during his lifetime, David invested his time and possessions in things that would minister to others for centuries to come. He collected materials for the temple. He organized the priests and Levites for their work there. We also need to look beyond ourselves and seek to assist others with their spiritual growth as well.

LEARNING TO ACCEPT NO FOR AN ANSWER
David had great plans for Israel. He was a dreamer; he could see great things ahead. But God had greater plans for David. While David assumed that he would build God's temple, God said no. Often, when God says no to us, we withdraw, argue, or feel rejected. Spiritual growth involves not only learning how to *say* no to those things outside God's will but also how to *accept* the no to our plans that might come from God himself or from his people.

Historical Records From Adam to Abraham

To Noah's Sons

1 Adam, Seth, Enosh, 2Kenan, Mahalalel, Jared, 3Enoch, Methuselah, Lamech, Noah.

4The sons of Noah:[a]
Shem, Ham and Japheth.

The Japhethites

5The sons[b] of Japheth:
Gomer, Magog, Madai, Javan, Tubal, Meshech and Tiras.
6The sons of Gomer:
Ashkenaz, Riphath[c] and Togarmah.
7The sons of Javan:
Elishah, Tarshish, the Kittim and the Rodanim.

The Hamites

8The sons of Ham:
Cush, Mizraim,[d] Put and Canaan.
9The sons of Cush:
Seba, Havilah, Sabta, Raamah and Sabteca.
The sons of Raamah:
Sheba and Dedan.
10Cush was the father[e] of
Nimrod, who grew to be a mighty warrior on earth.
11Mizraim was the father of
the Ludites, Anamites, Lehabites, Naphtuhites, 12Pathrusites, Casluhites (from whom the Philistines came) and Caphtorites.
13Canaan was the father of
Sidon his firstborn,[f] and of the Hittites, 14Jebusites, Amorites, Girgashites, 15Hivites, Arkites, Sinites, 16Arvadites, Zemarites and Hamathites.

The Semites

17The sons of Shem:
Elam, Asshur, Arphaxad, Lud and Aram.
The sons of Aram[g]:
Uz, Hul, Gether and Meshech.
18Arphaxad was the father of Shelah,
and Shelah the father of Eber.
19Two sons were born to Eber:
One was named Peleg,[h] because in his time the earth was divided; his brother was named Joktan.
20Joktan was the father of
Almodad, Sheleph, Hazarmaveth, Jerah, 21Hadoram, Uzal, Diklah, 22Obal,[i] Abimael, Sheba, 23Ophir, Havilah and Jobab. All these were sons of Joktan.

24Shem, Arphaxad,[j] Shelah,
25Eber, Peleg, Reu,
26Serug, Nahor, Terah
27and Abram (that is, Abraham).

The Family of Abraham

28The sons of Abraham:
Isaac and Ishmael.

Descendants of Hagar

29These were their descendants:
Nebaioth the firstborn of Ishmael, Kedar, Adbeel, Mibsam, 30Mishma, Dumah, Massa, Hadad, Tema, 31Jetur, Naphish and Kedemah. These were the sons of Ishmael.

Descendants of Keturah

32The sons born to Keturah, Abraham's concubine:
Zimran, Jokshan, Medan, Midian, Ishbak and Shuah.
The sons of Jokshan:
Sheba and Dedan.
33The sons of Midian:
Ephah, Epher, Hanoch, Abida and Eldaah.
All these were descendants of Keturah.

Descendants of Sarah

34Abraham was the father of Isaac.
The sons of Isaac:
Esau and Israel.

Esau's Sons

35The sons of Esau:

[a] 4 Septuagint; Hebrew does not have *The sons of Noah:*
[b] 5 *Sons* may mean *descendants* or *successors* or *nations;* also in verses 6-10, 17 and 20.
[c] 6 Many Hebrew manuscripts and Vulgate (see also Septuagint and Gen. 10:3); most Hebrew manuscripts *Diphath*
[d] 8 That is, Egypt; also in verse 11
[e] 10 *Father* may mean *ancestor* or *predecessor* or *founder;* also in verses 11, 13, 18 and 20.
[f] 13 Or *of the Sidonians, the foremost*
[g] 17 One Hebrew manuscript and some Septuagint manuscripts (see also Gen. 10:23); most Hebrew manuscripts do not have this line.
[h] 19 *Peleg* means *division.*
[i] 22 Some Hebrew manuscripts and Syriac (see also Gen. 10:28); most Hebrew manuscripts *Ebal*
[j] 24 Hebrew; some Septuagint manuscripts *Arphaxad, Cainan* (see also note at Gen. 11:10)

1:1 As the father of the human race, Adam is in a way the "head of our family." We often are prone to blame our environment or family background for the mistakes we make. Living in the perfect surroundings of Eden, Adam couldn't use his environment as an excuse for his sin (see Genesis 2). Adam had no choice but to take responsibility for his actions. Blaming our environment or circumstances for the sins we commit will never lead us to spiritual renewal. Each of us must accept responsibility for our sin and ask God to help us redirect our course to correct them.

1:1 "Adam, Seth, Enosh." Notice that neither Cain nor Abel followed Adam in the genealogy of Israel. Genesis 4 records how Cain committed the first murder by killing his brother Abel. One of the consequences of Adam and Eve's first sin was a deeply troubled family. Note, however, that despite Cain and Abel's failure to leave descendants in Israel's ancestry, God provided Adam's broken family with a new start in another son named Seth.

Eliphaz, Reuel, Jeush, Jalam and Korah.
36The sons of Eliphaz:
Teman, Omar, Zepho,[a] Gatam and Kenaz;
by Timna: Amalek.[b]
37The sons of Reuel:
Nahath, Zerah, Shammah and Mizzah.

The People of Seir in Edom

38The sons of Seir:
Lotan, Shobal, Zibeon, Anah, Dishon, Ezer and Dishan.
39The sons of Lotan:
Hori and Homam. Timna was Lotan's sister.
40The sons of Shobal:
Alvan,[c] Manahath, Ebal, Shepho and Onam.
The sons of Zibeon:
Aiah and Anah.
41The son of Anah:
Dishon.
The sons of Dishon:
Hemdan,[d] Eshban, Ithran and Keran.
42The sons of Ezer:
Bilhan, Zaavan and Akan.[e]
The sons of Dishan[f]:
Uz and Aran.

The Rulers of Edom

43These were the kings who reigned in Edom before any Israelite king reigned[g]:
Bela son of Beor, whose city was named Dinhabah.
44When Bela died, Jobab son of Zerah from Bozrah succeeded him as king.
45When Jobab died, Husham from the land of the Temanites succeeded him as king.
46When Husham died, Hadad son of Bedad, who defeated Midian in the country of Moab, succeeded him as king. His city was named Avith.
47When Hadad died, Samlah from Masrekah succeeded him as king.
48When Samlah died, Shaul from Rehoboth on the river[h] succeeded him as king.
49When Shaul died, Baal-Hanan son of Acbor succeeded him as king.
50When Baal-Hanan died, Hadad succeeded him as king. His city was named Pau,[i] and his wife's name was Mehetabel daughter of Matred, the daughter of Me-Zahab. 51Hadad also died.

The chiefs of Edom were:
Timna, Alvah, Jetheth, 52Oholibamah, Elah, Pinon, 53Kenaz, Teman, Mibzar, 54Magdiel and Iram. These were the chiefs of Edom.

Israel's Sons

2 These were the sons of Israel:
Reuben, Simeon, Levi, Judah, Issachar, Zebulun, 2Dan, Joseph, Benjamin, Naphtali, Gad and Asher.

Judah

To Hezron's Sons

3The sons of Judah:
Er, Onan and Shelah. These three were born to him by a Canaanite woman, the daughter of Shua. Er, Judah's firstborn, was wicked in the LORD's sight; so the LORD put him to death. 4Tamar, Judah's daughter-in-law, bore him Perez and Zerah. Judah had five sons in all.

5The sons of Perez:
Hezron and Hamul.
6The sons of Zerah:
Zimri, Ethan, Heman, Calcol and Darda[j]—five in all.
7The son of Carmi:
Achar,[k] who brought trouble on Israel by violating the ban on taking devoted things.[l]
8The son of Ethan:
Azariah.
9The sons born to Hezron were:
Jerahmeel, Ram and Caleb.[m]

[a]36 Many Hebrew manuscripts, some Septuagint manuscripts and Syriac (see also Gen. 36:11); most Hebrew manuscripts *Zephi* [b]36 Some Septuagint manuscripts (see also Gen. 36:12); Hebrew *Gatam, Kenaz, Timna and Amalek* [c]40 Many Hebrew manuscripts and some Septuagint manuscripts (see also Gen. 36:23); most Hebrew manuscripts *Alian* [d]41 Many Hebrew manuscripts and some Septuagint manuscripts (see also Gen. 36:26); most Hebrew manuscripts *Hamran* [e]42 Many Hebrew and Septuagint manuscripts (see also Gen. 36:27); most Hebrew manuscripts *Zaavan, Jaakan* [f]42 Hebrew *Dishon,* a variant of *Dishan* [g]43 Or *before an Israelite king reigned over them* [h]48 Possibly the Euphrates [i]50 Many Hebrew manuscripts, some Septuagint manuscripts, Vulgate and Syriac (see also Gen. 36:39); most Hebrew manuscripts *Pai* [j]6 Many Hebrew manuscripts, some Septuagint manuscripts and Syriac (see also 1 Kings 4:31); most Hebrew manuscripts *Dara* [k]7 *Achar* means *trouble; Achar* is called *Achan* in Joshua. [l]7 The Hebrew term refers to the irrevocable giving over of things or persons to the LORD, often by totally destroying them. [m]9 Hebrew *Kelubai,* a variant of *Caleb*

2:3–15 Many regard these verses as merely a boring list of people in David's ancestry, the family line of the promised Messiah. Among these names, however, are stories of God's grace. Notice that the Messiah's line comes through an illegitimate union between Judah and Tamar (2:4; see Genesis 38). Notice also that the line passes through Salmon, who fathered Boaz through Rahab, a former Canaanite prostitute from Jericho (see Joshua 2). Boaz bore Obed through Ruth, a Moabite woman (Ruth 1—4). God used numerous people, some less than ideal, to bring his Messiah into the world. God can also use us significantly in his plan, no matter what our past.

From Ram Son of Hezron

10Ram was the father of
Amminadab, and Amminadab the father of Nahshon, the leader of the people of Judah. 11Nahshon was the father
of Salmon,[a] Salmon the father of
Boaz, 12Boaz the father of Obed and
Obed the father of Jesse.
13Jesse was the father of
Eliab his firstborn; the second son was
Abinadab, the third Shimea, 14the
fourth Nethanel, the fifth Raddai,
15the sixth Ozem and the seventh David. 16Their sisters were Zeruiah and
Abigail. Zeruiah's three sons were
Abishai, Joab and Asahel. 17Abigail
was the mother of Amasa, whose father was Jether the Ishmaelite.

Caleb Son of Hezron

18Caleb son of Hezron had children by his
wife Azubah (and by Jerioth). These
were her sons: Jesher, Shobab and Ar-
don. 19When Azubah died, Caleb married Ephrath, who bore him Hur.
20Hur was the father of Uri, and Uri
the father of Bezalel.
21Later, Hezron lay with the daughter of
Makir the father of Gilead (he had
married her when he was sixty years
old), and she bore him Segub. 22Segub
was the father of Jair, who controlled
twenty-three towns in Gilead. 23(But
Geshur and Aram captured Havvoth
Jair,[b] as well as Kenath with its surrounding settlements—sixty towns.)
All these were descendants of Makir
the father of Gilead.

24After Hezron died in Caleb Ephrathah,
Abijah the wife of Hezron bore him
Ashhur the father[c] of Tekoa.

Jerahmeel Son of Hezron

25The sons of Jerahmeel the firstborn of
Hezron:
Ram his firstborn, Bunah, Oren, Ozem
and[d] Ahijah. 26Jerahmeel had another wife, whose name was Atarah; she
was the mother of Onam.
27The sons of Ram the firstborn of Jerahmeel:
Maaz, Jamin and Eker.
28The sons of Onam:
Shammai and Jada.
The sons of Shammai:
Nadab and Abishur.
29Abishur's wife was named Abihail, who
bore him Ahban and Molid.
30The sons of Nadab:
Seled and Appaim. Seled died without
children.
31The son of Appaim:
Ishi, who was the father of Sheshan.
Sheshan was the father of Ahlai.
32The sons of Jada, Shammai's brother:
Jether and Jonathan. Jether died without children.
33The sons of Jonathan:
Peleth and Zaza.
These were the descendants of Jerahmeel.
34Sheshan had no sons—only daughters.
He had an Egyptian servant named Jarha. 35Sheshan gave his daughter in
marriage to his servant Jarha, and she
bore him Attai.
36Attai was the father of Nathan,
Nathan the father of Zabad,
37Zabad the father of Ephlal,
Ephlal the father of Obed,
38Obed the father of Jehu,
Jehu the father of Azariah,
39Azariah the father of Helez,
Helez the father of Eleasah,
40Eleasah the father of Sismai,
Sismai the father of Shallum,
41Shallum the father of Jekamiah,
and Jekamiah the father of Elishama.

The Clans of Caleb

42The sons of Caleb the brother of Jerahmeel:
Mesha his firstborn, who was the father of Ziph, and his son Mareshah,[e]
who was the father of Hebron.
43The sons of Hebron:
Korah, Tappuah, Rekem and Shema.
44Shema was the father of Raham, and
Raham the father of Jorkeam. Rekem
was the father of Shammai. 45The son
of Shammai was Maon, and Maon was
the father of Beth Zur.
46Caleb's concubine Ephah was the mother
of Haran, Moza and Gazez. Haran was
the father of Gazez.
47The sons of Jahdai:
Regem, Jotham, Geshan, Pelet, Ephah
and Shaaph.
48Caleb's concubine Maacah was the mother of Sheber and Tirhanah. 49She also

[a] *11* Septuagint (see also Ruth 4:21); Hebrew *Salma*
[b] *23* Or *captured the settlements of Jair* [c] *24* *Father* may mean *civic leader* or *military leader*; also in verses 42, 45, 49-52 and possibly elsewhere. [d] *25* Or *Oren and Ozem, by* [e] *42* The meaning of the Hebrew for this phrase is uncertain.

2:42–55 God rewards faith. This entire section is devoted to the family of Caleb, one of the twelve spies sent by Moses into Canaan (see Numbers 13). Caleb, along with Joshua, brought a positive report based entirely upon his faith in God's provision. He refused to be discouraged by difficult obstacles, believing that God could overcome all of them. We need not be stopped by our difficult circumstances either. Like Caleb, we should remember that God is able to overcome anything we might face. God is the source of true victory.

gave birth to Shaaph the father of
Madmannah and to Sheva the father
of Macbenah and Gibea. Caleb's
daughter was Acsah. 50 These were the
descendants of Caleb.

The sons of Hur the firstborn of Ephra-
thah:
Shobal the father of Kiriath Jearim,
51 Salma the father of Bethlehem, and
Hareph the father of Beth Gader.
52 The descendants of Shobal the father of
Kiriath Jearim were:
Haroeh, half the Manahathites, 53 and
the clans of Kiriath Jearim: the Ithrites,
Puthites, Shumathites and Mishraites.
From these descended the Zorathites
and Eshtaolites.
54 The descendants of Salma:
Bethlehem, the Netophathites, Atroth
Beth Joab, half the Manahathites, the
Zorites, 55 and the clans of scribes[a]
who lived at Jabez: the Tirathites,
Shimeathites and Sucathites. These are
the Kenites who came from Hammath,
the father of the house of Recab.[b]

The Sons of David

3 These were the sons of David born to him
in Hebron:
The firstborn was Amnon the son of
Ahinoam of Jezreel;
the second, Daniel the son of Abigail
of Carmel;
2 the third, Absalom the son of Maacah
daughter of Talmai king of Geshur;
the fourth, Adonijah the son of Haggith;
3 the fifth, Shephatiah the son of Abital;
and the sixth, Ithream, by his wife
Eglah.
4 These six were born to David in Hebron, where he reigned seven years
and six months.
David reigned in Jerusalem thirty-three years,
5 and these were the children born to him there:
Shammua,[c] Shobab, Nathan and Sol-
omon. These four were by Bathsheba[d] daughter of Ammiel. 6 There were
also Ibhar, Elishua,[e] Eliphelet, 7 No-
gah, Nepheg, Japhia, 8 Elishama, Eliada
and Eliphelet—nine in all. 9 All these
were the sons of David, besides his
sons by his concubines. And Tamar
was their sister.

The Kings of Judah

10 Solomon's son was Rehoboam,
Abijah his son,
Asa his son,
Jehoshaphat his son,
11 Jehoram[f] his son,
Ahaziah his son,
Joash his son,
12 Amaziah his son,
Azariah his son,
Jotham his son,
13 Ahaz his son,
Hezekiah his son,
Manasseh his son,
14 Amon his son,
Josiah his son.
15 The sons of Josiah:
Johanan the firstborn,
Jehoiakim the second son,
Zedekiah the third,
Shallum the fourth.
16 The successors of Jehoiakim:
Jehoiachin[g] his son,
and Zedekiah.

The Royal Line After the Exile

17 The descendants of Jehoiachin the cap-
tive:
Shealtiel his son, 18 Malkiram, Pedaiah,
Shenazzar, Jekamiah, Hoshama and
Nedabiah.
19 The sons of Pedaiah:
Zerubbabel and Shimei.
The sons of Zerubbabel:
Meshullam and Hananiah.
Shelomith was their sister.
20 There were also five others:
Hashubah, Ohel, Berekiah, Hasadiah
and Jushab-Hesed.
21 The descendants of Hananiah:
Pelatiah and Jeshaiah, and the sons of
Rephaiah, of Arnan, of Obadiah and
of Shecaniah.
22 The descendants of Shecaniah:
Shemaiah and his sons:
Hattush, Igal, Bariah, Neariah and
Shaphat—six in all.
23 The sons of Neariah:
Elioenai, Hizkiah and Azrikam—three
in all.
24 The sons of Elioenai:
Hodaviah, Eliashib, Pelaiah, Akkub,
Johanan, Delaiah and Anani—seven in
all.

[a]55 Or *of the Sopherites* [b]55 Or *father of Beth Recab*
[c]5 Hebrew *Shimea,* a variant of *Shammua* [d]5 One Hebrew manuscript and Vulgate (see also Septuagint and 2 Samuel 11:3); most Hebrew manuscripts *Bathshua*
[e]6 Two Hebrew manuscripts (see also 2 Samuel 5:15 and 1 Chron. 14:5); most Hebrew manuscripts *Elishama*
[f]11 Hebrew *Joram,* a variant of *Jehoram* [g]16 Hebrew *Jeconiah,* a variant of *Jehoiachin;* also in verse 17

3:1–24 This chapter is devoted entirely to the family of David. It is the most important of the genealogies in that it contains the line of the promised Messiah. Many of these names are cited in the New Testament genealogies of Jesus in the books of Matthew and Luke. Just as the entire Old Testament looks forward to Jesus the Messiah, we also must look to Jesus if we hope to experience a meaningful future.

Other Clans of Judah

4 The descendants of Judah:
Perez, Hezron, Carmi, Hur and Shobal.
2 Reaiah son of Shobal was the father of
Jahath, and Jahath the father of Ahumai
and Lahad. These were the clans of
the Zorathites.
3 These were the sons[a] of Etam:
Jezreel, Ishma and Idbash. Their sister
was named Hazzelelponi. 4 Penuel was
the father of Gedor, and Ezer the father
of Hushah.
These were the descendants of Hur, the
firstborn of Ephrathah and father[b] of
Bethlehem.
5 Ashhur the father of Tekoa had two
wives, Helah and Naarah.
6 Naarah bore him Ahuzzam, Hepher,
Temeni and Haahashtari. These were
the descendants of Naarah.
7 The sons of Helah:
Zereth, Zohar, Ethnan, 8 and Koz, who
was the father of Anub and Hazzobebah
and of the clans of Aharhel son of
Harum.

9 Jabez was more honorable than his brothers.
His mother had named him Jabez,[c] saying,
"I gave birth to him in pain." 10 Jabez cried
out to the God of Israel, "Oh, that you would
bless me and enlarge my territory! Let your
hand be with me, and keep me from harm so
that I will be free from pain." And God granted
his request.

11 Kelub, Shuhah's brother, was the father
of Mehir, who was the father of Eshton.
12 Eshton was the father of Beth
Rapha, Paseah and Tehinnah the father
of Ir Nahash.[d] These were the
men of Recah.

13 The sons of Kenaz:
Othniel and Seraiah.
The sons of Othniel:
Hathath and Meonothai.[e] 14 Meonothai
was the father of Ophrah.
Seraiah was the father of Joab,
the father of Ge Harashim.[f] It was
called this because its people were
craftsmen.
15 The sons of Caleb son of Jephunneh:
Iru, Elah and Naam.
The son of Elah:
Kenaz.
16 The sons of Jehallelel:
Ziph, Ziphah, Tiria and Asarel.
17 The sons of Ezrah:
Jether, Mered, Epher and Jalon. One of
Mered's wives gave birth to Miriam,
Shammai and Ishbah the father of
Eshtemoa. 18 (His Judean wife gave
birth to Jered the father of Gedor, Heber
the father of Soco, and Jekuthiel
the father of Zanoah.) These were the
children of Pharaoh's daughter Bithiah,
whom Mered had married.
19 The sons of Hodiah's wife, the sister of
Naham:
the father of Keilah the Garmite, and
Eshtemoa the Maacathite.
20 The sons of Shimon:
Amnon, Rinnah, Ben-Hanan and Tilon.
The descendants of Ishi:
Zoheth and Ben-Zoheth.
21 The sons of Shelah son of Judah:
Er the father of Lecah, Laadah the father
of Mareshah and the clans of the
linen workers at Beth Ashbea, 22 Jokim,
the men of Cozeba, and Joash and Saraph,
who ruled in Moab and Jashubi
Lehem. (These records are from ancient
times.) 23 They were the potters
who lived at Netaim and Gederah;
they stayed there and worked for the
king.

Simeon

24 The descendants of Simeon:
Nemuel, Jamin, Jarib, Zerah and
Shaul;
25 Shallum was Shaul's son, Mibsam his
son and Mishma his son.
26 The descendants of Mishma:
Hammuel his son, Zaccur his son and
Shimei his son.

27 Shimei had sixteen sons and six daughters,
but his brothers did not have many children; so
their entire clan did not become as numerous as
the people of Judah. 28 They lived in Beersheba,
Moladah, Hazar Shual, 29 Bilhah, Ezem, Tolad,
30 Bethuel, Hormah, Ziklag, 31 Beth Marcaboth,
Hazar Susim, Beth Biri and Shaaraim. These
were their towns until the reign of David.
32 Their surrounding villages were Etam, Ain,
Rimmon, Token and Ashan—five towns— 33 and
all the villages around these towns as far as
Baalath.[g] These were their settlements. And
they kept a genealogical record.

34 Meshobab, Jamlech, Joshah son of Amaziah,
35 Joel, Jehu son of Joshibiah, the son
of Seraiah, the son of Asiel, 36 also Elioenai,
Jaakobah, Jeshohaiah, Asaiah, Adiel,
Jesimiel, Benaiah, 37 and Ziza son of Shiphi,
the son of Allon, the son of Jedaiah,
the son of Shimri, the son of Shemaiah.

38 The men listed above by name were leaders
of their clans. Their families increased greatly,

[a] 3 Some Septuagint manuscripts (see also Vulgate); Hebrew *father* [b] 4 *Father* may mean *civic leader* or *military leader*; also in verses 12, 14, 17, 18 and possibly elsewhere. [c] 9 *Jabez* sounds like the Hebrew for *pain*. [d] 12 Or *of the city of Nahash* [e] 13 Some Septuagint manuscripts and Vulgate; Hebrew does not have *and Meonothai*. [f] 14 *Ge Harashim* means *valley of craftsmen*. [g] 33 Some Septuagint manuscripts (see also Joshua 19:8); Hebrew *Baal*

39and they went to the outskirts of Gedor to the
east of the valley in search of pasture for their
flocks. 40They found rich, good pasture, and the
land was spacious, peaceful and quiet. Some
Hamites had lived there formerly.

41The men whose names were listed came in
the days of Hezekiah king of Judah. They attacked the Hamites in their dwellings and also
the Meunites who were there and completely
destroyed[a] them, as is evident to this day.
Then they settled in their place, because there
was pasture for their flocks. 42And five hundred
of these Simeonites, led by Pelatiah, Neariah,
Rephaiah and Uzziel, the sons of Ishi, invaded
the hill country of Seir. 43They killed the remaining Amalekites who had escaped, and they
have lived there to this day.

Reuben

5 The sons of Reuben the firstborn of Israel
(he was the firstborn, but when he defiled
his father's marriage bed, his rights as firstborn
were given to the sons of Joseph son of Israel;
so he could not be listed in the genealogical
record in accordance with his birthright, 2and
though Judah was the strongest of his brothers
and a ruler came from him, the rights of the
firstborn belonged to Joseph)— 3the sons of
Reuben the firstborn of Israel:

Hanoch, Pallu, Hezron and Carmi.

4The descendants of Joel:

Shemaiah his son, Gog his son,
Shimei his son, 5Micah his son,
Reaiah his son, Baal his son,
6and Beerah his son, whom Tiglath-
Pileser[b] king of Assyria took into exile. Beerah was a leader of the Reubenites.

7Their relatives by clans, listed according
to their genealogical records:

Jeiel the chief, Zechariah, 8and Bela
son of Azaz, the son of Shema, the son
of Joel. They settled in the area from
Aroer to Nebo and Baal Meon. 9To the
east they occupied the land up to the
edge of the desert that extends to
the Euphrates River, because their livestock had increased in Gilead.

10During Saul's reign they waged war
against the Hagrites, who were defeated
at their hands; they occupied the dwellings of the Hagrites throughout the entire
region east of Gilead.

Gad

11The Gadites lived next to them in Bashan,
as far as Salecah:

12Joel was the chief, Shapham the second, then Janai and Shaphat, in Bashan.

13Their relatives, by families, were:

Michael, Meshullam, Sheba, Jorai, Ja-
can, Zia and Eber—seven in all.

14These were the sons of Abihail son of
Huri, the son of Jaroah, the son of Gil-
ead, the son of Michael, the son of
Jeshishai, the son of Jahdo, the son of
Buz.

15Ahi son of Abdiel, the son of Guni, was
head of their family.

16The Gadites lived in Gilead, in Bashan
and its outlying villages, and on all the
pasturelands of Sharon as far as they
extended.

17All these were entered in the genealogical
records during the reigns of Jotham king of Judah and Jeroboam king of Israel.

18The Reubenites, the Gadites and the half-
tribe of Manasseh had 44,760 men ready for
military service—able-bodied men who could
handle shield and sword, who could use a bow,
and who were trained for battle. 19They waged
war against the Hagrites, Jetur, Naphish and
Nodab. 20They were helped in fighting them,
and God handed the Hagrites and all their allies
over to them, because they cried out to him
during the battle. He answered their prayers,
because they trusted in him. 21They seized the
livestock of the Hagrites—fifty thousand camels,
two hundred fifty thousand sheep and two
thousand donkeys. They also took one hundred
thousand people captive, 22and many others
fell slain, because the battle was God's. And
they occupied the land until the exile.

The Half-Tribe of Manasseh

23The people of the half-tribe of Manasseh
were numerous; they settled in the land from
Bashan to Baal Hermon, that is, to Senir
(Mount Hermon).

24These were the heads of their families:
Epher, Ishi, Eliel, Azriel, Jeremiah, Hodaviah
and Jahdiel. They were brave warriors, famous
men, and heads of their families. 25But they
were unfaithful to the God of their fathers and
prostituted themselves to the gods of the peoples of the land, whom God had destroyed before them. 26So the God of Israel stirred up the
spirit of Pul king of Assyria (that is, Tiglath-
Pileser king of Assyria), who took the Reubenites, the Gadites and the half-tribe of Manasseh

[a]41 The Hebrew term refers to the irrevocable giving over of things or persons to the LORD, often by totally destroying them. [b]6 Hebrew *Tilgath-Pilneser,* a variant of *Tiglath-Pileser;* also in verse 26

5:1 After plowing through all these names, people usually wonder, *Why are these lists in the Bible?* Each of these names represents an individual and, in some cases, an entire family. It is obvious from this that God values individuals; he uses them to work out his plan. Most of these people are not well remembered in history. Some of them had major faults. But in reading these lists we realize that God cares for us—no matter who we are or what we've done.

into exile. He took them to Halah, Habor, Hara and the river of Gozan, where they are to this day.

Levi

6 The sons of Levi:
Gershon, Kohath and Merari.
2The sons of Kohath:
Amram, Izhar, Hebron and Uzziel.
3The children of Amram:
Aaron, Moses and Miriam.
The sons of Aaron:
Nadab, Abihu, Eleazar and Ithamar.
4Eleazar was the father of Phinehas,
Phinehas the father of Abishua,
5Abishua the father of Bukki,
Bukki the father of Uzzi,
6Uzzi the father of Zerahiah,
Zerahiah the father of Meraioth,
7Meraioth the father of Amariah,
Amariah the father of Ahitub,
8Ahitub the father of Zadok,
Zadok the father of Ahimaaz,
9Ahimaaz the father of Azariah,
Azariah the father of Johanan,
10Johanan the father of Azariah (it was he who served as priest in the temple Solomon built in Jerusalem),
11Azariah the father of Amariah,
Amariah the father of Ahitub,
12Ahitub the father of Zadok,
Zadok the father of Shallum,
13Shallum the father of Hilkiah,
Hilkiah the father of Azariah,
14Azariah the father of Seraiah,
and Seraiah the father of Jehozadak.
15Jehozadak was deported when the LORD sent Judah and Jerusalem into exile by the hand of Nebuchadnezzar.

16The sons of Levi:
Gershon,[a] Kohath and Merari.
17These are the names of the sons of Gershon:
Libni and Shimei.
18The sons of Kohath:
Amram, Izhar, Hebron and Uzziel.
19The sons of Merari:
Mahli and Mushi.
These are the clans of the Levites listed according to their fathers:
20Of Gershon:
Libni his son, Jehath his son,
Zimmah his son, 21Joah his son,
Iddo his son, Zerah his son
and Jeatherai his son.
22The descendants of Kohath:
Amminadab his son, Korah his son,
Assir his son, 23Elkanah his son,
Ebiasaph his son, Assir his son,
24Tahath his son, Uriel his son,
Uzziah his son and Shaul his son.
25The descendants of Elkanah:
Amasai, Ahimoth,
26Elkanah his son,[b] Zophai his son,
Nahath his son, 27Eliab his son,
Jeroham his son, Elkanah his son
and Samuel his son.[c]
28The sons of Samuel:
Joel[d] the firstborn
and Abijah the second son.
29The descendants of Merari:
Mahli, Libni his son,
Shimei his son, Uzzah his son,
30Shimea his son, Haggiah his son
and Asaiah his son.

The Temple Musicians

31These are the men David put in charge of the music in the house of the LORD after the ark came to rest there. 32They ministered with music before the tabernacle, the Tent of Meeting, until Solomon built the temple of the LORD in Jerusalem. They performed their duties according to the regulations laid down for them.
33Here are the men who served, together with their sons:
From the Kohathites:
Heman, the musician,
the son of Joel, the son of Samuel,
34the son of Elkanah, the son of Jeroham,
the son of Eliel, the son of Toah,
35the son of Zuph, the son of Elkanah,
the son of Mahath, the son of Amasai,
36the son of Elkanah, the son of Joel,
the son of Azariah, the son of Zephaniah,
37the son of Tahath, the son of Assir,
the son of Ebiasaph, the son of Korah,
38the son of Izhar, the son of Kohath,
the son of Levi, the son of Israel;

[a]*16* Hebrew *Gershom*, a variant of *Gershon*; also in verses 17, 20, 43, 62 and 71 [b]*26* Some Hebrew manuscripts, Septuagint and Syriac; most Hebrew manuscripts *Ahimoth* [26]*and Elkanah. The sons of Elkanah:* [c]*27* Some Septuagint manuscripts (see also 1 Samuel 1:19,20 and 1 Chron. 6:33,34); Hebrew does not have *and Samuel his son.* [d]*28* Some Septuagint manuscripts and Syriac (see also 1 Samuel 8:2 and 1 Chron. 6:33); Hebrew does not have *Joel.*

6:1–30 This chapter contains the priestly genealogy. In the Old Testament, the priests represented the people before God. Whenever any breach in fellowship was committed, the priests had to serve as mediators to effect reconciliation. Access to God is vital for us too. In the New Testament, Jesus Christ stands before God as our Mediator. Spiritual renewal begins here, for Christ makes it possible for us to deal with our sin and draw close to God.

6:31–48 These verses contain a genealogy of the family that led the Israelites in worship. Music and singing were vital parts of serving God in the temple, calling the people to express their thanks joyfully to God. Our worship of God needs to contain the element of joy too. Joy is an aspect of worship that is often ignored. Worship must never become rote—it should be a happy response to a good and loving God. It does not need to be an elaborate ceremony but can merely be simple thanks for God's grace, power, and rich blessings in our lives.

[39]and Heman's associate Asaph, who
served at his right hand:
Asaph son of Berekiah, the son of
Shimea,
[40]the son of Michael, the son of Baase-
iah,[a]
the son of Malkijah, [41]the son of Ethni,
the son of Zerah, the son of Adaiah,
[42]the son of Ethan, the son of Zimmah,
the son of Shimei, [43]the son of Jahath,
the son of Gershon, the son of Levi;
[44]and from their associates, the Merarites,
at his left hand:
Ethan son of Kishi, the son of Abdi,
the son of Malluch, [45]the son of Hashabiah,
the son of Amaziah, the son of Hilkiah,
[46]the son of Amzi, the son of Bani,
the son of Shemer, [47]the son of Mahli,
the son of Mushi, the son of Merari,
the son of Levi.

[48]Their fellow Levites were assigned to all the
other duties of the tabernacle, the house of
God. [49]But Aaron and his descendants were the
ones who presented offerings on the altar of
burnt offering and on the altar of incense in
connection with all that was done in the Most
Holy Place, making atonement for Israel, in accordance with all that Moses the servant of God
had commanded.

[50]These were the descendants of Aaron:
Eleazar his son, Phinehas his son,
Abishua his son, [51]Bukki his son,
Uzzi his son, Zerahiah his son,
[52]Meraioth his son, Amariah his son,
Ahitub his son, [53]Zadok his son
and Ahimaaz his son.

[54]These were the locations of their settlements allotted as their territory (they were assigned to the descendants of Aaron who were
from the Kohathite clan, because the first lot
was for them):

[55]They were given Hebron in Judah
with its surrounding pasturelands. [56]But
the fields and villages around the city were
given to Caleb son of Jephunneh.
[57]So the descendants of Aaron were giv-
en Hebron (a city of refuge), and Libnah,[b] Jattir, Eshtemoa, [58]Hilen, Debir,
[59]Ashan, Juttah[c] and Beth Shemesh, together with their pasturelands. [60]And from
the tribe of Benjamin they were given Gibeon,[d] Geba, Alemeth and Anathoth, together with their pasturelands.

These towns, which were distributed
among the Kohathite clans, were thirteen
in all.

[61]The rest of Kohath's descendants were allotted ten towns from the clans of half the tribe
of Manasseh.
[62]The descendants of Gershon, clan by clan,
were allotted thirteen towns from the tribes of
Issachar, Asher and Naphtali, and from the part
of the tribe of Manasseh that is in Bashan.
[63]The descendants of Merari, clan by clan,
were allotted twelve towns from the tribes of
Reuben, Gad and Zebulun.
[64]So the Israelites gave the Levites these
towns and their pasturelands. [65]From the tribes
of Judah, Simeon and Benjamin they allotted
the previously named towns.
[66]Some of the Kohathite clans were given as
their territory towns from the tribe of Ephraim.

[67]In the hill country of Ephraim they
were given Shechem (a city of refuge), and
Gezer,[e] [68]Jokmeam, Beth Horon, [69]Aija-
lon and Gath Rimmon, together with their
pasturelands.
[70]And from half the tribe of Manasseh
the Israelites gave Aner and Bileam, together with their pasturelands, to the rest
of the Kohathite clans.

[71]The Gershonites received the following:
From the clan of the half-tribe of Manasseh
they received Golan in Bashan and
also Ashtaroth, together with their pasturelands;
[72]from the tribe of Issachar
they received Kedesh, Daberath, [73]Ra-
moth and Anem, together with their
pasturelands;
[74]from the tribe of Asher
they received Mashal, Abdon, [75]Hukok
and Rehob, together with their pasturelands;
[76]and from the tribe of Naphtali
they received Kedesh in Galilee, Hammon and Kiriathaim, together with
their pasturelands.

[77]The Merarites (the rest of the Levites) received the following:
From the tribe of Zebulun
they received Jokneam, Kartah,[f] Rim-
mono and Tabor, together with their
pasturelands;
[78]from the tribe of Reuben across the Jordan east of Jericho
they received Bezer in the desert, Jahzah, [79]Kedemoth and Mephaath, together with their pasturelands;
[80]and from the tribe of Gad
they received Ramoth in Gilead, Mahanaim, [81]Heshbon and Jazer, together with their pasturelands.

[a]*40* Most Hebrew manuscripts; some Hebrew manuscripts, one Septuagint manuscript and Syriac *Maaseiah* [b]*57* See Joshua 21:13; Hebrew *given the cities of refuge: Hebron, Libnah.* [c]*59* Syriac (see also Septuagint and Joshua 21:16); Hebrew does not have *Juttah.* [d]*60* See Joshua 21:17; Hebrew does not have *Gibeon.* [e]*67* See Joshua 21:21; Hebrew *given the cities of refuge: Shechem, Gezer.* [f]*77* See Septuagint and Joshua 21:34; Hebrew does not have *Jokneam, Kartah.*

Issachar

7 The sons of Issachar:
Tola, Puah, Jashub and Shimron—four in all.
2The sons of Tola:
Uzzi, Rephaiah, Jeriel, Jahmai, Ibsam and Samuel—heads of their families. During the reign of David, the descendants of Tola listed as fighting men in their genealogy numbered 22,600.
3The son of Uzzi:
Izrahiah.
The sons of Izrahiah:
Michael, Obadiah, Joel and Isshiah. All five of them were chiefs. 4According to their family genealogy, they had 36,000 men ready for battle, for they had many wives and children.
5The relatives who were fighting men belonging to all the clans of Issachar, as listed in their genealogy, were 87,000 in all.

Benjamin

6Three sons of Benjamin:
Bela, Beker and Jediael.
7The sons of Bela:
Ezbon, Uzzi, Uzziel, Jerimoth and Iri, heads of families—five in all. Their genealogical record listed 22,034 fighting men.
8The sons of Beker:
Zemirah, Joash, Eliezer, Elioenai, Omri, Jeremoth, Abijah, Anathoth and Alemeth. All these were the sons of Beker. 9Their genealogical record listed the heads of families and 20,200 fighting men.
10The son of Jediael:
Bilhan.
The sons of Bilhan:
Jeush, Benjamin, Ehud, Kenaanah, Zethan, Tarshish and Ahishahar. 11All these sons of Jediael were heads of families. There were 17,200 fighting men ready to go out to war.
12The Shuppites and Huppites were the descendants of Ir, and the Hushites the descendants of Aher.

Naphtali

13The sons of Naphtali:
Jahziel, Guni, Jezer and Shillem[a]—the descendants of Bilhah.

Manasseh

14The descendants of Manasseh:
Asriel was his descendant through his Aramean concubine. She gave birth to Makir the father of Gilead. 15Makir took a wife from among the Huppites and Shuppites. His sister's name was Maacah.
Another descendant was named Zelophehad, who had only daughters.
16Makir's wife Maacah gave birth to a son and named him Peresh. His brother was named Sheresh, and his sons were Ulam and Rakem.
17The son of Ulam:
Bedan.
These were the sons of Gilead son of Makir, the son of Manasseh. 18His sister Hammoleketh gave birth to Ishhod, Abiezer and Mahlah.
19The sons of Shemida were:
Ahian, Shechem, Likhi and Aniam.

Ephraim

20The descendants of Ephraim:
Shuthelah, Bered his son,
Tahath his son, Eleadah his son,
Tahath his son, 21Zabad his son
and Shuthelah his son.
Ezer and Elead were killed by the native-born men of Gath, when they went down to seize their livestock.
22Their father Ephraim mourned for them many days, and his relatives came to comfort him. 23Then he lay with his wife again, and she became pregnant and gave birth to a son. He named him Beriah,[b] because there had been misfortune in his family. 24His daughter was Sheerah, who built Lower and Upper Beth Horon as well as Uzzen Sheerah.
25Rephah was his son, Resheph his son,[c]
Telah his son, Tahan his son,
26Ladan his son, Ammihud his son,
Elishama his son, 27Nun his son
and Joshua his son.
28Their lands and settlements included Bethel and its surrounding villages, Naaran to the east, Gezer and its villages to the west, and Shechem and its villages all the way to Ayyah and its villages. 29Along the borders of Manasseh were Beth Shan, Taanach, Megiddo and Dor, together with their villages. The descendants of Joseph son of Israel lived in these towns.

Asher

30The sons of Asher:
Imnah, Ishvah, Ishvi and Beriah. Their sister was Serah.
31The sons of Beriah:
Heber and Malkiel, who was the father of Birzaith.
32Heber was the father of Japhlet, Shomer and Hotham and of their sister Shua.
33The sons of Japhlet:
Pasach, Bimhal and Ashvath.
These were Japhlet's sons.

[a]*13* Some Hebrew and Septuagint manuscripts (see also Gen. 46:24 and Num. 26:49); most Hebrew manuscripts *Shallum* [b]*23* *Beriah* sounds like the Hebrew for *misfortune.* [c]*25* Some Septuagint manuscripts; Hebrew does not have *his son.*

34The sons of Shomer:
Ahi, Rohgah,[a] Hubbah and Aram.
35The sons of his brother Helem:
Zophah, Imna, Shelesh and Amal.
36The sons of Zophah:
Suah, Harnepher, Shual, Beri, Imrah,
37Bezer, Hod, Shamma, Shilshah, Ithran[b] and Beera.
38The sons of Jether:
Jephunneh, Pispah and Ara.
39The sons of Ulla:
Arah, Hanniel and Rizia.
40All these were descendants of Asher—heads of families, choice men, brave warriors and outstanding leaders. The number of men ready for battle, as listed in their genealogy, was 26,000.

The Genealogy of Saul the Benjamite

8 Benjamin was the father of Bela his firstborn,
Ashbel the second son, Aharah the third,
2Nohah the fourth and Rapha the fifth.
3The sons of Bela were:
Addar, Gera, Abihud,[c] 4Abishua, Naaman, Ahoah, 5Gera, Shephuphan and Huram.
6These were the descendants of Ehud, who were heads of families of those living in Geba and were deported to Manahath:
7Naaman, Ahijah, and Gera, who deported them and who was the father of Uzza and Ahihud.
8Sons were born to Shaharaim in Moab after he had divorced his wives Hushim and Baara.
9By his wife Hodesh he had Jobab, Zibia, Mesha, Malcam,
10Jeuz, Sakia and Mirmah. These were his sons, heads of families.
11By Hushim he had Abitub and Elpaal.
12The sons of Elpaal:
Eber, Misham, Shemed (who built Ono and Lod with its surrounding villages),
13and Beriah and Shema, who were heads of families of those living in Aijalon and who drove out the inhabitants of Gath.
14Ahio, Shashak, Jeremoth,
15Zebadiah, Arad, Eder,
16Michael, Ishpah and Joha were the sons of Beriah.
17Zebadiah, Meshullam, Hizki, Heber,
18Ishmerai, Izliah and Jobab were the sons of Elpaal.
19Jakim, Zicri, Zabdi,
20Elienai, Zillethai, Eliel,
21Adaiah, Beraiah and Shimrath were the sons of Shimei.
22Ishpan, Eber, Eliel,
23Abdon, Zicri, Hanan,
24Hananiah, Elam, Anthothijah,
25Iphdeiah and Penuel were the sons of Shashak.
26Shamsherai, Shehariah, Athaliah,
27Jaareshiah, Elijah and Zicri were the sons of Jeroham.
28All these were heads of families, chiefs as listed in their genealogy, and they lived in Jerusalem.

29Jeiel[d] the father[e] of Gibeon lived in Gibeon.
His wife's name was Maacah,
30and his firstborn son was Abdon, followed by Zur, Kish, Baal, Ner,[f] Nadab,
31Gedor, Ahio, Zeker
32and Mikloth, who was the father of Shimeah. They too lived near their relatives in Jerusalem.
33Ner was the father of Kish, Kish the father of Saul, and Saul the father of Jonathan, Malki-Shua, Abinadab and Esh-Baal.[g]
34The son of Jonathan:
Merib-Baal,[h] who was the father of Micah.
35The sons of Micah:
Pithon, Melech, Tarea and Ahaz.
36Ahaz was the father of Jehoaddah, Jehoaddah was the father of Alemeth, Azmaveth and Zimri, and Zimri was the father of Moza.
37Moza was the father of Binea; Raphah was his son, Eleasah his son and Azel his son.
38Azel had six sons, and these were their names:
Azrikam, Bokeru, Ishmael, Sheariah, Obadiah and Hanan. All these were the sons of Azel.
39The sons of his brother Eshek:
Ulam his firstborn, Jeush the second son and Eliphelet the third.
40The sons of Ulam were brave warriors who could handle the bow. They had many sons and grandsons—150 in all.
All these were the descendants of Benjamin.

9 All Israel was listed in the genealogies recorded in the book of the kings of Israel.

[a]34 Or *of his brother Shomer: Rohgah* [b]37 Possibly a variant of *Jether* [c]3 Or *Gera the father of Ehud* [d]29 Some Septuagint manuscripts (see also 1 Chron. 9:35); Hebrew does not have *Jeiel.* [e]29 *Father* may mean *civic leader* or *military leader.* [f]30 Some Septuagint manuscripts (see also 1 Chron. 9:36); Hebrew does not have *Ner.* [g]33 Also known as *Ish-Bosheth* [h]34 Also known as *Mephibosheth*

8:1–33 When the people demanded a king, God gave them Saul (see 1 Samuel 8—10). These verses contain an account of Saul's personal genealogy. Even though he was well received by the people, it soon became obvious that Saul was attempting to build his kingdom by utilizing only human resources. God must bless any plan or project, on a personal, national or spiritual level, if anything lasting is to result.

9:1–44 This chapter contains a record of the Jews who returned to Judah after their seventy-year Babylonian exile (539 B.C.). The books of 1 and 2 Chronicles were written to encourage these people as they rebuilt their nation. The temple had been destroyed, and the Davidic line of kings had been discontinued. It must have been a great

The People in Jerusalem

The people of Judah were taken captive to Babylon because of their unfaithfulness. [2]Now the first to resettle on their own property in their own towns were some Israelites, priests, Levites and temple servants.

[3]Those from Judah, from Benjamin, and from Ephraim and Manasseh who lived in Jerusalem were:

[4]Uthai son of Ammihud, the son of Omri, the son of Imri, the son of Bani, a descendant of Perez son of Judah.

[5]Of the Shilonites:

Asaiah the firstborn and his sons.

[6]Of the Zerahites:

Jeuel.

The people from Judah numbered 690.

[7]Of the Benjamites:

Sallu son of Meshullam, the son of Hodaviah, the son of Hassenuah;

[8]Ibneiah son of Jeroham; Elah son of Uzzi, the son of Micri; and Meshullam son of Shephatiah, the son of Reuel, the son of Ibnijah.

[9]The people from Benjamin, as listed in their genealogy, numbered 956. All these men were heads of their families.

[10]Of the priests:

Jedaiah; Jehoiarib; Jakin;

[11]Azariah son of Hilkiah, the son of Meshullam, the son of Zadok, the son of Meraioth, the son of Ahitub, the official in charge of the house of God;

[12]Adaiah son of Jeroham, the son of Pashhur, the son of Malkijah; and Maasai son of Adiel, the son of Jahzerah, the son of Meshullam, the son of Meshillemith, the son of Immer.

[13]The priests, who were heads of families, numbered 1,760. They were able men, responsible for ministering in the house of God.

[14]Of the Levites:

Shemaiah son of Hasshub, the son of Azrikam, the son of Hashabiah, a Merarite; [15]Bakbakkar, Heresh, Galal and Mattaniah son of Mica, the son of Zicri, the son of Asaph; [16]Obadiah son of Shemaiah, the son of Galal, the son of Jeduthun; and Berekiah son of Asa, the son of Elkanah, who lived in the villages of the Netophathites.

[17]The gatekeepers:

Shallum, Akkub, Talmon, Ahiman and their brothers, Shallum their chief [18]being stationed at the King's Gate on the east, up to the present time. These were the gatekeepers belonging to the camp of the Levites. [19]Shallum son of Kore, the son of Ebiasaph, the son of Korah, and his fellow gatekeepers from his family (the Korahites) were responsible for guarding the thresholds of the Tent[a] just as their fathers had been responsible for guarding the entrance to the dwelling of the LORD. [20]In earlier times Phinehas son of Eleazar was in charge of the gatekeepers, and the LORD was with him. [21]Zechariah son of Meshelemiah was the gatekeeper at the entrance to the Tent of Meeting.

[22]Altogether, those chosen to be gatekeepers at the thresholds numbered 212. They were registered by genealogy in their villages. The gatekeepers had been assigned to their positions of trust by David and Samuel the seer. [23]They and their descendants were in charge of guarding the gates of the house of the LORD—the house called the Tent. [24]The gatekeepers were on the four sides: east, west, north and south. [25]Their brothers in their villages had to come from time to time and share their duties for seven-day periods. [26]But the four principal gatekeepers, who were Levites, were entrusted with the responsibility for the rooms and treasuries in the house of God. [27]They would spend the night stationed around the house of God, because they had to guard it; and they had charge of the key for opening it each morning.

[28]Some of them were in charge of the articles used in the temple service; they counted them when they were brought in and when they were taken out. [29]Others were assigned to take care of the furnishings and all the other articles of the sanctuary, as well as the flour and wine, and the oil, incense and spices. [30]But some of the priests took care of mixing the spices. [31]A Levite named Mattithiah, the firstborn son of Shallum the Korahite, was entrusted with the responsibility for baking the offering bread. [32]Some of their Kohathite brothers were in charge of preparing for every Sabbath the bread set out on the table.

[33]Those who were musicians, heads of Levite families, stayed in the rooms of the temple and

[a]19 That is, the temple; also in verses 21 and 23

encouragement for them to see that they were still God's people. God had made promises to their ancestors, and though they had sinned and suffered the consequences, God's promises were still valid for them. In the Bible, God gives many promises to his people. In Christ, God's promises are for all of us to embrace, no matter what we have done or suffered in the past (see 2 Corinthians 1:20). We, too, are the people of God.

9:1 This passage reminds us of the primary reason for Israel's exile—the people had turned from God and worshiped idols. Exile was their punishment. The idols in our lives often lead us into similar states of exile. When we worship anything other than God, our values get distorted. We forget about God, our families and the other important things in life. But just as Israel was restored, we also can find restoration from our spiritual exile. Even when our past is filled with sin and failure, God has the power to give us a new start. All we need to do is repent and ask him.

were exempt from other duties because they were responsible for the work day and night.

34All these were heads of Levite families, chiefs as listed in their genealogy, and they lived in Jerusalem.

The Genealogy of Saul

35Jeiel the father[a] of Gibeon lived in Gibeon.
His wife's name was Maacah, 36and his firstborn son was Abdon, followed by Zur, Kish, Baal, Ner, Nadab, 37Gedor, Ahio, Zechariah and Mikloth. 38Mikloth was the father of Shimeam. They too lived near their relatives in Jerusalem.

39Ner was the father of Kish, Kish the father of Saul, and Saul the father of Jonathan, Malki-Shua, Abinadab and Esh-Baal.[b]

40The son of Jonathan:
Merib-Baal,[c] who was the father of Micah.

41The sons of Micah:
Pithon, Melech, Tahrea and Ahaz.[d]
42Ahaz was the father of Jadah, Jadah[e] was the father of Alemeth, Azmaveth and Zimri, and Zimri was the father of Moza. 43Moza was the father of Binea; Rephaiah was his son, Eleasah his son and Azel his son.

44Azel had six sons, and these were their names:
Azrikam, Bokeru, Ishmael, Sheariah, Obadiah and Hanan. These were the sons of Azel.

Saul Takes His Life

10 Now the Philistines fought against Israel; the Israelites fled before them, and many fell slain on Mount Gilboa. 2The Philistines pressed hard after Saul and his sons, and they killed his sons Jonathan, Abinadab and Malki-Shua. 3The fighting grew fierce around Saul, and when the archers overtook him, they wounded him.

4Saul said to his armor-bearer, "Draw your sword and run me through, or these uncircumcised fellows will come and abuse me."

But his armor-bearer was terrified and would not do it; so Saul took his own sword and fell on it. 5When the armor-bearer saw that Saul was dead, he too fell on his sword and died. 6So Saul and his three sons died, and all his house died together.

7When all the Israelites in the valley saw that the army had fled and that Saul and his sons had died, they abandoned their towns and fled. And the Philistines came and occupied them.

8The next day, when the Philistines came to strip the dead, they found Saul and his sons fallen on Mount Gilboa. 9They stripped him and took his head and his armor, and sent messengers throughout the land of the Philistines to proclaim the news among their idols and their people. 10They put his armor in the temple of their gods and hung up his head in the temple of Dagon.

11When all the inhabitants of Jabesh Gilead heard of everything the Philistines had done to Saul, 12all their valiant men went and took the bodies of Saul and his sons and brought them to Jabesh. Then they buried their bones under the great tree in Jabesh, and they fasted seven days.

13Saul died because he was unfaithful to the LORD; he did not keep the word of the LORD and even consulted a medium for guidance, 14and did not inquire of the LORD. So the LORD put him to death and turned the kingdom over to David son of Jesse.

David Becomes King Over Israel

11 All Israel came together to David at Hebron and said, "We are your own flesh and blood. 2In the past, even while Saul was king, you were the one who led Israel on their military campaigns. And the LORD your God

[a]35 *Father* may mean *civic leader* or *military leader.*
[b]39 Also known as *Ish-Bosheth*
[c]40 Also known as *Mephibosheth*
[d]41 Vulgate and Syriac (see also Septuagint and 1 Chron. 8:35); Hebrew does not have *and Ahaz.*
[e]42 Some Hebrew manuscripts and Septuagint (see also 1 Chron. 8:36); most Hebrew manuscripts *Jarah, Jarah*

10:1–10 These verses are a horrifying account of personal defeat. Saul had started out well. He was humble, willing to follow the leadership of the prophet Samuel. But then Saul began to take matters into his own hands and merely added rebellion to rebellion in the course of his downward spiral. Saul's final outcome and defeat is described in these verses. We need to be careful! We can easily start down this same pathway toward complete disaster. We must seek God daily. And no matter how we may go astray, God can redirect our course back to his ways and redeem us.

10:11–12 In spite of Saul's failure and final downfall, the men of Jabesh Gilead remembered the kindness that Saul had shown toward them. They were loyal to his memory and, at great personal risk, rescued the bodies of Saul and his three sons. Faithfulness and loyalty are important traits that should characterize the life of every believer.

10:13–14 As we face problems in life, we must be careful about where we go for help. God is our true source of help. In many cases, looking elsewhere can prove fatal. This was true in Saul's case. Notice that Saul's sins, which cost him the throne, originated from his failure to seek God for help. Instead, Saul went to a source that was forbidden by God. God is waiting to help us too. We need to seek him and surrender to him. Looking to the occult or other sources for help will always spell disaster.

11:1–3 With every God-given opportunity comes a God-given responsibility. This is clear in the career of David, the man after God's own heart (see 1 Samuel 16:1–14). The people of Israel pledged themselves as subjects to David. In this relationship, the people had a perfect right to look to David for military leadership and personal protection. When God gives us opportunities to lead, we need to realize that with the position of leadership comes a responsibility to shepherd God's people.

said to you, 'You will shepherd my people Israel, and you will become their ruler.' "

3When all the elders of Israel had come to King David at Hebron, he made a compact with them at Hebron before the LORD, and they anointed David king over Israel, as the LORD had promised through Samuel.

David Conquers Jerusalem

4David and all the Israelites marched to Jerusalem (that is, Jebus). The Jebusites who lived there 5said to David, "You will not get in here." Nevertheless, David captured the fortress of Zion, the City of David.

6David had said, "Whoever leads the attack on the Jebusites will become commander-in-chief." Joab son of Zeruiah went up first, and so he received the command.

7David then took up residence in the fortress, and so it was called the City of David. 8He built up the city around it, from the supporting terraces[a] to the surrounding wall, while Joab restored the rest of the city. 9And David became more and more powerful, because the LORD Almighty was with him.

David's Mighty Men

10These were the chiefs of David's mighty men—they, together with all Israel, gave his kingship strong support to extend it over the whole land, as the LORD had promised— 11this is the list of David's mighty men:

Jashobeam,[b] a Hacmonite, was chief of the officers[c]; he raised his spear against three hundred men, whom he killed in one encounter.

12Next to him was Eleazar son of Dodai the Ahohite, one of the three mighty men. 13He was with David at Pas Dammim when the Philistines gathered there for battle. At a place where there was a field full of barley, the troops fled from the Philistines. 14But they took their stand in the middle of the field. They defended it and struck the Philistines down, and the LORD brought about a great victory.

15Three of the thirty chiefs came down to David to the rock at the cave of Adullam, while a band of Philistines was encamped in the Valley of Rephaim. 16At that time David was in the stronghold, and the Philistine garrison was at Bethlehem. 17David longed for water and said, "Oh, that someone would get me a drink of water from the well near the gate of Bethlehem!" 18So the Three broke through the Philistine lines, drew water from the well near the gate of Bethlehem and carried it back to David. But he refused to drink it; instead, he poured it out before the LORD. 19"God forbid that I should do this!" he said. "Should I drink the blood of these men who went at the risk of their lives?" Because they risked their lives to bring it back, David would not drink it.

Such were the exploits of the three mighty men.

20Abishai the brother of Joab was chief of the Three. He raised his spear against three hundred men, whom he killed, and so he became as famous as the Three. 21He was doubly honored above the Three and became their commander, even though he was not included among them.

22Benaiah son of Jehoiada was a valiant fighter from Kabzeel, who performed great exploits. He struck down two of Moab's best men. He also went down into a pit on a snowy day and killed a lion. 23And he struck down an Egyptian who was seven and a half feet[d] tall. Although the Egyptian had a spear like a weaver's rod in his hand, Benaiah went against him with a club. He snatched the spear from the Egyptian's hand and killed him with his own spear. 24Such were the exploits of Benaiah son of Jehoiada; he too was as famous as the three mighty men. 25He was held in greater honor than any of the Thirty, but he was not included among the Three. And David put him in charge of his bodyguard.

26The mighty men were:
Asahel the brother of Joab,
Elhanan son of Dodo from Bethlehem,
27Shammoth the Harorite,
Helez the Pelonite,
28Ira son of Ikkesh from Tekoa,
Abiezer from Anathoth,
29Sibbecai the Hushathite,
Ilai the Ahohite,
30Maharai the Netophathite,
Heled son of Baanah the Netophathite,
31Ithai son of Ribai from Gibeah in Benjamin,
Benaiah the Pirathonite,
32Hurai from the ravines of Gaash,
Abiel the Arbathite,
33Azmaveth the Baharumite,
Eliahba the Shaalbonite,
34the sons of Hashem the Gizonite,
Jonathan son of Shagee the Hararite,
35Ahiam son of Sacar the Hararite,
Eliphal son of Ur,

[a]8 Or *the Millo* [b]11 Possibly a variant of *Jashob-Baal* [c]11 Or *Thirty*; some Septuagint manuscripts *Three* (see also 2 Samuel 23:8) [d]23 Hebrew *five cubits* (about 2.3 meters)

11:4–7 These verses recount David's capture of the city of Jerusalem. He wanted to make this city the center of worship for Israel. This place remained the focal point for Israel's worship for centuries and is important in the thinking of Jews to this day. Today, God has provided his people with a community for worship—the church. Through the church, God encourages us, giving us the strength we need to persevere in our spiritual walk.

11:9 All of us desire success of one kind or another. When the Bible makes note of the success of any individual, it always attributes that success to a strong relationship with God. True success is possible only with God's help. If we achieve personal greatness but are spiritually bankrupt, our efforts will have been in vain.

[36]Hepher the Mekerathite,
Ahijah the Pelonite,
[37]Hezro the Carmelite,
Naarai son of Ezbai,
[38]Joel the brother of Nathan,
Mibhar son of Hagri,
[39]Zelek the Ammonite,
Naharai the Berothite, the armor-bearer of Joab son of Zeruiah,
[40]Ira the Ithrite,
Gareb the Ithrite,
[41]Uriah the Hittite,
Zabad son of Ahlai,
[42]Adina son of Shiza the Reubenite, who was chief of the Reubenites, and the thirty with him,
[43]Hanan son of Maacah,
Joshaphat the Mithnite,
[44]Uzzia the Ashterathite,
Shama and Jeiel the sons of Hotham the Aroerite,
[45]Jediael son of Shimri,
his brother Joha the Tizite,
[46]Eliel the Mahavite,
Jeribai and Joshaviah the sons of Elnaam,
Ithmah the Moabite,
[47]Eliel, Obed and Jaasiel the Mezobaite.

Warriors Join David

12 These were the men who came to David
at Ziklag, while he was banished from
the presence of Saul son of Kish (they were
among the warriors who helped him in battle;
[2]they were armed with bows and were able to
shoot arrows or to sling stones right-handed or
left-handed; they were kinsmen of Saul from
the tribe of Benjamin):

[3]Ahiezer their chief and Joash the sons of
Shemaah the Gibeathite; Jeziel and Pelet
the sons of Azmaveth; Beracah, Jehu the
Anathothite, [4]and Ishmaiah the Gibeon-
ite, a mighty man among the Thirty, who
was a leader of the Thirty; Jeremiah, Jahaziel, Johanan, Jozabad the Gederathite,
[5]Eluzai, Jerimoth, Bealiah, Shemariah and
Shephatiah the Haruphite; [6]Elkanah, Isshiah, Azarel, Joezer and Jashobeam the
Korahites; [7]and Joelah and Zebadiah the
sons of Jeroham from Gedor.

[8]Some Gadites defected to David at his
stronghold in the desert. They were brave warriors, ready for battle and able to handle the
shield and spear. Their faces were the faces of
lions, and they were as swift as gazelles in the
mountains.

[9]Ezer was the chief,
Obadiah the second in command, Eliab the third,
[10]Mishmannah the fourth, Jeremiah the fifth,
[11]Attai the sixth, Eliel the seventh,
[12]Johanan the eighth, Elzabad the ninth,
[13]Jeremiah the tenth and Macbannai the eleventh.

[14]These Gadites were army commanders; the
least was a match for a hundred, and the greatest for a thousand. [15]It was they who crossed the
Jordan in the first month when it was overflowing all its banks, and they put to flight everyone
living in the valleys, to the east and to the west.
[16]Other Benjamites and some men from Judah also came to David in his stronghold. [17]Da-
vid went out to meet them and said to them, "If
you have come to me in peace, to help me, I am
ready to have you unite with me. But if you
have come to betray me to my enemies when
my hands are free from violence, may the God
of our fathers see it and judge you."
[18]Then the Spirit came upon Amasai, chief of
the Thirty, and he said:

"We are yours, O David!
We are with you, O son of Jesse!
Success, success to you,
and success to those who help you,
for your God will help you."

So David received them and made them
leaders of his raiding bands.
[19]Some of the men of Manasseh defected to
David when he went with the Philistines to
fight against Saul. (He and his men did not help
the Philistines because, after consultation, their
rulers sent him away. They said, "It will cost
us our heads if he deserts to his master Saul.")
[20]When David went to Ziklag, these were the
men of Manasseh who defected to him: Adnah,
Jozabad, Jediael, Michael, Jozabad, Elihu and
Zillethai, leaders of units of a thousand in Manasseh. [21]They helped David against raiding
bands, for all of them were brave warriors, and
they were commanders in his army. [22]Day after

12:1–7 All the warriors mentioned here were well prepared for conflict. Proper preparation is necessary for winning any battle. The example of David's warriors should encourage us to be prepared as well. When we are armed with God's armor, we will be prepared to fight life's battles (see Ephesians 6:10–18).

12:16–18 This group of warriors came to David wanting to submit to his leadership. During the period of anarchy in Israel after Saul's death, many people desperately sought direction for their lives. These volunteers were not only anxious to serve, but they were also empowered by the Holy Spirit. David gave this band of warriors the direction they needed. We all desire meaningful lives. We must depend on the Holy Spirit to empower us, for it is " 'not by might nor by power, but by my Spirit,' says the LORD Almighty" (Zechariah 4:6). If we hope to move forward spiritually, we must do it with God's power.

12:18 Under spiritual direction, Amasai proclaimed peace to David. How can there be peace in the midst of conflict? The Hebrew word *shalom* conveys the idea of completeness. It is a peace based on the fact of God's presence, not on the surrounding circumstances. As such, this peace may be enjoyed even during warfare. No matter what personal conflicts we face, we can find peace and comfort in acknowledging that God is in complete control of our lives and our world.

day men came to help David, until he had a
great army, like the army of God.[a]

Others Join David at Hebron

23These are the numbers of the men armed
for battle who came to David at Hebron to turn
Saul's kingdom over to him, as the LORD had
said:

24men of Judah, carrying shield and spear—
6,800 armed for battle;
25men of Simeon, warriors ready for battle—7,100;
26men of Levi—4,600, 27including Jehoiada,
leader of the family of Aaron, with
3,700 men, 28and Zadok, a brave
young warrior, with 22 officers from
his family;
29men of Benjamin, Saul's kinsmen—3,000,
most of whom had remained loyal to
Saul's house until then;
30men of Ephraim, brave warriors, famous
in their own clans—20,800;
31men of half the tribe of Manasseh, designated by name to come and make David king—18,000;
32men of Issachar, who understood the
times and knew what Israel should
do—200 chiefs, with all their relatives
under their command;
33men of Zebulun, experienced soldiers
prepared for battle with every type of
weapon, to help David with undivided
loyalty—50,000;
34men of Naphtali—1,000 officers, together
with 37,000 men carrying shields and
spears;
35men of Dan, ready for battle—28,600;
36men of Asher, experienced soldiers prepared for battle—40,000;
37and from east of the Jordan, men of
Reuben, Gad and the half-tribe of Manasseh, armed with every type of
weapon—120,000.

38All these were fighting men who volunteered to serve in the ranks. They came to Hebron fully determined to make David king over
all Israel. All the rest of the Israelites were also
of one mind to make David king. 39The men
spent three days there with David, eating and
drinking, for their families had supplied provisions for them. 40Also, their neighbors from as
far away as Issachar, Zebulun and Naphtali
came bringing food on donkeys, camels, mules
and oxen. There were plentiful supplies of flour,
fig cakes, raisin cakes, wine, oil, cattle and
sheep, for there was joy in Israel.

Bringing Back the Ark

13 David conferred with each of his officers, the commanders of thousands and
commanders of hundreds. 2He then said to the
whole assembly of Israel, "If it seems good to
you and if it is the will of the LORD our God, let
us send word far and wide to the rest of our
brothers throughout the territories of Israel, and
also to the priests and Levites who are with
them in their towns and pasturelands, to come
and join us. 3Let us bring the ark of our God
back to us, for we did not inquire of[b] it[c]
during the reign of Saul." 4The whole assembly
agreed to do this, because it seemed right to all
the people.

5So David assembled all the Israelites, from
the Shihor River in Egypt to Lebo[d] Hamath, to
bring the ark of God from Kiriath Jearim. 6Da-
vid and all the Israelites with him went to Baalah of Judah (Kiriath Jearim) to bring up from
there the ark of God the LORD, who is enthroned between the cherubim—the ark that is
called by the Name.

7They moved the ark of God from Abinadab's house on a new cart, with Uzzah and Ahio
guiding it. 8David and all the Israelites were
celebrating with all their might before God,
with songs and with harps, lyres, tambourines,
cymbals and trumpets.

9When they came to the threshing floor of
Kidon, Uzzah reached out his hand to steady
the ark, because the oxen stumbled. 10The
LORD's anger burned against Uzzah, and he
struck him down because he had put his hand
on the ark. So he died there before God.

11Then David was angry because the LORD's
wrath had broken out against Uzzah, and to
this day that place is called Perez Uzzah.[e]

12David was afraid of God that day and
asked, "How can I ever bring the ark of God to
me?" 13He did not take the ark to be with him in

[a]22 Or *a great and mighty army* [b]3 Or *we neglected* [c]3 Or *him* [d]5 Or *to the entrance to* [e]11 *Perez Uzzah* means *outbreak against Uzzah.*

13:1–10 David did a good thing in a wrong way. God had prescribed exactly the method for moving the ark of God. David used a different way—the expedient way—and the results were catastrophic! God's clear guidelines were ignored. As we go about our lives, we can fall into the same trap. We must be extremely careful to obey God in everything. Spiritual growth is clearly within God's will, but we need to go about it in God's way. If we don't, we will have to suffer the consequences.

13:9–11 We must take great care as we deal with obstacles in our path. We are prone to do the first thing we think of—almost a knee-jerk reaction. But some things are absolutely forbidden by God. Uzzah discovered this basic principle too late. We must always be careful to do things God's way; otherwise, the results could be disastrous.

13:13–14 We sometimes experience setbacks when we attempt to accomplish something good. Such was the case in this passage. David wanted to bring the ark to Jerusalem, but the death of Uzzah brought his project to a standstill. The well-intentioned action remained unfinished because God's requirements were not observed. We often experience similar setbacks in our spiritual lives when we try to achieve spiritual goals in our own way. We must never forget to seek God's will and way. He is concerned that we not only reach the goal but also go about it in the right way.

the City of David. Instead, he took it aside to the house of Obed-Edom the Gittite. 14The ark of God remained with the family of Obed-Edom in his house for three months, and the LORD blessed his household and everything he had.

David's House and Family

14 Now Hiram king of Tyre sent messengers to David, along with cedar logs, stonemasons and carpenters to build a palace for him. 2And David knew that the LORD had established him as king over Israel and that his kingdom had been highly exalted for the sake of his people Israel.

3In Jerusalem David took more wives and became the father of more sons and daughters. 4These are the names of the children born to him there: Shammua, Shobab, Nathan, Solomon, 5Ibhar, Elishua, Elpelet, 6Nogah, Nepheg, Japhia, 7Elishama, Beeliada[a] and Eliphelet.

David Defeats the Philistines

8When the Philistines heard that David had been anointed king over all Israel, they went up in full force to search for him, but David heard about it and went out to meet them. 9Now the Philistines had come and raided the Valley of Rephaim; 10so David inquired of God: "Shall I go and attack the Philistines? Will you hand them over to me?"

The LORD answered him, "Go, I will hand them over to you."

11So David and his men went up to Baal Perazim, and there he defeated them. He said, "As waters break out, God has broken out against my enemies by my hand." So that place was called Baal Perazim.[b] 12The Philistines had abandoned their gods there, and David gave orders to burn them in the fire.

13Once more the Philistines raided the valley; 14so David inquired of God again, and God answered him, "Do not go straight up, but circle around them and attack them in front of the balsam trees. 15As soon as you hear the sound of marching in the tops of the balsam trees, move out to battle, because that will mean God has gone out in front of you to strike the Philistine army." 16So David did as God commanded him, and they struck down the Philistine army, all the way from Gibeon to Gezer.

17So David's fame spread throughout every land, and the LORD made all the nations fear him.

The Ark Brought to Jerusalem

15 After David had constructed buildings for himself in the City of David, he prepared a place for the ark of God and pitched a tent for it. 2Then David said, "No one but the Levites may carry the ark of God, because the LORD chose them to carry the ark of the LORD and to minister before him forever."

3David assembled all Israel in Jerusalem to bring up the ark of the LORD to the place he had prepared for it. 4He called together the descendants of Aaron and the Levites:

5From the descendants of Kohath,
Uriel the leader and 120 relatives;
6from the descendants of Merari,
Asaiah the leader and 220 relatives;
7from the descendants of Gershon,[c]
Joel the leader and 130 relatives;
8from the descendants of Elizaphan,
Shemaiah the leader and 200 relatives;
9from the descendants of Hebron,
Eliel the leader and 80 relatives;
10from the descendants of Uzziel,
Amminadab the leader and 112 relatives.

11Then David summoned Zadok and Abiathar the priests, and Uriel, Asaiah, Joel, Shemaiah, Eliel and Amminadab the Levites. 12He said to them, "You are the heads of the Levitical families; you and your fellow Levites are to consecrate yourselves and bring up the ark of the LORD, the God of Israel, to the place I have prepared for it. 13It was because you, the Levites, did not bring it up the first time that the LORD our God broke out in anger against us. We did not inquire of him about how to do it in the prescribed way." 14So the priests and Levites consecrated themselves in order to bring up the ark of the LORD, the God of Israel. 15And the Levites carried the ark of God with the poles on their shoulders, as Moses had commanded in accordance with the word of the LORD.

16David told the leaders of the Levites to appoint their brothers as singers to sing joyful songs, accompanied by musical instruments: lyres, harps and cymbals.

17So the Levites appointed Heman son of Joel; from his brothers, Asaph son of Berekiah; and from their brothers the Merarites, Ethan son of Kushaiah; 18and with them their brothers

[a]7 A variant of *Eliada* [b]11 *Baal Perazim* means *the lord who breaks out.* [c]7 Hebrew *Gershom,* a variant of *Gershon*

14:1–2 God gave great success to David. God blessed him so much because he also wanted to give joy to his people. By helping David, God was helping the whole nation of Israel. Often when God gives us success, we become a source of blessing and help to many others as well.

14:16–17 David did as God commanded, and God granted him success. Simple obedience was certainly the key to David's victory. Yet it is important that we do not misunderstand and begin to view God as a "push-button" deity who will act or react because of a set formula. Sometimes our obedience will be answered by new and more difficult circumstances. When hard times fall repeatedly upon us, we need not fear that God has rejected us. If we have been obedient to his will, these situations may be God's means to work his will in us in a new way. We can be sure that God will always stand with us, even if he doesn't always give us an immediate solution.

next in rank: Zechariah,[a] Jaaziel, Shemiramoth, Jehiel, Unni, Eliab, Benaiah, Maaseiah, Mattithiah, Eliphelehu, Mikneiah, Obed-Edom and Jeiel,[b] the gatekeepers.

19The musicians Heman, Asaph and Ethan were to sound the bronze cymbals; 20Zechariah, Aziel, Shemiramoth, Jehiel, Unni, Eliab, Maaseiah and Benaiah were to play the lyres according to *alamoth,*[c] 21and Mattithiah, Eliphelehu, Mikneiah, Obed-Edom, Jeiel and Azaziah were to play the harps, directing according to *sheminith.*[c] 22Kenaniah the head Levite was in charge of the singing; that was his responsibility because he was skillful at it.

23Berekiah and Elkanah were to be doorkeepers for the ark. 24Shebaniah, Joshaphat, Nethanel, Amasai, Zechariah, Benaiah and Eliezer the priests were to blow trumpets before the ark of God. Obed-Edom and Jehiah were also to be doorkeepers for the ark.

25So David and the elders of Israel and the commanders of units of a thousand went to bring up the ark of the covenant of the LORD from the house of Obed-Edom, with rejoicing. 26Because God had helped the Levites who were carrying the ark of the covenant of the LORD, seven bulls and seven rams were sacrificed. 27Now David was clothed in a robe of fine linen, as were all the Levites who were carrying the ark, and as were the singers, and Kenaniah, who was in charge of the singing of the choirs. David also wore a linen ephod. 28So all Israel brought up the ark of the covenant of the LORD with shouts, with the sounding of rams' horns and trumpets, and of cymbals, and the playing of lyres and harps.

29As the ark of the covenant of the LORD was entering the City of David, Michal daughter of Saul watched from a window. And when she saw King David dancing and celebrating, she despised him in her heart.

16 They brought the ark of God and set it inside the tent that David had pitched for it, and they presented burnt offerings and fellowship offerings[d] before God. 2After David had finished sacrificing the burnt offerings and fellowship offerings, he blessed the people in the name of the LORD. 3Then he gave a loaf of bread, a cake of dates and a cake of raisins to each Israelite man and woman.

4He appointed some of the Levites to minister before the ark of the LORD, to make petition, to give thanks, and to praise the LORD, the God of Israel: 5Asaph was the chief, Zechariah second, then Jeiel, Shemiramoth, Jehiel, Mattithiah, Eliab, Benaiah, Obed-Edom and Jeiel. They were to play the lyres and harps, Asaph was to sound the cymbals, 6and Benaiah and Jahaziel the priests were to blow the trumpets regularly before the ark of the covenant of God.

David's Psalm of Thanks

7That day David first committed to Asaph and his associates this psalm of thanks to the LORD:

8Give thanks to the LORD, call on his name;
make known among the nations what he
has done.
9Sing to him, sing praise to him;
tell of all his wonderful acts.
10Glory in his holy name;
let the hearts of those who seek the LORD
rejoice.
11Look to the LORD and his strength;
seek his face always.
12Remember the wonders he has done,
his miracles, and the judgments he
pronounced,
13O descendants of Israel his servant,
O sons of Jacob, his chosen ones.

14He is the LORD our God;
his judgments are in all the earth.
15He remembers[e] his covenant forever,

[a] *18* Three Hebrew manuscripts and most Septuagint manuscripts (see also verse 20 and 1 Chron. 16:5); most Hebrew manuscripts *Zechariah son and* or *Zechariah, Ben and*
[b] *18* Hebrew; Septuagint (see also verse 21) *Jeiel and Azaziah*
[c] *20,21* Probably a musical term
[d] *1* Traditionally *peace offerings;* also in verse 2
[e] *15* Some Septuagint manuscripts (see also Psalm 105:8); Hebrew *Remember*

15:25 What happens when victory is finally achieved? What are the emotions? What are the reactions? This verse says that these people did their work with rejoicing. The joy of accomplishing God's will is one of the sweetest joys of all.

15:27–28 Some Christians believe that they should be indifferent to what they are feeling. Contrary to this popular view, God's Word insists that we be honest about our feelings, releasing them to God. In this passage, David responded with an intense emotional outburst that was commended, rather than condemned, by God. Expressing our sorrow and joy to God should characterize our lives as Christians; both grieving and rejoicing are part of genuine spiritual growth.

16:1–3 When God's will is accomplished, celebration should be an automatic response. We should celebrate each victory we experience, no matter how small it may be. When David finally brought the ark to Jerusalem, he threw a great celebration. The whole city enjoyed a happy time of worship. This kind of appropriate celebration affirms our progress and encourages us to move forward once again.

16:8–13 In times of victory or defeat, turmoil or stability, God remains the same. Our response to him in all circumstances should include the elements of thanksgiving and praise. There is never a time when it is inappropriate to seek God.

16:14–22 Sometimes it is tempting for us to think that God has lost control of things. We are not the only ones who have felt this way. There were times during Israel's history when God seemed far away. God's plan for his people must have seemed obscure and distant. But as time passed, it became clear that God had been with Israel all along—even as they wandered in the wilderness. God used the difficult times to work out his plan. When we experience crises and emergencies, we can be sure that even in such times God is there and in control! During trying times we must learn to rest in our knowledge of God's sovereignty and love.

the word he commanded, for a thousand
generations,
16the covenant he made with Abraham,
the oath he swore to Isaac.
17He confirmed it to Jacob as a decree,
to Israel as an everlasting covenant:
18"To you I will give the land of Canaan
as the portion you will inherit."

19When they were but few in number,
few indeed, and strangers in it,
20they[a] wandered from nation to nation,
from one kingdom to another.
21He allowed no man to oppress them;
for their sake he rebuked kings:
22"Do not touch my anointed ones;
do my prophets no harm."

23Sing to the LORD, all the earth;
proclaim his salvation day after day.
24Declare his glory among the nations,
his marvelous deeds among all peoples.
25For great is the LORD and most worthy of
praise;
he is to be feared above all gods.
26For all the gods of the nations are idols,
but the LORD made the heavens.
27Splendor and majesty are before him;
strength and joy in his dwelling place.
28Ascribe to the LORD, O families of nations,
ascribe to the LORD glory and strength,
29 ascribe to the LORD the glory due his
name.
Bring an offering and come before him;
worship the LORD in the splendor of
his[b] holiness.
30Tremble before him, all the earth!
The world is firmly established; it cannot
be moved.
31Let the heavens rejoice, let the earth be
glad;
let them say among the nations, "The
LORD reigns!"
32Let the sea resound, and all that is in it;
let the fields be jubilant, and everything
in them!
33Then the trees of the forest will sing,
they will sing for joy before the LORD,
for he comes to judge the earth.

34Give thanks to the LORD, for he is good;
his love endures forever.
35Cry out, "Save us, O God our Savior;
gather us and deliver us from the
nations,
that we may give thanks to your holy
name,
that we may glory in your praise."
36Praise be to the LORD, the God of Israel,
from everlasting to everlasting.

Then all the people said "Amen" and "Praise the
LORD."

37David left Asaph and his associates before
the ark of the covenant of the LORD to minister
there regularly, according to each day's requirements. 38He also left Obed-Edom and his sixty-
eight associates to minister with them. Obed-
Edom son of Jeduthun, and also Hosah, were
gatekeepers.

39David left Zadok the priest and his fellow
priests before the tabernacle of the LORD at the
high place in Gibeon 40to present burnt offerings to the LORD on the altar of burnt offering
regularly, morning and evening, in accordance
with everything written in the Law of the LORD,
which he had given Israel. 41With them were
Heman and Jeduthun and the rest of those chosen and designated by name to give thanks to
the LORD, "for his love endures forever." 42He-
man and Jeduthun were responsible for the
sounding of the trumpets and cymbals and for
the playing of the other instruments for sacred
song. The sons of Jeduthun were stationed at
the gate.

43Then all the people left, each for his own
home, and David returned home to bless his
family.

God's Promise to David

17 After David was settled in his palace, he
said to Nathan the prophet, "Here I
am, living in a palace of cedar, while the ark of
the covenant of the LORD is under a tent."

2Nathan replied to David, "Whatever you
have in mind, do it, for God is with you."

3That night the word of God came to Nathan, saying:

4"Go and tell my servant David, 'This
is what the LORD says: You are not the one
to build me a house to dwell in. 5I have
not dwelt in a house from the day I
brought Israel up out of Egypt to this day.
I have moved from one tent site to another, from one dwelling place to another.
6Wherever I have moved with all the Israelites, did I ever say to any of their leaders[c] whom I commanded to shepherd

[a] *18-20* One Hebrew manuscript, Septuagint and Vulgate (see also Psalm 105:12); most Hebrew manuscripts *inherit, / 19though you are but few in number, / few indeed, and strangers in it." / 20They* [b] *29* Or *LORD with the splendor of* [c] *6* Traditionally *judges;* also in verse 10

17:1–2 In these verses, David had a wonderful idea: He wanted to build God a temple to house the ark. David's idea to build the temple was a good one, but, like all good ideas, it had to pass muster. David's idea needed to conform to God's will and timing. We must learn to seek God's will and submit to his plans in all that we wish to accomplish too.

17:3–4 As we make our plans, we must remember that God's will and timing always take precedence over ours. Nathan, who had earlier approved the idea of the temple, discovered that the timing was wrong in God's eyes. We tend to believe that if we desire a good thing, God's time for it is *now*! But we must learn that God knows what he is doing; his plans and timing are best.

THE SPIRITUAL DISCIPLINES

In the Life of David

We know more about the spiritual life of David than of any other person in the Bible. The extensive record of his life and his many psalms illustrate why David was known as "a man after [God's] own heart" (1 Samuel 13:14). A careful study of David's life shows that he practiced all of the spiritual disciplines highlighted in this study. David alludes to Bible study and meditation in Psalm 19 and fasting in Psalm 35:13. Stewardship was also a significant aspect of David's life, as evidenced by his incalculable offering for the building of the temple (29:3). In addition, David's entire life was yielded to God's service. He was an active man of God who knew how to maintain spiritual vitality by caring for his soul.

Among all the spiritual disciplines, however, two seem to stand out as those that David practiced most often: worship and prayer. These spiritual exercises brought consistent renewal to David's life.

WORSHIP. David's first role in Saul's court was as a musician. His music had a powerful, spiritual impact on Saul, relieving his misery when "an evil spirit from the LORD tormented him" (1 Samuel 16:14). David's ministry of worship and music touched the very heart of Saul—and of untold numbers across the centuries. His worship is so powerful because it combines honest human experience and emotion with an unwavering faith in a gracious, almighty God. (To learn more about worship, turn to Exodus 20.)

PRAYER. David's prayers sprang from his vibrant faith. We first witness David's deep faith during his encounter with Goliath. Here David was gripped by passion to honor the Lord's name. He couldn't stand Goliath's mockery and defiance of God. "You come against me with sword and spear and javelin, but I come against you in the name of the LORD Almighty, the God of the armies of Israel, whom you have defied. This day the LORD will hand you over to me, and I'll strike you down" (1 Samuel 17:45–46). This passionate desire to honor the Lord's name was evidenced through David's prayers throughout his eventful life.

David's prayers often begin with an honest confession of anger or despair or frustration. He didn't hide his feelings from God and pretend about his spiritual condition, for David knew that "the LORD is near to all who call on him, to all who call on him in truth" (Psalm 145:18). Spiritual renewal flows from the freedom to be totally honest with God (see Matthew 6:5–8). As Psalm 145 progresses, David's faith builds from a spark to a flame, from a whisper to a crescendo. As he releases the anxiety and cares of life, David regains his perspective and orientation. Assurance and the confidence of faith fill his heart. (To learn more about prayer, turn to Genesis 18.)

Lessons for Life

As we look at these two disciplines in David's life, we soon recognize that being a person after God's own heart does not mean that we will never fall. Rather, it means that when we do fall, we must also fall immediately to our knees. By faith we come before the living, gracious God and in prayer and worship our hearts cry out, "I will sing of the LORD's great love forever; with my mouth I will make your faithfulness known through all generations. I will declare that your love stands firm forever, that you established your faithfulness in heaven itself" (Psalm 89:1–2).

my people, "Why have you not built me a house of cedar?" '

7"Now then, tell my servant David, 'This is what the LORD Almighty says: I took you from the pasture and from following the flock, to be ruler over my people Israel. 8I have been with you wherever you have gone, and I have cut off all your enemies from before you. Now I will make your name like the names of the greatest men of the earth. 9And I will provide a place for my people Israel and will plant them so that they can have a home of their own and no longer be disturbed. Wicked people will not oppress them anymore, as they did at the beginning 10and have done ever since the time I appointed leaders over my people Israel. I will also subdue all your enemies.

" 'I declare to you that the LORD will build a house for you: 11When your days are over and you go to be with your fathers, I will raise up your offspring to succeed you, one of your own sons, and I will establish his kingdom. 12He is the one who will build a house for me, and I will establish his throne forever. 13I will be his father, and he will be my son. I will never take my love away from him, as I took it away from your predecessor. 14I will set him over my house and my kingdom forever; his throne will be established forever.' "

15Nathan reported to David all the words of this entire revelation.

David's Prayer

16Then King David went in and sat before the LORD, and he said:

"Who am I, O LORD God, and what is my family, that you have brought me this far? 17And as if this were not enough in your sight, O God, you have spoken about the future of the house of your servant. You have looked on me as though I were the most exalted of men, O LORD God.

18"What more can David say to you for honoring your servant? For you know your servant, 19O LORD. For the sake of your servant and according to your will, you have done this great thing and made known all these great promises.

20"There is no one like you, O LORD, and there is no God but you, as we have heard with our own ears. 21And who is like your people Israel—the one nation on earth whose God went out to redeem a people for himself, and to make a name for yourself, and to perform great and awesome wonders by driving out nations from before your people, whom you redeemed from Egypt? 22You made your people Israel your very own forever, and you, O LORD, have become their God.

23"And now, LORD, let the promise you have made concerning your servant and his house be established forever. Do as you promised, 24so that it will be established and that your name will be great forever. Then men will say, 'The LORD Almighty, the God over Israel, is Israel's God!' And the house of your servant David will be established before you.

25"You, my God, have revealed to your servant that you will build a house for him. So your servant has found courage to pray to you. 26O LORD, you are God! You have promised these good things to your servant. 27Now you have been pleased to bless the house of your servant, that it may continue forever in your sight; for you, O LORD, have blessed it, and it will be blessed forever."

David's Victories

18 In the course of time, David defeated the Philistines and subdued them, and he took Gath and its surrounding villages from the control of the Philistines.

2David also defeated the Moabites, and they became subject to him and brought tribute.

3Moreover, David fought Hadadezer king of Zobah, as far as Hamath, when he went to establish his control along the Euphrates River. 4David captured a thousand of his chariots, seven thousand charioteers and twenty thousand foot soldiers. He hamstrung all but a hundred of the chariot horses.

5When the Arameans of Damascus came to help Hadadezer king of Zobah, David struck down twenty-two thousand of them. 6He put garrisons in the Aramean kingdom of Damascus, and the Arameans became subject to him and brought tribute. The LORD gave David victory everywhere he went.

7David took the gold shields carried by the

17:9–10 David wanted to build God a house. That was a good idea. But it did not conform to God's plans. God assigned that job to Solomon, David's son. More importantly, God promised to build a "house" for David—a dynasty that would reign forever. From that dynasty came David's greater son, Jesus Christ, who provides salvation for all willing to receive it! This promise to David became a promise for all who need cleansing from the powerful effects of sin.

18:4 Why did David cripple the horses? God had commanded that Israel's kings never build up large stables of horses (see Deuteronomy 17:16). God wanted Israel to depend on him for protection, not on great armies of chariots and horses. This is an important principle for us to keep in mind. Only God can truly defend us and give us the power to overcome. We must be sure that as we build human relationships to support our spiritual growth, we don't forget to depend on God. Without his strength, our personal resources are never sufficient for success.

officers of Hadadezer and brought them to Jerusalem. 8From Tebah[a] and Cun, towns that belonged to Hadadezer, David took a great quantity of bronze, which Solomon used to make the bronze Sea, the pillars and various bronze articles.

9When Tou king of Hamath heard that David had defeated the entire army of Hadadezer king of Zobah, 10he sent his son Hadoram to King David to greet him and congratulate him on his victory in battle over Hadadezer, who had been at war with Tou. Hadoram brought all kinds of articles of gold and silver and bronze.

11King David dedicated these articles to the LORD, as he had done with the silver and gold he had taken from all these nations: Edom and Moab, the Ammonites and the Philistines, and Amalek.

12Abishai son of Zeruiah struck down eighteen thousand Edomites in the Valley of Salt. 13He put garrisons in Edom, and all the Edomites became subject to David. The LORD gave David victory everywhere he went.

David's Officials

14David reigned over all Israel, doing what was just and right for all his people. 15Joab son of Zeruiah was over the army; Jehoshaphat son of Ahilud was recorder; 16Zadok son of Ahitub and Ahimelech[b] son of Abiathar were priests; Shavsha was secretary; 17Benaiah son of Jehoiada was over the Kerethites and Pelethites; and David's sons were chief officials at the king's side.

The Battle Against the Ammonites

19 In the course of time, Nahash king of the Ammonites died, and his son succeeded him as king. 2David thought, "I will show kindness to Hanun son of Nahash, because his father showed kindness to me." So David sent a delegation to express his sympathy to Hanun concerning his father.

When David's men came to Hanun in the land of the Ammonites to express sympathy to him, 3the Ammonite nobles said to Hanun, "Do you think David is honoring your father by sending men to you to express sympathy? Haven't his men come to you to explore and spy out the country and overthrow it?" 4So Hanun seized David's men, shaved them, cut off their garments in the middle at the buttocks, and sent them away.

5When someone came and told David about the men, he sent messengers to meet them, for they were greatly humiliated. The king said, "Stay at Jericho till your beards have grown, and then come back."

6When the Ammonites realized that they had become a stench in David's nostrils, Hanun and the Ammonites sent a thousand talents[c] of silver to hire chariots and charioteers from Aram Naharaim,[d] Aram Maacah and Zobah. 7They hired thirty-two thousand chariots and charioteers, as well as the king of Maacah with his troops, who came and camped near Medeba, while the Ammonites were mustered from their towns and moved out for battle.

8On hearing this, David sent Joab out with the entire army of fighting men. 9The Ammonites came out and drew up in battle formation at the entrance to their city, while the kings who had come were by themselves in the open country.

10Joab saw that there were battle lines in front of him and behind him; so he selected some of the best troops in Israel and deployed them against the Arameans. 11He put the rest of the men under the command of Abishai his brother, and they were deployed against the Ammonites. 12Joab said, "If the Arameans are too strong for me, then you are to rescue me; but if the Ammonites are too strong for you, then I will rescue you. 13Be strong and let us fight bravely for our people and the cities of our God. The LORD will do what is good in his sight."

14Then Joab and the troops with him advanced to fight the Arameans, and they fled before him. 15When the Ammonites saw that the Arameans were fleeing, they too fled before his brother Abishai and went inside the city. So Joab went back to Jerusalem.

16After the Arameans saw that they had been routed by Israel, they sent messengers and had

[a]8 Hebrew *Tibhath*, a variant of *Tebah* [b]16 Some Hebrew manuscripts, Vulgate and Syriac (see also 2 Samuel 8:17); most Hebrew manuscripts *Abimelech*
[c]6 That is, about 37 tons (about 34 metric tons)
[d]6 That is, Northwest Mesopotamia

19:1–4 The distrust of Hanun's nobles caused them to misread David's friendly overtures. So instead of building a strong relationship with Israel, they created a destructive one. We often make the same mistake, especially when people we love have disappointed us. This can cause us to cut off even the healthy relationships offered to us. We must learn how to discern between the people we can trust and those we can't. Honest relationships are extremely important. We cannot afford to alienate the people who will encourage us in our spiritual growth.

19:5 In this very delicate situation, David showed deep sensitivity to the embarrassment of his ambassadors. He gave them time to recover their dignity before returning home. Surely there is a lesson here for all of us. Like David, we need to exhibit sensitivity to others as they deal with embarrassing issues. This is especially true when people confess sins to us. We must be trustworthy confidants and stand with them as they overcome these sins through the Lord's power.

19:13 Joab's words here are worth remembering. He began by calling his men to act, but he also recognized that ultimately God was in control. We need to keep the same principles before us. We are responsible to act and strike out boldly to seek God's will. Yet we don't have the power or resources to accomplish God's will on our own. We always need God's help. We need to continually leave things in God's hands, seek his will and surrender to him. As we face trials, we can be assured of God's powerful help. He will bring about the outcome he desires when we follow his will.

Arameans brought from beyond the River,[a] with Shophach the commander of Hadadezer's army leading them.

17When David was told of this, he gathered all Israel and crossed the Jordan; he advanced against them and formed his battle lines opposite them. David formed his lines to meet the Arameans in battle, and they fought against him. 18But they fled before Israel, and David killed seven thousand of their charioteers and forty thousand of their foot soldiers. He also killed Shophach the commander of their army.

19When the vassals of Hadadezer saw that they had been defeated by Israel, they made peace with David and became subject to him.

So the Arameans were not willing to help the Ammonites anymore.

The Capture of Rabbah

20 In the spring, at the time when kings go off to war, Joab led out the armed forces. He laid waste the land of the Ammonites and went to Rabbah and besieged it, but David remained in Jerusalem. Joab attacked Rabbah and left it in ruins. 2David took the crown from the head of their king[b]—its weight was found to be a talent[c] of gold, and it was set with precious stones—and it was placed on David's head. He took a great quantity of plunder from the city 3and brought out the people who were there, consigning them to labor with saws and with iron picks and axes. David did this to all the Ammonite towns. Then David and his entire army returned to Jerusalem.

War With the Philistines

4In the course of time, war broke out with the Philistines, at Gezer. At that time Sibbecai the Hushathite killed Sippai, one of the descendants of the Rephaites, and the Philistines were subjugated.

5In another battle with the Philistines, Elhanan son of Jair killed Lahmi the brother of Goliath the Gittite, who had a spear with a shaft like a weaver's rod.

6In still another battle, which took place at Gath, there was a huge man with six fingers on each hand and six toes on each foot—twenty-four in all. He also was descended from Rapha. 7When he taunted Israel, Jonathan son of Shimea, David's brother, killed him.

8These were descendants of Rapha in Gath, and they fell at the hands of David and his men.

David Numbers the Fighting Men

21 Satan rose up against Israel and incited David to take a census of Israel. 2So David said to Joab and the commanders of the troops, "Go and count the Israelites from Beersheba to Dan. Then report back to me so that I may know how many there are."

3But Joab replied, "May the LORD multiply his troops a hundred times over. My lord the king, are they not all my lord's subjects? Why does my lord want to do this? Why should he bring guilt on Israel?"

4The king's word, however, overruled Joab; so Joab left and went throughout Israel and then came back to Jerusalem. 5Joab reported the number of the fighting men to David: In all Israel there were one million one hundred thousand men who could handle a sword, including four hundred and seventy thousand in Judah.

6But Joab did not include Levi and Benjamin in the numbering, because the king's command was repulsive to him. 7This command was also evil in the sight of God; so he punished Israel.

8Then David said to God, "I have sinned greatly by doing this. Now, I beg you, take away the guilt of your servant. I have done a very foolish thing."

9The LORD said to Gad, David's seer, 10"Go and tell David, 'This is what the LORD says: I am giving you three options. Choose one of them for me to carry out against you.' "

11So Gad went to David and said to him, "This is what the LORD says: 'Take your choice: 12three years of famine, three months of being swept away[d] before your enemies, with their swords overtaking you, or three days of the sword of the LORD—days of plague in the land, with the angel of the LORD ravaging every part of Israel.' Now then, decide how I should answer the one who sent me."

13David said to Gad, "I am in deep distress. Let me fall into the hands of the LORD, for his mercy is very great; but do not let me fall into the hands of men."

14So the LORD sent a plague on Israel, and seventy thousand men of Israel fell dead. 15And God sent an angel to destroy Jerusalem. But as the angel was doing so, the LORD saw it and was grieved because of the calamity and said to the angel who was destroying the people,

[a]*16* That is, the Euphrates [b]*2* Or *of Milcom,* that is, Molech [c]*2* That is, about 75 pounds (about 34 kilograms) [d]*12* Hebrew; Septuagint and Vulgate (see also 2 Samuel 24:13) *of fleeing*

20:1–8 David knew who his enemies were, and he acted accordingly. With God's help he overcame each one in turn. We often make the mistake of allowing enemies into our lives—sinful behaviors that are dangerous to our spiritual health. We often treat these sins as our friends. David understood who his enemies were. In spiritual battle, we need to identify our enemies and act accordingly.

21:1 God had punished David for his acts of adultery and murder. But the punishment suffered for David's census was greater and more widespread because David counted the people to assess their human strength. He was putting his trust in Israel's numbers and the army that it could muster. He had forgotten that with God's help they needed no army at all to achieve victory. We often make the same mistake. We seek to do things in our own strength, rather than depend on God's. Seeking spiritual growth, or anything else, through human strength alone will end only in disaster.

"Enough! Withdraw your hand." The angel of
the LORD was then standing at the threshing
floor of Araunah[a] the Jebusite.
16David looked up and saw the angel of the
LORD standing between heaven and earth, with
a drawn sword in his hand extended over Jerusalem. Then David and the elders, clothed in
sackcloth, fell facedown.
17David said to God, "Was it not I who ordered the fighting men to be counted? I am the
one who has sinned and done wrong. These are
but sheep. What have they done? O LORD my
God, let your hand fall upon me and my family,
but do not let this plague remain on your people."
18Then the angel of the LORD ordered Gad to
tell David to go up and build an altar to the
LORD on the threshing floor of Araunah the Jebusite. 19So David went up in obedience to the
word that Gad had spoken in the name of the
LORD.
20While Araunah was threshing wheat, he
turned and saw the angel; his four sons who
were with him hid themselves. 21Then David
approached, and when Araunah looked and
saw him, he left the threshing floor and bowed
down before David with his face to the ground.
22David said to him, "Let me have the site of
your threshing floor so I can build an altar to
the LORD, that the plague on the people may be
stopped. Sell it to me at the full price."
23Araunah said to David, "Take it! Let my
lord the king do whatever pleases him. Look, I
will give the oxen for the burnt offerings, the
threshing sledges for the wood, and the wheat
for the grain offering. I will give all this."
24But King David replied to Araunah, "No, I
insist on paying the full price. I will not take for
the LORD what is yours, or sacrifice a burnt offering that costs me nothing."
25So David paid Araunah six hundred shekels[b] of gold for the site. 26David built an altar
to the LORD there and sacrificed burnt offerings
and fellowship offerings.[c] He called on the
LORD, and the LORD answered him with fire
from heaven on the altar of burnt offering.
27Then the LORD spoke to the angel, and he
put his sword back into its sheath. 28At that
time, when David saw that the LORD had answered him on the threshing floor of Araunah
the Jebusite, he offered sacrifices there. 29The
tabernacle of the LORD, which Moses had made
in the desert, and the altar of burnt offering
were at that time on the high place at Gibeon.
30But David could not go before it to inquire of
God, because he was afraid of the sword of the
angel of the LORD.

22 Then David said, "The house of the
LORD God is to be here, and also the
altar of burnt offering for Israel."

Preparations for the Temple

2So David gave orders to assemble the aliens
living in Israel, and from among them he appointed stonecutters to prepare dressed stone
for building the house of God. 3He provided a
large amount of iron to make nails for the doors
of the gateways and for the fittings, and more
bronze than could be weighed. 4He also provided more cedar logs than could be counted, for
the Sidonians and Tyrians had brought large
numbers of them to David.
5David said, "My son Solomon is young and
inexperienced, and the house to be built for the
LORD should be of great magnificence and fame
and splendor in the sight of all the nations.
Therefore I will make preparations for it." So
David made extensive preparations before his
death.
6Then he called for his son Solomon and
charged him to build a house for the LORD, the
God of Israel. 7David said to Solomon: "My
son, I had it in my heart to build a house for the
Name of the LORD my God. 8But this word of
the LORD came to me: 'You have shed much
blood and have fought many wars. You are not
to build a house for my Name, because you
have shed much blood on the earth in my sight.
9But you will have a son who will be a man of
peace and rest, and I will give him rest from all
his enemies on every side. His name will be
Solomon,[d] and I will grant Israel peace and
quiet during his reign. 10He is the one who will
build a house for my Name. He will be my son,
and I will be his father. And I will establish the
throne of his kingdom over Israel forever.'
11"Now, my son, the LORD be with you, and
may you have success and build the house of
the LORD your God, as he said you would.
12May the LORD give you discretion and understanding when he puts you in command over
Israel, so that you may keep the law of the LORD
your God. 13Then you will have success if you
are careful to observe the decrees and laws that

[a]15 Hebrew *Ornan*, a variant of *Araunah*; also in verses 18-28 [b]25 That is, about 15 pounds (about 7 kilograms) [c]26 Traditionally *peace offerings* [d]9 *Solomon* sounds like and may be derived from the Hebrew for *peace*.

21:17 Our personal sins may bring serious consequences to the lives of other people. David was aware that the people of his kingdom would suffer for his sin. It is heart-rending to hear David's admission of guilt. He saw the truth, confessed his sin and accepted full responsibility for it. Then he prayed diligently for the rescue of his people. When people close to us suffer because of our sins, we would be wise to pray that God would give them special grace to overcome the consequences of our failures.

22:1–5 Although David would never build the temple, he collected numerous materials for the project. A whole chapter is dedicated to David's preparations for building the temple. Any building project needs careful planning and the necessary materials and resources to get the job done. We need planning and preparation in our spiritual renewal too. We need to assess our needs and seek help and resources to support us throughout our spiritual growth process.

the LORD gave Moses for Israel. Be strong and
courageous. Do not be afraid or discouraged.
14 "I have taken great pains to provide for
the temple of the LORD a hundred thousand
talents[a] of gold, a million talents[b] of silver, quantities of bronze and iron too great to
be weighed, and wood and stone. And you
may add to them. 15 You have many workmen:
stonecutters, masons and carpenters, as well as
men skilled in every kind of work 16 in gold and
silver, bronze and iron—craftsmen beyond
number. Now begin the work, and the LORD be
with you."
17 Then David ordered all the leaders of Israel
to help his son Solomon. 18 He said to them, "Is
not the LORD your God with you? And has he
not granted you rest on every side? For he has
handed the inhabitants of the land over to me,
and the land is subject to the LORD and to his
people. 19 Now devote your heart and soul to
seeking the LORD your God. Begin to build the
sanctuary of the LORD God, so that you may
bring the ark of the covenant of the LORD and
the sacred articles belonging to God into the
temple that will be built for the Name of the
LORD."

The Levites

23 When David was old and full of years,
he made his son Solomon king over
Israel.
2 He also gathered together all the leaders of
Israel, as well as the priests and Levites. 3 The
Levites thirty years old or more were counted,
and the total number of men was thirty-eight
thousand. 4 David said, "Of these, twenty-four
thousand are to supervise the work of the temple of the LORD and six thousand are to be officials and judges. 5 Four thousand are to be gatekeepers and four thousand are to praise the
LORD with the musical instruments I have provided for that purpose."
6 David divided the Levites into groups corresponding to the sons of Levi: Gershon, Kohath
and Merari.

Gershonites

7 Belonging to the Gershonites:
Ladan and Shimei.
8 The sons of Ladan:
Jehiel the first, Zetham and Joel—three
in all.
9 The sons of Shimei:
Shelomoth, Haziel and Haran—three
in all.
These were the heads of the families of
Ladan.
10 And the sons of Shimei:
Jahath, Ziza,[c] Jeush and Beriah.
These were the sons of Shimei—four in
all.
11 Jahath was the first and Ziza the second, but Jeush and Beriah did not have
many sons; so they were counted as
one family with one assignment.

Kohathites

12 The sons of Kohath:
Amram, Izhar, Hebron and Uzziel—
four in all.
13 The sons of Amram:
Aaron and Moses.
Aaron was set apart, he and his descendants forever, to consecrate the most
holy things, to offer sacrifices before
the LORD, to minister before him and
to pronounce blessings in his name
forever. 14 The sons of Moses the man
of God were counted as part of the
tribe of Levi.
15 The sons of Moses:
Gershom and Eliezer.
16 The descendants of Gershom:
Shubael was the first.
17 The descendants of Eliezer:
Rehabiah was the first.
Eliezer had no other sons, but the sons
of Rehabiah were very numerous.
18 The sons of Izhar:
Shelomith was the first.
19 The sons of Hebron:
Jeriah the first, Amariah the second,
Jahaziel the third and Jekameam the
fourth.
20 The sons of Uzziel:
Micah the first and Isshiah the second.

Merarites

21 The sons of Merari:
Mahli and Mushi.
The sons of Mahli:
Eleazar and Kish.
22 Eleazar died without having sons: he
had only daughters. Their cousins, the
sons of Kish, married them.
23 The sons of Mushi:
Mahli, Eder and Jerimoth—three in all.
24 These were the descendants of Levi by their
families—the heads of families as they were reg-

[a]14 That is, about 3,750 tons (about 3,450 metric tons)
[b]14 That is, about 37,500 tons (about 34,500 metric tons)
[c]10 One Hebrew manuscript, Septuagint and Vulgate (see also verse 11); most Hebrew manuscripts *Zina*

23:1–2 At a certain point in his life, David stepped down from his position of responsibility. Since many of us derive our self-worth from our activities, this is often a difficult thing to do. But none of us can take responsibility for everything. There are some matters that we are not capable of handling. We may need to relinquish some of our burdens to others (see Galatians 6:2). This is important for maintaining the balance necessary to preserve spiritual gains. We need to determine our limits and then stand by them. Being loaded down with responsibilities can be just as destructive as being irresponsible.

istered under their names and counted individually, that is, the workers twenty years old or more who served in the temple of the LORD.
25For David had said, "Since the LORD, the God of Israel, has granted rest to his people and has come to dwell in Jerusalem forever, 26the Levites no longer need to carry the tabernacle or any of the articles used in its service." 27According to the last instructions of David, the Levites were counted from those twenty years old or more.

28The duty of the Levites was to help Aaron's descendants in the service of the temple of the LORD: to be in charge of the courtyards, the side rooms, the purification of all sacred things and the performance of other duties at the house of God. 29They were in charge of the bread set out on the table, the flour for the grain offerings, the unleavened wafers, the baking and the mixing, and all measurements of quantity and size.
30They were also to stand every morning to thank and praise the LORD. They were to do the same in the evening 31and whenever burnt offerings were presented to the LORD on Sabbaths and at New Moon festivals and at appointed feasts. They were to serve before the LORD regularly in the proper number and in the way prescribed for them.

32And so the Levites carried out their responsibilities for the Tent of Meeting, for the Holy Place and, under their brothers the descendants of Aaron, for the service of the temple of the LORD.

The Divisions of Priests

24 These were the divisions of the sons of Aaron:
The sons of Aaron were Nadab, Abihu, Eleazar and Ithamar. 2But Nadab and Abihu died before their father did, and they had no sons; so Eleazar and Ithamar served as the priests. 3With the help of Zadok a descendant of Eleazar and Ahimelech a descendant of Ithamar, David separated them into divisions for their appointed order of ministering. 4A larger number of leaders were found among Eleazar's descendants than among Ithamar's, and they were divided accordingly: sixteen heads of families from Eleazar's descendants and eight heads of families from Ithamar's descendants. 5They divided them impartially by drawing lots, for there were officials of the sanctuary and officials of God among the descendants of both Eleazar and Ithamar.

6The scribe Shemaiah son of Nethanel, a Levite, recorded their names in the presence of the king and of the officials: Zadok the priest, Ahimelech son of Abiathar and the heads of families of the priests and of the Levites—one family being taken from Eleazar and then one from Ithamar.

7The first lot fell to Jehoiarib,
the second to Jedaiah,
8the third to Harim,
the fourth to Seorim,
9the fifth to Malkijah,
the sixth to Mijamin,
10the seventh to Hakkoz,
the eighth to Abijah,
11the ninth to Jeshua,
the tenth to Shecaniah,
12the eleventh to Eliashib,
the twelfth to Jakim,
13the thirteenth to Huppah,
the fourteenth to Jeshebeab,
14the fifteenth to Bilgah,
the sixteenth to Immer,
15the seventeenth to Hezir,
the eighteenth to Happizzez,
16the nineteenth to Pethahiah,
the twentieth to Jehezkel,
17the twenty-first to Jakin,
the twenty-second to Gamul,
18the twenty-third to Delaiah
and the twenty-fourth to Maaziah.

19This was their appointed order of ministering when they entered the temple of the LORD, according to the regulations prescribed for them by their forefather Aaron, as the LORD, the God of Israel, had commanded him.

The Rest of the Levites

20As for the rest of the descendants of Levi:
from the sons of Amram: Shubael;
from the sons of Shubael: Jehdeiah.
21As for Rehabiah, from his sons:
Isshiah was the first.
22From the Izharites: Shelomoth;
from the sons of Shelomoth: Jahath.
23The sons of Hebron: Jeriah the first,[a]
Amariah the second, Jahaziel the third
and Jekameam the fourth.
24The son of Uzziel: Micah;
from the sons of Micah: Shamir.
25The brother of Micah: Isshiah;
from the sons of Isshiah: Zechariah.
26The sons of Merari: Mahli and Mushi.
The son of Jaaziah: Beno.
27The sons of Merari:
from Jaaziah: Beno, Shoham, Zaccur
and Ibri.
28From Mahli: Eleazar, who had no sons.
29From Kish: the son of Kish:
Jerahmeel.
30And the sons of Mushi: Mahli, Eder and
Jerimoth.

These were the Levites, according to their families. 31They also cast lots, just as their brothers the descendants of Aaron did, in the presence of King David and of Zadok, Ahimelech, and the heads of families of the priests and

[a]23 Two Hebrew manuscripts and some Septuagint manuscripts (see also 1 Chron. 23:19); most Hebrew manuscripts *The sons of Jeriah:*

of the Levites. The families of the oldest brother were treated the same as those of the youngest.

The Singers

25 David, together with the commanders of the army, set apart some of the sons of Asaph, Heman and Jeduthun for the ministry of prophesying, accompanied by harps, lyres and cymbals. Here is the list of the men who performed this service:

2From the sons of Asaph:
Zaccur, Joseph, Nethaniah and Asarelah. The sons of Asaph were under the supervision of Asaph, who prophesied under the king's supervision.
3As for Jeduthun, from his sons:
Gedaliah, Zeri, Jeshaiah, Shimei,[a] Hashabiah and Mattithiah, six in all, under the supervision of their father Jeduthun, who prophesied, using the harp in thanking and praising the LORD.
4As for Heman, from his sons:
Bukkiah, Mattaniah, Uzziel, Shubael and Jerimoth; Hananiah, Hanani, Eliathah, Giddalti and Romamti-Ezer; Joshbekashah, Mallothi, Hothir and Mahazioth.
5All these were sons of Heman the king's seer. They were given him through the promises of God to exalt him.[b] God gave Heman fourteen sons and three daughters.

6All these men were under the supervision of their fathers for the music of the temple of the LORD, with cymbals, lyres and harps, for the ministry at the house of God. Asaph, Jeduthun and Heman were under the supervision of the king.
7Along with their relatives—all of them trained and skilled in music for the LORD—they numbered 288.
8Young and old alike, teacher as well as student, cast lots for their duties.

9The first lot, which was for Asaph,
fell to Joseph,
his sons and relatives,[c] 12[d]
the second to Gedaliah,
he and his relatives and sons, 12
10the third to Zaccur,
his sons and relatives, 12
11the fourth to Izri,[e]
his sons and relatives, 12
12the fifth to Nethaniah,
his sons and relatives, 12
13the sixth to Bukkiah,
his sons and relatives, 12
14the seventh to Jesarelah,[f]
his sons and relatives, 12
15the eighth to Jeshaiah,
his sons and relatives, 12
16the ninth to Mattaniah,
his sons and relatives, 12
17the tenth to Shimei,
his sons and relatives, 12
18the eleventh to Azarel,[g]
his sons and relatives, 12
19the twelfth to Hashabiah,
his sons and relatives, 12
20the thirteenth to Shubael,
his sons and relatives, 12
21the fourteenth to Mattithiah,
his sons and relatives, 12
22the fifteenth to Jerimoth,
his sons and relatives, 12
23the sixteenth to Hananiah,
his sons and relatives, 12
24the seventeenth to
Joshbekashah,
his sons and relatives, 12
25the eighteenth to Hanani,
his sons and relatives, 12
26the nineteenth to Mallothi,
his sons and relatives, 12
27the twentieth to Eliathah,
his sons and relatives, 12
28the twenty-first to Hothir,
his sons and relatives, 12
29the twenty-second to Giddalti,
his sons and relatives, 12
30the twenty-third to Mahazioth,
his sons and relatives, 12
31the twenty-fourth to Romamti-Ezer,
his sons and relatives, 12

The Gatekeepers

26 The divisions of the gatekeepers:

From the Korahites: Meshelemiah son of Kore, one of the sons of Asaph.
2Meshelemiah had sons:
Zechariah the firstborn,
Jediael the second,
Zebadiah the third,
Jathniel the fourth,
3Elam the fifth,
Jehohanan the sixth
and Eliehoenai the seventh.
4Obed-Edom also had sons:
Shemaiah the firstborn,
Jehozabad the second,
Joah the third,
Sacar the fourth,
Nethanel the fifth,
5Ammiel the sixth,

[a]3 One Hebrew manuscript and some Septuagint manuscripts (see also verse 17); most Hebrew manuscripts do not have *Shimei.* [b]5 Hebrew *exalt the horn* [c]9 See Septuagint; Hebrew does not have *his sons and relatives.* [d]9 See the total in verse 7; Hebrew does not have *twelve.* [e]11 A variant of *Zeri* [f]14 A variant of *Asarelah* [g]18 A variant of *Uzziel*

26:1–32 God wants all kinds of people to serve him. Not everyone is a musician or worship leader. Not everyone is gifted with a golden tongue. Gatekeepers, ushers, financial officers, custodians and others essential to running the worship services are also valued by God. These duties, which we might consider mundane, are of great importance. God values our service even if few people ever become aware of it.

Issachar the seventh
and Peullethai the eighth.
(For God had blessed Obed-Edom.)

[6]His son Shemaiah also had sons, who
were leaders in their father's family because they were very capable men.
[7]The sons of Shemaiah: Othni, Repha-
el, Obed and Elzabad; his relatives Elihu and Semakiah were also able men.
[8]All these were descendants of Obed-
Edom; they and their sons and their
relatives were capable men with the
strength to do the work—descendants
of Obed-Edom, 62 in all.
[9]Meshelemiah had sons and relatives, who
were able men—18 in all.

[10]Hosah the Merarite had sons: Shimri the
first (although he was not the firstborn, his father had appointed him
the first), [11]Hilkiah the second, Tabali-
ah the third and Zechariah the fourth.
The sons and relatives of Hosah were
13 in all.

[12]These divisions of the gatekeepers, through
their chief men, had duties for ministering in
the temple of the LORD, just as their relatives
had. [13]Lots were cast for each gate, according to
their families, young and old alike.
[14]The lot for the East Gate fell to Shelemiah.[a] Then lots were cast for his son Zechariah,
a wise counselor, and the lot for the North Gate
fell to him. [15]The lot for the South Gate fell to
Obed-Edom, and the lot for the storehouse fell
to his sons. [16]The lots for the West Gate and the
Shalleketh Gate on the upper road fell to Shup-
pim and Hosah.
Guard was alongside of guard: [17]There were
six Levites a day on the east, four a day on the
north, four a day on the south and two at a time
at the storehouse. [18]As for the court to the west,
there were four at the road and two at the court
itself.
[19]These were the divisions of the gatekeepers
who were descendants of Korah and Merari.

The Treasurers and Other Officials

[20]Their fellow Levites were[b] in charge of the
treasuries of the house of God and the treasuries
for the dedicated things.
[21]The descendants of Ladan, who were Gershonites through Ladan and who were heads of
families belonging to Ladan the Gershonite,
were Jehieli, [22]the sons of Jehieli, Zetham and
his brother Joel. They were in charge of the
treasuries of the temple of the LORD.
[23]From the Amramites, the Izharites, the Hebronites and the Uzzielites:

[24]Shubael, a descendant of Gershom son of
Moses, was the officer in charge of the
treasuries. [25]His relatives through Eliezer: Rehabiah his son, Jeshaiah his
son, Joram his son, Zicri his son and
Shelomith his son. [26]Shelomith and
his relatives were in charge of all the
treasuries for the things dedicated by
King David, by the heads of families
who were the commanders of thousands and commanders of hundreds,
and by the other army commanders.
[27]Some of the plunder taken in battle
they dedicated for the repair of the
temple of the LORD. [28]And everything
dedicated by Samuel the seer and by
Saul son of Kish, Abner son of Ner and
Joab son of Zeruiah, and all the other
dedicated things were in the care of
Shelomith and his relatives.
[29]From the Izharites: Kenaniah and his
sons were assigned duties away from
the temple, as officials and judges over
Israel.
[30]From the Hebronites: Hashabiah and his
relatives—seventeen hundred able
men—were responsible in Israel west
of the Jordan for all the work of the
LORD and for the king's service. [31]As for
the Hebronites, Jeriah was their chief
according to the genealogical records
of their families. In the fortieth year of
David's reign a search was made in the
records, and capable men among the
Hebronites were found at Jazer in Gilead. [32]Jeriah had twenty-seven hundred
relatives, who were able men and
heads of families, and King David put
them in charge of the Reubenites, the
Gadites and the half-tribe of Manasseh
for every matter pertaining to God and
for the affairs of the king.

Army Divisions

27 This is the list of the Israelites—heads of
families, commanders of thousands
and commanders of hundreds, and their officers, who served the king in all that concerned
the army divisions that were on duty month by
month throughout the year. Each division consisted of 24,000 men.

[2]In charge of the first division, for the first
month, was Jashobeam son of Zabdiel.
There were 24,000 men in his division.
[3]He was a descendant of Perez and chief of
all the army officers for the first month.
[4]In charge of the division for the second
month was Dodai the Ahohite; Mikloth

[a]14 A variant of *Meshelemiah* [b]20 Septuagint; Hebrew *As for the Levites, Ahijah was*

27:1–34 This chapter details the proper lines of authority for the people of Israel. Recognizing and submitting to authority is important for God's people too (see Romans 13:1–5). Believers need to be accountable to others, including those in our local church body.

was the leader of his division. There were
24,000 men in his division.
5The third army commander, for the third
month, was Benaiah son of Jehoiada the
priest. He was chief and there were 24,000
men in his division. 6This was the Benaiah
who was a mighty man among the Thirty
and was over the Thirty. His son Ammiza-
bad was in charge of his division.
7The fourth, for the fourth month, was Asahel
the brother of Joab; his son Zebadiah was
his successor. There were 24,000 men in
his division.
8The fifth, for the fifth month, was the commander Shamhuth the Izrahite. There were
24,000 men in his division.
9The sixth, for the sixth month, was Ira the son
of Ikkesh the Tekoite. There were 24,000
men in his division.
10The seventh, for the seventh month, was Helez the Pelonite, an Ephraimite. There were
24,000 men in his division.
11The eighth, for the eighth month, was Sibbecai the Hushathite, a Zerahite. There were
24,000 men in his division.
12The ninth, for the ninth month, was Abiezer
the Anathothite, a Benjamite. There were
24,000 men in his division.
13The tenth, for the tenth month, was Maharai
the Netophathite, a Zerahite. There were
24,000 men in his division.
14The eleventh, for the eleventh month, was
Benaiah the Pirathonite, an Ephraimite.
There were 24,000 men in his division.
15The twelfth, for the twelfth month, was Heldai the Netophathite, from the family of
Othniel. There were 24,000 men in his division.

Officers of the Tribes

16The officers over the tribes of Israel:

over the Reubenites: Eliezer son of Zicri;
over the Simeonites: Shephatiah son of
Maacah;
17over Levi: Hashabiah son of Kemuel;
over Aaron: Zadok;
18over Judah: Elihu, a brother of David;
over Issachar: Omri son of Michael;
19over Zebulun: Ishmaiah son of Obadiah;
over Naphtali: Jerimoth son of Azriel;
20over the Ephraimites: Hoshea son of Azaziah;
over half the tribe of Manasseh: Joel son
of Pedaiah;
21over the half-tribe of Manasseh in Gilead:
Iddo son of Zechariah;
over Benjamin: Jaasiel son of Abner;
22over Dan: Azarel son of Jeroham.

These were the officers over the tribes of Israel.

23David did not take the number of the men
twenty years old or less, because the LORD had
promised to make Israel as numerous as the
stars in the sky. 24Joab son of Zeruiah began to
count the men but did not finish. Wrath came
on Israel on account of this numbering, and the
number was not entered in the book[a] of the
annals of King David.

The King's Overseers

25Azmaveth son of Adiel was in charge of the
royal storehouses.

Jonathan son of Uzziah was in charge of
the storehouses in the outlying districts, in the
towns, the villages and the watchtowers.

26Ezri son of Kelub was in charge of the field
workers who farmed the land.

27Shimei the Ramathite was in charge of the
vineyards.

Zabdi the Shiphmite was in charge of the
produce of the vineyards for the wine vats.

28Baal-Hanan the Gederite was in charge of
the olive and sycamore-fig trees in the western
foothills.

Joash was in charge of the supplies of olive
oil.

29Shitrai the Sharonite was in charge of
the herds grazing in Sharon.

Shaphat son of Adlai was in charge of the
herds in the valleys.

30Obil the Ishmaelite was in charge of the
camels.

Jehdeiah the Meronothite was in charge of
the donkeys.

31Jaziz the Hagrite was in charge of the
flocks.

All these were the officials in charge of King
David's property.

32Jonathan, David's uncle, was a counselor, a
man of insight and a scribe. Jehiel son of Hac-
moni took care of the king's sons.
33Ahithophel was the king's counselor.
Hushai the Arkite was the king's friend.
34Ahithophel was succeeded by Jehoiada son of
Benaiah and by Abiathar.

Joab was the commander of the royal army.

David's Plans for the Temple

28 David summoned all the officials of Israel to assemble at Jerusalem: the officers over the tribes, the commanders of the divisions in the service of the king, the commanders
of thousands and commanders of hundreds,
and the officials in charge of all the property
and livestock belonging to the king and his
sons, together with the palace officials, the
mighty men and all the brave warriors.
2King David rose to his feet and said: "Listen
to me, my brothers and my people. I had it in
my heart to build a house as a place of rest for
the ark of the covenant of the LORD, for the
footstool of our God, and I made plans to build
it. 3But God said to me, 'You are not to build a

[a]24 Septuagint; Hebrew *number*

house for my Name, because you are a warrior
and have shed blood.'
4"Yet the LORD, the God of Israel, chose me
from my whole family to be king over Israel
forever. He chose Judah as leader, and from the
house of Judah he chose my family, and from
my father's sons he was pleased to make me
king over all Israel. 5Of all my sons—and the
LORD has given me many—he has chosen my
son Solomon to sit on the throne of the kingdom of the LORD over Israel. 6He said to me:
'Solomon your son is the one who will build
my house and my courts, for I have chosen him
to be my son, and I will be his father. 7I will
establish his kingdom forever if he is unswerv-
ing in carrying out my commands and laws, as
is being done at this time.'
8"So now I charge you in the sight of all
Israel and of the assembly of the LORD, and in
the hearing of our God: Be careful to follow all
the commands of the LORD your God, that you
may possess this good land and pass it on as an
inheritance to your descendants forever.
9"And you, my son Solomon, acknowledge
the God of your father, and serve him with
wholehearted devotion and with a willing
mind, for the LORD searches every heart and
understands every motive behind the thoughts.
If you seek him, he will be found by you; but
if you forsake him, he will reject you forever.
10Consider now, for the LORD has chosen you to
build a temple as a sanctuary. Be strong and do
the work."
11Then David gave his son Solomon the
plans for the portico of the temple, its buildings, its storerooms, its upper parts, its inner
rooms and the place of atonement. 12He gave
him the plans of all that the Spirit had put in his
mind for the courts of the temple of the LORD
and all the surrounding rooms, for the treasuries of the temple of God and for the treasuries
for the dedicated things. 13He gave him instructions for the divisions of the priests and Levites,
and for all the work of serving in the temple of
the LORD, as well as for all the articles to be used
in its service. 14He designated the weight of gold
for all the gold articles to be used in various
kinds of service, and the weight of silver for all
the silver articles to be used in various kinds of
service: 15the weight of gold for the gold lampstands and their lamps, with the weight for each
lampstand and its lamps; and the weight of silver for each silver lampstand and its lamps, according to the use of each lampstand; 16the
weight of gold for each table for consecrated
bread; the weight of silver for the silver tables;
17the weight of pure gold for the forks, sprinkling bowls and pitchers; the weight of gold for
each gold dish; the weight of silver for each

28:8–10 David took the time to pass on to Solomon the wisdom he had received from God. David recognized that he and his descendants were responsible to obey God's commands. Likewise, we must recognize God's greatness and pass this knowledge on to our families, too.

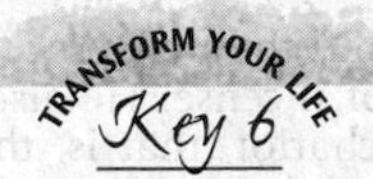

Faith to Build a New Life

1 Chronicles 28:1–21 Our past sometimes gets in the way of our vision for the future. If we let ourselves to dwell on the areas in which we have failed or on the losses and disappointments that have hurt us, we may find it difficult to look forward to the future God has for us.

King David dreamed of building a magnificent temple. In commissioning his son Solomon to do the work, he said, "Be strong and courageous, and do the work. Do not be afraid or discouraged, for the LORD God, my God, is with you. He will not fail you or forsake you" (28:20). Many years later the apostle Paul said, "You are no longer foreigners and aliens, but fellow citizens with God's people . . . built on the foundation of the apostles and prophets, with Christ Jesus himself as the chief cornerstone. In him the whole building is joined together and rises to become a holy temple in the Lord" (Ephesians 2:19–21).

Just as David dreamed of building a magnificent temple, we can dare to dream of building a magnificent new life. God has the blueprint already drawn up; all we have to do is follow it by faith. We may be afraid that we will start and fail, but we only need to "be strong and courageous, and do the work." We don't need to be frightened by the size of the task, for "he who began a good work in you will carry it on to completion until the day of Christ Jesus" (Philippians 1:6).

Turn to 2 Chronicles 15.

silver dish; [18]and the weight of the refined gold for the altar of incense. He also gave him the plan for the chariot, that is, the cherubim of gold that spread their wings and shelter the ark of the covenant of the LORD.

[19]"All this," David said, "I have in writing from the hand of the LORD upon me, and he gave me understanding in all the details of the plan."

[20]David also said to Solomon his son, "Be strong and courageous, and do the work. Do not be afraid or discouraged, for the LORD God, my God, is with you. He will not fail you or forsake you until all the work for the service of the temple of the LORD is finished. [21]The divisions of the priests and Levites are ready for all the work on the temple of God, and every willing man skilled in any craft will help you in all the work. The officials and all the people will obey your every command."

Gifts for Building the Temple

29 Then King David said to the whole assembly: "My son Solomon, the one whom God has chosen, is young and inexperienced. The task is great, because this palatial structure is not for man but for the LORD God. [2]With all my resources I have provided for the temple of my God—gold for the gold work, silver for the silver, bronze for the bronze, iron for the iron and wood for the wood, as well as onyx for the settings, turquoise,[a] stones of various colors, and all kinds of fine stone and marble—all of these in large quantities. [3]Besides, in my devotion to the temple of my God I now give my personal treasures of gold and silver for the temple of my God, over and above everything I have provided for this holy temple: [4]three thousand talents[b] of gold (gold of Ophir) and seven thousand talents[c] of refined silver, for the overlaying of the walls of the buildings, [5]for the gold work and the silver work, and for all the work to be done by the craftsmen. Now, who is willing to consecrate himself today to the LORD?"

[6]Then the leaders of families, the officers of the tribes of Israel, the commanders of thousands and commanders of hundreds, and the officials in charge of the king's work gave willingly. [7]They gave toward the work on the temple of God five thousand talents[d] and ten thousand darics[e] of gold, ten thousand talents[f] of silver, eighteen thousand talents[g] of bronze and a hundred thousand talents[h] of iron. [8]Any who had precious stones gave them to the treasury of the temple of the LORD in the custody of Jehiel the Gershonite. [9]The people rejoiced at the willing response of their leaders, for they had given freely and wholeheartedly to the LORD. David the king also rejoiced greatly.

David's Prayer

[10]David praised the LORD in the presence of the whole assembly, saying,

"Praise be to you, O LORD,
God of our father Israel,
from everlasting to everlasting.
[11]Yours, O LORD, is the greatness and the power
and the glory and the majesty and the splendor,
for everything in heaven and earth is yours.
Yours, O LORD, is the kingdom;
you are exalted as head over all.
[12]Wealth and honor come from you;
you are the ruler of all things.
In your hands are strength and power
to exalt and give strength to all.
[13]Now, our God, we give you thanks,
and praise your glorious name.

[14]"But who am I, and who are my people, that we should be able to give as generously as this? Everything comes from you, and we have given you only what comes from your hand. [15]We are aliens and strangers in your sight, as were all our forefathers. Our days on earth are like a shadow, without hope. [16]O LORD our God, as for all this abundance that we have provided for building you a temple for your Holy Name, it comes from your hand, and all of it belongs to you. [17]I know, my God, that you test the heart and are pleased with integrity. All these things have I given willingly and with honest intent. And now I have seen with joy

[a]2 The meaning of the Hebrew for this word is uncertain.
[b]4 That is, about 110 tons (about 100 metric tons)
[c]4 That is, about 260 tons (about 240 metric tons)
[d]7 That is, about 190 tons (about 170 metric tons)
[e]7 That is, about 185 pounds (about 84 kilograms)
[f]7 That is, about 375 tons (about 345 metric tons)
[g]7 That is, about 675 tons (about 610 metric tons)
[h]7 That is, about 3,750 tons (about 3,450 metric tons)

28:19 God had a plan for building the temple in Jerusalem. David passed that plan on to Solomon, who would complete the project. God also has a plan for each one of us. His blueprint includes our spiritual growth. Each of us is a "temple" for the Holy Spirit; God actually dwells inside his people (see 1 Corinthians 6:19). In light of this, our thoughts and behavior should reflect the character of the one who lives within us.

29:3 Proper priorities are necessary for aligning our lives with God's will. We need to put God first in our thinking. We also need to help others. David gave to God out of his own personal wealth and energy. His personal treasures would help support the work of God in Israel. His giving would also contribute to the blessings received by people worshiping at the temple for generations to come.

29:11–12 David's prayer of praise is filled with important truths. He recognizes that God is the source of all true success. His prayer ascribes all greatness, power, glory, victory and majesty to God. It recognizes that God is the source of all riches and honor and that God is sovereign over peoples, tongues and nations. These are essential truths. We must daily affirm these truths and recognize that God is our source of strength. We are helpless on our own, but God is more than able to help us overcome our struggles.

how willingly your people who are here have
given to you. 18O LORD, God of our fathers
Abraham, Isaac and Israel, keep this desire in
the hearts of your people forever, and keep their
hearts loyal to you. 19And give my son Solomon
the wholehearted devotion to keep your commands, requirements and decrees and to do everything to build the palatial structure for which
I have provided."

20Then David said to the whole assembly,
"Praise the LORD your God." So they all praised
the LORD, the God of their fathers; they bowed
low and fell prostrate before the LORD and the
king.

Solomon Acknowledged as King

21The next day they made sacrifices to the
LORD and presented burnt offerings to him: a
thousand bulls, a thousand rams and a thousand male lambs, together with their drink offerings, and other sacrifices in abundance for all
Israel. 22They ate and drank with great joy in the
presence of the LORD that day.

Then they acknowledged Solomon son of
David as king a second time, anointing him
before the LORD to be ruler and Zadok to be
priest. 23So Solomon sat on the throne of the
LORD as king in place of his father David. He
prospered and all Israel obeyed him. 24All the
officers and mighty men, as well as all of King
David's sons, pledged their submission to King
Solomon.

25The LORD highly exalted Solomon in the
sight of all Israel and bestowed on him royal
splendor such as no king over Israel ever had
before.

The Death of David

26David son of Jesse was king over all Israel.
27He ruled over Israel forty years—seven in Hebron and thirty-three in Jerusalem. 28He died at
a good old age, having enjoyed long life, wealth
and honor. His son Solomon succeeded him as
king.

29As for the events of King David's reign,
from beginning to end, they are written in the
records of Samuel the seer, the records of Nathan the prophet and the records of Gad the
seer, 30together with the details of his reign and
power, and the circumstances that surrounded
him and Israel and the kingdoms of all the other lands.

2 CHRONICLES

A. THE REIGN OF SOLOMON (1:1–9:31)

B. THE DOWNWARD SLIDE OF THE KINGS (10:1–36:4)

1. Rehoboam (10:1–13:22)
2. Asa (14:1–16:14)
3. Jehoshaphat (17:1–20:37)
4. Jehoram and Athaliah (21:1–22:12)
5. Joash (23:1–24:27)
6. Amaziah (25:1-28)
7. Uzziah (26:1-23)
8. Jotham (27:1-9)
9. Ahaz (28:1-27)
10. Hezekiah (29:1–32:33)
11. Manasseh (33:1-25)
12. Josiah (34:1–35:27)
13. Sons of Josiah (36:1-14)
    a. Jehoahaz (36:1-4)
    b. Jehoiakim (36:5-8)
    c. Grandson, Jehoiachin (36:9-10)
    d. Zedekiah (36:11-14)

C. JUDAH EXILED TO BABYLON (36:5-21)

D. THE DECREE OF HOPE (36:22-23)

The Big Picture

The book of 2 Chronicles was originally part of a larger book that also included 1 Chronicles. The larger work recorded Israel's history, starting with a genealogy of Adam's descendants and ending with Israel in Babylonian captivity. This condensed history was written to give Israel hope as they sought to rebuild their nation after the Babylonian exile.

Second Chronicles begins on a high note, recording Solomon's great success at building God's temple in Jerusalem. But after his good start, Solomon made some mistakes that were intensified by his son Rehoboam and ultimately led to the division of Israel into two kingdoms (931 B.C.). Second Chronicles focuses our attention on the southern kingdom of Judah. The succession of David's royal descendants in the southern kingdom exhibited varying degrees of accomplishment and failure during their reigns. Some attempted to break from the sinful patterns and lead the people to examine their lives and turn back to God. Through these kings, God brought revival and renewal to his people. But the kings who set their hearts against God led the people back into sinful ways. As a result, the southern kingdom of Judah was conquered, and the people were taken captive by Babylonian armies.

The account in 2 Chronicles follows David's royal line on a slow but steady decline toward destruction and exile. But when things look their darkest, the final verses leave us with a message of hope. Stirred by the spirit of God, King Cyrus of Persia issued a decree allowing the temple at Jerusalem to be rebuilt. This showed the Israelites who were seeking to rebuild their homeland that God had been working behind the scenes on their behalf. Despite their past failures and lack of faith, God was graciously working to bring about their restoration.

Spiritual Renewal Themes

THE NECESSITY OF FAITHFULNESS

When a king who was faithful to God was in power, the people often followed his lead and experienced restoration and spiritual renewal. But the victories of one day did not automatically guarantee winning the trials of the next. The people had to persevere in their faithfulness each day. When the path of faithfulness was forsaken, the people quickly returned to their false

gods. Their disobedience stood in sharp contrast to their earlier faithfulness. When the principles the people learned were not incorporated into their daily lives on a continual basis, their human resolve quickly eroded in the face of sin and temptation.

GOD MUST BE THE FOCUS OF OUR SPIRITUAL RENEWAL

This book was written to encourage the Israelites after their return from Babylonian exile. In their humiliating captivity, the people had come to the end of themselves. As they returned to rebuild their temple, land and nation, God wanted them to learn that any successful rebuilding plan must center around the true worship of God. A spiritual-growth plan that does not begin and end with God's power becomes empty and weak. We need to learn the lessons that the Israelites struggled to grasp throughout their history—genuine spiritual growth begins, survives and continues through dependence on God.

THE UPS AND DOWNS OF SPIRITUAL GROWTH

We might think that God is pleased with us only when we are making steady, forward progress in our spiritual growth. If we slip backward, even a little, it is easy to feel that we've lost everything. But spiritual growth has its ups and downs. In 2 Chronicles we see the Israelites following a pattern that will eventually lead to destruction. They take three steps backward and then only one step forward. If we can take more steps forward than we do backward, we will be on the right track. Our spiritual growth will progress as we depend on God for strength and guidance.

WITH GOD THERE IS ALWAYS HOPE

Even when things seem darkest, God is at work. When we are overwhelmed by circumstances and feel that God has forsaken us, it may help to remember that we are feeling what the people of Judah must have felt in Babylon! We should be encouraged as we look at the surprising reversal of their situation. In the midst of their despair, Cyrus granted a decree that allowed them to return to Jerusalem to rebuild their temple. When we continually seek God and surrender to him we can be confident that even in our darkest hour God is at work—and there is hope!

Essential Facts

PURPOSE:
To record the history of Judah's kings, both those who obeyed God and those who sinned against him. Their examples would encourage and admonish the people to rebuild their nation according to God's plan.

AUTHOR:
Unknown, but tradition attributes it to Ezra.

AUDIENCE:
The people of Israel after their return from exile in Babylon.

DATE WRITTEN:
Approximately 430 B.C.

SETTING:
The kingdom of Judah between Solomon's reign (979 B.C.) and the decree of Cyrus (539 B.C.).

KEY VERSE:
"If my people, who are called by my name, will humble themselves and pray and seek my face and turn from their wicked ways, then will I hear from heaven and will forgive their sin and will heal their land" (7:14).

KEY EVENTS:
The spiritual revivals that occurred under Asa, Jehoshaphat, Joash, Hezekiah and Josiah.

Solomon Asks for Wisdom

1 Solomon son of David established himself firmly over his kingdom, for the LORD his God was with him and made him exceedingly great.

2Then Solomon spoke to all Israel—to the commanders of thousands and commanders of hundreds, to the judges and to all the leaders in Israel, the heads of families— 3and Solomon and the whole assembly went to the high place at Gibeon, for God's Tent of Meeting was there, which Moses the LORD's servant had made in the desert. 4Now David had brought up the ark of God from Kiriath Jearim to the place he had prepared for it, because he had pitched a tent for it in Jerusalem. 5But the bronze altar that Bezalel son of Uri, the son of Hur, had made was in Gibeon in front of the tabernacle of the LORD; so Solomon and the assembly inquired of him there. 6Solomon went up to the bronze altar before the LORD in the Tent of Meeting and offered a thousand burnt offerings on it.

7That night God appeared to Solomon and said to him, "Ask for whatever you want me to give you."

8Solomon answered God, "You have shown great kindness to David my father and have made me king in his place. 9Now, LORD God, let your promise to my father David be confirmed, for you have made me king over a people who are as numerous as the dust of the earth. 10Give me wisdom and knowledge, that I may lead this people, for who is able to govern this great people of yours?"

11God said to Solomon, "Since this is your heart's desire and you have not asked for wealth, riches or honor, nor for the death of your enemies, and since you have not asked for a long life but for wisdom and knowledge to govern my people over whom I have made you king, 12therefore wisdom and knowledge will be given you. And I will also give you wealth, riches and honor, such as no king who was before you ever had and none after you will have."

13Then Solomon went to Jerusalem from the high place at Gibeon, from before the Tent of Meeting. And he reigned over Israel.

14Solomon accumulated chariots and horses; he had fourteen hundred chariots and twelve thousand horses,[a] which he kept in the chariot cities and also with him in Jerusalem. 15The king made silver and gold as common in Jerusalem as stones, and cedar as plentiful as sycamore-fig trees in the foothills. 16Solomon's horses were imported from Egypt[b] and from Kue[c]—the royal merchants purchased them from Kue. 17They imported a chariot from Egypt for six hundred shekels[d] of silver, and a horse for a hundred and fifty.[e] They also exported them to all the kings of the Hittites and of the Arameans.

Preparations for Building the Temple

2 Solomon gave orders to build a temple for the Name of the LORD and a royal palace for himself. 2He conscripted seventy thousand men as carriers and eighty thousand as stonecutters in the hills and thirty-six hundred as foremen over them.

3Solomon sent this message to Hiram[f] king of Tyre:

> "Send me cedar logs as you did for my father David when you sent him cedar to build a palace to live in. 4Now I am about to build a temple for the Name of the LORD my God and to dedicate it to him for burning fragrant incense before him, for setting out the consecrated bread regularly, and for making burnt offerings every morning and evening and on Sabbaths and New Moons and at the appointed feasts of the LORD our God. This is a lasting ordinance for Israel.
>
> 5"The temple I am going to build will be great, because our God is greater than all other gods. 6But who is able to build a

[a]14 Or *charioteers* [b]16 Or possibly *Muzur,* a region in Cilicia; also in verse 17 [c]16 Probably Cilicia
[d]17 That is, about 15 pounds (about 7 kilograms)
[e]17 That is, about 3 3/4 pounds (about 1.7 kilograms)
[f]3 Hebrew *Huram,* a variant of *Hiram;* also in verses 11 and 12

1:1 We all want to succeed, whether in spiritual or practical ways. At the outset of this book, God gave Solomon unprecedented success in everything he did. But notice that Solomon's success depended on God's presence with him. We, too, must recognize that true success depends on God's guiding presence in our lives.

1:7 What might we request if God made us this offer? Solomon asked for wisdom, passing over the opportunity to request wealth or power. He desired something that would serve the best interests of his people. God was pleased with Solomon's selfless attitude and rewarded him with more power and wealth than he could have wished for. We also need to ask God to give us his wisdom as well as whatever we need to fulfill his calling for us.

2:1 In order to move toward spiritual renewal and transformation, we must begin with the proper resolve. Solomon was anxious to fulfill the plans God had for him. He began by building the temple—a huge task—perhaps even an impossible one! God has certain tasks ordained for each of us (see Ephesians 2:10). Some of these tasks will be difficult; some may even seem impossible! But with God's help, we will be able to accomplish them.

2:5 Solomon's achievements for God were great. This passage tells us why: "This temple . . . will be great, because our God is greater than all other gods." The deeper our relationship with God, the more we will realize how much he deserves our obedience and service. The realization of God's great power and love for us should give us courage as we seek to grow spiritually.

2:6 This verse reminds us of how great God really is. He is far greater than we can even imagine or understand. Solomon's temple was magnificent, but even it was not good enough for God. God's greatness may discourage some of us and cause us to wonder why such a great God would even bother with us. Though God is great, he is also loving and gracious. He reaches out to sinful, weak

temple for him, since the heavens, even the highest heavens, cannot contain him? Who then am I to build a temple for him, except as a place to burn sacrifices before him?

7"Send me, therefore, a man skilled to work in gold and silver, bronze and iron, and in purple, crimson and blue yarn, and experienced in the art of engraving, to work in Judah and Jerusalem with my skilled craftsmen, whom my father David provided.

8"Send me also cedar, pine and algum[a] logs from Lebanon, for I know that your men are skilled in cutting timber there. My men will work with yours 9to provide me with plenty of lumber, because the temple I build must be large and magnificent. 10I will give your servants, the woodsmen who cut the timber, twenty thousand cors[b] of ground wheat, twenty thousand cors of barley, twenty thousand baths[c] of wine and twenty thousand baths of olive oil."

11Hiram king of Tyre replied by letter to Solomon:

"Because the LORD loves his people, he has made you their king."

12And Hiram added:

"Praise be to the LORD, the God of Israel, who made heaven and earth! He has given King David a wise son, endowed with intelligence and discernment, who will build a temple for the LORD and a palace for himself.

13"I am sending you Huram-Abi, a man of great skill, 14whose mother was from Dan and whose father was from Tyre. He is trained to work in gold and silver, bronze and iron, stone and wood, and with purple and blue and crimson yarn and fine linen. He is experienced in all kinds of engraving and can execute any design given to him. He will work with your craftsmen and with those of my lord, David your father.

15"Now let my lord send his servants the wheat and barley and the olive oil and wine he promised, 16and we will cut all the logs from Lebanon that you need and will float them in rafts by sea down to Joppa. You can then take them up to Jerusalem."

17Solomon took a census of all the aliens who were in Israel, after the census his father David had taken; and they were found to be 153,600. 18He assigned 70,000 of them to be carriers and 80,000 to be stonecutters in the hills, with 3,600 foremen over them to keep the people working.

Solomon Builds the Temple

3 Then Solomon began to build the temple of the LORD in Jerusalem on Mount Moriah, where the LORD had appeared to his father David. It was on the threshing floor of Araunah[d] the Jebusite, the place provided by David. 2He began building on the second day of the second month in the fourth year of his reign.

3The foundation Solomon laid for building the temple of God was sixty cubits long and twenty cubits wide[e] (using the cubit of the old standard). 4The portico at the front of the temple was twenty cubits[f] long across the width of the building and twenty cubits[g] high.

He overlaid the inside with pure gold. 5He paneled the main hall with pine and covered it with fine gold and decorated it with palm tree and chain designs. 6He adorned the temple with precious stones. And the gold he used was gold of Parvaim. 7He overlaid the ceiling beams, doorframes, walls and doors of the temple with gold, and he carved cherubim on the walls.

8He built the Most Holy Place, its length corresponding to the width of the temple—twenty cubits long and twenty cubits wide. He overlaid the inside with six hundred talents[h] of fine gold. 9The gold nails weighed fifty shekels.[i] He also overlaid the upper parts with gold.

10In the Most Holy Place he made a pair of sculptured cherubim and overlaid them with gold. 11The total wingspan of the cherubim was twenty cubits. One wing of the first cherub was five cubits[j] long and touched the temple wall, while its other wing, also five cubits long, touched the wing of the other cherub. 12Similarly one wing of the second cherub was five cubits long and touched the other temple wall, and its other wing, also five cubits long, touched the wing of the first cherub. 13The wings of these

[a]8 Probably a variant of *almug;* possibly juniper
[b]10 That is, probably about 125,000 bushels (about 4,400 kiloliters)
[c]10 That is, probably about 115,000 gallons (about 440 kiloliters)
[d]1 Hebrew *Ornan,* a variant of *Araunah*
[e]3 That is, about 90 feet (about 27 meters) long and 30 feet (about 9 meters) wide
[f]4 That is, about 30 feet (about 9 meters); also in verses 8, 11 and 13
[g]4 Some Septuagint and Syriac manuscripts; Hebrew *and a hundred and twenty*
[h]8 That is, about 23 tons (about 21 metric tons)
[i]9 That is, about 1 1/4 pounds (about 0.6 kilogram)
[j]11 That is, about 7 1/2 feet (about 2.3 meters); also in verse 15

people like us to bring about our restoration. And as great as God is, he certainly does not lack the power we need to accomplish anything he has called us to do.

3:3–17 This passage begins a description of the temple's specifications. The immense wealth required to build the temple is overwhelming. Large projects always require great resources. God is the only one with sufficient resources for the huge task of spiritual transformation. We need to learn to depend on his power.

cherubim extended twenty cubits. They stood on their feet, facing the main hall.[a]

14 He made the curtain of blue, purple and crimson yarn and fine linen, with cherubim worked into it.

15 In the front of the temple he made two pillars, which ⌞together⌟ were thirty-five cubits[b] long, each with a capital on top measuring five cubits. 16 He made interwoven chains[c] and put them on top of the pillars. He also made a hundred pomegranates and attached them to the chains. 17 He erected the pillars in the front of the temple, one to the south and one to the north. The one to the south he named Jakin[d] and the one to the north Boaz.[e]

The Temple's Furnishings

4 He made a bronze altar twenty cubits long, twenty cubits wide and ten cubits high.[f] 2 He made the Sea of cast metal, circular in shape, measuring ten cubits from rim to rim and five cubits[g] high. It took a line of thirty cubits[h] to measure around it. 3 Below the rim, figures of bulls encircled it—ten to a cubit.[i] The bulls were cast in two rows in one piece with the Sea.

4 The Sea stood on twelve bulls, three facing north, three facing west, three facing south and three facing east. The Sea rested on top of them, and their hindquarters were toward the center. 5 It was a handbreadth[j] in thickness, and its rim was like the rim of a cup, like a lily blossom. It held three thousand baths.[k]

6 He then made ten basins for washing and placed five on the south side and five on the north. In them the things to be used for the burnt offerings were rinsed, but the Sea was to be used by the priests for washing.

7 He made ten gold lampstands according to the specifications for them and placed them in the temple, five on the south side and five on the north.

8 He made ten tables and placed them in the temple, five on the south side and five on the north. He also made a hundred gold sprinkling bowls.

9 He made the courtyard of the priests, and the large court and the doors for the court, and overlaid the doors with bronze. 10 He placed the Sea on the south side, at the southeast corner.

11 He also made the pots and shovels and sprinkling bowls.

So Huram finished the work he had undertaken for King Solomon in the temple of God:

12 the two pillars;
the two bowl-shaped capitals on top of the pillars;
the two sets of network decorating the two bowl-shaped capitals on top of the pillars;
13 the four hundred pomegranates for the two sets of network (two rows of pomegranates for each network, decorating the bowl-shaped capitals on top of the pillars);
14 the stands with their basins;
15 the Sea and the twelve bulls under it;
16 the pots, shovels, meat forks and all related articles.

All the objects that Huram-Abi made for King Solomon for the temple of the LORD were of polished bronze. 17 The king had them cast in clay molds in the plain of the Jordan between Succoth and Zarethan.[l] 18 All these things that Solomon made amounted to so much that the weight of the bronze was not determined.

19 Solomon also made all the furnishings that were in God's temple:

the golden altar;
the tables on which was the bread of the Presence;
20 the lampstands of pure gold with their lamps, to burn in front of the inner sanctuary as prescribed;
21 the gold floral work and lamps and tongs (they were solid gold);
22 the pure gold wick trimmers, sprinkling bowls, dishes and censers; and the gold doors of the temple: the inner doors to the Most Holy Place and the doors of the main hall.

[a]13 Or *facing inward* [b]15 That is, about 52 feet (about 16 meters) [c]16 Or possibly *made chains in the inner sanctuary*; the meaning of the Hebrew for this phrase is uncertain. [d]17 *Jakin* probably means *he establishes.* [e]17 *Boaz* probably means *in him is strength.* [f]1 That is, about 30 feet (about 9 meters) long and wide, and about 15 feet (about 4.5 meters) high [g]2 That is, about 7 1/2 feet (about 2.3 meters) [h]2 That is, about 45 feet (about 13.5 meters) [i]3 That is, about 1 1/2 feet (about 0.5 meter) [j]5 That is, about 3 inches (about 8 centimeters) [k]5 That is, about 17,500 gallons (about 66 kiloliters) [l]17 Hebrew *Zeredatha,* a variant of *Zarethan*

4:1 Immediately upon entering the temple area, worshipers were confronted with the great bronze altar. This object would remind them that each individual was in great need of God's forgiveness. Many animal sacrifices were offered in payment for the people's sins. Forgiveness had to be achieved through sacrifice before any approach to God was possible. God made it possible for us to approach him, too—through the death and resurrection of his Son, Jesus Christ.

4:2 The sea of cast metal corresponded to the tabernacle's laver. As they did God's work, the priests became covered with the blood of the sacrificial animals. The priests needed immediate cleansing. Likewise, we need cleansing from the sinful pollution we encounter in our daily walk. How wonderful to remember that our sins can be forgiven daily through Christ!

4:20 The temple needed light in its darkened interior. Even as the Holy Place would have been dark were it not for the lampstand, so our lives would be in total darkness without the presence of the "Light of the World"—Jesus Christ (see John 8:12).

5 When all the work Solomon had done for the temple of the LORD was finished, he brought in the things his father David had dedicated—the silver and gold and all the furnishings—and he placed them in the treasuries of God's temple.

The Ark Brought to the Temple

[2]Then Solomon summoned to Jerusalem the elders of Israel, all the heads of the tribes and the chiefs of the Israelite families, to bring up the ark of the LORD's covenant from Zion, the City of David. [3]And all the men of Israel came together to the king at the time of the festival in the seventh month.

[4]When all the elders of Israel had arrived, the Levites took up the ark, [5]and they brought up the ark and the Tent of Meeting and all the sacred furnishings in it. The priests, who were Levites, carried them up; [6]and King Solomon and the entire assembly of Israel that had gathered about him were before the ark, sacrificing so many sheep and cattle that they could not be recorded or counted.

[7]The priests then brought the ark of the LORD's covenant to its place in the inner sanctuary of the temple, the Most Holy Place, and put it beneath the wings of the cherubim. [8]The cherubim spread their wings over the place of the ark and covered the ark and its carrying poles. [9]These poles were so long that their ends, extending from the ark, could be seen from in front of the inner sanctuary, but not from outside the Holy Place; and they are still there today. [10]There was nothing in the ark except the two tablets that Moses had placed in it at Horeb, where the LORD made a covenant with the Israelites after they came out of Egypt.

[11]The priests then withdrew from the Holy Place. All the priests who were there had consecrated themselves, regardless of their divisions. [12]All the Levites who were musicians—Asaph, Heman, Jeduthun and their sons and relatives—stood on the east side of the altar, dressed in fine linen and playing cymbals, harps and lyres. They were accompanied by 120 priests sounding trumpets. [13]The trumpeters and singers joined in unison, as with one voice, to give praise and thanks to the LORD. Accompanied by trumpets, cymbals and other instruments, they raised their voices in praise to the LORD and sang:

"He is good;
his love endures forever."

Then the temple of the LORD was filled with a cloud, [14]and the priests could not perform their service because of the cloud, for the glory of the LORD filled the temple of God.

6 Then Solomon said, "The LORD has said that he would dwell in a dark cloud; [2]I have built a magnificent temple for you, a place for you to dwell forever."

[3]While the whole assembly of Israel was standing there, the king turned around and blessed them. [4]Then he said:

"Praise be to the LORD, the God of Israel, who with his hands has fulfilled what he promised with his mouth to my father David. For he said, [5]'Since the day I brought my people out of Egypt, I have not chosen a city in any tribe of Israel to have a temple built for my Name to be there, nor have I chosen anyone to be the leader over my people Israel. [6]But now I have chosen Jerusalem for my Name to be there, and I have chosen David to rule my people Israel.'

[7]"My father David had it in his heart to build a temple for the Name of the LORD, the God of Israel. [8]But the LORD said to my father David, 'Because it was in your heart to build a temple for my Name, you did well to have this in your heart. [9]Nevertheless, you are not the one to build the temple, but your son, who is your own flesh and blood—he is the one who will build the temple for my Name.'

[10]"The LORD has kept the promise he made. I have succeeded David my father and now I sit on the throne of Israel, just as the LORD promised, and I have built the temple for the Name of the LORD, the God of Israel. [11]There I have placed the ark, in which is the covenant of the LORD that he made with the people of Israel."

Solomon's Prayer of Dedication

[12]Then Solomon stood before the altar of the LORD in front of the whole assembly of Israel and spread out his hands. [13]Now he had made a bronze platform, five cubits[a] long, five cubits wide and three cubits[b] high, and had placed it in the center of the outer court. He stood on the platform and then knelt down before the whole assembly of Israel and spread out his hands toward heaven. [14]He said:

[a]13 That is, about 7 1/2 feet (about 2.3 meters)
[b]13 That is, about 4 1/2 feet (about 1.3 meters)

5:13–14 The trumpets sounded with joy! The singers sang out their praises to God in a beautiful celebration! For the victories in life, we must remember to respond with thanksgiving and praise to God.

5:13–14 As the people praised him, God's visible presence appeared and entered the temple. No wonder God's people responded with such a joyful celebration. They were assured that God was with them! This fact alone gave them confidence in a future filled with joy and success. For us to experience spiritual growth, God must be present in our lives too. No matter what we set out to do, God's presence is essential for true success.

6:14 We are often impressed by trendy schemes that claim to be able to solve all our problems. New techniques or programs promise to accomplish great changes in our lives. Yet this verse reminds us that there is no substitute for God. He alone is able to transform us into the people he created us to be. Notice also that God's

"O LORD, God of Israel, there is no God like you in heaven or on earth—you who keep your covenant of love with your servants who continue wholeheartedly in your way. 15You have kept your promise to your servant David my father; with your mouth you have promised and with your hand you have fulfilled it—as it is today.

16"Now LORD, God of Israel, keep for your servant David my father the promises you made to him when you said, 'You shall never fail to have a man to sit before me on the throne of Israel, if only your sons are careful in all they do to walk before me according to my law, as you have done.' 17And now, O LORD, God of Israel, let your word that you promised your servant David come true.

18"But will God really dwell on earth with men? The heavens, even the highest heavens, cannot contain you. How much less this temple I have built! 19Yet give attention to your servant's prayer and his plea for mercy, O LORD my God. Hear the cry and the prayer that your servant is praying in your presence. 20May your eyes be open toward this temple day and night, this place of which you said you would put your Name there. May you hear the prayer your servant prays toward this place. 21Hear the supplications of your servant and of your people Israel when they pray toward this place. Hear from heaven, your dwelling place; and when you hear, forgive.

22"When a man wrongs his neighbor and is required to take an oath and he comes and swears the oath before your altar in this temple, 23then hear from heaven and act. Judge between your servants, repaying the guilty by bringing down on his own head what he has done. Declare the innocent not guilty and so establish his innocence.

24"When your people Israel have been defeated by an enemy because they have sinned against you and when they turn back and confess your name, praying and making supplication before you in this temple, 25then hear from heaven and forgive the sin of your people Israel and bring them back to the land you gave to them and their fathers.

26"When the heavens are shut up and there is no rain because your people have sinned against you, and when they pray toward this place and confess your name and turn from their sin because you have afflicted them, 27then hear from heaven and forgive the sin of your servants, your people Israel. Teach them the right way to live, and send rain on the land you gave your people for an inheritance.

28"When famine or plague comes to the land, or blight or mildew, locusts or grasshoppers, or when enemies besiege them in any of their cities, whatever disaster or disease may come, 29and when a prayer or plea is made by any of your people Israel—each one aware of his afflictions and pains, and spreading out his hands toward this temple— 30then hear from heaven, your dwelling place. Forgive, and deal with each man according to all he does, since you know his heart (for you alone know the hearts of men), 31so that they will fear you and walk in your ways all the time they live in the land you gave our fathers.

32"As for the foreigner who does not belong to your people Israel but has come from a distant land because of your great name and your mighty hand and your outstretched arm—when he comes and prays toward this temple, 33then hear from heaven, your dwelling place, and do whatever the foreigner asks of you, so that all the peoples of the earth may know your name and fear you, as do your own people Israel, and may know that this house I have built bears your Name.

34"When your people go to war against their enemies, wherever you send them, and when they pray to you toward this city you have chosen and the temple I have built for your Name, 35then hear from heaven their prayer and their plea, and uphold their cause.

36"When they sin against you—for there is no one who does not sin—and you become angry with them and give them over to the enemy, who takes them captive to a land far away or near; 37and if they have a change of heart in the land where they are held captive, and repent and plead with you in the land of their captivity and say, 'We have sinned, we have done wrong and acted wickedly'; 38and if they turn back to you with all their heart and soul in the land of their captivity where they were taken, and pray toward the land you gave their fathers, toward the city you have chosen and toward the temple I have built for your Name; 39then from heaven, your dwelling place, hear their prayer and their pleas, and uphold their cause. And forgive your people, who have sinned against you.

---

promises are realized only when we submit to his will. Though God empowers us to change, he also requires us to surrender to him.

6:18 As humans, we face many limitations: Our strength is limited; our money is limited; our time is limited; our opportunities are limited. But this verse reminds us that God is never limited. God's resources can be counted on in every situation and circumstance.

40"Now, my God, may your eyes be open and your ears attentive to the prayers offered in this place.

41"Now arise, O LORD God, and come
to your resting place,
you and the ark of your might.
May your priests, O LORD God, be
clothed with salvation,
may your saints rejoice in your
goodness.
42O LORD God, do not reject your
anointed one.
Remember the great love promised
to David your servant."

The Dedication of the Temple

7 When Solomon finished praying, fire came
down from heaven and consumed the
burnt offering and the sacrifices, and the glory
of the LORD filled the temple. 2The priests could
not enter the temple of the LORD because the
glory of the LORD filled it. 3When all the Israelites saw the fire coming down and the glory of
the LORD above the temple, they knelt on the
pavement with their faces to the ground, and
they worshiped and gave thanks to the LORD,
saying,

"He is good;
his love endures forever."

4Then the king and all the people offered sacrifices before the LORD. 5And King Solomon offered a sacrifice of twenty-two thousand head
of cattle and a hundred and twenty thousand
sheep and goats. So the king and all the people
dedicated the temple of God. 6The priests took
their positions, as did the Levites with the
LORD's musical instruments, which King David
had made for praising the LORD and which were
used when he gave thanks, saying, "His love
endures forever." Opposite the Levites, the
priests blew their trumpets, and all the Israelites
were standing.

7Solomon consecrated the middle part of the
courtyard in front of the temple of the LORD,
and there he offered burnt offerings and the
fat of the fellowship offerings,[a] because the
bronze altar he had made could not hold the
burnt offerings, the grain offerings and the fat
portions.

8So Solomon observed the festival at that
time for seven days, and all Israel with him—a
vast assembly, people from Lebo[b] Hamath to
the Wadi of Egypt. 9On the eighth day they held
an assembly, for they had celebrated the dedication of the altar for seven days and the festival
for seven days more. 10On the twenty-third day
of the seventh month he sent the people to their
homes, joyful and glad in heart for the good
things the LORD had done for David and Solomon and for his people Israel.

The LORD Appears to Solomon

11When Solomon had finished the temple of
the LORD and the royal palace, and had succeeded in carrying out all he had in mind to do in
the temple of the LORD and in his own palace,
12the LORD appeared to him at night and said:

"I have heard your prayer and have
chosen this place for myself as a temple
for sacrifices.

13"When I shut up the heavens so that
there is no rain, or command locusts to
devour the land or send a plague among
my people, 14if my people, who are called
by my name, will humble themselves and
pray and seek my face and turn from their
wicked ways, then will I hear from heaven
and will forgive their sin and will heal
their land. 15Now my eyes will be open
and my ears attentive to the prayers offered in this place. 16I have chosen and
consecrated this temple so that my Name
may be there forever. My eyes and my
heart will always be there.

17"As for you, if you walk before me as
David your father did, and do all I command, and observe my decrees and laws,
18I will establish your royal throne, as I
covenanted with David your father when
I said, 'You shall never fail to have a man
to rule over Israel.'

19"But if you[c] turn away and forsake
the decrees and commands I have given
you[c] and go off to serve other gods and
worship them, 20then I will uproot Israel
from my land, which I have given them,
and will reject this temple I have consecrated for my Name. I will make it a byword and an object of ridicule among all
peoples. 21And though this temple is now
so imposing, all who pass by will be appalled and say, 'Why has the LORD done
such a thing to this land and to this temple?' 22People will answer, 'Because they
have forsaken the LORD, the God of their
fathers, who brought them out of Egypt,
and have embraced other gods, worship-

[a]7 Traditionally *peace offerings* [b]8 Or *from the entrance to* [c]19 The Hebrew is plural.

7:1–3 A powerful response is needed when we achieve victory over a significant challenge. Solomon and the people had just finished a monumental task—the temple was now complete! In verse 3, the people's response was enthusiastic: "He is good!" They affirmed God's goodness as they thanked him for his help in building the temple. As we experience great victories, we also need to affirm God's goodness in our lives.

7:14 This verse contains one of God's greatest promises to Israel. Although this promise was given specifically to the Old Testament Israelites, we know that through Jesus Christ, God also listens to our prayers and forgives our sins as we confess them. It is part of God's nature to forgive repentant hearts. This fact should give us great comfort as we seek to deal with past sin and failure.

ing and serving them—that is why he brought all this disaster on them.' "

Solomon's Other Activities

8 At the end of twenty years, during which Solomon built the temple of the LORD and his own palace, 2Solomon rebuilt the villages that Hiram[a] had given him, and settled Israelites in them. 3Solomon then went to Hamath Zobah and captured it. 4He also built up Tadmor in the desert and all the store cities he had built in Hamath. 5He rebuilt Upper Beth Horon and Lower Beth Horon as fortified cities, with walls and with gates and bars, 6as well as Baalath and all his store cities, and all the cities for his chariots and for his horses[b]—whatever he desired to build in Jerusalem, in Lebanon and throughout all the territory he ruled.

7All the people left from the Hittites, Amorites, Perizzites, Hivites and Jebusites (these peoples were not Israelites), 8that is, their descendants remaining in the land, whom the Israelites had not destroyed—these Solomon conscripted for his slave labor force, as it is to this day. 9But Solomon did not make slaves of the Israelites for his work; they were his fighting men, commanders of his captains, and commanders of his chariots and charioteers. 10They were also King Solomon's chief officials—two hundred and fifty officials supervising the men.

11Solomon brought Pharaoh's daughter up from the City of David to the palace he had built for her, for he said, "My wife must not live in the palace of David king of Israel, because the places the ark of the LORD has entered are holy."

12On the altar of the LORD that he had built in front of the portico, Solomon sacrificed burnt offerings to the LORD, 13according to the daily requirement for offerings commanded by Moses for Sabbaths, New Moons and the three annual feasts—the Feast of Unleavened Bread, the Feast of Weeks and the Feast of Tabernacles. 14In keeping with the ordinance of his father David, he appointed the divisions of the priests for their duties, and the Levites to lead the praise and to assist the priests according to each day's requirement. He also appointed the gatekeepers by divisions for the various gates, because this was what David the man of God had ordered. 15They did not deviate from the king's commands to the priests or to the Levites in any matter, including that of the treasuries.

16All Solomon's work was carried out, from the day the foundation of the temple of the LORD was laid until its completion. So the temple of the LORD was finished.

17Then Solomon went to Ezion Geber and Elath on the coast of Edom. 18And Hiram sent him ships commanded by his own officers, men who knew the sea. These, with Solomon's men, sailed to Ophir and brought back four hundred and fifty talents[c] of gold, which they delivered to King Solomon.

The Queen of Sheba Visits Solomon

9 When the queen of Sheba heard of Solomon's fame, she came to Jerusalem to test him with hard questions. Arriving with a very great caravan—with camels carrying spices, large quantities of gold, and precious stones—she came to Solomon and talked with him about all she had on her mind. 2Solomon answered all her questions; nothing was too hard for him to explain to her. 3When the queen of Sheba saw the wisdom of Solomon, as well as the palace he had built, 4the food on his table, the seating of his officials, the attending servants in their robes, the cupbearers in their robes and the burnt offerings he made at[d] the temple of the LORD, she was overwhelmed.

5She said to the king, "The report I heard in my own country about your achievements and your wisdom is true. 6But I did not believe what they said until I came and saw with my own eyes. Indeed, not even half the greatness of your wisdom was told me; you have far exceeded the report I heard. 7How happy your men must be! How happy your officials, who continually stand before you and hear your wisdom! 8Praise be to the LORD your God, who has delighted in you and placed you on his throne as king to rule for the LORD your God. Because of the love of your God for Israel and his desire to uphold them forever, he has made you king over them, to maintain justice and righteousness."

9Then she gave the king 120 talents[e] of gold, large quantities of spices, and precious stones. There had never been such spices as those the queen of Sheba gave to King Solomon.

10(The men of Hiram and the men of Solomon brought gold from Ophir; they also

[a]2 Hebrew *Huram,* a variant of *Hiram;* also in verse 18
[b]6 Or *charioteers*
[c]18 That is, about 17 tons (about 16 metric tons)
[d]4 Or *the ascent by which he went up to*
[e]9 That is, about 4 1/2 tons (about 4 metric tons)

8:3 Solomon's name is derived from the Hebrew word meaning "to be quiet; peaceable; peaceful." Yet even peaceful Solomon encountered some conflict. We, too, will encounter conflict in life. God's Word tells us to expect troubles, trials and spiritual attacks (see John 16:33). We must recognize that we are in a constant state of warfare against the spiritual forces that stand against God and his people (see Ephesians 6:12). Then we can begin to prepare ourselves to overcome these struggles through the power of God.

8:11 In Solomon's day it was common for a ruler to confirm a treaty with another foreign ruler by marrying one of the foreigner's daughters. Solomon accepted this worldly practice and married numerous foreign wives to validate his treaties with the surrounding nations despite God's instructions not to do so (see Deuteronomy 17:16–17). Sadly, this practice eventually led Solomon into idolatry. We should learn from Solomon's mistake of being negatively influenced by those who do not know God.

brought algumwood[a] and precious stones. 11The king used the algumwood to make steps for the temple of the LORD and for the royal palace, and to make harps and lyres for the musicians. Nothing like them had ever been seen in Judah.)

12King Solomon gave the queen of Sheba all she desired and asked for; he gave her more than she had brought to him. Then she left and returned with her retinue to her own country.

Solomon's Splendor

13The weight of the gold that Solomon received yearly was 666 talents,[b] 14not including the revenues brought in by merchants and traders. Also all the kings of Arabia and the governors of the land brought gold and silver to Solomon.

15King Solomon made two hundred large shields of hammered gold; six hundred bekas[c] of hammered gold went into each shield. 16He also made three hundred small shields of hammered gold, with three hundred bekas[d] of gold in each shield. The king put them in the Palace of the Forest of Lebanon.

17Then the king made a great throne inlaid with ivory and overlaid with pure gold. 18The throne had six steps, and a footstool of gold was attached to it. On both sides of the seat were armrests, with a lion standing beside each of them. 19Twelve lions stood on the six steps, one at either end of each step. Nothing like it had ever been made for any other kingdom. 20All King Solomon's goblets were gold, and all the household articles in the Palace of the Forest of Lebanon were pure gold. Nothing was made of silver, because silver was considered of little value in Solomon's day. 21The king had a fleet of trading ships[e] manned by Hiram's[f] men. Once every three years it returned, carrying gold, silver and ivory, and apes and baboons.

22King Solomon was greater in riches and wisdom than all the other kings of the earth. 23All the kings of the earth sought audience with Solomon to hear the wisdom God had put in his heart. 24Year after year, everyone who came brought a gift—articles of silver and gold, and robes, weapons and spices, and horses and mules.

25Solomon had four thousand stalls for horses and chariots, and twelve thousand horses,[g] which he kept in the chariot cities and also with him in Jerusalem. 26He ruled over all the kings from the River[h] to the land of the Philistines, as far as the border of Egypt. 27The king made silver as common in Jerusalem as stones, and cedar as plentiful as sycamore-fig trees in the foothills. 28Solomon's horses were imported from Egypt[i] and from all other countries.

Solomon's Death

29As for the other events of Solomon's reign, from beginning to end, are they not written in the records of Nathan the prophet, in the prophecy of Ahijah the Shilonite and in the visions of Iddo the seer concerning Jeroboam son of Nebat? 30Solomon reigned in Jerusalem over all Israel forty years. 31Then he rested with his fathers and was buried in the city of David his father. And Rehoboam his son succeeded him as king.

Israel Rebels Against Rehoboam

10 Rehoboam went to Shechem, for all the Israelites had gone there to make him king. 2When Jeroboam son of Nebat heard this (he was in Egypt, where he had fled from King Solomon), he returned from Egypt. 3So they sent for Jeroboam, and he and all Israel went to Rehoboam and said to him: 4"Your father put a heavy yoke on us, but now lighten the harsh labor and the heavy yoke he put on us, and we will serve you."

5Rehoboam answered, "Come back to me in three days." So the people went away.

6Then King Rehoboam consulted the elders who had served his father Solomon during his lifetime. "How would you advise me to answer these people?" he asked.

7They replied, "If you will be kind to these people and please them and give them a favorable answer, they will always be your servants."

8But Rehoboam rejected the advice the elders gave him and consulted the young men who had grown up with him and were serving him. 9He asked them, "What is your advice? How should we answer these people who say to me, 'Lighten the yoke your father put on us'?"

10The young men who had grown up with him replied, "Tell the people who have said to you, 'Your father put a heavy yoke on us, but make our yoke lighter'—tell them, 'My little fin-

[a]10 Probably a variant of *almugwood* [b]13 That is, about 25 tons (about 23 metric tons) [c]15 That is, about 7 1/2 pounds (about 3.5 kilograms) [d]16 That is, about 3 3/4 pounds (about 1.7 kilograms) [e]21 Hebrew *of ships that could go to Tarshish* [f]21 Hebrew *Huram,* a variant of *Hiram* [g]25 Or *charioteers* [h]26 That is, the Euphrates [i]28 Or possibly *Muzur,* a region in Cilicia

9:28 When we seek security from any strategy or resource outside of God himself, we are in grave danger. For most of his reign, David had refused to trust in horses and the military advantages they offered (see Deuteronomy 17:16; 1 Chronicles 18:4). Unfortunately, Solomon did not follow his father's example. No matter how far we progress spiritually, we must always remind ourselves that God alone is capable of leading us to victory. No one else is capable of providing the support we need for life's trials.

10:1–14 Rehoboam followed some foolish advice in responding to what seemed a reasonable request. Advice is cheap. We will always have people trying to tell us how to live. Sometimes that advice will be godly; other times it will be foolish. Before heeding the advice of any individual, we should look at the fruits of their own life. Where have their decisions led them? Check to see whether or not their advice is in line with God's Word. Any advice that contradicts God's Word must be rejected.

ger is thicker than my father's waist. 11My father
laid on you a heavy yoke; I will make it even
heavier. My father scourged you with whips; I
will scourge you with scorpions.' "
12Three days later Jeroboam and all the people returned to Rehoboam, as the king had said,
"Come back to me in three days." 13The king
answered them harshly. Rejecting the advice of
the elders, 14he followed the advice of the
young men and said, "My father made your
yoke heavy; I will make it even heavier. My
father scourged you with whips; I will scourge
you with scorpions." 15So the king did not listen
to the people, for this turn of events was from
God, to fulfill the word the LORD had spoken to
Jeroboam son of Nebat through Ahijah the Shilonite.
16When all Israel saw that the king refused to
listen to them, they answered the king:

"What share do we have in David,
what part in Jesse's son?
To your tents, O Israel!
Look after your own house, O David!"

So all the Israelites went home. 17But as for the
Israelites who were living in the towns of Judah,
Rehoboam still ruled over them.
18King Rehoboam sent out Adoniram,[a] who
was in charge of forced labor, but the Israelites
stoned him to death. King Rehoboam, however,
managed to get into his chariot and escape to
Jerusalem. 19So Israel has been in rebellion
against the house of David to this day.

11 When Rehoboam arrived in Jerusalem,
he mustered the house of Judah and
Benjamin—a hundred and eighty thousand
fighting men—to make war against Israel and to
regain the kingdom for Rehoboam.
2But this word of the LORD came to Shemaiah
the man of God: 3"Say to Rehoboam son of
Solomon king of Judah and to all the Israelites
in Judah and Benjamin, 4'This is what the LORD
says: Do not go up to fight against your brothers. Go home, every one of you, for this is my
doing.' " So they obeyed the words of the LORD
and turned back from marching against Jeroboam.

Rehoboam Fortifies Judah

5Rehoboam lived in Jerusalem and built up
towns for defense in Judah: 6Bethlehem, Etam,
Tekoa, 7Beth Zur, Soco, Adullam, 8Gath, Mareshah, Ziph, 9Adoraim, Lachish, Azekah, 10Zo-
rah, Aijalon and Hebron. These were fortified
cities in Judah and Benjamin. 11He strengthened their defenses and put commanders in
them, with supplies of food, olive oil and wine.
12He put shields and spears in all the cities, and
made them very strong. So Judah and Benjamin
were his.
13The priests and Levites from all their districts throughout Israel sided with him. 14The
Levites even abandoned their pasturelands and
property, and came to Judah and Jerusalem because Jeroboam and his sons had rejected them
as priests of the LORD. 15And he appointed his
own priests for the high places and for the goat
and calf idols he had made. 16Those from every
tribe of Israel who set their hearts on seeking
the LORD, the God of Israel, followed the Levites
to Jerusalem to offer sacrifices to the LORD, the
God of their fathers. 17They strengthened the
kingdom of Judah and supported Rehoboam
son of Solomon three years, walking in the ways
of David and Solomon during this time.

Rehoboam's Family

18Rehoboam married Mahalath, who was the
daughter of David's son Jerimoth and of Abihail, the daughter of Jesse's son Eliab. 19She
bore him sons: Jeush, Shemariah and Zaham.
20Then he married Maacah daughter of Absa-

[a]18 Hebrew *Hadoram,* a variant of *Adoniram*

10:15–16 Responding to Rehoboam's foolish decision, the people rebelled and split the kingdom of Israel in two. However, two wrongs never make a right. The consequences that followed the people's rebellion and division were far more harmful to Israel than Rehoboam's foolish decision. The impulsive actions of the people eventually led the northern tribes away from God and toward destruction. Sometimes we are tempted to take rash measures when others mistreat us. Let us learn from this passage to be extremely cautious in our response to mistreatment.

11:1–12 Rehoboam was tempted to take matters into his own hands. He prepared to attack Jeroboam and the northern kingdom, but God's messenger came and warned him not to attack. To Rehoboam's credit, he listened to God and abandoned his plans. Our plans and programs need to be subject to God's leading too. We need to redirect our course based on the direction God gives us. If we try to do things our own way, the outcome will always be disastrous.

11:13–17 The priests of the northern kingdom found themselves in a difficult position when King Jeroboam ascended to Israel's throne. Jeroboam ousted the true priests of God and replaced them with priests who would support his rebellious plan. The true priests probably wanted to stay in the land of their childhood, but it was obvious that the northern kingdom had turned from God. The priests moved to the southern kingdom where true worship was still being maintained. We often face similar decisions. We may have to make difficult choices in order to follow God's plan. We would be wise to do as the priests did. They maintained their relationship with God at the cost of personal stability and comfort. Our relationship with God should shape all the decisions we face too.

11:15 Most of us try to justify our actions. It is sometimes tempting to use religious beliefs to do this. Jeroboam ordained false priests in order to provide religious respectability for his kingdom. When we face difficulties in our lives, we may attempt to justify our actions by finding something in the Bible to support our viewpoint or by quoting some religious authority figure who agrees with our position. When we do this, however, we usually only compound our problems by defending the sin in our lives. To grow spiritually, we must continually examine our lives, noting our sins, confessing them to God, accepting responsibility for them and seeking God's help to root them out.

lom, who bore him Abijah, Attai, Ziza and Shelomith. 21Rehoboam loved Maacah daughter of Absalom more than any of his other wives and concubines. In all, he had eighteen wives and sixty concubines, twenty-eight sons and sixty daughters.

22Rehoboam appointed Abijah son of Maacah to be the chief prince among his brothers, in order to make him king. 23He acted wisely, dispersing some of his sons throughout the districts of Judah and Benjamin, and to all the fortified cities. He gave them abundant provisions and took many wives for them.

Shishak Attacks Jerusalem

12 After Rehoboam's position as king was established and he had become strong, he and all Israel[a] with him abandoned the law of the LORD. 2Because they had been unfaithful to the LORD, Shishak king of Egypt attacked Jerusalem in the fifth year of King Rehoboam. 3With twelve hundred chariots and sixty thousand horsemen and the innumerable troops of Libyans, Sukkites and Cushites[b] that came with him from Egypt, 4he captured the fortified cities of Judah and came as far as Jerusalem.

5Then the prophet Shemaiah came to Rehoboam and to the leaders of Judah who had assembled in Jerusalem for fear of Shishak, and he said to them, "This is what the LORD says, 'You have abandoned me; therefore, I now abandon you to Shishak.' "

6The leaders of Israel and the king humbled themselves and said, "The LORD is just."

7When the LORD saw that they humbled themselves, this word of the LORD came to Shemaiah: "Since they have humbled themselves, I will not destroy them but will soon give them deliverance. My wrath will not be poured out on Jerusalem through Shishak. 8They will, however, become subject to him, so that they may learn the difference between serving me and serving the kings of other lands."

9When Shishak king of Egypt attacked Jerusalem, he carried off the treasures of the temple of the LORD and the treasures of the royal palace. He took everything, including the gold shields Solomon had made. 10So King Rehoboam made bronze shields to replace them and assigned these to the commanders of the guard on duty at the entrance to the royal palace. 11Whenever the king went to the LORD's temple, the guards went with him, bearing the shields, and afterward they returned them to the guardroom.

12Because Rehoboam humbled himself, the LORD's anger turned from him, and he was not totally destroyed. Indeed, there was some good in Judah.

13King Rehoboam established himself firmly in Jerusalem and continued as king. He was forty-one years old when he became king, and he reigned seventeen years in Jerusalem, the city the LORD had chosen out of all the tribes of Israel in which to put his Name. His mother's name was Naamah; she was an Ammonite. 14He did evil because he had not set his heart on seeking the LORD.

15As for the events of Rehoboam's reign, from beginning to end, are they not written in the records of Shemaiah the prophet and of Iddo the seer that deal with genealogies? There was continual warfare between Rehoboam and Jeroboam. 16Rehoboam rested with his fathers and was buried in the City of David. And Abijah his son succeeded him as king.

Abijah King of Judah

13 In the eighteenth year of the reign of Jeroboam, Abijah became king of Judah, 2and he reigned in Jerusalem three years. His mother's name was Maacah,[c] a daughter[d] of Uriel of Gibeah.

There was war between Abijah and Jeroboam. 3Abijah went into battle with a force of four hundred thousand able fighting men, and Jeroboam drew up a battle line against him with eight hundred thousand able troops.

4Abijah stood on Mount Zemaraim, in the hill country of Ephraim, and said, "Jeroboam and all Israel, listen to me! 5Don't you know

[a] 1 That is, Judah, as frequently in 2 Chronicles
[b] 3 That is, people from the upper Nile region
[c] 2 Most Septuagint manuscripts and Syriac (see also 2 Chron. 11:20 and 1 Kings 15:2); Hebrew *Micaiah*
[d] 2 Or *granddaughter*

12:1–4 With success comes the danger of pride and self-sufficiency. When Rehoboam was firmly established and began to feel secure, he forsook his obligation to lead the people closer to God. As a result, the whole nation fell into sin and was defeated by the Egyptians. The same thing tends to happen to us. When things are going well for us spiritually, we begin to relax. We need to stay alert, realizing that good times often make us more vulnerable to a fall.

12:5 Turning from God has its consequences. Rehoboam failed to lead his people in godly ways. As a result, God sent him a message: "You have abandoned me; therefore, I now abandon you to Shishak." God loves us and wants us to honor him. We cannot sin with impunity. Sin always brings destructive consequences.

12:13–16 How might our epitaph read? What have we done that is worth remembering? How will people remember our relationship with God when we die? Rehoboam's epitaph reads this way: "He did evil because he had not set his heart on seeking the LORD" (12:14). When we die, our wealth and achievements will soon be forgotten. But our relationship with God and what we do for his glory are everlasting and eternal. We would be wise to put our energy into things of eternal value.

13:1–9 Abijah was about to go into a battle in which his army was vastly outnumbered. Instead of giving in to fear, Abijah stood firm because of his faith in God's promises. As we grow spiritually, we will face many difficult situations. If we try to face them alone, we will fail. We need to stand on the many promises God has given us in the Bible and trust him to deliver us.

13:5–9 Taking God at his word is not always easy, especially when God's promises seem impossible. In the face of Jeroboam's massive armies, King Abijah of Judah had

that the LORD, the God of Israel, has given the
kingship of Israel to David and his descendants
forever by a covenant of salt? 6Yet Jeroboam son
of Nebat, an official of Solomon son of David,
rebelled against his master. 7Some worthless
scoundrels gathered around him and opposed
Rehoboam son of Solomon when he was young
and indecisive and not strong enough to resist
them.

8"And now you plan to resist the kingdom
of the LORD, which is in the hands of David's
descendants. You are indeed a vast army and
have with you the golden calves that Jeroboam
made to be your gods. 9But didn't you drive out
the priests of the LORD, the sons of Aaron, and
the Levites, and make priests of your own as the
peoples of other lands do? Whoever comes to
consecrate himself with a young bull and seven
rams may become a priest of what are not gods.

10"As for us, the LORD is our God, and we
have not forsaken him. The priests who serve
the LORD are sons of Aaron, and the Levites
assist them. 11Every morning and evening they
present burnt offerings and fragrant incense to
the LORD. They set out the bread on the ceremonially clean table and light the lamps on the
gold lampstand every evening. We are observing the requirements of the LORD our God. But
you have forsaken him. 12God is with us; he is
our leader. His priests with their trumpets will
sound the battle cry against you. Men of Israel,
do not fight against the LORD, the God of your
fathers, for you will not succeed."

13Now Jeroboam had sent troops around to
the rear, so that while he was in front of Judah
the ambush was behind them. 14Judah turned
and saw that they were being attacked at both
front and rear. Then they cried out to the LORD.
The priests blew their trumpets 15and the men
of Judah raised the battle cry. At the sound of
their battle cry, God routed Jeroboam and all
Israel before Abijah and Judah. 16The Israelites
fled before Judah, and God delivered them into
their hands. 17Abijah and his men inflicted
heavy losses on them, so that there were five
hundred thousand casualties among Israel's
able men. 18The men of Israel were subdued on
that occasion, and the men of Judah were victorious because they relied on the LORD, the God
of their fathers.

19Abijah pursued Jeroboam and took from
him the towns of Bethel, Jeshanah and Ephron,
with their surrounding villages. 20Jeroboam did
not regain power during the time of Abijah.
And the LORD struck him down and he died.

21But Abijah grew in strength. He married
fourteen wives and had twenty-two sons and
sixteen daughters.

22The other events of Abijah's reign, what he
did and what he said, are written in the annotations of the prophet Iddo.

14 And Abijah rested with his fathers and
was buried in the City of David. Asa his
son succeeded him as king, and in his days the
country was at peace for ten years.

Asa King of Judah

2Asa did what was good and right in the eyes
of the LORD his God. 3He removed the foreign
altars and the high places, smashed the sacred
stones and cut down the Asherah poles.[a] 4He
commanded Judah to seek the LORD, the God of
their fathers, and to obey his laws and commands. 5He removed the high places and incense altars in every town in Judah, and the
kingdom was at peace under him. 6He built up
the fortified cities of Judah, since the land was
at peace. No one was at war with him during
those years, for the LORD gave him rest.

7"Let us build up these towns," he said to
Judah, "and put walls around them, with towers, gates and bars. The land is still ours, because we have sought the LORD our God; we
sought him and he has given us rest on every
side." So they built and prospered.

8Asa had an army of three hundred thousand
men from Judah, equipped with large shields
and with spears, and two hundred and eighty
thousand from Benjamin, armed with small
shields and with bows. All these were brave
fighting men.

9Zerah the Cushite marched out against
them with a vast army[b] and three hundred
chariots, and came as far as Mareshah. 10Asa
went out to meet him, and they took up battle
positions in the Valley of Zephathah near Mareshah.

11Then Asa called to the LORD his God and
said, "LORD, there is no one like you to help the

[a]3 That is, symbols of the goddess Asherah; here and elsewhere in 2 Chronicles [b]9 Hebrew *with an army of a thousand thousands* or *with an army of thousands upon thousands*

---

good reason to doubt God's promises. Practically speaking, the army of Judah didn't stand a chance. But King Abijah trusted God's promises for the kingly line of David. The positive results of Abijah's trust should encourage us to do just as he did. When God makes a promise, we should have no doubt that he will keep it.

13:10–14 Abijah was able to say, "The LORD is our God, and we have not forsaken him" (13:10). Because of this, Abijah was assured that the Lord would watch over him as he fought against those who were disobedient. We, too, must always be certain that we are living in obedience to God as we continue to serve him.

13:18–20 There is great danger in rebelling against God. When people seem to get away with sinfulness, it may sometimes appear that God is not paying attention. But what we sow, we will eventually reap (see Galatians 6:7). Jeroboam seemed to be successful, but eventually his sins caught up with him. A small army from Judah, set firmly in God's hands, soundly defeated him. Sin has inevitable consequences. We must root sin out of our lives before it leads to our downfall.

14:9–15 Asa was facing a mighty enemy army, but he cried out to God. This was his first step toward victory. We, too, must be willing to surrender to God and trust him to deliver us from our struggles.

powerless against the mighty. Help us, O LORD
our God, for we rely on you, and in your name
we have come against this vast army. O LORD,
you are our God; do not let man prevail against
you."
12The LORD struck down the Cushites before
Asa and Judah. The Cushites fled, 13and Asa and
his army pursued them as far as Gerar. Such a
great number of Cushites fell that they could
not recover; they were crushed before the LORD
and his forces. The men of Judah carried off a
large amount of plunder. 14They destroyed all
the villages around Gerar, for the terror of the
LORD had fallen upon them. They plundered
all these villages, since there was much booty
there. 15They also attacked the camps of the
herdsmen and carried off droves of sheep and
goats and camels. Then they returned to Jerusalem.

Asa's Reform

15 The Spirit of God came upon Azariah
son of Oded. 2He went out to meet Asa
and said to him, "Listen to me, Asa and all
Judah and Benjamin. The LORD is with you
when you are with him. If you seek him, he will
be found by you, but if you forsake him, he will
forsake you. 3For a long time Israel was without
the true God, without a priest to teach and without the law. 4But in their distress they turned to
the LORD, the God of Israel, and sought him,
and he was found by them. 5In those days it was
not safe to travel about, for all the inhabitants
of the lands were in great turmoil. 6One nation
was being crushed by another and one city by
another, because God was troubling them with
every kind of distress. 7But as for you, be strong
and do not give up, for your work will be rewarded."
8When Asa heard these words and the prophecy of Azariah son of[a] Oded the prophet, he
took courage. He removed the detestable idols
from the whole land of Judah and Benjamin
and from the towns he had captured in the hills
of Ephraim. He repaired the altar of the LORD

[a]8 Vulgate and Syriac (see also Septuagint and verse 1); Hebrew does not have *Azariah son of.*

15:1–8 God sent a prophet to warn Asa, king of Judah, that sin would bring suffering to his kingdom. Asa responded to God's warning with appropriate action. He destroyed the idols in his kingdom and rebuilt the altar of God. We also receive warnings from God. He speaks to us through the Bible, through people and through our own mind and conscience. We need to listen for God's direction and then act appropriately. Regular times of prayer and meditation on God's Word can help us to become more sensitive to God's leading.

15:4 God is a forgiving God. No matter how deep the stain of sin upon the people of Israel, God forgave them when they chose to repent. We may have failed and sinned so often that we may believe we are beyond God's forgiveness. It is never too late to turn to God! When we cry out in repentance for help, God will respond with restoration and forgiveness and help us deal with the problems before us.

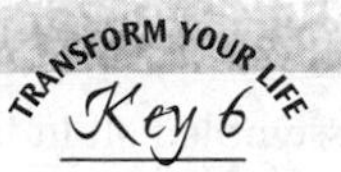

Tearing Down Old Idols

2 Chronicles 15:1–19 As we allow God to redeem our lives and work everything out for the best, it is important for us to continue to reject the idols we may have once worshiped. Idols are those things that come between us and God. They can be anything—people, money, power, possessions or even our dreams and aspirations. Idols, in whatever form they manifest themselves in our lives, can do us nothing but harm.

King Asa lived at a time when the people of Israel had given themselves over to the worship of idols. They had turned away from God and the way of life they knew to be right. But a messenger of God came and told the king, "The LORD is with you when you are with him. If you seek him, he will be found by you, but if you forsake him, he will forsake you" (15:2). When King Asa heard this message, he took courage and destroyed all the idols in the land. He also repaired the altar of the Lord. Asa even removed his mother from her position of power because she had been influential in Israel's idolatry.

As we continue to grow in our spiritual lives, we will need to crush and burn the "idols" we have served. God calls us to redirect our course to follow him, even if that means we have to go against the crowd and separate ourselves from those who don't contribute to our spiritual growth. As we seek to turn our lives around, God will empower and encourage us each step of the way.

Turn to Job 6.

that was in front of the portico of the LORD's temple.

9Then he assembled all Judah and Benjamin and the people from Ephraim, Manasseh and Simeon who had settled among them, for large numbers had come over to him from Israel when they saw that the LORD his God was with him.

10They assembled at Jerusalem in the third month of the fifteenth year of Asa's reign. 11At that time they sacrificed to the LORD seven hundred head of cattle and seven thousand sheep and goats from the plunder they had brought back. 12They entered into a covenant to seek the LORD, the God of their fathers, with all their heart and soul. 13All who would not seek the LORD, the God of Israel, were to be put to death, whether small or great, man or woman. 14They took an oath to the LORD with loud acclamation, with shouting and with trumpets and horns. 15All Judah rejoiced about the oath because they had sworn it wholeheartedly. They sought God eagerly, and he was found by them. So the LORD gave them rest on every side.

16King Asa also deposed his grandmother Maacah from her position as queen mother, because she had made a repulsive Asherah pole. Asa cut the pole down, broke it up and burned it in the Kidron Valley. 17Although he did not remove the high places from Israel, Asa's heart was fully committed ⌊to the LORD⌋ all his life. 18He brought into the temple of God the silver and gold and the articles that he and his father had dedicated.

19There was no more war until the thirty-fifth year of Asa's reign.

Asa's Last Years

16 In the thirty-sixth year of Asa's reign Baasha king of Israel went up against Judah and fortified Ramah to prevent anyone from leaving or entering the territory of Asa king of Judah.

2Asa then took the silver and gold out of the treasuries of the LORD's temple and of his own palace and sent it to Ben-Hadad king of Aram, who was ruling in Damascus. 3"Let there be a treaty between me and you," he said, "as there was between my father and your father. See, I am sending you silver and gold. Now break your treaty with Baasha king of Israel so he will withdraw from me."

4Ben-Hadad agreed with King Asa and sent the commanders of his forces against the towns of Israel. They conquered Ijon, Dan, Abel Maim[a] and all the store cities of Naphtali. 5When Baasha heard this, he stopped building Ramah and abandoned his work. 6Then King Asa brought all the men of Judah, and they carried away from Ramah the stones and timber Baasha had been using. With them he built up Geba and Mizpah.

7At that time Hanani the seer came to Asa king of Judah and said to him: "Because you relied on the king of Aram and not on the LORD your God, the army of the king of Aram has escaped from your hand. 8Were not the Cushites[b] and Libyans a mighty army with great numbers of chariots and horsemen[c]? Yet when you relied on the LORD, he delivered them into your hand. 9For the eyes of the LORD range throughout the earth to strengthen those whose hearts are fully committed to him. You have done a foolish thing, and from now on you will be at war."

10Asa was angry with the seer because of this; he was so enraged that he put him in prison. At the same time Asa brutally oppressed some of the people.

11The events of Asa's reign, from beginning to end, are written in the book of the kings of Judah and Israel. 12In the thirty-ninth year of his reign Asa was afflicted with a disease in his feet. Though his disease was severe, even in his illness he did not seek help from the LORD, but only from the physicians. 13Then in the forty-first year of his reign Asa died and rested with his fathers. 14They buried him in the tomb that he had cut out for himself in the City of David. They laid him on a bier covered with spices and various blended perfumes, and they made a huge fire in his honor.

Jehoshaphat King of Judah

17 Jehoshaphat his son succeeded him as king and strengthened himself against Israel. 2He stationed troops in all the fortified cities of Judah and put garrisons in Judah and in the towns of Ephraim that his father Asa had captured.

[a]4 Also known as *Abel Beth Maacah* [b]8 That is, people from the upper Nile region [c]8 Or *charioteers*

16:7–9 Hanani rebuked Asa for depending on the king of Aram instead of trusting in God. No matter what the odds, God could have delivered Asa without the help of a foreign army. We must learn that God is the only one who is truly able to deliver us. We need to put our trust in him.

16:10 When Hanani rebuked Asa for hiring the Arameans, the king immediately responded incorrectly—he punished Hanani. Asa would have been wise to listen and allow God to correct him through the insight of another. When someone honestly points out a problem or failure in our lives, we sometimes behave like Asa, responding in anger to the person who confronted us. As we grow spiritually, God may send us people who can see errors in our lives that we cannot see. We should humbly ask God to help us see the truth about ourselves. Then, instead of reacting in anger, we should accept responsibility for our sin and ask God to redirect our course.

16:12–14 King Asa's feet were seriously diseased, so he sought a human solution to his problem. Despite the measures he took, however, Asa's condition worsened, and he died. Asa failed to look to God for help. In times of trouble, God is often the last resource we turn to, and we are willing instead to try any scheme possible to solve our problems. Such solutions will never be able to give us true victory. God alone can do that. We would be wise to go to him first.

3The LORD was with Jehoshaphat because in
his early years he walked in the ways his father
David had followed. He did not consult the
Baals 4but sought the God of his father and
followed his commands rather than the practices of Israel. 5The LORD established the kingdom under his control; and all Judah brought
gifts to Jehoshaphat, so that he had great wealth
and honor. 6His heart was devoted to the ways
of the LORD; furthermore, he removed the high
places and the Asherah poles from Judah.

7In the third year of his reign he sent his
officials Ben-Hail, Obadiah, Zechariah, Nethanel and Micaiah to teach in the towns of
Judah. 8With them were certain Levites—Shemaiah, Nethaniah, Zebadiah, Asahel, Shemiramoth, Jehonathan, Adonijah, Tobijah and Tob-
Adonijah—and the priests Elishama and
Jehoram. 9They taught throughout Judah, taking with them the Book of the Law of the LORD;
they went around to all the towns of Judah and
taught the people.

10The fear of the LORD fell on all the kingdoms of the lands surrounding Judah, so that
they did not make war with Jehoshaphat.
11Some Philistines brought Jehoshaphat gifts
and silver as tribute, and the Arabs brought him
flocks: seven thousand seven hundred rams and
seven thousand seven hundred goats.

12Jehoshaphat became more and more powerful; he built forts and store cities in Judah
13and had large supplies in the towns of Judah.
He also kept experienced fighting men in Jerusalem. 14Their enrollment by families was as
follows:

From Judah, commanders of units of 1,000:
Adnah the commander, with 300,000 fighting men;
15next, Jehohanan the commander, with 280,000;
16next, Amasiah son of Zicri, who volunteered himself for the service of the LORD, with 200,000.

17From Benjamin:
Eliada, a valiant soldier, with 200,000 men armed with bows and shields;
18next, Jehozabad, with 180,000 men armed for battle.

19These were the men who served the king, besides those he stationed in the fortified cities
throughout Judah.

Micaiah Prophesies Against Ahab

18 Now Jehoshaphat had great wealth and
honor, and he allied himself with Ahab
by marriage. 2Some years later he went down to
visit Ahab in Samaria. Ahab slaughtered many
sheep and cattle for him and the people with
him and urged him to attack Ramoth Gilead.
3Ahab king of Israel asked Jehoshaphat king of
Judah, "Will you go with me against Ramoth
Gilead?"

Jehoshaphat replied, "I am as you are, and
my people as your people; we will join you in
the war." 4But Jehoshaphat also said to the king
of Israel, "First seek the counsel of the LORD."

5So the king of Israel brought together the
prophets—four hundred men—and asked them,
"Shall we go to war against Ramoth Gilead, or
shall I refrain?"

"Go," they answered, "for God will give it
into the king's hand."

6But Jehoshaphat asked, "Is there not a
prophet of the LORD here whom we can inquire of?"

7The king of Israel answered Jehoshaphat,
"There is still one man through whom we can
inquire of the LORD, but I hate him because he
never prophesies anything good about me, but
always bad. He is Micaiah son of Imlah."

"The king should not say that," Jehoshaphat
replied.

8So the king of Israel called one of his officials and said, "Bring Micaiah son of Imlah at
once."

9Dressed in their royal robes, the king of Israel and Jehoshaphat king of Judah were sitting

---

17:3–4 The role models we follow make a tremendous difference in how we respond to life's challenges. It is refreshing to discover that Jehoshaphat chose a positive role model as a guide for his life. Following his lead, Jehoshaphat instituted excellent reforms in Judah. We must be careful not to follow those whose paths lead away from the heart of God. We need to follow paths and mentors that lead us to seek God and surrender to him.

17:5–6 We can learn a lot about people by the way they achieve fulfillment in life. Jehoshaphat "was devoted to the ways of the LORD" (17:6). In following God's paths, Jehoshaphat led his kingdom away from idolatry and sin. Like Jehoshaphat, we need to find fulfillment in our lives by committing ourselves to the ways of the Lord.

17:7–9 Notice that Jehoshaphat used the Word of God as the foundation for his reforms. As we attempt to effect changes in our lives, we need God's Word to direct the changes we make. The Bible furnishes the only adequate foundation for change. We need to take time to study God's Word to discover God's will for our lives and learn about the power that God offers us.

18:3–5 Companions and allies must be chosen when any large project is attempted. Yet there is grave danger in choosing the wrong allies. Jehoshaphat's alliance with Ahab almost caused his undoing. In this verse, Jehoshaphat allied himself with Ahab and declared that he was in complete agreement with this godless king. Companions are necessary; it is difficult to accomplish spiritual growth alone. But choosing the wrong companions can be as destructive as having no companions at all.

18:3–7 Ahab called upon a false prophet; as a result, he got false information. Jehoshaphat wanted to discover what God had to say, so he looked for a true prophet. The false prophets told the people whatever they wanted to hear. True prophets spoke God's words whether the people liked it or not. As we seek God's will for our lives, we must be careful not to reject God's messages simply because we don't like them. God may call us to do things that we don't really want to do. Yet, in the long run, God's way is always the best way. Looking for quick and easy solutions to our problems will never yield permanent results.

on their thrones at the threshing floor by the entrance to the gate of Samaria, with all the prophets prophesying before them. 10Now Zedekiah son of Kenaanah had made iron horns, and he declared, "This is what the LORD says: 'With these you will gore the Arameans until they are destroyed.' "

11All the other prophets were prophesying the same thing. "Attack Ramoth Gilead and be victorious," they said, "for the LORD will give it into the king's hand."

12The messenger who had gone to summon Micaiah said to him, "Look, as one man the other prophets are predicting success for the king. Let your word agree with theirs, and speak favorably."

13But Micaiah said, "As surely as the LORD lives, I can tell him only what my God says."

14When he arrived, the king asked him, "Micaiah, shall we go to war against Ramoth Gilead, or shall I refrain?"

"Attack and be victorious," he answered, "for they will be given into your hand."

15The king said to him, "How many times must I make you swear to tell me nothing but the truth in the name of the LORD?"

16Then Micaiah answered, "I saw all Israel scattered on the hills like sheep without a shepherd, and the LORD said, 'These people have no master. Let each one go home in peace.' "

17The king of Israel said to Jehoshaphat, "Didn't I tell you that he never prophesies anything good about me, but only bad?"

18Micaiah continued, "Therefore hear the word of the LORD: I saw the LORD sitting on his throne with all the host of heaven standing on his right and on his left. 19And the LORD said, 'Who will entice Ahab king of Israel into attacking Ramoth Gilead and going to his death there?'

"One suggested this, and another that. 20Finally, a spirit came forward, stood before the LORD and said, 'I will entice him.'

" 'By what means?' the LORD asked.

21" 'I will go and be a lying spirit in the mouths of all his prophets,' he said.

" 'You will succeed in enticing him,' said the LORD. 'Go and do it.'

22"So now the LORD has put a lying spirit in the mouths of these prophets of yours. The LORD has decreed disaster for you."

23Then Zedekiah son of Kenaanah went up and slapped Micaiah in the face. "Which way did the spirit from[a] the LORD go when he went from me to speak to you?" he asked.

24Micaiah replied, "You will find out on the day you go to hide in an inner room."

25The king of Israel then ordered, "Take Micaiah and send him back to Amon the ruler of the city and to Joash the king's son, 26and say, 'This is what the king says: Put this fellow in prison and give him nothing but bread and water until I return safely.' "

27Micaiah declared, "If you ever return safely, the LORD has not spoken through me." Then he added, "Mark my words, all you people!"

Ahab Killed at Ramoth Gilead

28So the king of Israel and Jehoshaphat king of Judah went up to Ramoth Gilead. 29The king of Israel said to Jehoshaphat, "I will enter the battle in disguise, but you wear your royal robes." So the king of Israel disguised himself and went into battle.

30Now the king of Aram had ordered his chariot commanders, "Do not fight with anyone, small or great, except the king of Israel." 31When the chariot commanders saw Jehoshaphat, they thought, "This is the king of Israel." So they turned to attack him, but Jehoshaphat cried out, and the LORD helped him. God drew them away from him, 32for when the chariot commanders saw that he was not the king of Israel, they stopped pursuing him.

33But someone drew his bow at random and hit the king of Israel between the sections of his armor. The king told the chariot driver, "Wheel around and get me out of the fighting. I've been wounded." 34All day long the battle raged, and the king of Israel propped himself up in his chariot facing the Arameans until evening. Then at sunset he died.

19 When Jehoshaphat king of Judah returned safely to his palace in Jerusalem, 2Jehu the seer, the son of Hanani, went out to meet him and said to the king, "Should you help the wicked and love[b] those who hate the LORD? Because of this, the wrath of the LORD is upon you. 3There is, however, some good in

[a]23 Or *Spirit of* [b]2 Or *and make alliances with*

18:13–22 Often it is expensive to be absolutely faithful to God, but it is worth the cost. The prophet Micaiah knew that he would get into trouble if he told King Ahab to abandon his plans to attack Ramoth-Gilead. At first, Micaiah appeared to support Ahab's plans, but in the end Micaiah took a stand and told the truth. When God speaks to us in his Word or by some other means, we need to do things his way. We must stand for the truth no matter what the people around us are thinking and doing.

18:31–34 After hearing God's warning to abandon his plans, Ahab took precautions so he would not be killed in the battle. He dressed as a common soldier so that he wouldn't be a target of the enemy. In spite of his crafty preparations, a "random" arrow killed Ahab. In trying to escape God's will, Ahab sealed his own doom. When God directs us through his Word or through wise counsel, we should listen. Following God's will, no matter how hard that may be, is the only way that leads to life.

19:1–2 When we make wrong alliances and place our trust in human strength and ability, there will be consequences to pay. The prophet Jehu met Jehoshaphat to proclaim a message of judgment. Because of Jehoshaphat's cooperation with Ahab, Jehoshaphat would have to bear the consequences. Let this be a warning to us. Our strongest friendships should be with those who will encourage us to obey God's Word and follow his plan for our lives. Seeking help from anyone else will lead to negative consequences and suffering.

you, for you have rid the land of the Asherah
poles and have set your heart on seeking God."

Jehoshaphat Appoints Judges

4 Jehoshaphat lived in Jerusalem, and he
went out again among the people from Beersheba to the hill country of Ephraim and turned
them back to the LORD, the God of their fathers.
5 He appointed judges in the land, in each of the
fortified cities of Judah. 6 He told them, "Consider carefully what you do, because you are not
judging for man but for the LORD, who is with
you whenever you give a verdict. 7 Now let the
fear of the LORD be upon you. Judge carefully,
for with the LORD our God there is no injustice
or partiality or bribery."

8 In Jerusalem also, Jehoshaphat appointed
some of the Levites, priests and heads of Israelite families to administer the law of the LORD
and to settle disputes. And they lived in Jerusalem. 9 He gave them these orders: "You must
serve faithfully and wholeheartedly in the fear
of the LORD. 10 In every case that comes before
you from your fellow countrymen who live in
the cities—whether bloodshed or other concerns
of the law, commands, decrees or ordinances—
you are to warn them not to sin against the
LORD; otherwise his wrath will come on you
and your brothers. Do this, and you will not
sin.

11 "Amariah the chief priest will be over you
in any matter concerning the LORD, and Zebadiah son of Ishmael, the leader of the tribe of
Judah, will be over you in any matter concerning the king, and the Levites will serve as officials before you. Act with courage, and may the
LORD be with those who do well."

Jehoshaphat Defeats Moab and Ammon

20 After this, the Moabites and Ammonites with some of the Meunites[a] came
to make war on Jehoshaphat.

2 Some men came and told Jehoshaphat, "A
vast army is coming against you from Edom,[b]
from the other side of the Sea.[c] It is already in
Hazazon Tamar" (that is, En Gedi). 3 Alarmed,
Jehoshaphat resolved to inquire of the LORD,
and he proclaimed a fast for all Judah. 4 The
people of Judah came together to seek help
from the LORD; indeed, they came from every
town in Judah to seek him.

5 Then Jehoshaphat stood up in the assembly
of Judah and Jerusalem at the temple of the
LORD in the front of the new courtyard 6 and
said:

"O LORD, God of our fathers, are you
not the God who is in heaven? You rule
over all the kingdoms of the nations. Power and might are in your hand, and no one
can withstand you. 7 O our God, did you
not drive out the inhabitants of this land
before your people Israel and give it forever to the descendants of Abraham your
friend? 8 They have lived in it and have
built in it a sanctuary for your Name, saying, 9 'If calamity comes upon us, whether
the sword of judgment, or plague or famine, we will stand in your presence before
this temple that bears your Name and will
cry out to you in our distress, and you will
hear us and save us.'

10 "But now here are men from Ammon, Moab and Mount Seir, whose territory you would not allow Israel to invade
when they came from Egypt; so they
turned away from them and did not destroy them. 11 See how they are repaying us
by coming to drive us out of the possession you gave us as an inheritance.
12 O our God, will you not judge them?
For we have no power to face this vast
army that is attacking us. We do not know
what to do, but our eyes are upon you."

13 All the men of Judah, with their wives and
children and little ones, stood there before the
LORD.

14 Then the Spirit of the LORD came upon Jahaziel son of Zechariah, the son of Benaiah, the
son of Jeiel, the son of Mattaniah, a Levite and
descendant of Asaph, as he stood in the assembly.

15 He said: "Listen, King Jehoshaphat and all
who live in Judah and Jerusalem! This is what
the LORD says to you: 'Do not be afraid or dis-

[a]1 Some Septuagint manuscripts; Hebrew *Ammonites*
[b]2 One Hebrew manuscript; most Hebrew manuscripts, Septuagint and Vulgate *Aram* [c]2 That is, the Dead Sea

19:5–7 The judicial system in Judah was corrupt, but rather than give up in despair, Jehoshaphat challenged the judges to pay attention to God's way. He reminded them that the fear of God and his justice was the only proper motivation for action. God's ways should also direct our decisions. We must take time to seek his wisdom in the Bible.

19:11 Jehoshaphat appointed officials to carry out justice in the land. He wanted to make sure that the people would be treated fairly and that the truth would never be hidden. As we reflect on our lives, we must judge our past performance by God's standards of justice. We must look honestly at our sin and failures, avoiding any tendency to be defensive. If we are fearless in our stand for truth and honesty, we will build the foundation for true spiritual growth.

20:6–9 God is in charge of our world! He is the master over all peoples and nations! Trust in his sovereignty is the basis for our victory. As we learn to trust in God's control even when things aren't going our way, our lives can be serene in the midst of conflict. God desires what is best for us. Seeking his will and obeying his direction for our lives is always in our best interest.

20:15 If God is on our side, the greatest of life's difficulties will not stand in the way of victory. Just as the prophet spoke to the people of Israel, urging them to hope in God's power to deliver them, God speaks to us in the Bible. He calls upon us to trust in him. The most common command in all of Scripture is "Do not be afraid!" God shows us time and again that no matter how terrible the circumstances, he is able to give the victory. All we need to do is trust him.

THE SPIRITUAL DISCIPLINES

Fasting

Hungering for God's Deliverance

2 Chronicles 20:3 There are times when it is especially clear that we cannot save ourselves. These times may come when we are facing overwhelming pressures in our relationships, our jobs, our finances or even our health. Jehoshaphat was once under attack by three armies. When we feel besieged from all sides, we are tempted to either give in and surrender or muster every human resource we can find. Neither of these reactions, however, is pleasing to God. God wants these situations to remind us that we are sustained not by our own cleverness but by his power. We are delivered not by our ability but by his mercy.

Apparently King Jehoshaphat understood this truth, for his reaction to the threatening armies was to call everyone in Judah to fast. Instead of merely calling his people to military exercises and preparations, King Jehoshaphat called his people to spiritual exercises. Instead of fattening their bodies, he called them to nourish their souls. Instead of looking to their own defenses, he urged them to trust in God's protection.

As we look at the discipline of fasting in the Bible, we find that fasting reminds us of our dependence on God, who is more than able to provide what we truly need. Because we must have food to live, physical hunger is one of the most powerful drives of life. When we fast, however, we purposely seek to refocus our attention on nourishment that comes from doing the will of God (see John 4:34). We realize that all the food in the world can never satisfy the hunger of our souls. Only God himself can satisfy that longing.

Don't wait until you are overwhelmed by your enemies before you admit your dependence on God. Practice fasting as a means of sensitizing your heart to this total dependence so that you can grow in your understanding of God's gracious protection and provision.

For more on fasting, turn to Isaiah 58.

Putting It Into Practice

During a normal fast, a person abstains from food, but not from water, for a set period of time. A good starting place is to practice a twenty-four-hour fast from lunch one day to lunch the next. It's important to drink healthy quantities of water. For variety, you may want to flavor your water with a slice of lemon or lime or drops of lemon or lime juice. Don't be hard on yourself; a few shorter fasts will soon reduce the distractions of the physical discomfort and the strangeness of the whole experience.

During the fast, it is important to undertake some other specific disciplines, such as prayer and Bible reading, to support and direct your fast. You may want to use your normal meal times for personal worship and prayer. Keep a journal handy throughout the day. Let your food thoughts trigger thoughts about God. Those God thoughts can be helpful insights.

couraged because of this vast army. For the battle is not yours, but God's. [16]Tomorrow march down against them. They will be climbing up by the Pass of Ziz, and you will find them at the end of the gorge in the Desert of Jeruel. [17]You will not have to fight this battle. Take up your positions; stand firm and see the deliverance the LORD will give you, O Judah and Jerusalem. Do not be afraid; do not be discouraged. Go out to face them tomorrow, and the LORD will be with you.' "

[18]Jehoshaphat bowed with his face to the ground, and all the people of Judah and Jerusalem fell down in worship before the LORD. [19]Then some Levites from the Kohathites and Korahites stood up and praised the LORD, the God of Israel, with very loud voice.

[20]Early in the morning they left for the Desert of Tekoa. As they set out, Jehoshaphat stood and said, "Listen to me, Judah and people of Jerusalem! Have faith in the LORD your God and you will be upheld; have faith in his prophets and you will be successful." [21]After consulting the people, Jehoshaphat appointed men to sing to the LORD and to praise him for the splendor of his[a] holiness as they went out at the head of the army, saying:

"Give thanks to the LORD,
for his love endures forever."

[22]As they began to sing and praise, the LORD set ambushes against the men of Ammon and Moab and Mount Seir who were invading Judah, and they were defeated. [23]The men of Ammon and Moab rose up against the men from Mount Seir to destroy and annihilate them. After they finished slaughtering the men from Seir, they helped to destroy one another.

[24]When the men of Judah came to the place that overlooks the desert and looked toward the vast army, they saw only dead bodies lying on the ground; no one had escaped. [25]So Jehoshaphat and his men went to carry off their plunder, and they found among them a great amount of equipment and clothing[b] and also articles of value—more than they could take away. There was so much plunder that it took three days to collect it. [26]On the fourth day they assembled in the Valley of Beracah, where they praised the LORD. This is why it is called the Valley of Beracah[c] to this day.

[27]Then, led by Jehoshaphat, all the men of Judah and Jerusalem returned joyfully to Jerusalem, for the LORD had given them cause to rejoice over their enemies. [28]They entered Jerusalem and went to the temple of the LORD with harps and lutes and trumpets.

[29]The fear of God came upon all the kingdoms of the countries when they heard how the LORD had fought against the enemies of Israel. [30]And the kingdom of Jehoshaphat was at peace, for his God had given him rest on every side.

The End of Jehoshaphat's Reign

[31]So Jehoshaphat reigned over Judah. He was thirty-five years old when he became king of Judah, and he reigned in Jerusalem twenty-five years. His mother's name was Azubah daughter of Shilhi. [32]He walked in the ways of his father Asa and did not stray from them; he did what was right in the eyes of the LORD. [33]The high places, however, were not removed, and the people still had not set their hearts on the God of their fathers.

[34]The other events of Jehoshaphat's reign, from beginning to end, are written in the annals of Jehu son of Hanani, which are recorded in the book of the kings of Israel.

[35]Later, Jehoshaphat king of Judah made an alliance with Ahaziah king of Israel, who was guilty of wickedness. [36]He agreed with him to construct a fleet of trading ships.[d] After these were built at Ezion Geber, [37]Eliezer son of Dodavahu of Mareshah prophesied against Jehoshaphat, saying, "Because you have made an alliance with Ahaziah, the LORD will destroy what you have made." The ships were wrecked and were not able to set sail to trade.[e]

21 Then Jehoshaphat rested with his fathers and was buried with them in the City of David. And Jehoram his son succeeded him as king. [2]Jehoram's brothers, the sons of Jehoshaphat, were Azariah, Jehiel, Zechariah, Azariahu, Michael and Shephatiah. All these were sons of Jehoshaphat king of Israel.[f] [3]Their father had given them many gifts of silver and gold and articles of value, as well as fortified cities in Judah, but he had given the kingdom to Jehoram because he was his firstborn son.

Jehoram King of Judah

[4]When Jehoram established himself firmly over his father's kingdom, he put all his brothers to the sword along with some of the princes of Israel. [5]Jehoram was thirty-two years old when he became king, and he reigned in Jerusa-

[a]21 Or *him with the splendor of* [b]25 Some Hebrew manuscripts and Vulgate; most Hebrew manuscripts *corpses* [c]26 *Beracah* means *praise.* [d]36 Hebrew *of ships that could go to Tarshish* [e]37 Hebrew *sail for Tarshish* [f]2 That is, Judah, as frequently in 2 Chronicles

---

20:17 It is hard for some of us to give up control. We want to do things our own way, and often we want the credit for our success! God told the people of Judah to sit and watch as he gave them a great victory. We need to learn to give our battles to God. We cannot win them alone. With God's help, however, no enemy is too large or terrible for us to face. If we are willing to put our lives in his hands, God will give us the victory.

21:1–6 King Jehoshaphat of Judah gave his children great wealth, but apparently he did little to teach or guide them. A parent's role includes much more than merely supplying children's material needs. Children also need comfort, direction and the gift of godly values.

lem eight years. 6He walked in the ways of the
kings of Israel, as the house of Ahab had done,
for he married a daughter of Ahab. He did evil
in the eyes of the LORD. 7Nevertheless, because
of the covenant the LORD had made with David,
the LORD was not willing to destroy the house
of David. He had promised to maintain a lamp
for him and his descendants forever.

8In the time of Jehoram, Edom rebelled
against Judah and set up its own king. 9So Jehoram went there with his officers and all his chariots. The Edomites surrounded him and his
chariot commanders, but he rose up and broke
through by night. 10To this day Edom has been
in rebellion against Judah.

Libnah revolted at the same time, because
Jehoram had forsaken the LORD, the God of his
fathers. 11He had also built high places on the
hills of Judah and had caused the people of
Jerusalem to prostitute themselves and had led
Judah astray.

12Jehoram received a letter from Elijah the
prophet, which said:

"This is what the LORD, the God of your
father David, says: 'You have not walked
in the ways of your father Jehoshaphat
or of Asa king of Judah. 13But you have
walked in the ways of the kings of Israel,
and you have led Judah and the people of
Jerusalem to prostitute themselves, just as
the house of Ahab did. You have also murdered your own brothers, members of
your father's house, men who were better
than you. 14So now the LORD is about to
strike your people, your sons, your wives
and everything that is yours, with a heavy
blow. 15You yourself will be very ill with a
lingering disease of the bowels, until the
disease causes your bowels to come out.' "

16The LORD aroused against Jehoram the hostility of the Philistines and of the Arabs who
lived near the Cushites. 17They attacked Judah,
invaded it and carried off all the goods found in
the king's palace, together with his sons and
wives. Not a son was left to him except Ahaziah,[a] the youngest.

18After all this, the LORD afflicted Jehoram
with an incurable disease of the bowels. 19In the
course of time, at the end of the second year, his
bowels came out because of the disease, and he
died in great pain. His people made no fire in
his honor, as they had for his fathers.

20Jehoram was thirty-two years old when he
became king, and he reigned in Jerusalem eight
years. He passed away, to no one's regret, and
was buried in the City of David, but not in the
tombs of the kings.

Ahaziah King of Judah

22 The people of Jerusalem made Ahaziah,
Jehoram's youngest son, king in his
place, since the raiders, who came with the
Arabs into the camp, had killed all the older
sons. So Ahaziah son of Jehoram king of Judah
began to reign.

2Ahaziah was twenty-two[b] years old when
he became king, and he reigned in Jerusalem
one year. His mother's name was Athaliah, a
granddaughter of Omri.

3He too walked in the ways of the house of
Ahab, for his mother encouraged him in doing
wrong. 4He did evil in the eyes of the LORD, as
the house of Ahab had done, for after his father's death they became his advisers, to his
undoing. 5He also followed their counsel when
he went with Joram[c] son of Ahab king of Israel
to war against Hazael king of Aram at Ramoth
Gilead. The Arameans wounded Joram; 6so he
returned to Jezreel to recover from the wounds
they had inflicted on him at Ramoth[d] in his
battle with Hazael king of Aram.

Then Ahaziah[e] son of Jehoram king of Judah went down to Jezreel to see Joram son of
Ahab because he had been wounded.

7Through Ahaziah's visit to Joram, God
brought about Ahaziah's downfall. When Ahaziah arrived, he went out with Joram to meet
Jehu son of Nimshi, whom the LORD had
anointed to destroy the house of Ahab. 8While
Jehu was executing judgment on the house of
Ahab, he found the princes of Judah and the

[a]17 Hebrew *Jehoahaz,* a variant of *Ahaziah* [b]2 Some Septuagint manuscripts and Syriac (see also 2 Kings 8:26); Hebrew *forty-two* [c]5 Hebrew *Jehoram,* a variant of *Joram;* also in verses 6 and 7 [d]6 Hebrew *Ramah,* a variant of *Ramoth* [e]6 Some Hebrew manuscripts, Septuagint, Vulgate and Syriac (see also 2 Kings 8:29); most Hebrew manuscripts *Azariah*

21:6–7 What an amazing contrast between father and son! In this passage we read about the faithlessness of Jehoram. He patterned his reign after the kings of the northern kingdom and even married one of Ahab's wicked daughters. The consequences of turning away from God are exhibited in Jehoram's life. Jehoram's actions, however, never curtailed the faithfulness of God.

21:8–10 The book of Genesis records the feud between Jacob and Esau (see Genesis 27). Jacob's descendants became the Israelites, and Esau's descendants became the Edomites. In these verses we see that the families were still feuding hundreds of years later. The conflicts that we also fail to resolve may be passed on to our descendants. For their sake, we would be wise to restore our broken relationships now.

21:18–20 Jehoram's life of rebellion against God and his failure to fulfill his royal responsibilities led to a tragic end: He was disowned and unwanted by his own people. They didn't even give him an honorable burial. We can only wonder what would have happened if Jehoram had sought God, surrendered to him and reconciled himself with his people. Rejecting God's plan always leads to failure. God's way is the only way to success.

22:2–4 It is a terrible thing to follow a bad example and listen to foolish advice. Ahaziah's grandparents were Ahab and Jezebel. His mother was godless Athaliah, who served as his chief advisor. Sadly, Ahaziah never turned to God to receive the gift of forgiveness and reconciliation. Regardless of what our spiritual heritage has been, however, we must accept responsibility for our own lives and our relationship with God.

sons of Ahaziah's relatives, who had been attending Ahaziah, and he killed them. 9He then went in search of Ahaziah, and his men captured him while he was hiding in Samaria. He was brought to Jehu and put to death. They buried him, for they said, "He was a son of Jehoshaphat, who sought the LORD with all his heart." So there was no one in the house of Ahaziah powerful enough to retain the kingdom.

Athaliah and Joash

10When Athaliah the mother of Ahaziah saw that her son was dead, she proceeded to destroy the whole royal family of the house of Judah. 11But Jehosheba,[a] the daughter of King Jehoram, took Joash son of Ahaziah and stole him away from among the royal princes who were about to be murdered and put him and his nurse in a bedroom. Because Jehosheba,[a] the daughter of King Jehoram and wife of the priest Jehoiada, was Ahaziah's sister, she hid the child from Athaliah so she could not kill him. 12He remained hidden with them at the temple of God for six years while Athaliah ruled the land.

23 In the seventh year Jehoiada showed his strength. He made a covenant with the commanders of units of a hundred: Azariah son of Jeroham, Ishmael son of Jehohanan, Azariah son of Obed, Maaseiah son of Adaiah, and Elishaphat son of Zicri. 2They went throughout Judah and gathered the Levites and the heads of Israelite families from all the towns. When they came to Jerusalem, 3the whole assembly made a covenant with the king at the temple of God.

Jehoiada said to them, "The king's son shall reign, as the LORD promised concerning the descendants of David. 4Now this is what you are to do: A third of you priests and Levites who are going on duty on the Sabbath are to keep watch at the doors, 5a third of you at the royal palace and a third at the Foundation Gate, and all the other men are to be in the courtyards of the temple of the LORD. 6No one is to enter the temple of the LORD except the priests and Levites on duty; they may enter because they are consecrated, but all the other men are to guard what the LORD has assigned to them.[b] 7The Levites are to station themselves around the king, each man with his weapons in his hand. Anyone who enters the temple must be put to death. Stay close to the king wherever he goes."

8The Levites and all the men of Judah did just as Jehoiada the priest ordered. Each one took his men—those who were going on duty on the Sabbath and those who were going off duty—for Jehoiada the priest had not released any of the divisions. 9Then he gave the commanders of units of a hundred the spears and the large and small shields that had belonged to King David and that were in the temple of God. 10He stationed all the men, each with his weapon in his hand, around the king—near the altar and the temple, from the south side to the north side of the temple.

11Jehoiada and his sons brought out the king's son and put the crown on him; they presented him with a copy of the covenant and proclaimed him king. They anointed him and shouted, "Long live the king!"

12When Athaliah heard the noise of the people running and cheering the king, she went to them at the temple of the LORD. 13She looked, and there was the king, standing by his pillar at the entrance. The officers and the trumpeters were beside the king, and all the people of the land were rejoicing and blowing trumpets, and singers with musical instruments were leading the praises. Then Athaliah tore her robes and shouted, "Treason! Treason!"

14Jehoiada the priest sent out the commanders of units of a hundred, who were in charge of the troops, and said to them: "Bring her out between the ranks[c] and put to the sword anyone who follows her." For the priest had said, "Do not put her to death at the temple of the LORD." 15So they seized her as she reached the entrance of the Horse Gate on the palace grounds, and there they put her to death.

16Jehoiada then made a covenant that he and the people and the king[d] would be the LORD's people. 17All the people went to the temple of Baal and tore it down. They smashed the altars and idols and killed Mattan the priest of Baal in front of the altars.

18Then Jehoiada placed the oversight of the temple of the LORD in the hands of the priests, who were Levites, to whom David had made assignments in the temple, to present the burnt offerings of the LORD as written in the Law of Moses, with rejoicing and singing, as David had ordered. 19He also stationed doorkeepers at the gates of the LORD's temple so that no one who was in any way unclean might enter.

20He took with him the commanders of hun-

[a] 11 Hebrew *Jehoshabeath,* a variant of *Jehosheba* [b] 6 Or *to observe the LORD's command ⌊not to enter⌋* [c] 14 Or *out from the precincts* [d] 16 Or *covenant between ⌊the LORD⌋ and the people and the king that they* (see 2 Kings 11:17)

22:10–12 God is sovereign. Although it seemed as if everything was against Jehoiada and young Joash, they escaped the bloodbath of Jehu and avoided Athaliah's slaughter of Ahaziah's family. As we face difficult circumstances, we can be encouraged that God is ultimately in control. If we entrust our lives to him, he will lead us through even the worst situations.

23:1–11 In order to accomplish God's will, Jehoiada made painstaking plans. He did everything necessary to restore the Davidic line to Judah's throne. Sometimes doing the right thing requires careful planning.

23:15–17 After the overthrow of Athaliah, Jehoiada led the people of Judah in renewing their relationship with God. After times of rebellion, we also need to renew our commitment to God. He is always willing to offer a repentant heart a fresh start—no matter how serious our sins have been.

23:20–21 The results of conflict are not always negative. After the overthrow of Athaliah, the people rejoiced, and there was peace in Jerusalem. Conflicts can help us pin-

dreds, the nobles, the rulers of the people and all the people of the land and brought the king down from the temple of the LORD. They went into the palace through the Upper Gate and seated the king on the royal throne, 21and all the people of the land rejoiced. And the city was quiet, because Athaliah had been slain with the sword.

Joash Repairs the Temple

24 Joash was seven years old when he became king, and he reigned in Jerusalem forty years. His mother's name was Zibiah; she was from Beersheba. 2Joash did what was right in the eyes of the LORD all the years of Jehoiada the priest. 3Jehoiada chose two wives for him, and he had sons and daughters.

4Some time later Joash decided to restore the temple of the LORD. 5He called together the priests and Levites and said to them, "Go to the towns of Judah and collect the money due annually from all Israel, to repair the temple of your God. Do it now." But the Levites did not act at once.

6Therefore the king summoned Jehoiada the chief priest and said to him, "Why haven't you required the Levites to bring in from Judah and Jerusalem the tax imposed by Moses the servant of the LORD and by the assembly of Israel for the Tent of the Testimony?"

7Now the sons of that wicked woman Athaliah had broken into the temple of God and had used even its sacred objects for the Baals.

8At the king's command, a chest was made and placed outside, at the gate of the temple of the LORD. 9A proclamation was then issued in Judah and Jerusalem that they should bring to the LORD the tax that Moses the servant of God had required of Israel in the desert. 10All the officials and all the people brought their contributions gladly, dropping them into the chest until it was full. 11Whenever the chest was brought in by the Levites to the king's officials and they saw that there was a large amount of money, the royal secretary and the officer of the chief priest would come and empty the chest and carry it back to its place. They did this regularly and collected a great amount of money. 12The king and Jehoiada gave it to the men who carried out the work required for the temple of the LORD. They hired masons and carpenters to restore the LORD's temple, and also workers in iron and bronze to repair the temple.

13The men in charge of the work were diligent, and the repairs progressed under them. They rebuilt the temple of God according to its original design and reinforced it. 14When they had finished, they brought the rest of the money to the king and Jehoiada, and with it were made articles for the LORD's temple: articles for the service and for the burnt offerings, and also dishes and other objects of gold and silver. As long as Jehoiada lived, burnt offerings were presented continually in the temple of the LORD.

15Now Jehoiada was old and full of years, and he died at the age of a hundred and thirty. 16He was buried with the kings in the City of David, because of the good he had done in Israel for God and his temple.

The Wickedness of Joash

17After the death of Jehoiada, the officials of Judah came and paid homage to the king, and he listened to them. 18They abandoned the temple of the LORD, the God of their fathers, and worshiped Asherah poles and idols. Because of their guilt, God's anger came upon Judah and Jerusalem. 19Although the LORD sent prophets to the people to bring them back to him, and though they testified against them, they would not listen.

20Then the Spirit of God came upon Zechariah son of Jehoiada the priest. He stood before the people and said, "This is what God says: 'Why do you disobey the LORD's commands? You will not prosper. Because you have forsaken the LORD, he has forsaken you.' "

21But they plotted against him, and by order of the king they stoned him to death in the courtyard of the LORD's temple. 22King Joash did not remember the kindness Zechariah's father Jehoiada had shown him but killed his son, who said as he lay dying, "May the LORD see this and call you to account."

23At the turn of the year,[a] the army of Aram marched against Joash; it invaded Judah and Jerusalem and killed all the leaders of the people. They sent all the plunder to their king in Damascus. 24Although the Aramean army had come with only a few men, the LORD delivered

[a]23 Probably in the spring

---

point problems in our lives. Once we see these difficulties, we should accept responsibility for them and ask God to help us redirect our course.

24:1–2 When we are poorly equipped or unprepared for a certain role in life, it is important that we find a godly mentor to give us direction. The young boy-king Joash was greatly blessed to have Jehoiada help guide him in his early decisions. The old priest kept him moving in the right direction, leading him in the ways of God. All of us need the help of a godly mentor who can relate to what we are going through. We must avoid the tendency toward self-sufficiency. Others can help hold us accountable, help us grow and help preserve our spiritual gains.

24:4–5 We must be committed to doing God's will when God wants it done. Procrastinating when God has shown us what he requires is a form of disobedience. Plans to do God's will "tomorrow" should never be mistaken for obedience. If we know what God wants us to do, we need to do it!

24:17–20 After Jehoiada died, Joash turned away from God. Jehoiada's son Zechariah rebuked Joash for his failure to obey God's laws. Joash was unwilling to face the truth about his behavior and killed Zechariah to hide from it. When we are confronted with our own sin, it is tempting to deny its existence. Instead, we should admit our sin, repent of it and seek God's forgiveness. Then we can redirect our course and praise God for his redemption.

into their hands a much larger army. Because Judah had forsaken the LORD, the God of their fathers, judgment was executed on Joash. 25When the Arameans withdrew, they left Joash severely wounded. His officials conspired against him for murdering the son of Jehoiada the priest, and they killed him in his bed. So he died and was buried in the City of David, but not in the tombs of the kings.

26Those who conspired against him were Zabad,[a] son of Shimeath an Ammonite woman, and Jehozabad, son of Shimrith[b] a Moabite woman. 27The account of his sons, the many prophecies about him, and the record of the restoration of the temple of God are written in the annotations on the book of the kings. And Amaziah his son succeeded him as king.

Amaziah King of Judah

25 Amaziah was twenty-five years old when he became king, and he reigned in Jerusalem twenty-nine years. His mother's name was Jehoaddin[c]; she was from Jerusalem. 2He did what was right in the eyes of the LORD, but not wholeheartedly. 3After the kingdom was firmly in his control, he executed the officials who had murdered his father the king. 4Yet he did not put their sons to death, but acted in accordance with what is written in the Law, in the Book of Moses, where the LORD commanded: "Fathers shall not be put to death for their children, nor children put to death for their fathers; each is to die for his own sins."[d]

5Amaziah called the people of Judah together and assigned them according to their families to commanders of thousands and commanders of hundreds for all Judah and Benjamin. He then mustered those twenty years old or more and found that there were three hundred thousand men ready for military service, able to handle the spear and shield. 6He also hired a hundred thousand fighting men from Israel for a hundred talents[e] of silver.

7But a man of God came to him and said, "O king, these troops from Israel must not march with you, for the LORD is not with Israel—not with any of the people of Ephraim. 8Even if you go and fight courageously in battle, God will overthrow you before the enemy, for God has the power to help or to overthrow."

9Amaziah asked the man of God, "But what about the hundred talents I paid for these Israelite troops?"

The man of God replied, "The LORD can give you much more than that."

10So Amaziah dismissed the troops who had come to him from Ephraim and sent them home. They were furious with Judah and left for home in a great rage.

11Amaziah then marshaled his strength and led his army to the Valley of Salt, where he killed ten thousand men of Seir. 12The army of Judah also captured ten thousand men alive, took them to the top of a cliff and threw them down so that all were dashed to pieces.

13Meanwhile the troops that Amaziah had sent back and had not allowed to take part in the war raided Judean towns from Samaria to Beth Horon. They killed three thousand people and carried off great quantities of plunder.

14When Amaziah returned from slaughtering the Edomites, he brought back the gods of the people of Seir. He set them up as his own gods, bowed down to them and burned sacrifices to them. 15The anger of the LORD burned against Amaziah, and he sent a prophet to him, who said, "Why do you consult this people's gods, which could not save their own people from your hand?"

16While he was still speaking, the king said to him, "Have we appointed you an adviser to the king? Stop! Why be struck down?"

So the prophet stopped but said, "I know that God has determined to destroy you, because you have done this and have not listened to my counsel."

17After Amaziah king of Judah consulted his advisers, he sent this challenge to Jehoash[f] son of Jehoahaz, the son of Jehu, king of Israel: "Come, meet me face to face."

18But Jehoash king of Israel replied to Amaziah king of Judah: "A thistle in Lebanon sent a message to a cedar in Lebanon, 'Give your daughter to my son in marriage.' Then a wild beast in Lebanon came along and trampled the thistle underfoot. 19You say to yourself that you have defeated Edom, and now you are arrogant and proud. But stay at home! Why ask for trou-

[a]26 A variant of *Jozabad* [b]26 A variant of *Shomer*
[c]1 Hebrew *Jehoaddan,* a variant of *Jehoaddin*
[d]4 Deut. 24:16 [e]6 That is, about 3 3/4 tons (about 3.4 metric tons); also in verse 9 [f]17 Hebrew *Joash,* a variant of *Jehoash;* also in verses 18, 21, 23 and 25

25:1–2 Amaziah was a good king—but not great. He did the right things, but he failed to do them with the right attitude. As we follow God, we need to do so with our whole heart. We need to seek God sincerely. If we are just going through the motions of spirituality, hoping to receive God's blessings, our spiritual progress will be nonexistent.

25:4 This passage reminds us that we all must take responsibility for our sins. While we may sense that some of our suffering is a result of our parents' mistakes, we must not use this as an excuse for our own failures. We must take responsibility for how we choose to deal with the suffering brought into our lives by others. We alone are responsible before God for our actions and our reactions.

25:5–8 As Amaziah faced a powerful enemy, it seemed a good idea to hire a large contingent of mercenaries from the northern kingdom. But God told Amaziah to send all the foreign troops home and to trust him for the outcome instead. When we face difficult situations, we may be tempted to try every human resource available before we turn to God. We must always remember that God is our ultimate defender and provider. When we turn to him in times of need, he will provide abundantly for us. If we turn only to human resources, we are headed for trouble.

ble and cause your own downfall and that of Judah also?"

20Amaziah, however, would not listen, for God so worked that he might hand them over to ⌊Jehoash⌋, because they sought the gods of Edom. 21So Jehoash king of Israel attacked. He and Amaziah king of Judah faced each other at Beth Shemesh in Judah. 22Judah was routed by Israel, and every man fled to his home. 23Jehoash king of Israel captured Amaziah king of Judah, the son of Joash, the son of Ahaziah,[a] at Beth Shemesh. Then Jehoash brought him to Jerusalem and broke down the wall of Jerusalem from the Ephraim Gate to the Corner Gate—a section about six hundred feet[b] long. 24He took all the gold and silver and all the articles found in the temple of God that had been in the care of Obed-Edom, together with the palace treasures and the hostages, and returned to Samaria.

25Amaziah son of Joash king of Judah lived for fifteen years after the death of Jehoash son of Jehoahaz king of Israel. 26As for the other events of Amaziah's reign, from beginning to end, are they not written in the book of the kings of Judah and Israel? 27From the time that Amaziah turned away from following the LORD, they conspired against him in Jerusalem and he fled to Lachish, but they sent men after him to Lachish and killed him there. 28He was brought back by horse and was buried with his fathers in the City of Judah.

Uzziah King of Judah

26 Then all the people of Judah took Uzziah,[c] who was sixteen years old, and made him king in place of his father Amaziah. 2He was the one who rebuilt Elath and restored it to Judah after Amaziah rested with his fathers.

3Uzziah was sixteen years old when he became king, and he reigned in Jerusalem fifty-two years. His mother's name was Jecoliah; she was from Jerusalem. 4He did what was right in the eyes of the LORD, just as his father Amaziah had done. 5He sought God during the days of Zechariah, who instructed him in the fear[d] of God. As long as he sought the LORD, God gave him success.

6He went to war against the Philistines and broke down the walls of Gath, Jabneh and Ashdod. He then rebuilt towns near Ashdod and elsewhere among the Philistines. 7God helped him against the Philistines and against the Arabs who lived in Gur Baal and against the Meunites. 8The Ammonites brought tribute to Uzziah, and his fame spread as far as the border of Egypt, because he had become very powerful.

9Uzziah built towers in Jerusalem at the Corner Gate, at the Valley Gate and at the angle of the wall, and he fortified them. 10He also built towers in the desert and dug many cisterns, because he had much livestock in the foothills and in the plain. He had people working his fields and vineyards in the hills and in the fertile lands, for he loved the soil.

11Uzziah had a well-trained army, ready to go out by divisions according to their numbers as mustered by Jeiel the secretary and Maaseiah the officer under the direction of Hananiah, one of the royal officials. 12The total number of family leaders over the fighting men was 2,600. 13Under their command was an army of 307,500 men trained for war, a powerful force to support the king against his enemies. 14Uzziah provided shields, spears, helmets, coats of armor, bows and slingstones for the entire army. 15In Jerusalem he made machines designed by skillful men for use on the towers and on the corner defenses to shoot arrows and hurl large stones. His fame spread far and wide, for he was greatly helped until he became powerful.

16But after Uzziah became powerful, his pride led to his downfall. He was unfaithful to the LORD his God, and entered the temple of the LORD to burn incense on the altar of incense. 17Azariah the priest with eighty other courageous priests of the LORD followed him in. 18They confronted him and said, "It is not right for you, Uzziah, to burn incense to the LORD. That is for the priests, the descendants of Aaron, who have been consecrated to burn incense. Leave the sanctuary, for you have been unfaithful; and you will not be honored by the LORD God."

19Uzziah, who had a censer in his hand ready to burn incense, became angry. While he was raging at the priests in their presence before the incense altar in the LORD's temple, leprosy[e] broke out on his forehead. 20When Azariah the chief priest and all the other priests looked at him, they saw that he had leprosy on his forehead, so they hurried him out. Indeed, he himself was eager to leave, because the LORD had afflicted him.

21King Uzziah had leprosy until the day he died. He lived in a separate house[f]—leprous, and excluded from the temple of the LORD. Jotham his son had charge of the palace and governed the people of the land.

22The other events of Uzziah's reign, from

[a] 23 Hebrew *Jehoahaz,* a variant of *Ahaziah*
[b] 23 Hebrew *four hundred cubits* (about 180 meters)
[c] 1 Also called *Azariah*
[d] 5 Many Hebrew manuscripts, Septuagint and Syriac; other Hebrew manuscripts *vision*
[e] 19 The Hebrew word was used for various diseases affecting the skin—not necessarily leprosy; also in verses 20, 21 and 23.
[f] 21 Or *in a house where he was relieved of responsibilities*

26:16–18 Uzziah had begun his reign so well; he possessed the potential for being one of the greatest kings in Judah's history. God blessed him in almost everything he did. But then Uzziah became proud. He entered the temple sanctuary, something only the priests were allowed to do. And Uzziah discovered an important truth—we cannot sin without suffering the consequences.

beginning to end, are recorded by the prophet Isaiah son of Amoz. 23Uzziah rested with his fathers and was buried near them in a field for burial that belonged to the kings, for people said, "He had leprosy." And Jotham his son succeeded him as king.

Jotham King of Judah

27 Jotham was twenty-five years old when he became king, and he reigned in Jerusalem sixteen years. His mother's name was Jerusha daughter of Zadok. 2He did what was right in the eyes of the LORD, just as his father Uzziah had done, but unlike him he did not enter the temple of the LORD. The people, however, continued their corrupt practices. 3Jotham rebuilt the Upper Gate of the temple of the LORD and did extensive work on the wall at the hill of Ophel. 4He built towns in the Judean hills and forts and towers in the wooded areas.

5Jotham made war on the king of the Ammonites and conquered them. That year the Ammonites paid him a hundred talents[a] of silver, ten thousand cors[b] of wheat and ten thousand cors of barley. The Ammonites brought him the same amount also in the second and third years.

6Jotham grew powerful because he walked steadfastly before the LORD his God.

7The other events in Jotham's reign, including all his wars and the other things he did, are written in the book of the kings of Israel and Judah. 8He was twenty-five years old when he became king, and he reigned in Jerusalem sixteen years. 9Jotham rested with his fathers and was buried in the City of David. And Ahaz his son succeeded him as king.

Ahaz King of Judah

28 Ahaz was twenty years old when he became king, and he reigned in Jerusalem sixteen years. Unlike David his father, he did not do what was right in the eyes of the LORD. 2He walked in the ways of the kings of Israel and also made cast idols for worshiping the Baals. 3He burned sacrifices in the Valley of Ben Hinnom and sacrificed his sons in the fire, following the detestable ways of the nations the LORD had driven out before the Israelites. 4He offered sacrifices and burned incense at the high places, on the hilltops and under every spreading tree.

5Therefore the LORD his God handed him over to the king of Aram. The Arameans defeated him and took many of his people as prisoners and brought them to Damascus.

He was also given into the hands of the king of Israel, who inflicted heavy casualties on him. 6In one day Pekah son of Remaliah killed a hundred and twenty thousand soldiers in Judah—because Judah had forsaken the LORD, the God of their fathers. 7Zicri, an Ephraimite warrior, killed Maaseiah the king's son, Azrikam the officer in charge of the palace, and Elkanah, second to the king. 8The Israelites took captive from their kinsmen two hundred thousand wives, sons and daughters. They also took a great deal of plunder, which they carried back to Samaria.

9But a prophet of the LORD named Oded was there, and he went out to meet the army when it returned to Samaria. He said to them, "Because the LORD, the God of your fathers, was angry with Judah, he gave them into your hand. But you have slaughtered them in a rage that reaches to heaven. 10And now you intend to make the men and women of Judah and Jerusalem your slaves. But aren't you also guilty of sins against the LORD your God? 11Now listen to me! Send back your fellow countrymen you have taken as prisoners, for the LORD's fierce anger rests on you."

12Then some of the leaders in Ephraim—Azariah son of Jehohanan, Berekiah son of Meshillemoth, Jehizkiah son of Shallum, and Amasa son of Hadlai—confronted those who were arriving from the war. 13"You must not bring those prisoners here," they said, "or we will be guilty before the LORD. Do you intend to add to our sin and guilt? For our guilt is already great, and his fierce anger rests on Israel."

14So the soldiers gave up the prisoners and plunder in the presence of the officials and all the assembly. 15The men designated by name took the prisoners, and from the plunder they clothed all who were naked. They provided them with clothes and sandals, food and drink, and healing balm. All those who were weak they put on donkeys. So they took them back to their fellow countrymen at Jericho, the City of Palms, and returned to Samaria.

16At that time King Ahaz sent to the king[c] of Assyria for help. 17The Edomites had again come and attacked Judah and carried away prisoners, 18while the Philistines had raided towns in the foothills and in the Negev of Judah. They captured and occupied Beth Shemesh, Aijalon and Gederoth, as well as Soco, Timnah and Gimzo, with their surrounding villages. 19The LORD had humbled Judah because of Ahaz king of Israel,[d] for he had promoted wickedness in Judah and had been most unfaithful to the

[a]5 That is, about 3 3/4 tons (about 3.4 metric tons)
[b]5 That is, probably about 62,000 bushels (about 2,200 kiloliters)
[c]16 One Hebrew manuscript, Septuagint and Vulgate (see also 2 Kings 16:7); most Hebrew manuscripts *kings*
[d]19 That is, Judah, as frequently in 2 Chronicles

28:1–2 The northern kingdom of Israel was slowly dying. It had been conquered by the Assyrians; most of its people had been taken into captivity and would never return. How foolish for Ahaz of Judah to follow the example of the kings of the northern kingdom! He could see the results of their sinful behavior. We need to be careful about whom we choose to emulate too.

LORD. 20Tiglath-Pileser[a] king of Assyria came to him, but he gave him trouble instead of help. 21Ahaz took some of the things from the temple of the LORD and from the royal palace and from the princes and presented them to the king of Assyria, but that did not help him.

22In his time of trouble King Ahaz became even more unfaithful to the LORD. 23He offered sacrifices to the gods of Damascus, who had defeated him; for he thought, "Since the gods of the kings of Aram have helped them, I will sacrifice to them so they will help me." But they were his downfall and the downfall of all Israel.

24Ahaz gathered together the furnishings from the temple of God and took them away.[b] He shut the doors of the LORD's temple and set up altars at every street corner in Jerusalem. 25In every town in Judah he built high places to burn sacrifices to other gods and provoked the LORD, the God of his fathers, to anger.

26The other events of his reign and all his ways, from beginning to end, are written in the book of the kings of Judah and Israel. 27Ahaz rested with his fathers and was buried in the city of Jerusalem, but he was not placed in the tombs of the kings of Israel. And Hezekiah his son succeeded him as king.

Hezekiah Purifies the Temple

29 Hezekiah was twenty-five years old when he became king, and he reigned in Jerusalem twenty-nine years. His mother's name was Abijah daughter of Zechariah. 2He did what was right in the eyes of the LORD, just as his father David had done.

3In the first month of the first year of his reign, he opened the doors of the temple of the LORD and repaired them. 4He brought in the priests and the Levites, assembled them in the square on the east side 5and said: "Listen to me, Levites! Consecrate yourselves now and consecrate the temple of the LORD, the God of your fathers. Remove all defilement from the sanctuary. 6Our fathers were unfaithful; they did evil in the eyes of the LORD our God and forsook him. They turned their faces away from the LORD's dwelling place and turned their backs on him. 7They also shut the doors of the portico and put out the lamps. They did not burn incense or present any burnt offerings at the sanctuary to the God of Israel. 8Therefore, the anger of the LORD has fallen on Judah and Jerusalem; he has made them an object of dread and horror and scorn, as you can see with your own eyes. 9This is why our fathers have fallen by the sword and why our sons and daughters and our wives are in captivity. 10Now I intend to make a covenant with the LORD, the God of Israel, so that his fierce anger will turn away from us. 11My sons, do not be negligent now, for the LORD has chosen you to stand before him and serve him, to minister before him and to burn incense."

12Then these Levites set to work:
from the Kohathites,
Mahath son of Amasai and Joel son of Azariah;
from the Merarites,
Kish son of Abdi and Azariah son of Jehallelel;
from the Gershonites,
Joah son of Zimmah and Eden son of Joah;
13from the descendants of Elizaphan,
Shimri and Jeiel;
from the descendants of Asaph,
Zechariah and Mattaniah;
14from the descendants of Heman,
Jehiel and Shimei;
from the descendants of Jeduthun,
Shemaiah and Uzziel.

15When they had assembled their brothers and consecrated themselves, they went in to purify the temple of the LORD, as the king had ordered, following the word of the LORD. 16The priests went into the sanctuary of the LORD to purify it. They brought out to the courtyard of the LORD's temple everything unclean that they found in the temple of the LORD. The Levites took it and carried it out to the Kidron Valley. 17They began the consecration on the first day of the first month, and by the eighth day of the month they reached the portico of the LORD. For eight more days they consecrated the temple of the LORD itself, finishing on the sixteenth day of the first month.

18Then they went in to King Hezekiah and reported: "We have purified the entire temple of the LORD, the altar of burnt offering with all its utensils, and the table for setting out the consecrated bread, with all its articles. 19We have prepared and consecrated all the articles that King Ahaz removed in his unfaithfulness while he was king. They are now in front of the LORD's altar."

[a] 20 Hebrew *Tilgath-Pilneser,* a variant of *Tiglath-Pileser*
[b] 24 Or *and cut them up*

29:1–2 Hezekiah received a high commendation: He followed the example of his ancestor David. King David was continually used as the gauge for success as a king. As we seek to grow spiritually, we need to find worthy role models to emulate. David is an ideal role model. Though he made many mistakes, David was always willing to humbly confess his sins and seek reconciliation with God and other people.

29:3–5 Hezekiah began his reign in the right way—seeking for God. His father had closed the temple. Worship of the Lord had been discontinued and Judah was mired in sin and idolatry. Hezekiah recognized his father's failures and set out to make changes. He opened the temple's doors and enjoined the priests to cleanse themselves in order to reinstitute the proper worship activities. When our lives are filled with problems, refusing to see the truth and face reality is not the way to make things better. We need to act like Hezekiah, assessing our problems and doing what we can to change them.

[20]Early the next morning King Hezekiah
gathered the city officials together and went up
to the temple of the LORD. [21]They brought seven
bulls, seven rams, seven male lambs and seven
male goats as a sin offering for the kingdom, for
the sanctuary and for Judah. The king commanded the priests, the descendants of Aaron,
to offer these on the altar of the LORD. [22]So they
slaughtered the bulls, and the priests took the
blood and sprinkled it on the altar; next they
slaughtered the rams and sprinkled their blood
on the altar; then they slaughtered the lambs
and sprinkled their blood on the altar. [23]The
goats for the sin offering were brought before
the king and the assembly, and they laid their
hands on them. [24]The priests then slaughtered
the goats and presented their blood on the altar
for a sin offering to atone for all Israel, because
the king had ordered the burnt offering and the
sin offering for all Israel.

[25]He stationed the Levites in the temple of
the LORD with cymbals, harps and lyres in the
way prescribed by David and Gad the king's seer
and Nathan the prophet; this was commanded
by the LORD through his prophets. [26]So the Levites stood ready with David's instruments, and
the priests with their trumpets.

[27]Hezekiah gave the order to sacrifice the
burnt offering on the altar. As the offering began, singing to the LORD began also, accompanied by trumpets and the instruments of David
king of Israel. [28]The whole assembly bowed in
worship, while the singers sang and the trumpeters played. All this continued until the sacrifice of the burnt offering was completed.

[29]When the offerings were finished, the king
and everyone present with him knelt down and
worshiped. [30]King Hezekiah and his officials
ordered the Levites to praise the LORD with the
words of David and of Asaph the seer. So they
sang praises with gladness and bowed their
heads and worshiped.

[31]Then Hezekiah said, "You have now dedicated yourselves to the LORD. Come and bring
sacrifices and thank offerings to the temple of
the LORD." So the assembly brought sacrifices
and thank offerings, and all whose hearts were
willing brought burnt offerings.

[32]The number of burnt offerings the assembly brought was seventy bulls, a hundred rams
and two hundred male lambs—all of them for
burnt offerings to the LORD. [33]The animals consecrated as sacrifices amounted to six hundred
bulls and three thousand sheep and goats.
[34]The priests, however, were too few to skin all
the burnt offerings; so their kinsmen the Levites
helped them until the task was finished and
until other priests had been consecrated, for the
Levites had been more conscientious in consecrating themselves than the priests had been.
[35]There were burnt offerings in abundance, together with the fat of the fellowship offerings[a]
and the drink offerings that accompanied the
burnt offerings.

So the service of the temple of the LORD was
reestablished. [36]Hezekiah and all the people rejoiced at what God had brought about for his
people, because it was done so quickly.

Hezekiah Celebrates the Passover

30 Hezekiah sent word to all Israel and
Judah and also wrote letters to Ephraim
and Manasseh, inviting them to come to the
temple of the LORD in Jerusalem and celebrate
the Passover to the LORD, the God of Israel. [2]The
king and his officials and the whole assembly in
Jerusalem decided to celebrate the Passover in
the second month. [3]They had not been able
to celebrate it at the regular time because not
enough priests had consecrated themselves and
the people had not assembled in Jerusalem.
[4]The plan seemed right both to the king and to
the whole assembly. [5]They decided to send a
proclamation throughout Israel, from Beersheba to Dan, calling the people to come to Jerusalem and celebrate the Passover to the LORD, the
God of Israel. It had not been celebrated in large
numbers according to what was written.

[6]At the king's command, couriers went
throughout Israel and Judah with letters from
the king and from his officials, which read:

> "People of Israel, return to the LORD,
> the God of Abraham, Isaac and Israel, that
> he may return to you who are left, who
> have escaped from the hand of the kings
> of Assyria. [7]Do not be like your fathers
> and brothers, who were unfaithful to the
> LORD, the God of their fathers, so that he
> made them an object of horror, as you see.
> [8]Do not be stiff-necked, as your fathers
> were; submit to the LORD. Come to the
> sanctuary, which he has consecrated forev-
> er. Serve the LORD your God, so that his
> fierce anger will turn away from you. [9]If
> you return to the LORD, then your brothers
> and your children will be shown compas-
> sion by their captors and will come back
> to this land, for the LORD your God is gra-
> cious and compassionate. He will not turn
> his face from you if you return to him."

[10]The couriers went from town to town in
Ephraim and Manasseh, as far as Zebulun, but
the people scorned and ridiculed them. [11]Nev-
ertheless, some men of Asher, Manasseh and
Zebulun humbled themselves and went to Jeru-

[a]35 Traditionally *peace offerings*

30:6–8 Hezekiah urged his people to break from the sinful patterns set by their ancestors. Hezekiah had already broken from the sinful patterns set by his father. Now he called his people to do the same. He knew their situation well. Some people feel imprisoned by the sins and wrong patterns set by their parents. However, there is hope for all who repent and trust God. We don't need to be bound by our parents' failures. Spiritual renewal can begin any time we are willing to seek God and surrender to him.

salem. 12Also in Judah the hand of God was on the people to give them unity of mind to carry out what the king and his officials had ordered, following the word of the LORD.

13A very large crowd of people assembled in Jerusalem to celebrate the Feast of Unleavened Bread in the second month. 14They removed the altars in Jerusalem and cleared away the incense altars and threw them into the Kidron Valley.

15They slaughtered the Passover lamb on the fourteenth day of the second month. The priests and the Levites were ashamed and consecrated themselves and brought burnt offerings to the temple of the LORD. 16Then they took up their regular positions as prescribed in the Law of Moses the man of God. The priests sprinkled the blood handed to them by the Levites. 17Since many in the crowd had not consecrated themselves, the Levites had to kill the Passover lambs for all those who were not ceremonially clean and could not consecrate ⌞their lambs⌟ to the LORD. 18Although most of the many people who came from Ephraim, Manasseh, Issachar and Zebulun had not purified themselves, yet they ate the Passover, contrary to what was written. But Hezekiah prayed for them, saying, "May the LORD, who is good, pardon everyone 19who sets his heart on seeking God—the LORD, the God of his fathers—even if he is not clean according to the rules of the sanctuary." 20And the LORD heard Hezekiah and healed the people.

21The Israelites who were present in Jerusalem celebrated the Feast of Unleavened Bread for seven days with great rejoicing, while the Levites and priests sang to the LORD every day, accompanied by the LORD's instruments of praise.[a]

22Hezekiah spoke encouragingly to all the Levites, who showed good understanding of the service of the LORD. For the seven days they ate their assigned portion and offered fellowship offerings[b] and praised the LORD, the God of their fathers.

23The whole assembly then agreed to celebrate the festival seven more days; so for another seven days they celebrated joyfully. 24Hezekiah king of Judah provided a thousand bulls and seven thousand sheep and goats for the assembly, and the officials provided them with a thousand bulls and ten thousand sheep and goats. A great number of priests consecrated themselves. 25The entire assembly of Judah rejoiced, along with the priests and Levites and all who had assembled from Israel, including the aliens who had come from Israel and those who lived in Judah. 26There was great joy in Jerusalem, for since the days of Solomon son of David king of Israel there had been nothing like this in Jerusalem. 27The priests and the Levites stood to bless the people, and God heard them, for their prayer reached heaven, his holy dwelling place.

31 When all this had ended, the Israelites who were there went out to the towns of Judah, smashed the sacred stones and cut down the Asherah poles. They destroyed the high places and the altars throughout Judah and Benjamin and in Ephraim and Manasseh. After they had destroyed all of them, the Israelites returned to their own towns and to their own property.

Contributions for Worship

2Hezekiah assigned the priests and Levites to divisions—each of them according to their duties as priests or Levites—to offer burnt offerings and fellowship offerings,[b] to minister, to give thanks and to sing praises at the gates of the LORD's dwelling. 3The king contributed from his own possessions for the morning and evening burnt offerings and for the burnt offerings on the Sabbaths, New Moons and appointed feasts as written in the Law of the LORD. 4He ordered the people living in Jerusalem to give the portion due the priests and Levites so they could devote themselves to the Law of the LORD. 5As soon as the order went out, the Israelites generously gave the firstfruits of their grain, new wine, oil and honey and all that the fields produced. They brought a great amount, a tithe of everything. 6The men of Israel and Judah who lived in the towns of Judah also brought a tithe of their herds and flocks and a tithe of the holy things dedicated to the LORD their God, and they piled them in heaps. 7They began doing this in the third month and finished in the seventh month. 8When Hezekiah and his officials came and saw the heaps, they praised the LORD and blessed his people Israel.

9Hezekiah asked the priests and Levites about the heaps; 10and Azariah the chief priest, from the family of Zadok, answered, "Since the people began to bring their contributions to the

[a] 21 Or *priests praised the LORD every day with resounding instruments belonging to the LORD* [b] 22,2 Traditionally *peace offerings*

30:17–19 God is high and holy; he is sinless and perfect. We can approach him only because he graciously allows us to do so. In the Old Testament, seeking God was guided by definite procedures. Hezekiah prayed on behalf of those whose preparations were not as complete as they should have been. In the same way, though we have fallen short of perfection, we can come before God because of the sacrifice of his Son, Jesus Christ.

31:2 In this passage Hezekiah illustrates another important aspect of spiritual growth. He ensured constant praise to God by setting up programs and personnel to lead the people in worship. We must never forget to thank God for his help as we seek to overcome the powerful problems in our lives. Praising God is important for our spiritual renewal.

31:4–8 Hezekiah made certain that encouragement was given to the people who took part in Judah's restoration. When the people gave sacrificially to God, Hezekiah praised them for their generosity. How necessary it is for us to be a part of a comforting and strengthening fellowship! We need to remember to give and to receive the encouragement we all need.

temple of the LORD, we have had enough to
eat and plenty to spare, because the LORD has
blessed his people, and this great amount is left
over."
11Hezekiah gave orders to prepare storerooms in the temple of the LORD, and this was
done. 12Then they faithfully brought in the contributions, tithes and dedicated gifts. Conaniah,
a Levite, was in charge of these things, and his
brother Shimei was next in rank. 13Jehiel, Azaziah, Nahath, Asahel, Jerimoth, Jozabad, Eliel, Is-
makiah, Mahath and Benaiah were supervisors
under Conaniah and Shimei his brother, by appointment of King Hezekiah and Azariah the
official in charge of the temple of God.
14Kore son of Imnah the Levite, keeper of the
East Gate, was in charge of the freewill offerings
given to God, distributing the contributions
made to the LORD and also the consecrated gifts.
15Eden, Miniamin, Jeshua, Shemaiah, Amariah
and Shecaniah assisted him faithfully in the
towns of the priests, distributing to their fellow
priests according to their divisions, old and
young alike.
16In addition, they distributed to the males
three years old or more whose names were in
the genealogical records—all who would enter
the temple of the LORD to perform the daily
duties of their various tasks, according to their
responsibilities and their divisions. 17And they
distributed to the priests enrolled by their families in the genealogical records and likewise to
the Levites twenty years old or more, according
to their responsibilities and their divisions.
18They included all the little ones, the wives,
and the sons and daughters of the whole community listed in these genealogical records. For
they were faithful in consecrating themselves.
19As for the priests, the descendants of Aaron,
who lived on the farm lands around their towns
or in any other towns, men were designated
by name to distribute portions to every male
among them and to all who were recorded in
the genealogies of the Levites.
20This is what Hezekiah did throughout Judah, doing what was good and right and faithful before the LORD his God. 21In everything
that he undertook in the service of God's temple
and in obedience to the law and the commands, he sought his God and worked wholeheartedly. And so he prospered.

Sennacherib Threatens Jerusalem

32 After all that Hezekiah had so faithfully
done, Sennacherib king of Assyria came
and invaded Judah. He laid siege to the fortified
cities, thinking to conquer them for himself.
2When Hezekiah saw that Sennacherib had
come and that he intended to make war on
Jerusalem, 3he consulted with his officials and

32:3–6 Hezekiah gives us an excellent example of how we should act—with both faith and hard work. Hezekiah knew that only God could deliver Judah from the Assyrian

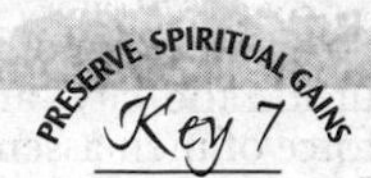

Repairing Our Boundaries

2 Chronicles 32:1–19 Boundaries are the limits that we set for the protection of ourselves and others. As we grow spiritually, we need to continually make sure our boundaries are in good shape. The limits we set will help to protect and preserve our spiritual growth. This may involve repairing or building healthy boundaries where they have become weak, defective or torn down.

In Bible times each city was fortified by boundary walls that gave its inhabitants protection from outside enemies. If these walls were weak or broken, there was grave danger of invasion and destruction. At one point in Israel's history, an enemy was threatening to attack Jerusalem, so King Hezekiah "worked hard repairing all the broken sections of the wall and building towers on it. He built another wall outside that one and reinforced the supporting terraces of the City of David" (32:5). Then Hezekiah encouraged the people by saying, "Be strong and courageous. Do not be afraid of discouraged because of the king of Assyria . . . for there is a greater power with us than with him. With him is only the arm of flesh, but with us is the LORD our God to help us and to fight our battles" (32:7–8).

Some of our boundaries may have deteriorated as we've let our guard down against our weaknesses toward sin. We may have let our commitments to live a balanced life slip so that we find ourselves exhausted or overtaxed. We need to check and repair our boundaries as a way to preserve our spiritual gains. We can also construct a second wall of defense by developing a strong support network of other believers around us. In all this we must remember that no matter what enemies or entanglements we face, our God is with us. He is far greater than any of our enemies. This should bring us great encouragement.

Turn to Psalm 65.

military staff about blocking off the water from the springs outside the city, and they helped him. 4A large force of men assembled, and they blocked all the springs and the stream that flowed through the land. "Why should the kings[a] of Assyria come and find plenty of water?" they said. 5Then he worked hard repairing all the broken sections of the wall and building towers on it. He built another wall outside that one and reinforced the supporting terraces[b] of the City of David. He also made large numbers of weapons and shields.

6He appointed military officers over the people and assembled them before him in the square at the city gate and encouraged them with these words: 7"Be strong and courageous. Do not be afraid or discouraged because of the king of Assyria and the vast army with him, for there is a greater power with us than with him. 8With him is only the arm of flesh, but with us is the LORD our God to help us and to fight our battles." And the people gained confidence from what Hezekiah the king of Judah said.

9Later, when Sennacherib king of Assyria and all his forces were laying siege to Lachish, he sent his officers to Jerusalem with this message for Hezekiah king of Judah and for all the people of Judah who were there:

> 10"This is what Sennacherib king of Assyria says: On what are you basing your confidence, that you remain in Jerusalem under siege? 11When Hezekiah says, 'The LORD our God will save us from the hand of the king of Assyria,' he is misleading you, to let you die of hunger and thirst. 12Did not Hezekiah himself remove this god's high places and altars, saying to Judah and Jerusalem, 'You must worship before one altar and burn sacrifices on it'?
>
> 13"Do you not know what I and my fathers have done to all the peoples of the other lands? Were the gods of those nations ever able to deliver their land from my hand? 14Who of all the gods of these nations that my fathers destroyed has been able to save his people from me? How then can your god deliver you from my hand? 15Now do not let Hezekiah deceive you and mislead you like this. Do not believe him, for no god of any nation or kingdom has been able to deliver his people from my hand or the hand of my fathers. How much less will your god deliver you from my hand!"

16Sennacherib's officers spoke further against the LORD God and against his servant Hezekiah. 17The king also wrote letters insulting the LORD, the God of Israel, and saying this against him: "Just as the gods of the peoples of the other lands did not rescue their people from my hand, so the god of Hezekiah will not rescue his people from my hand." 18Then they called out in Hebrew to the people of Jerusalem who were on the wall, to terrify them and make them afraid in order to capture the city. 19They spoke about the God of Jerusalem as they did about the gods of the other peoples of the world—the work of men's hands.

20King Hezekiah and the prophet Isaiah son of Amoz cried out in prayer to heaven about this. 21And the LORD sent an angel, who annihilated all the fighting men and the leaders and officers in the camp of the Assyrian king. So he withdrew to his own land in disgrace. And when he went into the temple of his god, some of his sons cut him down with the sword.

22So the LORD saved Hezekiah and the people of Jerusalem from the hand of Sennacherib king of Assyria and from the hand of all others. He took care of them[c] on every side. 23Many brought offerings to Jerusalem for the LORD and valuable gifts for Hezekiah king of Judah. From then on he was highly regarded by all the nations.

Hezekiah's Pride, Success and Death

24In those days Hezekiah became ill and was at the point of death. He prayed to the LORD, who answered him and gave him a miraculous sign. 25But Hezekiah's heart was proud and he did not respond to the kindness shown him; therefore the LORD's wrath was on him and on Judah and Jerusalem. 26Then Hezekiah repented of the pride of his heart, as did the people of Jerusalem; therefore the LORD's wrath did not come upon them during the days of Hezekiah.

27Hezekiah had very great riches and honor, and he made treasuries for his silver and gold and for his precious stones, spices, shields and all kinds of valuables. 28He also made buildings to store the harvest of grain, new wine and oil; and he made stalls for various kinds of cattle,

[a]4 Hebrew; Septuagint and Syriac *king* [b]5 Or *the Millo*
[c]22 Hebrew; Septuagint and Vulgate *He gave them rest*

---

invasion, but that didn't stop him from doing what he could to protect Jerusalem. Hezekiah built a great tunnel to bring water from a spring into the city, ensuring a steady supply during a siege. Hezekiah trusted God for victory, but he also prepared for the invasion.

32:7–8 King Hezekiah of Judah had made elaborate preparations for defense. But he didn't trust in his armies to bring him victory. Hezekiah looked only to God. We may have a tendency to depend on our own resources in a crisis. Yet our self-sufficiency and pride will not bring spiritual renewal or restoration; only God has the power we need for victory.

32:20–22 Prayer is essential to spiritual renewal. We cannot seek God and surrender to him without prayer. Every key to spiritual renewal involves prayer as our means of communication with God. And God does hear and answer the call of his people. He does not always send an immediate and miraculous rescue as he did for Hezekiah, but he always answers. God's intervention in this instance is clear. By human estimation, Sennacherib should have won this battle, but God gave Judah the victory. God is just as able to help us in our "impossible" situations.

and pens for the flocks. 29He built villages and acquired great numbers of flocks and herds, for God had given him very great riches.

30It was Hezekiah who blocked the upper outlet of the Gihon spring and channeled the water down to the west side of the City of David. He succeeded in everything he undertook. 31But when envoys were sent by the rulers of Babylon to ask him about the miraculous sign that had occurred in the land, God left him to test him and to know everything that was in his heart.

32The other events of Hezekiah's reign and his acts of devotion are written in the vision of the prophet Isaiah son of Amoz in the book of the kings of Judah and Israel. 33Hezekiah rested with his fathers and was buried on the hill where the tombs of David's descendants are. All Judah and the people of Jerusalem honored him when he died. And Manasseh his son succeeded him as king.

Manasseh King of Judah

33 Manasseh was twelve years old when he became king, and he reigned in Jerusalem fifty-five years. 2He did evil in the eyes of the LORD, following the detestable practices of the nations the LORD had driven out before the Israelites. 3He rebuilt the high places his father Hezekiah had demolished; he also erected altars to the Baals and made Asherah poles. He bowed down to all the starry hosts and worshiped them. 4He built altars in the temple of the LORD, of which the LORD had said, "My Name will remain in Jerusalem forever." 5In both courts of the temple of the LORD, he built altars to all the starry hosts. 6He sacrificed his sons in[a] the fire in the Valley of Ben Hinnom, practiced sorcery, divination and witchcraft, and consulted mediums and spiritists. He did much evil in the eyes of the LORD, provoking him to anger.

7He took the carved image he had made and put it in God's temple, of which God had said to David and to his son Solomon, "In this temple and in Jerusalem, which I have chosen out of all the tribes of Israel, I will put my Name forever. 8I will not again make the feet of the Israelites leave the land I assigned to your forefathers, if only they will be careful to do everything I commanded them concerning all the laws, decrees and ordinances given through Moses." 9But Manasseh led Judah and the people of Jerusalem astray, so that they did more evil than the nations the LORD had destroyed before the Israelites.

10The LORD spoke to Manasseh and his people, but they paid no attention. 11So the LORD brought against them the army commanders of the king of Assyria, who took Manasseh prisoner, put a hook in his nose, bound him with bronze shackles and took him to Babylon. 12In his distress he sought the favor of the LORD his God and humbled himself greatly before the God of his fathers. 13And when he prayed to him, the LORD was moved by his entreaty and listened to his plea; so he brought him back to Jerusalem and to his kingdom. Then Manasseh knew that the LORD is God.

14Afterward he rebuilt the outer wall of the City of David, west of the Gihon spring in the valley, as far as the entrance of the Fish Gate and encircling the hill of Ophel; he also made it much higher. He stationed military commanders in all the fortified cities in Judah.

15He got rid of the foreign gods and removed the image from the temple of the LORD, as well as all the altars he had built on the temple hill and in Jerusalem; and he threw them out of the city. 16Then he restored the altar of the LORD and sacrificed fellowship offerings[b] and thank offerings on it, and told Judah to serve the LORD, the God of Israel. 17The people, however, continued to sacrifice at the high places, but only to the LORD their God.

18The other events of Manasseh's reign, including his prayer to his God and the words the seers spoke to him in the name of the LORD, the God of Israel, are written in the annals of the kings of Israel.[c] 19His prayer and how God was moved by his entreaty, as well as all his sins and unfaithfulness, and the sites where he built high places and set up Asherah poles and idols before he humbled himself—all are written in the records of the seers.[d] 20Manasseh rested with his fathers and was buried in his palace. And Amon his son succeeded him as king.

Amon King of Judah

21Amon was twenty-two years old when he became king, and he reigned in Jerusalem two years. 22He did evil in the eyes of the LORD,

[a] 6 Or *He made his sons pass through* [b] 16 Traditionally *peace offerings* [c] 18 That is, Judah, as frequently in 2 Chronicles [d] 19 One Hebrew manuscript and Septuagint; most Hebrew manuscripts *of Hozai*

33:1–2 There is biting irony in these verses. Manasseh followed the patterns of the heathen nations—the very ones over whom God had demonstrated his superiority. Manasseh insisted on following a way that had already been proven inadequate. Some things will never bring about spiritual renewal and godly growth. Following them is only folly. We need to make sure that the way we proceed reflects God's truth as revealed in the Bible.

33:9 It is a terrible thing to do evil; it is terrible to lead others into evil too. King Manasseh of Judah was guilty on both counts. He was even worse than the heathen kings who lived nearby. We must be careful by our example to never lead others into evil.

33:12–13 God allowed Manasseh to fall into such dire straits that there was nothing else he could do but seek God. Even though Manasseh had been the worst of all Judah's kings, he was forgiven and restored when he recognized his desperate situation and cried out in repentance to God for help. God will do no less for each of us. Sin and failure ultimately lead us into difficult circumstances. When this happens, we need to let the hard times drive us into God's open and forgiving arms.

as his father Manasseh had done. Amon worshiped and offered sacrifices to all the idols Manasseh had made. 23But unlike his father Manasseh, he did not humble himself before the LORD; Amon increased his guilt.

24Amon's officials conspired against him and assassinated him in his palace. 25Then the people of the land killed all who had plotted against King Amon, and they made Josiah his son king in his place.

Josiah's Reforms

34 Josiah was eight years old when he became king, and he reigned in Jerusalem thirty-one years. 2He did what was right in the eyes of the LORD and walked in the ways of his father David, not turning aside to the right or to the left.

3In the eighth year of his reign, while he was still young, he began to seek the God of his father David. In his twelfth year he began to purge Judah and Jerusalem of high places, Asherah poles, carved idols and cast images. 4Under his direction the altars of the Baals were torn down; he cut to pieces the incense altars that were above them, and smashed the Asherah poles, the idols and the images. These he broke to pieces and scattered over the graves of those who had sacrificed to them. 5He burned the bones of the priests on their altars, and so he purged Judah and Jerusalem. 6In the towns of Manasseh, Ephraim and Simeon, as far as Naphtali, and in the ruins around them, 7he tore down the altars and the Asherah poles and crushed the idols to powder and cut to pieces all the incense altars throughout Israel. Then he went back to Jerusalem.

8In the eighteenth year of Josiah's reign, to purify the land and the temple, he sent Shaphan son of Azaliah and Maaseiah the ruler of the city, with Joah son of Joahaz, the recorder, to repair the temple of the LORD his God.

9They went to Hilkiah the high priest and gave him the money that had been brought into the temple of God, which the Levites who were the doorkeepers had collected from the people of Manasseh, Ephraim and the entire remnant of Israel and from all the people of Judah and Benjamin and the inhabitants of Jerusalem. 10Then they entrusted it to the men appointed to supervise the work on the LORD's temple. These men paid the workers who repaired and restored the temple. 11They also gave money to the carpenters and builders to purchase dressed stone, and timber for joists and beams for the buildings that the kings of Judah had allowed to fall into ruin.

12The men did the work faithfully. Over them to direct them were Jahath and Obadiah, Levites descended from Merari, and Zechariah and Meshullam, descended from Kohath. The Levites—all who were skilled in playing musical instruments— 13had charge of the laborers and supervised all the workers from job to job. Some of the Levites were secretaries, scribes and doorkeepers.

The Book of the Law Found

14While they were bringing out the money that had been taken into the temple of the LORD, Hilkiah the priest found the Book of the Law of the LORD that had been given through Moses. 15Hilkiah said to Shaphan the secretary, "I have found the Book of the Law in the temple of the LORD." He gave it to Shaphan.

16Then Shaphan took the book to the king and reported to him: "Your officials are doing everything that has been committed to them. 17They have paid out the money that was in the temple of the LORD and have entrusted it to the supervisors and workers." 18Then Shaphan the secretary informed the king, "Hilkiah the priest has given me a book." And Shaphan read from it in the presence of the king.

19When the king heard the words of the Law, he tore his robes. 20He gave these orders to Hilkiah, Ahikam son of Shaphan, Abdon son of Micah,[a] Shaphan the secretary and Asaiah the king's attendant: 21"Go and inquire of the LORD for me and for the remnant in Israel and Judah about what is written in this book that has been found. Great is the LORD's anger that is poured out on us because our fathers have not kept the word of the LORD; they have not acted in accordance with all that is written in this book."

22Hilkiah and those the king had sent with

[a]20 Also called *Acbor son of Micaiah*

34:8–11 When things are in ruin and disarray, it is necessary to rebuild, repair and clean up. During the godless years of King Manasseh and at the beginning of King Josiah's reign, worship of God had been discontinued at the temple in Jerusalem. The temple itself had fallen into disrepair. Josiah committed the resources of the nation to the restoration of the temple. We also need to set aside significant resources to devote to God and his kingdom. It will demand a great deal of commitment and sacrifice, but no matter what we give up, the gains will be well worth the cost.

34:14–19 Even the Book of the Law had been lost during the years of spiritual decline. Without it, the people didn't know how God wanted them to live. Over time, it became less and less apparent what they were doing wrong or what they needed to do to please God. We also need some definite standards of right and wrong. Without God's Word, such things become matters of individual opinion. Whole systems of faith have been based on personal opinions—what people want to hear rather than what God has to say. Our path to spiritual renewal must follow the way God has set out for us in the Bible.

34:21 As soon as Josiah heard what God expected of his people, he began to carefully consider the situation in Judah. He was willing to see how he and the people measured up against God's standards. The humility and honesty of Josiah are truly exemplary. He did not try to hide his sin or the sin of his nation. He was not defensive, but open to God and his direction. Josiah admitted his sin and failures and sought to change things immediately. As we carefully consider our lives, we need to display the same kind of honest humility.

him[a] went to speak to the prophetess Huldah, who was the wife of Shallum son of Tokhath,[b] the son of Hasrah,[c] keeper of the wardrobe. She lived in Jerusalem, in the Second District.

23She said to them, "This is what the LORD, the God of Israel, says: Tell the man who sent you to me, 24'This is what the LORD says: I am going to bring disaster on this place and its people—all the curses written in the book that has been read in the presence of the king of Judah. 25Because they have forsaken me and burned incense to other gods and provoked me to anger by all that their hands have made,[d] my anger will be poured out on this place and will not be quenched.' 26Tell the king of Judah, who sent you to inquire of the LORD, 'This is what the LORD, the God of Israel, says concerning the words you heard: 27Because your heart was responsive and you humbled yourself before God when you heard what he spoke against this place and its people, and because you humbled yourself before me and tore your robes and wept in my presence, I have heard you, declares the LORD. 28Now I will gather you to your fathers, and you will be buried in peace. Your eyes will not see all the disaster I am going to bring on this place and on those who live here.' "

So they took her answer back to the king.

29Then the king called together all the elders of Judah and Jerusalem. 30He went up to the temple of the LORD with the men of Judah, the people of Jerusalem, the priests and the Levites—all the people from the least to the greatest. He read in their hearing all the words of the Book of the Covenant, which had been found in the temple of the LORD. 31The king stood by his pillar and renewed the covenant in the presence of the LORD—to follow the LORD and keep his commands, regulations and decrees with all his heart and all his soul, and to obey the words of the covenant written in this book.

32Then he had everyone in Jerusalem and Benjamin pledge themselves to it; the people of Jerusalem did this in accordance with the covenant of God, the God of their fathers.

33Josiah removed all the detestable idols from all the territory belonging to the Israelites, and he had all who were present in Israel serve the LORD their God. As long as he lived, they did not fail to follow the LORD, the God of their fathers.

Josiah Celebrates the Passover

35 Josiah celebrated the Passover to the LORD in Jerusalem, and the Passover lamb was slaughtered on the fourteenth day of the first month. 2He appointed the priests to their duties and encouraged them in the service of the LORD's temple. 3He said to the Levites, who instructed all Israel and who had been consecrated to the LORD: "Put the sacred ark in the temple that Solomon son of David king of Israel built. It is not to be carried about on your shoulders. Now serve the LORD your God and his people Israel. 4Prepare yourselves by families in your divisions, according to the directions written by David king of Israel and by his son Solomon.

5"Stand in the holy place with a group of Levites for each subdivision of the families of your fellow countrymen, the lay people. 6Slaughter the Passover lambs, consecrate yourselves and prepare ⌞the lambs⌟ for your fellow countrymen, doing what the LORD commanded through Moses."

7Josiah provided for all the lay people who were there a total of thirty thousand sheep and goats for the Passover offerings, and also three thousand cattle—all from the king's own possessions.

8His officials also contributed voluntarily to the people and the priests and Levites. Hilkiah, Zechariah and Jehiel, the administrators of God's temple, gave the priests twenty-six hundred Passover offerings and three hundred cattle. 9Also Conaniah along with Shemaiah and Nethanel, his brothers, and Hashabiah, Jeiel and Jozabad, the leaders of the Levites, provided five thousand Passover offerings and five hundred head of cattle for the Levites.

10The service was arranged and the priests stood in their places with the Levites in their divisions as the king had ordered. 11The Passover lambs were slaughtered, and the priests sprinkled the blood handed to them, while the Levites skinned the animals. 12They set aside the burnt offerings to give them to the subdivisions of the families of the people to offer to the LORD, as is written in the Book of Moses. They did the same with the cattle. 13They roasted the Passover animals over the fire as prescribed, and boiled the holy offerings in pots, caldrons and pans and served them quickly to all the people. 14After this, they made preparations for themselves and for the priests, because the priests, the descendants of Aaron, were sacrificing the burnt offerings and the fat portions until

[a]22 One Hebrew manuscript, Vulgate and Syriac; most Hebrew manuscripts do not have *had sent with him.*
[b]22 Also called *Tikvah* [c]22 Also called *Harhas*
[d]25 Or *by everything they have done*

34:31–33 Hearing God's Word is important, but we must act on what we hear. If we refuse to act, the hearing is all in vain. After hearing the Scriptures, King Josiah pledged himself to obey God's revealed will. Not only did he do so as an individual, but he also called his people to follow. We, too, must hear the Word of God and then act on it.

35:1–2 Notice that Josiah took the time to encourage the priests in their temple activities. Encouragement is extremely important for anyone pursuing spiritual growth and a vibrant relationship with God. At this time, the priests were unaccustomed to leading the people in worship. They needed encouragement to face new and difficult tasks. As we seek to live as God says we should, we will need the encouragement and support of others. Our relationships with those who encourage our spiritual pursuits will help us preserve our spiritual gains.

nightfall. So the Levites made preparations for themselves and for the Aaronic priests.

15The musicians, the descendants of Asaph, were in the places prescribed by David, Asaph, Heman and Jeduthun the king's seer. The gatekeepers at each gate did not need to leave their posts, because their fellow Levites made the preparations for them.

16So at that time the entire service of the LORD was carried out for the celebration of the Passover and the offering of burnt offerings on the altar of the LORD, as King Josiah had ordered. 17The Israelites who were present celebrated the Passover at that time and observed the Feast of Unleavened Bread for seven days. 18The Passover had not been observed like this in Israel since the days of the prophet Samuel; and none of the kings of Israel had ever celebrated such a Passover as did Josiah, with the priests, the Levites and all Judah and Israel who were there with the people of Jerusalem. 19This Passover was celebrated in the eighteenth year of Josiah's reign.

The Death of Josiah

20After all this, when Josiah had set the temple in order, Neco king of Egypt went up to fight at Carchemish on the Euphrates, and Josiah marched out to meet him in battle. 21But Neco sent messengers to him, saying, "What quarrel is there between you and me, O king of Judah? It is not you I am attacking at this time, but the house with which I am at war. God has told me to hurry; so stop opposing God, who is with me, or he will destroy you."

22Josiah, however, would not turn away from him, but disguised himself to engage him in battle. He would not listen to what Neco had said at God's command but went to fight him on the plain of Megiddo.

23Archers shot King Josiah, and he told his officers, "Take me away; I am badly wounded." 24So they took him out of his chariot, put him in the other chariot he had and brought him to Jerusalem, where he died. He was buried in the tombs of his fathers, and all Judah and Jerusalem mourned for him.

25Jeremiah composed laments for Josiah, and to this day all the men and women singers commemorate Josiah in the laments. These became a tradition in Israel and are written in the Laments.

26The other events of Josiah's reign and his acts of devotion, according to what is written in the Law of the LORD— 27all the events, from beginning to end, are written in the book of the kings of Israel and Judah.

36 1And the people of the land took Jehoahaz son of Josiah and made him king in Jerusalem in place of his father.

Jehoahaz King of Judah

2Jehoahaz[a] was twenty-three years old when he became king, and he reigned in Jerusalem three months. 3The king of Egypt dethroned him in Jerusalem and imposed on Judah a levy of a hundred talents[b] of silver and a talent[c] of gold. 4The king of Egypt made Eliakim, a brother of Jehoahaz, king over Judah and Jerusalem and changed Eliakim's name to Jehoiakim. But Neco took Eliakim's brother Jehoahaz and carried him off to Egypt.

Jehoiakim King of Judah

5Jehoiakim was twenty-five years old when he became king, and he reigned in Jerusalem eleven years. He did evil in the eyes of the LORD his God. 6Nebuchadnezzar king of Babylon attacked him and bound him with bronze shackles to take him to Babylon. 7Nebuchadnezzar also took to Babylon articles from the temple of the LORD and put them in his temple[d] there.

8The other events of Jehoiakim's reign, the detestable things he did and all that was found against him, are written in the book of the kings of Israel and Judah. And Jehoiachin his son succeeded him as king.

Jehoiachin King of Judah

9Jehoiachin was eighteen[e] years old when he became king, and he reigned in Jerusalem three months and ten days. He did evil in the eyes of the LORD. 10In the spring, King Nebuchadnezzar sent for him and brought him to Babylon, together with articles of value from the temple of the LORD, and he made Jehoiachin's uncle,[f] Zedekiah, king over Judah and Jerusalem.

Zedekiah King of Judah

11Zedekiah was twenty-one years old when he became king, and he reigned in Jerusalem eleven years. 12He did evil in the eyes of the LORD his God and did not humble himself before Jeremiah the prophet, who spoke the word of the LORD. 13He also rebelled against King Nebuchadnezzar, who had made him take an oath in God's name. He became stiff-necked and hardened his heart and would not turn to the LORD, the God of Israel. 14Furthermore, all

[a]2 Hebrew *Joahaz,* a variant of *Jehoahaz;* also in verse 4
[b]3 That is, about 3 3/4 tons (about 3.4 metric tons)
[c]3 That is, about 75 pounds (about 34 kilograms)
[d]7 Or *palace* [e]9 One Hebrew manuscript, some Septuagint manuscripts and Syriac (see also 2 Kings 24:8); most Hebrew manuscripts *eight* [f]10 Hebrew *brother,* that is, relative (see 2 Kings 24:17)

36:4–8 In this final assessment, King Jehoiakim's reign is condemned as an evil one. By the world's standards, he might have been considered successful. He reigned eleven years through a very difficult time, and he weathered the change of world powers at the battle of Carchemish. But worldly success is never the final measure. If we refuse to live according to God's plan, we will not be truly successful in God's eyes.

36:14–20 We can never ignore God's will without suffering the consequences. Under Zedekiah the people ignored

the leaders of the priests and the people became
more and more unfaithful, following all the detestable practices of the nations and defiling the
temple of the LORD, which he had consecrated
in Jerusalem.

The Fall of Jerusalem

15 The LORD, the God of their fathers, sent
word to them through his messengers again and
again, because he had pity on his people and on
his dwelling place. 16 But they mocked God's
messengers, despised his words and scoffed at
his prophets until the wrath of the LORD was
aroused against his people and there was no
remedy. 17 He brought up against them the king
of the Babylonians,[a] who killed their young
men with the sword in the sanctuary, and
spared neither young man nor young woman,
old man or aged. God handed all of them over
to Nebuchadnezzar. 18 He carried to Babylon all
the articles from the temple of God, both large
and small, and the treasures of the LORD's temple and the treasures of the king and his officials. 19 They set fire to God's temple and broke
down the wall of Jerusalem; they burned all the
palaces and destroyed everything of value there.
20 He carried into exile to Babylon the remnant, who escaped from the sword, and they
became servants to him and his sons until the
kingdom of Persia came to power. 21 The land
enjoyed its sabbath rests; all the time of its desolation it rested, until the seventy years were
completed in fulfillment of the word of the
LORD spoken by Jeremiah.
22 In the first year of Cyrus king of Persia, in
order to fulfill the word of the LORD spoken by
Jeremiah, the LORD moved the heart of Cyrus
king of Persia to make a proclamation throughout his realm and to put it in writing:

23 "This is what Cyrus king of Persia says:
"'The LORD, the God of heaven, has
given me all the kingdoms of the earth
and he has appointed me to build a temple for him at Jerusalem in Judah. Anyone
of his people among you—may the LORD
his God be with him, and let him go up.'"

[a]17 Or *Chaldeans*

God's laws and even persecuted the prophets who were sent to remind them of their failure. Is it any wonder that the temple was destroyed and the people of Judah were exiled to Babylon? As we discover God's will in the Bible, we need to act on it, redirecting the course of our lives to align with his plan.

36:22–23 These books of woe and doom end with a note of amazing hope. They were written for people who had returned to rebuild their temple and nation. This final passage would show them that even though their ancestors had failed, God is faithful to his promises. He would help them to recover from centuries of failure. No matter what our past, God holds out the same opportunity for us. With his help, we too can find spiritual renewal and restoration.

EZRA

The Big Picture

A. REBUILDING THE PLACE (1:1–6:22)

1. The First Exiles Return (1:1–2:70)
2. The Attempt to Rebuild the Temple (3:1-13)
3. The Discouragement of the People (4:1-24)
4. The Joy of the People at the Rebuilt Temple (5:1–6:22)

B. REBUILDING THE PEOPLE (7:1–10:44)

1. The Second Group of Exiles Returns With Ezra (7:1–8:36)
2. The Sins of the People (9:1-15)
3. The People Confess Their Sins (10:1-44)

The book of Ezra records two great journeys toward restoration after the Babylonian exile. The first journey (1:1—6:22) took place immediately after the decree of Cyrus (538 B.C.) and was led by Zerubbabel, one of King David's descendants. Under his direction the temple was rebuilt over a twenty-three-year period (538–515 B.C.). The priest Joshua and the prophets Haggai and Zechariah encouraged the people in this task. Ezra led the second journey (7:1—10:44) almost sixty years after the temple's completion (458 B.C.). Under Ezra's leadership great spiritual restoration was accomplished in Israel.

Ezra was one of the great leaders and writers of the Old Testament. Tradition assigns most of Chronicles, Ezra, Nehemiah and Psalm 119 to his hand. The book of Ezra picks up Israel's history where 2 Chronicles leaves off, approximately forty-eight years after Babylon destroyed Jerusalem. After Nebuchadnezzar's glorious rule, Babylon slowly declined until Persia conquered it. It was under Cyrus of Persia that Zerubbabel was allowed to lead the first group of exiles home to rebuild the temple.

Ezra shows us what it means to surrender our lives to God. His desire to know God better motivated him to study God's Word and obey it. In the same way, we need to learn what God's will is through careful study of the Bible. We also need to take action to accomplish it. Ezra didn't stop once he had attained spiritual growth in his own life. He returned to Jerusalem and taught the returning exiles how to renew their lives as well. Ezra provides us with a model of how we should share our message of hope with others.

Spiritual Renewal Themes

GOD'S PROVISION FOR RESTORATION

God shows his mercy to every one of us. In his love, God desires our restoration—not only from our sins but also from the consequences of those sins. When we are in captivity to our sins, we are never far from God's love and mercy. God is waiting to help us. All we need to do is see the truth of our situation, confess our sins and come to him for forgiveness and restoration. When we admit that we do not have the power we need, we are then closest to his powerful arm. In the book of Ezra, we see

various examples of how God empowered his people to do what they could never have done without him. All they had to do was give themselves over to his plan.

RESISTANCE TO SPIRITUAL RENEWAL

There will always be those who do not want to see us redeemed from our "captivity." People who were associated with our old lifestyle may fight against our spiritual renewal, just as those within Jerusalem fought against the rebuilding of the temple. But the most dangerous form of opposition to renewal is often found within our own selves. Even though we may truly want to do the right thing, there is always a part of us that rebels against the good we want to do (see Romans 7:21–25). We need to be aware of this part of our inner self. We don't have to obey this sinful inclination. By surrendering our wills to God, we can become people who desire to obey God wholeheartedly.

STARTING OVER

In the face of opposition, the people of God were not only hindered in their work, they ultimately had to stop the rebuilding process. The same thing often happens to us as we seek spiritual renewal. Discouragement sets in. We begin to feel as if everything we've done has been to no avail. In the book of Ezra, the work stopped for ten years. To have our spiritual-growth process blocked for ten years could be devastating, leaving us with a feeling of hopelessness. But be encouraged; God is patient and long-suffering. He comes to the aid of those who seek him. As we look at the history of God's people, we see that the Lord is indeed the God of restoration!

THE IMPORTANCE OF ACTION

It is one thing to talk about renewal; it is quite another thing actually to do it! The main characters in this book were all people of action. They didn't just sit around and discuss rebuilding the temple; they organized themselves and started working. The task must have appeared overwhelming at first. But as they asked God for help and took things day by day, one task at a time, even daunting tasks became possible. The first step is always the most difficult, but the next step is almost as hard. Sometimes each step is difficult, but we must focus on today's task and take action, trusting that God will empower us along the way.

Essential Facts

PURPOSE:
To record how the people rebuilt their lives and nation after their exile in Babylon.

AUTHOR:
Not stated, but probably Ezra.

AUDIENCE:
The people of Israel after their return from exile in Babylon.

DATE WRITTEN:
Around the year 446 B.C.

SETTING:
Ezra picks up where 2 Chronicles left off, covering the period from the decree of Cyrus (538 B.C.) through Ezra's return and reformation (458–446 B.C.).

KEY VERSE:
"Rise up; this matter is in your hands. We will support you, so take courage and do it" (10:4).

KEY PEOPLE:
Zerubbabel, Haggai, Zechariah, Ezra.

Cyrus Helps the Exiles to Return

1 In the first year of Cyrus king of Persia, in
order to fulfill the word of the LORD spoken by Jeremiah, the LORD moved the heart of
Cyrus king of Persia to make a proclamation
throughout his realm and to put it in writing:

2"This is what Cyrus king of Persia says:
" 'The LORD, the God of heaven, has
given me all the kingdoms of the earth
and he has appointed me to build a temple for him at Jerusalem in Judah. 3Any-
one of his people among you—may his
God be with him, and let him go up to
Jerusalem in Judah and build the temple
of the LORD, the God of Israel, the God
who is in Jerusalem. 4And the people of
any place where survivors may now be living are to provide him with silver and
gold, with goods and livestock, and with
freewill offerings for the temple of God in
Jerusalem.' "

5Then the family heads of Judah and Benjamin, and the priests and Levites—everyone
whose heart God had moved—prepared to go
up and build the house of the LORD in Jerusalem. 6All their neighbors assisted them with articles of silver and gold, with goods and livestock, and with valuable gifts, in addition to all
the freewill offerings. 7Moreover, King Cyrus
brought out the articles belonging to the temple
of the LORD, which Nebuchadnezzar had carried away from Jerusalem and had placed in the
temple of his god.[a] 8Cyrus king of Persia had
them brought by Mithredath the treasurer, who
counted them out to Sheshbazzar the prince of
Judah.
9This was the inventory:

gold dishes	30
silver dishes	1,000
silver pans[b]	29
10gold bowls	30
matching silver bowls	410
other articles	1,000

11In all, there were 5,400 articles of gold and
of silver. Sheshbazzar brought all these along
when the exiles came up from Babylon to Jerusalem.

The List of the Exiles Who Returned

2 Now these are the people of the province
who came up from the captivity of the exiles, whom Nebuchadnezzar king of Babylon
had taken captive to Babylon (they returned to
Jerusalem and Judah, each to his own town, 2in
company with Zerubbabel, Jeshua, Nehemiah,
Seraiah, Reelaiah, Mordecai, Bilshan, Mispar,
Bigvai, Rehum and Baanah):

The list of the men of the people of Israel:

3the descendants of Parosh	2,172
4of Shephatiah	372
5of Arah	775
6of Pahath-Moab (through the line of Jeshua and Joab)	2,812
7of Elam	1,254
8of Zattu	945
9of Zaccai	760
10of Bani	642
11of Bebai	623
12of Azgad	1,222
13of Adonikam	666
14of Bigvai	2,056
15of Adin	454
16of Ater (through Hezekiah)	98
17of Bezai	323
18of Jorah	112
19of Hashum	223
20of Gibbar	95
21the men of Bethlehem	123
22of Netophah	56
23of Anathoth	128
24of Azmaveth	42
25of Kiriath Jearim,[c] Kephirah and Beeroth	743
26of Ramah and Geba	621
27of Micmash	122
28of Bethel and Ai	223
29of Nebo	52
30of Magbish	156
31of the other Elam	1,254
32of Harim	320
33of Lod, Hadid and Ono	725
34of Jericho	345
35of Senaah	3,630

36The priests:

[a]7 Or *gods* [b]9 The meaning of the Hebrew for this word is uncertain. [c]25 See Septuagint (see also Neh. 7:29); Hebrew *Kiriath Arim.*

1:1 All of us need something that we can count on. The Jews in exile counted on Jeremiah's prophecy that their captivity would last only seventy years. Today, God has promises for us too. If we know Jesus as our Savior, the Holy Spirit will comfort us and help us. We will become a new person—leaving our old ways behind (see 2 Corinthians 5:17). And though our problems may seem overwhelming today, God has given us promises of deliverance.

1:3 We need to make the most of every opportunity God brings our way. The Jews had been living in Babylonian exile for many years. King Cyrus gave them an open invitation to return to Jerusalem to rebuild their nation and their lives. Through the work of Jesus Christ, God has given us an open invitation to rebuild our lives as well.

1:4–6 It is important to have people encourage us in our spiritual growth. Even though many of the exiles remained in Persia, they encouraged and supported those who had chosen to return to Judah. Had those making the return trip not been given assistance, they might not have had the motivation or strength to finish their mission. In the same way, we should seek to encourage others in their journey toward spiritual maturity.

the descendants of Jedaiah
(through the family of Jeshua) 973
37of Immer 1,052
38of Pashhur 1,247
39of Harim 1,017

40The Levites:

the descendants of Jeshua and
Kadmiel (through the line of
Hodaviah) 74

41The singers:

the descendants of Asaph 128

42The gatekeepers of the temple:

the descendants of
Shallum, Ater, Talmon,
Akkub, Hatita and Shobai 139

43The temple servants:

the descendants of
Ziha, Hasupha, Tabbaoth,
44Keros, Siaha, Padon,
45Lebanah, Hagabah, Akkub,
46Hagab, Shalmai, Hanan,
47Giddel, Gahar, Reaiah,
48Rezin, Nekoda, Gazzam,
49Uzza, Paseah, Besai,
50Asnah, Meunim, Nephussim,
51Bakbuk, Hakupha, Harhur,
52Bazluth, Mehida, Harsha,
53Barkos, Sisera, Temah,
54Neziah and Hatipha

55The descendants of the servants of Solomon:

the descendants of
Sotai, Hassophereth, Peruda,
56Jaala, Darkon, Giddel,
57Shephatiah, Hattil,
Pokereth-Hazzebaim and Ami

58The temple servants and the
descendants of the servants of
Solomon 392

59The following came up from the
towns of Tel Melah, Tel Harsha, Kerub,
Addon and Immer, but they could not
show that their families were descended
from Israel:

60The descendants of
Delaiah, Tobiah and Nekoda 652

61And from among the priests:

The descendants of
Hobaiah, Hakkoz and Barzillai (a
man who had married a daughter
of Barzillai the Gileadite and was
called by that name).

62These searched for their family
records, but they could not find them and
so were excluded from the priesthood as
unclean. 63The governor ordered them not
to eat any of the most sacred food until
there was a priest ministering with the
Urim and Thummim.

64The whole company numbered
42,360, 65besides their 7,337 menservants
and maidservants; and they also had 200
men and women singers. 66They had 736
horses, 245 mules, 67435 camels and
6,720 donkeys.

68When they arrived at the house of the LORD
in Jerusalem, some of the heads of the families
gave freewill offerings toward the rebuilding of
the house of God on its site. 69According to
their ability they gave to the treasury for this
work 61,000 drachmas[a] of gold, 5,000 minas[b] of silver and 100 priestly garments.

70The priests, the Levites, the singers, the
gatekeepers and the temple servants settled in
their own towns, along with some of the other
people, and the rest of the Israelites settled in
their towns.

Rebuilding the Altar

3 When the seventh month came and the
Israelites had settled in their towns, the
people assembled as one man in Jerusalem.
2Then Jeshua son of Jozadak and his fellow
priests and Zerubbabel son of Shealtiel and his
associates began to build the altar of the God of
Israel to sacrifice burnt offerings on it, in accordance with what is written in the Law of Moses
the man of God. 3Despite their fear of the peoples around them, they built the altar on its
foundation and sacrificed burnt offerings on it
to the LORD, both the morning and evening
sacrifices. 4Then in accordance with what is
written, they celebrated the Feast of Tabernacles
with the required number of burnt offerings
prescribed for each day. 5After that, they presented the regular burnt offerings, the New
Moon sacrifices and the sacrifices for all the
appointed sacred feasts of the LORD, as well as
those brought as freewill offerings to the LORD.
6On the first day of the seventh month they
began to offer burnt offerings to the LORD,
though the foundation of the LORD's temple
had not yet been laid.

[a]69 That is, about 1,100 pounds (about 500 kilograms)
[b]69 That is, about 3 tons (about 2.9 metric tons)

3:1–2 The temple had been destroyed many years before, so there was no altar for burning sacrifices. The people's method of reconciliation with God had been discontinued; their spiritual life had been cut off. Before the people could proceed with the rebuilding process, they needed to straighten out their relationship with God. The Israelites reestablished the sacrifices as a means of reconciliation. We, too, need to reconcile ourselves to God through the sacrifice of Jesus Christ in order to progress spiritually.

Rebuilding the Temple

7Then they gave money to the masons and carpenters, and gave food and drink and oil to the people of Sidon and Tyre, so that they would bring cedar logs by sea from Lebanon to Joppa, as authorized by Cyrus king of Persia.

8In the second month of the second year after their arrival at the house of God in Jerusalem, Zerubbabel son of Shealtiel, Jeshua son of Jozadak and the rest of their brothers (the priests and the Levites and all who had returned from the captivity to Jerusalem) began the work, appointing Levites twenty years of age and older to supervise the building of the house of the LORD. 9Jeshua and his sons and brothers and Kadmiel and his sons (descendants of Hodaviah[a]) and the sons of Henadad and their sons and brothers—all Levites—joined together in supervising those working on the house of God.

10When the builders laid the foundation of the temple of the LORD, the priests in their vestments and with trumpets, and the Levites (the sons of Asaph) with cymbals, took their places to praise the LORD, as prescribed by David king of Israel. 11With praise and thanksgiving they sang to the LORD:

"He is good;
his love to Israel endures forever."

And all the people gave a great shout of praise to the LORD, because the foundation of the house of the LORD was laid. 12But many of the older priests and Levites and family heads, who had seen the former temple, wept aloud when they saw the foundation of this temple being laid, while many others shouted for joy. 13No one could distinguish the sound of the shouts of joy from the sound of weeping, because the people made so much noise. And the sound was heard far away.

Opposition to the Rebuilding

4 When the enemies of Judah and Benjamin heard that the exiles were building a temple for the LORD, the God of Israel, 2they came to Zerubbabel and to the heads of the families and said, "Let us help you build because, like you, we seek your God and have been sacrificing to him since the time of Esarhaddon king of Assyria, who brought us here."

3But Zerubbabel, Jeshua and the rest of the heads of the families of Israel answered, "You have no part with us in building a temple to our God. We alone will build it for the LORD, the God of Israel, as King Cyrus, the king of Persia, commanded us."

4Then the peoples around them set out to discourage the people of Judah and make them afraid to go on building.[b] 5They hired counselors to work against them and frustrate their plans during the entire reign of Cyrus king of Persia and down to the reign of Darius king of Persia.

Later Opposition Under Xerxes and Artaxerxes

6At the beginning of the reign of Xerxes,[c] they lodged an accusation against the people of Judah and Jerusalem.

7And in the days of Artaxerxes king of Persia, Bishlam, Mithredath, Tabeel and the rest of his associates wrote a letter to Artaxerxes. The letter was written in Aramaic script and in the Aramaic language.[d,e]

8Rehum the commanding officer and Shimshai the secretary wrote a letter against Jerusalem to Artaxerxes the king as follows:

9Rehum the commanding officer and Shimshai the secretary, together with the rest of their associates—the judges and officials over the men from Tripolis, Persia,[f] Erech and Babylon, the Elamites of Susa, 10and the other people whom the great and honorable Ashurbanipal[g] deported and settled in the city of Samaria and elsewhere in Trans-Euphrates.

11(This is a copy of the letter they sent him.)

To King Artaxerxes,

[a]9 Hebrew *Yehudah,* probably a variant of *Hodaviah* [b]4 Or *and troubled them as they built* [c]6 Hebrew *Ahasuerus,* a variant of Xerxes' Persian name [d]7 Or *written in Aramaic and translated* [e]7 The text of Ezra 4:8—6:18 is in Aramaic. [f]9 Or *officials, magistrates and governors over the men from* [g]10 Aramaic *Osnappar,* a variant of *Ashurbanipal*

3:10–11 Having already built an altar for the sacrifices, the people began the work of rebuilding the temple itself. Notice that they praised God and celebrated after having laid only the temple's foundation. Big jobs always seem easier and less intimidating when we break them up into smaller steps. When we face overwhelming or long-term projects, we should take time to celebrate the smaller victories. Realizing that we are making progress will encourage us to keep going.

3:12 Some of the old people compared this rebuilt temple with their memories of the former temple. This temple obviously would never match the glory of Solomon's temple built during Israel's golden age. The people's expectations were too high. Though Israel would never regain its previous status in the world, God promised that one day the new Jerusalem would be the center of God's eternal kingdom (see Revelation 21). Like the Israelites, we should look forward to what God is doing in our lives and not look back and become depressed (see Philippians 3:13–14). God has planned a new life for us that has yet to unfold. One day we will be sinless like Christ for all eternity.

4:1–3 When God's work kicks off in a great way, enemies invariably rise up against it. There will be adversaries against us as we seek to obey God's plan for our lives, but we must trust that the Lord will help us persevere in obedience to his will.

From your servants, the men of Trans-Euphrates:

12The king should know that the Jews who came up to us from you have gone to Jerusalem and are rebuilding that rebellious and wicked city. They are restoring the walls and repairing the foundations. 13Furthermore, the king should know that if this city is built and its walls are restored, no more taxes, tribute or duty will be paid, and the royal revenues will suffer. 14Now since we are under obligation to the palace and it is not proper for us to see the king dishonored, we are sending this message to inform the king, 15so that a search may be made in the archives of your predecessors. In these records you will find that this city is a rebellious city, troublesome to kings and provinces, a place of rebellion from ancient times. That is why this city was destroyed. 16We inform the king that if this city is built and its walls are restored, you will be left with nothing in Trans-Euphrates.

17The king sent this reply:

To Rehum the commanding officer, Shimshai the secretary and the rest of their associates living in Samaria and elsewhere in Trans-Euphrates:

Greetings.

18The letter you sent us has been read and translated in my presence. 19I issued an order and a search was made, and it was found that this city has a long history of revolt against kings and has been a place of rebellion and sedition. 20Jerusalem has had powerful kings ruling over the whole of Trans-Euphrates, and taxes, tribute and duty were paid to them. 21Now issue an order to these men to stop work, so that this city will not be rebuilt until I so order. 22Be careful not to neglect this matter. Why let this threat grow, to the detriment of the royal interests?

23As soon as the copy of the letter of King Artaxerxes was read to Rehum and Shimshai the secretary and their associates, they went immediately to the Jews in Jerusalem and compelled them by force to stop.

24Thus the work on the house of God in Jerusalem came to a standstill until the second year of the reign of Darius king of Persia.

Tattenai's Letter to Darius

5 Now Haggai the prophet and Zechariah the prophet, a descendant of Iddo, prophesied to the Jews in Judah and Jerusalem in the name of the God of Israel, who was over them. 2Then Zerubbabel son of Shealtiel and Jeshua son of Jozadak set to work to rebuild the house of God in Jerusalem. And the prophets of God were with them, helping them.

3At that time Tattenai, governor of Trans-Euphrates, and Shethar-Bozenai and their associates went to them and asked, "Who authorized you to rebuild this temple and restore this structure?" 4They also asked, "What are the names of the men constructing this building?"[a] 5But the eye of their God was watching over the elders of the Jews, and they were not stopped until a report could go to Darius and his written reply be received.

6This is a copy of the letter that Tattenai, governor of Trans-Euphrates, and Shethar-Bozenai and their associates, the officials of Trans-Euphrates, sent to King Darius. 7The report they sent him read as follows:

To King Darius:

Cordial greetings.

8The king should know that we went to the district of Judah, to the temple of the great God. The people are building it with large stones and placing the timbers in the walls. The work is being carried on with diligence and is making rapid progress under their direction.

9We questioned the elders and asked them, "Who authorized you to rebuild this temple and restore this structure?" 10We also asked them their names, so that we could write down the names of their leaders for your information.

11This is the answer they gave us:

"We are the servants of the God of heaven and earth, and we are rebuilding the temple that was built many years ago, one that a great king of Israel built and finished. 12But because our fathers angered the God of heaven, he handed them

[a] 4 See Septuagint; Aramaic 4*We told them the names of the men constructing this building.*

4:17–24 Often we find obstacles placed in the way of rebuilding. In this case, a work-restraining order from Artaxerxes ground the rebuilding to a halt. We must realize that some people will not be supportive of our new way of life. We must never allow such people to stand in the way of our spiritual transformation.

4:24 Whether it was for a legitimate reason or because the workers were taking an easy way out, the rebuilding work on God's temple ceased. How often in our own lives have outward difficulties stopped our positive progress? We need to guard against such interruptions. It is often hard to get back on track once we have stopped or slowed down.

5:3–5 The rebuilding was going smoothly; the people worked with enthusiasm and joy. But again, enemies tried to halt the rebuilding. This time, though, the people did not stop rebuilding. God was supervising their work. If God cared then about the rebuilding of Jerusalem's temple, surely he cares about the renewal of our lives—his temple—today.

over to Nebuchadnezzar the Chaldean,
king of Babylon, who destroyed this temple and deported the people to Babylon.
13"However, in the first year of Cyrus
king of Babylon, King Cyrus issued a decree to rebuild this house of God. 14He
even removed from the temple[a] of Babylon the gold and silver articles of the
house of God, which Nebuchadnezzar
had taken from the temple in Jerusalem
and brought to the temple[a] in Babylon.
"Then King Cyrus gave them to a man
named Sheshbazzar, whom he had appointed governor, 15and he told him,
'Take these articles and go and deposit
them in the temple in Jerusalem. And rebuild the house of God on its site.' 16So
this Sheshbazzar came and laid the foundations of the house of God in Jerusalem.
From that day to the present it has been
under construction but is not yet finished."

17Now if it pleases the king, let a search
be made in the royal archives of Babylon
to see if King Cyrus did in fact issue a
decree to rebuild this house of God in
Jerusalem. Then let the king send us his
decision in this matter.

The Decree of Darius

6 King Darius then issued an order, and they
searched in the archives stored in the treasury at Babylon. 2A scroll was found in the citadel of Ecbatana in the province of Media, and
this was written on it:

Memorandum:

3In the first year of King Cyrus, the king
issued a decree concerning the temple of
God in Jerusalem:

Let the temple be rebuilt as a place to
present sacrifices, and let its foundations
be laid. It is to be ninety feet[b] high and
ninety feet wide, 4with three courses of
large stones and one of timbers. The costs
are to be paid by the royal treasury. 5Also,
the gold and silver articles of the house of
God, which Nebuchadnezzar took from
the temple in Jerusalem and brought to
Babylon, are to be returned to their places
in the temple in Jerusalem; they are to be
deposited in the house of God.

6Now then, Tattenai, governor of
Trans-Euphrates, and Shethar-Bozenai and
you, their fellow officials of that province, stay away from there. 7Do not interfere with the work on this temple of God.
Let the governor of the Jews and the Jewish elders rebuild this house of God on its
site.

8Moreover, I hereby decree what you
are to do for these elders of the Jews in the
construction of this house of God:

The expenses of these men are to be
fully paid out of the royal treasury, from
the revenues of Trans-Euphrates, so that
the work will not stop. 9Whatever is needed—young bulls, rams, male lambs for
burnt offerings to the God of heaven, and
wheat, salt, wine and oil, as requested by
the priests in Jerusalem—must be given
them daily without fail, 10so that they may
offer sacrifices pleasing to the God of
heaven and pray for the well-being of the
king and his sons.

11Furthermore, I decree that if anyone
changes this edict, a beam is to be pulled
from his house and he is to be lifted up
and impaled on it. And for this crime his
house is to be made a pile of rubble.
12May God, who has caused his Name to
dwell there, overthrow any king or people
who lifts a hand to change this decree or
to destroy this temple in Jerusalem.

I Darius have decreed it. Let it be carried
out with diligence.

Completion and Dedication of the Temple

13Then, because of the decree King Darius
had sent, Tattenai, governor of Trans-Euphrates, and Shethar-Bozenai and their associates
carried it out with diligence. 14So the elders
of the Jews continued to build and prosper
under the preaching of Haggai the prophet and
Zechariah, a descendant of Iddo. They finished
building the temple according to the command
of the God of Israel and the decrees of Cyrus,
Darius and Artaxerxes, kings of Persia. 15The
temple was completed on the third day of the
month Adar, in the sixth year of the reign of
King Darius.

16Then the people of Israel—the priests, the
Levites and the rest of the exiles—celebrated the
dedication of the house of God with joy. 17For
the dedication of this house of God they offered
a hundred bulls, two hundred rams, four hundred male lambs and, as a sin offering for all
Israel, twelve male goats, one for each of the

[a] 14 Or *palace* [b] 3 Aramaic *sixty cubits* (about 27 meters)

6:14–15 It took more than twenty years, but the temple was finally finished. The long process had sometimes been tedious, sometimes disillusioning and sometimes actually heartbreaking. But now it was finished, and it was worth every minute of it! Spiritual transformation takes more time than we usually plan too. The spiritual renewal of our lives is not easy, but the end result will make the difficult process worth it.

6:16–19 After this long, drawn-out process was finally over, the people responded to their success by acknowledging God's assistance throughout the entire project. They also formally recognized the completion of the temple in a dedication ceremony that was celebrated with great joy. We need to celebrate our own spiritual progress. What is worth celebrating more than a life brought back into a right relationship with God and other people?

tribes of Israel. 18 And they installed the priests in their divisions and the Levites in their groups for the service of God at Jerusalem, according to what is written in the Book of Moses.

The Passover

19 On the fourteenth day of the first month, the exiles celebrated the Passover. 20 The priests and Levites had purified themselves and were all ceremonially clean. The Levites slaughtered the Passover lamb for all the exiles, for their brothers the priests and for themselves. 21 So the Israelites who had returned from the exile ate it, together with all who had separated themselves from the unclean practices of their Gentile neighbors in order to seek the LORD, the God of Israel. 22 For seven days they celebrated with joy the Feast of Unleavened Bread, because the LORD had filled them with joy by changing the attitude of the king of Assyria, so that he assisted them in the work on the house of God, the God of Israel.

Ezra Comes to Jerusalem

7 After these things, during the reign of Artaxerxes king of Persia, Ezra son of Seraiah, the son of Azariah, the son of Hilkiah, 2 the son of Shallum, the son of Zadok, the son of Ahitub, 3 the son of Amariah, the son of Azariah, the son of Meraioth, 4 the son of Zerahiah, the son of Uzzi, the son of Bukki, 5 the son of Abishua, the son of Phinehas, the son of Eleazar, the son of Aaron the chief priest— 6 this Ezra came up from Babylon. He was a teacher well versed in the Law of Moses, which the LORD, the God of Israel, had given. The king had granted him everything he asked, for the hand of the LORD his God was on him. 7 Some of the Israelites, including priests, Levites, singers, gatekeepers and temple servants, also came up to Jerusalem in the seventh year of King Artaxerxes.

8 Ezra arrived in Jerusalem in the fifth month of the seventh year of the king. 9 He had begun his journey from Babylon on the first day of the first month, and he arrived in Jerusalem on the first day of the fifth month, for the gracious hand of his God was on him. 10 For Ezra had devoted himself to the study and observance of the Law of the LORD, and to teaching its decrees and laws in Israel.

King Artaxerxes' Letter to Ezra

11 This is a copy of the letter King Artaxerxes had given to Ezra the priest and teacher, a man learned in matters concerning the commands and decrees of the LORD for Israel:

12 [a]Artaxerxes, king of kings,

To Ezra the priest, a teacher of the Law of the God of heaven:

Greetings.

13 Now I decree that any of the Israelites in my kingdom, including priests and Levites, who wish to go to Jerusalem with you, may go. 14 You are sent by the king and his seven advisers to inquire about Judah and Jerusalem with regard to the Law of your God, which is in your hand. 15 Moreover, you are to take with you the silver and gold that the king and his advisers have freely given to the God of Israel, whose dwelling is in Jerusalem, 16 together with all the silver and gold you may obtain from the province of Babylon, as well as the freewill offerings of the people and priests for the temple of their God in Jerusalem. 17 With this money be sure to buy bulls, rams and male lambs, together with their grain offerings and drink offerings, and sacrifice them on the altar of the temple of your God in Jerusalem.

18 You and your brother Jews may then do whatever seems best with the rest of the silver and gold, in accordance with the will of your God. 19 Deliver to the God of Jerusalem all the articles entrusted to you for worship in the temple of your God. 20 And anything else needed for the temple of your God that you may have occasion to supply, you may provide from the royal treasury.

21 Now I, King Artaxerxes, order all the treasurers of Trans-Euphrates to provide with diligence whatever Ezra the priest, a teacher of the Law of the God of heaven, may ask of you— 22 up to a hundred talents[b] of silver, a hundred cors[c] of wheat, a hundred baths[d] of wine, a hundred baths[d] of olive oil, and salt without limit. 23 Whatever the God of heaven has prescribed, let it be done with diligence for the temple of the God of heaven. Why should there be wrath against the realm of the king and of his sons? 24 You are also to know that you have no authority to impose taxes, tribute or duty on any of the priests, Levites, singers, gatekeepers, tem-

[a]12 The text of Ezra 7:12-26 is in Aramaic. [b]22 That is, about 3 3/4 tons (about 3.4 metric tons) [c]22 That is, probably about 600 bushels (about 22 kiloliters) [d]22 That is, probably about 600 gallons (about 2.2 kiloliters)

6:20 Before they could lead the people in worshiping God, it was necessary for the priests and Levites to purify themselves. They had to be ritually clean. Now, purification is available to all through Jesus Christ. When we place our trust in Jesus, he purifies us and allows us to come before God.

7:10 What a noble aspiration is recorded in this verse! Ezra prepared his heart to receive what God was saying through his Word. Then, he was obedient to its requirements. Ezra also wanted to teach the people the truth he had discovered and share God's laws with the people of Israel. It is natural for us to want to share something that we believe is worthwhile. We should share with others what God has done in our lives in order to encourage them to seek God and surrender to him.

ple servants or other workers at this house
of God.
[25]And you, Ezra, in accordance with the
wisdom of your God, which you possess,
appoint magistrates and judges to administer justice to all the people of Trans-Euphrates—all who know the laws of your
God. And you are to teach any who do not
know them. [26]Whoever does not obey the
law of your God and the law of the king
must surely be punished by death, banishment, confiscation of property, or imprisonment.

[27]Praise be to the LORD, the God of our fathers, who has put it into the king's heart to
bring honor to the house of the LORD in Jerusalem in this way [28]and who has extended his
good favor to me before the king and his advisers and all the king's powerful officials. Because
the hand of the LORD my God was on me, I took
courage and gathered leading men from Israel
to go up with me.

List of the Family Heads Returning With Ezra

8 These are the family heads and those registered with them who came up with me
from Babylon during the reign of King Artaxerxes:

[2]of the descendants of Phinehas, Gershom;
of the descendants of Ithamar, Daniel;
of the descendants of David, Hattush [3]of
the descendants of Shecaniah;

of the descendants of Parosh, Zechariah, and with him were registered 150 men;
[4]of the descendants of Pahath-Moab, Eliehoenai son of Zerahiah, and with him 200 men;
[5]of the descendants of Zattu,[a] Shecaniah son of Jahaziel, and with him 300 men;
[6]of the descendants of Adin, Ebed son of Jonathan, and with him 50 men;
[7]of the descendants of Elam, Jeshaiah son of Athaliah, and with him 70 men;
[8]of the descendants of Shephatiah, Zebadiah son of Michael, and with him 80 men;
[9]of the descendants of Joab, Obadiah son of Jehiel, and with him 218 men;
[10]of the descendants of Bani,[b] Shelomith son of Josiphiah, and with him 160 men;
[11]of the descendants of Bebai, Zechariah son of Bebai, and with him 28 men;
[12]of the descendants of Azgad, Johanan son of Hakkatan, and with him 110 men;
[13]of the descendants of Adonikam, the last ones, whose names were Eliphelet, Jeuel and Shemaiah, and with them 60 men;
[14]of the descendants of Bigvai, Uthai and Zaccur, and with them 70 men.

The Return to Jerusalem

[15]I assembled them at the canal that flows
toward Ahava, and we camped there three days.
When I checked among the people and the
priests, I found no Levites there. [16]So I summoned Eliezer, Ariel, Shemaiah, Elnathan,
Jarib, Elnathan, Nathan, Zechariah and Meshullam, who were leaders, and Joiarib and
Elnathan, who were men of learning, [17]and I
sent them to Iddo, the leader in Casiphia. I told
them what to say to Iddo and his kinsmen, the
temple servants in Casiphia, so that they might
bring attendants to us for the house of our God.
[18]Because the gracious hand of our God was on
us, they brought us Sherebiah, a capable man,
from the descendants of Mahli son of Levi, the
son of Israel, and Sherebiah's sons and brothers, 18 men; [19]and Hashabiah, together with
Jeshaiah from the descendants of Merari, and
his brothers and nephews, 20 men. [20]They also
brought 220 of the temple servants—a body that
David and the officials had established to assist
the Levites. All were registered by name.
[21]There, by the Ahava Canal, I proclaimed a
fast, so that we might humble ourselves before
our God and ask him for a safe journey for us
and our children, with all our possessions. [22]I
was ashamed to ask the king for soldiers and
horsemen to protect us from enemies on the
road, because we had told the king, "The gracious hand of our God is on everyone who
looks to him, but his great anger is against all
who forsake him." [23]So we fasted and petitioned
our God about this, and he answered our
prayer.
[24]Then I set apart twelve of the leading

[a]5 Some Septuagint manuscripts (also 1 Esdras 8:32); Hebrew does not have *Zattu*. [b]10 Some Septuagint manuscripts (also 1 Esdras 8:36); Hebrew does not have *Bani*.

7:27–28 Many obstacles stood in the way of Ezra's dream of teaching the people to learn and obey God's Word. The first obstacle was a governmental one, but God worked in the heart of Artaxerxes to provide permission and resources for Ezra's mission. These two verses record Ezra's prayer of thanks to God. The progress we make is due only to God's love for us. We should praise him for the good work he is accomplishing in our lives.

8:15–20 Our spiritual growth generally requires careful preparation and listening to the wise advice of godly people. Ezra knew that his primary task was a spiritual one. These verses detail some of the preparations he made. We also need God's help and the help of others who will encourage us in our spiritual growth.

8:24–30 Ezra's preparations for the safekeeping of money show that he understood the importance of accountability. We also must set up measures of accountability for ourselves. We need to establish spiritual goals and then find someone to hold us accountable to them.

priests, together with Sherebiah, Hashabiah and ten of their brothers, 25and I weighed out to them the offering of silver and gold and the articles that the king, his advisers, his officials and all Israel present there had donated for the house of our God. 26I weighed out to them 650 talents[a] of silver, silver articles weighing 100 talents,[b] 100 talents[b] of gold, 2720 bowls of gold valued at 1,000 darics,[c] and two fine articles of polished bronze, as precious as gold.

28I said to them, "You as well as these articles are consecrated to the LORD. The silver and gold are a freewill offering to the LORD, the God of your fathers. 29Guard them carefully until you weigh them out in the chambers of the house of the LORD in Jerusalem before the leading priests and the Levites and the family heads of Israel." 30Then the priests and Levites received the silver and gold and sacred articles that had been weighed out to be taken to the house of our God in Jerusalem.

31On the twelfth day of the first month we set out from the Ahava Canal to go to Jerusalem. The hand of our God was on us, and he protected us from enemies and bandits along the way. 32So we arrived in Jerusalem, where we rested three days.

33On the fourth day, in the house of our God, we weighed out the silver and gold and the sacred articles into the hands of Meremoth son of Uriah, the priest. Eleazar son of Phinehas was with him, and so were the Levites Jozabad son of Jeshua and Noadiah son of Binnui. 34Everything was accounted for by number and weight, and the entire weight was recorded at that time.

35Then the exiles who had returned from captivity sacrificed burnt offerings to the God of Israel: twelve bulls for all Israel, ninety-six rams, seventy-seven male lambs and, as a sin offering, twelve male goats. All this was a burnt offering to the LORD. 36They also delivered the king's orders to the royal satraps and to the governors of Trans-Euphrates, who then gave assistance to the people and to the house of God.

Ezra's Prayer About Intermarriage

9 After these things had been done, the leaders came to me and said, "The people of Israel, including the priests and the Levites, have not kept themselves separate from the neighboring peoples with their detestable practices, like those of the Canaanites, Hittites, Perizzites, Jebusites, Ammonites, Moabites, Egyptians and Amorites. 2They have taken some of their daughters as wives for themselves and their sons, and have mingled the holy race with the peoples around them. And the leaders and officials have led the way in this unfaithfulness."

3When I heard this, I tore my tunic and cloak, pulled hair from my head and beard and sat down appalled. 4Then everyone who trembled at the words of the God of Israel gathered around me because of this unfaithfulness of the exiles. And I sat there appalled until the evening sacrifice.

5Then, at the evening sacrifice, I rose from my self-abasement, with my tunic and cloak torn, and fell on my knees with my hands spread out to the LORD my God 6and prayed:

> "O my God, I am too ashamed and disgraced to lift up my face to you, my God, because our sins are higher than our heads and our guilt has reached to the heavens. 7From the days of our forefathers until now, our guilt has been great. Because of our sins, we and our kings and our priests have been subjected to the sword and captivity, to pillage and humiliation at the hand of foreign kings, as it is today.
>
> 8"But now, for a brief moment, the LORD our God has been gracious in leaving us a remnant and giving us a firm place in his sanctuary, and so our God gives light to our eyes and a little relief in our bondage. 9Though we are slaves, our God has not deserted us in our bondage. He has shown us kindness in the sight of

[a]26 That is, about 25 tons (about 22 metric tons)
[b]26 That is, about 3 3/4 tons (about 3.4 metric tons)
[c]27 That is, about 19 pounds (about 8.5 kilograms)

8:31–34 Ezra finally arrived at Jerusalem. He had overcome many obstacles, even facing considerable danger on the journey itself. Note that the first thing Ezra did upon arrival was to wait for three days. If we are exhausted or emotionally burned out when we begin a project, our task will seem much tougher than it really is. We need to slow down, develop patience and gain perspective.

9:1–2 God called Israel to be his chosen people. He set them apart to bring salvation to the world. He intended them to be holy—unique among all the other peoples on earth. Ezra discovered that the returning exiles were compromising their uniqueness through intermarriage with the pagan peoples living in the land. God has called us as believers to be his people too. We should not blend in with the unbelievers around us; we must remain clearly identifiable as God's chosen and holy people.

9:3 Upon realizing the people's sin, Ezra responded with deep mourning. He was heartbroken that the people had forgotten their calling and the special obligations it entailed. As people of God, we must remember that we also have certain responsibilities before God. There is a temptation to procrastinate in dealing with tough issues in our lives. But God wants us to tackle them head-on, remembering that he is there to give us strength and encouragement.

9:6–15 Ezra's prayer of confession followed his mourning. He freely admitted the sins of the people and pleaded with God for their restoration. He realized that until the people removed this major obstacle to their spiritual growth, they would never achieve the victory God had intended for them. Often we hold onto areas of our lives that prevent us from experiencing everything God has for us. We should act immediately and surrender these to God's control so that we can get on with our spiritual growth.

the kings of Persia: He has granted us new
life to rebuild the house of our God and
repair its ruins, and he has given us a wall
of protection in Judah and Jerusalem.
10"But now, O our God, what can we
say after this? For we have disregarded the
commands 11you gave through your servants the prophets when you said: 'The
land you are entering to possess is a land
polluted by the corruption of its peoples.
By their detestable practices they have
filled it with their impurity from one end
to the other. 12Therefore, do not give your
daughters in marriage to their sons or take
their daughters for your sons. Do not seek
a treaty of friendship with them at any
time, that you may be strong and eat the
good things of the land and leave it to
your children as an everlasting inheritance.'
13"What has happened to us is a result
of our evil deeds and our great guilt, and
yet, our God, you have punished us less
than our sins have deserved and have giv-
en us a remnant like this. 14Shall we again
break your commands and intermarry
with the peoples who commit such detestable practices? Would you not be angry
enough with us to destroy us, leaving us
no remnant or survivor? 15O LORD, God of
Israel, you are righteous! We are left this
day as a remnant. Here we are before you
in our guilt, though because of it not one
of us can stand in your presence."

The People's Confession of Sin

10 While Ezra was praying and confessing,
weeping and throwing himself down
before the house of God, a large crowd of Israelites—men, women and children—gathered
around him. They too wept bitterly. 2Then
Shecaniah son of Jehiel, one of the descendants
of Elam, said to Ezra, "We have been unfaithful
to our God by marrying foreign women from
the peoples around us. But in spite of this, there
is still hope for Israel. 3Now let us make a covenant before our God to send away all these
women and their children, in accordance with
the counsel of my lord and of those who fear
the commands of our God. Let it be done according to the Law. 4Rise up; this matter is in
your hands. We will support you, so take courage and do it."
5So Ezra rose up and put the leading priests
and Levites and all Israel under oath to do what
had been suggested. And they took the oath.
6Then Ezra withdrew from before the house of
God and went to the room of Jehohanan son of
Eliashib. While he was there, he ate no food and
drank no water, because he continued to mourn
over the unfaithfulness of the exiles.
7A proclamation was then issued throughout
Judah and Jerusalem for all the exiles to assemble in Jerusalem. 8Anyone who failed to appear
within three days would forfeit all his property,
in accordance with the decision of the officials
and elders, and would himself be expelled from
the assembly of the exiles.

9Within the three days, all the men of Judah
and Benjamin had gathered in Jerusalem. And
on the twentieth day of the ninth month, all the
people were sitting in the square before the
house of God, greatly distressed by the occasion
and because of the rain. 10Then Ezra the priest
stood up and said to them, "You have been
unfaithful; you have married foreign women,
adding to Israel's guilt. 11Now make confession
to the LORD, the God of your fathers, and do
his will. Separate yourselves from the peoples
around you and from your foreign wives."
12The whole assembly responded with a loud
voice: "You are right! We must do as you say.
13But there are many people here and it is the
rainy season; so we cannot stand outside. Besides, this matter cannot be taken care of in a
day or two, because we have sinned greatly in
this thing. 14Let our officials act for the whole
assembly. Then let everyone in our towns who
has married a foreign woman come at a set
time, along with the elders and judges of each
town, until the fierce anger of our God in this
matter is turned away from us." 15Only Jonathan
son of Asahel and Jahzeiah son of Tikvah, supported by Meshullam and Shabbethai the Levite, opposed this.
16So the exiles did as was proposed. Ezra the
priest selected men who were family heads, one
from each family division, and all of them designated by name. On the first day of the tenth
month they sat down to investigate the cases,
17and by the first day of the first month they
finished dealing with all the men who had married foreign women.

Those Guilty of Intermarriage

18Among the descendants of the priests,
the following had married foreign
women:

10:2 It was a good thing for Ezra to confess the sins of the people, but until the people acknowledged their sin, the victory could not take place. If we do not acknowledge the sin in our lives, we will never move forward. We must confess these sins to God and then take action against them.

10:3 The people did not stop at mere confession; they vowed to reform, redirecting the course of their lives back into alignment with God's commands. It is never enough just to acknowledge that we have sin in our lives. We must follow our confession with action, accepting responsibility for our sin and taking active steps to eliminate sinful and destructive behaviors from our lives.

10:10–12 Heartily, the people responded, "We must do as you say." The people recognized their responsibilities as God's people. When they admitted that they needed to obey God's will, they found victory! Ezra was successful in his mission to lead the nation to restoration. We, too, can know such victory if we follow God's will for our lives and trust him to see us through.

From the descendants of Jeshua son of Jozadak, and his brothers: Maaseiah, Eliezer, Jarib and Gedaliah. 19 (They all gave their hands in pledge to put away their wives, and for their guilt they each presented a ram from the flock as a guilt offering.)

20 From the descendants of Immer: Hanani and Zebadiah.

21 From the descendants of Harim: Maaseiah, Elijah, Shemaiah, Jehiel and Uzziah.

22 From the descendants of Pashhur: Elioenai, Maaseiah, Ishmael, Nethanel, Jozabad and Elasah.

23 Among the Levites:

Jozabad, Shimei, Kelaiah (that is, Kelita), Pethahiah, Judah and Eliezer.

24 From the singers: Eliashib.

From the gatekeepers: Shallum, Telem and Uri.

25 And among the other Israelites:

From the descendants of Parosh: Ramiah, Izziah, Malkijah, Mijamin, Eleazar, Malkijah and Benaiah.

26 From the descendants of Elam: Mattaniah, Zechariah, Jehiel, Abdi, Jeremoth and Elijah.

27 From the descendants of Zattu: Elioenai, Eliashib, Mattaniah, Jeremoth, Zabad and Aziza.

28 From the descendants of Bebai: Jehohanan, Hananiah, Zabbai and Athlai.

29 From the descendants of Bani: Meshullam, Malluch, Adaiah, Jashub, Sheal and Jeremoth.

30 From the descendants of Pahath-Moab: Adna, Kelal, Benaiah, Maaseiah, Mattaniah, Bezalel, Binnui and Manasseh.

31 From the descendants of Harim: Eliezer, Ishijah, Malkijah, Shemaiah, Shimeon,
32 Benjamin, Malluch and Shemariah.

33 From the descendants of Hashum: Mattenai, Mattattah, Zabad, Eliphelet, Jeremai, Manasseh and Shimei.

34 From the descendants of Bani: Maadai, Amram, Uel,
35 Benaiah, Bedeiah, Keluhi,
36 Vaniah, Meremoth, Eliashib,
37 Mattaniah, Mattenai and Jaasu.

38 From the descendants of Binnui:[a] Shimei,
39 Shelemiah, Nathan, Adaiah,
40 Macnadebai, Shashai, Sharai,
41 Azarel, Shelemiah, Shemariah,
42 Shallum, Amariah and Joseph.

43 From the descendants of Nebo: Jeiel, Mattithiah, Zabad, Zebina, Jaddai, Joel and Benaiah.

44 All these had married foreign women, and some of them had children by these wives.[b]

[a] *37,38* See Septuagint (also 1 Esdras 9:34); Hebrew *Jaasu* [38] *and Bani and Binnui,* [b] *44* Or *and they sent them away with their children*

NEHEMIAH

The Big Picture

A. REBUILDING THE WALL (1:1–7:73)

1. Nehemiah's Call (1:1–2:6)
2. Nehemiah's Preparations (2:7–3:32)
3. The Problems Faced by Nehemiah (4:1–6:14)
   a. Derision–answered by prayer (4:1-6)
   b. Discouragement–answered by communication (4:7-23)
   c. Greed–answered by confrontation (5:1-19)
   d. Personal attacks–answered by dependence on God (6:1-14)
4. Nehemiah Perseveres (6:15–7:73)

B. REBUILDING THE WORKERS (8:1–12:47)

1. Ezra Leads in Revival (8:1-18)
2. The Role of Confession (9:1-37)
3. The Response of the People (9:38–10:39)
4. Nehemiah Establishes Policies (11:1–12:47)

C. REBUILDING THE WORSHIP (13:1-31)

When we do not feel safe, it is difficult to concentrate on the job at hand. The people of Jerusalem possessed no physical security—their city wall had been in ruins for over a hundred years. The temple had been rebuilt many years before, but the wall around Jerusalem was still in disrepair. Walls are important boundaries. They protect and shelter the inhabitants who live inside; they repel destructive intruders attacking from the outside. In the ancient Near East, a city without a wall was vulnerable to raids and harassment of all kinds. A city without walls was unthinkable! In this unstable situation, Ezra was trying to encourage the Jews to rebuild their nation and lives.

At the same time, Nehemiah worked as the cupbearer for King Artaxerxes of Persia. When he heard about the situation that Ezra faced in Jerusalem, Nehemiah literally sat down and wept.

Nehemiah decided to approach King Artaxerxes about the problem and ask for his assistance. The king was sympathetic and gave Nehemiah permission to lead a third group of Jews back to Jerusalem. Nehemiah encouraged the people to rebuild Jerusalem's wall. His leadership abilities overcame both international and local resistance to this rebuilding project. In the end, by trusting God and working together, the people completed the task of rebuilding the wall.

When the work was completed, Nehemiah joined with Ezra to encourage the people to rebuild their lives, their culture and the proper worship of God. Nehemiah was skilled in organization and administration. He handled the logistics of organizing the Levites, the people and other officials. Ezra complemented Nehemiah's leadership abilities with his own skills as a teacher and scholar as he led the people in the restoration of their spiritual heritage.

Spiritual Renewal Themes

THE IMPORTANCE OF CONFRONTATION

Sometimes, directly confronting a blameworthy person is the best way to remedy a bad situation. Several times Nehemiah's enemies tried to undermine his work through their lies and deceit. Each time, Nehemiah directly confronted the lies, going straight to the source of the problem. He did not allow himself

to get discouraged or overwhelmed by the difficulties. Every time he encountered a potential roadblock to God's work, Nehemiah faced the issues squarely and honestly. Then he persisted in his course of action until the problem was resolved.

THE DANGER OF DISCOURAGEMENT

As a wise leader, Nehemiah knew that the people's discouragement was probably one of their biggest enemies. Discouragement is one of our biggest enemies too. When we get discouraged, we open ourselves up to defeat, giving the enemy an opportunity for victory for a period of time. The book of Nehemiah shows us that we need to be on guard against discouragement.

THE POWER OF CONFESSION AND WORSHIP

The book of Nehemiah presents a vivid picture of the power of confession and the role of worship in our spiritual renewal. Not many days after the end of the Feast of Booths (8:13–18), the people gathered together for another celebration (chapters 9—10). This celebration commemorated the restoration of both the temple and the city of Jerusalem. The people began this celebration by listening to the Word of God and confessing not only their own sins but also the sins of their ancestors. Confession brings healing and prepares us for true worship, genuine spiritual renewal and joyous celebration.

Essential Facts

PURPOSE:
To describe the rebuilding of Jerusalem's wall and the continued spiritual rebuilding of the people.

AUTHOR:
Nehemiah; Ezra probably served as an editor.

AUDIENCE:
The people of Israel after their return from exile in Babylon.

DATE WRITTEN:
The book was probably written during Nehemiah's first administration, sometime between 445–432 B.C.

SETTING:
The city of Jerusalem.

KEY VERSE:
"They stood where they were and read from the Book of the Law of the LORD their God for a quarter of the day, and spent another quarter in confession and in worshiping the LORD their God" (9:3).

KEY PEOPLE:
Ezra, Nehemiah.

Nehemiah's Prayer

1 The words of Nehemiah son of Hacaliah:

In the month of Kislev in the twentieth year, while I was in the citadel of Susa, 2Hanani, one of my brothers, came from Judah with some other men, and I questioned them about the Jewish remnant that survived the exile, and also about Jerusalem.

3They said to me, "Those who survived the exile and are back in the province are in great trouble and disgrace. The wall of Jerusalem is broken down, and its gates have been burned with fire."

4When I heard these things, I sat down and wept. For some days I mourned and fasted and prayed before the God of heaven. 5Then I said:

> "O LORD, God of heaven, the great and awesome God, who keeps his covenant of love with those who love him and obey his commands, 6let your ear be attentive and your eyes open to hear the prayer your servant is praying before you day and night for your servants, the people of Israel. I confess the sins we Israelites, including myself and my father's house, have committed against you. 7We have acted very wickedly toward you. We have not obeyed the commands, decrees and laws you gave your servant Moses.
>
> 8"Remember the instruction you gave your servant Moses, saying, 'If you are unfaithful, I will scatter you among the nations, 9but if you return to me and obey my commands, then even if your exiled people are at the farthest horizon, I will gather them from there and bring them to the place I have chosen as a dwelling for my Name.'
>
> 10"They are your servants and your people, whom you redeemed by your great strength and your mighty hand. 11O Lord, let your ear be attentive to the prayer of this your servant and to the prayer of your servants who delight in revering your name. Give your servant success today by granting him favor in the presence of this man."

I was cupbearer to the king.

Artaxerxes Sends Nehemiah to Jerusalem

2 In the month of Nisan in the twentieth year of King Artaxerxes, when wine was brought for him, I took the wine and gave it to the king. I had not been sad in his presence before; 2so the king asked me, "Why does your face look so sad when you are not ill? This can be nothing but sadness of heart."

I was very much afraid, 3but I said to the king, "May the king live forever! Why should my face not look sad when the city where my fathers are buried lies in ruins, and its gates have been destroyed by fire?"

4The king said to me, "What is it you want?"

Then I prayed to the God of heaven, 5and I answered the king, "If it pleases the king and if your servant has found favor in his sight, let him send me to the city in Judah where my fathers are buried so that I can rebuild it."

6Then the king, with the queen sitting beside him, asked me, "How long will your journey take, and when will you get back?" It pleased the king to send me; so I set a time.

7I also said to him, "If it pleases the king, may I have letters to the governors of Trans-Euphrates, so that they will provide me safe-conduct until I arrive in Judah? 8And may I have a letter to Asaph, keeper of the king's forest, so he will give me timber to make beams for the gates of the citadel by the temple and for the city wall and for the residence I will occupy?" And because the gracious hand of my God was upon me, the king granted my requests. 9So I went to the governors of Trans-Euphrates and gave them the king's letters. The king had also sent army officers and cavalry with me.

10When Sanballat the Horonite and Tobiah the Ammonite official heard about this, they

---

1:1–3 The walls in Jerusalem desperately needed rebuilding. When Nehemiah heard of the circumstances in Jerusalem, he was immediately touched. He wanted to do something about it. As we honestly reflect on our spiritual lives, we need to take careful note of what areas need specific work. Renewal cannot take place until we know where to begin.

1:4–11 For believers, prayer is often an untapped resource—the last resort after every other possibility has been exhausted. It is refreshing to notice that prayer was Nehemiah's immediate response. Nehemiah knew that in order to correct the situation, God would have to be the one to accomplish it! This is a powerful reminder for us—we should fall on our knees so that we don't fall on our faces.

1:11 Spiritual growth is never a solitary journey. Other people must be involved. In this case, Nehemiah recognized the need for the king's favor, so Nehemiah asked God to secure the necessary response from him. Like Nehemiah, we should determine whose help we need and then prayerfully ask God and other people for their assistance.

2:1–3 In the Bible, God's people openly expressed their emotions: Job revealed his emotions to his friends; King David poured his heart into his many psalms, pleading with God for his rescue; Jesus displayed emotions, even weeping on occasion (see John 11:35). God wants us to be open and honest in our expression of emotion. Too often, maybe because we fear appearing weak, we refuse to express our feelings and repress them. When this happens, our emotions sometimes only increase in intensity and haunt us for years to come. Releasing our emotions openly before God is a vital step toward moving forward and away from pain and despair.

2:4–8 In answer to Nehemiah's prayer, the king's immediate response was one of encouragement and assistance. One wonders how Artaxerxes would have responded if Nehemiah had not approached God first about this matter. God is sovereign, and he listens to our prayers. We would be foolish to neglect his help before we begin any new venture in our lives.

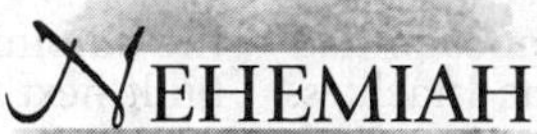

NEHEMIAH

Spiritual renewal is all about taking a life, often from the point of near destruction, and rebuilding it to God's specifications. Nehemiah, the great rebuilder of Jerusalem, grants us an excellent Biblical example of how to pursue and enhance our spiritual growth.

Nehemiah did not let the long-delayed restoration of Jerusalem discourage him. He realized that it was never too late for God's people to begin the process of rebuilding. Nehemiah's actions were direct and forceful, always based on the realities at hand. His faith, wisdom and courage kept him focused on his goal, despite considerable opposition. Leaders like Sanballat and Tobiah, who had dominated the land of Judah for some time, used various means to discourage the progress of Nehemiah and his workforce. The people also had to resolve painful differences among themselves along the way. But all of the obstacles were overcome as the people worked to build a new, more secure life.

The wall of Jerusalem was completed in a miraculous fifty-two days! Soon after this first victory, Nehemiah directed the people toward a second phase of restoration. He called upon the great teacher Ezra to lead the people in a study of the Law. Confronted by God's Word, the people were soon in tears because they could see the truth of how far they had strayed from God's law. They confessed their sins and the sins of their ancestors. They accepted responsibility for their unfaithfulness and grieved openly before God. Ezra, Nehemiah and the other leaders encouraged the people to be filled with joy because God was with them.

Even at this point, however, there were still some painful lessons of restoration to be learned. After Nehemiah returned to Babylon, the people reverted once again to their sinful ways. When Nehemiah returned to Jerusalem, he helped put the people back on the path toward restoration. Nehemiah's story ends on a very realistic note. The people's short-term restoration shows how prone we all are to drifting away from what is right if we are not held accountable by others. There will be times when we may fall back into familiar, though destructive, patterns. Nehemiah's experience should encourage us to realize that no matter how often we sin, there is always an opportunity for repentance, forgiveness and a restored life.

STRENGTHS AND ACCOMPLISHMENTS:

- Nehemiah was a man of prayer and unshakable commitment to God.
- He was an effective administrator and a great visionary.
- Secure in his calling, Nehemiah was able to withstand criticism.
- With faith and perseverance, Nehemiah completed the rebuilding process for Jerusalem and the nation.

LESSONS FROM HIS LIFE:

- Prayerful intervention, a realistic vision and commitment to God are necessary for continued spiritual growth.
- Confronting and overcoming obstacles to spiritual renewal can actually provide momentum for the process.
- The completion of one phase of restoration should motivate us to pursue the next step.
- Drifting back toward our old ways is to be expected. Holding each other accountable will help redirect our course whenever this begins to happen.

KEY VERSE:

"They realized that this work had been done with the help of our God" (6:16).

Nehemiah's story is told in the book of Nehemiah. He is also mentioned in Ezra 2:2.

were very much disturbed that someone had come to promote the welfare of the Israelites.

Nehemiah Inspects Jerusalem's Walls

11I went to Jerusalem, and after staying there three days 12I set out during the night with a few men. I had not told anyone what my God had put in my heart to do for Jerusalem. There were no mounts with me except the one I was riding on.

13By night I went out through the Valley Gate toward the Jackal[a] Well and the Dung Gate, examining the walls of Jerusalem, which had been broken down, and its gates, which had been destroyed by fire. 14Then I moved on toward the Fountain Gate and the King's Pool, but there was not enough room for my mount to get through; 15so I went up the valley by night, examining the wall. Finally, I turned back and reentered through the Valley Gate. 16The officials did not know where I had gone or what I was doing, because as yet I had said nothing to the Jews or the priests or nobles or officials or any others who would be doing the work.

17Then I said to them, "You see the trouble we are in: Jerusalem lies in ruins, and its gates have been burned with fire. Come, let us rebuild the wall of Jerusalem, and we will no longer be in disgrace." 18I also told them about the gracious hand of my God upon me and what the king had said to me.

They replied, "Let us start rebuilding." So they began this good work.

19But when Sanballat the Horonite, Tobiah the Ammonite official and Geshem the Arab heard about it, they mocked and ridiculed us. "What is this you are doing?" they asked. "Are you rebelling against the king?"

20I answered them by saying, "The God of heaven will give us success. We his servants will start rebuilding, but as for you, you have no share in Jerusalem or any claim or historic right to it."

Builders of the Wall

3 Eliashib the high priest and his fellow priests went to work and rebuilt the Sheep Gate. They dedicated it and set its doors in place, building as far as the Tower of the Hundred, which they dedicated, and as far as the Tower of Hananel. 2The men of Jericho built the adjoining section, and Zaccur son of Imri built next to them.

3The Fish Gate was rebuilt by the sons of Hassenaah. They laid its beams and put its doors and bolts and bars in place. 4Meremoth son of Uriah, the son of Hakkoz, repaired the next section. Next to him Meshullam son of Berekiah, the son of Meshezabel, made repairs, and next to him Zadok son of Baana also made repairs. 5The next section was repaired by the men of Tekoa, but their nobles would not put their shoulders to the work under their supervisors.[b]

6The Jeshanah[c] Gate was repaired by Joiada son of Paseah and Meshullam son of Besodeiah. They laid its beams and put its doors and bolts and bars in place. 7Next to them, repairs were made by men from Gibeon and Mizpah—Melatiah of Gibeon and Jadon of Meronoth—places under the authority of the governor of Trans-Euphrates. 8Uzziel son of Harhaiah, one of the goldsmiths, repaired the next section; and Hananiah, one of the perfume-makers, made repairs next to that. They restored[d] Jerusalem as far as the Broad Wall. 9Rephaiah son of Hur, ruler of a half-district of Jerusalem, repaired the next section. 10Adjoining this, Jedaiah son of Harumaph made repairs opposite his house, and Hattush son of Hashabneiah made repairs next to him. 11Malkijah son of Harim and Hasshub son of Pahath-Moab repaired another section and the Tower of the Ovens. 12Shallum son of Hallohesh, ruler of a half-district of Jerusalem, repaired the next section with the help of his daughters.

13The Valley Gate was repaired by Hanun and the residents of Zanoah. They rebuilt it and put its doors and bolts and bars in place. They also repaired five hundred yards[e] of the wall as far as the Dung Gate.

14The Dung Gate was repaired by Malkijah son of Recab, ruler of the district of Beth Hakkerem. He rebuilt it and put its doors and bolts and bars in place.

[a] 13 Or *Serpent* or *Fig* [b] 5 Or *their Lord* or *the governor* [c] 6 Or *Old* [d] 8 Or *They left out part of* [e] 13 Hebrew *a thousand cubits* (about 450 meters)

2:11–16 One of the first tasks in any rebuilding project is an honest evaluation of the situation. As soon as Nehemiah came to Jerusalem, he made a nighttime inspection of the city's broken wall. As we begin our journey toward spiritual renewal, each of us needs to take an honest look at the circumstances, problems and resources before us. Then, with God's help, we can execute a plan to reach our goal of spiritual renewal.

2:17–20 Nehemiah performed a ministry of encouragement to the people. He was completely honest about their problems; he didn't deny or underestimate their needs. But Nehemiah also took time to remind them of God's powerful hand and challenged them to get on with their work. Every one of us needs a Nehemiah—someone who will honestly tell us what needs to be fixed in our lives and then will stick close to help us complete the task.

3:1–32 Rebuilding the entire wall of Jerusalem was an enormous task. But Nehemiah had a plan to make it easier—he divided the work and assigned it to different groups of people. This way the people felt responsible for their section, and no one became overworked toiling on the entire task. There is a lesson here for us too. As we consider our lives and the work necessary to conform them to God's design, we may become discouraged by the immensity of the task. But if we break up the process into smaller steps—a day or week or month at a time—the task will look less intimidating.

15 The Fountain Gate was repaired by Shallun son of Col-Hozeh, ruler of the district of Mizpah. He rebuilt it, roofing it over and putting its doors and bolts and bars in place. He also repaired the wall of the Pool of Siloam,[a] by the King's Garden, as far as the steps going down from the City of David. 16 Beyond him, Nehemiah son of Azbuk, ruler of a half-district of Beth Zur, made repairs up to a point opposite the tombs[b] of David, as far as the artificial pool and the House of the Heroes.

17 Next to him, the repairs were made by the Levites under Rehum son of Bani. Beside him, Hashabiah, ruler of half the district of Keilah, carried out repairs for his district. 18 Next to him, the repairs were made by their countrymen under Binnui[c] son of Henadad, ruler of the other half-district of Keilah. 19 Next to him, Ezer son of Jeshua, ruler of Mizpah, repaired another section, from a point facing the ascent to the armory as far as the angle. 20 Next to him, Baruch son of Zabbai zealously repaired another section, from the angle to the entrance of the house of Eliashib the high priest. 21 Next to him, Meremoth son of Uriah, the son of Hakkoz, repaired another section, from the entrance of Eliashib's house to the end of it.

22 The repairs next to him were made by the priests from the surrounding region. 23 Beyond them, Benjamin and Hasshub made repairs in front of their house; and next to them, Azariah son of Maaseiah, the son of Ananiah, made repairs beside his house. 24 Next to him, Binnui son of Henadad repaired another section, from Azariah's house to the angle and the corner, 25 and Palal son of Uzai worked opposite the angle and the tower projecting from the upper palace near the court of the guard. Next to him, Pedaiah son of Parosh 26 and the temple servants living on the hill of Ophel made repairs up to a point opposite the Water Gate toward the east and the projecting tower. 27 Next to them, the men of Tekoa repaired another section, from the great projecting tower to the wall of Ophel.

28 Above the Horse Gate, the priests made repairs, each in front of his own house. 29 Next to them, Zadok son of Immer made repairs opposite his house. Next to him, Shemaiah son of Shecaniah, the guard at the East Gate, made repairs. 30 Next to him, Hananiah son of Shelemiah, and Hanun, the sixth son of Zalaph, repaired another section. Next to them, Meshullam son of Berekiah made repairs opposite his living quarters. 31 Next to him, Malkijah, one of the goldsmiths, made repairs as far as the house of the temple servants and the merchants, opposite the Inspection Gate, and as far as the room above the corner; 32 and between the room above the corner and the Sheep Gate the goldsmiths and merchants made repairs.

Opposition to the Rebuilding

4 When Sanballat heard that we were rebuilding the wall, he became angry and was greatly incensed. He ridiculed the Jews, 2 and in the presence of his associates and the army of Samaria, he said, "What are those feeble Jews doing? Will they restore their wall? Will they offer sacrifices? Will they finish in a day? Can they bring the stones back to life from those heaps of rubble—burned as they are?"

3 Tobiah the Ammonite, who was at his side, said, "What they are building—if even a fox climbed up on it, he would break down their wall of stones!"

4 Hear us, O our God, for we are despised. Turn their insults back on their own heads. Give them over as plunder in a land of captivity. 5 Do not cover up their guilt or blot out their sins from your sight, for they have thrown insults in the face of[d] the builders.

6 So we rebuilt the wall till all of it reached half its height, for the people worked with all their heart.

7 But when Sanballat, Tobiah, the Arabs, the Ammonites and the men of Ashdod heard that the repairs to Jerusalem's walls had gone ahead and that the gaps were being closed, they were very angry. 8 They all plotted together to come and fight against Jerusalem and stir up trouble against it. 9 But we prayed to our God and posted a guard day and night to meet this threat.

10 Meanwhile, the people in Judah said, "The strength of the laborers is giving out, and there is so much rubble that we cannot rebuild the wall."

11 Also our enemies said, "Before they know it or see us, we will be right there among them and will kill them and put an end to the work."

12 Then the Jews who lived near them came and told us ten times over, "Wherever you turn, they will attack us."

13 Therefore I stationed some of the people

[a] 15 Hebrew *Shelah,* a variant of *Shiloah,* that is, Siloam
[b] 16 Hebrew; Septuagint, some Vulgate manuscripts and Syriac *tomb*
[c] 18 Two Hebrew manuscripts and Syriac (see also Septuagint and verse 24); most Hebrew manuscripts *Bavvai*
[d] 5 Or *have provoked you to anger before*

4:1–4 Carrying out the will of God will always bring opposition; sometimes that opposition will be characterized by ridicule. Nehemiah's experience was no exception. The sarcasm expressed by Sanballat and Tobiah must have stung. But Nehemiah did not focus his attention on the ridicule; he continued to look to God. We, too, should look to God as we seek to obey God's plans for us and overlook the ridicule of unbelievers.

4:4–9 How do we counter ridicule and disdain? In these verses Nehemiah offers us a magnificent example: seek God and keep our guard up. Nehemiah countered ridicule with prayer. Not only did he pray, but Nehemiah also set a twenty-four-hour watch, guarding against an attack. Prayer and God-directed action set God's plan in motion for Nehemiah—and for us too.

behind the lowest points of the wall at the exposed places, posting them by families, with their swords, spears and bows. [14]After I looked things over, I stood up and said to the nobles, the officials and the rest of the people, "Don't be afraid of them. Remember the Lord, who is great and awesome, and fight for your brothers, your sons and your daughters, your wives and your homes."

[15]When our enemies heard that we were aware of their plot and that God had frustrated it, we all returned to the wall, each to his own work.

[16]From that day on, half of my men did the work, while the other half were equipped with spears, shields, bows and armor. The officers posted themselves behind all the people of Judah [17]who were building the wall. Those who carried materials did their work with one hand and held a weapon in the other, [18]and each of the builders wore his sword at his side as he worked. But the man who sounded the trumpet stayed with me.

[19]Then I said to the nobles, the officials and the rest of the people, "The work is extensive and spread out, and we are widely separated from each other along the wall. [20]Wherever you hear the sound of the trumpet, join us there. Our God will fight for us!"

[21]So we continued the work with half the men holding spears, from the first light of dawn till the stars came out. [22]At that time I also said to the people, "Have every man and his helper stay inside Jerusalem at night, so they can serve us as guards by night and workmen by day." [23]Neither I nor my brothers nor my men nor the guards with me took off our clothes; each had his weapon, even when he went for water.[a]

Nehemiah Helps the Poor

5 Now the men and their wives raised a great outcry against their Jewish brothers. [2]Some were saying, "We and our sons and daughters are numerous; in order for us to eat and stay alive, we must get grain."

[3]Others were saying, "We are mortgaging our fields, our vineyards and our homes to get grain during the famine."

[4]Still others were saying, "We have had to borrow money to pay the king's tax on our fields and vineyards. [5]Although we are of the same flesh and blood as our countrymen and though our sons are as good as theirs, yet we have to subject our sons and daughters to slavery. Some of our daughters have already been enslaved, but we are powerless, because our fields and our vineyards belong to others."

[6]When I heard their outcry and these charges, I was very angry. [7]I pondered them in my mind and then accused the nobles and officials. I told them, "You are exacting usury from your own countrymen!" So I called together a large meeting to deal with them [8]and said: "As far as possible, we have bought back our Jewish brothers who were sold to the Gentiles. Now you are selling your brothers, only for them to be sold back to us!" They kept quiet, because they could find nothing to say.

[9]So I continued, "What you are doing is not right. Shouldn't you walk in the fear of our God to avoid the reproach of our Gentile enemies? [10]I and my brothers and my men are also lending the people money and grain. But let the exacting of usury stop! [11]Give back to them immediately their fields, vineyards, olive groves and houses, and also the usury you are charging them—the hundredth part of the money, grain, new wine and oil."

[12]"We will give it back," they said. "And we will not demand anything more from them. We will do as you say."

Then I summoned the priests and made the nobles and officials take an oath to do what they had promised. [13]I also shook out the folds of my robe and said, "In this way may God shake out of his house and possessions every man who does not keep this promise. So may such a man be shaken out and emptied!"

At this the whole assembly said, "Amen," and praised the LORD. And the people did as they had promised.

[14]Moreover, from the twentieth year of King Artaxerxes, when I was appointed to be their governor in the land of Judah, until his thirty-second year—twelve years—neither I nor my brothers ate the food allotted to the governor. [15]But the earlier governors—those preceding me—placed a heavy burden on the people and took forty shekels[b] of silver from them in addition to food and wine. Their assistants also lorded it over the people. But out of reverence for God I did not act like that. [16]Instead, I devoted myself to the work on this wall. All my men were assembled there for the work; we[c] did not acquire any land.

[17]Furthermore, a hundred and fifty Jews and officials ate at my table, as well as those who came to us from the surrounding nations. [18]Each day one ox, six choice sheep and some poultry were prepared for me, and every ten days an abundant supply of wine of all kinds. In spite of all this, I never demanded the food

[a]*23* The meaning of the Hebrew for this clause is uncertain. [b]*15* That is, about 1 pound (about 0.5 kilogram) [c]*16* Most Hebrew manuscripts; some Hebrew manuscripts, Septuagint, Vulgate and Syriac *I*

5:1–5 The previous attack had come from the outside; now a new attack came from within. The rebuilding was costing too much! We may experience the same emotions the Jews felt. There is a cost to obeying God's plans, but we must remember that spiritual growth is worth the pain and sacrifice.

5:14–19 Leadership by example is difficult but very effective. Nehemiah gave up many of his rightful privileges in order to be a godly example. He did not insist on his own rights. Rather, as a part of his response to God, Nehemiah was willing to sacrifice his privileges for the good of the people.

allotted to the governor, because the demands were heavy on these people.

19 Remember me with favor, O my God, for all I have done for these people.

Further Opposition to the Rebuilding

6 When word came to Sanballat, Tobiah, Geshem the Arab and the rest of our enemies that I had rebuilt the wall and not a gap was left in it—though up to that time I had not set the doors in the gates— 2 Sanballat and Geshem sent me this message: "Come, let us meet together in one of the villages[a] on the plain of Ono."

But they were scheming to harm me; 3 so I sent messengers to them with this reply: "I am carrying on a great project and cannot go down. Why should the work stop while I leave it and go down to you?" 4 Four times they sent me the same message, and each time I gave them the same answer.

5 Then, the fifth time, Sanballat sent his aide to me with the same message, and in his hand was an unsealed letter 6 in which was written:

> "It is reported among the nations—and Geshem[b] says it is true—that you and the Jews are plotting to revolt, and therefore you are building the wall. Moreover, according to these reports you are about to become their king 7 and have even appointed prophets to make this proclamation about you in Jerusalem: 'There is a king in Judah!' Now this report will get back to the king; so come, let us confer together."

8 I sent him this reply: "Nothing like what you are saying is happening; you are just making it up out of your head."

9 They were all trying to frighten us, thinking, "Their hands will get too weak for the work, and it will not be completed."

⌞But I prayed,⌟ "Now strengthen my hands."

10 One day I went to the house of Shemaiah son of Delaiah, the son of Mehetabel, who was shut in at his home. He said, "Let us meet in the house of God, inside the temple, and let us close the temple doors, because men are coming to kill you—by night they are coming to kill you."

11 But I said, "Should a man like me run away? Or should one like me go into the temple to save his life? I will not go!" 12 I realized that God had not sent him, but that he had prophesied against me because Tobiah and Sanballat had hired him. 13 He had been hired to intimidate me so that I would commit a sin by doing this, and then they would give me a bad name to discredit me.

14 Remember Tobiah and Sanballat, O my God, because of what they have done; remember also the prophetess Noadiah and the rest of the prophets who have been trying to intimidate me.

The Completion of the Wall

15 So the wall was completed on the twenty-fifth of Elul, in fifty-two days. 16 When all our enemies heard about this, all the surrounding nations were afraid and lost their self-confidence, because they realized that this work had been done with the help of our God.

17 Also, in those days the nobles of Judah were sending many letters to Tobiah, and replies from Tobiah kept coming to them. 18 For many in Judah were under oath to him, since he was son-in-law to Shecaniah son of Arah, and his son Jehohanan had married the daughter of Meshullam son of Berekiah. 19 Moreover, they kept reporting to me his good deeds and then telling him what I said. And Tobiah sent letters to intimidate me.

7 After the wall had been rebuilt and I had set the doors in place, the gatekeepers and the singers and the Levites were appointed. 2 I put in charge of Jerusalem my brother Hanani, along with[c] Hananiah the commander of the citadel, because he was a man of integrity and feared God more than most men do. 3 I said to them, "The gates of Jerusalem are not to be opened until the sun is hot. While the gatekeepers are still on duty, have them shut the doors and bar them. Also appoint residents of Jerusa-

[a] 2 Or *in Kephirim* [b] 6 Hebrew *Gashmu,* a variant of *Geshem* [c] 2 Or *Hanani, that is,*

6:1–2 As the work neared completion, the enemies resorted to trickery under the guise of negotiation. As we seek to rebuild our lives according to God's design, enemies will oppose us too. We should not allow others to distract us from our goal of spiritual growth. We dare not compromise with those who are opposed to God and his plan for our lives.

6:3 Nehemiah set his mind to the task; he possessed a singleness of purpose. When his enemies tried to lure him away from the work, he answered with the ringing statement, "I am carrying on a great project and cannot go down." Nehemiah allowed nothing to turn him from his purpose. Each of us needs to seek God with such clear focus so that we, too, cannot be turned from God's purposes.

6:15–16 After overcoming all kinds of evil opposition, the workers completely rebuilt the wall in a record fifty-two days. The work was completed so quickly because God had helped the Israelites. A job that had languished for almost a hundred years was finished within two months. If we have delayed our spiritual renewal and now think it is too late to begin, we should take encouragement from this great feat. It is never too late or too difficult to begin our spiritual renewal if we do it in God's strength and with his help.

7:1–4 After the great project was completed, Nehemiah did not quit. Rather, he set up a careful organization for further reconstruction. He made careful provision for the further defense of the city. Nehemiah wanted to provide God's people with a safe environment for their individual building projects. Our spiritual growth requires ongoing attention. We must be on guard for lapses in our resolve that would allow us to slip back into sinful habits.

lem as guards, some at their posts and some near their own houses."

The List of the Exiles Who Returned

[4]Now the city was large and spacious, but there were few people in it, and the houses had not yet been rebuilt. [5]So my God put it into my heart to assemble the nobles, the officials and the common people for registration by families. I found the genealogical record of those who had been the first to return. This is what I found written there:

[6]These are the people of the province who came up from the captivity of the exiles whom Nebuchadnezzar king of Babylon had taken captive (they returned to Jerusalem and Judah, each to his own town, [7]in company with Zerubbabel, Jeshua, Nehemiah, Azariah, Raamiah, Nahamani, Mordecai, Bilshan, Mispereth, Bigvai, Nehum and Baanah):

The list of the men of Israel:

[8]the descendants of Parosh 2,172
[9]of Shephatiah 372
[10]of Arah 652
[11]of Pahath-Moab (through the line of Jeshua and Joab) 2,818
[12]of Elam 1,254
[13]of Zattu 845
[14]of Zaccai 760
[15]of Binnui 648
[16]of Bebai 628
[17]of Azgad 2,322
[18]of Adonikam 667
[19]of Bigvai 2,067
[20]of Adin 655
[21]of Ater (through Hezekiah) 98
[22]of Hashum 328
[23]of Bezai 324
[24]of Hariph 112
[25]of Gibeon 95

[26]the men of Bethlehem and Netophah 188
[27]of Anathoth 128
[28]of Beth Azmaveth 42
[29]of Kiriath Jearim, Kephirah and Beeroth 743
[30]of Ramah and Geba 621
[31]of Micmash 122
[32]of Bethel and Ai 123
[33]of the other Nebo 52
[34]of the other Elam 1,254
[35]of Harim 320
[36]of Jericho 345
[37]of Lod, Hadid and Ono 721
[38]of Senaah 3,930

[39]The priests:

the descendants of Jedaiah (through the family of Jeshua) 973
[40]of Immer 1,052
[41]of Pashhur 1,247
[42]of Harim 1,017

[43]The Levites:

the descendants of Jeshua (through Kadmiel through the line of Hodaviah) 74

[44]The singers:

the descendants of Asaph 148

[45]The gatekeepers:

the descendants of Shallum, Ater, Talmon, Akkub, Hatita and Shobai 138

[46]The temple servants:

the descendants of
Ziha, Hasupha, Tabbaoth,
[47]Keros, Sia, Padon,
[48]Lebana, Hagaba, Shalmai,
[49]Hanan, Giddel, Gahar,
[50]Reaiah, Rezin, Nekoda,
[51]Gazzam, Uzza, Paseah,
[52]Besai, Meunim, Nephussim,
[53]Bakbuk, Hakupha, Harhur,
[54]Bazluth, Mehida, Harsha,
[55]Barkos, Sisera, Temah,
[56]Neziah and Hatipha

[57]The descendants of the servants of Solomon:

the descendants of
Sotai, Sophereth, Perida,
[58]Jaala, Darkon, Giddel,
[59]Shephatiah, Hattil,
Pokereth-Hazzebaim and Amon

[60]The temple servants and the descendants of the servants of Solomon 392

[61]The following came up from the towns of Tel Melah, Tel Harsha, Kerub, Addon and Immer, but they could not show that their families were descended from Israel:

[62]the descendants of
Delaiah, Tobiah and Nekoda 642

[63]And from among the priests:

the descendants of
Hobaiah, Hakkoz and Barzillai (a man who had married a daughter of Barzillai the Gileadite and was called by that name).

[64]These searched for their family records, but they could not find them and so were excluded from the priesthood as unclean. [65]The governor, therefore, ordered them not to eat any of the most sacred food until there should be a priest ministering with the Urim and Thummim.

[66]The whole company numbered

42,360, 67 besides their 7,337 menservants and maidservants; and they also had 245 men and women singers. 68 There were 736 horses, 245 mules,[a] 69 435 camels and 6,720 donkeys.

70 Some of the heads of the families contributed to the work. The governor gave to the treasury 1,000 drachmas[b] of gold, 50 bowls and 530 garments for priests. 71 Some of the heads of the families gave to the treasury for the work 20,000 drachmas[c] of gold and 2,200 minas[d] of silver. 72 The total given by the rest of the people was 20,000 drachmas of gold, 2,000 minas[e] of silver and 67 garments for priests.

73 The priests, the Levites, the gatekeepers, the singers and the temple servants, along with certain of the people and the rest of the Israelites, settled in their own towns.

Ezra Reads the Law

When the seventh month came and the Israelites had settled in their towns, **8** 1 all the people assembled as one man in the square before the Water Gate. They told Ezra the scribe to bring out the Book of the Law of Moses, which the LORD had commanded for Israel.

2 So on the first day of the seventh month Ezra the priest brought the Law before the assembly, which was made up of men and women and all who were able to understand. 3 He read it aloud from daybreak till noon as he faced the square before the Water Gate in the presence of the men, women and others who could understand. And all the people listened attentively to the Book of the Law.

4 Ezra the scribe stood on a high wooden platform built for the occasion. Beside him on his right stood Mattithiah, Shema, Anaiah, Uriah, Hilkiah and Maaseiah; and on his left were Pedaiah, Mishael, Malkijah, Hashum, Hashbaddanah, Zechariah and Meshullam.

5 Ezra opened the book. All the people could see him because he was standing above them; and as he opened it, the people all stood up. 6 Ezra praised the LORD, the great God; and all the people lifted their hands and responded, "Amen! Amen!" Then they bowed down and worshiped the LORD with their faces to the ground.

7 The Levites—Jeshua, Bani, Sherebiah, Jamin, Akkub, Shabbethai, Hodiah, Maaseiah, Kelita, Azariah, Jozabad, Hanan and Pelaiah—instructed the people in the Law while the people were standing there. 8 They read from the Book of the Law of God, making it clear[f] and giving the meaning so that the people could understand what was being read.

9 Then Nehemiah the governor, Ezra the priest and scribe, and the Levites who were instructing the people said to them all, "This day is sacred to the LORD your God. Do not mourn or weep." For all the people had been weeping as they listened to the words of the Law.

10 Nehemiah said, "Go and enjoy choice food and sweet drinks, and send some to those who have nothing prepared. This day is sacred to our Lord. Do not grieve, for the joy of the LORD is your strength."

11 The Levites calmed all the people, saying, "Be still, for this is a sacred day. Do not grieve."

12 Then all the people went away to eat and drink, to send portions of food and to celebrate with great joy, because they now understood the words that had been made known to them.

13 On the second day of the month, the heads of all the families, along with the priests and the Levites, gathered around Ezra the scribe to give attention to the words of the Law. 14 They found written in the Law, which the LORD had commanded through Moses, that the Israelites were to live in booths during the feast of the seventh month 15 and that they should proclaim this word and spread it throughout their towns and in Jerusalem: "Go out into the hill country and bring back branches from olive and wild olive trees, and from myrtles, palms and shade trees, to make booths"—as it is written.[g]

16 So the people went out and brought back branches and built themselves booths on their own roofs, in their courtyards, in the courts of the house of God and in the square by the Water Gate and the one by the Gate of Ephraim. 17 The whole company that had returned from exile built booths and lived in them. From the

[a] 68 Some Hebrew manuscripts (see also Ezra 2:66); most Hebrew manuscripts do not have this verse. [b] 70 That is, about 19 pounds (about 8.5 kilograms) [c] 71 That is, about 375 pounds (about 170 kilograms); also in verse 72 [d] 71 That is, about 1 1/3 tons (about 1.2 metric tons) [e] 72 That is, about 1 1/4 tons (about 1.1 metric tons) [f] 8 Or *God, translating it* [g] 15 See Lev. 23:37-40.

8:1–5 Ezra took on the task of spiritual renewal in the lives of the citizens. Now that the wall of Jerusalem was rebuilt and its streets were safe, Ezra was able to give attention to the reading of the Law. It is imperative to remember that the Bible contains the directions and resources for rebuilding broken lives. Jesus Christ is the foundation upon which we must build the new life God gives us.

8:7–8 Not only did Ezra engage in the public reading of the Law, he also chose a team that was responsible for the public teaching of the Word. This group of men assisted the people in understanding what God's Word meant. The renewing of our mind also involves the study of God's Word and its application to life. Without the Bible, we would not know God's purpose for our lives or what he wants us to do.

8:12 The people expressed great joy at understanding God's words. They went out rejoicing. They weren't excited about just hearing God's words; they were excited because they *understood* God's words. When we understand God's Word—that he is all powerful, that he loves us, that he sent his Son to die for our sins—we will be filled with great joy too.

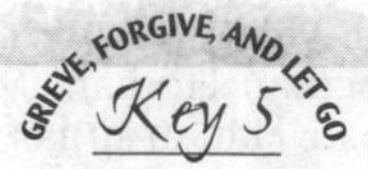

Releasing Our Sorrow Makes Way for Joy

Nehemiah 8:7–10 In order to release the past into God's hands, we must fully encounter our grief, and we must be willing to forgive ourselves and others for the pain that has occurred.

Many of the Jewish exiles who returned to Jerusalem after captivity in Babylon had forgotten the laws of God. During the exile, they hadn't been taught his laws, so, naturally, they hadn't practiced them either. After rebuilding the city wall and the temple, the priests gathered the people together to read the Book of the Law. The people were overwhelmed with grief and began sobbing because their lives in no way measured up. But the priests said to them:

> This day is sacred to the LORD your God. Do not mourn or weep . . . Go and enjoy choice food and sweet drinks, and send some to those who have nothing prepared. This day is sacred to our Lord. Do not grieve, for the joy of the LORD is your strength (8:9–10).

That day marked the beginning of the Feast of Booths, which celebrated the Jews' escape from bondage in Egypt and God's care for them while they wandered in the wilderness.

Although the process of releasing the past may require grief as well as forgiveness, we have been given the "joy of the LORD" as our strength. This joy comes from recognizing, even celebrating, God's ability to set us free from our past, and in doing so, to prepare us for a new way of life.

Turn to Job 14.

days of Joshua son of Nun until that day, the Israelites had not celebrated it like this. And their joy was very great.
18Day after day, from the first day to the last,
Ezra read from the Book of the Law of God. They celebrated the feast for seven days, and on the eighth day, in accordance with the regulation, there was an assembly.

The Israelites Confess Their Sins

9 On the twenty-fourth day of the same month, the Israelites gathered together, fasting and wearing sackcloth and having dust
on their heads. 2Those of Israelite descent had
separated themselves from all foreigners. They stood in their places and confessed their sins
and the wickedness of their fathers. 3They stood
where they were and read from the Book of the Law of the LORD their God for a quarter of the day, and spent another quarter in confession
and in worshiping the LORD their God. 4Stand-
ing on the stairs were the Levites—Jeshua, Bani, Kadmiel, Shebaniah, Bunni, Sherebiah, Bani and Kenani—who called with loud voices to the
LORD their God. 5And the Levites—Jeshua, Kad-
miel, Bani, Hashabneiah, Sherebiah, Hodiah, Shebaniah and Pethahiah—said: "Stand up and praise the LORD your God, who is from everlasting to everlasting.[a]"

"Blessed be your glorious name, and may it be exalted above all blessing and
praise. 6You alone are the LORD. You made
the heavens, even the highest heavens, and all their starry host, the earth and all that is on it, the seas and all that is in them. You give life to everything, and the multitudes of heaven worship you.
7"You are the LORD God, who chose
Abram and brought him out of Ur of the Chaldeans and named him Abraham.
8You found his heart faithful to you, and
you made a covenant with him to give to his descendants the land of the Canaanites, Hittites, Amorites, Perizzites, Jebusites and Girgashites. You have kept your promise because you are righteous.
9"You saw the suffering of our forefa-
thers in Egypt; you heard their cry at the
Red Sea.[b] 10You sent miraculous signs

[a]5 Or *God for ever and ever* [b]9 Hebrew *Yam Suph;* that is, Sea of Reeds

9:1–3 The people's fresh understanding of the Bible brought about their repentance. They confessed their sins and expressed deep sorrow for disobeying God. They also confessed the sins of their ancestors—a necessary step for us as well if we are to break sinful family patterns. When we repent, we recognize and admit our disobedience, and we resolve to change course and walk in God's paths. It is only by repenting that we can truly surrender our lives to God.

9:4–38 In these verses we read words of praise to God. As the Levites sang this beautiful hymn, they gloried in the person of God—who he is and what he has done. We can gain much by making these words of praise our own.

Repentance That Touches the Past

Nehemiah 9:1–38 Many Americans admire those who practice a rugged individualism. But in our emphasis upon individual freedoms, we often lose sight of our corporate responsibilities. As Christians, we are individuals who are also part of a greater people. We are called to benefit from the work of others, to suffer with others and to bear responsibility with others. While it may not seem fair, our ties reach back to Adam and Eve. Adam's sin brought condemnation upon everyone (see Romans 5:12). This principle of corporate connection not only makes our salvation necessary but also makes salvation possible through our unity with Christ. "Just as the result of one trespass was condemnation for all men, so also the result of one act of righteousness was justification that brings life for all men. For just as through the disobedience of the one man the many were made sinners, so also through the obedience of the one man the many will be made righteous" (Romans 5:18–19).

When the Israelites returned from exile, they had to rebuild not only their cities but also their relationship with God. Even as they had to clear the land in order to lay new foundations, so the people had to reestablish their relationship with God by clearing away the rubble of sin that had plagued them for generations. They had suffered not only because of their own sin but also because of the sin of their ancestors. Therefore, when they made confession, they repented not only for themselves but also for those who had gone before.

This repentance originated with instruction from God's Word. As the people understood what God required of them and realized how they had sinned, they were overcome with grief. In their repentant grief, however, the people heard the good news of grace. This revived and renewed their love for God and their desire to obey him.

For more on repentance and confession, turn to Psalm 32.

Putting It Into Practice

In light of this passage, we should gain a new sense of responsibility toward the larger communities to which we belong. Consider how you have been affected by the sins of your family, community or nation. Write a prayer of confession that enumerates these "we" sins, both past and present.

Also consider the sins of your own lifetime. In addition to confessing daily sins, strive to recognize and release significant life-pattern sins. It is often easiest to identify these by looking at the various stages of your life, possibly taking five to ten years at a time, and considering what struggles and mistakes you have repeatedly encountered. Ask God to bring to mind any sins you have committed so that you may confess and release them. Confession is a powerful, demanding exercise, not to be undertaken by the fainthearted. But seeing God's mercy cover all our sin can be one of the most liberating experiences of the soul.

and wonders against Pharaoh, against all his officials and all the people of his land, for you knew how arrogantly the Egyptians treated them. You made a name for yourself, which remains to this day. 11You divided the sea before them, so that they passed through it on dry ground, but you hurled their pursuers into the depths, like a stone into mighty waters. 12By day you led them with a pillar of cloud, and by night with a pillar of fire to give them light on the way they were to take.

13"You came down on Mount Sinai; you spoke to them from heaven. You gave them regulations and laws that are just and right, and decrees and commands that are good. 14You made known to them your holy Sabbath and gave them commands, decrees and laws through your servant Moses. 15In their hunger you gave them bread from heaven and in their thirst you brought them water from the rock; you told them to go in and take possession of the land you had sworn with uplifted hand to give them.

16"But they, our forefathers, became arrogant and stiff-necked, and did not obey your commands. 17They refused to listen and failed to remember the miracles you performed among them. They became stiff-necked and in their rebellion appointed a leader in order to return to their slavery. But you are a forgiving God, gracious and compassionate, slow to anger and abounding in love. Therefore you did not desert them, 18even when they cast for themselves an image of a calf and said, 'This is your god, who brought you up out of Egypt,' or when they committed awful blasphemies.

19"Because of your great compassion you did not abandon them in the desert. By day the pillar of cloud did not cease to guide them on their path, nor the pillar of fire by night to shine on the way they were to take. 20You gave your good Spirit to instruct them. You did not withhold your manna from their mouths, and you gave them water for their thirst. 21For forty years you sustained them in the desert; they lacked nothing, their clothes did not wear out nor did their feet become swollen.

22"You gave them kingdoms and nations, allotting to them even the remotest frontiers. They took over the country of Sihon[a] king of Heshbon and the country of Og king of Bashan. 23You made their sons as numerous as the stars in the sky, and you brought them into the land that you told their fathers to enter and possess. 24Their sons went in and took possession of the land. You subdued before them the Canaanites, who lived in the land; you handed the Canaanites over to them, along with their kings and the peoples of the land, to deal with them as they pleased. 25They captured fortified cities and fertile land; they took possession of houses filled with all kinds of good things, wells already dug, vineyards, olive groves and fruit trees in abundance. They ate to the full and were well-nourished; they reveled in your great goodness.

26"But they were disobedient and rebelled against you; they put your law behind their backs. They killed your prophets, who had admonished them in order to turn them back to you; they committed awful blasphemies. 27So you handed them over to their enemies, who oppressed them. But when they were oppressed they cried out to you. From heaven you heard them, and in your great compassion you gave them deliverers, who rescued them from the hand of their enemies.

28"But as soon as they were at rest, they again did what was evil in your sight. Then you abandoned them to the hand of their enemies so that they ruled over them. And when they cried out to you again, you heard from heaven, and in your compassion you delivered them time after time.

29"You warned them to return to your law, but they became arrogant and disobeyed your commands. They sinned against your ordinances, by which a man will live if he obeys them. Stubbornly they turned their backs on you, became stiff-necked and refused to listen. 30For many years you were patient with them. By your Spirit you admonished them through your prophets. Yet they paid no attention, so you handed them over to the neighboring peoples. 31But in your great mercy you did not put an end to them or abandon them, for you are a gracious and merciful God.

32"Now therefore, O our God, the great, mighty and awesome God, who keeps his covenant of love, do not let all this hardship seem trifling in your eyes—the hardship that has come upon us, upon our kings and leaders, upon our priests and prophets, upon our fathers and all your people, from the days of the kings of Assyria until today. 33In all that has happened to us, you have been just; you have acted faithfully, while we did wrong. 34Our kings, our leaders, our priests and our fathers did not follow your law; they did not pay attention to your commands or the warnings you gave them. 35Even while they were in their kingdom, enjoying your great goodness to them in the

[a] *22* One Hebrew manuscript and Septuagint; most Hebrew manuscripts *Sihon, that is, the country of the*

spacious and fertile land you gave them,
they did not serve you or turn from their
evil ways.
36"But see, we are slaves today, slaves
in the land you gave our forefathers so
they could eat its fruit and the other good
things it produces. 37Because of our sins,
its abundant harvest goes to the kings you
have placed over us. They rule over our
bodies and our cattle as they please. We
are in great distress.

The Agreement of the People

38"In view of all this, we are making a binding agreement, putting it in writing, and our
leaders, our Levites and our priests are affixing
their seals to it."

10 Those who sealed it were:

Nehemiah the governor, the son of Hacaliah.

Zedekiah, 2Seraiah, Azariah, Jeremiah,
3Pashhur, Amariah, Malkijah,
4Hattush, Shebaniah, Malluch,
5Harim, Meremoth, Obadiah,
6Daniel, Ginnethon, Baruch,
7Meshullam, Abijah, Mijamin,
8Maaziah, Bilgai and Shemaiah.
These were the priests.

9The Levites:

Jeshua son of Azaniah, Binnui of the sons of Henadad, Kadmiel,
10and their associates: Shebaniah,
Hodiah, Kelita, Pelaiah, Hanan,
11Mica, Rehob, Hashabiah,
12Zaccur, Sherebiah, Shebaniah,
13Hodiah, Bani and Beninu.

14The leaders of the people:

Parosh, Pahath-Moab, Elam, Zattu, Bani,
15Bunni, Azgad, Bebai,
16Adonijah, Bigvai, Adin,
17Ater, Hezekiah, Azzur,
18Hodiah, Hashum, Bezai,
19Hariph, Anathoth, Nebai,
20Magpiash, Meshullam, Hezir,
21Meshezabel, Zadok, Jaddua,
22Pelatiah, Hanan, Anaiah,
23Hoshea, Hananiah, Hasshub,
24Hallohesh, Pilha, Shobek,
25Rehum, Hashabnah, Maaseiah,
26Ahiah, Hanan, Anan,
27Malluch, Harim and Baanah.

28"The rest of the people—priests, Levites, gatekeepers, singers, temple servants
and all who separated themselves from
the neighboring peoples for the sake of
the Law of God, together with their wives
and all their sons and daughters who are
able to understand— 29all these now join
their brothers the nobles, and bind themselves with a curse and an oath to follow
the Law of God given through Moses the
servant of God and to obey carefully all
the commands, regulations and decrees of
the LORD our Lord.
30"We promise not to give our daughters in marriage to the peoples around us
or take their daughters for our sons.
31"When the neighboring peoples
bring merchandise or grain to sell on the
Sabbath, we will not buy from them on
the Sabbath or on any holy day. Every seventh year we will forgo working the land
and will cancel all debts.
32"We assume the responsibility for
carrying out the commands to give a third
of a shekel[a] each year for the service of
the house of our God: 33for the bread set
out on the table; for the regular grain offerings and burnt offerings; for the offerings on the Sabbaths, New Moon festivals
and appointed feasts; for the holy offerings; for sin offerings to make atonement
for Israel; and for all the duties of the
house of our God.
34"We—the priests, the Levites and the
people—have cast lots to determine when
each of our families is to bring to the
house of our God at set times each year a
contribution of wood to burn on the altar
of the LORD our God, as it is written in the
Law.
35"We also assume responsibility for
bringing to the house of the LORD each
year the firstfruits of our crops and of every fruit tree.
36"As it is also written in the Law, we
will bring the firstborn of our sons and of
our cattle, of our herds and of our flocks
to the house of our God, to the priests
ministering there.
37"Moreover, we will bring to the storerooms of the house of our God, to the
priests, the first of our ground meal, of our
⌊grain⌋ offerings, of the fruit of all our
trees and of our new wine and oil. And we
will bring a tithe of our crops to the Levites, for it is the Levites who collect the
tithes in all the towns where we work. 38A
priest descended from Aaron is to accompany the Levites when they receive the
tithes, and the Levites are to bring a tenth
of the tithes up to the house of our God,

[a]32 That is, about 1/8 ounce (about 4 grams)

9:38 God's people need a specific structure of accountability. To establish such accountability, the religious leaders in Israel formally wrote out this pact. The leaders pledged themselves to be accountable to God and to each other. We must not be isolated in our spiritual walk. We need others to encourage us, give us direction and pray for us.

to the storerooms of the treasury. 39 The people of Israel, including the Levites, are to bring their contributions of grain, new wine and oil to the storerooms where the articles for the sanctuary are kept and where the ministering priests, the gatekeepers and the singers stay.

"We will not neglect the house of our God."

The New Residents of Jerusalem

11 Now the leaders of the people settled in Jerusalem, and the rest of the people cast lots to bring one out of every ten to live in Jerusalem, the holy city, while the remaining nine were to stay in their own towns. 2 The people commended all the men who volunteered to live in Jerusalem.

3 These are the provincial leaders who settled in Jerusalem (now some Israelites, priests, Levites, temple servants and descendants of Solomon's servants lived in the towns of Judah, each on his own property in the various towns, 4 while other people from both Judah and Benjamin lived in Jerusalem):

From the descendants of Judah:

Athaiah son of Uzziah, the son of Zechariah, the son of Amariah, the son of Shephatiah, the son of Mahalalel, a descendant of Perez; 5 and Maaseiah son of Baruch, the son of Col-Hozeh, the son of Hazaiah, the son of Adaiah, the son of Joiarib, the son of Zechariah, a descendant of Shelah. 6 The descendants of Perez who lived in Jerusalem totaled 468 able men.

7 From the descendants of Benjamin:

Sallu son of Meshullam, the son of Joed, the son of Pedaiah, the son of Kolaiah, the son of Maaseiah, the son of Ithiel, the son of Jeshaiah, 8 and his followers, Gabbai and Sallai—928 men. 9 Joel son of Zicri was their chief officer, and Judah son of Hassenuah was over the Second District of the city.

10 From the priests:

Jedaiah; the son of Joiarib; Jakin; 11 Seraiah son of Hilkiah, the son of Meshullam, the son of Zadok, the son of Meraioth, the son of Ahitub, supervisor in the house of God, 12 and their associates, who carried on work for the temple—822 men; Adaiah son of Jeroham, the son of Pelaliah, the son of Amzi, the son of Zechariah, the son of Pashhur, the son of Malkijah, 13 and his associates, who were heads of families—242 men; Amashsai son of Azarel, the son of Ahzai, the son of Meshillemoth, the son of Immer, 14 and his[a] associates, who were able men—128. Their chief officer was Zabdiel son of Haggedolim.

15 From the Levites:

Shemaiah son of Hasshub, the son of Azrikam, the son of Hashabiah, the son of Bunni; 16 Shabbethai and Jozabad, two of the heads of the Levites, who had charge of the outside work of the house of God; 17 Mattaniah son of Mica, the son of Zabdi, the son of Asaph, the director who led in thanksgiving and prayer; Bakbukiah, second among his associates; and Abda son of Shammua, the son of Galal, the son of Jeduthun. 18 The Levites in the holy city totaled 284.

19 The gatekeepers:

Akkub, Talmon and their associates, who kept watch at the gates—172 men.

20 The rest of the Israelites, with the priests and Levites, were in all the towns of Judah, each on his ancestral property.

21 The temple servants lived on the hill of Ophel, and Ziha and Gishpa were in charge of them.

22 The chief officer of the Levites in Jerusalem was Uzzi son of Bani, the son of Hashabiah, the son of Mattaniah, the son of Mica. Uzzi was one of Asaph's descendants, who were the singers responsible for the service of the house of God. 23 The singers were under the king's orders, which regulated their daily activity.

24 Pethahiah son of Meshezabel, one of the descendants of Zerah son of Judah, was the king's agent in all affairs relating to the people.

25 As for the villages with their fields, some of the people of Judah lived in Kiriath Arba and its surrounding settlements, in Dibon and its settlements, in Jekabzeel and its villages, 26 in Jeshua, in Moladah, in Beth Pelet, 27 in Hazar Shual, in Beersheba and its settlements, 28 in Ziklag, in Meconah and its settlements, 29 in En Rimmon, in Zorah, in Jarmuth, 30 Zanoah, Adullam and their villages, in Lachish and its fields, and in Azekah and its settlements. So they were living all the way from Beersheba to the Valley of Hinnom.

31 The descendants of the Benjamites from Geba lived in Micmash, Aija, Bethel and its settlements, 32 in Anathoth, Nob and Ananiah, 33 in Hazor, Ramah and Gittaim, 34 in Hadid, Zeboim and Neballat, 35 in Lod and Ono, and in the Valley of the Craftsmen.

[a] 14 Most Septuagint manuscripts; Hebrew *their*

10:39 The people agreed not to neglect the temple, God's dwelling place among them. We have a temple to care for too—our body. "Do you not know that your body is a temple of the Holy Spirit, who is in you, whom you have received from God? You are not your own" (1 Corinthians 6:19). We should take care of our bodies and treat them with respect because the Holy Spirit lives in them. To mistreat our bodies is to mistreat God's own dwelling place.

36 Some of the divisions of the Levites of Judah settled in Benjamin.

Priests and Levites

12 These were the priests and Levites who
returned with Zerubbabel son of Shealtiel and with Jeshua:
Seraiah, Jeremiah, Ezra,
2 Amariah, Malluch, Hattush,
3 Shecaniah, Rehum, Meremoth,
4 Iddo, Ginnethon,[a] Abijah,
5 Mijamin,[b] Moadiah, Bilgah,
6 Shemaiah, Joiarib, Jedaiah,
7 Sallu, Amok, Hilkiah and Jedaiah.
These were the leaders of the priests and their
associates in the days of Jeshua.
8 The Levites were Jeshua, Binnui, Kadmiel,
Sherebiah, Judah, and also Mattaniah, who, together with his associates, was in charge of the
songs of thanksgiving. 9 Bakbukiah and Unni,
their associates, stood opposite them in the services.
10 Jeshua was the father of Joiakim, Joiakim
the father of Eliashib, Eliashib the father of Joiada, 11 Joiada the father of Jonathan, and Jonathan the father of Jaddua.
12 In the days of Joiakim, these were the heads
of the priestly families:
of Seraiah's family, Meraiah;
of Jeremiah's, Hananiah;
13 of Ezra's, Meshullam;
of Amariah's, Jehohanan;
14 of Malluch's, Jonathan;
of Shecaniah's,[c] Joseph;
15 of Harim's, Adna;
of Meremoth's,[d] Helkai;
16 of Iddo's, Zechariah;
of Ginnethon's, Meshullam;
17 of Abijah's, Zicri;
of Miniamin's and of Moadiah's, Piltai;
18 of Bilgah's, Shammua;
of Shemaiah's, Jehonathan;
19 of Joiarib's, Mattenai;
of Jedaiah's, Uzzi;
20 of Sallu's, Kallai;
of Amok's, Eber;
21 of Hilkiah's, Hashabiah;
of Jedaiah's, Nethanel.
22 The family heads of the Levites in the days
of Eliashib, Joiada, Johanan and Jaddua, as well
as those of the priests, were recorded in the
reign of Darius the Persian. 23 The family heads
among the descendants of Levi up to the time
of Johanan son of Eliashib were recorded in the
book of the annals. 24 And the leaders of the
Levites were Hashabiah, Sherebiah, Jeshua son
of Kadmiel, and their associates, who stood opposite them to give praise and thanksgiving,
one section responding to the other, as prescribed by David the man of God.
25 Mattaniah, Bakbukiah, Obadiah, Meshullam, Talmon and Akkub were gatekeepers who
guarded the storerooms at the gates. 26 They
served in the days of Joiakim son of Jeshua, the
son of Jozadak, and in the days of Nehemiah
the governor and of Ezra the priest and scribe.

Dedication of the Wall of Jerusalem

27 At the dedication of the wall of Jerusalem,
the Levites were sought out from where they
lived and were brought to Jerusalem to celebrate joyfully the dedication with songs of
thanksgiving and with the music of cymbals,
harps and lyres. 28 The singers also were brought
together from the region around Jerusalem—
from the villages of the Netophathites, 29 from
Beth Gilgal, and from the area of Geba and
Azmaveth, for the singers had built villages for
themselves around Jerusalem. 30 When the
priests and Levites had purified themselves ceremonially, they purified the people, the gates
and the wall.
31 I had the leaders of Judah go up on top[e]
of the wall. I also assigned two large choirs to
give thanks. One was to proceed on top[f] of the
wall to the right, toward the Dung Gate. 32 Hoshaiah and half the leaders of Judah followed
them, 33 along with Azariah, Ezra, Meshullam,
34 Judah, Benjamin, Shemaiah, Jeremiah, 35 as
well as some priests with trumpets, and also
Zechariah son of Jonathan, the son of Shemaiah, the son of Mattaniah, the son of Micaiah,
the son of Zaccur, the son of Asaph, 36 and his
associates—Shemaiah, Azarel, Milalai, Gilalai,
Maai, Nethanel, Judah and Hanani—with musical instruments ⌞prescribed by⌟ David the man
of God. Ezra the scribe led the procession. 37 At
the Fountain Gate they continued directly up
the steps of the City of David on the ascent to
the wall and passed above the house of David
to the Water Gate on the east.
38 The second choir proceeded in the opposite direction. I followed them on top[g] of the
wall, together with half the people—past the
Tower of the Ovens to the Broad Wall, 39 over
the Gate of Ephraim, the Jeshanah[h] Gate, the
Fish Gate, the Tower of Hananel and the Tower
of the Hundred, as far as the Sheep Gate. At the
Gate of the Guard they stopped.
40 The two choirs that gave thanks then took

[a] *4* Many Hebrew manuscripts and Vulgate (see also Neh. 12:16); most Hebrew manuscripts *Ginnethoi* [b] *5* A variant of *Miniamin* [c] *14* Very many Hebrew manuscripts, some Septuagint manuscripts and Syriac (see also Neh. 12:3); most Hebrew manuscripts *Shebaniah's* [d] *15* Some Septuagint manuscripts (see also Neh. 12:3); Hebrew *Meraioth's* [e] *31* Or *go alongside* [f] *31* Or *proceed alongside* [g] *38* Or *them alongside* [h] *39* Or *Old*

12:27 As God's people, we have the privilege and reason to celebrate. All of the worship leaders were called upon to come to Jerusalem to dedicate the new wall. This would be the most joyous occasion in Israel in over half a century! We should take time to joyfully celebrate what God has done in us too and to dedicate ourselves to his service.

their places in the house of God; so did I, together with half the officials, 41as well as the
priests—Eliakim, Maaseiah, Miniamin, Micaiah,
Elioenai, Zechariah and Hananiah with their
trumpets— 42and also Maaseiah, Shemaiah,
Eleazar, Uzzi, Jehohanan, Malkijah, Elam and
Ezer. The choirs sang under the direction of
Jezrahiah. 43And on that day they offered great
sacrifices, rejoicing because God had given
them great joy. The women and children also
rejoiced. The sound of rejoicing in Jerusalem
could be heard far away.

44At that time men were appointed to be in
charge of the storerooms for the contributions,
firstfruits and tithes. From the fields around the
towns they were to bring into the storerooms
the portions required by the Law for the priests
and the Levites, for Judah was pleased with the
ministering priests and Levites. 45They performed the service of their God and the service
of purification, as did also the singers and gatekeepers, according to the commands of David
and his son Solomon. 46For long ago, in the
days of David and Asaph, there had been direc-
tors for the singers and for the songs of praise
and thanksgiving to God. 47So in the days of
Zerubbabel and of Nehemiah, all Israel contributed the daily portions for the singers and gatekeepers. They also set aside the portion for the
other Levites, and the Levites set aside the portion for the descendants of Aaron.

Nehemiah's Final Reforms

13 On that day the Book of Moses was
read aloud in the hearing of the people
and there it was found written that no Ammonite or Moabite should ever be admitted into the
assembly of God, 2because they had not met the
Israelites with food and water but had hired
Balaam to call a curse down on them. (Our
God, however, turned the curse into a blessing.)
3When the people heard this law, they excluded
from Israel all who were of foreign descent.

4Before this, Eliashib the priest had been put
in charge of the storerooms of the house of our
God. He was closely associated with Tobiah,
5and he had provided him with a large room
formerly used to store the grain offerings and
incense and temple articles, and also the tithes
of grain, new wine and oil prescribed for the
Levites, singers and gatekeepers, as well as the
contributions for the priests.

6But while all this was going on, I was not in
Jerusalem, for in the thirty-second year of Artax-
erxes king of Babylon I had returned to the king.
Some time later I asked his permission 7and
came back to Jerusalem. Here I learned about
the evil thing Eliashib had done in providing
Tobiah a room in the courts of the house of
God. 8I was greatly displeased and threw all
Tobiah's household goods out of the room. 9I
gave orders to purify the rooms, and then I put
back into them the equipment of the house of
God, with the grain offerings and the incense.

10I also learned that the portions assigned to
the Levites had not been given to them, and that
all the Levites and singers responsible for the
service had gone back to their own fields. 11So
I rebuked the officials and asked them, "Why is
the house of God neglected?" Then I called them
together and stationed them at their posts.

12All Judah brought the tithes of grain, new
wine and oil into the storerooms. 13I put Shelemiah the priest, Zadok the scribe, and a Levite
named Pedaiah in charge of the storerooms and
made Hanan son of Zaccur, the son of Mattaniah, their assistant, because these men were considered trustworthy. They were made responsible for distributing the supplies to their
brothers.

14Remember me for this, O my God, and do
not blot out what I have so faithfully done for
the house of my God and its services.

15In those days I saw men in Judah treading
winepresses on the Sabbath and bringing in
grain and loading it on donkeys, together with
wine, grapes, figs and all other kinds of loads.
And they were bringing all this into Jerusalem
on the Sabbath. Therefore I warned them
against selling food on that day. 16Men from
Tyre who lived in Jerusalem were bringing in
fish and all kinds of merchandise and selling
them in Jerusalem on the Sabbath to the people
of Judah. 17I rebuked the nobles of Judah and
said to them, "What is this wicked thing you are
doing—desecrating the Sabbath day? 18Didn't
your forefathers do the same things, so that our
God brought all this calamity upon us and
upon this city? Now you are stirring up more
wrath against Israel by desecrating the Sabbath."

19When evening shadows fell on the gates of
Jerusalem before the Sabbath, I ordered the
doors to be shut and not opened until the Sabbath was over. I stationed some of my own men

---

13:1–3, 23–30 Through the nation of Israel, God intended to bring salvation to the world. It was necessary for the Israelites to remain pure. They were not to mix with the godless population around them; certain peoples were not to be allowed at the temple. However, over the years, some of the people had intermarried with foreign nations. Nehemiah had to remove the pagan people so that they would not lead Israel astray. Our spiritual growth is either strengthened or weakened by our relationships. We need to guard ourselves against relationships that draw us away from God's plans for us.

13:4–9 Open union with God's enemies is never an acceptable course of action. In this case, one of the temple administrators provided a room within the temple for Tobiah, one of Nehemiah's chief opponents. At this strategic location in the very heart of Jerusalem, Tobiah could have undermined God's authority and leadership in the Israelites' lives. We must be careful not to allow people into our lives who would lead us away from God.

13:14, 31 Nehemiah was a great rebuilder. He reconstructed the wall of Jerusalem and helped the people rebuild their broken lives too. God honored this good and faithful servant! God will honor our attempts to rebuild too.

at the gates so that no load could be brought in
on the Sabbath day. 20Once or twice the merchants and sellers of all kinds of goods spent the
night outside Jerusalem. 21But I warned them
and said, "Why do you spend the night by the
wall? If you do this again, I will lay hands on
you." From that time on they no longer came on
the Sabbath. 22Then I commanded the Levites
to purify themselves and go and guard the gates
in order to keep the Sabbath day holy.

Remember me for this also, O my God, and
show mercy to me according to your great love.

23Moreover, in those days I saw men of Judah
who had married women from Ashdod, Ammon and Moab. 24Half of their children spoke
the language of Ashdod or the language of one
of the other peoples, and did not know how to
speak the language of Judah. 25I rebuked them
and called curses down on them. I beat some of
the men and pulled out their hair. I made them
take an oath in God's name and said: "You are
not to give your daughters in marriage to their
sons, nor are you to take their daughters in
marriage for your sons or for yourselves. 26Was
it not because of marriages like these that Solomon king of Israel sinned? Among the many
nations there was no king like him. He was
loved by his God, and God made him king over
all Israel, but even he was led into sin by foreign
women. 27Must we hear now that you too are
doing all this terrible wickedness and are being
unfaithful to our God by marrying foreign
women?"

28One of the sons of Joiada son of Eliashib
the high priest was son-in-law to Sanballat the
Horonite. And I drove him away from me.

29Remember them, O my God, because they
defiled the priestly office and the covenant of
the priesthood and of the Levites.

30So I purified the priests and the Levites of
everything foreign, and assigned them duties,
each to his own task. 31I also made provision for
contributions of wood at designated times, and
for the firstfruits.

Remember me with favor, O my God.

Esther

The Big Picture

A. *ESTHER BECOMES QUEEN (1:1–2:23)*

1. Dethroning of Vashti (1:1-22)
2. Crowning of Esther (2:1-23)

B. *A THREAT AGAINST GOD'S PEOPLE (3:1–7:10)*

1. The Rise of the Enemy of God's People (3:1-15)
2. The Commitment of the Leader of God's People (4:1–5:14)
3. The Fall of the Enemy of God's People (6:1–7:10)

C. *MORDECAI SECURES THEIR FUTURE (8:1–10:3)*

1. The Plan of a Rescue Operation (8:1-17)
2. The Process of a Rescue Operation (9:1-32)
3. The Product of a Rescue Operation (10:1-3)

The book of Esther tells a story about God's loving care for his people during the Babylonian exile. Although a few Jews had returned to Jerusalem with Zerubbabel to rebuild the temple, the majority of exiled Jews remained in Babylonia. Esther was raised within this Jewish community in exile. King Xerxes deposed his queen because of her disobedience to him. The king later held a contest to find a new queen. Esther was chosen to fill that role.

Soon after Esther became queen, the king appointed Haman, an Agagite, to the position of second-in-command. All people in the empire were expected to bow down to him to show him respect. Mordecai, Esther's cousin, refused to bow down to Haman. This so enraged Haman that he persuaded the king to enact an irrevocable edict sentencing all Jews to death. Neither the king nor Haman knew that Esther was among the people doomed by the edict. Through Mordecai's prodding, Esther secured the king's favor to deliver her people and brought about Haman's demise.

In the Hebrew Bible, God's name never actually appears in this story. Yet throughout the book we see God's quiet, effective activity behind the scenes, working through different individuals who were willing to trust him. God brought Esther to a position of influence at the right time and gave her the courage to act. Esther could have remained selfishly silent. Instead, she risked her life and became an instrument of great deliverance. Even though God's presence is not always obvious in our lives, we can be sure that he is there, behind the scenes, working to lead us to the future he desires for us.

Spiritual Renewal Themes

HOPE FOR THE HELPLESS

When we recognize that we do not have the power to solve our problems alone, we are in a place of great opportunity. Facing our difficulties squarely, we are most likely to seek God and surrender to him. This was exactly the experience of Esther, Mordecai and the Jews during their exile under Persian rule. They were the captives. Their lives were out of their own control and under the control of Persian rulers. In the midst of this helpless situation, God worked through Esther and Mordecai to

bring amazing deliverance to his people. When we put ourselves in God's hands, we open the door to God's power.

GOD'S FAITHFULNESS
When we seek God and surrender our lives and our wills to him, we can take courage. We can expect him to carry out his will in our lives in spite of our doubts. One of the great lessons we can learn from the book of Esther is the realization that God acts on our behalf even when we are unaware of what he is doing. He is a God who can be trusted to underwrite our spiritual renewal. Even when we are faithless, he always remains faithful!

THE EMPTINESS OF HATRED
Racial prejudice and hatred were driving forces in Haman's life. In the blindness of his own hatred, Haman determined his own punishment and died the death he had planned for the one he despised—Mordecai. Racial hatred is always sinful because it denies the intrinsic value of God's creation. When we hate others in this way, we end up with an emptiness that brings about our own destruction through bitterness and isolation.

DEALING WITH PRESSURES
It takes great wisdom and patience to survive in a world that is not concerned about God or with our own health and welfare. Mordecai shows us how to live under the rule of a pagan government while resisting the pressures around us and refusing to compromise our integrity.

Essential Facts

PURPOSE:
To demonstrate God's loving care for his people and his sovereignty over history and to record the origins of the Jewish holiday of Purim.

AUTHOR:
Unknown, but Mordecai or Ezra may have written it.

AUDIENCE:
The people of Israel after the Babylonian exile.

DATE WRITTEN:
Approximately 470 B.C.; Esther became queen in 479 B.C.

SETTING:
In Susa, the capital of the Medo-Persian empire.

KEY VERSE:
"If you remain silent at this time, relief and deliverance for the Jews will arise from another place, but you and your father's family will perish. And who knows but that you have come to royal position for such a time as this?" (4:14).

KEY PEOPLE AND RELATIONSHIPS:
Esther and Mordecai, Haman, King Xerxes, Queen Vashti.

Queen Vashti Deposed

1 This is what happened during the time of Xerxes,[a] the Xerxes who ruled over 127 provinces stretching from India to Cush[b]: 2At that time King Xerxes reigned from his royal throne in the citadel of Susa, 3and in the third year of his reign he gave a banquet for all his nobles and officials. The military leaders of Persia and Media, the princes, and the nobles of the provinces were present.

4For a full 180 days he displayed the vast wealth of his kingdom and the splendor and glory of his majesty. 5When these days were over, the king gave a banquet, lasting seven days, in the enclosed garden of the king's palace, for all the people from the least to the greatest, who were in the citadel of Susa. 6The garden had hangings of white and blue linen, fastened with cords of white linen and purple material to silver rings on marble pillars. There were couches of gold and silver on a mosaic pavement of porphyry, marble, mother-of-pearl and other costly stones. 7Wine was served in goblets of gold, each one different from the other, and the royal wine was abundant, in keeping with the king's liberality. 8By the king's command each guest was allowed to drink in his own way, for the king instructed all the wine stewards to serve each man what he wished.

9Queen Vashti also gave a banquet for the women in the royal palace of King Xerxes.

10On the seventh day, when King Xerxes was in high spirits from wine, he commanded the seven eunuchs who served him—Mehuman, Biztha, Harbona, Bigtha, Abagtha, Zethar and Carcas— 11to bring before him Queen Vashti, wearing her royal crown, in order to display her beauty to the people and nobles, for she was lovely to look at. 12But when the attendants delivered the king's command, Queen Vashti refused to come. Then the king became furious and burned with anger.

13Since it was customary for the king to consult experts in matters of law and justice, he spoke with the wise men who understood the times 14and were closest to the king—Carshena, Shethar, Admatha, Tarshish, Meres, Marsena and Memucan, the seven nobles of Persia and Media who had special access to the king and were highest in the kingdom.

15"According to law, what must be done to Queen Vashti?" he asked. "She has not obeyed the command of King Xerxes that the eunuchs have taken to her."

16Then Memucan replied in the presence of the king and the nobles, "Queen Vashti has done wrong, not only against the king but also against all the nobles and the peoples of all the provinces of King Xerxes. 17For the queen's conduct will become known to all the women, and so they will despise their husbands and say, 'King Xerxes commanded Queen Vashti to be brought before him, but she would not come.' 18This very day the Persian and Median women of the nobility who have heard about the queen's conduct will respond to all the king's nobles in the same way. There will be no end of disrespect and discord.

19"Therefore, if it pleases the king, let him issue a royal decree and let it be written in the laws of Persia and Media, which cannot be repealed, that Vashti is never again to enter the presence of King Xerxes. Also let the king give her royal position to someone else who is better than she. 20Then when the king's edict is proclaimed throughout all his vast realm, all the women will respect their husbands, from the least to the greatest."

21The king and his nobles were pleased with this advice, so the king did as Memucan proposed. 22He sent dispatches to all parts of the kingdom, to each province in its own script and to each people in its own language, proclaiming in each people's tongue that every man should be ruler over his own household.

Esther Made Queen

2 Later when the anger of King Xerxes had subsided, he remembered Vashti and what she had done and what he had decreed about her. 2Then the king's personal attendants proposed, "Let a search be made for beautiful young virgins for the king. 3Let the king appoint commissioners in every province of his realm to bring all these beautiful girls into the harem at the citadel of Susa. Let them be placed under the care of Hegai, the king's eunuch, who is in charge of the women; and let beauty treatments be given to them. 4Then let the girl who pleases the king be queen instead of Vashti." This advice appealed to the king, and he followed it.

5Now there was in the citadel of Susa a Jew of the tribe of Benjamin, named Mordecai son of Jair, the son of Shimei, the son of Kish, 6who had been carried into exile from Jerusalem by Nebuchadnezzar king of Babylon, among those taken captive with Jehoiachin[c] king of Judah. 7Mordecai had a cousin named Hadassah, whom he had brought up because she had neither father nor mother. This girl, who was also known as Esther, was lovely in form and

[a] 1 Hebrew *Ahasuerus,* a variant of Xerxes' Persian name; here and throughout Esther [b] 1 That is, the upper Nile region [c] 6 Hebrew *Jeconiah,* a variant of *Jehoiachin*

1:16–22 Anxious to please his allies, King Xerxes had made an unwise request of Vashti and now had to live with the consequences of his impulsive demand. His advisers evaluated the situation regarding Vashti's disobedience and, realizing the far-reaching effects that such an act could have, suggested that quick and final action be taken at once. King Xerxes' situation provides a stirring example for us. We need to carefully evaluate the requests we make of others, realizing that we may be compromising their rights or desires.

THE SPIRITUAL DISCIPLINES

In the Life of Esther

Esther's life is an example of how employing the spiritual disciplines during a time of crisis can help us keep our eyes focused on God's desires. By remembering her true purpose and calling as one of God's people, Esther was able to save her people from total destruction.

Esther faced some significant disadvantages from the start. First, she was a Jew living in exile in Persia. This meant that Esther and her people were often at the mercy of their pagan rulers. Haman's decree to destroy the Jews would have meant the virtual annihilation of Esther's people. Also, she was a woman. In ancient Near Eastern society a woman was virtually powerless. In such situations, most of us would be too fearful or despondent to take action. But Esther, relying on spiritual disciplines she had learned as a child, placed her trust in God's sovereignty and depended on him to save her people.

FASTING. As Esther contemplated how best to help her people, her first move was to call for the spiritual discipline of a fast (see Esther 4:16). Esther's call for an extended fast of three days with neither food nor water immediately communicated the urgency of the situation. Presumably this fasting also involved prayer for Esther as she prepared to approach King Xerxes, that God would preserve her life and grant her people deliverance. (To learn more about fasting, turn to 2 Chronicles 20.)

SERVICE. Esther also practiced the discipline of service. As Esther served King Xerxes, she was actually serving her people and God, preparing the king to be receptive to her request to deliver her people. She combined the shrewdness of a snake with the innocence of a dove ultimately to accomplish God's purposes (see Matthew 10:16). Esther's intercession for her people could have brought about her death, but she selflessly responded, "If I perish, I perish" (Esther 4:16). This echoes Jesus' words in the New Testament: "Greater love has no one than this, that he lay down his life for his friends" (John 15:13).

Lessons for Life

What is your first response in a crisis? Esther reached out to her community, calling them to come together in fasting before the Lord. She then went forward in faith and served, trusting that God had brought her to this time and place for his purposes. We, too, can use these spiritual exercises to help bring us into deep fellowship with the living Lord, stripping away our anxiety and fear when facing difficult circumstances. Such exercises become the means to courage, deliverance and the discovery of God's grace and power.

features, and Mordecai had taken her as his own
daughter when her father and mother died.
8When the king's order and edict had been
proclaimed, many girls were brought to the citadel of Susa and put under the care of Hegai.
Esther also was taken to the king's palace and
entrusted to Hegai, who had charge of the harem. 9The girl pleased him and won his favor.
Immediately he provided her with her beauty
treatments and special food. He assigned to her
seven maids selected from the king's palace and
moved her and her maids into the best place in
the harem.
10Esther had not revealed her nationality and
family background, because Mordecai had forbidden her to do so. 11Every day he walked back
and forth near the courtyard of the harem to
find out how Esther was and what was happening to her.
12Before a girl's turn came to go in to King
Xerxes, she had to complete twelve months of
beauty treatments prescribed for the women, six
months with oil of myrrh and six with perfumes
and cosmetics. 13And this is how she would go
to the king: Anything she wanted was given her
to take with her from the harem to the king's
palace. 14In the evening she would go there and
in the morning return to another part of the
harem to the care of Shaashgaz, the king's eunuch who was in charge of the concubines. She
would not return to the king unless he was
pleased with her and summoned her by name.
15When the turn came for Esther (the girl
Mordecai had adopted, the daughter of his uncle Abihail) to go to the king, she asked for
nothing other than what Hegai, the king's eunuch who was in charge of the harem, suggested. And Esther won the favor of everyone who
saw her. 16She was taken to King Xerxes in the
royal residence in the tenth month, the month
of Tebeth, in the seventh year of his reign.
17Now the king was attracted to Esther more
than to any of the other women, and she won
his favor and approval more than any of the
other virgins. So he set a royal crown on her
head and made her queen instead of Vashti.
18And the king gave a great banquet, Esther's
banquet, for all his nobles and officials. He proclaimed a holiday throughout the provinces
and distributed gifts with royal liberality.

Mordecai Uncovers a Conspiracy

19When the virgins were assembled a second
time, Mordecai was sitting at the king's gate.
20But Esther had kept secret her family background and nationality just as Mordecai had
told her to do, for she continued to follow Mordecai's instructions as she had done when he
was bringing her up.
21During the time Mordecai was sitting at the
king's gate, Bigthana[a] and Teresh, two of the
king's officers who guarded the doorway, became angry and conspired to assassinate King
Xerxes. 22But Mordecai found out about the
plot and told Queen Esther, who in turn reported it to the king, giving credit to Mordecai.
23And when the report was investigated and
found to be true, the two officials were hanged
on a gallows.[b] All this was recorded in the
book of the annals in the presence of the king.

Haman's Plot to Destroy the Jews

3 After these events, King Xerxes honored
Haman son of Hammedatha, the Agagite,
elevating him and giving him a seat of honor
higher than that of all the other nobles. 2All the
royal officials at the king's gate knelt down and
paid honor to Haman, for the king had commanded this concerning him. But Mordecai
would not kneel down or pay him honor.
3Then the royal officials at the king's gate
asked Mordecai, "Why do you disobey the
king's command?" 4Day after day they spoke to
him but he refused to comply. Therefore they
told Haman about it to see whether Mordecai's
behavior would be tolerated, for he had told
them he was a Jew.
5When Haman saw that Mordecai would not
kneel down or pay him honor, he was enraged.
6Yet having learned who Mordecai's people
were, he scorned the idea of killing only Mordecai. Instead Haman looked for a way to destroy
all Mordecai's people, the Jews, throughout the
whole kingdom of Xerxes.

[a]21 Hebrew *Bigthan,* a variant of *Bigthana* [b]23 Or *were hung* (or *impaled*) *on poles;* similarly elsewhere in Esther

---

2:15–20 Esther wisely listened to Hegai (a man who knew the king well), taking his advice on how she might please the king. Hence, Esther succeeded in becoming the new queen (2:17). Esther sacrificed her own desires to follow her cousin Mordecai's wishes. Making a major life decision because someone else wants us to is very difficult; none of us want to give up control of our lives. The question we must ask when facing similar situations is whether or not what we are asked to do agrees with God's will. Mordecai's wishes were in keeping with God's will, so Esther agreed with them.

2:21–23 When Mordecai learned of the officers' plan to kill King Xerxes, he reported their plot to Queen Esther (2:22). Though he had done something worthy of great honor, Mordecai received no recognition at the time (see 6:1–11). Sometimes the good decisions we make are only rewarded by our own sense of integrity. Knowing that we made a right decision should be enough for us to continue on the right path.

3:1–6 When Haman heard that Mordecai refused to bow before him, he became furious. Haman wanted revenge for Mordecai's insubordination, so he sought the destruction of all the Jews. His desire to destroy the whole nation may be due to his family's (the Agagites) feud with Mordecai's tribe (the Benjamites; see 1 Samuel 15 for the story of King Saul and King Agag). If that was indeed the case, this story illustrates how a legacy of hatred can affect a person's judgment. Haman took drastic measures to settle a conflict that had begun over five hundred years earlier. Do we have unsettled disagreements with others? If so, we need to forgive them in order to help keep our descendants from inheriting our conflicts.

[7]In the twelfth year of King Xerxes, in the first
month, the month of Nisan, they cast the *pur*
(that is, the lot) in the presence of Haman to
select a day and month. And the lot fell on[a]
the twelfth month, the month of Adar.

[8]Then Haman said to King Xerxes, "There is
a certain people dispersed and scattered among
the peoples in all the provinces of your kingdom whose customs are different from those of
all other people and who do not obey the king's
laws; it is not in the king's best interest to tolerate them. [9]If it pleases the king, let a decree be
issued to destroy them, and I will put ten thousand talents[b] of silver into the royal treasury
for the men who carry out this business."

[10]So the king took his signet ring from his
finger and gave it to Haman son of Hammedatha, the Agagite, the enemy of the Jews. [11]"Keep
the money," the king said to Haman, "and do
with the people as you please."

[12]Then on the thirteenth day of the first
month the royal secretaries were summoned.
They wrote out in the script of each province
and in the language of each people all Haman's
orders to the king's satraps, the governors of the
various provinces and the nobles of the various
peoples. These were written in the name of King
Xerxes himself and sealed with his own ring.
[13]Dispatches were sent by couriers to all the
king's provinces with the order to destroy, kill
and annihilate all the Jews—young and old,
women and little children—on a single day, the
thirteenth day of the twelfth month, the month
of Adar, and to plunder their goods. [14]A copy of
the text of the edict was to be issued as law in
every province and made known to the people
of every nationality so they would be ready for
that day.

[15]Spurred on by the king's command, the
couriers went out, and the edict was issued in
the citadel of Susa. The king and Haman sat
down to drink, but the city of Susa was bewildered.

Mordecai Persuades Esther to Help

4 When Mordecai learned of all that had
been done, he tore his clothes, put on sackcloth and ashes, and went out into the city,
wailing loudly and bitterly. [2]But he went only
as far as the king's gate, because no one clothed
in sackcloth was allowed to enter it. [3]In every
province to which the edict and order of the
king came, there was great mourning among
the Jews, with fasting, weeping and wailing.
Many lay in sackcloth and ashes.

[4]When Esther's maids and eunuchs came and
told her about Mordecai, she was in great distress. She sent clothes for him to put on instead
of his sackcloth, but he would not accept them.
[5]Then Esther summoned Hathach, one of the
king's eunuchs assigned to attend her, and ordered him to find out what was troubling Mordecai and why.

[6]So Hathach went out to Mordecai in the
open square of the city in front of the king's
gate. [7]Mordecai told him everything that had
happened to him, including the exact amount
of money Haman had promised to pay into the
royal treasury for the destruction of the Jews.
[8]He also gave him a copy of the text of the edict
for their annihilation, which had been published in Susa, to show to Esther and explain it
to her, and he told him to urge her to go into
the king's presence to beg for mercy and plead
with him for her people.

[9]Hathach went back and reported to Esther
what Mordecai had said. [10]Then she instructed
him to say to Mordecai, [11]"All the king's officials and the people of the royal provinces
know that for any man or woman who approaches the king in the inner court without
being summoned the king has but one law: that
he be put to death. The only exception to this
is for the king to extend the gold scepter to him
and spare his life. But thirty days have passed
since I was called to go to the king."

[12]When Esther's words were reported to Mordecai, [13]he sent back this answer: "Do not think
that because you are in the king's house you
alone of all the Jews will escape. [14]For if you
remain silent at this time, relief and deliverance
for the Jews will arise from another place, but
you and your father's family will perish. And
who knows but that you have come to royal
position for such a time as this?"

[15]Then Esther sent this reply to Mordecai:

[a]7 Septuagint; Hebrew does not have *And the lot fell on.*
[b]9 That is, about 375 tons (about 345 metric tons)

3:8–15 Without mentioning the Jews by name, Haman convinced the king to allow their destruction because they followed different customs and disobeyed the king's laws (3:8). Irresponsibly, without investigating such a serious matter, the king gave Haman complete authority to implement his plan. We should always check into the requests of others, especially when those requests have major implications.

4:1–8 Mordecai and the Jews throughout the empire sensed the hopelessness of their situation and put on mourning clothes—sackcloth and ashes (4:1–3). When Esther learned that Mordecai was weeping, she dispatched a servant to determine the reasons for Mordecai's anguish (4:5–6). In a straightforward manner, Mordecai disclosed the gravity of the situation (4:7–8). Accepting the reality of our situation is vital to reaching out for God's help. Had Mordecai denied the truth of Haman's edict, he and the Jews would have faced certain death.

4:9–17 At first Esther denied the reality of the threat posed by Haman's edict. She focused instead on her fear that she might be killed for approaching the king uninvited. In doing so, Esther failed to see the long-term consequences that might result if she refused to act. Esther finally consented to help her people by approaching King Xerxes, not knowing if he would accept her or have her killed. Her statement "If I perish, I perish" (4:16) reveals her faith in God and her selflessness. We, too, need to trust in God to deliver us whenever we face dangerous situations. We also need to look to others for their support and prayer. Like Esther, we need people praying for us if we hope to succeed.

Esther & Mordecai

Many of us find ourselves in situations in which cruel and unfortunate experiences seem to be the norm. We may feel powerless to act, either to defend ourselves or to help anyone else. We may wonder how we got there, or why. Esther must have felt this way at times. Esther lived in a community of exiled Jews in Babylonia, far from her homeland of Israel. She was a Jewish foreigner; her people were dominated by pagan Persian rulers. She was also an orphan. Her cousin Mordecai, a prominent leader in the Jewish exilic community, had adopted her as a child.

When Esther was probably still in her late teens, King Xerxes, ruler of the empire, deposed his queen and held an empire-wide beauty contest to find a replacement. Esther competed in the contest and was selected to become the new queen. But she was instructed by Mordecai not to tell anyone of her Jewish background.

As queen to King Xerxes, Esther was in a difficult situation. She was one among many wives and concubines and would not see her husband for months at a time. King Xerxes was hardly an ideal husband. He was known to kill the people closest to him at a mere whim. Being close to King Xerxes was hardly a secure position. As one of God's people, Esther must have often wondered how she had ever become queen and why she was there in the first place.

About this time, a man named Haman rose to the position of prime minister in King Xerxes' court. Esther's cousin Mordecai enraged Haman by not bowing down to him. To get revenge, Haman sought the destruction of all the Jews in the Persian Empire. When Mordecai learned of Haman's plan to kill the Jews, he went to Esther for help. After much prayer and fasting, Esther risked her life by approaching King Xerxes without an appointment. Within a few days, Esther succeeded in delivering her people from sure destruction.

Initially Esther may not have known why she was chosen as queen, but God soon made his reasons known to her: She was there to save her people from sure destruction. God used Esther and Mordecai to work his will in a difficult situation. We may not know why we are placed in our situations, but God has a purpose and a plan for us. If we seek God and surrender to him in difficult circumstances, he will use us to work his will in the lives of many.

STRENGTHS AND ACCOMPLISHMENTS:

Both Esther and Mordecai showed great courage and careful planning.

Esther was open to wise advice from Mordecai.

Esther placed the lives of her people above her own.

Mordecai refused to worship Haman, disregarding the possible consequences.

LESSONS FROM THEIR LIVES:

Following God often means that we will have to sacrifice our own security.

We can trust that God will deliver his people.

God may allow certain circumstances to happen to us in order to benefit or even rescue others.

God often uses ordinary people in extraordinary ways to work his perfect will.

KEY VERSE:

"If you remain silent at this time, relief and deliverance for the Jews will arise from another place, but you and your father's family will perish. And who knows but that you have come to royal position for such a time as this?" (4:14).

Esther and Mordecai's story is told in the book of Esther.

16"Go, gather together all the Jews who are in
Susa, and fast for me. Do not eat or drink for
three days, night or day. I and my maids will
fast as you do. When this is done, I will go to
the king, even though it is against the law. And
if I perish, I perish."
17So Mordecai went away and carried out all
of Esther's instructions.

Esther's Request to the King

5 On the third day Esther put on her royal
robes and stood in the inner court of the
palace, in front of the king's hall. The king was
sitting on his royal throne in the hall, facing the
entrance. 2When he saw Queen Esther standing
in the court, he was pleased with her and held
out to her the gold scepter that was in his hand.
So Esther approached and touched the tip of the
scepter.
3Then the king asked, "What is it, Queen
Esther? What is your request? Even up to half
the kingdom, it will be given you."
4"If it pleases the king," replied Esther, "let
the king, together with Haman, come today to
a banquet I have prepared for him."
5"Bring Haman at once," the king said, "so
that we may do what Esther asks."
So the king and Haman went to the banquet
Esther had prepared. 6As they were drinking
wine, the king again asked Esther, "Now what
is your petition? It will be given you. And what
is your request? Even up to half the kingdom, it
will be granted."
7Esther replied, "My petition and my request
is this: 8If the king regards me with favor and if
it pleases the king to grant my petition and
fulfill my request, let the king and Haman come
tomorrow to the banquet I will prepare for
them. Then I will answer the king's question."

Haman's Rage Against Mordecai

9Haman went out that day happy and in high
spirits. But when he saw Mordecai at the king's
gate and observed that he neither rose nor
showed fear in his presence, he was filled with
rage against Mordecai. 10Nevertheless, Haman
restrained himself and went home.
Calling together his friends and Zeresh, his
wife, 11Haman boasted to them about his vast
wealth, his many sons, and all the ways the king
had honored him and how he had elevated him
above the other nobles and officials. 12"And
that's not all," Haman added. "I'm the only person Queen Esther invited to accompany the
king to the banquet she gave. And she has invited me along with the king tomorrow. 13But all
this gives me no satisfaction as long as I see that
Jew Mordecai sitting at the king's gate."
14His wife Zeresh and all his friends said to
him, "Have a gallows built, seventy-five feet[a]
high, and ask the king in the morning to have
Mordecai hanged on it. Then go with the king
to the dinner and be happy." This suggestion
delighted Haman, and he had the gallows built.

Mordecai Honored

6 That night the king could not sleep; so he
ordered the book of the chronicles, the
record of his reign, to be brought in and read to
him. 2It was found recorded there that Mordecai had exposed Bigthana and Teresh, two of the
king's officers who guarded the doorway, who
had conspired to assassinate King Xerxes.
3"What honor and recognition has Mordecai
received for this?" the king asked.
"Nothing has been done for him," his attendants answered.
4The king said, "Who is in the court?" Now
Haman had just entered the outer court of the
palace to speak to the king about hanging Mordecai on the gallows he had erected for him.
5His attendants answered, "Haman is standing in the court."
"Bring him in," the king ordered.
6When Haman entered, the king asked him,
"What should be done for the man the king
delights to honor?"
Now Haman thought to himself, "Who is
there that the king would rather honor than
me?" 7So he answered the king, "For the man
the king delights to honor, 8have them bring a
royal robe the king has worn and a horse the
king has ridden, one with a royal crest placed
on its head. 9Then let the robe and horse be
entrusted to one of the king's most noble
princes. Let them robe the man the king delights to honor, and lead him on the horse
through the city streets, proclaiming before
him, 'This is what is done for the man the king
delights to honor!' "
10"Go at once," the king commanded Haman.
"Get the robe and the horse and do just as you

[a]14 Hebrew *fifty cubits* (about 23 meters)

5:9–14 Haman, totally oblivious to Queen Esther's plan, was overjoyed at being so highly honored by her (5:9, 12). Yet even under such auspicious circumstances, Haman could not fully enjoy himself because he wanted still more. More than anything else, he still wanted Mordecai to bow down to him (5:9, 13). In fact, it became an obsession with him. We shouldn't allow what we don't have to overshadow what we do have; our desire to have everything might cost us the riches we already possess.

6:1–6 Even though some time had passed, the king felt a responsibility to acknowledge his gratitude to Mordecai for saving his life. Expressing gratitude is important; it shows others that we appreciate their help and also that we are not fooling ourselves by thinking our progress is accomplished on our own.

6:6–12 Thinking the king was going to honor him, Haman recommended a public display of honor. Haman must have been livid when he was ordered to honor Mordecai according to the plan he himself had outlined. Perhaps Haman's hatred of Mordecai was further sparked because showing respect to others would have been a blow to his ego. We should make sure our self-worth does not depend on what others think about us. Once we realize our self-worth is based on our acceptance by God, we can stop competing with others and appreciate them for who they are.

have suggested for Mordecai the Jew, who sits at the king's gate. Do not neglect anything you have recommended."

11So Haman got the robe and the horse. He robed Mordecai, and led him on horseback through the city streets, proclaiming before him, "This is what is done for the man the king delights to honor!"

12Afterward Mordecai returned to the king's gate. But Haman rushed home, with his head covered in grief, 13and told Zeresh his wife and all his friends everything that had happened to him.

His advisers and his wife Zeresh said to him, "Since Mordecai, before whom your downfall has started, is of Jewish origin, you cannot stand against him—you will surely come to ruin!" 14While they were still talking with him, the king's eunuchs arrived and hurried Haman away to the banquet Esther had prepared.

Haman Hanged

7 So the king and Haman went to dine with Queen Esther, 2and as they were drinking wine on that second day, the king again asked, "Queen Esther, what is your petition? It will be given you. What is your request? Even up to half the kingdom, it will be granted."

3Then Queen Esther answered, "If I have found favor with you, O king, and if it pleases your majesty, grant me my life—this is my petition. And spare my people—this is my request. 4For I and my people have been sold for destruction and slaughter and annihilation. If we had merely been sold as male and female slaves, I would have kept quiet, because no such distress would justify disturbing the king.[a]"

5King Xerxes asked Queen Esther, "Who is he? Where is the man who has dared to do such a thing?"

6Esther said, "The adversary and enemy is this vile Haman."

Then Haman was terrified before the king and queen. 7The king got up in a rage, left his wine and went out into the palace garden. But Haman, realizing that the king had already decided his fate, stayed behind to beg Queen Esther for his life.

8Just as the king returned from the palace garden to the banquet hall, Haman was falling on the couch where Esther was reclining.

The king exclaimed, "Will he even molest the queen while she is with me in the house?"

As soon as the word left the king's mouth, they covered Haman's face. 9Then Harbona, one of the eunuchs attending the king, said, "A gallows seventy-five feet[b] high stands by Haman's house. He had it made for Mordecai, who spoke up to help the king."

The king said, "Hang him on it!" 10So they hanged Haman on the gallows he had prepared for Mordecai. Then the king's fury subsided.

The King's Edict in Behalf of the Jews

8 That same day King Xerxes gave Queen Esther the estate of Haman, the enemy of the Jews. And Mordecai came into the presence of the king, for Esther had told how he was related to her. 2The king took off his signet ring, which he had reclaimed from Haman, and presented it to Mordecai. And Esther appointed him over Haman's estate.

3Esther again pleaded with the king, falling at his feet and weeping. She begged him to put an end to the evil plan of Haman the Agagite, which he had devised against the Jews. 4Then the king extended the gold scepter to Esther and she arose and stood before him.

5"If it pleases the king," she said, "and if he regards me with favor and thinks it the right thing to do, and if he is pleased with me, let an order be written overruling the dispatches that Haman son of Hammedatha, the Agagite, devised and wrote to destroy the Jews in all the king's provinces. 6For how can I bear to see disaster fall on my people? How can I bear to see the destruction of my family?"

7King Xerxes replied to Queen Esther and to Mordecai the Jew, "Because Haman attacked the Jews, I have given his estate to Esther, and they have hanged him on the gallows. 8Now write another decree in the king's name in behalf of the Jews as seems best to you, and seal it with the king's signet ring—for no document written in the king's name and sealed with his ring can be revoked."

9At once the royal secretaries were summoned—on the twenty-third day of the third month, the month of Sivan. They wrote out all Mordecai's orders to the Jews, and to the satraps, governors and nobles of the 127 provinces stretching from India to Cush.[c] These orders were written in the script of each province and the language of each people and also to the Jews in their own script and language. 10Mordecai wrote in the name of King Xerxes,

[a]4 Or *quiet, but the compensation our adversary offers cannot be compared with the loss the king would suffer*
[b]9 Hebrew *fifty cubits* (about 23 meters) [c]9 That is, the upper Nile region

7:1–6 Esther presented her petition to the king, seeking his help in saving her and her people from the edict ordering their death. She explained this life-threatening situation and wisely waited to see how the king would respond. Noting his rage, Esther boldly proceeded to denounce Haman as the enemy of her people. Wisely evaluating situations before moving forward is often necessary. Waiting for the proper timing is ultimately much easier than trying to repair the damage wreaked by impulsiveness.

8:1–6 Esther received Haman's property, and Mordecai became prime minister, but still the Jewish people were in danger. Once again Esther approached King Xerxes, this time asking for a reversal of Haman's decree. Like Esther, we shouldn't stop seeking God when our lives are out of danger. We should do what we can to help others seek God and escape the disastrous effects of sin too.

sealed the dispatches with the king's signet ring, and sent them by mounted couriers, who rode fast horses especially bred for the king.

11The king's edict granted the Jews in every city the right to assemble and protect themselves; to destroy, kill and annihilate any armed force of any nationality or province that might attack them and their women and children; and to plunder the property of their enemies. 12The day appointed for the Jews to do this in all the provinces of King Xerxes was the thirteenth day of the twelfth month, the month of Adar. 13A copy of the text of the edict was to be issued as law in every province and made known to the people of every nationality so that the Jews would be ready on that day to avenge themselves on their enemies.

14The couriers, riding the royal horses, raced out, spurred on by the king's command. And the edict was also issued in the citadel of Susa.

15Mordecai left the king's presence wearing royal garments of blue and white, a large crown of gold and a purple robe of fine linen. And the city of Susa held a joyous celebration. 16For the Jews it was a time of happiness and joy, gladness and honor. 17In every province and in every city, wherever the edict of the king went, there was joy and gladness among the Jews, with feasting and celebrating. And many people of other nationalities became Jews because fear of the Jews had seized them.

Triumph of the Jews

9 On the thirteenth day of the twelfth month, the month of Adar, the edict commanded by the king was to be carried out. On this day the enemies of the Jews had hoped to overpower them, but now the tables were turned and the Jews got the upper hand over those who hated them. 2The Jews assembled in their cities in all the provinces of King Xerxes to attack those seeking their destruction. No one could stand against them, because the people of all the other nationalities were afraid of them. 3And all the nobles of the provinces, the satraps, the governors and the king's administrators helped the Jews, because fear of Mordecai had seized them. 4Mordecai was prominent in the palace; his reputation spread throughout the provinces, and he became more and more powerful.

5The Jews struck down all their enemies with the sword, killing and destroying them, and they did what they pleased to those who hated them. 6In the citadel of Susa, the Jews killed and destroyed five hundred men. 7They also killed Parshandatha, Dalphon, Aspatha, 8Poratha, Adalia, Aridatha, 9Parmashta, Arisai, Aridai and Vaizatha, 10the ten sons of Haman son of Hammedatha, the enemy of the Jews. But they did not lay their hands on the plunder.

11The number of those slain in the citadel of Susa was reported to the king that same day. 12The king said to Queen Esther, "The Jews have killed and destroyed five hundred men and the ten sons of Haman in the citadel of Susa. What have they done in the rest of the king's provinces? Now what is your petition? It will be given you. What is your request? It will also be granted."

13"If it pleases the king," Esther answered, "give the Jews in Susa permission to carry out this day's edict tomorrow also, and let Haman's ten sons be hanged on gallows."

14So the king commanded that this be done. An edict was issued in Susa, and they hanged the ten sons of Haman. 15The Jews in Susa came together on the fourteenth day of the month of Adar, and they put to death in Susa three hundred men, but they did not lay their hands on the plunder.

16Meanwhile, the remainder of the Jews who were in the king's provinces also assembled to protect themselves and get relief from their enemies. They killed seventy-five thousand of them but did not lay their hands on the plunder. 17This happened on the thirteenth day of the month of Adar, and on the fourteenth they rested and made it a day of feasting and joy.

Purim Celebrated

18The Jews in Susa, however, had assembled on the thirteenth and fourteenth, and then on the fifteenth they rested and made it a day of feasting and joy.

19That is why rural Jews—those living in villages—observe the fourteenth of the month of Adar as a day of joy and feasting, a day for giving presents to each other.

20Mordecai recorded these events, and he sent letters to all the Jews throughout the provinces of King Xerxes, near and far, 21to have them celebrate annually the fourteenth and fifteenth days of the month of Adar 22as the time when the Jews got relief from their enemies, and as the month when their sorrow was turned

---

9:5–15 The Jews defended themselves from their enemies. The Jews exhibited self-control and did not plunder their enemies' goods even though they had the right to do so (see 8:11). This was a wise move: The Jews could not be accused of rationalizing their slaughter as a cover for becoming rich. We don't always have to embrace every advantage that the law allows. Sacrificing some of our rights may be wiser and may make a bolder statement about our motives.

9:16–19 Upon completing their task, the Jews throughout the empire spontaneously and joyfully celebrated their success. There is nothing wrong with celebrating a great victory, whether it is emotional, spiritual or physical. Not only is celebration fun, but it also helps us recharge our batteries for the battles ahead.

9:20–28 Mordecai instituted this celebration as an annual event to commemorate the deliverance of the Jews (9:20–21). He named this day *Purim.* It is often helpful for us to establish special days to commemorate the important victories in our lives too. Such days then will serve as reminders of how God is constantly working to help us in our spiritual renewal.

into joy and their mourning into a day of celebration. He wrote them to observe the days as
days of feasting and joy and giving presents of
food to one another and gifts to the poor.
[23]So the Jews agreed to continue the celebration they had begun, doing what Mordecai had
written to them. [24]For Haman son of Hammedatha, the Agagite, the enemy of all the Jews,
had plotted against the Jews to destroy them
and had cast the *pur* (that is, the lot) for their
ruin and destruction. [25]But when the plot came
to the king's attention,[a] he issued written orders that the evil scheme Haman had devised
against the Jews should come back onto his
own head, and that he and his sons should be
hanged on the gallows. [26](Therefore these days
were called Purim, from the word *pur*.) Because
of everything written in this letter and because
of what they had seen and what had happened
to them, [27]the Jews took it upon themselves to
establish the custom that they and their descendants and all who join them should without fail
observe these two days every year, in the way
prescribed and at the time appointed. [28]These
days should be remembered and observed in
every generation by every family, and in every
province and in every city. And these days of
Purim should never cease to be celebrated by
the Jews, nor should the memory of them die
out among their descendants.
[29]So Queen Esther, daughter of Abihail,
along with Mordecai the Jew, wrote with full
authority to confirm this second letter concerning Purim. [30]And Mordecai sent letters to all the
Jews in the 127 provinces of the kingdom of
Xerxes—words of goodwill and assurance— [31]to
establish these days of Purim at their designated
times, as Mordecai the Jew and Queen Esther
had decreed for them, and as they had established for themselves and their descendants in
regard to their times of fasting and lamentation.
[32]Esther's decree confirmed these regulations
about Purim, and it was written down in the
records.

The Greatness of Mordecai

10 King Xerxes imposed tribute throughout the empire, to its distant shores.
[2]And all his acts of power and might, together
with a full account of the greatness of Mordecai
to which the king had raised him, are they not
written in the book of the annals of the kings of
Media and Persia? [3]Mordecai the Jew was second in rank to King Xerxes, preeminent among
the Jews, and held in high esteem by his many
fellow Jews, because he worked for the good of
his people and spoke up for the welfare of all
the Jews.

[a]25 Or *when Esther came before the king*

10:1–3 Mordecai became known as a great prime minister, no doubt because of his fairness and godliness. God's name is never once mentioned in the original Hebrew in this entire book. Yet God's handiwork—his timing, his deliverance and his encouragement—can be seen throughout. The book of Esther ends with the Jews enjoying much success, proving that God truly works behind the scenes for the good of his people.

The Big Picture

The book of Job directly addresses the problem of the suffering of the innocent. At its opening, Job was a prosperous man, greatly blessed by God. But then God allowed one disaster after another to fall upon Job. We are told that Job's suffering was the consequence of a spiritual conflict, not because of any failure on Job's part. But Job, his wife and his friends were never made aware of this. They were left to struggle with the pain and to ask the age-old question, *Why?*

Job was confused by the devastating losses he had experienced. Even after humbly examining his moral condition, he could find nothing to warrant the punishment he had received. Amidst his confusion, however, Job displayed an amazing faith in God, despite short lapses of anger and despair. Job's wife reacted to Job's suffering as we often do in such situations—she pointed an angry finger at God. The four visiting friends approached Job's suffering with the popular theology of their day which considered all suffering to be the direct result of sin. They could think of no other reason for Job's suffering except that he was refusing to confess some hidden sin.

The book's prologue makes it clear that Job was innocent. The solution offered by Job's friends was clearly wrong. Why did God allow Job to suffer? Job was never given a clear answer. He did learn, however, to stand humbly before his Creator and trust the God who knew and understood the reasons behind Job's suffering. Life brings hurts, and there are no guarantees that we will escape them. But through suffering we can learn to live by faith rather than trying to get along on our own strength. We can learn that even when suffering causes us to question, God is still with us.

A. THE PAIN BEGINS (1:1–2:13)

1. The World of a Faithful Man (1:1-5)
2. The World of a Faithless Angel (1:6-7)
3. God's Choice for Faithfulness (1:8-12)
4. The Trial Begins (1:13–2:10)
5. The Only Friendly Visit (2:11-13)

B. A MAN FORSAKEN (3:1–37:24)

1. Round One: Undependable Friends (3:1–14:22)
2. Round Two: Unnerving Theologies (15:1–21:34)
3. Round Three: Misguided Cures (22:1–26:14)
4. A Painful Remembrance (27:1–31:40)
5. A Self-Appointed Spokesman (32:1–37:24)

C. A VOICE OUT OF THE STORM (38:1–41:34)

D. SPIRITUAL VISION: EYES THAT SEE GOD (42:1-6)

E. PHYSICAL RESTORATION: A NEW BEGINNING (42:7–17)

Spiritual Renewal Themes

DEALING WITH UNFAIRNESS

We live in a world filled with injustice and unfairness. The Bible recognizes this hard fact. Joseph suffered unfairly at the hands of his brothers and Potiphar's wife. David suffered unjustly for many years at the hands of King Saul. And here, through no fault of his own, Job lost his possessions, his family and his health. Job wondered why God allowed him to suffer, but he never got a clear answer. However, Job did come to know God

Essential Facts

PURPOSE:
To provide an intimate look into the struggles of a man dealing with the problem of innocent suffering.

AUTHOR:
The author is unknown, though either Job or Elihu may have written the initial record.

AUDIENCE:
The people of Israel.

DATE WRITTEN:
The date of the book's written completion is unknown. The events may belong to the patriarchal period (2000–1800 B.C.).

SETTING:
The land of Uz, probably located in either northeastern Israel or northwestern Arabia.

KEY VERSES:
"I know that my Redeemer lives, and that in the end he will stand upon the earth. And after my skin has been destroyed, yet in my flesh I will see God" (19:25–26).

KEY PEOPLE:
Job, his wife, and his friends Eliphaz, Bildad, Zophar and Elihu.

in a new and deeper way because of his struggles. When we face unfairness in our world, we can view it as an opportunity to learn more about trusting God.

HONESTY WITH OUR EMOTIONS

In the book of Job we discover that it is all right to cry, to doubt, to fear, to question, to need and to wrestle with the very essence of our existence. As our hearts cry out against injustice and pain, the book of Job reassures us of the importance of being honest with God. When we are angry, we should tell God how we feel. When we are afraid, we should reach out to him. God will understand our strong feelings. He is never put off or threatened by our emotions. In fact, God longs for us to be open and honest with him. He wants to be involved in the darkest hours of our lives too. Only then will we be able to relate completely to him. Only then can we receive the healing and hope he longs to give us.

GOD'S GOODNESS

God is all-knowing and all-powerful. His will for each of us is perfect. But God doesn't always act in ways we understand. Very often he does things that seem to contradict his justice. As Job suffered, his friends believed his pain was caused by something Job had done, that his suffering was a punishment for some sin. Job knew this was not the case. Yet he wondered why he had to suffer so much pain. It would have been easy for Job to wholeheartedly reject God for the apparent injustice of his situation. But Job knew categorically that God was good. Despite occasional lapses into anger and despair, Job trusted that God would ultimately deal with him justly.

THE IMPORTANCE OF TRUST

When life is going smoothly, trust is easy. The test of trust always comes when life stops making sense. Job's life is a clear example of how trust needs to work in our lives. Everything that Job enjoyed had been stripped away from him for no reason that he could understand or discover. In spite of this, however, Job never gave up on God. He never placed his hope for his deliverance in his experience, his wisdom, his friends or his wealth. Job's trust was in God. God alone is sufficient to help us deal with the ambiguities in life. We can trust in him.

Prologue

1 In the land of Uz there lived a man whose name was Job. This man was blameless and upright; he feared God and shunned evil. 2He had seven sons and three daughters, 3and he owned seven thousand sheep, three thousand camels, five hundred yoke of oxen and five hundred donkeys, and had a large number of servants. He was the greatest man among all the people of the East.

4His sons used to take turns holding feasts in their homes, and they would invite their three sisters to eat and drink with them. 5When a period of feasting had run its course, Job would send and have them purified. Early in the morning he would sacrifice a burnt offering for each of them, thinking, "Perhaps my children have sinned and cursed God in their hearts." This was Job's regular custom.

Job's First Test

6One day the angels[a] came to present themselves before the LORD, and Satan[b] also came with them. 7The LORD said to Satan, "Where have you come from?"

Satan answered the LORD, "From roaming through the earth and going back and forth in it."

8Then the LORD said to Satan, "Have you considered my servant Job? There is no one on earth like him; he is blameless and upright, a man who fears God and shuns evil."

9"Does Job fear God for nothing?" Satan replied. 10"Have you not put a hedge around him and his household and everything he has? You have blessed the work of his hands, so that his flocks and herds are spread throughout the land. 11But stretch out your hand and strike everything he has, and he will surely curse you to your face."

12The LORD said to Satan, "Very well, then, everything he has is in your hands, but on the man himself do not lay a finger."

Then Satan went out from the presence of the LORD.

13One day when Job's sons and daughters were feasting and drinking wine at the oldest brother's house, 14a messenger came to Job and said, "The oxen were plowing and the donkeys were grazing nearby, 15and the Sabeans attacked and carried them off. They put the servants to the sword, and I am the only one who has escaped to tell you!"

16While he was still speaking, another messenger came and said, "The fire of God fell from the sky and burned up the sheep and the servants, and I am the only one who has escaped to tell you!"

17While he was still speaking, another messenger came and said, "The Chaldeans formed three raiding parties and swept down on your camels and carried them off. They put the servants to the sword, and I am the only one who has escaped to tell you!"

18While he was still speaking, yet another messenger came and said, "Your sons and daughters were feasting and drinking wine at the oldest brother's house, 19when suddenly a mighty wind swept in from the desert and struck the four corners of the house. It collapsed on them and they are dead, and I am the only one who has escaped to tell you!"

20At this, Job got up and tore his robe and shaved his head. Then he fell to the ground in worship 21and said:

"Naked I came from my mother's womb,
    and naked I will depart.[c]
The LORD gave and the LORD has taken
    away;
  may the name of the LORD be praised."

22In all this, Job did not sin by charging God with wrongdoing.

Job's Second Test

2 On another day the angels[a] came to present themselves before the LORD, and

[a]6,1 Hebrew *the sons of God* [b]6 *Satan* means *accuser.*
[c]21 Or *will return there*

1:1–5 Job's heart and life are revealed to us in these introductory verses. Job loved God and desired to lead his children to do the same. Remembering these facts will help us understand the rest of the narrative properly. Job's innocence is established at the beginning of the book so we won't question it as his friends do.

1:8–12 God knew the heart of his servant Job and of Satan, Job's accuser. The stage was set as God volunteered Job to be the one who would prove Satan wrong. How could God have used Job in this seemingly cruel way? Perhaps the answer lies in the way we understand suffering. We usually view suffering as a crippling tragedy. But suffering can be a pathway to maturity (see 42:1–5; Romans 5:3–5; James 1:2–4). God allowed Job's suffering to bring him even greater blessings and strength in the end. We can be sure that God is working his good in our lives, even in the midst of our pain.

1:13–19 In what seems to be only a few hours' time, everything Job had held significant was stripped away. His pain must have seemed intolerable; his grief, beyond solace. Even though Job mourned his losses, however, his love for God was not dependent on his possessions. We can easily be caught in the trap of loving God for what he gives us—our home, car, job or wealth. Yet, if those things were taken away, how would we feel? Our love for God must be based on those things that can never be taken away—the fact that God loved us so much that he sent his Son, Jesus, to die for us while we were still sinners (see Romans 5:8).

1:20–22 We may never know how we'll respond to tragedy until we face it. Job chose to worship God, even in his grief. From Job's response we learn why God labeled him a man who was "blameless and upright, a man who fears God and shuns evil" (1:8). Job chose to praise God even after great loss. When we suffer a loss, praising God for his generosity in allowing us to have had the possessions or loved ones for a period of time is often the last thing we feel like doing—but it is the proper response to God's sovereignty.

2:1–3 Satan has no authority apart from God's consent.

*J*OB, *H*IS *F*AMILY & *F*RIENDS

Knowing how to respond to tragedy is never easy. Maybe it's the terrible sense of loss we feel. Perhaps it's the desire to know the reason for a tragedy that leaves us feeling alienated and alone. Was it something we did? Was it someone else's fault? Why did God allow it to happen? These questions often go unanswered. Some of our suffering may be a consequence of our own wrongdoing. But in Job's case this wasn't true. He was a godly man who hadn't done anything to deserve what had happened to him. When Job lost everything—wealth and family—in an overnight disaster, the question *why* was especially appropriate.

Even after his great losses, Job continued to glorify God. Yet, very soon after losing everything he owned, Job also lost his good health. Job, his wife and the friends who visited him in his misery all wondered why this was happening to such a good person. Such *why* questions are inevitably asked, but they are ultimately unanswerable from our limited human standpoint. We must face these questions with openness and honesty as we seek to navigate our way through the tragedies of life.

Though Job and the others had no idea what was happening in the unseen realm, we know from reading Job's story that his sufferings resulted from what the New Testament calls spiritual warfare (see Ephesians 6:10–18). But Job and the others could only guess or theorize about what was going on. Job's friends believed that he was hiding sins and refusing to confess or accept responsibility for the sins that they assumed had caused his suffering. Knowing that he had not sinned, Job disagreed with the explanations of his friends. But Job had no real answer either for the nagging question *why*. As time passed, Job grew increasingly upset and confused, until even he began to question God in regard to his suffering.

In the end, Job's arguments were silenced before God. While God never fully explained to Job why the disasters had befallen him, God did bring Job to a place of humble surrender. Job's understanding of God expanded and gave him the proper perspective to continue life. Neither Job nor any other person who has suffered a serious loss can ever fully understand why the catastrophe has happened. But if sufferers willingly seek God and surrender their lives into his powerful hands, restoration can take place as it did in Job's life.

STRENGTHS AND ACCOMPLISHMENTS:

Job was rightly known for his godliness.

Job proved himself to be a good father and husband.

Job is also famous for his patience and perseverance.

WEAKNESSES AND MISTAKES:

Job's friends made their judgments based on outward appearances without truly understanding the situation.

Job's wife let her losses come between her and God.

Job displayed a pride that needed to be dealt with.

LESSONS FROM THEIR LIVES:

Disasters touch the lives of everyone—even moral and godly people.

As we sustain any major loss, we should not deny our grief and anger; instead, we should honestly release these emotions to God.

In times of loss, we must not let pride stand in the way of seeking God and surrendering to him.

KEY VERSE:

"We consider blessed those who have persevered. You have heard of Job's perseverance and have seen what the Lord finally brought about. The Lord is full of compassion and mercy" (James 5:11).

The story of Job, his family and his friends is told in the book of Job. He is also referred to in Ezekiel 14:14, 20 and James 5:11.

Satan also came with them to present himself
before him. 2And the LORD said to Satan,
"Where have you come from?"
Satan answered the LORD, "From roaming through the earth and going back and forth in it."
3Then the LORD said to Satan, "Have you considered my servant Job? There is no one on earth like him; he is blameless and upright, a man who fears God and shuns evil. And he still maintains his integrity, though you incited me against him to ruin him without any reason."
4"Skin for skin!" Satan replied. "A man will
give all he has for his own life. 5But stretch out
your hand and strike his flesh and bones, and he will surely curse you to your face."
6The LORD said to Satan, "Very well, then, he is in your hands; but you must spare his life."
7So Satan went out from the presence of the LORD and afflicted Job with painful sores from
the soles of his feet to the top of his head. 8Then
Job took a piece of broken pottery and scraped himself with it as he sat among the ashes.
9His wife said to him, "Are you still holding on to your integrity? Curse God and die!"
10He replied, "You are talking like a foolish[a] woman. Shall we accept good from God, and not trouble?"

In all this, Job did not sin in what he said.

Job's Three Friends

11When Job's three friends, Eliphaz the Temanite, Bildad the Shuhite and Zophar the Naamathite, heard about all the troubles that had come upon him, they set out from their homes and met together by agreement to go and sympathize with him and comfort him. 12When
they saw him from a distance, they could hardly recognize him; they began to weep aloud, and they tore their robes and sprinkled dust on their heads. 13Then they sat on the ground with him for seven days and seven nights. No one said a word to him, because they saw how great his suffering was.

Job Speaks

3 After this, Job opened his mouth and cursed the day of his birth. 2He said:

3"May the day of my birth perish,
and the night it was said, 'A boy is born!'
4That day—may it turn to darkness;
may God above not care about it;
may no light shine upon it.
5May darkness and deep shadow[b] claim it once more;
may a cloud settle over it;
may blackness overwhelm its light.
6That night—may thick darkness seize it;
may it not be included among the days of the year
nor be entered in any of the months.
7May that night be barren;
may no shout of joy be heard in it.
8May those who curse days[c] curse that day,
those who are ready to rouse Leviathan.
9May its morning stars become dark;
may it wait for daylight in vain
and not see the first rays of dawn,
10for it did not shut the doors of the womb on me
to hide trouble from my eyes.

11"Why did I not perish at birth,
and die as I came from the womb?
12Why were there knees to receive me
and breasts that I might be nursed?
13For now I would be lying down in peace;
I would be asleep and at rest
14with kings and counselors of the earth,
who built for themselves places now lying in ruins,
15with rulers who had gold,
who filled their houses with silver.
16Or why was I not hidden in the ground like a stillborn child,
like an infant who never saw the light of day?

[a]10 The Hebrew word rendered *foolish* denotes moral deficiency. [b]5 Or *and the shadow of death* [c]8 Or *the sea*

When we undergo trials, we must realize that God is in control and will help us through them. He wants us to grow in our faith and glorify his name, no matter what difficulties we may be called upon to face.

2:4–6 Satan made a keen observation about human character. We are willing to give up all that we have to save our life, but when our life is confronted by physical illness, we often turn against God. It is difficult to maintain a proper perspective when we are physically afflicted. As we suffer physical pain, however, we should continue to praise God, for he is worthy to receive it, regardless of how we feel.

2:9–10 It is one thing to lose our comforts; it is quite another to lose the support of a spouse. The only mention of Job's wife comes at the start of his affliction. She was bitter and unable to share in his pain. Her words only added to Job's pain. In times of great loss, we desperately need the support of our loved ones. We need their vote of confidence when everyone else deserts us. And as our loved ones experience tough times, we need to be there to offer support.

2:11–13 Three friends observed Job's pain from a distance and were overwhelmed. But then they gave him the best gift they had to offer—they wept and shared in his grief. When others are suffering, we may feel that we have to say something comforting, offer them advice or sympathize with their grief. Often what those who are suffering really need may be just our presence with them to help share their pain.

3:1–19 Even though Job had known amazing success and happiness earlier in his life, he couldn't remember what it had been like. A common element in suffering is a loss of perspective. No matter how hard we try to maintain our point of view, it is difficult to see yesterday's celebration in the midst of today's devastation. But we can hold fast to the hope that someday God will give us reason to celebrate once again.

17There the wicked cease from turmoil,
and there the weary are at rest.
18Captives also enjoy their ease;
they no longer hear the slave driver's shout.
19The small and the great are there,
and the slave is freed from his master.

20"Why is light given to those in misery,
and life to the bitter of soul,
21to those who long for death that does not come,
who search for it more than for hidden treasure,
22who are filled with gladness
and rejoice when they reach the grave?
23Why is life given to a man
whose way is hidden,
whom God has hedged in?
24For sighing comes to me instead of food;
my groans pour out like water.
25What I feared has come upon me;
what I dreaded has happened to me.
26I have no peace, no quietness;
I have no rest, but only turmoil."

Eliphaz

4 Then Eliphaz the Temanite replied:

2"If someone ventures a word with you, will you be impatient?
But who can keep from speaking?
3Think how you have instructed many,
how you have strengthened feeble hands.
4Your words have supported those who stumbled;
you have strengthened faltering knees.
5But now trouble comes to you, and you are discouraged;
it strikes you, and you are dismayed.
6Should not your piety be your confidence
and your blameless ways your hope?

7"Consider now: Who, being innocent, has ever perished?
Where were the upright ever destroyed?
8As I have observed, those who plow evil
and those who sow trouble reap it.
9At the breath of God they are destroyed;
at the blast of his anger they perish.
10The lions may roar and growl,
yet the teeth of the great lions are broken.
11The lion perishes for lack of prey,
and the cubs of the lioness are scattered.

12"A word was secretly brought to me,
my ears caught a whisper of it.
13Amid disquieting dreams in the night,
when deep sleep falls on men,
14fear and trembling seized me
and made all my bones shake.
15A spirit glided past my face,
and the hair on my body stood on end.
16It stopped,
but I could not tell what it was.
A form stood before my eyes,
and I heard a hushed voice:
17'Can a mortal be more righteous than God?
Can a man be more pure than his Maker?
18If God places no trust in his servants,
if he charges his angels with error,
19how much more those who live in houses of clay,
whose foundations are in the dust,
who are crushed more readily than a moth!
20Between dawn and dusk they are broken to pieces;
unnoticed, they perish forever.
21Are not the cords of their tent pulled up,
so that they die without wisdom?'[a]

5 "Call if you will, but who will answer you?
To which of the holy ones will you turn?
2Resentment kills a fool,
and envy slays the simple.
3I myself have seen a fool taking root,
but suddenly his house was cursed.
4His children are far from safety,
crushed in court without a defender.
5The hungry consume his harvest,
taking it even from among thorns,
and the thirsty pant after his wealth.
6For hardship does not spring from the soil,

[a]21 Some interpreters end the quotation after verse 17.

3:20–23 Like most sufferers, Job asked *why*. Unfortunately, the answer to that question is often reserved for eternity. We must learn to trust God and remain faithful to him even if we never receive an explanation for our suffering. Sometimes we will never know why things happen the way they do. We can be sure, though, that God is with us in our pain.

4:7–11 We know that people reap what they sow (see Galatians 6:7), but we cannot offer this passage in Job as a universal reason for suffering. Suffering is not always a tool of God's judgment. Suffering can also be used to strengthen our faith. Just as gold must be melted to remove its impurities, so we must go through trials to purify our faith.

4:7–21 We can easily be frustrated by someone who always claims to know *what* is happening, *why* it is happening and *how* we should respond. Job wasn't disobedient and unwilling to follow God. Job was a sufferer, and he needed his friends to trust what they knew to be true about him. Job needed people to share his pain and help him grieve. When our friends face difficult times, we don't have to provide all their answers in order to comfort them. We only need to lovingly support them.

5:1–7 Eliphaz acted like he was God's prophet sent to straighten out Job's life. He claimed to know more about Job than even Job knew! Not all of Eliphaz's words were false, but he spoke about things that he didn't fully understand. It is always easier to analyze than to empathize, because to feel empathy means to put ourselves in the sufferer's position. This can be quite frightening—especially if our friend is suffering from things that could happen to us.

nor does trouble sprout from the ground.
7Yet man is born to trouble
as surely as sparks fly upward.

8"But if it were I, I would appeal to God;
I would lay my cause before him.
9He performs wonders that cannot be fathomed,
miracles that cannot be counted.
10He bestows rain on the earth;
he sends water upon the countryside.
11The lowly he sets on high,
and those who mourn are lifted to safety.
12He thwarts the plans of the crafty,
so that their hands achieve no success.
13He catches the wise in their craftiness,
and the schemes of the wily are swept away.
14Darkness comes upon them in the daytime;
at noon they grope as in the night.
15He saves the needy from the sword in their mouth;
he saves them from the clutches of the powerful.
16So the poor have hope,
and injustice shuts its mouth.

17"Blessed is the man whom God corrects;
so do not despise the discipline of the Almighty.[a]
18For he wounds, but he also binds up;
he injures, but his hands also heal.
19From six calamities he will rescue you;
in seven no harm will befall you.
20In famine he will ransom you from death,
and in battle from the stroke of the sword.
21You will be protected from the lash of the tongue,
and need not fear when destruction comes.
22You will laugh at destruction and famine,
and need not fear the beasts of the earth.
23For you will have a covenant with the stones of the field,
and the wild animals will be at peace with you.
24You will know that your tent is secure;
you will take stock of your property and find nothing missing.
25You will know that your children will be many,
and your descendants like the grass of the earth.
26You will come to the grave in full vigor,
like sheaves gathered in season.

27"We have examined this, and it is true.
So hear it and apply it to yourself."

Job

6 Then Job replied:

2"If only my anguish could be weighed
and all my misery be placed on the scales!
3It would surely outweigh the sand of the seas—
no wonder my words have been impetuous.
4The arrows of the Almighty are in me,
my spirit drinks in their poison;
God's terrors are marshaled against me.
5Does a wild donkey bray when it has grass,
or an ox bellow when it has fodder?
6Is tasteless food eaten without salt,
or is there flavor in the white of an egg[b]?
7I refuse to touch it;
such food makes me ill.

8"Oh, that I might have my request,
that God would grant what I hope for,
9that God would be willing to crush me,

[a]17 Hebrew *Shaddai*; here and throughout Job
[b]6 The meaning of the Hebrew for this phrase is uncertain.

5:8–16 As we seek to comfort others, we must be very careful before saying, "If I were you . . ." No matter what we have experienced in the past, we should not assume that we automatically know what someone else's course of action should be. Every situation is different, and it is difficult to know how we would respond if placed in another's situation.

5:17 Eliphaz assumed that Job was rejecting God's discipline. Though God was not disciplining Job in this instance, Eliphaz was correct in saying that we should welcome God's correction. God wants only the best for us. Sometimes God does discipline us in order to get us to redirect our course back into line with his will. But we shouldn't assume that every experience of suffering in our lives is an instance of God's correction.

5:18–26 Eliphaz's testimony about God was not incorrect, but it was insensitive. Job did not doubt God's sovereignty or faithfulness; he was simply mourning his loss. He had, after all, suddenly lost his children, his wealth and his health. We, like Job, need to grieve for a period of time. Grief and mourning are part of life and necessary if we are to progress in our spiritual life.

5:27 Eliphaz made the mistake of trying to play the role of the Holy Spirit in Job's life. As we seek to comfort our friends, we should not be as eager to tell them what to do as we are to sit quietly with them. Job's friends sat quietly with him at the start and ultimately were more sympathetic when their mouths were shut.

6:1–7 Suffering has a way of stripping us of the protective shields we create and hide behind. Job grieved deeply in these verses. He felt wounded by God and had no reason to pretend that his pain was insignificant. We should not hide our pain and pretend that things are all right. Rather, we should talk about our suffering and get our emotions out in the open where we can deal with them.

6:8–13 Job knew that he hadn't disobeyed God; he was able to take some comfort from that fact. Though he was in intense pain, Job was still concerned about his relationship with God. The opposite is often true with us. Our discouragement often touches our spiritual life rather quickly, and the more pain we feel, the more quickly we give up on God and his ways. But we can learn from Job that when we suffer, we should focus our thoughts on God. He is our only hope for salvation.

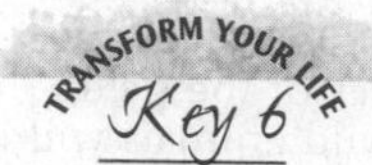

Hope in the Midst of Tragedy

Job 6:2–13 Tragedy can strike anyone. When it does, we may feel as if we have no hope. We may wish we could die and get it over with. But even though tragedy has devastated our lives, God can still redirect our course toward a good future.

Though he was a righteous man, Job lost everything. His children were killed; he lost his riches and his health. All this happened in a matter of days! Job was left with a despairing wife and three friends who blamed him for his own misfortune. Job cried out, "If only my anguish could be weighed and all my misery be placed on the scales! It would surely outweigh the sand of the seas . . . [Oh,] that God would be willing to crush me, to let loose his hand and cut me off! What strength do I have, that I should still hope? What prospects, that I should be patient?" (6:2–3, 9,11).

Job didn't know that the end of his life would be even better than the beginning. God restored everything Job had lost, and then some: "And so he died, old and full of years" (42:17). Even when we're pressed to the point of death, we can rightfully hope that God will eventually redirect the course of our lives.

Turn to Isaiah 61.

to let loose his hand and cut me off!
10 Then I would still have this consolation—
my joy in unrelenting pain—
that I had not denied the words of the Holy One.

11 "What strength do I have, that I should still hope?
What prospects, that I should be patient?
12 Do I have the strength of stone?
Is my flesh bronze?
13 Do I have any power to help myself,
now that success has been driven from me?

14 "A despairing man should have the devotion of his friends,
even though he forsakes the fear of the Almighty.
15 But my brothers are as undependable as intermittent streams,
as the streams that overflow
16 when darkened by thawing ice
and swollen with melting snow,
17 but that cease to flow in the dry season,
and in the heat vanish from their channels.
18 Caravans turn aside from their routes;
they go up into the wasteland and perish.
19 The caravans of Tema look for water,
the traveling merchants of Sheba look in hope.
20 They are distressed, because they had been confident;
they arrive there, only to be disappointed.
21 Now you too have proved to be of no help;
you see something dreadful and are afraid.
22 Have I ever said, 'Give something on my behalf,
pay a ransom for me from your wealth,
23 deliver me from the hand of the enemy,
ransom me from the clutches of the ruthless'?

24 "Teach me, and I will be quiet;
show me where I have been wrong.
25 How painful are honest words!
But what do your arguments prove?
26 Do you mean to correct what I say,
and treat the words of a despairing man as wind?
27 You would even cast lots for the fatherless
and barter away your friend.

6:14–21 Friends are very important. When we are hurting, we depend on them to listen, to weep, to support and to sit with us. Job needed his friends in all of these ways. Yet Job found his friends as undependable as a seasonal brook. He was deeply disappointed in their failure to support him in his pain. They were long on advice but short on compassion. When our friends try to comfort us, we should tell them how they could better help us. And if we are called upon to comfort others, we need to be sensitive to their needs.

28"But now be so kind as to look at me.
Would I lie to your face?
29Relent, do not be unjust;
reconsider, for my integrity is at stake.[a]
30Is there any wickedness on my lips?
Can my mouth not discern malice?

7 "Does not man have hard service on earth?
Are not his days like those of a hired man?
2Like a slave longing for the evening shadows,
or a hired man waiting eagerly for his wages,
3so I have been allotted months of futility,
and nights of misery have been assigned to me.
4When I lie down I think, 'How long before I get up?'
The night drags on, and I toss till dawn.
5My body is clothed with worms and scabs,
my skin is broken and festering.

6"My days are swifter than a weaver's shuttle,
and they come to an end without hope.
7Remember, O God, that my life is but a breath;
my eyes will never see happiness again.
8The eye that now sees me will see me no longer;
you will look for me, but I will be no more.
9As a cloud vanishes and is gone,
so he who goes down to the grave[b] does not return.
10He will never come to his house again;
his place will know him no more.

11"Therefore I will not keep silent;
I will speak out in the anguish of my spirit,
I will complain in the bitterness of my soul.
12Am I the sea, or the monster of the deep,
that you put me under guard?
13When I think my bed will comfort me
and my couch will ease my complaint,
14even then you frighten me with dreams
and terrify me with visions,
15so that I prefer strangling and death,
rather than this body of mine.
16I despise my life; I would not live forever.
Let me alone; my days have no meaning.

17"What is man that you make so much of him,
that you give him so much attention,
18that you examine him every morning
and test him every moment?
19Will you never look away from me,
or let me alone even for an instant?
20If I have sinned, what have I done to you,
O watcher of men?
Why have you made me your target?
Have I become a burden to you?[c]
21Why do you not pardon my offenses
and forgive my sins?
For I will soon lie down in the dust;
you will search for me, but I will be no more."

Bildad

8 Then Bildad the Shuhite replied:

2"How long will you say such things?
Your words are a blustering wind.
3Does God pervert justice?
Does the Almighty pervert what is right?
4When your children sinned against him,
he gave them over to the penalty of their sin.
5But if you will look to God
and plead with the Almighty,
6if you are pure and upright,
even now he will rouse himself on your behalf
and restore you to your rightful place.
7Your beginnings will seem humble,
so prosperous will your future be.

[a]29 Or *my righteousness still stands* [b]9 Hebrew *Sheol*
[c]20 A few manuscripts of the Masoretic Text, an ancient Hebrew scribal tradition and Septuagint; most manuscripts of the Masoretic Text *I have become a burden to myself.*

6:29–30 Job wanted to know what he had done to deserve punishment. He stated in these verses that if he had sinned, he would have admitted it. Job honestly reflected on his spiritual condition and couldn't find anything wrong. We, too, need to honestly review our spiritual condition. If there is sin in our lives, we need to confess it. If we have wronged someone, we need to make restitution. Denying the facts will not help our spiritual growth.

7:1–5 Whenever we suffer from physical pain, the loss of a spouse, a disappointing career, divorce, loneliness, depression, an estranged loved one or any other kind of trouble, nights can be a difficult time. During the daylight hours our work or other activities can take our minds off our situation. But when night falls and we are alone, the reality of our pain stares us in the face with no distractions. When this happens we must talk to God about our pain. He will listen and comfort us. We are never alone—we can always talk to God through prayer.

7:11–21 Job petitioned God. He recognized that God was the only one who could give him relief from his troubles (7:21). Whether or not the pain we feel is a result of our own sins, God is there to comfort us. His timing may not be what we would consider ideal, but God's perspective and timing are always best. We can trust God to deliver us, but in his time, not ours.

8:1–7 "You're getting what you deserve." This is perhaps the most unkind remark we might ever make to a sufferer. In some cases the observation may be true. Foolish choices do often lead to painful consequences. Yet, at times, our suffering is not at all a consequence of sin. Bildad showed his ignorance of God's ways when he tried to connect Job's loss to some hidden sin. We need to reserve judgment about someone who is suffering a setback, for we may not have the whole story. Only God truly knows and understands all the circumstances.

8"Ask the former generations
and find out what their fathers learned,
9for we were born only yesterday and know nothing,
and our days on earth are but a shadow.
10Will they not instruct you and tell you?
Will they not bring forth words from their understanding?
11Can papyrus grow tall where there is no marsh?
Can reeds thrive without water?
12While still growing and uncut,
they wither more quickly than grass.
13Such is the destiny of all who forget God;
so perishes the hope of the godless.
14What he trusts in is fragile[a];
what he relies on is a spider's web.
15He leans on his web, but it gives way;
he clings to it, but it does not hold.
16He is like a well-watered plant in the sunshine,
spreading its shoots over the garden;
17it entwines its roots around a pile of rocks
and looks for a place among the stones.
18But when it is torn from its spot,
that place disowns it and says, 'I never saw you.'
19Surely its life withers away,
and[b] from the soil other plants grow.

20"Surely God does not reject a blameless man
or strengthen the hands of evildoers.
21He will yet fill your mouth with laughter
and your lips with shouts of joy.
22Your enemies will be clothed in shame,
and the tents of the wicked will be no more."

Job

9 Then Job replied:

2"Indeed, I know that this is true.
But how can a mortal be righteous before God?
3Though one wished to dispute with him,
he could not answer him one time out of a thousand.
4His wisdom is profound, his power is vast.
Who has resisted him and come out unscathed?
5He moves mountains without their knowing it
and overturns them in his anger.
6He shakes the earth from its place
and makes its pillars tremble.
7He speaks to the sun and it does not shine;
he seals off the light of the stars.
8He alone stretches out the heavens
and treads on the waves of the sea.
9He is the Maker of the Bear and Orion,
the Pleiades and the constellations of the south.
10He performs wonders that cannot be fathomed,
miracles that cannot be counted.
11When he passes me, I cannot see him;
when he goes by, I cannot perceive him.
12If he snatches away, who can stop him?
Who can say to him, 'What are you doing?'
13God does not restrain his anger;
even the cohorts of Rahab cowered at his feet.

14"How then can I dispute with him?
How can I find words to argue with him?
15Though I were innocent, I could not answer him;
I could only plead with my Judge for mercy.
16Even if I summoned him and he responded,
I do not believe he would give me a hearing.
17He would crush me with a storm
and multiply my wounds for no reason.
18He would not let me regain my breath
but would overwhelm me with misery.
19If it is a matter of strength, he is mighty!
And if it is a matter of justice, who will summon him[c]?
20Even if I were innocent, my mouth would condemn me;
if I were blameless, it would pronounce me guilty.

21"Although I am blameless,
I have no concern for myself;
I despise my own life.
22It is all the same; that is why I say,
'He destroys both the blameless and the wicked.'
23When a scourge brings sudden death,
he mocks the despair of the innocent.
24When a land falls into the hands of the wicked,
he blindfolds its judges.
If it is not he, then who is it?

[a]14 The meaning of the Hebrew for this word is uncertain. [b]19 Or *Surely all the joy it has / is that* [c]19 See Septuagint; Hebrew *me.*

8:8–22 Bildad was correct about some of his theology, but he erred in the application of his knowledge. God viewed Job as blameless and upright (see 1:8; 2:3), not as unfaithful or disobedient. Job's suffering was not the result of a wayward life. We must be very careful before we claim to know the purpose of another person's pain. Our first concern should be to offer comfort and support.

9:1–20 Job knew more than he understood. He knew about God's sovereignty and mercy. He recognized that no one is blameless apart from God's gracious forgiveness. When we feel that God isn't being fair, we should remember that if God were "fair," we would never be able to enter his presence because of our sinful nature. When God seems "unfair," he is always on the side of mercy.

25"My days are swifter than a runner;
they fly away without a glimpse of joy.
26They skim past like boats of papyrus,
like eagles swooping down on their prey.
27If I say, 'I will forget my complaint,
I will change my expression, and smile,'
28I still dread all my sufferings,
for I know you will not hold me
innocent.
29Since I am already found guilty,
why should I struggle in vain?
30Even if I washed myself with soap[a]
and my hands with washing soda,
31you would plunge me into a slime pit
so that even my clothes would detest
me.

32"He is not a man like me that I might
answer him,
that we might confront each other in
court.
33If only there were someone to arbitrate
between us,
to lay his hand upon us both,
34someone to remove God's rod from me,
so that his terror would frighten me no
more.
35Then I would speak up without fear of
him,
but as it now stands with me, I cannot.

10 "I loathe my very life;
therefore I will give free rein to my
complaint
and speak out in the bitterness of my
soul.
2I will say to God: Do not condemn me,
but tell me what charges you have
against me.
3Does it please you to oppress me,
to spurn the work of your hands,
while you smile on the schemes of the
wicked?
4Do you have eyes of flesh?
Do you see as a mortal sees?
5Are your days like those of a mortal
or your years like those of a man,
6that you must search out my faults
and probe after my sin—
7though you know that I am not guilty
and that no one can rescue me from
your hand?

8"Your hands shaped me and made me.
Will you now turn and destroy me?
9Remember that you molded me like clay.
Will you now turn me to dust again?
10Did you not pour me out like milk
and curdle me like cheese,
11clothe me with skin and flesh
and knit me together with bones and
sinews?
12You gave me life and showed me kindness,
and in your providence watched over my
spirit.

13"But this is what you concealed in your
heart,
and I know that this was in your mind:
14If I sinned, you would be watching me
and would not let my offense go
unpunished.
15If I am guilty—woe to me!
Even if I am innocent, I cannot lift my
head,
for I am full of shame
and drowned in[b] my affliction.
16If I hold my head high, you stalk me like a
lion
and again display your awesome power
against me.
17You bring new witnesses against me
and increase your anger toward me;
your forces come against me wave upon
wave.

18"Why then did you bring me out of the
womb?
I wish I had died before any eye saw me.
19If only I had never come into being,
or had been carried straight from the
womb to the grave!
20Are not my few days almost over?
Turn away from me so I can have a
moment's joy
21before I go to the place of no return,
to the land of gloom and deep
shadow,[c]
22to the land of deepest night,
of deep shadow and disorder,
where even the light is like darkness."

Zophar

11 Then Zophar the Naamathite replied:

2"Are all these words to go unanswered?
Is this talker to be vindicated?
3Will your idle talk reduce men to silence?

[a]30 Or *snow* [b]15 Or *and aware of* [c]21 Or *and the shadow of death;* also in verse 22

9:32–35 Job lamented the absence of a mediator to stand between himself and God. We do have a such a mediator—Jesus Christ. We can take our case directly to God because Jesus' death and resurrection gives us access to God's presence.

10:1–17 Job put off measuring his pain and began to direct his thoughts toward God. This subtle shift in direction would become a catalyst for Job's growth though he was not yet able to sense immediate relief. So often in our pain we talk *about* God when we really need to release our feelings *to* God. He does not despise our grief; he welcomes the honest cries of our hearts.

10:18–22 Job couldn't imagine a future of light when he felt so enveloped in darkness. When we suffer, sometimes hope seems far away. Before leaving this world, Jesus gave a picture of hope to the disciples, knowing that they would be facing the grief of his death. He assured them, and us, that we all will have a place with him in eternity (see John 14:1–4). We can have hope because we have Jesus' promise.

Will no one rebuke you when you
mock?
4You say to God, 'My beliefs are flawless
and I am pure in your sight.'
5Oh, how I wish that God would speak,
that he would open his lips against you
6and disclose to you the secrets of wisdom,
for true wisdom has two sides.
Know this: God has even forgotten some
of your sin.

7"Can you fathom the mysteries of God?
Can you probe the limits of the
Almighty?
8They are higher than the heavens—what can
you do?
They are deeper than the depths of the
grave[a]—what can you know?
9Their measure is longer than the earth
and wider than the sea.

10"If he comes along and confines you in
prison
and convenes a court, who can oppose
him?
11Surely he recognizes deceitful men;
and when he sees evil, does he not take
note?
12But a witless man can no more become
wise
than a wild donkey's colt can be born a
man.[b]

13"Yet if you devote your heart to him
and stretch out your hands to him,
14if you put away the sin that is in your hand
and allow no evil to dwell in your tent,
15then you will lift up your face without
shame;
you will stand firm and without fear.
16You will surely forget your trouble,
recalling it only as waters gone by.
17Life will be brighter than noonday,
and darkness will become like morning.
18You will be secure, because there is hope;
you will look about you and take your
rest in safety.
19You will lie down, with no one to make
you afraid,
and many will court your favor.
20But the eyes of the wicked will fail,
and escape will elude them;
their hope will become a dying gasp."

Job

12 Then Job replied:

2"Doubtless you are the people,
and wisdom will die with you!
3But I have a mind as well as you;
I am not inferior to you.
Who does not know all these things?

4"I have become a laughingstock to my
friends,
though I called upon God and he
answered—
a mere laughingstock, though righteous
and blameless!
5Men at ease have contempt for misfortune
as the fate of those whose feet are
slipping.
6The tents of marauders are undisturbed,
and those who provoke God are secure—
those who carry their god in their
hands.[c]

7"But ask the animals, and they will teach
you,
or the birds of the air, and they will tell
you;
8or speak to the earth, and it will teach you,
or let the fish of the sea inform you.
9Which of all these does not know
that the hand of the LORD has done this?
10In his hand is the life of every creature
and the breath of all mankind.
11Does not the ear test words
as the tongue tastes food?
12Is not wisdom found among the aged?
Does not long life bring understanding?

[a]8 Hebrew *than Sheol* [b]12 Or *wild donkey can be born tame* [c]6 Or *secure / in what God's hand brings them*

11:7–12 Zophar knew something about God, but his knowledge was limited. God is indeed sovereign, and no one can oppose him and hope to win. But Job wasn't opposing God; he was trying to make sense of his suffering. Just as God allowed Job to meditate on his suffering, he will allow us time to try and understand why some things are happening to us. We may never find a clear answer, but our faith in God will grow if we learn from our trials to trust God through them rather than complain at each new trial.

11:13–20 As we devote our hearts to God, we will experience a deepening fellowship with him. Fellowship with God never eliminates all our suffering, because pain is part of life, whether we are close to God or rebellious against him. Zophar was mistaken in his theology because he could not believe that Job could suffer and still be righteous.

12:1–6 Job became wiser because of his pain. He understood the worldview of his companions. Theirs was a very comfortable theology: If we are good, God blesses with wealth and comfort. If we are bad, God punishes with poverty and suffering. But as we see here, Job's friends' assumptions were far from the truth. Job knew that he was innocent of wrongdoing, yet he still suffered greatly. His sufferings provided the perspective he needed for a better understanding of God and the way God works in our world. Unlike his friends, Job recognized that suffering was not always a punishment for sin. We, too, should let the difficult times in our lives lead us to a deeper understanding of God.

12:7–25 Job explored the sovereign nature of God. He recognized that God is powerful; humans are not. Herein lies one of the most difficult lessons for all of us to learn—God is in ultimate control. Humility does not come easily to those of us who place great value on power and independence. But the truth is that we are dependent upon God even for our very existence.

13 "To God belong wisdom and power;
counsel and understanding are his.
14 What he tears down cannot be rebuilt;
the man he imprisons cannot be released.
15 If he holds back the waters, there is drought;
if he lets them loose, they devastate the land.
16 To him belong strength and victory;
both deceived and deceiver are his.
17 He leads counselors away stripped
and makes fools of judges.
18 He takes off the shackles put on by kings
and ties a loincloth[a] around their waist.
19 He leads priests away stripped
and overthrows men long established.
20 He silences the lips of trusted advisers
and takes away the discernment of elders.
21 He pours contempt on nobles
and disarms the mighty.
22 He reveals the deep things of darkness
and brings deep shadows into the light.
23 He makes nations great, and destroys them;
he enlarges nations, and disperses them.
24 He deprives the leaders of the earth of their reason;
he sends them wandering through a trackless waste.
25 They grope in darkness with no light;
he makes them stagger like drunkards.

13 "My eyes have seen all this,
my ears have heard and understood it.
2 What you know, I also know;
I am not inferior to you.
3 But I desire to speak to the Almighty
and to argue my case with God.
4 You, however, smear me with lies;
you are worthless physicians, all of you!
5 If only you would be altogether silent!
For you, that would be wisdom.
6 Hear now my argument;
listen to the plea of my lips.
7 Will you speak wickedly on God's behalf?
Will you speak deceitfully for him?
8 Will you show him partiality?
Will you argue the case for God?
9 Would it turn out well if he examined you?
Could you deceive him as you might deceive men?
10 He would surely rebuke you
if you secretly showed partiality.
11 Would not his splendor terrify you?
Would not the dread of him fall on you?
12 Your maxims are proverbs of ashes;
your defenses are defenses of clay.

13 "Keep silent and let me speak;
then let come to me what may.
14 Why do I put myself in jeopardy
and take my life in my hands?
15 Though he slay me, yet will I hope in him;
I will surely[b] defend my ways to his face.
16 Indeed, this will turn out for my deliverance,
for no godless man would dare come before him!
17 Listen carefully to my words;
let your ears take in what I say.
18 Now that I have prepared my case,
I know I will be vindicated.
19 Can anyone bring charges against me?
If so, I will be silent and die.

20 "Only grant me these two things, O God,
and then I will not hide from you:
21 Withdraw your hand far from me,
and stop frightening me with your terrors.
22 Then summon me and I will answer,
or let me speak, and you reply.
23 How many wrongs and sins have I committed?
Show me my offense and my sin.
24 Why do you hide your face
and consider me your enemy?
25 Will you torment a windblown leaf?
Will you chase after dry chaff?
26 For you write down bitter things against me
and make me inherit the sins of my youth.
27 You fasten my feet in shackles;
you keep close watch on all my paths
by putting marks on the soles of my feet.

28 "So man wastes away like something rotten,
like a garment eaten by moths.

14 "Man born of woman
is of few days and full of trouble.

[a] 18 Or *shackles of kings / and ties a belt* [b] 15 Or *He will surely slay me; I have no hope — / yet I will*

13:1–12 Job was clearly angry with his accusers. He saw them as obstacles to his own conversation with God. Like Job's friends, we often find it easy to speak for God when deciding what someone else should do. We need to recognize that we never have the whole story on any one situation. God rarely appoints us as intercessors or spokespersons for himself. We must be sure that we do not presume to speak for God if he has not told us to do so.
13:14–19 Job continued to grow bolder about his case and decided to do something about his circumstances. God is never afraid of our strong feelings. He welcomes the honest expression of our emotions as we seek to draw closer to him. When suffering comes upon us, we can sit and wallow in our misery, or we can come before God with our thoughts and feelings.
14:1–12 We are blessed to live after the time of Jesus Christ. We have seen a demonstration of God's grace and have experienced the power of resurrection in the risen Christ. Job understood much, but he couldn't quite grasp the idea of eternal life. Our days on this earth are numbered and final, and this disturbed Job. Our hope in a future life with Christ should make our troubles here on earth more bearable. We can know with certainty that our sufferings here are not permanent.

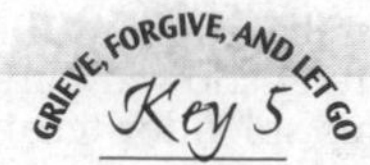

Bringing Our Hard Questions to God

Job 14:1–6 Life often seems unfair to us. Because of this, many of us, like Job, conclude that God is unreasonable in his demands. Of course, God is holy and does not have to answer to us, yet, in our humanness we may sometimes question God about the things in life that we cannot understand. In doing so, we release our angry feelings and are able to continue our search for spiritual renewal.

In the midst of his suffering, Job cried, "Man born of woman is of few days and full of trouble. He springs up like a flower and withers away; like a fleeting shadow, he does not endure. Do you fix your eye on such a one? Will you bring him before you for judgment? Who can bring what is pure from the impure?" (14:1–4). That is a good question—one that most of us have asked in one form or another. Job persisted in his questioning because deep inside he believed God to be good and fair, even though life wasn't. He was honest with his emotions and questions, but he never stopped seeking God.

While working through the pain and unfairness of life, we may have to be satisfied with trusting God, even though we simply don't understand. But be assured that if we trust God and seek him in the hard times, our good Father will respond and bless us for our faith.

Turn to Psalm 103.

2He springs up like a flower and withers away;
like a fleeting shadow, he does not endure.
3Do you fix your eye on such a one?
Will you bring him[a] before you for judgment?
4Who can bring what is pure from the impure?
No one!
5Man's days are determined;
you have decreed the number of his months
and have set limits he cannot exceed.
6So look away from him and let him alone,
till he has put in his time like a hired man.

7"At least there is hope for a tree:
If it is cut down, it will sprout again,
and its new shoots will not fail.
8Its roots may grow old in the ground
and its stump die in the soil,
9yet at the scent of water it will bud
and put forth shoots like a plant.
10But man dies and is laid low;
he breathes his last and is no more.
11As water disappears from the sea
or a riverbed becomes parched and dry,
12so man lies down and does not rise;
till the heavens are no more, men will not awake
or be roused from their sleep.

13"If only you would hide me in the grave[b]
and conceal me till your anger has passed!
If only you would set me a time
and then remember me!
14If a man dies, will he live again?
All the days of my hard service
I will wait for my renewal[c] to come.
15You will call and I will answer you;
you will long for the creature your hands have made.
16Surely then you will count my steps
but not keep track of my sin.

[a]3 Septuagint, Vulgate and Syriac; Hebrew *me*
[b]13 Hebrew *Sheol* [c]14 Or *release*

14:4 Job's insight in this verse reflects the very heart of God's message of grace. Who can make something pure out of something inherently impure? No one—at least no one on earth. Only our gracious God can do this, and he has done so through the death and resurrection of Jesus Christ. Through Christ we are made holy and pure.
14:13–19 We all face times when we simply want to hide from distress and defeat. Job was no exception. He pleaded with God for the chance to hide until his troubles were gone. We need to realize that God wasn't punishing Job or taking pleasure in his anguish. God was allowing Job to pass through a fiery trial. God knows the end result of our suffering and despair—a faith that is purer than gold (see 1 Peter 1:6–7). We must look past the difficult times with encouragement and trust God for the positive effects he desires to work in our lives.

17My offenses will be sealed up in a bag;
you will cover over my sin.

18"But as a mountain erodes and crumbles
and as a rock is moved from its place,
19as water wears away stones
and torrents wash away the soil,
so you destroy man's hope.
20You overpower him once for all, and he is gone;
you change his countenance and send him away.
21If his sons are honored, he does not know it;
if they are brought low, he does not see it.
22He feels but the pain of his own body
and mourns only for himself."

Eliphaz

15 Then Eliphaz the Temanite replied:

2"Would a wise man answer with empty notions
or fill his belly with the hot east wind?
3Would he argue with useless words,
with speeches that have no value?
4But you even undermine piety
and hinder devotion to God.
5Your sin prompts your mouth;
you adopt the tongue of the crafty.
6Your own mouth condemns you, not mine;
your own lips testify against you.

7"Are you the first man ever born?
Were you brought forth before the hills?
8Do you listen in on God's council?
Do you limit wisdom to yourself?
9What do you know that we do not know?
What insights do you have that we do not have?
10The gray-haired and the aged are on our side,
men even older than your father.
11Are God's consolations not enough for you,
words spoken gently to you?
12Why has your heart carried you away,
and why do your eyes flash,
13so that you vent your rage against God
and pour out such words from your mouth?

14"What is man, that he could be pure,
or one born of woman, that he could be righteous?
15If God places no trust in his holy ones,
if even the heavens are not pure in his eyes,
16how much less man, who is vile and corrupt,
who drinks up evil like water!

17"Listen to me and I will explain to you;
let me tell you what I have seen,
18what wise men have declared,
hiding nothing received from their fathers
19(to whom alone the land was given
when no alien passed among them):
20All his days the wicked man suffers torment,
the ruthless through all the years stored up for him.
21Terrifying sounds fill his ears;
when all seems well, marauders attack him.
22He despairs of escaping the darkness;
he is marked for the sword.
23He wanders about—food for vultures[a];
he knows the day of darkness is at hand.
24Distress and anguish fill him with terror;
they overwhelm him, like a king poised to attack,
25because he shakes his fist at God
and vaunts himself against the Almighty,
26defiantly charging against him
with a thick, strong shield.

27"Though his face is covered with fat
and his waist bulges with flesh,
28he will inhabit ruined towns
and houses where no one lives,
houses crumbling to rubble.
29He will no longer be rich and his wealth will not endure,
nor will his possessions spread over the land.
30He will not escape the darkness;
a flame will wither his shoots,
and the breath of God's mouth will carry him away.
31Let him not deceive himself by trusting what is worthless,
for he will get nothing in return.
32Before his time he will be paid in full,
and his branches will not flourish.
33He will be like a vine stripped of its unripe grapes,
like an olive tree shedding its blossoms.

[a]23 Or *about, looking for food*

15:1–16 Eliphaz didn't like Job's attitude. He mistook Job's words of grief for words of pride—foolish words. Be careful not to minimize the importance of expressed grief. Grieving is necessary in order to move from despair to hope and to proceed with life. We would do well to steer clear of the judgmental attitudes exhibited by Job's friends.

15:17–35 Eliphaz thought he had the sole explanation for Job's misery: Suffering was reserved for the ungodly. Therefore Job must be a wicked man, charging at God with a shield of his own making. Why would Eliphaz speak so to Job? What made him think Job was wicked? We may be tempted to adopt Eliphaz's theory as long as things are going well for us. But when things get tough for us and there is no clear cause for our suffering, his theory will no longer be a comfort. Hopefully we are not as callous about the pain of others as Eliphaz was, otherwise we will probably bring more harm than help to our friends.

34For the company of the godless will be
barren,
and fire will consume the tents of those
who love bribes.
35They conceive trouble and give birth to
evil;
their womb fashions deceit."

Job

16 Then Job replied:

2"I have heard many things like these;
miserable comforters are you all!
3Will your long-winded speeches never end?
What ails you that you keep on arguing?
4I also could speak like you,
if you were in my place;
I could make fine speeches against you
and shake my head at you.
5But my mouth would encourage you;
comfort from my lips would bring you
relief.

6"Yet if I speak, my pain is not relieved;
and if I refrain, it does not go away.
7Surely, O God, you have worn me out;
you have devastated my entire
household.
8You have bound me—and it has become a
witness;
my gauntness rises up and testifies
against me.
9God assails me and tears me in his anger
and gnashes his teeth at me;
my opponent fastens on me his piercing
eyes.
10Men open their mouths to jeer at me;
they strike my cheek in scorn
and unite together against me.
11God has turned me over to evil men
and thrown me into the clutches of the
wicked.
12All was well with me, but he shattered me;
he seized me by the neck and crushed
me.
He has made me his target;
13 his archers surround me.
Without pity, he pierces my kidneys
and spills my gall on the ground.
14Again and again he bursts upon me;
he rushes at me like a warrior.

15"I have sewed sackcloth over my skin
and buried my brow in the dust.
16My face is red with weeping,
deep shadows ring my eyes;
17yet my hands have been free of violence
and my prayer is pure.

18"O earth, do not cover my blood;
may my cry never be laid to rest!
19Even now my witness is in heaven;
my advocate is on high.
20My intercessor is my friend[a]
as my eyes pour out tears to God;
21on behalf of a man he pleads with God
as a man pleads for his friend.

22"Only a few years will pass
before I go on the journey of no return.

17 1My spirit is broken,
my days are cut short,
the grave awaits me.
2Surely mockers surround me;
my eyes must dwell on their hostility.

3"Give me, O God, the pledge you demand.
Who else will put up security for me?
4You have closed their minds to
understanding;
therefore you will not let them triumph.
5If a man denounces his friends for reward,
the eyes of his children will fail.

6"God has made me a byword to everyone,
a man in whose face people spit.
7My eyes have grown dim with grief;
my whole frame is but a shadow.
8Upright men are appalled at this;
the innocent are aroused against the
ungodly.
9Nevertheless, the righteous will hold to
their ways,
and those with clean hands will grow
stronger.

10"But come on, all of you, try again!
I will not find a wise man among you.
11My days have passed, my plans are
shattered,
and so are the desires of my heart.
12These men turn night into day;
in the face of darkness they say, 'Light is
near.'
13If the only home I hope for is the grave,[b]
if I spread out my bed in darkness,
14if I say to corruption, 'You are my father,'
and to the worm, 'My mother' or 'My
sister,'
15where then is my hope?
Who can see any hope for me?

[a]20 Or *My friends treat me with scorn* [b]13 Hebrew *Sheol*

16:1–5 Most of us have known "miserable comforters": those who give advice, those who offer solutions, those who lecture us concerning our failures and mistakes. These people generally mean well, but they know little about giving or receiving comfort. Paul tells us that the comfort we offer should grow out of the wealth of comfort we have received from God (see 2 Corinthians 1:3–7). We should take note of the ways we have been comforted by God and let his example guide us as we seek to console the people we love.

16:18—17:2 How frightening death can be to those who are unaware of God's glorious hope. Job knew God. He even knew that God was his advocate and friend. But Job did not completely realize that God's people would spend eternity in heaven. While it is all right to be concerned for our lives, we need never despair, for a home in eternity with God awaits those who believe in him.

16Will it go down to the gates of death[a]?
Will we descend together into the dust?"

Bildad

18 Then Bildad the Shuhite replied:

2"When will you end these speeches?
Be sensible, and then we can talk.
3Why are we regarded as cattle
and considered stupid in your sight?
4You who tear yourself to pieces in your anger,
is the earth to be abandoned for your sake?
Or must the rocks be moved from their place?

5"The lamp of the wicked is snuffed out;
the flame of his fire stops burning.
6The light in his tent becomes dark;
the lamp beside him goes out.
7The vigor of his step is weakened;
his own schemes throw him down.
8His feet thrust him into a net
and he wanders into its mesh.
9A trap seizes him by the heel;
a snare holds him fast.
10A noose is hidden for him on the ground;
a trap lies in his path.
11Terrors startle him on every side
and dog his every step.
12Calamity is hungry for him;
disaster is ready for him when he falls.
13It eats away parts of his skin;
death's firstborn devours his limbs.
14He is torn from the security of his tent
and marched off to the king of terrors.
15Fire resides[b] in his tent;
burning sulfur is scattered over his dwelling.
16His roots dry up below
and his branches wither above.
17The memory of him perishes from the earth;
he has no name in the land.
18He is driven from light into darkness
and is banished from the world.
19He has no offspring or descendants among his people,
no survivor where once he lived.
20Men of the west are appalled at his fate;
men of the east are seized with horror.
21Surely such is the dwelling of an evil man;
such is the place of one who knows not God."

Job

19 Then Job replied:

2"How long will you torment me
and crush me with words?
3Ten times now you have reproached me;
shamelessly you attack me.
4If it is true that I have gone astray,
my error remains my concern alone.
5If indeed you would exalt yourselves above me
and use my humiliation against me,
6then know that God has wronged me
and drawn his net around me.

7"Though I cry, 'I've been wronged!' I get no response;
though I call for help, there is no justice.
8He has blocked my way so I cannot pass;
he has shrouded my paths in darkness.
9He has stripped me of my honor
and removed the crown from my head.
10He tears me down on every side till I am gone;
he uproots my hope like a tree.
11His anger burns against me;
he counts me among his enemies.
12His troops advance in force;
they build a siege ramp against me
and encamp around my tent.

13"He has alienated my brothers from me;
my acquaintances are completely estranged from me.
14My kinsmen have gone away;
my friends have forgotten me.
15My guests and my maidservants count me a stranger;
they look upon me as an alien.
16I summon my servant, but he does not answer,
though I beg him with my own mouth.
17My breath is offensive to my wife;
I am loathsome to my own brothers.
18Even the little boys scorn me;
when I appear, they ridicule me.
19All my intimate friends detest me;
those I love have turned against me.
20I am nothing but skin and bones;
I have escaped with only the skin of my teeth.[c]

21"Have pity on me, my friends, have pity,
for the hand of God has struck me.

[a]16 Hebrew *Sheol* [b]15 Or *Nothing he had remains*
[c]20 Or *only my gums*

18:1–21 We can all sense Job's frustration as he longed for a little comfort from his friends. Bildad wanted to know why Job offered speeches and why he disregarded the words of his friends. The answer is fairly simple: Job's friends didn't know what they were talking about. We should never burden our suffering friends with unnecessary guilt. God is their ultimate judge. We should be a support for our friends in need.

19:1–22 Job's frustration reached the breaking point in these verses. His friends had repeatedly accused him of sin but had yet to prove any of it. Job believed that he was not being punished for some hidden, willful sin. He merely wanted some comfort and understanding. Sufferers long to be understood. Most of the time sufferers need comfort, not judgment. We need to keep this in mind as we seek to help our friends who are grieving a loss in their own lives.

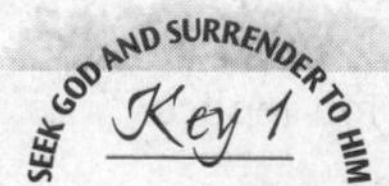

Surrendering in Times of Suffering

Job 19:8–27 When we experience pain and loss because of something beyond our control, we may feel as if God is our enemy. But the anger and confusion we may feel should not separate us from God. We may never fully understand why God allows such torment, but we can surrender to him, trusting that God is in control and always has our best interests in mind.

During his suffering, Job also experienced feelings of bitterness toward God, remarking, "He has blocked my way so I cannot pass; he has shrouded my paths in darkness. He has stripped me of my honor and removed the crown from my head . . . he uproots my hope like a tree . . . he counts me among his enemies . . . All my intimate friends detest me; those I love have turned against me. I am nothing but skin and bones; I have escaped with only the skin of my teeth" (19:8–20).

Despite Job's confusion and pain, however, he was able to conclude his despair with a statement of faith in God: "I know that my Redeemer lives, and that in the end he will stand upon the earth. And after my skin has been destroyed, yet in my flesh I will see God" (19:25–26). Like Job, we must remember that God is on our side even when we don't understand our suffering. We can always surrender to him in trust.

Turn to Psalm 111.

22Why do you pursue me as God does?
Will you never get enough of my flesh?

23"Oh, that my words were recorded,
that they were written on a scroll,
24that they were inscribed with an iron tool
on[a] lead,
or engraved in rock forever!
25I know that my Redeemer[b] lives,
and that in the end he will stand upon
the earth.[c]
26And after my skin has been destroyed,
yet[d] in[e] my flesh I will see God;
27I myself will see him
with my own eyes—I, and not another.
How my heart yearns within me!

28"If you say, 'How we will hound him,
since the root of the trouble lies in
him,[f]'
29you should fear the sword yourselves;
for wrath will bring punishment by the
sword,
and then you will know that there is
judgment.[g]"

Zophar

20 Then Zophar the Naamathite replied:

2"My troubled thoughts prompt me to
answer
because I am greatly disturbed.
3I hear a rebuke that dishonors me,
and my understanding inspires me to
reply.

4"Surely you know how it has been from of
old,
ever since man[h] was placed on the
earth,
5that the mirth of the wicked is brief,
the joy of the godless lasts but a
moment.
6Though his pride reaches to the heavens

[a]24 Or *and* [b]25 Or *defender* [c]25 Or *upon my grave* [d]26 Or *And after I awake, / though this ⌞body⌟ has been destroyed, / then* [e]26 Or */ apart from* [f]28 Many Hebrew manuscripts, Septuagint and Vulgate; most Hebrew manuscripts *me* [g]29 Or */ that you may come to know the Almighty* [h]4 Or *Adam*

19:23–27 Job's growth should encourage us as we struggle with our own pain. As we grieve over losses in this world, we learn to see the reality of eternity. Where once Job saw death as unrelenting darkness (see 10:20–22), here he gave testimony to a living Redeemer. Job's heart yearned for what he knew to be light and life. The Redeemer in whom Job took comfort is the person we call Jesus Christ. He is waiting to redeem us, just as he redeemed Job. All we have to do is believe in him, and he will rescue us from eternal darkness.

19:28–29 If we live by judgment and condemnation, Job reminds us that we will die by the same. It is critical that we live a life guided by grace. It is by grace that we are saved, and it is by grace that we live in this world (see Ephesians 2:5–10). We need to remember that we will be judged by the measure with which we judge others (see Matthew 7:1–5; James 2:12–13).

and his head touches the clouds,
[7]he will perish forever, like his own dung;
those who have seen him will say,
'Where is he?'
[8]Like a dream he flies away, no more to be found,
banished like a vision of the night.
[9]The eye that saw him will not see him again;
his place will look on him no more.
[10]His children must make amends to the poor;
his own hands must give back his wealth.
[11]The youthful vigor that fills his bones
will lie with him in the dust.

[12]"Though evil is sweet in his mouth
and he hides it under his tongue,
[13]though he cannot bear to let it go
and keeps it in his mouth,
[14]yet his food will turn sour in his stomach;
it will become the venom of serpents within him.
[15]He will spit out the riches he swallowed;
God will make his stomach vomit them up.
[16]He will suck the poison of serpents;
the fangs of an adder will kill him.
[17]He will not enjoy the streams,
the rivers flowing with honey and cream.
[18]What he toiled for he must give back uneaten;
he will not enjoy the profit from his trading.
[19]For he has oppressed the poor and left them destitute;
he has seized houses he did not build.

[20]"Surely he will have no respite from his craving;
he cannot save himself by his treasure.
[21]Nothing is left for him to devour;
his prosperity will not endure.
[22]In the midst of his plenty, distress will overtake him;
the full force of misery will come upon him.
[23]When he has filled his belly,
God will vent his burning anger against him
and rain down his blows upon him.
[24]Though he flees from an iron weapon,
a bronze-tipped arrow pierces him.
[25]He pulls it out of his back,
the gleaming point out of his liver.
Terrors will come over him;
[26] total darkness lies in wait for his treasures.
A fire unfanned will consume him
and devour what is left in his tent.
[27]The heavens will expose his guilt;
the earth will rise up against him.
[28]A flood will carry off his house,
rushing waters[a] on the day of God's wrath.
[29]Such is the fate God allots the wicked,
the heritage appointed for them by God."

Job

21

Then Job replied:

[2]"Listen carefully to my words;
let this be the consolation you give me.
[3]Bear with me while I speak,
and after I have spoken, mock on.

[4]"Is my complaint directed to man?
Why should I not be impatient?
[5]Look at me and be astonished;
clap your hand over your mouth.
[6]When I think about this, I am terrified;
trembling seizes my body.
[7]Why do the wicked live on,
growing old and increasing in power?
[8]They see their children established around them,
their offspring before their eyes.
[9]Their homes are safe and free from fear;
the rod of God is not upon them.
[10]Their bulls never fail to breed;
their cows calve and do not miscarry.
[11]They send forth their children as a flock;
their little ones dance about.
[12]They sing to the music of tambourine and harp;
they make merry to the sound of the flute.
[13]They spend their years in prosperity
and go down to the grave[b] in peace.[c]
[14]Yet they say to God, 'Leave us alone!
We have no desire to know your ways.
[15]Who is the Almighty, that we should serve him?
What would we gain by praying to him?'
[16]But their prosperity is not in their own hands,
so I stand aloof from the counsel of the wicked.

[17]"Yet how often is the lamp of the wicked snuffed out?
How often does calamity come upon them,

[a]28 Or *The possessions in his house will be carried off, / washed away* [b]13 Hebrew *Sheol* [c]13 Or *in an instant*

21:1–21 Job refuted Zophar's arguments by saying that the wicked often succeed, have large families, accumulate great wealth and live long lives. Sometimes it even seems that God skips the wicked when he angrily hands out sorrow and suffering (21:17). To a large extent, Job was right. Often the wicked do seem to prosper while the godly suffer. Yet we do not obey and worship God because of *what he can do* for us. Rather we worship and obey God because of *who he is*—the sovereign Creator, the only one worthy of our worship. At the same time, we can be comforted that one day the wicked will be judged and those who follow God will be blessed (see Luke 16:19–31).

the fate God allots in his anger?
18How often are they like straw before the wind,
like chaff swept away by a gale?
19⌊It is said,⌋ 'God stores up a man's punishment for his sons.'
Let him repay the man himself, so that he will know it!
20Let his own eyes see his destruction;
let him drink of the wrath of the Almighty.[a]
21For what does he care about the family he leaves behind
when his allotted months come to an end?

22"Can anyone teach knowledge to God,
since he judges even the highest?
23One man dies in full vigor,
completely secure and at ease,
24his body[b] well nourished,
his bones rich with marrow.
25Another man dies in bitterness of soul,
never having enjoyed anything good.
26Side by side they lie in the dust,
and worms cover them both.

27"I know full well what you are thinking,
the schemes by which you would wrong me.
28You say, 'Where now is the great man's house,
the tents where wicked men lived?'
29Have you never questioned those who travel?
Have you paid no regard to their accounts—
30that the evil man is spared from the day of calamity,
that he is delivered from[c] the day of wrath?
31Who denounces his conduct to his face?
Who repays him for what he has done?
32He is carried to the grave,
and watch is kept over his tomb.
33The soil in the valley is sweet to him;
all men follow after him,
and a countless throng goes[d] before him.

34"So how can you console me with your nonsense?
Nothing is left of your answers but falsehood!"

Eliphaz

22 Then Eliphaz the Temanite replied:

2"Can a man be of benefit to God?
Can even a wise man benefit him?
3What pleasure would it give the Almighty if you were righteous?
What would he gain if your ways were blameless?

4"Is it for your piety that he rebukes you
and brings charges against you?
5Is not your wickedness great?
Are not your sins endless?
6You demanded security from your brothers for no reason;
you stripped men of their clothing, leaving them naked.
7You gave no water to the weary
and you withheld food from the hungry,
8though you were a powerful man, owning land—
an honored man, living on it.
9And you sent widows away empty-handed
and broke the strength of the fatherless.
10That is why snares are all around you,
why sudden peril terrifies you,
11why it is so dark you cannot see,
and why a flood of water covers you.

12"Is not God in the heights of heaven?
And see how lofty are the highest stars!
13Yet you say, 'What does God know?
Does he judge through such darkness?
14Thick clouds veil him, so he does not see us
as he goes about in the vaulted heavens.'
15Will you keep to the old path
that evil men have trod?
16They were carried off before their time,
their foundations washed away by a flood.
17They said to God, 'Leave us alone!
What can the Almighty do to us?'
18Yet it was he who filled their houses with good things,
so I stand aloof from the counsel of the wicked.

19"The righteous see their ruin and rejoice;
the innocent mock them, saying,

[a]*17-20* Verses 17 and 18 may be taken as exclamations and 19 and 20 as declarations. [b]*24* The meaning of the Hebrew for this word is uncertain. [c]*30* Or *man is reserved for the day of calamity, / that he is brought forth to* [d]*33* Or */ as a countless throng went*

21:22–26 Job examined the futility of this world's treasures firsthand. His discovery was simple: Those who have known great prosperity meet the same end as those who have known poverty. All will die, all bodies will return to the dust, and the treasures we store up in this world will meet the same fate. Earthly conditions don't have an impact on eternal perspectives. We should store our treasures in heaven, not on earth (see Matthew 6:19–21).

22:1–10 Eliphaz fabricated a list of sins he was sure Job had committed at one time or another. The problem was that all of Eliphaz's accusations were unfounded. He did not know Job or the things he had done. We must be careful about our reactions to the problems or sins of others. We must not accuse others of things about which we are uninformed.

20'Surely our foes are destroyed,
and fire devours their wealth.'
21"Submit to God and be at peace with him;
in this way prosperity will come to you.
22Accept instruction from his mouth
and lay up his words in your heart.
23If you return to the Almighty, you will be restored:
If you remove wickedness far from your tent
24and assign your nuggets to the dust,
your gold of Ophir to the rocks in the ravines,
25then the Almighty will be your gold,
the choicest silver for you.
26Surely then you will find delight in the Almighty
and will lift up your face to God.
27You will pray to him, and he will hear you,
and you will fulfill your vows.
28What you decide on will be done,
and light will shine on your ways.
29When men are brought low and you say,
'Lift them up!'
then he will save the downcast.
30He will deliver even one who is not innocent,
who will be delivered through the cleanness of your hands."

Job

23 Then Job replied:

2"Even today my complaint is bitter;
his hand[a] is heavy in spite of[b] my groaning.
3If only I knew where to find him;
if only I could go to his dwelling!
4I would state my case before him
and fill my mouth with arguments.
5I would find out what he would answer me,
and consider what he would say.
6Would he oppose me with great power?
No, he would not press charges against me.
7There an upright man could present his case before him,
and I would be delivered forever from my judge.
8"But if I go to the east, he is not there;
if I go to the west, I do not find him.
9When he is at work in the north, I do not see him;
when he turns to the south, I catch no glimpse of him.
10But he knows the way that I take;
when he has tested me, I will come forth as gold.
11My feet have closely followed his steps;
I have kept to his way without turning aside.
12I have not departed from the commands of his lips;
I have treasured the words of his mouth
more than my daily bread.

13"But he stands alone, and who can oppose him?
He does whatever he pleases.
14He carries out his decree against me,
and many such plans he still has in store.
15That is why I am terrified before him;
when I think of all this, I fear him.
16God has made my heart faint;
the Almighty has terrified me.
17Yet I am not silenced by the darkness,
by the thick darkness that covers my face.

24 "Why does the Almighty not set times for judgment?
Why must those who know him look in vain for such days?
2Men move boundary stones;
they pasture flocks they have stolen.
3They drive away the orphan's donkey
and take the widow's ox in pledge.
4They thrust the needy from the path
and force all the poor of the land into hiding.
5Like wild donkeys in the desert,
the poor go about their labor of foraging food;
the wasteland provides food for their children.
6They gather fodder in the fields
and glean in the vineyards of the wicked.
7Lacking clothes, they spend the night naked;
they have nothing to cover themselves in the cold.
8They are drenched by mountain rains
and hug the rocks for lack of shelter.
9The fatherless child is snatched from the breast;
the infant of the poor is seized for a debt.
10Lacking clothes, they go about naked;

[a]2 Septuagint and Syriac; Hebrew / *the hand on me*
[b]2 Or *heavy on me in*

23:1–17 Throughout his trials, Job was honest about what he was thinking and feeling. God is not afraid of our feelings; strong emotions are a natural part of life. God is more concerned with how we choose to express our emotions and how we deal with them. An honest assessment of our feelings is important as we seek spiritual growth.
24:1–25 Why aren't the faithful rewarded or even protected? Why don't exploiters meet a speedy punishment? Where is God when we cry for help? When we face a momentous loss, we often review the foundations of our faith. Job probed the whole realm of God's justice, judgment and timing. And Job came to a humble conclusion: God's ways are just. His timing may confuse us, but God's ways are ultimately just.

they carry the sheaves, but still go hungry.
11They crush olives among the terraces[a];
they tread the winepresses, yet suffer thirst.
12The groans of the dying rise from the city,
and the souls of the wounded cry out for help.
But God charges no one with wrongdoing.

13"There are those who rebel against the light,
who do not know its ways
or stay in its paths.
14When daylight is gone, the murderer rises up
and kills the poor and needy;
in the night he steals forth like a thief.
15The eye of the adulterer watches for dusk;
he thinks, 'No eye will see me,'
and he keeps his face concealed.
16In the dark, men break into houses,
but by day they shut themselves in;
they want nothing to do with the light.
17For all of them, deep darkness is their morning[b];
they make friends with the terrors of darkness.[c]

18"Yet they are foam on the surface of the water;
their portion of the land is cursed,
so that no one goes to the vineyards.
19As heat and drought snatch away the melted snow,
so the grave[d] snatches away those who have sinned.
20The womb forgets them,
the worm feasts on them;
evil men are no longer remembered
but are broken like a tree.
21They prey on the barren and childless woman,
and to the widow show no kindness.
22But God drags away the mighty by his power;
though they become established, they have no assurance of life.
23He may let them rest in a feeling of security,
but his eyes are on their ways.
24For a little while they are exalted, and then they are gone;
they are brought low and gathered up like all others;
they are cut off like heads of grain.

25"If this is not so, who can prove me false
and reduce my words to nothing?"

Bildad

25 Then Bildad the Shuhite replied:

2"Dominion and awe belong to God;
he establishes order in the heights of heaven.
3Can his forces be numbered?
Upon whom does his light not rise?
4How then can a man be righteous before God?
How can one born of woman be pure?
5If even the moon is not bright
and the stars are not pure in his eyes,
6how much less man, who is but a maggot—
a son of man, who is only a worm!"

Job

26 Then Job replied:

2"How you have helped the powerless!
How you have saved the arm that is feeble!
3What advice you have offered to one without wisdom!
And what great insight you have displayed!
4Who has helped you utter these words?
And whose spirit spoke from your mouth?

5"The dead are in deep anguish,
those beneath the waters and all that live in them.
6Death[d] is naked before God;
Destruction[e] lies uncovered.
7He spreads out the northern ⌊skies⌋ over empty space;
he suspends the earth over nothing.
8He wraps up the waters in his clouds,
yet the clouds do not burst under their weight.
9He covers the face of the full moon,
spreading his clouds over it.
10He marks out the horizon on the face of the waters
for a boundary between light and darkness.
11The pillars of the heavens quake,
aghast at his rebuke.
12By his power he churned up the sea;
by his wisdom he cut Rahab to pieces.
13By his breath the skies became fair;
his hand pierced the gliding serpent.

[a] 11 Or *olives between the millstones;* the meaning of the Hebrew for this word is uncertain. [b] 17 Or *them, their morning is like the shadow of death* [c] 17 Or *of the shadow of death* [d] 19,6 Hebrew *Sheol* [e] 6 Hebrew *Abaddon*

24:22–25 Our need for security affects our decisions, attitudes and actions every day. Each of us operates under a working definition of security. We fear anything that threatens that security. Job's entire foundation in this world had been shaken, and yet he learned an important lesson: Real security doesn't lie in what this world has to offer; security lies in the consistency, justice, faithfulness, power and love of God.

14And these are but the outer fringe of his
works;
how faint the whisper we hear of him!
Who then can understand the thunder of
his power?"

27 And Job continued his discourse:
2"As surely as God lives, who has denied
me justice,
the Almighty, who has made me taste
bitterness of soul,
3as long as I have life within me,
the breath of God in my nostrils,
4my lips will not speak wickedness,
and my tongue will utter no deceit.
5I will never admit you are in the right;
till I die, I will not deny my integrity.
6I will maintain my righteousness and never
let go of it;
my conscience will not reproach me as
long as I live.

7"May my enemies be like the wicked,
my adversaries like the unjust!
8For what hope has the godless when he is
cut off,
when God takes away his life?
9Does God listen to his cry
when distress comes upon him?
10Will he find delight in the Almighty?
Will he call upon God at all times?

11"I will teach you about the power of God;
the ways of the Almighty I will not
conceal.
12You have all seen this yourselves.
Why then this meaningless talk?

13"Here is the fate God allots to the wicked,
the heritage a ruthless man receives from
the Almighty:
14However many his children, their fate is the
sword;
his offspring will never have enough to
eat.
15The plague will bury those who survive
him,
and their widows will not weep for
them.
16Though he heaps up silver like dust
and clothes like piles of clay,
17what he lays up the righteous will wear,
and the innocent will divide his silver.
18The house he builds is like a moth's
cocoon,
like a hut made by a watchman.
19He lies down wealthy, but will do so no
more;
when he opens his eyes, all is gone.
20Terrors overtake him like a flood;
a tempest snatches him away in the
night.
21The east wind carries him off, and he is
gone;
it sweeps him out of his place.
22It hurls itself against him without mercy
as he flees headlong from its power.
23It claps its hands in derision
and hisses him out of his place.

28 "There is a mine for silver
and a place where gold is refined.
2Iron is taken from the earth,
and copper is smelted from ore.
3Man puts an end to the darkness;
he searches the farthest recesses
for ore in the blackest darkness.
4Far from where people dwell he cuts a
shaft,
in places forgotten by the foot of man;
far from men he dangles and sways.
5The earth, from which food comes,
is transformed below as by fire;
6sapphires[a] come from its rocks,
and its dust contains nuggets of gold.
7No bird of prey knows that hidden path,
no falcon's eye has seen it.
8Proud beasts do not set foot on it,
and no lion prowls there.
9Man's hand assaults the flinty rock
and lays bare the roots of the mountains.
10He tunnels through the rock;
his eyes see all its treasures.
11He searches[b] the sources of the rivers
and brings hidden things to light.

12"But where can wisdom be found?
Where does understanding dwell?
13Man does not comprehend its worth;
it cannot be found in the land of the
living.
14The deep says, 'It is not in me';
the sea says, 'It is not with me.'
15It cannot be bought with the finest gold,
nor can its price be weighed in silver.
16It cannot be bought with the gold of
Ophir,
with precious onyx or sapphires.
17Neither gold nor crystal can compare with
it,
nor can it be had for jewels of gold.
18Coral and jasper are not worthy of
mention;
the price of wisdom is beyond rubies.
19The topaz of Cush cannot compare with it;
it cannot be bought with pure gold.

20"Where then does wisdom come from?
Where does understanding dwell?
21It is hidden from the eyes of every living
thing,
concealed even from the birds of the air.
22Destruction[c] and Death say,
'Only a rumor of it has reached our
ears.'
23God understands the way to it
and he alone knows where it dwells,

[a] 6 Or *lapis lazuli*; also in verse 16 [b] 11 Septuagint, Aquila and Vulgate; Hebrew *He dams up* [c] 22 Hebrew *Abaddon*

24for he views the ends of the earth
and sees everything under the heavens.
25When he established the force of the wind
and measured out the waters,
26when he made a decree for the rain
and a path for the thunderstorm,
27then he looked at wisdom and appraised it;
he confirmed it and tested it.
28And he said to man,
'The fear of the Lord—that is wisdom,
and to shun evil is understanding.' "

29 Job continued his discourse:

2"How I long for the months gone by,
for the days when God watched over me,
3when his lamp shone upon my head
and by his light I walked through darkness!
4Oh, for the days when I was in my prime,
when God's intimate friendship blessed my house,
5when the Almighty was still with me
and my children were around me,
6when my path was drenched with cream
and the rock poured out for me streams of olive oil.

7"When I went to the gate of the city
and took my seat in the public square,
8the young men saw me and stepped aside
and the old men rose to their feet;
9the chief men refrained from speaking
and covered their mouths with their hands;
10the voices of the nobles were hushed,
and their tongues stuck to the roof of their mouths.
11Whoever heard me spoke well of me,
and those who saw me commended me,
12because I rescued the poor who cried for help,
and the fatherless who had none to assist him.
13The man who was dying blessed me;
I made the widow's heart sing.
14I put on righteousness as my clothing;
justice was my robe and my turban.
15I was eyes to the blind
and feet to the lame.
16I was a father to the needy;
I took up the case of the stranger.
17I broke the fangs of the wicked
and snatched the victims from their teeth.

18"I thought, 'I will die in my own house,
my days as numerous as the grains of sand.
19My roots will reach to the water,
and the dew will lie all night on my branches.
20My glory will remain fresh in me,
the bow ever new in my hand.'

21"Men listened to me expectantly,
waiting in silence for my counsel.
22After I had spoken, they spoke no more;
my words fell gently on their ears.
23They waited for me as for showers
and drank in my words as the spring rain.
24When I smiled at them, they scarcely believed it;
the light of my face was precious to them.[a]
25I chose the way for them and sat as their chief;
I dwelt as a king among his troops;
I was like one who comforts mourners.

30 "But now they mock me,
men younger than I,
whose fathers I would have disdained
to put with my sheep dogs.
2Of what use was the strength of their hands to me,
since their vigor had gone from them?
3Haggard from want and hunger,
they roamed[b] the parched land
in desolate wastelands at night.
4In the brush they gathered salt herbs,
and their food[c] was the root of the broom tree.
5They were banished from their fellow men,
shouted at as if they were thieves.
6They were forced to live in the dry stream beds,
among the rocks and in holes in the ground.
7They brayed among the bushes
and huddled in the undergrowth.
8A base and nameless brood,
they were driven out of the land.

9"And now their sons mock me in song;

[a]24 The meaning of the Hebrew for this clause is uncertain. [b]3 Or *gnawed* [c]4 Or *fuel*

28:28 This is God's message to us: Wisdom is found only in God and his ways. But how do we know what God expects of us? God has given us his truth in the Bible. We are responsible to study it and discover what he expects of us. We should ask God to show us his truth, and then take the time to listen (see James 1:5–6, 22). As God reveals his truth to us, he will give us the strength and encouragement we need to follow his plan for our lives.
29:1–3 Job remembered the days when he was prosperous and God was blessing him. Those were days when Job felt secure. As hard as it is for us to believe, God continues to care for us when we suffer. Even when the suffering is brought about by our own actions, God is there, waiting for us to repent and call on him for deliverance.
29:18–19 Our lives may be very different from what we had hoped they would be. Accepting the reality of our lives as they are, not as we wish them to be, is the first step toward surrendering our lives to God. Only when we have surrendered to him can God begin the process of spiritual renewal that can completely transform us into what he wants us to be.

I have become a byword among them.
10They detest me and keep their distance;
they do not hesitate to spit in my face.
11Now that God has unstrung my bow and afflicted me,
they throw off restraint in my presence.
12On my right the tribe[a] attacks;
they lay snares for my feet,
they build their siege ramps against me.
13They break up my road;
they succeed in destroying me—
without anyone's helping them.[b]
14They advance as through a gaping breach;
amid the ruins they come rolling in.
15Terrors overwhelm me;
my dignity is driven away as by the wind,
my safety vanishes like a cloud.

16"And now my life ebbs away;
days of suffering grip me.
17Night pierces my bones;
my gnawing pains never rest.
18In his great power ⌞God⌟ becomes like clothing to me[c];
he binds me like the neck of my garment.
19He throws me into the mud,
and I am reduced to dust and ashes.

20"I cry out to you, O God, but you do not answer;
I stand up, but you merely look at me.
21You turn on me ruthlessly;
with the might of your hand you attack me.
22You snatch me up and drive me before the wind;
you toss me about in the storm.
23I know you will bring me down to death,
to the place appointed for all the living.

24"Surely no one lays a hand on a broken man
when he cries for help in his distress.
25Have I not wept for those in trouble?
Has not my soul grieved for the poor?
26Yet when I hoped for good, evil came;
when I looked for light, then came darkness.
27The churning inside me never stops;
days of suffering confront me.
28I go about blackened, but not by the sun;
I stand up in the assembly and cry for help.
29I have become a brother of jackals,
a companion of owls.
30My skin grows black and peels;
my body burns with fever.
31My harp is tuned to mourning,
and my flute to the sound of wailing.

31 "I made a covenant with my eyes
not to look lustfully at a girl.
2For what is man's lot from God above,
his heritage from the Almighty on high?
3Is it not ruin for the wicked,
disaster for those who do wrong?
4Does he not see my ways
and count my every step?

5"If I have walked in falsehood
or my foot has hurried after deceit—
6let God weigh me in honest scales
and he will know that I am blameless—
7if my steps have turned from the path,
if my heart has been led by my eyes,
or if my hands have been defiled,
8then may others eat what I have sown,
and may my crops be uprooted.

9"If my heart has been enticed by a woman,
or if I have lurked at my neighbor's door,
10then may my wife grind another man's grain,
and may other men sleep with her.
11For that would have been shameful,
a sin to be judged.
12It is a fire that burns to Destruction[d];
it would have uprooted my harvest.

13"If I have denied justice to my menservants and maidservants
when they had a grievance against me,
14what will I do when God confronts me?
What will I answer when called to account?
15Did not he who made me in the womb make them?
Did not the same one form us both within our mothers?

16"If I have denied the desires of the poor
or let the eyes of the widow grow weary,
17if I have kept my bread to myself,
not sharing it with the fatherless—
18but from my youth I reared him as would a father,
and from my birth I guided the widow—
19if I have seen anyone perishing for lack of clothing,
or a needy man without a garment,
20and his heart did not bless me
for warming him with the fleece from my sheep,
21if I have raised my hand against the fatherless,

[a] 12 The meaning of the Hebrew for this word is uncertain. [b] 13 Or *me.* / *'No one can help him,' ⌞they say⌟.* [c] 18 Hebrew; Septuagint *⌞God⌟ grasps my clothing* [d] 12 Hebrew *Abaddon*

30:20 As his suffering progressed, Job began to feel that God wasn't listening. Yet, if we look closely, Job hadn't given God the chance to answer. Often we, like Job, talk about God and even talk to God, but we don't stop our complaining long enough to let him respond. God speaks to us through the Bible and through our times of prayer and meditation. When we are facing difficulties, we need to sit still and wait for God to speak to our hearts.

knowing that I had influence in court,
22then let my arm fall from the shoulder,
let it be broken off at the joint.
23For I dreaded destruction from God,
and for fear of his splendor I could not do such things.

24"If I have put my trust in gold
or said to pure gold, 'You are my security,'
25if I have rejoiced over my great wealth,
the fortune my hands had gained,
26if I have regarded the sun in its radiance
or the moon moving in splendor,
27so that my heart was secretly enticed
and my hand offered them a kiss of homage,
28then these also would be sins to be judged,
for I would have been unfaithful to God on high.

29"If I have rejoiced at my enemy's misfortune
or gloated over the trouble that came to him—
30I have not allowed my mouth to sin
by invoking a curse against his life—
31if the men of my household have never said,
'Who has not had his fill of Job's meat?'—
32but no stranger had to spend the night in the street,
for my door was always open to the traveler—
33if I have concealed my sin as men do,[a]
by hiding my guilt in my heart
34because I so feared the crowd
and so dreaded the contempt of the clans
that I kept silent and would not go outside
35("Oh, that I had someone to hear me!
I sign now my defense—let the Almighty answer me;
let my accuser put his indictment in writing.
36Surely I would wear it on my shoulder,
I would put it on like a crown.
37I would give him an account of my every step;
like a prince I would approach him.)—
38"if my land cries out against me
and all its furrows are wet with tears,
39if I have devoured its yield without payment
or broken the spirit of its tenants,
40then let briers come up instead of wheat
and weeds instead of barley."

The words of Job are ended.

Elihu

32 So these three men stopped answering
Job, because he was righteous in his
own eyes. 2But Elihu son of Barakel the Buzite,
of the family of Ram, became very angry with
Job for justifying himself rather than God. 3He
was also angry with the three friends, because
they had found no way to refute Job, and yet
had condemned him.[b] 4Now Elihu had waited
before speaking to Job because they were older
than he. 5But when he saw that the three men
had nothing more to say, his anger was aroused.
6So Elihu son of Barakel the Buzite said:

"I am young in years,
and you are old;
that is why I was fearful,
not daring to tell you what I know.
7I thought, 'Age should speak;
advanced years should teach wisdom.'
8But it is the spirit[c] in a man,
the breath of the Almighty, that gives him understanding.
9It is not only the old[d] who are wise,
not only the aged who understand what is right.

10"Therefore I say: Listen to me;
I too will tell you what I know.
11I waited while you spoke,
I listened to your reasoning;
while you were searching for words,
12 I gave you my full attention.
But not one of you has proved Job wrong;
none of you has answered his arguments.
13Do not say, 'We have found wisdom;
let God refute him, not man.'
14But Job has not marshaled his words against me,
and I will not answer him with your arguments.

[a] 33 Or *as Adam did* [b] 3 Masoretic Text; an ancient Hebrew scribal tradition *Job, and so had condemned God* [c] 8 Or *Spirit*; also in verse 18 [d] 9 Or *many*; or *great*

31:35–36 Job wished that God would show him his failure. He was tired and wanted some kind of resolution to his suffering. He wanted God to explain what was going on. If God found Job guilty of something, Job was confident that he could stand up to the charges. Though Job was indeed innocent of sin, his attitude here is not acceptable. He arrogantly demanded that God answer him, instead of humbly acknowledging that God is righteous and just. Though we don't always understand why we are suffering, God welcomes our honest expressions of frustration. But we must guard ourselves against becoming arrogant.

32:6–20 We will always find people around us who think they have all the answers. They will give us reasons for our actions and will think that they alone have been granted wisdom. Job's friend Elihu was not that way. He carefully listened to all the arguments and weighed each person's words before he spoke. We need to follow Elihu's example and carefully weigh our words before we try to tell someone what to do or how to think about something.

15"They are dismayed and have no more to say;
words have failed them.
16Must I wait, now that they are silent,
now that they stand there with no reply?
17I too will have my say;
I too will tell what I know.
18For I am full of words,
and the spirit within me compels me;
19inside I am like bottled-up wine,
like new wineskins ready to burst.
20I must speak and find relief;
I must open my lips and reply.
21I will show partiality to no one,
nor will I flatter any man;
22for if I were skilled in flattery,
my Maker would soon take me away.

33 "But now, Job, listen to my words;
pay attention to everything I say.
2I am about to open my mouth;
my words are on the tip of my tongue.
3My words come from an upright heart;
my lips sincerely speak what I know.
4The Spirit of God has made me;
the breath of the Almighty gives me life.
5Answer me then, if you can;
prepare yourself and confront me.
6I am just like you before God;
I too have been taken from clay.
7No fear of me should alarm you,
nor should my hand be heavy upon you.

8"But you have said in my hearing—
I heard the very words—
9'I am pure and without sin;
I am clean and free from guilt.
10Yet God has found fault with me;
he considers me his enemy.
11He fastens my feet in shackles;
he keeps close watch on all my paths.'

12"But I tell you, in this you are not right,
for God is greater than man.
13Why do you complain to him
that he answers none of man's words[a]?
14For God does speak—now one way, now another—
though man may not perceive it.
15In a dream, in a vision of the night,
when deep sleep falls on men
as they slumber in their beds,
16he may speak in their ears
and terrify them with warnings,
17to turn man from wrongdoing
and keep him from pride,
18to preserve his soul from the pit,[b]
his life from perishing by the sword.[c]
19Or a man may be chastened on a bed of pain
with constant distress in his bones,
20so that his very being finds food repulsive
and his soul loathes the choicest meal.
21His flesh wastes away to nothing,
and his bones, once hidden, now stick out.
22His soul draws near to the pit,[d]
and his life to the messengers of death.[e]

23"Yet if there is an angel on his side
as a mediator, one out of a thousand,
to tell a man what is right for him,
24to be gracious to him and say,
'Spare him from going down to the pit[f];
I have found a ransom for him'—
25then his flesh is renewed like a child's;
it is restored as in the days of his youth.
26He prays to God and finds favor with him,
he sees God's face and shouts for joy;
he is restored by God to his righteous state.
27Then he comes to men and says,
'I sinned, and perverted what was right,
but I did not get what I deserved.
28He redeemed my soul from going down to the pit,[g]
and I will live to enjoy the light.'

29"God does all these things to a man—
twice, even three times—
30to turn back his soul from the pit,[h]
that the light of life may shine on him.

31"Pay attention, Job, and listen to me;
be silent, and I will speak.
32If you have anything to say, answer me;
speak up, for I want you to be cleared.
33But if not, then listen to me;
be silent, and I will teach you wisdom."

34 Then Elihu said:

2"Hear my words, you wise men;
listen to me, you men of learning.
3For the ear tests words
as the tongue tastes food.
4Let us discern for ourselves what is right;
let us learn together what is good.

5"Job says, 'I am innocent,
but God denies me justice.
6Although I am right,
I am considered a liar;
although I am guiltless,
his arrow inflicts an incurable wound.'
7What man is like Job,
who drinks scorn like water?
8He keeps company with evildoers;
he associates with wicked men.
9For he says, 'It profits a man nothing
when he tries to please God.'

10"So listen to me, you men of understanding.

a13 Or that he does not answer for any of his actions
b18 Or preserve him from the grave
c18 Or from crossing the River
d22 Or He draws near to the grave
e22 Or to the dead
f24 Or grave
g28 Or redeemed me from going down to the grave
h30 Or turn him back from the grave

Far be it from God to do evil,
from the Almighty to do wrong.
11 He repays a man for what he has done;
he brings upon him what his conduct deserves.
12 It is unthinkable that God would do wrong,
that the Almighty would pervert justice.
13 Who appointed him over the earth?
Who put him in charge of the whole world?
14 If it were his intention
and he withdrew his spirit[a] and breath,
15 all mankind would perish together
and man would return to the dust.

16 "If you have understanding, hear this;
listen to what I say.
17 Can he who hates justice govern?
Will you condemn the just and mighty One?
18 Is he not the One who says to kings, 'You are worthless,'
and to nobles, 'You are wicked,'
19 who shows no partiality to princes
and does not favor the rich over the poor,
for they are all the work of his hands?
20 They die in an instant, in the middle of the night;
the people are shaken and they pass away;
the mighty are removed without human hand.

21 "His eyes are on the ways of men;
he sees their every step.
22 There is no dark place, no deep shadow,
where evildoers can hide.
23 God has no need to examine men further,
that they should come before him for judgment.
24 Without inquiry he shatters the mighty
and sets up others in their place.
25 Because he takes note of their deeds,
he overthrows them in the night and they are crushed.
26 He punishes them for their wickedness
where everyone can see them,
27 because they turned from following him
and had no regard for any of his ways.
28 They caused the cry of the poor to come before him,
so that he heard the cry of the needy.
29 But if he remains silent, who can condemn him?
If he hides his face, who can see him?
Yet he is over man and nation alike,
30 to keep a godless man from ruling,
from laying snares for the people.

31 "Suppose a man says to God,
'I am guilty but will offend no more.
32 Teach me what I cannot see;
if I have done wrong, I will not do so again.'
33 Should God then reward you on your terms,
when you refuse to repent?
You must decide, not I;
so tell me what you know.

34 "Men of understanding declare,
wise men who hear me say to me,
35 'Job speaks without knowledge;
his words lack insight.'
36 Oh, that Job might be tested to the utmost
for answering like a wicked man!
37 To his sin he adds rebellion;
scornfully he claps his hands among us
and multiplies his words against God."

35

Then Elihu said:

2 "Do you think this is just?
You say, 'I will be cleared by God.[b]'
3 Yet you ask him, 'What profit is it to me,[c]
and what do I gain by not sinning?'

4 "I would like to reply to you
and to your friends with you.
5 Look up at the heavens and see;
gaze at the clouds so high above you.
6 If you sin, how does that affect him?
If your sins are many, what does that do to him?
7 If you are righteous, what do you give to him,
or what does he receive from your hand?
8 Your wickedness affects only a man like yourself,
and your righteousness only the sons of men.

9 "Men cry out under a load of oppression;
they plead for relief from the arm of the powerful.
10 But no one says, 'Where is God my Maker,
who gives songs in the night,
11 who teaches more to us than to[d] the beasts of the earth
and makes us wiser than[e] the birds of the air?'
12 He does not answer when men cry out
because of the arrogance of the wicked.
13 Indeed, God does not listen to their empty plea;
the Almighty pays no attention to it.
14 How much less, then, will he listen
when you say that you do not see him,
that your case is before him
and you must wait for him,
15 and further, that his anger never punishes
and he does not take the least notice of wickedness.[f]
16 So Job opens his mouth with empty talk;
without knowledge he multiplies words."

[a] 14 Or *Spirit* [b] 2 Or *My righteousness is more than God's* [c] 3 Or *you* [d] 11 Or *teaches us by* [e] 11 Or *us wise by* [f] 15 Symmachus, Theodotion and Vulgate; the meaning of the Hebrew for this word is uncertain.

36

Elihu continued:

2"Bear with me a little longer and I will show you
that there is more to be said in God's behalf.
3I get my knowledge from afar;
I will ascribe justice to my Maker.
4Be assured that my words are not false;
one perfect in knowledge is with you.

5"God is mighty, but does not despise men;
he is mighty, and firm in his purpose.
6He does not keep the wicked alive
but gives the afflicted their rights.
7He does not take his eyes off the righteous;
he enthrones them with kings
and exalts them forever.
8But if men are bound in chains,
held fast by cords of affliction,
9he tells them what they have done—
that they have sinned arrogantly.
10He makes them listen to correction
and commands them to repent of their evil.
11If they obey and serve him,
they will spend the rest of their days in prosperity
and their years in contentment.
12But if they do not listen,
they will perish by the sword[a]
and die without knowledge.

13"The godless in heart harbor resentment;
even when he fetters them, they do not cry for help.
14They die in their youth,
among male prostitutes of the shrines.
15But those who suffer he delivers in their suffering;
he speaks to them in their affliction.

16"He is wooing you from the jaws of distress
to a spacious place free from restriction,
to the comfort of your table laden with choice food.
17But now you are laden with the judgment due the wicked;
judgment and justice have taken hold of you.
18Be careful that no one entices you by riches;
do not let a large bribe turn you aside.
19Would your wealth
or even all your mighty efforts
sustain you so you would not be in distress?
20Do not long for the night,
to drag people away from their homes.[b]
21Beware of turning to evil,
which you seem to prefer to affliction.

22"God is exalted in his power.
Who is a teacher like him?
23Who has prescribed his ways for him,
or said to him, 'You have done wrong'?
24Remember to extol his work,
which men have praised in song.
25All mankind has seen it;
men gaze on it from afar.
26How great is God—beyond our understanding!
The number of his years is past finding out.

27"He draws up the drops of water,
which distill as rain to the streams[c];
28the clouds pour down their moisture
and abundant showers fall on mankind.
29Who can understand how he spreads out the clouds,
how he thunders from his pavilion?
30See how he scatters his lightning about him,
bathing the depths of the sea.
31This is the way he governs[d] the nations
and provides food in abundance.
32He fills his hands with lightning
and commands it to strike its mark.
33His thunder announces the coming storm;
even the cattle make known its approach.[e]

37

"At this my heart pounds
and leaps from its place.
2Listen! Listen to the roar of his voice,
to the rumbling that comes from his mouth.
3He unleashes his lightning beneath the whole heaven
and sends it to the ends of the earth.
4After that comes the sound of his roar;
he thunders with his majestic voice.
When his voice resounds,
he holds nothing back.
5God's voice thunders in marvelous ways;
he does great things beyond our understanding.
6He says to the snow, 'Fall on the earth,'
and to the rain shower, 'Be a mighty downpour.'
7So that all men he has made may know his work,
he stops every man from his labor.[f]
8The animals take cover;
they remain in their dens.
9The tempest comes out from its chamber,
the cold from the driving winds.
10The breath of God produces ice,

[a] 12 Or *will cross the River* [b] 20 The meaning of the Hebrew for verses 18-20 is uncertain. [c] 27 Or *distill from the mist as rain* [d] 31 Or *nourishes* [e] 33 Or *announces his coming— / the One zealous against evil* [f] 7 Or / *he fills all men with fear by his power*

37:1–24 God will soon deliver a speech similar to Elihu's. God is the Creator, the Almighty, but he is not beyond our reach. He has made himself available to us, even when we fall desperately short of his glorious ideals.

and the broad waters become frozen.
[11]He loads the clouds with moisture;
he scatters his lightning through them.
[12]At his direction they swirl around
over the face of the whole earth
to do whatever he commands them.
[13]He brings the clouds to punish men,
or to water his earth[a] and show his love.

[14]"Listen to this, Job;
stop and consider God's wonders.
[15]Do you know how God controls the clouds
and makes his lightning flash?
[16]Do you know how the clouds hang poised,
those wonders of him who is perfect in knowledge?
[17]You who swelter in your clothes
when the land lies hushed under the south wind,
[18]can you join him in spreading out the skies,
hard as a mirror of cast bronze?

[19]"Tell us what we should say to him;
we cannot draw up our case because of our darkness.
[20]Should he be told that I want to speak?
Would any man ask to be swallowed up?
[21]Now no one can look at the sun,
bright as it is in the skies
after the wind has swept them clean.
[22]Out of the north he comes in golden splendor;
God comes in awesome majesty.
[23]The Almighty is beyond our reach and exalted in power;
in his justice and great righteousness, he does not oppress.
[24]Therefore, men revere him,
for does he not have regard for all the wise in heart?[b]"

The LORD Speaks

38 Then the LORD answered Job out of the storm. He said:

[2]"Who is this that darkens my counsel
with words without knowledge?
[3]Brace yourself like a man;
I will question you,
and you shall answer me.

[4]"Where were you when I laid the earth's foundation?
Tell me, if you understand.
[5]Who marked off its dimensions? Surely you know!
Who stretched a measuring line across it?
[6]On what were its footings set,
or who laid its cornerstone—
[7]while the morning stars sang together
and all the angels[c] shouted for joy?

[8]"Who shut up the sea behind doors
when it burst forth from the womb,
[9]when I made the clouds its garment
and wrapped it in thick darkness,
[10]when I fixed limits for it
and set its doors and bars in place,
[11]when I said, 'This far you may come and no farther;
here is where your proud waves halt'?

[12]"Have you ever given orders to the morning,
or shown the dawn its place,
[13]that it might take the earth by the edges
and shake the wicked out of it?
[14]The earth takes shape like clay under a seal;
its features stand out like those of a garment.
[15]The wicked are denied their light,
and their upraised arm is broken.

[16]"Have you journeyed to the springs of the sea
or walked in the recesses of the deep?
[17]Have the gates of death been shown to you?
Have you seen the gates of the shadow of death[d]?
[18]Have you comprehended the vast expanses of the earth?
Tell me, if you know all this.

[19]"What is the way to the abode of light?
And where does darkness reside?
[20]Can you take them to their places?
Do you know the paths to their dwellings?
[21]Surely you know, for you were already born!
You have lived so many years!

[22]"Have you entered the storehouses of the snow
or seen the storehouses of the hail,
[23]which I reserve for times of trouble,
for days of war and battle?
[24]What is the way to the place where the lightning is dispersed,
or the place where the east winds are scattered over the earth?

[a]13 Or *to favor them* [b]24 Or *for he does not have regard for any who think they are wise.* [c]7 Hebrew *the sons of God* [d]17 Or *gates of deep shadows*

38:2—39:30 God used a series of questions to illustrate how little Job knew about creation and God's ways. If Job knew nothing of these mysteries, how could he question God? All Job could do was worship and trust God. We, too, may wonder why we suffer. We may wonder why bad things happen to us and to those we love. But we, like Job, are finite and cannot understand the ways of the infinite God. All we can do is praise him and await his deliverance.

25Who cuts a channel for the torrents of rain,
and a path for the thunderstorm,
26to water a land where no man lives,
a desert with no one in it,
27to satisfy a desolate wasteland
and make it sprout with grass?
28Does the rain have a father?
Who fathers the drops of dew?
29From whose womb comes the ice?
Who gives birth to the frost from the heavens
30when the waters become hard as stone,
when the surface of the deep is frozen?

31"Can you bind the beautiful[a] Pleiades?
Can you loose the cords of Orion?
32Can you bring forth the constellations in their seasons[b]
or lead out the Bear[c] with its cubs?
33Do you know the laws of the heavens?
Can you set up ⌊God's[d]⌋ dominion over the earth?

34"Can you raise your voice to the clouds
and cover yourself with a flood of water?
35Do you send the lightning bolts on their way?
Do they report to you, 'Here we are'?
36Who endowed the heart[e] with wisdom
or gave understanding to the mind[e]?
37Who has the wisdom to count the clouds?
Who can tip over the water jars of the heavens
38when the dust becomes hard
and the clods of earth stick together?

39"Do you hunt the prey for the lioness
and satisfy the hunger of the lions
40when they crouch in their dens
or lie in wait in a thicket?
41Who provides food for the raven
when its young cry out to God
and wander about for lack of food?

39 "Do you know when the mountain goats give birth?
Do you watch when the doe bears her fawn?
2Do you count the months till they bear?
Do you know the time they give birth?
3They crouch down and bring forth their young;
their labor pains are ended.
4Their young thrive and grow strong in the wilds;
they leave and do not return.

5"Who let the wild donkey go free?
Who untied his ropes?
6I gave him the wasteland as his home,
the salt flats as his habitat.
7He laughs at the commotion in the town;
he does not hear a driver's shout.
8He ranges the hills for his pasture
and searches for any green thing.

9"Will the wild ox consent to serve you?
Will he stay by your manger at night?
10Can you hold him to the furrow with a harness?
Will he till the valleys behind you?
11Will you rely on him for his great strength?
Will you leave your heavy work to him?
12Can you trust him to bring in your grain
and gather it to your threshing floor?

13"The wings of the ostrich flap joyfully,
but they cannot compare with the pinions and feathers of the stork.
14She lays her eggs on the ground
and lets them warm in the sand,
15unmindful that a foot may crush them,
that some wild animal may trample them.
16She treats her young harshly, as if they were not hers;
she cares not that her labor was in vain,
17for God did not endow her with wisdom
or give her a share of good sense.
18Yet when she spreads her feathers to run,
she laughs at horse and rider.

19"Do you give the horse his strength
or clothe his neck with a flowing mane?
20Do you make him leap like a locust,
striking terror with his proud snorting?
21He paws fiercely, rejoicing in his strength,
and charges into the fray.
22He laughs at fear, afraid of nothing;
he does not shy away from the sword.
23The quiver rattles against his side,
along with the flashing spear and lance.
24In frenzied excitement he eats up the ground;
he cannot stand still when the trumpet sounds.
25At the blast of the trumpet he snorts, 'Aha!'
He catches the scent of battle from afar,
the shout of commanders and the battle cry.

26"Does the hawk take flight by your wisdom
and spread his wings toward the south?
27Does the eagle soar at your command
and build his nest on high?
28He dwells on a cliff and stays there at night;
a rocky crag is his stronghold.
29From there he seeks out his food;
his eyes detect it from afar.
30His young ones feast on blood,
and where the slain are, there is he."

[a]31 *Or the twinkling; or the chains of the* [b]32 *Or the morning star in its season* [c]32 *Or out Leo* [d]33 *Or his; or their* [e]36 The meaning of the Hebrew for this word is uncertain.

40 The LORD said to Job:

2 "Will the one who contends with the
Almighty correct him?
Let him who accuses God answer him!"

3 Then Job answered the LORD:

4 "I am unworthy—how can I reply to you?
I put my hand over my mouth.
5 I spoke once, but I have no answer—
twice, but I will say no more."

6 Then the LORD spoke to Job out of the
storm:

7 "Brace yourself like a man;
I will question you,
and you shall answer me.

8 "Would you discredit my justice?
Would you condemn me to justify
yourself?
9 Do you have an arm like God's,
and can your voice thunder like his?
10 Then adorn yourself with glory and
splendor,
and clothe yourself in honor and
majesty.
11 Unleash the fury of your wrath,
look at every proud man and bring him
low,
12 look at every proud man and humble him,
crush the wicked where they stand.
13 Bury them all in the dust together;
shroud their faces in the grave.
14 Then I myself will admit to you
that your own right hand can save you.

15 "Look at the behemoth,[a]
which I made along with you
and which feeds on grass like an ox.
16 What strength he has in his loins,
what power in the muscles of his belly!
17 His tail[b] sways like a cedar;
the sinews of his thighs are close-knit.
18 His bones are tubes of bronze,
his limbs like rods of iron.
19 He ranks first among the works of God,
yet his Maker can approach him with his
sword.
20 The hills bring him their produce,
and all the wild animals play nearby.
21 Under the lotus plants he lies,
hidden among the reeds in the marsh.
22 The lotuses conceal him in their shadow;
the poplars by the stream surround him.
23 When the river rages, he is not alarmed;
he is secure, though the Jordan should
surge against his mouth.
24 Can anyone capture him by the eyes,[c]
or trap him and pierce his nose?

41 "Can you pull in the leviathan[d]
with a fishhook
or tie down his tongue with a rope?
2 Can you put a cord through his nose
or pierce his jaw with a hook?
3 Will he keep begging you for mercy?
Will he speak to you with gentle words?
4 Will he make an agreement with you
for you to take him as your slave for
life?
5 Can you make a pet of him like a bird
or put him on a leash for your girls?
6 Will traders barter for him?
Will they divide him up among the
merchants?
7 Can you fill his hide with harpoons
or his head with fishing spears?
8 If you lay a hand on him,
you will remember the struggle and
never do it again!
9 Any hope of subduing him is false;
the mere sight of him is overpowering.
10 No one is fierce enough to rouse him.
Who then is able to stand against me?
11 Who has a claim against me that I must pay?
Everything under heaven belongs to me.

12 "I will not fail to speak of his limbs,
his strength and his graceful form.
13 Who can strip off his outer coat?
Who would approach him with a bridle?
14 Who dares open the doors of his mouth,
ringed about with his fearsome teeth?
15 His back has[e] rows of shields
tightly sealed together;
16 each is so close to the next
that no air can pass between.
17 They are joined fast to one another;
they cling together and cannot be parted.
18 His snorting throws out flashes of light;
his eyes are like the rays of dawn.
19 Firebrands stream from his mouth;
sparks of fire shoot out.
20 Smoke pours from his nostrils
as from a boiling pot over a fire of reeds.
21 His breath sets coals ablaze,
and flames dart from his mouth.
22 Strength resides in his neck;
dismay goes before him.
23 The folds of his flesh are tightly joined;
they are firm and immovable.
24 His chest is hard as rock,

[a] 15 Possibly the hippopotamus or the elephant
[b] 17 Possibly trunk
[c] 24 Or *by a water hole*
[d] 1 Possibly the crocodile
[e] 15 Or *His pride is his*

40:1—41:34 God used the majesty and power of his creation to remind Job that God is the only one who can save. Everything under heaven belongs to God, and that included Job. God never gave Job an explanation for his suffering; God only reminded Job that he was sovereign. We also may suffer without ever knowing why we have to go through this pain. We may suffer because of the sins of others or simply because we live in a fallen world. But we need to realize that God is ultimately in control. Our faith in him will be rewarded—if not in this life, then in the next.

At a Loss for Words?

Job 42:3–5 Many of our toughest questions cannot be answered with words. Can words explain the depth of a person's love, the intensity of a heartache or the reasons for a noble sacrifice? Words often fail us. However, in times of deepest need, we can often find comfort and a sense of God's presence in silence.

The book of Job is arguably the most profound story of human suffering ever told. In the story, Job, a prosperous and thoroughly righteous man, suffers deeply when disaster strikes. Early in the narrative four tragedies assault Job like hammer blows: In one day he loses all his material possessions, his entire household of servants and his seven sons and three daughters. Job himself comes under physical attack too, and is covered with painful sores.

Initially Job suffered in silence, and four friends mourned with him. After a week of this silent mourning, the friends began to offer their answers to Job's suffering. Three of them sought to convince Job that he must be suffering as a punishment for sin, but Job correctly discerned no such sin in his life. The fourth friend asserted that Job was suffering in order to be humbled. While each of the friends' explanations contained nuggets of truth, none of the friends had been privy to the heavenly council in which God gave Satan permission to attack Job in order to display Job's faithfulness (see 1:6–12). Finally, God himself addressed Job, and all were silenced. God said nothing about Job's problems, never giving an explanation for his suffering. Instead, God revealed himself as the sovereign Creator, and Job was silenced in humility and awe: "I am unworthy—how can I reply to you? I put my hand over my mouth. I spoke once, but I have no answer—twice, but I will say no more" (40:4–5).

Job's story reminds us that silence can help us express our humility and awe before the sovereign God. Silence enables us to reflect and remember that God is in control whether we are given answers to our questions or not. Often there is much more to God's plans and our suffering than we can know from our finite perspective.

Putting It Into Practice

What problem has been weighing heavily on you? Write it out in a journal, then put down your pen, close your eyes, bow your head and be still before God. Listen for God's voice in your silence. Reflect on his words to Job. Reaffirm your belief that regardless of your limited perspective on your troubles, God is God, and you are not.

For more on silence, turn to Psalm 46.

hard as a lower millstone.
25When he rises up, the mighty are terrified;
they retreat before his thrashing.
26The sword that reaches him has no effect,
nor does the spear or the dart or the
javelin.
27Iron he treats like straw
and bronze like rotten wood.
28Arrows do not make him flee;
slingstones are like chaff to him.
29A club seems to him but a piece of straw;
he laughs at the rattling of the lance.
30His undersides are jagged potsherds,
leaving a trail in the mud like a
threshing sledge.
31He makes the depths churn like a boiling
caldron
and stirs up the sea like a pot of
ointment.
32Behind him he leaves a glistening wake;
one would think the deep had white
hair.
33Nothing on earth is his equal—
a creature without fear.
34He looks down on all that are haughty;
he is king over all that are proud."

Job

42 Then Job replied to the LORD:

2"I know that you can do all things;
no plan of yours can be thwarted.
3⌊You asked,⌋ 'Who is this that obscures my
counsel without knowledge?'
Surely I spoke of things I did not
understand,
things too wonderful for me to know.

4⌊"You said,⌋ 'Listen now, and I will speak;
I will question you,
and you shall answer me.'
5My ears had heard of you
but now my eyes have seen you.
6Therefore I despise myself
and repent in dust and ashes."

Epilogue

7After the LORD had said these things to Job,
he said to Eliphaz the Temanite, "I am angry
with you and your two friends, because you
have not spoken of me what is right, as my
servant Job has. 8So now take seven bulls and
seven rams and go to my servant Job and sacrifice a burnt offering for yourselves. My servant
Job will pray for you, and I will accept his
prayer and not deal with you according to your
folly. You have not spoken of me what is right,
as my servant Job has." 9So Eliphaz the Temanite, Bildad the Shuhite and Zophar the Naamathite did what the LORD told them; and the
LORD accepted Job's prayer.
10After Job had prayed for his friends, the
LORD made him prosperous again and gave him
twice as much as he had before. 11All his brothers and sisters and everyone who had known
him before came and ate with him in his house.
They comforted and consoled him over all the
trouble the LORD had brought upon him, and
each one gave him a piece of silver[a] and a gold
ring.
12The LORD blessed the latter part of Job's life
more than the first. He had fourteen thousand
sheep, six thousand camels, a thousand yoke of
oxen and a thousand donkeys. 13And he also
had seven sons and three daughters. 14The first
daughter he named Jemimah, the second Kezi-
ah and the third Keren-Happuch. 15Nowhere in
all the land were there found women as beautiful as Job's daughters, and their father granted
them an inheritance along with their brothers.
16After this, Job lived a hundred and forty
years; he saw his children and their children to
the fourth generation. 17And so he died, old and
full of years.

[a] *11* Hebrew *him a kesitah;* a kesitah was a unit of money of unknown weight and value.

42:1–6 Job's reply was filled with gratitude. Where Job had once only heard about God, here he actually saw him—the loving, merciful, all-powerful, majestic Creator (42:5). This man, who was blameless and full of integrity before his suffering, was now even stronger because of his suffering. God is good. All that he does is ultimately for our good. It is important to remember this as we go through painful times.

42:7–9 How thankful Job's friends must have been that God would deal with them graciously and not as they deserved. They had wrongly accused Job of sin. But Job interceded for them, and God forgave them. When we are disobedient to God and hurtful to others, we need to repent of our sin and seek forgiveness.

42:10–17 Even if Job's fortunes had not been restored and he had continued in his pain, God would still have been in control of the universe. The same is true for us. Whether our sins or the sins of other people have caused our pain, God is in control of our lives, and he will care for us.

PSALMS

The Big Picture

It is impossible to adequately summarize the richness and breadth contained in the book of Psalms. This book was Israel's hymnal, containing songs of praise to God for personal and national salvation. It was also a book of laments for God's people facing difficult situations. The book of Psalms was also Israel's prayer book. The psalmists looked to God in moments of private despair and times of national suffering. Amidst their difficulties, they found release by lifting their heartfelt laments and praises to God.

The book of Psalms is still applicable for us too, for we are God's people today. The Psalms brim with honest emotion. By embracing them as our own we can pour out our anguish and adoration, our suffering and confession, our hopes and fears. Through some we may ask God why he has or hasn't acted in a certain way. Through others we might express our pain, heartache and discouragement. Through still others we may praise God as he frees us from oppression and sin. Each psalm is an expression of the heart. None of them is a neat little package of answers tied up with a pretty bow. They are living documents, a collection of spiritual diaries from people who honestly sought God's gracious help.

The Psalms may be read in many different ways, depending on what situations, problems or circumstances we may face. They may function as deterrents to keep us out of trouble, as guides to help us through our problems, as reminders of the one who actually delivers us or as beacons of hope to encourage us in perplexing or painful situations. Through the book of Psalms we share in the hopes and failures of the entire human race. Yet as we read these hymns and prayers, we are also ushered into the very presence of our loving and merciful God.

A. PSALMS OF PREPARATION AND PROMISE (1–41)

B. PSALMS OF PETITION AND PRESERVATION (42–72)

C. PSALMS OF PROBLEMS AND POWER (73–89)

D. PSALMS OF PERIL AND PROTECTION (90–106)

E. PSALMS OF PERFECTION AND PRAISE (107–150)

Spiritual Renewal Themes

TRUTH BRINGS HEALING

The psalmists were honest about their experiences and feelings. Again and again they testified to God's faithfulness in listening and responding to their words of honest confession or praise. It is sometimes easy to compromise the truth, even when we pray to God. This, however, is always a dead end. Only the truth can bring us into the kind of relationship with God that will result

Essential Facts

PURPOSE:
To demonstrate that God is holy and loving and intimately involved in every aspect of our human experience.

AUTHORS:
David wrote seventy-three psalms; Asaph wrote twelve; the sons of Korah wrote nine; Solomon wrote two; Heman (with the sons of Korah), Ethan and Moses each wrote one; fifty-one psalms are anonymous.

AUDIENCE:
The people of Israel.

DATE WRITTEN:
The Psalms were written between the years 1440 and 440 B.C.

SETTING:
Though the Psalms are not generally concerned with recording history, many of them were inspired by historical events.

KEY VERSE:
"Let everything that has breath praise the LORD. Praise the LORD" (150:6).

KEY PEOPLE:
David, Asaph, Solomon, Heman, Ethan, Moses and the sons of Korah.

in true healing. When we face the truth about our sins, recognize that we don't have power over them and seek God's forgiveness, God will meet us and guide us in the path of spiritual renewal and healing.

LEGITIMATE QUESTIONS AND COMPLAINTS
Most of us act as though questioning God is an unforgivable sin. But God knows all about our questions, and he is not afraid of them. The psalmists were honest about their feelings and brought their questions straight to God. They were also honest in their complaints. There is a time and place for us to bring our disappointments and complaints to God too. It helps us grasp the truth about what is going on in our lives. But like the psalmists, we should move through our complaints to affirm our faith in God. If we hide our questions about God's way of doing things, we only make it easier to drift away from him. But if we honestly express our feelings, even bringing to God our disappointments about his apparent lack of action in our lives, we will discover that our faith can be renewed.

GOD'S POWERFUL PRESENCE
We can count on the fact that God is all-powerful. He always chooses to act at the best time possible. God is sovereign over every situation. The psalmists testify again and again that God is able to overcome the despair and pain in life and that he is always in control. This kind of faith didn't come easily to the psalmists. They struggled with this truth, often questioning God's presence in their lives, just as we do. But in the end, their questions were always replaced by praises that affirmed the fact of God's powerful presence.

THE NECESSITY OF FORGIVENESS
Many of the psalms are intense prayers seeking God's forgiveness. The psalmists discovered that they could be open and honest with God about their failures and sins; they counted on his forgiveness. As we experience God's forgiveness, we can release our guilt and move into an intimate and loving relationship with God too. No matter what our failures and sins, God is ready and willing to forgive those who repent and seek him.

BOOK I

Psalms 1–41

Psalm 1

1Blessed is the man
who does not walk in the counsel of the wicked
or stand in the way of sinners
or sit in the seat of mockers.
2But his delight is in the law of the LORD,
and on his law he meditates day and night.
3He is like a tree planted by streams of water,
which yields its fruit in season
and whose leaf does not wither.
Whatever he does prospers.

4Not so the wicked!
They are like chaff
that the wind blows away.
5Therefore the wicked will not stand in the judgment,
nor sinners in the assembly of the righteous.

6For the LORD watches over the way of the righteous,
but the way of the wicked will perish.

Psalm 2

1Why do the nations conspire[a]
and the peoples plot in vain?
2The kings of the earth take their stand
and the rulers gather together
against the LORD
and against his Anointed One.[b]
3"Let us break their chains," they say,
"and throw off their fetters."

4The One enthroned in heaven laughs;
the Lord scoffs at them.
5Then he rebukes them in his anger
and terrifies them in his wrath, saying,
6"I have installed my King[c]
on Zion, my holy hill."

7I will proclaim the decree of the LORD:
He said to me, "You are my Son[d];
today I have become your Father.[e]
8Ask of me,
and I will make the nations your inheritance,
the ends of the earth your possession.
9You will rule them with an iron scepter[f];
you will dash them to pieces like pottery."

10Therefore, you kings, be wise;
be warned, you rulers of the earth.
11Serve the LORD with fear
and rejoice with trembling.
12Kiss the Son, lest he be angry
and you be destroyed in your way,
for his wrath can flare up in a moment.
Blessed are all who take refuge in him.

Psalm 3

A psalm of David. When he fled from his son Absalom.

1O LORD, how many are my foes!
How many rise up against me!
2Many are saying of me,
"God will not deliver him." *Selah*[g]

3But you are a shield around me, O LORD;
you bestow glory on me and lift[h] up my head.
4To the LORD I cry aloud,
and he answers me from his holy hill. *Selah*

5I lie down and sleep;
I wake again, because the LORD sustains me.
6I will not fear the tens of thousands
drawn up against me on every side.

7Arise, O LORD!
Deliver me, O my God!
Strike all my enemies on the jaw;
break the teeth of the wicked.

[a]1 Hebrew; Septuagint *rage* [b]2 Or *anointed one* [c]6 Or *king* [d]7 Or *son;* also in verse 12 [e]7 Or *have begotten you* [f]9 Or *will break them with a rod of iron* [g]2 A word of uncertain meaning, occurring frequently in the Psalms; possibly a musical term [h]3 Or LORD, / *my Glorious One, who lifts*

1:1–6 One key to spiritual growth is turning toward God and turning away from people and situations that draw us into temptation. There is no better source for wisdom and direction than God's Word. When we fail to study and apply God's Word, we tend to drift through life or follow those who do not follow God. If we are not careful to let God's Word guide our lives, we will be tossed around by every new fad or philosophy that comes our way (see Ephesians 4:11–14).

2:1–6 If God is in charge of the world, why do we continually try to do things our own way? This passage tells us that fighting God's plan is foolishness. Many turn away from God because they don't want to be his slaves. But if we reject God's rule over us, we will invariably become slaves to someone or something else. The foolish man, in rejecting God's righteous rule, soon falls into a prison of sin and destructive habits. It is fruitless to challenge God. The only way we can be in tune with God's plan and receive his help is to surrender to him and accept his loving rule over our lives.

3:1–4 David faced enemies who mocked him, saying that there was no hope for him. But David didn't believe them and called out to God for help. We may encounter those who say there is no hope for us. We must not listen to them; rather, we should follow David's example and call out to God for help.

3:5–8 God comforted David so much that he could sleep peacefully in spite of his troubles. David's worries and anxieties vanished when he focused his thoughts fully on God. By placing his problems in God's hands, David had taken the most important step toward solving them. He could view his life as if all of his problems had been eliminated. When we surrender our lives to God, we can rest peacefully too, knowing that God is ultimately in control.

Bible Study and Meditation

Encountering the Word of God

Psalm 1 Because Satan fears our use of the spiritual disciplines, he tries to confuse us by distorting the spiritual disciplines and causing us to fear them. This tactic seems to be especially true of the discipline of meditation. There are so many misunderstandings surrounding meditation that many are afraid to practice it. Yet meditation upon God's truth is one of the chief avenues to spiritual renewal.

Christian meditation encounters the living Word through the written Word by utilizing our God-given faculties of reflection and imagination. Meditation builds on our mental understanding of God's Word; it does not replace it. Meditation means stopping long enough to turn a single thought or idea over and over in our minds, viewing it from many different angles. The goal of meditation is not quantity of facts but depth of understanding.

There are two primary approaches to Christian meditation: cognitive meditation or discursive meditation. Cognitive meditation involves reflection on God's Word that is largely analytical, logical and inductive. We ponder the text and its context and search out all possible meanings. We draw conclusions from the text and develop principles that we can apply to our lives. We think through God's Word as deeply as possible.

Discursive meditation emphasizes more of an intuitive, imaginative approach to God's Word. We enter into the text with few expectations and allow the text, in a sense, to search us. We use our "sanctified imagination," drawing upon all our senses as we approach a Bible passage. Such an exercise often leads a person to conclusions he or she may never have considered before. When great preachers and storytellers fill in the details and bring the Bible text to life, often they are sharing the fruit of discursive meditation.

Putting It Into Practice

To practice Biblical meditation, select a brief verse or passage that attracts your attention. You may want to do some basic study of the verse, such as defining its terms using a Bible dictionary or looking up its concepts in a commentary. At the same time, come to the passage as "fresh" as possible so that the Holy Spirit, not simply a Bible commentary, can guide your meditation.

To root the passage firmly in your mind, speak the passage aloud or write it down several times until you can do so without having to look at it.

Then, ponder the verse. Reflect on it from many different angles in order to uncover new insights into the verse's meaning for believers today. Since you are primarily seeking depth of insight, you need not be preoccupied with the quantity of thoughts. Or you may just want to consider the passage in light of one situation.

As you meditate, record your observations in your journal, summarizing both your experience and the insights God gives you.

For more on Bible study and meditation, turn to Isaiah 55.

8From the LORD comes deliverance.
May your blessing be on your people. *Selah*

Psalm 4

For the director of music. With stringed instruments. A psalm of David.

1Answer me when I call to you,
O my righteous God.
Give me relief from my distress;
be merciful to me and hear my prayer.

2How long, O men, will you turn my glory into shame[a]?
How long will you love delusions and seek false gods[b]? *Selah*
3Know that the LORD has set apart the godly for himself;
the LORD will hear when I call to him.

4In your anger do not sin;
when you are on your beds,
search your hearts and be silent. *Selah*
5Offer right sacrifices
and trust in the LORD.

6Many are asking, "Who can show us any good?"
Let the light of your face shine upon us, O LORD.
7You have filled my heart with greater joy
than when their grain and new wine abound.
8I will lie down and sleep in peace,
for you alone, O LORD,
make me dwell in safety.

Psalm 5

For the director of music. For flutes. A psalm of David.

1Give ear to my words, O LORD,
consider my sighing.
2Listen to my cry for help,
my King and my God,
for to you I pray.
3In the morning, O LORD, you hear my voice;
in the morning I lay my requests before you
and wait in expectation.

4You are not a God who takes pleasure in evil;
with you the wicked cannot dwell.
5The arrogant cannot stand in your presence;
you hate all who do wrong.
6You destroy those who tell lies;
bloodthirsty and deceitful men
the LORD abhors.

7But I, by your great mercy,
will come into your house;
in reverence will I bow down
toward your holy temple.
8Lead me, O LORD, in your righteousness
because of my enemies—
make straight your way before me.

9Not a word from their mouth can be trusted;
their heart is filled with destruction.
Their throat is an open grave;
with their tongue they speak deceit.
10Declare them guilty, O God!
Let their intrigues be their downfall.
Banish them for their many sins,
for they have rebelled against you.

11But let all who take refuge in you be glad;
let them ever sing for joy.
Spread your protection over them,
that those who love your name may rejoice in you.
12For surely, O LORD, you bless the righteous;
you surround them with your favor as with a shield.

Psalm 6

For the director of music. With stringed instruments. According to *sheminith.*[c] A psalm of David.

1O LORD, do not rebuke me in your anger
or discipline me in your wrath.
2Be merciful to me, LORD, for I am faint;

[a]2 Or *you dishonor my Glorious One* [b]2 Or *seek lies*
[c]Title: Probably a musical term

4:1–3 David rejoiced in God's powerful protection. In times of distress our merciful God is the perfect haven of rest. He is listening; he hears our cries for help. God wants us to put our trust in him. We insult God when we trust in our own resources, or anything else, to deliver us from our problems. When we surrender our lives to God, we become his own chosen ones. He promises to hear us when we call out to him.
4:6–8 Many of the people around us cannot see God at work in our lives. They view us only through the filter of our past failures. But as God transforms our lives, we can become living testimonies of his power. True joy comes from God—a joy that is greater than all the gladness the world can produce. Nothing will bring us more peace than the knowledge that God is with us.
5:1–7 David understood how foolish it was to look for help from anything or anyone else but God. One by one he brought his needs to God. Wherever we go and whatever we are doing, we can trust God to help us in our moment-by-moment walk of obedience.
5:8–12 David requested God's guidance because he knew that the Lord would see him through the many troubles he faced. Like David's enemies, some people will tell us that sin won't hurt us. Their words may sound good, but these people are headed for destruction. Their own lives prove their slavery to sin. Despite these worldly snares, we can find deliverance by trusting in God.
6:1–5 Life may bring anguish into our situation at times. And there are times when we bring anguish into our own lives because of our sin. In times of anguish, we need to pour out our hearts to God, confessing our sins, our sorrows and even our complaints. We can call on God's mer-

O LORD, heal me, for my bones are in agony.
[3]My soul is in anguish.
How long, O LORD, how long?

[4]Turn, O LORD, and deliver me;
save me because of your unfailing love.
[5]No one remembers you when he is dead.
Who praises you from the grave[a]?

[6]I am worn out from groaning;
all night long I flood my bed with weeping
and drench my couch with tears.
[7]My eyes grow weak with sorrow;
they fail because of all my foes.

[8]Away from me, all you who do evil,
for the LORD has heard my weeping.
[9]The LORD has heard my cry for mercy;
the LORD accepts my prayer.
[10]All my enemies will be ashamed and dismayed;
they will turn back in sudden disgrace.

Psalm 7

A *shiggaion*[b] of David, which he sang to the LORD concerning Cush, a Benjamite.

[1]O LORD my God, I take refuge in you;
save and deliver me from all who pursue me,
[2]or they will tear me like a lion
and rip me to pieces with no one to rescue me.

[3]O LORD my God, if I have done this
and there is guilt on my hands—
[4]if I have done evil to him who is at peace with me
or without cause have robbed my foe—
[5]then let my enemy pursue and overtake me;
let him trample my life to the ground
and make me sleep in the dust. *Selah*

[6]Arise, O LORD, in your anger;
rise up against the rage of my enemies.
Awake, my God; decree justice.
[7]Let the assembled peoples gather around you.
Rule over them from on high;
[8] let the LORD judge the peoples.
Judge me, O LORD, according to my righteousness,
according to my integrity, O Most High.
[9]O righteous God,
who searches minds and hearts,
bring to an end the violence of the wicked
and make the righteous secure.

[10]My shield[c] is God Most High,
who saves the upright in heart.
[11]God is a righteous judge,
a God who expresses his wrath every day.
[12]If he does not relent,
he[d] will sharpen his sword;
he will bend and string his bow.
[13]He has prepared his deadly weapons;
he makes ready his flaming arrows.

[14]He who is pregnant with evil
and conceives trouble gives birth to disillusionment.
[15]He who digs a hole and scoops it out
falls into the pit he has made.
[16]The trouble he causes recoils on himself;
his violence comes down on his own head.

[17]I will give thanks to the LORD because of his righteousness
and will sing praise to the name of the LORD Most High.

Psalm 8

For the director of music. According to *gittith*.[e] A psalm of David.

[1]O LORD, our Lord,
how majestic is your name in all the earth!

You have set your glory
above the heavens.
[2]From the lips of children and infants
you have ordained praise[f]
because of your enemies,
to silence the foe and the avenger.

[3]When I consider your heavens,

[a]5 Hebrew *Sheol* [b]Title: Probably a literary or musical term [c]10 Or *sovereign* [d]12 Or *If a man does not repent, / God* [e]Title: Probably a musical term [f]2 Or *strength*

---

cy and know that he will hear the honest cries of our hearts. He will preserve us and use our lives to demonstrate his mercy.

6:6–10 Even though we may suffer greatly, we can have confidence that God will answer our prayers. God always hears our petitions. We should be as bold as David, who claimed victory immediately after finishing his prayer. When we seek God and surrender our lives to him, we can pray with assurance and declare victory because God himself will overcome our enemies.

7:3–10 David looked to God to defend him against the slanderous judgments of his enemies. If we are doing what we can to avoid temptation, we can count on the Lord to deal with those who oppose us too. We must hate the things God hates. When we choose the right path, God promises to be our defense.

7:11–16 God is patient, but there is a limit to how long he will tolerate those who continue to rebel against him (see 2 Peter 3:9). When we choose to live in ways that counter God's plan, we will quickly discover that our problems only grow worse. The plans we make to achieve personal success at the expense of others will ultimately destroy us. We will only fall prey to our own schemes (see 9:15).

8:3–9 The God who created the universe in its awesome splendor also created us and considers us the crown of all creation. Knowing the greatness of our Creator should inspire us to seek him. As we see the truth of how God

the work of your fingers,
the moon and the stars,
which you have set in place,
4what is man that you are mindful of him,
the son of man that you care for him?
5You made him a little lower than the heavenly beings[a]
and crowned him with glory and honor.
6You made him ruler over the works of your hands;
you put everything under his feet:
7all flocks and herds,
and the beasts of the field,
8the birds of the air,
and the fish of the sea,
all that swim the paths of the seas.
9O LORD, our Lord,
how majestic is your name in all the earth!

Psalm 9[b]

For the director of music. To ⌊the tune of⌋ "The Death of the Son." A psalm of David.

1I will praise you, O LORD, with all my heart;
I will tell of all your wonders.
2I will be glad and rejoice in you;
I will sing praise to your name, O Most High.
3My enemies turn back;
they stumble and perish before you.
4For you have upheld my right and my cause;
you have sat on your throne, judging righteously.
5You have rebuked the nations and destroyed the wicked;
you have blotted out their name for ever and ever.
6Endless ruin has overtaken the enemy,
you have uprooted their cities;
even the memory of them has perished.
7The LORD reigns forever;

[a]5 Or *than God* [b]Psalms 9 and 10 may have been originally a single acrostic poem, the stanzas of which begin with the successive letters of the Hebrew alphabet. In the Septuagint they constitute one psalm.

SEE THE TRUTH

Key 2

Seeing Ourselves as God Sees Us

Psalm 8:1–9 We tend to view ourselves the way important people in our lives view us. If we grew up around people who didn't appreciate us, we may have trouble seeing ourselves as we truly are in God's eyes. Understanding how God sees us and how he values us can help us see the truth about ourselves.

David was amazed as he considered how much God valued him. He said, "What is man that you are mindful of him, the son of man that you care for him? You made him a little lower than the heavenly beings and crowned him with glory and honor" (8:4–5). He also rejoiced, "How precious to me are your thoughts, O God! How vast is the sum of them!" (139:17). The greatest demonstration of how precious we are to God is that his Son, Jesus Christ, gave his life for us.

God wants us to realize how precious we are to him. He wants us to see ourselves in the light of his love. Consider this: If God considered us worthy enough to give up the most precious thing he possessed (his only Son), what does that say about our value to God? Yes, we may be sinful and unworthy in our own merit, but we are priceless in God's sight.

Turn to Psalm 139.

loves us and has called us to be his people, we should be encouraged. We should long to grow closer to God so that he might transform us into all that he created us to be.
9:1–6 As we experience God's help and our lives begin to change for the better, we should share our experience of spiritual renewal with others so that their lives can be changed too. As God transforms our lives, others will see what God has done for us and will find hope for their own lives. Our struggles can also be a source of encouragement and guidance to others if we surrender to God in the midst of them and let others see God redirect the course of our lives.
9:7–14 David praised God for delivering him from powerful enemies. God is merciful; he is always ready to help

he has established his throne for
judgment.
8He will judge the world in righteousness;
he will govern the peoples with justice.
9The LORD is a refuge for the oppressed,
a stronghold in times of trouble.
10Those who know your name will trust in
you,
for you, LORD, have never forsaken those
who seek you.

11Sing praises to the LORD, enthroned in
Zion;
proclaim among the nations what he has
done.
12For he who avenges blood remembers;
he does not ignore the cry of the
afflicted.

13O LORD, see how my enemies persecute
me!
Have mercy and lift me up from the
gates of death,
14that I may declare your praises
in the gates of the Daughter of Zion
and there rejoice in your salvation.
15The nations have fallen into the pit they
have dug;
their feet are caught in the net they have
hidden.
16The LORD is known by his justice;
the wicked are ensnared by the work of
their hands. *Higgaion.*[a] *Selah*
17The wicked return to the grave,[b]
all the nations that forget God.
18But the needy will not always be forgotten,
nor the hope of the afflicted ever perish.

19Arise, O LORD, let not man triumph;
let the nations be judged in your
presence.
20Strike them with terror, O LORD;
let the nations know they are but men.
Selah

Psalm 10[c]

1Why, O LORD, do you stand far off?
Why do you hide yourself in times of
trouble?

2In his arrogance the wicked man hunts
down the weak,
who are caught in the schemes he
devises.
3He boasts of the cravings of his heart;
he blesses the greedy and reviles the
LORD.
4In his pride the wicked does not seek him;
in all his thoughts there is no room for
God.
5His ways are always prosperous;
he is haughty and your laws are far from
him;
he sneers at all his enemies.
6He says to himself, "Nothing will shake
me;
I'll always be happy and never have
trouble."
7His mouth is full of curses and lies and
threats;
trouble and evil are under his tongue.
8He lies in wait near the villages;
from ambush he murders the innocent,
watching in secret for his victims.
9He lies in wait like a lion in cover;
he lies in wait to catch the helpless;
he catches the helpless and drags them
off in his net.
10His victims are crushed, they collapse;
they fall under his strength.
11He says to himself, "God has forgotten;
he covers his face and never sees."

12Arise, LORD! Lift up your hand, O God.
Do not forget the helpless.
13Why does the wicked man revile God?
Why does he say to himself,
"He won't call me to account"?
14But you, O God, do see trouble and grief;
you consider it to take it in hand.
The victim commits himself to you;
you are the helper of the fatherless.
15Break the arm of the wicked and evil man;
call him to account for his wickedness
that would not be found out.

16The LORD is King for ever and ever;
the nations will perish from his land.

[a]*16* Or *Meditation;* possibly a musical notation
[b]*17* Hebrew *Sheol* [c]Psalms 9 and 10 may have been originally a single acrostic poem, the stanzas of which begin with the successive letters of the Hebrew alphabet. In the Septuagint they constitute one psalm.

---

those who are oppressed by their enemies. In God's perfect timing, those who are oppressed will find comfort and encouragement if they put their trust in God. Because God never forsakes those who trust him, we should praise him and tell others about God's powerful deliverance at work in our lives.

9:15–20 The people who set traps for others will ultimately be trapped themselves. Such people do not succeed in the long run. Those who realize they need God's help and turn to him will receive his aid. If we think we are in control of our own destiny and the destinies of others, we are misguided. One day God will step in and demonstrate who truly is in control.

10:1–11 God sometimes seems far away when the temptation to sin is strong. In truth, he is never far from us. We may think that those who do evil never get trapped, but actually they are headed for trouble; they just don't recognize it yet. Evildoers may appear to be doing well, but appearances are not always what they seem. We need to make sure that the apparent success of the wicked doesn't lead us away from God's plan for our lives.

10:13–18 Though it may appear that God is blind to the evil deeds of others, we can be sure that ultimately he will respond with judgment. Those who drag others into sin will be judged harshly by God (see Luke 17:1–2). God often works quietly behind the scenes, helping those who admit the reality of their situations to overcome the enemies and problems they face.

17 You hear, O LORD, the desire of the afflicted;
you encourage them, and you listen to their cry,
18 defending the fatherless and the oppressed,
in order that man, who is of the earth,
may terrify no more.

Psalm 11

For the director of music. Of David.

1 In the LORD I take refuge.
How then can you say to me:
"Flee like a bird to your mountain.
2 For look, the wicked bend their bows;
they set their arrows against the strings
to shoot from the shadows
at the upright in heart.
3 When the foundations are being destroyed,
what can the righteous do[a]?"

4 The LORD is in his holy temple;
the LORD is on his heavenly throne.
He observes the sons of men;
his eyes examine them.
5 The LORD examines the righteous,
but the wicked[b] and those who love violence
his soul hates.
6 On the wicked he will rain
fiery coals and burning sulfur;
a scorching wind will be their lot.

7 For the LORD is righteous,
he loves justice;
upright men will see his face.

Psalm 12

For the director of music. According to *sheminith.*[c] A psalm of David.

1 Help, LORD, for the godly are no more;
the faithful have vanished from among men.
2 Everyone lies to his neighbor;
their flattering lips speak with deception.

3 May the LORD cut off all flattering lips
and every boastful tongue
4 that says, "We will triumph with our tongues;
we own our lips[d]—who is our master?"

5 "Because of the oppression of the weak
and the groaning of the needy,
I will now arise," says the LORD.
"I will protect them from those who malign them."
6 And the words of the LORD are flawless,
like silver refined in a furnace of clay,
purified seven times.

7 O LORD, you will keep us safe
and protect us from such people forever.
8 The wicked freely strut about
when what is vile is honored among men.

Psalm 13

For the director of music. A psalm of David.

1 How long, O LORD? Will you forget me forever?
How long will you hide your face from me?
2 How long must I wrestle with my thoughts
and every day have sorrow in my heart?
How long will my enemy triumph over me?

3 Look on me and answer, O LORD my God.
Give light to my eyes, or I will sleep in death;
4 my enemy will say, "I have overcome him,"
and my foes will rejoice when I fall.

5 But I trust in your unfailing love;
my heart rejoices in your salvation.
6 I will sing to the LORD,
for he has been good to me.

Psalm 14

For the director of music. Of David.

1 The fool[e] says in his heart,
"There is no God."
They are corrupt, their deeds are vile;
there is no one who does good.

2 The LORD looks down from heaven

[a] 3 Or *what is the Righteous One doing* [b] 5 Or *The LORD, the Righteous One, examines the wicked, /* [c] Title: Probably a musical term [d] 4 Or */ our lips are our plowshares* [e] 1 The Hebrew words rendered *fool* in Psalms denote one who is morally deficient.

11:1–3 Security from temptation can be found in God; running elsewhere for help will never do any good. If we turn to some other resource for help, the people and problems that threaten to destroy us will lead us astray when we are most vulnerable. When our outside resources are unavailable, temptation will rush in to take advantage of us. God is always with us. If we put our trust in him, we will have the means to overcome temptation.

12:5–8 God has promised to deliver us from those who try to destroy us. People make a grave mistake if they don't understand that God is not like us—his promises are true. He never deceives, nor does he ever fail to keep his promises. God has offered to surround us with help if we ask for it.

13:1–6 There are times on our spiritual journey when we may be convinced that God has forgotten us. We may feel completely overwhelmed by our problems and baffled that God has done nothing to help. David began writing this psalm sharing feelings like these. But ultimately, David confidently recognized that the Lord would respond to his cry for help; David knew that the Lord is faithful. We, too, can depend on the Lord's unfailing love toward us, even though we may grow weary and discouraged.

14:1–3 Refusing to believe in God ensures ultimate failure. Unless we accept the fact that God is concerned about us, there is no hope for us. The psalmist labeled

on the sons of men
to see if there are any who understand,
any who seek God.
[3]All have turned aside,
they have together become corrupt;
there is no one who does good,
not even one.

[4]Will evildoers never learn—
those who devour my people as men eat bread
and who do not call on the LORD?
[5]There they are, overwhelmed with dread,
for God is present in the company of the righteous.
[6]You evildoers frustrate the plans of the poor,
but the LORD is their refuge.

[7]Oh, that salvation for Israel would come out of Zion!
When the LORD restores the fortunes of his people,
let Jacob rejoice and Israel be glad!

Psalm 15

A psalm of David.

[1]LORD, who may dwell in your sanctuary?
Who may live on your holy hill?

[2]He whose walk is blameless
and who does what is righteous,
who speaks the truth from his heart
[3] and has no slander on his tongue,
who does his neighbor no wrong
and casts no slur on his fellowman,
[4]who despises a vile man
but honors those who fear the LORD,
who keeps his oath
even when it hurts,
[5]who lends his money without usury
and does not accept a bribe against the innocent.

He who does these things
will never be shaken.

Psalm 16

A *miktam*[a] of David.

[1]Keep me safe, O God,
for in you I take refuge.

[2]I said to the LORD, "You are my Lord;
apart from you I have no good thing."
[3]As for the saints who are in the land,
they are the glorious ones in whom is all my delight.[b]
[4]The sorrows of those will increase
who run after other gods.
I will not pour out their libations of blood
or take up their names on my lips.

[5]LORD, you have assigned me my portion and my cup;
you have made my lot secure.
[6]The boundary lines have fallen for me in pleasant places;
surely I have a delightful inheritance.
[7]I will praise the LORD, who counsels me;
even at night my heart instructs me.
[8]I have set the LORD always before me.
Because he is at my right hand,
I will not be shaken.

[9]Therefore my heart is glad and my tongue rejoices;
my body also will rest secure,
[10]because you will not abandon me to the grave,[c]
nor will you let your Holy One[d] see decay.
[11]You have made[e] known to me the path of life;
you will fill me with joy in your presence,
with eternal pleasures at your right hand.

Psalm 17

A prayer of David.

[1]Hear, O LORD, my righteous plea;
listen to my cry.

[a]Title: Probably a literary or musical term [b]3 Or *As for the pagan priests who are in the land / and the nobles in whom all delight, I said:* [c]10 Hebrew *Sheol* [d]10 Or *your faithful one* [e]11 Or *You will make*

---

people who refuse to believe in God as fools. The world is filled with such fools, but we don't have to be like them. We can surrender to God, receive his forgiveness and follow his ways.

15:1–3 As God's people, we have been called to a life of honesty and integrity, refusing to lie about ourselves or others. We are also urged to build up God's people and to refrain from hurting other people. By practicing these disciplines, our lives will reflect the character of the God we serve.

15:1–5 Following God's plan leads to a life of stability and peace. If we want to progress spiritually, we must not give in to sin. No matter how painful it might be, we must confess the sin in our lives or sometimes even confront others with their sins. Many times our failures have caused a great deal of pain and loss to the people close to us. We must honestly reflect on our lives, recognize the wrongs we have committed and reconcile ourselves to those we have hurt.

16:1–6 Strength and security come from God. He alone is truly able to restore us. If we look to God as the source of our strength and joy, he will never disappoint us. We can also draw encouragement from others who are trying to find and do God's will too.

17:1–5 David honestly considered his heart's condition and confidently asserted that he was not harboring any sin within it. Honestly examining our spiritual condition is essential to spiritual renewal. If we refuse to examine our-

Give ear to my prayer—
it does not rise from deceitful lips.
2May my vindication come from you;
may your eyes see what is right.

3Though you probe my heart and examine me at night,
though you test me, you will find nothing;
I have resolved that my mouth will not sin.
4As for the deeds of men—
by the word of your lips
I have kept myself
from the ways of the violent.
5My steps have held to your paths;
my feet have not slipped.

6I call on you, O God, for you will answer me;
give ear to me and hear my prayer.
7Show the wonder of your great love,
you who save by your right hand
those who take refuge in you from their foes.
8Keep me as the apple of your eye;
hide me in the shadow of your wings
9from the wicked who assail me,
from my mortal enemies who surround me.

10They close up their callous hearts,
and their mouths speak with arrogance.
11They have tracked me down, they now surround me,
with eyes alert, to throw me to the ground.
12They are like a lion hungry for prey,
like a great lion crouching in cover.

13Rise up, O LORD, confront them, bring them down;
rescue me from the wicked by your sword.
14O LORD, by your hand save me from such men,
from men of this world whose reward is in this life.

You still the hunger of those you cherish;
their sons have plenty,
and they store up wealth for their children.
15And I—in righteousness I will see your face;
when I awake, I will be satisfied with seeing your likeness.

Psalm 18

For the director of music. Of David the servant of the LORD. He sang to the LORD the words of this song when the LORD delivered him from the hand of all his enemies and from the hand of Saul. He said:

1I love you, O LORD, my strength.

2The LORD is my rock, my fortress and my deliverer;
my God is my rock, in whom I take refuge.
He is my shield and the horn[a] of my salvation, my stronghold.
3I call to the LORD, who is worthy of praise,
and I am saved from my enemies.

4The cords of death entangled me;
the torrents of destruction overwhelmed me.
5The cords of the grave[b] coiled around me;
the snares of death confronted me.
6In my distress I called to the LORD;
I cried to my God for help.
From his temple he heard my voice;
my cry came before him, into his ears.

7The earth trembled and quaked,
and the foundations of the mountains shook;
they trembled because he was angry.
8Smoke rose from his nostrils;
consuming fire came from his mouth,
burning coals blazed out of it.
9He parted the heavens and came down;
dark clouds were under his feet.
10He mounted the cherubim and flew;
he soared on the wings of the wind.
11He made darkness his covering, his canopy around him—
the dark rain clouds of the sky.
12Out of the brightness of his presence clouds advanced,
with hailstones and bolts of lightning.
13The LORD thundered from heaven;
the voice of the Most High resounded.[c]
14He shot his arrows and scattered ⌞the enemies⌟,
great bolts of lightning and routed them.
15The valleys of the sea were exposed
and the foundations of the earth laid bare

[a]2 *Horn* here symbolizes strength. [b]5 Hebrew *Sheol*
[c]13 Some Hebrew manuscripts and Septuagint (see also 2 Samuel 22:14); most Hebrew manuscripts *resounded, / amid hailstones and bolts of lightning*

selves, we will encounter numerous obstacles to our spiritual growth.

18:1–5 David wrote this psalm soon after God delivered him from his enemies. God is more than able to deliver us from those who oppose his will, just as he delivered David. God is our source of strength, our rock, the one on whom we must rely for help.

18:6–15 David used very descriptive language in these verses to show us how serious God is about helping those who turn to him for aid. The psalmist knew that he would be delivered, not because he was strong or deserving of God's help, but because God loved him and was powerful enough to stir up all the forces of nature to come to his aid. When God is on our side, no enemy is too powerful for God to overcome. We can only experience victory by depending on God's delivering hand.

at your rebuke, O LORD,
at the blast of breath from your nostrils.
16He reached down from on high and took hold of me;
he drew me out of deep waters.
17He rescued me from my powerful enemy,
from my foes, who were too strong for me.
18They confronted me in the day of my disaster,
but the LORD was my support.
19He brought me out into a spacious place;
he rescued me because he delighted in me.

20The LORD has dealt with me according to my righteousness;
according to the cleanness of my hands he has rewarded me.
21For I have kept the ways of the LORD;
I have not done evil by turning from my God.
22All his laws are before me;
I have not turned away from his decrees.
23I have been blameless before him
and have kept myself from sin.
24The LORD has rewarded me according to my righteousness,
according to the cleanness of my hands in his sight.

25To the faithful you show yourself faithful,
to the blameless you show yourself blameless,
26to the pure you show yourself pure,
but to the crooked you show yourself shrewd.
27You save the humble
but bring low those whose eyes are haughty.
28You, O LORD, keep my lamp burning;
my God turns my darkness into light.
29With your help I can advance against a troop[a];
with my God I can scale a wall.

30As for God, his way is perfect;
the word of the LORD is flawless.
He is a shield
for all who take refuge in him.
31For who is God besides the LORD?
And who is the Rock except our God?
32It is God who arms me with strength
and makes my way perfect.
33He makes my feet like the feet of a deer;
he enables me to stand on the heights.
34He trains my hands for battle;
my arms can bend a bow of bronze.
35You give me your shield of victory,
and your right hand sustains me;
you stoop down to make me great.
36You broaden the path beneath me,
so that my ankles do not turn.

37I pursued my enemies and overtook them;
I did not turn back till they were destroyed.
38I crushed them so that they could not rise;
they fell beneath my feet.
39You armed me with strength for battle;
you made my adversaries bow at my feet.
40You made my enemies turn their backs in flight,
and I destroyed my foes.
41They cried for help, but there was no one to save them—
to the LORD, but he did not answer.
42I beat them as fine as dust borne on the wind;
I poured them out like mud in the streets.

43You have delivered me from the attacks of the people;
you have made me the head of nations;
people I did not know are subject to me.
44As soon as they hear me, they obey me;
foreigners cringe before me.
45They all lose heart;
they come trembling from their strongholds.

46The LORD lives! Praise be to my Rock!
Exalted be God my Savior!

[a]29 Or *can run through a barricade*

18:16–19 When the psalmist realized his helplessness and surrendered his life to the Lord, God came to his aid. Many of us know this theological truth in principle, but we must also experience it in our own lives. These verses give us a clear warning. Enemies and temptations always attack us when we are most vulnerable. An honest review of our spiritual lives will help us recognize what our weaknesses are and when we might be most susceptible to temptation. We must surrender these areas to God and depend on him to help us stand firm.

18:25–29 David recognized God's desire to bestow mercy on those who are repentant of their sins and merciful toward others. When we admit our sin to God, and when we show mercy to others, God is merciful toward us. We do great harm to ourselves and to others when we are too proud to admit our sins and failures. Such pride fears acknowledging and confessing the truth of our wrongdoing. And this kind of pride keeps us from truly seeking God. But God is quick to redirect our course when we acknowledge our pride as sin.

18:30–36 David praised God for rescuing those who looked to God for help. God will also deliver us if we are willing to admit our weaknesses, repent of our sins and depend on him. He will give us both the power to do what is right in difficult situations and the ability to walk without stumbling, even when the path is slippery.

18:43–50 The successes that God gives to us can become a strong encouragement to others. We are urged to share our victories with others and encourage them to press on in their spiritual journey. They will see God's transforming power at work in our lives and realize that God can do the same for them. Because of who God is and what he does for us, we should constantly give him thanks and praise.

47He is the God who avenges me,
who subdues nations under me,
48 who saves me from my enemies.
You exalted me above my foes;
from violent men you rescued me.
49Therefore I will praise you among the nations, O LORD;
I will sing praises to your name.
50He gives his king great victories;
he shows unfailing kindness to his anointed,
to David and his descendants forever.

Psalm 19

For the director of music. A psalm of David.

1The heavens declare the glory of God;
the skies proclaim the work of his hands.
2Day after day they pour forth speech;
night after night they display knowledge.
3There is no speech or language
where their voice is not heard.[a]
4Their voice[b] goes out into all the earth,
their words to the ends of the world.

In the heavens he has pitched a tent for the sun,
5 which is like a bridegroom coming forth from his pavilion,
like a champion rejoicing to run his course.
6It rises at one end of the heavens
and makes its circuit to the other;
nothing is hidden from its heat.

7The law of the LORD is perfect,
reviving the soul.
The statutes of the LORD are trustworthy,
making wise the simple.
8The precepts of the LORD are right,
giving joy to the heart.
The commands of the LORD are radiant,
giving light to the eyes.
9The fear of the LORD is pure,
enduring forever.
The ordinances of the LORD are sure
and altogether righteous.
10They are more precious than gold,
than much pure gold;
they are sweeter than honey,
than honey from the comb.
11By them is your servant warned;
in keeping them there is great reward.

12Who can discern his errors?
Forgive my hidden faults.
13Keep your servant also from willful sins;
may they not rule over me.
Then will I be blameless,
innocent of great transgression.

14May the words of my mouth and the meditation of my heart
be pleasing in your sight,
O LORD, my Rock and my Redeemer.

Psalm 20

For the director of music. A psalm of David.

1May the LORD answer you when you are in distress;
may the name of the God of Jacob protect you.
2May he send you help from the sanctuary
and grant you support from Zion.
3May he remember all your sacrifices
and accept your burnt offerings. *Selah*
4May he give you the desire of your heart
and make all your plans succeed.
5We will shout for joy when you are victorious
and will lift up our banners in the name of our God.
May the LORD grant all your requests.

6Now I know that the LORD saves his anointed;
he answers him from his holy heaven
with the saving power of his right hand.
7Some trust in chariots and some in horses,
but we trust in the name of the LORD our God.
8They are brought to their knees and fall,
but we rise up and stand firm.

9O LORD, save the king!
Answer[c] us when we call!

[a]3 Or *They have no speech, there are no words; / no sound is heard from them* [b]4 Septuagint, Jerome and Syriac; Hebrew *line* [c]9 Or *save! / O King, answer*

19:1–6 No one can truly say that they have no knowledge about God (see Romans 1:18–20). His power can be seen throughout our physical world. Though the sun does not speak aloud, it declares every day what God has done. All humans benefit from the sun, and we cannot hide from the message it declares to the entire world: God is not a figment of our imagination. He is with us right now, and he desires to help us.
19:7–11 God's laws guide us in the right way to live. They are not a burden that robs us of the good things of life (see Matthew 11:29–30). Instead, his laws transform us, causing us to reflect God's image all the more.
19:12–14 David asked God to reveal any hidden sins in his life so that he might see the truth. David was aware that he needed to honestly examine his heart, and he asked God to help him do this. We often are blind to our sins. We need God's help to clarify our thinking—to reveal the sin that deceives us and keeps us deliberately doing wrong. When our hearts are right with God, our actions will be right also.
20:1–3 The psalmist counted on God's presence at all times to protect him, especially when his problems were intense. If God could help David with all his troubles, he can also help us.

Psalm 21

For the director of music. A psalm of David.

[1]O LORD, the king rejoices in your strength.
How great is his joy in the victories you give!
[2]You have granted him the desire of his heart
and have not withheld the request of his lips. *Selah*
[3]You welcomed him with rich blessings
and placed a crown of pure gold on his head.
[4]He asked you for life, and you gave it to him—
length of days, for ever and ever.
[5]Through the victories you gave, his glory is great;
you have bestowed on him splendor and majesty.
[6]Surely you have granted him eternal blessings
and made him glad with the joy of your presence.
[7]For the king trusts in the LORD;
through the unfailing love of the Most High
he will not be shaken.

[8]Your hand will lay hold on all your enemies;
your right hand will seize your foes.
[9]At the time of your appearing
you will make them like a fiery furnace.
In his wrath the LORD will swallow them up,
and his fire will consume them.
[10]You will destroy their descendants from the earth,
their posterity from mankind.
[11]Though they plot evil against you
and devise wicked schemes, they cannot succeed;
[12]for you will make them turn their backs
when you aim at them with drawn bow.

[13]Be exalted, O LORD, in your strength;
we will sing and praise your might.

Psalm 22

For the director of music. To ⌞the tune of⌟ "The Doe of the Morning." A psalm of David.

[1]My God, my God, why have you forsaken me?
Why are you so far from saving me,
so far from the words of my groaning?
[2]O my God, I cry out by day, but you do not answer,
by night, and am not silent.

[3]Yet you are enthroned as the Holy One;
you are the praise of Israel.[a]
[4]In you our fathers put their trust;
they trusted and you delivered them.
[5]They cried to you and were saved;
in you they trusted and were not disappointed.

[6]But I am a worm and not a man,
scorned by men and despised by the people.
[7]All who see me mock me;
they hurl insults, shaking their heads:
[8]"He trusts in the LORD;
let the LORD rescue him.
Let him deliver him,
since he delights in him."

[9]Yet you brought me out of the womb;
you made me trust in you
even at my mother's breast.
[10]From birth I was cast upon you;
from my mother's womb you have been my God.
[11]Do not be far from me,
for trouble is near
and there is no one to help.

[12]Many bulls surround me;
strong bulls of Bashan encircle me.
[13]Roaring lions tearing their prey
open their mouths wide against me.
[14]I am poured out like water,
and all my bones are out of joint.
My heart has turned to wax;
it has melted away within me.

[a]3 Or *Yet you are holy, / enthroned on the praises of Israel*

21:1–6 As we honestly reflect on our spiritual condition, we realize that God's strength comes to us as we seek him through prayer and meditation on his Word. God wants each of us to live a life that has eternal value and meaning. As we experience such a life, we recognize that true joy is an outgrowth of being in God's presence. We need to draw close to God, not just for what he can do for us, but for who he is. This realization should motivate us to spend time with God, seeking him through prayer and meditation on his Word.

22:1–5 Jesus Christ repeated the words in the first verse of this psalm as he hung on the cross, indicating his feelings of isolation from God the Father (see Matthew 27:46; Mark 15:34). We all have felt such times of abandonment. When we feel cut off from God, we may be tempted to question his existence or even doubt that he is able to deliver us. At such times, we must not rely on feelings but rather on facts. We must remember who God is and what he has done for his people in the past.

22:6–11 When things aren't going well, we may feel like a "worm," just as David did. But God cares for us and will help us. Others may mock us, doubting that God can really save us. We should ignore these people because we know God is there to deliver us. He has helped us before, ever since our birth, and he will surely help us now.

22:12–21 God understands our pain. Jesus Christ experienced the most terrible conditions imaginable during his earthly life and sacrificial death on the cross. He was beaten, crucified and stripped of his dignity. Jesus knows how we feel when we suffer physical and emotional pain. He knows what it feels like to be betrayed and rejected by those we love. He is always with us (see Matthew 28:20), and he will help us when we are suffering.

15My strength is dried up like a potsherd,
and my tongue sticks to the roof of my mouth;
you lay me[a] in the dust of death.
16Dogs have surrounded me;
a band of evil men has encircled me,
they have pierced[b] my hands and my feet.
17I can count all my bones;
people stare and gloat over me.
18They divide my garments among them
and cast lots for my clothing.

19But you, O LORD, be not far off;
O my Strength, come quickly to help me.
20Deliver my life from the sword,
my precious life from the power of the dogs.
21Rescue me from the mouth of the lions;
save[c] me from the horns of the wild oxen.

22I will declare your name to my brothers;
in the congregation I will praise you.
23You who fear the LORD, praise him!
All you descendants of Jacob, honor him!
Revere him, all you descendants of Israel!
24For he has not despised or disdained
the suffering of the afflicted one;
he has not hidden his face from him
but has listened to his cry for help.

25From you comes the theme of my praise in the great assembly;
before those who fear you[d] will I fulfill my vows.
26The poor will eat and be satisfied;
they who seek the LORD will praise him—
may your hearts live forever!
27All the ends of the earth
will remember and turn to the LORD,
and all the families of the nations
will bow down before him,
28for dominion belongs to the LORD
and he rules over the nations.

29All the rich of the earth will feast and worship;
all who go down to the dust will kneel before him—
those who cannot keep themselves alive.
30Posterity will serve him;
future generations will be told about the Lord.
31They will proclaim his righteousness
to a people yet unborn—
for he has done it.

Psalm 23

A psalm of David.

1The LORD is my shepherd, I shall not be in want.
2 He makes me lie down in green pastures,
he leads me beside quiet waters,
3 he restores my soul.
He guides me in paths of righteousness
for his name's sake.
4Even though I walk
through the valley of the shadow of death,[e]
I will fear no evil,
for you are with me;
your rod and your staff,
they comfort me.

5You prepare a table before me
in the presence of my enemies.
You anoint my head with oil;
my cup overflows.
6Surely goodness and love will follow me
all the days of my life,
and I will dwell in the house of the LORD
forever.

Psalm 24

Of David. A psalm.

1The earth is the LORD's, and everything in it,
the world, and all who live in it;
2for he founded it upon the seas
and established it upon the waters.

3Who may ascend the hill of the LORD?
Who may stand in his holy place?
4He who has clean hands and a pure heart,
who does not lift up his soul to an idol
or swear by what is false.[f]
5He will receive blessing from the LORD
and vindication from God his Savior.
6Such is the generation of those who seek him,
who seek your face, O God of Jacob.[g] *Selah*

[a]15 Or */ I am laid* [b]16 Some Hebrew manuscripts, Septuagint and Syriac; most Hebrew manuscripts */ like the lion,* [c]21 Or */ you have heard* [d]25 Hebrew *him* [e]4 Or *through the darkest valley* [f]4 Or *swear falsely* [g]6 Two Hebrew manuscripts and Syriac (see also Septuagint); most Hebrew manuscripts *face, Jacob*

23:1–6 The Lord is our shepherd, and he knows what we need better than we do. God wants us to have what is best for us. As long as we trust him as our shepherd, he will lead us to places of blessing. He can direct us away from places where we will stumble. Yet even when we fall, he can still rescue us.

24:1–2 Sometimes we may feel that there is no way out of the terrible circumstances into which we have fallen. In these verses, however, we glimpse God's power over the entire universe. With such power available to us from God's outstretched hand there is always a way out of our problems. The Bible tells us that God has provided a way for our sins to be paid and for us to be delivered from sin's grip (see 2 Corinthians 1:10).

[7]Lift up your heads, O you gates;
be lifted up, you ancient doors,
that the King of glory may come in.
[8]Who is this King of glory?
The LORD strong and mighty,
the LORD mighty in battle.
[9]Lift up your heads, O you gates;
lift them up, you ancient doors,
that the King of glory may come in.
[10]Who is he, this King of glory?
The LORD Almighty—
he is the King of glory. *Selah*

Psalm 25[a]

Of David.

[1]To you, O LORD, I lift up my soul;
[2] in you I trust, O my God.
Do not let me be put to shame,
nor let my enemies triumph over me.
[3]No one whose hope is in you
will ever be put to shame,
but they will be put to shame
who are treacherous without excuse.

[4]Show me your ways, O LORD,
teach me your paths;
[5]guide me in your truth and teach me,
for you are God my Savior,
and my hope is in you all day long.
[6]Remember, O LORD, your great mercy and love,
for they are from of old.
[7]Remember not the sins of my youth
and my rebellious ways;
according to your love remember me,
for you are good, O LORD.

[8]Good and upright is the LORD;
therefore he instructs sinners in his ways.
[9]He guides the humble in what is right
and teaches them his way.
[10]All the ways of the LORD are loving and faithful
for those who keep the demands of his covenant.
[11]For the sake of your name, O LORD,
forgive my iniquity, though it is great.
[12]Who, then, is the man that fears the LORD?
He will instruct him in the way chosen for him.
[13]He will spend his days in prosperity,
and his descendants will inherit the land.
[14]The LORD confides in those who fear him;
he makes his covenant known to them.
[15]My eyes are ever on the LORD,
for only he will release my feet from the snare.

[16]Turn to me and be gracious to me,
for I am lonely and afflicted.
[17]The troubles of my heart have multiplied;
free me from my anguish.
[18]Look upon my affliction and my distress
and take away all my sins.
[19]See how my enemies have increased
and how fiercely they hate me!
[20]Guard my life and rescue me;
let me not be put to shame,
for I take refuge in you.
[21]May integrity and uprightness protect me,
because my hope is in you.

[22]Redeem Israel, O God,
from all their troubles!

Psalm 26

Of David.

[1]Vindicate me, O LORD,
for I have led a blameless life;
I have trusted in the LORD
without wavering.
[2]Test me, O LORD, and try me,
examine my heart and my mind;
[3]for your love is ever before me,
and I walk continually in your truth.
[4]I do not sit with deceitful men,
nor do I consort with hypocrites;
[5]I abhor the assembly of evildoers
and refuse to sit with the wicked.
[6]I wash my hands in innocence,
and go about your altar, O LORD,
[7]proclaiming aloud your praise
and telling of all your wonderful deeds.
[8]I love the house where you live, O LORD,
the place where your glory dwells.

[9]Do not take away my soul along with sinners,
my life with bloodthirsty men,
[10]in whose hands are wicked schemes,
whose right hands are full of bribes.
[11]But I lead a blameless life;
redeem me and be merciful to me.

[12]My feet stand on level ground;
in the great assembly I will praise the LORD.

Psalm 27

Of David.

[1]The LORD is my light and my salvation—
whom shall I fear?

[a]This psalm is an acrostic poem, the verses of which begin with the successive letters of the Hebrew alphabet.

25:1–7 When we place our faith in God, we can trust him to care for us and help us overcome the things in our lives that would destroy us. We need to ask God to forgive our sins and show us how to live according to his will.
27:1–6 David praised God for the help and hope he provided. We have nothing to fear in this life if we put our complete trust in God as our guide, deliverer and protector. If we continually seek God, we can be assured that when problems arise, he will watch over us, make our way secure and draw us closer to himself.

The LORD is the stronghold of my life—
of whom shall I be afraid?
2 When evil men advance against me
to devour my flesh,[a]
when my enemies and my foes attack me,
they will stumble and fall.
3 Though an army besiege me,
my heart will not fear;
though war break out against me,
even then will I be confident.

4 One thing I ask of the LORD,
this is what I seek:
that I may dwell in the house of the LORD
all the days of my life,
to gaze upon the beauty of the LORD
and to seek him in his temple.
5 For in the day of trouble
he will keep me safe in his dwelling;
he will hide me in the shelter of his tabernacle
and set me high upon a rock.
6 Then my head will be exalted
above the enemies who surround me;
at his tabernacle will I sacrifice with shouts of joy;
I will sing and make music to the LORD.

7 Hear my voice when I call, O LORD;
be merciful to me and answer me.
8 My heart says of you, "Seek his[b] face!"
Your face, LORD, I will seek.
9 Do not hide your face from me,
do not turn your servant away in anger;
you have been my helper.
Do not reject me or forsake me,
O God my Savior.
10 Though my father and mother forsake me,
the LORD will receive me.
11 Teach me your way, O LORD;
lead me in a straight path
because of my oppressors.
12 Do not turn me over to the desire of my foes,
for false witnesses rise up against me,
breathing out violence.

13 I am still confident of this:
I will see the goodness of the LORD
in the land of the living.
14 Wait for the LORD;
be strong and take heart
and wait for the LORD.

Psalm 28

Of David.

1 To you I call, O LORD my Rock;
do not turn a deaf ear to me.
For if you remain silent,
I will be like those who have gone down to the pit.
2 Hear my cry for mercy
as I call to you for help,
as I lift up my hands
toward your Most Holy Place.

3 Do not drag me away with the wicked,
with those who do evil,
who speak cordially with their neighbors
but harbor malice in their hearts.
4 Repay them for their deeds
and for their evil work;
repay them for what their hands have done
and bring back upon them what they deserve.
5 Since they show no regard for the works of the LORD
and what his hands have done,
he will tear them down
and never build them up again.

6 Praise be to the LORD,
for he has heard my cry for mercy.
7 The LORD is my strength and my shield;
my heart trusts in him, and I am helped.
My heart leaps for joy
and I will give thanks to him in song.

8 The LORD is the strength of his people,
a fortress of salvation for his anointed one.
9 Save your people and bless your inheritance;
be their shepherd and carry them forever.

Psalm 29

A psalm of David.

1 Ascribe to the LORD, O mighty ones,
ascribe to the LORD glory and strength.
2 Ascribe to the LORD the glory due his name;
worship the LORD in the splendor of his[c] holiness.

[a] 2 Or *to slander me* [b] 8 Or *To you, O my heart, he has said, "Seek my* [c] 2 Or *LORD with the splendor of*

27:11–14 Because temptations are pressing in around us, we must learn to depend on God to guide us. Apart from God we have no power against the things that seek to destroy us. We must determine every day to follow God, patiently and confidently waiting for him to care for us and lead us.

28:1–5 We won't find the answers to life's problems among those who practice evil. Such people are headed for ultimate judgment. If we don't avoid the people and situations of our former sins, the same old temptations will trap us again.

28:6–9 God can empower us to stand against the pressures that drive us back into sinful habits. Knowing that God is on our side should be a source of great joy and encouragement. Even when we feel we can't go on, God is always there to lift us up and support us.

29:1–9 In this psalm, we are reminded of God's power over nature. Yet despite God's awe-inspiring power, he knows and loves each one of us. He is able to conquer any struggle we face. God's personal concern for us should inspire us to surrender to him.

3The voice of the LORD is over the waters;
the God of glory thunders,
the LORD thunders over the mighty
waters.
4The voice of the LORD is powerful;
the voice of the LORD is majestic.
5The voice of the LORD breaks the cedars;
the LORD breaks in pieces the cedars of
Lebanon.
6He makes Lebanon skip like a calf,
Sirion[a] like a young wild ox.
7The voice of the LORD strikes
with flashes of lightning.
8The voice of the LORD shakes the desert;
the LORD shakes the Desert of Kadesh.
9The voice of the LORD twists the oaks[b]
and strips the forests bare.
And in his temple all cry, "Glory!"
10The LORD sits[c] enthroned over the flood;
the LORD is enthroned as King forever.
11The LORD gives strength to his people;
the LORD blesses his people with peace.

Psalm 30

A psalm. A song. For the dedication of the temple.[d] Of David.

1I will exalt you, O LORD,
for you lifted me out of the depths
and did not let my enemies gloat over
me.
2O LORD my God, I called to you for help
and you healed me.
3O LORD, you brought me up from the
grave[e];
you spared me from going down into
the pit.

4Sing to the LORD, you saints of his;
praise his holy name.
5For his anger lasts only a moment,
but his favor lasts a lifetime;
weeping may remain for a night,
but rejoicing comes in the morning.

6When I felt secure, I said,
"I will never be shaken."
7O LORD, when you favored me,
you made my mountain[f] stand firm;
but when you hid your face,
I was dismayed.

8To you, O LORD, I called;
to the Lord I cried for mercy:
9"What gain is there in my destruction,[g]
in my going down into the pit?
Will the dust praise you?
Will it proclaim your faithfulness?
10Hear, O LORD, and be merciful to me;
O LORD, be my help."

11You turned my wailing into dancing;
you removed my sackcloth and clothed
me with joy,
12that my heart may sing to you and not be
silent.
O LORD my God, I will give you thanks
forever.

Psalm 31

For the director of music. A psalm of David.

1In you, O LORD, I have taken refuge;
let me never be put to shame;
deliver me in your righteousness.
2Turn your ear to me,
come quickly to my rescue;
be my rock of refuge,
a strong fortress to save me.
3Since you are my rock and my fortress,
for the sake of your name lead and guide
me.
4Free me from the trap that is set for me,
for you are my refuge.
5Into your hands I commit my spirit;
redeem me, O LORD, the God of truth.

6I hate those who cling to worthless idols;
I trust in the LORD.
7I will be glad and rejoice in your love,
for you saw my affliction
and knew the anguish of my soul.
8You have not handed me over to the
enemy
but have set my feet in a spacious place.

[a]6 That is, Mount Hermon [b]9 Or *LORD makes the deer give birth* [c]10 Or *sat* [d]Title: Or *palace* [e]3 Hebrew *Sheol* [f]7 Or *hill country* [g]9 Or *there if I am silenced*

30:1–5 What joy and gratitude we feel when God lifts us up and does not let our problems defeat or destroy us! We all go through long, dark nights struggling with temptation. These are times we must wait on the Lord. But when, in his power, we overcome those temptations, we will experience victory and the joy of success that is so sweet.

30:6–9 We are often in the most danger when everything in our lives is progressing smoothly. At those times, we tend to get overconfident and think nothing can happen to us. But pride and overconfidence usually come before a fall (see Proverbs 16:8). We must always remember that we can't make it alone.

30:10–12 David concluded his request for deliverance with words of praise to God. Staying close to God, seeking him through prayer, meditating on his Word and worshiping him are key spiritual disciplines that will help us preserve our spiritual gains. God wants us to grow spiritually—to live lives filled with purpose and joy. When God helps us, we should not hesitate to praise him. Praising God aloud is an excellent way to tell others about God's work in our lives. Our praise will encourage others to seek God and will give us added strength to persevere in our own spiritual growth.

31:1–5 David's words exhibit his dependence on God in a time of stress. God is our strong refuge, our rock of safety, the one we should turn to when we feel overwhelmed by temptation and danger. Because we know God is such a strong refuge for us, we can surrender our lives to him each day with confidence.

9Be merciful to me, O LORD, for I am in
distress;
my eyes grow weak with sorrow,
my soul and my body with grief.
10My life is consumed by anguish
and my years by groaning;
my strength fails because of my affliction,[a]
and my bones grow weak.
11Because of all my enemies,
I am the utter contempt of my
neighbors;
I am a dread to my friends—
those who see me on the street flee from
me.
12I am forgotten by them as though I were
dead;
I have become like broken pottery.
13For I hear the slander of many;
there is terror on every side;
they conspire against me
and plot to take my life.

14But I trust in you, O LORD;
I say, "You are my God."
15My times are in your hands;
deliver me from my enemies
and from those who pursue me.
16Let your face shine on your servant;
save me in your unfailing love.
17Let me not be put to shame, O LORD,
for I have cried out to you;
but let the wicked be put to shame
and lie silent in the grave.[b]
18Let their lying lips be silenced,
for with pride and contempt
they speak arrogantly against the
righteous.

19How great is your goodness,
which you have stored up for those who
fear you,
which you bestow in the sight of men
on those who take refuge in you.
20In the shelter of your presence you hide
them
from the intrigues of men;
in your dwelling you keep them safe
from accusing tongues.

21Praise be to the LORD,
for he showed his wonderful love to me
when I was in a besieged city.
22In my alarm I said,
"I am cut off from your sight!"
Yet you heard my cry for mercy
when I called to you for help.
23Love the LORD, all his saints!
The LORD preserves the faithful,
but the proud he pays back in full.
24Be strong and take heart,
all you who hope in the LORD.

Psalm 32

Of David. A *maskil*.[c]

1Blessed is he
whose transgressions are forgiven,
whose sins are covered.
2Blessed is the man
whose sin the LORD does not count
against him
and in whose spirit is no deceit.

3When I kept silent,
my bones wasted away
through my groaning all day long.
4For day and night
your hand was heavy upon me;
my strength was sapped
as in the heat of summer. *Selah*
5Then I acknowledged my sin to you
and did not cover up my iniquity.
I said, "I will confess
my transgressions to the LORD"—
and you forgave
the guilt of my sin. *Selah*
6Therefore let everyone who is godly pray to
you
while you may be found;
surely when the mighty waters rise,
they will not reach him.
7You are my hiding place;
you will protect me from trouble
and surround me with songs of
deliverance. *Selah*
8I will instruct you and teach you in the way
you should go;
I will counsel you and watch over you.
9Do not be like the horse or the mule,
which have no understanding
but must be controlled by bit and bridle
or they will not come to you.
10Many are the woes of the wicked,

[a]10 Or *guilt* [b]17 Hebrew *Sheol* [c]Title: Probably a literary or musical term

31:14–18 David shared his confidence that God alone could deliver him from his troubles. David also realized that without God's help he would suffer great humiliation. God is the only one able to solve our problems. He is willing to help us overcome the people and situations that once troubled us. We need to make sure God is at the center of our lives.

32:1–4 We notice in this psalm that we suffer unnecessary guilt by refusing to confess our sin. Making restitution for our past failures and reconciling our relationships is an important part of our spiritual growth. As David declared, we can know great joy when we receive forgiveness for our sins.

32:5–9 Like David, we need to confess our sins before God and receive forgiveness. When we do so, we set a good example for others who have difficulty admitting their sin to God. We also set our own hearts free from the destructive grip of guilt and restore our relationship with God. With our relationship restored, we can learn to live in obedience to the Lord's will and respond willingly to his instruction.

The Fever of Guilt

Psalm 32 Guilt is like a fever of the soul. Like a warning light, our guilt alerts us to our actions that conflict with God's will, ourselves and maybe even others. When we sense the alarm of guilt, many of us descend into deep depression, condemning ourselves or imagining various ways that God will punish us. Wallowing in feelings of guilt, however, only leaves us discouraged and spiritually drained.

David understood the fever of guilt, but he also knew the recovery that could come with forgiveness. Both guilt and forgiveness are described in Psalm 32. It is very possible that David wrote this psalm around the same time as Psalm 51. Psalm 51 pertains to his adultery with Bathsheba. David initially covered up his adultery with Bathsheba and contrived the murder of Bathsheba's husband, Uriah. David didn't confess his sin until Nathan the prophet confronted him several months later. Psalm 32 gives us an insight into the painful, physical and spiritual symptoms that were generated by David's guilty conscience. These symptoms were resolved only through David's confession of sin and his forgiveness from God.

Sometimes we believe we can make up for our sin because of the suffering we endure from our accusing conscience. But guilt itself cannot atone for our sin. We can only rid ourselves of guilt by dealing with its *cause.* Once we have treated the root cause of our sin, guilt takes care of itself. In this way, guilt can help bring us to God, prompting us to confess our sins and find forgiveness and restoration. Hiding our sins only gives them increasing power over us. Instead, we must break sin's power by confessing our sin to God and seeking his forgiveness. And God may also lead us to confess our sin to those we have harmed and seek their forgiveness as well.

Putting It Into Practice

What are some of the sins you are hiding from God? How has this affected your spiritual vitality? What holds you back from confessing these sins?

Ask God to help you confess them, both to him and to those you have hurt, so that you may receive God's gracious forgiveness.

For more on repentance and confession, turn to Psalm 51.

but the LORD's unfailing love
surrounds the man who trusts in him.

11Rejoice in the LORD and be glad, you righteous;
sing, all you who are upright in heart!

Psalm 33

1Sing joyfully to the LORD, you righteous;
it is fitting for the upright to praise him.
2Praise the LORD with the harp;
make music to him on the ten-stringed lyre.
3Sing to him a new song;
play skillfully, and shout for joy.

4For the word of the LORD is right and true;
he is faithful in all he does.
5The LORD loves righteousness and justice;
the earth is full of his unfailing love.

6By the word of the LORD were the heavens made,
their starry host by the breath of his mouth.
7He gathers the waters of the sea into jars[a];
he puts the deep into storehouses.
8Let all the earth fear the LORD;
let all the people of the world revere him.
9For he spoke, and it came to be;
he commanded, and it stood firm.
10The LORD foils the plans of the nations;
he thwarts the purposes of the peoples.
11But the plans of the LORD stand firm forever,
the purposes of his heart through all generations.

12Blessed is the nation whose God is the LORD,
the people he chose for his inheritance.
13From heaven the LORD looks down
and sees all mankind;
14from his dwelling place he watches
all who live on earth—
15he who forms the hearts of all,
who considers everything they do.
16No king is saved by the size of his army;
no warrior escapes by his great strength.
17A horse is a vain hope for deliverance;
despite all its great strength it cannot save.
18But the eyes of the LORD are on those who fear him,
on those whose hope is in his unfailing love,
19to deliver them from death
and keep them alive in famine.

20We wait in hope for the LORD;
he is our help and our shield.
21In him our hearts rejoice,
for we trust in his holy name.
22May your unfailing love rest upon us, O LORD,
even as we put our hope in you.

Psalm 34[b]

Of David. When he pretended to be insane before Abimelech, who drove him away, and he left.

1I will extol the LORD at all times;
his praise will always be on my lips.
2My soul will boast in the LORD;
let the afflicted hear and rejoice.
3Glorify the LORD with me;
let us exalt his name together.

4I sought the LORD, and he answered me;
he delivered me from all my fears.
5Those who look to him are radiant;
their faces are never covered with shame.
6This poor man called, and the LORD heard him;
he saved him out of all his troubles.
7The angel of the LORD encamps around those who fear him,
and he delivers them.

8Taste and see that the LORD is good;
blessed is the man who takes refuge in him.
9Fear the LORD, you his saints,
for those who fear him lack nothing.
10The lions may grow weak and hungry,
but those who seek the LORD lack no good thing.
11Come, my children, listen to me;
I will teach you the fear of the LORD.
12Whoever of you loves life
and desires to see many good days,
13keep your tongue from evil
and your lips from speaking lies.
14Turn from evil and do good;
seek peace and pursue it.

15The eyes of the LORD are on the righteous
and his ears are attentive to their cry;

[a]7 Or *sea as into a heap* [b]This psalm is an acrostic poem, the verses of which begin with the successive letters of the Hebrew alphabet.

34:1–7 When we experience deliverance through God's power, we should praise him and share our good news with others. If we care about others who suffer from problems similar to our own, we would be selfish not to tell them how we found help. Boasting about our God and the help he has given us is something we should do. This type of godly boasting will encourage others and strengthen our faith in God as well.

34:8–14 If we have spent our lives trusting our own judgment, we may find it hard to surrender to God and his plan for us. But if we refuse to seek God's help and direction, we will never know how good he can be to us. God has the power and the wisdom we need to gain victory in our struggles with sin and temptation.

16the face of the LORD is against those who do evil,
to cut off the memory of them from the earth.
17The righteous cry out, and the LORD hears them;
he delivers them from all their troubles.
18The LORD is close to the brokenhearted
and saves those who are crushed in spirit.

19A righteous man may have many troubles,
but the LORD delivers him from them all;
20he protects all his bones,
not one of them will be broken.

21Evil will slay the wicked;
the foes of the righteous will be condemned.
22The LORD redeems his servants;
no one will be condemned who takes refuge in him.

Psalm 35

Of David.

1Contend, O LORD, with those who contend with me;
fight against those who fight against me.
2Take up shield and buckler;
arise and come to my aid.
3Brandish spear and javelin[a]
against those who pursue me.
Say to my soul,
"I am your salvation."

4May those who seek my life
be disgraced and put to shame;
may those who plot my ruin
be turned back in dismay.
5May they be like chaff before the wind,
with the angel of the LORD driving them away;
6may their path be dark and slippery,
with the angel of the LORD pursuing them.
7Since they hid their net for me without cause
and without cause dug a pit for me,
8may ruin overtake them by surprise—
may the net they hid entangle them,
may they fall into the pit, to their ruin.
9Then my soul will rejoice in the LORD
and delight in his salvation.
10My whole being will exclaim,
"Who is like you, O LORD?
You rescue the poor from those too strong for them,
the poor and needy from those who rob them."
11Ruthless witnesses come forward;
they question me on things I know nothing about.
12They repay me evil for good
and leave my soul forlorn.
13Yet when they were ill, I put on sackcloth
and humbled myself with fasting.
When my prayers returned to me unanswered,
14I went about mourning
as though for my friend or brother.
I bowed my head in grief
as though weeping for my mother.
15But when I stumbled, they gathered in glee;
attackers gathered against me when I was unaware.
They slandered me without ceasing.
16Like the ungodly they maliciously mocked[b];
they gnashed their teeth at me.
17O Lord, how long will you look on?
Rescue my life from their ravages,
my precious life from these lions.
18I will give you thanks in the great assembly;
among throngs of people I will praise you.

19Let not those gloat over me
who are my enemies without cause;
let not those who hate me without reason
maliciously wink the eye.
20They do not speak peaceably,
but devise false accusations
against those who live quietly in the land.
21They gape at me and say, "Aha! Aha!
With our own eyes we have seen it."

22O LORD, you have seen this; be not silent.
Do not be far from me, O Lord.
23Awake, and rise to my defense!
Contend for me, my God and Lord.
24Vindicate me in your righteousness, O LORD my God;
do not let them gloat over me.
25Do not let them think, "Aha, just what we wanted!"
or say, "We have swallowed him up."

26May all who gloat over my distress
be put to shame and confusion;
may all who exalt themselves over me
be clothed with shame and disgrace.
27May those who delight in my vindication
shout for joy and gladness;
may they always say, "The LORD be exalted,
who delights in the well-being of his servant."

[a]3 Or *and block the way* [b]16 Septuagint; Hebrew may mean *ungodly circle of mockers.*

35:17–28 In this psalm, David expressed feelings of desperation; it seemed to him that God had forgotten him. At times we may feel the same way. But when relief comes, we should act like David and encourage others who have the same desperate feelings. We should cry out to God for his wisdom and power, knowing that he hears us when we pray.

[28]My tongue will speak of your righteousness
and of your praises all day long.

Psalm 36

For the director of music. Of David the servant of the LORD.

[1]An oracle is within my heart
concerning the sinfulness of the wicked:[a]
There is no fear of God
before his eyes.
[2]For in his own eyes he flatters himself
too much to detect or hate his sin.
[3]The words of his mouth are wicked and deceitful;
he has ceased to be wise and to do good.
[4]Even on his bed he plots evil;
he commits himself to a sinful course
and does not reject what is wrong.

[5]Your love, O LORD, reaches to the heavens,
your faithfulness to the skies.
[6]Your righteousness is like the mighty mountains,
your justice like the great deep.
O LORD, you preserve both man and beast.
[7] How priceless is your unfailing love!
Both high and low among men
find[b] refuge in the shadow of your wings.
[8]They feast on the abundance of your house;
you give them drink from your river of delights.
[9]For with you is the fountain of life;
in your light we see light.

[10]Continue your love to those who know you,
your righteousness to the upright in heart.
[11]May the foot of the proud not come against me,
nor the hand of the wicked drive me away.
[12]See how the evildoers lie fallen—
thrown down, not able to rise!

Psalm 37[c]

Of David.

[1]Do not fret because of evil men
or be envious of those who do wrong;
[2]for like the grass they will soon wither,
like green plants they will soon die away.

[3]Trust in the LORD and do good;
dwell in the land and enjoy safe pasture.
[4]Delight yourself in the LORD
and he will give you the desires of your heart.

[5]Commit your way to the LORD;
trust in him and he will do this:
[6]He will make your righteousness shine like the dawn,
the justice of your cause like the noonday sun.

[7]Be still before the LORD and wait patiently for him;
do not fret when men succeed in their ways,
when they carry out their wicked schemes.

[8]Refrain from anger and turn from wrath;
do not fret—it leads only to evil.
[9]For evil men will be cut off,
but those who hope in the LORD will inherit the land.

[10]A little while, and the wicked will be no more;
though you look for them, they will not be found.
[11]But the meek will inherit the land
and enjoy great peace.

[12]The wicked plot against the righteous
and gnash their teeth at them;
[13]but the Lord laughs at the wicked,
for he knows their day is coming.

[14]The wicked draw the sword
and bend the bow
to bring down the poor and needy,
to slay those whose ways are upright.
[15]But their swords will pierce their own hearts,
and their bows will be broken.

[16]Better the little that the righteous have
than the wealth of many wicked;
[17]for the power of the wicked will be broken,
but the LORD upholds the righteous.

[18]The days of the blameless are known to the LORD,
and their inheritance will endure forever.
[19]In times of disaster they will not wither;
in days of famine they will enjoy plenty.

[20]But the wicked will perish:

[a]1 Or *heart: / Sin proceeds from the wicked.* [b]7 Or *love, O God! / Men find*; or *love! / Both heavenly beings and men / find* [c]This psalm is an acrostic poem, the stanzas of which begin with the successive letters of the Hebrew alphabet.

37:1–7 We do not need to worry about or be jealous of those who seem to be getting away with doing wrong things. Their day in the sun is short; their moment of glory will soon be over. We need to live a life of lasting value—faithfully serving our God and helping the people around us. God wants us to develop a close relationship with him and serve him in everything we do. Then, in God's perfect timing, everyone will see that God's way is right.

The LORD's enemies will be like the
beauty of the fields,
they will vanish—vanish like smoke.

21The wicked borrow and do not repay,
but the righteous give generously;
22those the LORD blesses will inherit the land,
but those he curses will be cut off.

23If the LORD delights in a man's way,
he makes his steps firm;
24though he stumble, he will not fall,
for the LORD upholds him with his hand.

25I was young and now I am old,
yet I have never seen the righteous
forsaken
or their children begging bread.
26They are always generous and lend freely;
their children will be blessed.

27Turn from evil and do good;
then you will dwell in the land forever.
28For the LORD loves the just
and will not forsake his faithful ones.

They will be protected forever,
but the offspring of the wicked will be
cut off;
29the righteous will inherit the land
and dwell in it forever.

30The mouth of the righteous man utters
wisdom,
and his tongue speaks what is just.
31The law of his God is in his heart;
his feet do not slip.

32The wicked lie in wait for the righteous,
seeking their very lives;
33but the LORD will not leave them in their
power
or let them be condemned when brought
to trial.

34Wait for the LORD
and keep his way.
He will exalt you to inherit the land;
when the wicked are cut off, you will see
it.

35I have seen a wicked and ruthless man
flourishing like a green tree in its native
soil,
36but he soon passed away and was no more;
though I looked for him, he could not
be found.

37Consider the blameless, observe the
upright;
there is a future[a] for the man of peace.
38But all sinners will be destroyed;
the future[b] of the wicked will be cut
off.

39The salvation of the righteous comes from
the LORD;
he is their stronghold in time of trouble.
40The LORD helps them and delivers them;
he delivers them from the wicked and
saves them,
because they take refuge in him.

Psalm 38

A psalm of David. A petition.

1O LORD, do not rebuke me in your anger
or discipline me in your wrath.
2For your arrows have pierced me,
and your hand has come down upon
me.
3Because of your wrath there is no health in
my body;
my bones have no soundness because of
my sin.
4My guilt has overwhelmed me
like a burden too heavy to bear.
5My wounds fester and are loathsome
because of my sinful folly.
6I am bowed down and brought very low;
all day long I go about mourning.
7My back is filled with searing pain;
there is no health in my body.
8I am feeble and utterly crushed;
I groan in anguish of heart.
9All my longings lie open before you,
O Lord;
my sighing is not hidden from you.
10My heart pounds, my strength fails me;
even the light has gone from my eyes.
11My friends and companions avoid me
because of my wounds;
my neighbors stay far away.
12Those who seek my life set their traps,
those who would harm me talk of my
ruin;
all day long they plot deception.

13I am like a deaf man, who cannot hear,
like a mute, who cannot open his
mouth;
14I have become like a man who does not
hear,

[a]37 Or *there will be posterity* [b]38 Or *posterity*

38:1–8 God's judgment against our sinful habits may seem harsh, but he intends it for our ultimate good. Our sin has consequences. God allows these painful results to remind us that our suffering will only worsen until we turn from our sin and surrender to him. Only God can help us overcome our sinful habits and reestablish our relationships. We should learn from our suffering rather than be destroyed by it.

38:9–16 David lamented his sinful state and turned to the only one who was listening—the only one able to help—God. The longer we remain in our sin, the more our hearts pound in fear, our energies ebb away, and our ability to see ourselves becomes distorted. Even David's closest friends and family members deserted him. In such times, we need to repent and turn to God for help. He is able and willing to help us when we repent and ask him to do so.

whose mouth can offer no reply.
15I wait for you, O LORD;
you will answer, O Lord my God.
16For I said, "Do not let them gloat
or exalt themselves over me when my foot slips."
17For I am about to fall,
and my pain is ever with me.
18I confess my iniquity;
I am troubled by my sin.
19Many are those who are my vigorous enemies;
those who hate me without reason are numerous.
20Those who repay my good with evil
slander me when I pursue what is good.

21O LORD, do not forsake me;
be not far from me, O my God.
22Come quickly to help me,
O Lord my Savior.

Psalm 39

For the director of music. For Jeduthun. A psalm of David.

1I said, "I will watch my ways
and keep my tongue from sin;
I will put a muzzle on my mouth
as long as the wicked are in my presence."
2But when I was silent and still,
not even saying anything good,
my anguish increased.
3My heart grew hot within me,
and as I meditated, the fire burned;
then I spoke with my tongue:

4"Show me, O LORD, my life's end
and the number of my days;
let me know how fleeting is my life.
5You have made my days a mere handbreadth;
the span of my years is as nothing before you.
Each man's life is but a breath. *Selah*
6Man is a mere phantom as he goes to and fro:
He bustles about, but only in vain;
he heaps up wealth, not knowing who will get it.

7"But now, Lord, what do I look for?
My hope is in you.
8Save me from all my transgressions;
do not make me the scorn of fools.
9I was silent; I would not open my mouth,
for you are the one who has done this.
10Remove your scourge from me;
I am overcome by the blow of your hand.
11You rebuke and discipline men for their sin;
you consume their wealth like a moth—
each man is but a breath. *Selah*

12"Hear my prayer, O LORD,
listen to my cry for help;
be not deaf to my weeping.
For I dwell with you as an alien,
a stranger, as all my fathers were.
13Look away from me, that I may rejoice again
before I depart and am no more."

Psalm 40

For the director of music. Of David. A psalm.

1I waited patiently for the LORD;
he turned to me and heard my cry.
2He lifted me out of the slimy pit,
out of the mud and mire;
he set my feet on a rock
and gave me a firm place to stand.
3He put a new song in my mouth,
a hymn of praise to our God.
Many will see and fear
and put their trust in the LORD.

4Blessed is the man
who makes the LORD his trust,
who does not look to the proud,
to those who turn aside to false gods.[a]
5Many, O LORD my God,
are the wonders you have done.
The things you planned for us
no one can recount to you;
were I to speak and tell of them,
they would be too many to declare.

6Sacrifice and offering you did not desire,
but my ears you have pierced[b,c];
burnt offerings and sin offerings
you did not require.
7Then I said, "Here I am, I have come—
it is written about me in the scroll.[d]
8I desire to do your will, O my God;
your law is within my heart."

[a]4 Or *to falsehood* [b]6 Hebrew; Septuagint *but a body you have prepared for me* (see also Symmachus and Theodotion) [c]6 Or *opened* [d]7 Or *come / with the scroll written for me*

39:8–13 God will punish us for our sins. There is no point in trying to escape it. Rather than trying to rationalize our sins, we need to confess them. God is ready and willing to forgive anyone who comes to him with a humble heart. In confessing our sins and failures to God, we move toward spiritual renewal.

40:1–5 God's timing is worth waiting for. If we look to God for help, he will deliver us from destruction and despair and from the things that imprison us. God will help us move forward with confidence and joy. God's best for our lives far exceeds all we can imagine (see Ephesians 3:20). To experience God's best for us, we need to rely on him alone and avoid any entanglements with those who will lead us away from God and his plan for us.

[9]I proclaim righteousness in the great
assembly;
I do not seal my lips,
as you know, O LORD.
[10]I do not hide your righteousness in my
heart;
I speak of your faithfulness and
salvation.
I do not conceal your love and your truth
from the great assembly.

[11]Do not withhold your mercy from me,
O LORD;
may your love and your truth always
protect me.
[12]For troubles without number surround me;
my sins have overtaken me, and I cannot
see.
They are more than the hairs of my head,
and my heart fails within me.

[13]Be pleased, O LORD, to save me;
O LORD, come quickly to help me.
[14]May all who seek to take my life
be put to shame and confusion;
may all who desire my ruin
be turned back in disgrace.
[15]May those who say to me, "Aha! Aha!"
be appalled at their own shame.
[16]But may all who seek you
rejoice and be glad in you;
may those who love your salvation always
say,
"The LORD be exalted!"

[17]Yet I am poor and needy;
may the Lord think of me.
You are my help and my deliverer;
O my God, do not delay.

Psalm 41

For the director of music. A psalm of David.

[1]Blessed is he who has regard for the weak;
the LORD delivers him in times of
trouble.
[2]The LORD will protect him and preserve his
life;
he will bless him in the land
and not surrender him to the desire of
his foes.
[3]The LORD will sustain him on his sickbed
and restore him from his bed of illness.

[4]I said, "O LORD, have mercy on me;
heal me, for I have sinned against you."
[5]My enemies say of me in malice,
"When will he die and his name perish?"
[6]Whenever one comes to see me,
he speaks falsely, while his heart gathers
slander;
then he goes out and spreads it abroad.

[7]All my enemies whisper together against
me;
they imagine the worst for me, saying,
[8]"A vile disease has beset him;
he will never get up from the place
where he lies."
[9]Even my close friend, whom I trusted,
he who shared my bread,
has lifted up his heel against me.

[10]But you, O LORD, have mercy on me;
raise me up, that I may repay them.
[11]I know that you are pleased with me,
for my enemy does not triumph over
me.
[12]In my integrity you uphold me
and set me in your presence forever.

[13]Praise be to the LORD, the God of Israel,
from everlasting to everlasting.
Amen and Amen.

BOOK II

Psalms 42–72

Psalm 42[a]

For the director of music. A *maskil*[b] of the Sons of Korah.

[1]As the deer pants for streams of water,
so my soul pants for you, O God.

[a]In many Hebrew manuscripts Psalms 42 and 43 constitute one psalm. [b]Title: Probably a literary or musical term

40:9–10 After experiencing God's deliverance, David spoke about sharing his good news with others. Those who are struggling need some good news too, and we have some to share. God is righteous, faithful and able to deliver others from their bondage, just as he has delivered us. As we share this good news with others, they will be encouraged and we will be strengthened as well.

40:11–17 Spiritual renewal is not a permanent experience. The psalmist apparently experienced deliverance of some kind (see 40:1), but later expressed frustration at his continued troubles (40:12). Yet every time he felt trapped, he called out to God for help. This is an important lesson for us: God will respond as many times as we call out to him. However, we should never use God's willingness to help us as an excuse to sin time and time again. We need to do what we can to avoid the people and situations that we know will lead us into trouble.

41:1–3 We can become blinded to the needs of others if we focus only on our own needs and feelings. We must reach out to help others in need. As we do, we will experience God's help when we face difficult situations or when we are emotionally or physically troubled.

41:4–9 There may be people in our lives who hope we will fail in our spiritual journey. We may feel pressure from these people when our relationship with God is weak. We need to keep our eyes focused on God; he will never let us down.

42:1–3 The psalmist paints a beautiful picture of a person who aches to be close to God. We need to realize that only God can satisfy our real needs. Other things may temporarily soothe us, but in the end we will lose our contentment with them. If we seek God sincerely, he will help us change our desires. We must make him the object of our heart's deepest longing.

[2]My soul thirsts for God, for the living
God.
When can I go and meet with God?
[3]My tears have been my food
day and night,
while men say to me all day long,
"Where is your God?"
[4]These things I remember
as I pour out my soul:
how I used to go with the multitude,
leading the procession to the house
of God,
with shouts of joy and thanksgiving
among the festive throng.

[5]Why are you downcast, O my soul?
Why so disturbed within me?
Put your hope in God,
for I will yet praise him,
my Savior and [6]my God.

My[a] soul is downcast within me;
therefore I will remember you
from the land of the Jordan,
the heights of Hermon—from Mount
Mizar.
[7]Deep calls to deep
in the roar of your waterfalls;
all your waves and breakers
have swept over me.

[8]By day the LORD directs his love,
at night his song is with me—
a prayer to the God of my life.

[9]I say to God my Rock,
"Why have you forgotten me?
Why must I go about mourning,
oppressed by the enemy?"
[10]My bones suffer mortal agony
as my foes taunt me,
saying to me all day long,
"Where is your God?"

[11]Why are you downcast, O my soul?
Why so disturbed within me?
Put your hope in God,
for I will yet praise him,
my Savior and my God.

[a]5,6 A few Hebrew manuscripts, Septuagint and Syriac; most Hebrew manuscripts *praise him for his saving help.* / [6]O *my God, my*

42:4–11 The writer of this psalm honestly shared his feelings of depression about his suffering, but he declared his faith in God and recognized God's power to deliver him. The psalmist struggled back and forth between despair and faith, yet he was always honest about what he was feeling. We will all experience times of deep despair. But God wants us to remember that even as floods of trouble sweep over us, we should keep trusting in him. We should feel free to express our feelings to God; he will answer us.

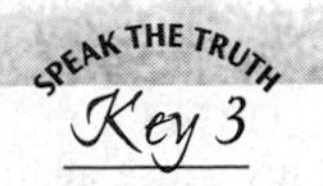

Truthful in Depression

Psalm 42:1–11 When we are feeling depressed, it is vital that we speak the truth—God's truth—to ourselves and to others. Everyone goes through ups and downs. As we strive for spiritual renewal, we will struggle with conflicting emotions, sometimes teetering between the extremes of despair and hope. Confessing God's truth aloud can remind us that his truth supercedes anything we may feel or think on our own.

The psalmist spoke the truth to himself when he was feeling down, saying, "Why are you downcast, O my soul? Why so disturbed within me? Put your hope in God, for I will yet praise him, my Savior and my God. My soul is downcast within me; therefore I will remember you . . . By day the LORD directs his love, at night his song is with me—a prayer to the God of my life" (42:5–6, 8).

Despite his troublesome situation and distress, the psalmist remembered the reality of the Lord's goodness. He spoke the truth about God to himself, and he recorded it openly so that others could hear it too. The greatest truth we can speak is that the Lord has been good to us in the past and that he is still good to us today. As we confess this aloud to others, we will be encouraged and will keep ourselves from despairing over our present circumstances.

Turn to Isaiah 57.

Psalm 43[a]

[1]Vindicate me, O God,
and plead my cause against an ungodly nation;
rescue me from deceitful and wicked men.
[2]You are God my stronghold.
Why have you rejected me?
Why must I go about mourning,
oppressed by the enemy?
[3]Send forth your light and your truth,
let them guide me;
let them bring me to your holy mountain,
to the place where you dwell.
[4]Then will I go to the altar of God,
to God, my joy and my delight.
I will praise you with the harp,
O God, my God.

[5]Why are you downcast, O my soul?
Why so disturbed within me?
Put your hope in God,
for I will yet praise him,
my Savior and my God.

Psalm 44

For the director of music. Of the Sons of Korah. A *maskil.*[b]

[1]We have heard with our ears, O God;
our fathers have told us
what you did in their days,
in days long ago.
[2]With your hand you drove out the nations
and planted our fathers;
you crushed the peoples
and made our fathers flourish.
[3]It was not by their sword that they won the land,
nor did their arm bring them victory;
it was your right hand, your arm,
and the light of your face, for you loved them.
[4]You are my King and my God,
who decrees[c] victories for Jacob.
[5]Through you we push back our enemies;
through your name we trample our foes.
[6]I do not trust in my bow,
my sword does not bring me victory;
[7]but you give us victory over our enemies,
you put our adversaries to shame.
[8]In God we make our boast all day long,
and we will praise your name forever.
Selah

[9]But now you have rejected and humbled us;
you no longer go out with our armies.
[10]You made us retreat before the enemy,
and our adversaries have plundered us.
[11]You gave us up to be devoured like sheep
and have scattered us among the nations.
[12]You sold your people for a pittance,
gaining nothing from their sale.

[13]You have made us a reproach to our neighbors,
the scorn and derision of those around us.
[14]You have made us a byword among the nations;
the peoples shake their heads at us.
[15]My disgrace is before me all day long,
and my face is covered with shame
[16]at the taunts of those who reproach and revile me,
because of the enemy, who is bent on revenge.

[17]All this happened to us,
though we had not forgotten you
or been false to your covenant.
[18]Our hearts had not turned back;
our feet had not strayed from your path.
[19]But you crushed us and made us a haunt for jackals
and covered us over with deep darkness.

[20]If we had forgotten the name of our God
or spread out our hands to a foreign god,
[21]would not God have discovered it,
since he knows the secrets of the heart?
[22]Yet for your sake we face death all day long;
we are considered as sheep to be slaughtered.

[23]Awake, O Lord! Why do you sleep?
Rouse yourself! Do not reject us forever.
[24]Why do you hide your face
and forget our misery and oppression?

[25]We are brought down to the dust;
our bodies cling to the ground.
[26]Rise up and help us;
redeem us because of your unfailing love.

[a]In many Hebrew manuscripts Psalms 42 and 43 constitute one psalm. [b]Title: Probably a literary or musical term [c]4 Septuagint, Aquila and Syriac; Hebrew *King, O God; / command*

43:1–5 People may sometimes treat us unfairly. During such times we must remember to look to God for strength and encouragement. As we surrender our lives to him, we will find the help we need and be able to burst into praise for our Savior and our God.

44:1–7 There are always valuable lessons to be learned from our spiritual predecessors. Those who have progressed in their spiritual journey can share how God has transformed their lives. The victory God has given others should encourage us as we put into practice the principles they share.

Psalm 45

For the director of music. To ⌊the tune of⌋ "Lilies." Of the Sons of Korah. A *maskil*.[a] A wedding song.

1My heart is stirred by a noble theme
as I recite my verses for the king;
my tongue is the pen of a skillful writer.

2You are the most excellent of men
and your lips have been anointed with grace,
since God has blessed you forever.
3Gird your sword upon your side, O mighty one;
clothe yourself with splendor and majesty.
4In your majesty ride forth victoriously
in behalf of truth, humility and righteousness;
let your right hand display awesome deeds.
5Let your sharp arrows pierce the hearts of the king's enemies;
let the nations fall beneath your feet.
6Your throne, O God, will last for ever and ever;
a scepter of justice will be the scepter of your kingdom.
7You love righteousness and hate wickedness;
therefore God, your God, has set you above your companions
by anointing you with the oil of joy.
8All your robes are fragrant with myrrh and aloes and cassia;
from palaces adorned with ivory
the music of the strings makes you glad.
9Daughters of kings are among your honored women;
at your right hand is the royal bride in gold of Ophir.

10Listen, O daughter, consider and give ear:
Forget your people and your father's house.
11The king is enthralled by your beauty;
honor him, for he is your lord.
12The Daughter of Tyre will come with a gift,[b]
men of wealth will seek your favor.

13All glorious is the princess within ⌊her chamber⌋;
her gown is interwoven with gold.
14In embroidered garments she is led to the king;
her virgin companions follow her
and are brought to you.
15They are led in with joy and gladness;
they enter the palace of the king.

16Your sons will take the place of your fathers;
you will make them princes throughout the land.
17I will perpetuate your memory through all generations;
therefore the nations will praise you for ever and ever.

Psalm 46

For the director of music. Of the Sons of Korah. According to *alamoth*.[c] A song.

1God is our refuge and strength,
an ever-present help in trouble.
2Therefore we will not fear, though the earth give way
and the mountains fall into the heart of the sea,
3though its waters roar and foam
and the mountains quake with their surging. *Selah*

4There is a river whose streams make glad the city of God,
the holy place where the Most High dwells.
5God is within her, she will not fall;
God will help her at break of day.
6Nations are in uproar, kingdoms fall;
he lifts his voice, the earth melts.

7The LORD Almighty is with us;
the God of Jacob is our fortress. *Selah*

8Come and see the works of the LORD,
the desolations he has brought on the earth.
9He makes wars cease to the ends of the earth;
he breaks the bow and shatters the spear,
he burns the shields[d] with fire.
10"Be still, and know that I am God;
I will be exalted among the nations,
I will be exalted in the earth."

11The LORD Almighty is with us;
the God of Jacob is our fortress. *Selah*

[a]Title: Probably a literary or musical term [b]12 Or *A Tyrian robe is among the gifts* [c]Title: Probably a musical term [d]9 Or *chariots*

46:1–6 God is more than able to protect us no matter what troubles assail us. If we try to resist temptation in our own strength, we have good reason to fear. But when God is with us, his rivers of mercy and strength refresh us when we are weak and thirsty. No power can draw us out of the circle of his protection once we take refuge in him.

46:7–11 The Lord Almighty is with us. If we put our lives in his hands, we can be sure that he will take care of us. He knows our weaknesses and can strengthen us, helping us overcome the attacks we face each day. Our enemies may be strong, but God is far more powerful than anything that might assail us.

Silence

Silencing All Unholy Sounds

Psalm 46:10 Silence inspires a sense of stability and safety. Psalm 46 is filled with the imagery of great turmoil and tumult. Yet in the midst of earthquakes, fire, flood and warfare, God commands all the earth to be silent. The psalmist declares that God is our fortress (46:11). These verses inspired Luther to write his famous hymn "A Mighty Fortress Is Our God." And as we read the whole passage we come full circle from this fortress back to the opening verse that declares God to be our refuge in the midst of trouble. But how do we find refuge in such a frenzied world?

We will never find true refuge by trying to escape from the world and its concerns because it is impossible to remove ourselves completely from either of them. But we can learn to be silent in the midst of this world and its trouble and by our silence acknowledge that the Lord is God. No words, no explanations, no actions. Simply be silent.

Through silence we honor God above all else. We take a break from the constant chatter of the world that ceaselessly cries out, "Doom, doom" or "Peace, peace." In place of the noise and chatter we hear God's comforting words, breaking through the power of fear. Silence also makes us aware of God's presence, reassuring us of his mercy. Silence heightens our senses to glimpse God's preserving power. And in silence, we learn to hear God, whose greatness muffles the din of the world.

Putting It Into Practice

Reread Psalm 46. Concentrate on the last two verses. Sit quietly with your eyes closed and repeat several times to yourself, Be still, and know that the Lord is God!

Do not attempt to do any critical study on the verse. Simply let your heart rest in this humbling thought.

For more on silence, turn to Proverbs 10.

Psalm 47

For the director of music. Of the Sons of Korah. A psalm.

1Clap your hands, all you nations;
shout to God with cries of joy.
2How awesome is the LORD Most High,
the great King over all the earth!
3He subdued nations under us,
peoples under our feet.
4He chose our inheritance for us,
the pride of Jacob, whom he loved. *Selah*

5God has ascended amid shouts of joy,
the LORD amid the sounding of trumpets.
6Sing praises to God, sing praises;
sing praises to our King, sing praises.

7For God is the King of all the earth;
sing to him a psalm[a] of praise.
8God reigns over the nations;
God is seated on his holy throne.
9The nobles of the nations assemble
as the people of the God of Abraham,
for the kings[b] of the earth belong to God;
he is greatly exalted.

Psalm 48

A song. A psalm of the Sons of Korah.

1Great is the LORD, and most worthy of praise,
in the city of our God, his holy mountain.
2It is beautiful in its loftiness,
the joy of the whole earth.
Like the utmost heights of Zaphon[c] is Mount Zion,
the[d] city of the Great King.
3God is in her citadels;
he has shown himself to be her fortress.

4When the kings joined forces,
when they advanced together,
5they saw ⌊her⌋ and were astounded;
they fled in terror.
6Trembling seized them there,
pain like that of a woman in labor.
7You destroyed them like ships of Tarshish
shattered by an east wind.

8As we have heard,
so have we seen
in the city of the LORD Almighty,
in the city of our God:
God makes her secure forever. *Selah*

9Within your temple, O God,
we meditate on your unfailing love.
10Like your name, O God,
your praise reaches to the ends of the earth;
your right hand is filled with righteousness.
11Mount Zion rejoices,
the villages of Judah are glad
because of your judgments.

12Walk about Zion, go around her,
count her towers,
13consider well her ramparts,
view her citadels,
that you may tell of them to the next generation.
14For this God is our God for ever and ever;
he will be our guide even to the end.

Psalm 49

For the director of music. Of the Sons of Korah. A psalm.

1Hear this, all you peoples;
listen, all who live in this world,
2both low and high,
rich and poor alike:
3My mouth will speak words of wisdom;
the utterance from my heart will give understanding.
4I will turn my ear to a proverb;
with the harp I will expound my riddle:

5Why should I fear when evil days come,
when wicked deceivers surround me—
6those who trust in their wealth
and boast of their great riches?
7No man can redeem the life of another
or give to God a ransom for him—
8the ransom for a life is costly,
no payment is ever enough—
9that he should live on forever
and not see decay.
10For all can see that wise men die;
the foolish and the senseless alike perish
and leave their wealth to others.
11Their tombs will remain their houses[e] forever,
their dwellings for endless generations,
though they had[f] named lands after themselves.

12But man, despite his riches, does not endure;
he is[g] like the beasts that perish.

13This is the fate of those who trust in themselves,
and of their followers, who approve their sayings. *Selah*

[a]7 Or *a maskil* (probably a literary or musical term) [b]9 Or *shields* [c]2 *Zaphon* can refer to a sacred mountain or the direction north. [d]2 Or *earth, / Mount Zion, on the northern side / of the* [e]11 Septuagint and Syriac; Hebrew *In their thoughts their houses will remain* [f]11 Or */ for they have* [g]12 Hebrew; Septuagint and Syriac read verse 12 the same as verse 20.

47:1–9 Victories great and small should be celebrated. The psalmist made it a goal to encourage others, reminding them about God's goodness and power and inviting them to join him in praising God.

14Like sheep they are destined for the grave,[a]
and death will feed on them.
The upright will rule over them in the morning;
their forms will decay in the grave,[a]
far from their princely mansions.
15But God will redeem my life[b] from the grave;
he will surely take me to himself. *Selah*

16Do not be overawed when a man grows rich,
when the splendor of his house increases;
17for he will take nothing with him when he dies,
his splendor will not descend with him.
18Though while he lived he counted himself blessed—
and men praise you when you prosper—
19he will join the generation of his fathers,
who will never see the light ⌊of life⌋.

20A man who has riches without understanding
is like the beasts that perish.

Psalm 50

A psalm of Asaph.

1The Mighty One, God, the LORD,
speaks and summons the earth
from the rising of the sun to the place where it sets.
2From Zion, perfect in beauty,
God shines forth.
3Our God comes and will not be silent;
a fire devours before him,
and around him a tempest rages.
4He summons the heavens above,
and the earth, that he may judge his people:
5"Gather to me my consecrated ones,
who made a covenant with me by sacrifice."
6And the heavens proclaim his righteousness,
for God himself is judge. *Selah*

7"Hear, O my people, and I will speak,
O Israel, and I will testify against you:
I am God, your God.
8I do not rebuke you for your sacrifices
or your burnt offerings, which are ever before me.
9I have no need of a bull from your stall
or of goats from your pens,
10for every animal of the forest is mine,
and the cattle on a thousand hills.
11I know every bird in the mountains,
and the creatures of the field are mine.
12If I were hungry I would not tell you,
for the world is mine, and all that is in it.
13Do I eat the flesh of bulls
or drink the blood of goats?
14Sacrifice thank offerings to God,
fulfill your vows to the Most High,
15and call upon me in the day of trouble;
I will deliver you, and you will honor me."

16But to the wicked, God says:

"What right have you to recite my laws
or take my covenant on your lips?
17You hate my instruction
and cast my words behind you.
18When you see a thief, you join with him;
you throw in your lot with adulterers.
19You use your mouth for evil
and harness your tongue to deceit.
20You speak continually against your brother
and slander your own mother's son.
21These things you have done and I kept silent;
you thought I was altogether[c] like you.
But I will rebuke you
and accuse you to your face.

22"Consider this, you who forget God,
or I will tear you to pieces, with none to rescue:
23He who sacrifices thank offerings honors me,
and he prepares the way
so that I may show him[d] the salvation of God."

Psalm 51

For the director of music. A psalm of David. When the prophet Nathan came to him after David had committed adultery with Bathsheba.

1Have mercy on me, O God,
according to your unfailing love;
according to your great compassion
blot out my transgressions.

[a]14 Hebrew *Sheol;* also in verse 15 [b]15 Or *soul*
[c]21 Or *thought the 'I AM' was* [d]23 Or *and to him who considers his way / I will show*

50:1–6 Judgment is coming to those who refuse to recognize God's authority. God is loving, but he will deal with those who have chosen to rebel against him. We need to reflect honestly on our lives and ask God to remove any sinful or rebellious ways in us and to forgive us for the wrongs we have committed.

50:16–23 God will not tolerate hypocrites who claim to believe his Word yet blatantly disobey the instructions found there. God knows what is happening. While his silence may seem to indicate that he doesn't care, eventually God will present his case against such deceivers. Instead of practicing hypocrisy, we ought to worship God with thanksgiving and follow his ways.

Repentance and Confession

Releasing Our Sins to God

Psalm 51 Psalm 51 poignantly records David's confession of his sin of adultery with Bathsheba. Confession is the appropriate response to guilt. Confession does not earn forgiveness, however. Forgiveness is purely a work of God's grace. Confession simply prepares us to receive God's gracious forgiveness. When we refuse to admit our sin, God's grace is untouched, much like a healing ointment left unused. We refuse to be restored to spiritual health when we refuse to admit our sin.

Confession comes from the Latin *con fateri* meaning "to acknowledge together; to agree together." When we confess our sins to God, we agree that we have violated his standards and that we deserve to be punished. We release our sins and repent of them, asking God to change our hearts. Confession is needed for our spiritual growth, not because God desires to hear us admit our sin, but rather because when we confess our sin we accept responsibility for our actions.

There are various types of confession. Many times we practice immediate confession, which is made as soon as we recognize our sin. This can involve simple thought prayers that focus on letting go of the sin: "*Lord, forgive me. I surrender this sin to your grace and mercy. Guard my steps and deliver me from evil.*" Such a prayer moves beyond acknowledgment of wrong. It focuses us on repentance and restoration as well.

Another common practice is to confess at the end of the day. As we prepare for sleep, a few moments in prayerful reflection on the day can help bring our sins to mind. Here again, we agree with God that we have lived against him in ways unworthy of his eternal kingdom. Then we release these sins with prayers of thanksgiving and praise for God's infinite mercy.

One practice of confession that is more sweeping could be labeled whole-life confession. This practice focuses on releasing significant life-patterns of sin to God. This often occurs in seasons of crisis or during a significant spiritual awakening, and may be found both individually or corporately.

Putting It Into Practice

In what ways are you practicing confession throughout the day? If you struggle with guilt, reflect on the reasons for your guilt feelings. Think of specific sins that need to be released to God. Confess these sins to him and repent of them, asking God to help you overcome these sins and their temptations.

For more on repentance and confession, turn to Matthew 5.

2Wash away all my iniquity
and cleanse me from my sin.

3For I know my transgressions,
and my sin is always before me.
4Against you, you only, have I sinned
and done what is evil in your sight,
so that you are proved right when you speak
and justified when you judge.
5Surely I was sinful at birth,
sinful from the time my mother conceived me.
6Surely you desire truth in the inner parts[a];
you teach[b] me wisdom in the inmost place.

7Cleanse me with hyssop, and I will be clean;
wash me, and I will be whiter than snow.
8Let me hear joy and gladness;
let the bones you have crushed rejoice.
9Hide your face from my sins
and blot out all my iniquity.

10Create in me a pure heart, O God,
and renew a steadfast spirit within me.
11Do not cast me from your presence
or take your Holy Spirit from me.
12Restore to me the joy of your salvation
and grant me a willing spirit, to sustain me.

13Then I will teach transgressors your ways,
and sinners will turn back to you.
14Save me from bloodguilt, O God,
the God who saves me,
and my tongue will sing of your righteousness.
15O Lord, open my lips,
and my mouth will declare your praise.
16You do not delight in sacrifice, or I would bring it;
you do not take pleasure in burnt offerings.
17The sacrifices of God are[c] a broken spirit;
a broken and contrite heart,
O God, you will not despise.

18In your good pleasure make Zion prosper;
build up the walls of Jerusalem.
19Then there will be righteous sacrifices,
whole burnt offerings to delight you;
then bulls will be offered on your altar.

Psalm 52

For the director of music. A *maskil*[d] of David. When Doeg the Edomite had gone to Saul and told him: "David has gone to the house of Ahimelech."

1Why do you boast of evil, you mighty man?
Why do you boast all day long,
you who are a disgrace in the eyes of God?
2Your tongue plots destruction;
it is like a sharpened razor,
you who practice deceit.
3You love evil rather than good,
falsehood rather than speaking the truth. *Selah*
4You love every harmful word,
O you deceitful tongue!

5Surely God will bring you down to everlasting ruin:
He will snatch you up and tear you from your tent;
he will uproot you from the land of the living. *Selah*
6The righteous will see and fear;
they will laugh at him, saying,
7"Here now is the man
who did not make God his stronghold
but trusted in his great wealth
and grew strong by destroying others!"

8But I am like an olive tree
flourishing in the house of God;
I trust in God's unfailing love
for ever and ever.
9I will praise you forever for what you have done;
in your name I will hope, for your name is good.
I will praise you in the presence of your saints.

[a]6 The meaning of the Hebrew for this phrase is uncertain. [b]6 Or *you desired . . . ; / you taught* [c]17 Or *My sacrifice, O God, is* [d]Title: Probably a literary or musical term

51:5–9 If we fail to admit and confess our sin, it will continue to burden us with destructive guilt. We should confess and repent of our sin and seek God's wisdom to make amends with the people we have wronged. Seeking forgiveness is essential for spiritual growth. We can be sure that God will forgive us when we humbly come to him.

51:10–13 David wrote this psalm of repentance after he had committed adultery with Bathsheba and then conspired to murder her husband (see 2 Samuel 11—12). Why did God forgive David and offer him restoration? David was humble and repentant about his sin. He admitted his sin and asked for God's forgiveness. If we confess our sin and humbly seek God's forgiveness, there is hope for us, no matter how great our failures (see 1 John 1:9).

51:16–19 David realized that God would grant him forgiveness if he honestly admitted his sin. God desires true, heartfelt repentance rather than mere gestures or rituals. We don't have to earn forgiveness from God. God is looking for people with humble hearts, not perfect records, who are willing to take responsibility for their sins and earnestly desire restoration. He will graciously grant forgiveness when we repent and confess our sins. There is always hope for us if we are willing to confront our sins and seek God's forgiveness.

Psalm 53

For the director of music. According to *mahalath.*[a] A *maskil*[b] of David.

[1]The fool says in his heart,
"There is no God."
They are corrupt, and their ways are vile;
there is no one who does good.

[2]God looks down from heaven
on the sons of men
to see if there are any who understand,
any who seek God.
[3]Everyone has turned away,
they have together become corrupt;
there is no one who does good,
not even one.

[4]Will the evildoers never learn—
those who devour my people as men eat bread
and who do not call on God?
[5]There they were, overwhelmed with dread,
where there was nothing to dread.
God scattered the bones of those who attacked you;
you put them to shame, for God despised them.

[6]Oh, that salvation for Israel would come out of Zion!
When God restores the fortunes of his people,
let Jacob rejoice and Israel be glad!

Psalm 54

For the director of music. With stringed instruments. A *maskil*[b] of David. When the Ziphites had gone to Saul and said, "Is not David hiding among us?"

[1]Save me, O God, by your name;
vindicate me by your might.
[2]Hear my prayer, O God;
listen to the words of my mouth.

[3]Strangers are attacking me;
ruthless men seek my life—
men without regard for God. *Selah*

[4]Surely God is my help;
the Lord is the one who sustains me.

[5]Let evil recoil on those who slander me;
in your faithfulness destroy them.

[6]I will sacrifice a freewill offering to you;
I will praise your name, O LORD,
for it is good.
[7]For he has delivered me from all my troubles,
and my eyes have looked in triumph on my foes.

Psalm 55

For the director of music. With stringed instruments. A *maskil*[b] of David.

[1]Listen to my prayer, O God,
do not ignore my plea;
[2] hear me and answer me.
My thoughts trouble me and I am distraught
[3] at the voice of the enemy,
at the stares of the wicked;
for they bring down suffering upon me
and revile me in their anger.

[4]My heart is in anguish within me;
the terrors of death assail me.
[5]Fear and trembling have beset me;
horror has overwhelmed me.
[6]I said, "Oh, that I had the wings of a dove!
I would fly away and be at rest—
[7]I would flee far away
and stay in the desert; *Selah*
[8]I would hurry to my place of shelter,
far from the tempest and storm."

[9]Confuse the wicked, O Lord, confound their speech,
for I see violence and strife in the city.
[10]Day and night they prowl about on its walls;
malice and abuse are within it.
[11]Destructive forces are at work in the city;
threats and lies never leave its streets.

[12]If an enemy were insulting me,
I could endure it;
if a foe were raising himself against me,
I could hide from him.
[13]But it is you, a man like myself,
my companion, my close friend,
[14]with whom I once enjoyed sweet fellowship
as we walked with the throng at the house of God.

[15]Let death take my enemies by surprise;
let them go down alive to the grave,[c]
for evil finds lodging among them.

[16]But I call to God,

[a]Title: Probably a musical term [b]Title: Probably a literary or musical term [c]*15* Hebrew *Sheol*

53:1–6 All people are inclined toward evil; not one of us is good apart from the transforming power of God (see Romans 3:23). But God can restore us, and he will do so when we repent and ask his forgiveness.
54:1–7 We will probably face opposition from people who don't understand our spiritual pursuits or who feel threatened by them. The words of this psalm should be our prayer for deliverance at such times. God is our deliverer and sustainer. He will cause our enemies to fall into their own traps. Our response to God's deliverance from those who are against us should be worship and thanksgiving.
55:16–19 At times, God may be the only friend we possess. David was confident that God would rescue and deliver him from his problems. He depended on God to keep him safe from others who desired his destruction.

and the LORD saves me.
17Evening, morning and noon
I cry out in distress,
and he hears my voice.
18He ransoms me unharmed
from the battle waged against me,
even though many oppose me.
19God, who is enthroned forever,
will hear them and afflict them— *Selah*
men who never change their ways
and have no fear of God.

20My companion attacks his friends;
he violates his covenant.
21His speech is smooth as butter,
yet war is in his heart;
his words are more soothing than oil,
yet they are drawn swords.

22Cast your cares on the LORD
and he will sustain you;
he will never let the righteous fall.
23But you, O God, will bring down the wicked
into the pit of corruption;
bloodthirsty and deceitful men
will not live out half their days.

But as for me, I trust in you.

Psalm 56

For the director of music. To ⌊the tune of⌋ "A Dove on Distant Oaks." Of David. A *miktam.*[a] When the Philistines had seized him in Gath.

1Be merciful to me, O God, for men hotly pursue me;
all day long they press their attack.
2My slanderers pursue me all day long;
many are attacking me in their pride.

3When I am afraid,
I will trust in you.
4In God, whose word I praise,
in God I trust; I will not be afraid.
What can mortal man do to me?

5All day long they twist my words;
they are always plotting to harm me.
6They conspire, they lurk,
they watch my steps,
eager to take my life.

7On no account let them escape;
in your anger, O God, bring down the nations.

8Record my lament;
list my tears on your scroll[b]—
are they not in your record?
9Then my enemies will turn back
when I call for help.
By this I will know that God is for me.
10In God, whose word I praise,
in the LORD, whose word I praise—
11in God I trust; I will not be afraid.
What can man do to me?

12I am under vows to you, O God;
I will present my thank offerings to you.
13For you have delivered me[c] from death
and my feet from stumbling,
that I may walk before God
in the light of life.[d]

Psalm 57

For the director of music. ⌊To the tune of⌋ "Do Not Destroy." Of David. A *miktam.*[a] When he had fled from Saul into the cave.

1Have mercy on me, O God, have mercy on me,
for in you my soul takes refuge.
I will take refuge in the shadow of your wings
until the disaster has passed.

2I cry out to God Most High,
to God, who fulfills ⌊his purpose⌋ for me.
3He sends from heaven and saves me,
rebuking those who hotly pursue me; *Selah*
God sends his love and his faithfulness.

4I am in the midst of lions;
I lie among ravenous beasts—
men whose teeth are spears and arrows,
whose tongues are sharp swords.

5Be exalted, O God, above the heavens;
let your glory be over all the earth.

6They spread a net for my feet—
I was bowed down in distress.
They dug a pit in my path—
but they have fallen into it themselves. *Selah*

7My heart is steadfast, O God,

[a]Title: Probably a literary or musical term [b]8 Or / *put my tears in your wineskin* [c]13 Or *my soul* [d]13 Or *the land of the living*

With God as our friend and helper, there is hope for spiritual renewal no matter what circumstances we have to face.

56:1–7 David trusted God to take care of him during a time of great danger. When we are troubled by tempting or dangerous circumstances, we need to turn our lives and our wills over to God. We need to trust his promises. He is able to strengthen us and bring us through such trials.

56:8–13 In these verses we can learn a helpful lesson from the psalmist—we should keep our thoughts focused on God and trust him. We will find, as the psalmist did, that God will strengthen us even during our difficult struggles. However, we must be obedient to God's will. Ultimately, his plan is always best for us.

57:1–3 We can find comfort in turning to God in times of trouble, for we know that he will surround us with his care until the storm is past. God cares about us; understanding and acting upon this truth is essential to our spiritual growth.

57:7–11 The psalmist demonstrates an important principle in these verses: After receiving God's help, we need to

my heart is steadfast;
I will sing and make music.
8Awake, my soul!
Awake, harp and lyre!
I will awaken the dawn.

9I will praise you, O Lord, among the nations;
I will sing of you among the peoples.
10For great is your love, reaching to the heavens;
your faithfulness reaches to the skies.

11Be exalted, O God, above the heavens;
let your glory be over all the earth.

Psalm 58

For the director of music. ⌊To the tune of⌋ "Do Not Destroy." Of David. A *miktam*.[a]

1Do you rulers indeed speak justly?
Do you judge uprightly among men?
2No, in your heart you devise injustice,
and your hands mete out violence on the earth.
3Even from birth the wicked go astray;
from the womb they are wayward and speak lies.
4Their venom is like the venom of a snake,
like that of a cobra that has stopped its ears,
5that will not heed the tune of the charmer,
however skillful the enchanter may be.

6Break the teeth in their mouths, O God;
tear out, O LORD, the fangs of the lions!
7Let them vanish like water that flows away;
when they draw the bow, let their arrows be blunted.
8Like a slug melting away as it moves along,
like a stillborn child, may they not see the sun.

9Before your pots can feel ⌊the heat of⌋ the thorns—
whether they be green or dry—the wicked will be swept away.[b]
10The righteous will be glad when they are avenged,
when they bathe their feet in the blood of the wicked.
11Then men will say,
"Surely the righteous still are rewarded;
surely there is a God who judges the earth."

Psalm 59

For the director of music. ⌊To the tune of⌋ "Do Not Destroy." Of David. A *miktam*.[a] When Saul had sent men to watch David's house in order to kill him.

1Deliver me from my enemies, O God;
protect me from those who rise up against me.
2Deliver me from evildoers
and save me from bloodthirsty men.

3See how they lie in wait for me!
Fierce men conspire against me
for no offense or sin of mine, O LORD.
4I have done no wrong, yet they are ready to attack me.
Arise to help me; look on my plight!
5O LORD God Almighty, the God of Israel,
rouse yourself to punish all the nations;
show no mercy to wicked traitors. *Selah*

6They return at evening,
snarling like dogs,
and prowl about the city.
7See what they spew from their mouths—
they spew out swords from their lips,
and they say, "Who can hear us?"
8But you, O LORD, laugh at them;
you scoff at all those nations.

9O my Strength, I watch for you;
you, O God, are my fortress, 10my loving God.

God will go before me
and will let me gloat over those who slander me.
11But do not kill them, O Lord our shield,[c]
or my people will forget.
In your might make them wander about,
and bring them down.
12For the sins of their mouths,
for the words of their lips,
let them be caught in their pride.
For the curses and lies they utter,
13 consume them in wrath,
consume them till they are no more.
Then it will be known to the ends of the earth
that God rules over Jacob. *Selah*

14They return at evening,
snarling like dogs,
and prowl about the city.
15They wander about for food
and howl if not satisfied.

[a]Title: Probably a literary or musical term
[b]9 The meaning of the Hebrew for this verse is uncertain.
[c]11 Or *sovereign*

---

share our experience with others. In fact, our witness should be the natural response of a grateful heart. Our words will not only encourage others, but will also further our own spiritual growth.

59:1–4 There are times when we will be surrounded by enemies. At those times we must seek God and surrender to his care. Whenever we face those who oppose us, whether or not we have done them harm, the best thing we can do is call out to God. He is able to help us; he is our place of refuge.

16But I will sing of your strength,
in the morning I will sing of your love;
for you are my fortress,
my refuge in times of trouble.

17O my Strength, I sing praise to you;
you, O God, are my fortress, my loving God.

Psalm 60

For the director of music. To ⌊the tune of⌋ "The Lily of the Covenant." A *miktam*[a] of David. For teaching. When he fought Aram Naharaim[b] and Aram Zobah,[c] and when Joab returned and struck down twelve thousand Edomites in the Valley of Salt.

1You have rejected us, O God, and burst forth upon us;
you have been angry—now restore us!
2You have shaken the land and torn it open;
mend its fractures, for it is quaking.
3You have shown your people desperate times;
you have given us wine that makes us stagger.

4But for those who fear you, you have raised a banner
to be unfurled against the bow. *Selah*
5Save us and help us with your right hand,
that those you love may be delivered.
6God has spoken from his sanctuary:
"In triumph I will parcel out Shechem
and measure off the Valley of Succoth.
7Gilead is mine, and Manasseh is mine;
Ephraim is my helmet,
Judah my scepter.
8Moab is my washbasin,
upon Edom I toss my sandal;
over Philistia I shout in triumph."

9Who will bring me to the fortified city?
Who will lead me to Edom?
10Is it not you, O God, you who have rejected us
and no longer go out with our armies?
11Give us aid against the enemy,
for the help of man is worthless.
12With God we will gain the victory,
and he will trample down our enemies.

Psalm 61

For the director of music. With stringed instruments. Of David.

1Hear my cry, O God;
listen to my prayer.

2From the ends of the earth I call to you,
I call as my heart grows faint;
lead me to the rock that is higher than I.
3For you have been my refuge,
a strong tower against the foe.

4I long to dwell in your tent forever
and take refuge in the shelter of your wings. *Selah*
5For you have heard my vows, O God;
you have given me the heritage of those who fear your name.

6Increase the days of the king's life,
his years for many generations.
7May he be enthroned in God's presence forever;
appoint your love and faithfulness to protect him.

8Then will I ever sing praise to your name
and fulfill my vows day after day.

Psalm 62

For the director of music. For Jeduthun. A psalm of David.

1My soul finds rest in God alone;
my salvation comes from him.
2He alone is my rock and my salvation;
he is my fortress, I will never be shaken.

3How long will you assault a man?
Would all of you throw him down—
this leaning wall, this tottering fence?
4They fully intend to topple him
from his lofty place;
they take delight in lies.
With their mouths they bless,
but in their hearts they curse. *Selah*

5Find rest, O my soul, in God alone;
my hope comes from him.
6He alone is my rock and my salvation;

[a]Title: Probably a literary or musical term [b]Title: That is, Arameans of Northwest Mesopotamia [c]Title: That is, Arameans of central Syria

---

60:1–5 When God shows his anger because of our sin, we may feel abandoned and overwhelmed. In these times, we need to seek forgiveness and restoration in our relationship with God. We are able to do this through Christ, for his perfect sacrifice has taken away our sins (see Hebrews 10:10).

60:6–12 David wrote this psalm during a time of war and affirmed that his help came from God alone. We can turn to God for deliverance because he has promised to help us. God reminds us that we belong to him, no matter how great our sin and weakness. He will give us victory if we call upon him to fight our battles.

61:1–8 Wherever we are, whatever circumstances we face, we can turn to God for help. He is always watching over us. We can confidently ask him for help because he has repeatedly delivered his people. He is our loving provider, who blesses us and gives us meaningful lives, helping us fulfill our vows to live for him day by day.

62:1–8 Whenever we face problems that we cannot overcome alone, the wisest thing to do is call upon God to help us. We will never totally escape our problems and temptations, but God is always with us. He is more than able to overcome our most powerful adversaries.

he is my fortress, I will not be shaken.
7My salvation and my honor depend on
God[a];
he is my mighty rock, my refuge.
8Trust in him at all times, O people;
pour out your hearts to him,
for God is our refuge. *Selah*

9Lowborn men are but a breath,
the highborn are but a lie;
if weighed on a balance, they are nothing;
together they are only a breath.
10Do not trust in extortion
or take pride in stolen goods;
though your riches increase,
do not set your heart on them.

11One thing God has spoken,
two things have I heard:
that you, O God, are strong,
12 and that you, O Lord, are loving.
Surely you will reward each person
according to what he has done.

Psalm 63

A psalm of David. When he was in the Desert of Judah.

1O God, you are my God,
earnestly I seek you;
my soul thirsts for you,
my body longs for you,
in a dry and weary land
where there is no water.

2I have seen you in the sanctuary
and beheld your power and your glory.
3Because your love is better than life,
my lips will glorify you.
4I will praise you as long as I live,
and in your name I will lift up my
hands.
5My soul will be satisfied as with the richest
of foods;
with singing lips my mouth will praise
you.

6On my bed I remember you;
I think of you through the watches of
the night.
7Because you are my help,
I sing in the shadow of your wings.
8My soul clings to you;
your right hand upholds me.

9They who seek my life will be destroyed;
they will go down to the depths of the
earth.
10They will be given over to the sword
and become food for jackals.
11But the king will rejoice in God;
all who swear by God's name will praise
him,
while the mouths of liars will be
silenced.

Psalm 64

For the director of music. A psalm of David.

1Hear me, O God, as I voice my complaint;
protect my life from the threat of the
enemy.
2Hide me from the conspiracy of the wicked,
from that noisy crowd of evildoers.

3They sharpen their tongues like swords
and aim their words like deadly arrows.
4They shoot from ambush at the innocent
man;
they shoot at him suddenly, without
fear.

5They encourage each other in evil plans,
they talk about hiding their snares;
they say, "Who will see them[b]?"
6They plot injustice and say,
"We have devised a perfect plan!"
Surely the mind and heart of man are
cunning.

7But God will shoot them with arrows;
suddenly they will be struck down.
8He will turn their own tongues against
them
and bring them to ruin;
all who see them will shake their heads
in scorn.

9All mankind will fear;
they will proclaim the works of God
and ponder what he has done.
10Let the righteous rejoice in the LORD
and take refuge in him;
let all the upright in heart praise him!

Psalm 65

For the director of music. A psalm of David. A song.

1Praise awaits[c] you, O God, in Zion;
to you our vows will be fulfilled.
2O you who hear prayer,
to you all men will come.
3When we were overwhelmed by sins,
you forgave[d] our transgressions.

[a]7 Or / *God Most High is my salvation and my honor*
[b]5 Or *us* [c]1 Or *befits;* the meaning of the Hebrew for this word is uncertain. [d]3 Or *made atonement for*

63:1–5 The more difficulties and temptations we face in life, the more we realize how much we need God. When we are at our weakest, God's power takes on added significance for us. As we sense how precious God's compassionate care toward us really is, we will begin to praise him for his goodness toward us.

64:7–10 God knows exactly where our enemies are, and he is able to help us thwart their attacks. As we call upon God to help us, others will be awed at what he does for us. And as we share the good news of God's marvelous deeds, our victory will fill others with hope and celebration too.

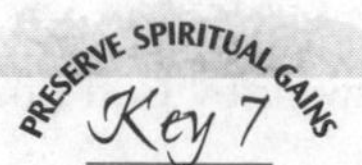

Joy in God's Presence

Psalm 65:1–4 Spending time in God's presence by praying, singing praises to him and bowing before him in silent worship are exercises that can help us preserve our spiritual gains. By practicing these observances, we are reminded of God's greatness and his holiness. We gain a new appreciation for how gracious God is to forgive us and allow us into his presence. At the same time, these spiritual disciplines encourage us to seek God with our whole heart, for we see that he loves us very much.

This psalm of David should give us hope, for David was a man who recognized his own sinfulness yet was able to sing, "Blessed are those you choose and bring near to live in your courts! We are filled with the good things of your house, of your holy temple" (65:4). God wants us to experience the joys of those who lived and served in his temple, where God's presence dwelt. He wants us to know that we are welcome and valued before him (see Matthew 10:29–31).

The joy we find daily in God's presence can help us stay attuned to God's desires for us. In this way, the progress we have made in our spiritual lives will be reinforced, and we can continue to be transformed into the image of Christ.

Turn to Proverbs 15.

4 Blessed are those you choose
and bring near to live in your courts!
We are filled with the good things of your house,
of your holy temple.

5 You answer us with awesome deeds of righteousness,
O God our Savior,
the hope of all the ends of the earth
and of the farthest seas,
6 who formed the mountains by your power,
having armed yourself with strength,
7 who stilled the roaring of the seas,
the roaring of their waves,
and the turmoil of the nations.
8 Those living far away fear your wonders;
where morning dawns and evening fades
you call forth songs of joy.

9 You care for the land and water it;
you enrich it abundantly.
The streams of God are filled with water
to provide the people with grain,
for so you have ordained it.[a]
10 You drench its furrows
and level its ridges;
you soften it with showers
and bless its crops.
11 You crown the year with your bounty,
and your carts overflow with abundance.
12 The grasslands of the desert overflow;
the hills are clothed with gladness.
13 The meadows are covered with flocks
and the valleys are mantled with grain;
they shout for joy and sing.

Psalm 66

For the director of music. A song. A psalm.

1 Shout with joy to God, all the earth!
2 Sing the glory of his name;
make his praise glorious!
3 Say to God, "How awesome are your deeds!
So great is your power
that your enemies cringe before you.
4 All the earth bows down to you;
they sing praise to you,
they sing praise to your name." *Selah*

5 Come and see what God has done,

[a] 9 Or *for that is how you prepare the land*

65:5–13 God is more than able to help us because he is the same God who made this world with its majestic mountains. If God can control the rainfall and the waters of the earth, we can be sure he can take care of us.
66:1–7 When God demonstrates his power and his care for us, we need to share our experiences with others. We are not alone in our trouble. Some of our struggling friends face the same problems we do. Our thanks to God for his deliverance can become a source of their hope and inspiration too.

how awesome his works in man's
behalf!
6He turned the sea into dry land,
they passed through the waters on foot—
come, let us rejoice in him.
7He rules forever by his power,
his eyes watch the nations—
let not the rebellious rise up against him.
Selah

8Praise our God, O peoples,
let the sound of his praise be heard;
9he has preserved our lives
and kept our feet from slipping.
10For you, O God, tested us;
you refined us like silver.
11You brought us into prison
and laid burdens on our backs.
12You let men ride over our heads;
we went through fire and water,
but you brought us to a place of
abundance.

13I will come to your temple with burnt
offerings
and fulfill my vows to you—
14vows my lips promised and my mouth
spoke
when I was in trouble.
15I will sacrifice fat animals to you
and an offering of rams;
I will offer bulls and goats. *Selah*

16Come and listen, all you who fear God;
let me tell you what he has done for me.
17I cried out to him with my mouth;
his praise was on my tongue.
18If I had cherished sin in my heart,
the Lord would not have listened;
19but God has surely listened
and heard my voice in prayer.
20Praise be to God,
who has not rejected my prayer
or withheld his love from me!

Psalm 67

For the director of music. With stringed instruments. A psalm. A song.

1May God be gracious to us and bless us
and make his face shine upon us, *Selah*
2that your ways may be known on earth,
your salvation among all nations.

3May the peoples praise you, O God;
may all the peoples praise you.
4May the nations be glad and sing for joy,
for you rule the peoples justly
and guide the nations of the earth. *Selah*
5May the peoples praise you, O God;
may all the peoples praise you.

6Then the land will yield its harvest,
and God, our God, will bless us.
7God will bless us,
and all the ends of the earth will fear
him.

Psalm 68

For the director of music. Of David. A psalm. A song.

1May God arise, may his enemies be
scattered;
may his foes flee before him.
2As smoke is blown away by the wind,
may you blow them away;
as wax melts before the fire,
may the wicked perish before God.
3But may the righteous be glad
and rejoice before God;
may they be happy and joyful.

4Sing to God, sing praise to his name,
extol him who rides on the clouds[a]—
his name is the LORD—
and rejoice before him.
5A father to the fatherless, a defender of
widows,
is God in his holy dwelling.
6God sets the lonely in families,[b]
he leads forth the prisoners with singing;
but the rebellious live in a sun-scorched
land.

7When you went out before your people, O
God,
when you marched through the
wasteland, *Selah*
8the earth shook,
the heavens poured down rain,
before God, the One of Sinai,
before God, the God of Israel.
9You gave abundant showers, O God;
you refreshed your weary inheritance.
10Your people settled in it,
and from your bounty, O God, you
provided for the poor.

11The Lord announced the word,
and great was the company of those who
proclaimed it:
12"Kings and armies flee in haste;
in the camps men divide the plunder.

[a]4 Or / *prepare the way for him who rides through the deserts*
[b]6 Or *the desolate in a homeland*

67:1–7 God tells us to share his love and good news with others. This should not be a chore, but rather a natural expression of our joy at being delivered from forces too powerful for us to handle alone. Without God's help we could never resist the temptations that could destroy our lives. But with God's help we can live a life of freedom and joy. Let us celebrate and spread the news of God's powerful deliverance!

68:1–6 There is no security for those who act in opposition to God, but God watches over those who call upon him. He is our Father, a loving deliverer who sets us free from the traps of sin into which we have fallen.

13Even while you sleep among the campfires,[a]
the wings of ⌊my⌋ dove are sheathed with silver,
its feathers with shining gold."
14When the Almighty[b] scattered the kings in the land,
it was like snow fallen on Zalmon.

15The mountains of Bashan are majestic mountains;
rugged are the mountains of Bashan.
16Why gaze in envy, O rugged mountains,
at the mountain where God chooses to reign,
where the LORD himself will dwell forever?
17The chariots of God are tens of thousands
and thousands of thousands;
the Lord ⌊has come⌋ from Sinai into his sanctuary.
18When you ascended on high,
you led captives in your train;
you received gifts from men,
even from[c] the rebellious—
that you,[d] O LORD God, might dwell there.

19Praise be to the Lord, to God our Savior,
who daily bears our burdens. *Selah*
20Our God is a God who saves;
from the Sovereign LORD comes escape from death.

21Surely God will crush the heads of his enemies,
the hairy crowns of those who go on in their sins.
22The Lord says, "I will bring them from Bashan;
I will bring them from the depths of the sea,
23that you may plunge your feet in the blood of your foes,
while the tongues of your dogs have their share."

24Your procession has come into view, O God,
the procession of my God and King into the sanctuary.
25In front are the singers, after them the musicians;
with them are the maidens playing tambourines.
26Praise God in the great congregation;
praise the LORD in the assembly of Israel.
27There is the little tribe of Benjamin, leading them,
there the great throng of Judah's princes,
and there the princes of Zebulun and of Naphtali.

28Summon your power, O God[e];
show us your strength, O God, as you have done before.
29Because of your temple at Jerusalem
kings will bring you gifts.
30Rebuke the beast among the reeds,
the herd of bulls among the calves of the nations.
Humbled, may it bring bars of silver.
Scatter the nations who delight in war.
31Envoys will come from Egypt;
Cush[f] will submit herself to God.

32Sing to God, O kingdoms of the earth,
sing praise to the Lord, *Selah*
33to him who rides the ancient skies above,
who thunders with mighty voice.
34Proclaim the power of God,
whose majesty is over Israel,
whose power is in the skies.
35You are awesome, O God, in your sanctuary;
the God of Israel gives power and strength to his people.

Praise be to God!

Psalm 69

For the director of music. To ⌊the tune of⌋ "Lilies." Of David.

1Save me, O God,
for the waters have come up to my neck.
2I sink in the miry depths,
where there is no foothold.
I have come into the deep waters;
the floods engulf me.
3I am worn out calling for help;
my throat is parched.
My eyes fail,
looking for my God.
4Those who hate me without reason
outnumber the hairs of my head;
many are my enemies without cause,
those who seek to destroy me.
I am forced to restore
what I did not steal.

5You know my folly, O God;
my guilt is not hidden from you.

6May those who hope in you

[a]13 Or *saddlebags* [b]14 Hebrew *Shaddai* [c]18 Or *gifts for men, / even* [d]18 Or *they* [e]28 Many Hebrew manuscripts, Septuagint and Syriac; most Hebrew manuscripts *Your God has summoned power for you* [f]31 That is, the upper Nile region

68:24–31 When God delivers us from trials, praise should naturally flow from our lips. As we thank God for transforming our lives, others will be encouraged to admit their need for God and begin seeking him too.
69:1–4, 13 As he wrote this psalm, David felt as though his problems were closing in on him. It seemed that no one supported him. We may also have experienced this feeling. When faced with times like these, we should do what David did—repent and cry out to God for help, submit to his will and entrust our lives to his care.

not be disgraced because of me,
O Lord, the LORD Almighty;
may those who seek you
not be put to shame because of me,
O God of Israel.
7For I endure scorn for your sake,
and shame covers my face.
8I am a stranger to my brothers,
an alien to my own mother's sons;
9for zeal for your house consumes me,
and the insults of those who insult you
fall on me.
10When I weep and fast,
I must endure scorn;
11when I put on sackcloth,
people make sport of me.
12Those who sit at the gate mock me,
and I am the song of the drunkards.

13But I pray to you, O LORD,
in the time of your favor;
in your great love, O God,
answer me with your sure salvation.
14Rescue me from the mire,
do not let me sink;
deliver me from those who hate me,
from the deep waters.
15Do not let the floodwaters engulf me
or the depths swallow me up
or the pit close its mouth over me.
16Answer me, O LORD, out of the goodness of
your love;
in your great mercy turn to me.
17Do not hide your face from your servant;
answer me quickly, for I am in trouble.
18Come near and rescue me;
redeem me because of my foes.

19You know how I am scorned, disgraced and
shamed;
all my enemies are before you.
20Scorn has broken my heart
and has left me helpless;
I looked for sympathy, but there was none,
for comforters, but I found none.
21They put gall in my food
and gave me vinegar for my thirst.

22May the table set before them become a
snare;
may it become retribution and[a] a trap.
23May their eyes be darkened so they cannot
see,
and their backs be bent forever.
24Pour out your wrath on them;
let your fierce anger overtake them.
25May their place be deserted;
let there be no one to dwell in their
tents.
26For they persecute those you wound
and talk about the pain of those you
hurt.
27Charge them with crime upon crime;
do not let them share in your salvation.
28May they be blotted out of the book of life
and not be listed with the righteous.

29I am in pain and distress;
may your salvation, O God, protect me.

30I will praise God's name in song
and glorify him with thanksgiving.
31This will please the LORD more than an ox,
more than a bull with its horns and
hoofs.
32The poor will see and be glad—
you who seek God, may your hearts live!
33The LORD hears the needy
and does not despise his captive people.

34Let heaven and earth praise him,
the seas and all that move in them,
35for God will save Zion
and rebuild the cities of Judah.
Then people will settle there and possess it;
36 the children of his servants will inherit
it,
and those who love his name will dwell
there.

Psalm 70

For the director of music. Of David. A petition.

1Hasten, O God, to save me;
O LORD, come quickly to help me.
2May those who seek my life
be put to shame and confusion;
may all who desire my ruin
be turned back in disgrace.
3May those who say to me, "Aha! Aha!"
turn back because of their shame.
4But may all who seek you
rejoice and be glad in you;
may those who love your salvation always
say,
"Let God be exalted!"

5Yet I am poor and needy;
come quickly to me, O God.
You are my help and my deliverer;
O LORD, do not delay.

[a]22 Or *snare / and their fellowship become*

69:9–12 David's visible repentance and desire to change his life brought him intense ridicule. He became a laughingstock among those who were opposed to God. Even the town drunks derided him. As we confess our failures and surrender our lives to God, we may experience similar scorn. During such trials we should remember that God's judgment matters most; he highly honors such repentance.

70:1–5 This prayer is short and to the point. The psalmist cried out for help in an emergency. It is possible to pray at any time, and it is especially appropriate to pray when faced with a sudden concern. For many of us, prayer is a last resort in times of trouble. We will seek any number of human solutions before looking to God for help. We would be wise to keep prayer always on the tip of our tongue.

Psalm 71

1In you, O LORD, I have taken refuge;
let me never be put to shame.
2Rescue me and deliver me in your
righteousness;
turn your ear to me and save me.
3Be my rock of refuge,
to which I can always go;
give the command to save me,
for you are my rock and my fortress.
4Deliver me, O my God, from the hand of
the wicked,
from the grasp of evil and cruel men.

5For you have been my hope, O Sovereign
LORD,
my confidence since my youth.
6From birth I have relied on you;
you brought me forth from my mother's
womb.
I will ever praise you.
7I have become like a portent to many,
but you are my strong refuge.
8My mouth is filled with your praise,
declaring your splendor all day long.

9Do not cast me away when I am old;
do not forsake me when my strength is
gone.
10For my enemies speak against me;
those who wait to kill me conspire
together.
11They say, "God has forsaken him;
pursue him and seize him,
for no one will rescue him."
12Be not far from me, O God;
come quickly, O my God, to help me.
13May my accusers perish in shame;
may those who want to harm me
be covered with scorn and disgrace.

14But as for me, I will always have hope;
I will praise you more and more.
15My mouth will tell of your righteousness,
of your salvation all day long,
though I know not its measure.
16I will come and proclaim your mighty acts,
O Sovereign LORD;
I will proclaim your righteousness, yours
alone.
17Since my youth, O God, you have taught
me,
and to this day I declare your marvelous
deeds.
18Even when I am old and gray,
do not forsake me, O God,
till I declare your power to the next
generation,
your might to all who are to come.

19Your righteousness reaches to the skies,
O God,
you who have done great things.
Who, O God, is like you?
20Though you have made me see troubles,
many and bitter,
you will restore my life again;
from the depths of the earth
you will again bring me up.
21You will increase my honor
and comfort me once again.

22I will praise you with the harp
for your faithfulness, O my God;
I will sing praise to you with the lyre,
O Holy One of Israel.
23My lips will shout for joy
when I sing praise to you—
I, whom you have redeemed.
24My tongue will tell of your righteous acts
all day long,
for those who wanted to harm me
have been put to shame and confusion.

Psalm 72

Of Solomon.

1Endow the king with your justice, O God,
the royal son with your righteousness.
2He will[a] judge your people in
righteousness,
your afflicted ones with justice.
3The mountains will bring prosperity to the
people,
the hills the fruit of righteousness.
4He will defend the afflicted among the
people
and save the children of the needy;
he will crush the oppressor.

5He will endure[b] as long as the sun,
as long as the moon, through all
generations.
6He will be like rain falling on a mown
field,
like showers watering the earth.
7In his days the righteous will flourish;
prosperity will abound till the moon is
no more.

8He will rule from sea to sea
and from the River[c] to the ends of the
earth.[d]
9The desert tribes will bow before him
and his enemies will lick the dust.
10The kings of Tarshish and of distant shores

[a]2 Or *May he*; similarly in verses 3-11 and 17
[b]5 Septuagint; Hebrew *You will be feared*
[c]8 That is, the Euphrates
[d]8 Or *the end of the land*

71:1–8 The psalmist often described God as his refuge or protecting rock—a place of safety in times of difficulty and trial. The psalmist praised God for the shelter he provided. Let us learn from the psalmist and give God praise for being our rock and our refuge too.

71:9–12 We all face difficult times. As we struggle with the difficulties of life, our strength often ebbs to its lowest level. During these times of weakness we must look to God for strength. He is able to overcome even the most devastating problems.

will bring tribute to him;
the kings of Sheba and Seba
will present him gifts.
11All kings will bow down to him
and all nations will serve him.

12For he will deliver the needy who cry out,
the afflicted who have no one to help.
13He will take pity on the weak and the needy
and save the needy from death.
14He will rescue them from oppression and violence,
for precious is their blood in his sight.

15Long may he live!
May gold from Sheba be given him.
May people ever pray for him
and bless him all day long.
16Let grain abound throughout the land;
on the tops of the hills may it sway.
Let its fruit flourish like Lebanon;
let it thrive like the grass of the field.
17May his name endure forever;
may it continue as long as the sun.

All nations will be blessed through him,
and they will call him blessed.

18Praise be to the LORD God, the God of Israel,
who alone does marvelous deeds.
19Praise be to his glorious name forever;
may the whole earth be filled with his glory.
Amen and Amen.

20This conclude the prayers of David son of Jesse.

BOOK III

Psalms 73–89

Psalm 73

A psalm of Asaph.

1Surely God is good to Israel,
to those who are pure in heart.

2But as for me, my feet had almost slipped;
I had nearly lost my foothold.
3For I envied the arrogant
when I saw the prosperity of the wicked.

4They have no struggles;
their bodies are healthy and strong.[a]
5They are free from the burdens common to man;
they are not plagued by human ills.
6Therefore pride is their necklace;
they clothe themselves with violence.
7From their callous hearts comes iniquity[b];
the evil conceits of their minds know no limits.
8They scoff, and speak with malice;
in their arrogance they threaten oppression.
9Their mouths lay claim to heaven,
and their tongues take possession of the earth.
10Therefore their people turn to them
and drink up waters in abundance.[c]
11They say, "How can God know?
Does the Most High have knowledge?"

12This is what the wicked are like—
always carefree, they increase in wealth.

13Surely in vain have I kept my heart pure;
in vain have I washed my hands in innocence.
14All day long I have been plagued;
I have been punished every morning.

15If I had said, "I will speak thus,"
I would have betrayed your children.
16When I tried to understand all this,
it was oppressive to me
17till I entered the sanctuary of God;
then I understood their final destiny.

18Surely you place them on slippery ground;
you cast them down to ruin.
19How suddenly are they destroyed,
completely swept away by terrors!
20As a dream when one awakes,
so when you arise, O Lord,
you will despise them as fantasies.

21When my heart was grieved
and my spirit embittered,
22I was senseless and ignorant;
I was a brute beast before you.

23Yet I am always with you;
you hold me by my right hand.

[a]4 With a different word division of the Hebrew; Masoretic Text *struggles at their death; / their bodies are healthy* [b]7 Syriac (see also Septuagint); Hebrew *Their eyes bulge with fat* [c]10 The meaning of the Hebrew for this verse is uncertain.

72:12–14 God acts on behalf of those who have no power to free themselves from their problems. He also helps those who suffer under great burdens and have no other source of help. God has great love and compassion for those who are needy. With God's help, there is always hope. He alone has the power to overcome any of the problems we may face.

73:13–20 The psalmist wondered whether following God's plan was worth it. Life didn't seem to make sense. It seemed that evil people were happy and prosperous. In these verses, however, the psalmist came to his senses. Ultimately, God's ways will prevail. We would be wise to follow his plan no matter how difficult it may seem to us at present.

73:21–24 The psalmist thought that God was unjust. He couldn't believe that God was loving and good. In these verses, however, the psalmist realized how foolish he had been. God was waiting to restore his relationship with the doubting psalmist. If we cannot believe that God is good, we will be afraid to surrender our lives to him. Like the psalmist, we need to realize that God does love us and that his plan for us is always the best.

24You guide me with your counsel,
and afterward you will take me into glory.
25Whom have I in heaven but you?
And earth has nothing I desire besides you.
26My flesh and my heart may fail,
but God is the strength of my heart
and my portion forever.

27Those who are far from you will perish;
you destroy all who are unfaithful to you.
28But as for me, it is good to be near God.
I have made the Sovereign LORD my refuge;
I will tell of all your deeds.

Psalm 74

A *maskil*[a] of Asaph.

1Why have you rejected us forever, O God?
Why does your anger smolder against the sheep of your pasture?
2Remember the people you purchased of old,
the tribe of your inheritance, whom you redeemed—
Mount Zion, where you dwelt.
3Turn your steps toward these everlasting ruins,
all this destruction the enemy has brought on the sanctuary.

4Your foes roared in the place where you met with us;
they set up their standards as signs.
5They behaved like men wielding axes
to cut through a thicket of trees.
6They smashed all the carved paneling
with their axes and hatchets.
7They burned your sanctuary to the ground;
they defiled the dwelling place of your Name.
8They said in their hearts, "We will crush them completely!"
They burned every place where God was worshiped in the land.
9We are given no miraculous signs;
no prophets are left,
and none of us knows how long this will be.
10How long will the enemy mock you, O God?
Will the foe revile your name forever?
11Why do you hold back your hand, your right hand?
Take it from the folds of your garment and destroy them!
12But you, O God, are my king from of old;
you bring salvation upon the earth.
13It was you who split open the sea by your power;
you broke the heads of the monster in the waters.
14It was you who crushed the heads of Leviathan
and gave him as food to the creatures of the desert.
15It was you who opened up springs and streams;
you dried up the ever flowing rivers.
16The day is yours, and yours also the night;
you established the sun and moon.
17It was you who set all the boundaries of the earth;
you made both summer and winter.

18Remember how the enemy has mocked you, O LORD,
how foolish people have reviled your name.
19Do not hand over the life of your dove to wild beasts;
do not forget the lives of your afflicted people forever.
20Have regard for your covenant,
because haunts of violence fill the dark places of the land.
21Do not let the oppressed retreat in disgrace;
may the poor and needy praise your name.

22Rise up, O God, and defend your cause;
remember how fools mock you all day long.
23Do not ignore the clamor of your adversaries,
the uproar of your enemies, which rises continually.

Psalm 75

For the director of music. ⌞To the tune of⌟ "Do Not Destroy." A psalm of Asaph. A song.

1We give thanks to you, O God,
we give thanks, for your Name is near;
men tell of your wonderful deeds.

2You say, "I choose the appointed time;
it is I who judge uprightly.
3When the earth and all its people quake,
it is I who hold its pillars firm. *Selah*

[a]Title: Probably a literary or musical term

74:12–23 God has proven himself over and over as our deliverer. We therefore can call on him and be confident that he is able to overcome all the problems we may face. He will be faithful, watching over us even as we walk through the darkest valleys in this life.
75:1–5 Pride is a powerful enemy. It keeps us from turning to God and makes us believe we control our fate. One day God will bring judgment against the proud and arrogant. We were created by God to fit into his plan for the universe. We must always be careful to recognize our dependence upon him.

4To the arrogant I say, 'Boast no more,'
and to the wicked, 'Do not lift up your horns.
5Do not lift your horns against heaven;
do not speak with outstretched neck.' "

6No one from the east or the west
or from the desert can exalt a man.
7But it is God who judges:
He brings one down, he exalts another.
8In the hand of the LORD is a cup
full of foaming wine mixed with spices;
he pours it out, and all the wicked of the earth
drink it down to its very dregs.

9As for me, I will declare this forever;
I will sing praise to the God of Jacob.
10I will cut off the horns of all the wicked,
but the horns of the righteous will be lifted up.

Psalm 76

For the director of music. With stringed instruments. A psalm of Asaph. A song.

1In Judah God is known;
his name is great in Israel.
2His tent is in Salem,
his dwelling place in Zion.
3There he broke the flashing arrows,
the shields and the swords, the weapons of war. *Selah*

4You are resplendent with light,
more majestic than mountains rich with game.
5Valiant men lie plundered,
they sleep their last sleep;
not one of the warriors
can lift his hands.
6At your rebuke, O God of Jacob,
both horse and chariot lie still.
7You alone are to be feared.
Who can stand before you when you are angry?
8From heaven you pronounced judgment,
and the land feared and was quiet—
9when you, O God, rose up to judge,
to save all the afflicted of the land. *Selah*
10Surely your wrath against men brings you praise,
and the survivors of your wrath are restrained.[a]
11Make vows to the LORD your God and fulfill them;
let all the neighboring lands
bring gifts to the One to be feared.
12He breaks the spirit of rulers;
he is feared by the kings of the earth.

Psalm 77

For the director of music. For Jeduthun. Of Asaph. A psalm.

1I cried out to God for help;
I cried out to God to hear me.
2When I was in distress, I sought the Lord;
at night I stretched out untiring hands
and my soul refused to be comforted.

3I remembered you, O God, and I groaned;
I mused, and my spirit grew faint. *Selah*
4You kept my eyes from closing;
I was too troubled to speak.
5I thought about the former days,
the years of long ago;
6I remembered my songs in the night.
My heart mused and my spirit inquired:

7"Will the Lord reject forever?
Will he never show his favor again?
8Has his unfailing love vanished forever?
Has his promise failed for all time?
9Has God forgotten to be merciful?
Has he in anger withheld his compassion?" *Selah*

10Then I thought, "To this I will appeal:
the years of the right hand of the Most High."
11I will remember the deeds of the LORD;
yes, I will remember your miracles of long ago.
12I will meditate on all your works
and consider all your mighty deeds.

13Your ways, O God, are holy.
What god is so great as our God?
14You are the God who performs miracles;
you display your power among the peoples.
15With your mighty arm you redeemed your people,
the descendants of Jacob and Joseph. *Selah*

16The waters saw you, O God,

[a]10 Or *Surely the wrath of men brings you praise, / and with the remainder of wrath you arm yourself*

75:6–10 The psalmist understood that it was God who lifts up one person and humbles another. The promise of God's punishment of the wicked is given to warn people away from their sin. It is also a reminder for those who suffer at the hands of wicked people that God hasn't forgotten them.
76:1–12 The writer of this psalm recognized that God is able to overcome the most powerful opposition we might face. He is even able to use evil deeds to bring about his own plans for good. God's power is far greater than we can ever imagine (see Ephesians 3:20). He is able to overcome even our greatest problems.
77:1–4 As he wrote these verses, the psalmist was feeling such deep anguish that he didn't feel like praying. The same thing often happens to us. When we are discouraged, we need to be persistent in our prayers, for God is more than able to help us.

the waters saw you and writhed;
the very depths were convulsed.
17The clouds poured down water,
the skies resounded with thunder;
your arrows flashed back and forth.
18Your thunder was heard in the whirlwind,
your lightning lit up the world;
the earth trembled and quaked.
19Your path led through the sea,
your way through the mighty waters,
though your footprints were not seen.

20You led your people like a flock
by the hand of Moses and Aaron.

Psalm 78

A *maskil*[a] of Asaph.

1O my people, hear my teaching;
listen to the words of my mouth.
2I will open my mouth in parables,
I will utter hidden things, things from of old—
3what we have heard and known,
what our fathers have told us.
4We will not hide them from their children;
we will tell the next generation
the praiseworthy deeds of the LORD,
his power, and the wonders he has done.
5He decreed statutes for Jacob
and established the law in Israel,
which he commanded our forefathers
to teach their children,
6so the next generation would know them,
even the children yet to be born,
and they in turn would tell their children.
7Then they would put their trust in God
and would not forget his deeds
but would keep his commands.
8They would not be like their forefathers—
a stubborn and rebellious generation,
whose hearts were not loyal to God,
whose spirits were not faithful to him.

9The men of Ephraim, though armed with bows,
turned back on the day of battle;
10they did not keep God's covenant
and refused to live by his law.
11They forgot what he had done,
the wonders he had shown them.
12He did miracles in the sight of their fathers
in the land of Egypt, in the region of Zoan.
13He divided the sea and led them through;
he made the water stand firm like a wall.
14He guided them with the cloud by day
and with light from the fire all night.
15He split the rocks in the desert
and gave them water as abundant as the seas;
16he brought streams out of a rocky crag
and made water flow down like rivers.

17But they continued to sin against him,
rebelling in the desert against the Most High.
18They willfully put God to the test
by demanding the food they craved.
19They spoke against God, saying,
"Can God spread a table in the desert?
20When he struck the rock, water gushed out,
and streams flowed abundantly.
But can he also give us food?
Can he supply meat for his people?"
21When the LORD heard them, he was very angry;
his fire broke out against Jacob,
and his wrath rose against Israel,
22for they did not believe in God
or trust in his deliverance.
23Yet he gave a command to the skies above
and opened the doors of the heavens;
24he rained down manna for the people to eat,
he gave them the grain of heaven.
25Men ate the bread of angels;
he sent them all the food they could eat.
26He let loose the east wind from the heavens
and led forth the south wind by his power.
27He rained meat down on them like dust,
flying birds like sand on the seashore.
28He made them come down inside their camp,
all around their tents.
29They ate till they had more than enough,
for he had given them what they craved.
30But before they turned from the food they craved,
even while it was still in their mouths,
31God's anger rose against them;
he put to death the sturdiest among them,
cutting down the young men of Israel.

32In spite of all this, they kept on sinning;
in spite of his wonders, they did not believe.

[a]Title: Probably a literary or musical term

78:9–12 God's people, although well equipped to defeat their enemies in the promised land, failed to completely carry out God's commands. When the people should have boldly pressed forward, they ran from the conflict like cowards. Their cowardice was undoubtedly brought about because they did not consider the full significance of God's prior powerful acts on their behalf. When we fail to count on God's power, either because of unbelief or because of pride, we are bound to fail. Instead, we should confidently trust in God's strength to overcome our struggles.

78:17–33 God's anger grew against his rebellious people because they continually complained and refused to trust him to deliver them from their wilderness experience. We should remember their example and pray that this won't happen to us.

33So he ended their days in futility
and their years in terror.
34Whenever God slew them, they would seek him;
they eagerly turned to him again.
35They remembered that God was their Rock,
that God Most High was their Redeemer.
36But then they would flatter him with their mouths,
lying to him with their tongues;
37their hearts were not loyal to him,
they were not faithful to his covenant.
38Yet he was merciful;
he forgave their iniquities
and did not destroy them.
Time after time he restrained his anger
and did not stir up his full wrath.
39He remembered that they were but flesh,
a passing breeze that does not return.

40How often they rebelled against him in the desert
and grieved him in the wasteland!
41Again and again they put God to the test;
they vexed the Holy One of Israel.
42They did not remember his power—
the day he redeemed them from the oppressor,
43the day he displayed his miraculous signs in Egypt,
his wonders in the region of Zoan.
44He turned their rivers to blood;
they could not drink from their streams.
45He sent swarms of flies that devoured them,
and frogs that devastated them.
46He gave their crops to the grasshopper,
their produce to the locust.
47He destroyed their vines with hail
and their sycamore-figs with sleet.
48He gave over their cattle to the hail,
their livestock to bolts of lightning.
49He unleashed against them his hot anger,
his wrath, indignation and hostility—
a band of destroying angels.
50He prepared a path for his anger;
he did not spare them from death
but gave them over to the plague.
51He struck down all the firstborn of Egypt,
the firstfruits of manhood in the tents of Ham.
52But he brought his people out like a flock;
he led them like sheep through the desert.
53He guided them safely, so they were unafraid;
but the sea engulfed their enemies.
54Thus he brought them to the border of his holy land,
to the hill country his right hand had taken.
55He drove out nations before them
and allotted their lands to them as an inheritance;
he settled the tribes of Israel in their homes.

56But they put God to the test
and rebelled against the Most High;
they did not keep his statutes.
57Like their fathers they were disloyal and faithless,
as unreliable as a faulty bow.
58They angered him with their high places;
they aroused his jealousy with their idols.
59When God heard them, he was very angry;
he rejected Israel completely.
60He abandoned the tabernacle of Shiloh,
the tent he had set up among men.
61He sent ⌊the ark of⌋ his might into captivity,
his splendor into the hands of the enemy.
62He gave his people over to the sword;
he was very angry with his inheritance.
63Fire consumed their young men,
and their maidens had no wedding songs;
64their priests were put to the sword,
and their widows could not weep.

65Then the Lord awoke as from sleep,
as a man wakes from the stupor of wine.
66He beat back his enemies;
he put them to everlasting shame.
67Then he rejected the tents of Joseph,
he did not choose the tribe of Ephraim;
68but he chose the tribe of Judah,
Mount Zion, which he loved.
69He built his sanctuary like the heights,
like the earth that he established forever.
70He chose David his servant
and took him from the sheep pens;
71from tending the sheep he brought him
to be the shepherd of his people Jacob,
of Israel his inheritance.
72And David shepherded them with integrity of heart;
with skillful hands he led them.

Psalm 79

A psalm of Asaph.

1O God, the nations have invaded your inheritance;

78:34–39 God knows that we are human and prone to disobedience, yet he is compassionate toward us, forgiving our sins, just as he did for his people in the wilderness. God's goodness should encourage us to surrender our lives to him continually.

78:59–64 Sin has devastating consequences. God loves us, but continued disobedience will eventually bring judgment. If we are wise, we will understand our error, admit our sin and commit our lives again to God.

they have defiled your holy temple,
they have reduced Jerusalem to rubble.
[2]They have given the dead bodies of your servants
as food to the birds of the air,
the flesh of your saints to the beasts of the earth.
[3]They have poured out blood like water
all around Jerusalem,
and there is no one to bury the dead.
[4]We are objects of reproach to our neighbors,
of scorn and derision to those around us.

[5]How long, O LORD? Will you be angry forever?
How long will your jealousy burn like fire?
[6]Pour out your wrath on the nations
that do not acknowledge you,
on the kingdoms
that do not call on your name;
[7]for they have devoured Jacob
and destroyed his homeland.
[8]Do not hold against us the sins of the fathers;
may your mercy come quickly to meet us,
for we are in desperate need.

[9]Help us, O God our Savior,
for the glory of your name;
deliver us and forgive our sins
for your name's sake.
[10]Why should the nations say,
"Where is their God?"
Before our eyes, make known among the nations
that you avenge the outpoured blood of your servants.
[11]May the groans of the prisoners come before you;
by the strength of your arm
preserve those condemned to die.

[12]Pay back into the laps of our neighbors seven times
the reproach they have hurled at you, O Lord.
[13]Then we your people, the sheep of your pasture,
will praise you forever;
from generation to generation
we will recount your praise.

Psalm 80

For the director of music. To ⌊the tune of⌋ "The Lilies of the Covenant." Of Asaph. A psalm.

[1]Hear us, O Shepherd of Israel,
you who lead Joseph like a flock;
you who sit enthroned between the cherubim, shine forth
[2] before Ephraim, Benjamin and Manasseh.
Awaken your might;
come and save us.

[3]Restore us, O God;
make your face shine upon us,
that we may be saved.

[4]O LORD God Almighty,
how long will your anger smolder
against the prayers of your people?
[5]You have fed them with the bread of tears;
you have made them drink tears by the bowlful.
[6]You have made us a source of contention to our neighbors,
and our enemies mock us.

[7]Restore us, O God Almighty;
make your face shine upon us,
that we may be saved.

[8]You brought a vine out of Egypt;
you drove out the nations and planted it.
[9]You cleared the ground for it,
and it took root and filled the land.
[10]The mountains were covered with its shade,
the mighty cedars with its branches.
[11]It sent out its boughs to the Sea,[a]
its shoots as far as the River.[b]

[12]Why have you broken down its walls
so that all who pass by pick its grapes?
[13]Boars from the forest ravage it
and the creatures of the field feed on it.
[14]Return to us, O God Almighty!
Look down from heaven and see!
Watch over this vine,
[15] the root your right hand has planted,
the son[c] you have raised up for yourself.
[16]Your vine is cut down, it is burned with fire;
at your rebuke your people perish.
[17]Let your hand rest on the man at your right hand,

[a]11 Probably the Mediterranean [b]11 That is, the Euphrates [c]15 Or *branch*

79:5–13 There are times when we will feel persecuted, times we need God to come to our defense. We need to be able to recognize these times, seeing the truth of our situation and admitting our need for God's help. God is ready to come to our aid when we call on him.

80:14–19 When we are beaten down, we need to plead for God's mercy and ask him to restore us. Though we may feel overwhelmed by our suffering, we should remember that God can bring us through any trial.

the son of man you have raised up for
yourself.
18Then we will not turn away from you;
revive us, and we will call on your name.
19Restore us, O LORD God Almighty;
make your face shine upon us,
that we may be saved.

Psalm 81

For the director of music. According to *gittith.*[a] Of Asaph.

1Sing for joy to God our strength;
shout aloud to the God of Jacob!
2Begin the music, strike the tambourine,
play the melodious harp and lyre.
3Sound the ram's horn at the New Moon,
and when the moon is full, on the day
of our Feast;
4this is a decree for Israel,
an ordinance of the God of Jacob.
5He established it as a statute for Joseph
when he went out against Egypt,
where we heard a language we did not
understand.[b]
6He says, "I removed the burden from their
shoulders;
their hands were set free from the basket.
7In your distress you called and I rescued
you,
I answered you out of a thundercloud;
I tested you at the waters of Meribah.
Selah
8"Hear, O my people, and I will warn you—
if you would but listen to me, O Israel!
9You shall have no foreign god among you;
you shall not bow down to an alien god.
10I am the LORD your God,
who brought you up out of Egypt.
Open wide your mouth and I will fill it.
11"But my people would not listen to me;
Israel would not submit to me.
12So I gave them over to their stubborn
hearts
to follow their own devices.
13"If my people would but listen to me,
if Israel would follow my ways,
14how quickly would I subdue their enemies
and turn my hand against their foes!
15Those who hate the LORD would cringe
before him,
and their punishment would last forever.
16But you would be fed with the finest of
wheat;
with honey from the rock I would satisfy
you."

Psalm 82

A psalm of Asaph.

1God presides in the great assembly;
he gives judgment among the "gods":
2"How long will you[c] defend the unjust
and show partiality to the wicked? *Selah*
3Defend the cause of the weak and
fatherless;
maintain the rights of the poor and
oppressed.
4Rescue the weak and needy;
deliver them from the hand of the
wicked.
5"They know nothing, they understand
nothing.
They walk about in darkness;
all the foundations of the earth are
shaken.
6"I said, 'You are "gods";
you are all sons of the Most High.'
7But you will die like mere men;
you will fall like every other ruler."
8Rise up, O God, judge the earth,
for all the nations are your inheritance.

Psalm 83

A song. A psalm of Asaph.

1O God, do not keep silent;
be not quiet, O God, be not still.
2See how your enemies are astir,
how your foes rear their heads.
3With cunning they conspire against your
people;
they plot against those you cherish.
4"Come," they say, "let us destroy them as a
nation,

[a]Title: Probably a musical term [b]5 Or / *and we heard a voice we had not known* [c]2 The Hebrew is plural.

81:6–10 With great power, God delivered his people and took away their burdens when they relied on him. God warns us over and over not to let any person or thing take his place in our lives. Trusting any resource or power other than God is foolishness. He is far more powerful than any other possible means of deliverance. Only God can satisfy our deepest needs; all we need to do is look to him for help.
82:1–4 God executes judgment among his people and holds them accountable. Those who deal unfairly with the innocent and destitute will eventually have to answer to God for what they have done. As Christians we should stand up for the cause of the innocent and seek justice for them.
83:1–8 When we encounter problems, we should immediately call out to God for help. All the forces of evil seem to conspire against us as we face temptation. God doesn't want us to fail; he is there to help us. But we need to become aware of the things that weaken and defeat us. By avoiding them, we will find temptation easier to deal with.

that the name of Israel be remembered
no more."

5With one mind they plot together;
they form an alliance against you—
6the tents of Edom and the Ishmaelites,
of Moab and the Hagrites,
7Gebal,[a] Ammon and Amalek,
Philistia, with the people of Tyre.
8Even Assyria has joined them
to lend strength to the descendants of
Lot. *Selah*

9Do to them as you did to Midian,
as you did to Sisera and Jabin at the
river Kishon,
10who perished at Endor
and became like refuse on the ground.
11Make their nobles like Oreb and Zeeb,
all their princes like Zebah and
Zalmunna,
12who said, "Let us take possession
of the pasturelands of God."

13Make them like tumbleweed, O my God,
like chaff before the wind.
14As fire consumes the forest
or a flame sets the mountains ablaze,
15so pursue them with your tempest
and terrify them with your storm.
16Cover their faces with shame
so that men will seek your name,
O LORD.

17May they ever be ashamed and dismayed;
may they perish in disgrace.
18Let them know that you, whose name is
the LORD—
that you alone are the Most High over
all the earth.

Psalm 84

For the director of music. According to *gittith.*[b] Of the Sons of Korah. A psalm.

1How lovely is your dwelling place,
O LORD Almighty!
2My soul yearns, even faints,
for the courts of the LORD;
my heart and my flesh cry out
for the living God.

3Even the sparrow has found a home,
and the swallow a nest for herself,
where she may have her young—
a place near your altar,
O LORD Almighty, my King and my God.
4Blessed are those who dwell in your house;
they are ever praising you. *Selah*

5Blessed are those whose strength is in you,
who have set their hearts on pilgrimage.
6As they pass through the Valley of Baca,
they make it a place of springs;
the autumn rains also cover it with
pools.[c]
7They go from strength to strength,
till each appears before God in Zion.

8Hear my prayer, O LORD God Almighty;
listen to me, O God of Jacob. *Selah*
9Look upon our shield,[d] O God;
look with favor on your anointed one.

10Better is one day in your courts
than a thousand elsewhere;
I would rather be a doorkeeper in the
house of my God
than dwell in the tents of the wicked.
11For the LORD God is a sun and shield;
the LORD bestows favor and honor;
no good thing does he withhold
from those whose walk is blameless.

12O LORD Almighty,
blessed is the man who trusts in you.

Psalm 85

For the director of music. Of the Sons of Korah. A psalm.

1You showed favor to your land, O LORD;
you restored the fortunes of Jacob.
2You forgave the iniquity of your people
and covered all their sins. *Selah*
3You set aside all your wrath
and turned from your fierce anger.

4Restore us again, O God our Savior,
and put away your displeasure toward
us.
5Will you be angry with us forever?
Will you prolong your anger through all
generations?
6Will you not revive us again,
that your people may rejoice in you?
7Show us your unfailing love, O LORD,
and grant us your salvation.

8I will listen to what God the LORD will say;
he promises peace to his people, his
saints—
but let them not return to folly.

[a]7 That is, Byblos [b]Title: Probably a musical term [c]6 Or *blessings* [d]9 Or *sovereign*

83:13–18 Nothing can stand against God. He created everything that exists, and he alone is sovereign over all the world. When we live according to his plan, our enemies are his enemies; we can count on him to deal with them as such.

84:8–12 Spending a little time in the presence of God is better than spending a lifetime apart from him. The security, peace and love that God offers are greater than anything we could receive from other people.

85:1–3 What a wonderful blessing—God has forgiven our sins! We have all fallen short of God's standard and deserve punishment (see Romans 3:23). But God has been gracious to us by granting forgiveness through his Son, Jesus Christ. Let us thank God for this gift and praise him for our restoration.

9Surely his salvation is near those who fear
him,
that his glory may dwell in our land.

10Love and faithfulness meet together;
righteousness and peace kiss each other.
11Faithfulness springs forth from the earth,
and righteousness looks down from
heaven.
12The LORD will indeed give what is good,
and our land will yield its harvest.
13Righteousness goes before him
and prepares the way for his steps.

Psalm 86

A prayer of David.

1Hear, O LORD, and answer me,
for I am poor and needy.
2Guard my life, for I am devoted to you.
You are my God; save your servant
who trusts in you.
3Have mercy on me, O Lord,
for I call to you all day long.
4Bring joy to your servant,
for to you, O Lord,
I lift up my soul.

5You are forgiving and good, O Lord,
abounding in love to all who call to you.
6Hear my prayer, O LORD;
listen to my cry for mercy.
7In the day of my trouble I will call to you,
for you will answer me.

8Among the gods there is none like you,
O Lord;
no deeds can compare with yours.
9All the nations you have made
will come and worship before you,
O Lord;
they will bring glory to your name.
10For you are great and do marvelous deeds;
you alone are God.

11Teach me your way, O LORD,
and I will walk in your truth;
give me an undivided heart,
that I may fear your name.
12I will praise you, O Lord my God, with all
my heart;
I will glorify your name forever.
13For great is your love toward me;
you have delivered me from the depths
of the grave.[a]

14The arrogant are attacking me, O God;
a band of ruthless men seeks my life—
men without regard for you.
15But you, O Lord, are a compassionate and
gracious God,
slow to anger, abounding in love and
faithfulness.
16Turn to me and have mercy on me;
grant your strength to your servant
and save the son of your maidservant.[b]
17Give me a sign of your goodness,
that my enemies may see it and be put
to shame,
for you, O LORD, have helped me and
comforted me.

Psalm 87

Of the Sons of Korah. A psalm. A song.

1He has set his foundation on the holy
mountain;
2 the LORD loves the gates of Zion
more than all the dwellings of Jacob.
3Glorious things are said of you,
O city of God: *Selah*
4"I will record Rahab[c] and Babylon
among those who acknowledge me—
Philistia too, and Tyre, along with Cush[d]—
and will say, 'This[e] one was born in
Zion.' "

5Indeed, of Zion it will be said,
"This one and that one were born in
her,
and the Most High himself will establish
her."
6The LORD will write in the register of the
peoples:
"This one was born in Zion." *Selah*
7As they make music they will sing,
"All my fountains are in you."

[a]13 Hebrew *Sheol* [b]16 Or *save your faithful son*
[c]4 A poetic name for Egypt [d]4 That is, the upper Nile region [e]4 Or *"O Rahab and Babylon, / Philistia, Tyre and Cush, / I will record concerning those who acknowledge me: / 'This*

86:1–5 Though we follow God, we will still be faced with grave difficulties. Sometimes the answers won't come quickly, and though we pray long and diligently, nothing will happen immediately. We may become impatient and begin to wonder whether God will ever act. However, God will respond with goodness, forgiveness and compassion to all who will repent and call on him.

86:11–13 We learn more about God's will as we seek him through prayer and the study of his Word. The more we know about God, the more we will know what he expects of us. And as we get to know God better, we will discover that he not only gives us direction, but he also gives us the strength and encouragement we need to walk down the path he has chosen for us.

87:1–7 In God's eyes we are like Jerusalem, his beloved city. In the Old Testament, Jerusalem was known as God's dwelling place on earth and the site of his rule. Since the coming of Jesus Christ and the outpouring of the Holy Spirit, God dwells in our hearts (see John 14:16; Acts 2). God loves us and longs to direct our decisions and actions. It is a privilege to be called God's beloved and to be considered citizens of his kingdom (see Ephesians 2:18–19). He cares for us and wants us to enjoy living in his presence.

Psalm 88

A song. A psalm of the Sons of Korah. For the director of music. According to *mahalath leannoth.*[a] A *maskil*[b] of Heman the Ezrahite.

1O LORD, the God who saves me,
day and night I cry out before you.
2May my prayer come before you;
turn your ear to my cry.

3For my soul is full of trouble
and my life draws near the grave.[c]
4I am counted among those who go down to the pit;
I am like a man without strength.
5I am set apart with the dead,
like the slain who lie in the grave,
whom you remember no more,
who are cut off from your care.

6You have put me in the lowest pit,
in the darkest depths.
7Your wrath lies heavily upon me;
you have overwhelmed me with all your waves. *Selah*
8You have taken from me my closest friends
and have made me repulsive to them.
I am confined and cannot escape;
9 my eyes are dim with grief.

I call to you, O LORD, every day;
I spread out my hands to you.
10Do you show your wonders to the dead?
Do those who are dead rise up and praise you? *Selah*
11Is your love declared in the grave,
your faithfulness in Destruction[d]?
12Are your wonders known in the place of darkness,
or your righteous deeds in the land of oblivion?
13But I cry to you for help, O LORD;
in the morning my prayer comes before you.
14Why, O LORD, do you reject me
and hide your face from me?

15From my youth I have been afflicted and close to death;
I have suffered your terrors and am in despair.
16Your wrath has swept over me;
your terrors have destroyed me.
17All day long they surround me like a flood;
they have completely engulfed me.
18You have taken my companions and loved ones from me;
the darkness is my closest friend.

Psalm 89

A *maskil*[b] of Ethan the Ezrahite.

1I will sing of the LORD's great love forever;
with my mouth I will make your faithfulness known through all generations.
2I will declare that your love stands firm forever,
that you established your faithfulness in heaven itself.

3You said, "I have made a covenant with my chosen one,
I have sworn to David my servant,
4'I will establish your line forever
and make your throne firm through all generations.' " *Selah*

5The heavens praise your wonders, O LORD,
your faithfulness too, in the assembly of the holy ones.
6For who in the skies above can compare with the LORD?
Who is like the LORD among the heavenly beings?
7In the council of the holy ones God is greatly feared;
he is more awesome than all who surround him.
8O LORD God Almighty, who is like you?
You are mighty, O LORD, and your faithfulness surrounds you.

9You rule over the surging sea;
when its waves mount up, you still them.
10You crushed Rahab like one of the slain;
with your strong arm you scattered your enemies.
11The heavens are yours, and yours also the earth;
you founded the world and all that is in it.
12You created the north and the south;
Tabor and Hermon sing for joy at your name.
13Your arm is endued with power;
your hand is strong, your right hand exalted.

14Righteousness and justice are the foundation of your throne;
love and faithfulness go before you.

[a]Title: Possibly a tune, "The Suffering of Affliction" [b]Title: Probably a literary or musical term [c]3 Hebrew *Sheol* [d]11 Hebrew *Abaddon*

88:1–5 Everyone feels hopeless and overwhelmed by troubles at some time. It is comforting to know that God is listening to our cries. No situation is hopeless for those who call out to God.
88:6–12 In these verses, the psalmist wrote that God had abandoned him to his problems. It is important to remember that God allows us to stumble and fall. When we do, we personally learn about the consequences of sin. But it is also important to remember that God does not cause us to fall. Temptation is a tool of the enemy, and yielding to temptation will result in painful consequences. When we suffer for our sins, we should learn our lesson, redirect our course with repentance and surrender again to God.

15Blessed are those who have learned to
acclaim you,
who walk in the light of your presence,
O LORD.
16They rejoice in your name all day long;
they exult in your righteousness.
17For you are their glory and strength,
and by your favor you exalt our horn.[a]
18Indeed, our shield[b] belongs to the LORD,
our king to the Holy One of Israel.

19Once you spoke in a vision,
to your faithful people you said:
"I have bestowed strength on a warrior;
I have exalted a young man from among
the people.
20I have found David my servant;
with my sacred oil I have anointed him.
21My hand will sustain him;
surely my arm will strengthen him.
22No enemy will subject him to tribute;
no wicked man will oppress him.
23I will crush his foes before him
and strike down his adversaries.
24My faithful love will be with him,
and through my name his horn[c] will be
exalted.
25I will set his hand over the sea,
his right hand over the rivers.
26He will call out to me, 'You are my Father,
my God, the Rock my Savior.'
27I will also appoint him my firstborn,
the most exalted of the kings of the
earth.
28I will maintain my love to him forever,
and my covenant with him will never
fail.
29I will establish his line forever,
his throne as long as the heavens endure.

30"If his sons forsake my law
and do not follow my statutes,
31if they violate my decrees
and fail to keep my commands,
32I will punish their sin with the rod,
their iniquity with flogging;
33but I will not take my love from him,
nor will I ever betray my faithfulness.
34I will not violate my covenant
or alter what my lips have uttered.
35Once for all, I have sworn by my holiness—
and I will not lie to David—
36that his line will continue forever
and his throne endure before me like the
sun;
37it will be established forever like the moon,
the faithful witness in the sky." *Selah*
38But you have rejected, you have spurned,
you have been very angry with your
anointed one.
39You have renounced the covenant with
your servant
and have defiled his crown in the dust.
40You have broken through all his walls
and reduced his strongholds to ruins.
41All who pass by have plundered him;
he has become the scorn of his
neighbors.
42You have exalted the right hand of his foes;
you have made all his enemies rejoice.
43You have turned back the edge of his sword
and have not supported him in battle.
44You have put an end to his splendor
and cast his throne to the ground.
45You have cut short the days of his youth;
you have covered him with a mantle of
shame. *Selah*

46How long, O LORD? Will you hide yourself
forever?
How long will your wrath burn like fire?
47Remember how fleeting is my life.
For what futility you have created all
men!
48What man can live and not see death,
or save himself from the power of the
grave[d]? *Selah*
49O Lord, where is your former great love,
which in your faithfulness you swore to
David?
50Remember, Lord, how your servant has[e]
been mocked,
how I bear in my heart the taunts of all
the nations,
51the taunts with which your enemies have
mocked, O LORD,
with which they have mocked every step
of your anointed one.

52Praise be to the LORD forever!
Amen and Amen.

BOOK IV

Psalms 90–106

Psalm 90

A prayer of Moses the man of God.

1Lord, you have been our dwelling place
throughout all generations.
2Before the mountains were born
or you brought forth the earth and the
world,
from everlasting to everlasting you are
God.

3You turn men back to dust,
saying, "Return to dust, O sons of men."
4For a thousand years in your sight
are like a day that has just gone by,
or like a watch in the night.
5You sweep men away in the sleep of death;
they are like the new grass of the
morning—

[a]17 *Horn* here symbolizes strong one. [b]18 Or *sovereign* [c]24 *Horn* here symbolizes strength. [d]48 Hebrew *Sheol* [e]50 Or *your servants have*

[6]though in the morning it springs up new,
by evening it is dry and withered.

[7]We are consumed by your anger
and terrified by your indignation.
[8]You have set our iniquities before you,
our secret sins in the light of your presence.
[9]All our days pass away under your wrath;
we finish our years with a moan.
[10]The length of our days is seventy years—
or eighty, if we have the strength;
yet their span[a] is but trouble and sorrow,
for they quickly pass, and we fly away.
[11]Who knows the power of your anger?
For your wrath is as great as the fear that is due you.
[12]Teach us to number our days aright,
that we may gain a heart of wisdom.

[13]Relent, O LORD! How long will it be?
Have compassion on your servants.
[14]Satisfy us in the morning with your unfailing love,
that we may sing for joy and be glad all our days.
[15]Make us glad for as many days as you have afflicted us,
for as many years as we have seen trouble.
[16]May your deeds be shown to your servants,
your splendor to their children.
[17]May the favor[b] of the Lord our God rest upon us;
establish the work of our hands for us—
yes, establish the work of our hands.

Psalm 91

[1]He who dwells in the shelter of the Most High
will rest in the shadow of the Almighty.[c]
[2]I will say[d] of the LORD, "He is my refuge and my fortress,
my God, in whom I trust."

[3]Surely he will save you from the fowler's snare
and from the deadly pestilence.
[4]He will cover you with his feathers,
and under his wings you will find refuge;
his faithfulness will be your shield and rampart.
[5]You will not fear the terror of night,
nor the arrow that flies by day,
[6]nor the pestilence that stalks in the darkness,
nor the plague that destroys at midday.
[7]A thousand may fall at your side,
ten thousand at your right hand,
but it will not come near you.
[8]You will only observe with your eyes
and see the punishment of the wicked.

[9]If you make the Most High your dwelling—
even the LORD, who is my refuge—
[10]then no harm will befall you,
no disaster will come near your tent.
[11]For he will command his angels concerning you
to guard you in all your ways;
[12]they will lift you up in their hands,
so that you will not strike your foot against a stone.
[13]You will tread upon the lion and the cobra;
you will trample the great lion and the serpent.

[14]"Because he loves me," says the LORD, "I will rescue him;
I will protect him, for he acknowledges my name.
[15]He will call upon me, and I will answer him;
I will be with him in trouble,
I will deliver him and honor him.
[16]With long life will I satisfy him
and show him my salvation."

Psalm 92

A psalm. A song. For the Sabbath day.

[1]It is good to praise the LORD
and make music to your name, O Most High,
[2]to proclaim your love in the morning
and your faithfulness at night,
[3]to the music of the ten-stringed lyre
and the melody of the harp.

[4]For you make me glad by your deeds, O LORD;

[a]10 Or *yet the best of them* [b]17 Or *beauty*
[c]1 Hebrew *Shaddai* [d]2 Or *He says*

90:13–17 Only God can give us the power to be what we ought to be; yet God won't force those changes on us. We must be willing to change. Prayer is the gateway to change. We can ask God to make us willing to change and then to give us the strength to follow through with action.
91:1–4 When we recognize God as our refuge, our deliverer, we will be eager to seek him and surrender our lives to his care. How comforting to know that when we cry out, God cares for us as a mother bird cares for her young. Our powerful defender is always there when we turn to him for shelter and comfort.
91:10–16 God watches over us, his chosen ones. Sometimes his deliverance will come in the form of angels who care for us and rescue us (see Matthew 4:6). At other times God may use more natural means to deliver us. But his help will come. As we cry out to him, he will be with us in our troubles and deliver us.
92:1–4 We should praise God for all that he has done for us. Part of our offering should be a declaration of praise for God's marvelous compassion and unceasing goodness to us. God truly is the one who brings joy to our lives. As we experience his faithfulness, praise and thanks should be our natural response to him, and others will be drawn to him as well.

I sing for joy at the works of your hands.
5How great are your works, O LORD,
how profound your thoughts!
6The senseless man does not know,
fools do not understand,
7that though the wicked spring up like grass
and all evildoers flourish,
they will be forever destroyed.

8But you, O LORD, are exalted forever.

9For surely your enemies, O LORD,
surely your enemies will perish;
all evildoers will be scattered.
10You have exalted my horn[a] like that of a wild ox;
fine oils have been poured upon me.
11My eyes have seen the defeat of my adversaries;
my ears have heard the rout of my wicked foes.

12The righteous will flourish like a palm tree,
they will grow like a cedar of Lebanon;
13planted in the house of the LORD,
they will flourish in the courts of our God.
14They will still bear fruit in old age,
they will stay fresh and green,
15proclaiming, "The LORD is upright;
he is my Rock, and there is no wickedness in him."

Psalm 93

1The LORD reigns, he is robed in majesty;
the LORD is robed in majesty
and is armed with strength.
The world is firmly established;
it cannot be moved.
2Your throne was established long ago;
you are from all eternity.

3The seas have lifted up, O LORD,
the seas have lifted up their voice;
the seas have lifted up their pounding waves.
4Mightier than the thunder of the great waters,
mightier than the breakers of the sea—
the LORD on high is mighty.

5Your statutes stand firm;
holiness adorns your house
for endless days, O LORD.

Psalm 94

1O LORD, the God who avenges,
O God who avenges, shine forth.
2Rise up, O Judge of the earth;
pay back to the proud what they deserve.
3How long will the wicked, O LORD,
how long will the wicked be jubilant?

4They pour out arrogant words;
all the evildoers are full of boasting.
5They crush your people, O LORD;
they oppress your inheritance.
6They slay the widow and the alien;
they murder the fatherless.
7They say, "The LORD does not see;
the God of Jacob pays no heed."

8Take heed, you senseless ones among the people;
you fools, when will you become wise?
9Does he who implanted the ear not hear?
Does he who formed the eye not see?
10Does he who disciplines nations not punish?
Does he who teaches man lack knowledge?
11The LORD knows the thoughts of man;
he knows that they are futile.

12Blessed is the man you discipline, O LORD,
the man you teach from your law;
13you grant him relief from days of trouble,
till a pit is dug for the wicked.
14For the LORD will not reject his people;
he will never forsake his inheritance.
15Judgment will again be founded on righteousness,
and all the upright in heart will follow it.

16Who will rise up for me against the wicked?
Who will take a stand for me against evildoers?
17Unless the LORD had given me help,
I would soon have dwelt in the silence of death.
18When I said, "My foot is slipping,"
your love, O LORD, supported me.
19When anxiety was great within me,
your consolation brought joy to my soul.

20Can a corrupt throne be allied with you—
one that brings on misery by its decrees?
21They band together against the righteous
and condemn the innocent to death.
22But the LORD has become my fortress,
and my God the rock in whom I take refuge.

a10 *Horn* here symbolizes strength.

94:8–10 The voice of the tempter says, "No one will know or care if you commit this one sin." This passage reminds us that God is neither deaf nor blind. Remembering that God knows what we are doing and that he cares about us should encourage us to stand against the temptations we face (see Jeremiah 23:23–24).

94:16–23 We can count on God to support us against our enemies. When we stumble into temptation or trials, God is there to keep us from falling (see Jude 24). Because he is our defender, God does not allow sin to destroy us beyond hope. Knowing that God is involved in our lives should encourage us to live for him.

23He will repay them for their sins
and destroy them for their wickedness;
the LORD our God will destroy them.

Psalm 95

1Come, let us sing for joy to the LORD;
let us shout aloud to the Rock of our salvation.
2Let us come before him with thanksgiving
and extol him with music and song.

3For the LORD is the great God,
the great King above all gods.
4In his hand are the depths of the earth,
and the mountain peaks belong to him.
5The sea is his, for he made it,
and his hands formed the dry land.

6Come, let us bow down in worship,
let us kneel before the LORD our Maker;
7for he is our God
and we are the people of his pasture,
the flock under his care.

Today, if you hear his voice,
8 do not harden your hearts as you did at Meribah,[a]
as you did that day at Massah[b] in the desert,
9where your fathers tested and tried me,
though they had seen what I did.
10For forty years I was angry with that generation;
I said, "They are a people whose hearts go astray,
and they have not known my ways."
11So I declared on oath in my anger,
"They shall never enter my rest."

Psalm 96

1Sing to the LORD a new song;
sing to the LORD, all the earth.
2Sing to the LORD, praise his name;
proclaim his salvation day after day.
3Declare his glory among the nations,
his marvelous deeds among all peoples.

4For great is the LORD and most worthy of praise;
he is to be feared above all gods.
5For all the gods of the nations are idols,
but the LORD made the heavens.
6Splendor and majesty are before him;
strength and glory are in his sanctuary.

7Ascribe to the LORD, O families of nations,
ascribe to the LORD glory and strength.
8Ascribe to the LORD the glory due his name;
bring an offering and come into his courts.
9Worship the LORD in the splendor of his[c] holiness;
tremble before him, all the earth.

10Say among the nations, "The LORD reigns."
The world is firmly established, it cannot be moved;
he will judge the peoples with equity.
11Let the heavens rejoice, let the earth be glad;
let the sea resound, and all that is in it;
12 let the fields be jubilant, and everything in them.
Then all the trees of the forest will sing for joy;
13 they will sing before the LORD, for he comes,
he comes to judge the earth.
He will judge the world in righteousness
and the peoples in his truth.

Psalm 97

1The LORD reigns, let the earth be glad;
let the distant shores rejoice.

2Clouds and thick darkness surround him;
righteousness and justice are the foundation of his throne.
3Fire goes before him
and consumes his foes on every side.
4His lightning lights up the world;
the earth sees and trembles.
5The mountains melt like wax before the LORD,
before the Lord of all the earth.
6The heavens proclaim his righteousness,
and all the peoples see his glory.

7All who worship images are put to shame,
those who boast in idols—
worship him, all you gods!

8Zion hears and rejoices
and the villages of Judah are glad
because of your judgments, O LORD.
9For you, O LORD, are the Most High over all the earth;
you are exalted far above all gods.

10Let those who love the LORD hate evil,
for he guards the lives of his faithful ones
and delivers them from the hand of the wicked.
11Light is shed upon the righteous
and joy on the upright in heart.
12Rejoice in the LORD, you who are righteous,
and praise his holy name.

[a]8 *Meribah* means *quarreling.* [b]8 *Massah* means *testing.*
[c]9 Or *LORD with the splendor of*

97:10–12 God is always quick to help those who hate evil and want to please him. God has linked our happiness to our holiness. If we want real joy, we need to surrender our lives to God.

Psalm 98

A psalm.

[1]Sing to the LORD a new song,
for he has done marvelous things;
his right hand and his holy arm
have worked salvation for him.
[2]The LORD has made his salvation known
and revealed his righteousness to the nations.
[3]He has remembered his love
and his faithfulness to the house of Israel;
all the ends of the earth have seen
the salvation of our God.

[4]Shout for joy to the LORD, all the earth,
burst into jubilant song with music;
[5]make music to the LORD with the harp,
with the harp and the sound of singing,
[6]with trumpets and the blast of the ram's horn—
shout for joy before the LORD, the King.

[7]Let the sea resound, and everything in it,
the world, and all who live in it.
[8]Let the rivers clap their hands,
let the mountains sing together for joy;
[9]let them sing before the LORD,
for he comes to judge the earth.
He will judge the world in righteousness
and the peoples with equity.

Psalm 99

[1]The LORD reigns,
let the nations tremble;
he sits enthroned between the cherubim,
let the earth shake.
[2]Great is the LORD in Zion;
he is exalted over all the nations.
[3]Let them praise your great and awesome name—
he is holy.

[4]The King is mighty, he loves justice—
you have established equity;
in Jacob you have done
what is just and right.
[5]Exalt the LORD our God
and worship at his footstool;
he is holy.

[6]Moses and Aaron were among his priests,
Samuel was among those who called on his name;
they called on the LORD
and he answered them.
[7]He spoke to them from the pillar of cloud;
they kept his statutes and the decrees he gave them.

[8]O LORD our God,
you answered them;
you were to Israel[a] a forgiving God,
though you punished their misdeeds.[b]
[9]Exalt the LORD our God
and worship at his holy mountain,
for the LORD our God is holy.

Psalm 100

A psalm. For giving thanks.

[1]Shout for joy to the LORD, all the earth.
[2] Worship the LORD with gladness;
come before him with joyful songs.
[3]Know that the LORD is God.
It is he who made us, and we are his[c];
we are his people, the sheep of his pasture.

[4]Enter his gates with thanksgiving
and his courts with praise;
give thanks to him and praise his name.
[5]For the LORD is good and his love endures forever;
his faithfulness continues through all generations.

Psalm 101

Of David. A psalm.

[1]I will sing of your love and justice;
to you, O LORD, I will sing praise.
[2]I will be careful to lead a blameless life—
when will you come to me?

I will walk in my house
with blameless heart.
[3]I will set before my eyes
no vile thing.

The deeds of faithless men I hate;
they will not cling to me.
[4]Men of perverse heart shall be far from me;
I will have nothing to do with evil.

[5]Whoever slanders his neighbor in secret,
him will I put to silence;

[a]8 Hebrew *them* [b]8 Or / *an avenger of the wrongs done to them* [c]3 Or *and not we ourselves*

98:1–3 God revealed his power to the whole world by rescuing the people of Israel. We are able to win seemingly impossible battles, just as the Israelites did, because God is powerfully active in our lives. Having found victory, we can share our story of God's deliverance with others. Our witness can give them the hope and wisdom they need to experience God's help in their own lives.
99:1–9 God is loving and holy. His love causes him to show mercy toward us, but we can't please him if we continue in sin, because God is also holy. We must not presume upon God's loving and forgiving nature, for he also loves justice. Continuing in sin will only result in terrible consequences.
100:1–5 We have many reasons to rejoice: We live in God's favor, under his continual care, and we experience his love each day. Such a realization should fill us with gratitude and praise each time we come before God in prayer. God never stops showering us with his compassion; he always keeps his promises to help us when we repent and call on him.

whoever has haughty eyes and a proud
heart,
him will I not endure.

6My eyes will be on the faithful in the land,
that they may dwell with me;
he whose walk is blameless
will minister to me.

7No one who practices deceit
will dwell in my house;
no one who speaks falsely
will stand in my presence.

8Every morning I will put to silence
all the wicked in the land;
I will cut off every evildoer
from the city of the LORD.

Psalm 102

A prayer of an afflicted man. When he is faint and pours out his lament before the LORD.

1Hear my prayer, O LORD;
let my cry for help come to you.
2Do not hide your face from me
when I am in distress.
Turn your ear to me;
when I call, answer me quickly.
3For my days vanish like smoke;
my bones burn like glowing embers.
4My heart is blighted and withered like
grass;
I forget to eat my food.
5Because of my loud groaning
I am reduced to skin and bones.
6I am like a desert owl,
like an owl among the ruins.
7I lie awake; I have become
like a bird alone on a roof.
8All day long my enemies taunt me;
those who rail against me use my name
as a curse.
9For I eat ashes as my food
and mingle my drink with tears
10because of your great wrath,
for you have taken me up and thrown
me aside.
11My days are like the evening shadow;
I wither away like grass.

12But you, O LORD, sit enthroned forever;
your renown endures through all
generations.
13You will arise and have compassion on
Zion,
for it is time to show favor to her;
the appointed time has come.
14For her stones are dear to your servants;
her very dust moves them to pity.
15The nations will fear the name of the LORD,
all the kings of the earth will revere your
glory.
16For the LORD will rebuild Zion
and appear in his glory.
17He will respond to the prayer of the
destitute;
he will not despise their plea.

18Let this be written for a future generation,
that a people not yet created may praise
the LORD:
19"The LORD looked down from his sanctuary
on high,
from heaven he viewed the earth,
20to hear the groans of the prisoners
and release those condemned to death."
21So the name of the LORD will be declared
in Zion
and his praise in Jerusalem
22when the peoples and the kingdoms
assemble to worship the LORD.

23In the course of my life[a] he broke my
strength;
he cut short my days.
24So I said:
"Do not take me away, O my God, in
the midst of my days;
your years go on through all generations.
25In the beginning you laid the foundations
of the earth,
and the heavens are the work of your
hands.
26They will perish, but you remain;
they will all wear out like a garment.
Like clothing you will change them
and they will be discarded.
27But you remain the same,
and your years will never end.
28The children of your servants will live in
your presence;
their descendants will be established
before you."

Psalm 103

Of David.

1Praise the LORD, O my soul;
all my inmost being, praise his holy
name.

[a]23 Or *By his power*

102:1–7 When we are beaten down by life's trials, we can call upon God to help us. In such times we may feel as if our lives are withering like grass under the scorching sun. Like the psalmist, our agony may be so great that we have no desire even to eat. When there is no apparent solution to be found, we need to admit our lack of power and trust God to help us through the pain. No matter the situation, God is still able to deliver us.

102:17–22 God responds to people who are downtrodden and in distress. Sometimes we may feel that God is too busy or distant, but he is always intimately concerned for us. God wants us to have a joyful and meaningful life. When we seek God and surrender to him, he will reach out to us. Our natural response to him should be one of joyful praise; we should want to tell others about what God has done for us.

²Praise the LORD, O my soul,
and forget not all his benefits—
³who forgives all your sins
and heals all your diseases,
⁴who redeems your life from the pit
and crowns you with love and
compassion,
⁵who satisfies your desires with good things
so that your youth is renewed like the
eagle's.

⁶The LORD works righteousness
and justice for all the oppressed.

⁷He made known his ways to Moses,
his deeds to the people of Israel:
⁸The LORD is compassionate and gracious,
slow to anger, abounding in love.
⁹He will not always accuse,
nor will he harbor his anger forever;
¹⁰he does not treat us as our sins deserve
or repay us according to our iniquities.
¹¹For as high as the heavens are above the
earth,
so great is his love for those who fear
him;
¹²as far as the east is from the west,
so far has he removed our transgressions
from us.
¹³As a father has compassion on his children,
so the LORD has compassion on those
who fear him;
¹⁴for he knows how we are formed,
he remembers that we are dust.
¹⁵As for man, his days are like grass,
he flourishes like a flower of the field;
¹⁶the wind blows over it and it is gone,
and its place remembers it no more.
¹⁷But from everlasting to everlasting
the LORD's love is with those who fear
him,
and his righteousness with their
children's children—
¹⁸with those who keep his covenant
and remember to obey his precepts.

¹⁹The LORD has established his throne in
heaven,
and his kingdom rules over all.

²⁰Praise the LORD, you his angels,
you mighty ones who do his bidding,
who obey his word.
²¹Praise the LORD, all his heavenly hosts,
you his servants who do his will.

103:8–12 David praised God for his great love and kindness. We have all failed, and our sins have hurt other people and damaged or destroyed our relationships. When we seek to make restitution, others may have a hard time forgiving us. God, on the other hand, is waiting to forgive us. All we have to do is repent of our sin and surrender our lives to him. We should be encouraged by this wonderful truth.

103:13–18 In the same manner that a loving father cares about his children, God has compassion on all who call on him. God's love never ceases. We can be assured that he will be faithful to all his promises to us.

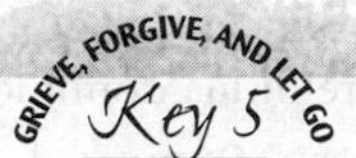

Trusting in God's Forgiveness

Psalm 103:1–22 Many of us have a hard time believing that God can truly forgive us. We may think, *After all I've done, no one can completely forgive me.* Maybe we feel that we have done such horrible things or hurt people so badly that there would be no way to completely erase our sins. Yet if we could be forgiven, who could ever *forget* the things we have done?

When we think of people we have hurt, perhaps our fears are well founded. But when it comes to God, we need to remember that his ways are higher than our ways (see Isaiah 55:8–9). The psalmist wrote, "[God] does not treat us as our sins deserve or repay us according to our iniquities. For as high as the heavens are above the earth, so great is his love for those who fear him; as far as the east is from the west, so far has he removed our transgressions from us" (Psalm 103:10–12). God also promised his people, "Come now, let us reason together,' says the LORD. 'Though your sins are like scarlet, they shall be as white as snow; though they are red as crimson, they shall be like wool" (Isaiah 1:18). And again, God asserts, "I, even I, am he who blots out your transgressions, for my own sake, and remembers your sins no more" (Isaiah 43:25).

When we fully trust that God can completely forgive us, we pave the way for true spiritual renewal. We can come to God because of the blood of Jesus Christ, whose death on the cross provided the payment for all our sins. We may keep track of our own failures, adding every sin to the long list we have written out against ourselves. But God doesn't remember our past sins once we have been forgiven; in his eyes we are clean. And believing that God forgives us completely will enable us to forgive others as well.

Turn to Proverbs 3.

22Praise the LORD, all his works
everywhere in his dominion.

Praise the LORD, O my soul.

Psalm 104

1Praise the LORD, O my soul.

O LORD my God, you are very great;
you are clothed with splendor and majesty.
2He wraps himself in light as with a garment;
he stretches out the heavens like a tent
3 and lays the beams of his upper chambers on their waters.
He makes the clouds his chariot
and rides on the wings of the wind.
4He makes winds his messengers,[a]
flames of fire his servants.

5He set the earth on its foundations;
it can never be moved.
6You covered it with the deep as with a garment;
the waters stood above the mountains.
7But at your rebuke the waters fled,
at the sound of your thunder they took to flight;
8they flowed over the mountains,
they went down into the valleys,
to the place you assigned for them.
9You set a boundary they cannot cross;
never again will they cover the earth.

10He makes springs pour water into the ravines;
it flows between the mountains.
11They give water to all the beasts of the field;
the wild donkeys quench their thirst.
12The birds of the air nest by the waters;
they sing among the branches.
13He waters the mountains from his upper chambers;
the earth is satisfied by the fruit of his work.
14He makes grass grow for the cattle,
and plants for man to cultivate—
bringing forth food from the earth:
15wine that gladdens the heart of man,
oil to make his face shine,
and bread that sustains his heart.
16The trees of the LORD are well watered,
the cedars of Lebanon that he planted.
17There the birds make their nests;
the stork has its home in the pine trees.
18The high mountains belong to the wild goats;
the crags are a refuge for the coneys.[b]
19The moon marks off the seasons,
and the sun knows when to go down.
20You bring darkness, it becomes night,
and all the beasts of the forest prowl.
21The lions roar for their prey
and seek their food from God.
22The sun rises, and they steal away;
they return and lie down in their dens.
23Then man goes out to his work,
to his labor until evening.

24How many are your works, O LORD!
In wisdom you made them all;
the earth is full of your creatures.
25There is the sea, vast and spacious,
teeming with creatures beyond number—
living things both large and small.
26There the ships go to and fro,
and the leviathan, which you formed to frolic there.

27These all look to you
to give them their food at the proper time.
28When you give it to them,
they gather it up;
when you open your hand,
they are satisfied with good things.
29When you hide your face,
they are terrified;
when you take away their breath,
they die and return to the dust.
30When you send your Spirit,
they are created,
and you renew the face of the earth.

31May the glory of the LORD endure forever;
may the LORD rejoice in his works—
32he who looks at the earth, and it trembles,
who touches the mountains, and they smoke.

33I will sing to the LORD all my life;
I will sing praise to my God as long as I live.
34May my meditation be pleasing to him,
as I rejoice in the LORD.

[a]4 Or *angels* [b]18 That is, the hyrax or rock badger

104:1–24 God created the world to function according to his good plan. God also created us to live joyful and healthy lives. But to do so we must obey his instructions. When we go our own way, we will suffer painful consequences. If we seek to live according to God's plan revealed in the Bible, we will discover peace and harmony with God and with others around us.

104:19–24 The writer of this psalm praised God for his amazing control over the created world. God uses the sun to regulate the days and the moon to mark the months. Through these stars God also defines the seasons of the year and the movement of the tides. Such power and control over the world should reassure us that we are under the keeping of someone who is more than able to take care of us.

104:25–35 God is sovereign over everything. Every living thing depends on him for food and life. We must realize that if we remove ourselves from God's presence, from his control and care, we are without hope, just as the earth would be without hope if God should withdraw himself from it.

35But may sinners vanish from the earth
and the wicked be no more.

Praise the LORD, O my soul.

Praise the LORD.[a]

Psalm 105

1Give thanks to the LORD, call on his name;
make known among the nations what he
has done.
2Sing to him, sing praise to him;
tell of all his wonderful acts.
3Glory in his holy name;
let the hearts of those who seek the LORD
rejoice.
4Look to the LORD and his strength;
seek his face always.

5Remember the wonders he has done,
his miracles, and the judgments he
pronounced,
6O descendants of Abraham his servant,
O sons of Jacob, his chosen ones.
7He is the LORD our God;
his judgments are in all the earth.

8He remembers his covenant forever,
the word he commanded, for a thousand
generations,
9the covenant he made with Abraham,
the oath he swore to Isaac.
10He confirmed it to Jacob as a decree,
to Israel as an everlasting covenant:
11"To you I will give the land of Canaan
as the portion you will inherit."

12When they were but few in number,
few indeed, and strangers in it,
13they wandered from nation to nation,
from one kingdom to another.
14He allowed no one to oppress them;
for their sake he rebuked kings:
15"Do not touch my anointed ones;
do my prophets no harm."

16He called down famine on the land
and destroyed all their supplies of food;
17and he sent a man before them—
Joseph, sold as a slave.
18They bruised his feet with shackles,
his neck was put in irons,
19till what he foretold came to pass,
till the word of the LORD proved him
true.
20The king sent and released him,
the ruler of peoples set him free.
21He made him master of his household,
ruler over all he possessed,
22to instruct his princes as he pleased
and teach his elders wisdom.

23Then Israel entered Egypt;
Jacob lived as an alien in the land of
Ham.
24The LORD made his people very fruitful;
he made them too numerous for their
foes,
25whose hearts he turned to hate his people,
to conspire against his servants.
26He sent Moses his servant,
and Aaron, whom he had chosen.
27They performed his miraculous signs
among them,
his wonders in the land of Ham.
28He sent darkness and made the land dark—
for had they not rebelled against his
words?
29He turned their waters into blood,
causing their fish to die.
30Their land teemed with frogs,
which went up into the bedrooms of
their rulers.
31He spoke, and there came swarms of flies,
and gnats throughout their country.
32He turned their rain into hail,
with lightning throughout their land;
33he struck down their vines and fig trees
and shattered the trees of their country.
34He spoke, and the locusts came,
grasshoppers without number;
35they ate up every green thing in their land,
ate up the produce of their soil.
36Then he struck down all the firstborn in
their land,
the firstfruits of all their manhood.

37He brought out Israel, laden with silver and
gold,
and from among their tribes no one
faltered.
38Egypt was glad when they left,
because dread of Israel had fallen on
them.
39He spread out a cloud as a covering,
and a fire to give light at night.
40They asked, and he brought them quail
and satisfied them with the bread of
heaven.
41He opened the rock, and water gushed out;
like a river it flowed in the desert.

42For he remembered his holy promise
given to his servant Abraham.
43He brought out his people with rejoicing,
his chosen ones with shouts of joy;

[a]35 Hebrew *Hallelu Yah*; in the Septuagint this line stands at the beginning of Psalm 105.

105:5–15 God always keeps his word. When he makes a promise, he fulfills it. God promised Abraham that his descendants would inherit the land of Canaan. Generations after Abraham's death, the Israelites entered Canaan under Joshua's leadership. Sometimes God takes time to fulfill his promises. We may grow impatient or be tempted to give up on God. But just because we don't see immediate results we shouldn't conclude that God isn't working.
105:39–45 God is able to care for his people. He responds to our prayers—even our complaints—and meets all our needs. When we surrender our lives to God, we can be sure we are in good hands.

44he gave them the lands of the nations,
and they fell heir to what others had toiled for—
45that they might keep his precepts
and observe his laws.

Praise the LORD.[a]

Psalm 106

1Praise the LORD.[b]

Give thanks to the LORD, for he is good;
his love endures forever.
2Who can proclaim the mighty acts of the LORD
or fully declare his praise?
3Blessed are they who maintain justice,
who constantly do what is right.
4Remember me, O LORD, when you show favor to your people,
come to my aid when you save them,
5that I may enjoy the prosperity of your chosen ones,
that I may share in the joy of your nation
and join your inheritance in giving praise.

6We have sinned, even as our fathers did;
we have done wrong and acted wickedly.
7When our fathers were in Egypt,
they gave no thought to your miracles;
they did not remember your many kindnesses,
and they rebelled by the sea, the Red Sea.[c]
8Yet he saved them for his name's sake,
to make his mighty power known.
9He rebuked the Red Sea, and it dried up;
he led them through the depths as through a desert.
10He saved them from the hand of the foe;
from the hand of the enemy he redeemed them.
11The waters covered their adversaries;
not one of them survived.
12Then they believed his promises
and sang his praise.

13But they soon forgot what he had done
and did not wait for his counsel.
14In the desert they gave in to their craving;
in the wasteland they put God to the test.
15So he gave them what they asked for,
but sent a wasting disease upon them.

16In the camp they grew envious of Moses
and of Aaron, who was consecrated to the LORD.
17The earth opened up and swallowed Dathan;
it buried the company of Abiram.
18Fire blazed among their followers;
a flame consumed the wicked.

19At Horeb they made a calf
and worshiped an idol cast from metal.
20They exchanged their Glory
for an image of a bull, which eats grass.
21They forgot the God who saved them,
who had done great things in Egypt,
22miracles in the land of Ham
and awesome deeds by the Red Sea.
23So he said he would destroy them—
had not Moses, his chosen one,
stood in the breach before him
to keep his wrath from destroying them.

24Then they despised the pleasant land;
they did not believe his promise.
25They grumbled in their tents
and did not obey the LORD.
26So he swore to them with uplifted hand
that he would make them fall in the desert,
27make their descendants fall among the nations
and scatter them throughout the lands.
28They yoked themselves to the Baal of Peor
and ate sacrifices offered to lifeless gods;
29they provoked the LORD to anger by their wicked deeds,
and a plague broke out among them.
30But Phinehas stood up and intervened,
and the plague was checked.
31This was credited to him as righteousness
for endless generations to come.
32By the waters of Meribah they angered the LORD,
and trouble came to Moses because of them;
33for they rebelled against the Spirit of God,
and rash words came from Moses' lips.[d]

34They did not destroy the peoples
as the LORD had commanded them,
35but they mingled with the nations
and adopted their customs.
36They worshiped their idols,
which became a snare to them.
37They sacrificed their sons
and their daughters to demons.
38They shed innocent blood,

[a]45 Hebrew *Hallelu Yah* [b]1 Hebrew *Hallelu Yah;* also in verse 48 [c]7 Hebrew *Yam Suph;* that is, Sea of Reeds; also in verses 9 and 22 [d]33 Or *against his spirit, / and rash words came from his lips*

106:6–9 The psalmist reflects on the failures of the past and present generations in Israel. He notes that God was good to his people, often delivering them from their troubles despite their sin and rebelliousness. As we look back over our lives, we need to honestly assess our sins, taking responsibility for them and seeking forgiveness from those we have hurt. Just as God helped the Israelites redirect their course, he will forgive us and redeem our lives as well.

the blood of their sons and daughters,
whom they sacrificed to the idols of
Canaan,
and the land was desecrated by their
blood.
39They defiled themselves by what they did;
by their deeds they prostituted
themselves.

40Therefore the LORD was angry with his
people
and abhorred his inheritance.
41He handed them over to the nations,
and their foes ruled over them.
42Their enemies oppressed them
and subjected them to their power.
43Many times he delivered them,
but they were bent on rebellion
and they wasted away in their sin.
44But he took note of their distress
when he heard their cry;
45for their sake he remembered his covenant
and out of his great love he relented.
46He caused them to be pitied
by all who held them captive.

47Save us, O LORD our God,
and gather us from the nations,
that we may give thanks to your holy name
and glory in your praise.

48Praise be to the LORD, the God of Israel,
from everlasting to everlasting.
Let all the people say, "Amen!"
Praise the LORD.

BOOK V

Psalms 107–150

Psalm 107

1Give thanks to the LORD, for he is good;
his love endures forever.
2Let the redeemed of the LORD say this—
those he redeemed from the hand of the
foe,
3those he gathered from the lands,
from east and west, from north and
south.[a]
4Some wandered in desert wastelands,
finding no way to a city where they
could settle.
5They were hungry and thirsty,
and their lives ebbed away.
6Then they cried out to the LORD in their
trouble,
and he delivered them from their
distress.
7He led them by a straight way
to a city where they could settle.
8Let them give thanks to the LORD for his
unfailing love
and his wonderful deeds for men,
9for he satisfies the thirsty
and fills the hungry with good things.

10Some sat in darkness and the deepest
gloom,
prisoners suffering in iron chains,
11for they had rebelled against the words of
God
and despised the counsel of the Most
High.
12So he subjected them to bitter labor;
they stumbled, and there was no one to
help.
13Then they cried to the LORD in their
trouble,
and he saved them from their distress.
14He brought them out of darkness and the
deepest gloom
and broke away their chains.
15Let them give thanks to the LORD for his
unfailing love
and his wonderful deeds for men,
16for he breaks down gates of bronze
and cuts through bars of iron.

17Some became fools through their rebellious
ways
and suffered affliction because of their
iniquities.
18They loathed all food
and drew near the gates of death.
19Then they cried to the LORD in their
trouble,
and he saved them from their distress.
20He sent forth his word and healed them;
he rescued them from the grave.
21Let them give thanks to the LORD for his
unfailing love
and his wonderful deeds for men.
22Let them sacrifice thank offerings
and tell of his works with songs of joy.

23Others went out on the sea in ships;
they were merchants on the mighty
waters.
24They saw the works of the LORD,
his wonderful deeds in the deep.
25For he spoke and stirred up a tempest
that lifted high the waves.

[a]3 Hebrew *north and the sea*

107:10–16 When we reject God and his plan, we live in spiritual darkness and suffer the consequences of disobedience. Yet, as the psalmist notes, we should not despair. God can deliver us from our bondage to sin. If we repent of our sins and seek God's forgiveness, he will redeem us.
107:23–32 Sometimes we may feel that we are sailing in a small ship, plowing through stormy seas and about to sink. The world around us can seem dark and friendless. The longer the storm rages, the more we lose all hope of rescue. But God can turn our stormy lives into calm and peaceful seas; he can restore our joy in the midst of trouble.

26They mounted up to the heavens and went down to the depths;
in their peril their courage melted away.
27They reeled and staggered like drunken men;
they were at their wits' end.
28Then they cried out to the LORD in their trouble,
and he brought them out of their distress.
29He stilled the storm to a whisper;
the waves of the sea were hushed.
30They were glad when it grew calm,
and he guided them to their desired haven.
31Let them give thanks to the LORD for his unfailing love
and his wonderful deeds for men.
32Let them exalt him in the assembly of the people
and praise him in the council of the elders.

33He turned rivers into a desert,
flowing springs into thirsty ground,
34and fruitful land into a salt waste,
because of the wickedness of those who lived there.
35He turned the desert into pools of water
and the parched ground into flowing springs;
36there he brought the hungry to live,
and they founded a city where they could settle.
37They sowed fields and planted vineyards
that yielded a fruitful harvest;
38he blessed them, and their numbers greatly increased,
and he did not let their herds diminish.

39Then their numbers decreased, and they were humbled
by oppression, calamity and sorrow;
40he who pours contempt on nobles
made them wander in a trackless waste.
41But he lifted the needy out of their affliction
and increased their families like flocks.
42The upright see and rejoice,
but all the wicked shut their mouths.

43Whoever is wise, let him heed these things
and consider the great love of the LORD.

Psalm 108

A song. A psalm of David.

1My heart is steadfast, O God;
I will sing and make music with all my soul.
2Awake, harp and lyre!
I will awaken the dawn.
3I will praise you, O LORD, among the nations;
I will sing of you among the peoples.
4For great is your love, higher than the heavens;
your faithfulness reaches to the skies.
5Be exalted, O God, above the heavens,
and let your glory be over all the earth.

6Save us and help us with your right hand,
that those you love may be delivered.
7God has spoken from his sanctuary:
"In triumph I will parcel out Shechem
and measure off the Valley of Succoth.
8Gilead is mine, Manasseh is mine;
Ephraim is my helmet,
Judah my scepter.
9Moab is my washbasin,
upon Edom I toss my sandal;
over Philistia I shout in triumph."

10Who will bring me to the fortified city?
Who will lead me to Edom?
11Is it not you, O God, you who have rejected us
and no longer go out with our armies?
12Give us aid against the enemy,
for the help of man is worthless.
13With God we will gain the victory,
and he will trample down our enemies.

Psalm 109

For the director of music. Of David. A psalm.

1O God, whom I praise,
do not remain silent,
2for wicked and deceitful men
have opened their mouths against me;
they have spoken against me with lying tongues.
3With words of hatred they surround me;
they attack me without cause.
4In return for my friendship they accuse me,
but I am a man of prayer.
5They repay me evil for good,
and hatred for my friendship.

108:1–6 We should let the joy of our salvation spill out, releasing our praise to God and sharing our message of hope with others in need. Our word of testimony may lead others to experience the joy we feel as we draw closer to God.

108:7–13 There is no resource for true spiritual renewal other than the strength offered by our gracious God. It is futile to trust anyone else for our victory. God alone can give us the power to overcome our sins. Ultimately he is the one who conquers for us. We must see the truth of our desperate situation, turn from our wicked ways, confess our need for help and surrender our lives to his care. Then God will redirect the course of our lives as he redeems and restores us.

109:1–5 We all know what it feels like to be condemned by others—sometimes unjustly. When feeling condemnation, we need to seek relief from God. He will fill our hearts with his love and help us forgive those who are speaking out against us. We can rest in him and try to reconcile with the people who are hurting us.

6Appoint[a] an evil man[b] to oppose him;
let an accuser[c] stand at his right hand.
7When he is tried, let him be found guilty,
and may his prayers condemn him.
8May his days be few;
may another take his place of leadership.
9May his children be fatherless
and his wife a widow.
10May his children be wandering beggars;
may they be driven[d] from their ruined homes.
11May a creditor seize all he has;
may strangers plunder the fruits of his labor.
12May no one extend kindness to him
or take pity on his fatherless children.
13May his descendants be cut off,
their names blotted out from the next generation.
14May the iniquity of his fathers be remembered before the LORD;
may the sin of his mother never be blotted out.
15May their sins always remain before the LORD,
that he may cut off the memory of them from the earth.

16For he never thought of doing a kindness,
but hounded to death the poor
and the needy and the brokenhearted.
17He loved to pronounce a curse—
may it[e] come on him;
he found no pleasure in blessing—
may it be[f] far from him.
18He wore cursing as his garment;
it entered into his body like water,
into his bones like oil.
19May it be like a cloak wrapped about him,
like a belt tied forever around him.
20May this be the LORD's payment to my accusers,
to those who speak evil of me.

21But you, O Sovereign LORD,
deal well with me for your name's sake;
out of the goodness of your love, deliver me.
22For I am poor and needy,
and my heart is wounded within me.
23I fade away like an evening shadow;
I am shaken off like a locust.
24My knees give way from fasting;
my body is thin and gaunt.
25I am an object of scorn to my accusers;
when they see me, they shake their heads.

26Help me, O LORD my God;
save me in accordance with your love.
27Let them know that it is your hand,
that you, O LORD, have done it.
28They may curse, but you will bless;
when they attack they will be put to shame,
but your servant will rejoice.
29My accusers will be clothed with disgrace
and wrapped in shame as in a cloak.

30With my mouth I will greatly extol the LORD;
in the great throng I will praise him.
31For he stands at the right hand of the needy one,
to save his life from those who condemn him.

Psalm 110

Of David. A psalm.

1The LORD says to my Lord:
"Sit at my right hand
until I make your enemies
a footstool for your feet."

2The LORD will extend your mighty scepter from Zion;
you will rule in the midst of your enemies.
3Your troops will be willing
on your day of battle.
Arrayed in holy majesty,
from the womb of the dawn
you will receive the dew of your youth.[g]

4The LORD has sworn
and will not change his mind:
"You are a priest forever,
in the order of Melchizedek."

5The Lord is at your right hand;
he will crush kings on the day of his wrath.
6He will judge the nations, heaping up the dead
and crushing the rulers of the whole earth.

[a]6 Or *⌞They say:⌟ "Appoint* (with quotation marks at the end of verse 19) [b]6 Or *the Evil One* [c]6 Or *let Satan* [d]10 Septuagint; Hebrew *sought* [e]17 Or *curse, / and it has* [f]17 Or *blessing, / and it is* [g]3 Or */ your young men will come to you like the dew*

109:16–20 David spoke to God about the undeserved attacks he had endured. All of us have suffered injustice; we all know the feelings that accompany innocent suffering. When we are hurt without just cause, we may be tempted to lash out in revenge. Revenge never resolves our pain or hurt. We need to release our anger; it will only lead to more suffering. We can trust God to bring justice according to his timetable.

109:21–31 As God's children, we don't need to pretend to be strong and self-sufficient. When we are weak, God is still strong (see 2 Corinthians 12:9). Rather than try to hide our weakness, we should seek God and admit the truth of our situation. God will rescue us whenever we call on him with a repentant heart. If we allow our pride to keep us from calling out to God when we are weak, we are in greater danger than we realize.

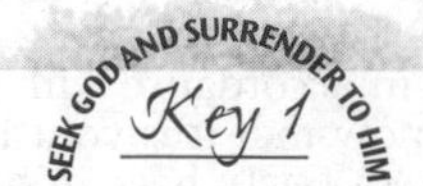

The Starting Point

Psalm 111:1–10 Where do we begin in our search for spiritual renewal? We must start with the realization that spiritual renewal comes from God. It is not so much that we seek the *experience* of spiritual renewal as we seek the *one* who renews our spirits.

When needy people came to Jesus, he often redirected their thinking. He taught them to lift their eyes off of their own daily necessities and seek God first. He told them, "Seek first his kingdom and his righteousness, and all these things will be given to you as well" (Matthew 6:33). We cannot seek the kingdom of God without bowing to the King himself. In the same way, the psalmist encourages his listeners to look to God first. God will then meet their needs: "He has caused his wonders to be remembered; the LORD is gracious and compassionate. He provides food for those who fear him; he remembers his covenant forever" (111:4–5).

So it is with our spiritual hunger. Spiritual renewal does not come from merely seeking spiritual renewal. Seeking renewal results in a temporary emotional high, lacking the true substance that God alone can provide. Instead, we must seek God and surrender to his rule in our lives if we are to find true spiritual renewal.

Turn to Jeremiah 17.

7He will drink from a brook beside the way[a];
therefore he will lift up his head.

Psalm 111[b]

1Praise the LORD.[c]

I will extol the LORD with all my heart
in the council of the upright and in the assembly.

2Great are the works of the LORD;
they are pondered by all who delight in them.
3Glorious and majestic are his deeds,
and his righteousness endures forever.
4He has caused his wonders to be remembered;
the LORD is gracious and compassionate.
5He provides food for those who fear him;
he remembers his covenant forever.
6He has shown his people the power of his works,
giving them the lands of other nations.
7The works of his hands are faithful and just;
all his precepts are trustworthy.
8They are steadfast for ever and ever,
done in faithfulness and uprightness.
9He provided redemption for his people;
he ordained his covenant forever—
holy and awesome is his name.

10The fear of the LORD is the beginning of wisdom;
all who follow his precepts have good understanding.
To him belongs eternal praise.

Psalm 112[b]

1Praise the LORD.[c]

Blessed is the man who fears the LORD,
who finds great delight in his commands.

[a]7 Or / *The One who grants succession will set him in authority* [b]This psalm is an acrostic poem, the lines of which begin with the successive letters of the Hebrew alphabet. [c]1 Hebrew *Hallelu Yah*

111:1–8 Through these words the psalmist illustrates that God's work in our lives has a twofold purpose—to accomplish our deliverance from bondage and to demonstrate God's power to others who need his help. Sharing our testimony of God's goodness will not only help others; it will also strengthen us spiritually.

111:9–10 We must never forget the ransom price God paid so that we might have access to him. God offered his only Son as a sacrifice so that we, unworthy as we are, can be restored to a godly and joyful life. God wants us to come to him! We can safely surrender our lives into his hands.

112:1–5 When we choose to surrender our lives to God and commit ourselves to doing his will, we enter into the joy that this passage is talking about. When difficulties arise and we are unsure about what to do, God will reveal his path to us and give us reason to rejoice.

2His children will be mighty in the land;
the generation of the upright will be blessed.
3Wealth and riches are in his house,
and his righteousness endures forever.
4Even in darkness light dawns for the upright,
for the gracious and compassionate and righteous man.[a]
5Good will come to him who is generous and lends freely,
who conducts his affairs with justice.
6Surely he will never be shaken;
a righteous man will be remembered forever.
7He will have no fear of bad news;
his heart is steadfast, trusting in the LORD.
8His heart is secure, he will have no fear;
in the end he will look in triumph on his foes.
9He has scattered abroad his gifts to the poor,
his righteousness endures forever;
his horn[b] will be lifted high in honor.

10The wicked man will see and be vexed,
he will gnash his teeth and waste away;
the longings of the wicked will come to nothing.

Psalm 113

1Praise the LORD.[c]

Praise, O servants of the LORD,
praise the name of the LORD.
2Let the name of the LORD be praised,
both now and forevermore.
3From the rising of the sun to the place where it sets,
the name of the LORD is to be praised.

4The LORD is exalted over all the nations,
his glory above the heavens.
5Who is like the LORD our God,
the One who sits enthroned on high,
6who stoops down to look
on the heavens and the earth?

7He raises the poor from the dust
and lifts the needy from the ash heap;
8he seats them with princes,
with the princes of their people.
9He settles the barren woman in her home
as a happy mother of children.

Praise the LORD.

Psalm 114

1When Israel came out of Egypt,
the house of Jacob from a people of foreign tongue,
2Judah became God's sanctuary,
Israel his dominion.

3The sea looked and fled,
the Jordan turned back;
4the mountains skipped like rams,
the hills like lambs.

5Why was it, O sea, that you fled,
O Jordan, that you turned back,
6you mountains, that you skipped like rams,
you hills, like lambs?

7Tremble, O earth, at the presence of the Lord,
at the presence of the God of Jacob,
8who turned the rock into a pool,
the hard rock into springs of water.

Psalm 115

1Not to us, O LORD, not to us
but to your name be the glory,
because of your love and faithfulness.

2Why do the nations say,
"Where is their God?"
3Our God is in heaven;
he does whatever pleases him.
4But their idols are silver and gold,
made by the hands of men.
5They have mouths, but cannot speak,
eyes, but they cannot see;
6they have ears, but cannot hear,
noses, but they cannot smell;
7they have hands, but cannot feel,
feet, but they cannot walk;
nor can they utter a sound with their throats.
8Those who make them will be like them,
and so will all who trust in them.

9O house of Israel, trust in the LORD—
he is their help and shield.

a4 Or / *for* ⌊*the* LORD⌋ *is gracious and compassionate and righteous* b9 *Horn* here symbolizes dignity.
c1 Hebrew *Hallelu Yah;* also in verse 9

112:6–10 Making changes in our lives to follow God's way won't make everyone happy. Some people will wonder why we no longer relate to them as we did in the past. Others may even criticize us or think we are being snobbish. But God is always with us, and with his help we will find strength to persevere in our spiritual journey.
114:1–6 God can perform amazing miracles on behalf of those who seek refuge in him. To bring courage to his readers, the psalmist lists some of God's amazing acts of deliverance throughout Israel's history. As we face difficulties in our lives, it is often helpful to recall events of God's deliverance—in Biblical history or in our own lives. These remembrances will give us hope to persevere and help us surrender our lives to God without reservation. God is truly awesome. He is worthy of our respect, obedience and praise.
115:1–8 Sometimes we look for help in places where it will never be found. If we don't ask God for help, all of these other resources are useless—they are only human inventions. God alone knows what we need and has the power to fill our lives with meaning and joy.

10O house of Aaron, trust in the LORD—
he is their help and shield.
11You who fear him, trust in the LORD—
he is their help and shield.

12The LORD remembers us and will bless us:
He will bless the house of Israel,
he will bless the house of Aaron,
13he will bless those who fear the LORD—
small and great alike.

14May the LORD make you increase,
both you and your children.
15May you be blessed by the LORD,
the Maker of heaven and earth.

16The highest heavens belong to the LORD,
but the earth he has given to man.
17It is not the dead who praise the LORD,
those who go down to silence;
18it is we who extol the LORD,
both now and forevermore.

Praise the LORD.[a]

Psalm 116

1I love the LORD, for he heard my voice;
he heard my cry for mercy.
2Because he turned his ear to me,
I will call on him as long as I live.

3The cords of death entangled me,
the anguish of the grave[b] came upon me;
I was overcome by trouble and sorrow.
4Then I called on the name of the LORD:
"O LORD, save me!"

5The LORD is gracious and righteous;
our God is full of compassion.
6The LORD protects the simplehearted;
when I was in great need, he saved me.

7Be at rest once more, O my soul,
for the LORD has been good to you.

8For you, O LORD, have delivered my soul from death,
my eyes from tears,
my feet from stumbling,
9that I may walk before the LORD
in the land of the living.
10I believed; therefore[c] I said,
"I am greatly afflicted."
11And in my dismay I said,
"All men are liars."

12How can I repay the LORD
for all his goodness to me?
13I will lift up the cup of salvation
and call on the name of the LORD.
14I will fulfill my vows to the LORD
in the presence of all his people.

15Precious in the sight of the LORD
is the death of his saints.
16O LORD, truly I am your servant;
I am your servant, the son of your maidservant[d];
you have freed me from my chains.

17I will sacrifice a thank offering to you
and call on the name of the LORD.
18I will fulfill my vows to the LORD
in the presence of all his people,
19in the courts of the house of the LORD—
in your midst, O Jerusalem.

Praise the LORD.[a]

Psalm 117

1Praise the LORD, all you nations;
extol him, all you peoples.
2For great is his love toward us,
and the faithfulness of the LORD endures forever.

Praise the LORD.[a]

Psalm 118

1Give thanks to the LORD, for he is good;
his love endures forever.

2Let Israel say:
"His love endures forever."
3Let the house of Aaron say:
"His love endures forever."
4Let those who fear the LORD say:
"His love endures forever."

5In my anguish I cried to the LORD,
and he answered by setting me free.
6The LORD is with me; I will not be afraid.
What can man do to me?
7The LORD is with me; he is my helper.
I will look in triumph on my enemies.

8It is better to take refuge in the LORD
than to trust in man.
9It is better to take refuge in the LORD
than to trust in princes.

10All the nations surrounded me,
but in the name of the LORD I cut them off.
11They surrounded me on every side,
but in the name of the LORD I cut them off.
12They swarmed around me like bees,
but they died out as quickly as burning thorns;
in the name of the LORD I cut them off.

13I was pushed back and about to fall,
but the LORD helped me.

[a] 18,19,2 Hebrew *Hallelu Yah* [b] 3 Hebrew *Sheol* [c] 10 Or *believed even when* [d] 16 Or *servant, your faithful son*

116:10–19 We could never repay God for what he has done to help us. But we can show our gratitude to God by fulfilling our promises to him and by praising him for restoring our lives.

14The LORD is my strength and my song;
he has become my salvation.

15Shouts of joy and victory
resound in the tents of the righteous:
"The LORD's right hand has done mighty
things!
16 The LORD's right hand is lifted high;
the LORD's right hand has done mighty
things!"

17I will not die but live,
and will proclaim what the LORD has
done.
18The LORD has chastened me severely,
but he has not given me over to death.

19Open for me the gates of righteousness;
I will enter and give thanks to the LORD.
20This is the gate of the LORD
through which the righteous may enter.
21I will give you thanks, for you answered
me;
you have become my salvation.

22The stone the builders rejected
has become the capstone;
23the LORD has done this,
and it is marvelous in our eyes.
24This is the day the LORD has made;
let us rejoice and be glad in it.

25O LORD, save us;
O LORD, grant us success.
26Blessed is he who comes in the name of
the LORD.
From the house of the LORD we bless
you.[a]
27The LORD is God,
and he has made his light shine upon
us.
With boughs in hand, join in the festal
procession
up[b] to the horns of the altar.

28You are my God, and I will give you
thanks;
you are my God, and I will exalt you.

29Give thanks to the LORD, for he is good;
his love endures forever.

Psalm 119[c]

א Aleph

1Blessed are they whose ways are blameless,
who walk according to the law of the
LORD.
2Blessed are they who keep his statutes
and seek him with all their heart.
3They do nothing wrong;
they walk in his ways.
4You have laid down precepts
that are to be fully obeyed.
5Oh, that my ways were steadfast
in obeying your decrees!
6Then I would not be put to shame
when I consider all your commands.
7I will praise you with an upright heart
as I learn your righteous laws.
8I will obey your decrees;
do not utterly forsake me.

ב Beth

9How can a young man keep his way pure?
By living according to your word.
10I seek you with all my heart;
do not let me stray from your
commands.
11I have hidden your word in my heart
that I might not sin against you.
12Praise be to you, O LORD;
teach me your decrees.
13With my lips I recount
all the laws that come from your mouth.
14I rejoice in following your statutes
as one rejoices in great riches.
15I meditate on your precepts
and consider your ways.
16I delight in your decrees;
I will not neglect your word.

ג Gimel

17Do good to your servant, and I will live;
I will obey your word.
18Open my eyes that I may see
wonderful things in your law.
19I am a stranger on earth;
do not hide your commands from me.
20My soul is consumed with longing
for your laws at all times.
21You rebuke the arrogant, who are cursed
and who stray from your commands.
22Remove from me scorn and contempt,
for I keep your statutes.
23Though rulers sit together and slander me,
your servant will meditate on your
decrees.
24Your statutes are my delight;
they are my counselors.

[a]26 The Hebrew is plural. [b]27 Or *Bind the festal sacrifice with ropes / and take it* [c]This psalm is an acrostic poem; the verses of each stanza begin with the same letter of the Hebrew alphabet.

118:22–25 God's ways are not the same as our ways (see Isaiah 55:8). What some people may cast aside as unfit for use, God uses for awe-inspiring work. We may feel that we, too, are beyond repair. We may think that God will never use us for anything significant. Yet God often uses the most unlikely people to work his greatest miracles, showing the world that he is indeed at work in our lives. As willing vessels of God's power, we can be transformed to make an impact on others that can exceed our wildest dreams.

119:9–16 As we learn about God through his Word, we learn about his ways. It seems only logical that we should do all we can to follow his plan. In the Bible, God has left clear guidelines telling us how he expects us to live. He has also promised that he will help us carry out his will if only we will ask him. Studying, pondering and applying God's Word should become a joyful experience that will implant God's truth firmly in our hearts and minds.

Hiding God's Word in Our Hearts

Psalm 119:1–11 What sorts of things find their way into our hearts and minds? We are not taking full responsibility for our lives when we expose ourselves to a constant barrage of ungodly words, music, or images. On the other hand, we can fill our hearts and minds with God's Word, and therefore create a defense against some of the evil messages the world sends our way.

The writer of Psalm 119 declared, "I seek you with all my heart; do not let me stray from your commands. I have hidden your word in my heart that I might not sin against you" (119:10–11). For us, "hiding" God's Word in our hearts essentially means memorizing and meditating on the Bible, which God uses to speak to us and to show us how we ought to live.

We have been given the responsibility to guard our hearts and to keep track of the things that we hide inside it. Hiding God's Word in our heart fosters spiritual growth by helping us guard against those things that displease God.

Turn to Hosea 3.

ד Daleth

25I am laid low in the dust;
preserve my life according to your word.
26I recounted my ways and you answered me;
teach me your decrees.
27Let me understand the teaching of your
precepts;
then I will meditate on your wonders.
28My soul is weary with sorrow;
strengthen me according to your word.
29Keep me from deceitful ways;
be gracious to me through your law.
30I have chosen the way of truth;
I have set my heart on your laws.
31I hold fast to your statutes, O LORD;
do not let me be put to shame.
32I run in the path of your commands,
for you have set my heart free.

ה He

33Teach me, O LORD, to follow your decrees;
then I will keep them to the end.
34Give me understanding, and I will keep
your law
and obey it with all my heart.
35Direct me in the path of your commands,
for there I find delight.
36Turn my heart toward your statutes
and not toward selfish gain.
37Turn my eyes away from worthless things;
preserve my life according to your
word.[a]
38Fulfill your promise to your servant,
so that you may be feared.
39Take away the disgrace I dread,
for your laws are good.
40How I long for your precepts!
Preserve my life in your righteousness.

ו Waw

41May your unfailing love come to me,
O LORD,
your salvation according to your
promise;
42then I will answer the one who taunts me,
for I trust in your word.
43Do not snatch the word of truth from my
mouth,
for I have put my hope in your laws.
44I will always obey your law,
for ever and ever.
45I will walk about in freedom,
for I have sought out your precepts.
46I will speak of your statutes before kings
and will not be put to shame,
47for I delight in your commands
because I love them.
48I lift up my hands to[b] your commands,
which I love,
and I meditate on your decrees.

[a]37 Two manuscripts of the Masoretic Text and Dead Sea Scrolls; most manuscripts of the Masoretic Text *life in your way* [b]48 Or *for*

ז Zayin

49Remember your word to your servant,
for you have given me hope.
50My comfort in my suffering is this:
Your promise preserves my life.
51The arrogant mock me without restraint,
but I do not turn from your law.
52I remember your ancient laws, O LORD,
and I find comfort in them.
53Indignation grips me because of the wicked,
who have forsaken your law.
54Your decrees are the theme of my song
wherever I lodge.
55In the night I remember your name,
O LORD,
and I will keep your law.
56This has been my practice:
I obey your precepts.

ח Heth

57You are my portion, O LORD;
I have promised to obey your words.
58I have sought your face with all my heart;
be gracious to me according to your
promise.
59I have considered my ways
and have turned my steps to your
statutes.
60I will hasten and not delay
to obey your commands.
61Though the wicked bind me with ropes,
I will not forget your law.
62At midnight I rise to give you thanks
for your righteous laws.
63I am a friend to all who fear you,
to all who follow your precepts.
64The earth is filled with your love, O LORD;
teach me your decrees.

ט Teth

65Do good to your servant
according to your word, O LORD.
66Teach me knowledge and good judgment,
for I believe in your commands.
67Before I was afflicted I went astray,
but now I obey your word.
68You are good, and what you do is good;
teach me your decrees.
69Though the arrogant have smeared me with
lies,
I keep your precepts with all my heart.
70Their hearts are callous and unfeeling,
but I delight in your law.
71It was good for me to be afflicted
so that I might learn your decrees.
72The law from your mouth is more precious
to me
than thousands of pieces of silver and
gold.

י Yodh

73Your hands made me and formed me;
give me understanding to learn your
commands.
74May those who fear you rejoice when they
see me,
for I have put my hope in your word.
75I know, O LORD, that your laws are
righteous,
and in faithfulness you have afflicted me.
76May your unfailing love be my comfort,
according to your promise to your
servant.
77Let your compassion come to me that I
may live,
for your law is my delight.
78May the arrogant be put to shame for
wronging me without cause;
but I will meditate on your precepts.
79May those who fear you turn to me,
those who understand your statutes.
80May my heart be blameless toward your
decrees,
that I may not be put to shame.

כ Kaph

81My soul faints with longing for your
salvation,
but I have put my hope in your word.
82My eyes fail, looking for your promise;
I say, "When will you comfort me?"
83Though I am like a wineskin in the smoke,
I do not forget your decrees.
84How long must your servant wait?
When will you punish my persecutors?
85The arrogant dig pitfalls for me,
contrary to your law.
86All your commands are trustworthy;
help me, for men persecute me without
cause.
87They almost wiped me from the earth,
but I have not forsaken your precepts.
88Preserve my life according to your love,
and I will obey the statutes of your
mouth.

119:57–64 We are called to seek out God's will for our lives. The Bible should be the first place we look to discover it. Once we have been given direction, we must not be merely hearers of God's Word (see James 1:22–25). We also need to take appropriate action once God's will is known; otherwise, we are no better off than we were before.

119:71–72 We should be thankful when God disciplines us for our sin. As painful as it may be, discipline drives us back to his truth, a truth far more valuable than all the riches of this world. God wants only what is best for us. We would be wise to learn from God's discipline rather than fight it. Discipline is given for our betterment, not our destruction.

119:73–80 As we obey God's revealed will, people will begin to see the changes in our lives and praise God. All of God's work—even his discipline—is accomplished because of his goodness and faithfulness. God wants us to live joyful lives. Our responsibility is to seek out God's will and follow it. Then, as God transforms us, we will be a living testimony of God's power.

ל Lamedh

89Your word, O LORD, is eternal;
it stands firm in the heavens.
90Your faithfulness continues through all generations;
you established the earth, and it endures.
91Your laws endure to this day,
for all things serve you.
92If your law had not been my delight,
I would have perished in my affliction.
93I will never forget your precepts,
for by them you have preserved my life.
94Save me, for I am yours;
I have sought out your precepts.
95The wicked are waiting to destroy me,
but I will ponder your statutes.
96To all perfection I see a limit;
but your commands are boundless.

מ Mem

97Oh, how I love your law!
I meditate on it all day long.
98Your commands make me wiser than my enemies,
for they are ever with me.
99I have more insight than all my teachers,
for I meditate on your statutes.
100I have more understanding than the elders,
for I obey your precepts.
101I have kept my feet from every evil path
so that I might obey your word.
102I have not departed from your laws,
for you yourself have taught me.
103How sweet are your words to my taste,
sweeter than honey to my mouth!
104I gain understanding from your precepts;
therefore I hate every wrong path.

נ Nun

105Your word is a lamp to my feet
and a light for my path.
106I have taken an oath and confirmed it,
that I will follow your righteous laws.
107I have suffered much;
preserve my life, O LORD, according to your word.
108Accept, O LORD, the willing praise of my mouth,
and teach me your laws.
109Though I constantly take my life in my hands,
I will not forget your law.
110The wicked have set a snare for me,
but I have not strayed from your precepts.
111Your statutes are my heritage forever;
they are the joy of my heart.
112My heart is set on keeping your decrees
to the very end.

ס Samekh

113I hate double-minded men,
but I love your law.
114You are my refuge and my shield;
I have put my hope in your word.
115Away from me, you evildoers,
that I may keep the commands of my God!
116Sustain me according to your promise, and I will live;
do not let my hopes be dashed.
117Uphold me, and I will be delivered;
I will always have regard for your decrees.
118You reject all who stray from your decrees,
for their deceitfulness is in vain.
119All the wicked of the earth you discard like dross;
therefore I love your statutes.
120My flesh trembles in fear of you;
I stand in awe of your laws.

ע Ayin

121I have done what is righteous and just;
do not leave me to my oppressors.
122Ensure your servant's well-being;
let not the arrogant oppress me.
123My eyes fail, looking for your salvation,
looking for your righteous promise.
124Deal with your servant according to your love
and teach me your decrees.
125I am your servant; give me discernment
that I may understand your statutes.
126It is time for you to act, O LORD;
your law is being broken.
127Because I love your commands
more than gold, more than pure gold,
128and because I consider all your precepts right,
I hate every wrong path.

פ Pe

129Your statutes are wonderful;
therefore I obey them.
130The unfolding of your words gives light;
it gives understanding to the simple.
131I open my mouth and pant,
longing for your commands.
132Turn to me and have mercy on me,
as you always do to those who love your name.
133Direct my footsteps according to your word;
let no sin rule over me.
134Redeem me from the oppression of men,

119:124–128 God gives us sure guidance for our lives. Following God's plan may not be easy, but we can count on his help. The psalmist asked God to help him follow God's ways. We should do the same. When we are under pressure, we may be tempted to follow our own path. Instead, we should turn to God, asking him to help us do what is right. God wants us to grow and is willing to provide not only the plan but also the encouragement we need to do so.

that I may obey your precepts.
135Make your face shine upon your servant
and teach me your decrees.
136Streams of tears flow from my eyes,
for your law is not obeyed.

צ Tsadhe

137Righteous are you, O LORD,
and your laws are right.
138The statutes you have laid down are
righteous;
they are fully trustworthy.
139My zeal wears me out,
for my enemies ignore your words.
140Your promises have been thoroughly
tested,
and your servant loves them.
141Though I am lowly and despised,
I do not forget your precepts.
142Your righteousness is everlasting
and your law is true.
143Trouble and distress have come upon me,
but your commands are my delight.
144Your statutes are forever right;
give me understanding that I may live.

ק Qoph

145I call with all my heart; answer me,
O LORD,
and I will obey your decrees.
146I call out to you; save me
and I will keep your statutes.
147I rise before dawn and cry for help;
I have put my hope in your word.
148My eyes stay open through the watches of
the night,
that I may meditate on your promises.
149Hear my voice in accordance with your
love;
preserve my life, O LORD, according to
your laws.
150Those who devise wicked schemes are
near,
but they are far from your law.
151Yet you are near, O LORD,
and all your commands are true.
152Long ago I learned from your statutes
that you established them to last forever.

ר Resh

153Look upon my suffering and deliver me,
for I have not forgotten your law.
154Defend my cause and redeem me;
preserve my life according to your
promise.
155Salvation is far from the wicked,
for they do not seek out your decrees.
156Your compassion is great, O LORD;
preserve my life according to your laws.
157Many are the foes who persecute me,
but I have not turned from your statutes.
158I look on the faithless with loathing,
for they do not obey your word.
159See how I love your precepts;
preserve my life, O LORD, according to
your love.
160All your words are true;
all your righteous laws are eternal.

ש Sin and Shin

161Rulers persecute me without cause,
but my heart trembles at your word.
162I rejoice in your promise
like one who finds great spoil.
163I hate and abhor falsehood
but I love your law.
164Seven times a day I praise you
for your righteous laws.
165Great peace have they who love your law,
and nothing can make them stumble.
166I wait for your salvation, O LORD,
and I follow your commands.
167I obey your statutes,
for I love them greatly.
168I obey your precepts and your statutes,
for all my ways are known to you.

ת Taw

169May my cry come before you, O LORD;
give me understanding according to your
word.
170May my supplication come before you;
deliver me according to your promise.
171May my lips overflow with praise,
for you teach me your decrees.
172May my tongue sing of your word,
for all your commands are righteous.
173May your hand be ready to help me,
for I have chosen your precepts.
174I long for your salvation, O LORD,
and your law is my delight.
175Let me live that I may praise you,
and may your laws sustain me.
176I have strayed like a lost sheep.
Seek your servant,
for I have not forgotten your commands.

Psalm 120

A song of ascents.

1I call on the LORD in my distress,
and he answers me.
2Save me, O LORD, from lying lips
and from deceitful tongues.

3What will he do to you,
and what more besides, O deceitful
tongue?

119:153–160 As we seek God's will through his Word, we will discover these wonderful truths: When we surrender our lives to God, he willingly restores and renews us. God's compassion for us will never cease. We can expect him to encourage us when life becomes difficult or painful.

4He will punish you with a warrior's sharp arrows,
with burning coals of the broom tree.

5Woe to me that I dwell in Meshech,
that I live among the tents of Kedar!
6Too long have I lived
among those who hate peace.
7I am a man of peace;
but when I speak, they are for war.

Psalm 121

A song of ascents.

1I lift up my eyes to the hills—
where does my help come from?
2My help comes from the LORD,
the Maker of heaven and earth.

3He will not let your foot slip—
he who watches over you will not slumber;
4indeed, he who watches over Israel
will neither slumber nor sleep.

5The LORD watches over you—
the LORD is your shade at your right hand;
6the sun will not harm you by day,
nor the moon by night.

7The LORD will keep you from all harm—
he will watch over your life;
8the LORD will watch over your coming and going
both now and forevermore.

Psalm 122

A song of ascents. Of David.

1I rejoiced with those who said to me,
"Let us go to the house of the LORD."
2Our feet are standing
in your gates, O Jerusalem.

3Jerusalem is built like a city
that is closely compacted together.
4That is where the tribes go up,
the tribes of the LORD,
to praise the name of the LORD
according to the statute given to Israel.
5There the thrones for judgment stand,
the thrones of the house of David.

6Pray for the peace of Jerusalem:
"May those who love you be secure.
7May there be peace within your walls
and security within your citadels."
8For the sake of my brothers and friends,
I will say, "Peace be within you."
9For the sake of the house of the LORD our God,
I will seek your prosperity.

Psalm 123

A song of ascents.

1I lift up my eyes to you,
to you whose throne is in heaven.
2As the eyes of slaves look to the hand of their master,
as the eyes of a maid look to the hand of her mistress,
so our eyes look to the LORD our God,
till he shows us his mercy.

3Have mercy on us, O LORD, have mercy on us,
for we have endured much contempt.
4We have endured much ridicule from the proud,
much contempt from the arrogant.

Psalm 124

A song of ascents. Of David.

1If the LORD had not been on our side—
let Israel say—
2if the LORD had not been on our side
when men attacked us,
3when their anger flared against us,
they would have swallowed us alive;
4the flood would have engulfed us,
the torrent would have swept over us,
5the raging waters
would have swept us away.

6Praise be to the LORD,
who has not let us be torn by their teeth.
7We have escaped like a bird
out of the fowler's snare;
the snare has been broken,
and we have escaped.
8Our help is in the name of the LORD,
the Maker of heaven and earth.

Psalm 125

A song of ascents.

1Those who trust in the LORD are like Mount Zion,
which cannot be shaken but endures forever.
2As the mountains surround Jerusalem,
so the LORD surrounds his people
both now and forevermore.

121:1–8 God watches over us, placing us under his umbrella of refuge. He preserves us from the evils that threaten to destroy our lives. Simply put, God exercises great care over us day and night.
124:1–8 Without God, there is no hope in the midst of life's battles. If he does not fight our battles for us, we will be overwhelmed by the spiritual forces arrayed against us. We should respond to God's gracious help by praising him for what he has done for us.

[3]The scepter of the wicked will not remain
over the land allotted to the righteous,
for then the righteous might use
their hands to do evil.

[4]Do good, O LORD, to those who are good,
to those who are upright in heart.
[5]But those who turn to crooked ways
the LORD will banish with the evildoers.

Peace be upon Israel.

Psalm 126

A song of ascents.

[1]When the LORD brought back the captives
to[a] Zion,
we were like men who dreamed.[b]
[2]Our mouths were filled with laughter,
our tongues with songs of joy.
Then it was said among the nations,
"The LORD has done great things for
them."
[3]The LORD has done great things for us,
and we are filled with joy.

[4]Restore our fortunes,[c] O LORD,
like streams in the Negev.
[5]Those who sow in tears
will reap with songs of joy.
[6]He who goes out weeping,
carrying seed to sow,
will return with songs of joy,
carrying sheaves with him.

Psalm 127

A song of ascents. Of Solomon.

[1]Unless the LORD builds the house,
its builders labor in vain.
Unless the LORD watches over the city,
the watchmen stand guard in vain.
[2]In vain you rise early
and stay up late,
toiling for food to eat—
for he grants sleep to[d] those he loves.

[3]Sons are a heritage from the LORD,
children a reward from him.
[4]Like arrows in the hands of a warrior
are sons born in one's youth.
[5]Blessed is the man
whose quiver is full of them.
They will not be put to shame
when they contend with their enemies in
the gate.

Psalm 128

A song of ascents.

[1]Blessed are all who fear the LORD,
who walk in his ways.
[2]You will eat the fruit of your labor;
blessings and prosperity will be yours.
[3]Your wife will be like a fruitful vine
within your house;
your sons will be like olive shoots
around your table.
[4]Thus is the man blessed
who fears the LORD.

[5]May the LORD bless you from Zion
all the days of your life;
may you see the prosperity of Jerusalem,
[6] and may you live to see your children's
children.

Peace be upon Israel.

Psalm 129

A song of ascents.

[1]They have greatly oppressed me from my
youth—
let Israel say—
[2]they have greatly oppressed me from my
youth,
but they have not gained the victory over
me.
[3]Plowmen have plowed my back
and made their furrows long.
[4]But the LORD is righteous;
he has cut me free from the cords of the
wicked.

[5]May all who hate Zion
be turned back in shame.
[6]May they be like grass on the roof,
which withers before it can grow;
[7]with it the reaper cannot fill his hands,
nor the one who gathers fill his arms.
[8]May those who pass by not say,
"The blessing of the LORD be upon
you;
we bless you in the name of the LORD."

[a]1 Or *LORD restored the fortunes of* [b]1 Or *men restored to health* [c]4 Or *Bring back our captives* [d]2 Or *eat— / for while they sleep he provides for*

126:1–6 This psalm was written in response to the return of Jewish exiles from captivity as they admitted their sins and returned to God. This can be our story too. Regardless of how far we have strayed from God's plan into sin, God can redeem us. And as we experience God's restoration, our tears will turn to joy, and we can sing songs of praise. Change never comes overnight, but God promises to continually transform us to reflect his image if we will only repent of our sins.

127:1 As we seek spiritual renewal, we need to make sure that God directs the process. Without him, we have no hope for success. The forces that tear down our lives are too strong for us to handle alone. Yet God is able to protect us, and he will direct us each step of the way. Our failure to keep God at the center of our lives will only lead to disappointment and deeper suffering.

Psalm 130

A song of ascents.

[1]Out of the depths I cry to you, O LORD;
[2] O Lord, hear my voice.
Let your ears be attentive
to my cry for mercy.

[3]If you, O LORD, kept a record of sins,
O Lord, who could stand?
[4]But with you there is forgiveness;
therefore you are feared.

[5]I wait for the LORD, my soul waits,
and in his word I put my hope.
[6]My soul waits for the Lord
more than watchmen wait for the morning,
more than watchmen wait for the morning.

[7]O Israel, put your hope in the LORD,
for with the LORD is unfailing love
and with him is full redemption.
[8]He himself will redeem Israel
from all their sins.

Psalm 131

A song of ascents. Of David.

[1]My heart is not proud, O LORD,
my eyes are not haughty;
I do not concern myself with great matters
or things too wonderful for me.
[2]But I have stilled and quieted my soul;
like a weaned child with its mother,
like a weaned child is my soul within me.
[3]O Israel, put your hope in the LORD
both now and forevermore.

Psalm 132

A song of ascents.

[1]O LORD, remember David
and all the hardships he endured.

[2]He swore an oath to the LORD
and made a vow to the Mighty One of Jacob:
[3]"I will not enter my house
or go to my bed—
[4]I will allow no sleep to my eyes,
no slumber to my eyelids,
[5]till I find a place for the LORD,
a dwelling for the Mighty One of Jacob."

[6]We heard it in Ephrathah,
we came upon it in the fields of Jaar[a:b]
[7]"Let us go to his dwelling place;
let us worship at his footstool—
[8]arise, O LORD, and come to your resting place,
you and the ark of your might.
[9]May your priests be clothed with righteousness;
may your saints sing for joy."

[10]For the sake of David your servant,
do not reject your anointed one.

[11]The LORD swore an oath to David,
a sure oath that he will not revoke:
"One of your own descendants
I will place on your throne—
[12]if your sons keep my covenant
and the statutes I teach them,
then their sons will sit
on your throne for ever and ever."

[13]For the LORD has chosen Zion,
he has desired it for his dwelling:
[14]"This is my resting place for ever and ever;
here I will sit enthroned, for I have desired it—
[15]I will bless her with abundant provisions;
her poor will I satisfy with food.
[16]I will clothe her priests with salvation,
and her saints will ever sing for joy.

[17]"Here I will make a horn[c] grow for David
and set up a lamp for my anointed one.
[18]I will clothe his enemies with shame,
but the crown on his head will be resplendent."

Psalm 133

A song of ascents. Of David.

[1]How good and pleasant it is
when brothers live together in unity!
[2]It is like precious oil poured on the head,
running down on the beard,
running down on Aaron's beard,
down upon the collar of his robes.
[3]It is as if the dew of Hermon
were falling on Mount Zion.
For there the LORD bestows his blessing,
even life forevermore.

[a]6 That is, Kiriath Jearim [b]6 Or *heard of it in Ephrathah, / we found it in the fields of Jaar.* (And no quotes around verses 7-9) [c]17 *Horn* here symbolizes strong one, that is, king.

130:1–8 We should be thankful that God has forgiven our sins. Despite the many ways we have turned from him, he responds to our cries of repentance, and we can depend on him to deliver us. Considering his loving forgiveness, we ought to worship God with thankful hearts.

133:1–3 There is nothing quite like human fellowship and friendship. Reconciling our human relationships is an important part of our spiritual growth. God wants to bless us through other people. The friendships most helpful to our spiritual growth will be with people who are trying to live according to God's plan too.

Psalm 134

A song of ascents.

1Praise the LORD, all you servants of the LORD
who minister by night in the house of the LORD.
2Lift up your hands in the sanctuary
and praise the LORD.

3May the LORD, the Maker of heaven and earth,
bless you from Zion.

Psalm 135

1Praise the LORD.[a]

Praise the name of the LORD;
praise him, you servants of the LORD,
2you who minister in the house of the LORD,
in the courts of the house of our God.

3Praise the LORD, for the LORD is good;
sing praise to his name, for that is pleasant.
4For the LORD has chosen Jacob to be his own,
Israel to be his treasured possession.

5I know that the LORD is great,
that our Lord is greater than all gods.
6The LORD does whatever pleases him,
in the heavens and on the earth,
in the seas and all their depths.
7He makes clouds rise from the ends of the earth;
he sends lightning with the rain
and brings out the wind from his storehouses.

8He struck down the firstborn of Egypt,
the firstborn of men and animals.
9He sent his signs and wonders into your midst, O Egypt,
against Pharaoh and all his servants.
10He struck down many nations
and killed mighty kings—
11Sihon king of the Amorites,
Og king of Bashan
and all the kings of Canaan—
12and he gave their land as an inheritance,
an inheritance to his people Israel.

13Your name, O LORD, endures forever,
your renown, O LORD, through all generations.
14For the LORD will vindicate his people
and have compassion on his servants.

15The idols of the nations are silver and gold,
made by the hands of men.
16They have mouths, but cannot speak,
eyes, but they cannot see;
17they have ears, but cannot hear,
nor is there breath in their mouths.
18Those who make them will be like them,
and so will all who trust in them.

19O house of Israel, praise the LORD;
O house of Aaron, praise the LORD;
20O house of Levi, praise the LORD;
you who fear him, praise the LORD.
21Praise be to the LORD from Zion,
to him who dwells in Jerusalem.

Praise the LORD.

Psalm 136

1Give thanks to the LORD, for he is good.
His love endures forever.
2Give thanks to the God of gods.
His love endures forever.
3Give thanks to the Lord of lords:
His love endures forever.

4to him who alone does great wonders,
His love endures forever.
5who by his understanding made the heavens,
His love endures forever.
6who spread out the earth upon the waters,
His love endures forever.
7who made the great lights—
His love endures forever.
8the sun to govern the day,
His love endures forever.
9the moon and stars to govern the night;
His love endures forever.

10to him who struck down the firstborn of Egypt
His love endures forever.
11and brought Israel out from among them
His love endures forever.
12with a mighty hand and outstretched arm;
His love endures forever.

13to him who divided the Red Sea[b] asunder
His love endures forever.
14and brought Israel through the midst of it,
His love endures forever.
15but swept Pharaoh and his army into the Red Sea;
His love endures forever.

16to him who led his people through the desert,
His love endures forever.

[a]1 Hebrew *Hallelu Yah;* also in verses 3 and 21
[b]13 Hebrew *Yam Suph;* that is, Sea of Reeds; also in verse 15

135:1–12 Knowing that God has chosen us as his own should give us confidence to call on him. All through the Old Testament we see evidence of God's power at work to save his people. If God is powerful and caring enough to do all these miracles, he can help us when we call on him. No problem is too great for him to solve.

136:16–26 Moving through life can sometimes be like a lonely walk through a wilderness. But God is able to lead

17who struck down great kings,
His love endures forever.
18and killed mighty kings—
His love endures forever.
19Sihon king of the Amorites
His love endures forever.
20and Og king of Bashan—
His love endures forever.
21and gave their land as an inheritance,
His love endures forever.
22an inheritance to his servant Israel;
His love endures forever.

23to the One who remembered us in our low estate
His love endures forever.
24and freed us from our enemies,
His love endures forever.
25and who gives food to every creature.
His love endures forever.

26Give thanks to the God of heaven.
His love endures forever.

Psalm 137

1By the rivers of Babylon we sat and wept
when we remembered Zion.
2There on the poplars
we hung our harps,
3for there our captors asked us for songs,
our tormentors demanded songs of joy;
they said, "Sing us one of the songs of Zion!"

4How can we sing the songs of the LORD
while in a foreign land?
5If I forget you, O Jerusalem,
may my right hand forget ⌊its skill⌋.
6May my tongue cling to the roof of my mouth
if I do not remember you,
if I do not consider Jerusalem
my highest joy.

7Remember, O LORD, what the Edomites did
on the day Jerusalem fell.
"Tear it down," they cried,
"tear it down to its foundations!"

8O Daughter of Babylon, doomed to destruction,
happy is he who repays you
for what you have done to us—
9he who seizes your infants
and dashes them against the rocks.

Psalm 138

Of David.

1I will praise you, O LORD, with all my heart;
before the "gods" I will sing your praise.
2I will bow down toward your holy temple
and will praise your name
for your love and your faithfulness,
for you have exalted above all things
your name and your word.
3When I called, you answered me;
you made me bold and stouthearted.

4May all the kings of the earth praise you, O LORD,
when they hear the words of your mouth.
5May they sing of the ways of the LORD,
for the glory of the LORD is great.
6Though the LORD is on high, he looks upon the lowly,
but the proud he knows from afar.
7Though I walk in the midst of trouble,
you preserve my life;
you stretch out your hand against the anger of my foes,
with your right hand you save me.
8The LORD will fulfill ⌊his purpose⌋ for me;
your love, O LORD, endures forever—
do not abandon the works of your hands.

Psalm 139

For the director of music. Of David. A psalm.

1O LORD, you have searched me
and you know me.
2You know when I sit and when I rise;
you perceive my thoughts from afar.
3You discern my going out and my lying down;
you are familiar with all my ways.
4Before a word is on my tongue
you know it completely, O LORD.

5You hem me in—behind and before;
you have laid your hand upon me.
6Such knowledge is too wonderful for me,
too lofty for me to attain.

7Where can I go from your Spirit?
Where can I flee from your presence?
8If I go up to the heavens, you are there;

---

us out of the wilderness if we are willing to surrender our lives to him. He will never abandon us, because "his love endures forever."

138:6–8 God responds favorably to humility; he sets himself against the proud, who think they do not need him. When we remain humble and seek God, he is quick to renew our strength and to help us against our enemies. He will never fail us, because he is good.

139:6–12 God is everywhere. We could never run away from him even if we tried to. Such knowledge should keep us from falling into sin and encourage us to follow God, knowing he is there to help us. God is not limited by space or time. He works with us day and night to strengthen and encourage us.

if I make my bed in the depths,[a] you
are there.
9If I rise on the wings of the dawn,
if I settle on the far side of the sea,
10even there your hand will guide me,
your right hand will hold me fast.

11If I say, "Surely the darkness will hide
me
and the light become night around
me,"
12even the darkness will not be dark to
you;
the night will shine like the day,
for darkness is as light to you.

13For you created my inmost being;
you knit me together in my mother's
womb.
14I praise you because I am fearfully and
wonderfully made;
your works are wonderful,
I know that full well.
15My frame was not hidden from you
when I was made in the secret place.
When I was woven together in the depths
of the earth,
16 your eyes saw my unformed body.
All the days ordained for me
were written in your book
before one of them came to be.

17How precious to[b] me are your thoughts,
O God!
How vast is the sum of them!
18Were I to count them,
they would outnumber the grains of
sand.
When I awake,
I am still with you.

19If only you would slay the wicked, O God!
Away from me, you bloodthirsty men!
20They speak of you with evil intent;
your adversaries misuse your name.
21Do I not hate those who hate you, O LORD,
and abhor those who rise up against
you?
22I have nothing but hatred for them;
I count them my enemies.

23Search me, O God, and know my heart;
test me and know my anxious thoughts.
24See if there is any offensive way in me,
and lead me in the way everlasting.

Key 2

Accepting Ourselves

Psalm 139:1–16 Most of us wish we were different somehow, perhaps in personality, appearance or physical abilities. While it is all right to admire good traits in others, often this desire to be like someone else is actually a form of envy, or covetousness, which God condemns (see Exodus 20:17). God wants us to accept ourselves just the way he has made us. Before we can truly accept ourselves, however, we must first see the truth about ourselves, recognizing both the gifts God has given us and the limitations of our human nature. If we do not look at ourselves in this way, we will constantly be struggling to be someone we were never created to be. We can obtain a better appreciation for the way that God made us by reading Psalm 139. The psalmist rejoices, "I praise you because I am fearfully and wonderfully made; your works are wonderful, I know that full well" (139:14). As God's "workmanship," we are beautiful masterpieces—works of his divine hands that ought to be highly valued.

Each one of us is unique and special, embraced and accepted by God, even though not one of us is perfect. Spiritual renewal cannot begin until we are willing to accept ourselves as God made us (see 100:3). Once we accept the truth about ourselves, we can bring great glory to God and begin the process of true spiritual renewal to our hearts.

Turn to Ecclesiastes 3.

[a]8 Hebrew *Sheol* [b]17 Or *concerning*

139:13–18 These verses reveal an exciting fact: Each one of us is an amazing creation—wonderfully made! And God is thinking about us at all times! Anytime we view ourselves as worthless, we are not looking at the truth. We need to begin to see ourselves as God sees us. When we grasp the truth that we are wonderfully made by God himself, we will gladly surrender our lives to him so that he can transform us into the people he created us to be.

Psalm 140

For the director of music. A psalm of David.

[1]Rescue me, O LORD, from evil men;
protect me from men of violence,
[2]who devise evil plans in their hearts
and stir up war every day.
[3]They make their tongues as sharp as a serpent's;
the poison of vipers is on their lips. *Selah*
[4]Keep me, O LORD, from the hands of the wicked;
protect me from men of violence
who plan to trip my feet.
[5]Proud men have hidden a snare for me;
they have spread out the cords of their net
and have set traps for me along my path. *Selah*
[6]O LORD, I say to you, "You are my God."
Hear, O LORD, my cry for mercy.
[7]O Sovereign LORD, my strong deliverer,
who shields my head in the day of battle—
[8]do not grant the wicked their desires, O LORD;
do not let their plans succeed,
or they will become proud. *Selah*
[9]Let the heads of those who surround me
be covered with the trouble their lips have caused.
[10]Let burning coals fall upon them;
may they be thrown into the fire,
into miry pits, never to rise.
[11]Let slanderers not be established in the land;
may disaster hunt down men of violence.
[12]I know that the LORD secures justice for the poor
and upholds the cause of the needy.
[13]Surely the righteous will praise your name
and the upright will live before you.

Psalm 141

A psalm of David.

[1]O LORD, I call to you; come quickly to me.
Hear my voice when I call to you.
[2]May my prayer be set before you like incense;
may the lifting up of my hands be like the evening sacrifice.
[3]Set a guard over my mouth, O LORD;
keep watch over the door of my lips.
[4]Let not my heart be drawn to what is evil,
to take part in wicked deeds
with men who are evildoers;
let me not eat of their delicacies.
[5]Let a righteous man[a] strike me—it is a kindness;
let him rebuke me—it is oil on my head.
My head will not refuse it.

Yet my prayer is ever against the deeds of evildoers;
6 their rulers will be thrown down from the cliffs,
and the wicked will learn that my words were well spoken.
[7]⌊They will say,⌋ "As one plows and breaks up the earth,
so our bones have been scattered at the mouth of the grave.[b]"
[8]But my eyes are fixed on you, O Sovereign LORD;
in you I take refuge—do not give me over to death.
[9]Keep me from the snares they have laid for me,
from the traps set by evildoers.
[10]Let the wicked fall into their own nets,
while I pass by in safety.

Psalm 142

A *maskil*[c] of David. When he was in the cave. A prayer.

[1]I cry aloud to the LORD;
I lift up my voice to the LORD for mercy.
[2]I pour out my complaint before him;
before him I tell my trouble.

[3]When my spirit grows faint within me,
it is you who know my way.
In the path where I walk
men have hidden a snare for me.
[4]Look to my right and see;
no one is concerned for me.

[a]5 Or *Let the Righteous One* [b]7 Hebrew *Sheol*
[c]Title: Probably a literary or musical term

140:1–5 Some people like to stir up trouble and may try to lead us astray into sin. We need God to keep us from being caught in their hidden snares. We will never totally escape the siren call of sin as long as we live in these human bodies. Therefore, we must commit ourselves to stay close to God, the only one who can guard us from sin. We should also be accountable to others who are committed to obeying God's Word and to helping us do likewise.
141:1–10 During times of stress, when we desire to go our own way, we need to call upon God for help. We need to ask him to protect us from the snares that surround us. God has assured us that he will help us find a way to escape temptation (see 1 Corinthians 10:13). We should also encourage our friends to strengthen us when we feel weak.
142:1–7 Suffering should drive us to God, not to despair. Because God cares about us, we can release our feelings about the trials we are experiencing to him. God can release us from our bondage and surround us with people who can encourage and strengthen us.

I have no refuge;
no one cares for my life.

5I cry to you, O LORD;
I say, "You are my refuge,
my portion in the land of the living."
6Listen to my cry,
for I am in desperate need;
rescue me from those who pursue me,
for they are too strong for me.
7Set me free from my prison,
that I may praise your name.

Then the righteous will gather about me
because of your goodness to me.

Psalm 143

A psalm of David.

1O LORD, hear my prayer,
listen to my cry for mercy;
in your faithfulness and righteousness
come to my relief.
2Do not bring your servant into judgment,
for no one living is righteous before you.

3The enemy pursues me,
he crushes me to the ground;
he makes me dwell in darkness
like those long dead.
4So my spirit grows faint within me;
my heart within me is dismayed.

5I remember the days of long ago;
I meditate on all your works
and consider what your hands have done.
6I spread out my hands to you;
my soul thirsts for you like a parched land. *Selah*

7Answer me quickly, O LORD;
my spirit fails.
Do not hide your face from me
or I will be like those who go down to the pit.
8Let the morning bring me word of your unfailing love,
for I have put my trust in you.
Show me the way I should go,
for to you I lift up my soul.
9Rescue me from my enemies, O LORD,
for I hide myself in you.
10Teach me to do your will,
for you are my God;
may your good Spirit
lead me on level ground.

11For your name's sake, O LORD, preserve my life;
in your righteousness, bring me out of trouble.
12In your unfailing love, silence my enemies;
destroy all my foes,
for I am your servant.

Psalm 144

Of David.

1Praise be to the LORD my Rock,
who trains my hands for war,
my fingers for battle.
2He is my loving God and my fortress,
my stronghold and my deliverer,
my shield, in whom I take refuge,
who subdues peoples[a] under me.

3O LORD, what is man that you care for him,
the son of man that you think of him?
4Man is like a breath;
his days are like a fleeting shadow.

5Part your heavens, O LORD, and come down;
touch the mountains, so that they smoke.
6Send forth lightning and scatter ⌊the enemies⌋;
shoot your arrows and rout them.
7Reach down your hand from on high;
deliver me and rescue me
from the mighty waters,
from the hands of foreigners
8whose mouths are full of lies,
whose right hands are deceitful.

9I will sing a new song to you, O God;
on the ten-stringed lyre I will make music to you,
10to the One who gives victory to kings,
who delivers his servant David from the deadly sword.

11Deliver me and rescue me
from the hands of foreigners
whose mouths are full of lies,
whose right hands are deceitful.

12Then our sons in their youth
will be like well-nurtured plants,
and our daughters will be like pillars
carved to adorn a palace.

[a]2 Many manuscripts of the Masoretic Text, Dead Sea Scrolls, Aquila, Jerome and Syriac; most manuscripts of the Masoretic Text *subdues my people*

143:5–12 Even though we pursue spiritual growth, there will be times when we will get discouraged. In our discouragement, it is important to recall the times when God has helped us in the past. We also need to remind ourselves of God's promises for the future. Viewing our present situation in the light of God's past faithfulness and his promises for the future will help us see our circumstances in a true light and redirect the course of our lives toward the plan God has for us.

144:3–8 One mystery we will never understand in this life is why God would ever concern himself with us. Why would he show such great mercy to us? Why does he go out of his way to rescue us? Though we may not understand *why*, we can praise him for being merciful and loving and for delivering us from sin.

13Our barns will be filled
with every kind of provision.
Our sheep will increase by thousands,
by tens of thousands in our fields;
14 our oxen will draw heavy loads.[a]
There will be no breaching of walls,
no going into captivity,
no cry of distress in our streets.

15Blessed are the people of whom this is true;
blessed are the people whose God is the
LORD.

Psalm 145[b]

A psalm of praise. Of David.

1I will exalt you, my God the King;
I will praise your name for ever and ever.
2Every day I will praise you
and extol your name for ever and ever.

3Great is the LORD and most worthy of
praise;
his greatness no one can fathom.
4One generation will commend your works
to another;
they will tell of your mighty acts.
5They will speak of the glorious splendor of
your majesty,
and I will meditate on your wonderful
works.[c]
6They will tell of the power of your
awesome works,
and I will proclaim your great deeds.
7They will celebrate your abundant goodness
and joyfully sing of your righteousness.

8The LORD is gracious and compassionate,
slow to anger and rich in love.
9The LORD is good to all;
he has compassion on all he has made.
10All you have made will praise you, O LORD;
your saints will extol you.
11They will tell of the glory of your kingdom
and speak of your might,
12so that all men may know of your mighty
acts
and the glorious splendor of your
kingdom.
13Your kingdom is an everlasting kingdom,
and your dominion endures through all
generations.

The LORD is faithful to all his promises
and loving toward all he has made.[d]
14The LORD upholds all those who fall
and lifts up all who are bowed down.
15The eyes of all look to you,
and you give them their food at the
proper time.
16You open your hand
and satisfy the desires of every living
thing.

17The LORD is righteous in all his ways
and loving toward all he has made.
18The LORD is near to all who call on him,
to all who call on him in truth.
19He fulfills the desires of those who fear
him;
he hears their cry and saves them.
20The LORD watches over all who love him,
but all the wicked he will destroy.

21My mouth will speak in praise of the LORD.
Let every creature praise his holy name
for ever and ever.

Psalm 146

1Praise the LORD.[e]

Praise the LORD, O my soul.
2 I will praise the LORD all my life;
I will sing praise to my God as long as I
live.

3Do not put your trust in princes,
in mortal men, who cannot save.
4When their spirit departs, they return to the
ground;
on that very day their plans come to
nothing.

5Blessed is he whose help is the God of
Jacob,
whose hope is in the LORD his God,
6the Maker of heaven and earth,
the sea, and everything in them—
the LORD, who remains faithful forever.
7He upholds the cause of the oppressed
and gives food to the hungry.
The LORD sets prisoners free,
8 the LORD gives sight to the blind,

[a]14 Or *our chieftains will be firmly established* [b]This psalm is an acrostic poem, the verses of which (including verse 13b) begin with the successive letters of the Hebrew alphabet. [c]5 Dead Sea Scrolls and Syriac (see also Septuagint); Masoretic Text *On the glorious splendor of your majesty / and on your wonderful works I will meditate* [d]13 One manuscript of the Masoretic Text, Dead Sea Scrolls and Syriac (see also Septuagint); most manuscripts of the Masoretic Text do not have the last two lines of verse 13. [e]1 Hebrew *Hallelu Yah;* also in verse 10

145:1–7 Praise is one of our spiritual weapons. As we praise God for his deliverance, our minds are fixed on the one who can deliver us. Anything that keeps our minds focused on God is helpful to our spiritual growth. And our praise for God's work in our lives can also be an encouragement to others.

145:8–13 God showers us with his gifts and does not give us the punishment we deserve. Instead, he shows us great compassion. One day, all people will recognize this and will praise God. Believers are part of the host that will be a testimony to his great power, especially to his work of deliverance in our own lives.

146:5–9 God remains faithful forever. God made all things and cares about all his creation. He cares for the downtrodden, feeds the hungry and liberates the captives. We may think no one else cares about us, but we can be assured that God does; he watches over those who have no one else to care for them.

the LORD lifts up those who are bowed
down,
the LORD loves the righteous.
9The LORD watches over the alien
and sustains the fatherless and the
widow,
but he frustrates the ways of the wicked.

10The LORD reigns forever,
your God, O Zion, for all generations.

Praise the LORD.

Psalm 147

1Praise the LORD.[a]

How good it is to sing praises to our God,
how pleasant and fitting to praise him!

2The LORD builds up Jerusalem;
he gathers the exiles of Israel.
3He heals the brokenhearted
and binds up their wounds.

4He determines the number of the stars
and calls them each by name.
5Great is our Lord and mighty in power;
his understanding has no limit.
6The LORD sustains the humble
but casts the wicked to the ground.

7Sing to the LORD with thanksgiving;
make music to our God on the harp.
8He covers the sky with clouds;
he supplies the earth with rain
and makes grass grow on the hills.
9He provides food for the cattle
and for the young ravens when they call.

10His pleasure is not in the strength of the
horse,
nor his delight in the legs of a man;
11the LORD delights in those who fear him,
who put their hope in his unfailing love.

12Extol the LORD, O Jerusalem;
praise your God, O Zion,
13for he strengthens the bars of your gates
and blesses your people within you.
14He grants peace to your borders
and satisfies you with the finest of
wheat.

15He sends his command to the earth;
his word runs swiftly.
16He spreads the snow like wool
and scatters the frost like ashes.
17He hurls down his hail like pebbles.
Who can withstand his icy blast?
18He sends his word and melts them;
he stirs up his breezes, and the waters
flow.

19He has revealed his word to Jacob,
his laws and decrees to Israel.
20He has done this for no other nation;
they do not know his laws.

Praise the LORD.

Psalm 148

1Praise the LORD.[b]

Praise the LORD from the heavens,
praise him in the heights above.
2Praise him, all his angels,
praise him, all his heavenly hosts.
3Praise him, sun and moon,
praise him, all you shining stars.
4Praise him, you highest heavens
and you waters above the skies.
5Let them praise the name of the LORD,
for he commanded and they were
created.
6He set them in place for ever and ever;
he gave a decree that will never pass
away.

7Praise the LORD from the earth,
you great sea creatures and all ocean
depths,
8lightning and hail, snow and clouds,
stormy winds that do his bidding,
9you mountains and all hills,
fruit trees and all cedars,
10wild animals and all cattle,
small creatures and flying birds,
11kings of the earth and all nations,
you princes and all rulers on earth,
12young men and maidens,
old men and children.

13Let them praise the name of the LORD,
for his name alone is exalted;
his splendor is above the earth and the
heavens.
14He has raised up for his people a horn,[c]
the praise of all his saints,
of Israel, the people close to his heart.

Praise the LORD.

Psalm 149

1Praise the LORD.[d]

Sing to the LORD a new song,
his praise in the assembly of the saints.

2Let Israel rejoice in their Maker;

a1 Hebrew *Hallelu Yah;* also in verse 20 b1 Hebrew *Hallelu Yah;* also in verse 14 c14 *Horn* here symbolizes strong one, that is, king. d1 Hebrew *Hallelu Yah;* also in verse 9

147:2–11 God can restore what has been destroyed. There is always hope because God created everything and watches over his creation. He is able to provide for all our needs and is never overwhelmed by anything or anyone.
147:12–20 God is our defender and our peacemaker, the one who meets all of our needs. Since he is the Creator, we should have no doubt about his ability to care for us once we surrender our lives to him. He is worthy of our trust.

let the people of Zion be glad in their
King.
3Let them praise his name with dancing
and make music to him with tambourine
and harp.
4For the LORD takes delight in his people;
he crowns the humble with salvation.
5Let the saints rejoice in this honor
and sing for joy on their beds.

6May the praise of God be in their mouths
and a double-edged sword in their
hands,
7to inflict vengeance on the nations
and punishment on the peoples,
8to bind their kings with fetters,
their nobles with shackles of iron,
9to carry out the sentence written against
them.
This is the glory of all his saints.

Praise the LORD.

Psalm 150

1Praise the LORD.[a]

Praise God in his sanctuary;
praise him in his mighty heavens.
2Praise him for his acts of power;
praise him for his surpassing greatness.
3Praise him with the sounding of the
trumpet,
praise him with the harp and lyre,
4praise him with tambourine and dancing,
praise him with the strings and flute,
5praise him with the clash of cymbals,
praise him with resounding cymbals.

6Let everything that has breath praise the
LORD.

Praise the LORD.

[a] 1 Hebrew *Hallelu Yah;* also in verse 6

150:1–6 Some of the best ways to praise God are by the way we live, by the means with which we share the Good News with others, and by our continual surrender to his will for us. All of us are recipients of God's loving forgiveness and restoration. Every living creature—each of us—has ample reason to praise our wonderful and gracious God. "Praise the LORD."

PROVERBS

The Big Picture

Common sense—the idea sounds so folksy and simple. Oddly enough, however, we seem to exhibit less and less of it. Perhaps we are too busy or too far removed to learn natural wisdom from our parents and grandparents. But as rare as common sense is, godly wisdom is also hard to find. The wisdom found in Proverbs can be a helpful resource to fill the lack in our own culture. By reading and heeding Proverbs' wise words, we will avoid many common, destructive mistakes that flow so naturally from ignorance, spiritual blindness and pride.

Although he made many costly mistakes, Solomon was the wisest person who ever lived. Because Solomon valued wisdom so highly, he collected many wise proverbs and recorded them as a guidebook of insight and counsel. Solomon was by no means the only wise man of his day. Agur and Lemuel, also known for their wisdom, are credited with the book's final chapters.

Solomon was particularly aware of the need for young people to acquire wisdom and develop proper behavior patterns. However, young people were not Solomon's only concern. His collection of wisdom is invaluable to people of all ages and occupations. King Hezekiah later found wisdom so important that he assigned his men to compile a collection of Solomon's proverbs.

As our society continues to follow its own sinful paths, we desperately need the wise guidance and direction offered by the book of Proverbs. Its precious nuggets of life-changing counsel are there for us to discover and apply.

A. ***PROLOGUE: THE PURPOSE AND WAY OF WISDOM (1:1-7)***

B. ***SOLOMON CHALLENGES YOUNG PEOPLE TO WISE BEHAVIOR (1:8–9:18)***

C. ***SOLOMON CHALLENGES ALL PEOPLE TO WISE LIVING (10:1–24:34)***

D. ***WISDOM FOR PEOPLE IN LEADERSHIP (25:1–31:9)***

E. ***EPILOGUE: THE WOMAN OF WISDOM (31:10-31)***

Spiritual Renewal Themes

THE IMPORTANCE OF COMMON SENSE

A good plan for spiritual renewal is filled with common sense and wisdom. The book of Proverbs is a primary source for these nuggets of wisdom. Proverbs uses contrast, comparing a person with common sense with a fool—a stubborn person who either hates or ignores God. The wise ones in Proverbs, on the other hand, quickly learn that they must fear God.

Essential Facts

PURPOSE:
To offer God-given wisdom for protection against sinful behaviors and ungodly practices.

AUTHOR:
Solomon collected or wrote most of the book; Agur and Lemuel were responsible for the final chapters.

AUDIENCE:
The people of Israel.

DATE WRITTEN:
Much of the book was compiled during Solomon's reign (970–930 B.C.); it probably took its final form during Hezekiah's reign (715–686 B.C.).

KEY VERSE:
"The fear of the LORD is the beginning of knowledge, but fools despise wisdom and discipline" (1:7).

KEY PEOPLE AND RELATIONSHIPS:
Parents and children, husbands and wives, leaders and citizens, people and God.

PROPER PRIORITIES

Whether we're aware of our priorities, we all have them. A large part of our spiritual renewal involves straightening out our priorities—sorting them out in accordance with God's will. The book of Proverbs is concerned with establishing priorities that please God. As our priorities reflect God's will, our spiritual growth will progress.

PROPER BOUNDARIES

Setting personal boundaries in our lives requires knowing how and when to say no. Solomon recorded numerous situations where saying no is the wisest option—in family situations, sexual situations, monetary situations, business situations and others.

HEALTHY RELATIONSHIPS

The book of Proverbs gives us sound advice for building healthy relationships with friends, family and coworkers. We are urged to be consistent and tactful and to use discipline. If we hope to build the kind of relationships that will help us love and follow God, high moral standards are essential, both for us and for those close to us.

Prologue: Purpose and Theme

1 The proverbs of Solomon son of David, king of Israel:

2 for attaining wisdom and discipline;
for understanding words of insight;
3 for acquiring a disciplined and prudent life,
doing what is right and just and fair;
4 for giving prudence to the simple,
knowledge and discretion to the young—
5 let the wise listen and add to their learning,
and let the discerning get guidance—
6 for understanding proverbs and parables,
the sayings and riddles of the wise.

7 The fear of the LORD is the beginning of knowledge,
but fools[a] despise wisdom and discipline.

Exhortations to Embrace Wisdom

Warning Against Enticement

8 Listen, my son, to your father's instruction
and do not forsake your mother's teaching.
9 They will be a garland to grace your head
and a chain to adorn your neck.

10 My son, if sinners entice you,
do not give in to them.
11 If they say, "Come along with us;
let's lie in wait for someone's blood,
let's waylay some harmless soul;
12 let's swallow them alive, like the grave,[b]
and whole, like those who go down to the pit;
13 we will get all sorts of valuable things
and fill our houses with plunder;
14 throw in your lot with us,
and we will share a common purse"—
15 my son, do not go along with them,
do not set foot on their paths;
16 for their feet rush into sin,
they are swift to shed blood.
17 How useless to spread a net
in full view of all the birds!
18 These men lie in wait for their own blood;
they waylay only themselves!
19 Such is the end of all who go after ill-gotten gain;
it takes away the lives of those who get it.

Warning Against Rejecting Wisdom

20 Wisdom calls aloud in the street,
she raises her voice in the public squares;
21 at the head of the noisy streets[c] she cries out,
in the gateways of the city she makes her speech:

22 "How long will you simple ones[d] love your simple ways?
How long will mockers delight in mockery
and fools hate knowledge?
23 If you had responded to my rebuke,
I would have poured out my heart to you
and made my thoughts known to you.
24 But since you rejected me when I called
and no one gave heed when I stretched out my hand,
25 since you ignored all my advice
and would not accept my rebuke,
26 I in turn will laugh at your disaster;
I will mock when calamity overtakes you—
27 when calamity overtakes you like a storm,
when disaster sweeps over you like a whirlwind,
when distress and trouble overwhelm you.

28 "Then they will call to me but I will not answer;
they will look for me but will not find me.
29 Since they hated knowledge
and did not choose to fear the LORD,
30 since they would not accept my advice
and spurned my rebuke,
31 they will eat the fruit of their ways
and be filled with the fruit of their schemes.
32 For the waywardness of the simple will kill them,
and the complacency of fools will destroy them;
33 but whoever listens to me will live in safety
and be at ease, without fear of harm."

[a] 7 The Hebrew words rendered *fool* in Proverbs, and often elsewhere in the Old Testament, denote one who is morally deficient. [b] 12 Hebrew *Sheol* [c] 21 Hebrew; Septuagint / *on the tops of the walls* [d] 22 The Hebrew word rendered *simple* in Proverbs generally denotes one without moral direction and inclined to evil.

1:2–7 The purpose for writing down these proverbs was to teach people foundational principles about living a good life and dealing with the problems that they would encounter in life. The first step to attaining this kind of wisdom is often the hardest: trusting and showing reverence for God. Ultimately this means admitting that we need help and then allowing God to guide us (see 9:10; 14:26–27; 15:16, 33; 19:23).

1:20–23 Wisdom is personified here, urging all to follow her. There is no real secret to obtaining wisdom; all we have to do is ask God for it (see James 1:5). Unlike experience, which we never get until *after* we need it, God's wisdom is available to us as soon as we are willing to listen to him and obey his plan for our lives.

1:29–33 Many people choose to live life as they please. They give in to their sinful impulses without thinking about the consequences or God's will for them. It is foolish to let ourselves fall prey to temptations. Temptation will lead us away from God, and only he can really satisfy our deepest needs. The path to secure freedom and peace is narrow. We must listen to God's wisdom and exercise self-control to stay on that path.

Moral Benefits of Wisdom

2 My son, if you accept my words
and store up my commands within you,
2turning your ear to wisdom
and applying your heart to
understanding,
3and if you call out for insight
and cry aloud for understanding,
4and if you look for it as for silver
and search for it as for hidden treasure,
5then you will understand the fear of the
LORD
and find the knowledge of God.
6For the LORD gives wisdom,
and from his mouth come knowledge
and understanding.
7He holds victory in store for the upright,
he is a shield to those whose walk is
blameless,
8for he guards the course of the just
and protects the way of his faithful ones.

9Then you will understand what is right and
just
and fair—every good path.
10For wisdom will enter your heart,
and knowledge will be pleasant to your
soul.
11Discretion will protect you,
and understanding will guard you.

12Wisdom will save you from the ways of
wicked men,
from men whose words are perverse,
13who leave the straight paths
to walk in dark ways,
14who delight in doing wrong
and rejoice in the perverseness of evil,
15whose paths are crooked
and who are devious in their ways.

16It will save you also from the adulteress,
from the wayward wife with her
seductive words,
17who has left the partner of her youth
and ignored the covenant she made
before God.[a]
18For her house leads down to death
and her paths to the spirits of the dead.
19None who go to her return
or attain the paths of life.

20Thus you will walk in the ways of good
men
and keep to the paths of the righteous.
21For the upright will live in the land,
and the blameless will remain in it;
22but the wicked will be cut off from the
land,
and the unfaithful will be torn from it.

Further Benefits of Wisdom

3 My son, do not forget my teaching,
but keep my commands in your heart,
2for they will prolong your life many years
and bring you prosperity.

3Let love and faithfulness never leave you;
bind them around your neck,
write them on the tablet of your heart.
4Then you will win favor and a good name
in the sight of God and man.

5Trust in the LORD with all your heart
and lean not on your own
understanding;
6in all your ways acknowledge him,
and he will make your paths straight.[b]

7Do not be wise in your own eyes;
fear the LORD and shun evil.
8This will bring health to your body
and nourishment to your bones.

9Honor the LORD with your wealth,
with the firstfruits of all your crops;
10then your barns will be filled to
overflowing,
and your vats will brim over with new
wine.

11My son, do not despise the LORD's
discipline
and do not resent his rebuke,
12because the LORD disciplines those he loves,
as a father[c] the son he delights in.

13Blessed is the man who finds wisdom,
the man who gains understanding,
14for she is more profitable than silver
and yields better returns than gold.
15She is more precious than rubies;
nothing you desire can compare with
her.

[a]17 Or *covenant of her God* [b]6 Or *will direct your paths*
[c]12 Hebrew; Septuagint / *and he punishes*

2:1–9 Wisdom is like a hidden treasure that is found only by those who search for it. God will grant us wisdom and good sense. He will also care for us and instruct us about making good decisions. We may not have made great decisions in the past, and we may now be suffering the consequences of those decisions. But when we repent and put our trust in God, he will show us the decisions we need to make in keeping with his will.

2:20–22 There is a good path that leads to a full life. It is the path that God marks out for us in his Word. As we let God redirect the course of our lives, he will lead us on the right path. If we refuse to follow God's path, we will miss out on the good things God has for us. We need to follow those who follow God and stay away from those who follow evil. That path leads to destruction.

3:5–6 What a promise! God will direct us and crown our efforts with success if we put our trust in him rather than trying to do it on our own. Putting God first means turning our lives and wills over to him. Surrendering to his lordship may seem humbling, but God will bless us as a result.

3:11–12 When God reproves us, he is not doing so because he likes to see people suffer. God corrects us because he loves us and doesn't want us to fall any further into sin. God has our best interests in mind when he corrects us.

16Long life is in her right hand;
in her left hand are riches and honor.
17Her ways are pleasant ways,
and all her paths are peace.
18She is a tree of life to those who embrace her;
those who lay hold of her will be blessed.

19By wisdom the LORD laid the earth's foundations,
by understanding he set the heavens in place;
20by his knowledge the deeps were divided,
and the clouds let drop the dew.

21My son, preserve sound judgment and discernment,
do not let them out of your sight;
22they will be life for you,
an ornament to grace your neck.
23Then you will go on your way in safety,
and your foot will not stumble;
24when you lie down, you will not be afraid;
when you lie down, your sleep will be sweet.
25Have no fear of sudden disaster
or of the ruin that overtakes the wicked,
26for the LORD will be your confidence
and will keep your foot from being snared.

27Do not withhold good from those who deserve it,
when it is in your power to act.
28Do not say to your neighbor,
"Come back later; I'll give it tomorrow"—
when you now have it with you.

29Do not plot harm against your neighbor,
who lives trustfully near you.
30Do not accuse a man for no reason—
when he has done you no harm.

31Do not envy a violent man
or choose any of his ways,
32for the LORD detests a perverse man
but takes the upright into his confidence.

33The LORD's curse is on the house of the wicked,
but he blesses the home of the righteous.
34He mocks proud mockers
but gives grace to the humble.
35The wise inherit honor,
but fools he holds up to shame.

Wisdom Is Supreme

4 Listen, my sons, to a father's instruction;
pay attention and gain understanding.
2I give you sound learning,
so do not forsake my teaching.
3When I was a boy in my father's house,
still tender, and an only child of my mother,
4he taught me and said,

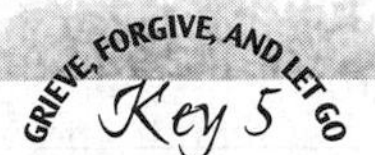

Releasing Past Failures

Proverbs 3:13–26 Some of us go through life excusing our shortcomings. We may feel that because of various disadvantages in our environment life has been stacked against us. Some people grow up in families in which wisdom is modeled and taught by godly parents. These people have the privilege of receiving wise advice at home. If we were deprived of such guidance, we may feel as if we have been shortchanged. We may become angry, resentful or ashamed. We may ask ourselves, *Shouldn't someone have shown us the way?*

We need to let go of any resentment we may feel because of the past failures of others. Resentment only breeds envy, accomplishing nothing constructive. God is the great Redeemer. Regardless of what we have lacked in the past, he has provided us with guidance for today in his Word. Ideally, all of us should receive wise and godly instruction as children. But even if we haven't, the book of Proverbs is filled with wisdom that is always available to us. "Blessed is the man who finds wisdom, the man who gains understanding . . . She is a tree of life to those who embrace her; those who lay hold of her will be blessed" (3:13, 18).

Regardless of our upbringing or background, we have a Father in heaven who loves us and is eager to give us the wisdom we need. James promises, "If any of you lacks wisdom, he should ask God, who gives generously to all without finding fault, and it will be given to him" (James 1:5). We must release any resentment we may harbor about the failures of others to help us in the past, and instead take hold of God's words of wisdom.

Turn to Lamentations 3.

"Lay hold of my words with all your
heart;
keep my commands and you will live.
5Get wisdom, get understanding;
do not forget my words or swerve from
them.
6Do not forsake wisdom, and she will
protect you;
love her, and she will watch over you.
7Wisdom is supreme; therefore get wisdom.
Though it cost all you have,[a] get
understanding.
8Esteem her, and she will exalt you;
embrace her, and she will honor you.
9She will set a garland of grace on your
head
and present you with a crown of
splendor."

10Listen, my son, accept what I say,
and the years of your life will be many.
11I guide you in the way of wisdom
and lead you along straight paths.
12When you walk, your steps will not be
hampered;
when you run, you will not stumble.
13Hold on to instruction, do not let it go;
guard it well, for it is your life.
14Do not set foot on the path of the wicked
or walk in the way of evil men.
15Avoid it, do not travel on it;
turn from it and go on your way.
16For they cannot sleep till they do evil;
they are robbed of slumber till they
make someone fall.
17They eat the bread of wickedness
and drink the wine of violence.

18The path of the righteous is like the first
gleam of dawn,
shining ever brighter till the full light of
day.
19But the way of the wicked is like deep
darkness;
they do not know what makes them
stumble.

20My son, pay attention to what I say;
listen closely to my words.
21Do not let them out of your sight,
keep them within your heart;
22for they are life to those who find them
and health to a man's whole body.
23Above all else, guard your heart,
for it is the wellspring of life.
24Put away perversity from your mouth;
keep corrupt talk far from your lips.
25Let your eyes look straight ahead,
fix your gaze directly before you.
26Make level[b] paths for your feet
and take only ways that are firm.
27Do not swerve to the right or the left;
keep your foot from evil.

Warning Against Adultery

5 My son, pay attention to my wisdom,
listen well to my words of insight,
2that you may maintain discretion
and your lips may preserve knowledge.
3For the lips of an adulteress drip honey,
and her speech is smoother than oil;
4but in the end she is bitter as gall,
sharp as a double-edged sword.
5Her feet go down to death;
her steps lead straight to the grave.[c]
6She gives no thought to the way of life;
her paths are crooked, but she knows it
not.

7Now then, my sons, listen to me;
do not turn aside from what I say.
8Keep to a path far from her,
do not go near the door of her house,
9lest you give your best strength to others
and your years to one who is cruel,
10lest strangers feast on your wealth
and your toil enrich another man's
house.
11At the end of your life you will groan,
when your flesh and body are spent.
12You will say, "How I hated discipline!
How my heart spurned correction!
13I would not obey my teachers
or listen to my instructors.
14I have come to the brink of utter ruin
in the midst of the whole assembly."

15Drink water from your own cistern,
running water from your own well.
16Should your springs overflow in the streets,
your streams of water in the public
squares?
17Let them be yours alone,
never to be shared with strangers.
18May your fountain be blessed,

[a]7 Or *Whatever else you get* [b]26 Or *Consider the*
[c]5 Hebrew *Sheol*

4:11–19 Everyone can be influenced by their environment. That is why we are warned to stay away from those who do wicked deeds. If we spend too much time with people who have few moral boundaries, we will begin to think and act as they do. However, by spending time with godly people, we will find the encouragement we need to stay on the right path and enjoy the life God intends for us.

4:23–27 The warning to guard our heart is also a warning to resist the temptation of sinful pleasures of all kinds. Indulging in sin seems pleasurable at first, but in the end its promise is empty and bitter. Sin may satisfy short-term desires, but it brings about long-term consequences and impedes our spiritual growth.

5:1–23 Sexual temptation is often hard to resist, even when we are aware of the dangers and consequences. Throughout the book of Proverbs are warnings against promiscuity (see 2:16–19; 6:25–35; 7:6–27; 9:13–18; 22:14; 23:26–28). Infidelity violates God's laws. It can destroy our family life, ruin our physical health, and result in an unwanted pregnancy. If we are enticed by sexual sin, we must *run* from any situation where we might be tempted. Also, we should seek help from other believers.

and may you rejoice in the wife of your
youth.
19 A loving doe, a graceful deer—
may her breasts satisfy you always,
may you ever be captivated by her love.
20 Why be captivated, my son, by an
adulteress?
Why embrace the bosom of another
man's wife?

21 For a man's ways are in full view of the
LORD,
and he examines all his paths.
22 The evil deeds of a wicked man ensnare
him;
the cords of his sin hold him fast.
23 He will die for lack of discipline,
led astray by his own great folly.

Warnings Against Folly

6 My son, if you have put up security for
your neighbor,
if you have struck hands in pledge for
another,
2 if you have been trapped by what you said,
ensnared by the words of your mouth,
3 then do this, my son, to free yourself,
since you have fallen into your
neighbor's hands:
Go and humble yourself;
press your plea with your neighbor!
4 Allow no sleep to your eyes,
no slumber to your eyelids.
5 Free yourself, like a gazelle from the hand
of the hunter,
like a bird from the snare of the fowler.

6 Go to the ant, you sluggard;
consider its ways and be wise!
7 It has no commander,
no overseer or ruler,
8 yet it stores its provisions in summer
and gathers its food at harvest.

9 How long will you lie there, you sluggard?
When will you get up from your sleep?
10 A little sleep, a little slumber,
a little folding of the hands to rest—
11 and poverty will come on you like a bandit
and scarcity like an armed man.[a]

12 A scoundrel and villain,
who goes about with a corrupt mouth,
13 who winks with his eye,
signals with his feet
and motions with his fingers,
14 who plots evil with deceit in his heart—
he always stirs up dissension.
15 Therefore disaster will overtake him in an
instant;
he will suddenly be destroyed—without
remedy.

16 There are six things the LORD hates,
seven that are detestable to him:
17 haughty eyes,
a lying tongue,
hands that shed innocent blood,
18 a heart that devises wicked schemes,
feet that are quick to rush into evil,
19 a false witness who pours out lies
and a man who stirs up dissension
among brothers.

Warning Against Adultery

20 My son, keep your father's commands
and do not forsake your mother's
teaching.
21 Bind them upon your heart forever;
fasten them around your neck.
22 When you walk, they will guide you;
when you sleep, they will watch over
you;
when you awake, they will speak to you.
23 For these commands are a lamp,
this teaching is a light,
and the corrections of discipline
are the way to life,
24 keeping you from the immoral woman,
from the smooth tongue of the wayward
wife.
25 Do not lust in your heart after her beauty
or let her captivate you with her eyes,
26 for the prostitute reduces you to a loaf of
bread,
and the adulteress preys upon your very
life.
27 Can a man scoop fire into his lap
without his clothes being burned?
28 Can a man walk on hot coals
without his feet being scorched?
29 So is he who sleeps with another man's
wife;
no one who touches her will go
unpunished.

30 Men do not despise a thief if he steals
to satisfy his hunger when he is starving.
31 Yet if he is caught, he must pay sevenfold,
though it costs him all the wealth of his
house.
32 But a man who commits adultery lacks
judgment;
whoever does so destroys himself.
33 Blows and disgrace are his lot,
and his shame will never be wiped away;
34 for jealousy arouses a husband's fury,
and he will show no mercy when he
takes revenge.
35 He will not accept any compensation;
he will refuse the bribe, however great it
is.

Warning Against the Adulteress

7 My son, keep my words
and store up my commands within you.
2 Keep my commands and you will live;

[a] 11 Or *like a vagrant / and scarcity like a beggar*

guard my teachings as the apple of your
eye.
3Bind them on your fingers;
write them on the tablet of your heart.
4Say to wisdom, "You are my sister,"
and call understanding your kinsman;
5they will keep you from the adulteress,
from the wayward wife with her
seductive words.

6At the window of my house
I looked out through the lattice.
7I saw among the simple,
I noticed among the young men,
a youth who lacked judgment.
8He was going down the street near her
corner,
walking along in the direction of her
house
9at twilight, as the day was fading,
as the dark of night set in.

10Then out came a woman to meet him,
dressed like a prostitute and with crafty
intent.
11(She is loud and defiant,
her feet never stay at home;
12now in the street, now in the squares,
at every corner she lurks.)
13She took hold of him and kissed him
and with a brazen face she said:

14"I have fellowship offerings[a] at home;
today I fulfilled my vows.
15So I came out to meet you;
I looked for you and have found you!
16I have covered my bed
with colored linens from Egypt.
17I have perfumed my bed
with myrrh, aloes and cinnamon.
18Come, let's drink deep of love till morning;
let's enjoy ourselves with love!
19My husband is not at home;
he has gone on a long journey.
20He took his purse filled with money
and will not be home till full moon."

21With persuasive words she led him astray;
she seduced him with her smooth talk.
22All at once he followed her
like an ox going to the slaughter,
like a deer[b] stepping into a noose[c]
23 till an arrow pierces his liver,
like a bird darting into a snare,
little knowing it will cost him his life.

24Now then, my sons, listen to me;
pay attention to what I say.
25Do not let your heart turn to her ways
or stray into her paths.
26Many are the victims she has brought
down;
her slain are a mighty throng.
27Her house is a highway to the grave,[d]
leading down to the chambers of death.

Wisdom's Call

8 Does not wisdom call out?
Does not understanding raise her voice?
2On the heights along the way,
where the paths meet, she takes her
stand;
3beside the gates leading into the city,
at the entrances, she cries aloud:
4"To you, O men, I call out;
I raise my voice to all mankind.
5You who are simple, gain prudence;
you who are foolish, gain understanding.
6Listen, for I have worthy things to say;
I open my lips to speak what is right.
7My mouth speaks what is true,
for my lips detest wickedness.
8All the words of my mouth are just;
none of them is crooked or perverse.
9To the discerning all of them are right;
they are faultless to those who have
knowledge.
10Choose my instruction instead of silver,
knowledge rather than choice gold,
11for wisdom is more precious than rubies,
and nothing you desire can compare
with her.

12"I, wisdom, dwell together with prudence;
I possess knowledge and discretion.
13To fear the LORD is to hate evil;
I hate pride and arrogance,
evil behavior and perverse speech.
14Counsel and sound judgment are mine;
I have understanding and power.
15By me kings reign
and rulers make laws that are just;
16by me princes govern,
and all nobles who rule on earth.[e]
17I love those who love me,
and those who seek me find me.
18With me are riches and honor,
enduring wealth and prosperity.
19My fruit is better than fine gold;
what I yield surpasses choice silver.
20I walk in the way of righteousness,
along the paths of justice,
21bestowing wealth on those who love me
and making their treasuries full.

22"The LORD brought me forth as the first of
his works,[f,g]
before his deeds of old;
23I was appointed[h] from eternity,
from the beginning, before the world
began.
24When there were no oceans, I was given
birth,

[a]14 Traditionally *peace offerings* [b]22 Syriac (see also Septuagint); Hebrew *fool* [c]22 The meaning of the Hebrew for this line is uncertain. [d]27 Hebrew *Sheol* [e]16 Many Hebrew manuscripts and Septuagint; most Hebrew manuscripts *and nobles—all righteous rulers* [f]22 Or *way;* or *dominion* [g]22 Or *The LORD possessed me at the beginning of his work;* or *The LORD brought me forth at the beginning of his work* [h]23 Or *fashioned*

when there were no springs abounding
with water;
25before the mountains were settled in place,
before the hills, I was given birth,
26before he made the earth or its fields
or any of the dust of the world.
27I was there when he set the heavens in
place,
when he marked out the horizon on the
face of the deep,
28when he established the clouds above
and fixed securely the fountains of the
deep,
29when he gave the sea its boundary
so the waters would not overstep his
command,
and when he marked out the foundations
of the earth.
30 Then I was the craftsman at his side.
I was filled with delight day after day,
rejoicing always in his presence,
31rejoicing in his whole world
and delighting in mankind.

32"Now then, my sons, listen to me;
blessed are those who keep my ways.
33Listen to my instruction and be wise;
do not ignore it.
34Blessed is the man who listens to me,
watching daily at my doors,
waiting at my doorway.
35For whoever finds me finds life
and receives favor from the LORD.
36But whoever fails to find me harms
himself;
all who hate me love death."

Invitations of Wisdom and of Folly

9 Wisdom has built her house;
she has hewn out its seven pillars.
2She has prepared her meat and mixed her
wine;
she has also set her table.
3She has sent out her maids, and she calls
from the highest point of the city.
4"Let all who are simple come in here!"
she says to those who lack judgment.
5"Come, eat my food
and drink the wine I have mixed.
6Leave your simple ways and you will live;
walk in the way of understanding.

7"Whoever corrects a mocker invites insult;
whoever rebukes a wicked man incurs
abuse.
8Do not rebuke a mocker or he will hate
you;
rebuke a wise man and he will love you.
9Instruct a wise man and he will be wiser
still;
teach a righteous man and he will add to
his learning.

10"The fear of the LORD is the beginning of
wisdom,
and knowledge of the Holy One is
understanding.
11For through me your days will be many,
and years will be added to your life.
12If you are wise, your wisdom will reward
you;
if you are a mocker, you alone will
suffer."

13The woman Folly is loud;
she is undisciplined and without
knowledge.
14She sits at the door of her house,
on a seat at the highest point of the city,
15calling out to those who pass by,
who go straight on their way.
16"Let all who are simple come in here!"
she says to those who lack judgment.
17"Stolen water is sweet;
food eaten in secret is delicious!"
18But little do they know that the dead are
there,
that her guests are in the depths of the
grave.[a]

Proverbs of Solomon

10 The proverbs of Solomon:

A wise son brings joy to his father,
but a foolish son grief to his mother.

2Ill-gotten treasures are of no value,
but righteousness delivers from death.

3The LORD does not let the righteous go
hungry
but he thwarts the craving of the wicked.

4Lazy hands make a man poor,
but diligent hands bring wealth.

5He who gathers crops in summer is a wise
son,
but he who sleeps during harvest is a
disgraceful son.

[a]18 Hebrew *Sheol*

9:7–8 When someone tries to help us and correct us, we have two choices. We can either listen and learn, as the wise do, or we can get angry and rebel, as the mockers do. To mock and hate those who are concerned for us is to deny that we have a problem. The wise are honest enough to admit that they have a problem and need help. Mockers will reject good advice, and their sins will overtake them. The wise will learn from advice and prosper.

10:4–5 According to these verses, there is little hope for people who are not willing to work hard. Spiritual growth requires perseverance as well as devotion to God. But effort alone will not bring about our spiritual renewal. We need to reach out in faith and seize the opportunities that God brings our way. God shows his grace to us by providing chances for us to exercise our faith. He will also provide us with his spiritual support, wisdom and encouragement as we seek to obey his will.

[6]Blessings crown the head of the righteous,
but violence overwhelms the mouth of the wicked.[a]

[7]The memory of the righteous will be a blessing,
but the name of the wicked will rot.

[8]The wise in heart accept commands,
but a chattering fool comes to ruin.

[9]The man of integrity walks securely,
but he who takes crooked paths will be found out.

[10]He who winks maliciously causes grief,
and a chattering fool comes to ruin.

[11]The mouth of the righteous is a fountain of life,
but violence overwhelms the mouth of the wicked.

[12]Hatred stirs up dissension,
but love covers over all wrongs.

[13]Wisdom is found on the lips of the discerning,
but a rod is for the back of him who lacks judgment.

[14]Wise men store up knowledge,
but the mouth of a fool invites ruin.

[15]The wealth of the rich is their fortified city,
but poverty is the ruin of the poor.

[16]The wages of the righteous bring them life,
but the income of the wicked brings them punishment.

[17]He who heeds discipline shows the way to life,
but whoever ignores correction leads others astray.

[18]He who conceals his hatred has lying lips,
and whoever spreads slander is a fool.

[19]When words are many, sin is not absent,
but he who holds his tongue is wise.

[20]The tongue of the righteous is choice silver,
but the heart of the wicked is of little value.

[21]The lips of the righteous nourish many,
but fools die for lack of judgment.

[22]The blessing of the LORD brings wealth,
and he adds no trouble to it.

[23]A fool finds pleasure in evil conduct,
but a man of understanding delights in wisdom.

[24]What the wicked dreads will overtake him;
what the righteous desire will be granted.

[25]When the storm has swept by, the wicked are gone,
but the righteous stand firm forever.

[26]As vinegar to the teeth and smoke to the eyes,
so is a sluggard to those who send him.

[27]The fear of the LORD adds length to life,
but the years of the wicked are cut short.

[28]The prospect of the righteous is joy,
but the hopes of the wicked come to nothing.

[29]The way of the LORD is a refuge for the righteous,
but it is the ruin of those who do evil.

[30]The righteous will never be uprooted,
but the wicked will not remain in the land.

[31]The mouth of the righteous brings forth wisdom,
but a perverse tongue will be cut out.

[32]The lips of the righteous know what is fitting,
but the mouth of the wicked only what is perverse.

11 The LORD abhors dishonest scales,
but accurate weights are his delight.

[2]When pride comes, then comes disgrace,
but with humility comes wisdom.

[3]The integrity of the upright guides them,
but the unfaithful are destroyed by their duplicity.

[4]Wealth is worthless in the day of wrath,
but righteousness delivers from death.

[5]The righteousness of the blameless makes a straight way for them,
but the wicked are brought down by their own wickedness.

[6]The righteousness of the upright delivers them,
but the unfaithful are trapped by evil desires.

[7]When a wicked man dies, his hope perishes;

[a]6 Or *but the mouth of the wicked conceals violence*; also in verse 11

10:6 In this and in many of the following proverbs, Solomon contrasts good people and evil people by the way they live and the consequences they suffer. A basic principle is repeated again and again: Moral living is good for us.

10:25 When we encounter difficulties in life, it is a real challenge to be content, weather the storm and learn what God is teaching us through it. For people of faith, trials become an opportunity for personal growth (see 24:10).

11:1–3 These proverbs underscore the importance of being honest. We need to be honest—with ourselves and with others. We need to honestly admit our sins and reflect on the condition of our spiritual lives in light of God's Word.

A Caution About Words

Proverbs 10:19 Have you ever hung up the telephone and felt as if you had said too much? Have you ever wished you could have taken back something you said? We often learn the hard way that words can cause pain and create problems. Too much talking often clutters and consumes precious time. One way to refine our use of words is by routinely practicing the discipline of silence.

When we are quiet—listening to others or reflecting on our own conversations—we can glimpse more clearly the ways that we use and abuse words. We may use words to rationalize, to lie, to deceive or to manipulate. In silence, we remember the words we often speak quickly in anger but slowly in apology, words spoken arrogantly in accusation or humbly in confession. In silence, we become aware of the wicked world's noise and confusion that masks the quiet, gentle whisper of the Lord.

Often those who have achieved great things for God are the ones who have spent significant time in intentional silence. In that silence, God has spoken to them and renewed them. Silence can help break the power of words so that we can listen to the Word himself and be renewed as well.

For more on silence, turn to Habakkuk 2.

Putting It Into Practice

Consider taking a day to monitor your conversations. Spend some time in silence reflecting upon your use or abuse of words. Begin to make changes where necessary.

Heart attack survivors are often counseled to bring quiet into their lives by speaking less often and speaking more slowly when they do speak. Such discipline has been proven to reduce stress and ease tension; it can also help us use our words in ways that encourage others and please God.

all he expected from his power comes to
nothing.

8 The righteous man is rescued from trouble,
and it comes on the wicked instead.

9 With his mouth the godless destroys his
neighbor,
but through knowledge the righteous
escape.

10 When the righteous prosper, the city
rejoices;
when the wicked perish, there are shouts
of joy.

11 Through the blessing of the upright a city is
exalted,
but by the mouth of the wicked it is
destroyed.

12 A man who lacks judgment derides his
neighbor,
but a man of understanding holds his
tongue.

13 A gossip betrays a confidence,
but a trustworthy man keeps a secret.

14 For lack of guidance a nation falls,
but many advisers make victory sure.

15 He who puts up security for another will
surely suffer,
but whoever refuses to strike hands in
pledge is safe.

16 A kindhearted woman gains respect,
but ruthless men gain only wealth.

17 A kind man benefits himself,
but a cruel man brings trouble on
himself.

18 The wicked man earns deceptive wages,
but he who sows righteousness reaps a
sure reward.

19 The truly righteous man attains life,
but he who pursues evil goes to his
death.

20 The LORD detests men of perverse heart
but he delights in those whose ways are
blameless.

21 Be sure of this: The wicked will not go
unpunished,
but those who are righteous will go free.

22 Like a gold ring in a pig's snout
is a beautiful woman who shows no
discretion.

23 The desire of the righteous ends only in
good,
but the hope of the wicked only in
wrath.

24 One man gives freely, yet gains even more;
another withholds unduly, but comes to
poverty.

25 A generous man will prosper;
he who refreshes others will himself be
refreshed.

26 People curse the man who hoards grain,
but blessing crowns him who is willing
to sell.

27 He who seeks good finds goodwill,
but evil comes to him who searches for
it.

28 Whoever trusts in his riches will fall,
but the righteous will thrive like a green
leaf.

29 He who brings trouble on his family will
inherit only wind,
and the fool will be servant to the wise.

30 The fruit of the righteous is a tree of life,
and he who wins souls is wise.

31 If the righteous receive their due on earth,
how much more the ungodly and the
sinner!

12 Whoever loves discipline loves
knowledge,
but he who hates correction is stupid.

2 A good man obtains favor from the LORD,
but the LORD condemns a crafty man.

3 A man cannot be established through
wickedness,
but the righteous cannot be uprooted.

4 A wife of noble character is her husband's
crown,
but a disgraceful wife is like decay in his
bones.

5 The plans of the righteous are just,
but the advice of the wicked is deceitful.

6 The words of the wicked lie in wait for
blood,
but the speech of the upright rescues
them.

7 Wicked men are overthrown and are no
more,
but the house of the righteous stands
firm.

8 A man is praised according to his wisdom,
but men with warped minds are
despised.

9 Better to be a nobody and yet have a
servant
than pretend to be somebody and have
no food.

11:24–25 One of the things we can give away is encouragement. When we share our victories as well as our failures, others will be strengthened for the battles ahead. Sharing our experience of spiritual renewal with others will also give them added insight and encouragement.

[10]A righteous man cares for the needs of his
animal,
but the kindest acts of the wicked are
cruel.

[11]He who works his land will have abundant
food,
but he who chases fantasies lacks
judgment.

[12]The wicked desire the plunder of evil men,
but the root of the righteous flourishes.

[13]An evil man is trapped by his sinful talk,
but a righteous man escapes trouble.

[14]From the fruit of his lips a man is filled
with good things
as surely as the work of his hands
rewards him.

[15]The way of a fool seems right to him,
but a wise man listens to advice.

[16]A fool shows his annoyance at once,
but a prudent man overlooks an insult.

[17]A truthful witness gives honest testimony,
but a false witness tells lies.

[18]Reckless words pierce like a sword,
but the tongue of the wise brings
healing.

[19]Truthful lips endure forever,
but a lying tongue lasts only a moment.

[20]There is deceit in the hearts of those who
plot evil,
but joy for those who promote peace.

[21]No harm befalls the righteous,
but the wicked have their fill of trouble.

[22]The LORD detests lying lips,
but he delights in men who are truthful.

[23]A prudent man keeps his knowledge to
himself,
but the heart of fools blurts out folly.

[24]Diligent hands will rule,
but laziness ends in slave labor.

[25]An anxious heart weighs a man down,
but a kind word cheers him up.

[26]A righteous man is cautious in
friendship,[a]
but the way of the wicked leads them
astray.

[27]The lazy man does not roast[b] his game,
but the diligent man prizes his
possessions.

[28]In the way of righteousness there is life;
along that path is immortality.

13 A wise son heeds his father's
instruction,
but a mocker does not listen to rebuke.

[2]From the fruit of his lips a man enjoys
good things,
but the unfaithful have a craving for
violence.

[3]He who guards his lips guards his life,
but he who speaks rashly will come to
ruin.

[4]The sluggard craves and gets nothing,
but the desires of the diligent are fully
satisfied.

[5]The righteous hate what is false,
but the wicked bring shame and
disgrace.

[6]Righteousness guards the man of integrity,
but wickedness overthrows the sinner.

[7]One man pretends to be rich, yet has
nothing;
another pretends to be poor, yet has
great wealth.

[8]A man's riches may ransom his life,
but a poor man hears no threat.

[9]The light of the righteous shines brightly,
but the lamp of the wicked is snuffed
out.

[10]Pride only breeds quarrels,
but wisdom is found in those who take
advice.

[11]Dishonest money dwindles away,

[a]26 Or *man is a guide to his neighbor* [b]27 The meaning of the Hebrew for this word is uncertain.

12:15 Changing sinful patterns of behavior may require the help of people we trust and respect (see 12:26; 15:22; 19:20). We cannot live life successfully all by ourselves. Growing toward spiritual and emotional maturity requires the help of trustworthy people who can guide us with care and hold us accountable as we try to make changes in our lives.

12:16 It is foolish for us to lose our tempers when we are insulted. We demonstrate maturity by staying self-controlled and finding other ways of expressing our anger without sinning.

12:25 This verse reminds us of the value of encouragement. When people are feeling troubled or burdened, we can let them know we support them and that we love them.

13:6 It should not surprise us that evil deeds destroy people. Painful consequences are often a direct result of sin. Substance abuse will destroy the body; lying will ruin a person's reputation; gambling will put one in the poorhouse. To avoid the inevitable results of sinful behavior, we need to obediently follow God.

13:9 Leaving a sinful past and entering God's kingdom is like walking out of the darkness and into the light. Those of us who enter the light recognize our need for help and glimpse the reality of a loving God who wants to help us. When we come into the light of God's kingdom, we can no longer hide our deeds in the darkness. The light of God's truth causes us to see the truth and helps us deal honestly with the sins the light has exposed.

13:11 This verse emphasizes the importance of hard work. Hard work not only produces material riches—it also can produce spiritual riches. Physical discipline and

but he who gathers money little by little
makes it grow.

12Hope deferred makes the heart sick,
but a longing fulfilled is a tree of life.

13He who scorns instruction will pay for it,
but he who respects a command is
rewarded.

14The teaching of the wise is a fountain of
life,
turning a man from the snares of death.

15Good understanding wins favor,
but the way of the unfaithful is hard.[a]

16Every prudent man acts out of knowledge,
but a fool exposes his folly.

17A wicked messenger falls into trouble,
but a trustworthy envoy brings healing.

18He who ignores discipline comes to poverty
and shame,
but whoever heeds correction is honored.

19A longing fulfilled is sweet to the soul,
but fools detest turning from evil.

20He who walks with the wise grows wise,
but a companion of fools suffers harm.

21Misfortune pursues the sinner,
but prosperity is the reward of the
righteous.

22A good man leaves an inheritance for his
children's children,
but a sinner's wealth is stored up for the
righteous.

23A poor man's field may produce abundant
food,
but injustice sweeps it away.

24He who spares the rod hates his son,
but he who loves him is careful to
discipline him.

25The righteous eat to their hearts' content,
but the stomach of the wicked goes
hungry.

14 The wise woman builds her house,
but with her own hands the foolish
one tears hers down.

2He whose walk is upright fears the LORD,
but he whose ways are devious despises
him.

3A fool's talk brings a rod to his back,
but the lips of the wise protect them.

4Where there are no oxen, the manger is
empty,
but from the strength of an ox comes an
abundant harvest.

5A truthful witness does not deceive,
but a false witness pours out lies.

6The mocker seeks wisdom and finds none,
but knowledge comes easily to the
discerning.

7Stay away from a foolish man,
for you will not find knowledge on his
lips.

8The wisdom of the prudent is to give
thought to their ways,
but the folly of fools is deception.

9Fools mock at making amends for sin,
but goodwill is found among the
upright.

10Each heart knows its own bitterness,
and no one else can share its joy.

11The house of the wicked will be destroyed,
but the tent of the upright will flourish.

12There is a way that seems right to a man,
but in the end it leads to death.

13Even in laughter the heart may ache,
and joy may end in grief.

14The faithless will be fully repaid for their
ways,
and the good man rewarded for his.

15A simple man believes anything,
but a prudent man gives thought to his
steps.

16A wise man fears the LORD and shuns evil,
but a fool is hotheaded and reckless.

17A quick-tempered man does foolish things,
and a crafty man is hated.

18The simple inherit folly,

[a]15 Or *unfaithful does not endure*

---

exercise strengthen our bodies and preserve our physical lives. Likewise, spiritual disciplines such as prayer and meditation on God's Word serve to strengthen our spiritual lives and help us grow.

13:16 As we see in this verse, it is wise to process our thoughts and feelings before we act (see 14:8). Acting solely on impulse can get us into trouble. We may give in to impulses that make us feel good at the moment but that will ultimately undermine our long-term health and welfare.

13:20 Since we become like the company we keep, it is important to have friends we respect who have also surrendered their lives to God. It is helpful to see others modeling the things that will help us preserve spiritual gains.

14:2 If we are truly seeking after God, we will want to obey and honor him. Like children who want to please their parents, we should want to please God, our heavenly Father, with our obedience.

14:15 Trusting God to direct us through the advice of others is an important aspect of our spiritual growth. Solomon, however, gave a wise note of caution in this matter: Don't blindly trust others. A healthy trust in others is developed gradually and carefully, and any advice that is contrary to the truth revealed in the Bible should be disregarded, no matter who gives it.

but the prudent are crowned with knowledge.

19 Evil men will bow down in the presence of the good,
and the wicked at the gates of the righteous.

20 The poor are shunned even by their neighbors,
but the rich have many friends.

21 He who despises his neighbor sins,
but blessed is he who is kind to the needy.

22 Do not those who plot evil go astray?
But those who plan what is good find[a] love and faithfulness.

23 All hard work brings a profit,
but mere talk leads only to poverty.

24 The wealth of the wise is their crown,
but the folly of fools yields folly.

25 A truthful witness saves lives,
but a false witness is deceitful.

26 He who fears the LORD has a secure fortress,
and for his children it will be a refuge.

27 The fear of the LORD is a fountain of life,
turning a man from the snares of death.

28 A large population is a king's glory,
but without subjects a prince is ruined.

29 A patient man has great understanding,
but a quick-tempered man displays folly.

30 A heart at peace gives life to the body,
but envy rots the bones.

31 He who oppresses the poor shows contempt for their Maker,
but whoever is kind to the needy honors God.

32 When calamity comes, the wicked are brought down,
but even in death the righteous have a refuge.

33 Wisdom reposes in the heart of the discerning
and even among fools she lets herself be known.[b]

34 Righteousness exalts a nation,
but sin is a disgrace to any people.

35 A king delights in a wise servant,
but a shameful servant incurs his wrath.

15

A gentle answer turns away wrath,
but a harsh word stirs up anger.

2 The tongue of the wise commends knowledge,
but the mouth of the fool gushes folly.

3 The eyes of the LORD are everywhere,
keeping watch on the wicked and the good.

4 The tongue that brings healing is a tree of life,
but a deceitful tongue crushes the spirit.

5 A fool spurns his father's discipline,
but whoever heeds correction shows prudence.

6 The house of the righteous contains great treasure,
but the income of the wicked brings them trouble.

7 The lips of the wise spread knowledge;
not so the hearts of fools.

8 The LORD detests the sacrifice of the wicked,
but the prayer of the upright pleases him.

9 The LORD detests the way of the wicked
but he loves those who pursue righteousness.

10 Stern discipline awaits him who leaves the path;
he who hates correction will die.

11 Death and Destruction[c] lie open before the LORD—
how much more the hearts of men!

12 A mocker resents correction;
he will not consult the wise.

13 A happy heart makes the face cheerful,
but heartache crushes the spirit.

14 The discerning heart seeks knowledge,
but the mouth of a fool feeds on folly.

15 All the days of the oppressed are wretched,
but the cheerful heart has a continual feast.

16 Better a little with the fear of the LORD
than great wealth with turmoil.

17 Better a meal of vegetables where there is love
than a fattened calf with hatred.

18 A hot-tempered man stirs up dissension,
but a patient man calms a quarrel.

[a] 22 Or *show* [b] 33 Hebrew; Septuagint and Syriac / *but in the heart of fools she is not known* [c] 11 Hebrew *Sheol and Abaddon*

14:26–27 God will give us security, strength and life if we fear him. If we haven't given our lives to him yet, now is the time to do so. Any hope of spiritual renewal depends on our relationship with him.

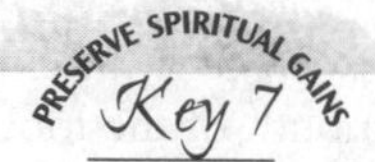

Wise Counselors Can Help

Proverbs 15:22–33 As we seek to grow spiritually, we will need wise counselors. Even Solomon, the wisest man who ever lived, recognized the need for wise and godly counsel. Turning to trustworthy counselors in times of confusion or uncertainty can help us preserve our spiritual gains.

In the book of Proverbs, Solomon gave this advice, "Plans fail for lack of counsel, but with many advisers they succeed" (15:22), and also, "For lack of guidance a nation falls, but many advisers make victory sure" (11:14). David looked to God's Word for advice, saying, "Your statutes are my delight; they are my counselors" (Psalm 119:24). Isaiah made it clear that the Messiah himself would be our great counselor when he came: "For to us a child is born, to us a son is given, and the government will be on his shoulders. And he will be called Wonderful Counselor, Mighty God, Everlasting Father, Prince of Peace" (Isaiah 9:6).

Good counsel can come from the Bible and from godly people. It can come from professionally trained ministers or from people who understand our specific problems and what the Bible has to say about them. Whatever the case, we do ourselves a great service when we seek wise counsel throughout life.

Turn to Isaiah 40.

19The way of the sluggard is blocked with thorns,
but the path of the upright is a highway.

20A wise son brings joy to his father,
but a foolish man despises his mother.

21Folly delights a man who lacks judgment,
but a man of understanding keeps a straight course.

22Plans fail for lack of counsel,
but with many advisers they succeed.

23A man finds joy in giving an apt reply—
and how good is a timely word!

24The path of life leads upward for the wise
to keep him from going down to the grave.[a]

25The LORD tears down the proud man's house
but he keeps the widow's boundaries intact.

26The LORD detests the thoughts of the wicked,
but those of the pure are pleasing to him.

27A greedy man brings trouble to his family,
but he who hates bribes will live.

28The heart of the righteous weighs its answers,
but the mouth of the wicked gushes evil.

29The LORD is far from the wicked
but he hears the prayer of the righteous.

30A cheerful look brings joy to the heart,
and good news gives health to the bones.

31He who listens to a life-giving rebuke
will be at home among the wise.

32He who ignores discipline despises himself,
but whoever heeds correction gains understanding.

33The fear of the LORD teaches a man wisdom,[b]
and humility comes before honor.

16 To man belong the plans of the heart,
but from the LORD comes the reply of the tongue.

[a]24 Hebrew *Sheol* [b]33 Or *Wisdom teaches the fear of the LORD*

15:31–32 If we really want to learn and grow, we must be willing to be held accountable by receiving constructive criticism from others (see 10:8; 13:18; 15:5; 25:12). It is hard for many of us to receive reproof because even when it is shared in love, criticism hurts. We may try to ignore correction in order to avoid being hurt by such criticism. But we would be wise to ask for feedback from people we respect so that we can learn from our mistakes and grow in maturity.

2All a man's ways seem innocent to him,
but motives are weighed by the LORD.

3Commit to the LORD whatever you do,
and your plans will succeed.

4The LORD works out everything for his own ends—
even the wicked for a day of disaster.

5The LORD detests all the proud of heart.
Be sure of this: They will not go unpunished.

6Through love and faithfulness sin is atoned for;
through the fear of the LORD a man avoids evil.

7When a man's ways are pleasing to the LORD,
he makes even his enemies live at peace with him.

8Better a little with righteousness
than much gain with injustice.

9In his heart a man plans his course,
but the LORD determines his steps.

10The lips of a king speak as an oracle,
and his mouth should not betray justice.

11Honest scales and balances are from the LORD;
all the weights in the bag are of his making.

12Kings detest wrongdoing,
for a throne is established through righteousness.

13Kings take pleasure in honest lips;
they value a man who speaks the truth.

14A king's wrath is a messenger of death,
but a wise man will appease it.

15When a king's face brightens, it means life;
his favor is like a rain cloud in spring.

16How much better to get wisdom than gold,
to choose understanding rather than silver!

17The highway of the upright avoids evil;
he who guards his way guards his life.

18Pride goes before destruction,
a haughty spirit before a fall.

19Better to be lowly in spirit and among the oppressed
than to share plunder with the proud.

20Whoever gives heed to instruction prospers,
and blessed is he who trusts in the LORD.

21The wise in heart are called discerning,
and pleasant words promote instruction.[a]

22Understanding is a fountain of life to those who have it,
but folly brings punishment to fools.

23A wise man's heart guides his mouth,
and his lips promote instruction.[b]

24Pleasant words are a honeycomb,
sweet to the soul and healing to the bones.

25There is a way that seems right to a man,
but in the end it leads to death.

26The laborer's appetite works for him;
his hunger drives him on.

27A scoundrel plots evil,
and his speech is like a scorching fire.

28A perverse man stirs up dissension,
and a gossip separates close friends.

29A violent man entices his neighbor
and leads him down a path that is not good.

30He who winks with his eye is plotting perversity;
he who purses his lips is bent on evil.

31Gray hair is a crown of splendor;
it is attained by a righteous life.

32Better a patient man than a warrior,
a man who controls his temper than one who takes a city.

33The lot is cast into the lap,
but its every decision is from the LORD.

17 Better a dry crust with peace and quiet
than a house full of feasting,[c] with strife.

2A wise servant will rule over a disgraceful son,
and will share the inheritance as one of the brothers.

3The crucible for silver and the furnace for gold,
but the LORD tests the heart.

4A wicked man listens to evil lips;
a liar pays attention to a malicious tongue.

5He who mocks the poor shows contempt for their Maker;

[a]21 Or *words make a man persuasive* [b]23 Or *mouth / and makes his lips persuasive* [c]1 Hebrew *sacrifices*

16:33 There is no such thing as luck. All that happens in our lives, even the seemingly random toss of a coin, is under the watchful eye and guiding hand of our sovereign God. It is a challenge for our faith to trust that God is truly in control and that he cares about all the details of our lives. But we must remember that "we know that in all things God works for the good of those who love him, who have been called according to his purpose" (Romans 8:28).

whoever gloats over disaster will not go
unpunished.

6 Children's children are a crown to the aged,
and parents are the pride of their
children.

7 Arrogant[a] lips are unsuited to a fool—
how much worse lying lips to a ruler!

8 A bribe is a charm to the one who gives it;
wherever he turns, he succeeds.

9 He who covers over an offense promotes
love,
but whoever repeats the matter separates
close friends.

10 A rebuke impresses a man of discernment
more than a hundred lashes a fool.

11 An evil man is bent only on rebellion;
a merciless official will be sent against
him.

12 Better to meet a bear robbed of her cubs
than a fool in his folly.

13 If a man pays back evil for good,
evil will never leave his house.

14 Starting a quarrel is like breaching a dam;
so drop the matter before a dispute
breaks out.

15 Acquitting the guilty and condemning the
innocent—
the LORD detests them both.

16 Of what use is money in the hand of a
fool,
since he has no desire to get wisdom?

17 A friend loves at all times,
and a brother is born for adversity.

18 A man lacking in judgment strikes hands in
pledge
and puts up security for his neighbor.

19 He who loves a quarrel loves sin;
he who builds a high gate invites
destruction.

20 A man of perverse heart does not prosper;
he whose tongue is deceitful falls into
trouble.

21 To have a fool for a son brings grief;
there is no joy for the father of a fool.

22 A cheerful heart is good medicine,
but a crushed spirit dries up the bones.

23 A wicked man accepts a bribe in secret
to pervert the course of justice.

24 A discerning man keeps wisdom in view,
but a fool's eyes wander to the ends of
the earth.

25 A foolish son brings grief to his father
and bitterness to the one who bore him.

26 It is not good to punish an innocent man,
or to flog officials for their integrity.

27 A man of knowledge uses words with
restraint,
and a man of understanding is
even-tempered.

28 Even a fool is thought wise if he keeps
silent,
and discerning if he holds his tongue.

18 An unfriendly man pursues selfish
ends;
he defies all sound judgment.

2 A fool finds no pleasure in understanding
but delights in airing his own opinions.

3 When wickedness comes, so does contempt,
and with shame comes disgrace.

4 The words of a man's mouth are deep
waters,
but the fountain of wisdom is a
bubbling brook.

5 It is not good to be partial to the wicked
or to deprive the innocent of justice.

6 A fool's lips bring him strife,
and his mouth invites a beating.

7 A fool's mouth is his undoing,
and his lips are a snare to his soul.

8 The words of a gossip are like choice
morsels;
they go down to a man's inmost parts.

9 One who is slack in his work
is brother to one who destroys.

10 The name of the LORD is a strong tower;
the righteous run to it and are safe.

11 The wealth of the rich is their fortified city;
they imagine it an unscalable wall.

12 Before his downfall a man's heart is proud,
but humility comes before honor.

13 He who answers before listening—
that is his folly and his shame.

14 A man's spirit sustains him in sickness,
but a crushed spirit who can bear?

[a] 7 Or *Eloquent*

17:17 A true friend will support us during the hard times. Building such relationships will help us in our spiritual growth. We all need to be able to express our needs and concerns to someone who will care about us and encourage us in our path toward change.

18:12 When we are filled with pride, we cannot see our weaknesses clearly. If we cannot admit our faults, they will never be corrected, and we will suffer the consequences. On the other hand, humility lets us surrender to God, opening the way for him to correct us and redirect the course of our lives.

15The heart of the discerning acquires
knowledge;
the ears of the wise seek it out.

16A gift opens the way for the giver
and ushers him into the presence of the
great.

17The first to present his case seems right,
till another comes forward and questions
him.

18Casting the lot settles disputes
and keeps strong opponents apart.

19An offended brother is more unyielding
than a fortified city,
and disputes are like the barred gates of
a citadel.

20From the fruit of his mouth a man's
stomach is filled;
with the harvest from his lips he is
satisfied.

21The tongue has the power of life and death,
and those who love it will eat its fruit.

22He who finds a wife finds what is good
and receives favor from the LORD.

23A poor man pleads for mercy,
but a rich man answers harshly.

24A man of many companions may come to
ruin,
but there is a friend who sticks closer
than a brother.

19 Better a poor man whose walk is
blameless
than a fool whose lips are perverse.

2It is not good to have zeal without
knowledge,
nor to be hasty and miss the way.

3A man's own folly ruins his life,
yet his heart rages against the LORD.

4Wealth brings many friends,
but a poor man's friend deserts him.

5A false witness will not go unpunished,
and he who pours out lies will not go
free.

6Many curry favor with a ruler,
and everyone is the friend of a man who
gives gifts.

7A poor man is shunned by all his relatives—
how much more do his friends avoid
him!
Though he pursues them with pleading,
they are nowhere to be found.[a]

8He who gets wisdom loves his own soul;
he who cherishes understanding
prospers.

9A false witness will not go unpunished,
and he who pours out lies will perish.

10It is not fitting for a fool to live in luxury—
how much worse for a slave to rule over
princes!

11A man's wisdom gives him patience;
it is to his glory to overlook an offense.

12A king's rage is like the roar of a lion,
but his favor is like dew on the grass.

13A foolish son is his father's ruin,
and a quarrelsome wife is like a constant
dripping.

14Houses and wealth are inherited from
parents,
but a prudent wife is from the LORD.

15Laziness brings on deep sleep,
and the shiftless man goes hungry.

16He who obeys instructions guards his life,
but he who is contemptuous of his ways
will die.

17He who is kind to the poor lends to the
LORD,
and he will reward him for what he has
done.

18Discipline your son, for in that there is
hope;
do not be a willing party to his death.

19A hot-tempered man must pay the penalty;
if you rescue him, you will have to do it
again.

20Listen to advice and accept instruction,
and in the end you will be wise.

21Many are the plans in a man's heart,
but it is the LORD's purpose that prevails.

22What a man desires is unfailing love[b];
better to be poor than a liar.

23The fear of the LORD leads to life:
Then one rests content, untouched by
trouble.

24The sluggard buries his hand in the dish;
he will not even bring it back to his
mouth!

25Flog a mocker, and the simple will learn
prudence;
rebuke a discerning man, and he will
gain knowledge.

26He who robs his father and drives out his
mother
is a son who brings shame and disgrace.

27Stop listening to instruction, my son,
and you will stray from the words of
knowledge.

28A corrupt witness mocks at justice,

[a]7 The meaning of the Hebrew for this sentence is uncertain. [b]22 Or *A man's greed is his shame*

and the mouth of the wicked gulps
down evil.

29Penalties are prepared for mockers,
and beatings for the backs of fools.

20 Wine is a mocker and beer a brawler;
whoever is led astray by them is not
wise.

2A king's wrath is like the roar of a lion;
he who angers him forfeits his life.

3It is to a man's honor to avoid strife,
but every fool is quick to quarrel.

4A sluggard does not plow in season;
so at harvest time he looks but finds
nothing.

5The purposes of a man's heart are deep
waters,
but a man of understanding draws them
out.

6Many a man claims to have unfailing love,
but a faithful man who can find?

7The righteous man leads a blameless life;
blessed are his children after him.

8When a king sits on his throne to judge,
he winnows out all evil with his eyes.

9Who can say, "I have kept my heart pure;
I am clean and without sin"?

10Differing weights and differing measures—
the LORD detests them both.

11Even a child is known by his actions,
by whether his conduct is pure and right.

12Ears that hear and eyes that see—
the LORD has made them both.

13Do not love sleep or you will grow poor;
stay awake and you will have food to
spare.

14"It's no good, it's no good!" says the buyer;
then off he goes and boasts about his
purchase.

15Gold there is, and rubies in abundance,
but lips that speak knowledge are a rare
jewel.

16Take the garment of one who puts up
security for a stranger;
hold it in pledge if he does it for a
wayward woman.

17Food gained by fraud tastes sweet to a man,
but he ends up with a mouth full of
gravel.

18Make plans by seeking advice;
if you wage war, obtain guidance.

19A gossip betrays a confidence;
so avoid a man who talks too much.

20If a man curses his father or mother,
his lamp will be snuffed out in pitch
darkness.

21An inheritance quickly gained at the
beginning
will not be blessed at the end.

22Do not say, "I'll pay you back for this
wrong!"
Wait for the LORD, and he will deliver
you.

23The LORD detests differing weights,
and dishonest scales do not please him.

24A man's steps are directed by the LORD.
How then can anyone understand his
own way?

25It is a trap for a man to dedicate something
rashly
and only later to consider his vows.

26A wise king winnows out the wicked;
he drives the threshing wheel over them.

27The lamp of the LORD searches the spirit of
a man[a];
it searches out his inmost being.

28Love and faithfulness keep a king safe;
through love his throne is made secure.

29The glory of young men is their strength,
gray hair the splendor of the old.

30Blows and wounds cleanse away evil,
and beatings purge the inmost being.

21 The king's heart is in the hand of the
LORD;
he directs it like a watercourse wherever
he pleases.

2All a man's ways seem right to him,
but the LORD weighs the heart.

3To do what is right and just
is more acceptable to the LORD than
sacrifice.

[a]27 Or *The spirit of man is the LORD's lamp*

20:9 None of us is without sin, but we can receive forgiveness as we confess our sins to God and repent of them. Since we are inclined to sin, constant soul-searching will help us rid ourselves of sinful thoughts and behaviors.
20:22 Seeking revenge against someone who has hurt us will never satisfy our anger; it will only add fuel to the fire of retribution. The cycle of retaliation often continues for years after both parties have forgotten the origin of the conflict. To overcome our anger, we need to start the process of forgiveness right away. We may need to confront those who have offended us and seek resolution. If reconciliation is not possible, then it is best to surrender the matter to God and his ultimate justice. Either way, we need to put the matter behind us and move on with life.
20:25 Counting the cost involves seriously examining what is required of us and then being willing to fulfill that requirement. However, if we don't want to change but realize that we need to, we should ask God to make us willing to change.

4Haughty eyes and a proud heart,
the lamp of the wicked, are sin!

5The plans of the diligent lead to profit
as surely as haste leads to poverty.

6A fortune made by a lying tongue
is a fleeting vapor and a deadly snare.[a]

7The violence of the wicked will drag them away,
for they refuse to do what is right.

8The way of the guilty is devious,
but the conduct of the innocent is upright.

9Better to live on a corner of the roof
than share a house with a quarrelsome wife.

10The wicked man craves evil;
his neighbor gets no mercy from him.

11When a mocker is punished, the simple gain wisdom;
when a wise man is instructed, he gets knowledge.

12The Righteous One[b] takes note of the house of the wicked
and brings the wicked to ruin.

13If a man shuts his ears to the cry of the poor,
he too will cry out and not be answered.

14A gift given in secret soothes anger,
and a bribe concealed in the cloak pacifies great wrath.

15When justice is done, it brings joy to the righteous
but terror to evildoers.

16A man who strays from the path of understanding
comes to rest in the company of the dead.

17He who loves pleasure will become poor;
whoever loves wine and oil will never be rich.

18The wicked become a ransom for the righteous,
and the unfaithful for the upright.

19Better to live in a desert
than with a quarrelsome and ill-tempered wife.

20In the house of the wise are stores of choice food and oil,
but a foolish man devours all he has.

21He who pursues righteousness and love
finds life, prosperity[c] and honor.

22A wise man attacks the city of the mighty
and pulls down the stronghold in which they trust.

23He who guards his mouth and his tongue
keeps himself from calamity.

24The proud and arrogant man—"Mocker" is his name;
he behaves with overweening pride.

25The sluggard's craving will be the death of him,
because his hands refuse to work.

26All day long he craves for more,
but the righteous give without sparing.

27The sacrifice of the wicked is detestable—
how much more so when brought with evil intent!

28A false witness will perish,
and whoever listens to him will be destroyed forever.[d]

29A wicked man puts up a bold front,
but an upright man gives thought to his ways.

30There is no wisdom, no insight, no plan
that can succeed against the LORD.

31The horse is made ready for the day of battle,
but victory rests with the LORD.

22

A good name is more desirable than great riches;
to be esteemed is better than silver or gold.

2Rich and poor have this in common:
The LORD is the Maker of them all.

3A prudent man sees danger and takes refuge,
but the simple keep going and suffer for it.

4Humility and the fear of the LORD
bring wealth and honor and life.

5In the paths of the wicked lie thorns and snares,
but he who guards his soul stays far from them.

6Train[e] a child in the way he should go,
and when he is old he will not turn from it.

7The rich rule over the poor,
and the borrower is servant to the lender.

[a]6 Some Hebrew manuscripts, Septuagint and Vulgate; most Hebrew manuscripts *vapor for those who seek death*
[b]12 Or *The righteous man* [c]21 Or *righteousness*
[d]28 Or / *but the words of an obedient man will live on*
[e]6 Or *Start*

22:6 A parent's ultimate goal is to train children to lead godly lives. If children learn to respect authority, love others and obey God while they are young, there is a good chance they will stay on that path when they are older.

8He who sows wickedness reaps trouble,
and the rod of his fury will be destroyed.

9A generous man will himself be blessed,
for he shares his food with the poor.

10Drive out the mocker, and out goes strife;
quarrels and insults are ended.

11He who loves a pure heart and whose speech is gracious
will have the king for his friend.

12The eyes of the LORD keep watch over knowledge,
but he frustrates the words of the unfaithful.

13The sluggard says, "There is a lion outside!"
or, "I will be murdered in the streets!"

14The mouth of an adulteress is a deep pit;
he who is under the LORD's wrath will fall into it.

15Folly is bound up in the heart of a child,
but the rod of discipline will drive it far from him.

16He who oppresses the poor to increase his wealth
and he who gives gifts to the rich—both come to poverty.

Sayings of the Wise

17Pay attention and listen to the sayings of the wise;
apply your heart to what I teach,
18for it is pleasing when you keep them in your heart
and have all of them ready on your lips.
19So that your trust may be in the LORD,
I teach you today, even you.
20Have I not written thirty[a] sayings for you,
sayings of counsel and knowledge,
21teaching you true and reliable words,
so that you can give sound answers
to him who sent you?

22Do not exploit the poor because they are poor
and do not crush the needy in court,
23for the LORD will take up their case
and will plunder those who plunder them.

24Do not make friends with a hot-tempered man,
do not associate with one easily angered,
25or you may learn his ways
and get yourself ensnared.

26Do not be a man who strikes hands in pledge
or puts up security for debts;
27if you lack the means to pay,
your very bed will be snatched from under you.

28Do not move an ancient boundary stone
set up by your forefathers.

29Do you see a man skilled in his work?
He will serve before kings;
he will not serve before obscure men.

23 When you sit to dine with a ruler,
note well what[b] is before you,
2and put a knife to your throat
if you are given to gluttony.
3Do not crave his delicacies,
for that food is deceptive.

4Do not wear yourself out to get rich;
have the wisdom to show restraint.
5Cast but a glance at riches, and they are gone,
for they will surely sprout wings
and fly off to the sky like an eagle.

6Do not eat the food of a stingy man,
do not crave his delicacies;
7for he is the kind of man
who is always thinking about the cost.[c]
"Eat and drink," he says to you,
but his heart is not with you.
8You will vomit up the little you have eaten
and will have wasted your compliments.

9Do not speak to a fool,
for he will scorn the wisdom of your words.

10Do not move an ancient boundary stone
or encroach on the fields of the fatherless,
11for their Defender is strong;
he will take up their case against you.

12Apply your heart to instruction
and your ears to words of knowledge.

13Do not withhold discipline from a child;
if you punish him with the rod, he will not die.
14Punish him with the rod
and save his soul from death.[d]

15My son, if your heart is wise,
then my heart will be glad;

[a]20 Or *not formerly written;* or *not written excellent*
[b]1 Or *who*
[c]7 Or *for as he thinks within himself, / so he is;* or *for as he puts on a feast, / so he is*
[d]14 Hebrew *Sheol*

22:17–19 In this passage Solomon repeated one of his favorite themes: It is wise to put our trust in God. God alone is the source of perfect love and truth. It is only by surrendering to him that we can experience true love and discover how our lives should be lived.

23:4–5 Perhaps the most common—and most subtle—sin in our culture today is greed, or materialism. Many people weary themselves trying to get more money so that they can buy more things and do more things. There is nothing wrong with money itself; it's the endless pursuit of our own pleasure that God condemns. True joy comes from serving God and others with the things God has given us.

16my inmost being will rejoice
when your lips speak what is right.

17Do not let your heart envy sinners,
but always be zealous for the fear of the LORD.
18There is surely a future hope for you,
and your hope will not be cut off.

19Listen, my son, and be wise,
and keep your heart on the right path.
20Do not join those who drink too much wine
or gorge themselves on meat,
21for drunkards and gluttons become poor,
and drowsiness clothes them in rags.

22Listen to your father, who gave you life,
and do not despise your mother when she is old.
23Buy the truth and do not sell it;
get wisdom, discipline and understanding.
24The father of a righteous man has great joy;
he who has a wise son delights in him.
25May your father and mother be glad;
may she who gave you birth rejoice!

26My son, give me your heart
and let your eyes keep to my ways,
27for a prostitute is a deep pit
and a wayward wife is a narrow well.
28Like a bandit she lies in wait,
and multiplies the unfaithful among men.

29Who has woe? Who has sorrow?
Who has strife? Who has complaints?
Who has needless bruises? Who has bloodshot eyes?
30Those who linger over wine,
who go to sample bowls of mixed wine.
31Do not gaze at wine when it is red,
when it sparkles in the cup,
when it goes down smoothly!
32In the end it bites like a snake
and poisons like a viper.
33Your eyes will see strange sights
and your mind imagine confusing things.
34You will be like one sleeping on the high seas,
lying on top of the rigging.
35"They hit me," you will say, "but I'm not hurt!
They beat me, but I don't feel it!
When will I wake up
so I can find another drink?"

24 Do not envy wicked men,
do not desire their company;
2for their hearts plot violence,
and their lips talk about making trouble.

3By wisdom a house is built,
and through understanding it is established;
4through knowledge its rooms are filled
with rare and beautiful treasures.

5A wise man has great power,
and a man of knowledge increases strength;
6for waging war you need guidance,
and for victory many advisers.

7Wisdom is too high for a fool;
in the assembly at the gate he has nothing to say.

8He who plots evil
will be known as a schemer.
9The schemes of folly are sin,
and men detest a mocker.

10If you falter in times of trouble,
how small is your strength!

11Rescue those being led away to death;
hold back those staggering toward slaughter.
12If you say, "But we knew nothing about this,"
does not he who weighs the heart perceive it?
Does not he who guards your life know it?
Will he not repay each person according to what he has done?

13Eat honey, my son, for it is good;
honey from the comb is sweet to your taste.
14Know also that wisdom is sweet to your soul;
if you find it, there is a future hope for you,
and your hope will not be cut off.

15Do not lie in wait like an outlaw against a righteous man's house,
do not raid his dwelling place;
16for though a righteous man falls seven times, he rises again,
but the wicked are brought down by calamity.

17Do not gloat when your enemy falls;

23:17–18 We often look with envy at people who indulge themselves in sinful pleasures. Such people seem to do whatever they choose without regard for how their actions affect others (see 24:1, 19–20). It seems they have an easy and pleasurable life, while those who live righteously seem to have it harder. But in God's eternal economy, those who follow God will receive the greater blessings, and those who live only for themselves will face judgment.

23:26–35 Three thousand years haven't changed the fact that alcohol and sex are two of the most alluring and destructive enticements. They promise pleasure and escape from our troubles, but in the end they release a poison of shame and embarrassment. The only real solution to our sin and temptation is Jesus Christ. When we surrender our lives to him and turn from our sins, we are freed to lead godly and fulfilling lives. The temptations will still be there, but God will work with us to help us resist them. He will help us to grow and mature in our spiritual walk.

when he stumbles, do not let your heart
rejoice,
18or the LORD will see and disapprove
and turn his wrath away from him.

19Do not fret because of evil men
or be envious of the wicked,
20for the evil man has no future hope,
and the lamp of the wicked will be
snuffed out.

21Fear the LORD and the king, my son,
and do not join with the rebellious,
22for those two will send sudden destruction
upon them,
and who knows what calamities they can
bring?

Further Sayings of the Wise

23These also are sayings of the wise:

To show partiality in judging is not good:
24Whoever says to the guilty, "You are
innocent"—
peoples will curse him and nations
denounce him.
25But it will go well with those who convict
the guilty,
and rich blessing will come upon them.

26An honest answer
is like a kiss on the lips.

27Finish your outdoor work
and get your fields ready;
after that, build your house.

28Do not testify against your neighbor
without cause,
or use your lips to deceive.
29Do not say, "I'll do to him as he has done
to me;
I'll pay that man back for what he did."

30I went past the field of the sluggard,
past the vineyard of the man who lacks
judgment;
31thorns had come up everywhere,
the ground was covered with weeds,
and the stone wall was in ruins.
32I applied my heart to what I observed
and learned a lesson from what I saw:
33A little sleep, a little slumber,
a little folding of the hands to rest—
34and poverty will come on you like a bandit
and scarcity like an armed man.[a]

More Proverbs of Solomon

25 These are more proverbs of Solomon,
copied by the men of Hezekiah king of
Judah:

2It is the glory of God to conceal a matter;
to search out a matter is the glory of
kings.
3As the heavens are high and the earth is
deep,
so the hearts of kings are unsearchable.

4Remove the dross from the silver,
and out comes material for[b] the
silversmith;
5remove the wicked from the king's
presence,
and his throne will be established
through righteousness.

6Do not exalt yourself in the king's presence,
and do not claim a place among great
men;
7it is better for him to say to you, "Come
up here,"
than for him to humiliate you before a
nobleman.

What you have seen with your eyes
8 do not bring[c] hastily to court,
for what will you do in the end
if your neighbor puts you to shame?

9If you argue your case with a neighbor,
do not betray another man's confidence,
10or he who hears it may shame you
and you will never lose your bad
reputation.

11A word aptly spoken
is like apples of gold in settings of silver.

12Like an earring of gold or an ornament of
fine gold
is a wise man's rebuke to a listening ear.

13Like the coolness of snow at harvest time
is a trustworthy messenger to those who
send him;
he refreshes the spirit of his masters.

14Like clouds and wind without rain
is a man who boasts of gifts he does not
give.

15Through patience a ruler can be persuaded,
and a gentle tongue can break a bone.

16If you find honey, eat just enough—
too much of it, and you will vomit.
17Seldom set foot in your neighbor's house—
too much of you, and he will hate you.

18Like a club or a sword or a sharp arrow
is the man who gives false testimony
against his neighbor.

19Like a bad tooth or a lame foot
is reliance on the unfaithful in times of
trouble.

[a]34 Or *like a vagrant / and scarcity like a beggar* [b]4 Or *comes a vessel from* [c]7,8 Or *nobleman / on whom you had set your eyes. / 8Do not go*

20Like one who takes away a garment on a
cold day,
or like vinegar poured on soda,
is one who sings songs to a heavy heart.

21If your enemy is hungry, give him food to
eat;
if he is thirsty, give him water to drink.
22In doing this, you will heap burning coals
on his head,
and the LORD will reward you.

23As a north wind brings rain,
so a sly tongue brings angry looks.

24Better to live on a corner of the roof
than share a house with a quarrelsome
wife.

25Like cold water to a weary soul
is good news from a distant land.

26Like a muddied spring or a polluted well
is a righteous man who gives way to the
wicked.

27It is not good to eat too much honey,
nor is it honorable to seek one's own
honor.

28Like a city whose walls are broken down
is a man who lacks self-control.

26 Like snow in summer or rain in
harvest,
honor is not fitting for a fool.

2Like a fluttering sparrow or a darting
swallow,
an undeserved curse does not come to
rest.

3A whip for the horse, a halter for the
donkey,
and a rod for the backs of fools!

4Do not answer a fool according to his folly,
or you will be like him yourself.

5Answer a fool according to his folly,
or he will be wise in his own eyes.

6Like cutting off one's feet or drinking
violence
is the sending of a message by the hand
of a fool.

7Like a lame man's legs that hang limp
is a proverb in the mouth of a fool.

8Like tying a stone in a sling
is the giving of honor to a fool.

9Like a thornbush in a drunkard's hand
is a proverb in the mouth of a fool.

10Like an archer who wounds at random
is he who hires a fool or any passer-by.

11As a dog returns to its vomit,
so a fool repeats his folly.

12Do you see a man wise in his own eyes?
There is more hope for a fool than for
him.

13The sluggard says, "There is a lion in the
road,
a fierce lion roaming the streets!"

14As a door turns on its hinges,
so a sluggard turns on his bed.

15The sluggard buries his hand in the dish;
he is too lazy to bring it back to his
mouth.

16The sluggard is wiser in his own eyes
than seven men who answer discreetly.

17Like one who seizes a dog by the ears
is a passer-by who meddles in a quarrel
not his own.

18Like a madman shooting
firebrands or deadly arrows
19is a man who deceives his neighbor
and says, "I was only joking!"

20Without wood a fire goes out;
without gossip a quarrel dies down.

21As charcoal to embers and as wood to fire,
so is a quarrelsome man for kindling
strife.

22The words of a gossip are like choice
morsels;
they go down to a man's inmost parts.

23Like a coating of glaze[a] over earthenware
are fervent lips with an evil heart.

24A malicious man disguises himself with his
lips,
but in his heart he harbors deceit.
25Though his speech is charming, do not
believe him,
for seven abominations fill his heart.
26His malice may be concealed by deception,
but his wickedness will be exposed in
the assembly.

27If a man digs a pit, he will fall into it;
if a man rolls a stone, it will roll back
on him.

28A lying tongue hates those it hurts,
and a flattering mouth works ruin.

27 Do not boast about tomorrow,
for you do not know what a day may
bring forth.

[a]23 With a different word division of the Hebrew; Masoretic Text *of silver dross*

25:20 People who are troubled need empathy, not just carefree attempts to make their sadness go away. By indicating that we understand and care about their feelings, we can bring comfort to others and give them strength.

26:11 We almost invariably repeat the patterns of the past; our old problems often revisit us. It is easy to slip back into familiar sinful patterns; that is why we need to be diligent in order to preserve our spiritual gains.

2Let another praise you, and not your own mouth;
someone else, and not your own lips.

3Stone is heavy and sand a burden,
but provocation by a fool is heavier than both.

4Anger is cruel and fury overwhelming,
but who can stand before jealousy?

5Better is open rebuke
than hidden love.

6Wounds from a friend can be trusted,
but an enemy multiplies kisses.

7He who is full loathes honey,
but to the hungry even what is bitter tastes sweet.

8Like a bird that strays from its nest
is a man who strays from his home.

9Perfume and incense bring joy to the heart,
and the pleasantness of one's friend
springs from his earnest counsel.

10Do not forsake your friend and the friend of your father,
and do not go to your brother's house when disaster strikes you—
better a neighbor nearby than a brother far away.

11Be wise, my son, and bring joy to my heart;
then I can answer anyone who treats me with contempt.

12The prudent see danger and take refuge,
but the simple keep going and suffer for it.

13Take the garment of one who puts up security for a stranger;
hold it in pledge if he does it for a wayward woman.

14If a man loudly blesses his neighbor early in the morning,
it will be taken as a curse.

15A quarrelsome wife is like
a constant dripping on a rainy day;
16restraining her is like restraining the wind
or grasping oil with the hand.

17As iron sharpens iron,
so one man sharpens another.

18He who tends a fig tree will eat its fruit,
and he who looks after his master will be honored.

19As water reflects a face,
so a man's heart reflects the man.

20Death and Destruction[a] are never satisfied,
and neither are the eyes of man.

21The crucible for silver and the furnace for gold,
but man is tested by the praise he receives.

22Though you grind a fool in a mortar,
grinding him like grain with a pestle,
you will not remove his folly from him.

23Be sure you know the condition of your flocks,
give careful attention to your herds;
24for riches do not endure forever,
and a crown is not secure for all generations.
25When the hay is removed and new growth appears
and the grass from the hills is gathered in,
26the lambs will provide you with clothing,
and the goats with the price of a field.
27You will have plenty of goats' milk
to feed you and your family
and to nourish your servant girls.

28

The wicked man flees though no one pursues,
but the righteous are as bold as a lion.

2When a country is rebellious, it has many rulers,
but a man of understanding and knowledge maintains order.

3A ruler[b] who oppresses the poor
is like a driving rain that leaves no crops.

4Those who forsake the law praise the wicked,
but those who keep the law resist them.

5Evil men do not understand justice,
but those who seek the LORD understand it fully.

6Better a poor man whose walk is blameless
than a rich man whose ways are perverse.

7He who keeps the law is a discerning son,
but a companion of gluttons disgraces his father.

8He who increases his wealth by exorbitant interest

[a] 20 Hebrew *Sheol and Abaddon* [b] 3 Or *A poor man*

27:10 Friends are an important resource for our spiritual growth. We need people to whom we can be accountable and to whom we can turn in times of need. We need them to be honest with us and have our best interests at heart. And just as we want our friends to stick by us in times of our crises, we should also support our friends when they need our help.

27:20 The word "destruction" here refers to lust or greed. This includes things like sexual gratification, materialism and an insatiable desire for power or prestige. Although gratifying these desires can be pleasurable, such gratification is not fulfilling in the long run. The more we seek God to fulfill our real needs, the more we will be truly satisfied.

amasses it for another, who will be kind
to the poor.

9If anyone turns a deaf ear to the law,
even his prayers are detestable.

10He who leads the upright along an evil
path
will fall into his own trap,
but the blameless will receive a good
inheritance.

11A rich man may be wise in his own eyes,
but a poor man who has discernment
sees through him.

12When the righteous triumph, there is great
elation;
but when the wicked rise to power, men
go into hiding.

13He who conceals his sins does not prosper,
but whoever confesses and renounces
them finds mercy.

14Blessed is the man who always fears the
LORD,
but he who hardens his heart falls into
trouble.

15Like a roaring lion or a charging bear
is a wicked man ruling over a helpless
people.

16A tyrannical ruler lacks judgment,
but he who hates ill-gotten gain will
enjoy a long life.

17A man tormented by the guilt of murder
will be a fugitive till death;
let no one support him.

18He whose walk is blameless is kept safe,
but he whose ways are perverse will
suddenly fall.

19He who works his land will have abundant
food,
but the one who chases fantasies will
have his fill of poverty.

20A faithful man will be richly blessed,
but one eager to get rich will not go
unpunished.

21To show partiality is not good—
yet a man will do wrong for a piece of
bread.

22A stingy man is eager to get rich
and is unaware that poverty awaits him.

23He who rebukes a man will in the end gain
more favor
than he who has a flattering tongue.

24He who robs his father or mother
and says, "It's not wrong"—
he is partner to him who destroys.

25A greedy man stirs up dissension,
but he who trusts in the LORD will
prosper.

26He who trusts in himself is a fool,
but he who walks in wisdom is kept
safe.

27He who gives to the poor will lack nothing,
but he who closes his eyes to them
receives many curses.

28When the wicked rise to power, people go
into hiding;
but when the wicked perish, the
righteous thrive.

29 A man who remains stiff-necked after
many rebukes
will suddenly be destroyed—without
remedy.

2When the righteous thrive, the people
rejoice;
when the wicked rule, the people groan.

3A man who loves wisdom brings joy to his
father,
but a companion of prostitutes
squanders his wealth.

4By justice a king gives a country stability,
but one who is greedy for bribes tears it
down.

5Whoever flatters his neighbor
is spreading a net for his feet.

6An evil man is snared by his own sin,
but a righteous one can sing and be
glad.

7The righteous care about justice for the
poor,
but the wicked have no such concern.

8Mockers stir up a city,
but wise men turn away anger.

9If a wise man goes to court with a fool,
the fool rages and scoffs, and there is no
peace.

10Bloodthirsty men hate a man of integrity
and seek to kill the upright.

11A fool gives full vent to his anger,
but a wise man keeps himself under
control.

12If a ruler listens to lies,
all his officials become wicked.

13The poor man and the oppressor have this
in common:
The LORD gives sight to the eyes of both.

14If a king judges the poor with fairness,
his throne will always be secure.

28:13 This verse contains wisdom essential to our spiritual growth and transformation. We must honestly assess our mistakes, confess our wrongs to one another and to God and strive to avoid such mistakes in the future.

15The rod of correction imparts wisdom,
but a child left to himself disgraces his mother.

16When the wicked thrive, so does sin,
but the righteous will see their downfall.

17Discipline your son, and he will give you peace;
he will bring delight to your soul.

18Where there is no revelation, the people cast off restraint;
but blessed is he who keeps the law.

19A servant cannot be corrected by mere words;
though he understands, he will not respond.

20Do you see a man who speaks in haste?
There is more hope for a fool than for him.

21If a man pampers his servant from youth,
he will bring grief[a] in the end.

22An angry man stirs up dissension,
and a hot-tempered one commits many sins.

23A man's pride brings him low,
but a man of lowly spirit gains honor.

24The accomplice of a thief is his own enemy;
he is put under oath and dare not testify.

25Fear of man will prove to be a snare,
but whoever trusts in the LORD is kept safe.

26Many seek an audience with a ruler,
but it is from the LORD that man gets justice.

27The righteous detest the dishonest;
the wicked detest the upright.

Sayings of Agur

30 The sayings of Agur son of Jakeh—an oracle[b]:

This man declared to Ithiel,
to Ithiel and to Ucal:[c]

2"I am the most ignorant of men;
I do not have a man's understanding.
3I have not learned wisdom,
nor have I knowledge of the Holy One.
4Who has gone up to heaven and come down?
Who has gathered up the wind in the hollow of his hands?
Who has wrapped up the waters in his cloak?
Who has established all the ends of the earth?
What is his name, and the name of his son?
Tell me if you know!

5"Every word of God is flawless;
he is a shield to those who take refuge in him.
6Do not add to his words,
or he will rebuke you and prove you a liar.

7"Two things I ask of you, O LORD;
do not refuse me before I die:
8Keep falsehood and lies far from me;
give me neither poverty nor riches,
but give me only my daily bread.
9Otherwise, I may have too much and disown you
and say, 'Who is the LORD?'
Or I may become poor and steal,
and so dishonor the name of my God.

10"Do not slander a servant to his master,
or he will curse you, and you will pay for it.

11"There are those who curse their fathers
and do not bless their mothers;
12those who are pure in their own eyes
and yet are not cleansed of their filth;

[a] *21* The meaning of the Hebrew for this word is uncertain. [b] *1* Or *Jakeh of Massa* [c] *1* Masoretic Text; with a different word division of the Hebrew *declared, "I am weary, O God; / I am weary, O God, and faint.*

29:15, 17 Children cannot grow up to be responsible adults if they are never disciplined, corrected or held accountable for their actions. Children who are not held accountable fail to learn from the negative consequences of sin, so they continue to develop sinful patterns of behavior. Discipline is an essential part of a child's spiritual development.

29:23 Pride always sets us up for a fall. Pride tells us, "I'm strong; I don't need anyone's help." Pride blinds us to our weaknesses and leads us away from seeking the help we need. Humility says, "I need improvement; could you help me?" Those of us who maintain a humble perspective, realizing that we are weak and vulnerable, will look for the help and support we need for successful spiritual growth.

30:5 The words of God, including these principles in Proverbs, are true and offer deliverance to those who live by them. Living by God's truth demands that we honestly admit our need for God's wisdom and that we seek to live by it. This will not be easy, and it probably won't be popular. But walking in God's light will place us under God's direction and care.

30:11–12 It is easy to blame others for our problems. Some of our problems do have roots in the failures of others. But often our problems have been compounded by bad decisions that we ourselves have made. Our suffering is usually caused by a combination of factors—the sins of others and sins of our own. We cannot change the failures of others, and blame does nothing to speed our spiritual growth. We can, however, change our own attitudes and actions that have perpetuated our suffering. Maturity comes as we take responsibility for our problems by forgiving those who have wronged us and by seeking forgiveness for our own sins.

[13]those whose eyes are ever so haughty,
whose glances are so disdainful;
[14]those whose teeth are swords
and whose jaws are set with knives
to devour the poor from the earth,
the needy from among mankind.

[15]"The leech has two daughters.
'Give! Give!' they cry.

"There are three things that are never
satisfied,
four that never say, 'Enough!':
[16]the grave,[a] the barren womb,
land, which is never satisfied with water,
and fire, which never says, 'Enough!'

[17]"The eye that mocks a father,
that scorns obedience to a mother,
will be pecked out by the ravens of the
valley,
will be eaten by the vultures.

[18]"There are three things that are too
amazing for me,
four that I do not understand:
[19]the way of an eagle in the sky,
the way of a snake on a rock,
the way of a ship on the high seas,
and the way of a man with a maiden.

[20]"This is the way of an adulteress:
She eats and wipes her mouth
and says, 'I've done nothing wrong.'

[21]"Under three things the earth trembles,
under four it cannot bear up:
[22]a servant who becomes king,
a fool who is full of food,
[23]an unloved woman who is married,
and a maidservant who displaces her
mistress.

[24]"Four things on earth are small,
yet they are extremely wise:
[25]Ants are creatures of little strength,
yet they store up their food in the
summer;
[26]coneys[b] are creatures of little power,
yet they make their home in the crags;
[27]locusts have no king,
yet they advance together in ranks;
[28]a lizard can be caught with the hand,
yet it is found in kings' palaces.

[29]"There are three things that are stately in
their stride,
four that move with stately bearing:
[30]a lion, mighty among beasts,
who retreats before nothing;
[31]a strutting rooster, a he-goat,
and a king with his army around him.[c]

[32]"If you have played the fool and exalted
yourself,
or if you have planned evil,
clap your hand over your mouth!
[33]For as churning the milk produces butter,
and as twisting the nose produces blood,
so stirring up anger produces strife."

Sayings of King Lemuel

31 The sayings of King Lemuel—an oracle[d] his mother taught him:

[2]"O my son, O son of my womb,
O son of my vows,[e]
[3]do not spend your strength on women,
your vigor on those who ruin kings.

[4]"It is not for kings, O Lemuel—
not for kings to drink wine,
not for rulers to crave beer,
[5]lest they drink and forget what the law
decrees,
and deprive all the oppressed of their
rights.
[6]Give beer to those who are perishing,
wine to those who are in anguish;
[7]let them drink and forget their poverty
and remember their misery no more.

[8]"Speak up for those who cannot speak for
themselves,
for the rights of all who are destitute.
[9]Speak up and judge fairly;
defend the rights of the poor and needy."

Epilogue: The Wife of Noble Character

[10][f]A wife of noble character who can find?
She is worth far more than rubies.
[11]Her husband has full confidence in her
and lacks nothing of value.
[12]She brings him good, not harm,
all the days of her life.
[13]She selects wool and flax
and works with eager hands.
[14]She is like the merchant ships,
bringing her food from afar.
[15]She gets up while it is still dark;
she provides food for her family

[a]16 Hebrew *Sheol* [b]26 That is, the hyrax or rock badger [c]31 Or *king secure against revolt* [d]1 Or *of Lemuel king of Massa, which* [e]2 Or / *the answer to my prayers* [f]10 Verses 10-31 are an acrostic, each verse beginning with a successive letter of the Hebrew alphabet.

31:10–31 Some women compare themselves to the wife in this chapter and feel inadequate. Actually, the woman of Proverbs 31 presents a description of the ideal wife. No wife ever has or ever will completely measure up to all these standards. A wife should not fall into the perfectionist's trap of striving to measure up to these ideal standards. This will inevitably lead to frustration and despair. Instead, a woman should accept herself for who she is and commit herself to God, asking him to transform her into his likeness. As she grows to be more like him, she will naturally exhibit many of the characteristics of this "wife of noble character" (31:10).

and portions for her servant girls.
16She considers a field and buys it;
out of her earnings she plants a vineyard.
17She sets about her work vigorously;
her arms are strong for her tasks.
18She sees that her trading is profitable,
and her lamp does not go out at night.
19In her hand she holds the distaff
and grasps the spindle with her fingers.
20She opens her arms to the poor
and extends her hands to the needy.
21When it snows, she has no fear for her
household;
for all of them are clothed in scarlet.
22She makes coverings for her bed;
she is clothed in fine linen and purple.
23Her husband is respected at the city gate,
where he takes his seat among the elders
of the land.
24She makes linen garments and sells them,
and supplies the merchants with sashes.
25She is clothed with strength and dignity;
she can laugh at the days to come.
26She speaks with wisdom,
and faithful instruction is on her tongue.
27She watches over the affairs of her
household
and does not eat the bread of idleness.
28Her children arise and call her blessed;
her husband also, and he praises her:
29"Many women do noble things,
but you surpass them all."
30Charm is deceptive, and beauty is fleeting;
but a woman who fears the LORD is to
be praised.
31Give her the reward she has earned,
and let her works bring her praise at the
city gate.

ECCLESIASTES

The Big Picture

- A. *PROLOGUE: THE FUTILITY OF LIFE (1:1-2)*
- B. *PROOF OF THE FUTILITY OF LIFE IN A FALLEN WORLD (1:3–6:12)*
- C. *COPING WITH LIFE IN A FALLEN WORLD (7:1–12:8)*
- D. *EPILOGUE: LIFE IN A FALLEN WORLD BEGINS AND ENDS WITH GOD (12:9-14)*

Sometimes the events of life don't seem to fit together into a coherent, meaningful pattern. How can we make sense of experiences that have damaged our lives? Why does God sometimes allow us to be hurt by the irresponsible actions of others? How do pain and heartbreak play a part in God's plan? When faced with difficulties beyond our control we may hold on to our grief, grudges and bitterness instead of releasing these to God. This failure to set ourselves free can perpetuate a pattern that leads to destruction rather than to spiritual renewal.

The Teacher in Ecclesiastes sought for the key that would unlock the door to life's meaning. The first part of Ecclesiastes states the Teacher's conclusion that "under the sun"—that is, on this side of eternity—some things just don't make sense. After he recognized this basic truth, the Teacher advised his listeners to enjoy life as much as possible because life is God's good gift to us all. The Teacher's final conclusion, which admonishes us to reverence God and obey his commands, puts life back into perspective. Reverence for God will create the necessary boundaries to hold us back from a life of selfish hedonism while still allowing us to enjoy the good things in life.

Since life is God's good gift to be enjoyed rather than a puzzle to be solved, Ecclesiastes helps us cope with our humanity. While on this side of eternity, we will never be able to comprehend some things in life. Rather than attempt to understand them, we need to entrust these situations to God's care.

Spiritual Renewal Themes

THE PARALYSIS OF ANALYSIS

The Teacher's search for meaning was almost like a scientific experiment. He seemed desperate to explain life's ambiguities, and he tried every human solution available before finally realizing that only God truly understands life. We need to beware of the paralysis that can set in when we get caught up in analyzing our situations and seeking human solutions to our problems. When we are stuck in the cycle of analysis it's too easy to get lost on the way and to never reach the right conclusion: Our lives and wills must be surrendered to God. Only by such a surrender will we be able to make true progress in spiritual growth.

Essential Facts

PURPOSE:
To show us that life is God's good gift to be responsibly enjoyed, not a puzzle that must be solved.

AUTHOR:
Attributed to Solomon, although the Hebrew text doesn't clearly name him as the author.

AUDIENCE:
The people of Israel.

DATE WRITTEN:
Possibly written toward the end of Solomon's life, around 935 B.C.

SETTING:
The writer evaluates what he has done in life and ponders the relative value of his activities and accomplishments.

KEY VERSE:
"Now all has been heard: here is the conclusion of the matter: Fear God and keep his commandments, for this is the whole ⌞duty⌟ of man" (12:13).

SPECIAL FEATURES:
The book uses a variety of literary forms: poems, proverbs, parables, pointed questions and couplets.

SOME THINGS WILL NEVER MAKE SENSE

The Teacher's diligent search for understanding and meaning was ultimately futile. There are some things in life that we will never understand. We need to stop trying to make sense of it all. We need to take responsible steps toward spiritual renewal and seek God's help now. If God wills, someday in eternity our whole life will make sense. We need to recognize, however, that in this life some things will remain a puzzle. We can only trust that God will love and care for us through the difficult and apparently meaningless problems we are forced to deal with in this life.

ONLY GOD CAN FILL OUR EMPTINESS

The Teacher provides us with an accurate picture of the emptiness of our search for answers and meaning apart from God. All around us, people are still pursuing the same empty search, looking at wealth, pleasure and success as the answers to life's problems. We may have been sidetracked in our spiritual growth by the same kinds of futile searching. The Teacher's experience shows us that until we surrender our lives to God, our search will lead only to emptiness. God is the only one who can fill our restless and searching hearts.

LIFE IS TO BE ENJOYED RESPONSIBLY

The Teacher assessed life very honestly. He was not depressed by life—only by the futility of seeking happiness and fulfillment apart from God. The Teacher affirmed the value of knowledge, relationships, work and pleasure as long as they are put in their proper perspective. We should seek balance in our lives, knowing that meaning can be found only through a relationship with God. Our spiritual growth will be enhanced when we see that life is a gift from God. When God is at the center of all we do—including our pursuit of spiritual renewal—we will find joy during the short time we are given to live "under the sun."

Everything Is Meaningless

1 The words of the Teacher,[a] son of David, king in Jerusalem:

2"Meaningless! Meaningless!"
says the Teacher.
"Utterly meaningless!
Everything is meaningless."

3What does man gain from all his labor
at which he toils under the sun?
4Generations come and generations go,
but the earth remains forever.
5The sun rises and the sun sets,
and hurries back to where it rises.
6The wind blows to the south
and turns to the north;
round and round it goes,
ever returning on its course.
7All streams flow into the sea,
yet the sea is never full.
To the place the streams come from,
there they return again.
8All things are wearisome,
more than one can say.
The eye never has enough of seeing,
nor the ear its fill of hearing.
9What has been will be again,
what has been done will be done again;
there is nothing new under the sun.
10Is there anything of which one can say,
"Look! This is something new"?
It was here already, long ago;
it was here before our time.
11There is no remembrance of men of old,
and even those who are yet to come
will not be remembered
by those who follow.

Wisdom Is Meaningless

12I, the Teacher, was king over Israel in Jerusalem. 13I devoted myself to study and to explore by wisdom all that is done under heaven.
What a heavy burden God has laid on men! 14I
have seen all the things that are done under the
sun; all of them are meaningless, a chasing after
the wind.

15What is twisted cannot be straightened;
what is lacking cannot be counted.

16I thought to myself, "Look, I have grown
and increased in wisdom more than anyone
who has ruled over Jerusalem before me; I have
experienced much of wisdom and knowledge."
17Then I applied myself to the understanding
of wisdom, and also of madness and folly, but
I learned that this, too, is a chasing after the
wind.

18For with much wisdom comes much
sorrow;
the more knowledge, the more grief.

Pleasures Are Meaningless

2 I thought in my heart, "Come now, I will
test you with pleasure to find out what is
good." But that also proved to be meaningless.
2"Laughter," I said, "is foolish. And what does
pleasure accomplish?" 3I tried cheering myself
with wine, and embracing folly—my mind still
guiding me with wisdom. I wanted to see what
was worthwhile for men to do under heaven
during the few days of their lives.
4I undertook great projects: I built houses for
myself and planted vineyards. 5I made gardens
and parks and planted all kinds of fruit trees
in them. 6I made reservoirs to water groves of
flourishing trees. 7I bought male and female
slaves and had other slaves who were born in
my house. I also owned more herds and flocks
than anyone in Jerusalem before me. 8I amassed
silver and gold for myself, and the treasure of
kings and provinces. I acquired men and wom-

[a] 1 Or *leader of the assembly;* also in verses 2 and 12

1:2 Throughout Ecclesiastes, the Teacher makes several absolute statements about the seeming meaninglessness of life and its various activities. But the Teacher is not necessarily opposed to these activities; he is simply decrying the futility of making them the ultimate goal and end of our existence. For example, work is not wholly worthless (see 2:17–24); elsewhere in Ecclesiastes the Teacher encourages us to enjoy our work (see 3:9–11, 22). But work becomes meaningless if we try to use it to make sense out of life. Only God can give true meaning to all our activities "under the sun."

1:3–11 The Teacher began his search for meaning in life by looking at the world of nature. He concluded from nature that life is a wearying grind, filled with seemingly endless repetition. Though life may often seem like this, we know that God is indeed sovereign and that he is working out his will among those who follow him (see Romans 8:28). Knowing that God is in control should give us a new, hopeful perspective that looks beyond the bounds of our natural world and enables us to cope with the difficulties of daily life.

1:12–16 The Teacher continued his search for meaning by trying to acquire understanding and wisdom. Instead of finding meaning, however, he only discovered the limits of knowledge. The Teacher also found pain in his search for wisdom because he recognized the realities of this fallen world. Only by trusting God and obeying his will can we find meaningful direction and joy in life.

2:1–3 The Teacher tried the pleasurable escapes of laughter and alcohol to find meaning for his life. If mind-altering drugs had been available in his day as they are now, the Teacher may also have used them in his search. But none of these so-called pleasures could satisfy his search for meaning. Seeking to escape our painful existence through the pursuit of pleasure will not ultimately satisfy us. Only God can give us strength and purpose for a meaningful life. We need to trust him and patiently follow his plan revealed in the Bible.

2:1–11 The Teacher illustrates that living for personal success will ultimately cause us to come up empty too. Notice how the first-person pronouns—*I, me, my*—dominate this section. The Teacher was committed to self-interest as a means of making sense of life. The ultimate failure of this approach to discovering meaning is an important lesson for us to learn. We need to realize that living for self is ultimately self-destructive. Until we learn this lesson, we will find it difficult to reach out to others or make sense of our own lives.

en singers, and a harem[a] as well—the delights
of the heart of man. 9I became greater by far
than anyone in Jerusalem before me. In all this
my wisdom stayed with me.

10I denied myself nothing my eyes desired;
  I refused my heart no pleasure.
 My heart took delight in all my work,
  and this was the reward for all my labor.
11Yet when I surveyed all that my hands had
    done
  and what I had toiled to achieve,
 everything was meaningless, a chasing after
    the wind;
  nothing was gained under the sun.

Wisdom and Folly Are Meaningless

12Then I turned my thoughts to consider
    wisdom,
  and also madness and folly.
 What more can the king's successor do
  than what has already been done?
13I saw that wisdom is better than folly,
  just as light is better than darkness.
14The wise man has eyes in his head,
  while the fool walks in the darkness;
 but I came to realize
  that the same fate overtakes them both.

15Then I thought in my heart,

"The fate of the fool will overtake me also.
  What then do I gain by being wise?"
 I said in my heart,
  "This too is meaningless."
16For the wise man, like the fool, will not be
    long remembered;
  in days to come both will be forgotten.
 Like the fool, the wise man too must die!

Toil Is Meaningless

17So I hated life, because the work that is
done under the sun was grievous to me. All of
it is meaningless, a chasing after the wind. 18I
hated all the things I had toiled for under the
sun, because I must leave them to the one who
comes after me. 19And who knows whether he
will be a wise man or a fool? Yet he will have
control over all the work into which I have
poured my effort and skill under the sun. This
too is meaningless. 20So my heart began to despair over all my toilsome labor under the sun.
21For a man may do his work with wisdom,
knowledge and skill, and then he must leave all
he owns to someone who has not worked for it.
This too is meaningless and a great misfortune.
22What does a man get for all the toil and anxious striving with which he labors under the
sun? 23All his days his work is pain and grief;
even at night his mind does not rest. This too is
meaningless.

24A man can do nothing better than to eat
and drink and find satisfaction in his work. This
too, I see, is from the hand of God, 25for without him, who can eat or find enjoyment? 26To
the man who pleases him, God gives wisdom,
knowledge and happiness, but to the sinner he
gives the task of gathering and storing up wealth
to hand it over to the one who pleases God.
This too is meaningless, a chasing after the
wind.

A Time for Everything

3

There is a time for everything,
  and a season for every activity under
    heaven:

2 a time to be born and a time to die,
  a time to plant and a time to uproot,
3 a time to kill and a time to heal,
  a time to tear down and a time to build,
4 a time to weep and a time to laugh,
  a time to mourn and a time to dance,
5 a time to scatter stones and a time to
    gather them,
  a time to embrace and a time to refrain,
6 a time to search and a time to give up,
  a time to keep and a time to throw
    away,
7 a time to tear and a time to mend,
  a time to be silent and a time to speak,
8 a time to love and a time to hate,
  a time for war and a time for peace.

9What does the worker gain from his toil? 10I
have seen the burden God has laid on men.
11He has made everything beautiful in its time.

[a]8 The meaning of the Hebrew for this phrase is uncertain.

2:17–23 The Teacher's frustration here is a lesson for those whose approach to work is out of balance. Work is valuable, even necessary, to our welfare (see 2:24; Genesis 2:15), yet a disproportionate commitment to work can cause problems in our personal and spiritual lives. The Teacher gives us a number of reasons why pursuing work as the ultimate meaning in life is a fruitless endeavor: (1) We don't know who will succeed us in our work (2:17–19); (2) the one who inherits our work will not have the same passion for it as we did (2:19); and (3) a disproportionate commitment to work carries a high emotional and physical cost and does not reap positive benefits (2:22–23).

2:24–26 The alternative to being a workaholic is to be someone who enjoys life as God's good gift. This includes enjoying our work while not allowing it to become the key to meaning in our lives. This is the first of the Teacher's admonitions to take life less seriously and enjoy it more. Life is too short to waste it on the treadmill of ever-increasing, professional accomplishments. We need to take the time to enjoy the gifts that God gives us.

3:1–8 To analyze each of these "times" would mean we would most likely miss the Teacher's point. These are mere figures of speech that present two opposite extremes and the entire spectrum that lies between them. There is a time for everything because God has set the times. When we follow God's plan and timing for our own lives, we assist his process of our spiritual growth.

3:11 God has placed eternity in our hearts. This probably refers to our innate human desire for ultimate meaning in life. Yet in this life, our perspective and understanding are limited. We can't always understand why things happen as they do. Looking at life is like looking at the underside of an Oriental rug. Most of what we see are knots and loose ends. We can only faintly determine the rug's pattern. But

He has also set eternity in the hearts of men; yet they cannot fathom what God has done from beginning to end. 12I know that there is nothing better for men than to be happy and do good while they live. 13That everyone may eat and drink, and find satisfaction in all his toil—this is the gift of God. 14I know that everything God does will endure forever; nothing can be added to it and nothing taken from it. God does it so that men will revere him.

15Whatever is has already been,
and what will be has been before;
and God will call the past to account.[a]

16And I saw something else under the sun:

In the place of judgment—wickedness was there,
in the place of justice—wickedness was there.

17I thought in my heart,

"God will bring to judgment
both the righteous and the wicked,
for there will be a time for every activity,
a time for every deed."

18I also thought, "As for men, God tests them so that they may see that they are like the animals. 19Man's fate is like that of the animals; the same fate awaits them both: As one dies, so dies the other. All have the same breath[b]; man has no advantage over the animal. Everything is meaningless. 20All go to the same place; all come from dust, and to dust all return. 21Who knows if the spirit of man rises upward and if the spirit of the animal[c] goes down into the earth?"

22So I saw that there is nothing better for a man than to enjoy his work, because that is his lot. For who can bring him to see what will happen after him?

Oppression, Toil, Friendlessness

4 Again I looked and saw all the oppression that was taking place under the sun:

I saw the tears of the oppressed—

*a*15 Or *God calls back the past* *b*19 Or *spirit* *c*21 Or *Who knows the spirit of man, which rises upward, or the spirit of the animal, which*

God sees both the underside and the topside of our life's pattern. We must not let the things we can't understand—the knots and loose ends of life—drag us down. God tells us enough in the Bible to direct us to a life filled with joy and meaning.

3:12–15 The Teacher proposes a practical alternative to his frustrating search for ultimate meaning in life. He calls for responsible enjoyment of life as God's good gift. The Teacher wants to enjoy life more and spend less time and energy trying to make sense of it all. Notice that 3:14 sets parameters around the enjoyment of life. Everything we do must be done with the recognition that God is in charge. We must act in ways that demonstrate our respect for him. This will prevent our enjoyment of life from becoming selfish sensuality.

We Can't Right Every Wrong

Ecclesiastes 3:16–17 Our zealousness to set the world aright can be a means for avoiding the truth about our own lives. Rather than look at ourselves, we sometimes spend our time trying to fix the world, right every wrong, heal every wound, and point out every injustice. We work long and hard to see the world system reformed. We may also dedicate ourselves to rescuing and reforming those we love.

The Teacher of Ecclesiastes said, "I saw something else under the sun: In the place of judgment—wickedness was there, in the place of justice—wickedness was there. I thought in my heart, 'God will bring to judgment both the righteous and the wicked, for there will be a time for every activity, a time for every deed' " (3:16–17). The Teacher saw that the world was not as it should be, but he also recognized that it was ultimately God's job to judge the injustices in our world.

When we set out to save the world, we err by taking on a role that belongs to God. All we gain by trying to "save the world" is the guarantee that we will always be busy. And that probably means we will never have the time or energy to face our own issues. The Bible makes it clear that the world will never be completely right until Jesus Christ returns to make it so. Helping others and making a difference is important, but we need to balance this with a healthy concern for ourselves. We need to see and accept the problems in our own lives rather than trying to be in charge of everyone else.

Move on to Key 3 and turn to Genesis 38.

and they have no comforter;
power was on the side of their oppressors—
and they have no comforter.
2And I declared that the dead,
who had already died,
are happier than the living,
who are still alive.
3But better than both
is he who has not yet been,
who has not seen the evil
that is done under the sun.

4And I saw that all labor and all achievement
spring from man's envy of his neighbor. This
too is meaningless, a chasing after the wind.

5The fool folds his hands
and ruins himself.
6Better one handful with tranquillity
than two handfuls with toil
and chasing after the wind.

7Again I saw something meaningless under
the sun:

8There was a man all alone;
he had neither son nor brother.
There was no end to his toil,
yet his eyes were not content with his
wealth.
"For whom am I toiling," he asked,
"and why am I depriving myself of
enjoyment?"
This too is meaningless—
a miserable business!

9Two are better than one,
because they have a good return for their
work:
10If one falls down,
his friend can help him up.
But pity the man who falls
and has no one to help him up!
11Also, if two lie down together, they will
keep warm.
But how can one keep warm alone?
12Though one may be overpowered,
two can defend themselves.
A cord of three strands is not quickly
broken.

Advancement Is Meaningless

13Better a poor but wise youth than an old
but foolish king who no longer knows how
to take warning. 14The youth may have come
from prison to the kingship, or he may have
been born in poverty within his kingdom. 15I
saw that all who lived and walked under the
sun followed the youth, the king's successor.
16There was no end to all the people who were
before them. But those who came later were not
pleased with the successor. This too is meaningless, a chasing after the wind.

Stand in Awe of God

5 Guard your steps when you go to the house
of God. Go near to listen rather than to
offer the sacrifice of fools, who do not know
that they do wrong.

2Do not be quick with your mouth,
do not be hasty in your heart
to utter anything before God.
God is in heaven
and you are on earth,
so let your words be few.
3As a dream comes when there are many
cares,
so the speech of a fool when there are
many words.

4When you make a vow to God, do not delay
in fulfilling it. He has no pleasure in fools; fulfill your vow. 5It is better not to vow than to
make a vow and not fulfill it. 6Do not let your
mouth lead you into sin. And do not protest to
the ⌊temple⌋ messenger, "My vow was a mistake." Why should God be angry at what you say
and destroy the work of your hands? 7Much
dreaming and many words are meaningless.
Therefore stand in awe of God.

Riches Are Meaningless

8If you see the poor oppressed in a district,
and justice and rights denied, do not be surprised at such things; for one official is eyed by
a higher one, and over them both are others
higher still. 9The increase from the land is taken
by all; the king himself profits from the fields.

10Whoever loves money never has money
enough;

4:7–8 These verses make it clear that if we allow work to dominate our lives, we are headed for trouble. This unbalanced commitment to work will cut us off from the significant relationships necessary to enjoy life.

4:9–12 Supportive friendships are absolutely necessary for our spiritual growth. When we fall down, we need help getting up again. We must learn to trust others, to reach out to others and to admit our need for support. This will give us added strength and wisdom in our spiritual journey.

4:13–16 Climbing the ladder of success in either business or leadership will not bring ultimate fulfillment in life. Success in these areas is always temporary. Someone will inherit our work, and ultimately we will be forgotten. Our relationships with God and other people are of far greater importance, for they will lead to true, lasting success and a joyful life.

5:4–7 We are reminded here that our commitments are very important. When we make a commitment to God or to another person, we need to take it very seriously. If we fail to keep our commitments, we will hurt the people close to us and cause them to mistrust us. God takes the commitments we make very seriously, and we should too.

5:10–17 The Teacher notes here that for those who love money, enough is never enough. Wealth is not the key to meaning in life. We are given additional reasons to avoid a passionate search for wealth: (1) The more money we have, the more money we spend, saving nothing (5:11); (2) the greater our empire, the more we will worry about it (5:12); and (3) we can't take any of our wealth with us

whoever loves wealth is never satisfied
with his income.
This too is meaningless.

[11]As goods increase,
so do those who consume them.
And what benefit are they to the owner
except to feast his eyes on them?

[12]The sleep of a laborer is sweet,
whether he eats little or much,
but the abundance of a rich man
permits him no sleep.

[13]I have seen a grievous evil under the sun:

wealth hoarded to the harm of its owner,
[14] or wealth lost through some misfortune,
so that when he has a son
there is nothing left for him.
[15]Naked a man comes from his mother's
womb,
and as he comes, so he departs.
He takes nothing from his labor
that he can carry in his hand.

[16]This too is a grievous evil:

As a man comes, so he departs,
and what does he gain,
since he toils for the wind?
[17]All his days he eats in darkness,
with great frustration, affliction and
anger.

[18]Then I realized that it is good and proper
for a man to eat and drink, and to find satisfaction in his toilsome labor under the sun during
the few days of life God has given him—for this
is his lot. [19]Moreover, when God gives any man
wealth and possessions, and enables him to enjoy them, to accept his lot and be happy in his
work—this is a gift of God. [20]He seldom reflects
on the days of his life, because God keeps him
occupied with gladness of heart.

6 I have seen another evil under the sun, and
it weighs heavily on men: [2]God gives a
man wealth, possessions and honor, so that he
lacks nothing his heart desires, but God does
not enable him to enjoy them, and a stranger
enjoys them instead. This is meaningless, a
grievous evil.
[3]A man may have a hundred children and
live many years; yet no matter how long he
lives, if he cannot enjoy his prosperity and does
not receive proper burial, I say that a stillborn
child is better off than he. [4]It comes without
meaning, it departs in darkness, and in darkness
its name is shrouded. [5]Though it never saw the
sun or knew anything, it has more rest than
does that man— [6]even if he lives a thousand
years twice over but fails to enjoy his prosperity.
Do not all go to the same place?

[7]All man's efforts are for his mouth,
yet his appetite is never satisfied.
[8]What advantage has a wise man
over a fool?
What does a poor man gain
by knowing how to conduct himself
before others?
[9]Better what the eye sees
than the roving of the appetite.
This too is meaningless,
a chasing after the wind.

[10]Whatever exists has already been named,
and what man is has been known;
no man can contend
with one who is stronger than he.
[11]The more the words,
the less the meaning,
and how does that profit anyone?

[12]For who knows what is good for a man in
life, during the few and meaningless days he
passes through like a shadow? Who can tell him
what will happen under the sun after he is
gone?

Wisdom

7 A good name is better than fine perfume,
and the day of death better than the day
of birth.
[2]It is better to go to a house of mourning
than to go to a house of feasting,
for death is the destiny of every man;
the living should take this to heart.
[3]Sorrow is better than laughter,
because a sad face is good for the heart.
[4]The heart of the wise is in the house of
mourning,
but the heart of fools is in the house of
pleasure.
[5]It is better to heed a wise man's rebuke
than to listen to the song of fools.
[6]Like the crackling of thorns under the pot,
so is the laughter of fools.
This too is meaningless.

---

when we die (5:13–17). God never intended for us to live for our possessions. We need to make relationships with God and others the primary concerns in our lives.
5:18–20 The alternative to materialism is a celebration of the beauty of God's gift of life and its simple pleasures. If we are content with what we have, we need very little material wealth to really enjoy life. The Teacher shows that contentment is important by stating that those who are discontent are worse off than a stillborn child (see 6:3). Though the Teacher probably exaggerated to make his point, his message is clear. The celebration and enjoyment of life are extremely important. We need to take the time to enjoy life's simple pleasures to gain strength for the battles we face.
6:12 Sometimes our situation in life seems hopeless. No matter where we turn, everything seems painful and ultimately meaningless. But God certainly can give us hope for the future. We need to begin by placing our lives in his hands.
7:1 The approach of Ecclesiastes radically changes here, as does the emphasis of the Teacher. The message is now presented by using proverbs—short pithy statements of wisdom to help cope with everyday life in our fallen world.

7Extortion turns a wise man into a fool,
and a bribe corrupts the heart.
8The end of a matter is better than its beginning,
and patience is better than pride.
9Do not be quickly provoked in your spirit,
for anger resides in the lap of fools.

10Do not say, "Why were the old days better than these?"
For it is not wise to ask such questions.

11Wisdom, like an inheritance, is a good thing
and benefits those who see the sun.
12Wisdom is a shelter
as money is a shelter,
but the advantage of knowledge is this:
that wisdom preserves the life of its possessor.

13Consider what God has done:

Who can straighten
what he has made crooked?
14When times are good, be happy;
but when times are bad, consider:
God has made the one
as well as the other.
Therefore, a man cannot discover
anything about his future.

15In this meaningless life of mine I have seen
both of these:

a righteous man perishing in his righteousness,
and a wicked man living long in his wickedness.
16Do not be overrighteous,
neither be overwise—
why destroy yourself?
17Do not be overwicked,
and do not be a fool—
why die before your time?
18It is good to grasp the one
and not let go of the other.
The man who fears God will avoid all ⌊extremes⌋.[a]

19Wisdom makes one wise man more powerful
than ten rulers in a city.

20There is not a righteous man on earth
who does what is right and never sins.

21Do not pay attention to every word people say,
or you may hear your servant cursing you—
22for you know in your heart
that many times you yourself have cursed others.

23All this I tested by wisdom and I said,

"I am determined to be wise"—
but this was beyond me.
24Whatever wisdom may be,
it is far off and most profound—
who can discover it?
25So I turned my mind to understand,
to investigate and to search out wisdom
and the scheme of things
and to understand the stupidity of wickedness
and the madness of folly.

26I find more bitter than death
the woman who is a snare,
whose heart is a trap
and whose hands are chains.
The man who pleases God will escape her,
but the sinner she will ensnare.

27"Look," says the Teacher,[b] "this is what I
have discovered:

"Adding one thing to another to discover
the scheme of things—
28 while I was still searching
but not finding—
I found one ⌊upright⌋ man among a thousand,
but not one ⌊upright⌋ woman among them all.
29This only have I found:
God made mankind upright,
but men have gone in search of many schemes."

8 Who is like the wise man?
Who knows the explanation of things?
Wisdom brightens a man's face
and changes its hard appearance.

Obey the King

2Obey the king's command, I say, because
you took an oath before God. 3Do not be in a
hurry to leave the king's presence. Do not stand
up for a bad cause, for he will do whatever he
pleases. 4Since a king's word is supreme, who
can say to him, "What are you doing?"

[a] 18 Or *will follow them both* [b] 27 Or *leader of the assembly*

7:13–14 God is in control of our world. Since God created the world and the laws that govern it, we should follow his plan. Doing things God's way will lead us to live in harmony with him, with other people and with the world we live in. Though we will never understand everything about our world or why things happen the way they do, God is in control. By trusting him and obeying his Word, we can live productive and joyful lives. Living at odds with God's plan will ultimately only hurt us.

7:15–17 The Teacher does not suggest that we compromise our commitment to righteousness. Sin is destructive. This warning was probably the Teacher's way of suggesting that we avoid extremes in all areas of our lives. But it also serves as a literal admonition against being so caught up in religious things that we miss what's going on around us. We must always be careful to keep in touch with the concerns and needs of others.

5 Whoever obeys his command will come to
no harm,
and the wise heart will know the proper
time and procedure.
6 For there is a proper time and procedure
for every matter,
though a man's misery weighs heavily
upon him.

7 Since no man knows the future,
who can tell him what is to come?
8 No man has power over the wind to
contain it[a];
so no one has power over the day of his
death.
As no one is discharged in time of war,
so wickedness will not release those who
practice it.

9 All this I saw, as I applied my mind to everything done under the sun. There is a time when
a man lords it over others to his own[b] hurt.
10 Then too, I saw the wicked buried—those who
used to come and go from the holy place and
receive praise[c] in the city where they did this.
This too is meaningless.
11 When the sentence for a crime is not quickly carried out, the hearts of the people are filled
with schemes to do wrong. 12 Although a wicked
man commits a hundred crimes and still lives a
long time, I know that it will go better with
God-fearing men, who are reverent before God.
13 Yet because the wicked do not fear God, it will
not go well with them, and their days will not
lengthen like a shadow.
14 There is something else meaningless that
occurs on earth: righteous men who get what
the wicked deserve, and wicked men who get
what the righteous deserve. This too, I say, is
meaningless. 15 So I commend the enjoyment of
life, because nothing is better for a man under
the sun than to eat and drink and be glad. Then
joy will accompany him in his work all the days
of the life God has given him under the sun.
16 When I applied my mind to know wisdom
and to observe man's labor on earth—his eyes
not seeing sleep day or night— 17 then I saw all
that God has done. No one can comprehend
what goes on under the sun. Despite all his
efforts to search it out, man cannot discover its
meaning. Even if a wise man claims he knows,
he cannot really comprehend it.

A Common Destiny for All

9 So I reflected on all this and concluded that
the righteous and the wise and what they
do are in God's hands, but no man knows
whether love or hate awaits him. 2 All share
a common destiny—the righteous and the
wicked, the good and the bad,[d] the clean
and the unclean, those who offer sacrifices and
those who do not.

As it is with the good man,
so with the sinner;
as it is with those who take oaths,
so with those who are afraid to take
them.

3 This is the evil in everything that happens
under the sun: The same destiny overtakes all.
The hearts of men, moreover, are full of evil and
there is madness in their hearts while they live,
and afterward they join the dead. 4 Anyone who
is among the living has hope[e]—even a live dog
is better off than a dead lion!

5 For the living know that they will die,
but the dead know nothing;
they have no further reward,
and even the memory of them is
forgotten.
6 Their love, their hate
and their jealousy have long since
vanished;
never again will they have a part
in anything that happens under the sun.

7 Go, eat your food with gladness, and drink
your wine with a joyful heart, for it is now that
God favors what you do. 8 Always be clothed in
white, and always anoint your head with oil.
9 Enjoy life with your wife, whom you love, all
the days of this meaningless life that God has
given you under the sun—all your meaningless
days. For this is your lot in life and in your
toilsome labor under the sun. 10 Whatever your
hand finds to do, do it with all your might, for
in the grave,[f] where you are going, there is
neither working nor planning nor knowledge
nor wisdom.

11 I have seen something else under the sun:

The race is not to the swift
or the battle to the strong,
nor does food come to the wise
or wealth to the brilliant
or favor to the learned;
but time and chance happen to them all.

12 Moreover, no man knows when his hour
will come:

As fish are caught in a cruel net,
or birds are taken in a snare,
so men are trapped by evil times
that fall unexpectedly upon them.

[a]8 Or *over his spirit to retain it* [b]9 Or *to their*
[c]10 Some Hebrew manuscripts and Septuagint (Aquila); most Hebrew manuscripts *and are forgotten*
[d]2 Septuagint (Aquila), Vulgate and Syriac; Hebrew does not have *and the bad.* [e]4 Or *What then is to be chosen? With all who live, there is hope* [f]10 Hebrew *Sheol*

8:14 The Teacher noticed something that didn't make sense. Some good people suffer, and some wicked people prosper. Here we are advised not to trouble our minds with problems we cannot solve. We will never have the whole picture. Only God can understand the reasons behind everything; we need to trust him.

Wisdom Better Than Folly

13I also saw under the sun this example of
wisdom that greatly impressed me: 14There was
once a small city with only a few people in it.
And a powerful king came against it, surrounded it and built huge siegeworks against it.
15Now there lived in that city a man poor but
wise, and he saved the city by his wisdom. But
nobody remembered that poor man. 16So I said,
"Wisdom is better than strength." But the poor
man's wisdom is despised, and his words are no
longer heeded.

17The quiet words of the wise are more to be heeded
than the shouts of a ruler of fools.
18Wisdom is better than weapons of war,
but one sinner destroys much good.

10 As dead flies give perfume a bad smell,
so a little folly outweighs wisdom and honor.
2The heart of the wise inclines to the right,
but the heart of the fool to the left.
3Even as he walks along the road,
the fool lacks sense
and shows everyone how stupid he is.
4If a ruler's anger rises against you,
do not leave your post;
calmness can lay great errors to rest.

5There is an evil I have seen under the sun,
the sort of error that arises from a ruler:
6Fools are put in many high positions,
while the rich occupy the low ones.
7I have seen slaves on horseback,
while princes go on foot like slaves.

8Whoever digs a pit may fall into it;
whoever breaks through a wall may be bitten by a snake.
9Whoever quarries stones may be injured by them;
whoever splits logs may be endangered by them.

10If the ax is dull
and its edge unsharpened,
more strength is needed
but skill will bring success.

11If a snake bites before it is charmed,
there is no profit for the charmer.

12Words from a wise man's mouth are gracious,
but a fool is consumed by his own lips.
13At the beginning his words are folly;
at the end they are wicked madness—
14 and the fool multiplies words.

No one knows what is coming—
who can tell him what will happen after him?

15A fool's work wearies him;
he does not know the way to town.

16Woe to you, O land whose king was a servant[a]
and whose princes feast in the morning.
17Blessed are you, O land whose king is of noble birth
and whose princes eat at a proper time—
for strength and not for drunkenness.

18If a man is lazy, the rafters sag;
if his hands are idle, the house leaks.

19A feast is made for laughter,
and wine makes life merry,
but money is the answer for everything.

20Do not revile the king even in your thoughts,
or curse the rich in your bedroom,
because a bird of the air may carry your words,
and a bird on the wing may report what you say.

Bread Upon the Waters

11 Cast your bread upon the waters,
for after many days you will find it again.
2Give portions to seven, yes to eight,
for you do not know what disaster may come upon the land.

3If clouds are full of water,
they pour rain upon the earth.
Whether a tree falls to the south or to the north,
in the place where it falls, there will it lie.
4Whoever watches the wind will not plant;
whoever looks at the clouds will not reap.

5As you do not know the path of the wind,
or how the body is formed[b] in a mother's womb,
so you cannot understand the work of God,
the Maker of all things.

6Sow your seed in the morning,
and at evening let not your hands be idle,
for you do not know which will succeed,

[a]16 Or *king is a child* [b]5 Or *know how life* (or *the spirit*) / *enters the body being formed*

9:13–18 Even though wisdom in itself cannot give meaning to our lives, wisdom is still clearly to be desired over foolishness. Wisdom is not meaningless in an absolute sense, but it is limited for the purpose of putting together the pieces of the puzzle of life.
11:5–6 For the last time in the book of Ecclesiastes, the Teacher reminds us of the limits of our understanding. He counsels diligence, since we do not know the outcome of our labor. We will never understand all the events of our lives. But God has given us instructions to follow. We need to be diligent as we obey the will of our faithful and loving God.

whether this or that,
or whether both will do equally well.

Remember Your Creator While Young

7Light is sweet,
and it pleases the eyes to see the sun.
8However many years a man may live,
let him enjoy them all.
But let him remember the days of darkness,
for they will be many.
Everything to come is meaningless.

9Be happy, young man, while you are young,
and let your heart give you joy in the days of your youth.
Follow the ways of your heart
and whatever your eyes see,
but know that for all these things
God will bring you to judgment.
10So then, banish anxiety from your heart
and cast off the troubles of your body,
for youth and vigor are meaningless.

12 Remember your Creator
in the days of your youth,
before the days of trouble come
and the years approach when you will say,
"I find no pleasure in them"—
2before the sun and the light
and the moon and the stars grow dark,
and the clouds return after the rain;
3when the keepers of the house tremble,
and the strong men stoop,
when the grinders cease because they are few,
and those looking through the windows grow dim;
4when the doors to the street are closed
and the sound of grinding fades;
when men rise up at the sound of birds,
but all their songs grow faint;
5when men are afraid of heights
and of dangers in the streets;
when the almond tree blossoms
and the grasshopper drags himself along
and desire no longer is stirred.
Then man goes to his eternal home
and mourners go about the streets.

6Remember him—before the silver cord is severed,
or the golden bowl is broken;
before the pitcher is shattered at the spring,
or the wheel broken at the well,
7and the dust returns to the ground it came from,
and the spirit returns to God who gave it.

8"Meaningless! Meaningless!" says the Teacher.[a]
"Everything is meaningless!"

The Conclusion of the Matter

9Not only was the Teacher wise, but also he
imparted knowledge to the people. He pondered and searched out and set in order many
proverbs. 10The Teacher searched to find just
the right words, and what he wrote was upright
and true.
11The words of the wise are like goads, their
collected sayings like firmly embedded nails—
given by one Shepherd. 12Be warned, my son, of
anything in addition to them.
Of making many books there is no end, and
much study wearies the body.

13Now all has been heard;
here is the conclusion of the matter:
Fear God and keep his commandments,
for this is the whole ⌊duty⌋ of man.
14For God will bring every deed into judgment,
including every hidden thing,
whether it is good or evil.

[a]8 Or *the leader of the assembly;* also in verses 9 and 10

12:1 Our relationship with God is foundational for coping with life in a fallen world. We are encouraged to remember God in our youth before we grow old and no longer have the ambition to carry out his will.

12:13–14 These final verses remind us of the importance of our relationship with God as we live in a fallen world. Life is filled with ambiguity; there are many things that we will never understand. But God sees the big picture; he knows what will happen in the future. If we follow his plan—obeying his commandments with his help—we will discover joy amidst the ambiguity.

SONG OF SONGS

The Big Picture

A. COURTSHIP (1:1–3:5)

B. MARRIAGE CEREMONY AND CONSUMMATION (3:6–5:1)

C. SEPARATION (5:2–6:13)

D. RESOLUTION AND STRENGTHENING OF LOVE (7:1–8:14)

No other book in the Bible describes the sexual relationship in such detail and with such affirmation. Ironically, in our society the Bible is often thought to deny the importance of the sexual relationship. God is clearly not embarrassed by the topic. In fact, he is the one who created sex in the first place! It stands to reason that God is also the best qualified to tell us how to experience sex with the greatest fulfillment.

The Song of Songs is characterized by the use of rich, figurative language that helps the lovers express the inexpressible about each other. The words are full of passion and emotion, and the figures of speech are designed to paint visual pictures so we can share in the emotional experience of the lovers.

The song develops a history of the relationship between Solomon and his lover. It is not a continuous history but a series of seemingly isolated snapshots. The couple meets, and their love matures through courtship. Then the reader is taken to the wedding ceremony and the wedding night. In an unspecified later time, the couple encounters separation, and then they passionately renew their love for each other.

The words of each lover clearly focus on the physical aspects of married love. Even the way Solomon and his bride praise each other is focused almost exclusively on their physical attributes. They have come to see each other as thoroughly beautiful. Marriage symbolically illustrates the love relationship between Christ and the church (see Ephesians 5:23–33), and Solomon's song has often been used as an illustration of God's love for his people. However, the primary focus of the Song of Songs is the celebration of sexual love in the context of marriage.

Spiritual Renewal Themes

THE BEAUTY OF GOD'S CREATION

Our past experiences may have limited our ability to see the many beautiful things that God has created for us to enjoy. If we have been sexually abused, our legitimate personal boundaries have been destroyed. This has soiled the beautiful sexual experience God intended. When misused, sex can become an experience of pain and fear. The Song of Songs helps us see sexuality as God intended it—a physical love that is shameless and beautiful in God's eyes. If we have misused our sexuality or

have been sexually abused, God can restore us so that we can see the beauty in what he has created.

THE BEAUTY OF PEOPLE

At several points in the poem, Solomon described his bride's appearance using beautiful metaphors from nature. She may not have been considered attractive by the general public or even by herself (see 1:6), but Solomon saw her as exquisitely beautiful—no doubt due to his biased perspective as her lover. In much the same way, God sees everyone as beautiful because he sees us through the filter of Christ's work on our behalf. We should all practice viewing each other as God views us—immensely beautiful.

THE JOY OF COMMITTED LOVE

Our culture's understanding of love is largely distorted and twisted. It is a form of love that is driven by selfish desires, and it often involves some form of exploitation or abuse of those involved. In the Song of Songs we see the beauty of committed love, a love that is protected by God-given boundaries. God designed sexual intercourse as a holy means of celebrating love, producing children and experiencing pleasure. As we seek to follow God's design for our lives, we need to rediscover God's design for our sexuality. God's Word makes it clear that sexual intercourse is to be kept holy, within the boundaries of marriage.

Essential Facts

PURPOSE:
To tell of the love between a bridegroom and his bride, affirming the sanctity of marriage and the richness of physical love.

AUTHOR:
Solomon.

AUDIENCE:
The people of Israel.

DATE WRITTEN:
Probably during the early part of Solomon's reign.

SETTING:
Jerusalem and the surrounding countryside.

KEY VERSE:
"I am my lover's and my lover is mine; he browses among the lilies" (6:3).

KEY PEOPLE AND RELATIONSHIPS:
Solomon, his bride and the young women of Jerusalem.

1 Solomon's Song of Songs.

Beloved[a]

2Let him kiss me with the kisses of his mouth—
for your love is more delightful than wine.
3Pleasing is the fragrance of your perfumes;
your name is like perfume poured out.
No wonder the maidens love you!
4Take me away with you—let us hurry!
Let the king bring me into his chambers.

Friends

We rejoice and delight in you[b];
we will praise your love more than wine.

Beloved

How right they are to adore you!

5Dark am I, yet lovely,
O daughters of Jerusalem,
dark like the tents of Kedar,
like the tent curtains of Solomon.[c]
6Do not stare at me because I am dark,
because I am darkened by the sun.
My mother's sons were angry with me
and made me take care of the vineyards;
my own vineyard I have neglected.
7Tell me, you whom I love, where you graze your flock
and where you rest your sheep at midday.
Why should I be like a veiled woman
beside the flocks of your friends?

Friends

8If you do not know, most beautiful of women,
follow the tracks of the sheep
and graze your young goats
by the tents of the shepherds.

Lover

9I liken you, my darling, to a mare
harnessed to one of the chariots of Pharaoh.
10Your cheeks are beautiful with earrings,
your neck with strings of jewels.
11We will make you earrings of gold,
studded with silver.

Beloved

12While the king was at his table,
my perfume spread its fragrance.
13My lover is to me a sachet of myrrh
resting between my breasts.
14My lover is to me a cluster of henna blossoms
from the vineyards of En Gedi.

Lover

15How beautiful you are, my darling!
Oh, how beautiful!
Your eyes are doves.

Beloved

16How handsome you are, my lover!
Oh, how charming!
And our bed is verdant.

Lover

17The beams of our house are cedars;
our rafters are firs.

Beloved[d]

2 I am a rose[e] of Sharon,
a lily of the valleys.

Lover

2Like a lily among thorns
is my darling among the maidens.

Beloved

3Like an apple tree among the trees of the forest
is my lover among the young men.
I delight to sit in his shade,
and his fruit is sweet to my taste.
4He has taken me to the banquet hall,
and his banner over me is love.
5Strengthen me with raisins,
refresh me with apples,
for I am faint with love.
6His left arm is under my head,
and his right arm embraces me.
7Daughters of Jerusalem, I charge you
by the gazelles and by the does of the field:
Do not arouse or awaken love
until it so desires.

[a]Primarily on the basis of the gender of the Hebrew pronouns used, male and female speakers are indicated in the margins by the captions *Lover* and *Beloved* respectively. The words of others are marked *Friends*. In some instances the divisions and their captions are debatable.
[b]4 The Hebrew is masculine singular. [c]5 Or *Salma*
[d]1 Or *Lover* [e]1 Possibly a member of the crocus family

1:6 Because of our appearance, we may feel unacceptable. But God wants us to know that no matter how ugly or unacceptable we feel, he loves us and accepts us. We need to learn to trust him, obey his loving plan for our lives and grow to respect ourselves.

1:9–17 This is the first of many sections of mutual praise and admiration between the bride and groom. There is no hint of criticism or sarcasm, two common elements in a deteriorating relationship. Notice especially the creative ways in which the lovers compliment each other. Our relationships are extremely important to our spiritual growth. We might learn a few lessons here that will help us maintain the relationships God has given us.

2:7 Though she delighted in being with her groom, the bride desired sexual restraint until the proper time—until marriage. It is easy to see how difficult this restraint was for her, which is why she implored her friends for their help in keeping her desire under control until the wedding night. The assumption of the book is that sex should occur only within the parameters of marriage.

8Listen! My lover!
Look! Here he comes,
leaping across the mountains,
bounding over the hills.
9My lover is like a gazelle or a young stag.
Look! There he stands behind our wall,
gazing through the windows,
peering through the lattice.
10My lover spoke and said to me,
"Arise, my darling,
my beautiful one, and come with me.
11See! The winter is past;
the rains are over and gone.
12Flowers appear on the earth;
the season of singing has come,
the cooing of doves
is heard in our land.
13The fig tree forms its early fruit;
the blossoming vines spread their fragrance.
Arise, come, my darling;
my beautiful one, come with me."

Lover

14My dove in the clefts of the rock,
in the hiding places on the mountainside,
show me your face,
let me hear your voice;
for your voice is sweet,
and your face is lovely.
15Catch for us the foxes,
the little foxes
that ruin the vineyards,
our vineyards that are in bloom.

Beloved

16My lover is mine and I am his;
he browses among the lilies.
17Until the day breaks
and the shadows flee,
turn, my lover,
and be like a gazelle
or like a young stag
on the rugged hills.[a]

3 All night long on my bed
I looked for the one my heart loves;
I looked for him but did not find him.
2I will get up now and go about the city,
through its streets and squares;
I will search for the one my heart loves.
So I looked for him but did not find him.
3The watchmen found me
as they made their rounds in the city.
"Have you seen the one my heart loves?"
4Scarcely had I passed them
when I found the one my heart loves.
I held him and would not let him go
till I had brought him to my mother's house,
to the room of the one who conceived me.
5Daughters of Jerusalem, I charge you
by the gazelles and by the does of the field:
Do not arouse or awaken love
until it so desires.

6Who is this coming up from the desert
like a column of smoke,
perfumed with myrrh and incense
made from all the spices of the merchant?
7Look! It is Solomon's carriage,
escorted by sixty warriors,
the noblest of Israel,
8all of them wearing the sword,
all experienced in battle,
each with his sword at his side,
prepared for the terrors of the night.
9King Solomon made for himself the carriage;
he made it of wood from Lebanon.
10Its posts he made of silver,
its base of gold.
Its seat was upholstered with purple,
its interior lovingly inlaid
by[b] the daughters of Jerusalem.
11Come out, you daughters of Zion,
and look at King Solomon wearing the crown,
the crown with which his mother crowned him
on the day of his wedding,
the day his heart rejoiced.

Lover

4 How beautiful you are, my darling!
Oh, how beautiful!
Your eyes behind your veil are doves.
Your hair is like a flock of goats
descending from Mount Gilead.
2Your teeth are like a flock of sheep just shorn,
coming up from the washing.
Each has its twin;

[a]17 Or *the hills of Bether* [b]10 Or *its inlaid interior a gift of love / from*

3:6–11 As was customary in ancient Israel, the groom would travel to the home of the bride via an elaborate procession. After the ceremony and wedding feast, the newly married couple would then go to the groom's home to consummate the marriage. They were not to live with his parents, as was typical of other cultures of the ancient Near East, but were to follow God's injunction and form a new household (see Genesis 2:24).

4:1–7 In perhaps the most sensual part of the book, Solomon described his bride from a lover's perspective. Though she may not have been considered attractive by the general public, or even by herself (see 1:6), he saw her as exquisitely beautiful. In the same way, no matter how broken and sinful our lives are, God sees past our flaws. Jesus Christ paid for all our sins by dying for us. Because of this, God can look on us as this lover looks on his bride.

not one of them is alone.
3Your lips are like a scarlet ribbon;
your mouth is lovely.
Your temples behind your veil
are like the halves of a pomegranate.
4Your neck is like the tower of David,
built with elegance[a];
on it hang a thousand shields,
all of them shields of warriors.
5Your two breasts are like two fawns,
like twin fawns of a gazelle
that browse among the lilies.
6Until the day breaks
and the shadows flee,
I will go to the mountain of myrrh
and to the hill of incense.
7All beautiful you are, my darling;
there is no flaw in you.

8Come with me from Lebanon, my bride,
come with me from Lebanon.
Descend from the crest of Amana,
from the top of Senir, the summit of Hermon,
from the lions' dens
and the mountain haunts of the leopards.
9You have stolen my heart, my sister, my bride;
you have stolen my heart
with one glance of your eyes,
with one jewel of your necklace.
10How delightful is your love, my sister, my bride!
How much more pleasing is your love than wine,
and the fragrance of your perfume than any spice!
11Your lips drop sweetness as the honeycomb, my bride;
milk and honey are under your tongue.
The fragrance of your garments is like that of Lebanon.
12You are a garden locked up, my sister, my bride;
you are a spring enclosed, a sealed fountain.
13Your plants are an orchard of pomegranates
with choice fruits,
with henna and nard,
14 nard and saffron,
calamus and cinnamon,
with every kind of incense tree,
with myrrh and aloes
and all the finest spices.
15You are[b] a garden fountain,
a well of flowing water
streaming down from Lebanon.

Beloved

16Awake, north wind,
and come, south wind!
Blow on my garden,
that its fragrance may spread abroad.
Let my lover come into his garden
and taste its choice fruits.

Lover

5 I have come into my garden, my sister, my bride;
I have gathered my myrrh with my spice.
I have eaten my honeycomb and my honey;
I have drunk my wine and my milk.

Friends

Eat, O friends, and drink;
drink your fill, O lovers.

Beloved

2I slept but my heart was awake.
Listen! My lover is knocking:
"Open to me, my sister, my darling,
my dove, my flawless one.
My head is drenched with dew,
my hair with the dampness of the night."
3I have taken off my robe—
must I put it on again?
I have washed my feet—
must I soil them again?
4My lover thrust his hand through the latch-opening;
my heart began to pound for him.
5I arose to open for my lover,
and my hands dripped with myrrh,
my fingers with flowing myrrh,
on the handles of the lock.
6I opened for my lover,
but my lover had left; he was gone.
My heart sank at his departure.[c]
I looked for him but did not find him.
I called him but he did not answer.
7The watchmen found me
as they made their rounds in the city.

[a]4 The meaning of the Hebrew for this word is uncertain.
[b]15 Or *I am* (spoken by the *Beloved*)
[c]6 Or *heart had gone out to him when he spoke*

4:12–15 The bride is compared to a garden, a spring and a fountain, which have been inaccessible to Solomon until now. The sexual enjoyment of the couple is compared to choice fruits that have come out of her garden. Many of us may suffer from the pain of having been violated by others. We may feel that our sexuality has been spoiled. But God, who created our sexuality, is capable of restoring it. Notice that each of the symbols used here—the garden, the spring and the fountain—are symbols of recurring freshness. Even after a dormant season, they soon return to their original condition. With God's help, our sexuality can also be restored.

5:1 Solomon delighted in his sexual relationship with his bride. He realized that people were created to enjoy sexual intimacy, and he celebrated that truth. God has given us the sexual relationship between a man and a woman as a gift to be enjoyed within marriage. Sexual intimacy can seem very ugly when practiced outside these proper bounds. If our sexuality has been violated in this way, we need to look to God for healing and restoration. He will help us rebuild the boundaries we need for a healthy and enjoyable sexual relationship.

They beat me, they bruised me;
they took away my cloak,
those watchmen of the walls!
8O daughters of Jerusalem, I charge you—
if you find my lover,
what will you tell him?
Tell him I am faint with love.

Friends

9How is your beloved better than others,
most beautiful of women?
How is your beloved better than others,
that you charge us so?

Beloved

10My lover is radiant and ruddy,
outstanding among ten thousand.
11His head is purest gold;
his hair is wavy
and black as a raven.
12His eyes are like doves
by the water streams,
washed in milk,
mounted like jewels.
13His cheeks are like beds of spice
yielding perfume.
His lips are like lilies
dripping with myrrh.
14His arms are rods of gold
set with chrysolite.
His body is like polished ivory
decorated with sapphires.[a]
15His legs are pillars of marble
set on bases of pure gold.
His appearance is like Lebanon,
choice as its cedars.
16His mouth is sweetness itself;
he is altogether lovely.
This is my lover, this my friend,
O daughters of Jerusalem.

Friends

6 Where has your lover gone,
most beautiful of women?
Which way did your lover turn,
that we may look for him with you?

Beloved

2My lover has gone down to his garden,
to the beds of spices,
to browse in the gardens
and to gather lilies.
3I am my lover's and my lover is mine;
he browses among the lilies.

Lover

4You are beautiful, my darling, as Tirzah,
lovely as Jerusalem,
majestic as troops with banners.
5Turn your eyes from me;
they overwhelm me.
Your hair is like a flock of goats
descending from Gilead.
6Your teeth are like a flock of sheep
coming up from the washing.
Each has its twin,
not one of them is alone.
7Your temples behind your veil
are like the halves of a pomegranate.
8Sixty queens there may be,
and eighty concubines,
and virgins beyond number;
9but my dove, my perfect one, is unique,
the only daughter of her mother,
the favorite of the one who bore her.
The maidens saw her and called her
blessed;
the queens and concubines praised
her.

Friends

10Who is this that appears like the dawn,
fair as the moon, bright as the sun,
majestic as the stars in procession?

Lover

11I went down to the grove of nut trees
to look at the new growth in the valley,
to see if the vines had budded
or the pomegranates were in bloom.
12Before I realized it,
my desire set me among the royal
chariots of my people.[b]

Friends

13Come back, come back, O Shulammite;
come back, come back, that we may gaze
on you!

Lover

Why would you gaze on the Shulammite
as on the dance of Mahanaim?

7 How beautiful your sandaled feet,
O prince's daughter!
Your graceful legs are like jewels,
the work of a craftsman's hands.

[a]14 Or *lapis lazuli* [b]12 Or *among the chariots of Amminadab;* or *among the chariots of the people of the prince*

5:9–16 The young women of Jerusalem urged the young bride to remind herself of all the things she loved about her husband. Her description began with his physical attributes; it concluded with her calling him both her lover and her friend (5:16). Even though the descriptions in the Song of Songs emphasize the physical relationship, the two lovers had apparently also cultivated a solid friendship.

7:1–9 Solomon's praise of his bride continues. As the couple matured in their love, their passion did not diminish. Yet in all relationships there are times of indifference and rejection. But this passage indicates that passionate love can last as a marriage matures. Maintaining our relationships through the periods of ebb and flow of life is vital to our spiritual growth.

2Your navel is a rounded goblet
that never lacks blended wine.
Your waist is a mound of wheat
encircled by lilies.
3Your breasts are like two fawns,
twins of a gazelle.
4Your neck is like an ivory tower.
Your eyes are the pools of Heshbon
by the gate of Bath Rabbim.
Your nose is like the tower of Lebanon
looking toward Damascus.
5Your head crowns you like Mount Carmel.
Your hair is like royal tapestry;
the king is held captive by its tresses.
6How beautiful you are and how pleasing,
O love, with your delights!
7Your stature is like that of the palm,
and your breasts like clusters of fruit.
8I said, "I will climb the palm tree;
I will take hold of its fruit."
May your breasts be like the clusters of the
vine,
the fragrance of your breath like apples,
9 and your mouth like the best wine.

Beloved

May the wine go straight to my lover,
flowing gently over lips and teeth.[a]
10I belong to my lover,
and his desire is for me.
11Come, my lover, let us go to the
countryside,
let us spend the night in the villages.[b]
12Let us go early to the vineyards
to see if the vines have budded,
if their blossoms have opened,
and if the pomegranates are in bloom—
there I will give you my love.
13The mandrakes send out their fragrance,
and at our door is every delicacy,
both new and old,
that I have stored up for you, my lover.

8 If only you were to me like a brother,
who was nursed at my mother's breasts!
Then, if I found you outside,
I would kiss you,
and no one would despise me.
2I would lead you
and bring you to my mother's house—
she who has taught me.
I would give you spiced wine to drink,
the nectar of my pomegranates.
3His left arm is under my head
and his right arm embraces me.
4Daughters of Jerusalem, I charge you:
Do not arouse or awaken love
until it so desires.

Friends

5Who is this coming up from the desert
leaning on her lover?

Beloved

Under the apple tree I roused you;
there your mother conceived you,
there she who was in labor gave you
birth.
6Place me like a seal over your heart,
like a seal on your arm;
for love is as strong as death,
its jealousy[c] unyielding as the grave.[d]
It burns like blazing fire,
like a mighty flame.[e]
7Many waters cannot quench love;
rivers cannot wash it away.
If one were to give
all the wealth of his house for love,
it[f] would be utterly scorned.

Friends

8We have a young sister,
and her breasts are not yet grown.
What shall we do for our sister
for the day she is spoken for?
9If she is a wall,
we will build towers of silver on her.
If she is a door,
we will enclose her with panels of
cedar.

[a]9 Septuagint, Aquila, Vulgate and Syriac; Hebrew *lips of sleepers* [b]11 Or *henna bushes* [c]6 Or *ardor* [d]6 Hebrew *Sheol* [e]6 Or / *like the very flame of the LORD* [f]7 Or *he*

7:10–13 The couple returned to the countryside villages to renew their love. They celebrated their renewal in the same place that they had met—in the vineyards (7:12). This would have reminded them of the tender moments they had shared when they first fell in love, almost re-creating some of those moments as they were together. The example of Solomon and his bride should inspire us to do what we can to put some sparkle back into our own marriage relationship.

8:6–7 This eloquent statement describing committed love shows the renewed fervor of a love that endures and resolves conflict. The seal, or signet ring, was symbolic of Solomon's commitment to his bride. The jealousy mentioned in 8:6 is a positive emotion; it speaks of the accountability shared between Solomon and his bride. Their commitment was so strong that there would be serious consequences for anyone who threatened it. Given his vast wealth, Solomon could speak from experience about the value of love over riches. True love can never be bought; it must be cultivated. Relationships characterized by commitment, love and accountability need to be cultivated in order to help us preserve our spiritual gains.

8:8–12 These verses assume the fact that sexual expression is to be limited to the marriage relationship. The girl's brothers desired to protect their sister from sexual activity prior to her marriage. Sexual activity outside the safety of marriage commitment is always destructive. It may bring pleasure for a while, but it will never lead to a life of stability and fulfillment. We need to build relationships characterized by trust and honesty and keep sexual activity in the proper context—marriage.

Beloved

10I am a wall,
and my breasts are like towers.
Thus I have become in his eyes
like one bringing contentment.
11Solomon had a vineyard in Baal Hamon;
he let out his vineyard to tenants.
Each was to bring for its fruit
a thousand shekels[a] of silver.
12But my own vineyard is mine to give;
the thousand shekels are for you,
O Solomon,
and two hundred[b] are for those who
tend its fruit.

Lover

13You who dwell in the gardens
with friends in attendance,
let me hear your voice!

Beloved

14Come away, my lover,
and be like a gazelle
or like a young stag
on the spice-laden mountains.

[a] *11* That is, about 25 pounds (about 11.5 kilograms); also in verse 12 [b] *12* That is, about 5 pounds (about 2.3 kilograms)

ISAIAH

The Big Picture

Though it is never easy, facing the truth brings healing. God spoke through Isaiah to address the sins of the people of Judah. Over the centuries the people of Judah had turned away from God and practiced idolatry. They had developed corrupt and oppressive behaviors. And, though repeatedly confronted by Isaiah, the people refused to admit their sin. Instead, they blamed God for their sufferings and wondered why he refused to bless them.

The first part of Isaiah (1:1—39:8) is dominated by Isaiah's message of judgment. The Assyrians had recently destroyed the northern kingdom of Israel and now threatened to destroy Judah as well. God told the people of Judah that deliverance would come, but only if they repented of their sins and turned to him for help. The people of Judah only trusted in God superficially. They sought to save themselves through clever political alliances with Assyria and Egypt. Their human attempts to escape the suffering of exile could never bring about their permanent deliverance. God allowed Judah to survive the attacks of Egypt and Assyria, but a few generations later, Judah was ultimately crushed by Babylon.

The second part of Isaiah (40:1—66:24) is dominated by God's message of hope. In spite of Judah's unworthiness, God promised that he would lead his people out of their Babylonian captivity. He foretold the ministry of his suffering servant and his ultimate victory that would culminate in a new heaven and a new earth. Through the words of Isaiah we discover that God's ultimate purpose for his people is blessing and restoration.

Spiritual Renewal Themes

TRUTH BRINGS HEALING

Because the truth often hurts, we may try to protect ourselves from it. When Isaiah told the people of Judah the truth about their sin, they chose to hide from the truth too. They refused to admit that they had failed. By failing to face the truth, they also refused to experience healing. Our spiritual renewal can only progress to the degree that we open ourselves to the truth, regardless of how painful that might be.

SPIRITUAL BLINDNESS LEADS TO BLAMING

Instead of admitting their sin and responding to the truth, the people of Judah blamed God for the terrible consequences of their sin. If we continue in our spiritual blindness, we will also become expert at shifting blame. The painful circumstances we may suffer as a result will be a direct consequence of our own failures and refusal to see the truth. We must take responsibility for our actions if we desire to progress spiritually.

SPIRITUAL RENEWAL THROUGH CONFRONTATION

God wanted to restore the people of Judah. Through Isaiah, God confronted them with the truth of their sin. Isaiah's words of confrontation, however, were punctuated by the message of God's love and hope. The model of confrontation found in the book of Isaiah can help us as we intervene in the lives of the people we love who are trapped in ongoing cycles of sin. Our words of confrontation need to be balanced by words and actions that demonstrate our love and forgiveness. Confrontation rendered in anger will only bring about greater conflict and deeper destruction.

Essential Facts

PURPOSE:
To confront the people of Judah with their sin and to lead them to rebuild their lives based on God's promises.

AUTHOR:
The prophet Isaiah.

AUDIENCE:
Isaiah 1–39 was spoken to the people of Judah before their exile; Isaiah 40–66 records a message of hope for future generations of exiled Jews.

DATE WRITTEN:
The book includes oracles given throughout Isaiah's ministry (740–681 B.C.).

SETTING:
The land of Judah before its destruction by Babylon.

KEY VERSE:
"But he was pierced for our transgressions, he was crushed for our iniquities; the punishment that brought us peace was upon him, and by his wounds we are healed" (53:5).

KEY PLACES:
Judah, Egypt, Assyria, Babylonia and Persia.

KEY PEOPLE AND RELATIONSHIPS:
Isaiah with kings Ahaz and Hezekiah of Judah and with King Cyrus of Persia.

1 The vision concerning Judah and Jerusalem that Isaiah son of Amoz saw during the reigns of Uzziah, Jotham, Ahaz and Hezekiah, kings of Judah.

A Rebellious Nation

2Hear, O heavens! Listen, O earth!
For the LORD has spoken:
"I reared children and brought them up,
but they have rebelled against me.
3The ox knows his master,
the donkey his owner's manger,
but Israel does not know,
my people do not understand."

4Ah, sinful nation,
a people loaded with guilt,
a brood of evildoers,
children given to corruption!
They have forsaken the LORD;
they have spurned the Holy One of Israel
and turned their backs on him.

5Why should you be beaten anymore?
Why do you persist in rebellion?
Your whole head is injured,
your whole heart afflicted.
6From the sole of your foot to the top of your head
there is no soundness—
only wounds and welts
and open sores,
not cleansed or bandaged
or soothed with oil.

7Your country is desolate,
your cities burned with fire;
your fields are being stripped by foreigners
right before you,
laid waste as when overthrown by strangers.
8The Daughter of Zion is left
like a shelter in a vineyard,
like a hut in a field of melons,
like a city under siege.
9Unless the LORD Almighty
had left us some survivors,
we would have become like Sodom,
we would have been like Gomorrah.

10Hear the word of the LORD,
you rulers of Sodom;
listen to the law of our God,
you people of Gomorrah!
11"The multitude of your sacrifices—
what are they to me?" says the LORD.
"I have more than enough of burnt offerings,
of rams and the fat of fattened animals;
I have no pleasure
in the blood of bulls and lambs and goats.
12When you come to appear before me,
who has asked this of you,
this trampling of my courts?
13Stop bringing meaningless offerings!
Your incense is detestable to me.
New Moons, Sabbaths and convocations—
I cannot bear your evil assemblies.
14Your New Moon festivals and your appointed feasts
my soul hates.
They have become a burden to me;
I am weary of bearing them.
15When you spread out your hands in prayer,
I will hide my eyes from you;
even if you offer many prayers,
I will not listen.
Your hands are full of blood;
16 wash and make yourselves clean.
Take your evil deeds
out of my sight!
Stop doing wrong,
17 learn to do right!
Seek justice,
encourage the oppressed.[a]
Defend the cause of the fatherless,
plead the case of the widow.

18"Come now, let us reason together,"
says the LORD.
"Though your sins are like scarlet,
they shall be as white as snow;
though they are red as crimson,
they shall be like wool.
19If you are willing and obedient,
you will eat the best from the land;
20but if you resist and rebel,
you will be devoured by the sword."
For the mouth of the LORD has spoken.

21See how the faithful city
has become a harlot!

[a]17 Or / *rebuke the oppressor*

1:2–4 Despite God's attempts to lead the people of Judah, they still went wrong. They were responsible for their sins and the consequences that would surely follow. Even though some of our problems may be inherited from our parents, we are ultimately held accountable for our actions. Taking responsibility for our problems is an essential part of our spiritual renewal and growth.

1:5–6 Because the people of Judah refused to see the truth and admit the seriousness of their sin, they continued to suffer unnecessarily. When we refuse to see the truth about our sin and do not admit we need God's cleansing and forgiveness, we often suffer the destructive consequences of trying to manage our own lives. God wants us to know that we can safely deal with truth and admit our sin in his presence. We must then trust him to bring healing and forgiveness.

1:9–20 Although the people of Judah were very religious, Isaiah said they were as evil as the people of Sodom and Gomorrah had been. Though they gave sacrifices to pay for their sins, they felt no remorse. The people needed to see the truth about their spiritual condition, acknowledge the depth of their sin and turn to God for cleansing and renewal. Religious activity is no substitute for a genuine life of faith with God. Only when we honestly confess our sins and ask God to help us will he make us "as white as snow" (1:18).

She once was full of justice;
righteousness used to dwell in her—
but now murderers!
22Your silver has become dross,
your choice wine is diluted with water.
23Your rulers are rebels,
companions of thieves;
they all love bribes
and chase after gifts.
They do not defend the cause of the fatherless;
the widow's case does not come before them.
24Therefore the Lord, the LORD Almighty,
the Mighty One of Israel, declares:
"Ah, I will get relief from my foes
and avenge myself on my enemies.
25I will turn my hand against you;
I will thoroughly purge away your dross
and remove all your impurities.
26I will restore your judges as in days of old,
your counselors as at the beginning.
Afterward you will be called
the City of Righteousness,
the Faithful City."

27Zion will be redeemed with justice,
her penitent ones with righteousness.
28But rebels and sinners will both be broken,
and those who forsake the LORD will perish.

29"You will be ashamed because of the sacred oaks
in which you have delighted;
you will be disgraced because of the gardens
that you have chosen.
30You will be like an oak with fading leaves,
like a garden without water.
31The mighty man will become tinder
and his work a spark;
both will burn together,
with no one to quench the fire."

The Mountain of the LORD

2 This is what Isaiah son of Amoz saw concerning Judah and Jerusalem:

2In the last days
the mountain of the LORD's temple will be established
as chief among the mountains;
it will be raised above the hills,
and all nations will stream to it.

3Many peoples will come and say,
"Come, let us go up to the mountain of the LORD,
to the house of the God of Jacob.
He will teach us his ways,
so that we may walk in his paths."
The law will go out from Zion,
the word of the LORD from Jerusalem.
4He will judge between the nations
and will settle disputes for many peoples.
They will beat their swords into plowshares
and their spears into pruning hooks.
Nation will not take up sword against nation,
nor will they train for war anymore.

5Come, O house of Jacob,
let us walk in the light of the LORD.

The Day of the LORD

6You have abandoned your people,
the house of Jacob.
They are full of superstitions from the East;
they practice divination like the Philistines
and clasp hands with pagans.
7Their land is full of silver and gold;
there is no end to their treasures.
Their land is full of horses;
there is no end to their chariots.
8Their land is full of idols;
they bow down to the work of their hands,
to what their fingers have made.
9So man will be brought low
and mankind humbled—
do not forgive them.[a]

10Go into the rocks,
hide in the ground
from dread of the LORD
and the splendor of his majesty!
11The eyes of the arrogant man will be humbled
and the pride of men brought low;
the LORD alone will be exalted in that day.

12The LORD Almighty has a day in store
for all the proud and lofty,
for all that is exalted
(and they will be humbled),
13for all the cedars of Lebanon, tall and lofty,
and all the oaks of Bashan,
14for all the towering mountains
and all the high hills,
15for every lofty tower

[a] 9 Or *not raise them up*

2:1–5 At the end of history, people will finally acknowledge that God is supreme. Judah was urged to live in light of that future reality. We, too, are called to give up our sins and other distractions that draw our attention from God. We need to seek out, and then live according to, God's will for us. When we do this, we will restore our present lives and also share in God's eternal kingdom.

2:6–22 Isaiah declared that those who have put their trust in anything other than God will be humbled and hide in fear when God sets up his kingdom. By trusting God rather than human programs or plans, we will not be ashamed or afraid when he fully reveals his awesome power. Any human solution we choose to trust will one day be destroyed. We would be foolish to depend on things like money, position or anything else that excludes God and his power.

and every fortified wall,
16for every trading ship[a]
and every stately vessel.
17The arrogance of man will be brought low
and the pride of men humbled;
the LORD alone will be exalted in that day,
18 and the idols will totally disappear.

19Men will flee to caves in the rocks
and to holes in the ground
from dread of the LORD
and the splendor of his majesty,
when he rises to shake the earth.
20In that day men will throw away
to the rodents and bats
their idols of silver and idols of gold,
which they made to worship.
21They will flee to caverns in the rocks
and to the overhanging crags
from dread of the LORD
and the splendor of his majesty,
when he rises to shake the earth.
22Stop trusting in man,
who has but a breath in his nostrils.
Of what account is he?

Judgment on Jerusalem and Judah

3 See now, the Lord,
the LORD Almighty,
is about to take from Jerusalem and Judah
both supply and support:
all supplies of food and all supplies of
water,
2 the hero and warrior,
the judge and prophet,
the soothsayer and elder,
3the captain of fifty and man of rank,
the counselor, skilled craftsman and
clever enchanter.

4I will make boys their officials;
mere children will govern them.
5People will oppress each other—
man against man, neighbor against
neighbor.
The young will rise up against the old,
the base against the honorable.

6A man will seize one of his brothers
at his father's home, and say,
"You have a cloak, you be our leader;
take charge of this heap of ruins!"
7But in that day he will cry out,
"I have no remedy.
I have no food or clothing in my house;
do not make me the leader of the
people."
8Jerusalem staggers,
Judah is falling;
their words and deeds are against the LORD,
defying his glorious presence.
9The look on their faces testifies against
them;
they parade their sin like Sodom;
they do not hide it.
Woe to them!
They have brought disaster upon
themselves.

10Tell the righteous it will be well with them,
for they will enjoy the fruit of their
deeds.
11Woe to the wicked! Disaster is upon them!
They will be paid back for what their hands
have done.

12Youths oppress my people,
women rule over them.
O my people, your guides lead you astray;
they turn you from the path.

13The LORD takes his place in court;
he rises to judge the people.
14The LORD enters into judgment
against the elders and leaders of his
people:
"It is you who have ruined my vineyard;
the plunder from the poor is in your
houses.
15What do you mean by crushing my people
and grinding the faces of the poor?"
declares the Lord,
the LORD Almighty.

16The LORD says,
"The women of Zion are haughty,
walking along with outstretched necks,
flirting with their eyes,
tripping along with mincing steps,
with ornaments jingling on their ankles.
17Therefore the Lord will bring sores on the
heads of the women of Zion;
the LORD will make their scalps bald."

18In that day the Lord will snatch away their
finery: the bangles and headbands and crescent
necklaces, 19the earrings and bracelets and veils,
20the headdresses and ankle chains and sashes,
the perfume bottles and charms, 21the signet
rings and nose rings, 22the fine robes and the

[a]16 Hebrew *every ship of Tarshish*

3:1–8 God would crush the people of Judah to show them that life is unmanageable without him. The people refused to listen to God's warnings, so drastic action was needed to awaken them to their true condition. If we ignore God's warnings, he may need to send a pressing trial to help us see the truth and get back on the right track. God wants us to have a joyful and meaningful life. We need to pay attention to his warnings before it is too late.
3:9–26 The wickedness of Sodom and Gomorrah was well known to the people of Judah; God had utterly destroyed those cities because of their sin (see Genesis 19). Being compared to wicked Sodom should have alerted the people to their wickedness, but it didn't. The people didn't deny their sins; they delighted in them. We are in serious spiritual danger any time that we fail to be concerned about our sinfulness. Humility and a contrite spirit are signs that we are in right relationship with God.

capes and cloaks, the purses [23]and mirrors, and the linen garments and tiaras and shawls.

[24]Instead of fragrance there will be a stench;
instead of a sash, a rope;
instead of well-dressed hair, baldness;
instead of fine clothing, sackcloth;
instead of beauty, branding.
[25]Your men will fall by the sword,
your warriors in battle.
[26]The gates of Zion will lament and mourn;
destitute, she will sit on the ground.

4 In that day seven women
will take hold of one man
and say, "We will eat our own food
and provide our own clothes;
only let us be called by your name.
Take away our disgrace!"

The Branch of the LORD

[2]In that day the Branch of the LORD will be
beautiful and glorious, and the fruit of the land
will be the pride and glory of the survivors in
Israel. [3]Those who are left in Zion, who remain
in Jerusalem, will be called holy, all who are
recorded among the living in Jerusalem. [4]The
Lord will wash away the filth of the women of
Zion; he will cleanse the bloodstains from Jerusalem by a spirit[a] of judgment and a spirit[a]
of fire. [5]Then the LORD will create over all of
Mount Zion and over those who assemble there
a cloud of smoke by day and a glow of flaming
fire by night; over all the glory will be a canopy.
[6]It will be a shelter and shade from the heat of
the day, and a refuge and hiding place from the
storm and rain.

The Song of the Vineyard

5 I will sing for the one I love
a song about his vineyard:
My loved one had a vineyard
on a fertile hillside.
[2]He dug it up and cleared it of stones
and planted it with the choicest vines.
He built a watchtower in it
and cut out a winepress as well.
Then he looked for a crop of good grapes,
but it yielded only bad fruit.

[3]"Now you dwellers in Jerusalem and men
of Judah,
judge between me and my vineyard.
[4]What more could have been done for my
vineyard
than I have done for it?
When I looked for good grapes,
why did it yield only bad?
[5]Now I will tell you
what I am going to do to my vineyard:
I will take away its hedge,
and it will be destroyed;
I will break down its wall,
and it will be trampled.
[6]I will make it a wasteland,
neither pruned nor cultivated,
and briers and thorns will grow there.
I will command the clouds
not to rain on it."

[7]The vineyard of the LORD Almighty
is the house of Israel,
and the men of Judah
are the garden of his delight.
And he looked for justice, but saw
bloodshed;
for righteousness, but heard cries of
distress.

Woes and Judgments

[8]Woe to you who add house to house
and join field to field
till no space is left
and you live alone in the land.

[9]The LORD Almighty has declared in my hearing:

"Surely the great houses will become
desolate,
the fine mansions left without occupants.
[10]A ten-acre[b] vineyard will produce only a
bath[c] of wine,
a homer[d] of seed only an ephah[e] of
grain."

[11]Woe to those who rise early in the morning
to run after their drinks,
who stay up late at night
till they are inflamed with wine.
[12]They have harps and lyres at their
banquets,
tambourines and flutes and wine,
but they have no regard for the deeds of
the LORD,
no respect for the work of his hands.
[13]Therefore my people will go into exile
for lack of understanding;

[a]4 Or *the Spirit* [b]10 Hebrew *ten-yoke,* that is, the land plowed by 10 yoke of oxen in one day [c]10 That is, probably about 6 gallons (about 22 liters) [d]10 That is, probably about 6 bushels (about 220 liters) [e]10 That is, probably about 3/5 bushel (about 22 liters)

4:2–4 God wants his people to be known for their self-respect, honor and righteousness. Achieving these character traits, however, sometimes includes a scorching purification process. Dealing with the reality of our inadequacies, sins and disobedience to God is not easy or painless. But God's plan for us is worth the price of the process.

4:5–6 Isaiah used the imagery of the cloud of smoke and fire to remind the people of God's protection of their ancestors in the desert wanderings (see Exodus 13:21—14:31). Though we may not see a pillar of cloud and fire, God is still with us to guide us and deliver us throughout our lives if we will continue to seek him.

5:1–7 God provides us with all we need for a fruitful life. If we reject him and abandon his way, our lives will be unfruitful and troubled. If we will seek God and surrender our lives to him, he can cultivate a new way of life that will be fulfilling and fruitful.

their men of rank will die of hunger
and their masses will be parched with thirst.
14Therefore the grave[a] enlarges its appetite
and opens its mouth without limit;
into it will descend their nobles and masses
with all their brawlers and revelers.
15So man will be brought low
and mankind humbled,
the eyes of the arrogant humbled.
16But the LORD Almighty will be exalted by his justice,
and the holy God will show himself holy by his righteousness.
17Then sheep will graze as in their own pasture;
lambs will feed[b] among the ruins of the rich.

18Woe to those who draw sin along with cords of deceit,
and wickedness as with cart ropes,
19to those who say, "Let God hurry,
let him hasten his work
so we may see it.
Let it approach,
let the plan of the Holy One of Israel come,
so we may know it."

20Woe to those who call evil good
and good evil,
who put darkness for light
and light for darkness,
who put bitter for sweet
and sweet for bitter.

21Woe to those who are wise in their own eyes
and clever in their own sight.

22Woe to those who are heroes at drinking wine
and champions at mixing drinks,
23who acquit the guilty for a bribe,
but deny justice to the innocent.
24Therefore, as tongues of fire lick up straw
and as dry grass sinks down in the flames,
so their roots will decay
and their flowers blow away like dust;
for they have rejected the law of the LORD Almighty
and spurned the word of the Holy One of Israel.
25Therefore the LORD's anger burns against his people;
his hand is raised and he strikes them down.
The mountains shake,
and the dead bodies are like refuse in the streets.

Yet for all this, his anger is not turned away,
his hand is still upraised.

26He lifts up a banner for the distant nations,
he whistles for those at the ends of the earth.
Here they come,
swiftly and speedily!
27Not one of them grows tired or stumbles,
not one slumbers or sleeps;
not a belt is loosened at the waist,
not a sandal thong is broken.
28Their arrows are sharp,
all their bows are strung;
their horses' hoofs seem like flint,
their chariot wheels like a whirlwind.
29Their roar is like that of the lion,
they roar like young lions;
they growl as they seize their prey
and carry it off with no one to rescue.
30In that day they will roar over it
like the roaring of the sea.
And if one looks at the land,
he will see darkness and distress;
even the light will be darkened by the clouds.

Isaiah's Commission

6 In the year that King Uzziah died, I saw the
Lord seated on a throne, high and exalted,
and the train of his robe filled the temple.
2Above him were seraphs, each with six wings:
With two wings they covered their faces, with
two they covered their feet, and with two they
were flying. 3And they were calling to one another:

"Holy, holy, holy is the LORD Almighty;
the whole earth is full of his glory."

4At the sound of their voices the doorposts and
thresholds shook and the temple was filled with
smoke.

[a]14 Hebrew *Sheol* [b]17 Septuagint; Hebrew / *strangers will eat*

5:20–23 When we reject God, our perception of reality becomes distorted. We cannot see the truth if we reject the one who is truth. To see things in the proper light again, we need to read the Bible—God's Word to us—and talk to God through prayer. As we become familiar with God and his Word, we will discover his will for our lives and gain a clearer understanding of God's truth.
5:24–30 God had given the people of Israel his laws and a promise of life if they would obey them. But the people refused to obey God. They chose to worship the idols of the surrounding nations and looked to their pagan neighbors for protection. This rejection of God's laws led to God's judgment and Israel's invasion by the Assyrian army. God has given us his Word to follow. He offers to provide our needs and deliver us from our enemies. However, if we stubbornly refuse to obey God's will, he may allow outside enemies to drive us back to him.
6:1–8 Isaiah's recognition of his own uncleanness did not disqualify him from a relationship with God and a life of service to him. In contrast, Isaiah's attitude set the stage for his cleansing and commissioning into service. When we hide our sins and failures, God will not use us in his service. But when we admit our sins, God can cleanse, restore and use us.

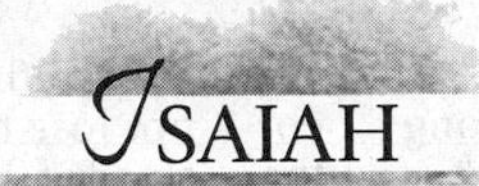

ISAIAH

God called Isaiah to be a prophet in "the year that King Uzziah died" (6:1). Isaiah's ministry extended over more than forty years (740–681 B.C.). Isaiah prophesied during the reigns of four kings of Judah: Uzziah, Jotham, Ahaz and Hezekiah. Isaiah's name means "the LORD saves," a meaning especially appropriate since Isaiah speaks throughout his book of God's promises to his people of comfort and deliverance.

Isaiah was married and had a family. His sons were given symbolic names: *Shear-Jashub* means "a remnant will return"; *Maher-Shalal-Hash-Baz* means "quick to the plunder, swift to the spoil." These names carried messages of warning from God to the people of Judah.

Though we do not know much about Isaiah, what we do know about him indicates that he was one of the great people of his time. His book is a masterpiece, suggesting that Isaiah possessed considerable intelligence and education. Tradition holds that Isaiah belonged to a family of some rank, thus explaining his easy access to the king. Isaiah was a statesman and a man of God. He had the soul of an artist, and he was steadfast in his obedience to God.

Although Isaiah had many gifts, his success resulted primarily from his humility and faithfulness to God's will for his life. When God called him, Isaiah was overcome with an overwhelming sense of his own sinfulness. Isaiah began where we need to begin: He admitted his sin and sought God for cleansing and renewal. Then, when God revealed his will for Isaiah, the prophet pursued God's plan with determination. He spoke and lived out God's plan despite the opposition that he faced. As a result, God used Isaiah to confront his people with their sin and to comfort his people as they faced a painful future. Through his words and life, Isaiah blazed a trail for our spiritual growth.

STRENGTHS AND ACCOMPLISHMENTS:

Isaiah was a gifted statesman, speaker and author.

He recognized his personal need for healing and received God's help.

Though strong in his convictions, Isaiah was also sensitive.

Despite great opposition and discouragement, Isaiah was faithful to God's call.

LESSONS FROM HIS LIFE:

Our healing begins when we admit our sin and turn to God.

When we decide to follow God's will, we must remain faithful to our decision.

God will help us and lead us as we place our trust in him.

KEY VERSE:

"Then I heard the voice of the Lord saying, 'Whom shall I send? And who will go for us?' And I said, 'Here am I. Send me!'" (6:8)

The story of Isaiah is told in the book of Isaiah. He is also mentioned in 2 Kings 19—20. His name is also found in the New Testament gospels, where he is recognized for having foretold the coming of the Messiah. Isaiah is also mentioned in Acts 8; 28; Romans 9; 10 and 15:12.

5"Woe to me!" I cried. "I am ruined! For I am
a man of unclean lips, and I live among a people of unclean lips, and my eyes have seen the
King, the LORD Almighty."
6Then one of the seraphs flew to me with a
live coal in his hand, which he had taken with
tongs from the altar. 7With it he touched my
mouth and said, "See, this has touched your
lips; your guilt is taken away and your sin
atoned for."
8Then I heard the voice of the Lord saying,
"Whom shall I send? And who will go for us?"
And I said, "Here am I. Send me!"
9He said, "Go and tell this people:

" 'Be ever hearing, but never
understanding;
be ever seeing, but never perceiving.'
10Make the heart of this people calloused;
make their ears dull
and close their eyes.[a]
Otherwise they might see with their eyes,
hear with their ears,
understand with their hearts,
and turn and be healed."

11Then I said, "For how long, O Lord?"
And he answered:

"Until the cities lie ruined
and without inhabitant,
until the houses are left deserted
and the fields ruined and ravaged,
12until the LORD has sent everyone far away
and the land is utterly forsaken.
13And though a tenth remains in the land,
it will again be laid waste.
But as the terebinth and oak
leave stumps when they are cut down,
so the holy seed will be the stump in the
land."

The Sign of Immanuel

7 When Ahaz son of Jotham, the son of Uzziah, was king of Judah, King Rezin of Aram
and Pekah son of Remaliah king of Israel
marched up to fight against Jerusalem, but they
could not overpower it.
2Now the house of David was told, "Aram
has allied itself with[b] Ephraim"; so the hearts of
Ahaz and his people were shaken, as the trees of
the forest are shaken by the wind.
3Then the LORD said to Isaiah, "Go out, you
and your son Shear-Jashub,[c] to meet Ahaz at
the end of the aqueduct of the Upper Pool, on
the road to the Washerman's Field. 4Say to him,
'Be careful, keep calm and don't be afraid. Do
not lose heart because of these two smoldering
stubs of firewood—because of the fierce anger of
Rezin and Aram and of the son of Remaliah.
5Aram, Ephraim and Remaliah's son have plotted your ruin, saying, 6"Let us invade Judah; let
us tear it apart and divide it among ourselves,
and make the son of Tabeel king over it." 7Yet
this is what the Sovereign LORD says:

" 'It will not take place,
it will not happen,
8for the head of Aram is Damascus,
and the head of Damascus is only Rezin.
Within sixty-five years
Ephraim will be too shattered to be a
people.
9The head of Ephraim is Samaria,
and the head of Samaria is only
Remaliah's son.
If you do not stand firm in your faith,
you will not stand at all.' "

10Again the LORD spoke to Ahaz, 11"Ask the
LORD your God for a sign, whether in the deepest depths or in the highest heights."
12But Ahaz said, "I will not ask; I will not put
the LORD to the test."
13Then Isaiah said, "Hear now, you house of
David! Is it not enough to try the patience of
men? Will you try the patience of my God also?
14Therefore the Lord himself will give you[d] a
sign: The virgin will be with child and will give
birth to a son, and[e] will call him Immanuel.[f]
15He will eat curds and honey when he knows
enough to reject the wrong and choose the
right. 16But before the boy knows enough to
reject the wrong and choose the right, the land
of the two kings you dread will be laid waste.
17The LORD will bring on you and on your people and on the house of your father a time
unlike any since Ephraim broke away from Judah—he will bring the king of Assyria."
18In that day the LORD will whistle for flies
from the distant streams of Egypt and for bees
from the land of Assyria. 19They will all come
and settle in the steep ravines and in the crevices
in the rocks, on all the thornbushes and at all

[a]9,10 Hebrew; Septuagint *'You will be ever hearing, but never understanding; / you will be ever seeing, but never perceiving.' / 10This people's heart has become calloused; / they hardly hear with their ears, / and they have closed their eyes*
[b]2 Or *has set up camp in* [c]3 *Shear-Jashub* means *a remnant will return.* [d]14 The Hebrew is plural.
[e]14 Masoretic Text; Dead Sea Scrolls *and he* or *and they*
[f]14 *Immanuel* means *God with us.*

6:8 God is not looking for people who are perfect or who pretend to be perfect. He is looking for people who can say with Isaiah, "Here am I. Send me!" (6:8). If we are willing to surrender our weaknesses to God, he will not allow them to stand in the way of our future.

6:9–13 Being fruitful does not necessarily mean we have to be a great success. We don't need to overachieve or look good to others; Isaiah certainly did not. To be fruitful, we should aim to be faithful to God's calling, not to measure up to the world's standards.

7:17–25 Confronted with the challenge of invasion from the coalition of Israel and Syria, Ahaz rejected Isaiah's call to trust God and tried to solve his problems his own way: He called on Assyria for protection. Later Assyria turned on Judah and damaged God's nation and people. The things we use to help us cope with our problems may ultimately take over our lives and destroy us. It is never too late to call on the one we should have turned to in the first place—God.

the water holes. 20In that day the Lord will use a razor hired from beyond the River[a]—the king of Assyria—to shave your head and the hair of your legs, and to take off your beards also. 21In that day, a man will keep alive a young cow and two goats. 22And because of the abundance of the milk they give, he will have curds to eat. All who remain in the land will eat curds and honey. 23In that day, in every place where there were a thousand vines worth a thousand silver shekels,[b] there will be only briers and thorns. 24Men will go there with bow and arrow, for the land will be covered with briers and thorns. 25As for all the hills once cultivated by the hoe, you will no longer go there for fear of the briers and thorns; they will become places where cattle are turned loose and where sheep run.

Assyria, the LORD's Instrument

8 The LORD said to me, "Take a large scroll and write on it with an ordinary pen: Maher-Shalal-Hash-Baz.[c] 2And I will call in Uriah the priest and Zechariah son of Jeberekiah as reliable witnesses for me."

3Then I went to the prophetess, and she conceived and gave birth to a son. And the LORD said to me, "Name him Maher-Shalal-Hash-Baz. 4Before the boy knows how to say 'My father' or 'My mother,' the wealth of Damascus and the plunder of Samaria will be carried off by the king of Assyria."

5The LORD spoke to me again:

6"Because this people has rejected
the gently flowing waters of Shiloah
and rejoices over Rezin
the son of Remaliah,
7therefore the Lord is about to bring against them
the mighty floodwaters of the River[a]—
the king of Assyria with all his pomp.
It will overflow all its channels,
run over all its banks
8and sweep on into Judah, swirling over it,
passing through it and reaching up to the neck.
Its outspread wings will cover the breadth of your land,
O Immanuel[d]!"

9Raise the war cry,[e] you nations, and be shattered!
Listen, all you distant lands.
Prepare for battle, and be shattered!
Prepare for battle, and be shattered!
10Devise your strategy, but it will be thwarted;
propose your plan, but it will not stand,
for God is with us.[f]

Fear God

11The LORD spoke to me with his strong hand upon me, warning me not to follow the way of this people. He said:

12"Do not call conspiracy
everything that these people call conspiracy[g];
do not fear what they fear,
and do not dread it.
13The LORD Almighty is the one you are to regard as holy,
he is the one you are to fear,
he is the one you are to dread,
14and he will be a sanctuary;
but for both houses of Israel he will be
a stone that causes men to stumble
and a rock that makes them fall.
And for the people of Jerusalem he will be
a trap and a snare.
15Many of them will stumble;
they will fall and be broken,
they will be snared and captured."

16Bind up the testimony
and seal up the law among my disciples.
17I will wait for the LORD,
who is hiding his face from the house of Jacob.
I will put my trust in him.

18Here am I, and the children the LORD has given me. We are signs and symbols in Israel from the LORD Almighty, who dwells on Mount Zion.

19When men tell you to consult mediums and spiritists, who whisper and mutter, should not a people inquire of their God? Why consult the dead on behalf of the living? 20To the law and to the testimony! If they do not speak according to this word, they have no light of dawn. 21Distressed and hungry, they will roam through the land; when they are famished, they will become enraged and, looking upward, will

[a]20,7 That is, the Euphrates [b]23 That is, about 25 pounds (about 11.5 kilograms) [c]1 *Maher-Shalal-Hash-Baz* means *quick to the plunder, swift to the spoil*; also in verse 3. [d]8 *Immanuel* means *God with us.* [e]9 Or *Do your worst* [f]10 Hebrew *Immanuel* [g]12 Or *Do not call for a treaty / every time these people call for a treaty*

8:6–8 To the leaders of Judah, asking a stronger, neighboring army for protection seemed like a good solution, but the long-term consequences proved to be disastrous. The Assyrian armies eventually attacked Judah and destroyed the land. If the leaders had heeded God's warning they could have avoided Assyria's attacks. If our spiritual renewal is grounded in anything other than God and his instructions for our lives, we may wind up in greater peril than before.

8:11–15 Isaiah was pressured to go along with the king's plan—a plan of human origin. To reject the king's plan, however, amounted to treason. The king's advisers probably stressed this to Isaiah to get him to go along with the plan. We, too, will face pressure to follow ungodly plans that might lead us back into our old ways. When others try to coerce us to follow their ways, we shouldn't fear their rejection if we resist. God says that if we fear him, we need not fear anything else—not friends, coworkers or family.

curse their king and their God. 22Then they will look toward the earth and see only distress and darkness and fearful gloom, and they will be thrust into utter darkness.

To Us a Child Is Born

9 Nevertheless, there will be no more gloom for those who were in distress. In the past he humbled the land of Zebulun and the land of Naphtali, but in the future he will honor Galilee of the Gentiles, by the way of the sea, along the Jordan—

2The people walking in darkness
have seen a great light;
on those living in the land of the shadow of death[a]
a light has dawned.
3You have enlarged the nation
and increased their joy;
they rejoice before you
as people rejoice at the harvest,
as men rejoice
when dividing the plunder.
4For as in the day of Midian's defeat,
you have shattered
the yoke that burdens them,
the bar across their shoulders,
the rod of their oppressor.
5Every warrior's boot used in battle
and every garment rolled in blood
will be destined for burning,
will be fuel for the fire.
6For to us a child is born,
to us a son is given,
and the government will be on his shoulders.
And he will be called
Wonderful Counselor,[b] Mighty God,
Everlasting Father, Prince of Peace.
7Of the increase of his government and peace
there will be no end.
He will reign on David's throne
and over his kingdom,
establishing and upholding it
with justice and righteousness
from that time on and forever.
The zeal of the LORD Almighty
will accomplish this.

The LORD's Anger Against Israel

8The Lord has sent a message against Jacob;
it will fall on Israel.
9All the people will know it—
Ephraim and the inhabitants of Samaria—
who say with pride
and arrogance of heart,
10"The bricks have fallen down,
but we will rebuild with dressed stone;
the fig trees have been felled,
but we will replace them with cedars."
11But the LORD has strengthened Rezin's foes against them
and has spurred their enemies on.
12Arameans from the east and Philistines from the west
have devoured Israel with open mouth.

Yet for all this, his anger is not turned away,
his hand is still upraised.

13But the people have not returned to him who struck them,
nor have they sought the LORD Almighty.
14So the LORD will cut off from Israel both head and tail,
both palm branch and reed in a single day;
15the elders and prominent men are the head,
the prophets who teach lies are the tail.
16Those who guide this people mislead them,
and those who are guided are led astray.
17Therefore the Lord will take no pleasure in the young men,
nor will he pity the fatherless and widows,
for everyone is ungodly and wicked,
every mouth speaks vileness.

Yet for all this, his anger is not turned away,
his hand is still upraised.

18Surely wickedness burns like a fire;
it consumes briers and thorns,
it sets the forest thickets ablaze,
so that it rolls upward in a column of smoke.
19By the wrath of the LORD Almighty
the land will be scorched
and the people will be fuel for the fire;
no one will spare his brother.
20On the right they will devour,
but still be hungry;
on the left they will eat,
but not be satisfied.

[a]2 Or *land of darkness* [b]6 Or *Wonderful, Counselor*

9:6 God is the one to whom we can turn for deep healing and restoration. He is the Wonderful Counselor, who will help us sort through our inner struggles and guide us into truth and reality. He is the Mighty God, who supplies us with the power we need to follow his path for life. He is the Everlasting Father, who loves us more deeply than any earthly father can. He is the Prince of Peace, who can fill our minds with peace and our lives with wholeness.

9:7 God brings justice and peace to the world and to troubled people. Though injustice seems to prevail and we may suffer from problems that are not our fault, we can be assured that justice will one day be served—if not in this lifetime, then in the next. We can have God's peace if we trust him and give him all our worries, cares, hopes and ambitions. We need to ask God to help us find true peace as we face the everyday problems of life.

Each will feed on the flesh of his own
offspring[a]:
21 Manasseh will feed on Ephraim, and
Ephraim on Manasseh;
together they will turn against Judah.

Yet for all this, his anger is not turned
away,
his hand is still upraised.

10 Woe to those who make unjust laws,
to those who issue oppressive decrees,
2 to deprive the poor of their rights
and withhold justice from the oppressed
of my people,
making widows their prey
and robbing the fatherless.
3 What will you do on the day of reckoning,
when disaster comes from afar?
To whom will you run for help?
Where will you leave your riches?
4 Nothing will remain but to cringe among
the captives
or fall among the slain.

Yet for all this, his anger is not turned
away,
his hand is still upraised.

God's Judgment on Assyria

5 "Woe to the Assyrian, the rod of my anger,
in whose hand is the club of my wrath!
6 I send him against a godless nation,
I dispatch him against a people who
anger me,
to seize loot and snatch plunder,
and to trample them down like mud in
the streets.
7 But this is not what he intends,
this is not what he has in mind;
his purpose is to destroy,
to put an end to many nations.
8 'Are not my commanders all kings?' he
says.
9 'Has not Calno fared like Carchemish?
Is not Hamath like Arpad,
and Samaria like Damascus?
10 As my hand seized the kingdoms of the
idols,
kingdoms whose images excelled those
of Jerusalem and Samaria—
11 shall I not deal with Jerusalem and her
images
as I dealt with Samaria and her idols?' "

12 When the Lord has finished all his work
against Mount Zion and Jerusalem, he will say,
"I will punish the king of Assyria for the willful
pride of his heart and the haughty look in his
eyes. 13 For he says:

" 'By the strength of my hand I have done
this,
and by my wisdom, because I have
understanding.
I removed the boundaries of nations,
I plundered their treasures;
like a mighty one I subdued[b] their
kings.
14 As one reaches into a nest,
so my hand reached for the wealth of
the nations;
as men gather abandoned eggs,
so I gathered all the countries;
not one flapped a wing,
or opened its mouth to chirp.' "

15 Does the ax raise itself above him who
swings it,
or the saw boast against him who uses
it?
As if a rod were to wield him who lifts it
up,
or a club brandish him who is not
wood!
16 Therefore, the Lord, the LORD Almighty,
will send a wasting disease upon his
sturdy warriors;
under his pomp a fire will be kindled
like a blazing flame.
17 The Light of Israel will become a fire,
their Holy One a flame;
in a single day it will burn and consume
his thorns and his briers.
18 The splendor of his forests and fertile fields
it will completely destroy,
as when a sick man wastes away.
19 And the remaining trees of his forests will
be so few
that a child could write them down.

The Remnant of Israel

20 In that day the remnant of Israel,
the survivors of the house of Jacob,
will no longer rely on him
who struck them down
but will truly rely on the LORD,
the Holy One of Israel.
21 A remnant will return,[c] a remnant of
Jacob
will return to the Mighty God.
22 Though your people, O Israel, be like the
sand by the sea,
only a remnant will return.
Destruction has been decreed,
overwhelming and righteous.
23 The Lord, the LORD Almighty, will carry out

[a] 20 Or *arm* [b] 13 Or / *I subdued the mighty,*
[c] 21 Hebrew *shear-jashub;* also in verse 22

10:1–19 This passage brings us comfort when we recognize that God sometimes uses evil people to work his plan and bring about good: God used Assyria to discipline Judah. Yet it is also comforting to realize that God will someday punish all who do evil, including the wicked nation of Assyria (10:12–19). God is sovereign and can use even the evil actions of others for our ultimate good (see Romans 8:28).

the destruction decreed upon the whole
land.

24Therefore, this is what the Lord, the LORD
Almighty, says:

"O my people who live in Zion,
do not be afraid of the Assyrians,
who beat you with a rod
and lift up a club against you, as Egypt
did.
25Very soon my anger against you will end
and my wrath will be directed to their
destruction."

26The LORD Almighty will lash them with a
whip,
as when he struck down Midian at the
rock of Oreb;
and he will raise his staff over the waters,
as he did in Egypt.
27In that day their burden will be lifted from
your shoulders,
their yoke from your neck;
the yoke will be broken
because you have grown so fat.[a]

28They enter Aiath;
they pass through Migron;
they store supplies at Micmash.
29They go over the pass, and say,
"We will camp overnight at Geba."
Ramah trembles;
Gibeah of Saul flees.
30Cry out, O Daughter of Gallim!
Listen, O Laishah!
Poor Anathoth!
31Madmenah is in flight;
the people of Gebim take cover.
32This day they will halt at Nob;
they will shake their fist
at the mount of the Daughter of Zion,
at the hill of Jerusalem.

33See, the Lord, the LORD Almighty,
will lop off the boughs with great power.
The lofty trees will be felled,
the tall ones will be brought low.
34He will cut down the forest thickets with
an ax;
Lebanon will fall before the Mighty One.

The Branch From Jesse

11 A shoot will come up from the stump
of Jesse;
from his roots a Branch will bear fruit.
2The Spirit of the LORD will rest on him—
the Spirit of wisdom and of
understanding,
the Spirit of counsel and of power,
the Spirit of knowledge and of the fear
of the LORD—
3and he will delight in the fear of the LORD.

He will not judge by what he sees with his
eyes,
or decide by what he hears with his ears;
4but with righteousness he will judge the
needy,
with justice he will give decisions for the
poor of the earth.
He will strike the earth with the rod of his
mouth;
with the breath of his lips he will slay
the wicked.
5Righteousness will be his belt
and faithfulness the sash around his
waist.

6The wolf will live with the lamb,
the leopard will lie down with the goat,
the calf and the lion and the yearling[b]
together;
and a little child will lead them.
7The cow will feed with the bear,
their young will lie down together,
and the lion will eat straw like the ox.
8The infant will play near the hole of the
cobra,
and the young child put his hand into
the viper's nest.
9They will neither harm nor destroy
on all my holy mountain,
for the earth will be full of the knowledge
of the LORD
as the waters cover the sea.

10In that day the Root of Jesse will stand as
a banner for the peoples; the nations will rally
to him, and his place of rest will be glorious.
11In that day the Lord will reach out his hand a
second time to reclaim the remnant that is left
of his people from Assyria, from Lower Egypt,
from Upper Egypt,[c] from Cush,[d] from Elam,
from Babylonia,[e] from Hamath and from the
islands of the sea.

12He will raise a banner for the nations
and gather the exiles of Israel;
he will assemble the scattered people of
Judah

[a]27 Hebrew; Septuagint *broken / from your shoulders*
[b]6 Hebrew; Septuagint *lion will feed* [c]11 Hebrew *from Pathros* [d]11 That is, the upper Nile region
[e]11 Hebrew *Shinar*

11:1–10 We may feel deep insecurity and hurt about injustices we have suffered at the hands of others. Our hope should be in God, who will come again and rule the world in justice and truth. He will resolve all the inequities of the past. When his kingdom is established, we will have nothing to fear because "they will neither harm nor destroy on all [God's] holy mountain" (11:9).
11:11–16 God is powerful enough to restore disintegrated families. The family of Israel had fallen. Many had been scattered among the nations during the exile. The nations of Israel and Judah were locked in destructive patterns of jealousy. Yet, despite this mess, God promised to bring restoration and unity. He can do the same for us too. If our family is divided, God can unite it. Restoration begins with repentance, open communication and complete trust in God.

from the four quarters of the earth.
13Ephraim's jealousy will vanish,
and Judah's enemies[a] will be cut off;
Ephraim will not be jealous of Judah,
nor Judah hostile toward Ephraim.
14They will swoop down on the slopes of Philistia to the west;
together they will plunder the people to the east.
They will lay hands on Edom and Moab,
and the Ammonites will be subject to them.
15The LORD will dry up
the gulf of the Egyptian sea;
with a scorching wind he will sweep his hand
over the Euphrates River.[b]
He will break it up into seven streams
so that men can cross over in sandals.
16There will be a highway for the remnant of his people
that is left from Assyria,
as there was for Israel
when they came up from Egypt.

Songs of Praise

12 In that day you will say:

"I will praise you, O LORD.
Although you were angry with me,
your anger has turned away
and you have comforted me.
2Surely God is my salvation;
I will trust and not be afraid.
The LORD, the LORD, is my strength and my song;
he has become my salvation."
3With joy you will draw water
from the wells of salvation.

4In that day you will say:

"Give thanks to the LORD, call on his name;
make known among the nations what he has done,
and proclaim that his name is exalted.
5Sing to the LORD, for he has done glorious things;
let this be known to all the world.
6Shout aloud and sing for joy, people of Zion,
for great is the Holy One of Israel
among you."

A Prophecy Against Babylon

13 An oracle concerning Babylon that Isaiah son of Amoz saw:

2Raise a banner on a bare hilltop,
shout to them;
beckon to them
to enter the gates of the nobles.
3I have commanded my holy ones;
I have summoned my warriors to carry out my wrath—
those who rejoice in my triumph.

4Listen, a noise on the mountains,
like that of a great multitude!
Listen, an uproar among the kingdoms,
like nations massing together!
The LORD Almighty is mustering
an army for war.
5They come from faraway lands,
from the ends of the heavens—
the LORD and the weapons of his wrath—
to destroy the whole country.

6Wail, for the day of the LORD is near;
it will come like destruction from the Almighty.[c]
7Because of this, all hands will go limp,
every man's heart will melt.
8Terror will seize them,
pain and anguish will grip them;
they will writhe like a woman in labor.
They will look aghast at each other,
their faces aflame.

9See, the day of the LORD is coming
—a cruel day, with wrath and fierce anger—
to make the land desolate
and destroy the sinners within it.
10The stars of heaven and their constellations
will not show their light.
The rising sun will be darkened
and the moon will not give its light.
11I will punish the world for its evil,
the wicked for their sins.
I will put an end to the arrogance of the haughty
and will humble the pride of the ruthless.
12I will make man scarcer than pure gold,
more rare than the gold of Ophir.
13Therefore I will make the heavens tremble;

[a]13 Or *hostility* [b]15 Hebrew *the River* [c]6 Hebrew *Shaddai*

12:1–6 Once we surrender our lives to God, we can rejoice in his salvation. Sin separates us from God, but when we repent, he comforts, heals, and strengthens us. We will want to share with others our joy and the story of how God has helped us.
13:1—14:2 Babylon would ultimately come under God's judgment. God will display his anger toward unrepentant sinners. But God's anger is not abusive or irresponsible. God's judgment is just. Yet to those who believe in him, repent, and ask his forgiveness, God will show his gracious compassion (14:1).
13:1—23:18 These chapters deal with God's judgment against unbelieving nations and reveal that evildoers will eventually come under God's judgment. If people have hurt us, we can release these situations to God and not seek revenge, because we know that God will deal with them. Also, those who reject God and think they can handle their lives alone will eventually discover their error. We must surrender our lives to God so we can be saved now and for all eternity.

and the earth will shake from its place
at the wrath of the LORD Almighty,
in the day of his burning anger.

14 Like a hunted gazelle,
like sheep without a shepherd,
each will return to his own people,
each will flee to his native land.
15 Whoever is captured will be thrust through;
all who are caught will fall by the sword.
16 Their infants will be dashed to pieces
before their eyes;
their houses will be looted and their
wives ravished.

17 See, I will stir up against them the Medes,
who do not care for silver
and have no delight in gold.
18 Their bows will strike down the young
men;
they will have no mercy on infants
nor will they look with compassion on
children.
19 Babylon, the jewel of kingdoms,
the glory of the Babylonians'[a] pride,
will be overthrown by God
like Sodom and Gomorrah.
20 She will never be inhabited
or lived in through all generations;
no Arab will pitch his tent there,
no shepherd will rest his flocks there.
21 But desert creatures will lie there,
jackals will fill her houses;
there the owls will dwell,
and there the wild goats will leap about.
22 Hyenas will howl in her strongholds,
jackals in her luxurious palaces.
Her time is at hand,
and her days will not be prolonged.

14 The LORD will have compassion on
Jacob;
once again he will choose Israel
and will settle them in their own land.
Aliens will join them
and unite with the house of Jacob.
2 Nations will take them
and bring them to their own place.
And the house of Israel will possess the
nations
as menservants and maidservants in the
LORD's land.
They will make captives of their captors
and rule over their oppressors.

3 On the day the LORD gives you relief from
suffering and turmoil and cruel bondage, 4 you
will take up this taunt against the king of Babylon:

How the oppressor has come to an end!
How his fury[b] has ended!
5 The LORD has broken the rod of the
wicked,
the scepter of the rulers,
6 which in anger struck down peoples
with unceasing blows,
and in fury subdued nations
with relentless aggression.
7 All the lands are at rest and at peace;
they break into singing.
8 Even the pine trees and the cedars of
Lebanon
exult over you and say,
"Now that you have been laid low,
no woodsman comes to cut us down."

9 The grave[c] below is all astir
to meet you at your coming;
it rouses the spirits of the departed to greet
you—
all those who were leaders in the world;
it makes them rise from their thrones—
all those who were kings over the
nations.
10 They will all respond,
they will say to you,
"You also have become weak, as we are;
you have become like us."
11 All your pomp has been brought down to
the grave,
along with the noise of your harps;
maggots are spread out beneath you
and worms cover you.

12 How you have fallen from heaven,
O morning star, son of the dawn!
You have been cast down to the earth,
you who once laid low the nations!
13 You said in your heart,
"I will ascend to heaven;
I will raise my throne
above the stars of God;
I will sit enthroned on the mount of
assembly,
on the utmost heights of the sacred
mountain.[d]
14 I will ascend above the tops of the clouds;
I will make myself like the Most High."
15 But you are brought down to the grave,
to the depths of the pit.

16 Those who see you stare at you,
they ponder your fate:
"Is this the man who shook the earth
and made kingdoms tremble,
17 the man who made the world a desert,
who overthrew its cities
and would not let his captives go home?"

[a] 19 Or *Chaldeans'* [b] 4 Dead Sea Scrolls, Septuagint and Syriac; the meaning of the word in the Masoretic Text is uncertain. [c] 9 Hebrew *Sheol*; also in verses 11 and 15 [d] 13 Or *the north*; Hebrew *Zaphon*

14:12–20 Pride was the root of Babylon's sin. We, too, must beware of this deadly sin. Healthy self-esteem is proper. But the sin of pride leads us to believe that we are better than others. Our pride may even be an unhealthy attempt to cover up deep insecurities that can be dealt with only by the love and grace of God.

18All the kings of the nations lie in state,
each in his own tomb.
19But you are cast out of your tomb
like a rejected branch;
you are covered with the slain,
with those pierced by the sword,
those who descend to the stones of the pit.
Like a corpse trampled underfoot,
20 you will not join them in burial,
for you have destroyed your land
and killed your people.

The offspring of the wicked
will never be mentioned again.
21Prepare a place to slaughter his sons
for the sins of their forefathers;
they are not to rise to inherit the land
and cover the earth with their cities.

22"I will rise up against them,"
declares the LORD Almighty.
"I will cut off from Babylon her name and survivors,
her offspring and descendants,"
declares the LORD.
23"I will turn her into a place for owls
and into swampland;
I will sweep her with the broom of destruction,"
declares the LORD Almighty.

A Prophecy Against Assyria

24The LORD Almighty has sworn,

"Surely, as I have planned, so it will be,
and as I have purposed, so it will stand.
25I will crush the Assyrian in my land;
on my mountains I will trample him down.
His yoke will be taken from my people,
and his burden removed from their shoulders."

26This is the plan determined for the whole world;
this is the hand stretched out over all nations.
27For the LORD Almighty has purposed, and who can thwart him?
His hand is stretched out, and who can turn it back?

A Prophecy Against the Philistines

28This oracle came in the year King Ahaz died:

29Do not rejoice, all you Philistines,
that the rod that struck you is broken;
from the root of that snake will spring up a viper,
its fruit will be a darting, venomous serpent.
30The poorest of the poor will find pasture,
and the needy will lie down in safety.
But your root I will destroy by famine;
it will slay your survivors.

31Wail, O gate! Howl, O city!
Melt away, all you Philistines!
A cloud of smoke comes from the north,
and there is not a straggler in its ranks.
32What answer shall be given
to the envoys of that nation?
"The LORD has established Zion,
and in her his afflicted people will find refuge."

A Prophecy Against Moab

15 An oracle concerning Moab:

Ar in Moab is ruined,
destroyed in a night!
Kir in Moab is ruined,
destroyed in a night!
2Dibon goes up to its temple,
to its high places to weep;
Moab wails over Nebo and Medeba.
Every head is shaved
and every beard cut off.
3In the streets they wear sackcloth;
on the roofs and in the public squares
they all wail,
prostrate with weeping.
4Heshbon and Elealeh cry out,
their voices are heard all the way to Jahaz.
Therefore the armed men of Moab cry out,
and their hearts are faint.

5My heart cries out over Moab;
her fugitives flee as far as Zoar,
as far as Eglath Shelishiyah.
They go up the way to Luhith,
weeping as they go;
on the road to Horonaim
they lament their destruction.
6The waters of Nimrim are dried up
and the grass is withered;
the vegetation is gone
and nothing green is left.
7So the wealth they have acquired and stored up
they carry away over the Ravine of the Poplars.

14:26–27 We would only be fooling ourselves if we believed that we could ignore God and his moral laws and expect life to go well anyway. The Assyrians believed that, denied reality and suffered the consequences. God is sovereign over the whole earth. He will uphold his moral laws and purposes whether we believe them or not. Even if we have ignored God all our lives, it is not too late to seek him now and start following his plan.

15:2–3 The Moabites lamented about their suffering, but they never acknowledged their sins and asked God to forgive them. We may face a similar danger. Unless we admit our sins to God, we may never get beyond feeling sorry for ourselves. Bemoaning the suffering brought on by our sins is helpful only if it leads us to redirect our lives according to God's will and plan.

8Their outcry echoes along the border of
Moab;
their wailing reaches as far as Eglaim,
their lamentation as far as Beer Elim.
9Dimon's[a] waters are full of blood,
but I will bring still more upon
Dimon[a]—
a lion upon the fugitives of Moab
and upon those who remain in the land.

16 Send lambs as tribute
to the ruler of the land,
from Sela, across the desert,
to the mount of the Daughter of Zion.
2Like fluttering birds
pushed from the nest,
so are the women of Moab
at the fords of the Arnon.

3"Give us counsel,
render a decision.
Make your shadow like night—
at high noon.
Hide the fugitives,
do not betray the refugees.
4Let the Moabite fugitives stay with you;
be their shelter from the destroyer."

The oppressor will come to an end,
and destruction will cease;
the aggressor will vanish from the land.
5In love a throne will be established;
in faithfulness a man will sit on it—
one from the house[b] of David—
one who in judging seeks justice
and speeds the cause of righteousness.

6We have heard of Moab's pride—
her overweening pride and conceit,
her pride and her insolence—
but her boasts are empty.
7Therefore the Moabites wail,
they wail together for Moab.
Lament and grieve
for the men[c] of Kir Hareseth.
8The fields of Heshbon wither,
the vines of Sibmah also.
The rulers of the nations
have trampled down the choicest vines,
which once reached Jazer
and spread toward the desert.
Their shoots spread out
and went as far as the sea.
9So I weep, as Jazer weeps,
for the vines of Sibmah.
O Heshbon, O Elealeh,
I drench you with tears!
The shouts of joy over your ripened fruit
and over your harvests have been stilled.
10Joy and gladness are taken away from the
orchards;
no one sings or shouts in the vineyards;
no one treads out wine at the presses,
for I have put an end to the shouting.
11My heart laments for Moab like a harp,
my inmost being for Kir Hareseth.
12When Moab appears at her high place,
she only wears herself out;
when she goes to her shrine to pray,
it is to no avail.

13This is the word the LORD has already spoken concerning Moab. 14But now the LORD says:
"Within three years, as a servant bound by contract would count them, Moab's splendor and
all her many people will be despised, and her
survivors will be very few and feeble."

An Oracle Against Damascus

17 An oracle concerning Damascus:

"See, Damascus will no longer be a city
but will become a heap of ruins.
2The cities of Aroer will be deserted
and left to flocks, which will lie down,
with no one to make them afraid.
3The fortified city will disappear from
Ephraim,
and royal power from Damascus;
the remnant of Aram will be
like the glory of the Israelites,"
declares the LORD Almighty.

4"In that day the glory of Jacob will fade;
the fat of his body will waste away.
5It will be as when a reaper gathers the
standing grain
and harvests the grain with his arm—
as when a man gleans heads of grain
in the Valley of Rephaim.
6Yet some gleanings will remain,
as when an olive tree is beaten,
leaving two or three olives on the topmost
branches,
four or five on the fruitful boughs,"
declares the LORD,
the God of Israel.

[a]9 Masoretic Text; Dead Sea Scrolls, some Septuagint manuscripts and Vulgate *Dibon* [b]5 Hebrew *tent* [c]7 Or *"raisin cakes,"* a wordplay

---

16:3–5 Moab's request for Judah's help echoes our own communities and their dealings with suffering people. Have we opened our doors to those who are troubled so they can find refuge, counsel and help in an environment of love and grace? As God's people, governed by the rule of Christ, we have much to offer our hurting world.
16:12 Judgment would humble Moab and force her to deal with the truth of her sin. Yet instead of turning to God, Moab turned to idols that had no power to help. We may be like Moab. We need God's help but refuse it. His help is available to all who will accept it. Instead of turning to God, we may turn to our work, perfectionism, substance abuse or any number of pursuits. However, turning to these solutions instead of God will only add to our trouble.
17:3–7 It took almost total destruction before Israel turned back to God and followed him. If we are wise, we won't wait until our lives are destroyed before turning to God for help. The sooner we admit that we need God's powerful help, the sooner God can deliver us.

7In that day men will look to their Maker
and turn their eyes to the Holy One of Israel.
8They will not look to the altars,
the work of their hands,
and they will have no regard for the Asherah poles[a]
and the incense altars their fingers have made.

9In that day their strong cities, which they left
because of the Israelites, will be like places
abandoned to thickets and undergrowth. And
all will be desolation.

10You have forgotten God your Savior;
you have not remembered the Rock,
your fortress.
Therefore, though you set out the finest plants
and plant imported vines,
11though on the day you set them out, you make them grow,
and on the morning when you plant them, you bring them to bud,
yet the harvest will be as nothing
in the day of disease and incurable pain.
12Oh, the raging of many nations—
they rage like the raging sea!
Oh, the uproar of the peoples—
they roar like the roaring of great waters!
13Although the peoples roar like the roar of surging waters,
when he rebukes them they flee far away,
driven before the wind like chaff on the hills,
like tumbleweed before a gale.
14In the evening, sudden terror!
Before the morning, they are gone!
This is the portion of those who loot us,
the lot of those who plunder us.

A Prophecy Against Cush

18 Woe to the land of whirring wings[b]
along the rivers of Cush,[c]
2which sends envoys by sea
in papyrus boats over the water.

Go, swift messengers,
to a people tall and smooth-skinned,
to a people feared far and wide,
an aggressive nation of strange speech,
whose land is divided by rivers.

3All you people of the world,
you who live on the earth,
when a banner is raised on the mountains,
you will see it,
and when a trumpet sounds,
you will hear it.
4This is what the LORD says to me:

"I will remain quiet and will look on
from my dwelling place,
like shimmering heat in the sunshine,
like a cloud of dew in the heat of harvest."
5For, before the harvest, when the blossom is gone
and the flower becomes a ripening grape,
he will cut off the shoots with pruning knives,
and cut down and take away the spreading branches.
6They will all be left to the mountain birds of prey
and to the wild animals;
the birds will feed on them all summer,
the wild animals all winter.

7At that time gifts will be brought to the LORD
Almighty

from a people tall and smooth-skinned,
from a people feared far and wide,
an aggressive nation of strange speech,
whose land is divided by rivers—

the gifts will be brought to Mount Zion, the
place of the Name of the LORD Almighty.

A Prophecy About Egypt

19 An oracle concerning Egypt:

See, the LORD rides on a swift cloud
and is coming to Egypt.
The idols of Egypt tremble before him,
and the hearts of the Egyptians melt within them.

2"I will stir up Egyptian against Egyptian—
brother will fight against brother,
neighbor against neighbor,
city against city,
kingdom against kingdom.
3The Egyptians will lose heart,
and I will bring their plans to nothing;
they will consult the idols and the spirits of the dead,
the mediums and the spiritists.
4I will hand the Egyptians over
to the power of a cruel master,
and a fierce king will rule over them,"
declares the Lord, the LORD Almighty.

5The waters of the river will dry up,
and the riverbed will be parched and dry.
6The canals will stink;
the streams of Egypt will dwindle and dry up.
The reeds and rushes will wither,

[a]8 That is, symbols of the goddess Asherah [b]1 Or *of locusts* [c]1 That is, the upper Nile region

18:7 This passage tells us that the enemy nation of Ethiopia would one day come to Jerusalem to worship God. God can do the unexpected and seemingly impossible. What things in our lives appear impossible? Whatever the situation, God can bring healing. "Is anything too hard for the LORD?" (Genesis 18:14).

7 also the plants along the Nile,
at the mouth of the river.
Every sown field along the Nile
will become parched, will blow away
and be no more.
8The fishermen will groan and lament,
all who cast hooks into the Nile;
those who throw nets on the water
will pine away.
9Those who work with combed flax will
despair,
the weavers of fine linen will lose hope.
10The workers in cloth will be dejected,
and all the wage earners will be sick at
heart.

11The officials of Zoan are nothing but fools;
the wise counselors of Pharaoh give
senseless advice.
How can you say to Pharaoh,
"I am one of the wise men,
a disciple of the ancient kings"?

12Where are your wise men now?
Let them show you and make known
what the LORD Almighty
has planned against Egypt.
13The officials of Zoan have become fools,
the leaders of Memphis[a] are deceived;
the cornerstones of her peoples
have led Egypt astray.
14The LORD has poured into them
a spirit of dizziness;
they make Egypt stagger in all that she
does,
as a drunkard staggers around in his
vomit.
15There is nothing Egypt can do—
head or tail, palm branch or reed.

16In that day the Egyptians will be like wom-
en. They will shudder with fear at the uplifted
hand that the LORD Almighty raises against
them. 17And the land of Judah will bring terror
to the Egyptians; everyone to whom Judah is
mentioned will be terrified, because of what the
LORD Almighty is planning against them.
18In that day five cities in Egypt will speak the
language of Canaan and swear allegiance to the
LORD Almighty. One of them will be called
the City of Destruction.[b]
19In that day there will be an altar to the
LORD in the heart of Egypt, and a monument to
the LORD at its border. 20It will be a sign and
witness to the LORD Almighty in the land of
Egypt. When they cry out to the LORD because
of their oppressors, he will send them a savior
and defender, and he will rescue them. 21So the
LORD will make himself known to the Egyptians, and in that day they will acknowledge the
LORD. They will worship with sacrifices and
grain offerings; they will make vows to the LORD
and keep them. 22The LORD will strike Egypt
with a plague; he will strike them and heal
them. They will turn to the LORD, and he will
respond to their pleas and heal them.
23In that day there will be a highway from
Egypt to Assyria. The Assyrians will go to Egypt
and the Egyptians to Assyria. The Egyptians and
Assyrians will worship together. 24In that day
Israel will be the third, along with Egypt and
Assyria, a blessing on the earth. 25The LORD Almighty will bless them, saying, "Blessed be
Egypt my people, Assyria my handiwork, and
Israel my inheritance."

A Prophecy Against Egypt and Cush

20 In the year that the supreme commander, sent by Sargon king of Assyria, came
to Ashdod and attacked and captured it— 2at
that time the LORD spoke through Isaiah son of
Amoz. He said to him, "Take off the sackcloth
from your body and the sandals from your feet."
And he did so, going around stripped and barefoot.
3Then the LORD said, "Just as my servant Isaiah has gone stripped and barefoot for three
years, as a sign and portent against Egypt and
Cush,[c] 4so the king of Assyria will lead away
stripped and barefoot the Egyptian captives and
Cushite exiles, young and old, with buttocks
bared—to Egypt's shame. 5Those who trusted in
Cush and boasted in Egypt will be afraid and
put to shame. 6In that day the people who live
on this coast will say, 'See what has happened
to those we relied on, those we fled to for help
and deliverance from the king of Assyria! How
then can we escape?' "

A Prophecy Against Babylon

21 An oracle concerning the Desert by the
Sea:

Like whirlwinds sweeping through the
southland,
an invader comes from the desert,
from a land of terror.

2A dire vision has been shown to me:
The traitor betrays, the looter takes loot.
Elam, attack! Media, lay siege!
I will bring to an end all the groaning
she caused.

3At this my body is racked with pain,
pangs seize me, like those of a woman
in labor;
I am staggered by what I hear,
I am bewildered by what I see.

[a]13 Hebrew *Noph* [b]18 Most manuscripts of the Masoretic Text; some manuscripts of the Masoretic Text, Dead Sea Scrolls and Vulgate *City of the Sun* (that is, Heliopolis) [c]3 That is, the upper Nile region; also in verse 5

19:11–15 The wisdom of the Egyptians turned out to be foolishness. True wisdom comes from God alone. The wise men counted on their own logic and were deceived. Our plans will succeed only if we ask God for assistance and rely on him to show us the proper way to go.

4My heart falters,
fear makes me tremble;
the twilight I longed for
has become a horror to me.

5They set the tables,
they spread the rugs,
they eat, they drink!
Get up, you officers,
oil the shields!

6This is what the Lord says to me:

"Go, post a lookout
and have him report what he sees.
7When he sees chariots
with teams of horses,
riders on donkeys
or riders on camels,
let him be alert,
fully alert."

8And the lookout[a] shouted,

"Day after day, my lord, I stand on the watchtower;
every night I stay at my post.
9Look, here comes a man in a chariot
with a team of horses.
And he gives back the answer:
'Babylon has fallen, has fallen!
All the images of its gods
lie shattered on the ground!' "

10O my people, crushed on the threshing floor,
I tell you what I have heard
from the LORD Almighty,
from the God of Israel.

A Prophecy Against Edom

11An oracle concerning Dumah[b]:

Someone calls to me from Seir,
"Watchman, what is left of the night?
Watchman, what is left of the night?"
12The watchman replies,
"Morning is coming, but also the night.
If you would ask, then ask;
and come back yet again."

A Prophecy Against Arabia

13An oracle concerning Arabia:

You caravans of Dedanites,
who camp in the thickets of Arabia,
14 bring water for the thirsty;
you who live in Tema,
bring food for the fugitives.
15They flee from the sword,
from the drawn sword,
from the bent bow
and from the heat of battle.

16This is what the Lord says to me: "Within
one year, as a servant bound by contract would
count it, all the pomp of Kedar will come to an
end. 17The survivors of the bowmen, the warriors of Kedar, will be few." The LORD, the God
of Israel, has spoken.

A Prophecy About Jerusalem

22 An oracle concerning the Valley of Vision:

What troubles you now,
that you have all gone up on the roofs,
2O town full of commotion,
O city of tumult and revelry?
Your slain were not killed by the sword,
nor did they die in battle.
3All your leaders have fled together;
they have been captured without using the bow.
All you who were caught were taken prisoner together,
having fled while the enemy was still far away.
4Therefore I said, "Turn away from me;
let me weep bitterly.
Do not try to console me
over the destruction of my people."

5The Lord, the LORD Almighty, has a day
of tumult and trampling and terror
in the Valley of Vision,
a day of battering down walls
and of crying out to the mountains.
6Elam takes up the quiver,
with her charioteers and horses;
Kir uncovers the shield.
7Your choicest valleys are full of chariots,
and horsemen are posted at the city gates;
8 the defenses of Judah are stripped away.

And you looked in that day
to the weapons in the Palace of the Forest;
9you saw that the City of David
had many breaches in its defenses;
you stored up water
in the Lower Pool.

[a]8 Dead Sea Scrolls and Syriac; Masoretic Text *A lion*
[b]11 *Dumah* means *silence* or *stillness,* a wordplay on *Edom.*

21:5 The Babylonians were blind to the truth. Their destruction was imminent, but they refused to face reality. They were feasting when they should have been preparing for battle. As a result, the Babylonians fell to the Medes and Persians without a fight (see Daniel 5). Pursuing sinful pleasures will result in destructive consequences. We won't know when major catastrophes are about to strike. But we can avoid these painful disasters if we will surrender our lives to God.

22:1–11 Judah was threatened with destruction. The people responded by taking inventory of their situation and weaponry, but they overlooked one thing—God. The people still believed they could hold off the enemy on their own. We often do the same thing. We look within ourselves for the resources to handle our own difficult situations. We forget to turn to the only resource who can truly help—God. We should always look to God first in times of need.

10You counted the buildings in Jerusalem
and tore down houses to strengthen the wall.
11You built a reservoir between the two walls
for the water of the Old Pool,
but you did not look to the One who made it,
or have regard for the One who planned it long ago.
12The Lord, the LORD Almighty,
called you on that day
to weep and to wail,
to tear out your hair and put on sackcloth.
13But see, there is joy and revelry,
slaughtering of cattle and killing of sheep,
eating of meat and drinking of wine!
"Let us eat and drink," you say,
"for tomorrow we die!"

14The LORD Almighty has revealed this in my
hearing: "Till your dying day this sin will not be
atoned for," says the Lord, the LORD Almighty.

15This is what the Lord, the LORD Almighty,
says:

"Go, say to this steward,
to Shebna, who is in charge of the palace:
16What are you doing here and who gave you permission
to cut out a grave for yourself here,
hewing your grave on the height
and chiseling your resting place in the rock?

17"Beware, the LORD is about to take firm hold of you
and hurl you away, O you mighty man.
18He will roll you up tightly like a ball
and throw you into a large country.
There you will die
and there your splendid chariots will remain—
you disgrace to your master's house!
19I will depose you from your office,
and you will be ousted from your position.

20"In that day I will summon my servant,
Eliakim son of Hilkiah. 21I will clothe him with
your robe and fasten your sash around him and
hand your authority over to him. He will be a
father to those who live in Jerusalem and to the
house of Judah. 22I will place on his shoulder
the key to the house of David; what he opens no
one can shut, and what he shuts no one can
open. 23I will drive him like a peg into a firm
place; he will be a seat[a] of honor for the house
of his father. 24All the glory of his family will
hang on him: its offspring and offshoots—all its
lesser vessels, from the bowls to all the jars.

25"In that day," declares the LORD Almighty,
"the peg driven into the firm place will give
way; it will be sheared off and will fall, and the
load hanging on it will be cut down." The LORD
has spoken.

A Prophecy About Tyre

23 An oracle concerning Tyre:

Wail, O ships of Tarshish!
For Tyre is destroyed
and left without house or harbor.
From the land of Cyprus[b]
word has come to them.

2Be silent, you people of the island
and you merchants of Sidon,
whom the seafarers have enriched.
3On the great waters
came the grain of the Shihor;
the harvest of the Nile[c] was the revenue of Tyre,
and she became the marketplace of the nations.

4Be ashamed, O Sidon, and you, O fortress of the sea,
for the sea has spoken:
"I have neither been in labor nor given birth;
I have neither reared sons nor brought up daughters."
5When word comes to Egypt,
they will be in anguish at the report from Tyre.

6Cross over to Tarshish;
wail, you people of the island.
7Is this your city of revelry,
the old, old city,
whose feet have taken her
to settle in far-off lands?
8Who planned this against Tyre,
the bestower of crowns,
whose merchants are princes,
whose traders are renowned in the earth?
9The LORD Almighty planned it,

[a]23 Or *throne* [b]1 Hebrew *Kittim* [c]2,3 Masoretic Text; one Dead Sea Scroll *Sidon, / who cross over the sea; / your envoys* 3*are on the great waters. / The grain of the Shihor, / the harvest of the Nile,*

22:12–14 Ignoring our problems doesn't make them go away. Rather, the opposite is true—problems get worse when we delay dealing with them. Whenever we turn to anything or anyone as a substitute for God's help, we have only compounded our original problems. Instead of giving up hope, as Judah did, we should repent and turn to God and seek his help. If we trust the promises he has given us in the Bible, there is no reason to give up—God is faithful!

23:1–12 God pronounced judgment on the prosperous merchant city of Tyre because of her pride. The prideful arrogance of Tyre was not positive self-esteem. Tyre said, in effect, "I don't need God. I can prosper by my own efforts." We need to constantly watch out for pride and make sure we have not replaced our dependence on God with unrealistic confidence in ourselves.

to bring low the pride of all glory
and to humble all who are renowned on the earth.

10Till[a] your land as along the Nile,
O Daughter of Tarshish,
for you no longer have a harbor.
11The LORD has stretched out his hand over the sea
and made its kingdoms tremble.
He has given an order concerning Phoenicia[b]
that her fortresses be destroyed.
12He said, "No more of your reveling,
O Virgin Daughter of Sidon, now crushed!

"Up, cross over to Cyprus[c];
even there you will find no rest."
13Look at the land of the Babylonians,[d]
this people that is now of no account!
The Assyrians have made it
a place for desert creatures;
they raised up their siege towers,
they stripped its fortresses bare
and turned it into a ruin.

14Wail, you ships of Tarshish;
your fortress is destroyed!

15At that time Tyre will be forgotten for seventy years, the span of a king's life. But at the end of these seventy years, it will happen to Tyre as in the song of the prostitute:

16"Take up a harp, walk through the city,
O prostitute forgotten;
play the harp well, sing many a song,
so that you will be remembered."

17At the end of seventy years, the LORD will deal with Tyre. She will return to her hire as a prostitute and will ply her trade with all the kingdoms on the face of the earth. 18Yet her profit and her earnings will be set apart for the LORD; they will not be stored up or hoarded. Her profits will go to those who live before the LORD, for abundant food and fine clothes.

The LORD's Devastation of the Earth

24 See, the LORD is going to lay waste the earth
and devastate it;
he will ruin its face
and scatter its inhabitants—
2it will be the same
for priest as for people,
for master as for servant,
for mistress as for maid,
for seller as for buyer,
for borrower as for lender,
for debtor as for creditor.
3The earth will be completely laid waste
and totally plundered.
The LORD has spoken this word.

4The earth dries up and withers,
the world languishes and withers,
the exalted of the earth languish.
5The earth is defiled by its people;
they have disobeyed the laws,
violated the statutes
and broken the everlasting covenant.
6Therefore a curse consumes the earth;
its people must bear their guilt.
Therefore earth's inhabitants are burned up,
and very few are left.
7The new wine dries up and the vine withers;
all the merrymakers groan.
8The gaiety of the tambourines is stilled,
the noise of the revelers has stopped,
the joyful harp is silent.
9No longer do they drink wine with a song;
the beer is bitter to its drinkers.
10The ruined city lies desolate;
the entrance to every house is barred.
11In the streets they cry out for wine;
all joy turns to gloom,
all gaiety is banished from the earth.
12The city is left in ruins,
its gate is battered to pieces.
13So will it be on the earth
and among the nations,
as when an olive tree is beaten,
or as when gleanings are left after the grape harvest.

14They raise their voices, they shout for joy;
from the west they acclaim the LORD's majesty.
15Therefore in the east give glory to the LORD;
exalt the name of the LORD, the God of Israel,
in the islands of the sea.
16From the ends of the earth we hear singing:
"Glory to the Righteous One."

But I said, "I waste away, I waste away!
Woe to me!
The treacherous betray!

[a]10 Dead Sea Scrolls and some Septuagint manuscripts; Masoretic Text *Go through* [b]11 Hebrew *Canaan* [c]12 Hebrew *Kittim* [d]13 Or *Chaldeans*

23:13–18 At the end of seventy years Tyre would rebuild and return to her old ways of seducing the nations to materialism and idolatry. Without genuine renewal, we may also go back to the old, destructive patterns of our lives. We not only need to be freed from whatever held us captive in the past, but we also need a whole new life with God as our foundation. As Jesus said, when we follow him we are like a person who builds a house on solid rock. Even though the storms of life constantly assail us, we will stand firm (see Matthew 7:24–27).

24:4–7 Our sins affect not only us, but they also affect our family, our friends, our nation, and even the earth itself. Our spiritual renewal is important, but not just to us and to those close to us. What we do has a serious impact on the health of our larger communities, our nation and our world. If each individual on earth chose to live God's way, just imagine the transformation we would experience!

With treachery the treacherous betray!"
17Terror and pit and snare await you,
O people of the earth.
18Whoever flees at the sound of terror
will fall into a pit;
whoever climbs out of the pit
will be caught in a snare.

The floodgates of the heavens are opened,
the foundations of the earth shake.
19The earth is broken up,
the earth is split asunder,
the earth is thoroughly shaken.
20The earth reels like a drunkard,
it sways like a hut in the wind;
so heavy upon it is the guilt of its rebellion
that it falls—never to rise again.

21In that day the LORD will punish
the powers in the heavens above
and the kings on the earth below.
22They will be herded together
like prisoners bound in a dungeon;
they will be shut up in prison
and be punished[a] after many days.
23The moon will be abashed, the sun
ashamed;
for the LORD Almighty will reign
on Mount Zion and in Jerusalem,
and before its elders, gloriously.

Praise to the LORD

25 O LORD, you are my God;
I will exalt you and praise your name,
for in perfect faithfulness
you have done marvelous things,
things planned long ago.
2You have made the city a heap of rubble,
the fortified town a ruin,
the foreigners' stronghold a city no more;
it will never be rebuilt.
3Therefore strong peoples will honor you;
cities of ruthless nations will revere you.
4You have been a refuge for the poor,
a refuge for the needy in his distress,
a shelter from the storm
and a shade from the heat.
For the breath of the ruthless
is like a storm driving against a wall
5 and like the heat of the desert.
You silence the uproar of foreigners;
as heat is reduced by the shadow of a
cloud,
so the song of the ruthless is stilled.

6On this mountain the LORD Almighty will
prepare
a feast of rich food for all peoples,
a banquet of aged wine—
the best of meats and the finest of wines.
7On this mountain he will destroy
the shroud that enfolds all peoples,
the sheet that covers all nations;
8 he will swallow up death forever.
The Sovereign LORD will wipe away the
tears
from all faces;
he will remove the disgrace of his people
from all the earth.
The LORD has spoken.

9In that day they will say,

"Surely this is our God;
we trusted in him, and he saved us.
This is the LORD, we trusted in him;
let us rejoice and be glad in his
salvation."

10The hand of the LORD will rest on this
mountain;
but Moab will be trampled under him
as straw is trampled down in the
manure.
11They will spread out their hands in it,
as a swimmer spreads out his hands to
swim.
God will bring down their pride
despite the cleverness[b] of their hands.
12He will bring down your high fortified
walls
and lay them low;
he will bring them down to the ground,
to the very dust.

A Song of Praise

26 In that day this song will be sung in the
land of Judah:

We have a strong city;
God makes salvation
its walls and ramparts.
2Open the gates
that the righteous nation may enter,
the nation that keeps faith.
3You will keep in perfect peace
him whose mind is steadfast,
because he trusts in you.
4Trust in the LORD forever,

[a]22 Or *released* [b]11 The meaning of the Hebrew for this word is uncertain.

24:17–20 The people refused to see the truth of their sin, so Isaiah declared that they would get what they deserved. When we ignore the warning signs and refuse to see the truth of our sinful behavior, we are inviting disaster. We must be honest with ourselves, see what we are doing wrong and confess this to God. Then we can take steps to redirect our course.
25:1–5 God will comfort those who trust in him and punish those who ignore him. No matter what we have done in the past, when we repent we can rely on God to strengthen us and keep us from sin. And if we haven't yet asked God to take control of our lives, there is still time. No one is too sinful to receive God's mercy.
26:3 When we are absorbed with sinful distractions or pain from the past, our inner lives fill with anxiety and turmoil. But when we turn from our sins or let go of our painful past, God can change our perspectives, helping us to fix our minds on him. With God as our focus, the turmoil around us will fade, and we will be flooded with his peace.

for the LORD, the LORD, is the Rock
eternal.
5He humbles those who dwell on high,
he lays the lofty city low;
he levels it to the ground
and casts it down to the dust.
6Feet trample it down—
the feet of the oppressed,
the footsteps of the poor.

7The path of the righteous is level;
O upright One, you make the way of the
righteous smooth.
8Yes, LORD, walking in the way of your
laws,[a]
we wait for you;
your name and renown
are the desire of our hearts.
9My soul yearns for you in the night;
in the morning my spirit longs for you.
When your judgments come upon the
earth,
the people of the world learn
righteousness.
10Though grace is shown to the wicked,
they do not learn righteousness;
even in a land of uprightness they go on
doing evil
and regard not the majesty of the LORD.
11O LORD, your hand is lifted high,
but they do not see it.
Let them see your zeal for your people and
be put to shame;
let the fire reserved for your enemies
consume them.

12LORD, you establish peace for us;
all that we have accomplished you have
done for us.
13O LORD, our God, other lords besides you
have ruled over us,
but your name alone do we honor.
14They are now dead, they live no more;
those departed spirits do not rise.
You punished them and brought them to
ruin;
you wiped out all memory of them.
15You have enlarged the nation, O LORD;
you have enlarged the nation.
You have gained glory for yourself;
you have extended all the borders of the
land.

16LORD, they came to you in their distress;
when you disciplined them,
they could barely whisper a prayer.[b]
17As a woman with child and about to give
birth
writhes and cries out in her pain,
so were we in your presence, O LORD.
18We were with child, we writhed in pain,
but we gave birth to wind.
We have not brought salvation to the earth;
we have not given birth to people of the
world.

19But your dead will live;
their bodies will rise.
You who dwell in the dust,
wake up and shout for joy.
Your dew is like the dew of the morning;
the earth will give birth to her dead.

20Go, my people, enter your rooms
and shut the doors behind you;
hide yourselves for a little while
until his wrath has passed by.
21See, the LORD is coming out of his dwelling
to punish the people of the earth for
their sins.
The earth will disclose the blood shed upon
her;
she will conceal her slain no longer.

Deliverance of Israel

27 In that day,

the LORD will punish with his sword,
his fierce, great and powerful sword,
Leviathan the gliding serpent,
Leviathan the coiling serpent;
he will slay the monster of the sea.

2In that day—

"Sing about a fruitful vineyard:
3 I, the LORD, watch over it;
I water it continually.
I guard it day and night
so that no one may harm it.
4 I am not angry.
If only there were briers and thorns
confronting me!
I would march against them in battle;
I would set them all on fire.
5Or else let them come to me for refuge;
let them make peace with me,
yes, let them make peace with me."

6In days to come Jacob will take root,
Israel will bud and blossom
and fill all the world with fruit.

7Has ⌊the LORD⌋ struck her
as he struck down those who struck her?
Has she been killed
as those were killed who killed her?

[a]8 Or *judgments* [b]16 The meaning of the Hebrew for this clause is uncertain.

27:1 Leviathan was a mythical, wicked sea monster. Its mention here is symbolic; God will destroy his enemies, especially Satan. God can overcome all the forces of darkness that threaten our spiritual lives and growth. And eventually, Satan will be vanquished forever.

27:2–3 God said he would take care of his people just as a farmer takes care of his vineyard. God would provide nourishment and keep enemies away. That is still true for us today. God will care for us if we surrender to his power. Once we repent of our sins, he will help us escape the destructive pull of our sinful nature.

[8]By warfare[a] and exile you contend with
her—
with his fierce blast he drives her out,
as on a day the east wind blows.
[9]By this, then, will Jacob's guilt be atoned
for,
and this will be the full fruitage of the
removal of his sin:
When he makes all the altar stones
to be like chalk stones crushed to pieces,
no Asherah poles[b] or incense altars
will be left standing.
[10]The fortified city stands desolate,
an abandoned settlement, forsaken like
the desert;
there the calves graze,
there they lie down;
they strip its branches bare.
[11]When its twigs are dry, they are broken off
and women come and make fires with
them.
For this is a people without understanding;
so their Maker has no compassion on
them,
and their Creator shows them no favor.

[12]In that day the LORD will thresh from the
flowing Euphrates[c] to the Wadi of Egypt, and
you, O Israelites, will be gathered up one by
one. [13]And in that day a great trumpet will
sound. Those who were perishing in Assyria
and those who were exiled in Egypt will come
and worship the LORD on the holy mountain in
Jerusalem.

Woe to Ephraim

28 Woe to that wreath, the pride of
Ephraim's drunkards,
to the fading flower, his glorious beauty,
set on the head of a fertile valley—
to that city, the pride of those laid low
by wine!
[2]See, the Lord has one who is powerful and
strong.
Like a hailstorm and a destructive wind,
like a driving rain and a flooding
downpour,
he will throw it forcefully to the ground.
[3]That wreath, the pride of Ephraim's
drunkards,
will be trampled underfoot.
[4]That fading flower, his glorious beauty,
set on the head of a fertile valley,
will be like a fig ripe before harvest—
as soon as someone sees it and takes it
in his hand,
he swallows it.

[5]In that day the LORD Almighty
will be a glorious crown,
a beautiful wreath
for the remnant of his people.
[6]He will be a spirit of justice
to him who sits in judgment,
a source of strength
to those who turn back the battle at the
gate.

[7]And these also stagger from wine
and reel from beer:
Priests and prophets stagger from beer
and are befuddled with wine;
they reel from beer,
they stagger when seeing visions,
they stumble when rendering decisions.
[8]All the tables are covered with vomit
and there is not a spot without filth.

[9]"Who is it he is trying to teach?
To whom is he explaining his message?
To children weaned from their milk,
to those just taken from the breast?
[10]For it is:
Do and do, do and do,
rule on rule, rule on rule[d];
a little here, a little there."

[11]Very well then, with foreign lips and
strange tongues
God will speak to this people,
[12]to whom he said,
"This is the resting place, let the weary
rest";
and, "This is the place of repose"—
but they would not listen.
[13]So then, the word of the LORD to them will
become:
Do and do, do and do,
rule on rule, rule on rule;
a little here, a little there—
so that they will go and fall backward,
be injured and snared and captured.

[14]Therefore hear the word of the LORD, you
scoffers

[a]*8* See Septuagint; the meaning of the Hebrew for this word is uncertain. [b]*9* That is, symbols of the goddess Asherah [c]*12* Hebrew *River* [d]*10* Hebrew */ sav lasav sav lasav / kav lakav kav lakav* (possibly meaningless sounds; perhaps a mimicking of the prophet's words); also in verse 13

28:1–6 The rewards of sinful pleasure are like a crown of flowers whose beauty quickly fades. The intense feeling we experience won't last and leaves us wanting. In contrast, God is an unfading crown of glory to those who obey his commands. He can fill our lives completely and grant us pleasures that will last throughout eternity.
28:7–13 Judah's leaders belittled Isaiah's message, declaring it was infantile (28:9–10). By doing so, Judah's leaders rejected God's salvation and rest. We, too, may belittle God's way, saying it is too simplistic, elementary or old-fashioned. The simplicity of God's message does not negate its truth. As we obey God's simple truth, we are protected from the consequences of disobedience.
28:14–22 The rulers of Jerusalem refused to see the truth. They thought they could withstand Assyria's destruction. In reality, though, Assyria's attack was God's judgment on their sin, and there was no escape from this punishment. We also commit a fatal error when God confronts us with our sin and we refuse to see the truth or admit that there is any problem we cannot handle alone.

who rule this people in Jerusalem.
15You boast, "We have entered into a
covenant with death,
with the grave[a] we have made an
agreement.
When an overwhelming scourge sweeps by,
it cannot touch us,
for we have made a lie our refuge
and falsehood[b] our hiding place."

16So this is what the Sovereign LORD says:

"See, I lay a stone in Zion,
a tested stone,
a precious cornerstone for a sure
foundation;
the one who trusts will never be
dismayed.
17I will make justice the measuring line
and righteousness the plumb line;
hail will sweep away your refuge, the lie,
and water will overflow your hiding
place.
18Your covenant with death will be annulled;
your agreement with the grave will not
stand.
When the overwhelming scourge sweeps by,
you will be beaten down by it.
19As often as it comes it will carry you away;
morning after morning, by day and by
night,
it will sweep through."

The understanding of this message
will bring sheer terror.
20The bed is too short to stretch out on,
the blanket too narrow to wrap around
you.
21The LORD will rise up as he did at Mount
Perazim,
he will rouse himself as in the Valley of
Gibeon—
to do his work, his strange work,
and perform his task, his alien task.
22Now stop your mocking,
or your chains will become heavier;
the Lord, the LORD Almighty, has told me
of the destruction decreed against the
whole land.
23Listen and hear my voice;
pay attention and hear what I say.
24When a farmer plows for planting, does he
plow continually?
Does he keep on breaking up and
harrowing the soil?
25When he has leveled the surface,
does he not sow caraway and scatter
cummin?
Does he not plant wheat in its place,[c]
barley in its plot,[c]
and spelt in its field?
26His God instructs him
and teaches him the right way.

27Caraway is not threshed with a sledge,
nor is a cartwheel rolled over cummin;
caraway is beaten out with a rod,
and cummin with a stick.
28Grain must be ground to make bread;
so one does not go on threshing it
forever.
Though he drives the wheels of his
threshing cart over it,
his horses do not grind it.
29All this also comes from the LORD
Almighty,
wonderful in counsel and magnificent in
wisdom.

Woe to David's City

29 Woe to you, Ariel, Ariel,
the city where David settled!
Add year to year
and let your cycle of festivals go on.
2Yet I will besiege Ariel;
she will mourn and lament,
she will be to me like an altar hearth.[d]
3I will encamp against you all around;
I will encircle you with towers
and set up my siege works against you.
4Brought low, you will speak from the
ground;
your speech will mumble out of the
dust.
Your voice will come ghostlike from the
earth;
out of the dust your speech will whisper.

5But your many enemies will become like
fine dust,
the ruthless hordes like blown chaff.
Suddenly, in an instant,
6 the LORD Almighty will come
with thunder and earthquake and great
noise,
with windstorm and tempest and flames
of a devouring fire.
7Then the hordes of all the nations that
fight against Ariel,
that attack her and her fortress and
besiege her,
will be as it is with a dream,
with a vision in the night—

[a]15 Hebrew *Sheol*; also in verse 18 [b]15 Or *false gods*
[c]25 The meaning of the Hebrew for this word is uncertain. [d]2 The Hebrew for *altar hearth* sounds like the Hebrew for *Ariel*.

When King David sinned and faced judgment, he said, "Let us fall into the hands of the LORD, for his mercy is great; but do not let me fall into the hands of men" (2 Samuel 24:14). God will show us mercy if we truly repent and turn from our sins.

29:5–8 When all hope was lost, God miraculously saved Jerusalem from its attackers. He will miraculously intervene on our behalf too. All we have to do is ask him and trust him. If God can save an entire nation from annihilation and save the whole world from the consequences of sin, he certainly can deliver us from the troubles we face.

8 as when a hungry man dreams that he is eating,
but he awakens, and his hunger remains;
as when a thirsty man dreams that he is drinking,
but he awakens faint, with his thirst unquenched.
So will it be with the hordes of all the nations
that fight against Mount Zion.

9 Be stunned and amazed,
blind yourselves and be sightless;
be drunk, but not from wine,
stagger, but not from beer.
10 The LORD has brought over you a deep sleep:
He has sealed your eyes (the prophets);
he has covered your heads (the seers).

11 For you this whole vision is nothing but
words sealed in a scroll. And if you give the
scroll to someone who can read, and say to
him, "Read this, please," he will answer, "I
can't; it is sealed." 12 Or if you give the scroll to
someone who cannot read, and say, "Read this,
please," he will answer, "I don't know how to
read."

13 The Lord says:

"These people come near to me with their mouth
and honor me with their lips,
but their hearts are far from me.
Their worship of me
is made up only of rules taught by men.[a]
14 Therefore once more I will astound these people
with wonder upon wonder;
the wisdom of the wise will perish,
the intelligence of the intelligent will vanish."
15 Woe to those who go to great depths
to hide their plans from the LORD,
who do their work in darkness and think,
"Who sees us? Who will know?"
16 You turn things upside down,
as if the potter were thought to be like the clay!
Shall what is formed say to him who formed it,
"He did not make me"?
Can the pot say of the potter,
"He knows nothing"?

17 In a very short time, will not Lebanon be turned into a fertile field
and the fertile field seem like a forest?
18 In that day the deaf will hear the words of the scroll,
and out of gloom and darkness
the eyes of the blind will see.
19 Once more the humble will rejoice in the LORD;
the needy will rejoice in the Holy One of Israel.
20 The ruthless will vanish,
the mockers will disappear,
and all who have an eye for evil will be cut down—
21 those who with a word make a man out to be guilty,
who ensnare the defender in court
and with false testimony deprive the innocent of justice.

22 Therefore this is what the LORD, who redeemed Abraham, says to the house of Jacob:

"No longer will Jacob be ashamed;
no longer will their faces grow pale.
23 When they see among them their children,
the work of my hands,
they will keep my name holy;
they will acknowledge the holiness of the Holy One of Jacob,
and will stand in awe of the God of Israel.
24 Those who are wayward in spirit will gain understanding;
those who complain will accept instruction."

Woe to the Obstinate Nation

30 "Woe to the obstinate children,"
declares the LORD,
"to those who carry out plans that are not mine,
forming an alliance, but not by my Spirit,
heaping sin upon sin;
2 who go down to Egypt
without consulting me;
who look for help to Pharaoh's protection,
to Egypt's shade for refuge.
3 But Pharaoh's protection will be to your shame,
Egypt's shade will bring you disgrace.
4 Though they have officials in Zoan

[a] 13 Hebrew; Septuagint *They worship me in vain; / their teachings are but rules taught by men*

29:15–16 We can't hide anything from God; he knows about everything we've done, are doing and will do. We must honestly examine our lives and admit our weaknesses to God and ourselves. We tell God, not to inform him of something he doesn't already know, but to hand over our lives to him. We also may need to admit our weaknesses to others so that they can help us stand firm against these problem areas in our lives.

30:1–5 In their quest for protection, Judah sought help from Egypt, not from God. God warned Judah's leaders that their plan would only bring defeat because Egypt wouldn't be able to save them. God alone had the power to deliver them. When we put our trust in people or anything that excludes God, we will fail. To attempt anything apart from God will only lead to increased suffering.

and their envoys have arrived in Hanes,
5everyone will be put to shame
because of a people useless to them,
who bring neither help nor advantage,
but only shame and disgrace."

6An oracle concerning the animals of the Negev:

Through a land of hardship and distress,
of lions and lionesses,
of adders and darting snakes,
the envoys carry their riches on donkeys' backs,
their treasures on the humps of camels,
to that unprofitable nation,
7 to Egypt, whose help is utterly useless.
Therefore I call her
Rahab the Do-Nothing.

8Go now, write it on a tablet for them,
inscribe it on a scroll,
that for the days to come
it may be an everlasting witness.
9These are rebellious people, deceitful children,
children unwilling to listen to the LORD's instruction.
10They say to the seers,
"See no more visions!"
and to the prophets,
"Give us no more visions of what is right!
Tell us pleasant things,
prophesy illusions.
11Leave this way,
get off this path,
and stop confronting us
with the Holy One of Israel!"

12Therefore, this is what the Holy One of Israel says:

"Because you have rejected this message,
relied on oppression
and depended on deceit,
13this sin will become for you
like a high wall, cracked and bulging,
that collapses suddenly, in an instant.
14It will break in pieces like pottery,
shattered so mercilessly
that among its pieces not a fragment will be found
for taking coals from a hearth
or scooping water out of a cistern."

15This is what the Sovereign LORD, the Holy One of Israel, says:

"In repentance and rest is your salvation,
in quietness and trust is your strength,
but you would have none of it.
16You said, 'No, we will flee on horses.'
Therefore you will flee!
You said, 'We will ride off on swift horses.'
Therefore your pursuers will be swift!
17A thousand will flee
at the threat of one;
at the threat of five
you will all flee away,
till you are left
like a flagstaff on a mountaintop,
like a banner on a hill."

18Yet the LORD longs to be gracious to you;
he rises to show you compassion.
For the LORD is a God of justice.
Blessed are all who wait for him!

19O people of Zion, who live in Jerusalem,
you will weep no more. How gracious he will be
when you cry for help! As soon as he hears, he
will answer you. 20Although the Lord gives you
the bread of adversity and the water of affliction, your teachers will be hidden no more;
with your own eyes you will see them. 21Wheth-
er you turn to the right or to the left, your ears
will hear a voice behind you, saying, "This is
the way; walk in it." 22Then you will defile your
idols overlaid with silver and your images covered with gold; you will throw them away like
a menstrual cloth and say to them, "Away with
you!"

23He will also send you rain for the seed you
sow in the ground, and the food that comes
from the land will be rich and plentiful. In that
day your cattle will graze in broad meadows.
24The oxen and donkeys that work the soil will
eat fodder and mash, spread out with fork and
shovel. 25In the day of great slaughter, when the
towers fall, streams of water will flow on every
high mountain and every lofty hill. 26The moon
will shine like the sun, and the sunlight will be
seven times brighter, like the light of seven full
days, when the LORD binds up the bruises of his
people and heals the wounds he inflicted.

27See, the Name of the LORD comes from afar,
with burning anger and dense clouds of smoke;

30:6–11 When we sin, we try to avoid what God has to say about our sin. Intrinsically we know what God thinks about sinful behavior. But admitting our sin only brings conviction, guilt and the recognition that we need to change. We would rather hear people say that we are doing all right, that we have no problems. To continue in this state of self-imposed spiritual deafness eventually leads to ruin. We may even reach a point when we no longer accept the truth of God's Word. It is important to accept the truth from God; a little pain now is better than much pain later.

30:12–17 We are often like Judah, frantically turning to every source of help except God to find instant relief from our problems. We know we should admit our need for God and return to him, trusting him for deliverance. The Bible clearly states which choice will lead to spiritual renewal and which will lead to ruin. Which way will we choose?

30:18 "Blessed are all who wait for him!" God will bless us, but God's ways take time. We may need to wait! Trying to hurry the process only leads to disaster.

his lips are full of wrath,
and his tongue is a consuming fire.
28His breath is like a rushing torrent,
rising up to the neck.
He shakes the nations in the sieve of destruction;
he places in the jaws of the peoples
a bit that leads them astray.
29And you will sing
as on the night you celebrate a holy festival;
your hearts will rejoice
as when people go up with flutes
to the mountain of the LORD,
to the Rock of Israel.
30The LORD will cause men to hear his majestic voice
and will make them see his arm coming down
with raging anger and consuming fire,
with cloudburst, thunderstorm and hail.
31The voice of the LORD will shatter Assyria;
with his scepter he will strike them down.
32Every stroke the LORD lays on them
with his punishing rod
will be to the music of tambourines and harps,
as he fights them in battle with the blows of his arm.
33Topheth has long been prepared;
it has been made ready for the king.
Its fire pit has been made deep and wide,
with an abundance of fire and wood;
the breath of the LORD,
like a stream of burning sulfur,
sets it ablaze.

Woe to Those Who Rely on Egypt

31 Woe to those who go down to Egypt for help,
who rely on horses,
who trust in the multitude of their chariots
and in the great strength of their horsemen,
but do not look to the Holy One of Israel,
or seek help from the LORD.
2Yet he too is wise and can bring disaster;
he does not take back his words.
He will rise up against the house of the wicked,
against those who help evildoers.
3But the Egyptians are men and not God;
their horses are flesh and not spirit.
When the LORD stretches out his hand,
he who helps will stumble,
he who is helped will fall;
both will perish together.

4This is what the LORD says to me:

"As a lion growls,
a great lion over his prey—
and though a whole band of shepherds
is called together against him,
he is not frightened by their shouts
or disturbed by their clamor—
so the LORD Almighty will come down
to do battle on Mount Zion and on its heights.
5Like birds hovering overhead,
the LORD Almighty will shield Jerusalem;
he will shield it and deliver it,
he will 'pass over' it and will rescue it."

6Return to him you have so greatly revolted
against, O Israelites. 7For in that day every one
of you will reject the idols of silver and gold
your sinful hands have made.

8"Assyria will fall by a sword that is not of man;
a sword, not of mortals, will devour them.
They will flee before the sword
and their young men will be put to forced labor.
9Their stronghold will fall because of terror;
at sight of the battle standard their commanders will panic,"
declares the LORD,
whose fire is in Zion,
whose furnace is in Jerusalem.

The Kingdom of Righteousness

32 See, a king will reign in righteousness
and rulers will rule with justice.
2Each man will be like a shelter from the wind
and a refuge from the storm,
like streams of water in the desert
and the shadow of a great rock in a thirsty land.

3Then the eyes of those who see will no longer be closed,
and the ears of those who hear will listen.

31:1–5 Judah turned to Egypt instead of to God for help. Destruction quickly followed. Egypt can symbolize for us all those things we use to gain relief from our inner pain: work, illicit sex, alcohol, drugs, food, unhealthy relationships and the like. These appear to give us relief and help, just as the mighty chariots of Egypt appeared to help Israel. But such help is illusory; only God can bring us true deliverance.

31:6–9 We might think that with such rebellion and stubbornness, God would have given up on his people. But incredibly, God continually invited them to return to him and find his blessings. What an encouragement this is for us. We may wonder whether God still cares about us after our repeated failures. This passage reassures us that God wants all of us to turn to him and find salvation.

32:1–2 The king mentioned here is Jesus. We don't have to wait for him any longer. The future blessings described in these verses are available to us now. We can trust that he will help us. To claim God's aid, we need to confess Jesus as our Savior, realize that he died for our sins and rose again, request forgiveness for our sins and surrender our lives to God so that he can purify us.

4The mind of the rash will know and
understand,
and the stammering tongue will be
fluent and clear.
5No longer will the fool be called noble
nor the scoundrel be highly respected.
6For the fool speaks folly,
his mind is busy with evil:
He practices ungodliness
and spreads error concerning the LORD;
the hungry he leaves empty
and from the thirsty he withholds water.
7The scoundrel's methods are wicked,
he makes up evil schemes
to destroy the poor with lies,
even when the plea of the needy is just.
8But the noble man makes noble plans,
and by noble deeds he stands.

The Women of Jerusalem

9You women who are so complacent,
rise up and listen to me;
you daughters who feel secure,
hear what I have to say!
10In little more than a year
you who feel secure will tremble;
the grape harvest will fail,
and the harvest of fruit will not come.
11Tremble, you complacent women;
shudder, you daughters who feel secure!
Strip off your clothes,
put sackcloth around your waists.
12Beat your breasts for the pleasant fields,
for the fruitful vines
13and for the land of my people,
a land overgrown with thorns and
briers—
yes, mourn for all houses of merriment
and for this city of revelry.
14The fortress will be abandoned,
the noisy city deserted;
citadel and watchtower will become a
wasteland forever,
the delight of donkeys, a pasture for
flocks,
15till the Spirit is poured upon us from on
high,
and the desert becomes a fertile field,
and the fertile field seems like a forest.
16Justice will dwell in the desert
and righteousness live in the fertile field.
17The fruit of righteousness will be peace;
the effect of righteousness will be
quietness and confidence forever.
18My people will live in peaceful dwelling
places,
in secure homes,
in undisturbed places of rest.
19Though hail flattens the forest
and the city is leveled completely,
20how blessed you will be,
sowing your seed by every stream,
and letting your cattle and donkeys range
free.

Distress and Help

33 Woe to you, O destroyer,
you who have not been destroyed!
Woe to you, O traitor,
you who have not been betrayed!
When you stop destroying,
you will be destroyed;
when you stop betraying,
you will be betrayed.

2O LORD, be gracious to us;
we long for you.
Be our strength every morning,
our salvation in time of distress.
3At the thunder of your voice, the peoples
flee;
when you rise up, the nations scatter.
4Your plunder, O nations, is harvested as by
young locusts;
like a swarm of locusts men pounce on
it.

5The LORD is exalted, for he dwells on high;
he will fill Zion with justice and
righteousness.
6He will be the sure foundation for your
times,
a rich store of salvation and wisdom and
knowledge;
the fear of the LORD is the key to this
treasure.[a]

7Look, their brave men cry aloud in the
streets;
the envoys of peace weep bitterly.
8The highways are deserted,
no travelers are on the roads.
The treaty is broken,
its witnesses[b] are despised,
no one is respected.
9The land mourns[c] and wastes away,
Lebanon is ashamed and withers;
Sharon is like the Arabah,
and Bashan and Carmel drop their
leaves.

10"Now will I arise," says the LORD.
"Now will I be exalted;
now will I be lifted up.
11You conceive chaff,
you give birth to straw;
your breath is a fire that consumes you.
12The peoples will be burned as if to lime;

[a]6 Or *is a treasure from him* [b]8 Dead Sea Scrolls; Masoretic Text / *the cities* [c]9 Or *dries up*

33:1 Assyria's foreign policy was based on a double standard: those who broke their promises to Assyria were punished, while Assyria's own broken promises were overlooked. God would judge this hypocrisy. God hates broken promises just as much today as he did then. We will be held responsible by God for our promises, so we must be certain to fulfill them.

like cut thornbushes they will be set
ablaze."

13You who are far away, hear what I have
done;
you who are near, acknowledge my
power!
14The sinners in Zion are terrified;
trembling grips the godless:
"Who of us can dwell with the consuming
fire?
Who of us can dwell with everlasting
burning?"
15He who walks righteously
and speaks what is right,
who rejects gain from extortion
and keeps his hand from accepting
bribes,
who stops his ears against plots of murder
and shuts his eyes against contemplating
evil—
16this is the man who will dwell on the
heights,
whose refuge will be the mountain
fortress.
His bread will be supplied,
and water will not fail him.

17Your eyes will see the king in his beauty
and view a land that stretches afar.
18In your thoughts you will ponder the
former terror:
"Where is that chief officer?
Where is the one who took the revenue?
Where is the officer in charge of the
towers?"
19You will see those arrogant people no
more,
those people of an obscure speech,
with their strange, incomprehensible
tongue.

20Look upon Zion, the city of our festivals;
your eyes will see Jerusalem,
a peaceful abode, a tent that will not be
moved;
its stakes will never be pulled up,
nor any of its ropes broken.
21There the LORD will be our Mighty One.
It will be like a place of broad rivers and
streams.
No galley with oars will ride them,
no mighty ship will sail them.
22For the LORD is our judge,
the LORD is our lawgiver,
the LORD is our king;
it is he who will save us.

23Your rigging hangs loose:
The mast is not held secure,
the sail is not spread.
Then an abundance of spoils will be
divided
and even the lame will carry off plunder.
24No one living in Zion will say, "I am ill";
and the sins of those who dwell there
will be forgiven.

Judgment Against the Nations

34 Come near, you nations, and listen;
pay attention, you peoples!
Let the earth hear, and all that is in it,
the world, and all that comes out of it!
2The LORD is angry with all nations;
his wrath is upon all their armies.
He will totally destroy[a] them,
he will give them over to slaughter.
3Their slain will be thrown out,
their dead bodies will send up a stench;
the mountains will be soaked with their
blood.
4All the stars of the heavens will be
dissolved
and the sky rolled up like a scroll;
all the starry host will fall
like withered leaves from the vine,
like shriveled figs from the fig tree.

5My sword has drunk its fill in the heavens;
see, it descends in judgment on Edom,
the people I have totally destroyed.
6The sword of the LORD is bathed in blood,
it is covered with fat—
the blood of lambs and goats,
fat from the kidneys of rams.
For the LORD has a sacrifice in Bozrah
and a great slaughter in Edom.
7And the wild oxen will fall with them,
the bull calves and the great bulls.
Their land will be drenched with blood,
and the dust will be soaked with fat.

8For the LORD has a day of vengeance,
a year of retribution, to uphold Zion's
cause.
9Edom's streams will be turned into pitch,
her dust into burning sulfur;
her land will become blazing pitch!
10It will not be quenched night and day;
its smoke will rise forever.
From generation to generation it will lie
desolate;
no one will ever pass through it again.

[a] *2* The Hebrew term refers to the irrevocable giving over of things or persons to the LORD, often by totally destroying them; also in verse 5.

33:24 God says he will heal the sick and helpless people who turn to him. All of us have committed sins, some of which we did to escape our guilt. God longs to heal us, forgive our sins, and bless us. Once God has forgiven us, we are freed from guilt. Our sins are gone—God will never remember them again.

34:1–17 God's judgment on Edom reminds us that rejecting him brings disaster. Rejecting him may bring deteriorating health, emotional destruction or even eternal destruction if we continue down such a destructive path. Accepting God's plan for our lives ensures that we will finish life on the right path and will enjoy God's presence throughout eternity.

11The desert owl[a] and screech owl[a] will
possess it;
the great owl[a] and the raven will nest
there.
God will stretch out over Edom
the measuring line of chaos
and the plumb line of desolation.
12Her nobles will have nothing there to be
called a kingdom,
all her princes will vanish away.
13Thorns will overrun her citadels,
nettles and brambles her strongholds.
She will become a haunt for jackals,
a home for owls.
14Desert creatures will meet with hyenas,
and wild goats will bleat to each other;
there the night creatures will also repose
and find for themselves places of rest.
15The owl will nest there and lay eggs,
she will hatch them, and care for her
young under the shadow of her
wings;
there also the falcons will gather,
each with its mate.

16Look in the scroll of the LORD and read:
None of these will be missing,
not one will lack her mate.
For it is his mouth that has given the order,
and his Spirit will gather them together.
17He allots their portions;
his hand distributes them by measure.
They will possess it forever
and dwell there from generation to
generation.

Joy of the Redeemed

35 The desert and the parched land will
be glad;
the wilderness will rejoice and blossom.
Like the crocus, 2it will burst into bloom;
it will rejoice greatly and shout for joy.
The glory of Lebanon will be given to it,
the splendor of Carmel and Sharon;
they will see the glory of the LORD,
the splendor of our God.

3Strengthen the feeble hands,
steady the knees that give way;
4say to those with fearful hearts,
"Be strong, do not fear;
your God will come,
he will come with vengeance;
with divine retribution
he will come to save you."
5Then will the eyes of the blind be opened
and the ears of the deaf unstopped.
6Then will the lame leap like a deer,
and the mute tongue shout for joy.
Water will gush forth in the wilderness
and streams in the desert.
7The burning sand will become a pool,
the thirsty ground bubbling springs.
In the haunts where jackals once lay,
grass and reeds and papyrus will grow.

8And a highway will be there;
it will be called the Way of Holiness.
The unclean will not journey on it;
it will be for those who walk in that
Way;
wicked fools will not go about on it.[b]
9No lion will be there,
nor will any ferocious beast get up on it;
they will not be found there.
But only the redeemed will walk there,
10 and the ransomed of the LORD will
return.
They will enter Zion with singing;
everlasting joy will crown their heads.
Gladness and joy will overtake them,
and sorrow and sighing will flee away.

Sennacherib Threatens Jerusalem

36 In the fourteenth year of King Hezekiah's reign, Sennacherib king of Assyria
attacked all the fortified cities of Judah and captured them. 2Then the king of Assyria sent his
field commander with a large army from Lachish to King Hezekiah at Jerusalem. When the
commander stopped at the aqueduct of the Upper Pool, on the road to the Washerman's Field,
3Eliakim son of Hilkiah the palace administrator, Shebna the secretary, and Joah son of Asaph
the recorder went out to him.
4The field commander said to them, "Tell
Hezekiah,

"'This is what the great king, the king
of Assyria, says: On what are you basing
this confidence of yours? 5You say you
have strategy and military strength—but
you speak only empty words. On whom

[a]11 The precise identification of these birds is uncertain.
[b]8 Or / *the simple will not stray from it*

35:3–7 God proclaims a message of hope to those who are discouraged, frightened and injured. God will save and heal; that is his promise. Part of this prophecy was fulfilled through Jesus' healing ministry when he was here on earth. Today we can still ask God for salvation and healing too. And following God means that we can ask him for help in this lifetime and share eternal glory with him in the next.

35:8–10 This "Way of Holiness" would provide a route for God's people to return from exile. God also provides us with a passageway through the desert of our pain and suffering. The road we must travel holds no threat because God is traveling with us. We are not alone as we fight our sinful nature—God is with us, strengthening us to resist temptation.

36:1–12 The Assyrians besieged Jerusalem and mocked Judah for thinking they could find deliverance through trust in God. In a similar way, people may mock us for believing we can find hope in God. "That's a religious cop-out," they may say. "Face reality." The truth is that God loves us, cares about us and wants what is best for us. And God is the only one who can effectively transform our lives. To trust in anything else is to deny reality.

are you depending, that you rebel against
me? 6Look now, you are depending on
Egypt, that splintered reed of a staff, which
pierces a man's hand and wounds him if
he leans on it! Such is Pharaoh king of
Egypt to all who depend on him. 7And if
you say to me, "We are depending on the
LORD our God"—isn't he the one whose
high places and altars Hezekiah removed,
saying to Judah and Jerusalem, "You must
worship before this altar"?
8" 'Come now, make a bargain with
my master, the king of Assyria: I will give
you two thousand horses—if you can put
riders on them! 9How then can you repulse one officer of the least of my master's officials, even though you are depending on Egypt for chariots and
horsemen? 10Furthermore, have I come to
attack and destroy this land without the
LORD? The LORD himself told me to march
against this country and destroy it.' "

11Then Eliakim, Shebna and Joah said to the
field commander, "Please speak to your servants in Aramaic, since we understand it. Don't
speak to us in Hebrew in the hearing of the
people on the wall."
12But the commander replied, "Was it only
to your master and you that my master sent me
to say these things, and not to the men sitting
on the wall—who, like you, will have to eat their
own filth and drink their own urine?"
13Then the commander stood and called out
in Hebrew, "Hear the words of the great king,
the king of Assyria! 14This is what the king says:
Do not let Hezekiah deceive you. He cannot
deliver you! 15Do not let Hezekiah persuade
you to trust in the LORD when he says, 'The
LORD will surely deliver us; this city will not be
given into the hand of the king of Assyria.'
16"Do not listen to Hezekiah. This is what
the king of Assyria says: Make peace with me
and come out to me. Then every one of you will
eat from his own vine and fig tree and drink
water from his own cistern, 17until I come and
take you to a land like your own—a land of grain
and new wine, a land of bread and vineyards.
18"Do not let Hezekiah mislead you when he
says, 'The LORD will deliver us.' Has the god of
any nation ever delivered his land from the
hand of the king of Assyria? 19Where are the
gods of Hamath and Arpad? Where are the gods
of Sepharvaim? Have they rescued Samaria
from my hand? 20Who of all the gods of these
countries has been able to save his land from
me? How then can the LORD deliver Jerusalem
from my hand?"
21But the people remained silent and said
nothing in reply, because the king had commanded, "Do not answer him."
22Then Eliakim son of Hilkiah the palace administrator, Shebna the secretary, and Joah son
of Asaph the recorder went to Hezekiah, with
their clothes torn, and told him what the field
commander had said.

Jerusalem's Deliverance Foretold

37 When King Hezekiah heard this, he tore
his clothes and put on sackcloth and
went into the temple of the LORD. 2He sent Eliakim the palace administrator, Shebna the secretary, and the leading priests, all wearing sackcloth, to the prophet Isaiah son of Amoz. 3They
told him, "This is what Hezekiah says: This day
is a day of distress and rebuke and disgrace, as
when children come to the point of birth and
there is no strength to deliver them. 4It may be
that the LORD your God will hear the words of
the field commander, whom his master, the
king of Assyria, has sent to ridicule the living
God, and that he will rebuke him for the words
the LORD your God has heard. Therefore pray
for the remnant that still survives."
5When King Hezekiah's officials came to Isaiah, 6Isaiah said to them, "Tell your master,
'This is what the LORD says: Do not be afraid of
what you have heard—those words with which
the underlings of the king of Assyria have blasphemed me. 7Listen! I am going to put a spirit
in him so that when he hears a certain report,
he will return to his own country, and there I
will have him cut down with the sword.' "
8When the field commander heard that the
king of Assyria had left Lachish, he withdrew
and found the king fighting against Libnah.
9Now Sennacherib received a report that
Tirhakah, the Cushite[a] king ⌞of Egypt⌟, was
marching out to fight against him. When he
heard it, he sent messengers to Hezekiah with
this word: 10"Say to Hezekiah king of Judah: Do
not let the god you depend on deceive you

[a]9 That is, from the upper Nile region

36:13–22 Would the three little pigs have trusted the big, bad wolf and let him into their house? The king of Assyria's appeal to the people of Judah to place their trust in him instead of God sounds a lot like that big, bad wolf. In the same way, our sinful nature entices us to trust ourselves for our own satisfaction and protection instead of turning to God for help. Our sinful nature is only a big, bad wolf that will lead us to destruction. We must stop believing the lies that sin tells us and begin trusting God.

37:1–4 Hezekiah showed us the right thing to do when faced with overwhelming trouble: He humbled himself before God, prayed about the problem and sought help from a godly person. Too often we deny the seriousness of our problems and refuse to turn to God for help. Spiritual growth is impossible without asking God for help and without the encouragement and instruction of godly friends.

37:8–20 The king of Assyria tried to convince Hezekiah to abandon his trust in God. He compared the God of Israel with the false gods of the nations he had already conquered. Hezekiah recognized that those gods were man-made but that Israel's God was real and able to rescue his people. When we are in trouble, there are many places we may go for help, but only God has the power to deliver us. We should look to God to help us for he alone has the power to transform our lives.

when he says, 'Jerusalem will not be handed
over to the king of Assyria.' 11Surely you have
heard what the kings of Assyria have done to all
the countries, destroying them completely. And
will you be delivered? 12Did the gods of the
nations that were destroyed by my forefathers
deliver them—the gods of Gozan, Haran, Rezeph and the people of Eden who were in Tel
Assar? 13Where is the king of Hamath, the king
of Arpad, the king of the city of Sepharvaim, or
of Hena or Ivvah?"

Hezekiah's Prayer

14Hezekiah received the letter from the messengers and read it. Then he went up to the
temple of the LORD and spread it out before the
LORD. 15And Hezekiah prayed to the LORD:
16"O LORD Almighty, God of Israel, enthroned
between the cherubim, you alone are God over
all the kingdoms of the earth. You have made
heaven and earth. 17Give ear, O LORD, and hear;
open your eyes, O LORD, and see; listen to all
the words Sennacherib has sent to insult the
living God.

18"It is true, O LORD, that the Assyrian kings
have laid waste all these peoples and their
lands. 19They have thrown their gods into the
fire and destroyed them, for they were not gods
but only wood and stone, fashioned by human
hands. 20Now, O LORD our God, deliver us
from his hand, so that all kingdoms on earth
may know that you alone, O LORD, are God.[a]"

Sennacherib's Fall

21Then Isaiah son of Amoz sent a message to
Hezekiah: "This is what the LORD, the God of
Israel, says: Because you have prayed to me concerning Sennacherib king of Assyria, 22this is the
word the LORD has spoken against him:

"The Virgin Daughter of Zion
despises and mocks you.
The Daughter of Jerusalem
tosses her head as you flee.
23Who is it you have insulted and
blasphemed?
Against whom have you raised your
voice
and lifted your eyes in pride?
Against the Holy One of Israel!
24By your messengers
you have heaped insults on the Lord.
And you have said,
'With my many chariots
I have ascended the heights of the
mountains,
the utmost heights of Lebanon.
I have cut down its tallest cedars,
the choicest of its pines.
I have reached its remotest heights,
the finest of its forests.
25I have dug wells in foreign lands[b]
and drunk the water there.
With the soles of my feet
I have dried up all the streams of Egypt.'

26"Have you not heard?
Long ago I ordained it.
In days of old I planned it;
now I have brought it to pass,
that you have turned fortified cities
into piles of stone.
27Their people, drained of power,
are dismayed and put to shame.
They are like plants in the field,
like tender green shoots,
like grass sprouting on the roof,
scorched[c] before it grows up.

28"But I know where you stay
and when you come and go
and how you rage against me.
29Because you rage against me
and because your insolence has reached
my ears,
I will put my hook in your nose
and my bit in your mouth,
and I will make you return
by the way you came.

30"This will be the sign for you, O Hezekiah:

"This year you will eat what grows by
itself,
and the second year what springs from
that.
But in the third year sow and reap,
plant vineyards and eat their fruit.
31Once more a remnant of the house of
Judah
will take root below and bear fruit
above.
32For out of Jerusalem will come a remnant,
and out of Mount Zion a band of
survivors.
The zeal of the LORD Almighty
will accomplish this.

33"Therefore this is what the LORD says concerning the king of Assyria:

"He will not enter this city
or shoot an arrow here.
He will not come before it with shield
or build a siege ramp against it.
34By the way that he came he will return;

[a]20 Dead Sea Scrolls (see also 2 Kings 19:19); Masoretic Text *alone are the LORD* [b]25 Dead Sea Scrolls (see also 2 Kings 19:24); Masoretic Text does not have *in foreign lands.* [c]27 Some manuscripts of the Masoretic Text, Dead Sea Scrolls and some Septuagint manuscripts (see also 2 Kings 19:26); most manuscripts of the Masoretic Text *roof / and terraced fields*

37:33–38 What an impossible situation! The army of the largest empire on earth had totally surrounded Jerusalem. If the Assyrians had been patient and had waited, all of Jerusalem eventually would have starved and the Assyrians would have been victorious. But God is not bound by human impossibilities. He can bring deliverance to those who trust in him in the most hopeless of situations.

he will not enter this city,"
declares the LORD.
35 "I will defend this city and save it,
for my sake and for the sake of David
my servant!"

36 Then the angel of the LORD went out and
put to death a hundred and eighty-five thousand men in the Assyrian camp. When the people got up the next morning—there were all the
dead bodies! 37 So Sennacherib king of Assyria
broke camp and withdrew. He returned to Nineveh and stayed there.
38 One day, while he was worshiping in the
temple of his god Nisroch, his sons Adramme-
lech and Sharezer cut him down with the
sword, and they escaped to the land of Ararat.
And Esarhaddon his son succeeded him as king.

Hezekiah's Illness

38 In those days Hezekiah became ill and
was at the point of death. The prophet
Isaiah son of Amoz went to him and said, "This
is what the LORD says: Put your house in order,
because you are going to die; you will not recover."
2 Hezekiah turned his face to the wall and
prayed to the LORD, 3 "Remember, O LORD,
how I have walked before you faithfully and
with wholehearted devotion and have done
what is good in your eyes." And Hezekiah wept
bitterly.
4 Then the word of the LORD came to Isaiah:
5 "Go and tell Hezekiah, 'This is what the LORD,
the God of your father David, says: I have heard
your prayer and seen your tears; I will add fifteen years to your life. 6 And I will deliver you
and this city from the hand of the king of Assyria. I will defend this city.
7 " 'This is the LORD's sign to you that the
LORD will do what he has promised: 8 I will
make the shadow cast by the sun go back the
ten steps it has gone down on the stairway of
Ahaz.' " So the sunlight went back the ten steps
it had gone down.
9 A writing of Hezekiah king of Judah after his
illness and recovery:

10 I said, "In the prime of my life
must I go through the gates of death[a]
and be robbed of the rest of my years?"
11 I said, "I will not again see the LORD,
the LORD, in the land of the living;
no longer will I look on mankind,
or be with those who now dwell in this
world.[b]
12 Like a shepherd's tent my house
has been pulled down and taken from
me.
Like a weaver I have rolled up my life,
and he has cut me off from the loom;
day and night you made an end of me.
13 I waited patiently till dawn,
but like a lion he broke all my bones;
day and night you made an end of me.
14 I cried like a swift or thrush,
I moaned like a mourning dove.
My eyes grew weak as I looked to the
heavens.
I am troubled; O Lord, come to my aid!"

15 But what can I say?
He has spoken to me, and he himself
has done this.
I will walk humbly all my years
because of this anguish of my soul.
16 Lord, by such things men live;
and my spirit finds life in them too.
You restored me to health
and let me live.
17 Surely it was for my benefit
that I suffered such anguish.
In your love you kept me
from the pit of destruction;
you have put all my sins
behind your back.
18 For the grave[a] cannot praise you,
death cannot sing your praise;
those who go down to the pit
cannot hope for your faithfulness.
19 The living, the living—they praise you,
as I am doing today;
fathers tell their children
about your faithfulness.

20 The LORD will save me,
and we will sing with stringed
instruments
all the days of our lives
in the temple of the LORD.

21 Isaiah had said, "Prepare a poultice of figs
and apply it to the boil, and he will recover."
22 Hezekiah had asked, "What will be the
sign that I will go up to the temple of the LORD?"

Envoys From Babylon

39 At that time Merodach-Baladan son of
Baladan king of Babylon sent Hezekiah
letters and a gift, because he had heard of his

[a] 10,18 Hebrew *Sheol* [b] 11 A few Hebrew manuscripts; most Hebrew manuscripts *in the place of cessation*

38:1–8 Hezekiah's situation seemed hopeless. He had received a word from God that his life was over. Yet no situation is so hopeless that it is beyond God's ability to help. Hezekiah turned to God in prayer, and God spared his life. We are never without hope because God is merciful. When we admit our sin and ask him to forgive us, he will respond.

38:10–22 Hezekiah recognized that his illness was good for him because through it he found God's deliverance. Often our suffering works good in our lives too because it breaks into our lifestyle and causes us to realize we need God. We should honestly examine our lives to see whether we are living for God or ourselves. If God is not our priority, we need to confess this and give God his proper place.

39:1–8 Hezekiah foolishly received the Babylonians and showed them the extent of his treasures. He failed to understand that they would be the next conquerors of Judah. We also often fail to discern the things that are our

illness and recovery. 2Hezekiah received the envoys gladly and showed them what was in his
storehouses—the silver, the gold, the spices, the
fine oil, his entire armory and everything found
among his treasures. There was nothing in his
palace or in all his kingdom that Hezekiah did
not show them.
3Then Isaiah the prophet went to King Hezekiah and asked, "What did those men say, and
where did they come from?"
"From a distant land," Hezekiah replied.
"They came to me from Babylon."
4The prophet asked, "What did they see in
your palace?"
"They saw everything in my palace," Hezekiah said. "There is nothing among my treasures
that I did not show them."
5Then Isaiah said to Hezekiah, "Hear the
word of the LORD Almighty: 6The time will surely come when everything in your palace, and all
that your fathers have stored up until this day,
will be carried off to Babylon. Nothing will be
left, says the LORD. 7And some of your descendants, your own flesh and blood who will be
born to you, will be taken away, and they will
become eunuchs in the palace of the king of
Babylon."
8"The word of the LORD you have spoken is
good," Hezekiah replied. For he thought, "There
will be peace and security in my lifetime."

Comfort for God's People

40 Comfort, comfort my people,
says your God.
2Speak tenderly to Jerusalem,
and proclaim to her
that her hard service has been completed,
that her sin has been paid for,
that she has received from the LORD's hand
double for all her sins.

3A voice of one calling:
"In the desert prepare
the way for the LORD[a];
make straight in the wilderness
a highway for our God.[b]
4Every valley shall be raised up,
every mountain and hill made low;
the rough ground shall become level,
the rugged places a plain.
5And the glory of the LORD will be revealed,
and all mankind together will see it.
For the mouth of the LORD
has spoken."

6A voice says, "Cry out."
And I said, "What shall I cry?"

"All men are like grass,
and all their glory is like the flowers of
the field.
7The grass withers and the flowers fall,
because the breath of the LORD blows on
them.
Surely the people are grass.
8The grass withers and the flowers fall,
but the word of our God stands forever."

9You who bring good tidings to Zion,
go up on a high mountain.
You who bring good tidings to Jerusalem,[c]
lift up your voice with a shout,
lift it up, do not be afraid;
say to the towns of Judah,
"Here is your God!"
10See, the Sovereign LORD comes with power,
and his arm rules for him.
See, his reward is with him,
and his recompense accompanies him.
11He tends his flock like a shepherd:
He gathers the lambs in his arms
and carries them close to his heart;
he gently leads those that have young.

12Who has measured the waters in the
hollow of his hand,
or with the breadth of his hand marked
off the heavens?
Who has held the dust of the earth in a
basket,
or weighed the mountains on the scales
and the hills in a balance?
13Who has understood the mind[d] of the
LORD,
or instructed him as his counselor?
14Whom did the LORD consult to enlighten
him,
and who taught him the right way?
Who was it that taught him knowledge
or showed him the path of
understanding?

15Surely the nations are like a drop in a
bucket;
they are regarded as dust on the scales;

[a]3 Or *A voice of one calling in the desert: / "Prepare the way for the LORD* [b]3 Hebrew; Septuagint *make straight the paths of our God* [c]9 Or *O Zion, bringer of good tidings, / go up on a high mountain. / O Jerusalem, bringer of good tidings* [d]13 Or *Spirit*; or *spirit*

---

true enemies. We often make unhealthy alliances or participate in activities that can destroy us. To avoid this pitfall, we need to ask ourselves: *Would God approve of this relationship, activity, habit or environment?*

40:1–5 After the judgments of chapters 1—39, God's message to his people becomes one of comfort and blessing. God never gives up on us, no matter how sinful we have been. Our punishment will end, and God will restore us to a loving relationship with himself. We must clear out the obstacles in our lives: sin, pride, hypocrisy and greed. When those obstacles are gone, we are free to become the people God wants us to be.

40:10–17 Whenever we doubt God's power, we need to reread these verses. He is the Creator. He will rule with power. His wisdom is greater than that of any person. When we doubt that God can really help us, we need to remember that he is more powerful than anything on earth. Our God is also compassionate and loving. He will carry his sheep (that's us!) in his arms and "gently lead" us (40:11).

he weighs the islands as though they
were fine dust.
16Lebanon is not sufficient for altar fires,
nor its animals enough for burnt
offerings.
17Before him all the nations are as nothing;
they are regarded by him as worthless
and less than nothing.

18To whom, then, will you compare God?
What image will you compare him to?
19As for an idol, a craftsman casts it,
and a goldsmith overlays it with gold
and fashions silver chains for it.
20A man too poor to present such an offering
selects wood that will not rot.
He looks for a skilled craftsman
to set up an idol that will not topple.

21Do you not know?
Have you not heard?
Has it not been told you from the
beginning?
Have you not understood since the earth
was founded?
22He sits enthroned above the circle of the
earth,
and its people are like grasshoppers.
He stretches out the heavens like a canopy,
and spreads them out like a tent to live
in.
23He brings princes to naught
and reduces the rulers of this world to
nothing.
24No sooner are they planted,
no sooner are they sown,
no sooner do they take root in the
ground,
than he blows on them and they wither,
and a whirlwind sweeps them away like
chaff.

25"To whom will you compare me?
Or who is my equal?" says the Holy One.
26Lift your eyes and look to the heavens:
Who created all these?
He who brings out the starry host one by
one,
and calls them each by name.
Because of his great power and mighty
strength,
not one of them is missing.

27Why do you say, O Jacob,
and complain, O Israel,
"My way is hidden from the LORD;
my cause is disregarded by my God"?
28Do you not know?
Have you not heard?
The LORD is the everlasting God,
the Creator of the ends of the earth.
He will not grow tired or weary,
and his understanding no one can
fathom.
29He gives strength to the weary
and increases the power of the weak.
30Even youths grow tired and weary,
and young men stumble and fall;
31but those who hope in the LORD
will renew their strength.
They will soar on wings like eagles;
they will run and not grow weary,
they will walk and not be faint.

The Helper of Israel

41 "Be silent before me, you islands!
Let the nations renew their strength!
Let them come forward and speak;
let us meet together at the place of
judgment.

2"Who has stirred up one from the east,
calling him in righteousness to his
service[a]?
He hands nations over to him
and subdues kings before him.
He turns them to dust with his sword,
to windblown chaff with his bow.
3He pursues them and moves on unscathed,
by a path his feet have not traveled
before.
4Who has done this and carried it through,
calling forth the generations from the
beginning?
I, the LORD—with the first of them
and with the last—I am he."

5The islands have seen it and fear;
the ends of the earth tremble.
They approach and come forward;
6 each helps the other
and says to his brother, "Be strong!"
7The craftsman encourages the goldsmith,
and he who smooths with the hammer
spurs on him who strikes the anvil.
He says of the welding, "It is good."
He nails down the idol so it will not
topple.

8"But you, O Israel, my servant,
Jacob, whom I have chosen,
you descendants of Abraham my friend,
9I took you from the ends of the earth,
from its farthest corners I called you.
I said, 'You are my servant';
I have chosen you and have not rejected
you.
10So do not fear, for I am with you;
do not be dismayed, for I am your God.
I will strengthen you and help you;

[a]2 Or / *whom victory meets at every step*

40:27–31 God knows everything and understands all our pain. Our process of spiritual growth will take time, and we may suffer some setbacks. We may grow weary trying to live as God wants us to. We may want to give up and go back to old habits. Yet if we endure and keep faith in God he will renew our strength so that we can continue on in our spiritual growth.

I will uphold you with my righteous
right hand.

11"All who rage against you
will surely be ashamed and disgraced;
those who oppose you
will be as nothing and perish.
12Though you search for your enemies,
you will not find them.
Those who wage war against you
will be as nothing at all.
13For I am the LORD, your God,
who takes hold of your right hand
and says to you, Do not fear;
I will help you.
14Do not be afraid, O worm Jacob,
O little Israel,
for I myself will help you," declares the
LORD,
your Redeemer, the Holy One of Israel.
15"See, I will make you into a threshing
sledge,
new and sharp, with many teeth.
You will thresh the mountains and crush
them,
and reduce the hills to chaff.
16You will winnow them, the wind will pick
them up,
and a gale will blow them away.
But you will rejoice in the LORD
and glory in the Holy One of Israel.

17"The poor and needy search for water,
but there is none;
their tongues are parched with thirst.
But I the LORD will answer them;
I, the God of Israel, will not forsake
them.
18I will make rivers flow on barren heights,
and springs within the valleys.
I will turn the desert into pools of water,
and the parched ground into springs.
19I will put in the desert
the cedar and the acacia, the myrtle and
the olive.
I will set pines in the wasteland,
the fir and the cypress together,
20so that people may see and know,
may consider and understand,
that the hand of the LORD has done this,
that the Holy One of Israel has created
it.

21"Present your case," says the LORD.
"Set forth your arguments," says Jacob's
King.

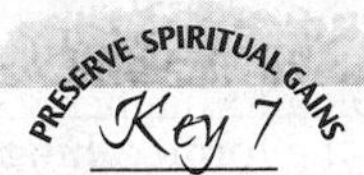

Waiting for the Lord to Renew Us

Isaiah 40:28–31 No matter how far we have progressed in our spiritual growth it is a continual challenge to wait patiently for the Lord. In order to preserve our spiritual gains, we must constantly practice the *first* key to renewal: seek God and surrender to him.

The prophet Isaiah gave us this promise: "Those who hope in the LORD will renew their strength. They will soar on wings like eagles; they will run and not grow weary, they will walk and not be faint" (40:31). Jeremiah said, "The LORD is good to those whose hope is in him, to the one who seeks him; it is good to wait quietly for the salvation of the LORD" (Lamentations 3:25–26).

The Lord will reward us for waiting upon him. We can remain calm when it appears that nothing is happening in our spiritual lives. As we learn to respond to life in new ways, the winds of difficulty will lift us up instead of knocking us down. We will rise up on the winds of adversity like the eagle rises on the updrafts. As we develop a patient faith in God, we will be able to endure to the end of the race—and win. As we seek God and wait on him to complete his work in our lives, we will be continually renewed.

This is the last devotion in the Old Testament reading plan. Now begin the New Testament reading plan by turning to Matthew 11.

41:11–14 God promised that he would crush Judah's enemies. They would be unable to destroy them on their own. God will take care of us too, helping us all the way. Though others may ridicule us now for the way we live, God will redeem us and make us whole again.
41:17–20 God wants us to come to him to receive wholeness in life, pictured here by the images of water and trees in a dry, barren land. Receiving God's fullness, however, requires that we admit we are sinful and needy, unable to control our lives without him.

22"Bring in ⌞your idols⌟ to tell us
what is going to happen.
Tell us what the former things were,
so that we may consider them
and know their final outcome.
Or declare to us the things to come,
23 tell us what the future holds,
so we may know that you are gods.
Do something, whether good or bad,
so that we will be dismayed and filled
with fear.
24But you are less than nothing
and your works are utterly worthless;
he who chooses you is detestable.

25"I have stirred up one from the north, and
he comes—
one from the rising sun who calls on my
name.
He treads on rulers as if they were mortar,
as if he were a potter treading the clay.
26Who told of this from the beginning, so we
could know,
or beforehand, so we could say, 'He was
right'?
No one told of this,
no one foretold it,
no one heard any words from you.
27I was the first to tell Zion, 'Look, here they
are!'
I gave to Jerusalem a messenger of good
tidings.
28I look but there is no one—
no one among them to give counsel,
no one to give answer when I ask them.
29See, they are all false!
Their deeds amount to nothing;
their images are but wind and confusion.

The Servant of the LORD

42 "Here is my servant, whom I uphold,
my chosen one in whom I delight;
I will put my Spirit on him
and he will bring justice to the nations.
2He will not shout or cry out,
or raise his voice in the streets.
3A bruised reed he will not break,
and a smoldering wick he will not snuff
out.
In faithfulness he will bring forth justice;
4 he will not falter or be discouraged
till he establishes justice on earth.
In his law the islands will put their
hope."

5This is what God the LORD says—
he who created the heavens and stretched
them out,
who spread out the earth and all that
comes out of it,
who gives breath to its people,
and life to those who walk on it:
6"I, the LORD, have called you in
righteousness;
I will take hold of your hand.
I will keep you and will make you
to be a covenant for the people
and a light for the Gentiles,
7to open eyes that are blind,
to free captives from prison
and to release from the dungeon those
who sit in darkness.

8"I am the LORD; that is my name!
I will not give my glory to another
or my praise to idols.
9See, the former things have taken place,
and new things I declare;
before they spring into being
I announce them to you."

Song of Praise to the LORD

10Sing to the LORD a new song,
his praise from the ends of the earth,
you who go down to the sea, and all that is
in it,
you islands, and all who live in them.
11Let the desert and its towns raise their
voices;
let the settlements where Kedar lives
rejoice.
Let the people of Sela sing for joy;
let them shout from the mountaintops.
12Let them give glory to the LORD
and proclaim his praise in the islands.
13The LORD will march out like a mighty
man,
like a warrior he will stir up his zeal;
with a shout he will raise the battle cry
and will triumph over his enemies.

14"For a long time I have kept silent,
I have been quiet and held myself back.
But now, like a woman in childbirth,
I cry out, I gasp and pant.
15I will lay waste the mountains and hills
and dry up all their vegetation;
I will turn rivers into islands
and dry up the pools.
16I will lead the blind by ways they have not
known,
along unfamiliar paths I will guide them;
I will turn the darkness into light before
them
and make the rough places smooth.
These are the things I will do;
I will not forsake them.

42:1–4 This servant song describes Jesus the Messiah and his ministry. No description could be more encouraging to us as we seek spiritual renewal. He is gentle. He will not shame us. He will encourage us and bring about justice for the oppressed. We may have endured abuse or wrongdoing that we did not deserve. But Jesus will deal with the people who have hurt us. We need to ask God to help us grieve, forgive and let go of any bitterness we may feel so that we can get on with our lives.

[17]But those who trust in idols,
who say to images, 'You are our gods,'
will be turned back in utter shame.

Israel Blind and Deaf

[18]"Hear, you deaf;
look, you blind, and see!
[19]Who is blind but my servant,
and deaf like the messenger I send?
Who is blind like the one committed to
me,
blind like the servant of the LORD?
[20]You have seen many things, but have paid
no attention;
your ears are open, but you hear
nothing."
[21]It pleased the LORD
for the sake of his righteousness
to make his law great and glorious.
[22]But this is a people plundered and looted,
all of them trapped in pits
or hidden away in prisons.
They have become plunder,
with no one to rescue them;
they have been made loot,
with no one to say, "Send them back."

[23]Which of you will listen to this
or pay close attention in time to come?
[24]Who handed Jacob over to become loot,
and Israel to the plunderers?
Was it not the LORD,
against whom we have sinned?
For they would not follow his ways;
they did not obey his law.
[25]So he poured out on them his burning
anger,
the violence of war.
It enveloped them in flames, yet they did
not understand;
it consumed them, but they did not take
it to heart.

Israel's Only Savior

43 But now, this is what the LORD says—
he who created you, O Jacob,
he who formed you, O Israel:
"Fear not, for I have redeemed you;
I have summoned you by name; you are
mine.
[2]When you pass through the waters,
I will be with you;
and when you pass through the rivers,
they will not sweep over you.
When you walk through the fire,
you will not be burned;
the flames will not set you ablaze.
[3]For I am the LORD, your God,
the Holy One of Israel, your Savior;
I give Egypt for your ransom,
Cush[a] and Seba in your stead.
[4]Since you are precious and honored in my
sight,
and because I love you,
I will give men in exchange for you,
and people in exchange for your life.
[5]Do not be afraid, for I am with you;
I will bring your children from the east
and gather you from the west.
[6]I will say to the north, 'Give them up!'
and to the south, 'Do not hold them
back.'
Bring my sons from afar
and my daughters from the ends of the
earth—
[7]everyone who is called by my name,
whom I created for my glory,
whom I formed and made."

[8]Lead out those who have eyes but are
blind,
who have ears but are deaf.
[9]All the nations gather together
and the peoples assemble.
Which of them foretold this
and proclaimed to us the former things?
Let them bring in their witnesses to prove
they were right,
so that others may hear and say, "It is
true."
[10]"You are my witnesses," declares the LORD,
"and my servant whom I have chosen,
so that you may know and believe me
and understand that I am he.
Before me no god was formed,
nor will there be one after me.
[11]I, even I, am the LORD,
and apart from me there is no savior.
[12]I have revealed and saved and proclaimed—
I, and not some foreign god among you.
You are my witnesses," declares the LORD,
"that I am God.
[13] Yes, and from ancient days I am he.
No one can deliver out of my hand.
When I act, who can reverse it?"

God's Mercy and Israel's Unfaithfulness

[14]This is what the LORD says—
your Redeemer, the Holy One of Israel:

[a]3 That is, the upper Nile region

42:20–23 God encourages us to do two things: Do what we know is right; learn lessons from our past experiences. Israel ridiculed God's righteous laws. Her attitudes enslaved her and led to her ruin. Haven't we been enslaved by our sins too? We can be set free only when we accept reality and confess our sins to God.
43:1–3 God loves us and will support us in times of trouble. As we "pass through the rivers" (43:2) of difficulty, we have a choice. We can trust in our own ability and drown, or trust in God and be delivered. If we are honest, we will realize that God is the only one who can redeem us.
43:9–13 When we experience doubt or feel like giving in to temptation, we need encouragement from those who have encountered God's power in similar situations. They can share how God helped them overcome sin and temptation as well as show us God's ability to transform a broken life.

"For your sake I will send to Babylon
and bring down as fugitives all the
Babylonians,[a]
in the ships in which they took pride.
15I am the LORD, your Holy One,
Israel's Creator, your King."

16This is what the LORD says—
he who made a way through the sea,
a path through the mighty waters,
17who drew out the chariots and horses,
the army and reinforcements together,
and they lay there, never to rise again,
extinguished, snuffed out like a wick:
18"Forget the former things;
do not dwell on the past.
19See, I am doing a new thing!
Now it springs up; do you not perceive
it?
I am making a way in the desert
and streams in the wasteland.
20The wild animals honor me,
the jackals and the owls,
because I provide water in the desert
and streams in the wasteland,
to give drink to my people, my chosen,
21 the people I formed for myself
that they may proclaim my praise.

22"Yet you have not called upon me,
O Jacob,
you have not wearied yourselves for me,
O Israel.
23You have not brought me sheep for burnt
offerings,
nor honored me with your sacrifices.
I have not burdened you with grain
offerings
nor wearied you with demands for
incense.
24You have not bought any fragrant calamus
for me,
or lavished on me the fat of your
sacrifices.
But you have burdened me with your sins
and wearied me with your offenses.

25"I, even I, am he who blots out
your transgressions, for my own sake,
and remembers your sins no more.
26Review the past for me,
let us argue the matter together;
state the case for your innocence.
27Your first father sinned;
your spokesmen rebelled against me.
28So I will disgrace the dignitaries of your
temple,
and I will consign Jacob to destruction[b]
and Israel to scorn.

Israel the Chosen

44 "But now listen, O Jacob, my servant,
Israel, whom I have chosen.
2This is what the LORD says—
he who made you, who formed you in
the womb,
and who will help you:
Do not be afraid, O Jacob, my servant,
Jeshurun, whom I have chosen.
3For I will pour water on the thirsty land,
and streams on the dry ground;
I will pour out my Spirit on your offspring,
and my blessing on your descendants.
4They will spring up like grass in a meadow,
like poplar trees by flowing streams.
5One will say, 'I belong to the LORD';
another will call himself by the name of
Jacob;
still another will write on his hand, 'The
LORD's,'
and will take the name Israel.

The LORD, Not Idols

6"This is what the LORD says—
Israel's King and Redeemer, the LORD
Almighty:
I am the first and I am the last;
apart from me there is no God.
7Who then is like me? Let him proclaim it.
Let him declare and lay out before me
what has happened since I established my
ancient people,
and what is yet to come—
yes, let him foretell what will come.
8Do not tremble, do not be afraid.
Did I not proclaim this and foretell it
long ago?
You are my witnesses. Is there any God
besides me?
No, there is no other Rock; I know not
one."

9All who make idols are nothing,
and the things they treasure are
worthless.
Those who would speak up for them are
blind;
they are ignorant, to their own shame.

[a]14 Or *Chaldeans* [b]28 The Hebrew term refers to the irrevocable giving over of things or persons to the LORD, often by totally destroying them.

43:25–28 We may be afraid to come to God because we think we've been too sinful. We may be afraid God won't forgive us. But God promises to blot out our sins when we come to him, forgetting them and cleansing us. Approaching God in humility is the only way to have the shame of our sin removed.

44:6–8 God is our Redeemer and the rock on which we should build our lives. He has promised to save us from our sins and the sure penalty of death. When we have such a promise from the all-powerful God, why should we look to any other source?

44:9–20 All man-made gods will fail us, whether they are money, success, perfectionism, alcohol, drugs or false religions with their trinkets, crystals and charms. If we believe that such things will deliver us, we are not seeing the truth. We need to examine our lives in light of God's commands and trust only him. Any other allegiance means disaster.

[10]Who shapes a god and casts an idol,
which can profit him nothing?
[11]He and his kind will be put to shame;
craftsmen are nothing but men.
Let them all come together and take their stand;
they will be brought down to terror and infamy.

[12]The blacksmith takes a tool
and works with it in the coals;
he shapes an idol with hammers,
he forges it with the might of his arm.
He gets hungry and loses his strength;
he drinks no water and grows faint.
[13]The carpenter measures with a line
and makes an outline with a marker;
he roughs it out with chisels
and marks it with compasses.
He shapes it in the form of man,
of man in all his glory,
that it may dwell in a shrine.
[14]He cut down cedars,
or perhaps took a cypress or oak.
He let it grow among the trees of the forest,
or planted a pine, and the rain made it grow.
[15]It is man's fuel for burning;
some of it he takes and warms himself,
he kindles a fire and bakes bread.
But he also fashions a god and worships it;
he makes an idol and bows down to it.
[16]Half of the wood he burns in the fire;
over it he prepares his meal,
he roasts his meat and eats his fill.
He also warms himself and says,
"Ah! I am warm; I see the fire."
[17]From the rest he makes a god, his idol;
he bows down to it and worships.
He prays to it and says,
"Save me; you are my god."
[18]They know nothing, they understand nothing;
their eyes are plastered over so they cannot see,
and their minds closed so they cannot understand.
[19]No one stops to think,
no one has the knowledge or understanding to say,
"Half of it I used for fuel;
I even baked bread over its coals,
I roasted meat and I ate.
Shall I make a detestable thing from what is left?
Shall I bow down to a block of wood?"
[20]He feeds on ashes, a deluded heart misleads him;
he cannot save himself, or say,
"Is not this thing in my right hand a lie?"

[21]"Remember these things, O Jacob,
for you are my servant, O Israel.
I have made you, you are my servant;
O Israel, I will not forget you.
[22]I have swept away your offenses like a cloud,
your sins like the morning mist.
Return to me,
for I have redeemed you."

[23]Sing for joy, O heavens, for the LORD has done this;
shout aloud, O earth beneath.
Burst into song, you mountains,
you forests and all your trees,
for the LORD has redeemed Jacob,
he displays his glory in Israel.

Jerusalem to Be Inhabited

[24]"This is what the LORD says—
your Redeemer, who formed you in the womb:

I am the LORD,
who has made all things,
who alone stretched out the heavens,
who spread out the earth by myself,

[25]who foils the signs of false prophets
and makes fools of diviners,
who overthrows the learning of the wise
and turns it into nonsense,
[26]who carries out the words of his servants
and fulfills the predictions of his messengers,

who says of Jerusalem, 'It shall be inhabited,'
of the towns of Judah, 'They shall be built,'
and of their ruins, 'I will restore them,'
[27]who says to the watery deep, 'Be dry,
and I will dry up your streams,'
[28]who says of Cyrus, 'He is my shepherd
and will accomplish all that I please;
he will say of Jerusalem, "Let it be rebuilt,"
and of the temple, "Let its foundations be laid." '

45 "This is what the LORD says to his anointed,

44:21–28 Through Isaiah, God foretold that Cyrus would free God's people from captivity. But Cyrus did not rise to power until 150 years *after* Isaiah's ministry! If God could name the king who would allow Israel to rebuild Jerusalem 150 years before he came to the throne, God can do anything. He can provide for us and care for our needs, leading us to a fulfilling life. We only need to surrender our lives to him and trust him to fulfill what he has promised.

45:1–6 God used a pagan king like Cyrus for his purposes even though Cyrus never realized God was doing it. There are great possibilities with God. If he can use a pagan king—someone who doesn't even know God—to fulfill his plans, imagine how much more God could do with those who trust him. We only need the faith to follow him.

to Cyrus, whose right hand I take hold
of
to subdue nations before him
and to strip kings of their armor,
to open doors before him
so that gates will not be shut:
2I will go before you
and will level the mountains[a];
I will break down gates of bronze
and cut through bars of iron.
3I will give you the treasures of darkness,
riches stored in secret places,
so that you may know that I am the LORD,
the God of Israel, who summons you by
name.
4For the sake of Jacob my servant,
of Israel my chosen,
I summon you by name
and bestow on you a title of honor,
though you do not acknowledge me.
5I am the LORD, and there is no other;
apart from me there is no God.
I will strengthen you,
though you have not acknowledged me,
6so that from the rising of the sun
to the place of its setting
men may know there is none besides me.
I am the LORD, and there is no other.
7I form the light and create darkness,
I bring prosperity and create disaster;
I, the LORD, do all these things.

8"You heavens above, rain down
righteousness;
let the clouds shower it down.
Let the earth open wide,
let salvation spring up,
let righteousness grow with it;
I, the LORD, have created it.

9"Woe to him who quarrels with his Maker,
to him who is but a potsherd among the
potsherds on the ground.
Does the clay say to the potter,
'What are you making?'
Does your work say,
'He has no hands'?
10Woe to him who says to his father,
'What have you begotten?'
or to his mother,
'What have you brought to birth?'

11"This is what the LORD says—
the Holy One of Israel, and its Maker:
Concerning things to come,
do you question me about my children,
or give me orders about the work of my
hands?
12It is I who made the earth
and created mankind upon it.
My own hands stretched out the heavens;
I marshaled their starry hosts.
13I will raise up Cyrus[b] in my righteousness:
I will make all his ways straight.
He will rebuild my city
and set my exiles free,
but not for a price or reward,
says the LORD Almighty."

14This is what the LORD says:

"The products of Egypt and the
merchandise of Cush,[c]
and those tall Sabeans—
they will come over to you
and will be yours;
they will trudge behind you,
coming over to you in chains.
They will bow down before you
and plead with you, saying,
'Surely God is with you, and there is no
other;
there is no other god.' "

15Truly you are a God who hides himself,
O God and Savior of Israel.
16All the makers of idols will be put to
shame and disgraced;
they will go off into disgrace together.
17But Israel will be saved by the LORD
with an everlasting salvation;
you will never be put to shame or
disgraced,
to ages everlasting.

18For this is what the LORD says—
he who created the heavens,
he is God;
he who fashioned and made the earth,
he founded it;
he did not create it to be empty,
but formed it to be inhabited—
he says:
"I am the LORD,
and there is no other.
19I have not spoken in secret,
from somewhere in a land of darkness;
I have not said to Jacob's descendants,
'Seek me in vain.'
I, the LORD, speak the truth;
I declare what is right.

20"Gather together and come;
assemble, you fugitives from the nations.

[a]2 Dead Sea Scrolls and Septuagint; the meaning of the word in the Masoretic Text is uncertain. [b]13 Hebrew *him* [c]14 That is, the upper Nile region

45:9–13 The psalmist proved that it is acceptable to pour out our complaints and questions to God as we wrestle with the problems of life. What Isaiah rebuked in this passage is the stubborn, chronic unbelief of God's people. They charged God with mishandling his control of history by allowing Cyrus to come to power. They believed that God was assisting their enemy. But their limited view of life did not let them see God's true purpose. Likewise, we may not understand why God allows certain things to happen. But we can trust that God is working according to his perfect plan.

Ignorant are those who carry about idols of wood,
who pray to gods that cannot save.
21Declare what is to be, present it—
let them take counsel together.
Who foretold this long ago,
who declared it from the distant past?
Was it not I, the LORD?
And there is no God apart from me,
a righteous God and a Savior;
there is none but me.

22"Turn to me and be saved,
all you ends of the earth;
for I am God, and there is no other.
23By myself I have sworn,
my mouth has uttered in all integrity
a word that will not be revoked:
Before me every knee will bow;
by me every tongue will swear.
24They will say of me, 'In the LORD alone
are righteousness and strength.' "
All who have raged against him
will come to him and be put to shame.
25But in the LORD all the descendants of Israel
will be found righteous and will exult.

Gods of Babylon

46 Bel bows down, Nebo stoops low;
their idols are borne by beasts of burden.[a]
The images that are carried about are burdensome,
a burden for the weary.
2They stoop and bow down together;
unable to rescue the burden,
they themselves go off into captivity.

3"Listen to me, O house of Jacob,
all you who remain of the house of Israel,
you whom I have upheld since you were conceived,
and have carried since your birth.
4Even to your old age and gray hairs
I am he, I am he who will sustain you.
I have made you and I will carry you;
I will sustain you and I will rescue you.

5"To whom will you compare me or count me equal?
To whom will you liken me that we may be compared?
6Some pour out gold from their bags
and weigh out silver on the scales;
they hire a goldsmith to make it into a god,
and they bow down and worship it.
7They lift it to their shoulders and carry it;
they set it up in its place, and there it stands.
From that spot it cannot move.
Though one cries out to it, it does not answer;
it cannot save him from his troubles.

8"Remember this, fix it in mind,
take it to heart, you rebels.
9Remember the former things, those of long ago;
I am God, and there is no other;
I am God, and there is none like me.
10I make known the end from the beginning,
from ancient times, what is still to come.
I say: My purpose will stand,
and I will do all that I please.
11From the east I summon a bird of prey;
from a far-off land, a man to fulfill my purpose.
What I have said, that will I bring about;
what I have planned, that will I do.
12Listen to me, you stubborn-hearted,
you who are far from righteousness.
13I am bringing my righteousness near,
it is not far away;
and my salvation will not be delayed.
I will grant salvation to Zion,
my splendor to Israel.

The Fall of Babylon

47 "Go down, sit in the dust,
Virgin Daughter of Babylon;
sit on the ground without a throne,
Daughter of the Babylonians.[b]
No more will you be called
tender or delicate.
2Take millstones and grind flour;
take off your veil.
Lift up your skirts, bare your legs,
and wade through the streams.
3Your nakedness will be exposed
and your shame uncovered.
I will take vengeance;
I will spare no one."

4Our Redeemer—the LORD Almighty is his name—
is the Holy One of Israel.

5"Sit in silence, go into darkness,

[a] 1 Or *are but beasts and cattle* [b] 1 Or *Chaldeans*; also in verse 5

46:1–13 God calls us to reality and truth. People turn to many things to fill their inner needs. But anything other than God will fail. God is the everlasting, sovereign Lord of history who can, and will, do what he says. Putting our hope in God's hands is the only way to find true fulfillment.

47:1–15 Babylon can be compared to those who ruthlessly oppress or mistreat us. Though they may believe they have gotten away with their evil deeds, God has kept track of their sins. He will punish them. We don't need to plot our revenge; God will bring about justice. We need to release our desire for vengeance to God, focus on our other concerns and deal with the damage that has been done. Then he can redirect our course and redeem our lives.

Daughter of the Babylonians;
no more will you be called
queen of kingdoms.
6I was angry with my people
and desecrated my inheritance;
I gave them into your hand,
and you showed them no mercy.
Even on the aged
you laid a very heavy yoke.
7You said, 'I will continue forever—
the eternal queen!'
But you did not consider these things
or reflect on what might happen.

8"Now then, listen, you wanton creature,
lounging in your security
and saying to yourself,
'I am, and there is none besides me.
I will never be a widow
or suffer the loss of children.'
9Both of these will overtake you
in a moment, on a single day:
loss of children and widowhood.
They will come upon you in full measure,
in spite of your many sorceries
and all your potent spells.
10You have trusted in your wickedness
and have said, 'No one sees me.'
Your wisdom and knowledge mislead you
when you say to yourself,
'I am, and there is none besides me.'
11Disaster will come upon you,
and you will not know how to conjure it
away.
A calamity will fall upon you
that you cannot ward off with a ransom;
a catastrophe you cannot foresee
will suddenly come upon you.

12"Keep on, then, with your magic spells
and with your many sorceries,
which you have labored at since
childhood.
Perhaps you will succeed,
perhaps you will cause terror.
13All the counsel you have received has only
worn you out!
Let your astrologers come forward,
those stargazers who make predictions
month by month,
let them save you from what is coming
upon you.
14Surely they are like stubble;
the fire will burn them up.
They cannot even save themselves
from the power of the flame.
Here are no coals to warm anyone;
here is no fire to sit by.
15That is all they can do for you—
these you have labored with
and trafficked with since childhood.
Each of them goes on in his error;
there is not one that can save you.

Stubborn Israel

48 "Listen to this, O house of Jacob,
you who are called by the name of
Israel
and come from the line of Judah,
you who take oaths in the name of the
LORD
and invoke the God of Israel—
but not in truth or righteousness—
2you who call yourselves citizens of the holy
city
and rely on the God of Israel—
the LORD Almighty is his name:
3I foretold the former things long ago,
my mouth announced them and I made
them known;
then suddenly I acted, and they came to
pass.
4For I knew how stubborn you were;
the sinews of your neck were iron,
your forehead was bronze.
5Therefore I told you these things long ago;
before they happened I announced them
to you
so that you could not say,
'My idols did them;
my wooden image and metal god
ordained them.'
6You have heard these things; look at them
all.
Will you not admit them?

"From now on I will tell you of new
things,
of hidden things unknown to you.
7They are created now, and not long ago;
you have not heard of them before
today.
So you cannot say,
'Yes, I knew of them.'
8You have neither heard nor understood;
from of old your ear has not been open.
Well do I know how treacherous you are;
you were called a rebel from birth.
9For my own name's sake I delay my wrath;
for the sake of my praise I hold it back
from you,
so as not to cut you off.
10See, I have refined you, though not as
silver;
I have tested you in the furnace of
affliction.
11For my own sake, for my own sake, I do
this.
How can I let myself be defamed?
I will not yield my glory to another.

48:1–11 Once we have committed our lives to God, we belong to him. He then promises to bring us spiritual blessings. Our stubborn rebellion and spiritual incompetence will not keep God's grace away. Even when we fail, he will still love us and willingly forgive us when we repent.

Israel Freed

12 "Listen to me, O Jacob,
Israel, whom I have called:
I am he;
I am the first and I am the last.
13 My own hand laid the foundations of the earth,
and my right hand spread out the heavens;
when I summon them,
they all stand up together.

14 "Come together, all of you, and listen:
Which of ⌊the idols⌋ has foretold these things?
The LORD's chosen ally
will carry out his purpose against Babylon;
his arm will be against the Babylonians.[a]
15 I, even I, have spoken;
yes, I have called him.
I will bring him,
and he will succeed in his mission.

16 "Come near me and listen to this:

"From the first announcement I have not spoken in secret;
at the time it happens, I am there."

And now the Sovereign LORD has sent me,
with his Spirit.

17 This is what the LORD says—
your Redeemer, the Holy One of Israel:
"I am the LORD your God,
who teaches you what is best for you,
who directs you in the way you should go.
18 If only you had paid attention to my commands,
your peace would have been like a river,
your righteousness like the waves of the sea.
19 Your descendants would have been like the sand,
your children like its numberless grains;
their name would never be cut off
nor destroyed from before me."

20 Leave Babylon,
flee from the Babylonians!
Announce this with shouts of joy
and proclaim it.
Send it out to the ends of the earth;
say, "The LORD has redeemed his servant Jacob."
21 They did not thirst when he led them through the deserts;
he made water flow for them from the rock;
he split the rock
and water gushed out.

22 "There is no peace," says the LORD, "for the wicked."

The Servant of the LORD

49 Listen to me, you islands;
hear this, you distant nations:
Before I was born the LORD called me;
from my birth he has made mention of my name.
2 He made my mouth like a sharpened sword,
in the shadow of his hand he hid me;
he made me into a polished arrow
and concealed me in his quiver.
3 He said to me, "You are my servant,
Israel, in whom I will display my splendor."
4 But I said, "I have labored to no purpose;
I have spent my strength in vain and for nothing.
Yet what is due me is in the LORD's hand,
and my reward is with my God."

5 And now the LORD says—
he who formed me in the womb to be his servant
to bring Jacob back to him
and gather Israel to himself,
for I am honored in the eyes of the LORD
and my God has been my strength—
6 he says:
"It is too small a thing for you to be my servant
to restore the tribes of Jacob
and bring back those of Israel I have kept.
I will also make you a light for the Gentiles,
that you may bring my salvation to the ends of the earth."

7 This is what the LORD says—

[a] 14 Or *Chaldeans;* also in verse 20

48:12–15 Amid the uncertainties of life, we can derive comfort from knowing who God is. He is the God of the past, who knows all of the troubles that have brought the pain we experience today. He is the God of the future, who knows what lies ahead and can be trusted to guide us in the right path. He is the God of today, who has power over all of his creation and sovereignty over all that happens. We can surely trust a God this powerful to complete his work of transformation in our lives.

48:16–22 The people of Judah would forfeit peace of mind because of their resistance to God. But despite their unworthiness, God would eventually deliver the people of Judah from Babylon. We, too, can have a relationship with God and be assured of eternal peace, but we will sacrifice God's peace if we continue in sin. To achieve a peaceful and stable life we must give up our sinful way of life and the turmoil it brings.

49:1–7 Sometimes it seems as though our resolve to grow spiritually results in continual hardship. We may lose some old friends or strain some relationships in our pursuit of God. There may even be times when we struggle with our own temptations and our spiritual growth seems to have come to a halt. But if we persevere in our faith, we honor God; in due time he will reward us.

the Redeemer and Holy One of Israel—
to him who was despised and abhorred by the nation,
to the servant of rulers:
"Kings will see you and rise up,
princes will see and bow down,
because of the LORD, who is faithful,
the Holy One of Israel, who has chosen you."

Restoration of Israel

8This is what the LORD says:

"In the time of my favor I will answer you,
and in the day of salvation I will help you;
I will keep you and will make you
to be a covenant for the people,
to restore the land
and to reassign its desolate inheritances,
9to say to the captives, 'Come out,'
and to those in darkness, 'Be free!'

"They will feed beside the roads
and find pasture on every barren hill.
10They will neither hunger nor thirst,
nor will the desert heat or the sun beat upon them.
He who has compassion on them will guide them
and lead them beside springs of water.
11I will turn all my mountains into roads,
and my highways will be raised up.
12See, they will come from afar—
some from the north, some from the west,
some from the region of Aswan.[a]"

13Shout for joy, O heavens;
rejoice, O earth;
burst into song, O mountains!
For the LORD comforts his people
and will have compassion on his afflicted ones.

14But Zion said, "The LORD has forsaken me,
the Lord has forgotten me."

15"Can a mother forget the baby at her breast
and have no compassion on the child she has borne?
Though she may forget,
I will not forget you!
16See, I have engraved you on the palms of my hands;
your walls are ever before me.
17Your sons hasten back,
and those who laid you waste depart from you.
18Lift up your eyes and look around;
all your sons gather and come to you.
As surely as I live," declares the LORD,
"you will wear them all as ornaments;
you will put them on, like a bride.

19"Though you were ruined and made desolate
and your land laid waste,
now you will be too small for your people,
and those who devoured you will be far away.
20The children born during your bereavement
will yet say in your hearing,
'This place is too small for us;
give us more space to live in.'
21Then you will say in your heart,
'Who bore me these?
I was bereaved and barren;
I was exiled and rejected.
Who brought these up?
I was left all alone,
but these—where have they come from?' "

22This is what the Sovereign LORD says:

"See, I will beckon to the Gentiles,
I will lift up my banner to the peoples;
they will bring your sons in their arms
and carry your daughters on their shoulders.
23Kings will be your foster fathers,
and their queens your nursing mothers.
They will bow down before you with their faces to the ground;
they will lick the dust at your feet.
Then you will know that I am the LORD;
those who hope in me will not be disappointed."

24Can plunder be taken from warriors,
or captives rescued from the fierce[b]?

25But this is what the LORD says:

"Yes, captives will be taken from warriors,
and plunder retrieved from the fierce;
I will contend with those who contend with you,
and your children I will save.
26I will make your oppressors eat their own flesh;

[a]12 Dead Sea Scrolls; Masoretic Text *Sinim* [b]24 Dead Sea Scrolls, Vulgate and Syriac (see also Septuagint and verse 25); Masoretic Text *righteous*

49:8–12 We see in this passage what God offers to the downtrodden through his Messiah. To those who are in spiritual and emotional bondage and depression, the Messiah offers freedom. To those who feel inner emptiness and aimlessness, he offers guidance, care and fulfillment. To those who feel battered by life, he offers comfort. To those who are ensnared by sin, he offers liberation and salvation.

49:13–26 The people of Judah felt abandoned by God because they were suffering. We can be assured that even though we might *feel* abandoned by God because of our troubles, God will never abandon us. In spite of appearances, God is working out his plan for us and will bring deliverance.

they will be drunk on their own blood,
as with wine.
Then all mankind will know
that I, the LORD, am your Savior,
your Redeemer, the Mighty One of
Jacob."

Israel's Sin and the Servant's Obedience

50 This is what the LORD says:

"Where is your mother's certificate of
divorce
with which I sent her away?
Or to which of my creditors
did I sell you?
Because of your sins you were sold;
because of your transgressions your
mother was sent away.
2When I came, why was there no one?
When I called, why was there no one to
answer?
Was my arm too short to ransom you?
Do I lack the strength to rescue you?
By a mere rebuke I dry up the sea,
I turn rivers into a desert;
their fish rot for lack of water
and die of thirst.
3I clothe the sky with darkness
and make sackcloth its covering."

4The Sovereign LORD has given me an
instructed tongue,
to know the word that sustains the
weary.
He wakens me morning by morning,
wakens my ear to listen like one being
taught.
5The Sovereign LORD has opened my ears,
and I have not been rebellious;
I have not drawn back.
6I offered my back to those who beat me,
my cheeks to those who pulled out my
beard;
I did not hide my face
from mocking and spitting.
7Because the Sovereign LORD helps me,
I will not be disgraced.
Therefore have I set my face like flint,
and I know I will not be put to shame.
8He who vindicates me is near.
Who then will bring charges against me?
Let us face each other!
Who is my accuser?
Let him confront me!
9It is the Sovereign LORD who helps me.
Who is he that will condemn me?
They will all wear out like a garment;
the moths will eat them up.

10Who among you fears the LORD
and obeys the word of his servant?
Let him who walks in the dark,
who has no light,
trust in the name of the LORD
and rely on his God.
11But now, all you who light fires
and provide yourselves with flaming
torches,
go, walk in the light of your fires
and of the torches you have set ablaze.
This is what you shall receive from my
hand:
You will lie down in torment.

Everlasting Salvation for Zion

51 "Listen to me, you who pursue
righteousness
and who seek the LORD:
Look to the rock from which you were cut
and to the quarry from which you were
hewn;
2look to Abraham, your father,
and to Sarah, who gave you birth.
When I called him he was but one,
and I blessed him and made him many.
3The LORD will surely comfort Zion
and will look with compassion on all
her ruins;
he will make her deserts like Eden,
her wastelands like the garden of the
LORD.
Joy and gladness will be found in her,
thanksgiving and the sound of singing.

4"Listen to me, my people;
hear me, my nation:

50:1–2 When trouble fills our lives, we may be tempted to think that God has turned on us or is unable to help. But Isaiah made it clear that Judah's problems had been brought about by the people's sins, not by God's injustice. Our own sins, or the sins of others, bring on most of our problems too. Our trials and suffering are not allowed by God to abuse us. Sometimes we suffer because we live in a world corrupted by sin. Yet the God who controls all nature can certainly care for us if we turn to him in the midst of our trouble.

50:4–6 The Messiah speaks in this passage about following God's call despite the hardships involved. He serves as a model to us when we need courage to follow God's will when it is difficult to do so. We may receive rebuke, suffer shame, or be misunderstood by those who reject God's ways. We may face opposition if our spiritual growth causes some people to lose their influence over us. They may feel threatened by our change in lifestyle. We must stand up to them and follow through with God's plan.

50:7–9 We are encouraged to persevere because God is close to us, defending us from our enemies. Whenever we surrender to God, others who have not surrendered to him may feel uncomfortable. They may resist us or tempt us to fall back into old patterns of behavior. If we stand firm in our resolve to follow God, he will see to it that we triumph.

51:1–6 When the people of Judah looked to their own strength, they could see no hope for deliverance. But when they looked to God, they remembered that he was able to bring a whole nation out of one man, Abraham. Therefore, God could certainly bring joy, comfort, and deliverance to them. When we try to solve our difficulties through our own strength, our hope vanishes. When we look to God, that hope can return. Trusting anyone or anything other than God is a plan destined for failure. True success will come from relying on God alone.

The law will go out from me;
my justice will become a light to the nations.
5My righteousness draws near speedily,
my salvation is on the way,
and my arm will bring justice to the nations.
The islands will look to me
and wait in hope for my arm.
6Lift up your eyes to the heavens,
look at the earth beneath;
the heavens will vanish like smoke,
the earth will wear out like a garment
and its inhabitants die like flies.
But my salvation will last forever,
my righteousness will never fail.

7"Hear me, you who know what is right,
you people who have my law in your hearts:
Do not fear the reproach of men
or be terrified by their insults.
8For the moth will eat them up like a garment;
the worm will devour them like wool.
But my righteousness will last forever,
my salvation through all generations."

9Awake, awake! Clothe yourself with strength,
O arm of the LORD;
awake, as in days gone by,
as in generations of old.
Was it not you who cut Rahab to pieces,
who pierced that monster through?
10Was it not you who dried up the sea,
the waters of the great deep,
who made a road in the depths of the sea
so that the redeemed might cross over?
11The ransomed of the LORD will return.
They will enter Zion with singing;
everlasting joy will crown their heads.
Gladness and joy will overtake them,
and sorrow and sighing will flee away.

12"I, even I, am he who comforts you.
Who are you that you fear mortal men,
the sons of men, who are but grass,
13that you forget the LORD your Maker,
who stretched out the heavens
and laid the foundations of the earth,
that you live in constant terror every day
because of the wrath of the oppressor,
who is bent on destruction?
For where is the wrath of the oppressor?
14 The cowering prisoners will soon be set free;
they will not die in their dungeon,
nor will they lack bread.
15For I am the LORD your God,
who churns up the sea so that its waves roar—
the LORD Almighty is his name.
16I have put my words in your mouth
and covered you with the shadow of my hand—
I who set the heavens in place,
who laid the foundations of the earth,
and who say to Zion, 'You are my people.' "

The Cup of the LORD's Wrath

17Awake, awake!
Rise up, O Jerusalem,
you who have drunk from the hand of the LORD
the cup of his wrath,
you who have drained to its dregs
the goblet that makes men stagger.
18Of all the sons she bore
there was none to guide her;
of all the sons she reared
there was none to take her by the hand.
19These double calamities have come upon you—
who can comfort you?—
ruin and destruction, famine and sword—
who can[a] console you?
20Your sons have fainted;
they lie at the head of every street,
like antelope caught in a net.
They are filled with the wrath of the LORD
and the rebuke of your God.

21Therefore hear this, you afflicted one,
made drunk, but not with wine.
22This is what your Sovereign LORD says,
your God, who defends his people:
"See, I have taken out of your hand
the cup that made you stagger;
from that cup, the goblet of my wrath,
you will never drink again.
23I will put it into the hands of your tormentors,
who said to you,
'Fall prostrate that we may walk over you.'
And you made your back like the ground,
like a street to be walked over."

[a]19 Dead Sea Scrolls, Septuagint, Vulgate and Syriac; Masoretic Text / *how can I*

51:7–8 When we devote ourselves to obedience to God we may experience scorn and slander from those who do not share our devotion. Though their rejection will hurt us, we need to see the bigger picture. People, and eventually the entire earth, will pass away. But God's justice, mercy and salvation will last. We should concentrate on pleasing God, not people. God is permanent—people and their criticism are not.

51:12–23 God actually controls our lives, yet we don't fear him as we should. Instead, we fear people—people who don't have any authority over us. We are tempted to retreat from God's ways and lapse back into sinful ways just to please others. We should strive to please God because he has the power to bless us for seeking his will and to discipline us for disobeying.

52 Awake, awake, O Zion,
clothe yourself with strength.
Put on your garments of splendor,
O Jerusalem, the holy city.
The uncircumcised and defiled
will not enter you again.
2Shake off your dust;
rise up, sit enthroned, O Jerusalem.
Free yourself from the chains on your neck,
O captive Daughter of Zion.

3For this is what the LORD says:

"You were sold for nothing,
and without money you will be
redeemed."

4For this is what the Sovereign LORD says:

"At first my people went down to Egypt to
live;
lately, Assyria has oppressed them.

5"And now what do I have here?" declares the
LORD.

"For my people have been taken away for
nothing,
and those who rule them mock,[a]"
declares the LORD.
"And all day long
my name is constantly blasphemed.
6Therefore my people will know my name;
therefore in that day they will know
that it is I who foretold it.
Yes, it is I."

7How beautiful on the mountains
are the feet of those who bring good
news,
who proclaim peace,
who bring good tidings,
who proclaim salvation,
who say to Zion,
"Your God reigns!"
8Listen! Your watchmen lift up their voices;
together they shout for joy.
When the LORD returns to Zion,
they will see it with their own eyes.
9Burst into songs of joy together,
you ruins of Jerusalem,
for the LORD has comforted his people,
he has redeemed Jerusalem.
10The LORD will lay bare his holy arm
in the sight of all the nations,
and all the ends of the earth will see
the salvation of our God.

11Depart, depart, go out from there!
Touch no unclean thing!
Come out from it and be pure,
you who carry the vessels of the LORD.
12But you will not leave in haste
or go in flight;
for the LORD will go before you,
the God of Israel will be your rear guard.

The Suffering and Glory of the Servant

13See, my servant will act wisely[b];
he will be raised and lifted up and
highly exalted.
14Just as there were many who were appalled
at him[c]—
his appearance was so disfigured beyond
that of any man
and his form marred beyond human
likeness—
15so will he sprinkle many nations,[d]
and kings will shut their mouths because
of him.
For what they were not told, they will see,
and what they have not heard, they will
understand.

53 Who has believed our message
and to whom has the arm of the
LORD been revealed?
2He grew up before him like a tender shoot,
and like a root out of dry ground.
He had no beauty or majesty to attract us
to him,
nothing in his appearance that we
should desire him.
3He was despised and rejected by men,
a man of sorrows, and familiar with
suffering.
Like one from whom men hide their faces
he was despised, and we esteemed him
not.

4Surely he took up our infirmities

[a]5 Dead Sea Scrolls and Vulgate; Masoretic Text *wail*
[b]13 Or *will prosper* [c]14 Hebrew *you* [d]15 Hebrew; Septuagint *so will many nations marvel at him*

52:1–6 We know what it feels like to be a slave to the appetites of our sinful natures. When we seek God and surrender to him, God promises to free us from our enslavement; he wants to remove our chains and set us free from our bondage.

52:7–10 God's message of deliverance is so wonderful that it deserves to be shared near and far. "Beautiful" are the feet of those who make the effort to share such news with others (52:7). Just as the message of Judah's deliverance from captivity deserved to be shared abroad, our message of salvation and spiritual renewal through Christ deserves to be shared with others too.

52:12 As we progress along the path to spiritual growth, it is comforting to know that God is with us, bringing us out of our slavery to sin. He goes ahead of us, showing us the way to a productive, normal life. And he watches over us from behind, guarding us from attack by the enemy of our souls.

52:13—53:12 This marvelous passage describes in detail the atoning death of Jesus the Messiah, God's suffering servant. His death for us is the basis of our redemption. Because he died for our sins, we do not have to pay the penalty for our sins, which is eternal death (see Romans 6:23), but we do have to endure the consequences of whatever we have done, and we do have to make restitution.

53:4–6 Isaiah described the Messiah who would come and suffer on our behalf. Jesus Christ fulfilled Isaiah's prophecy. He came, not because *some* of us needed to be saved from sin, but because *all* of us have strayed from

and carried our sorrows,
yet we considered him stricken by God,
smitten by him, and afflicted.
5But he was pierced for our transgressions,
he was crushed for our iniquities;
the punishment that brought us peace was upon him,
and by his wounds we are healed.
6We all, like sheep, have gone astray,
each of us has turned to his own way;
and the LORD has laid on him
the iniquity of us all.

7He was oppressed and afflicted,
yet he did not open his mouth;
he was led like a lamb to the slaughter,
and as a sheep before her shearers is silent,
so he did not open his mouth.
8By oppression[a] and judgment he was taken away.
And who can speak of his descendants?
For he was cut off from the land of the living;
for the transgression of my people he was stricken.[b]
9He was assigned a grave with the wicked,
and with the rich in his death,
though he had done no violence,
nor was any deceit in his mouth.

10Yet it was the LORD's will to crush him and cause him to suffer,
and though the LORD makes[c] his life a guilt offering,
he will see his offspring and prolong his days,
and the will of the LORD will prosper in his hand.
11After the suffering of his soul,
he will see the light ⌞of life⌟[d] and be satisfied[e];
by his knowledge[f] my righteous servant will justify many,
and he will bear their iniquities.
12Therefore I will give him a portion among the great,[g]
and he will divide the spoils with the strong,[h]
because he poured out his life unto death,
and was numbered with the transgressors.
For he bore the sin of many,
and made intercession for the transgressors.

The Future Glory of Zion

54 "Sing, O barren woman,
you who never bore a child;
burst into song, shout for joy,
you who were never in labor;
because more are the children of the desolate woman
than of her who has a husband,"
says the LORD.
2"Enlarge the place of your tent,
stretch your tent curtains wide,
do not hold back;
lengthen your cords,
strengthen your stakes.
3For you will spread out to the right and to the left;
your descendants will dispossess nations
and settle in their desolate cities.

4"Do not be afraid; you will not suffer shame.
Do not fear disgrace; you will not be humiliated.
You will forget the shame of your youth
and remember no more the reproach of your widowhood.
5For your Maker is your husband—
the LORD Almighty is his name—
the Holy One of Israel is your Redeemer;
he is called the God of all the earth.
6The LORD will call you back
as if you were a wife deserted and distressed in spirit—
a wife who married young,
only to be rejected," says your God.
7"For a brief moment I abandoned you,
but with deep compassion I will bring you back.
8In a surge of anger
I hid my face from you for a moment,
but with everlasting kindness
I will have compassion on you,"
says the LORD your Redeemer.

[a]8 Or *From arrest* [b]8 Or *away. / Yet who of his generation considered / that he was cut off from the land of the living / for the transgression of my people, / to whom the blow was due?* [c]10 Hebrew *though you make* [d]11 Dead Sea Scrolls (see also Septuagint); Masoretic Text does not have *the light ⌞of life⌟.* [e]11 Or (with Masoretic Text) *11He will see the result of the suffering of his soul / and be satisfied* [f]11 Or *by knowledge of him* [g]12 Or *many* [h]12 Or *numerous*

God's path and need salvation (see Romans 3:23). Jesus suffered the punishment for our sins. He can completely understand what the pain we suffer feels like. We can confess our anguish and feelings of hatred, shame and sorrow to Jesus. He will sympathize with us and send us comfort.

53:7–12 It was not easy for Jesus the Messiah to bear such undeserved abuse and shame. The outcome, however, was a blessing that would change the world. When we suffer for doing what is right, we can be assured that God will use it to be a blessing. He will also vindicate us in due time.

54:1–8 Israel strayed from God, and God punished them. He wanted them to see the error of their ways and return to him. But God promised he would restore them to himself and bless them. We also will suffer punishment for our sins. Our suffering should warn us of the dangers of making sinful choices. We need God's help to redirect our course. When we make a decision to seek God, we must surrender to him, follow his ways and turn from our old lifestyle. Then God can work in us and give us his blessings.

9"To me this is like the days of Noah,
when I swore that the waters of Noah
would never again cover the earth.
So now I have sworn not to be angry with
you,
never to rebuke you again.
10Though the mountains be shaken
and the hills be removed,
yet my unfailing love for you will not be
shaken
nor my covenant of peace be removed,"
says the LORD, who has compassion on
you.

11"O afflicted city, lashed by storms and not
comforted,
I will build you with stones of
turquoise,[a]
your foundations with sapphires.[b]
12I will make your battlements of rubies,
your gates of sparkling jewels,
and all your walls of precious stones.
13All your sons will be taught by the LORD,
and great will be your children's peace.
14In righteousness you will be established:
Tyranny will be far from you;
you will have nothing to fear.
Terror will be far removed;
it will not come near you.
15If anyone does attack you, it will not be my
doing;
whoever attacks you will surrender to
you.

16"See, it is I who created the blacksmith
who fans the coals into flame
and forges a weapon fit for its work.
And it is I who have created the destroyer
to work havoc;
17 no weapon forged against you will
prevail,
and you will refute every tongue that
accuses you.
This is the heritage of the servants of the
LORD,
and this is their vindication from me,"
declares the LORD.

Invitation to the Thirsty

55 "Come, all you who are thirsty,
come to the waters;
and you who have no money,
come, buy and eat!
Come, buy wine and milk
without money and without cost.
2Why spend money on what is not bread,
and your labor on what does not satisfy?
Listen, listen to me, and eat what is good,
and your soul will delight in the richest
of fare.
3Give ear and come to me;
hear me, that your soul may live.
I will make an everlasting covenant with
you,
my faithful love promised to David.
4See, I have made him a witness to the
peoples,
a leader and commander of the peoples.
5Surely you will summon nations you know
not,
and nations that do not know you will
hasten to you,
because of the LORD your God,
the Holy One of Israel,
for he has endowed you with splendor."

6Seek the LORD while he may be found;
call on him while he is near.
7Let the wicked forsake his way
and the evil man his thoughts.
Let him turn to the LORD, and he will have
mercy on him,
and to our God, for he will freely
pardon.

8"For my thoughts are not your thoughts,
neither are your ways my ways,"
declares the LORD.
9"As the heavens are higher than the earth,
so are my ways higher than your ways
and my thoughts than your thoughts.
10As the rain and the snow
come down from heaven,

[a]11 The meaning of the Hebrew for this word is uncertain. [b]11 Or *lapis lazuli*

54:10 This verse is a promise we can count on during those times when everything seems to be falling apart. Though mountains and hills may appear permanent, they will not last as long as God's mercy for his people. God's promise of kindness and peace in the midst of our troubles stands forever.

54:11–17 This passage gives us a vision of what lies ahead for those who look to God for forgiveness and deliverance. In God's messianic kingdom there will be blessing, fairness and justice. As we struggle with sins that may entangle us, the oppression of cruel people and the injustice that pervades our society, we can take comfort that no matter how rough life gets we will have security and peace with God throughout eternity.

55:1–5 God alone can satisfy our soul's hunger and thirst. He urges us to stop seeking fulfillment in things that cannot satisfy—work, sex, false religions, material possessions or other obsessions. We spend our time chasing after "what does not satisfy" (55:2) when we should be seeking God and his will, the only real nourishment for our souls.

55:6 We need to seek God while we have the opportunity. God is available to us. He wants to be found by us. If we will only repent and call out to God, he will answer us. True spiritual renewal begins when we seek God wholeheartedly. If we don't seek God, we will miss out on his presence in our lives and the blessings that are ours when we live our lives in his presence.

55:7–9 As long as God is calling out to us, it is never too late to begin to follow him. No matter how great our sins, no matter how unlikely it seems that God could forgive us, God offers forgiveness to repentant hearts. While people may give up on us, God doesn't. God's ways are not our ways. He is in the business of granting salvation to hopeless sinners (see Luke 19:1–10; 23:32–43; Acts 9:1–19). To receive his help we only need to repent and ask.

Bible Study and Meditation

Reading God's Mind

Isaiah 55:1–13 You may have said to yourself, *If only I knew God's thoughts!* Some people act as though they *do* know God's thoughts. They are full of advice and seem to believe that they understand exactly what God thinks and what he would do in every situation. Such people need to recognize that God's thoughts and ways are far beyond our ability to fully understand. No one can read minds—especially God's.

On the other hand, God's Word does give us a glimpse into God's thoughts and desires. God has called us to forsake our worldly thought patterns and assumptions and to learn instead his principles for life. Conventional worldly wisdom is often the exact opposite of God's ways. By saturating our minds with God's Word, we begin to see both God's message and God's method. As we read, we consider questions such as: *How has God worked in history? How does he work in our lives? What are the great concerns of God's heart? What should be our great concerns?*

God's word to Isaiah gives us great hope. Through it we learn to see life through God's eyes. We learn to think God's thoughts.

Putting It Into Practice

Make a list titled "God's Way Is Different." Divide the list into two columns. At the top of the left-hand column, write The World's Way; label the right-hand column God's Way. List as many concepts as you can for each column, showing the contrast between the two. Use the Bible as much as possible. For example:

GOD'S WAY IS DIFFERENT

The World's Way	*God's Way*
1) Get even with someone who hurts you.	*1) Forgive someone who hurts you (Matthew 6:14–15).*
2) Place your security in your savings.	*2) Place your trust in God and act responsibly with your money (Psalm 33:16–22; Luke 12:13-21).*

Use this list to highlight areas where you need to be especially careful in your spiritual life. Let God's Word guide your thinking; think God's thoughts instead of the world's.

For more on Bible study and meditation, turn to Colossians 3.

and do not return to it
without watering the earth
and making it bud and flourish,
so that it yields seed for the sower and bread for the eater,
11so is my word that goes out from my mouth:
It will not return to me empty,
but will accomplish what I desire
and achieve the purpose for which I sent it.
12You will go out in joy
and be led forth in peace;
the mountains and hills
will burst into song before you,
and all the trees of the field
will clap their hands.
13Instead of the thornbush will grow the pine tree,
and instead of briers the myrtle will grow.
This will be for the LORD's renown,
for an everlasting sign,
which will not be destroyed."

Salvation for Others

56 This is what the LORD says:

"Maintain justice
and do what is right,
for my salvation is close at hand
and my righteousness will soon be revealed.
2Blessed is the man who does this,
the man who holds it fast,
who keeps the Sabbath without desecrating it,
and keeps his hand from doing any evil."

3Let no foreigner who has bound himself to the LORD say,
"The LORD will surely exclude me from his people."
And let not any eunuch complain,
"I am only a dry tree."

4For this is what the LORD says:

"To the eunuchs who keep my Sabbaths,
who choose what pleases me
and hold fast to my covenant—
5to them I will give within my temple and its walls
a memorial and a name
better than sons and daughters;
I will give them an everlasting name
that will not be cut off.
6And foreigners who bind themselves to the LORD
to serve him,
to love the name of the LORD,
and to worship him,
all who keep the Sabbath without desecrating it
and who hold fast to my covenant—
7these I will bring to my holy mountain
and give them joy in my house of prayer.
Their burnt offerings and sacrifices
will be accepted on my altar;
for my house will be called
a house of prayer for all nations."
8The Sovereign LORD declares—
he who gathers the exiles of Israel:
"I will gather still others to them
besides those already gathered."

God's Accusation Against the Wicked

9Come, all you beasts of the field,
come and devour, all you beasts of the forest!
10Israel's watchmen are blind,
they all lack knowledge;
they are all mute dogs,
they cannot bark;
they lie around and dream,
they love to sleep.
11They are dogs with mighty appetites;
they never have enough.
They are shepherds who lack understanding;
they all turn to their own way,
each seeks his own gain.
12"Come," each one cries, "let me get wine!
Let us drink our fill of beer!
And tomorrow will be like today,
or even far better."

57 The righteous perish,
and no one ponders it in his heart;
devout men are taken away,
and no one understands
that the righteous are taken away
to be spared from evil.
2Those who walk uprightly

56:1–2 God rescues us free of charge; salvation is a gift. It is not something we can earn by being good. Yet our good deeds are an important demonstration of our faith in God. By following God's instructions for living, we demonstrate our respect for God. Observing God's laws will lead to a rich, full life. Since he created the world and its people, he knows what will work best for us.

56:3–8 Both Gentiles and eunuchs were excluded from full participation in the worship ceremonies in Israel. The Jews generally despised both groups because of this. But this passage says we are all welcome to join God's family regardless of our heritage or past. God loves everyone and wants the whole world to believe in him (see 1 Timothy 2:4). And all who believe are welcome in his love.

57:1–14 In this passage God judges those who turn their backs on him and plunge headlong into sin. These people deliberately reject God and don't care about following his ways. God knows our hearts. He knows that sometimes we struggle with doing what is right and fail. Sin is common to all of us because we are not perfect. We will make mistakes and encounter failures. But by asking for forgiveness and help from God we can continue toward our goal—spiritual renewal.

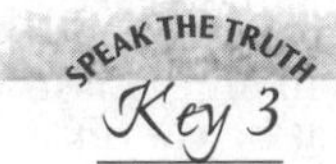

Clearing the Way for Restoration

Isaiah 57:12–19 God wants us to confess our sins because confession clears the way for spiritual renewal and restoration. When we verbally admit that we have sinned, we prepare our hearts to be transformed by God's grace.

Through his prophet Isaiah, the Lord called the Israelites to do the same: "Build up, build up, prepare the road! Remove the obstacles out of the way of my people . . . I live in a high and holy place, but also with him who is contrite and lowly in spirit, to revive the spirit of the lowly and to revive the heart of the contrite . . . I have seen his ways, but I will heal him; I will guide him and restore comfort to him" (57:14–15, 18).

God wants to clear the way to a better future for his people. When we come to him in humility, admitting to ourselves and to others that we are sinful and weak, God responds by healing us and restoring us so that we can follow him once again.

Turn to Hosea 11.

enter into peace;
they find rest as they lie in death.

3 "But you—come here, you sons of a sorceress,
you offspring of adulterers and prostitutes!
4 Whom are you mocking?
At whom do you sneer
and stick out your tongue?
Are you not a brood of rebels,
the offspring of liars?
5 You burn with lust among the oaks
and under every spreading tree;
you sacrifice your children in the ravines
and under the overhanging crags.
6 ⌊The idols⌋ among the smooth stones of the ravines are your portion;
they, they are your lot.
Yes, to them you have poured out drink offerings
and offered grain offerings.
In the light of these things, should I relent?
7 You have made your bed on a high and lofty hill;
there you went up to offer your sacrifices.
8 Behind your doors and your doorposts
you have put your pagan symbols.
Forsaking me, you uncovered your bed,
you climbed into it and opened it wide;
you made a pact with those whose beds you love,
and you looked on their nakedness.
9 You went to Molech[a] with olive oil
and increased your perfumes.
You sent your ambassadors[b] far away;
you descended to the grave[c] itself!
10 You were wearied by all your ways,
but you would not say, 'It is hopeless.'
You found renewal of your strength,
and so you did not faint.

11 "Whom have you so dreaded and feared
that you have been false to me,
and have neither remembered me
nor pondered this in your hearts?
Is it not because I have long been silent
that you do not fear me?
12 I will expose your righteousness and your works,
and they will not benefit you.
13 When you cry out for help,
let your collection ⌊of idols⌋ save you!
The wind will carry all of them off,
a mere breath will blow them away.
But the man who makes me his refuge
will inherit the land
and possess my holy mountain."

Comfort for the Contrite

14 And it will be said:

[a] 9 Or *to the king* [b] 9 Or *idols* [c] 9 Hebrew *Sheol*

"Build up, build up, prepare the road!
Remove the obstacles out of the way of my people."
15 For this is what the high and lofty One says—
he who lives forever, whose name is holy:
"I live in a high and holy place,
but also with him who is contrite and lowly in spirit,
to revive the spirit of the lowly
and to revive the heart of the contrite.
16 I will not accuse forever,
nor will I always be angry,
for then the spirit of man would grow faint before me—
the breath of man that I have created.
17 I was enraged by his sinful greed;
I punished him, and hid my face in anger,
yet he kept on in his willful ways.
18 I have seen his ways, but I will heal him;
I will guide him and restore comfort to him,
19 creating praise on the lips of the mourners in Israel.
Peace, peace, to those far and near,"
says the LORD. "And I will heal them."
20 But the wicked are like the tossing sea,
which cannot rest,
whose waves cast up mire and mud.
21 "There is no peace," says my God, "for the wicked."

True Fasting

58 "Shout it aloud, do not hold back.
Raise your voice like a trumpet.
Declare to my people their rebellion
and to the house of Jacob their sins.
2 For day after day they seek me out;
they seem eager to know my ways,
as if they were a nation that does what is right
and has not forsaken the commands of its God.
They ask me for just decisions
and seem eager for God to come near them.
3 'Why have we fasted,' they say,
'and you have not seen it?
Why have we humbled ourselves,
and you have not noticed?'

"Yet on the day of your fasting, you do as you please
and exploit all your workers.
4 Your fasting ends in quarreling and strife,
and in striking each other with wicked fists.
You cannot fast as you do today
and expect your voice to be heard on high.
5 Is this the kind of fast I have chosen,
only a day for a man to humble himself?
Is it only for bowing one's head like a reed
and for lying on sackcloth and ashes?
Is that what you call a fast,
a day acceptable to the LORD?

6 "Is not this the kind of fasting I have chosen:
to loose the chains of injustice
and untie the cords of the yoke,
to set the oppressed free
and break every yoke?
7 Is it not to share your food with the hungry
and to provide the poor wanderer with shelter—
when you see the naked, to clothe him,
and not to turn away from your own flesh and blood?
8 Then your light will break forth like the dawn,
and your healing will quickly appear;
then your righteousness[a] will go before you,
and the glory of the LORD will be your rear guard.
9 Then you will call, and the LORD will answer;
you will cry for help, and he will say: Here am I.

"If you do away with the yoke of oppression,
with the pointing finger and malicious talk,
10 and if you spend yourselves in behalf of the hungry
and satisfy the needs of the oppressed,
then your light will rise in the darkness,
and your night will become like the noonday.

[a] 8 Or *your righteous One*

57:15 God's blessings are available to all who will humbly admit their sins and weaknesses and repent of their wrongs. If there is willingness on our part, we will find that God's arms are open wide to accept us.

57:17–21 God is gracious and will bless us beyond what we deserve. Even though we may have lived a sinful lifestyle for years, God's healing is available to us if we will repent. He promises to help us in our spiritual growth. Those who persist in their sins and refuse to repent, however, will eventually lose their opportunity to receive God's peace.

58:1–5 The people of Judah were busy with religious activities, but for most of the people these observances were mere ritual. They lived sinful lives, devoid of obedience to God or concern for his laws. Not realizing that their own empty religious acts were at fault for their suffering, the people of Judah blamed God for not helping them. Sometimes we also may go through the motions of being religious. But if we don't truly seek God, he will ignore our false religious acts.

58:6–12 Spiritual renewal includes carrying out compassionate acts for others. If we focus our attention on our own lives and ignore others, we will not progress in our spiritual growth. God urges us to love others and treat them justly.

Fasting

A Fast That Satisfies God's Hunger

Isaiah 58:1 – 14 Fasting does not automatically honor God. As with any other spiritual discipline, if we simply go through the motions, we will not only waste time and effort, but we will also dishonor God and may even harm others.

Isaiah clearly states that there is a vital link between devotion to God and concern for those around us, between spiritual concerns and our responsibility to the world. The people of Israel falsely assumed that God was most concerned with getting something *from* us. They mistakenly believed that mere rituals would please God. In reality, God wants something *for* us—and for his creation. He desires that our hearts be filled with compassion so that we might care for the world around us. God warned Israel about the danger of empty asceticism. He urged them to fast from self-concern in order to care for others: "Is it not to share your food with the hungry and to provide the poor wanderer with shelter—when you see the naked, to clothe him, and not to turn away from your own flesh and blood?" (58:7).

God blesses those who bless others in his name. Note the promises of rest and renewal that come with obedience to God's will. When we bless others, God promises to heal and protect us and lead us forward (58:8). He responds to our prayers (58:9). He blesses our children and our cities (58:12). As always with God, what we give up in a fast cannot compare with what God gives us in return.

For more on fasting, turn to Daniel 10.

Putting It Into Practice

In the book of Isaiah, God calls for a fast in which we choose to say no to ourselves in order to say yes to acts of mercy and compassion for others.

Read Isaiah 58 again and prayerfully choose one group that you believe God wants to use you to touch. From what could you fast in order to serve them? A fast of your time? Your money? Your energy? Make specific plans to do this.

Note in your journal your preparations, your experiences and your reflections on what you learn through this process.

[11]The LORD will guide you always;
he will satisfy your needs in a sun-scorched land
and will strengthen your frame.
You will be like a well-watered garden,
like a spring whose waters never fail.
[12]Your people will rebuild the ancient ruins
and will raise up the age-old foundations;
you will be called Repairer of Broken Walls,
Restorer of Streets with Dwellings.

[13]"If you keep your feet from breaking the Sabbath
and from doing as you please on my holy day,
if you call the Sabbath a delight
and the LORD's holy day honorable,
and if you honor it by not going your own way
and not doing as you please or speaking idle words,
[14]then you will find your joy in the LORD,
and I will cause you to ride on the heights of the land
and to feast on the inheritance of your father Jacob."
The mouth of the LORD has spoken.

Sin, Confession and Redemption

59 Surely the arm of the LORD is not too short to save,
nor his ear too dull to hear.
[2]But your iniquities have separated
you from your God;
your sins have hidden his face from you,
so that he will not hear.
[3]For your hands are stained with blood,
your fingers with guilt.
Your lips have spoken lies,
and your tongue mutters wicked things.
[4]No one calls for justice;
no one pleads his case with integrity.
They rely on empty arguments and speak lies;
they conceive trouble and give birth to evil.
[5]They hatch the eggs of vipers
and spin a spider's web.
Whoever eats their eggs will die,
and when one is broken, an adder is hatched.
[6]Their cobwebs are useless for clothing;
they cannot cover themselves with what they make.
Their deeds are evil deeds,
and acts of violence are in their hands.
[7]Their feet rush into sin;
they are swift to shed innocent blood.
Their thoughts are evil thoughts;
ruin and destruction mark their ways.
[8]The way of peace they do not know;
there is no justice in their paths.
They have turned them into crooked roads;
no one who walks in them will know peace.

[9]So justice is far from us,
and righteousness does not reach us.
We look for light, but all is darkness;
for brightness, but we walk in deep shadows.
[10]Like the blind we grope along the wall,
feeling our way like men without eyes.
At midday we stumble as if it were twilight;
among the strong, we are like the dead.
[11]We all growl like bears;
we moan mournfully like doves.
We look for justice, but find none;
for deliverance, but it is far away.

[12]For our offenses are many in your sight,
and our sins testify against us.
Our offenses are ever with us,
and we acknowledge our iniquities:
[13]rebellion and treachery against the LORD,
turning our backs on our God,
fomenting oppression and revolt,
uttering lies our hearts have conceived.
[14]So justice is driven back,
and righteousness stands at a distance;
truth has stumbled in the streets,
honesty cannot enter.
[15]Truth is nowhere to be found,
and whoever shuns evil becomes a prey.

The LORD looked and was displeased
that there was no justice.
[16]He saw that there was no one,

58:13–14 The Old Testament Sabbath regulation provided a structure within which people would regularly take a rest from the pressures of life. They would use this time to worship God. We are still called to worship God in this way today. Not only does observing a Sabbath honor God, but it also physically refreshes us.

59:1–14 The people of Judah blamed God for failing to deliver them from their troubles. Sometimes we do the same thing. We get mad at God because we believe he has failed to follow through on his promises to us. God never fails us, but sometimes we fail God. If it seems that God isn't walking closely with us anymore, we should honestly examine our lives to see if there is any sin blocking our relationship. We need to ask God to show us the truth about our lives. When we recognize what the problem is, we can confess our sin and ask God to help us redirect our course.

59:13 We often fear dealing honestly with our sins. We may be afraid to start opening ourselves up to the truth. So we cover up the truth and begin to lie to ourselves and others about our sin. Before long we may even be taken in by our own lies. Honesty with God, with ourselves and with others is essential for our spiritual growth. If we refuse to see the truth, we can never confess it, accept responsibility for our lives or allow God to redirect our course.

59:15 Many people oppose those who try to improve themselves. Some may not want us to deal truthfully with our sins because we might cause them to feel guilty about their own. The world stands contrary to God's plan and exercises a resistance against our spiritual growth. We must resist what the world says and live for God, making God's kingdom our primary concern.

59:16 God doesn't tolerate inaction. If we don't help

he was appalled that there was no one to
intervene;
so his own arm worked salvation for him,
and his own righteousness sustained
him.
17He put on righteousness as his breastplate,
and the helmet of salvation on his head;
he put on the garments of vengeance
and wrapped himself in zeal as in a
cloak.
18According to what they have done,
so will he repay
wrath to his enemies
and retribution to his foes;
he will repay the islands their due.
19From the west, men will fear the name of
the LORD,
and from the rising of the sun, they will
revere his glory.
For he will come like a pent-up flood
that the breath of the LORD drives
along.[a]

20"The Redeemer will come to Zion,
to those in Jacob who repent of their
sins,"
declares the LORD.

21"As for me, this is my covenant with them,"
says the LORD. "My Spirit, who is on you, and
my words that I have put in your mouth will
not depart from your mouth, or from the
mouths of your children, or from the mouths of
their descendants from this time on and forever," says the LORD.

The Glory of Zion

60 "Arise, shine, for your light has
come,
and the glory of the LORD rises upon
you.
2See, darkness covers the earth
and thick darkness is over the peoples,
but the LORD rises upon you
and his glory appears over you.
3Nations will come to your light,
and kings to the brightness of your
dawn.

4"Lift up your eyes and look about you:
All assemble and come to you;
your sons come from afar,
and your daughters are carried on the
arm.
5Then you will look and be radiant,
your heart will throb and swell with joy;
the wealth on the seas will be brought to
you,
to you the riches of the nations will
come.
6Herds of camels will cover your land,
young camels of Midian and Ephah.
And all from Sheba will come,
bearing gold and incense
and proclaiming the praise of the LORD.
7All Kedar's flocks will be gathered to you,
the rams of Nebaioth will serve you;
they will be accepted as offerings on my
altar,
and I will adorn my glorious temple.

8"Who are these that fly along like clouds,
like doves to their nests?
9Surely the islands look to me;
in the lead are the ships of Tarshish,[b]
bringing your sons from afar,
with their silver and gold,
to the honor of the LORD your God,
the Holy One of Israel,
for he has endowed you with splendor.

10"Foreigners will rebuild your walls,
and their kings will serve you.
Though in anger I struck you,
in favor I will show you compassion.
11Your gates will always stand open,
they will never be shut, day or night,
so that men may bring you the wealth of
the nations—
their kings led in triumphal procession.
12For the nation or kingdom that will not
serve you will perish;
it will be utterly ruined.

13"The glory of Lebanon will come to you,
the pine, the fir and the cypress together,
to adorn the place of my sanctuary;
and I will glorify the place of my feet.
14The sons of your oppressors will come
bowing before you;
all who despise you will bow down at
your feet
and will call you the City of the LORD,
Zion of the Holy One of Israel.

[a]19 Or *When the enemy comes in like a flood, / the Spirit of the LORD will put him to flight* [b]9 Or *the trading ships*

those who suffer, our apathy is as bad in God's eyes as the direct cause for their misery. God makes it clear that his plan for us includes our helping one another. We need to pray for others and help them when they need our support.

59:20–21 Isaiah clearly states that God desires to indwell us with his Spirit. His desire is to change us and to begin a pattern of spiritual renewal that will be passed on to future generations.

60:1–3 God urged his people to let their light shine to the nations. God wants to transform us and then to use us to bring his truth to others. Part of our spiritual growth involves sharing our lives as living proof that transformation is possible with God's help.

60:4–22 These verses describe the restoration and exaltation of Israel at the end of history. How unbelievable this description must have seemed to the Jews of Isaiah's day. They lived under the threat of Assyrian domination. Subsequent generations were held captive in Babylon. But God can do the seemingly impossible. He could restore them, and he can restore us too (see Ephesians 3:20–21).

15 "Although you have been forsaken and
hated,
with no one traveling through,
I will make you the everlasting pride
and the joy of all generations.
16 You will drink the milk of nations
and be nursed at royal breasts.
Then you will know that I, the LORD, am
your Savior,
your Redeemer, the Mighty One of
Jacob.
17 Instead of bronze I will bring you gold,
and silver in place of iron.
Instead of wood I will bring you bronze,
and iron in place of stones.
I will make peace your governor
and righteousness your ruler.
18 No longer will violence be heard in your
land,
nor ruin or destruction within your
borders,
but you will call your walls Salvation
and your gates Praise.
19 The sun will no more be your light by day,
nor will the brightness of the moon
shine on you,
for the LORD will be your everlasting light,
and your God will be your glory.
20 Your sun will never set again,
and your moon will wane no more;
the LORD will be your everlasting light,
and your days of sorrow will end.
21 Then will all your people be righteous
and they will possess the land forever.
They are the shoot I have planted,
the work of my hands,
for the display of my splendor.
22 The least of you will become a thousand,
the smallest a mighty nation.
I am the LORD;
in its time I will do this swiftly."

The Year of the LORD's Favor

61 The Spirit of the Sovereign LORD is on
me,
because the LORD has anointed me
to preach good news to the poor.
He has sent me to bind up the
brokenhearted,
to proclaim freedom for the captives
and release from darkness for the
prisoners,[a]

[a]1 Hebrew; Septuagint *the blind*

60:17 This is a wonderful verse for meditation. God longs to exchange all that is worthless in our lives with things of value. He wants to lead us with peace and righteousness. In order to experience this exchange, we need to surrender our lives fully to God.
61:1–3 This prophecy of the Messiah's healing ministry was quoted by Jesus as a description of himself (see Luke 4:18–19). He is the Anointed One, the Christ, who calls all sufferers to come to him and find comfort, healing, joy and beauty. There is nothing we can do to earn these gifts from Christ; they are free to all who ask.

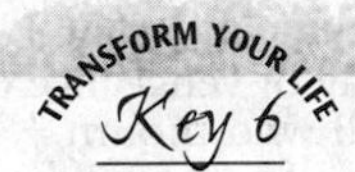

Fulfilling Our Mission

Isaiah 61:1–3 A life set free from sin is a beautiful sight. When we turn from our sins and follow God's plan for us, we testify to the glory of God and give others hope that he can change their lives as well. We may have learned from experience the suffering, affliction and brokenness that come from going our own way. We may also know what it is like to be enslaved to our passions. Yet we also recognize that there is more to life than bondage. There is healing and freedom; there is beauty and joy; there is love and mercy. And we have the wonderful privilege of proclaiming this news to those around us.

Jesus was commissioned with this same task—to bring Good News to those who are broken. He began his ministry by quoting these verses from Isaiah: "The Spirit of the Sovereign LORD is on me, because the LORD has anointed me to preach good news to the poor. He has sent me to bind up the brokenhearted, to proclaim freedom for the captives and release from darkness for the prisoners, to proclaim the year of the LORD's favor and the day of vengeance of our God, to comfort all who mourn" (61:1–2).

We were once on our way to destruction too, but God redirected us toward Jesus Christ. When we surrendered our lives to Jesus, we started on the path to heaven. Now we are called to bring this Good News to others, urging them to turn from their own way and follow the Lord.

Turn to Ezekiel 33.

2to proclaim the year of the LORD's favor
and the day of vengeance of our God,
to comfort all who mourn,
3 and provide for those who grieve in Zion—
to bestow on them a crown of beauty
instead of ashes,
the oil of gladness
instead of mourning,
and a garment of praise
instead of a spirit of despair.
They will be called oaks of righteousness,
a planting of the LORD
for the display of his splendor.

4They will rebuild the ancient ruins
and restore the places long devastated;
they will renew the ruined cities
that have been devastated for generations.
5Aliens will shepherd your flocks;
foreigners will work your fields and vineyards.
6And you will be called priests of the LORD,
you will be named ministers of our God.
You will feed on the wealth of nations,
and in their riches you will boast.

7Instead of their shame
my people will receive a double portion,
and instead of disgrace
they will rejoice in their inheritance;
and so they will inherit a double portion in their land,
and everlasting joy will be theirs.

8"For I, the LORD, love justice;
I hate robbery and iniquity.
In my faithfulness I will reward them
and make an everlasting covenant with them.
9Their descendants will be known among the nations
and their offspring among the peoples.
All who see them will acknowledge
that they are a people the LORD has blessed."

10I delight greatly in the LORD;
my soul rejoices in my God.
For he has clothed me with garments of salvation
and arrayed me in a robe of righteousness,
as a bridegroom adorns his head like a priest,
and as a bride adorns herself with her jewels.
11For as the soil makes the sprout come up
and a garden causes seeds to grow,
so the Sovereign LORD will make
righteousness and praise
spring up before all nations.

Zion's New Name

62 For Zion's sake I will not keep silent,
for Jerusalem's sake I will not remain quiet,
till her righteousness shines out like the dawn,
her salvation like a blazing torch.
2The nations will see your righteousness,
and all kings your glory;
you will be called by a new name
that the mouth of the LORD will bestow.
3You will be a crown of splendor in the LORD's hand,
a royal diadem in the hand of your God.
4No longer will they call you Deserted,
or name your land Desolate.
But you will be called Hephzibah,[a]
and your land Beulah[b];
for the LORD will take delight in you,
and your land will be married.
5As a young man marries a maiden,
so will your sons[c] marry you;
as a bridegroom rejoices over his bride,
so will your God rejoice over you.

6I have posted watchmen on your walls,
O Jerusalem;
they will never be silent day or night.
You who call on the LORD,
give yourselves no rest,

[a]4 *Hephzibah* means *my delight is in her.* [b]4 *Beulah* means *married.* [c]5 Or *Builder*

61:4–7 God promised rebuilding, prosperity, ministry and honor to his people in their final restoration at the end of history. Right now God promises these same things, though in different forms, to all of his children, whether Jew or Gentile. He wants to rebuild our broken lives, make us spiritually prosperous, give our lives significance through ministry to others and fill us with honor through his love and grace.

61:8–9 God hates injustice, so he himself is not going to treat us unjustly. When others have mistreated us, we are often afraid that everyone, even God, will treat us in the same manner. But Isaiah assures us that God will treat his people justly and will reward them for their undue suffering.

61:10 In this passage the Messiah is overwhelmed with joy at the fact that God has promised future blessings for his people. God is not stingy. He does not give begrudgingly, as some people we know may do. He wants to bless us! He is happy when people find salvation in him. He wants everyone to trust him and no one to suffer eternal judgment (see 1 Timothy 2:4).

62:1–5 God promised a glorious future restoration for Jerusalem and for her people. The city that had been degraded and devastated by conquerors would be lifted up and honored. This is God's desire for us too. God desires to lift us up, transform our lives, cleanse us and restore us to spiritual health and honor. He can do this if we believe in him, repent from our sins and ask him to save us.

62:6–7 The intercessors were asked to cry out to God, reminding him of his promises to Jerusalem. And they were to keep praying until God had fulfilled his word. We should not neglect prayer. It is not just a way to bring us peace of mind; it is also a way to preserve our spiritual gains and bring change in the world.

7and give him no rest till he establishes
Jerusalem
and makes her the praise of the earth.

8The LORD has sworn by his right hand
and by his mighty arm:
"Never again will I give your grain
as food for your enemies,
and never again will foreigners drink the
new wine
for which you have toiled;
9but those who harvest it will eat it
and praise the LORD,
and those who gather the grapes will drink
it
in the courts of my sanctuary."
10Pass through, pass through the gates!
Prepare the way for the people.
Build up, build up the highway!
Remove the stones.
Raise a banner for the nations.
11The LORD has made proclamation
to the ends of the earth:
"Say to the Daughter of Zion,
'See, your Savior comes!
See, his reward is with him,
and his recompense accompanies him.'"
12They will be called the Holy People,
the Redeemed of the LORD;
and you will be called Sought After,
the City No Longer Deserted.

God's Day of Vengeance and Redemption

63 Who is this coming from Edom,
from Bozrah, with his garments
stained crimson?
Who is this, robed in splendor,
striding forward in the greatness of his
strength?

"It is I, speaking in righteousness,
mighty to save."

2Why are your garments red,
like those of one treading the winepress?

3"I have trodden the winepress alone;
from the nations no one was with me.
I trampled them in my anger
and trod them down in my wrath;
their blood spattered my garments,
and I stained all my clothing.
4For the day of vengeance was in my heart,
and the year of my redemption has
come.
5I looked, but there was no one to help,
I was appalled that no one gave support;
so my own arm worked salvation for me,
and my own wrath sustained me.
6I trampled the nations in my anger;
in my wrath I made them drunk
and poured their blood on the ground."

Praise and Prayer

7I will tell of the kindnesses of the LORD,
the deeds for which he is to be praised,
according to all the LORD has done for
us—
yes, the many good things he has done
for the house of Israel,
according to his compassion and many
kindnesses.
8He said, "Surely they are my people,
sons who will not be false to me";
and so he became their Savior.
9In all their distress he too was distressed,
and the angel of his presence saved
them.
In his love and mercy he redeemed them;
he lifted them up and carried them
all the days of old.
10Yet they rebelled
and grieved his Holy Spirit.
So he turned and became their enemy
and he himself fought against them.

11Then his people recalled[a] the days of old,
the days of Moses and his people—
where is he who brought them through the
sea,
with the shepherd of his flock?
Where is he who set
his Holy Spirit among them,
12who sent his glorious arm of power
to be at Moses' right hand,
who divided the waters before them,
to gain for himself everlasting renown,
13who led them through the depths?
Like a horse in open country,
they did not stumble;
14like cattle that go down to the plain,
they were given rest by the Spirit of the
LORD.
This is how you guided your people
to make for yourself a glorious name.

15Look down from heaven and see

[a]11 Or *But may he recall*

63:1–6 God is pictured as a victorious warrior returning from a battle that he has had to fight alone against the enemies of his people. Because of the troubles we encounter and the pain we bear, we sometimes wonder whether God is for us or against us. As we see in these verses, God is definitely on our side. He loves us so much that he is willing to fight to deliver us.

63:10–14 Isaiah recounted the history of Israel. Despite God's miraculous deliverance of Israel from the Egyptians, Israel rebelled against God, worshiped idols, and then wondered why their lives were not blessed. We may also do the same thing if we believe that trusting God is only a temporary step in our spiritual growth. If we believe that we can achieve a certain level of spiritual maturity at which we can stop depending on God and take care of things ourselves, we will only experience disaster. Seeking God and surrendering to him is critical throughout our lives.

63:15–16 When we fall away from God, we should seek him again. Even if our own parents would disown us be-

from your lofty throne, holy and
glorious.
Where are your zeal and your might?
Your tenderness and compassion are
withheld from us.
16But you are our Father,
though Abraham does not know us
or Israel acknowledge us;
you, O LORD, are our Father,
our Redeemer from of old is your name.
17Why, O LORD, do you make us wander
from your ways
and harden our hearts so we do not
revere you?
Return for the sake of your servants,
the tribes that are your inheritance.
18For a little while your people possessed
your holy place,
but now our enemies have trampled
down your sanctuary.
19We are yours from of old;
but you have not ruled over them,
they have not been called by your
name.[a]

64 Oh, that you would rend the heavens
and come down,
that the mountains would tremble before
you!
2As when fire sets twigs ablaze
and causes water to boil,
come down to make your name known to
your enemies
and cause the nations to quake before
you!
3For when you did awesome things that we
did not expect,
you came down, and the mountains
trembled before you.
4Since ancient times no one has heard,
no ear has perceived,
no eye has seen any God besides you,
who acts on behalf of those who wait for
him.
5You come to the help of those who gladly
do right,
who remember your ways.
But when we continued to sin against
them,
you were angry.
How then can we be saved?
6All of us have become like one who is
unclean,
and all our righteous acts are like filthy
rags;
we all shrivel up like a leaf,
and like the wind our sins sweep us
away.
7No one calls on your name
or strives to lay hold of you;
for you have hidden your face from us
and made us waste away because of our
sins.

8Yet, O LORD, you are our Father.
We are the clay, you are the potter;
we are all the work of your hand.
9Do not be angry beyond measure, O LORD;
do not remember our sins forever.
Oh, look upon us, we pray,
for we are all your people.
10Your sacred cities have become a desert;
even Zion is a desert, Jerusalem a
desolation.
11Our holy and glorious temple, where our
fathers praised you,
has been burned with fire,
and all that we treasured lies in ruins.
12After all this, O LORD, will you hold
yourself back?
Will you keep silent and punish us
beyond measure?

Judgment and Salvation

65 "I revealed myself to those who did
not ask for me;

[a]19 Or *We are like those you have never ruled, / like those never called by your name*

---

cause of our sinful state, God will welcome us back to himself and love us if we will only repent (see Luke 15:11–32).

63:17–19 Turning back to God and renewing our relationship with him is not a push-button experience that happens instantly. If our hearts have been hardened, it will take time for them to be softened again. As we begin the process of restoration, God may not seem immediately close to us. Yet as we call upon God to help us, our relationship with him will eventually blossom. God is always there; we may just have trouble seeing him.

64:1–4 In this passage, we glimpse two key elements that are essential to spiritual renewal: faith and patience. The people of Judah looked at the awesome nature of their glorious, powerful, incomparable God. This increased their faith. Then they patiently waited for him to bring about their deliverance. Such events do not happen instantly or according to our timetable. But if we persevere, God will bring about the results in due time. If we are faithful and trust God, he will help us preserve our spiritual gains.

64:5 Isaiah admitted that he and all of his people were sinners. He asked God how they all could be saved. Though Isaiah was God's prophet, he included himself as a sinner before God. He remained humble, continually looking to God to forgive his sins. We need to be careful not to become so confident in our spiritual progress that we no longer acknowledge our own sins before God.

64:8–12 The people of Judah asked God to act graciously toward them. They had admitted their sin. They recognized that their punishment was deserved. But now they asked God to turn away his wrath and forget their sins. God acts graciously toward us too. When we trust Jesus the Messiah, his blood cleanses us from all our sin. Then we can spend eternity in God's presence.

65:1–2 When we consider all of our sins and failures, we may think that God wants nothing to do with us. This passage shows us that God stands with open arms, ready to receive us in spite of our sins. He welcomes all who repent—those who have never sought him before as well as those who have strayed from his side.

I was found by those who did not seek
me.
To a nation that did not call on my name,
I said, 'Here am I, here am I.'
2All day long I have held out my hands
to an obstinate people,
who walk in ways not good,
pursuing their own imaginations—
3a people who continually provoke me
to my very face,
offering sacrifices in gardens
and burning incense on altars of brick;
4who sit among the graves
and spend their nights keeping secret
vigil;
who eat the flesh of pigs,
and whose pots hold broth of unclean
meat;
5who say, 'Keep away; don't come near me,
for I am too sacred for you!'
Such people are smoke in my nostrils,
a fire that keeps burning all day.

6"See, it stands written before me:
I will not keep silent but will pay back
in full;
I will pay it back into their laps—
7both your sins and the sins of your fathers,"
says the LORD.
"Because they burned sacrifices on the
mountains
and defied me on the hills,
I will measure into their laps
the full payment for their former deeds."

8This is what the LORD says:

"As when juice is still found in a cluster of
grapes
and men say, 'Don't destroy it,
there is yet some good in it,'
so will I do in behalf of my servants;
I will not destroy them all.
9I will bring forth descendants from Jacob,
and from Judah those who will possess
my mountains;
my chosen people will inherit them,
and there will my servants live.
10Sharon will become a pasture for flocks,
and the Valley of Achor a resting place
for herds,
for my people who seek me.

11"But as for you who forsake the LORD
and forget my holy mountain,
who spread a table for Fortune
and fill bowls of mixed wine for Destiny,
12I will destine you for the sword,
and you will all bend down for the
slaughter;
for I called but you did not answer,
I spoke but you did not listen.
You did evil in my sight
and chose what displeases me."

13Therefore this is what the Sovereign LORD
says:

"My servants will eat,
but you will go hungry;
my servants will drink,
but you will go thirsty;
my servants will rejoice,
but you will be put to shame.
14My servants will sing
out of the joy of their hearts,
but you will cry out
from anguish of heart
and wail in brokenness of spirit.
15You will leave your name
to my chosen ones as a curse;
the Sovereign LORD will put you to death,
but to his servants he will give another
name.
16Whoever invokes a blessing in the land
will do so by the God of truth;
he who takes an oath in the land
will swear by the God of truth.
For the past troubles will be forgotten
and hidden from my eyes.

New Heavens and a New Earth

17"Behold, I will create
new heavens and a new earth.
The former things will not be remembered,
nor will they come to mind.
18But be glad and rejoice forever
in what I will create,
for I will create Jerusalem to be a delight
and its people a joy.
19I will rejoice over Jerusalem
and take delight in my people;
the sound of weeping and of crying
will be heard in it no more.

20"Never again will there be in it
an infant who lives but a few days,
or an old man who does not live out his
years;
he who dies at a hundred
will be thought a mere youth;

65:8–10 God deals righteously with each individual, preserving those who seek him. We need not fear that God will treat us unfairly. God is both just and merciful when he deals with his people.
65:11–15 The people of Judah abandoned the true God and dabbled in occult practices. They worshiped pagan gods called Fortune and Destiny, hoping to influence their own future. Yet the suffering and judgment they were trying to avoid by worshiping these pagan gods came upon them anyway because they sought help from these idols instead of from God. God is our only reliable source of help. Seeking any other source of assistance will ultimately bring disaster.
65:16–25 The new heaven and new earth will be wonderful; there will be no pain, suffering, sorrow or want. God will answer our prayers while we are still speaking them. There will be peace everywhere, even among the animals. While this level of blessing will not be achieved in this earthly lifetime, we can look forward to it in the next life if we are God's children.

he who fails to reach[a] a hundred
will be considered accursed.
21 They will build houses and dwell in them;
they will plant vineyards and eat their fruit.
22 No longer will they build houses and others live in them,
or plant and others eat.
For as the days of a tree,
so will be the days of my people;
my chosen ones will long enjoy
the works of their hands.
23 They will not toil in vain
or bear children doomed to misfortune;
for they will be a people blessed by the LORD,
they and their descendants with them.
24 Before they call I will answer;
while they are still speaking I will hear.
25 The wolf and the lamb will feed together,
and the lion will eat straw like the ox,
but dust will be the serpent's food.
They will neither harm nor destroy
on all my holy mountain,"
says the LORD.

Judgment and Hope

66 This is what the LORD says:
"Heaven is my throne,
and the earth is my footstool.
Where is the house you will build for me?
Where will my resting place be?
2 Has not my hand made all these things,
and so they came into being?"
declares the LORD.

"This is the one I esteem:
he who is humble and contrite in spirit,
and trembles at my word.
3 But whoever sacrifices a bull
is like one who kills a man,
and whoever offers a lamb,
like one who breaks a dog's neck;
whoever makes a grain offering
is like one who presents pig's blood,
and whoever burns memorial incense,
like one who worships an idol.
They have chosen their own ways,
and their souls delight in their abominations;
4 so I also will choose harsh treatment for them
and will bring upon them what they dread.
For when I called, no one answered,
when I spoke, no one listened.
They did evil in my sight
and chose what displeases me."
5 Hear the word of the LORD,
you who tremble at his word:
"Your brothers who hate you,
and exclude you because of my name,
have said,
'Let the LORD be glorified,
that we may see your joy!'
Yet they will be put to shame.
6 Hear that uproar from the city,
hear that noise from the temple!
It is the sound of the LORD
repaying his enemies all they deserve.

7 "Before she goes into labor,
she gives birth;
before the pains come upon her,
she delivers a son.
8 Who has ever heard of such a thing?
Who has ever seen such things?
Can a country be born in a day
or a nation be brought forth in a moment?
Yet no sooner is Zion in labor
than she gives birth to her children.
9 Do I bring to the moment of birth
and not give delivery?" says the LORD.
"Do I close up the womb
when I bring to delivery?" says your God.
10 "Rejoice with Jerusalem and be glad for her,
all you who love her;
rejoice greatly with her,
all you who mourn over her.
11 For you will nurse and be satisfied
at her comforting breasts;
you will drink deeply
and delight in her overflowing abundance."

12 For this is what the LORD says:

"I will extend peace to her like a river,
and the wealth of nations like a flooding stream;
you will nurse and be carried on her arm
and dandled on her knees.
13 As a mother comforts her child,
so will I comfort you;

[a] 20 Or / *the sinner who reaches*

66:2 God will respond to us when we follow these key principles: (1) humbly acknowledge our faults; (2) willingly turn from and deal with our sin; and (3) willingly desire to do what is right, no matter how difficult. When we follow these principles, there is a double blessing for us: We can overcome our sins and we can share in God's kingdom.

66:3–4 God is not fooled by our religious games. If we have no real desire to follow God and merely follow a set of worship rituals, we will be judged. God's deliverance comes from seeking his will and honoring and trusting him. Our spiritual growth is ensured when we truly depend on God, not just go through the motions of following him.

66:7–9 God will fulfill his promises, including his promise to transform us. Knowing that God will carry out his promise of spiritual renewal in our lives should give us the courage to continue with the process no matter how difficult the steps may be at times.

and you will be comforted over
Jerusalem."

14When you see this, your heart will rejoice
and you will flourish like grass;
the hand of the LORD will be made known
to his servants,
but his fury will be shown to his foes.
15See, the LORD is coming with fire,
and his chariots are like a whirlwind;
he will bring down his anger with fury,
and his rebuke with flames of fire.
16For with fire and with his sword
the LORD will execute judgment upon all
men,
and many will be those slain by the
LORD.

17"Those who consecrate and purify themselves to go into the gardens, following the one in the midst of[a] those who eat the flesh of pigs and rats and other abominable things—they will meet their end together," declares the LORD.
18"And I, because of their actions and their imaginations, am about to come[b] and gather all nations and tongues, and they will come and see my glory.
19"I will set a sign among them, and I will send some of those who survive to the nations—to Tarshish, to the Libyans[c] and Lydians (famous as archers), to Tubal and Greece, and to the distant islands that have not heard of my fame or seen my glory. They will proclaim my glory among the nations.
20And they will bring all your brothers, from all the nations, to my holy mountain in Jerusalem as an offering to the LORD—on horses, in chariots and wagons, and on mules and camels," says the LORD. "They will bring them, as the Israelites bring their grain offerings, to the temple of the LORD in ceremonially clean vessels.
21And I will select some of them also to be priests and Levites," says the LORD.

22"As the new heavens and the new earth that I make will endure before me," declares the LORD, "so will your name and descendants endure.
23From one New Moon to another and from one Sabbath to another, all mankind will come and bow down before me," says the LORD.
24"And they will go out and look upon the dead bodies of those who rebelled against me; their worm will not die, nor will their fire be quenched, and they will be loathsome to all mankind."

[a]17 Or *gardens behind one of your temples, and*
[b]18 The meaning of the Hebrew for this clause is uncertain.
[c]19 Some Septuagint manuscripts *Put* (Libyans); Hebrew *Pul*

66:22–24 Isaiah ends his book with a twofold promise: Those who follow God will live with him forever and their names will endure; those who oppose God and his people will suffer eternal punishment. The choice is clear. We may either follow God and experience healing and blessing, or we may rebel against God and experience turmoil and pain.

JEREMIAH

The Big Picture

A. JEREMIAH'S SPECIAL APPOINTMENT (1:1-19)

B. THE PROPHET DELIVERS GOD'S MESSAGES (2:1–45:5)

1. God's Warnings to Judah (2:1–29:32)
2. The Coming Exile and Restoration (30:1–33:26)
3. The Fall of Jerusalem (34:1–45:5)

C. GOD'S JUDGMENT ON THE NATIONS (46:1–51:64)

D. A PAINFUL REMINDER OF PAINFUL DAYS (52:1-34)

When we think of the future, most of us dream that we will be needed, loved, successful and sought after. Rarely do we hope for deep sorrow, thankless service or unwarranted persecution at the hands of the people we care about. When God called him, Jeremiah probably dreamed of people listening and responding to his words. He probably hoped that his ministry would inspire the spiritual renewal of the people of Judah. However, Jeremiah's hopes for success never came to be—at least not in his lifetime.

Jeremiah faithfully warned the Israelites of the punishment that would come because of their sin, but the people ignored his passionate pleas. Instead of admitting their sins and failures, they rejected, imprisoned and abused God's messenger. No one wanted to hear what Jeremiah had to say. King Zedekiah put Jeremiah into an empty cistern where the prophet sank not only into the mud but also into a mire of rejection. Virtually no one respected Jeremiah or the messages he spoke. The consequences of rejecting Jeremiah and his message were great: Judah fell deeper into sin and eventually suffered destruction and exile.

From a human standpoint, Jeremiah was not a successful prophet. But in the eyes of God, he was one of the most successful people in all history. Jeremiah remained faithful despite the opposition he faced. We may also experience opposition and suffering. God will fulfill his purposes for us, just as he did for Jeremiah, if we are faithful to God and his plan.

Spiritual Renewal Themes

FAITHFULNESS OVERCOMES FAILURE

From our human perspective, Jeremiah was a failure. But from God's point of view, Jeremiah was one of the greatest success stories in the Bible. Jeremiah remained faithful to God and God's commands despite the powerful opposition that he faced. When we feel discouraged, we need to remember that God simply calls us to be faithful—to keep on going. We don't have to be a success. We only need to be faithful. God will honor our faithfulness by providing us with strength when we need it.

GOD'S WAY MAY BE PAINFUL

In order to avoid facing their sin, the people of Judah refused to listen to Jeremiah's call for repentance. At times we may be tempted to avoid the truth and necessary changes we must make to our lives, but such avoidance will only stunt our spiritual growth. When we refuse to hear God's message of truth, we only create suffering that cuts even deeper than the pain we are trying to avoid. We should face the truth of our sin and allow it to redirect our course toward righteous living.

GOD UNDERSTANDS OUR EMOTIONS

Jeremiah has often been called the weeping prophet. But he did more than weep—at times Jeremiah was bitter, angry, discouraged, depressed and lonely. We have all experienced those feelings. Jeremiah even complained to God, "Why is my pain unending and my wound grievous and incurable? Will you be to me like a deceptive brook, like a spring that fails?" (15:18). God accepted Jeremiah's emotional tirades. His understanding of Jeremiah's emotions frees us to bring all of our strong feelings straight to God. God accepts us just as we are, and he is ready to heal our pain. We simply need to be honest with him.

HOPE DESPITE DISASTER

Jeremiah's warnings of impending judgment are punctuated by promises of ultimate deliverance. Jeremiah told the people about a new covenant that God had in store for them (see 31:1–40). Despite their impending doom, Jeremiah also reminded the people that God loved them and had a wonderful future planned for them: " 'For I know the plans I have for you,' declares the LORD, 'plans to prosper you and not to harm you, plans to give you hope and a future' " (29:11). When God confronts us with the truth about our sin, he also desires to give us a message of hope. He truly is the God of hope and restoration.

Essential Facts

PURPOSE:
To warn the people of Judah to turn from their sin and to obey God's good plan for them.

AUTHOR:
The prophet Jeremiah.

AUDIENCE:
The people of Judah, before and during the Babylonian exile.

DATE WRITTEN:
The book includes oracles given throughout Jeremiah's ministry (626-585 B.C.).

SETTING:
The land of Judah, from the initial threats of Assyria and Egypt (627 B.C.) until after Judah's eventual destruction by Babylon (586 B.C.).

KEY VERSE:
"When your words came, I ate them; they were my joy and my heart's delight, for I bear your name, O LORD God Almighty" (15:16).

KEY PEOPLE AND RELATIONSHIPS:
Jeremiah with God and with the people of Judah.

1

The words of Jeremiah son of Hilkiah, one of the priests at Anathoth in the territory of Benjamin. 2 The word of the LORD came to him in the thirteenth year of the reign of Josiah son of Amon king of Judah, 3 and through the reign of Jehoiakim son of Josiah king of Judah, down to the fifth month of the eleventh year of Zedekiah son of Josiah king of Judah, when the people of Jerusalem went into exile.

The Call of Jeremiah

4 The word of the LORD came to me, saying,

5 "Before I formed you in the womb I knew[a] you,
before you were born I set you apart;
I appointed you as a prophet to the nations."

6 "Ah, Sovereign LORD," I said, "I do not know how to speak; I am only a child."

7 But the LORD said to me, "Do not say, 'I am only a child.' You must go to everyone I send you to and say whatever I command you. 8 Do not be afraid of them, for I am with you and will rescue you," declares the LORD.

9 Then the LORD reached out his hand and touched my mouth and said to me, "Now, I have put my words in your mouth. 10 See, today I appoint you over nations and kingdoms to uproot and tear down, to destroy and overthrow, to build and to plant."

11 The word of the LORD came to me: "What do you see, Jeremiah?"

"I see the branch of an almond tree," I replied.

12 The LORD said to me, "You have seen correctly, for I am watching[b] to see that my word is fulfilled."

13 The word of the LORD came to me again: "What do you see?"

"I see a boiling pot, tilting away from the north," I answered.

14 The LORD said to me, "From the north disaster will be poured out on all who live in the land. 15 I am about to summon all the peoples of the northern kingdoms," declares the LORD.

"Their kings will come and set up their thrones
in the entrance of the gates of Jerusalem;
they will come against all her surrounding walls
and against all the towns of Judah.
16 I will pronounce my judgments on my people
because of their wickedness in forsaking me,
in burning incense to other gods
and in worshiping what their hands have made.

17 "Get yourself ready! Stand up and say to them whatever I command you. Do not be terrified by them, or I will terrify you before them. 18 Today I have made you a fortified city, an iron pillar and a bronze wall to stand against the whole land—against the kings of Judah, its officials, its priests and the people of the land. 19 They will fight against you but will not overcome you, for I am with you and will rescue you," declares the LORD.

Israel Forsakes God

2

The word of the LORD came to me: 2 "Go and proclaim in the hearing of Jerusalem:

" 'I remember the devotion of your youth,
how as a bride you loved me
and followed me through the desert,

[a] 5 Or *chose* [b] 12 The Hebrew for *watching* sounds like the Hebrew for *almond tree.*

1:1–3 Some of Jeremiah's messages warned the Jews of the impending Babylonian captivity; other messages were communiqués given after Judah had already fallen to Babylon. God often tries to warn us of the consequences of our sins; we would be wise to listen when he does. But we should be grateful that God also reaches out to help us even after we have sinned.

1:4–5 God has a plan for us. He may want us to be prophets like Jeremiah, or he may not. But it is our responsibility to cooperate with God so that he can work his plan in our lives. We need to seek out God's will and then follow it. God will help and encourage us as we do.

1:6–8 God asked his prophet to do some difficult things. God asks us to do some difficult things, too. He asks us to put our past sins behind us and live according to his will. But in his love, God never sends us into battle alone. He is always with us, encouraging us and showing us the way.

1:11–16 God used signs to illustrate to Jeremiah that Judah would be judged for her continued idolatry. We may also have idols. Power, wealth, comfort, prestige, and possessions are only a few of the idols we tend to protect and to which we give our time and energy. When our idols cease to satisfy us, it may be because God is showing us the weakness of the gods we worship. Those who worship the true God will find complete satisfaction. No false god can promise that.

1:16 Our idols may take on a different form than the idols of the people of Judah, but they are just as sinful. Though the people of Judah worshiped gods that were handmade statues of clay or precious metals, our idols tend to come in the form of money, prestige or pleasure. Idolatry of all kinds will destroy our relationship with God and ultimately ruin our lives. We must rid ourselves of it.

2:1—3:5 This message was intended for the people of Judah. Judah had forsaken God to create her own idols (2:13), and God's heart had been broken. The idols in our lives never bring satisfaction. Careful and honest reflection will reveal the things that take first place in our lives besides God. These "idols" need to be confessed and forsaken before we can move forward in our relationship with God and in our spiritual growth.

2:2–3 In marriage, people speak of a honeymoon period—a time during which each spouse is eager to please the other. Disillusionment often sets in when the honeymoon period is over. God recalled a time when Israel was his eager bride, happy to be faithful to him. We also have a honeymoon period in our relationship with God—a time when we are eager to please him and focus on him. By taking time daily to seek God and surrender to him, we can keep our love relationship growing. Temptations will lose their power to divert us if we daily surrender our lives to God's control.

through a land not sown.
[3]Israel was holy to the LORD,
the firstfruits of his harvest;
all who devoured her were held guilty,
and disaster overtook them,' "
declares the LORD.

[4]Hear the word of the LORD, O house of Jacob,
all you clans of the house of Israel.

[5]This is what the LORD says:

"What fault did your fathers find in me,
that they strayed so far from me?
They followed worthless idols
and became worthless themselves.
[6]They did not ask, 'Where is the LORD,
who brought us up out of Egypt
and led us through the barren wilderness,
through a land of deserts and rifts,
a land of drought and darkness,[a]
a land where no one travels and no one lives?'
[7]I brought you into a fertile land
to eat its fruit and rich produce.
But you came and defiled my land
and made my inheritance detestable.
[8]The priests did not ask,
'Where is the LORD?'
Those who deal with the law did not know me;
the leaders rebelled against me.
The prophets prophesied by Baal,
following worthless idols.

[9]"Therefore I bring charges against you again,"
declares the LORD.
"And I will bring charges against your children's children.
[10]Cross over to the coasts of Kittim[b] and look,
send to Kedar[c] and observe closely;
see if there has ever been anything like this:
[11]Has a nation ever changed its gods?
(Yet they are not gods at all.)
But my people have exchanged their[d] Glory
for worthless idols.
[12]Be appalled at this, O heavens,
and shudder with great horror,"
declares the LORD.
[13]"My people have committed two sins:
They have forsaken me,
the spring of living water,
and have dug their own cisterns,
broken cisterns that cannot hold water.
[14]Is Israel a servant, a slave by birth?
Why then has he become plunder?
[15]Lions have roared;
they have growled at him.
They have laid waste his land;
his towns are burned and deserted.
[16]Also, the men of Memphis[e] and Tahpanhes
have shaved the crown of your head.[f]
[17]Have you not brought this on yourselves
by forsaking the LORD your God
when he led you in the way?
[18]Now why go to Egypt
to drink water from the Shihor[g]?
And why go to Assyria
to drink water from the River[h]?
[19]Your wickedness will punish you;
your backsliding will rebuke you.
Consider then and realize
how evil and bitter it is for you
when you forsake the LORD your God
and have no awe of me,"
declares the Lord,
the LORD Almighty.

[20]"Long ago you broke off your yoke
and tore off your bonds;
you said, 'I will not serve you!'
Indeed, on every high hill
and under every spreading tree
you lay down as a prostitute.
[21]I had planted you like a choice vine
of sound and reliable stock.
How then did you turn against me
into a corrupt, wild vine?
[22]Although you wash yourself with soda
and use an abundance of soap,
the stain of your guilt is still before me,"
declares the Sovereign LORD.
[23]"How can you say, 'I am not defiled;
I have not run after the Baals'?
See how you behaved in the valley;
consider what you have done.

[a]6 Or *and the shadow of death* [b]10 That is, Cyprus and western coastlands [c]10 The home of Bedouin tribes in the Syro-Arabian desert [d]11 Masoretic Text; an ancient Hebrew scribal tradition *my* [e]16 Hebrew *Noph* [f]16 Or *have cracked your skull* [g]18 That is, a branch of the Nile [h]18 That is, the Euphrates

2:6–8 Jeremiah recalled how the people of Israel soon forgot who had saved them from their bondage in Egypt. As a result, they wandered for years in the wilderness. Without God, we also will find ourselves wandering in a terrible wilderness. Drifting into sinful, selfish ways is a certainty without God's help to keep us on the right path.
2:9 God was persistent in his efforts to deliver Israel from the bondage of Egypt and their slavery to sin. He never gave up on them; neither will he give up on us. He will continue to seek us out. As we wander from him and try to take control of our lives, he pleads for us to return to him. We would be wise to listen and respond with loving obedience.
2:13 The practice of idolatry involves two grave mistakes: a turning away from our powerful God, the only one who can really help us, and a turning toward idols that have no power to help us. When we turn away from God, we are turning instead to something else to help deal with a pain that only God can heal. These temporary solutions only deepen and lengthen our pain. God wants us to put these things away and return to his loving care.

You are a swift she-camel
running here and there,
24a wild donkey accustomed to the desert,
sniffing the wind in her craving—
in her heat who can restrain her?
Any males that pursue her need not tire
themselves;
at mating time they will find her.
25Do not run until your feet are bare
and your throat is dry.
But you said, 'It's no use!
I love foreign gods,
and I must go after them.'

26"As a thief is disgraced when he is caught,
so the house of Israel is disgraced—
they, their kings and their officials,
their priests and their prophets.
27They say to wood, 'You are my father,'
and to stone, 'You gave me birth.'
They have turned their backs to me
and not their faces;
yet when they are in trouble, they say,
'Come and save us!'
28Where then are the gods you made for
yourselves?
Let them come if they can save you
when you are in trouble!
For you have as many gods
as you have towns, O Judah.

29"Why do you bring charges against me?
You have all rebelled against me,"
declares the LORD.
30"In vain I punished your people;
they did not respond to correction.
Your sword has devoured your prophets
like a ravening lion.

31"You of this generation, consider the word
of the LORD:

"Have I been a desert to Israel
or a land of great darkness?
Why do my people say, 'We are free to
roam;
we will come to you no more'?
32Does a maiden forget her jewelry,
a bride her wedding ornaments?
Yet my people have forgotten me,
days without number.
33How skilled you are at pursuing love!
Even the worst of women can learn from
your ways.
34On your clothes men find
the lifeblood of the innocent poor,
though you did not catch them breaking
in.
Yet in spite of all this
35 you say, 'I am innocent;
he is not angry with me.'
But I will pass judgment on you
because you say, 'I have not sinned.'
36Why do you go about so much,
changing your ways?
You will be disappointed by Egypt
as you were by Assyria.
37You will also leave that place
with your hands on your head,
for the LORD has rejected those you trust;
you will not be helped by them.

3 "If a man divorces his wife
and she leaves him and marries another
man,
should he return to her again?
Would not the land be completely
defiled?
But you have lived as a prostitute with
many lovers—
would you now return to me?"
declares the LORD.
2"Look up to the barren heights and see.
Is there any place where you have not
been ravished?
By the roadside you sat waiting for lovers,
sat like a nomad[a] in the desert.
You have defiled the land
with your prostitution and wickedness.
3Therefore the showers have been withheld,
and no spring rains have fallen.
Yet you have the brazen look of a
prostitute;
you refuse to blush with shame.
4Have you not just called to me:
'My Father, my friend from my youth,
5will you always be angry?
Will your wrath continue forever?'
This is how you talk,
but you do all the evil you can."

[a]2 Or *an Arab*

2:24–25 Jeremiah compared Israel to a female donkey at mating time, running from one male donkey to another to satisfy her lusts. Israel was willing to try any god without even thinking about the results—she was out of control! When we reject God's control in our lives, we will also find ourselves out of control, mindlessly chasing after sinful attractions. We need to recognize our helplessness against the pull of sin. Once we surrender to God, he will help us overcome our sinful desires.

2:26–27 Often we feel guilty only if we get caught doing wrong. Suffering the consequences of our sins can be instructive, helping us understand and admit our true condition. Feeling shame, seeing our lives destroyed—these consequences show us our need for God. If we turn to him, we can know the wonderful joy that there is still hope for us.

2:34–35 When we fail to surrender our lives to God, we may commit sins that hurt innocent people. What better reason to repent and turn to the only true God who can redeem us and change us.

3:1 Because of his unlimited grace, no matter how far we have wandered, no matter how many other false gods we have worshiped, God will forgive us if we truly repent. When we stop living life in our own power, God invites us to receive his power. No sin is so awful that God's love won't forgive it.

Unfaithful Israel

6During the reign of King Josiah, the LORD
said to me, "Have you seen what faithless Israel
has done? She has gone up on every high hill
and under every spreading tree and has committed adultery there. 7I thought that after she
had done all this she would return to me but
she did not, and her unfaithful sister Judah saw
it. 8I gave faithless Israel her certificate of divorce and sent her away because of all her adulteries. Yet I saw that her unfaithful sister Judah
had no fear; she also went out and committed
adultery. 9Because Israel's immorality mattered
so little to her, she defiled the land and committed adultery with stone and wood. 10In spite of
all this, her unfaithful sister Judah did not return to me with all her heart, but only in pretense," declares the LORD.

11The LORD said to me, "Faithless Israel is
more righteous than unfaithful Judah. 12Go,
proclaim this message toward the north:

" 'Return, faithless Israel,' declares the
LORD,
'I will frown on you no longer,
for I am merciful,' declares the LORD,
'I will not be angry forever.
13Only acknowledge your guilt—
you have rebelled against the LORD your
God,
you have scattered your favors to foreign
gods
under every spreading tree,
and have not obeyed me,' "
declares the LORD.

14"Return, faithless people," declares the
LORD, "for I am your husband. I will choose
you—one from a town and two from a clan—
and bring you to Zion. 15Then I will give you
shepherds after my own heart, who will lead
you with knowledge and understanding. 16In
those days, when your numbers have increased
greatly in the land," declares the LORD, "men
will no longer say, 'The ark of the covenant
of the LORD.' It will never enter their minds
or be remembered; it will not be missed, nor
will another one be made. 17At that time they
will call Jerusalem The Throne of the LORD,
and all nations will gather in Jerusalem to
honor the name of the LORD. No longer will
they follow the stubbornness of their evil
hearts. 18In those days the house of Judah will
join the house of Israel, and together they will
come from a northern land to the land I gave
your forefathers as an inheritance.

19"I myself said,

" 'How gladly would I treat you like sons
and give you a desirable land,
the most beautiful inheritance of any
nation.'
I thought you would call me 'Father'
and not turn away from following me.
20But like a woman unfaithful to her
husband,
so you have been unfaithful to me,
O house of Israel,"
declares the LORD.

21A cry is heard on the barren heights,
the weeping and pleading of the people
of Israel,
because they have perverted their ways
and have forgotten the LORD their God.

22"Return, faithless people;
I will cure you of backsliding."

"Yes, we will come to you,
for you are the LORD our God.
23Surely the ⌊idolatrous⌋ commotion on the
hills
and mountains is a deception;
surely in the LORD our God
is the salvation of Israel.
24From our youth shameful gods have
consumed
the fruits of our fathers' labor—
their flocks and herds,
their sons and daughters.
25Let us lie down in our shame,
and let our disgrace cover us.
We have sinned against the LORD our God,

3:6—4:4 God is portrayed as feeling intense emotion, hurt deeply by the sin of Israel and Judah. God longed for his people to return to him and receive his forgiveness. Sin is painful to everyone it touches, yet no one grieves over sin's devastating consequences more than God does. He wants us to turn to him for deliverance from the grip of sin; he wants to set us free from the painful consequences sin creates in our lives each passing day.

3:8 God likens our worship of other gods to prostitution. When we worship money, success, power or prestige, we are like a well-loved wife who searches for others to satisfy her sexual desire instead of remaining faithful to her loving husband. We intrinsically realize that these false gods can never really satisfy us. We would be wise to surrender our lives to the only true God. He will care for us and love us as a faithful and loving husband would.

3:9–10 The people of Israel refused to see the truth and took their sins lightly. We often do the same thing, perhaps because the consequences of our sins don't always follow immediately. Nothing bad happens for a while, and we can be lulled into thinking that we can get away with our destructive behavior. If sin's consequences struck us instantly, we might take our actions more seriously. But regardless, we must realize that God does not take our sin lightly. The consequences for sinful behavior will inevitably come, sooner or later.

3:12–13 This passage represents God's plan for change. He expects us to see the truth, admit our guilt and confess that we have been following someone or something other than God. God will not change us until we are willing to confess our sins. Our spiritual renewal can begin today the same way it did thousands of years ago if only we will repent.

3:19–20 God reminded his people that he had longed to be a loving father to them. Few of us understand the depth of God's fatherly love. What a wonderful God who waits patiently for the day when we turn to him and utter the word *Father!* As his children, we are privileged to enjoy God's presence and come before him with our requests.

both we and our fathers;
from our youth till this day
we have not obeyed the LORD our God."

4

"If you will return, O Israel,
return to me,"
declares the LORD.
"If you put your detestable idols out of my sight
and no longer go astray,
2 and if in a truthful, just and righteous way
you swear, 'As surely as the LORD lives,'
then the nations will be blessed by him
and in him they will glory."

3 This is what the LORD says to the men of
Judah and to Jerusalem:

"Break up your unplowed ground
and do not sow among thorns.
4 Circumcise yourselves to the LORD,
circumcise your hearts,
you men of Judah and people of Jerusalem,
or my wrath will break out and burn like fire
because of the evil you have done—
burn with no one to quench it.

Disaster From the North

5 "Announce in Judah and proclaim in Jerusalem and say:
'Sound the trumpet throughout the land!'
Cry aloud and say:
'Gather together!
Let us flee to the fortified cities!'
6 Raise the signal to go to Zion!
Flee for safety without delay!
For I am bringing disaster from the north,
even terrible destruction."

7 A lion has come out of his lair;
a destroyer of nations has set out.
He has left his place
to lay waste your land.
Your towns will lie in ruins
without inhabitant.
8 So put on sackcloth,
lament and wail,
for the fierce anger of the LORD
has not turned away from us.
9 "In that day," declares the LORD,
"the king and the officials will lose heart,
the priests will be horrified,
and the prophets will be appalled."

10 Then I said, "Ah, Sovereign LORD, how
completely you have deceived this people and
Jerusalem by saying, 'You will have peace,'
when the sword is at our throats."
11 At that time this people and Jerusalem will
be told, "A scorching wind from the barren
heights in the desert blows toward my people,
but not to winnow or cleanse; 12 a wind too
strong for that comes from me.[a] Now I pronounce my judgments against them."

13 Look! He advances like the clouds,
his chariots come like a whirlwind,
his horses are swifter than eagles.
Woe to us! We are ruined!
14 O Jerusalem, wash the evil from your heart
and be saved.
How long will you harbor wicked thoughts?
15 A voice is announcing from Dan,
proclaiming disaster from the hills of Ephraim.
16 "Tell this to the nations,
proclaim it to Jerusalem:
'A besieging army is coming from a distant land,
raising a war cry against the cities of Judah.
17 They surround her like men guarding a field,
because she has rebelled against me,' "
declares the LORD.
18 "Your own conduct and actions
have brought this upon you.
This is your punishment.
How bitter it is!
How it pierces to the heart!"

19 Oh, my anguish, my anguish!
I writhe in pain.
Oh, the agony of my heart!
My heart pounds within me,
I cannot keep silent.
For I have heard the sound of the trumpet;
I have heard the battle cry.
20 Disaster follows disaster;

[a] 12 Or *comes at my command*

4:1–2 God always planned for his people to be living proof of his power and goodness. He wanted others to believe in him because of what they saw among his people, Israel. God also wants to use us as a testimony to his loving power. When we surrender our lives to God, our increasing purity and honesty will stand out as a testimony to the kind of life that is possible through God's power. What an honor it is for us to be used by our Creator to touch the lives of others! Our spiritual renewal can help bring hope and encouragement to others as they begin to seek God for themselves.

4:5—6:30 No parent enjoys disciplining his or her child, but without it, love is incomplete. God allows his people to suffer the consequences of their sins (see 4:18; 5:3, 19; 6:18–19), yet his heart is heavy. He suffers when we suffer. But the suffering in our lives is designed to lead us back to God, to healing, and to spiritual growth.

4:14 It isn't easy to rid our minds of deeply ingrained sinful thought patterns. But as we surrender our lives to God, spend time with him in prayer and ask him to lead us, God will reveal his will for us and begin to reshape the way we think. As we continue to meditate on his Word, God's thoughts will become our own. He will replace our evil thoughts with godly ones. Developing God-honoring thought patterns is an essential part of our spiritual renewal.

the whole land lies in ruins.
In an instant my tents are destroyed,
my shelter in a moment.
21How long must I see the battle standard
and hear the sound of the trumpet?

22"My people are fools;
they do not know me.
They are senseless children;
they have no understanding.
They are skilled in doing evil;
they know not how to do good."

23I looked at the earth,
and it was formless and empty;
and at the heavens,
and their light was gone.
24I looked at the mountains,
and they were quaking;
all the hills were swaying.
25I looked, and there were no people;
every bird in the sky had flown away.
26I looked, and the fruitful land was a desert;
all its towns lay in ruins
before the LORD, before his fierce anger.

27This is what the LORD says:

"The whole land will be ruined,
though I will not destroy it completely.
28Therefore the earth will mourn
and the heavens above grow dark,
because I have spoken and will not relent,
I have decided and will not turn back."

29At the sound of horsemen and archers
every town takes to flight.
Some go into the thickets;
some climb up among the rocks.
All the towns are deserted;
no one lives in them.

30What are you doing, O devastated one?
Why dress yourself in scarlet
and put on jewels of gold?
Why shade your eyes with paint?
You adorn yourself in vain.
Your lovers despise you;
they seek your life.

31I hear a cry as of a woman in labor,
a groan as of one bearing her first child—
the cry of the Daughter of Zion gasping for
breath,
stretching out her hands and saying,
"Alas! I am fainting;
my life is given over to murderers."

Not One Is Upright

5 "Go up and down the streets of
Jerusalem,
look around and consider,
search through her squares.
If you can find but one person
who deals honestly and seeks the truth,
I will forgive this city.
2Although they say, 'As surely as the LORD
lives,'
still they are swearing falsely."

3O LORD, do not your eyes look for truth?
You struck them, but they felt no pain;
you crushed them, but they refused
correction.
They made their faces harder than stone
and refused to repent.
4I thought, "These are only the poor;
they are foolish,
for they do not know the way of the LORD,
the requirements of their God.
5So I will go to the leaders
and speak to them;
surely they know the way of the LORD,
the requirements of their God."
But with one accord they too had broken
off the yoke
and torn off the bonds.
6Therefore a lion from the forest will attack
them,
a wolf from the desert will ravage them,
a leopard will lie in wait near their towns
to tear to pieces any who venture out,
for their rebellion is great
and their backslidings many.

7"Why should I forgive you?
Your children have forsaken me
and sworn by gods that are not gods.
I supplied all their needs,
yet they committed adultery
and thronged to the houses of
prostitutes.
8They are well-fed, lusty stallions,
each neighing for another man's wife.
9Should I not punish them for this?"
declares the LORD.
"Should I not avenge myself
on such a nation as this?

10"Go through her vineyards and ravage
them,
but do not destroy them completely.
Strip off her branches,

4:30 Facing imminent destruction, the people of Israel sought to make external changes that they hoped would bring about their deliverance. We sometimes do the same thing, making external changes to our lifestyle instead of making internal changes of the heart. We may go to more church services or carry a bigger Bible, trying to look good and cover the terrible pain we feel. Yet covering up our sin and failures this way only hides the truth. Spiritual renewal begins when we open our hearts to God and admit our wrongs. God can then change us on the inside. If we are too concerned about what we look like to others, we may not deal with the real problems hiding in our hearts.

5:1 If only one person had been honest and seeking the truth, the course of Israel's history could have been changed. We can change history today too. Our honesty can profoundly impact the people around us and maybe even generations to come. Our failure in seeking the truth or living honestly, however, will only hurt ourselves and others.

for these people do not belong to the
LORD.
11The house of Israel and the house of Judah
have been utterly unfaithful to me,"
declares the LORD.

12They have lied about the LORD;
they said, "He will do nothing!
No harm will come to us;
we will never see sword or famine.
13The prophets are but wind
and the word is not in them;
so let what they say be done to them."

14Therefore this is what the LORD God Almighty says:

"Because the people have spoken these
words,
I will make my words in your mouth a
fire
and these people the wood it consumes.
15O house of Israel," declares the LORD,
"I am bringing a distant nation against
you—
an ancient and enduring nation,
a people whose language you do not
know,
whose speech you do not understand.
16Their quivers are like an open grave;
all of them are mighty warriors.
17They will devour your harvests and food,
devour your sons and daughters;
they will devour your flocks and herds,
devour your vines and fig trees.
With the sword they will destroy
the fortified cities in which you trust.

18"Yet even in those days," declares the LORD,
"I will not destroy you completely. 19And when
the people ask, 'Why has the LORD our God
done all this to us?' you will tell them, 'As you
have forsaken me and served foreign gods in
your own land, so now you will serve foreigners
in a land not your own.'

20"Announce this to the house of Jacob
and proclaim it in Judah:
21Hear this, you foolish and senseless people,
who have eyes but do not see,
who have ears but do not hear:
22Should you not fear me?" declares the LORD.
"Should you not tremble in my
presence?
I made the sand a boundary for the sea,
an everlasting barrier it cannot cross.
The waves may roll, but they cannot
prevail;
they may roar, but they cannot cross it.
23But these people have stubborn and
rebellious hearts;
they have turned aside and gone away.
24They do not say to themselves,
'Let us fear the LORD our God,
who gives autumn and spring rains in
season,
who assures us of the regular weeks of
harvest.'
25Your wrongdoings have kept these away;
your sins have deprived you of good.

26"Among my people are wicked men
who lie in wait like men who snare birds
and like those who set traps to catch
men.
27Like cages full of birds,
their houses are full of deceit;
they have become rich and powerful
28 and have grown fat and sleek.
Their evil deeds have no limit;
they do not plead the case of the
fatherless to win it,
they do not defend the rights of the
poor.
29Should I not punish them for this?"
declares the LORD.
"Should I not avenge myself
on such a nation as this?

30"A horrible and shocking thing
has happened in the land:
31The prophets prophesy lies,
the priests rule by their own authority,
and my people love it this way.
But what will you do in the end?

Jerusalem Under Siege

6 "Flee for safety, people of Benjamin!
Flee from Jerusalem!
Sound the trumpet in Tekoa!
Raise the signal over Beth Hakkerem!
For disaster looms out of the north,
even terrible destruction.
2I will destroy the Daughter of Zion,
so beautiful and delicate.
3Shepherds with their flocks will come
against her;
they will pitch their tents around her,
each tending his own portion."

4"Prepare for battle against her!
Arise, let us attack at noon!

5:11–13 Jeremiah's audience refused to see the truth that sin brings devastating consequences. The prophet warned the people, but they refused to listen. We often do the same thing. When confronted with the consequences of our behavior, we foolishly rationalize our actions. The next time someone confronts us, we should listen to them, honestly examining our lives and asking God to change us where we need to change.

5:19 Everyone who refuses to serve God will become a slave to something else. When we rebel against God's control, we are controlled by our sinful natures. The only way to escape from this type of slavery is to relinquish control of our lives to God. He is a kind and loving master, and we can trust him with our lives.

5:21–22 A proper reverence for God inspires us to trust God and obey his will for our lives. Disregard for God leaves us grappling with life's difficulties in our own strength, utilizing our own limited resources and understanding. Such a path is a guaranteed formula for failure.

But, alas, the daylight is fading,
and the shadows of evening grow long.
5So arise, let us attack at night
and destroy her fortresses!"

6This is what the LORD Almighty says:

"Cut down the trees
and build siege ramps against Jerusalem.
This city must be punished;
it is filled with oppression.
7As a well pours out its water,
so she pours out her wickedness.
Violence and destruction resound in her;
her sickness and wounds are ever before me.
8Take warning, O Jerusalem,
or I will turn away from you
and make your land desolate
so no one can live in it."

9This is what the LORD Almighty says:

"Let them glean the remnant of Israel
as thoroughly as a vine;
pass your hand over the branches again,
like one gathering grapes."

10To whom can I speak and give warning?
Who will listen to me?
Their ears are closed[a]
so they cannot hear.
The word of the LORD is offensive to them;
they find no pleasure in it.
11But I am full of the wrath of the LORD,
and I cannot hold it in.

"Pour it out on the children in the street
and on the young men gathered together;
both husband and wife will be caught in it,
and the old, those weighed down with years.
12Their houses will be turned over to others,
together with their fields and their wives,
when I stretch out my hand
against those who live in the land,"
declares the LORD.
13"From the least to the greatest,
all are greedy for gain;
prophets and priests alike,
all practice deceit.
14They dress the wound of my people
as though it were not serious.
'Peace, peace,' they say,
when there is no peace.
15Are they ashamed of their loathsome conduct?
No, they have no shame at all;
they do not even know how to blush.
So they will fall among the fallen;
they will be brought down when I punish them,"
says the LORD.

16This is what the LORD says:

"Stand at the crossroads and look;
ask for the ancient paths,
ask where the good way is, and walk in it,
and you will find rest for your souls.
But you said, 'We will not walk in it.'
17I appointed watchmen over you and said,
'Listen to the sound of the trumpet!'
But you said, 'We will not listen.'
18Therefore hear, O nations;
observe, O witnesses,
what will happen to them.
19Hear, O earth:
I am bringing disaster on this people,
the fruit of their schemes,
because they have not listened to my words
and have rejected my law.
20What do I care about incense from Sheba
or sweet calamus from a distant land?
Your burnt offerings are not acceptable;
your sacrifices do not please me."

21Therefore this is what the LORD says:

"I will put obstacles before this people.
Fathers and sons alike will stumble over them;
neighbors and friends will perish."

22This is what the LORD says:

"Look, an army is coming
from the land of the north;
a great nation is being stirred up
from the ends of the earth.
23They are armed with bow and spear;
they are cruel and show no mercy.
They sound like the roaring sea
as they ride on their horses;
they come like men in battle formation
to attack you, O Daughter of Zion."

24We have heard reports about them,
and our hands hang limp.
Anguish has gripped us,
pain like that of a woman in labor.
25Do not go out to the fields
or walk on the roads,
for the enemy has a sword,
and there is terror on every side.
26O my people, put on sackcloth
and roll in ashes;
mourn with bitter wailing

[a]10 Hebrew *uncircumcised*

6:16 God promises rest for our souls if we are willing to do things his way; rejecting God's laws will only drain our resources, leaving us exhausted and distant from God. The road back to God is always the right road to travel. Traveling the road back to God lets our souls experience the peace and rest available only for those who surrender their lives to him.

6:26 The grief felt over the loss of an only son is too painful to imagine. Yet our misguided lives should cause us just as much grief and sorrow as the death of a loved one. These words of warning remind us that we have opportunities each day to make good choices that will lead us away from the destructive consequences of sin.

as for an only son,
for suddenly the destroyer
will come upon us.

27"I have made you a tester of metals
and my people the ore,
that you may observe
and test their ways.
28They are all hardened rebels,
going about to slander.
They are bronze and iron;
they all act corruptly.
29The bellows blow fiercely
to burn away the lead with fire,
but the refining goes on in vain;
the wicked are not purged out.
30They are called rejected silver,
because the LORD has rejected them."

False Religion Worthless

7 This is the word that came to Jeremiah
from the LORD: 2"Stand at the gate of the
LORD's house and there proclaim this message:
" 'Hear the word of the LORD, all you people
of Judah who come through these gates to worship the LORD. 3This is what the LORD Almighty,
the God of Israel, says: Reform your ways and
your actions, and I will let you live in this place.
4Do not trust in deceptive words and say, "This
is the temple of the LORD, the temple of the
LORD, the temple of the LORD!" 5If you really
change your ways and your actions and deal
with each other justly, 6if you do not oppress
the alien, the fatherless or the widow and do
not shed innocent blood in this place, and if
you do not follow other gods to your own
harm, 7then I will let you live in this place, in
the land I gave your forefathers for ever and
ever. 8But look, you are trusting in deceptive
words that are worthless.
9" 'Will you steal and murder, commit adultery and perjury,[a] burn incense to Baal and
follow other gods you have not known, 10and
then come and stand before me in this house,
which bears my Name, and say, "We are safe"—
safe to do all these detestable things? 11Has this
house, which bears my Name, become a den of
robbers to you? But I have been watching! declares the LORD.
12" 'Go now to the place in Shiloh where I
first made a dwelling for my Name, and see
what I did to it because of the wickedness of my
people Israel. 13While you were doing all these
things, declares the LORD, I spoke to you again
and again, but you did not listen; I called you,
but you did not answer. 14Therefore, what I did
to Shiloh I will now do to the house that bears
my Name, the temple you trust in, the place I
gave to you and your fathers. 15I will thrust you
from my presence, just as I did all your brothers,
the people of Ephraim.'
16"So do not pray for this people nor offer
any plea or petition for them; do not plead with
me, for I will not listen to you. 17Do you not see
what they are doing in the towns of Judah and
in the streets of Jerusalem? 18The children gather wood, the fathers light the fire, and the wom-
en knead the dough and make cakes of bread
for the Queen of Heaven. They pour out drink
offerings to other gods to provoke me to anger.
19But am I the one they are provoking? declares
the LORD. Are they not rather harming themselves, to their own shame?
20" 'Therefore this is what the Sovereign
LORD says: My anger and my wrath will be
poured out on this place, on man and beast, on
the trees of the field and on the fruit of the
ground, and it will burn and not be quenched.
21" 'This is what the LORD Almighty, the God
of Israel, says: Go ahead, add your burnt offerings to your other sacrifices and eat the meat
yourselves! 22For when I brought your forefathers out of Egypt and spoke to them, I did not
just give them commands about burnt offerings
and sacrifices, 23but I gave them this command:
Obey me, and I will be your God and you will
be my people. Walk in all the ways I command
you, that it may go well with you. 24But they did
not listen or pay attention; instead, they followed the stubborn inclinations of their evil
hearts. They went backward and not forward.
25From the time your forefathers left Egypt until
now, day after day, again and again I sent you
my servants the prophets. 26But they did not
listen to me or pay attention. They were stiff-
necked and did more evil than their forefathers.'
27"When you tell them all this, they will not
listen to you; when you call to them, they will
not answer. 28Therefore say to them, 'This is the
nation that has not obeyed the LORD its God or
responded to correction. Truth has perished; it
has vanished from their lips. 29Cut off your hair
and throw it away; take up a lament on the
barren heights, for the LORD has rejected and
abandoned this generation that is under his
wrath.

The Valley of Slaughter

30" 'The people of Judah have done evil in

[a]9 Or *and swear by false gods*

7:8–11 Many of God's chosen people believed that God's presence in the temple would protect them from enemy attack, regardless of whether or not they obeyed God's laws. This assumption was incorrect. The people of Judah were not excused from obedience; neither are we.

7:12 By examining the lives of our ancestors, we can see the blessings experienced by those who obeyed God and the terrible consequences suffered by those who rebelled against him. Greed, denial and the pursuit of pleasure have destroyed the lives of thousands of our ancestors. If we willingly act upon our findings, we can make changes in our lives and avoid their terrible fate.

7:30–34 Judah had sunk into the depths of depravity. The people practiced the sacrifice of children, a heinous act that God had clearly forbidden. How could God's people have grown so distant from God's plan for them? How

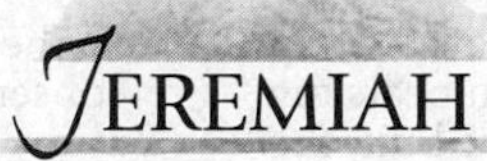

JEREMIAH

Jeremiah was born into a priestly clan and was called to the prophetic ministry when he was just a youth. Even though he was young, Jeremiah was humble and eager to serve God. Jeremiah's ministry stretched from the thirteenth year of King Josiah's reign (626 B.C.) until after the destruction of Jerusalem (585 B.C.).

Josiah's reign was the last high point in Judah's spiritual history, and Jeremiah was an ally in the king's reforms. After Josiah's death, Judah quickly declined spiritually, causing great sorrow to Jeremiah. During those years, Jeremiah preached against the hypocrisy and corruption of prophets, priests and government officials alike. He also prophesied that the nation faced sure destruction as a consequence of her sins—a message that few believed. The people preferred to believe the false prophets who predicted a rosy future for Judah.

During his years of ministry, Jeremiah suffered intense persecution. He was thrown into a dungeon, beaten, put in stocks, threatened and almost killed. Tradition holds that Jeremiah was ultimately stoned to death. As a man of prayer and deep spirituality, Jeremiah faced his trials with courage. Despite the opposition he faced, Jeremiah remained true to the messages God had given to him. He confronted God's people with their rebellion and called them to confess their sins and turn from them, accept responsibility for their actions and ask God for forgiveness. As God directed him, Jeremiah also spoke words of comfort to a people facing disaster.

Because Jeremiah openly expressed his grief over the sinfulness of his people, he is known as the weeping prophet. He also shed many tears for the destructive consequences he knew his people would face. After Jerusalem was destroyed and the people were exiled, Jeremiah wrote the book of Lamentations to express his sorrow about the suffering of his nation. There were times when Jeremiah openly and honestly complained to God about the work that God had given him to do. Yet even in the midst of his despair, Jeremiah never lost faith in God's power to judge righteously, to reward liberally and to restore his broken and sinful people.

STRENGTHS AND ACCOMPLISHMENTS:

Jeremiah was faithful to God's call despite the persecution that he suffered.

He showed great compassion for his people even though they mistreated him.

He was open and honest with God regarding his feelings.

He fearlessly confronted God's people about their sins.

LESSONS FROM HIS LIFE:

Sin is always accompanied by painful consequences.

No matter how great our sin, God still loves us and desires our redemption.

God is not shocked when we openly share our feelings with him, releasing our grief, anger and disappointment.

True spiritual renewal is evidenced by our faithfulness to God's plan for our lives.

KEY VERSES:

"' *Today I have made you a fortified city, an iron pillar and a bronze wall to stand against the whole land—against the kings of Judah, its officials, its priests and the people of the land. They will fight against you but will not overcome you, for I am with you and will rescue you,' declares the LORD*" (1:18–19).

Jeremiah's story is told primarily in the book of Jeremiah. He is also mentioned in 2 Chronicles 35:25; 36; Ezra 1:1; Daniel 9:2; Matthew 2:17; 16:14 and 27:9.

my eyes, declares the LORD. They have set up
their detestable idols in the house that bears my
Name and have defiled it. 31They have built the
high places of Topheth in the Valley of Ben
Hinnom to burn their sons and daughters in the
fire—something I did not command, nor did it
enter my mind. 32So beware, the days are coming, declares the LORD, when people will no
longer call it Topheth or the Valley of Ben Hinnom, but the Valley of Slaughter, for they will
bury the dead in Topheth until there is no more
room. 33Then the carcasses of this people will
become food for the birds of the air and the
beasts of the earth, and there will be no one to
frighten them away. 34I will bring an end to the
sounds of joy and gladness and to the voices of
bride and bridegroom in the towns of Judah
and the streets of Jerusalem, for the land will
become desolate.

8 " 'At that time, declares the LORD, the
bones of the kings and officials of Judah,
the bones of the priests and prophets, and the
bones of the people of Jerusalem will be removed from their graves. 2They will be exposed
to the sun and the moon and all the stars of the
heavens, which they have loved and served and
which they have followed and consulted and
worshiped. They will not be gathered up or buried, but will be like refuse lying on the ground.
3Wherever I banish them, all the survivors of
this evil nation will prefer death to life, declares
the LORD Almighty.'

Sin and Punishment

4"Say to them, 'This is what the LORD says:

" 'When men fall down, do they not get
 up?
When a man turns away, does he not
 return?
5Why then have these people turned away?
 Why does Jerusalem always turn away?
They cling to deceit;
 they refuse to return.
6I have listened attentively,
 but they do not say what is right.
No one repents of his wickedness,
 saying, "What have I done?"
Each pursues his own course
 like a horse charging into battle.
7Even the stork in the sky
 knows her appointed seasons,
and the dove, the swift and the thrush
 observe the time of their migration.
But my people do not know
 the requirements of the LORD.

8" 'How can you say, "We are wise,
 for we have the law of the LORD,"
when actually the lying pen of the scribes
 has handled it falsely?
9The wise will be put to shame;
 they will be dismayed and trapped.
Since they have rejected the word of the
 LORD,
 what kind of wisdom do they have?
10Therefore I will give their wives to other
 men
 and their fields to new owners.
From the least to the greatest,
 all are greedy for gain;
prophets and priests alike,
 all practice deceit.
11They dress the wound of my people
 as though it were not serious.
"Peace, peace," they say,
 when there is no peace.
12Are they ashamed of their loathsome
 conduct?
No, they have no shame at all;
 they do not even know how to blush.
So they will fall among the fallen;
 they will be brought down when they
 are punished,
 says the LORD.

13" 'I will take away their harvest,
 declares the LORD.
There will be no grapes on the vine.
There will be no figs on the tree,
 and their leaves will wither.
What I have given them
 will be taken from them.[a]' "

14"Why are we sitting here?
 Gather together!
Let us flee to the fortified cities
 and perish there!
For the LORD our God has doomed us to
 perish
 and given us poisoned water to drink,
 because we have sinned against him.
15We hoped for peace

[a]13 The meaning of the Hebrew for this sentence is uncertain.

---

are we lured so far from God's plan for us? One sin casually leads to another. As we continue to sin, we become blind to our wrongs, and they grow ever greater. When we honestly examine our lives, asking God to reveal the truth, we can see our sin and ask God to forgive us and change us, rooting out our problems before they lead us to greater ones.

8:4—10:22 This passage is filled with predictions of God's judgment. God's people no longer spoke the truth. There seemed to be nothing good left to salvage in the land of Judah, so the people would soon suffer terrible punishment. We may reach a point in life at which God allows the consequences of our sins to catch up to us too. Instead of waiting until we reach this low point, we should turn from our sins now and seek God's forgiveness.

8:7 When we refuse to accept God's direction for living and foolishly seek to find truth and meaning apart from him, we are headed for trouble. Even the animals know that God's way is best. We would be wise to follow their lead.

8:14–15 No matter how hard we struggle in our pursuits, health and peace can only be found where God says they will be found. Spiritual renewal can begin only if we seek God and surrender to him, following his intended plan for us.

but no good has come,
for a time of healing
but there was only terror.
16The snorting of the enemy's horses
is heard from Dan;
at the neighing of their stallions
the whole land trembles.
They have come to devour
the land and everything in it,
the city and all who live there."

17"See, I will send venomous snakes among you,
vipers that cannot be charmed,
and they will bite you,"
declares the LORD.

18O my Comforter[a] in sorrow,
my heart is faint within me.
19Listen to the cry of my people
from a land far away:
"Is the LORD not in Zion?
Is her King no longer there?"

"Why have they provoked me to anger
with their images,
with their worthless foreign idols?"

20"The harvest is past,
the summer has ended,
and we are not saved."

21Since my people are crushed, I am crushed;
I mourn, and horror grips me.
22Is there no balm in Gilead?
Is there no physician there?
Why then is there no healing
for the wound of my people?

9 1Oh, that my head were a spring of water
and my eyes a fountain of tears!
I would weep day and night
for the slain of my people.
2Oh, that I had in the desert
a lodging place for travelers,
so that I might leave my people
and go away from them;
for they are all adulterers,
a crowd of unfaithful people.

3"They make ready their tongue
like a bow, to shoot lies;
it is not by truth
that they triumph[b] in the land.
They go from one sin to another;
they do not acknowledge me,"
declares the LORD.
4"Beware of your friends;
do not trust your brothers.
For every brother is a deceiver,[c]
and every friend a slanderer.
5Friend deceives friend,
and no one speaks the truth.
They have taught their tongues to lie;
they weary themselves with sinning.
6You[d] live in the midst of deception;
in their deceit they refuse to
acknowledge me,"
declares the LORD.

7Therefore this is what the LORD Almighty says:

"See, I will refine and test them,
for what else can I do
because of the sin of my people?
8Their tongue is a deadly arrow;
it speaks with deceit.
With his mouth each speaks cordially to his neighbor,
but in his heart he sets a trap for him.
9Should I not punish them for this?"
declares the LORD.
"Should I not avenge myself
on such a nation as this?"

10I will weep and wail for the mountains
and take up a lament concerning the desert pastures.
They are desolate and untraveled,
and the lowing of cattle is not heard.
The birds of the air have fled
and the animals are gone.

11"I will make Jerusalem a heap of ruins,
a haunt of jackals;
and I will lay waste the towns of Judah
so no one can live there."

12What man is wise enough to understand
this? Who has been instructed by the LORD and
can explain it? Why has the land been ruined
and laid waste like a desert that no one can
cross?
13The LORD said, "It is because they have
forsaken my law, which I set before them; they

[a]18 The meaning of the Hebrew for this word is uncertain. [b]3 Or *lies; / they are not valiant for truth* [c]4 Or *a deceiving Jacob* [d]6 That is, Jeremiah (the Hebrew is singular)

8:18–19 The people of Judah had disobediently strayed from God and then complained that God had deserted them. We often do the same thing. If we are no longer walking side by side with God, who moved? God promises never to leave us. Any sense of desertion we feel must be caused by our own disobedience. Restoration can only come as we ask God to take control of our lives and transform us. God is eager to help those who humbly turn to him in repentance.

9:4–6 Jeremiah warned his people about the power of others to lead them astray. We also need to remain obedient to the truth and steadfast in our relationship with God so that we can overcome the temptation of sin around us.

9:7–8 The people of Judah had ignored God's warnings and continued to disobey his will for them. God now had to bring punishment upon them. Notice, however, that their punishment was designed to better them. God would "refine and test them" (9:7), melting them down through their exile and reshaping them into a nation that he could use for his glory. In much the same way, God uses the trials in our lives to refine and test us. We often try to escape such testing, but God wants our trials to remind us of how much we need him.

have not obeyed me or followed my law. [14]In-
stead, they have followed the stubbornness of
their hearts; they have followed the Baals, as
their fathers taught them." [15]Therefore, this is
what the LORD Almighty, the God of Israel, says:
"See, I will make this people eat bitter food and
drink poisoned water. [16]I will scatter them
among nations that neither they nor their fathers have known, and I will pursue them with
the sword until I have destroyed them."

[17]This is what the LORD Almighty says:

"Consider now! Call for the wailing
women to come;
send for the most skillful of them.
[18]Let them come quickly
and wail over us
till our eyes overflow with tears
and water streams from our eyelids.
[19]The sound of wailing is heard from Zion:
'How ruined we are!
How great is our shame!
We must leave our land
because our houses are in ruins.' "
[20]Now, O women, hear the word of the
LORD;
open your ears to the words of his
mouth.
Teach your daughters how to wail;
teach one another a lament.
[21]Death has climbed in through our windows
and has entered our fortresses;
it has cut off the children from the streets
and the young men from the public
squares.

[22]Say, "This is what the LORD declares:

" 'The dead bodies of men will lie
like refuse on the open field,
like cut grain behind the reaper,
with no one to gather them.' "

[23]This is what the LORD says:

"Let not the wise man boast of his wisdom
or the strong man boast of his strength
or the rich man boast of his riches,
[24]but let him who boasts boast about this:
that he understands and knows me,
that I am the LORD, who exercises kindness,
justice and righteousness on earth,
for in these I delight,"
declares the LORD.

[25]"The days are coming," declares the LORD,
"when I will punish all who are circumcised
only in the flesh— [26]Egypt, Judah, Edom, Ammon, Moab and all who live in the desert in
distant places.[a] For all these nations are really
uncircumcised, and even the whole house of
Israel is uncircumcised in heart."

God and Idols

10 Hear what the LORD says to you,
O house of Israel. [2]This is what the
LORD says:

"Do not learn the ways of the nations
or be terrified by signs in the sky,
though the nations are terrified by them.
[3]For the customs of the peoples are
worthless;
they cut a tree out of the forest,
and a craftsman shapes it with his chisel.
[4]They adorn it with silver and gold;
they fasten it with hammer and nails
so it will not totter.
[5]Like a scarecrow in a melon patch,
their idols cannot speak;
they must be carried
because they cannot walk.
Do not fear them;
they can do no harm
nor can they do any good."

[6]No one is like you, O LORD;
you are great,
and your name is mighty in power.
[7]Who should not revere you,
O King of the nations?
This is your due.
Among all the wise men of the nations
and in all their kingdoms,
there is no one like you.
[8]They are all senseless and foolish;
they are taught by worthless wooden
idols.
[9]Hammered silver is brought from Tarshish
and gold from Uphaz.
What the craftsman and goldsmith have
made
is then dressed in blue and purple—
all made by skilled workers.
[10]But the LORD is the true God;
he is the living God, the eternal King.
When he is angry, the earth trembles;
the nations cannot endure his wrath.

[11]"Tell them this: 'These gods, who did not
make the heavens and the earth, will perish
from the earth and from under the heavens.' "[b]

[12]But God made the earth by his power;
he founded the world by his wisdom
and stretched out the heavens by his
understanding.
[13]When he thunders, the waters in the
heavens roar;
he makes clouds rise from the ends of
the earth.
He sends lightning with the rain

[a]26 Or *desert and who clip the hair by their foreheads*
[b]11 The text of this verse is in Aramaic.

10:2–3 Using a horoscope or relying on astrology is a way of seeking for truth apart from God. It is a bad substitute for a personal relationship with him. Instead of looking at the stars to find God's will for our lives, we should look to the Creator of the stars and listen to his words to us.

and brings out the wind from his
storehouses.
14Everyone is senseless and without
knowledge;
every goldsmith is shamed by his idols.
His images are a fraud;
they have no breath in them.
15They are worthless, the objects of mockery;
when their judgment comes, they will
perish.
16He who is the Portion of Jacob is not like
these,
for he is the Maker of all things,
including Israel, the tribe of his
inheritance—
the LORD Almighty is his name.

Coming Destruction

17Gather up your belongings to leave the
land,
you who live under siege.
18For this is what the LORD says:
"At this time I will hurl out
those who live in this land;
I will bring distress on them
so that they may be captured."

19Woe to me because of my injury!
My wound is incurable!
Yet I said to myself,
"This is my sickness, and I must endure
it."
20My tent is destroyed;
all its ropes are snapped.
My sons are gone from me and are no
more;
no one is left now to pitch my tent
or to set up my shelter.
21The shepherds are senseless
and do not inquire of the LORD;
so they do not prosper
and all their flock is scattered.
22Listen! The report is coming—
a great commotion from the land of the
north!
It will make the towns of Judah desolate,
a haunt of jackals.

Jeremiah's Prayer

23I know, O LORD, that a man's life is not his
own;
it is not for man to direct his steps.
24Correct me, LORD, but only with justice—
not in your anger,
lest you reduce me to nothing.
25Pour out your wrath on the nations
that do not acknowledge you,
on the peoples who do not call on your
name.
For they have devoured Jacob;
they have devoured him completely
and destroyed his homeland.

The Covenant Is Broken

11 This is the word that came to Jeremiah
from the LORD: 2"Listen to the terms of
this covenant and tell them to the people of
Judah and to those who live in Jerusalem. 3Tell
them that this is what the LORD, the God of
Israel, says: 'Cursed is the man who does not
obey the terms of this covenant— 4the terms I
commanded your forefathers when I brought
them out of Egypt, out of the iron-smelting
furnace.' I said, 'Obey me and do everything I
command you, and you will be my people, and
I will be your God. 5Then I will fulfill the oath
I swore to your forefathers, to give them a land
flowing with milk and honey'—the land you
possess today."

I answered, "Amen, LORD."

6The LORD said to me, "Proclaim all these
words in the towns of Judah and in the streets
of Jerusalem: 'Listen to the terms of this covenant and follow them. 7From the time I
brought your forefathers up from Egypt until
today, I warned them again and again, saying,
"Obey me." 8But they did not listen or pay attention; instead, they followed the stubbornness of
their evil hearts. So I brought on them all the
curses of the covenant I had commanded them
to follow but that they did not keep.' "

9Then the LORD said to me, "There is a conspiracy among the people of Judah and those
who live in Jerusalem. 10They have returned to
the sins of their forefathers, who refused to listen to my words. They have followed other gods
to serve them. Both the house of Israel and the
house of Judah have broken the covenant I
made with their forefathers. 11Therefore this is
what the LORD says: 'I will bring on them a
disaster they cannot escape. Although they cry
out to me, I will not listen to them. 12The towns
of Judah and the people of Jerusalem will go
and cry out to the gods to whom they burn
incense, but they will not help them at all when
disaster strikes. 13You have as many gods as you

10:23–25 The prophet acknowledged his inability to map out his life and recognized his lack of power. This acknowledgment is the first step toward spiritual renewal. Sadly, the people of Judah didn't share Jeremiah's sentiments. Punishment was God's only recourse for their refusal to obey him.

11:1–17 God revealed to his people the terms for their restoration: He asked for their obedience. We can see from this passage that God already knew that his people would refuse to repent. They had enjoyed their ancestors' sins and preferred their idols to the true God. We may consider God's price of obedience too high to give up the pleasures of our sin. Yet if this is our attitude, we will ultimately reap a harvest of suffering. Keeping a long-term perspective helps us to choose God's way.

11:5 God is waiting to do wonderful things for those who simply trust and obey him. When we reject God's plan, we reap the consequences of our rebellion and sin. Turning away from God will always end in disappointment. But God promises that wonderful blessings will be ours if we decide to obey him.

have towns, O Judah; and the altars you have
set up to burn incense to that shameful god Baal
are as many as the streets of Jerusalem.'
14"Do not pray for this people nor offer any
plea or petition for them, because I will not
listen when they call to me in the time of their
distress.

15"What is my beloved doing in my temple
as she works out her evil schemes with many?
Can consecrated meat avert ⌊your punishment⌋?
When you engage in your wickedness,
then you rejoice.[a]"
16The LORD called you a thriving olive tree
with fruit beautiful in form.
But with the roar of a mighty storm
he will set it on fire,
and its branches will be broken.

17The LORD Almighty, who planted you, has decreed disaster for you, because the house of Israel and the house of Judah have done evil and
provoked me to anger by burning incense to
Baal.

Plot Against Jeremiah

18Because the LORD revealed their plot to me,
I knew it, for at that time he showed me what
they were doing. 19I had been like a gentle lamb
led to the slaughter; I did not realize that they
had plotted against me, saying,

"Let us destroy the tree and its fruit;
let us cut him off from the land of the living,
that his name be remembered no more."
20But, O LORD Almighty, you who judge righteously
and test the heart and mind,
let me see your vengeance upon them,
for to you I have committed my cause.

21"Therefore this is what the LORD says about
the men of Anathoth who are seeking your life
and saying, 'Do not prophesy in the name of
the LORD or you will die by our hands'— 22there-
fore this is what the LORD Almighty says: 'I will
punish them. Their young men will die by the
sword, their sons and daughters by famine.
23Not even a remnant will be left to them, because I will bring disaster on the men of Anathoth in the year of their punishment.' "

Jeremiah's Complaint

12 You are always righteous, O LORD,
when I bring a case before you.
Yet I would speak with you about your justice:
Why does the way of the wicked prosper?
Why do all the faithless live at ease?
2You have planted them, and they have taken root;
they grow and bear fruit.
You are always on their lips
but far from their hearts.
3Yet you know me, O LORD;
you see me and test my thoughts about you.
Drag them off like sheep to be butchered!
Set them apart for the day of slaughter!
4How long will the land lie parched[b]
and the grass in every field be withered?
Because those who live in it are wicked,
the animals and birds have perished.
Moreover, the people are saying,
"He will not see what happens to us."

God's Answer

5"If you have raced with men on foot
and they have worn you out,
how can you compete with horses?
If you stumble in safe country,[c]
how will you manage in the thickets by[d] the Jordan?
6Your brothers, your own family—
even they have betrayed you;
they have raised a loud cry against you.
Do not trust them,
though they speak well of you.

7"I will forsake my house,
abandon my inheritance;
I will give the one I love
into the hands of her enemies.
8My inheritance has become to me
like a lion in the forest.
She roars at me;
therefore I hate her.
9Has not my inheritance become to me
like a speckled bird of prey
that other birds of prey surround and attack?
Go and gather all the wild beasts;
bring them to devour.
10Many shepherds will ruin my vineyard
and trample down my field;
they will turn my pleasant field
into a desolate wasteland.
11It will be made a wasteland,
parched and desolate before me;
the whole land will be laid waste

[a]15 Or *Could consecrated meat avert your punishment? / Then you would rejoice* [b]4 Or *land mourn* [c]5 Or *If you put your trust in a land of safety* [d]5 Or *the flooding of*

12:1–17 Jeremiah struggled deeply with his calling. He lived in the midst of Judah's sin; he could see the godless lifestyle of the people; he knew God's concern about their sin. And Jeremiah asked the question we often ask, *Why do the wicked prosper?* God responded to his query by revealing that the wicked never prosper for long. We should not allow ourselves to be bothered by their apparent success. If we do, we are the ones who will stumble (see Psalm 37:1; 73:2–3). As difficult as it is to be patient, God's truth and righteousness do prevail—always.

because there is no one who cares.
12Over all the barren heights in the desert
destroyers will swarm,
for the sword of the LORD will devour
from one end of the land to the other;
no one will be safe.
13They will sow wheat but reap thorns;
they will wear themselves out but gain
nothing.
So bear the shame of your harvest
because of the LORD's fierce anger."

14This is what the LORD says: "As for all my
wicked neighbors who seize the inheritance I
gave my people Israel, I will uproot them from
their lands and I will uproot the house of Judah
from among them. 15But after I uproot them, I
will again have compassion and will bring each
of them back to his own inheritance and his
own country. 16And if they learn well the ways
of my people and swear by my name, saying,
'As surely as the LORD lives'—even as they once
taught my people to swear by Baal—then they
will be established among my people. 17But if
any nation does not listen, I will completely
uproot and destroy it," declares the LORD.

A Linen Belt

13 This is what the LORD said to me: "Go
and buy a linen belt and put it around
your waist, but do not let it touch water." 2So I
bought a belt, as the LORD directed, and put it
around my waist.

3Then the word of the LORD came to me a
second time: 4"Take the belt you bought and
are wearing around your waist, and go now to
Perath[a] and hide it there in a crevice in the
rocks." 5So I went and hid it at Perath, as the
LORD told me.

6Many days later the LORD said to me, "Go
now to Perath and get the belt I told you to hide
there." 7So I went to Perath and dug up the belt
and took it from the place where I had hidden
it, but now it was ruined and completely useless.

8Then the word of the LORD came to me:
9"This is what the LORD says: 'In the same way
I will ruin the pride of Judah and the great pride
of Jerusalem. 10These wicked people, who refuse to listen to my words, who follow the stubbornness of their hearts and go after other gods
to serve and worship them, will be like this
belt—completely useless! 11For as a belt is
bound around a man's waist, so I bound the
whole house of Israel and the whole house of
Judah to me,' declares the LORD, 'to be my people for my renown and praise and honor. But
they have not listened.'

Wineskins

12"Say to them: 'This is what the LORD, the
God of Israel, says: Every wineskin should be
filled with wine.' And if they say to you, 'Don't
we know that every wineskin should be filled
with wine?' 13then tell them, 'This is what the
LORD says: I am going to fill with drunkenness
all who live in this land, including the kings
who sit on David's throne, the priests, the
prophets and all those living in Jerusalem. 14I
will smash them one against the other, fathers
and sons alike, declares the LORD. I will allow
no pity or mercy or compassion to keep me
from destroying them.' "

Threat of Captivity

15Hear and pay attention,
do not be arrogant,
for the LORD has spoken.
16Give glory to the LORD your God
before he brings the darkness,
before your feet stumble
on the darkening hills.
You hope for light,
but he will turn it to thick darkness
and change it to deep gloom.
17But if you do not listen,
I will weep in secret
because of your pride;
my eyes will weep bitterly,
overflowing with tears,
because the LORD's flock will be taken
captive.

18Say to the king and to the queen mother,
"Come down from your thrones,
for your glorious crowns
will fall from your heads."
19The cities in the Negev will be shut up,
and there will be no one to open them.
All Judah will be carried into exile,
carried completely away.

20Lift up your eyes and see
those who are coming from the north.
Where is the flock that was entrusted to
you,

[a] 4 Or possibly *the Euphrates;* also in verses 5-7

12:13 Our sinful actions often result in shame, but God can turn our shameful experiences into meaningful lessons if we are willing to surrender to him. We must take our failure and shame to God and ask him to forgive us and change our hearts. Then, with renewed humility and faith, we can make significant progress in our spiritual growth.

13:1–11 God used an object lesson to prepare Jeremiah for the devastation that was coming. In this illustration God compared himself to Jeremiah and compared his people to Jeremiah's new linen belt. Jeremiah was told to bury the belt and, after a period of time, dig it up again. When Jeremiah retrieved the belt, it was rotten. This illustrated how the people of Judah had become spiritually rotten by following their own way in life. Following our selfish inclinations always leads to painful consequences, while following God's will leads to health and spiritual renewal.

13:15 Pride is one of the greatest barriers to our spiritual growth. When we finally turn over our pride to God, we become compliant to his will for us and experience true spiritual renewal.

the sheep of which you boasted?
21What will you say when ⌊the LORD⌋ sets
over you
those you cultivated as your special
allies?
Will not pain grip you
like that of a woman in labor?
22And if you ask yourself,
"Why has this happened to me?"—
it is because of your many sins
that your skirts have been torn off
and your body mistreated.
23Can the Ethiopian[a] change his skin
or the leopard its spots?
Neither can you do good
who are accustomed to doing evil.

24"I will scatter you like chaff
driven by the desert wind.
25This is your lot,
the portion I have decreed for you,"
declares the LORD,
"because you have forgotten me
and trusted in false gods.
26I will pull up your skirts over your face
that your shame may be seen—
27your adulteries and lustful neighings,
your shameless prostitution!
I have seen your detestable acts
on the hills and in the fields.
Woe to you, O Jerusalem!
How long will you be unclean?"

Drought, Famine, Sword

14 This is the word of the LORD to Jeremiah concerning the drought:

2"Judah mourns,
her cities languish;
they wail for the land,
and a cry goes up from Jerusalem.
3The nobles send their servants for water;
they go to the cisterns
but find no water.
They return with their jars unfilled;
dismayed and despairing,
they cover their heads.
4The ground is cracked
because there is no rain in the land;
the farmers are dismayed
and cover their heads.
5Even the doe in the field
deserts her newborn fawn
because there is no grass.
6Wild donkeys stand on the barren heights
and pant like jackals;
their eyesight fails
for lack of pasture."

7Although our sins testify against us,
O LORD, do something for the sake of
your name.
For our backsliding is great;
we have sinned against you.
8O Hope of Israel,
its Savior in times of distress,
why are you like a stranger in the land,
like a traveler who stays only a night?
9Why are you like a man taken by surprise,
like a warrior powerless to save?
You are among us, O LORD,
and we bear your name;
do not forsake us!

10This is what the LORD says about this people:

"They greatly love to wander;
they do not restrain their feet.
So the LORD does not accept them;
he will now remember their wickedness
and punish them for their sins."

11Then the LORD said to me, "Do not pray for
the well-being of this people. 12Although they
fast, I will not listen to their cry; though they
offer burnt offerings and grain offerings, I will
not accept them. Instead, I will destroy them
with the sword, famine and plague."
13But I said, "Ah, Sovereign LORD, the prophets keep telling them, 'You will not see the
sword or suffer famine. Indeed, I will give you
lasting peace in this place.' "
14Then the LORD said to me, "The prophets
are prophesying lies in my name. I have not
sent them or appointed them or spoken to
them. They are prophesying to you false visions,
divinations, idolatries[b] and the delusions of
their own minds. 15Therefore, this is what the
LORD says about the prophets who are prophesying in my name: I did not send them, yet they
are saying, 'No sword or famine will touch this
land.' Those same prophets will perish by sword
and famine. 16And the people they are prophesying to will be thrown out into the streets of

[a]23 Hebrew *Cushite* (probably a person from the upper Nile region) [b]14 Or *visions, worthless divinations*

13:23 We often try to change our own lives by making resolutions to do what we know to be right. But change doesn't happen overnight, and we don't have the power to make these changes alone. If we set out to change in our own power, we will be sure to fail. We must admit that we are unable to change without God's help in order to begin the process of allowing God to transform our hearts and lives from the inside out. If we are willing to cooperate, God can and will make permanent changes in our lives.
14:1–10 As the people of Judah faced a period of drought, they turned to God in desperation. How quickly we turn to God when something goes wrong in our lives! Where yesterday's happiness found us only vaguely aware of God's power and grace, today's pain finds us begging for his mercy. We would be wiser to remain close to God even when things are going well for us.
14:13 We often refuse to see the truth of a difficult situation, somehow hoping that God will protect us from it. But sin leads to painful consequences. The sooner we accept that fact, the sooner we will seek God and surrender to him. God may allow us to experience the consequences of our sin in order to wake us up and lead us back to himself.

Jerusalem because of the famine and sword. There will be no one to bury them or their wives, their sons or their daughters. I will pour out on them the calamity they deserve.

17"Speak this word to them:

" 'Let my eyes overflow with tears
night and day without ceasing;
for my virgin daughter—my people—
has suffered a grievous wound,
a crushing blow.
18If I go into the country,
I see those slain by the sword;
if I go into the city,
I see the ravages of famine.
Both prophet and priest
have gone to a land they know not.' "

19Have you rejected Judah completely?
Do you despise Zion?
Why have you afflicted us
so that we cannot be healed?
We hoped for peace
but no good has come,
for a time of healing
but there is only terror.
20O LORD, we acknowledge our wickedness
and the guilt of our fathers;
we have indeed sinned against you.
21For the sake of your name do not despise us;
do not dishonor your glorious throne.
Remember your covenant with us
and do not break it.
22Do any of the worthless idols of the nations bring rain?
Do the skies themselves send down showers?
No, it is you, O LORD our God.
Therefore our hope is in you,
for you are the one who does all this.

15 Then the LORD said to me: "Even if Moses and Samuel were to stand before
me, my heart would not go out to this people.
Send them away from my presence! Let them
go! 2And if they ask you, 'Where shall we go?'
tell them, 'This is what the LORD says:

" 'Those destined for death, to death;
those for the sword, to the sword;
those for starvation, to starvation;
those for captivity, to captivity.'

3"I will send four kinds of destroyers against
them," declares the LORD, "the sword to kill and
the dogs to drag away and the birds of the air
and the beasts of the earth to devour and destroy. 4I will make them abhorrent to all the
kingdoms of the earth because of what Manasseh son of Hezekiah king of Judah did in Jerusalem.

5"Who will have pity on you, O Jerusalem?
Who will mourn for you?
Who will stop to ask how you are?
6You have rejected me," declares the LORD.
"You keep on backsliding.
So I will lay hands on you and destroy you;
I can no longer show compassion.
7I will winnow them with a winnowing fork
at the city gates of the land.
I will bring bereavement and destruction on my people,
for they have not changed their ways.
8I will make their widows more numerous
than the sand of the sea.
At midday I will bring a destroyer
against the mothers of their young men;
suddenly I will bring down on them
anguish and terror.
9The mother of seven will grow faint
and breathe her last.
Her sun will set while it is still day;
she will be disgraced and humiliated.
I will put the survivors to the sword
before their enemies,"
declares the LORD.

10Alas, my mother, that you gave me birth,
a man with whom the whole land strives and contends!
I have neither lent nor borrowed,
yet everyone curses me.

11The LORD said,

"Surely I will deliver you for a good purpose;
surely I will make your enemies plead with you
in times of disaster and times of distress.
12"Can a man break iron—
iron from the north—or bronze?
13Your wealth and your treasures
I will give as plunder, without charge,
because of all your sins
throughout your country.
14I will enslave you to your enemies
in[a] a land you do not know,
for my anger will kindle a fire
that will burn against you."

15You understand, O LORD;
remember me and care for me.
Avenge me on my persecutors.

[a]14 Some Hebrew manuscripts, Septuagint and Syriac (see also Jer. 17:4); most Hebrew manuscripts *I will cause your enemies to bring you / into*

15:3–9 God blamed King Manasseh as the person primarily responsible for Judah's great suffering. Manasseh had died several generations before the ministry of Jeremiah began, yet his sinful lifestyle had infected the entire nation of Judah. Generations of God's people would suffer the consequences of his behavior. Our behavior is important not only to us but also for our descendants and all the people who will come in contact with them. Knowing this truth should motivate us to follow God's plan for our lives. If we do things God's way, we will pass on peace and joy to future generations instead of sorrow and suffering.

You are long-suffering—do not take me
away;
think of how I suffer reproach for your
sake.
16When your words came, I ate them;
they were my joy and my heart's delight,
for I bear your name,
O LORD God Almighty.
17I never sat in the company of revelers,
never made merry with them;
I sat alone because your hand was on me
and you had filled me with indignation.
18Why is my pain unending
and my wound grievous and incurable?
Will you be to me like a deceptive brook,
like a spring that fails?

19Therefore this is what the LORD says:

"If you repent, I will restore you
that you may serve me;
if you utter worthy, not worthless, words,
you will be my spokesman.
Let this people turn to you,
but you must not turn to them.
20I will make you a wall to this people,
a fortified wall of bronze;
they will fight against you
but will not overcome you,
for I am with you
to rescue and save you,"
declares the LORD.
21"I will save you from the hands of the
wicked
and redeem you from the grasp of the
cruel."

Day of Disaster

16 Then the word of the LORD came to me:
2"You must not marry and have sons or
daughters in this place." 3For this is what the
LORD says about the sons and daughters born in
this land and about the women who are their
mothers and the men who are their fathers:
4"They will die of deadly diseases. They will not
be mourned or buried but will be like refuse
lying on the ground. They will perish by sword
and famine, and their dead bodies will become
food for the birds of the air and the beasts of the
earth."
5For this is what the LORD says: "Do not
enter a house where there is a funeral meal; do
not go to mourn or show sympathy, because I
have withdrawn my blessing, my love and my
pity from this people," declares the LORD. 6"Both
high and low will die in this land. They will not
be buried or mourned, and no one will cut himself or shave his head for them. 7No one will
offer food to comfort those who mourn for the
dead—not even for a father or a mother—nor
will anyone give them a drink to console them.
8"And do not enter a house where there is
feasting and sit down to eat and drink. 9For this
is what the LORD Almighty, the God of Israel,
says: Before your eyes and in your days I will
bring an end to the sounds of joy and gladness
and to the voices of bride and bridegroom in
this place.
10"When you tell these people all this and
they ask you, 'Why has the LORD decreed such
a great disaster against us? What wrong have we
done? What sin have we committed against the
LORD our God?' 11then say to them, 'It is because your fathers forsook me,' declares the
LORD, 'and followed other gods and served and
worshiped them. They forsook me and did not
keep my law. 12But you have behaved more
wickedly than your fathers. See how each of you
is following the stubbornness of his evil heart
instead of obeying me. 13So I will throw you out
of this land into a land neither you nor your
fathers have known, and there you will serve
other gods day and night, for I will show you no
favor.'
14"However, the days are coming," declares
the LORD, "when men will no longer say, 'As
surely as the LORD lives, who brought the Israelites up out of Egypt,' 15but they will say, 'As
surely as the LORD lives, who brought the Israelites up out of the land of the north and out of
all the countries where he had banished them.'
For I will restore them to the land I gave their
forefathers.
16"But now I will send for many fishermen,"
declares the LORD, "and they will catch them.

16:1–13 God contended with his people for centuries, warning them, forgiving them and healing them; but the people continued to ignore God and follow their own selfish ways. As a result, God withdrew his blessings from his people. Painful discipline often gets our attention when everything else fails. We should learn from our painful experiences and turn to God; we should never allow punishment to drive us away from him. His discipline is a sign that he loves us and wants to have a close relationship with us.

16:8 In this verse, God told Jeremiah not to ignore the sinfulness of the people. The prophet was told to confront them by his refusal to celebrate with them. It takes a great deal of courage to confront loved ones who fail to admit the sinfulness of their ways. They may question our choices and may even actively pressure us to join them in their sin. Sometimes we can help the people we love by gently showing them that they are in need of repentance. Often, though, a more direct approach may become necessary. Jesus was hardly gentle when he threw the moneychangers out of the temple! If the situation calls for it and God directs it, straightforward confrontation may be the best approach.

16:14–15 Tucked away in a long passage describing God's judgment we find words that reveal God's forgiving heart. The sins of Judah would lead to punishment in exile, but God's plans for his people didn't stop there. God wanted his people to persevere through their suffering, recognize their sin and look to God for deliverance. God then redeemed his people from exile and led them back to the promised land. No matter how badly we have sinned and how terrible the consequences we have suffered for those sins, God desires to work good in our lives. If we admit our sin and repent, he will be faithful to restore us.

16:16—17:13 We may be able to fool others with our

After that I will send for many hunters, and they will hunt them down on every mountain and hill and from the crevices of the rocks. [17]My eyes are on all their ways; they are not hidden from me, nor is their sin concealed from my eyes. [18]I will repay them double for their wickedness and their sin, because they have defiled my land with the lifeless forms of their vile images and have filled my inheritance with their detestable idols."

[19]O LORD, my strength and my fortress,
my refuge in time of distress,
to you the nations will come
from the ends of the earth and say,
"Our fathers possessed nothing but false gods,
worthless idols that did them no good.
[20]Do men make their own gods?
Yes, but they are not gods!"
[21]"Therefore I will teach them—
this time I will teach them
my power and might.
Then they will know
that my name is the LORD.

17 "Judah's sin is engraved with an iron tool,
inscribed with a flint point,
on the tablets of their hearts
and on the horns of their altars.
[2]Even their children remember
their altars and Asherah poles[a]
beside the spreading trees
and on the high hills.
[3]My mountain in the land
and your[b] wealth and all your treasures
I will give away as plunder,
together with your high places,
because of sin throughout your country.
[4]Through your own fault you will lose
the inheritance I gave you.
I will enslave you to your enemies
in a land you do not know,
for you have kindled my anger,
and it will burn forever."
[5]This is what the LORD says:
"Cursed is the one who trusts in man,
who depends on flesh for his strength
and whose heart turns away from the LORD.
[6]He will be like a bush in the wastelands;
he will not see prosperity when it comes.

[a]2 That is, symbols of the goddess Asherah [b]2,3 Or *hills* / [3]*and the mountains of the land.* / *Your*

actions, but we can never fool God. Judgment came to Judah not only because the people's sins were grievous, but also because their hearts were unrepentant. God searches our innermost thoughts. He knows our hearts. He cares about who we are, not just about what we do. For this reason, our spiritual renewal does not begin with a heroic act. It begins with a humble and repentant heart.

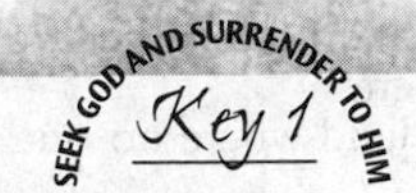

Hope and Confidence in God

Jeremiah 17:5–14 The human heart cannot thrive without something to hope for and someone in whom we can place our confidence. God alone is able to perfectly fulfill both needs. Placing our hope and confidence in him will cause our spiritual lives to flourish.

The Lord declared these truths to his people long ago. As enemies threatened the nation of Judah, many turned to Egypt and other human powers for deliverance. But the Lord said:

Cursed is the one who trusts in man, who depends on flesh for his strength and whose heart turns away from the LORD. He will be like a bush in the wastelands; he will not see prosperity when it comes. He will dwell in the parched places of the desert, in a salt land where no one lives. But blessed is the man who trusts in the LORD, whose confidence is in him. He will be like a tree planted by the water that sends out its roots by the stream. It does not fear when heat comes; its leaves are always green. It has no worries in a year of drought and never fails to bear fruit. (17:5–8).

Placing our hope and confidence in anything or anyone but God is like expecting a tree to flourish in a barren desert. Our thirst will only continue because people and possessions are unable to satisfy our deepest needs. But placing our hope in the Lord alone changes everything, for Jesus said, "Whoever drinks the water I give him will never thirst. Indeed, the water I give him will become in him a spring of water welling up to eternal life" (John 4:14).

Move on to Key 2 and turn to Genesis 31.

He will dwell in the parched places of the
desert,
in a salt land where no one lives.

7"But blessed is the man who trusts in the
LORD,
whose confidence is in him.
8He will be like a tree planted by the water
that sends out its roots by the stream.
It does not fear when heat comes;
its leaves are always green.
It has no worries in a year of drought
and never fails to bear fruit."

9The heart is deceitful above all things
and beyond cure.
Who can understand it?

10"I the LORD search the heart
and examine the mind,
to reward a man according to his conduct,
according to what his deeds deserve."

11Like a partridge that hatches eggs it did not
lay
is the man who gains riches by unjust
means.
When his life is half gone, they will desert
him,
and in the end he will prove to be a
fool.

12A glorious throne, exalted from the
beginning,
is the place of our sanctuary.
13O LORD, the hope of Israel,
all who forsake you will be put to
shame.
Those who turn away from you will be
written in the dust
because they have forsaken the LORD,
the spring of living water.

14Heal me, O LORD, and I will be healed;
save me and I will be saved,
for you are the one I praise.
15They keep saying to me,
"Where is the word of the LORD?
Let it now be fulfilled!"
16I have not run away from being your
shepherd;
you know I have not desired the day of
despair.
What passes my lips is open before you.
17Do not be a terror to me;
you are my refuge in the day of disaster.
18Let my persecutors be put to shame,
but keep me from shame;
let them be terrified,
but keep me from terror.
Bring on them the day of disaster;
destroy them with double destruction.

Keeping the Sabbath Holy

19This is what the LORD said to me: "Go and
stand at the gate of the people, through which
the kings of Judah go in and out; stand also at
all the other gates of Jerusalem. 20Say to them,
'Hear the word of the LORD, O kings of Judah
and all people of Judah and everyone living in
Jerusalem who come through these gates. 21This
is what the LORD says: Be careful not to carry a
load on the Sabbath day or bring it through the
gates of Jerusalem. 22Do not bring a load out of
your houses or do any work on the Sabbath, but
keep the Sabbath day holy, as I commanded
your forefathers. 23Yet they did not listen or pay
attention; they were stiff-necked and would not
listen or respond to discipline. 24But if you are
careful to obey me, declares the LORD, and bring
no load through the gates of this city on the
Sabbath, but keep the Sabbath day holy by not
doing any work on it, 25then kings who sit on
David's throne will come through the gates of
this city with their officials. They and their officials will come riding in chariots and on horses,
accompanied by the men of Judah and those
living in Jerusalem, and this city will be inhabited forever. 26People will come from the towns
of Judah and the villages around Jerusalem,
from the territory of Benjamin and the western
foothills, from the hill country and the Negev,
bringing burnt offerings and sacrifices, grain offerings, incense and thank offerings to the
house of the LORD. 27But if you do not obey me
to keep the Sabbath day holy by not carrying
any load as you come through the gates of Jerusalem on the Sabbath day, then I will kindle an
unquenchable fire in the gates of Jerusalem that
will consume her fortresses.' "

At the Potter's House

18 This is the word that came to Jeremiah
from the LORD: 2"Go down to the potter's house, and there I will give you my message." 3So I went down to the potter's house, and
I saw him working at the wheel. 4But the pot he
was shaping from the clay was marred in his
hands; so the potter formed it into another pot,
shaping it as seemed best to him.
5Then the word of the LORD came to me:
6"O house of Israel, can I not do with you as
this potter does?" declares the LORD. "Like clay in
the hand of the potter, so are you in my hand,
O house of Israel. 7If at any time I announce
that a nation or kingdom is to be uprooted,
torn down and destroyed, 8and if that nation I

17:14 When we cry to God for help we are also crying out for spiritual renewal. When we acknowledge that only God can save us and heal us, we can begin a new life. Hope doesn't come from within; we don't have the power to produce it. Only God can give us hope and then provide the help we need.

17:19–27 When we focus on the laws of God, we often lose sight of God's purpose behind those laws. The people of Judah had forsaken the Sabbath day, not realizing that the day had been set aside for their benefit. God's laws were not given to inconvenience us. God loves us; his laws were given in our best interest. Following God's plan is the only way to experience fulfillment and freedom in this life.

warned repents of its evil, then I will relent and
not inflict on it the disaster I had planned. 9And
if at another time I announce that a nation or
kingdom is to be built up and planted, 10and if
it does evil in my sight and does not obey me,
then I will reconsider the good I had intended
to do for it.

11"Now therefore say to the people of Judah
and those living in Jerusalem, 'This is what the
LORD says: Look! I am preparing a disaster for
you and devising a plan against you. So turn
from your evil ways, each one of you, and reform your ways and your actions.' 12But they
will reply, 'It's no use. We will continue with
our own plans; each of us will follow the stubbornness of his evil heart.' "

13Therefore this is what the LORD says:

"Inquire among the nations:
Who has ever heard anything like this?
A most horrible thing has been done
by Virgin Israel.
14Does the snow of Lebanon
ever vanish from its rocky slopes?
Do its cool waters from distant sources
ever cease to flow?[a]
15Yet my people have forgotten me;
they burn incense to worthless idols,
which made them stumble in their ways
and in the ancient paths.
They made them walk in bypaths
and on roads not built up.
16Their land will be laid waste,
an object of lasting scorn;
all who pass by will be appalled
and will shake their heads.
17Like a wind from the east,
I will scatter them before their enemies;
I will show them my back and not my face
in the day of their disaster."

18They said, "Come, let's make plans against
Jeremiah; for the teaching of the law by the
priest will not be lost, nor will counsel from the
wise, nor the word from the prophets. So come,
let's attack him with our tongues and pay no
attention to anything he says."

19Listen to me, O LORD;
hear what my accusers are saying!
20Should good be repaid with evil?
Yet they have dug a pit for me.
Remember that I stood before you
and spoke in their behalf
to turn your wrath away from them.
21So give their children over to famine;
hand them over to the power of the sword.
Let their wives be made childless and widows;
let their men be put to death,
their young men slain by the sword in battle.
22Let a cry be heard from their houses
when you suddenly bring invaders against them,
for they have dug a pit to capture me
and have hidden snares for my feet.
23But you know, O LORD,
all their plots to kill me.
Do not forgive their crimes
or blot out their sins from your sight.
Let them be overthrown before you;
deal with them in the time of your anger.

19 This is what the LORD says: "Go and
buy a clay jar from a potter. Take along
some of the elders of the people and of the
priests 2and go out to the Valley of Ben Hinnom, near the entrance of the Potsherd Gate.
There proclaim the words I tell you, 3and say,
'Hear the word of the LORD, O kings of Judah
and people of Jerusalem. This is what the LORD
Almighty, the God of Israel, says: Listen! I am
going to bring a disaster on this place that will
make the ears of everyone who hears of it tingle.
4For they have forsaken me and made this a
place of foreign gods; they have burned sacrifices in it to gods that neither they nor their
fathers nor the kings of Judah ever knew, and
they have filled this place with the blood of the
innocent. 5They have built the high places of
Baal to burn their sons in the fire as offerings to
Baal—something I did not command or mention, nor did it enter my mind. 6So beware, the
days are coming, declares the LORD, when people will no longer call this place Topheth or the
Valley of Ben Hinnom, but the Valley of Slaughter.

7" 'In this place I will ruin[b] the plans of

[a] 14 The meaning of the Hebrew for this sentence is uncertain. [b] 7 The Hebrew for *ruin* sounds like the Hebrew for *jar* (see verses 1 and 10).

18:11–17 God warned the people of Judah to turn from their sin or face judgment, but they would not respond. They preferred their own sinful ways to God's ways. God's ways are simple; his paths are straight; his burden is light. But we sometimes become stubborn, proud and arrogant, choosing to do things our own way—a way that leads ultimately to despair and pain.

18:12–15 The people of Judah were aware of their sin and admitted it openly, yet in their pride they refused to repent. God's only recourse was the destruction of his holy nation and the exile of his people. God's love and holiness meant that the people would be punished for their sin. But God wanted them to respond to him in repentance. We are most hopeless when we admit we have a problem and still continue on the path toward destruction. Admission without change is meaningless. The more we know about ourselves, the greater our responsibility to seek God's forgiveness.

19:1–15 It is hard to imagine God's people sacrificing their own children on an altar. For those who had turned away from the true God, turning to Baal and other false gods was the next step. The hideous sacrifices were inevitable once their path had turned away from God. One mistake almost always leads to another. When we turn to any resource other than the true God, many problems and sins gradually creep into our lives.

Judah and Jerusalem. I will make them fall by
the sword before their enemies, at the hands of
those who seek their lives, and I will give their
carcasses as food to the birds of the air and the
beasts of the earth. 8 I will devastate this city and
make it an object of scorn; all who pass by will
be appalled and will scoff because of all its
wounds. 9 I will make them eat the flesh of their
sons and daughters, and they will eat one another's flesh during the stress of the siege imposed on them by the enemies who seek their
lives.'

10 "Then break the jar while those who go
with you are watching, 11 and say to them, 'This
is what the LORD Almighty says: I will smash
this nation and this city just as this potter's jar
is smashed and cannot be repaired. They will
bury the dead in Topheth until there is no more
room. 12 This is what I will do to this place and
to those who live here, declares the LORD. I will
make this city like Topheth. 13 The houses in
Jerusalem and those of the kings of Judah will
be defiled like this place, Topheth—all the
houses where they burned incense on the roofs
to all the starry hosts and poured out drink
offerings to other gods.' "

14 Jeremiah then returned from Topheth,
where the LORD had sent him to prophesy, and
stood in the court of the LORD's temple and said
to all the people, 15 "This is what the LORD Almighty, the God of Israel, says: 'Listen! I am
going to bring on this city and the villages
around it every disaster I pronounced against
them, because they were stiff-necked and
would not listen to my words.' "

Jeremiah and Pashhur

20 When the priest Pashhur son of Immer,
the chief officer in the temple of the
LORD, heard Jeremiah prophesying these things,
2 he had Jeremiah the prophet beaten and put in
the stocks at the Upper Gate of Benjamin at the
LORD's temple. 3 The next day, when Pashhur
released him from the stocks, Jeremiah said to
him, "The LORD's name for you is not Pashhur,
but Magor-Missabib.[a] 4 For this is what the
LORD says: 'I will make you a terror to yourself
and to all your friends; with your own eyes you
will see them fall by the sword of their enemies.
I will hand all Judah over to the king of Babylon, who will carry them away to Babylon or
put them to the sword. 5 I will hand over to their
enemies all the wealth of this city—all its products, all its valuables and all the treasures of the
kings of Judah. They will take it away as plunder
and carry it off to Babylon. 6 And you, Pashhur,
and all who live in your house will go into exile
to Babylon. There you will die and be buried,
you and all your friends to whom you have
prophesied lies.' "

Jeremiah's Complaint

7 O LORD, you deceived[b] me, and I was
    deceived[b];
  you overpowered me and prevailed.
I am ridiculed all day long;
  everyone mocks me.
8 Whenever I speak, I cry out
  proclaiming violence and destruction.
So the word of the LORD has brought me
  insult and reproach all day long.
9 But if I say, "I will not mention him
  or speak any more in his name,"
his word is in my heart like a fire,
  a fire shut up in my bones.
I am weary of holding it in;
  indeed, I cannot.
10 I hear many whispering,
  "Terror on every side!
  Report him! Let's report him!"
All my friends
  are waiting for me to slip, saying,
"Perhaps he will be deceived;
  then we will prevail over him
  and take our revenge on him."

11 But the LORD is with me like a mighty
    warrior;
  so my persecutors will stumble and not
    prevail.
They will fail and be thoroughly disgraced;
  their dishonor will never be forgotten.
12 O LORD Almighty, you who examine the
    righteous
  and probe the heart and mind,
let me see your vengeance upon them,
  for to you I have committed my cause.

13 Sing to the LORD!
  Give praise to the LORD!
He rescues the life of the needy
  from the hands of the wicked.

14 Cursed be the day I was born!
  May the day my mother bore me not be
    blessed!
15 Cursed be the man who brought my father
    the news,
  who made him very glad, saying,
  "A child is born to you—a son!"
16 May that man be like the towns
  the LORD overthrew without pity.
May he hear wailing in the morning,
  a battle cry at noon.
17 For he did not kill me in the womb,

[a]3 *Magor-Missabib* means *terror on every side.* [b]7 Or *persuaded*

20:7–18 The beauty of the prophet's relationship with God lies in his freedom to question and to lament, or to praise God for his faithfulness even when hope seemed far away. God longs for such a freedom of exchange with each of us. He longs for open and honest communication.

20:14–18 In our moments of greatest despair, we sometimes regret we were ever born. Knowing that God cares for us, however, can help give us hope. Despite our feelings of loss and despair, God does love us. He is with us even when we cannot sense his presence.

with my mother as my grave,
her womb enlarged forever.
18Why did I ever come out of the womb
to see trouble and sorrow
and to end my days in shame?

God Rejects Zedekiah's Request

21 The word came to Jeremiah from the
LORD when King Zedekiah sent to him
Pashhur son of Malkijah and the priest Zephaniah son of Maaseiah. They said: 2"Inquire now
of the LORD for us because Nebuchadnezzar[a]
king of Babylon is attacking us. Perhaps the
LORD will perform wonders for us as in times
past so that he will withdraw from us."
3But Jeremiah answered them, "Tell Zedekiah, 4'This is what the LORD, the God of Israel,
says: I am about to turn against you the weapons of war that are in your hands, which you are
using to fight the king of Babylon and the Babylonians[b] who are outside the wall besieging
you. And I will gather them inside this city. 5I
myself will fight against you with an outstretched hand and a mighty arm in anger and
fury and great wrath. 6I will strike down those
who live in this city—both men and animals—
and they will die of a terrible plague. 7After that,
declares the LORD, I will hand over Zedekiah
king of Judah, his officials and the people in
this city who survive the plague, sword and
famine, to Nebuchadnezzar king of Babylon
and to their enemies who seek their lives. He
will put them to the sword; he will show them
no mercy or pity or compassion.'
8"Furthermore, tell the people, 'This is what
the LORD says: See, I am setting before you the
way of life and the way of death. 9Whoever stays
in this city will die by the sword, famine or
plague. But whoever goes out and surrenders to
the Babylonians who are besieging you will live;
he will escape with his life. 10I have determined
to do this city harm and not good, declares the
LORD. It will be given into the hands of the king
of Babylon, and he will destroy it with fire.'
11"Moreover, say to the royal house of Judah, 'Hear the word of the LORD; 12O house of
David, this is what the LORD says:

" 'Administer justice every morning;
rescue from the hand of his oppressor
the one who has been robbed,
or my wrath will break out and burn like
fire
because of the evil you have done—
burn with no one to quench it.
13I am against you, ⌞Jerusalem,⌟
you who live above this valley
on the rocky plateau,
declares the LORD—
you who say, "Who can come against us?
Who can enter our refuge?"
14I will punish you as your deeds deserve,
declares the LORD.
I will kindle a fire in your forests
that will consume everything around
you.' "

Judgment Against Evil Kings

22 This is what the LORD says: "Go down
to the palace of the king of Judah and
proclaim this message there: 2'Hear the word of
the LORD, O king of Judah, you who sit on
David's throne—you, your officials and your
people who come through these gates. 3This is
what the LORD says: Do what is just and right.
Rescue from the hand of his oppressor the one
who has been robbed. Do no wrong or violence
to the alien, the fatherless or the widow, and do
not shed innocent blood in this place. 4For if
you are careful to carry out these commands,
then kings who sit on David's throne will come
through the gates of this palace, riding in chariots and on horses, accompanied by their officials and their people. 5But if you do not obey
these commands, declares the LORD, I swear by
myself that this palace will become a ruin.' "
6For this is what the LORD says about the
palace of the king of Judah:

"Though you are like Gilead to me,
like the summit of Lebanon,
I will surely make you like a desert,
like towns not inhabited.
7I will send destroyers against you,
each man with his weapons,
and they will cut up your fine cedar beams
and throw them into the fire.

8"People from many nations will pass by
this city and will ask one another, 'Why has the
LORD done such a thing to this great city?' 9And
the answer will be: 'Because they have forsaken
the covenant of the LORD their God and have
worshiped and served other gods.' "

10Do not weep for the dead ⌞king⌟ or mourn
his loss;

[a]2 Hebrew *Nebuchadrezzar,* of which *Nebuchadnezzar* is a variant; here and often in Jeremiah and Ezekiel [b]4 Or *Chaldeans;* also in verse 9

21:1–14 Judgment will come. Eventually people will reap the painful consequences of their sin. As Nebuchadnezzar bore down on Jerusalem, King Zedekiah wanted Jeremiah to petition God for help. God responded by telling his people that it was too late. Since they had failed to respond to God's numerous warnings through his prophets, the people would have to endure incredible devastation. We would be wise to listen to the warnings we receive before it's too late for us too.

22:1–30 All of us are responsible for our own actions, but leaders and teachers are held to even greater degrees of responsibility. In this chapter, Jeremiah confronted the leaders of Judah about their sins. He urged the kings to rule as David had ruled, but they refused, encouraging their people to turn to idols instead. As a result of their disobedience, the entire nation suffered destruction. We are all leaders in some context. Like it or not, whether we interact with children, employees, neighbors or friends, what we do and say does affect others.

rather, weep bitterly for him who is exiled,
because he will never return
nor see his native land again.

11For this is what the LORD says about Shallum[a] son of Josiah, who succeeded his father as king of Judah but has gone from this place: "He will never return. 12He will die in the place where they have led him captive; he will not see this land again."

13"Woe to him who builds his palace by unrighteousness,
his upper rooms by injustice,
making his countrymen work for nothing,
not paying them for their labor.
14He says, 'I will build myself a great palace
with spacious upper rooms.'
So he makes large windows in it,
panels it with cedar
and decorates it in red.

15"Does it make you a king
to have more and more cedar?
Did not your father have food and drink?
He did what was right and just,
so all went well with him.
16He defended the cause of the poor and needy,
and so all went well.
Is that not what it means to know me?"
declares the LORD.
17"But your eyes and your heart
are set only on dishonest gain,
on shedding innocent blood
and on oppression and extortion."

18Therefore this is what the LORD says about Jehoiakim son of Josiah king of Judah:

"They will not mourn for him:
'Alas, my brother! Alas, my sister!'
They will not mourn for him:
'Alas, my master! Alas, his splendor!'
19He will have the burial of a donkey—
dragged away and thrown
outside the gates of Jerusalem."

20"Go up to Lebanon and cry out,
let your voice be heard in Bashan,
cry out from Abarim,
for all your allies are crushed.
21I warned you when you felt secure,
but you said, 'I will not listen!'
This has been your way from your youth;
you have not obeyed me.
22The wind will drive all your shepherds away,
and your allies will go into exile.
Then you will be ashamed and disgraced
because of all your wickedness.
23You who live in 'Lebanon,[b]'
who are nestled in cedar buildings,
how you will groan when pangs come upon you,
pain like that of a woman in labor!

24"As surely as I live," declares the LORD,
"even if you, Jehoiachin[c] son of Jehoiakim
king of Judah, were a signet ring on my right
hand, I would still pull you off. 25I will hand
you over to those who seek your life, those you
fear—to Nebuchadnezzar king of Babylon and
to the Babylonians.[d] 26I will hurl you and the
mother who gave you birth into another country, where neither of you was born, and there
you both will die. 27You will never come back
to the land you long to return to."

28Is this man Jehoiachin a despised, broken pot,
an object no one wants?
Why will he and his children be hurled out,
cast into a land they do not know?
29O land, land, land,
hear the word of the LORD!
30This is what the LORD says:
"Record this man as if childless,
a man who will not prosper in his lifetime,
for none of his offspring will prosper,
none will sit on the throne of David
or rule anymore in Judah."

The Righteous Branch

23 "Woe to the shepherds who are destroying and scattering the sheep of my
pasture!" declares the LORD. 2Therefore this is
what the LORD, the God of Israel, says to the
shepherds who tend my people: "Because you
have scattered my flock and driven them away
and have not bestowed care on them, I will
bestow punishment on you for the evil you
have done," declares the LORD. 3"I myself will
gather the remnant of my flock out of all the
countries where I have driven them and will
bring them back to their pasture, where they

[a]11 Also called *Jehoahaz* [b]23 That is, the palace in Jerusalem (see 1 Kings 7:2) [c]24 Hebrew *Coniah,* a variant of *Jehoiachin;* also in verse 28 [d]25 Or *Chaldeans*

22:21 When the people of Judah were prosperous, they refused to listen to God's warnings. When life is going well for us, we may also assume that we don't need God's help. As we experience success, we may begin to grow confident in our own ability and forget that we are dependent on God. But self-sufficiency and pride will lead to a downfall. We need God to help us—even when things are going well!

23:1–4 The "shepherds" were supposed to care for God's people. Since Judah's leaders had only led God's people astray, God himself promised to guide his people back to safety and vowed to place them in the care of shepherds who would love them and tend them. Jesus is the Good Shepherd, loving us and tending us as his flock (see John 10:1–18). If we are willing to follow his will for our lives, there is always hope for us, no matter how far we may have strayed.

will be fruitful and increase in number. 4I will
place shepherds over them who will tend them,
and they will no longer be afraid or terrified,
nor will any be missing," declares the LORD.

5"The days are coming," declares the LORD,
"when I will raise up to David[a] a
righteous Branch,
a King who will reign wisely
and do what is just and right in the
land.
6In his days Judah will be saved
and Israel will live in safety.
This is the name by which he will be
called:
The LORD Our Righteousness.

7"So then, the days are coming," declares the
LORD, "when people will no longer say, 'As
surely as the LORD lives, who brought the Israelites up out of Egypt,' 8but they will say, 'As
surely as the LORD lives, who brought the
descendants of Israel up out of the land of the
north and out of all the countries where he had
banished them.' Then they will live in their own
land."

Lying Prophets

9Concerning the prophets:

My heart is broken within me;
all my bones tremble.
I am like a drunken man,
like a man overcome by wine,
because of the LORD
and his holy words.
10The land is full of adulterers;
because of the curse[b] the land lies
parched[c]
and the pastures in the desert are
withered.
The ⌊prophets⌋ follow an evil course
and use their power unjustly.
11"Both prophet and priest are godless;
even in my temple I find their
wickedness,"
declares the LORD.
12"Therefore their path will become slippery;
they will be banished to darkness
and there they will fall.
I will bring disaster on them
in the year they are punished,"
declares the LORD.

13"Among the prophets of Samaria
I saw this repulsive thing:
They prophesied by Baal
and led my people Israel astray.
14And among the prophets of Jerusalem
I have seen something horrible:
They commit adultery and live a lie.
They strengthen the hands of evildoers,
so that no one turns from his
wickedness.
They are all like Sodom to me;
the people of Jerusalem are like
Gomorrah."

15Therefore, this is what the LORD Almighty
says concerning the prophets:

"I will make them eat bitter food
and drink poisoned water,
because from the prophets of Jerusalem
ungodliness has spread throughout the
land."

16This is what the LORD Almighty says:

"Do not listen to what the prophets are
prophesying to you;
they fill you with false hopes.
They speak visions from their own minds,
not from the mouth of the LORD.
17They keep saying to those who despise me,
'The LORD says: You will have peace.'
And to all who follow the stubbornness of
their hearts
they say, 'No harm will come to you.'
18But which of them has stood in the council
of the LORD
to see or to hear his word?
Who has listened and heard his word?
19See, the storm of the LORD
will burst out in wrath,
a whirlwind swirling down
on the heads of the wicked.
20The anger of the LORD will not turn back
until he fully accomplishes
the purposes of his heart.
In days to come
you will understand it clearly.
21I did not send these prophets,
yet they have run with their message;
I did not speak to them,

[a]5 Or *up from David's line* [b]10 Or *because of these things* [c]10 Or *land mourns*

23:5–8 The people of Judah faced a future filled with suffering, but Jeremiah offered them hope that after the destruction there would be a time of rebuilding. Even in the darkest times, when judgment seems most severe, God reminds us that a better day is coming. How sweet these promises must have sounded to the weary prophet! As we face suffering in our own lives, we can know that God desires to restore us and give us a hopeful future.

23:9–40 Throughout the Bible there are warnings for God's people to watch out for false prophets and false teachers. In this passage the false prophets of Judah claimed that the people had nothing to fear. They said that God's presence with them in the temple was a guarantee of protection. Their words only supported the people's spiritual blindness. It is never easy to see the truth of our own failure and the pain caused by our sins. But God urges us to repent of our sins and receive the forgiveness and restoration that only he can give.

23:21–22 The people of Judah hoped they would escape destruction. The false prophets supported their hope with false predictions of deliverance so that they continued in their sin with no thought of the consequences. Jeremiah, however, called the people to face reality. He warned them of the inevitable consequences of their sin. Yet the people were upset by his words and rejected his message. Unlike the people of Judah, we must accept the truth

yet they have prophesied.
22But if they had stood in my council,
they would have proclaimed my words
to my people
and would have turned them from their
evil ways
and from their evil deeds.
23"Am I only a God nearby,"
declares the LORD,
"and not a God far away?
24Can anyone hide in secret places
so that I cannot see him?"
declares the LORD.
"Do not I fill heaven and earth?"
declares the LORD.

25"I have heard what the prophets say who
prophesy lies in my name. They say, 'I had a
dream! I had a dream!' 26How long will this
continue in the hearts of these lying prophets,
who prophesy the delusions of their own
minds? 27They think the dreams they tell one
another will make my people forget my name,
just as their fathers forgot my name through
Baal worship. 28Let the prophet who has a
dream tell his dream, but let the one who has
my word speak it faithfully. For what has straw
to do with grain?" declares the LORD. 29"Is not
my word like fire," declares the LORD, "and like
a hammer that breaks a rock in pieces?

30"Therefore," declares the LORD, "I am
against the prophets who steal from one another words supposedly from me. 31Yes," declares
the LORD, "I am against the prophets who wag
their own tongues and yet declare, 'The LORD
declares.' 32Indeed, I am against those who
prophesy false dreams," declares the LORD.
"They tell them and lead my people astray with
their reckless lies, yet I did not send or appoint
them. They do not benefit these people in the
least," declares the LORD.

False Oracles and False Prophets

33"When these people, or a prophet or a
priest, ask you, 'What is the oracle[a] of the
LORD?' say to them, 'What oracle?[b] I will forsake you, declares the LORD.' 34If a prophet or a
priest or anyone else claims, 'This is the oracle
of the LORD,' I will punish that man and his
household. 35This is what each of you keeps on
saying to his friend or relative: 'What is the
LORD's answer?' or 'What has the LORD spoken?'
36But you must not mention 'the oracle of the
LORD' again, because every man's own word becomes his oracle and so you distort the words
of the living God, the LORD Almighty, our God.
37This is what you keep saying to a prophet:
'What is the LORD's answer to you?' or 'What
has the LORD spoken?' 38Although you claim,
'This is the oracle of the LORD,' this is what the
LORD says: You used the words, 'This is the
oracle of the LORD,' even though I told you that
you must not claim, 'This is the oracle of the
LORD.' 39Therefore, I will surely forget you and
cast you out of my presence along with the city
I gave to you and your fathers. 40I will bring
upon you everlasting disgrace—everlasting
shame that will not be forgotten."

Two Baskets of Figs

24 After Jehoiachin[c] son of Jehoiakim
king of Judah and the officials, the
craftsmen and the artisans of Judah were carried
into exile from Jerusalem to Babylon by Nebuchadnezzar king of Babylon, the LORD showed
me two baskets of figs placed in front of the
temple of the LORD. 2One basket had very good
figs, like those that ripen early; the other basket
had very poor figs, so bad they could not be
eaten.

3Then the LORD asked me, "What do you see,
Jeremiah?"

"Figs," I answered. "The good ones are very
good, but the poor ones are so bad they cannot
be eaten."

4Then the word of the LORD came to me:
5"This is what the LORD, the God of Israel, says:
'Like these good figs, I regard as good the exiles
from Judah, whom I sent away from this place
to the land of the Babylonians.[d] 6My eyes will
watch over them for their good, and I will bring
them back to this land. I will build them up and
not tear them down; I will plant them and not
uproot them. 7I will give them a heart to know
me, that I am the LORD. They will be my people,
and I will be their God, for they will return to
me with all their heart.

8" 'But like the poor figs, which are so bad
they cannot be eaten,' says the LORD, 'so will I
deal with Zedekiah king of Judah, his officials
and the survivors from Jerusalem, whether they
remain in this land or live in Egypt. 9I will make
them abhorrent and an offense to all the king-

[a]33 Or *burden* (see Septuagint and Vulgate)
[b]33 Hebrew; Septuagint and Vulgate *'You are the burden.* (The Hebrew for *oracle* and *burden* is the same.)
[c]1 Hebrew *Jeconiah,* a variant of *Jehoiachin*
[d]5 Or *Chaldeans*

---

about our sinful behavior and ask God to change us.

23:23–24 It is often easier to be led astray when we think no one is watching. Although we may hide our behavior from others, we can never hide it from God. Knowing that God is aware of all our thoughts and actions should help us stand against temptation. Despite the fact that he knows all about us, God still loves us and wants to grant repentant hearts his healing and grace.

24:1–10 God gave Jeremiah another illustration to help him understand the fate of the Jews taken into captivity. The exiles who followed God would be like good figs, full of nourishment. They would be well treated in exile and would be allowed to return to their homeland. King Zedekiah and those who had led the people falsely would be like bad figs, tasteless and fit only for destruction. God made it clear that the exile was intended to bring healing to his shattered and sin-scarred people. In the same way, God can use our suffering to draw us closer to himself and bring spiritual renewal to our lives.

doms of the earth, a reproach and a byword, an object of ridicule and cursing, wherever I banish them. 10I will send the sword, famine and plague against them until they are destroyed from the land I gave to them and their fathers.' "

Seventy Years of Captivity

25 The word came to Jeremiah concerning all the people of Judah in the fourth year of Jehoiakim son of Josiah king of Judah, which was the first year of Nebuchadnezzar king of Babylon. 2So Jeremiah the prophet said to all the people of Judah and to all those living in Jerusalem: 3For twenty-three years—from the thirteenth year of Josiah son of Amon king of Judah until this very day—the word of the LORD has come to me and I have spoken to you again and again, but you have not listened.

4And though the LORD has sent all his servants the prophets to you again and again, you have not listened or paid any attention. 5They said, "Turn now, each of you, from your evil ways and your evil practices, and you can stay in the land the LORD gave to you and your fathers for ever and ever. 6Do not follow other gods to serve and worship them; do not provoke me to anger with what your hands have made. Then I will not harm you."

7"But you did not listen to me," declares the LORD, "and you have provoked me with what your hands have made, and you have brought harm to yourselves."

8Therefore the LORD Almighty says this: "Because you have not listened to my words, 9I will summon all the peoples of the north and my servant Nebuchadnezzar king of Babylon," declares the LORD, "and I will bring them against this land and its inhabitants and against all the surrounding nations. I will completely destroy[a] them and make them an object of horror and scorn, and an everlasting ruin. 10I will banish from them the sounds of joy and gladness, the voices of bride and bridegroom, the sound of millstones and the light of the lamp. 11This whole country will become a desolate wasteland, and these nations will serve the king of Babylon seventy years.

12"But when the seventy years are fulfilled, I will punish the king of Babylon and his nation, the land of the Babylonians,[b] for their guilt," declares the LORD, "and will make it desolate forever. 13I will bring upon that land all the things I have spoken against it, all that are written in this book and prophesied by Jeremiah against all the nations. 14They themselves will be enslaved by many nations and great kings; I will repay them according to their deeds and the work of their hands."

The Cup of God's Wrath

15This is what the LORD, the God of Israel, said to me: "Take from my hand this cup filled with the wine of my wrath and make all the nations to whom I send you drink it. 16When they drink it, they will stagger and go mad because of the sword I will send among them."

17So I took the cup from the LORD's hand and made all the nations to whom he sent me drink it: 18Jerusalem and the towns of Judah, its kings and officials, to make them a ruin and an object of horror and scorn and cursing, as they are today; 19Pharaoh king of Egypt, his attendants, his officials and all his people, 20and all the foreign people there; all the kings of Uz; all the kings of the Philistines (those of Ashkelon, Gaza, Ekron, and the people left at Ashdod); 21Edom, Moab and Ammon; 22all the kings of Tyre and Sidon; the kings of the coastlands across the sea; 23Dedan, Tema, Buz and all who are in distant places[c]; 24all the kings of Arabia and all the kings of the foreign people who live in the desert; 25all the kings of Zimri, Elam and Media; 26and all the kings of the north, near and far, one after the other—all the kingdoms on the face of the earth. And after all of them, the king of Sheshach[d] will drink it too.

27"Then tell them, 'This is what the LORD Almighty, the God of Israel, says: Drink, get drunk and vomit, and fall to rise no more because of the sword I will send among you.' 28But if they refuse to take the cup from your hand and drink, tell them, 'This is what the LORD Almighty says: You must drink it! 29See, I am beginning to bring disaster on the city that bears my Name, and will you indeed go unpunished? You will not go unpunished, for I am calling down a sword upon all who live on the earth, declares the LORD Almighty.'

30"Now prophesy all these words against them and say to them:

" 'The LORD will roar from on high;
he will thunder from his holy dwelling
and roar mightily against his land.
He will shout like those who tread the
grapes,
shout against all who live on the earth.

[a]9 The Hebrew term refers to the irrevocable giving over of things or persons to the LORD, often by totally destroying them. [b]12 Or *Chaldeans* [c]23 Or *who clip the hair by their foreheads* [d]26 *Sheshach* is a cryptogram for Babylon.

25:1–14 How impatient we become when the consequences of our sins last for a long time. The Israelites were in exile for seventy years! Many of them finally learned to honor God in the midst of their captivity. It is important for us to face the consequences of our behavior too. One way we can honor God is to accept his discipline and build upon the lessons we learn from it.

25:15–38 Sometimes it seems that God allows people to prosper who care nothing about him or his ways. In these verses we are reminded that God will bring about justice in his time. All people and all nations are subject to God, and he will reward those who sincerely seek him (see Hebrews 11:6).

[31]The tumult will resound to the ends of the
earth,
for the LORD will bring charges against
the nations;
he will bring judgment on all mankind
and put the wicked to the sword,' "
declares the LORD.

[32]This is what the LORD Almighty says:

"Look! Disaster is spreading
from nation to nation;
a mighty storm is rising
from the ends of the earth."

[33]At that time those slain by the LORD will be everywhere—from one end of the earth to the other. They will not be mourned or gathered up or buried, but will be like refuse lying on the ground.

[34]Weep and wail, you shepherds;
roll in the dust, you leaders of the flock.
For your time to be slaughtered has come;
you will fall and be shattered like fine
pottery.
[35]The shepherds will have nowhere to flee,
the leaders of the flock no place to
escape.
[36]Hear the cry of the shepherds,
the wailing of the leaders of the flock,
for the LORD is destroying their pasture.
[37]The peaceful meadows will be laid waste
because of the fierce anger of the LORD.
[38]Like a lion he will leave his lair,
and their land will become desolate
because of the sword[a] of the oppressor
and because of the LORD's fierce anger.

Jeremiah Threatened With Death

26 Early in the reign of Jehoiakim son of
Josiah king of Judah, this word came
from the LORD: [2]"This is what the LORD says:
Stand in the courtyard of the LORD's house and
speak to all the people of the towns of Judah
who come to worship in the house of the LORD.
Tell them everything I command you; do not
omit a word. [3]Perhaps they will listen and each
will turn from his evil way. Then I will relent
and not bring on them the disaster I was planning because of the evil they have done. [4]Say to
them, 'This is what the LORD says: If you do not
listen to me and follow my law, which I have set
before you, [5]and if you do not listen to the
words of my servants the prophets, whom I
have sent to you again and again (though you
have not listened), [6]then I will make this house
like Shiloh and this city an object of cursing
among all the nations of the earth.' "
[7]The priests, the prophets and all the people
heard Jeremiah speak these words in the house
of the LORD. [8]But as soon as Jeremiah finished
telling all the people everything the LORD had
commanded him to say, the priests, the prophets and all the people seized him and said,
"You must die! [9]Why do you prophesy in the
LORD's name that this house will be like Shiloh
and this city will be desolate and deserted?" And
all the people crowded around Jeremiah in the
house of the LORD.
[10]When the officials of Judah heard about
these things, they went up from the royal palace
to the house of the LORD and took their places
at the entrance of the New Gate of the LORD's
house. [11]Then the priests and the prophets said
to the officials and all the people, "This man
should be sentenced to death because he has
prophesied against this city. You have heard it
with your own ears!"
[12]Then Jeremiah said to all the officials and
all the people: "The LORD sent me to prophesy
against this house and this city all the things
you have heard. [13]Now reform your ways and
your actions and obey the LORD your God. Then
the LORD will relent and not bring the disaster
he has pronounced against you. [14]As for me, I
am in your hands; do with me whatever you
think is good and right. [15]Be assured, however,
that if you put me to death, you will bring the
guilt of innocent blood on yourselves and on
this city and on those who live in it, for in truth
the LORD has sent me to you to speak all these
words in your hearing."
[16]Then the officials and all the people said to
the priests and the prophets, "This man should
not be sentenced to death! He has spoken to us
in the name of the LORD our God."
[17]Some of the elders of the land stepped forward and said to the entire assembly of people,
[18]"Micah of Moresheth prophesied in the days
of Hezekiah king of Judah. He told all the people of Judah, 'This is what the LORD Almighty
says:

" 'Zion will be plowed like a field,
Jerusalem will become a heap of rubble,
the temple hill a mound overgrown with
thickets.'[b]

[19]"Did Hezekiah king of Judah or anyone else

[a]38 Some Hebrew manuscripts and Septuagint (see also Jer. 46:16 and 50:16); most Hebrew manuscripts *anger*
[b]18 Micah 3:12

26:1–24 It can be difficult to serve God when others mock, question or tempt us to doubt. The rulers of Judah tried to silence Jeremiah. Finally they threatened him with physical death. Though threats can discourage us, sometimes they can also fuel the fire of our commitment (see Philippians 1:12–14). As we experience God's power in our lives, we need to share the Good News of freedom in Christ. Some people may laugh at us; others may oppose us. But we should not allow this to stop us. God's deliverance needs to be made known to everyone.

26:12–15 Because of Jeremiah's faith, he was able to speak boldly for God even when his life was threatened. Anyone can claim to have faith when life is going smoothly. The depth of our faith is measured when we are under pressure. We should never allow the opinions of others to keep us from speaking out boldly for God and sharing what we know about God's power to deliver us from the bondage of sin.

in Judah put him to death? Did not Hezekiah fear the LORD and seek his favor? And did not the LORD relent, so that he did not bring the disaster he pronounced against them? We are about to bring a terrible disaster on ourselves!"

20(Now Uriah son of Shemaiah from Kiriath Jearim was another man who prophesied in the name of the LORD; he prophesied the same things against this city and this land as Jeremiah did. 21When King Jehoiakim and all his officers and officials heard his words, the king sought to put him to death. But Uriah heard of it and fled in fear to Egypt. 22King Jehoiakim, however, sent Elnathan son of Acbor to Egypt, along with some other men. 23They brought Uriah out of Egypt and took him to King Jehoiakim, who had him struck down with a sword and his body thrown into the burial place of the common people.)

24Furthermore, Ahikam son of Shaphan supported Jeremiah, and so he was not handed over to the people to be put to death.

Judah to Serve Nebuchadnezzar

27 Early in the reign of Zedekiah[a] son of Josiah king of Judah, this word came to Jeremiah from the LORD: 2This is what the LORD said to me: "Make a yoke out of straps and crossbars and put it on your neck. 3Then send word to the kings of Edom, Moab, Ammon, Tyre and Sidon through the envoys who have come to Jerusalem to Zedekiah king of Judah. 4Give them a message for their masters and say, 'This is what the LORD Almighty, the God of Israel, says: "Tell this to your masters: 5With my great power and outstretched arm I made the earth and its people and the animals that are on it, and I give it to anyone I please. 6Now I will hand all your countries over to my servant Nebuchadnezzar king of Babylon; I will make even the wild animals subject to him. 7All nations will serve him and his son and his grandson until the time for his land comes; then many nations and great kings will subjugate him.

8" ' "If, however, any nation or kingdom will not serve Nebuchadnezzar king of Babylon or bow its neck under his yoke, I will punish that nation with the sword, famine and plague, declares the LORD, until I destroy it by his hand. 9So do not listen to your prophets, your diviners, your interpreters of dreams, your mediums or your sorcerers who tell you, 'You will not serve the king of Babylon.' 10They prophesy lies to you that will only serve to remove you far from your lands; I will banish you and you will perish. 11But if any nation will bow its neck under the yoke of the king of Babylon and serve him, I will let that nation remain in its own land to till it and to live there, declares the LORD." ' "

12I gave the same message to Zedekiah king of Judah. I said, "Bow your neck under the yoke of the king of Babylon; serve him and his people, and you will live. 13Why will you and your people die by the sword, famine and plague with which the LORD has threatened any nation that will not serve the king of Babylon? 14Do not listen to the words of the prophets who say to you, 'You will not serve the king of Babylon,' for they are prophesying lies to you. 15'I have not sent them,' declares the LORD. 'They are prophesying lies in my name. Therefore, I will banish you and you will perish, both you and the prophets who prophesy to you.' "

16Then I said to the priests and all these people, "This is what the LORD says: Do not listen to the prophets who say, 'Very soon now the articles from the LORD's house will be brought back from Babylon.' They are prophesying lies to you. 17Do not listen to them. Serve the king of Babylon, and you will live. Why should this city become a ruin? 18If they are prophets and have the word of the LORD, let them plead with the LORD Almighty that the furnishings remaining in the house of the LORD and in the palace of the king of Judah and in Jerusalem not be taken to Babylon. 19For this is what the LORD Almighty says about the pillars, the Sea, the movable stands and the other furnishings that are left in this city, 20which Nebuchadnezzar king of Babylon did not take away when he carried Jehoiachin[b] son of Jehoiakim king of Judah into exile from Jerusalem to Babylon, along with all the nobles of Judah and Jerusalem— 21yes, this is what the LORD Almighty, the God of Israel, says about the things that are left in the house of the LORD and in the palace of the king of Judah and in Jerusalem: 22'They will be taken to Babylon and there they will remain until the day I come for them,' declares the LORD. 'Then I will bring them back and restore them to this place.' "

[a] *1* A few Hebrew manuscripts and Syriac (see also Jer. 27:3, 12 and 28:1); most Hebrew manuscripts *Jehoiakim* (Most Septuagint manuscripts do not have this verse.)
[b] *20* Hebrew *Jeconiah,* a variant of *Jehoiachin*

27:1–15 Sometimes God uses the unrighteous to achieve his righteous plan. Nebuchadnezzar was not the kind of king God would normally honor, yet God used him to discipline the people of Judah and lead them to repentance. God wanted what was best for his people and used an ungodly king to carry out his will. When we suffer at the hands of people who care nothing for God, we should realize that God is with us. If we listen for his voice in the midst of our suffering, we may learn some important things about ourselves and about our loving God.

27:16–22 The people of Judah chose to listen to the pleasant messages of the false prophets, but this only blinded them to their sin and its inevitable consequences. All of us are extremely impressionable when we are going through difficult times. It is important that we build our lives on truth rather than on convenient or pleasant messages. God calls us to a challenging lifestyle. He requires that we take an honest look at our lives, admit our sin and humbly seek his forgiveness.

The False Prophet Hananiah

28 In the fifth month of that same year, the fourth year, early in the reign of Zedekiah king of Judah, the prophet Hananiah son of Azzur, who was from Gibeon, said to me in the house of the LORD in the presence of the priests and all the people: 2"This is what the LORD Almighty, the God of Israel, says: 'I will break the yoke of the king of Babylon. 3Within two years I will bring back to this place all the articles of the LORD's house that Nebuchadnezzar king of Babylon removed from here and took to Babylon. 4I will also bring back to this place Jehoiachin[a] son of Jehoiakim king of Judah and all the other exiles from Judah who went to Babylon,' declares the LORD, 'for I will break the yoke of the king of Babylon.' "

5Then the prophet Jeremiah replied to the prophet Hananiah before the priests and all the people who were standing in the house of the LORD. 6He said, "Amen! May the LORD do so! May the LORD fulfill the words you have prophesied by bringing the articles of the LORD's house and all the exiles back to this place from Babylon. 7Nevertheless, listen to what I have to say in your hearing and in the hearing of all the people: 8From early times the prophets who preceded you and me have prophesied war, disaster and plague against many countries and great kingdoms. 9But the prophet who prophesies peace will be recognized as one truly sent by the LORD only if his prediction comes true."

10Then the prophet Hananiah took the yoke off the neck of the prophet Jeremiah and broke it, 11and he said before all the people, "This is what the LORD says: 'In the same way will I break the yoke of Nebuchadnezzar king of Babylon off the neck of all the nations within two years.' " At this, the prophet Jeremiah went on his way.

12Shortly after the prophet Hananiah had broken the yoke off the neck of the prophet Jeremiah, the word of the LORD came to Jeremiah: 13"Go and tell Hananiah, 'This is what the LORD says: You have broken a wooden yoke, but in its place you will get a yoke of iron. 14This is what the LORD Almighty, the God of Israel, says: I will put an iron yoke on the necks of all these nations to make them serve Nebuchadnezzar king of Babylon, and they will serve him. I will even give him control over the wild animals.' "

15Then the prophet Jeremiah said to Hananiah the prophet, "Listen, Hananiah! The LORD has not sent you, yet you have persuaded this nation to trust in lies. 16Therefore, this is what the LORD says: 'I am about to remove you from the face of the earth. This very year you are going to die, because you have preached rebellion against the LORD.' "

17In the seventh month of that same year, Hananiah the prophet died.

A Letter to the Exiles

29 This is the text of the letter that the prophet Jeremiah sent from Jerusalem to the surviving elders among the exiles and to the priests, the prophets and all the other people Nebuchadnezzar had carried into exile from Jerusalem to Babylon. 2(This was after King Jehoiachin[a] and the queen mother, the court officials and the leaders of Judah and Jerusalem, the craftsmen and the artisans had gone into exile from Jerusalem.) 3He entrusted the letter to Elasah son of Shaphan and to Gemariah son of Hilkiah, whom Zedekiah king of Judah sent to King Nebuchadnezzar in Babylon. It said:

4This is what the LORD Almighty, the God of Israel, says to all those I carried into exile from Jerusalem to Babylon: 5"Build houses and settle down; plant gardens and eat what they produce. 6Marry and have sons and daughters; find wives for your sons and give your daughters in marriage, so that they too may have sons and daughters. Increase in number there; do not decrease. 7Also, seek the peace and prosperity of the city to which I have carried you into exile. Pray to the LORD for it, because if it prospers, you too will prosper." 8Yes, this is what the LORD Almighty, the God of Israel, says: "Do not let the prophets and diviners among you deceive you. Do not listen to the dreams you encourage them to have. 9They are prophesying lies to you in my name. I have not sent them," declares the LORD.

10This is what the LORD says: "When seventy years are completed for Babylon, I will come to you and fulfill my gracious promise to bring you back to this place. 11For I know the plans I have for you," declares the LORD, "plans to prosper you and not to harm you, plans to give you hope and a future. 12Then you will call upon me and come and pray to me, and I will listen to you. 13You will seek me and find me when you seek me with all your heart. 14I will be found by you," declares the LORD, "and will bring you back from captivity.[b] I will gather you from all the nations and places where I have banished you," declares the LORD, "and will bring you back to the place from which I carried you into exile."

15You may say, "The LORD has raised up prophets for us in Babylon," 16but this

[a] 4,2 Hebrew *Jeconiah,* a variant of *Jehoiachin* [b] 14 Or *will restore your fortunes*

29:11 What comfort this verse offers us! In our moments of despair, we can remember that God has a plan for his people and that his plan is filled with blessing. We can be sure that our spiritual growth is an important part of God's will for us. Realizing these things will give us hope for the future.

is what the LORD says about the king who
sits on David's throne and all the people
who remain in this city, your countrymen
who did not go with you into exile— 17yes,
this is what the LORD Almighty says: "I
will send the sword, famine and plague
against them and I will make them like
poor figs that are so bad they cannot be
eaten. 18I will pursue them with the
sword, famine and plague and will make
them abhorrent to all the kingdoms of the
earth and an object of cursing and horror,
of scorn and reproach, among all the nations where I drive them. 19For they have
not listened to my words," declares the
LORD, "words that I sent to them again
and again by my servants the prophets.
And you exiles have not listened either,"
declares the LORD.

20Therefore, hear the word of the LORD,
all you exiles whom I have sent away from
Jerusalem to Babylon. 21This is what the
LORD Almighty, the God of Israel, says
about Ahab son of Kolaiah and Zedekiah
son of Maaseiah, who are prophesying lies
to you in my name: "I will hand them
over to Nebuchadnezzar king of Babylon,
and he will put them to death before your
very eyes. 22Because of them, all the exiles
from Judah who are in Babylon will use
this curse: 'The LORD treat you like Zedekiah and Ahab, whom the king of Babylon
burned in the fire.' 23For they have done
outrageous things in Israel; they have
committed adultery with their neighbors'
wives and in my name have spoken lies,
which I did not tell them to do. I know it
and am a witness to it," declares the LORD.

Message to Shemaiah

24Tell Shemaiah the Nehelamite, 25"This is
what the LORD Almighty, the God of Israel, says:
You sent letters in your own name to all the
people in Jerusalem, to Zephaniah son of Maaseiah the priest, and to all the other priests. You
said to Zephaniah, 26'The LORD has appointed
you priest in place of Jehoiada to be in charge
of the house of the LORD; you should put any
madman who acts like a prophet into the stocks
and neck-irons. 27So why have you not repri-
manded Jeremiah from Anathoth, who poses as
a prophet among you? 28He has sent this message to us in Babylon: It will be a long time.
Therefore build houses and settle down; plant
gardens and eat what they produce.' "

29Zephaniah the priest, however, read the letter to Jeremiah the prophet. 30Then the word of
the LORD came to Jeremiah: 31"Send this message to all the exiles: 'This is what the LORD says
about Shemaiah the Nehelamite: Because Shemaiah has prophesied to you, even though I did
not send him, and has led you to believe a lie,
32this is what the LORD says: I will surely punish
Shemaiah the Nehelamite and his descendants.
He will have no one left among this people, nor
will he see the good things I will do for my
people, declares the LORD, because he has
preached rebellion against me.' "

Restoration of Israel

30 This is the word that came to Jeremiah
from the LORD: 2"This is what the LORD,
the God of Israel, says: 'Write in a book all the
words I have spoken to you. 3The days are coming,' declares the LORD, 'when I will bring my
people Israel and Judah back from captivity[a]
and restore them to the land I gave their forefathers to possess,' says the LORD."

4These are the words the LORD spoke concerning Israel and Judah: 5"This is what the
LORD says:

" 'Cries of fear are heard—
terror, not peace.
6Ask and see:
Can a man bear children?
Then why do I see every strong man
with his hands on his stomach like a
woman in labor,
every face turned deathly pale?
7How awful that day will be!
None will be like it.
It will be a time of trouble for Jacob,
but he will be saved out of it.

8" 'In that day,' declares the LORD Almighty,
'I will break the yoke off their necks
and will tear off their bonds;
no longer will foreigners enslave them.
9Instead, they will serve the LORD their God
and David their king,
whom I will raise up for them.

10" 'So do not fear, O Jacob my servant;
do not be dismayed, O Israel,'
declares the LORD.
'I will surely save you out of a distant
place,
your descendants from the land of their
exile.
Jacob will again have peace and security,
and no one will make him afraid.
11I am with you and will save you,'
declares the LORD.
'Though I completely destroy all the
nations
among which I scatter you,
I will not completely destroy you.

[a]3 Or *will restore the fortunes of my people Israel and Judah*

30:1–24 The people of Judah wanted God's judgment to end quickly. Before his wrath was fully poured out upon them, God told his people that they would be renewed and restored. Such a promise unveils the unfailing love God has for his people. Punishment is uncomfortable, but it is necessary for our healing and true restoration. If we repent and follow God's will for our lives, he will use our chastisement as part of his plan to redeem us.

I will discipline you but only with justice;
I will not let you go entirely
unpunished.'

12"This is what the LORD says:

" 'Your wound is incurable,
your injury beyond healing.
13There is no one to plead your cause,
no remedy for your sore,
no healing for you.
14All your allies have forgotten you;
they care nothing for you.
I have struck you as an enemy would
and punished you as would the cruel,
because your guilt is so great
and your sins so many.
15Why do you cry out over your wound,
your pain that has no cure?
Because of your great guilt and many sins
I have done these things to you.

16" 'But all who devour you will be
devoured;
all your enemies will go into exile.
Those who plunder you will be plundered;
all who make spoil of you I will despoil.
17But I will restore you to health
and heal your wounds,'
declares the LORD,
'because you are called an outcast,
Zion for whom no one cares.'

18"This is what the LORD says:

" 'I will restore the fortunes of Jacob's tents
and have compassion on his dwellings;
the city will be rebuilt on her ruins,
and the palace will stand in its proper
place.
19From them will come songs of thanksgiving
and the sound of rejoicing.
I will add to their numbers,
and they will not be decreased;
I will bring them honor,
and they will not be disdained.
20Their children will be as in days of old,
and their community will be established
before me;
I will punish all who oppress them.
21Their leader will be one of their own;
their ruler will arise from among them.
I will bring him near and he will come
close to me,
for who is he who will devote himself
to be close to me?'
declares the LORD.
22" 'So you will be my people,
and I will be your God.' "

23See, the storm of the LORD
will burst out in wrath,
a driving wind swirling down
on the heads of the wicked.
24The fierce anger of the LORD will not turn
back
until he fully accomplishes
the purposes of his heart.
In days to come
you will understand this.

31 "At that time," declares the LORD, "I will
be the God of all the clans of Israel, and
they will be my people."

2This is what the LORD says:

"The people who survive the sword
will find favor in the desert;
I will come to give rest to Israel."

3The LORD appeared to us in the past,[a] saying:

"I have loved you with an everlasting love;
I have drawn you with loving-kindness.
4I will build you up again
and you will be rebuilt, O Virgin Israel.
Again you will take up your tambourines
and go out to dance with the joyful.
5Again you will plant vineyards
on the hills of Samaria;
the farmers will plant them
and enjoy their fruit.
6There will be a day when watchmen cry out
on the hills of Ephraim,
'Come, let us go up to Zion,
to the LORD our God.' "

7This is what the LORD says:

"Sing with joy for Jacob;
shout for the foremost of the nations.
Make your praises heard, and say,
'O LORD, save your people,
the remnant of Israel.'
8See, I will bring them from the land of the
north
and gather them from the ends of the
earth.
Among them will be the blind and the
lame,
expectant mothers and women in labor;
a great throng will return.
9They will come with weeping;
they will pray as I bring them back.
I will lead them beside streams of water
on a level path where they will not
stumble,
because I am Israel's father,
and Ephraim is my firstborn son.

10"Hear the word of the LORD, O nations;

[a]3 Or *LORD has appeared to us from afar*

31:1–40 God paints a joyful picture of renewal in this passage, with all the details of repentance, sorrow, forgiveness, laughter, restoration and hope. God's picture showed his people following his plan for their lives and worshiping and praising him. We can experience this kind of restoration too by admitting our need for God's healing touch in our lives. God desires to rebuild his relationship with us no matter how far we may have strayed from him.

proclaim it in distant coastlands:
'He who scattered Israel will gather them
and will watch over his flock like a shepherd.'
11For the LORD will ransom Jacob
and redeem them from the hand of those stronger than they.
12They will come and shout for joy on the heights of Zion;
they will rejoice in the bounty of the LORD—
the grain, the new wine and the oil,
the young of the flocks and herds.
They will be like a well-watered garden,
and they will sorrow no more.
13Then maidens will dance and be glad,
young men and old as well.
I will turn their mourning into gladness;
I will give them comfort and joy instead of sorrow.
14I will satisfy the priests with abundance,
and my people will be filled with my bounty,"
declares the LORD.

15This is what the LORD says:

"A voice is heard in Ramah,
mourning and great weeping,
Rachel weeping for her children
and refusing to be comforted,
because her children are no more."

16This is what the LORD says:

"Restrain your voice from weeping
and your eyes from tears,
for your work will be rewarded,"
declares the LORD.
"They will return from the land of the enemy.
17So there is hope for your future,"
declares the LORD.
"Your children will return to their own land.

18"I have surely heard Ephraim's moaning:
'You disciplined me like an unruly calf,
and I have been disciplined.
Restore me, and I will return,
because you are the LORD my God.
19After I strayed,
I repented;
after I came to understand,
I beat my breast.
I was ashamed and humiliated
because I bore the disgrace of my youth.'
20Is not Ephraim my dear son,
the child in whom I delight?
Though I often speak against him,
I still remember him.
Therefore my heart yearns for him;
I have great compassion for him,"
declares the LORD.
21"Set up road signs;
put up guideposts.
Take note of the highway,
the road that you take.
Return, O Virgin Israel,
return to your towns.
22How long will you wander,
O unfaithful daughter?
The LORD will create a new thing on earth—
a woman will surround[a] a man."

23This is what the LORD Almighty, the God of
Israel, says: "When I bring them back from captivity,[b] the people in the land of Judah and in
its towns will once again use these words: 'The
LORD bless you, O righteous dwelling, O sacred
mountain.' 24People will live together in Judah
and all its towns—farmers and those who move
about with their flocks. 25I will refresh the weary
and satisfy the faint."

26At this I awoke and looked around. My
sleep had been pleasant to me.

27"The days are coming," declares the LORD,
"when I will plant the house of Israel and the
house of Judah with the offspring of men and
of animals. 28Just as I watched over them to
uproot and tear down, and to overthrow, destroy and bring disaster, so I will watch over
them to build and to plant," declares the LORD.
29"In those days people will no longer say,

'The fathers have eaten sour grapes,
and the children's teeth are set on edge.'

30Instead, everyone will die for his own sin;
whoever eats sour grapes—his own teeth will be
set on edge.

31"The time is coming," declares the LORD,
"when I will make a new covenant
with the house of Israel
and with the house of Judah.
32It will not be like the covenant
I made with their forefathers
when I took them by the hand
to lead them out of Egypt,
because they broke my covenant,
though I was a husband to[c] them,[d]"
declares the LORD.
33"This is the covenant I will make with the house of Israel
after that time," declares the LORD.
"I will put my law in their minds
and write it on their hearts.
I will be their God,
and they will be my people.
34No longer will a man teach his neighbor,
or a man his brother, saying, 'Know the LORD,'
because they will all know me,
from the least of them to the greatest,"
declares the LORD.
"For I will forgive their wickedness
and will remember their sins no more."

[a]22 Or *will go about ⌞seeking⌟*; or *will protect* [b]23 Or *I restore their fortunes* [c]32 Hebrew; Septuagint and Syriac */ and I turned away from* [d]32 Or *was their master*

35This is what the LORD says,

he who appoints the sun
to shine by day,
who decrees the moon and stars
to shine by night,
who stirs up the sea
so that its waves roar—
the LORD Almighty is his name:
36"Only if these decrees vanish from my
sight,"
declares the LORD,
"will the descendants of Israel ever cease
to be a nation before me."

37This is what the LORD says:

"Only if the heavens above can be
measured
and the foundations of the earth below
be searched out
will I reject all the descendants of Israel
because of all they have done,"
declares the LORD.

38"The days are coming," declares the LORD,
"when this city will be rebuilt for me from the
Tower of Hananel to the Corner Gate. 39The
measuring line will stretch from there straight
to the hill of Gareb and then turn to Goah.
40The whole valley where dead bodies and
ashes are thrown, and all the terraces out to the
Kidron Valley on the east as far as the corner of
the Horse Gate, will be holy to the LORD. The
city will never again be uprooted or demolished."

Jeremiah Buys a Field

32 This is the word that came to Jeremiah
from the LORD in the tenth year of Zedekiah king of Judah, which was the eighteenth
year of Nebuchadnezzar. 2The army of the king
of Babylon was then besieging Jerusalem, and
Jeremiah the prophet was confined in the courtyard of the guard in the royal palace of Judah.
3Now Zedekiah king of Judah had imprisoned him there, saying, "Why do you prophesy
as you do? You say, 'This is what the LORD says:
I am about to hand this city over to the king of
Babylon, and he will capture it. 4Zedekiah king
of Judah will not escape out of the hands of the
Babylonians[a] but will certainly be handed
over to the king of Babylon, and will speak with
him face to face and see him with his own eyes.
5He will take Zedekiah to Babylon, where he
will remain until I deal with him, declares the
LORD. If you fight against the Babylonians, you
will not succeed.' "
6Jeremiah said, "The word of the LORD came
to me: 7Hanamel son of Shallum your uncle is
going to come to you and say, 'Buy my field at
Anathoth, because as nearest relative it is your
right and duty to buy it.'
8"Then, just as the LORD had said, my cousin
Hanamel came to me in the courtyard of the
guard and said, 'Buy my field at Anathoth in the
territory of Benjamin. Since it is your right to
redeem it and possess it, buy it for yourself.'
"I knew that this was the word of the LORD;
9so I bought the field at Anathoth from my
cousin Hanamel and weighed out for him seventeen shekels[b] of silver. 10I signed and sealed
the deed, had it witnessed, and weighed out the
silver on the scales. 11I took the deed of purchase—the sealed copy containing the terms and
conditions, as well as the unsealed copy— 12and
I gave this deed to Baruch son of Neriah, the son
of Mahseiah, in the presence of my cousin Hanamel and of the witnesses who had signed the
deed and of all the Jews sitting in the courtyard
of the guard.
13"In their presence I gave Baruch these instructions: 14'This is what the LORD Almighty,
the God of Israel, says: Take these documents,
both the sealed and unsealed copies of the deed
of purchase, and put them in a clay jar so they
will last a long time. 15For this is what the LORD
Almighty, the God of Israel, says: Houses, fields
and vineyards will again be bought in this land.'
16"After I had given the deed of purchase to
Baruch son of Neriah, I prayed to the LORD:

17"Ah, Sovereign LORD, you have made
the heavens and the earth by your great
power and outstretched arm. Nothing is
too hard for you. 18You show love to thousands but bring the punishment for the
fathers' sins into the laps of their children
after them. O great and powerful God,
whose name is the LORD Almighty, 19great
are your purposes and mighty are your
deeds. Your eyes are open to all the ways
of men; you reward everyone according
to his conduct and as his deeds deserve.
20You performed miraculous signs and
wonders in Egypt and have continued

[a]4 Or *Chaldeans;* also in verses 5, 24, 25, 28, 29 and 43
[b]9 That is, about 7 ounces (about 200 grams)

32:1–5 Even though King Zedekiah could see Jeremiah's prophecies coming to pass, he still ignored Jeremiah's warnings and brought suffering upon himself and his people for his failure to see the truth. We can also be very good at hiding from the truth. We may work out schemes to hide our sins and problems from others. But we cannot be freed from our sin until we admit that we are sinful. Once we repent and receive God's forgiveness, then we can seek God and follow his plan for our lives.

32:6–15 God instructed Jeremiah to buy land even though the Babylonians would soon conquer Judah and the laws of ownership would no longer apply. God used Jeremiah's actions to show the people that there was still hope. Despite the losses they would soon experience, God's people would once again be returned to their homeland. Jeremiah's investment in real estate would someday be valuable again. We may also face the devastating consequences of our sins and see little hope for our future. But God has invested in our future through the atoning death of Jesus Christ. God greatly values our lives and will work to restore us when we repent and seek him.

them to this day, both in Israel and among all mankind, and have gained the renown that is still yours. 21You brought your people Israel out of Egypt with signs and wonders, by a mighty hand and an outstretched arm and with great terror. 22You gave them this land you had sworn to give their forefathers, a land flowing with milk and honey. 23They came in and took possession of it, but they did not obey you or follow your law; they did not do what you commanded them to do. So you brought all this disaster upon them.

24"See how the siege ramps are built up to take the city. Because of the sword, famine and plague, the city will be handed over to the Babylonians who are attacking it. What you said has happened, as you now see. 25And though the city will be handed over to the Babylonians, you, O Sovereign LORD, say to me, 'Buy the field with silver and have the transaction witnessed.' "

26Then the word of the LORD came to Jeremiah: 27"I am the LORD, the God of all mankind. Is anything too hard for me? 28Therefore, this is what the LORD says: I am about to hand this city over to the Babylonians and to Nebuchadnezzar king of Babylon, who will capture it. 29The Babylonians who are attacking this city will come in and set it on fire; they will burn it down, along with the houses where the people provoked me to anger by burning incense on the roofs to Baal and by pouring out drink offerings to other gods.

30"The people of Israel and Judah have done nothing but evil in my sight from their youth; indeed, the people of Israel have done nothing but provoke me with what their hands have made, declares the LORD. 31From the day it was built until now, this city has so aroused my anger and wrath that I must remove it from my sight. 32The people of Israel and Judah have provoked me by all the evil they have done—they, their kings and officials, their priests and prophets, the men of Judah and the people of Jerusalem. 33They turned their backs to me and not their faces; though I taught them again and again, they would not listen or respond to discipline. 34They set up their abominable idols in the house that bears my Name and defiled it. 35They built high places for Baal in the Valley of Ben Hinnom to sacrifice their sons and daughters[a] to Molech, though I never commanded, nor did it enter my mind, that they should do such a detestable thing and so make Judah sin.

36"You are saying about this city, 'By the sword, famine and plague it will be handed over to the king of Babylon'; but this is what the LORD, the God of Israel, says: 37I will surely gather them from all the lands where I banish them in my furious anger and great wrath; I will bring them back to this place and let them live in safety. 38They will be my people, and I will be their God. 39I will give them singleness of heart and action, so that they will always fear me for their own good and the good of their children after them. 40I will make an everlasting covenant with them: I will never stop doing good to them, and I will inspire them to fear me, so that they will never turn away from me. 41I will rejoice in doing them good and will assuredly plant them in this land with all my heart and soul.

42"This is what the LORD says: As I have brought all this great calamity on this people, so I will give them all the prosperity I have promised them. 43Once more fields will be bought in this land of which you say, 'It is a desolate waste, without men or animals, for it has been handed over to the Babylonians.' 44Fields will be bought for silver, and deeds will be signed, sealed and witnessed in the territory of Benjamin, in the villages around Jerusalem, in the towns of Judah and in the towns of the hill country, of the western foothills and of the Negev, because I will restore their fortunes,[b] declares the LORD."

Promise of Restoration

33 While Jeremiah was still confined in the courtyard of the guard, the word of the LORD came to him a second time: 2"This is what the LORD says, he who made the earth, the LORD who formed it and established it—the LORD is his name: 3'Call to me and I will answer you and tell you great and unsearchable things you do not know.' 4For this is what the LORD, the God of Israel, says about the houses in this city and the royal palaces of Judah that have been torn down to be used against the siege ramps and the sword 5in the fight with the Babylonians[c]: 'They will be filled with the dead bodies of the men I will slay in my anger and wrath. I will hide my face from this city because of all its wickedness.

6" 'Nevertheless, I will bring health and

[a]35 Or *to make their sons and daughters pass through ⌊the fire⌋* [b]44 Or *will bring them back from captivity*
[c]5 Or *Chaldeans*

32:26–39 God wanted his people to accept responsibility for their sins, bad choices and failures; their suffering in exile would force them to honestly reflect on their wayward lives. But God promised that he would deliver his people from captivity, restore them to their homeland and reconcile them to himself. These promises must have sounded impossible to a people facing the devastation of warfare, famine and disease. In answer to their doubt, God asked the people a question: "Is anything too hard for me?" (32:27). As we face problems that are beyond our control, we can cling to the hope that nothing is too hard for God!

33:1–26 When everything in life seems to be heading for disaster, we can still rely on God. He is faithful, and he will see us through. No matter how dark our future may seem, our loving and faithful God can restore our hope and redirect our course.

healing to it; I will heal my people and will let
them enjoy abundant peace and security. 7I will
bring Judah and Israel back from captivity[a]
and will rebuild them as they were before. 8I
will cleanse them from all the sin they have
committed against me and will forgive all their
sins of rebellion against me. 9Then this city will
bring me renown, joy, praise and honor before
all nations on earth that hear of all the good
things I do for it; and they will be in awe and
will tremble at the abundant prosperity and
peace I provide for it.'

10"This is what the LORD says: 'You say about
this place, "It is a desolate waste, without men
or animals." Yet in the towns of Judah and the
streets of Jerusalem that are deserted, inhabited
by neither men nor animals, there will be heard
once more 11the sounds of joy and gladness, the
voices of bride and bridegroom, and the voices
of those who bring thank offerings to the house
of the LORD, saying,

"Give thanks to the LORD Almighty,
for the LORD is good;
his love endures forever."

For I will restore the fortunes of the land as they
were before,' says the LORD.

12"This is what the LORD Almighty says: 'In
this place, desolate and without men or animals—in all its towns there will again be pastures for shepherds to rest their flocks. 13In the
towns of the hill country, of the western foothills and of the Negev, in the territory of Benjamin, in the villages around Jerusalem and in the
towns of Judah, flocks will again pass under the
hand of the one who counts them,' says
the LORD.

14" 'The days are coming,' declares the LORD,
'when I will fulfill the gracious promise I made
to the house of Israel and to the house of Judah.

15" 'In those days and at that time
I will make a righteous Branch sprout
from David's line;
he will do what is just and right in the
land.
16In those days Judah will be saved
and Jerusalem will live in safety.
This is the name by which it[b] will be
called:
The LORD Our Righteousness.'

17For this is what the LORD says: 'David will
never fail to have a man to sit on the throne of
the house of Israel, 18nor will the priests, who
are Levites, ever fail to have a man to stand
before me continually to offer burnt offerings,
to burn grain offerings and to present sacrifices.' "

19The word of the LORD came to Jeremiah:
20"This is what the LORD says: 'If you can break
my covenant with the day and my covenant
with the night, so that day and night no longer
come at their appointed time, 21then my covenant with David my servant—and my covenant
with the Levites who are priests ministering before me—can be broken and David will no longer have a descendant to reign on his throne. 22I
will make the descendants of David my servant
and the Levites who minister before me as
countless as the stars of the sky and as measure-
less as the sand on the seashore.' "

23The word of the LORD came to Jeremiah:
24"Have you not noticed that these people are
saying, 'The LORD has rejected the two kingdoms[c] he chose'? So they despise my people
and no longer regard them as a nation. 25This is
what the LORD says: 'If I have not established
my covenant with day and night and the fixed
laws of heaven and earth, 26then I will reject the
descendants of Jacob and David my servant and
will not choose one of his sons to rule over the
descendants of Abraham, Isaac and Jacob. For I
will restore their fortunes[d] and have compassion on them.' "

Warning to Zedekiah

34 While Nebuchadnezzar king of Babylon and all his army and all the kingdoms and peoples in the empire he ruled were
fighting against Jerusalem and all its surrounding towns, this word came to Jeremiah from the
LORD: 2"This is what the LORD, the God of Israel, says: Go to Zedekiah king of Judah and tell
him, 'This is what the LORD says: I am about to
hand this city over to the king of Babylon, and
he will burn it down. 3You will not escape from
his grasp but will surely be captured and handed over to him. You will see the king of Babylon
with your own eyes, and he will speak with you
face to face. And you will go to Babylon.

4" 'Yet hear the promise of the LORD,
O Zedekiah king of Judah. This is what the
LORD says concerning you: You will not die by
the sword; 5you will die peacefully. As people
made a funeral fire in honor of your fathers, the
former kings who preceded you, so they will
make a fire in your honor and lament, "Alas,
O master!" I myself make this promise, declares
the LORD.' "

6Then Jeremiah the prophet told all this to
Zedekiah king of Judah, in Jerusalem, 7while
the army of the king of Babylon was fighting
against Jerusalem and the other cities of Judah
that were still holding out—Lachish and Azekah.
These were the only fortified cities left in Judah.

[a]7 Or *will restore the fortunes of Judah and Israel*
[b]16 Or *he* [c]24 Or *families* [d]26 Or *will bring them back from captivity*

34:1–7 Though King Zedekiah's deed brought suffering to many, God promised grace to Zedekiah. The king would not die by the sword; God would let him live. In the same way, we deserve punishment for our sinfulness, but God has offered us grace instead. No matter what we have done in the past, there is still hope. If we honestly admit our sins and turn to God, he will be gracious to us.

Freedom for Slaves

8The word came to Jeremiah from the LORD after King Zedekiah had made a covenant with all the people in Jerusalem to proclaim freedom for the slaves. 9Everyone was to free his Hebrew slaves, both male and female; no one was to hold a fellow Jew in bondage. 10So all the officials and people who entered into this covenant agreed that they would free their male and female slaves and no longer hold them in bondage. They agreed, and set them free. 11But afterward they changed their minds and took back the slaves they had freed and enslaved them again.

12Then the word of the LORD came to Jeremiah: 13"This is what the LORD, the God of Israel, says: I made a covenant with your forefathers when I brought them out of Egypt, out of the land of slavery. I said, 14'Every seventh year each of you must free any fellow Hebrew who has sold himself to you. After he has served you six years, you must let him go free.'[a] Your fathers, however, did not listen to me or pay attention to me. 15Recently you repented and did what is right in my sight: Each of you proclaimed freedom to his countrymen. You even made a covenant before me in the house that bears my Name. 16But now you have turned around and profaned my name; each of you has taken back the male and female slaves you had set free to go where they wished. You have forced them to become your slaves again.

17"Therefore, this is what the LORD says: You have not obeyed me; you have not proclaimed freedom for your fellow countrymen. So I now proclaim 'freedom' for you, declares the LORD—'freedom' to fall by the sword, plague and famine. I will make you abhorrent to all the kingdoms of the earth. 18The men who have violated my covenant and have not fulfilled the terms of the covenant they made before me, I will treat like the calf they cut in two and then walked between its pieces. 19The leaders of Judah and Jerusalem, the court officials, the priests and all the people of the land who walked between the pieces of the calf, 20I will hand over to their enemies who seek their lives. Their dead bodies will become food for the birds of the air and the beasts of the earth.

21"I will hand Zedekiah king of Judah and his officials over to their enemies who seek their lives, to the army of the king of Babylon, which has withdrawn from you. 22I am going to give the order, declares the LORD, and I will bring them back to this city. They will fight against it, take it and burn it down. And I will lay waste the towns of Judah so no one can live there."

The Recabites

35 This is the word that came to Jeremiah from the LORD during the reign of Jehoiakim son of Josiah king of Judah: 2"Go to the Recabite family and invite them to come to one of the side rooms of the house of the LORD and give them wine to drink."

3So I went to get Jaazaniah son of Jeremiah, the son of Habazziniah, and his brothers and all his sons—the whole family of the Recabites. 4I brought them into the house of the LORD, into the room of the sons of Hanan son of Igdaliah the man of God. It was next to the room of the officials, which was over that of Maaseiah son of Shallum the doorkeeper. 5Then I set bowls full of wine and some cups before the men of the Recabite family and said to them, "Drink some wine."

6But they replied, "We do not drink wine, because our forefather Jonadab son of Recab gave us this command: 'Neither you nor your descendants must ever drink wine. 7Also you must never build houses, sow seed or plant vineyards; you must never have any of these things, but must always live in tents. Then you will live a long time in the land where you are nomads.' 8We have obeyed everything our forefather Jonadab son of Recab commanded us. Neither we nor our wives nor our sons and daughters have ever drunk wine 9or built houses to live in or had vineyards, fields or crops. 10We have lived in tents and have fully obeyed everything our forefather Jonadab commanded us. 11But when Nebuchadnezzar king of Babylon invaded this land, we said, 'Come, we must go to Jerusalem to escape the Babylonian[b] and Aramean armies.' So we have remained in Jerusalem."

12Then the word of the LORD came to Jeremiah, saying: 13"This is what the LORD Almighty, the God of Israel, says: Go and tell the men of Judah and the people of Jerusalem, 'Will you not learn a lesson and obey my words?' declares the LORD. 14'Jonadab son of Recab ordered his sons not to drink wine and this command has been kept. To this day they do not drink wine, because they obey their forefather's command. But I have spoken to you again and again, yet you have not obeyed me. 15Again and again I sent all my servants the prophets to you. They

[a] 14 Deut. 15:12 [b] 11 Or *Chaldean*

34:8–22 Zedekiah accepted God's grace and, in turn, extended grace to others. He urged his people to free their Hebrew slaves, which was a requirement of God's law. While the people initially responded well to Zedekiah's request, they soon went back to their old ways of disobedience. As a result, they soon lost all the gains they had made toward healing and restoration. Likewise, spiritual renewal is a long-term process. If we fail to persevere in our spiritual gains, we may lose ground. When God calls us to change, he calls us to change permanently.

35:1–19 This chapter contains a fascinating story about a family that faithfully obeyed the direction of its ancestors, choosing to submit to God's plan. God used this family as an example for the people of Judah. He longed for his people to obey him, just as the Recabites followed the direction of their leaders. Trusting God and obeying his will for our lives is always the best decision we can make.

said, "Each of you must turn from your wicked
ways and reform your actions; do not follow
other gods to serve them. Then you will live in
the land I have given to you and your fathers."
But you have not paid attention or listened to
me. 16The descendants of Jonadab son of Recab have carried out the command their forefather gave them, but these people have not
obeyed me.'

17"Therefore, this is what the LORD God Almighty, the God of Israel, says: 'Listen! I am
going to bring on Judah and on everyone living in Jerusalem every disaster I pronounced
against them. I spoke to them, but they did not
listen; I called to them, but they did not answer.' "

18Then Jeremiah said to the family of the
Recabites, "This is what the LORD Almighty, the
God of Israel, says: 'You have obeyed the command of your forefather Jonadab and have followed all his instructions and have done everything he ordered.' 19Therefore, this is what the
LORD Almighty, the God of Israel, says: 'Jonadab son of Recab will never fail to have a man
to serve me.' "

Jehoiakim Burns Jeremiah's Scroll

36 In the fourth year of Jehoiakim son of
Josiah king of Judah, this word came to
Jeremiah from the LORD: 2"Take a scroll and
write on it all the words I have spoken to you
concerning Israel, Judah and all the other nations from the time I began speaking to you in
the reign of Josiah till now. 3Perhaps when the
people of Judah hear about every disaster I plan
to inflict on them, each of them will turn from
his wicked way; then I will forgive their wickedness and their sin."

4So Jeremiah called Baruch son of Neriah,
and while Jeremiah dictated all the words the
LORD had spoken to him, Baruch wrote them on
the scroll. 5Then Jeremiah told Baruch, "I am
restricted; I cannot go to the LORD's temple. 6So
you go to the house of the LORD on a day of
fasting and read to the people from the scroll
the words of the LORD that you wrote as I dictated. Read them to all the people of Judah who
come in from their towns. 7Perhaps they will
bring their petition before the LORD, and each
will turn from his wicked ways, for the anger
and wrath pronounced against this people by
the LORD are great."

8Baruch son of Neriah did everything Jeremiah the prophet told him to do; at the LORD's
temple he read the words of the LORD from the
scroll. 9In the ninth month of the fifth year of
Jehoiakim son of Josiah king of Judah, a time of
fasting before the LORD was proclaimed for all
the people in Jerusalem and those who had
come from the towns of Judah. 10From the
room of Gemariah son of Shaphan the secretary, which was in the upper courtyard at the
entrance of the New Gate of the temple, Baruch
read to all the people at the LORD's temple the
words of Jeremiah from the scroll.

11When Micaiah son of Gemariah, the son of
Shaphan, heard all the words of the LORD from
the scroll, 12he went down to the secretary's
room in the royal palace, where all the officials
were sitting: Elishama the secretary, Delaiah
son of Shemaiah, Elnathan son of Acbor, Gemariah son of Shaphan, Zedekiah son of Hananiah, and all the other officials. 13After Micaiah
told them everything he had heard Baruch read
to the people from the scroll, 14all the officials
sent Jehudi son of Nethaniah, the son of Shelemiah, the son of Cushi, to say to Baruch, "Bring
the scroll from which you have read to the people and come." So Baruch son of Neriah went to
them with the scroll in his hand. 15They said to
him, "Sit down, please, and read it to us."

So Baruch read it to them. 16When they heard
all these words, they looked at each other in fear
and said to Baruch, "We must report all these
words to the king." 17Then they asked Baruch,
"Tell us, how did you come to write all this?
Did Jeremiah dictate it?"

18"Yes," Baruch replied, "he dictated all these
words to me, and I wrote them in ink on the
scroll."

19Then the officials said to Baruch, "You and
Jeremiah, go and hide. Don't let anyone know
where you are."

20After they put the scroll in the room of
Elishama the secretary, they went to the king in
the courtyard and reported everything to him.
21The king sent Jehudi to get the scroll, and
Jehudi brought it from the room of Elishama
the secretary and read it to the king and all the
officials standing beside him. 22It was the ninth
month and the king was sitting in the winter
apartment, with a fire burning in the firepot in
front of him. 23Whenever Jehudi had read three
or four columns of the scroll, the king cut them
off with a scribe's knife and threw them into the
firepot, until the entire scroll was burned in the
fire. 24The king and all his attendants who
heard all these words showed no fear, nor did
they tear their clothes. 25Even though Elnathan,
Delaiah and Gemariah urged the king not to
burn the scroll, he would not listen to them.
26Instead, the king commanded Jerahmeel, a
son of the king, Seraiah son of Azriel and Shelemiah son of Abdeel to arrest Baruch the scribe
and Jeremiah the prophet. But the LORD had
hidden them.

27After the king burned the scroll containing

36:1–32 King Jehoiakim refused to listen to Jeremiah's predictions of a coming destruction. He preferred the comforting lies of the false prophets to the terrifying truth of God's prophet. Jehoiakim tried to deny his sin and its consequences by ignoring them. Refusing to see our problems can never solve them; it only compounds them. When we are willing to see the truth, admit our sins, repent and allow God to redirect the course of our lives, we will find hope.

the words that Baruch had written at Jeremiah's
dictation, the word of the LORD came to Jeremiah: 28"Take another scroll and write on it all the
words that were on the first scroll, which Jehoiakim king of Judah burned up. 29Also tell Jehoiakim king of Judah, 'This is what the LORD says:
You burned that scroll and said, "Why did you
write on it that the king of Babylon would certainly come and destroy this land and cut off
both men and animals from it?" 30Therefore, this
is what the LORD says about Jehoiakim king of
Judah: He will have no one to sit on the throne
of David; his body will be thrown out and exposed to the heat by day and the frost by night.
31I will punish him and his children and his
attendants for their wickedness; I will bring on
them and those living in Jerusalem and the people of Judah every disaster I pronounced against
them, because they have not listened.' "

32So Jeremiah took another scroll and gave it
to the scribe Baruch son of Neriah, and as Jeremiah dictated, Baruch wrote on it all the words
of the scroll that Jehoiakim king of Judah had
burned in the fire. And many similar words
were added to them.

Jeremiah in Prison

37 Zedekiah son of Josiah was made king
of Judah by Nebuchadnezzar king of
Babylon; he reigned in place of Jehoiachin[a]
son of Jehoiakim. 2Neither he nor his attendants nor the people of the land paid any attention to the words the LORD had spoken through
Jeremiah the prophet.

3King Zedekiah, however, sent Jehucal son
of Shelemiah with the priest Zephaniah son
of Maaseiah to Jeremiah the prophet with this
message: "Please pray to the LORD our God
for us."

4Now Jeremiah was free to come and go
among the people, for he had not yet been put
in prison. 5Pharaoh's army had marched out of
Egypt, and when the Babylonians[b] who were
besieging Jerusalem heard the report about
them, they withdrew from Jerusalem.

6Then the word of the LORD came to Jeremiah the prophet: 7"This is what the LORD, the
God of Israel, says: Tell the king of Judah, who
sent you to inquire of me, 'Pharaoh's army,
which has marched out to support you, will go
back to its own land, to Egypt. 8Then the Babylonians will return and attack this city; they
will capture it and burn it down.'

9"This is what the LORD says: Do not deceive
yourselves, thinking, 'The Babylonians will
surely leave us.' They will not! 10Even if you
were to defeat the entire Babylonian[c] army
that is attacking you and only wounded men
were left in their tents, they would come out
and burn this city down."

11After the Babylonian army had withdrawn
from Jerusalem because of Pharaoh's army,
12Jeremiah started to leave the city to go to the
territory of Benjamin to get his share of the
property among the people there. 13But when
he reached the Benjamin Gate, the captain of
the guard, whose name was Irijah son of Shelemiah, the son of Hananiah, arrested him and
said, "You are deserting to the Babylonians!"

14"That's not true!" Jeremiah said. "I am not
deserting to the Babylonians." But Irijah would
not listen to him; instead, he arrested Jeremiah
and brought him to the officials. 15They were
angry with Jeremiah and had him beaten and
imprisoned in the house of Jonathan the secretary, which they had made into a prison.

16Jeremiah was put into a vaulted cell in a
dungeon, where he remained a long time.
17Then King Zedekiah sent for him and had
him brought to the palace, where he asked him
privately, "Is there any word from the LORD?"

"Yes," Jeremiah replied, "you will be handed
over to the king of Babylon."

18Then Jeremiah said to King Zedekiah,
"What crime have I committed against you or
your officials or this people, that you have put
me in prison? 19Where are your prophets who
prophesied to you, 'The king of Babylon will
not attack you or this land'? 20But now, my lord
the king, please listen. Let me bring my petition
before you: Do not send me back to the house
of Jonathan the secretary, or I will die there."

21King Zedekiah then gave orders for Jeremiah to be placed in the courtyard of the guard
and given bread from the street of the bakers
each day until all the bread in the city was gone.
So Jeremiah remained in the courtyard of the
guard.

Jeremiah Thrown Into a Cistern

38 Shephatiah son of Mattan, Gedaliah
son of Pashhur, Jehucal[d] son of Shelemiah, and Pashhur son of Malkijah heard what
Jeremiah was telling all the people when he
said, 2"This is what the LORD says: 'Whoever
stays in this city will die by the sword, famine
or plague, but whoever goes over to the Babylonians[e] will live. He will escape with his life; he
will live.' 3And this is what the LORD says: 'This
city will certainly be handed over to the army of
the king of Babylon, who will capture it.' "

4Then the officials said to the king, "This
man should be put to death. He is discouraging
the soldiers who are left in this city, as well as
all the people, by the things he is saying to
them. This man is not seeking the good of these
people but their ruin."

5"He is in your hands," King Zedekiah answered. "The king can do nothing to oppose
you."

6So they took Jeremiah and put him into the
cistern of Malkijah, the king's son, which was in
the courtyard of the guard. They lowered Jere-

[a]*1* Hebrew *Coniah,* a variant of *Jehoiachin* [b]*5* Or *Chaldeans;* also in verses 8, 9, 13 and 14 [c]*10* Or *Chaldean;* also in verse 11 [d]*1* Hebrew *Jucal,* a variant of *Jehucal* [e]*2* Or *Chaldeans;* also in verses 18, 19 and 23

miah by ropes into the cistern; it had no water in it, only mud, and Jeremiah sank down into the mud.

7But Ebed-Melech, a Cushite,[a] an official[b] in the royal palace, heard that they had put Jeremiah into the cistern. While the king was sitting in the Benjamin Gate, 8Ebed-Melech went out of the palace and said to him, 9"My lord the king, these men have acted wickedly in all they have done to Jeremiah the prophet. They have thrown him into a cistern, where he will starve to death when there is no longer any bread in the city."

10Then the king commanded Ebed-Melech the Cushite, "Take thirty men from here with you and lift Jeremiah the prophet out of the cistern before he dies."

11So Ebed-Melech took the men with him and went to a room under the treasury in the palace. He took some old rags and worn-out clothes from there and let them down with ropes to Jeremiah in the cistern. 12Ebed-Melech the Cushite said to Jeremiah, "Put these old rags and worn-out clothes under your arms to pad the ropes." Jeremiah did so, 13and they pulled him up with the ropes and lifted him out of the cistern. And Jeremiah remained in the courtyard of the guard.

Zedekiah Questions Jeremiah Again

14Then King Zedekiah sent for Jeremiah the prophet and had him brought to the third entrance to the temple of the LORD. "I am going to ask you something," the king said to Jeremiah. "Do not hide anything from me."

15Jeremiah said to Zedekiah, "If I give you an answer, will you not kill me? Even if I did give you counsel, you would not listen to me."

16But King Zedekiah swore this oath secretly to Jeremiah: "As surely as the LORD lives, who has given us breath, I will neither kill you nor hand you over to those who are seeking your life."

17Then Jeremiah said to Zedekiah, "This is what the LORD God Almighty, the God of Israel, says: 'If you surrender to the officers of the king of Babylon, your life will be spared and this city will not be burned down; you and your family will live. 18But if you will not surrender to the officers of the king of Babylon, this city will be handed over to the Babylonians and they will burn it down; you yourself will not escape from their hands.' "

19King Zedekiah said to Jeremiah, "I am afraid of the Jews who have gone over to the Babylonians, for the Babylonians may hand me over to them and they will mistreat me."

20"They will not hand you over," Jeremiah replied. "Obey the LORD by doing what I tell you. Then it will go well with you, and your life will be spared. 21But if you refuse to surrender, this is what the LORD has revealed to me: 22All the women left in the palace of the king of Judah will be brought out to the officials of the king of Babylon. Those women will say to you:

" 'They misled you and overcame you—
those trusted friends of yours.
Your feet are sunk in the mud;
your friends have deserted you.'

23"All your wives and children will be brought out to the Babylonians. You yourself will not escape from their hands but will be captured by the king of Babylon; and this city will[c] be burned down."

24Then Zedekiah said to Jeremiah, "Do not let anyone know about this conversation, or you may die. 25If the officials hear that I talked with you, and they come to you and say, 'Tell us what you said to the king and what the king said to you; do not hide it from us or we will kill you,' 26then tell them, 'I was pleading with the king not to send me back to Jonathan's house to die there.' "

27All the officials did come to Jeremiah and question him, and he told them everything the king had ordered him to say. So they said no more to him, for no one had heard his conversation with the king.

28And Jeremiah remained in the courtyard of the guard until the day Jerusalem was captured.

The Fall of Jerusalem

39 This is how Jerusalem was taken: 1In the ninth year of Zedekiah king of Judah, in the tenth month, Nebuchadnezzar king of Babylon marched against Jerusalem with his whole army and laid siege to it. 2And on the ninth day of the fourth month of Zedekiah's eleventh year, the city wall was broken through. 3Then all the officials of the king of Babylon came and took seats in the Middle Gate: Nergal-Sharezer of Samgar, Nebo-Sarsekim[d] a chief officer, Nergal-Sharezer a high official and all the other officials of the king of Babylon. 4When Zedekiah king of Judah and all the soldiers saw them, they fled; they left the city at night by way of the king's garden, through the

[a]7 Probably from the upper Nile region [b]7 Or *a eunuch* [c]23 Or *and you will cause this city to* [d]3 Or *Nergal-Sharezer, Samgar-Nebo, Sarsekim*

38:14–28 Jeremiah shared God's clear direction with Zedekiah, but the king was too afraid to follow the prophet's advice. We often fall into the same trap. God gives us clear indications in his Word of how he wants us to live, but sometimes we fail to act on what he says because we are afraid of what others will think, or we may not want to do it. Seeking God's will for our lives is only part of the task. We must act on what we learn before it will become effective in our lives.

39:1–18 Jeremiah's prophecy became a reality. Tragic scenes of murder and destruction filled the city of Jerusalem. Even when we know the consequences of our sin are coming, the resulting pain is no less difficult to bear. God doesn't enjoy our pain; he longs for us to learn from the devastation and turn to him.

gate between the two walls, and headed toward the Arabah.[a]

5But the Babylonian[b] army pursued them and overtook Zedekiah in the plains of Jericho. They captured him and took him to Nebuchadnezzar king of Babylon at Riblah in the land of Hamath, where he pronounced sentence on him. 6There at Riblah the king of Babylon slaughtered the sons of Zedekiah before his eyes and also killed all the nobles of Judah. 7Then he put out Zedekiah's eyes and bound him with bronze shackles to take him to Babylon.

8The Babylonians[c] set fire to the royal palace and the houses of the people and broke down the walls of Jerusalem. 9Nebuzaradan commander of the imperial guard carried into exile to Babylon the people who remained in the city, along with those who had gone over to him, and the rest of the people. 10But Nebuzaradan the commander of the guard left behind in the land of Judah some of the poor people, who owned nothing; and at that time he gave them vineyards and fields.

11Now Nebuchadnezzar king of Babylon had given these orders about Jeremiah through Nebuzaradan commander of the imperial guard: 12"Take him and look after him; don't harm him but do for him whatever he asks." 13So Nebuzaradan the commander of the guard, Nebushazban a chief officer, Nergal-Sharezer a high official and all the other officers of the king of Babylon 14sent and had Jeremiah taken out of the courtyard of the guard. They turned him over to Gedaliah son of Ahikam, the son of Shaphan, to take him back to his home. So he remained among his own people.

15While Jeremiah had been confined in the courtyard of the guard, the word of the LORD came to him: 16"Go and tell Ebed-Melech the Cushite, 'This is what the LORD Almighty, the God of Israel, says: I am about to fulfill my words against this city through disaster, not prosperity. At that time they will be fulfilled before your eyes. 17But I will rescue you on that day, declares the LORD; you will not be handed over to those you fear. 18I will save you; you will not fall by the sword but will escape with your life, because you trust in me, declares the LORD.' "

Jeremiah Freed

40 The word came to Jeremiah from the LORD after Nebuzaradan commander of the imperial guard had released him at Ramah. He had found Jeremiah bound in chains among all the captives from Jerusalem and Judah who were being carried into exile to Babylon. 2When the commander of the guard found Jeremiah, he said to him, "The LORD your God decreed this disaster for this place. 3And now the LORD has brought it about; he has done just as he said he would. All this happened because you people sinned against the LORD and did not obey him. 4But today I am freeing you from the chains on your wrists. Come with me to Babylon, if you like, and I will look after you; but if you do not want to, then don't come. Look, the whole country lies before you; go wherever you please." 5However, before Jeremiah turned to go,[d] Nebuzaradan added, "Go back to Gedaliah son of Ahikam, the son of Shaphan, whom the king of Babylon has appointed over the towns of Judah, and live with him among the people, or go anywhere else you please."

Then the commander gave him provisions and a present and let him go. 6So Jeremiah went to Gedaliah son of Ahikam at Mizpah and stayed with him among the people who were left behind in the land.

Gedaliah Assassinated

7When all the army officers and their men who were still in the open country heard that the king of Babylon had appointed Gedaliah son of Ahikam as governor over the land and had put him in charge of the men, women and children who were the poorest in the land and who had not been carried into exile to Babylon, 8they came to Gedaliah at Mizpah—Ishmael son of Nethaniah, Johanan and Jonathan the sons of Kareah, Seraiah son of Tanhumeth, the sons of Ephai the Netophathite, and Jaazaniah[e] the son of the Maacathite, and their men. 9Gedaliah son of Ahikam, the son of Shaphan, took an oath to reassure them and their men. "Do not be afraid to serve the Babylonians,[f]" he said. "Settle down in the land and serve the king of Babylon, and it will go well with you. 10I myself will stay at Mizpah to represent you before the Babylonians who come to us, but you are to harvest the wine, summer fruit and oil, and put them in your storage jars, and live in the towns you have taken over."

11When all the Jews in Moab, Ammon, Edom and all the other countries heard that the king of Babylon had left a remnant in Judah and had appointed Gedaliah son of Ahikam, the son of Shaphan, as governor over them, 12they all came back to the land of Judah, to Gedaliah at Mizpah, from all the countries where they had been scattered. And they harvested an abundance of wine and summer fruit.

13Johanan son of Kareah and all the army officers still in the open country came to Gedali-

[a]4 Or *the Jordan Valley* [b]5 Or *Chaldean* [c]8 Or *Chaldeans* [d]5 Or *Jeremiah answered* [e]8 Hebrew *Jezaniah,* a variant of *Jaazaniah* [f]9 Or *Chaldeans;* also in verse 10

40:1–12 For the first time since Jeremiah's prophetic work began, we glimpse peace and harmony in the lives of God's people. The reason was simple. They were following God's directive to serve Nebuchadnezzar. They were obedient to God. The same holds true for us today: The best way is always God's way.

40:13—43:13 When turmoil threatened the security of the people, they chose to take matters back into their

ah at Mizpah 14and said to him, "Don't you know that Baalis king of the Ammonites has sent Ishmael son of Nethaniah to take your life?" But Gedaliah son of Ahikam did not believe them.

15Then Johanan son of Kareah said privately to Gedaliah in Mizpah, "Let me go and kill Ishmael son of Nethaniah, and no one will know it. Why should he take your life and cause all the Jews who are gathered around you to be scattered and the remnant of Judah to perish?"

16But Gedaliah son of Ahikam said to Johanan son of Kareah, "Don't do such a thing! What you are saying about Ishmael is not true."

41 In the seventh month Ishmael son of Nethaniah, the son of Elishama, who was of royal blood and had been one of the king's officers, came with ten men to Gedaliah son of Ahikam at Mizpah. While they were eating together there, 2Ishmael son of Nethaniah and the ten men who were with him got up and struck down Gedaliah son of Ahikam, the son of Shaphan, with the sword, killing the one whom the king of Babylon had appointed as governor over the land. 3Ishmael also killed all the Jews who were with Gedaliah at Mizpah, as well as the Babylonian[a] soldiers who were there.

4The day after Gedaliah's assassination, before anyone knew about it, 5eighty men who had shaved off their beards, torn their clothes and cut themselves came from Shechem, Shiloh and Samaria, bringing grain offerings and incense with them to the house of the LORD. 6Ishmael son of Nethaniah went out from Mizpah to meet them, weeping as he went. When he met them, he said, "Come to Gedaliah son of Ahikam." 7When they went into the city, Ishmael son of Nethaniah and the men who were with him slaughtered them and threw them into a cistern. 8But ten of them said to Ishmael, "Don't kill us! We have wheat and barley, oil and honey, hidden in a field." So he let them alone and did not kill them with the others. 9Now the cistern where he threw all the bodies of the men he had killed along with Gedaliah was the one King Asa had made as part of his defense against Baasha king of Israel. Ishmael son of Nethaniah filled it with the dead.

10Ishmael made captives of all the rest of the people who were in Mizpah—the king's daughters along with all the others who were left there, over whom Nebuzaradan commander of the imperial guard had appointed Gedaliah son of Ahikam. Ishmael son of Nethaniah took them captive and set out to cross over to the Ammonites.

11When Johanan son of Kareah and all the army officers who were with him heard about all the crimes Ishmael son of Nethaniah had committed, 12they took all their men and went to fight Ishmael son of Nethaniah. They caught up with him near the great pool in Gibeon. 13When all the people Ishmael had with him saw Johanan son of Kareah and the army officers who were with him, they were glad. 14All the people Ishmael had taken captive at Mizpah turned and went over to Johanan son of Kareah. 15But Ishmael son of Nethaniah and eight of his men escaped from Johanan and fled to the Ammonites.

Flight to Egypt

16Then Johanan son of Kareah and all the army officers who were with him led away all the survivors from Mizpah whom he had recovered from Ishmael son of Nethaniah after he had assassinated Gedaliah son of Ahikam: the soldiers, women, children and court officials he had brought from Gibeon. 17And they went on, stopping at Geruth Kimham near Bethlehem on their way to Egypt 18to escape the Babylonians.[b] They were afraid of them because Ishmael son of Nethaniah had killed Gedaliah son of Ahikam, whom the king of Babylon had appointed as governor over the land.

42 Then all the army officers, including Johanan son of Kareah and Jezaniah[c] son of Hoshaiah, and all the people from the least to the greatest approached 2Jeremiah the prophet and said to him, "Please hear our petition and pray to the LORD your God for this entire remnant. For as you now see, though we were once many, now only a few are left. 3Pray that the LORD your God will tell us where we should go and what we should do."

4"I have heard you," replied Jeremiah the prophet. "I will certainly pray to the LORD your God as you have requested; I will tell you everything the LORD says and will keep nothing back from you."

5Then they said to Jeremiah, "May the LORD be a true and faithful witness against us if we do not act in accordance with everything the LORD your God sends you to tell us. 6Whether it is favorable or unfavorable, we will obey the LORD our God, to whom we are sending you, so that it will go well with us, for we will obey the LORD our God."

7Ten days later the word of the LORD came to Jeremiah. 8So he called together Johanan son of Kareah and all the army officers who were with him and all the people from the least to the greatest. 9He said to them, "This is what the LORD, the God of Israel, to whom you sent me to present your petition, says: 10'If you stay in this land, I will build you up and not tear you down; I will plant you and not uproot you, for

[a] 3 Or *Chaldean* [b] 18 Or *Chaldeans* [c] 1 Hebrew; Septuagint (see also 43:2) *Azariah*

own hands. When things begin to go well for us, we may forget our need for God and try to control things on our own. This forgetfulness leads only to our downfall. When we forget God and try to go it alone, there is little hope for spiritual progress.

I am grieved over the disaster I have inflicted on you. [11]Do not be afraid of the king of Babylon, whom you now fear. Do not be afraid of him, declares the LORD, for I am with you and will save you and deliver you from his hands. [12]I will show you compassion so that he will have compassion on you and restore you to your land.'

[13]"However, if you say, 'We will not stay in this land,' and so disobey the LORD your God, [14]and if you say, 'No, we will go and live in Egypt, where we will not see war or hear the trumpet or be hungry for bread,' [15]then hear the word of the LORD, O remnant of Judah. This is what the LORD Almighty, the God of Israel, says: 'If you are determined to go to Egypt and you do go to settle there, [16]then the sword you fear will overtake you there, and the famine you dread will follow you into Egypt, and there you will die. [17]Indeed, all who are determined to go to Egypt to settle there will die by the sword, famine and plague; not one of them will survive or escape the disaster I will bring on them.' [18]This is what the LORD Almighty, the God of Israel, says: 'As my anger and wrath have been poured out on those who lived in Jerusalem, so will my wrath be poured out on you when you go to Egypt. You will be an object of cursing and horror, of condemnation and reproach; you will never see this place again.'

[19]"O remnant of Judah, the LORD has told you, 'Do not go to Egypt.' Be sure of this: I warn you today [20]that you made a fatal mistake[a] when you sent me to the LORD your God and said, 'Pray to the LORD our God for us; tell us everything he says and we will do it.' [21]I have told you today, but you still have not obeyed the LORD your God in all he sent me to tell you. [22]So now, be sure of this: You will die by the sword, famine and plague in the place where you want to go to settle."

43 When Jeremiah finished telling the people all the words of the LORD their God—everything the LORD had sent him to tell them— [2]Azariah son of Hoshaiah and Johanan son of Kareah and all the arrogant men said to Jeremiah, "You are lying! The LORD our God has not sent you to say, 'You must not go to Egypt to settle there.' [3]But Baruch son of Neriah is inciting you against us to hand us over to the Babylonians,[b] so they may kill us or carry us into exile to Babylon."

[4]So Johanan son of Kareah and all the army officers and all the people disobeyed the LORD's command to stay in the land of Judah. [5]Instead, Johanan son of Kareah and all the army officers led away all the remnant of Judah who had come back to live in the land of Judah from all the nations where they had been scattered. [6]They also led away all the men, women and children and the king's daughters whom Nebuzaradan commander of the imperial guard had left with Gedaliah son of Ahikam, the son of Shaphan, and Jeremiah the prophet and Baruch son of Neriah. [7]So they entered Egypt in disobedience to the LORD and went as far as Tahpanhes.

[8]In Tahpanhes the word of the LORD came to Jeremiah: [9]"While the Jews are watching, take some large stones with you and bury them in clay in the brick pavement at the entrance to Pharaoh's palace in Tahpanhes. [10]Then say to them, 'This is what the LORD Almighty, the God of Israel, says: I will send for my servant Nebuchadnezzar king of Babylon, and I will set his throne over these stones I have buried here; he will spread his royal canopy above them. [11]He will come and attack Egypt, bringing death to those destined for death, captivity to those destined for captivity, and the sword to those destined for the sword. [12]He[c] will set fire to the temples of the gods of Egypt; he will burn their temples and take their gods captive. As a shepherd wraps his garment around him, so will he wrap Egypt around himself and depart from there unscathed. [13]There in the temple of the sun[d] in Egypt he will demolish the sacred pillars and will burn down the temples of the gods of Egypt.' "

Disaster Because of Idolatry

44 This word came to Jeremiah concerning all the Jews living in Lower Egypt—in Migdol, Tahpanhes and Memphis[e]—and in Upper Egypt[f]: [2]"This is what the LORD Almighty, the God of Israel, says: You saw the great disaster I brought on Jerusalem and on all the towns of Judah. Today they lie deserted and in ruins [3]because of the evil they have done. They provoked me to anger by burning incense and by worshiping other gods that neither they nor you nor your fathers ever knew. [4]Again and again I sent my servants the prophets, who said, 'Do not do this detestable thing that I hate!' [5]But they did not listen or pay attention; they did not turn from their wickedness or stop burning incense to other gods. [6]Therefore, my fierce anger was poured out; it raged against the towns of Judah and the streets of Jerusalem and made them the desolate ruins they are today.

[7]"Now this is what the LORD God Almighty, the God of Israel, says: Why bring such great

[a]20 Or *you erred in your hearts* [b]3 Or *Chaldeans* [c]12 Or *I* [d]13 Or *in Heliopolis* [e]1 Hebrew *Noph* [f]1 Hebrew *in Pathros*

44:1–30 Jeremiah encouraged the remnant in Egypt to heed the lessons learned from Judah's recent fall and to turn away from their idolatry. But sadly, their love for God was conditional. Unless God rewarded them in the ways they expected, they refused to obey him. Our response should not echo the Egyptian remnant's. God is worthy of our love and obedience whether or not he gives us what we want.

disaster on yourselves by cutting off from Judah the men and women, the children and infants, and so leave yourselves without a remnant? [8]Why provoke me to anger with what your hands have made, burning incense to other gods in Egypt, where you have come to live? You will destroy yourselves and make yourselves an object of cursing and reproach among all the nations on earth. [9]Have you forgotten the wickedness committed by your fathers and by the kings and queens of Judah and the wickedness committed by you and your wives in the land of Judah and the streets of Jerusalem? [10]To this day they have not humbled themselves or shown reverence, nor have they followed my law and the decrees I set before you and your fathers.

[11]"Therefore, this is what the LORD Almighty, the God of Israel, says: I am determined to bring disaster on you and to destroy all Judah. [12]I will take away the remnant of Judah who were determined to go to Egypt to settle there. They will all perish in Egypt; they will fall by the sword or die from famine. From the least to the greatest, they will die by sword or famine. They will become an object of cursing and horror, of condemnation and reproach. [13]I will punish those who live in Egypt with the sword, famine and plague, as I punished Jerusalem. [14]None of the remnant of Judah who have gone to live in Egypt will escape or survive to return to the land of Judah, to which they long to return and live; none will return except a few fugitives."

[15]Then all the men who knew that their wives were burning incense to other gods, along with all the women who were present—a large assembly—and all the people living in Lower and Upper Egypt,[a] said to Jeremiah, [16]"We will not listen to the message you have spoken to us in the name of the LORD! [17]We will certainly do everything we said we would: We will burn incense to the Queen of Heaven and will pour out drink offerings to her just as we and our fathers, our kings and our officials did in the towns of Judah and in the streets of Jerusalem. At that time we had plenty of food and were well off and suffered no harm. [18]But ever since we stopped burning incense to the Queen of Heaven and pouring out drink offerings to her, we have had nothing and have been perishing by sword and famine."

[19]The women added, "When we burned incense to the Queen of Heaven and poured out drink offerings to her, did not our husbands know that we were making cakes like her image and pouring out drink offerings to her?"

[20]Then Jeremiah said to all the people, both men and women, who were answering him, [21]"Did not the LORD remember and think about the incense burned in the towns of Judah and the streets of Jerusalem by you and your fathers, your kings and your officials and the people of the land? [22]When the LORD could no longer endure your wicked actions and the detestable things you did, your land became an object of cursing and a desolate waste without inhabitants, as it is today. [23]Because you have burned incense and have sinned against the LORD and have not obeyed him or followed his law or his decrees or his stipulations, this disaster has come upon you, as you now see."

[24]Then Jeremiah said to all the people, including the women, "Hear the word of the LORD, all you people of Judah in Egypt. [25]This is what the LORD Almighty, the God of Israel, says: You and your wives have shown by your actions what you promised when you said, 'We will certainly carry out the vows we made to burn incense and pour out drink offerings to the Queen of Heaven.'

"Go ahead then, do what you promised! Keep your vows! [26]But hear the word of the LORD, all Jews living in Egypt: 'I swear by my great name,' says the LORD, 'that no one from Judah living anywhere in Egypt will ever again invoke my name or swear, "As surely as the Sovereign LORD lives." [27]For I am watching over them for harm, not for good; the Jews in Egypt will perish by sword and famine until they are all destroyed. [28]Those who escape the sword and return to the land of Judah from Egypt will be very few. Then the whole remnant of Judah who came to live in Egypt will know whose word will stand—mine or theirs.

[29]" 'This will be the sign to you that I will punish you in this place,' declares the LORD, 'so that you will know that my threats of harm against you will surely stand.' [30]This is what the LORD says: 'I am going to hand Pharaoh Hophra king of Egypt over to his enemies who seek his life, just as I handed Zedekiah king of Judah over to Nebuchadnezzar king of Babylon, the enemy who was seeking his life.' "

A Message to Baruch

45 This is what Jeremiah the prophet told Baruch son of Neriah in the fourth year of Jehoiakim son of Josiah king of Judah, after Baruch had written on a scroll the words Jeremiah was then dictating: [2]"This is what the LORD, the God of Israel, says to you, Baruch: [3]You said, 'Woe to me! The LORD has added sorrow to my pain; I am worn out with groaning and find no rest.' "

[4]⌊The LORD said,⌋ "Say this to him: 'This is what the LORD says: I will overthrow what I have built and uproot what I have planted, throughout the land. [5]Should you then seek great things for yourself? Seek them not. For I will bring disaster on all people, declares the LORD, but wherever you go I will let you escape with your life.' "

[a]15 *Hebrew in Egypt and Pathros*

A Message About Egypt

46 This is the word of the LORD that came to Jeremiah the prophet concerning the nations:

[2]Concerning Egypt:

This is the message against the army of Pharaoh Neco king of Egypt, which was defeated at Carchemish on the Euphrates River by Nebuchadnezzar king of Babylon in the fourth year of Jehoiakim son of Josiah king of Judah:

[3]"Prepare your shields, both large and small,
and march out for battle!
[4]Harness the horses,
mount the steeds!
Take your positions
with helmets on!
Polish your spears,
put on your armor!
[5]What do I see?
They are terrified,
they are retreating,
their warriors are defeated.
They flee in haste
without looking back,
and there is terror on every side,"
declares the LORD.
[6]"The swift cannot flee
nor the strong escape.
In the north by the River Euphrates
they stumble and fall.
[7]"Who is this that rises like the Nile,
like rivers of surging waters?
[8]Egypt rises like the Nile,
like rivers of surging waters.
She says, 'I will rise and cover the earth;
I will destroy cities and their people.'
[9]Charge, O horses!
Drive furiously, O charioteers!
March on, O warriors—
men of Cush[a] and Put who carry shields,
men of Lydia who draw the bow.
[10]But that day belongs to the Lord, the LORD Almighty—
a day of vengeance, for vengeance on his foes.
The sword will devour till it is satisfied,
till it has quenched its thirst with blood.
For the Lord, the LORD Almighty, will offer sacrifice
in the land of the north by the River Euphrates.
[11]"Go up to Gilead and get balm,
O Virgin Daughter of Egypt.
But you multiply remedies in vain;
there is no healing for you.
[12]The nations will hear of your shame;
your cries will fill the earth.
One warrior will stumble over another;
both will fall down together."

[13]This is the message the LORD spoke to Jeremiah the prophet about the coming of Nebuchadnezzar king of Babylon to attack Egypt:

[14]"Announce this in Egypt, and proclaim it in Migdol;
proclaim it also in Memphis[b] and Tahpanhes:
'Take your positions and get ready,
for the sword devours those around you.'
[15]Why will your warriors be laid low?
They cannot stand, for the LORD will push them down.
[16]They will stumble repeatedly;
they will fall over each other.
They will say, 'Get up, let us go back
to our own people and our native lands,
away from the sword of the oppressor.'
[17]There they will exclaim,
'Pharaoh king of Egypt is only a loud noise;
he has missed his opportunity.'
[18]"As surely as I live," declares the King,
whose name is the LORD Almighty,
"one will come who is like Tabor among the mountains,
like Carmel by the sea.
[19]Pack your belongings for exile,
you who live in Egypt,
for Memphis will be laid waste
and lie in ruins without inhabitant.
[20]"Egypt is a beautiful heifer,
but a gadfly is coming
against her from the north.
[21]The mercenaries in her ranks
are like fattened calves.
They too will turn and flee together,
they will not stand their ground,
for the day of disaster is coming upon them,
the time for them to be punished.
[22]Egypt will hiss like a fleeing serpent
as the enemy advances in force;
they will come against her with axes,
like men who cut down trees.
[23]They will chop down her forest,"
declares the LORD,
"dense though it be.
They are more numerous than locusts,

[a]9 That is, the upper Nile region [b]14 Hebrew *Noph;* also in verse 19

46:1—51:64 Jeremiah pronounced words of judgment on all the nations who had mistreated God's people. Without exception, Egypt, Philistia, Moab, Ammon, Edom, Damascus, Kedar, Hazor, Elam, and Babylon would all experience God's judgment for their wicked and ungodly practices. The wicked never prosper for long, though it may appear that they do for a time (see Psalm 37:1). We can rely on God's righteousness to prevail. He may discipline us, but that discipline is always just and designed for our good.

they cannot be counted.
24The Daughter of Egypt will be put to shame,
handed over to the people of the north."

25The LORD Almighty, the God of Israel, says:
"I am about to bring punishment on Amon god
of Thebes,[a] on Pharaoh, on Egypt and her
gods and her kings, and on those who rely on
Pharaoh. 26I will hand them over to those who
seek their lives, to Nebuchadnezzar king of Babylon and his officers. Later, however, Egypt will
be inhabited as in times past," declares the LORD.

27"Do not fear, O Jacob my servant;
do not be dismayed, O Israel.
I will surely save you out of a distant place,
your descendants from the land of their exile.
Jacob will again have peace and security,
and no one will make him afraid.
28Do not fear, O Jacob my servant,
for I am with you," declares the LORD.
"Though I completely destroy all the nations
among which I scatter you,
I will not completely destroy you.
I will discipline you but only with justice;
I will not let you go entirely unpunished."

A Message About the Philistines

47 This is the word of the LORD that came
to Jeremiah the prophet concerning the
Philistines before Pharaoh attacked Gaza:

2This is what the LORD says:

"See how the waters are rising in the north;
they will become an overflowing torrent.
They will overflow the land and everything in it,
the towns and those who live in them.
The people will cry out;
all who dwell in the land will wail
3at the sound of the hoofs of galloping steeds,
at the noise of enemy chariots
and the rumble of their wheels.
Fathers will not turn to help their children;
their hands will hang limp.
4For the day has come
to destroy all the Philistines
and to cut off all survivors
who could help Tyre and Sidon.
The LORD is about to destroy the Philistines,
the remnant from the coasts of Caphtor.[b]
5Gaza will shave her head in mourning;
Ashkelon will be silenced.
O remnant on the plain,
how long will you cut yourselves?

6" 'Ah, sword of the LORD,' ⌊you cry,⌋
'how long till you rest?
Return to your scabbard;
cease and be still.'
7But how can it rest
when the LORD has commanded it,
when he has ordered it
to attack Ashkelon and the coast?"

A Message About Moab

48 Concerning Moab:

This is what the LORD Almighty, the God of
Israel, says:

"Woe to Nebo, for it will be ruined.
Kiriathaim will be disgraced and captured;
the stronghold[c] will be disgraced and shattered.
2Moab will be praised no more;
in Heshbon[d] men will plot her downfall:
'Come, let us put an end to that nation.'
You too, O Madmen,[e] will be silenced;
the sword will pursue you.
3Listen to the cries from Horonaim,
cries of great havoc and destruction.
4Moab will be broken;
her little ones will cry out.[f]
5They go up the way to Luhith,
weeping bitterly as they go;
on the road down to Horonaim
anguished cries over the destruction are heard.
6Flee! Run for your lives;
become like a bush[g] in the desert.
7Since you trust in your deeds and riches,
you too will be taken captive,
and Chemosh will go into exile,
together with his priests and officials.
8The destroyer will come against every town,
and not a town will escape.
The valley will be ruined
and the plateau destroyed,
because the LORD has spoken.
9Put salt on Moab,
for she will be laid waste[h];
her towns will become desolate,
with no one to live in them.

10"A curse on him who is lax in doing the LORD's work!
A curse on him who keeps his sword from bloodshed!

11"Moab has been at rest from youth,
like wine left on its dregs,
not poured from one jar to another—
she has not gone into exile.
So she tastes as she did,
and her aroma is unchanged.
12But days are coming,"

[a]25 Hebrew *No* [b]4 That is, Crete [c]1 Or / *Misgab* [d]2 The Hebrew for *Heshbon* sounds like the Hebrew for *plot.* [e]2 The name of the Moabite town Madmen sounds like the Hebrew for *be silenced.* [f]4 Hebrew; Septuagint / *proclaim it to Zoar* [g]6 Or *like Aroer* [h]9 Or *Give wings to Moab, / for she will fly away*

declares the LORD,
"when I will send men who pour from jars,
and they will pour her out;
they will empty her jars
and smash her jugs.
13Then Moab will be ashamed of Chemosh,
as the house of Israel was ashamed
when they trusted in Bethel.

14"How can you say, 'We are warriors,
men valiant in battle'?
15Moab will be destroyed and her towns invaded;
her finest young men will go down in the slaughter,"
declares the King, whose name is the LORD Almighty.
16"The fall of Moab is at hand;
her calamity will come quickly.
17Mourn for her, all who live around her,
all who know her fame;
say, 'How broken is the mighty scepter,
how broken the glorious staff!'

18"Come down from your glory
and sit on the parched ground,
O inhabitants of the Daughter of Dibon,
for he who destroys Moab
will come up against you
and ruin your fortified cities.
19Stand by the road and watch,
you who live in Aroer.
Ask the man fleeing and the woman escaping,
ask them, 'What has happened?'
20Moab is disgraced, for she is shattered.
Wail and cry out!
Announce by the Arnon
that Moab is destroyed.
21Judgment has come to the plateau—
to Holon, Jahzah and Mephaath,
22 to Dibon, Nebo and Beth Diblathaim,
23 to Kiriathaim, Beth Gamul and Beth Meon,
24 to Kerioth and Bozrah—
to all the towns of Moab, far and near.
25Moab's horn[a] is cut off;
her arm is broken,"
declares the LORD.

26"Make her drunk,
for she has defied the LORD.
Let Moab wallow in her vomit;
let her be an object of ridicule.
27Was not Israel the object of your ridicule?
Was she caught among thieves,
that you shake your head in scorn
whenever you speak of her?
28Abandon your towns and dwell among the rocks,
you who live in Moab.
Be like a dove that makes its nest
at the mouth of a cave.

29"We have heard of Moab's pride—
her overweening pride and conceit,
her pride and arrogance
and the haughtiness of her heart.
30I know her insolence but it is futile,"
declares the LORD,
"and her boasts accomplish nothing.
31Therefore I wail over Moab,
for all Moab I cry out,
I moan for the men of Kir Hareseth.
32I weep for you, as Jazer weeps,
O vines of Sibmah.
Your branches spread as far as the sea;
they reached as far as the sea of Jazer.
The destroyer has fallen
on your ripened fruit and grapes.
33Joy and gladness are gone
from the orchards and fields of Moab.
I have stopped the flow of wine from the presses;
no one treads them with shouts of joy.
Although there are shouts,
they are not shouts of joy.

34"The sound of their cry rises
from Heshbon to Elealeh and Jahaz,
from Zoar as far as Horonaim and Eglath Shelishiyah,
for even the waters of Nimrim are dried up.
35In Moab I will put an end
to those who make offerings on the high places
and burn incense to their gods,"
declares the LORD.
36"So my heart laments for Moab like a flute;
it laments like a flute for the men of Kir Hareseth.
The wealth they acquired is gone.
37Every head is shaved
and every beard cut off;
every hand is slashed
and every waist is covered with sackcloth.
38On all the roofs in Moab
and in the public squares
there is nothing but mourning,
for I have broken Moab
like a jar that no one wants,"
declares the LORD.
39"How shattered she is! How they wail!
How Moab turns her back in shame!
Moab has become an object of ridicule,
an object of horror to all those around her."

40This is what the LORD says:

"Look! An eagle is swooping down,
spreading its wings over Moab.
41Kerioth[b] will be captured
and the strongholds taken.
In that day the hearts of Moab's warriors
will be like the heart of a woman in labor.

[a]25 *Horn* here symbolizes strength. [b]41 Or *The cities*

42Moab will be destroyed as a nation
because she defied the LORD.
43Terror and pit and snare await you,
O people of Moab,"
declares the LORD.
44"Whoever flees from the terror
will fall into a pit,
whoever climbs out of the pit
will be caught in a snare;
for I will bring upon Moab
the year of her punishment,"
declares the LORD.

45"In the shadow of Heshbon
the fugitives stand helpless,
for a fire has gone out from Heshbon,
a blaze from the midst of Sihon;
it burns the foreheads of Moab,
the skulls of the noisy boasters.
46Woe to you, O Moab!
The people of Chemosh are destroyed;
your sons are taken into exile
and your daughters into captivity.

47"Yet I will restore the fortunes of Moab
in days to come,"
declares the LORD.

Here ends the judgment on Moab.

A Message About Ammon

49 Concerning the Ammonites:

This is what the LORD says:

"Has Israel no sons?
Has she no heirs?
Why then has Molech[a] taken possession
of Gad?
Why do his people live in its towns?
2But the days are coming,"
declares the LORD,
"when I will sound the battle cry
against Rabbah of the Ammonites;
it will become a mound of ruins,
and its surrounding villages will be set
on fire.
Then Israel will drive out
those who drove her out,"
says the LORD.
3"Wail, O Heshbon, for Ai is destroyed!
Cry out, O inhabitants of Rabbah!
Put on sackcloth and mourn;
rush here and there inside the walls,
for Molech will go into exile,
together with his priests and officials.
4Why do you boast of your valleys,
boast of your valleys so fruitful?
O unfaithful daughter,
you trust in your riches and say,
'Who will attack me?'
5I will bring terror on you
from all those around you,"
declares the Lord,
the LORD Almighty.
"Every one of you will be driven away,
and no one will gather the fugitives.

6"Yet afterward, I will restore the fortunes of
the Ammonites,"
declares the LORD.

A Message About Edom

7Concerning Edom:

This is what the LORD Almighty says:

"Is there no longer wisdom in Teman?
Has counsel perished from the prudent?
Has their wisdom decayed?
8Turn and flee, hide in deep caves,
you who live in Dedan,
for I will bring disaster on Esau
at the time I punish him.
9If grape pickers came to you,
would they not leave a few grapes?
If thieves came during the night,
would they not steal only as much as
they wanted?
10But I will strip Esau bare;
I will uncover his hiding places,
so that he cannot conceal himself.
His children, relatives and neighbors will
perish,
and he will be no more.
11Leave your orphans; I will protect their lives.
Your widows too can trust in me."

12This is what the LORD says: "If those who
do not deserve to drink the cup must drink it,
why should you go unpunished? You will not
go unpunished, but must drink it. 13I swear by
myself," declares the LORD, "that Bozrah will become a ruin and an object of horror, of reproach and of cursing; and all its towns will be
in ruins forever."

14I have heard a message from the LORD:
An envoy was sent to the nations to say,
"Assemble yourselves to attack it!
Rise up for battle!"

15"Now I will make you small among the
nations,
despised among men.
16The terror you inspire
and the pride of your heart have
deceived you,
you who live in the clefts of the rocks,
who occupy the heights of the hill.
Though you build your nest as high as the
eagle's,
from there I will bring you down,"
declares the LORD.
17"Edom will become an object of horror;
all who pass by will be appalled and will
scoff
because of all its wounds.
18As Sodom and Gomorrah were overthrown,
along with their neighboring towns,"
says the LORD,

[a]1 Or *their king*; Hebrew *malcam*; also in verse 3

"so no one will live there;
no man will dwell in it.

19 "Like a lion coming up from Jordan's thickets
to a rich pastureland,
I will chase Edom from its land in an instant.
Who is the chosen one I will appoint for this?
Who is like me and who can challenge me?
And what shepherd can stand against me?"
20 Therefore, hear what the LORD has planned against Edom,
what he has purposed against those who live in Teman:
The young of the flock will be dragged away;
he will completely destroy their pasture because of them.
21 At the sound of their fall the earth will tremble;
their cry will resound to the Red Sea.[a]
22 Look! An eagle will soar and swoop down,
spreading its wings over Bozrah.
In that day the hearts of Edom's warriors
will be like the heart of a woman in labor.

A Message About Damascus

23 Concerning Damascus:

"Hamath and Arpad are dismayed,
for they have heard bad news.
They are disheartened,
troubled like[b] the restless sea.
24 Damascus has become feeble,
she has turned to flee
and panic has gripped her;
anguish and pain have seized her,
pain like that of a woman in labor.
25 Why has the city of renown not been abandoned,
the town in which I delight?
26 Surely, her young men will fall in the streets;
all her soldiers will be silenced in that day,"
declares the LORD Almighty.
27 "I will set fire to the walls of Damascus;
it will consume the fortresses of Ben-Hadad."

A Message About Kedar and Hazor

28 Concerning Kedar and the kingdoms of Hazor, which Nebuchadnezzar king of Babylon attacked:

This is what the LORD says:

"Arise, and attack Kedar
and destroy the people of the East.
29 Their tents and their flocks will be taken;
their shelters will be carried off
with all their goods and camels.
Men will shout to them,
'Terror on every side!'
30 "Flee quickly away!
Stay in deep caves, you who live in Hazor,"
declares the LORD.
"Nebuchadnezzar king of Babylon has plotted against you;
he has devised a plan against you.

31 "Arise and attack a nation at ease,
which lives in confidence,"
declares the LORD,
"a nation that has neither gates nor bars;
its people live alone.
32 Their camels will become plunder,
and their large herds will be booty.
I will scatter to the winds those who are in distant places[c]
and will bring disaster on them from every side,"
declares the LORD.
33 "Hazor will become a haunt of jackals,
a desolate place forever.
No one will live there;
no man will dwell in it."

A Message About Elam

34 This is the word of the LORD that came to Jeremiah the prophet concerning Elam, early in the reign of Zedekiah king of Judah:

35 This is what the LORD Almighty says:

"See, I will break the bow of Elam,
the mainstay of their might.
36 I will bring against Elam the four winds
from the four quarters of the heavens;
I will scatter them to the four winds,
and there will not be a nation
where Elam's exiles do not go.
37 I will shatter Elam before their foes,
before those who seek their lives;
I will bring disaster upon them,
even my fierce anger,"
declares the LORD.
"I will pursue them with the sword
until I have made an end of them.
38 I will set my throne in Elam
and destroy her king and officials,"
declares the LORD.

39 "Yet I will restore the fortunes of Elam
in days to come,"
declares the LORD.

A Message About Babylon

50 This is the word the LORD spoke through Jeremiah the prophet concerning Babylon and the land of the Babylonians[d]:

[a] 21 Hebrew *Yam Suph;* that is, Sea of Reeds
[b] 23 Hebrew *on* or *by*
[c] 32 Or *who clip the hair by their foreheads*
[d] 1 Or *Chaldeans;* also in verses 8, 25, 35 and 45

2"Announce and proclaim among the nations,
lift up a banner and proclaim it;
keep nothing back, but say,
'Babylon will be captured;
Bel will be put to shame,
Marduk filled with terror.
Her images will be put to shame
and her idols filled with terror.'
3A nation from the north will attack her
and lay waste her land.
No one will live in it;
both men and animals will flee away.

4"In those days, at that time,"
declares the LORD,
"the people of Israel and the people of Judah together
will go in tears to seek the LORD their God.
5They will ask the way to Zion
and turn their faces toward it.
They will come and bind themselves to the LORD
in an everlasting covenant
that will not be forgotten.

6"My people have been lost sheep;
their shepherds have led them astray
and caused them to roam on the mountains.
They wandered over mountain and hill
and forgot their own resting place.
7Whoever found them devoured them;
their enemies said, 'We are not guilty,
for they sinned against the LORD, their true pasture,
the LORD, the hope of their fathers.'

8"Flee out of Babylon;
leave the land of the Babylonians,
and be like the goats that lead the flock.
9For I will stir up and bring against Babylon
an alliance of great nations from the land of the north.
They will take up their positions against her,
and from the north she will be captured.
Their arrows will be like skilled warriors
who do not return empty-handed.
10So Babylonia[a] will be plundered;
all who plunder her will have their fill,"
declares the LORD.

11"Because you rejoice and are glad,
you who pillage my inheritance,
because you frolic like a heifer threshing grain
and neigh like stallions,
12your mother will be greatly ashamed;
she who gave you birth will be disgraced.
She will be the least of the nations—
a wilderness, a dry land, a desert.
13Because of the LORD's anger she will not be inhabited
but will be completely desolate.
All who pass Babylon will be horrified and scoff
because of all her wounds.

14"Take up your positions around Babylon,
all you who draw the bow.
Shoot at her! Spare no arrows,
for she has sinned against the LORD.
15Shout against her on every side!
She surrenders, her towers fall,
her walls are torn down.
Since this is the vengeance of the LORD,
take vengeance on her;
do to her as she has done to others.
16Cut off from Babylon the sower,
and the reaper with his sickle at harvest.
Because of the sword of the oppressor
let everyone return to his own people,
let everyone flee to his own land.

17"Israel is a scattered flock
that lions have chased away.
The first to devour him
was the king of Assyria;
the last to crush his bones
was Nebuchadnezzar king of Babylon."

18Therefore this is what the LORD Almighty, the God of Israel, says:

"I will punish the king of Babylon and his land
as I punished the king of Assyria.
19But I will bring Israel back to his own pasture
and he will graze on Carmel and Bashan;
his appetite will be satisfied
on the hills of Ephraim and Gilead.
20In those days, at that time,"
declares the LORD,
"search will be made for Israel's guilt,
but there will be none,
and for the sins of Judah,
but none will be found,
for I will forgive the remnant I spare.

21"Attack the land of Merathaim
and those who live in Pekod.
Pursue, kill and completely destroy[b] them,"
declares the LORD.
"Do everything I have commanded you.
22The noise of battle is in the land,
the noise of great destruction!
23How broken and shattered
is the hammer of the whole earth!
How desolate is Babylon
among the nations!
24I set a trap for you, O Babylon,
and you were caught before you knew it;

a10 Or *Chaldea* b21 The Hebrew term refers to the irrevocable giving over of things or persons to the LORD, often by totally destroying them; also in verse 26.

you were found and captured
because you opposed the LORD.
25 The LORD has opened his arsenal
and brought out the weapons of his wrath,
for the Sovereign LORD Almighty has work to do
in the land of the Babylonians.
26 Come against her from afar.
Break open her granaries;
pile her up like heaps of grain.
Completely destroy her
and leave her no remnant.
27 Kill all her young bulls;
let them go down to the slaughter!
Woe to them! For their day has come,
the time for them to be punished.
28 Listen to the fugitives and refugees from Babylon
declaring in Zion
how the LORD our God has taken vengeance,
vengeance for his temple.

29 "Summon archers against Babylon,
all those who draw the bow.
Encamp all around her;
let no one escape.
Repay her for her deeds;
do to her as she has done.
For she has defied the LORD,
the Holy One of Israel.
30 Therefore, her young men will fall in the streets;
all her soldiers will be silenced in that day,"
declares the LORD.
31 "See, I am against you, O arrogant one,"
declares the Lord, the LORD Almighty,
"for your day has come,
the time for you to be punished.
32 The arrogant one will stumble and fall
and no one will help her up;
I will kindle a fire in her towns
that will consume all who are around her."

33 This is what the LORD Almighty says:

"The people of Israel are oppressed,
and the people of Judah as well.
All their captors hold them fast,
refusing to let them go.
34 Yet their Redeemer is strong;
the LORD Almighty is his name.
He will vigorously defend their cause
so that he may bring rest to their land,
but unrest to those who live in Babylon.

35 "A sword against the Babylonians!"
declares the LORD—
"against those who live in Babylon
and against her officials and wise men!
36 A sword against her false prophets!
They will become fools.
A sword against her warriors!
They will be filled with terror.
37 A sword against her horses and chariots
and all the foreigners in her ranks!
They will become women.
A sword against her treasures!
They will be plundered.
38 A drought on[a] her waters!
They will dry up.
For it is a land of idols,
idols that will go mad with terror.

39 "So desert creatures and hyenas will live there,
and there the owl will dwell.
It will never again be inhabited
or lived in from generation to generation.
40 As God overthrew Sodom and Gomorrah
along with their neighboring towns,"
declares the LORD,
"so no one will live there;
no man will dwell in it.

41 "Look! An army is coming from the north;
a great nation and many kings
are being stirred up from the ends of the earth.
42 They are armed with bows and spears;
they are cruel and without mercy.
They sound like the roaring sea
as they ride on their horses;
they come like men in battle formation
to attack you, O Daughter of Babylon.
43 The king of Babylon has heard reports about them,
and his hands hang limp.
Anguish has gripped him,
pain like that of a woman in labor.
44 Like a lion coming up from Jordan's thickets
to a rich pastureland,
I will chase Babylon from its land in an instant.
Who is the chosen one I will appoint for this?
Who is like me and who can challenge me?
And what shepherd can stand against me?"
45 Therefore, hear what the LORD has planned against Babylon,
what he has purposed against the land of the Babylonians:
The young of the flock will be dragged away;
he will completely destroy their pasture because of them.
46 At the sound of Babylon's capture the earth will tremble;
its cry will resound among the nations.

51 This is what the LORD says:

"See, I will stir up the spirit of a destroyer

[a]38 Or *A sword against*

against Babylon and the people of Leb
Kamai.[a]
2I will send foreigners to Babylon
to winnow her and to devastate her land;
they will oppose her on every side
in the day of her disaster.
3Let not the archer string his bow,
nor let him put on his armor.
Do not spare her young men;
completely destroy[b] her army.
4They will fall down slain in Babylon,[c]
fatally wounded in her streets.
5For Israel and Judah have not been
forsaken
by their God, the LORD Almighty,
though their land[d] is full of guilt
before the Holy One of Israel.

6"Flee from Babylon!
Run for your lives!
Do not be destroyed because of her sins.
It is time for the LORD's vengeance;
he will pay her what she deserves.
7Babylon was a gold cup in the LORD's
hand;
she made the whole earth drunk.
The nations drank her wine;
therefore they have now gone mad.
8Babylon will suddenly fall and be broken.
Wail over her!
Get balm for her pain;
perhaps she can be healed.

9" 'We would have healed Babylon,
but she cannot be healed;
let us leave her and each go to his own
land,
for her judgment reaches to the skies,
it rises as high as the clouds.'

10" 'The LORD has vindicated us;
come, let us tell in Zion
what the LORD our God has done.'

11"Sharpen the arrows,
take up the shields!
The LORD has stirred up the kings of the
Medes,
because his purpose is to destroy
Babylon.
The LORD will take vengeance,
vengeance for his temple.
12Lift up a banner against the walls of
Babylon!
Reinforce the guard,
station the watchmen,
prepare an ambush!
The LORD will carry out his purpose,
his decree against the people of Babylon.
13You who live by many waters
and are rich in treasures,
your end has come,
the time for you to be cut off.
14The LORD Almighty has sworn by himself:
I will surely fill you with men, as with a
swarm of locusts,
and they will shout in triumph over you.

15"He made the earth by his power;
he founded the world by his wisdom
and stretched out the heavens by his
understanding.
16When he thunders, the waters in the
heavens roar;
he makes clouds rise from the ends of
the earth.
He sends lightning with the rain
and brings out the wind from his
storehouses.

17"Every man is senseless and without
knowledge;
every goldsmith is shamed by his idols.
His images are a fraud;
they have no breath in them.
18They are worthless, the objects of mockery;
when their judgment comes, they will
perish.
19He who is the Portion of Jacob is not like
these,
for he is the Maker of all things,
including the tribe of his inheritance—
the LORD Almighty is his name.

20"You are my war club,
my weapon for battle—
with you I shatter nations,
with you I destroy kingdoms,
21with you I shatter horse and rider,
with you I shatter chariot and driver,
22with you I shatter man and woman,
with you I shatter old man and youth,
with you I shatter young man and
maiden,
23with you I shatter shepherd and flock,
with you I shatter farmer and oxen,
with you I shatter governors and
officials.

24"Before your eyes I will repay Babylon and all who live in Babylonia[e] for all the wrong they have done in Zion," declares the LORD.

25"I am against you, O destroying mountain,
you who destroy the whole earth,"
declares the LORD.
"I will stretch out my hand against you,
roll you off the cliffs,
and make you a burned-out mountain.
26No rock will be taken from you for a
cornerstone,
nor any stone for a foundation,
for you will be desolate forever,"
declares the LORD.

[a]1 *Leb Kamai* is a cryptogram for Chaldea, that is, Babylonia. [b]3 The Hebrew term refers to the irrevocable giving over of things or persons to the LORD, often by totally destroying them. [c]4 Or *Chaldea* [d]5 Or / *and the land* ⌞*of the Babylonians*⌟ [e]24 Or *Chaldea;* also in verse 35

27"Lift up a banner in the land!
Blow the trumpet among the nations!
Prepare the nations for battle against her;
summon against her these kingdoms:
Ararat, Minni and Ashkenaz.
Appoint a commander against her;
send up horses like a swarm of locusts.
28Prepare the nations for battle against her—
the kings of the Medes,
their governors and all their officials,
and all the countries they rule.
29The land trembles and writhes,
for the LORD's purposes against Babylon
stand—
to lay waste the land of Babylon
so that no one will live there.
30Babylon's warriors have stopped fighting;
they remain in their strongholds.
Their strength is exhausted;
they have become like women.
Her dwellings are set on fire;
the bars of her gates are broken.
31One courier follows another
and messenger follows messenger
to announce to the king of Babylon
that his entire city is captured,
32the river crossings seized,
the marshes set on fire,
and the soldiers terrified."

33This is what the LORD Almighty, the God of Israel, says:

"The Daughter of Babylon is like a
threshing floor
at the time it is trampled;
the time to harvest her will soon come."
34"Nebuchadnezzar king of Babylon has
devoured us,
he has thrown us into confusion,
he has made us an empty jar.
Like a serpent he has swallowed us
and filled his stomach with our
delicacies,
and then has spewed us out.
35May the violence done to our flesh[a] be
upon Babylon,"
say the inhabitants of Zion.
"May our blood be on those who live in
Babylonia,"
says Jerusalem.

36Therefore, this is what the LORD says:

"See, I will defend your cause
and avenge you;
I will dry up her sea
and make her springs dry.
37Babylon will be a heap of ruins,
a haunt of jackals,
an object of horror and scorn,
a place where no one lives.
38Her people all roar like young lions,
they growl like lion cubs.
39But while they are aroused,
I will set out a feast for them
and make them drunk,
so that they shout with laughter—
then sleep forever and not awake,"
declares the LORD.
40"I will bring them down
like lambs to the slaughter,
like rams and goats.

41"How Sheshach[b] will be captured,
the boast of the whole earth seized!
What a horror Babylon will be
among the nations!
42The sea will rise over Babylon;
its roaring waves will cover her.
43Her towns will be desolate,
a dry and desert land,
a land where no one lives,
through which no man travels.
44I will punish Bel in Babylon
and make him spew out what he has
swallowed.
The nations will no longer stream to him.
And the wall of Babylon will fall.

45"Come out of her, my people!
Run for your lives!
Run from the fierce anger of the LORD.
46Do not lose heart or be afraid
when rumors are heard in the land;
one rumor comes this year, another the
next,
rumors of violence in the land
and of ruler against ruler.
47For the time will surely come
when I will punish the idols of Babylon;
her whole land will be disgraced
and her slain will all lie fallen within
her.
48Then heaven and earth and all that is in
them
will shout for joy over Babylon,
for out of the north
destroyers will attack her,"
declares the LORD.
49"Babylon must fall because of Israel's slain,
just as the slain in all the earth
have fallen because of Babylon.
50You who have escaped the sword,
leave and do not linger!
Remember the LORD in a distant land,
and think on Jerusalem."

51"We are disgraced,
for we have been insulted
and shame covers our faces,
because foreigners have entered
the holy places of the LORD's house."

52"But days are coming," declares the LORD,
"when I will punish her idols,
and throughout her land
the wounded will groan.

[a]35 Or *done to us and to our children* [b]41 *Sheshach* is a cryptogram for Babylon.

53 Even if Babylon reaches the sky
and fortifies her lofty stronghold,
I will send destroyers against her,"
declares the LORD.

54 "The sound of a cry comes from Babylon,
the sound of great destruction
from the land of the Babylonians.[a]
55 The LORD will destroy Babylon;
he will silence her noisy din.
Waves ⌞of enemies⌟ will rage like great
waters;
the roar of their voices will resound.
56 A destroyer will come against Babylon;
her warriors will be captured,
and their bows will be broken.
For the LORD is a God of retribution;
he will repay in full.
57 I will make her officials and wise men
drunk,
her governors, officers and warriors as
well;
they will sleep forever and not awake,"
declares the King, whose name is the
LORD Almighty.

58 This is what the LORD Almighty says:

"Babylon's thick wall will be leveled
and her high gates set on fire;
the peoples exhaust themselves for nothing,
the nations' labor is only fuel for the
flames."

59 This is the message Jeremiah gave to the staff officer Seraiah son of Neriah, the son of Mahseiah, when he went to Babylon with Zedekiah king of Judah in the fourth year of his reign. 60 Jeremiah had written on a scroll about all the disasters that would come upon Babylon—all that had been recorded concerning Babylon. 61 He said to Seraiah, "When you get to Babylon, see that you read all these words aloud. 62 Then say, 'O LORD, you have said you will destroy this place, so that neither man nor animal will live in it; it will be desolate forever.' 63 When you finish reading this scroll, tie a stone to it and throw it into the Euphrates. 64 Then say, 'So will Babylon sink to rise no more because of the disaster I will bring upon her. And her people will fall.' "

The words of Jeremiah end here.

The Fall of Jerusalem

52 Zedekiah was twenty-one years old when he became king, and he reigned in Jerusalem eleven years. His mother's name was Hamutal daughter of Jeremiah; she was from Libnah. 2 He did evil in the eyes of the LORD, just as Jehoiakim had done. 3 It was because of the LORD's anger that all this happened to Jerusalem and Judah, and in the end he thrust them from his presence.

Now Zedekiah rebelled against the king of Babylon.

4 So in the ninth year of Zedekiah's reign, on the tenth day of the tenth month, Nebuchadnezzar king of Babylon marched against Jerusalem with his whole army. They camped outside the city and built siege works all around it. 5 The city was kept under siege until the eleventh year of King Zedekiah.

6 By the ninth day of the fourth month the famine in the city had become so severe that there was no food for the people to eat. 7 Then the city wall was broken through, and the whole army fled. They left the city at night through the gate between the two walls near the king's garden, though the Babylonians[b] were surrounding the city. They fled toward the Arabah,[c] 8 but the Babylonian[d] army pursued King Zedekiah and overtook him in the plains of Jericho. All his soldiers were separated from him and scattered, 9 and he was captured.

He was taken to the king of Babylon at Riblah in the land of Hamath, where he pronounced sentence on him. 10 There at Riblah the king of Babylon slaughtered the sons of Zedekiah before his eyes; he also killed all the officials of Judah. 11 Then he put out Zedekiah's eyes, bound him with bronze shackles and took him to Babylon, where he put him in prison till the day of his death.

12 On the tenth day of the fifth month, in the nineteenth year of Nebuchadnezzar king of Babylon, Nebuzaradan commander of the imperial guard, who served the king of Babylon, came to Jerusalem. 13 He set fire to the temple of the LORD, the royal palace and all the houses of Jerusalem. Every important building he burned down. 14 The whole Babylonian army under the commander of the imperial guard broke down all the walls around Jerusalem. 15 Nebuzaradan the commander of the guard carried into exile some of the poorest people and those who remained in the city, along with the rest of the craftsmen[e] and those who had gone over to the king of Babylon. 16 But Nebuzaradan left behind the rest of the poorest people of the land to work the vineyards and fields.

[a] 54 Or *Chaldeans* [b] 7 Or *Chaldeans;* also in verse 17 [c] 7 Or *the Jordan Valley* [d] 8 Or *Chaldean;* also in verse 14 [e] 15 Or *populace*

52:1–34 As Jerusalem fell, the people could no longer avoid the destructive consequences of their sin. The memories of Jerusalem's broken walls would resurrect the memories of their past failures and haunt them again and again. What a burden to carry into exile! As we remember our past sin and rebellion against God, we may have to face the devastation brought about by our poor choices and selfish actions. At such times we can turn to God and hope for restoration. God loves us as no one else can. He desires a relationship with us more than we can know. The pain of our sin is grievous to us and to God, but God always desires our restoration and wants to give us a chance to begin again.

17The Babylonians broke up the bronze pillars, the movable stands and the bronze Sea
that were at the temple of the LORD and they
carried all the bronze to Babylon. 18They also
took away the pots, shovels, wick trimmers,
sprinkling bowls, dishes and all the bronze articles used in the temple service. 19The commander of the imperial guard took away the
basins, censers, sprinkling bowls, pots, lampstands, dishes and bowls used for drink offerings—all that were made of pure gold or silver.
20The bronze from the two pillars, the Sea
and the twelve bronze bulls under it, and the
movable stands, which King Solomon had
made for the temple of the LORD, was more
than could be weighed. 21Each of the pillars was
eighteen cubits high and twelve cubits in circumference[a]; each was four fingers thick, and
hollow. 22The bronze capital on top of the one
pillar was five cubits[b] high and was decorated
with a network and pomegranates of bronze all
around. The other pillar, with its pomegranates,
was similar. 23There were ninety-six pomegranates on the sides; the total number of pomegranates above the surrounding network was a
hundred.
24The commander of the guard took as prisoners Seraiah the chief priest, Zephaniah the
priest next in rank and the three doorkeepers.
25Of those still in the city, he took the officer in
charge of the fighting men, and seven royal advisers. He also took the secretary who was chief
officer in charge of conscripting the people of
the land and sixty of his men who were found
in the city. 26Nebuzaradan the commander took
them all and brought them to the king of Babylon at Riblah. 27There at Riblah, in the land of
Hamath, the king had them executed.

So Judah went into captivity, away from her
land. 28This is the number of the people Nebuchadnezzar carried into exile:

in the seventh year, 3,023 Jews;
29in Nebuchadnezzar's eighteenth year,
832 people from Jerusalem;
30in his twenty-third year,
745 Jews taken into exile by Nebuzaradan the commander of the imperial
guard.
There were 4,600 people in all.

Jehoiachin Released

31In the thirty-seventh year of the exile of
Jehoiachin king of Judah, in the year Evil-
Merodach[c] became king of Babylon, he released Jehoiachin king of Judah and freed him
from prison on the twenty-fifth day of the
twelfth month. 32He spoke kindly to him and
gave him a seat of honor higher than those of
the other kings who were with him in Babylon.
33So Jehoiachin put aside his prison clothes and
for the rest of his life ate regularly at the king's
table. 34Day by day the king of Babylon gave
Jehoiachin a regular allowance as long as he
lived, till the day of his death.

[a] *21* That is, about 27 feet (about 8.1 meters) high and 18 feet (about 5.4 meters) in circumference [b] *22* That is, about 7 1/2 feet (about 2.3 meters) [c] *31* Also called *Amel-Marduk*

LAMENTATIONS

The Big Picture

- **A. *JEREMIAH'S GRIEF IS EXPRESSED (1:1-22)***
- **B. *THE AGONY OF THE CONSEQUENCES (2:1-22)***
- **C. *THE PROPHET'S DEEP PAIN AND CONSOLATION (3:1-66)***
- **D. *THE PAST AND THE PRESENT IN FULL VIEW (4:1-22)***
- **E. *AN IMPASSIONED PRAYER FOR FORGIVENESS (5:1-22)***

With head bowed in humility and pain, Jeremiah penned the words of Lamentations. His heart was broken. He wept to see the great city of Jerusalem destroyed and God's people sent into exile.

Jeremiah's pain was similar to that of a father with an errant child. The prophet had lived with God's people and pleaded with them to return to God. But his pleas fell on deaf ears. Jeremiah's tears were God's tears, for God weeps for our sin and mourns with us in our loss. Jeremiah didn't mince his words or hide his pain. He wept openly and fully, releasing his emotions to God. His example can help us as we grieve over our own losses.

Lamentations does not provide pat answers for the suffering we experience. As we read, we discover that it is all right to be real in our emotions—to be angry, to be disappointed with life or to be concerned about what tomorrow holds for us. God accepted Jeremiah as he was—angry, tired, discouraged—and God will accept us as well.

Jeremiah gives us a model for expressing our pain to God. In response to his honest cries, God listened to Jeremiah and comforted him. In the midst of his agony, Jeremiah found one ray of hope despite the destruction around him—"Because of the LORD's great love we are not consumed, for his compassions never fail" (3:22). As we face great pain in our lives, we can tell God what we are feeling and also can find hope that he really does hear us and care for us.

Spiritual Renewal Themes

THE IMPORTANCE OF GRIEF

Grief is the process that helps us release our pain and losses to God. In grief we come to terms with our past and find freedom to live in the reality of the present. Grief also lays the groundwork for our hope for the future. When we harden our hearts and refuse to grieve over our pain, we make it difficult to progress in our spiritual renewal. We see that God honored the tears and grief of Jeremiah. He will also reward our honesty as we share our pain with him, bringing healing for the present and hope for the future.

THE PAIN OF CONSEQUENCES

God does not always protect us from the consequences of our attitudes and behaviors. Through them we learn to accept responsibility for the sins we have committed and the mistakes we have made. Only then can our spiritual growth continue.

THE GIFT OF OUR EMOTIONS

Emotions flow from the core of our being. If we develop a pattern of denying or hiding our feelings, we lose some of the sense of who we are—emotional beings, created by God. Jeremiah's honesty in his writing style shows us that we have nothing to fear in bringing even our most raw or embarrassing emotions to God. The more honest we are about how we feel, the more completely we will become involved in our relationships with God and with others.

FORGIVENESS—A WAY OF LIFE

Jeremiah finished grieving and turned to God to seek forgiveness. The book of Lamentations ends with an emotional statement that shows a wavering in Jeremiah's confidence in God (see 5:22). Behind this statement is Jeremiah's humility, coupled with his hope that God will start the process toward reconciliation and forgiveness. Jeremiah knew God's heart. He knew that God would forgive. If we truly repent of our sin, we can be sure that God will forgive us, too, no matter how great our sins and failures. We need to come humbly before God and place our lives in his strong, gentle hands.

Essential Facts

PURPOSE:
To lament the destruction of Jerusalem and the sins of Judah and to pray for restoration.

AUTHOR:
The prophet Jeremiah.

AUDIENCE:
The people of Judah after they were exiled to Babylon.

DATE WRITTEN:
Soon after the fall of Jerusalem (approximately 586 B.C.).

SETTING:
Jeremiah, amidst the ruins of Jerusalem, lamenting for the exiled Jews.

KEY VERSES:
"Yet this I call to mind and therefore I have hope: Because of the LORD's great love we are not consumed, for his compassions never fail" (3:21-22).

SPECIAL FEATURES:
Lamentations is written in the rhythm and style of ancient Jewish funeral songs and chants. Each chapter contains an acrostic poem: Each new verse opens with the next letter of the Hebrew alphabet.

1[a] How deserted lies the city,
once so full of people!
How like a widow is she,
who once was great among the nations!
She who was queen among the provinces
has now become a slave.

2Bitterly she weeps at night,
tears are upon her cheeks.
Among all her lovers
there is none to comfort her.
All her friends have betrayed her;
they have become her enemies.

3After affliction and harsh labor,
Judah has gone into exile.
She dwells among the nations;
she finds no resting place.
All who pursue her have overtaken her
in the midst of her distress.

4The roads to Zion mourn,
for no one comes to her appointed feasts.
All her gateways are desolate,
her priests groan,
her maidens grieve,
and she is in bitter anguish.

5Her foes have become her masters;
her enemies are at ease.
The LORD has brought her grief
because of her many sins.
Her children have gone into exile,
captive before the foe.

6All the splendor has departed
from the Daughter of Zion.
Her princes are like deer
that find no pasture;
in weakness they have fled
before the pursuer.

7In the days of her affliction and wandering
Jerusalem remembers all the treasures
that were hers in days of old.
When her people fell into enemy hands,
there was no one to help her.
Her enemies looked at her
and laughed at her destruction.

8Jerusalem has sinned greatly
and so has become unclean.
All who honored her despise her,
for they have seen her nakedness;
she herself groans
and turns away.

9Her filthiness clung to her skirts;
she did not consider her future.
Her fall was astounding;
there was none to comfort her.
"Look, O LORD, on my affliction,
for the enemy has triumphed."

10The enemy laid hands
on all her treasures;
she saw pagan nations
enter her sanctuary—
those you had forbidden
to enter your assembly.

11All her people groan
as they search for bread;
they barter their treasures for food
to keep themselves alive.
"Look, O LORD, and consider,
for I am despised."

12"Is it nothing to you, all you who pass by?
Look around and see.
Is any suffering like my suffering
that was inflicted on me,
that the LORD brought on me
in the day of his fierce anger?

13"From on high he sent fire,
sent it down into my bones.
He spread a net for my feet
and turned me back.
He made me desolate,
faint all the day long.

14"My sins have been bound into a yoke[b];
by his hands they were woven together.
They have come upon my neck
and the Lord has sapped my strength.
He has handed me over
to those I cannot withstand.

15"The Lord has rejected
all the warriors in my midst;
he has summoned an army against me
to[c] crush my young men.
In his winepress the Lord has trampled
the Virgin Daughter of Judah.

16"This is why I weep
and my eyes overflow with tears.
No one is near to comfort me,
no one to restore my spirit.
My children are destitute
because the enemy has prevailed."

17Zion stretches out her hands,
but there is no one to comfort her.
The LORD has decreed for Jacob
that his neighbors become his foes;

[a]This chapter is an acrostic poem, the verses of which begin with the successive letters of the Hebrew alphabet.
[b]14 Most Hebrew manuscripts; Septuagint *He kept watch over my sins*
[c]15 Or *has set a time for me / when he will*

1:1–11 Because of their sins, the people of Judah faced destruction and exile. The once prosperous nation was now only a memory. Its capital city, Jerusalem, lay in ruins. Solomon's magnificent temple had been leveled. The people felt abandoned by God. The prophet Jeremiah mourned these terrible losses, acknowledging that the people's sins had brought them about. Our sin will also bring devastating consequences if we allow it to continue unchecked. When we suffer terrible losses, we should evaluate our lives to assess whether sin is responsible for them. Spiritual renewal requires that we repent of our sin and seek forgiveness from God.

Jerusalem has become
  an unclean thing among them.

18 "The LORD is righteous,
  yet I rebelled against his command.
Listen, all you peoples;
  look upon my suffering.
My young men and maidens
  have gone into exile.

19 "I called to my allies
  but they betrayed me.
My priests and my elders
  perished in the city
while they searched for food
  to keep themselves alive.

20 "See, O LORD, how distressed I am!
  I am in torment within,
and in my heart I am disturbed,
  for I have been most rebellious.
Outside, the sword bereaves;
  inside, there is only death.

21 "People have heard my groaning,
  but there is no one to comfort me.
All my enemies have heard of my distress;
  they rejoice at what you have done.
May you bring the day you have announced
  so they may become like me.

22 "Let all their wickedness come before you;
  deal with them
as you have dealt with me
  because of all my sins.
My groans are many
  and my heart is faint."

2[a] How the Lord has covered the Daughter of Zion
  with the cloud of his anger[b]!
He has hurled down the splendor of Israel
  from heaven to earth;
he has not remembered his footstool
  in the day of his anger.

2 Without pity the Lord has swallowed up
  all the dwellings of Jacob;
in his wrath he has torn down
  the strongholds of the Daughter of Judah.
He has brought her kingdom and its princes
  down to the ground in dishonor.

3 In fierce anger he has cut off
  every horn[c] of Israel.
He has withdrawn his right hand
  at the approach of the enemy.
He has burned in Jacob like a flaming fire
  that consumes everything around it.

4 Like an enemy he has strung his bow;
  his right hand is ready.
Like a foe he has slain
  all who were pleasing to the eye;
he has poured out his wrath like fire
  on the tent of the Daughter of Zion.

5 The Lord is like an enemy;
  he has swallowed up Israel.
He has swallowed up all her palaces
  and destroyed her strongholds.
He has multiplied mourning and lamentation
  for the Daughter of Judah.

6 He has laid waste his dwelling like a garden;
  he has destroyed his place of meeting.
The LORD has made Zion forget
  her appointed feasts and her Sabbaths;
in his fierce anger he has spurned
  both king and priest.

7 The Lord has rejected his altar
  and abandoned his sanctuary.
He has handed over to the enemy
  the walls of her palaces;
they have raised a shout in the house of the LORD
  as on the day of an appointed feast.

8 The LORD determined to tear down
  the wall around the Daughter of Zion.
He stretched out a measuring line
  and did not withhold his hand from destroying.
He made ramparts and walls lament;
  together they wasted away.

9 Her gates have sunk into the ground;
  their bars he has broken and destroyed.
Her king and her princes are exiled among the nations,
  the law is no more,
and her prophets no longer find
  visions from the LORD.

10 The elders of the Daughter of Zion
  sit on the ground in silence;

[a] This chapter is an acrostic poem, the verses of which begin with the successive letters of the Hebrew alphabet.
[b] 1 Or *How the Lord in his anger / has treated the Daughter of Zion with contempt*
[c] 3 Or / *all the strength;* or *every king; horn* here symbolizes strength.

1:18–22 After suffering through Jerusalem's devastation and exile, many of the Jews were forced to recognize that they had indeed sinned. Before Jerusalem's destruction, many believed that God would protect Jerusalem and the temple regardless of their lifestyle. The destruction of Jerusalem forced the people to face reality. They had sinned, and their sins brought terrible consequences. Accepting responsibility for our sin is an essential part of the spiritual growth process.

2:1–18 God's anger and the devastating consequences of that anger are described in detail in these verses. Notice that God is always slow to anger and quick to forgive. God's prophets had warned the Israelites to turn from their wickedness for centuries before Jerusalem was finally destroyed. God's anger is prompted by his love; it is his last resort to get our attention. His purpose is not to destroy us but to bring us to repentance and restoration.

they have sprinkled dust on their heads
and put on sackcloth.
The young women of Jerusalem
have bowed their heads to the ground.

11My eyes fail from weeping,
I am in torment within,
my heart is poured out on the ground
because my people are destroyed,
because children and infants faint
in the streets of the city.

12They say to their mothers,
"Where is bread and wine?"
as they faint like wounded men
in the streets of the city,
as their lives ebb away
in their mothers' arms.

13What can I say for you?
With what can I compare you,
O Daughter of Jerusalem?
To what can I liken you,
that I may comfort you,
O Virgin Daughter of Zion?
Your wound is as deep as the sea.
Who can heal you?

14The visions of your prophets
were false and worthless;
they did not expose your sin
to ward off your captivity.
The oracles they gave you
were false and misleading.

15All who pass your way
clap their hands at you;
they scoff and shake their heads
at the Daughter of Jerusalem:
"Is this the city that was called
the perfection of beauty,
the joy of the whole earth?"

16All your enemies open their mouths
wide against you;
they scoff and gnash their teeth
and say, "We have swallowed her up.
This is the day we have waited for;
we have lived to see it."

17The LORD has done what he planned;
he has fulfilled his word,
which he decreed long ago.
He has overthrown you without pity,
he has let the enemy gloat over you,
he has exalted the horn[a] of your foes.

18The hearts of the people
cry out to the Lord.
O wall of the Daughter of Zion,
let your tears flow like a river
day and night;
give yourself no relief,
your eyes no rest.

19Arise, cry out in the night,
as the watches of the night begin;
pour out your heart like water
in the presence of the Lord.
Lift up your hands to him
for the lives of your children,
who faint from hunger
at the head of every street.

20"Look, O LORD, and consider:
Whom have you ever treated like this?
Should women eat their offspring,
the children they have cared for?
Should priest and prophet be killed
in the sanctuary of the Lord?

21"Young and old lie together
in the dust of the streets;
my young men and maidens
have fallen by the sword.
You have slain them in the day of your
anger;
you have slaughtered them without pity.

22"As you summon to a feast day,
so you summoned against me terrors on
every side.
In the day of the LORD's anger
no one escaped or survived;
those I cared for and reared,
my enemy has destroyed."

3 [b]I am the man who has seen affliction
by the rod of his wrath.
2He has driven me away and made me walk
in darkness rather than light;
3indeed, he has turned his hand against me
again and again, all day long.

4He has made my skin and my flesh grow
old
and has broken my bones.
5He has besieged me and surrounded me
with bitterness and hardship.
6He has made me dwell in darkness
like those long dead.

[a]17 *Horn* here symbolizes strength. [b]This chapter is an acrostic poem; the verses of each stanza begin with the successive letters of the Hebrew alphabet, and the verses within each stanza begin with the same letter.

2:19–22 Jeremiah urged the people to admit their helplessness and turn to God for deliverance. Some of us can relate to the terrible losses that the Jews had experienced. Many of us can point to sins in our lives that have brought about our suffering. All of us, no matter what our problems, can recognize our helpless situation and turn to God for help. Doing this will set the process of spiritual growth in motion.

3:1–20 The prophet's words took a personal turn in this chapter. He was heartbroken and weary, discouraged and completely undone. He felt alone and helpless, very much afflicted by God. Notice that Jeremiah spoke frankly with God; he didn't hide his despair or anger. Expressing his feelings was an important part of his healing and restoration (see 3:21). Sometimes we hide our feelings from God, fearing that he will condemn us for them. God is never provoked by our honest emotions. Until we recognize what is truly in our hearts, we cannot deal with it and move on in our spiritual renewal.

7He has walled me in so I cannot escape;
he has weighed me down with chains.
8Even when I call out or cry for help,
he shuts out my prayer.
9He has barred my way with blocks of stone;
he has made my paths crooked.

10Like a bear lying in wait,
like a lion in hiding,
11he dragged me from the path and mangled me
and left me without help.
12He drew his bow
and made me the target for his arrows.

13He pierced my heart
with arrows from his quiver.
14I became the laughingstock of all my people;
they mock me in song all day long.
15He has filled me with bitter herbs
and sated me with gall.

16He has broken my teeth with gravel;
he has trampled me in the dust.
17I have been deprived of peace;
I have forgotten what prosperity is.
18So I say, "My splendor is gone
and all that I had hoped from the LORD."

19I remember my affliction and my wandering,
the bitterness and the gall.
20I well remember them,
and my soul is downcast within me.
21Yet this I call to mind
and therefore I have hope:

22Because of the LORD's great love we are not consumed,
for his compassions never fail.
23They are new every morning;
great is your faithfulness.
24I say to myself, "The LORD is my portion;
therefore I will wait for him."

25The LORD is good to those whose hope is in him,
to the one who seeks him;
26it is good to wait quietly
for the salvation of the LORD.
27It is good for a man to bear the yoke
while he is young.

3:21–26 After Jeremiah shared his pain with God, he reflected upon God's faithfulness. What could possibly save him from his terrible anguish? Nothing—except the compassion of a gracious, loving God. God's love is unfailing, his purposes clear, his righteousness unquestionable. When we come to God with our pain, we can be certain that he is listening. And God, in his mercy and grace, will give us the help we need to overcome our struggles.
3:27–39 God disciplines us because he loves us. When we follow a dangerous path, we need to be stopped. Sometimes the only way God can get our attention is by allowing us to suffer the consequences of our sin. Though we may get angry at God for such discipline, God's correction presents us an opportunity for change. We should

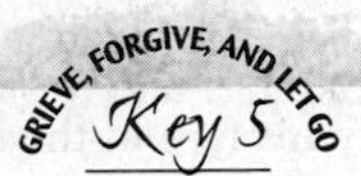

Help for the Brokenhearted

Lamentations 3:1–26 Even though we may seek God and pursue spiritual renewal, we will not be exempt from suffering. We may encounter personal tragedy, or we may suffer by watching loved ones bear the consequences of their own sins. Whenever our hearts are breaking, we should release our grief and sorrow to God. Only he can mend our broken hearts.

Jeremiah watched as his beloved nation was taken captive, ravished and almost completely destroyed because of its refusal to surrender to God. No wonder Jeremiah is known as the weeping prophet. Lamentations records Jeremiah's sorrow over the shameful fate of God's people. He cried:

My splendor is gone and all that I had hoped from the LORD. I remember my affliction and my wandering, the bitterness and the gall. I well remember them, and my soul is downcast within me. Yet this I call to mind and therefore I have hope: Because of the LORD's great love we are not consumed, for his compassions never fail. They are new every morning; great is your faithfulness. I say to myself, "The LORD is my portion; therefore I will wait for him." The LORD is good to those whose hope is in him, to the one who seeks him (3:18–25).

Releasing our lives to God also means forgiving those who have contributed to our pain and giving that pain and suffering over to God. In our times of grief and shame, we can trust that God will overcome the problems we face. God is strong enough to lift our burdens and loving enough to mend our broken hearts. We must remind ourselves of God's love for us.

Turn to Jonah 4.

28Let him sit alone in silence,
for the LORD has laid it on him.
29Let him bury his face in the dust—
there may yet be hope.
30Let him offer his cheek to one who would strike him,
and let him be filled with disgrace.

31For men are not cast off
by the Lord forever.
32Though he brings grief, he will show compassion,
so great is his unfailing love.
33For he does not willingly bring affliction
or grief to the children of men.

34To crush underfoot
all prisoners in the land,
35to deny a man his rights
before the Most High,
36to deprive a man of justice—
would not the Lord see such things?

37Who can speak and have it happen
if the Lord has not decreed it?
38Is it not from the mouth of the Most High
that both calamities and good things come?
39Why should any living man complain
when punished for his sins?

40Let us examine our ways and test them,
and let us return to the LORD.
41Let us lift up our hearts and our hands
to God in heaven, and say:
42"We have sinned and rebelled
and you have not forgiven.

43"You have covered yourself with anger and pursued us;
you have slain without pity.
44You have covered yourself with a cloud
so that no prayer can get through.
45You have made us scum and refuse
among the nations.

46"All our enemies have opened their mouths
wide against us.
47We have suffered terror and pitfalls,
ruin and destruction."
48Streams of tears flow from my eyes
because my people are destroyed.

49My eyes will flow unceasingly,
without relief,
50until the LORD looks down
from heaven and sees.
51What I see brings grief to my soul
because of all the women of my city.

52Those who were my enemies without cause
hunted me like a bird.
53They tried to end my life in a pit
and threw stones at me;
54the waters closed over my head,
and I thought I was about to be cut off.

55I called on your name, O LORD,
from the depths of the pit.
56You heard my plea: "Do not close your ears
to my cry for relief."
57You came near when I called you,
and you said, "Do not fear."

58O Lord, you took up my case;
you redeemed my life.
59You have seen, O LORD, the wrong done to me.
Uphold my cause!
60You have seen the depth of their vengeance,
all their plots against me.

61O LORD, you have heard their insults,
all their plots against me—
62what my enemies whisper and mutter
against me all day long.
63Look at them! Sitting or standing,
they mock me in their songs.

64Pay them back what they deserve, O LORD,
for what their hands have done.
65Put a veil over their hearts,
and may your curse be on them!
66Pursue them in anger and destroy them
from under the heavens of the LORD.

4 [a]How the gold has lost its luster,
the fine gold become dull!
The sacred gems are scattered
at the head of every street.

2How the precious sons of Zion,
once worth their weight in gold,
are now considered as pots of clay,
the work of a potter's hands!

3Even jackals offer their breasts
to nurse their young,
but my people have become heartless
like ostriches in the desert.

4Because of thirst the infant's tongue

[a]This chapter is an acrostic poem, the verses of which begin with the successive letters of the Hebrew alphabet.

---

honestly examine our lives, asking God to help us see our sins. Then we must repent of them, receive God's forgiveness and seek to live according to his plan. When we face the pain of discipline, we would be wise to ask Jeremiah's question: "Why should any living man complain when punished for his sins?" (3:39).

4:1–22 In this chapter, Jeremiah took a moment to reflect on the ravaged city of Jerusalem. He recalled a time when Jerusalem existed in splendor and majesty, when no one would have believed that Jerusalem could be destroyed. But now the holy city lay in ruins; children were begging for bread. We may believe that our lives are safe from destruction if we give lip service to God. However, if we are controlled by our sins rather than by God, we are in danger. We must take steps toward spiritual renewal while there is still time.

sticks to the roof of its mouth;
the children beg for bread,
but no one gives it to them.

5Those who once ate delicacies
are destitute in the streets.
Those nurtured in purple
now lie on ash heaps.

6The punishment of my people
is greater than that of Sodom,
which was overthrown in a moment
without a hand turned to help her.

7Their princes were brighter than snow
and whiter than milk,
their bodies more ruddy than rubies,
their appearance like sapphires.[a]

8But now they are blacker than soot;
they are not recognized in the streets.
Their skin has shriveled on their bones;
it has become as dry as a stick.

9Those killed by the sword are better off
than those who die of famine;
racked with hunger, they waste away
for lack of food from the field.

10With their own hands compassionate women
have cooked their own children,
who became their food
when my people were destroyed.

11The LORD has given full vent to his wrath;
he has poured out his fierce anger.
He kindled a fire in Zion
that consumed her foundations.

12The kings of the earth did not believe,
nor did any of the world's people,
that enemies and foes could enter
the gates of Jerusalem.

13But it happened because of the sins of her prophets
and the iniquities of her priests,
who shed within her
the blood of the righteous.

14Now they grope through the streets
like men who are blind.
They are so defiled with blood
that no one dares to touch their garments.

15"Go away! You are unclean!" men cry to them.
"Away! Away! Don't touch us!"
When they flee and wander about,
people among the nations say,
"They can stay here no longer."

16The LORD himself has scattered them;
he no longer watches over them.
The priests are shown no honor,
the elders no favor.

17Moreover, our eyes failed,
looking in vain for help;
from our towers we watched
for a nation that could not save us.

18Men stalked us at every step,
so we could not walk in our streets.
Our end was near, our days were numbered,
for our end had come.

19Our pursuers were swifter
than eagles in the sky;
they chased us over the mountains
and lay in wait for us in the desert.

20The LORD's anointed, our very life breath,
was caught in their traps.
We thought that under his shadow
we would live among the nations.

21Rejoice and be glad, O Daughter of Edom,
you who live in the land of Uz.
But to you also the cup will be passed;
you will be drunk and stripped naked.

22O Daughter of Zion, your punishment will end;
he will not prolong your exile.
But, O Daughter of Edom, he will punish your sin
and expose your wickedness.

5 Remember, O LORD, what has happened to us;
look, and see our disgrace.
2Our inheritance has been turned over to aliens,
our homes to foreigners.
3We have become orphans and fatherless,
our mothers like widows.
4We must buy the water we drink;
our wood can be had only at a price.
5Those who pursue us are at our heels;
we are weary and find no rest.
6We submitted to Egypt and Assyria
to get enough bread.
7Our fathers sinned and are no more,
and we bear their punishment.
8Slaves rule over us,
and there is none to free us from their hands.
9We get our bread at the risk of our lives
because of the sword in the desert.
10Our skin is hot as an oven,
feverish from hunger.

[a]7 Or *lapis lazuli*

5:1–18 The prophet asked God to remember the sufferings of his people and carefully listed the sufferings that they had endured. Notice how bold Jeremiah was in his relationship with God. When we feel upset about the situations we face, we often remain silent or complain under our breath, allowing our relationship with God to grow distant. Jeremiah went directly to God with his complaints, strengthening his relationship with God in the process. God does hear, and he does care. We need to share our feelings and struggles with him.

[11]Women have been ravished in Zion,
and virgins in the towns of Judah.
[12]Princes have been hung up by their hands;
elders are shown no respect.
[13]Young men toil at the millstones;
boys stagger under loads of wood.
[14]The elders are gone from the city gate;
the young men have stopped their
music.
[15]Joy is gone from our hearts;
our dancing has turned to mourning.
[16]The crown has fallen from our head.
Woe to us, for we have sinned!
[17]Because of this our hearts are faint,
because of these things our eyes grow
dim
[18]for Mount Zion, which lies desolate,
with jackals prowling over it.

[19]You, O LORD, reign forever;
your throne endures from generation to
generation.
[20]Why do you always forget us?
Why do you forsake us so long?
[21]Restore us to yourself, O LORD, that we
may return;
renew our days as of old
[22]unless you have utterly rejected us
and are angry with us beyond measure.

5:19–22 Jeremiah made a final, impassioned plea asking God to remember and restore his broken people. God did restore Israel after the years of Babylonian captivity. Under the leadership of men like Zerubbabel, Ezra and Nehemiah, God led his people home to rebuild Jerusalem and the temple. God still restores his people today. Regardless of the intensity of our pain, he is able to bring deep and abiding comfort.

Ezekiel

The Big Picture

Discouragement. Despair. Disillusionment. These are just a few of the feelings experienced by Ezekiel's audience. Ezekiel was deported with other Jews to Babylonia about ten years before the destruction of Jerusalem. He prophesied to the Jewish exiles at the Kebar River during the last years of Jerusalem's survival and in the years closely following its fall. He was called by God to confront and then to comfort his people.

As the book of Ezekiel begins, one hope for the exiles still remained. Jerusalem was still standing; there was hope that the holy city and temple would yet be spared. God's people, however, were spiritually blind. The popular theology of the day assumed that God's presence in the temple would protect Jerusalem from destruction. The people refused to see the truth that there was no escaping the painful consequences of their sins. During this time of false hope, God called Ezekiel to proclaim the sure destruction of Jerusalem. The people needed to realize that their sins brought about painful consequences and that humble repentance was required.

The final chapters of the book (25:1—48:35) are filled with words of hope for God's broken people. With the fall of Jerusalem (24:1–27), the predicted consequences of the people's sins had come to pass. The people of Judah now could no longer deny their sin; they finally took responsibility for it and turned to God for help. God responded with a promise of future restoration and peace. Through a vision of dry bones coming to life, the exiled Jews saw hope for a new life. God could do the impossible! He would lead his people home, restore what was totally ruined and rebuild his nation.

A. CONDEMNATION FOR JUDAH (1:1–24:27)

1. God's Glory in Ezekiel's Vision and Commission (1:1–3:27)
2. Messages of Gloom for Israel (4:1–24:27)

B. CONSOLATION FOR JUDAH (25:1–48:35)

1. Judgment Against Foreign Nations (25:1–32:32)
2. Messages of Hope for Judah (33:1–39:29)
3. The New Temple in Jerusalem (40:1–48:35)

Spiritual Renewal Themes

SPIRITUAL RENEWAL THROUGH CONFRONTATION

Throughout the opening chapters of Ezekiel, God's people were spiritually blind. They believed that God would preserve Jerusalem regardless of how they behaved. So God's plan for Judah's spiritual renewal came through the words of Ezekiel in the form of direct confrontation. Ezekiel told the Jews the truth about their sin and that the nation would soon suffer the consequence of complete destruction. When we are spiritually blind, direct confrontation may be the last resort and only way to get

Essential Facts

PURPOSE:
To help the people in exile understand that God's glory and righteousness made their present judgment necessary and their future restoration certain.

AUTHOR:
The prophet Ezekiel.

AUDIENCE:
The Jews of the Babylonian exile, before and after the fall of Jerusalem.

DATE WRITTEN:
The book was probably written shortly after the time period it covers, during the time of Ezekiel's ministry (593–570 B.C.).

SETTING:
Ezekiel lived near the Kebar River in Babylon and ministered to the Jews in exile there.

KEY VERSE:
"I will give you a new heart and put a new spirit in you; I will remove from you your heart of stone and give you a heart of flesh" (36:26).

KEY PLACES:
Jerusalem, Babylon and Egypt.

KEY PEOPLE:
Ezekiel, his wife, Israel's leaders and Nebuchadnezzar.

our attention. If we fail to see or listen to the truth, God may let us suffer the consequences. We would be wise to listen and take action when we are confronted with our sin.

HOPE IN FAILURE

Whenever the consequences of our sin overtake us, we may feel that all is lost, that nothing good can happen. After the destruction of Jerusalem, God's people felt like this. Ezekiel's message of judgment came true. The people realized too late that they were sinful and that their suffering was a consequence of their sin. As the people grasped the severity of their situation, God sent them a message of hope. When we feel defeated because of our sin, God brings us a message of hope too. He is our strength and our hope for spiritual renewal.

GOD IS ALWAYS WITH US

The exiles in Babylon lived in a location that daily reminded them of their failure and shame. They felt abandoned by God. Yet God, who isn't limited by geographical boundaries, was present in Babylon with them. He met Ezekiel on foreign soil, and spoke to his disheartened people through him. God wants to meet us where we are, even when we are at our worst. And when God comes, he comes in glory, bringing light to the darkness and hope for spiritual renewal. God is always with us—even in the midst of our mistakes and failures.

NO SITUATION IS HOPELESS

Some of us suffer the consequences of having been raised in families that didn't follow God's ways. The results of their bad decisions, and our own, may affect our lives for a long period of time. We may share the feelings of the Jewish exiles in Babylon. Many of them were suffering in exile because of the sins of their ancestors. They felt overwhelmed and helpless. But God entered their hopeless situation and transformed it into something that brought honor and glory to his name. God hasn't changed. He still wants to come into our hopeless situations and transform them. He wants to free us from our bondage to sin and failure.

The Living Creatures and the Glory of the LORD

1 In the[a] thirtieth year, in the fourth month on the fifth day, while I was among the exiles by the Kebar River, the heavens were opened and I saw visions of God.

2On the fifth of the month—it was the fifth year of the exile of King Jehoiachin— 3the word of the LORD came to Ezekiel the priest, the son of Buzi,[b] by the Kebar River in the land of the Babylonians.[c] There the hand of the LORD was upon him.

4I looked, and I saw a windstorm coming out of the north—an immense cloud with flashing lightning and surrounded by brilliant light. The center of the fire looked like glowing metal, 5and in the fire was what looked like four living creatures. In appearance their form was that of a man, 6but each of them had four faces and four wings. 7Their legs were straight; their feet were like those of a calf and gleamed like burnished bronze. 8Under their wings on their four sides they had the hands of a man. All four of them had faces and wings, 9and their wings touched one another. Each one went straight ahead; they did not turn as they moved.

10Their faces looked like this: Each of the four had the face of a man, and on the right side each had the face of a lion, and on the left the face of an ox; each also had the face of an eagle. 11Such were their faces. Their wings were spread out upward; each had two wings, one touching the wing of another creature on either side, and two wings covering its body. 12Each one went straight ahead. Wherever the spirit would go, they would go, without turning as they went. 13The appearance of the living creatures was like burning coals of fire or like torches. Fire moved back and forth among the creatures; it was bright, and lightning flashed out of it. 14The creatures sped back and forth like flashes of lightning.

15As I looked at the living creatures, I saw a wheel on the ground beside each creature with its four faces. 16This was the appearance and structure of the wheels: They sparkled like chrysolite, and all four looked alike. Each appeared to be made like a wheel intersecting a wheel. 17As they moved, they would go in any one of the four directions the creatures faced; the wheels did not turn about[d] as the creatures went. 18Their rims were high and awesome, and all four rims were full of eyes all around.

19When the living creatures moved, the wheels beside them moved; and when the living creatures rose from the ground, the wheels also rose. 20Wherever the spirit would go, they would go, and the wheels would rise along with them, because the spirit of the living creatures was in the wheels. 21When the creatures moved, they also moved; when the creatures stood still, they also stood still; and when the creatures rose from the ground, the wheels rose along with them, because the spirit of the living creatures was in the wheels.

22Spread out above the heads of the living creatures was what looked like an expanse, sparkling like ice, and awesome. 23Under the expanse their wings were stretched out one toward the other, and each had two wings covering its body. 24When the creatures moved, I heard the sound of their wings, like the roar of rushing waters, like the voice of the Almighty,[e] like the tumult of an army. When they stood still, they lowered their wings.

25Then there came a voice from above the expanse over their heads as they stood with lowered wings. 26Above the expanse over their heads was what looked like a throne of sapphire,[f] and high above on the throne was a figure like that of a man. 27I saw that from what appeared to be his waist up he looked like glowing metal, as if full of fire, and that from there down he looked like fire; and brilliant light surrounded him. 28Like the appearance of a rainbow in the clouds on a rainy day, so was the radiance around him.

This was the appearance of the likeness of the glory of the LORD. When I saw it, I fell facedown, and I heard the voice of one speaking.

[a] 1 Or ⌊my⌋ [b] 3 Or *Ezekiel son of Buzi the priest* [c] 3 Or *Chaldeans* [d] 17 Or *aside* [e] 24 Hebrew *Shaddai* [f] 26 Or *lapis lazuli*

1:1–3 Ezekiel was one of the people of Judah exiled to Babylon about ten years prior to Jerusalem's destruction. Though the people had lost their homeland and property, in the early chapters of this book (1:1—24:27) they still clung to a slim measure of hope. Jerusalem and its temple still stood; complete destruction had not yet taken place. Because of this, many of the people continued in their spiritual blindness, believing that God would not allow their homeland to be destroyed. They refused to admit their sins and the sins of their ancestors. In the early chapters of this book, the prophet confronted the exiles with their sins and predicted Jerusalem's ultimate destruction. Ezekiel's early ministry was one of confrontation.

1:1–3 Having been trained as a priest, Ezekiel would have naturally associated God's presence with the temple in Jerusalem. But Ezekiel and his companions had been uprooted from their land and from their temple. Many wondered whether or not they would ever experience God's presence in Babylon. Through Ezekiel's visions, it became clear to the people that God was not limited by geography. He could even reveal himself in godless Babylon! God can reach out to us no matter where we are or what we have done. If we surrender our lives to him, there is always hope for restoration.

1:4–28 What a magnificent vision! The glory of God was revealed to God's people in captivity. Many of them doubted whether God was with them in this foreign land. Some even believed that when Babylon defeated the Israelite armies, the gods of Babylon had defeated God too. To counteract this confusion and to help the people trust him, God revealed his glory to his exiled people in Babylon.

Ezekiel's Call

2 He said to me, "Son of man, stand up on your feet and I will speak to you." 2As he spoke, the Spirit came into me and raised me to my feet, and I heard him speaking to me.

3He said: "Son of man, I am sending you to the Israelites, to a rebellious nation that has rebelled against me; they and their fathers have been in revolt against me to this very day. 4The people to whom I am sending you are obstinate and stubborn. Say to them, 'This is what the Sovereign LORD says.' 5And whether they listen or fail to listen—for they are a rebellious house—they will know that a prophet has been among them. 6And you, son of man, do not be afraid of them or their words. Do not be afraid, though briers and thorns are all around you and you live among scorpions. Do not be afraid of what they say or terrified by them, though they are a rebellious house. 7You must speak my words to them, whether they listen or fail to listen, for they are rebellious. 8But you, son of man, listen to what I say to you. Do not rebel like that rebellious house; open your mouth and eat what I give you."

9Then I looked, and I saw a hand stretched out to me. In it was a scroll, 10which he unrolled before me. On both sides of it were written words of lament and mourning and woe.

3 And he said to me, "Son of man, eat what is before you, eat this scroll; then go and speak to the house of Israel." 2So I opened my mouth, and he gave me the scroll to eat.

3Then he said to me, "Son of man, eat this scroll I am giving you and fill your stomach with it." So I ate it, and it tasted as sweet as honey in my mouth.

4He then said to me: "Son of man, go now to the house of Israel and speak my words to them. 5You are not being sent to a people of obscure speech and difficult language, but to the house of Israel— 6not to many peoples of obscure speech and difficult language, whose words you cannot understand. Surely if I had sent you to them, they would have listened to you. 7But the house of Israel is not willing to listen to you because they are not willing to listen to me, for the whole house of Israel is hardened and obstinate. 8But I will make you as unyielding and hardened as they are. 9I will make your forehead like the hardest stone, harder than flint. Do not be afraid of them or terrified by them, though they are a rebellious house."

10And he said to me, "Son of man, listen carefully and take to heart all the words I speak to you. 11Go now to your countrymen in exile and speak to them. Say to them, 'This is what the Sovereign LORD says,' whether they listen or fail to listen."

12Then the Spirit lifted me up, and I heard behind me a loud rumbling sound—May the glory of the LORD be praised in his dwelling place!— 13the sound of the wings of the living creatures brushing against each other and the sound of the wheels beside them, a loud rumbling sound. 14The Spirit then lifted me up and took me away, and I went in bitterness and in the anger of my spirit, with the strong hand of the LORD upon me. 15I came to the exiles who lived at Tel Abib near the Kebar River. And there, where they were living, I sat among them for seven days—overwhelmed.

Warning to Israel

16At the end of seven days the word of the LORD came to me: 17"Son of man, I have made

---

2:1–2 Ezekiel was awestruck by God's glory and found himself facedown on the ground, unable to stand in God's presence. When we realize our sinfulness and begin to understand God's holiness, we may also find ourselves falling facedown before him. But notice that God's Spirit lifted Ezekiel back to his feet and prepared the stricken prophet to receive God's message. We, too, need to throw ourselves on the mercy of God. As we surrender our lives to him, God will lift us up and set us on the right road. When we are unable to help ourselves, God will give us the strength we need to take the next step.

2:3–5 Why did God send a message of judgment to a group of people already suffering in exile? At the time of this message, Jerusalem still stood. A majority of the Israelites still lived in their homeland. Ezekiel was one of a small group that had been exiled in 597 B.C. Many of these early exiles believed that their captivity would be short. God called Ezekiel to make it clear to the first group of exiles that the consequences of their sins had not yet fully fallen upon them. Jerusalem would be destroyed. The people would need to admit their sins and turn to God in repentance. We may also refuse to see the truth even though we have begun to feel the destructive consequences of our sins. We must honestly admit our sin and ask God to forgive us and change us.

2:6 God warned Ezekiel about the great difficulties that he would face as he obeyed God's will for his life. But God also made it clear that he would be with Ezekiel if the prophet trusted and obeyed him. When we seek to follow God's will, we can know that God will be with us. That doesn't mean life will always be easy for us. Sometimes situations may even get worse before they get better. Close friends may reject us or ridicule us. But God's promise to Ezekiel should give us courage to follow God's will.

3:1–3 Ezekiel was commanded to eat the scroll that contained God's Word. This act enabled Ezekiel to perform his difficult ministry. He was sustained and directed by the words he received from God. As we face trials, God's sustaining words in the Bible can provide us with the direction and strength we need to keep going and growing in our faith. As we read and meditate on God's truths, we will discover God's power helping us progress in the spiritual growth process.

3:7–8 Interpersonal confrontation is never comfortable, yet Ezekiel was warned that his ministry would be filled with it. If God's work was to be accomplished, Ezekiel would have to speak directly to God's people and condemn them for their sins. Times of confrontation are seldom pleasant for us either, but sometimes they are necessary. We need to remember that what we fail to deal with today often becomes a much bigger problem tomorrow.

3:17–21 What is our responsibility to other individuals? Are we responsible to warn them of impending danger? People who live sinful lives are often blind to the danger of God's judgment. Ezekiel was commissioned as a guard

EZEKIEL

Little is known of Ezekiel's personal life. He was a priest who faithfully obeyed God's laws and was called by God to be a prophet. Ezekiel began his ministry at age thirty, five years after he had been taken into Babylonian captivity. He had settled near the Kebar River, where he prophesied to the exiles during the years prior to and closely following Jerusalem's destruction.

Ezekiel's reticence to tell us more about himself may indicate his humility. A prophet's work was certainly humbling. God called on Ezekiel to publicly act out God's message for his people. On one occasion Ezekiel was told to lie on his left side for 390 days, symbolizing the years of Israel's sin, and then to lie on his right side for 40 days to depict the years of Judah's sin. When his wife died, Ezekiel was forbidden to mourn her death, illustrating the lack of mourners for Jerusalem after her impending demise.

Ezekiel's name means "God will strengthen," a name appropriate to the man and his message. Ezekiel needed God's strength as he carried a message of judgment to a people who did not want to hear it. God wanted his people to know that they could not escape the consequences of their sins. Ezekiel's message was intended to break through their spiritual blindness. But Ezekiel also carried a message of hope following Jerusalem's destruction. God wanted his people to realize that his mercy was available to those who would admit their sins and turn to him for his strength. Suffering was designed to bring about his people's restoration, not their destruction.

Ezekiel's messages of confrontation and comfort are applicable for us too. If we ignore the sin in our lives, Ezekiel's words warn us that our spiritual blindness will only lead to suffering and destruction. When we surrender our lives to God, Ezekiel's words of comfort are meant for us as well. God can rebuild our lives, no matter how broken or painful they have become. Ezekiel glimpsed a vision in which God reassembled the scattered, dry bones of his people and brought them back to life. God can do the same thing for us too and restore us to spiritual vitality.

STRENGTHS AND ACCOMPLISHMENTS:

Ezekiel was completely dedicated to God.
He communlcated God's message clearly despite opposition.
He did not complain about the difficult task that God had given him.
Ezekiel was willing to be humiliated for God's cause.

LESSONS FROM HIS LIFE:

Sin and the refusal to see the truth will lead to suffering and destruction.
Through repentance we can receive forgiveness and restoration.
God may call us to do difficult things to accomplish his will.
When God urges us to speak, we must not be swayed by the opposition.

KEY VERSES:

"And he said to me, 'Son of man, listen carefully and take to heart all the words I speak to you. Go now to your countrymen in exile and speak to them. Say to them, "This is what the Sovereign LORD says," whether they listen or fail to listen'" (3:10–11).

Ezekiel's story is told in the book of Ezekiel.

you a watchman for the house of Israel; so hear the word I speak and give them warning from me. 18When I say to a wicked man, 'You will surely die,' and you do not warn him or speak out to dissuade him from his evil ways in order to save his life, that wicked man will die for[a] his sin, and I will hold you accountable for his blood. 19But if you do warn the wicked man and he does not turn from his wickedness or from his evil ways, he will die for his sin; but you will have saved yourself.

20"Again, when a righteous man turns from his righteousness and does evil, and I put a stumbling block before him, he will die. Since you did not warn him, he will die for his sin. The righteous things he did will not be remembered, and I will hold you accountable for his blood. 21But if you do warn the righteous man not to sin and he does not sin, he will surely live because he took warning, and you will have saved yourself."

22The hand of the LORD was upon me there, and he said to me, "Get up and go out to the plain, and there I will speak to you." 23So I got up and went out to the plain. And the glory of the LORD was standing there, like the glory I had seen by the Kebar River, and I fell facedown.

24Then the Spirit came into me and raised me to my feet. He spoke to me and said: "Go, shut yourself inside your house. 25And you, son of man, they will tie with ropes; you will be bound so that you cannot go out among the people. 26I will make your tongue stick to the roof of your mouth so that you will be silent and unable to rebuke them, though they are a rebellious house. 27But when I speak to you, I will open your mouth and you shall say to them, 'This is what the Sovereign LORD says.' Whoever will listen let him listen, and whoever will refuse let him refuse; for they are a rebellious house.

Siege of Jerusalem Symbolized

4 "Now, son of man, take a clay tablet, put it in front of you and draw the city of Jerusalem on it. 2Then lay siege to it: Erect siege works against it, build a ramp up to it, set up camps against it and put battering rams around it. 3Then take an iron pan, place it as an iron wall between you and the city and turn your face toward it. It will be under siege, and you shall besiege it. This will be a sign to the house of Israel.

4"Then lie on your left side and put the sin of the house of Israel upon yourself.[b] You are to bear their sin for the number of days you lie on your side. 5I have assigned you the same number of days as the years of their sin. So for 390 days you will bear the sin of the house of Israel.

6"After you have finished this, lie down again, this time on your right side, and bear the sin of the house of Judah. I have assigned you 40 days, a day for each year. 7Turn your face toward the siege of Jerusalem and with bared arm prophesy against her. 8I will tie you up with ropes so that you cannot turn from one side to the other until you have finished the days of your siege.

9"Take wheat and barley, beans and lentils, millet and spelt; put them in a storage jar and use them to make bread for yourself. You are to eat it during the 390 days you lie on your side. 10Weigh out twenty shekels[c] of food to eat each day and eat it at set times. 11Also measure out a sixth of a hin[d] of water and drink it at set times. 12Eat the food as you would a barley cake; bake it in the sight of the people, using human excrement for fuel." 13The LORD said, "In this way the people of Israel will eat defiled food among the nations where I will drive them."

14Then I said, "Not so, Sovereign LORD! I have never defiled myself. From my youth until now I have never eaten anything found dead or torn by wild animals. No unclean meat has ever entered my mouth."

15"Very well," he said, "I will let you bake your bread over cow manure instead of human excrement."

16He then said to me: "Son of man, I will cut off the supply of food in Jerusalem. The people will eat rationed food in anxiety and drink rationed water in despair, 17for food and water will be scarce. They will be appalled at the sight of each other and will waste away because of[e] their sin.

5 "Now, son of man, take a sharp sword and use it as a barber's razor to shave your head and your beard. Then take a set of scales and divide up the hair. 2When the days of your siege

[a] 18 Or *in;* also in verses 19 and 20 [b] 4 Or *your side* [c] 10 That is, about 8 ounces (about 0.2 kilogram) [d] 11 That is, about 2/3 quart (about 0.6 liter) [e] 17 Or *away in*

---

to warn his people of approaching danger. We should love others enough to warn them of the danger they face before it is too late.

3:24 Ezekiel had just been commissioned as God's prophet. His task was immense, and he was overwhelmed by the scope of it. At this point, God's Spirit empowered him for the work he had to do. We also need God's help to perform the tasks he gives us to do. And as we examine our lives, we should rejoice in the small miracles God has performed for us.

4:1–3 Ezekiel made it clear to the Jewish exiles that their troubles were not over. Many refused to see the truth about their sin and hoped they would soon return to Jerusalem. Ezekiel told them that their beloved homeland would soon be destroyed. The people had to recognize their sin before God could help them resolve it. Seeing the truth of our sinfulness may sometimes be unpleasant, but it is essential if we want to overcome sin and continue in our spiritual growth.

4:9–11 In this little drama, Ezekiel illustrated what it would be like for God's people during the coming siege. Though things were already bad, the situation was only going to get worse. God knew that as long as the people had any reason for hope they would never admit their sin and trust him for restoration. It is essential that we recognize our need for God and daily surrender to him.

come to an end, burn a third of the hair with fire inside the city. Take a third and strike it with the sword all around the city. And scatter a third to the wind. For I will pursue them with drawn sword. 3But take a few strands of hair and tuck them away in the folds of your garment. 4Again, take a few of these and throw them into the fire and burn them up. A fire will spread from there to the whole house of Israel.

5"This is what the Sovereign LORD says: This is Jerusalem, which I have set in the center of the nations, with countries all around her. 6Yet in her wickedness she has rebelled against my laws and decrees more than the nations and countries around her. She has rejected my laws and has not followed my decrees.

7"Therefore this is what the Sovereign LORD says: You have been more unruly than the nations around you and have not followed my decrees or kept my laws. You have not even[a] conformed to the standards of the nations around you.

8"Therefore this is what the Sovereign LORD says: I myself am against you, Jerusalem, and I will inflict punishment on you in the sight of the nations. 9Because of all your detestable idols, I will do to you what I have never done before and will never do again. 10Therefore in your midst fathers will eat their children, and children will eat their fathers. I will inflict punishment on you and will scatter all your survivors to the winds. 11Therefore as surely as I live, declares the Sovereign LORD, because you have defiled my sanctuary with all your vile images and detestable practices, I myself will withdraw my favor; I will not look on you with pity or spare you. 12A third of your people will die of the plague or perish by famine inside you; a third will fall by the sword outside your walls; and a third I will scatter to the winds and pursue with drawn sword.

13"Then my anger will cease and my wrath against them will subside, and I will be avenged. And when I have spent my wrath upon them, they will know that I the LORD have spoken in my zeal.

14"I will make you a ruin and a reproach among the nations around you, in the sight of all who pass by. 15You will be a reproach and a taunt, a warning and an object of horror to the nations around you when I inflict punishment on you in anger and in wrath and with stinging rebuke. I the LORD have spoken. 16When I shoot at you with my deadly and destructive arrows of famine, I will shoot to destroy you. I will bring more and more famine upon you and cut off your supply of food. 17I will send famine and wild beasts against you, and they will leave you childless. Plague and bloodshed will sweep through you, and I will bring the sword against you. I the LORD have spoken."

A Prophecy Against the Mountains of Israel

6 The word of the LORD came to me: 2"Son of man, set your face against the mountains of Israel; prophesy against them 3and say: 'O mountains of Israel, hear the word of the Sovereign LORD. This is what the Sovereign LORD says to the mountains and hills, to the ravines and valleys: I am about to bring a sword against you, and I will destroy your high places. 4Your altars will be demolished and your incense altars will be smashed; and I will slay your people in front of your idols. 5I will lay the dead bodies of the Israelites in front of their idols, and I will scatter your bones around your altars. 6Wherever you live, the towns will be laid waste and the high places demolished, so that your altars will be laid waste and devastated, your idols smashed and ruined, your incense altars broken down, and what you have made wiped out. 7Your people will fall slain among you, and you will know that I am the LORD.

8" 'But I will spare some, for some of you will escape the sword when you are scattered among the lands and nations. 9Then in the nations where they have been carried captive, those who escape will remember me—how I have been grieved by their adulterous hearts, which have turned away from me, and by their eyes, which have lusted after their idols. They will loathe themselves for the evil they have done and for all their detestable practices. 10And they will know that I am the LORD; I did not threaten in vain to bring this calamity on them.

11" 'This is what the Sovereign LORD says: Strike your hands together and stamp your feet and cry out "Alas!" because of all the wicked and

[a]7 Most Hebrew manuscripts; some Hebrew manuscripts and Syriac *You have*

5:8–10 God's judgment is righteous and inevitable, Ezekiel announced. Sin brings terrible and unavoidable consequences. If we refuse to repent, we also must face God's punishment for our sin. We cannot live a life of sin and hope to slip past the consequences of our rebellion. God loves us and will restore us if we confess our sins to him and ask his forgiveness. But this does not mean we can do whatever we want. God is just and will discipline his people if they continue to sin.

5:14–15 God punished the people of Israel for their rebellion in order to show the world what happens to those who disobey him. Rebellion against God brings painful consequences. We would be wise to learn from the pain of the Israelites rather than repeat their mistakes. If we don't, we may also be used as an object lesson to show others what happens to those who rebel against God and his ways.

6:8–10 God rebuked his people for their sins and assured them of coming judgment, but he did not leave them in despair. He promised to spare a remnant who would eventually rebuild the nation. Yet, in order to rebuild, it was necessary for God to first tear down. People who experience destruction find new hope as they turn to God. No matter how great our present suffering, there is always hope for the future. We must view our pain as God's tool for our spiritual growth. Then we must turn to God for the forgiveness and healing he promises.

detestable practices of the house of Israel, for they will fall by the sword, famine and plague. 12He that is far away will die of the plague, and he that is near will fall by the sword, and he that survives and is spared will die of famine. So will I spend my wrath upon them. 13And they will know that I am the LORD, when their people lie slain among their idols around their altars, on every high hill and on all the mountaintops, under every spreading tree and every leafy oak—places where they offered fragrant incense to all their idols. 14And I will stretch out my hand against them and make the land a desolate waste from the desert to Diblah[a]—wherever they live. Then they will know that I am the LORD.' "

The End Has Come

7 The word of the LORD came to me: 2"Son of man, this is what the Sovereign LORD says to the land of Israel: The end! The end has come upon the four corners of the land. 3The end is now upon you and I will unleash my anger against you. I will judge you according to your conduct and repay you for all your detestable practices. 4I will not look on you with pity or spare you; I will surely repay you for your conduct and the detestable practices among you. Then you will know that I am the LORD.

5"This is what the Sovereign LORD says: Disaster! An unheard-of[b] disaster is coming. 6The end has come! The end has come! It has roused itself against you. It has come! 7Doom has come upon you—you who dwell in the land. The time has come, the day is near; there is panic, not joy, upon the mountains. 8I am about to pour out my wrath on you and spend my anger against you; I will judge you according to your conduct and repay you for all your detestable practices. 9I will not look on you with pity or spare you; I will repay you in accordance with your conduct and the detestable practices among you. Then you will know that it is I the LORD who strikes the blow.

10"The day is here! It has come! Doom has burst forth, the rod has budded, arrogance has blossomed! 11Violence has grown into[c] a rod to punish wickedness; none of the people will be left, none of that crowd—no wealth, nothing of value. 12The time has come, the day has arrived. Let not the buyer rejoice nor the seller grieve, for wrath is upon the whole crowd. 13The seller will not recover the land he has sold as long as both of them live, for the vision concerning the whole crowd will not be reversed. Because of their sins, not one of them will preserve his life. 14Though they blow the trumpet and get everything ready, no one will go into battle, for my wrath is upon the whole crowd.

15"Outside is the sword, inside are plague and famine; those in the country will die by the sword, and those in the city will be devoured by famine and plague. 16All who survive and escape will be in the mountains, moaning like doves of the valleys, each because of his sins. 17Every hand will go limp, and every knee will become as weak as water. 18They will put on sackcloth and be clothed with terror. Their faces will be covered with shame and their heads will be shaved. 19They will throw their silver into the streets, and their gold will be an unclean thing. Their silver and gold will not be able to save them in the day of the LORD's wrath. They will not satisfy their hunger or fill their stomachs with it, for it has made them stumble into sin. 20They were proud of their beautiful jewelry and used it to make their detestable idols and vile images. Therefore I will turn these into an unclean thing for them. 21I will hand it all over as plunder to foreigners and as loot to the wicked of the earth, and they will defile it. 22I will turn my face away from them, and they will desecrate my treasured place; robbers will enter it and desecrate it.

23"Prepare chains, because the land is full of bloodshed and the city is full of violence. 24I will bring the most wicked of the nations to take possession of their houses; I will put an end to the pride of the mighty, and their sanctuaries will be desecrated. 25When terror comes, they will seek peace, but there will be none. 26Calamity upon calamity will come, and rumor upon rumor. They will try to get a vision from the prophet; the teaching of the law by the priest will be lost, as will the counsel of the elders. 27The king will mourn, the prince will be clothed with despair, and the hands of the people of the land will tremble. I will deal with them according to their conduct, and by their

[a]14 Most Hebrew manuscripts; a few Hebrew manuscripts *Riblah* [b]5 Most Hebrew manuscripts; some Hebrew manuscripts and Syriac *Disaster after* [c]11 Or *The violent one has become*

6:14 "Then they will know that I am the LORD." The people of Israel needed to learn this lesson if they hoped to recover from their punishment in exile. Each of us must also discover who God is and what he requires of us if we desire true spiritual renewal and transformation. When we give God control of our lives and follow his will, we establish ourselves on a firm foundation.

7:5–11 Until we recognize where we are, we can never take measures to get where we should be. The people of Israel refused to admit their sinful past and were therefore unable to receive God's forgiveness, healing and direction. God awakened them to the sinfulness of their lives by allowing them to suffer. We would be wise to admit our sins and humbly turn to God for help before we experience sin's painful consequences too.

7:19 The people of Israel couldn't use their wealth or other human resources to escape their inevitable punishment. Only God was able to deliver them. But since the people refused to admit and forsake their sin, there was no hope of deliverance. When it comes to dealing with our sinful nature, human resources alone are of no avail. God is our only hope. If we depend on any other resource, we are headed for sure destruction.

own standards I will judge them. Then they will know that I am the LORD."

Idolatry in the Temple

8 In the sixth year, in the sixth month on the fifth day, while I was sitting in my house and the elders of Judah were sitting before me, the hand of the Sovereign LORD came upon me there. [2]I looked, and I saw a figure like that of a man.[a] From what appeared to be his waist down he was like fire, and from there up his appearance was as bright as glowing metal. [3]He stretched out what looked like a hand and took me by the hair of my head. The Spirit lifted me up between earth and heaven and in visions of God he took me to Jerusalem, to the entrance to the north gate of the inner court, where the idol that provokes to jealousy stood. [4]And there before me was the glory of the God of Israel, as in the vision I had seen in the plain.

[5]Then he said to me, "Son of man, look toward the north." So I looked, and in the entrance north of the gate of the altar I saw this idol of jealousy.

[6]And he said to me, "Son of man, do you see what they are doing—the utterly detestable things the house of Israel is doing here, things that will drive me far from my sanctuary? But you will see things that are even more detestable."

[7]Then he brought me to the entrance to the court. I looked, and I saw a hole in the wall. [8]He said to me, "Son of man, now dig into the wall." So I dug into the wall and saw a doorway there.

[9]And he said to me, "Go in and see the wicked and detestable things they are doing here." [10]So I went in and looked, and I saw portrayed all over the walls all kinds of crawling things and detestable animals and all the idols of the house of Israel. [11]In front of them stood seventy elders of the house of Israel, and Jaazaniah son of Shaphan was standing among them. Each had a censer in his hand, and a fragrant cloud of incense was rising.

[12]He said to me, "Son of man, have you seen what the elders of the house of Israel are doing in the darkness, each at the shrine of his own idol? They say, 'The LORD does not see us; the LORD has forsaken the land.' " [13]Again, he said, "You will see them doing things that are even more detestable."

[14]Then he brought me to the entrance to the north gate of the house of the LORD, and I saw women sitting there, mourning for Tammuz. [15]He said to me, "Do you see this, son of man? You will see things that are even more detestable than this."

[16]He then brought me into the inner court of the house of the LORD, and there at the entrance to the temple, between the portico and the altar, were about twenty-five men. With their backs toward the temple of the LORD and their faces toward the east, they were bowing down to the sun in the east.

[17]He said to me, "Have you seen this, son of man? Is it a trivial matter for the house of Judah to do the detestable things they are doing here? Must they also fill the land with violence and continually provoke me to anger? Look at them putting the branch to their nose! [18]Therefore I will deal with them in anger; I will not look on them with pity or spare them. Although they shout in my ears, I will not listen to them."

Idolaters Killed

9 Then I heard him call out in a loud voice, "Bring the guards of the city here, each with a weapon in his hand." [2]And I saw six men coming from the direction of the upper gate, which faces north, each with a deadly weapon in his hand. With them was a man clothed in linen who had a writing kit at his side. They came in and stood beside the bronze altar.

[3]Now the glory of the God of Israel went up from above the cherubim, where it had been, and moved to the threshold of the temple. Then the LORD called to the man clothed in linen who had the writing kit at his side [4]and said to him, "Go throughout the city of Jerusalem and put a mark on the foreheads of those who grieve and lament over all the detestable things that are done in it."

[5]As I listened, he said to the others, "Follow him through the city and kill, without showing pity or compassion. [6]Slaughter old men, young men and maidens, women and children, but do not touch anyone who has the mark. Begin at my sanctuary." So they began with the elders who were in front of the temple.

[7]Then he said to them, "Defile the temple and fill the courts with the slain. Go!" So they went out and began killing throughout the city. [8]While they were killing and I was left alone, I fell facedown, crying out, "Ah, Sovereign LORD! Are you going to destroy the entire remnant of

[a]2 Or *saw a fiery figure*

8:1–18 The religious leaders in Ezekiel's day were involved in idolatrous, pagan practices. They either mistakenly believed that God didn't see what they were doing or that he had gone away. We sometimes share this misconception and think that we can actually hide our sins from God. We might even believe that he looks the other way when we sin. Such a belief is false and extremely dangerous. God is deeply concerned about our sinful behavior. The terrible fate of Israel's leaders should serve as a warning to us.

9:1–6 In Ezekiel's day many in Israel believed they had nothing to fear because of their favored status as God's people. They thought that God's presence in the temple guaranteed their safety. From these verses, however, it is clear that God was concerned about the people's blatant disregard for his laws. He would make sure the offenders were punished. God will not stand idly by and allow people to rebel against him forever. We would be wise to listen and take appropriate action before it is too late.

Israel in this outpouring of your wrath on Jerusalem?"

9 He answered me, "The sin of the house of Israel and Judah is exceedingly great; the land is full of bloodshed and the city is full of injustice. They say, 'The LORD has forsaken the land; the LORD does not see.' 10 So I will not look on them with pity or spare them, but I will bring down on their own heads what they have done."

11 Then the man in linen with the writing kit at his side brought back word, saying, "I have done as you commanded."

The Glory Departs From the Temple

10 I looked, and I saw the likeness of a throne of sapphire[a] above the expanse that was over the heads of the cherubim. 2 The LORD said to the man clothed in linen, "Go in among the wheels beneath the cherubim. Fill your hands with burning coals from among the cherubim and scatter them over the city." And as I watched, he went in.

3 Now the cherubim were standing on the south side of the temple when the man went in, and a cloud filled the inner court. 4 Then the glory of the LORD rose from above the cherubim and moved to the threshold of the temple. The cloud filled the temple, and the court was full of the radiance of the glory of the LORD. 5 The sound of the wings of the cherubim could be heard as far away as the outer court, like the voice of God Almighty[b] when he speaks.

6 When the LORD commanded the man in linen, "Take fire from among the wheels, from among the cherubim," the man went in and stood beside a wheel. 7 Then one of the cherubim reached out his hand to the fire that was among them. He took up some of it and put it into the hands of the man in linen, who took it and went out. 8 (Under the wings of the cherubim could be seen what looked like the hands of a man.)

9 I looked, and I saw beside the cherubim four wheels, one beside each of the cherubim; the wheels sparkled like chrysolite. 10 As for their appearance, the four of them looked alike; each was like a wheel intersecting a wheel. 11 As they moved, they would go in any one of the four directions the cherubim faced; the wheels did not turn about[c] as the cherubim went. The cherubim went in whatever direction the head faced, without turning as they went. 12 Their entire bodies, including their backs, their hands and their wings, were completely full of eyes, as were their four wheels. 13 I heard the wheels being called "the whirling wheels." 14 Each of the cherubim had four faces: One face was that of a cherub, the second the face of a man, the third the face of a lion, and the fourth the face of an eagle.

15 Then the cherubim rose upward. These were the living creatures I had seen by the Kebar River. 16 When the cherubim moved, the wheels beside them moved; and when the cherubim spread their wings to rise from the ground, the wheels did not leave their side. 17 When the cherubim stood still, they also stood still; and when the cherubim rose, they rose with them, because the spirit of the living creatures was in them.

18 Then the glory of the LORD departed from over the threshold of the temple and stopped above the cherubim. 19 While I watched, the cherubim spread their wings and rose from the ground, and as they went, the wheels went with them. They stopped at the entrance to the east gate of the LORD's house, and the glory of the God of Israel was above them.

20 These were the living creatures I had seen beneath the God of Israel by the Kebar River, and I realized that they were cherubim. 21 Each had four faces and four wings, and under their wings was what looked like the hands of a man. 22 Their faces had the same appearance as those I had seen by the Kebar River. Each one went straight ahead.

Judgment on Israel's Leaders

11 Then the Spirit lifted me up and brought me to the gate of the house of the LORD that faces east. There at the entrance to the gate were twenty-five men, and I saw among them Jaazaniah son of Azzur and Pelatiah son of Benaiah, leaders of the people. 2 The LORD said to me, "Son of man, these are the men who are plotting evil and giving wicked advice in this city. 3 They say, 'Will it not soon be time to build houses?[d] This city is a cooking pot, and we are the meat.' 4 Therefore prophesy against them; prophesy, son of man."

5 Then the Spirit of the LORD came upon me, and he told me to say: "This is what the LORD says: That is what you are saying, O house of Israel, but I know what is going through your mind. 6 You have killed many people in this city and filled its streets with the dead.

7 "Therefore this is what the Sovereign LORD says: The bodies you have thrown there are the meat and this city is the pot, but I will drive you out of it. 8 You fear the sword, and the sword is what I will bring against you, declares the Sovereign LORD. 9 I will drive you out of the city and

[a] 1 Or *lapis lazuli* [b] 5 Hebrew *El-Shaddai* [c] 11 Or *aside* [d] 3 Or *This is not the time to build houses.*

10:1–22 Many of the Jews believed they were immune to enemy attack because of God's presence among them. This attitude made them deaf to Ezekiel's condemnation of their sin and his predictions of Jerusalem's destruction. In chapters 9—11 God's glory departed from the temple. God left the temple and Jerusalem by moving to the entrance of the temple (see 9:3), then to the south side of the temple (10:3), to the east gate (10:18–19; 11:1) and finally to the mountain east of the temple (see 11:23). When God left the temple, the people could no longer claim his divine presence. Their sin was real, and God's judgment was imminent.

hand you over to foreigners and inflict punishment on you. 10You will fall by the sword, and I will execute judgment on you at the borders of Israel. Then you will know that I am the LORD. 11This city will not be a pot for you, nor will you be the meat in it; I will execute judgment on you at the borders of Israel. 12And you will know that I am the LORD, for you have not followed my decrees or kept my laws but have conformed to the standards of the nations around you."

13Now as I was prophesying, Pelatiah son of Benaiah died. Then I fell facedown and cried out in a loud voice, "Ah, Sovereign LORD! Will you completely destroy the remnant of Israel?"

14The word of the LORD came to me: 15"Son of man, your brothers—your brothers who are your blood relatives[a] and the whole house of Israel—are those of whom the people of Jerusalem have said, 'They are[b] far away from the LORD; this land was given to us as our possession.'

Promised Return of Israel

16"Therefore say: 'This is what the Sovereign LORD says: Although I sent them far away among the nations and scattered them among the countries, yet for a little while I have been a sanctuary for them in the countries where they have gone.'

17"Therefore say: 'This is what the Sovereign LORD says: I will gather you from the nations and bring you back from the countries where you have been scattered, and I will give you back the land of Israel again.'

18"They will return to it and remove all its vile images and detestable idols. 19I will give them an undivided heart and put a new spirit in them; I will remove from them their heart of stone and give them a heart of flesh. 20Then they will follow my decrees and be careful to keep my laws. They will be my people, and I will be their God. 21But as for those whose hearts are devoted to their vile images and detestable idols, I will bring down on their own heads what they have done, declares the Sovereign LORD."

22Then the cherubim, with the wheels beside them, spread their wings, and the glory of the God of Israel was above them. 23The glory of the LORD went up from within the city and stopped above the mountain east of it. 24The Spirit lifted me up and brought me to the exiles in Babylonia[c] in the vision given by the Spirit of God.

Then the vision I had seen went up from me, 25and I told the exiles everything the LORD had shown me.

The Exile Symbolized

12 The word of the LORD came to me: 2"Son of man, you are living among a rebellious people. They have eyes to see but do not see and ears to hear but do not hear, for they are a rebellious people.

3"Therefore, son of man, pack your belongings for exile and in the daytime, as they watch, set out and go from where you are to another place. Perhaps they will understand, though they are a rebellious house. 4During the daytime, while they watch, bring out your belongings packed for exile. Then in the evening, while they are watching, go out like those who go into exile. 5While they watch, dig through the wall and take your belongings out through it. 6Put them on your shoulder as they are watching and carry them out at dusk. Cover your face so that you cannot see the land, for I have made you a sign to the house of Israel."

7So I did as I was commanded. During the day I brought out my things packed for exile. Then in the evening I dug through the wall with my hands. I took my belongings out at dusk, carrying them on my shoulders while they watched.

8In the morning the word of the LORD came to me: 9"Son of man, did not that rebellious house of Israel ask you, 'What are you doing?'

10"Say to them, 'This is what the Sovereign LORD says: This oracle concerns the prince in Jerusalem and the whole house of Israel who are there.' 11Say to them, 'I am a sign to you.'

"As I have done, so it will be done to them. They will go into exile as captives.

12"The prince among them will put his things on his shoulder at dusk and leave, and a hole will be dug in the wall for him to go through. He will cover his face so that he cannot see the land. 13I will spread my net for him, and he will be caught in my snare; I will bring him to Babylonia, the land of the Chaldeans, but he will not see it, and there he will die. 14I will scatter to the winds all those around him—his staff and all his troops—and I will pursue them with drawn sword.

15"They will know that I am the LORD, when I disperse them among the nations and scatter them through the countries. 16But I will spare a few of them from the sword, famine and

[a]15 Or *are in exile with you* (see Septuagint and Syriac)
[b]15 Or *those to whom the people of Jerusalem have said, 'Stay*
[c]24 Or *Chaldea*

11:16–21 Destruction fell on God's people as a means for getting their attention. God wanted to change their hearts. We are often as stubborn as the people of Israel. God may let us suffer in order to get our attention too. Yet, just as the exile transformed the Israelites into a people who loved God, Ezekiel's words about restoration can come true for us too. As we admit our sins to God, he will bring us forgiveness and healing. We can become God's own people too.

12:1–3 The people referred to in these verses were totally unaware of their spiritual condition. When people are spiritually blind, only God can open their eyes to their sinfulness. We all need to humbly ask God to show us the sins in our own lives so that we can confess them and forsake them.

plague, so that in the nations where they go they may acknowledge all their detestable practices. Then they will know that I am the LORD."

17The word of the LORD came to me: 18"Son of man, tremble as you eat your food, and shudder in fear as you drink your water. 19Say to the people of the land: 'This is what the Sovereign LORD says about those living in Jerusalem and in the land of Israel: They will eat their food in anxiety and drink their water in despair, for their land will be stripped of everything in it because of the violence of all who live there. 20The inhabited towns will be laid waste and the land will be desolate. Then you will know that I am the LORD.' "

21The word of the LORD came to me: 22"Son of man, what is this proverb you have in the land of Israel: 'The days go by and every vision comes to nothing'? 23Say to them, 'This is what the Sovereign LORD says: I am going to put an end to this proverb, and they will no longer quote it in Israel.' Say to them, 'The days are near when every vision will be fulfilled. 24For there will be no more false visions or flattering divinations among the people of Israel. 25But I the LORD will speak what I will, and it shall be fulfilled without delay. For in your days, you rebellious house, I will fulfill whatever I say, declares the Sovereign LORD.' "

26The word of the LORD came to me: 27"Son of man, the house of Israel is saying, 'The vision he sees is for many years from now, and he prophesies about the distant future.'

28"Therefore say to them, 'This is what the Sovereign LORD says: None of my words will be delayed any longer; whatever I say will be fulfilled, declares the Sovereign LORD.' "

False Prophets Condemned

13 The word of the LORD came to me: 2"Son of man, prophesy against the prophets of Israel who are now prophesying. Say to those who prophesy out of their own imagination: 'Hear the word of the LORD! 3This is what the Sovereign LORD says: Woe to the foolish[a] prophets who follow their own spirit and have seen nothing! 4Your prophets, O Israel, are like jackals among ruins. 5You have not gone up to the breaks in the wall to repair it for the house of Israel so that it will stand firm in the battle on the day of the LORD. 6Their visions are false and their divinations a lie. They say, "The LORD declares," when the LORD has not sent them; yet they expect their words to be fulfilled. 7Have you not seen false visions and uttered lying divinations when you say, "The LORD declares," though I have not spoken?

8" 'Therefore this is what the Sovereign LORD says: Because of your false words and lying visions, I am against you, declares the Sovereign LORD. 9My hand will be against the prophets who see false visions and utter lying divinations. They will not belong to the council of my people or be listed in the records of the house of Israel, nor will they enter the land of Israel. Then you will know that I am the Sovereign LORD.

10" 'Because they lead my people astray, saying, "Peace," when there is no peace, and because, when a flimsy wall is built, they cover it with whitewash, 11therefore tell those who cover it with whitewash that it is going to fall. Rain will come in torrents, and I will send hailstones hurtling down, and violent winds will burst forth. 12When the wall collapses, will people not ask you, "Where is the whitewash you covered it with?"

13" 'Therefore this is what the Sovereign LORD says: In my wrath I will unleash a violent wind, and in my anger hailstones and torrents of rain will fall with destructive fury. 14I will tear down the wall you have covered with whitewash and will level it to the ground so that its foundation will be laid bare. When it[b] falls, you will be destroyed in it; and you will know that I am the LORD. 15So I will spend my wrath against the wall and against those who covered it with whitewash. I will say to you, "The wall is gone and so are those who whitewashed it, 16those prophets of Israel who prophesied to Jerusalem and saw visions of peace for her when there was no peace, declares the Sovereign LORD." '

17"Now, son of man, set your face against the daughters of your people who prophesy out of their own imagination. Prophesy against them 18and say, 'This is what the Sovereign LORD says: Woe to the women who sew magic

[a]3 Or *wicked* [b]14 Or *the city*

12:18–20 In these verses Ezekiel prophesied, through symbolic actions, the coming destruction of Jerusalem. We tend to ignore dire predictions as mere gloom and doom. But Ezekiel's harsh predictions were driven by God's truth, not merely Ezekiel's gloomy disposition. Repeatedly Ezekiel attempted to turn the people's focus from hope in Jerusalem's survival to hope in God—the only means for their ultimate deliverance. The people needed to face the truth about their sin and make some changes.

13:2–3 Following ungodly leaders can be very dangerous for anyone. The people of Israel faced terrible destruction, and God's truth was their only pathway to deliverance. False prophets loudly claimed that the people had nothing to worry about—a message the people were glad to believe. But these prophets offered an easy way out when such a way didn't exist. If someone claims that we can just ignore our sins, we need to steer clear of them and their message. God calls us to examine our lives in light of his Word. When we recognize areas in our lives that are not in keeping with God's commands, we must face our sin and its consequences and take responsibility for them.

13:10 It is unwise to proclaim peace when there is no peace. We may face significant problems in our lives, but claiming everything is all right will never solve them. Our refusal to see the truth will only make things worse. If problems exist, we need to admit them and respond with appropriate action. Looking the other way, pretending everything is all right, will only lead us deeper into slavery and eventual destruction.

charms on all their wrists and make veils of various lengths for their heads in order to ensnare people. Will you ensnare the lives of my people but preserve your own? 19You have profaned me among my people for a few handfuls of barley and scraps of bread. By lying to my people, who listen to lies, you have killed those who should not have died and have spared those who should not live.

20" 'Therefore this is what the Sovereign LORD says: I am against your magic charms with which you ensnare people like birds and I will tear them from your arms; I will set free the people that you ensnare like birds. 21I will tear off your veils and save my people from your hands, and they will no longer fall prey to your power. Then you will know that I am the LORD. 22Because you disheartened the righteous with your lies, when I had brought them no grief, and because you encouraged the wicked not to turn from their evil ways and so save their lives, 23therefore you will no longer see false visions or practice divination. I will save my people from your hands. And then you will know that I am the LORD.' "

Idolaters Condemned

14 Some of the elders of Israel came to me and sat down in front of me. 2Then the word of the LORD came to me: 3"Son of man, these men have set up idols in their hearts and put wicked stumbling blocks before their faces. Should I let them inquire of me at all? 4Therefore speak to them and tell them, 'This is what the Sovereign LORD says: When any Israelite sets up idols in his heart and puts a wicked stumbling block before his face and then goes to a prophet, I the LORD will answer him myself in keeping with his great idolatry. 5I will do this to recapture the hearts of the people of Israel, who have all deserted me for their idols.'

6"Therefore say to the house of Israel, 'This is what the Sovereign LORD says: Repent! Turn from your idols and renounce all your detestable practices!

7" 'When any Israelite or any alien living in Israel separates himself from me and sets up idols in his heart and puts a wicked stumbling block before his face and then goes to a prophet to inquire of me, I the LORD will answer him myself. 8I will set my face against that man and make him an example and a byword. I will cut him off from my people. Then you will know that I am the LORD.

9" 'And if the prophet is enticed to utter a prophecy, I the LORD have enticed that prophet, and I will stretch out my hand against him and destroy him from among my people Israel. 10They will bear their guilt—the prophet will be as guilty as the one who consults him. 11Then the people of Israel will no longer stray from me, nor will they defile themselves anymore with all their sins. They will be my people, and I will be their God, declares the Sovereign LORD.' "

Judgment Inescapable

12The word of the LORD came to me: 13"Son of man, if a country sins against me by being unfaithful and I stretch out my hand against it to cut off its food supply and send famine upon it and kill its men and their animals, 14even if these three men—Noah, Daniel[a] and Job—were in it, they could save only themselves by their righteousness, declares the Sovereign LORD.

15"Or if I send wild beasts through that country and they leave it childless and it becomes desolate so that no one can pass through it because of the beasts, 16as surely as I live, declares the Sovereign LORD, even if these three men were in it, they could not save their own sons or daughters. They alone would be saved, but the land would be desolate.

17"Or if I bring a sword against that country and say, 'Let the sword pass throughout the land,' and I kill its men and their animals, 18as surely as I live, declares the Sovereign LORD, even if these three men were in it, they could not save their own sons or daughters. They alone would be saved.

19"Or if I send a plague into that land and pour out my wrath upon it through bloodshed, killing its men and their animals, 20as surely as I live, declares the Sovereign LORD, even if Noah, Daniel and Job were in it, they could save neither son nor daughter. They would save only themselves by their righteousness.

21"For this is what the Sovereign LORD says: How much worse will it be when I send against Jerusalem my four dreadful judgments—sword and famine and wild beasts and plague—to kill its men and their animals! 22Yet there will be some survivors—sons and daughters who will be brought out of it. They will come to you, and when you see their conduct and their actions, you will be consoled regarding the disaster I have brought upon Jerusalem—every disaster I have brought upon it. 23You will be consoled when you see their conduct and their actions, for you will know that I have done nothing in it without cause, declares the Sovereign LORD."

[a] 14 Or *Danel*; the Hebrew spelling may suggest a person other than the prophet Daniel; also in verse 20.

14:1–5 Very often a third party is responsible for the breakdown of important relationships. For example, a third party may come between a husband and wife. Our relationship with God suffers in a similar way when the third party is an idol. We should allow nothing to come between us and God.

14:21–23 Ezekiel struggled with the impending destruction of Jerusalem. He couldn't understand how God could destroy his holy city. In these verses, God told Ezekiel that judgment would come, just as he had predicted. Ezekiel was also assured that the judgments on Jerusalem were completely just. We can trust God; his actions are always right. Even when we don't fully understand our situations, we can trust God to do the right thing.

Jerusalem, A Useless Vine

15 The word of the LORD came to me: 2"Son of man, how is the wood of a vine better than that of a branch on any of the trees in the forest? 3Is wood ever taken from it to make anything useful? Do they make pegs from it to hang things on? 4And after it is thrown on the fire as fuel and the fire burns both ends and chars the middle, is it then useful for anything? 5If it was not useful for anything when it was whole, how much less can it be made into something useful when the fire has burned it and it is charred?

6"Therefore this is what the Sovereign LORD says: As I have given the wood of the vine among the trees of the forest as fuel for the fire, so will I treat the people living in Jerusalem. 7I will set my face against them. Although they have come out of the fire, the fire will yet consume them. And when I set my face against them, you will know that I am the LORD. 8I will make the land desolate because they have been unfaithful, declares the Sovereign LORD."

An Allegory of Unfaithful Jerusalem

16 The word of the LORD came to me: 2"Son of man, confront Jerusalem with her detestable practices 3and say, 'This is what the Sovereign LORD says to Jerusalem: Your ancestry and birth were in the land of the Canaanites; your father was an Amorite and your mother a Hittite. 4On the day you were born your cord was not cut, nor were you washed with water to make you clean, nor were you rubbed with salt or wrapped in cloths. 5No one looked on you with pity or had compassion enough to do any of these things for you. Rather, you were thrown out into the open field, for on the day you were born you were despised.

6" 'Then I passed by and saw you kicking about in your blood, and as you lay there in your blood I said to you, "Live!"[a] 7I made you grow like a plant of the field. You grew up and developed and became the most beautiful of jewels.[b] Your breasts were formed and your hair grew, you who were naked and bare.

8" 'Later I passed by, and when I looked at you and saw that you were old enough for love, I spread the corner of my garment over you and covered your nakedness. I gave you my solemn oath and entered into a covenant with you, declares the Sovereign LORD, and you became mine.

9" 'I bathed[c] you with water and washed the blood from you and put ointments on you. 10I clothed you with an embroidered dress and put leather sandals on you. I dressed you in fine linen and covered you with costly garments. 11I adorned you with jewelry: I put bracelets on your arms and a necklace around your neck, 12and I put a ring on your nose, earrings on your ears and a beautiful crown on your head. 13So you were adorned with gold and silver; your clothes were of fine linen and costly fabric and embroidered cloth. Your food was fine flour, honey and olive oil. You became very beautiful and rose to be a queen. 14And your fame spread among the nations on account of your beauty, because the splendor I had given you made your beauty perfect, declares the Sovereign LORD.

15" 'But you trusted in your beauty and used your fame to become a prostitute. You lavished your favors on anyone who passed by and your beauty became his.[d] 16You took some of your garments to make gaudy high places, where you carried on your prostitution. Such things should not happen, nor should they ever occur. 17You also took the fine jewelry I gave you, the jewelry made of my gold and silver, and you made for yourself male idols and engaged in prostitution with them. 18And you took your embroidered clothes to put on them, and you offered my oil and incense before them. 19Also the food I provided for you—the fine flour, olive oil and honey I gave you to eat—you offered as fragrant incense before them. That is what happened, declares the Sovereign LORD.

20" 'And you took your sons and daughters whom you bore to me and sacrificed them as food to the idols. Was your prostitution not enough? 21You slaughtered my children and sacrificed them[e] to the idols. 22In all your detestable practices and your prostitution you did not remember the days of your youth, when you were naked and bare, kicking about in your blood.

23" 'Woe! Woe to you, declares the Sovereign LORD. In addition to all your other wickedness, 24you built a mound for yourself and made a lofty shrine in every public square. 25At the head of every street you built your lofty shrines and degraded your beauty, offering your body with increasing promiscuity to anyone who passed by. 26You engaged in prostitution with the Egyptians, your lustful neighbors, and

[a]6 A few Hebrew manuscripts, Septuagint and Syriac; most Hebrew manuscripts *"Live!" And as you lay there in your blood I said to you, "Live!"*
[b]7 Or *became mature*
[c]9 Or *I had bathed*
[d]15 Most Hebrew manuscripts; one Hebrew manuscript (see some Septuagint manuscripts) *by. Such a thing should not happen*
[e]21 Or *and made them pass through ⌊the fire⌋*

16:6–15 In this passage, Ezekiel compared God's people to a young, helpless slave girl. God strengthened her in power and beauty and trained her to be a queen. He made a covenant with her, similar in many respects to a marriage covenant. But rather than being devoted to her provider, she became a prostitute and gave herself to others. Indeed, God had taken Israel from Egyptian slavery and made her into one of the great nations of the world. She responded by making alliances with pagan nations and worshiping their gods. In our lives, we may drift away from a love relationship with God. We may not feel as if we need God as much as we did initially. But God is the one who freed us from our past and strengthened us. Our relationship with him is a key to our spiritual vitality.

provoked me to anger with your increasing promiscuity. 27So I stretched out my hand against you and reduced your territory; I gave you over to the greed of your enemies, the daughters of the Philistines, who were shocked by your lewd conduct. 28You engaged in prostitution with the Assyrians too, because you were insatiable; and even after that, you still were not satisfied. 29Then you increased your promiscuity to include Babylonia,[a] a land of merchants, but even with this you were not satisfied.

30" 'How weak-willed you are, declares the Sovereign LORD, when you do all these things, acting like a brazen prostitute! 31When you built your mounds at the head of every street and made your lofty shrines in every public square, you were unlike a prostitute, because you scorned payment.

32" 'You adulterous wife! You prefer strangers to your own husband! 33Every prostitute receives a fee, but you give gifts to all your lovers, bribing them to come to you from everywhere for your illicit favors. 34So in your prostitution you are the opposite of others; no one runs after you for your favors. You are the very opposite, for you give payment and none is given to you.

35" 'Therefore, you prostitute, hear the word of the LORD! 36This is what the Sovereign LORD says: Because you poured out your wealth[b] and exposed your nakedness in your promiscuity with your lovers, and because of all your detestable idols, and because you gave them your children's blood, 37therefore I am going to gather all your lovers, with whom you found pleasure, those you loved as well as those you hated. I will gather them against you from all around and will strip you in front of them, and they will see all your nakedness. 38I will sentence you to the punishment of women who commit adultery and who shed blood; I will bring upon you the blood vengeance of my wrath and jealous anger. 39Then I will hand you over to your lovers, and they will tear down your mounds and destroy your lofty shrines. They will strip you of your clothes and take your fine jewelry and leave you naked and bare. 40They will bring a mob against you, who will stone you and hack you to pieces with their swords. 41They will burn down your houses and inflict punishment on you in the sight of many women. I will put a stop to your prostitution, and you will no longer pay your lovers. 42Then my wrath against you will subside and my jealous anger will turn away from you; I will be calm and no longer angry.

43" 'Because you did not remember the days of your youth but enraged me with all these things, I will surely bring down on your head what you have done, declares the Sovereign LORD. Did you not add lewdness to all your other detestable practices?

44" 'Everyone who quotes proverbs will quote this proverb about you: "Like mother, like daughter." 45You are a true daughter of your mother, who despised her husband and her children; and you are a true sister of your sisters, who despised their husbands and their children. Your mother was a Hittite and your father an Amorite. 46Your older sister was Samaria, who lived to the north of you with her daughters; and your younger sister, who lived to the south of you with her daughters, was Sodom. 47You not only walked in their ways and copied their detestable practices, but in all your ways you soon became more depraved than they. 48As surely as I live, declares the Sovereign LORD, your sister Sodom and her daughters never did what you and your daughters have done.

49" 'Now this was the sin of your sister Sodom: She and her daughters were arrogant, overfed and unconcerned; they did not help the poor and needy. 50They were haughty and did detestable things before me. Therefore I did away with them as you have seen. 51Samaria did not commit half the sins you did. You have done more detestable things than they, and have made your sisters seem righteous by all these things you have done. 52Bear your disgrace, for you have furnished some justification for your sisters. Because your sins were more vile than theirs, they appear more righteous than you. So then, be ashamed and bear your disgrace, for you have made your sisters appear righteous.

53" 'However, I will restore the fortunes of Sodom and her daughters and of Samaria and her daughters, and your fortunes along with them, 54so that you may bear your disgrace and be ashamed of all you have done in giving them comfort. 55And your sisters, Sodom with her daughters and Samaria with her daughters, will return to what they were before; and you and your daughters will return to what you were before. 56You would not even mention your sister Sodom in the day of your pride, 57before your wickedness was uncovered. Even so, you are now scorned by the daughters of Edom[c] and all her neighbors and the daughters of the Philistines—all those around you who despise you. 58You will bear the consequences of your lewdness and your detestable practices, declares the LORD.

59" 'This is what the Sovereign LORD says: I will deal with you as you deserve, because you

[a] 29 Or *Chaldea* [b] 36 Or *lust* [c] 57 Many Hebrew manuscripts and Syriac; most Hebrew manuscripts, Septuagint and Vulgate *Aram*

16:59–63 Even though Israel had sinned and her punishment was certain, God's promises of blessing for Israel would still be fulfilled. Israel's punishment was designed to help her redirect her course. The same is true for us. As we face the consequences of our sins, we must acknowledge that we have failed God and others. Yet we can still hope for a future restoration if we are willing to learn from our sufferings and let God use them to redirect the course of our lives.

have despised my oath by breaking the covenant. 60 Yet I will remember the covenant I made with you in the days of your youth, and I will establish an everlasting covenant with you. 61 Then you will remember your ways and be ashamed when you receive your sisters, both those who are older than you and those who are younger. I will give them to you as daughters, but not on the basis of my covenant with you. 62 So I will establish my covenant with you, and you will know that I am the LORD. 63 Then, when I make atonement for you for all you have done, you will remember and be ashamed and never again open your mouth because of your humiliation, declares the Sovereign LORD.' "

Two Eagles and a Vine

17 The word of the LORD came to me: 2 "Son of man, set forth an allegory and tell the house of Israel a parable. 3 Say to them, 'This is what the Sovereign LORD says: A great eagle with powerful wings, long feathers and full plumage of varied colors came to Lebanon. Taking hold of the top of a cedar, 4 he broke off its topmost shoot and carried it away to a land of merchants, where he planted it in a city of traders.

5 " 'He took some of the seed of your land and put it in fertile soil. He planted it like a willow by abundant water, 6 and it sprouted and became a low, spreading vine. Its branches turned toward him, but its roots remained under it. So it became a vine and produced branches and put out leafy boughs.

7 " 'But there was another great eagle with powerful wings and full plumage. The vine now sent out its roots toward him from the plot where it was planted and stretched out its branches to him for water. 8 It had been planted in good soil by abundant water so that it would produce branches, bear fruit and become a splendid vine.'

9 "Say to them, 'This is what the Sovereign LORD says: Will it thrive? Will it not be uprooted and stripped of its fruit so that it withers? All its new growth will wither. It will not take a strong arm or many people to pull it up by the roots. 10 Even if it is transplanted, will it thrive? Will it not wither completely when the east wind strikes it—wither away in the plot where it grew?' "

11 Then the word of the LORD came to me: 12 "Say to this rebellious house, 'Do you not know what these things mean?' Say to them: 'The king of Babylon went to Jerusalem and carried off her king and her nobles, bringing them back with him to Babylon. 13 Then he took a member of the royal family and made a treaty with him, putting him under oath. He also carried away the leading men of the land, 14 so that the kingdom would be brought low, unable to rise again, surviving only by keeping his treaty. 15 But the king rebelled against him by sending his envoys to Egypt to get horses and a large army. Will he succeed? Will he who does such things escape? Will he break the treaty and yet escape?

16 " 'As surely as I live, declares the Sovereign LORD, he shall die in Babylon, in the land of the king who put him on the throne, whose oath he despised and whose treaty he broke. 17 Pharaoh with his mighty army and great horde will be of no help to him in war, when ramps are built and siege works erected to destroy many lives. 18 He despised the oath by breaking the covenant. Because he had given his hand in pledge and yet did all these things, he shall not escape.

19 " 'Therefore this is what the Sovereign LORD says: As surely as I live, I will bring down on his head my oath that he despised and my covenant that he broke. 20 I will spread my net for him, and he will be caught in my snare. I will bring him to Babylon and execute judgment upon him there because he was unfaithful to me. 21 All his fleeing troops will fall by the sword, and the survivors will be scattered to the winds. Then you will know that I the LORD have spoken.

22 " 'This is what the Sovereign LORD says: I myself will take a shoot from the very top of a cedar and plant it; I will break off a tender sprig from its topmost shoots and plant it on a high and lofty mountain. 23 On the mountain heights of Israel I will plant it; it will produce branches and bear fruit and become a splendid cedar. Birds of every kind will nest in it; they will find shelter in the shade of its branches. 24 All the trees of the field will know that I the LORD bring down the tall tree and make the low tree grow tall. I dry up the green tree and make the dry tree flourish.

" 'I the LORD have spoken, and I will do it.' "

The Soul Who Sins Will Die

18 The word of the LORD came to me: 2 "What do you people mean by quoting this proverb about the land of Israel:

17:1–24 This chapter contains a review of Judah's final years, noting the Israelite's exile to Babylon and predicting Jerusalem's ultimate destruction. The exiles who heard Ezekiel's words had been among those exiled during the events he had described; yet they still hoped that his final prediction about Jerusalem's destruction would not take place. They still refused to see the truth. We often resist the truth about our situations and ourselves just as the people of Judah did. Such blindness will not solve our problems. We must humbly repent of our sins and seek forgiveness.

18:2–4 This passage reminds us that God holds us accountable for our actions. Many of us have suffered innocently at the hands of others. We cannot change the behavior of others, but we must forgive them and put the pain of these experiences behind us. Though others may have hurt us, we must never blame them for the mistakes we have made. Spiritual renewal requires that we accept responsibility for our own failures and do what we can to make restitution with those we have harmed.

" 'The fathers eat sour grapes,
and the children's teeth are set on edge'?

[3]"As surely as I live, declares the Sovereign
LORD, you will no longer quote this proverb in
Israel. [4]For every living soul belongs to me, the
father as well as the son—both alike belong to
me. The soul who sins is the one who will die.

[5]"Suppose there is a righteous man
who does what is just and right.
[6]He does not eat at the mountain shrines
or look to the idols of the house of
Israel.
He does not defile his neighbor's wife
or lie with a woman during her period.
[7]He does not oppress anyone,
but returns what he took in pledge for a
loan.
He does not commit robbery
but gives his food to the hungry
and provides clothing for the naked.
[8]He does not lend at usury
or take excessive interest.[a]
He withholds his hand from doing wrong
and judges fairly between man and man.
[9]He follows my decrees
and faithfully keeps my laws.
That man is righteous;
he will surely live,
declares the Sovereign LORD.

[10]"Suppose he has a violent son, who sheds
blood or does any of these other things[b]
[11](though the father has done none of them):

"He eats at the mountain shrines.
He defiles his neighbor's wife.
[12]He oppresses the poor and needy.
He commits robbery.
He does not return what he took in pledge.
He looks to the idols.
He does detestable things.
[13]He lends at usury and takes excessive
interest.

Will such a man live? He will not! Because he
has done all these detestable things, he will
surely be put to death and his blood will be on
his own head.

[14]"But suppose this son has a son who sees
all the sins his father commits, and though he
sees them, he does not do such things:

[15]"He does not eat at the mountain shrines
or look to the idols of the house of
Israel.
He does not defile his neighbor's wife.
[16]He does not oppress anyone
or require a pledge for a loan.
He does not commit robbery
but gives his food to the hungry
and provides clothing for the naked.
[17]He withholds his hand from sin[c]
and takes no usury or excessive interest.
He keeps my laws and follows my decrees.

He will not die for his father's sin; he will surely
live. [18]But his father will die for his own sin,
because he practiced extortion, robbed his
brother and did what was wrong among his
people.

[19]"Yet you ask, 'Why does the son not share
the guilt of his father?' Since the son has done
what is just and right and has been careful to
keep all my decrees, he will surely live. [20]The
soul who sins is the one who will die. The son
will not share the guilt of the father, nor will the
father share the guilt of the son. The righteousness of the righteous man will be credited to
him, and the wickedness of the wicked will be
charged against him.

[21]"But if a wicked man turns away from all
the sins he has committed and keeps all my
decrees and does what is just and right, he will
surely live; he will not die. [22]None of the offenses he has committed will be remembered
against him. Because of the righteous things he
has done, he will live. [23]Do I take any pleasure
in the death of the wicked? declares the Sovereign LORD. Rather, am I not pleased when they
turn from their ways and live?

[24]"But if a righteous man turns from his righteousness and commits sin and does the same
detestable things the wicked man does, will he
live? None of the righteous things he has done
will be remembered. Because of the unfaithfulness he is guilty of and because of the sins he
has committed, he will die.

[25]"Yet you say, 'The way of the Lord is not
just.' Hear, O house of Israel: Is my way unjust?
Is it not your ways that are unjust? [26]If a righteous man turns from his righteousness and
commits sin, he will die for it; because of the sin
he has committed he will die. [27]But if a wicked
man turns away from the wickedness he has
committed and does what is just and right, he
will save his life. [28]Because he considers all the
offenses he has committed and turns away from
them, he will surely live; he will not die. [29]Yet
the house of Israel says, 'The way of the Lord is
not just.' Are my ways unjust, O house of Israel?
Is it not your ways that are unjust?

[30]"Therefore, O house of Israel, I will judge
you, each one according to his ways, declares
the Sovereign LORD. Repent! Turn away from all
your offenses; then sin will not be your downfall. [31]Rid yourselves of all the offenses you
have committed, and get a new heart and a new
spirit. Why will you die, O house of Israel?

[a]8 Or *take interest*; similarly in verses 13 and 17
[b]10 Or *things to a brother* [c]17 Septuagint (see also verse 8); Hebrew *from the poor*

18:30–32 Some believe that God is too loving to punish anyone. Certainly, it is true that God takes no pleasure in the death of the wicked (see 18:23). But if people choose not to turn from their sins, they separate themselves from God by their rejection of his ways. Let us heed the Lord's passionate call to turn from our sins and live.

[32]For I take no pleasure in the death of anyone, declares the Sovereign LORD. Repent and live!

A Lament for Israel's Princes

19 "Take up a lament concerning the princes of Israel [2]and say:

" 'What a lioness was your mother
among the lions!
She lay down among the young lions
and reared her cubs.
[3]She brought up one of her cubs,
and he became a strong lion.
He learned to tear the prey
and he devoured men.
[4]The nations heard about him,
and he was trapped in their pit.
They led him with hooks
to the land of Egypt.

[5]" 'When she saw her hope unfulfilled,
her expectation gone,
she took another of her cubs
and made him a strong lion.
[6]He prowled among the lions,
for he was now a strong lion.
He learned to tear the prey
and he devoured men.
[7]He broke down[a] their strongholds
and devastated their towns.
The land and all who were in it
were terrified by his roaring.
[8]Then the nations came against him,
those from regions round about.
They spread their net for him,
and he was trapped in their pit.
[9]With hooks they pulled him into a cage
and brought him to the king of Babylon.
They put him in prison,
so his roar was heard no longer
on the mountains of Israel.

[10]" 'Your mother was like a vine in your
vineyard[b]
planted by the water;
it was fruitful and full of branches
because of abundant water.
[11]Its branches were strong,
fit for a ruler's scepter.
It towered high
above the thick foliage,
conspicuous for its height
and for its many branches.
[12]But it was uprooted in fury
and thrown to the ground.
The east wind made it shrivel,
it was stripped of its fruit;
its strong branches withered
and fire consumed them.
[13]Now it is planted in the desert,
in a dry and thirsty land.
[14]Fire spread from one of its main[c]
branches
and consumed its fruit.
No strong branch is left on it
fit for a ruler's scepter.'

This is a lament and is to be used as a lament."

Rebellious Israel

20 In the seventh year, in the fifth month
on the tenth day, some of the elders of
Israel came to inquire of the LORD, and they sat
down in front of me.
[2]Then the word of the LORD came to me:
[3]"Son of man, speak to the elders of Israel and
say to them, 'This is what the Sovereign LORD
says: Have you come to inquire of me? As surely
as I live, I will not let you inquire of me, declares the Sovereign LORD.'
[4]"Will you judge them? Will you judge them,
son of man? Then confront them with the detestable practices of their fathers [5]and say to
them: 'This is what the Sovereign LORD says: On
the day I chose Israel, I swore with uplifted
hand to the descendants of the house of Jacob
and revealed myself to them in Egypt. With uplifted hand I said to them, "I am the LORD your
God." [6]On that day I swore to them that I would
bring them out of Egypt into a land I had
searched out for them, a land flowing with milk
and honey, the most beautiful of all lands. [7]And
I said to them, "Each of you, get rid of the vile
images you have set your eyes on, and do not
defile yourselves with the idols of Egypt. I am
the LORD your God."
[8]" 'But they rebelled against me and would
not listen to me; they did not get rid of the vile
images they had set their eyes on, nor did they
forsake the idols of Egypt. So I said I would
pour out my wrath on them and spend my anger against them in Egypt. [9]But for the sake of
my name I did what would keep it from being
profaned in the eyes of the nations they lived
among and in whose sight I had revealed myself
to the Israelites by bringing them out of Egypt.
[10]Therefore I led them out of Egypt and brought
them into the desert. [11]I gave them my decrees
and made known to them my laws, for the man
who obeys them will live by them. [12]Also I gave
them my Sabbaths as a sign between us, so they
would know that I the LORD made them holy.
[13]" 'Yet the people of Israel rebelled against
me in the desert. They did not follow my decrees but rejected my laws—although the man
who obeys them will live by them—and they
utterly desecrated my Sabbaths. So I said I

[a]7 Targum (see Septuagint); Hebrew *He knew*
[b]10 Two Hebrew manuscripts; most Hebrew manuscripts *your blood* [c]14 Or *from under its*

20:1–8 The experiences of the people of Judah clearly point out that God alone defines his plan. He sets up the terms; we don't. If we want to come to God, we must come on his terms and enter his kingdom his way. As the one who created us and loves us, God knows how we ought to live. If we try to do things our own way, we are only heading for trouble.

would pour out my wrath on them and destroy them in the desert. 14But for the sake of my name I did what would keep it from being profaned in the eyes of the nations in whose sight I had brought them out. 15Also with uplifted hand I swore to them in the desert that I would not bring them into the land I had given them—a land flowing with milk and honey, most beautiful of all lands— 16because they rejected my laws and did not follow my decrees and desecrated my Sabbaths. For their hearts were devoted to their idols. 17Yet I looked on them with pity and did not destroy them or put an end to them in the desert. 18I said to their children in the desert, "Do not follow the statutes of your fathers or keep their laws or defile yourselves with their idols. 19I am the LORD your God; follow my decrees and be careful to keep my laws. 20Keep my Sabbaths holy, that they may be a sign between us. Then you will know that I am the LORD your God."

21" 'But the children rebelled against me: They did not follow my decrees, they were not careful to keep my laws—although the man who obeys them will live by them—and they desecrated my Sabbaths. So I said I would pour out my wrath on them and spend my anger against them in the desert. 22But I withheld my hand, and for the sake of my name I did what would keep it from being profaned in the eyes of the nations in whose sight I had brought them out. 23Also with uplifted hand I swore to them in the desert that I would disperse them among the nations and scatter them through the countries, 24because they had not obeyed my laws but had rejected my decrees and desecrated my Sabbaths, and their eyes ⌊lusted⌋ after their fathers' idols. 25I also gave them over to statutes that were not good and laws they could not live by; 26I let them become defiled through their gifts—the sacrifice of every firstborn[a]—that I might fill them with horror so they would know that I am the LORD.'

27"Therefore, son of man, speak to the people of Israel and say to them, 'This is what the Sovereign LORD says: In this also your fathers blasphemed me by forsaking me: 28When I brought them into the land I had sworn to give them and they saw any high hill or any leafy tree, there they offered their sacrifices, made offerings that provoked me to anger, presented their fragrant incense and poured out their drink offerings. 29Then I said to them: What is this high place you go to?' " (It is called Bamah[b] to this day.)

Judgment and Restoration

30"Therefore say to the house of Israel: 'This is what the Sovereign LORD says: Will you defile yourselves the way your fathers did and lust after their vile images? 31When you offer your gifts—the sacrifice of your sons in[c] the fire—you continue to defile yourselves with all your idols to this day. Am I to let you inquire of me, O house of Israel? As surely as I live, declares the Sovereign LORD, I will not let you inquire of me.

32" 'You say, "We want to be like the nations, like the peoples of the world, who serve wood and stone." But what you have in mind will never happen. 33As surely as I live, declares the Sovereign LORD, I will rule over you with a mighty hand and an outstretched arm and with outpoured wrath. 34I will bring you from the nations and gather you from the countries where you have been scattered—with a mighty hand and an outstretched arm and with outpoured wrath. 35I will bring you into the desert of the nations and there, face to face, I will execute judgment upon you. 36As I judged your fathers in the desert of the land of Egypt, so I will judge you, declares the Sovereign LORD. 37I will take note of you as you pass under my rod, and I will bring you into the bond of the covenant. 38I will purge you of those who revolt and rebel against me. Although I will bring them out of the land where they are living, yet they will not enter the land of Israel. Then you will know that I am the LORD.

39" 'As for you, O house of Israel, this is what the Sovereign LORD says: Go and serve your idols, every one of you! But afterward you will surely listen to me and no longer profane my holy name with your gifts and idols. 40For on my holy mountain, the high mountain of Israel, declares the Sovereign LORD, there in the land the entire house of Israel will serve me, and there I will accept them. There I will require your offerings and your choice gifts,[d] along with all your holy sacrifices. 41I will accept you as fragrant incense when I bring you out from the nations and gather you from the countries where you have been scattered, and I will show myself holy among you in the sight of the nations. 42Then you will know that I am the LORD, when I bring you into the land of Israel, the land I had sworn with uplifted hand to give to your fathers. 43There you will remember your conduct and all the actions by which you have defiled yourselves, and you will loathe yourselves for all the evil you have done. 44You will know that I am the LORD, when I deal with you for my name's sake and not according to your evil ways and your corrupt practices, O house of Israel, declares the Sovereign LORD.' "

[a]26 Or *—making every firstborn pass through ⌊the fire⌋* [b]29 *Bamah* means *high place.* [c]31 Or *—making your sons pass through* [d]40 Or *and the gifts of your firstfruits*

20:40–42 Ezekiel gave God's exiled people a precious promise for the future: After a period of suffering, the people would repent, experience God's cleansing and be restored to the promised land. But, of even greater significance, the people would also be restored to God's fellowship. Doing things God's way—admitting our sin and seeking his plan for us—is the beginning of our spiritual growth and the foundation for our hope for the future.

Prophecy Against the South

45The word of the LORD came to me: 46"Son of man, set your face toward the south; preach against the south and prophesy against the forest of the southland. 47Say to the southern forest: 'Hear the word of the LORD. This is what the Sovereign LORD says: I am about to set fire to you, and it will consume all your trees, both green and dry. The blazing flame will not be quenched, and every face from south to north will be scorched by it. 48Everyone will see that I the LORD have kindled it; it will not be quenched.' "

49Then I said, "Ah, Sovereign LORD! They are saying of me, 'Isn't he just telling parables?' "

Babylon, God's Sword of Judgment

21 The word of the LORD came to me: 2"Son of man, set your face against Jerusalem and preach against the sanctuary. Prophesy against the land of Israel 3and say to her: 'This is what the LORD says: I am against you. I will draw my sword from its scabbard and cut off from you both the righteous and the wicked. 4Because I am going to cut off the righteous and the wicked, my sword will be unsheathed against everyone from south to north. 5Then all people will know that I the LORD have drawn my sword from its scabbard; it will not return again.'

6"Therefore groan, son of man! Groan before them with broken heart and bitter grief. 7And when they ask you, 'Why are you groaning?' you shall say, 'Because of the news that is coming. Every heart will melt and every hand go limp; every spirit will become faint and every knee become as weak as water.' It is coming! It will surely take place, declares the Sovereign LORD."

8The word of the LORD came to me: 9"Son of man, prophesy and say, 'This is what the Lord says:

" 'A sword, a sword,
    sharpened and polished—
10sharpened for the slaughter,
    polished to flash like lightning!

" 'Shall we rejoice in the scepter of my son ⌊Judah⌋? The sword despises every such stick.

11" 'The sword is appointed to be polished,
    to be grasped with the hand;
it is sharpened and polished,
    made ready for the hand of the slayer.
12Cry out and wail, son of man,
    for it is against my people;
    it is against all the princes of Israel.
They are thrown to the sword
    along with my people.
Therefore beat your breast.

13" 'Testing will surely come. And what if the scepter ⌊of Judah⌋, which the sword despises, does not continue? declares the Sovereign LORD.'

14"So then, son of man, prophesy
    and strike your hands together.
Let the sword strike twice,
    even three times.
It is a sword for slaughter—
    a sword for great slaughter,
    closing in on them from every side.
15So that hearts may melt
    and the fallen be many,
I have stationed the sword for slaughter[a]
    at all their gates.
Oh! It is made to flash like lightning,
    it is grasped for slaughter.
16O sword, slash to the right,
    then to the left,
    wherever your blade is turned.
17I too will strike my hands together,
    and my wrath will subside.
I the LORD have spoken."

18The word of the LORD came to me: 19"Son of man, mark out two roads for the sword of the king of Babylon to take, both starting from the same country. Make a signpost where the road branches off to the city. 20Mark out one road for the sword to come against Rabbah of the Ammonites and another against Judah and fortified Jerusalem. 21For the king of Babylon will stop at the fork in the road, at the junction of the two roads, to seek an omen: He will cast lots with arrows, he will consult his idols, he will examine the liver. 22Into his right hand will come the lot for Jerusalem, where he is to set up battering rams, to give the command to slaughter, to sound the battle cry, to set battering rams against the gates, to build a ramp and to erect siege works. 23It will seem like a false omen to those who have sworn allegiance to him, but he will remind them of their guilt and take them captive.

24"Therefore this is what the Sovereign LORD says: 'Because you people have brought to mind your guilt by your open rebellion, revealing your sins in all that you do—because you have done this, you will be taken captive.

25" 'O profane and wicked prince of Israel, whose day has come, whose time of punishment has reached its climax, 26this is what the Sovereign LORD says: Take off the turban, re-

[a] *15* Septuagint; the meaning of the Hebrew for this word is uncertain.

21:3 These ominous words are addressed to the nation of Israel. Notice that God promises punishment on the entire nation, including the few good people. Our sin always brings consequences. Very often those consequences affect innocent people around us. Our mistakes and sinful ways can cause undeserved pain for spouses, children, coworkers and friends. Knowing this should motivate us to seek changes in our lives and make restitution to those we have hurt.

move the crown. It will not be as it was: The
lowly will be exalted and the exalted will be
brought low. 27A ruin! A ruin! I will make it a
ruin! It will not be restored until he comes to
whom it rightfully belongs; to him I will
give it.'

28"And you, son of man, prophesy and say,
'This is what the Sovereign LORD says about the
Ammonites and their insults:

" 'A sword, a sword,
drawn for the slaughter,
polished to consume
and to flash like lightning!
29Despite false visions concerning you
and lying divinations about you,
it will be laid on the necks
of the wicked who are to be slain,
whose day has come,
whose time of punishment has reached
its climax.
30Return the sword to its scabbard.
In the place where you were created,
in the land of your ancestry,
I will judge you.
31I will pour out my wrath upon you
and breathe out my fiery anger against
you;
I will hand you over to brutal men,
men skilled in destruction.
32You will be fuel for the fire,
your blood will be shed in your land,
you will be remembered no more;
for I the LORD have spoken.' "

Jerusalem's Sins

22 The word of the LORD came to me:
2"Son of man, will you judge her? Will
you judge this city of bloodshed? Then confront
her with all her detestable practices 3and say:
'This is what the Sovereign LORD says: O city
that brings on herself doom by shedding blood
in her midst and defiles herself by making idols,
4you have become guilty because of the blood
you have shed and have become defiled by the
idols you have made. You have brought your
days to a close, and the end of your years has
come. Therefore I will make you an object of
scorn to the nations and a laughingstock to all
the countries. 5Those who are near and those
who are far away will mock you, O infamous
city, full of turmoil.

6" 'See how each of the princes of Israel who
are in you uses his power to shed blood. 7In you
they have treated father and mother with contempt; in you they have oppressed the alien and
mistreated the fatherless and the widow. 8You
have despised my holy things and desecrated
my Sabbaths. 9In you are slanderous men bent
on shedding blood; in you are those who eat at
the mountain shrines and commit lewd acts.
10In you are those who dishonor their fathers'
bed; in you are those who violate women during their period, when they are ceremonially
unclean. 11In you one man commits a detestable offense with his neighbor's wife, another
shamefully defiles his daughter-in-law, and another violates his sister, his own father's daughter. 12In you men accept bribes to shed blood;
you take usury and excessive interest[a] and
make unjust gain from your neighbors by extortion. And you have forgotten me, declares the
Sovereign LORD.

13" 'I will surely strike my hands together at
the unjust gain you have made and at the blood
you have shed in your midst. 14Will your courage endure or your hands be strong in the day
I deal with you? I the LORD have spoken, and I
will do it. 15I will disperse you among the nations and scatter you through the countries; and
I will put an end to your uncleanness. 16When
you have been defiled[b] in the eyes of the nations, you will know that I am the LORD.' "

17Then the word of the LORD came to me:
18"Son of man, the house of Israel has become
dross to me; all of them are the copper, tin, iron
and lead left inside a furnace. They are but the
dross of silver. 19Therefore this is what the Sovereign LORD says: 'Because you have all become
dross, I will gather you into Jerusalem. 20As men
gather silver, copper, iron, lead and tin into a
furnace to melt it with a fiery blast, so will I
gather you in my anger and my wrath and put
you inside the city and melt you. 21I will gather
you and I will blow on you with my fiery wrath,
and you will be melted inside her. 22As silver is
melted in a furnace, so you will be melted inside her, and you will know that I the LORD have
poured out my wrath upon you.' "

23Again the word of the LORD came to me:
24"Son of man, say to the land, 'You are a land
that has had no rain or showers[c] in the day of
wrath.' 25There is a conspiracy of her princes[d]
within her like a roaring lion tearing its prey;
they devour people, take treasures and precious
things and make many widows within her.
26Her priests do violence to my law and profane
my holy things; they do not distinguish between the holy and the common; they teach
that there is no difference between the unclean
and the clean; and they shut their eyes to the
keeping of my Sabbaths, so that I am profaned
among them. 27Her officials within her are like

[a]12 Or *usury and interest* [b]16 Or *When I have allotted you your inheritance* [c]24 Septuagint; Hebrew *has not been cleansed or rained on* [d]25 Septuagint; Hebrew *prophets*

22:2–4 In contemporary culture personal guilt is often treated as an illusion. Some suggest we should ignore the guilt we feel rather than deal with the sin that lies at its root. Any teaching or philosophy that denies the existence of sin and tries to excuse it rather than remedy it is not in agreement with God's Word. God has provided salvation from the guilt of sin. There is no reason for us to hide or ignore it. We must choose God's remedy by recognizing our guilt, confessing our sins and depending on God for true forgiveness.

wolves tearing their prey; they shed blood and kill people to make unjust gain. 28Her prophets whitewash these deeds for them by false visions and lying divinations. They say, 'This is what the Sovereign LORD says'—when the LORD has not spoken. 29The people of the land practice extortion and commit robbery; they oppress the poor and needy and mistreat the alien, denying them justice.

30"I looked for a man among them who would build up the wall and stand before me in the gap on behalf of the land so I would not have to destroy it, but I found none. 31So I will pour out my wrath on them and consume them with my fiery anger, bringing down on their own heads all they have done, declares the Sovereign LORD."

Two Adulterous Sisters

23 The word of the LORD came to me: 2"Son of man, there were two women, daughters of the same mother. 3They became prostitutes in Egypt, engaging in prostitution from their youth. In that land their breasts were fondled and their virgin bosoms caressed. 4The older was named Oholah, and her sister was Oholibah. They were mine and gave birth to sons and daughters. Oholah is Samaria, and Oholibah is Jerusalem.

5"Oholah engaged in prostitution while she was still mine; and she lusted after her lovers, the Assyrians—warriors 6clothed in blue, governors and commanders, all of them handsome young men, and mounted horsemen. 7She gave herself as a prostitute to all the elite of the Assyrians and defiled herself with all the idols of everyone she lusted after. 8She did not give up the prostitution she began in Egypt, when during her youth men slept with her, caressed her virgin bosom and poured out their lust upon her.

9"Therefore I handed her over to her lovers, the Assyrians, for whom she lusted. 10They stripped her naked, took away her sons and daughters and killed her with the sword. She became a byword among women, and punishment was inflicted on her.

11"Her sister Oholibah saw this, yet in her lust and prostitution she was more depraved than her sister. 12She too lusted after the Assyrians—governors and commanders, warriors in full dress, mounted horsemen, all handsome young men. 13I saw that she too defiled herself; both of them went the same way.

14"But she carried her prostitution still further. She saw men portrayed on a wall, figures of Chaldeans[a] portrayed in red, 15with belts around their waists and flowing turbans on their heads; all of them looked like Babylonian chariot officers, natives of Chaldea.[b] 16As soon as she saw them, she lusted after them and sent messengers to them in Chaldea. 17Then the Babylonians came to her, to the bed of love, and in their lust they defiled her. After she had been defiled by them, she turned away from them in disgust. 18When she carried on her prostitution openly and exposed her nakedness, I turned away from her in disgust, just as I had turned away from her sister. 19Yet she became more and more promiscuous as she recalled the days of her youth, when she was a prostitute in Egypt. 20There she lusted after her lovers, whose genitals were like those of donkeys and whose emission was like that of horses. 21So you longed for the lewdness of your youth, when in Egypt your bosom was caressed and your young breasts fondled.[c]

22"Therefore, Oholibah, this is what the Sovereign LORD says: I will stir up your lovers against you, those you turned away from in disgust, and I will bring them against you from every side— 23the Babylonians and all the Chaldeans, the men of Pekod and Shoa and Koa, and all the Assyrians with them, handsome young men, all of them governors and commanders, chariot officers and men of high rank, all mounted on horses. 24They will come against you with weapons,[d] chariots and wagons and with a throng of people; they will take up positions against you on every side with large and small shields and with helmets. I will turn you over to them for punishment, and they will punish you according to their standards. 25I will direct my jealous anger against you, and they will deal with you in fury. They will cut off your noses and your ears, and those of you who are left will fall by the sword. They will take away your sons and daughters, and those of you who are left will be consumed by fire. 26They will also strip you of your clothes and take your fine jewelry. 27So I will put a stop to the lewdness and prostitution you began in Egypt. You will not look on these things with longing or remember Egypt anymore.

28"For this is what the Sovereign LORD says: I am about to hand you over to those you hate, to those you turned away from in disgust. 29They will deal with you in hatred and take away everything you have worked for. They will leave you naked and bare, and the shame of your prostitution will be exposed. Your lewdness and promiscuity 30have brought this upon you, because you lusted after the nations and defiled yourself with their idols. 31You have

[a] *14* Or *Babylonians* [b] *15* Or *Babylonia*; also in verse 16
[c] *21* Syriac (see also verse 3); Hebrew *caressed because of your young breasts* [d] *24* The meaning of the Hebrew for this word is uncertain.

23:1–49 Ezekiel compared the kingdoms of Judah and Israel to two adulterous sisters. Despite all the blessings God had given them, they sold themselves to idolatry and thus were guilty of spiritual prostitution. We are guilty of this same sin when we allow anything in our lives to take God's place. Whatever idols we have begun to serve, they must be removed if we hope to maintain a relationship with the true God.

gone the way of your sister; so I will put her cup into your hand.

32"This is what the Sovereign LORD says:

"You will drink your sister's cup,
a cup large and deep;
it will bring scorn and derision,
for it holds so much.
33You will be filled with drunkenness and sorrow,
the cup of ruin and desolation,
the cup of your sister Samaria.
34You will drink it and drain it dry;
you will dash it to pieces
and tear your breasts.

I have spoken, declares the Sovereign LORD.

35"Therefore this is what the Sovereign LORD says: Since you have forgotten me and thrust me behind your back, you must bear the consequences of your lewdness and prostitution."

36The LORD said to me: "Son of man, will you judge Oholah and Oholibah? Then confront them with their detestable practices, 37for
they have committed adultery and blood is on their hands. They committed adultery with their idols; they even sacrificed their children, whom they bore to me,[a] as food for them. 38They
have also done this to me: At that same time they defiled my sanctuary and desecrated my Sabbaths. 39On the very day they sacrificed their
children to their idols, they entered my sanctuary and desecrated it. That is what they did in my house.

40"They even sent messengers for men who came from far away, and when they arrived you bathed yourself for them, painted your eyes and put on your jewelry. 41You sat on an elegant
couch, with a table spread before it on which you had placed the incense and oil that belonged to me.

42"The noise of a carefree crowd was around her; Sabeans[b] were brought from the desert along with men from the rabble, and they put bracelets on the arms of the woman and her sister and beautiful crowns on their heads.
43Then I said about the one worn out by adultery, 'Now let them use her as a prostitute, for that is all she is.' 44And they slept with her. As
men sleep with a prostitute, so they slept with those lewd women, Oholah and Oholibah.
45But righteous men will sentence them to the punishment of women who commit adultery and shed blood, because they are adulterous and blood is on their hands.

46"This is what the Sovereign LORD says: Bring a mob against them and give them over to terror and plunder. 47The mob will stone them
and cut them down with their swords; they will kill their sons and daughters and burn down their houses.

48"So I will put an end to lewdness in the land, that all women may take warning and not imitate you. 49You will suffer the penalty for
your lewdness and bear the consequences of your sins of idolatry. Then you will know that I am the Sovereign LORD."

The Cooking Pot

24 In the ninth year, in the tenth month on the tenth day, the word of the LORD came to me: 2"Son of man, record this date, this
very date, because the king of Babylon has laid siege to Jerusalem this very day. 3Tell this rebellious house a parable and say to them: 'This is what the Sovereign LORD says:

" 'Put on the cooking pot; put it on
and pour water into it.
4Put into it the pieces of meat,
all the choice pieces—the leg and the shoulder.
Fill it with the best of these bones;
5 take the pick of the flock.
Pile wood beneath it for the bones;
bring it to a boil
and cook the bones in it.

6" 'For this is what the Sovereign LORD says:

" 'Woe to the city of bloodshed,
to the pot now encrusted,
whose deposit will not go away!
Empty it piece by piece
without casting lots for them.

7" 'For the blood she shed is in her midst:
She poured it on the bare rock;
she did not pour it on the ground,
where the dust would cover it.
8To stir up wrath and take revenge
I put her blood on the bare rock,
so that it would not be covered.

9" 'Therefore this is what the Sovereign LORD says:

" 'Woe to the city of bloodshed!
I, too, will pile the wood high.
10So heap on the wood
and kindle the fire.
Cook the meat well,
mixing in the spices;
and let the bones be charred.
11Then set the empty pot on the coals
till it becomes hot and its copper glows
so its impurities may be melted
and its deposit burned away.
12It has frustrated all efforts;

[a]37 Or *even made the children they bore to me pass through ⌊the fire⌋* [b]42 Or *drunkards*

24:1–14 In these verses God predicted the destruction of Jerusalem. God had delayed his punishment for many years, giving his people ample opportunity to repent and seek forgiveness. However, his people had refused, and the time of their final destruction had arrived. God gives us many opportunities to admit our sin and ask his forgiveness before he allows our punishment. We would be wise to listen before it is too late.

its heavy deposit has not been removed,
not even by fire.

13" 'Now your impurity is lewdness. Because I tried to cleanse you but you would not be cleansed from your impurity, you will not be clean again until my wrath against you has subsided.

14" 'I the LORD have spoken. The time has come for me to act. I will not hold back; I will not have pity, nor will I relent. You will be judged according to your conduct and your actions, declares the Sovereign LORD.' "

Ezekiel's Wife Dies

15The word of the LORD came to me: 16"Son of man, with one blow I am about to take away from you the delight of your eyes. Yet do not lament or weep or shed any tears. 17Groan quietly; do not mourn for the dead. Keep your turban fastened and your sandals on your feet; do not cover the lower part of your face or eat the customary food ⌞of mourners⌟."

18So I spoke to the people in the morning, and in the evening my wife died. The next morning I did as I had been commanded.

19Then the people asked me, "Won't you tell us what these things have to do with us?"

20So I said to them, "The word of the LORD came to me: 21Say to the house of Israel, 'This is what the Sovereign LORD says: I am about to desecrate my sanctuary—the stronghold in which you take pride, the delight of your eyes, the object of your affection. The sons and daughters you left behind will fall by the sword. 22And you will do as I have done. You will not cover the lower part of your face or eat the customary food ⌞of mourners⌟. 23You will keep your turbans on your heads and your sandals on your feet. You will not mourn or weep but will waste away because of[a] your sins and groan among yourselves. 24Ezekiel will be a sign to you; you will do just as he has done. When this happens, you will know that I am the Sovereign LORD.'

25"And you, son of man, on the day I take away their stronghold, their joy and glory, the delight of their eyes, their heart's desire, and their sons and daughters as well— 26on that day a fugitive will come to tell you the news. 27At that time your mouth will be opened; you will speak with him and will no longer be silent. So you will be a sign to them, and they will know that I am the LORD."

A Prophecy Against Ammon

25 The word of the LORD came to me: 2"Son of man, set your face against the Ammonites and prophesy against them. 3Say to them, 'Hear the word of the Sovereign LORD. This is what the Sovereign LORD says: Because you said "Aha!" over my sanctuary when it was desecrated and over the land of Israel when it was laid waste and over the people of Judah when they went into exile, 4therefore I am going to give you to the people of the East as a possession. They will set up their camps and pitch their tents among you; they will eat your fruit and drink your milk. 5I will turn Rabbah into a pasture for camels and Ammon into a resting place for sheep. Then you will know that I am the LORD. 6For this is what the Sovereign LORD says: Because you have clapped your hands and stamped your feet, rejoicing with all the malice of your heart against the land of Israel, 7therefore I will stretch out my hand against you and give you as plunder to the nations. I will cut you off from the nations and exterminate you from the countries. I will destroy you, and you will know that I am the LORD.' "

A Prophecy Against Moab

8"This is what the Sovereign LORD says: 'Because Moab and Seir said, "Look, the house of Judah has become like all the other nations," 9therefore I will expose the flank of Moab, beginning at its frontier towns—Beth Jeshimoth, Baal Meon and Kiriathaim—the glory of that land. 10I will give Moab along with the Ammonites to the people of the East as a possession, so that the Ammonites will not be remembered among the nations; 11and I will inflict punishment on Moab. Then they will know that I am the LORD.' "

A Prophecy Against Edom

12"This is what the Sovereign LORD says: 'Because Edom took revenge on the house of Judah and became very guilty by doing so, 13therefore this is what the Sovereign LORD says: I will stretch out my hand against Edom and kill its men and their animals. I will lay it waste, and from Teman to Dedan they will fall by the sword. 14I will take vengeance on Edom by the hand of my people Israel, and they will deal with Edom in accordance with my anger and my wrath; they will know my vengeance, declares the Sovereign LORD.' "

A Prophecy Against Philistia

15"This is what the Sovereign LORD says: 'Because the Philistines acted in vengeance and took revenge with malice in their hearts, and

[a]23 Or *away in*

24:25–27 These verses conclude the long section of judgment (1:1—24:27). The people already in exile in Babylon would soon hear news of Jerusalem's destruction. They would discover that Ezekiel's predictions had all come true, confirming the truth of his words and reinforcing his condemnation of the people's sin. Their response could only be one of mourning and repentance, humbling themselves before their Judge and Redeemer. Yet from this point on Ezekiel brings a message of hope to the exiled Jews. The foreign nations would be judged for their sin (see 25:1—32:32) and God's people would one day be restored to their homeland, Israel (see 33:1—39:29).

with ancient hostility sought to destroy Judah,
16therefore this is what the Sovereign LORD says:
I am about to stretch out my hand against the
Philistines, and I will cut off the Kerethites and
destroy those remaining along the coast. 17I will
carry out great vengeance on them and punish
them in my wrath. Then they will know that I
am the LORD, when I take vengeance on them.' "

A Prophecy Against Tyre

26 In the eleventh year, on the first day of
the month, the word of the LORD came
to me: 2"Son of man, because Tyre has said of
Jerusalem, 'Aha! The gate to the nations is broken, and its doors have swung open to me; now
that she lies in ruins I will prosper,' 3therefore
this is what the Sovereign LORD says: I am
against you, O Tyre, and I will bring many nations against you, like the sea casting up its
waves. 4They will destroy the walls of Tyre and
pull down her towers; I will scrape away her
rubble and make her a bare rock. 5Out in the sea
she will become a place to spread fishnets, for
I have spoken, declares the Sovereign LORD. She
will become plunder for the nations, 6and her
settlements on the mainland will be ravaged by
the sword. Then they will know that I am the
LORD.

7"For this is what the Sovereign LORD says:
From the north I am going to bring against Tyre
Nebuchadnezzar[a] king of Babylon, king of
kings, with horses and chariots, with horsemen
and a great army. 8He will ravage your settlements on the mainland with the sword; he will
set up siege works against you, build a ramp up
to your walls and raise his shields against you.
9He will direct the blows of his battering rams
against your walls and demolish your towers
with his weapons. 10His horses will be so many
that they will cover you with dust. Your walls
will tremble at the noise of the war horses, wagons and chariots when he enters your gates as
men enter a city whose walls have been broken
through. 11The hoofs of his horses will trample
all your streets; he will kill your people with the
sword, and your strong pillars will fall to the
ground. 12They will plunder your wealth and
loot your merchandise; they will break down
your walls and demolish your fine houses and
throw your stones, timber and rubble into the
sea. 13I will put an end to your noisy songs, and
the music of your harps will be heard no more.
14I will make you a bare rock, and you will
become a place to spread fishnets. You will never be rebuilt, for I the LORD have spoken, declares the Sovereign LORD.

15"This is what the Sovereign LORD says to
Tyre: Will not the coastlands tremble at the
sound of your fall, when the wounded groan
and the slaughter takes place in you? 16Then all
the princes of the coast will step down from
their thrones and lay aside their robes and take
off their embroidered garments. Clothed with
terror, they will sit on the ground, trembling
every moment, appalled at you. 17Then they
will take up a lament concerning you and say to
you:

" 'How you are destroyed, O city of
renown,
peopled by men of the sea!
You were a power on the seas,
you and your citizens;
you put your terror
on all who lived there.
18Now the coastlands tremble
on the day of your fall;
the islands in the sea
are terrified at your collapse.'

19"This is what the Sovereign LORD says:
When I make you a desolate city, like cities no
longer inhabited, and when I bring the ocean
depths over you and its vast waters cover you,
20then I will bring you down with those who go
down to the pit, to the people of long ago. I will
make you dwell in the earth below, as in ancient ruins, with those who go down to the pit,
and you will not return or take your place[b] in
the land of the living. 21I will bring you to a
horrible end and you will be no more. You will
be sought, but you will never again be found,
declares the Sovereign LORD."

A Lament for Tyre

27 The word of the LORD came to me:
2"Son of man, take up a lament concerning Tyre. 3Say to Tyre, situated at the gateway to the sea, merchant of peoples on many
coasts, 'This is what the Sovereign LORD says:

" 'You say, O Tyre,
"I am perfect in beauty."
4Your domain was on the high seas;

[a]7 Hebrew *Nebuchadrezzar,* of which *Nebuchadnezzar* is a variant; here and often in Ezekiel and Jeremiah
[b]20 Septuagint; Hebrew *return, and I will give glory*

26:1–21 This entire chapter focuses on God's judgment of the city of Tyre. In the ancient world, Tyre was considered to be impregnable. The main body of the city was surrounded by water and was very difficult to attack. Tyre's ships could keep her continually supplied with food and water. Her people believed that no one could conquer her and that her future was secure. But God had other plans, and her destruction was assured. We may also think we are strong enough to stand on our own and go our own way without God. This is not true. Ultimately we must recognize our dependence on him for everything.

27:3–25 Tyre congratulated herself on her beauty (27:3–7), her military might (27:8–11) and her wealth (27:12–25), but none of these would be able to avert the disaster she would soon face. When we are gifted with intelligence, beauty, strength or wealth, it is easy to deceive ourselves into thinking that we don't need God's help. If we possess this attitude, however, our strengths become our liabilities. We must never let our strengths blind us to our weaknesses and lead us away from dependence on God.

your builders brought your beauty to
perfection.
5They made all your timbers
of pine trees from Senir[a];
they took a cedar from Lebanon
to make a mast for you.
6Of oaks from Bashan
they made your oars;
of cypress wood[b] from the coasts of
Cyprus[c]
they made your deck, inlaid with ivory.
7Fine embroidered linen from Egypt was
your sail
and served as your banner;
your awnings were of blue and purple
from the coasts of Elishah.
8Men of Sidon and Arvad were your
oarsmen;
your skilled men, O Tyre, were aboard as
your seamen.
9Veteran craftsmen of Gebal[d] were on
board
as shipwrights to caulk your seams.
All the ships of the sea and their sailors
came alongside to trade for your wares.

10" 'Men of Persia, Lydia and Put
served as soldiers in your army.
They hung their shields and helmets on
your walls,
bringing you splendor.
11Men of Arvad and Helech
manned your walls on every side;
men of Gammad
were in your towers.
They hung their shields around your walls;
they brought your beauty to perfection.

12" 'Tarshish did business with you because
of your great wealth of goods; they exchanged
silver, iron, tin and lead for your merchandise.
13" 'Greece, Tubal and Meshech traded with
you; they exchanged slaves and articles of
bronze for your wares.
14" 'Men of Beth Togarmah exchanged work
horses, war horses and mules for your merchandise.
15" 'The men of Rhodes[e] traded with you,
and many coastlands were your customers; they
paid you with ivory tusks and ebony.
16" 'Aram[f] did business with you because
of your many products; they exchanged turquoise, purple fabric, embroidered work, fine
linen, coral and rubies for your merchandise.
17" 'Judah and Israel traded with you; they
exchanged wheat from Minnith and confec-
tions,[g] honey, oil and balm for your wares.
18" 'Damascus, because of your many products and great wealth of goods, did business
with you in wine from Helbon and wool from
Zahar.
19" 'Danites and Greeks from Uzal bought
your merchandise; they exchanged wrought
iron, cassia and calamus for your wares.
20" 'Dedan traded in saddle blankets with
you.
21" 'Arabia and all the princes of Kedar were
your customers; they did business with you in
lambs, rams and goats.
22" 'The merchants of Sheba and Raamah
traded with you; for your merchandise they exchanged the finest of all kinds of spices and
precious stones, and gold.
23" 'Haran, Canneh and Eden and merchants of Sheba, Asshur and Kilmad traded with
you. 24In your marketplace they traded with you
beautiful garments, blue fabric, embroidered
work and multicolored rugs with cords twisted
and tightly knotted.

25" 'The ships of Tarshish serve
as carriers for your wares.
You are filled with heavy cargo
in the heart of the sea.
26Your oarsmen take you
out to the high seas.
But the east wind will break you to pieces
in the heart of the sea.
27Your wealth, merchandise and wares,
your mariners, seamen and shipwrights,
your merchants and all your soldiers,
and everyone else on board
will sink into the heart of the sea
on the day of your shipwreck.
28The shorelands will quake
when your seamen cry out.
29All who handle the oars
will abandon their ships;
the mariners and all the seamen
will stand on the shore.
30They will raise their voice
and cry bitterly over you;
they will sprinkle dust on their heads
and roll in ashes.
31They will shave their heads because of you
and will put on sackcloth.
They will weep over you with anguish of
soul
and with bitter mourning.
32As they wail and mourn over you,
they will take up a lament concerning
you:
"Who was ever silenced like Tyre,

[a]5 That is, Hermon [b]6 Targum; the Masoretic Text has a different division of the consonants. [c]6 Hebrew *Kittim* [d]9 That is, Byblos [e]15 Septuagint; Hebrew *Dedan* [f]16 Most Hebrew manuscripts; some Hebrew manuscripts and Syriac *Edom* [g]17 The meaning of the Hebrew for this word is uncertain.

27:26–36 Tyre had achieved success—except the type of success that really mattered. She believed that she could handle any crisis on her own. This city had stood for centuries against many different invaders, but ultimately Tyre was destroyed. No matter how successful we may appear, we are headed for destruction if our lives are not in line with God's will.

surrounded by the sea?"
33When your merchandise went out on the seas,
you satisfied many nations;
with your great wealth and your wares
you enriched the kings of the earth.
34Now you are shattered by the sea
in the depths of the waters;
your wares and all your company
have gone down with you.
35All who live in the coastlands
are appalled at you;
their kings shudder with horror
and their faces are distorted with fear.
36The merchants among the nations hiss at you;
you have come to a horrible end
and will be no more.' "

A Prophecy Against the King of Tyre

28 The word of the LORD came to me: 2"Son of man, say to the ruler of Tyre, 'This is what the Sovereign LORD says:

" 'In the pride of your heart
you say, "I am a god;
I sit on the throne of a god
in the heart of the seas."
But you are a man and not a god,
though you think you are as wise as a god.
3Are you wiser than Daniel[a]?
Is no secret hidden from you?
4By your wisdom and understanding
you have gained wealth for yourself
and amassed gold and silver
in your treasuries.
5By your great skill in trading
you have increased your wealth,
and because of your wealth
your heart has grown proud.

6" 'Therefore this is what the Sovereign LORD says:

" 'Because you think you are wise,
as wise as a god,
7I am going to bring foreigners against you,
the most ruthless of nations;
they will draw their swords against your beauty and wisdom
and pierce your shining splendor.
8They will bring you down to the pit,
and you will die a violent death
in the heart of the seas.
9Will you then say, "I am a god,"
in the presence of those who kill you?
You will be but a man, not a god,
in the hands of those who slay you.
10You will die the death of the uncircumcised
at the hands of foreigners.
I have spoken, declares the Sovereign LORD.' "

11The word of the LORD came to me: 12"Son of man, take up a lament concerning the king of Tyre and say to him: 'This is what the Sovereign LORD says:

" 'You were the model of perfection,
full of wisdom and perfect in beauty.
13You were in Eden,
the garden of God;
every precious stone adorned you:
ruby, topaz and emerald,
chrysolite, onyx and jasper,
sapphire,[b] turquoise and beryl.[c]
Your settings and mountings[d] were made of gold;
on the day you were created they were prepared.
14You were anointed as a guardian cherub,
for so I ordained you.
You were on the holy mount of God;
you walked among the fiery stones.
15You were blameless in your ways
from the day you were created
till wickedness was found in you.
16Through your widespread trade
you were filled with violence,
and you sinned.
So I drove you in disgrace from the mount of God,
and I expelled you, O guardian cherub,
from among the fiery stones.
17Your heart became proud
on account of your beauty,
and you corrupted your wisdom
because of your splendor.
So I threw you to the earth;
I made a spectacle of you before kings.
18By your many sins and dishonest trade
you have desecrated your sanctuaries.
So I made a fire come out from you,
and it consumed you,
and I reduced you to ashes on the ground
in the sight of all who were watching.
19All the nations who knew you
are appalled at you;
you have come to a horrible end
and will be no more.' "

A Prophecy Against Sidon

20The word of the LORD came to me: 21"Son

[a]3 Or *Danel*; the Hebrew spelling may suggest a person other than the prophet Daniel. [b]13 Or *lapis lazuli* [c]13 The precise identification of some of these precious stones is uncertain. [d]13 The meaning of the Hebrew for this phrase is uncertain.

28:2–10 The first lie ever told was Satan's promise to Eve: "You will be like God" (Genesis 3:5). It seems that the prince of Tyre believed that same, recycled falsehood. If we choose to live according to our sinful natures and the desires of our flesh, we are believing the same lie as well. Doing things our own way sets us up as our own god. We should surrender the throne of our lives to the only one who can give us lives filled with meaning and freedom—God himself.

of man, set your face against Sidon; prophesy
against her 22and say: 'This is what the Sovereign LORD says:

" 'I am against you, O Sidon,
and I will gain glory within you.
They will know that I am the LORD,
when I inflict punishment on her
and show myself holy within her.
23I will send a plague upon her
and make blood flow in her streets.
The slain will fall within her,
with the sword against her on every side.
Then they will know that I am the LORD.

24" 'No longer will the people of Israel have
malicious neighbors who are painful briers and
sharp thorns. Then they will know that I am the
Sovereign LORD.
25" 'This is what the Sovereign LORD says:
When I gather the people of Israel from the
nations where they have been scattered, I will
show myself holy among them in the sight of
the nations. Then they will live in their own
land, which I gave to my servant Jacob. 26They
will live there in safety and will build houses
and plant vineyards; they will live in safety
when I inflict punishment on all their neighbors who maligned them. Then they will know
that I am the LORD their God.' "

A Prophecy Against Egypt

29 In the tenth year, in the tenth month on
the twelfth day, the word of the LORD
came to me: 2"Son of man, set your face against
Pharaoh king of Egypt and prophesy against
him and against all Egypt. 3Speak to him and
say: 'This is what the Sovereign LORD says:

" 'I am against you, Pharaoh king of Egypt,
you great monster lying among your
streams.
You say, "The Nile is mine;
I made it for myself."
4But I will put hooks in your jaws
and make the fish of your streams stick
to your scales.
I will pull you out from among your
streams,
with all the fish sticking to your scales.
5I will leave you in the desert,
you and all the fish of your streams.
You will fall on the open field
and not be gathered or picked up.
I will give you as food
to the beasts of the earth and the birds
of the air.

6Then all who live in Egypt will know that I am
the LORD.

" 'You have been a staff of reed for the house
of Israel. 7When they grasped you with their
hands, you splintered and you tore open their
shoulders; when they leaned on you, you broke
and their backs were wrenched.[a]
8" 'Therefore this is what the Sovereign LORD
says: I will bring a sword against you and kill
your men and their animals. 9Egypt will become a desolate wasteland. Then they will
know that I am the LORD.
" 'Because you said, "The Nile is mine; I
made it," 10therefore I am against you and
against your streams, and I will make the land
of Egypt a ruin and a desolate waste from Migdol to Aswan, as far as the border of Cush.[b]
11No foot of man or animal will pass through
it; no one will live there for forty years. 12I will
make the land of Egypt desolate among devastated lands, and her cities will lie desolate forty
years among ruined cities. And I will disperse
the Egyptians among the nations and scatter
them through the countries.
13" 'Yet this is what the Sovereign LORD says:
At the end of forty years I will gather the Egyptians from the nations where they were scattered. 14I will bring them back from captivity
and return them to Upper Egypt,[c] the land of
their ancestry. There they will be a lowly kingdom. 15It will be the lowliest of kingdoms and
will never again exalt itself above the other nations. I will make it so weak that it will never
again rule over the nations. 16Egypt will no
longer be a source of confidence for the people
of Israel but will be a reminder of their sin in
turning to her for help. Then they will know
that I am the Sovereign LORD.' "

17In the twenty-seventh year, in the first
month on the first day, the word of the LORD
came to me: 18"Son of man, Nebuchadnezzar
king of Babylon drove his army in a hard campaign against Tyre; every head was rubbed bare

[a]7 Syriac (see also Septuagint and Vulgate); Hebrew *and you caused their backs to stand* [b]10 That is, the upper Nile region [c]14 Hebrew *to Pathros*

28:25–26 By every human measure, the day of Israel's success was in the past. The elite of Israel's population had lived in forced captivity for years. Jerusalem was on the verge of destruction. But no matter how far a nation or a person falls, God always controls the final outcome. God can restore such a nation or individual and bring victory when defeat seems a certainty.

29:2–16 When Israel was in trouble, her leaders often turned to Egypt for help. Their dependence on Egypt, however, was always in vain. Egypt lacked the power necessary to bring true and permanent deliverance for Israel. We often make the same mistake. When we face terrible problems, we may turn to strategies that provide only temporary relief or fail altogether. We must be careful to bring our problems to the only one able to bring true deliverance—God.

29:18–21 God used King Nebuchadnezzar of Babylon as his agent to achieve his sovereign will. It may be hard for us to understand why God would use an evil dictator as a part of his plan. Nebuchadnezzar disposed of people and treaties without giving a thought to the consequences. He once even considered himself a god. Sometimes God may use hostile forces to accomplish his purposes in our lives too. We may wonder how God could allow such a thing to happen. But we must trust God's sovereignty and believe that we will eventually receive his best for us.

and every shoulder made raw. Yet he and his
army got no reward from the campaign he led
against Tyre. 19Therefore this is what the Sovereign LORD says: I am going to give Egypt to
Nebuchadnezzar king of Babylon, and he will
carry off its wealth. He will loot and plunder the
land as pay for his army. 20I have given him
Egypt as a reward for his efforts because he and
his army did it for me, declares the Sovereign
LORD.

21"On that day I will make a horn[a] grow for
the house of Israel, and I will open your mouth
among them. Then they will know that I am the
LORD."

A Lament for Egypt

30 The word of the LORD came to me:
2"Son of man, prophesy and say: 'This
is what the Sovereign LORD says:

" 'Wail and say,
"Alas for that day!"
3For the day is near,
the day of the LORD is near—
a day of clouds,
a time of doom for the nations.
4A sword will come against Egypt,
and anguish will come upon Cush.[b]
When the slain fall in Egypt,
her wealth will be carried away
and her foundations torn down.

5Cush and Put, Lydia and all Arabia, Libya[c]
and the people of the covenant land will fall by
the sword along with Egypt.

6" 'This is what the LORD says:

" 'The allies of Egypt will fall
and her proud strength will fail.
From Migdol to Aswan
they will fall by the sword within her,
declares the Sovereign LORD.
7" 'They will be desolate
among desolate lands,
and their cities will lie
among ruined cities.
8Then they will know that I am the LORD,
when I set fire to Egypt
and all her helpers are crushed.

9" 'On that day messengers will go out from
me in ships to frighten Cush out of her complacency. Anguish will take hold of them on the
day of Egypt's doom, for it is sure to come.

10" 'This is what the Sovereign LORD says:

" 'I will put an end to the hordes of Egypt
by the hand of Nebuchadnezzar king of
Babylon.
11He and his army—the most ruthless of
nations—
will be brought in to destroy the land.
They will draw their swords against Egypt
and fill the land with the slain.
12I will dry up the streams of the Nile
and sell the land to evil men;
by the hand of foreigners
I will lay waste the land and everything
in it.

I the LORD have spoken.

13" 'This is what the Sovereign LORD says:

" 'I will destroy the idols
and put an end to the images in
Memphis.[d]
No longer will there be a prince in Egypt,
and I will spread fear throughout the
land.
14I will lay waste Upper Egypt,[e]
set fire to Zoan
and inflict punishment on Thebes.[f]
15I will pour out my wrath on Pelusium,[g]
the stronghold of Egypt,
and cut off the hordes of Thebes.
16I will set fire to Egypt;
Pelusium will writhe in agony.
Thebes will be taken by storm;
Memphis will be in constant distress.
17The young men of Heliopolis[h] and
Bubastis[i]
will fall by the sword,
and the cities themselves will go into
captivity.
18Dark will be the day at Tahpanhes
when I break the yoke of Egypt;
there her proud strength will come to an
end.
She will be covered with clouds,
and her villages will go into captivity.
19So I will inflict punishment on Egypt,
and they will know that I am the LORD.' "

20In the eleventh year, in the first month on
the seventh day, the word of the LORD came to
me: 21"Son of man, I have broken the arm of
Pharaoh king of Egypt. It has not been bound
up for healing or put in a splint so as to become
strong enough to hold a sword. 22Therefore this
is what the Sovereign LORD says: I am against
Pharaoh king of Egypt. I will break both his
arms, the good arm as well as the broken one,
and make the sword fall from his hand. 23I will

[a] 21 *Horn* here symbolizes strength. [b] 4 That is, the upper Nile region; also in verses 5 and 9 [c] 5 Hebrew *Cub* [d] 13 Hebrew *Noph;* also in verse 16 [e] 14 Hebrew *waste Pathros* [f] 14 Hebrew *No;* also in verses 15 and 16 [g] 15 Hebrew *Sin;* also in verse 16 [h] 17 Hebrew *Awen* (or *On*) [i] 17 Hebrew *Pi Beseth*

30:21–26 God is sovereign in international affairs. If God can work his will among hostile superpowers, how simple it must be for him to do so in willing individuals! God wants us to grow spiritually. If we willingly submit to his will for us, he will bring it to pass. God is both willing and able to work miraculous changes in this world. If we surrender our lives to him, we can become a part of God's plan for the redemption of both his people and this world.

disperse the Egyptians among the nations and scatter them through the countries. 24I will strengthen the arms of the king of Babylon and put my sword in his hand, but I will break the arms of Pharaoh, and he will groan before him like a mortally wounded man. 25I will strengthen the arms of the king of Babylon, but the arms of Pharaoh will fall limp. Then they will know that I am the LORD, when I put my sword into the hand of the king of Babylon and he brandishes it against Egypt. 26I will disperse the Egyptians among the nations and scatter them through the countries. Then they will know that I am the LORD."

A Cedar in Lebanon

31 In the eleventh year, in the third month on the first day, the word of the LORD came to me: 2"Son of man, say to Pharaoh king of Egypt and to his hordes:

" 'Who can be compared with you in
majesty?
3Consider Assyria, once a cedar in Lebanon,
with beautiful branches overshadowing
the forest;
it towered on high,
its top above the thick foliage.
4The waters nourished it,
deep springs made it grow tall;
their streams flowed
all around its base
and sent their channels
to all the trees of the field.
5So it towered higher
than all the trees of the field;
its boughs increased
and its branches grew long,
spreading because of abundant waters.
6All the birds of the air
nested in its boughs,
all the beasts of the field
gave birth under its branches;
all the great nations
lived in its shade.
7It was majestic in beauty,
with its spreading boughs,
for its roots went down
to abundant waters.
8The cedars in the garden of God
could not rival it,
nor could the pine trees
equal its boughs,
nor could the plane trees
compare with its branches—
no tree in the garden of God
could match its beauty.
9I made it beautiful
with abundant branches,
the envy of all the trees of Eden
in the garden of God.

10" 'Therefore this is what the Sovereign LORD says: Because it towered on high, lifting its top above the thick foliage, and because it was proud of its height, 11I handed it over to the ruler of the nations, for him to deal with according to its wickedness. I cast it aside, 12and the most ruthless of foreign nations cut it down and left it. Its boughs fell on the mountains and in all the valleys; its branches lay broken in all the ravines of the land. All the nations of the earth came out from under its shade and left it. 13All the birds of the air settled on the fallen tree, and all the beasts of the field were among its branches. 14Therefore no other trees by the waters are ever to tower proudly on high, lifting their tops above the thick foliage. No other trees so well-watered are ever to reach such a height; they are all destined for death, for the earth below, among mortal men, with those who go down to the pit.

15" 'This is what the Sovereign LORD says: On the day it was brought down to the grave[a] I covered the deep springs with mourning for it; I held back its streams, and its abundant waters were restrained. Because of it I clothed Lebanon with gloom, and all the trees of the field withered away. 16I made the nations tremble at the sound of its fall when I brought it down to the grave with those who go down to the pit. Then all the trees of Eden, the choicest and best of Lebanon, all the trees that were well-watered, were consoled in the earth below. 17Those who lived in its shade, its allies among the nations, had also gone down to the grave with it, joining those killed by the sword.

18" 'Which of the trees of Eden can be compared with you in splendor and majesty? Yet you, too, will be brought down with the trees of Eden to the earth below; you will lie among the uncircumcised, with those killed by the sword.

" 'This is Pharaoh and all his hordes, declares the Sovereign LORD.' "

A Lament for Pharaoh

32 In the twelfth year, in the twelfth month on the first day, the word of the

[a]15 Hebrew *Sheol*; also in verses 16 and 17

31:2–9 In Ezekiel's day Egypt's pharaoh was one of the most powerful rulers in the world. Only Nebuchadnezzar of Babylon was greater than the pharaoh. The pharaoh was reminded that Babylon had already destroyed the great empire of Assyria, once the greatest power on earth. Pharaoh needed to learn that no one, not even a powerful nation like Egypt, could stand against God's ultimate plan for the world. God has created all people and things to live in a close relationship with himself. Only as we conform our lives to God's will can we find hope and blessing.

31:18 God's measurement of greatness was certainly different from Pharaoh's. Pharaoh thought he possessed great strength and glory. But as magnificent as Pharaoh and his nation were, they would soon be cut down and destroyed. No one can reject God and hope to succeed forever. Pride always comes before a fall (see Proverbs 16:18). As soon as we believe we can do things our way and in our own power, we are headed for trouble.

LORD came to me: [2]"Son of man, take up a lament concerning Pharaoh king of Egypt and say to him:

" 'You are like a lion among the nations;
you are like a monster in the seas
thrashing about in your streams,
churning the water with your feet
and muddying the streams.

[3]" 'This is what the Sovereign LORD says:

" 'With a great throng of people
I will cast my net over you,
and they will haul you up in my net.
[4]I will throw you on the land
and hurl you on the open field.
I will let all the birds of the air settle on you
and all the beasts of the earth gorge themselves on you.
[5]I will spread your flesh on the mountains
and fill the valleys with your remains.
[6]I will drench the land with your flowing blood
all the way to the mountains,
and the ravines will be filled with your flesh.
[7]When I snuff you out, I will cover the heavens
and darken their stars;
I will cover the sun with a cloud,
and the moon will not give its light.
[8]All the shining lights in the heavens
I will darken over you;
I will bring darkness over your land,
declares the Sovereign LORD.
[9]I will trouble the hearts of many peoples
when I bring about your destruction among the nations,
among[a] lands you have not known.
[10]I will cause many peoples to be appalled at you,
and their kings will shudder with horror because of you
when I brandish my sword before them.
On the day of your downfall
each of them will tremble
every moment for his life.

[11]" 'For this is what the Sovereign LORD says:

" 'The sword of the king of Babylon
will come against you.
[12]I will cause your hordes to fall
by the swords of mighty men—
the most ruthless of all nations.
They will shatter the pride of Egypt,
and all her hordes will be overthrown.
[13]I will destroy all her cattle
from beside abundant waters
no longer to be stirred by the foot of man
or muddied by the hoofs of cattle.
[14]Then I will let her waters settle
and make her streams flow like oil,
declares the Sovereign LORD.
[15]When I make Egypt desolate
and strip the land of everything in it,
when I strike down all who live there,
then they will know that I am the LORD.'

[16]"This is the lament they will chant for her.
The daughters of the nations will chant it; for
Egypt and all her hordes they will chant it, de-
clares the Sovereign LORD."

[17]In the twelfth year, on the fifteenth day of
the month, the word of the LORD came to me:
[18]"Son of man, wail for the hordes of Egypt and
consign to the earth below both her and the
daughters of mighty nations, with those who
go down to the pit. [19]Say to them, 'Are you
more favored than others? Go down and be
laid among the uncircumcised.' [20]They will fall
among those killed by the sword. The sword
is drawn; let her be dragged off with all her
hordes. [21]From within the grave[b] the mighty
leaders will say of Egypt and her allies, 'They
have come down and they lie with the uncircumcised, with those killed by the sword.'

[22]"Assyria is there with her whole army; she
is surrounded by the graves of all her slain, all
who have fallen by the sword. [23]Their graves
are in the depths of the pit and her army lies
around her grave. All who had spread terror in
the land of the living are slain, fallen by the
sword.

[24]"Elam is there, with all her hordes around
her grave. All of them are slain, fallen by the
sword. All who had spread terror in the land
of the living went down uncircumcised to the
earth below. They bear their shame with those
who go down to the pit. [25]A bed is made for her
among the slain, with all her hordes around her
grave. All of them are uncircumcised, killed by
the sword. Because their terror had spread in the
land of the living, they bear their shame with
those who go down to the pit; they are laid
among the slain.

[26]"Meshech and Tubal are there, with all

[a]9 Hebrew; Septuagint *bring you into captivity among the nations, / to* [b]21 Hebrew *Sheol*; also in verse 27

32:2–8 It is always dangerous when we begin to think of ourselves more highly than we ought. Pharaoh thought he was a lion, spreading fear among all who saw him. But these verses reveal just how vulnerable he actually was. If we begin to think we can go it alone, we will reject the help and support offered by God and others. Yet not one of us is strong enough to endure the pull of our sinful nature without God's help. We need to be reminded that we need God's power continually.

32:9–10 There is something terrifying about the demise of a great person or nation. Pharaoh's authority had been absolute; his was a powerful nation. And when Pharaoh was judged and fell, the rest of the world was horrified and fearful. We would be wise to learn from such failure. People with far greater strength than ours have been destroyed when they rebelled against God. We must not reject God and believe that we are strong enough to stand against him and his purposes. No one is strong enough to resist God and win.

their hordes around their graves. All of them are uncircumcised, killed by the sword because they spread their terror in the land of the living. 27Do they not lie with the other uncircumcised warriors who have fallen, who went down to the grave with their weapons of war, whose swords were placed under their heads? The punishment for their sins rested on their bones, though the terror of these warriors had stalked through the land of the living.

28"You too, O Pharaoh, will be broken and will lie among the uncircumcised, with those killed by the sword.

29"Edom is there, her kings and all her princes; despite their power, they are laid with those killed by the sword. They lie with the uncircumcised, with those who go down to the pit.

30"All the princes of the north and all the Sidonians are there; they went down with the slain in disgrace despite the terror caused by their power. They lie uncircumcised with those killed by the sword and bear their shame with those who go down to the pit.

31"Pharaoh—he and all his army—will see them and he will be consoled for all his hordes that were killed by the sword, declares the Sovereign LORD. 32Although I had him spread terror in the land of the living, Pharaoh and all his hordes will be laid among the uncircumcised, with those killed by the sword, declares the Sovereign LORD."

Ezekiel a Watchman

33 The word of the LORD came to me: 2"Son of man, speak to your countrymen and say to them: 'When I bring the sword against a land, and the people of the land choose one of their men and make him their watchman, 3and he sees the sword coming against the land and blows the trumpet to warn the people, 4then if anyone hears the trumpet but does not take warning and the sword comes and takes his life, his blood will be on his own head. 5Since he heard the sound of the trumpet but did not take warning, his blood will be on his own head. If he had taken warning, he would have saved himself. 6But if the watchman sees the sword coming and does not blow the trumpet to warn the people and the sword comes and takes the life of one of them, that man will be taken away because of his sin, but I will hold the watchman accountable for his blood.'

7"Son of man, I have made you a watchman for the house of Israel; so hear the word I speak and give them warning from me. 8When I say to the wicked, 'O wicked man, you will surely die,' and you do not speak out to dissuade him from his ways, that wicked man will die for[a] his sin, and I will hold you accountable for his blood. 9But if you do warn the wicked man to turn from his ways and he does not do so, he will die for his sin, but you will have saved yourself.

10"Son of man, say to the house of Israel, 'This is what you are saying: "Our offenses and sins weigh us down, and we are wasting away because of[b] them. How then can we live?" ' 11Say to them, 'As surely as I live, declares the Sovereign LORD, I take no pleasure in the death of the wicked, but rather that they turn from their ways and live. Turn! Turn from your evil ways! Why will you die, O house of Israel?'

12"Therefore, son of man, say to your countrymen, 'The righteousness of the righteous man will not save him when he disobeys, and the wickedness of the wicked man will not cause him to fall when he turns from it. The righteous man, if he sins, will not be allowed to live because of his former righteousness.' 13If I tell the righteous man that he will surely live, but then he trusts in his righteousness and does evil, none of the righteous things he has done will be remembered; he will die for the evil he has done. 14And if I say to the wicked man, 'You will surely die,' but he then turns away from his sin and does what is just and right— 15if he gives back what he took in pledge for a loan, returns what he has stolen, follows the decrees that give life, and does no evil, he will surely live; he will not die. 16None of the sins he has committed will be remembered against him. He has done what is just and right; he will surely live.

17"Yet your countrymen say, 'The way of the Lord is not just.' But it is their way that is not just. 18If a righteous man turns from his righteousness and does evil, he will die for it. 19And if a wicked man turns away from his wickedness and does what is just and right, he will live by doing so. 20Yet, O house of Israel, you say, 'The way of the Lord is not just.' But I will judge each of you according to his own ways."

Jerusalem's Fall Explained

21In the twelfth year of our exile, in the tenth month on the fifth day, a man who had escaped from Jerusalem came to me and said, "The city has fallen!" 22Now the evening before the man arrived, the hand of the LORD was upon me, and he opened my mouth before the man came to me in the morning. So my mouth was opened and I was no longer silent.

[a]8 Or *in;* also in verse 9 [b]10 Or *away in*

33:2–6 The solemn responsibility of an Old Testament town watchman was to warn the citizens of impending danger. If the watchman failed to warn them, the result would be the tragic loss of life and property. We are watchmen for others as well. Like Ezekiel, we should be careful not to lead others astray or fail to warn them of the dangers of disobeying God.

33:10–16 When we suffer the consequences for our failures and sins, we can be sure that if we repent God will forgive us. God does not punish us in anger or because of vengeance; he punishes us because he loves us. He doesn't desire our destruction; he desires our spiritual renewal and restoration.

23Then the word of the LORD came to me:
24"Son of man, the people living in those ruins
in the land of Israel are saying, 'Abraham was
only one man, yet he possessed the land. But we
are many; surely the land has been given to us
as our possession.' 25Therefore say to them,
'This is what the Sovereign LORD says: Since you
eat meat with the blood still in it and look to
your idols and shed blood, should you then
possess the land? 26You rely on your sword, you
do detestable things, and each of you defiles his
neighbor's wife. Should you then possess the
land?'
27"Say this to them: 'This is what the Sovereign LORD says: As surely as I live, those who are
left in the ruins will fall by the sword, those out
in the country I will give to the wild animals
to be devoured, and those in strongholds and
caves will die of a plague. 28I will make the land
a desolate waste, and her proud strength will
come to an end, and the mountains of Israel
will become desolate so that no one will cross
them. 29Then they will know that I am the
LORD, when I have made the land a desolate
waste because of all the detestable things they
have done.'
30"As for you, son of man, your countrymen
are talking together about you by the walls and
at the doors of the houses, saying to each other,
'Come and hear the message that has come
from the LORD.' 31My people come to you, as
they usually do, and sit before you to listen to
your words, but they do not put them into practice. With their mouths they express devotion,
but their hearts are greedy for unjust gain. 32In-
deed, to them you are nothing more than one
who sings love songs with a beautiful voice and
plays an instrument well, for they hear your
words but do not put them into practice.
33"When all this comes true—and it surely
will—then they will know that a prophet has
been among them."

Shepherds and Sheep

34 The word of the LORD came to me:
2"Son of man, prophesy against the

33:33 There is an inescapable certainty to God's pronouncements. When God's Word is faithfully proclaimed, as it was by Ezekiel, then the message and messenger are vindicated when the declarations come to pass. God declares much of his will for us in the Bible, and we can be assured that God's Word will be fulfilled. We would be wise to listen to what he has to say and act on it. Doing anything less will lead to painful consequences.

34:2–10 The spiritual leaders of Israel were like evil shepherds who did not care for their flocks. Since God holds leaders accountable for their actions, God pronounced judgment on these opportunists because they took advantage of the people under their care. As we grow spiritually, we must be aware of our leadership responsibilities too. All of us touch the lives of others in some way. We must be careful to follow God's Word. If we don't, we will suffer painful consequences and cause others to suffer too. If we have failed in providing godly leadership, we need to take immediate action to correct any damage we might have done.

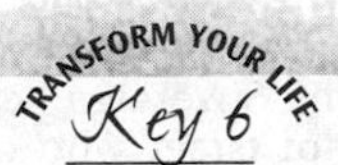

God Offers a Blessed Future

Ezekiel 33:10–16 The Bible tells us that all have sinned and gone their own way (see Psalm 14:3; Isaiah 53:6; Romans 3:23). But no matter how far we have gone in the wrong direction, if we repent and turn around, God always welcomes us back. His arms are open, and his promises are sure—he will transform our broken lives and grant us a blessed future if only we will ask him to. Even in the Old Testament God offered hope to those who chose to repent of their sins and follow the Lord:

> Say to them, "As surely as I live, declares the Sovereign LORD, I take no pleasure in the death of the wicked, but rather that they turn from their ways and live. Turn! Turn from your evil ways! Why will you die, O house of Israel?" Therefore, son of man, say to your countrymen, "The righteousness of the righteous man will not save him when he disobeys, and the wickedness of the wicked man will not cause him to fall when he turns from it" (33:11–12).

There is hope for all who turn from their sin and ask God to redeem their lives. God is gracious and will forgive us no matter what we have done. He will even redirect our course and create a new life—a life of hope, peace and ongoing relationship with him.

Move on to Key 7 and turn to Exodus 31.

shepherds of Israel; prophesy and say to them:
'This is what the Sovereign LORD says: Woe to
the shepherds of Israel who only take care of
themselves! Should not shepherds take care of
the flock? 3You eat the curds, clothe yourselves
with the wool and slaughter the choice animals,
but you do not take care of the flock. 4You have
not strengthened the weak or healed the sick or
bound up the injured. You have not brought
back the strays or searched for the lost. You
have ruled them harshly and brutally. 5So they
were scattered because there was no shepherd,
and when they were scattered they became food
for all the wild animals. 6My sheep wandered
over all the mountains and on every high hill.
They were scattered over the whole earth, and
no one searched or looked for them.

7" 'Therefore, you shepherds, hear the word
of the LORD: 8As surely as I live, declares the
Sovereign LORD, because my flock lacks a shepherd and so has been plundered and has become food for all the wild animals, and because
my shepherds did not search for my flock but
cared for themselves rather than for my flock,
9therefore, O shepherds, hear the word of the
LORD: 10This is what the Sovereign LORD says: I
am against the shepherds and will hold them
accountable for my flock. I will remove them
from tending the flock so that the shepherds
can no longer feed themselves. I will rescue my
flock from their mouths, and it will no longer
be food for them.

11" 'For this is what the Sovereign LORD says:
I myself will search for my sheep and look after
them. 12As a shepherd looks after his scattered
flock when he is with them, so will I look after
my sheep. I will rescue them from all the places
where they were scattered on a day of clouds
and darkness. 13I will bring them out from the
nations and gather them from the countries,
and I will bring them into their own land. I will
pasture them on the mountains of Israel, in the
ravines and in all the settlements in the land. 14I
will tend them in a good pasture, and the
mountain heights of Israel will be their grazing
land. There they will lie down in good grazing
land, and there they will feed in a rich pasture
on the mountains of Israel. 15I myself will tend
my sheep and have them lie down, declares the
Sovereign LORD. 16I will search for the lost and
bring back the strays. I will bind up the injured
and strengthen the weak, but the sleek and the
strong I will destroy. I will shepherd the flock
with justice.

17" 'As for you, my flock, this is what the
Sovereign LORD says: I will judge between one
sheep and another, and between rams and
goats. 18Is it not enough for you to feed on the
good pasture? Must you also trample the rest of
your pasture with your feet? Is it not enough for
you to drink clear water? Must you also muddy
the rest with your feet? 19Must my flock feed on
what you have trampled and drink what you
have muddied with your feet?

20" 'Therefore this is what the Sovereign
LORD says to them: See, I myself will judge between the fat sheep and the lean sheep. 21Be-
cause you shove with flank and shoulder, but-
ting all the weak sheep with your horns until
you have driven them away, 22I will save my
flock, and they will no longer be plundered. I
will judge between one sheep and another. 23I
will place over them one shepherd, my servant
David, and he will tend them; he will tend them
and be their shepherd. 24I the LORD will be their
God, and my servant David will be prince
among them. I the LORD have spoken.

25" 'I will make a covenant of peace with
them and rid the land of wild beasts so that they
may live in the desert and sleep in the forests in
safety. 26I will bless them and the places surrounding my hill.[a] I will send down showers
in season; there will be showers of blessing.
27The trees of the field will yield their fruit and
the ground will yield its crops; the people will
be secure in their land. They will know that I am
the LORD, when I break the bars of their yoke
and rescue them from the hands of those who
enslaved them. 28They will no longer be plundered by the nations, nor will wild animals devour them. They will live in safety, and no one
will make them afraid. 29I will provide for them
a land renowned for its crops, and they will no
longer be victims of famine in the land or bear
the scorn of the nations. 30Then they will know
that I, the LORD their God, am with them and
that they, the house of Israel, are my people,
declares the Sovereign LORD. 31You my sheep,
the sheep of my pasture, are people, and I am
your God, declares the Sovereign LORD.' "

A Prophecy Against Edom

35 The word of the LORD came to me:
2"Son of man, set your face against
Mount Seir; prophesy against it 3and say: 'This
is what the Sovereign LORD says: I am against
you, Mount Seir, and I will stretch out my hand
against you and make you a desolate waste. 4I
will turn your towns into ruins and you will be
desolate. Then you will know that I am the
LORD.

[a]26 Or *I will make them and the places surrounding my hill a blessing*

34:11–16 Even though Israel was a conquered nation, Jerusalem had fallen, the nation's population had been deported and the people had no real hope left, God had given his people a promise they could count on. No matter what our circumstances, no matter how bleak our situation, we can be assured of God's constant care and concern for us.

34:23–24 God had promised David that he would provide someone from David's family line to rule his people in peace. This promise would eventually be fulfilled in the person of Jesus the Messiah. He is the Good Shepherd. We can trust him for guidance in every situation in our lives. He promises to help us and give us power to overcome the areas in our lives that draw us toward destruction.

5" 'Because you harbored an ancient hostility and delivered the Israelites over to the sword
at the time of their calamity, the time their punishment reached its climax, 6therefore as surely
as I live, declares the Sovereign LORD, I will give
you over to bloodshed and it will pursue you.
Since you did not hate bloodshed, bloodshed
will pursue you. 7I will make Mount Seir a desolate waste and cut off from it all who come and
go. 8I will fill your mountains with the slain;
those killed by the sword will fall on your hills
and in your valleys and in all your ravines. 9I
will make you desolate forever; your towns will
not be inhabited. Then you will know that I am
the LORD.

10" 'Because you have said, "These two nations and countries will be ours and we will take
possession of them," even though I the LORD was
there, 11therefore as surely as I live, declares the
Sovereign LORD, I will treat you in accordance
with the anger and jealousy you showed in your
hatred of them and I will make myself known
among them when I judge you. 12Then you will
know that I the LORD have heard all the contemptible things you have said against the
mountains of Israel. You said, "They have been
laid waste and have been given over to us to
devour." 13You boasted against me and spoke
against me without restraint, and I heard it.
14This is what the Sovereign LORD says: While
the whole earth rejoices, I will make you desolate. 15Because you rejoiced when the inheritance of the house of Israel became desolate,
that is how I will treat you. You will be desolate,
O Mount Seir, you and all of Edom. Then they
will know that I am the LORD.' "

A Prophecy to the Mountains of Israel

36 "Son of man, prophesy to the mountains of Israel and say, 'O mountains of
Israel, hear the word of the LORD. 2This is what
the Sovereign LORD says: The enemy said of you,
"Aha! The ancient heights have become our
possession." ' 3Therefore prophesy and say, 'This
is what the Sovereign LORD says: Because they
ravaged and hounded you from every side so
that you became the possession of the rest of
the nations and the object of people's malicious
talk and slander, 4therefore, O mountains of
Israel, hear the word of the Sovereign LORD:
This is what the Sovereign LORD says to the
mountains and hills, to the ravines and valleys,
to the desolate ruins and the deserted towns
that have been plundered and ridiculed by the
rest of the nations around you— 5this is what
the Sovereign LORD says: In my burning zeal I
have spoken against the rest of the nations, and
against all Edom, for with glee and with malice
in their hearts they made my land their own
possession so that they might plunder its pastureland.' 6Therefore prophesy concerning the
land of Israel and say to the mountains and
hills, to the ravines and valleys: 'This is what the
Sovereign LORD says: I speak in my jealous
wrath because you have suffered the scorn of
the nations. 7Therefore this is what the Sovereign LORD says: I swear with uplifted hand that
the nations around you will also suffer scorn.

8" 'But you, O mountains of Israel, will produce branches and fruit for my people Israel, for
they will soon come home. 9I am concerned for
you and will look on you with favor; you will
be plowed and sown, 10and I will multiply the
number of people upon you, even the whole
house of Israel. The towns will be inhabited and
the ruins rebuilt. 11I will increase the number of
men and animals upon you, and they will be
fruitful and become numerous. I will settle people on you as in the past and will make you
prosper more than before. Then you will know
that I am the LORD. 12I will cause people, my
people Israel, to walk upon you. They will possess you, and you will be their inheritance; you
will never again deprive them of their children.

13" 'This is what the Sovereign LORD says:
Because people say to you, "You devour men
and deprive your nation of its children," 14there-
fore you will no longer devour men or make
your nation childless, declares the Sovereign
LORD. 15No longer will I make you hear the
taunts of the nations, and no longer will you
suffer the scorn of the peoples or cause your
nation to fall, declares the Sovereign LORD.' "

16Again the word of the LORD came to me:
17"Son of man, when the people of Israel were
living in their own land, they defiled it by their
conduct and their actions. Their conduct was
like a woman's monthly uncleanness in my
sight. 18So I poured out my wrath on them because they had shed blood in the land and because they had defiled it with their idols. 19I
dispersed them among the nations, and they
were scattered through the countries; I judged
them according to their conduct and their actions. 20And wherever they went among the nations they profaned my holy name, for it was
said of them, 'These are the LORD's people, and
yet they had to leave his land.' 21I had concern
for my holy name, which the house of Israel
profaned among the nations where they had
gone.

22"Therefore say to the house of Israel, 'This
is what the Sovereign LORD says: It is not for
your sake, O house of Israel, that I am going to
do these things, but for the sake of my holy
name, which you have profaned among the na-

36:17–24 God promised the people of Israel that their nation would be restored. The people truly deserved destruction, but God had promised to reveal himself to the world through the nation of Israel; and God's will would not be thwarted. God promised to deliver his people from exile and rebuild his nation so that the whole world would be blessed. The Messiah would come from this tiny nation and change the face of history as he transformed all who would give their lives to him. We should gratefully take advantage of God's gift of forgiveness and restoration through Jesus the Messiah.

tions where you have gone. 23I will show the holiness of my great name, which has been profaned among the nations, the name you have profaned among them. Then the nations will know that I am the LORD, declares the Sovereign LORD, when I show myself holy through you before their eyes.

24" 'For I will take you out of the nations; I will gather you from all the countries and bring you back into your own land. 25I will sprinkle clean water on you, and you will be clean; I will cleanse you from all your impurities and from all your idols. 26I will give you a new heart and put a new spirit in you; I will remove from you your heart of stone and give you a heart of flesh. 27And I will put my Spirit in you and move you to follow my decrees and be careful to keep my laws. 28You will live in the land I gave your forefathers; you will be my people, and I will be your God. 29I will save you from all your uncleanness. I will call for the grain and make it plentiful and will not bring famine upon you. 30I will increase the fruit of the trees and the crops of the field, so that you will no longer suffer disgrace among the nations because of famine. 31Then you will remember your evil ways and wicked deeds, and you will loathe yourselves for your sins and detestable practices. 32I want you to know that I am not doing this for your sake, declares the Sovereign LORD. Be ashamed and disgraced for your conduct, O house of Israel!

33" 'This is what the Sovereign LORD says: On the day I cleanse you from all your sins, I will resettle your towns, and the ruins will be rebuilt. 34The desolate land will be cultivated instead of lying desolate in the sight of all who pass through it. 35They will say, "This land that was laid waste has become like the garden of Eden; the cities that were lying in ruins, desolate and destroyed, are now fortified and inhabited." 36Then the nations around you that remain will know that I the LORD have rebuilt what was destroyed and have replanted what was desolate. I the LORD have spoken, and I will do it.'

37"This is what the Sovereign LORD says: Once again I will yield to the plea of the house of Israel and do this for them: I will make their people as numerous as sheep, 38as numerous as the flocks for offerings at Jerusalem during her appointed feasts. So will the ruined cities be filled with flocks of people. Then they will know that I am the LORD."

The Valley of Dry Bones

37 The hand of the LORD was upon me, and he brought me out by the Spirit of the LORD and set me in the middle of a valley; it was full of bones. 2He led me back and forth among them, and I saw a great many bones on the floor of the valley, bones that were very dry. 3He asked me, "Son of man, can these bones live?"

I said, "O Sovereign LORD, you alone know."

4Then he said to me, "Prophesy to these bones and say to them, 'Dry bones, hear the word of the LORD! 5This is what the Sovereign LORD says to these bones: I will make breath[a] enter you, and you will come to life. 6I will attach tendons to you and make flesh come upon you and cover you with skin; I will put breath in you, and you will come to life. Then you will know that I am the LORD.' "

7So I prophesied as I was commanded. And as I was prophesying, there was a noise, a rattling sound, and the bones came together, bone to bone. 8I looked, and tendons and flesh appeared on them and skin covered them, but there was no breath in them.

9Then he said to me, "Prophesy to the breath; prophesy, son of man, and say to it, 'This is what the Sovereign LORD says: Come from the four winds, O breath, and breathe into these slain, that they may live.' " 10So I prophesied as he commanded me, and breath entered them; they came to life and stood up on their feet—a vast army.

11Then he said to me: "Son of man, these bones are the whole house of Israel. They say, 'Our bones are dried up and our hope is gone; we are cut off.' 12Therefore prophesy and say to them: 'This is what the Sovereign LORD says: O my people, I am going to open your graves and bring you up from them; I will bring you back to the land of Israel. 13Then you, my people, will know that I am the LORD, when I open your graves and bring you up from them. 14I will put my Spirit in you and you will live, and I will settle you in your own land. Then you will know that I the LORD have spoken, and I have done it, declares the LORD.' "

One Nation Under One King

15The word of the LORD came to me: 16"Son

[a]5 The Hebrew for this word can also mean *wind* or *spirit* (see verses 6-14).

36:25–27 How can any individual please God? We are helpless against sin, but these verses should fill us with hope. As we repent and respond to God's gracious provision of forgiveness and restoration, God promises to give us a new heart and fill us with his Spirit so that we can obey him.

36:33 Before the nation of Israel could be rebuilt, it had to be cleansed of sin. Sin separates us from God and leads to destructive consequences. Let us repent, receive God's gracious forgiveness and cleansing and experience his power at work in our lives.

37:1–10 Ezekiel saw a vision of an old battlefield filled with dry bones. There was no life in them whatsoever. What a marvelous illustration of our complete lack of power apart from God! The bones were helpless to act for themselves. The dry bones pictured our complete need, but God's Spirit pictured an inexhaustible supply for any need. When God entered the picture, defeat became uncompromising victory. Our lives may appear hopeless, but when God restores us people will be amazed at the new life they see in us.

of man, take a stick of wood and write on it,
'Belonging to Judah and the Israelites associated with him.' Then take another stick of wood,
and write on it, 'Ephraim's stick, belonging to
Joseph and all the house of Israel associated
with him.' 17 Join them together into one stick
so that they will become one in your hand.
18 "When your countrymen ask you, 'Won't
you tell us what you mean by this?' 19 say to
them, 'This is what the Sovereign LORD says: I
am going to take the stick of Joseph—which is in
Ephraim's hand—and of the Israelite tribes associated with him, and join it to Judah's stick,
making them a single stick of wood, and they
will become one in my hand.' 20 Hold before
their eyes the sticks you have written on 21 and
say to them, 'This is what the Sovereign LORD
says: I will take the Israelites out of the nations
where they have gone. I will gather them from
all around and bring them back into their own
land. 22 I will make them one nation in the land,
on the mountains of Israel. There will be one
king over all of them and they will never again
be two nations or be divided into two kingdoms. 23 They will no longer defile themselves
with their idols and vile images or with any of
their offenses, for I will save them from all their
sinful backsliding,[a] and I will cleanse them.
They will be my people, and I will be their God.
24 " 'My servant David will be king over
them, and they will all have one shepherd. They
will follow my laws and be careful to keep my
decrees. 25 They will live in the land I gave to my
servant Jacob, the land where your fathers lived.
They and their children and their children's
children will live there forever, and David my
servant will be their prince forever. 26 I will make
a covenant of peace with them; it will be an
everlasting covenant. I will establish them and
increase their numbers, and I will put my sanctuary among them forever. 27 My dwelling place
will be with them; I will be their God, and they
will be my people. 28 Then the nations will
know that I the LORD make Israel holy, when
my sanctuary is among them forever.' "

A Prophecy Against Gog

38 The word of the LORD came to me:
2 "Son of man, set your face against
Gog, of the land of Magog, the chief prince of[b]
Meshech and Tubal; prophesy against him 3 and
say: 'This is what the Sovereign LORD says: I am
against you, O Gog, chief prince of[c] Meshech
and Tubal. 4 I will turn you around, put hooks
in your jaws and bring you out with your whole
army—your horses, your horsemen fully armed,
and a great horde with large and small shields,
all of them brandishing their swords. 5 Persia,
Cush[d] and Put will be with them, all with
shields and helmets, 6 also Gomer with all its
troops, and Beth Togarmah from the far north
with all its troops—the many nations with you.
7 " 'Get ready; be prepared, you and all the
hordes gathered about you, and take command
of them. 8 After many days you will be called to
arms. In future years you will invade a land that
has recovered from war, whose people were
gathered from many nations to the mountains
of Israel, which had long been desolate. They
had been brought out from the nations, and
now all of them live in safety. 9 You and all your
troops and the many nations with you will go
up, advancing like a storm; you will be like a
cloud covering the land.
10 " 'This is what the Sovereign LORD says: On
that day thoughts will come into your mind and
you will devise an evil scheme. 11 You will say,
"I will invade a land of unwalled villages; I will
attack a peaceful and unsuspecting people—all
of them living without walls and without gates
and bars. 12 I will plunder and loot and turn my
hand against the resettled ruins and the people
gathered from the nations, rich in livestock and
goods, living at the center of the land." 13 Sheba
and Dedan and the merchants of Tarshish
and all her villages[e] will say to you, "Have
you come to plunder? Have you gathered your
hordes to loot, to carry off silver and gold, to
take away livestock and goods and to seize
much plunder?" '
14 "Therefore, son of man, prophesy and say
to Gog: 'This is what the Sovereign LORD says:
In that day, when my people Israel are living in
safety, will you not take notice of it? 15 You will
come from your place in the far north, you and
many nations with you, all of them riding on
horses, a great horde, a mighty army. 16 You will
advance against my people Israel like a cloud
that covers the land. In days to come, O Gog, I
will bring you against my land, so that the nations may know me when I show myself holy
through you before their eyes.
17 " 'This is what the Sovereign LORD says:
Are you not the one I spoke of in former days
by my servants the prophets of Israel? At that
time they prophesied for years that I would
bring you against them. 18 This is what will hap-

[a]23 Many Hebrew manuscripts (see also Septuagint); most Hebrew manuscripts *all their dwelling places where they sinned* [b]2 Or *the prince of Rosh,* [c]3 Or *Gog, prince of Rosh,* [d]5 That is, the upper Nile region [e]13 Or *her strong lions*

37:24–28 God promised that one day he would make his home among his people. This prophecy was fulfilled when God became a man in the person of Jesus Christ. As we study the life of Jesus on earth, we can discover a lot about God—what he is really like and who he really is. God still lives among us in the person of his Spirit. Though our world is sinful and imperfect, we can look forward to the day when Jesus Christ, the Good Shepherd, will return to guide his people in righteousness and truth.

38:17–23 In these verses God declared his power. The greatest military and political powers of the world would array themselves against God and his people. But when God intervened, his powerful hand would destroy even the greatest enemies. God is powerful enough to handle any struggles we may face. All we need to do is trust and obey him.

pen in that day: When Gog attacks the land of Israel, my hot anger will be aroused, declares the Sovereign LORD. 19In my zeal and fiery wrath I declare that at that time there shall be a great earthquake in the land of Israel. 20The fish of the sea, the birds of the air, the beasts of the field, every creature that moves along the ground, and all the people on the face of the earth will tremble at my presence. The mountains will be overturned, the cliffs will crumble and every wall will fall to the ground. 21I will summon a sword against Gog on all my mountains, declares the Sovereign LORD. Every man's sword will be against his brother. 22I will execute judgment upon him with plague and bloodshed; I will pour down torrents of rain, hailstones and burning sulfur on him and on his troops and on the many nations with him. 23And so I will show my greatness and my holiness, and I will make myself known in the sight of many nations. Then they will know that I am the LORD.'

39 "Son of man, prophesy against Gog and say: 'This is what the Sovereign LORD says: I am against you, O Gog, chief prince of[a] Meshech and Tubal. 2I will turn you around and drag you along. I will bring you from the far north and send you against the mountains of Israel. 3Then I will strike your bow from your left hand and make your arrows drop from your right hand. 4On the mountains of Israel you will fall, you and all your troops and the nations with you. I will give you as food to all kinds of carrion birds and to the wild animals. 5You will fall in the open field, for I have spoken, declares the Sovereign LORD. 6I will send fire on Magog and on those who live in safety in the coastlands, and they will know that I am the LORD.

7" 'I will make known my holy name among my people Israel. I will no longer let my holy name be profaned, and the nations will know that I the LORD am the Holy One in Israel. 8It is coming! It will surely take place, declares the Sovereign LORD. This is the day I have spoken of.

9" 'Then those who live in the towns of Israel will go out and use the weapons for fuel and burn them up—the small and large shields, the bows and arrows, the war clubs and spears. For seven years they will use them for fuel. 10They will not need to gather wood from the fields or cut it from the forests, because they will use the weapons for fuel. And they will plunder those who plundered them and loot those who looted them, declares the Sovereign LORD.

11" 'On that day I will give Gog a burial place in Israel, in the valley of those who travel east toward[b] the Sea.[c] It will block the way of travelers, because Gog and all his hordes will be buried there. So it will be called the Valley of Hamon Gog.[d]

12" 'For seven months the house of Israel will be burying them in order to cleanse the land. 13All the people of the land will bury them, and the day I am glorified will be a memorable day for them, declares the Sovereign LORD.

14" 'Men will be regularly employed to cleanse the land. Some will go throughout the land and, in addition to them, others will bury those that remain on the ground. At the end of the seven months they will begin their search. 15As they go through the land and one of them sees a human bone, he will set up a marker beside it until the gravediggers have buried it in the Valley of Hamon Gog. 16(Also a town called Hamonah[e] will be there.) And so they will cleanse the land.'

17"Son of man, this is what the Sovereign LORD says: Call out to every kind of bird and all the wild animals: 'Assemble and come together from all around to the sacrifice I am preparing for you, the great sacrifice on the mountains of Israel. There you will eat flesh and drink blood. 18You will eat the flesh of mighty men and drink the blood of the princes of the earth as if they were rams and lambs, goats and bulls—all of them fattened animals from Bashan. 19At the sacrifice I am preparing for you, you will eat fat till you are glutted and drink blood till you are drunk. 20At my table you will eat your fill of horses and riders, mighty men and soldiers of every kind,' declares the Sovereign LORD.

21"I will display my glory among the nations, and all the nations will see the punishment I inflict and the hand I lay upon them. 22From that day forward the house of Israel will know that I am the LORD their God. 23And the nations will know that the people of Israel went into exile for their sin, because they were unfaithful to me. So I hid my face from them and handed them over to their enemies, and they all fell by the sword. 24I dealt with them according to their uncleanness and their offenses, and I hid my face from them.

25"Therefore this is what the Sovereign LORD says: I will now bring Jacob back from captivi-

[a]1 Or *Gog, prince of Rosh,* [b]11 Or *of* [c]11 That is, the Dead Sea [d]11 *Hamon Gog* means *hordes of Gog.* [e]16 *Hamonah* means *horde.*

39:1–6 God was at odds with Gog, but it must be remembered that Gog stood against God first. Gog had arrayed his mighty forces against God's people; he had rejected God and his divine will. Ezekiel's prophecy of Gog's destruction reveals the consequences of standing against God and his will. We should take this warning to heart and admit our own sin and rebellion and follow God's will for our lives.

39:25–29 Without God, Israel's future was hopeless and bleak. But the people could still hope for the future, knowing that God had promised great things for them. God is a God of restoration. He wants sin's power to be broken and sin's destruction to be reversed. God restored his people so that his promise of a Redeemer—Jesus the Messiah—could be fulfilled. Through this Redeemer, our lives can be restored, no matter how terrible our sin or

ty[a] and will have compassion on all the people of Israel, and I will be zealous for my holy name. 26They will forget their shame and all the unfaithfulness they showed toward me when they lived in safety in their land with no one to make them afraid. 27When I have brought them back from the nations and have gathered them from the countries of their enemies, I will show myself holy through them in the sight of many nations. 28Then they will know that I am the LORD their God, for though I sent them into exile among the nations, I will gather them to their own land, not leaving any behind. 29I will no longer hide my face from them, for I will pour out my Spirit on the house of Israel, declares the Sovereign LORD."

The New Temple Area

40 In the twenty-fifth year of our exile, at the beginning of the year, on the tenth of the month, in the fourteenth year after the fall of the city—on that very day the hand of the LORD was upon me and he took me there. 2In visions of God he took me to the land of Israel and set me on a very high mountain, on whose south side were some buildings that looked like a city. 3He took me there, and I saw a man whose appearance was like bronze; he was standing in the gateway with a linen cord and a measuring rod in his hand. 4The man said to me, "Son of man, look with your eyes and hear with your ears and pay attention to everything I am going to show you, for that is why you have been brought here. Tell the house of Israel everything you see."

The East Gate to the Outer Court

5I saw a wall completely surrounding the temple area. The length of the measuring rod in the man's hand was six long cubits, each of which was a cubit[b] and a handbreadth.[c] He measured the wall; it was one measuring rod thick and one rod high.

6Then he went to the gate facing east. He climbed its steps and measured the threshold of the gate; it was one rod deep.[d] 7The alcoves for the guards were one rod long and one rod wide, and the projecting walls between the alcoves were five cubits thick. And the threshold of the gate next to the portico facing the temple was one rod deep.

8Then he measured the portico of the gateway; 9it[e] was eight cubits deep and its jambs were two cubits thick. The portico of the gateway faced the temple.

10Inside the east gate were three alcoves on each side; the three had the same measurements, and the faces of the projecting walls on each side had the same measurements. 11Then he measured the width of the entrance to the gateway; it was ten cubits and its length was thirteen cubits. 12In front of each alcove was a wall one cubit high, and the alcoves were six cubits square. 13Then he measured the gateway from the top of the rear wall of one alcove to the top of the opposite one; the distance was twenty-five cubits from one parapet opening to the opposite one. 14He measured along the faces of the projecting walls all around the inside of the gateway—sixty cubits. The measurement was up to the portico[f] facing the courtyard.[g] 15The distance from the entrance of the gateway to the far end of its portico was fifty cubits. 16The alcoves and the projecting walls inside the gateway were surmounted by narrow parapet openings all around, as was the portico; the openings all around faced inward. The faces of the projecting walls were decorated with palm trees.

The Outer Court

17Then he brought me into the outer court. There I saw some rooms and a pavement that had been constructed all around the court; there were thirty rooms along the pavement. 18It abutted the sides of the gateways and was as wide as they were long; this was the lower pavement. 19Then he measured the distance from the inside of the lower gateway to the outside of the inner court; it was a hundred cubits on the east side as well as on the north.

The North Gate

20Then he measured the length and width of the gate facing north, leading into the outer court. 21Its alcoves—three on each side—its projecting walls and its portico had the same mea-

[a]25 Or *now restore the fortunes of Jacob*
[b]5 The common cubit was about 1 1/2 feet (about 0.5 meter).
[c]5 That is, about 3 inches (about 8 centimeters)
[d]6 Septuagint; Hebrew *deep, the first threshold, one rod deep*
[e]8,9 Many Hebrew manuscripts, Septuagint, Vulgate and Syriac; most Hebrew manuscripts *gateway facing the temple; it was one rod deep. 9Then he measured the portico of the gateway; it*
[f]14 Septuagint; Hebrew *projecting wall*
[g]14 The meaning of the Hebrew for this verse is uncertain.

present circumstances.

40:1 Notice that God spoke to his people through Ezekiel while they were still in exile. Where we are or what we have done never limits God. Ezekiel discovered that even under the adverse circumstances of exile, God still communicated with his people. We may face terrible circumstances because of our sin. We may feel that we have sinned too deeply and are ineligible for God's help or forgiveness. But God is always reaching out to us. He desires to help us; all we need to do is repent and admit that we need him.

40:1—48:35 The final chapters of Ezekiel contain a description of a new temple in a new Jerusalem. The restoration of the temple symbolized the restoration of the proper worship of God. God considers worship one of the most important activities of life. In fact, our life ought to be an expression of worship. Our hope for future restoration must involve a restoration of our relationship with God and our proper worship of him. Without a healthy relationship with God, spiritual transformation is impossible.

surements as those of the first gateway. It was fifty cubits long and twenty-five cubits wide. 22Its openings, its portico and its palm tree decorations had the same measurements as those of the gate facing east. Seven steps led up to it, with its portico opposite them. 23There was a gate to the inner court facing the north gate, just as there was on the east. He measured from one gate to the opposite one; it was a hundred cubits.

The South Gate

24Then he led me to the south side and I saw a gate facing south. He measured its jambs and its portico, and they had the same measurements as the others. 25The gateway and its portico had narrow openings all around, like the openings of the others. It was fifty cubits long and twenty-five cubits wide. 26Seven steps led up to it, with its portico opposite them; it had palm tree decorations on the faces of the projecting walls on each side. 27The inner court also had a gate facing south, and he measured from this gate to the outer gate on the south side; it was a hundred cubits.

Gates to the Inner Court

28Then he brought me into the inner court through the south gate, and he measured the south gate; it had the same measurements as the others. 29Its alcoves, its projecting walls and its portico had the same measurements as the others. The gateway and its portico had openings all around. It was fifty cubits long and twenty-five cubits wide. 30(The porticoes of the gateways around the inner court were twenty-five cubits wide and five cubits deep.) 31Its portico faced the outer court; palm trees decorated its jambs, and eight steps led up to it.

32Then he brought me to the inner court on the east side, and he measured the gateway; it had the same measurements as the others. 33Its alcoves, its projecting walls and its portico had the same measurements as the others. The gateway and its portico had openings all around. It was fifty cubits long and twenty-five cubits wide. 34Its portico faced the outer court; palm trees decorated the jambs on either side, and eight steps led up to it.

35Then he brought me to the north gate and measured it. It had the same measurements as the others, 36as did its alcoves, its projecting walls and its portico, and it had openings all around. It was fifty cubits long and twenty-five cubits wide. 37Its portico[a] faced the outer court; palm trees decorated the jambs on either side, and eight steps led up to it.

The Rooms for Preparing Sacrifices

38A room with a doorway was by the portico in each of the inner gateways, where the burnt offerings were washed. 39In the portico of the gateway were two tables on each side, on which the burnt offerings, sin offerings and guilt offerings were slaughtered. 40By the outside wall of the portico of the gateway, near the steps at the entrance to the north gateway were two tables, and on the other side of the steps were two tables. 41So there were four tables on one side of the gateway and four on the other—eight tables in all—on which the sacrifices were slaughtered. 42There were also four tables of dressed stone for the burnt offerings, each a cubit and a half long, a cubit and a half wide and a cubit high. On them were placed the utensils for slaughtering the burnt offerings and the other sacrifices. 43And double-pronged hooks, each a handbreadth long, were attached to the wall all around. The tables were for the flesh of the offerings.

Rooms for the Priests

44Outside the inner gate, within the inner court, were two rooms, one[b] at the side of the north gate and facing south, and another at the side of the south[c] gate and facing north. 45He said to me, "The room facing south is for the priests who have charge of the temple, 46and the room facing north is for the priests who have charge of the altar. These are the sons of Zadok, who are the only Levites who may draw near to the LORD to minister before him."

47Then he measured the court: It was square—a hundred cubits long and a hundred cubits wide. And the altar was in front of the temple.

The Temple

48He brought me to the portico of the temple and measured the jambs of the portico; they were five cubits wide on either side. The width of the entrance was fourteen cubits and its projecting walls were[d] three cubits wide on either side. 49The portico was twenty cubits wide, and twelve[e] cubits from front to back. It was reached by a flight of stairs,[f] and there were pillars on each side of the jambs.

41 Then the man brought me to the outer sanctuary and measured the jambs; the width of the jambs was six cubits[g] on each side.[h] 2The entrance was ten cubits wide, and the projecting walls on each side of it were five cubits wide. He also measured the outer sanctuary; it was forty cubits long and twenty cubits wide.

3Then he went into the inner sanctuary and measured the jambs of the entrance; each was two cubits wide. The entrance was six cubits wide, and the projecting walls on each side of it were seven cubits wide. 4And he measured the length of the inner sanctuary; it was twenty cu-

[a]37 Septuagint (see also verses 31 and 34); Hebrew *jambs*
[b]44 Septuagint; Hebrew *were rooms for singers, which were*
[c]44 Septuagint; Hebrew *east* [d]48 Septuagint; Hebrew *entrance was* [e]49 Septuagint; Hebrew *eleven*
[f]49 Hebrew; Septuagint *Ten steps led up to it*
[g]1 The common cubit was about 1 1/2 feet (about 0.5 meter). [h]1 One Hebrew manuscript and Septuagint; most Hebrew manuscripts *side, the width of the tent*

bits, and its width was twenty cubits across the end of the outer sanctuary. He said to me, "This is the Most Holy Place."

5Then he measured the wall of the temple; it was six cubits thick, and each side room around the temple was four cubits wide. 6The side rooms were on three levels, one above another, thirty on each level. There were ledges all around the wall of the temple to serve as supports for the side rooms, so that the supports were not inserted into the wall of the temple. 7The side rooms all around the temple were wider at each successive level. The structure surrounding the temple was built in ascending stages, so that the rooms widened as one went upward. A stairway went up from the lowest floor to the top floor through the middle floor.

8I saw that the temple had a raised base all around it, forming the foundation of the side rooms. It was the length of the rod, six long cubits. 9The outer wall of the side rooms was five cubits thick. The open area between the side rooms of the temple 10and the ⌊priests'⌋ rooms was twenty cubits wide all around the temple. 11There were entrances to the side rooms from the open area, one on the north and another on the south; and the base adjoining the open area was five cubits wide all around.

12The building facing the temple courtyard on the west side was seventy cubits wide. The wall of the building was five cubits thick all around, and its length was ninety cubits.

13Then he measured the temple; it was a hundred cubits long, and the temple courtyard and the building with its walls were also a hundred cubits long. 14The width of the temple courtyard on the east, including the front of the temple, was a hundred cubits.

15Then he measured the length of the building facing the courtyard at the rear of the temple, including its galleries on each side; it was a hundred cubits.

The outer sanctuary, the inner sanctuary and the portico facing the court, 16as well as the thresholds and the narrow windows and galleries around the three of them—everything beyond and including the threshold was covered with wood. The floor, the wall up to the windows, and the windows were covered. 17In the space above the outside of the entrance to the inner sanctuary and on the walls at regular intervals all around the inner and outer sanctuary 18were carved cherubim and palm trees. Palm trees alternated with cherubim. Each cherub had two faces: 19the face of a man toward the palm tree on one side and the face of a lion toward the palm tree on the other. They were carved all around the whole temple. 20From the floor to the area above the entrance, cherubim and palm trees were carved on the wall of the outer sanctuary.

21The outer sanctuary had a rectangular doorframe, and the one at the front of the Most Holy Place was similar. 22There was a wooden altar three cubits high and two cubits square[a]; its corners, its base[b] and its sides were of wood. The man said to me, "This is the table that is before the LORD." 23Both the outer sanctuary and the Most Holy Place had double doors. 24Each door had two leaves—two hinged leaves for each door. 25And on the doors of the outer sanctuary were carved cherubim and palm trees like those carved on the walls, and there was a wooden overhang on the front of the portico. 26On the sidewalls of the portico were narrow windows with palm trees carved on each side. The side rooms of the temple also had overhangs.

Rooms for the Priests

42 Then the man led me northward into the outer court and brought me to the rooms opposite the temple courtyard and opposite the outer wall on the north side. 2The building whose door faced north was a hundred cubits[c] long and fifty cubits wide. 3Both in the section twenty cubits from the inner court and in the section opposite the pavement of the outer court, gallery faced gallery at the three levels. 4In front of the rooms was an inner passageway ten cubits wide and a hundred cubits[d] long. Their doors were on the north. 5Now the upper rooms were narrower, for the galleries took more space from them than from the rooms on the lower and middle floors of the building. 6The rooms on the third floor had no pillars, as the courts had; so they were smaller in floor space than those on the lower and middle floors. 7There was an outer wall parallel to the rooms and the outer court; it extended in front of the rooms for fifty cubits. 8While the row of rooms on the side next to the outer court was fifty cubits long, the row on the side nearest the sanctuary was a hundred cubits long. 9The lower rooms had an entrance on the east side as one enters them from the outer court.

10On the south side[e] along the length of the wall of the outer court, adjoining the temple courtyard and opposite the outer wall, were rooms 11with a passageway in front of them. These were like the rooms on the north; they had the same length and width, with similar exits and dimensions. Similar to the doorways on the north 12were the doorways of the rooms on the south. There was a doorway at the beginning of the passageway that was parallel to the corresponding wall extending eastward, by which one enters the rooms.

13Then he said to me, "The north and south rooms facing the temple courtyard are the priests' rooms, where the priests who approach the LORD will eat the most holy offerings. There they will put the most holy offerings—the grain offerings, the sin offerings and the guilt offer-

[a]22 Septuagint; Hebrew *long* [b]22 Septuagint; Hebrew *length* [c]2 The common cubit was about 1 1/2 feet (about 0.5 meter). [d]4 Septuagint and Syriac; Hebrew *and one cubit* [e]10 Septuagint; Hebrew *Eastward*

ings—for the place is holy. **14**Once the priests enter the holy precincts, they are not to go into the outer court until they leave behind the garments in which they minister, for these are holy. They are to put on other clothes before they go near the places that are for the people."

15When he had finished measuring what was inside the temple area, he led me out by the east gate and measured the area all around: **16**He measured the east side with the measuring rod; it was five hundred cubits.[a] **17**He measured the north side; it was five hundred cubits[b] by the measuring rod. **18**He measured the south side; it was five hundred cubits by the measuring rod. **19**Then he turned to the west side and measured; it was five hundred cubits by the measuring rod. **20**So he measured the area on all four sides. It had a wall around it, five hundred cubits long and five hundred cubits wide, to separate the holy from the common.

The Glory Returns to the Temple

43 Then the man brought me to the gate facing east, **2**and I saw the glory of the God of Israel coming from the east. His voice was like the roar of rushing waters, and the land was radiant with his glory. **3**The vision I saw was like the vision I had seen when he[c] came to destroy the city and like the visions I had seen by the Kebar River, and I fell facedown. **4**The glory of the LORD entered the temple through the gate facing east. **5**Then the Spirit lifted me up and brought me into the inner court, and the glory of the LORD filled the temple.

6While the man was standing beside me, I heard someone speaking to me from inside the temple. **7**He said: "Son of man, this is the place of my throne and the place for the soles of my feet. This is where I will live among the Israelites forever. The house of Israel will never again defile my holy name—neither they nor their kings—by their prostitution[d] and the lifeless idols[e] of their kings at their high places. **8**When they placed their threshold next to my threshold and their doorposts beside my doorposts, with only a wall between me and them, they defiled my holy name by their detestable practices. So I destroyed them in my anger. **9**Now let them put away from me their prostitution and the lifeless idols of their kings, and I will live among them forever.

10"Son of man, describe the temple to the people of Israel, that they may be ashamed of their sins. Let them consider the plan, **11**and if they are ashamed of all they have done, make known to them the design of the temple—its arrangement, its exits and entrances—its whole design and all its regulations[f] and laws. Write these down before them so that they may be faithful to its design and follow all its regulations.

12"This is the law of the temple: All the surrounding area on top of the mountain will be most holy. Such is the law of the temple.

The Altar

13"These are the measurements of the altar in long cubits, that cubit being a cubit[g] and a handbreadth[h]: Its gutter is a cubit deep and a cubit wide, with a rim of one span[i] around the edge. And this is the height of the altar: **14**From the gutter on the ground up to the lower ledge it is two cubits high and a cubit wide, and from the smaller ledge up to the larger ledge it is four cubits high and a cubit wide. **15**The altar hearth is four cubits high, and four horns project upward from the hearth. **16**The altar hearth is square, twelve cubits long and twelve cubits wide. **17**The upper ledge also is square, fourteen cubits long and fourteen cubits wide, with a rim of half a cubit and a gutter of a cubit all around. The steps of the altar face east."

18Then he said to me, "Son of man, this is what the Sovereign LORD says: These will be the regulations for sacrificing burnt offerings and sprinkling blood upon the altar when it is built: **19**You are to give a young bull as a sin offering to the priests, who are Levites, of the family of Zadok, who come near to minister before me, declares the Sovereign LORD. **20**You are to take some of its blood and put it on the four horns of the altar and on the four corners of the upper ledge and all around the rim, and so purify the altar and make atonement for it. **21**You are to take the bull for the sin offering and burn it in the designated part of the temple area outside the sanctuary.

22"On the second day you are to offer a male goat without defect for a sin offering, and the altar is to be purified as it was purified with the bull. **23**When you have finished purifying it, you

[a]*16* See Septuagint of verse 17; Hebrew *rods;* also in verses 18 and 19. [b]*17* Septuagint; Hebrew *rods* [c]*3* Some Hebrew manuscripts and Vulgate; most Hebrew manuscripts *I* [d]*7* Or *their spiritual adultery;* also in verse 9 [e]*7* Or *the corpses;* also in verse 9 [f]*11* Some Hebrew manuscripts and Septuagint; most Hebrew manuscripts *regulations and its whole design* [g]*13* The common cubit was about 1 1/2 feet (about 0.5 meter). [h]*13* That is, about 3 inches (about 8 centimeters) [i]*13* That is, about 9 inches (about 22 centimeters)

43:1–5 Ezekiel had seen the glory of God leave the temple in Jerusalem early in his prophetic career (10:1—11:23). In this passage Ezekiel joyously saw God's presence return. What an encouragement this vision must have been for Ezekiel. God's presence would be renewed among his people, and there would be hope for their restoration. God did restore his people and then came to live among us in the person of his Son, Jesus the Messiah. Through our relationship with him, we are assured of God's presence with us as we continue in our spiritual renewal. God promises us his transforming presence through his Spirit, giving us hope and help to make the changes needed to conform to his will for our lives.

are to offer a young bull and a ram from the flock, both without defect. 24You are to offer them before the LORD, and the priests are to sprinkle salt on them and sacrifice them as a burnt offering to the LORD.

25"For seven days you are to provide a male goat daily for a sin offering; you are also to provide a young bull and a ram from the flock, both without defect. 26For seven days they are to make atonement for the altar and cleanse it; thus they will dedicate it. 27At the end of these days, from the eighth day on, the priests are to present your burnt offerings and fellowship offerings[a] on the altar. Then I will accept you, declares the Sovereign LORD."

The Prince, the Levites, the Priests

44 Then the man brought me back to the outer gate of the sanctuary, the one facing east, and it was shut. 2The LORD said to me, "This gate is to remain shut. It must not be opened; no one may enter through it. It is to remain shut because the LORD, the God of Israel, has entered through it. 3The prince himself is the only one who may sit inside the gateway to eat in the presence of the LORD. He is to enter by way of the portico of the gateway and go out the same way."

4Then the man brought me by way of the north gate to the front of the temple. I looked and saw the glory of the LORD filling the temple of the LORD, and I fell facedown.

5The LORD said to me, "Son of man, look carefully, listen closely and give attention to everything I tell you concerning all the regulations regarding the temple of the LORD. Give attention to the entrance of the temple and all the exits of the sanctuary. 6Say to the rebellious house of Israel, 'This is what the Sovereign LORD says: Enough of your detestable practices, O house of Israel! 7In addition to all your other detestable practices, you brought foreigners uncircumcised in heart and flesh into my sanctuary, desecrating my temple while you offered me food, fat and blood, and you broke my covenant. 8Instead of carrying out your duty in regard to my holy things, you put others in charge of my sanctuary. 9This is what the Sovereign LORD says: No foreigner uncircumcised in heart and flesh is to enter my sanctuary, not even the foreigners who live among the Israelites.

10" 'The Levites who went far from me when Israel went astray and who wandered from me after their idols must bear the consequences of their sin. 11They may serve in my sanctuary, having charge of the gates of the temple and serving in it; they may slaughter the burnt offerings and sacrifices for the people and stand before the people and serve them. 12But because they served them in the presence of their idols and made the house of Israel fall into sin, therefore I have sworn with uplifted hand that they must bear the consequences of their sin, declares the Sovereign LORD. 13They are not to come near to serve me as priests or come near any of my holy things or my most holy offerings; they must bear the shame of their detestable practices. 14Yet I will put them in charge of the duties of the temple and all the work that is to be done in it.

15" 'But the priests, who are Levites and descendants of Zadok and who faithfully carried out the duties of my sanctuary when the Israelites went astray from me, are to come near to minister before me; they are to stand before me to offer sacrifices of fat and blood, declares the Sovereign LORD. 16They alone are to enter my sanctuary; they alone are to come near my table to minister before me and perform my service.

17" 'When they enter the gates of the inner court, they are to wear linen clothes; they must not wear any woolen garment while ministering at the gates of the inner court or inside the temple. 18They are to wear linen turbans on their heads and linen undergarments around their waists. They must not wear anything that makes them perspire. 19When they go out into the outer court where the people are, they are to take off the clothes they have been ministering in and are to leave them in the sacred rooms, and put on other clothes, so that they do not consecrate the people by means of their garments.

20" 'They must not shave their heads or let their hair grow long, but they are to keep the hair of their heads trimmed. 21No priest is to drink wine when he enters the inner court. 22They must not marry widows or divorced women; they may marry only virgins of Israelite descent or widows of priests. 23They are to teach my people the difference between the holy and the common and show them how to distinguish between the unclean and the clean.

24" 'In any dispute, the priests are to serve as judges and decide it according to my ordinances. They are to keep my laws and my decrees for all my appointed feasts, and they are to keep my Sabbaths holy.

25" 'A priest must not defile himself by going near a dead person; however, if the dead person was his father or mother, son or daughter, brother or unmarried sister, then he may defile himself. 26After he is cleansed, he must wait seven days. 27On the day he goes into the inner court of the sanctuary to minister in the sanctu-

[a] 27 Traditionally *peace offerings*

44:6–7 God had clearly revealed his will for his people, but they had ignored the guidelines God had graciously provided. They had rebelled against the plan God had laid out for them. God has clearly revealed much of his will for us in the Bible. It is our responsibility to follow it. Since there are painful consequences for failing to obey God's will, we would be wise to seek God's will for our lives and do whatever is necessary to carry it out.

ary, he is to offer a sin offering for himself, declares the Sovereign LORD.

28 " 'I am to be the only inheritance the priests have. You are to give them no possession in Israel; I will be their possession. 29 They will eat the grain offerings, the sin offerings and the guilt offerings; and everything in Israel devoted[a] to the LORD will belong to them. 30 The best of all the firstfruits and of all your special gifts will belong to the priests. You are to give them the first portion of your ground meal so that a blessing may rest on your household. 31 The priests must not eat anything, bird or animal, found dead or torn by wild animals.

Division of the Land

45 " 'When you allot the land as an inheritance, you are to present to the LORD a portion of the land as a sacred district, 25,000 cubits long and 20,000[b] cubits wide; the entire area will be holy. 2 Of this, a section 500 cubits square is to be for the sanctuary, with 50 cubits around it for open land. 3 In the sacred district, measure off a section 25,000 cubits[c] long and 10,000 cubits[d] wide. In it will be the sanctuary, the Most Holy Place. 4 It will be the sacred portion of the land for the priests, who minister in the sanctuary and who draw near to minister before the LORD. It will be a place for their houses as well as a holy place for the sanctuary. 5 An area 25,000 cubits long and 10,000 cubits wide will belong to the Levites, who serve in the temple, as their possession for towns to live in.[e]

6 " 'You are to give the city as its property an area 5,000 cubits wide and 25,000 cubits long, adjoining the sacred portion; it will belong to the whole house of Israel.

7 " 'The prince will have the land bordering each side of the area formed by the sacred district and the property of the city. It will extend westward from the west side and eastward from the east side, running lengthwise from the western to the eastern border parallel to one of the tribal portions. 8 This land will be his possession in Israel. And my princes will no longer oppress my people but will allow the house of Israel to possess the land according to their tribes.

9 " 'This is what the Sovereign LORD says: You have gone far enough, O princes of Israel! Give up your violence and oppression and do what is just and right. Stop dispossessing my people, declares the Sovereign LORD. 10 You are to use accurate scales, an accurate ephah[f] and an accurate bath.[g] 11 The ephah and the bath are to be the same size, the bath containing a tenth of a homer[h] and the ephah a tenth of a homer; the homer is to be the standard measure for both. 12 The shekel[i] is to consist of twenty gerahs. Twenty shekels plus twenty-five shekels plus fifteen shekels equal one mina.[j]

Offerings and Holy Days

13 " 'This is the special gift you are to offer: a sixth of an ephah from each homer of wheat and a sixth of an ephah from each homer of barley. 14 The prescribed portion of oil, measured by the bath, is a tenth of a bath from each cor (which consists of ten baths or one homer, for ten baths are equivalent to a homer). 15 Also one sheep is to be taken from every flock of two hundred from the well-watered pastures of Israel. These will be used for the grain offerings, burnt offerings and fellowship offerings[k] to make atonement for the people, declares the Sovereign LORD. 16 All the people of the land will participate in this special gift for the use of the prince in Israel. 17 It will be the duty of the prince to provide the burnt offerings, grain offerings and drink offerings at the festivals, the New Moons and the Sabbaths—at all the appointed feasts of the house of Israel. He will provide the sin offerings, grain offerings, burnt offerings and fellowship offerings to make atonement for the house of Israel.

18 " 'This is what the Sovereign LORD says: In the first month on the first day you are to take a young bull without defect and purify the sanctuary. 19 The priest is to take some of the blood of the sin offering and put it on the doorposts of the temple, on the four corners of the upper ledge of the altar and on the gateposts of the inner court. 20 You are to do the same on the seventh day of the month for anyone who sins unintentionally or through ignorance; so you are to make atonement for the temple.

21 " 'In the first month on the fourteenth day you are to observe the Passover, a feast lasting seven days, during which you shall eat bread made without yeast. 22 On that day the prince is to provide a bull as a sin offering for himself and for all the people of the land. 23 Every day during the seven days of the Feast he is to provide seven bulls and seven rams without defect as a burnt offering to the LORD, and a male goat for a sin offering. 24 He is to provide as a grain offering an ephah for each bull and an ephah for each ram, along with a hin[l] of oil for each ephah.

25 " 'During the seven days of the Feast, which begins in the seventh month on the fifteenth day, he is to make the same provision for sin offerings, burnt offerings, grain offerings and oil.

[a] *29* The Hebrew term refers to the irrevocable giving over of things or persons to the LORD. [b] *1* Septuagint (see also verses 3 and 5 and 48:9); Hebrew *10,000* [c] *3* That is, about 7 miles (about 12 kilometers) [d] *3* That is, about 3 miles (about 5 kilometers) [e] *5* Septuagint; Hebrew *temple; they will have as their possession 20 rooms* [f] *10* An ephah was a dry measure. [g] *10* A bath was a liquid measure. [h] *11* A homer was a dry measure. [i] *12* A shekel weighed about 2/5 ounce (about 11.5 grams). [j] *12* That is, 60 shekels; the common mina was 50 shekels. [k] *15* Traditionally *peace offerings;* also in verse 17 [l] *24* That is, probably about 4 quarts (about 4 liters)

46 " 'This is what the Sovereign LORD says: The gate of the inner court facing east is to be shut on the six working days, but on the Sabbath day and on the day of the New Moon it is to be opened. 2The prince is to enter from the outside through the portico of the gateway and stand by the gatepost. The priests are to sacrifice his burnt offering and his fellowship offerings.[a] He is to worship at the threshold of the gateway and then go out, but the gate will not be shut until evening. 3On the Sabbaths and New Moons the people of the land are to worship in the presence of the LORD at the entrance to that gateway. 4The burnt offering the prince brings to the LORD on the Sabbath day is to be six male lambs and a ram, all without defect. 5The grain offering given with the ram is to be an ephah,[b] and the grain offering with the lambs is to be as much as he pleases, along with a hin[c] of oil for each ephah. 6On the day of the New Moon he is to offer a young bull, six lambs and a ram, all without defect. 7He is to provide as a grain offering one ephah with the bull, one ephah with the ram, and with the lambs as much as he wants to give, along with a hin of oil with each ephah. 8When the prince enters, he is to go in through the portico of the gateway, and he is to come out the same way.

9" 'When the people of the land come before the LORD at the appointed feasts, whoever enters by the north gate to worship is to go out the south gate; and whoever enters by the south gate is to go out the north gate. No one is to return through the gate by which he entered, but each is to go out the opposite gate. 10The prince is to be among them, going in when they go in and going out when they go out.

11" 'At the festivals and the appointed feasts, the grain offering is to be an ephah with a bull, an ephah with a ram, and with the lambs as much as one pleases, along with a hin of oil for each ephah. 12When the prince provides a freewill offering to the LORD—whether a burnt offering or fellowship offerings—the gate facing east is to be opened for him. He shall offer his burnt offering or his fellowship offerings as he does on the Sabbath day. Then he shall go out, and after he has gone out, the gate will be shut.

13" 'Every day you are to provide a year-old lamb without defect for a burnt offering to the LORD; morning by morning you shall provide it. 14You are also to provide with it morning by morning a grain offering, consisting of a sixth of an ephah with a third of a hin of oil to moisten the flour. The presenting of this grain offering to the LORD is a lasting ordinance. 15So the lamb and the grain offering and the oil shall be provided morning by morning for a regular burnt offering.

16" 'This is what the Sovereign LORD says: If the prince makes a gift from his inheritance to one of his sons, it will also belong to his descendants; it is to be their property by inheritance. 17If, however, he makes a gift from his inheritance to one of his servants, the servant may keep it until the year of freedom; then it will revert to the prince. His inheritance belongs to his sons only; it is theirs. 18The prince must not take any of the inheritance of the people, driving them off their property. He is to give his sons their inheritance out of his own property, so that none of my people will be separated from his property.' "

19Then the man brought me through the entrance at the side of the gate to the sacred rooms facing north, which belonged to the priests, and showed me a place at the western end. 20He said to me, "This is the place where the priests will cook the guilt offering and the sin offering and bake the grain offering, to avoid bringing them into the outer court and consecrating the people."

21He then brought me to the outer court and led me around to its four corners, and I saw in each corner another court. 22In the four corners of the outer court were enclosed[d] courts, forty cubits long and thirty cubits wide; each of the courts in the four corners was the same size. 23Around the inside of each of the four courts was a ledge of stone, with places for fire built all around under the ledge. 24He said to me, "These are the kitchens where those who minister at the temple will cook the sacrifices of the people."

The River From the Temple

47 The man brought me back to the entrance of the temple, and I saw water

[a] 2 Traditionally *peace offerings;* also in verse 12
[b] 5 That is, probably about 3/5 bushel (about 22 liters)
[c] 5 That is, probably about 4 quarts (about 4 liters)
[d] 22 The meaning of the Hebrew for this word is uncertain.

46:1–24 This chapter contains a long list of regulations relating to the offering of sacrifices. Sacrifices were a means of reestablishing the people's relationship with God. Slaughtering animals for our sins may seem terribly barbaric, and we may wonder why God chose to do things this way. Our negative reactions to this practice, however, simply underscore the awfulness of sin. Yet, notice that God provided a way to pay for the people's sins without bringing their complete destruction. They had to admit their sins, receive his forgiveness and live in obedience to him. Since Ezekiel's day, God has provided the ultimate sacrifice, Jesus Christ, to pay for our sins and provide a means for our redemption. We must accept the gift he has provided.

47:1–12 These verses describe a healing river that flows throughout the land, restoring the arid landscape with vitality and life. The land had been destroyed because of the sins of God's people, but God will restore what they had destroyed. This is also our hope in the coming of Jesus the Messiah. Jesus made our personal restoration possible through the power of his miraculous resurrection. We now look forward to his second coming when God will restore all of creation. Humanity's sin has perverted God's perfect plan for the world. However, God's plan of peace and prosperity on earth will ultimately come to pass. God will restore us and the universe we live in from the devastating consequences of sin.

coming out from under the threshold of the
temple toward the east (for the temple faced
east). The water was coming down from under
the south side of the temple, south of the altar.
2He then brought me out through the north
gate and led me around the outside to the outer
gate facing east, and the water was flowing from
the south side.

3As the man went eastward with a measuring
line in his hand, he measured off a thousand
cubits[a] and then led me through water that
was ankle-deep. 4He measured off another
thousand cubits and led me through water that
was knee-deep. He measured off another thousand and led me through water that was up to
the waist. 5He measured off another thousand,
but now it was a river that I could not cross,
because the water had risen and was deep
enough to swim in—a river that no one could
cross. 6He asked me, "Son of man, do you see
this?"

Then he led me back to the bank of the river.
7When I arrived there, I saw a great number of
trees on each side of the river. 8He said to me,
"This water flows toward the eastern region and
goes down into the Arabah,[b] where it enters
the Sea.[c] When it empties into the Sea,[c] the
water there becomes fresh. 9Swarms of living
creatures will live wherever the river flows.
There will be large numbers of fish, because this
water flows there and makes the salt water fresh;
so where the river flows everything will live.
10Fishermen will stand along the shore; from
En Gedi to En Eglaim there will be places for
spreading nets. The fish will be of many kinds—
like the fish of the Great Sea.[d] 11But the
swamps and marshes will not become fresh;
they will be left for salt. 12Fruit trees of all kinds
will grow on both banks of the river. Their
leaves will not wither, nor will their fruit fail.
Every month they will bear, because the water
from the sanctuary flows to them. Their fruit
will serve for food and their leaves for healing."

The Boundaries of the Land

13This is what the Sovereign LORD says:
"These are the boundaries by which you are to
divide the land for an inheritance among the
twelve tribes of Israel, with two portions for
Joseph. 14You are to divide it equally among
them. Because I swore with uplifted hand to
give it to your forefathers, this land will become
your inheritance.

15"This is to be the boundary of the land:

"On the north side it will run from the Great
Sea by the Hethlon road past Lebo[e] Hamath to Zedad, 16Berothah[f] and Sibraim
(which lies on the border between Damascus and Hamath), as far as Hazer Hatticon,
which is on the border of Hauran. 17The
boundary will extend from the sea to Hazar Enan,[g] along the northern border of
Damascus, with the border of Hamath to
the north. This will be the north boundary.
18"On the east side the boundary will run between Hauran and Damascus, along the
Jordan between Gilead and the land of Israel, to the eastern sea and as far as Tamar.[h] This will be the east boundary.
19"On the south side it will run from Tamar as
far as the waters of Meribah Kadesh, then
along the Wadi ⌞of Egypt⌟ to the Great Sea.
This will be the south boundary.
20"On the west side, the Great Sea will be the
boundary to a point opposite Lebo[i] Hamath. This will be the west boundary.

21"You are to distribute this land among
yourselves according to the tribes of Israel.
22You are to allot it as an inheritance for yourselves and for the aliens who have settled
among you and who have children. You are to
consider them as native-born Israelites; along
with you they are to be allotted an inheritance
among the tribes of Israel. 23In whatever tribe
the alien settles, there you are to give him his
inheritance," declares the Sovereign LORD.

The Division of the Land

48 "These are the tribes, listed by name: At
the northern frontier, Dan will have
one portion; it will follow the Hethlon road to
Lebo[j] Hamath; Hazar Enan and the northern
border of Damascus next to Hamath will be
part of its border from the east side to the west
side.

2"Asher will have one portion; it will border
the territory of Dan from east to west.

3"Naphtali will have one portion; it will border the territory of Asher from east to west.

4"Manasseh will have one portion; it will
border the territory of Naphtali from east to
west.

5"Ephraim will have one portion; it will border the territory of Manasseh from east to west.

6"Reuben will have one portion; it will border the territory of Ephraim from east to west.

7"Judah will have one portion; it will border
the territory of Reuben from east to west.

8"Bordering the territory of Judah from east
to west will be the portion you are to present as
a special gift. It will be 25,000 cubits[k] wide,
and its length from east to west will equal one
of the tribal portions; the sanctuary will be in
the center of it.

9"The special portion you are to offer to the

[a]3 That is, about 1,500 feet (about 450 meters)
[b]8 Or *the Jordan Valley* [c]8 That is, the Dead Sea
[d]10 That is, the Mediterranean; also in verses 15, 19 and 20 [e]15 Or *past the entrance to* [f]15,16 See Septuagint and Ezekiel 48:1; Hebrew *road to go into Zedad, 16Hamath, Berothah* [g]17 Hebrew *Enon,* a variant of *Enan* [h]18 Septuagint and Syriac; Hebrew *Israel. You will measure to the eastern sea* [i]20 Or *opposite the entrance to* [j]1 Or *to the entrance to* [k]8 That is, about 7 miles (about 12 kilometers)

LORD will be 25,000 cubits long and 10,000
cubits[a] wide. **10**This will be the sacred portion
for the priests. It will be 25,000 cubits long on
the north side, 10,000 cubits wide on the west
side, 10,000 cubits wide on the east side and
25,000 cubits long on the south side. In the
center of it will be the sanctuary of the LORD.
11This will be for the consecrated priests, the
Zadokites, who were faithful in serving me and
did not go astray as the Levites did when the
Israelites went astray. **12**It will be a special gift to
them from the sacred portion of the land, a
most holy portion, bordering the territory of
the Levites.

13"Alongside the territory of the priests, the
Levites will have an allotment 25,000 cubits
long and 10,000 cubits wide. Its total length
will be 25,000 cubits and its width 10,000 cubits. **14**They must not sell or exchange any of it.
This is the best of the land and must not pass
into other hands, because it is holy to the LORD.

15"The remaining area, 5,000 cubits wide
and 25,000 cubits long, will be for the common
use of the city, for houses and for pastureland.
The city will be in the center of it **16**and will have
these measurements: the north side 4,500 cubits, the south side 4,500 cubits, the east side
4,500 cubits, and the west side 4,500 cubits.
17The pastureland for the city will be 250 cubits
on the north, 250 cubits on the south, 250 cubits on the east, and 250 cubits on the west.
18What remains of the area, bordering on the
sacred portion and running the length of it, will
be 10,000 cubits on the east side and 10,000
cubits on the west side. Its produce will supply
food for the workers of the city. **19**The workers
from the city who farm it will come from all the
tribes of Israel. **20**The entire portion will be a
square, 25,000 cubits on each side. As a special
gift you will set aside the sacred portion, along
with the property of the city.

21"What remains on both sides of the area
formed by the sacred portion and the city property will belong to the prince. It will extend
eastward from the 25,000 cubits of the sacred
portion to the eastern border, and westward
from the 25,000 cubits to the western border.
Both these areas running the length of the tribal
portions will belong to the prince, and the sacred portion with the temple sanctuary will be
in the center of them. **22**So the property of the Levites and the property of the city will lie in the center of the area that belongs to the prince. The
area belonging to the prince will lie between the
border of Judah and the border of Benjamin.

23"As for the rest of the tribes: Benjamin will
have one portion; it will extend from the east
side to the west side.

24"Simeon will have one portion; it will border the territory of Benjamin from east to west.

25"Issachar will have one portion; it will border the territory of Simeon from east to west.

26"Zebulun will have one portion; it will
border the territory of Issachar from east to
west.

27"Gad will have one portion; it will border
the territory of Zebulun from east to west.

28"The southern boundary of Gad will run
south from Tamar to the waters of Meribah Kadesh, then along the Wadi ⌞of Egypt⌟ to the
Great Sea.[b]

29"This is the land you are to allot as an
inheritance to the tribes of Israel, and these will
be their portions," declares the Sovereign LORD.

The Gates of the City

30"These will be the exits of the city: Beginning on the north side, which is 4,500 cubits
long, **31**the gates of the city will be named after
the tribes of Israel. The three gates on the north
side will be the gate of Reuben, the gate of Judah and the gate of Levi.

32"On the east side, which is 4,500 cubits
long, will be three gates: the gate of Joseph, the
gate of Benjamin and the gate of Dan.

33"On the south side, which measures 4,500
cubits, will be three gates: the gate of Simeon,
the gate of Issachar and the gate of Zebulun.

34"On the west side, which is 4,500 cubits
long, will be three gates: the gate of Gad, the
gate of Asher and the gate of Naphtali.

35"The distance all around will be 18,000
cubits.

"And the name of the city from that time on
will be:

THE LORD IS THERE."

[a]9 That is, about 3 miles (about 5 kilometers)
[b]28 That is, the Mediterranean

DANIEL

The Big Picture

A. *EXPERIENCES OF DANIEL AND HIS FRIENDS (1:1–6:28)*

1. In Nebuchadnezzar's Court (1:1–4:37)
2. Daniel Explains the Writing on the Wall (5:1-30)
3. Daniel in the Lions' Den (6:1-28)

B. *DANIEL'S VISIONS AND PRAYER (7:1–12:13)*

The mistakes and crimes of other people often injure innocent bystanders. Natural disasters may haunt us for life even though we have no direct responsibility for the events that have taken place. The best way to handle these setbacks, however, is to accept them and make the best of the situation.

Daniel and his friends were innocent bystanders. They suffered a lifelong exile to Babylon because of Judah's prolonged disobedience to God. But Daniel and his friends did not let their misfortune destroy their relationship with God. With courage and faith in God, they faced the realities of exile and lived successful lives—even by Babylonian standards. Their lives give us insight into how we, too, can deal with tragedy.

After being taken from Jerusalem to Babylon, Daniel and his three friends were trained for service in the king's court. Part of their training required adherence to standards that stood in opposition to God's revealed will for these young men's lives. To protect their relationship with God, Daniel and his friends set clear boundaries for their behavior. They followed God's plan for their lives, despite its conflict with the commands of their strong-willed captors and the life-threatening consequences that resulted from these choices. God protected these faithful young men from the foreign laws and unstable tyrants who ruled over them.

Daniel and his friends were exiled to Babylon because of the sins of their ancestors, but they did not use those past sins as excuses for continued failure. Instead, they trusted God to redeem their lives and determined to live according to his will. Because of their faith and courage, God not only repeatedly delivered Daniel and his friends from difficult circumstances, but God also used them to prove his existence and power to others who might otherwise never have had the opportunity to know him.

Spiritual Renewal Themes

LIFE IS UNFAIR

When we experience injustice in life, the examples of Daniel and his three friends give us some encouragement and direction. Despite his life of obedience, Daniel was not protected from God's judgment on the people of Judah. Innocence does

not automatically protect us from tragedy. But we do have the assurance that God is concerned about what we are doing. He will honor our faithfulness and obedience.

GOD IS IN CONTROL EVEN WHEN LIFE IS OUT OF CONTROL
Daniel's life was controlled by a powerful group of people. He had no say in his future. Even though Daniel's life was out of his control, he trusted that God was still sovereign. Daniel was not merely the hapless pawn of a selfish and unstable foreign ruler. He was in God's powerful and protecting hand. As Daniel faithfully obeyed God's commands, God delivered him from terrible situations, giving him freedom in the midst of his exile and bondage.

GOD CAN DO ANYTHING
If Daniel and his friends had not believed that God was sovereign, they might have decided that compromising their beliefs was better than risking their lives. But if these young men had compromised, they would not have experienced God's glorious victories. God is greater than anything we might face. We must be willing to hand our lives over to him and follow his will.

PAIN IN THE PROCESS OF RENEWAL
Daniel and his friends sought to live according to God's plan, but they found that others opposed their efforts. This led them all initially into great danger. Shadrach, Meshach and Abednego had to walk through a fiery furnace because they obeyed God's will. Daniel was thrown into a den of lions. Yet the obedience of these young men ultimately led to glorious victory. Only the ropes that bound Shadrach, Meshach and Abednego were burned by fire; they escaped unharmed. Daniel walked out of the lion's den unscathed because of his faithful obedience. God used these trials to bring blessings to his servants and glory to himself. As we seek to do God's will we may face some difficult situations. God can use such trials to bless us. We need to continually seek God and surrender to him, no matter what difficulties we face.

Essential Facts

PURPOSE:
To show that God humbles proud oppressors and vindicates those who trust him through their days of suffering.

AUTHOR:
The prophet Daniel.

AUDIENCE:
God's people during and after the Babylonian exile.

DATE WRITTEN:
The book was probably written around 535 B.C., recording events that happened between 605 and 535 B.C.

SETTING:
The land of Babylon after Daniel and his friends were exiled there in 605 B.C.

KEY VERSE:
"Those who are wise will shine like the brightness of the heavens, and those who lead many to righteousness, like the stars for ever and ever" (12:3).

KEY PLACES:
Jerusalem, Babylon and Susa.

KEY PEOPLE AND RELATIONSHIPS:
Daniel, Shadrach, Meshach and Abednego; and foreign rulers Nebuchadnezzar, Belshazzar and Darius.

Daniel's Training in Babylon

1 In the third year of the reign of Jehoiakim king of Judah, Nebuchadnezzar king of Babylon came to Jerusalem and besieged it. 2And the Lord delivered Jehoiakim king of Judah into his hand, along with some of the articles from the temple of God. These he carried off to the temple of his god in Babylonia[a] and put in the treasure house of his god.

3Then the king ordered Ashpenaz, chief of his court officials, to bring in some of the Israelites from the royal family and the nobility— 4young men without any physical defect, handsome, showing aptitude for every kind of learning, well informed, quick to understand, and qualified to serve in the king's palace. He was to teach them the language and literature of the Babylonians.[b] 5The king assigned them a daily amount of food and wine from the king's table. They were to be trained for three years, and after that they were to enter the king's service.

6Among these were some from Judah: Daniel, Hananiah, Mishael and Azariah. 7The chief official gave them new names: to Daniel, the name Belteshazzar; to Hananiah, Shadrach; to Mishael, Meshach; and to Azariah, Abednego.

8But Daniel resolved not to defile himself with the royal food and wine, and he asked the chief official for permission not to defile himself this way. 9Now God had caused the official to show favor and sympathy to Daniel, 10but the official told Daniel, "I am afraid of my lord the king, who has assigned your[c] food and drink. Why should he see you looking worse than the other young men your age? The king would then have my head because of you."

11Daniel then said to the guard whom the chief official had appointed over Daniel, Hananiah, Mishael and Azariah, 12"Please test your servants for ten days: Give us nothing but vegetables to eat and water to drink. 13Then compare our appearance with that of the young men who eat the royal food, and treat your servants in accordance with what you see." 14So he agreed to this and tested them for ten days.

15At the end of the ten days they looked healthier and better nourished than any of the young men who ate the royal food. 16So the guard took away their choice food and the wine they were to drink and gave them vegetables instead.

17To these four young men God gave knowledge and understanding of all kinds of literature and learning. And Daniel could understand visions and dreams of all kinds.

18At the end of the time set by the king to bring them in, the chief official presented them to Nebuchadnezzar. 19The king talked with them, and he found none equal to Daniel, Hananiah, Mishael and Azariah; so they entered the king's service. 20In every matter of wisdom and understanding about which the king questioned them, he found them ten times better than all the magicians and enchanters in his whole kingdom.

21And Daniel remained there until the first year of King Cyrus.

Nebuchadnezzar's Dream

2 In the second year of his reign, Nebuchadnezzar had dreams; his mind was troubled and he could not sleep. 2So the king summoned the magicians, enchanters, sorcerers and astrologers[d] to tell him what he had dreamed. When they came in and stood before the king, 3he said to them, "I have had a dream that troubles me and I want to know what it means.[e]"

4Then the astrologers answered the king in Aramaic,[f] "O king, live forever! Tell your servants the dream, and we will interpret it."

5The king replied to the astrologers, "This is what I have firmly decided: If you do not tell me what my dream was and interpret it, I will have you cut into pieces and your houses turned into piles of rubble. 6But if you tell me the dream and explain it, you will receive from me gifts and rewards and great honor. So tell me the dream and interpret it for me."

7Once more they replied, "Let the king tell his servants the dream, and we will interpret it."

8Then the king answered, "I am certain that you are trying to gain time, because you realize that this is what I have firmly decided: 9If you do not tell me the dream, there is just one penalty for you. You have conspired to tell me misleading and wicked things, hoping the situation will change. So then, tell me the dream, and I will know that you can interpret it for me."

10The astrologers answered the king, "There

[a] 2 Hebrew *Shinar* [b] 4 Or *Chaldeans* [c] 10 The Hebrew for *your* and *you* in this verse is plural.
[d] 2 Or *Chaldeans;* also in verses 4, 5 and 10 [e] 3 Or *was*
[f] 4 The text from here through chapter 7 is in Aramaic.

1:1–6 Daniel, Hananiah, Mishael and Azariah faced troubled times: Their city was conquered; they were captured by the enemy and marched across the desert to Babylon. Life must have seemed over for the four young men. But then the direction of their life changed. After a three-year training period these four young men were chosen to be King Nebuchadnezzar's counselors. No one ever knows what the future holds. Our bad times may be only temporary; God's blessings may be just around the corner. And God may even use our hard times to prepare us for his greater service.

1:7–16 When people try to squeeze us into their mold and make us compromise our values, we need to remain strong in our faith. We must set godly boundaries on our behavior, just as Daniel did by not eating food that was contrary to God's laws. With proper boundaries, we will be less tempted to yield to compromise and our spiritual growth will be enhanced.

1:17–21 When we use the talents and abilities God has given us, others will notice. King Nebuchadnezzar saw that Daniel and his friends possessed more insight than any of his other magicians or enchanters. The wisdom of these young men—God's wisdom—set them apart from the other advisers and allowed them to triumph.

is not a man on earth who can do what the king
asks! No king, however great and mighty, has
ever asked such a thing of any magician or enchanter or astrologer. 11What the king asks is
too difficult. No one can reveal it to the king
except the gods, and they do not live among
men."
12This made the king so angry and furious
that he ordered the execution of all the wise
men of Babylon. 13So the decree was issued to
put the wise men to death, and men were sent
to look for Daniel and his friends to put them
to death.
14When Arioch, the commander of the king's
guard, had gone out to put to death the wise
men of Babylon, Daniel spoke to him with wisdom and tact. 15He asked the king's officer,
"Why did the king issue such a harsh decree?"
Arioch then explained the matter to Daniel. 16At
this, Daniel went in to the king and asked for
time, so that he might interpret the dream for
him.
17Then Daniel returned to his house and explained the matter to his friends Hananiah,
Mishael and Azariah. 18He urged them to plead
for mercy from the God of heaven concerning
this mystery, so that he and his friends might
not be executed with the rest of the wise men of
Babylon. 19During the night the mystery was
revealed to Daniel in a vision. Then Daniel
praised the God of heaven 20and said:

"Praise be to the name of God for ever and
ever;
wisdom and power are his.
21He changes times and seasons;
he sets up kings and deposes them.
He gives wisdom to the wise
and knowledge to the discerning.
22He reveals deep and hidden things;
he knows what lies in darkness,
and light dwells with him.
23I thank and praise you, O God of my
fathers:
You have given me wisdom and power,
you have made known to me what we
asked of you,
you have made known to us the dream
of the king."

Daniel Interprets the Dream

24Then Daniel went to Arioch, whom the
king had appointed to execute the wise men of
Babylon, and said to him, "Do not execute the
wise men of Babylon. Take me to the king, and
I will interpret his dream for him."
25Arioch took Daniel to the king at once and
said, "I have found a man among the exiles
from Judah who can tell the king what his
dream means."
26The king asked Daniel (also called Belteshazzar), "Are you able to tell me what I saw in
my dream and interpret it?"
27Daniel replied, "No wise man, enchanter,
magician or diviner can explain to the king the
mystery he has asked about, 28but there is a God
in heaven who reveals mysteries. He has shown
King Nebuchadnezzar what will happen in days
to come. Your dream and the visions that
passed through your mind as you lay on your
bed are these:
29"As you were lying there, O king, your
mind turned to things to come, and the revealer
of mysteries showed you what is going to happen. 30As for me, this mystery has been revealed
to me, not because I have greater wisdom than
other living men, but so that you, O king, may
know the interpretation and that you may understand what went through your mind.
31"You looked, O king, and there before you
stood a large statue—an enormous, dazzling
statue, awesome in appearance. 32The head of
the statue was made of pure gold, its chest and
arms of silver, its belly and thighs of bronze,
33its legs of iron, its feet partly of iron and partly
of baked clay. 34While you were watching, a
rock was cut out, but not by human hands. It
struck the statue on its feet of iron and clay and
smashed them. 35Then the iron, the clay, the
bronze, the silver and the gold were broken to
pieces at the same time and became like chaff
on a threshing floor in the summer. The wind
swept them away without leaving a trace. But
the rock that struck the statue became a huge
mountain and filled the whole earth.
36"This was the dream, and now we will interpret it to the king. 37You, O king, are the king
of kings. The God of heaven has given you dominion and power and might and glory; 38in
your hands he has placed mankind and the
beasts of the field and the birds of the air. Wherever they live, he has made you ruler over them
all. You are that head of gold.
39"After you, another kingdom will rise, infe-

2:16–23 When we are in trouble and need a model for action, we should remember Daniel. Daniel needed help, so he gathered his godly friends and prayed. Then, after their request was granted, Daniel praised God for his blessings. Praying with others is essential to our spiritual growth. It is easy to forget that God is sovereign and that we do not have to accomplish everything on our own. Thanking God when he grants our requests helps us maintain a proper focus on him.

2:26–28 Daniel wisely gave God the credit for the interpretation of the dream. Daniel could easily have told Nebuchadnezzar that *he* had interpreted the dream, thereby elevating himself above all the counselors. But Daniel acknowledged God and God's power. God works in our lives too, bringing new life where once there was pain and despair. Have we given God the credit for our spiritual growth, or have we stolen the credit for ourselves? We need to follow Daniel's example and give credit where credit is due.

2:29–45 In this vision, we see a prominent theme of the book of Daniel: God's ultimate control, even over seemingly unshakable human power. This passage provides the framework for interpreting all of the prophetic visions of Daniel, but it also tells us that God will ultimately defeat those who stand against his people. God will establish his kingdom for those who follow him.

rior to yours. Next, a third kingdom, one of bronze, will rule over the whole earth. 40Finally, there will be a fourth kingdom, strong as iron—for iron breaks and smashes everything—and as iron breaks things to pieces, so it will crush and break all the others. 41Just as you saw that the feet and toes were partly of baked clay and partly of iron, so this will be a divided kingdom; yet it will have some of the strength of iron in it, even as you saw iron mixed with clay. 42As the toes were partly iron and partly clay, so this kingdom will be partly strong and partly brittle. 43And just as you saw the iron mixed with baked clay, so the people will be a mixture and will not remain united, any more than iron mixes with clay.

44"In the time of those kings, the God of heaven will set up a kingdom that will never be destroyed, nor will it be left to another people. It will crush all those kingdoms and bring them to an end, but it will itself endure forever. 45This is the meaning of the vision of the rock cut out of a mountain, but not by human hands—a rock that broke the iron, the bronze, the clay, the silver and the gold to pieces.

"The great God has shown the king what will take place in the future. The dream is true and the interpretation is trustworthy."

46Then King Nebuchadnezzar fell prostrate before Daniel and paid him honor and ordered that an offering and incense be presented to him. 47The king said to Daniel, "Surely your God is the God of gods and the Lord of kings and a revealer of mysteries, for you were able to reveal this mystery."

48Then the king placed Daniel in a high position and lavished many gifts on him. He made him ruler over the entire province of Babylon and placed him in charge of all its wise men. 49Moreover, at Daniel's request the king appointed Shadrach, Meshach and Abednego administrators over the province of Babylon, while Daniel himself remained at the royal court.

The Image of Gold and the Fiery Furnace

3 King Nebuchadnezzar made an image of gold, ninety feet high and nine feet[a] wide, and set it up on the plain of Dura in the province of Babylon. 2He then summoned the satraps, prefects, governors, advisers, treasurers, judges, magistrates and all the other provincial officials to come to the dedication of the image he had set up. 3So the satraps, prefects, governors, advisers, treasurers, judges, magistrates and all the other provincial officials assembled for the dedication of the image that King Nebuchadnezzar had set up, and they stood before it.

4Then the herald loudly proclaimed, "This is what you are commanded to do, O peoples, nations and men of every language: 5As soon as you hear the sound of the horn, flute, zither, lyre, harp, pipes and all kinds of music, you must fall down and worship the image of gold that King Nebuchadnezzar has set up. 6Whoever does not fall down and worship will immediately be thrown into a blazing furnace."

7Therefore, as soon as they heard the sound of the horn, flute, zither, lyre, harp and all kinds of music, all the peoples, nations and men of every language fell down and worshiped the image of gold that King Nebuchadnezzar had set up.

8At this time some astrologers[b] came forward and denounced the Jews. 9They said to King Nebuchadnezzar, "O king, live forever! 10You have issued a decree, O king, that everyone who hears the sound of the horn, flute, zither, lyre, harp, pipes and all kinds of music must fall down and worship the image of gold, 11and that whoever does not fall down and worship will be thrown into a blazing furnace. 12But there are some Jews whom you have set over the affairs of the province of Babylon—Shadrach, Meshach and Abednego—who pay no attention to you, O king. They neither serve your gods nor worship the image of gold you have set up."

13Furious with rage, Nebuchadnezzar summoned Shadrach, Meshach and Abednego. So these men were brought before the king, 14and Nebuchadnezzar said to them, "Is it true, Shadrach, Meshach and Abednego, that you do not serve my gods or worship the image of gold I have set up? 15Now when you hear the sound of the horn, flute, zither, lyre, harp, pipes and all kinds of music, if you are ready to fall down and worship the image I made, very good. But if you do not worship it, you will be thrown immediately into a blazing furnace. Then what god will be able to rescue you from my hand?"

16Shadrach, Meshach and Abednego replied to the king, "O Nebuchadnezzar, we do not need to defend ourselves before you in this matter. 17If we are thrown into the blazing furnace, the God we serve is able to save us from it, and he will rescue us from your hand, O king. 18But even if he does not, we want you to know,

[a]1 Aramaic *sixty cubits high and six cubits wide* (about 27 meters high and 2.7 meters wide) [b]8 Or *Chaldeans*

3:1–30 We all face situations in which we are tempted to do things that are wrong. Sometimes there are consequences for not going along with the crowd. This fact is clearly illustrated in the story of the fiery furnace. The penalty for not following the crowd was death—a horrible death of being burned alive. When we stand for what is right and refuse to yield to peer pressure, we may suffer persecution, but we must stand firm in our faith. God will reward those who remain faithful to him.

3:16–23 Shadrach, Meshach and Abednego refused to give in to Nebuchadnezzar's threats. They risked their lives in obedience to God's will. To die was better than to live with the guilt and shame of disobeying God. Like these three friends, we must determine to stand up against those who tempt us to turn from God's plan. We must follow God—no matter what the cost.

NEBUCHADNEZZAR

Nebuchadnezzar was one of the greatest conquerors in the history of our world. He dominated the people of many nations, including Judah. Nebuchadnezzar possessed power, fame and wealth. At one point, he even considered himself to be a god. But, like so many powerful people, Nebuchadnezzar lacked the one thing he needed the most: peace. His insecurities would not allow him to be at peace with himself or with others. Nebuchadnezzar was unhappy with himself and hostile toward the people around him.

Nebuchadnezzar never truly discovered the peace that could have been found by surrendering his life to God. He did everything he could to maintain his power over others. But still peace eluded him. Daniel and his friends found success and peace through complete dependence on God and surrender to his will. After Shadrach, Meshach and Abednego walked out of the fiery furnace unscathed, Nebuchadnezzar realized that God had thwarted his plans. He also saw that the three friends, who had surrendered their lives to God, had far greater power at their disposal than he had as the mighty ruler of Babylon. Despite this recognition of God's power, however, Nebuchadnezzar's pride continued to get the best of him.

Bragging about his greatness and claiming that he alone was responsible for the great city of Babylon, Nebuchadnezzar refused to acknowledge that all power—even his kingly power—was granted by God. So God judged Nebuchadnezzar's pride by afflicting him with insanity, forcing the king from his throne. After a time, God restored Nebuchadnezzar's sanity. The king of Babylon turned to God and admitted his sin of pride, and God restored his reign as well. Yet Nebuchadnezzar had been reminded once again that he was not ultimately in control of the world.

Sadly, it seems that Nebuchadnezzar never completely understood the nature of submission to God. He watched God working in the lives of others, and in his own life. He clearly believed in God's presence and power. Yet Nebuchadnezzar's pride seemed to keep him from completely surrendering his life to God. Although he may have experienced conviction, it seems that Nebuchadnezzar never experienced spiritual conversion and transformation.

STRENGTHS AND ACCOMPLISHMENTS:

Nebuchadnezzar achieved great success and accumulated astounding wealth.

He was used by God, in spite of himself, to accomplish God's purposes.

WEAKNESSES AND MISTAKES:

Nebuchadnezzar wanted his people to worship him as if he were a god.

He failed to act on his knowledge that God was ultimately in control.

His pride kept him from submitting to God.

LESSONS FROM HIS LIFE:

Submitting to God's will is the first step toward true success.

Refusing to trust in God often results in fear.

True peace can be found only by entrusting our lives to God.

Healing comes when we admit our sin to God and look to him for help.

KEY VERSES:

"[Nebuchadnezzar] said, 'Is not this the great Babylon I have built as the royal residence, by my mighty power and for the glory of my majesty?' The words were still on his lips when a voice came from heaven, 'This is what is decreed for you, King Nebuchadnezzar: Your royal authority has been taken from you'" (4:30–31).

Nebuchadnezzar's story is told in Daniel 1—5. He is also mentioned in 2 Kings 24—25; 2 Chronicles 36; Ezra 1:7; 2:1; 5; 6:5; Nehemiah 7:6; Esther 2:6; Jeremiah 21—52; Ezekiel 26:7; 29 and 30:10.

O king, that we will not serve your gods or worship the image of gold you have set up."

19Then Nebuchadnezzar was furious with Shadrach, Meshach and Abednego, and his attitude toward them changed. He ordered the furnace heated seven times hotter than usual 20and commanded some of the strongest soldiers in his army to tie up Shadrach, Meshach and Abednego and throw them into the blazing furnace. 21So these men, wearing their robes, trousers, turbans and other clothes, were bound and thrown into the blazing furnace. 22The king's command was so urgent and the furnace so hot that the flames of the fire killed the soldiers who took up Shadrach, Meshach and Abednego, 23and these three men, firmly tied, fell into the blazing furnace.

24Then King Nebuchadnezzar leaped to his feet in amazement and asked his advisers, "Weren't there three men that we tied up and threw into the fire?"

They replied, "Certainly, O king."

25He said, "Look! I see four men walking around in the fire, unbound and unharmed, and the fourth looks like a son of the gods."

26Nebuchadnezzar then approached the opening of the blazing furnace and shouted, "Shadrach, Meshach and Abednego, servants of the Most High God, come out! Come here!"

So Shadrach, Meshach and Abednego came out of the fire, 27and the satraps, prefects, governors and royal advisers crowded around them. They saw that the fire had not harmed their bodies, nor was a hair of their heads singed; their robes were not scorched, and there was no smell of fire on them.

28Then Nebuchadnezzar said, "Praise be to the God of Shadrach, Meshach and Abednego, who has sent his angel and rescued his servants! They trusted in him and defied the king's command and were willing to give up their lives rather than serve or worship any god except their own God. 29Therefore I decree that the people of any nation or language who say anything against the God of Shadrach, Meshach and Abednego be cut into pieces and their houses be turned into piles of rubble, for no other god can save in this way."

30Then the king promoted Shadrach, Meshach and Abednego in the province of Babylon.

Nebuchadnezzar's Dream of a Tree

4 King Nebuchadnezzar,

To the peoples, nations and men of every language, who live in all the world:

May you prosper greatly!

2It is my pleasure to tell you about the miraculous signs and wonders that the Most High God has performed for me.

3How great are his signs,
how mighty his wonders!
His kingdom is an eternal kingdom;
his dominion endures from
generation to generation.

4I, Nebuchadnezzar, was at home in my palace, contented and prosperous. 5I had a dream that made me afraid. As I was lying in my bed, the images and visions that passed through my mind terrified me. 6So I commanded that all the wise men of Babylon be brought before me to interpret the dream for me. 7When the magicians, enchanters, astrologers[a] and diviners came, I told them the dream, but they could not interpret it for me. 8Finally, Daniel came into my presence and I told him the dream. (He is called Belteshazzar, after the name of my god, and the spirit of the holy gods is in him.)

9I said, "Belteshazzar, chief of the magicians, I know that the spirit of the holy gods is in you, and no mystery is too difficult for you. Here is my dream; interpret it for me. 10These are the visions I saw while lying in my bed: I looked, and there before me stood a tree in the middle of the land. Its height was enormous. 11The tree grew large and strong and its top touched the sky; it was visible to the ends of the earth. 12Its leaves were beautiful, its fruit abundant, and on it was food for all. Under it the beasts of the field found shelter, and the birds of the air lived in its branches; from it every creature was fed.

13"In the visions I saw while lying in my bed, I looked, and there before me was a messenger,[b] a holy one, coming down from heaven. 14He called in a loud voice: 'Cut down the tree and trim off its branches; strip off its leaves and scatter its fruit. Let the animals flee from under it and the birds from its branches. 15But let the stump and its roots, bound with iron and bronze, remain in the ground, in the grass of the field.

" 'Let him be drenched with the dew of heaven, and let him live with the animals among the plants of the earth. 16Let his mind be changed from that of a man and let him be given the mind of an animal, till seven times[c] pass by for him.

17" 'The decision is announced by mes-

[a]7 Or *Chaldeans* [b]13 Or *watchman;* also in verses 17 and 23 [c]16 Or *years;* also in verses 23, 25 and 32

3:24–30 Nebuchadnezzar was amazed at what he saw and immediately worshiped the God of Shadrach, Meshach and Abednego. If these young men had not stood up to Nebuchadnezzar, he never would have seen the great power of God. The best way we can tell others about God is to demonstrate his power in our lives. Seeing God at work in our lives will encourage them to seek him and surrender their lives to him.

sengers, the holy ones declare the verdict, so that the living may know that the Most High is sovereign over the kingdoms of men and gives them to anyone he wishes and sets over them the lowliest of men.'

18"This is the dream that I, King Nebuchadnezzar, had. Now, Belteshazzar, tell me what it means, for none of the wise men in my kingdom can interpret it for me. But you can, because the spirit of the holy gods is in you."

Daniel Interprets the Dream

19Then Daniel (also called Belteshazzar) was greatly perplexed for a time, and his thoughts terrified him. So the king said, "Belteshazzar, do not let the dream or its meaning alarm you."

Belteshazzar answered, "My lord, if only the dream applied to your enemies and its meaning to your adversaries! 20The tree you saw, which grew large and strong, with its top touching the sky, visible to the whole earth, 21with beautiful leaves and abundant fruit, providing food for all, giving shelter to the beasts of the field, and having nesting places in its branches for the birds of the air— 22you, O king, are that tree! You have become great and strong; your greatness has grown until it reaches the sky, and your dominion extends to distant parts of the earth.

23"You, O king, saw a messenger, a holy one, coming down from heaven and saying, 'Cut down the tree and destroy it, but leave the stump, bound with iron and bronze, in the grass of the field, while its roots remain in the ground. Let him be drenched with the dew of heaven; let him live like the wild animals, until seven times pass by for him.'

24"This is the interpretation, O king, and this is the decree the Most High has issued against my lord the king: 25You will be driven away from people and will live with the wild animals; you will eat grass like cattle and be drenched with the dew of heaven. Seven times will pass by for you until you acknowledge that the Most High is sovereign over the kingdoms of men and gives them to anyone he wishes. 26The command to leave the stump of the tree with its roots means that your kingdom will be restored to you when you acknowledge that Heaven rules. 27Therefore, O king, be pleased to accept my advice: Renounce your sins by doing what is right, and your wickedness by being kind to the oppressed. It may be that then your prosperity will continue."

The Dream Is Fulfilled

28All this happened to King Nebuchadnezzar. 29Twelve months later, as the king was walking on the roof of the royal palace of Babylon, 30he said, "Is not this the great Babylon I have built as the royal residence, by my mighty power and for the glory of my majesty?"

31The words were still on his lips when a voice came from heaven, "This is what is decreed for you, King Nebuchadnezzar: Your royal authority has been taken from you. 32You will be driven away from people and will live with the wild animals; you will eat grass like cattle. Seven times will pass by for you until you acknowledge that the Most High is sovereign over the kingdoms of men and gives them to anyone he wishes."

33Immediately what had been said about Nebuchadnezzar was fulfilled. He was driven away from people and ate grass like cattle. His body was drenched with the dew of heaven until his hair grew like the feathers of an eagle and his nails like the claws of a bird.

34At the end of that time, I, Nebuchadnezzar, raised my eyes toward heaven, and my sanity was restored. Then I praised the Most High; I honored and glorified him who lives forever.

His dominion is an eternal dominion;
 his kingdom endures from generation to generation.
35All the peoples of the earth
 are regarded as nothing.
He does as he pleases
 with the powers of heaven
 and the peoples of the earth.
No one can hold back his hand
 or say to him: "What have you done?"

36At the same time that my sanity was restored, my honor and splendor were returned to me for the glory of my kingdom. My advisers and nobles sought me out, and I was restored to my throne and became even greater than before. 37Now I, Nebuchadnezzar, praise and exalt and glo-

4:18–27 Daniel (Belteshazzar) interpreted Nebuchadnezzar's dream because of the wisdom given to him by God's Spirit (4:18). The king's tragic breakdown would soon take place unless he made some drastic changes in his life. We also may be heading for a humbling experience if we continue to think we are in control of our lives. Our spiritual growth is dependent upon our trust in God and our obedience to his will for our lives.

4:28–37 Even after Daniel's warning, Nebuchadnezzar did not change his lifestyle or give God the credit for his power. His arrogance resulted in seven years of humiliating insanity. But God restored Nebuchadnezzar to the throne when he finally turned toward heaven for deliverance. Notice that the king praised and honored God; Nebuchadnezzar didn't curse God for his many years of madness. When we experience painful setbacks, we need to consider what we can learn from our trials and how we can honor God in them.

rify the King of heaven, because everything he does is right and all his ways are
just. And those who walk in pride he is
able to humble.

The Writing on the Wall

5 King Belshazzar gave a great banquet for
a thousand of his nobles and drank wine
with them. 2While Belshazzar was drinking his
wine, he gave orders to bring in the gold and
silver goblets that Nebuchadnezzar his father[a]
had taken from the temple in Jerusalem, so that
the king and his nobles, his wives and his concubines might drink from them. 3So they
brought in the gold goblets that had been taken
from the temple of God in Jerusalem, and the
king and his nobles, his wives and his concubines drank from them. 4As they drank the
wine, they praised the gods of gold and silver,
of bronze, iron, wood and stone.

5Suddenly the fingers of a human hand appeared and wrote on the plaster of the wall,
near the lampstand in the royal palace. The king
watched the hand as it wrote. 6His face turned
pale and he was so frightened that his knees
knocked together and his legs gave way.

7The king called out for the enchanters, astrologers[b] and diviners to be brought and said
to these wise men of Babylon, "Whoever reads
this writing and tells me what it means will be
clothed in purple and have a gold chain placed
around his neck, and he will be made the third
highest ruler in the kingdom."

8Then all the king's wise men came in, but
they could not read the writing or tell the king
what it meant. 9So King Belshazzar became
even more terrified and his face grew more pale.
His nobles were baffled.

10The queen,[c] hearing the voices of the king
and his nobles, came into the banquet hall.
"O king, live forever!" she said. "Don't be
alarmed! Don't look so pale! 11There is a man
in your kingdom who has the spirit of the holy
gods in him. In the time of your father he was
found to have insight and intelligence and wisdom like that of the gods. King Nebuchadnezzar your father—your father the king, I say—appointed him chief of the magicians, enchanters,
astrologers and diviners. 12This man Daniel,
whom the king called Belteshazzar, was found
to have a keen mind and knowledge and understanding, and also the ability to interpret
dreams, explain riddles and solve difficult problems. Call for Daniel, and he will tell you what
the writing means."

13So Daniel was brought before the king, and
the king said to him, "Are you Daniel, one of
the exiles my father the king brought from Judah? 14I have heard that the spirit of the gods is
in you and that you have insight, intelligence
and outstanding wisdom. 15The wise men and
enchanters were brought before me to read this
writing and tell me what it means, but they
could not explain it. 16Now I have heard that
you are able to give interpretations and to solve
difficult problems. If you can read this writing
and tell me what it means, you will be clothed
in purple and have a gold chain placed around
your neck, and you will be made the third highest ruler in the kingdom."

17Then Daniel answered the king, "You may
keep your gifts for yourself and give your rewards to someone else. Nevertheless, I will read
the writing for the king and tell him what it
means.

18"O king, the Most High God gave your father Nebuchadnezzar sovereignty and greatness
and glory and splendor. 19Because of the high
position he gave him, all the peoples and nations and men of every language dreaded and
feared him. Those the king wanted to put to
death, he put to death; those he wanted to
spare, he spared; those he wanted to promote,
he promoted; and those he wanted to humble,
he humbled. 20But when his heart became arrogant and hardened with pride, he was deposed
from his royal throne and stripped of his glory.
21He was driven away from people and given
the mind of an animal; he lived with the wild
donkeys and ate grass like cattle; and his body
was drenched with the dew of heaven, until he
acknowledged that the Most High God is sovereign over the kingdoms of men and sets over
them anyone he wishes.

22"But you his son,[d] O Belshazzar, have
not humbled yourself, though you knew all
this. 23Instead, you have set yourself up against
the Lord of heaven. You had the goblets from
his temple brought to you, and you and your
nobles, your wives and your concubines drank
wine from them. You praised the gods of silver
and gold, of bronze, iron, wood and stone,
which cannot see or hear or understand. But
you did not honor the God who holds in his
hand your life and all your ways. 24Therefore he
sent the hand that wrote the inscription.

25"This is the inscription that was written:

MENE, MENE, TEKEL, PARSIN[e]

26"This is what these words mean:

Mene[f]: God has numbered the days
of your reign and brought it to
an end.

[a]2 Or *ancestor;* or *predecessor;* also in verses 11, 13 and 18
[b]7 Or *Chaldeans;* also in verse 11
[c]10 Or *queen mother*
[d]22 Or *descendant;* or *successor*
[e]25 Aramaic *UPARSIN* (that is, *AND PARSIN*)
[f]26 *Mene* can mean *numbered* or *mina* (a unit of money).

5:18–31 Belshazzar did not learn from the experiences of his ancestor Nebuchadnezzar. Now his time had run out. He, too, would reap the consequences of his pride and arrogance: He would die before the night was over. It is a sad thing when someone reaps the consequences of their sin. We must make certain that we repent and seek forgiveness so that we will not encounter Belshazzar's sad fate.

27*Tekel*[a]: You have been weighed on
the scales and found wanting.
28*Peres*[b]: Your kingdom is divided
and given to the Medes and
Persians."

29Then at Belshazzar's command, Daniel was
clothed in purple, a gold chain was placed
around his neck, and he was proclaimed the
third highest ruler in the kingdom.
30That very night Belshazzar, king of the Babylonians,[c] was slain, 31and Darius the Mede
took over the kingdom, at the age of sixty-two.

Daniel in the Den of Lions

6 It pleased Darius to appoint 120 satraps to
rule throughout the kingdom, 2with three
administrators over them, one of whom was
Daniel. The satraps were made accountable to
them so that the king might not suffer loss.
3Now Daniel so distinguished himself among
the administrators and the satraps by his excep-
tional qualities that the king planned to set him
over the whole kingdom. 4At this, the administrators and the satraps tried to find grounds for
charges against Daniel in his conduct of government affairs, but they were unable to do so.
They could find no corruption in him, because
he was trustworthy and neither corrupt nor negligent. 5Finally these men said, "We will never
find any basis for charges against this man Daniel unless it has something to do with the law
of his God."
6So the administrators and the satraps went
as a group to the king and said: "O King Darius,
live forever! 7The royal administrators, prefects,
satraps, advisers and governors have all agreed
that the king should issue an edict and enforce
the decree that anyone who prays to any god or
man during the next thirty days, except to you,
O king, shall be thrown into the lions' den.
8Now, O king, issue the decree and put it in
writing so that it cannot be altered—in accordance with the laws of the Medes and Persians,
which cannot be repealed." 9So King Darius put
the decree in writing.
10Now when Daniel learned that the decree
had been published, he went home to his upstairs room where the windows opened toward
Jerusalem. Three times a day he got down on his
knees and prayed, giving thanks to his God, just
as he had done before. 11Then these men went
as a group and found Daniel praying and asking
God for help. 12So they went to the king and
spoke to him about his royal decree: "Did you
not publish a decree that during the next thirty
days anyone who prays to any god or man except to you, O king, would be thrown into the
lions' den?"
The king answered, "The decree stands—in
accordance with the laws of the Medes and Persians, which cannot be repealed."
13Then they said to the king, "Daniel, who is
one of the exiles from Judah, pays no attention
to you, O king, or to the decree you put in
writing. He still prays three times a day." 14When
the king heard this, he was greatly distressed; he
was determined to rescue Daniel and made every effort until sundown to save him.
15Then the men went as a group to the king
and said to him, "Remember, O king, that according to the law of the Medes and Persians
no decree or edict that the king issues can be
changed."
16So the king gave the order, and they
brought Daniel and threw him into the lions'
den. The king said to Daniel, "May your God,
whom you serve continually, rescue you!"
17A stone was brought and placed over the
mouth of the den, and the king sealed it with
his own signet ring and with the rings of his
nobles, so that Daniel's situation might not be
changed. 18Then the king returned to his palace
and spent the night without eating and without
any entertainment being brought to him. And
he could not sleep.
19At the first light of dawn, the king got up
and hurried to the lions' den. 20When he came
near the den, he called to Daniel in an anguished voice, "Daniel, servant of the living
God, has your God, whom you serve continually, been able to rescue you from the lions?"
21Daniel answered, "O king, live forever!
22My God sent his angel, and he shut the

[a]27 *Tekel* can mean *weighed* or *shekel*. [b]28 *Peres* (the singular of *Parsin*) can mean *divided* or *Persia* or *a half mina* or *a half shekel*. [c]30 Or *Chaldeans*

6:1–4 Spirituality doesn't guarantee popularity or acceptance by those around us. Spiritual strength and wholeness, especially if matched with natural ability, can be quite intimidating to others who lack true spirituality. There will always be those who are threatened by our spiritual progress. They may even try to impede our growth. Nevertheless, we must set our minds and hearts to follow God and depend on his strength so that we will not be swayed by their intimidation.

6:6–10 Daniel chose to ignore the manipulation of his rivals and continued to worship the God who had cared for Daniel throughout his life. Though prayer may not earn the death penalty for most of us, there are other drawbacks to following God. We can be ridiculed or discriminated against by people who feel threatened by our faith. No matter what conflicts we face, however, God is still worthy of our trust. We must remain true to him despite opposition.

6:11–17 We must always consider how our actions will affect others. The king satisfied his ego but failed to realize that this new law would put his close advisor, Daniel, in a dangerous position. Before making decisions of major significance we must ask ourselves several questions. Will anyone be hurt by our decision? Is what we are about to do morally wrong? Will we regret the outcome? If any of these questions can be answered in the positive, we need to consider another plan of action.

6:19–23 God rescued Daniel from what seemed to be a sure death. The lions didn't harm Daniel, just as the fire hadn't touched Shadrach, Meshach and Abednego (see 3:1–30). Clearly, God watches over those who obey his will. He alone can deliver us. Even when we face situations with no apparent hope of escape, we need to continue to trust God. He is still able to deliver us.

THE SPIRITUAL DISCIPLINES

In the Life of Daniel

We sometimes tend to view spiritual renewal as being dependent upon external circumstances: When conditions are favorable, spiritual growth goes forward. When difficulties arise, spiritual growth stagnates. Daniel, however, maintained spiritual vitality in the midst of a world that was often hostile to his faith. No doubt a key factor to Daniel's healthy faith was his regular practice of the spiritual disciplines.

When he was a young man, Daniel was exiled over nine hundred miles from his home in Jerusalem to Babylon, the capital city of the Babylonian empire. The Babylonians worshiped a multitude of gods and even considered their king to be a god. Though living in this place of spiritual darkness, Daniel and his friends remained true to their faith. Even though they were exiled from their homeland, they were not cut off from God's presence. In fact, in this strange land they discovered a deeper sense of God's closeness. Daniel strengthened his faith during this time by practicing at least six spiritual disciplines on a regular basis.

FASTING. When he arrived in Babylon, Daniel refused to eat the rich foods of the king's table and requested a simple diet of vegetables and water (Daniel 1:12). While this was not a complete fast, Daniel restricted his food intake in order to maintain his spiritual focus. Later, he even fasted while interceding for the restoration of Jerusalem (9:3). In Daniel 10:3 we read again of a partial fast from rich food, meat, wine and the use of fragrant oils over a three-week period of mourning following a vision of coming war and hardship. (To learn more about fasting, turn to 2 Chronicles 20.)

PRAYER. Daniel prayed three times a day (Daniel 6:10), presumably upon waking in the morning, at midday and before retiring at night. He also prayed when called upon to interpret dreams for the king (2:18). Daniel's wisdom and education were no substitute for his vital fellowship with God in prayer. (To learn more about prayer, turn to Genesis 18.)

WORSHIP. We know little about Daniel's specific worship practices. The Israelites in exile had to adjust to the lack of a temple or place of meeting and the prohibition of sacrifices in Babylon. Nevertheless, we see evidences of Daniel's worship and thanksgiving when God revealed to him the answers to dreams (Daniel 2:19–23). (To learn more about worship, turn to Exodus 20.)

BIBLE STUDY. The study of the Scriptures also undergirded Daniel's life. His insistence on a strict dietary code shows that he was familiar with the laws of purity, such as those in Leviticus. Daniel 9:2 records that Daniel studied the writings of the prophets, especially Jeremiah, his contemporary, who had remained in Jerusalem. (To learn more about Bible study, turn to Deuteronomy 17.)

REPENTANCE AND CONFESSION. Repentance and confession also characterized Daniel's life, as evidenced by his prayer in chapter 9. In this prayer he identified not only with his own sin but also with the sin of his people. (To learn more about repentance and confession, turn to Exodus 20.)

SERVICE. Daniel also practiced the spiritual discipline of service, regarding his work as the king's political adviser as a ministry from the Lord. Daniel never compromised his beliefs, and his faith was evidenced in his work on countless occasions. Daniel shows us that faithful believers can thrive in the midst of difficult work environments. Their lives can shine as testimonies to their faith in God. (To learn more about service, turn to Mark 10.)

Lessons for Life

The root concept of holiness is that of being "set apart" from the world. Daniel's spiritual disciplines set him apart as God's person from the very beginning of his time in Babylon. The Babylonians constantly tried to assimilate God's people into their culture, even changing their Hebrew names to Babylonian ones. Despite these efforts, Daniel's spiritual disciplines helped him retain his true identity as a follower of the one true God and kept him from compromising his faith.

Daniel's spiritual exercises also helped him look to God for strength when all other supports were stripped away from him. In the king's court, Daniel lacked a favorable consensus about right and wrong. Instead, Daniel drew his strength and support directly from God. We, too, can use these spiritual disciplines to help us draw strength from God whenever we face opposition.

mouths of the lions. They have not hurt me, because I was found innocent in his sight. Nor have I ever done any wrong before you, O king."
23The king was overjoyed and gave orders to lift Daniel out of the den. And when Daniel was lifted from the den, no wound was found on him, because he had trusted in his God.
24At the king's command, the men who had falsely accused Daniel were brought in and thrown into the lions' den, along with their wives and children. And before they reached the floor of the den, the lions overpowered them and crushed all their bones.
25Then King Darius wrote to all the peoples, nations and men of every language throughout the land:

"May you prosper greatly!

26"I issue a decree that in every part of my kingdom people must fear and reverence the God of Daniel.

"For he is the living God
and he endures forever;
his kingdom will not be destroyed,
his dominion will never end.
27He rescues and he saves;
he performs signs and wonders
in the heavens and on the earth.
He has rescued Daniel
from the power of the lions."

28So Daniel prospered during the reign of Darius and the reign of Cyrus[a] the Persian.

Daniel's Dream of Four Beasts

7 In the first year of Belshazzar king of Babylon, Daniel had a dream, and visions passed through his mind as he was lying on his bed. He wrote down the substance of his dream.
2Daniel said: "In my vision at night I looked, and there before me were the four winds of heaven churning up the great sea. 3Four great beasts, each different from the others, came up out of the sea.
4"The first was like a lion, and it had the wings of an eagle. I watched until its wings were torn off and it was lifted from the ground so that it stood on two feet like a man, and the heart of a man was given to it.
5"And there before me was a second beast, which looked like a bear. It was raised up on one of its sides, and it had three ribs in its mouth between its teeth. It was told, 'Get up and eat your fill of flesh!'
6"After that, I looked, and there before me was another beast, one that looked like a leopard. And on its back it had four wings like those of a bird. This beast had four heads, and it was given authority to rule.
7"After that, in my vision at night I looked, and there before me was a fourth beast—terrifying and frightening and very powerful. It had large iron teeth; it crushed and devoured its victims and trampled underfoot whatever was left. It was different from all the former beasts, and it had ten horns.
8"While I was thinking about the horns, there before me was another horn, a little one, which came up among them; and three of the first horns were uprooted before it. This horn had eyes like the eyes of a man and a mouth that spoke boastfully.
9"As I looked,

"thrones were set in place,
and the Ancient of Days took his seat.
His clothing was as white as snow;
the hair of his head was white like wool.
His throne was flaming with fire,
and its wheels were all ablaze.
10A river of fire was flowing,
coming out from before him.
Thousands upon thousands attended him;
ten thousand times ten thousand stood
before him.
The court was seated,
and the books were opened.

11"Then I continued to watch because of the boastful words the horn was speaking. I kept looking until the beast was slain and its body destroyed and thrown into the blazing fire.
12(The other beasts had been stripped of their authority, but were allowed to live for a period of time.)
13"In my vision at night I looked, and there before me was one like a son of man, coming with the clouds of heaven. He approached the Ancient of Days and was led into his presence.
14He was given authority, glory and sovereign power; all peoples, nations and men of every language worshiped him. His dominion is an everlasting dominion that will not pass away, and his kingdom is one that will never be destroyed.

The Interpretation of the Dream

15"I, Daniel, was troubled in spirit, and the visions that passed through my mind disturbed me. 16I approached one of those standing there and asked him the true meaning of all this.
"So he told me and gave me the interpretation of these things: 17'The four great beasts are four kingdoms that will rise from the earth.
18But the saints of the Most High will receive the

[a]28 Or *Darius, that is, the reign of Cyrus*

6:25–27 When God is at work in our lives, not only will we reap the benefits of his grace—so will others. Darius recognized the awesome power of Daniel's God and was freed from the guilt he felt for sentencing Daniel to death. As we patiently endure our sufferings, we may find that God uses situations to reach others. Those who mistreat or persecute us, whether or not they mean to, need God as much as we do. When God reveals himself to them through us, their lives can change, and they can share their own experiences of God's power with others.

kingdom and will possess it forever—yes, for ever and ever.'

19"Then I wanted to know the true meaning of the fourth beast, which was different from all the others and most terrifying, with its iron teeth and bronze claws—the beast that crushed and devoured its victims and trampled underfoot whatever was left. 20I also wanted to know about the ten horns on its head and about the other horn that came up, before which three of them fell—the horn that looked more imposing than the others and that had eyes and a mouth that spoke boastfully. 21As I watched, this horn was waging war against the saints and defeating them, 22until the Ancient of Days came and pronounced judgment in favor of the saints of the Most High, and the time came when they possessed the kingdom.

23"He gave me this explanation: 'The fourth beast is a fourth kingdom that will appear on earth. It will be different from all the other kingdoms and will devour the whole earth, trampling it down and crushing it. 24The ten horns are ten kings who will come from this kingdom. After them another king will arise, different from the earlier ones; he will subdue three kings. 25He will speak against the Most High and oppress his saints and try to change the set times and the laws. The saints will be handed over to him for a time, times and half a time.[a]

26" 'But the court will sit, and his power will be taken away and completely destroyed forever. 27Then the sovereignty, power and greatness of the kingdoms under the whole heaven will be handed over to the saints, the people of the Most High. His kingdom will be an everlasting kingdom, and all rulers will worship and obey him.'

28"This is the end of the matter. I, Daniel, was deeply troubled by my thoughts, and my face turned pale, but I kept the matter to myself."

Daniel's Vision of a Ram and a Goat

8 In the third year of King Belshazzar's reign, I, Daniel, had a vision, after the one that had already appeared to me. 2In my vision I saw myself in the citadel of Susa in the province of Elam; in the vision I was beside the Ulai Canal. 3I looked up, and there before me was a ram with two horns, standing beside the canal, and the horns were long. One of the horns was longer than the other but grew up later. 4I watched the ram as he charged toward the west and the north and the south. No animal could stand against him, and none could rescue from his power. He did as he pleased and became great.

5As I was thinking about this, suddenly a goat with a prominent horn between his eyes came from the west, crossing the whole earth without touching the ground. 6He came toward the two-horned ram I had seen standing beside the canal and charged at him in great rage. 7I saw him attack the ram furiously, striking the ram and shattering his two horns. The ram was powerless to stand against him; the goat knocked him to the ground and trampled on him, and none could rescue the ram from his power. 8The goat became very great, but at the height of his power his large horn was broken off, and in its place four prominent horns grew up toward the four winds of heaven.

9Out of one of them came another horn, which started small but grew in power to the south and to the east and toward the Beautiful Land. 10It grew until it reached the host of the heavens, and it threw some of the starry host down to the earth and trampled on them. 11It set itself up to be as great as the Prince of the host; it took away the daily sacrifice from him, and the place of his sanctuary was brought low. 12Because of rebellion, the host ⌞of the saints⌟[b] and the daily sacrifice were given over to it. It prospered in everything it did, and truth was thrown to the ground.

13Then I heard a holy one speaking, and another holy one said to him, "How long will it take for the vision to be fulfilled—the vision concerning the daily sacrifice, the rebellion that causes desolation, and the surrender of the sanctuary and of the host that will be trampled underfoot?"

14He said to me, "It will take 2,300 evenings and mornings; then the sanctuary will be reconsecrated."

The Interpretation of the Vision

15While I, Daniel, was watching the vision and trying to understand it, there before me stood one who looked like a man. 16And I heard a man's voice from the Ulai calling, "Gabriel, tell this man the meaning of the vision."

17As he came near the place where I was standing, I was terrified and fell prostrate. "Son of man," he said to me, "understand that the vision concerns the time of the end."

18While he was speaking to me, I was in a

[a] 25 Or *for a year, two years and half a year* [b] 12 Or *rebellion, the armies*

8:5–8, 21 One of the figures in this vision of the future is Alexander the Great, the "first king" of Greece (8:21). We can see from this passage that while oppressors may seem to be invincible and possess great power, God is ultimately in control of their fate. All who are in authority have been allowed by God to rise to power (see Romans 13:1). When God deems the time is right, he will cause such rulers to stand or fall.

8:9–14, 25 This prophetic description of the reign of an evil leader carries with it an important point. This leader was allowed to practice his atrocities only for a period of time. The days of his domination were numbered, and true temple worship would begin again (8:14, 25). Likewise, God sees the mistreatment we suffer. He has set a limit on the amount of pain we will have to endure. Whenever we suffer, we can pray to God for comfort, guidance and help to persevere through our anguish until he delivers us.

deep sleep, with my face to the ground. Then he
touched me and raised me to my feet.
19He said: "I am going to tell you what will
happen later in the time of wrath, because the
vision concerns the appointed time of the
end.[a] 20The two-horned ram that you saw represents the kings of Media and Persia. 21The
shaggy goat is the king of Greece, and the large
horn between his eyes is the first king. 22The
four horns that replaced the one that was broken off represent four kingdoms that will
emerge from his nation but will not have the
same power.
23"In the latter part of their reign, when
rebels have become completely wicked, a stern-
faced king, a master of intrigue, will arise. 24He
will become very strong, but not by his own
power. He will cause astounding devastation
and will succeed in whatever he does. He will
destroy the mighty men and the holy people.
25He will cause deceit to prosper, and he will
consider himself superior. When they feel secure, he will destroy many and take his stand
against the Prince of princes. Yet he will be destroyed, but not by human power.
26"The vision of the evenings and mornings
that has been given you is true, but seal up the
vision, for it concerns the distant future."
27I, Daniel, was exhausted and lay ill for several days. Then I got up and went about the
king's business. I was appalled by the vision; it
was beyond understanding.

Daniel's Prayer

9 In the first year of Darius son of Xerxes[b]
(a Mede by descent), who was made ruler
over the Babylonian[c] kingdom— 2in the first
year of his reign, I, Daniel, understood from the
Scriptures, according to the word of the LORD
given to Jeremiah the prophet, that the desolation of Jerusalem would last seventy years. 3So
I turned to the Lord God and pleaded with him
in prayer and petition, in fasting, and in sackcloth and ashes.
4I prayed to the LORD my God and confessed:

"O Lord, the great and awesome God,
who keeps his covenant of love with all
who love him and obey his commands,
5we have sinned and done wrong. We
have been wicked and have rebelled; we
have turned away from your commands
and laws. 6We have not listened to your
servants the prophets, who spoke in your
name to our kings, our princes and our
fathers, and to all the people of the land.
7"Lord, you are righteous, but this day
we are covered with shame—the men of
Judah and people of Jerusalem and all Israel, both near and far, in all the countries
where you have scattered us because of
our unfaithfulness to you. 8O LORD, we
and our kings, our princes and our fathers
are covered with shame because we have
sinned against you. 9The Lord our God is
merciful and forgiving, even though we
have rebelled against him; 10we have not
obeyed the LORD our God or kept the laws
he gave us through his servants the prophets. 11All Israel has transgressed your law
and turned away, refusing to obey you.
"Therefore the curses and sworn judgments written in the Law of Moses, the
servant of God, have been poured out on
us, because we have sinned against you.
12You have fulfilled the words spoken
against us and against our rulers by bringing upon us great disaster. Under the
whole heaven nothing has ever been done
like what has been done to Jerusalem.
13Just as it is written in the Law of Moses,
all this disaster has come upon us, yet we
have not sought the favor of the LORD our
God by turning from our sins and giving
attention to your truth. 14The LORD did
not hesitate to bring the disaster upon us,
for the LORD our God is righteous in everything he does; yet we have not obeyed
him.
15"Now, O Lord our God, who
brought your people out of Egypt with a
mighty hand and who made for yourself a
name that endures to this day, we have
sinned, we have done wrong. 16O Lord, in
keeping with all your righteous acts, turn
away your anger and your wrath from
Jerusalem, your city, your holy hill. Our

[a] 19 Or *because the end will be at the appointed time*
[b] 1 Hebrew *Ahasuerus* [c] 1 Or *Chaldean*

9:1–3 Daniel and his friends suffered as a consequence of the sins of others. Because of his nation's sins, Daniel and other "innocent bystanders" were forced into captivity. Often we, too, suffer from the injustices of others. When this happens, we would do well to follow Daniel's example and not waste time or energy merely blaming others and complaining about the injustice. We should confess our sins and the sins of those who have caused our injustice and ask God for comfort and deliverance.

9:7–9 Everyone is guilty of sinning against God, and we all need redemption from sin's eternal consequence—death (see Romans 6:23). Daniel admitted his sins, asked for God's mercy and surrendered his life to God. We need to do the same thing with the sins that entangle us. Twenty-five centuries have not changed the way God works in people's lives.

9:10–14 Refusing to see the truth about our own sins blinds us to the dangers about us. Daniel recognized that the people of Israel had suffered the consequences that God had promised to send for their disobedience. Yet, despite their suffering, the people still wouldn't obey God. If the Israelites had been spiritually honest, they would have seen their mistakes and could have corrected the situation and avoided much of their severe punishment. We must be careful to recognize the truth that we are sinful, or a dangerous spiritual blindness can result. We need to be honest with ourselves and God and ask him to forgive our sins.

sins and the iniquities of our fathers have
made Jerusalem and your people an object of scorn to all those around us.
17"Now, our God, hear the prayers and
petitions of your servant. For your sake,
O Lord, look with favor on your desolate
sanctuary. 18Give ear, O God, and hear;
open your eyes and see the desolation of
the city that bears your Name. We do not
make requests of you because we are righteous, but because of your great mercy.
19O Lord, listen! O Lord, forgive! O Lord,
hear and act! For your sake, O my God, do
not delay, because your city and your people bear your Name."

The Seventy "Sevens"

20While I was speaking and praying, confessing my sin and the sin of my people Israel and
making my request to the LORD my God for his
holy hill— 21while I was still in prayer, Gabriel,
the man I had seen in the earlier vision, came
to me in swift flight about the time of the evening sacrifice. 22He instructed me and said to
me, "Daniel, I have now come to give you insight and understanding. 23As soon as you began to pray, an answer was given, which I have
come to tell you, for you are highly esteemed.
Therefore, consider the message and understand the vision:
24"Seventy 'sevens'[a] are decreed for your
people and your holy city to finish[b] transgression, to put an end to sin, to atone for wickedness, to bring in everlasting righteousness, to
seal up vision and prophecy and to anoint the
most holy.[c]
25"Know and understand this: From the issu-
ing of the decree[d] to restore and rebuild Jerusalem until the Anointed One,[e] the ruler, comes,
there will be seven 'sevens,' and sixty-two 'sevens.' It will be rebuilt with streets and a trench,
but in times of trouble. 26After the sixty-two
'sevens,' the Anointed One will be cut off and
will have nothing.[f] The people of the ruler
who will come will destroy the city and the
sanctuary. The end will come like a flood: War
will continue until the end, and desolations
have been decreed. 27He will confirm a covenant with many for one 'seven.'[g] In the middle of the 'seven'[g] he will put an end to sacrifice and offering. And on a wing ⌊of the temple⌋
he will set up an abomination that causes desolation, until the end that is decreed is poured
out on him.[h]"[i]

Daniel's Vision of a Man

10 In the third year of Cyrus king of Persia,
a revelation was given to Daniel (who
was called Belteshazzar). Its message was true
and it concerned a great war.[j] The understanding of the message came to him in a vision.
2At that time I, Daniel, mourned for three
weeks. 3I ate no choice food; no meat or wine
touched my lips; and I used no lotions at all
until the three weeks were over.
4On the twenty-fourth day of the first
month, as I was standing on the bank of the
great river, the Tigris, 5I looked up and there
before me was a man dressed in linen, with a
belt of the finest gold around his waist. 6His
body was like chrysolite, his face like lightning,
his eyes like flaming torches, his arms and legs
like the gleam of burnished bronze, and his
voice like the sound of a multitude.
7I, Daniel, was the only one who saw the
vision; the men with me did not see it, but such
terror overwhelmed them that they fled and hid
themselves. 8So I was left alone, gazing at this
great vision; I had no strength left, my face
turned deathly pale and I was helpless. 9Then I
heard him speaking, and as I listened to him, I
fell into a deep sleep, my face to the ground.
10A hand touched me and set me trembling
on my hands and knees. 11He said, "Daniel,
you who are highly esteemed, consider carefully
the words I am about to speak to you, and stand
up, for I have now been sent to you." And when
he said this to me, I stood up trembling.
12Then he continued, "Do not be afraid,
Daniel. Since the first day that you set your
mind to gain understanding and to humble
yourself before your God, your words were
heard, and I have come in response to them.
13But the prince of the Persian kingdom resisted
me twenty-one days. Then Michael, one of the
chief princes, came to help me, because I was
detained there with the king of Persia. 14Now I
have come to explain to you what will happen
to your people in the future, for the vision concerns a time yet to come."
15While he was saying this to me, I bowed
with my face toward the ground and was
speechless. 16Then one who looked like a

[a]24 Or *'weeks'*; also in verses 25 and 26 [b]24 Or *restrain* [c]24 Or *Most Holy Place*; or *most holy One* [d]25 Or *word* [e]25 Or *an anointed one*; also in verse 26 [f]26 Or *off and will have no one*; or *off, but not for himself* [g]27 Or *'week'* [h]27 Or *it* [i]27 Or *And one who causes desolation will come upon the pinnacle of the abominable ⌊temple⌋, until the end that is decreed is poured out on the desolated ⌊city⌋* [j]1 Or *true and burdensome*

9:20–27 Though Daniel was worried about his people and nation, God had a plan for their restoration. There would be many years of pain ahead, but God's time to judge their enemies would come. God hasn't abandoned us in our hour of need either. He is with us, waiting to work his plan for our lives. We need to follow God and trust his timing for our complete redemption.

10:11, 18 God twice assured Daniel of his great, personal love. God also loves each one of us. When we realize that the Creator of the universe finds value in us, we begin to understand that our identity isn't wrapped up in our jobs, possessions or power. If we truly believe this, we no longer need to gain our sense of worth from what we do or what we have, but we can begin to feel good about ourselves because God loves us.

Keeping a Partial Fast

Daniel 10:3 Fasting can be an effective means to keep us from being swallowed up by our culture. Daniel was one of the leading Jewish young men who were exiled to Babylon when Nebuchadnezzar first conquered Judah (605 B.C.). Placed into service in the king's court, Daniel undertook several spiritual disciplines to sustain his faith and identity as one of God's chosen people in the midst of a pagan culture. Daniel's decision to fast was one of the most visible ways in which he avoided being fully absorbed into the pagan, Babylonian culture.

Daniel frequently practiced partial fasts, abstaining from certain items but not from food altogether. For example, when Daniel mourned because of a vision of war and hardship that awaited his people, he observed a partial fast to help him focus on interceding for his people in prayer. His prayers were answered when an angel appeared to him and assured him of God's care. " 'Do not be afraid, O man highly esteemed,' he said. 'Peace! Be strong now; be strong' " (Daniel 10:19).

A partial fast helps to remind us of our spiritual commitments yet allows us to remain fully engaged in our ordinary routine. A normal fast can often be more disruptive to daily life—and that is a good thing at times. But at other times we may sense the need to support our prayers or spiritual activities with fasting, yet still feel the need to sustain ourselves with food. In such times, we may give up other items so that our thoughts will repeatedly be drawn to God, just as Daniel gave up rich foods, meat and wine in his partial fast.

For more on fasting, turn to Matthew 4.

Putting It Into Practice

A partial fast limits food or drink but does not completely abstain from all of them. A good way to develop the discipline of partial fasting is to begin with a fast from lunch one day until lunch the next. During that time period you may choose to give up such things as flavored drinks or certain types of food that you would normally eat.

As you prepare to fast, take some time to consider how you will use your meal times and what specific Bible reading and prayer you will undertake.

During your fast, pay attention to how you respond to this discipline. Note what you learn about the role that food plays in your life. Also use your thoughts about food to trigger thoughts about spiritual concerns.

man[a] touched my lips, and I opened my
mouth and began to speak. I said to the one
standing before me, "I am overcome with anguish because of the vision, my lord, and I am
helpless. 17How can I, your servant, talk with
you, my lord? My strength is gone and I can
hardly breathe."
18Again the one who looked like a man
touched me and gave me strength. 19"Do not
be afraid, O man highly esteemed," he said.
"Peace! Be strong now; be strong."
When he spoke to me, I was strengthened
and said, "Speak, my lord, since you have given
me strength."
20So he said, "Do you know why I have
come to you? Soon I will return to fight against
the prince of Persia, and when I go, the prince
of Greece will come; 21but first I will tell you
what is written in the Book of Truth. (No one
supports me against them except Michael, your
11 prince. 1And in the first year of Darius
the Mede, I took my stand to support
and protect him.)

The Kings of the South and the North

2"Now then, I tell you the truth: Three more
kings will appear in Persia, and then a fourth,
who will be far richer than all the others. When
he has gained power by his wealth, he will stir
up everyone against the kingdom of Greece.
3Then a mighty king will appear, who will rule
with great power and do as he pleases. 4After he
has appeared, his empire will be broken up and
parceled out toward the four winds of heaven.
It will not go to his descendants, nor will it have
the power he exercised, because his empire will
be uprooted and given to others.
5"The king of the South will become strong,
but one of his commanders will become even
stronger than he and will rule his own kingdom
with great power. 6After some years, they will
become allies. The daughter of the king of the
South will go to the king of the North to make
an alliance, but she will not retain her power,
and he and his power[b] will not last. In those
days she will be handed over, together with her
royal escort and her father[c] and the one who
supported her.
7"One from her family line will arise to take
her place. He will attack the forces of the king
of the North and enter his fortress; he will fight
against them and be victorious. 8He will also
seize their gods, their metal images and their
valuable articles of silver and gold and carry
them off to Egypt. For some years he will leave
the king of the North alone. 9Then the king of
the North will invade the realm of the king of
the South but will retreat to his own country.
10His sons will prepare for war and assemble a
great army, which will sweep on like an irresist-
ible flood and carry the battle as far as his fortress.
11"Then the king of the South will march out
in a rage and fight against the king of the North,
who will raise a large army, but it will be defeated. 12When the army is carried off, the king
of the South will be filled with pride and will
slaughter many thousands, yet he will not remain triumphant. 13For the king of the North
will muster another army, larger than the first;
and after several years, he will advance with a
huge army fully equipped.
14"In those times many will rise against the
king of the South. The violent men among your
own people will rebel in fulfillment of the vision, but without success. 15Then the king of the
North will come and build up siege ramps and
will capture a fortified city. The forces of the
South will be powerless to resist; even their best
troops will not have the strength to stand. 16The
invader will do as he pleases; no one will be
able to stand against him. He will establish
himself in the Beautiful Land and will have the
power to destroy it. 17He will determine to
come with the might of his entire kingdom and
will make an alliance with the king of the
South. And he will give him a daughter in marriage in order to overthrow the kingdom, but
his plans[d] will not succeed or help him.
18Then he will turn his attention to the coastlands and will take many of them, but a commander will put an end to his insolence and
will turn his insolence back upon him. 19After
this, he will turn back toward the fortresses of
his own country but will stumble and fall, to be
seen no more.
20"His successor will send out a tax collector
to maintain the royal splendor. In a few years,
however, he will be destroyed, yet not in anger
or in battle.
21"He will be succeeded by a contemptible
person who has not been given the honor of
royalty. He will invade the kingdom when its
people feel secure, and he will seize it through
intrigue. 22Then an overwhelming army will be
swept away before him; both it and a prince of
the covenant will be destroyed. 23After coming
to an agreement with him, he will act deceitfully, and with only a few people he will rise to
power. 24When the richest provinces feel secure,
he will invade them and will achieve what nei-

[a]16 Most manuscripts of the Masoretic Text; one manuscript of the Masoretic Text, Dead Sea Scrolls and Septuagint *Then something that looked like a man's hand*
[b]6 Or *offspring* [c]6 Or *child* (see Vulgate and Syriac)
[d]17 Or *but she*

11:12 The king of Egypt's success would be short-lived, probably the result of God's judgment against his pride. God usually refuses to help proud people who believe all success is a result of their own efforts. God effects the changes within us. When we begin to take credit for our successes and believe that we have made progress because of our own efforts, we only distance ourselves from God and lose ground in our spiritual growth. Remembering to thank God for the work he is doing in us and giving him the credit he deserves will help us progress in our spiritual renewal and keep us dependent on God.

ther his fathers nor his forefathers did. He will distribute plunder, loot and wealth among his followers. He will plot the overthrow of fortresses—but only for a time.

25 "With a large army he will stir up his strength and courage against the king of the South. The king of the South will wage war with a large and very powerful army, but he will not be able to stand because of the plots devised against him. 26 Those who eat from the king's provisions will try to destroy him; his army will be swept away, and many will fall in battle. 27 The two kings, with their hearts bent on evil, will sit at the same table and lie to each other, but to no avail, because an end will still come at the appointed time. 28 The king of the North will return to his own country with great wealth, but his heart will be set against the holy covenant. He will take action against it and then return to his own country.

29 "At the appointed time he will invade the South again, but this time the outcome will be different from what it was before. 30 Ships of the western coastlands[a] will oppose him, and he will lose heart. Then he will turn back and vent his fury against the holy covenant. He will return and show favor to those who forsake the holy covenant.

31 "His armed forces will rise up to desecrate the temple fortress and will abolish the daily sacrifice. Then they will set up the abomination that causes desolation. 32 With flattery he will corrupt those who have violated the covenant, but the people who know their God will firmly resist him.

33 "Those who are wise will instruct many, though for a time they will fall by the sword or be burned or captured or plundered. 34 When they fall, they will receive a little help, and many who are not sincere will join them. 35 Some of the wise will stumble, so that they may be refined, purified and made spotless until the time of the end, for it will still come at the appointed time.

The King Who Exalts Himself

36 "The king will do as he pleases. He will exalt and magnify himself above every god and will say unheard-of things against the God of gods. He will be successful until the time of wrath is completed, for what has been determined must take place. 37 He will show no regard for the gods of his fathers or for the one desired by women, nor will he regard any god, but will exalt himself above them all. 38 Instead of them, he will honor a god of fortresses; a god unknown to his fathers he will honor with gold and silver, with precious stones and costly gifts. 39 He will attack the mightiest fortresses with the help of a foreign god and will greatly honor those who acknowledge him. He will make them rulers over many people and will distribute the land at a price.[b]

40 "At the time of the end the king of the South will engage him in battle, and the king of the North will storm out against him with chariots and cavalry and a great fleet of ships. He will invade many countries and sweep through them like a flood. 41 He will also invade the Beautiful Land. Many countries will fall, but Edom, Moab and the leaders of Ammon will be delivered from his hand. 42 He will extend his power over many countries; Egypt will not escape. 43 He will gain control of the treasures of gold and silver and all the riches of Egypt, with the Libyans and Nubians in submission. 44 But reports from the east and the north will alarm him, and he will set out in a great rage to destroy and annihilate many. 45 He will pitch his royal tents between the seas at[c] the beautiful holy mountain. Yet he will come to his end, and no one will help him.

The End Times

12 "At that time Michael, the great prince who protects your people, will arise. There will be a time of distress such as has not happened from the beginning of nations until then. But at that time your people—everyone whose name is found written in the book—will be delivered. 2 Multitudes who sleep in the dust of the earth will awake: some to everlasting life, others to shame and everlasting contempt. 3 Those who are wise[d] will shine like the brightness of the heavens, and those who lead many to righteousness, like the stars for ever and ever. 4 But you, Daniel, close up and seal the words of the scroll until the time of the end. Many will go here and there to increase knowledge."

5 Then I, Daniel, looked, and there before me stood two others, one on this bank of the river and one on the opposite bank. 6 One of them said to the man clothed in linen, who was above the waters of the river, "How long will it be before these astonishing things are fulfilled?"

7 The man clothed in linen, who was above the waters of the river, lifted his right hand and

[a] 30 Hebrew *of Kittim* [b] 39 Or *land for a reward*
[c] 45 Or *the sea and* [d] 3 Or *who impart wisdom*

11:35 Persevering through suffering in our spiritual walk will refine and strengthen us. We should view our struggles as a weight lifter looks at weights. If weights weren't difficult to lift, the athlete wouldn't gain any muscle. In our spiritual walk we may stumble frequently at first, but as we struggle, we will grow stronger. Eventually, with God's grace we will be able to resist greater and greater temptations where we once would have fallen.

12:1–4, 13 When we seek God and surrender to him, we sometimes hope that life will never again be painful. A painless life, however, is not guaranteed. There will be times of trouble for God's people (see John 16:33; Acts 14:22). There will also be times when we may not have all the answers to our questions. But through it all, we have the assurance that God will be with us and will ultimately bring us peace.

his left hand toward heaven, and I heard him
swear by him who lives forever, saying, "It will
be for a time, times and half a time.[a] When the
power of the holy people has been finally broken, all these things will be completed."
8I heard, but I did not understand. So I asked,
"My lord, what will the outcome of all this be?"
9He replied, "Go your way, Daniel, because
the words are closed up and sealed until the
time of the end. 10Many will be purified, made
spotless and refined, but the wicked will continue to be wicked. None of the wicked will understand, but those who are wise will understand.
11"From the time that the daily sacrifice is
abolished and the abomination that causes desolation is set up, there will be 1,290 days.
12Blessed is the one who waits for and reaches
the end of the 1,335 days.
13"As for you, go your way till the end. You
will rest, and then at the end of the days you
will rise to receive your allotted inheritance."

[a]7 *Or a year, two years and half a year*

12:10 Those who have surrendered their lives to God may have to endure suffering. But that suffering can have a very positive effect. Difficult trials can teach us lessons that will help us in the future. Yet for those who deny the truth, there will be no knowledge, no cleansing, no redemption. Through our openness, honesty and self-examination, God can use our trials and suffering to purify our faith and shape us into the people he wants us to be.

Hosea

The Big Picture

God called Hosea to reveal through word and deed that God loved his people and desired to restore his relationship with them. God initiated this message by commanding Hosea to marry an unfaithful woman, Gomer. As soon as Hosea's and his wife's children were born, she became a prostitute and ultimately also a slave. In response to God's command, Hosea redeemed his wife from slavery and restored her to the family. Through this demonstration of unconditional love, God symbolized his own love for the people of Israel.

The book of Hosea tells the story of God's stormy relationship with his people. God treated them with mercy and compassion even though they repeatedly rejected him and his will for their lives. God did not condone their sin but allowed Israel to suffer the consequences of their disobedience. Though God was angered by the unfaithfulness of his people, he never rejected them completely. He ultimately promised to restore them if they repented.

While the story of Hosea's gracious love for Gomer is the story of God's love for the wayward Israelites, it is also the story of God's love for us. We may sometimes choose the way of disobedience that leads inevitably toward suffering and exile. God may use the pain of our suffering to awaken us and lead us back to him. Because of God's unfailing love, we can be restored and enjoy an intimate relationship with him.

A. *HOSEA'S MARRIAGE: A PICTURE OF GOD'S UNFAILING LOVE (1:1–3:5)*

1. Hosea's Troubled Family (1:1–2:1)
2. The Unfaithful Wife and Mother (2:2-13)
3. The Reconciliation of Husband and Wife (2:14-23)
4. The Restoration of the Unfaithful Wife (3:1-5)

B. *HOSEA'S MESSAGES: TEACHING ABOUT GOD'S UNFAILING LOVE (4:1–14:9)*

1. God's Complaints Against Israel (4:1-19)
2. Israel's Refusal to Return to God (5:1–8:14)
3. God Uses "Tough Love" (9:1-9)
4. Israel's History of Rejecting God's Love (9:10–13:16)
5. The Reconciliation of God and Israel (14:1-9)

Spiritual Renewal Themes

THE POWER OF COMMITTED LOVE

It is hard to love people when we feel they don't deserve it. But God says these are the people we need to love the most. The kind of love that God pours out on us is unconditional. Throughout the book of Hosea we hear this message again and again: God loves us and reaches out to us no matter how unworthy we are. Understanding this fact is foundational for spiritual renewal.

GOD'S DISCIPLINE LEADS TO RESTORATION

God revealed his love for his people by allowing them to suffer the pain of captivity in a foreign land. God never condones sin. He often allows us to suffer the painful consequences of our sins to bring us to our senses.

Essential Facts

PURPOSE:
To reveal God's unending love for his sinful people and God's desire to restore their relationship with him.

AUTHOR:
The prophet Hosea.

AUDIENCE:
The people of the northern kingdom of Israel.

DATE WRITTEN:
Approximately 715 B.C., at the end of Hosea's ministry (755–715 B.C.).

SETTING:
The northern kingdom of Israel just prior to its conquest by Assyria in 722 B.C.

KEY VERSE:
"Sow for yourselves righteousness, reap the fruit of unfailing love, and break up your unplowed ground; for it is time to seek the LORD, until he comes and showers righteousness on you" (10:12).

KEY PEOPLE AND RELATIONSHIPS:
Hosea, his wife, Gomer, and their children.

GOD IS MERCIFUL

When Hosea found Gomer, his ultimate intent was a merciful restoration. When God allowed Israel to be conquered by Assyria, his ultimate desire was to bring restoration to his people. When we suffer the consequences of our sin, we can be confident that God desires the same for us.

NEVER "TOO FAR GONE" FOR GOD

Gomer was a failure; she sold herself into slavery in order to survive. But Hosea did not give up on her. Israel also was a failure; she turned to other gods in her rebellion. But God did not give up on her. If we have become slaves to sin, we can be certain that God has not given up on us either. He will receive us if only we will repent and call upon him.

1 The word of the LORD that came to Hosea son of Beeri during the reigns of Uzziah, Jotham, Ahaz and Hezekiah, kings of Judah, and during the reign of Jeroboam son of Jehoash[a] king of Israel:

Hosea's Wife and Children

2When the LORD began to speak through Hosea, the LORD said to him, "Go, take to yourself an adulterous wife and children of unfaithfulness, because the land is guilty of the vilest adultery in departing from the LORD." 3So he married Gomer daughter of Diblaim, and she conceived and bore him a son.

4Then the LORD said to Hosea, "Call him Jezreel, because I will soon punish the house of Jehu for the massacre at Jezreel, and I will put an end to the kingdom of Israel. 5In that day I will break Israel's bow in the Valley of Jezreel."

6Gomer conceived again and gave birth to a daughter. Then the LORD said to Hosea, "Call her Lo-Ruhamah,[b] for I will no longer show love to the house of Israel, that I should at all forgive them. 7Yet I will show love to the house of Judah; and I will save them—not by bow, sword or battle, or by horses and horsemen, but by the LORD their God."

8After she had weaned Lo-Ruhamah, Gomer had another son. 9Then the LORD said, "Call him Lo-Ammi,[c] for you are not my people, and I am not your God.

10"Yet the Israelites will be like the sand on the seashore, which cannot be measured or counted. In the place where it was said to them, 'You are not my people,' they will be called 'sons of the living God.' 11The people of Judah and the people of Israel will be reunited, and they will appoint one leader and will come up out of the land, for great will be the day of Jezreel.

2 "Say of your brothers, 'My people,' and of your sisters, 'My loved one.'

Israel Punished and Restored

2"Rebuke your mother, rebuke her,
for she is not my wife,
and I am not her husband.
Let her remove the adulterous look from her face
and the unfaithfulness from between her breasts.
3Otherwise I will strip her naked
and make her as bare as on the day she was born;
I will make her like a desert,
turn her into a parched land,
and slay her with thirst.
4I will not show my love to her children,
because they are the children of adultery.
5Their mother has been unfaithful
and has conceived them in disgrace.
She said, 'I will go after my lovers,
who give me my food and my water,
my wool and my linen, my oil and my drink.'
6Therefore I will block her path with thornbushes;
I will wall her in so that she cannot find her way.
7She will chase after her lovers but not catch them;
she will look for them but not find them.
Then she will say,
'I will go back to my husband as at first,
for then I was better off than now.'
8She has not acknowledged that I was the one
who gave her the grain, the new wine and oil,
who lavished on her the silver and gold—
which they used for Baal.

9"Therefore I will take away my grain when it ripens,
and my new wine when it is ready.
I will take back my wool and my linen,
intended to cover her nakedness.
10So now I will expose her lewdness
before the eyes of her lovers;

[a]1 Hebrew *Joash*, a variant of *Jehoash* [b]6 *Lo-Ruhamah* means *not loved.* [c]9 *Lo-Ammi* means *not my people.*

1:2–3 God told Hosea to marry an unfaithful woman. Their relationship would symbolize God's relationship with Israel, who prostituted herself to the false gods of her pagan neighbors. Understanding this analogy shows us how it must hurt God when we forsake him and seek after other "gods" in our attempts to satisfy our desires. These other gods will ultimately hurt us. Let us be faithful to God, the one who truly loves us.

1:6 Naming Hosea's daughter *Lo-Ruhamah* ("not loved") indicated a change was coming for the nation of Israel. God had shown mercy to them in the past despite Israel's unrepentant condition. Now genuine love demanded that God withdraw his mercy, allowing Israel to suffer the consequences of her sin and bringing her to abandon all of her false hopes. Letting others experience the consequences of their actions is often hard for us to do. Yet when people keep falling into sin, often the best thing we can do for them is to refuse to catch them. They may need to fall so that they can learn the painful lessons of responsibility and accountability for their sinful actions and then seek God on their own.

1:7—2:1 Hosea was told to name his third child *Lo-Ammi*, which means "not my people." In essence, God granted Israel a divorce because of her unfaithfulness. God's rejection, however, was only a temporary condition. The punishment and exile that were soon to arrive would someday be replaced with complete restoration and healing. That is the hope for all who follow God's path. Today's pain and suffering last only for a season, "but rejoicing comes in the morning" (Psalm 30:5).

2:5–13 Our desire to seek spiritual fulfillment apart from God compares to Israel's worship of foreign gods. Our joy and fulfillment can only be found in God. Though God is patient with us, if we refuse to devote our lives to him, he will often allow us to suffer the consequences of our disobedience. But his love is still available to us. God loves us; we don't have to die in our sins. If we turn to God, we will be redeemed.

no one will take her out of my hands.
11I will stop all her celebrations:
her yearly festivals, her New Moons,
her Sabbath days—all her appointed feasts.
12I will ruin her vines and her fig trees,
which she said were her pay from her lovers;
I will make them a thicket,
and wild animals will devour them.
13I will punish her for the days
she burned incense to the Baals;
she decked herself with rings and jewelry,
and went after her lovers,
but me she forgot,"
declares the LORD.

14"Therefore I am now going to allure her;
I will lead her into the desert
and speak tenderly to her.
15There I will give her back her vineyards,
and will make the Valley of Achor[a] a door of hope.
There she will sing[b] as in the days of her youth,
as in the day she came up out of Egypt.

16"In that day," declares the LORD,
"you will call me 'my husband';
you will no longer call me 'my master.[c]'
17I will remove the names of the Baals from her lips;
no longer will their names be invoked.
18In that day I will make a covenant for them
with the beasts of the field and the birds of the air
and the creatures that move along the ground.
Bow and sword and battle
I will abolish from the land,
so that all may lie down in safety.
19I will betroth you to me forever;
I will betroth you in[d] righteousness and justice,
in[e] love and compassion.
20I will betroth you in faithfulness,
and you will acknowledge the LORD.

21"In that day I will respond,"
declares the LORD—
"I will respond to the skies,
and they will respond to the earth;
22and the earth will respond to the grain,
the new wine and oil,
and they will respond to Jezreel.[f]
23I will plant her for myself in the land;
I will show my love to the one I called 'Not my loved one.[g]'
I will say to those called 'Not my people,[h]' 'You are my people';
and they will say, 'You are my God.'"

Hosea's Reconciliation With His Wife

3 The LORD said to me, "Go, show your love
to your wife again, though she is loved by
another and is an adulteress. Love her as the
LORD loves the Israelites, though they turn to
other gods and love the sacred raisin cakes."
2So I bought her for fifteen shekels[i] of silver
and about a homer and a lethek[j] of barley.
3Then I told her, "You are to live with[k] me
many days; you must not be a prostitute or be
intimate with any man, and I will live with[k]
you."
4For the Israelites will live many days without king or prince, without sacrifice or sacred
stones, without ephod or idol. 5Afterward the
Israelites will return and seek the LORD their
God and David their king. They will come trembling to the LORD and to his blessings in the last
days.

The Charge Against Israel

4 Hear the word of the LORD, you Israelites,
because the LORD has a charge to bring
against you who live in the land:
"There is no faithfulness, no love,
no acknowledgment of God in the land.
2There is only cursing,[l] lying and murder,
stealing and adultery;
they break all bounds,
and bloodshed follows bloodshed.
3Because of this the land mourns,[m]

[a] 15 *Achor* means *trouble.* [b] 15 Or *respond* [c] 16 Hebrew *baal* [d] 19 Or *with;* also in verse 20 [e] 19 Or *with* [f] 22 *Jezreel* means *God plants.* [g] 23 Hebrew *Lo-Ruhamah* [h] 23 Hebrew *Lo-Ammi* [i] 2 That is, about 6 ounces (about 170 grams) [j] 2 That is, probably about 10 bushels (about 330 liters) [k] 3 Or *wait for* [l] 2 That is, to pronounce a curse upon [m] 3 Or *dries up*

2:21–22 God controls his creation, and his creation praises him. Since God can control the rain and the growth of plants, he certainly can control the events of our lives. Like creation, we must proclaim the greatness of God. Without his help, we would still be in a spiritual wilderness of sin. As we sing out our story of deliverance, we will not only encourage others to persevere, but we will also find renewed strength for our spiritual journey.

3:1–2 Hosea healed his broken family by redeeming, or buying back, his wife from slavery. When Gomer did not come back to him, Hosea went to her and paid money to get her back. Hosea's unexpected act of extraordinary love symbolizes God's love, which is even more extraordinary. While we were still sinners, God sent his Son, Jesus, to give his life for us (see Romans 5:8). We can experience spiritual renewal by admitting our sin, accepting this gift of Jesus' sacrifice for us and becoming a part of the community of believers.

4:1–2 God wanted his people to honestly examine their lives. They had ignored the boundaries set up by the Ten Commandments (see Exodus 20:1–17; Deuteronomy 5:6–21). Their lack of commitment to God formed the root of such sinful behaviors as cursing, lying, murdering, stealing and committing adultery. We also should honestly reflect on our lives to recognize our sins and repent of them. If we are honest in our self-examination and confession, God will grant us the healing and forgiveness we need.

and all who live in it waste away;
the beasts of the field and the birds of the air
and the fish of the sea are dying.

4"But let no man bring a charge,
let no man accuse another,
for your people are like those
who bring charges against a priest.
5You stumble day and night,
and the prophets stumble with you.
So I will destroy your mother—
6 my people are destroyed from lack of knowledge.

"Because you have rejected knowledge,
I also reject you as my priests;
because you have ignored the law of your God,
I also will ignore your children.
7The more the priests increased,
the more they sinned against me;
they exchanged[a] their[b] Glory for something disgraceful.
8They feed on the sins of my people
and relish their wickedness.
9And it will be: Like people, like priests.
I will punish both of them for their ways
and repay them for their deeds.

10"They will eat but not have enough;
they will engage in prostitution but not increase,
because they have deserted the LORD
to give themselves 11to prostitution,
to old wine and new,
which take away the understanding 12of my people.
They consult a wooden idol
and are answered by a stick of wood.
A spirit of prostitution leads them astray;
they are unfaithful to their God.
13They sacrifice on the mountaintops
and burn offerings on the hills,
under oak, poplar and terebinth,
where the shade is pleasant.

[a]7 Syriac and an ancient Hebrew scribal tradition; Masoretic Text *I will exchange* [b]7 Masoretic Text; an ancient Hebrew scribal tradition *my*

4:6 A healthy relationship with God requires an intimate knowledge of the Bible. This knowledge goes beyond a mere acquaintance with the facts of God's Word, however. God wants us to get to know him personally. The priests of Israel were well acquainted with the laws of God, but they lived an immoral lifestyle because they didn't really know God personally. In order to progress in our spiritual growth, we must have a personal, growing relationship with God himself.

4:7–9 Spiritual leaders bear a responsibility not only for their own spiritual lives but also for the spiritual welfare of those who follow them. If we share the good news of God's deliverance in our lives with others, we must be sure to stay on the right path and not lapse back into sin. Those who look to us for guidance will follow our example, whether good or bad. To help others stay on the road to spiritual growth, we need to stay on the right path too.

Patience for Restoration

Hosea 3:1–5 Restoration of human relationships does not happen instantaneously. If we have broken someone's heart or broken trust with a loved one, we have a responsibility to face our failures in the situation while refusing to blame others for the problems we have caused. It may take some time before we are able to face up to our failures. In the same way, we should expect that the process of restoration and regaining trust will take time.

God told the prophet Hosea to marry a prostitute. This marriage was to be a living example to the nation of Israel illustrating her infidelity toward God. It probably hurt Hosea deeply when Gomer returned to her life of prostitution. Hosea said, "The LORD said to me, 'Go, show your love to your wife again, though she is loved by another and is an adulteress. Love her as the LORD loves the Israelites, though they turn to other gods and love the sacred raisin cakes' " (3:1). But Hosea needed some time before he could be close to his wife again, for such deep restoration takes time.

It is our responsibility to wait patiently while God helps us restore our broken relationships and the hearts we may have hurt. God can restore love when love has been lost; he can help us trust and become trustworthy again, but these things take time.

Move on to Key 5 and turn to Genesis 23.

Therefore your daughters turn to
prostitution
and your daughters-in-law to adultery.

14 "I will not punish your daughters
when they turn to prostitution,
nor your daughters-in-law
when they commit adultery,
because the men themselves consort with
harlots
and sacrifice with shrine prostitutes—
a people without understanding will
come to ruin!

15 "Though you commit adultery, O Israel,
let not Judah become guilty.

"Do not go to Gilgal;
do not go up to Beth Aven.[a]
And do not swear, 'As surely as the LORD
lives!'
16 The Israelites are stubborn,
like a stubborn heifer.
How then can the LORD pasture them
like lambs in a meadow?
17 Ephraim is joined to idols;
leave him alone!
18 Even when their drinks are gone,
they continue their prostitution;
their rulers dearly love shameful ways.
19 A whirlwind will sweep them away,
and their sacrifices will bring them
shame.

Judgment Against Israel

5 "Hear this, you priests!
Pay attention, you Israelites!
Listen, O royal house!
This judgment is against you:
You have been a snare at Mizpah,
a net spread out on Tabor.
2 The rebels are deep in slaughter.
I will discipline all of them.
3 I know all about Ephraim;
Israel is not hidden from me.
Ephraim, you have now turned to
prostitution;
Israel is corrupt.

4 "Their deeds do not permit them
to return to their God.
A spirit of prostitution is in their heart;
they do not acknowledge the LORD.
5 Israel's arrogance testifies against them;
the Israelites, even Ephraim, stumble in
their sin;
Judah also stumbles with them.
6 When they go with their flocks and herds
to seek the LORD,
they will not find him;
he has withdrawn himself from them.
7 They are unfaithful to the LORD;
they give birth to illegitimate children.
Now their New Moon festivals
will devour them and their fields.

8 "Sound the trumpet in Gibeah,
the horn in Ramah.
Raise the battle cry in Beth Aven[a];
lead on, O Benjamin.
9 Ephraim will be laid waste
on the day of reckoning.
Among the tribes of Israel
I proclaim what is certain.
10 Judah's leaders are like those
who move boundary stones.
I will pour out my wrath on them
like a flood of water.
11 Ephraim is oppressed,
trampled in judgment,
intent on pursuing idols.[b]
12 I am like a moth to Ephraim,
like rot to the people of Judah.

13 "When Ephraim saw his sickness,
and Judah his sores,
then Ephraim turned to Assyria,
and sent to the great king for help.
But he is not able to cure you,
not able to heal your sores.
14 For I will be like a lion to Ephraim,
like a great lion to Judah.
I will tear them to pieces and go away;
I will carry them off, with no one to
rescue them.
15 Then I will go back to my place
until they admit their guilt.
And they will seek my face;
in their misery they will earnestly seek
me."

Israel Unrepentant

6 "Come, let us return to the LORD.
He has torn us to pieces

[a] 15,8 *Beth Aven* means *house of wickedness* (a name for Bethel, which means *house of God*). [b] 11 The meaning of the Hebrew for this word is uncertain.

4:15–19 Judah was warned to stay away from Israel, lest she be tempted to follow her unfaithful sister nation into sin. We must also heed this warning. Since we tend to conform to the people around us, it makes sense for us to stay away from those who engage in sinful behavior. To stay on God's path, we must develop deep relationships with people who are following God and obeying his Word.

5:3–4 Because God's people clung to their idolatry and refused to admit their wrongdoing and surrender their lives to God, they could not enjoy a relationship with him. Though the pleasures of sin may bring us a temporary thrill, we can never escape their destructive consequences. We must turn from our sin and receive God's forgiveness in order to enjoy a restored relationship with him.

5:13 The people of Israel and Judah recognized their need for help, but they turned to the wrong source. And they suffered as a result of their poor choice. If we are honest in our self-examination, we will recognize that no one can heal the disease of sin except God. Let us turn to him and be delivered from sin's deadly grip.

6:1–3 In this passage the people finally saw the truth and admitted their helplessness, regarding themselves as torn and wounded. They surrendered their lives to God, deciding to "return to the LORD" (6:1). Asking God to

but he will heal us;
he has injured us
but he will bind up our wounds.
2After two days he will revive us;
on the third day he will restore us,
that we may live in his presence.
3Let us acknowledge the LORD;
let us press on to acknowledge him.
As surely as the sun rises,
he will appear;
he will come to us like the winter rains,
like the spring rains that water the earth."

4"What can I do with you, Ephraim?
What can I do with you, Judah?
Your love is like the morning mist,
like the early dew that disappears.
5Therefore I cut you in pieces with my
prophets,
I killed you with the words of my
mouth;
my judgments flashed like lightning
upon you.
6For I desire mercy, not sacrifice,
and acknowledgment of God rather than
burnt offerings.
7Like Adam,[a] they have broken the
covenant—
they were unfaithful to me there.
8Gilead is a city of wicked men,
stained with footprints of blood.
9As marauders lie in ambush for a man,
so do bands of priests;
they murder on the road to Shechem,
committing shameful crimes.
10I have seen a horrible thing
in the house of Israel.
There Ephraim is given to prostitution
and Israel is defiled.
11"Also for you, Judah,
a harvest is appointed.

"Whenever I would restore the fortunes of
my people,
7 1whenever I would heal Israel,
the sins of Ephraim are exposed
and the crimes of Samaria revealed.
They practice deceit,
thieves break into houses,
bandits rob in the streets;
2but they do not realize
that I remember all their evil deeds.
Their sins engulf them;
they are always before me.

3"They delight the king with their
wickedness,
the princes with their lies.
4They are all adulterers,
burning like an oven
whose fire the baker need not stir
from the kneading of the dough till it
rises.
5On the day of the festival of our king
the princes become inflamed with wine,
and he joins hands with the mockers.
6Their hearts are like an oven;
they approach him with intrigue.
Their passion smolders all night;
in the morning it blazes like a flaming
fire.
7All of them are hot as an oven;
they devour their rulers.
All their kings fall,
and none of them calls on me.

8"Ephraim mixes with the nations;
Ephraim is a flat cake not turned over.
9Foreigners sap his strength,
but he does not realize it.
His hair is sprinkled with gray,
but he does not notice.
10Israel's arrogance testifies against him,
but despite all this
he does not return to the LORD his God
or search for him.

11"Ephraim is like a dove,
easily deceived and senseless—
now calling to Egypt,
now turning to Assyria.
12When they go, I will throw my net over
them;
I will pull them down like birds of the
air.
When I hear them flocking together,
I will catch them.
13Woe to them,
because they have strayed from me!

[a]7 Or *As at Adam;* or *Like men*

---

change them, the people affirmed that God would heal and bandage their wounds. They sought a relationship with God, saying, "Let us acknowledge the LORD; let us press on to acknowledge him" (6:3). These actions exemplify many of the keys to spiritual renewal.

6:4–5 The people of Israel started down the right path, but they soon turned back to sin. Why did they fail? Perhaps the Israelites were never really committed to following God and his will for them. Although they turned away from God, however, he never turned away from them or stopped loving them. We should remember that even though we may turn away from God at times, he will never turn away from us or stop loving us.

6:6 Sometimes we perform our religious acts of worship without any true feeling. Our worship may be mere ritual. God values our sincere acts of worship. And if our worship is sincere, it will be manifested in our compassion for others. Acting kindly toward others and forgiving those who have hurt us not only gives us a good idea of how committed we are to God but also proves that we are growing spiritually.

7:10 Pride is a destructive sin. Pride tells us to take credit for our successes and blame others for our failures. The sin of pride causes us to assume the place of God in our own lives and robs us of God's help because we won't admit we have a problem. To grow spiritually and see God's transforming power change our lives, we need to come to God with humble hearts, admitting our sin and seeking change.

7:13 God longs to redeem us and transform our lives. But hearts hardened by rebellion and a refusal to see the truth hinder him from his mission of redemption. If we

Destruction to them,
because they have rebelled against me!
I long to redeem them
but they speak lies against me.
14They do not cry out to me from their hearts
but wail upon their beds.
They gather together[a] for grain and new wine
but turn away from me.
15I trained them and strengthened them,
but they plot evil against me.
16They do not turn to the Most High;
they are like a faulty bow.
Their leaders will fall by the sword
because of their insolent words.
For this they will be ridiculed
in the land of Egypt.

Israel to Reap the Whirlwind

8 "Put the trumpet to your lips!
An eagle is over the house of the LORD
because the people have broken my covenant
and rebelled against my law.
2Israel cries out to me,
'O our God, we acknowledge you!'
3But Israel has rejected what is good;
an enemy will pursue him.
4They set up kings without my consent;
they choose princes without my approval.
With their silver and gold
they make idols for themselves
to their own destruction.
5Throw out your calf-idol, O Samaria!
My anger burns against them.
How long will they be incapable of purity?
6 They are from Israel!
This calf—a craftsman has made it;
it is not God.
It will be broken in pieces,
that calf of Samaria.

7"They sow the wind
and reap the whirlwind.
The stalk has no head;
it will produce no flour.
Were it to yield grain,
foreigners would swallow it up.
8Israel is swallowed up;
now she is among the nations
like a worthless thing.
9For they have gone up to Assyria
like a wild donkey wandering alone.
Ephraim has sold herself to lovers.
10Although they have sold themselves among the nations,
I will now gather them together.
They will begin to waste away
under the oppression of the mighty king.

11"Though Ephraim built many altars for sin offerings,
these have become altars for sinning.
12I wrote for them the many things of my law,
but they regarded them as something alien.
13They offer sacrifices given to me
and they eat the meat,
but the LORD is not pleased with them.
Now he will remember their wickedness
and punish their sins:
They will return to Egypt.
14Israel has forgotten his Maker
and built palaces;
Judah has fortified many towns.
But I will send fire upon their cities
that will consume their fortresses."

Punishment for Israel

9 Do not rejoice, O Israel;
do not be jubilant like the other nations.
For you have been unfaithful to your God;
you love the wages of a prostitute
at every threshing floor.
2Threshing floors and winepresses will not feed the people;
the new wine will fail them.
3They will not remain in the LORD's land;
Ephraim will return to Egypt
and eat unclean[b] food in Assyria.
4They will not pour out wine offerings to the LORD,
nor will their sacrifices please him.
Such sacrifices will be to them like the bread of mourners;
all who eat them will be unclean.
This food will be for themselves;

[a] *14* Most Hebrew manuscripts; some Hebrew manuscripts and Septuagint *They slash themselves* [b] *3* That is, ceremonially unclean

want God's powerful help, we must surrender ourselves to him, accept the reality of our sins and faults and open our lives up to God so that he can help us.

8:5–6 Jeroboam feared losing control of the northern kingdom of Israel if everyone went to worship God in the southern city of Jerusalem. In an attempt to consolidate his power, Jeroboam set up two golden calves in Bethel and Dan and told his people that these were the gods who had led the people out of Egypt (see 1 Kings 12:28–30). Though God had promised to give Jeroboam the kingdom of Israel, Jeroboam sought another source to secure God's promise. This disobedience led to Jeroboam's destruction (see 1 Kings 13:33–34). When God promises us something, we can trust him to complete it in his way and in his time. Taking matters into our own hands is always harmful and will impede our spiritual growth.

8:12 God's laws apply to everyone, even unbelievers. Those who contend that God's laws apply only to others are merely harming themselves. If we drive faster than the speed limit and are stopped by the police, the officer will not let us go free if we claim, "I saw the speed limit sign, but speed limit laws don't apply to me." God will not let us go free if we refuse to obey his laws either. Knowing that God holds us accountable to know and obey his will should motivate us to read and understand his Word.

it will not come into the temple of the
LORD.

5What will you do on the day of your
appointed feasts,
on the festival days of the LORD?
6Even if they escape from destruction,
Egypt will gather them,
and Memphis will bury them.
Their treasures of silver will be taken over
by briers,
and thorns will overrun their tents.
7The days of punishment are coming,
the days of reckoning are at hand.
Let Israel know this.
Because your sins are so many
and your hostility so great,
the prophet is considered a fool,
the inspired man a maniac.
8The prophet, along with my God,
is the watchman over Ephraim,[a]
yet snares await him on all his paths,
and hostility in the house of his God.
9They have sunk deep into corruption,
as in the days of Gibeah.
God will remember their wickedness
and punish them for their sins.

10"When I found Israel,
it was like finding grapes in the desert;
when I saw your fathers,
it was like seeing the early fruit on the
fig tree.
But when they came to Baal Peor,
they consecrated themselves to that
shameful idol
and became as vile as the thing they
loved.
11Ephraim's glory will fly away like a bird—
no birth, no pregnancy, no conception.
12Even if they rear children,
I will bereave them of every one.
Woe to them
when I turn away from them!
13I have seen Ephraim, like Tyre,
planted in a pleasant place.
But Ephraim will bring out
their children to the slayer."

14Give them, O LORD—
what will you give them?
Give them wombs that miscarry
and breasts that are dry.

15"Because of all their wickedness in Gilgal,
I hated them there.
Because of their sinful deeds,
I will drive them out of my house.
I will no longer love them;
all their leaders are rebellious.
16Ephraim is blighted,
their root is withered,
they yield no fruit.
Even if they bear children,
I will slay their cherished offspring."

17My God will reject them
because they have not obeyed him;
they will be wanderers among the
nations.

10 Israel was a spreading vine;
he brought forth fruit for himself.
As his fruit increased,
he built more altars;
as his land prospered,
he adorned his sacred stones.
2Their heart is deceitful,
and now they must bear their guilt.
The LORD will demolish their altars
and destroy their sacred stones.

3Then they will say, "We have no king
because we did not revere the LORD.
But even if we had a king,
what could he do for us?"
4They make many promises,
take false oaths
and make agreements;
therefore lawsuits spring up
like poisonous weeds in a plowed field.
5The people who live in Samaria fear
for the calf-idol of Beth Aven.[b]
Its people will mourn over it,
and so will its idolatrous priests,
those who had rejoiced over its splendor,
because it is taken from them into exile.
6It will be carried to Assyria
as tribute for the great king.
Ephraim will be disgraced;
Israel will be ashamed of its wooden
idols.[c]
7Samaria and its king will float away
like a twig on the surface of the waters.
8The high places of wickedness[d] will be
destroyed—
it is the sin of Israel.
Thorns and thistles will grow up
and cover their altars.

[a]8 Or *The prophet is the watchman over Ephraim, / the people of my God* [b]5 *Beth Aven* means *house of wickedness* (a name for Bethel, which means *house of God*). [c]6 Or *its counsel* [d]8 Hebrew *aven,* a reference to Beth Aven (a derogatory name for Bethel)

10:1 The more prosperous the people of Israel became, the further away from God they moved. Many people think that success is measured in direct proportion to wealth. Even if we are spiritually bankrupt, we may think everything is all right if we are financially successful. Yet money is never the key to a successful life. Our relationship with God is our measure of true success. Living a godly life and receiving eternal wealth is worth far more than possessing earthly riches.

10:8 When we begin to experience the painful consequences of our sinful choices, it may seem as if a quick death would be better than redirecting the course of our lives. A quick end to our pain may be the easiest way out, but it is never the best way. There is always hope for a good future, no matter how terrible things may seem in the present. We can begin to end our pain by surrendering our lives to our merciful God. He wants all of us to come to him, no matter how great our failures.

Then they will say to the mountains,
"Cover us!"
and to the hills, "Fall on us!"

9"Since the days of Gibeah, you have
sinned, O Israel,
and there you have remained.[a]
Did not war overtake
the evildoers in Gibeah?
10When I please, I will punish them;
nations will be gathered against them
to put them in bonds for their double
sin.
11Ephraim is a trained heifer
that loves to thresh;
so I will put a yoke
on her fair neck.
I will drive Ephraim,
Judah must plow,
and Jacob must break up the ground.
12Sow for yourselves righteousness,
reap the fruit of unfailing love,
and break up your unplowed ground;
for it is time to seek the LORD,
until he comes
and showers righteousness on you.
13But you have planted wickedness,
you have reaped evil,
you have eaten the fruit of deception.
Because you have depended on your own
strength
and on your many warriors,
14the roar of battle will rise against your
people,
so that all your fortresses will be
devastated—
as Shalman devastated Beth Arbel on the
day of battle,
when mothers were dashed to the
ground with their children.
15Thus will it happen to you, O Bethel,
because your wickedness is great.
When that day dawns,
the king of Israel will be completely
destroyed.

God's Love for Israel

11 "When Israel was a child, I loved
him,
and out of Egypt I called my son.
2But the more I[b] called Israel,
the further they went from me.[c]
They sacrificed to the Baals
and they burned incense to images.
3It was I who taught Ephraim to walk,
taking them by the arms;
but they did not realize
it was I who healed them.
4I led them with cords of human kindness,
with ties of love;
I lifted the yoke from their neck
and bent down to feed them.

5"Will they not return to Egypt
and will not Assyria rule over them
because they refuse to repent?
6Swords will flash in their cities,
will destroy the bars of their gates
and put an end to their plans.
7My people are determined to turn from me.
Even if they call to the Most High,
he will by no means exalt them.

8"How can I give you up, Ephraim?
How can I hand you over, Israel?
How can I treat you like Admah?
How can I make you like Zeboiim?
My heart is changed within me;
all my compassion is aroused.
9I will not carry out my fierce anger,
nor will I turn and devastate Ephraim.
For I am God, and not man—
the Holy One among you.
I will not come in wrath.[d]
10They will follow the LORD;
he will roar like a lion.
When he roars,
his children will come trembling from
the west.
11They will come trembling
like birds from Egypt,
like doves from Assyria.
I will settle them in their homes,"
declares the LORD.

Israel's Sin

12Ephraim has surrounded me with lies,
the house of Israel with deceit.
And Judah is unruly against God,
even against the faithful Holy One.

12 1Ephraim feeds on the wind;
he pursues the east wind all day
and multiplies lies and violence.
He makes a treaty with Assyria
and sends olive oil to Egypt.

[a]9 Or *there a stand was taken* [b]2 Some Septuagint manuscripts; Hebrew *they* [c]2 Septuagint; Hebrew *them* [d]9 Or *come against any city*

10:12 In this verse, God expressed his desire to restore his relationship with Israel. The people had sinned and then reaped the chaotic and painful consequences (see 8:7). Here they were urged to plant righteousness and reap the unfailing love of God.

11:1–3 Hosea compared God's love for Israel to a father's love for his son. He painted a poignant picture of their complete dependence on God. God had raised his child correctly, but Israel had rebelled against God and had sought the favor of false gods who could not protect her from the coming destruction. We should learn from Israel's catastrophe and accept the guidance of our heavenly Father before our lives are destroyed by the consequences of our own sin and rebellion.

11:8–11 This passage shows us how painful it is for God when people stray from him and seek out false sources of security. Even though sins that entangle us may almost destroy our lives, we will never suffer what we truly deserve because of God's compassion on us, his wayward people. What a wonderful God he is! He shows us mercy and provides healing and restoration in our relationship with him.

[2]The LORD has a charge to bring against
Judah;
he will punish Jacob[a] according to his
ways
and repay him according to his deeds.
[3]In the womb he grasped his brother's heel;
as a man he struggled with God.
[4]He struggled with the angel and overcame
him;
he wept and begged for his favor.
He found him at Bethel
and talked with him there—
[5]the LORD God Almighty,
the LORD is his name of renown!
[6]But you must return to your God;
maintain love and justice,
and wait for your God always.

[7]The merchant uses dishonest scales;
he loves to defraud.
[8]Ephraim boasts,
"I am very rich; I have become wealthy.
With all my wealth they will not find in
me
any iniquity or sin."

[9]"I am the LORD your God,
⌞who brought you⌟ out of[b] Egypt;
I will make you live in tents again,
as in the days of your appointed feasts.
[10]I spoke to the prophets,
gave them many visions
and told parables through them."

[11]Is Gilead wicked?
Its people are worthless!
Do they sacrifice bulls in Gilgal?
Their altars will be like piles of stones
on a plowed field.
[12]Jacob fled to the country of Aram[c];
Israel served to get a wife,
and to pay for her he tended sheep.
[13]The LORD used a prophet to bring Israel up
from Egypt,
by a prophet he cared for him.
[14]But Ephraim has bitterly provoked him to
anger;
his Lord will leave upon him the guilt of
his bloodshed
and will repay him for his contempt.

[a]2 *Jacob* means *he grasps the heel* (figuratively, *he deceives*).
[b]9 Or *God / ever since you were in* [c]12 That is, Northwest Mesopotamia

12:2–5 Jacob changed from being a deceiver to one who sought God's blessing. In his struggles with God he finally faced his need and earnestly sought God's favor. Healing and growth are found only through honest communion with God.

12:6 God asks his people to love him by loving others. We must seek the best interests of others in a manner consistent with God's revealed will. When we are tempted to take advantage of others for personal gain, we need to ask for God's help to be just and loving. Then we can treat others as he wants us to treat them.

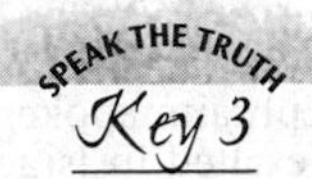

Unending Love

Hosea 11:8–11 We may hesitate to honestly confess our sins and shortcomings because of fear. Maybe we tried to share our secrets with someone at another time, only to find ourselves rejected because of what we said. Even though people may have let us down, God will never turn away from our honest confessions. Because of the sacrifice of Jesus Christ, there is nothing we could admit to God that would cause him to stop loving and accepting us.

Hosea prophesied to the rebellious nation of Israel. God used Hosea's life as a demonstration of his unconditional love for us. The Lord told Hosea to marry a prostitute. Hosea married her, loved her and devoted himself to her. Yet eventually she went back to her old ways, broke Hosea's heart and shamed their family. Ultimately Hosea's unfaithful wife ended up as a slave. God baffled Hosea by telling him, "Go, show your love to your wife again, though she is loved by another and is an adulteress. Love her as the LORD loves the Israelites, though they turn to other gods" (3:1).

God loves us this deeply as well. Though the way we have behaved may make us wonder how God could still love us, God asks, "How can I give you up . . . My heart is changed within me; all my compassion is aroused . . . For I am God, and not man—the Holy One among you. I will not come in wrath" (11:8–9).

Like Hosea's unfaithful wife, we may have committed sins that seem unforgivable. Yet these verses give us hope: There is absolutely nothing we can do or admit that would cause God to stop loving us (see Romans 8:38–39). Knowing this, we should confess our sins to God and accept his forgiveness and restoration.

Turn to Amos 7.

The LORD's Anger Against Israel

13 When Ephraim spoke, men trembled;
he was exalted in Israel.
But he became guilty of Baal worship
and died.
2Now they sin more and more;
they make idols for themselves from
their silver,
cleverly fashioned images,
all of them the work of craftsmen.
It is said of these people,
"They offer human sacrifice
and kiss[a] the calf-idols."
3Therefore they will be like the morning
mist,
like the early dew that disappears,
like chaff swirling from a threshing floor,
like smoke escaping through a window.

4"But I am the LORD your God,
⌞who brought you⌟ out of[b] Egypt.
You shall acknowledge no God but me,
no Savior except me.
5I cared for you in the desert,
in the land of burning heat.
6When I fed them, they were satisfied;
when they were satisfied, they became
proud;
then they forgot me.
7So I will come upon them like a lion,
like a leopard I will lurk by the path.
8Like a bear robbed of her cubs,
I will attack them and rip them open.
Like a lion I will devour them;
a wild animal will tear them apart.

9"You are destroyed, O Israel,
because you are against me, against your
helper.
10Where is your king, that he may save you?
Where are your rulers in all your towns,
of whom you said,
'Give me a king and princes'?
11So in my anger I gave you a king,
and in my wrath I took him away.
12The guilt of Ephraim is stored up,
his sins are kept on record.
13Pains as of a woman in childbirth come to
him,
but he is a child without wisdom;
when the time arrives,
he does not come to the opening of the
womb.

14"I will ransom them from the power of the
grave[c];
I will redeem them from death.
Where, O death, are your plagues?
Where, O grave,[c] is your destruction?

"I will have no compassion,
15 even though he thrives among his
brothers.
An east wind from the LORD will come,
blowing in from the desert;
his spring will fail
and his well dry up.
His storehouse will be plundered
of all its treasures.
16The people of Samaria must bear their
guilt,
because they have rebelled against their
God.
They will fall by the sword;
their little ones will be dashed to the
ground,
their pregnant women ripped open."

Repentance to Bring Blessing

14 Return, O Israel, to the LORD your
God.
Your sins have been your downfall!
2Take words with you
and return to the LORD.
Say to him:
"Forgive all our sins
and receive us graciously,
that we may offer the fruit of our lips.[d]
3Assyria cannot save us;
we will not mount war-horses.
We will never again say 'Our gods'
to what our own hands have made,
for in you the fatherless find
compassion."

4"I will heal their waywardness
and love them freely,

[a]2 Or *"Men who sacrifice / kiss* [b]4 Or *God / ever since you were in* [c]14 Hebrew *Sheol* [d]2 Or *offer our lips as sacrifices of bulls*

13:1–3 Israel's downfall came *after* the people had forsaken God and gone after false gods. We may also find that our willful choices to forsake God and go our own way are the source of our problems. We cannot blame God for our situations if we have abandoned him. He lovingly cares for us. When we recognize that our problems began when we willfully went our own way, we can begin to remedy those problems by turning back to God. We must admit our sin and ask God to direct us back to obedience to his will. He will lovingly forgive us and redirect the course of our lives.

13:4, 13 The God of the Bible offers salvation to all who will accept it (see John 3:3, 16; Romans 1:16). Anyone who refuses this offer and looks to another source for salvation is like a stubborn child who resists being born, not wanting the life being offered. Are we resisting God's offer, or have we gladly accepted the new life God has in store for us?

14:1–4 These verses contain a model for spiritual renewal. The people were urged to admit their helplessness apart from God and to examine themselves, taking responsibility for their condition. They were advised to let God change them, renouncing any further dealings with gods of their own making, and to commit their lives to God alone. We can follow these same directions in our spiritual renewal, renouncing our own false gods and surrendering our lives to God by obeying his will.

14:4–8 God promised that his people would experience unprecedented spiritual growth as they committed their lives completely to him. As they allowed God to heal them, they would realize that he was the source of their nourishment and growth. We can have the same hope to-

for my anger has turned away from
them.
[5]I will be like the dew to Israel;
he will blossom like a lily.
Like a cedar of Lebanon
he will send down his roots;
[6] his young shoots will grow.
His splendor will be like an olive tree,
his fragrance like a cedar of Lebanon.
[7]Men will dwell again in his shade.
He will flourish like the grain.
He will blossom like a vine,
and his fame will be like the wine from
Lebanon.

[8]O Ephraim, what more have I[a] to do with
idols?
I will answer him and care for him.
I am like a green pine tree;
your fruitfulness comes from me."

[9]Who is wise? He will realize these things.
Who is discerning? He will understand
them.
The ways of the LORD are right;
the righteous walk in them,
but the rebellious stumble in them.

[a]8 Or *What more has Ephraim*

---

day. The problems caused by our sins can be resolved as we repent and accept God's mercy on our behalf.

14:9 The prophet Hosea spoke often of sin and judgment, but he also pointed the way to salvation through humble repentance. Wise people will listen and learn from the prophet's words and find the inherent truth in all that God asks of them. God cares about our welfare and wants us to be healed because he loves us.

JOEL

The Big Picture

A. A LOCUST PLAGUE: FROM CATASTROPHE TO SPIRITUAL RENEWAL (1:1–2:27)

1. Locusts Terrify the Land (1:1-15)
2. God Judges the Land (1:16–2:11)
3. God Has Mercy on the Land (2:12-27)

B. THE DAY OF THE LORD: JUDGMENT OR SPIRITUAL RENEWAL (2:28–3:21)

1. Power to Live Uprightly: The Gift of the Spirit (2:28-29)
2. Terror on the Earth: The Day of the Lord (2:30-31)
3. Deliverance From Judgment: An Invitation to All (2:32)
4. Judgment on the Earth: The Wars of God (3:1-16)
5. Restoration of the Land: God's Kingdom (3:17-21)

Earthquakes, hurricanes, floods, tornadoes. Natural catastrophes of various kinds make us feel helpless. We can't stop them. We can only try to avoid them and then pick up the pieces after they have passed. The first part of Joel's prophecy concerns two natural disasters that led to great suffering for God's people: a major drought and a plague of locusts. God used these natural events to warn his people of their impending destruction if they refused to recognize their need for him.

Disasters sometimes result because of our own behavior. Joel realized that Judah's natural disasters were God's way of getting his people's attention. Centuries earlier, Moses had warned God's people that disobedience to God's plan would lead to such catastrophes (see Deuteronomy 28:38–39). God sought to restore his people to himself. Using these natural disasters, God broke through their illusions of security and self-sufficiency and showed them the importantance of their relationship with him.

Some of us have suffered from disasters in our own lives. We may suffer painful consequences because of our own mistakes and find ourselves unable to combat the powers that assail us. As we recognize our own limitations and accept responsibility for our sins, we should realize that this turmoil is a wonderful opportunity for a new start! Recognizing our need for God's power in our lives will lead us to seek God afresh and surrender to him again. This will help us continue with the ongoing process of spiritual renewal.

Spiritual Renewal Themes

THE POWER OF CONFRONTATION

God's people had lost sight of their need for God. They had become complacent about following the plan God had laid out for them. To break through their spiritual blindness, God let them suffer a series of disasters. Through their sufferings and the words of the prophet Joel, God let his people know that they were headed for disaster and needed to make some changes in their lives. God often intervenes in our lives in similar ways. He may allow us to suffer the consequences of our sinfulness in order to awaken us from our spiritual blindness and complacency. He may confront us with the painful reality of our

choices and actions. We should find comfort in this process because God confronts us not to destroy us but to initiate our restoration.

THE IMPORTANCE OF FORGIVENESS

Joel stated that "the day of the Lord" was coming. But along with his message of warning and judgment, Joel also brought his listeners hope. By confessing their sins, accepting responsibility for their wrongdoing and seeking to redirect their course, God's people could experience the healing available to them through God's forgiveness. Some of us want to undo some of our past actions and choices. Rather than change the past, God provides a means of resolving our past sin and failure through forgiveness. Our spiritual renewal is built upon the foundation of both receiving and granting forgiveness.

THE LIMITLESSNESS OF GOD'S POWER

We can easily be overwhelmed by the power of nature when it unleashes its fury in an earthquake, volcano or hurricane. When we look at the coastline and see how the waves have carved out cliffs and caves, we marvel at the power of the ocean. But none of these powerful acts of nature can compare to the overwhelming power of God. When we feel powerless, God invites us to repent and come to him for help. In him we have all the power we need to overcome our weaknesses.

GOD'S POWER WITHIN US

Joel predicted a time when the limitless power of God would be poured out upon us through the Holy Spirit. God would then be directly available to his people. This prophecy was fulfilled when God's Spirit was poured out after Jesus' ascension into heaven. In the process of spiritual renewal we must remember that God is with us. His power is always available to us as we persevere in our struggle to grow.

Essential Facts

PURPOSE:
To warn God's people of impending judgment and to urge them to admit their sins and turn back to God.

AUTHOR:
The prophet Joel.

AUDIENCE:
The people of the southern kingdom of Judah.

DATE WRITTEN:
Though Joel does not give us historical markers to help assign a date for the book, some believe Joel penned these words about 800 B.C. during the reign of young King Joash (see 2 Kings 11; 2 Chronicles 23–24).

SETTING:
Jerusalem during a period of prosperity; the people had become complacent about their relationship with God.

KEY VERSE:
"Rend your heart and not your garments. Return to the Lord your God, for he is gracious and compassionate, slow to anger and abounding in love, and he relents from sending calamity" (2:13).

KEY PEOPLE AND RELATIONSHIPS:
Political and religious leaders, parents and children, bride and groom, Joel and God's people.

1 The word of the LORD that came to Joel son of Pethuel.

An Invasion of Locusts

2Hear this, you elders;
listen, all who live in the land.
Has anything like this ever happened in your days
or in the days of your forefathers?
3Tell it to your children,
and let your children tell it to their children,
and their children to the next generation.
4What the locust swarm has left
the great locusts have eaten;
what the great locusts have left
the young locusts have eaten;
what the young locusts have left
other locusts[a] have eaten.

5Wake up, you drunkards, and weep!
Wail, all you drinkers of wine;
wail because of the new wine,
for it has been snatched from your lips.
6A nation has invaded my land,
powerful and without number;
it has the teeth of a lion,
the fangs of a lioness.
7It has laid waste my vines
and ruined my fig trees.
It has stripped off their bark
and thrown it away,
leaving their branches white.

8Mourn like a virgin[b] in sackcloth
grieving for the husband[c] of her youth.
9Grain offerings and drink offerings
are cut off from the house of the LORD.
The priests are in mourning,
those who minister before the LORD.
10The fields are ruined,
the ground is dried up[d];
the grain is destroyed,
the new wine is dried up,
the oil fails.
11Despair, you farmers,
wail, you vine growers;
grieve for the wheat and the barley,
because the harvest of the field is destroyed.
12The vine is dried up
and the fig tree is withered;
the pomegranate, the palm and the apple tree—
all the trees of the field—are dried up.
Surely the joy of mankind
is withered away.

A Call to Repentance

13Put on sackcloth, O priests, and mourn;
wail, you who minister before the altar.
Come, spend the night in sackcloth,
you who minister before my God;
for the grain offerings and drink offerings
are withheld from the house of your God.
14Declare a holy fast;
call a sacred assembly.
Summon the elders
and all who live in the land
to the house of the LORD your God,
and cry out to the LORD.
15Alas for that day!
For the day of the LORD is near;
it will come like destruction from the Almighty.[e]

16Has not the food been cut off
before our very eyes—
joy and gladness
from the house of our God?
17The seeds are shriveled
beneath the clods.[f]
The storehouses are in ruins,
the granaries have been broken down,
for the grain has dried up.
18How the cattle moan!
The herds mill about
because they have no pasture;
even the flocks of sheep are suffering.
19To you, O LORD, I call,
for fire has devoured the open pastures
and flames have burned up all the trees of the field.
20Even the wild animals pant for you;
the streams of water have dried up
and fire has devoured the open pastures.

An Army of Locusts

2 Blow the trumpet in Zion;
sound the alarm on my holy hill.
Let all who live in the land tremble,
for the day of the LORD is coming.
It is close at hand—
2 a day of darkness and gloom,
a day of clouds and blackness.
Like dawn spreading across the mountains
a large and mighty army comes,
such as never was of old
nor ever will be in ages to come.

a4 The precise meaning of the four Hebrew words used here for locusts is uncertain. b8 Or *young woman* c8 Or *betrothed* d10 Or *ground mourns* e15 Hebrew *Shaddai* f17 The meaning of the Hebrew for this word is uncertain.

1:4—2:11 The people faced a hopeless situation. Their physical resources had been depleted by the locust plague and drought (1:4–12). They were spiritually destitute and separated from God despite offering their sacrifices (1:13–20). And the locusts were such a great foe to overcome that the people lacked courage and a means of self-defense. Yet the people needed to admit their helplessness before God could intervene on their behalf. We must also admit that we cannot do anything to save ourselves. Then God can mercifully rescue us from our pain.

[3]Before them fire devours,
behind them a flame blazes.
Before them the land is like the garden of Eden,
behind them, a desert waste—
nothing escapes them.
[4]They have the appearance of horses;
they gallop along like cavalry.
[5]With a noise like that of chariots
they leap over the mountaintops,
like a crackling fire consuming stubble,
like a mighty army drawn up for battle.

[6]At the sight of them, nations are in anguish;
every face turns pale.
[7]They charge like warriors;
they scale walls like soldiers.
They all march in line,
not swerving from their course.
[8]They do not jostle each other;
each marches straight ahead.
They plunge through defenses
without breaking ranks.
[9]They rush upon the city;
they run along the wall.
They climb into the houses;
like thieves they enter through the windows.

[10]Before them the earth shakes,
the sky trembles,
the sun and moon are darkened,
and the stars no longer shine.
[11]The LORD thunders
at the head of his army;
his forces are beyond number,
and mighty are those who obey his command.
The day of the LORD is great;
it is dreadful.
Who can endure it?

Rend Your Heart

[12]"Even now," declares the LORD,
"return to me with all your heart,
with fasting and weeping and mourning."

[13]Rend your heart
and not your garments.
Return to the LORD your God,
for he is gracious and compassionate,
slow to anger and abounding in love,
and he relents from sending calamity.
[14]Who knows? He may turn and have pity
and leave behind a blessing—
grain offerings and drink offerings
for the LORD your God.

[15]Blow the trumpet in Zion,
declare a holy fast,
call a sacred assembly.
[16]Gather the people,
consecrate the assembly;
bring together the elders,
gather the children,
those nursing at the breast.
Let the bridegroom leave his room
and the bride her chamber.
[17]Let the priests, who minister before the LORD,
weep between the temple porch and the altar.
Let them say, "Spare your people, O LORD.
Do not make your inheritance an object of scorn,
a byword among the nations.
Why should they say among the peoples,
'Where is their God?' "

The LORD's Answer

[18]Then the LORD will be jealous for his land
and take pity on his people.
[19]The LORD will reply[a] to them:

"I am sending you grain, new wine and oil,
enough to satisfy you fully;
never again will I make you
an object of scorn to the nations.

[20]"I will drive the northern army far from you,
pushing it into a parched and barren land,
with its front columns going into the eastern sea[b]
and those in the rear into the western sea.[c]
And its stench will go up;
its smell will rise."

Surely he has done great things.[d]
[21] Be not afraid, O land;
be glad and rejoice.
Surely the LORD has done great things.
[22] Be not afraid, O wild animals,
for the open pastures are becoming green.

[a]18,19 Or *LORD was jealous . . . / and took pity . . . / [19]The LORD replied* [b]20 That is, the Dead Sea [c]20 That is, the Mediterranean [d]20 Or *rise. / Surely it has done great things."*

2:12–17 God wanted the people of Judah to come to him with torn hearts, admitting their guilt and helplessness, rather than responding to God's judgment with the ritual tearing of their garments. The people needed to commit themselves to God, examine themselves, and ask God to change them. Since God is gracious and compassionate (2:13), we should surrender our lives to him so that he can change our pain into joy.

2:18–27 If the people of Judah admitted their sin, God would take away their disgrace and replace it with his blessing. When we also accept reality, admit our sins, accept responsibility for our lives and surrender them to God, he will free us from the bondage of sin and grant us mercy. The parched, barren areas of our lives will flourish, and our lives will bring glory to God.

The trees are bearing their fruit;
the fig tree and the vine yield their riches.
23Be glad, O people of Zion,
rejoice in the LORD your God,
for he has given you
the autumn rains in righteousness.[a]
He sends you abundant showers,
both autumn and spring rains, as before.
24The threshing floors will be filled with grain;
the vats will overflow with new wine and oil.

25"I will repay you for the years the locusts have eaten—
the great locust and the young locust,
the other locusts and the locust swarm[b]—
my great army that I sent among you.
26You will have plenty to eat, until you are full,
and you will praise the name of the LORD your God,
who has worked wonders for you;
never again will my people be shamed.
27Then you will know that I am in Israel,
that I am the LORD your God,
and that there is no other;
never again will my people be shamed.

The Day of the LORD

28"And afterward,
I will pour out my Spirit on all people.
Your sons and daughters will prophesy,
your old men will dream dreams,
your young men will see visions.
29Even on my servants, both men and women,
I will pour out my Spirit in those days.
30I will show wonders in the heavens
and on the earth,
blood and fire and billows of smoke.
31The sun will be turned to darkness
and the moon to blood
before the coming of the great and dreadful day of the LORD.
32And everyone who calls
on the name of the LORD will be saved;
for on Mount Zion and in Jerusalem
there will be deliverance,
as the LORD has said,
among the survivors
whom the LORD calls.

The Nations Judged

3 "In those days and at that time,
when I restore the fortunes of Judah and Jerusalem,
2I will gather all nations
and bring them down to the Valley of Jehoshaphat.[c]
There I will enter into judgment against them
concerning my inheritance, my people Israel,
for they scattered my people among the nations
and divided up my land.
3They cast lots for my people
and traded boys for prostitutes;
they sold girls for wine
that they might drink.

4"Now what have you against me, O Tyre
and Sidon and all you regions of Philistia? Are
you repaying me for something I have done?
If you are paying me back, I will swiftly and
speedily return on your own heads what you
have done. 5For you took my silver and my gold
and carried off my finest treasures to your temples. 6You sold the people of Judah and Jerusalem to the Greeks, that you might send them far
from their homeland.

7"See, I am going to rouse them out of the
places to which you sold them, and I will return
on your own heads what you have done. 8I will
sell your sons and daughters to the people of
Judah, and they will sell them to the Sabeans, a
nation far away." The LORD has spoken.

9Proclaim this among the nations:
Prepare for war!
Rouse the warriors!
Let all the fighting men draw near and attack.
10Beat your plowshares into swords
and your pruning hooks into spears.
Let the weakling say,
"I am strong!"
11Come quickly, all you nations from every side,
and assemble there.

Bring down your warriors, O LORD!

12"Let the nations be roused;

[a]23 Or / *the teacher for righteousness:* [b]25 The precise meaning of the four Hebrew words used here for locusts is uncertain. [c]2 *Jehoshaphat* means *the LORD judges;* also in verse 12.

2:28–29 This prophecy was fulfilled at Pentecost (see Acts 2). The Bible tells us that the Holy Spirit has changed many sinful and troubled lives: Peter and the apostles (see Acts 2), Paul (see Acts 9), a demon-possessed slave girl and a prison guard (see Acts 16) and others. The Spirit prophesied about in Joel and experienced by first-century Christians is available to us, too. We can trust the God of the Old and New Testaments to heal our broken lives and bring about our complete redemption.

2:32 When we call on the Lord's name we will find deliverance. No failure or sin is too great to prevent this. No disadvantage or lack can keep us from God's grace. When God comes to judge the world, his grace will still be available to us.

let them advance into the Valley of
Jehoshaphat,
for there I will sit
to judge all the nations on every side.
13 Swing the sickle,
for the harvest is ripe.
Come, trample the grapes,
for the winepress is full
and the vats overflow—
so great is their wickedness!"

14 Multitudes, multitudes
in the valley of decision!
For the day of the LORD is near
in the valley of decision.
15 The sun and moon will be darkened,
and the stars no longer shine.
16 The LORD will roar from Zion
and thunder from Jerusalem;
the earth and the sky will tremble.
But the LORD will be a refuge for his
people,
a stronghold for the people of Israel.

Blessings for God's People

17 "Then you will know that I, the LORD your
God,
dwell in Zion, my holy hill.
Jerusalem will be holy;
never again will foreigners invade her.

18 "In that day the mountains will drip new
wine,
and the hills will flow with milk;
all the ravines of Judah will run with
water.
A fountain will flow out of the LORD's
house
and will water the valley of acacias.[a]
19 But Egypt will be desolate,
Edom a desert waste,
because of violence done to the people of
Judah,
in whose land they shed innocent blood.
20 Judah will be inhabited forever
and Jerusalem through all generations.
21 Their bloodguilt, which I have not
pardoned,
I will pardon."

The LORD dwells in Zion!

[a] 18 Or *Valley of Shittim*

3:16–21 Ultimately God has a wonderful future planned for all who trust in him. Restoration will be complete; salvation will last forever. With this hope for the future, we can find the courage we need to persevere through our problems today (see Romans 8:18–21). Our final destination is assured and God promises to stay with us throughout life. With this in mind, we need not fear the path we must walk, even if it winds through uncertain territory.

Amos

The Big Picture

A. *THINGS THAT OFFEND GOD (1:1–2:16)*

1. Inhumane Conduct Between Nations (1:1–2:3)
2. Rejecting God and His Laws (2:4-5)
3. Oppressing the Poor and Helpless (2:6-8)
4. Rejecting God's Pleas to Repent (2:9-16)

B. *WARNINGS FROM GOD (3:1–6:14)*

1. The People Break the Covenant (3:1-15)
2. The People Refuse to Change Their Behavior (4:1-13)
3. The People Must Choose Life or Death (5:1-27)
4. Danger in Putting Confidence in the Wrong Things (6:1-14)

C. *GOD'S LOVING PUNISHMENT (7:1–9:15)*

1. The Context for Punishment: Merciful Love (7:1-6)
2. The Time for Punishment: The Near Future (7:7–8:14)
3. The Extent of Punishment: The Entire Nation (9:1-6)
4. The Result of Punishment: Restoration (9:7-15)

God is righteous and just, yet he always expresses his justice in the context of his love and compassion. God expects us to act in the same way toward others, showing mercy and understanding. In Amos's day, Israel was a prosperous nation. But with Israel's prosperity came corruption, injustice toward the helpless and religious apostasy. God had given his people laws for governing human relationships, but they had refused to obey these laws.

God called Amos, a shepherd from Tekoa, to awaken his people from their spiritual sleep. Sadly, their sinful behavior was worse than that of some of their pagan neighbors! Amos warned them of the painful consequences that would follow their sinful behavior. He confronted the people of Israel with their ill treatment of the poor and oppressed. God warned his people of their impending punishment so that they might change. They were reminded of their responsibilities as God's chosen people. He wanted them to act mercifully and with justice.

But God's people refused to repent. So Amos's predictions for Israel's future were dark and dismal. God would allow his people to suffer a period of destruction and exile. Despite his predictions of doom, however, Amos also spoke about a hopeful future. If only the people would admit their sin and ask for forgiveness, God would purify and restore them completely. It is never too late to seek spiritual renewal. God eagerly waits for us to repent and recognize how helpless we are and to call out to him for his loving help.

Spiritual Renewal Themes

COMPLACENCY LEADS TO A DOWNFALL

When life is going smoothly, we must be careful. An easy life makes us ripe for complacency and a downfall. In Amos's day, the people of Israel were prosperous and began to think they could succeed without God. This attitude led them down a path toward destruction. Even when our lives are successful, we still need God. He is the source of our spiritual renewal; all success must be attributed to him. A complacent, self-sufficient attitude will lead only to a fall.

CREATED FOR RELATIONSHIP

The people in Amos's time believed they did not need other people. They exploited the weak and poor and were indifferent to the pain of those around them. They enslaved the helpless through extortion and heavy taxation. God has created us to live in relationship *with* others, not in isolation *from* others. God urges us to recognize our need for others and do what we can to make restitution to those we may have hurt.

GOD HONORS UPRIGHT HEARTS

Many of the people of Israel kept up the outward appearances of religion even though they had abandoned their faith in God. There is the danger that we may fall into the same trap. We may perform religious rituals to obtain the approval of others but never allow a genuine internal change to take place. We may hide our sins from others, pretending we are faithfully following God's way when we are not. God wants us to have genuine hearts that seek to know and trust him. He is not as concerned with how we appear on the surface; he sees through our false appearances even if other people don't. God cares about the attitudes of our hearts.

SPIRITUAL RENEWAL BEGINS WITH SURRENDER

When the people of Israel went into captivity, their lives were crumbling about them. They could finally see the truth. They knew that they needed God. The dark times of life often lead us to recognize our need for God too. Our helplessness breaks apart our spiritual blindness, opening our eyes to reality. When our lives are out of control and crumbling around us, our attempts to deny that we need God are futile. We must acknowledge our need and be open to his saving power before true spiritual renewal can begin.

Essential Facts

PURPOSE:
To confront the people of Israel with their sin, calling them to confession and repentance.

AUTHOR:
The prophet Amos.

AUDIENCE:
The people of the northern kingdom of Israel.

DATE WRITTEN:
Between 760 and 750 B.C., when Jeroboam II was king of Israel and Uzziah was king of Judah.

SETTING:
The northern kingdom of Israel during a time of material prosperity and spiritual complacency.

KEY VERSE:
"In that day I will restore David's fallen tent. I will repair its broken places, restore its ruins, and build it as it used to be" (9:11).

KEY PLACES:
Samaria, the northern kingdom's capital and the temple at Bethel.

KEY PEOPLE AND RELATIONSHIPS:
Amos, Amaziah the priest at Bethel, the people of Israel and the Edomites.

1 The words of Amos, one of the shepherds of Tekoa—what he saw concerning Israel two years before the earthquake, when Uzziah was king of Judah and Jeroboam son of Jehoash[a] was king of Israel.

[2]He said:

"The LORD roars from Zion
and thunders from Jerusalem;
the pastures of the shepherds dry up,[b]
and the top of Carmel withers."

Judgment on Israel's Neighbors

[3]This is what the LORD says:

"For three sins of Damascus,
even for four, I will not turn back ⌞my wrath⌟.
Because she threshed Gilead
with sledges having iron teeth,
[4]I will send fire upon the house of Hazael
that will consume the fortresses of Ben-Hadad.
[5]I will break down the gate of Damascus;
I will destroy the king who is in[c] the Valley of Aven[d]
and the one who holds the scepter in Beth Eden.
The people of Aram will go into exile to Kir,"
says the LORD.

[6]This is what the LORD says:

"For three sins of Gaza,
even for four, I will not turn back ⌞my wrath⌟.
Because she took captive whole communities
and sold them to Edom,
[7]I will send fire upon the walls of Gaza
that will consume her fortresses.
[8]I will destroy the king[e] of Ashdod
and the one who holds the scepter in Ashkelon.
I will turn my hand against Ekron,
till the last of the Philistines is dead,"
says the Sovereign LORD.

[9]This is what the LORD says:

"For three sins of Tyre,
even for four, I will not turn back ⌞my wrath⌟.
Because she sold whole communities of captives to Edom,
disregarding a treaty of brotherhood,
[10]I will send fire upon the walls of Tyre
that will consume her fortresses."

[11]This is what the LORD says:

"For three sins of Edom,
even for four, I will not turn back ⌞my wrath⌟.
Because he pursued his brother with a sword,
stifling all compassion,[f]
because his anger raged continually
and his fury flamed unchecked,
[12]I will send fire upon Teman
that will consume the fortresses of Bozrah."

[13]This is what the LORD says:

"For three sins of Ammon,
even for four, I will not turn back ⌞my wrath⌟.
Because he ripped open the pregnant women of Gilead
in order to extend his borders,
[14]I will set fire to the walls of Rabbah
that will consume her fortresses
amid war cries on the day of battle,
amid violent winds on a stormy day.
[15]Her king[g] will go into exile,
he and his officials together,"
says the LORD.

2 This is what the LORD says:

"For three sins of Moab,
even for four, I will not turn back ⌞my wrath⌟.
Because he burned, as if to lime,
the bones of Edom's king,
[2]I will send fire upon Moab
that will consume the fortresses of Kerioth.[h]
Moab will go down in great tumult
amid war cries and the blast of the trumpet.
[3]I will destroy her ruler
and kill all her officials with him,"
says the LORD.

[4]This is what the LORD says:

"For three sins of Judah,

[a]1 Hebrew *Joash,* a variant of *Jehoash* [b]2 Or *shepherds mourn* [c]5 Or *the inhabitants of* [d]5 *Aven* means *wickedness.* [e]8 Or *inhabitants* [f]11 Or *sword / and destroyed his allies* [g]15 Or / *Molech;* Hebrew *malcam* [h]2 Or *of her cities*

1:3—2:3 All people are accountable to God for their actions. There are certain boundaries of human behavior that God requires of everyone. If anyone crosses these boundaries, God will punish them. God will send judgment, but only after giving all people time to repent and change their ways (see 2 Peter 3:9). We may seem to prosper while going our own way, but this will last only a short while. If we do not admit our sin and turn back to God, we will eventually suffer the consequences for our actions.

2:4–8 The sins of the Israelites stemmed from their rejection of God's laws. The Israelite leaders oppressed and took advantage of the poor, accepted bribes, engaged in sexual sins, and disregarded God's laws in many other ways. Obeying God's regulations would have brought them blessing, but their evil deeds ensured their punishment. While our world and our societal standards may have changed since Bible times, God and his laws have not. These immoral behaviors will still result in punishment from God.

even for four, I will not turn back ⌊my wrath⌋.
Because they have rejected the law of the LORD
and have not kept his decrees,
because they have been led astray by false gods,[a]
the gods[b] their ancestors followed,
5I will send fire upon Judah
that will consume the fortresses of Jerusalem."

Judgment on Israel

6This is what the LORD says:

"For three sins of Israel,
even for four, I will not turn back ⌊my wrath⌋.
They sell the righteous for silver,
and the needy for a pair of sandals.
7They trample on the heads of the poor
as upon the dust of the ground
and deny justice to the oppressed.
Father and son use the same girl
and so profane my holy name.
8They lie down beside every altar
on garments taken in pledge.
In the house of their god
they drink wine taken as fines.

9"I destroyed the Amorite before them,
though he was tall as the cedars
and strong as the oaks.
I destroyed his fruit above
and his roots below.

10"I brought you up out of Egypt,
and I led you forty years in the desert
to give you the land of the Amorites.
11I also raised up prophets from among your sons
and Nazirites from among your young men.
Is this not true, people of Israel?"
declares the LORD.
12"But you made the Nazirites drink wine
and commanded the prophets not to prophesy.

13"Now then, I will crush you
as a cart crushes when loaded with grain.
14The swift will not escape,
the strong will not muster their strength,
and the warrior will not save his life.
15The archer will not stand his ground,
the fleet-footed soldier will not get away,
and the horseman will not save his life.
16Even the bravest warriors
will flee naked on that day,"
declares the LORD.

Witnesses Summoned Against Israel

3 Hear this word the LORD has spoken
against you, O people of Israel—against the
whole family I brought up out of Egypt:

2"You only have I chosen
of all the families of the earth;
therefore I will punish you
for all your sins."

3Do two walk together
unless they have agreed to do so?
4Does a lion roar in the thicket
when he has no prey?
Does he growl in his den
when he has caught nothing?
5Does a bird fall into a trap on the ground
where no snare has been set?
Does a trap spring up from the earth
when there is nothing to catch?
6When a trumpet sounds in a city,
do not the people tremble?
When disaster comes to a city,
has not the LORD caused it?

7Surely the Sovereign LORD does nothing
without revealing his plan
to his servants the prophets.

8The lion has roared—
who will not fear?
The Sovereign LORD has spoken—
who can but prophesy?

9Proclaim to the fortresses of Ashdod
and to the fortresses of Egypt:
"Assemble yourselves on the mountains of Samaria;
see the great unrest within her
and the oppression among her people."

10"They do not know how to do right,"
declares the LORD,
"who hoard plunder and loot in their fortresses."

11Therefore this is what the Sovereign LORD
says:

"An enemy will overrun the land;

[a]4 Or *by lies* [b]4 Or *lies*

3:2 The people of Israel knew what God wanted them to do and how he wanted them to live. They knew the laws and the consequences for disobedience, yet they chose to sin anyway. God's response to their disobedience was to send the curses outlined in his laws. We also know the dangers and consequences for our sins. To continue in sin and ignore sin's consequences is a mark of spiritual blindness. The only way to avoid the consequences of our sins is to repent and confess our sins, surrendering our lives to God. Then God can grant us mercy and redirect the course of our lives.

3:3–8 God's prophets had issued warnings to the people of Israel on a regular basis, reminding them of their ancestors' disobedience and subsequent suffering. We receive regular warnings about our sinful choices too. Continuing in our sins and ignoring the warnings can be compared to hearing a smoke alarm go off and then waiting around to be burned up in the fire. We should listen to the warnings we receive and respond before it is too late.

he will pull down your strongholds
and plunder your fortresses."

12This is what the LORD says:

"As a shepherd saves from the lion's mouth
only two leg bones or a piece of an ear,
so will the Israelites be saved,
those who sit in Samaria
on the edge of their beds
and in Damascus on their couches.[a]"

13"Hear this and testify against the house
of Jacob," declares the Lord, the LORD God Almighty.

14"On the day I punish Israel for her sins,
I will destroy the altars of Bethel;
the horns of the altar will be cut off
and fall to the ground.
15I will tear down the winter house
along with the summer house;
the houses adorned with ivory will be destroyed
and the mansions will be demolished,"
declares the LORD.

Israel Has Not Returned to God

4 Hear this word, you cows of Bashan on Mount Samaria,
you women who oppress the poor and crush the needy
and say to your husbands, "Bring us some drinks!"
2The Sovereign LORD has sworn by his holiness:
"The time will surely come
when you will be taken away with hooks,
the last of you with fishhooks.
3You will each go straight out
through breaks in the wall,
and you will be cast out toward Harmon,[b]"
declares the LORD.

4"Go to Bethel and sin;
go to Gilgal and sin yet more.
Bring your sacrifices every morning,
your tithes every three years.[c]
5Burn leavened bread as a thank offering
and brag about your freewill offerings—
boast about them, you Israelites,
for this is what you love to do,"
declares the Sovereign LORD.

6"I gave you empty stomachs[d] in every city
and lack of bread in every town,
yet you have not returned to me,"
declares the LORD.

7"I also withheld rain from you
when the harvest was still three months away.
I sent rain on one town,
but withheld it from another.
One field had rain;
another had none and dried up.
8People staggered from town to town for water
but did not get enough to drink,
yet you have not returned to me,"
declares the LORD.

9"Many times I struck your gardens and vineyards,
I struck them with blight and mildew.
Locusts devoured your fig and olive trees,
yet you have not returned to me,"
declares the LORD.

10"I sent plagues among you
as I did to Egypt.
I killed your young men with the sword,
along with your captured horses.
I filled your nostrils with the stench of your camps,
yet you have not returned to me,"
declares the LORD.

11"I overthrew some of you
as I[e] overthrew Sodom and Gomorrah.
You were like a burning stick snatched from the fire,
yet you have not returned to me,"
declares the LORD.

12"Therefore this is what I will do to you, Israel,
and because I will do this to you,
prepare to meet your God, O Israel."

13He who forms the mountains,
creates the wind,
and reveals his thoughts to man,
he who turns dawn to darkness,
and treads the high places of the earth—
the LORD God Almighty is his name.

A Lament and Call to Repentance

5 Hear this word, O house of Israel, this lament I take up concerning you:

2"Fallen is Virgin Israel,
never to rise again,
deserted in her own land,
with no one to lift her up."

[a]12 The meaning of the Hebrew for this line is uncertain.
[b]3 Masoretic Text; with a different word division of the Hebrew (see Septuagint) *out, O mountain of oppression*
[c]4 Or *tithes on the third day* [d]6 Hebrew *you cleanness of teeth* [e]11 Hebrew *God*

4:4–5 Finding a substitute for a genuine relationship with God is fairly easy. A tempting substitute is religious activity. If we go to church regularly, perhaps even sing in the choir, we sometimes feel we have done all we can to build a relationship with God. God requires more than tithes, offerings and time spent in worship. God really wants our heartfelt devotion.

4:6–11 Even though the Israelites possessed much, without God they still felt empty inside. Yet they refused to give up their sins. The negative effects of our sins should also be signs for us to turn back to God, the giver of all that is good and perfect (see James 1:17).

3 This is what the Sovereign LORD says:

"The city that marches out a thousand
strong for Israel
will have only a hundred left;
the town that marches out a hundred
strong
will have only ten left."

4 This is what the LORD says to the house of
Israel:

"Seek me and live;
5 do not seek Bethel,
do not go to Gilgal,
do not journey to Beersheba.
For Gilgal will surely go into exile,
and Bethel will be reduced to nothing.[a]"
6 Seek the LORD and live,
or he will sweep through the house of
Joseph like a fire;
it will devour,
and Bethel will have no one to quench
it.

7 You who turn justice into bitterness
and cast righteousness to the ground
8 (he who made the Pleiades and Orion,
who turns blackness into dawn
and darkens day into night,
who calls for the waters of the sea
and pours them out over the face of the
land—
the LORD is his name—
9 he flashes destruction on the stronghold
and brings the fortified city to ruin),
10 you hate the one who reproves in court
and despise him who tells the truth.

11 You trample on the poor
and force him to give you grain.
Therefore, though you have built stone
mansions,
you will not live in them;
though you have planted lush vineyards,
you will not drink their wine.
12 For I know how many are your offenses
and how great your sins.

You oppress the righteous and take bribes
and you deprive the poor of justice in
the courts.
13 Therefore the prudent man keeps quiet in
such times,
for the times are evil.

14 Seek good, not evil,
that you may live.
Then the LORD God Almighty will be with
you,
just as you say he is.
15 Hate evil, love good;
maintain justice in the courts.
Perhaps the LORD God Almighty will have
mercy
on the remnant of Joseph.

16 Therefore this is what the Lord, the LORD
God Almighty, says:

"There will be wailing in all the streets
and cries of anguish in every public
square.
The farmers will be summoned to weep
and the mourners to wail.
17 There will be wailing in all the vineyards,
for I will pass through your midst,"
says the LORD.

The Day of the LORD

18 Woe to you who long
for the day of the LORD!
Why do you long for the day of the LORD?
That day will be darkness, not light.
19 It will be as though a man fled from a lion
only to meet a bear,
as though he entered his house
and rested his hand on the wall
only to have a snake bite him.
20 Will not the day of the LORD be darkness,
not light—
pitch-dark, without a ray of brightness?

21 "I hate, I despise your religious feasts;
I cannot stand your assemblies.

[a] 5 Or *grief*; or *wickedness*; Hebrew *aven,* a reference to Beth Aven (a derogatory name for Bethel)

5:4–5 Israel was warned not to worship idols. They were repeatedly told that those who did would face trouble. We may not worship carved images, but when we look to other things to receive what only God can provide, we are serving a false god. God doesn't want us chasing after things that will lead only to disappointment and death. Instead, he calls out to us: "Seek me and live" (5:4).

5:6, 14 Life comes from God alone and nowhere else. To seek God means to surrender our lives to him, letting him change us. But how do we avoid the various failures mentioned in these verses? God reveals himself uniquely in the Bible; it is our infallible guide to the truth. We need to seek out God's will in his Word and then seek his help to live by it.

5:8–9 When we seek God, we seek the Creator of all things. He is all-powerful, controlling both day and night. He pours out the sea like water from a pitcher. He cannot be stopped by the best efforts of the human race. When we commit our lives to him, we can be sure that he can transform us.

5:18–20 We may fool ourselves into believing we are spiritually right with God when we are not. Amos calls here for an honest self-examination. When Jesus Christ returns, it will be a time of joy for those whose faith is genuine. Those who have not been honest with themselves and who have not surrendered their lives to God through Jesus Christ will be lost forever (see Matthew 7:21–23). Let us honestly reflect on our lives and determine where we stand with God. What must we change to be more like he wants us to be?

5:21–24 No amount of religious activity will make up for a sinful lifestyle. We may fool others, leading them to believe that we are spiritually on track because we go to church three times a week or give twenty percent of our income to the church. But God will not look favorably upon our religious behavior if our hearts are not right with him.

22Even though you bring me burnt offerings
and grain offerings,
I will not accept them.
Though you bring choice fellowship
offerings,[a]
I will have no regard for them.
23Away with the noise of your songs!
I will not listen to the music of your
harps.
24But let justice roll on like a river,
righteousness like a never-failing stream!

25"Did you bring me sacrifices and offerings
forty years in the desert, O house of
Israel?
26You have lifted up the shrine of your king,
the pedestal of your idols,
the star of your god[b]—
which you made for yourselves.
27Therefore I will send you into exile beyond
Damascus,"
says the LORD, whose name is God
Almighty.

Woe to the Complacent

6 Woe to you who are complacent in Zion,
and to you who feel secure on Mount
Samaria,
you notable men of the foremost nation,
to whom the people of Israel come!
2Go to Calneh and look at it;
go from there to great Hamath,
and then go down to Gath in Philistia.
Are they better off than your two
kingdoms?
Is their land larger than yours?
3You put off the evil day
and bring near a reign of terror.
4You lie on beds inlaid with ivory
and lounge on your couches.
You dine on choice lambs
and fattened calves.
5You strum away on your harps like David
and improvise on musical instruments.
6You drink wine by the bowlful
and use the finest lotions,
but you do not grieve over the ruin of
Joseph.
7Therefore you will be among the first to go
into exile;
your feasting and lounging will end.

The LORD Abhors the Pride of Israel

8The Sovereign LORD has sworn by himself—
the LORD God Almighty declares:

"I abhor the pride of Jacob
and detest his fortresses;
I will deliver up the city
and everything in it."

9If ten men are left in one house, they too
will die. 10And if a relative who is to burn the
bodies comes to carry them out of the house
and asks anyone still hiding there, "Is anyone
with you?" and he says, "No," then he will say,
"Hush! We must not mention the name of the
LORD."

11For the LORD has given the command,
and he will smash the great house into
pieces
and the small house into bits.

12Do horses run on the rocky crags?
Does one plow there with oxen?
But you have turned justice into poison
and the fruit of righteousness into
bitterness—
13you who rejoice in the conquest of
Lo Debar[c]
and say, "Did we not take Karnaim[d] by
our own strength?"

14For the LORD God Almighty declares,
"I will stir up a nation against you,
O house of Israel,
that will oppress you all the way
from Lebo[e] Hamath to the valley of the
Arabah."

Locusts, Fire and a Plumb Line

7 This is what the Sovereign LORD showed
me: He was preparing swarms of locusts
after the king's share had been harvested and
just as the second crop was coming up. 2When
they had stripped the land clean, I cried out,
"Sovereign LORD, forgive! How can Jacob survive? He is so small!"
3So the LORD relented.
"This will not happen," the LORD said.
4This is what the Sovereign LORD showed me:
The Sovereign LORD was calling for judgment by
fire; it dried up the great deep and devoured the
land. 5Then I cried out, "Sovereign LORD, I beg
you, stop! How can Jacob survive? He is so
small!"
6So the LORD relented.
"This will not happen either," the Sovereign
LORD said.

7This is what he showed me: The Lord was

[a]22 Traditionally *peace offerings* [b]26 Or *lifted up Sakkuth your king / and Kaiwan your idols, / your star-gods;* Septuagint *lifted up the shrine of Molech / and the star of your god Rephan, / their idols* [c]13 *Lo Debar* means *nothing.* [d]13 *Karnaim* means *horns; horn* here symbolizes strength. [e]14 Or *from the entrance to*

6:4–7 God wants his people to enjoy the good things he provides for them. However, the Israelites craved these good things so much that they no longer cared about anyone or anything else. Many of us are in the same situation, wrapped up in our pleasures and too busy for God or those around us. We may even have ruined our family life or our friendships in the pursuit of more "things." If we surrender these areas to God, he can restore our lives and our relationships.

7:7–9 God would not withhold his judgment any longer. He held a plumb line up to Israel to see how Israel measured up to his righteous standards. God holds his plumb

standing by a wall that had been built true to
plumb, with a plumb line in his hand. 8And the
LORD asked me, "What do you see, Amos?"

"A plumb line," I replied.

Then the Lord said, "Look, I am setting a plumb line among my people Israel; I will spare them no longer.

9"The high places of Isaac will be destroyed
and the sanctuaries of Israel will be ruined;
with my sword I will rise against the house of Jeroboam."

Amos and Amaziah

10Then Amaziah the priest of Bethel sent a
message to Jeroboam king of Israel: "Amos is
raising a conspiracy against you in the very
heart of Israel. The land cannot bear all his
words. 11For this is what Amos is saying:

" 'Jeroboam will die by the sword,
and Israel will surely go into exile,
away from their native land.' "

12Then Amaziah said to Amos, "Get out, you
seer! Go back to the land of Judah. Earn your
bread there and do your prophesying there.
13Don't prophesy anymore at Bethel, because
this is the king's sanctuary and the temple of the
kingdom."

14Amos answered Amaziah, "I was neither a
prophet nor a prophet's son, but I was a shepherd, and I also took care of sycamore-fig trees.
15But the LORD took me from tending the flock
and said to me, 'Go, prophesy to my people
Israel.' 16Now then, hear the word of the LORD.
You say,

" 'Do not prophesy against Israel,
and stop preaching against the house of Isaac.'

17"Therefore this is what the LORD says:

" 'Your wife will become a prostitute in the city,
and your sons and daughters will fall by the sword.
Your land will be measured and divided up,

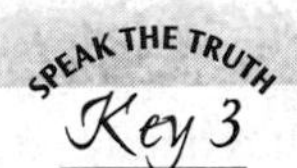

The Plumb Line

Amos 7:7–8 When we assess our moral character, we must base our measurements on truth. If we measure ourselves against a faulty standard, we won't be able to see the truth and make an honest confession of our sins to God.

The Lord wanted the Israelites to acknowledge their sin and used the analogy of a plumb line to get their attention. "I am setting a plumb line among my people Israel; I will spare them no longer" (7:8). A plumb line is a length of string with a weight tied to one end. When the string is held next to a building or structure with the weighted end hanging down, gravity ensures that the string is perfectly vertical. This vertical plumb line provides a sure standard by which to measure the building's position. Unless a building is built in line with the plumb line, the walls will not stand as straight and true as they should.

In the spiritual realm, God's Word is our spiritual plumb line. We can't change the spiritual laws revealed in the Bible. It is to our advantage to measure our lives by the plumb line of God's Word. When things don't measure up, it is important that we admit there is a problem and start rebuilding accordingly.

Turn to Zechariah 9.

---

line of the Bible against our lives. When we look at ourselves, we may appear straight and true. But measured alongside God's plumb line, we can easily see that our lives are weak and leaning toward sin. A prayer to God for help is the best way to begin anew a life in line with God's plan.

7:10–17 Amos was sure of his commitment to God. He courageously faced the opposition of the people and persevered in what he knew to be God's will. We may also face opposition to our spiritual growth, especially when we openly repent from sin. People may feel threatened by our progress. They might even want us to fail so they won't feel guilty about their own lifestyles. When we suffer opposition, we may feel like giving up and giving in to others. But we must persevere, trusting God for guidance and strength.

and you yourself will die in a pagan[a]
country.
And Israel will certainly go into exile,
away from their native land.' "

A Basket of Ripe Fruit

8 This is what the Sovereign LORD showed
me: a basket of ripe fruit. 2"What do you
see, Amos?" he asked.

"A basket of ripe fruit," I answered.

Then the LORD said to me, "The time is ripe
for my people Israel; I will spare them no
longer.

3"In that day," declares the Sovereign LORD,
"the songs in the temple will turn to wailing.[b]
Many, many bodies—flung everywhere! Silence!"

4Hear this, you who trample the needy
and do away with the poor of the land,

5saying,

"When will the New Moon be over
that we may sell grain,
and the Sabbath be ended
that we may market wheat?"—
skimping the measure,
boosting the price
and cheating with dishonest scales,
6buying the poor with silver
and the needy for a pair of sandals,
selling even the sweepings with the
wheat.

7The LORD has sworn by the Pride of Jacob:
"I will never forget anything they have done.

8"Will not the land tremble for this,
and all who live in it mourn?
The whole land will rise like the Nile;
it will be stirred up and then sink
like the river of Egypt.

9"In that day," declares the Sovereign LORD,

"I will make the sun go down at noon
and darken the earth in broad daylight.
10I will turn your religious feasts into
mourning
and all your singing into weeping.
I will make all of you wear sackcloth
and shave your heads.
I will make that time like mourning for an
only son
and the end of it like a bitter day.

11"The days are coming," declares the
Sovereign LORD,
"when I will send a famine through the
land—
not a famine of food or a thirst for water,
but a famine of hearing the words of the
LORD.
12Men will stagger from sea to sea
and wander from north to east,
searching for the word of the LORD,
but they will not find it.

13"In that day

"the lovely young women and strong
young men
will faint because of thirst.
14They who swear by the shame[c] of
Samaria,
or say, 'As surely as your god lives,
O Dan,'
or, 'As surely as the god[d] of Beersheba
lives'—
they will fall,
never to rise again."

Israel to Be Destroyed

9 I saw the Lord standing by the altar, and he
said:

"Strike the tops of the pillars
so that the thresholds shake.
Bring them down on the heads of all the
people;
those who are left I will kill with the
sword.
Not one will get away,
none will escape.
2Though they dig down to the depths of the
grave,[e]
from there my hand will take them.
Though they climb up to the heavens,
from there I will bring them down.
3Though they hide themselves on the top of
Carmel,
there I will hunt them down and seize
them.
Though they hide from me at the bottom
of the sea,

[a]17 Hebrew *an unclean* [b]3 Or *"the temple singers will wail* [c]14 Or *by Ashima;* or *by the idol* [d]14 Or *power* [e]2 Hebrew *to Sheol*

8:4–6 Instead of serving God, the Israelites served material wealth. They were not honest about this, however. They went through the rituals of worship but spent the time thinking up new ways to cheat their customers. Serving wealth has become quite common in our society and has even become a way of life for many. But if we are devoted to money, we cannot be devoted to God (see Matthew 6:24). We must decide whether our master will be God, who offers eternal life and peace, or whether our master will be money, which can never satisfy us.

8:11–14 Why wouldn't the people be able to find "the words of the LORD"? God was still speaking through other prophets: Hosea, Isaiah, Micah, and many others. The people couldn't find God's words because they were looking for revelations from pagan idols. God's people would not be able to hear God speaking to them until they admitted their sin. They needed to seek God alone and nothing else. We, too, need to stop trusting the "idols" we count on daily in order to hear the truth of God's Word. Only God's Word can offer us a true hope that satisfies.

9:1–4 If we desire spiritual renewal, we must surrender our lives to God. Amos tells us the terrible consequences reserved for those who refuse to do so (see Revelation 6:15–17). Earthly and eternal redemption are available to all who ask God to deliver them from their sins.

there I will command the serpent to bite
them.
[4]Though they are driven into exile by their
enemies,
there I will command the sword to slay
them.
I will fix my eyes upon them
for evil and not for good."

[5]The Lord, the LORD Almighty,
he who touches the earth and it melts,
and all who live in it mourn—
the whole land rises like the Nile,
then sinks like the river of Egypt—
[6]he who builds his lofty palace[a] in the
heavens
and sets its foundation[b] on the earth,
who calls for the waters of the sea
and pours them out over the face of the
land—
the LORD is his name.

[7]"Are not you Israelites
the same to me as the Cushites[c]?"
declares the LORD.
"Did I not bring Israel up from Egypt,
the Philistines from Caphtor[d]
and the Arameans from Kir?

[8]"Surely the eyes of the Sovereign LORD
are on the sinful kingdom.
I will destroy it
from the face of the earth—
yet I will not totally destroy
the house of Jacob,"
declares the LORD.

[9]"For I will give the command,
and I will shake the house of Israel
among all the nations
as grain is shaken in a sieve,
and not a pebble will reach the ground.
[10]All the sinners among my people
will die by the sword,
all those who say,
'Disaster will not overtake or meet us.'

Israel's Restoration

[11]"In that day I will restore
David's fallen tent.
I will repair its broken places,
restore its ruins,
and build it as it used to be,
[12]so that they may possess the remnant of
Edom
and all the nations that bear my name,[e]"
declares the LORD,
who will do these things.

[13]"The days are coming," declares the LORD,
"when the reaper will be overtaken by the
plowman
and the planter by the one treading
grapes.
New wine will drip from the mountains
and flow from all the hills.
[14]I will bring back my exiled[f] people Israel;
they will rebuild the ruined cities and
live in them.
They will plant vineyards and drink their
wine;
they will make gardens and eat their
fruit.
[15]I will plant Israel in their own land,
never again to be uprooted
from the land I have given them,"
says the LORD your God.

[a]6 The meaning of the Hebrew for this phrase is uncertain. [b]6 The meaning of the Hebrew for this word is uncertain. [c]7 That is, people from the upper Nile region [d]7 That is, Crete [e]12 Hebrew; Septuagint *so that the remnant of men / and all the nations that bear my name may seek ⌊the Lord⌋* [f]14 Or *will restore the fortunes of my*

9:10 Refusing to admit the truth can be dangerous. Outward appearances denied the truth of Amos's message. The nation was prosperous. Enemies were weak; the military was strong. Alliances had been made with Egypt and other nations. Yet inwardly the Israelites were diseased, and their spiritual sickness would ultimately lead to their destruction. Their refusal to see the truth resulted in their destruction and captivity at the hands of Assyria. Our refusal to see the truth can also cost us our lives and happiness. Let's admit the truth to ourselves and to God so we can enjoy the fulfillment he offers.

9:11–15 God has committed himself to redeeming and restoring his people. He wants to restore what is broken and ruined, changing barren land to a place of fruitfulness. This can happen only when we recognize how helpless we are without God's help and commit our lives into his hands. The process of our spiritual growth may be painful, but the end result will be worth it.

OBADIAH

The Big Picture

Betrayal produces feelings of agony. The closer our relationship with someone, the greater the pain we feel when that person betrays us. In this short book, Obadiah condemned the people of Edom for betraying their relatives when the Babylonian armies attacked Judah. The people of Judah were the descendants of Jacob, while the Edomites were descended from Jacob's twin brother, Esau. The two nations were closely related, yet Edom's acts of aggression toward Judah over the years had been intense.

When Judah needed help to stand against the armies of Babylon, the Edomites stood by and encouraged the Babylonian attackers, cheering the enemy on. The Edomites gloated while the Babylonians sacked Jerusalem. And when the Babylonians left, the Edomites entered the city, helped themselves to the remaining plunder, captured all the runaway citizens they could find and turned them over to the Babylonians.

Obadiah reassured the people of Judah that God would bring about justice. In God's timing, Edom would experience a devastation similar to Judah's. God promised that the people of Judah would someday be victorious. When we have been betrayed and struggle with the desire to get even, we must leave our desire for justice in God's hands. Someday he will right all wrongs. As we release our burden of anger and bitterness to God, we can continue with our spiritual growth.

Spiritual Renewal Themes

JUSTICE BELONGS TO GOD

When we have been betrayed by someone we trusted and realize the enormity of their offense, we may become obsessed with the desire for revenge. But God makes it very clear that we are not to seek such revenge. Hatred and revenge only bring more pain and devastation into our lives. We must confidently place all injustice in God's hands. He can be trusted to bring about true and total justice. Then we can be free from the destructive hatred of revenge that can only impede our spiritual growth.

THE DANGER OF SELF-SUFFICIENCY

The Edomites were proud of their self-sufficiency. They felt secure in their mountain fortress. However, there is no lasting security apart from God. Success can subtly lead us to think we can go it alone, an attitude that invariably leads to our downfall. As we begin to see spiritual growth, we must remember that God is the one who empowers us. We cannot stand on our own; we need God's constant sustenance and strength.

THE IMPORTANCE OF RECONCILIATION

The Edomites and Israelites were descendants of Esau and Jacob, the twin sons of the patriarch Isaac. Throughout their lives these brothers had lived in conflict. Though they were partially reconciled later in life, both men were never able to live together for long. Down through the centuries, the anger between the two families continued. Unresolved conflict always brings long-term consequences. We may also have suffered because of the conflicts of our ancestors; we may carry their traits and sinful tendencies within us. We need to resolve such conflicts and painful issues in our own lives and avoid passing them on to future generations.

Essential Facts

PURPOSE:
To demonstrate how God would accomplish restoration for his people after their allies had betrayed them.

AUTHOR:
The prophet Obadiah.

AUDIENCE:
The people of Judah and the Edomites.

DATE WRITTEN:
Either shortly after Judah and Jerusalem fell to the Babylonians in 586 B.C., or perhaps much earlier when Jehoram was king of Judah in 845 B.C.

SETTING:
The prophet speaks alternately to the nation of Edom and to the people of Judah in Jerusalem.

KEY VERSE:
"Deliverers will go up on Mount Zion to govern the mountains of Esau. And the kingdom will be the LORD's" (21).

KEY PEOPLE AND RELATIONSHIPS:
The book focuses on the relationship between the descendants of Isaac's twin sons: Jacob (the ancestor of the people of Judah) and Esau (the ancestor of the nation of Edom).

1The vision of Obadiah.

This is what the Sovereign LORD says about Edom—

We have heard a message from the LORD:
An envoy was sent to the nations to say,
"Rise, and let us go against her for battle"—
2"See, I will make you small among the nations;
you will be utterly despised.
3The pride of your heart has deceived you,
you who live in the clefts of the rocks[a]
and make your home on the heights,
you who say to yourself,
'Who can bring me down to the ground?'
4Though you soar like the eagle
and make your nest among the stars,
from there I will bring you down,"
declares the LORD.
5"If thieves came to you,
if robbers in the night—
Oh, what a disaster awaits you—
would they not steal only as much as they wanted?
If grape pickers came to you,
would they not leave a few grapes?
6But how Esau will be ransacked,
his hidden treasures pillaged!
7All your allies will force you to the border;
your friends will deceive and overpower you;
those who eat your bread will set a trap for you,[b]
but you will not detect it.
8"In that day," declares the LORD,
"will I not destroy the wise men of Edom,
men of understanding in the mountains of Esau?
9Your warriors, O Teman, will be terrified,
and everyone in Esau's mountains
will be cut down in the slaughter.
10Because of the violence against your brother Jacob,
you will be covered with shame;
you will be destroyed forever.
11On the day you stood aloof
while strangers carried off his wealth
and foreigners entered his gates
and cast lots for Jerusalem,
you were like one of them.
12You should not look down on your brother
in the day of his misfortune,
nor rejoice over the people of Judah
in the day of their destruction,
nor boast so much
in the day of their trouble.
13You should not march through the gates of my people
in the day of their disaster,
nor look down on them in their calamity
in the day of their disaster,
nor seize their wealth
in the day of their disaster.
14You should not wait at the crossroads
to cut down their fugitives,
nor hand over their survivors
in the day of their trouble.
15"The day of the LORD is near
for all nations.
As you have done, it will be done to you;
your deeds will return upon your own head.
16Just as you drank on my holy hill,
so all the nations will drink continually;
they will drink and drink
and be as if they had never been.
17But on Mount Zion will be deliverance;
it will be holy,
and the house of Jacob
will possess its inheritance.
18The house of Jacob will be a fire
and the house of Joseph a flame;
the house of Esau will be stubble,
and they will set it on fire and consume it.
There will be no survivors
from the house of Esau."
The LORD has spoken.

19People from the Negev will occupy
the mountains of Esau,
and people from the foothills will possess
the land of the Philistines.
They will occupy the fields of Ephraim and Samaria,
and Benjamin will possess Gilead.
20This company of Israelite exiles who are in Canaan

[a]3 Or *of Sela* [b]7 The meaning of the Hebrew for this clause is uncertain.

3–4 Pride had twisted the thinking of the Edomites. They believed they were so great and powerful that they didn't need God, but God let them know that no one is beyond the reach of his power. We may think that we don't need God because of our status in society or because of our wealth and prestige. Harboring such pride is destructive. Whether or not we like it, we are helpless without God. If we cannot admit the fact that we need God, there is little hope for our spiritual growth.

10–15 God held the Edomites accountable for taking advantage of the helpless Israelites. People who undergo troubles are precious to God. He will not tolerate those who gain from others' misfortune—God will make certain that justice is served. We may have suffered unjustly at the hands of others. If so, we must release our feelings of bitterness because God is ultimately in control of the situation. And if we have taken unfair advantage of others, God will not allow such sin to go unpunished. We need to admit our failures to God and seek to make restitution.

17–21 Obadiah's words were meant to comfort God's people in Israel, but they also apply to all people who suffer. While we may experience troubles now, God's promises offer us assurance of his preservation and hope for our future restoration.

will possess ⌞the land⌟ as far as
Zarephath;
the exiles from Jerusalem who are in
Sepharad
will possess the towns of the Negev.

21 Deliverers will go up on[a] Mount Zion
to govern the mountains of Esau.
And the kingdom will be the LORD's.

[a]21 Or *from*

Jonah

The Big Picture

A. *JONAH REJECTS GOD'S PLAN (1:1-17)*

B. *JONAH IS DELIVERED FROM THE CONSEQUENCES (2:1-10)*

C. *GOD SPARES THE PEOPLE OF NINEVEH (3:1-10)*

D. *THE DEBATE BETWEEN GOD AND JONAH (4:1-11)*

God wanted Jonah to warn the people of Nineveh of their sure destruction if they failed to repent of their sins. But Jonah would rather have died than obey God's command to confront the Ninevites with their sin. Jonah wanted God to destroy the wicked Ninevites; he didn't want the people of that Assyrian capital to repent and receive God's forgiveness. So Jonah boarded a ship and headed in the opposite direction.

When Jonah chose to disobey God's call, his disobedience endangered the life of everyone on the ship. God sent a great storm that threatened to swamp the ship. Terrified, the sailors sought out the guilty party, and Jonah quickly volunteered to be thrown overboard. Jonah seemed to prefer death to the prospect of preaching to the godless Ninevites.

Once bitterness has taken hold of a heart, it is difficult to reverse the process and begin to forgive. God placed Jonah inside a great fish for three days to get his attention. Jonah finally sought God and surrendered to him, begging God to preserve his life. He ultimately went to Nineveh and warned the people of their impending punishment, but Jonah was not happy with their response. The Ninevites repented, and God responded to their humility with mercy.

Even though Jonah disobeyed God, God never gave up on Jonah. Forgiving someone is never easy. God used several object lessons—a storm, a great fish, a large bush, a small worm, a scorching wind—to teach Jonah about compassion and forgiveness. And in spite of Jonah's resistance to God's call, God used him to spread the good news that God desires to save the entire human race.

Spiritual Renewal Themes

GOD DELIVERS THOSE WHO CALL OUT TO HIM

None of us likes to admit we need help. However, it is only when we acknowledge our need for God and his power that our spiritual renewal can begin. In the darkness inside the great fish, Jonah came to realize how desperately he needed God's help. He finally surrendered to God and agreed to follow his plan. As we recognize our sin and disobedience, we too can receive the help God offers. Only he can redeem and deliver us from overwhelming troubles. If we try to go it alone, we are headed for sure disaster.

KEEPING GOD'S PRIORITIES

Since Jonah was a prophet of God, we might have expected him to share God's priorities. But when God told him to go to Nineveh, Jonah's response reflected his cultural heritage rather than God's values. Jonah hated the people of Nineveh just as most Israelites of his day did. They were the enemy. But God had compassion on this wicked, bloodthirsty people. Jonah had to get his priorities in line with God's. God desires the salvation of all people regardless of their race, religion, nationality or apparent wickedness. We need to ask God to reveal any prejudices that might keep us from sharing his love with others.

GOD'S PATIENCE

There are many painful aspects of the spiritual growth process. We, like Jonah, are often tempted to drag our feet when God asks us to do something we are hesitant to do. We may even pout when we must face struggles in our lives. But God is patient with us, just as he was with Jonah. Instead of running away *from* God and trying to avoid the pain of spiritual growth, we need to run *toward* God who is in control of everything and worthy of our trust. He will walk with us all the way.

FORGIVENESS FOR EVERYONE

Jonah was so bitter toward the people of Nineveh that he chose to die rather than proclaim God's good news to them. Our desire for revenge can be destructive in our lives too. Bitterness destroys our peace, takes away our joy and impedes our spiritual growth. But God is merciful to our enemies, even as he has been merciful to us. It may not be natural to seek God's forgiveness for those who have hurt us, but forgiveness is God's way of restoring lives. When we experience God's forgiveness, we should respond with joy when someone else receives the same. God may even use us to be an instrument of healing to the people who have hurt us in the past.

Essential Facts

PURPOSE:
To show that God has compassion not only for the Israelites but also for all peoples and nations.

AUTHOR:
The prophet Jonah.

AUDIENCE:
The people of God in Israel's northern and southern kingdoms.

DATE WRITTEN:
Probably around 760 B.C.

SETTING:
Jonah was a prophet in Israel during the time of Jeroboam II, one of the northern kingdom's most powerful kings. He was sent to preach to the people of Nineveh, the capital of Assyria. This same nation would conquer the northern kingdom in 722 B.C.

KEY VERSE:
"In my distress I called to the LORD, and he answered me. From the depths of the grave I called for help, and you listened to my cry" (2:2).

KEY PEOPLE AND RELATIONSHIPS:
Jonah, the ship's captain, the ship's crew and the people of Nineveh.

Jonah Flees From the LORD

1 The word of the LORD came to Jonah son of
Amittai: 2"Go to the great city of Nineveh
and preach against it, because its wickedness
has come up before me."
3But Jonah ran away from the LORD and
headed for Tarshish. He went down to Joppa,
where he found a ship bound for that port. After
paying the fare, he went aboard and sailed for
Tarshish to flee from the LORD.
4Then the LORD sent a great wind on the sea,
and such a violent storm arose that the ship
threatened to break up. 5All the sailors were
afraid and each cried out to his own god. And
they threw the cargo into the sea to lighten the
ship.
But Jonah had gone below deck, where he lay
down and fell into a deep sleep. 6The captain
went to him and said, "How can you sleep? Get
up and call on your god! Maybe he will take
notice of us, and we will not perish."
7Then the sailors said to each other, "Come,
let us cast lots to find out who is responsible for
this calamity." They cast lots and the lot fell on
Jonah.
8So they asked him, "Tell us, who is responsible for making all this trouble for us? What do
you do? Where do you come from? What is
your country? From what people are you?"
9He answered, "I am a Hebrew and I worship the LORD, the God of heaven, who made
the sea and the land."
10This terrified them and they asked, "What
have you done?" (They knew he was running
away from the LORD, because he had already
told them so.)
11The sea was getting rougher and rougher.
So they asked him, "What should we do to you
to make the sea calm down for us?"
12"Pick me up and throw me into the sea," he
replied, "and it will become calm. I know that
it is my fault that this great storm has come
upon you."
13Instead, the men did their best to row back
to land. But they could not, for the sea grew
even wilder than before. 14Then they cried to
the LORD, "O LORD, please do not let us die for
taking this man's life. Do not hold us accountable for killing an innocent man, for you,
O LORD, have done as you pleased." 15Then they
took Jonah and threw him overboard, and the
raging sea grew calm. 16At this the men greatly
feared the LORD, and they offered a sacrifice to
the LORD and made vows to him.
17But the LORD provided a great fish to swallow Jonah, and Jonah was inside the fish three
days and three nights.

Jonah's Prayer

2 From inside the fish Jonah prayed to the
LORD his God. 2He said:

"In my distress I called to the LORD,
 and he answered me.
From the depths of the grave[a] I called for
 help,
 and you listened to my cry.
3You hurled me into the deep,
 into the very heart of the seas,
 and the currents swirled about me;
all your waves and breakers
 swept over me.
4I said, 'I have been banished
 from your sight;
yet I will look again
 toward your holy temple.'
5The engulfing waters threatened me,[b]
 the deep surrounded me;
 seaweed was wrapped around my head.
6To the roots of the mountains I sank down;
 the earth beneath barred me in forever.
But you brought my life up from the pit,
 O LORD my God.

7"When my life was ebbing away,
 I remembered you, LORD,
and my prayer rose to you,
 to your holy temple.

8"Those who cling to worthless idols
 forfeit the grace that could be theirs.
9But I, with a song of thanksgiving,
 will sacrifice to you.
What I have vowed I will make good.
 Salvation comes from the LORD."

[a]2 Hebrew *Sheol* [b]5 Or *waters were at my throat*

1:1–3 God's ways are not always our ways. God gave Jonah a message that he didn't want to hear, much less accept and obey. Jonah might have been afraid to confront these wicked people with the truth about their sin. But as we read Jonah's story we see the real reason for his reticence (see 4:1–2). Jonah was afraid that the Ninevites would repent and that God would spare them. The prophet was bitter against the Ninevites and wanted them to be destroyed. Yet God desires that everyone should repent and receive his forgiveness and restoration (see 2 Peter 3:9). We should desire the same, no matter how wicked those persons may be.

1:4–17 Because of Jonah's disobedience, God allowed a great storm to come up, putting the sailors in an uncontrollable, dangerous position. Yet Jonah, who was responsible for their plight, was asleep in the hold of the boat. Often our irresponsible actions and refusal to obey God bring pain, and sometimes long-term consequences, into the lives of others. Like Jonah, we need to wake up from our disobedience, take responsibility for our failures and do what we can to make restitution to those we have hurt.

2:1–10 Jonah spent three days in the fish's stomach before he agreed to follow God's plan for his life. God had called Jonah to do something he didn't want to do. Jonah tried to do things his own way and suffered the consequences for his disobedience. We also can do things God's way and receive his help and blessing, or we can do things our way and suffer the painful consequences. Those consequences just might be a path that will lead down to the depths if that's what it takes to show us that God's way is the only way.

10And the LORD commanded the fish, and it
vomited Jonah onto dry land.

Jonah Goes to Nineveh

3 Then the word of the LORD came to Jonah
a second time: 2"Go to the great city of
Nineveh and proclaim to it the message I give
you."
3Jonah obeyed the word of the LORD and
went to Nineveh. Now Nineveh was a very important city—a visit required three days. 4On the
first day, Jonah started into the city. He proclaimed: "Forty more days and Nineveh will be
overturned." 5The Ninevites believed God. They
declared a fast, and all of them, from the greatest to the least, put on sackcloth.
6When the news reached the king of Nineveh, he rose from his throne, took off his royal
robes, covered himself with sackcloth and sat
down in the dust. 7Then he issued a proclamation in Nineveh:

"By the decree of the king and his nobles:

Do not let any man or beast, herd or
flock, taste anything; do not let them eat
or drink. 8But let man and beast be covered with sackcloth. Let everyone call urgently on God. Let them give up their evil
ways and their violence. 9Who knows?
God may yet relent and with compassion
turn from his fierce anger so that we will
not perish."

10When God saw what they did and how
they turned from their evil ways, he had compassion and did not bring upon them the destruction he had threatened.

Jonah's Anger at the LORD's Compassion

4 But Jonah was greatly displeased and became angry. 2He prayed to the LORD,
"O LORD, is this not what I said when I was still
at home? That is why I was so quick to flee to

3:1–3 God once again commanded Jonah to go to Nineveh and proclaim his message. This time Jonah obeyed God and preached to those despised people of Nineveh. Sometimes God may ask us to do things that we would rather not do. The easy road is often the wrong road; the right road usually costs us something. Ultimately, however, the right way always leads to spiritual growth, blessing and deliverance.

3:4–9 God's message penetrated all of Nineveh. The people admitted their faults before God and dressed in mourning clothes. The king then took responsibility for his people, making sure that they understood how serious their situation was. He called both great and small to humble themselves before God. We need to bring God's truth to the world today as well, for God can bring even the most sinful, rebellious people to repentance.

4:1–3 Jonah's message was a success. So why was he so agitated? The prophet became incensed because God decided to forgive the wicked Ninevites. God often chooses to answer our prayers in ways we would never imagine but that bring a much greater good. We need to submit to God's ways, for he knows what is best.

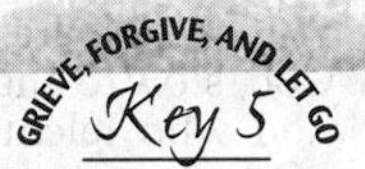

Relinquishing Prejudice

Jonah 4:1–4 Sometimes we allow our upbringing or experiences to prejudice us against a particular group of people. Prejudice often leads to hatred and a lack of compassion toward others. God's people, however, should be known as loving, accepting, compassionate people. Surrendering our lives to God involves recognizing and relinquishing our prejudices.

Jonah hated the people of Nineveh. The Ninevites had been cruel to the Israelites. Jonah would have taken great pleasure in going to Nineveh to declare God's judgment against such a wicked city. But God told Jonah to go to Nineveh and warn them of their impending destruction so that they might avert God's wrath. Jonah did not want to participate in such a mission of mercy. He tried to run away by boarding a ship and sailing in the opposite direction. God sent some very difficult circumstances to get Jonah's attention so that finally Jonah went to Nineveh and preached to the people. Surprisingly, they changed their ways, and God suspended his plans for their destruction. Jonah was upset by God's mercy toward the Ninevites. But God corrected Jonah for his prejudice, pointing out that "Nineveh has more than a hundred and twenty thousand people who cannot tell their right hand from their left, and many cattle as well. Should I not be concerned about that great city?" (4:11).

God practically had to force Jonah to let go of his prejudice and hatred in order to get him to share God's message of mercy with the Ninevites. Our spiritual transformation cannot be complete until we have relinquished our prejudices toward other people. This is not an easy task. We need to ask God and those close to us to help us recognize our prejudices, confess these to God and ask him to change our hearts.

Move on to Key 6 and turn to Joshua 1.

Tarshish. I knew that you are a gracious and
compassionate God, slow to anger and abounding in love, a God who relents from sending
calamity. 3Now, O LORD, take away my life, for
it is better for me to die than to live."
4But the LORD replied, "Have you any right
to be angry?"
5Jonah went out and sat down at a place east
of the city. There he made himself a shelter, sat
in its shade and waited to see what would happen to the city. 6Then the LORD God provided
a vine and made it grow up over Jonah to give
shade for his head to ease his discomfort, and
Jonah was very happy about the vine. 7But at
dawn the next day God provided a worm,
which chewed the vine so that it withered.
8When the sun rose, God provided a scorching
east wind, and the sun blazed on Jonah's head
so that he grew faint. He wanted to die, and
said, "It would be better for me to die than to
live."
9But God said to Jonah, "Do you have a right
to be angry about the vine?"
"I do," he said. "I am angry enough to die."
10But the LORD said, "You have been concerned about this vine, though you did not tend
it or make it grow. It sprang up overnight and
died overnight. 11But Nineveh has more than a
hundred and twenty thousand people who cannot tell their right hand from their left, and
many cattle as well. Should I not be concerned
about that great city?"

4:4–11 God was very patient with Jonah. Rather than condemn him for his anger or punish him for his actions, God taught Jonah another lesson. God used a fast-growing vine to give Jonah some deliverance from the scorching sun and heat of the day. When the vine died and the hot desert wind and sun beat fiercely against Jonah, he wanted to die. God reminded Jonah that he seemed more concerned about a silly little plant than he did for an entire city of people loved by God. We, too, must make certain that we align our priorities and concerns to match God's priorities.

MICAH

The Big Picture

The people of Micah's day were not much different from people today. Many of them lived self-centered lives driven by greed and false pride. They spent their nights plotting against the helpless and their days taking advantage of the weak. Religion was a tool for personal gain, and hypocrisy marked their spiritual lives. They lied to make themselves look good and deceived others to cover their corruption. The kingdoms of Israel and Judah had wandered far from God's plan. The people would soon suffer the painful consequences.

Centuries before, God had agreed to bless the people of Israel in a unique way in return for their faithfulness (see Deuteronomy 28:1–15). The people had agreed to follow God's will, but they had never kept their promise. Through his prophet Micah, God took his wayward people to court. God was the prosecutor and plaintiff; Micah was the plaintiff's spokesman; Israel was the defendant; the witnesses were heaven and earth. God could do nothing but judge his people guilty as charged. Their punishment would be exile. The northern kingdom of Israel fell to Assyria soon after this prophecy; the southern kingdom of Judah fell to Babylon a few centuries later.

Micah made it clear that no satisfaction in this life can be found apart from God. Only when we acknowledge our weaknesses, accept responsibility for our actions and submit to God's will can we hope to escape judgment. Through our repentance God will offer us his forgiveness, compassion and unfailing love.

A. *THE DOWNFALL OF THE PROUD (1:1–2:13)*

1. Judgment Comes to the Sinful (1:1–2:11)
2. Hope Comes to the Faithful (2:12-13)

B. *THE DELIVERANCE OF THE HELPLESS (3:1–5:15)*

1. Judgment Comes to Those Who Serve Themselves (3:1-12)
2. Hope Comes From the One Who Serves Others (4:1–5:15)

C. *THE DEFEAT OF THE OPPRESSORS (6:1–7:20)*

1. Judgment Comes to Those Who Give Misery to Others (6:1–7:13)
2. Hope Ultimately Comes for God's People (7:14-20)

Spiritual Renewal Themes

THE DANGERS OF PRETENSE

The people in Micah's day were extremely hypocritical. All their religious activities were designed only to make them look good to others. Honestly assessing our actions and doing away with pretense are necessary if we want to progress spiritually. To mix selfish motives with an empty display of religious activity will pervert the meaning of faith. But to turn to God in our need and to honestly repent of our sins will signify a genuine change of heart that will lead to healing. Anything less will only set us up for failure.

Essential Facts

PURPOSE:
To warn God's people of the destructive consequences of disobedience and to offer a life of peace to those willing to obey God's revealed will.

AUTHOR:
The prophet Micah.

AUDIENCE:
The people of God in Israel's northern and southern kingdoms.

DATE WRITTEN:
Sometime between 742 and 687 B.C.

SETTING:
Micah spoke to God's people in the northern and southern kingdoms during the period described in 2 Kings 15–20 and 2 Chronicles 26–30.

KEY VERSE:
"He has showed you, O man, what is good. And what does the LORD require of you? To act justly and to love mercy and to walk humbly with your God" (6:8).

KEY PLACES:
Samaria, Jerusalem and Bethlehem.

KEY PEOPLE AND RELATIONSHIPS:
Micah and the people of Samaria and Jerusalem.

GOD DELIVERS THE POWERLESS

Though God's judgment against his rebellious people was sure, he promised that a remnant would trust him and survive the trials ahead. God can bring hope into our hopeless situations. God's ways are different from the ways of the world. He brings deliverance in unexpected ways. Micah made it clear that when we acknowledge our sins, God will step in and deliver us.

GOD CARES FOR THE HURTING

God cares for those who are hurting and helpless. He shows tenderness to those who suffer and have been rejected. He reaches out in love and mercy to bring healing and hope. And he calls on us to do the same. As we progress spiritually, we can become God's instruments to bring healing to others. An important part of our spiritual growth is sharing God's promise of freedom with those who are still in bondage. As we do this, we give hope to others and also experience renewed encouragement to persevere in our own spiritual growth.

1 The word of the LORD that came to Micah of Moresheth during the reigns of Jotham, Ahaz and Hezekiah, kings of Judah—the vision he saw concerning Samaria and Jerusalem.

2Hear, O peoples, all of you,
listen, O earth and all who are in it,
that the Sovereign LORD may witness
against you,
the Lord from his holy temple.

Judgment Against Samaria and Jerusalem

3Look! The LORD is coming from his
dwelling place;
he comes down and treads the high
places of the earth.
4The mountains melt beneath him
and the valleys split apart,
like wax before the fire,
like water rushing down a slope.
5All this is because of Jacob's transgression,
because of the sins of the house of Israel.
What is Jacob's transgression?
Is it not Samaria?
What is Judah's high place?
Is it not Jerusalem?

6"Therefore I will make Samaria a heap of
rubble,
a place for planting vineyards.
I will pour her stones into the valley
and lay bare her foundations.
7All her idols will be broken to pieces;
all her temple gifts will be burned with
fire;
I will destroy all her images.
Since she gathered her gifts from the wages
of prostitutes,
as the wages of prostitutes they will
again be used."

Weeping and Mourning

8Because of this I will weep and wail;
I will go about barefoot and naked.
I will howl like a jackal
and moan like an owl.
9For her wound is incurable;
it has come to Judah.
It[a] has reached the very gate of my people,
even to Jerusalem itself.
10Tell it not in Gath[b];
weep not at all.[c]
In Beth Ophrah[d]
roll in the dust.
11Pass on in nakedness and shame,
you who live in Shaphir.[e]
Those who live in Zaanan[f]
will not come out.
Beth Ezel is in mourning;
its protection is taken from you.
12Those who live in Maroth[g] writhe in pain,
waiting for relief,
because disaster has come from the LORD,
even to the gate of Jerusalem.
13You who live in Lachish,[h]
harness the team to the chariot.
You were the beginning of sin
to the Daughter of Zion,
for the transgressions of Israel
were found in you.
14Therefore you will give parting gifts
to Moresheth Gath.
The town of Aczib[i] will prove deceptive
to the kings of Israel.
15I will bring a conqueror against you
who live in Mareshah.[j]
He who is the glory of Israel
will come to Adullam.
16Shave your heads in mourning
for the children in whom you delight;
make yourselves as bald as the vulture,
for they will go from you into exile.

Man's Plans and God's

2 Woe to those who plan iniquity,
to those who plot evil on their beds!
At morning's light they carry it out
because it is in their power to do it.
2They covet fields and seize them,
and houses, and take them.
They defraud a man of his home,
a fellowman of his inheritance.

3Therefore, the LORD says:

"I am planning disaster against this people,

[a]9 Or *He* [b]10 *Gath* sounds like the Hebrew for *tell.* [c]10 Hebrew; Septuagint may suggest *not in Acco.* The Hebrew for *in Acco* sounds like the Hebrew for *weep.* [d]10 *Beth Ophrah* means *house of dust.* [e]11 *Shaphir* means *pleasant.* [f]11 *Zaanan* sounds like the Hebrew for *come out.* [g]12 *Maroth* sounds like the Hebrew for *bitter.* [h]13 *Lachish* sounds like the Hebrew for *team.* [i]14 *Aczib* means *deception.* [j]15 *Mareshah* sounds like the Hebrew for *conqueror.*

1:2–7 God announced the coming of a sudden and intense judgment on his people. They had refused to trust and obey him. They had rebelled and sought help from powerless idols. But their idol worship was useless, and God allowed them to suffer the consequences of seeking help from a source that could not deliver it. Anything we turn to in the place of God may become an idol. If we pursue help from idols, however, we will only be disappointed. Only God has the power to help us and satisfy our hearts' true desires.

1:12–16 Sin is contagious. When there is no repentance, its effects are far-reaching. Notice that even the innocent children of the Israelites would be sold into slavery because of their parents' sins. We often fail to realize that our sins may cause great suffering for generations into the future. We need to act now, admitting our sins and surrendering our lives into God's gracious hands and thereby freeing countless generations from a painful future.

2:1–5 Many of Israel's influential people sought personal wealth and influence, often at the expense of others. The more they took for themselves, the more they hurt those around them. These leaders were blind to the pain they caused others and were unaware of the judgment they piled up for themselves. Our sins often cause us to make the same mistake. As we reflect honestly on our lives, we should think clearly about those we may have hurt and seek ways to make restitution.

from which you cannot save yourselves.
You will no longer walk proudly,
for it will be a time of calamity.
4In that day men will ridicule you;
they will taunt you with this mournful song:
'We are utterly ruined;
my people's possession is divided up.
He takes it from me!
He assigns our fields to traitors.' "
5Therefore you will have no one in the assembly of the LORD
to divide the land by lot.

False Prophets

6"Do not prophesy," their prophets say.
"Do not prophesy about these things;
disgrace will not overtake us."
7Should it be said, O house of Jacob:
"Is the Spirit of the LORD angry?
Does he do such things?"

"Do not my words do good
to him whose ways are upright?
8Lately my people have risen up
like an enemy.
You strip off the rich robe
from those who pass by without a care,
like men returning from battle.
9You drive the women of my people
from their pleasant homes.
You take away my blessing
from their children forever.
10Get up, go away!
For this is not your resting place,
because it is defiled,
it is ruined, beyond all remedy.
11If a liar and deceiver comes and says,
'I will prophesy for you plenty of wine and beer,'
he would be just the prophet for this people!

Deliverance Promised

12"I will surely gather all of you, O Jacob;
I will surely bring together the remnant of Israel.
I will bring them together like sheep in a pen,
like a flock in its pasture;
the place will throng with people.
13One who breaks open the way will go up before them;
they will break through the gate and go out.
Their king will pass through before them,
the LORD at their head."

Leaders and Prophets Rebuked

3 Then I said,

"Listen, you leaders of Jacob,
you rulers of the house of Israel.
Should you not know justice,
2 you who hate good and love evil;
who tear the skin from my people
and the flesh from their bones;
3who eat my people's flesh,
strip off their skin
and break their bones in pieces;
who chop them up like meat for the pan,
like flesh for the pot?"

4Then they will cry out to the LORD,
but he will not answer them.
At that time he will hide his face from them
because of the evil they have done.

5This is what the LORD says:

"As for the prophets
who lead my people astray,
if one feeds them,
they proclaim 'peace';
if he does not,
they prepare to wage war against him.
6Therefore night will come over you,
without visions,
and darkness, without divination.
The sun will set for the prophets,
and the day will go dark for them.
7The seers will be ashamed
and the diviners disgraced.
They will all cover their faces
because there is no answer from God."

8But as for me, I am filled with power,
with the Spirit of the LORD,
and with justice and might,
to declare to Jacob his transgression,
to Israel his sin.

2:6–7 The people of Israel did not want to face up to their sins. They tried to ignore Micah's predictions of God's punishment. But their refusal to listen to God's warnings meant they would have to face the consequences of their actions. Notice that God told his people that he planned to punish them because he loved them. He did not want vengeance; God wanted his people to have a restored relationship with him. The painful consequences we suffer for our sins are one way God calls us back into a right relationship with him. Sometimes our refusal to see the truth can be so strong that only a disaster can get our attention. Yet no matter how much pain we feel now, God still loves us and desires the best for us.

2:12–13 Even though God warned his people of a sure destruction to come, he also gave them a reason to hope for the future: Someday he would restore the nation he was about to punish. As we face the inescapable consequences of our sinful actions, we can still have hope for the future. Even though there may be hard times ahead, if we repent, trust God and obey his will for our lives, there is always hope. No matter how great our sin, God is always able to bring about our forgiveness and restoration if only we will repent.

3:1–4 The leaders of Israel failed to fulfill their responsibilities to defend the poor and helpless in society. In fact, they took advantage of the very people they were supposed to protect. They could expect only punishment from God for such actions. If we have harmed the innocent people in our charge, it is time to repent and make restitution.

9Hear this, you leaders of the house of
Jacob,
you rulers of the house of Israel,
who despise justice
and distort all that is right;
10who build Zion with bloodshed,
and Jerusalem with wickedness.
11Her leaders judge for a bribe,
her priests teach for a price,
and her prophets tell fortunes for
money.
Yet they lean upon the LORD and say,
"Is not the LORD among us?
No disaster will come upon us."
12Therefore because of you,
Zion will be plowed like a field,
Jerusalem will become a heap of rubble,
the temple hill a mound overgrown with
thickets.

The Mountain of the LORD

4 In the last days

the mountain of the LORD's temple will be
established
as chief among the mountains;
it will be raised above the hills,
and peoples will stream to it.
2Many nations will come and say,

"Come, let us go up to the mountain of
the LORD,
to the house of the God of Jacob.
He will teach us his ways,
so that we may walk in his paths."
The law will go out from Zion,
the word of the LORD from Jerusalem.
3He will judge between many peoples
and will settle disputes for strong nations
far and wide.
They will beat their swords into plowshares
and their spears into pruning hooks.
Nation will not take up sword against
nation,
nor will they train for war anymore.
4Every man will sit under his own vine
and under his own fig tree,
and no one will make them afraid,
for the LORD Almighty has spoken.
5All the nations may walk
in the name of their gods;
we will walk in the name of the LORD
our God for ever and ever.

The LORD's Plan

6"In that day," declares the LORD,

"I will gather the lame;
I will assemble the exiles
and those I have brought to grief.
7I will make the lame a remnant,
those driven away a strong nation.
The LORD will rule over them in Mount
Zion
from that day and forever.
8As for you, O watchtower of the flock,
O stronghold[a] of the Daughter of Zion,
the former dominion will be restored to
you;
kingship will come to the Daughter of
Jerusalem."

9Why do you now cry aloud—
have you no king?
Has your counselor perished,
that pain seizes you like that of a
woman in labor?
10Writhe in agony, O Daughter of Zion,
like a woman in labor,
for now you must leave the city
to camp in the open field.
You will go to Babylon;
there you will be rescued.
There the LORD will redeem you
out of the hand of your enemies.

11But now many nations
are gathered against you.
They say, "Let her be defiled,
let our eyes gloat over Zion!"
12But they do not know
the thoughts of the LORD;
they do not understand his plan,
he who gathers them like sheaves to the
threshing floor.

13"Rise and thresh, O Daughter of Zion,
for I will give you horns of iron;
I will give you hoofs of bronze

[a]8 Or *hill*

4:1–5 If everyone obeyed God's will, life would be filled with peace and prosperity, meaning and joy. However, we continually reject God's plan and continue to do things our own way. We live for personal gratification and remain blind to the needs of others. As we recognize the destruction and pain we cause by doing things our own way, we should remember how things could be if we did things God's way. God wants us to live in a world of joy and harmony. When we admit our sin and seek to live according to his will for us, our corner of the world can reflect God's good intentions for joy and peace.

4:6–7 God consistently shows deep tenderness for hurting people—those rejected by society. God also demonstrates a fatherly concern for those that he has disciplined. In fact, God's discipline is a clear sign of his love (see Hebrews 12:6–7). Although God's discipline may hurt, it will help us recognize our sin and redirect the course of our lives. We need to remember that God will never forget us. He seeks only to restore us to himself.

4:9–13 God's people needed to accept the consequences of their actions. God removed their world of false security and sent them into exile so that they would realize their need for him and become a stronger and more righteous people. God's punishments were meant to restore and heal them. God works the same way in our lives. The painful consequences we may face now for our sin are only a small part of God's plan for our spiritual growth. God's judgments can become a source of great blessing for us if we will trust God and obey his plan for our lives.

and you will break to pieces many nations."
You will devote their ill-gotten gains to the LORD,
their wealth to the Lord of all the earth.

A Promised Ruler From Bethlehem

5 Marshal your troops, O city of troops,[a]
for a siege is laid against us.
They will strike Israel's ruler
on the cheek with a rod.

2"But you, Bethlehem Ephrathah,
though you are small among the clans[b] of Judah,
out of you will come for me
one who will be ruler over Israel,
whose origins[c] are from of old,
from ancient times.[d]"

3Therefore Israel will be abandoned
until the time when she who is in labor gives birth
and the rest of his brothers return
to join the Israelites.

4He will stand and shepherd his flock
in the strength of the LORD,
in the majesty of the name of the LORD his God.
And they will live securely, for then his greatness
will reach to the ends of the earth.
5 And he will be their peace.

Deliverance and Destruction

When the Assyrian invades our land
and marches through our fortresses,
we will raise against him seven shepherds,
even eight leaders of men.
6They will rule[e] the land of Assyria with the sword,
the land of Nimrod with drawn sword.[f]
He will deliver us from the Assyrian
when he invades our land
and marches into our borders.

7The remnant of Jacob will be
in the midst of many peoples
like dew from the LORD,
like showers on the grass,
which do not wait for man
or linger for mankind.
8The remnant of Jacob will be among the nations,
in the midst of many peoples,
like a lion among the beasts of the forest,
like a young lion among flocks of sheep,
which mauls and mangles as it goes,
and no one can rescue.
9Your hand will be lifted up in triumph over your enemies,
and all your foes will be destroyed.

10"In that day," declares the LORD,

"I will destroy your horses from among you
and demolish your chariots.
11I will destroy the cities of your land
and tear down all your strongholds.
12I will destroy your witchcraft
and you will no longer cast spells.
13I will destroy your carved images
and your sacred stones from among you;
you will no longer bow down
to the work of your hands.
14I will uproot from among you your Asherah poles[g]
and demolish your cities.
15I will take vengeance in anger and wrath
upon the nations that have not obeyed me."

The LORD's Case Against Israel

6 Listen to what the LORD says:

"Stand up, plead your case before the mountains;
let the hills hear what you have to say.
2Hear, O mountains, the LORD's accusation;
listen, you everlasting foundations of the earth.
For the LORD has a case against his people;
he is lodging a charge against Israel.

3"My people, what have I done to you?
How have I burdened you? Answer me.
4I brought you up out of Egypt

[a]1 Or *Strengthen your walls, O walled city* [b]2 Or *rulers* [c]2 Hebrew *goings out* [d]2 Or *from days of eternity* [e]6 Or *crush* [f]6 Or *Nimrod in its gates* [g]14 That is, symbols of the goddess Asherah

5:1–5 Out of an insignificant place, God would bring greatness. God chose Bethlehem as the birthplace of his Messiah and made this tiny town an internationally famous place. God often uses "insignificant" people and places to achieve great things. Though we may feel insignificant, God can use us to bring great blessing to others. Sharing our story of God's deliverance in our lives can bring blessing to others as they experience hope that God can do the same for them.

5:10–15 God promised to destroy all the useless things his people had depended on for security: weapons and walled cities for protection, astrology and idol worship for spiritual guidance. God's people discovered that the strengths of these things were only illusions—these things could never help them. When we turn to our own devices for a sense of security we are only being led away from the one true source of help—God.

6:4–5 The people of Israel became smug and self-sufficient, forgetting that they were helpless without God's power. When we begin to experience significant spiritual growth, we can easily forget that God delivered us from our problems. We may take some of the credit and place less importance on our relationship with God. When we fail to acknowledge God's help in our successes, we may experience a setback. God is the only one who can deliver us from bondage, and he is the only one able to sustain our spiritual growth.

and redeemed you from the land of
slavery.
I sent Moses to lead you,
also Aaron and Miriam.
5My people, remember
what Balak king of Moab counseled
and what Balaam son of Beor answered.
Remember ⌞your journey⌟ from Shittim to
Gilgal,
that you may know the righteous acts of
the LORD."
6With what shall I come before the LORD
and bow down before the exalted God?
Shall I come before him with burnt
offerings,
with calves a year old?
7Will the LORD be pleased with thousands of
rams,
with ten thousand rivers of oil?
Shall I offer my firstborn for my
transgression,
the fruit of my body for the sin of my
soul?
8He has showed you, O man, what is good.
And what does the LORD require of you?
To act justly and to love mercy
and to walk humbly with your God.

Israel's Guilt and Punishment

9Listen! The LORD is calling to the city—
and to fear your name is wisdom—
"Heed the rod and the One who
appointed it.[a]
10Am I still to forget, O wicked house,
your ill-gotten treasures
and the short ephah,[b] which is
accursed?
11Shall I acquit a man with dishonest scales,
with a bag of false weights?
12Her rich men are violent;
her people are liars
and their tongues speak deceitfully.
13Therefore, I have begun to destroy you,
to ruin you because of your sins.
14You will eat but not be satisfied;
your stomach will still be empty.[c]
You will store up but save nothing,
because what you save I will give to the
sword.
15You will plant but not harvest;
you will press olives but not use the oil
on yourselves,
you will crush grapes but not drink the
wine.
16You have observed the statutes of Omri
and all the practices of Ahab's house,
and you have followed their traditions.
Therefore I will give you over to ruin
and your people to derision;
you will bear the scorn of the nations.[d]"

Israel's Misery

7 What misery is mine!
I am like one who gathers summer fruit
at the gleaning of the vineyard;
there is no cluster of grapes to eat,
none of the early figs that I crave.
2The godly have been swept from the land;
not one upright man remains.
All men lie in wait to shed blood;
each hunts his brother with a net.
3Both hands are skilled in doing evil;
the ruler demands gifts,
the judge accepts bribes,
the powerful dictate what they desire—
they all conspire together.
4The best of them is like a brier,
the most upright worse than a thorn
hedge.
The day of your watchmen has come,
the day God visits you.
Now is the time of their confusion.
5Do not trust a neighbor;
put no confidence in a friend.
Even with her who lies in your embrace
be careful of your words.
6For a son dishonors his father,
a daughter rises up against her mother,
a daughter-in-law against her
mother-in-law—
a man's enemies are the members of his
own household.

7But as for me, I watch in hope for the
LORD,
I wait for God my Savior;
my God will hear me.

Israel Will Rise

8Do not gloat over me, my enemy!
Though I have fallen, I will rise.
Though I sit in darkness,

[a]9 The meaning of the Hebrew for this line is uncertain.
[b]10 An ephah was a dry measure. [c]14 The meaning of the Hebrew for this word is uncertain.
[d]16 Septuagint; Hebrew *scorn due my people*

6:6–8 When we consider who God is and who we are, we realize that there is nothing we can truly give to him—neither our possessions nor our most prized treasures—that will impress him or win his favor. God does not desire our religious acts of worship unless those acts are accompanied by lives that are also pleasing to him. He wants us to treat others responsibly, demonstrate compassion toward them and exhibit a full reliance on him.
6:10–16 The prophet clearly stated that God despises those who are dishonest and seek their own personal gain (see Deuteronomy 25:13–16; Proverbs 11:1; 20:10, 23). God brings dryness to the souls of such people. They will experience an emptiness that cannot be satisfied by the things of this world.
7:1–6 The leaders of the government became corrupt, and no one could be trusted. When people live for personal gain and turn away from God, the results are always disastrous. Seeking only personal gratification leads to sin and selfishness. Following God's plan leads to peace and blessing. Instead of following our selfish inclinations, we should obey God's will for our lives.

the LORD will be my light.
9Because I have sinned against him,
I will bear the LORD's wrath,
until he pleads my case
and establishes my right.
He will bring me out into the light;
I will see his righteousness.
10Then my enemy will see it
and will be covered with shame,
she who said to me,
"Where is the LORD your God?"
My eyes will see her downfall;
even now she will be trampled underfoot
like mire in the streets.

11The day for building your walls will come,
the day for extending your boundaries.
12In that day people will come to you
from Assyria and the cities of Egypt,
even from Egypt to the Euphrates
and from sea to sea
and from mountain to mountain.
13The earth will become desolate because of its inhabitants,
as the result of their deeds.

Prayer and Praise

14Shepherd your people with your staff,
the flock of your inheritance,
which lives by itself in a forest,
in fertile pasturelands.[a]
Let them feed in Bashan and Gilead
as in days long ago.
15"As in the days when you came out of Egypt,
I will show them my wonders."
16Nations will see and be ashamed,
deprived of all their power.
They will lay their hands on their mouths
and their ears will become deaf.
17They will lick dust like a snake,
like creatures that crawl on the ground.
They will come trembling out of their dens;
they will turn in fear to the LORD our God
and will be afraid of you.
18Who is a God like you,
who pardons sin and forgives the transgression
of the remnant of his inheritance?
You do not stay angry forever
but delight to show mercy.
19You will again have compassion on us;
you will tread our sins underfoot
and hurl all our iniquities into the depths of the sea.
20You will be true to Jacob,
and show mercy to Abraham,
as you pledged on oath to our fathers
in days long ago.

[a]14 *Or in the middle of Carmel*

7:9–13 Micah spoke for God's people, recognizing that they had sinned and that their suffering was a part of God's plan for their restoration. Instead of trying to escape the well-deserved consequences for our sins, we should surrender our lives to God. He will use our pain to help us grow. Just as he redeemed his people from the exile, he desires to redeem us from our bondage and give us a life filled with meaning and joy.
7:14–20 What beautiful words of comfort! No matter how terrible our sin, there is always hope for the future when we repent and surrender our lives to God. As we follow God's will for us, we will begin to experience God's full pardon and perfect compassion. God will free us from the clutches of our sinful nature and make us a blessing to others. We can be assured that God will fulfill his promises for our healing as we look back and remember how he has kept his promises in the past. We can depend on God to redeem us.

NAHUM

The Big Picture

The prophet Nahum ministered in Judah during a time of great fear. Judah had barely survived attacks from the brutal Assyrians. This enemy was indifferent to their suffering and well known for its cruelty and oppression. Assyria's bloodthirsty armies had long since destroyed Judah's sister nation, the kingdom of Israel. The people of Judah now lived in constant fear of being overrun.

Nahum, whose name means "comfort," was God's prophet of consolation during these troubled times. His words were meant to lift the hearts of Judah's oppressed people and to address their unspoken doubts. Nahum reminded the people that God is a powerful refuge for those in trouble. He told them that God would judge Judah's cruel oppressors and that Judah would someday regain her status of significance and wholeness.

Nahum's words were also intended for the people of Nineveh, Assyria's capital. Nahum predicted Nineveh's imminent doom, and God's judgment arrived soon after the prophet spoke. The Medes and Babylonians plundered Nineveh, and the Assyrian empire soon crumbled. Nineveh's demise was a consequence of her harsh treatment of others, especially the people of God.

A century earlier, the prophet Jonah had gone to Nineveh. At that time the city had been spared destruction because her people had repented. But their failure to follow God led to severe consequences in Nahum's day. Repentance is never a one-time thing. We must continually redirect our course back into line with God's plan. True repentance means that we will follow through on our promises to obey and will do so by the power of the Holy Spirit.

A. JUDAH'S COMFORT IN GOD'S CHARACTER (1:1-15)

1. God's Justice (1:1-3)
2. God's Sovereignty (1:4-6)
3. God's Mercy Toward His People (1:7)
4. God's Judgment Toward His Enemies (1:8)
5. God's Good News of Restoration and Spiritual Renewal (1:9-15)

B. ASSYRIA'S FEAR AT GOD'S JUDGMENT (2:1–3:19)

1. Judgment Predicted (2:1-2)
2. Judgment Described (2:3-10)
3. Judgment Justified (2:11–3:19)

Spiritual Renewal Themes

RESCUED FROM FEAR

Our fears can destroy us if we allow them to control our lives. The people of Judah lived under the threat of Assyrian attack for many years. Nahum comforted them by turning their eyes away from their cruel enemy and toward their powerful and loving God. He urged them to make God their source of strength. God will help us in all our spiritual battles too. Our enemies are the spiritual forces that try to deter us from follow-

Essential Facts

PURPOSE:
To prophesy the overthrow of Assyria, illustrating that God is all-powerful, that he hates wickedness and that he is able to help those who are oppressed and in trouble.

AUTHOR:
The prophet Nahum.

AUDIENCE:
The people of Judah and Nineveh.

DATE WRITTEN:
Sometime between 663 and 612 B.C., during the period preceding Nineveh's fall in 612 B.C.

SETTING:
In Nahum's day, Assyria controlled most of the ancient Near East and had already destroyed the northern kingdom of Israel (722 B.C.).

KEY VERSE:
"The LORD is good, a refuge in times of trouble. He cares for those who trust in him" (1:7).

KEY PLACE:
The Assyrian capital city of Nineveh.

KEY PEOPLE AND RELATIONSHIPS:
Nahum, the people of Judah and the people of Nineveh.

ing God's plan for our lives. If we focus our attention solely on the struggles we face, we could feel overwhelmed. But if we keep our eyes fixed upon God, who loves us and desires our best, our fear will melt away. We can count on God to help us in all our spiritual battles.

LIVING LIFE GOD'S WAY

God created us to function best when we do things his way. The people of Nineveh broke all of God's laws and commands. They continued in their destructive behavior for quite some time before the consequences caught up with them. But God's inevitable judgment did come. We need to live life within the boundaries of God's revealed will. Rejecting God's commands will always lead to pain and devastation.

THE IMPORTANCE OF PERSEVERANCE

Nahum was not the first of God's prophets to warn Nineveh of impending destruction. Over one hundred years earlier Jonah had called the Ninevites to repentance. At that time the city had responded to Jonah's message and was spared destruction. But apparently the Ninevites failed to follow through on their initial promises. Their behavior reverted to their original wicked ways and quickly deteriorated even further. Spiritual growth doesn't happen all at once. It is a growing, continual process requiring perseverance. Spiritual growth also demands action. We need to follow through on our promises to change, or we will end up as Nineveh did—wrecked beyond recognition.

1

An oracle concerning Nineveh. The book of the vision of Nahum the Elkoshite.

The LORD's Anger Against Nineveh

2The LORD is a jealous and avenging God;
the LORD takes vengeance and is filled with wrath.
The LORD takes vengeance on his foes
and maintains his wrath against his enemies.
3The LORD is slow to anger and great in power;
the LORD will not leave the guilty unpunished.
His way is in the whirlwind and the storm,
and clouds are the dust of his feet.
4He rebukes the sea and dries it up;
he makes all the rivers run dry.
Bashan and Carmel wither
and the blossoms of Lebanon fade.
5The mountains quake before him
and the hills melt away.
The earth trembles at his presence,
the world and all who live in it.
6Who can withstand his indignation?
Who can endure his fierce anger?
His wrath is poured out like fire;
the rocks are shattered before him.

7The LORD is good,
a refuge in times of trouble.
He cares for those who trust in him,
8 but with an overwhelming flood
he will make an end of ⌊Nineveh⌋;
he will pursue his foes into darkness.

9Whatever they plot against the LORD
he[a] will bring to an end;
trouble will not come a second time.
10They will be entangled among thorns
and drunk from their wine;
they will be consumed like dry stubble.[b]
11From you, ⌊O Nineveh,⌋ has one come forth
who plots evil against the LORD
and counsels wickedness.

12This is what the LORD says:

"Although they have allies and are numerous,
they will be cut off and pass away.
Although I have afflicted you, ⌊O Judah,⌋
I will afflict you no more.
13Now I will break their yoke from your neck
and tear your shackles away."

14The LORD has given a command concerning you, ⌊Nineveh⌋:
"You will have no descendants to bear your name.
I will destroy the carved images and cast idols
that are in the temple of your gods.
I will prepare your grave,
for you are vile."

15Look, there on the mountains,
the feet of one who brings good news,
who proclaims peace!
Celebrate your festivals, O Judah,
and fulfill your vows.
No more will the wicked invade you;
they will be completely destroyed.

Nineveh to Fall

2

An attacker advances against you, ⌊Nineveh⌋.
Guard the fortress,
watch the road,
brace yourselves,
marshal all your strength!

2The LORD will restore the splendor of Jacob
like the splendor of Israel,
though destroyers have laid them waste
and have ruined their vines.

3The shields of his soldiers are red;
the warriors are clad in scarlet.
The metal on the chariots flashes
on the day they are made ready;
the spears of pine are brandished.[c]
4The chariots storm through the streets,
rushing back and forth through the squares.
They look like flaming torches;
they dart about like lightning.

5He summons his picked troops,
yet they stumble on their way.
They dash to the city wall;
the protective shield is put in place.
6The river gates are thrown open
and the palace collapses.
7It is decreed[d] that ⌊the city⌋

[a] 9 Or *What do you foes plot against the LORD? / He*
[b] 10 The meaning of the Hebrew for this verse is uncertain.
[c] 3 Hebrew; Septuagint and Syriac / *the horsemen rush to and fro*
[d] 7 The meaning of the Hebrew for this word is uncertain.

1:15 Isaiah used this same word picture of heralds poised on the hills shouting the good news of Judah's liberation (see Isaiah 52:7). Assyria had already destroyed the kingdom of Israel, and Judah had lived under the continual threat of attack for many years. The conquest in 612 B.C. of the Assyrian capital city of Nineveh by the Babylonians and Medes would have been good news to the desperate people of Judah. Nahum 2:3–10 records an account of Nineveh's defeat.

2:2 Assyria had rendered God's people powerless. However, because of God's righteous character and his faithfulness to his people, Nahum spoke God's promise that the past glories of Judah and Israel would be restored and God's enemies defeated. There is always hope for those who trust in God.

be exiled and carried away.
Its slave girls moan like doves
and beat upon their breasts.
8Nineveh is like a pool,
and its water is draining away.
"Stop! Stop!" they cry,
but no one turns back.
9Plunder the silver!
Plunder the gold!
The supply is endless,
the wealth from all its treasures!
10She is pillaged, plundered, stripped!
Hearts melt, knees give way,
bodies tremble, every face grows pale.

11Where now is the lions' den,
the place where they fed their young,
where the lion and lioness went,
and the cubs, with nothing to fear?
12The lion killed enough for his cubs
and strangled the prey for his mate,
filling his lairs with the kill
and his dens with the prey.

13"I am against you,"
declares the LORD Almighty.
"I will burn up your chariots in smoke,
and the sword will devour your young lions.
I will leave you no prey on the earth.
The voices of your messengers
will no longer be heard."

Woe to Nineveh

3 Woe to the city of blood,
full of lies,
full of plunder,
never without victims!
2The crack of whips,
the clatter of wheels,
galloping horses
and jolting chariots!
3Charging cavalry,
flashing swords
and glittering spears!
Many casualties,
piles of dead,
bodies without number,
people stumbling over the corpses—
4all because of the wanton lust of a harlot,
alluring, the mistress of sorceries,
who enslaved nations by her prostitution
and peoples by her witchcraft.

5"I am against you," declares the LORD Almighty.
"I will lift your skirts over your face.
I will show the nations your nakedness
and the kingdoms your shame.
6I will pelt you with filth,
I will treat you with contempt
and make you a spectacle.
7All who see you will flee from you and say,
'Nineveh is in ruins—who will mourn for her?'
Where can I find anyone to comfort you?"
8Are you better than Thebes,[a]
situated on the Nile,
with water around her?
The river was her defense,
the waters her wall.
9Cush[b] and Egypt were her boundless strength;
Put and Libya were among her allies.
10Yet she was taken captive
and went into exile.
Her infants were dashed to pieces
at the head of every street.
Lots were cast for her nobles,
and all her great men were put in chains.
11You too will become drunk;
you will go into hiding
and seek refuge from the enemy.

12All your fortresses are like fig trees
with their first ripe fruit;
when they are shaken,
the figs fall into the mouth of the eater.
13Look at your troops—
they are all women!
The gates of your land
are wide open to your enemies;
fire has consumed their bars.

14Draw water for the siege,
strengthen your defenses!
Work the clay,
tread the mortar,
repair the brickwork!
15There the fire will devour you;
the sword will cut you down
and, like grasshoppers, consume you.
Multiply like grasshoppers,
multiply like locusts!
16You have increased the number of your merchants
till they are more than the stars of the sky,
but like locusts they strip the land
and then fly away.
17Your guards are like locusts,
your officials like swarms of locusts
that settle in the walls on a cold day—

[a] 8 Hebrew *No Amon* [b] 9 That is, the upper Nile region

2:13—3:1 Assyria's defeat was certain. God's people would be delivered, and those who supported Assyria would be silenced forever. God's justice is always administered according to his timetable. We may become discouraged when we see injustice happening all around us. We may wonder why God seems to be doing so little about it. This passage assures us that God will ultimately hold unjust people accountable for their actions.

but when the sun appears they fly away,
and no one knows where.

18 O king of Assyria, your shepherds[a]
slumber;
your nobles lie down to rest.
Your people are scattered on the mountains
with no one to gather them.

19 Nothing can heal your wound;
your injury is fatal.
Everyone who hears the news about you
claps his hands at your fall,
for who has not felt
your endless cruelty?

[a] 18 Or *rulers*

HABAKKUK

The Big Picture

A. *HABAKKUK'S PERPLEXITY AND DOUBT (1:1-17)*

B. *HABAKKUK PERCEIVES GOD'S PURPOSES (2:1-20)*

C. *HABAKKUK PRAISES GOD (3:1-19)*

Habakkuk was troubled by the evil he saw running rampant in Judah. He brought his honest concern to God but was not prepared for God's answer. God planned to use the cruel and violent Babylonians to punish Judah! Judah, even with all her sin, was far more righteous than Babylon. How could God support Babylon's success while bringing destruction on Judah?

Life is filled with such questions. Injustice is a familiar occurrence in our society; the bad guys seem to win more often than the good guys. Why does God allow these things to happen? The words of Habakkuk's prophecy assure us that no matter what we face in life, God never changes his personality or his promises. His holy and loving character remains the same even when everything seems to be falling apart. God will fulfill all the good promises of his Word, even when our future seems to hold nothing but pain. God is powerful enough to use even our painful circumstances to bring about his good will for us.

This book is unique because the prophet never assumed the role of God's spokesman. Instead, Habakkuk recorded God's responses to the prophet's honest questions about life. God wants us to come to him with our questions. If we listen to God's reply, our hearts can be stirred to a renewed trust and hope in God just as Habakkuk's heart was. Habakkuk remembered past displays of God's power and gained faith in God for future struggles. As we share our stories of deliverance with others and remember how God has worked in our lives, we will be strengthened for the conflicts yet to come.

Spiritual Renewal Themes

THE VALUE OF DOUBT

Habakkuk's prophecy centers around a question posed to God. We all have questions; they are a part of life. We may not always find the answers, but God does not condemn us for asking our questions. Habakkuk felt free to ask such questions of God. God cares about us, and he wants us to come freely to him with our doubts. It is often during times of doubt that our spiritual growth can surge forward. In these times of honest reflection, we can seek God afresh, asking him to help us see the truth as we surrender our lives to him.

GOD NEVER CHANGES

Everyone experiences some hard times. The prophet Habakkuk was greatly encouraged as he remembered all that God had done for his people. When we face hard times, we can find a continual source of strength by remembering God's faithfulness to us in the past. Because God never changes, we can be confident that what he has done in the past, he will continue to do in the future. Sharing our story and telling others about what God has done for us will give them a reason to believe that he can help them as well.

GOD IS OUR SOURCE OF HOPE

Our hope must be built upon our powerful and loving God. Because Habakkuk's hope was in God, he could patiently wait for God to bring the day of judgment against Babylon. We live—really live—by trusting God. We will make progress spiritually as we improve our relationship with him and continually seek him. He is our strength and sure deliverer. He is the basis of our hope for ongoing spiritual renewal.

Essential Facts

PURPOSE:
To deal with doubt by affirming that despite the world's evil, God has not changed in his person or purpose.

AUTHOR:
The prophet Habakkuk.

AUDIENCE:
The people of the southern kingdom of Judah.

DATE WRITTEN:
Between 612 and 589 B.C.

SETTING:
The kingdom of Judah, just prior to the beginning of the Babylonian invasions and the destruction of Jerusalem.

KEY VERSE:
"See, he is puffed up; his desires are not upright—but the righteous will live by his faith" (2:4).

KEY PEOPLE AND RELATIONSHIPS:
Habakkuk and the Babylonians, Habakkuk and God.

1 The oracle that Habakkuk the prophet received.

Habakkuk's Complaint

2How long, O LORD, must I call for help,
but you do not listen?
Or cry out to you, "Violence!"
but you do not save?
3Why do you make me look at injustice?
Why do you tolerate wrong?
Destruction and violence are before me;
there is strife, and conflict abounds.
4Therefore the law is paralyzed,
and justice never prevails.
The wicked hem in the righteous,
so that justice is perverted.

The LORD's Answer

5"Look at the nations and watch—
and be utterly amazed.
For I am going to do something in your days
that you would not believe,
even if you were told.
6I am raising up the Babylonians,[a]
that ruthless and impetuous people,
who sweep across the whole earth
to seize dwelling places not their own.
7They are a feared and dreaded people;
they are a law to themselves
and promote their own honor.
8Their horses are swifter than leopards,
fiercer than wolves at dusk.
Their cavalry gallops headlong;
their horsemen come from afar.
They fly like a vulture swooping to devour;
9 they all come bent on violence.
Their hordes[b] advance like a desert wind
and gather prisoners like sand.
10They deride kings
and scoff at rulers.
They laugh at all fortified cities;
they build earthen ramps and capture them.
11Then they sweep past like the wind and go on—
guilty men, whose own strength is their god."

Habakkuk's Second Complaint

12O LORD, are you not from everlasting?
My God, my Holy One, we will not die.
O LORD, you have appointed them to execute judgment;
O Rock, you have ordained them to punish.
13Your eyes are too pure to look on evil;
you cannot tolerate wrong.
Why then do you tolerate the treacherous?
Why are you silent while the wicked
swallow up those more righteous than themselves?
14You have made men like fish in the sea,
like sea creatures that have no ruler.
15The wicked foe pulls all of them up with hooks,
he catches them in his net,
he gathers them up in his dragnet;
and so he rejoices and is glad.
16Therefore he sacrifices to his net
and burns incense to his dragnet,
for by his net he lives in luxury
and enjoys the choicest food.
17Is he to keep on emptying his net,
destroying nations without mercy?

2 I will stand at my watch
and station myself on the ramparts;
I will look to see what he will say to me,
and what answer I am to give to this complaint.[c]

The LORD's Answer

2Then the LORD replied:

"Write down the revelation
and make it plain on tablets
so that a herald[d] may run with it.
3For the revelation awaits an appointed time;
it speaks of the end
and will not prove false.
Though it linger, wait for it;
it[e] will certainly come and will not delay.

[a]6 Or *Chaldeans* [b]9 The meaning of the Hebrew for this word is uncertain. [c]1 Or *and what to answer when I am rebuked* [d]2 Or *so that whoever reads it* [e]3 Or *Though he linger, wait for him; / he*

1:1–4 Habakkuk, a contemporary of the prophets Jeremiah, Daniel and Ezekiel, was appalled at the wickedness swirling about him like a windstorm. As he called out to God, lawlessness and injustice were rampant in the nation of Judah. Today's society is not much different. We may wonder, *Will this ever end?* Habakkuk's words provide an answer to this question.

1:5–11 God's solution for Judah's sin was punishment through exile in Babylon. The destruction of Judah and Jerusalem was a reminder that disobedience to God carries a high price. Yet this punishment was also God's way of helping his people devote themselves to him again and experience God's redemption and restoration. God often does the same thing with us. He allows us to live in our sins for a while before the consequences catch up with us. When faced with sin's consequences, we finally realize that we truly need God's help and mercy. We must repent and surrender our lives to God in order to experience his redemption and restoration.

1:12—2:3 God said the Babylonians would attack and win. To Habakkuk it seemed that God's cure was worse than the disease. How could God let the godless Babylonians destroy his own people? Like Habakkuk, we sometimes wonder how wicked people can be allowed to prosper. Rather than turn away in confusion, we would be wise to turn to God, honestly asking him to help us understand. God will deal with the wicked when the time is right. He is still in control.

[4]"See, he is puffed up;
his desires are not upright—
but the righteous will live by his faith[a]—
[5]indeed, wine betrays him;
he is arrogant and never at rest.
Because he is as greedy as the grave[b]
and like death is never satisfied,
he gathers to himself all the nations
and takes captive all the peoples.

[6]"Will not all of them taunt him with ridicule and scorn, saying,

" 'Woe to him who piles up stolen goods
and makes himself wealthy by extortion!
How long must this go on?'
[7]Will not your debtors[c] suddenly arise?
Will they not wake up and make you tremble?
Then you will become their victim.
[8]Because you have plundered many nations,
the peoples who are left will plunder you.
For you have shed man's blood;
you have destroyed lands and cities and everyone in them.

[9]"Woe to him who builds his realm by unjust gain
to set his nest on high,
to escape the clutches of ruin!
[10]You have plotted the ruin of many peoples,
shaming your own house and forfeiting your life.
[11]The stones of the wall will cry out,
and the beams of the woodwork will echo it.

[12]"Woe to him who builds a city with bloodshed
and establishes a town by crime!
[13]Has not the LORD Almighty determined
that the people's labor is only fuel for the fire,
that the nations exhaust themselves for nothing?
[14]For the earth will be filled with the
knowledge of the glory of the LORD,
as the waters cover the sea.

[15]"Woe to him who gives drink to his neighbors,
pouring it from the wineskin till they are drunk,
so that he can gaze on their naked bodies.
[16]You will be filled with shame instead of glory.
Now it is your turn! Drink and be exposed[d]!
The cup from the LORD's right hand is coming around to you,
and disgrace will cover your glory.
[17]The violence you have done to Lebanon will overwhelm you,
and your destruction of animals will terrify you.
For you have shed man's blood;
you have destroyed lands and cities and everyone in them.

[18]"Of what value is an idol, since a man has carved it?
Or an image that teaches lies?
For he who makes it trusts in his own creation;
he makes idols that cannot speak.
[19]Woe to him who says to wood, 'Come to life!'
Or to lifeless stone, 'Wake up!'
Can it give guidance?
It is covered with gold and silver;
there is no breath in it.
[20]But the LORD is in his holy temple;
let all the earth be silent before him."

Habakkuk's Prayer

3 A prayer of Habakkuk the prophet. On *shigionoth.*[e]

[2]LORD, I have heard of your fame;
I stand in awe of your deeds, O LORD.
Renew them in our day,
in our time make them known;
in wrath remember mercy.

[3]God came from Teman,

[a]4 Or *faithfulness* [b]5 Hebrew *Sheol* [c]7 Or *creditors* [d]16 Masoretic Text; Dead Sea Scrolls, Aquila, Vulgate and Syriac (see also Septuagint) *and stagger* [e]1 Probably a literary or musical term

---

2:4 Wicked people are characterized by the fact that they trust in themselves. They proudly believe they can make their own way in the world under their own power. Most of us have experienced the sad consequences of such an attitude. God alone knows what is best for us; we can trust him to lead us in the right way. Being righteous does not depend on our *doing* the right things. We can be righteous, no matter how terrible our past, by trusting and following God's plan for us.

3:1–2 Habakkuk praised God, not only for answering his questions, but also for the knowledge he had gained about God's nature. Habakkuk realized how much his people needed God's discipline (see Hebrews 12:5–7). He acknowledged God's righteousness in God's choice for their punishment. Then Habakkuk looked toward a future time of restoration. God's punishment of his people was meted out for the purpose of their growth and blessing. If we recognize our need for God and follow his good plans for us, we can experience the blessings God intends for us even in the midst of our painful experiences.

3:3–15 Remembering the powerful acts of God in the past can give us confidence in what God can do in the future. When we read about God's work in the lives of his people, we can receive encouragement from their experiences (see Romans 15:4; 1 Corinthians 10:11). God's work in our own lives can also be of great help to others. As we share how God has delivered us, not only will others receive new hope, but we also will find encouragement by remembering what God has already done for us.

In Awe of God

Habakkuk 2:20 We live in a noisy world. Whether we hear the loud throbbing of the neighbor's rock music or the incessant din of background noise, we are constantly assaulted by sound. While some of this noise cannot be avoided, we often use constant sound to cover our true thoughts and feelings.

Being confined in an elevator is so uncomfortable for most people that music is piped in over a loudspeaker to distract them from their discomfort. Many public places such as restaurants and waiting rooms play background music so that people won't feel uncomfortable because of the silence. In a similar way, people often use noise to hide from God. Noise and activity cover the nagging sense that we ought to be paying more attention to our spiritual lives. Noise may even distract us from worshiping God. But what happens when all noise is silenced? Suddenly, there's nowhere to hide. This is why the prophet Habakkuk called all the earth to silence during God's time of judgment (2:20).

Habakkuk condemned those who foolishly worshiped idols. Their speechless idols could not help; they could not give guidance and direction or comfort and hope. Because of this, the people themselves were speechless, having nothing worthwhile to reiterate from their idols. Therefore, the whole earth was called to silence in reverence for the Lord, who lives in his temple.

Unlike those who worship idols, however, we need not fear silence if we have a relationship with God. Silence can inspire a sense of awe at God's presence within us. The half hour of silence in heaven before the great trumpet blasts (see Revelation 8:1) or the pause in Handel's *Messiah* just before the final "Hallelujah!" of the "Hallelujah Chorus," are both moments of silence that allow us to center our attention and prepare for what will come next. Silence in our time with God helps us focus on him and prepares us for what he is about to do. Such silence becomes a resting time, a time for renewing strength: "In quietness and trust is your strength" (Isaiah 30:15).

Putting It Into Practice

What inspires your worship? Is it a favorite hymn or song? A favorite picture or painting? A special place? Listen to that piece of music, view that picture or visit that place, but then be still and savor the wonder of God that comes to you in those moments. Do not strain for thoughts, but simply welcome the stillness as a gift. And give your silence back to God as a gift of praise.

For more on silence, turn to James 3.

the Holy One from Mount Paran.
Selah[a]
His glory covered the heavens
and his praise filled the earth.
4His splendor was like the sunrise;
rays flashed from his hand,
where his power was hidden.
5Plague went before him;
pestilence followed his steps.
6He stood, and shook the earth;
he looked, and made the nations
tremble.
The ancient mountains crumbled
and the age-old hills collapsed.
His ways are eternal.
7I saw the tents of Cushan in distress,
the dwellings of Midian in anguish.
8Were you angry with the rivers, O LORD?
Was your wrath against the streams?
Did you rage against the sea
when you rode with your horses
and your victorious chariots?
9You uncovered your bow,
you called for many arrows. *Selah*
You split the earth with rivers;
10 the mountains saw you and writhed.
Torrents of water swept by;
the deep roared
and lifted its waves on high.
11Sun and moon stood still in the heavens
at the glint of your flying arrows,
at the lightning of your flashing spear.
12In wrath you strode through the earth
and in anger you threshed the nations.
13You came out to deliver your people,
to save your anointed one.
You crushed the leader of the land of
wickedness,
you stripped him from head to foot.
Selah
14With his own spear you pierced his head
when his warriors stormed out to scatter
us,
gloating as though about to devour
the wretched who were in hiding.
15You trampled the sea with your horses,
churning the great waters.

16I heard and my heart pounded,
my lips quivered at the sound;
decay crept into my bones,
and my legs trembled.
Yet I will wait patiently for the day of
calamity
to come on the nation invading us.
17Though the fig tree does not bud
and there are no grapes on the vines,
though the olive crop fails
and the fields produce no food,
though there are no sheep in the pen
and no cattle in the stalls,
18yet I will rejoice in the LORD,
I will be joyful in God my Savior.

19The Sovereign LORD is my strength;
he makes my feet like the feet of a deer,
he enables me to go on the heights.

For the director of music. On my stringed
instruments.

[a] 3 A word of uncertain meaning; possibly a musical term; also in verses 9 and 13

3:17–19 Habakkuk's prayer came to a climax in a beautiful affirmation of faith. Though there would be hard times ahead, Habakkuk knew that he could trust God to provide him with the strength he needed to persevere. Habakkuk's final words provide a stunning picture of the surefooted confidence we can have in our God of strength and safety. What a great assurance for all who seek God!

ZEPHANIAH

The Big Picture

A. PROPHECIES OF JUDGMENT AGAINST JUDAH (1:1–2:3)

1. Judah's Moral and Spiritual Irresponsibility (1:1-13)
2. Judah's Accountability Before God (1:14-18)
3. Judah's Opportunity for Restoration (2:1-3)

B. PROPHECIES OF JUDGMENT AGAINST THE NATIONS (2:4-15)

C. PROPHECIES OF JUDGMENT AGAINST JERUSALEM (3:1-8)

D. PROMISES OF BLESSING TO THOSE WHO TRUST IN GOD (3:9-20)

"*If only . . .*" is a haunting phrase. It implies that we have failed—that we wish we could go back in time and do things differently. As we see the truth and accept responsibility for our lives, we may be saddened and ashamed when we reflect on our past. We may regret our irresponsible and destructive behaviors and wish we could erase past mistakes. This must have been how the people of Judah felt when they heard the prophetic words of Zephaniah. *If only* they had obeyed and trusted God!

God called Zephaniah to be his prophet during the days of King Josiah, the last of Judah's good kings. The prophet's condemnation of Judah's idol worship and self-centered living echoed the young king's disdain for these sinful practices. Zephaniah's prophetic words would have bolstered support of Josiah's purges against idolatry during the early years of his reign. However, the apostasy of Judah's previous kings, Manasseh and Amon, had left deep spiritual wounds in the land of Judah. Despite Zephaniah's ministry and Josiah's noble reforms, these scars remained visible in Judah throughout his reign.

The people of Judah needed to make some major changes. They had seen the exile of the northern kingdom of Israel, but they falsely assumed that the presence of God in the Jerusalem temple would protect them from foreign invaders. Their spiritual indifference blinded them to their true situation. Zephaniah warned the people that Judah would be destroyed if they didn't repent right away. He also informed them that spiritual renewal was still possible. Spiritual awakening could still occur if they would admit their sins and trust in God. Josiah and the people listened to Zephaniah, responded and experienced revival.

Spiritual Renewal Themes

THE CONSEQUENCES OF IRRESPONSIBILITY

Many of our troubles come as direct consequences of our irresponsibility. Judah was irresponsible in her covenant relationship with God. Judah worshiped false gods and ignored God's laws—laws that were intended for her own good. Zephaniah clearly stated that the nation's irresponsibility would carry heavy consequences. Encouraged by Zephaniah and led by

Josiah, the people of Judah confessed their sins, took responsibility for their lives and turned back to God. As a result, they received substantial healing and restoration. When we are irresponsible in our relationships with God and others, our situations will grow progressively worse. But as we learn to live responsible lives, we will begin to experience the blessings of God.

COMPLACENCY LEADS TO A DOWNFALL

Prosperity and success often lead to complacency. Josiah's great-grandfather Hezekiah had been one of Judah's greatest kings. Hezekiah had led his people back to God, and God had greatly blessed them. However, Judah's next two kings, Manasseh and Amon, led their people into a period of spiritual complacency and sin. And with time, those sins brought about grievous consequences. Josiah followed in the footsteps of Hezekiah and helped lead the people back to God. Sometimes our greatest failures will follow our greatest victories. In order to prevent a downfall, we need to continually seek God and honestly reflect on our spiritual condition. Our hearts must always be vulnerable and dependent on God, regardless of how far we have progressed spiritually.

SPIRITUAL RENEWAL LEADS TO JOY

The process of spiritual renewal may contain some painful steps. When we confess the truth about ourselves, it can hurt. But as we begin to speak the truth and accept responsibility for our own lives, we can discover the great relief and hope that God offers. As we release our hold on our lives and begin to follow God's will for us, we find joy. Then we can truly celebrate God's goodness as it filters into every area of our lives, bringing joy where there was once only sorrow and pain.

Essential Facts

PURPOSE:
To shake the people of Judah out of their complacency and get them back on the path of spiritual renewal.

AUTHOR:
The prophet Zephaniah.

AUDIENCE:
The people of the southern kingdom of Judah.

DATE WRITTEN:
Sometime between 640 and 621 B.C., just prior to King Josiah's great reformation.

SETTING:
The kingdom of Judah during the years of King Josiah; Zephaniah's ministry may have helped to motivate the young king's reforms.

KEY VERSE:
"On that day you will not be put to shame for all the wrongs you have done to me, because I will remove from this city those who rejoice in their pride. Never again will you be haughty on my holy hill" (3:11).

KEY PLACE:
Jerusalem.

KEY PEOPLE AND RELATIONSHIPS:
Zephaniah and the people of Judah.

1 The word of the LORD that came to Zephaniah son of Cushi, the son of Gedaliah, the
son of Amariah, the son of Hezekiah, during the
reign of Josiah son of Amon king of Judah:

Warning of Coming Destruction

2"I will sweep away everything
from the face of the earth,"
declares the LORD.
3"I will sweep away both men and animals;
I will sweep away the birds of the air
and the fish of the sea.
The wicked will have only heaps of
rubble[a]
when I cut off man from the face of the
earth,"
declares the LORD.

Against Judah

4"I will stretch out my hand against Judah
and against all who live in Jerusalem.
I will cut off from this place every remnant
of Baal,
the names of the pagan and the
idolatrous priests—
5those who bow down on the roofs
to worship the starry host,
those who bow down and swear by the
LORD
and who also swear by Molech,[b]
6those who turn back from following the
LORD
and neither seek the LORD nor inquire of
him.
7Be silent before the Sovereign LORD,
for the day of the LORD is near.
The LORD has prepared a sacrifice;
he has consecrated those he has invited.
8On the day of the LORD's sacrifice
I will punish the princes
and the king's sons
and all those clad
in foreign clothes.
9On that day I will punish
all who avoid stepping on the
threshold,[c]
who fill the temple of their gods
with violence and deceit.

10"On that day," declares the LORD,
"a cry will go up from the Fish Gate,
wailing from the New Quarter,
and a loud crash from the hills.
11Wail, you who live in the market district[d];
all your merchants will be wiped out,
all who trade with[e] silver will be
ruined.
12At that time I will search Jerusalem with
lamps
and punish those who are complacent,
who are like wine left on its dregs,
who think, 'The LORD will do nothing,
either good or bad.'
13Their wealth will be plundered,
their houses demolished.
They will build houses
but not live in them;
they will plant vineyards
but not drink the wine.

The Great Day of the LORD

14"The great day of the LORD is near—
near and coming quickly.
Listen! The cry on the day of the LORD will
be bitter,
the shouting of the warrior there.
15That day will be a day of wrath,
a day of distress and anguish,
a day of trouble and ruin,
a day of darkness and gloom,
a day of clouds and blackness,
16a day of trumpet and battle cry
against the fortified cities
and against the corner towers.
17I will bring distress on the people
and they will walk like blind men,
because they have sinned against the
LORD.
Their blood will be poured out like dust
and their entrails like filth.
18Neither their silver nor their gold
will be able to save them
on the day of the LORD's wrath.
In the fire of his jealousy
the whole world will be consumed,
for he will make a sudden end
of all who live in the earth."

2 Gather together, gather together,
O shameful nation,
2before the appointed time arrives

[a]3 The meaning of the Hebrew for this line is uncertain. [b]5 Hebrew *Malcam,* that is, Milcom [c]9 See 1 Samuel 5:5. [d]11 Or *the Mortar* [e]11 Or *in*

1:4–13 Through Zephaniah, God condemned the irresponsible behavior of Judah's wicked leaders, probably referring to the recent reigns of Manasseh and Amon. During their reigns the people of Judah had become increasingly dependent upon false gods, had ceased to worship the true God and had built a society in which deceitful and immoral people could prosper. The progression is clear: When we turn from the true God, our society and its members begin to deteriorate. We all need God. Unless we recognize this fact our lives will continue on a downhill path.

1:14–18 The prophet warned of the coming "day of the LORD"—a day of reckoning with God. Judah would be conquered and her people led away as slaves to Babylon. God mercifully offered his people many opportunities to repent, but Zephaniah warned that there would come a time when judgment would fall. We should be thankful that God will not allow us to reject his way forever either. When we do things our own way, we only hurt ourselves and the people we love. If we listen to the early warnings we receive and act appropriately, we need not fear a future day of reckoning.

2:1–3 God's warning of impending judgment was intended to encourage the people of Judah to return to him. The prophet urged the people to repent, hoping that they would be spared the coming devastation. The people re-

and that day sweeps on like chaff,
before the fierce anger of the LORD comes upon you,
before the day of the LORD's wrath comes upon you.
3Seek the LORD, all you humble of the land,
you who do what he commands.
Seek righteousness, seek humility;
perhaps you will be sheltered
on the day of the LORD's anger.

Against Philistia

4Gaza will be abandoned
and Ashkelon left in ruins.
At midday Ashdod will be emptied
and Ekron uprooted.
5Woe to you who live by the sea,
O Kerethite people;
the word of the LORD is against you,
O Canaan, land of the Philistines.

"I will destroy you,
and none will be left."

6The land by the sea, where the Kerethites[a] dwell,
will be a place for shepherds and sheep pens.
7It will belong to the remnant of the house of Judah;
there they will find pasture.
In the evening they will lie down
in the houses of Ashkelon.
The LORD their God will care for them;
he will restore their fortunes.[b]

Against Moab and Ammon

8"I have heard the insults of Moab
and the taunts of the Ammonites,
who insulted my people
and made threats against their land.
9Therefore, as surely as I live,"
declares the LORD Almighty, the God of Israel,
"surely Moab will become like Sodom,
the Ammonites like Gomorrah—
a place of weeds and salt pits,
a wasteland forever.
The remnant of my people will plunder them;
the survivors of my nation will inherit their land."
10This is what they will get in return for their pride,
for insulting and mocking the people of the LORD Almighty.
11The LORD will be awesome to them
when he destroys all the gods of the land.
The nations on every shore will worship him,
every one in its own land.

Against Cush

12"You too, O Cushites,[c]
will be slain by my sword."

Against Assyria

13He will stretch out his hand against the north
and destroy Assyria,
leaving Nineveh utterly desolate
and dry as the desert.
14Flocks and herds will lie down there,
creatures of every kind.
The desert owl and the screech owl
will roost on her columns.
Their calls will echo through the windows,
rubble will be in the doorways,
the beams of cedar will be exposed.
15This is the carefree city
that lived in safety.
She said to herself,
"I am, and there is none besides me."
What a ruin she has become,
a lair for wild beasts!
All who pass by her scoff
and shake their fists.

The Future of Jerusalem

3 Woe to the city of oppressors,
rebellious and defiled!
2She obeys no one,
she accepts no correction.
She does not trust in the LORD,
she does not draw near to her God.
3Her officials are roaring lions,
her rulers are evening wolves,
who leave nothing for the morning.

[a]6 The meaning of the Hebrew for this word is uncertain.
[b]7 Or *will bring back their captives*
[c]12 That is, people from the upper Nile region

---

sponded favorably to Zephaniah's message. King Josiah led them in a great reformation—the last high point in Judah's history. Though the day of reckoning did come, it was delayed for several generations. Like the people of Zephaniah's day, we must respond to the warnings we receive, admit our sin and ask God to help us.

2:4–15 Zephaniah listed the nations that had influenced Judah in their idolatrous practices. These nations would come under God's judgment and ultimately lose their power and influence. God gives us opportunities to influence others for good. Sometimes, however, we end up leading others in the wrong direction. Taking responsibility for those we have led astray is part of accepting responsibility for our lives. Part of making restitution with such people is doing what we can to get them back on the right track.

3:1–5 Judah's destructive behavior, though influenced by other nations, was ultimately her responsibility. The people refused to admit their sins to God. They rejected all his warnings and attempts to correct them. Others may have negatively influenced us too. But pointing the finger of blame at them will only slow our spiritual progress. They are responsible for dealing with their problems; we are responsible for our own. As we take responsibility for our actions we will recognize how much we need God to help redirect the course of our lives. If we continue to blame others for our problems, we are headed for destruction.

4Her prophets are arrogant;
they are treacherous men.
Her priests profane the sanctuary
and do violence to the law.
5The LORD within her is righteous;
he does no wrong.
Morning by morning he dispenses his
justice,
and every new day he does not fail,
yet the unrighteous know no shame.

6"I have cut off nations;
their strongholds are demolished.
I have left their streets deserted,
with no one passing through.
Their cities are destroyed;
no one will be left—no one at all.
7I said to the city,
'Surely you will fear me
and accept correction!'
Then her dwelling would not be cut off,
nor all my punishments come upon her.
But they were still eager
to act corruptly in all they did.
8Therefore wait for me," declares the LORD,
"for the day I will stand up to testify.[a]
I have decided to assemble the nations,
to gather the kingdoms
and to pour out my wrath on them—
all my fierce anger.
The whole world will be consumed
by the fire of my jealous anger.

9"Then will I purify the lips of the peoples,
that all of them may call on the name of
the LORD
and serve him shoulder to shoulder.
10From beyond the rivers of Cush[b]
my worshipers, my scattered people,
will bring me offerings.
11On that day you will not be put to shame
for all the wrongs you have done to me,
because I will remove from this city
those who rejoice in their pride.
Never again will you be haughty
on my holy hill.
12But I will leave within you
the meek and humble,
who trust in the name of the LORD.
13The remnant of Israel will do no wrong;
they will speak no lies,
nor will deceit be found in their mouths.
They will eat and lie down
and no one will make them afraid."

14Sing, O Daughter of Zion;
shout aloud, O Israel!
Be glad and rejoice with all your heart,
O Daughter of Jerusalem!
15The LORD has taken away your punishment,
he has turned back your enemy.
The LORD, the King of Israel, is with you;
never again will you fear any harm.
16On that day they will say to Jerusalem,
"Do not fear, O Zion;
do not let your hands hang limp.
17The LORD your God is with you,
he is mighty to save.
He will take great delight in you,
he will quiet you with his love,
he will rejoice over you with singing."

18"The sorrows for the appointed feasts
I will remove from you;
they are a burden and a reproach to
you.[c]
19At that time I will deal
with all who oppressed you;
I will rescue the lame
and gather those who have been
scattered.
I will give them praise and honor
in every land where they were put to
shame.
20At that time I will gather you;
at that time I will bring you home.
I will give you honor and praise
among all the peoples of the earth
when I restore your fortunes[d]
before your very eyes,"
says the LORD.

[a]8 Septuagint and Syriac; Hebrew *will rise up to plunder* [b]10 That is, the upper Nile region [c]18 Or *"I will gather you who mourn for the appointed feasts; / your reproach is a burden to you* [d]20 Or *I bring back your captives*

3:9–20 Zephaniah described a future age that would follow the ultimate "day of the LORD." This age of blessing will ultimately be marked by honest and pure worship of God. Sorrows and burdens will no longer exist, and the nation of Israel will finally be restored to its land of hope and security. We can rejoice in this great promise for God's people.

HAGGAI

The Big Picture

- *A. INTRODUCTION (1:1)*
- *B. THE FIRST SERMON: REBUKE (1:2-15)*
  1. The Prophet's Challenge to Rebuild the Temple (1:2-11)
  2. The People Respond With Action (1:12-15)
- *C. THE SECOND SERMON: RENEWAL (2:1-9)*
- *D. THE THIRD SERMON: RESTORATION (2:10-19)*
- *E. THE FOURTH SERMON: REASSURANCE (2:20-23)*

Haggai was called to encourage the people of Jerusalem to return to the task of rebuilding God's house. About eighteen years had passed since Cyrus had released Zerubbabel and a group of Jewish exiles to Jerusalem to rebuild the temple. The people had begun the project filled with hope, but pressure from the local authorities and selfish decisions led them to quit the task and turn instead to building their own homes. Their priorities were out of order.

Over a six-month period, Haggai delivered four messages designed to motivate the people to complete the task of rebuilding God's temple and redirecting the course of their lives. Haggai told the people to stop making excuses and get back to work. He told them that their present sufferings were a result of their failure to put God first in their lives. They needed to get their spiritual lives back in line with God's will. Their actions needed to prove their change of heart before they could expect God's blessings. Haggai's messages concluded with encouragement by promising God's help as they continued the task.

The task of rebuilding the temple was difficult; so is the task of rebuilding our lives. There will always be obstacles to any rebuilding project, but we don't have to let those obstacles stop us. We must remember the message of Haggai. God is there to help us each step of the way. Just as God's people had to reassess their spiritual lives in the rebuilding process, we also need to examine our lives and prove our change of heart by our actions. We can then respond, like the people of Jerusalem, to Haggai's message and move forward with God's help in our own rebuilding and restoration process.

Spiritual Renewal Themes

GOD'S PLAN MUST COME FIRST

The people of Jerusalem started rebuilding God's temple. But when they met with stiff opposition, instead of trusting God and standing up to the opposition, the people turned away from the rebuilding project God had set out for them and built their own homes instead. We tend to make the same mistake. When we face obstacles to God's plan for our spiritual growth, we may get sidetracked from our primary mission and follow the way of

Essential Facts

PURPOSE:
To challenge the people to complete the rebuilding of God's temple, their community and their lives.

AUTHOR:
The prophet Haggai.

AUDIENCE:
The people living in Jerusalem, including those who had returned from Babylonian exile.

DATE WRITTEN:
Between August and December 520 B.C.

SETTING:
Jerusalem had been in ruins since her destruction by the Babylonians in 586 B.C. The people had started to rebuild the temple but had failed to complete the task.

KEY VERSES:
"This is what the LORD Almighty says: 'Give careful thought to your ways. Go up into the mountains and bring down timber and build the house, so that I may take pleasure in it and be honored,' says the LORD" (1:7–8).

KEY PLACES:
Jerusalem and the temple.

KEY PEOPLE AND RELATIONSHIPS:
Zerubbabel (the political leader), Joshua (the priestly leader) and the prophets Haggai and Zechariah.

least resistance. We may lower our standards, give in to sin, avoid confession, stop seeking God and neglect relationships with those who hold us accountable. We may even look for a spiritual path that looks easier because it excludes God or removes the voice of a nagging conscience. But when we reject God's plan, we also reject his power and blessing in our lives. Even though God's way may not always be easy, we cannot experience spiritual renewal and fulfillment apart from following God's will.

WE WILL FACE OBSTACLES

The rebuilding process is never easy. Satan will rear his ugly head time and again as we seek God and surrender to him. The people of Jerusalem faced numerous obstacles as they sought to rebuild the temple. Local leaders repeatedly tried to stop the work. The people became afraid and gave up on the task God had given them to do. With God's help and Haggai's encouragement, however, the rebuilding of God's temple was completed. God wants us to grow spiritually, and he will help us to overcome the obstacles to our spiritual renewal if we look to him for help.

SPIRITUAL RENEWAL REQUIRES ACTION

It is much easier to recognize a problem than it is to do something about it. God's people in Jerusalem knew the temple needed to be rebuilt. Their national strength and spiritual lives depended on it. They had begun the task but had become discouraged and failed to follow through. This failure to act brought continued suffering to God's people. Haggai urged the people to act; he calls us to do the same. When seeking spiritual renewal, we must not merely recognize our need. We must also use the keys God gives us to move toward reconciliation with God, ourselves and others. As painful as this process can be at times, our spiritual renewal will also be moving us toward restoration and peace.

A Call to Build the House of the LORD

1 In the second year of King Darius, on the first day of the sixth month, the word of the LORD came through the prophet Haggai to Zerubbabel son of Shealtiel, governor of Judah, and to Joshua[a] son of Jehozadak, the high priest:

2This is what the LORD Almighty says: "These people say, 'The time has not yet come for the LORD's house to be built.' "

3Then the word of the LORD came through the prophet Haggai: 4"Is it a time for you yourselves to be living in your paneled houses, while this house remains a ruin?"

5Now this is what the LORD Almighty says: "Give careful thought to your ways. 6You have planted much, but have harvested little. You eat, but never have enough. You drink, but never have your fill. You put on clothes, but are not warm. You earn wages, only to put them in a purse with holes in it."

7This is what the LORD Almighty says: "Give careful thought to your ways. 8Go up into the mountains and bring down timber and build the house, so that I may take pleasure in it and be honored," says the LORD. 9"You expected much, but see, it turned out to be little. What you brought home, I blew away. Why?" declares the LORD Almighty. "Because of my house, which remains a ruin, while each of you is busy with his own house. 10Therefore, because of you the heavens have withheld their dew and the earth its crops. 11I called for a drought on the fields and the mountains, on the grain, the new wine, the oil and whatever the ground produces, on men and cattle, and on the labor of your hands."

12Then Zerubbabel son of Shealtiel, Joshua son of Jehozadak, the high priest, and the whole remnant of the people obeyed the voice of the LORD their God and the message of the prophet Haggai, because the LORD their God had sent him. And the people feared the LORD.

13Then Haggai, the LORD's messenger, gave this message of the LORD to the people: "I am with you," declares the LORD. 14So the LORD stirred up the spirit of Zerubbabel son of Shealtiel, governor of Judah, and the spirit of Joshua son of Jehozadak, the high priest, and the spirit of the whole remnant of the people. They came and began to work on the house of the LORD Almighty, their God, 15on the twenty-fourth day of the sixth month in the second year of King Darius.

The Promised Glory of the New House

2 On the twenty-first day of the seventh month, the word of the LORD came through the prophet Haggai: 2"Speak to Zerubbabel son of Shealtiel, governor of Judah, to Joshua son of Jehozadak, the high priest, and to the remnant of the people. Ask them, 3'Who of you is left who saw this house in its former glory? How does it look to you now? Does it not seem to you like nothing? 4But now be strong, O Zerubbabel,' declares the LORD. 'Be strong, O Joshua son of Jehozadak, the high priest. Be strong, all you people of the land,' declares the LORD, 'and work. For I am with you,' declares the LORD Almighty. 5'This is what I covenanted with you when you came out of Egypt. And my Spirit remains among you. Do not fear.'

6"This is what the LORD Almighty says: 'In a little while I will once more shake the heavens and the earth, the sea and the dry land. 7I will shake all nations, and the desired of all nations will come, and I will fill this house with glory,' says the LORD Almighty. 8'The silver is mine and the gold is mine,' declares the LORD Almighty. 9'The glory of this present house will be greater than the glory of the former house,' says the LORD Almighty. 'And in this place I will grant peace,' declares the LORD Almighty."

Blessings for a Defiled People

10On the twenty-fourth day of the ninth month, in the second year of Darius, the word of the LORD came to the prophet Haggai: 11"This is what the LORD Almighty says: 'Ask the priests what the law says: 12If a person carries consecrated meat in the fold of his garment,

[a]1 A variant of *Jeshua;* here and elsewhere in Haggai

1:2–8 God wanted the people in Jerusalem to reflect on their lives and reconsider their priorities. The people had returned from exile and started to rebuild the temple. But when they faced opposition to the rebuilding project, they chose to build beautiful homes for themselves instead of finishing God's house. Their actions proved that they considered their personal comfort more important than God. We must make sure that our priorities are in keeping with God's Word. God must be first in our lives.

1:13–15 The people in Haggai's day knew God's will for them—they were to rebuild God's temple. Their problem was that they needed to act on their knowledge. In this passage we see that the people finally took concrete steps to complete the task God had given them. As we honestly reflect on our lives we will become aware of the things we need to change, and we will have a good idea of what we should do. When we reach this point, it is time to take responsibility for what we have done and ask forgiveness. Then we need to take concrete, active steps to make real spiritual progress.

2:3–9 The temple in Jerusalem had been destroyed over sixty years earlier, so there were few alive who could remember it. The older people who had seen Solomon's temple were sad because the new temple would never match the old one's splendor. God made it clear, however, that their rebuilding project would result in a temple even more glorious than Solomon's. In our lives, too, regardless of our past, God has a glorious future planned for us. When we surrender our lives to God, he will guide us through our present circumstances to the glorious future he has planned.

2:12–13 Purity does not rub off; impurity does. This is true not only in a physical sense, but in a spiritual sense as well. We need to guard against being influenced by sinful people. If we are not prepared for them, they will likely lead us astray.

and that fold touches some bread or stew, some
wine, oil or other food, does it become consecrated?' "

The priests answered, "No."

13Then Haggai said, "If a person defiled by
contact with a dead body touches one of these
things, does it become defiled?"

"Yes," the priests replied, "it becomes defiled."

14Then Haggai said, " 'So it is with this people and this nation in my sight,' declares the
LORD. 'Whatever they do and whatever they offer there is defiled.

15" 'Now give careful thought to this from
this day on[a]—consider how things were before
one stone was laid on another in the LORD's
temple. 16When anyone came to a heap of
twenty measures, there were only ten. When
anyone went to a wine vat to draw fifty measures, there were only twenty. 17I struck all the
work of your hands with blight, mildew and
hail, yet you did not turn to me,' declares the
LORD. 18'From this day on, from this twenty-
fourth day of the ninth month, give careful
thought to the day when the foundation of the
LORD's temple was laid. Give careful thought:
19Is there yet any seed left in the barn? Until
now, the vine and the fig tree, the pomegranate
and the olive tree have not borne fruit.

" 'From this day on I will bless you.' "

Zerubbabel the LORD's Signet Ring

20The word of the LORD came to Haggai a
second time on the twenty-fourth day of the
month: 21"Tell Zerubbabel governor of Judah
that I will shake the heavens and the earth. 22I
will overturn royal thrones and shatter the power of the foreign kingdoms. I will overthrow
chariots and their drivers; horses and their riders will fall, each by the sword of his brother.

23" 'On that day,' declares the LORD Almighty, 'I will take you, my servant Zerubbabel
son of Shealtiel,' declares the LORD, 'and I will
make you like my signet ring, for I have chosen
you,' declares the LORD Almighty."

[a]15 Or *to the days past*

ZECHARIAH

The Big Picture

A past filled with difficulty and broken relationships can overshadow the present. Though we have been forgiven for our sins and have turned away from them, we are not automatically freed from the struggles with sin. If we are not careful, these struggles can sap our enthusiasm for life and douse our hope for the future.

God's people in Judah probably experienced such a lack of hope. As a result of the repeated sins of their fathers, their families had been exiled from the promised land to Assyria and Babylonia. Seventy years later, because of a decree issued by King Cyrus, a remnant of Jews returned to Jerusalem under the leadership of Zerubbabel. Their first goal was to rebuild God's house, but opposition from local residents dampened their initial enthusiasm. The work of rebuilding the temple was soon stopped.

To counter this hopelessness, God appointed the elderly Haggai and the young Zechariah to bring a message of encouragement to the returned exiles. They needed to continue rebuilding God's temple in Jerusalem. Zechariah, whose name means "God remembers," reminded the Jews that God had not forgotten them. Rather, God had a certain and dynamic plan for their restoration.

Hope for future blessing can provide great encouragement for persevering through present suffering. The promise of deliverance makes it possible for us to continue in the process of spiritual renewal. The book of Zechariah is a fascinating study of how God, through his prophets, led his hurting people from hopelessness to commitment, from self-examination and transformation to a deepening spiritual perception. Zechariah is an uplifting account of rebuilding and spiritual renewal.

A. THE PROPHET'S INTRODUCTION (1:1-6)

B. A PLAN FOR THE PEOPLE'S RESTORATION (1:7–6:15)

1. A Vision of Preparation (1:7-17)
2. A Vision of Reflection (1:18-21)
3. A Vision of Reconstruction (2:1-13)
4. A Vision of Justification (3:1-10)
5. A Vision of Evangelization (4:1-14)
6. A Vision of Liberation (5:1-11)
7. A Vision of Retribution (6:1-8)
8. The Coronation of Joshua (6:9-15)

C. A SPIRITUAL PROBLEM IN THE PEOPLE'S RESTORATION (7:1–8:23)

1. The Problem of Religious Formality (7:1-14)
2. The Solution of Genuine Spirituality (8:1-23)

D. A SPECIFIC PROCESS IN THE PEOPLE'S RESTORATION (9:1–14:21)

1. The Way of Failure: Rejection of the Savior (9:1–11:17)
2. The Way of Deliverance: Receiving the Savior (12:1–14:21)

Spiritual Renewal Themes

DISAPPOINTMENT CAN LEAD TO DESPAIR

When faced with disappointment we have a choice: We can nurture our negative feelings, or we can confront them and find a solution. The people of God chose to hold on to their disappointments. This led to despair. To avoid despair we need to release our disappointments to God and confront those aspects of our pain that we can change. As we utilize the keys to spiri-

Essential Facts

PURPOSE:
To encourage God's people to complete the task of rebuilding God's temple, their community and their lives.

AUTHOR:
The prophet Zechariah.

AUDIENCE:
The people living in Jerusalem, including those who had returned from Babylonian exile.

DATE WRITTEN:
Chapters 1–8 were written between 528 and 520 B.C.; chapters 9–14 were written around 480 B.C.

SETTING:
The people had started to rebuild God's temple in Jerusalem but had failed to complete the task.

KEY VERSE:
"Return to your fortress, O prisoners of hope; even now I announce that I will restore twice as much to you" (9:12).

KEY PLACES:
Jerusalem and the temple.

KEY PEOPLE AND RELATIONSHIPS:
Zerubbabel, Joshua the priest and the prophets Haggai and Zechariah.

tual renewal, our feelings of despair will pass. But we cannot just passively wait for our transformation. We need to become actively involved in God's plan for our spiritual renewal.

HOPE ENCOURAGES US TODAY

Zechariah's visions of the future gave hope to the people, helping them meet the tasks they faced each day. Our hope of God's complete transformation in our lives can encourage us to endure the pain that may be part of our spiritual growth today. If we follow God's will for us in faith, we will experience his transforming power, our hurt and confusion will fade, and we will discover the joy that only he can give.

SPIRITUAL RENEWAL INVOLVES THE HEART

Zechariah told the people that God did not care about their fasts or religious observances. What concerned God greatly were the attitudes of their hearts. Just as this was true for the people in Jerusalem in Zechariah's day, it is true for us today. Our spiritual renewal is not a matter of just doing and saying the right things either. Spiritual renewal can only occur as God changes our minds and hearts. As our hearts are transformed, our attitudes and actions will also be transformed. If we go through the motions without experiencing inner change, our spiritual renewal will be superficial. We need to be changed from the inside out.

A Call to Return to the LORD

1 In the eighth month of the second year of Darius, the word of the LORD came to the prophet Zechariah son of Berekiah, the son of Iddo:

2 "The LORD was very angry with your forefathers. 3 Therefore tell the people: This is what the LORD Almighty says: 'Return to me,' declares the LORD Almighty, 'and I will return to you,' says the LORD Almighty. 4 Do not be like your forefathers, to whom the earlier prophets proclaimed: This is what the LORD Almighty says: 'Turn from your evil ways and your evil practices.' But they would not listen or pay attention to me, declares the LORD. 5 Where are your forefathers now? And the prophets, do they live forever? 6 But did not my words and my decrees, which I commanded my servants the prophets, overtake your forefathers?

"Then they repented and said, 'The LORD Almighty has done to us what our ways and practices deserve, just as he determined to do.' "

The Man Among the Myrtle Trees

7 On the twenty-fourth day of the eleventh month, the month of Shebat, in the second year of Darius, the word of the LORD came to the prophet Zechariah son of Berekiah, the son of Iddo.

8 During the night I had a vision—and there before me was a man riding a red horse! He was standing among the myrtle trees in a ravine. Behind him were red, brown and white horses.

9 I asked, "What are these, my lord?"

The angel who was talking with me answered, "I will show you what they are."

10 Then the man standing among the myrtle trees explained, "They are the ones the LORD has sent to go throughout the earth."

11 And they reported to the angel of the LORD, who was standing among the myrtle trees, "We have gone throughout the earth and found the whole world at rest and in peace."

12 Then the angel of the LORD said, "LORD Almighty, how long will you withhold mercy from Jerusalem and from the towns of Judah, which you have been angry with these seventy years?" 13 So the LORD spoke kind and comforting words to the angel who talked with me.

14 Then the angel who was speaking to me said, "Proclaim this word: This is what the LORD Almighty says: 'I am very jealous for Jerusalem and Zion, 15 but I am very angry with the nations that feel secure. I was only a little angry, but they added to the calamity.'

16 "Therefore, this is what the LORD says: 'I will return to Jerusalem with mercy, and there my house will be rebuilt. And the measuring line will be stretched out over Jerusalem,' declares the LORD Almighty.

17 "Proclaim further: This is what the LORD Almighty says: 'My towns will again overflow with prosperity, and the LORD will again comfort Zion and choose Jerusalem.' "

Four Horns and Four Craftsmen

18 Then I looked up—and there before me were four horns! 19 I asked the angel who was speaking to me, "What are these?"

He answered me, "These are the horns that scattered Judah, Israel and Jerusalem."

20 Then the LORD showed me four craftsmen. 21 I asked, "What are these coming to do?"

He answered, "These are the horns that scattered Judah so that no one could raise his head, but the craftsmen have come to terrify them and throw down these horns of the nations who lifted up their horns against the land of Judah to scatter its people."

A Man With a Measuring Line

2 Then I looked up—and there before me was a man with a measuring line in his hand! 2 I asked, "Where are you going?"

He answered me, "To measure Jerusalem, to find out how wide and how long it is."

3 Then the angel who was speaking to me left, and another angel came to meet him 4 and said to him: "Run, tell that young man, 'Jerusalem will be a city without walls because of the great number of men and livestock in it. 5 And I myself will be a wall of fire around it,' declares the LORD, 'and I will be its glory within.'

6 "Come! Come! Flee from the land of the north," declares the LORD, "for I have scattered you to the four winds of heaven," declares the LORD.

7 "Come, O Zion! Escape, you who live in the Daughter of Babylon!" 8 For this is what the LORD Almighty says: "After he has honored me and has sent me against the nations that have plundered you—for whoever touches you touches the apple of his eye— 9 I will surely raise my hand against them so that their slaves will

---

1:1–6 Zechariah confronted the people with their sin. Though they had recently returned from exile, the prophet reminded them that God would deal with their sins just as he had punished their ancestors. It is never safe to ignore such a call to turn back to God. Hearing demands heeding! God's promises of future comfort, victory and deliverance must not lead us to a false sense of security. Neglected spiritual opportunities are lost opportunities.

1:18–21 Similar to one of Daniel's visions, the vision of the four horns (the horn being a symbol of power) and the four craftsmen gave hope to the Jewish people. Eventually their oppressors would be overthrown. Today we, too, can find courage and hope in the fact that God will eventually overthrow the oppressive powers that dominate us.

2:1–13 The vision of the man with a measuring line concerned the reconstruction and repatriation of Israel. Many of God's people were comfortable in exile and reluctant to return to their homeland. They were probably afraid of what they might find there. Yet there was no need to fear, for God had promised a future of prosperity and peace. We also are given the assurance of God's special care. If we want to escape our bondage, we need to trust God and follow his plan for our deliverance.

plunder them.[a] Then you will know that the
LORD Almighty has sent me.
10"Shout and be glad, O Daughter of Zion.
For I am coming, and I will live among you,"
declares the LORD. 11"Many nations will be
joined with the LORD in that day and will become my people. I will live among you and you
will know that the LORD Almighty has sent me
to you. 12The LORD will inherit Judah as his
portion in the holy land and will again choose
Jerusalem. 13Be still before the LORD, all mankind, because he has roused himself from his
holy dwelling."

Clean Garments for the High Priest

3 Then he showed me Joshua[b] the high
priest standing before the angel of the
LORD, and Satan[c] standing at his right side to
accuse him. 2The LORD said to Satan, "The LORD
rebuke you, Satan! The LORD, who has chosen
Jerusalem, rebuke you! Is not this man a burning stick snatched from the fire?"
3Now Joshua was dressed in filthy clothes as
he stood before the angel. 4The angel said to
those who were standing before him, "Take off
his filthy clothes."
Then he said to Joshua, "See, I have taken
away your sin, and I will put rich garments on
you."
5Then I said, "Put a clean turban on his
head." So they put a clean turban on his head
and clothed him, while the angel of the LORD
stood by.
6The angel of the LORD gave this charge to
Joshua: 7"This is what the LORD Almighty says:
'If you will walk in my ways and keep my requirements, then you will govern my house and
have charge of my courts, and I will give you a
place among these standing here.
8" 'Listen, O high priest Joshua and your associates seated before you, who are men symbolic of things to come: I am going to bring my
servant, the Branch. 9See, the stone I have set in
front of Joshua! There are seven eyes[d] on that
one stone, and I will engrave an inscription on
it,' says the LORD Almighty, 'and I will remove
the sin of this land in a single day.
10" 'In that day each of you will invite his
neighbor to sit under his vine and fig tree,' declares the LORD Almighty."

The Gold Lampstand and the Two Olive Trees

4 Then the angel who talked with me returned and wakened me, as a man is wakened from his sleep. 2He asked me, "What do
you see?"
I answered, "I see a solid gold lampstand
with a bowl at the top and seven lights on it,
with seven channels to the lights. 3Also there
are two olive trees by it, one on the right of the
bowl and the other on its left."
4I asked the angel who talked with me,
"What are these, my lord?"
5He answered, "Do you not know what these
are?"
"No, my lord," I replied.
6So he said to me, "This is the word of the
LORD to Zerubbabel: 'Not by might nor by power, but by my Spirit,' says the LORD Almighty.
7"What[e] are you, O mighty mountain? Before Zerubbabel you will become level ground.
Then he will bring out the capstone to shouts of
'God bless it! God bless it!' "
8Then the word of the LORD came to me:
9"The hands of Zerubbabel have laid the foundation of this temple; his hands will also complete it. Then you will know that the LORD Almighty has sent me to you.
10"Who despises the day of small things?
Men will rejoice when they see the plumb line
in the hand of Zerubbabel.
"(These seven are the eyes of the LORD,
which range throughout the earth.)"
11Then I asked the angel, "What are these

[a] 8,9 Or *says after . . . eye:* 9"*I . . . plunder them."*
[b] 1 A variant of *Jeshua;* here and elsewhere in Zechariah
[c] 1 *Satan* means *accuser.* [d] 9 Or *facets* [e] 7 Or *Who*

3:1–4 This vision of Jeshua the high priest teaches us much about God's merciful forgiveness. The historical figure Joshua son of Jehozadak, the high priest at that time, appeared here in soiled garments. Satan stood at his right, accusing him of many things. The filthy high priest symbolized what Israel looked like to God in their sinful state. We still wrestle with sin today, and Satan is always there to accuse us before God for things in our lives that have demoralized and immobilized us. Yet God is always there to defend us if we have come to him for forgiveness and cleansing.

3:5–10 God would purify the high priest Joshua. He would be a living illustration of the good leadership the people would experience under the Messiah's rule. What a word of hope! When God's restoration is complete, hurting people will experience healing. Joy and true fellowship with friends and neighbors will replace sorrow and isolation. As we experience God's powerful deliverance in our lives, we can be an illustration, like Joshua was, to others of a life that is ruled and directed by God. As we share with others through both word and deed the news of God's deliverance, they can experience the healing power he offers too.

4:1–6 This strange vision of the gold lampstand and the olive trees points to God's sustaining provision and the inauguration of the Messiah's kingdom through the power of the Holy Spirit (4:6).

4:6–14 Zerubbabel had brought a contingent of exiles to Jerusalem to rebuild the temple, but political opposition had stopped their efforts. The people were discouraged and wondered if God was with them. God gave Zechariah a message of encouragement for his people. They needed to remember that success was not due to human strength or ingenuity but came as a result of the Holy Spirit's power. With his power, the difficult task of rebuilding could still be accomplished. We may become discouraged when we face the task of rebuilding our lives. If we experience regular opposition from people, emotions and temptations, the task may seem too big for us. But God's power is more than sufficient to bring full redemption and restoration to our lives.

two olive trees on the right and the left of the lampstand?"

12Again I asked him, "What are these two olive branches beside the two gold pipes that pour out golden oil?"

13He replied, "Do you not know what these are?"

"No, my lord," I said.

14So he said, "These are the two who are anointed to[a] serve the Lord of all the earth."

The Flying Scroll

5 I looked again—and there before me was a flying scroll!

2He asked me, "What do you see?"

I answered, "I see a flying scroll, thirty feet long and fifteen feet wide.[b]"

3And he said to me, "This is the curse that is going out over the whole land; for according to what it says on one side, every thief will be banished, and according to what it says on the other, everyone who swears falsely will be banished. 4The LORD Almighty declares, 'I will send it out, and it will enter the house of the thief and the house of him who swears falsely by my name. It will remain in his house and destroy it, both its timbers and its stones.' "

The Woman in a Basket

5Then the angel who was speaking to me came forward and said to me, "Look up and see what this is that is appearing."

6I asked, "What is it?"

He replied, "It is a measuring basket.[c]" And he added, "This is the iniquity[d] of the people throughout the land."

7Then the cover of lead was raised, and there in the basket sat a woman! 8He said, "This is wickedness," and he pushed her back into the basket and pushed the lead cover down over its mouth.

9Then I looked up—and there before me were two women, with the wind in their wings! They had wings like those of a stork, and they lifted up the basket between heaven and earth.

10"Where are they taking the basket?" I asked the angel who was speaking to me.

11He replied, "To the country of Babylonia[e] to build a house for it. When it is ready, the basket will be set there in its place."

Four Chariots

6 I looked up again—and there before me were four chariots coming out from between two mountains—mountains of bronze! 2The first chariot had red horses, the second black, 3the third white, and the fourth dappled—all of them powerful. 4I asked the angel who was speaking to me, "What are these, my lord?"

5The angel answered me, "These are the four spirits[f] of heaven, going out from standing in the presence of the Lord of the whole world. 6The one with the black horses is going toward the north country, the one with the white horses toward the west,[g] and the one with the dappled horses toward the south."

7When the powerful horses went out, they were straining to go throughout the earth. And he said, "Go throughout the earth!" So they went throughout the earth.

8Then he called to me, "Look, those going toward the north country have given my Spirit[h] rest in the land of the north."

A Crown for Joshua

9The word of the LORD came to me: 10"Take ⌊silver and gold⌋ from the exiles Heldai, Tobijah and Jedaiah, who have arrived from Babylon. Go the same day to the house of Josiah son of Zephaniah. 11Take the silver and gold and make a crown, and set it on the head of the high priest, Joshua son of Jehozadak. 12Tell him this is what the LORD Almighty says: 'Here is the man whose name is the Branch, and he will branch out from his place and build the temple of the LORD. 13It is he who will build the temple of the LORD, and he will be clothed with majesty and will sit and rule on his throne. And he will be a priest on his throne. And there will be harmony between the two.' 14The crown will be given to Heldai,[i] Tobijah, Jedaiah and Hen[j] son of Zephaniah as a memorial in the temple of the LORD. 15Those who are far away will come and help to build the temple of the LORD, and you will know that the LORD Almighty has sent me to you. This will happen if you diligently obey the LORD your God."

Justice and Mercy, Not Fasting

7 In the fourth year of King Darius, the word of the LORD came to Zechariah on the fourth day of the ninth month, the month of

[a] 14 Or *two who bring oil and* [b] 2 Hebrew *twenty cubits long and ten cubits wide* (about 9 meters long and 4.5 meters wide) [c] 6 Hebrew *an ephah;* also in verses 7-11 [d] 6 Or *appearance* [e] 11 Hebrew *Shinar* [f] 5 Or *winds* [g] 6 Or *horses after them* [h] 8 Or *spirit* [i] 14 Syriac; Hebrew *Helem* [j] 14 Or *and the gracious one, the*

5:5–11 The vision of the measuring basket was a revelation about liberation. The strange imagery graphically portrays the liberation of God's people from a long-standing curse of materialism. We who are controlled by sins that enslave us need to realize that deliverance comes when we ask God to change us.

6:9–15 Zechariah was instructed to receive gifts designated for the work of rebuilding the temple from a delegation of Jews from Babylon. From the silver and gold, Zechariah was to make a crown that he would set upon Joshua's head, foreshadowing the royal priesthood that the Messiah would bring (see Psalm 110:1–4; Hebrews 7:1–3). The obligation upon God's people was clear. There would be no blessing from God unless they were willing to follow his will for them. The same is true for us. There is little hope for spiritual renewal unless we recognize our need for God and do things his way.

7:1–7 Two years had elapsed since Zechariah had received the visions of the first six chapters. Since then, the work on the temple had progressed, and the minds of the

Kislev. 2The people of Bethel had sent Sharezer and Regem-Melech, together with their men, to entreat the LORD 3by asking the priests of the house of the LORD Almighty and the prophets, "Should I mourn and fast in the fifth month, as I have done for so many years?"

4Then the word of the LORD Almighty came to me: 5"Ask all the people of the land and the priests, 'When you fasted and mourned in the fifth and seventh months for the past seventy years, was it really for me that you fasted? 6And when you were eating and drinking, were you not just feasting for yourselves? 7Are these not the words the LORD proclaimed through the earlier prophets when Jerusalem and its surrounding towns were at rest and prosperous, and the Negev and the western foothills were settled?' "

8And the word of the LORD came again to Zechariah: 9"This is what the LORD Almighty says: 'Administer true justice; show mercy and compassion to one another. 10Do not oppress the widow or the fatherless, the alien or the poor. In your hearts do not think evil of each other.'

11"But they refused to pay attention; stubbornly they turned their backs and stopped up their ears. 12They made their hearts as hard as flint and would not listen to the law or to the words that the LORD Almighty had sent by his Spirit through the earlier prophets. So the LORD Almighty was very angry.

13" 'When I called, they did not listen; so when they called, I would not listen,' says the LORD Almighty. 14'I scattered them with a whirlwind among all the nations, where they were strangers. The land was left so desolate behind them that no one could come or go. This is how they made the pleasant land desolate.' "

The LORD Promises to Bless Jerusalem

8 Again the word of the LORD Almighty came to me. 2This is what the LORD Almighty says: "I am very jealous for Zion; I am burning with jealousy for her."

3This is what the LORD says: "I will return to Zion and dwell in Jerusalem. Then Jerusalem will be called the City of Truth, and the mountain of the LORD Almighty will be called the Holy Mountain."

4This is what the LORD Almighty says: "Once again men and women of ripe old age will sit in the streets of Jerusalem, each with cane in hand because of his age. 5The city streets will be filled with boys and girls playing there."

6This is what the LORD Almighty says: "It may seem marvelous to the remnant of this people at that time, but will it seem marvelous to me?" declares the LORD Almighty.

7This is what the LORD Almighty says: "I will save my people from the countries of the east and the west. 8I will bring them back to live in Jerusalem; they will be my people, and I will be faithful and righteous to them as their God."

9This is what the LORD Almighty says: "You who now hear these words spoken by the prophets who were there when the foundation was laid for the house of the LORD Almighty, let your hands be strong so that the temple may be built. 10Before that time there were no wages for man or beast. No one could go about his business safely because of his enemy, for I had turned every man against his neighbor. 11But now I will not deal with the remnant of this people as I did in the past," declares the LORD Almighty.

12"The seed will grow well, the vine will yield its fruit, the ground will produce its crops, and the heavens will drop their dew. I will give all these things as an inheritance to the remnant of this people. 13As you have been an object of cursing among the nations, O Judah and Israel, so will I save you, and you will be a blessing. Do not be afraid, but let your hands be strong."

14This is what the LORD Almighty says: "Just as I had determined to bring disaster upon you and showed no pity when your fathers angered me," says the LORD Almighty, 15"so now I have determined to do good again to Jerusalem and Judah. Do not be afraid. 16These are the things you are to do: Speak the truth to each other, and render true and sound judgment in your courts; 17do not plot evil against your neighbor, and do not love to swear falsely. I hate all this," declares the LORD.

---

people had turned back toward God. The citizens of Bethel sent a delegation to Jerusalem asking whether they should continue with the traditional ceremonies of fasting that commemorated the destruction of Jerusalem, especially since the temple was being rebuilt. God's answer made it clear that he was more concerned about the attitudes of their hearts than whether or not they observed the ceremonies. Many of us realize that true spiritual renewal and transformation must involve deep internal change. Only as God changes our hearts can real renewal and transformation occur.

7:8–10 For the exiles, the test of their faith was simple: love for others, especially widows, orphans, foreigners and the poor (see Leviticus 19:18). The final step and ultimate proof of our spiritual renewal is our desire to help others who are suffering. As we reach out to offer them the second chance we have been granted, we will discover the joy of loving others, and our own spiritual lives will be strengthened as a result.

7:11–14 The ancestors of Zechariah's audience had ignored all of God's appeals to show compassion to the poor and helpless. Because they would not listen to God, he refused to listen to their prayers. Merely attending church or performing religious acts will be of no profit if we do not obey God and surrender our lives to him. True emotional and spiritual healing always involves obedience to God's revealed will.

8:1–17 True religion affects our daily lives. God promised wonderful blessings if his people completed the task of rebuilding his temple. Rebuilding God's house would prove their commitment to his plan. Once we have examined our lives and have found areas of sin or disobedience to God's will, we must take appropriate action. Our obedience to God's will proves that we trust his plan and will shape our lives around it.

[18]Again the word of the LORD Almighty came
to me. [19]This is what the LORD Almighty says:
"The fasts of the fourth, fifth, seventh and tenth months will become joyful and glad occasions and happy festivals for Judah. Therefore love truth and peace."

[20]This is what the LORD Almighty says:
"Many peoples and the inhabitants of many
cities will yet come, [21]and the inhabitants of
one city will go to another and say, 'Let us go at once to entreat the LORD and seek the LORD
Almighty. I myself am going.' [22]And many peo-
ples and powerful nations will come to Jerusalem to seek the LORD Almighty and to entreat him."

[23]This is what the LORD Almighty says: "In
those days ten men from all languages and nations will take firm hold of one Jew by the hem of his robe and say, 'Let us go with you, because we have heard that God is with you.' "

Judgment on Israel's Enemies

An Oracle

9 The word of the LORD is against the land
of Hadrach
and will rest upon Damascus—
for the eyes of men and all the tribes of
Israel
are on the LORD—[a]
[2]and upon Hamath too, which borders on
it,
and upon Tyre and Sidon, though they
are very skillful.
[3]Tyre has built herself a stronghold;
she has heaped up silver like dust,
and gold like the dirt of the streets.
[4]But the Lord will take away her possessions
and destroy her power on the sea,
and she will be consumed by fire.
[5]Ashkelon will see it and fear;
Gaza will writhe in agony,
and Ekron too, for her hope will wither.
Gaza will lose her king
and Ashkelon will be deserted.
[6]Foreigners will occupy Ashdod,
and I will cut off the pride of the
Philistines.
[7]I will take the blood from their mouths,
the forbidden food from between their
teeth.
Those who are left will belong to our God
and become leaders in Judah,
and Ekron will be like the Jebusites.
[8]But I will defend my house
against marauding forces.
Never again will an oppressor overrun my
people,
for now I am keeping watch.

The Coming of Zion's King

[9]Rejoice greatly, O Daughter of Zion!
Shout, Daughter of Jerusalem!
See, your king[b] comes to you,
righteous and having salvation,
gentle and riding on a donkey,
on a colt, the foal of a donkey.
[10]I will take away the chariots from Ephraim
and the war-horses from Jerusalem,
and the battle bow will be broken.
He will proclaim peace to the nations.
His rule will extend from sea to sea
and from the River[c] to the ends of the
earth.[d]
[11]As for you, because of the blood of my
covenant with you,
I will free your prisoners from the
waterless pit.
[12]Return to your fortress, O prisoners of
hope;
even now I announce that I will restore
twice as much to you.
[13]I will bend Judah as I bend my bow
and fill it with Ephraim.
I will rouse your sons, O Zion,
against your sons, O Greece,
and make you like a warrior's sword.

The LORD Will Appear

[14]Then the LORD will appear over them;
his arrow will flash like lightning.
The Sovereign LORD will sound the trumpet;
he will march in the storms of the south,
[15] and the LORD Almighty will shield them.
They will destroy

[a]1 Or *Damascus. / For the eye of the LORD is on all mankind, / as well as on the tribes of Israel,* [b]9 Or *King* [c]10 That is, the Euphrates [d]10 Or *the end of the land*

9:1–8 These verses introduce God's long indictment against the Gentile nations. Israel's neighbors would be overrun, yet God would protect his land from the invading armies. This prophecy probably foretold the conquests of Alexander the Great—nearly two centuries before they happened. In 334–332 B.C., Alexander conquered Syria, Phoenicia and Philistia. But God stopped Alexander from destroying the temple in Jerusalem. This word would have given hope to God's people. For years they had lived with the threat of invading armies. God's assurance of his protection would have given them courage. As we face difficulties in life, God's promise to stay with us should give us the courage to persevere.
9:9–10 At the very center of Israel's hope was the Messiah. His promised coming was a source of great joy. His credentials were righteousness, salvation and lowliness, distinguishing him from all other earthly rulers. The one who demonstrated these credentials perfectly was Jesus of Nazareth. Clearly, God's people must not place their hope primarily in human sources but in their personal relationship with God through Jesus Christ. If we put our hope in God, no problem will be too great for us to overcome.
9:14—10:1 Spiritual renewal involves surrendering our lives to God and patiently waiting for his timely intervention. The Jews' victory over the Greek tyrants is described here in a series of rapidly changing metaphors. God's people were instruments of conquest: the bow and arrow, a hero's sword. God would give his people victory over the oppressive powers that assailed them.

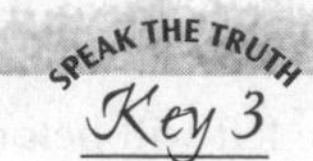

Speaking the Truth About Our Future

Zechariah 9:9–17 No one knows what tomorrow may bring. We will go through many battles in our pursuit of spiritual renewal. There will be days when we face tremendous challenges, and we may lose courage and become fearful of our future. But we can find security in the future God has waiting for us by knowing the truth of God's promises and confessing this truth to ourselves and others.

Five hundred years before the birth of Jesus, the prophet Zechariah wrote: "Rejoice greatly, O Daughter of Zion! Shout, Daughter of Jerusalem! See, your king comes to you, righteous and having salvation, gentle and riding on a donkey, on a colt, the foal of a donkey" (9:9). This prophecy was fulfilled in Jesus Christ (see Matthew 21:4–11). The prophet continued:

> I will take away the chariots from Ephraim and the war-horses from Jerusalem, and the battle bow will be broken. He will proclaim peace to the nations. His rule will extend from sea to sea and from the River to the ends of the earth. As for you, because of the blood of my covenant with you, I will free your prisoners from the waterless pit (9:10–11).

Jesus fulfilled part of these prophecies when he came and lived on earth with his disciples. He delivered us from death by shedding his own blood to seal our pardon. And Jesus will come again, just as he promised (see John 14:3; Acts 1:11). When he comes, Jesus will bring peace on earth. Reminding ourselves of these truths and speaking these truths to others will give us courage to persevere through our spiritual battles.

Move on to Key 4 and turn to Genesis 33.

and overcome with slingstones.
They will drink and roar as with wine;
they will be full like a bowl
used for sprinkling[a] the corners of the altar.
16The LORD their God will save them on that day
as the flock of his people.
They will sparkle in his land
like jewels in a crown.
17How attractive and beautiful they will be!
Grain will make the young men thrive,
and new wine the young women.

The LORD Will Care for Judah

10 Ask the LORD for rain in the springtime;
it is the LORD who makes the storm clouds.
He gives showers of rain to men,
and plants of the field to everyone.
2The idols speak deceit,
diviners see visions that lie;
they tell dreams that are false,
they give comfort in vain.
Therefore the people wander like sheep
oppressed for lack of a shepherd.

3"My anger burns against the shepherds,
and I will punish the leaders;
for the LORD Almighty will care
for his flock, the house of Judah,
and make them like a proud horse in battle.
4From Judah will come the cornerstone,
from him the tent peg,
from him the battle bow,
from him every ruler.
5Together they[b] will be like mighty men
trampling the muddy streets in battle.
Because the LORD is with them,
they will fight and overthrow the horsemen.

6"I will strengthen the house of Judah
and save the house of Joseph.
I will restore them
because I have compassion on them.
They will be as though
I had not rejected them,
for I am the LORD their God
and I will answer them.
7The Ephraimites will become like mighty men,
and their hearts will be glad as with wine.
Their children will see it and be joyful;
their hearts will rejoice in the LORD.
8I will signal for them

[a]15 Or *bowl, / like* [b]4,5 Or *ruler, all of them together. / 5They*

10:8–12 Like a shepherd who signals to his flocks, God called his people back from exile. Political restoration was a good start, but the people needed to return in faith to

and gather them in.
Surely I will redeem them;
they will be as numerous as before.
9Though I scatter them among the peoples,
yet in distant lands they will remember
me.
They and their children will survive,
and they will return.
10I will bring them back from Egypt
and gather them from Assyria.
I will bring them to Gilead and Lebanon,
and there will not be room enough for
them.
11They will pass through the sea of trouble;
the surging sea will be subdued
and all the depths of the Nile will dry
up.
Assyria's pride will be brought down
and Egypt's scepter will pass away.
12I will strengthen them in the LORD
and in his name they will walk,"
declares the LORD.

11 Open your doors, O Lebanon,
so that fire may devour your cedars!
2Wail, O pine tree, for the cedar has fallen;
the stately trees are ruined!
Wail, oaks of Bashan;
the dense forest has been cut down!
3Listen to the wail of the shepherds;
their rich pastures are destroyed!
Listen to the roar of the lions;
the lush thicket of the Jordan is ruined!

Two Shepherds

4This is what the LORD my God says: "Pasture the flock marked for slaughter. 5Their buy-
ers slaughter them and go unpunished. Those
who sell them say, 'Praise the LORD, I am rich!'
Their own shepherds do not spare them. 6For I
will no longer have pity on the people of the
land," declares the LORD. "I will hand everyone
over to his neighbor and his king. They will
oppress the land, and I will not rescue them
from their hands."

7So I pastured the flock marked for slaughter,
particularly the oppressed of the flock. Then I
took two staffs and called one Favor and the
other Union, and I pastured the flock. 8In one
month I got rid of the three shepherds.

The flock detested me, and I grew weary of
them 9and said, "I will not be your shepherd.
Let the dying die, and the perishing perish. Let
those who are left eat one another's flesh."

10Then I took my staff called Favor and broke
it, revoking the covenant I had made with all
the nations. 11It was revoked on that day, and so
the afflicted of the flock who were watching me
knew it was the word of the LORD.

12I told them, "If you think it best, give me
my pay; but if not, keep it." So they paid me
thirty pieces of silver.

13And the LORD said to me, "Throw it to
the potter"—the handsome price at which they
priced me! So I took the thirty pieces of silver
and threw them into the house of the LORD to
the potter.

14Then I broke my second staff called Union,
breaking the brotherhood between Judah and
Israel.

15Then the LORD said to me, "Take again the
equipment of a foolish shepherd. 16For I am
going to raise up a shepherd over the land who
will not care for the lost, or seek the young, or
heal the injured, or feed the healthy, but will eat
the meat of the choice sheep, tearing off their
hoofs.

17"Woe to the worthless shepherd,
who deserts the flock!
May the sword strike his arm and his right
eye!
May his arm be completely withered,
his right eye totally blinded!"

Jerusalem's Enemies to Be Destroyed

An Oracle

12 This is the word of the LORD concerning
Israel. The LORD, who stretches out the
heavens, who lays the foundation of the earth,
and who forms the spirit of man within him,
declares: 2"I am going to make Jerusalem a cup
that sends all the surrounding peoples reeling.
Judah will be besieged as well as Jerusalem. 3On
that day, when all the nations of the earth are
gathered against her, I will make Jerusalem an
immovable rock for all the nations. All who try
to move it will injure themselves. 4On that day
I will strike every horse with panic and its rider
with madness," declares the LORD. "I will keep a
watchful eye over the house of Judah, but I will
blind all the horses of the nations. 5Then the
leaders of Judah will say in their hearts, 'The
people of Jerusalem are strong, because the
LORD Almighty is their God.'

6"On that day I will make the leaders of Judah like a firepot in a woodpile, like a flaming
torch among sheaves. They will consume right
and left all the surrounding peoples, but Jerusalem will remain intact in her place.

7"The LORD will save the dwellings of Judah
first, so that the honor of the house of David
and of Jerusalem's inhabitants may not be
greater than that of Judah. 8On that day the
LORD will shield those who live in Jerusalem, so
that the feeblest among them will be like David,
and the house of David will be like God, like
the Angel of the LORD going before them. 9On
that day I will set out to destroy all the nations
that attack Jerusalem.

---

their God as well. God has a perfect plan for his people, and he will not rest until it is accomplished (see Romans 8:30–32). We must seek out God's will for us and follow it. When we do, he promises to help us all along the way.

Mourning for the One They Pierced

10"And I will pour out on the house of David
and the inhabitants of Jerusalem a spirit[a] of
grace and supplication. They will look on[b] me,
the one they have pierced, and they will mourn
for him as one mourns for an only child, and
grieve bitterly for him as one grieves for a firstborn son. 11On that day the weeping in Jerusalem will be great, like the weeping of Hadad
Rimmon in the plain of Megiddo. 12The land
will mourn, each clan by itself, with their wives
by themselves: the clan of the house of David
and their wives, the clan of the house of Nathan and their wives, 13the clan of the house of
Levi and their wives, the clan of Shimei and their
wives, 14and all the rest of the clans and their
wives.

Cleansing From Sin

13 "On that day a fountain will be opened
to the house of David and the inhabitants of Jerusalem, to cleanse them from sin and
impurity.

2"On that day, I will banish the names of the
idols from the land, and they will be remembered no more," declares the LORD Almighty. "I
will remove both the prophets and the spirit of
impurity from the land. 3And if anyone still
prophesies, his father and mother, to whom he
was born, will say to him, 'You must die, because you have told lies in the LORD's name.'
When he prophesies, his own parents will stab
him.

4"On that day every prophet will be
ashamed of his prophetic vision. He will not
put on a prophet's garment of hair in order to
deceive. 5He will say, 'I am not a prophet. I am
a farmer; the land has been my livelihood since
my youth.[c]' 6If someone asks him, 'What are
these wounds on your body[d]?' he will answer,
'The wounds I was given at the house of my
friends.'

The Shepherd Struck, the Sheep Scattered

7"Awake, O sword, against my shepherd,
against the man who is close to me!"
declares the LORD Almighty.
"Strike the shepherd,
and the sheep will be scattered,
and I will turn my hand against the little
ones.
8In the whole land," declares the LORD,
"two-thirds will be struck down and
perish;
yet one-third will be left in it.
9This third I will bring into the fire;
I will refine them like silver
and test them like gold.
They will call on my name
and I will answer them;
I will say, 'They are my people,'
and they will say, 'The LORD is our
God.' "

The LORD Comes and Reigns

14 A day of the LORD is coming when your
plunder will be divided among you.
2I will gather all the nations to Jerusalem to
fight against it; the city will be captured, the
houses ransacked, and the women raped. Half
of the city will go into exile, but the rest of the
people will not be taken from the city.

3Then the LORD will go out and fight against
those nations, as he fights in the day of battle.
4On that day his feet will stand on the Mount
of Olives, east of Jerusalem, and the Mount of
Olives will be split in two from east to west,
forming a great valley, with half of the mountain moving north and half moving south. 5You
will flee by my mountain valley, for it will extend to Azel. You will flee as you fled from the
earthquake[e] in the days of Uzziah king of Judah. Then the LORD my God will come, and all
the holy ones with him.

6On that day there will be no light, no cold
or frost. 7It will be a unique day, without daytime or nighttime—a day known to the LORD.
When evening comes, there will be light.

8On that day living water will flow out from

[a] 10 Or *the Spirit* [b] 10 Or *to* [c] 5 Or *farmer; a man sold me in my youth* [d] 6 Or *wounds between your hands* [e] 5 Or *5My mountain valley will be blocked and will extend to Azel. It will be blocked as it was blocked because of the earthquake*

12:10—13:1 These verses describe a national conversion in Israel and also form an outline for our own spiritual conversion. We must recognize our helplessness without God and depend on him to show us the areas of sin and failure in our lives (12:10). We need to admit our failures and seek to follow God's will for our lives (12:11–14). Then we must accept the cleansing that God offers us (13:1). Because of what Jesus Christ has done on our behalf, we can be confident of God's total forgiveness of all our sins.

13:2–4 The people had placed their trust in teachings and objects that had no power to deliver. God would remove those sources of false hope so that the people could learn to depend on him alone. We, too, are often guilty of trusting in idols or following false teachings. False prophets, teachings and religions all lead us away from true dependence on God.

14:1–7 Zechariah foresaw a time of terrible desolation. Yet in the midst of the horrible suffering God would step in to deliver his people. Throughout the Bible God changed terrible situations into amazing victories. This prophecy looks forward to a time in the future when God will do this in a final sense. We all have experienced deep pain. Yet God is able to heal our deepest hurts. We must see the truth of our desperate situation and realize how useless it is to go on alone. God is able to restore our lives, no matter how terrible our past, if we will only admit our need and call out to him.

14:8–15 In this revelation of the Messianic kingdom Zechariah reached the climax of his prophecy, and of all history. The Messiah will be king over all the earth. All of earth's inhabitants will know, worship and serve him. When the whole world runs according to God's will, peace and joy will characterize everyone's life. If we want to enjoy God's full blessings today and in the future, we must live according to God's will. When God occupies the place

Jerusalem, half to the eastern sea[a] and half to
the western sea,[b] in summer and in winter.
9The LORD will be king over the whole earth.
On that day there will be one LORD, and his
name the only name.
10The whole land, from Geba to Rimmon,
south of Jerusalem, will become like the Arabah. But Jerusalem will be raised up and remain
in its place, from the Benjamin Gate to the site
of the First Gate, to the Corner Gate, and from
the Tower of Hananel to the royal winepresses.
11It will be inhabited; never again will it be
destroyed. Jerusalem will be secure.
12This is the plague with which the LORD will
strike all the nations that fought against Jerusalem: Their flesh will rot while they are still
standing on their feet, their eyes will rot in their
sockets, and their tongues will rot in their
mouths. 13On that day men will be stricken by
the LORD with great panic. Each man will seize
the hand of another, and they will attack each
other. 14Judah too will fight at Jerusalem. The
wealth of all the surrounding nations will be
collected—great quantities of gold and silver
and clothing. 15A similar plague will strike the
horses and mules, the camels and donkeys, and
all the animals in those camps.
16Then the survivors from all the nations that
have attacked Jerusalem will go up year after
year to worship the King, the LORD Almighty,
and to celebrate the Feast of Tabernacles. 17If
any of the peoples of the earth do not go up to
Jerusalem to worship the King, the LORD Almighty, they will have no rain. 18If the Egyptian
people do not go up and take part, they will
have no rain. The LORD[c] will bring on them
the plague he inflicts on the nations that do not
go up to celebrate the Feast of Tabernacles.
19This will be the punishment of Egypt and the
punishment of all the nations that do not go up
to celebrate the Feast of Tabernacles.
20On that day HOLY TO THE LORD will be inscribed on the bells of the horses, and the cooking pots in the LORD's house will be like the
sacred bowls in front of the altar. 21Every pot in
Jerusalem and Judah will be holy to the LORD
Almighty, and all who come to sacrifice will
take some of the pots and cook in them. And on
that day there will no longer be a Canaanite[d]
in the house of the LORD Almighty.

[a]8 That is, the Dead Sea [b]8 That is, the Mediterranean [c]18 Or *part, then the LORD* [d]21 Or *merchant*

---

of absolute authority, radical changes will take place. Our lives will be transformed, taking on a new beauty and peace as we see God fulfill his promise of restoration.

14:16–21 When the Messiah rules, Israel will be sanctified as God's priestly nation, holy and set apart. Nothing unclean will defile the temple precincts. God wants his people to be holy just as he is holy. We are made holy by accepting God's work on our behalf through Jesus Christ. Because God dwells in us through his Holy Spirit, our body becomes his temple. Nothing unclean should be allowed to enter it (see 1 Corinthians 6:19–20). This should be a strong motivation for us to stay free of the sins that enslave us.

MALACHI

The Big Picture

A. DESCRIPTION OF THE BOOK (1:1)

B. DIALOGUES ABOUT FAILURE (1:2-14)

1. A Dialogue About Love (1:2-5)
2. A Dialogue About Faithlessness (1:6-10)
3. A Dialogue About Holiness (1:11-14)

C. SERMONS ABOUT FAILURE (2:1-17)

1. The Failure of the Priests (2:1-9)
2. The Failure of the People (2:10-17)

D. A MESSAGE OF HOPE: GOD'S PROMISED MESSIAH (3:1-5)

E. ANOTHER MESSAGE TO THOSE SEEKING SPIRITUAL RENEWAL (3:6-18)

1. Failure in Fiscal Responsibility (3:6-15)
2. Success of the Remnant (3:16-18)

F. A MESSAGE OF JUDGMENT: GOD'S PROMISED INTERVENTION (4:1-6)

When spiritual growth brings only external changes without internal change, there is the constant threat of slipping back into sinful habits. This seemed to be the case with the people in Jerusalem. Under Nehemiah's leadership, the people had rebuilt the walls of the city. They had begun to follow God's plan and rebuild their lives. But when Nehemiah returned to Persia, all the positive changes and attitudes that he had encouraged in them disappeared.

Malachi preached to a nation of backsliders—a people who had slipped back into their old ways. Even the spiritual leaders had fallen into old sinful patterns. As a result, the people suffered from economic problems, poor crops and the attacks of foreign marauders. Family life was in shambles; divorce was rampant. Religious life was cold and filled with empty formalism.

Malachi brought a message of hope to a nation that knew repeated failure. After being restored to their homeland, the Jews had forgotten the one who had delivered them. We often make the same kind of mistake. As soon as we overcome our pressing problems, we forget the one who delivered us from them—God. Without a continued relationship with God, we have no hope of sustaining our spiritual growth. We need to keep our eyes on God, for he alone is the source and means for our continued spiritual growth.

Although Malachi presented a long list of the people's failures, woven throughout his words of judgment rings a clear message of hope and forgiveness. As the final book of the Old Testament, Malachi forms a bridge with the New Testament. Malachi concludes with a promise of Elijah's coming (see 4:5–6). Jesus said this promise was fulfilled in the coming of John the Baptist, who prepared the way for the Messiah—Jesus Christ himself (see Matthew 11:7–14). With God, there is always hope!

Spiritual Renewal Themes

GOD ALWAYS LOVES US

God's love for the people of Jerusalem and for us cannot be explained. God knows the depth of our sin; he knows how weak we are; yet he still loves us. There is nothing that we can do to

lose this love that we never deserved in the first place (see Romans 8:38–39). God's love has the power to heal all the broken places in our lives. Our failures, setbacks and defenses cannot stop God from wanting to heal us. This fact should give us hope, no matter how terrible our sins and failures.

FORGIVENESS BRINGS RENEWAL

The way of forgiveness redirects us back to a relationship with God. God wants us not only to receive his forgiveness but also to forgive others, passing on what he has so freely given to us (see Matthew 10:8; Colossians 3:13). If we can receive God's forgiveness and grant forgiveness to others, we have learned a key to spiritual growth that will serve us well.

GOD IS ALWAYS WITH US

God wants us to turn to him for healing and forgiveness. He was patient with the people of Israel for hundreds of years in spite of their sin. In his grace, God is patient with us now as well (see 2 Peter 3:9). When he spoke through the prophets, God wove a message of hope into his warnings of judgment. In Malachi 4:5, God continued this theme of hope by promising the "prophet Elijah" would come and bring forgiveness and freedom to all people. God is with us even now to help us. We can receive his help by repenting of our sins, trusting him and seeking to obey his will for our lives.

Essential Facts

PURPOSE:
To confront the people about getting back on track after they had slipped back into old patterns of sin.

AUTHOR:
The prophet Malachi.

AUDIENCE:
The people in Judah shortly after Nehemiah rebuilt Jerusalem's walls.

DATE WRITTEN:
Sometime between 432 and 420 B.C.

SETTING:
After the temple and Jerusalem's walls were rebuilt, the people began to fall back into destructive behavior patterns. Malachi confronted God's people with their sins, urging them to restore their relationship with God.

KEY VERSE:
"I the LORD do not change. So you, O descendants of Jacob, are not destroyed" (3:6).

KEY PLACES:
Jerusalem and the temple.

KEY PEOPLE:
Malachi and the priests.

1

An oracle: The word of the LORD to Israel through Malachi.[a]

Jacob Loved, Esau Hated

2"I have loved you," says the LORD.

"But you ask, 'How have you loved us?'

"Was not Esau Jacob's brother?" the LORD says. "Yet I have loved Jacob, 3but Esau I have hated, and I have turned his mountains into a wasteland and left his inheritance to the desert jackals."

4Edom may say, "Though we have been crushed, we will rebuild the ruins."

But this is what the LORD Almighty says: "They may build, but I will demolish. They will be called the Wicked Land, a people always under the wrath of the LORD. 5You will see it with your own eyes and say, 'Great is the LORD—even beyond the borders of Israel!'

Blemished Sacrifices

6"A son honors his father, and a servant his master. If I am a father, where is the honor due me? If I am a master, where is the respect due me?" says the LORD Almighty. "It is you, O priests, who show contempt for my name.

"But you ask, 'How have we shown contempt for your name?'

7"You place defiled food on my altar.

"But you ask, 'How have we defiled you?'

"By saying that the LORD's table is contemptible. 8When you bring blind animals for sacrifice, is that not wrong? When you sacrifice crippled or diseased animals, is that not wrong? Try offering them to your governor! Would he be pleased with you? Would he accept you?" says the LORD Almighty.

9"Now implore God to be gracious to us. With such offerings from your hands, will he accept you?"—says the LORD Almighty.

10"Oh, that one of you would shut the temple doors, so that you would not light useless fires on my altar! I am not pleased with you," says the LORD Almighty, "and I will accept no offering from your hands. 11My name will be great among the nations, from the rising to the setting of the sun. In every place incense and pure offerings will be brought to my name, because my name will be great among the nations," says the LORD Almighty.

12"But you profane it by saying of the Lord's table, 'It is defiled,' and of its food, 'It is contemptible.' 13And you say, 'What a burden!' and you sniff at it contemptuously," says the LORD Almighty.

"When you bring injured, crippled or diseased animals and offer them as sacrifices, should I accept them from your hands?" says the LORD. 14"Cursed is the cheat who has an acceptable male in his flock and vows to give it, but then sacrifices a blemished animal to the Lord. For I am a great king," says the LORD Almighty, "and my name is to be feared among the nations.

Admonition for the Priests

2

"And now this admonition is for you, O priests. 2If you do not listen, and if you do not set your heart to honor my name," says the LORD Almighty, "I will send a curse upon you, and I will curse your blessings. Yes, I have already cursed them, because you have not set your heart to honor me.

3"Because of you I will rebuke[b] your descendants[c]; I will spread on your faces the offal from your festival sacrifices, and you will be carried off with it. 4And you will know that I have sent you this admonition so that my covenant with Levi may continue," says the LORD Almighty. 5"My covenant was with him, a covenant of life and peace, and I gave them to him; this called for reverence and he revered me and stood in awe of my name. 6True instruction was in his mouth and nothing false was found on his lips. He walked with me in peace and uprightness, and turned many from sin.

7"For the lips of a priest ought to preserve knowledge, and from his mouth men should seek instruction—because he is the messenger of the LORD Almighty. 8But you have turned from the way and by your teaching have caused many to stumble; you have violated the covenant with Levi," says the LORD Almighty. 9"So I have caused you to be despised and humiliated be-

[a]1 *Malachi* means *my messenger.* [b]3 Or *cut off* (see Septuagint) [c]3 Or *will blight your grain*

1:5 Through God's power the people of Judah had experienced many triumphs. God had returned them to the promised land after years in exile. Then, with God's help, they overcame great obstacles and rebuilt the temple and the city of Jerusalem. The people had many reasons to be thankful to God for his powerful acts of restoration. However, despite these great triumphs, the people quickly returned to doing things their own way. After we have experienced great victories with God's help, we often fall back into old sinful patterns too. We need to be reminded on a regular basis of what God has done and can do.

1:7–14 God did not desire mere words of repentance; he wanted the people to back up their words with appropriate actions. If the people were really sorry for their sins and honored God in their hearts, they should have brought their best offerings to God. Yet they exposed their insincerity by bringing blemished sacrifices and keeping the best for themselves. When we seek God and surrender our lives to him, we also need to change our lifestyle. When we truly are devoted to God, we will gladly offer him the best we have.

2:1–9 Israel's religious leaders failed to show God proper respect. God singled out these people for special punishment because they used their influence to hurt rather than help the people subordinate to them. We all influence people at one level or another. Some of us are responsible for many; others of us influence only our families, spouses or a few friends. Yet regardless of our position, we all can influence people for either good or evil. If we have led others astray, we must acknowledge our failure and do what we can to make restitution. This may mean doing what we can to help these people redirect the course of their lives.

fore all the people, because you have not followed my ways but have shown partiality in
matters of the law."

Judah Unfaithful

10Have we not all one Father[a]? Did not one
God create us? Why do we profane the covenant
of our fathers by breaking faith with one another?
11Judah has broken faith. A detestable thing
has been committed in Israel and in Jerusalem:
Judah has desecrated the sanctuary the LORD
loves, by marrying the daughter of a foreign
god. 12As for the man who does this, whoever
he may be, may the LORD cut him off from the
tents of Jacob[b]—even though he brings offerings to the LORD Almighty.
13Another thing you do: You flood the
LORD's altar with tears. You weep and wail because he no longer pays attention to your offerings or accepts them with pleasure from your
hands. 14You ask, "Why?" It is because the LORD
is acting as the witness between you and the
wife of your youth, because you have broken
faith with her, though she is your partner, the
wife of your marriage covenant.
15Has not ⌊the LORD⌋ made them one? In
flesh and spirit they are his. And why one? Because he was seeking godly offspring.[c] So
guard yourself in your spirit, and do not break
faith with the wife of your youth.
16"I hate divorce," says the LORD God of Israel, "and I hate a man's covering himself[d] with
violence as well as with his garment," says the
LORD Almighty.

So guard yourself in your spirit, and do not
break faith.

The Day of Judgment

17You have wearied the LORD with your
words.

"How have we wearied him?" you ask.

By saying, "All who do evil are good in the
eyes of the LORD, and he is pleased with them"
or "Where is the God of justice?"

3 "See, I will send my messenger, who will
prepare the way before me. Then suddenly
the Lord you are seeking will come to his temple; the messenger of the covenant, whom you
desire, will come," says the LORD Almighty.
2But who can endure the day of his coming?
Who can stand when he appears? For he will be
like a refiner's fire or a launderer's soap. 3He
will sit as a refiner and purifier of silver; he will
purify the Levites and refine them like gold and
silver. Then the LORD will have men who will
bring offerings in righteousness, 4and the offerings of Judah and Jerusalem will be acceptable
to the LORD, as in days gone by, as in former
years.
5"So I will come near to you for judgment. I
will be quick to testify against sorcerers, adulterers and perjurers, against those who defraud
laborers of their wages, who oppress the widows and the fatherless, and deprive aliens of
justice, but do not fear me," says the LORD Almighty.

Robbing God

6"I the LORD do not change. So you,
O descendants of Jacob, are not destroyed.
7Ever since the time of your forefathers you
have turned away from my decrees and have
not kept them. Return to me, and I will return
to you," says the LORD Almighty.

"But you ask, 'How are we to return?'
8"Will a man rob God? Yet you rob me.

"But you ask, 'How do we rob you?'

"In tithes and offerings. 9You are under a
curse—the whole nation of you—because you
are robbing me. 10Bring the whole tithe into
the storehouse, that there may be food in my
house. Test me in this," says the LORD Almighty,
"and see if I will not throw open the floodgates
of heaven and pour out so much blessing that
you will not have room enough for it. 11I will
prevent pests from devouring your crops, and
the vines in your fields will not cast their fruit,"
says the LORD Almighty. 12"Then all the nations

[a]10 Or *father* [b]12 Or *12May the LORD cut off from the tents of Jacob anyone who gives testimony in behalf of the man who does this* [c]15 Or *15But the one ⌊who is our father⌋ did not do this, not as long as life remained in him. And what was he seeking? An offspring from God* [d]16 Or *his wife*

2:14–16 Some of the returned exiles had divorced their wives without cause. In a society where these women had no means of supporting themselves, this practice was not only unethical, it was also terribly cruel. God hates divorce. He intended marriage commitments to be binding. Some of us may have experienced the pain of a broken marriage. A broken family can seriously hinder spiritual growth. Yet with God's help we can build strong relationships that will hold us accountable and keep us on the right track.

2:17 God's standards cannot be ignored with impunity. The people had deceived themselves into believing that their evil deeds were upright. However, a refusal to recognize and respect God's standards will lead to severe consequences. Our spiritual renewal is possible only if we recognize our need for God and the value of his plan. Without God, we will face a steady decline leading to disaster. But if we trust God and follow his will, he will strengthen us as we continue to seek him.

3:3–4 The searing heat of the furnace refines precious metals. Caustic soap cleanses filthy fabric. God often uses the fire of difficult times to ready us for his work. God uses the cleansing work of suffering to awaken us to our need for him. When we recognize this and turn to God for help, he will deliver us, encourage us and redirect the course of our lives to walk in his ways.

3:7 God's people refused to see the truth. God confronted them directly about their sin, but they still refused to acknowledge their failure. Our sinful nature can blind us to the truth. As long as we try to hide our sins, we cannot receive God's help. We can receive help only after we acknowledge that we have a problem and repent from our sin.

will call you blessed, for yours will be a delightful land," says the LORD Almighty.
13 "You have said harsh things against me,"
says the LORD.
"Yet you ask, 'What have we said against
you?'
14 "You have said, 'It is futile to serve God.
What did we gain by carrying out his requirements and going about like mourners before
the LORD Almighty? 15 But now we call the arrogant blessed. Certainly the evildoers prosper,
and even those who challenge God escape.' "
16 Then those who feared the LORD talked
with each other, and the LORD listened and
heard. A scroll of remembrance was written in
his presence concerning those who feared the
LORD and honored his name.
17 "They will be mine," says the LORD Almighty, "in the day when I make up my
treasured possession.[a] I will spare them, just
as in compassion a man spares his son who
serves him. 18 And you will again see the distinction between the righteous and the wicked,
between those who serve God and those who
do not.

The Day of the LORD

4 "Surely the day is coming; it will burn like
a furnace. All the arrogant and every evildoer will be stubble, and that day that is coming
will set them on fire," says the LORD Almighty.
"Not a root or a branch will be left to them.
2 But for you who revere my name, the sun of
righteousness will rise with healing in its wings.
And you will go out and leap like calves released from the stall. 3 Then you will trample
down the wicked; they will be ashes under the
soles of your feet on the day when I do these
things," says the LORD Almighty.
4 "Remember the law of my servant Moses,
the decrees and laws I gave him at Horeb for all
Israel.
5 "See, I will send you the prophet Elijah before that great and dreadful day of the LORD
comes. 6 He will turn the hearts of the fathers to
their children, and the hearts of the children to
their fathers; or else I will come and strike the
land with a curse."

[a]17 Or *Almighty, "my treasured possession, in the day when I act*

4:1 The Bible is filled with warnings against proud and sinful people. People who think they don't need God are doomed to destruction. We may react negatively to God's warnings because we don't understand his heart. God warns us of impending destruction because he wants us to change the course of our lives. If we continue in our selfish ways, we will risk destroying not only our own lives but also the lives of those with whom we come into contact. And if we follow our own sinful ways, we will never experience the meaningful lives that God wants for us.

4:2–6 Fear is never a pleasant subject, but healthy fear gives us a proper view of God. As we recognize God's goodness and power, we learn to trust him and willingly follow his plan. A proper view of God leads to healing in our lives. Wholeness and peace will characterize our life in God's kingdom. We must put God in charge of our lives in order to experience his healing in our own corner of the world. As we give God the respect he deserves, we can joyfully follow his perfect plan for us.

THE NEW TESTAMENT

MATTHEW

The Big Picture

Many Jews in Jesus' day cherished some form of "Messianic hope." The Romans were oppressive rulers, and the Jews suffered miserably under their control. God's people clung to the belief that a Savior would emerge to deliver them. Based on the Old Testament promises of a delivering king, the people eagerly awaited the Messiah's coming.

God wanted people to accept Jesus as their Messiah and Savior. Through Jesus' ancestry, virgin birth, fulfillment of Old Testament prophecies, teachings and miracles, God demonstrated who Jesus was. But during Jesus' earthly ministry most people were unwilling to face the reality of his identity. Instead of viewing him as their long-awaited Messiah, the people crucified him. Instead of finding deliverance, they remained bound in sin.

To deal with our problems, we sometimes focus our hope on various means of deliverance. Some of us may still look to sin to meet our needs. Some of us long for freedom through people or plans rather than Jesus and his way. The Gospel of Matthew makes it clear that our only hope for spiritual renewal lies in Jesus the Messiah.

In order to experience freedom from the power of sin we must place our trust in Jesus. When we rely on the forgiveness gained through his death and the hope for new life found in his resurrection, we gain true hope for a genuine spiritual renewal. Letting go of our self-sufficiency and pride, we must place our hope in God and make Jesus the king of our lives. He alone is worthy of that honor and responsibility.

A. JESUS' INTRODUCTION AS THE PROMISED KING (1:1–4:11)

1. His Family History (1:1-17)
2. His Birth and Development (1:18–2:23)
3. His Baptism and Temptation (3:1–4:11)

B. JESUS' KINGLY MINISTRY AND MESSAGE (4:12–20:34)

1. Jesus' Early Ministry (4:12-25)
2. Jesus' Sermon on the Mount (5:1–7:29)
3. Jesus' Many Miracles (8:1–10:42)
4. Jesus' Teachings About His Kingdom (11:1–20:34)

C. JESUS, THE REJECTED REDEEMER (21:1–27:66)

1. Jesus the King Enters Jerusalem (21:1-17)
2. Jesus Teaches His Disciples (21:18–25:46)
3. Jesus Is Rejected and Crucified (26:1–27:66)

D. JESUS, THE RESURRECTED SAVIOR (28:1-20)

Spiritual Renewal Themes

THE POWER OF THE RESURRECTION

We sometimes believe we can find the power for our spiritual renewal within ourselves. We don't want to depend on something outside of us. But the power within us can be only as strong as we are, and we all have inherent weaknesses. God demonstrated his power in many ways in the Gospels. God's power was ultimately exemplified in the resurrection of Jesus Christ. In his victory over sin and death, Jesus established his credentials as king and his power and authority over all evil.

Essential Facts

PURPOSE:
To prove that Jesus was the promised Messiah and to show that God offers salvation to all through him.

AUTHOR:
Matthew, a disciple and former tax collector.

AUDIENCE:
Matthew wrote primarily for Jewish Christian readers.

DATE WRITTEN:
Probably between A.D. 60 and 65.

SETTING:
Matthew emphasized the fulfillment of Old Testament prophecy in the person of Jesus Christ, making this Gospel the connecting link between the Old and New Testaments.

KEY VERSE:
"Do not think that I have come to abolish the Law or the Prophets; I have not come to abolish them but to fulfill them" (5:17).

KEY PEOPLE AND RELATIONSHIPS:
Jesus in relationship with his ancestors, Mary and Joseph, John the Baptist, his disciples, and the Jewish and Roman leaders.

That's the kind of power we need, and it is available when we surrender our lives to God.

THE IMPORTANCE OF HOPE

Without hope, we are miserable. Hope is the driving force behind our spiritual renewal. If we had no hope, there would be no reason to seek spiritual growth. Understanding who Jesus is gives each of us hope that transcends even the deepest despair. In the Gospel of Matthew, we see and hear the message of a hope available to everyone, not just to a select group of people. Jesus' resurrection forms the basis of our hope because through it God demonstrated his control over the power of death.

THE DANGERS OF SPIRITUAL BLINDNESS

Often people claim that if they could just witness a miracle, they would believe in God. But as we see throughout Matthew's Gospel, many people denied the truth about Jesus despite the miracles he performed in their presence. Spiritually blinded people cannot glimpse the truth even when it is right before their eyes. God can handle our doubts and our fears, but our cynicism and unbelief blind us and effectively shut us off from his transforming power. Let us be like the disciples who stood in awe and wondered what kind of man Jesus was (see 8:27). Such an open, receptive heart will cause us to seek God more and more.

The Genealogy of Jesus

‰ See Ruth 4:18–22; 1 Chronicles 3:10–17; Luke 3:23–38

1 A record of the genealogy of Jesus Christ the son of David, the son of Abraham:

2Abraham was the father of Isaac,
Isaac the father of Jacob,
Jacob the father of Judah and his brothers,
3Judah the father of Perez and Zerah, whose mother was Tamar,
Perez the father of Hezron,
Hezron the father of Ram,
4Ram the father of Amminadab,
Amminadab the father of Nahshon,
Nahshon the father of Salmon,
5Salmon the father of Boaz, whose mother was Rahab,
Boaz the father of Obed, whose mother was Ruth,
Obed the father of Jesse,
6and Jesse the father of King David.

David was the father of Solomon, whose mother had been Uriah's wife,
7Solomon the father of Rehoboam,
Rehoboam the father of Abijah,
Abijah the father of Asa,
8Asa the father of Jehoshaphat,
Jehoshaphat the father of Jehoram,
Jehoram the father of Uzziah,
9Uzziah the father of Jotham,
Jotham the father of Ahaz,
Ahaz the father of Hezekiah,
10Hezekiah the father of Manasseh,
Manasseh the father of Amon,
Amon the father of Josiah,
11and Josiah the father of Jeconiah[a] and his brothers at the time of the exile to Babylon.

12After the exile to Babylon:
Jeconiah was the father of Shealtiel,
Shealtiel the father of Zerubbabel,
13Zerubbabel the father of Abiud,
Abiud the father of Eliakim,
Eliakim the father of Azor,
14Azor the father of Zadok,
Zadok the father of Akim,
Akim the father of Eliud,
15Eliud the father of Eleazar,
Eleazar the father of Matthan,
Matthan the father of Jacob,
16and Jacob the father of Joseph, the husband of Mary, of whom was born Jesus, who is called Christ.

17Thus there were fourteen generations in all from Abraham to David, fourteen from David to the exile to Babylon, and fourteen from the exile to the Christ.[b]

The Birth of Jesus Christ

18This is how the birth of Jesus Christ came
about: His mother Mary was pledged to be married to Joseph, but before they came together,
she was found to be with child through the
Holy Spirit. 19Because Joseph her husband was
a righteous man and did not want to expose her to public disgrace, he had in mind to divorce her quietly.
20But after he had considered this, an angel
of the Lord appeared to him in a dream and
said, "Joseph son of David, do not be afraid to
take Mary home as your wife, because what is
conceived in her is from the Holy Spirit. 21She
will give birth to a son, and you are to give him
the name Jesus,[c] because he will save his people from their sins."
22All this took place to fulfill what the Lord
had said through the prophet: 23"The virgin
will be with child and will give birth to a son,
and they will call him Immanuel"[d]—which means, "God with us."
24When Joseph woke up, he did what the
angel of the Lord had commanded him and
took Mary home as his wife. 25But he had no
union with her until she gave birth to a son.
And he gave him the name Jesus.

The Visit of the Magi

2 After Jesus was born in Bethlehem in Judea, during the time of King Herod, Magi[e]
from the east came to Jerusalem 2and asked,
"Where is the one who has been born king of
the Jews? We saw his star in the east[f] and have come to worship him."
3When King Herod heard this he was disturbed, and all Jerusalem with him. 4When he
had called together all the people's chief priests
and teachers of the law, he asked them where
the Christ[g] was to be born. 5"In Bethlehem in

[a]11 That is, Jehoiachin; also in verse 12 [b]17 Or *Messiah.* "The Christ" (Greek) and "the Messiah" (Hebrew) both mean "the Anointed One." [c]21 *Jesus* is the Greek form of *Joshua,* which means *the LORD saves.* [d]23 Isaiah 7:14 [e]1 Traditionally *Wise Men* [f]2 Or *star when it rose* [g]4 Or *Messiah*

1:1–16 Notice that the family tree of Jesus, the sinless God-man, was far from perfect. Judah fathered Perez through his daughter-in-law Tamar, thinking she was a prostitute (1:3; see Genesis 38); Salmon married Rahab, the former prostitute of Jericho (1:5; see Joshua 6); David had an adulterous affair with Uriah's wife, Bathsheba (1:6; see 2 Samuel 11). Throughout history God has used imperfect people to work his will. God is well aware of people's past mistakes. But God can redeem the lives of repentant people so that they can do great things for him. God can also grant us a productive future no matter how sinful our past if only we will repent.

1:5–16 The mention of Rahab, Ruth and Bathsheba in Jesus' lineage is significant. Though each of these women came from different backgrounds, God used them to prepare for the coming of the Messiah. Similarly, God often employs people from diverse and unusual backgrounds to accomplish his purposes. His grace is greater than the presumed limitations of our past. He can use us regardless of our background.

Herod & Family

There are certain historical names that immediately bring to mind images of horror, violence, greed and cruelty. This is true in the Bible as well. The name "Herod" evoked terror in the hearts of those living in New Testament times. Herod the Great earned the appellation "great" because of his ambitious and lavish building projects, including the rebuilding of the temple in Jerusalem. His character, however, was anything but great. He was known for his cruelty, jealousy and an insatiable lust for power and wealth.

The Romans appointed Herod as king, but many of his Jewish subjects never really accepted him as a legitimate ruler. Herod was not really of Jewish descent; he was an Idumean from the land south of Judea. Because of this, Herod was uneasy about any threat to his position and responded with swift cruelty to the slightest rumor of disloyalty. The ruling Herods didn't hesitate to have even their own family members murdered if it would be to their own advantage.

Herod Antipas, Herod the Great's son, is well known for his role in killing John the Baptist. Another descendant, Herod Agrippa I, was responsible for the death of the apostle James. A grandson, Herod Agrippa II, heard the truth of the gospel directly from the apostle Paul. In fact, each of the Herods had an encounter with a messenger from God but each, in turn, refused to respond to the truth.

The inability of this ruling family to respond to God's truth grew out of their greed and insecurity. As a result, each successive King Herod left his children a legacy of greed and cruelty. It is important that we ask ourselves what heritage we are leaving for those who come after us. We can refuse to see the truth and thereby pass along our sins and their consequences to others. Or we can choose God's path and build a happy and meaningful future for our descendants. There is a great deal at stake. We are fighting for our own lives and the lives of countless descendants as well.

STRENGTHS AND ACCOMPLISHMENTS:

Herod and his family were industrious builders.

They were extremely clever at political maneuvering.

WEAKNESSES AND MISTAKES:

Herod and his family lusted after power and possessions.

They didn't hesitate to destroy innocent people who stood in their way.

LESSONS FROM THEIR LIVES:

Having power and wealth doesn't guarantee success and happiness.

We must carefully consider the heritage we will leave our children.

Those who live for themselves at the expense of others will pay the price in the end.

KEY VERSE:

"When Herod realized that he had been outwitted by the Magi, he was furious, and he gave orders to kill all the boys in Bethlehem and its vicinity who were two years old and under, in accordance with the time he had learned from the Magi" (2:16).

Herod and members of his family are mentioned in Matthew 2:1–22; Mark 6:14–29; Luke 1:5; 3:1–20; 23:7–15; Acts 4:27; 12:1–23; 13:1 and 25:13—26:32.

Judea," they replied, "for this is what the prophet has written:

6 " 'But you, Bethlehem, in the land of
Judah,
are by no means least among the rulers
of Judah;
for out of you will come a ruler
who will be the shepherd of my people
Israel.'[a] "

7 Then Herod called the Magi secretly and
found out from them the exact time the star had
appeared. 8 He sent them to Bethlehem and
said, "Go and make a careful search for the
child. As soon as you find him, report to me, so
that I too may go and worship him."

9 After they had heard the king, they went on
their way, and the star they had seen in the
east[b] went ahead of them until it stopped over
the place where the child was. 10 When they saw
the star, they were overjoyed. 11 On coming to
the house, they saw the child with his mother
Mary, and they bowed down and worshiped
him. Then they opened their treasures and presented him with gifts of gold and of incense and
of myrrh. 12 And having been warned in a dream
not to go back to Herod, they returned to their
country by another route.

The Escape to Egypt

13 When they had gone, an angel of the Lord
appeared to Joseph in a dream. "Get up," he
said, "take the child and his mother and escape
to Egypt. Stay there until I tell you, for Herod is
going to search for the child to kill him."

14 So he got up, took the child and his mother
during the night and left for Egypt, 15 where he
stayed until the death of Herod. And so was
fulfilled what the Lord had said through the
prophet: "Out of Egypt I called my son."[c]

16 When Herod realized that he had been outwitted by the Magi, he was furious, and he gave
orders to kill all the boys in Bethlehem and its
vicinity who were two years old and under, in
accordance with the time he had learned from
the Magi. 17 Then what was said through the
prophet Jeremiah was fulfilled:

18 "A voice is heard in Ramah,
weeping and great mourning,
Rachel weeping for her children
and refusing to be comforted,
because they are no more."[d]

The Return to Nazareth

19 After Herod died, an angel of the Lord appeared in a dream to Joseph in Egypt 20 and said,
"Get up, take the child and his mother and go
to the land of Israel, for those who were trying
to take the child's life are dead."

21 So he got up, took the child and his mother
and went to the land of Israel. 22 But when he
heard that Archelaus was reigning in Judea in
place of his father Herod, he was afraid to go
there. Having been warned in a dream, he withdrew to the district of Galilee, 23 and he went
and lived in a town called Nazareth. So was
fulfilled what was said through the prophets:
"He will be called a Nazarene."

John the Baptist Prepares the Way

‰ See Mark 1:3–8; Luke 3:2–17

3 In those days John the Baptist came,
preaching in the Desert of Judea 2 and saying, "Repent, for the kingdom of heaven is
near." 3 This is he who was spoken of through the
prophet Isaiah:

"A voice of one calling in the desert,
'Prepare the way for the Lord,
make straight paths for him.' "[e]

4 John's clothes were made of camel's hair,
and he had a leather belt around his waist. His
food was locusts and wild honey. 5 People went
out to him from Jerusalem and all Judea and
the whole region of the Jordan. 6 Confessing
their sins, they were baptized by him in the
Jordan River.

7 But when he saw many of the Pharisees and
Sadducees coming to where he was baptizing,
he said to them: "You brood of vipers! Who
warned you to flee from the coming wrath?
8 Produce fruit in keeping with repentance. 9 And
do not think you can say to yourselves, 'We
have Abraham as our father.' I tell you that out
of these stones God can raise up children for

[a] 6 Micah 5:2 [b] 9 Or *seen when it rose*
[c] 15 Hosea 11:1 [d] 18 Jer. 31:15 [e] 3 Isaiah 40:3

3:1–2 John the Baptist preached an age-old message: repentance. People could have easily dismissed his message. But John's presentation carried with it an urgency for an immediate moral U–turn: "The kingdom of heaven is near." The urgency in John's message still holds true for us today. Repentance requires our honest self-examination. There is no time like the present to face reality and turn from our sinful behavior.

3:5–9 Clearly not everyone who went to listen to John the Baptist wanted to repent and find new life. John recognized that the Pharisees, and others like them, were merely observing religious rituals, trusting external appearances for their salvation. We must make sure that we do not seek spiritual renewal merely for the sake of appearances or try to earn our salvation by what we do. It is not our outward appearance that matters most to God, but our inner person of the heart. We must honestly assess our inner lives before God will transform our behavior.

3:7–11 John the Baptist confronted the Pharisees with their refusal to see the truth. These religious leaders were spiritually blinded to their sins. They believed they were beyond the reach of God's judgment. Perhaps we have also believed the consequences of our sins would never catch up with us. Our spiritual blindness may have been so severe that we weren't even aware that there were serious consequences to our sinful lifestyle. As a good gardener, God will take an ax to unproductive trees—those who do not follow him. But for those of us willing to repent, God will fuel our spiritual growth through the power of his Holy Spirit. We may either continue in our sin, awaiting God's judgment, or turn from our present lifestyle and repent, counting on God's Spirit to help us change.

Abraham. 10The ax is already at the root of the trees, and every tree that does not produce good fruit will be cut down and thrown into the fire.

11"I baptize you with[a] water for repentance. But after me will come one who is more powerful than I, whose sandals I am not fit to carry. He will baptize you with the Holy Spirit and with fire. 12His winnowing fork is in his hand, and he will clear his threshing floor, gathering his wheat into the barn and burning up the chaff with unquenchable fire."

The Baptism of Jesus

‰ See Mark 1:9–11; Luke 3:21–22; John 1:31–34

13Then Jesus came from Galilee to the Jordan to be baptized by John. 14But John tried to deter him, saying, "I need to be baptized by you, and do you come to me?"

15Jesus replied, "Let it be so now; it is proper for us to do this to fulfill all righteousness." Then John consented.

16As soon as Jesus was baptized, he went up out of the water. At that moment heaven was opened, and he saw the Spirit of God descending like a dove and lighting on him. 17And a voice from heaven said, "This is my Son, whom I love; with him I am well pleased."

The Temptation of Jesus

‰ See Mark 1:12–13; Luke 4:1–13

4 Then Jesus was led by the Spirit into the desert to be tempted by the devil. 2After fasting forty days and forty nights, he was hungry. 3The tempter came to him and said, "If you are the Son of God, tell these stones to become bread."

4Jesus answered, "It is written: 'Man does not live on bread alone, but on every word that comes from the mouth of God.'[b]"

5Then the devil took him to the holy city and had him stand on the highest point of the temple. 6"If you are the Son of God," he said, "throw yourself down. For it is written:

" 'He will command his angels concerning you,
and they will lift you up in their hands,
so that you will not strike your foot against a stone.'[c]"

7Jesus answered him, "It is also written: 'Do not put the Lord your God to the test.'[d]"

8Again, the devil took him to a very high mountain and showed him all the kingdoms of the world and their splendor. 9"All this I will give you," he said, "if you will bow down and worship me."

10Jesus said to him, "Away from me, Satan! For it is written: 'Worship the Lord your God, and serve him only.'[e]"

11Then the devil left him, and angels came and attended him.

Jesus Begins to Preach

12When Jesus heard that John had been put in prison, he returned to Galilee. 13Leaving Nazareth, he went and lived in Capernaum, which was by the lake in the area of Zebulun and Naphtali— 14to fulfill what was said through the prophet Isaiah:

15"Land of Zebulun and land of Naphtali,
the way to the sea, along the Jordan,
Galilee of the Gentiles—
16the people living in darkness
have seen a great light;
on those living in the land of the shadow of death
a light has dawned."[f]

17From that time on Jesus began to preach, "Repent, for the kingdom of heaven is near."

The Calling of the First Disciples

‰ See Mark 1:16–20; Luke 5:2–11; John 1:35–42

18As Jesus was walking beside the Sea of

[a]11 Or *in* [b]4 Deut. 8:3 [c]6 Psalm 91:11,12
[d]7 Deut. 6:16 [e]10 Deut. 6:13 [f]16 Isaiah 9:1,2

3:13–15 Jesus did not need to follow John's call to baptism because he had never sinned. He had no reason to repent. However, Jesus proceeded to be baptized anyway because it was the right thing to do. Jesus' actions modeled the importance of baptism to others. We all need to have role models who live a balanced life and do the right things for the right reasons. As we continue growing spiritually, we can become role models for others to follow too.

3:16–17 After Jesus' baptism, the Holy Spirit appeared from heaven in visible form, and people heard the voice of the Father commending the Son. Jesus was thus shown to be in perfect harmony with his Father and the Holy Spirit. While we will never have perfect unity in our earthly relationships, we can draw support from those who affirm us and trust that God's great love for us will never end.

4:1–2 When we seek God and surrender to him, we should not mistakenly think that our faith will insulate us from further temptation. Jesus was actually led into the wilderness by the Holy Spirit for a prolonged siege of temptation. We should be warned that temptation may follow quickly on the heels of a spiritual blessing. God can use such trials in our lives to remind us how helpless we are without him.

4:3–10 Satan did not doubt Jesus' identity as the Son of God. Rather, his temptations appealed to real needs and possible doubts that were common to all people. Jesus, as a human being, needed food, security and protection. If Jesus had faltered at the point of his humanity, Satan could have called into question Jesus' perfection and his right to rule as the unique God-man. Similarly Satan and his forces will attack those of us who pursue spiritual growth at our most vulnerable points. We must be on guard against these attacks, filling our minds with Scripture and calling upon the Lord to help us.

4:12–16 The way of salvation through Jesus Christ is open to everyone. Jesus can redeem anyone, regardless of that person's background or sinful past. Jesus proved this by spending his early years in the cosmopolitan region of Galilee. The Jews in Galilee had dealings with the Gentiles who also lived in Galilee. The Judean Jews considered this contact a type of corruption. But Jesus showed God's love to the Galileans. And he continues to show his love to all who trust him, no matter who we are or how great our sin and failure.

Fasting

Keeping Our Appetites in Check

Matthew 4:1–11 Fasting may drain the body but it feeds the soul. Some have said that fasting is praying with the body. Fasting is abstaining from things that are good for you in order to give greater attention to spiritual concerns. Fasting is also one of the most frequently illustrated spiritual exercises in the Bible, occurring in a great variety of situations.

Following Jesus' baptism, the Holy Spirit led him into the wilderness. There, Jesus fasted for forty days and nights, identifying himself with Israel hungering in the wilderness, both spiritually and physically. But when temptation came, another issue came to the fore: What forces would control Jesus and his mission? He was tempted to let his own appetites control him and to put his own desires before God's will.

We often use food as a source of pleasure, to reward ourselves, to distract ourselves from sadness or even sometimes as a display of prosperity. Once we recognize the many messages food can convey, we can easily see that food affects us not only physically but also spiritually. If we are not careful, our hunger for food and our other appetites can completely control us. When we lose control over our use of time or money, or over purity of thought, speech or actions, we open ourselves up to all sorts of trouble. The spiritual discipline of Biblical fasting can help us overcome the magnetic pull of our appetites and align our lives with God's purposes and values.

At the end of Jesus' fast, his response to Satan's temptations clarified his proper outlook on life, giving us also a proper outlook on food: "It is written: 'Man does not live on bread alone, but on every word that comes from the mouth of God' " (4:4). Jesus obeyed the will of God before he obeyed his stomach, and so should we.

Putting It Into Practice

An extended fast, meaning one that lasts beyond twenty-four hours, can sometimes be helpful in realigning our priorities with God's desires. Typical lengths of time for such fasts are thirty-six hours, forty-eight hours or seventy-two hours. Such extended fasts definitely require more physical stamina and spiritual preparation. As with any exercise, it is wise to start small and work your way up. To attempt an extended fast before you are truly ready can be unhealthy and possibly end in failure and discouragement in your spiritual walk. Thought should be given to functioning with a reduced energy level. Breaking such fasts also requires intentional planning. When you begin eating again, eat foods that are easily digestible. Avoid spicy or greasy foods. Eat smaller quantities so your system can readjust more easily.

Your fast should always be accompanied by the practice of other disciplines such as prayer and Bible study so that proper focus is maintained throughout this special time. Be sure to enter your thoughts and reflections in a journal.

For more on fasting, turn to Matthew 6.

Galilee, he saw two brothers, Simon called Peter
and his brother Andrew. They were casting a
net into the lake, for they were fishermen.
19 "Come, follow me," Jesus said, "and I will
make you fishers of men." 20 At once they left
their nets and followed him.

21 Going on from there, he saw two other
brothers, James son of Zebedee and his brother
John. They were in a boat with their father Zebedee, preparing their nets. Jesus called them,
22 and immediately they left the boat and their
father and followed him.

Jesus Heals the Sick

23 Jesus went throughout Galilee, teaching in
their synagogues, preaching the good news of
the kingdom, and healing every disease and
sickness among the people. 24 News about him
spread all over Syria, and people brought to
him all who were ill with various diseases, those
suffering severe pain, the demon-possessed,
those having seizures, and the paralyzed, and
he healed them. 25 Large crowds from Galilee,
the Decapolis,[a] Jerusalem, Judea and the region across the Jordan followed him.

The Beatitudes

‰ See Luke 6:20–23

5 Now when he saw the crowds, he went up
on a mountainside and sat down. His disciples came to him, 2 and he began to teach
them, saying:

3 "Blessed are the poor in spirit,
for theirs is the kingdom of heaven.
4 Blessed are those who mourn,
for they will be comforted.
5 Blessed are the meek,
for they will inherit the earth.
6 Blessed are those who hunger and thirst for
righteousness,
for they will be filled.
7 Blessed are the merciful,
for they will be shown mercy.
8 Blessed are the pure in heart,
for they will see God.
9 Blessed are the peacemakers,
for they will be called sons of God.
10 Blessed are those who are persecuted
because of righteousness,
for theirs is the kingdom of heaven.

11 "Blessed are you when people insult you,
persecute you and falsely say all kinds of evil
against you because of me. 12 Rejoice and be
glad, because great is your reward in heaven, for
in the same way they persecuted the prophets
who were before you.

Salt and Light

13 "You are the salt of the earth. But if the salt
loses its saltiness, how can it be made salty
again? It is no longer good for anything, except
to be thrown out and trampled by men.

14 "You are the light of the world. A city on
a hill cannot be hidden. 15 Neither do people
light a lamp and put it under a bowl. Instead
they put it on its stand, and it gives light to
everyone in the house. 16 In the same way, let
your light shine before men, that they may see
your good deeds and praise your Father in
heaven.

The Fulfillment of the Law

17 "Do not think that I have come to abolish
the Law or the Prophets; I have not come to
abolish them but to fulfill them. 18 I tell you the
truth, until heaven and earth disappear, not the
smallest letter, not the least stroke of a pen, will
by any means disappear from the Law until everything is accomplished. 19 Anyone who breaks
one of the least of these commandments and
teaches others to do the same will be called least
in the kingdom of heaven, but whoever practices and teaches these commands will be called
great in the kingdom of heaven. 20 For I tell you
that unless your righteousness surpasses that of
the Pharisees and the teachers of the law, you
will certainly not enter the kingdom of heaven.

Murder

21 "You have heard that it was said to the

[a] *25* That is, the Ten Cities

5:1–12 The Beatitudes contain much of God's plan for us as we follow his will for our lives. The lifestyle advocated by the Beatitudes affirms God's perspective, priorities and boundaries. Yet as we look over God's plan in this passage, we may wonder how anyone could live up to it. The truth is, no one can live this way without God's help. Following God's plan requires his wisdom and grace.

5:3–5 We cannot experience spiritual renewal and God's transformation without true humility. Pride stands in the way of recognizing our painful problems and sins. If we cannot admit our problems and failures, there can be no real cure for us. When we humble ourselves before God, we may need to grieve over our mistakes and losses. As we do this, we can then experience the wonderful comfort that only God can offer (see 2 Corinthians 1:3–5).

5:10–12 Persecution can be a true problem for us when we try to live by God's principles. People may try to intimidate us into quitting our spiritual journey. Family members may be threatened by the lifestyle changes we make. They may try to discourage us. We need to realize that it is more important to please God than to please other people. When we do things God's way, we will be set free from our sinful ways. We can begin to build healthy relationships with others and continue to strengthen our relationship with God.

5:13–16 If we have been delivered by God's power, we need to be witnesses to others of his power to save and carry the light of this good news to people imprisoned in the darkness of sin. Sinful behaviors and warped relationships abound. People desperately seek truth and light. We can make a significant impact on individuals, relationships and societal structures if we will shine our spiritual light for others to see. As we experience God's deliverance in our lives, we can share God's love with others and extend hope to hurting people.

5:21–22, 27–29 Intense emotions and desires threaten all of us in one way or another. They must be dealt with from the inside out. Those of us burning within with rage,

THE SPIRITUAL DISCIPLINES

Repentance and Confession

A Higher Standard, A Richer Grace

Matthew 5:48 As we grow in our spiritual lives, the high calling and exacting standards of God become increasingly clearer. Some of the most challenging mountains to climb do not look very imposing from a distance. It's only when you begin climbing the mountain itself that you sense the difficulty of the ascent. Likewise, the difficulty of God's call to holiness only becomes clear as we embark on the ascent of faithfulness.

In his Sermon on the Mount, Jesus presented a vision of a new level of obedience to God. God judges not simply murder but anger, not simply adultery but lust, not simply religious ritual but heart motivation. Jesus taught that God's standards rise far above the mere letter of the law. Human effort alone can never satisfy them (see Romans 3:23). These facts should drive us into the arms of grace, however, not into the depths of despair.

In Matthew 5:48, the Greek word translated as "perfect" is *teleios.* Indeed, *teleios* means "complete in labor, growth, mental and moral character; the goal, the final purpose toward which we are moving." This fits with Jesus' elevation of the law to an unattainable plane. Yet the word also carries with it the sense of being complete and mature. For example, a blossoming tree can be "perfect," even though there is no fruit, because it is at the appropriate stage for fruit to be produced in time. Likewise, we can be *teleios,* mature, even when we are green in the practices of spiritual living. What matters to God is our journey, not just the arrival at the goal. God's concern is not that we've arrived but that we continue to travel in the right direction, for his grace both empowers our obedience and forgives our sin.

For more on repentance and confession, turn to Romans 7.

Putting It Into Practice

Our spiritual lives are energized when we remind ourselves of the two facets of faith in Christ: a higher standard for our behavior and a richer mercy for our sin. Neglecting either can lead to spiritual weakness and discouragement. Some become careless through forgetting this higher standard. Others are oppressed by their failure to meet this standard on their own, losing sight of God's forgiveness through Christ.

Which facet of faith are you most comfortable with? What do you need to learn from the other? Cultivating a balanced view of both a higher standard and a richer mercy will prepare our hearts for further spiritual growth.

people long ago, 'Do not murder,[a] and anyone who murders will be subject to judgment.' 22 But I tell you that anyone who is angry with his brother[b] will be subject to judgment. Again, anyone who says to his brother, 'Raca,[c]' is answerable to the Sanhedrin. But anyone who says, 'You fool!' will be in danger of the fire of hell.

23 "Therefore, if you are offering your gift at the altar and there remember that your brother has something against you, 24 leave your gift there in front of the altar. First go and be reconciled to your brother; then come and offer your gift.

25 "Settle matters quickly with your adversary who is taking you to court. Do it while you are still with him on the way, or he may hand you over to the judge, and the judge may hand you over to the officer, and you may be thrown into prison. 26 I tell you the truth, you will not get out until you have paid the last penny.[d]

Adultery

27 "You have heard that it was said, 'Do not commit adultery.'[e] 28 But I tell you that anyone who looks at a woman lustfully has already committed adultery with her in his heart. 29 If your right eye causes you to sin, gouge it out and throw it away. It is better for you to lose one part of your body than for your whole body to be thrown into hell. 30 And if your right hand causes you to sin, cut it off and throw it away. It is better for you to lose one part of your body than for your whole body to go into hell.

Divorce

31 "It has been said, 'Anyone who divorces his wife must give her a certificate of divorce.'[f] 32 But I tell you that anyone who divorces his wife, except for marital unfaithfulness, causes her to become an adulteress, and anyone who marries the divorced woman commits adultery.

Oaths

33 "Again, you have heard that it was said to the people long ago, 'Do not break your oath, but keep the oaths you have made to the Lord.' 34 But I tell you, Do not swear at all: either by heaven, for it is God's throne; 35 or by the earth, for it is his footstool; or by Jerusalem, for it is the city of the Great King. 36 And do not swear by your head, for you cannot make even one hair white or black. 37 Simply let your 'Yes' be 'Yes,' and your 'No,' 'No'; anything beyond this comes from the evil one.

An Eye for an Eye

38 "You have heard that it was said, 'Eye for eye, and tooth for tooth.'[g] 39 But I tell you, Do not resist an evil person. If someone strikes you on the right cheek, turn to him the other also. 40 And if someone wants to sue you and take your tunic, let him have your cloak as well. 41 If someone forces you to go one mile, go with him two miles. 42 Give to the one who asks you, and do not turn away from the one who wants to borrow from you.

Love for Enemies

43 "You have heard that it was said, 'Love your neighbor[h] and hate your enemy.' 44 But I tell you: Love your enemies[i] and pray for those who persecute you, 45 that you may be sons of your Father in heaven. He causes his sun to rise on the evil and the good, and sends rain on the righteous and the unrighteous. 46 If you love those who love you, what reward will you get? Are not even the tax collectors doing that? 47 And if you greet only your brothers, what are you doing more than others? Do not even pagans do that? 48 Be perfect, therefore, as your heavenly Father is perfect.

Giving to the Needy

6 "Be careful not to do your 'acts of righteousness' before men, to be seen by them. If you do, you will have no reward from your Father in heaven.

2 "So when you give to the needy, do not announce it with trumpets, as the hypocrites do in the synagogues and on the streets, to be honored by men. I tell you the truth, they have received their reward in full. 3 But when you give

[a] *21* Exodus 20:13 [b] *22* Some manuscripts *brother without cause* [c] *22* An Aramaic term of contempt [d] *26* Greek *kodrantes* [e] *27* Exodus 20:14 [f] *31* Deut. 24:1 [g] *38* Exodus 21:24; Lev. 24:20; Deut. 19:21 [h] *43* Lev. 19:18 [i] *44* Some late manuscripts *enemies, bless those who curse you, do good to those who hate you*

---

lust or other intense, driving forces may think we can control those desires from the outside. But eventually we lose control. Jesus knows that the patterns of anger and lust are serious and far too powerful for us to control alone. We need to recognize that we are unable to control such forces on our own, confess this truth to God and ask for his powerful help.

5:43–48 Loving our enemies doesn't come naturally. Yet when we find ourselves able to love our enemies, we can be sure that we are making spiritual progress. Loving our enemies means forgiving them and desiring what is best for them. If we harbor anger and bitterness toward others, we only hurt ourselves; such emotions keep us from making progress in our spiritual growth. God loved us while we were still his enemies (see Romans 5:8); and he loves us now even though we are far from perfect. Spiritual growth is not perfectionism; it is the development of the ability to follow God and shape our actions according to his good plans for us.

6:1–4 God's priorities are different from ours (see Isaiah 55:8–9). All of us live both public and private lives, but the reward systems for each are very different. God is clearly more interested in our quiet service to others than our outward, worldly success. While we may succeed to some degree by becoming famous or wealthy, we will never receive further reward from God for our public success. However, if we humbly seek to help others, our heavenly Father will openly reward us. What may seem unnoticed by others is often center stage before God.

Just Between You and God

Matthew 6:6 Did you ever long for someone who would listen as you poured out your heart? For someone who would listen without interrupting, without condemning, without discounting your story? God is such a listener, and prayer gives us this opportunity. In fact, honest prayer is one of the most important means to spiritual renewal and continuing spiritual vitality.

One of Jesus' themes in his Sermon on the Mount was the problem of spiritual pride and competition. He condemned benevolence merely for the sake of impressing others rather than as an expression of faith and love for God.

This attitude is of particular interest in prayer. Who's our audience? If our focus in prayer is on others who may be listening, we will continually be editing, censoring and measuring our sentences and expressions. We will be more concerned about what others think about our words than about sharing our hearts with God.

Here is Jesus' invitation: Come as you are! There's no sense in trying to impress God. While we should always approach God with reverence, we don't need to censor our feelings or "clean up our act" when we come to him. "The LORD is near to all who call on him, to all who call on him in truth" (Psalm 145:18).

This freedom to be honest is especially valuable for our private prayers. Even when we're alone, we may be more concerned with getting the words right than with simply conversing with God. But God invites us to come just as we are. Many of the psalms express blunt honesty and emotional expressions before God. Some of these hymns make us truly uncomfortable in their candor, anger and vexation. Yet God receives them all. One of the greatest blessings in prayer is the freedom to be totally honest with God.

For more on prayer, turn to Matthew 6.

Putting It Into Practice

When we are truly being honest about our thoughts and feelings, God is ready to hear anything we have to say. What do you need to talk about with him? Whether you take a long walk or go for a drive or write in your journal, come to your Father, who is always listening, and share your heart with him.

not let your left hand know
hand is doing, 4so that your
secret. Then your Father, who
in secret, will reward you.

5"And when you pray, do not be like the
hypocrites, for they love to pray standing in the
synagogues and on the street corners to be seen
by men. I tell you the truth, they have received
their reward in full. 6But when you pray, go into
your room, close the door and pray to your
Father, who is unseen. Then your Father, who
sees what is done in secret, will reward you.
7And when you pray, do not keep on babbling
like pagans, for they think they will be heard
because of their many words. 8Do not be like
them, for your Father knows what you need
before you ask him.
9"This, then, is how you should pray:

" 'Our Father in heaven,
hallowed be your name,
10your kingdom come,
your will be done
on earth as it is in heaven.
11Give us today our daily bread.
12Forgive us our debts,
as we also have forgiven our debtors.
13And lead us not into temptation,
but deliver us from the evil one.[a]'

14For if you forgive men when they sin against
you, your heavenly Father will also forgive you.
15But if you do not forgive men their sins, your
Father will not forgive your sins.

Fasting

16"When you fast, do not look somber as the
hypocrites do, for they disfigure their faces to
show men they are fasting. I tell you the truth,
they have received their reward in full. 17But
when you fast, put oil on your head and wash
your face, 18so that it will not be obvious to men
that you are fasting, but only to your Father,
who is unseen; and your Father, who sees what
is done in secret, will reward you.

Treasures in Heaven

19"Do not store up for yourselves treasures
on earth, where moth and rust destroy, and
where thieves break in and steal. 20But store up
for yourselves treasures in heaven, where moth
and rust do not destroy, and where thieves do
not break in and steal. 21For where your treasure
is, there your heart will be also.
22"The eye is the lamp of the body. If your
eyes are good, your whole body will be full of
light. 23But if your eyes are bad, your whole
body will be full of darkness. If then the light
within you is darkness, how great is that darkness!
24"No one can serve two masters. Either he
will hate the one and love the other, or he will
be devoted to the one and despise the other.
You cannot serve both God and Money.

Do Not Worry

‰ See Luke 12:22–31

25"Therefore I tell you, do not worry about
your life, what you will eat or drink; or about
your body, what you will wear. Is not life more
important than food, and the body more important than clothes? 26Look at the birds of the
air; they do not sow or reap or store away in
barns, and yet your heavenly Father feeds them.
Are you not much more valuable than they?
27Who of you by worrying can add a single hour
to his life[b]?
28"And why do you worry about clothes? See
how the lilies of the field grow. They do not
labor or spin. 29Yet I tell you that not even
Solomon in all his splendor was dressed like
one of these. 30If that is how God clothes the
grass of the field, which is here today and tomorrow is thrown into the fire, will he not

[a]13 Or *from evil*; some late manuscripts *one, / for yours is the kingdom and the power and the glory forever. Amen.*
[b]27 Or *single cubit to his height*

6:5–8 Public prayer has been distorted and abused. Some individuals use majestic, religious jargon that often impresses people but doesn't impress God. Others think that the key to receiving an answer to prayer is repetition, using the same words and phrases over and over. Such an attitude reduces prayer to the level of a chant or mantra. Both attitudes assume that prayer has more to do with technique than heart attitudes. True heart-to-heart communication with God, whether private or public, is rewarded and will have a profound effect on our spiritual growth.

6:9–13 Jesus gave his disciples a model prayer to follow. This prayer, however, is more than just a model for our *prayers*; it is also a model for our *lives.* We must acknowledge and praise God's supremacy and desire that his kingdom enter our world. We are to ask for God's will to be accomplished, both in our lives and in our world. Looking to God for our daily provision, we must also ask for forgiveness of our sins while forgiving those who have wronged us. God also wants us to ask for protection from the evil temptations that we face each day. Let us seek to serve God by both praying these things and living them out in our daily lives.

6:12, 14–15 True forgiveness is an essential part of our obedience to God. We often experience difficulty in releasing our anger and bitterness toward those who have mistreated us. Yet asking God to forgive our personal shortcomings and sins is hypocritical unless we are willing to forgive others (see Colossians 3:13). We forfeit forgiveness from God by denying forgiveness to others. Such an attitude is selfish and self-destructive.

6:19–34 Jesus made it clear that living for personal gain only leads to great anxiety. Materialism and anxiety are two enemies to spiritual growth, working together to lead us away from a balanced life. We need to realize that the essence of life is not found in the possession of things or that worry about the future is never helpful. We have little power to change the future, so we must trust God to take care of us. God promises to provide our needs, for he loves us and gives his children good gifts (see Luke 11:13). Therefore, those who learn to trust God have no need to worry about anything.

THE SPIRITUAL DISCIPLINES

Prayer

The Lord's Prayer

Matthew 6:7–15 The few words of the Lord's Prayer span the spectrum of God's purpose and concern for humanity. They sweep from the majesty of God in heaven to the earthly details of daily need. Upholding the highest ideals while recognizing the realistic obstacles of human temptation and failure, the Lord's Prayer searches us, instructs us, inspires us and empowers us.

Jesus gave us the Lord's Prayer not only as a specific text to be recited but also as a model for our own prayers. God is not manipulated by rote exercises or mechanical prayers, but the Lord's Prayer does give us a basic pattern that will deepen and enrich all of our prayers:

"Our Father in heaven . . ." (6:9). Prayer begins with the assurance of our adoption and acceptance as God's children. The Creator loves us and desires to answer the requests of his children.

"Hallowed be your name . . ." (6:9). The third commandment speaks against misusing God's name (see Exodus 20:7). This refers to more than just using his name as an expletive. It includes associating God's name with anything that demeans, devalues or dishonors him. We sometimes do this not only with our lips but also with our lives.

"Your kingdom come, your will be done on earth as it is in heaven" (6:10). This is our highest goal, that for which we should pray and strive. God's agenda must set our agenda.

"Give us today our daily bread" (6:11). Jesus assures us that if God's kingdom is our primary concern, he will provide for our needs from day to day (see 6:33).

"Forgive us our debts, as we also have forgiven our debtors" (6:12). The grace of God shown *to* us must show *through* us to others. If we hold grudges, our hands and hearts are not free to receive God's mercy.

"And lead us not into temptation, but deliver us from the evil one" (6:13). God is the great guardian of our lives. He is more powerful that anything that can come against us. He will not allow us to experience anything beyond our ability to bear it (see 1 Corinthians 10:13).

These few words of the Lord's Prayer provide us with a comprehensive pattern for prayer that can help us thoughtfully bring our requests before God.

Putting It Into Practice

In light of the comments above, reflect on the following questions: What limits have you put on God that weaken your faith and hinder your prayers? How does your way of life honor God's name? What situations are currently dishonoring it? In what ways is God working through you now? How can God's kingdom be advanced through your life? What do you need today? Whom do you need to forgive? What do you need to confess? Where are you vulnerable to temptation?

Rewrite the Lord's Prayer in your own words, using the pattern presented above. Record specific requests in each area so that your prayer is very personal. Do this on a regular basis, and you will be surprised at the variety and richness it brings to your prayer time.

For more on prayer, turn to Matthew 26.

much more clothe you, O you of little faith?
31So do not worry, saying, 'What shall we eat?'
or 'What shall we drink?' or 'What shall we
wear?' 32For the pagans run after all these
things, and your heavenly Father knows that
you need them. 33But seek first his kingdom
and his righteousness, and all these things will
be given to you as well. 34Therefore do not worry about tomorrow, for tomorrow will worry
about itself. Each day has enough trouble of its
own.

Judging Others

‰ See Luke 6:41–42

7 "Do not judge, or you too will be judged.
2For in the same way you judge others, you
will be judged, and with the measure you use,
it will be measured to you.
3"Why do you look at the speck of sawdust
in your brother's eye and pay no attention to
the plank in your own eye? 4How can you say
to your brother, 'Let me take the speck out of
your eye,' when all the time there is a plank in
your own eye? 5You hypocrite, first take the
plank out of your own eye, and then you will
see clearly to remove the speck from your brother's eye.
6"Do not give dogs what is sacred; do not
throw your pearls to pigs. If you do, they may
trample them under their feet, and then turn
and tear you to pieces.

Ask, Seek, Knock

‰ See Luke 11:9–13

7"Ask and it will be given to you; seek and
you will find; knock and the door will be
opened to you. 8For everyone who asks receives;
he who seeks finds; and to him who knocks, the
door will be opened.
9"Which of you, if his son asks for bread, will
give him a stone? 10Or if he asks for a fish, will
give him a snake? 11If you, then, though you are
evil, know how to give good gifts to your children, how much more will your Father in heav-
en give good gifts to those who ask him! 12So in
everything, do to others what you would have
them do to you, for this sums up the Law and
the Prophets.

The Narrow and Wide Gates

13"Enter through the narrow gate. For wide is
the gate and broad is the road that leads to
destruction, and many enter through it. 14But
small is the gate and narrow the road that leads
to life, and only a few find it.

A Tree and Its Fruit

15"Watch out for false prophets. They come
to you in sheep's clothing, but inwardly they are
ferocious wolves. 16By their fruit you will recognize them. Do people pick grapes from thornbushes, or figs from thistles? 17Likewise every
good tree bears good fruit, but a bad tree bears
bad fruit. 18A good tree cannot bear bad fruit,
and a bad tree cannot bear good fruit. 19Every
tree that does not bear good fruit is cut down
and thrown into the fire. 20Thus, by their fruit
you will recognize them.
21"Not everyone who says to me, 'Lord,
Lord,' will enter the kingdom of heaven, but
only he who does the will of my Father who is
in heaven. 22Many will say to me on that day,
'Lord, Lord, did we not prophesy in your name,
and in your name drive out demons and perform many miracles?' 23Then I will tell them
plainly, 'I never knew you. Away from me, you
evildoers!'

The Wise and Foolish Builders

‰ See Luke 6:47–49

24"Therefore everyone who hears these
words of mine and puts them into practice is
like a wise man who built his house on the rock.
25The rain came down, the streams rose, and
the winds blew and beat against that house; yet
it did not fall, because it had its foundation on
the rock. 26But everyone who hears these words
of mine and does not put them into practice is
like a foolish man who built his house on sand.
27The rain came down, the streams rose, and

7:1–5 Jesus warned against judging others. It is often easy to hide from the sin ("plank") in our own lives by pointing out the failure ("speck") in others' lives. This refusal to see the truth destroys the relationships we need for spiritual growth and blinds us to our own sin and its consequences. To be truly helpful to others, we must first recognize the sin in our own lives and deal with that sin. After humbling ourselves in this way, we will be ready to lovingly confront others about the sin in their lives.

7:7–11 Prayer is an opportunity for perseverance. Each of the three commands in this passage is a positive habit we should develop. We can persist in prayer with realistic hope once we fully appreciate the Father who hears our prayers. Some of us may have had abusive parents who offered us metaphorical "stones" and "snakes" instead of providing for our true needs. If so, we must gain a right concept of God as a Father who gives good gifts to his children. When we discover God's loving character, we will be encouraged to ask him for the good gifts that he promises us in his Word.

7:15–20 Our lives should evidence the good fruit of the Holy Spirit: "love, joy, peace, patience, kindness, goodness, faithfulness, gentleness and self-control" (Galatians 5:22–23). When we are enslaved to our sins, however, we are unfruitful. As we honestly reflect on our spiritual lives, we need to examine the fruit of our lives. If we do not evidence the fruit of the Holy Spirit, we need to confess this to God and ask him how to produce such fruit.

7:24–27 There are two kinds of foundations upon which we can build our lives. One foundation is as solid as rock—the foundation of faith in Jesus Christ. The other foundation is like shifting sand—the foundation of human pride and selfish endeavor. Our lives might be outwardly impressive, but if they are built on the wrong foundation difficult circumstances will soon level what we have built. Like a fragile house of cards, our lives will come crashing down. We should build our lives on the solid foundation of faith in Jesus Christ. Then when the inevitable storms of life come, we will not be moved.

Fasting for Whom?

Matthew 6:16 Motives form a significant aspect of spirituality. We need to remind ourselves continually to seek God's praise, not the praise of other people. And spiritual activities can sometimes make us more vulnerable to the lure of spiritual pride.

Jesus warns his followers against using spiritual practices, such as fasting, to gain praise from people. When we try to impress others with our spirituality, we forfeit all hope of pleasing God. Fasting, done properly, frees us from the desires that control us so that we come more fully under God's control. To care what others think when we follow a spiritual discipline such as fasting contradicts the essential purpose of fasting.

At the same time, it may not be practical to keep your fast a total secret, especially in a family setting. Often it is best to explain to your family or close friends that you are fasting for spiritual reasons, so that you do not concern or inconvenience them by your actions. You might choose to sit at the table while the others eat, or you might spend the time alone in prayer. If you are married, tell your spouse in advance about your fasting, so that meals and family plans can be adjusted accordingly.

Putting It Into Practice

Consider regular fasting, such as weekly, monthly or annually. For many, fasting becomes more effective as a regular practice. Their bodies adjust to fasting, so they aren't as distracted by the physical discomforts. Some practice a partial fast weekly for someone else's spiritual welfare. Others commit to a season of fasting when faced with a major decision. Whatever the practice, keep a careful watch on your heart and motives. Don't allow fasting to degenerate into an empty routine devoid of spiritual meaning.

For more on fasting, turn to 1 Corinthians 7.

the winds blew and beat against that house, and
it fell with a great crash."

28When Jesus had finished saying these
things, the crowds were amazed at his teaching,
29because he taught as one who had authority,
and not as their teachers of the law.

The Man With Leprosy

‰ See Mark 1:40–44; Luke 5:12–14

8 When he came down from the mountainside, large crowds followed him. 2A man
with leprosy[a] came and knelt before him and
said, "Lord, if you are willing, you can make me
clean."

3Jesus reached out his hand and touched the
man. "I am willing," he said. "Be clean!" Immediately he was cured[b] of his leprosy. 4Then
Jesus said to him, "See that you don't tell anyone. But go, show yourself to the priest and
offer the gift Moses commanded, as a testimony
to them."

The Faith of the Centurion

‰ See Luke 7:1–10

5When Jesus had entered Capernaum, a centurion came to him, asking for help. 6"Lord," he
said, "my servant lies at home paralyzed and in
terrible suffering."

7Jesus said to him, "I will go and heal him."

8The centurion replied, "Lord, I do not deserve to have you come under my roof. But just
say the word, and my servant will be healed.
9For I myself am a man under authority, with
soldiers under me. I tell this one, 'Go,' and he
goes; and that one, 'Come,' and he comes. I say
to my servant, 'Do this,' and he does it."

10When Jesus heard this, he was astonished
and said to those following him, "I tell you the
truth, I have not found anyone in Israel with
such great faith. 11I say to you that many will
come from the east and the west, and will take
their places at the feast with Abraham, Isaac and
Jacob in the kingdom of heaven. 12But the subjects of the kingdom will be thrown outside,
into the darkness, where there will be weeping
and gnashing of teeth."

13Then Jesus said to the centurion, "Go! It
will be done just as you believed it would." And
his servant was healed at that very hour.

Jesus Heals Many

‰ See Mark 1:29–34; Luke 4:38–41

14When Jesus came into Peter's house, he saw
Peter's mother-in-law lying in bed with a fever.
15He touched her hand and the fever left her,
and she got up and began to wait on him.

16When evening came, many who were
demon-possessed were brought to him, and he
drove out the spirits with a word and healed all
the sick. 17This was to fulfill what was spoken
through the prophet Isaiah:

"He took up our infirmities
and carried our diseases."[c]

The Cost of Following Jesus

‰ See Luke 9:57–60

18When Jesus saw the crowd around him, he
gave orders to cross to the other side of the lake.
19Then a teacher of the law came to him and
said, "Teacher, I will follow you wherever
you go."

20Jesus replied, "Foxes have holes and birds
of the air have nests, but the Son of Man has no
place to lay his head."

21Another disciple said to him, "Lord, first
let me go and bury my father."

22But Jesus told him, "Follow me, and let the
dead bury their own dead."

Jesus Calms the Storm

‰ See Mark 4:36–41; Luke 8:22–25

23Then he got into the boat and his disciples
followed him. 24Without warning, a furious
storm came up on the lake, so that the waves
swept over the boat. But Jesus was sleeping.
25The disciples went and woke him, saying,
"Lord, save us! We're going to drown!"

26He replied, "You of little faith, why are you
so afraid?" Then he got up and rebuked the
winds and the waves, and it was completely
calm.

27The men were amazed and asked, "What
kind of man is this? Even the winds and the
waves obey him!"

[a]2 The Greek word was used for various diseases affecting the skin—not necessarily leprosy. [b]3 Greek *made clean* [c]17 Isaiah 53:4

8:2–4 When Jesus healed the leper, he demonstrated his ability to bring about instant, physical healing in response to faith. Emotional and spiritual healing is often more of a prolonged process rather than an instant healing. Yet both processes of healing have the same starting and ending points. The same Jesus who can effect instant healing is also the one who will bring about our emotional and spiritual healing.

8:5–13 The healing of the Roman centurion's servant can teach all of us a valuable lesson. The centurion understood and humbly admitted his need, believing that Jesus could heal his servant even at a distance. Jesus marveled because such faith was rare, even among God's chosen people. Because of Jesus' interest in this Roman, we see here that Jesus came to bring deliverance to all people, whether Jew or Gentile, man or woman, rich or poor, religious or secular. With God's help we all can have hope, no matter who we are.

8:23–32 In this passage Jesus exhibited power over both the weather and the demonic realm. In both cases the disciples learned lessons about faith in God's incredible power. Since Jesus calmed a mighty storm and rid people of demonic influence, he can certainly calm the storms we encounter and overcome any forces of evil that come against us.

The Healing of Two Demon-possessed Men

‰ See Mark 5:1–17; Luke 8:26–37

28When he arrived at the other side in the
region of the Gadarenes,[a] two demon-
possessed men coming from the tombs met
him. They were so violent that no one could
pass that way. 29"What do you want with us,
Son of God?" they shouted. "Have you come
here to torture us before the appointed time?"
30Some distance from them a large herd of
pigs was feeding. 31The demons begged Jesus,
"If you drive us out, send us into the herd of
pigs."
32He said to them, "Go!" So they came out
and went into the pigs, and the whole herd
rushed down the steep bank into the lake and
died in the water. 33Those tending the pigs ran
off, went into the town and reported all this,
including what had happened to the demon-
possessed men. 34Then the whole town went
out to meet Jesus. And when they saw him, they
pleaded with him to leave their region.

Jesus Heals a Paralytic

‰ See Mark 2:3–12; Luke 5:18–26

9 Jesus stepped into a boat, crossed over and
came to his own town. 2Some men
brought to him a paralytic, lying on a mat.
When Jesus saw their faith, he said to the paralytic, "Take heart, son; your sins are forgiven."
3At this, some of the teachers of the law said
to themselves, "This fellow is blaspheming!"
4Knowing their thoughts, Jesus said, "Why
do you entertain evil thoughts in your hearts?
5Which is easier: to say, 'Your sins are forgiven,'
or to say, 'Get up and walk'? 6But so that you
may know that the Son of Man has authority on
earth to forgive sins . . . ." Then he said to the
paralytic, "Get up, take your mat and go home."
7And the man got up and went home. 8When
the crowd saw this, they were filled with awe;
and they praised God, who had given such authority to men.

The Calling of Matthew

‰ See Mark 2:14–17; Luke 5:27–32

9As Jesus went on from there, he saw a man
named Matthew sitting at the tax collector's
booth. "Follow me," he told him, and Matthew
got up and followed him.
10While Jesus was having dinner at Matthew's house, many tax collectors and "sinners"
came and ate with him and his disciples.
11When the Pharisees saw this, they asked his
disciples, "Why does your teacher eat with tax
collectors and 'sinners'?"
12On hearing this, Jesus said, "It is not the
healthy who need a doctor, but the sick. 13But
go and learn what this means: 'I desire mercy,
not sacrifice.'[b] For I have not come to call the
righteous, but sinners."

Jesus Questioned About Fasting

‰ See Mark 2:18–22; Luke 5:33–39

14Then John's disciples came and asked him,
"How is it that we and the Pharisees fast, but
your disciples do not fast?"
15Jesus answered, "How can the guests of the
bridegroom mourn while he is with them? The
time will come when the bridegroom will be
taken from them; then they will fast.
16"No one sews a patch of unshrunk cloth
on an old garment, for the patch will pull away
from the garment, making the tear worse. 17Nei-
ther do men pour new wine into old wineskins.
If they do, the skins will burst, the wine will run
out and the wineskins will be ruined. No, they
pour new wine into new wineskins, and both
are preserved."

A Dead Girl and a Sick Woman

‰ See Mark 5:22–43; Luke 8:41–56

18While he was saying this, a ruler came and
knelt before him and said, "My daughter has
just died. But come and put your hand on her,
and she will live." 19Jesus got up and went with
him, and so did his disciples.
20Just then a woman who had been subject to
bleeding for twelve years came up behind him
and touched the edge of his cloak. 21She said to
herself, "If I only touch his cloak, I will be
healed."
22Jesus turned and saw her. "Take heart,
daughter," he said, "your faith has healed you."
And the woman was healed from that moment.

[a] 28 Some manuscripts *Gergesenes;* others *Gerasenes*
[b] 13 Hosea 6:6

9:1–7 The Jewish religious leaders thought Jesus' claim to forgive sins was blasphemous. So by doing the impossible—healing the paralytic—Jesus made it clear to his critics that he also had the power to forgive sins. Implicit in his actions was a claim to deity, because only God is able to heal and forgive sins. We should courageously turn to Jesus for help, for as God's own Son, he has the power to offer forgiveness and healing to all who trust in him.

9:9–13 The tax collectors in Judea during the time of Jesus were viewed as traitors working for the oppressive Roman government. They also were hated by the Jews because they used their position to extort money from their own people. Many people were surprised that Jesus would even speak to a tax collector. Yet as sinful as many of the tax collectors were, some admitted their need and responded to Jesus with humility. By contrast, many of the Pharisees clung to their self-righteousness and did not recognize their own desperate need for redemption. It is not our appearance to others that matters. We should concern ourselves with a willingness to be redeemed from the power of sin in our lives.

9:18–33 Jesus restored life to a dead girl and stopped a woman's chronic hemorrhage. He healed two blind men and a demon-possessed man who was unable to speak. No matter what our need or how desperate our situation, we can always bring our needs to Christ and trust him to meet them completely. His unlimited power is sufficient for any situation we could possibly face.

23When Jesus entered the ruler's house and
saw the flute players and the noisy crowd, 24he
said, "Go away. The girl is not dead but asleep."
But they laughed at him. 25After the crowd had
been put outside, he went in and took the girl
by the hand, and she got up. 26News of this
spread through all that region.

Jesus Heals the Blind and Mute

27As Jesus went on from there, two blind
men followed him, calling out, "Have mercy
on us, Son of David!"

28When he had gone indoors, the blind men
came to him, and he asked them, "Do you
believe that I am able to do this?"

"Yes, Lord," they replied.

29Then he touched their eyes and said, "According to your faith will it be done to you";
30and their sight was restored. Jesus warned
them sternly, "See that no one knows about
this." 31But they went out and spread the news
about him all over that region.

32While they were going out, a man who
was demon-possessed and could not talk was
brought to Jesus. 33And when the demon was
driven out, the man who had been mute spoke.
The crowd was amazed and said, "Nothing like
this has ever been seen in Israel."

34But the Pharisees said, "It is by the prince
of demons that he drives out demons."

The Workers Are Few

35Jesus went through all the towns and villages, teaching in their synagogues, preaching
the good news of the kingdom and healing every disease and sickness. 36When he saw the
crowds, he had compassion on them, because
they were harassed and helpless, like sheep
without a shepherd. 37Then he said to his disciples, "The harvest is plentiful but the workers
are few. 38Ask the Lord of the harvest, therefore,
to send out workers into his harvest field."

Jesus Sends Out the Twelve

‰ See Mark 6:8–11; Luke 9:3–5; 10:4–12

10 He called his twelve disciples to him
and gave them authority to drive out
evil[a] spirits and to heal every disease and sickness.

2These are the names of the twelve apostles:
first, Simon (who is called Peter) and his brother Andrew; James son of Zebedee, and his
brother John; 3Philip and Bartholomew; Thomas and Matthew the tax collector; James son of
Alphaeus, and Thaddaeus; 4Simon the Zealot
and Judas Iscariot, who betrayed him.

5These twelve Jesus sent out with the following instructions: "Do not go among the Gentiles or enter any town of the Samaritans. 6Go
rather to the lost sheep of Israel. 7As you go,
preach this message: 'The kingdom of heaven
is near.' 8Heal the sick, raise the dead, cleanse
those who have leprosy,[b] drive out demons.
Freely you have received, freely give. 9Do not
take along any gold or silver or copper in your
belts; 10take no bag for the journey, or extra
tunic, or sandals or a staff; for the worker is
worth his keep.

11"Whatever town or village you enter,
search for some worthy person there and stay at
his house until you leave. 12As you enter the
home, give it your greeting. 13If the home is
deserving, let your peace rest on it; if it is not,
let your peace return to you. 14If anyone will not
welcome you or listen to your words, shake the
dust off your feet when you leave that home or
town. 15I tell you the truth, it will be more bearable for Sodom and Gomorrah on the day of
judgment than for that town. 16I am sending
you out like sheep among wolves. Therefore be
as shrewd as snakes and as innocent as doves.

17"Be on your guard against men; they will
hand you over to the local councils and flog you
in their synagogues. 18On my account you will
be brought before governors and kings as witnesses to them and to the Gentiles. 19But when
they arrest you, do not worry about what to say
or how to say it. At that time you will be given
what to say, 20for it will not be you speaking,
but the Spirit of your Father speaking through
you.

21"Brother will betray brother to death, and
a father his child; children will rebel against
their parents and have them put to death. 22All
men will hate you because of me, but he who
stands firm to the end will be saved. 23When
you are persecuted in one place, flee to another.
I tell you the truth, you will not finish going
through the cities of Israel before the Son of
Man comes.

[a]1 Greek *unclean* [b]8 The Greek word was used for various diseases affecting the skin—not necessarily leprosy.

9:36—10:8 Jesus felt great compassion for those who had no protection or guidance. Jesus also trained his closest disciples to help fill the need. He wanted them to go out and use God's power to spread the Good News of God's kingdom to the Jewish people. Jesus knew they would not reach everyone, but they were supposed to make a difference among the Jews. As we seek to share our experience of renewal with others, we cannot expect to reach everyone with our good news. We can, however, share the message with a few. They can then share it with others. By reaching out to a few, we will start a chain reaction that can touch the lives of many.

10:14–15 Spiritual blindness carries with it eternal ramifications. Those who refuse the offer of redemption in Christ make a huge mistake. Yet while this passage may seem threatening, it is also meant to bring peace to those who serve God. There will always be some who will not welcome our message, but God will take care of those situations. We must simply do what he has called us to do.

10:16–26 Those of us who seek God and have surrendered our lives to him may feel like sheep in the presence of wolves. We must remember, however, that Jesus suffered much at the hands of godless people. Those who are committed to him can expect similar treatment. Yet if we persevere in following God's will for us, we will receive a tremendous reward (see 5:11–12).

24"A student is not above his teacher, nor a
servant above his master. 25It is enough for the
student to be like his teacher, and the servant
like his master. If the head of the house has
been called Beelzebub,[a] how much more the
members of his household!

26"So do not be afraid of them. There is
nothing concealed that will not be disclosed, or
hidden that will not be made known. 27What I
tell you in the dark, speak in the daylight; what
is whispered in your ear, proclaim from the
roofs. 28Do not be afraid of those who kill the
body but cannot kill the soul. Rather, be afraid
of the One who can destroy both soul and body
in hell. 29Are not two sparrows sold for a penny[b]? Yet not one of them will fall to the
ground apart from the will of your Father.
30And even the very hairs of your head are all
numbered. 31So don't be afraid; you are worth
more than many sparrows.

32"Whoever acknowledges me before men, I
will also acknowledge him before my Father in
heaven. 33But whoever disowns me before men,
I will disown him before my Father in heaven.

34"Do not suppose that I have come to bring
peace to the earth. I did not come to bring
peace, but a sword. 35For I have come to turn

" 'a man against his father,
a daughter against her mother,
a daughter-in-law against her
mother-in-law—
36 a man's enemies will be the members of
his own household.'[c]

37"Anyone who loves his father or mother
more than me is not worthy of me; anyone who
loves his son or daughter more than me is not
worthy of me; 38and anyone who does not take
his cross and follow me is not worthy of me.
39Whoever finds his life will lose it, and whoever loses his life for my sake will find it.

40"He who receives you receives me, and he
who receives me receives the one who sent me.
41Anyone who receives a prophet because he is
a prophet will receive a prophet's reward, and
anyone who receives a righteous man because
he is a righteous man will receive a righteous
man's reward. 42And if anyone gives even a cup
of cold water to one of these little ones because
he is my disciple, I tell you the truth, he will
certainly not lose his reward."

Jesus and John the Baptist

‰ See Luke 7:18–35

11 After Jesus had finished instructing his
twelve disciples, he went on from there
to teach and preach in the towns of Galilee.[d]

2When John heard in prison what Christ was
doing, he sent his disciples 3to ask him, "Are
you the one who was to come, or should we
expect someone else?"

4Jesus replied, "Go back and report to John
what you hear and see: 5The blind receive sight,
the lame walk, those who have leprosy[e] are
cured, the deaf hear, the dead are raised, and the
good news is preached to the poor. 6Blessed is
the man who does not fall away on account
of me."

7As John's disciples were leaving, Jesus began
to speak to the crowd about John: "What did
you go out into the desert to see? A reed swayed
by the wind? 8If not, what did you go out to see?
A man dressed in fine clothes? No, those who
wear fine clothes are in kings' palaces. 9Then
what did you go out to see? A prophet? Yes, I tell
you, and more than a prophet. 10This is the one
about whom it is written:

" 'I will send my messenger ahead of you,
who will prepare your way before you.'[f]

11I tell you the truth: Among those born of
women there has not risen anyone greater than
John the Baptist; yet he who is least in the kingdom of heaven is greater than he. 12From the
days of John the Baptist until now, the kingdom
of heaven has been forcefully advancing, and
forceful men lay hold of it. 13For all the Prophets and the Law prophesied until John. 14And
if you are willing to accept it, he is the Elijah
who was to come. 15He who has ears, let him
hear.

16"To what can I compare this generation?
They are like children sitting in the marketplaces and calling out to others:

[a]25 Greek *Beezeboul* or *Beelzeboul* [b]29 Greek *an assarion* [c]36 Micah 7:6 [d]1 Greek *in their towns* [e]5 The Greek word was used for various diseases affecting the skin—not necessarily leprosy. [f]10 Mal. 3:1

10:39 The only way to find true fulfillment in our lives is to submit ourselves to God through Jesus Christ. By living for ourselves, we become slaves to ourselves and to sin, for we are sinful people by nature. By yielding our lives to Jesus, we allow him to cleanse us of the sins that enslave us and show us the way to real life—a life free from the grip of sin.

11:2–6 Doubt is a troubling reality. We may even doubt ourselves and others. John the Baptist had his doubts too. He even doubted that Jesus was the promised Messiah, the one who would come to offer physical and spiritual redemption to his people. Jesus reassured John by pointing to the good things that had been accomplished—the miraculous healings and the spread of the Good News. In the same way, looking around and seeing what Jesus has done and is doing in the lives of his followers can quiet our doubts too.

11:16–19 The religious leaders of Jesus' day wanted God to fit their expectations. They were not willing to repent because of the message of John the Baptist or Jesus. To avoid having to obey God's message, the religious leaders found excuses for rejecting God's messenger and God's Son. Anytime we find ourselves making excuses for not accepting God's message we must beware. God's Word cannot be adapted to fit our view of life. We should never reject God's Word just because it does not agree with our lifestyle or expectations. When our lives do not agree with God's Word, we should ask God to help us see the truth and help us change.

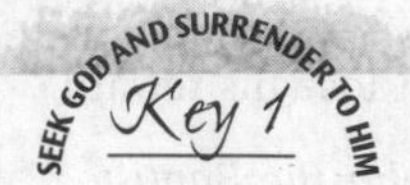

Rest for the Weary Soul

Matthew 11:27–30 Many roads promise to lead us to spiritual renewal and transformation, but not all roads lead in the right direction. Some of us have grown weary of traveling down one such road after another. We have exhausted ourselves seeking spiritual refreshment. Some of us have worked hard at building a good life, but instead of finding joy in the journey, we feel weighted down by life. We need rest for our souls.

Proverbs 14:12 tells us, "There is a way that seems right to a man, but in the end it leads to death." The mere fact that a direction seems right doesn't always mean that path is leading toward true spiritual renewal; it could be leading to a dead end. Those of us who have taken many wrong paths find ourselves weary and need to come to Jesus. He said, "Come to me, all you who are weary and burdened, and I will give you rest. Take my yoke upon you and learn from me, for I am gentle and humble in heart, and you will find rest for your souls. For my yoke is easy and my burden is light" (11:28–30).

Any spiritual path that does not lead us to Jesus Christ will not lead us to true spiritual renewal either—no matter how right it seems at first. Jesus Christ himself is our way (see John 14:6). The burden he calls us to bear on our journey is light; the yoke of his expectations fits us perfectly. Following Christ's way, we are promised rest for our souls. Then we can experience true spiritual renewal.

Turn to Acts 9.

17" 'We played the flute for you,
and you did not dance;
we sang a dirge,
and you did not mourn.'

18For John came neither eating nor drinking,
and they say, 'He has a demon.' 19The Son of
Man came eating and drinking, and they say,
'Here is a glutton and a drunkard, a friend of tax
collectors and "sinners." ' But wisdom is proved
right by her actions."

Woe on Unrepentant Cities

‰ See Luke 10:13–15

20Then Jesus began to denounce the cities
in which most of his miracles had been performed, because they did not repent. 21"Woe to
you, Korazin! Woe to you, Bethsaida! If the
miracles that were performed in you had been
performed in Tyre and Sidon, they would have
repented long ago in sackcloth and ashes. 22But
I tell you, it will be more bearable for Tyre and
Sidon on the day of judgment than for you.
23And you, Capernaum, will you be lifted up
to the skies? No, you will go down to the
depths.[a] If the miracles that were performed in
you had been performed in Sodom, it would
have remained to this day. 24But I tell you that
it will be more bearable for Sodom on the day
of judgment than for you."

Rest for the Weary

‰ See Luke 10:21–22

25At that time Jesus said, "I praise you, Father, Lord of heaven and earth, because you
have hidden these things from the wise and
learned, and revealed them to little children.
26Yes, Father, for this was your good pleasure.
27"All things have been committed to me by
my Father. No one knows the Son except the
Father, and no one knows the Father except the
Son and those to whom the Son chooses to
reveal him.
28"Come to me, all you who are weary and
burdened, and I will give you rest. 29Take my
yoke upon you and learn from me, for I am
gentle and humble in heart, and you will find
rest for your souls. 30For my yoke is easy and my
burden is light."

[a]23 Greek *Hades*

11:25–30 Only when we come to Jesus as little children can we find redemption and relief. Many of us think we can work things out our own way. In doing this, however, we miss the simple truth that God alone has the power to redeem us. Children are very aware of the fact that they do not have power over their own lives. As a result, they entrust themselves to parents, teachers or other authority figures each and every day. When we acknowledge our powerlessness over the sins that entangle us, we can surrender ourselves to God's loving care. He has all the power we need—power to redeem us and to help us break free from sinful habits.

Lord of the Sabbath

‰ See Mark 2:23—3:6; Luke 6:1–11

12 At that time Jesus went through the
grainfields on the Sabbath. His disciples were hungry and began to pick some heads
of grain and eat them. 2When the Pharisees saw
this, they said to him, "Look! Your disciples are
doing what is unlawful on the Sabbath."
3He answered, "Haven't you read what David did when he and his companions were hungry? 4He entered the house of God, and he and
his companions ate the consecrated bread—
which was not lawful for them to do, but only
for the priests. 5Or haven't you read in the Law
that on the Sabbath the priests in the temple
desecrate the day and yet are innocent? 6I tell
you that one[a] greater than the temple is here.
7If you had known what these words mean, 'I
desire mercy, not sacrifice,'[b] you would not
have condemned the innocent. 8For the Son of
Man is Lord of the Sabbath."
9Going on from that place, he went into their
synagogue, 10and a man with a shriveled hand
was there. Looking for a reason to accuse Jesus,
they asked him, "Is it lawful to heal on the
Sabbath?"
11He said to them, "If any of you has a sheep
and it falls into a pit on the Sabbath, will you
not take hold of it and lift it out? 12How much
more valuable is a man than a sheep! Therefore
it is lawful to do good on the Sabbath."
13Then he said to the man, "Stretch out your
hand." So he stretched it out and it was completely restored, just as sound as the other. 14But
the Pharisees went out and plotted how they
might kill Jesus.

God's Chosen Servant

15Aware of this, Jesus withdrew from that
place. Many followed him, and he healed all
their sick, 16warning them not to tell who he
was. 17This was to fulfill what was spoken
through the prophet Isaiah:

18"Here is my servant whom I have chosen,
the one I love, in whom I delight;
I will put my Spirit on him,
and he will proclaim justice to the
nations.
19He will not quarrel or cry out;
no one will hear his voice in the streets.
20A bruised reed he will not break,
and a smoldering wick he will not snuff
out,
till he leads justice to victory.
21 In his name the nations will put their
hope."[c]

Jesus and Beelzebub

‰ See Mark 3:23–27; Luke 11:17–22

22Then they brought him a demon-
possessed man who was blind and mute, and
Jesus healed him, so that he could both talk and
see. 23All the people were astonished and said,
"Could this be the Son of David?"
24But when the Pharisees heard this, they
said, "It is only by Beelzebub,[d] the prince of
demons, that this fellow drives out demons."
25Jesus knew their thoughts and said to
them, "Every kingdom divided against itself
will be ruined, and every city or household divided against itself will not stand. 26If Satan
drives out Satan, he is divided against himself.
How then can his kingdom stand? 27And if I
drive out demons by Beelzebub, by whom do
your people drive them out? So then, they will
be your judges. 28But if I drive out demons by
the Spirit of God, then the kingdom of God has
come upon you.
29"Or again, how can anyone enter a strong
man's house and carry off his possessions unless he first ties up the strong man? Then he can
rob his house.
30"He who is not with me is against me, and

[a]6 Or *something;* also in verses 41 and 42
[b]7 Hosea 6:6 [c]21 Isaiah 42:1-4 [d]24 Greek *Beezeboul* or *Beelzeboul*; also in verse 27

12:1–8 God's standards are intended for our good; his standards mercifully meet the needs of his people. But God's laws can be abused through legalism. By seeking to follow God's laws to the letter we can easily violate the very reasons that God gave his laws in the first place. God provided the Sabbath as a reminder of the covenant he had made with his people. The Pharisees were so caught up in the Sabbath rules and regulations that they forgot its intended purpose. They employed God's Word for restrictive and enslaving purposes rather than for spiritual freedom and health. People do the same thing today. Yet God wants to be merciful, offering us hope instead of condemnation. If God had intended to crush us with legalism, he would never have sent Jesus to die for us. He would have let us die in our sins.

12:9–12 People who refuse to admit their own need for God sometimes stand in the way of another's spiritual renewal. Instead of praising God for the miracle that Jesus had performed, the Pharisees judged Jesus for breaking the Sabbath laws. To the Pharisees, the preservation of their legalistic observances was more important than the healing of a deformed man. The Pharisees measured everything by their interpretations of the law, and they rejected the compassionate Jesus. People may also oppose our pursuit of spiritual renewal, hoping instead to keep us enslaved to sin. We should follow God's will for our lives regardless of the pressures from people around us. No obstacles are too great to overcome with God's help.

12:17–21 Centuries earlier the prophet Isaiah had described the Messiah (see Isaiah 42:1–4). Matthew recognized that Jesus fulfilled Isaiah's prophecy. This passage offers a powerful message of hope. Jesus is the Messiah. He is both our servant and our leader. He is strong enough to judge the nations yet tender enough to care for the weak and helpless. Jesus is the world's only hope for salvation.

12:22–32 Only God through Jesus Christ can offer us salvation and transformation. There is no other source. Tragically, many who need salvation or spiritual growth do not trust Jesus Christ and look to him for their transformation. God's way of salvation comes only through Jesus Christ. It is through him that we can be saved, empowered and restored.

he who does not gather with me scatters. 31And so I tell you, every sin and blasphemy will be forgiven men, but the blasphemy against the Spirit will not be forgiven. 32Anyone who speaks a word against the Son of Man will be forgiven, but anyone who speaks against the Holy Spirit will not be forgiven, either in this age or in the age to come.

33"Make a tree good and its fruit will be good, or make a tree bad and its fruit will be bad, for a tree is recognized by its fruit. 34You brood of vipers, how can you who are evil say anything good? For out of the overflow of the heart the mouth speaks. 35The good man brings good things out of the good stored up in him, and the evil man brings evil things out of the evil stored up in him. 36But I tell you that men will have to give account on the day of judgment for every careless word they have spoken. 37For by your words you will be acquitted, and by your words you will be condemned."

The Sign of Jonah

‰ See Luke 11:29–32

38Then some of the Pharisees and teachers of the law said to him, "Teacher, we want to see a miraculous sign from you."

39He answered, "A wicked and adulterous generation asks for a miraculous sign! But none will be given it except the sign of the prophet Jonah. 40For as Jonah was three days and three nights in the belly of a huge fish, so the Son of Man will be three days and three nights in the heart of the earth. 41The men of Nineveh will stand up at the judgment with this generation and condemn it; for they repented at the preaching of Jonah, and now one[a] greater than Jonah is here. 42The Queen of the South will rise at the judgment with this generation and condemn it; for she came from the ends of the earth to listen to Solomon's wisdom, and now one greater than Solomon is here.

43"When an evil[b] spirit comes out of a man, it goes through arid places seeking rest and does not find it. 44Then it says, 'I will return to the house I left.' When it arrives, it finds the house unoccupied, swept clean and put in order. 45Then it goes and takes with it seven other spirits more wicked than itself, and they go in and live there. And the final condition of that man is worse than the first. That is how it will be with this wicked generation."

Jesus' Mother and Brothers

‰ See Mark 3:31–35; Luke 8:19–21

46While Jesus was still talking to the crowd, his mother and brothers stood outside, wanting to speak to him. 47Someone told him, "Your mother and brothers are standing outside, wanting to speak to you."[c]

48He replied to him, "Who is my mother, and who are my brothers?" 49Pointing to his disciples, he said, "Here are my mother and my brothers. 50For whoever does the will of my Father in heaven is my brother and sister and mother."

The Parable of the Sower

‰ See Mark 4:1–20; Luke 8:4–15

13 That same day Jesus went out of the house and sat by the lake. 2Such large crowds gathered around him that he got into a boat and sat in it, while all the people stood on the shore. 3Then he told them many things in parables, saying: "A farmer went out to sow his seed. 4As he was scattering the seed, some fell along the path, and the birds came and ate it up. 5Some fell on rocky places, where it did not have much soil. It sprang up quickly, because the soil was shallow. 6But when the sun came up, the plants were scorched, and they withered because they had no root. 7Other seed fell among thorns, which grew up and choked the plants. 8Still other seed fell on good soil, where it produced a crop—a hundred, sixty or thirty times what was sown. 9He who has ears, let him hear."

10The disciples came to him and asked, "Why do you speak to the people in parables?"

11He replied, "The knowledge of the secrets of the kingdom of heaven has been given to you, but not to them. 12Whoever has will be given more, and he will have an abundance. Whoever does not have, even what he has will be taken from him. 13This is why I speak to them in parables:

"Though seeing, they do not see;
  though hearing, they do not hear or
    understand.

14In them is fulfilled the prophecy of Isaiah:

[a]41 Or *something;* also in verse 42 [b]43 Greek *unclean*
[c]47 Some manuscripts do not have verse 47.

12:43–45 Spiritual forces can invade and overtake our lives in dangerous ways. Ridding ourselves of evil without allowing the Holy Spirit to fill our emptiness will only leave us worse off than before. Removing the affliction and evil is only half the battle. We must fill the void in our lives with God's Spirit, God's truth and godly attitudes and actions. God wants our hearts to be devoted to him and filled with his Holy Spirit.

13:2–8, 18–23 Our receptivity to the gospel will determine how fruitful our lives will be. Some of us seeking spiritual renewal do so wholeheartedly. Some only seek halfheartedly or temporarily, and some pass up the opportunity all together, denying they even need it. If we hope to bear spiritual fruit, we must let God plow up the soil of our hearts and make it ready to receive his Word.

13:10–17 Jesus understood our limited ability to see the truth. His stories and illustrations were designed to help us understand his message. When we respond in faith to what we already know, we will be given more insight to make further spiritual progress. But if we do not respond properly, we will become spiritually blind and unable to see the truth. We must ask God to give us eyes to see his will and hearts that are willing to obey it.

"'You will be ever hearing but never
understanding;
you will be ever seeing but never
perceiving.
15 For this people's heart has become
calloused;
they hardly hear with their ears,
and they have closed their eyes.
Otherwise they might see with their eyes,
hear with their ears,
understand with their hearts
and turn, and I would heal them.'[a]

16 But blessed are your eyes because they see,
and your ears because they hear. 17 For I tell you
the truth, many prophets and righteous men
longed to see what you see but did not see it,
and to hear what you hear but did not hear it.

18 "Listen then to what the parable of the
sower means: 19 When anyone hears the message about the kingdom and does not understand it, the evil one comes and snatches away
what was sown in his heart. This is the seed
sown along the path. 20 The one who received
the seed that fell on rocky places is the man who
hears the word and at once receives it with joy.
21 But since he has no root, he lasts only a short
time. When trouble or persecution comes because of the word, he quickly falls away. 22 The
one who received the seed that fell among the
thorns is the man who hears the word, but the
worries of this life and the deceitfulness of
wealth choke it, making it unfruitful. 23 But the
one who received the seed that fell on good soil
is the man who hears the word and understands
it. He produces a crop, yielding a hundred, sixty
or thirty times what was sown."

The Parable of the Weeds

24 Jesus told them another parable: "The
kingdom of heaven is like a man who sowed
good seed in his field. 25 But while everyone was
sleeping, his enemy came and sowed weeds
among the wheat, and went away. 26 When the
wheat sprouted and formed heads, then the
weeds also appeared.

27 "The owner's servants came to him and
said, 'Sir, didn't you sow good seed in your
field? Where then did the weeds come from?'

28 " 'An enemy did this,' he replied.

"The servants asked him, 'Do you want us to
go and pull them up?'

29 " 'No,' he answered, 'because while you
are pulling the weeds, you may root up the
wheat with them. 30 Let both grow together until
the harvest. At that time I will tell the harvesters:
First collect the weeds and tie them in bundles
to be burned; then gather the wheat and bring
it into my barn.' "

The Parables of the Mustard Seed and the Yeast

‰ See Mark 4:30–32; Luke 13:18–21

31 He told them another parable: "The kingdom of heaven is like a mustard seed, which a
man took and planted in his field. 32 Though it
is the smallest of all your seeds, yet when it
grows, it is the largest of garden plants and becomes a tree, so that the birds of the air come
and perch in its branches."

33 He told them still another parable: "The
kingdom of heaven is like yeast that a woman
took and mixed into a large amount[b] of flour
until it worked all through the dough."

34 Jesus spoke all these things to the crowd in
parables; he did not say anything to them without using a parable. 35 So was fulfilled what was
spoken through the prophet:

"I will open my mouth in parables,
I will utter things hidden since the
creation of the world."[c]

The Parable of the Weeds Explained

36 Then he left the crowd and went into the
house. His disciples came to him and said, "Explain to us the parable of the weeds in the field."

37 He answered, "The one who sowed the
good seed is the Son of Man. 38 The field is the
world, and the good seed stands for the sons of
the kingdom. The weeds are the sons of the evil
one, 39 and the enemy who sows them is the
devil. The harvest is the end of the age, and the
harvesters are angels.

40 "As the weeds are pulled up and burned in
the fire, so it will be at the end of the age. 41 The
Son of Man will send out his angels, and they
will weed out of his kingdom everything that
causes sin and all who do evil. 42 They will
throw them into the fiery furnace, where there
will be weeping and gnashing of teeth. 43 Then
the righteous will shine like the sun in the kingdom of their Father. He who has ears, let him
hear.

The Parables of the Hidden Treasure and the Pearl

44 "The kingdom of heaven is like treasure
hidden in a field. When a man found it, he hid
it again, and then in his joy went and sold all
he had and bought that field.

45 "Again, the kingdom of heaven is like a
merchant looking for fine pearls. 46 When he
found one of great value, he went away and
sold everything he had and bought it.

[a] 15 Isaiah 6:9,10 [b] 33 Greek *three satas* (probably about 1/2 bushel or 22 liters) [c] 35 Psalm 78:2

13:24–30, 36–43 The story about the wheat and the weeds applies to those who claim to seek God. Ultimately, there are two kinds of people in the world. Some submit to God's will and experience the restoration he offers in Jesus Christ. Others, whether they realize it or not, submit themselves to the control of Satan. This stark but realistic contrast shows us that if we do not follow Christ, we have chosen by default to follow Satan.

The Parable of the Net

47"Once again, the kingdom of heaven is like a net that was let down into the lake and caught all kinds of fish. 48When it was full, the fishermen pulled it up on the shore. Then they sat down and collected the good fish in baskets, but threw the bad away. 49This is how it will be at the end of the age. The angels will come and separate the wicked from the righteous 50and throw them into the fiery furnace, where there will be weeping and gnashing of teeth.

51"Have you understood all these things?" Jesus asked.

"Yes," they replied.

52He said to them, "Therefore every teacher of the law who has been instructed about the kingdom of heaven is like the owner of a house who brings out of his storeroom new treasures as well as old."

A Prophet Without Honor

‰ See Mark 6:1–6

53When Jesus had finished these parables, he moved on from there. 54Coming to his hometown, he began teaching the people in their synagogue, and they were amazed. "Where did this man get this wisdom and these miraculous powers?" they asked. 55"Isn't this the carpenter's son? Isn't his mother's name Mary, and aren't his brothers James, Joseph, Simon and Judas? 56Aren't all his sisters with us? Where then did this man get all these things?" 57And they took offense at him.

But Jesus said to them, "Only in his hometown and in his own house is a prophet without honor."

58And he did not do many miracles there because of their lack of faith.

John the Baptist Beheaded

‰ See Mark 6:14–29

14 At that time Herod the tetrarch heard the reports about Jesus, 2and he said to his attendants, "This is John the Baptist; he has risen from the dead! That is why miraculous powers are at work in him."

3Now Herod had arrested John and bound him and put him in prison because of Herodias, his brother Philip's wife, 4for John had been saying to him: "It is not lawful for you to have her." 5Herod wanted to kill John, but he was afraid of the people, because they considered him a prophet.

6On Herod's birthday the daughter of Herodias danced for them and pleased Herod so much 7that he promised with an oath to give her whatever she asked. 8Prompted by her mother, she said, "Give me here on a platter the head of John the Baptist." 9The king was distressed, but because of his oaths and his dinner guests, he ordered that her request be granted 10and had John beheaded in the prison. 11His head was brought in on a platter and given to the girl, who carried it to her mother. 12John's disciples came and took his body and buried it. Then they went and told Jesus.

Jesus Feeds the Five Thousand

‰ See Mark 6:32–44; Luke 9:10–17; John 6:1–13

13When Jesus heard what had happened, he withdrew by boat privately to a solitary place. Hearing of this, the crowds followed him on foot from the towns. 14When Jesus landed and saw a large crowd, he had compassion on them and healed their sick.

15As evening approached, the disciples came to him and said, "This is a remote place, and it's already getting late. Send the crowds away, so they can go to the villages and buy themselves some food."

16Jesus replied, "They do not need to go away. You give them something to eat."

17"We have here only five loaves of bread and two fish," they answered.

18"Bring them here to me," he said. 19And he directed the people to sit down on the grass. Taking the five loaves and the two fish and looking up to heaven, he gave thanks and broke the loaves. Then he gave them to the disciples, and the disciples gave them to the people. 20They all ate and were satisfied, and the disciples picked up twelve basketfuls of broken pieces that were left over. 21The number of those who ate was about five thousand men, besides women and children.

13:53–58 Sometimes people will ignore or discount God's work in and through our lives, commenting that we are still the same people we have always been. They refuse to acknowledge the changes in our lives because they fail to see God's grace at work in our lives. When we share what God has done in our lives with those who are familiar with our sinful past, it may take some time to convince them of our sincerity and prove to them the validity of our claims.

14:1–11 John the Baptist had been arrested because he had condemned Herod Antipas for marrying his brother's wife, Herodias. Rather than admit his sin, Herod placed John in prison, hoping to silence him. Herodias wanted John silenced too. She viciously demanded John's execution. Herod was too weak to refuse his wife's request, and the prophet was beheaded. Our shame from one sin often leads us to commit greater sins. To avoid this downward spiral, we must courageously admit our sins before we build upon them. As we turn from our sins and repent to God, we can be confident that we will receive his healing help and forgiveness.

14:15–21 Jesus fed large groups of hungry people on more than one occasion, illustrating his ability to work miracles as well as his concern with our pressing human needs (see 15:32–39). Since Jesus is committed to meeting our most basic, physical needs, imagine how much more he is committed to meeting our spiritual needs! Note that in this passage Jesus did not do everything himself; he used his disciples to help meet the people's needs. Jesus may choose to meet our needs through others too. God may well be working through concerned friends or others who, like us, are hurting. And as we encourage others, we can be thankful that God has chosen to use us.

Jesus Walks on the Water

‰ See Mark 6:45–51; John 6:15–21

22Immediately Jesus made the disciples get
into the boat and go on ahead of him to the
other side, while he dismissed the crowd. 23After
he had dismissed them, he went up on a
mountainside by himself to pray. When evening
came, he was there alone, 24but the boat
was already a considerable distance[a] from
land, buffeted by the waves because the wind
was against it.
25During the fourth watch of the night Jesus
went out to them, walking on the lake. 26When
the disciples saw him walking on the lake, they
were terrified. "It's a ghost," they said, and cried
out in fear.
27But Jesus immediately said to them: "Take
courage! It is I. Don't be afraid."
28"Lord, if it's you," Peter replied, "tell me to
come to you on the water."
29"Come," he said.
Then Peter got down out of the boat, walked
on the water and came toward Jesus. 30But
when he saw the wind, he was afraid and, beginning
to sink, cried out, "Lord, save me!"
31Immediately Jesus reached out his hand
and caught him. "You of little faith," he said,
"why did you doubt?"
32And when they climbed into the boat, the
wind died down. 33Then those who were in the
boat worshiped him, saying, "Truly you are
the Son of God."
34When they had crossed over, they landed at
Gennesaret. 35And when the men of that place
recognized Jesus, they sent word to all the surrounding
country. People brought all their sick
to him 36and begged him to let the sick just
touch the edge of his cloak, and all who
touched him were healed.

Clean and Unclean

‰ See Mark 7:1–23

15 Then some Pharisees and teachers of
the law came to Jesus from Jerusalem

[a]24 Greek *many stadia*

14:22–24 We must find time alone to focus on our tasks and pray if we want to preserve our spiritual gains. Though we may feel we are wasting time, recharging our batteries physically, emotionally and spiritually through solitude and rest is essential. If we don't allow ourselves time to pray and rest, we will experience burnout. Jesus took time out to pray and recharge; we should never feel guilty for doing the same.

14:25–33 Jesus walked on water and then empowered Peter, through faith, to do the same. Life will always have occasional storms. However, when we trust God, we can receive God's power to make it through the storm just like Peter did. As long as we trust and keep our eyes on Jesus, we will not be overcome by the storms of life. But when we focus on the troubled waters around us and forget God's assistance, we will start to sink. To make continued progress, we need to keep our eyes on God.

15:1–20 There are those who assume a self-righteous posture because they fulfill all the proper "religious" obli-

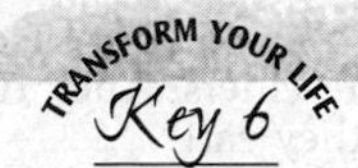

Courage to Take a Step

Matthew 14:23–33 Transforming our lives means stepping out in faith, believing that God is able to turn even the watery depths of the ocean into a pathway toward himself and his plan for us. We may have taken other "safe" paths in the past and found that these didn't take us where we truly longed to go spiritually, but their familiarity made us feel comfortable. But now, with our eyes fixed on Jesus, we will have to face our fear of the unknown and get beyond it.

If we wait for all our fear to go away before we begin to transform our lives, we will never make significant spiritual progress. Courage isn't the absence of fear. Courage means that we take advantage of the little strength we find within us, that we find little ways to encourage ourselves, and that we stubbornly follow God's direction. It means that we find enough strength to take a step in the right direction.

In the account where Jesus walked on the water, the disciples were terrified when they saw him (14:28–31). "'Lord, if it's you,' Peter replied, 'tell me to come to you on the water'" (14:28). Jesus told him to come, so Peter went over the side of the boat and walked on the water toward Jesus. Peter became terrified and began to sink, but Jesus reached out his hand and lifted him up.

Peter gathered up enough courage to take one step in the Lord's direction when the Lord called to him. He ventured out into a new experience. When he got in over his head, Peter called out and found the help he needed. We, too, need only to summon the courage to take a step in the right direction whether or not we feel afraid or need help. With God's help we will make it when we step out in faith.

Turn to Acts 8.

and asked, 2"Why do your disciples break the tradition of the elders? They don't wash their hands before they eat!"

3Jesus replied, "And why do you break the command of God for the sake of your tradition? 4For God said, 'Honor your father and mother'[a] and 'Anyone who curses his father or mother must be put to death.'[b] 5But you say that if a man says to his father or mother, 'Whatever help you might otherwise have received from me is a gift devoted to God,' 6he is not to 'honor his father[c]' with it. Thus you nullify the word of God for the sake of your tradition. 7You hypocrites! Isaiah was right when he prophesied about you:

8" 'These people honor me with their lips,
but their hearts are far from me.
9They worship me in vain;
their teachings are but rules taught by men.'[d]"

10Jesus called the crowd to him and said, "Listen and understand. 11What goes into a man's mouth does not make him 'unclean,' but what comes out of his mouth, that is what makes him 'unclean.' "

12Then the disciples came to him and asked, "Do you know that the Pharisees were offended when they heard this?"

13He replied, "Every plant that my heavenly Father has not planted will be pulled up by the roots. 14Leave them; they are blind guides.[e] If a blind man leads a blind man, both will fall into a pit."

15Peter said, "Explain the parable to us."

16"Are you still so dull?" Jesus asked them. 17"Don't you see that whatever enters the mouth goes into the stomach and then out of the body? 18But the things that come out of the mouth come from the heart, and these make a man 'unclean.' 19For out of the heart come evil thoughts, murder, adultery, sexual immorality, theft, false testimony, slander. 20These are what make a man 'unclean'; but eating with unwashed hands does not make him 'unclean.' "

The Faith of the Canaanite Woman

See Mark 7:24–30

21Leaving that place, Jesus withdrew to the region of Tyre and Sidon. 22A Canaanite woman from that vicinity came to him, crying out, "Lord, Son of David, have mercy on me! My daughter is suffering terribly from demon-possession."

23Jesus did not answer a word. So his disciples came to him and urged him, "Send her away, for she keeps crying out after us."

24He answered, "I was sent only to the lost sheep of Israel."

25The woman came and knelt before him. "Lord, help me!" she said.

26He replied, "It is not right to take the children's bread and toss it to their dogs."

27"Yes, Lord," she said, "but even the dogs eat the crumbs that fall from their masters' table."

28Then Jesus answered, "Woman, you have great faith! Your request is granted." And her daughter was healed from that very hour.

Jesus Feeds the Four Thousand

See Mark 8:1–10

29Jesus left there and went along the Sea of Galilee. Then he went up on a mountainside and sat down. 30Great crowds came to him, bringing the lame, the blind, the crippled, the mute and many others, and laid them at his feet; and he healed them. 31The people were amazed when they saw the mute speaking, the crippled made well, the lame walking and the blind seeing. And they praised the God of Israel.

32Jesus called his disciples to him and said, "I have compassion for these people; they have already been with me three days and have nothing to eat. I do not want to send them away hungry, or they may collapse on the way."

33His disciples answered, "Where could we get enough bread in this remote place to feed such a crowd?"

34"How many loaves do you have?" Jesus asked.

"Seven," they replied, "and a few small fish."

35He told the crowd to sit down on the ground. 36Then he took the seven loaves and the fish, and when he had given thanks, he broke them and gave them to the disciples, and they in turn to the people. 37They all ate and were satisfied. Afterward the disciples picked up seven basketfuls of broken pieces that were left over. 38The number of those who ate was four thousand, besides women and children. 39After Jesus had sent the crowd away, he got into the boat and went to the vicinity of Magadan.

[a] 4 Exodus 20:12; Deut. 5:16 [b] 4 Exodus 21:17; Lev. 20:9 [c] 6 Some manuscripts *father or his mother* [d] 9 Isaiah 29:13 [e] 14 Some manuscripts *guides of the blind*

gations, while others do not appear to be model believers. However, Jesus says that those who go through all the right motions may not necessarily be righteous on the inside. If we do all the right things but have proud and selfish hearts, God will judge us. But if we have repented of our sin and received forgiveness in Christ, he is pleased with us no matter what others may say.

15:32–38 The feeding of the four thousand is both similar to and different from the feeding of the five thousand (see 14:15–21). In both cases Jesus pitied those in need, took a small amount of food and fed a large number of people, then used the disciples to distribute the resources and collect the leftovers. Since the location and number of people fed were different, Jesus tailored his resources to meet each specific situation. God will show similar concern for us and lend his unlimited resources to provide for us in times of need.

The Demand for a Sign

‰ See Mark 8:11–21

16 The Pharisees and Sadducees came to
Jesus and tested him by asking him to
show them a sign from heaven.
2He replied,[a] "When evening comes, you
say, 'It will be fair weather, for the sky is red,'
3and in the morning, 'Today it will be stormy,
for the sky is red and overcast.' You know how
to interpret the appearance of the sky, but you
cannot interpret the signs of the times. 4A wicked and adulterous generation looks for a miraculous sign, but none will be given it except the
sign of Jonah." Jesus then left them and went
away.

The Yeast of the Pharisees and Sadducees

5When they went across the lake, the disciples forgot to take bread. 6"Be careful," Jesus
said to them. "Be on your guard against the
yeast of the Pharisees and Sadducees."
7They discussed this among themselves and
said, "It is because we didn't bring any bread."
8Aware of their discussion, Jesus asked, "You
of little faith, why are you talking among yourselves about having no bread? 9Do you still not
understand? Don't you remember the five
loaves for the five thousand, and how many
basketfuls you gathered? 10Or the seven loaves
for the four thousand, and how many basketfuls you gathered? 11How is it you don't understand that I was not talking to you about bread?
But be on your guard against the yeast of the
Pharisees and Sadducees." 12Then they understood that he was not telling them to guard
against the yeast used in bread, but against the
teaching of the Pharisees and Sadducees.

Peter's Confession of Christ

‰ See Mark 8:27–29; Luke 9:18–20

13When Jesus came to the region of Caesarea
Philippi, he asked his disciples, "Who do people say the Son of Man is?"
14They replied, "Some say John the Baptist;
others say Elijah; and still others, Jeremiah or
one of the prophets."
15"But what about you?" he asked. "Who do
you say I am?"
16Simon Peter answered, "You are the
Christ,[b] the Son of the living God."
17Jesus replied, "Blessed are you, Simon son
of Jonah, for this was not revealed to you by
man, but by my Father in heaven. 18And I tell
you that you are Peter,[c] and on this rock I will
build my church, and the gates of Hades[d] will
not overcome it.[e] 19I will give you the keys of
the kingdom of heaven; whatever you bind on
earth will be[f] bound in heaven, and whatever
you loose on earth will be[f] loosed in heaven."
20Then he warned his disciples not to tell anyone that he was the Christ.

Jesus Predicts His Death

‰ See Mark 8:31—9:1; Luke 9:22–27

21From that time on Jesus began to explain to
his disciples that he must go to Jerusalem and
suffer many things at the hands of the elders,
chief priests and teachers of the law, and that he
must be killed and on the third day be raised to
life.
22Peter took him aside and began to rebuke
him. "Never, Lord!" he said. "This shall never
happen to you!"
23Jesus turned and said to Peter, "Get behind
me, Satan! You are a stumbling block to me;
you do not have in mind the things of God, but
the things of men."
24Then Jesus said to his disciples, "If anyone
would come after me, he must deny himself
and take up his cross and follow me. 25For whoever wants to save his life[g] will lose it, but
whoever loses his life for me will find it. 26What
good will it be for a man if he gains the whole
world, yet forfeits his soul? Or what can a man
give in exchange for his soul? 27For the Son of
Man is going to come in his Father's glory with
his angels, and then he will reward each person
according to what he has done. 28I tell you the
truth, some who are standing here will not taste
death before they see the Son of Man coming in
his kingdom."

The Transfiguration

‰ See Mark 9:2–13; Luke 9:28–36

17 After six days Jesus took with him Peter,
James and John the brother of James,
and led them up a high mountain by themselves. 2There he was transfigured before them.
His face shone like the sun, and his clothes
became as white as the light. 3Just then there

[a]2 Some early manuscripts do not have the rest of verse 2 and all of verse 3. [b]16 Or *Messiah;* also in verse 20 [c]18 *Peter* means *rock.* [d]18 Or *hell* [e]18 Or *not prove stronger than it* [f]19 Or *have been* [g]25 The Greek word means either *life* or *soul;* also in verse 26.

16:1–4 The Pharisees' attitude hinders true spiritual growth. They wanted Jesus to perform a miracle to prove that he was the Messiah. We make the same mistake today when we demand an instant cure or supernatural intervention before we will trust God with our lives. Looking for a quick fix to a lifelong problem is tantamount to seeking "a sign from heaven" (16:1). We must willingly trust God regardless of how long it takes for him to work in our lives. The same God who may choose to perform an immediate miracle also has the prerogative to transform our lives a little bit, day by day. Our part is to seek him and surrender our lives to him. His part is to choose change our lives—however long he decides that will take.

16:13–17 Who is Jesus? Jesus is the promised Messiah and the Son of God. That truth comes from God himself. It doesn't come from any human source. If we are not assured that Jesus is the promised Messiah and the source of our spiritual renewal, we need to ask God to reveal the truth to us. Recognizing this truth is foundational to our spiritual renewal.

appeared before them Moses and Elijah, talking with Jesus.

4Peter said to Jesus, "Lord, it is good for us to be here. If you wish, I will put up three shelters—one for you, one for Moses and one for Elijah."

5While he was still speaking, a bright cloud enveloped them, and a voice from the cloud said, "This is my Son, whom I love; with him I am well pleased. Listen to him!"

6When the disciples heard this, they fell facedown to the ground, terrified. 7But Jesus came and touched them. "Get up," he said. "Don't be afraid." 8When they looked up, they saw no one except Jesus.

9As they were coming down the mountain, Jesus instructed them, "Don't tell anyone what you have seen, until the Son of Man has been raised from the dead."

10The disciples asked him, "Why then do the teachers of the law say that Elijah must come first?"

11Jesus replied, "To be sure, Elijah comes and will restore all things. 12But I tell you, Elijah has already come, and they did not recognize him, but have done to him everything they wished. In the same way the Son of Man is going to suffer at their hands." 13Then the disciples understood that he was talking to them about John the Baptist.

The Healing of a Boy With a Demon

‰ See Mark 9:14–28; Luke 9:37–42

14When they came to the crowd, a man approached Jesus and knelt before him. 15"Lord, have mercy on my son," he said. "He has seizures and is suffering greatly. He often falls into the fire or into the water. 16I brought him to your disciples, but they could not heal him."

17"O unbelieving and perverse generation," Jesus replied, "how long shall I stay with you? How long shall I put up with you? Bring the boy here to me." 18Jesus rebuked the demon, and it came out of the boy, and he was healed from that moment.

19Then the disciples came to Jesus in private and asked, "Why couldn't we drive it out?"

20He replied, "Because you have so little faith. I tell you the truth, if you have faith as small as a mustard seed, you can say to this mountain, 'Move from here to there' and it will move. Nothing will be impossible for you.[a]"

22When they came together in Galilee, he said to them, "The Son of Man is going to be betrayed into the hands of men. 23They will kill him, and on the third day he will be raised to life." And the disciples were filled with grief.

The Temple Tax

24After Jesus and his disciples arrived in Capernaum, the collectors of the two-drachma tax came to Peter and asked, "Doesn't your teacher pay the temple tax[b]?"

25"Yes, he does," he replied.

When Peter came into the house, Jesus was the first to speak. "What do you think, Simon?" he asked. "From whom do the kings of the earth collect duty and taxes—from their own sons or from others?"

26"From others," Peter answered.

"Then the sons are exempt," Jesus said to him. 27"But so that we may not offend them, go to the lake and throw out your line. Take the first fish you catch; open its mouth and you will find a four-drachma coin. Take it and give it to them for my tax and yours."

The Greatest in the Kingdom of Heaven

‰ See Mark 9:33–37; Luke 9:46–48

18 At that time the disciples came to Jesus and asked, "Who is the greatest in the kingdom of heaven?"

2He called a little child and had him stand among them. 3And he said: "I tell you the truth, unless you change and become like little children, you will never enter the kingdom of heaven. 4Therefore, whoever humbles himself like this child is the greatest in the kingdom of heaven.

5"And whoever welcomes a little child like this in my name welcomes me. 6But if anyone causes one of these little ones who believe in me to sin, it would be better for him to have a large millstone hung around his neck and to be drowned in the depths of the sea.

7"Woe to the world because of the things that cause people to sin! Such things must come, but woe to the man through whom they come! 8If your hand or your foot causes you to sin, cut it off and throw it away. It is better for you to enter life maimed or crippled than to have two hands or two feet and be thrown into eternal fire. 9And if your eye causes you to sin, gouge it out and throw it away. It is better for you to enter life with one eye than to have two eyes and be thrown into the fire of hell.

The Parable of the Lost Sheep

‰ See Luke 15:4–7

10"See that you do not look down on one of these little ones. For I tell you that their angels

[a]20 Some manuscripts *you.* [21]*But this kind does not go out except by prayer and fasting.* [b]24 Greek *the two drachmas*

17:14–21 Jesus criticized the disciples for their lack of faith in God's powerful ability to heal the boy. Their failure to cast out this demon teaches us a crucial lesson about faith. We don't need large amounts of faith for God to work in us; we need only a small amount, "as small as a mustard seed," to effect change (17:20). Prayer and faith in God are enough to move mountains!

18:10–14 Many people believe that they are worthless to others and insignificant to God. Jesus indicated that his mission was to save the lost, no matter how few or insignificant they were considered to be. God the Father does not want anyone to miss the opportunity for salvation in Jesus Christ. God values each one of us. If we admit our need for him, repent from our sin and seek to follow his

in heaven always see the face of my Father in
heaven.[a]
12 "What do you think? If a man owns a hundred sheep, and one of them wanders away, will
he not leave the ninety-nine on the hills and go
to look for the one that wandered off? 13 And if
he finds it, I tell you the truth, he is happier
about that one sheep than about the ninety-
nine that did not wander off. 14 In the same way
your Father in heaven is not willing that any of
these little ones should be lost.

A Brother Who Sins Against You

15 "If your brother sins against you,[b] go and
show him his fault, just between the two of you.
If he listens to you, you have won your brother
over. 16 But if he will not listen, take one or two
others along, so that 'every matter may be established by the testimony of two or three witnesses.'[c] 17 If he refuses to listen to them, tell it
to the church; and if he refuses to listen even to
the church, treat him as you would a pagan or
a tax collector.
18 "I tell you the truth, whatever you bind on
earth will be[d] bound in heaven, and whatever
you loose on earth will be[d] loosed in heaven.
19 "Again, I tell you that if two of you on
earth agree about anything you ask for, it will be
done for you by my Father in heaven. 20 For
where two or three come together in my name,
there am I with them."

The Parable of the Unmerciful Servant

21 Then Peter came to Jesus and asked, "Lord,
how many times shall I forgive my brother
when he sins against me? Up to seven times?"
22 Jesus answered, "I tell you, not seven
times, but seventy-seven times.[e]
23 "Therefore, the kingdom of heaven is like
a king who wanted to settle accounts with his
servants. 24 As he began the settlement, a man
who owed him ten thousand talents[f] was
brought to him. 25 Since he was not able to pay,
the master ordered that he and his wife and his
children and all that he had be sold to repay the
debt.
26 "The servant fell on his knees before him.
'Be patient with me,' he begged, 'and I will pay
back everything.' 27 The servant's master took
pity on him, canceled the debt and let him go.
28 "But when that servant went out, he found
one of his fellow servants who owed him a
hundred denarii.[g] He grabbed him and began
to choke him. 'Pay back what you owe me!' he
demanded.
29 "His fellow servant fell to his knees and

[a] 10 Some manuscripts *heaven.* 11 *The Son of Man came to save what was lost.* [b] 15 Some manuscripts do not have *against you.* [c] 16 Deut. 19:15 [d] 18 Or *have been* [e] 22 Or *seventy times seven* [f] 24 That is, millions of dollars [g] 28 That is, a few dollars

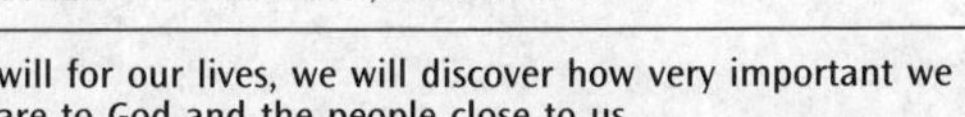
will for our lives, we will discover how very important we are to God and the people close to us.

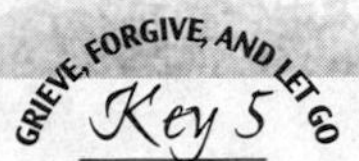

Relinquishing the Debts Owed Us

Matthew 18:23–35 We sometimes keep a running list of the wrongs others have done against us. And besides the internal list of wrongs suffered, we usually keep another kind of list—an accounting of what we think others *owe* us for what they have done. We may feel they owe us an apology, a sum of money or perhaps something larger. In our minds, every time we suffer hurt, the ones who hurt us owe us a moral debt to make things right. Relinquishing these accounts to God and forgiving the debts we feel others owe us is essential to our spiritual growth.

Jesus told a story: "A king . . . wanted to settle accounts with his servants. As he began the settlement, a man who owed him ten thousand talents was brought to him" (18:23–24). The man begged for forgiveness. The king was filled with pity for him, canceled the debt and let him go. But when the man left the king, he went to "one of his fellow servants who owed him a hundred denarii. He grabbed him and began to choke him" (18:27–28). He demanded immediate payment of the debt. When the other servant was unable to pay, the first man had him sent to prison. This incident was reported to the king. The king called in the man he had forgiven. " 'You wicked servant,' he said, 'I canceled all that debt of yours because you begged me to. Shouldn't you have had mercy on your fellow servant just as I had on you?' In anger his master turned him over to the jailers to be tortured, until he should pay back all he owed. This is how my heavenly Father will treat each of you unless you forgive your brother from your heart" (18:32–35).

When we look at the enormous moral debt God has forgiven us in Christ, we should be compelled to forgive others. This will free us from the torture of festering resentment. We can't change what others have done to us, but we can write off their debts by handing our accounting process over to God.

Turn to John 21.

Maintaining Our Relationships

Matthew 18:15–20 Good relationships are essential to good spiritual health. Conflict and disharmony drain our energy and distract us from practicing other disciplines that foster spiritual vitality. In Matthew 18, Jesus gives directions for the discipline of maintaining our relationships with other believers.

Jesus spoke these words in the context of forgiveness and caring for the integrity of fellowship. He makes it clear that we will have disappointments and conflict within the fellowship of believers. Yet Jesus was concerned with our response to these conflicts. If we refuse to face the problem, it will not go away; it will simply go underground and fester, giving the evil one a foothold to bring disharmony within the body of Christ (see Ephesians 4:25–27).

We are called to live in the light of God's presence, which includes bringing our conflicts into the open so that we can properly deal with them. Some people call this practice "keeping short accounts." This means that we address an offense or problem (committed by us or against us) as soon as possible. We don't let a "debt" accumulate the interest of bitterness by waiting to see whether the other person will do something to correct the situation. The simple fact of viewing this confrontation as a spiritual discipline moves it from being an option to being an important exercise of love.

Putting It Into Practice

Are there relationships you have allowed to deteriorate because of differences or conflicts? What specific issues have come between you and another? What steps could you take to clear your relationship of the debris? A good first step is to write an honest letter in your journal, expressing your feelings. This gives you the freedom to be open and explore your true feelings. God may give you insight and specific ideas for moving forward. If the relationship is especially strained, however, it may be good to seek counsel from trusted believers before making direct contact with the person.

For more on spiritual friendship, turn to Acts 4.

begged him, 'Be patient with me, and I will pay you back.'

30"But he refused. Instead, he went off and had the man thrown into prison until he could pay the debt. 31When the other servants saw what had happened, they were greatly distressed and went and told their master everything that had happened.

32"Then the master called the servant in. 'You wicked servant,' he said, 'I canceled all that debt of yours because you begged me to. 33Shouldn't you have had mercy on your fellow servant just as I had on you?' 34In anger his master turned him over to the jailers to be tortured, until he should pay back all he owed.

35"This is how my heavenly Father will treat each of you unless you forgive your brother from your heart."

Divorce

‰ See Mark 10:1–12

19 When Jesus had finished saying these things, he left Galilee and went into the region of Judea to the other side of the Jordan. 2Large crowds followed him, and he healed them there.

3Some Pharisees came to him to test him. They asked, "Is it lawful for a man to divorce his wife for any and every reason?"

4"Haven't you read," he replied, "that at the beginning the Creator 'made them male and female,'[a] 5and said, 'For this reason a man will leave his father and mother and be united to his wife, and the two will become one flesh'[b]? 6So they are no longer two, but one. Therefore what God has joined together, let man not separate."

7"Why then," they asked, "did Moses command that a man give his wife a certificate of divorce and send her away?"

8Jesus replied, "Moses permitted you to divorce your wives because your hearts were hard. But it was not this way from the beginning. 9I tell you that anyone who divorces his wife, except for marital unfaithfulness, and marries another woman commits adultery."

10The disciples said to him, "If this is the situation between a husband and wife, it is better not to marry."

11Jesus replied, "Not everyone can accept this word, but only those to whom it has been given. 12For some are eunuchs because they were born that way; others were made that way by men; and others have renounced marriage[c] because of the kingdom of heaven. The one who can accept this should accept it."

The Little Children and Jesus

‰ See Mark 10:13–16; Luke 18:15–17

13Then little children were brought to Jesus for him to place his hands on them and pray for them. But the disciples rebuked those who brought them.

14Jesus said, "Let the little children come to me, and do not hinder them, for the kingdom of heaven belongs to such as these." 15When he had placed his hands on them, he went on from there.

The Rich Young Man

‰ See Mark 10:17–30; Luke 18:18–30

16Now a man came up to Jesus and asked, "Teacher, what good thing must I do to get eternal life?"

17"Why do you ask me about what is good?" Jesus replied. "There is only One who is good. If you want to enter life, obey the commandments."

18"Which ones?" the man inquired.

Jesus replied, " 'Do not murder, do not commit adultery, do not steal, do not give false testimony, 19honor your father and mother,'[d] and 'love your neighbor as yourself.'[e]"

20"All these I have kept," the young man said. "What do I still lack?"

21Jesus answered, "If you want to be perfect, go, sell your possessions and give to the poor, and you will have treasure in heaven. Then come, follow me."

22When the young man heard this, he went away sad, because he had great wealth.

23Then Jesus said to his disciples, "I tell you the truth, it is hard for a rich man to enter the kingdom of heaven. 24Again I tell you, it is easier for a camel to go through the eye of a needle than for a rich man to enter the kingdom of God."

25When the disciples heard this, they were greatly astonished and asked, "Who then can be saved?"

[a]4 Gen. 1:27 [b]5 Gen. 2:24 [c]12 Or *have made themselves eunuchs* [d]19 Exodus 20:12-16; Deut. 5:16-20 [e]19 Lev. 19:18

19:3–12 Jesus affirmed the importance of the marriage relationship. There is no escape clause in marriage. While we may find that confining, God always intended marriage to be a lifelong relationship. Realizing that marriage is permanent and that a husband and wife become one through marriage should cause us to consider how much our sins affect our spouses. The sins that enslave us also harm our mates in one way or another. Though divorce may end the immediate conflict, it will not correct the attitudes or behaviors that brought about the conflict. Unless we correct the root problems in our marriage, we will face the same conflicts in the future.

19:16–24 This rich young man was trying to work his way into heaven. Jesus accepted this man's shortsighted claim to perfection. But it soon became clear that this young man was dependent upon his material wealth and the security it bought him. He valued his possessions more than he valued God. We must guard against materialism, for it often keeps people from humbling themselves and trusting Jesus Christ alone for salvation.

19:25–26 Left on our own, we would only fall deeper into enslavement to sin. But with God's help, the inconceivable is made possible. He can lift us out of our sinful state and bring hope and health where there was once only despair and pain. Surrendering our lives to God is the only way to freedom from the sins that enslave us.

26Jesus looked at them and said, "With man
this is impossible, but with God all things are
possible."
27Peter answered him, "We have left everything to follow you! What then will there be
for us?"
28Jesus said to them, "I tell you the truth, at
the renewal of all things, when the Son of Man
sits on his glorious throne, you who have followed me will also sit on twelve thrones, judging the twelve tribes of Israel. 29And everyone
who has left houses or brothers or sisters or
father or mother[a] or children or fields for my
sake will receive a hundred times as much and
will inherit eternal life. 30But many who are first
will be last, and many who are last will be first.

The Parable of the Workers in the Vineyard

20 "For the kingdom of heaven is like a
landowner who went out early in the
morning to hire men to work in his vineyard.
2He agreed to pay them a denarius for the day
and sent them into his vineyard.
3"About the third hour he went out and saw
others standing in the marketplace doing nothing. 4He told them, 'You also go and work in
my vineyard, and I will pay you whatever is
right.' 5So they went.
"He went out again about the sixth hour and
the ninth hour and did the same thing. 6About
the eleventh hour he went out and found still
others standing around. He asked them, 'Why
have you been standing here all day long doing
nothing?'
7" 'Because no one has hired us,' they answered.
"He said to them, 'You also go and work in
my vineyard.'
8"When evening came, the owner of the
vineyard said to his foreman, 'Call the workers
and pay them their wages, beginning with the
last ones hired and going on to the first.'
9"The workers who were hired about the
eleventh hour came and each received a denarius. 10So when those came who were hired first,
they expected to receive more. But each one of
them also received a denarius. 11When they received it, they began to grumble against the
landowner. 12'These men who were hired last
worked only one hour,' they said, 'and you
have made them equal to us who have borne
the burden of the work and the heat of the day.'
13"But he answered one of them, 'Friend, I
am not being unfair to you. Didn't you agree to
work for a denarius? 14Take your pay and go. I
want to give the man who was hired last the
same as I gave you. 15Don't I have the right to
do what I want with my own money? Or are
you envious because I am generous?'
16"So the last will be first, and the first will
be last."

Jesus Again Predicts His Death

‰ See Mark 10:32–34; Luke 18:31–33

17Now as Jesus was going up to Jerusalem, he
took the twelve disciples aside and said to them,
18"We are going up to Jerusalem, and the Son
of Man will be betrayed to the chief priests and
the teachers of the law. They will condemn him
to death 19and will turn him over to the Gentiles to be mocked and flogged and crucified.
On the third day he will be raised to life!"

A Mother's Request

‰ See Mark 10:35–45

20Then the mother of Zebedee's sons came to
Jesus with her sons and, kneeling down, asked
a favor of him.
21"What is it you want?" he asked.
She said, "Grant that one of these two sons
of mine may sit at your right and the other at
your left in your kingdom."
22"You don't know what you are asking,"
Jesus said to them. "Can you drink the cup I am
going to drink?"
"We can," they answered.
23Jesus said to them, "You will indeed drink
from my cup, but to sit at my right or left is not
for me to grant. These places belong to those for
whom they have been prepared by my Father."
24When the ten heard about this, they were
indignant with the two brothers. 25Jesus called
them together and said, "You know that the
rulers of the Gentiles lord it over them, and
their high officials exercise authority over them.
26Not so with you. Instead, whoever wants to
become great among you must be your servant,
27and whoever wants to be first must be your
slave— 28just as the Son of Man did not come to
be served, but to serve, and to give his life as a
ransom for many."

Two Blind Men Receive Sight

‰ See Mark 10:46–52; Luke 18:35–43

29As Jesus and his disciples were leaving Jericho, a large crowd followed him. 30Two blind

[a]29 Some manuscripts *mother or wife*

20:1–16 The story about the workers and their pay speaks strongly about the grace of God. No matter when we begin to follow Jesus, we all receive the same amount of grace from God. That may seem unfair to some. Yet God in his mercy accepts all people who turn to him for salvation, no matter how early (or late) in life.

20:20–28 The disciples were indignant at James and John's request for special recognition. They, too, wanted to achieve a high position of honor in God's kingdom. But their prideful attitude was contrary to what Jesus taught. Such an attitude is detrimental to our spiritual growth too. The path to greatness in God's sight is through humble service for others. When we receive God's grace and experience his restoration, we should share God's message with others and do what we can to help them grow spiritually.

20:29–34 Jesus' sensitivity to the needs of two blind men in the midst of a huge crowd shows us that God cares very much for individuals who need him. Jesus healed the blind men because they believed in him and asked him to

men were sitting by the roadside, and when
they heard that Jesus was going by, they shouted, "Lord, Son of David, have mercy on us!"
31 The crowd rebuked them and told them to
be quiet, but they shouted all the louder, "Lord,
Son of David, have mercy on us!"
32 Jesus stopped and called them. "What do
you want me to do for you?" he asked.
33 "Lord," they answered, "we want our sight."
34 Jesus had compassion on them and
touched their eyes. Immediately they received
their sight and followed him.

The Triumphal Entry

‰ See Mark 11:1–10; Luke 19:29–38; John 12:12–15

21 As they approached Jerusalem and
came to Bethphage on the Mount of
Olives, Jesus sent two disciples, 2 saying to them,
"Go to the village ahead of you, and at once
you will find a donkey tied there, with her colt
by her. Untie them and bring them to me. 3 If
anyone says anything to you, tell him that the
Lord needs them, and he will send them right
away."
4 This took place to fulfill what was spoken
through the prophet:

5 "Say to the Daughter of Zion,
'See, your king comes to you,
gentle and riding on a donkey,
on a colt, the foal of a donkey.' "[a]

6 The disciples went and did as Jesus had instructed them. 7 They brought the donkey and
the colt, placed their cloaks on them, and Jesus
sat on them. 8 A very large crowd spread their
cloaks on the road, while others cut branches
from the trees and spread them on the road.
9 The crowds that went ahead of him and those
that followed shouted,

"Hosanna[b] to the Son of David!"

"Blessed is he who comes in the name of
the Lord!"[c]

"Hosanna[b] in the highest!"

10 When Jesus entered Jerusalem, the whole
city was stirred and asked, "Who is this?"
11 The crowds answered, "This is Jesus, the
prophet from Nazareth in Galilee."

Jesus at the Temple

‰ See Mark 11:15–18; Luke 19:45–47

12 Jesus entered the temple area and drove out
all who were buying and selling there. He overturned the tables of the money changers and the
benches of those selling doves. 13 "It is written,"
he said to them, " 'My house will be called a
house of prayer,'[d] but you are making it a 'den
of robbers.'[e] "

14 The blind and the lame
the temple, and he healed then
chief priests and the teachers c
wonderful things he did and th
ing in the temple area, "Hosa
David," they were indignant.
16 "Do you hear what these
ing?" they asked him.
"Yes," replied Jesus, "have you never read,

" 'From the lips of children and infants
you have ordained praise'[f]?"

17 And he left them and went out of the city
to Bethany, where he spent the night.

The Fig Tree Withers

‰ See Mark 11:12–14,20–24

18 Early in the morning, as he was on his way
back to the city, he was hungry. 19 Seeing a fig
tree by the road, he went up to it but found
nothing on it except leaves. Then he said to it,
"May you never bear fruit again!" Immediately
the tree withered.
20 When the disciples saw this, they were
amazed. "How did the fig tree wither so quickly?" they asked.
21 Jesus replied, "I tell you the truth, if you
have faith and do not doubt, not only can you
do what was done to the fig tree, but also
you can say to this mountain, 'Go, throw
yourself into the sea,' and it will be done.
22 If you believe, you will receive whatever
you ask for in prayer."

The Authority of Jesus Questioned

‰ See Mark 11:27–33; Luke 20:1–8

23 Jesus entered the temple courts, and, while
he was teaching, the chief priests and the elders
of the people came to him. "By what authority
are you doing these things?" they asked. "And
who gave you this authority?"
24 Jesus replied, "I will also ask you one question. If you answer me, I will tell you by what
authority I am doing these things. 25 John's baptism—where did it come from? Was it from
heaven, or from men?"
They discussed it among themselves and
said, "If we say, 'From heaven,' he will ask,
'Then why didn't you believe him?' 26 But if we
say, 'From men'—we are afraid of the people, for
they all hold that John was a prophet."
27 So they answered Jesus, "We don't know."
Then he said, "Neither will I tell you by what
authority I am doing these things.

[a] 5 Zech. 9:9 [b] 9 A Hebrew expression meaning "Save!" which became an exclamation of praise; also in verse 15 [c] 9 Psalm 118:26 [d] 13 Isaiah 56:7 [e] 13 Jer. 7:11 [f] 16 Psalm 8:2

---

help them. Notice that they did not listen to the discouraging remarks of the bystanders. These blind men persevered despite opposition and continued with their humble pleas for help. As we continue to grow spiritually, we may encounter similar opposition. If this happens, we may need to swallow our pride and just keep going. We can be sure that even if others ridicule us, God is listening and will help us.

arable of the Two Sons

28"What do you think? There was a man who
ıad two sons. He went to the first and said,
'Son, go and work today in the vineyard.'
29" 'I will not,' he answered, but later he
changed his mind and went.
30"Then the father went to the other son and
said the same thing. He answered, 'I will, sir,'
but he did not go.
31"Which of the two did what his father
wanted?"
"The first," they answered.
Jesus said to them, "I tell you the truth, the
tax collectors and the prostitutes are entering
the kingdom of God ahead of you. 32For John
came to you to show you the way of righteousness, and you did not believe him, but the tax
collectors and the prostitutes did. And even after you saw this, you did not repent and believe
him.

The Parable of the Tenants

‰ See Mark 12:1–12; Luke 20:9–19

33"Listen to another parable: There was a
landowner who planted a vineyard. He put a
wall around it, dug a winepress in it and built
a watchtower. Then he rented the vineyard to
some farmers and went away on a journey.
34When the harvest time approached, he sent
his servants to the tenants to collect his fruit.
35"The tenants seized his servants; they beat
one, killed another, and stoned a third. 36Then
he sent other servants to them, more than the
first time, and the tenants treated them the
same way. 37Last of all, he sent his son to them.
'They will respect my son,' he said.
38"But when the tenants saw the son, they
said to each other, 'This is the heir. Come, let's
kill him and take his inheritance.' 39So they
took him and threw him out of the vineyard
and killed him.
40"Therefore, when the owner of the vineyard comes, what will he do to those tenants?"
41"He will bring those wretches to a wretched end," they replied, "and he will rent the vineyard to other tenants, who will give him his
share of the crop at harvest time."
42Jesus said to them, "Have you never read in
the Scriptures:

" 'The stone the builders rejected
has become the capstone[a];
the Lord has done this,
and it is marvelous in our eyes'[b]?

43"Therefore I tell you that the kingdom of
God will be taken away from you and given to
a people who will produce its fruit. 44He who
falls on this stone will be broken to pieces, but
he on whom it falls will be crushed."[c]
45When the chief priests and the Pharisees
heard Jesus' parables, they knew he was talking
about them. 46They looked for a way to arrest
him, but they were afraid of the crowd because
the people held that he was a prophet.

The Parable of the Wedding Banquet

22 Jesus spoke to them again in parables,
saying: 2"The kingdom of heaven is
like a king who prepared a wedding banquet for
his son. 3He sent his servants to those who had
been invited to the banquet to tell them to
come, but they refused to come.
4"Then he sent some more servants and said,
'Tell those who have been invited that I have
prepared my dinner: My oxen and fattened cattle have been butchered, and everything is
ready. Come to the wedding banquet.'
5"But they paid no attention and went off—
one to his field, another to his business. 6The
rest seized his servants, mistreated them and
killed them. 7The king was enraged. He sent
his army and destroyed those murderers and
burned their city.
8"Then he said to his servants, 'The wedding
banquet is ready, but those I invited did not
deserve to come. 9Go to the street corners and
invite to the banquet anyone you find.' 10So the
servants went out into the streets and gathered
all the people they could find, both good and
bad, and the wedding hall was filled with
guests.
11"But when the king came in to see the
guests, he noticed a man there who was not
wearing wedding clothes. 12'Friend,' he asked,
'how did you get in here without wedding
clothes?' The man was speechless.
13"Then the king told the attendants, 'Tie
him hand and foot, and throw him outside,
into the darkness, where there will be weeping
and gnashing of teeth.'
14"For many are invited, but few are chosen."

Paying Taxes to Caesar

‰ See Mark 12:13–17; Luke 20:20–26

15Then the Pharisees went out and laid plans
to trap him in his words. 16They sent their disci-

[a]42 Or *cornerstone* [b]42 Psalm 118:22,23
[c]44 Some manuscripts do not have verse 44.

21:28–32 Before we surrendered our lives to God, we were like the first son, disobeying his father's wishes and indulging our sinful desires. But later, recognizing where we were headed, we may have changed our mind and obeyed our Father. Although we may have gone our own way at times, God wants us to change our ways and truly obey him. He doesn't want only a verbal agreement like the other son who said he would obey and then didn't. Our change of lifestyle will reflect our spiritual condition.

22:1–10 When the king's servants brought everyone they could find, there were both good people and bad people. The offer for the banquet was open to anyone who wanted to come. So it is with heaven: Everyone is invited, and anyone can either accept or turn down the offer. Will we be like the first group of guests and suffer for our decision? Or will we be like the second and enjoy what God has to offer us?

ples to him along with the Herodians. "Teacher," they said, "we know you are a man of integrity and that you teach the way of God in
accordance with the truth. You aren't swayed by
men, because you pay no attention to who they
are. 17Tell us then, what is your opinion? Is it
right to pay taxes to Caesar or not?"
18But Jesus, knowing their evil intent, said,
"You hypocrites, why are you trying to trap me?
19Show me the coin used for paying the tax."
They brought him a denarius, 20and he asked
them, "Whose portrait is this? And whose inscription?"
21"Caesar's," they replied.
Then he said to them, "Give to Caesar what
is Caesar's, and to God what is God's."
22When they heard this, they were amazed.
So they left him and went away.

Marriage at the Resurrection

‰ See Mark 12:18–27; Luke 20:27–40

23That same day the Sadducees, who say
there is no resurrection, came to him with a
question. 24"Teacher," they said, "Moses told us
that if a man dies without having children, his
brother must marry the widow and have children for him. 25Now there were seven brothers
among us. The first one married and died, and
since he had no children, he left his wife to his
brother. 26The same thing happened to the second and third brother, right on down to the
seventh. 27Finally, the woman died. 28Now
then, at the resurrection, whose wife will she be
of the seven, since all of them were married to
her?"
29Jesus replied, "You are in error because you
do not know the Scriptures or the power of
God. 30At the resurrection people will neither
marry nor be given in marriage; they will be like
the angels in heaven. 31But about the resurrection of the dead—have you not read what God
said to you, 32'I am the God of Abraham, the
God of Isaac, and the God of Jacob'[a]? He is
not the God of the dead but of the living."
33When the crowds heard this, they were astonished at his teaching.

The Greatest Commandment

‰ See Mark 12:28–31

34Hearing that Jesus had silenced the Sadducees, the Pharisees got together. 35One of them,
an expert in the law, tested him with this question: 36"Teacher, which is the greatest commandment in the Law?"
37Jesus replied: " 'Love the Lord your God
with all your heart and with all your soul and
with all your mind.'[b] 38This is the first and
greatest commandment. 39And the second is
like it: 'Love your neighbor as yourself.'[c] 40All
the Law and the Prophets hang on these two
commandments."

Whose Son Is the Christ?

‰ See Mark 12:35–37; Luke 20:41–44

41While the Pharisees were gathered together, Jesus asked them, 42"What do you think
about the Christ[d]? Whose son is he?"
"The son of David," they replied.
43He said to them, "How is it then that David, speaking by the Spirit, calls him 'Lord'? For
he says,

44" 'The Lord said to my Lord:
"Sit at my right hand
until I put your enemies
under your feet." '[e]

45If then David calls him 'Lord,' how can he be
his son?" 46No one could say a word in reply,
and from that day on no one dared to ask him
any more questions.

Seven Woes

‰ See Mark 12:38–39; Luke 20:45–46

23 Then Jesus said to the crowds and to his
disciples: 2"The teachers of the law and
the Pharisees sit in Moses' seat. 3So you must
obey them and do everything they tell you. But
do not do what they do, for they do not practice
what they preach. 4They tie up heavy loads and
put them on men's shoulders, but they themselves are not willing to lift a finger to move
them.
5"Everything they do is done for men to see:
They make their phylacteries[f] wide and the
tassels on their garments long; 6they love the
place of honor at banquets and the most important seats in the synagogues; 7they love to be
greeted in the marketplaces and to have men
call them 'Rabbi.'
8"But you are not to be called 'Rabbi,' for
you have only one Master and you are all brothers. 9And do not call anyone on earth 'father,'
for you have one Father, and he is in heaven.
10Nor are you to be called 'teacher,' for you
have one Teacher, the Christ.[d] 11The greatest
among you will be your servant. 12For whoever

a32 Exodus 3:6 b37 Deut. 6:5 c39 Lev. 19:18
d42,10 Or *Messiah* e44 Psalm 110:1 f5 That is,
boxes containing Scripture verses, worn on forehead
and arm

22:33–40 To simplify our priorities, Jesus boiled down the six-hundred-plus interpretations of the Law of Moses into two foundational truths: We are to love God with everything we are and have, and we are to love our neighbors as ourselves. If we do these consistently, we will obey every other law.

23:1–12 The Pharisees and Jewish leaders were classic examples of people who lived by a double standard. They set the standards of behavior for others so high that they could not keep these stipulations themselves. In spite of their shortcomings, the religious leaders demanded that they be addressed with distinguished titles. They did not realize that true greatness begins with humility and is proven by a willingness to help others. The Pharisees' pride kept them from seeing their true need for God.

exalts himself will be humbled, and whoever humbles himself will be exalted.

13"Woe to you, teachers of the law and Pharisees, you hypocrites! You shut the kingdom of heaven in men's faces. You yourselves do not enter, nor will you let those enter who are trying to.[a]

15"Woe to you, teachers of the law and Pharisees, you hypocrites! You travel over land and sea to win a single convert, and when he becomes one, you make him twice as much a son of hell as you are.

16"Woe to you, blind guides! You say, 'If anyone swears by the temple, it means nothing; but if anyone swears by the gold of the temple, he is bound by his oath.' 17You blind fools! Which is greater: the gold, or the temple that makes the gold sacred? 18You also say, 'If anyone swears by the altar, it means nothing; but if anyone swears by the gift on it, he is bound by his oath.' 19You blind men! Which is greater: the gift, or the altar that makes the gift sacred? 20Therefore, he who swears by the altar swears by it and by everything on it. 21And he who swears by the temple swears by it and by the one who dwells in it. 22And he who swears by heaven swears by God's throne and by the one who sits on it.

23"Woe to you, teachers of the law and Pharisees, you hypocrites! You give a tenth of your spices—mint, dill and cummin. But you have neglected the more important matters of the law—justice, mercy and faithfulness. You should have practiced the latter, without neglecting the former. 24You blind guides! You strain out a gnat but swallow a camel.

25"Woe to you, teachers of the law and Pharisees, you hypocrites! You clean the outside of the cup and dish, but inside they are full of greed and self-indulgence. 26Blind Pharisee! First clean the inside of the cup and dish, and then the outside also will be clean.

27"Woe to you, teachers of the law and Pharisees, you hypocrites! You are like whitewashed tombs, which look beautiful on the outside but on the inside are full of dead men's bones and everything unclean. 28In the same way, on the outside you appear to people as righteous but on the inside you are full of hypocrisy and wickedness.

29"Woe to you, teachers of the law and Pharisees, you hypocrites! You build tombs for the prophets and decorate the graves of the righteous. 30And you say, 'If we had lived in the days of our forefathers, we would not have taken part with them in shedding the blood of the prophets.' 31So you testify against yourselves that you are the descendants of those who murdered the prophets. 32Fill up, then, the measure of the sin of your forefathers!

33"You snakes! You brood of vipers! How will you escape being condemned to hell? 34Therefore I am sending you prophets and wise men and teachers. Some of them you will kill and crucify; others you will flog in your synagogues and pursue from town to town. 35And so upon you will come all the righteous blood that has been shed on earth, from the blood of righteous Abel to the blood of Zechariah son of Berekiah, whom you murdered between the temple and the altar. 36I tell you the truth, all this will come upon this generation.

37"O Jerusalem, Jerusalem, you who kill the prophets and stone those sent to you, how often I have longed to gather your children together, as a hen gathers her chicks under her wings, but you were not willing. 38Look, your house is left to you desolate. 39For I tell you, you will not see me again until you say, 'Blessed is he who comes in the name of the Lord.'[b]"

Signs of the End of the Age

‰ See Mark 13:1–37; Luke 21:5–36

24 Jesus left the temple and was walking away when his disciples came up to him to call his attention to its buildings. 2"Do you see all these things?" he asked. "I tell you the truth, not one stone here will be left on another; every one will be thrown down."

3As Jesus was sitting on the Mount of Olives, the disciples came to him privately. "Tell us," they said, "when will this happen, and what will be the sign of your coming and of the end of the age?"

4Jesus answered: "Watch out that no one deceives you. 5For many will come in my name, claiming, 'I am the Christ,[c]' and will deceive many. 6You will hear of wars and rumors of wars, but see to it that you are not alarmed. Such things must happen, but the end is still to come. 7Nation will rise against nation, and kingdom against kingdom. There will be famines and earthquakes in various places. 8All these are the beginning of birth pains.

9"Then you will be handed over to be persecuted and put to death, and you will be hated by all nations because of me. 10At that time many will turn away from the faith and will betray and hate each other, 11and many false prophets will appear and deceive many people. 12Because of the increase of wickedness, the

[a] *13* Some manuscripts *to.* *14Woe to you, teachers of the law and Pharisees, you hypocrites! You devour widows' houses and for a show make lengthy prayers. Therefore you will be punished more severely.* [b] *39* Psalm 118:26 [c] *5* Or *Messiah*; also in verse 23

23:13–36 As a result of their hypocritical behavior, Jesus pronounced judgment on all the spiritually blind religious leaders. Their external rhetoric and ritual observances were mere pretense—all show with no inner reality. Such people cause great pain to others and themselves. However, there is hope for everyone—even hypocrites! Both Joseph of Arimathea and Nicodemus, once numbered with the hypocrites, eventually found new life through faith in Jesus (see John 19:38–42). If we search for Jesus, we will find him. And if we have been hypocrites and repent, he will change us, making our faith genuine.

love of most will grow cold, 13but he who
stands firm to the end will be saved. 14And this
gospel of the kingdom will be preached in the
whole world as a testimony to all nations, and
then the end will come.
15"So when you see standing in the holy
place 'the abomination that causes desolation,'[a] spoken of through the prophet Daniel—
let the reader understand— 16then let those who
are in Judea flee to the mountains. 17Let no one
on the roof of his house go down to take anything out of the house. 18Let no one in the field
go back to get his cloak. 19How dreadful it will
be in those days for pregnant women and nursing mothers! 20Pray that your flight will not
take place in winter or on the Sabbath. 21For
then there will be great distress, unequaled
from the beginning of the world until now—and
never to be equaled again. 22If those days had
not been cut short, no one would survive, but
for the sake of the elect those days will be shortened. 23At that time if anyone says to you,
'Look, here is the Christ!' or, 'There he is!' do
not believe it. 24For false Christs and false
prophets will appear and perform great signs
and miracles to deceive even the elect—if that
were possible. 25See, I have told you ahead of
time.
26"So if anyone tells you, 'There he is, out in
the desert,' do not go out; or, 'Here he is, in the
inner rooms,' do not believe it. 27For as lightning that comes from the east is visible even in
the west, so will be the coming of the Son of
Man. 28Wherever there is a carcass, there the
vultures will gather.
29"Immediately after the distress of those
days

" 'the sun will be darkened,
and the moon will not give its light;
the stars will fall from the sky,
and the heavenly bodies will be
shaken.'[b]

30"At that time the sign of the Son of Man
will appear in the sky, and all the nations of the
earth will mourn. They will see the Son of Man
coming on the clouds of the sky, with power
and great glory. 31And he will send his angels
with a loud trumpet call, and they will gather
his elect from the four winds, from one end of
the heavens to the other.
32"Now learn this lesson from the fig tree: As
soon as its twigs get tender and its leaves come
out, you know that summer is near. 33Even so,
when you see all these things, you know that
it[c] is near, right at the door. 34I tell you the
truth, this generation[d] will certainly not pass
away until all these things have happened.
35Heaven and earth will pass away, but my
words will never pass away.

The Day and Hour Unknown

‰ See Luke 12:42–46; 17:26–27

36"No one knows about that day or hour,
not even the angels in heaven, nor the Son,[e]
but only the Father. 37As it was in the days of
Noah, so it will be at the coming of the Son of
Man. 38For in the days before the flood, people
were eating and drinking, marrying and giving
in marriage, up to the day Noah entered the ark;
39and they knew nothing about what would
happen until the flood came and took them all
away. That is how it will be at the coming of the
Son of Man. 40Two men will be in the field; one
will be taken and the other left. 41Two women
will be grinding with a hand mill; one will be
taken and the other left.
42"Therefore keep watch, because you do not
know on what day your Lord will come. 43But
understand this: If the owner of the house had
known at what time of night the thief was coming, he would have kept watch and would not
have let his house be broken into. 44So you also
must be ready, because the Son of Man will
come at an hour when you do not expect him.
45"Who then is the faithful and wise servant,
whom the master has put in charge of the servants in his household to give them their food
at the proper time? 46It will be good for that
servant whose master finds him doing so when
he returns. 47I tell you the truth, he will put him
in charge of all his possessions. 48But suppose
that servant is wicked and says to himself, 'My
master is staying away a long time,' 49and he
then begins to beat his fellow servants and to
eat and drink with drunkards. 50The master of
that servant will come on a day when he does
not expect him and at an hour he is not aware
of. 51He will cut him to pieces and assign him
a place with the hypocrites, where there will be
weeping and gnashing of teeth.

The Parable of the Ten Virgins

25 "At that time the kingdom of heaven
will be like ten virgins who took their
lamps and went out to meet the bridegroom.
2Five of them were foolish and five were wise.
3The foolish ones took their lamps but did not
take any oil with them. 4The wise, however,
took oil in jars along with their lamps. 5The
bridegroom was a long time in coming, and
they all became drowsy and fell asleep.

[a]15 Daniel 9:27; 11:31; 12:11 [b]29 Isaiah 13:10; 34:4
[c]33 Or *he* [d]34 Or *race* [e]36 Some manuscripts do
not have *nor the Son.*

24:36–51 Jesus did not tell us when the final redemption of this evil world would come. In the meantime, we are to make good use of our time here, daily conforming our lives to God's will. None of us is perfect, so we need to constantly seek God's help to live God's way.

25:1–13 The story of the ten bridesmaids reinforces the need for wise preparation and readiness for Christ's second coming. Those who have readied themselves for the return of Jesus, the heavenly bridegroom—by faith, commitment and righteous living—will not be ashamed.

6"At midnight the cry rang out: 'Here's the bridegroom! Come out to meet him!'

7"Then all the virgins woke up and trimmed their lamps. 8The foolish ones said to the wise, 'Give us some of your oil; our lamps are going out.'

9" 'No,' they replied, 'there may not be enough for both us and you. Instead, go to those who sell oil and buy some for yourselves.'

10"But while they were on their way to buy the oil, the bridegroom arrived. The virgins who were ready went in with him to the wedding banquet. And the door was shut.

11"Later the others also came. 'Sir! Sir!' they said. 'Open the door for us!'

12"But he replied, 'I tell you the truth, I don't know you.'

13"Therefore keep watch, because you do not know the day or the hour.

The Parable of the Talents

14"Again, it will be like a man going on a journey, who called his servants and entrusted his property to them. 15To one he gave five talents[a] of money, to another two talents, and to another one talent, each according to his ability. Then he went on his journey. 16The man who had received the five talents went at once and put his money to work and gained five more. 17So also, the one with the two talents gained two more. 18But the man who had received the one talent went off, dug a hole in the ground and hid his master's money.

19"After a long time the master of those servants returned and settled accounts with them. 20The man who had received the five talents brought the other five. 'Master,' he said, 'you entrusted me with five talents. See, I have gained five more.'

21"His master replied, 'Well done, good and faithful servant! You have been faithful with a few things; I will put you in charge of many things. Come and share your master's happiness!'

22"The man with the two talents also came. 'Master,' he said, 'you entrusted me with two talents; see, I have gained two more.'

23"His master replied, 'Well done, good and faithful servant! You have been faithful with a few things; I will put you in charge of many things. Come and share your master's happiness!'

24"Then the man who had received the one talent came. 'Master,' he said, 'I knew that you are a hard man, harvesting where you have not sown and gathering where you have not scattered seed. 25So I was afraid and went out and hid your talent in the ground. See, here is what belongs to you.'

26"His master replied, 'You wicked, lazy servant! So you knew that I harvest where I have not sown and gather where I have not scattered seed? 27Well then, you should have put my money on deposit with the bankers, so that when I returned I would have received it back with interest.

28" 'Take the talent from him and give it to the one who has the ten talents. 29For everyone who has will be given more, and he will have an abundance. Whoever does not have, even what he has will be taken from him. 30And throw that worthless servant outside, into the darkness, where there will be weeping and gnashing of teeth.'

The Sheep and the Goats

31"When the Son of Man comes in his glory, and all the angels with him, he will sit on his throne in heavenly glory. 32All the nations will be gathered before him, and he will separate the people one from another as a shepherd separates the sheep from the goats. 33He will put the sheep on his right and the goats on his left.

34"Then the King will say to those on his right, 'Come, you who are blessed by my Father; take your inheritance, the kingdom prepared for you since the creation of the world. 35For I was hungry and you gave me something to eat, I was thirsty and you gave me something to drink, I was a stranger and you invited me in, 36I needed clothes and you clothed me, I was sick and you looked after me, I was in prison and you came to visit me.'

37"Then the righteous will answer him, 'Lord, when did we see you hungry and feed you, or thirsty and give you something to drink? 38When did we see you a stranger and invite you in, or needing clothes and clothe you? 39When did we see you sick or in prison and go to visit you?'

40"The King will reply, 'I tell you the truth, whatever you did for one of the least of these brothers of mine, you did for me.'

41"Then he will say to those on his left, 'Depart from me, you who are cursed, into the eternal fire prepared for the devil and his angels. 42For I was hungry and you gave me nothing to eat, I was thirsty and you gave me nothing to drink, 43I was a stranger and you did not invite me in, I needed clothes and you did not clothe me, I was sick and in prison and you did not look after me.'

[a]15 A talent was worth more than a thousand dollars.

25:14–30 This story encourages us to use our gifts wisely, reminding us about our accountability to God. Even though this parable is about money, it can, by extension, also refer to God-given abilities. God has given everyone abilities of various kinds; no one is untalented or worthless. That fact should encourage us to use our abilities for God.

25:31–46 We will all ultimately be accountable to God on judgment day. Not only will we be responsible for our own conduct; we will also be responsible for how we have helped others. Since Jesus identifies himself with those who suffer, we should follow his example and be especially alert to the needs of others too.

44“They also will answer, ‘Lord, when did we see you hungry or thirsty or a stranger or needing clothes or sick or in prison, and did not help you?’

45“He will reply, ‘I tell you the truth, whatever you did not do for one of the least of these, you did not do for me.’

46“Then they will go away to eternal punishment, but the righteous to eternal life.”

The Plot Against Jesus

‰ See Mark 14:1–2; Luke 22:1–2

26 When Jesus had finished saying all these things, he said to his disciples, 2“As you know, the Passover is two days away—and the Son of Man will be handed over to be crucified.”

3Then the chief priests and the elders of the people assembled in the palace of the high priest, whose name was Caiaphas, 4and they plotted to arrest Jesus in some sly way and kill him. 5“But not during the Feast,” they said, “or there may be a riot among the people.”

Jesus Anointed at Bethany

‰ See Mark 14:3–9

6While Jesus was in Bethany in the home of a man known as Simon the Leper, 7a woman came to him with an alabaster jar of very expensive perfume, which she poured on his head as he was reclining at the table.

8When the disciples saw this, they were indignant. “Why this waste?” they asked. 9“This perfume could have been sold at a high price and the money given to the poor.”

10Aware of this, Jesus said to them, “Why are you bothering this woman? She has done a beautiful thing to me. 11The poor you will always have with you, but you will not always have me. 12When she poured this perfume on my body, she did it to prepare me for burial. 13I tell you the truth, wherever this gospel is preached throughout the world, what she has done will also be told, in memory of her.”

Judas Agrees to Betray Jesus

‰ See Mark 14:10–11; Luke 22:3–6

14Then one of the Twelve—the one called Judas Iscariot—went to the chief priests 15and asked, “What are you willing to give me if I hand him over to you?” So they counted out for him thirty silver coins. 16From then on Judas watched for an opportunity to hand him over.

The Lord’s Supper

‰ See Mark 14:12–25; Luke 22:7–13

17On the first day of the Feast of Unleavened Bread, the disciples came to Jesus and asked, “Where do you want us to make preparations for you to eat the Passover?”

18He replied, “Go into the city to a certain man and tell him, ‘The Teacher says: My appointed time is near. I am going to celebrate the Passover with my disciples at your house.’ ” 19So the disciples did as Jesus had directed them and prepared the Passover.

20When evening came, Jesus was reclining at the table with the Twelve. 21And while they were eating, he said, “I tell you the truth, one of you will betray me.”

22They were very sad and began to say to him one after the other, “Surely not I, Lord?”

23Jesus replied, “The one who has dipped his hand into the bowl with me will betray me. 24The Son of Man will go just as it is written about him. But woe to that man who betrays the Son of Man! It would be better for him if he had not been born.”

25Then Judas, the one who would betray him, said, “Surely not I, Rabbi?”

Jesus answered, “Yes, it is you.”[a]

26While they were eating, Jesus took bread, gave thanks and broke it, and gave it to his disciples, saying, “Take and eat; this is my body.”

27Then he took the cup, gave thanks and offered it to them, saying, “Drink from it, all of you. 28This is my blood of the[b] covenant, which is poured out for many for the forgiveness of sins. 29I tell you, I will not drink of this fruit of the vine from now on until that day when I drink it anew with you in my Father’s kingdom.”

30When they had sung a hymn, they went out to the Mount of Olives.

[a]25 Or *“You yourself have said it”* [b]28 Some manuscripts *the new*

26:6–13 This woman expressed her love for Jesus the best way she knew how. The disciples criticized her wastefulness, but Jesus commended her action. There will always be someone who thinks we are foolish for expressing our gratitude to God. But we should continue to praise him because our praise reminds us that our love for Jesus should take precedence over all other good deeds. Our love and devotion for Jesus should motivate all that we do, regardless of the reactions of others. When we do what we can to show our love and gratitude to the Lord, he will commend our lives too.

26:14–16, 20–25 Judas thought he could hide his dealings with the chief priests, but Jesus discreetly yet openly made Judas aware that he knew exactly what was going on. Judas passed up the opportunity to confess his actions and restore his relationship with Jesus. When we are confronted with our sin, will we do as Judas did and continue in our sin, or will we use the chance to turn to God?

26:26–28 Through the activities of the Last Supper, Jesus communicated his reason for coming to earth. His body would be broken, he said, like the bread, so that we could receive continued spiritual sustenance. His blood, represented by the wine, was the eternal payment for our sins. When we acknowledge Jesus as the Lord of our lives, we become members of his body, forgiven through his blood. There are no restrictions on race, sex, occupation or past mistakes. All who look to Jesus are forgiven through the blood he shed on the cross.

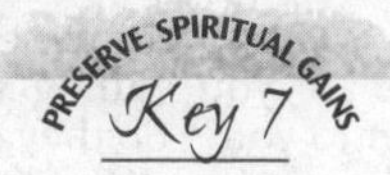

At the Cross

Matthew 26:36–39 Our spiritual journey is not always an easy one. As we travel the long, difficult road that God calls us to walk, we must bear a cross. That cross represents our death to our sinful desires and ways of life. But the way of the cross always leads to a resurrection and new life. When we think about the cross we must bear, we need to surrender to God so that we won't give up or stumble beneath the weight.

As God leads us to do his will instead of our own, we may wish there were some other way. We may feel fear, a lack of confidence, deep anguish, and a host of other emotions that threaten to stop us in our tracks. Regardless of our feelings, we must not let them cause us to turn away from the path God sets before us.

Jesus understands our fears and our struggle to persevere. He had similar emotions the night he was arrested. He told his disciples, "My soul is overwhelmed with sorrow to the point of death" (26:38). As Jesus realized the enormity of the pain he would face, he wondered if there was some other way. He struggled and prayed the same basic prayer three times, "My Father, if it is possible, may this cup be taken from me. Yet not as I will, but as you will" (26:39). As we can see from the end of his prayer, however, Jesus found the grace to accept God's plan.

We may be overwhelmed as we consider the cross we will have to bear on the way to a new life. But during such times of struggle, we can go to Jesus for encouragement and express our deepest emotions. As we cry out for help, we can be confident that we will be given the strength we need to do God's will rather than our own.

Turn to John 15.

Jesus Predicts Peter's Denial

‰ See Mark 14:27–31; Luke 22:31–34

31Then Jesus told them, "This very night you
will all fall away on account of me, for it is
written:

" 'I will strike the shepherd,
and the sheep of the flock will be
scattered.'[a]

32But after I have risen, I will go ahead of you
into Galilee."
33Peter replied, "Even if all fall away on account of you, I never will."
34"I tell you the truth," Jesus answered, "this
very night, before the rooster crows, you will
disown me three times."
35But Peter declared, "Even if I have to die
with you, I will never disown you." And all the
other disciples said the same.

Gethsemane

‰ See Mark 14:32–42; Luke 22:40–46

36Then Jesus went with his disciples to a
place called Gethsemane, and he said to them,
"Sit here while I go over there and pray." 37He
took Peter and the two sons of Zebedee along
with him, and he began to be sorrowful and
troubled. 38Then he said to them, "My soul is
overwhelmed with sorrow to the point of death.
Stay here and keep watch with me."
39Going a little farther, he fell with his face to
the ground and prayed, "My Father, if it is possible, may this cup be taken from me. Yet not as
I will, but as you will."
40Then he returned to his disciples and
found them sleeping. "Could you men not
keep watch with me for one hour?" he asked
Peter. 41"Watch and pray so that you will not
fall into temptation. The spirit is willing, but
the body is weak."
42He went away a second time and prayed,
"My Father, if it is not possible for this cup to
be taken away unless I drink it, may your will
be done."
43When he came back, he again found them
sleeping, because their eyes were heavy. 44So he
left them and went away once more and prayed
the third time, saying the same thing.
45Then he returned to the disciples and said
to them, "Are you still sleeping and resting?
Look, the hour is near, and the Son of Man is
betrayed into the hands of sinners. 46Rise, let us
go! Here comes my betrayer!"

[a]31 Zech. 13:7

26:31–75 Like Peter, we often go through several stages as we fall prey to our weaknesses. We proclaim we will never fail in a certain way (26:31–35). Yet we often find ourselves doing exactly what we promised we wouldn't do (26:56, 69–74). And we realize that we have failed miserably (26:75). But we have two options: We can work to overcome our weakness and learn from the experience, as Peter did, or we can flounder in our sin and never allow ourselves to be restored.

THE SPIRITUAL DISCIPLINES

Prayer

Letting Go and Taking Hold

Matthew 26:36–46 A common misconception among believers is the thought that if you are truly spiritually oriented, you will not struggle with following God's will. Jesus' own actions teach that this belief just isn't so. Jesus' final moments before his crucifixion were spent in prayer in the Garden of Gethsemane. Gethsemane in Aramaic means "oil press." This garden area on the Mount of Olives was used to press the olives grown on the mountain into olive oil. And this garden was a fitting image for the pressure Jesus underwent as he faced the call to the cross.

In Gethsemane, Jesus prayed three times. Each prayer was a step toward releasing the things that could hold him back from taking hold of God's will. The first prayer, an outburst of grief, was the step of realization, of feeling the full impact of his mission. Jesus shuddered in the chill of death's dark shadow. Prayer was his only refuge. He longed for his companions to comfort and support him, but they slept.

The second prayer was one of release. Jesus was faced with two choices: If he saved his own life, he would lose us because he would not have achieved salvation for us. But if he lost his life, he would save us. Jesus desired to do the will of his Father, so he accepted his calling to die for us. The Father's will became Jesus' will.

The third prayer strengthened his resolve. Like the tempering of steel when refined metal is heated a second time to increase its strength or like a soldier getting ready for battle or a patient preparing for a difficult surgery, so Jesus gathered strength from his Father for his upcoming task. Jesus left all his anxiety with him.

What we keep from God also keeps us from God. What we give to God becomes a channel for giving ourselves to God. Prayer enables us to travel the journey from realization to release and from release to resolve. We see this same process at work in the apostle Paul. He also prayed three times for relief from his thorn in the flesh. Each time God told him, "My grace is sufficient for you, for my power is made perfect in weakness" (2 Corinthians 12:9). This word enabled Paul to accept his situation and allow the power of Christ in his life to be made clear to all.

Putting It Into Practice

Is there something God is asking of you that weighs heavily on your heart? Ask God to help you move through the stages of realization, release and resolve. Allow yourself to feel the full impact of what God seems to be asking. This may lead to tears or other expressions of pain, but trust that God will see you through it. Then, let go, trusting that the Lord wants his best for you. Finally, boldly affirm your desire to honor God. You will likely experience a growing sense of grace and power as you do.

For more on prayer, turn to Ephesians 6.

Jesus Arrested

‰ See Mark 14:43–50; Luke 22:47–53

47While he was still speaking, Judas, one of the Twelve, arrived. With him was a large crowd armed with swords and clubs, sent from the chief priests and the elders of the people. 48Now the betrayer had arranged a signal with them: "The one I kiss is the man; arrest him." 49Going at once to Jesus, Judas said, "Greetings, Rabbi!" and kissed him.

50Jesus replied, "Friend, do what you came for."[a]

Then the men stepped forward, seized Jesus and arrested him. 51With that, one of Jesus' companions reached for his sword, drew it out and struck the servant of the high priest, cutting off his ear.

52"Put your sword back in its place," Jesus said to him, "for all who draw the sword will die by the sword. 53Do you think I cannot call on my Father, and he will at once put at my disposal more than twelve legions of angels? 54But how then would the Scriptures be fulfilled that say it must happen in this way?"

55At that time Jesus said to the crowd, "Am I leading a rebellion, that you have come out with swords and clubs to capture me? Every day I sat in the temple courts teaching, and you did not arrest me. 56But this has all taken place that the writings of the prophets might be fulfilled." Then all the disciples deserted him and fled.

Before the Sanhedrin

‰ See Mark 14:53–65; John 18:12–13,19–24

57Those who had arrested Jesus took him to Caiaphas, the high priest, where the teachers of the law and the elders had assembled. 58But Peter followed him at a distance, right up to the courtyard of the high priest. He entered and sat down with the guards to see the outcome.

59The chief priests and the whole Sanhedrin were looking for false evidence against Jesus so that they could put him to death. 60But they did not find any, though many false witnesses came forward.

Finally two came forward 61and declared, "This fellow said, 'I am able to destroy the temple of God and rebuild it in three days.' "

62Then the high priest stood up and said to Jesus, "Are you not going to answer? What is this testimony that these men are bringing against you?" 63But Jesus remained silent.

The high priest said to him, "I charge you under oath by the living God: Tell us if you are the Christ,[b] the Son of God."

64"Yes, it is as you say," Jesus replied. "But I say to all of you: In the future you will see the Son of Man sitting at the right hand of the Mighty One and coming on the clouds of heaven."

65Then the high priest tore his clothes and said, "He has spoken blasphemy! Why do we need any more witnesses? Look, now you have heard the blasphemy. 66What do you think?"

"He is worthy of death," they answered.

67Then they spit in his face and struck him with their fists. Others slapped him 68and said, "Prophesy to us, Christ. Who hit you?"

Peter Disowns Jesus

‰ See Mark 14:66–72; Luke 22:52–62; John 18:16–18,25–27

69Now Peter was sitting out in the courtyard, and a servant girl came to him. "You also were with Jesus of Galilee," she said.

70But he denied it before them all. "I don't know what you're talking about," he said.

71Then he went out to the gateway, where another girl saw him and said to the people there, "This fellow was with Jesus of Nazareth."

72He denied it again, with an oath: "I don't know the man!"

73After a little while, those standing there went up to Peter and said, "Surely you are one of them, for your accent gives you away."

74Then he began to call down curses on himself and he swore to them, "I don't know the man!"

Immediately a rooster crowed. 75Then Peter remembered the word Jesus had spoken: "Before the rooster crows, you will disown me three times." And he went outside and wept bitterly.

Judas Hangs Himself

27 Early in the morning, all the chief priests and the elders of the people came to the decision to put Jesus to death. 2They bound him, led him away and handed him over to Pilate, the governor.

3When Judas, who had betrayed him, saw that Jesus was condemned, he was seized with remorse and returned the thirty silver coins to the chief priests and the elders. 4"I have sinned," he said, "for I have betrayed innocent blood."

"What is that to us?" they replied. "That's your responsibility."

5So Judas threw the money into the temple and left. Then he went away and hanged himself.

6The chief priests picked up the coins and said, "It is against the law to put this into the treasury, since it is blood money." 7So they decided to use the money to buy the potter's field as a burial place for foreigners. 8That is why it has been called the Field of Blood to this day.

[a]50 Or *"Friend, why have you come?"* [b]63 Or *Messiah;* also in verse 68

27:3–8 The religious leaders refused to accept the blood money that Judas tried to return. It was probably their way of denying that they were responsible for Jesus' death. If we are not careful, we can fall into this kind of hypocrisy. Sometimes we hide behind righteous activities to conceal terrible sins. We must honestly examine our lives to see which actions do not line up with God's desires. Then we must confess our sins and ask God to help us change. Denying sin in even one area of our lives undermines our entire spiritual growth.

9Then what was spoken by Jeremiah the prophet was fulfilled: "They took the thirty silver
coins, the price set on him by the people of
Israel, 10and they used them to buy the potter's
field, as the Lord commanded me."[a]

Jesus Before Pilate

‰ See Mark 15:2–15; Luke 23:2–3,18–25; John 18:29—19:16

11Meanwhile Jesus stood before the governor, and the governor asked him, "Are you the
king of the Jews?"
"Yes, it is as you say," Jesus replied.
12When he was accused by the chief priests
and the elders, he gave no answer. 13Then Pilate
asked him, "Don't you hear the testimony they
are bringing against you?" 14But Jesus made no
reply, not even to a single charge—to the great
amazement of the governor.
15Now it was the governor's custom at the
Feast to release a prisoner chosen by the crowd.
16At that time they had a notorious prisoner,
called Barabbas. 17So when the crowd had gathered, Pilate asked them, "Which one do you
want me to release to you: Barabbas, or Jesus
who is called Christ?" 18For he knew it was out
of envy that they had handed Jesus over to him.
19While Pilate was sitting on the judge's seat,
his wife sent him this message: "Don't have
anything to do with that innocent man, for I
have suffered a great deal today in a dream because of him."
20But the chief priests and the elders persuaded the crowd to ask for Barabbas and to have
Jesus executed.
21"Which of the two do you want me to
release to you?" asked the governor.
"Barabbas," they answered.
22"What shall I do, then, with Jesus who is
called Christ?" Pilate asked.
They all answered, "Crucify him!"
23"Why? What crime has he committed?"
asked Pilate.
But they shouted all the louder, "Crucify
him!"
24When Pilate saw that he was getting nowhere, but that instead an uproar was starting,
he took water and washed his hands in front of
the crowd. "I am innocent of this man's blood,"
he said. "It is your responsibility!"
25All the people answered, "Let his blood be
on us and on our children!"
26Then he released Barabbas to them. But he
had Jesus flogged, and handed him over to be
crucified.

The Soldiers Mock Jesus

‰ See Mark 15:16–20

27Then the governor's soldiers took Jesus
into the Praetorium and gathered the whole
company of soldiers around him. 28They
stripped him and put a scarlet robe on him,
29and then twisted together a crown of thorns
and set it on his head. They put a staff in his
right hand and knelt in front of him and
mocked him. "Hail, king of the Jews!" they said.
30They spit on him, and took the staff and
struck him on the head again and again. 31After
they had mocked him, they took off the robe
and put his own clothes on him. Then they led
him away to crucify him.

The Crucifixion

‰ See Mark 15:22–32; Luke 23:33–43; John 19:17–24

32As they were going out, they met a man
from Cyrene, named Simon, and they forced
him to carry the cross. 33They came to a place
called Golgotha (which means The Place of the
Skull). 34There they offered Jesus wine to drink,
mixed with gall; but after tasting it, he refused
to drink it. 35When they had crucified him, they
divided up his clothes by casting lots.[b] 36And
sitting down, they kept watch over him there.
37Above his head they placed the written charge
against him: THIS IS JESUS, THE KING OF THE JEWS.
38Two robbers were crucified with him, one on
his right and one on his left. 39Those who
passed by hurled insults at him, shaking their
heads 40and saying, "You who are going to destroy the temple and build it in three days, save
yourself! Come down from the cross, if you are
the Son of God!"
41In the same way the chief priests, the teachers of the law and the elders mocked him.
42"He saved others," they said, "but he can't
save himself! He's the King of Israel! Let him
come down now from the cross, and we will
believe in him. 43He trusts in God. Let God
rescue him now if he wants him, for he said, 'I
am the Son of God.' " 44In the same way the
robbers who were crucified with him also
heaped insults on him.

[a] *10* See Zech. 11:12,13; Jer. 19:1-13; 32:6-9.
[b] *35* A few late manuscripts *lots that the word spoken by the prophet might be fulfilled: "They divided my garments among themselves and cast lots for my clothing"* (Psalm 22:18)

27:11–26 Although he was convinced that Jesus was innocent and righteous, Pilate bowed to public opinion and political pressure (27:24). Pilate exemplified someone in need of redemption who knew the right thing to do but did not have the courage to follow through and risk angering others. Since it is impossible to please everyone all the time, we must make sure that what we are doing is honest and pleasing to God. We should ultimately be more concerned about our sinning against God than about our angering others.

27:26–54 The narrative of Jesus' crucifixion and death records one act of brutal torture after another. Jesus was beaten, ridiculed, tortured and killed. He can directly identify with others who have suffered or have been oppressed. Jesus can also redeem the oppressors who come to faith, as did the soldiers and their centurion at the cross. Jesus' death and resurrection bring deliverance for everyone.

The Death of Jesus

‰ See Mark 15:33–41; Luke 23:44–49; John 19:29–30

45 From the sixth hour until the ninth hour
darkness came over all the land. 46 About the
ninth hour Jesus cried out in a loud voice, *"Eloi,
Eloi,*[a] *lama sabachthani?"*—which means, "My
God, my God, why have you forsaken me?"[b]
47 When some of those standing there heard
this, they said, "He's calling Elijah."
48 Immediately one of them ran and got a
sponge. He filled it with wine vinegar, put it on
a stick, and offered it to Jesus to drink. 49 The
rest said, "Now leave him alone. Let's see if
Elijah comes to save him."
50 And when Jesus had cried out again in a
loud voice, he gave up his spirit.
51 At that moment the curtain of the temple
was torn in two from top to bottom. The earth
shook and the rocks split. 52 The tombs broke
open and the bodies of many holy people who
had died were raised to life. 53 They came out of
the tombs, and after Jesus' resurrection they
went into the holy city and appeared to many
people.
54 When the centurion and those with him
who were guarding Jesus saw the earthquake
and all that had happened, they were terrified,
and exclaimed, "Surely he was the Son[c] of
God!"
55 Many women were there, watching from a
distance. They had followed Jesus from Galilee
to care for his needs. 56 Among them were Mary
Magdalene, Mary the mother of James and Joses, and the mother of Zebedee's sons.

The Burial of Jesus

‰ See Mark 15:42–47; Luke 23:50–56; John 19:38–42

57 As evening approached, there came a rich
man from Arimathea, named Joseph, who had
himself become a disciple of Jesus. 58 Going to
Pilate, he asked for Jesus' body, and Pilate ordered that it be given to him. 59 Joseph took the
body, wrapped it in a clean linen cloth, 60 and
placed it in his own new tomb that he had cut
out of the rock. He rolled a big stone in front
of the entrance to the tomb and went away.
61 Mary Magdalene and the other Mary were sitting there opposite the tomb.

The Guard at the Tomb

62 The next day, the one after Preparation
Day, the chief priests and the Pharisees went to
Pilate. 63 "Sir," they said, "we remember that
while he was still alive that deceiver said, 'After
three days I will rise again.' 64 So give the order
for the tomb to be made secure until the third
day. Otherwise, his disciples may come and
steal the body and tell the people that he has
been raised from the dead. This last deception
will be worse than the first."
65 "Take a guard," Pilate answered. "Go, make
the tomb as secure as you know how." 66 So they
went and made the tomb secure by putting a
seal on the stone and posting the guard.

The Resurrection

‰ See Mark 16:1–8; Luke 24:1–10; John 20:1–8

28 After the Sabbath, at dawn on the first
day of the week, Mary Magdalene and
the other Mary went to look at the tomb.
2 There was a violent earthquake, for an angel
of the Lord came down from heaven and, going
to the tomb, rolled back the stone and sat on
it. 3 His appearance was like lightning, and his
clothes were white as snow. 4 The guards were so
afraid of him that they shook and became like
dead men.
5 The angel said to the women, "Do not be
afraid, for I know that you are looking for Jesus,
who was crucified. 6 He is not here; he has risen,
just as he said. Come and see the place where he
lay. 7 Then go quickly and tell his disciples: 'He
has risen from the dead and is going ahead of
you into Galilee. There you will see him.' Now
I have told you."
8 So the women hurried away from the tomb,
afraid yet filled with joy, and ran to tell his
disciples. 9 Suddenly Jesus met them. "Greetings," he said. They came to him, clasped his feet
and worshiped him. 10 Then Jesus said to them,
"Do not be afraid. Go and tell my brothers to
go to Galilee; there they will see me."

The Guards' Report

11 While the women were on their way, some
of the guards went into the city and reported to
the chief priests everything that had happened.
12 When the chief priests had met with the elders
and devised a plan, they gave the soldiers a large
sum of money, 13 telling them, "You are to say,
'His disciples came during the night and stole

[a]46 Some manuscripts *Eli, Eli* [b]46 Psalm 22:1
[c]54 Or *a son*

27:57–60 Joseph of Arimathea was a secret disciple who revealed his faith at a crisis point (see John 19:38). Joseph's willingness to approach Pilate, as well as his generous burial of Jesus, indicates that he took an outward step toward a stronger faith and commitment. What kind of crisis will it take to inspire us to devote our lives wholeheartedly to God?

27:62—28:15 The religious leaders wanted to be free of Jesus' message. They tried everything they could think of. They attempted to discredit him in front of the crowds. They plotted his murder. And when they arrested him, the religious leader bribed witnesses in order to convince Rome that Jesus was worthy of death. Yet once Jesus was dead, the leaders feared he would come back to life. They were granted permission to seal and guard the tomb. Finally, they had to come up with a story to explain the disappearance of Jesus' body. Obviously the easier path would have been to accept Jesus' message in the first place and make the appropriate changes in their lives and beliefs. We must make sure we don't become so hardened to God's plan that we, like the Jewish leaders, go to great lengths to avoid accepting the lifesaving message of the gospel.

him away while we were asleep.' 14If this report
gets to the governor, we will satisfy him and
keep you out of trouble." 15So the soldiers took
the money and did as they were instructed. And
this story has been widely circulated among the
Jews to this very day.

The Great Commission

16Then the eleven disciples went to Galilee,
to the mountain where Jesus had told them to
go. 17When they saw him, they worshiped him;
but some doubted. 18Then Jesus came to them
and said, "All authority in heaven and on earth
has been given to me. 19Therefore go and make
disciples of all nations, baptizing them in[a] the
name of the Father and of the Son and of the
Holy Spirit, 20and teaching them to obey everything I have commanded you. And surely I am
with you always, to the very end of the age."

[a]*19* Or *into;* see Acts 8:16; 19:5; Romans 6:3; 1 Cor. 1:13; 10:2 and Gal. 3:27.

28:16–20 Some disciples received the news of Jesus' resurrection quite readily while others were more reticent. But Jesus' resurrection was not an end in itself. Nor was salvation granted to just his closest disciples. The message of new life through faith in the crucified and resurrected Christ was to be offered to everyone. And continual instruction in the faith will help us grow and preserve our spiritual gains.

MARK

The Big Picture

A. JESUS PREPARES FOR SERVICE (1:1-13)

B. JESUS SERVES THROUGH WORD AND DEED (1:14–13:37)

1. Jesus Serves in Galilee (1:14–9:50)
2. Jesus Serves Beyond Jerusalem (10:1-45)
3. Jesus Serves in Jerusalem (10:46–13:37)

C. JESUS SERVES THROUGH SELF-SACRIFICE (14:1–16:20)

When we desire spiritual renewal, we are usually looking for something that will make a real difference in our lives. Perhaps we were raised in a church or a godly family and know all the rules of godly behavior but have never felt God's power in our daily lives. The Gospel of Mark is written for people like us, giving us a glimpse of a powerful God who wants to help us.

In Mark's Gospel, Jesus' power is displayed again and again: He raised the dead, gave sight to the blind, restored deformed limbs, made lame people walk, cast out demons, healed incurable skin diseases and quieted stormy waters. Though Mark is the shortest of the Gospels, it records more miracles than the other three gospels. Mark shows us Jesus as a powerful Savior who is more than able to help suffering people.

Mark also emphasizes Jesus' desire to help us. By recording a rapid succession of vivid pictures, Mark shows us Jesus in action, spending his energy to the point of exhaustion in order to heal those who came to him for help. Jesus came to help us too. And this truth is driven home by Jesus' willingness to suffer a painful death to free us from our bondage to sin.

Jesus has power over sin, demonic powers and nature. He demonstrated this power when he walked on earth, and he possesses the same power today. Whatever problems we may face or needs we may have, Jesus has the power to help us. We only need to look to him and admit that we need his help.

Spiritual Renewal Themes

JESUS AS THE SERVANT

True spiritual renewal should encourage us to be servants and to share our experience with others. Greatness in God's eyes is measured by a willingness to serve and to sacrifice for others. Jesus didn't come to earth as a conquering king; he came as a servant. He chose to obey his Father and die for us. Following Jesus' example, we must not let personal ambition or a hunger for power control our lives. Instead we should humbly seek to follow God's will and serve others.

THE POWER OF GOD

The Gospel of Mark is filled with amazing events that display the awesome power of God in Jesus life. Mark recorded more of Jesus' miracles than his sermons, thereby emphasizing God's power in action. The more we believe that Jesus is God, the more we will witness his power and love in our own lives. Jesus' greatest miracles are still those that involve forgiveness, healing of relationships and restoration. The power we see in Mark's Gospel is still available to us.

SHARING THE MESSAGE

Discipleship and spiritual growth take place within relationships. There is no such thing as a secret disciple or private spiritual growth. As we share the joys and struggles of our own spiritual growth, we encourage others in theirs. Such a message transcends national, racial and economic barriers, reaching out to those who desire to seek God and surrender to him. God's Good News and the message of our spiritual renewal are meant to be shared with others.

Essential Facts

PURPOSE:
To encourage us to continue trusting and serving God, even through life's difficulties.

AUTHOR:
John Mark.

AUDIENCE:
The Christians in Rome.

DATE WRITTEN:
Probably between A.D. 55 and 65.

SETTING:
The known world was united under the Roman Empire, and its common language made conditions ideal for spreading the Gospel in written form.

KEY VERSE:
"For even the Son of Man did not come to be served, but to serve, and to give his life as a ransom for many" (10:45).

KEY PEOPLE AND RELATIONSHIPS:
Jesus with his disciples, especially Peter.

SPECIAL FEATURES:
A fast-paced narrative characterizes the Gospel of Mark.

John the Baptist Prepares the Way

‰ See Matthew 3:1–11; Luke 3:2–16

1 The beginning of the gospel about Jesus
Christ, the Son of God.[a]

2It is written in Isaiah the prophet:

"I will send my messenger ahead of you,
who will prepare your way"[b]—
3"a voice of one calling in the desert,
'Prepare the way for the Lord,
make straight paths for him.' "[c]

4And so John came, baptizing in the desert region and preaching a baptism of repentance
for the forgiveness of sins. 5The whole Judean
countryside and all the people of Jerusalem
went out to him. Confessing their sins, they
were baptized by him in the Jordan River. 6John
wore clothing made of camel's hair, with a
leather belt around his waist, and he ate locusts
and wild honey. 7And this was his message:
"After me will come one more powerful than I,
the thongs of whose sandals I am not worthy to
stoop down and untie. 8I baptize you with[d]
water, but he will baptize you with the Holy
Spirit."

The Baptism and Temptation of Jesus

‰ See Matthew 3:13–17; 4:1–11; Luke 3:21–22; 4:1–13

9At that time Jesus came from Nazareth in
Galilee and was baptized by John in the Jordan.
10As Jesus was coming up out of the water, he
saw heaven being torn open and the Spirit descending on him like a dove. 11And a voice
came from heaven: "You are my Son, whom I
love; with you I am well pleased."
12At once the Spirit sent him out into the
desert, 13and he was in the desert forty days,
being tempted by Satan. He was with the wild
animals, and angels attended him.

The Calling of the First Disciples

‰ See Matthew 4:18–22; Luke 5:2–11; John 1:35–42

14After John was put in prison, Jesus went
into Galilee, proclaiming the good news of
God. 15"The time has come," he said. "The kingdom of God is near. Repent and believe the
good news!"
16As Jesus walked beside the Sea of Galilee,
he saw Simon and his brother Andrew casting
a net into the lake, for they were fishermen.
17"Come, follow me," Jesus said, "and I will
make you fishers of men." 18At once they left
their nets and followed him.
19When he had gone a little farther, he saw
James son of Zebedee and his brother John in
a boat, preparing their nets. 20Without delay he
called them, and they left their father Zebedee
in the boat with the hired men and followed
him.

Jesus Drives Out an Evil Spirit

‰ See Luke 4:31–37

21They went to Capernaum, and when the
Sabbath came, Jesus went into the synagogue
and began to teach. 22The people were amazed
at his teaching, because he taught them as one
who had authority, not as the teachers of the
law. 23Just then a man in their synagogue who
was possessed by an evil[e] spirit cried out,
24"What do you want with us, Jesus of Nazareth? Have you come to destroy us? I know who
you are—the Holy One of God!"
25"Be quiet!" said Jesus sternly. "Come out of
him!" 26The evil spirit shook the man violently
and came out of him with a shriek.
27The people were all so amazed that they
asked each other, "What is this? A new teaching—and with authority! He even gives orders
to evil spirits and they obey him." 28News
about him spread quickly over the whole region of Galilee.

Jesus Heals Many

‰ See Matthew 8:14–17; Luke 4:38–41

29As soon as they left the synagogue, they
went with James and John to the home of Simon and Andrew. 30Simon's mother-in-law
was in bed with a fever, and they told Jesus
about her. 31So he went to her, took her hand
and helped her up. The fever left her and she
began to wait on them.
32That evening after sunset the people
brought to Jesus all the sick and demon-
possessed. 33The whole town gathered at the
door, 34and Jesus healed many who had various
diseases. He also drove out many demons, but
he would not let the demons speak because
they knew who he was.

a1 Some manuscripts do not have *the Son of God.*
b2 Mal. 3:1 c3 Isaiah 40:3 d8 Or *in*
e23 Greek *unclean;* also in verses 26 and 27

1:1–13 Jesus demonstrated his great power through his victory over Satan and his temptations. Jesus' victory over temptation can encourage us as we face temptation in our own lives. With his help, we can stand up to anything. Under our own power, we are helpless against the sins that enslave us. We can only tap into God's power by making a conscious decision to turn our backs on sin and by surrendering our lives to God.

1:16–20 We are not sure how many times Jesus had to summon Simon Peter, Andrew, James and John to follow him. On two other occasions, a similar call went out to these four fishermen (see Luke 5:1–11; John 1:35–42). Their initial response to Jesus' call seems to have been immediate. But it appears that they soon went back to their old occupations and ways of life. Sometimes our faith in God grows that way over time, at uneven rates, with uncertain steps. Each step of faith we take requires that we drop whatever else we are doing and follow Jesus wholeheartedly.

1:21–28 God's power to change lives was demonstrated as Jesus cast out an evil spirit. Since Jesus has the power to cast out evil spirits, he certainly has enough power to free us from the sins that entangle us. We need to recognize our sins, confess them honestly and call out to him for help.

Jesus Prays in a Solitary Place

‰ See Luke 4:42–43

[35]Very early in the morning, while it was still dark, Jesus got up, left the house and went off to a solitary place, where he prayed. [36]Simon and his companions went to look for him, [37]and when they found him, they exclaimed: "Everyone is looking for you!"

[38]Jesus replied, "Let us go somewhere else—to the nearby villages—so I can preach there also. That is why I have come." [39]So he traveled throughout Galilee, preaching in their synagogues and driving out demons.

A Man With Leprosy

‰ See Matthew 8:2–4; Luke 5:12–14

[40]A man with leprosy[a] came to him and begged him on his knees, "If you are willing, you can make me clean."

[41]Filled with compassion, Jesus reached out his hand and touched the man. "I am willing," he said. "Be clean!" [42]Immediately the leprosy left him and he was cured.

[43]Jesus sent him away at once with a strong warning: [44]"See that you don't tell this to anyone. But go, show yourself to the priest and offer the sacrifices that Moses commanded for your cleansing, as a testimony to them." [45]Instead he went out and began to talk freely, spreading the news. As a result, Jesus could no longer enter a town openly but stayed outside in lonely places. Yet the people still came to him from everywhere.

Jesus Heals a Paralytic

‰ See Matthew 9:2–8; Luke 5:18–26

2 A few days later, when Jesus again entered Capernaum, the people heard that he had come home. [2]So many gathered that there was no room left, not even outside the door, and he preached the word to them. [3]Some men came, bringing to him a paralytic, carried by four of them. [4]Since they could not get him to Jesus because of the crowd, they made an opening in the roof above Jesus and, after digging through it, lowered the mat the paralyzed man was lying on. [5]When Jesus saw their faith, he said to the paralytic, "Son, your sins are forgiven."

[6]Now some teachers of the law were sitting there, thinking to themselves, [7]"Why does this fellow talk like that? He's blaspheming! Who can forgive sins but God alone?"

[8]Immediately Jesus knew in his spirit that this was what they were thinking in their hearts, and he said to them, "Why are you thinking these things? [9]Which is easier: to say to the paralytic, 'Your sins are forgiven,' or to say, 'Get up, take your mat and walk'? [10]But that you may know that the Son of Man has authority on earth to forgive sins . . . ." He said to the paralytic, [11]"I tell you, get up, take your mat and go home." [12]He got up, took his mat and walked out in full view of them all. This amazed everyone and they praised God, saying, "We have never seen anything like this!"

The Calling of Levi

‰ See Matthew 9:9–13; Luke 5:27–32

[13]Once again Jesus went out beside the lake. A large crowd came to him, and he began to teach them. [14]As he walked along, he saw Levi son of Alphaeus sitting at the tax collector's booth. "Follow me," Jesus told him, and Levi got up and followed him.

[15]While Jesus was having dinner at Levi's house, many tax collectors and "sinners" were eating with him and his disciples, for there were many who followed him. [16]When the teachers of the law who were Pharisees saw him eating with the "sinners" and tax collectors, they asked his disciples: "Why does he eat with tax collectors and 'sinners'?"

[17]On hearing this, Jesus said to them, "It is not the healthy who need a doctor, but the sick.

[a]*40* The Greek word was used for various diseases affecting the skin—not necessarily leprosy.

1:35–39 If Jesus, the Son of God, took time from his busy schedule to pray, how much more do we need to do so. By placing a high priority on prayer, Jesus was able to persevere in his ministry and keep from becoming exhausted. We who seek spiritual growth for ourselves and redemption for others, must pray. The busier the day ahead, the more we need to meditate on God's Word and pray for his strength and wisdom.

1:40–45 Jesus displayed his power by healing a man with leprosy. Leprosy is a progressive, infectious, crippling disease that affects the skin and superficial nerves. In ancient times, the disease of leprosy was often considered a form of divine retribution (see Numbers 12:9–10; 2 Chronicles 26:16–23). There was no cure except a miracle from God. We also are infected by an incurable disease—the disease of sin. Sin has made us ugly and left us spiritually deformed. Yet there is hope for us. We can be restored to healthy living and fellowship through the healing touch of Jesus. First, like the lepers, we must realize our inability to cure ourselves. Then we can trust Jesus' power and love to cleanse and renew us.

2:1–12 Jesus came not only to heal physical problems, but also to solve the sin problem. When we do not know Jesus we are paralyzed in spirit, as powerless to help ourselves as was this paralyzed man. If our faith is still too weak to carry us to the point of healing, the faith of our friends may help get us there. Notice that Jesus did more than simply mouth the words of forgiveness; he also showed his authority and intent with his actions. In the same way, we need to do more than mouth our words of faith. We should also act on what God has called us to do.

2:13–17 Because of their unethical practices and support of the pagan Romans, the Jews considered tax collectors notorious sinners. But it was for people like these tax collectors that Jesus came to bring salvation. Levi (Matthew) proved he meant business with Jesus by bringing him his friends, colleagues and collaborators in sin. Some may question whether a person so new and immature in his faith should be telling his story to others. But the account here illustrates the truth that our spiritual lives are strengthened when we share the news of God's love with others, no matter what the extent of our knowledge, skill or experience.

Solitude

Overcoming Expectations

Mark 1:35 One of the subtlest enemies to spiritual vitality is the influence of others and their expectations of us. The world expects us to continually seek possessions or prestige or to always fill our time with busy activity, whether meaningful or not. How often do we let the world's expectations of us dictate our spiritual lives as well? How often do we do something that will please others rather than what will please God? Sometimes pleasing God may actually require that we disappoint others because we cannot fulfill their demands on us.

Solitude helps us break free from the expectations of others. In solitude we can see more clearly what the world is asking of us. We can more easily evaluate these expectations in relation to God's desires for us and decide which demands should and should not be fulfilled.

Following one of the busiest days—and nights—of his ministry, "very early in the morning, while it was still dark, Jesus got up, left the house and went off to a solitary place, where he prayed" (1:35). The people began asking to see Jesus. When the disciples came looking for him to take him back to town, Jesus told them that they must instead go on to other towns. Opportunity and success didn't dictate Jesus' direction; God did. Jesus' time spent alone helped him to be directed by God alone.

Putting It Into Practice

When do you feel most vulnerable to others' expectations? What specifically do you feel others expect of you? What do you do when the world's demands press in on you? Spend some time alone in prayerful reflection and respond to each of those expectations as you feel God would want you to respond. You may realize, for example, that others expect you to solve their problems for them. But as you reflect on that expectation, you may see that God wants to solve other people's problems in his own way. Sometimes God may desire to use you to encourage and support others; at other times he may wish you to leave them alone so that they would turn to him.

For more on solitude, turn to Luke 4.

I have not come to call the righteous, but sinners."

Jesus Questioned About Fasting

‰ See Matthew 9:14–17; Luke 5:33–38

18 Now John's disciples and the Pharisees were fasting. Some people came and asked Jesus, "How is it that John's disciples and the disciples of the Pharisees are fasting, but yours are not?"

19 Jesus answered, "How can the guests of the bridegroom fast while he is with them? They cannot, so long as they have him with them. 20 But the time will come when the bridegroom will be taken from them, and on that day they will fast.

21 "No one sews a patch of unshrunk cloth on an old garment. If he does, the new piece will pull away from the old, making the tear worse. 22 And no one pours new wine into old wineskins. If he does, the wine will burst the skins, and both the wine and the wineskins will be ruined. No, he pours new wine into new wineskins."

Lord of the Sabbath

‰ See Matthew 12:1–14; Luke 6:1–11

23 One Sabbath Jesus was going through the grainfields, and as his disciples walked along, they began to pick some heads of grain. 24 The Pharisees said to him, "Look, why are they doing what is unlawful on the Sabbath?"

25 He answered, "Have you never read what David did when he and his companions were hungry and in need? 26 In the days of Abiathar the high priest, he entered the house of God and ate the consecrated bread, which is lawful only for priests to eat. And he also gave some to his companions."

27 Then he said to them, "The Sabbath was made for man, not man for the Sabbath. 28 So the Son of Man is Lord even of the Sabbath."

3 Another time he went into the synagogue, and a man with a shriveled hand was there. 2 Some of them were looking for a reason to accuse Jesus, so they watched him closely to see if he would heal him on the Sabbath. 3 Jesus said to the man with the shriveled hand, "Stand up in front of everyone."

4 Then Jesus asked them, "Which is lawful on the Sabbath: to do good or to do evil, to save life or to kill?" But they remained silent.

5 He looked around at them in anger and, deeply distressed at their stubborn hearts, said to the man, "Stretch out your hand." He stretched it out, and his hand was completely restored. 6 Then the Pharisees went out and began to plot with the Herodians how they might kill Jesus.

Crowds Follow Jesus

‰ See Matthew 12:15–16; Luke 6:17–19

7 Jesus withdrew with his disciples to the lake, and a large crowd from Galilee followed. 8 When they heard all he was doing, many people came to him from Judea, Jerusalem, Idumea, and the regions across the Jordan and around Tyre and Sidon. 9 Because of the crowd he told his disciples to have a small boat ready for him, to keep the people from crowding him. 10 For he had healed many, so that those with diseases were pushing forward to touch him. 11 Whenever the evil[a] spirits saw him, they fell down before him and cried out, "You are the Son of God." 12 But he gave them strict orders not to tell who he was.

The Appointing of the Twelve Apostles

13 Jesus went up on a mountainside and called to him those he wanted, and they came to him. 14 He appointed twelve—designating them apostles[b]—that they might be with him and that he might send them out to preach 15 and to have authority to drive out demons. 16 These are the twelve he appointed: Simon (to whom he gave the name Peter); 17 James son

[a] 11 Greek *unclean;* also in verse 30 [b] 14 Some manuscripts do not have *designating them apostles.*

2:18–22 The old wineskins of Jewish religious practice were too rigid to carry the expansive, life-changing message of God's love in Jesus Christ. In a similar way, religious activities are never enough unless they are coupled with genuine repentance. We must recognize the failures in our lives and then look to the only one who is able to make things right again—God in Jesus Christ. If we look to him for help, he is more than able to forgive us and get us back on the right track. God will make our hard hearts open and pliable, like fresh wineskins, so that we can receive his gifts of grace.

2:23–28 All of God's laws were intended for the good of his people. When the disciples picked grain at the edge of a farmer's field, they were actually utilizing one of the provisions God had prescribed in his law (see Leviticus 19:9–10). Yet the Pharisees, with their regulations and assumptions, accused Jesus of breaking God's law by working on the Sabbath. Sadly, as they pretended to uphold the law, the Pharisees actually stood counter to God's intentions. We must guard against religious legalism, keeping in mind that God's ultimate desire is to help.

3:1–6 This Sabbath controversy revealed two ways of dealing with anger. Anger itself is a morally neutral human emotion; how we handle our anger is what really matters. Jesus was angry at the Pharisees for making up rules about the Sabbath that stood counter to God's real intentions in the law. He used his anger constructively, not to tear people down, but to heal a man's deformed hand. The Pharisees and supporters of Herod, however, used their anger to plan Jesus' execution. Anger expressed in selfish or harmful ways is always a destructive thing.

3:7–19 Despite his rejection by the religious leaders, Jesus enjoyed a growing following, even from among outlying districts. Jesus' popularity reached a high point nearly halfway through his three years of public ministry. The great demands on Jesus for his service and ministry may have prompted him to summon and appoint the twelve disciples who helped him carry out his ministry. Not even Jesus attempted to minister alone. In the same way, our work for Christ can be multiplied through the help of other believers.

Avoiding the Legalism Trap

Mark 2:27 A practice that begins as a good exercise can become faulty and worthless when we lose sight of its original purpose. God's command to keep the Sabbath was given as a gracious gift to remind his people of his covenant with them. But the observance of the Sabbath soon became a burden to Israel. Instead of focusing on the true purpose for the day, the religious leaders of Israel became sidetracked with the legalistic concerns about *how* to keep the Sabbath. They became more concerned about specific definitions of right and wrong than about their devotion to God. The religious leaders even carefully detailed which knots could be tied on the Sabbath and which knots were considered work. Knots that could be tied and untied with one hand were legal, but those involving both hands were not. This slavish attention to strict regulations made dressing, drawing water from a well and a number of other practices a legal nightmare.

These interpretations of God's laws took people's attention off God and robbed them of the gift God originally intended for them in the Sabbath. This is seen clearly in Mark 2:23–27. Jesus and his disciples were gleaning in the fields for their daily meal—an act fully appropriate with the spirit of the Sabbath as God originally intended it. But the Pharisees interpreted such gleaning as work and therefore a violation of God's law. Jesus confronted their misinterpretation by declaring the original intent of the Sabbath: "The Sabbath was made for man, not man for the Sabbath" (2:27). Legalistic concerns had perverted the good gift that God had given his people and made it a burden to them. The Sabbath was not a principle to be served by the people; it was a gift to serve them.

This legalism plagued the early church as well. In Colossians 2:16–23, Paul confronted those who were relying on their performance to please God. We are not immune from this emphasis on works either. In our performance-based culture, many find it difficult to simply trust God's transforming power. We want to achieve everything ourselves. But worship helps us readjust our perspective and understand that it is not what we *do* but who we *are* in Christ that matters most.

Yet in Christian obedience, there is a difference between legalism and discipline. Legalism is practiced for the sake of keeping the law. Guilt or fear or a desire to earn favor with God often motivates such legalistic practices. Love and gratitude for the gracious relationship the Lord has given us, on the other hand, motivate discipline. Legalism boasts in its achievements. Discipline rejoices in what God has done through Christ. Legalism thinks it must pay God back. Discipline recognizes its debt to grace. As you consider your pace of life and your "rules of conduct," avoid the legalism trap that can smother spiritual vitality.

Putting It Into Practice

Observing the Sabbath is important for our spiritual health. A Sabbath observance reminds us of the covenant God has established with us, his people. One way we can observe the Sabbath is through worshiping God with other believers. Are you involved in corporate worship on a weekly basis? If not, why not? Hebrews 10:25 reminds us to "not give up meeting together, as some are in the habit of doing, but let us encourage one another." How do you prepare yourself for worship? Many find it helpful to make special efforts the evening before, such as getting clothes ready, getting enough sleep, preparing their financial gifts and so on. Read the Bible passage associated with the sermon; pray for your church leaders and teachers. Then, after worship, ask yourself, What did the Lord say to me? Write your reflections in your journal. Always keep in mind, however, that these practices are ultimately for the purpose of honoring the Lord and remembering his covenant with us.

For more on worship, turn to Romans 12.

of Zebedee and his brother John (to them he gave the name Boanerges, which means Sons of Thunder); 18 Andrew, Philip, Bartholomew, Matthew, Thomas, James son of Alphaeus, Thaddaeus, Simon the Zealot 19 and Judas Iscariot, who betrayed him.

Jesus and Beelzebub

‰ See Matthew 12:25–29; Luke 11:17–22

20 Then Jesus entered a house, and again a crowd gathered, so that he and his disciples were not even able to eat. 21 When his family heard about this, they went to take charge of him, for they said, "He is out of his mind."

22 And the teachers of the law who came down from Jerusalem said, "He is possessed by Beelzebub[a]! By the prince of demons he is driving out demons."

23 So Jesus called them and spoke to them in parables: "How can Satan drive out Satan? 24 If a kingdom is divided against itself, that kingdom cannot stand. 25 If a house is divided against itself, that house cannot stand. 26 And if Satan opposes himself and is divided, he cannot stand; his end has come. 27 In fact, no one can enter a strong man's house and carry off his possessions unless he first ties up the strong man. Then he can rob his house. 28 I tell you the truth, all the sins and blasphemies of men will be forgiven them. 29 But whoever blasphemes against the Holy Spirit will never be forgiven; he is guilty of an eternal sin."

30 He said this because they were saying, "He has an evil spirit."

Jesus' Mother and Brothers

‰ See Matthew 12:46–50; Luke 8:19–21

31 Then Jesus' mother and brothers arrived. Standing outside, they sent someone in to call him. 32 A crowd was sitting around him, and they told him, "Your mother and brothers are outside looking for you."

33 "Who are my mother and my brothers?" he asked.

34 Then he looked at those seated in a circle around him and said, "Here are my mother and my brothers! 35 Whoever does God's will is my brother and sister and mother."

The Parable of the Sower

‰ See Matthew 13:1–15,18–23; Luke 8:4–15

4 Again Jesus began to teach by the lake. The crowd that gathered around him was so large that he got into a boat and sat in it out on the lake, while all the people were along the shore at the water's edge. 2 He taught them many things by parables, and in his teaching said: 3 "Listen! A farmer went out to sow his seed. 4 As he was scattering the seed, some fell along the path, and the birds came and ate it up. 5 Some fell on rocky places, where it did not have much soil. It sprang up quickly, because the soil was shallow. 6 But when the sun came up, the plants were scorched, and they withered because they had no root. 7 Other seed fell among thorns, which grew up and choked the plants, so that they did not bear grain. 8 Still other seed fell on good soil. It came up, grew and produced a crop, multiplying thirty, sixty, or even a hundred times."

9 Then Jesus said, "He who has ears to hear, let him hear."

10 When he was alone, the Twelve and the others around him asked him about the parables. 11 He told them, "The secret of the kingdom of God has been given to you. But to those on the outside everything is said in parables 12 so that,

" 'they may be ever seeing but never
perceiving,
and ever hearing but never
understanding;
otherwise they might turn and be
forgiven!'[b] "

13 Then Jesus said to them, "Don't you understand this parable? How then will you understand any parable? 14 The farmer sows the word. 15 Some people are like seed along the path, where the word is sown. As soon as they hear it, Satan comes and takes away the word that was sown in them. 16 Others, like seed sown on rocky places, hear the word and at once receive it with joy. 17 But since they have no root, they last only a short time. When trouble or persecution comes because of the word, they quickly fall away. 18 Still others, like seed sown among thorns, hear the word; 19 but the worries of this life, the deceitfulness of wealth and the desires for other things come in and choke the word, making it unfruitful. 20 Others, like seed sown on good soil, hear the word, accept it, and produce a crop—thirty, sixty or even a hundred times what was sown."

A Lamp on a Stand

21 He said to them, "Do you bring in a lamp to put it under a bowl or a bed? Instead, don't you put it on its stand? 22 For whatever is hidden is meant to be disclosed, and whatever is con-

[a] 22 Greek *Beezeboul* or *Beelzeboul*   [b] 12 Isaiah 6:9,10

4:1–20 Some welcomed Christ's message of redemption while others rejected it. Jesus told the people stories to help communicate further truth about the nature of God's kingdom. Four of these stories about the kingdom are given in this chapter. Together these stories portray the amazing growth of God's kingdom, which will one day reach to all nations when Christ returns.

4:21–25 The lamp in this illustration represents the truth about Jesus. We hide Jesus' light every time we fail to openly share our faith with others. God wants us to openly share his love, his truth and what he has done for us with others. If we discover that we are hiding our light, we need to confess this to God and ask him to help us share our faith more openly.

James & John

Sons of Thunder! Why would Jesus use such a powerful description for two Galilean fishermen? We are given a glimpse of their fiery personalities when, after the people of a Samaritan village rejected them, James and John asked Jesus if they should call down fire from heaven to consume the village. Jesus rebuked them for their impulse to retaliate.

Yet Jesus worked in these brothers' lives so that they ultimately became known for their love and forgiveness, not for anger and revenge. John, "the disciple whom Jesus loved" (John 13:23), wrote powerful words on the importance of love. He discovered that he didn't have to earn God's love but that he could freely receive it and pass it on to others. John became an important leader in the church of Asia Minor and was later exiled to the island of Patmos, where he wrote the book of Revelation. He apparently outlived the rest of the twelve disciples. James was the first of the twelve disciples to give his life for his faith. He was killed in Jerusalem by order of Herod Agrippa I.

Though the two brothers had once been ambitious for personal advancement, they became ambitious to advance the lives of others by sharing God's love with them. The brothers discovered that when we understand and experience God's love, we are free to live and grow. And as we grow and share our discovery with others, God can use us to touch the lives of others who need God's healing help.

STRENGTHS AND ACCOMPLISHMENTS:

With Peter, James and John formed the inner circle of Jesus' disciples.

Both men were important leaders in the early church.

John was inspired to write five New Testament books (The Gospel of John; 1, 2, 3 John and Revelation).

WEAKNESSES AND MISTAKES:

James and John tended to react in anger to anyone who opposed them.

They selfishly tried to promote themselves ahead of the other disciples.

LESSONS FROM THEIR LIVES:

It is important to experience God's love and act with love toward others.

God can take our weaknesses and mold them into strengths.

KEY VERSES:

"He appointed twelve—designating them apostles—that they might be with him and that he might send them out to preach . . . These are the twelve he appointed: . . . James son of Zebedee and his brother John (to them he gave the name Boanerges, which means Sons of Thunder)" (3:14, 16–17).

The stories of James and John are told in Matthew 4:21–22; 20:20–28; Mark 1:19–20; 3:13–19; 9:2–9; 10:35–40; Luke 9:49–56 and Acts 12:2. John is also mentioned in John 13:23–25; 19:26–27; 21:20–24; Acts 4:1–23; 8:14–25; Revelation 1:1–2, 9; 22:8.

cealed is meant to be brought out into the open. 23If anyone has ears to hear, let him hear."

24"Consider carefully what you hear," he continued. "With the measure you use, it will be measured to you—and even more. 25Whoever has will be given more; whoever does not have, even what he has will be taken from him."

The Parable of the Growing Seed

26He also said, "This is what the kingdom of God is like. A man scatters seed on the ground. 27Night and day, whether he sleeps or gets up, the seed sprouts and grows, though he does not know how. 28All by itself the soil produces grain—first the stalk, then the head, then the full kernel in the head. 29As soon as the grain is ripe, he puts the sickle to it, because the harvest has come."

The Parable of the Mustard Seed

‰ See Matthew 13:31–32; Luke 13:18–19

30Again he said, "What shall we say the kingdom of God is like, or what parable shall we use to describe it? 31It is like a mustard seed, which is the smallest seed you plant in the ground. 32Yet when planted, it grows and becomes the largest of all garden plants, with such big branches that the birds of the air can perch in its shade."

33With many similar parables Jesus spoke the word to them, as much as they could understand. 34He did not say anything to them without using a parable. But when he was alone with his own disciples, he explained everything.

Jesus Calms the Storm

‰ See Matthew 8:18,23–27; Luke 8:22–25

35That day when evening came, he said to his disciples, "Let us go over to the other side." 36Leaving the crowd behind, they took him along, just as he was, in the boat. There were also other boats with him. 37A furious squall came up, and the waves broke over the boat, so that it was nearly swamped. 38Jesus was in the stern, sleeping on a cushion. The disciples woke him and said to him, "Teacher, don't you care if we drown?"

39He got up, rebuked the wind and said to the waves, "Quiet! Be still!" Then the wind died down and it was completely calm.

40He said to his disciples, "Why are you so afraid? Do you still have no faith?"

41They were terrified and asked each other, "Who is this? Even the wind and the waves obey him!"

The Healing of a Demon-possessed Man

‰ See Matthew 8:28–34; Luke 8:26–39

5 They went across the lake to the region of the Gerasenes.[a] 2When Jesus got out of the boat, a man with an evil[b] spirit came from the tombs to meet him. 3This man lived in the tombs, and no one could bind him any more, not even with a chain. 4For he had often been chained hand and foot, but he tore the chains apart and broke the irons on his feet. No one was strong enough to subdue him. 5Night and day among the tombs and in the hills he would cry out and cut himself with stones.

6When he saw Jesus from a distance, he ran and fell on his knees in front of him. 7He shouted at the top of his voice, "What do you want with me, Jesus, Son of the Most High God? Swear to God that you won't torture me!" 8For Jesus had said to him, "Come out of this man, you evil spirit!"

9Then Jesus asked him, "What is your name?"

"My name is Legion," he replied, "for we are many." 10And he begged Jesus again and again not to send them out of the area.

11A large herd of pigs was feeding on the nearby hillside. 12The demons begged Jesus, "Send us among the pigs; allow us to go into them." 13He gave them permission, and the evil spirits came out and went into the pigs. The herd, about two thousand in number, rushed down the steep bank into the lake and were drowned.

14Those tending the pigs ran off and reported

[a] 1 Some manuscripts *Gadarenes;* other manuscripts *Gergesenes* [b] 2 Greek *unclean;* also in verses 8 and 13

4:26–29 Just as seeds silently grow in the soil, so God gradually prepares people for their transformation by his grace. We may not see God working in the lives of those we pray for, but often God is bringing them to a realization of their need for him. Ultimately we cannot change people—God does the changing. He has the power to grant new life and spiritual growth.

4:30–34 Jesus used the illustration of the mustard seed to make another point about how God works in our lives. God's healing work may start small. We may even wonder if anything has happened at all. But as God's power and grace begin to work in our lives, we will experience significant changes for the better. In time, our transformation will be complete (see Philippians 1:6). Just as the mustard seed grew into a large plant that cast a refreshing patch of shade, God's grace at work in our lives will leave a profound impact for good on the lives of the people around us.

4:35–41 Jesus demonstrated his power over nature: Even the wind and the seas obeyed him! The disciples were awed by such power. And we should be too. Just as he was able to calm the stormy sea, Jesus has the power to calm the storms of our lives. We need not fear, for there is no storm so powerful that Jesus is unable to handle it. We should never hesitate to cry out to him in our desperation.

5:1–20 After healing the demon-possessed man, Jesus faced opposition from the townspeople. The demons had left the man and entered a herd of pigs, causing them to run wildly into the lake and drown. The townspeople were frightened by this and begged Jesus to leave. We may experience similar opposition when God begins to make changes in our lives. Friends and family members may feel threatened by such changes and try to stop us. If we experience such opposition, we should simply continue trusting God to change us so that we will be able to help our friends and family in ways they may never have imagined possible.

THE SPIRITUAL DISCIPLINES

In the Life of Jesus

We may hesitate to speak about the spirituality of Jesus, regarding him as a person with whom we could never identify. Yet the author of Hebrews reminds us that "he had to be made like his brothers in every way . . . that he might make atonement for the sins of the people" (Hebrews 2:17). By the mystery of God, Jesus was fully human as well as fully divine. Hebrews goes on to say, "he learned obedience from what he suffered" (Hebrews 5:8). If Jesus "learned" and grew in obedience, it makes sense that he would have also employed spiritual exercises to cultivate his soul. We see numerous examples of the disciplines consistently practiced in Jesus' life:

PRAYER. The discipline of prayer was a central part of Jesus' life. The Gospels record specific prayers of Jesus, including the Lord's Prayer (see Matthew 6:9–13; Luke 11:1–4), Jesus' prayer of thanksgiving (see Matthew 11:25–26), and what is often called Jesus' High Priestly Prayer (see John 17:1–26). The Gospels also note that Jesus prayed regularly (see 1:35; Luke 6:12) and that his heavenly Father showed him what to do (see John 5:19–20). (To learn more about prayer, turn to Genesis 18.)

WORSHIP. Jesus worshiped regularly in the synagogue (see Luke 4:16). He also taught at the temple and observed the festivals of Israel (see John 7:14). Jesus' aim both in his life and ministry was to glorify his Father (see John 17:1–4). (To learn more about worship, turn to Exodus 20.)

BIBLE STUDY. Bible study and meditation were central parts of Jesus' life. When he was tempted, he gained victory through God's Word (see Matthew 4:1–11). His parables also arose from meditation on the Scriptures: His parable of the vine (see John 15:1–8) has its roots in Isaiah 5:1–7. Jesus applied the prophets' old images to his own time. (To learn more about Bible study, turn to Deuteronomy 30.)

FASTING. At the outset of his ministry, Jesus fasted for forty days in the wilderness. Such an extensive fast typically requires the preparation and conditioning of regular fasting. Jesus taught about fasting in Matthew 6:16–18, but he also limited the fasting of his disciples during his earthly ministry (see Matthew 9:14–17). (To learn more about fasting, turn to 2 Chronicles 20.)

SILENCE AND SOLITUDE. Jesus occasionally withdrew to quiet places to rest and regain perspective (see Luke 5:16). He observed silence before his accusers (Matthew 27:12), displaying his control and security in the situation. (To learn more about solitude, turn to Exodus 3.)

STEWARDSHIP. Jesus' stewardship was seen in his lifestyle. With no permanent place to call home (see Luke 9:58) and presumably no wealth, Jesus urged his disciples to give and receive daily as God provided, fulfilling their obligations both to God and to the government. (To learn more about stewardship, turn to Deuteronomy 8.)

SERVICE. Service to others was a hallmark of Jesus' daily ministry. He continually taught, preached and healed, ministering to the needs of the whole person. (To learn more about service, turn to Mark 10.)

SPIRITUAL FRIENDSHIP. We may be tempted to think that Jesus wouldn't really have needed friends—after all, he had God the Father! But Jesus called twelve disciples to be with him and called them his "friends" (John 15:15). Three of these men apparently were Jesus' closest friends, those with whom he shared his most intimate times, such as the transfiguration (see Luke 9:28–36) and Gethsemane (see Matthew 26:36–46). (To learn more about spiritual friendship, turn to Genesis 2.)

Lessons for Life

In one of the most intriguing promises in Scripture, Jesus says, "I tell you the truth, anyone who has faith in me will do what I have been doing" (John 14:12). If Jesus practiced the spiritual disciplines in his life, how much more should we practice these same spiritual principles?

this in the town and countryside, and the people went out to see what had happened. 15When they came to Jesus, they saw the man who had been possessed by the legion of demons, sitting there, dressed and in his right mind; and they were afraid. 16Those who had seen it told the people what had happened to the demon-possessed man—and told about the pigs as well. 17Then the people began to plead with Jesus to leave their region.

18As Jesus was getting into the boat, the man who had been demon-possessed begged to go with him. 19Jesus did not let him, but said, "Go home to your family and tell them how much the Lord has done for you, and how he has had mercy on you." 20So the man went away and began to tell in the Decapolis[a] how much Jesus had done for him. And all the people were amazed.

A Dead Girl and a Sick Woman

‰ See Matthew 9:18–26; Luke 8:41–56

21When Jesus had again crossed over by boat to the other side of the lake, a large crowd gathered around him while he was by the lake. 22Then one of the synagogue rulers, named Jairus, came there. Seeing Jesus, he fell at his feet 23and pleaded earnestly with him, "My little daughter is dying. Please come and put your hands on her so that she will be healed and live." 24So Jesus went with him.

A large crowd followed and pressed around him. 25And a woman was there who had been subject to bleeding for twelve years. 26She had suffered a great deal under the care of many doctors and had spent all she had, yet instead of getting better she grew worse. 27When she heard about Jesus, she came up behind him in the crowd and touched his cloak, 28because she thought, "If I just touch his clothes, I will be healed." 29Immediately her bleeding stopped and she felt in her body that she was freed from her suffering.

30At once Jesus realized that power had gone out from him. He turned around in the crowd and asked, "Who touched my clothes?"

31"You see the people crowding against you," his disciples answered, "and yet you can ask, 'Who touched me?' "

32But Jesus kept looking around to see who had done it. 33Then the woman, knowing what had happened to her, came and fell at his feet and, trembling with fear, told him the whole truth. 34He said to her, "Daughter, your faith has healed you. Go in peace and be freed from your suffering."

35While Jesus was still speaking, some men came from the house of Jairus, the synagogue ruler. "Your daughter is dead," they said. "Why bother the teacher any more?"

36Ignoring what they said, Jesus told the synagogue ruler, "Don't be afraid; just believe."

37He did not let anyone follow him except Peter, James and John the brother of James. 38When they came to the home of the synagogue ruler, Jesus saw a commotion, with people crying and wailing loudly. 39He went in and said to them, "Why all this commotion and wailing? The child is not dead but asleep." 40But they laughed at him.

After he put them all out, he took the child's father and mother and the disciples who were with him, and went in where the child was. 41He took her by the hand and said to her, *"Talitha koum!"* (which means, "Little girl, I say to you, get up!"). 42Immediately the girl stood up and walked around (she was twelve years old). At this they were completely astonished. 43He gave strict orders not to let anyone know about this, and told them to give her something to eat.

A Prophet Without Honor

‰ See Matthew 13:54–58

6 Jesus left there and went to his hometown, accompanied by his disciples. 2When the Sabbath came, he began to teach in the synagogue, and many who heard him were amazed.

[a] *20* That is, the Ten Cities

5:21–43 Jairus was one of the few Jewish leaders who responded positively to Jesus. Driven by love for his daughter and by faith that Jesus could help her, Jairus risked the scorn of his peers by publicly seeking Jesus' help. His humble faith was rewarded. We may avoid coming to Jesus because we are ashamed to admit we have a problem. Yet if we cannot humbly admit our sin and failures, there is little hope for our healing. We must, like Jairus, risk the scorn of friends and enemies and admit our failures and mistakes. We can be sure that Jesus will be there to help us. With his help, no problem is too great to solve; no wound is too deep to heal.

5:25–34 Sometimes we may feel so ashamed of our situation that we believe God's opinion of us must mirror the social ostracism we have experienced or the self-loathing we feel. Such was the case of the woman who had hemorrhaged for twelve years. This problem was likely a menstrual or uterine disorder, which would have made the woman "unclean" (see Leviticus 15:25–27). According to Jewish law, anyone who touched her would also be rendered unclean. This woman had likely lived as an outcast for some time. But she reached out to Jesus in faith and was miraculously healed. We must never allow fear or shame to keep us from approaching God for forgiveness and healing. He is waiting for us to reach out and touch him.

6:1–6 During Jesus' visit to his hometown, he was viewed as a mere man, a carpenter, Joseph and Mary's boy. Jesus was just a regular guy to this hometown crowd. This attitude of unbelief effectively hindered Jesus from accomplishing a more extensive ministry in Nazareth. For the people of Nazareth, their familiarity with Jesus bred contempt for his message. Fortunately for us, Jesus left and ministered to those who would believe in his miracles and message. Many in our world have passed Jesus off as just another man, a good teacher, a wise prophet. Yet anyone who focuses on Jesus' humanity to the exclusion of his divinity makes a grave mistake. If Jesus is not the Son of God, there is no hope for our redemption.

"Where did this man get these things?" they asked. "What's this wisdom that has been given him, that he even does miracles! 3Isn't this the carpenter? Isn't this Mary's son and the brother of James, Joseph,[a] Judas and Simon? Aren't his sisters here with us?" And they took offense at him.

4Jesus said to them, "Only in his hometown, among his relatives and in his own house is a prophet without honor." 5He could not do any miracles there, except lay his hands on a few sick people and heal them. 6And he was amazed at their lack of faith.

Jesus Sends Out the Twelve

‰ See Matthew 10:1,9–14; Luke 9:1,3–5

Then Jesus went around teaching from village to village. 7Calling the Twelve to him, he sent them out two by two and gave them authority over evil[b] spirits.

8These were his instructions: "Take nothing for the journey except a staff—no bread, no bag, no money in your belts. 9Wear sandals but not an extra tunic. 10Whenever you enter a house, stay there until you leave that town. 11And if any place will not welcome you or listen to you, shake the dust off your feet when you leave, as a testimony against them."

12They went out and preached that people should repent. 13They drove out many demons and anointed many sick people with oil and healed them.

John the Baptist Beheaded

‰ See Matthew 14:1–12

14King Herod heard about this, for Jesus' name had become well known. Some were saying,[c] "John the Baptist has been raised from the dead, and that is why miraculous powers are at work in him."

15Others said, "He is Elijah."

And still others claimed, "He is a prophet, like one of the prophets of long ago."

16But when Herod heard this, he said, "John, the man I beheaded, has been raised from the dead!"

17For Herod himself had given orders to have John arrested, and he had him bound and put in prison. He did this because of Herodias, his brother Philip's wife, whom he had married. 18For John had been saying to Herod, "It is not lawful for you to have your brother's wife." 19So Herodias nursed a grudge against John and wanted to kill him. But she was not able to, 20because Herod feared John and protected him, knowing him to be a righteous and holy man. When Herod heard John, he was greatly puzzled[d]; yet he liked to listen to him.

21Finally the opportune time came. On his birthday Herod gave a banquet for his high officials and military commanders and the leading men of Galilee. 22When the daughter of Herodias came in and danced, she pleased Herod and his dinner guests.

The king said to the girl, "Ask me for anything you want, and I'll give it to you." 23And he promised her with an oath, "Whatever you ask I will give you, up to half my kingdom."

24She went out and said to her mother, "What shall I ask for?"

"The head of John the Baptist," she answered.

25At once the girl hurried in to the king with the request: "I want you to give me right now the head of John the Baptist on a platter."

26The king was greatly distressed, but because of his oaths and his dinner guests, he did not want to refuse her. 27So he immediately sent an executioner with orders to bring John's head. The man went, beheaded John in the prison, 28and brought back his head on a platter. He presented it to the girl, and she gave it to her mother. 29On hearing of this, John's disciples came and took his body and laid it in a tomb.

Jesus Feeds the Five Thousand

‰ See Matthew 14:13–21; Luke 9:10–17; John 6:5–13

30The apostles gathered around Jesus and reported to him all they had done and taught. 31Then, because so many people were coming and going that they did not even have a chance to eat, he said to them, "Come with me by yourselves to a quiet place and get some rest."

32So they went away by themselves in a boat

[a]3 Greek *Joses,* a variant of *Joseph* [b]7 Greek *unclean* [c]14 Some early manuscripts *He was saying* [d]20 Some early manuscripts *he did many things*

6:7–13 When we experience the joy of redemption, we naturally want to share our news with others. Yet we are not always well received. So it was with the disciples, who were paired off and sent out to share the Good News of the Messiah's coming. They were told what to take, where to stay and for how long and what to do when rejected. In the face of rejection, the disciples kept on preaching repentance, deliverance and healing. As we share God's hand at work in our lives, not everyone will respond positively. When ridiculed or rejected, we should still press on to share our hope with others. Sharing our message may make the difference between life and death for someone in need.

6:14–29 Herod Antipas did not like being rebuked. So when John the Baptist confronted him concerning his immoral marriage to his brother's wife, the prophet paid for it with his life. Herod refused to see the truth about his sin. He did not want to be reminded of what he had done. But Herod's attitude only led to an even greater sin—murder. We need to learn that our refusal to see the truth about our lives will never help things; it will only lead to even greater suffering and devastation. We would be wise to immediately act on the warnings we receive. If we don't, we are headed for even greater trouble.

6:30–34 Jesus encouraged his disciples to take care of themselves by withdrawing for rest and solitude. The disciples needed time apart for personal reflection and refreshment in order to be able to continue helping others. We need to make sure that our lives are balanced too. We need time apart to recharge our spiritual and emotional batteries. As we take time to reflect, we will learn the lessons of humility and dependence on God that are necessary for our continued spiritual progress.

to a solitary place. 33But many who saw them leaving recognized them and ran on foot from all the towns and got there ahead of them. 34When Jesus landed and saw a large crowd, he had compassion on them, because they were like sheep without a shepherd. So he began teaching them many things.

35By this time it was late in the day, so his disciples came to him. "This is a remote place," they said, "and it's already very late. 36Send the people away so they can go to the surrounding countryside and villages and buy themselves something to eat."

37But he answered, "You give them something to eat."

They said to him, "That would take eight months of a man's wages[a]! Are we to go and spend that much on bread and give it to them to eat?"

38"How many loaves do you have?" he asked. "Go and see."

When they found out, they said, "Five—and two fish."

39Then Jesus directed them to have all the people sit down in groups on the green grass. 40So they sat down in groups of hundreds and fifties. 41Taking the five loaves and the two fish and looking up to heaven, he gave thanks and broke the loaves. Then he gave them to his disciples to set before the people. He also divided the two fish among them all. 42They all ate and were satisfied, 43and the disciples picked up twelve basketfuls of broken pieces of bread and fish. 44The number of the men who had eaten was five thousand.

Jesus Walks on the Water

‰ See Matthew 14:22–32; John 6:15–21

45Immediately Jesus made his disciples get into the boat and go on ahead of him to Bethsaida, while he dismissed the crowd. 46After leaving them, he went up on a mountainside to pray.

47When evening came, the boat was in the middle of the lake, and he was alone on land. 48He saw the disciples straining at the oars, because the wind was against them. About the fourth watch of the night he went out to them, walking on the lake. He was about to pass by them, 49but when they saw him walking on the lake, they thought he was a ghost. They cried out, 50because they all saw him and were terrified.

Immediately he spoke to them and said, "Take courage! It is I. Don't be afraid." 51Then he climbed into the boat with them, and the wind died down. They were completely amazed, 52for they had not understood about the loaves; their hearts were hardened.

53When they had crossed over, they landed at Gennesaret and anchored there. 54As soon as they got out of the boat, people recognized Jesus. 55They ran throughout that whole region and carried the sick on mats to wherever they heard he was. 56And wherever he went—into villages, towns or countryside—they placed the sick in the marketplaces. They begged him to let them touch even the edge of his cloak, and all who touched him were healed.

Clean and Unclean

‰ See Matthew 15:1–20

7 The Pharisees and some of the teachers of the law who had come from Jerusalem gathered around Jesus and 2saw some of his disciples eating food with hands that were "unclean," that is, unwashed. 3(The Pharisees and all the Jews do not eat unless they give their hands a ceremonial washing, holding to the tradition of the elders. 4When they come from the marketplace they do not eat unless they wash. And they observe many other traditions, such as the washing of cups, pitchers and kettles.[b])

5So the Pharisees and teachers of the law asked Jesus, "Why don't your disciples live according to the tradition of the elders instead of eating their food with 'unclean' hands?"

6He replied, "Isaiah was right when he prophesied about you hypocrites; as it is written:

" 'These people honor me with their lips,
but their hearts are far from me.
7They worship me in vain;
their teachings are but rules taught by men.'[c]

[a]37 Greek *take two hundred denarii*
[b]4 Some early manuscripts *pitchers, kettles and dining couches*
[c]6,7 Isaiah 29:13

6:35–44 This miraculous supply of food for more than five thousand people demonstrates an important principle: Our needs are never greater than God's supply. The twelve disciples should have learned this lesson through Jesus' ample provision, but they failed to do so (see 6:52). They should have learned that when confronted with an impossible situation, Jesus could be trusted to meet that need. We also need to remember that no obstacle is too great for God. He is more than able to meet all of our needs.

6:45–52 We may lose sight of Jesus, but Jesus never loses sight of us. In this threefold miracle Jesus walked on water, calmed the storm and saw the disciples' boat safely to shore (see John 6:21). Despite many such miracles, the disciples still had not realized just how powerful Jesus was or how concerned he was with their welfare. All of us can recall some time when Jesus intervened in our lives to show us that we are still in his care. When we begin to waver in our faith and lose sight of God, we should recall the times when God has helped us in the past. This should give us the courage to submit our lives once again to his loving care.

7:1–13 For many of the Jewish leaders, human tradition superseded God's revealed Word. Ritual replaced a relationship with God; reputation was more important than godliness. Jesus labeled these attitudes as hypocrisy. Our spiritual growth can succeed only if we are willing to have our hearts and outward actions changed according to God's Word.

8You have let go of the commands of God and are holding on to the traditions of men."

9And he said to them: "You have a fine way of setting aside the commands of God in order to observe[a] your own traditions! 10For Moses said, 'Honor your father and your mother,'[b] and, 'Anyone who curses his father or mother must be put to death.'[c] 11But you say that if a man says to his father or mother: 'Whatever help you might otherwise have received from me is Corban' (that is, a gift devoted to God), 12then you no longer let him do anything for his father or mother. 13Thus you nullify the word of God by your tradition that you have handed down. And you do many things like that."

14Again Jesus called the crowd to him and said, "Listen to me, everyone, and understand this. 15Nothing outside a man can make him 'unclean' by going into him. Rather, it is what comes out of a man that makes him 'unclean.'[d]"

17After he had left the crowd and entered the house, his disciples asked him about this parable. 18"Are you so dull?" he asked. "Don't you see that nothing that enters a man from the outside can make him 'unclean'? 19For it doesn't go into his heart but into his stomach, and then out of his body." (In saying this, Jesus declared all foods "clean.")

20He went on: "What comes out of a man is what makes him 'unclean.' 21For from within, out of men's hearts, come evil thoughts, sexual immorality, theft, murder, adultery, 22greed, malice, deceit, lewdness, envy, slander, arrogance and folly. 23All these evils come from inside and make a man 'unclean.' "

The Faith of a Syrophoenician Woman

‰ See Matthew 15:21–28

24Jesus left that place and went to the vicinity of Tyre.[e] He entered a house and did not want anyone to know it; yet he could not keep his presence secret. 25In fact, as soon as she heard about him, a woman whose little daughter was possessed by an evil[f] spirit came and fell at his feet. 26The woman was a Greek, born in Syrian Phoenicia. She begged Jesus to drive the demon out of her daughter.

27"First let the children eat all they want," he told her, "for it is not right to take the children's bread and toss it to their dogs."

28"Yes, Lord," she replied, "but even the dogs under the table eat the children's crumbs."

29Then he told her, "For such a reply, you may go; the demon has left your daughter."

30She went home and found her child lying on the bed, and the demon gone.

The Healing of a Deaf and Mute Man

‰ See Matthew 15:29–31

31Then Jesus left the vicinity of Tyre and went through Sidon, down to the Sea of Galilee and into the region of the Decapolis.[g] 32There some people brought to him a man who was deaf and could hardly talk, and they begged him to place his hand on the man.

33After he took him aside, away from the crowd, Jesus put his fingers into the man's ears. Then he spit and touched the man's tongue. 34He looked up to heaven and with a deep sigh said to him, "*Ephphatha!*" (which means, "Be opened!"). 35At this, the man's ears were opened, his tongue was loosened and he began to speak plainly.

36Jesus commanded them not to tell anyone. But the more he did so, the more they kept talking about it. 37People were overwhelmed with amazement. "He has done everything well," they said. "He even makes the deaf hear and the mute speak."

Jesus Feeds the Four Thousand

‰ See Matthew 15:32–39

8 During those days another large crowd gathered. Since they had nothing to eat, Jesus called his disciples to him and said, 2"I have compassion for these people; they have already been with me three days and have

[a]9 Some manuscripts *set up* [b]10 Exodus 20:12; Deut. 5:16 [c]10 Exodus 21:17; Lev. 20:9 [d]15 Some early manuscripts *'unclean.'* [16]*If anyone has ears to hear, let him hear.* [e]24 Many early manuscripts *Tyre and Sidon* [f]25 Greek *unclean* [g]31 That is, the Ten Cities

7:14–23 Jesus explained that defilement does not begin on the outside but comes from within our hearts. Most of us have tried to control our sinful natures by changing various aspects of our external behavior. But these changes never last for long because our real problem lies within. How encouraging that God goes right to the root of the problem; he works his healing from the inside out. By recognizing our need for internal healing, we open our lives to God's healing power.

7:24–30 By helping this Gentile woman, Jesus made it clear that his message of hope was for everyone, not just a privileged few. Jesus responded not only to the woman's humility and accurate self-perception but also to her great faith and perseverance. The more we trust God, the more he can do for us and through us. Conversely, a lack of faith and perseverance will keep us from experiencing God's healing in our lives and in the lives of our loved ones.

7:31–37 Another person may have led us to seek God and get the help we needed. In this account, a group of people apparently cared enough for this deaf man to do something about his problem. They brought their friend to Jesus and then begged Jesus to heal him. We may be the one God will use to bring another hurting person hope and direction. As we share how God has helped us and tell others the Good News of God's power for bringing new life, we can share the gift of salvation.

8:1–9 We sometimes feel as if our prayers never get beyond the ceiling. We wonder if the hot line to God is busy and if we have been left indefinitely on hold. The truth is, God is never too busy to concern himself with our daily needs. Jesus was moved by compassion to feed four thousand hungry people, even though he was very busy with other things. There is no need too small or request too large that God will not hear and respond to.

Simon Peter

Simon was a fisherman. We would probably never nickname such a reckless, vacillating and often thoughtless person *Peter,* which means "Rock." But Jesus did. What greater evidence could there be that Jesus accepted Simon as he was but also had a vision for the man he would become? By the end of Simon's life, his nickname, Peter, appropriately described his steadfast maturity. What an amazing transformation took place in that burly fisherman!

Most of us readily identify with Simon Peter. His intentions were usually good, but he was impetuous in speech and impulsive in action. Instead of standing in awe at the transfiguration, Simon Peter blurted out the first idea that came into his head. When Jesus revealed that his divine mission would involve a painful death, Peter rashly told Jesus to stop talking that way. At the Last Supper, Simon Peter brazenly objected to letting Jesus wash his feet. When Jesus was arrested, Peter bravely but brashly cut off the ear of the high priest's servant. And at a turning point in his life, Peter denied Jesus three times. Yet even as Jesus restored Peter from this failure, Peter's attention was on John rather than on what God was doing for him.

Later in Simon's life we glimpse what Jesus recognized when he nicknamed him "Rock." Peter presided over the meeting to select a successor to Judas. At Pentecost he preached publicly about Jesus despite the opposition he knew he would face. God used Peter to work several miracles. Peter was miraculously rescued from prison too. With a spiritual insight gained from a close relationship with God, Peter proclaimed a great confession at Caesarea Philippi, stating clearly that Jesus Christ was the only means to salvation.

In Simon Peter's life we see hope for our spiritual renewal and transformation. While Peter was amazingly transformed by God, we should remember that he was never made perfect. In fact, the apostle Paul's word in Galatians 2:11–14 described Peter's hypocritical actions as one of the early church leaders. Despite his imperfections, Peter's transformation had a profound effect on the world around him. His words, actions and letters became a significant part of the early church's spiritual foundation.

STRENGTHS AND ACCOMPLISHMENTS:

Simon's natural boldness was used to spread the Good News of Jesus Christ.

He was the recognized leader and spokesman for the twelve disciples.

Simon Peter was inspired to write letters to encourage believers (1 and 2 Peter).

Peter's natural enthusiasm was later channeled into disciplined courage.

WEAKNESSES AND MISTAKES:

Simon often spoke and acted before he thought about the consequences.

Simon Peter's temperament was mercurial, quickly moving from professing loyalty to Christ to denying him before a servant girl.

Even after his transformation, Peter sometimes still made wrong decisions and actions (Galatians 2:11–14).

LESSONS FROM HIS LIFE:

Jesus Christ has enough power to transform even the most unlikely people.

God can transform our faults into powerful tools for use in his kingdom.

When people make themselves available, God can always use them.

KEY VERSE:

"I tell you that you are Peter, and on this rock I will build my church, and the gates of Hades will not overcome it" (Matthew 16:18).

There is extensive Biblical material on Simon Peter throughout the Gospels and Acts 1—15. In Paul's letters, Peter is mentioned in 1 Corinthians 15:5; Galatians 1:18 and 2:7–14. Some material about him may also be gleaned from his two letters, 1 and 2 Peter.

nothing to eat. 3If I send them home hungry,
they will collapse on the way, because some of
them have come a long distance."
4His disciples answered, "But where in this
remote place can anyone get enough bread to
feed them?"
5"How many loaves do you have?" Jesus
asked.
"Seven," they replied.
6He told the crowd to sit down on the
ground. When he had taken the seven loaves
and given thanks, he broke them and gave them
to his disciples to set before the people, and
they did so. 7They had a few small fish as well;
he gave thanks for them also and told the disciples to distribute them. 8The people ate and
were satisfied. Afterward the disciples picked up
seven basketfuls of broken pieces that were left
over. 9About four thousand men were present.
And having sent them away, 10he got into the
boat with his disciples and went to the region
of Dalmanutha.
11The Pharisees came and began to question
Jesus. To test him, they asked him for a sign
from heaven. 12He sighed deeply and said,
"Why does this generation ask for a miraculous
sign? I tell you the truth, no sign will be given
to it." 13Then he left them, got back into the boat
and crossed to the other side.

The Yeast of the Pharisees and Herod

14The disciples had forgotten to bring bread,
except for one loaf they had with them in the
boat. 15"Be careful," Jesus warned them. "Watch
out for the yeast of the Pharisees and that of
Herod."
16They discussed this with one another and
said, "It is because we have no bread."
17Aware of their discussion, Jesus asked
them: "Why are you talking about having no
bread? Do you still not see or understand? Are
your hearts hardened? 18Do you have eyes but
fail to see, and ears but fail to hear? And don't
you remember? 19When I broke the five loaves
for the five thousand, how many basketfuls of
pieces did you pick up?"
"Twelve," they replied.
20"And when I broke the seven loaves for the
four thousand, how many basketfuls of pieces
did you pick up?"
They answered, "Seven."
21He said to them, "Do you still not understand?"

The Healing of a Blind Man at Bethsaida

22They came to Bethsaida, and some people
brought a blind man and begged Jesus to touch
him. 23He took the blind man by the hand and
led him outside the village. When he had spit
on the man's eyes and put his hands on him,
Jesus asked, "Do you see anything?"
24He looked up and said, "I see people; they
look like trees walking around."
25Once more Jesus put his hands on the
man's eyes. Then his eyes were opened, his sight
was restored, and he saw everything clearly.
26Jesus sent him home, saying, "Don't go into
the village.[a]"

Peter's Confession of Christ

‰ See Matthew 16:13–16; Luke 9:18–20

27Jesus and his disciples went on to the villages around Caesarea Philippi. On the way he
asked them, "Who do people say I am?"
28They replied, "Some say John the Baptist;
others say Elijah; and still others, one of the
prophets."
29"But what about you?" he asked. "Who do
you say I am?"
Peter answered, "You are the Christ.[b]"
30Jesus warned them not to tell anyone about
him.

Jesus Predicts His Death

‰ See Matthew 16:21–28; Luke 9:22–27

31He then began to teach them that the Son
of Man must suffer many things and be rejected
by the elders, chief priests and teachers of the
law, and that he must be killed and after three
days rise again. 32He spoke plainly about this,
and Peter took him aside and began to rebuke
him.
33But when Jesus turned and looked at his
disciples, he rebuked Peter. "Get behind me,
Satan!" he said. "You do not have in mind the
things of God, but the things of men."
34Then he called the crowd to him along
with his disciples and said: "If anyone would
come after me, he must deny himself and take
up his cross and follow me. 35For whoever
wants to save his life[c] will lose it, but whoever
loses his life for me and for the gospel will save
it. 36What good is it for a man to gain the whole

[a] 26 Some manuscripts *Don't go and tell anyone in the village* [b] 29 Or *Messiah.* "The Christ" (Greek) and "the Messiah" (Hebrew) both mean "the Anointed One." [c] 35 The Greek word means either *life* or *soul*; also in verse 36.

8:10–21 Jesus was troubled by his disciples' lack of faith and their seeming inability to learn the basic lessons he was trying to teach them. Yet, even though they were slow learners, Jesus still nurtured them in faith. Our spiritual progress may be marked with a series of lurches and falls. When we fail, we can recover by admitting our limitations, accepting God's forgiveness and continuing to depend on his power day by day. God will be patient with us if we continue to follow him and return to him whenever we stray.

8:31—9:1 Jesus told his disciples that his ministry would lead to suffering and death. There would be no resurrection if there were no cross. Jesus had to suffer to overcome the power of sin in our world. We should be grateful that Jesus has already paid the price for our sins. When we admit our failures and accept God's forgiveness, we can be sure that God will free us from the destructive hold of sin.

world, yet forfeit his soul? [37]Or what can a man give in exchange for his soul? [38]If anyone is ashamed of me and my words in this adulterous and sinful generation, the Son of Man will be ashamed of him when he comes in his Father's glory with the holy angels."

9 And he said to them, "I tell you the truth, some who are standing here will not taste death before they see the kingdom of God come with power."

The Transfiguration

‰ See Matthew 17:1–13; Luke 9:28–36

[2]After six days Jesus took Peter, James and John with him and led them up a high mountain, where they were all alone. There he was transfigured before them. [3]His clothes became dazzling white, whiter than anyone in the world could bleach them. [4]And there appeared before them Elijah and Moses, who were talking with Jesus.

[5]Peter said to Jesus, "Rabbi, it is good for us to be here. Let us put up three shelters—one for you, one for Moses and one for Elijah." [6](He did not know what to say, they were so frightened.)

[7]Then a cloud appeared and enveloped them, and a voice came from the cloud: "This is my Son, whom I love. Listen to him!"

[8]Suddenly, when they looked around, they no longer saw anyone with them except Jesus.

[9]As they were coming down the mountain, Jesus gave them orders not to tell anyone what they had seen until the Son of Man had risen from the dead. [10]They kept the matter to themselves, discussing what "rising from the dead" meant.

[11]And they asked him, "Why do the teachers of the law say that Elijah must come first?"

[12]Jesus replied, "To be sure, Elijah does come first, and restores all things. Why then is it written that the Son of Man must suffer much and be rejected? [13]But I tell you, Elijah has come, and they have done to him everything they wished, just as it is written about him."

The Healing of a Boy With an Evil Spirit

‰ See Matthew 17:14–19,22–23; Luke 9:37–45

[14]When they came to the other disciples, they saw a large crowd around them and the teachers of the law arguing with them. [15]As soon as all the people saw Jesus, they were overwhelmed with wonder and ran to greet him.

[16]"What are you arguing with them about?" he asked.

[17]A man in the crowd answered, "Teacher, I brought you my son, who is possessed by a spirit that has robbed him of speech. [18]Whenever it seizes him, it throws him to the ground. He foams at the mouth, gnashes his teeth and becomes rigid. I asked your disciples to drive out the spirit, but they could not."

[19]"O unbelieving generation," Jesus replied, "how long shall I stay with you? How long shall I put up with you? Bring the boy to me."

[20]So they brought him. When the spirit saw Jesus, it immediately threw the boy into a convulsion. He fell to the ground and rolled around, foaming at the mouth.

[21]Jesus asked the boy's father, "How long has he been like this?"

"From childhood," he answered. [22]"It has often thrown him into fire or water to kill him. But if you can do anything, take pity on us and help us."

[23]" 'If you can'?" said Jesus. "Everything is possible for him who believes."

[24]Immediately the boy's father exclaimed, "I do believe; help me overcome my unbelief!"

[25]When Jesus saw that a crowd was running to the scene, he rebuked the evil[a] spirit. "You deaf and mute spirit," he said, "I command you, come out of him and never enter him again."

[26]The spirit shrieked, convulsed him violently and came out. The boy looked so much like a corpse that many said, "He's dead." [27]But Jesus took him by the hand and lifted him to his feet, and he stood up.

[28]After Jesus had gone indoors, his disciples asked him privately, "Why couldn't we drive it out?"

[29]He replied, "This kind can come out only by prayer.[b]"

[30]They left that place and passed through Galilee. Jesus did not want anyone to know where they were, [31]because he was teaching his disciples. He said to them, "The Son of Man is

[a]25 Greek *unclean* [b]29 Some manuscripts *prayer and fasting*

9:2–13 In this amazing event, we are given a picture of what we can hope for in our own lives. Someday we will be changed to be like Christ; we will be made perfect. Yet God wants to begin the process of leading us toward a godly and productive life right now. During times of struggle and despair, we can reflect on who we will become when God completes our transformation.

9:14–29 In a moment of honest reflection, the father of the demon-possessed boy acknowledged both belief and unbelief. He believed that Jesus could restore his son to health, but he questioned whether Jesus would do so. Sometimes we feel the same way. We recognize that God has delivered others and believe he is able to help, but we are afraid that God will refuse to help *us*. We may believe that God feels we are unworthy of his deliverance. Yet God never works that way. Not only is he able to help us, but he also wants to help us. We must turn to him in faith, repent of our sin, ask for his forgiveness and follow his plan for us. God will do the rest.

9:30–37 The argument over who would be the greatest in God's kingdom countered everything Jesus stood for. True greatness is measured in our service to others. For the disciples, such service included loving all people, even a little child. We may not be tempted to turn away from children in need, but what about the many adults who need our help? Do we turn away from the poor, homeless, hungry and needy? God heals our hurts so we can help others find the healing they need, not so we can rise to a higher position in society. If we fail to help others in need, we have missed an important part of Jesus' message.

going to be betrayed into the hands of men. They will kill him, and after three days he will rise." [32]But they did not understand what he meant and were afraid to ask him about it.

Who Is the Greatest?

‰ See Matthew 18:1–5; Luke 9:46–48

[33]They came to Capernaum. When he was in the house, he asked them, "What were you arguing about on the road?" [34]But they kept quiet because on the way they had argued about who was the greatest.

[35]Sitting down, Jesus called the Twelve and said, "If anyone wants to be first, he must be the very last, and the servant of all."

[36]He took a little child and had him stand among them. Taking him in his arms, he said to them, [37]"Whoever welcomes one of these little children in my name welcomes me; and whoever welcomes me does not welcome me but the one who sent me."

Whoever Is Not Against Us Is for Us

‰ See Luke 9:49–50

[38]"Teacher," said John, "we saw a man driving out demons in your name and we told him to stop, because he was not one of us."

[39]"Do not stop him," Jesus said. "No one who does a miracle in my name can in the next moment say anything bad about me, [40]for whoever is not against us is for us. [41]I tell you the truth, anyone who gives you a cup of water in my name because you belong to Christ will certainly not lose his reward.

Causing to Sin

[42]"And if anyone causes one of these little ones who believe in me to sin, it would be better for him to be thrown into the sea with a large millstone tied around his neck. [43]If your hand causes you to sin, cut it off. It is better for you to enter life maimed than with two hands to go into hell, where the fire never goes out.[a] [45]And if your foot causes you to sin, cut it off. It is better for you to enter life crippled than to have two feet and be thrown into hell.[b] [47]And if your eye causes you to sin, pluck it out. It is better for you to enter the kingdom of God with one eye than to have two eyes and be thrown into hell, [48]where

" 'their worm does not die,
and the fire is not quenched.'[c]

[49]Everyone will be salted with fire.

[50]"Salt is good, but if it loses its saltiness, how can you make it salty again? Have salt in yourselves, and be at peace with each other."

Divorce

‰ See Matthew 19:1–9

10 Jesus then left that place and went into the region of Judea and across the Jordan. Again crowds of people came to him, and as was his custom, he taught them.

[2]Some Pharisees came and tested him by asking, "Is it lawful for a man to divorce his wife?"

[3]"What did Moses command you?" he replied.

[4]They said, "Moses permitted a man to write a certificate of divorce and send her away."

[5]"It was because your hearts were hard that Moses wrote you this law," Jesus replied. [6]"But at the beginning of creation God 'made them male and female.'[d] [7]'For this reason a man will leave his father and mother and be united to his wife,[e] [8]and the two will become one flesh.'[f] So they are no longer two, but one. [9]Therefore what God has joined together, let man not separate."

[10]When they were in the house again, the disciples asked Jesus about this. [11]He answered, "Anyone who divorces his wife and marries another woman commits adultery against her. [12]And if she divorces her husband and marries another man, she commits adultery."

The Little Children and Jesus

‰ See Matthew 19:13–15; Luke 18:15–17

[13]People were bringing little children to Jesus to have him touch them, but the disciples re-

[a]43 Some manuscripts *out,* [44]*where / " 'their worm does not die, / and the fire is not quenched.'* [b]45 Some manuscripts *hell,* [46]*where / " 'their worm does not die, / and the fire is not quenched.'* [c]48 Isaiah 66:24 [d]6 Gen. 1:27 [e]7 Some early manuscripts do not have *and be united to his wife.* [f]8 Gen. 2:24

9:38–42 Cooperation and peace, not cutthroat competition, must characterize our interpersonal relationships. Notice that Jesus instructed his disciples to fully and peacefully accept others who ministered in his name. He accepted those who were not in the immediate circle of disciples but were building up the kingdom of God. So must we. If we fail to do so and cause others to lose faith, then we will suffer the painful consequences.

9:43–50 Through a series of startling statements, Jesus admonished his disciples to get rid of anything in their lives that might draw them away from God. Jesus' statements showed that it is vital to our spiritual welfare to cut sin out of our lives. When we see areas of sin in our lives, we must bring them to God. We must ask him to help us do whatever it takes to rid our lives of sin.

10:1–12 The Pharisees were not looking for guidance when they asked Jesus about divorce; they were only looking for a way to discredit him. Jesus offered no grounds for divorce, with the possible exception of infidelity (see Matthew 19:9). In our society, many believe divorce is a good option for dealing with conflict. Most of us have discovered, however, that interpersonal conflict follows us wherever we go because such conflict is only an evidence of much deeper problems. Marriage is not easy; neither is spiritual growth. But both can be of great help to the other. Marriage gives us a context of accountability and loving support that can help us through the process of spiritual growth. As we grow spiritually, seeking God and surrendering to him, he gives us the help we need for personal growth and for reestablishing our family and marriage relationships.

10:13–22 These verses contrast two kinds of people: those who are like the little children, coming to Jesus with innocent trust, and those who are like the wealthy young

buked them. [14]When Jesus saw this, he was indignant. He said to them, "Let the little children come to me, and do not hinder them, for the kingdom of God belongs to such as these. [15]I tell you the truth, anyone who will not receive the kingdom of God like a little child will never enter it." [16]And he took the children in his arms, put his hands on them and blessed them.

The Rich Young Man

‰ See Matthew 19:16–30; Luke 18:18–30

[17]As Jesus started on his way, a man ran up to him and fell on his knees before him. "Good teacher," he asked, "what must I do to inherit eternal life?"

[18]"Why do you call me good?" Jesus answered. "No one is good—except God alone. [19]You know the commandments: 'Do not murder, do not commit adultery, do not steal, do not give false testimony, do not defraud, honor your father and mother.'[a]"

[20]"Teacher," he declared, "all these I have kept since I was a boy."

[21]Jesus looked at him and loved him. "One thing you lack," he said. "Go, sell everything you have and give to the poor, and you will have treasure in heaven. Then come, follow me."

[22]At this the man's face fell. He went away sad, because he had great wealth.

[23]Jesus looked around and said to his disciples, "How hard it is for the rich to enter the kingdom of God!"

[24]The disciples were amazed at his words. But Jesus said again, "Children, how hard it is[b] to enter the kingdom of God! [25]It is easier for a camel to go through the eye of a needle than for a rich man to enter the kingdom of God."

[26]The disciples were even more amazed, and said to each other, "Who then can be saved?"

[27]Jesus looked at them and said, "With man this is impossible, but not with God; all things are possible with God."

[28]Peter said to him, "We have left everything to follow you!"

[29]"I tell you the truth," Jesus replied, "no one who has left home or brothers or sisters or mother or father or children or fields for me and the gospel [30]will fail to receive a hundred times as much in this present age (homes, brothers, sisters, mothers, children and fields—and with them, persecutions) and in the age to come, eternal life. [31]But many who are first will be last, and the last first."

Jesus Again Predicts His Death

‰ See Matthew 20:17–19; Luke 18:31–33

[32]They were on their way up to Jerusalem, with Jesus leading the way, and the disciples were astonished, while those who followed were afraid. Again he took the Twelve aside and told them what was going to happen to him. [33]"We are going up to Jerusalem," he said, "and the Son of Man will be betrayed to the chief priests and teachers of the law. They will condemn him to death and will hand him over to the Gentiles, [34]who will mock him and spit on him, flog him and kill him. Three days later he will rise."

The Request of James and John

‰ See Matthew 20:20–28

[35]Then James and John, the sons of Zebedee, came to him. "Teacher," they said, "we want you to do for us whatever we ask."

[36]"What do you want me to do for you?" he asked.

[37]They replied, "Let one of us sit at your right and the other at your left in your glory."

[38]"You don't know what you are asking," Jesus said. "Can you drink the cup I drink or be baptized with the baptism I am baptized with?"

[39]"We can," they answered.

Jesus said to them, "You will drink the cup I drink and be baptized with the baptism I am baptized with, [40]but to sit at my right or left is not for me to grant. These places belong to those for whom they have been prepared."

[41]When the ten heard about this, they became indignant with James and John. [42]Jesus called them together and said, "You know that those who are regarded as rulers of the Gentiles lord it over them, and their high officials exercise authority over them. [43]Not so with you. Instead, whoever wants to become great among you must be your servant, [44]and whoever wants to be first must be slave of all. [45]For even the Son of Man did not come to be served, but to serve, and to give his life as a ransom for many."

[a] *19* Exodus 20:12-16; Deut. 5:16-20 [b] *24* Some manuscripts *is for those who trust in riches*

---

man, trusting in his wealth and unwilling to follow Jesus. The only way we can enter the kingdom of God is through childlike trust. As long as we think we can make it on our own, we will fail. We must begin by assuming that we are like little children. We must not trust in our abilities or wealth, but rather put our lives into the hands of God. Only God can give us entrance into his kingdom.

10:23–31 Most people in Jesus' day believed that wealth was a reward from God for righteous living. The wealthy usually enjoyed a measure of prestige. Jesus amazed his audience by stating how difficult it was for the rich to enter God's kingdom. Sometimes wealth and achievements can blind us to our need for God. Whenever we recognize this attitude in ourselves, we need to confess it to God as sin. The rich young man needed to see his helplessness before he could be helped. Yet God has ways of getting the attention of even the proud and self-sufficient. God can change our attitudes before they keep us from receiving the treasures he longs to give us.

10:32–45 Immediately after Jesus warned his disciples of his impending suffering and death, James and John requested positions of honor and authority. They did not realize that the call to follow Jesus would involve suffering and persecution. Following Jesus is never the easiest path, but it is the only path that leads to a life of restoration, joy and fulfillment.

THE SPIRITUAL DISCIPLINES

Service

Leading Through Serving

Mark 10:41–45 When attempting to describe God, human beings have often conjured up an image of a hostile being who must be appeased or a disinterested deity who is uninvolved in our lives or possibly a magical entity who can be manipulated through superstitious ritual. The Bible, however, reveals the most astonishing truth about God: Though he is the sovereign Creator and worthy of honor, God has come to us in the form of a servant, Jesus Christ. He became a suffering servant for his people (see Isaiah 53).

Immediately after Jesus' teaching about going to the cross, the disciples began arguing about their place around Jesus' throne. They wanted the places of honor and prestige. Jesus offered them places of humility and sacrifice.

In Mark 10, Jesus clearly teaches that the way of faith is also the way of service. Like the disciples, too many of us think that leadership equals power and prestige. Jesus teaches us, both by his life and words, that humility and servanthood characterize true leaders in his kingdom. In the eyes of God, greatness is measured not by where we stand but by where we kneel.

Putting It Into Practice

Where are you most tempted to seek the places of honor? At church? At school? At work? In a community organization? What one step could you take to free yourself from seeking your own interests and to begin focusing on serving others?

For more on service, turn to Acts 6.

Blind Bartimaeus Receives His Sight

‰ See Matthew 20:29–34; Luke 18:35–43

[46]Then they came to Jericho. As Jesus and his
disciples, together with a large crowd, were leaving the city, a blind man, Bartimaeus (that is,
the Son of Timaeus), was sitting by the roadside
begging. [47]When he heard that it was Jesus of
Nazareth, he began to shout, "Jesus, Son of
David, have mercy on me!"

[48]Many rebuked him and told him to be quiet, but he shouted all the more, "Son of David,
have mercy on me!"

[49]Jesus stopped and said, "Call him."

So they called to the blind man, "Cheer up!
On your feet! He's calling you." [50]Throwing his
cloak aside, he jumped to his feet and came to
Jesus.

[51]"What do you want me to do for you?" Jesus
asked him.

The blind man said, "Rabbi, I want to see."

[52]"Go," said Jesus, "your faith has healed
you." Immediately he received his sight and followed Jesus along the road.

The Triumphal Entry

‰ See Matthew 21:1–9; Luke 19:29–38; John 12:12–15

11 As they approached Jerusalem and
came to Bethphage and Bethany at the
Mount of Olives, Jesus sent two of his disciples,
[2]saying to them, "Go to the village ahead of
you, and just as you enter it, you will find a colt
tied there, which no one has ever ridden. Untie
it and bring it here. [3]If anyone asks you, 'Why
are you doing this?' tell him, 'The Lord needs it
and will send it back here shortly.' "

[4]They went and found a colt outside in the
street, tied at a doorway. As they untied it,
[5]some people standing there asked, "What are
you doing, untying that colt?" [6]They answered as
Jesus had told them to, and the people let them
go. [7]When they brought the colt to Jesus and
threw their cloaks over it, he sat on it. [8]Many
people spread their cloaks on the road, while
others spread branches they had cut in the
fields. [9]Those who went ahead and those who
followed shouted,

"Hosanna![a]"

"Blessed is he who comes in the name of
the Lord!"[b]

[10]"Blessed is the coming kingdom of our
father David!"

"Hosanna in the highest!"

[11]Jesus entered Jerusalem and went to the
temple. He looked around at everything, but
since it was already late, he went out to Bethany
with the Twelve.

Jesus Clears the Temple

‰ See Matthew 21:12–16; Luke 19:45–47; John 2:13–16

[12]The next day as they were leaving Bethany,
Jesus was hungry. [13]Seeing in the distance a fig
tree in leaf, he went to find out if it had any
fruit. When he reached it, he found nothing but
leaves, because it was not the season for figs.
[14]Then he said to the tree, "May no one ever eat
fruit from you again." And his disciples heard
him say it.

[15]On reaching Jerusalem, Jesus entered the
temple area and began driving out those who
were buying and selling there. He overturned
the tables of the money changers and the
benches of those selling doves, [16]and would not
allow anyone to carry merchandise through the
temple courts. [17]And as he taught them, he said,
"Is it not written:

" 'My house will be called
a house of prayer for all nations'[c]?

But you have made it 'a den of robbers.'[d]"

[18]The chief priests and the teachers of the law
heard this and began looking for a way to kill
him, for they feared him, because the whole
crowd was amazed at his teaching.

[19]When evening came, they[e] went out of
the city.

The Withered Fig Tree

‰ See Matthew 21:19–22

[20]In the morning, as they went along, they
saw the fig tree withered from the roots. [21]Peter

a9 A Hebrew expression meaning "Save!" which became an exclamation of praise; also in verse 10
b9 Psalm 118:25,26 *c17* Isaiah 56:7 *d17* Jer. 7:11
e19 Some early manuscripts *he*

10:46–52 Faith brought recovery of sight to blind Bartimaeus. He had to persevere in faith despite the initial opposition that he experienced from Jesus' followers. In ancient times, blindness was often viewed as a divine curse for sin (see John 9:2). Jesus refuted this notion by both word and deed. We sometimes face opposition to our spiritual growth. Sometimes those who claim to be God's people reject us and make us feel unwelcome because we are still enslaved by our sins. Even when others have rejected us, we can be sure that Jesus will never turn us away. We should persevere as Bartimaeus did, knowing that Jesus has the power to help us overcome the sins that enslave us and to heal us.

11:11–19 The barren fig tree is analogous to spiritually bankrupt people. If the fig tree did not produce fruit as it was supposed to do, then it had no real reason to exist. So also if our lives are not bearing the fruit of the Spirit, then our faith has no substance, and our attempt at spirituality is only a pretense. We need to ask God's Spirit to change us and cause us to become the people he wants us to be.

11:19–25 God wants us to pray for his will to be done in our lives, much as he wants us to pray for fruitfulness in his kingdom work. The God we serve is the God of the impossible. He has the power to do miracles. We are invited to participate in bringing God's miracle-working power into everyday life. We do this by taking him at his word, truly believing his offer to intervene in our lives and praying to him. And when we pray, we must make certain that we forgive others, for God desires to forgive us.

remembered and said to Jesus, "Rabbi, look! The fig tree you cursed has withered!"

22"Have[a] faith in God," Jesus answered. 23"I tell you the truth, if anyone says to this mountain, 'Go, throw yourself into the sea,' and does not doubt in his heart but believes that what he says will happen, it will be done for him. 24Therefore I tell you, whatever you ask for in prayer, believe that you have received it, and it will be yours. 25And when you stand praying, if you hold anything against anyone, forgive him, so that your Father in heaven may forgive you your sins.[b]"

The Authority of Jesus Questioned

‰ See Matthew 21:23–27; Luke 20:1–8

27They arrived again in Jerusalem, and while Jesus was walking in the temple courts, the chief priests, the teachers of the law and the elders came to him. 28"By what authority are you doing these things?" they asked. "And who gave you authority to do this?"

29Jesus replied, "I will ask you one question. Answer me, and I will tell you by what authority I am doing these things. 30John's baptism—was it from heaven, or from men? Tell me!"

31They discussed it among themselves and said, "If we say, 'From heaven,' he will ask, 'Then why didn't you believe him?' 32But if we say, 'From men' . . . ." (They feared the people, for everyone held that John really was a prophet.)

33So they answered Jesus, "We don't know."

Jesus said, "Neither will I tell you by what authority I am doing these things."

The Parable of the Tenants

‰ See Matthew 21:33–46; Luke 20:9–19

12 He then began to speak to them in parables: "A man planted a vineyard. He put a wall around it, dug a pit for the winepress and built a watchtower. Then he rented the vineyard to some farmers and went away on a journey. 2At harvest time he sent a servant to the tenants to collect from them some of the fruit of the vineyard. 3But they seized him, beat him and sent him away empty-handed. 4Then he sent another servant to them; they struck this man on the head and treated him shamefully. 5He sent still another, and that one they killed. He sent many others; some of them they beat, others they killed.

6"He had one left to send, a son, whom he loved. He sent him last of all, saying, 'They will respect my son.'

7"But the tenants said to one another, 'This is the heir. Come, let's kill him, and the inheritance will be ours.' 8So they took him and killed him, and threw him out of the vineyard.

9"What then will the owner of the vineyard do? He will come and kill those tenants and give the vineyard to others. 10Haven't you read this scripture:

" 'The stone the builders rejected
has become the capstone[c];
11the Lord has done this,
and it is marvelous in our eyes'[d]?"

12Then they looked for a way to arrest him because they knew he had spoken the parable against them. But they were afraid of the crowd; so they left him and went away.

Paying Taxes to Caesar

‰ See Matthew 22:15–22; Luke 20:20–26

13Later they sent some of the Pharisees and Herodians to Jesus to catch him in his words. 14They came to him and said, "Teacher, we know you are a man of integrity. You aren't swayed by men, because you pay no attention to who they are; but you teach the way of God in accordance with the truth. Is it right to pay taxes to Caesar or not? 15Should we pay or shouldn't we?"

But Jesus knew their hypocrisy. "Why are you trying to trap me?" he asked. "Bring me a denarius and let me look at it." 16They brought the coin, and he asked them, "Whose portrait is this? And whose inscription?"

"Caesar's," they replied.

17Then Jesus said to them, "Give to Caesar what is Caesar's and to God what is God's."

And they were amazed at him.

Marriage at the Resurrection

‰ See Matthew 22:23–33; Luke 20:27–38

18Then the Sadducees, who say there is no resurrection, came to him with a question. 19"Teacher," they said, "Moses wrote for us that if a man's brother dies and leaves a wife but no children, the man must marry the widow and have children for his brother. 20Now there were

[a]22 Some early manuscripts *If you have* [b]25 Some manuscripts *sins. 26But if you do not forgive, neither will your Father who is in heaven forgive your sins.* [c]10 Or *cornerstone* [d]11 Psalm 118:22,23

12:1–12 By telling this story, Jesus confronted the religious leaders with their hypocrisy. Jesus likened the religious leaders to the wicked farmers who had rejected God and had not tended the vineyard (God's people). These leaders had pretended to be in touch with God, but their actions and attitudes proved otherwise. Jesus confronted them, hoping they would listen and change. God often brings people into our lives who can help us hear and receive the truth. We would be wise to listen to them, for if we refuse to admit our sins and mistakes like the proud Pharisees, we will never be able to receive the help God willingly offers us.

12:18–27 Jesus answered this trick question posed by the Sadducees, who did not believe in the possibility of resurrection from the dead. Jesus cleverly exposed the moral shortcomings of those who possessed a form of religion but denied its power. Knowledge alone, even of the Bible, is not enough to keep us from sin or help us break free from the sins that enslave us. We must know the living God personally and accept the help he offers. The God of the patriarchs is not a God of philosophical speculation. He is our God, active in our lives.

seven brothers. The first one married and died without leaving any children. 21The second one married the widow, but he also died, leaving no child. It was the same with the third. 22In fact, none of the seven left any children. Last of all, the woman died too. 23At the resurrection[a] whose wife will she be, since the seven were married to her?"

24Jesus replied, "Are you not in error because you do not know the Scriptures or the power of God? 25When the dead rise, they will neither marry nor be given in marriage; they will be like the angels in heaven. 26Now about the dead rising—have you not read in the book of Moses, in the account of the bush, how God said to him, 'I am the God of Abraham, the God of Isaac, and the God of Jacob'[b]? 27He is not the God of the dead, but of the living. You are badly mistaken!"

The Greatest Commandment

‰ See Matthew 22:34–40

28One of the teachers of the law came and heard them debating. Noticing that Jesus had given them a good answer, he asked him, "Of all the commandments, which is the most important?"

29"The most important one," answered Jesus, "is this: 'Hear, O Israel, the Lord our God, the Lord is one.[c] 30Love the Lord your God with all your heart and with all your soul and with all your mind and with all your strength.'[d] 31The second is this: 'Love your neighbor as yourself.'[e] There is no commandment greater than these."

32"Well said, teacher," the man replied. "You are right in saying that God is one and there is no other but him. 33To love him with all your heart, with all your understanding and with all your strength, and to love your neighbor as yourself is more important than all burnt offerings and sacrifices."

34When Jesus saw that he had answered wisely, he said to him, "You are not far from the kingdom of God." And from then on no one dared ask him any more questions.

Whose Son Is the Christ?

‰ See Matthew 22:41–46; Luke 20:41–47

35While Jesus was teaching in the temple courts, he asked, "How is it that the teachers of the law say that the Christ[f] is the son of David? 36David himself, speaking by the Holy Spirit, declared:

" 'The Lord said to my Lord:
"Sit at my right hand
until I put your enemies
under your feet." '[g]

37David himself calls him 'Lord.' How then can he be his son?"

The large crowd listened to him with delight.

38As he taught, Jesus said, "Watch out for the teachers of the law. They like to walk around in flowing robes and be greeted in the marketplaces, 39and have the most important seats in the synagogues and the places of honor at banquets. 40They devour widows' houses and for a show make lengthy prayers. Such men will be punished most severely."

The Widow's Offering

‰ See Luke 21:1–4

41Jesus sat down opposite the place where the offerings were put and watched the crowd putting their money into the temple treasury. Many rich people threw in large amounts. 42But a poor widow came and put in two very small copper coins,[h] worth only a fraction of a penny.[i]

43Calling his disciples to him, Jesus said, "I tell you the truth, this poor widow has put more into the treasury than all the others. 44They all gave out of their wealth; but she, out of her poverty, put in everything—all she had to live on."

Signs of the End of the Age

‰ See Matthew 24:1–51; Luke 21:5–36

13 As he was leaving the temple, one of his disciples said to him, "Look, Teacher! What massive stones! What magnificent buildings!"

2"Do you see all these great buildings?" replied Jesus. "Not one stone here will be left on another; every one will be thrown down."

3As Jesus was sitting on the Mount of Olives opposite the temple, Peter, James, John and Andrew asked him privately, 4"Tell us, when will these things happen? And what will be the sign that they are all about to be fulfilled?"

5Jesus said to them: "Watch out that no one deceives you. 6Many will come in my name, claiming, 'I am he,' and will deceive many. 7When you hear of wars and rumors of wars, do not be alarmed. Such things must happen, but the end is still to come. 8Nation will rise against nation, and kingdom against kingdom. There

[a]23 Some manuscripts *resurrection, when men rise from the dead,* [b]26 Exodus 3:6 [c]29 Or *the Lord our God is one Lord* [d]30 Deut. 6:4,5 [e]31 Lev. 19:18 [f]35 Or *Messiah* [g]36 Psalm 110:1 [h]42 Greek *two lepta* [i]42 Greek *kodrantes*

12:28–34 Many think of the law as a burdensome straitjacket, antithetical to true spiritual freedom and renewal. This may have been true, in some sense, of the regulations for implementing God's law in Jesus' day. The religious legalism of the day made God's laws oppressive. Jesus wanted to correct this wrong understanding of true faith. He summed up the numerous Jewish regulations in two simple but profound commandments: We are to love God totally, and we are to love others as ourselves. If these two truths rule our hearts and minds, the rest of the law will fall into its proper place in our lives.

will be earthquakes in various places, and famines. These are the beginning of birth pains.
9 "You must be on your guard. You will be
handed over to the local councils and flogged in
the synagogues. On account of me you will
stand before governors and kings as witnesses
to them. 10 And the gospel must first be
preached to all nations. 11 Whenever you are arrested and brought to trial, do not worry beforehand about what to say. Just say whatever is
given you at the time, for it is not you speaking,
but the Holy Spirit.
12 "Brother will betray brother to death, and
a father his child. Children will rebel against
their parents and have them put to death. 13 All
men will hate you because of me, but he who
stands firm to the end will be saved.
14 "When you see 'the abomination that
causes desolation'[a] standing where it[b] does
not belong—let the reader understand—then let
those who are in Judea flee to the mountains.
15 Let no one on the roof of his house go down
or enter the house to take anything out. 16 Let no
one in the field go back to get his cloak. 17 How
dreadful it will be in those days for pregnant
women and nursing mothers! 18 Pray that this
will not take place in winter, 19 because those
will be days of distress unequaled from the beginning, when God created the world, until
now—and never to be equaled again. 20 If the
Lord had not cut short those days, no one
would survive. But for the sake of the elect,
whom he has chosen, he has shortened them.
21 At that time if anyone says to you, 'Look, here
is the Christ[c]!' or, 'Look, there he is!' do not
believe it. 22 For false Christs and false prophets
will appear and perform signs and miracles to
deceive the elect—if that were possible. 23 So be
on your guard; I have told you everything ahead
of time.
24 "But in those days, following that distress,

" 'the sun will be darkened,
and the moon will not give its light;
25 the stars will fall from the sky,
and the heavenly bodies will be
shaken.'[d]

26 "At that time men will see the Son of Man
coming in clouds with great power and glory.
27 And he will send his angels and gather his
elect from the four winds, from the ends of the
earth to the ends of the heavens.
28 "Now learn this lesson from the fig tree: As
soon as its twigs get tender and its leaves come
out, you know that summer is near. 29 Even so,
when you see these things happening, you
know that it is near, right at the door. 30 I tell you
the truth, this generation[e] will certainly not
pass away until all these things have happened.
31 Heaven and earth will pass away, but my
words will never pass away.

The Day and Hour Unknown

32 "No one knows about that day or hour,
not even the angels in heaven, nor the Son, but
only the Father. 33 Be on guard! Be alert[f]! You
do not know when that time will come. 34 It's
like a man going away: He leaves his house and
puts his servants in charge, each with his assigned task, and tells the one at the door to keep
watch.
35 "Therefore keep watch because you do not
know when the owner of the house will come
back—whether in the evening, or at midnight,
or when the rooster crows, or at dawn. 36 If he
comes suddenly, do not let him find you sleeping. 37 What I say to you, I say to everyone:
'Watch!' "

Jesus Anointed at Bethany

‰ See Matthew 26:2–16; Luke 22:1–6

14 Now the Passover and the Feast of Unleavened Bread were only two days
away, and the chief priests and the teachers of
the law were looking for some sly way to arrest
Jesus and kill him. 2 "But not during the Feast,"
they said, "or the people may riot."
3 While he was in Bethany, reclining at the
table in the home of a man known as Simon the
Leper, a woman came with an alabaster jar of
very expensive perfume, made of pure nard. She
broke the jar and poured the perfume on his
head.
4 Some of those present were saying indig-
nantly to one another, "Why this waste of perfume? 5 It could have been sold for more than
a year's wages[g] and the money given to the
poor." And they rebuked her harshly.
6 "Leave her alone," said Jesus. "Why are you
bothering her? She has done a beautiful thing to
me. 7 The poor you will always have with you,
and you can help them any time you want. But
you will not always have me. 8 She did what she
could. She poured perfume on my body before-

[a]14 Daniel 9:27; 11:31; 12:11 [b]14 Or *he;* also in verse 29 [c]21 Or *Messiah* [d]25 Isaiah 13:10; 34:4 [e]30 Or *race* [f]33 Some manuscripts *alert and pray* [g]5 Greek *than three hundred denarii*

13:21–37 Jesus did not reveal when the end of the world would come, but this should motivate us to remain alert and watchful until the end. There are also uncertainties concerning the timing and difficulties we will face in our own lives. We cannot calculate the day of his return and then plan to change just before the final event. We must make continual preparation for his return, recognizing that we will be completely transformed only after Jesus has returned to make us into new people.

14:1–9 Here a woman showed her devotion to Jesus by anointing him with expensive perfume (equal in value to a year's wages), as if preparing a king for burial. Some of the disciples mocked her devotion, but Jesus praised her and said she would be an example for all believers to follow. Our faith in God and commitment to spiritual growth may often receive the criticism of others. Sometimes family members will not believe our lifestyle changes are lasting. Our friends may feel threatened by the changes they see in our lives. No matter what others might say, Jesus is in favor of our devotion and commitment to him.

hand to prepare for my burial. 9I tell you the
truth, wherever the gospel is preached throughout the world, what she has done will also be
told, in memory of her."
10Then Judas Iscariot, one of the Twelve,
went to the chief priests to betray Jesus to them.
11They were delighted to hear this and promised to give him money. So he watched for an
opportunity to hand him over.

The Lord's Supper

‰ See Matthew 26:17–30; Luke 22:7–23

12On the first day of the Feast of Unleavened
Bread, when it was customary to sacrifice the
Passover lamb, Jesus' disciples asked him,
"Where do you want us to go and make preparations for you to eat the Passover?"
13So he sent two of his disciples, telling
them, "Go into the city, and a man carrying a
jar of water will meet you. Follow him. 14Say to
the owner of the house he enters, 'The Teacher
asks: Where is my guest room, where I may eat
the Passover with my disciples?' 15He will show
you a large upper room, furnished and ready.
Make preparations for us there."
16The disciples left, went into the city and
found things just as Jesus had told them. So
they prepared the Passover.
17When evening came, Jesus arrived with the
Twelve. 18While they were reclining at the table
eating, he said, "I tell you the truth, one of you
will betray me—one who is eating with me."
19They were saddened, and one by one they
said to him, "Surely not I?"
20"It is one of the Twelve," he replied, "one
who dips bread into the bowl with me. 21The
Son of Man will go just as it is written about
him. But woe to that man who betrays the Son
of Man! It would be better for him if he had not
been born."
22While they were eating, Jesus took bread,
gave thanks and broke it, and gave it to his
disciples, saying, "Take it; this is my body."
23Then he took the cup, gave thanks and offered it to them, and they all drank from it.
24"This is my blood of the[a] covenant,
which is poured out for many," he said to them.
25"I tell you the truth, I will not drink again of
the fruit of the vine until that day when I drink
it anew in the kingdom of God."

[a]24 Some manuscripts *the new*

14:10–25 We are often shocked by the story of Judas's betrayal of Jesus. Since Judas had spent about three years in close friendship with Jesus, we wonder what could have prompted him to act as he did. Yet if we are honest, we may recognize the same potential in our own hearts. Whenever we refuse to give Jesus authority over a certain area of our lives, we are acting like Judas. Whenever we promise to do one thing and then do another, we are following Judas's example. We all have betrayed God in one way or another. We should use Judas's failure as an opportunity to take a hard look at our own lives. In what ways are we betraying God now?

Humility and Wisdom

Mark 14:3–9 Matthew 26:6–13 also records this event and the disciples' negative response to this woman's actions. Yet Jesus' rebuke of their negative attitude shows us that we need God's help to see the truth in every situation. We need a humble willingness to receive God's wisdom and an openness to the Holy Spirit, who promises to guide us into all truth.

Solomon wrote, "Wisdom is supreme; therefore get wisdom. Though it cost all you have, get understanding" (Proverbs 4:7). The apostle Paul prayed constantly for fellow believers, "asking that the God of our Lord Jesus Christ, the glorious Father, may give you the Spirit of wisdom and revelation, so that you may know him better" (Ephesians 1:17). And James wrote, "If any of you lacks wisdom, he should ask God, who gives generously to all without finding fault, and it will be given to him" (James 1:5).

We must recognize that we are sometimes spiritually blind to our own faults and often misinterpret life. We must not assume that we can always recognize the truth—ignorance, deception, or denial sometimes obscures truth. Seeing the truth requires God's wisdom, which is available to all his children. We must recognize our sin, open ourselves to God, ask him to give us his wisdom and believe that he will. He will help us see the truth from his perspective.

Turn to John 3.

26When they had sung a hymn, they went out
to the Mount of Olives.

Jesus Predicts Peter's Denial

‰ See Matthew 26:31–35

27"You will all fall away," Jesus told them,
"for it is written:

" 'I will strike the shepherd,
and the sheep will be scattered.'[a]

28But after I have risen, I will go ahead of you
into Galilee."
29Peter declared, "Even if all fall away, I will
not."
30"I tell you the truth," Jesus answered, "today—yes, tonight—before the rooster crows
twice[b] you yourself will disown me three
times."
31But Peter insisted emphatically, "Even if I
have to die with you, I will never disown you."
And all the others said the same.

Gethsemane

‰ See Matthew 26:36–46; Luke 22:40–46

32They went to a place called Gethsemane,
and Jesus said to his disciples, "Sit here while I
pray." 33He took Peter, James and John along
with him, and he began to be deeply distressed
and troubled. 34"My soul is overwhelmed with
sorrow to the point of death," he said to them.
"Stay here and keep watch."
35Going a little farther, he fell to the ground
and prayed that if possible the hour might pass
from him. 36"*Abba*,[c] Father," he said, "everything is possible for you. Take this cup from me.
Yet not what I will, but what you will."
37Then he returned to his disciples and
found them sleeping. "Simon," he said to Peter,
"are you asleep? Could you not keep watch for
one hour? 38Watch and pray so that you will not
fall into temptation. The spirit is willing, but
the body is weak."
39Once more he went away and prayed the
same thing. 40When he came back, he again
found them sleeping, because their eyes were
heavy. They did not know what to say to him.
41Returning the third time, he said to them,
"Are you still sleeping and resting? Enough!
The hour has come. Look, the Son of Man is
betrayed into the hands of sinners. 42Rise! Let
us go! Here comes my betrayer!"

Jesus Arrested

‰ See Matthew 26:47–56; Luke 22:47–50; John 18:3–11

43Just as he was speaking, Judas, one of the
Twelve, appeared. With him was a crowd armed
with swords and clubs, sent from the chief
priests, the teachers of the law, and the elders.
44Now the betrayer had arranged a signal
with them: "The one I kiss is the man; arrest
him and lead him away under guard." 45Going
at once to Jesus, Judas said, "Rabbi!" and kissed
him. 46The men seized Jesus and arrested him.
47Then one of those standing near drew his
sword and struck the servant of the high priest,
cutting off his ear.
48"Am I leading a rebellion," said Jesus, "that
you have come out with swords and clubs to
capture me? 49Every day I was with you, teaching in the temple courts, and you did not arrest
me. But the Scriptures must be fulfilled." 50Then
everyone deserted him and fled.
51A young man, wearing nothing but a linen
garment, was following Jesus. When they seized
him, 52he fled naked, leaving his garment behind.

Before the Sanhedrin

‰ See Matthew 26:57–68; John 18:12–13,19–24

53They took Jesus to the high priest, and all
the chief priests, elders and teachers of the law
came together. 54Peter followed him at a distance, right into the courtyard of the high priest.
There he sat with the guards and warmed himself at the fire.
55The chief priests and the whole Sanhedrin

[a] *27* Zech. 13:7 [b] *30* Some early manuscripts do not have *twice.* [c] *36* Aramaic for *Father*

14:27–31 Peter wasn't realistic with himself when he promised that he would stay with Jesus no matter what the cost. He still did not realize that following Jesus would lead him to the foot of the cross. When things got tough, Peter backed out of his commitment. We often do the same thing. We would be wise to consider the difficulties we may face along our spiritual journey. Jesus never promised us an easy trip; he only promised to help us along the way.

14:32–42 Jesus opened his heart to Peter, James and John: "My soul is overwhelmed with sorrow to the point of death" (14:34). In this way, Jesus demonstrated his honesty, transparency and trust. Jesus needed others for support in this hour of agony before his death. If Jesus needed human support to face his trials, we need it even more. We must develop a network of relationships that hold us accountable to our commitments. When we develop and maintain meaningful human relationships, we create a network of support that can help us sustain our spiritual growth.

14:35–36 Jesus expressed his true feelings as he prayed for his Father to remove the cup of suffering that he faced. Yet Jesus never rebelled against God's will. He was willing to suffer and die so that we could experience forgiveness from sin and redemption from its painful effects. As much as we might want to escape certain occasions of suffering, we must submit to God's will. God may lead us into some tough experiences. As painful as they may be, we can be assured that he has our best in mind, and he will stand with us throughout the process.

14:53–65 Jesus himself endured injustice: He was lied about, falsely accused, convicted and physically tortured. But, instead of returning words or blows in kind, Jesus entrusted himself to his Father's care (see 1 Peter 2:23). Jesus modeled the trust in God that we should have when we are treated unjustly. As we experience the pain that comes from persecution, physical harm, injustice or the sins others commit against us, it is normal to feel anger, sorrow, fear and violation. Yet we need to release these feelings to God. As we surrender the injustices we endure to God, he can take vengeance where vengeance is due.

were looking for evidence against Jesus so that they could put him to death, but they did not find any. 56Many testified falsely against him, but their statements did not agree.

57Then some stood up and gave this false testimony against him: 58"We heard him say, 'I will destroy this man-made temple and in three days will build another, not made by man.' " 59Yet even then their testimony did not agree. 60Then the high priest stood up before them and asked Jesus, "Are you not going to answer? What is this testimony that these men are bringing against you?" 61But Jesus remained silent and gave no answer.

Again the high priest asked him, "Are you the Christ,[a] the Son of the Blessed One?"

62"I am," said Jesus. "And you will see the Son of Man sitting at the right hand of the Mighty One and coming on the clouds of heaven."

63The high priest tore his clothes. "Why do we need any more witnesses?" he asked. 64"You have heard the blasphemy. What do you think?"

They all condemned him as worthy of death. 65Then some began to spit at him; they blindfolded him, struck him with their fists, and said, "Prophesy!" And the guards took him and beat him.

Peter Disowns Jesus

‰ See Matthew 26:69–75; Luke 22:56–62; John 18:16–18,25–27

66While Peter was below in the courtyard, one of the servant girls of the high priest came by. 67When she saw Peter warming himself, she looked closely at him.

"You also were with that Nazarene, Jesus," she said.

68But he denied it. "I don't know or understand what you're talking about," he said, and went out into the entryway.[b]

69When the servant girl saw him there, she said again to those standing around, "This fellow is one of them." 70Again he denied it.

After a little while, those standing near said to Peter, "Surely you are one of them, for you are a Galilean."

71He began to call down curses on himself, and he swore to them, "I don't know this man you're talking about."

72Immediately the rooster crowed the second time.[c] Then Peter remembered the word Jesus had spoken to him: "Before the rooster crows twice[d] you will disown me three times." And he broke down and wept.

Jesus Before Pilate

‰ See Matthew 27:11–26; Luke 23:2–3,18–25; John 18:29—19:16

15 Very early in the morning, the chief priests, with the elders, the teachers of the law and the whole Sanhedrin, reached a decision. They bound Jesus, led him away and handed him over to Pilate.

2"Are you the king of the Jews?" asked Pilate.

"Yes, it is as you say," Jesus replied.

3The chief priests accused him of many things. 4So again Pilate asked him, "Aren't you going to answer? See how many things they are accusing you of."

5But Jesus still made no reply, and Pilate was amazed.

6Now it was the custom at the Feast to release a prisoner whom the people requested. 7A man called Barabbas was in prison with the insurrectionists who had committed murder in the uprising. 8The crowd came up and asked Pilate to do for them what he usually did.

9"Do you want me to release to you the king of the Jews?" asked Pilate, 10knowing it was out of envy that the chief priests had handed Jesus over to him. 11But the chief priests stirred up the crowd to have Pilate release Barabbas instead.

12"What shall I do, then, with the one you call the king of the Jews?" Pilate asked them.

13"Crucify him!" they shouted.

14"Why? What crime has he committed?" asked Pilate.

But they shouted all the louder, "Crucify him!"

15Wanting to satisfy the crowd, Pilate released Barabbas to them. He had Jesus flogged, and handed him over to be crucified.

The Soldiers Mock Jesus

‰ See Matthew 27:27–31

16The soldiers led Jesus away into the palace (that is, the Praetorium) and called together the whole company of soldiers. 17They put a purple robe on him, then twisted together a crown of thorns and set it on him. 18And they began to call out to him, "Hail, king of the Jews!" 19Again and again they struck him on the head with a staff and spit on him. Falling on their knees, they paid homage to him. 20And when they had mocked him, they took off the purple robe and

[a] 61 Or *Messiah* [b] 68 Some early manuscripts *entryway and the rooster crowed* [c] 72 Some early manuscripts do not have *the second time.* [d] 72 Some early manuscripts do not have *twice.*

15:1–15 Pilate stated at least three times that he found no guilt in Jesus, yet he handed Jesus over for execution. Strong emotions on the part of the Jews and Pilate's desire to pacify them at all cost led to the punishment of an innocent man. We often have a lot in common with Pilate and sacrifice the truth in order to please the crowd. Our challenge is to stand firm in our faith and not succumb to the world's sinful demands.

15:16–32 Jesus suffered the ultimate in humiliation and torture when he was spat upon, beaten, mocked and nailed to a cross. Knowing that Jesus endured all this to provide for our redemption should cause us to be grateful. No matter how terrible our past, no matter how great our mistakes in the future, Jesus has paid the penalty for all our sins. Because of his suffering, we can have a restored relationship with God.

put his own clothes on him. Then they led him out to crucify him.

The Crucifixion

‰ See Matthew 27:33–44; Luke 23:33–43; John 19:17–24

21A certain man from Cyrene, Simon, the father of Alexander and Rufus, was passing by on his way in from the country, and they forced him to carry the cross. 22They brought Jesus to the place called Golgotha (which means The Place of the Skull). 23Then they offered him wine mixed with myrrh, but he did not take it. 24And they crucified him. Dividing up his clothes, they cast lots to see what each would get.

25It was the third hour when they crucified him. 26The written notice of the charge against him read: THE KING OF THE JEWS. 27They crucified two robbers with him, one on his right and one on his left.[a] 29Those who passed by hurled insults at him, shaking their heads and saying, "So! You who are going to destroy the temple and build it in three days, 30come down from the cross and save yourself!"

31In the same way the chief priests and the teachers of the law mocked him among themselves. "He saved others," they said, "but he can't save himself! 32Let this Christ,[b] this King of Israel, come down now from the cross, that we may see and believe." Those crucified with him also heaped insults on him.

The Death of Jesus

‰ See Matthew 27:45–56; Luke 23:44–49; John 19:29–30

33At the sixth hour darkness came over the whole land until the ninth hour. 34And at the ninth hour Jesus cried out in a loud voice, *"Eloi, Eloi, lama sabachthani?"*—which means, "My God, my God, why have you forsaken me?"[c]

35When some of those standing near heard this, they said, "Listen, he's calling Elijah."

36One man ran, filled a sponge with wine vinegar, put it on a stick, and offered it to Jesus to drink. "Now leave him alone. Let's see if Elijah comes to take him down," he said.

37With a loud cry, Jesus breathed his last.

38The curtain of the temple was torn in two from top to bottom. 39And when the centurion, who stood there in front of Jesus, heard his cry and[d] saw how he died, he said, "Surely this man was the Son[e] of God!"

40Some women were watching from a distance. Among them were Mary Magdalene, Mary the mother of James the younger and of Joses, and Salome. 41In Galilee these women had followed him and cared for his needs. Many other women who had come up with him to Jerusalem were also there.

The Burial of Jesus

‰ See Matthew 27:57–61; Luke 23:50–56; John 19:38–42

42It was Preparation Day (that is, the day before the Sabbath). So as evening approached, 43Joseph of Arimathea, a prominent member of the Council, who was himself waiting for the kingdom of God, went boldly to Pilate and asked for Jesus' body. 44Pilate was surprised to hear that he was already dead. Summoning the centurion, he asked him if Jesus had already died. 45When he learned from the centurion that it was so, he gave the body to Joseph. 46So Joseph bought some linen cloth, took down the body, wrapped it in the linen, and placed it in a tomb cut out of rock. Then he rolled a stone against the entrance of the tomb. 47Mary Magdalene and Mary the mother of Joses saw where he was laid.

The Resurrection

‰ See Matthew 28:1–8; Luke 24:1–10

16 When the Sabbath was over, Mary Magdalene, Mary the mother of James, and Salome bought spices so that they might go to anoint Jesus' body. 2Very early on the first day of the week, just after sunrise, they were on their way to the tomb 3and they asked each other, "Who will roll the stone away from the entrance of the tomb?"

4But when they looked up, they saw that the stone, which was very large, had been rolled away. 5As they entered the tomb, they saw a young man dressed in a white robe sitting on the right side, and they were alarmed.

6"Don't be alarmed," he said. "You are looking for Jesus the Nazarene, who was crucified. He has risen! He is not here. See the place where they laid him. 7But go, tell his disciples and Peter, 'He is going ahead of you into Galilee. There you will see him, just as he told you.' "

8Trembling and bewildered, the women went out and fled from the tomb. They said nothing to anyone, because they were afraid.

[a] 27 Some manuscripts *left, 28and the scripture was fulfilled which says, "He was counted with the lawless ones"* (Isaiah 53:12) [b] 32 Or *Messiah* [c] 34 Psalm 22:1
[d] 39 Some manuscripts do not have *heard his cry and*
[e] 39 Or *a son*

15:33–41 Jesus came to "give his life as a ransom for many" (10:45). Jesus' ultimate purpose on this earth was his sacrificial death as a payment for our sins. At this excruciating moment, the Savior bore the pain and punishment for all the sins ever committed (see John 1:29). This is truly good news! Although we are never good enough by our own merit to gain God's favor, Jesus' sacrifice provides for our redemption.

16:3–7 The women wondered how they would ever roll the great stone away from the tomb entrance when, to their amazement, they found it had already been moved. The tomb was empty! Notice that the women had only wanted to open the tomb. But God had accomplished so much more: He had raised Jesus from the dead! If God can give life to a dead body, he surely can restore our lives. There is always hope. With God, all things are possible! God specializes in rolling away burdens too great for our feeble human strength to handle. When we set out to do all we can, we will likely discover that God has already accomplished our goals—and much more!

[The earliest manuscripts and some other
ancient witnesses do not have
Mark 16:9–20.]

9When Jesus rose early on the first day of the
week, he appeared first to Mary Magdalene, out
of whom he had driven seven demons. 10She
went and told those who had been with him
and who were mourning and weeping. 11When
they heard that Jesus was alive and that she had
seen him, they did not believe it.

12Afterward Jesus appeared in a different
form to two of them while they were walking in
the country. 13These returned and reported it to
the rest; but they did not believe them either.

14Later Jesus appeared to the Eleven as they
were eating; he rebuked them for their lack of
faith and their stubborn refusal to believe those
who had seen him after he had risen.

15He said to them, "Go into all the world
and preach the good news to all creation.
16Whoever believes and is baptized will be
saved, but whoever does not believe will be
condemned. 17And these signs will accompany
those who believe: In my name they will drive
out demons; they will speak in new tongues;
18they will pick up snakes with their hands; and
when they drink deadly poison, it will not hurt
them at all; they will place their hands on sick
people, and they will get well."

19After the Lord Jesus had spoken to them, he
was taken up into heaven and he sat at the right
hand of God. 20Then the disciples went out and
preached everywhere, and the Lord worked
with them and confirmed his word by the signs
that accompanied it.

16:9–20 Many of the disciples refused to believe that Jesus had risen from the dead. When they finally met the resurrected Jesus, he rebuked them for their unbelief. Faith is foundational for our salvation and redemption. As we grow in our faith in Jesus, we will discover that the power of his resurrection will touch and transform our lives. Then we can become a source of encouragement to others as we share the story of God's transforming power.

LUKE

The Big Picture

A. THE SAVIOR'S BIRTH AND PREPARATION (1:1–4:13)

B. THE SAVIOR'S MINISTRY IN WORD AND DEED (4:14–21:38)

1. Jesus' Ministry in Galilee (4:14–9:50)
2. Jesus' Ministry on the Way to Jerusalem (9:51–19:27)
3. Jesus' Ministry in Jerusalem (19:28–21:38)

C. THE SAVIOR'S DEATH AND RESURRECTION (22:1–24:53)

Tradition maintains that Luke was a physician as well as a historian. Luke pictured Jesus as a man who cared greatly for suffering and downtrodden people, a man who brought healing to the hurting. Through Jesus' genealogy, Luke traced Jesus' human ancestors back to Adam, the father of the human race. Luke's stories about Jesus focused on his relationships with individual people. Jesus paid special attention to people who were often ignored in society—women, children, the poor, prostitutes, despised tax collectors and sinners of every sort.

Jesus offered salvation, strength and restoration to everyone he met. But by far Jesus' greatest concern was for the outcasts of society. Luke stressed Jesus' humanity and compassion more than any of the other gospel writers did. Luke's narrative clearly shows God, through his Son Jesus, reaching out in love to the unlovable of our world. Ever since Adam and Eve's first sin in the Garden of Eden, God has desired and pursued the restoration of sinful people. His love and concern for us are unstoppable!

As we dare to see the truth of our lives, many of us discover just how terrible and destructive our mistakes have been. As we seek God and ask him to illuminate our lives, we may begin to see how sinful and broken we really are. We may wonder whether there is any hope for us at all. How could God care for us when we fall so far short of his perfect will? The Gospel of Luke gives us hope as we see God's compassion toward people who are a lot like us. God wants to show us how much he loves us, regardless of our sin or how far we fall short of his perfect will.

Spiritual Renewal Themes

JESUS LOVES THE OUTCAST

Jesus paid special attention to the poor, the despised, the hurt and the sinful. He rejected no one; he ignored no one. And no one today is beyond the scope of Jesus' love or ability to help—including us. Jesus cares for us no matter what we have done, what we have failed to do, what we have suffered or what suffering we have caused others. Only Jesus' deep love can satisfy our needs and draw us to God himself. When we face our weakness, we may feel that no one can understand us or care for us.

Luke shows us that God both understands and cares. We can safely surrender our lives to him!

THE POWER OF THE RESURRECTION

Paul wrote to the Philippians and rejoiced that he could "know Christ and the power of his resurrection and the fellowship of sharing in his sufferings" (Philippians 3:10). Like the other gospel writers, Luke recorded in detail the events surrounding the death and resurrection of Jesus. There is no greater example of God's power at work than that of bringing the dead back to life. God specializes in demonstrating that kind of power as we experience his work within us. With God, nothing is too difficult.

GOD'S PASSION FOR OUR SPIRITUAL RENEWAL

God cares about our spiritual renewal even more than we do—that's how much he loves and cares for us. Jesus showed us this aspect of God's nature through his interest in people and relationships. Jesus cared for his followers and friends. He was interested in all types of people—men, women and children. His concern transcended all barriers and extended to all that he met. Jesus wanted people to be spiritually alive, growing and fruitful. As we come to know him and share his heart, we will experience his passion for our spiritual renewal. He died that we might live.

THE POWER OF THE HOLY SPIRIT

Jesus lived his life in complete dependence on the Holy Spirit. The Holy Spirit was present at Jesus' birth, his baptism, in his ministry and in his resurrection. The Father sent the Holy Spirit to confirm Jesus' authority. Today the Holy Spirit is given to empower us to live as God wants us to live. By faith, we can have the Holy Spirit's presence and power within us.

Essential Facts

PURPOSE:
To confirm the historical record of the life of Jesus Christ and to present his message of hope and salvation to all who turn to him.

AUTHOR:
Luke the physician.

AUDIENCE:
Theophilus, whose name means "lover of God."

DATE WRITTEN:
Probably about A.D. 60.

KEY VERSES:
"Jesus said to him, 'Today salvation has come to this house, because this man, too, is a son of Abraham. For the Son of Man came to seek and to save what was lost'" (19:9–10).

KEY PEOPLE AND RELATIONSHIPS:
Jesus and his disciples; Zechariah and Elizabeth; Mary, Mary Magdalene and John the Baptist.

SPECIAL FEATURES:
Luke focused on Jesus' relationships with people, particularly those who were in need, placing special emphasis on the role of women.

Introduction

1 Many have undertaken to draw up an account of the things that have been fulfilled[a] among us, 2just as they were handed
down to us by those who from the first were
eyewitnesses and servants of the word. 3There-
fore, since I myself have carefully investigated
everything from the beginning, it seemed good
also to me to write an orderly account for you,
most excellent Theophilus, 4so that you may
know the certainty of the things you have been
taught.

The Birth of John the Baptist Foretold

5In the time of Herod king of Judea there was
a priest named Zechariah, who belonged to the
priestly division of Abijah; his wife Elizabeth
was also a descendant of Aaron. 6Both of them
were upright in the sight of God, observing all
the Lord's commandments and regulations
blamelessly. 7But they had no children, because
Elizabeth was barren; and they were both well
along in years.

8Once when Zechariah's division was on
duty and he was serving as priest before God,
9he was chosen by lot, according to the custom
of the priesthood, to go into the temple of the
Lord and burn incense. 10And when the time for
the burning of incense came, all the assembled
worshipers were praying outside.

11Then an angel of the Lord appeared to him,
standing at the right side of the altar of incense.
12When Zechariah saw him, he was startled and
was gripped with fear. 13But the angel said to
him: "Do not be afraid, Zechariah; your prayer
has been heard. Your wife Elizabeth will bear
you a son, and you are to give him the name
John. 14He will be a joy and delight to you, and
many will rejoice because of his birth, 15for he
will be great in the sight of the Lord. He is never
to take wine or other fermented drink, and he
will be filled with the Holy Spirit even from
birth.[b] 16Many of the people of Israel will he
bring back to the Lord their God. 17And he will
go on before the Lord, in the spirit and power
of Elijah, to turn the hearts of the fathers to their
children and the disobedient to the wisdom of
the righteous—to make ready a people prepared
for the Lord."

18Zechariah asked the angel, "How can I be
sure of this? I am an old man and my wife is
well along in years."

19The angel answered, "I am Gabriel. I stand
in the presence of God, and I have been sent to
speak to you and to tell you this good news.
20And now you will be silent and not able to
speak until the day this happens, because you
did not believe my words, which will come true
at their proper time."

21Meanwhile, the people were waiting for
Zechariah and wondering why he stayed so
long in the temple. 22When he came out, he
could not speak to them. They realized he had
seen a vision in the temple, for he kept making
signs to them but remained unable to speak.

23When his time of service was completed, he
returned home. 24After this his wife Elizabeth
became pregnant and for five months remained
in seclusion. 25"The Lord has done this for me,"
she said. "In these days he has shown his favor
and taken away my disgrace among the people."

The Birth of Jesus Foretold

26In the sixth month, God sent the angel Gabriel to Nazareth, a town in Galilee, 27to a virgin
pledged to be married to a man named Joseph,
a descendant of David. The virgin's name was
Mary. 28The angel went to her and said, "Greetings, you who are highly favored! The Lord is
with you."

29Mary was greatly troubled at his words and
wondered what kind of greeting this might be.
30But the angel said to her, "Do not be afraid,
Mary, you have found favor with God. 31You
will be with child and give birth to a son, and
you are to give him the name Jesus. 32He will be
great and will be called the Son of the Most
High. The Lord God will give him the throne of
his father David, 33and he will reign over the
house of Jacob forever; his kingdom will never
end."

34"How will this be," Mary asked the angel,
"since I am a virgin?"

[a] 1 Or *been surely believed* [b] 15 Or *from his mother's womb*

1:1–4 In this preface, Luke testified that the gospel of Jesus is based on historical facts and not on theories or myths. Speculative religions, secular philosophies and political leaders cannot meet the deepest needs of the human heart. History is filled with people who aspired to be gods, but only one was truly God. Jesus alone can meet our deepest needs.

1:5–7 Though Zechariah and Elizabeth were godly people, they were childless. Elizabeth was well past normal childbearing years. Their situation was discouraging, as many couples in our society can attest. To make matters worse, in ancient cultures, childlessness was typically taken as a sign of God's curse or displeasure. Yet Zechariah and Elizabeth faithfully trusted God even though God seemed to be against them. Their patient perseverance is a good example for those of us who seek to grow spiritually.

1:16–17 John the Baptist's ministry would turn the hearts of parents to their children (see Malachi 4:5–6). His message called for personal repentance and the restoration of broken family relationships. This principle has always been true. When God is at work, resistant hearts can be softened and families restored.

1:18–20 As godly as Zechariah was, he still could not believe the angel's promise. From a natural perspective, it was impossible that he and Elizabeth could conceive a child in their old age. The consequence of Zechariah's short-term unbelief was substantial and tragic—Zechariah could not speak throughout Elizabeth's entire miraculous pregnancy. Unbelief can numb our spiritual progress as well. Confession of faith, before God and others, will help our faith grow (see Romans 9:9–10). Honestly admitting our doubts is a good place to start.

ELIZABETH & ZECHARIAH

Many loving couples long for children but are physically unable to have them. Often, as each month passes, their attempts to conceive a child are met with a painful progression from hope, to fear, to terrible disappointment. As the years roll by, their lingering hopes for a child disappear, leaving them with feelings of emptiness and resignation.

This is what it was like for Elizabeth and Zechariah. Their desire for children had not been fulfilled. It seemed they would remain childless for the rest of their lives. But suddenly something changed. While Zechariah served in the Jerusalem temple, an angel visited him and announced that Zechariah and Elizabeth would have a son. This son was to be named John. He would prepare the way for the Messiah.

Understandably shocked, Zechariah doubted the words of the angel. Because of his unbelief, God rendered Zechariah speechless until the child's birth. But when Elizabeth heard the news, she believed the angel's message and was excited about her pregnancy. In her sixth month, Elizabeth was visited by her cousin Mary, who was pregnant with the child Jesus. Filled with the Holy Spirit, Elizabeth praised Mary's faith.

When Elizabeth's baby was born, Zechariah, who still could not speak, wrote down the name the angel had given him for his new son—John. God then restored Zechariah's voice. With his first joyful words, Zechariah praised God for the great gift of a son and for God's intimate concern with the pain of their infertility. Whether God blesses the childless with a child or the helpless with his powerful presence, we can see from the lives of Elizabeth and Zechariah that God is intimately involved in our pain. He desires to fill the empty places in our lives.

STRENGTHS AND ACCOMPLISHMENTS:

Zechariah and Elizabeth were known as godly people.

Zechariah overcame his doubt and praised God for his power.

Zechariah obeyed the angel and named his son John.

WEAKNESSES AND MISTAKES:

Zechariah initially doubted God's ability to give them a child in their older years.

LESSONS FROM THEIR LIVES:

God is fully aware of the painful disappointment that childless couples face.

God is intimately aware of the pain of all hurting people.

All things are possible with God.

God can use older people to make significant contributions to his plan.

KEY VERSES:

"There was a priest named Zechariah, who belonged to the priestly division of Abijah; his wife Elizabeth was also a descendant of Aaron. Both of them were upright in the sight of God, observing all the Lord's commandments and regulations blamelessly" (1:5–6).

The story of Elizabeth and Zechariah is told in Luke 1:5–80.

35The angel answered, "The Holy Spirit will
come upon you, and the power of the Most
High will overshadow you. So the holy one to
be born will be called[a] the Son of God. 36Even
Elizabeth your relative is going to have a child
in her old age, and she who was said to be
barren is in her sixth month. 37For nothing is
impossible with God."
38"I am the Lord's servant," Mary answered.
"May it be to me as you have said." Then the
angel left her.

Mary Visits Elizabeth

39At that time Mary got ready and hurried to
a town in the hill country of Judea, 40where she
entered Zechariah's home and greeted Elizabeth. 41When Elizabeth heard Mary's greeting,
the baby leaped in her womb, and Elizabeth
was filled with the Holy Spirit. 42In a loud voice
she exclaimed: "Blessed are you among wom-
en, and blessed is the child you will bear! 43But
why am I so favored, that the mother of my
Lord should come to me? 44As soon as the
sound of your greeting reached my ears, the
baby in my womb leaped for joy. 45Blessed is
she who has believed that what the Lord has
said to her will be accomplished!"

Mary's Song

‰ See 1 Samuel 2:1–10

46And Mary said:

"My soul glorifies the Lord
47 and my spirit rejoices in God my Savior,
48for he has been mindful
of the humble state of his servant.
From now on all generations will call me
blessed,
49 for the Mighty One has done great things
for me—
holy is his name.
50His mercy extends to those who fear him,
from generation to generation.
51He has performed mighty deeds with his
arm;
he has scattered those who are proud in
their inmost thoughts.
52He has brought down rulers from their
thrones
but has lifted up the humble.
53He has filled the hungry with good things
but has sent the rich away empty.
54He has helped his servant Israel,
remembering to be merciful
55to Abraham and his descendants forever,
even as he said to our fathers."

56Mary stayed with Elizabeth for about three
months and then returned home.

The Birth of John the Baptist

57When it was time for Elizabeth to have her
baby, she gave birth to a son. 58Her neighbors
and relatives heard that the Lord had shown her
great mercy, and they shared her joy.
59On the eighth day they came to circumcise
the child, and they were going to name him
after his father Zechariah, 60but his mother
spoke up and said, "No! He is to be called
John."
61They said to her, "There is no one among
your relatives who has that name."
62Then they made signs to his father, to find
out what he would like to name the child. 63He
asked for a writing tablet, and to everyone's astonishment he wrote, "His name is John." 64Im-
mediately his mouth was opened and his
tongue was loosed, and he began to speak,
praising God. 65The neighbors were all filled
with awe, and throughout the hill country of
Judea people were talking about all these
things. 66Everyone who heard this wondered
about it, asking, "What then is this child going
to be?" For the Lord's hand was with him.

Zechariah's Song

67His father Zechariah was filled with the
Holy Spirit and prophesied:

68"Praise be to the Lord, the God of Israel,
because he has come and has redeemed
his people.
69He has raised up a horn[b] of salvation for
us
in the house of his servant David
70(as he said through his holy prophets of
long ago),
71salvation from our enemies
and from the hand of all who hate us—
72to show mercy to our fathers
and to remember his holy covenant,
73 the oath he swore to our father
Abraham:
74to rescue us from the hand of our enemies,
and to enable us to serve him without
fear
75 in holiness and righteousness before him
all our days.

76And you, my child, will be called a prophet
of the Most High;

[a]35 Or *So the child to be born will be called holy,*
[b]69 *Horn* here symbolizes strength.

1:51–55 These words from Mary's song reflect God's priorities set in stark contrast to the way our world thinks. When life seems unfair and does not turn out the way we might have chosen, we must realize that God's ways are not our ways (see Isaiah 55:8). True greatness is not measured by human success or achievement but rather by the depth of our humility and service for others.

1:76–79 In this passage Jesus Christ is portrayed as light shining on those living in darkness. Picture a group of ancient travelers overtaken by darkness and left in danger by the roadside all night. Such people, helpless to defend themselves against the attacks of robbers, would have welcomed the light of the rising sun. Those of us trapped in the darkness of sin can move from darkness into light as we receive God's gift of forgiveness and make a personal commitment to him. As we experience a new hope in

for you will go on before the Lord to
prepare the way for him,
77to give his people the knowledge of
salvation
through the forgiveness of their sins,
78because of the tender mercy of our God,
by which the rising sun will come to us
from heaven
79to shine on those living in darkness
and in the shadow of death,
to guide our feet into the path of peace."

80And the child grew and became strong in
spirit; and he lived in the desert until he appeared publicly to Israel.

The Birth of Jesus

2 In those days Caesar Augustus issued a decree that a census should be taken of the
entire Roman world. 2(This was the first census
that took place while Quirinius was governor of
Syria.) 3And everyone went to his own town to
register.

4So Joseph also went up from the town of
Nazareth in Galilee to Judea, to Bethlehem the
town of David, because he belonged to the
house and line of David. 5He went there to
register with Mary, who was pledged to be married to him and was expecting a child. 6While
they were there, the time came for the baby to
be born, 7and she gave birth to her firstborn, a
son. She wrapped him in cloths and placed him
in a manger, because there was no room for
them in the inn.

The Shepherds and the Angels

8And there were shepherds living out in the
fields nearby, keeping watch over their flocks at
night. 9An angel of the Lord appeared to them,
and the glory of the Lord shone around them,
and they were terrified. 10But the angel said to
them, "Do not be afraid. I bring you good news
of great joy that will be for all the people. 11To-
day in the town of David a Savior has been born
to you; he is Christ[a] the Lord. 12This will be a
sign to you: You will find a baby wrapped in
cloths and lying in a manger."

13Suddenly a great company of the heavenly
host appeared with the angel, praising God and
saying,

14"Glory to God in the highest,
and on earth peace to men on whom his
favor rests."

15When the angels had left them and gone
into heaven, the shepherds said to one another,
"Let's go to Bethlehem and see this thing that
has happened, which the Lord has told us
about."

16So they hurried off and found Mary and
Joseph, and the baby, who was lying in the
manger. 17When they had seen him, they spread
the word concerning what had been told them
about this child, 18and all who heard it were
amazed at what the shepherds said to them.
19But Mary treasured up all these things and
pondered them in her heart. 20The shepherds
returned, glorifying and praising God for all the
things they had heard and seen, which were just
as they had been told.

Jesus Presented in the Temple

21On the eighth day, when it was time to
circumcise him, he was named Jesus, the name
the angel had given him before he had been
conceived.

22When the time of their purification according to the Law of Moses had been completed,
Joseph and Mary took him to Jerusalem to
present him to the Lord 23(as it is written in the
Law of the Lord, "Every firstborn male is to be
consecrated to the Lord"[b]), 24and to offer a sacrifice in keeping with what is said in the Law of
the Lord: "a pair of doves or two young pigeons."[c]

25Now there was a man in Jerusalem called
Simeon, who was righteous and devout. He was
waiting for the consolation of Israel, and the
Holy Spirit was upon him. 26It had been revealed to him by the Holy Spirit that he would
not die before he had seen the Lord's Christ.
27Moved by the Spirit, he went into the temple
courts. When the parents brought in the child
Jesus to do for him what the custom of the Law
required, 28Simeon took him in his arms and
praised God, saying:

29"Sovereign Lord, as you have promised,

[a] 11 Or *Messiah.* "The Christ" (Greek) and "the Messiah" (Hebrew) both mean "the Anointed One"; also in verse 26. [b] 23 Exodus 13:2,12 [c] 24 Lev. 12:8

Jesus, we can tell others about the light we have seen too.

2:6–7 The welcome that Jesus received as a newborn in Bethlehem is a good illustration of how most people respond to him today. His birthplace was hardly an idyllic location like the ones pictured on our beautiful Christmas cards. It may have been a cold, damp, dark, dirty cave with a hollowed-out feeding trough, or manger. Jesus' willingness to enter our world, darkened and dirtied by sin and unfit for his royal presence, is a reason for us to be thankful. We don't have to already be clean in order to make room for him. When Jesus comes into our lives, he accepts us as we are—then he works his transformation in us.

2:8–12 Encounters with the living God often elicit fear. The angels reassured the shepherds: "Do not be afraid" (2:10). Once the shepherds realized that God wanted to communicate with them, they were free to worship the Christ child. The fact that Jesus came to earth as a human being reassures us that our holy and almighty God is also a personal God. When we put our faith in the living God, his perfect love expels all fear (see 1 John 4:18).

2:29–32 Simeon's words reflect the universality of God's plan of salvation. It was a rare thing for a Jew to declare that the Messiah would bring deliverance to the whole world, not just the Jews. God reaches out to all people, not just one ethnic group. He brings light, life and contentment to all who put their faith in him through Jesus Christ. God will accept any of us who are willing to turn to him for salvation, regardless of our background or situation in life. He is our universal Savior.

you now dismiss[a] your servant in
peace.
30For my eyes have seen your salvation,
31 which you have prepared in the sight of
all people,
32a light for revelation to the Gentiles
and for glory to your people Israel."

33The child's father and mother marveled at what was said about him. 34Then Simeon blessed them and said to Mary, his mother: "This child is destined to cause the falling and rising of many in Israel, and to be a sign that will be spoken against, 35so that the thoughts of many hearts will be revealed. And a sword will pierce your own soul too."

36There was also a prophetess, Anna, the daughter of Phanuel, of the tribe of Asher. She was very old; she had lived with her husband seven years after her marriage, 37and then was a widow until she was eighty-four.[b] She never left the temple but worshiped night and day, fasting and praying. 38Coming up to them at that very moment, she gave thanks to God and spoke about the child to all who were looking forward to the redemption of Jerusalem.

39When Joseph and Mary had done everything required by the Law of the Lord, they returned to Galilee to their own town of Nazareth. 40And the child grew and became strong; he was filled with wisdom, and the grace of God was upon him.

The Boy Jesus at the Temple

41Every year his parents went to Jerusalem for the Feast of the Passover. 42When he was twelve years old, they went up to the Feast, according to the custom. 43After the Feast was over, while his parents were returning home, the boy Jesus stayed behind in Jerusalem, but they were unaware of it. 44Thinking he was in their company, they traveled on for a day. Then they began looking for him among their relatives and friends. 45When they did not find him, they went back to Jerusalem to look for him. 46After three days they found him in the temple courts, sitting among the teachers, listening to them and asking them questions. 47Everyone who heard him was amazed at his understanding and his answers. 48When his parents saw him, they were astonished. His mother said to him, "Son, why have you treated us like this? Your father and I have been anxiously searching for you."

49"Why were you searching for me?" he asked. "Didn't you know I had to be in my Father's house?" 50But they did not understand what he was saying to them.

51Then he went down to Nazareth with them and was obedient to them. But his mother treasured all these things in her heart. 52And Jesus grew in wisdom and stature, and in favor with God and men.

John the Baptist Prepares the Way

‰ See Matthew 3:1–10; Mark 1:3–5

3 In the fifteenth year of the reign of Tiberius Caesar—when Pontius Pilate was governor of Judea, Herod tetrarch of Galilee, his brother Philip tetrarch of Iturea and Traconitis, and Lysanias tetrarch of Abilene— 2during the high priesthood of Annas and Caiaphas, the word of God came to John son of Zechariah in the desert. 3He went into all the country around the Jordan, preaching a baptism of repentance for the forgiveness of sins. 4As is written in the book of the words of Isaiah the prophet:

"A voice of one calling in the desert,
'Prepare the way for the Lord,
make straight paths for him.
5Every valley shall be filled in,
every mountain and hill made low.
The crooked roads shall become straight,
the rough ways smooth.
6And all mankind will see God's
salvation.' "[c]

7John said to the crowds coming out to be baptized by him, "You brood of vipers! Who warned you to flee from the coming wrath? 8Produce fruit in keeping with repentance. And do not begin to say to yourselves, 'We have Abraham as our father.' For I tell you that out of these stones God can raise up children for Abraham. 9The ax is already at the root of the trees, and every tree that does not produce good fruit will be cut down and thrown into the fire."

10"What should we do then?" the crowd asked.

11John answered, "The man with two tunics should share with him who has none, and the one who has food should do the same."

12Tax collectors also came to be baptized. "Teacher," they asked, "what should we do?"

13"Don't collect any more than you are required to," he told them.

14Then some soldiers asked him, "And what should we do?"

He replied, "Don't extort money and don't

[a]29 Or *promised, / now dismiss* [b]37 Or *widow for eighty-four years* [c]6 Isaiah 40:3-5

2:36–38 Anna's life showed that faith in God can bring meaning to our lives, regardless of our situation. After a relatively short marriage and the loss of a husband, many of us would have become bitter. Not Anna. She used her time and energy to serve God in the temple. She prayed and fasted and was given the gift of prophecy. Anna accepted God's plan for her, which included seeing the Messiah she had eagerly been longing for.

2:52 Jesus did not need redemption because he was the sinless God-man. Yet it is clear that he lived a balanced life from childhood to adulthood. Jesus developed physically, intellectually, spiritually and socially. He displayed both personal and interpersonal growth. No dimension of his life was overemphasized, underdeveloped or rejected. Our own lives need to be balanced in a similar way.

accuse people falsely—be content with your pay."
15The people were waiting expectantly and
were all wondering in their hearts if John might
possibly be the Christ.[a] 16John answered them
all, "I baptize you with[b] water. But one more
powerful than I will come, the thongs of whose
sandals I am not worthy to untie. He will baptize you with the Holy Spirit and with fire. 17His
winnowing fork is in his hand to clear his
threshing floor and to gather the wheat into his
barn, but he will burn up the chaff with unquenchable fire." 18And with many other words
John exhorted the people and preached the
good news to them.
19But when John rebuked Herod the tetrarch
because of Herodias, his brother's wife, and all
the other evil things he had done, 20Herod added this to them all: He locked John up in prison.

The Baptism and Genealogy of Jesus

‰ See Matthew 1:1–17; 3:13–17; Mark 1:9–11

21When all the people were being baptized,
Jesus was baptized too. And as he was praying,
heaven was opened 22and the Holy Spirit descended on him in bodily form like a dove. And
a voice came from heaven: "You are my Son,
whom I love; with you I am well pleased."
23Now Jesus himself was about thirty years
old when he began his ministry. He was the
son, so it was thought, of Joseph,

the son of Heli, 24the son of Matthat,
the son of Levi, the son of Melki,
the son of Jannai, the son of Joseph,
25the son of Mattathias, the son of Amos,
the son of Nahum, the son of Esli,
the son of Naggai, 26the son of Maath,
the son of Mattathias, the son of Semein,
the son of Josech, the son of Joda,
27the son of Joanan, the son of Rhesa,
the son of Zerubbabel, the son of Shealtiel,
the son of Neri, 28the son of Melki,
the son of Addi, the son of Cosam,
the son of Elmadam, the son of Er,
29the son of Joshua, the son of Eliezer,
the son of Jorim, the son of Matthat,
the son of Levi, 30the son of Simeon,
the son of Judah, the son of Joseph,
the son of Jonam, the son of Eliakim,
31the son of Melea, the son of Menna,
the son of Mattatha, the son of Nathan,
the son of David, 32the son of Jesse,
the son of Obed, the son of Boaz,
the son of Salmon,[c] the son of Nahshon,
33the son of Amminadab, the son of
Ram,[d]
the son of Hezron, the son of Perez,
the son of Judah, 34the son of Jacob,
the son of Isaac, the son of Abraham,
the son of Terah, the son of Nahor,
35the son of Serug, the son of Reu,
the son of Peleg, the son of Eber,
the son of Shelah, 36the son of Cainan,
the son of Arphaxad, the son of Shem,
the son of Noah, the son of Lamech,
37the son of Methuselah, the son of Enoch,
the son of Jared, the son of Mahalalel,
the son of Kenan, 38the son of Enosh,
the son of Seth, the son of Adam,
the son of God.

The Temptation of Jesus

‰ See Matthew 4:1–11; Mark 1:12–13

4 Jesus, full of the Holy Spirit, returned from
the Jordan and was led by the Spirit in the
desert, 2where for forty days he was tempted by
the devil. He ate nothing during those days, and
at the end of them he was hungry.
3The devil said to him, "If you are the Son of
God, tell this stone to become bread."
4Jesus answered, "It is written: 'Man does
not live on bread alone.'[e]"
5The devil led him up to a high place and

[a]15 Or *Messiah* [b]16 Or *in* [c]32 Some early manuscripts *Sala* [d]33 Some manuscripts *Amminadab, the son of Admin, the son of Arni*; other manuscripts vary widely. [e]4 Deut. 8:3

3:21–22 By settling upon him in the form of a dove, the Holy Spirit visibly identified with Jesus and indicated that God's power was with him as well. God also loves us. In Jesus, we can experience God's heavenly power upon us, his fatherly love for us and his supreme identification with us.

3:23 Even though Jesus apparently knew from his youth what his mission on earth would be, he patiently persevered as an obscure carpenter in Nazareth until the age of thirty. He was never in a rush to accomplish his ambitious, God-given task. Jesus modeled for us the need for patience and trust in God's timing as we progress spiritually.

3:23–38 Luke's genealogy of Jesus traces his roots to the very beginning of the human race, illustrating Jesus' close identification with all humanity. Jesus' genealogy is sprinkled with people well known for their mistakes. Judah fathered Perez through an illicit relationship with his daughter-in-law Tamar. Salmon fathered Boaz through his marriage with Rahab, a former prostitute from Jericho. David fathered Nathan through Bathsheba, the rightful wife of another man (see 1 Chronicles 3:5; Matthew 1:1–17). From Jesus' genealogy we discover that God in Jesus Christ became fully human, ultimately suffering death for us. And Jesus can truly understand the difficulties we face.

4:1–2 Jesus was sorely tempted for forty days, alone in the Judean wilderness. Yet, as in every aspect of his life, he overcame adversity by depending on the Holy Spirit's power at work in his life. This same Holy Spirit is available for believers today, for he dwells in us (see Ephesians 1:13–14). The Holy Spirit helps us resist the most tempting of sins (see 1 John 2:16; 4:4).

4:3–13 Though Jesus did not succumb to temptation, he fully experienced, in one form or another, every temptation known to humanity. Jesus did not sin, but in his humanity he still faced struggle in his obedience to his Father. In this way, Jesus is truly able to sympathize with our weaknesses (see Hebrews 4:15). When we experience temptation and recognize our human weakness, we can remember that Jesus understands and will help us overcome temptation.

THE SPIRITUAL DISCIPLINES

Solitude

Maintaining a Rhythm of Renewal

Luke 4:1–14 There is a profound link between solitude and spiritual power. As we trace Jesus' life on earth we notice that he seemed to follow an alternating rhythm of involvement and withdrawal from the very outset of his ministry to the time of his death.

Jesus' baptism, typically hailed as the inauguration of his ministry, was followed immediately by a lengthy period of solitude. Luke's account tells us that Jesus, "full of the Holy Spirit, returned from the Jordan and was led by the Spirit in the desert" (4:1). Following his victory over temptation during this time, Jesus returned from the wilderness "in the power of the Spirit" (4:14). The Greek word for power, *dunamis* (from which we get the word *dynamite*), is the same term Paul used for the power of the gospel (see Romans 1:16).

Luke 5:16 says, "Jesus often withdrew to lonely places and prayed." By getting away, Jesus could more easily recognize evil influences, clarify his priorities and motives and reflect on God's Word and its requirements. These times of soul searching brought Jesus strength and spiritual refreshment so that he could then serve God and those people around him. No doubt Jesus' time with others also helped to direct his prayers in his times of solitude.

This principle is still applicable for all believers. Even as the disciples embarked on their ministry after Jesus' resurrection by waiting in the upper room until the coming of the Holy Spirit at Pentecost, so we are called to take special times to withdraw from activity and wait upon the Lord. Then he can fill us with his power and prepare us to serve him.

For more on solitude, turn to Exodus 3.

Putting It Into Practice

Depending on your personality, you may prefer more involvement with others or more solitary time. Regardless of your personal preference, how would you assess your balance of involvement and withdrawal? How can you build times of solitude and reflection into your day? What is the best time and place for you to do this? Plan a regular time so that you may be renewed and energized to serve God.

showed him in an instant all the kingdoms of
the world. 6And he said to him, "I will give you
all their authority and splendor, for it has been
given to me, and I can give it to anyone I want
to. 7So if you worship me, it will all be yours."
8Jesus answered, "It is written: 'Worship the
Lord your God and serve him only.'[a]"
9The devil led him to Jerusalem and had him
stand on the highest point of the temple. "If
you are the Son of God," he said, "throw yourself down from here. 10For it is written:

" 'He will command his angels concerning
you
to guard you carefully;
11they will lift you up in their hands,
so that you will not strike your foot
against a stone.'[b]"

12Jesus answered, "It says: 'Do not put the
Lord your God to the test.'[c]"
13When the devil had finished all this tempting, he left him until an opportune time.

Jesus Rejected at Nazareth

14Jesus returned to Galilee in the power of
the Spirit, and news about him spread through
the whole countryside. 15He taught in their synagogues, and everyone praised him.
16He went to Nazareth, where he had been
brought up, and on the Sabbath day he went
into the synagogue, as was his custom. And he
stood up to read. 17The scroll of the prophet
Isaiah was handed to him. Unrolling it, he
found the place where it is written:

18"The Spirit of the Lord is on me,
because he has anointed me
to preach good news to the poor.
He has sent me to proclaim freedom for
the prisoners
and recovery of sight for the blind,
to release the oppressed,
19 to proclaim the year of the Lord's
favor."[d]

20Then he rolled up the scroll, gave it back to
the attendant and sat down. The eyes of everyone in the synagogue were fastened on him,
21and he began by saying to them, "Today this
scripture is fulfilled in your hearing."
22All spoke well of him and were amazed
at the gracious words that came from his lips.
"Isn't this Joseph's son?" they asked.
23Jesus said to them, "Surely you will quote
this proverb to me: 'Physician, heal yourself!
Do here in your hometown what we have heard
that you did in Capernaum.' "
24"I tell you the truth," he continued, "no
prophet is accepted in his hometown. 25I assure
you that there were many widows in Israel in
Elijah's time, when the sky was shut for three
and a half years and there was a severe famine
throughout the land. 26Yet Elijah was not sent
to any of them, but to a widow in Zarephath in
the region of Sidon. 27And there were many in
Israel with leprosy[e] in the time of Elisha the
prophet, yet not one of them was cleansed—
only Naaman the Syrian."
28All the people in the synagogue were furious when they heard this. 29They got up, drove
him out of the town, and took him to the brow
of the hill on which the town was built, in order
to throw him down the cliff. 30But he walked
right through the crowd and went on his way.

Jesus Drives Out an Evil Spirit

31Then he went down to Capernaum, a town
in Galilee, and on the Sabbath began to teach
the people. 32They were amazed at his teaching,
because his message had authority.
33In the synagogue there was a man possessed by a demon, an evil[f] spirit. He cried out
at the top of his voice, 34"Ha! What do you
want with us, Jesus of Nazareth? Have you
come to destroy us? I know who you are—the
Holy One of God!"
35"Be quiet!" Jesus said sternly. "Come out of
him!" Then the demon threw the man down

[a] *8* Deut. 6:13 [b] *11* Psalm 91:11,12 [c] *12* Deut. 6:16
[d] *19* Isaiah 61:1,2 [e] *27* The Greek word was used for
various diseases affecting the skin—not necessarily leprosy.
[f] *33* Greek *unclean*; also in verse 36

4:13 Temptation from the devil is an ongoing reality. After tempting Jesus in the wilderness, Satan gave up, but only temporarily. He saved his best temptation for the cross. Having exhausted his most compelling temptations, Satan had to admit defeat this time. But throughout Jesus' ministry the devil continued to try to undermine Jesus, especially through the people around him. Similarly, if we withstand temptation at one point, Satan will eventually try again, either in the same area or in another. We need to constantly ask God to help us.

4:18–21 When Jesus said that the words of Isaiah 61 had come true that very day, he was making a direct claim to being Israel's long-awaited Messiah. Isaiah's words beautifully characterized a major focus of the Messiah's ministry. The Messiah would heal people who were brokenhearted and in distress and deliver those who were captives to sin. He would give sight to the physically and spiritually blind and bring triumph to the downcast. What a wonderful promise for all who believe in him.

4:28–30 The response of this hardhearted, hometown crowd in Nazareth to Jesus' remarks is a classic example of what happens when spiritual pride and doubt mix with anger. When Jesus challenged their unbelief, the townspeople's surface appreciation for his ministry gave way to outrage. They wondered how this local boy could claim to be a prophet. Their riot attempt illustrated how resistant to the truth people can be. We need to overcome pride and doubt if we want to receive all God has promised us. God will not heal us until we put our faith in Jesus Christ.

4:33–37 Jesus demonstrated his ability to deliver people from demon possession. Luke and the other gospel writers repeatedly affirmed Jesus' power in this area. In Jesus' day, demonic possession was considered the greatest infirmity one could suffer. Through his absolute control over demons, Jesus overruled all the adversity that could trouble humanity. Even today, no evil or adversity is too great for God's power to overcome.

before them all and came out without injuring him.

36All the people were amazed and said to each other, "What is this teaching? With authority and power he gives orders to evil spirits and they come out!" 37And the news about him spread throughout the surrounding area.

Jesus Heals Many

‰ See Matthew 8:14–17; Mark 1:29–38

38Jesus left the synagogue and went to the home of Simon. Now Simon's mother-in-law was suffering from a high fever, and they asked Jesus to help her. 39So he bent over her and rebuked the fever, and it left her. She got up at once and began to wait on them.

40When the sun was setting, the people brought to Jesus all who had various kinds of sickness, and laying his hands on each one, he healed them. 41Moreover, demons came out of many people, shouting, "You are the Son of God!" But he rebuked them and would not allow them to speak, because they knew he was the Christ.[a]

42At daybreak Jesus went out to a solitary place. The people were looking for him and when they came to where he was, they tried to keep him from leaving them. 43But he said, "I must preach the good news of the kingdom of God to the other towns also, because that is why I was sent." 44And he kept on preaching in the synagogues of Judea.[b]

The Calling of the First Disciples

‰ See Matthew 4:18–22; Mark 1:16–20; John 1:40–42

5 One day as Jesus was standing by the Lake of Gennesaret,[c] with the people crowding around him and listening to the word of God, 2he saw at the water's edge two boats, left there by the fishermen, who were washing their nets. 3He got into one of the boats, the one belonging to Simon, and asked him to put out a little from shore. Then he sat down and taught the people from the boat.

4When he had finished speaking, he said to Simon, "Put out into deep water, and let down[d] the nets for a catch."

5Simon answered, "Master, we've worked hard all night and haven't caught anything. But because you say so, I will let down the nets."

6When they had done so, they caught such a large number of fish that their nets began to break. 7So they signaled their partners in the other boat to come and help them, and they came and filled both boats so full that they began to sink.

8When Simon Peter saw this, he fell at Jesus' knees and said, "Go away from me, Lord; I am a sinful man!" 9For he and all his companions were astonished at the catch of fish they had taken, 10and so were James and John, the sons of Zebedee, Simon's partners.

Then Jesus said to Simon, "Don't be afraid; from now on you will catch men." 11So they pulled their boats up on shore, left everything and followed him.

The Man With Leprosy

‰ See Matthew 8:2–4; Mark 1:40–44

12While Jesus was in one of the towns, a man came along who was covered with leprosy.[e] When he saw Jesus, he fell with his face to the ground and begged him, "Lord, if you are willing, you can make me clean."

13Jesus reached out his hand and touched the man. "I am willing," he said. "Be clean!" And immediately the leprosy left him.

14Then Jesus ordered him, "Don't tell anyone, but go, show yourself to the priest and offer the sacrifices that Moses commanded for your cleansing, as a testimony to them."

15Yet the news about him spread all the more, so that crowds of people came to hear him and to be healed of their sicknesses. 16But Jesus often withdrew to lonely places and prayed.

Jesus Heals a Paralytic

‰ See Matthew 9:2–8; Mark 2:3–12

17One day as he was teaching, Pharisees and teachers of the law, who had come from every village of Galilee and from Judea and Jerusalem, were sitting there. And the power of the Lord was present for him to heal the sick. 18Some men came carrying a paralytic on a mat and tried to take him into the house to lay him before Jesus. 19When they could not find a way to do this because of the crowd, they went up on the roof and lowered him on his mat through the tiles into the middle of the crowd, right in front of Jesus.

20When Jesus saw their faith, he said, "Friend, your sins are forgiven."

21The Pharisees and the teachers of the law began thinking to themselves, "Who is this fellow who speaks blasphemy? Who can forgive sins but God alone?"

22Jesus knew what they were thinking and

[a] 41 Or *Messiah* [b] 44 Or *the land of the Jews*; some manuscripts *Galilee* [c] 1 That is, Sea of Galilee [d] 4 The Greek verb is plural. [e] 12 The Greek word was used for various diseases affecting the skin—not necessarily leprosy.

5:4–10 The disciples were certainly persistent in their fishing, but not very successful. Doing things their way just wasn't enough. As soon as they followed Jesus' unusual advice, the disciples experienced abundant success. We may be diligent, hardworking and disciplined, struggling along on our own. However, if we don't do things God's way, no amount of hard work will bring the desired results. We may think the truth found in God's Word seems crazy. But as we obediently follow God's plan, with his gracious help we will experience the abundant life he promises.

asked, "Why are you thinking these things in your hearts? 23Which is easier: to say, 'Your sins are forgiven,' or to say, 'Get up and walk'? 24But that you may know that the Son of Man has authority on earth to forgive sins . . . ." He said to the paralyzed man, "I tell you, get up, take your mat and go home." 25Immediately he stood up in front of them, took what he had been lying on and went home praising God. 26Everyone was amazed and gave praise to God. They were filled with awe and said, "We have seen remarkable things today."

The Calling of Levi

‰ See Matthew 9:9–13; Mark 2:14–17

27After this, Jesus went out and saw a tax collector by the name of Levi sitting at his tax booth. "Follow me," Jesus said to him, 28and Levi got up, left everything and followed him.

29Then Levi held a great banquet for Jesus at his house, and a large crowd of tax collectors and others were eating with them. 30But the Pharisees and the teachers of the law who belonged to their sect complained to his disciples, "Why do you eat and drink with tax collectors and 'sinners'?"

31Jesus answered them, "It is not the healthy who need a doctor, but the sick. 32I have not come to call the righteous, but sinners to repentance."

Jesus Questioned About Fasting

‰ See Matthew 9:14–17; Mark 2:18–22

33They said to him, "John's disciples often fast and pray, and so do the disciples of the Pharisees, but yours go on eating and drinking."

34Jesus answered, "Can you make the guests of the bridegroom fast while he is with them? 35But the time will come when the bridegroom will be taken from them; in those days they will fast."

36He told them this parable: "No one tears a patch from a new garment and sews it on an old one. If he does, he will have torn the new garment, and the patch from the new will not match the old. 37And no one pours new wine into old wineskins. If he does, the new wine will burst the skins, the wine will run out and the wineskins will be ruined. 38No, new wine must be poured into new wineskins. 39And no one after drinking old wine wants the new, for he says, 'The old is better.' "

Lord of the Sabbath

‰ See Matthew 12:1–14; Mark 2:23—3:6

6 One Sabbath Jesus was going through the grainfields, and his disciples began to pick some heads of grain, rub them in their hands and eat the kernels. 2Some of the Pharisees asked, "Why are you doing what is unlawful on the Sabbath?"

3Jesus answered them, "Have you never read what David did when he and his companions were hungry? 4He entered the house of God, and taking the consecrated bread, he ate what is lawful only for priests to eat. And he also gave some to his companions." 5Then Jesus said to them, "The Son of Man is Lord of the Sabbath."

6On another Sabbath he went into the synagogue and was teaching, and a man was there whose right hand was shriveled. 7The Pharisees and the teachers of the law were looking for a reason to accuse Jesus, so they watched him closely to see if he would heal on the Sabbath. 8But Jesus knew what they were thinking and said to the man with the shriveled hand, "Get up and stand in front of everyone." So he got up and stood there.

9Then Jesus said to them, "I ask you, which is lawful on the Sabbath: to do good or to do evil, to save life or to destroy it?"

10He looked around at them all, and then said to the man, "Stretch out your hand." He did so, and his hand was completely restored. 11But they were furious and began to discuss with one another what they might do to Jesus.

The Twelve Apostles

‰ See Matthew 10:2–4; Mark 3:16–19; Acts 1:13

12One of those days Jesus went out to a mountainside to pray, and spent the night praying to God. 13When morning came, he called his disciples to him and chose twelve of them, whom he also designated apostles: 14Simon (whom he named Peter), his brother Andrew, James, John, Philip, Bartholomew, 15Matthew, Thomas, James son of Alphaeus, Simon who was called the Zealot, 16Judas son of James, and Judas Iscariot, who became a traitor.

5:30–32 In order to receive Jesus' help, we must first repent from our sin and admit how helpless we are on our own. Jesus' greatest ministry priority was to the so-called notorious sinners (social outcasts) because they admitted their lowly, helpless position. The Pharisees were also sinners, but they refused to admit their sin. Because of their self-righteousness, pride and self-sufficiency, Jesus could do nothing for them. When we recognize our need and admit our sin to God, he will reach out and help us.

6:6–11 Jesus healed people on the Sabbath, and this angered his religious opponents. The religious leaders viewed healing as a violation of God's command that they rest on the Sabbath. While we are to maintain balance in our lives and take a day to rest each week, God never rests from his healing work in our lives. God wants to heal us every day. As we continually seek God, we must always be open to the healing touch he wants to give us.

6:12–16 Jesus spent an entire night in prayer before choosing his twelve disciples. Despite his prayerful preparation, however, one among them, Judas Iscariot, would betray him. But Jesus did not make a mistake; Judas was chosen purposely and prayerfully. In the same way, when we carefully follow what we know to be God's will and pray earnestly about our decisions, we can be certain that God will use our decisions for his ultimate good, though it may sometimes seem as if things are turning out all wrong.

Matthew & Simon the Zealot

If you have ever played with magnets, you may have learned that the opposite poles of two magnets are attracted to each other, while the similarly charged poles will repel one another. However, personal attraction differs greatly from magnetic attraction. In personal relationships, the differences between two personalities can result in a complementary relationship in which the strengths of one make up for the weaknesses of the other. In some cases, however, the differences can lead to continual strife. Relationships composed of two opposites can result either in great teamwork or terrible conflict.

Two of Jesus' twelve disciples, Matthew and Simon the Zealot, were opposites. Matthew was a Jew who worked for the Roman government as a tax collector. Tax collectors were usually corrupt. They grew rich by extorting excess taxes from their own people. Tax collectors typically were hated and despised as traitors by their countrymen.

Simon was probably a religious fanatic. The term *Zealot* was sometimes used to label people with intense zeal for the Law of Moses and Jewish religious tradition. This term was also used to identify someone who belonged to the religious and political party known as the Zealots. The Zealots wanted to overthrow the Roman government. If Simon were a member, he would have been strongly opposed to the Roman occupation of Judea, while Matthew had signed on as an integral part of its government. These men were clearly opposites.

But both Matthew and Simon met Jesus and were transformed. Both gave up their lifestyles in order to follow Christ in faith and experience new life in him. Both were transformed by God into people who could love and accept those who were very different from themselves.

STRENGTHS AND ACCOMPLISHMENTS:

Both Matthew and Simon apparently were capable men.

Both men were willing to recognize that they needed to change.

Both men made Jesus the center of their lives, enabling them to work with people who differed from themselves.

WEAKNESSES AND MISTAKES:

Both had been driven by shortsighted motivations before following Jesus.

As a tax collector, Matthew had probably used his position to extort money from the poor.

As a Zealot, Simon had probably condoned the use of violence to achieve his political ends.

LESSONS FROM THEIR LIVES:

Financial success cannot replace our need for a relationship with God.

If Christ is at the center of a relationship, no differences are too great to overcome.

Differences can strengthen a relationship and should not be used as an excuse to destroy it.

KEY VERSE:

"When [the disciples] arrived, they went upstairs to the room where they were staying. Those present were . . . Matthew . . . and Simon the Zealot" (Acts 1:13).

The story of the apostles Matthew and Simon the Zealot is found in the Gospels. Both men are also mentioned in Acts 1:13.

Blessings and Woes

‰ See Matthew 5:3–12

17He went down with them and stood on a
level place. A large crowd of his disciples was
there and a great number of people from all
over Judea, from Jerusalem, and from the coast
of Tyre and Sidon, 18who had come to hear him
and to be healed of their diseases. Those troubled by evil[a] spirits were cured, 19and the people all tried to touch him, because power was
coming from him and healing them all.
20Looking at his disciples, he said:

"Blessed are you who are poor,
for yours is the kingdom of God.
21Blessed are you who hunger now,
for you will be satisfied.
Blessed are you who weep now,
for you will laugh.
22Blessed are you when men hate you,
when they exclude you and insult you
and reject your name as evil,
because of the Son of Man.

23"Rejoice in that day and leap for joy, because great is your reward in heaven. For that is
how their fathers treated the prophets.

24"But woe to you who are rich,
for you have already received your
comfort.
25Woe to you who are well fed now,
for you will go hungry.
Woe to you who laugh now,
for you will mourn and weep.
26Woe to you when all men speak well of
you,
for that is how their fathers treated the
false prophets.

Love for Enemies

27"But I tell you who hear me: Love your
enemies, do good to those who hate you,
28bless those who curse you, pray for those who
mistreat you. 29If someone strikes you on one
cheek, turn to him the other also. If someone
takes your cloak, do not stop him from taking
your tunic. 30Give to everyone who asks you,
and if anyone takes what belongs to you, do not
demand it back. 31Do to others as you would
have them do to you.
32"If you love those who love you, what
credit is that to you? Even 'sinners' love those
who love them. 33And if you do good to those
who are good to you, what credit is that to you?
Even 'sinners' do that. 34And if you lend to
those from whom you expect repayment, what
credit is that to you? Even 'sinners' lend to 'sinners,' expecting to be repaid in full. 35But love
your enemies, do good to them, and lend to
them without expecting to get anything back.
Then your reward will be great, and you will be
sons of the Most High, because he is kind to the
ungrateful and wicked. 36Be merciful, just as
your Father is merciful.

Judging Others

‰ See Matthew 7:1–5

37"Do not judge, and you will not be judged.
Do not condemn, and you will not be condemned. Forgive, and you will be forgiven.
38Give, and it will be given to you. A good measure, pressed down, shaken together and running over, will be poured into your lap. For with
the measure you use, it will be measured to you."
39He also told them this parable: "Can a
blind man lead a blind man? Will they not both
fall into a pit? 40A student is not above his
teacher, but everyone who is fully trained will
be like his teacher.
41"Why do you look at the speck of sawdust
in your brother's eye and pay no attention to
the plank in your own eye? 42How can you say
to your brother, 'Brother, let me take the speck
out of your eye,' when you yourself fail to see
the plank in your own eye? You hypocrite, first
take the plank out of your eye, and then you
will see clearly to remove the speck from your
brother's eye.

A Tree and Its Fruit

‰ See Matthew 7:16,18,20

43"No good tree bears bad fruit, nor does a
bad tree bear good fruit. 44Each tree is recognized by its own fruit. People do not pick figs
from thornbushes, or grapes from briers. 45The
good man brings good things out of the good
stored up in his heart, and the evil man brings
evil things out of the evil stored up in his heart.
For out of the overflow of his heart his mouth
speaks.

The Wise and Foolish Builders

‰ See Matthew 7:24–27

46"Why do you call me, 'Lord, Lord,' and do
not do what I say? 47I will show you what he is
like who comes to me and hears my words and
puts them into practice. 48He is like a man
building a house, who dug down deep and laid
the foundation on rock. When a flood came,
the torrent struck that house but could not
shake it, because it was well built. 49But the one
who hears my words and does not put them
into practice is like a man who built a house on

[a]18 Greek *unclean*

6:20–26 When Jesus spoke about kingdom values, he left no question about the importance of priorities in life. He pronounced sorrows to shake people out of their selfishness and disobedience to God. He pronounced blessings to awaken joy and gratitude in those who depended on God. Through his strong words, Jesus helped people see their true spiritual condition. How we live our lives on earth will determine our eternal wealth or lack. We must make sure that we do not seek the satisfaction of earthly riches to the neglect of our heavenly rewards.

the ground without a foundation. The moment
the torrent struck that house, it collapsed and its
destruction was complete."

The Faith of the Centurion

‰ See Matthew 8:5–13

7 When Jesus had finished saying all this in
the hearing of the people, he entered Capernaum. 2There a centurion's servant, whom
his master valued highly, was sick and about
to die. 3The centurion heard of Jesus and sent
some elders of the Jews to him, asking him to
come and heal his servant. 4When they came to
Jesus, they pleaded earnestly with him, "This
man deserves to have you do this, 5because he
loves our nation and has built our synagogue."
6So Jesus went with them.
He was not far from the house when the
centurion sent friends to say to him: "Lord,
don't trouble yourself, for I do not deserve to
have you come under my roof. 7That is why I
did not even consider myself worthy to come to
you. But say the word, and my servant will be
healed. 8For I myself am a man under authority,
with soldiers under me. I tell this one, 'Go,' and
he goes; and that one, 'Come,' and he comes. I
say to my servant, 'Do this,' and he does it."
9When Jesus heard this, he was amazed at
him, and turning to the crowd following him,
he said, "I tell you, I have not found such great
faith even in Israel." 10Then the men who had
been sent returned to the house and found the
servant well.

Jesus Raises a Widow's Son

11Soon afterward, Jesus went to a town called
Nain, and his disciples and a large crowd went
along with him. 12As he approached the town
gate, a dead person was being carried out—the
only son of his mother, and she was a widow.
And a large crowd from the town was with her.
13When the Lord saw her, his heart went out to
her and he said, "Don't cry."
14Then he went up and touched the coffin,
and those carrying it stood still. He said,
"Young man, I say to you, get up!" 15The dead
man sat up and began to talk, and Jesus gave
him back to his mother.
16They were all filled with awe and praised
God. "A great prophet has appeared among us,"
they said. "God has come to help his people."
17This news about Jesus spread throughout Judea[a] and the surrounding country.

Jesus and John the Baptist

‰ See Matthew 11:2–19

18John's disciples told him about all these
things. Calling two of them, 19he sent them to
the Lord to ask, "Are you the one who was to
come, or should we expect someone else?"
20When the men came to Jesus, they said,
"John the Baptist sent us to you to ask, 'Are you
the one who was to come, or should we expect
someone else?' "
21At that very time Jesus cured many who
had diseases, sicknesses and evil spirits, and
gave sight to many who were blind. 22So he
replied to the messengers, "Go back and report
to John what you have seen and heard: The
blind receive sight, the lame walk, those who
have leprosy[b] are cured, the deaf hear, the
dead are raised, and the good news is preached
to the poor. 23Blessed is the man who does not
fall away on account of me."
24After John's messengers left, Jesus began to
speak to the crowd about John: "What did you
go out into the desert to see? A reed swayed by
the wind? 25If not, what did you go out to see?
A man dressed in fine clothes? No, those who
wear expensive clothes and indulge in luxury
are in palaces. 26But what did you go out to see?
A prophet? Yes, I tell you, and more than a
prophet. 27This is the one about whom it is
written:

[a]17 Or *the land of the Jews* [b]22 The Greek word was used for various diseases affecting the skin—not necessarily leprosy.

7:1–10 The centurion possessed certain qualities that are key elements for anyone wishing to receive God's greatest blessings in life. The centurion was compassionate to people of a lower social class or another race and religion. He was humble and recognized his own unworthiness despite being a man of authority. Nonetheless, the centurion wholeheartedly placed his faith in Jesus. Jesus himself marveled at such faith and answered the centurion's request. Sometimes true faith is best found in places we least expect it: among the irreligious and the outcasts, those who recognize their need for help and cry out to God in their helplessness. It is this kind of faith that is necessary for true spiritual growth.

7:11–15 When he raised the young boy from the dead, Jesus showed his compassion for people experiencing great loss. This woman had previously lost her husband. Now her only son was dead. This miracle illustrates that no situation in our lives is beyond God's restoring power. The God who can raise the dead can certainly bring health and restoration to our lives.

7:18–19 This account of John the Baptist shows that even the strongest believers may go through times of discouragement and doubt. John had been imprisoned and was facing death (see Matthew 11:2–3; Mark 6:17). Though John may have had his doubts about Jesus, Jesus had deep respect for John (see 7:28). John's questions were asked honestly, in a time of acute suffering, so Jesus affirmed him and answered him accordingly. God invites us to do as John did and bring our questions to Jesus. He will direct us to the truth that can inspire our faith and confidence.

7:24–28 Because of his strength of character, John the Baptist did not allow himself to be squeezed into anyone else's mold. Rather, John knew the boundaries of his role and committed himself to fulfilling his God-given role as a prophet and forerunner of the Messiah. John is a good example for us in this regard. God has a purpose for each one of us. As we learn what our role in his plan is, following his plan for us will bring us contentment. As we follow his will, God will always be with us, guiding and strengthening us along the way. Trying to become someone we were never intended to be will only slow our spiritual growth.

" 'I will send my messenger ahead of you,
who will prepare your way before you.'[a]

28I tell you, among those born of women there is no one greater than John; yet the one who is least in the kingdom of God is greater than he."

29(All the people, even the tax collectors, when they heard Jesus' words, acknowledged that God's way was right, because they had been baptized by John. 30But the Pharisees and experts in the law rejected God's purpose for themselves, because they had not been baptized by John.)

31"To what, then, can I compare the people of this generation? What are they like? 32They are like children sitting in the marketplace and calling out to each other:

" 'We played the flute for you,
and you did not dance;
we sang a dirge,
and you did not cry.'

33For John the Baptist came neither eating bread nor drinking wine, and you say, 'He has a demon.' 34The Son of Man came eating and drinking, and you say, 'Here is a glutton and a drunkard, a friend of tax collectors and "sinners." ' 35But wisdom is proved right by all her children."

Jesus Anointed by a Sinful Woman

36Now one of the Pharisees invited Jesus to have dinner with him, so he went to the Pharisee's house and reclined at the table. 37When a woman who had lived a sinful life in that town learned that Jesus was eating at the Pharisee's house, she brought an alabaster jar of perfume, 38and as she stood behind him at his feet weeping, she began to wet his feet with her tears. Then she wiped them with her hair, kissed them and poured perfume on them.

39When the Pharisee who had invited him saw this, he said to himself, "If this man were a prophet, he would know who is touching him and what kind of woman she is—that she is a sinner."

40Jesus answered him, "Simon, I have something to tell you."

"Tell me, teacher," he said.

41"Two men owed money to a certain moneylender. One owed him five hundred denarii,[b] and the other fifty. 42Neither of them had the money to pay him back, so he canceled the debts of both. Now which of them will love him more?"

43Simon replied, "I suppose the one who had the bigger debt canceled."

"You have judged correctly," Jesus said.

44Then he turned toward the woman and said to Simon, "Do you see this woman? I came into your house. You did not give me any water for my feet, but she wet my feet with her tears and wiped them with her hair. 45You did not give me a kiss, but this woman, from the time I entered, has not stopped kissing my feet. 46You did not put oil on my head, but she has poured perfume on my feet. 47Therefore, I tell you, her many sins have been forgiven—for she loved much. But he who has been forgiven little loves little."

48Then Jesus said to her, "Your sins are forgiven."

49The other guests began to say among themselves, "Who is this who even forgives sins?"

50Jesus said to the woman, "Your faith has saved you; go in peace."

The Parable of the Sower

‰ See Matthew 13:2–23; Mark 4:1–20

8 After this, Jesus traveled about from one town and village to another, proclaiming the good news of the kingdom of God. The Twelve were with him, 2and also some women who had been cured of evil spirits and diseases: Mary (called Magdalene) from whom seven demons had come out; 3Joanna the wife of Cuza, the manager of Herod's household; Susanna; and many others. These women were helping to support them out of their own means.

4While a large crowd was gathering and people were coming to Jesus from town after town, he told this parable: 5"A farmer went out to sow his seed. As he was scattering the seed, some fell along the path; it was trampled on, and the birds of the air ate it up. 6Some fell on rock, and when it came up, the plants withered because they had no moisture. 7Other seed fell among thorns, which grew up with it and choked the plants. 8Still other seed fell on good soil. It came up and yielded a crop, a hundred times more than was sown."

When he said this, he called out, "He who has ears to hear, let him hear."

9His disciples asked him what this parable meant. 10He said, "The knowledge of the secrets of the kingdom of God has been given to you, but to others I speak in parables, so that,

" 'though seeing, they may not see;
though hearing, they may not
understand.'[c]

11"This is the meaning of the parable: The seed is the word of God. 12Those along the path are the ones who hear, and then the devil comes and takes away the word from their hearts, so that they may not believe and be saved. 13Those on the rock are the ones who receive the word with joy when they hear it, but they have no root. They believe for a while, but in the time of testing they fall away. 14The seed that fell among thorns stands for those who hear, but as they go on their way they are choked by life's worries, riches and pleasures, and they do not mature. 15But the seed on good soil stands for those with a noble and good heart, who hear

[a]27 Mal. 3:1 [b]41 A denarius was a coin worth about a day's wages. [c]10 Isaiah 6:9

the word, retain it, and by persevering produce a crop.

A Lamp on a Stand

16"No one lights a lamp and hides it in a jar or puts it under a bed. Instead, he puts it on a stand, so that those who come in can see the light. 17For there is nothing hidden that will not be disclosed, and nothing concealed that will not be known or brought out into the open. 18Therefore consider carefully how you listen. Whoever has will be given more; whoever does not have, even what he thinks he has will be taken from him."

Jesus' Mother and Brothers

‰ See Matthew 12:46–50; Mark 3:31–35

19Now Jesus' mother and brothers came to see him, but they were not able to get near him because of the crowd. 20Someone told him, "Your mother and brothers are standing outside, wanting to see you."

21He replied, "My mother and brothers are those who hear God's word and put it into practice."

Jesus Calms the Storm

‰ See Matthew 8:23–27; Mark 4:36–41

22One day Jesus said to his disciples, "Let's go over to the other side of the lake." So they got into a boat and set out. 23As they sailed, he fell asleep. A squall came down on the lake, so that the boat was being swamped, and they were in great danger.

24The disciples went and woke him, saying, "Master, Master, we're going to drown!"

He got up and rebuked the wind and the raging waters; the storm subsided, and all was calm. 25"Where is your faith?" he asked his disciples.

In fear and amazement they asked one another, "Who is this? He commands even the winds and the water, and they obey him."

The Healing of a Demon-possessed Man

‰ See Matthew 8:28–34; Mark 5:1–20

26They sailed to the region of the Gerasenes,[a] which is across the lake from Galilee. 27When Jesus stepped ashore, he was met by a demon-possessed man from the town. For a long time this man had not worn clothes or lived in a house, but had lived in the tombs. 28When he saw Jesus, he cried out and fell at his feet, shouting at the top of his voice, "What do you want with me, Jesus, Son of the Most High God? I beg you, don't torture me!" 29For Jesus had commanded the evil[b] spirit to come out of the man. Many times it had seized him, and though he was chained hand and foot and kept under guard, he had broken his chains and had been driven by the demon into solitary places.

30Jesus asked him, "What is your name?"

"Legion," he replied, because many demons had gone into him. 31And they begged him repeatedly not to order them to go into the Abyss.

32A large herd of pigs was feeding there on the hillside. The demons begged Jesus to let them go into them, and he gave them permission. 33When the demons came out of the man, they went into the pigs, and the herd rushed down the steep bank into the lake and was drowned.

34When those tending the pigs saw what had happened, they ran off and reported this in the town and countryside, 35and the people went out to see what had happened. When they came to Jesus, they found the man from whom the demons had gone out, sitting at Jesus' feet, dressed and in his right mind; and they were afraid. 36Those who had seen it told the people how the demon-possessed man had been cured. 37Then all the people of the region of the Gerasenes asked Jesus to leave them, because they were overcome with fear. So he got into the boat and left.

38The man from whom the demons had gone out begged to go with him, but Jesus sent him away, saying, 39"Return home and tell how much God has done for you." So the man went away and told all over town how much Jesus had done for him.

A Dead Girl and a Sick Woman

‰ See Matthew 9:18–26; Mark 5:22–43

40Now when Jesus returned, a crowd welcomed him, for they were all expecting him. 41Then a man named Jairus, a ruler of the synagogue, came and fell at Jesus' feet, pleading with him to come to his house 42because his only daughter, a girl of about twelve, was dying.

As Jesus was on his way, the crowds almost crushed him. 43And a woman was there who

[a] 26 Some manuscripts *Gadarenes;* other manuscripts *Gergesenes;* also in verse 37 [b] 29 Greek *unclean*

8:16–17 Lamps expose everything nearby to the light; so God will someday bring our thoughts out into the open. Our thoughts and habits are already known to God (see Psalm 139:1–4). As we are open, honest and transparent in confessing our sin, God will work to transform our thought life and behavior. Then when our lives are exposed to all, we will bring glory to God instead of shame.

8:26–37 The life of this demon-possessed man was a complete disaster. Desperately in need of healing from demonic influence, he was a physical and emotional wreck, an embarrassing social outcast. As hopeless as his case was, Jesus powerfully broke Satan's bonds and freed him. No matter what obstacles we face, Jesus desires our complete freedom from the influence of the evil one. He will help us progress toward that goal if we repent and ask for his help.

8:43–44 Luke, with his background in medicine, noted that medical doctors had been able to do nothing for this woman's chronic illness. By faith, God's power performed the impossible. As with many of Jesus' miracles, this incident reveals that one who trusts God can find hope where previously there had been despair. Even problems beyond the scope of medical advances are well within the normal range of miracles that God can perform for people who

had been subject to bleeding for twelve years,[a] but no one could heal her. 44She came up behind him and touched the edge of his cloak, and immediately her bleeding stopped.

45"Who touched me?" Jesus asked.

When they all denied it, Peter said, "Master, the people are crowding and pressing against you."

46But Jesus said, "Someone touched me; I know that power has gone out from me."

47Then the woman, seeing that she could not go unnoticed, came trembling and fell at his feet. In the presence of all the people, she told why she had touched him and how she had been instantly healed. 48Then he said to her, "Daughter, your faith has healed you. Go in peace."

49While Jesus was still speaking, someone came from the house of Jairus, the synagogue ruler. "Your daughter is dead," he said. "Don't bother the teacher any more."

50Hearing this, Jesus said to Jairus, "Don't be afraid; just believe, and she will be healed."

51When he arrived at the house of Jairus, he did not let anyone go in with him except Peter, John and James, and the child's father and mother. 52Meanwhile, all the people were wailing and mourning for her. "Stop wailing," Jesus said. "She is not dead but asleep."

53They laughed at him, knowing that she was dead. 54But he took her by the hand and said, "My child, get up!" 55Her spirit returned, and at once she stood up. Then Jesus told them to give her something to eat. 56Her parents were astonished, but he ordered them not to tell anyone what had happened.

Jesus Sends Out the Twelve

‰ See Matthew 10:9–15; Mark 6:8–11

9 When Jesus had called the Twelve together, he gave them power and authority to drive out all demons and to cure diseases, 2and he sent them out to preach the kingdom of God and to heal the sick. 3He told them: "Take nothing for the journey—no staff, no bag, no bread, no money, no extra tunic. 4Whatever house you enter, stay there until you leave that town. 5If people do not welcome you, shake the dust off your feet when you leave their town, as a testimony against them." 6So they set out and went from village to village, preaching the gospel and healing people everywhere.

7Now Herod the tetrarch heard about all that was going on. And he was perplexed, because some were saying that John had been raised from the dead, 8others that Elijah had appeared, and still others that one of the prophets of long ago had come back to life. 9But Herod said, "I beheaded John. Who, then, is this I hear such things about?" And he tried to see him.

Jesus Feeds the Five Thousand

‰ See Matthew 14:13–21; Mark 6:32–44; John 6:5–13

10When the apostles returned, they reported to Jesus what they had done. Then he took them with him and they withdrew by themselves to a town called Bethsaida, 11but the crowds learned about it and followed him. He welcomed them and spoke to them about the kingdom of God, and healed those who needed healing.

12Late in the afternoon the Twelve came to him and said, "Send the crowd away so they can go to the surrounding villages and countryside and find food and lodging, because we are in a remote place here."

13He replied, "You give them something to eat."

They answered, "We have only five loaves of bread and two fish—unless we go and buy food for all this crowd." 14(About five thousand men were there.)

But he said to his disciples, "Have them sit down in groups of about fifty each." 15The disciples did so, and everybody sat down. 16Taking the five loaves and the two fish and looking up to heaven, he gave thanks and broke them. Then he gave them to the disciples to set before the people. 17They all ate and were satisfied, and the disciples picked up twelve basketfuls of broken pieces that were left over.

Peter's Confession of Christ

‰ See Matthew 16:13–16; Mark 8:27–29

18Once when Jesus was praying in private and his disciples were with him, he asked them, "Who do the crowds say I am?"

19They replied, "Some say John the Baptist; others say Elijah; and still others, that one of the prophets of long ago has come back to life."

20"But what about you?" he asked. "Who do you say I am?"

Peter answered, "The Christ[b] of God."

21Jesus strictly warned them not to tell this to anyone. 22And he said, "The Son of Man must suffer many things and be rejected by the elders, chief priests and teachers of the law, and he must be killed and on the third day be raised to life."

23Then he said to them all: "If anyone would

[a]43 Many manuscripts *years, and she had spent all she had on doctors* [b]20 Or *Messiah*

---

look to him in faith.

9:10–17 This episode demonstrates, once again, Jesus' desire to meet our daily needs. In feeding the five thousand Jesus supplied a most basic need—food. Before this incident, Jesus had dealt primarily with problems of physical healing. Notice also that Jesus met the intellectual and emotional needs of his disciples. God will ultimately meet our spiritual need for a right relationship with him. The restoration that Jesus the Messiah offers will touch every area of our lives.

9:23–27 In this classic confrontation of wills, Jesus illustrated the critical importance of submitting our wills to God's will. Jesus' claim on the lives of his followers supersedes all personal conveniences or desires. Clinging to the conveniences of our world and the desires of the flesh will ultimately destroy our lives. Yet giving up control of our

come after me, he must deny himself and take
up his cross daily and follow me. 24For whoever
wants to save his life will lose it, but whoever
loses his life for me will save it. 25What good is
it for a man to gain the whole world, and yet
lose or forfeit his very self? 26If anyone is
ashamed of me and my words, the Son of Man
will be ashamed of him when he comes in his
glory and in the glory of the Father and of the
holy angels. 27I tell you the truth, some who are
standing here will not taste death before they
see the kingdom of God."

The Transfiguration

‰ See Matthew 17:1–8; Mark 9:2–8

28About eight days after Jesus said this, he
took Peter, John and James with him and went
up onto a mountain to pray. 29As he was praying, the appearance of his face changed, and his
clothes became as bright as a flash of lightning.
30Two men, Moses and Elijah, 31appeared in
glorious splendor, talking with Jesus. They
spoke about his departure, which he was about
to bring to fulfillment at Jerusalem. 32Peter and
his companions were very sleepy, but when
they became fully awake, they saw his glory and
the two men standing with him. 33As the men
were leaving Jesus, Peter said to him, "Master,
it is good for us to be here. Let us put up three
shelters—one for you, one for Moses and one for
Elijah." (He did not know what he was saying.)
34While he was speaking, a cloud appeared
and enveloped them, and they were afraid as
they entered the cloud. 35A voice came from the
cloud, saying, "This is my Son, whom I have
chosen; listen to him." 36When the voice had
spoken, they found that Jesus was alone. The
disciples kept this to themselves, and told no
one at that time what they had seen.

The Healing of a Boy With an Evil Spirit

‰ See Matthew 17:14–18,22–23; Mark 9:14–27,30–32

37The next day, when they came down from
the mountain, a large crowd met him. 38A man
in the crowd called out, "Teacher, I beg you to
look at my son, for he is my only child. 39A
spirit seizes him and he suddenly screams; it
throws him into convulsions so that he foams
at the mouth. It scarcely ever leaves him and
is destroying him. 40I begged your disciples to
drive it out, but they could not."
41"O unbelieving and perverse generation,"
Jesus replied, "how long shall I stay with you
and put up with you? Bring your son here."
42Even while the boy was coming, the demon
threw him to the ground in a convulsion. But
Jesus rebuked the evil[a] spirit, healed the boy
and gave him back to his father. 43And they
were all amazed at the greatness of God.

While everyone was marveling at all that
Jesus did, he said to his disciples, 44"Listen carefully to what I am about to tell you: The Son of
Man is going to be betrayed into the hands of
men." 45But they did not understand what this
meant. It was hidden from them, so that they
did not grasp it, and they were afraid to ask him
about it.

Who Will Be the Greatest?

‰ See Matthew 18:1–5; Mark 9:33–40

46An argument started among the disciples as
to which of them would be the greatest. 47Jesus,
knowing their thoughts, took a little child and
had him stand beside him. 48Then he said to
them, "Whoever welcomes this little child in
my name welcomes me; and whoever welcomes
me welcomes the one who sent me. For he who
is least among you all—he is the greatest."
49"Master," said John, "we saw a man driving
out demons in your name and we tried to stop
him, because he is not one of us."
50"Do not stop him," Jesus said, "for whoever
is not against you is for you."

Samaritan Opposition

51As the time approached for him to be taken
up to heaven, Jesus resolutely set out for Jerusalem. 52And he sent messengers on ahead, who
went into a Samaritan village to get things ready
for him; 53but the people there did not welcome
him, because he was heading for Jerusalem.
54When the disciples James and John saw this,
they asked, "Lord, do you want us to call fire
down from heaven to destroy them[b]?" 55But
Jesus turned and rebuked them, 56and[c] they
went to another village.

The Cost of Following Jesus

‰ See Matthew 8:19–22

57As they were walking along the road, a man
said to him, "I will follow you wherever
you go."
58Jesus replied, "Foxes have holes and birds
of the air have nests, but the Son of Man has no
place to lay his head."
59He said to another man, "Follow me."

[a]42 Greek *unclean* [b]54 Some manuscripts *them, even as Elijah did* [c]55,56 Some manuscripts *them. And he said, "You do not know what kind of spirit you are of, for the Son of Man did not come to destroy men's lives, but to save them."* 56*And*

---

lives for a relationship with God through Jesus is the only sure way of finding ultimate meaning and purpose. This teaching goes against our natural inclinations and can only be accepted by faith. But if we willingly submit our wills to God's will, we will begin to experience the meaningful life that God wants us to have.

9:28–36 While initial impressions do mean a lot, appearances can be deceiving. At the transfiguration, Peter relied so much on first impressions and outward appearances that he jumped to some foolish conclusions. Two of the great Old Testament prophets appeared to be on a par with Jesus. Yet God's voice and later events confirmed that Jesus, unlike Moses and Elijah, was God himself, not merely a great prophet or leader. To progress spiritually, we need to suspend our human judgment and listen to God.

But the man replied, "Lord, first let me go
and bury my father."
60Jesus said to him, "Let the dead bury their
own dead, but you go and proclaim the kingdom of God."
61Still another said, "I will follow you, Lord;
but first let me go back and say good-by to my
family."
62Jesus replied, "No one who puts his hand
to the plow and looks back is fit for service in
the kingdom of God."

Jesus Sends Out the Seventy-two

‰ See Luke 9:3–5

10 After this the Lord appointed seventy-
two[a] others and sent them two by two
ahead of him to every town and place where he
was about to go. 2He told them, "The harvest is
plentiful, but the workers are few. Ask the Lord
of the harvest, therefore, to send out workers
into his harvest field. 3Go! I am sending you out
like lambs among wolves. 4Do not take a purse
or bag or sandals; and do not greet anyone on
the road.
5"When you enter a house, first say, 'Peace
to this house.' 6If a man of peace is there, your
peace will rest on him; if not, it will return to
you. 7Stay in that house, eating and drinking
whatever they give you, for the worker deserves
his wages. Do not move around from house to
house.
8"When you enter a town and are welcomed,
eat what is set before you. 9Heal the sick who
are there and tell them, 'The kingdom of God
is near you.' 10But when you enter a town and
are not welcomed, go into its streets and say,
11'Even the dust of your town that sticks to our
feet we wipe off against you. Yet be sure of this:
The kingdom of God is near.' 12I tell you, it will
be more bearable on that day for Sodom than
for that town.
13"Woe to you, Korazin! Woe to you, Bethsaida! For if the miracles that were performed in
you had been performed in Tyre and Sidon,
they would have repented long ago, sitting in
sackcloth and ashes. 14But it will be more bearable for Tyre and Sidon at the judgment than
for you. 15And you, Capernaum, will you be
lifted up to the skies? No, you will go down to
the depths.[b]
16"He who listens to you listens to me; he
who rejects you rejects me; but he who rejects
me rejects him who sent me."
17The seventy-two returned with joy and
said, "Lord, even the demons submit to us in
your name."
18He replied, "I saw Satan fall like lightning
from heaven. 19I have given you authority to
trample on snakes and scorpions and to overcome all the power of the enemy; nothing will
harm you. 20However, do not rejoice that the
spirits submit to you, but rejoice that your
names are written in heaven."
21At that time Jesus, full of joy through the
Holy Spirit, said, "I praise you, Father, Lord of
heaven and earth, because you have hidden
these things from the wise and learned, and
revealed them to little children. Yes, Father, for
this was your good pleasure.
22"All things have been committed to me by
my Father. No one knows who the Son is except
the Father, and no one knows who the Father is
except the Son and those to whom the Son
chooses to reveal him."
23Then he turned to his disciples and said
privately, "Blessed are the eyes that see what
you see. 24For I tell you that many prophets and
kings wanted to see what you see but did not
see it, and to hear what you hear but did not
hear it."

The Parable of the Good Samaritan

‰ See Matthew 22:34–40; Mark 12:28–31

25On one occasion an expert in the law stood
up to test Jesus. "Teacher," he asked, "what must
I do to inherit eternal life?"
26"What is written in the Law?" he replied.
"How do you read it?"
27He answered: "'Love the Lord your God
with all your heart and with all your soul and
with all your strength and with all your
mind'[c]; and, 'Love your neighbor as yourself.'[d]"

[a]1 Some manuscripts *seventy;* also in verse 17
[b]15 Greek *Hades* [c]27 Deut. 6:5 [d]27 Lev. 19:18

10:10–16 Jesus gave the disciples the ambitious task and privilege of sharing the message of the Messiah throughout Israel. Their ministry would not always be well received. Today, one who follows Jesus will encounter similar setbacks, rejection, opposition or ridicule. As we begin to share our faith with others, we may find our words are not always welcome. We should not be concerned, however, for the Lord calls us to persevere. He will bless our efforts among other people.

10:21 Some of us have spent years looking for wisdom. It often seems hard, if not impossible, to come by. Often the reason that true wisdom is so elusive is that it is divinely and simply revealed to those with a simple spirit. The greatest wisdom comes from God himself. God's wisdom can be gained by simply trusting him day by day, as children easily to do.

10:25–37 The story of the Good Samaritan teaches that true love for God will express itself in caring for the needs of others. According to the religious leaders in Jesus' day, the person least likely to help a wounded man was the Samaritan. When the despised Samaritan proved to be the good neighbor, Jesus story turned the tables on conventional wisdom and showed that concern for others has no boundaries. When God transforms our lives, we become the most effective instruments to reach others with similar needs. Sharing the Good News is a responsibility we receive when we experience God's help in our lives. As we share his Good News, we will experience great joy as others gain hope and find new life in Christ. We will also find our own faith strengthened as we remember what God has done on our behalf.

In the Life of Mary, Martha's Sister

Whenever the Bible shows us a glimpse of Mary, we find her at the feet of Jesus. In Luke 10:38–42 she is seated at Jesus' feet as a student. In John 11:32 Mary falls down at Jesus' feet in grief over her brother's death. In John 12:3 Mary once again bows at Jesus' feet, worshiping him and anointing and wiping his feet with her hair. Through these glimpses into Mary's life, we see that she practiced several spiritual exercises:

BIBLE STUDY. Mary carefully listened to the words of Jesus. In Mary's time, women were not allowed to be taught by anyone other than their father or husband. To be allowed to sit and listen and learn at the feet of Jesus was a tremendous privilege for Mary. Jesus commended her and assured her that he would not keep her from her desire to learn from him (see Luke 10:42). (To learn more about Bible study, turn to Deuteronomy 17.)

SERVICE. Mary and her sister Martha provided hospitality for Jesus and his disciples (see Luke 10:38; John 12). There were no motels or restaurants in the ancient Middle East, so hospitality was a societal obligation. Guests were viewed as being sent by God, and sharing food was a way of establishing peace with your guests. While other women also provided hospitality to Jesus and his disciples, Mary, Martha and their brother, Lazarus, seem to have made an extra effort to serve Jesus and his disciples in practical ways (see Luke 8:3). (To learn more about service, turn to Mark 10.)

WORSHIP. As Mary anointed Jesus' feet, she offered him heartfelt worship. Though it was not the formal worship of a gathered congregation, it was worship nonetheless. The ointment Mary used was a sacrificial offering equal to a year's wages. She humbly bowed herself at Jesus' feet before an entire roomful of people. While Judas protested Mary's extravagant generosity, Jesus said her deed would be talked about throughout the world (see Matthew 26:10–13). (To learn more about worship, turn to Exodus 20.)

Lessons for Life

The disciplines Mary practiced brought her eternal benefits. Mary's attentiveness to the words of Jesus filled her mind with timeless truths that would never pass away. Her service and hospitality to Jesus and his disciples would bring her great treasures in heaven, "where moth and rust do not destroy, and where thieves do not break in and steal" (Matthew 6:20). Jesus also promised that Mary's act of worship would be remembered throughout the world wherever the gospel is preached (see Mark 14:9). Like Mary, we should regularly practice the spiritual disciplines and thereby invest our time and energy in practices that will yield eternal rewards.

28"You have answered correctly," Jesus replied. "Do this and you will live."
29But he wanted to justify himself, so he
asked Jesus, "And who is my neighbor?"
30In reply Jesus said: "A man was going
down from Jerusalem to Jericho, when he fell
into the hands of robbers. They stripped him of
his clothes, beat him and went away, leaving
him half dead. 31A priest happened to be going
down the same road, and when he saw the man,
he passed by on the other side. 32So too, a Levite, when he came to the place and saw him,
passed by on the other side. 33But a Samaritan,
as he traveled, came where the man was; and
when he saw him, he took pity on him. 34He
went to him and bandaged his wounds, pouring on oil and wine. Then he put the man on his
own donkey, took him to an inn and took care
of him. 35The next day he took out two silver
coins[a] and gave them to the innkeeper. 'Look
after him,' he said, 'and when I return, I will
reimburse you for any extra expense you may
have.'
36"Which of these three do you think was a
neighbor to the man who fell into the hands of
robbers?"
37The expert in the law replied, "The one
who had mercy on him."
Jesus told him, "Go and do likewise."

At the Home of Martha and Mary

38As Jesus and his disciples were on their
way, he came to a village where a woman
named Martha opened her home to him. 39She
had a sister called Mary, who sat at the Lord's
feet listening to what he said. 40But Martha was
distracted by all the preparations that had to be
made. She came to him and asked, "Lord, don't
you care that my sister has left me to do the
work by myself? Tell her to help me!"
41"Martha, Martha," the Lord answered, "you
are worried and upset about many things, 42but
only one thing is needed.[b] Mary has chosen
what is better, and it will not be taken away
from her."

Jesus' Teaching on Prayer

‰ See Matthew 6:9–13; 7:7–11

11 One day Jesus was praying in a certain
place. When he finished, one of his disciples said to him, "Lord, teach us to pray, just
as John taught his disciples."
2He said to them, "When you pray, say:

" 'Father,[c]
hallowed be your name,
your kingdom come.[d]
3Give us each day our daily bread.
4Forgive us our sins,
for we also forgive everyone who sins
against us.[e]
And lead us not into temptation.[f]' "

5Then he said to them, "Suppose one of you
has a friend, and he goes to him at midnight
and says, 'Friend, lend me three loaves of bread,
6because a friend of mine on a journey has
come to me, and I have nothing to set before
him.'
7"Then the one inside answers, 'Don't bother me. The door is already locked, and my children are with me in bed. I can't get up and give
you anything.' 8I tell you, though he will not get
up and give him the bread because he is his
friend, yet because of the man's boldness[g] he
will get up and give him as much as he needs.
9"So I say to you: Ask and it will be given to
you; seek and you will find; knock and the door
will be opened to you. 10For everyone who asks
receives; he who seeks finds; and to him who
knocks, the door will be opened.
11"Which of you fathers, if your son asks
for[h] a fish, will give him a snake instead? 12Or
if he asks for an egg, will give him a scorpion?
13If you then, though you are evil, know how to
give good gifts to your children, how much

[a]35 Greek *two denarii* [b]42 Some manuscripts *but few things are needed—or only one* [c]2 Some manuscripts *Our Father in heaven* [d]2 Some manuscripts *come. May your will be done on earth as it is in heaven.* [e]4 Greek *everyone who is indebted to us* [f]4 Some manuscripts *temptation but deliver us from the evil one* [g]8 Or *persistence* [h]11 Some manuscripts *for bread, will give him a stone; or if he asks for*

10:38–42 This story about Mary and Martha illustrates the difference between being spiritually committed to God and being preoccupied with religious practices. Martha was so busy serving others that she had no time or energy left to be with Jesus. Mary, on the other hand, took time out from her serving to listen to Jesus. Martha was irritated at Mary for not being equally busy. Our religious practice needs to be born of love for Jesus from a devoted heart. We should not just keep busy doing good things if it means we will have no time to sit at Jesus' feet and listen to him.

11:4 God's forgiveness of us and our forgiveness of others are linked together. To fully experience God's forgiveness, we must forgive others. Conversely, an unforgiving spirit will hinder our ability to enjoy the freedom we can find in God's forgiveness. To harbor anger and an unforgiving spirit when God has forgiven us so much is not only hypocritical; it is a roadblock to our spiritual growth.

11:4 This honest prayer recognizes our own weakness and vulnerability to temptation. The prayer of faith asks for life's circumstances to lead away from rather than through temptation. As a model prayer, this principle is especially important when we are seeking victory over an area of our lives where sin has gained a foothold. Spiritual renewal involves not only recognizing our own shortcomings and sins but also avoiding situations that might lead to temptation and a fall.

11:8–13 God wants us to approach him with shameless persistence. The commands to ask, seek and knock are all given in the present tense, emphasizing continuous, persistent action on our part. To practice this persistence in our prayer life, we must first have a personal relationship with God. Through faith, we can have great expectations from our relationship with God. He is good—gentler and kinder than any human father—and he wants us to be redeemed.

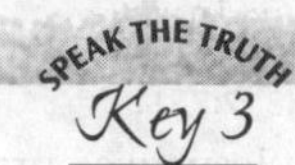

Honestly Admitting Our Needs

Luke 11:5–13 Part of speaking the truth to ourselves and others involves admitting that we have needs. We must rid ourselves of the pride and self-sufficiency that inhibit our confession of vulnerability or need for others. Confessing our needs can be just as important as confessing our sins and shortcomings.

God wants us to ask him for what we need. In fact, Jesus urged his followers, "Ask and it will be given to you; seek and you will find; knock and the door will be opened to you. For everyone who asks receives; he who seeks finds; and to him who knocks, the door will be opened" (11:9–10). Jesus also said, "Which of you, if his son asks for bread, will give him a stone? Or if he asks for a fish, will give him a snake? If you, then, though you are evil, know how to give good gifts to your children, how much more will your Father in heaven give good gifts to those who ask him!" (Matthew 7:9–11).

God wants to give us good things. But we must humbly admit that we have needs. We must even be willing, if God directs us to do so, to ask others for help. But we can't ask God for help just once and be done with it. We must be persistent and ask whenever we have needs, bringing them to him as they arise. We can be assured that our loving heavenly Father will respond lovingly—perhaps even through the generosity of others.

Turn to Acts 26.

more will your Father in heaven give the Holy Spirit to those who ask him!"

Jesus and Beelzebub

‰ See Matthew 12:22,24–29,43–45; Mark 3:23–27

14 Jesus was driving out a demon that was mute. When the demon left, the man who had been mute spoke, and the crowd was amazed. 15 But some of them said, "By Beelzebub,[a] the prince of demons, he is driving out demons." 16 Others tested him by asking for a sign from heaven.

17 Jesus knew their thoughts and said to them: "Any kingdom divided against itself will be ruined, and a house divided against itself will fall. 18 If Satan is divided against himself, how can his kingdom stand? I say this because you claim that I drive out demons by Beelzebub. 19 Now if I drive out demons by Beelzebub, by whom do your followers drive them out? So then, they will be your judges. 20 But if I drive out demons by the finger of God, then the kingdom of God has come to you.

21 "When a strong man, fully armed, guards his own house, his possessions are safe. 22 But when someone stronger attacks and overpowers him, he takes away the armor in which the man trusted and divides up the spoils.

23 "He who is not with me is against me, and he who does not gather with me, scatters.

24 "When an evil[b] spirit comes out of a man, it goes through arid places seeking rest and does not find it. Then it says, 'I will return to the house I left.' 25 When it arrives, it finds the house swept clean and put in order. 26 Then it goes and takes seven other spirits more wicked than itself, and they go in and live there. And the final condition of that man is worse than the first."

27 As Jesus was saying these things, a woman in the crowd called out, "Blessed is the mother who gave you birth and nursed you."

28 He replied, "Blessed rather are those who hear the word of God and obey it."

The Sign of Jonah

‰ See Matthew 12:39–42

29 As the crowds increased, Jesus said, "This is a wicked generation. It asks for a miraculous sign, but none will be given it except the sign of Jonah. 30 For as Jonah was a sign to the Nine-

[a] *15* Greek *Beezeboul* or *Beelzeboul*; also in verses 18 and 19 [b] *24* Greek *unclean*

11:14–23 In these verses, Jesus was accused of being an ally of Satan. Through Jesus' words and actions, however, it became clear that these accusations were false. Unseen powers of darkness are agents of Satan's kingdom and are responsible for a great deal of human bondage. When we understand this, then "straddling the fence" between living for God and living for ourselves is no longer an option. When we seek God and surrender to him, we leave no room for neutrality or living lives of moral compromise. To refuse God in Jesus Christ is to accept Satan and bondage to sin. Only through uncompromising faith in Jesus Christ can we achieve victory.

vites, so also will the Son of Man be to this generation. 31The Queen of the South will rise at the judgment with the men of this generation and condemn them; for she came from the ends of the earth to listen to Solomon's wisdom, and now one[a] greater than Solomon is here. 32The men of Nineveh will stand up at the judgment with this generation and condemn it; for they repented at the preaching of Jonah, and now one greater than Jonah is here.

The Lamp of the Body

‰ See Matthew 6:22–23

33"No one lights a lamp and puts it in a place where it will be hidden, or under a bowl. Instead he puts it on its stand, so that those who come in may see the light. 34Your eye is the lamp of your body. When your eyes are good, your whole body also is full of light. But when they are bad, your body also is full of darkness. 35See to it, then, that the light within you is not darkness. 36Therefore, if your whole body is full of light, and no part of it dark, it will be completely lighted, as when the light of a lamp shines on you."

Six Woes

37When Jesus had finished speaking, a Pharisee invited him to eat with him; so he went in and reclined at the table. 38But the Pharisee, noticing that Jesus did not first wash before the meal, was surprised.

39Then the Lord said to him, "Now then, you Pharisees clean the outside of the cup and dish, but inside you are full of greed and wickedness. 40You foolish people! Did not the one who made the outside make the inside also? 41But give what is inside ⌞the dish⌟[b] to the poor, and everything will be clean for you.

42"Woe to you Pharisees, because you give God a tenth of your mint, rue and all other kinds of garden herbs, but you neglect justice and the love of God. You should have practiced the latter without leaving the former undone.

43"Woe to you Pharisees, because you love the most important seats in the synagogues and greetings in the marketplaces.

44"Woe to you, because you are like unmarked graves, which men walk over without knowing it."

45One of the experts in the law answered him, "Teacher, when you say these things, you insult us also."

46Jesus replied, "And you experts in the law, woe to you, because you load people down with burdens they can hardly carry, and you yourselves will not lift one finger to help them.

47"Woe to you, because you build tombs for the prophets, and it was your forefathers who killed them. 48So you testify that you approve of what your forefathers did; they killed the prophets, and you build their tombs. 49Because of this, God in his wisdom said, 'I will send them prophets and apostles, some of whom they will kill and others they will persecute.' 50Therefore this generation will be held responsible for the blood of all the prophets that has been shed since the beginning of the world, 51from the blood of Abel to the blood of Zechariah, who was killed between the altar and the sanctuary. Yes, I tell you, this generation will be held responsible for it all.

52"Woe to you experts in the law, because you have taken away the key to knowledge. You yourselves have not entered, and you have hindered those who were entering."

53When Jesus left there, the Pharisees and the teachers of the law began to oppose him fiercely and to besiege him with questions, 54waiting to catch him in something he might say.

Warnings and Encouragements

‰ See Matthew 10:26–33

12 Meanwhile, when a crowd of many thousands had gathered, so that they were trampling on one another, Jesus began to speak first to his disciples, saying: "Be on your guard against the yeast of the Pharisees, which is hypocrisy. 2There is nothing concealed that will not be disclosed, or hidden that will not be made known. 3What you have said in the dark will be heard in the daylight, and what you have whispered in the ear in the inner rooms will be proclaimed from the roofs.

4"I tell you, my friends, do not be afraid of those who kill the body and after that can do no more. 5But I will show you whom you should fear: Fear him who, after the killing of the body, has power to throw you into hell. Yes, I tell you, fear him. 6Are not five sparrows sold for two pennies[c]? Yet not one of them is forgotten by God. 7Indeed, the very hairs of your head are all numbered. Don't be afraid; you are worth more than many sparrows.

8"I tell you, whoever acknowledges me before men, the Son of Man will also acknowledge him before the angels of God. 9But he who disowns me before men will be disowned before the angels of God. 10And everyone who speaks a word against the Son of Man will be forgiven, but anyone who blasphemes against the Holy Spirit will not be forgiven.

11"When you are brought before synagogues, rulers and authorities, do not worry about how you will defend yourselves or what

[a]31 Or *something;* also in verse 32 [b]41 Or *what you have* [c]6 Greek *two assaria*

12:6–7 If God cares about the smallest sparrow, how much more will he care for us! If he cares enough to count the hairs on our heads, then he will also be concerned about the thoughts and feelings inside. When we feel depressed or lonely, we can remember that the most powerful and important person in the universe cares deeply and personally for us.

you will say, 12for the Holy Spirit will teach you
at that time what you should say."

The Parable of the Rich Fool

13Someone in the crowd said to him,
"Teacher, tell my brother to divide the inheritance with me."
14Jesus replied, "Man, who appointed me a
judge or an arbiter between you?" 15Then he said
to them, "Watch out! Be on your guard against
all kinds of greed; a man's life does not consist
in the abundance of his possessions."
16And he told them this parable: "The
ground of a certain rich man produced a good
crop. 17He thought to himself, 'What shall I do?
I have no place to store my crops.'
18"Then he said, 'This is what I'll do. I will
tear down my barns and build bigger ones, and
there I will store all my grain and my goods.
19And I'll say to myself, "You have plenty of
good things laid up for many years. Take life
easy; eat, drink and be merry." '
20"But God said to him, 'You fool! This very
night your life will be demanded from you.
Then who will get what you have prepared for
yourself?'
21"This is how it will be with anyone who
stores up things for himself but is not rich toward God."

Do Not Worry

‰ See Matthew 6:25–33

22Then Jesus said to his disciples: "Therefore
I tell you, do not worry about your life, what
you will eat; or about your body, what you will
wear. 23Life is more than food, and the body
more than clothes. 24Consider the ravens: They
do not sow or reap, they have no storeroom or
barn; yet God feeds them. And how much more
valuable you are than birds! 25Who of you by
worrying can add a single hour to his life[a]?
26Since you cannot do this very little thing, why
do you worry about the rest?
27"Consider how the lilies grow. They do not
labor or spin. Yet I tell you, not even Solomon
in all his splendor was dressed like one of these.
28If that is how God clothes the grass of the
field, which is here today, and tomorrow is
thrown into the fire, how much more will he
clothe you, O you of little faith! 29And do not
set your heart on what you will eat or drink; do
not worry about it. 30For the pagan world runs
after all such things, and your Father knows that
you need them. 31But seek his kingdom, and
these things will be given to you as well.
32"Do not be afraid, little flock, for your Father has been pleased to give you the kingdom.
33Sell your possessions and give to the poor.
Provide purses for yourselves that will not wear
out, a treasure in heaven that will not be exhausted, where no thief comes near and no
moth destroys. 34For where your treasure is,
there your heart will be also.

Watchfulness

‰ See Matthew 24:43–51; Mark 13:33–37

35"Be dressed ready for service and keep your
lamps burning, 36like men waiting for their
master to return from a wedding banquet, so
that when he comes and knocks they can immediately open the door for him. 37It will be good
for those servants whose master finds them
watching when he comes. I tell you the truth, he
will dress himself to serve, will have them re-
cline at the table and will come and wait on
them. 38It will be good for those servants whose
master finds them ready, even if he comes in the
second or third watch of the night. 39But understand this: If the owner of the house had known
at what hour the thief was coming, he would
not have let his house be broken into. 40You
also must be ready, because the Son of Man will
come at an hour when you do not expect him."
41Peter asked, "Lord, are you telling this parable to us, or to everyone?"
42The Lord answered, "Who then is the faithful and wise manager, whom the master puts in
charge of his servants to give them their food
allowance at the proper time? 43It will be good
for that servant whom the master finds doing so
when he returns. 44I tell you the truth, he will
put him in charge of all his possessions. 45But
suppose the servant says to himself, 'My master
is taking a long time in coming,' and he then
begins to beat the menservants and maidservants and to eat and drink and get drunk. 46The
master of that servant will come on a day when
he does not expect him and at an hour he is not
aware of. He will cut him to pieces and assign
him a place with the unbelievers.
47"That servant who knows his master's will

[a]25 Or *single cubit to his height*

12:13–21 Jesus continually emphasized the dangers of materialism. Materialism is not just a problem for rich people or for the characters in Jesus' stories. Our tendency to want more of everything is endemic to human nature. Notice that Jesus was not as concerned with how much wealth we possess but with how much our wealth possesses us. True freedom and contentment cannot be found in the things we own. Freedom and contentment are freely given to us as we humbly turn to God for his gracious help.

12:22–31 True freedom and contentment are found by depending exclusively on God. The argument here confronts the worthlessness of time spent worrying about things God has already taken care of. Since neither animals nor plants worry about food and clothing, neither should we. As God takes care of them from day to day, so also God will take care of us while we seek his kingdom.

12:32–34 The things we value most and spend time and money pursuing demonstrate where our heartfelt attachments are. Our checkbooks and date books are barometers of our hearts. If we truly value God's kingdom and trust God to provide for our needs, we will willingly give generously to those in need. If we are afraid or unwilling to give to others, we need to confess this to God and ask him to help us trust his provision of our needs.

THE SPIRITUAL DISCIPLINES

Stewardship

Our Hearts Follow Our Money

Luke 12:34 Money often plays an important role in our spiritual lives. Scholars have noted that nearly one-fourth of Jesus' teaching mentions money in some way. Jesus recognized that our financial attitudes and practices influence our spiritual health. Money touches the heart of our lives.

The order of Jesus' words in this passage may surprise us. We often suppose that our heart's desire will direct our financial investments. But Jesus intimates that money itself has the power to direct our hearts. If we carelessly invest in worldly treasures, our hearts will be drawn to those things. But if we intentionally direct our financial resources toward spiritual priorities, our hearts will follow along.

Jesus gives us a principle of spiritual investment: We gain freedom from money's power by using money for his kingdom's priorities. Instead of trying to serve God and money, we need only use our money to serve God.

For more on stewardship, turn to 1 Corinthians 16.

Putting It Into Practice

Review your financial expenditures over the last week, month and year. What do they reveal about your heart? Do they include investments in the church and in other ministries to the world? Are there areas in which your heart could be drawn away from God by your investments? If you were to set up a spiritual investment account, in what would you invest? Are there ways you can begin to invest your treasure for some of these purposes now?

and does not get ready or does not do what his master wants will be beaten with many blows. [48]But the one who does not know and does things deserving punishment will be beaten with few blows. From everyone who has been given much, much will be demanded; and from the one who has been entrusted with much, much more will be asked.

Not Peace but Division

‰ See Matthew 10:34–36

[49]"I have come to bring fire on the earth, and how I wish it were already kindled! [50]But I have a baptism to undergo, and how distressed I am until it is completed! [51]Do you think I came to bring peace on earth? No, I tell you, but division. [52]From now on there will be five in one family divided against each other, three against two and two against three. [53]They will be divided, father against son and son against father, mother against daughter and daughter against mother, mother-in-law against daughter-in-law and daughter-in-law against mother-in-law."

Interpreting the Times

[54]He said to the crowd: "When you see a cloud rising in the west, immediately you say, 'It's going to rain,' and it does. [55]And when the south wind blows, you say, 'It's going to be hot,' and it is. [56]Hypocrites! You know how to interpret the appearance of the earth and the sky. How is it that you don't know how to interpret this present time?

[57]"Why don't you judge for yourselves what is right? [58]As you are going with your adversary to the magistrate, try hard to be reconciled to him on the way, or he may drag you off to the judge, and the judge turn you over to the officer, and the officer throw you into prison. [59]I tell you, you will not get out until you have paid the last penny.[a]"

Repent or Perish

13 Now there were some present at that time who told Jesus about the Galileans whose blood Pilate had mixed with their sacrifices. [2]Jesus answered, "Do you think that these Galileans were worse sinners than all the other Galileans because they suffered this way? [3]I tell you, no! But unless you repent, you too will all perish. [4]Or those eighteen who died when the tower in Siloam fell on them—do you think they were more guilty than all the others living in Jerusalem? [5]I tell you, no! But unless you repent, you too will all perish."

[6]Then he told this parable: "A man had a fig tree, planted in his vineyard, and he went to look for fruit on it, but did not find any. [7]So he said to the man who took care of the vineyard, 'For three years now I've been coming to look for fruit on this fig tree and haven't found any. Cut it down! Why should it use up the soil?'

[8]" 'Sir,' the man replied, 'leave it alone for one more year, and I'll dig around it and fertilize it. [9]If it bears fruit next year, fine! If not, then cut it down.' "

A Crippled Woman Healed on the Sabbath

[10]On a Sabbath Jesus was teaching in one of the synagogues, [11]and a woman was there who had been crippled by a spirit for eighteen years. She was bent over and could not straighten up at all. [12]When Jesus saw her, he called her forward and said to her, "Woman, you are set free from your infirmity." [13]Then he put his hands on her, and immediately she straightened up and praised God.

[14]Indignant because Jesus had healed on the Sabbath, the synagogue ruler said to the people, "There are six days for work. So come and be healed on those days, not on the Sabbath."

[15]The Lord answered him, "You hypocrites! Doesn't each of you on the Sabbath untie his ox or donkey from the stall and lead it out to give it water? [16]Then should not this woman, a daughter of Abraham, whom Satan has kept bound for eighteen long years, be set free on the Sabbath day from what bound her?"

[17]When he said this, all his opponents were humiliated, but the people were delighted with all the wonderful things he was doing.

The Parables of the Mustard Seed and the Yeast

‰ See Matthew 13:31–33; Mark 4:30–32

[18]Then Jesus asked, "What is the kingdom of God like? What shall I compare it to? [19]It is like a mustard seed, which a man took and planted in his garden. It grew and became a tree, and the birds of the air perched in its branches."

[20]Again he asked, "What shall I compare the kingdom of God to? [21]It is like yeast that a woman took and mixed into a large amount[b] of flour until it worked all through the dough."

The Narrow Door

[22]Then Jesus went through the towns and villages, teaching as he made his way to Jerusa-

[a]59 Greek *lepton* [b]21 Greek *three satas* (probably about 1/2 bushel or 22 liters)

13:10–13 Jesus cared for social outcasts, for those who were afflicted and for those in spiritual bondage. This handicapped woman was hurting in all these respects and had given up all hope for a new life. Yet Jesus healed her. He can do the same for us as we repent, seek God and surrender to him.

13:22–30 Appearances can be deceiving. But God is not fooled—he knows the intent of our hearts. Like the religious hypocrites of Jesus' day, we can go to church, teach Sunday school or sing in the choir yet still lack a real relationship with God. Being real, not merely religious, is what God desires of us. God will judge religious hypocrisy, and he will honor honest attempts to obey him and know him better.

lem. 23Someone asked him, "Lord, are only a few people going to be saved?"

He said to them, 24"Make every effort to enter through the narrow door, because many, I tell you, will try to enter and will not be able to. 25Once the owner of the house gets up and closes the door, you will stand outside knocking and pleading, 'Sir, open the door for us.'

"But he will answer, 'I don't know you or where you come from.'

26"Then you will say, 'We ate and drank with you, and you taught in our streets.'

27"But he will reply, 'I don't know you or where you come from. Away from me, all you evildoers!'

28"There will be weeping there, and gnashing of teeth, when you see Abraham, Isaac and Jacob and all the prophets in the kingdom of God, but you yourselves thrown out. 29People will come from east and west and north and south, and will take their places at the feast in the kingdom of God. 30Indeed there are those who are last who will be first, and first who will be last."

Jesus' Sorrow for Jerusalem

‰ See Matthew 23:37–39

31At that time some Pharisees came to Jesus and said to him, "Leave this place and go somewhere else. Herod wants to kill you."

32He replied, "Go tell that fox, 'I will drive out demons and heal people today and tomorrow, and on the third day I will reach my goal.' 33In any case, I must keep going today and tomorrow and the next day—for surely no prophet can die outside Jerusalem!

34"O Jerusalem, Jerusalem, you who kill the prophets and stone those sent to you, how often I have longed to gather your children together, as a hen gathers her chicks under her wings, but you were not willing! 35Look, your house is left to you desolate. I tell you, you will not see me again until you say, 'Blessed is he who comes in the name of the Lord.'[a]"

Jesus at a Pharisee's House

14 One Sabbath, when Jesus went to eat in the house of a prominent Pharisee, he was being carefully watched. 2There in front of him was a man suffering from dropsy. 3Jesus asked the Pharisees and experts in the law, "Is it lawful to heal on the Sabbath or not?" 4But they remained silent. So taking hold of the man, he healed him and sent him away.

5Then he asked them, "If one of you has a son[b] or an ox that falls into a well on the Sabbath day, will you not immediately pull him out?" 6And they had nothing to say.

7When he noticed how the guests picked the places of honor at the table, he told them this parable: 8"When someone invites you to a wedding feast, do not take the place of honor, for a person more distinguished than you may have been invited. 9If so, the host who invited both of you will come and say to you, 'Give this man your seat.' Then, humiliated, you will have to take the least important place. 10But when you are invited, take the lowest place, so that when your host comes, he will say to you, 'Friend, move up to a better place.' Then you will be honored in the presence of all your fellow guests. 11For everyone who exalts himself will be humbled, and he who humbles himself will be exalted."

12Then Jesus said to his host, "When you give a luncheon or dinner, do not invite your friends, your brothers or relatives, or your rich neighbors; if you do, they may invite you back and so you will be repaid. 13But when you give a banquet, invite the poor, the crippled, the lame, the blind, 14and you will be blessed. Although they cannot repay you, you will be repaid at the resurrection of the righteous."

The Parable of the Great Banquet

15When one of those at the table with him heard this, he said to Jesus, "Blessed is the man who will eat at the feast in the kingdom of God."

16Jesus replied: "A certain man was preparing a great banquet and invited many guests. 17At the time of the banquet he sent his servant to tell those who had been invited, 'Come, for everything is now ready.'

18"But they all alike began to make excuses. The first said, 'I have just bought a field, and I must go and see it. Please excuse me.'

19"Another said, 'I have just bought five yoke of oxen, and I'm on my way to try them out. Please excuse me.'

20"Still another said, 'I just got married, so I can't come.'

21"The servant came back and reported this to his master. Then the owner of the house became angry and ordered his servant, 'Go out quickly into the streets and alleys of the town and bring in the poor, the crippled, the blind and the lame.'

22" 'Sir,' the servant said, 'what you ordered has been done, but there is still room.'

23"Then the master told his servant, 'Go out to the roads and country lanes and make them come in, so that my house will be full. 24I tell you, not one of those men who were invited will get a taste of my banquet.' "

[a]35 Psalm 118:26 [b]5 Some manuscripts *donkey*

14:12–24 This story about the great feast illustrates one of the major themes in Luke's Gospel. God extends his grace and blessing to the poor and the afflicted of society, those who are most always ignored or rejected by others. God will reward us for extending mercy to such people. An important step in following Jesus is our willingness to help others less fortunate than we are.

The Cost of Being a Disciple

25 Large crowds were traveling with Jesus, and
turning to them he said: 26 "If anyone comes to
me and does not hate his father and mother, his
wife and children, his brothers and sisters—yes,
even his own life—he cannot be my disciple.
27 And anyone who does not carry his cross and
follow me cannot be my disciple.

28 "Suppose one of you wants to build a tower. Will he not first sit down and estimate the
cost to see if he has enough money to complete
it? 29 For if he lays the foundation and is not able
to finish it, everyone who sees it will ridicule
him, 30 saying, 'This fellow began to build and
was not able to finish.'

31 "Or suppose a king is about to go to war
against another king. Will he not first sit down
and consider whether he is able with ten thousand men to oppose the one coming against
him with twenty thousand? 32 If he is not able,
he will send a delegation while the other is still
a long way off and will ask for terms of peace.
33 In the same way, any of you who does not
give up everything he has cannot be my disciple.

34 "Salt is good, but if it loses its saltiness,
how can it be made salty again? 35 It is fit neither
for the soil nor for the manure pile; it is thrown
out.

"He who has ears to hear, let him hear."

The Parable of the Lost Sheep

‰ See Matthew 18:12–14

15 Now the tax collectors and "sinners"
were all gathering around to hear him.
2 But the Pharisees and the teachers of the law
muttered, "This man welcomes sinners and
eats with them."

3 Then Jesus told them this parable: 4 "Suppose one of you has a hundred sheep and loses
one of them. Does he not leave the ninety-nine
in the open country and go after the lost sheep
until he finds it? 5 And when he finds it, he
joyfully puts it on his shoulders 6 and goes
home. Then he calls his friends and neighbors
together and says, 'Rejoice with me; I have
found my lost sheep.' 7 I tell you that in the
same way there will be more rejoicing in heaven
over one sinner who repents than over ninety-
nine righteous persons who do not need to repent.

The Parable of the Lost Coin

8 "Or suppose a woman has ten silver coins[a]
and loses one. Does she not light a lamp, sweep
the house and search carefully until she finds it?
9 And when she finds it, she calls her friends and
neighbors together and says, 'Rejoice with me;
I have found my lost coin.' 10 In the same way,
I tell you, there is rejoicing in the presence of
the angels of God over one sinner who repents."

The Parable of the Lost Son

11 Jesus continued: "There was a man who
had two sons. 12 The younger one said to his
father, 'Father, give me my share of the estate.'
So he divided his property between them.

13 "Not long after that, the younger son got
together all he had, set off for a distant country
and there squandered his wealth in wild living.
14 After he had spent everything, there was a severe famine in that whole country, and he began to be in need. 15 So he went and hired himself out to a citizen of that country, who sent
him to his fields to feed pigs. 16 He longed to fill
his stomach with the pods that the pigs were
eating, but no one gave him anything.

17 "When he came to his senses, he said,
'How many of my father's hired men have food
to spare, and here I am starving to death! 18 I
will set out and go back to my father and say to
him: Father, I have sinned against heaven and
against you. 19 I am no longer worthy to be
called your son; make me like one of your hired
men.' 20 So he got up and went to his father.

[a] 8 Greek *ten drachmas,* each worth about a day's wages

14:26–33 We need to count the cost regarding our decision to follow Jesus and our commitment to discipleship. If commitment to Jesus is more valuable to us than our sins, we will be motivated to seek him and ask him to redirect the course of our lives. If we cannot give up the pleasures of sin, we will end up compromising our commitment to Christ and undermining our spiritual growth.

15:1–2 Jesus attracted many of the outcasts of Jewish religious and social life. Perhaps this was because he was the only one who did not despise and reject them. Jesus chose to spend time with these downcast people because they were aware of their sinfulness and approached God with humility. In contrast, the religious leaders were outwardly moral but inwardly proud and not at all attracted to Jesus. Even today, religious pride and self-righteousness can hinder true spiritual growth by prohibiting us from humbling ourselves to seek God and surrender to him.

15:3–10 The stories of the lost coin and the lost sheep show God's grace extended toward those who have strayed and reflect his great joy in finding them. Though we may have a sordid past, we are extremely valuable in God's eyes. Both the coin and the sheep were valuable commodities in their day. The fact that the owner would stop everything else to search for the lost one illustrates how valuable we are to the one who owns us.

15:11–32 The story of the lost son wonderfully illustrates the keys to spiritual renewal and the theme of Luke's Gospel (see 19:9–10). We may have been like the younger son, who chose a life of sinful pleasure. Yet in time we may have discovered that our lives were not what we or God had hoped for—enslaved to sin and selfish lifestyles. Recognizing that truth may have caused us to repent and ask God to redirect the course of our lives. Or, then again, we may have been more like the older brother who spent his life trying to earn the love that was freely offered all along. We need to recognize that God loves all his children. We must forgive and accept those who have been forgiven for things we might never have dared to do wrong. And we must humble ourselves to admit our own sins of self-righteousness and pride that can separate us from the Father's love as much as any sins of the flesh.

15:20–24 The father's great compassion for his younger son portrays God's response to anyone who repents. God actively seeks those who have strayed in their walk of

“But while he was still a long way off, his
father saw him and was filled with compassion
for him; he ran to his son, threw his arms
around him and kissed him.
21“The son said to him, ‘Father, I have
sinned against heaven and against you. I am no
longer worthy to be called your son.[a]’
22“But the father said to his servants, ‘Quick!
Bring the best robe and put it on him. Put a ring
on his finger and sandals on his feet. 23Bring the
fattened calf and kill it. Let’s have a feast and
celebrate. 24For this son of mine was dead and
is alive again; he was lost and is found.’ So they
began to celebrate.
25“Meanwhile, the older son was in the field.
When he came near the house, he heard music
and dancing. 26So he called one of the servants
and asked him what was going on. 27‘Your
brother has come,’ he replied, ‘and your father
has killed the fattened calf because he has him
back safe and sound.’
28“The older brother became angry and refused to go in. So his father went out and pleaded with him. 29But he answered his father,
‘Look! All these years I’ve been slaving for you
and never disobeyed your orders. Yet you never
gave me even a young goat so I could celebrate
with my friends. 30But when this son of yours
who has squandered your property with prostitutes comes home, you kill the fattened calf for
him!’
31“ ‘My son,’ the father said, ‘you are always
with me, and everything I have is yours. 32But
we had to celebrate and be glad, because this
brother of yours was dead and is alive again; he
was lost and is found.’ ”

The Parable of the Shrewd Manager

16 Jesus told his disciples: “There was a
rich man whose manager was accused
of wasting his possessions. 2So he called him in
and asked him, ‘What is this I hear about you?
Give an account of your management, because
you cannot be manager any longer.’
3“The manager said to himself, ‘What shall
I do now? My master is taking away my job. I’m
not strong enough to dig, and I’m ashamed to
beg— 4I know what I’ll do so that, when I lose
my job here, people will welcome me into their
houses.’
5“So he called in each one of his master’s
debtors. He asked the first, ‘How much do you
owe my master?’
6“ ‘Eight hundred gallons[b] of olive oil,’ he
replied.
“The manager told him, ‘Take your bill, sit
down quickly, and make it four hundred.’
7“Then he asked the second, ‘And how
much do you owe?’
“ ‘A thousand bushels[c] of wheat,’ he replied.
“He told him, ‘Take your bill and make it
eight hundred.’
8“The master commended the dishonest
manager because he had acted shrewdly. For the
people of this world are more shrewd in dealing
with their own kind than are the people of the
light. 9I tell you, use worldly wealth to gain
friends for yourselves, so that when it is gone,
you will be welcomed into eternal dwellings.
10“Whoever can be trusted with very little
can also be trusted with much, and whoever is
dishonest with very little will also be dishonest
with much. 11So if you have not been trustworthy in handling worldly wealth, who will trust
you with true riches? 12And if you have not been
trustworthy with someone else’s property, who
will give you property of your own?
13“No servant can serve two masters. Either
he will hate the one and love the other, or he
will be devoted to the one and despise the other. You cannot serve both God and Money.”
14The Pharisees, who loved money, heard all
this and were sneering at Jesus. 15He said to
them, “You are the ones who justify yourselves
in the eyes of men, but God knows your hearts.
What is highly valued among men is detestable
in God’s sight.

Additional Teachings

16“The Law and the Prophets were proclaimed until John. Since that time, the good
news of the kingdom of God is being preached,
and everyone is forcing his way into it. 17It is
easier for heaven and earth to disappear than
for the least stroke of a pen to drop out of the
Law.
18“Anyone who divorces his wife and mar-

[a]21 Some early manuscripts *son. Make me like one of your hired men.* [b]6 Greek *one hundred batous* (probably about 3 kiloliters) [c]7 Greek *one hundred korous* (probably about 35 kiloliters)

---

faith. Like the father in this story, God waits for the sinner to come to his senses and return to him of his own volition. The father, however, does not wait for his returning son to clean himself up. He welcomes him back as he is, running to meet him with hugs and kisses and joyful celebration.

15:25–30 God asks us to share his great concern for those who are helpless and lost. He wants us to be willing to carry the message of hope to them. The older brother in this story is a significant character because his attitude is sinful and self-centered. The father in this story demonstrates God’s attitude toward people who are lost. God desires our restoration more than anything, whether the people around us like it or not.

16:1–13 This story teaches the importance of using our material possessions for good purposes. If the shrewd accountant is commended for cleverly using his talent for winning friends and influencing people, how much more the honest steward will be commended for dedicating all to God. Using material possessions and God-given talents merely for personal enjoyment, with no concern for others, is wrong. When we find ourselves in such a situation it may mean that our possessions have possessed us or that our goods have become our gods.

ries another woman commits adultery, and the man who marries a divorced woman commits adultery.

The Rich Man and Lazarus

19 "There was a rich man who was dressed in purple and fine linen and lived in luxury every day. 20 At his gate was laid a beggar named Lazarus, covered with sores 21 and longing to eat what fell from the rich man's table. Even the dogs came and licked his sores.

22 "The time came when the beggar died and the angels carried him to Abraham's side. The rich man also died and was buried. 23 In hell,[a] where he was in torment, he looked up and saw Abraham far away, with Lazarus by his side. 24 So he called to him, 'Father Abraham, have pity on me and send Lazarus to dip the tip of his finger in water and cool my tongue, because I am in agony in this fire.'

25 "But Abraham replied, 'Son, remember that in your lifetime you received your good things, while Lazarus received bad things, but now he is comforted here and you are in agony. 26 And besides all this, between us and you a great chasm has been fixed, so that those who want to go from here to you cannot, nor can anyone cross over from there to us.'

27 "He answered, 'Then I beg you, father, send Lazarus to my father's house, 28 for I have five brothers. Let him warn them, so that they will not also come to this place of torment.'

29 "Abraham replied, 'They have Moses and the Prophets; let them listen to them.'

30 " 'No, father Abraham,' he said, 'but if someone from the dead goes to them, they will repent.'

31 "He said to him, 'If they do not listen to Moses and the Prophets, they will not be convinced even if someone rises from the dead.' "

Sin, Faith, Duty

17 Jesus said to his disciples: "Things that cause people to sin are bound to come, but woe to that person through whom they come. 2 It would be better for him to be thrown into the sea with a millstone tied around his neck than for him to cause one of these little ones to sin. 3 So watch yourselves.

"If your brother sins, rebuke him, and if he repents, forgive him. 4 If he sins against you seven times in a day, and seven times comes back to you and says, 'I repent,' forgive him."

5 The apostles said to the Lord, "Increase our faith!"

6 He replied, "If you have faith as small as a mustard seed, you can say to this mulberry tree, 'Be uprooted and planted in the sea,' and it will obey you.

7 "Suppose one of you had a servant plowing or looking after the sheep. Would he say to the servant when he comes in from the field, 'Come along now and sit down to eat'? 8 Would he not rather say, 'Prepare my supper, get yourself ready and wait on me while I eat and drink; after that you may eat and drink'? 9 Would he thank the servant because he did what he was told to do? 10 So you also, when you have done everything you were told to do, should say, 'We are unworthy servants; we have only done our duty.' "

Ten Healed of Leprosy

11 Now on his way to Jerusalem, Jesus traveled along the border between Samaria and Galilee. 12 As he was going into a village, ten men who had leprosy[b] met him. They stood at a distance 13 and called out in a loud voice, "Jesus, Master, have pity on us!"

14 When he saw them, he said, "Go, show yourselves to the priests." And as they went, they were cleansed.

15 One of them, when he saw he was healed, came back, praising God in a loud voice. 16 He threw himself at Jesus' feet and thanked him—and he was a Samaritan.

17 Jesus asked, "Were not all ten cleansed? Where are the other nine? 18 Was no one found to return and give praise to God except this foreigner?" 19 Then he said to him, "Rise and go; your faith has made you well."

The Coming of the Kingdom of God

20 Once, having been asked by the Pharisees when the kingdom of God would come, Jesus replied, "The kingdom of God does not come with your careful observation, 21 nor will people say, 'Here it is,' or 'There it is,' because the kingdom of God is within[c] you."

[a] 23 Greek *Hades* [b] 12 The Greek word was used for various diseases affecting the skin—not necessarily leprosy. [c] 21 Or *among*

16:19–31 In this story we see the consequences of selfishness. Insulated by all the material comforts of life, the rich man never reflected on his spiritual needs or shortcomings. Ultimately, he was consigned to hell. The beggar Lazarus lacked basic material needs and suffered physical pain in his lifetime, but he was prepared for eternity. Death proved to be the great equalizer, effecting a reversal of fortunes for these two. God wants us to have the proper attitude toward money and possessions and to use them unselfishly to help others.

17:1–4 Knowing when to forgive and when to confront is critical. Jesus taught that we should forgive others freely and frequently, with no strings attached. If our friends behave in ways clearly counter to God's will, we need to confront them for their own good. However, it will be terrible for the one who puts temptation in the way of others. God will hold those who lead others astray accountable.

17:11–19 The story of the ten lepers illustrates Jesus' great compassion for the hurting and his desire to make them whole. Only one of the ten lepers returned to say thanks. That leper was a Samaritan. While God freely offers his healing and restoration to us, we should never take it for granted. Part of maintaining our spiritual gains is to regularly thank God specifically for all the ways he has blessed us.

[22]Then he said to his disciples, "The time is
coming when you will long to see one of the
days of the Son of Man, but you will not see it.
[23]Men will tell you, 'There he is!' or 'Here he is!'
Do not go running off after them. [24]For the Son
of Man in his day[a] will be like the lightning,
which flashes and lights up the sky from one
end to the other. [25]But first he must suffer many
things and be rejected by this generation.
[26]"Just as it was in the days of Noah, so also
will it be in the days of the Son of Man. [27]People
were eating, drinking, marrying and being given
in marriage up to the day Noah entered the ark.
Then the flood came and destroyed them all.
[28]"It was the same in the days of Lot. People
were eating and drinking, buying and selling,
planting and building. [29]But the day Lot left
Sodom, fire and sulfur rained down from heav-
en and destroyed them all.
[30]"It will be just like this on the day the Son
of Man is revealed. [31]On that day no one who
is on the roof of his house, with his goods inside, should go down to get them. Likewise, no
one in the field should go back for anything.
[32]Remember Lot's wife! [33]Whoever tries to keep
his life will lose it, and whoever loses his life
will preserve it. [34]I tell you, on that night two
people will be in one bed; one will be taken and
the other left. [35]Two women will be grinding
grain together; one will be taken and the other
left.[b]"
[37]"Where, Lord?" they asked.
He replied, "Where there is a dead body,
there the vultures will gather."

The Parable of the Persistent Widow

18 Then Jesus told his disciples a parable
to show them that they should always
pray and not give up. [2]He said: "In a certain
town there was a judge who neither feared God
nor cared about men. [3]And there was a widow
in that town who kept coming to him with the
plea, 'Grant me justice against my adversary.'
[4]"For some time he refused. But finally he
said to himself, 'Even though I don't fear God
or care about men, [5]yet because this widow
keeps bothering me, I will see that she gets justice, so that she won't eventually wear me out
with her coming!' "
[6]And the Lord said, "Listen to what the unjust judge says. [7]And will not God bring about
justice for his chosen ones, who cry out to him
day and night? Will he keep putting them off?
[8]I tell you, he will see that they get justice, and
quickly. However, when the Son of Man comes,
will he find faith on the earth?"

The Parable of the Pharisee and the Tax Collector

[9]To some who were confident of their own
righteousness and looked down on everybody
else, Jesus told this parable: [10]"Two men went
up to the temple to pray, one a Pharisee and the
other a tax collector. [11]The Pharisee stood up
and prayed about[c] himself: 'God, I thank you
that I am not like other men—robbers, evildoers, adulterers—or even like this tax collector.
[12]I fast twice a week and give a tenth of all I get.'
[13]"But the tax collector stood at a distance.
He would not even look up to heaven, but beat
his breast and said, 'God, have mercy on me, a
sinner.'
[14]"I tell you that this man, rather than the
other, went home justified before God. For everyone who exalts himself will be humbled, and
he who humbles himself will be exalted."

The Little Children and Jesus

‰ See Matthew 19:13–15; Mark 10:13–16

[15]People were also bringing babies to Jesus to
have him touch them. When the disciples saw
this, they rebuked them. [16]But Jesus called the
children to him and said, "Let the little children
come to me, and do not hinder them, for the
kingdom of God belongs to such as these. [17]I
tell you the truth, anyone who will not receive
the kingdom of God like a little child will never
enter it."

The Rich Ruler

‰ See Matthew 19:16–29; Mark 10:17–30

[18]A certain ruler asked him, "Good teacher,
what must I do to inherit eternal life?"
[19]"Why do you call me good?" Jesus an-

[a]24 Some manuscripts do not have *in his day.*
[b]35 Some manuscripts *left.* [36]*Two men will be in the field; one will be taken and the other left.*
[c]11 Or *to*

18:1–8 Many of us have experienced injustice at the hands of some authority figure. This story contrasts God with the unfair judge and makes the point that even if life is unfair, at least God is just. If an unjust judge will answer the pleas of a persistent widow, how much more will a just God respond to those in need who pray to him in faith. When trials and challenges make life seem unfair, we can still trust God to deliver us. Seeking God in prayer requires patience and persistence, but it always pays off.

18:10–14 The Pharisee in these verses did not possess an accurate self-perception. He viewed himself as better than others; his pride hindered him from viewing others as God did. We are often just like this Pharisee when we refuse to see the truth. Most of us ignore our own sins and point a hypocritical finger at others we deem worse off than we are. Some of us hide behind the respect we command in our community. But God sees the heart and will forgive us, heal us and aid us in spiritual growth according to our humble faith. The tax collector in this story, with humble and honest self-awareness, was heading for true spiritual renewal. The Pharisee was heading for spiritual disaster.

18:15–17 Most children possess a trusting nature, and God wants our relationship with him to possess that kind of simple trust. Any other "faith" is inappropriate and ineffective. Childlike faith is a gift from God. It may take time for God to restore such faith in us, especially if we have been hurt by others. If this faith is hindered because of past hurts, we need to release these to God and ask him to make our hearts childlike once more, so that he can usher us into the abundant life he has for us.

18:18–23 Our true spiritual condition is not so much evidenced by our religious activities as by what we depend

swered. "No one is good—except God alone. 20You know the commandments: 'Do not commit adultery, do not murder, do not steal, do not give false testimony, honor your father and mother.'[a]"

21"All these I have kept since I was a boy," he said.

22When Jesus heard this, he said to him, "You still lack one thing. Sell everything you have and give to the poor, and you will have treasure in heaven. Then come, follow me."

23When he heard this, he became very sad, because he was a man of great wealth. 24Jesus looked at him and said, "How hard it is for the rich to enter the kingdom of God! 25Indeed, it is easier for a camel to go through the eye of a needle than for a rich man to enter the kingdom of God."

26Those who heard this asked, "Who then can be saved?"

27Jesus replied, "What is impossible with men is possible with God."

28Peter said to him, "We have left all we had to follow you!"

29"I tell you the truth," Jesus said to them, "no one who has left home or wife or brothers or parents or children for the sake of the kingdom of God 30will fail to receive many times as much in this age and, in the age to come, eternal life."

Jesus Again Predicts His Death

‰ See Matthew 20:17–19; Mark 10:32–34

31Jesus took the Twelve aside and told them, "We are going up to Jerusalem, and everything that is written by the prophets about the Son of Man will be fulfilled. 32He will be handed over to the Gentiles. They will mock him, insult him, spit on him, flog him and kill him. 33On the third day he will rise again."

34The disciples did not understand any of this. Its meaning was hidden from them, and they did not know what he was talking about.

A Blind Beggar Receives His Sight

‰ See Matthew 20:29–34; Mark 10:46–52

35As Jesus approached Jericho, a blind man was sitting by the roadside begging. 36When he heard the crowd going by, he asked what was happening. 37They told him, "Jesus of Nazareth is passing by."

38He called out, "Jesus, Son of David, have mercy on me!"

39Those who led the way rebuked him and told him to be quiet, but he shouted all the more, "Son of David, have mercy on me!"

40Jesus stopped and ordered the man to be brought to him. When he came near, Jesus asked him, 41"What do you want me to do for you?"

"Lord, I want to see," he replied.

42Jesus said to him, "Receive your sight; your faith has healed you." 43Immediately he received his sight and followed Jesus, praising God. When all the people saw it, they also praised God.

Zacchaeus the Tax Collector

19 Jesus entered Jericho and was passing through. 2A man was there by the name of Zacchaeus; he was a chief tax collector and was wealthy. 3He wanted to see who Jesus was, but being a short man he could not, because of the crowd. 4So he ran ahead and climbed a sycamore-fig tree to see him, since Jesus was coming that way.

5When Jesus reached the spot, he looked up and said to him, "Zacchaeus, come down immediately. I must stay at your house today." 6So he came down at once and welcomed him gladly.

7All the people saw this and began to mutter, "He has gone to be the guest of a 'sinner.' "

8But Zacchaeus stood up and said to the Lord, "Look, Lord! Here and now I give half of my possessions to the poor, and if I have cheated anybody out of anything, I will pay back four times the amount."

9Jesus said to him, "Today salvation has come to this house, because this man, too, is a

a20 Exodus 20:12-16; Deut. 5:16-20

---

on for security. In this passage Jesus exposed a wealthy young man's dependence upon his possessions. Jesus brought him face to face with a common human problem—loving the things of this world more than God. Though we don't know whether or not this young man ever repented of his attachment to his belongings, we all are faced with the same choice. Only by renouncing our dependence on earthly wealth will we be able to receive lasting, spiritual treasure.

18:31–34 Jesus predicted the suffering he would go through on the way to the cross. While the pain and disgrace he would experience were extreme, Jesus was willing to accept them as necessary parts of the process toward the goal. The process of spiritual growth often involves pain and sacrifice, but God promises that joy will follow. Reversing patterns of sinful behavior can be difficult and discouraging. Focusing on God's promised joy can make the pain we face in our lives worth the sacrifices we may have to make.

18:40–43 Jesus would not have healed the blind man if the man had not trusted in Jesus' power to do so. The man's healing involved two parts: the man's faith and God's power. Yet when our faith is weak, God's power is still strong. Our redemption is not based on our own ability or faith but on our love for God, who has the power and desire to heal us. Our part is to repent and look to him for help.

19:1–10 The story of Zacchaeus beautifully illustrates God's acceptance and restoration of a repentant sinner. After admitting his failures to God, to himself and to others, Zacchaeus was willing to repay the people he had wronged. Making restitution to those we have harmed or cheated is crucial to our spiritual growth. However, if making restitution will only cause further injury to people we have wronged, it is enough to admit our wrongdoing to God, to ourselves and to another person.

son of Abraham. 10For the Son of Man came to
seek and to save what was lost."

The Parable of the Ten Minas

11While they were listening to this, he went
on to tell them a parable, because he was near
Jerusalem and the people thought that the kingdom of God was going to appear at once. 12He
said: "A man of noble birth went to a distant
country to have himself appointed king and
then to return. 13So he called ten of his servants
and gave them ten minas.[a] 'Put this money to
work,' he said, 'until I come back.'

14"But his subjects hated him and sent a delegation after him to say, 'We don't want this
man to be our king.'

15"He was made king, however, and returned home. Then he sent for the servants to
whom he had given the money, in order to find
out what they had gained with it.

16"The first one came and said, 'Sir, your
mina has earned ten more.'

17" 'Well done, my good servant!' his master
replied. 'Because you have been trustworthy in
a very small matter, take charge of ten cities.'

18"The second came and said, 'Sir, your
mina has earned five more.'

19"His master answered, 'You take charge of
five cities.'

20"Then another servant came and said, 'Sir,
here is your mina; I have kept it laid away in a
piece of cloth. 21I was afraid of you, because you
are a hard man. You take out what you did not
put in and reap what you did not sow.'

22"His master replied, 'I will judge you by
your own words, you wicked servant! You
knew, did you, that I am a hard man, taking out
what I did not put in, and reaping what I did
not sow? 23Why then didn't you put my money
on deposit, so that when I came back, I could
have collected it with interest?'

24"Then he said to those standing by, 'Take
his mina away from him and give it to the one
who has ten minas.'

25" 'Sir,' they said, 'he already has ten!'

[a]13 A mina was about three months' wages.

19:9–10 A central theme of Luke's Gospel is Jesus' passion to find and restore those who are lost and alienated from God. This has been God's priority since the first sin in the Garden of Eden. Immediately after Adam and Eve sinned, God sought them out as they hid in fear. He restored fellowship to them and offered them a way of redemption from their sin (see Genesis 3). The work of Jesus on the cross represents the culmination of God's plan for forgiveness, hope and restored fellowship with him.

19:11–27 This story teaches us the principle of stewardship—our accountability before God to wisely use the gifts, abilities and possessions he has entrusted to us. To wisely use what God has given will result in generous reward; to refuse to do so will bring a stern reprimand from God. Whatever opportunities and resources God gives us—whether time, money, talents or relationships—we are to multiply these in the lives of others.

Responsible to God in Business

Luke 19:1–10 The "rules" practiced in today's business world are not always the same as God's rules. We may get caught up in the game of business, trying to accumulate as much as we can or cheating others by not giving them their fair share. God will hold us accountable for this, and we must take responsibility if we have sinned in this way.

Zacchaeus's hunger for riches drove him to take more than his fair share of the money while collecting taxes from the Jews for the Roman government. His own people hated him as an extortionist and a traitor. But when Jesus reached out to him, Zacchaeus changed dramatically. "Zacchaeus stood up and said to the Lord, 'Look, Lord! Here and now I give half of my possessions to the poor, and if I have cheated anybody out of anything, I will pay back four times the amount.' Jesus said to him, 'Today salvation has come to this house' " (19:8–9).

True spiritual growth will be evidenced in practical ways. When we honestly reflect on our lives, we must consider whether we have taken more than our fair share in our dealings—business and personal. If so, it is our responsibility to give back whatever we have taken unjustly. We are responsible to God for our financial dealings as well as our spiritual choices and lifestyle.

Turn to Romans 6.

26"He replied, 'I tell you that to everyone who has, more will be given, but as for the one who has nothing, even what he has will be taken away. 27But those enemies of mine who did not want me to be king over them—bring them here and kill them in front of me.' "

The Triumphal Entry

‰ See Matthew 21:1–9; Mark 11:1–10; John 12:12–15

28After Jesus had said this, he went on ahead, going up to Jerusalem. 29As he approached Bethphage and Bethany at the hill called the Mount of Olives, he sent two of his disciples, saying to them, 30"Go to the village ahead of you, and as you enter it, you will find a colt tied there, which no one has ever ridden. Untie it and bring it here. 31If anyone asks you, 'Why are you untying it?' tell him, 'The Lord needs it.' "

32Those who were sent ahead went and found it just as he had told them. 33As they were untying the colt, its owners asked them, "Why are you untying the colt?"

34They replied, "The Lord needs it."

35They brought it to Jesus, threw their cloaks on the colt and put Jesus on it. 36As he went along, people spread their cloaks on the road.

37When he came near the place where the road goes down the Mount of Olives, the whole crowd of disciples began joyfully to praise God in loud voices for all the miracles they had seen:

38"Blessed is the king who comes in the
name of the Lord!"[a]

"Peace in heaven and glory in the highest!"

39Some of the Pharisees in the crowd said to Jesus, "Teacher, rebuke your disciples!"

40"I tell you," he replied, "if they keep quiet, the stones will cry out."

41As he approached Jerusalem and saw the city, he wept over it 42and said, "If you, even you, had only known on this day what would bring you peace—but now it is hidden from your eyes. 43The days will come upon you when your enemies will build an embankment against you and encircle you and hem you in on every side. 44They will dash you to the ground, you and the children within your walls. They will not leave one stone on another, because you did not recognize the time of God's coming to you."

Jesus at the Temple

‰ See Matthew 21:12–16; Mark 11:15–18; John 2:13–16

45Then he entered the temple area and began driving out those who were selling. 46"It is written," he said to them, " 'My house will be a house of prayer'[b]; but you have made it 'a den of robbers.'[c]"

47Every day he was teaching at the temple. But the chief priests, the teachers of the law and the leaders among the people were trying to kill him. 48Yet they could not find any way to do it, because all the people hung on his words.

The Authority of Jesus Questioned

‰ See Matthew 21:23–27; Mark 11:27–33

20 One day as he was teaching the people in the temple courts and preaching the gospel, the chief priests and the teachers of the law, together with the elders, came up to him. 2"Tell us by what authority you are doing these things," they said. "Who gave you this authority?"

3He replied, "I will also ask you a question. Tell me, 4John's baptism—was it from heaven, or from men?"

5They discussed it among themselves and said, "If we say, 'From heaven,' he will ask, 'Why didn't you believe him?' 6But if we say, 'From men,' all the people will stone us, because they are persuaded that John was a prophet."

7So they answered, "We don't know where it was from."

8Jesus said, "Neither will I tell you by what authority I am doing these things."

The Parable of the Tenants

‰ See Matthew 21:33–46; Mark 12:1–12

9He went on to tell the people this parable: "A man planted a vineyard, rented it to some farmers and went away for a long time. 10At harvest time he sent a servant to the tenants so they would give him some of the fruit of the vineyard. But the tenants beat him and sent him away empty-handed. 11He sent another servant, but that one also they beat and treated shamefully and sent away empty-handed. 12He sent still a third, and they wounded him and threw him out.

13"Then the owner of the vineyard said,

[a]38 Psalm 118:26 [b]46 Isaiah 56:7 [c]46 Jer. 7:11

19:45–48 Jesus came to show God's love for the world. However, this same Jesus who would eventually give his own life to demonstrate God's love did not tolerate sin. Jesus openly expressed his anger toward the sin of those who misused the temple. Love and accountability are compatible. God loves us enough to send Jesus to die on the cross. God also loves us enough to chastise us for our sins. If we sin or misuse our bodies (the temple of God's Holy Spirit) God will hold us accountable. We must confess our sins and forsake them.

20:9–18 No one likes being confronted. The Jewish religious leaders were no exception. They didn't appreciate God's message, so they killed the messenger. When we choose to deny the truth, there is not much others can do for us. Sometimes the truth can break through when someone speaks plainly but indirectly. Nathan used this tactic effectively with David by telling him a story that motivated David to repent of his sin (see 2 Samuel 12). Yet some people who refuse to see the truth, like Jesus' listeners, will continue in their spiritual blindness to their dying day.

'What shall I do? I will send my son, whom I love; perhaps they will respect him.'

14"But when the tenants saw him, they talked the matter over. 'This is the heir,' they said. 'Let's kill him, and the inheritance will be ours.' 15So they threw him out of the vineyard and killed him.

"What then will the owner of the vineyard do to them? 16He will come and kill those tenants and give the vineyard to others."

When the people heard this, they said, "May this never be!"

17Jesus looked directly at them and asked, "Then what is the meaning of that which is written:

" 'The stone the builders rejected
has become the capstone[a]'[b]?

18Everyone who falls on that stone will be broken to pieces, but he on whom it falls will be crushed."

19The teachers of the law and the chief priests looked for a way to arrest him immediately, because they knew he had spoken this parable against them. But they were afraid of the people.

Paying Taxes to Caesar

‰ See Matthew 22:15–22; Mark 12:13–17

20Keeping a close watch on him, they sent spies, who pretended to be honest. They hoped to catch Jesus in something he said so that they might hand him over to the power and authority of the governor. 21So the spies questioned him: "Teacher, we know that you speak and teach what is right, and that you do not show partiality but teach the way of God in accordance with the truth. 22Is it right for us to pay taxes to Caesar or not?"

23He saw through their duplicity and said to them, 24"Show me a denarius. Whose portrait and inscription are on it?"

25"Caesar's," they replied.

He said to them, "Then give to Caesar what is Caesar's, and to God what is God's."

26They were unable to trap him in what he had said there in public. And astonished by his answer, they became silent.

The Resurrection and Marriage

‰ See Matthew 22:23–33; Mark 12:18–27

27Some of the Sadducees, who say there is no resurrection, came to Jesus with a question. 28"Teacher," they said, "Moses wrote for us that if a man's brother dies and leaves a wife but no children, the man must marry the widow and have children for his brother. 29Now there were seven brothers. The first one married a woman and died childless. 30The second 31and then the third married her, and in the same way the seven died, leaving no children. 32Finally, the woman died too. 33Now then, at the resurrection whose wife will she be, since the seven were married to her?"

34Jesus replied, "The people of this age marry and are given in marriage. 35But those who are considered worthy of taking part in that age and in the resurrection from the dead will neither marry nor be given in marriage, 36and they can no longer die; for they are like the angels. They are God's children, since they are children of the resurrection. 37But in the account of the bush, even Moses showed that the dead rise, for he calls the Lord 'the God of Abraham, and the God of Isaac, and the God of Jacob.'[c] 38He is not the God of the dead, but of the living, for to him all are alive."

39Some of the teachers of the law responded, "Well said, teacher!" 40And no one dared to ask him any more questions.

Whose Son Is the Christ?

‰ See Matthew 22:41—23:7; Mark 12:35–40

41Then Jesus said to them, "How is it that they say the Christ[d] is the Son of David? 42David himself declares in the Book of Psalms:

" 'The Lord said to my Lord:
"Sit at my right hand
43until I make your enemies
a footstool for your feet." '[e]

44David calls him 'Lord.' How then can he be his son?"

45While all the people were listening, Jesus said to his disciples, 46"Beware of the teachers of the law. They like to walk around in flowing robes and love to be greeted in the marketplaces and have the most important seats in the synagogues and the places of honor at banquets. 47They devour widows' houses and for a show make lengthy prayers. Such men will be punished most severely."

The Widow's Offering

‰ See Mark 12:41–44

21 As he looked up, Jesus saw the rich putting their gifts into the temple treasury. 2He also saw a poor widow put in two very small copper coins.[f] 3"I tell you the truth," he said, "this poor widow has put in more than all the others. 4All these people gave their gifts out of their wealth; but she out of her poverty put in all she had to live on."

a17 Or *cornerstone* b17 Psalm 118:22
c37 Exodus 3:6 d41 Or *Messiah* e43 Psalm 110:1
f2 Greek *two lepta*

21:1–4 God uses a different standard when he measures giving and givers. With God, attitude counts more than amount, so Jesus praised this widow. A generous person is not one who gives conveniently and comfortably out of abundance. A generous person in God's eyes is one who risks all, sacrifices cheerfully and gives without demanding attention or expecting a reward. Whether it's our time, talents or money, God wants us to give everything to him.

Signs of the End of the Age

‰ See Matthew 24; Mark 13

[5]Some of his disciples were remarking about
how the temple was adorned with beautiful
stones and with gifts dedicated to God. But
Jesus said, [6]"As for what you see here, the time
will come when not one stone will be left on
another; every one of them will be thrown
down."

[7]"Teacher," they asked, "when will these
things happen? And what will be the sign that
they are about to take place?"

[8]He replied: "Watch out that you are not
deceived. For many will come in my name,
claiming, 'I am he,' and, 'The time is near.' Do
not follow them. [9]When you hear of wars and
revolutions, do not be frightened. These things
must happen first, but the end will not come
right away."

[10]Then he said to them: "Nation will rise
against nation, and kingdom against kingdom.
[11]There will be great earthquakes, famines and
pestilences in various places, and fearful events
and great signs from heaven.

[12]"But before all this, they will lay hands on
you and persecute you. They will deliver you
to synagogues and prisons, and you will be
brought before kings and governors, and all on
account of my name. [13]This will result in your
being witnesses to them. [14]But make up your
mind not to worry beforehand how you will
defend yourselves. [15]For I will give you words
and wisdom that none of your adversaries will
be able to resist or contradict. [16]You will be
betrayed even by parents, brothers, relatives
and friends, and they will put some of you to
death. [17]All men will hate you because of me.
[18]But not a hair of your head will perish. [19]By
standing firm you will gain life.

[20]"When you see Jerusalem being surrounded by armies, you will know that its desolation
is near. [21]Then let those who are in Judea flee to
the mountains, let those in the city get out, and
let those in the country not enter the city. [22]For
this is the time of punishment in fulfillment of
all that has been written. [23]How dreadful it will
be in those days for pregnant women and nursing mothers! There will be great distress in the
land and wrath against this people. [24]They will
fall by the sword and will be taken as prisoners
to all the nations. Jerusalem will be trampled
on by the Gentiles until the times of the Gentiles are fulfilled.

[25]"There will be signs in the sun, moon and
stars. On the earth, nations will be in anguish
and perplexity at the roaring and tossing of the
sea. [26]Men will faint from terror, apprehensive
of what is coming on the world, for the heavenly bodies will be shaken. [27]At that time they will
see the Son of Man coming in a cloud with
power and great glory. [28]When these things begin to take place, stand up and lift up your
heads, because your redemption is drawing
near."

[29]He told them this parable: "Look at the fig
tree and all the trees. [30]When they sprout leaves,
you can see for yourselves and know that summer is near. [31]Even so, when you see these
things happening, you know that the kingdom
of God is near.

[32]"I tell you the truth, this generation[a] will
certainly not pass away until all these things
have happened. [33]Heaven and earth will pass
away, but my words will never pass away.

[34]"Be careful, or your hearts will be weighed
down with dissipation, drunkenness and the
anxieties of life, and that day will close on you
unexpectedly like a trap. [35]For it will come upon
all those who live on the face of the whole
earth. [36]Be always on the watch, and pray that
you may be able to escape all that is about to
happen, and that you may be able to stand
before the Son of Man."

[37]Each day Jesus was teaching at the temple,
and each evening he went out to spend the
night on the hill called the Mount of Olives,
[38]and all the people came early in the morning
to hear him at the temple.

Judas Agrees to Betray Jesus

‰ See Matthew 26:2–5; Mark 14:1–2,10–11

22 Now the Feast of Unleavened Bread,
called the Passover, was approaching,
[2]and the chief priests and the teachers of the law
were looking for some way to get rid of Jesus,
for they were afraid of the people. [3]Then Satan

[a]32 Or *race*

21:16–17 What happened to Jesus leading up to the cross, and what would happen to his disciples afterwards, illustrates an important principle. The people around us are not always pleased about our changed lives. Our faith in Jesus, as well as our freedom from sin, may threaten their status quo. As they resist what we know is best for us, those closest to us may even become our greatest source of hurt and misunderstanding. As we become aware of this, we should not allow them to slow us down. In time, our faithful example may lead them to seek spiritual renewal too.

21:34–36 This charge follows a lengthy prophecy about the coming days of destruction (see 21:5–31) and illustrates the Biblical purpose of prophecy. Prophecy is not meant to satisfy the curiosity of those who wonder about God's plan for the future. Prophecy is given to urge God's people to repent, stay alert and prepare their hearts spiritually. As we await Christ's return, God warns about the danger of a life controlled by sin. We only fool ourselves if we believe we have all the time in the world to get ready. If we continue to delay our repentance, we will be sorry one day!

22:3–6 At the deepest level, brokenness, bondage and temptation to sin are a result of Satan's influence. But Satan's involvement does not excuse our sin. Whatever role Satan may have in enticing us to sin, we are still accountable for our choices. God offers us a way of escape if we turn to him in times of temptation (see 1 Corinthians 10:13). No matter what Satan does to harm us, God is able to use those evil plans to work God's good plan of deliverance. God's plan is never thwarted (see Job 42:2). Jesus' death at the hands of Satan was part of God's plan

entered Judas, called Iscariot, one of the Twelve.
[4]And Judas went to the chief priests and the
officers of the temple guard and discussed with
them how he might betray Jesus. [5]They were
delighted and agreed to give him money. [6]He
consented, and watched for an opportunity to
hand Jesus over to them when no crowd was
present.

The Last Supper

‰ See Matthew 26:17–19,26–29; Mark 14:12–16,22–25

[7]Then came the day of Unleavened Bread on
which the Passover lamb had to be sacrificed.
[8]Jesus sent Peter and John, saying, "Go and
make preparations for us to eat the Passover."
[9]"Where do you want us to prepare for it?"
they asked.
[10]He replied, "As you enter the city, a man
carrying a jar of water will meet you. Follow
him to the house that he enters, [11]and say to the
owner of the house, 'The Teacher asks: Where is
the guest room, where I may eat the Passover
with my disciples?' [12]He will show you a large
upper room, all furnished. Make preparations
there."
[13]They left and found things just as Jesus had
told them. So they prepared the Passover.
[14]When the hour came, Jesus and his apostles reclined at the table. [15]And he said to them,
"I have eagerly desired to eat this Passover with
you before I suffer. [16]For I tell you, I will not eat
it again until it finds fulfillment in the kingdom
of God."
[17]After taking the cup, he gave thanks and
said, "Take this and divide it among you. [18]For
I tell you I will not drink again of the fruit of the
vine until the kingdom of God comes."
[19]And he took bread, gave thanks and broke
it, and gave it to them, saying, "This is my body
given for you; do this in remembrance of me."
[20]In the same way, after the supper he took
the cup, saying, "This cup is the new covenant
in my blood, which is poured out for you. [21]But
the hand of him who is going to betray me is
with mine on the table. [22]The Son of Man will
go as it has been decreed, but woe to that man
who betrays him." [23]They began to question
among themselves which of them it might be
who would do this.
[24]Also a dispute arose among them as to
which of them was considered to be greatest.
[25]Jesus said to them, "The kings of the Gentiles
lord it over them; and those who exercise authority over them call themselves Benefactors.
[26]But you are not to be like that. Instead, the
greatest among you should be like the youngest,
and the one who rules like the one who serves.
[27]For who is greater, the one who is at the table
or the one who serves? Is it not the one who is
at the table? But I am among you as one who
serves. [28]You are those who have stood by me
in my trials. [29]And I confer on you a kingdom,
just as my Father conferred one on me, [30]so that
you may eat and drink at my table in my kingdom and sit on thrones, judging the twelve
tribes of Israel.
[31]"Simon, Simon, Satan has asked to sift
you[a] as wheat. [32]But I have prayed for you,
Simon, that your faith may not fail. And when
you have turned back, strengthen your brothers."
[33]But he replied, "Lord, I am ready to go with
you to prison and to death."
[34]Jesus answered, "I tell you, Peter, before
the rooster crows today, you will deny three
times that you know me."
[35]Then Jesus asked them, "When I sent you
without purse, bag or sandals, did you lack anything?"
"Nothing," they answered.
[36]He said to them, "But now if you have a
purse, take it, and also a bag; and if you don't
have a sword, sell your cloak and buy one. [37]It
is written: 'And he was numbered with the
transgressors'[b]; and I tell you that this must be
fulfilled in me. Yes, what is written about me is
reaching its fulfillment."
[38]The disciples said, "See, Lord, here are two
swords."
"That is enough," he replied.

Jesus Prays on the Mount of Olives

‰ See Matthew 26:36–46; Mark 14:32–42

[39]Jesus went out as usual to the Mount of

[a]31 The Greek is plural. [b]37 Isaiah 53:12

---

all along (see Isaiah 46:10–11). Since Jesus defeated Satan at the cross, we now have access to God's power to resist Satan's temptations. We should seek God and surrender to him each time we are tempted to sin.

22:20 The cup of wine that Jesus and his disciples shared symbolized the blood of Jesus, which would institute the new covenant (see Jeremiah 31:31–34). Jesus Christ was the sacrificial Lamb of God, who removes the sins of the world (see John 1:29). Without this provision for sin, we have no peace or serenity. But with it, we have an open invitation to receive God's gracious forgiveness. We can now rest secure in God's grace, which allows us to remove the guilt of our sin.

22:24–30 This upper room discourse contrasts Jesus' humility and servant's heart with the selfish intentions of his twelve closest followers. In going to the cross, Jesus illustrated what it meant to be a servant-leader. The disciples' desire for a special place at God's table was not what Jesus wanted to teach them. Jesus calls us to put the needs of others first and serve others rather than expect to be served. Our lives should be characterized and motivated by humility and service.

22:31–34 Simon Peter and Judas were both influenced by Satan (see 22:3–6). Peter broke his commitment to Jesus and found his life careening out of control. Yet Jesus held out to Peter the hope of repentance and restoration. Jesus knows we will betray or deny him too, and he makes gracious provision for that. Though we may have been "sifted" by Satan, it is never too late to turn back to Jesus.

22:39–46 Jesus' prayer in the Garden of Gethsemane reflected the awesome task before him: He would shoulder the sins of the world. Jesus' commitment and faith to submit to God's sovereign will is an example for us of prayer

Olives, and his disciples followed him. **40**On reaching the place, he said to them, "Pray that you will not fall into temptation." **41**He withdrew about a stone's throw beyond them, knelt down and prayed, **42**"Father, if you are willing, take this cup from me; yet not my will, but yours be done." **43**An angel from heaven appeared to him and strengthened him. **44**And being in anguish, he prayed more earnestly, and his sweat was like drops of blood falling to the ground.[a]

45When he rose from prayer and went back to the disciples, he found them asleep, exhausted from sorrow. **46**"Why are you sleeping?" he asked them. "Get up and pray so that you will not fall into temptation."

Jesus Arrested

‰ See Matthew 26:47–56; Mark 14:43–50; John 18:3–11

47While he was still speaking a crowd came up, and the man who was called Judas, one of the Twelve, was leading them. He approached Jesus to kiss him, **48**but Jesus asked him, "Judas, are you betraying the Son of Man with a kiss?"

49When Jesus' followers saw what was going to happen, they said, "Lord, should we strike with our swords?" **50**And one of them struck the servant of the high priest, cutting off his right ear.

51But Jesus answered, "No more of this!" And he touched the man's ear and healed him.

52Then Jesus said to the chief priests, the officers of the temple guard, and the elders, who had come for him, "Am I leading a rebellion, that you have come with swords and clubs? **53**Every day I was with you in the temple courts, and you did not lay a hand on me. But this is your hour—when darkness reigns."

Peter Disowns Jesus

‰ See Matthew 26:69–75; Mark 14:66–72; John 18:16–18,25–27

54Then seizing him, they led him away and took him into the house of the high priest. Peter followed at a distance. **55**But when they had kindled a fire in the middle of the courtyard and had sat down together, Peter sat down with them. **56**A servant girl saw him seated there in the firelight. She looked closely at him and said, "This man was with him."

57But he denied it. "Woman, I don't know him," he said.

58A little later someone else saw him and said, "You also are one of them."

"Man, I am not!" Peter replied.

59About an hour later another asserted, "Certainly this fellow was with him, for he is a Galilean."

60Peter replied, "Man, I don't know what you're talking about!" Just as he was speaking, the rooster crowed. **61**The Lord turned and looked straight at Peter. Then Peter remembered the word the Lord had spoken to him: "Before the rooster crows today, you will disown me three times." **62**And he went outside and wept bitterly.

The Guards Mock Jesus

‰ See Matthew 26:67–68; Mark 14:65; John 18:22–23

63The men who were guarding Jesus began mocking and beating him. **64**They blindfolded him and demanded, "Prophesy! Who hit you?" **65**And they said many other insulting things to him.

Jesus Before Pilate and Herod

‰ See Matthew 26:63–66; Mark 14:61–63; John 18:19–21

66At daybreak the council of the elders of the people, both the chief priests and teachers of the law, met together, and Jesus was led before them. **67**"If you are the Christ,[b]" they said, "tell us."

Jesus answered, "If I tell you, you will not believe me, **68**and if I asked you, you would not answer. **69**But from now on, the Son of Man will be seated at the right hand of the mighty God."

70They all asked, "Are you then the Son of God?"

He replied, "You are right in saying I am."

71Then they said, "Why do we need any more testimony? We have heard it from his own lips."

23 Then the whole assembly rose and led him off to Pilate. **2**And they began to accuse him, saying, "We have found this man subverting our nation. He opposes payment of taxes to Caesar and claims to be Christ,[c] a king."

3So Pilate asked Jesus, "Are you the king of the Jews?"

"Yes, it is as you say," Jesus replied.

[a] 44 Some early manuscripts do not have verses 43 and 44. [b] 67 Or *Messiah* [c] 2 Or *Messiah;* also in verses 35 and 39

---

and perseverance. Jesus could have selfishly seized the privileges of deity and avoided the cross (see Philippians 2:6–8). Instead, he was willing to surrender to the will of his Father in heaven to accomplish this difficult task. Although our challenges in life will never be of this magnitude, there will be times when what God calls us to do may seem more than we can face. At such times, we must surrender our wills and accept the will of our Father in heaven. God will help us with the task and will reward us with new life.

22:54–62 Though Peter promised undying loyalty (see 22:31–34), he denied Jesus completely when things got difficult. Peter not only disappointed Jesus; he also disappointed himself. But all was not lost. Peter's threefold denial was followed by a threefold affirmation. Peter's experience led to his genuine sorrow, repentance and restoration to full-fledged service (see John 21:15–19). Eventually, Peter became the leading spokesman of the early church, powerfully proclaiming the message of the risen Christ. Only by God's complete forgiveness could Peter have so effectively recovered from the depths of despair.

4Then Pilate announced to the chief priests and the crowd, "I find no basis for a charge against this man."

5But they insisted, "He stirs up the people all over Judea[a] by his teaching. He started in Galilee and has come all the way here."

6On hearing this, Pilate asked if the man was a Galilean. 7When he learned that Jesus was under Herod's jurisdiction, he sent him to Herod, who was also in Jerusalem at that time.

8When Herod saw Jesus, he was greatly pleased, because for a long time he had been wanting to see him. From what he had heard about him, he hoped to see him perform some miracle. 9He plied him with many questions, but Jesus gave him no answer. 10The chief priests and the teachers of the law were standing there, vehemently accusing him. 11Then Herod and his soldiers ridiculed and mocked him. Dressing him in an elegant robe, they sent him back to Pilate. 12That day Herod and Pilate became friends—before this they had been enemies.

13Pilate called together the chief priests, the rulers and the people, 14and said to them, "You brought me this man as one who was inciting the people to rebellion. I have examined him in your presence and have found no basis for your charges against him. 15Neither has Herod, for he sent him back to us; as you can see, he has done nothing to deserve death. 16Therefore, I will punish him and then release him.[b]"

18With one voice they cried out, "Away with this man! Release Barabbas to us!" 19(Barabbas had been thrown into prison for an insurrection in the city, and for murder.)

20Wanting to release Jesus, Pilate appealed to them again. 21But they kept shouting, "Crucify him! Crucify him!"

22For the third time he spoke to them: "Why? What crime has this man committed? I have found in him no grounds for the death penalty. Therefore I will have him punished and then release him."

23But with loud shouts they insistently demanded that he be crucified, and their shouts prevailed. 24So Pilate decided to grant their demand. 25He released the man who had been thrown into prison for insurrection and murder, the one they asked for, and surrendered Jesus to their will.

The Crucifixion

‰ See Matthew 27:33–44; Mark 15:22–32; John 19:17–24

26As they led him away, they seized Simon from Cyrene, who was on his way in from the country, and put the cross on him and made him carry it behind Jesus. 27A large number of people followed him, including women who mourned and wailed for him. 28Jesus turned and said to them, "Daughters of Jerusalem, do not weep for me; weep for yourselves and for your children. 29For the time will come when you will say, 'Blessed are the barren women, the wombs that never bore and the breasts that never nursed!' 30Then

" 'they will say to the mountains, "Fall on us!"
and to the hills, "Cover us!" '[c]

31For if men do these things when the tree is green, what will happen when it is dry?"

32Two other men, both criminals, were also led out with him to be executed. 33When they came to the place called the Skull, there they crucified him, along with the criminals—one on his right, the other on his left. 34Jesus said, "Father, forgive them, for they do not know what they are doing."[d] And they divided up his clothes by casting lots.

35The people stood watching, and the rulers even sneered at him. They said, "He saved others; let him save himself if he is the Christ of God, the Chosen One."

36The soldiers also came up and mocked him. They offered him wine vinegar 37and said, "If you are the king of the Jews, save yourself."

38There was a written notice above him, which read: THIS IS THE KING OF THE JEWS.

39One of the criminals who hung there hurled insults at him: "Aren't you the Christ? Save yourself and us!"

40But the other criminal rebuked him. "Don't you fear God," he said, "since you are under the same sentence? 41We are punished justly, for we are getting what our deeds deserve. But this man has done nothing wrong."

[a]5 Or *over the land of the Jews* [b]16 Some manuscripts *him." 17Now he was obliged to release one man to them at the Feast.* [c]30 Hosea 10:8 [d]34 Some early manuscripts do not have this sentence.

23:13–25 Pilate recognized that the members of the Sanhedrin were lying to get what they wanted. Yet he did not act on his convictions but rather acquiesced to political expediency and moral compromise to save his job. Perceiving Jesus as a political threat, Pilate denied him his human dignity and rights. The truth often comes out, vindicating the innocent person, but not before a price has been paid. Telling the truth and doing the right thing are always crucial to our spiritual renewal.

23:32–34 In the most unjust situation in history, Jesus extended forgiveness without limit to those who nailed him to the cross. If Christ forgave in this way from the cross, surely no sin of ours is too great for his forgiveness. And as we experience his forgiveness, we are free to forgive those who have sinned against us. Christ enables us to release our bitterness and resentment, which can only imprison us. His forgiveness empowers us to be forgiving people—forgiving ourselves as well as those who have hurt us.

23:40–43 The piercing self-examination of the criminal crucified alongside Jesus was the prelude to his salvation. His attitude stands in stark contrast to the self-sufficient, bitter cynicism of the other criminal, who died in bondage to sin and despair. It is never too late to choose to turn to Jesus for salvation.

42 Then he said, "Jesus, remember me when you come into your kingdom.[a]"

43 Jesus answered him, "I tell you the truth, today you will be with me in paradise."

Jesus' Death

‰ See Matthew 27:45–56; Mark 15:33–41; John 19:29–30

44 It was now about the sixth hour, and darkness came over the whole land until the ninth hour, 45 for the sun stopped shining. And the curtain of the temple was torn in two. 46 Jesus called out with a loud voice, "Father, into your hands I commit my spirit." When he had said this, he breathed his last.

47 The centurion, seeing what had happened, praised God and said, "Surely this was a righteous man." 48 When all the people who had gathered to witness this sight saw what took place, they beat their breasts and went away. 49 But all those who knew him, including the women who had followed him from Galilee, stood at a distance, watching these things.

Jesus' Burial

‰ See Matthew 27:57–61; Mark 15:42–47; John 19:38–42

50 Now there was a man named Joseph, a member of the Council, a good and upright man, 51 who had not consented to their decision and action. He came from the Judean town of Arimathea and he was waiting for the kingdom of God. 52 Going to Pilate, he asked for Jesus' body. 53 Then he took it down, wrapped it in linen cloth and placed it in a tomb cut in the rock, one in which no one had yet been laid. 54 It was Preparation Day, and the Sabbath was about to begin.

55 The women who had come with Jesus from Galilee followed Joseph and saw the tomb and how his body was laid in it. 56 Then they went home and prepared spices and perfumes. But they rested on the Sabbath in obedience to the commandment.

The Resurrection

‰ See Matthew 28:1–8; Mark 16:1–8; John 20:1–8

24 On the first day of the week, very early in the morning, the women took the spices they had prepared and went to the tomb. 2 They found the stone rolled away from the tomb, 3 but when they entered, they did not find the body of the Lord Jesus. 4 While they were wondering about this, suddenly two men in clothes that gleamed like lightning stood beside them. 5 In their fright the women bowed down with their faces to the ground, but the men said to them, "Why do you look for the living among the dead? 6 He is not here; he has risen! Remember how he told you, while he was still with you in Galilee: 7 'The Son of Man must be delivered into the hands of sinful men, be crucified and on the third day be raised again.' " 8 Then they remembered his words.

9 When they came back from the tomb, they told all these things to the Eleven and to all the others. 10 It was Mary Magdalene, Joanna, Mary the mother of James, and the others with them who told this to the apostles. 11 But they did not believe the women, because their words seemed to them like nonsense. 12 Peter, however, got up and ran to the tomb. Bending over, he saw the strips of linen lying by themselves, and he went away, wondering to himself what had happened.

On the Road to Emmaus

13 Now that same day two of them were going to a village called Emmaus, about seven miles[b] from Jerusalem. 14 They were talking with each other about everything that had happened. 15 As they talked and discussed these things with each other, Jesus himself came up and walked along with them; 16 but they were kept from recognizing him.

17 He asked them, "What are you discussing together as you walk along?"

They stood still, their faces downcast. 18 One of them, named Cleopas, asked him, "Are you only a visitor to Jerusalem and do not know the things that have happened there in these days?"

19 "What things?" he asked.

"About Jesus of Nazareth," they replied. "He was a prophet, powerful in word and deed before God and all the people. 20 The chief priests and our rulers handed him over to be sentenced to death, and they crucified him; 21 but we had hoped that he was the one who was going to redeem Israel. And what is more, it is the third day since all this took place. 22 In addition, some of our women amazed us. They went to the tomb early this morning 23 but didn't find his body. They came and told us that they had seen a vision of angels, who said he was alive. 24 Then some of our companions went to the tomb and

[a] 42 Some manuscripts *come with your kingly power*
[b] 13 Greek *sixty stadia* (about 11 kilometers)

24:1–12 During Jesus' arrest and trial, most of the disciples ran away. They lacked the power and courage to face those who crucified Jesus. After the resurrection, the book of Acts records that the disciples were filled with a new power, giving them both the courage and strength to go into the world with God's Good News. The power of the Holy Spirit is greater than death itself and is more than able to help us overcome the sins that enslave us (see John 16:7–8). As we experience Christ's resurrection in our lives, we will enjoy victory over temptation and power to live lives free of bondage.

24:13–24 The disciples on the road to Emmaus were deeply discouraged and grieved by the events of the past few days. They did not fully comprehend who Jesus was or how God could turn their pain into joy. When Jesus revealed himself, they were lifted out of their grief to become people who could help change the world. By meeting and speaking with the resurrected Messiah, the disciples' despair turned to joy, their doubt to faith and their confusion to confidence in the fulfillment of God's Word.

found it just as the women had said, but him they did not see."

[25]He said to them, "How foolish you are, and how slow of heart to believe all that the prophets have spoken! [26]Did not the Christ[a] have to suffer these things and then enter his glory?" [27]And beginning with Moses and all the Prophets, he explained to them what was said in all the Scriptures concerning himself.

[28]As they approached the village to which they were going, Jesus acted as if he were going farther. [29]But they urged him strongly, "Stay with us, for it is nearly evening; the day is almost over." So he went in to stay with them.

[30]When he was at the table with them, he took bread, gave thanks, broke it and began to give it to them. [31]Then their eyes were opened and they recognized him, and he disappeared from their sight. [32]They asked each other, "Were not our hearts burning within us while he talked with us on the road and opened the Scriptures to us?"

[33]They got up and returned at once to Jerusalem. There they found the Eleven and those with them, assembled together [34]and saying, "It is true! The Lord has risen and has appeared to Simon." [35]Then the two told what had happened on the way, and how Jesus was recognized by them when he broke the bread.

Jesus Appears to the Disciples

[36]While they were still talking about this, Jesus himself stood among them and said to them, "Peace be with you."

[37]They were startled and frightened, thinking they saw a ghost. [38]He said to them, "Why are you troubled, and why do doubts rise in your minds? [39]Look at my hands and my feet. It is I myself! Touch me and see; a ghost does not have flesh and bones, as you see I have."

[40]When he had said this, he showed them his hands and feet. [41]And while they still did not believe it because of joy and amazement, he asked them, "Do you have anything here to eat?" [42]They gave him a piece of broiled fish, [43]and he took it and ate it in their presence.

[44]He said to them, "This is what I told you while I was still with you: Everything must be fulfilled that is written about me in the Law of Moses, the Prophets and the Psalms."

[45]Then he opened their minds so they could understand the Scriptures. [46]He told them, "This is what is written: The Christ will suffer and rise from the dead on the third day, [47]and repentance and forgiveness of sins will be preached in his name to all nations, beginning at Jerusalem. [48]You are witnesses of these things. [49]I am going to send you what my Father has promised; but stay in the city until you have been clothed with power from on high."

The Ascension

[50]When he had led them out to the vicinity of Bethany, he lifted up his hands and blessed them. [51]While he was blessing them, he left them and was taken up into heaven. [52]Then they worshiped him and returned to Jerusalem with great joy. [53]And they stayed continually at the temple, praising God.

[a]26 Or *Messiah;* also in verse 46

24:36–49 Jesus is alive and well, yet this was not immediately evident to his first followers in the upper room. They were banded together in their grief and pain when the living Christ appeared to them. Jesus is still alive. He can calm our fears and doubts. The task of spreading the Good News was an overwhelming job for the first-century believers. Through the promised Holy Spirit, the believers received the power to spread the Good News and become living witnesses of God's transforming work (see Acts 2). We have the same power available to us today through the Holy Spirit.

JOHN

The Big Picture

A. THE GLORIOUS SOURCE OF NEW LIFE REVEALED (1:1-18)

B. JESUS GIVES NEW LIFE (1:19–3:36)

C. SATISFYING THE LONGINGS OF YOUR SOUL (4:1–7:53)

D. COMING INTO THE LIGHT FOR FREEDOM FROM A PAINFUL PAST (8:1–9:41)

E. EMBRACING AND CELEBRATING AN ABUNDANT LIFE (10:1–12:50)

F. LOVING OTHERS AS JESUS HAS LOVED US (13:1–17:26)

G. THE CRUCIFIXION: EVERYTHING SEEMS TO FALL APART (18:1–19:42)

H. THE RESURRECTION (20:1–21:25)

From the vast stretches of eternity to the confines of time the Son of God came. The Creator of the world immersed himself in his creation, and Jesus entered this world. Jesus, the Son of God, became a man and willingly sacrificed himself so that all who would receive him could have forgiveness and redemption. This is the message of John's gospel.

In a number of different ways John illustrated who Jesus is and how he gives us eternal life. He showed us images of Jesus as the unblemished lamb sacrificed for us, the bread who satisfies our spiritual hunger and the living water who satisfies our spiritual thirst. We also see Jesus as the light who guides us, the shepherd who leads us, the vine who gives us life, and the counselor who comforts and teaches us. Through these images, John illustrated that Jesus provides all we need for new, abundant lives.

John also recorded Jesus' miracles to show us Jesus' power to transform lives. This Gospel is filled with examples of God's power in those needing new life. With God's help, we can drink the new wine of a changed life. We can accept responsibility for our lives, walk away from the sin that paralyzes us, recover from our sicknesses, be healed of our blindness to the truth, escape from bondage to sin, be protected from condemnation and be raised from a dead and empty existence to new life.

John penned these images and miracles to help us see Jesus for who he is—the Son of God. When we acknowledge the truth about Jesus' identity and character, we can begin to experience the new life that he offers to all who believe.

Spiritual Renewal Themes

THE POWER OF GOD

John records more miracles than any of the other gospel narratives, including six which are not recorded elsewhere. In each miracle God's power is clearly demonstrated. Jesus healed a man born blind; Jesus walked on water and then calmed a storm. John also records that Jesus healed a nobleman's son without even being present, and he raised Lazarus from the dead after Lazarus had been buried for more than three days. John did more than tell us about the life of Christ—he emphasized that Jesus is the embodiment of all of God's power. God's

power is promised to us when we recognize our weakness and call upon Jesus to help us.

GOD'S POWER CAN BE WITHIN US

Our spiritual renewal results from God's power at work within us. Jesus pictured God's power in our lives as a branch attached to the trunk of a vine, drawing life and power from it. Jesus told us that he is the bread of life and that we are to eat that bread. He said that he has water for us to drink that will quench our thirst forever. Each of these images illustrated his promise given in the upper room of the Holy Spirit's presence in our lives. When we surrender our lives to God, the Holy Spirit comes to live within us, to teach us, comfort us, guide us, transform us and empower us daily.

THE DANGERS OF SPIRITUAL BLINDNESS

In Jesus' early ministry, large crowds followed him. But as Jesus confronted the people with their sin, the crowds gradually thinned out. The people were unwilling to face the sin that Jesus exposed in their lives, and they rejected the only one who could help them. Times have changed, but the pattern of spiritual blindness remains the same: We may question the truth and eventually develop a rigid resistance to it. Our hearts become hardened to the obvious truth. As he confronted the crowds in John's day, so Jesus also confronts us with the changes we need to make. It takes courage to be open and willing to face the truth about ourselves, but doing so is essential to our spiritual renewal.

THE INVITATION TO RELATIONSHIP

Although each of the Gospels reveals Jesus' love, John presented love as a central theme in his narrative. In the upper room, Jesus said that the mark of following him is having love for others (see 13:34–35). Jesus prayed that we would be united in love as he and the Father are (see 17:21–26). John referred to himself in this Gospel as "the disciple whom Jesus loved" (21:20). In one of his later letters, he wrote that the greatest evidence of God's presence in our lives is our love for others (see 1 John 4:11–12, 20–21). Recognizing God's love for us and valuing and respecting others is central to our relationship with God and our ongoing spiritual growth.

Essential Facts

PURPOSE:
To reveal Jesus as the Son of God and to show that by faith in him we can experience true love, forgiveness and spiritual renewal.

AUTHOR:
John, a disciple and brother of James; both were called "Sons of Thunder" (Mark 3:17).

AUDIENCE:
All people everywhere.

DATE WRITTEN:
Probably between A.D. 80 and 90.

SETTING:
After many years of reflecting on his experience as a disciple of Jesus, the apostle John recorded this unique gospel narrative.

KEY VERSE:
"These [things] are written that you may believe that Jesus is the Christ, the Son of God, and that by believing you may have life in his name" (20:31).

KEY PEOPLE AND RELATIONSHIPS:
Jesus with John the Baptist, the disciples, Mary, Martha, Lazarus, the religious leaders, Pilate and Mary Magdalene.

The Word Became Flesh

1 In the beginning was the Word, and the Word was with God, and the Word was God. 2He was with God in the beginning.

3Through him all things were made; without him nothing was made that has been made. 4In him was life, and that life was the light of men. 5The light shines in the darkness, but the darkness has not understood[a] it.

6There came a man who was sent from God; his name was John. 7He came as a witness to testify concerning that light, so that through him all men might believe. 8He himself was not the light; he came only as a witness to the light. 9The true light that gives light to every man was coming into the world.[b]

10He was in the world, and though the world was made through him, the world did not recognize him. 11He came to that which was his own, but his own did not receive him. 12Yet to all who received him, to those who believed in his name, he gave the right to become children of God— 13children born not of natural descent,[c] nor of human decision or a husband's will, but born of God.

14The Word became flesh and made his dwelling among us. We have seen his glory, the glory of the One and Only,[d] who came from the Father, full of grace and truth.

15John testifies concerning him. He cries out, saying, "This was he of whom I said, 'He who comes after me has surpassed me because he was before me.'" 16From the fullness of his grace we have all received one blessing after another. 17For the law was given through Moses; grace and truth came through Jesus Christ. 18No one has ever seen God, but God the One and Only,[d,e] who is at the Father's side, has made him known.

John the Baptist Denies Being the Christ

19Now this was John's testimony when the Jews of Jerusalem sent priests and Levites to ask him who he was. 20He did not fail to confess, but confessed freely, "I am not the Christ.[f]"

21They asked him, "Then who are you? Are you Elijah?"

He said, "I am not."

"Are you the Prophet?"

He answered, "No."

22Finally they said, "Who are you? Give us an answer to take back to those who sent us. What do you say about yourself?"

23John replied in the words of Isaiah the prophet, "I am the voice of one calling in the desert, 'Make straight the way for the Lord.'"[g]

24Now some Pharisees who had been sent 25questioned him, "Why then do you baptize if you are not the Christ, nor Elijah, nor the Prophet?"

26"I baptize with[h] water," John replied, "but among you stands one you do not know. 27He is the one who comes after me, the thongs of whose sandals I am not worthy to untie."

28This all happened at Bethany on the other side of the Jordan, where John was baptizing.

Jesus the Lamb of God

29The next day John saw Jesus coming toward him and said, "Look, the Lamb of God, who takes away the sin of the world! 30This is the one I meant when I said, 'A man who comes after me has surpassed me because he was before me.' 31I myself did not know him, but the reason I came baptizing with water was that he might be revealed to Israel."

32Then John gave this testimony: "I saw the Spirit come down from heaven as a dove and remain on him. 33I would not have known him, except that the one who sent me to baptize with water told me, 'The man on whom you see the Spirit come down and remain is he who will baptize with the Holy Spirit.' 34I have seen and I testify that this is the Son of God."

Jesus' First Disciples

35The next day John was there again with two

[a]5 Or *darkness, and the darkness has not overcome*
[b]9 Or *This was the true light that gives light to every man who comes into the world* [c]13 Greek *of bloods*
[d]14,18 Or *the Only Begotten* [e]18 Some manuscripts *but the only* (or *only begotten*) *Son* [f]20 Or *Messiah.* "The Christ" (Greek) and "the Messiah" (Hebrew) both mean "the Anointed One"; also in verse 25.
[g]23 Isaiah 40:3 [h]26 Or *in;* also in verses 31 and 33

1:1–13 The same God who created the universe is able to create new life within us. The light of life that exposes and drives away the darkness of the human race is the same light that brightens the dark corners of our world. This true light of the world and source of all life is also the source of our spiritual renewal.

1:14–18 The true light of the world became a human being, Jesus Christ (see 1:1–9). Jesus was both fully God and fully human. Through Jesus we can know what God is like and can enjoy a relationship with him. Jesus Christ came to provide a way of redemption for us and to reveal God's truth to us. God, in his mercy, forgives us, loves us and accepts us and longs to restore his relationship with us.

1:19–28 John the Baptist was a messenger of repentance. He himself was not the true light; he merely pointed to the one who was (see 1:6–8, 26–27, 30–31, 34). Likewise, those of us who have received Christ should reflect God's light and point others to him, the true light. We are mere beggars telling other beggars where to find food. When we lay aside pride in our achievements and abilities, as John the Baptist did, we are better able to serve Christ by showing others the way to him.

1:29–31 Jesus was a perfect picture of God and a perfect teacher of God's truth. He was also the perfect sacrifice—the Lamb of God. The Old Testament sacrificial system required that an unblemished lamb be slain on the altar. Through the lamb's death the people could be forgiven of their sins and given a fresh start. By dying on the cross, Jesus fulfilled the requirements of that Old Testament sacrificial system completely and forever. He is the Lamb of God who takes away our sin and gives us a chance for a new start.

In the Life of John the Baptist

John the Baptist is often overlooked as one of the significant spiritual leaders of Israel. John's primary mission was to prepare the way for Jesus the Messiah. Jesus' influence would not have been as immediately widespread were it not for the work of his cousin John. People came from all over Judea to hear John preach and to be baptized by him (see Mark 1:5). John even baptized Jesus himself. Given John's extensive ministry and accomplishments, it would have been very easy for him to feel proud or self-important. Yet when it became apparent that Jesus' ministry was beginning to overshadow his own, John freely confessed, "He must become greater; I must become less" (John 3:30).

How did John remain so properly focused in his spiritual walk? Part of his success seems to originate from his spiritual practices or what we now call ascetic disciplines:

FASTING. John lived in the desert, wearing abrasive camel's hair and a leather belt and eating only locusts and wild honey. John's menu and apparel choices are noted in this section under fasting because the function and purpose of his lifestyle choices were the same: to practice self-denial and abstinence in order to stimulate spiritual growth. (To learn more about fasting, turn to 2 Chronicles 20.)

REPENTANCE. This word most vividly expresses John the Baptist's ministry and message. He came preaching a baptism of repentance to prepare the way for the Lord (see Mark 1:3–4). Isaiah 40:3 portrays sin not only as a detour from salvation, but also as a roadblock to the way God comes to his people. John's baptism prepared people for the Messiah by challenging them to clear away the obstacles of sin and self-righteous living. (To learn more about repentance, turn to Exodus 20.)

Lessons for Life

Throughout the course of Christian history, ascetic practices have ranged from poverty to self-inflicted physical punishment. Biblical asceticism traces its roots to the Nazirite tradition first described in Numbers 6:1–8. Nazirites were people who had made a vow to set themselves apart for God for a specific purpose and a specific time. They vowed to abstain from wine, from cutting their hair and from going near a dead body. Each of these abstentions was made for various reasons, but the ultimate purpose was clear: The Nazirites were to be holy, set apart and available to God so that God's power could flow through them.

Ascetic practices do not focus on what is *given up* but rather what is *gained* by being more fully available to God. By constantly checking the normal tendency to follow our own ways and desires, spiritual asceticism can nurture our spiritual renewal. John the Baptist wore camel's hair and ate locusts as a vivid reminder that God's power and resources are more valuable than any comforts or resources this world may offer. How have you kept yourself from being overcome by the world? Are there any areas in your life in which you could set yourself apart to God with respect to your clothing, diet, transportation, housing or stewardship?

When properly managed, ascetic practices can be a powerful witness to the world. John's austere lifestyle stood in stark contrast to worldly ways. It gave a visible expression to his message of repentance and preparation for the coming of the Lord. Are there choices you can make in your lifestyle that may stir others' interest and prepare their hearts to receive the Lord?

We must be careful, however, that our attentions to these ascetic practices do not divert our attention away from God. When spiritual disciplines become a matter of merit to achieve God's favor or become a basis for spiritual pride, they serve no useful purpose whatsoever (see Colossians 2:16–23).

of his disciples. 36 When he saw Jesus passing by, he said, "Look, the Lamb of God!"

37 When the two disciples heard him say this, they followed Jesus. 38 Turning around, Jesus saw them following and asked, "What do you want?"

They said, "Rabbi" (which means Teacher), "where are you staying?"

39 "Come," he replied, "and you will see."

So they went and saw where he was staying, and spent that day with him. It was about the tenth hour.

40 Andrew, Simon Peter's brother, was one of the two who heard what John had said and who had followed Jesus. 41 The first thing Andrew did was to find his brother Simon and tell him, "We have found the Messiah" (that is, the Christ). 42 And he brought him to Jesus.

Jesus looked at him and said, "You are Simon son of John. You will be called Cephas" (which, when translated, is Peter[a]).

Jesus Calls Philip and Nathanael

43 The next day Jesus decided to leave for Galilee. Finding Philip, he said to him, "Follow me."

44 Philip, like Andrew and Peter, was from the town of Bethsaida. 45 Philip found Nathanael and told him, "We have found the one Moses wrote about in the Law, and about whom the prophets also wrote—Jesus of Nazareth, the son of Joseph."

46 "Nazareth! Can anything good come from there?" Nathanael asked.

"Come and see," said Philip.

47 When Jesus saw Nathanael approaching, he said of him, "Here is a true Israelite, in whom there is nothing false."

48 "How do you know me?" Nathanael asked.

Jesus answered, "I saw you while you were still under the fig tree before Philip called you."

49 Then Nathanael declared, "Rabbi, you are the Son of God; you are the King of Israel."

50 Jesus said, "You believe[b] because I told you I saw you under the fig tree. You shall see greater things than that." 51 He then added, "I tell you[c] the truth, you[c] shall see heaven open, and the angels of God ascending and descending on the Son of Man."

Jesus Changes Water to Wine

2 On the third day a wedding took place at Cana in Galilee. Jesus' mother was there, 2 and Jesus and his disciples had also been invited to the wedding. 3 When the wine was gone, Jesus' mother said to him, "They have no more wine."

4 "Dear woman, why do you involve me?" Jesus replied. "My time has not yet come."

5 His mother said to the servants, "Do whatever he tells you."

6 Nearby stood six stone water jars, the kind used by the Jews for ceremonial washing, each holding from twenty to thirty gallons.[d]

7 Jesus said to the servants, "Fill the jars with water"; so they filled them to the brim.

8 Then he told them, "Now draw some out and take it to the master of the banquet."

They did so, 9 and the master of the banquet tasted the water that had been turned into wine. He did not realize where it had come from, though the servants who had drawn the water knew. Then he called the bridegroom aside 10 and said, "Everyone brings out the choice wine first and then the cheaper wine after the guests have had too much to drink; but you have saved the best till now."

11 This, the first of his miraculous signs, Jesus performed at Cana in Galilee. He thus revealed his glory, and his disciples put their faith in him.

Jesus Clears the Temple

‰ See Matthew 21:12–13; Mark 11:15–17; Luke 19:45–46

12 After this he went down to Capernaum with his mother and brothers and his disciples. There they stayed for a few days.

13 When it was almost time for the Jewish Passover, Jesus went up to Jerusalem. 14 In the temple courts he found men selling cattle, sheep and doves, and others sitting at tables exchanging money. 15 So he made a whip out of cords, and drove all from the temple area, both sheep and cattle; he scattered the coins of the money changers and overturned their tables.

[a] 42 Both *Cephas* (Aramaic) and *Peter* (Greek) mean *rock.*
[b] 50 Or *Do you believe . . . ?*
[c] 51 The Greek is plural.
[d] 6 Greek *two to three metretes* (probably about 75 to 115 liters)

1:40–42 Once Andrew had met Jesus and realized who he was, he quickly shared the Good News with others. Rushing off to find his brother Simon, Andrew immediately brought him to Jesus. When we experience God's power in our lives, we should be just as eager to share our new-found hope with others. This is an essential part of our spiritual growth. As we share God's Good News, we will give great hope to others. We will also be encouraged to persevere when we remember all the great things God has done for us.

2:1–12 Jesus attended a wedding celebration with family and friends. But the wine ran out. So Jesus turned the water from six stone water jars into enough wine for the rest of the celebration. This abundance of wine might seem dangerous to some. But one truth should be encouraging for us all: Jesus wanted the people at this wedding to enjoy themselves. Even though his life's mission was a very sobering one, he valued people's joy at a wedding feast. God wants us to live joyful lives as well. We may have to face some painful things in the process of life, but God's ultimate goal for us is joy.

2:13–16 Jesus was angry with those who turned the temple courts into a marketplace of unjust profit. People were forced to buy "approved" sacrificial animals at exorbitant prices. They also were required to exchange their currency for temple currency at inflated rates. Jesus cleared the temple with a whip to demonstrate God's anger at those who abused the public trust and mocked holy worship. Sometimes righteous anger that is measured and authorized by God's purposes is justified.

16To those who sold doves he said, "Get these
out of here! How dare you turn my Father's
house into a market!"
17His disciples remembered that it is written:
"Zeal for your house will consume me."[a]
18Then the Jews demanded of him, "What
miraculous sign can you show us to prove your
authority to do all this?"
19Jesus answered them, "Destroy this temple, and I will raise it again in three days."
20The Jews replied, "It has taken forty-six
years to build this temple, and you are going to
raise it in three days?" 21But the temple he had
spoken of was his body. 22After he was raised
from the dead, his disciples recalled what he
had said. Then they believed the Scripture and
the words that Jesus had spoken.
23Now while he was in Jerusalem at the Passover Feast, many people saw the miraculous
signs he was doing and believed in his name.[b]
24But Jesus would not entrust himself to them,
for he knew all men. 25He did not need man's
testimony about man, for he knew what was in
a man.

Jesus Teaches Nicodemus

3 Now there was a man of the Pharisees
named Nicodemus, a member of the Jewish ruling council. 2He came to Jesus at night
and said, "Rabbi, we know you are a teacher
who has come from God. For no one could
perform the miraculous signs you are doing if
God were not with him."
3In reply Jesus declared, "I tell you the truth,
no one can see the kingdom of God unless he
is born again.[c]"
4"How can a man be born when he is old?"
Nicodemus asked. "Surely he cannot enter a
second time into his mother's womb to be
born!"
5Jesus answered, "I tell you the truth, no one
can enter the kingdom of God unless he is born
of water and the Spirit. 6Flesh gives birth to
flesh, but the Spirit[d] gives birth to spirit. 7You
should not be surprised at my saying, 'You[e]
must be born again.' 8The wind blows wherever
it pleases. You hear its sound, but you cannot
tell where it comes from or where it
it is with everyone born of the Spi
9"How can this be?" Nicodemus
10"You are Israel's teacher," said
do you not understand these things? 11I tell you
the truth, we speak of what we know, and we
testify to what we have seen, but still you people
do not accept our testimony. 12I have spoken to
you of earthly things and you do not believe;
how then will you believe if I speak of heavenly
things? 13No one has ever gone into heaven
except the one who came from heaven—the Son
of Man.[f] 14Just as Moses lifted up the snake in
the desert, so the Son of Man must be lifted up,
15that everyone who believes in him may have
eternal life.[g]
16"For God so loved the world that he gave
his one and only Son,[h] that whoever believes
in him shall not perish but have eternal life.
17For God did not send his Son into the world
to condemn the world, but to save the world
through him. 18Whoever believes in him is not
condemned, but whoever does not believe
stands condemned already because he has not
believed in the name of God's one and only
Son.[i] 19This is the verdict: Light has come into
the world, but men loved darkness instead of
light because their deeds were evil. 20Everyone
who does evil hates the light, and will not come
into the light for fear that his deeds will be
exposed. 21But whoever lives by the truth comes
into the light, so that it may be seen plainly that
what he has done has been done through
God."[j]

John the Baptist's Testimony About Jesus

22After this, Jesus and his disciples went out
into the Judean countryside, where he spent
some time with them, and baptized. 23Now
John also was baptizing at Aenon near Salim,
because there was plenty of water, and people
were constantly coming to be baptized. 24(This

[a]17 Psalm 69:9 [b]23 Or *and believed in him* [c]3 Or *born from above;* also in verse 7 [d]6 Or *but spirit* [e]7 The Greek is plural. [f]13 Some manuscripts *Man, who is in heaven* [g]15 Or *believes may have eternal life in him* [h]16 Or *his only begotten Son* [i]18 Or *God's only begotten Son* [j]21 Some interpreters end the quotation after verse 15.

2:17–25 Those who witnessed Jesus' actions and words had to choose between belief and unbelief. We also must choose to accept or reject what Jesus' actions indicate about his mission and authority. Was he just a fascinating man who accomplished amazing deeds? Was he just a good teacher with an interesting message? Was he a madman with delusions of grandeur? Or is Jesus actually God, who came to live among us? According to the Bible, Jesus is God. He has the power to offer us a new life. The disciples discovered this truth and were transformed into some of the greatest leaders of their day. God has the power to transform us too.

3:1–12 Spiritual rebirth is necessary to enter God's kingdom. Being born again is the easy, passive part—just as a baby goes through the birth process. The challenge comes as we grow up and choose to submit our wills to God's control. When we surrender our lives to God, we grow up spiritually and are transformed by God. We cannot be transformed by trying harder to live a better life. As we yield our will to God's will over the course of our lives, the cleansing work of the Holy Spirit will transform us. Our transformation will come through the grace of God that is bestowed on us as we surrender our lives to him.

3:16–18 Faith says yes to God's loving overtures to us. God cared enough to send his own Son—Jesus Christ—to pay for our sin. True faith has nothing to do with our human efforts, social achievements or material wealth. Saving faith admits our helplessness and vulnerability to sin to God and trusts his forgiveness offered in Jesus Christ. That kind of faith in God delivers us from the ultimate consequences of our sins—eternal separation from God. Faith also empowers us to change our lifestyles and begin new ones.

Openness to God's Light

John 3:18–21 Our openness to God's light will affect our ability to see the truth. God offers us all the light we need, but there may be some aspects of the truth we would rather not see, some areas of our lives we would rather not open up to God's light. We may want to hide our areas of shame, areas of compromise that we know will look different under God's light or areas where we hide the secret sins we aren't ready to give up. Darkness hides many things, but we need light to see the truth.

Jesus knew that some refused to trust him with their lives. He said, "Light has come into the world, but men loved darkness instead of light because their deeds were evil. Everyone who does evil hates the light, and will not come into the light for fear that his deeds will be exposed" (3:19–20). Later, in one of his talks, Jesus said to the people, "I am the light of the world. Whoever follows me will never walk in darkness, but will have the light of life" (8:12).

We cannot fully see the truth unless we open our lives to God's light. But opening ourselves to his light is not a fearful process. God has already offered to forgive us for anything we may be hiding in the shadows. Jesus Christ is the light of the world. His light dispels all the darkness in our souls.

Turn to 1 Corinthians 10.

was before John was put in prison.) 25An argument developed between some of John's disciples and a certain Jew[a] over the matter of ceremonial washing. 26They came to John and said
to him, "Rabbi, that man who was with you on
the other side of the Jordan—the one you testified about—well, he is baptizing, and everyone
is going to him."

27To this John replied, "A man can receive
only what is given him from heaven. 28You
yourselves can testify that I said, 'I am not the
Christ[b] but am sent ahead of him.' 29The bride
belongs to the bridegroom. The friend who at-
tends the bridegroom waits and listens for him,
and is full of joy when he hears the bridegroom's voice. That joy is mine, and it is now
complete. 30He must become greater; I must
become less.

31"The one who comes from above is above
all; the one who is from the earth belongs to the
earth, and speaks as one from the earth. The one
who comes from heaven is above all. 32He testifies to what he has seen and heard, but no one
accepts his testimony. 33The man who has accepted it has certified that God is truthful. 34For
the one whom God has sent speaks the words
of God, for God[c] gives the Spirit without limit.
35The Father loves the Son and has placed everything in his hands. 36Whoever believes in the
Son has eternal life, but whoever rejects the Son
will not see life, for God's wrath remains on
him."[d]

Jesus Talks With a Samaritan Woman

4 The Pharisees heard that Jesus was gaining
and baptizing more disciples than John,
2although in fact it was not Jesus who baptized,
but his disciples. 3When the Lord learned of
this, he left Judea and went back once more to
Galilee.

4Now he had to go through Samaria. 5So he
came to a town in Samaria called Sychar, near
the plot of ground Jacob had given to his son
Joseph. 6Jacob's well was there, and Jesus, tired
as he was from the journey, sat down by the
well. It was about the sixth hour.

7When a Samaritan woman came to draw
water, Jesus said to her, "Will you give me a

[a]25 Some manuscripts *and certain Jews* [b]28 Or *Messiah* [c]34 Greek *he* [d]36 Some interpreters end the quotation after verse 30.

4:4–27 The disciples were surprised to find Jesus speaking with the woman at the well for a number of reasons: She was a Samaritan (half Jew and half Gentile), she was a woman and she possessed a questionable history. Any one of these factors would have disqualified her from speaking with a "righteous" Jewish man. But Jesus broke down all the traditional barriers to accept this woman as she was and gave her a chance to experience a fresh start in life. In doing this, Jesus demonstrated God's love for all who have been rejected or condemned. No matter what we have done in the past, God still offers us his unconditional acceptance through Jesus. With his powerful help, nothing can stand in the way of our salvation.

drink?" 8(His disciples had gone into the town
to buy food.)
9The Samaritan woman said to him, "You
are a Jew and I am a Samaritan woman. How
can you ask me for a drink?" (For Jews do not
associate with Samaritans.[a])
10Jesus answered her, "If you knew the gift of
God and who it is that asks you for a drink, you
would have asked him and he would have given
you living water."
11"Sir," the woman said, "you have nothing
to draw with and the well is deep. Where can
you get this living water? 12Are you greater than
our father Jacob, who gave us the well and
drank from it himself, as did also his sons and
his flocks and herds?"
13Jesus answered, "Everyone who drinks this
water will be thirsty again, 14but whoever drinks
the water I give him will never thirst. Indeed,
the water I give him will become in him a spring
of water welling up to eternal life."
15The woman said to him, "Sir, give me this
water so that I won't get thirsty and have to keep
coming here to draw water."
16He told her, "Go, call your husband and
come back."
17"I have no husband," she replied.
Jesus said to her, "You are right when you
say you have no husband. 18The fact is, you
have had five husbands, and the man you now
have is not your husband. What you have just
said is quite true."
19"Sir," the woman said, "I can see that you
are a prophet. 20Our fathers worshiped on this
mountain, but you Jews claim that the place
where we must worship is in Jerusalem."
21Jesus declared, "Believe me, woman, a
time is coming when you will worship the Father neither on this mountain nor in Jerusalem.
22You Samaritans worship what you do not
know; we worship what we do know, for salvation is from the Jews. 23Yet a time is coming and
has now come when the true worshipers will
worship the Father in spirit and truth, for they
are the kind of worshipers the Father seeks.
24God is spirit, and his worshipers must worship in spirit and in truth."
25The woman said, "I know that Messiah"
(called Christ) "is coming. When he comes, he
will explain everything to us."
26Then Jesus declared, "I who speak to you
am he."

The Disciples Rejoin Jesus

27Just then his disciples returned and were
surprised to find him talking with a woman.
But no one asked, "What do you want?" or
"Why are you talking with her?"
28Then, leaving her water jar, the woman
went back to the town and said to the people,
29"Come, see a man who told me everything I
ever did. Could this be the Christ[b]?" 30They
came out of the town and made their way toward him.
31Meanwhile his disciples urged him, "Rabbi, eat something."
32But he said to them, "I have food to eat
that you know nothing about."
33Then his disciples said to each other,
"Could someone have brought him food?"
34"My food," said Jesus, "is to do the will of
him who sent me and to finish his work. 35Do
you not say, 'Four months more and then the
harvest'? I tell you, open your eyes and look at
the fields! They are ripe for harvest. 36Even now
the reaper draws his wages, even now he harvests the crop for eternal life, so that the sower
and the reaper may be glad together. 37Thus the
saying 'One sows and another reaps' is true. 38I
sent you to reap what you have not worked for.
Others have done the hard work, and you have
reaped the benefits of their labor."

Many Samaritans Believe

39Many of the Samaritans from that town
believed in him because of the woman's testimony, "He told me everything I ever did." 40So
when the Samaritans came to him, they urged
him to stay with them, and he stayed two days.
41And because of his words many more became
believers.
42They said to the woman, "We no longer
believe just because of what you said; now we
have heard for ourselves, and we know that this
man really is the Savior of the world."

Jesus Heals the Official's Son

43After the two days he left for Galilee.
44(Now Jesus himself had pointed out that a
prophet has no honor in his own country.)
45When he arrived in Galilee, the Galileans welcomed him. They had seen all that he had done
in Jerusalem at the Passover Feast, for they also
had been there.
46Once more he visited Cana in Galilee,
where he had turned the water into wine. And
there was a certain royal official whose son lay

[a]9 Or *do not use dishes Samaritans have used* [b]29 Or *Messiah*

4:39–42 The Samaritan woman put her faith in Jesus. He knew all about her faults, yet he still loved and respected her. She responded to God's gracious forgiveness by immediately sharing her story with others. She told her neighbors about the Messiah, who had offered her a new life. As a result, many were blessed with the benefits of faith in Jesus Christ. As we experience the reality of Christ's love in our lives, it is important that we share the Good News with others. The message we share may make the difference between life and death for someone we know. And when we share our story, we will experience anew the great joy of knowing Christ.

4:46–53 The royal official demonstrated his faith by humbly asking Jesus to heal his son and then by taking him at his word. He believed Jesus' word to be true even though he hadn't yet seen the results. Our faith can be expressed in similar ways. We can begin by humbly repenting of our sins and honestly seeking God's help. He

sick at Capernaum. 47When this man heard that
Jesus had arrived in Galilee from Judea, he went
to him and begged him to come and heal his
son, who was close to death.
48"Unless you people see miraculous signs
and wonders," Jesus told him, "you will never
believe."
49The royal official said, "Sir, come down
before my child dies."
50Jesus replied, "You may go. Your son will
live."
The man took Jesus at his word and departed. 51While he was still on the way, his servants
met him with the news that his boy was living.
52When he inquired as to the time when his son
got better, they said to him, "The fever left him
yesterday at the seventh hour."
53Then the father realized that this was the
exact time at which Jesus had said to him,
"Your son will live." So he and all his household
believed.
54This was the second miraculous sign that
Jesus performed, having come from Judea to
Galilee.

The Healing at the Pool

5 Some time later, Jesus went up to Jerusalem for a feast of the Jews. 2Now there is in
Jerusalem near the Sheep Gate a pool, which in
Aramaic is called Bethesda[a] and which is surrounded by five covered colonnades. 3Here a
great number of disabled people used to lie—the
blind, the lame, the paralyzed.[b] 5One who was
there had been an invalid for thirty-eight years.
6When Jesus saw him lying there and learned
that he had been in this condition for a long
time, he asked him, "Do you want to get well?"
7"Sir," the invalid replied, "I have no one to
help me into the pool when the water is stirred.
While I am trying to get in, someone else goes
down ahead of me."
8Then Jesus said to him, "Get up! Pick up
your mat and walk." 9At once the man was cured;
he picked up his mat and walked.
The day on which this took place was a Sabbath, 10and so the Jews said to the man who had
been healed, "It is the Sabbath; the law forbids
you to carry your mat."
11But he replied, "The man who made me
well said to me, 'Pick up your mat and walk.' "
12So they asked him, "Who is this fellow
who told you to pick it up and walk?"
13The man who was healed had no idea who
it was, for Jesus had slipped away into the
crowd that was there.
14Later Jesus found him at the temple and
said to him, "See, you are well again. Stop sinning or something worse may happen to you."
15The man went away and told the Jews that it
was Jesus who had made him well.

Life Through the Son

16So, because Jesus was doing these things on
the Sabbath, the Jews persecuted him. 17Jesus
said to them, "My Father is always at his work
to this very day, and I, too, am working." 18For
this reason the Jews tried all the harder to kill
him; not only was he breaking the Sabbath, but
he was even calling God his own Father, making himself equal with God.
19Jesus gave them this answer: "I tell you the
truth, the Son can do nothing by himself; he
can do only what he sees his Father doing, because whatever the Father does the Son also
does. 20For the Father loves the Son and shows
him all he does. Yes, to your amazement he will
show him even greater things than these. 21For
just as the Father raises the dead and gives them
life, even so the Son gives life to whom he is
pleased to give it. 22Moreover, the Father judges
no one, but has entrusted all judgment to the
Son, 23that all may honor the Son just as they
honor the Father. He who does not honor the
Son does not honor the Father, who sent him.
24"I tell you the truth, whoever hears my
word and believes him who sent me has eternal
life and will not be condemned; he has crossed
over from death to life. 25I tell you the truth, a
time is coming and has now come when the
dead will hear the voice of the Son of God and
those who hear will live. 26For as the Father has
life in himself, so he has granted the Son to
have life in himself. 27And he has given him
authority to judge because he is the Son of Man.
28"Do not be amazed at this, for a time is
coming when all who are in their graves will
hear his voice 29and come out—those who have
done good will rise to live, and those who have
done evil will rise to be condemned. 30By myself I can do nothing; I judge only as I hear, and
my judgment is just, for I seek not to please
myself but him who sent me.

Testimonies About Jesus

31"If I testify about myself, my testimony is
not valid. 32There is another who testifies in my
favor, and I know that his testimony about me
is valid.
33"You have sent to John and he has testified
to the truth. 34Not that I accept human testimony; but I mention it that you may be saved.
35John was a lamp that burned and gave light,
and you chose for a time to enjoy his light.
36"I have testimony weightier than that of
John. For the very work that the Father has giv-
en me to finish, and which I am doing, testifies

[a]2 Some manuscripts *Bethzatha;* other manuscripts *Bethsaida* [b]3 Some less important manuscripts *paralyzed—and they waited for the moving of the waters. 4From time to time an angel of the Lord would come down and stir up the waters. The first one into the pool after each such disturbance would be cured of whatever disease he had.*

has promised to help us, but spiritual growth takes time. Even when the results of God's work are not immediately evident in our lives, we must persevere. God is working.

that the Father has sent me. 37And the Father who sent me has himself testified concerning me. You have never heard his voice nor seen his form, 38nor does his word dwell in you, for you do not believe the one he sent. 39You diligently study[a] the Scriptures because you think that by them you possess eternal life. These are the Scriptures that testify about me, 40yet you refuse to come to me to have life.

41"I do not accept praise from men, 42but I know you. I know that you do not have the love of God in your hearts. 43I have come in my Father's name, and you do not accept me; but if someone else comes in his own name, you will accept him. 44How can you believe if you accept praise from one another, yet make no effort to obtain the praise that comes from the only God[b]?

45"But do not think I will accuse you before the Father. Your accuser is Moses, on whom your hopes are set. 46If you believed Moses, you would believe me, for he wrote about me. 47But since you do not believe what he wrote, how are you going to believe what I say?"

Jesus Feeds the Five Thousand

‰ See Matthew 14:13–21; Mark 6:32–44; Luke 9:10–17

6 Some time after this, Jesus crossed to the far shore of the Sea of Galilee (that is, the Sea of Tiberias), 2and a great crowd of people followed him because they saw the miraculous signs he had performed on the sick. 3Then Jesus went up on a mountainside and sat down with his disciples. 4The Jewish Passover Feast was near.

5When Jesus looked up and saw a great crowd coming toward him, he said to Philip, "Where shall we buy bread for these people to eat?" 6He asked this only to test him, for he already had in mind what he was going to do. 7Philip answered him, "Eight months' wages[c] would not buy enough bread for each one to have a bite!"

8Another of his disciples, Andrew, Simon Peter's brother, spoke up, 9"Here is a boy with five small barley loaves and two small fish, but how far will they go among so many?"

10Jesus said, "Have the people sit down." There was plenty of grass in that place, and the men sat down, about five thousand of them. 11Jesus then took the loaves, gave thanks, and distributed to those who were seated as much as they wanted. He did the same with the fish.

12When they had all had enough to eat, he said to his disciples, "Gather the pieces that are left over. Let nothing be wasted." 13So they gathered them and filled twelve baskets with the pieces of the five barley loaves left over by those who had eaten.

14After the people saw the miraculous sign that Jesus did, they began to say, "Surely this is the Prophet who is to come into the world." 15Jesus, knowing that they intended to come and make him king by force, withdrew again to a mountain by himself.

Jesus Walks on the Water

‰ See Matthew 14:22–33; Mark 6:47–51

16When evening came, his disciples went down to the lake, 17where they got into a boat and set off across the lake for Capernaum. By now it was dark, and Jesus had not yet joined them. 18A strong wind was blowing and the waters grew rough. 19When they had rowed three or three and a half miles,[d] they saw Jesus approaching the boat, walking on the water; and they were terrified. 20But he said to them, "It is I; don't be afraid." 21Then they were willing to take him into the boat, and immediately the boat reached the shore where they were heading.

22The next day the crowd that had stayed on the opposite shore of the lake realized that only one boat had been there, and that Jesus had not entered it with his disciples, but that they had gone away alone. 23Then some boats from Tiberias landed near the place where the people had eaten the bread after the Lord had given thanks. 24Once the crowd realized that neither Jesus nor his disciples were there, they got into the boats and went to Capernaum in search of Jesus.

Jesus the Bread of Life

25When they found him on the other side of the lake, they asked him, "Rabbi, when did you get here?"

26Jesus answered, "I tell you the truth, you are looking for me, not because you saw mirac-

[a]39 Or *Study diligently* (the imperative) [b]44 Some early manuscripts *the Only One* [c]7 Greek *two hundred denarii* [d]19 Greek *rowed twenty-five or thirty stadia* (about 5 or 6 kilometers)

5:39–40 The Jewish religious leaders knew all about the Scriptures, yet these people were spiritually dead. They had missed the whole purpose of the Scriptures: to bring people into a vital relationship with God. Intellectual knowledge about the Bible will not bring us into a transforming relationship with God. We must act on that knowledge and apply it to our lives. Real spiritual growth comes by knowing God through the person of Jesus Christ.
5:41–44 Jesus took the Pharisees to task for being more concerned with people's opinions about them than God's opinions about them. At times we may have to do things that are neither understood nor approved by others. The bottom line for us should be God's approval of what we are doing, not the approval of others. As we honestly reflect on our lives, God and his Word—not the opinions of our peers—will be the guidelines for our behavior.
6:1–15 Jesus often used people as channels of his grace. In feeding five thousand people, Jesus used what a young boy provided. God lets us have a part in what he does too. When we willingly dedicate our own small resources of time, talents or possessions to God, he can work miracles for us and others. God can use our limited resources and multiply them beyond our wildest expectations.

ulous signs but because you ate the loaves and
had your fill. 27 Do not work for food that
spoils, but for food that endures to eternal life,
which the Son of Man will give you. On him
God the Father has placed his seal of approval."
28 Then they asked him, "What must we do
to do the works God requires?"
29 Jesus answered, "The work of God is this:
to believe in the one he has sent."
30 So they asked him, "What miraculous sign
then will you give that we may see it and believe
you? What will you do? 31 Our forefathers ate
the manna in the desert; as it is written: 'He
gave them bread from heaven to eat.'[a]"
32 Jesus said to them, "I tell you the truth, it
is not Moses who has given you the bread from
heaven, but it is my Father who gives you the
true bread from heaven. 33 For the bread of God
is he who comes down from heaven and gives
life to the world."
34 "Sir," they said, "from now on give us this
bread."
35 Then Jesus declared, "I am the bread of
life. He who comes to me will never go hungry,
and he who believes in me will never be thirsty.
36 But as I told you, you have seen me and still
you do not believe. 37 All that the Father gives
me will come to me, and whoever comes to me
I will never drive away. 38 For I have come down
from heaven not to do my will but to do the
will of him who sent me. 39 And this is the will
of him who sent me, that I shall lose none of all
that he has given me, but raise them up at the
last day. 40 For my Father's will is that everyone
who looks to the Son and believes in him shall
have eternal life, and I will raise him up at the
last day."
41 At this the Jews began to grumble about
him because he said, "I am the bread that came
down from heaven." 42 They said, "Is this not
Jesus, the son of Joseph, whose father and
mother we know? How can he now say, 'I came
down from heaven'?"
43 "Stop grumbling among yourselves," Jesus
answered. 44 "No one can come to me unless
the Father who sent me draws him, and I will
raise him up at the last day. 45 It is written in the
Prophets: 'They will all be taught by God.'[b]
Everyone who listens to the Father and learns
from him comes to me. 46 No one has seen the
Father except the one who is from God; only he
has seen the Father. 47 I tell you the truth, he
who believes has everlasting life. 48 I am the
bread of life. 49 Your forefathers ate the manna
in the desert, yet they died. 50 But here is the
bread that comes down from heaven, which a
man may eat and not die. 51 I am the living
bread that came down from heaven. If anyone
eats of this bread, he will live forever. This bread
is my flesh, which I will give for the life of the
world."
52 Then the Jews began to argue sharply
among themselves, "How can this man give us
his flesh to eat?"
53 Jesus said to them, "I tell you the truth,
unless you eat the flesh of the Son of Man and
drink his blood, you have no life in you. 54 Whoever eats my flesh and drinks my blood has
eternal life, and I will raise him up at the last
day. 55 For my flesh is real food and my blood
is real drink. 56 Whoever eats my flesh and
drinks my blood remains in me, and I in him.
57 Just as the living Father sent me and I live
because of the Father, so the one who feeds on
me will live because of me. 58 This is the bread
that came down from heaven. Your forefathers
ate manna and died, but he who feeds on this
bread will live forever." 59 He said this while
teaching in the synagogue in Capernaum.

Many Disciples Desert Jesus

60 On hearing it, many of his disciples said,
"This is a hard teaching. Who can accept it?"
61 Aware that his disciples were grumbling
about this, Jesus said to them, "Does this offend you? 62 What if you see the Son of Man
ascend to where he was before! 63 The Spirit
gives life; the flesh counts for nothing. The
words I have spoken to you are spirit[c] and they
are life. 64 Yet there are some of you who do not
believe." For Jesus had known from the beginning which of them did not believe and who
would betray him. 65 He went on to say, "This
is why I told you that no one can come to me
unless the Father has enabled him."
66 From this time many of his disciples turned
back and no longer followed him.
67 "You do not want to leave too, do you?"
Jesus asked the Twelve.

[a] *31* Exodus 16:4; Neh. 9:15; Psalm 78:24,25
[b] *45* Isaiah 54:13 [c] *63* Or *Spirit*

6:28–29 "What does God want us to do?" Many of us live by a list of "shoulds" and "should nots" in our effort to earn God's acceptance. But the good news is that we don't have to do anything to receive God's help and forgiveness! God in Jesus Christ has taken all the initiative; we simply repent and receive him by faith. Each step of our growth begins as we respond to God's love for us.

6:32–40 After feeding more than five thousand hungry people with five loaves of bread and two fish, Jesus explained that he himself is the bread of life. Jesus feeds the hungry with himself. He satisfies the deepest longings of our souls and fulfills our needs. Until the end of time, Jesus will work toward the redemption of all the sinful people in his world. Our part is to repent and turn to him and believe in his power to help us.

6:53–58 Jesus' imagery of eating his flesh and drinking his blood to obtain eternal life jars most of us. His words may offend some people, but they remind us of some important points. Jesus' flesh reminds us that he was fully human. As one of us, Jesus understands our temptations and struggles. Jesus' mention of his blood anticipated his death on the cross, in our place, for our sins. The call to partake of his flesh and blood is a call for us to make him and his teachings the very center of our being—emotional, spiritual and physical. As we feed our bodies with food, we are to feed our souls with the spiritual reality represented by the body and blood of Christ.

68Simon Peter answered him, "Lord, to
whom shall we go? You have the words of eternal life. 69We believe and know that you are the
Holy One of God."

70Then Jesus replied, "Have I not chosen
you, the Twelve? Yet one of you is a devil!" 71(He
meant Judas, the son of Simon Iscariot, who,
though one of the Twelve, was later to betray
him.)

Jesus Goes to the Feast of Tabernacles

7 After this, Jesus went around in Galilee,
purposely staying away from Judea because
the Jews there were waiting to take his life. 2But
when the Jewish Feast of Tabernacles was near,
3Jesus' brothers said to him, "You ought to
leave here and go to Judea, so that your disciples may see the miracles you do. 4No one who
wants to become a public figure acts in secret.
Since you are doing these things, show yourself
to the world." 5For even his own brothers did not
believe in him.

6Therefore Jesus told them, "The right time
for me has not yet come; for you any time is
right. 7The world cannot hate you, but it hates
me because I testify that what it does is evil.
8You go to the Feast. I am not yet[a] going up to
this Feast, because for me the right time has not
yet come." 9Having said this, he stayed in Galilee.

10However, after his brothers had left for the
Feast, he went also, not publicly, but in secret.
11Now at the Feast the Jews were watching for
him and asking, "Where is that man?"

12Among the crowds there was widespread
whispering about him. Some said, "He is a
good man."

Others replied, "No, he deceives the people."
13But no one would say anything publicly about
him for fear of the Jews.

Jesus Teaches at the Feast

14Not until halfway through the Feast did
Jesus go up to the temple courts and begin to
teach. 15The Jews were amazed and asked,
"How did this man get such learning without
having studied?"

16Jesus answered, "My teaching is not my
own. It comes from him who sent me. 17If anyone chooses to do God's will, he will find out
whether my teaching comes from God or
whether I speak on my own. 18He who speaks
on his own does so to gain honor for himself,
but he who works for the honor of the one who
sent him is a man of truth; there is nothing false
about him. 19Has not Moses given you the law?
Yet not one of you keeps the law. Why are you
trying to kill me?"

20"You are demon-possessed," the crowd answered. "Who is trying to kill you?"

21Jesus said to them, "I did one miracle, and
you are all astonished. 22Yet, because Moses
gave you circumcision (though actually it did
not come from Moses, but from the patriarchs),
you circumcise a child on the Sabbath. 23Now
if a child can be circumcised on the Sabbath so
that the law of Moses may not be broken, why
are you angry with me for healing the whole
man on the Sabbath? 24Stop judging by mere
appearances, and make a right judgment."

Is Jesus the Christ?

25At that point some of the people of Jerusalem began to ask, "Isn't this the man they are
trying to kill? 26Here he is, speaking publicly,
and they are not saying a word to him. Have
the authorities really concluded that he is the
Christ[b]? 27But we know where this man is
from; when the Christ comes, no one will know
where he is from."

28Then Jesus, still teaching in the temple
courts, cried out, "Yes, you know me, and you
know where I am from. I am not here on my
own, but he who sent me is true. You do not
know him, 29but I know him because I am from
him and he sent me."

30At this they tried to seize him, but no one
laid a hand on him, because his time had not
yet come. 31Still, many in the crowd put their
faith in him. They said, "When the Christ
comes, will he do more miraculous signs than
this man?"

32The Pharisees heard the crowd whispering
such things about him. Then the chief priests
and the Pharisees sent temple guards to arrest
him.

[a] 8 Some early manuscripts do not have *yet*. [b] 26 Or *Messiah*; also in verses 27, 31, 41 and 42

6:68–69 We see sales pitches for enticing products every day. Lottery games, television specials, political causes and religious gurus all vie for our time, money and devotion. They all promise to give us what we need and desire. Yet, when all is said and done, none of these things can satisfy us. Jesus is our only answer. He alone can deliver us from powerful sins that entangle us; he alone deserves our total commitment.

7:2–9 Jesus experienced ridicule and rejection from his family. His brothers did not understand what God was doing in or through Jesus. Therefore, Jesus obeyed the will of his Father in heaven instead of bowing to the pressure of those in his family. Like Jesus, we need to make sure that we are following God's plan for our lives rather than following the dictates of people who do not know what God has planned for us. We must know God's Word and have a close relationship with God, nurtured by prayer and Bible study. Staying close to God and remaining focused on his purpose for our lives will help us make good decisions and preserve our spiritual growth.

7:10–15, 25–27, 40–49 In this chapter some people believed that Jesus was a good man (7:12). Others thought he was a fraud or possessed by a demon (7:12, 20). Still others conceded he might be the Christ or the Prophet (7:26, 40). A powerful minority viewed Jesus as a political threat and wanted him arrested, even killed (7:1, 20, 44). We, too, must decide who Jesus is and what he means to us. Our decision about Jesus is very important. It will have eternal consequences (see 8:24).

33Jesus said, "I am with you for only a short time, and then I go to the one who sent me. 34You will look for me, but you will not find me; and where I am, you cannot come."

35The Jews said to one another, "Where does this man intend to go that we cannot find him? Will he go where our people live scattered among the Greeks, and teach the Greeks? 36What did he mean when he said, 'You will look for me, but you will not find me,' and 'Where I am, you cannot come'?"

37On the last and greatest day of the Feast, Jesus stood and said in a loud voice, "If anyone is thirsty, let him come to me and drink. 38Whoever believes in me, as[a] the Scripture has said, streams of living water will flow from within him." 39By this he meant the Spirit, whom those who believed in him were later to receive. Up to that time the Spirit had not been given, since Jesus had not yet been glorified.

40On hearing his words, some of the people said, "Surely this man is the Prophet."

41Others said, "He is the Christ."

Still others asked, "How can the Christ come from Galilee? 42Does not the Scripture say that the Christ will come from David's family[b] and from Bethlehem, the town where David lived?" 43Thus the people were divided because of Jesus. 44Some wanted to seize him, but no one laid a hand on him.

Unbelief of the Jewish Leaders

45Finally the temple guards went back to the chief priests and Pharisees, who asked them, "Why didn't you bring him in?"

46"No one ever spoke the way this man does," the guards declared.

47"You mean he has deceived you also?" the Pharisees retorted. 48"Has any of the rulers or of the Pharisees believed in him? 49No! But this mob that knows nothing of the law—there is a curse on them."

50Nicodemus, who had gone to Jesus earlier and who was one of their own number, asked, 51"Does our law condemn anyone without first hearing him to find out what he is doing?"

52They replied, "Are you from Galilee, too? Look into it, and you will find that a prophet[c] does not come out of Galilee."

[The earliest manuscripts and many other ancient witnesses do not have John 7:53–8:11.]

53Then each went to his own home.

8 But Jesus went to the Mount of Olives. 2At dawn he appeared again in the temple courts, where all the people gathered around him, and he sat down to teach them. 3The teachers of the law and the Pharisees brought in a woman caught in adultery. They made her stand before the group 4and said to Jesus, "Teacher, this woman was caught in the act of adultery. 5In the Law Moses commanded us to stone such women. Now what do you say?" 6They were using this question as a trap, in order to have a basis for accusing him.

But Jesus bent down and started to write on the ground with his finger. 7When they kept on questioning him, he straightened up and said to them, "If any one of you is without sin, let him be the first to throw a stone at her." 8Again he stooped down and wrote on the ground.

9At this, those who heard began to go away one at a time, the older ones first, until only Jesus was left, with the woman still standing there. 10Jesus straightened up and asked her, "Woman, where are they? Has no one condemned you?"

11"No one, sir," she said.

"Then neither do I condemn you," Jesus declared. "Go now and leave your life of sin."

The Validity of Jesus' Testimony

12When Jesus spoke again to the people, he said, "I am the light of the world. Whoever

[a]37,38 Or / *If anyone is thirsty, let him come to me. / And let him drink,* 38*who believes in me. / As* [b]42 Greek *seed* [c]52 Two early manuscripts *the Prophet*

7:37–39 Jesus is the living water who satisfies our thirst (see 4:10). When we put our faith in him and ask for a drink, he gives us his Spirit. The Holy Spirit becomes an inexhaustible stream of living water, welling up in us and flowing through us. The indwelling, eternal Holy Spirit goes with us wherever we go and quenches even our strongest spiritual thirst. Having this water available is the key to resisting the temptation to follow sinful pursuits. While sinful pleasures seem to satisfy for the moment, in the long run they will leave us thirstier than ever.

8:1–11 The Pharisees brought to Jesus a woman who had been caught in the act of adultery. Jewish law required capital punishment for persons guilty of adultery (see Leviticus 20:10; Deuteronomy 22:22). In asking Jesus to judge the situation, the Pharisees hoped to trap him. If Jesus had told them to stone her, they could have brought him before the Roman authorities, because the Romans did not allow the Jews to implement the death penalty. Yet, if Jesus had granted this woman a pardon, the Pharisees could have claimed he was a false prophet for ignoring God's laws. Jesus wisely escaped the trap by showing the Pharisees that they had no grounds for judging since they, too, were sinful. Then Jesus told the woman to go and leave her life of sin. Jesus did not ignore this woman's sin, but he forgave her and gave her a new start in life. Jesus will do the same for us when we turn to him.

8:12 As the light of the world, Jesus exposes what has been hidden and guides us down the path of life. To live in the light is to be honest and vulnerable with others and walk in fellowship with God (see 1 John 1:5–7). As we express to trusted people our needs and feelings, our sins and struggles, light will fall on our failures and strengths, giving us the direction we need to make significant spiritual progress (see 1:4–9; 3:19–21; 12:35, 46).

follows me will never walk in darkness, but will
have the light of life."
13 The Pharisees challenged him, "Here you
are, appearing as your own witness; your testimony is not valid."
14 Jesus answered, "Even if I testify on my
own behalf, my testimony is valid, for I know
where I came from and where I am going. But
you have no idea where I come from or where
I am going. 15 You judge by human standards; I
pass judgment on no one. 16 But if I do judge,
my decisions are right, because I am not alone.
I stand with the Father, who sent me. 17 In your
own Law it is written that the testimony of two
men is valid. 18 I am one who testifies for myself;
my other witness is the Father, who sent me."
19 Then they asked him, "Where is your father?"
"You do not know me or my Father," Jesus
replied. "If you knew me, you would know my
Father also." 20 He spoke these words while
teaching in the temple area near the place where
the offerings were put. Yet no one seized him,
because his time had not yet come.
21 Once more Jesus said to them, "I am going
away, and you will look for me, and you will die
in your sin. Where I go, you cannot come."
22 This made the Jews ask, "Will he kill himself? Is that why he says, 'Where I go, you cannot come'?"
23 But he continued, "You are from below; I
am from above. You are of this world; I am not
of this world. 24 I told you that you would die in
your sins; if you do not believe that I am ⌊the
one I claim to be⌋,[a] you will indeed die in your
sins."
25 "Who are you?" they asked.
"Just what I have been claiming all along,"
Jesus replied. 26 "I have much to say in judgment of you. But he who sent me is reliable, and
what I have heard from him I tell the world."
27 They did not understand that he was telling
them about his Father. 28 So Jesus said, "When
you have lifted up the Son of Man, then you
will know that I am ⌊the one I claim to be⌋ and
that I do nothing on my own but speak just
what the Father has taught me. 29 The one who
sent me is with me; he has not left me alone, for
I always do what pleases him." 30 Even as he
spoke, many put their faith in him.

The Children of Abraham

31 To the Jews who had believed him, Jesus
said, "If you hold to my teaching, you are really
my disciples. 32 Then you will know the truth,
and the truth will set you free."
33 They answered him, "We are Abraham's
descendants[b] and have never been slaves of
anyone. How can you say that we shall be set
free?"
34 Jesus replied, "I tell you the truth, everyone
who sins is a slave to sin. 35 Now a slave has no
permanent place in the family, but a son belongs to it forever. 36 So if the Son sets you free,
you will be free indeed. 37 I know you are Abraham's descendants. Yet you are ready to kill me,
because you have no room for my word. 38 I am
telling you what I have seen in the Father's presence, and you do what you have heard from
your father.[c]"
39 "Abraham is our father," they answered.
"If you were Abraham's children," said Jesus,
"then you would[d] do the things Abraham did.
40 As it is, you are determined to kill me, a man
who has told you the truth that I heard from
God. Abraham did not do such things. 41 You
are doing the things your own father does."
"We are not illegitimate children," they protested. "The only Father we have is God himself."

The Children of the Devil

42 Jesus said to them, "If God were your Father, you would love me, for I came from God
and now am here. I have not come on my own;
but he sent me. 43 Why is my language not clear
to you? Because you are unable to hear what I
say. 44 You belong to your father, the devil, and
you want to carry out your father's desire. He
was a murderer from the beginning, not holding to the truth, for there is no truth in him.
When he lies, he speaks his native language, for
he is a liar and the father of lies. 45 Yet because
I tell the truth, you do not believe me! 46 Can
any of you prove me guilty of sin? If I am telling
the truth, why don't you believe me? 47 He who
belongs to God hears what God says. The reason you do not hear is that you do not belong
to God."

The Claims of Jesus About Himself

48 The Jews answered him, "Aren't we right in
saying that you are a Samaritan and demon-
possessed?"
49 "I am not possessed by a demon," said
Jesus, "but I honor my Father and you dishonor
me. 50 I am not seeking glory for myself; but
there is one who seeks it, and he is the judge. 51 I
tell you the truth, if anyone keeps my word, he
will never see death."
52 At this the Jews exclaimed, "Now we know
that you are demon-possessed! Abraham died

[a] 24 Or *I am he;* also in verse 28 [b] 33 Greek *seed;* also in verse 37 [c] 38 Or *presence. Therefore do what you have heard from the Father.* [d] 39 Some early manuscripts *"If you are Abraham's children," said Jesus, "then*

8:31–36 To be set free is to know the truth about ourselves and Jesus our liberator. We are all slaves to our sinful natures. But with God's truth as the standard for our moral conduct, we can recognize and confess our struggles and our sins. Seeing the truth and speaking the truth in this way frees us. And when we turn our broken lives over to God, who alone can make us whole, we again acknowledge the truth.

and so did the prophets, yet you say that if anyone keeps your word, he will never taste death. 53Are you greater than our father Abraham? He died, and so did the prophets. Who do you think you are?"

54Jesus replied, "If I glorify myself, my glory means nothing. My Father, whom you claim as your God, is the one who glorifies me. 55Though you do not know him, I know him. If I said I did not, I would be a liar like you, but I do know him and keep his word. 56Your father Abraham rejoiced at the thought of seeing my day; he saw it and was glad."

57"You are not yet fifty years old," the Jews said to him, "and you have seen Abraham!"

58"I tell you the truth," Jesus answered, "before Abraham was born, I am!" 59At this, they picked up stones to stone him, but Jesus hid himself, slipping away from the temple grounds.

Jesus Heals a Man Born Blind

9 As he went along, he saw a man blind from birth. 2His disciples asked him, "Rabbi, who sinned, this man or his parents, that he was born blind?"

3"Neither this man nor his parents sinned," said Jesus, "but this happened so that the work of God might be displayed in his life. 4As long as it is day, we must do the work of him who sent me. Night is coming, when no one can work. 5While I am in the world, I am the light of the world."

6Having said this, he spit on the ground, made some mud with the saliva, and put it on the man's eyes. 7"Go," he told him, "wash in the Pool of Siloam" (this word means Sent). So the man went and washed, and came home seeing.

8His neighbors and those who had formerly seen him begging asked, "Isn't this the same man who used to sit and beg?" 9Some claimed that he was.

Others said, "No, he only looks like him."

But he himself insisted, "I am the man."

10"How then were your eyes opened?" they demanded.

11He replied, "The man they call Jesus made some mud and put it on my eyes. He told me to go to Siloam and wash. So I went and washed, and then I could see."

12"Where is this man?" they asked him.

"I don't know," he said.

The Pharisees Investigate the Healing

13They brought to the Pharisees the man who had been blind. 14Now the day on which Jesus had made the mud and opened the man's eyes was a Sabbath. 15Therefore the Pharisees also asked him how he had received his sight. "He put mud on my eyes," the man replied, "and I washed, and now I see."

16Some of the Pharisees said, "This man is not from God, for he does not keep the Sabbath."

But others asked, "How can a sinner do such miraculous signs?" So they were divided.

17Finally they turned again to the blind man, "What have you to say about him? It was your eyes he opened."

The man replied, "He is a prophet."

18The Jews still did not believe that he had been blind and had received his sight until they sent for the man's parents. 19"Is this your son?" they asked. "Is this the one you say was born blind? How is it that now he can see?"

20"We know he is our son," the parents answered, "and we know he was born blind. 21But how he can see now, or who opened his eyes, we don't know. Ask him. He is of age; he will speak for himself." 22His parents said this because they were afraid of the Jews, for already the Jews had decided that anyone who acknowledged that Jesus was the Christ[a] would be put out of the synagogue. 23That was why his parents said, "He is of age; ask him."

24A second time they summoned the man who had been blind. "Give glory to God,[b]" they said. "We know this man is a sinner."

25He replied, "Whether he is a sinner or not, I don't know. One thing I do know. I was blind but now I see!"

26Then they asked him, "What did he do to you? How did he open your eyes?"

27He answered, "I have told you already and you did not listen. Why do you want to hear it again? Do you want to become his disciples, too?"

28Then they hurled insults at him and said, "You are this fellow's disciple! We are disciples of Moses! 29We know that God spoke to Moses, but as for this fellow, we don't even know where he comes from."

30The man answered, "Now that is remark-

[a]22 Or *Messiah* [b]24 A solemn charge to tell the truth (see Joshua 7:19)

9:1–12, 35–41 Imagine being blind from birth, not being able to see the people we love and the world around us. Further imagine that people insinuate we are blind because of our personal sin or the sins of our parents! Jesus healed this man's blindness, but the real miracle occurred later when the man's spiritual blindness was healed. He learned to see through eyes of faith that Jesus truly was the Messiah, the Savior of the world. When we recognize Jesus as our deliverer, we have begun to gain our spiritual sight too.

9:13–34 Some people are so blinded by their legalistic attitudes that they cannot comprehend a wonderful miracle of healing taking place right in front of them. This was true of the Pharisees. They were more concerned about the letter of the law and the threat Jesus posed to their authority than about the amazing healing that had taken place. Even though they were exposed to the power of God, they chose to remain blind to the truth. Those who are teachable and humble will discover that God can heal even the most terrible afflictions. Often the very people we think least likely to make spiritual progress are the ones who experience healing and deliverance; they are the ones humble enough to ask God for help.

able! You don't know where he comes from, yet he opened my eyes. 31We know that God does not listen to sinners. He listens to the godly man who does his will. 32Nobody has ever heard of opening the eyes of a man born blind. 33If this man were not from God, he could do nothing."

34To this they replied, "You were steeped in sin at birth; how dare you lecture us!" And they threw him out.

Spiritual Blindness

35Jesus heard that they had thrown him out, and when he found him, he said, "Do you believe in the Son of Man?"

36"Who is he, sir?" the man asked. "Tell me so that I may believe in him."

37Jesus said, "You have now seen him; in fact, he is the one speaking with you."

38Then the man said, "Lord, I believe," and he worshiped him.

39Jesus said, "For judgment I have come into this world, so that the blind will see and those who see will become blind."

40Some Pharisees who were with him heard him say this and asked, "What? Are we blind too?"

41Jesus said, "If you were blind, you would not be guilty of sin; but now that you claim you can see, your guilt remains.

The Shepherd and His Flock

10 "I tell you the truth, the man who does not enter the sheep pen by the gate, but climbs in by some other way, is a thief and a robber. 2The man who enters by the gate is the shepherd of his sheep. 3The watchman opens the gate for him, and the sheep listen to his voice. He calls his own sheep by name and leads them out. 4When he has brought out all his own, he goes on ahead of them, and his sheep follow him because they know his voice. 5But they will never follow a stranger; in fact, they will run away from him because they do not recognize a stranger's voice." 6Jesus used this figure of speech, but they did not understand what he was telling them.

7Therefore Jesus said again, "I tell you the truth, I am the gate for the sheep. 8All who ever came before me were thieves and robbers, but the sheep did not listen to them. 9I am the gate; whoever enters through me will be saved.[a] He will come in and go out, and find pasture. 10The thief comes only to steal and kill and destroy; I have come that they may have life, and have it to the full.

11"I am the good shepherd. The good shepherd lays down his life for the sheep. 12The hired hand is not the shepherd who owns the sheep. So when he sees the wolf coming, he abandons the sheep and runs away. Then the wolf attacks the flock and scatters it. 13The man runs away because he is a hired hand and cares nothing for the sheep.

14"I am the good shepherd; I know my sheep and my sheep know me— 15just as the Father knows me and I know the Father—and I lay down my life for the sheep. 16I have other sheep that are not of this sheep pen. I must bring them also. They too will listen to my voice, and there shall be one flock and one shepherd. 17The reason my Father loves me is that I lay down my life—only to take it up again. 18No one takes it from me, but I lay it down of my own accord. I have authority to lay it down and authority to take it up again. This command I received from my Father."

19At these words the Jews were again divided. 20Many of them said, "He is demon-possessed and raving mad. Why listen to him?"

21But others said, "These are not the sayings of a man possessed by a demon. Can a demon open the eyes of the blind?"

The Unbelief of the Jews

22Then came the Feast of Dedication[b] at Jerusalem. It was winter, 23and Jesus was in the temple area walking in Solomon's Colonnade. 24The Jews gathered around him, saying, "How long will you keep us in suspense? If you are the Christ,[c] tell us plainly."

25Jesus answered, "I did tell you, but you do not believe. The miracles I do in my Father's name speak for me, 26but you do not believe because you are not my sheep. 27My sheep listen to my voice; I know them, and they follow me. 28I give them eternal life, and they shall never perish; no one can snatch them out of my hand. 29My Father, who has given them to me,

[a]9 Or *kept safe* [b]22 That is, Hanukkah [c]24 Or *Messiah*

10:1–5 The shepherd knows each of his sheep by name, and they know and respond only to his voice. In like manner, Jesus knows our personalities, needs, feelings and desires. He even knows our faults and our sins, yet he still loves us! He calls out to us and leads us in the way that is best for us. To be set free from the pain of our past, we need to respond to Jesus' guiding voice—the voice of one who knows us fully and loves us completely.

10:7–18 At night, shepherds in Bible times led their flocks to a natural sheep pen (an area boxed in by brush or rock). The shepherd slept in the opening and literally became the gate to the sheepfold. With his own body he would protect the sheep from wild animals and robbers. This is what Jesus, the gate and the good shepherd, does for us. By sacrificing his life he has provided the means for our protection from the evil one. In Jesus Christ we can find security, knowing that he is watching over us.

10:27–29 When we surrender our lives to Jesus, we can feel safe and secure. No one can take us away from him and his care, not even the devil! Such security is sometimes hard for us to grasp. Life often seems very unsafe, especially when we have been hurt in the past. Some of us may try to protect ourselves by keeping everyone at a distance—even God. Yet God can care for us far better than we can care for ourselves. When we surrender our lives to him, he will surround us with his peace and even redeem our past hurts.

is greater than all[a]; no one can snatch them out of my Father's hand. 30I and the Father are one."

31Again the Jews picked up stones to stone him, 32but Jesus said to them, "I have shown you many great miracles from the Father. For which of these do you stone me?"

33"We are not stoning you for any of these," replied the Jews, "but for blasphemy, because you, a mere man, claim to be God."

34Jesus answered them, "Is it not written in your Law, 'I have said you are gods'[b]? 35If he called them 'gods,' to whom the word of God came—and the Scripture cannot be broken—36what about the one whom the Father set apart as his very own and sent into the world? Why then do you accuse me of blasphemy because I said, 'I am God's Son'? 37Do not believe me unless I do what my Father does. 38But if I do it, even though you do not believe me, believe the miracles, that you may know and understand that the Father is in me, and I in the Father." 39Again they tried to seize him, but he escaped their grasp.

40Then Jesus went back across the Jordan to the place where John had been baptizing in the early days. Here he stayed 41and many people came to him. They said, "Though John never performed a miraculous sign, all that John said about this man was true." 42And in that place many believed in Jesus.

The Death of Lazarus

11 Now a man named Lazarus was sick. He was from Bethany, the village of Mary and her sister Martha. 2This Mary, whose brother Lazarus now lay sick, was the same one who poured perfume on the Lord and wiped his feet with her hair. 3So the sisters sent word to Jesus, "Lord, the one you love is sick."

4When he heard this, Jesus said, "This sickness will not end in death. No, it is for God's glory so that God's Son may be glorified through it." 5Jesus loved Martha and her sister and Lazarus. 6Yet when he heard that Lazarus was sick, he stayed where he was two more days.

7Then he said to his disciples, "Let us go back to Judea."

8"But Rabbi," they said, "a short while ago the Jews tried to stone you, and yet you are going back there?"

9Jesus answered, "Are there not twelve hours of daylight? A man who walks by day will not stumble, for he sees by this world's light. 10It is when he walks by night that he stumbles, for he has no light."

11After he had said this, he went on to tell them, "Our friend Lazarus has fallen asleep; but I am going there to wake him up."

12His disciples replied, "Lord, if he sleeps, he will get better." 13Jesus had been speaking of his death, but his disciples thought he meant natural sleep.

14So then he told them plainly, "Lazarus is dead, 15and for your sake I am glad I was not there, so that you may believe. But let us go to him."

16Then Thomas (called Didymus) said to the rest of the disciples, "Let us also go, that we may die with him."

Jesus Comforts the Sisters

17On his arrival, Jesus found that Lazarus had already been in the tomb for four days. 18Bethany was less than two miles[c] from Jerusalem, 19and many Jews had come to Martha and Mary to comfort them in the loss of their brother. 20When Martha heard that Jesus was coming, she went out to meet him, but Mary stayed at home.

21"Lord," Martha said to Jesus, "if you had been here, my brother would not have died. 22But I know that even now God will give you whatever you ask."

23Jesus said to her, "Your brother will rise again."

24Martha answered, "I know he will rise again in the resurrection at the last day."

25Jesus said to her, "I am the resurrection and the life. He who believes in me will live, even though he dies; 26and whoever lives and believes in me will never die. Do you believe this?"

27"Yes, Lord," she told him, "I believe that you are the Christ,[d] the Son of God, who was to come into the world."

28And after she had said this, she went back and called her sister Mary aside. "The Teacher is here," she said, "and is asking for you." 29When Mary heard this, she got up quickly and went to him. 30Now Jesus had not yet entered the village, but was still at the place where Martha had met him. 31When the Jews who had been with Mary in the house, comforting her, noticed how quickly she got up and went out, they followed

[a]29 Many early manuscripts *What my Father has given me is greater than all* [b]34 Psalm 82:6 [c]18 Greek *fifteen stadia* (about 3 kilometers) [d]27 Or *Messiah*

10:30–38 For Jesus to claim that he and the Father were one was a clear claim to divinity (see 1:1–2; 8:58). Jesus was God in human flesh (see 1:14). He was one with his Father in essence, in purpose, in word and in thought. All of Scripture and all of Jesus' miracles attest to his divine authority (see 5:39; 10:37–38) Only such a God-man could perfectly understand our human weaknesses yet still command our complete trust.

11:3–4 When faced with a critical illness or a hopeless situation, we have two basic options: We can complain and blame God, or we can view the crisis as an opportunity to make a request of God. Mary and Martha asked Jesus to help them with their great loss. Then they gave him the glory for the amazing miracle he performed—raising their brother, Lazarus, from the dead. Since God can raise someone from the dead, God is more than able to help us, if we humbly ask him for help.

her, supposing she was going to the tomb to mourn there.

32When Mary reached the place where Jesus was and saw him, she fell at his feet and said, "Lord, if you had been here, my brother would not have died."

33When Jesus saw her weeping, and the Jews who had come along with her also weeping, he was deeply moved in spirit and troubled. 34"Where have you laid him?" he asked.

"Come and see, Lord," they replied.

35Jesus wept.

36Then the Jews said, "See how he loved him!"

37But some of them said, "Could not he who opened the eyes of the blind man have kept this man from dying?"

Jesus Raises Lazarus From the Dead

38Jesus, once more deeply moved, came to the tomb. It was a cave with a stone laid across the entrance. 39"Take away the stone," he said.

"But, Lord," said Martha, the sister of the dead man, "by this time there is a bad odor, for he has been there four days."

40Then Jesus said, "Did I not tell you that if you believed, you would see the glory of God?"

41So they took away the stone. Then Jesus looked up and said, "Father, I thank you that you have heard me. 42I knew that you always hear me, but I said this for the benefit of the people standing here, that they may believe that you sent me."

43When he had said this, Jesus called in a loud voice, "Lazarus, come out!" 44The dead man came out, his hands and feet wrapped with strips of linen, and a cloth around his face.

Jesus said to them, "Take off the grave clothes and let him go."

The Plot to Kill Jesus

45Therefore many of the Jews who had come to visit Mary, and had seen what Jesus did, put their faith in him. 46But some of them went to the Pharisees and told them what Jesus had done. 47Then the chief priests and the Pharisees called a meeting of the Sanhedrin.

"What are we accomplishing?" they asked. "Here is this man performing many miraculous signs. 48If we let him go on like this, everyone will believe in him, and then the Romans will come and take away both our place[a] and our nation."

49Then one of them, named Caiaphas, who was high priest that year, spoke up, "You know nothing at all! 50You do not realize that it is better for you that one man die for the people than that the whole nation perish."

51He did not say this on his own, but as high priest that year he prophesied that Jesus would die for the Jewish nation, 52and not only for that nation but also for the scattered children of God, to bring them together and make them one. 53So from that day on they plotted to take his life.

54Therefore Jesus no longer moved about publicly among the Jews. Instead he withdrew to a region near the desert, to a village called Ephraim, where he stayed with his disciples.

55When it was almost time for the Jewish Passover, many went up from the country to Jerusalem for their ceremonial cleansing before the Passover. 56They kept looking for Jesus, and as they stood in the temple area they asked one another, "What do you think? Isn't he coming to the Feast at all?" 57But the chief priests and Pharisees had given orders that if anyone found out where Jesus was, he should report it so that they might arrest him.

Jesus Anointed at Bethany

12 Six days before the Passover, Jesus arrived at Bethany, where Lazarus lived, whom Jesus had raised from the dead. 2Here a dinner was given in Jesus' honor. Martha served, while Lazarus was among those reclining at the table with him. 3Then Mary took about a pint[b] of pure nard, an expensive perfume; she poured it on Jesus' feet and wiped his feet with her hair. And the house was filled with the fragrance of the perfume.

4But one of his disciples, Judas Iscariot, who was later to betray him, objected, 5"Why wasn't this perfume sold and the money given to the poor? It was worth a year's wages.[c]" 6He did not say this because he cared about the poor but because he was a thief; as keeper of the money bag, he used to help himself to what was put into it.

7"Leave her alone," Jesus replied. "⌊It was intended⌋ that she should save this perfume for the day of my burial. 8You will always have the poor among you, but you will not always have me."

9Meanwhile a large crowd of Jews found out that Jesus was there and came, not only because of him but also to see Lazarus, whom he had

[a]48 Or *temple* [b]3 Greek *a litra* (probably about 0.5 liter) [c]5 Greek *three hundred denarii*

11:37–44 Imagine the scene when Jesus raised Lazarus from the dead. The man had been dead and buried for four days. Yet he responded to Jesus' voice and walked out of the tomb, wrapped in grave clothes! The one who has power over the grave has power to bring new life to us, too (see 11:25–26). Jesus Christ can set us free from the bondage of sin and death.

12:1–8 Mary's faith in Jesus is a testimony for us all. The Bible records three instances where Mary was at Jesus' feet: She sat at Jesus' feet listening to what he taught (see Luke 10:39); she threw herself at his feet crying and seeking comfort (see 11:32); in this passage she knelt to clean and anoint his feet with expensive perfume. Jesus was first in Mary's heart, and she surrendered herself to him. The decision to surrender all we are and have to God is crucial. When we do this, God can help us with the problems we face.

Mary & Martha

As with all siblings, Mary and Martha each possessed her own unique gifts and personalities. Martha was industrious and concerned about detail; Mary was studious and contemplative, relishing the opportunity to study and learn.

Yet we are given a glimpse into Mary's heart when we see her anoint Jesus with costly perfume shortly before his death. Judas hypocritically criticized Mary's extravagant act of love and devotion. As we seek God and surrender our lives to him, fully devoting all that we have to his service, others will criticize us. We must remember that pleasing God is what truly matters.

Both Mary and Martha grew in their understanding of Jesus because of the events surrounding the death of their brother, Lazarus. Jesus knew that if he delayed coming to Mary and Martha's home, he wouldn't arrive until after Lazarus's death. If he had come before Lazarus died, Jesus certainly could have healed him, but by coming later, Jesus was able to do something even more glorious—raise him from the dead!

For Mary and Martha, the delay was painful. The ultimate outcome, however, was a deeper faith and a fuller experience of the joy that comes from trusting God with the details of life. As we go through our own difficult times, we may not always understand what God is doing, but we will grow in strength and faith as we persevere. There is always hope when the God who can raise the dead is on our side.

STRENGTHS AND ACCOMPLISHMENTS:

Both were devoted followers of Jesus.

Martha was hardworking, efficient and conscientious.

Mary attentively listened to the words of Jesus.

WEAKNESSES AND MISTAKES:

Martha was so worried about the details of her ministry that she missed spending time with Jesus.

LESSONS FROM THEIR LIVES:

We may get so busy doing things that relate to spiritual growth—even good things—that we forget to spend time with Jesus.

Jesus valued the contribution of both of these women.

KEY VERSES:

"Martha was distracted by all the preparations that had to be made. She came to him and asked, 'Lord, don't you care that my sister has left me to do the work by myself? Tell her to help me!' 'Martha, Martha,' the Lord answered, 'you are worried and upset about many things, but only one thing is needed. Mary has chosen what is better, and it will not be taken away from her' " (Luke 10:40–42).

The story of Mary and Martha is found in Matthew 26:6–13; Luke 10:38–42; John 11:1–45 and 12:1–8.

raised from the dead. 10So the chief priests made plans to kill Lazarus as well, 11for on account of him many of the Jews were going over to Jesus and putting their faith in him.

The Triumphal Entry

‰ See Matthew 21:4–9; Mark 11:7–10; Luke 19:35–38

12The next day the great crowd that had come for the Feast heard that Jesus was on his way to Jerusalem. 13They took palm branches and went out to meet him, shouting,

"Hosanna![a]"

"Blessed is he who comes in the name of
the Lord!"[b]

"Blessed is the King of Israel!"

14Jesus found a young donkey and sat upon it, as it is written,

15"Do not be afraid, O Daughter of Zion;
see, your king is coming,
seated on a donkey's colt."[c]

16At first his disciples did not understand all this. Only after Jesus was glorified did they realize that these things had been written about him and that they had done these things to him.

17Now the crowd that was with him when he called Lazarus from the tomb and raised him from the dead continued to spread the word. 18Many people, because they had heard that he had given this miraculous sign, went out to meet him. 19So the Pharisees said to one another, "See, this is getting us nowhere. Look how the whole world has gone after him!"

Jesus Predicts His Death

20Now there were some Greeks among those who went up to worship at the Feast. 21They came to Philip, who was from Bethsaida in Galilee, with a request. "Sir," they said, "we would like to see Jesus." 22Philip went to tell Andrew; Andrew and Philip in turn told Jesus.

23Jesus replied, "The hour has come for the Son of Man to be glorified. 24I tell you the truth, unless a kernel of wheat falls to the ground and dies, it remains only a single seed. But if it dies, it produces many seeds. 25The man who loves his life will lose it, while the man who hates his life in this world will keep it for eternal life. 26Whoever serves me must follow me; and where I am, my servant also will be. My Father will honor the one who serves me.

27"Now my heart is troubled, and what shall I say? 'Father, save me from this hour'? No, it was for this very reason I came to this hour. 28Father, glorify your name!"

Then a voice came from heaven, "I have glorified it, and will glorify it again." 29The crowd that was there and heard it said it had thundered; others said an angel had spoken to him.

30Jesus said, "This voice was for your benefit, not mine. 31Now is the time for judgment on this world; now the prince of this world will be driven out. 32But I, when I am lifted up from the earth, will draw all men to myself." 33He said this to show the kind of death he was going to die.

34The crowd spoke up, "We have heard from the Law that the Christ[d] will remain forever, so how can you say, 'The Son of Man must be lifted up'? Who is this 'Son of Man'?"

35Then Jesus told them, "You are going to have the light just a little while longer. Walk while you have the light, before darkness overtakes you. The man who walks in the dark does not know where he is going. 36Put your trust in the light while you have it, so that you may become sons of light." When he had finished speaking, Jesus left and hid himself from them.

The Jews Continue in Their Unbelief

37Even after Jesus had done all these miraculous signs in their presence, they still would not believe in him. 38This was to fulfill the word of Isaiah the prophet:

"Lord, who has believed our message
and to whom has the arm of the Lord
been revealed?"[e]

39For this reason they could not believe, because, as Isaiah says elsewhere:

40"He has blinded their eyes
and deadened their hearts,
so they can neither see with their eyes,
nor understand with their hearts,
nor turn—and I would heal them."[f]

41Isaiah said this because he saw Jesus' glory and spoke about him.

42Yet at the same time many even among the

[a]13 A Hebrew expression meaning "Save!" which became an exclamation of praise [b]13 Psalm 118:25, 26 [c]15 Zech. 9:9 [d]34 Or *Messiah* [e]38 Isaiah 53:1 [f]40 Isaiah 6:10

12:12–19 Jesus had just raised Lazarus from the dead in front of many witnesses. The people hailed him as their Messiah. In a few days, however, they would stand back in apathy as the Jewish leaders and Roman governors crowned Jesus with thorns and executed him as a pretentious "king of the Jews" (18:39—19:22). The world's affections for God blow hot and cold. But we are called to follow Jesus even when it is not the popular thing to do.

12:23–25 Instead of pronouncing a king's acceptance speech, Jesus explained that he would have to die to bring new life to his followers. One must die to an old life before a new life can begin. We are therefore called to move from brokenness to healing, from guilt to forgiveness and from isolation to intimacy.

12:42–43 Many of the Jewish leaders believed in Jesus, but their faith was rendered ineffective because of their fear and isolation. They were more concerned about what their peers thought of them than about what God thought about them. This kind of faith is very limiting. To make real spiritual progress, we need to share our belief in God with others. When we tell others what we believe, we are inviting them to hold us accountable. Accountability for

leaders believed in him. But because of the Pharisees they would not confess their faith for fear they would be put out of the synagogue; 43for they loved praise from men more than praise from God.

44Then Jesus cried out, "When a man believes in me, he does not believe in me only, but in the one who sent me. 45When he looks at me, he sees the one who sent me. 46I have come into the world as a light, so that no one who believes in me should stay in darkness.

47"As for the person who hears my words but does not keep them, I do not judge him. For I did not come to judge the world, but to save it. 48There is a judge for the one who rejects me and does not accept my words; that very word which I spoke will condemn him at the last day. 49For I did not speak of my own accord, but the Father who sent me commanded me what to say and how to say it. 50I know that his command leads to eternal life. So whatever I say is just what the Father has told me to say."

Jesus Washes His Disciples' Feet

13 It was just before the Passover Feast. Jesus knew that the time had come for him to leave this world and go to the Father. Having loved his own who were in the world, he now showed them the full extent of his love.[a]

2The evening meal was being served, and the devil had already prompted Judas Iscariot, son of Simon, to betray Jesus. 3Jesus knew that the Father had put all things under his power, and that he had come from God and was returning to God; 4so he got up from the meal, took off his outer clothing, and wrapped a towel around his waist. 5After that, he poured water into a basin and began to wash his disciples' feet, drying them with the towel that was wrapped around him.

6He came to Simon Peter, who said to him, "Lord, are you going to wash my feet?"

7Jesus replied, "You do not realize now what I am doing, but later you will understand."

8"No," said Peter, "you shall never wash my feet."

Jesus answered, "Unless I wash you, you have no part with me."

9"Then, Lord," Simon Peter replied, "not just my feet but my hands and my head as well!"

10Jesus answered, "A person who has had a bath needs only to wash his feet; his whole body is clean. And you are clean, though not every one of you." 11For he knew who was going to betray him, and that was why he said not every one was clean.

12When he had finished washing their feet, he put on his clothes and returned to his place. "Do you understand what I have done for you?" he asked them. 13"You call me 'Teacher' and 'Lord,' and rightly so, for that is what I am. 14Now that I, your Lord and Teacher, have washed your feet, you also should wash one another's feet. 15I have set you an example that you should do as I have done for you. 16I tell you the truth, no servant is greater than his master, nor is a messenger greater than the one who sent him. 17Now that you know these things, you will be blessed if you do them.

Jesus Predicts His Betrayal

18"I am not referring to all of you; I know those I have chosen. But this is to fulfill the scripture: 'He who shares my bread has lifted up his heel against me.'[b]

19"I am telling you now before it happens, so that when it does happen you will believe that I am He. 20I tell you the truth, whoever accepts anyone I send accepts me; and whoever accepts me accepts the one who sent me."

21After he had said this, Jesus was troubled in spirit and testified, "I tell you the truth, one of you is going to betray me."

22His disciples stared at one another, at a loss to know which of them he meant. 23One of them, the disciple whom Jesus loved, was reclining next to him. 24Simon Peter motioned to this disciple and said, "Ask him which one he means."

25Leaning back against Jesus, he asked him, "Lord, who is it?"

26Jesus answered, "It is the one to whom I will give this piece of bread when I have dipped it in the dish." Then, dipping the piece of bread, he gave it to Judas Iscariot, son of Simon. 27As soon as Judas took the bread, Satan entered into him.

"What you are about to do, do quickly," Jesus told him, 28but no one at the meal understood why Jesus said this to him. 29Since Judas had charge of the money, some thought Jesus was

[a]1 Or *he loved them to the last* [b]18 Psalm 41:9

---

our intentions, attitudes and actions will help our spiritual development.

13:1–7 The Son of God came, not as a proud master who demanded service from others, but as a humble servant who delighted in helping others. In stooping down to wash his disciples' feet, Jesus showed them that true leaders serve their followers. To follow Jesus' example, we must start by allowing him to serve us. As we experience his cleansing in our lives, we can help others by serving them—sharing our faith, listening to their confessions, encouraging them and standing by them in tough times. As we support others, we will be strengthened as well.

13:20 God expresses himself to us primarily through chosen messengers and makes our relationships with others sacred. We experience God's healing love through the godly people he brings into our lives. And as we reach out to others in the name of Jesus, we become his messengers too. God can use us to bring his powerful healing love into their lives as well.

13:23; 19:26; 21:20 Throughout this book, the apostle John referred to himself as "the disciple whom Jesus loved." John understood God's unconditional love for him. We, too, need to see ourselves as God does—as deeply loved. This will then pave the way for further spiritual growth.

telling him to buy what was needed for the Feast, or to give something to the poor. 30As soon as Judas had taken the bread, he went out. And it was night.

Jesus Predicts Peter's Denial

‰ See Matthew 26:33–35; Mark 14:29–31; Luke 22:33–34

31When he was gone, Jesus said, "Now is the Son of Man glorified and God is glorified in him. 32If God is glorified in him,[a] God will glorify the Son in himself, and will glorify him at once.

33"My children, I will be with you only a little longer. You will look for me, and just as I told the Jews, so I tell you now: Where I am going, you cannot come.

34"A new command I give you: Love one another. As I have loved you, so you must love one another. 35By this all men will know that you are my disciples, if you love one another."

36Simon Peter asked him, "Lord, where are you going?"

Jesus replied, "Where I am going, you cannot follow now, but you will follow later."

37Peter asked, "Lord, why can't I follow you now? I will lay down my life for you."

38Then Jesus answered, "Will you really lay down your life for me? I tell you the truth, before the rooster crows, you will disown me three times!

Jesus Comforts His Disciples

14 "Do not let your hearts be troubled. Trust in God[b]; trust also in me. 2In my Father's house are many rooms; if it were not so, I would have told you. I am going there to prepare a place for you. 3And if I go and prepare a place for you, I will come back and take you to be with me that you also may be where I am. 4You know the way to the place where I am going."

Jesus the Way to the Father

5Thomas said to him, "Lord, we don't know where you are going, so how can we know the way?"

6Jesus answered, "I am the way and the truth and the life. No one comes to the Father except through me. 7If you really knew me, you would know[c] my Father as well. From now on, you do know him and have seen him."

8Philip said, "Lord, show us the Father and that will be enough for us."

9Jesus answered: "Don't you know me, Philip, even after I have been among you such a long time? Anyone who has seen me has seen the Father. How can you say, 'Show us the Father'? 10Don't you believe that I am in the Father, and that the Father is in me? The words I say to you are not just my own. Rather, it is the Father, living in me, who is doing his work. 11Believe me when I say that I am in the Father and the Father is in me; or at least believe on the evidence of the miracles themselves. 12I tell you the truth, anyone who has faith in me will do what I have been doing. He will do even greater things than these, because I am going to the Father. 13And I will do whatever you ask in my name, so that the Son may bring glory to the Father. 14You may ask me for anything in my name, and I will do it.

Jesus Promises the Holy Spirit

15"If you love me, you will obey what I command. 16And I will ask the Father, and he will give you another Counselor to be with you forever— 17the Spirit of truth. The world cannot accept him, because it neither sees him nor knows him. But you know him, for he lives with you and will be[d] in you. 18I will not leave you as orphans; I will come to you. 19Before long, the world will not see me anymore, but you will see me. Because I live, you also will live. 20On that day you will realize that I am in my Father, and you are in me, and I am in you. 21Whoever has my commands and obeys them, he is the one who loves me. He who loves me will be loved by my Father, and I too will love him and show myself to him."

22Then Judas (not Judas Iscariot) said, "But, Lord, why do you intend to show yourself to us and not to the world?"

23Jesus replied, "If anyone loves me, he will obey my teaching. My Father will love him, and we will come to him and make our home with him. 24He who does not love me will not obey my teaching. These words you hear are not my own; they belong to the Father who sent me.

25"All this I have spoken while still with you. 26But the Counselor, the Holy Spirit, whom the Father will send in my name, will teach you all things and will remind you of everything I have said to you. 27Peace I leave with you; my peace I give you. I do not give to you as the world

[a]32 Many early manuscripts do not have *If God is glorified in him.* [b]1 Or *You trust in God* [c]7 Some early manuscripts *If you really have known me, you will know* [d]17 Some early manuscripts *and is*

14:5–11 Faith in Jesus is the only way to truly know God and receive the meaningful life he wants for each of us. Many people know all about God and Jesus Christ, but they don't know God personally. Genuine faith is personal and relational. Faith is based on the truth that can be known about God through Jesus Christ, who is the way, the truth and the life.

14:15–18 God desires to have a special relationship with us. When Jesus ascended to the Father in heaven, he sent his Spirit to live within his followers. This spirit serves as our Counselor, ministering God's compassion to us, bringing to mind Jesus' teachings, guiding us into all truth and bringing our needs before God the Father (see 14:26; 15:26; 16:7–15). The Holy Spirit will never leave us or forsake us. He is with us at all times, and he has the power to help us overcome the problems in our lives.

14:27 Many of us deal with stress and anxiety, grief and loss; we long for peace of mind and heart. So did the early disciples. They were about to lose their best friend, their Messiah. Their souls were troubled, and they were

Gently and Humbly Correcting Each Other

John 15:5–15 We all need a network of support and accountability. Within this safe haven there will be times when we will need to correct others regarding sin; sometimes others will need to correct us as well. When touching on such deep and sensitive issues, it is important to speak in the language of love, not condemnation. While this is a delicate matter, our willingness to correct others and to be corrected in accordance with God's Word will help preserve our spiritual gains.

The Bible tells us that "if someone is caught in a sin, you who are spiritual should restore him gently. But watch yourself, or you also may be tempted. Carry each other's burdens, and in this way you will fulfill the law of Christ" (Galatians 6:1–2). This command of Paul's echoes a similar command that Jesus taught his disciples: "A new command I give you: Love one another. As I have loved you, so you must love one another" (John 13:34). Jesus reiterated this instruction later, saying, "My command is this: Love each other as I have loved you. Greater love has no one than this, that he lay down his life for his friends" (15:12–13).

We must love others as our Savior has loved us. Love doesn't just speak words of righteousness. Sometimes love is spoken in our silence as we hold back our condemnation of someone who comes to us looking for help. Love may help carry the weight of others' burdens. Or love may require that we compassionately confront others with the truth of their sin. We can be part of a support network that lovingly confronts others just as they lovingly confront us and help us preserve our spiritual gains.

Turn to 1 Corinthians 6.

gives. Do not let your hearts be troubled and do
not be afraid.
28"You heard me say, 'I am going away and
I am coming back to you.' If you loved me, you
would be glad that I am going to the Father, for
the Father is greater than I. 29I have told you
now before it happens, so that when it does
happen you will believe. 30I will not speak with
you much longer, for the prince of this world is
coming. He has no hold on me, 31but the world
must learn that I love the Father and that I do
exactly what my Father has commanded me.
"Come now; let us leave.

The Vine and the Branches

15 "I am the true vine, and my Father is
the gardener. 2He cuts off every branch
in me that bears no fruit, while every branch
that does bear fruit he prunes[a] so that it will
be even more fruitful. 3You are already clean
because of the word I have spoken to you. 4Re-
main in me, and I will remain in you. No
branch can bear fruit by itself; it must remain in
the vine. Neither can you bear fruit unless you
remain in me.
5"I am the vine; you are the branches. If a
man remains in me and I in him, he will bear
much fruit; apart from me you can do nothing.
6If anyone does not remain in me, he is like a
branch that is thrown away and withers; such
branches are picked up, thrown into the fire and
burned. 7If you remain in me and my words
remain in you, ask whatever you wish, and it
will be given you. 8This is to my Father's glory,
that you bear much fruit, showing yourselves to
be my disciples.
9"As the Father has loved me, so have I loved
you. Now remain in my love. 10If you obey my
commands, you will remain in my love, just as
I have obeyed my Father's commands and remain in his love. 11I have told you this so that
my joy may be in you and that your joy may be
complete. 12My command is this: Love each
other as I have loved you. 13Greater love has no
one than this, that he lay down his life for his

[a]2 The Greek for *prunes* also means *cleans.*

looking for something to fill the void. Yet Jesus said he would give them peace. Unlike worldly peace, which is merely an absence of conflict, God can bring us peace even in the midst of our troubles (see 16:33).

15:1–8 God wants our lives to be like the fruitful branches of a grapevine. The only way to be fruitful is to remain connected to Jesus, the vine, and to let God, the gardener, prune our lives in ways that will stimulate growth and fruitfulness. God's work of cultivating, weeding and pruning in our lives yields spiritual fruit. Just as sustenance comes through the vine, so fullness of life comes through faith in Jesus Christ. We need to stay close to God in Jesus Christ, the source of our spiritual growth and fruitfulness.

15:9–12 Genuine, unconditional love overflows from the abundant love God has given us. Only when we experience and remain in God's love can we genuinely love ourselves and others. God's joy is made complete in us as we experience his love in our lives.

friends. 14You are my friends if you do what I command. 15I no longer call you servants, because a servant does not know his master's business. Instead, I have called you friends, for everything that I learned from my Father I have made known to you. 16You did not choose me, but I chose you and appointed you to go and bear fruit—fruit that will last. Then the Father will give you whatever you ask in my name. 17This is my command: Love each other.

The World Hates the Disciples

18"If the world hates you, keep in mind that it hated me first. 19If you belonged to the world, it would love you as its own. As it is, you do not belong to the world, but I have chosen you out of the world. That is why the world hates you. 20Remember the words I spoke to you: 'No servant is greater than his master.'[a] If they persecuted me, they will persecute you also. If they obeyed my teaching, they will obey yours also. 21They will treat you this way because of my name, for they do not know the One who sent me. 22If I had not come and spoken to them, they would not be guilty of sin. Now, however, they have no excuse for their sin. 23He who hates me hates my Father as well. 24If I had not done among them what no one else did, they would not be guilty of sin. But now they have seen these miracles, and yet they have hated both me and my Father. 25But this is to fulfill what is written in their Law: 'They hated me without reason.'[b]

26"When the Counselor comes, whom I will send to you from the Father, the Spirit of truth who goes out from the Father, he will testify about me. 27And you also must testify, for you have been with me from the beginning.

16 "All this I have told you so that you will not go astray. 2They will put you out of the synagogue; in fact, a time is coming when anyone who kills you will think he is offering a service to God. 3They will do such things because they have not known the Father or me. 4I have told you this, so that when the time comes you will remember that I warned you. I did not tell you this at first because I was with you.

The Work of the Holy Spirit

5"Now I am going to him who sent me, yet none of you asks me, 'Where are you going?' 6Because I have said these things, you are filled with grief. 7But I tell you the truth: It is for your good that I am going away. Unless I go away, the Counselor will not come to you; but if I go, I will send him to you. 8When he comes, he will convict the world of guilt[c] in regard to sin and righteousness and judgment: 9in regard to sin, because men do not believe in me; 10in regard to righteousness, because I am going to the Father, where you can see me no longer; 11and in regard to judgment, because the prince of this world now stands condemned.

12"I have much more to say to you, more than you can now bear. 13But when he, the Spirit of truth, comes, he will guide you into all truth. He will not speak on his own; he will speak only what he hears, and he will tell you what is yet to come. 14He will bring glory to me by taking from what is mine and making it known to you. 15All that belongs to the Father is mine. That is why I said the Spirit will take from what is mine and make it known to you.

16"In a little while you will see me no more, and then after a little while you will see me."

The Disciples' Grief Will Turn to Joy

17Some of his disciples said to one another, "What does he mean by saying, 'In a little while you will see me no more, and then after a little while you will see me,' and 'Because I am going to the Father'?" 18They kept asking, "What does he mean by 'a little while'? We don't understand what he is saying."

19Jesus saw that they wanted to ask him about this, so he said to them, "Are you asking one another what I meant when I said, 'In a little while you will see me no more, and then after a little while you will see me'? 20I tell you the truth, you will weep and mourn while the world rejoices. You will grieve, but your grief will turn to joy. 21A woman giving birth to a child has pain because her time has come; but when her baby is born she forgets the anguish because of her joy that a child is born into the world. 22So with you: Now is your time of grief, but I will see you again and you will rejoice, and no one will take away your joy. 23In that day you will no longer ask me anything. I tell you the truth, my Father will give you whatever you ask in my name. 24Until now you have not asked for anything in my name. Ask and you will receive, and your joy will be complete.

25"Though I have been speaking figuratively, a time is coming when I will no longer use this kind of language but will tell you plainly about my Father. 26In that day you will ask in my name. I am not saying that I will ask the Father on your behalf. 27No, the Father himself loves you because you have loved me and have believed that I came from God. 28I came from the Father and entered the world; now I am leaving the world and going back to the Father."

29Then Jesus' disciples said, "Now you are speaking clearly and without figures of speech.

[a]20 John 13:16 [b]25 Psalms 35:19; 69:4 [c]8 Or *will expose the guilt of the world*

15:26–27 As the "Spirit of truth," the Holy Spirit gives wisdom to help us examine our lives and see past our self-deception. The Holy Spirit reveals the truth of God's Word, holds us accountable to other believers and conforms us to the image of God's Son. He can guide us to an accurate perception of ourselves. The result will be convicting, but so fulfilling that we cannot help but share the Good News with others.

30Now we can see that you know all things and
that you do not even need to have anyone ask
you questions. This makes us believe that you
came from God."
31"You believe at last!"[a] Jesus answered.
32"But a time is coming, and has come, when
you will be scattered, each to his own home.
You will leave me all alone. Yet I am not alone,
for my Father is with me.
33"I have told you these things, so that in me
you may have peace. In this world you will have
trouble. But take heart! I have overcome the
world."

Jesus Prays for Himself

17 After Jesus said this, he looked toward
heaven and prayed:

"Father, the time has come. Glorify
your Son, that your Son may glorify you.
2For you granted him authority over all
people that he might give eternal life to all
those you have given him. 3Now this is
eternal life: that they may know you, the
only true God, and Jesus Christ, whom
you have sent. 4I have brought you glory
on earth by completing the work you gave
me to do. 5And now, Father, glorify me in
your presence with the glory I had with
you before the world began.

Jesus Prays for His Disciples

6"I have revealed you[b] to those whom
you gave me out of the world. They were
yours; you gave them to me and they have
obeyed your word. 7Now they know that
everything you have given me comes from
you. 8For I gave them the words you gave
me and they accepted them. They knew
with certainty that I came from you, and
they believed that you sent me. 9I pray for
them. I am not praying for the world, but
for those you have given me, for they are
yours. 10All I have is yours, and all you
have is mine. And glory has come to me
through them. 11I will remain in the world
no longer, but they are still in the world,
and I am coming to you. Holy Father, protect them by the power of your name—the
name you gave me—so that they may be
one as we are one. 12While I was with
them, I protected them and kept them safe
by that name you gave me. None has been
lost except the one doomed to destruction
so that Scripture would be fulfilled.
13"I am coming to you now, but I say
these things while I am still in the world,
so that they may have the full measure of
my joy within them. 14I have given them
your word and the world has hated them,
for they are not of the world any more
than I am of the world. 15My prayer is not
that you take them out of the world but
that you protect them from the evil one.
16They are not of the world, even as I am
not of it. 17Sanctify[c] them by the truth;
your word is truth. 18As you sent me into
the world, I have sent them into the world.
19For them I sanctify myself, that they too
may be truly sanctified.

Jesus Prays for All Believers

20"My prayer is not for them alone. I
pray also for those who will believe in me
through their message, 21that all of them
may be one, Father, just as you are in me
and I am in you. May they also be in us so
that the world may believe that you have
sent me. 22I have given them the glory that
you gave me, that they may be one as we
are one: 23I in them and you in me. May
they be brought to complete unity to let
the world know that you sent me and have
loved them even as you have loved me.
24"Father, I want those you have given
me to be with me where I am, and to see
my glory, the glory you have given me
because you loved me before the creation
of the world.
25"Righteous Father, though the world
does not know you, I know you, and they
know that you have sent me. 26I have
made you known to them, and will continue to make you known in order that the
love you have for me may be in them and
that I myself may be in them."

Jesus Arrested

‰ See Matthew 26:47–56; Mark 14:43–50; Luke 22:47–53

18 When he had finished praying, Jesus
left with his disciples and crossed the

[a]31 Or *"Do you now believe?"* [b]6 Greek *your name*; also in verse 26 [c]17 Greek *hagiazo (set apart for sacred use* or *make holy)*; also in verse 19

16:33 In this world, we will encounter many problems and troubles. Some of these difficulties are inevitable and beyond our control. Yet these can be endured with God's help. Some of our suffering, however, is self-inflicted and can be avoided. In such situations, God still offers us peace as we muster the courage to repent. God's forgiveness and loving acceptance give us peace even when the trials and sorrows we face come as a result of our own sinfulness. God is powerful enough to lead us down the path of life; he has already overcome all the obstacles that stand in our way!

17:1–26 Jesus is our high priest and intercessor: He makes God's will known to us and our heartfelt needs known to God. Through his words and deeds Jesus reveals to us God's mercy, justice, glory and truth and his desire to establish a personal relationship with us. Jesus also intercedes with God the Father on our behalf, bringing our needs and requests continually before his throne. He prays that we will know his perfect joy, be guarded from all evil, grow in truth and holiness and show love toward all people. Jesus prayed this prayer for his twelve disciples when they faced his imminent death. Yet this prayer is applicable to all who follow Jesus.

Kidron Valley. On the other side there was an olive grove, and he and his disciples went into it.

2Now Judas, who betrayed him, knew the place, because Jesus had often met there with his disciples. 3So Judas came to the grove, guiding a detachment of soldiers and some officials from the chief priests and Pharisees. They were carrying torches, lanterns and weapons.

4Jesus, knowing all that was going to happen to him, went out and asked them, "Who is it you want?"

5"Jesus of Nazareth," they replied.

"I am he," Jesus said. (And Judas the traitor was standing there with them.) 6When Jesus said, "I am he," they drew back and fell to the ground.

7Again he asked them, "Who is it you want?"

And they said, "Jesus of Nazareth."

8"I told you that I am he," Jesus answered. "If you are looking for me, then let these men go." 9This happened so that the words he had spoken would be fulfilled: "I have not lost one of those you gave me."[a]

10Then Simon Peter, who had a sword, drew it and struck the high priest's servant, cutting off his right ear. (The servant's name was Malchus.)

11Jesus commanded Peter, "Put your sword away! Shall I not drink the cup the Father has given me?"

Jesus Taken to Annas

‰ See Matthew 26:57

12Then the detachment of soldiers with its commander and the Jewish officials arrested Jesus. They bound him 13and brought him first to Annas, who was the father-in-law of Caiaphas, the high priest that year. 14Caiaphas was the one who had advised the Jews that it would be good if one man died for the people.

Peter's First Denial

‰ See Matthew 26:69–70; Mark 14:66–68; Luke 22:55–57

15Simon Peter and another disciple were following Jesus. Because this disciple was known to the high priest, he went with Jesus into the high priest's courtyard, 16but Peter had to wait outside at the door. The other disciple, who was known to the high priest, came back, spoke to the girl on duty there and brought Peter in.

17"You are not one of his disciples, are you?" the girl at the door asked Peter.

He replied, "I am not."

18It was cold, and the servants and officials stood around a fire they had made to keep warm. Peter also was standing with them, warming himself.

The High Priest Questions Jesus

‰ See Matthew 26:59–68; Mark 14:55–65; Luke 22:63–71

19Meanwhile, the high priest questioned Jesus about his disciples and his teaching.

20"I have spoken openly to the world," Jesus replied. "I always taught in synagogues or at the temple, where all the Jews come together. I said nothing in secret. 21Why question me? Ask those who heard me. Surely they know what I said."

22When Jesus said this, one of the officials nearby struck him in the face. "Is this the way you answer the high priest?" he demanded.

23"If I said something wrong," Jesus replied, "testify as to what is wrong. But if I spoke the truth, why did you strike me?" 24Then Annas sent him, still bound, to Caiaphas the high priest.[b]

Peter's Second and Third Denials

‰ See Matthew 26:71–75; Mark 14:69–72; Luke 22:58–62

25As Simon Peter stood warming himself, he was asked, "You are not one of his disciples, are you?"

He denied it, saying, "I am not."

26One of the high priest's servants, a relative of the man whose ear Peter had cut off, challenged him, "Didn't I see you with him in the olive grove?" 27Again Peter denied it, and at that moment a rooster began to crow.

Jesus Before Pilate

‰ See Matthew 27:11–18,20–23; Mark 15:2–15; Luke 23:2–3,18–25

28Then the Jews led Jesus from Caiaphas to the palace of the Roman governor. By now it was early morning, and to avoid ceremonial uncleanness the Jews did not enter the palace; they wanted to be able to eat the Passover. 29So Pilate came out to them and asked, "What charges are you bringing against this man?"

30"If he were not a criminal," they replied, "we would not have handed him over to you."

31Pilate said, "Take him yourselves and judge him by your own law."

"But we have no right to execute anyone," the Jews objected. 32This happened so that the words Jesus had spoken indicating the kind of death he was going to die would be fulfilled.

33Pilate then went back inside the palace,

[a]9 John 6:39 [b]24 Or *(Now Annas had sent him, still bound, to Caiaphas the high priest.)*

18:15–18, 25–27 The arrest, trial and crucifixion of Jesus unfold over several chapters. The injustice of the situation may make us angry. We may find ourselves blaming the religious leaders who instigated Jesus' execution. We watch Peter's denial of Jesus not only once but three times, despite his earlier assurances of loyalty. Yet we have often done the same thing. We have made steps of faith, only to turn around and deny Christ's lordship over a crucial area of our lives. Peter meant well when he assured Jesus of his loyalty, but he still failed. Yet his denial of Christ was not the end of Peter's story (see 21:15–19). When we turn back from following Christ, we are not disqualified from his love either. With Jesus Christ, there is always the opportunity for restoration.

summoned Jesus and asked him, “Are you the king of the Jews?”

34“Is that your own idea,” Jesus asked, “or did others talk to you about me?”

35“Am I a Jew?” Pilate replied. “It was your people and your chief priests who handed you over to me. What is it you have done?”

36Jesus said, “My kingdom is not of this world. If it were, my servants would fight to prevent my arrest by the Jews. But now my kingdom is from another place.”

37“You are a king, then!” said Pilate.

Jesus answered, “You are right in saying I am a king. In fact, for this reason I was born, and for this I came into the world, to testify to the truth. Everyone on the side of truth listens to me.”

38“What is truth?” Pilate asked. With this he went out again to the Jews and said, “I find no basis for a charge against him. 39But it is your custom for me to release to you one prisoner at the time of the Passover. Do you want me to release ‘the king of the Jews’?”

40They shouted back, “No, not him! Give us Barabbas!” Now Barabbas had taken part in a rebellion.

Jesus Sentenced to Be Crucified

‰ See Matthew 27:27–31; Mark 15:16–20

19 Then Pilate took Jesus and had him flogged. 2The soldiers twisted together a crown of thorns and put it on his head. They clothed him in a purple robe 3and went up to him again and again, saying, “Hail, king of the Jews!” And they struck him in the face.

4Once more Pilate came out and said to the Jews, “Look, I am bringing him out to you to let you know that I find no basis for a charge against him.” 5When Jesus came out wearing the crown of thorns and the purple robe, Pilate said to them, “Here is the man!”

6As soon as the chief priests and their officials saw him, they shouted, “Crucify! Crucify!”

But Pilate answered, “You take him and crucify him. As for me, I find no basis for a charge against him.”

7The Jews insisted, “We have a law, and according to that law he must die, because he claimed to be the Son of God.”

8When Pilate heard this, he was even more afraid, 9and he went back inside the palace. “Where do you come from?” he asked Jesus, but Jesus gave him no answer. 10“Do you refuse to speak to me?” Pilate said. “Don’t you realize I have power either to free you or to crucify you?”

11Jesus answered, “You would have no power over me if it were not given to you from above. Therefore the one who handed me over to you is guilty of a greater sin.”

12From then on, Pilate tried to set Jesus free, but the Jews kept shouting, “If you let this man go, you are no friend of Caesar. Anyone who claims to be a king opposes Caesar.”

13When Pilate heard this, he brought Jesus out and sat down on the judge’s seat at a place known as the Stone Pavement (which in Aramaic is Gabbatha). 14It was the day of Preparation of Passover Week, about the sixth hour.

“Here is your king,” Pilate said to the Jews.

15But they shouted, “Take him away! Take him away! Crucify him!”

“Shall I crucify your king?” Pilate asked.

“We have no king but Caesar,” the chief priests answered.

16Finally Pilate handed him over to them to be crucified.

The Crucifixion

‰ See Matthew 27:33–44; Mark 15:22–32; Luke 23:33–43

So the soldiers took charge of Jesus. 17Carrying his own cross, he went out to the place of the Skull (which in Aramaic is called Golgotha). 18Here they crucified him, and with him two others—one on each side and Jesus in the middle.

19Pilate had a notice prepared and fastened to the cross. It read: JESUS OF NAZARETH, THE KING OF THE JEWS. 20Many of the Jews read this sign, for the place where Jesus was crucified was near the city, and the sign was written in Aramaic, Latin and Greek. 21The chief priests of the Jews protested to Pilate, “Do not write ‘The King of the Jews,’ but that this man claimed to be king of the Jews.”

22Pilate answered, “What I have written, I have written.”

23When the soldiers crucified Jesus, they took his clothes, dividing them into four shares, one for each of them, with the undergarment remaining. This garment was seamless, woven in one piece from top to bottom.

19:1–3 When we are ridiculed, rejected or abused, we should look up and remember Jesus’ experiences leading to the cross. Jesus suffered the shame and humiliation of ridicule, a crown of thorns and physical violence. He was shamefully exposed on the cross, yet was able to clearly state, “It is finished” (see 19:30). Because of the shame Jesus suffered, we can hold our heads high as we look to God. We have been forgiven for our sins and failures. Through Jesus, our sin and shame are removed, and we have been offered another chance at life.

19:4–16 The people who were shouting “Crucify! Crucify!” (19:6) had only days before hailed Jesus as their King (see 12:12–13). Sometimes we are tempted to do the same thing. We may have surrendered our lives to God only to discover that following Christ comes at a price we may not be willing to pay. We may have wanted a quick fix for our problems, but God wanted our full surrender. The people in Jerusalem gave up hope as Jesus hung on the cross. But three days later, these same people discovered that even death gives way to God’s power! The path of pain and death led to the victory of the resurrection! God calls us to take up our cross and follow Christ, signifying the death of our old life. But the cross we carry leads to the resurrected lives God desires for us. Our new lives in Christ are well worth the sacrifices God calls us to make.

24“Let’s not tear it,” they said to one another.
“Let’s decide by lot who will get it.”
This happened that the scripture might be
fulfilled which said,

“They divided my garments among them
and cast lots for my clothing.”[a]

So this is what the soldiers did.
25Near the cross of Jesus stood his mother,
his mother’s sister, Mary the wife of Clopas, and
Mary Magdalene. 26When Jesus saw his mother
there, and the disciple whom he loved standing
nearby, he said to his mother, “Dear woman,
here is your son,” 27and to the disciple, “Here is
your mother.” From that time on, this disciple
took her into his home.

The Death of Jesus

‰ See Matthew 27:48,50; Mark 15:36–37; Luke 23:36

28Later, knowing that all was now completed, and so that the Scripture would be fulfilled,
Jesus said, “I am thirsty.” 29A jar of wine vinegar
was there, so they soaked a sponge in it, put the
sponge on a stalk of the hyssop plant, and lifted
it to Jesus’ lips. 30When he had received the
drink, Jesus said, “It is finished.” With that, he
bowed his head and gave up his spirit.
31Now it was the day of Preparation, and the
next day was to be a special Sabbath. Because
the Jews did not want the bodies left on the
crosses during the Sabbath, they asked Pilate
to have the legs broken and the bodies taken
down. 32The soldiers therefore came and broke
the legs of the first man who had been crucified
with Jesus, and then those of the other. 33But
when they came to Jesus and found that he was
already dead, they did not break his legs. 34In-
stead, one of the soldiers pierced Jesus’ side
with a spear, bringing a sudden flow of blood
and water. 35The man who saw it has given
testimony, and his testimony is true. He knows
that he tells the truth, and he testifies so that
you also may believe. 36These things happened
so that the scripture would be fulfilled: “Not
one of his bones will be broken,”[b] 37and, as
another scripture says, “They will look on the
one they have pierced.”[c]

The Burial of Jesus

‰ See Matthew 27:57–61; Mark 15:42–47; Luke 23:50–56

38Later, Joseph of Arimathea asked Pilate for
the body of Jesus. Now Joseph was a disciple of
Jesus, but secretly because he feared the Jews.
With Pilate’s permission, he came and took the
body away. 39He was accompanied by Nicodemus, the man who earlier had visited Jesus at
night. Nicodemus brought a mixture of myrrh
and aloes, about seventy-five pounds.[d] 40Tak-
ing Jesus’ body, the two of them wrapped it,
with the spices, in strips of linen. This was in
accordance with Jewish burial customs. 41At the
place where Jesus was crucified, there was a garden, and in the garden a new tomb, in which no
one had ever been laid. 42Because it was the
Jewish day of Preparation and since the tomb
was nearby, they laid Jesus there.

The Empty Tomb

‰ See Matthew 28:1–8; Mark 16:1–8; Luke 24:1–10

20 Early on the first day of the week, while
it was still dark, Mary Magdalene went
to the tomb and saw that the stone had been
removed from the entrance. 2So she came running to Simon Peter and the other disciple, the
one Jesus loved, and said, “They have taken the
Lord out of the tomb, and we don’t know where
they have put him!”
3So Peter and the other disciple started for
the tomb. 4Both were running, but the other
disciple outran Peter and reached the tomb first.
5He bent over and looked in at the strips of
linen lying there but did not go in. 6Then Simon Peter, who was behind him, arrived and
went into the tomb. He saw the strips of linen
lying there, 7as well as the burial cloth that had
been around Jesus’ head. The cloth was folded
up by itself, separate from the linen. 8Finally the
other disciple, who had reached the tomb first,
also went inside. He saw and believed. 9(They
still did not understand from Scripture that
Jesus had to rise from the dead.)

Jesus Appears to Mary Magdalene

10Then the disciples went back to their
homes, 11but Mary stood outside the tomb crying. As she wept, she bent over to look into the
tomb 12and saw two angels in white, seated
where Jesus’ body had been, one at the head
and the other at the foot.
13They asked her, “Woman, why are you crying?”
“They have taken my Lord away,” she said,
“and I don’t know where they have put him.”
14At this, she turned around and saw Jesus

[a]24 Psalm 22:18 [b]36 Exodus 12:46; Num. 9:12; Psalm 34:20 [c]37 Zech. 12:10 [d]39 Greek *a hundred litrai* (about 34 kilograms)

19:28–30 When Jesus uttered his final words, what did he actually finish? On the cross, Jesus finished the work he was sent to do (see 17:4). He paid in full for our sin (see 1 Peter 3:18). In the greatest act of love in all history, and as fulfillment of a complicated, centuries-old system of sacrifices, Jesus became the perfect, sacrificial Lamb of God (see 1:29; Hebrews 8:1—10:18). The miracle of the resurrection confirmed that Jesus is the Savior who can bring forgiveness and new life to all of us (see 20:1–9).

20:11–18 Once healed of seven demons, Mary was a faithful follower of Jesus and had supported his ministry financially from the very start (see Mark 16:9; Luke 8:2–3). Jesus rewarded her faithfulness by appearing to her and speaking to her before he spoke to anyone else! After seeing him, Mary went immediately and told the disciples about his resurrection. When we finally begin to realize the power of the risen Christ, we can pay our debt of gratitude by doing as Mary did and sharing the Good News with others.

MARY MAGDALENE

People who have been healed of the worst afflictions are often the most grateful for their new lease on life. Once enslaved by seven demons but freed by Jesus, Mary Magdalene was a shining example of one whose life was filled with gratitude and loyalty to Jesus.

We know few details about Mary's life. She apparently came from Magdala in Galilee and was an early follower of Jesus. Her life was dramatically changed when Jesus released her from demons. She traveled with Jesus and the disciples and helped meet their practical needs. During Jesus' crucifixion, when many of the disciples went into hiding, Mary Magdalene was courageous enough to stay at the foot of the cross. She was also one of the women who wanted to make sure Jesus had a proper burial.

Some have suggested that since the twelve disciples were all men, Jesus must not have considered women very important to his ministry. But the role of Mary Magdalene and the other women who followed Jesus shows that this was definitely not the case. Jesus treated women in a deferential manner far beyond the cultural expectation of the day, respecting them fully as persons and considering them a necessary part of his ministry.

We may identify with Mary Magdalene, either as a woman or as one who has been delivered from a life of total bondage. She was an outcast in society, a woman of ill repute. But because of her desire for healing and her trusting obedience of Jesus she became a significant person in history. Mary Magdalene's life encourages us to come boldly before God, knowing that his love extends to all of us, regardless of our situation. He specializes in tough cases.

STRENGTHS AND ACCOMPLISHMENTS:

Mary supported the work of Jesus and his disciples.

She remained with Jesus throughout his crucifixion.

She was the first person to see the risen Jesus and was given the responsibility of telling the disciples about the resurrection.

WEAKNESSES AND MISTAKES:

Before her encounter with Jesus, demonic forces had somehow enslaved Mary.

LESSONS FROM HER LIFE:

Those who receive the most from God are often the most grateful.

God intends that women play an essential role in his ministry.

The forgiveness we experience can motivate us to live our lives for God.

KEY VERSE:

"When Jesus rose early on the first day of the week, he appeared first to Mary Magdalene, out of whom he had driven seven demons" (Mark 16:9).

Mary Magdalene's story is found in Matthew 27:55—28:10; Mark 15:40—16:11; Luke 8:1–3; 24:10; John 19:25 and 20:1–18.

standing there, but she did not realize that it
was Jesus.
15"Woman," he said, "why are you crying?
Who is it you are looking for?"
Thinking he was the gardener, she said, "Sir,
if you have carried him away, tell me where you
have put him, and I will get him."
16Jesus said to her, "Mary."
She turned toward him and cried out in Aramaic, "Rabboni!" (which means Teacher).
17Jesus said, "Do not hold on to me, for I
have not yet returned to the Father. Go instead
to my brothers and tell them, 'I am returning to
my Father and your Father, to my God and your
God.' "
18Mary Magdalene went to the disciples with
the news: "I have seen the Lord!" And she told
them that he had said these things to her.

Jesus Appears to His Disciples

19On the evening of that first day of the week,
when the disciples were together, with the
doors locked for fear of the Jews, Jesus came
and stood among them and said, "Peace be
with you!" 20After he said this, he showed them
his hands and side. The disciples were overjoyed when they saw the Lord.
21Again Jesus said, "Peace be with you! As
the Father has sent me, I am sending you." 22And
with that he breathed on them and said, "Receive the Holy Spirit. 23If you forgive anyone his
sins, they are forgiven; if you do not forgive
them, they are not forgiven."

Jesus Appears to Thomas

24Now Thomas (called Didymus), one of the
Twelve, was not with the disciples when Jesus
came. 25So the other disciples told him, "We
have seen the Lord!"
But he said to them, "Unless I see the nail
marks in his hands and put my finger where the
nails were, and put my hand into his side, I will
not believe it."
26A week later his disciples were in the house
again, and Thomas was with them. Though the
doors were locked, Jesus came and stood
among them and said, "Peace be with you!"
27Then he said to Thomas, "Put your finger
here; see my hands. Reach out your hand and
put it into my side. Stop doubting and believe."
28Thomas said to him, "My Lord and my
God!"
29Then Jesus told him, "Because you have
seen me, you have believed; blessed are those
who have not seen and yet have believed."
30Jesus did many other miraculous signs in
the presence of his disciples, which are not recorded in this book. 31But these are written that
you may[a] believe that Jesus is the Christ, the
Son of God, and that by believing you may have
life in his name.

Jesus and the Miraculous Catch of Fish

21 Afterward Jesus appeared again to his
disciples, by the Sea of Tiberias.[b] It
happened this way: 2Simon Peter, Thomas
(called Didymus), Nathanael from Cana in Galilee, the sons of Zebedee, and two other disciples were together. 3"I'm going out to fish," Simon Peter told them, and they said, "We'll go
with you." So they went out and got into the
boat, but that night they caught nothing.
4Early in the morning, Jesus stood on the
shore, but the disciples did not realize that it
was Jesus.
5He called out to them, "Friends, haven't
you any fish?"
"No," they answered.
6He said, "Throw your net on the right side
of the boat and you will find some." When they
did, they were unable to haul the net in because
of the large number of fish.
7Then the disciple whom Jesus loved said to
Peter, "It is the Lord!" As soon as Simon Peter
heard him say, "It is the Lord," he wrapped his
outer garment around him (for he had taken it
off) and jumped into the water. 8The other disciples followed in the boat, towing the net full
of fish, for they were not far from shore, about

[a] 31 Some manuscripts *may continue to* [b] 1 That is, Sea of Galilee

---

20:22–23 The risen Christ did as he had promised and breathed his Spirit into his disciples (see 14:16–20; 15:26; 16:7). This life-giving, truth-revealing, sin-convicting, comfort-giving Spirit is also a Spirit of forgiveness. Just as we receive God's forgiveness for our sins, so we are exhorted and empowered to forgive those who sin against us (see Matthew 6:12–15). If we refuse to forgive others, we will miss the blessing of healing that God offers us. Our healing comes only when we have worked through our hurt and anger, released these feelings to God and forgiven those who have hurt us. Then God can redirect our course and redeem our lives.

20:24–29 Thomas earned his reputation as a doubter from this passage of Scripture. He refused to believe in Jesus' resurrection until he saw and felt the risen Christ with his own eyes and hands. Some of us may have a hard time believing God is at work in our lives too, especially when we don't see immediate changes or miraculous results. God's working may not be immediately visible; but when we persevere in faith, we will experience the peace that comes from trusting God with our present problems and our unknown future.

21:1–14 Just imagine what the disciples must have felt. They were professional fishermen who had spent an entire night fishing but still hadn't caught anything. Then Jesus called out to them and told them to throw the net on the other side of the boat! The disciples' first response must have been to laugh. But when they did as Jesus said, they caught so many fish that the net began to break. God will sometimes let us try to do things on our own, using all our resources and exerting all our strength without reaping any rewards. At such times we would do well to turn to Jesus and ask him what we should do. Peter offered his empty boat to Jesus as a pulpit. God wants us to offer what we have for his service too. When we do, God will gladly reward us. His abundance will overflow into our emptiness, and everyone will know that God is at work in our lives.

Though wavering in our faith happens to most of us, it is painful for us to be labeled a "doubting Thomas." We might wonder what it felt like for Thomas, Jesus' disciple who is best known for his lack of faith. Thomas simply did not believe that Jesus had risen from the dead. But that is not all there is to his story.

Thomas did not doubt Jesus' resurrection because of fear. He continued to meet with the followers of Jesus in the upper room. Thomas just happened to be absent when the risen Jesus first appeared to them. He wanted some kind of proof that his companions had not just been seeing things. When Jesus appeared a second time, Thomas was given the undeniable evidence that he asked for, permanently dispelling his doubts.

We also have evidence that proves the resurrection; we can experience God's transforming power in our own lives. We can overcome our troubling doubts as we continue to trust God to show his power in our lives. When Thomas overcame his doubts, he set out on a ministry that exhibited extraordinary faith. As we experience God's deliverance, it will motivate us to minister to others.

STRENGTHS AND ACCOMPLISHMENTS:

Thomas was a keen thinker and analyst of events.

Thomas was willing to admit his mistake.

WEAKNESSES AND MISTAKES:

At first Thomas did not believe the reports that Jesus had risen from the dead.

Thomas wanted undeniable evidence before he was willing to believe.

LESSONS FROM HIS LIFE:

Doubt can lead to deeper faith when faced honestly.

Undeniable evidence is not necessary to begin a life of faith.

God's work in our lives can lead to deeper faith.

KEY VERSE:

"Then Jesus told [Thomas], 'Because you have seen me, you have believed; blessed are those who have not seen and yet have believed' " (20:29).

Thomas's story is told in Matthew 10:3; Mark 3:17–18; Luke 6:15; John 11:16; 14:5; 20; 21:2; and Acts 1:13.

a hundred yards.[a] 9When they landed, they
saw a fire of burning coals there with fish on it,
and some bread.
10Jesus said to them, "Bring some of the fish
you have just caught."
11Simon Peter climbed aboard and dragged
the net ashore. It was full of large fish, 153, but
even with so many the net was not torn. 12Jesus
said to them, "Come and have breakfast." None
of the disciples dared ask him, "Who are you?"
They knew it was the Lord. 13Jesus came, took
the bread and gave it to them, and did the same
with the fish. 14This was now the third time
Jesus appeared to his disciples after he was
raised from the dead.

Jesus Reinstates Peter

15When they had finished eating, Jesus said
to Simon Peter, "Simon son of John, do you
truly love me more than these?"

"Yes, Lord," he said, "you know that I love
you."

Jesus said, "Feed my lambs."

16Again Jesus said, "Simon son of John, do
you truly love me?"

He answered, "Yes, Lord, you know that I
love you."

Jesus said, "Take care of my sheep."

17The third time he said to him, "Simon son
of John, do you love me?"

Peter was hurt because Jesus asked him the
third time, "Do you love me?" He said, "Lord,
you know all things; you know that I love you."

Jesus said, "Feed my sheep. 18I tell you the
truth, when you were younger you dressed
yourself and went where you wanted; but when
you are old you will stretch out your hands, and
someone else will dress you and lead you where
you do not want to go." 19Jesus said this to indicate the kind of death by which Peter would
glorify God. Then he said to him, "Follow me!"

20Peter turned and saw that the disciple
whom Jesus loved was following them. (This

[a]8 Greek *about two hundred cubits* (about 90 meters)

21:15–17 Just as Peter had denied Jesus three times, Jesus now let Peter declare his love for Jesus three times. Each time, Jesus affirmed his confidence in Peter by commissioning him to feed his flock. Peter was later able to fulfill this commission when he received the mighty power of the Holy Spirit at Pentecost and became a key leader in the early church. Though we may experience times of failure, God is willing and able to restore us and possibly even use us as models for others.

21:20–25 Peter compared himself with John. Comparison is an easy trap to fall into. We may look at others and become jealous of how quickly they seem to have progressed spiritually. Or we may take comfort in comparing ourselves with someone who is clearly not following God's way. Focusing on the failures and successes of others easily distracts us from our own lives. God doesn't want us to compare ourselves with others. He wants us to look to him and his Word. We are to take responsibility for our own lives and reflect on our own lives in light of his Word. Then we can progress spiritually and fulfill God's plan for our lives.

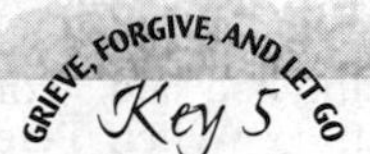

Forgiving Ourselves

John 21:14–25 For most of the sins we commit, we are grateful and eager to accept God's forgiveness. But sometimes we are so shocked at our own behavior, so ashamed of the way we have behaved, so heartbroken about the way we have hurt others that we find it hard to believe that God could really forgive us. Yet God *is* willing to forgive us. Even more, he desires to restore us, to transform us and to redeem our lives for his service. But this restoration cannot begin until we receive God's forgiveness and forgive ourselves.

Peter had once sworn his love and loyalty to Jesus. He pledged even to die with Jesus if necessary. Yet the same night that Jesus was arrested, Peter sheepishly protected himself by denying that he even knew Jesus. Jesus wasn't surprised; he had already told Peter that Peter would deny him three times before the night was out. Jesus was ready to forgive Peter even before he had committed the sins. But Peter had a hard time forgiving himself. After Jesus rose from the dead, he had this conversation with Peter:

> When they had finished eating, Jesus said to Simon Peter, "Simon son of John, do you truly love me more than these?" "Yes, Lord," he said, "you know that I love you." Jesus said, "Feed my lambs." Again Jesus said, "Simon son of John, do you truly love me?" He answered, "Yes, Lord, you know that I love you." Jesus said, "Take care of my sheep." The third time he said to him, "Simon son of John, do you love me?" Peter was hurt because Jesus asked him the third time, "Do you love me?" He said, "Lord, you know all things; you know that I love you." Jesus said, "Feed my sheep" (21:15–17).

Peter denied Jesus three times, and Jesus gave Peter the chance to reaffirm his love three times. Jesus reached out to Peter when Peter didn't feel worthy to reach out to him. When we are disheartened by our own sinfulness, it is difficult for us to receive God's forgiveness. But God is reaching out to forgive us of all our sins. Once we confess our sins, we need to let go of them and realize that Jesus paid for each and every one. Then we can accept God's forgiveness and get on with our lives. At times like these, it also helps to reaffirm our love for God.

Turn to 2 Corinthians 2.

was the one who had leaned back against Jesus
at the supper and had said, "Lord, who is going
to betray you?") 21When Peter saw him, he
asked, "Lord, what about him?"

22Jesus answered, "If I want him to remain
alive until I return, what is that to you? You
must follow me." 23Because of this, the rumor
spread among the brothers that this disciple
would not die. But Jesus did not say that he
would not die; he only said, "If I want him to
remain alive until I return, what is that to you?"

24This is the disciple who testifies to these
things and who wrote them down. We know
that his testimony is true.

25Jesus did many other things as well. If every
one of them were written down, I suppose that
even the whole world would not have room for
the books that would be written.

ACTS

The Big Picture

What occurred during the brief years of Jesus' earthly life was limited to a small corner of the world. Most of civilization never noticed Jesus bringing hope to a hurting and seemingly forsaken group of people. But just as Jesus predicted, the small band of disciples that met in Jerusalem following his death and resurrection turned the world upside down. And life on planet Earth has never been the same since.

Written by Luke as a sequel to his gospel account, the book of Acts records a history of the early believers and the beginnings of the church. Through the examples of these early believers, we see that the Holy Spirit can powerfully change lives. We learn that God can transform us and help us live at peace with him and with others.

The first half of this book focuses on the ministry of Peter—how he was transformed from an impulsive and unreliable, though well-intentioned, follower of Jesus to a bold and dedicated leader. The second half of the book presents us with the life and ministry of Paul. He and his companions faced difficulties and opposition, but through the power of God these missionaries spread the Good News about Jesus throughout the Mediterranean world.

These men should be an encouragement to us. Both made serious mistakes as younger men, but as they surrendered their lives to God, they gradually were changed. As an angry young man, Paul helped kill the first Christian martyr, Stephen. But later Paul became a selfless and dedicated missionary. Peter, whose cockiness often prevented him from overcoming his weaknesses, became a humble and effective leader in the new church. The changes in both men demonstrate what God can do in our lives too.

A. TO JERUSALEM: TELLING THEIR STORY AT HOME (1:1–8:40)

B. TO JUDEA AND SAMARIA: TRANSITION TO OUTSIDERS (9:1–12:25)

C. TO THE WHOLE WORLD: HOW OUTSIDERS BECOME INSIDERS (13:1–21:40)

D. JERUSALEM TO ROME: THE COST OF FOLLOWING JESUS (22:1–28:31)

Spiritual Renewal Themes

THE POWER OF THE HOLY SPIRIT

Jesus promised the disciples that after he left, the Holy Spirit would bring them power (see 1:8). Little did they know what kind of power that would be! As these men learned firsthand, the Holy Spirit and his power are real. When we compare Peter's life in the gospel narratives with his life and attitudes in the book of Acts, we can tell that Peter's life had been changed

Essential Facts

PURPOSE:
To trace the history of Christianity from its predominantly Jewish roots to a worldwide faith through the impetus of the Holy Spirit.

AUTHOR:
Luke, the physician.

AUDIENCE:
Theophilus, whose name means "lover of God."

DATE WRITTEN:
Sometime between A.D. 63 and 70.

SETTING:
Acts provides a history of the events that followed the resurrection of Jesus.

KEY VERSE:
"But you will receive power when the Holy Spirit comes on you; and you will be my witnesses in Jerusalem, and in all Judea and Samaria, and to the ends of the earth" (1:8).

KEY PEOPLE:
Peter, John, Stephen, Philip, Paul, Barnabas, Silas, Timothy and Luke.

SPECIAL FEATURES:
The book of Acts is a sequel to the Gospel of Luke.

by the Holy Spirit's power. When we look at Saul trying to destroy the early church and then see his dedicated missionary service, we can tell that God had radically transformed him. The power of God changed their hearts, giving them confidence to tell the truth about him. In our powerlessness, God makes his power available to us through the Holy Spirit. With God's help, no problem is too great to overcome; no life is so far gone that it cannot be made new.

COMMITMENT THAT OVERCOMES OPPOSITION

Luke did not idealize the people of the early church. They did not have an easy task, nor did they swiftly move toward their objective. Instead, the early believers struggled with controversy, opposition and discouragement. Religious and irreligious people alike misunderstood them. But a common thread was their commitment to God at any cost. As we commit our lives to God, we will also face obstacles, but we can expect to overcome any problems or opposing forces with God's powerful help.

LIVING BEYOND CIRCUMSTANCES

When we read about the early Christians and how they shared their possessions and took care of one another, it is easy to think that somehow they were spared the kinds of problems we experience. That perception is incorrect, because life for the early believers was very difficult. Rather than experiencing an easier lifestyle, these believers learned how to live above their circumstances. They were more conscious of God than they were of their problems. When we focus on the problems we face in our lives, we lose sight of our power source. We may try to succeed on our own power, only to fail and become discouraged. Denying or ignoring our circumstances will not help us, but trusting God and surrendering the circumstances of our lives to him will help us live above our problems too.

SHARING THE MESSAGE

As Peter, John, Philip, Paul, Barnabas and others came to faith in Jesus, they shared the Good News with more people. As we share our own experience of spiritual awakening and God's healing power with others in need, we will find that our faith in God grows stronger and others have the opportunity for spiritual renewal.

Jesus Taken Up Into Heaven

1 In my former book, Theophilus, I wrote
about all that Jesus began to do and to
teach 2until the day he was taken up to heaven,
after giving instructions through the Holy Spirit
to the apostles he had chosen. 3After his suffering, he showed himself to these men and gave
many convincing proofs that he was alive. He
appeared to them over a period of forty days
and spoke about the kingdom of God. 4On one
occasion, while he was eating with them, he
gave them this command: "Do not leave Jerusalem, but wait for the gift my Father promised,
which you have heard me speak about. 5For
John baptized with[a] water, but in a few days
you will be baptized with the Holy Spirit."

6So when they met together, they asked him,
"Lord, are you at this time going to restore the
kingdom to Israel?"

7He said to them: "It is not for you to know
the times or dates the Father has set by his own
authority. 8But you will receive power when the
Holy Spirit comes on you; and you will be my
witnesses in Jerusalem, and in all Judea and
Samaria, and to the ends of the earth."

9After he said this, he was taken up before
their very eyes, and a cloud hid him from their
sight.

10They were looking intently up into the sky
as he was going, when suddenly two men
dressed in white stood beside them. 11"Men
of Galilee," they said, "why do you stand here
looking into the sky? This same Jesus, who has
been taken from you into heaven, will come
back in the same way you have seen him go into
heaven."

Matthias Chosen to Replace Judas

12Then they returned to Jerusalem from the
hill called the Mount of Olives, a Sabbath day's
walk[b] from the city. 13When they arrived, they
went upstairs to the room where they were staying. Those present were Peter, John, James and
Andrew; Philip and Thomas, Bartholomew and
Matthew; James son of Alphaeus and Simon
the Zealot, and Judas son of James. 14They all
joined together constantly in prayer, along with
the women and Mary the mother of Jesus, and
with his brothers.

15In those days Peter stood up among the
believers[c] (a group numbering about a hundred and twenty) 16and said, "Brothers, the
Scripture had to be fulfilled which the Holy
Spirit spoke long ago through the mouth of
David concerning Judas, who served as guide
for those who arrested Jesus— 17he was one of
our number and shared in this ministry."

18(With the reward he got for his wickedness,
Judas bought a field; there he fell headlong, his
body burst open and all his intestines spilled
out. 19Everyone in Jerusalem heard about this,
so they called that field in their language Akel-
dama, that is, Field of Blood.)

20"For," said Peter, "it is written in the book
of Psalms,

" 'May his place be deserted;
let there be no one to dwell in it,'[d]

and,

" 'May another take his place of
leadership.'[e]

21Therefore it is necessary to choose one of the
men who have been with us the whole time the
Lord Jesus went in and out among us, 22begin-
ning from John's baptism to the time when
Jesus was taken up from us. For one of these
must become a witness with us of his resurrection."

23So they proposed two men: Joseph called
Barsabbas (also known as Justus) and Matthias.
24Then they prayed, "Lord, you know everyone's heart. Show us which of these two you
have chosen 25to take over this apostolic ministry, which Judas left to go where he belongs."
26Then they cast lots, and the lot fell to Matthias; so he was added to the eleven apostles.

The Holy Spirit Comes at Pentecost

2 When the day of Pentecost came, they were
all together in one place. 2Suddenly a
sound like the blowing of a violent wind came
from heaven and filled the whole house where
they were sitting. 3They saw what seemed to be
tongues of fire that separated and came to rest

[a]*5* Or *in* [b]*12* That is, about 3/4 mile (about 1,100 meters) [c]*15* Greek *brothers* [d]*20* Psalm 69:25 [e]*20* Psalm 109:8

1:1–5 This book is the sequel to Luke's Gospel. The story in Acts picks up where Luke's Gospel left off, recording the activities of the apostles soon after Jesus' resurrection. Before ascending to heaven, Jesus assured his followers that the promised Holy Spirit would come upon them as they waited in Jerusalem. At the appointed time, the early Christians received the power they needed to reach the world with the Good News of Jesus Christ. God offers us the same power for our spiritual renewal today.

1:6–11 When the disciples asked Jesus about the coming of his earthly kingdom, they displayed a deep yearning for the Messiah's reign of freedom and peace. Jesus responded by telling them not to worry about the future. Instead, he turned their eyes to the present. With the power of the Holy Spirit, they were to share the Good News of salvation in Jesus Christ with others. Sometimes we make the mistake the disciples did, looking forward to a time of complete freedom and peace while we could be taking productive steps of action here and now. Through the Holy Spirit, we can share the Good News with others as we await Christ's return.

2:1–4 On the day of Pentecost, the disciples waited in Jerusalem just as Jesus had told them to. Suddenly the Holy Spirit manifested his presence by sound (wind), sight (fire) and speech (new languages). The believers were filled with the Holy Spirit. God's renewing power began its work of transforming them from the inside out. This event marked a new era in history as God's powerful presence entered the lives of all believers. The Holy Spirit still works in the lives of believers, transforming them, healing their wounds, empowering them to be witnesses for Jesus and equipping them to do God's work in the world.

on each of them. 4All of them were filled with
the Holy Spirit and began to speak in other
tongues[a] as the Spirit enabled them.
5Now there were staying in Jerusalem God-
fearing Jews from every nation under heaven.
6When they heard this sound, a crowd came
together in bewilderment, because each one
heard them speaking in his own language. 7Ut-
terly amazed, they asked: "Are not all these
men who are speaking Galileans? 8Then how is
it that each of us hears them in his own native
language? 9Parthians, Medes and Elamites; residents of Mesopotamia, Judea and Cappadocia,
Pontus and Asia, 10Phrygia and Pamphylia,
Egypt and the parts of Libya near Cyrene; visitors from Rome 11(both Jews and converts to
Judaism); Cretans and Arabs—we hear them declaring the wonders of God in our own tongues!"
12Amazed and perplexed, they asked one another, "What does this mean?"
13Some, however, made fun of them and
said, "They have had too much wine.[b]"

Peter Addresses the Crowd

14Then Peter stood up with the Eleven, raised
his voice and addressed the crowd: "Fellow
Jews and all of you who live in Jerusalem, let me
explain this to you; listen carefully to what I say.
15These men are not drunk, as you suppose. It's
only nine in the morning! 16No, this is what
was spoken by the prophet Joel:

17" 'In the last days, God says,
I will pour out my Spirit on all people.
Your sons and daughters will prophesy,
your young men will see visions,
your old men will dream dreams.
18Even on my servants, both men and
women,
I will pour out my Spirit in those days,
and they will prophesy.
19I will show wonders in the heaven above
and signs on the earth below,
blood and fire and billows of smoke.
20The sun will be turned to darkness
and the moon to blood
before the coming of the great and
glorious day of the Lord.
21And everyone who calls
on the name of the Lord will be
saved.'[c]

22"Men of Israel, listen to this: Jesus of Nazareth was a man accredited by God to you by
miracles, wonders and signs, which God did
among you through him, as you yourselves
know. 23This man was handed over to you by
God's set purpose and foreknowledge; and you,
with the help of wicked men,[d] put him to
death by nailing him to the cross. 24But God
raised him from the dead, freeing him from the
agony of death, because it was impossible for
death to keep its hold on him. 25David said
about him:

" 'I saw the Lord always before me.
Because he is at my right hand,
I will not be shaken.
26Therefore my heart is glad and my tongue
rejoices;
my body also will live in hope,
27because you will not abandon me to the
grave,
nor will you let your Holy One see
decay.
28You have made known to me the paths of
life;
you will fill me with joy in your
presence.'[e]

29"Brothers, I can tell you confidently that
the patriarch David died and was buried, and
his tomb is here to this day. 30But he was a
prophet and knew that God had promised him
on oath that he would place one of his descendants on his throne. 31Seeing what was ahead,
he spoke of the resurrection of the Christ,[f] that
he was not abandoned to the grave, nor did his
body see decay. 32God has raised this Jesus to
life, and we are all witnesses of the fact. 33Exalt-
ed to the right hand of God, he has received
from the Father the promised Holy Spirit and
has poured out what you now see and hear.
34For David did not ascend to heaven, and yet
he said,

" 'The Lord said to my Lord:
"Sit at my right hand
35until I make your enemies
a footstool for your feet." '[g]

36"Therefore let all Israel be assured of this:
God has made this Jesus, whom you crucified,
both Lord and Christ."

[a]4 Or *languages;* also in verse 11 [b]13 Or *sweet wine*
[c]21 Joel 2:28-32 [d]23 Or *of those not having the law*
(that is, Gentiles) [e]28 Psalm 16:8-11 [f]31 Or
Messiah. "The Christ" (Greek) and "the Messiah" (Hebrew)
both mean "the Anointed One"; also in verse 36.
[g]35 Psalm 110:1

2:5–15 When the Holy Spirit came in power, the results were immediately apparent in the apostles, especially Peter. This man, who had previously denied even knowing Christ (see Luke 22:54–62), was now confidently preaching and helping others discover this new power for living. When we experience God's power in our lives, we will never be the same, nor will we be able to keep the Good News to ourselves.

2:14–21 After asserting his sobriety, Peter told the crowd about the power behind his transformation. The prophet Joel had promised the amazing power of the Holy Spirit centuries earlier (see Joel 2:28–32). By quoting Joel's words, Peter stressed the universal impact of the Holy Spirit. The Holy Spirit would be given to all God's people—young and old, men and women, masters and servants. God's power for living is available for everyone who recognizes their helpless state and asks for God's mercy (2:21). No one with a humble heart—regardless of race, gender or social class—is beyond the reach of God's powerful help.

37When the people heard this, they were cut
to the heart and said to Peter and the other
apostles, "Brothers, what shall we do?"
38Peter replied, "Repent and be baptized, every one of you, in the name of Jesus Christ for
the forgiveness of your sins. And you will receive the gift of the Holy Spirit. 39The promise
is for you and your children and for all who are
far off—for all whom the Lord our God will call."
40With many other words he warned them;
and he pleaded with them, "Save yourselves
from this corrupt generation." 41Those who accepted his message were baptized, and about
three thousand were added to their number that
day.

The Fellowship of the Believers

42They devoted themselves to the apostles'
teaching and to the fellowship, to the breaking
of bread and to prayer. 43Everyone was filled
with awe, and many wonders and miraculous
signs were done by the apostles. 44All the believers were together and had everything in common. 45Selling their possessions and goods,
they gave to anyone as he had need. 46Every day
they continued to meet together in the temple
courts. They broke bread in their homes and ate
together with glad and sincere hearts, 47praising
God and enjoying the favor of all the people.
And the Lord added to their number daily those
who were being saved.

Peter Heals the Crippled Beggar

3 One day Peter and John were going up to
the temple at the time of prayer—at three in
the afternoon. 2Now a man crippled from birth
was being carried to the temple gate called
Beautiful, where he was put every day to beg
from those going into the temple courts. 3When
he saw Peter and John about to enter, he asked
them for money. 4Peter looked straight at him,
as did John. Then Peter said, "Look at us!" 5So
the man gave them his attention, expecting to
get something from them.
6Then Peter said, "Silver or gold I do not
have, but what I have I give you. In the name of
Jesus Christ of Nazareth, walk." 7Taking him by
the right hand, he helped him up, and instantly
the man's feet and ankles became strong. 8He
jumped to his feet and began to walk. Then he
went with them into the temple courts, walking
and jumping, and praising God. 9When all the
people saw him walking and praising God,
10they recognized him as the same man who
used to sit begging at the temple gate called
Beautiful, and they were filled with wonder and
amazement at what had happened to him.

Peter Speaks to the Onlookers

11While the beggar held on to Peter and
John, all the people were astonished and came
running to them in the place called Solomon's
Colonnade. 12When Peter saw this, he said to
them: "Men of Israel, why does this surprise
you? Why do you stare at us as if by our own
power or godliness we had made this man
walk? 13The God of Abraham, Isaac and Jacob,
the God of our fathers, has glorified his servant
Jesus. You handed him over to be killed, and
you disowned him before Pilate, though he had
decided to let him go. 14You disowned the Holy
and Righteous One and asked that a murderer
be released to you. 15You killed the author of
life, but God raised him from the dead. We are
witnesses of this. 16By faith in the name of Jesus,
this man whom you see and know was made
strong. It is Jesus' name and the faith that comes
through him that has given this complete healing to him, as you can all see.
17"Now, brothers, I know that you acted in
ignorance, as did your leaders. 18But this is how
God fulfilled what he had foretold through all
the prophets, saying that his Christ[a] would
suffer. 19Repent, then, and turn to God, so that
your sins may be wiped out, that times of refreshing may come from the Lord, 20and that he
may send the Christ, who has been appointed
for you—even Jesus. 21He must remain in heav-
en until the time comes for God to restore everything, as he promised long ago through his
holy prophets. 22For Moses said, 'The Lord your

a18 Or *Messiah;* also in verse 20

2:37–39 Peter's words encouraged the people to examine their lives and ask the apostle what they should do. They readily recognized their need for salvation in Christ and went on to receive God's powerful help. Peter assured them that by turning from their sins and surrendering their lives to God, they would be forgiven and would receive the powerful presence of the Holy Spirit. We can expect the same blessings when we bring our sins before God. His forgiveness will set us free from our bondage to sin. The presence of his Holy Spirit will give us the power to persevere as we follow Christ. Then we can fully experience the transformation and blessing he longs to bring into our lives.

2:42–47 In these verses, Luke mentioned a number of activities that characterized the early Christian community. Early believers committed themselves to follow the teaching of the apostles, to fellowship together, to share in the Lord's Supper and to pray together. They helped those in need by sharing their food, clothing and even their homes. The faith, joy and loving support of the early believers were so contagious that large numbers soon joined them. Spiritual growth does not take place in isolation. We need people to walk along with us, encouraging us when we become discouraged and holding us accountable when we stray. This common bond helps us preserve our spiritual gains.

3:1–11 This crippled man was truly helpless, a prime candidate for God's powerful help. Notice the steps in this healing. Peter established personal contact by asking the man to look directly at him. Next, Peter awakened the man's hope by telling him that Jesus Christ could heal him. Then, at Peter's command and touch, the man was suddenly on his feet, leaping and praising God. Our healing often comes as God touches our lives through the ministry of others. As we experience healing in our own lives and share our faith, we can bestow the same blessings on others by leading them to Jesus Christ.

God will raise up for you a prophet like me from among your own people; you must listen to everything he tells you. 23Anyone who does not listen to him will be completely cut off from among his people.'[a]

24"Indeed, all the prophets from Samuel on, as many as have spoken, have foretold these days. 25And you are heirs of the prophets and of the covenant God made with your fathers. He said to Abraham, 'Through your offspring all peoples on earth will be blessed.'[b] 26When God raised up his servant, he sent him first to you to bless you by turning each of you from your wicked ways."

Peter and John Before the Sanhedrin

4 The priests and the captain of the temple guard and the Sadducees came up to Peter and John while they were speaking to the people. 2They were greatly disturbed because the apostles were teaching the people and proclaiming in Jesus the resurrection of the dead. 3They seized Peter and John, and because it was evening, they put them in jail until the next day. 4But many who heard the message believed, and the number of men grew to about five thousand.

5The next day the rulers, elders and teachers of the law met in Jerusalem. 6Annas the high priest was there, and so were Caiaphas, John, Alexander and the other men of the high priest's family. 7They had Peter and John brought before them and began to question them: "By what power or what name did you do this?"

8Then Peter, filled with the Holy Spirit, said to them: "Rulers and elders of the people! 9If we are being called to account today for an act of kindness shown to a cripple and are asked how he was healed, 10then know this, you and all the people of Israel: It is by the name of Jesus Christ of Nazareth, whom you crucified but whom God raised from the dead, that this man stands before you healed. 11He is

" 'the stone you builders rejected,
which has become the capstone.'[c,d]

12Salvation is found in no one else, for there is no other name under heaven given to men by which we must be saved."

13When they saw the courage of Peter and John and realized that they were unschooled, ordinary men, they were astonished and they took note that these men had been with Jesus. 14But since they could see the man who had been healed standing there with them, there was nothing they could say. 15So they ordered them to withdraw from the Sanhedrin and then conferred together. 16"What are we going to do with these men?" they asked. "Everybody living in Jerusalem knows they have done an outstanding miracle, and we cannot deny it. 17But to stop this thing from spreading any further among the people, we must warn these men to speak no longer to anyone in this name."

18Then they called them in again and commanded them not to speak or teach at all in the name of Jesus. 19But Peter and John replied, "Judge for yourselves whether it is right in God's sight to obey you rather than God. 20For we cannot help speaking about what we have seen and heard."

21After further threats they let them go. They could not decide how to punish them, because all the people were praising God for what had happened. 22For the man who was miraculously healed was over forty years old.

The Believers' Prayer

23On their release, Peter and John went back to their own people and reported all that the chief priests and elders had said to them. 24When they heard this, they raised their voices together in prayer to God. "Sovereign Lord," they said, "you made the heaven and the earth and the sea, and everything in them. 25You spoke by the Holy Spirit through the mouth of your servant, our father David:

" 'Why do the nations rage
and the peoples plot in vain?
26The kings of the earth take their stand
and the rulers gather together
against the Lord
and against his Anointed One.'[e,f]

27Indeed Herod and Pontius Pilate met together

[a] 23 Deut. 18:15,18,19 [b] 25 Gen. 22:18; 26:4
[c] 11 Or *cornerstone* [d] 11 Psalm 118:22 [e] 26 That is, Christ or Messiah [f] 26 Psalm 2:1,2

4:1–12 Peter consistently held his listeners accountable for their actions (see 2:36; 3:12–23). But he never concluded his messages on a negative note. Peter always went on to declare that God can do what we are powerless to do—deliver us from the destructive grip of sin. We all need the forgiveness and redemption offered only through Jesus Christ. Jesus desires our complete redemption—spiritual, emotional and physical. He alone has the power to bring it about.

4:13–22 Peter's courage and power took the religious leaders by surprise. They were uncertain about how they should proceed, so they commanded Peter to stop his preaching and healing ministry. But Peter refused to obey, affirming his commitment to God's authority. The leaders were unable to stop the spread of Jesus' message in Jerusalem and beyond. God wants everyone to find forgiveness and freedom, despite what the government authorities might say. Once we have experienced the reality of God's power and direction in our lives, no one can take that away from us.

4:23–31 When the religious leaders released Peter and John, the two disciples returned to their circle of friends and fellow believers. There they dealt with their difficulties by discussing the issues, worshiping God and spending time in prayer. This dedication resulted in a new manifestation of God's presence among them and a new empowering of boldness by the Holy Spirit. We can learn from these early believers that the way to deal with the obstacles before us is through prayer for one another. We, too, can find help through a group of believers in whom we can confide and with whom we can pray.

Spiritual Friendship

Touching Heart, Soul and Body

Acts 4:23–36 Love is the soil of spiritual vitality and revival. In the book of Acts we see a direct correlation between unity and power, between generosity and grace. The love within the Christian community empowered their witness to the gospel and fulfilled Jesus' earnest prayer for a distinctive unity among his followers (see John 17:23). Love and unity among believers is our most effective witness to the world (see John 13:35).

Love includes admitting that we have needs, not pretending to be completely self-sufficient. Love is also practical in its concern for others. Barnabas was moved to donate land because he saw the needs of his fellow believers (see 4:36–37).

If we want to develop deep, meaningful spiritual friendships, we will have to admit our need for love and learn how to receive it. Most of us are far more comfortable keeping our needs to ourselves and helping to supply the needs of others. But even Paul testifies to the power of admitting our personal needs and receiving help from others (see Galatians 4:13–14; Philippians 4:10–19).

For more on spiritual friendship, turn to Ephesians 5.

Putting It Into Practice

Do you have personal needs that you have yet to share with your spiritual friends? What keeps you from sharing? If a close friend shared a deep need with you, how would you respond? How does this help you as you consider disclosing your need to others?

with the Gentiles and the people[a] of Israel in this city to conspire against your holy servant Jesus, whom you anointed. 28They did what your power and will had decided beforehand should happen. 29Now, Lord, consider their threats and enable your servants to speak your word with great boldness. 30Stretch out your hand to heal and perform miraculous signs and wonders through the name of your holy servant Jesus."

31After they prayed, the place where they were meeting was shaken. And they were all filled with the Holy Spirit and spoke the word of God boldly.

The Believers Share Their Possessions

32All the believers were one in heart and mind. No one claimed that any of his possessions was his own, but they shared everything they had. 33With great power the apostles continued to testify to the resurrection of the Lord Jesus, and much grace was upon them all. 34There were no needy persons among them. For from time to time those who owned lands or houses sold them, brought the money from the sales 35and put it at the apostles' feet, and it was distributed to anyone as he had need.

36Joseph, a Levite from Cyprus, whom the apostles called Barnabas (which means Son of Encouragement), 37sold a field he owned and brought the money and put it at the apostles' feet.

Ananias and Sapphira

5 Now a man named Ananias, together with his wife Sapphira, also sold a piece of property. 2With his wife's full knowledge he kept back part of the money for himself, but brought the rest and put it at the apostles' feet.

3Then Peter said, "Ananias, how is it that Satan has so filled your heart that you have lied to the Holy Spirit and have kept for yourself some of the money you received for the land? 4Didn't it belong to you before it was sold? And after it was sold, wasn't the money at your disposal? What made you think of doing such a thing? You have not lied to men but to God."

5When Ananias heard this, he fell down and died. And great fear seized all who heard what had happened. 6Then the young men came forward, wrapped up his body, and carried him out and buried him.

7About three hours later his wife came in, not knowing what had happened. 8Peter asked her, "Tell me, is this the price you and Ananias got for the land?"

"Yes," she said, "that is the price."

9Peter said to her, "How could you agree to test the Spirit of the Lord? Look! The feet of the men who buried your husband are at the door, and they will carry you out also."

10At that moment she fell down at his feet and died. Then the young men came in and, finding her dead, carried her out and buried her beside her husband. 11Great fear seized the whole church and all who heard about these events.

The Apostles Heal Many

12The apostles performed many miraculous signs and wonders among the people. And all the believers used to meet together in Solomon's Colonnade. 13No one else dared join them, even though they were highly regarded by the people. 14Nevertheless, more and more men and women believed in the Lord and were added to their number. 15As a result, people brought the sick into the streets and laid them on beds and mats so that at least Peter's shadow might fall on some of them as he passed by. 16Crowds gathered also from the towns around Jerusalem, bringing their sick and those tormented by evil[b] spirits, and all of them were healed.

The Apostles Persecuted

17Then the high priest and all his associates, who were members of the party of the Sadducees, were filled with jealousy. 18They arrested the apostles and put them in the public jail. 19But during the night an angel of the Lord

[a]*27* The Greek is plural. [b]*16* Greek *unclean*

4:32–37 The early Christians grew spiritually by caring for each other, by meeting each other's basic needs and by carrying the Good News to people who hadn't yet heard. Even in the exemplary community, Barnabas was a model believer. His original name was Joseph, but the apostles renamed him Barnabas, which means "Son of Encouragement." When God transforms our lives, we may find that our personalities will also reflect the changes Christ makes in our lives. We might even become beacons of encouragement for others.

5:1–11 God's punishment of Ananias and Sapphira with immediate death makes this a unique event in the history of the church. But this account also carries a universal message by reminding us that we cannot pretend total devotion to God and get away with it. God desires that we willingly surrender our lives to him; he knows the extent of our true devotion. Trying to lie to God or appear more spiritual than we are reveals a serious problem in our spiritual lives. If we see these attitudes and actions in ourselves, we need to confess them to God and ask him to help us be truthful with him and with others.

5:9–11 Peter confronted Ananias and Sapphira about their dishonesty, holding them accountable for their sins. This kind of honest confrontation is as necessary today as it was in this early Christian community. Confrontation and discipline are vital components in any community, whether within a Christian church, a support group or a family. When we are confronted with the truth, we need to humbly and honestly admit our mistakes and sins. As we do this, God will give us the help we need to overcome them.

5:12–16 In the early church, God worked in people's lives through the help of other people. God channels his power through people like us so others can experience his powerful help. God may have touched our lives through the help of an individual or a group. As we share the Good News in both word and deed, we can be used to bring hope and healing to others too.

opened the doors of the jail and brought them out. 20"Go, stand in the temple courts," he said, "and tell the people the full message of this new life."

21At daybreak they entered the temple courts, as they had been told, and began to teach the people.

When the high priest and his associates arrived, they called together the Sanhedrin—the full assembly of the elders of Israel—and sent to the jail for the apostles. 22But on arriving at the jail, the officers did not find them there. So they went back and reported, 23"We found the jail securely locked, with the guards standing at the doors; but when we opened them, we found no one inside." 24On hearing this report, the captain of the temple guard and the chief priests were puzzled, wondering what would come of this.

25Then someone came and said, "Look! The men you put in jail are standing in the temple courts teaching the people." 26At that, the captain went with his officers and brought the apostles. They did not use force, because they feared that the people would stone them.

27Having brought the apostles, they made them appear before the Sanhedrin to be questioned by the high priest. 28"We gave you strict orders not to teach in this name," he said. "Yet you have filled Jerusalem with your teaching and are determined to make us guilty of this man's blood."

29Peter and the other apostles replied: "We must obey God rather than men! 30The God of our fathers raised Jesus from the dead—whom you had killed by hanging him on a tree. 31God exalted him to his own right hand as Prince and Savior that he might give repentance and forgiveness of sins to Israel. 32We are witnesses of these things, and so is the Holy Spirit, whom God has given to those who obey him."

33When they heard this, they were furious and wanted to put them to death. 34But a Pharisee named Gamaliel, a teacher of the law, who was honored by all the people, stood up in the Sanhedrin and ordered that the men be put outside for a little while. 35Then he addressed them: "Men of Israel, consider carefully what you intend to do to these men. 36Some time ago Theudas appeared, claiming to be somebody, and about four hundred men rallied to him. He was killed, all his followers were dispersed, and it all came to nothing. 37After him, Judas the Galilean appeared in the days of the census and led a band of people in revolt. He too was killed, and all his followers were scattered. 38Therefore, in the present case I advise you: Leave these men alone! Let them go! For if their purpose or activity is of human origin, it will fail. 39But if it is from God, you will not be able to stop these men; you will only find yourselves fighting against God."

40His speech persuaded them. They called the apostles in and had them flogged. Then they ordered them not to speak in the name of Jesus, and let them go.

41The apostles left the Sanhedrin, rejoicing because they had been counted worthy of suffering disgrace for the Name. 42Day after day, in the temple courts and from house to house, they never stopped teaching and proclaiming the good news that Jesus is the Christ.[a]

The Choosing of the Seven

6 In those days when the number of disciples was increasing, the Grecian Jews among them complained against the Hebraic Jews because their widows were being overlooked in the daily distribution of food. 2So the Twelve gathered all the disciples together and said, "It would not be right for us to neglect the ministry of the word of God in order to wait on tables. 3Brothers, choose seven men from among you who are known to be full of the Spirit and wisdom. We will turn this responsibility over to them 4and will give our attention to prayer and the ministry of the word."

5This proposal pleased the whole group. They chose Stephen, a man full of faith and of the Holy Spirit; also Philip, Procorus, Nicanor, Timon, Parmenas, and Nicolas from Antioch, a convert to Judaism. 6They presented these men to the apostles, who prayed and laid their hands on them.

7So the word of God spread. The number of disciples in Jerusalem increased rapidly, and a large number of priests became obedient to the faith.

[a]42 Or *Messiah*

5:24–42 This power struggle between the religious establishment and the apostles is instructive. People may try to oppose us as we grow in our relationship with God. But if our lives are centered on God and his will for us, nothing will be able to stop our progress.

6:1 As the Christian community grew, various problems arose. One such problem was the distribution of food to needy widows. The conflict was apparently rooted in the cultural differences between the various church members. Most of the church members were Aramaic-speaking Jewish Christians, but there were also Greek-speaking Jewish Christians among them. Apparently, the Aramaic-speaking Jews were neglecting the Greek-speaking Jews. Relationships within the church can be broken if members refuse to accept one another. As we humbly recognize our own need for God's gracious forgiveness, we will have less trouble accepting others who are different from us.

6:2–6 Conflict resolution is vital to our spiritual health, just as it was to the health of the early church. The early believers acknowledged their limitations, set their priorities and laid out specific tasks that would fulfill their needs. They sought God's wisdom and let the congregation select seven new leaders to better represent the cultural mix in their community. By delegating leadership to Spirit-filled, Greek-speaking Jews, the early believers overcame their food distribution problem. With God's wisdom and a godly network of support, we can find ways to overcome the problems we face and meet the needs of the people around us.

Full of the Spirit and Wisdom

Acts 6:1–6 When we consider acts of service, there are two kinds of people in the world: guests and hosts. The guests are those who expect to be taken care of; the hosts are those who do the caring. The discipline of service builds on the premise that we, as Christ's followers, are God's hosts in this world.

Division threatened the early church community because not everyone was being cared for adequately. The apostles' response was to call forth a group of hosts who could serve the practical needs of the community. These hosts, later called "deacons" (see 1 Timothy 3:8–10), did not simply perform menial chores. They were also "full of the Spirit and wisdom" (6:3). Whether administering a food program or proclaiming God's truth, these hosts showed God's love in practical ways. Two of them, Stephen and Philip, presented powerful testimonies to the living Lord Jesus Christ (see chapters 7—8).

No matter what our task, we should seek to be "full of the Spirit and wisdom" as we go about our work. Then others will hear and see the love of Christ in practical ways.

Putting It Into Practice

Do you view yourself as a guest or a host? How does picturing yourself as a host affect your view of service? Think of a situation in which you could make a significant impact by being a host. What actions can you take? Ask God to fill you with the Holy Spirit and wisdom as you enter this situation.

For more on service, turn to Romans 12.

Stephen Seized

8Now Stephen, a man full of God's grace and power, did great wonders and miraculous signs among the people. 9Opposition arose, however, from members of the Synagogue of the Freedmen (as it was called)—Jews of Cyrene and Alexandria as well as the provinces of Cilicia and Asia. These men began to argue with Stephen, 10but they could not stand up against his wisdom or the Spirit by whom he spoke.

11Then they secretly persuaded some men to say, "We have heard Stephen speak words of blasphemy against Moses and against God."

12So they stirred up the people and the elders and the teachers of the law. They seized Stephen and brought him before the Sanhedrin. 13They produced false witnesses, who testified, "This fellow never stops speaking against this holy place and against the law. 14For we have heard him say that this Jesus of Nazareth will destroy this place and change the customs Moses handed down to us."

15All who were sitting in the Sanhedrin looked intently at Stephen, and they saw that his face was like the face of an angel.

Stephen's Speech to the Sanhedrin

7 Then the high priest asked him, "Are these charges true?"

2To this he replied: "Brothers and fathers, listen to me! The God of glory appeared to our father Abraham while he was still in Mesopotamia, before he lived in Haran. 3'Leave your country and your people,' God said, 'and go to the land I will show you.'[a]

4"So he left the land of the Chaldeans and settled in Haran. After the death of his father, God sent him to this land where you are now living. 5He gave him no inheritance here, not even a foot of ground. But God promised him that he and his descendants after him would possess the land, even though at that time Abraham had no child. 6God spoke to him in this way: 'Your descendants will be strangers in a country not their own, and they will be enslaved and mistreated four hundred years. 7But I will punish the nation they serve as slaves,' God said, 'and afterward they will come out of that country and worship me in this place.'[b] 8Then he gave Abraham the covenant of circumcision. And Abraham became the father of Isaac and circumcised him eight days after his birth. Later Isaac became the father of Jacob, and Jacob became the father of the twelve patriarchs.

9"Because the patriarchs were jealous of Joseph, they sold him as a slave into Egypt. But God was with him 10and rescued him from all his troubles. He gave Joseph wisdom and enabled him to gain the goodwill of Pharaoh king of Egypt; so he made him ruler over Egypt and all his palace.

11"Then a famine struck all Egypt and Canaan, bringing great suffering, and our fathers could not find food. 12When Jacob heard that there was grain in Egypt, he sent our fathers on their first visit. 13On their second visit, Joseph told his brothers who he was, and Pharaoh learned about Joseph's family. 14After this, Joseph sent for his father Jacob and his whole family, seventy-five in all. 15Then Jacob went down to Egypt, where he and our fathers died. 16Their bodies were brought back to Shechem and placed in the tomb that Abraham had bought from the sons of Hamor at Shechem for a certain sum of money.

17"As the time drew near for God to fulfill his promise to Abraham, the number of our people in Egypt greatly increased. 18Then another king, who knew nothing about Joseph, became ruler of Egypt. 19He dealt treacherously with our people and oppressed our forefathers by forcing them to throw out their newborn babies so that they would die.

20"At that time Moses was born, and he was no ordinary child.[c] For three months he was cared for in his father's house. 21When he was placed outside, Pharaoh's daughter took him and brought him up as her own son. 22Moses was educated in all the wisdom of the Egyptians and was powerful in speech and action.

23"When Moses was forty years old, he decided to visit his fellow Israelites. 24He saw one of them being mistreated by an Egyptian, so he went to his defense and avenged him by killing the Egyptian. 25Moses thought that his own people would realize that God was using him to rescue them, but they did not. 26The next day Moses came upon two Israelites who were fighting. He tried to reconcile them by saying, 'Men, you are brothers; why do you want to hurt each other?'

27"But the man who was mistreating the other pushed Moses aside and said, 'Who made you ruler and judge over us? 28Do you want to

a3 Gen. 12:1 b7 Gen. 15:13,14 c20 Or *was fair in the sight of God*

6:8–15 Stephen was noted for his courage, boldness and faith. He dedicated himself to sharing the message of Jesus Christ with the people around him. The Jewish establishment accused Stephen of attacking their institutions, especially the Law of Moses and the Jerusalem temple. Stephen confronted the Jewish leaders directly with their refusal to see the truth. We may need to do the same for some of the people we know. If confrontation becomes necessary, we should seek God's wisdom, just as Stephen did, surrendering our lives to God and following his ways.

7:1–53 Stephen was not defensive about the accusations of his fellow Jews. Instead, he controlled the situation by sharing his faith with them. Like Stephen, we do not need to be defensive about our faith. When we experience God's healing power in our lives, we can boldly share that message with others without apology, fear or shame. Others may try to harm us, as they did Stephen, but that does not negate the reality of God's power in our lives.

STEPHEN

Stephen was filled with the Holy Spirit and exhibited God's power and love in everything he did. Known for performing spectacular miracles and helping people in need, Stephen was called to be one of the first deacons in the early church. His job was to make sure that no one (even a helpless widow) was overlooked in the distribution of food. Stephen also proclaimed the Good News of Jesus with boldness and power. As religious fanatics stoned him to death, God's hand was clearly upon Stephen.

Stephen demonstrated God's message publicly through the miracles that he performed in Jesus' name. Those who tried to disprove the truth about Jesus Christ could not stand against Stephen's wisdom and spirit. So they lied about him in order to have Stephen arrested and brought before the council of Jewish leaders.

Stephen responded to the inquisition by reciting the history of the Jewish people, beginning with Abraham, progressing through Moses, and ending with the coming of Jesus, the Messiah. Stephen concluded his remarks with a scathing attack on the religious leaders who, like many of their ancestors, refused to see God's truth and resisted the Holy Spirit.

Stephen's words angered the Jewish leaders so much that they rushed him out of the city and stoned him to death. As he stumbled under the rain of stones, Stephen called upon God to receive his spirit and to forgive the people who were killing him. Unlike Stephen, many of us hold on to grudges and past hurts and allow them to control our lives. We refuse to release our grudges to God, making our complete healing and spiritual renewal impossible. If we entrust our lives to God's hands, we can both live and die with joy, knowing that God will take care of the details we cannot control or change.

STRENGTHS AND ACCOMPLISHMENTS:

Stephen really knew God, both personally and through the Scriptures.

Because he trusted God, Stephen was able to rise above his circumstances.

Stephen possessed a passion for God and compassion for others.

He used his many gifts to serve the poor and helpless.

LESSONS FROM HIS LIFE:

Serving others is a natural activity when we have given our lives to God.

If we can trust God in our daily lives, we will be able to face death with joy.

We can face even the most terrible circumstances if God is with us.

KEY VERSE:

"Now Stephen, a man full of God's grace and power, did great wonders and miraculous signs among the people" (6:8).

Stephen's story is told in Acts 6—8, 11:19 and 22:20.

kill me as you killed the Egyptian yesterday?'[a]
29When Moses heard this, he fled to Midian,
where he settled as a foreigner and had two
sons.
30"After forty years had passed, an angel appeared to Moses in the flames of a burning bush
in the desert near Mount Sinai. 31When he saw
this, he was amazed at the sight. As he went
over to look more closely, he heard the Lord's
voice: 32'I am the God of your fathers, the God
of Abraham, Isaac and Jacob.'[b] Moses trembled with fear and did not dare to look.
33"Then the Lord said to him, 'Take off your
sandals; the place where you are standing is
holy ground. 34I have indeed seen the oppression of my people in Egypt. I have heard their
groaning and have come down to set them free.
Now come, I will send you back to Egypt.'[c]
35"This is the same Moses whom they had
rejected with the words, 'Who made you ruler
and judge?' He was sent to be their ruler and
deliverer by God himself, through the angel
who appeared to him in the bush. 36He led
them out of Egypt and did wonders and miraculous signs in Egypt, at the Red Sea[d] and for
forty years in the desert.
37"This is that Moses who told the Israelites,
'God will send you a prophet like me from your
own people.'[e] 38He was in the assembly in the
desert, with the angel who spoke to him on
Mount Sinai, and with our fathers; and he received living words to pass on to us.
39"But our fathers refused to obey him. Instead, they rejected him and in their hearts
turned back to Egypt. 40They told Aaron, 'Make
us gods who will go before us. As for this fellow
Moses who led us out of Egypt—we don't know
what has happened to him!'[f] 41That was the
time they made an idol in the form of a calf.
They brought sacrifices to it and held a celebration in honor of what their hands had made.
42But God turned away and gave them over
to the worship of the heavenly bodies. This
agrees with what is written in the book of the
prophets:

" 'Did you bring me sacrifices and offerings
forty years in the desert, O house of
Israel?
43You have lifted up the shrine of Molech
and the star of your god Rephan,
the idols you made to worship.
Therefore I will send you into exile'[g]
beyond Babylon.

44"Our forefathers had the tabernacle of the
Testimony with them in the desert. It had been
made as God directed Moses, according to the
pattern he had seen. 45Having received the tabernacle, our fathers under Joshua brought it
with them when they took the land from the
nations God drove out before them. It remained in the land until the time of David,
46who enjoyed God's favor and asked that he
might provide a dwelling place for the God of
Jacob.[h] 47But it was Solomon who built the
house for him.
48"However, the Most High does not live in
houses made by men. As the prophet says:

49" 'Heaven is my throne,
and the earth is my footstool.
What kind of house will you build for me?
says the Lord.
Or where will my resting place be?
50Has not my hand made all these things?'[i]

51"You stiff-necked people, with uncircumcised hearts and ears! You are just like your
fathers: You always resist the Holy Spirit! 52Was
there ever a prophet your fathers did not persecute? They even killed those who predicted the
coming of the Righteous One. And now you
have betrayed and murdered him— 53you who
have received the law that was put into effect
through angels but have not obeyed it."

The Stoning of Stephen

54When they heard this, they were furious
and gnashed their teeth at him. 55But Stephen,
full of the Holy Spirit, looked up to heaven and
saw the glory of God, and Jesus standing at the
right hand of God. 56"Look," he said, "I see
heaven open and the Son of Man standing at
the right hand of God."
57At this they covered their ears and, yelling
at the top of their voices, they all rushed at him,
58dragged him out of the city and began to
stone him. Meanwhile, the witnesses laid their
clothes at the feet of a young man named Saul.
59While they were stoning him, Stephen
prayed, "Lord Jesus, receive my spirit." 60Then
he fell on his knees and cried out, "Lord, do not

[a]28 Exodus 2:14 [b]32 Exodus 3:6
[c]34 Exodus 3:5,7,8,10 [d]36 That is, Sea of Reeds
[e]37 Deut. 18:15 [f]40 Exodus 32:1 [g]43 Amos 5:25-27 [h]46 Some early manuscripts *the house of Jacob*
[i]50 Isaiah 66:1,2

7:44–50 Stephen's discussion about the temple is important to us as well. Temple walls do not bind God, the Creator of the universe. Sometimes we mistakenly limit God to what we can understand and control. We shape him with our theological systems, our church dogmas, our political presuppositions and our personal experience. But God is much bigger than any conception we could ever have of him. He fills the entire universe! As we more accurately view God and his power, we will discover that he is far bigger than the problems that trouble us.

7:51–60 Through the power of the Holy Spirit, Stephen confronted the religious leaders with their refusal to see the truth. We might have expected these leaders to make some kind of honest self-assessment in response to Stephen's words. But the leaders resisted Stephen's rebuke and responded in anger, wanting to kill him. Despite their rage, Stephen did not react in anger. Instead, he kept his focus on Christ and forgave the people who stoned him. Stephen's peace and self-control were obvious blessings from the Holy Spirit and are available to us today through faith as we continue growing in our relationship with God.

hold this sin against them." When he had said this, he fell asleep.

8 And Saul was there, giving approval to his death.

The Church Persecuted and Scattered

On that day a great persecution broke out against the church at Jerusalem, and all except the apostles were scattered throughout Judea and Samaria. 2Godly men buried Stephen and mourned deeply for him. 3But Saul began to destroy the church. Going from house to house, he dragged off men and women and put them in prison.

Philip in Samaria

4Those who had been scattered preached the word wherever they went. 5Philip went down to a city in Samaria and proclaimed the Christ[a] there. 6When the crowds heard Philip and saw the miraculous signs he did, they all paid close attention to what he said. 7With shrieks, evil[b] spirits came out of many, and many paralytics and cripples were healed. 8So there was great joy in that city.

Simon the Sorcerer

9Now for some time a man named Simon had practiced sorcery in the city and amazed all the people of Samaria. He boasted that he was someone great, 10and all the people, both high and low, gave him their attention and exclaimed, "This man is the divine power known as the Great Power." 11They followed him because he had amazed them for a long time with his magic. 12But when they believed Philip as he preached the good news of the kingdom of God and the name of Jesus Christ, they were baptized, both men and women. 13Simon himself believed and was baptized. And he followed Philip everywhere, astonished by the great signs and miracles he saw.

14When the apostles in Jerusalem heard that Samaria had accepted the word of God, they sent Peter and John to them. 15When they arrived, they prayed for them that they might receive the Holy Spirit, 16because the Holy Spirit had not yet come upon any of them; they had simply been baptized into[c] the name of the Lord Jesus. 17Then Peter and John placed their hands on them, and they received the Holy Spirit.

18When Simon saw that the Spirit was given at the laying on of the apostles' hands, he offered them money 19and said, "Give me also this ability so that everyone on whom I lay my hands may receive the Holy Spirit."

20Peter answered: "May your money perish with you, because you thought you could buy the gift of God with money! 21You have no part or share in this ministry, because your heart is not right before God. 22Repent of this wickedness and pray to the Lord. Perhaps he will forgive you for having such a thought in your heart. 23For I see that you are full of bitterness and captive to sin."

24Then Simon answered, "Pray to the Lord for me so that nothing you have said may happen to me."

25When they had testified and proclaimed the word of the Lord, Peter and John returned to Jerusalem, preaching the gospel in many Samaritan villages.

Philip and the Ethiopian

26Now an angel of the Lord said to Philip, "Go south to the road—the desert road—that

[a]5 Or *Messiah* [b]7 Greek *unclean* [c]16 Or *in*

8:1–3 The people who may seem to us to be the most unlikely candidates for salvation are often at the top of God's list. Saul of Tarsus was one such candidate. Saul was a dreaded enemy of the early Christian church. He went from house to house, arresting believers in his mission to search and destroy. Yet Saul's story is really a story of God's amazing grace. Saul the persecutor became Paul the apostle, one of the greatest leaders in Christian history. Many of us may have begun our relationships with God as unlikely candidates too. Yet there is no limit to what we can become with God's powerful and gracious help.

8:4–8 God used the terrible circumstances of persecution to bring himself glory. Though the believers were driven from their homes in Jerusalem, they used the opportunity to share the Good News wherever they went. God often uses the painful circumstances in our lives for his glory too. Some of us would not have begun to seek God if we had not faced suffering or trouble. God sometimes allows us to suffer in order to awaken us to an opportunity to build our faith or give us a second chance at life.

8:9–17 The Samaritans were considered by the Jews to be no better than Gentiles because of their mixed ancestry. Philip preached boldly to the Samaritans, and they responded to the gospel message in great numbers. Hearing about the successful ministry in Samaria, Peter and John came to join Philip, and the Samaritan believers received the Holy Spirit. This proved that the Good News of salvation in Christ was not just for the Jews; it was available to all people. The Good News of Jesus Christ is available for us, too, no matter who we are or what we have done.

8:18–25 When Simon the sorcerer saw Peter and John's powerful ministry, he wanted to buy the secret of their power. Simon's attitude proved to Peter that Simon did not understand Peter's relationship with God. Simon sought God only for personal gain. Perhaps he wanted to regain the prestige he had lost when Philip came to town (see 8:9–13). Peter warned Simon that by harboring such an attitude Simon was heading for disaster. He needed to examine himself and repent. We need to guard against selfish motives in our walk with Christ too. We should consider, like John the Baptist, how we can become less and Christ can become greater (see John 3:30).

8:26–40 Philip's dealing with an Ethiopian eunuch serves as an excellent model of how we can effectively share the Good News with others. Philip didn't rush in and start preaching. He took time to understand where the Ethiopian was in his faith. Then, Philip proceeded humbly and confidently to share what he knew to be true—that Jesus is the Messiah and that through him we can experience deliverance from sin and its power. Sharing our faith this way takes time; it requires patience and sensitivity. But as we follow Philip's example, we will become more effective communicators of God's message of salvation.

goes down from Jerusalem to Gaza." [27]So he
started out, and on his way he met an Ethiopian[a] eunuch, an important official in charge of
all the treasury of Candace, queen of the Ethio-
pians. This man had gone to Jerusalem to worship, [28]and on his way home was sitting in his
chariot reading the book of Isaiah the prophet.
[29]The Spirit told Philip, "Go to that chariot and
stay near it."
[30]Then Philip ran up to the chariot and heard
the man reading Isaiah the prophet. "Do you
understand what you are reading?" Philip asked.
[31]"How can I," he said, "unless someone explains it to me?" So he invited Philip to come up
and sit with him.
[32]The eunuch was reading this passage of
Scripture:

"He was led like a sheep to the slaughter,
and as a lamb before the shearer is
silent,
so he did not open his mouth.
[33]In his humiliation he was deprived of
justice.
Who can speak of his descendants?
For his life was taken from the earth."[b]

[34]The eunuch asked Philip, "Tell me, please,
who is the prophet talking about, himself or
someone else?" [35]Then Philip began with that
very passage of Scripture and told him the good
news about Jesus.
[36]As they traveled along the road, they came
to some water and the eunuch said, "Look, here
is water. Why shouldn't I be baptized?"[c] [38]And
he gave orders to stop the chariot. Then both
Philip and the eunuch went down into the water and Philip baptized him. [39]When they came
up out of the water, the Spirit of the Lord suddenly took Philip away, and the eunuch did not
see him again, but went on his way rejoicing.
[40]Philip, however, appeared at Azotus and traveled about, preaching the gospel in all the
towns until he reached Caesarea.

Saul's Conversion

9 Meanwhile, Saul was still breathing out
murderous threats against the Lord's disciples. He went to the high priest [2]and asked him
for letters to the synagogues in Damascus, so
that if he found any there who belonged to the
Way, whether men or women, he might take
them as prisoners to Jerusalem. [3]As he neared

[a]27 That is, from the upper Nile region
[b]33 Isaiah 53:7,8 [c]36 Some late manuscripts *baptized?" 37Philip said, "If you believe with all your heart, you may." The eunuch answered, "I believe that Jesus Christ is the Son of God."*

9:3–9 Saul traveled to Damascus to persecute the Christians there. As he neared his destination, Saul was suddenly blinded by light from the risen Christ. Blind and helpless, Saul was led to Damascus to await further instructions from God. For three days he ate and drank nothing, using the time as a period of rigorous self-examination. Whether our moment of decision occurs with

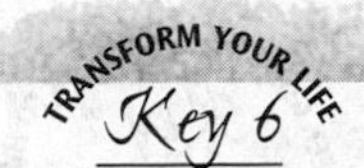

Sharing God's Message

Acts 8:26–40 When God begins to transform our lives, we may become so excited that we want to rush right out and tell everyone about the exciting changes in our lives. God will lead us to people with whom we can share this Good News. We can make the most of these opportunities by paying attention to God's leading by communicating his message effectively.

God led the evangelist Philip to an influential traveler who had gone to Jerusalem to worship and was returning to his native land. When Philip found him, the traveler was sitting in his chariot, reading from the book of Isaiah.

The Spirit told Philip, "Go to that chariot and stay near it." Then Philip ran up to the chariot and heard the man reading Isaiah the prophet. "Do you understand what you are reading?" Philip asked. "How can I," he said, "unless someone explains it to me?" So he invited Philip to come up and sit with him . . . Then Philip began with that very passage of Scripture and told him the good news about Jesus (8:29–31, 35).

The way Philip communicated the Good News is a model for us to follow. He allowed God to lead him to someone who was ready to receive the Good News. Then Philip listened carefully to the man's needs and interests and showed him how Christ could fulfill them. The man gladly received the message, was baptized immediately and went home a changed man. Whether we are zealous or shy, following this model can help us communicate our message in a way that people will receive and understand. In this way, God can use us to transform their lives as well as our own.

Turn to Ephesians 2.

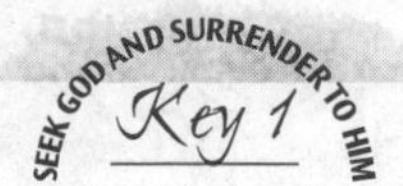

A Time to Surrender

Acts 9:1–9 There are important moments in life when we must choose whether or not we will surrender to God. These are usually times of crisis, situations that can bring about changes in our entire life direction. These moments can either destroy us or they can forever turn the course of our lives in a much better direction.

Saul of Tarsus faced such a moment. After Jesus' ascension, Saul set out to rid the world of Christians.

As he neared Damascus on his journey, suddenly a light from heaven flashed around him. He fell to the ground and heard a voice say to him, "Saul, Saul, why do you persecute me?" "Who are you, Lord?" Saul asked. "I am Jesus, whom you are persecuting," he replied. "Now get up and go into the city, and you will be told what you must do." . . . Saul got up from the ground, but when he opened his eyes he could see nothing. So they led him by the hand into Damascus. For three days he was blind, and did not eat or drink anything (9:3–6, 8–9).

This event produced a severe crisis for Saul. He had been certain that his religious zeal against Jesus and his followers was what God had expected of him. But suddenly the risen Messiah, Jesus, spoke to him, and then Saul was blind! In his physical blindness, Saul came to see that he had been spiritually blind to the truth about God. In response, Saul sought God. And God healed not only Saul's physical blindness but also the spiritual blindness that had kept him from accepting Jesus as his Messiah. The persecutor Saul became the apostle Paul, one of the greatest leaders of the Christian faith.

When we sincerely seek God, he promises to reveal himself to us, showing us where we have been blind to the truth. At such moments of crisis, we need to surrender to God. Then he can heal our blindness and lead us to spiritual renewal.

Turn to 2 Corinthians 4.

Damascus on his journey, suddenly a light from
heaven flashed around him. 4He fell to the
ground and heard a voice say to him, "Saul,
Saul, why do you persecute me?"
5"Who are you, Lord?" Saul asked.
"I am Jesus, whom you are persecuting," he
replied. 6"Now get up and go into the city, and
you will be told what you must do."
7The men traveling with Saul stood there
speechless; they heard the sound but did not see
anyone. 8Saul got up from the ground, but
when he opened his eyes he could see nothing.
So they led him by the hand into Damascus.
9For three days he was blind, and did not eat or
drink anything.
10In Damascus there was a disciple named
Ananias. The Lord called to him in a vision,
"Ananias!"
"Yes, Lord," he answered.
11The Lord told him, "Go to the house of
Judas on Straight Street and ask for a man from
Tarsus named Saul, for he is praying. 12In a
vision he has seen a man named Ananias come
and place his hands on him to restore his sight."
13"Lord," Ananias answered, "I have heard
many reports about this man and all the harm
he has done to your saints in Jerusalem. 14And
he has come here with authority from the chief
priests to arrest all who call on your name."
15But the Lord said to Ananias, "Go! This
man is my chosen instrument to carry my name
before the Gentiles and their kings and before
the people of Israel. 16I will show him how
much he must suffer for my name."
17Then Ananias went to the house and entered it. Placing his hands on Saul, he said,
"Brother Saul, the Lord—Jesus, who appeared to
you on the road as you were coming here—has
sent me so that you may see again and be filled
with the Holy Spirit." 18Immediately, something
like scales fell from Saul's eyes, and he could see
again. He got up and was baptized, 19and after
taking some food, he regained his strength.

Saul in Damascus and Jerusalem

Saul spent several days with the disciples in
Damascus. 20At once he began to preach in the

---

a bang or a whisper, we all must come face to face with our sins. Spiritual renewal begins when we are willing to see the truth, confess it to God and allow him to change our lives.

9:10–16 During Saul's intense self-examination, God sent Ananias to befriend him, pray for him and restore his sight. Ananias was initially afraid because he wasn't sure that Saul had really changed. When he met with Saul, however, Ananias discovered that no one is too far gone for God. By coming to help Saul, Ananias discovered an important truth. When we reach out to others and share the Good News, God not only uses us to help them; he also strengthens our own faith.

9:20–25 Saul quickly joined the Christians in Damascus and began to share the Good News of salvation in Jesus Christ. In this way, he demonstrated that his transformation was real. Both Jews and Christians were astounded at the changes in Saul. The Jews quickly turned against him

synagogues that Jesus is the Son of God. 21All those who heard him were astonished and asked, "Isn't he the man who raised havoc in Jerusalem among those who call on this name? And hasn't he come here to take them as prisoners to the chief priests?" 22Yet Saul grew more and more powerful and baffled the Jews living in Damascus by proving that Jesus is the Christ.[a]

23After many days had gone by, the Jews conspired to kill him, 24but Saul learned of their plan. Day and night they kept close watch on the city gates in order to kill him. 25But his followers took him by night and lowered him in a basket through an opening in the wall.

26When he came to Jerusalem, he tried to join the disciples, but they were all afraid of him, not believing that he really was a disciple. 27But Barnabas took him and brought him to the apostles. He told them how Saul on his journey had seen the Lord and that the Lord had spoken to him, and how in Damascus he had preached fearlessly in the name of Jesus. 28So Saul stayed with them and moved about freely in Jerusalem, speaking boldly in the name of the Lord. 29He talked and debated with the Grecian Jews, but they tried to kill him. 30When the brothers learned of this, they took him down to Caesarea and sent him off to Tarsus.

31Then the church throughout Judea, Galilee and Samaria enjoyed a time of peace. It was strengthened; and encouraged by the Holy Spirit, it grew in numbers, living in the fear of the Lord.

Aeneas and Dorcas

32As Peter traveled about the country, he went to visit the saints in Lydda. 33There he found a man named Aeneas, a paralytic who had been bedridden for eight years. 34"Aeneas," Peter said to him, "Jesus Christ heals you. Get up and take care of your mat." Immediately Aeneas got up. 35All those who lived in Lydda and Sharon saw him and turned to the Lord.

36In Joppa there was a disciple named Tabitha (which, when translated, is Dorcas[b]), who was always doing good and helping the poor. 37About that time she became sick and died, and her body was washed and placed in an upstairs room. 38Lydda was near Joppa; so when the disciples heard that Pe[...] da, they sent two men to him a[...] "Please come at once!"

39Peter went with them, and [...] he was taken upstairs to the roo[...] ows stood around him, crying and showing him the robes and other clothing that Dorcas had made while she was still with them.

40Peter sent them all out of the room; then he got down on his knees and prayed. Turning toward the dead woman, he said, "Tabitha, get up." She opened her eyes, and seeing Peter she sat up. 41He took her by the hand and helped her to her feet. Then he called the believers and the widows and presented her to them alive. 42This became known all over Joppa, and many people believed in the Lord. 43Peter stayed in Joppa for some time with a tanner named Simon.

Cornelius Calls for Peter

10 At Caesarea there was a man named Cornelius, a centurion in what was known as the Italian Regiment. 2He and all his family were devout and God-fearing; he gave generously to those in need and prayed to God regularly. 3One day at about three in the afternoon he had a vision. He distinctly saw an angel of God, who came to him and said, "Cornelius!"

4Cornelius stared at him in fear. "What is it, Lord?" he asked.

The angel answered, "Your prayers and gifts to the poor have come up as a memorial offering before God. 5Now send men to Joppa to bring back a man named Simon who is called Peter. 6He is staying with Simon the tanner, whose house is by the sea."

7When the angel who spoke to him had gone, Cornelius called two of his servants and a devout soldier who was one of his attendants. 8He told them everything that had happened and sent them to Joppa.

Peter's Vision

9About noon the following day as they were on their journey and approaching the city, Peter

[a]22 Or *Messiah* [b]36 Both *Tabitha* (Aramaic) and *Dorcas* (Greek) mean *gazelle.*

---

and sought to kill him, but his new Christian friends helped him escape. We also may experience opposition from our old associates when we surrender our lives to God and begin to share the Good News of Jesus Christ. They may begin to feel guilty about their own sins, or they may be afraid they are about to lose our friendship. Whatever the reason, they may try to thwart our spiritual growth. Our relationships with other believers are essential during these difficult times because they can help guide us through such times.

9:26–30 When Saul returned to Jerusalem and tried to join the Christian movement, he was immediately met with suspicion. The believers in Jerusalem couldn't believe that such a cruel enemy could have changed so quickly. In time, though, Saul proved his sincerity and was accepted. When we begin to seek God, we may meet similar skepticism from others. As we seek to follow God's plan for our lives, friends and family members may turn away. In time, however, if we continue to follow God's will, we can establish better relationships with our loved ones.

9:36–43 Peter received a call for help from grieving friends in nearby Joppa. Dorcas, a disciple who constantly served the poor and widows, had just died. Those who loved her had sent for Peter. Imitating Jesus and implementing God's power over death, Peter brought this woman back to life (see Luke 8:41–42, 49–56). When God's power is at work within us, nothing is impossible. God's power can revive us and give us new lives in Jesus Christ.

10:9–20 God sent Peter a special vision to help instruct him about things clean and unclean. In this vision, Peter

Cornelius & Family

Spiritual transformation usually doesn't happen overnight; spiritual growth is a process that takes time. When Cornelius and his family came into the spotlight in Acts 10, their spiritual renewal had already begun. Out of a Roman religious and military background, this centurion and his family had become "God-fearing." They worshiped the God of Israel and lived godly lives. They were deeply reverent and generous and were also people of prayer.

Cornelius's family had undoubtedly changed many of the habits and perspectives they had learned through their pagan background. At this point, God intervened so that Cornelius's family could move on to a deeper level of relationship with him. God met them at their point of need by sending them the apostle Peter, who came to this family with the spiritual insight they needed.

The scene in Cornelius's home reveals a family seeking God in their willingness to surrender to him. As Cornelius and his family came to believe in the redemption of Jesus, they also received the power of the Holy Spirit. But by no means was this the end of their spiritual growth. They were well on their way because they had established healthy relationships with each other and with God.

When Cornelius's family received the gift of the Holy Spirit, a new era of Christian history was born. God illustrated that all people were acceptable to him through Jesus Christ—even "unclean" Gentiles. Because of his cultural prejudices, Peter found it difficult to accept this truth. But when Cornelius and his family received the Holy Spirit, Peter could no longer deny God's free gift of grace for all. God desires to make the Holy Spirit's power a part of all our lives. If we accept God's forgiveness on the basis of the work of Jesus Christ, we can experience God's power, too. With God's help, no problem or prejudice is too great to overcome.

STRENGTHS AND ACCOMPLISHMENTS:

Cornelius believed in God and acted on what he knew about him.

He led his family to know God the best way he knew how.

Cornelius was not satisfied with his level of maturity and sought to grow further.

He and his family were open to change and embraced new life in Jesus Christ.

WEAKNESSES AND MISTAKES:

Because Cornelius's understanding was limited, he initially worshiped Peter.

LESSONS FROM THEIR LIVES:

God reaches out to those who want to know him better.

The power of Jesus is for everyone, regardless of race or background.

Spiritual growth often requires guidance from others.

KEY VERSE:

"Everyone who believes in [Jesus Christ] receives forgiveness of sins through his name" (10:43).

The story of Cornelius and his family is told in Acts 10—11.

went up on the roof to pray. 10 He became hungry and wanted something to eat, and while the meal was being prepared, he fell into a trance. 11 He saw heaven opened and something like a large sheet being let down to earth by its four corners. 12 It contained all kinds of four-footed animals, as well as reptiles of the earth and birds of the air. 13 Then a voice told him, "Get up, Peter. Kill and eat."

14 "Surely not, Lord!" Peter replied. "I have never eaten anything impure or unclean."

15 The voice spoke to him a second time, "Do not call anything impure that God has made clean."

16 This happened three times, and immediately the sheet was taken back to heaven.

17 While Peter was wondering about the meaning of the vision, the men sent by Cornelius found out where Simon's house was and stopped at the gate. 18 They called out, asking if Simon who was known as Peter was staying there.

19 While Peter was still thinking about the vision, the Spirit said to him, "Simon, three[a] men are looking for you. 20 So get up and go downstairs. Do not hesitate to go with them, for I have sent them."

21 Peter went down and said to the men, "I'm the one you're looking for. Why have you come?"

22 The men replied, "We have come from Cornelius the centurion. He is a righteous and God-fearing man, who is respected by all the Jewish people. A holy angel told him to have you come to his house so that he could hear what you have to say." 23 Then Peter invited the men into the house to be his guests.

Peter at Cornelius' House

The next day Peter started out with them, and some of the brothers from Joppa went along. 24 The following day he arrived in Caesarea. Cornelius was expecting them and had called together his relatives and close friends. 25 As Peter entered the house, Cornelius met him and fell at his feet in reverence. 26 But Peter made him get up. "Stand up," he said, "I am only a man myself."

27 Talking with him, Peter went inside and found a large gathering of people. 28 He said to them: "You are well aware that it is against our law for a Jew to associate with a Gentile or visit him. But God has shown me that I should not call any man impure or unclean. 29 So when I was sent for, I came without raising any objection. May I ask why you sent for me?"

30 Cornelius answered: "Four days ago I was in my house praying at this hour, at three in the afternoon. Suddenly a man in shining clothes stood before me 31 and said, 'Cornelius, God has heard your prayer and remembered your gifts to the poor. 32 Send to Joppa for Simon who is called Peter. He is a guest in the home of Simon the tanner, who lives by the sea.' 33 So I sent for you immediately, and it was good of you to come. Now we are all here in the presence of God to listen to everything the Lord has commanded you to tell us."

34 Then Peter began to speak: "I now realize how true it is that God does not show favoritism 35 but accepts men from every nation who fear him and do what is right. 36 You know the message God sent to the people of Israel, telling the good news of peace through Jesus Christ, who is Lord of all. 37 You know what has happened throughout Judea, beginning in Galilee after the baptism that John preached— 38 how God anointed Jesus of Nazareth with the Holy Spirit and power, and how he went around doing good and healing all who were under the power of the devil, because God was with him.

39 "We are witnesses of everything he did in the country of the Jews and in Jerusalem. They killed him by hanging him on a tree, 40 but God raised him from the dead on the third day and caused him to be seen. 41 He was not seen by all the people, but by witnesses whom God had already chosen—by us who ate and drank with him after he rose from the dead. 42 He commanded us to preach to the people and to testify that he is the one whom God appointed as judge of the living and the dead. 43 All the prophets testify about him that everyone who believes in him receives forgiveness of sins through his name."

44 While Peter was still speaking these words, the Holy Spirit came on all who heard the message. 45 The circumcised believers who had come with Peter were astonished that the gift of the Holy Spirit had been poured out even on

a 19 One early manuscript *two;* other manuscripts do not have the number.

---

saw a sheet holding all sorts of animals that, according to Jewish law, were unclean. Peter refused to have anything to do with them. But God sent the vision three times and challenged Peter's view of what was clean or unclean. Through the vision God was preparing Peter to carry the Good News into the "unclean" home of a Gentile named Cornelius. Peter needed to realize that in Christ all people are acceptable to God. This truth is important for us as well. As we share the Good News with others, we must not let our prejudices stand in the way of God's will for us. If God opens a door for us to share his hope with someone, we need to step through that door in faith.

10:21–33 Peter didn't want to visit the home of this "unclean" Gentile. But when Peter and Cornelius got together, they excitedly shared with each other the unusual things they had just seen and heard. God helped cut away the barriers that would have kept them from speaking to each other. Then the Holy Spirit filled all the Gentiles who were in the home of Cornelius, and God was able to draw people close who had once been separated by immense barriers. There may be relationships in our lives that seem broken beyond repair. Though such relationships might appear hopeless, as we surrender our lives to God and seek to follow his will, God can work to soften our defenses and enhance our communication.

the Gentiles. 46For they heard them speaking in tongues[a] and praising God.

Then Peter said, 47"Can anyone keep these people from being baptized with water? They have received the Holy Spirit just as we have." 48So he ordered that they be baptized in the name of Jesus Christ. Then they asked Peter to stay with them for a few days.

Peter Explains His Actions

11 The apostles and the brothers throughout Judea heard that the Gentiles also had received the word of God. 2So when Peter went up to Jerusalem, the circumcised believers criticized him 3and said, "You went into the house of uncircumcised men and ate with them."

4Peter began and explained everything to them precisely as it had happened: 5"I was in the city of Joppa praying, and in a trance I saw a vision. I saw something like a large sheet being let down from heaven by its four corners, and it came down to where I was. 6I looked into it and saw four-footed animals of the earth, wild beasts, reptiles, and birds of the air. 7Then I heard a voice telling me, 'Get up, Peter. Kill and eat.'

8"I replied, 'Surely not, Lord! Nothing impure or unclean has ever entered my mouth.'

9"The voice spoke from heaven a second time, 'Do not call anything impure that God has made clean.' 10This happened three times, and then it was all pulled up to heaven again.

11"Right then three men who had been sent to me from Caesarea stopped at the house where I was staying. 12The Spirit told me to have no hesitation about going with them. These six brothers also went with me, and we entered the man's house. 13He told us how he had seen an angel appear in his house and say, 'Send to Joppa for Simon who is called Peter. 14He will bring you a message through which you and all your household will be saved.'

15"As I began to speak, the Holy Spirit came on them as he had come on us at the beginning. 16Then I remembered what the Lord had said: 'John baptized with[b] water, but you will be baptized with the Holy Spirit.' 17So if God gave them the same gift as he gave us, who believed in the Lord Jesus Christ, who was I to think that I could oppose God?"

18When they heard this, they had no further objections and praised God, saying, "So then, God has granted even the Gentiles repentance unto life."

The Church in Antioch

19Now those who had been scattered by the persecution in connection with Stephen traveled as far as Phoenicia, Cyprus and Antioch, telling the message only to Jews. 20Some of them, however, men from Cyprus and Cyrene, went to Antioch and began to speak to Greeks also, telling them the good news about the Lord Jesus. 21The Lord's hand was with them, and a great number of people believed and turned to the Lord.

22News of this reached the ears of the church at Jerusalem, and they sent Barnabas to Antioch. 23When he arrived and saw the evidence of the grace of God, he was glad and encouraged them all to remain true to the Lord with all their hearts. 24He was a good man, full of the Holy Spirit and faith, and a great number of people were brought to the Lord.

25Then Barnabas went to Tarsus to look for Saul, 26and when he found him, he brought him to Antioch. So for a whole year Barnabas and Saul met with the church and taught great numbers of people. The disciples were called Christians first at Antioch.

27During this time some prophets came down from Jerusalem to Antioch. 28One of them, named Agabus, stood up and through the Spirit predicted that a severe famine would spread over the entire Roman world. (This happened during the reign of Claudius.) 29The disciples, each according to his ability, decided to provide help for the brothers living in Judea. 30This they did, sending their gift to the elders by Barnabas and Saul.

Peter's Miraculous Escape From Prison

12 It was about this time that King Herod arrested some who belonged to the church, intending to persecute them. 2He had James, the brother of John, put to death with the sword. 3When he saw that this pleased the Jews, he proceeded to seize Peter also. This happened during the Feast of Unleavened Bread. 4After arresting him, he put him in prison, handing him over to be guarded by four squads

[a]46 Or *other languages* [b]16 Or *in*

11:1–3 Even before Peter returned home, the Jewish believers heard that Gentiles had believed in Christ. Because of their prejudice, these Jewish believers could not believe this. They immediately confronted Peter. When faced with opposition before Christ's death, Peter had been afraid to speak the truth and stand up for what he believed (see Luke 22:54–62). But since Pentecost, Peter had become a courageous man. He faced the Jewish believers without concern for what it might cost him and defended the truth that had been revealed to him. We may be afraid to speak the truth at times, especially when there is a threat of dire consequences. However, the same Holy Spirit who gave Peter courage is available for us today; he will help us overcome our fears.

12:1–11 Peter's escape from prison shows us that nothing can thwart God's plan for our lives. This does not mean we will never face difficulties in our walk with God. Even as the early church enjoyed phenomenal success, it still suffered severe trials. Yet God can always overcome the obstacles in our way. He may even use supernatural means to deliver us—against all human odds and in response to prayer. God's plan will prevail. If we are fulfilling God's will, ultimately there is nothing that can stand in our way.

of four soldiers each. Herod intended to bring him out for public trial after the Passover.

[5]So Peter was kept in prison, but the church was earnestly praying to God for him.

[6]The night before Herod was to bring him to trial, Peter was sleeping between two soldiers, bound with two chains, and sentries stood guard at the entrance. [7]Suddenly an angel of the Lord appeared and a light shone in the cell. He struck Peter on the side and woke him up. "Quick, get up!" he said, and the chains fell off Peter's wrists.

[8]Then the angel said to him, "Put on your clothes and sandals." And Peter did so. "Wrap your cloak around you and follow me," the angel told him. [9]Peter followed him out of the prison, but he had no idea that what the angel was doing was really happening; he thought he was seeing a vision. [10]They passed the first and second guards and came to the iron gate leading to the city. It opened for them by itself, and they went through it. When they had walked the length of one street, suddenly the angel left him.

[11]Then Peter came to himself and said, "Now I know without a doubt that the Lord sent his angel and rescued me from Herod's clutches and from everything the Jewish people were anticipating."

[12]When this had dawned on him, he went to the house of Mary the mother of John, also called Mark, where many people had gathered and were praying. [13]Peter knocked at the outer entrance, and a servant girl named Rhoda came to answer the door. [14]When she recognized Peter's voice, she was so overjoyed she ran back without opening it and exclaimed, "Peter is at the door!"

[15]"You're out of your mind," they told her. When she kept insisting that it was so, they said, "It must be his angel."

[16]But Peter kept on knocking, and when they opened the door and saw him, they were astonished. [17]Peter motioned with his hand for them to be quiet and described how the Lord had brought him out of prison. "Tell James and the brothers about this," he said, and then he left for another place.

[18]In the morning, there was no small commotion among the soldiers as to what had become of Peter. [19]After Herod had a thorough search made for him and did not find him, he cross-examined the guards and ordered that they be executed.

Herod's Death

Then Herod went from Judea to Caesarea and stayed there a while. [20]He had been quarreling with the people of Tyre and Sidon; they now joined together and sought an audience with him. Having secured the support of Blastus, a trusted personal servant of the king, they asked for peace, because they depended on the king's country for their food supply.

[21]On the appointed day Herod, wearing his royal robes, sat on his throne and delivered a public address to the people. [22]They shouted, "This is the voice of a god, not of a man." [23]Immediately, because Herod did not give praise to God, an angel of the Lord struck him down, and he was eaten by worms and died.

[24]But the word of God continued to increase and spread.

[25]When Barnabas and Saul had finished their mission, they returned from[a] Jerusalem, taking with them John, also called Mark.

Barnabas and Saul Sent Off

13 In the church at Antioch there were prophets and teachers: Barnabas, Simeon called Niger, Lucius of Cyrene, Manaen (who had been brought up with Herod the tetrarch) and Saul. [2]While they were worshiping the Lord and fasting, the Holy Spirit said, "Set apart for me Barnabas and Saul for the work to which I have called them." [3]So after they had fasted and prayed, they placed their hands on them and sent them off.

On Cyprus

[4]The two of them, sent on their way by the Holy Spirit, went down to Seleucia and sailed from there to Cyprus. [5]When they arrived at Salamis, they proclaimed the word of God in the Jewish synagogues. John was with them as their helper.

[6]They traveled through the whole island until they came to Paphos. There they met a Jewish sorcerer and false prophet named Bar-Jesus, [7]who was an attendant of the proconsul, Sergius Paulus. The proconsul, an intelligent man, sent for Barnabas and Saul because he wanted to hear the word of God. [8]But Elymas the sorcerer (for that is what his name means) opposed them and tried to turn the proconsul from the faith. [9]Then Saul, who was also called Paul, filled with the Holy Spirit, looked straight at Elymas and said, [10]"You are a child of the devil and an enemy of everything that is right! You are full of all kinds of deceit and trickery. Will you never stop perverting the right ways of the Lord? [11]Now the hand of the Lord is against you. You are going to be blind, and for a time you will be unable to see the light of the sun."

Immediately mist and darkness came over

[a]25 Some manuscripts *to*

13:1–3 However reluctant the church in Antioch may have been to lose Paul and Barnabas, they immediately submitted to the voice of the Holy Spirit. Although it meant a major change, the believers fasted, prayed and laid hands on these leaders, releasing and commissioning them to missionary service. We can also support one another's growth and times of change for the better as we pray for each other and encourage each other to do God's will.

Barnabas & John Mark

Discouragement drains our energy, especially when we face various trials. At such times, we need to spend time with people who know how to encourage. Some people know just what to do or say to remind us that life is worthwhile even in the midst of pain and failure. These people inspire hope when there seems to be nothing to hope for. Barnabas, whose name means "Son of Encouragement" (Acts 4:36), was just that kind of person.

Barnabas demonstrated his gift of encouragement through his financial generosity, his leadership, his teaching of new believers at Antioch and his acceptance of Paul when others were afraid of him and doubted his conversion. Barnabas also shaped the course of church history by persevering in his encouragement of John Mark.

Unfortunately, John Mark abandoned his responsibilities on the first missionary journey with Paul and Barnabas. Barnabas was willing to give the younger man another chance by including him in a second journey, but Paul wouldn't hear of it. The disagreement between the two missionaries was so great that Barnabas and Paul parted company. Paul went back to Asia Minor with his new partner, Silas; Barnabas went on his own missionary journey with John Mark at his side (see 15:36–41).

With Barnabas's encouragement, John Mark was faithful in his missionary ministry and soon regained Paul's respect. Later, John Mark would also work with the apostle Peter (see 1 Peter 5:13). He authored the Gospel of Mark, which encouraged others to consider faith in Jesus Christ. John Mark's initial failure was not the end of his usefulness to God's kingdom. Our failures do not need to be the end for us either. Jesus Christ offers us forgiveness and gives each of us the chance for a new start. As we experience spiritual renewal, we also have the privilege of encouraging others along the way.

STRENGTHS AND ACCOMPLISHMENTS:

Barnabas was a gifted encourager.

Barnabas was willing to invest in John Mark even after his failure.

John Mark became a great minister and writer.

WEAKNESSES AND MISTAKES:

John Mark gave up and went home during Paul's first missionary journey.

LESSONS FROM THEIR LIVES:

As we seek to preserve spiritual gains, we need encouragers to help give us perspective; others need our encouragement too.

At times, we may need to make personal sacrifices to encourage others.

Though it may lead to disappointment, encouragement can pay huge dividends for those we encourage.

KEY VERSES:

"Barnabas wanted to take John, also called Mark, with them, but Paul did not think it wise to take him, because he had deserted them in Pamphylia and had not continued with them in the work. They had such a sharp disagreement that they parted company. Barnabas took Mark and sailed for Cyprus" (15:37–39).

The story of Barnabas and John Mark is told in Acts 12:25—15:39. Both also are mentioned in Colossians 4:10. Barnabas is also referred to in Acts 4:36, 9:27 and 11; 1 Corinthians 9:6 and Galatians 2. John Mark is referred to in Colossians 4:10; 2 Timothy 4:11; Philemon 24 and 1 Peter 5:13.

him, and he groped about, seeking someone to lead him by the hand. 12When the proconsul saw what had happened, he believed, for he was amazed at the teaching about the Lord.

In Pisidian Antioch

13From Paphos, Paul and his companions sailed to Perga in Pamphylia, where John left them to return to Jerusalem. 14From Perga they went on to Pisidian Antioch. On the Sabbath they entered the synagogue and sat down. 15After the reading from the Law and the Prophets, the synagogue rulers sent word to them, saying, "Brothers, if you have a message of encouragement for the people, please speak."

16Standing up, Paul motioned with his hand and said: "Men of Israel and you Gentiles who worship God, listen to me! 17The God of the people of Israel chose our fathers; he made the people prosper during their stay in Egypt, with mighty power he led them out of that country, 18he endured their conduct[a] for about forty years in the desert, 19he overthrew seven nations in Canaan and gave their land to his people as their inheritance. 20All this took about 450 years.

"After this, God gave them judges until the time of Samuel the prophet. 21Then the people asked for a king, and he gave them Saul son of Kish, of the tribe of Benjamin, who ruled forty years. 22After removing Saul, he made David their king. He testified concerning him: 'I have found David son of Jesse a man after my own heart; he will do everything I want him to do.'

23"From this man's descendants God has brought to Israel the Savior Jesus, as he promised. 24Before the coming of Jesus, John preached repentance and baptism to all the people of Israel. 25As John was completing his work, he said: 'Who do you think I am? I am not that one. No, but he is coming after me, whose sandals I am not worthy to untie.'

26"Brothers, children of Abraham, and you God-fearing Gentiles, it is to us that this message of salvation has been sent. 27The people of Jerusalem and their rulers did not recognize Jesus, yet in condemning him they fulfilled the words of the prophets that are read every Sabbath. 28Though they found no proper ground for a death sentence, they asked Pilate to have him executed. 29When they had carried out all that was written about him, they took him down from the tree and laid him in a tomb. 30But God raised him from the dead, 31and for many days he was seen by those who had traveled with him from Galilee to Jerusalem. They are now his witnesses to our people.

32"We tell you the good news: What God promised our fathers 33he has fulfilled for us, their children, by raising up Jesus. As it is written in the second Psalm:

" 'You are my Son;
today I have become your Father.[b][c]

34The fact that God raised him from the dead, never to decay, is stated in these words:

" 'I will give you the holy and sure
blessings promised to David.'[d]

35So it is stated elsewhere:

" 'You will not let your Holy One see
decay.'[e]

36"For when David had served God's purpose in his own generation, he fell asleep; he was buried with his fathers and his body decayed. 37But the one whom God raised from the dead did not see decay.

38"Therefore, my brothers, I want you to know that through Jesus the forgiveness of sins is proclaimed to you. 39Through him everyone who believes is justified from everything you could not be justified from by the law of Moses. 40Take care that what the prophets have said does not happen to you:

41" 'Look, you scoffers,
wonder and perish,
for I am going to do something in your days
that you would never believe,
even if someone told you.'[f]"

42As Paul and Barnabas were leaving the synagogue, the people invited them to speak further about these things on the next Sabbath. 43When the congregation was dismissed, many of the Jews and devout converts to Judaism followed Paul and Barnabas, who talked with them and urged them to continue in the grace of God.

44On the next Sabbath almost the whole city gathered to hear the word of the Lord. 45When the Jews saw the crowds, they were filled with

[a] 18 Some manuscripts *and cared for them* [b] 33 Or *have begotten you* [c] 33 Psalm 2:7 [d] 34 Isaiah 55:3 [e] 35 Psalm 16:10 [f] 41 Hab. 1:5

13:13–14 John Mark left the missionary team and returned home to Jerusalem. We aren't told the reasons for his departure. Perhaps it was due to a lack of faith, a conflict with Paul's leadership, culture shock, homesickness or fear. Most of our spiritual journeys will be marked with interruptions. There may be times when we, like John Mark, turn back from our commitments or even from God. It is encouraging to see that later John Mark was restored to fellowship with Barnabas and Paul. Barnabas took John Mark under his wing, even when Paul rejected him (see 15:37–39). From Paul's letters a decade later we know that John Mark became a faithful minister and trusted colleague of Paul (see Colossians 4:10; 2 Timothy 4:11). Our failures can become opportunities to start over and to keep growing if we ask God to redirect our course and restore us.

13:45—14:6 Paul and Barnabas experienced jealousy, rejection, ridicule, revenge, physical abuse, murder plots and more as they preached the Good News to others. Sometimes Paul and Barnabas stayed in a town for weeks, but sometimes they had to run for their lives after only a short stay. When we reach out to others, we may need

jealousy and talked abusively against what Paul
was saying.
46Then Paul and Barnabas answered them
boldly: "We had to speak the word of God to
you first. Since you reject it and do not consider
yourselves worthy of eternal life, we now turn
to the Gentiles. 47For this is what the Lord has
commanded us:

" 'I have made you[a] a light for the
Gentiles,
that you[a] may bring salvation to the
ends of the earth.'[b] "

48When the Gentiles heard this, they were
glad and honored the word of the Lord; and all
who were appointed for eternal life believed.
49The word of the Lord spread through the
whole region. 50But the Jews incited the God-
fearing women of high standing and the leading
men of the city. They stirred up persecution
against Paul and Barnabas, and expelled them
from their region. 51So they shook the dust
from their feet in protest against them and went
to Iconium. 52And the disciples were filled with
joy and with the Holy Spirit.

In Iconium

14 At Iconium Paul and Barnabas went as
usual into the Jewish synagogue. There
they spoke so effectively that a great number of
Jews and Gentiles believed. 2But the Jews who
refused to believe stirred up the Gentiles and
poisoned their minds against the brothers. 3So
Paul and Barnabas spent considerable time
there, speaking boldly for the Lord, who confirmed the message of his grace by enabling
them to do miraculous signs and wonders. 4The
people of the city were divided; some sided with
the Jews, others with the apostles. 5There was a
plot afoot among the Gentiles and Jews, together with their leaders, to mistreat them and stone
them. 6But they found out about it and fled to
the Lycaonian cities of Lystra and Derbe and to
the surrounding country, 7where they continued to preach the good news.

In Lystra and Derbe

8In Lystra there sat a man crippled in his
feet, who was lame from birth and had never
walked. 9He listened to Paul as he was speaking.
Paul looked directly at him, saw that he had
faith to be healed 10and called out, "Stand up
on your feet!" At that, the man jumped up and
began to walk.
11When the crowd saw what Paul had done,
they shouted in the Lycaonian language, "The
gods have come down to us in human form!"
12Barnabas they called Zeus, and Paul they
called Hermes because he was the chief speaker.
13The priest of Zeus, whose temple was just outside the city, brought bulls and wreaths to the
city gates because he and the crowd wanted to
offer sacrifices to them.
14But when the apostles Barnabas and Paul
heard of this, they tore their clothes and rushed
out into the crowd, shouting: 15"Men, why are
you doing this? We too are only men, human
like you. We are bringing you good news, telling you to turn from these worthless things to
the living God, who made heaven and earth
and sea and everything in them. 16In the past,
he let all nations go their own way. 17Yet he has
not left himself without testimony: He has
shown kindness by giving you rain from heaven
and crops in their seasons; he provides you with
plenty of food and fills your hearts with joy."
18Even with these words, they had difficulty
keeping the crowd from sacrificing to them.
19Then some Jews came from Antioch and
Iconium and won the crowd over. They stoned
Paul and dragged him outside the city, thinking
he was dead. 20But after the disciples had gathered around him, he got up and went back into
the city. The next day he and Barnabas left for
Derbe.

The Return to Antioch in Syria

21They preached the good news in that city
and won a large number of disciples. Then they
returned to Lystra, Iconium and Antioch,
22strengthening the disciples and encouraging
them to remain true to the faith. "We must go
through many hardships to enter the kingdom
of God," they said. 23Paul and Barnabas appointed elders[c] for them in each church and, with
prayer and fasting, committed them to the Lord,
in whom they had put their trust. 24After going
through Pisidia, they came into Pamphylia,
25and when they had preached the word in Perga, they went down to Attalia.
26From Attalia they sailed back to Antioch,
where they had been committed to the grace of
God for the work they had now completed.
27On arriving there, they gathered the church
together and reported all that God had done
through them and how he had opened the door

[a]47 The Greek is singular. [b]47 Isaiah 49:6 [c]23 Or *Barnabas ordained elders*; or *Barnabas had elders elected*

---

courage to persevere when unreceptive people challenge our message. At other times we may need to accept their rejection and move on. Only God can give us the wisdom to know how to react in each situation.

14:14–20 The crowds at Lystra erroneously believed that Paul and Barnabas were Greek gods. Such mistaken identification and misplaced worship horrified the two missionaries, who quickly sought to clear up the misunderstanding. Soon after this, Jews from Iconium persuaded the locals that Paul was a charlatan. As a result, Paul was nearly killed, but God intervened to spare his life. The people at Lystra changed their attitudes and opinions about God very quickly because they followed outward signs and the influence of persuasive people. Our spiritual growth cannot be dictated by such unreliable influences. While our emotions will be touched by our spiritual renewal, we must make sure that our faith is centered on the truth found in God's Word.

In the Life of Paul

Paul was an intense man. Whatever he did, he did with all his heart. Paul was also an apostle and helped lay the foundation for much of our theology and Christian practice today. Such a person could easily intimidate us were it not for the glimpses we have of his spiritual struggles. Like all of us, Paul was human and vulnerable to failure whenever he took his eyes off Jesus Christ. In order to guard against failure, Paul employed many of the spiritual disciplines. These practices strengthened him in his walk with God and reminded Paul of his dependence on God.

SOLITUDE. Immediately following Paul's conversion, he withdrew into the Arabian wilderness for a time of solitude (see Galatians 1:16–17), meditating intensely on God's Word and spending much time in prayer. Evidently, this was when he received his gospel message "by revelation from Jesus Christ" (Galatians 1:12). This time away equipped him for the lifetime of involvement and service that has changed the world even to this very day. (To learn more about solitude, turn to Exodus 3.)

PRAYER. Paul mentioned that he was given "a thorn" in his flesh (2 Corinthians 12:7). We are never told anything specific about the thorn. But we are given the specifics of Paul's response to it: Paul prayed. In fact, he prayed three times concerning this thorn much as Jesus prayed three times in Gethsemane (see Matthew 26:36–45; 2 Corinthians 12:8). Each time that Paul prayed, God answered him clearly, "My grace is sufficient for you, for my power is made perfect in weakness" (2 Corinthians 12:9). Prayer brought Paul the strength and reassurance he needed. (To learn more about prayer, turn to Genesis 18.)

SERVICE. We see Paul's practice of service as he committed himself "to preach the gospel where Christ was not known" (Romans 15:20). He made countless sacrifices for the sake of the gospel as well (see 2 Corinthians 11:23–33). We see by this that the practice of service set the agenda for Paul's life. (To learn more about service, turn to Mark 10.)

STEWARDSHIP. Paul was never wasteful and even refused to receive payment for preaching to the Corinthian church (see 1 Corinthians 9:1–18). Paul also encouraged all the churches he had planted to participate in an offering for the Jerusalem believers, who had been devastated by famine and poverty. He taught all believers to regularly set aside a certain amount to be given to the Lord's work (see 2 Corinthians 8—9). (To learn more about stewardship, turn to Deuteronomy 8.)

BIBLE STUDY. Paul was a student of God's Word. But Paul's study was not simply a matter of academic curiosity—it was an act of worship. Paul's theology bore the fruit of praise: "Oh, the depth of the riches of the wisdom and knowledge of God! How unsearchable his judgments, and his paths beyond tracing out! . . . To him be the glory forever! Amen" (Romans 11:33, 36). (To learn more about Bible study, turn to Deuteronomy 17.)

SPIRITUAL FRIENDSHIP. Paul's deep concern for people is reflected in his constant references to special friends whom he cherished in Christ. Friendship often lays the foundation for discipleship, as with Paul's relationships both with Timothy and Titus (see 2 Timothy 1:2–4; Titus 1:4). (To learn more about spiritual friendship, turn to Genesis 2.)

Lessons for Life

Even extraordinary people such as Paul are incapable of living the Christian life apart from the power of the Holy Spirit. As we undertake God's high calling in our lives, we must heed Paul's admonition, "After beginning with the Spirit, are you now trying to attain your goal by human effort?" (Galatians 3:3). We, like Paul, can employ the spiritual disciplines to help remind us of our dependence on God and form channels through which his Spirit can work in us.

of faith to the Gentiles. 28And they stayed there
a long time with the disciples.

The Council at Jerusalem

15 Some men came down from Judea to
Antioch and were teaching the brothers: "Unless you are circumcised, according to
the custom taught by Moses, you cannot be
saved." 2This brought Paul and Barnabas into
sharp dispute and debate with them. So Paul
and Barnabas were appointed, along with some
other believers, to go up to Jerusalem to see the
apostles and elders about this question. 3The
church sent them on their way, and as they
traveled through Phoenicia and Samaria, they
told how the Gentiles had been converted. This
news made all the brothers very glad. 4When
they came to Jerusalem, they were welcomed
by the church and the apostles and elders, to
whom they reported everything God had done
through them.

5Then some of the believers who belonged to
the party of the Pharisees stood up and said,
"The Gentiles must be circumcised and required to obey the law of Moses."

6The apostles and elders met to consider this
question. 7After much discussion, Peter got up
and addressed them: "Brothers, you know that
some time ago God made a choice among you
that the Gentiles might hear from my lips the
message of the gospel and believe. 8God, who
knows the heart, showed that he accepted them
by giving the Holy Spirit to them, just as he did
to us. 9He made no distinction between us and
them, for he purified their hearts by faith.
10Now then, why do you try to test God by
putting on the necks of the disciples a yoke that
neither we nor our fathers have been able to
bear? 11No! We believe it is through the grace of
our Lord Jesus that we are saved, just as they are."

12The whole assembly became silent as they
listened to Barnabas and Paul telling about the
miraculous signs and wonders God had done
among the Gentiles through them. 13When they
finished, James spoke up: "Brothers, listen to
me. 14Simon[a] has described to us how God at
first showed his concern by taking from the
Gentiles a people for himself. 15The words of
the prophets are in agreement with this, as it is
written:

16" 'After this I will return
  and rebuild David's fallen tent.
Its ruins I will rebuild,
  and I will restore it,
17that the remnant of men may seek the
  Lord,
  and all the Gentiles who bear my name,
says the Lord, who does these things'[b]
18 that have been known for ages.[c]

19"It is my judgment, therefore, that we
should not make it difficult for the Gentiles
who are turning to God. 20Instead we should
write to them, telling them to abstain from food
polluted by idols, from sexual immorality, from
the meat of strangled animals and from blood.
21For Moses has been preached in every city
from the earliest times and is read in the synagogues on every Sabbath."

The Council's Letter to Gentile Believers

22Then the apostles and elders, with the
whole church, decided to choose some of their
own men and send them to Antioch with Paul
and Barnabas. They chose Judas (called Barsabbas) and Silas, two men who were leaders
among the brothers. 23With them they sent the
following letter:

The apostles and elders, your brothers,

To the Gentile believers in Antioch, Syria
and Cilicia:
Greetings.

24We have heard that some went out
from us without our authorization and
disturbed you, troubling your minds by
what they said. 25So we all agreed to
choose some men and send them to you
with our dear friends Barnabas and Paul—
26men who have risked their lives for the
name of our Lord Jesus Christ. 27Therefore

[a]14 Greek *Simeon,* a variant of *Simon;* that is, Peter
[b]17 Amos 9:11,12 [c]17,18 Some manuscripts *things'— / 18known to the Lord for ages is his work*

15:1–5 The Jerusalem council marked a crisis point in the history of Christianity. At the center of this crisis was the issue of the Jewish law. Jewish Christians thought Gentile Christians should have to comply with the Law of Moses, including the rite of circumcision. In essence, the gospel of grace was at stake in this crisis. The council members needed to determine whether Christ's work alone was sufficient for our salvation or whether believers also had to follow the Law of Moses. The council's answer would affect the faith, fellowship, outreach and leadership of the church. Ultimately, Christ's sufficiency was defended. While there are specific keys to spiritual renewal that we can implement in our lives, our salvation is not based on anything that we do. God's grace delivers us and redirects the course of our lives.

15:12–21 At this council meeting in Jerusalem, James concluded the discussion by confirming Peter's view that Gentiles were acceptable to God in Christ without adhering to Jewish law. James defended his view by appealing to the Scriptures as his final authority for faith and practice. Henceforth, Gentile believers did not have to keep the Jewish law in order to be accepted in the Christian community. However, Gentile Christians agreed to follow some key Jewish practices such as refraining from sexual immorality (see 15:29). Just as the Jews did not add legalistic requirements for salvation in Christ, so we should not add our legalism to God's message of grace. Such an addition would only deny God's grace and undermine our spiritual freedom. Yet we should be sensitive to the differing beliefs of other Christians and not use our freedom in ways that can cause friction. As we continue to submit to God's will, he will show us what is essential for our faith and what is not.

we are sending Judas and Silas to confirm by word of mouth what we are writing. 28It seemed good to the Holy Spirit and to us not to burden you with anything beyond the following requirements: 29You are to abstain from food sacrificed to idols, from blood, from the meat of strangled animals and from sexual immorality. You will do well to avoid these things.

Farewell.

30The men were sent off and went down to Antioch, where they gathered the church together and delivered the letter. 31The people read it and were glad for its encouraging message. 32Judas and Silas, who themselves were prophets, said much to encourage and strengthen the brothers. 33After spending some time there, they were sent off by the brothers with the blessing of peace to return to those who had sent them.[a] 35But Paul and Barnabas remained in Antioch, where they and many others taught and preached the word of the Lord.

Disagreement Between Paul and Barnabas

36Some time later Paul said to Barnabas, "Let us go back and visit the brothers in all the towns where we preached the word of the Lord and see how they are doing." 37Barnabas wanted to take John, also called Mark, with them, 38but Paul did not think it wise to take him, because he had deserted them in Pamphylia and had not continued with them in the work. 39They had such a sharp disagreement that they parted company. Barnabas took Mark and sailed for Cyprus, 40but Paul chose Silas and left, commended by the brothers to the grace of the Lord. 41He went through Syria and Cilicia, strengthening the churches.

Timothy Joins Paul and Silas

16 He came to Derbe and then to Lystra, where a disciple named Timothy lived, whose mother was a Jewess and a believer, but whose father was a Greek. 2The brothers at Lystra and Iconium spoke well of him. 3Paul wanted to take him along on the journey, so he circumcised him because of the Jews who lived in that area, for they all knew that his father was a Greek. 4As they traveled from town to town, they delivered the decisions reached by the apostles and elders in Jerusalem for the people to obey. 5So the churches were strengthened in the faith and grew daily in numbers.

Paul's Vision of the Man of Macedonia

6Paul and his companions traveled throughout the region of Phrygia and Galatia, having been kept by the Holy Spirit from preaching the word in the province of Asia. 7When they came to the border of Mysia, they tried to enter Bithynia, but the Spirit of Jesus would not allow them to. 8So they passed by Mysia and went down to Troas. 9During the night Paul had a vision of a man of Macedonia standing and begging him, "Come over to Macedonia and help us." 10After Paul had seen the vision, we got ready at once to leave for Macedonia, concluding that God had called us to preach the gospel to them.

Lydia's Conversion in Philippi

11From Troas we put out to sea and sailed straight for Samothrace, and the next day on to Neapolis. 12From there we traveled to Philippi, a Roman colony and the leading city of that district of Macedonia. And we stayed there several days.

13On the Sabbath we went outside the city gate to the river, where we expected to find a place of prayer. We sat down and began to speak to the women who had gathered there. 14One of those listening was a woman named Lydia, a dealer in purple cloth from the city of Thyatira, who was a worshiper of God. The Lord opened her heart to respond to Paul's message. 15When she and the members of her household were baptized, she invited us to her home. "If you consider me a believer in the Lord," she said,

[a]33 Some manuscripts *them, 34but Silas decided to remain there*

15:36–41 In this life, we will always be prone to human weaknesses that can hurt our relationships. Note the conflict between Paul and Barnabas over John Mark. Paul did not want to work with John Mark because he had abandoned them on the first missionary journey (see 13:13–14). Paul's reluctance to take John Mark resulted in a sharp disagreement between Paul and Barnabas. Even as mature men of faith, Paul and Barnabas dealt with conflict. Yet we know from Paul's letters that all three men later reconciled. Like these godly men, no matter how mature in our faith we may become, we will encounter conflict with other godly people. When this happens, we must be careful to respond in a way that furthers God's kingdom.

16:1–3 Paul advised Timothy to submit to the Jewish practice of circumcision even though the Jerusalem council had established that it wasn't necessary for his salvation (see 15:12–21). By willingly following Paul's advice, Timothy removed any possible stumbling block to his communicating with a Jewish audience. As we seek to share God's Good News with others, we may need to remove cultural or social barriers to communicate more effectively. Whenever we have an opportunity to reach across racial or cultural lines, we should ask God to show us how to identify with that group of people. If we can do something in accordance with God's Word that will make people more receptive to God's message, we should do it.

16:11–18 In Macedonia Paul's first converts were women. One was a businesswoman named Lydia who sold expensive purple cloth to the wealthy. Another female convert was a slave girl who had been demon-possessed. These two women from entirely different economic and social levels both played key roles in the growth of the Philippian church. While we may be tempted to discriminate on the basis of gender, age, social class, employment status, marital status or disabilities, God does not. God welcomes everyone who is willing to follow him. And so should we.

"come and stay at my house." And she persuaded us.

Paul and Silas in Prison

16Once when we were going to the place of prayer, we were met by a slave girl who had a spirit by which she predicted the future. She earned a great deal of money for her owners by fortune-telling. 17This girl followed Paul and the rest of us, shouting, "These men are servants of the Most High God, who are telling you the way to be saved." 18She kept this up for many days. Finally Paul became so troubled that he turned around and said to the spirit, "In the name of Jesus Christ I command you to come out of her!" At that moment the spirit left her.

19When the owners of the slave girl realized that their hope of making money was gone, they seized Paul and Silas and dragged them into the marketplace to face the authorities. 20They brought them before the magistrates and said, "These men are Jews, and are throwing our city into an uproar 21by advocating customs unlawful for us Romans to accept or practice."

22The crowd joined in the attack against Paul and Silas, and the magistrates ordered them to be stripped and beaten. 23After they had been severely flogged, they were thrown into prison, and the jailer was commanded to guard them carefully. 24Upon receiving such orders, he put them in the inner cell and fastened their feet in the stocks.

25About midnight Paul and Silas were praying and singing hymns to God, and the other prisoners were listening to them. 26Suddenly there was such a violent earthquake that the foundations of the prison were shaken. At once all the prison doors flew open, and everybody's chains came loose. 27The jailer woke up, and when he saw the prison doors open, he drew his sword and was about to kill himself because he thought the prisoners had escaped. 28But Paul shouted, "Don't harm yourself! We are all here!"

29The jailer called for lights, rushed in and fell trembling before Paul and Silas. 30He then brought them out and asked, "Sirs, what must I do to be saved?"

31They replied, "Believe in the Lord Jesus, and you will be saved—you and your household." 32Then they spoke the word of the Lord to him and to all the others in his house. 33At that hour of the night the jailer took them and washed their wounds; then immediately he and all his family were baptized. 34The jailer brought them into his house and set a meal before them; he was filled with joy because he had come to believe in God—he and his whole family.

35When it was daylight, the magistrates sent their officers to the jailer with the order: "Release those men." 36The jailer told Paul, "The magistrates have ordered that you and Silas be released. Now you can leave. Go in peace."

37But Paul said to the officers: "They beat us publicly without a trial, even though we are Roman citizens, and threw us into prison. And now do they want to get rid of us quietly? No! Let them come themselves and escort us out."

38The officers reported this to the magistrates, and when they heard that Paul and Silas were Roman citizens, they were alarmed. 39They came to appease them and escorted them from the prison, requesting them to leave the city. 40After Paul and Silas came out of the prison, they went to Lydia's house, where they met with the brothers and encouraged them. Then they left.

In Thessalonica

17 When they had passed through Amphipolis and Apollonia, they came to Thessalonica, where there was a Jewish synagogue. 2As his custom was, Paul went into the synagogue, and on three Sabbath days he reasoned with them from the Scriptures, 3explaining and proving that the Christ[a] had to suffer and rise from the dead. "This Jesus I am proclaiming to you is the Christ,[a]" he said. 4Some of the Jews were persuaded and joined Paul and Silas, as did a large number of God-fearing Greeks and not a few prominent women.

5But the Jews were jealous; so they rounded up some bad characters from the marketplace, formed a mob and started a riot in the city. They rushed to Jason's house in search of Paul and Silas in order to bring them out to the crowd.[b] 6But when they did not find them, they dragged Jason and some other brothers before the city officials, shouting: "These men who have caused trouble all over the world have now come here, 7and Jason has welcomed them into

[a]3 Or *Messiah* [b]5 Or *the assembly of the people*

16:25–34 Paul and Silas were beaten and jailed in violation of their rights as Roman citizens. Yet they sang praises to God despite their painful circumstances, and God delivered them from this abusive situation. God's deliverance of Paul and Silas taught the Philippian rulers a clear lesson: God is able to deliver and sustain his followers even in difficult circumstances. When we keep our focus on God and all that he has done for us, our identity and inner strength will be sustained. God's power will be evidenced in our inner joy and ability to praise God in the midst of hardship. Such attitudes may even result in our enemies admitting their need for God.

17:1–9 At Thessalonica, Paul presented the Good News in a way that acknowledged the questions and needs of his predominantly Jewish audience. As a result, many people surrendered their lives to God. However, many more Jews objected to Paul's message because of jealousy. They incited the crowds and city officials to run Paul out of town—not just out of Thessalonica, but out of Berea too—complaining that Paul and Silas worshiped a king other than their earthly ruler. In our society, while people may be tolerant of discussions about spirituality, often they will object when we talk about Jesus as our King and the rightful ruler of all kingdoms. Yet we cannot be afraid of speaking the truth and clearly honoring Jesus. Opposition should not deter us from speaking the truth.

his house. They are all defying Caesar's decrees, saying that there is another king, one called Jesus." 8When they heard this, the crowd and the city officials were thrown into turmoil. 9Then they made Jason and the others post bond and let them go.

In Berea

10As soon as it was night, the brothers sent Paul and Silas away to Berea. On arriving there, they went to the Jewish synagogue. 11Now the Bereans were of more noble character than the Thessalonians, for they received the message with great eagerness and examined the Scriptures every day to see if what Paul said was true. 12Many of the Jews believed, as did also a number of prominent Greek women and many Greek men.

13When the Jews in Thessalonica learned that Paul was preaching the word of God at Berea, they went there too, agitating the crowds and stirring them up. 14The brothers immediately sent Paul to the coast, but Silas and Timothy stayed at Berea. 15The men who escorted Paul brought him to Athens and then left with instructions for Silas and Timothy to join him as soon as possible.

In Athens

16While Paul was waiting for them in Athens, he was greatly distressed to see that the city was full of idols. 17So he reasoned in the synagogue with the Jews and the God-fearing Greeks, as well as in the marketplace day by day with those who happened to be there. 18A group of Epicurean and Stoic philosophers began to dispute with him. Some of them asked, "What is this babbler trying to say?" Others remarked, "He seems to be advocating foreign gods." They said this because Paul was preaching the good news about Jesus and the resurrection. 19Then they took him and brought him to a meeting of the Areopagus, where they said to him, "May we know what this new teaching is that you are presenting? 20You are bringing some strange ideas to our ears, and we want to know what they mean." 21(All the Athenians and the foreigners who lived there spent their time doing nothing but talking about and listening to the latest ideas.)

22Paul then stood up in the meeting of the Areopagus and said: "Men of Athens! I see that in every way you are very religious. 23For as I walked around and looked carefully at your objects of worship, I even found an altar with this inscription: TO AN UNKNOWN GOD. Now what you worship as something unknown I am going to proclaim to you.

24"The God who made the world and everything in it is the Lord of heaven and earth and does not live in temples built by hands. 25And he is not served by human hands, as if he needed anything, because he himself gives all men life and breath and everything else. 26From one man he made every nation of men, that they should inhabit the whole earth; and he determined the times set for them and the exact places where they should live. 27God did this so that men would seek him and perhaps reach out for him and find him, though he is not far from each one of us. 28'For in him we live and move and have our being.' As some of your own poets have said, 'We are his offspring.'

29"Therefore since we are God's offspring, we should not think that the divine being is like gold or silver or stone—an image made by man's design and skill. 30In the past God overlooked such ignorance, but now he commands all people everywhere to repent. 31For he has set a day when he will judge the world with justice by the man he has appointed. He has given proof of this to all men by raising him from the dead."

32When they heard about the resurrection of the dead, some of them sneered, but others said, "We want to hear you again on this subject." 33At that, Paul left the Council. 34A few men became followers of Paul and believed. Among them was Dionysius, a member of the Areopagus, also a woman named Damaris, and a number of others.

In Corinth

18 After this, Paul left Athens and went to Corinth. 2There he met a Jew named Aquila, a native of Pontus, who had recently come from Italy with his wife Priscilla, because

---

17:10–12 At Berea, Paul enjoyed a most eager response from the Jewish community. The Bereans searched the Scriptures to confirm Paul's testimonial experience and anecdotal evidence about God. How exciting when someone is ready to hear the Good News of God's plan of salvation. But no one should have to simply take our word alone as truth. The Bible should back up every claim we make about God. As we seek God, we would do well to have the kind of attitude shown by the Bereans. We should eagerly seek God by studying his Word and making that the standard for our faith and conduct.

17:22–31 In Athens, Paul did not preach in the synagogue as he normally did upon entering a new town. Instead, he took a tour through Athens and then shared the Good News with intellectuals and philosophers in the marketplace. Paul acknowledged their belief in an unknown god and described that unknown god as the Creator of everything and our future judge as well. Thanks to Jesus and his messengers, we can know God personally (see John 1:18; 1 John 1:1–3). We don't have to look to some unknown god. We can trust in the powerful, loving and personal God who reveals himself through Jesus Christ.

18:1–9 Paul apparently felt discouraged about his ministry. Maybe there had been very few converts in Athens. Maybe his attempts to persuade the Corinthians to trust Christ fell on deaf ears. Whatever prompted the discouragement he felt, these verses show us the direct encouragement Paul received from God. We all go through hard times in life. However, if we continually seek God and surrender to his will, he will encourage us when times get tough. God doesn't bring us to a certain point just to let us flounder and be destroyed. He will come to us if we continue to seek him (see John 14:18).

Priscilla & Aquila

Priscilla and Aquila were united not only in marriage but also in ministry. In writing about this godly couple, Paul and Luke never mentioned one without the other. Their abilities and talents were complementary: Together, Priscilla and Aquila were able to enrich the lives of the people around them.

Priscilla and Aquila moved to Greece to build a new life after the Jews were commanded to leave the city of Rome. They settled in the cosmopolitan city of Corinth. While adjusting to this move, Priscilla and Aquila opened their home to the apostle Paul. He had recently experienced intense trials in his ministry and needed a place to rest and recuperate. In Priscilla and Aquila's home, Paul found not only acceptance and love but also a livelihood as he joined them in their tentmaking business.

Paul rested and was greatly encouraged during his time with Priscilla and Aquila. Paul then responded to God's challenge and entered new territories of ministry. Aquila and Priscilla moved to Ephesus with Paul and helped him in his ministry. Their faithful friendship provided Paul with both accountability and encouragement.

When Paul left Ephesus, Aquila and Priscilla oversaw the ministry there. They became aware that a young Jew, Apollos, was speaking with great zeal but with incomplete knowledge of the truth. They solved this problem by patiently explaining the things of God to him. Apollos soon became one of the most gifted preachers in the early church.

As a result of their perseverance in God's work, Priscilla and Aquila hosted a growing church in their home. Their strong relationship and godly example made them ideal leaders for new believers. Though they were never famous preachers or leaders themselves, God used Priscilla and Aquila to minister to some of the greatest leaders of the early church.

STRENGTHS AND ACCOMPLISHMENTS:

Priscilla and Aquila shared responsibilities in their marriage.

They were willing to take risks and accept new challenges.

By opening their home, Priscilla and Aquila gave help and encouragement to others.

LESSONS FROM THEIR LIVES:

A healthy marriage allows both husband and wife opportunities to exercise their gifts.

A godly and healthy home is always open to minister to others in need.

Rest is often needed before and after a time of stress and change.

KEY VERSES:

"Greet Priscilla and Aquila, my fellow workers in Christ Jesus. They risked their lives for me. Not only I but all the churches of the Gentiles are grateful to them" (Romans 16:3–4).

Priscilla and Aquila's story is told in Acts 18. Both are also mentioned in Romans 16:3; 1 Corinthians 16:19 and 2 Timothy 4:19.

Claudius had ordered all the Jews to leave
Rome. Paul went to see them, 3and because he
was a tentmaker as they were, he stayed and
worked with them. 4Every Sabbath he reasoned
in the synagogue, trying to persuade Jews and
Greeks.
5When Silas and Timothy came from Macedonia, Paul devoted himself exclusively to
preaching, testifying to the Jews that Jesus was
the Christ.[a] 6But when the Jews opposed Paul
and became abusive, he shook out his clothes
in protest and said to them, "Your blood be on
your own heads! I am clear of my responsibility. From now on I will go to the Gentiles."
7Then Paul left the synagogue and went next
door to the house of Titius Justus, a worshiper
of God. 8Crispus, the synagogue ruler, and his
entire household believed in the Lord; and
many of the Corinthians who heard him believed and were baptized.
9One night the Lord spoke to Paul in a vision: "Do not be afraid; keep on speaking, do
not be silent. 10For I am with you, and no one
is going to attack and harm you, because I have
many people in this city." 11So Paul stayed for a
year and a half, teaching them the word of God.
12While Gallio was proconsul of Achaia, the
Jews made a united attack on Paul and brought
him into court. 13"This man," they charged, "is
persuading the people to worship God in ways
contrary to the law."
14Just as Paul was about to speak, Gallio said
to the Jews, "If you Jews were making a complaint about some misdemeanor or serious
crime, it would be reasonable for me to listen to
you. 15But since it involves questions about
words and names and your own law—settle the
matter yourselves. I will not be a judge of such
things." 16So he had them ejected from the court.
17Then they all turned on Sosthenes the synagogue ruler and beat him in front of the court.
But Gallio showed no concern whatever.

Priscilla, Aquila and Apollos

18Paul stayed on in Corinth for some time.
Then he left the brothers and sailed for Syria,
accompanied by Priscilla and Aquila. Before he
sailed, he had his hair cut off at Cenchrea because of a vow he had taken. 19They arrived at
Ephesus, where Paul left Priscilla and Aquila.
He himself went into the synagogue and reasoned with the Jews. 20When they asked him to
spend more time with them, he declined. 21But
as he left, he promised, "I will come back if it
is God's will." Then he set sail from Ephesus.
22When he landed at Caesarea, he went up and
greeted the church and then went down to Antioch.
23After spending some time in Antioch, Paul
set out from there and traveled from place to
place throughout the region of Galatia and
Phrygia, strengthening all the disciples.
24Meanwhile a Jew named Apollos, a native
of Alexandria, came to Ephesus. He was a
learned man, with a thorough knowledge of the
Scriptures. 25He had been instructed in the way
of the Lord, and he spoke with great fervor[b]
and taught about Jesus accurately, though he
knew only the baptism of John. 26He began to
speak boldly in the synagogue. When Priscilla
and Aquila heard him, they invited him to their
home and explained to him the way of God
more adequately.
27When Apollos wanted to go to Achaia, the
brothers encouraged him and wrote to the disciples there to welcome him. On arriving, he was
a great help to those who by grace had believed.
28For he vigorously refuted the Jews in public
debate, proving from the Scriptures that Jesus
was the Christ.

Paul in Ephesus

19 While Apollos was at Corinth, Paul
took the road through the interior and
arrived at Ephesus. There he found some disciples 2and asked them, "Did you receive the
Holy Spirit when[c] you believed?"
They answered, "No, we have not even heard
that there is a Holy Spirit."
3So Paul asked, "Then what baptism did you
receive?"
"John's baptism," they replied.
4Paul said, "John's baptism was a baptism of
repentance. He told the people to believe in the
one coming after him, that is, in Jesus." 5On
hearing this, they were baptized into[d] the
name of the Lord Jesus. 6When Paul placed his
hands on them, the Holy Spirit came on them,
and they spoke in tongues[e] and prophesied.
7There were about twelve men in all.
8Paul entered the synagogue and spoke boldly there for three months, arguing persuasively
about the kingdom of God. 9But some of them
became obstinate; they refused to believe and
publicly maligned the Way. So Paul left them.
He took the disciples with him and had discussions daily in the lecture hall of Tyrannus.
10This went on for two years, so that all the Jews

[a]5 Or *Messiah;* also in verse 28 [b]25 Or *with fervor in the Spirit* [c]2 Or *after* [d]5 Or *in* [e]6 Or *other languages*

18:24–28 Apollos was very well educated, both in philosophy and in the Scriptures. He was also a skilled orator. Yet after hearing Apollos speak in the synagogue, Priscilla and Aquila realized that he still needed to know more about Jesus Christ. They invited Apollos home and explained the gospel to him, filling him in on the things he didn't yet know or understand. We may know people who appear happy and successful, yet they seem to be missing an essential element to a healthy life—a true understanding of and relationship with God. Their giftedness need not deter us from sharing the truth with them. We may find that they also sense a need for God and are ready to respond to our message.

APOLLOS

Apollos was a Jewish Bible teacher and skilled orator from Alexandria. He had heard about John the Baptist's message concerning the coming Messiah. Because he had studied the Scriptures seriously, Apollos knew John's message was true. Apollos traveled north to Ephesus, preaching the message of God's kingdom and zealously debating the skeptics.

Priscilla and Aquila heard Apollos preach in Ephesus. They were two devoted followers of Christ who had been greatly affected by Paul's ministry. Though they appreciated Apollos's zeal, they discerned that he had incomplete knowledge of the Scriptures. Priscilla and Aquila invited Apollos to their home and more fully explained the truth about Jesus Christ, the salvation he brings and the Holy Spirit who lives in and empowers believers. For the first time, Apollos understood the complete message of the Good News!

With this new understanding, Apollos ministered in the city of Corinth. He was such an effective speaker that Paul had to warn the believers there to keep their eyes on Christ rather than on Apollos or himself. Apollos continued to travel and speak throughout Greece. Paul came to appreciate Apollos so much that he encouraged Titus to support Apollos as much as possible.

The story of Apollos demonstrates the tremendous value of wise counsel in our lives. Some of us stumble through life with a limited view of the love and power available in Jesus Christ. The more we are exposed to truth through wise counsel, the more we will comprehend Christ's work on our behalf. We must study God's Word so that we can grow to know him better and become better equipped to minister to others in need.

STRENGTHS AND ACCOMPLISHMENTS:

Apollos believed God and was committed to him.

He used his strengths and abilities for the kingdom of God.

Apollos was teachable when confronted with the truth.

WEAKNESSES AND MISTAKES:

Initially, Apollos operated on an incomplete understanding of the truth.

LESSONS FROM HIS LIFE:

God's wisdom and truth are available for our personal healing and spiritual growth.

As we discover God's truth and experience his power, we are better able to help others.

If we are willing to act on what we know, God will help us learn the full truth.

KEY VERSE:

"When Priscilla and Aquila heard him, they invited him to their home and explained to him the way of God more adequately" (18:26).

The story of Apollos is told in Acts 18:24—19:1. He is also mentioned in 1 Corinthians 1:12; 3:4–6, 22; 4:6; 16:12 and Titus 3:13.

and Greeks who lived in the province of Asia
heard the word of the Lord.
11God did extraordinary miracles through
Paul, 12so that even handkerchiefs and aprons
that had touched him were taken to the sick,
and their illnesses were cured and the evil spirits
left them.
13Some Jews who went around driving out
evil spirits tried to invoke the name of the Lord
Jesus over those who were demon-possessed.
They would say, "In the name of Jesus, whom
Paul preaches, I command you to come out."
14Seven sons of Sceva, a Jewish chief priest, were
doing this. 15⌞One day⌟ the evil spirit answered
them, "Jesus I know, and I know about Paul,
but who are you?" 16Then the man who had the
evil spirit jumped on them and overpowered
them all. He gave them such a beating that they
ran out of the house naked and bleeding.
17When this became known to the Jews and
Greeks living in Ephesus, they were all seized
with fear, and the name of the Lord Jesus was
held in high honor. 18Many of those who believed now came and openly confessed their
evil deeds. 19A number who had practiced sorcery brought their scrolls together and burned
them publicly. When they calculated the value
of the scrolls, the total came to fifty thousand
drachmas.[a] 20In this way the word of the Lord
spread widely and grew in power.
21After all this had happened, Paul decided
to go to Jerusalem, passing through Macedonia
and Achaia. "After I have been there," he said, "I
must visit Rome also." 22He sent two of his helpers, Timothy and Erastus, to Macedonia, while
he stayed in the province of Asia a little longer.

The Riot in Ephesus

23About that time there arose a great disturbance about the Way. 24A silversmith named
Demetrius, who made silver shrines of Artemis,
brought in no little business for the craftsmen.
25He called them together, along with the workmen in related trades, and said: "Men, you
know we receive a good income from this business. 26And you see and hear how this fellow
Paul has convinced and led astray large numbers of people here in Ephesus and in practically the whole province of Asia. He says that man-
made gods are no gods at all. 27There is danger
not only that our trade will lose its good name,
but also that the temple of the great goddess
Artemis will be discredited, and the goddess
herself, who is worshiped throughout the province of Asia and the world, will be robbed of her
divine majesty."
28When they heard this, they were furious
and began shouting: "Great is Artemis of the
Ephesians!" 29Soon the whole city was in an uproar. The people seized Gaius and Aristarchus,
Paul's traveling companions from Macedonia,
and rushed as one man into the theater. 30Paul
wanted to appear before the crowd, but the disciples would not let him. 31Even some of the
officials of the province, friends of Paul, sent
him a message begging him not to venture into
the theater.
32The assembly was in confusion: Some were
shouting one thing, some another. Most of the
people did not even know why they were there.
33The Jews pushed Alexander to the front, and
some of the crowd shouted instructions to him.
He motioned for silence in order to make a
defense before the people. 34But when they realized he was a Jew, they all shouted in unison for
about two hours: "Great is Artemis of the Ephesians!"
35The city clerk quieted the crowd and said:
"Men of Ephesus, doesn't all the world know
that the city of Ephesus is the guardian of the
temple of the great Artemis and of her image,
which fell from heaven? 36Therefore, since these
facts are undeniable, you ought to be quiet and
not do anything rash. 37You have brought these
men here, though they have neither robbed
temples nor blasphemed our goddess. 38If,
then, Demetrius and his fellow craftsmen have
a grievance against anybody, the courts are
open and there are proconsuls. They can press
charges. 39If there is anything further you want
to bring up, it must be settled in a legal assembly. 40As it is, we are in danger of being charged
with rioting because of today's events. In that
case we would not be able to account for this
commotion, since there is no reason for it." 41Af-
ter he had said this, he dismissed the assembly.

Through Macedonia and Greece

20 When the uproar had ended, Paul sent
for the disciples and, after encouraging
them, said good-by and set out for Macedonia.
2He traveled through that area, speaking many

[a]*19* A drachma was a silver coin worth about a day's wages.

19:11–20 The people of Ephesus were bound by their fear of the spiritual realm. The seven sons of Sceva made their living by allaying these fears. Yet when confronted by a real demon, the sons of Sceva were powerless. The demon recognized God's authority at work in Jesus Christ and Paul, but the demon attacked the seven sons of Sceva because he did not recognize them or their power. The evil one is more powerful than we are. He works in opposition to God's will. We need God's power at work in our lives so that when we encounter opposition from the devil we can resist and he will flee from us (see James 4:7). But we dare not resist in our own strength; we need and have the power of God's Spirit.

20:1–6 Paul was accountable to and responsible for others. He cared for new converts and helped guide them in their spiritual journey. When we share God's message of hope with others, we must do more than just share the Good News. We need to introduce new converts into a community of believers where they can grow in their new-found faith. Paul's entourage pulled together as a team for the sake of growing believers. So we also can join hands with other believers to strengthen one another in the faith.

words of encouragement to the people, and finally arrived in Greece, 3where he stayed three months. Because the Jews made a plot against him just as he was about to sail for Syria, he decided to go back through Macedonia. 4He was accompanied by Sopater son of Pyrrhus from Berea, Aristarchus and Secundus from Thessalonica, Gaius from Derbe, Timothy also, and Tychicus and Trophimus from the province of Asia. 5These men went on ahead and waited for us at Troas. 6But we sailed from Philippi after the Feast of Unleavened Bread, and five days later joined the others at Troas, where we stayed seven days.

Eutychus Raised From the Dead at Troas

7On the first day of the week we came together to break bread. Paul spoke to the people and, because he intended to leave the next day, kept on talking until midnight. 8There were many lamps in the upstairs room where we were meeting. 9Seated in a window was a young man named Eutychus, who was sinking into a deep sleep as Paul talked on and on. When he was sound asleep, he fell to the ground from the third story and was picked up dead. 10Paul went down, threw himself on the young man and put his arms around him. "Don't be alarmed," he said. "He's alive!" 11Then he went upstairs again and broke bread and ate. After talking until daylight, he left. 12The people took the young man home alive and were greatly comforted.

Paul's Farewell to the Ephesian Elders

13We went on ahead to the ship and sailed for Assos, where we were going to take Paul aboard. He had made this arrangement because he was going there on foot. 14When he met us at Assos, we took him aboard and went on to Mitylene. 15The next day we set sail from there and arrived off Kios. The day after that we crossed over to Samos, and on the following day arrived at Miletus. 16Paul had decided to sail past Ephesus to avoid spending time in the province of Asia, for he was in a hurry to reach Jerusalem, if possible, by the day of Pentecost.

17From Miletus, Paul sent to Ephesus for the elders of the church. 18When they arrived, he said to them: "You know how I lived the whole time I was with you, from the first day I came into the province of Asia. 19I served the Lord with great humility and with tears, although I was severely tested by the plots of the Jews. 20You know that I have not hesitated to preach anything that would be helpful to you but have taught you publicly and from house to house. 21I have declared to both Jews and Greeks that they must turn to God in repentance and have faith in our Lord Jesus.

22"And now, compelled by the Spirit, I am going to Jerusalem, not knowing what will happen to me there. 23I only know that in every city the Holy Spirit warns me that prison and hardships are facing me. 24However, I consider my life worth nothing to me, if only I may finish the race and complete the task the Lord Jesus has given me—the task of testifying to the gospel of God's grace.

25"Now I know that none of you among whom I have gone about preaching the kingdom will ever see me again. 26Therefore, I declare to you today that I am innocent of the blood of all men. 27For I have not hesitated to proclaim to you the whole will of God. 28Keep watch over yourselves and all the flock of which the Holy Spirit has made you overseers.[a] Be shepherds of the church of God,[b] which he bought with his own blood. 29I know that after I leave, savage wolves will come in among you and will not spare the flock. 30Even from your own number men will arise and distort the truth in order to draw away disciples after them. 31So be on your guard! Remember that for three years I never stopped warning each of you night and day with tears.

32"Now I commit you to God and to the word of his grace, which can build you up and give you an inheritance among all those who are sanctified. 33I have not coveted anyone's silver or gold or clothing. 34You yourselves know that these hands of mine have supplied my own needs and the needs of my companions. 35In everything I did, I showed you that by this kind of hard work we must help the weak, remembering the words the Lord Jesus himself said: 'It is more blessed to give than to receive.' "

36When he had said this, he knelt down with all of them and prayed. 37They all wept as they embraced him and kissed him. 38What grieved them most was his statement that they would never see his face again. Then they accompanied him to the ship.

[a]28 Traditionally *bishops* [b]28 Many manuscripts *of the Lord*

20:7–12 Eutychus fell asleep while Paul was preaching, and he fell to his death. However, God used Paul to bring Eutychus back to life. When we know the happy outcome, this story can seem somewhat humorous—especially if, like Eutychus, we have ever fallen asleep during a sermon. Yet Luke recounts this event to remind us of an important lesson: God has the power to restore the dead to new life. God works beyond our own natural capabilities, performing what we would consider impossible. He can do the same for those of us who are dead in sin. We can find hope for restoration in this amazing story.

20:22–38 Paul met with the Ephesian elders and told them of his plans to return to Jerusalem. Paul sensed a clear leading by the Holy Spirit and was determined to follow it. Paul was probably aware that God's plan might lead him through difficult circumstances. Yet this knowledge didn't slow him down. Following God's plan may not always be easy for us either. We may face loneliness and loss or conflict with our friends and family members. Even though following God's will can be hard, Paul's example encourages us to pray for clear knowledge of God's will and the power to obey it.

On to Jerusalem

21 After we had torn ourselves away from
them, we put out to sea and sailed
straight to Cos. The next day we went to Rhodes
and from there to Patara. 2We found a ship
crossing over to Phoenicia, went on board and
set sail. 3After sighting Cyprus and passing to
the south of it, we sailed on to Syria. We landed
at Tyre, where our ship was to unload its cargo.
4Finding the disciples there, we stayed with
them seven days. Through the Spirit they urged
Paul not to go on to Jerusalem. 5But when our
time was up, we left and continued on our way.
All the disciples and their wives and children
accompanied us out of the city, and there on the
beach we knelt to pray. 6After saying good-by to
each other, we went aboard the ship, and they
returned home.

7We continued our voyage from Tyre and
landed at Ptolemais, where we greeted the
brothers and stayed with them for a day. 8Leav-
ing the next day, we reached Caesarea and
stayed at the house of Philip the evangelist, one
of the Seven. 9He had four unmarried daughters
who prophesied.

10After we had been there a number of days,
a prophet named Agabus came down from Judea. 11Coming over to us, he took Paul's belt,
tied his own hands and feet with it and said,
"The Holy Spirit says, 'In this way the Jews of
Jerusalem will bind the owner of this belt and
will hand him over to the Gentiles.' "

12When we heard this, we and the people
there pleaded with Paul not to go up to Jerusalem. 13Then Paul answered, "Why are you
weeping and breaking my heart? I am ready not
only to be bound, but also to die in Jerusalem
for the name of the Lord Jesus." 14When he
would not be dissuaded, we gave up and said,
"The Lord's will be done."

15After this, we got ready and went up to
Jerusalem. 16Some of the disciples from Caesarea accompanied us and brought us to the
home of Mnason, where we were to stay. He
was a man from Cyprus and one of the early
disciples.

Paul's Arrival at Jerusalem

17When we arrived at Jerusalem, the brothers
received us warmly. 18The next day Paul and the
rest of us went to see James, and all the elders
were present. 19Paul greeted them and reported
in detail what God had done among the Gentiles through his ministry.
20When they heard this, they praised God.
Then they said to Paul: "You see, brother, how
many thousands of Jews have believed, and all
of them are zealous for the law. 21They have
been informed that you teach all the Jews who
live among the Gentiles to turn away from Moses, telling them not to circumcise their children
or live according to our customs. 22What shall
we do? They will certainly hear that you have
come, 23so do what we tell you. There are four
men with us who have made a vow. 24Take
these men, join in their purification rites and
pay their expenses, so that they can have their
heads shaved. Then everybody will know there
is no truth in these reports about you, but that
you yourself are living in obedience to the law.
25As for the Gentile believers, we have written
to them our decision that they should abstain
from food sacrificed to idols, from blood, from
the meat of strangled animals and from sexual
immorality."

26The next day Paul took the men and purified himself along with them. Then he went to
the temple to give notice of the date when the
days of purification would end and the offering
would be made for each of them.

Paul Arrested

27When the seven days were nearly over,
some Jews from the province of Asia saw Paul
at the temple. They stirred up the whole crowd
and seized him, 28shouting, "Men of Israel,
help us! This is the man who teaches all men
everywhere against our people and our law and
this place. And besides, he has brought Greeks
into the temple area and defiled this holy place."
29(They had previously seen Trophimus the
Ephesian in the city with Paul and assumed that
Paul had brought him into the temple area.)

30The whole city was aroused, and the people
came running from all directions. Seizing Paul,
they dragged him from the temple, and immediately the gates were shut. 31While they were
trying to kill him, news reached the commander
of the Roman troops that the whole city of Jerusalem was in an uproar. 32He at once took some
officers and soldiers and ran down to the
crowd. When the rioters saw the commander
and his soldiers, they stopped beating Paul.

33The commander came up and arrested him
and ordered him to be bound with two chains.

21:7–9 The last recorded event involving Philip had taken place many years earlier while he traveled to Caesarea (see 8:40). After that time, Philip apparently not only continued in ministry but also married and had a family. This passage records that Philip had a godly family and four gifted daughters. Philip had instilled in them his faith in Christ and God's power for life and ministry. Faith in Christ resulted in Philip's transformed life. Philip's perseverance and fruitfulness can be ours too, if we put our faith in Christ.

21:18–26 Paul had been accused of encouraging Jews to live a Gentile lifestyle. James suggested that Paul participate in a special vow to show the Jews that he took his Jewish heritage seriously. Because of Paul's love for his brothers and sisters in Christ, he wanted to remove anything that might destroy the faith of a Jewish believer. Thus, Paul followed James's advice and participated in the prescribed temple worship. Like Paul, we may need to make some personal sacrifices in order to avoid unnecessary conflicts. As we learn to give up our own rights for the sake of others, we will discover the joy that comes from serving God and his people.

Then he asked who he was and what he had done. 34Some in the crowd shouted one thing and some another, and since the commander could not get at the truth because of the uproar, he ordered that Paul be taken into the barracks. 35When Paul reached the steps, the violence of the mob was so great he had to be carried by the soldiers. 36The crowd that followed kept shouting, "Away with him!"

Paul Speaks to the Crowd

37As the soldiers were about to take Paul into the barracks, he asked the commander, "May I say something to you?"

"Do you speak Greek?" he replied. 38"Aren't you the Egyptian who started a revolt and led four thousand terrorists out into the desert some time ago?"

39Paul answered, "I am a Jew, from Tarsus in Cilicia, a citizen of no ordinary city. Please let me speak to the people."

40Having received the commander's permission, Paul stood on the steps and motioned to the crowd. When they were all silent, he said to

22 them in Aramaic[a]: 1"Brothers and fathers, listen now to my defense."

2When they heard him speak to them in Aramaic, they became very quiet.

Then Paul said: 3"I am a Jew, born in Tarsus of Cilicia, but brought up in this city. Under Gamaliel I was thoroughly trained in the law of our fathers and was just as zealous for God as any of you are today. 4I persecuted the followers of this Way to their death, arresting both men and women and throwing them into prison, 5as also the high priest and all the Council can testify. I even obtained letters from them to their brothers in Damascus, and went there to bring these people as prisoners to Jerusalem to be punished.

6"About noon as I came near Damascus, suddenly a bright light from heaven flashed around me. 7I fell to the ground and heard a voice say to me, 'Saul! Saul! Why do you persecute me?'

8" 'Who are you, Lord?' I asked.

" 'I am Jesus of Nazareth, whom you are persecuting,' he replied. 9My companions saw the light, but they did not understand the voice of him who was speaking to me.

10" 'What shall I do, Lord?' I asked.

" 'Get up,' the Lord said, 'and go into Damascus. There you will be told all that you have been assigned to do.' 11My companions led me by the hand into Damascus, because the brilliance of the light had blinded me.

12"A man named Ananias came to see me. He was a devout observer of the law and highly respected by all the Jews living there. 13He stood beside me and said, 'Brother Saul, receive your sight!' And at that very moment I was able to see him.

14"Then he said: 'The God of our fathers has chosen you to know his will and to see the Righteous One and to hear words from his mouth. 15You will be his witness to all men of what you have seen and heard. 16And now what are you waiting for? Get up, be baptized and wash your sins away, calling on his name.'

17"When I returned to Jerusalem and was praying at the temple, I fell into a trance 18and saw the Lord speaking. 'Quick!' he said to me. 'Leave Jerusalem immediately, because they will not accept your testimony about me.'

19" 'Lord,' I replied, 'these men know that I went from one synagogue to another to imprison and beat those who believe in you. 20And when the blood of your martyr[b] Stephen was shed, I stood there giving my approval and guarding the clothes of those who were killing him.'

21"Then the Lord said to me, 'Go; I will send you far away to the Gentiles.' "

Paul the Roman Citizen

22The crowd listened to Paul until he said this. Then they raised their voices and shouted, "Rid the earth of him! He's not fit to live!"

23As they were shouting and throwing off their cloaks and flinging dust into the air, 24the commander ordered Paul to be taken into the barracks. He directed that he be flogged and questioned in order to find out why the people were shouting at him like this. 25As they stretched him out to flog him, Paul said to the centurion standing there, "Is it legal for you to flog a Roman citizen who hasn't even been found guilty?"

26When the centurion heard this, he went to the commander and reported it. "What are you going to do?" he asked. "This man is a Roman citizen."

27The commander went to Paul and asked, "Tell me, are you a Roman citizen?"

"Yes, I am," he answered.

28Then the commander said, "I had to pay a big price for my citizenship."

"But I was born a citizen," Paul replied.

29Those who were about to question him

[a] 40 Or possibly *Hebrew*; also in 22:2 [b] 20 Or *witness*

22:1–21 This passage provides a second account of Paul's conversion (see 9:1–18). In these verses we learn an additional detail about Paul's life: He had studied under the great rabbinical scholar Gamaliel. But despite Paul's former prestige, he quickly admitted his helplessness when Jesus appeared to him in a blinding light. Others had to lead him by the hand due to his temporary blindness. This momentous occasion was a crossroad for Paul. From this point on, God completely redirected the course of his life. Fortunately, we don't all need such a dramatic event to force us to see our need for God. However, without God we cannot overcome our spiritual blindness. When we surrender our lives to God, we must put aside our sinful pride and willingly follow him wherever he leads. Then he can redirect the course of our lives to fulfill the plans he has for us.

withdrew immediately. The commander himself was alarmed when he realized that he had put Paul, a Roman citizen, in chains.

Before the Sanhedrin

30 The next day, since the commander wanted to find out exactly why Paul was being accused by the Jews, he released him and ordered the chief priests and all the Sanhedrin to assemble. Then he brought Paul and had him stand before them.

23 Paul looked straight at the Sanhedrin and said, "My brothers, I have fulfilled my duty to God in all good conscience to this day." 2 At this the high priest Ananias ordered those standing near Paul to strike him on the mouth. 3 Then Paul said to him, "God will strike you, you whitewashed wall! You sit there to judge me according to the law, yet you yourself violate the law by commanding that I be struck!"

4 Those who were standing near Paul said, "You dare to insult God's high priest?"

5 Paul replied, "Brothers, I did not realize that he was the high priest; for it is written: 'Do not speak evil about the ruler of your people.'[a]"

6 Then Paul, knowing that some of them were Sadducees and the others Pharisees, called out in the Sanhedrin, "My brothers, I am a Pharisee, the son of a Pharisee. I stand on trial because of my hope in the resurrection of the dead." 7 When he said this, a dispute broke out between the Pharisees and the Sadducees, and the assembly was divided. 8 (The Sadducees say that there is no resurrection, and that there are neither angels nor spirits, but the Pharisees acknowledge them all.)

9 There was a great uproar, and some of the teachers of the law who were Pharisees stood up and argued vigorously. "We find nothing wrong with this man," they said. "What if a spirit or an angel has spoken to him?" 10 The dispute became so violent that the commander was afraid Paul would be torn to pieces by them. He ordered the troops to go down and take him away from them by force and bring him into the barracks.

11 The following night the Lord stood near Paul and said, "Take courage! As you have testified about me in Jerusalem, so you must also testify in Rome."

The Plot to Kill Paul

12 The next morning the Jews formed a conspiracy and bound themselves with an oath not to eat or drink until they had killed Paul. 13 More than forty men were involved in this plot. 14 They went to the chief priests and elders and said, "We have taken a solemn oath not to eat anything until we have killed Paul. 15 Now then, you and the Sanhedrin petition the commander to bring him before you on the pretext of wanting more accurate information about his case. We are ready to kill him before he gets here."

16 But when the son of Paul's sister heard of this plot, he went into the barracks and told Paul.

17 Then Paul called one of the centurions and said, "Take this young man to the commander; he has something to tell him." 18 So he took him to the commander.

The centurion said, "Paul, the prisoner, sent for me and asked me to bring this young man to you because he has something to tell you."

19 The commander took the young man by the hand, drew him aside and asked, "What is it you want to tell me?"

20 He said: "The Jews have agreed to ask you to bring Paul before the Sanhedrin tomorrow on the pretext of wanting more accurate information about him. 21 Don't give in to them, because more than forty of them are waiting in ambush for him. They have taken an oath not to eat or drink until they have killed him. They are ready now, waiting for your consent to their request."

22 The commander dismissed the young man and cautioned him, "Don't tell anyone that you have reported this to me."

Paul Transferred to Caesarea

23 Then he called two of his centurions and ordered them, "Get ready a detachment of two hundred soldiers, seventy horsemen and two hundred spearmen[b] to go to Caesarea at nine tonight. 24 Provide mounts for Paul so that he may be taken safely to Governor Felix."

25 He wrote a letter as follows:

26 Claudius Lysias,

To His Excellency, Governor Felix:

Greetings.

27 This man was seized by the Jews and they were about to kill him, but I came with my troops and rescued him, for I had learned that he is a Roman citizen. 28 I wanted to know why they were accusing him, so I brought him to their Sanhedrin. 29 I found that the accusation had to do

[a]5 Exodus 22:28 [b]23 The meaning of the Greek for this word is uncertain.

23:12–35 This chapter in Paul's life features the courage of a young man. Paul's young nephew risked his life to warn his uncle of a plot against his life. With this information, the Roman commander made adjustments in his plan and moved Paul safely to Caesarea. A military escort accompanied Paul on his journey that very night, and a letter to Felix, the governor, won Paul another chance to speak for himself and God. Thus God providentially worked through a variety of people to move Paul one step closer to Rome. God uses people—little children and governors alike—to accomplish his divine will.

with questions about their law, but there was no charge against him that deserved death or imprisonment. 30When I was informed of a plot to be carried out against the man, I sent him to you at once. I also ordered his accusers to present to you their case against him.

31So the soldiers, carrying out their orders, took Paul with them during the night and brought him as far as Antipatris. 32The next day they let the cavalry go on with him, while they returned to the barracks. 33When the cavalry arrived in Caesarea, they delivered the letter to the governor and handed Paul over to him. 34The governor read the letter and asked what province he was from. Learning that he was from Cilicia, 35he said, "I will hear your case when your accusers get here." Then he ordered that Paul be kept under guard in Herod's palace.

The Trial Before Felix

24 Five days later the high priest Ananias went down to Caesarea with some of the elders and a lawyer named Tertullus, and they brought their charges against Paul before the governor. 2When Paul was called in, Tertullus presented his case before Felix: "We have enjoyed a long period of peace under you, and your foresight has brought about reforms in this nation. 3Everywhere and in every way, most excellent Felix, we acknowledge this with profound gratitude. 4But in order not to weary you further, I would request that you be kind enough to hear us briefly.

5"We have found this man to be a troublemaker, stirring up riots among the Jews all over the world. He is a ringleader of the Nazarene sect 6and even tried to desecrate the temple; so we seized him. 8By[a] examining him yourself you will be able to learn the truth about all these charges we are bringing against him."

9The Jews joined in the accusation, asserting that these things were true.

10When the governor motioned for him to speak, Paul replied: "I know that for a number of years you have been a judge over this nation; so I gladly make my defense. 11You can easily verify that no more than twelve days ago I went up to Jerusalem to worship. 12My accusers did not find me arguing with anyone at the temple, or stirring up a crowd in the synagogues or anywhere else in the city. 13And they cannot prove to you the charges they are now making against me. 14However, I admit that I worship the God of our fathers as a follower of the Way, which they call a sect. I believe everything that agrees with the Law and that is written in the Prophets, 15and I have the same hope in God as these men, that there will be a resurrection of both the righteous and the wicked. 16So I strive always to keep my conscience clear before God and man.

17"After an absence of several years, I came to Jerusalem to bring my people gifts for the poor and to present offerings. 18I was ceremonially clean when they found me in the temple courts doing this. There was no crowd with me, nor was I involved in any disturbance. 19But there are some Jews from the province of Asia, who ought to be here before you and bring charges if they have anything against me. 20Or these who are here should state what crime they found in me when I stood before the Sanhedrin— 21unless it was this one thing I shouted as I stood in their presence: 'It is concerning the resurrection of the dead that I am on trial before you today.' "

22Then Felix, who was well acquainted with the Way, adjourned the proceedings. "When Lysias the commander comes," he said, "I will decide your case." 23He ordered the centurion to keep Paul under guard but to give him some freedom and permit his friends to take care of his needs.

24Several days later Felix came with his wife Drusilla, who was a Jewess. He sent for Paul and listened to him as he spoke about faith in Christ Jesus. 25As Paul discoursed on righteousness, self-control and the judgment to come, Felix was afraid and said, "That's enough for now! You may leave. When I find it convenient, I will send for you." 26At the same time he was hoping that Paul would offer him a bribe, so he sent for him frequently and talked with him.

27When two years had passed, Felix was succeeded by Porcius Festus, but because Felix wanted to grant a favor to the Jews, he left Paul in prison.

The Trial Before Festus

25 Three days after arriving in the province, Festus went up from Caesarea to Jerusalem, 2where the chief priests and Jewish leaders appeared before him and presented the charges against Paul. 3They urgently requested Festus, as a favor to them, to have Paul transferred to Jerusalem, for they were preparing an ambush to kill him along the way. 4Festus answered, "Paul is being held at Caesarea, and I

[a] 6-8 Some manuscripts *him and wanted to judge him according to our law. 7But the commander, Lysias, came and with the use of much force snatched him from our hands 8and ordered his accusers to come before you. By*

24:26–27 Felix made no decision on Paul's case. He might have been afraid that if he set Paul free, the Jews would respond in open rebellion. So Felix left Paul in prison for at least two years. Perhaps he hoped that by leaving Paul in prison for such a long time Paul would muster a bribe and buy his release. By the grace of God Paul endured his long stay with incredible patience. He continued growing spiritually. There are times when we may also feel stuck, not knowing what God is doing in our lives. During these times, we need to ask God for patience and continue to practice our spiritual disciplines so that we will grow and preserve our spiritual gains, regardless of our circumstances.

myself am going there soon. 5Let some of your leaders come with me and press charges against the man there, if he has done anything wrong."

6After spending eight or ten days with them, he went down to Caesarea, and the next day he convened the court and ordered that Paul be brought before him. 7When Paul appeared, the Jews who had come down from Jerusalem stood around him, bringing many serious charges against him, which they could not prove.

8Then Paul made his defense: "I have done nothing wrong against the law of the Jews or against the temple or against Caesar."

9Festus, wishing to do the Jews a favor, said to Paul, "Are you willing to go up to Jerusalem and stand trial before me there on these charges?"

10Paul answered: "I am now standing before Caesar's court, where I ought to be tried. I have not done any wrong to the Jews, as you yourself know very well. 11If, however, I am guilty of doing anything deserving death, I do not refuse to die. But if the charges brought against me by these Jews are not true, no one has the right to hand me over to them. I appeal to Caesar!"

12After Festus had conferred with his council, he declared: "You have appealed to Caesar. To Caesar you will go!"

Festus Consults King Agrippa

13A few days later King Agrippa and Bernice arrived at Caesarea to pay their respects to Festus. 14Since they were spending many days there, Festus discussed Paul's case with the king. He said: "There is a man here whom Felix left as a prisoner. 15When I went to Jerusalem, the chief priests and elders of the Jews brought charges against him and asked that he be condemned.

16"I told them that it is not the Roman custom to hand over any man before he has faced his accusers and has had an opportunity to defend himself against their charges. 17When they came here with me, I did not delay the case, but convened the court the next day and ordered the man to be brought in. 18When his accusers got up to speak, they did not charge him with any of the crimes I had expected. 19Instead, they had some points of dispute with him about their own religion and about a dead man named Jesus who Paul claimed was alive. 20I was at a loss how to investigate such matters; so I asked if he would be willing to go to Jerusalem and stand trial there on these charges. 21When Paul made his appeal to be held over for the Emperor's decision, I ordered him held until I could send him to Caesar."

22Then Agrippa said to Festus, "I would like to hear this man myself."

He replied, "Tomorrow you will hear him."

Paul Before Agrippa

23The next day Agrippa and Bernice came with great pomp and entered the audience room with the high ranking officers and the leading men of the city. At the command of Festus, Paul was brought in. 24Festus said: "King Agrippa, and all who are present with us, you see this man! The whole Jewish community has petitioned me about him in Jerusalem and here in Caesarea, shouting that he ought not to live any longer. 25I found he had done nothing deserving of death, but because he made his appeal to the Emperor I decided to send him to Rome. 26But I have nothing definite to write to His Majesty about him. Therefore I have brought him before all of you, and especially before you, King Agrippa, so that as a result of this investigation I may have something to write. 27For I think it is unreasonable to send on a prisoner without specifying the charges against him."

26 Then Agrippa said to Paul, "You have permission to speak for yourself."

So Paul motioned with his hand and began his defense: 2"King Agrippa, I consider myself fortunate to stand before you today as I make my defense against all the accusations of the Jews, 3and especially so because you are well acquainted with all the Jewish customs and controversies. Therefore, I beg you to listen to me patiently.

4"The Jews all know the way I have lived ever since I was a child, from the beginning of my life in my own country, and also in Jerusalem. 5They have known me for a long time and can testify, if they are willing, that according to the strictest sect of our religion, I lived as a Pharisee. 6And now it is because of my hope in what God has promised our fathers that I am on trial today. 7This is the promise our twelve tribes are hoping to see fulfilled as they earnestly serve God day and night. O king, it is because of this hope that the Jews are accusing me. 8Why should any of you consider it incredible that God raises the dead?

9"I too was convinced that I ought to do all that was possible to oppose the name of Jesus of Nazareth. 10And that is just what I did in Jerusalem. On the authority of the chief priests I put many of the saints in prison, and when they were put to death, I cast my vote against them. 11Many a time I went from one synagogue to another to have them punished, and I tried to force them to blaspheme. In my obses-

---

26:1–23 This is the third account of Paul's conversion in the book of Acts (see 9:1–18; 22:1–21). Paul had become quite skilled at sharing the testimony of God's powerful changes in his life. Before meeting Christ, Paul had been a powerful enemy of the Christian faith and had tried to stop its growth (see 26:9–11). Paul then met Jesus in a dramatic way, leading to his spiritual awakening (see 26:12–16). Paul went on to share his testimony before King Agrippa, who also needed to hear the message of salvation (see 26:18–19). No person is so important or great in this earthly realm that they do not need to hear God's message of salvation.

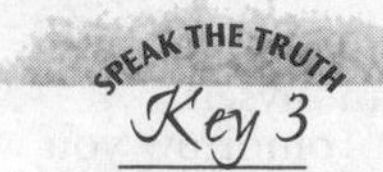

Receiving Forgiveness

Acts 26:12–18 Confessing our sins to God and to others humbles us and allows us to share our weaknesses. We should encourage others to do likewise. In doing so, we can help others live in the light and speak the truth before God.

Jesus appointed the apostle Paul as his servant and sent him as a witness to the Gentiles. Jesus wanted Paul to "open their eyes and turn them from darkness to light, and from the power of Satan to God, so that they may receive forgiveness of sins and a place among those who are sanctified by faith in me" (26:18).

Once we are honest before God and admit our wrongs, we will begin to dispel the darkness in our lives. God wants us to live in the light and receive immediate forgiveness based on the finished work of Jesus Christ. A restored relationship with God awaits us right now if we will confess our sins and receive his forgiveness.

Turn to Romans 2.

sion against them, I even went to foreign cities
to persecute them.
12"On one of these journeys I was going to
Damascus with the authority and commission
of the chief priests. 13About noon, O king, as I
was on the road, I saw a light from heaven,
brighter than the sun, blazing around me and
my companions. 14We all fell to the ground,
and I heard a voice saying to me in Aramaic,[a]
'Saul, Saul, why do you persecute me? It is hard
for you to kick against the goads.'
15"Then I asked, 'Who are you, Lord?'
" 'I am Jesus, whom you are persecuting,' the
Lord replied. 16'Now get up and stand on your
feet. I have appeared to you to appoint you as
a servant and as a witness of what you have seen
of me and what I will show you. 17I will rescue
you from your own people and from the Gentiles. I am sending you to them 18to open their
eyes and turn them from darkness to light, and
from the power of Satan to God, so that they
may receive forgiveness of sins and a place
among those who are sanctified by faith in me.'
19"So then, King Agrippa, I was not disobedient to the vision from heaven. 20First to those in
Damascus, then to those in Jerusalem and in all
Judea, and to the Gentiles also, I preached that
they should repent and turn to God and prove
their repentance by their deeds. 21That is why
the Jews seized me in the temple courts and
tried to kill me. 22But I have had God's help to
this very day, and so I stand here and testify to
small and great alike. I am saying nothing beyond what the prophets and Moses said would
happen— 23that the Christ[b] would suffer and,
as the first to rise from the dead, would proclaim light to his own people and to the Gentiles."
24At this point Festus interrupted Paul's defense. "You are out of your mind, Paul!" he
shouted. "Your great learning is driving you
insane."
25"I am not insane, most excellent Festus,"
Paul replied. "What I am saying is true and
reasonable. 26The king is familiar with these
things, and I can speak freely to him. I am con-

[a]14 Or *Hebrew* [b]23 Or *Messiah*

26:19–23 Paul assured King Agrippa that he was being persecuted, not because he had done anything wrong, but because he now espoused the faith he had once tried to destroy. Paul showed that what he was preaching as a Christian was really in agreement with the Old Testament Scriptures. The basic teaching of both the Old and New Testaments is that God desires to deliver people from the power of sin and has done so perfectly through the work of God's anointed one—Jesus. The message of God's desire to save us is essential to all spiritual renewal.

26:24–29 Paul was so concerned about the salvation of other people that he had little time to worry about his own problems. In this passage Paul risked his life to share his testimony with a man who had the power to kill him. This conversation with Herod Agrippa II shows Paul's burning desire to soften and reclaim even the most hardened heart. It can also be helpful for us to get our eyes off our own afflictions and focus on the needs of others.

vinced that none of this has escaped his notice,
because it was not done in a corner. 27King
Agrippa, do you believe the prophets? I know
you do."

28Then Agrippa said to Paul, "Do you think
that in such a short time you can persuade me
to be a Christian?"

29Paul replied, "Short time or long—I pray
God that not only you but all who are listening
to me today may become what I am, except for
these chains."

30The king rose, and with him the governor
and Bernice and those sitting with them. 31They
left the room, and while talking with one another, they said, "This man is not doing anything that deserves death or imprisonment."
32Agrippa said to Festus, "This man could
have been set free if he had not appealed to
Caesar."

Paul Sails for Rome

27 When it was decided that we would sail
for Italy, Paul and some other prisoners
were handed over to a centurion named Julius,
who belonged to the Imperial Regiment. 2We
boarded a ship from Adramyttium about to sail
for ports along the coast of the province of Asia,
and we put out to sea. Aristarchus, a Macedonian from Thessalonica, was with us.

3The next day we landed at Sidon; and Julius,
in kindness to Paul, allowed him to go to his
friends so they might provide for his needs.
4From there we put out to sea again and passed
to the lee of Cyprus because the winds were
against us. 5When we had sailed across the open
sea off the coast of Cilicia and Pamphylia, we
landed at Myra in Lycia. 6There the centurion
found an Alexandrian ship sailing for Italy and
put us on board. 7We made slow headway for
many days and had difficulty arriving off Cnidus. When the wind did not allow us to hold
our course, we sailed to the lee of Crete, opposite Salmone. 8We moved along the coast with
difficulty and came to a place called Fair Havens, near the town of Lasea.

9Much time had been lost, and sailing had
already become dangerous because by now it
was after the Fast.[a] So Paul warned them,
10"Men, I can see that our voyage is going to be
disastrous and bring great loss to ship and cargo, and to our own lives also." 11But the centurion, instead of listening to what Paul said, followed the advice of the pilot and of the owner
of the ship. 12Since the harbor was unsuitable to
winter in, the majority decided that we should
sail on, hoping to reach Phoenix and winter
there. This was a harbor in Crete, facing both
southwest and northwest.

The Storm

13When a gentle south wind began to blow,
they thought they had obtained what they
wanted; so they weighed anchor and sailed
along the shore of Crete. 14Before very long, a
wind of hurricane force, called the "northeast-
er," swept down from the island. 15The ship was
caught by the storm and could not head into
the wind; so we gave way to it and were driven
along. 16As we passed to the lee of a small island
called Cauda, we were hardly able to make the
lifeboat secure. 17When the men had hoisted it
aboard, they passed ropes under the ship itself
to hold it together. Fearing that they would run
aground on the sandbars of Syrtis, they lowered
the sea anchor and let the ship be driven along.
18We took such a violent battering from the
storm that the next day they began to throw the
cargo overboard. 19On the third day, they threw
the ship's tackle overboard with their own
hands. 20When neither sun nor stars appeared
for many days and the storm continued raging,
we finally gave up all hope of being saved.

21After the men had gone a long time without food, Paul stood up before them and said:
"Men, you should have taken my advice not to
sail from Crete; then you would have spared
yourselves this damage and loss. 22But now I
urge you to keep up your courage, because not
one of you will be lost; only the ship will be
destroyed. 23Last night an angel of the God
whose I am and whom I serve stood beside me
24and said, 'Do not be afraid, Paul. You must
stand trial before Caesar; and God has graciously given you the lives of all who sail with you.'
25So keep up your courage, men, for I have faith
in God that it will happen just as he told me.
26Nevertheless, we must run aground on some
island."

The Shipwreck

27On the fourteenth night we were still being

[a]9 That is, the Day of Atonement (Yom Kippur)

27:1–15 God determined that Paul must travel to Rome. But Paul's journey there was hardly uneventful. He had no control over the means or timing of getting to his destination. After years in prison, Paul was finally put on a ship bound for Rome. He knew God wanted him in Rome, and he was confident he would eventually get there despite the life-threatening storm and shipwreck that occurred along the way. Similarly, we can be sure that God wants us to make spiritual progress. Like Paul, we may have little control over the route we will take to get there. And our faithfulness will not ensure a life without storms or shipwrecks. Yet God does guarantee that his presence and power will be there with us and that we will ultimately arrive at our destination.

27:13–37 After two storm-tossed weeks, the ship had begun to fall apart. The sailors had given up hope. Everyone was hungry and terrified. Yet Paul urged all to believe God's promise that they would survive. The fate of 276 people—passengers and crew—hung in the balance. Paul's courageous faith was met with God's assurance that he would reach Rome and would face more hardships. Life can be like that. We must persevere through difficult times to attain faith's positive outcome.

27:27–42 Paul assured the soldiers that even though the ship would be destroyed, all the passengers would reach land safely. The next day the ship ran aground on a sand-

LUKE

Luke was one of the most prolific writers of the New Testament. He gave a detailed account of the life of Jesus in his Gospel and a description of the early church in Acts. Luke was a physician by profession, and his writing reveals his compassion for people. Even his efforts in authoring his two books were motivated by a concern to help a friend grow in the faith. Consistent with this, Luke pointed his readers to the healing work and person of Jesus, the Great Physician.

Luke's concern for the spiritual health of others was matched by his concern for their physical welfare. Throughout his books Luke noticed the physical suffering of people and the care that those people received. He recounted how Jesus and his apostles again and again brought physical and spiritual healing to hurting and broken lives. Luke also noted how Jesus paid special attention to the helpless in society. Though Jesus also helped the wealthy and religious, he made a special point of helping the diseased outcasts, prostitutes and hated tax collectors. As he wrote his account, Luke's compassionate heart emphasized Jesus' compassion for those rejected by society.

Luke was also loyally committed to the apostle Paul. They traveled together spreading the gospel in Asia Minor and Greece. In prison, near the end of his life, Paul wrote of his appreciation for Luke. He called Luke a dear friend, for he had stayed with Paul even when most of Paul's friends had deserted him (see Colossians 4:14). Luke was willing to follow God, even when it led him to share in Paul's sufferings.

Luke did not aspire to greatness. His goal in life was to serve and care for others. We need people like Luke in our lives and should do what we can to establish relationships with compassionate, godly people. Perhaps even more, however, we should become instruments of healing in the lives of the people around us. Sharing what God has done in our lives in order to help others should be one of the goals of our spiritual renewal.

STRENGTHS AND ACCOMPLISHMENTS:

Luke proclaimed the merits of Jesus without promoting himself.

He used his talents to serve God and help others.

Luke possessed great compassion for the physical and spiritual needs of others.

He was a loyal and faithful friend to the apostle Paul.

Even when he encountered tough times, Luke persevered in following God.

LESSONS FROM HIS LIFE:

Our care for others should meet spiritual, emotional and physical needs.

Being loyal to our friends during hard times is very important.

God's good will for us sometimes leads us through difficult times.

If we offer our abilities to God, he will use them to do something of eternal significance.

KEY VERSES:

"Demas, because he loved this world, has deserted me and has gone to Thessalonica. Crescens has gone to Galatia, and Titus to Dalmatia. Only Luke is with me" (2 Timothy 4:10–11).

Luke included himself in the "we" sections of Acts 16:10—28:16. He is also mentioned in Colossians 4:14; 2 Timothy 4:11 and Philemon 24.

driven across the Adriatic[a] Sea, when about
midnight the sailors sensed they were approaching land. 28They took soundings and
found that the water was a hundred and twenty
feet[b] deep. A short time later they took soundings again and found it was ninety feet[c] deep.
29Fearing that we would be dashed against the
rocks, they dropped four anchors from the stern
and prayed for daylight. 30In an attempt to escape from the ship, the sailors let the lifeboat
down into the sea, pretending they were going
to lower some anchors from the bow. 31Then
Paul said to the centurion and the soldiers,
"Unless these men stay with the ship, you cannot be saved." 32So the soldiers cut the ropes that
held the lifeboat and let it fall away.

33Just before dawn Paul urged them all to eat.
"For the last fourteen days," he said, "you have
been in constant suspense and have gone without food—you haven't eaten anything. 34Now I
urge you to take some food. You need it to
survive. Not one of you will lose a single hair
from his head." 35After he said this, he took
some bread and gave thanks to God in front of
them all. Then he broke it and began to eat.
36They were all encouraged and ate some food
themselves. 37Altogether there were 276 of us
on board. 38When they had eaten as much as
they wanted, they lightened the ship by throwing the grain into the sea.

39When daylight came, they did not recognize the land, but they saw a bay with a sandy
beach, where they decided to run the ship
aground if they could. 40Cutting loose the anchors, they left them in the sea and at the same
time untied the ropes that held the rudders.
Then they hoisted the foresail to the wind and
made for the beach. 41But the ship struck a
sandbar and ran aground. The bow stuck fast
and would not move, and the stern was broken
to pieces by the pounding of the surf.

42The soldiers planned to kill the prisoners to
prevent any of them from swimming away and
escaping. 43But the centurion wanted to spare
Paul's life and kept them from carrying out their
plan. He ordered those who could swim to
jump overboard first and get to land. 44The rest
were to get there on planks or on pieces of the
ship. In this way everyone reached land in
safety.

Ashore on Malta

28 Once safely on shore, we found out that
the island was called Malta. 2The islanders showed us unusual kindness. They built
a fire and welcomed us all because it was rain-
ing and cold. 3Paul gathered a pile of brush-
wood and, as he put it on the fire, a viper,
driven out by the heat, fastened itself on his
hand. 4When the islanders saw the snake hanging from his hand, they said to each other,
"This man must be a murderer; for though he
escaped from the sea, Justice has not allowed
him to live." 5But Paul shook the snake off into
the fire and suffered no ill effects. 6The people
expected him to swell up or suddenly fall dead,
but after waiting a long time and seeing nothing
unusual happen to him, they changed their
minds and said he was a god.

7There was an estate nearby that belonged to
Publius, the chief official of the island. He welcomed us to his home and for three days entertained us hospitably. 8His father was sick in
bed, suffering from fever and dysentery. Paul
went in to see him and, after prayer, placed his
hands on him and healed him. 9When this had
happened, the rest of the sick on the island
came and were cured. 10They honored us in
many ways and when we were ready to sail, they
furnished us with the supplies we needed.

Arrival at Rome

11After three months we put out to sea in a
ship that had wintered in the island. It was an
Alexandrian ship with the figurehead of the
twin gods Castor and Pollux. 12We put in at
Syracuse and stayed there three days. 13From
there we set sail and arrived at Rhegium. The
next day the south wind came up, and on the
following day we reached Puteoli. 14There we
found some brothers who invited us to spend a
week with them. And so we came to Rome.
15The brothers there had heard that we were
coming, and they traveled as far as the Forum of
Appius and the Three Taverns to meet us. At the
sight of these men Paul thanked God and was
encouraged. 16When we got to Rome, Paul was
allowed to live by himself, with a soldier to
guard him.

Paul Preaches at Rome Under Guard

17Three days later he called together the leaders of the Jews. When they had assembled, Paul
said to them: "My brothers, although I have
done nothing against our people or against the

[a]27 In ancient times the name referred to an area extending well south of Italy. [b]28 Greek *twenty orguias* (about 37 meters) [c]28 Greek *fifteen orguias* (about 27 meters)

---

bar and was destroyed by the winds and waves, but all the passengers safely reached shore. Few of us have been given a glimpse into the future like Paul's vision. But we can possess Paul's confidence in the power of God to deliver us when we follow his will, walking obediently by faith.

28:1–10 Safe on the island of Malta the ship's crew and passengers spent the winter there. A short time after landing on the island, a deadly snake bit Paul, yet he suffered no ill effects. Though Paul was deterred from reaching Rome because of the shipwreck and faced obstacles like the poisonous snake, he did not let these things keep him from using his time and talents to help the people around him. To Paul, even obstacles were opportunities to serve others and share his faith. If we will surrender to God, he can turn our obstacles into wonderful opportunities to share our faith.

customs of our ancestors, I was arrested in Jerusalem and handed over to the Romans. 18They
examined me and wanted to release me, because I was not guilty of any crime deserving
death. 19But when the Jews objected, I was compelled to appeal to Caesar—not that I had any
charge to bring against my own people. 20For
this reason I have asked to see you and talk with
you. It is because of the hope of Israel that I am
bound with this chain."

21They replied, "We have not received any
letters from Judea concerning you, and none
of the brothers who have come from there
has reported or said anything bad about you.
22But we want to hear what your views are,
for we know that people everywhere are talking against this sect."

23They arranged to meet Paul on a certain
day, and came in even larger numbers to the
place where he was staying. From morning till
evening he explained and declared to them the
kingdom of God and tried to convince them
about Jesus from the Law of Moses and from
the Prophets. 24Some were convinced by what
he said, but others would not believe. 25They
disagreed among themselves and began to leave
after Paul had made this final statement: "The
Holy Spirit spoke the truth to your forefathers
when he said through Isaiah the prophet:

26" 'Go to this people and say,
"You will be ever hearing but never
understanding;
you will be ever seeing but never
perceiving."
27For this people's heart has become
calloused;
they hardly hear with their ears,
and they have closed their eyes.
Otherwise they might see with their eyes,
hear with their ears,
understand with their hearts
and turn, and I would heal them.'[a]

28"Therefore I want you to know that God's
salvation has been sent to the Gentiles, and they
will listen!"[b]

30For two whole years Paul stayed there in his
own rented house and welcomed all who came
to see him. 31Boldly and without hindrance he
preached the kingdom of God and taught about
the Lord Jesus Christ.

[a]27 Isaiah 6:9,10 [b]28 Some manuscripts *listen!" 29After he said this, the Jews left, arguing vigorously among themselves.*

28:30–31 Even under house arrest, Paul experienced the peace and contentment that come only by following God's will. Paul used his time in prison to carry the message of salvation to people in need. The apostle Paul's life is an example to each of us, showing the importance and benefits of persisting in our relationship with God and sharing our faith even in the midst of difficulties. Regardless of our limitations, God can use our lives if we repent and surrender to him. God can use us right where we are if we will accept responsibility for our lives and use our talents to glorify God.

ROMANS

The Big Picture

The church in Rome was a testimony to God's power. This church had flourished despite the obstacles posed by the surrounding pagan culture. Yet the Roman believers were not perfect; they had some serious problems. Though they were well established in their faith, racial and cultural division threatened their convictions and unity as a group.

The main topic in this letter is the gospel message—the Good News that salvation from sin is available through Jesus Christ. At the core of this message is the truth that God is bigger than our sin. No matter who we are or what we have done, we can be saved by grace (undeserved favor from God) through faith (complete trust) in Christ. We can stand before God justified—declared "not guilty." That's the Good News!

In Romans, Paul explains four major points. First, God makes no distinction between us as individuals—we are all guilty, and we are all offered his free gift of salvation (see 1:18—4:25). Second, we can all be freed from sin's power through God's grace and the Holy Spirit inside us (see 5:1—8:39). Third, we are dependent upon God and have no grounds for arrogance (see 9:1—11:36). And finally, because of God's mercy, we all must respect one another, despite the differences between us (see 12:1—15:13).

Many people have called this letter to the Romans the greatest theological treatise ever written. But Romans is really a practical letter that tells us how to live, how to deal with our sinful behavior and how to get back on the right track. Paul's letter has direct application to us, illustrating how to overcome the effects of sin and let God redirect the course of our lives to align with his will for us.

A. GREETINGS AND THANKS (1:1-15)

B. THE THEME OF THE LETTER (1:16-17)

C. OUR NEED FOR GOD'S GRACE (1:18–4:25)

D. GOD'S POWER FOR OUR DELIVERANCE (5:1–8:39)

E. QUESTIONS ABOUT ISRAEL'S RESTORATION (9:1–11:36)

F. CONDUCT THAT REFLECTS SPIRITUAL RENEWAL (12:1–15:13)

G. CONCLUSION (15:14–16:27)

Spiritual Renewal Themes

OUR UNIVERSAL NEED

All of us have sinned; we have each fallen short of God's standards (see 3:23). Regardless of how great or terrible our lives have been, we are all in need of forgiveness and cleansing from sin. Ever since Adam and Eve rebelled against God, our natures have been flawed, bent on disobeying God. Sometimes we simply seek our own way instead of following his. Sometimes we blatantly violate his commands. And at other times we fail to

Essential Facts

PURPOSE:
To introduce Paul to the church at Rome and summarize his message before his arrival there.

AUTHOR:
The apostle Paul.

AUDIENCE:
The church at Rome.

DATE WRITTEN:
Just before Paul's return to Jerusalem from Corinth in A.D. 57.

SETTING:
Paul wrote this letter in anticipation of a future visit to the believers in Rome.

KEY VERSES:
"For I am convinced that neither death nor life, neither angels nor demons, neither the present nor the future, nor any powers, neither height nor depth, nor anything else in all creation, will be able to separate us from the love of God that is in Christ Jesus our Lord" (8:38–39).

KEY PEOPLE AND RELATIONSHIPS:
Paul with the believers in Rome and with Phoebe, who helped Paul in his ministry.

fulfill what he has told us to do. Whether our transgressions are sins of commission or omission, we do not have the power to live sinless lives. We all need God to save us and forgive us our sins.

GOD'S POWER TO DELIVER
Our need for spiritual renewal involves our need to be forgiven and to forgive, as well as to be cleansed from the effects of our sin. We are unable to help ourselves and have no grounds on which to demand divine help. And yet God, in his love, reaches out to us, offering to forgive us, cleanse us and empower us to become what he wants us to be. This is truly Good News! Our part is to see the truth of our need for God's power and to surrender our lives and will to this loving God.

SPIRITUAL RENEWAL LEADS TO FREEDOM
Because God has attacked our sin problem at the roots, he has made it possible for us to be freed from the grip of sin. Through God's power, our lives can come under his righteous rule. Though the process is never easy, we can become more and more like Christ as we walk with God each day. The better we get to know him, the more his Holy Spirit can empower us. By continuing to reflect on our spiritual condition, confessing our sins to God and seeking to make restitution to those whom we have wronged, we can experience true freedom and ongoing spiritual renewal.

THE ROLE OF FAITH
Much of this letter is a description of the importance of faith and trust in God: "The righteous will live by faith" (1:17). There is no other way to be renewed by God; the role of faith is central to spiritual growth. Our spiritual renewal began with faith when we sought God and surrendered to him. Each key to spiritual renewal requires faith. There is no magic formula for this—it is a daily act of trusting God by surrendering our wills and our lives to him. By doing so, we put ourselves in the hand of the all-powerful God, who promises never to forsake us and always to love us, no matter how unlovable we feel (see Deuteronomy 31:8).

1 Paul, a servant of Christ Jesus, called to be an apostle and set apart for the gospel of God— 2the gospel he promised beforehand through his prophets in the Holy Scriptures 3regarding his Son, who as to his human nature was a descendant of David, 4and who through the Spirit[a] of holiness was declared with power to be the Son of God[b] by his resurrection from the dead: Jesus Christ our Lord. 5Through him and for his name's sake, we received grace and apostleship to call people from among all the Gentiles to the obedience that comes from faith. 6And you also are among those who are called to belong to Jesus Christ.

7To all in Rome who are loved by God and called to be saints:

Grace and peace to you from God our Father and from the Lord Jesus Christ.

Paul's Longing to Visit Rome

8First, I thank my God through Jesus Christ for all of you, because your faith is being reported all over the world. 9God, whom I serve with my whole heart in preaching the gospel of his Son, is my witness how constantly I remember you 10in my prayers at all times; and I pray that now at last by God's will the way may be opened for me to come to you.

11I long to see you so that I may impart to you some spiritual gift to make you strong— 12that is, that you and I may be mutually encouraged by each other's faith. 13I do not want you to be unaware, brothers, that I planned many times to come to you (but have been prevented from doing so until now) in order that I might have a harvest among you, just as I have had among the other Gentiles.

14I am obligated both to Greeks and non-Greeks, both to the wise and the foolish. 15That is why I am so eager to preach the gospel also to you who are at Rome.

16I am not ashamed of the gospel, because it is the power of God for the salvation of everyone who believes: first for the Jew, then for the Gentile. 17For in the gospel a righteousness from God is revealed, a righteousness that is by faith from first to last,[c] just as it is written: "The righteous will live by faith."[d]

God's Wrath Against Mankind

18The wrath of God is being revealed from heaven against all the godlessness and wickedness of men who suppress the truth by their wickedness, 19since what may be known about God is plain to them, because God has made it plain to them. 20For since the creation of the world God's invisible qualities—his eternal power and divine nature—have been clearly seen, being understood from what has been made, so that men are without excuse.

21For although they knew God, they neither glorified him as God nor gave thanks to him, but their thinking became futile and their foolish hearts were darkened. 22Although they claimed to be wise, they became fools 23and exchanged the glory of the immortal God for images made to look like mortal man and birds and animals and reptiles.

24Therefore God gave them over in the sinful desires of their hearts to sexual impurity for the degrading of their bodies with one another. 25They exchanged the truth of God for a lie, and worshiped and served created things rather than the Creator—who is forever praised. Amen.

26Because of this, God gave them over to shameful lusts. Even their women exchanged natural relations for unnatural ones. 27In the same way the men also abandoned natural relations with women and were inflamed with lust for one another. Men committed indecent acts with other men, and received in themselves the due penalty for their perversion.

28Furthermore, since they did not think it worthwhile to retain the knowledge of God, he gave them over to a depraved mind, to do what ought not to be done. 29They have become filled with every kind of wickedness, evil, greed

[a]4 Or *who as to his spirit* [b]4 Or *was appointed to be the Son of God with power* [c]17 Or *is from faith to faith* [d]17 Hab. 2:4

1:1 In this letter, Paul introduced himself as a slave of Jesus Christ. For a Roman citizen a life of slavery was normally unthinkable. But Paul, a Roman citizen, purposely used this word to demonstrate his humility and dependence upon God. We all need this type of humility so that we can surrender our lives to God and experience the spiritual renewal he offers.

1:1–5 For the apostle Paul, the Good News was more than just an account of the events of Christ's death, burial and resurrection. The Good News moves beyond the amazing events of Jesus' life into our own sinful and broken lives, revealing that we can die to the power of sin because of what Jesus has done. We can be resurrected to new life! The Good News is a promise that there is power available to change our lives, no matter what we have done in the past. The Good News is the story of God's kindness to us through Jesus Christ. As we put our lives in God's hands, he will empower us to change. As we grow in him, we will experience God's joy in our lives and desire to share the Good News with others.

1:16–17 We all know what shame feels like. We may be ashamed of our failures, our bad habits or even the sinful thoughts we hide from others. Paul tells us that the Good News of Jesus Christ is God's power to deliver us from all the shameful things in our lives. God has the power to deliver and transform us when we surrender our lives to him. The Good News is certainly nothing to be ashamed of!

1:21–32 When we exchange our worship of the living God for a willful, sinful worship of things and other people, we follow the downward path that Paul describes here. If we go our own way apart from God, we enter a state of spiritual blindness where we believe lies and reject truth. This passage describes the natural consequence of pride and self-sufficiency. Whenever God reveals these attitudes in our lives, we must take it very seriously. When we confess these sins, God can break their power over us, allowing us to see the truth and freeing us to worship the true and living God.

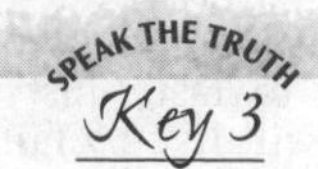

Freedom Through Confession

Romans 2:12–15 In order to put the past behind us, we must stop rationalizing our failures and start telling ourselves the truth. All of us struggle with our consciences, trying to make peace within our own hearts. In order to gain this peace, we may deny what we have done, find excuses or try to squirm out from under the full weight of our sin. We may work hard to be "good," attempting to counteract our wrongs. We will try everything we can to even up the score. But until we confess our sins to God, we will get nowhere.

God holds everyone accountable, "since they show that the requirements of the law are written on their hearts, their consciences also bearing witness, and their thoughts now accusing, now even defending them" (2:15). We are like people who have committed crimes but who refuse to accept the charges brought against them. We may have spent our energies constructing alibis, coming up with excuses and trying to plea-bargain. But if we sincerely seek spiritual renewal, now is the time to admit what we know deep down inside to be true: we are guilty.

By speaking the truth about our sinfulness, we stop fighting and admit that we are wrong. We agree with God and our own consciences that we have done wrong, and we confess these sins to him. Without confession there is no real freedom. But what a relief it is to finally admit our sinfulness to God. When we do confess, we regain internal peace, and our spirits will be renewed.

Turn to Galatians 6.

and depravity. They are full of envy, murder,
strife, deceit and malice. They are gossips,
30slanderers, God-haters, insolent, arrogant and
boastful; they invent ways of doing evil; they
disobey their parents; 31they are senseless, faithless, heartless, ruthless. 32Although they know
God's righteous decree that those who do such
things deserve death, they not only continue to
do these very things but also approve of those
who practice them.

God's Righteous Judgment

2 You, therefore, have no excuse, you who
pass judgment on someone else, for at
whatever point you judge the other, you are
condemning yourself, because you who pass
judgment do the same things. 2Now we know
that God's judgment against those who do such
things is based on truth. 3So when you, a mere
man, pass judgment on them and yet do the
same things, do you think you will escape God's
judgment? 4Or do you show contempt for the
riches of his kindness, tolerance and patience,
not realizing that God's kindness leads you toward repentance?

5But because of your stubbornness and your
unrepentant heart, you are storing up wrath
against yourself for the day of God's wrath,
when his righteous judgment will be revealed.
6God "will give to each person according to
what he has done."[a] 7To those who by persistence in doing good seek glory, honor and immortality, he will give eternal life. 8But for those
who are self-seeking and who reject the truth
and follow evil, there will be wrath and anger.
9There will be trouble and distress for every
human being who does evil: first for the Jew,
then for the Gentile; 10but glory, honor and
peace for everyone who does good: first for the
Jew, then for the Gentile. 11For God does not
show favoritism.

12All who sin apart from the law will also
perish apart from the law, and all who sin under
the law will be judged by the law. 13For it is not
those who hear the law who are righteous in

[a]6 Psalm 62:12; Prov. 24:12

2:1–4 In the previous chapter Paul described a life that was completely given over to sin. Reading through that description, we may find it easy to see these traits in someone else. Paul quickly corrects us by illustrating that everyone is in the same boat. We all do things that are wrong. We all hide our sins and failures. Spiritual growth will not come by condemning others. Only by honestly reflecting on our own lives, confessing our own sins and surrendering to God will we find spiritual renewal.

2:6–16 God is impartial in his judgments. He doesn't judge us merely by the way we talk, walk or dress, but rather God judges us by whether or not we obey his will. No group of people is favored over another in God's eyes. The Jewish people of Paul's day believed that God granted them special privileges purely because of their lineage. In this passage we find that God makes the same offer to all people. If we confess our sins and seek God's forgiveness, we can become his chosen people.

God's sight, but it is those who obey the law
who will be declared righteous. 14 (Indeed,
when Gentiles, who do not have the law, do by
nature things required by the law, they are a law
for themselves, even though they do not have
the law, 15 since they show that the requirements of the law are written on their hearts,
their consciences also bearing witness, and their
thoughts now accusing, now even defending
them.) 16 This will take place on the day when
God will judge men's secrets through Jesus
Christ, as my gospel declares.

The Jews and the Law

17 Now you, if you call yourself a Jew; if you
rely on the law and brag about your relationship to God; 18 if you know his will and approve
of what is superior because you are instructed
by the law; 19 if you are convinced that you are
a guide for the blind, a light for those who are
in the dark, 20 an instructor of the foolish, a
teacher of infants, because you have in the law
the embodiment of knowledge and truth—
21 you, then, who teach others, do you not teach
yourself? You who preach against stealing, do
you steal? 22 You who say that people should
not commit adultery, do you commit adultery?
You who abhor idols, do you rob temples?
23 You who brag about the law, do you dishonor
God by breaking the law? 24 As it is written:
"God's name is blasphemed among the Gentiles because of you."[a]

25 Circumcision has value if you observe the
law, but if you break the law, you have become
as though you had not been circumcised. 26 If
those who are not circumcised keep the law's
requirements, will they not be regarded as
though they were circumcised? 27 The one who
is not circumcised physically and yet obeys the
law will condemn you who, even though you
have the[b] written code and circumcision, are a
lawbreaker.

28 A man is not a Jew if he is only one outwardly, nor is circumcision merely outward and
physical. 29 No, a man is a Jew if he is one inwardly; and circumcision is circumcision of the
heart, by the Spirit, not by the written code.
Such a man's praise is not from men, but from
God.

God's Faithfulness

3 What advantage, then, is there in being a
Jew, or what value is there in circumcision?
2 Much in every way! First of all, they have been
entrusted with the very words of God.

3 What if some did not have faith? Will their
lack of faith nullify God's faithfulness? 4 Not at
all! Let God be true, and every man a liar. As it
is written:

> "So that you may be proved right when
> you speak
> and prevail when you judge."[c]

5 But if our unrighteousness brings out God's
righteousness more clearly, what shall we say?
That God is unjust in bringing his wrath on us?
(I am using a human argument.) 6 Certainly
not! If that were so, how could God judge the
world? 7 Someone might argue, "If my falsehood enhances God's truthfulness and so increases his glory, why am I still condemned as
a sinner?" 8 Why not say—as we are being slander-
ously reported as saying and as some claim that
we say—"Let us do evil that good may result"?
Their condemnation is deserved.

No One Is Righteous

9 What shall we conclude then? Are we any
better[d]? Not at all! We have already made the
charge that Jews and Gentiles alike are all under
sin. 10 As it is written:

> "There is no one righteous, not even one;
> 11 there is no one who understands,
> no one who seeks God.
> 12 All have turned away,
> they have together become worthless;
> there is no one who does good,
> not even one."[e]
> 13 "Their throats are open graves;
> their tongues practice deceit."[f]
> "The poison of vipers is on their lips."[g]
> 14 "Their mouths are full of cursing and
> bitterness."[h]
> 15 "Their feet are swift to shed blood;
> 16 ruin and misery mark their ways,
> 17 and the way of peace they do not know."[i]
> 18 "There is no fear of God before their
> eyes."[j]

19 Now we know that whatever the law says,
it says to those who are under the law, so that
every mouth may be silenced and the whole

[a] 24 Isaiah 52:5; Ezek. 36:22 [b] 27 Or *who, by means of a*
[c] 4 Psalm 51:4 [d] 9 Or *worse* [e] 12 Psalms 14:1-3;
53:1-3; Eccles. 7:20 [f] 13 Psalm 5:9
[g] 13 Psalm 140:3 [h] 14 Psalm 10:7
[i] 17 Isaiah 59:7,8 [j] 18 Psalm 36:1

2:28–29 Paul made an important point in these verses: God wants our hearts to be open and obedient to him. Our outward religious activities are important only if they reflect our love for God and others. We can fake our behavior and sometimes even outwardly fake our relationship with God. Yet if we only observe religious practices and make no real commitment to God, we cannot make spiritual progress. But if we are motivated by our love for God and other people, our outward behavior will reflect our inner devotion.

3:9–10 Paul summarized his earlier discussion by concluding, "There is no one righteous, not even one" (3:10). No one is exempt—we all have fallen and are sinful; we are all in need of salvation. If we pretend to be sinless and without defect, we only prove our refusal to see the truth. Spiritual renewal can begin only after we have seen the truth about ourselves and admitted it. When we recognize that we are broken and helpless, God can step in and provide the power we need.

world held accountable to God. [20]Therefore no one will be declared righteous in his sight by observing the law; rather, through the law we become conscious of sin.

Righteousness Through Faith

[21]But now a righteousness from God, apart from law, has been made known, to which the Law and the Prophets testify. [22]This righteousness from God comes through faith in Jesus Christ to all who believe. There is no difference, [23]for all have sinned and fall short of the glory of God, [24]and are justified freely by his grace through the redemption that came by Christ Jesus. [25]God presented him as a sacrifice of atonement,[a] through faith in his blood. He did this to demonstrate his justice, because in his forbearance he had left the sins committed beforehand unpunished— [26]he did it to demonstrate his justice at the present time, so as to be just and the one who justifies those who have faith in Jesus.

[27]Where, then, is boasting? It is excluded. On what principle? On that of observing the law? No, but on that of faith. [28]For we maintain that a man is justified by faith apart from observing the law. [29]Is God the God of Jews only? Is he not the God of Gentiles too? Yes, of Gentiles too, [30]since there is only one God, who will justify the circumcised by faith and the uncircumcised through that same faith. [31]Do we, then, nullify the law by this faith? Not at all! Rather, we uphold the law.

Abraham Justified by Faith

4 What then shall we say that Abraham, our forefather, discovered in this matter? [2]If, in fact, Abraham was justified by works, he had something to boast about—but not before God. [3]What does the Scripture say? "Abraham believed God, and it was credited to him as righteousness."[b]

[4]Now when a man works, his wages are not credited to him as a gift, but as an obligation. [5]However, to the man who does not work but trusts God who justifies the wicked, his faith is credited as righteousness. [6]David says the same thing when he speaks of the blessedness of the man to whom God credits righteousness apart from works:

[7]"Blessed are they
whose transgressions are forgiven,
whose sins are covered.
[8]Blessed is the man
whose sin the Lord will never count
against him."[c]

[9]Is this blessedness only for the circumcised, or also for the uncircumcised? We have been saying that Abraham's faith was credited to him as righteousness. [10]Under what circumstances was it credited? Was it after he was circumcised, or before? It was not after, but before! [11]And he received the sign of circumcision, a seal of the righteousness that he had by faith while he was still uncircumcised. So then, he is the father of all who believe but have not been circumcised, in order that righteousness might be credited to them. [12]And he is also the father of the circumcised who not only are circumcised but who also walk in the footsteps of the faith that our father Abraham had before he was circumcised.

[13]It was not through law that Abraham and his offspring received the promise that he would be heir of the world, but through the righteousness that comes by faith. [14]For if those who live by law are heirs, faith has no value and the promise is worthless, [15]because law brings wrath. And where there is no law there is no transgression.

[16]Therefore, the promise comes by faith, so

[a]25 Or *as the one who would turn aside his wrath, taking away sin* [b]3 Gen. 15:6; also in verse 22
[c]8 Psalm 32:1,2

3:20 The more we know about God's laws, God's heart and God's claim on our lives, the clearer it becomes that we don't measure up to his standards. God's laws in the Old Testament reflect God's will for us. Following these laws would lead to a healthy life. But none of us can follow these ideals under our own power. We need God's gracious forgiveness and power on a daily basis to help us follow his plan for right living. God will give us the forgiveness and power we need as we continually confess our sins and ask for his help.

3:21–26 This is one of the richest sections in the Bible to help us understand why Jesus died on the cross. Not one of us is so good that we don't need God's help; not one of us is so bad that we are beyond the reach of God's loving help. We are all made right with God through faith in Jesus Christ. Paul says that Jesus has set us free from God's wrath against sin. Although God freely gave us our salvation, he purchased it at great cost!

3:27 Again Paul emphasized that God deals with all people on the same basis. All must come to God through faith. We have nothing to boast about; none of us can be saved by anything we can do or say. And there is no reason for us to hide from God, for there is nothing so bad in our lives that it cannot be forgiven completely by our merciful God.

4:1–3 Paul referred to Abraham as an example of a faithful man. As we look at Abraham in the book of Genesis, we find a man who was set apart for God. Despite his mistakes, Abraham was a spiritual man who had a close relationship with God. But Abraham had to come to God the same way we do—through faith. We can do nothing to earn the promises of forgiveness and redemption that God offers us. No good deed can make us deserving of God's gracious forgiveness, and yet no failure is too great an obstacle for God's restoring power. When we entrust our lives to God and believe that he can help us, God can give us the power and courage to progress in our spiritual lives.

4:6–8 Many of us have failed desperately; we have hurt others in ways that cannot easily be repaired. King David was guilty of serious sins—adultery, deceit and murder. Yet when David acknowledged his guilt, confessed it to God and experienced God's forgiveness, he found joy. Each of these steps was an act of faith, but the final result was joy. Acknowledging our sin and confessing it also take an act of faith on our part. But as we follow these steps, we will receive God's forgiveness and joy.

that it may be by grace and may be guaranteed
to all Abraham's offspring—not only to those
who are of the law but also to those who are of
the faith of Abraham. He is the father of us all.
17As it is written: "I have made you a father of
many nations."[a] He is our father in the sight of
God, in whom he believed—the God who gives
life to the dead and calls things that are not as
though they were.

18Against all hope, Abraham in hope believed and so became the father of many nations, just as it had been said to him, "So shall
your offspring be."[b] 19Without weakening in
his faith, he faced the fact that his body was as
good as dead—since he was about a hundred
years old—and that Sarah's womb was also
dead. 20Yet he did not waver through unbelief
regarding the promise of God, but was strengthened in his faith and gave glory to God, 21being
fully persuaded that God had power to do what
he had promised. 22This is why "it was credited
to him as righteousness." 23The words "it was
credited to him" were written not for him alone,
24but also for us, to whom God will credit righteousness—for us who believe in him who
raised Jesus our Lord from the dead. 25He was
delivered over to death for our sins and was
raised to life for our justification.

Peace and Joy

5 Therefore, since we have been justified
through faith, we[c] have peace with God
through our Lord Jesus Christ, 2through whom
we have gained access by faith into this grace in
which we now stand. And we[c] rejoice in the
hope of the glory of God. 3Not only so, but
we[c] also rejoice in our sufferings, because we
know that suffering produces perseverance;
4perseverance, character; and character, hope.
5And hope does not disappoint us, because God
has poured out his love into our hearts by the
Holy Spirit, whom he has given us.

6You see, at just the right time, when we were
still powerless, Christ died for the ungodly.
7Very rarely will anyone die for a righteous
man, though for a good man someone might
possibly dare to die. 8But God demonstrates his
own love for us in this: While we were still
sinners, Christ died for us.

9Since we have now been justified by his
blood, how much more shall we be saved from
God's wrath through him! 10For if, when we
were God's enemies, we were reconciled to him
through the death of his Son, how much more,
having been reconciled, shall we be saved
through his life! 11Not only is this so, but we
also rejoice in God through our Lord Jesus
Christ, through whom we have now received
reconciliation.

Death Through Adam, Life Through Christ

12Therefore, just as sin entered the world
through one man, and death through sin, and
in this way death came to all men, because all
sinned— 13for before the law was given, sin was
in the world. But sin is not taken into account
when there is no law. 14Nevertheless, death
reigned from the time of Adam to the time of
Moses, even over those who did not sin by
breaking a command, as did Adam, who was a
pattern of the one to come.

15But the gift is not like the trespass. For if the
many died by the trespass of the one man, how
much more did God's grace and the gift that
came by the grace of the one man, Jesus Christ,
overflow to the many! 16Again, the gift of God
is not like the result of the one man's sin: The
judgment followed one sin and brought condemnation, but the gift followed many tres-
passes and brought justification. 17For if, by the
trespass of the one man, death reigned through
that one man, how much more will those who
receive God's abundant provision of grace and
of the gift of righteousness reign in life through
the one man, Jesus Christ.

18Consequently, just as the result of one trespass was condemnation for all men, so also the
result of one act of righteousness was justification that brings life for all men. 19For just as
through the disobedience of the one man the

[a]*17* Gen. 17:5 [b]*18* Gen. 15:5 [c]*1,2,3* Or *let us*

4:23–25 When we believe in God and the restoration he offers in Jesus Christ, an exchange takes place. We turn our unmanageable, sinful lives over to God, and he gives us his goodness and forgiveness in return. When Jesus died on the cross, he took away our sins and guilt. When Jesus rose from the grave, God demonstrated his power to transform us and fill us with his goodness. As we follow God's plan for restoration, we die to our sins and then rise to new and better lives.

5:1–11 Paul used several phrases to describe our painful condition: "We were still powerless" (5:6); we were "sinners" (5:8) and we were "God's enemies" (5:10). It was precisely when we were powerless, sinful and enemies that God decided to solve our sin problem for us. He loved us so much that he sent his Son to die on the cross to set us free from the power of sin. With a Savior like that, we can confidently surrender our lives to him.

5:12–13 Many of us find it easy to point a finger at others, blaming them for our problems. In these verses Paul made it clear that Adam's failure and the failures of our ancestors should not be our primary concern. Our problems may have started with the mistakes and sins of others, but we have all solidly aligned ourselves with Adam by repeatedly making the same mistakes. We are prone to rebel against God and his ways. If God doesn't intervene, we will suffer the consequences for the sins we have committed. We don't need fairness from God; we need his mercy. And that is what God provides for all who look to him in faith.

5:15–21 Paul had asserted that we stand justified and joyful in God's grace (see 5:1–2). In this passage he added to that reality. God's grace rules over the presence of sin and death in our world. While Adam's failure brought us the reign of sin and death, Jesus Christ has brought the reign of life through his grace for all who are willing to receive it. Our old lives represent the rule of death through Adam. Our new lives in Jesus Christ represent the rule of God's grace, kindness and love. As we surrender our lives to God, we can begin to receive the wonderful lives that he offers.

Unable to Remove Sinfulness

Romans 6:5–11 We must take responsibility for our lives and stop passing the blame for our sins to others. Yet we are not responsible for transforming our sinful nature. Most of us have made numerous attempts at self-improvement. Perhaps we have consciously tried to improve our attitudes, our education, our appearance or our habits. All these improvements are good. We may even have experienced some success in these areas. However, when it comes to our struggle with our sinful natures, chances are we have only experienced deep frustration whenever we have tried to change ourselves.

There is a reason for our failure to transform our lives by our own power: Only God can transform our sinful nature. The Bible tells us that our sinful nature must be put to death, as Jesus was, if we hope to find new life. The apostle Paul wrote, "Our old self was crucified with him so that the body of sin might be done away with, that we should no longer be slaves to sin" (6:6). And again, "Those who belong to Christ Jesus have crucified the sinful nature with its passions and desires" (Galatians 5:24).

There is no quick fix for our sinful nature, and we are not responsible to improve it. We are only responsible to repent and allow God to put our old nature to death daily. When we stop trying to improve that part of us that cannot be improved, God can crucify our old nature and resurrect a new life in its place. That is true spiritual renewal.

Turn to 1 Corinthians 13.

many were made sinners, so also through the
obedience of the one man the many will be
made righteous.
20 The law was added so that the trespass
might increase. But where sin increased, grace
increased all the more, 21 so that, just as sin
reigned in death, so also grace might reign
through righteousness to bring eternal life
through Jesus Christ our Lord.

Dead to Sin, Alive in Christ

6 What shall we say, then? Shall we go on
sinning so that grace may increase? 2 By no
means! We died to sin; how can we live in it any
longer? 3 Or don't you know that all of us who
were baptized into Christ Jesus were baptized
into his death? 4 We were therefore buried with
him through baptism into death in order that,
just as Christ was raised from the dead through
the glory of the Father, we too may live a new
life.
5 If we have been united with him like this in
his death, we will certainly also be united with
him in his resurrection. 6 For we know that our
old self was crucified with him so that the body
of sin might be done away with,[a] that we
should no longer be slaves to sin— 7 because
anyone who has died has been freed from sin.
8 Now if we died with Christ, we believe that
we will also live with him. 9 For we know that
since Christ was raised from the dead, he cannot die again; death no longer has mastery over
him. 10 The death he died, he died to sin once
for all; but the life he lives, he lives to God.
11 In the same way, count yourselves dead to
sin but alive to God in Christ Jesus. 12 Therefore
do not let sin reign in your mortal body so that

[a] 6 Or *be rendered powerless*

6:1–3 If God loves to forgive, why not sin to give him added opportunities to forgive us? Such an attitude presumes upon God's grace and makes light of the tremendous cost of our salvation. It is unthinkable that we would continue to allow sin to be our master when we have surrendered our lives to God.
6:2–11 Paul examined how we can receive new life through the death and resurrection of Jesus Christ. He traced the stages of Jesus' life, noting that his earthly body was subject to death, and reminded his readers of Jesus' death, burial and resurrection. Paul also noted that Jesus' resurrection body was no longer under the power of death. Next, Paul showed how our own lives parallel Jesus' life. While we begin our lives under the mastery of sin and death, we can identify with Jesus' death, burial and resurrection and receive new lives that are free from the power of sin and death. God has the power to take people destined for destruction and set them on the road to new life.
6:12–14 Paul recognized that temptation would be an ongoing reality, so he issued this warning: "Do not let sin reign in your mortal body" (6:12). The temptations we experience are extensions of the sinful natures that exist in each of us. Though we cannot overcome our sinful natures alone, we can ask God to help us. We must consider our sinful natures crucified with Christ. As we call on him, we have access to the Holy Spirit, who will help us overcome the powerful temptations in our lives.

you obey its evil desires. [13]Do not offer the parts of your body to sin, as instruments of wickedness, but rather offer yourselves to God, as those who have been brought from death to life; and offer the parts of your body to him as instruments of righteousness. [14]For sin shall not be your master, because you are not under law, but under grace.

Slaves to Righteousness

[15]What then? Shall we sin because we are not under law but under grace? By no means! [16]Don't you know that when you offer yourselves to someone to obey him as slaves, you are slaves to the one whom you obey—whether you are slaves to sin, which leads to death, or to obedience, which leads to righteousness? [17]But thanks be to God that, though you used to be slaves to sin, you wholeheartedly obeyed the form of teaching to which you were entrusted. [18]You have been set free from sin and have become slaves to righteousness.

[19]I put this in human terms because you are weak in your natural selves. Just as you used to offer the parts of your body in slavery to impurity and to ever-increasing wickedness, so now offer them in slavery to righteousness leading to holiness. [20]When you were slaves to sin, you were free from the control of righteousness. [21]What benefit did you reap at that time from the things you are now ashamed of? Those things result in death! [22]But now that you have been set free from sin and have become slaves to God, the benefit you reap leads to holiness, and the result is eternal life. [23]For the wages of sin is death, but the gift of God is eternal life in[a] Christ Jesus our Lord.

An Illustration From Marriage

7 Do you not know, brothers—for I am speaking to men who know the law—that the law has authority over a man only as long as he lives? [2]For example, by law a married woman is bound to her husband as long as he is alive, but if her husband dies, she is released from the law of marriage. [3]So then, if she marries another man while her husband is still alive, she is called an adulteress. But if her husband dies, she is released from that law and is not an adulteress, even though she marries another man.

[4]So, my brothers, you also died to the law through the body of Christ, that you might belong to another, to him who was raised from the dead, in order that we might bear fruit to God. [5]For when we were controlled by the sinful nature,[b] the sinful passions aroused by the law were at work in our bodies, so that we bore fruit for death. [6]But now, by dying to what once bound us, we have been released from the law so that we serve in the new way of the Spirit, and not in the old way of the written code.

Struggling With Sin

[7]What shall we say, then? Is the law sin? Certainly not! Indeed I would not have known what sin was except through the law. For I would not have known what coveting really was if the law had not said, "Do not covet."[c] [8]But sin, seizing the opportunity afforded by the commandment, produced in me every kind of covetous desire. For apart from law, sin is dead. [9]Once I was alive apart from law; but when the commandment came, sin sprang to life and I died. [10]I found that the very commandment that was intended to bring life actually brought death. [11]For sin, seizing the opportunity afforded by the commandment, deceived me, and through the commandment put me to death. [12]So then, the law is holy, and the commandment is holy, righteous and good.

[13]Did that which is good, then, become death to me? By no means! But in order that sin might be recognized as sin, it produced death in me through what was good, so that through the commandment sin might become utterly sinful.

[14]We know that the law is spiritual; but I am unspiritual, sold as a slave to sin. [15]I do not understand what I do. For what I want to do I

[a]23 Or *through* [b]5 Or *the flesh;* also in verse 25
[c]7 Exodus 20:17; Deut. 5:21

6:19–22 It is impossible to be neutral when dealing with the spiritual realm. We all have a master—either sin or God. Making sin our master may seem fun for a while, but sin only leads to a life that is painfully out of control. When we surrender our lives to God, we affirm that God is our master. Only by surrendering to him can we experience the restoration of our lives. At first God's way may look harder than the way of sin, but in time we will discover that God's way is the only way to a joyful and meaningful life.

7:13 Paul didn't want to give us the impression that God's laws are unsound. God's laws were meant to lead us to a meaningful life in close fellowship with him. But we, in our own strength, are unable to live up to God's standards. By nature we are flawed and sinful. And if we follow the dictates of our sinful natures, we will become enslaved to sin. Thankfully, God has made a provision for our weaknesses, solving the sin problem through the finished work of Jesus Christ. When we surrender our lives to God, we can experience his transforming power, bringing us the help we need to break free from our sinful natures and be ruled by the Holy Spirit.

7:14–17 In these verses, Paul described a struggle we can all identify with. We long to do what is good, healthy and right, but we end up committing the same old sins. As we honestly reflect on our lives, we admit our failures and seek to change, but often we fall back into our old habits once again. But we must not let this struggle discourage us. We need to continue confessing our sins to God, even if we've confessed the same sin numerous times. God promises to forgive us and cleanse us from all unrighteousness (see 1 John 1:9). It would also be wise to establish some relationships with people who will hold us accountable and help us set some limits for ourselves in order to guard against sin. Through this process, our tendency to fall back into the same old sins will be lessened as God transforms us.

THE SPIRITUAL DISCIPLINES

Repentance and Confession

Remembering What We Haven't Done

Romans 7:15 Many liturgical prayers of confession include the admission that we have not done those things we should have done. By confessing this, we affirm that sin consists not only of those things we do that are wrong, but also of those things we neglect to do that are right. In other words, there are sins of commission and sins of omission. It isn't enough simply to avoid the evil things of life. We must also do the right things.

Paul gives us a clear picture of this in Romans 12. We are exhorted not only to avoid conflict with our enemies but also to feed them. We are supposed to defend ourselves against evil but also go on the offensive for doing good.

As we examine our lives, we must look not only at our mistakes but also at the times when we had an opportunity to do right and didn't do it. Confessing these sins of omission helps make us more aware of such opportunities in the future so that we might serve God and others more faithfully.

For more on repentance and confession, turn to James 5.

Putting It Into Practice

Reflect on the commands outlined in Romans 12. Also consider the great commandments to love the Lord your God with all your heart, soul and mind, and to love your neighbor as yourself (see Matthew 22:37–39). In light of these commands, assess your recent behavior. What good things do you often neglect to do? Confess these sins of omission to God and ask his forgiveness. Then consider how you can stimulate yourself to do such things the next time an opportunity arises.

do not do, but what I hate I do. 16And if I do what I do not want to do, I agree that the law is good. 17As it is, it is no longer I myself who do it, but it is sin living in me. 18I know that nothing good lives in me, that is, in my sinful nature.[a] For I have the desire to do what is good, but I cannot carry it out. 19For what I do is not the good I want to do; no, the evil I do not want to do—this I keep on doing. 20Now if I do what I do not want to do, it is no longer I who do it, but it is sin living in me that does it.

21So I find this law at work: When I want to do good, evil is right there with me. 22For in my inner being I delight in God's law; 23but I see another law at work in the members of my body, waging war against the law of my mind and making me a prisoner of the law of sin at work within my members. 24What a wretched man I am! Who will rescue me from this body of death? 25Thanks be to God—through Jesus Christ our Lord!

So then, I myself in my mind am a slave to God's law, but in the sinful nature a slave to the law of sin.

Life Through the Spirit

8 Therefore, there is now no condemnation for those who are in Christ Jesus,[b] 2because through Christ Jesus the law of the Spirit of life set me free from the law of sin and death. 3For what the law was powerless to do in that it was weakened by the sinful nature,[c] God did by sending his own Son in the likeness of sinful man to be a sin offering.[d] And so he condemned sin in sinful man,[e] 4in order that the righteous requirements of the law might be fully met in us, who do not live according to the sinful nature but according to the Spirit.

5Those who live according to the sinful nature have their minds set on what that nature desires; but those who live in accordance with the Spirit have their minds set on what the Spirit desires. 6The mind of sinful man[f] is death, but the mind controlled by the Spirit is life and peace; 7the sinful mind[g] is hostile to God. It does not submit to God's law, nor can it do so. 8Those controlled by the sinful nature cannot please God.

9You, however, are controlled not by the sinful nature but by the Spirit, if the Spirit of God lives in you. And if anyone does not have the Spirit of Christ, he does not belong to Christ. 10But if Christ is in you, your body is dead because of sin, yet your spirit is alive because of righteousness. 11And if the Spirit of him who raised Jesus from the dead is living in you, he who raised Christ from the dead will also give life to your mortal bodies through his Spirit, who lives in you.

12Therefore, brothers, we have an obligation—but it is not to the sinful nature, to live according to it. 13For if you live according to the sinful nature, you will die; but if by the Spirit you put to death the misdeeds of the body, you will live, 14because those who are led by the Spirit of God are sons of God. 15For you did not receive a spirit that makes you a slave again to fear, but you received the Spirit of sonship.[h] And by him we cry, *"Abba,*[i] Father." 16The Spirit himself testifies with our spirit that we are God's children. 17Now if we are children, then we are heirs—heirs of God and co-heirs with Christ, if indeed we share in his sufferings in order that we may also share in his glory.

Future Glory

18I consider that our present sufferings are not worth comparing with the glory that will be revealed in us. 19The creation waits in eager expectation for the sons of God to be revealed.

[a]18 Or *my flesh* [b]1 Some later manuscripts *Jesus, who do not live according to the sinful nature but according to the Spirit,* [c]3 Or *the flesh;* also in verses 4, 5, 8, 9, 12 and 13 [d]3 Or *man, for sin* [e]3 Or *in the flesh* [f]6 Or *mind set on the flesh* [g]7 Or *the mind set on the flesh* [h]15 Or *adoption* [i]15 Aramaic for *Father*

7:18–20 Paul recognized the power of sin in his life and admitted his helplessness against it. When we admit our helplessness to overcome the sin that entangles us, we make a significant step toward spiritual renewal. Only when we are willing to accept the powerful help that God offers will we be able to overcome the temptations we face.

8:1 This verse is one of the great affirmations of the Bible: God will never condemn us for our sins because Jesus Christ has paid the price once and for all. When we decide to surrender our lives to God, we can be confident that he will not condemn us. If we have accepted God's offer of forgiveness in Christ, there is "no condemnation."

8:2–4 Once we recognize how helpless we are to fight our own sinful natures, the next step is to look beyond ourselves to God for the power we need. The life-giving Spirit that Paul mentioned in these verses is the Holy Spirit. He was present at the creation of the world (see Genesis 1—2). And the Holy Spirit is available to us as we allow God to recreate our lives according to his design. We cannot overcome the sins that entangle us by ourselves, but God is more than able to help us. He sent his Son and destroyed the power of sin through Jesus' death and resurrection. And now the Holy Spirit is always with us, empowering us to obey God's plan.

8:5–6 Paul places people into two categories—those who are controlled by their self-serving, sinful natures and those who follow after the Holy Spirit. Once we have made the decision to surrender our lives to God, we must also make a daily decision to consciously follow his way. We need to continually seek God, surrender our lives to him, honestly reflect on our lives in order to see the truth, speak the truth, accept responsibility for our lives, confess our sins, let go of the past, allow God to redirect our course and continue growing spiritually.

8:9–11 Either we have the Spirit of God living in us, or we don't. The Spirit of God comes to live within us by our act of faith in surrendering our lives to God and by our acceptance of the work of Christ on our behalf. Sometimes we can feel God's Spirit within us. But he is always with us, whether or not we feel his presence. When we turned our lives over to him, God gave us the same Holy Spirit who raised Jesus from the dead. God will put his power to work in us to bring about our spiritual renewal and transformation.

20For the creation was subjected to frustration, not by its own choice, but by the will of the one who subjected it, in hope 21that[a] the creation itself will be liberated from its bondage to decay and brought into the glorious freedom of the children of God.

22We know that the whole creation has been groaning as in the pains of childbirth right up to the present time. 23Not only so, but we ourselves, who have the firstfruits of the Spirit, groan inwardly as we wait eagerly for our adoption as sons, the redemption of our bodies. 24For in this hope we were saved. But hope that is seen is no hope at all. Who hopes for what he already has? 25But if we hope for what we do not yet have, we wait for it patiently.

26In the same way, the Spirit helps us in our weakness. We do not know what we ought to pray for, but the Spirit himself intercedes for us with groans that words cannot express. 27And he who searches our hearts knows the mind of the Spirit, because the Spirit intercedes for the saints in accordance with God's will.

More Than Conquerors

28And we know that in all things God works for the good of those who love him,[b] who[c] have been called according to his purpose. 29For those God foreknew he also predestined to be conformed to the likeness of his Son, that he might be the firstborn among many brothers. 30And those he predestined, he also called; those he called, he also justified; those he justified, he also glorified.

31What, then, shall we say in response to this? If God is for us, who can be against us? 32He who did not spare his own Son, but gave him up for us all—how will he not also, along with him, graciously give us all things? 33Who will bring any charge against those whom God has chosen? It is God who justifies. 34Who is he that condemns? Christ Jesus, who died—more than that, who was raised to life—is at the right hand of God and is also interceding for us. 35Who shall separate us from the love of Christ? Shall trouble or hardship or persecution or famine or nakedness or danger or sword? 36As it is written:

"For your sake we face death all day long;
we are considered as sheep to be
slaughtered."[d]

37No, in all these things we are more than conquerors through him who loved us. 38For I am convinced that neither death nor life, neither angels nor demons,[e] neither the present nor the future, nor any powers, 39neither height nor depth, nor anything else in all creation, will be able to separate us from the love of God that is in Christ Jesus our Lord.

God's Sovereign Choice

9 I speak the truth in Christ—I am not lying, my conscience confirms it in the Holy Spirit— 2I have great sorrow and unceasing anguish in my heart. 3For I could wish that I myself were cursed and cut off from Christ for the sake of my brothers, those of my own race, 4the people of Israel. Theirs is the adoption as sons; theirs the divine glory, the covenants, the receiving of the law, the temple worship and the promises. 5Theirs are the patriarchs, and from them is traced the human ancestry of Christ, who is God over all, forever praised![f] Amen.

6It is not as though God's word had failed. For not all who are descended from Israel are Israel. 7Nor because they are his descendants are they all Abraham's children. On the contrary, "It is through Isaac that your offspring will be reckoned."[g] 8In other words, it is not the natural children who are God's children, but it is the children of the promise who are regarded as Abraham's offspring. 9For this was how the promise was stated: "At the appointed time I will return, and Sarah will have a son."[h]

10Not only that, but Rebekah's children had one and the same father, our father Isaac. 11Yet, before the twins were born or had done anything good or bad—in order that God's purpose in election might stand: 12not by works but by him who calls—she was told, "The older will serve the younger."[i] 13Just as it is written: "Jacob I loved, but Esau I hated."[j]

14What then shall we say? Is God unjust? Not at all! 15For he says to Moses,

"I will have mercy on whom I have mercy,
and I will have compassion on whom I
have compassion."[k]

16It does not, therefore, depend on man's desire or effort, but on God's mercy. 17For the Scripture says to Pharaoh: "I raised you up for this very purpose, that I might display my power in

[a]20,21 Or *subjected it in hope.* [21]*For* [b]28 Some manuscripts *And we know that all things work together for good to those who love God* [c]28 Or *works together with those who love him to bring about what is good—with those who* [d]36 Psalm 44:22 [e]38 Or *nor heavenly rulers* [f]5 Or *Christ, who is over all. God be forever praised!* Or *Christ. God who is over all be forever praised!* [g]7 Gen. 21:12 [h]9 Gen. 18:10,14 [i]12 Gen. 25:23 [j]13 Mal. 1:2,3 [k]15 Exodus 33:19

8:26–28 We draw closer to God through prayer and preserve our spiritual gains through communication with God. Paul assures us that the indwelling power of the Holy Spirit is at work within us as we pray. We are not left alone to work out our own problems. As we entrust our lives to God, he directs the events of our lives and brings everything about for our good. He can turn even our mistakes and failures into the means for our growth and blessing.

8:31–39 Our security should be based on God's unshakable love for us. God's love for us is not just an emotion but an actual fact. God proved his love for us by willingly sending his Son to suffer and die. In fact, there is nothing in the whole universe that can separate us from God's love! What more could God say to us to make us more secure in his love?

you and that my name might be proclaimed in all the earth."[a] 18 Therefore God has mercy on whom he wants to have mercy, and he hardens whom he wants to harden.

19 One of you will say to me: "Then why does God still blame us? For who resists his will?" 20 But who are you, O man, to talk back to God? "Shall what is formed say to him who formed it, 'Why did you make me like this?' "[b] 21 Does not the potter have the right to make out of the same lump of clay some pottery for noble purposes and some for common use?

22 What if God, choosing to show his wrath and make his power known, bore with great patience the objects of his wrath—prepared for destruction? 23 What if he did this to make the riches of his glory known to the objects of his mercy, whom he prepared in advance for glory— 24 even us, whom he also called, not only from the Jews but also from the Gentiles? 25 As he says in Hosea:

"I will call them 'my people' who are not
my people;
and I will call her 'my loved one' who is
not my loved one,"[c]

26 and,

"It will happen that in the very place
where it was said to them,
'You are not my people,'
they will be called 'sons of the living
God.' "[d]

27 Isaiah cries out concerning Israel:

"Though the number of the Israelites be
like the sand by the sea,
only the remnant will be saved.
28 For the Lord will carry out
his sentence on earth with speed and
finality."[e]

29 It is just as Isaiah said previously:

"Unless the Lord Almighty
had left us descendants,
we would have become like Sodom,
we would have been like Gomorrah."[f]

Israel's Unbelief

30 What then shall we say? That the Gentiles, who did not pursue righteousness, have obtained it, a righteousness that is by faith; 31 but Israel, who pursued a law of righteousness, has not attained it. 32 Why not? Because they pursued it not by faith but as if it were by works. They stumbled over the "stumbling stone." 33 As it is written:

"See, I lay in Zion a stone that causes men
to stumble
and a rock that makes them fall,
and the one who trusts in him will never
be put to shame."[g]

10 Brothers, my heart's desire and prayer to God for the Israelites is that they may be saved. 2 For I can testify about them that they are zealous for God, but their zeal is not based on knowledge. 3 Since they did not know the righteousness that comes from God and sought to establish their own, they did not submit to God's righteousness. 4 Christ is the end of the law so that there may be righteousness for everyone who believes.

5 Moses describes in this way the righteousness that is by the law: "The man who does these things will live by them."[h] 6 But the righteousness that is by faith says: "Do not say in your heart, 'Who will ascend into heaven?'[i]" (that is, to bring Christ down) 7 "or 'Who will descend into the deep?'[j]" (that is, to bring Christ up from the dead). 8 But what does it say? "The word is near you; it is in your mouth and in your heart,"[k] that is, the word of faith we are proclaiming: 9 That if you confess with your mouth, "Jesus is Lord," and believe in your heart that God raised him from the dead, you will be saved. 10 For it is with your heart that you believe and are justified, and it is with your mouth that you confess and are saved. 11 As the Scripture says, "Anyone who trusts in him will never be put to shame."[l] 12 For there is no difference between Jew and Gentile—the same Lord is Lord of all and richly blesses all who call on him, 13 for, "Everyone who calls on the name of the Lord will be saved."[m]

14 How, then, can they call on the one they have not believed in? And how can they believe in the one of whom they have not heard? And

[a] *17* Exodus 9:16 [b] *20* Isaiah 29:16; 45:9
[c] *25* Hosea 2:23 [d] *26* Hosea 1:10
[e] *28* Isaiah 10:22,23 [f] *29* Isaiah 1:9
[g] *33* Isaiah 8:14; 28:16 [h] *5* Lev. 18:5
[i] *6* Deut. 30:12 [j] *7* Deut. 30:13 [k] *8* Deut. 30:14
[l] *11* Isaiah 28:16 [m] *13* Joel 2:32

9:25–26 God specializes in loving those who are unlovely and undeserving. The fact is, because of our sinful natures, not one of us deserves God's love. Yet God's love is bestowed on all who admit their need and respond to his love for them. Sometimes those who are despised by society are the first to admit their need for God. That is why such people often possess the most dramatic stories of God's transforming power in their lives. No one is innocent of wrongdoing; yet no sin is too great for God to forgive. Thus, those who have admitted their sinfulness are better off than "respectable" people who refuse to see the truth about their need for God. Admitting that we have failed and that we need God is essential to our spiritual renewal. We must not allow pride and social standing to keep us from admitting our need for God at any point in our spiritual growth process.

10:8–15 Our salvation comes by trusting Jesus Christ; there is nothing we can do to earn it. We may have spent our entire lives trying to earn the approval of others. Thankfully God does not accept us on the basis of our performance. No matter how great our successes or failures, God accepts us because of what Christ has done on our behalf. We have no reason to hide our mistakes from God; he wants to relieve us of the burdens we carry. He invites us to surrender our lives to him and receive his forgiveness.

how can they hear without someone preaching
to them? 15And how can they preach unless
they are sent? As it is written, "How beautiful
are the feet of those who bring good news!"[a]
16But not all the Israelites accepted the good
news. For Isaiah says, "Lord, who has believed
our message?"[b] 17Consequently, faith comes
from hearing the message, and the message is
heard through the word of Christ. 18But I ask:
Did they not hear? Of course they did:

"Their voice has gone out into all the
earth,
their words to the ends of the world."[c]

19Again I ask: Did Israel not understand? First,
Moses says,

"I will make you envious by those who are
not a nation;
I will make you angry by a nation that
has no understanding."[d]

20And Isaiah boldly says,

"I was found by those who did not seek
me;
I revealed myself to those who did not
ask for me."[e]

21But concerning Israel he says,

"All day long I have held out my hands
to a disobedient and obstinate people."[f]

The Remnant of Israel

11 I ask then: Did God reject his people?
By no means! I am an Israelite myself,
a descendant of Abraham, from the tribe of
Benjamin. 2God did not reject his people,
whom he foreknew. Don't you know what the
Scripture says in the passage about Elijah—how
he appealed to God against Israel: 3"Lord, they
have killed your prophets and torn down your
altars; I am the only one left, and they are trying
to kill me"[g]? 4And what was God's answer to
him? "I have reserved for myself seven thousand who have not bowed the knee to Baal."[h]
5So too, at the present time there is a remnant
chosen by grace. 6And if by grace, then it is no
longer by works; if it were, grace would no longer be grace.[i]
7What then? What Israel sought so earnestly
it did not obtain, but the elect did. The others
were hardened, 8as it is written:

"God gave them a spirit of stupor,
eyes so that they could not see
and ears so that they could not hear,
to this very day."[j]

9And David says:

"May their table become a snare and a
trap,
a stumbling block and a retribution for
them.
10May their eyes be darkened so they cannot
see,
and their backs be bent forever."[k]

Ingrafted Branches

11Again I ask: Did they stumble so as to fall
beyond recovery? Not at all! Rather, because of
their transgression, salvation has come to the
Gentiles to make Israel envious. 12But if their
transgression means riches for the world, and
their loss means riches for the Gentiles, how
much greater riches will their fullness bring!
13I am talking to you Gentiles. Inasmuch as
I am the apostle to the Gentiles, I make much
of my ministry 14in the hope that I may somehow arouse my own people to envy and save
some of them. 15For if their rejection is the reconciliation of the world, what will their acceptance be but life from the dead? 16If the part of
the dough offered as firstfruits is holy, then the
whole batch is holy; if the root is holy, so are
the branches.
17If some of the branches have been broken
off, and you, though a wild olive shoot, have
been grafted in among the others and now
share in the nourishing sap from the olive root,
18do not boast over those branches. If you do,
consider this: You do not support the root, but
the root supports you. 19You will say then,
"Branches were broken off so that I could be
grafted in." 20Granted. But they were broken off
because of unbelief, and you stand by faith. Do
not be arrogant, but be afraid. 21For if God did
not spare the natural branches, he will not spare
you either.
22Consider therefore the kindness and sternness of God: sternness to those who fell, but
kindness to you, provided that you continue in
his kindness. Otherwise, you also will be cut
off. 23And if they do not persist in unbelief, they
will be grafted in, for God is able to graft them
in again. 24After all, if you were cut out of an
olive tree that is wild by nature, and contrary to
nature were grafted into a cultivated olive tree,
how much more readily will these, the natural
branches, be grafted into their own olive tree!

[a] *15* Isaiah 52:7 [b] *16* Isaiah 53:1 [c] *18* Psalm 19:4 [d] *19* Deut. 32:21 [e] *20* Isaiah 65:1 [f] *21* Isaiah 65:2 [g] *3* 1 Kings 19:10,14 [h] *4* 1 Kings 19:18 [i] *6* Some manuscripts *by grace. But if by works, then it is no longer grace; if it were, work would no longer be work.* [j] *8* Deut. 29:4; Isaiah 29:10 [k] *10* Psalm 69:22,23

11:1–10 Even though a majority of Jews had rejected Jesus' Messianic claims, Paul stated that they could still surrender their lives to God and experience his healing power and grace. We can still ask for God's help and forgiveness too. Yet an extended period of spiritual blindness is always costly. During our refusal to see the truth we may cause great pain to others and to ourselves. The longer we wait, the more difficult it will be to confess our sins, accept responsibility for what we have done and ask God to change us. The time to seek God and let him redirect the course of our lives is now!

THE SPIRITUAL DISCIPLINES

Service

Your Altar Ego

Romans 12:1 Service is a way of saying thanks to God for all that he has done for us. We can never truly pay back the overwhelming love and support our friends and family may have shown us, but we can pass their love on to others. In the same way, we can never repay God for granting us life in Christ and for blessing us, but we can pass his love on to others in practical ways.

One of the greatest barriers to service, however, is pride. Sinful pride causes us to scoff at the thought of putting others first. Pride teaches us to calculate how every action will further our own reputation or advance us toward our goals. Pride carefully keeps records of who is next in line for something good.

Paul's letter to the Romans leaves no room for pride. Those who understand their unworthiness and sinfulness, as well as the priceless sacrifice of Christ and the new life of faith he gives by grace, will place their ego on the altar. Sinful pride must die when faith comes alive.

Romans 12 illustrates several specific areas in which we can be living sacrifices and serve God in the world. As living sacrifices, we surrender the use of our gifts solely for our own advancement. We seek to bless others instead and sacrifice our time and resources for their benefit. In the process, our lives are shaped into the image of Christ.

For more on service, turn to 1 Corinthians 12.

Putting It Into Practice

Have you determined to offer your life as a living sacrifice to God? What will this entail? Where do you sense God is calling you to serve? Let your motivation for service flow from a heart that is thankful to God for the grace he has shown you.

All Israel Will Be Saved

25I do not want you to be ignorant of this mystery, brothers, so that you may not be conceited: Israel has experienced a hardening in part until the full number of the Gentiles has come in. 26And so all Israel will be saved, as it is written:

"The deliverer will come from Zion;
he will turn godlessness away from Jacob.
27And this is[a] my covenant with them
when I take away their sins."[b]

28As far as the gospel is concerned, they are enemies on your account; but as far as election is concerned, they are loved on account of the patriarchs, 29for God's gifts and his call are irrevocable. 30Just as you who were at one time disobedient to God have now received mercy as a result of their disobedience, 31so they too have now become disobedient in order that they too may now[c] receive mercy as a result of God's mercy to you. 32For God has bound all men over to disobedience so that he may have mercy on them all.

Doxology

33Oh, the depth of the riches of the wisdom
and[d] knowledge of God!
How unsearchable his judgments,
and his paths beyond tracing out!
34"Who has known the mind of the Lord?
Or who has been his counselor?"[e]
35"Who has ever given to God,
that God should repay him?"[f]
36For from him and through him and to him
are all things.
To him be the glory forever! Amen.

Living Sacrifices

12 Therefore, I urge you, brothers, in view of God's mercy, to offer your bodies as living sacrifices, holy and pleasing to God—this is your spiritual[g] act of worship. 2Do not conform any longer to the pattern of this world, but be transformed by the renewing of your mind. Then you will be able to test and approve what God's will is—his good, pleasing and perfect will.

3For by the grace given me I say to every one of you: Do not think of yourself more highly than you ought, but rather think of yourself with sober judgment, in accordance with the measure of faith God has given you. 4Just as each of us has one body with many members, and these members do not all have the same function, 5so in Christ we who are many form one body, and each member belongs to all the others. 6We have different gifts, according to the grace given us. If a man's gift is prophesying, let him use it in proportion to his[h] faith. 7If it is serving, let him serve; if it is teaching, let him teach; 8if it is encouraging, let him encourage; if it is contributing to the needs of others, let him give generously; if it is leadership, let him govern diligently; if it is showing mercy, let him do it cheerfully.

Love

9Love must be sincere. Hate what is evil; cling to what is good. 10Be devoted to one another in brotherly love. Honor one another above yourselves. 11Never be lacking in zeal, but keep your spiritual fervor, serving the Lord. 12Be joyful in hope, patient in affliction, faithful in prayer. 13Share with God's people who are in need. Practice hospitality.

14Bless those who persecute you; bless and do not curse. 15Rejoice with those who rejoice; mourn with those who mourn. 16Live in harmony with one another. Do not be proud, but be willing to associate with people of low position.[i] Do not be conceited.

17Do not repay anyone evil for evil. Be care-

[a]27 Or *will be* [b]27 Isaiah 59:20,21; 27:9; Jer. 31:33,34 [c]31 Some manuscripts do not have *now.* [d]33 Or *riches and the wisdom and the* [e]34 Isaiah 40:13 [f]35 Job 41:11 [g]1 Or *reasonable* [h]6 Or *in agreement with the* [i]16 Or *willing to do menial work*

11:33–36 After sketching out the broad contours of God's plan for us, Paul could only fall on his knees in worship of God's majesty. God's plan, wisdom, knowledge and ways are all so far beyond ours that we have only one option: to humbly give him the praise he deserves! For those of us who recognize how helpless we are, God's love for us and desire to empower us and give us his wisdom can be a great encouragement.

12:1–2 These verses urge us to offer our bodies to God as living sacrifices. We are exhorted to make the decision to lay our lives on the altar before God so he can use us for his work. We are called to follow God's plan, utilizing the power he offers. Our lives can then become a showcase to others of what God's power can do. As we grow, we will discover the joy and meaning that we can experience when we offer our lives to God.

12:3 This verse is a call to honesty and true humility. We are to honestly reflect on our lives, making an assessment of both our strengths and weaknesses. This will teach us humility as we uncover our faults and confess them to God. It will also help us develop a grateful attitude toward God as we discover the many gifts he has given us.

12:4–8 God has an important task for each of us. We all have special gifts for building up other believers. Each of us can be used by God to accomplish something significant. As we surrender our lives to God as living sacrifices, we should further seek him to see how we can use our talents, resources and abilities to serve others. As we do, God will further reveal our spiritual gifts so that we can continue to bless others.

12:9–21 We are urged to let love govern our attitudes and actions. We must love even those we consider our enemies. Others may have wronged us. Yet God's love urges us to forgive them and seek reconciliation. We also may have hurt others. Love requires us to seek their forgiveness and do what we can to make up for the trouble and pain we have caused. Often we need to make a special effort to reach out to immediate family members—parents, siblings, children, a spouse. Love sometimes may call us to swallow our pride and admit our wrongs to others. Then God can heal our relationships, and our own spiritual condition can be improved.

THE SPIRITUAL DISCIPLINES

Worship

Worship Isn't Just for Church

Romans 12:1–2 Worship is a way of life. Worship is not simply what we *do* for God in church; it is also who we *are* for God in the world. Our behavior can inspire others to praise and thank the Lord (see Matthew 5:16; 2 Corinthians 9:11–13). This entire chapter demonstrates how we can bring worship into our daily lives. Worship becomes our way of life as we

- Allow God to transform our minds. In this way our allegiance is transferred from the world to God.
- Serve others with our gifts. God is honored by the full exercise of our gifts, for it displays his glory as our Creator. We should rejoice in these gifts and use them to accomplish God's purposes.
- Reflect God's love and grace to those around us. This is the second great commandment: that we love others as ourselves (see Matthew 22:39). In Romans 12:9–21, Paul gives us numerous examples that illustrate how we are to obey this commandment. Note that these are not simply humanitarian gestures. They are acts of worship, acts that please and honor God.

For more on worship, turn to 1 Corinthians 14.

Putting It Into Practice

Review Romans 12. Have you offered your entire self for the daily worship of God? If not, what has kept you from doing so? This is the starting place for our walk with God. Spiritual renewal begins with giving ourselves completely to God. Consider the three primary ways mentioned here to bring worship into daily life. Which of these ways least characterizes your behavior? Make specific plans for worshiping God more fully in this area in your life.

ful to do what is right in the eyes of everybody. 18If it is possible, as far as it depends on you, live at peace with everyone. 19Do not take revenge, my friends, but leave room for God's wrath, for it is written: "It is mine to avenge; I will repay,"[a] says the Lord. 20On the contrary:

"If your enemy is hungry, feed him;
if he is thirsty, give him something to drink.
In doing this, you will heap burning coals on his head."[b]

21Do not be overcome by evil, but overcome evil with good.

Submission to the Authorities

13 Everyone must submit himself to the governing authorities, for there is no authority except that which God has established. The authorities that exist have been established by God. 2Consequently, he who rebels against the authority is rebelling against what God has instituted, and those who do so will bring judgment on themselves. 3For rulers hold no terror for those who do right, but for those who do wrong. Do you want to be free from fear of the one in authority? Then do what is right and he will commend you. 4For he is God's servant to do you good. But if you do wrong, be afraid, for he does not bear the sword for nothing. He is God's servant, an agent of wrath to bring punishment on the wrongdoer. 5Therefore, it is necessary to submit to the authorities, not only because of possible punishment but also because of conscience.

6This is also why you pay taxes, for the authorities are God's servants, who give their full time to governing. 7Give everyone what you owe him: If you owe taxes, pay taxes; if revenue, then revenue; if respect, then respect; if honor, then honor.

Love, for the Day Is Near

8Let no debt remain outstanding, except the continuing debt to love one another, for he who loves his fellowman has fulfilled the law. 9The commandments, "Do not commit adultery," "Do not murder," "Do not steal," "Do not covet,"[c] and whatever other commandment there may be, are summed up in this one rule: "Love your neighbor as yourself."[d] 10Love does no harm to its neighbor. Therefore love is the fulfillment of the law.

11And do this, understanding the present time. The hour has come for you to wake up from your slumber, because our salvation is nearer now than when we first believed. 12The night is nearly over; the day is almost here. So let us put aside the deeds of darkness and put on the armor of light. 13Let us behave decently, as in the daytime, not in orgies and drunkenness, not in sexual immorality and debauchery, not in dissension and jealousy. 14Rather, clothe yourselves with the Lord Jesus Christ, and do not think about how to gratify the desires of the sinful nature.[e]

The Weak and the Strong

14 Accept him whose faith is weak, without passing judgment on disputable matters. 2One man's faith allows him to eat everything, but another man, whose faith is weak, eats only vegetables. 3The man who eats everything must not look down on him who does not, and the man who does not eat everything must not condemn the man who does, for God has accepted him. 4Who are you to judge someone else's servant? To his own master he stands or falls. And he will stand, for the Lord is able to make him stand.

5One man considers one day more sacred than another; another man considers every day alike. Each one should be fully convinced in his own mind. 6He who regards one day as special,

[a] 19 Deut. 32:35 [b] 20 Prov. 25:21,22
[c] 9 Exodus 20:13-15,17; Deut. 5:17-19,21
[d] 9 Lev. 19:18 [e] 14 Or *the flesh*

13:1–7 Paul pointed out that government exists because God allows it to exist. Therefore, we are told to submit to the government as we would submit to God himself. When authorities do not act with perfect justice, there is sometimes a place for civil disobedience (see Acts 4:13–22). Sometimes we need to resist evil, even if the governing authorities sanction it (see Daniel 6:7–14). But we are called to support and obey authorities that seek to uphold justice. When governing authorities stand in direct contradiction to God's will, we need to seek the support of others and try to change the situation.

13:8–10 Spiritual progress can take place only as we learn to love others. Godly love is not just an emotion we feel; it is an attitude of unselfish concern for others. If we love God and the people around us, we will treat others with respect. We would never harm them, steal from them or deprive them in any way to satisfy our own selfish desires. Love is the opposite of selfishness. As we continue to reflect honestly on our lives, we can use love as the standard by which we judge our behavior. If we measure all our actions against the measuring stick of love and correct them when they do not exemplify love, we will experience true spiritual progress.

13:12–14 When we surrender our lives to God, we are given new identities; we become children of the light. People who live in the light are awake—their eyes are open. They are not in the darkness of spiritual blindness. In other words, they have the ability to see and admit the truth about themselves. One way we can make sure we are walking in the light is to continually take in God's Word and examine our lives in its light. This will keep our eyes open to the truth.

14:1–4 We may find it easy to judge others who are still struggling spiritually. We might even be tempted to show them how strong we are by participating in activities that might cause them to stumble, tempt them to sin or even offend their consciences. Though we may have progressed spiritually to the point that certain activities no longer trouble us, we still need to be sensitive to the fact that our friends may be led astray by our actions. Our love for others should cause us to avoid anything that might lead to their downfall. The more spiritually mature we are, the more responsible we will be to respond to others in a loving way.

does so to the Lord. He who eats meat, eats to
the Lord, for he gives thanks to God; and he
who abstains, does so to the Lord and gives
thanks to God. 7For none of us lives to himself
alone and none of us dies to himself alone. 8If
we live, we live to the Lord; and if we die, we die
to the Lord. So, whether we live or die, we belong to the Lord.

9For this very reason, Christ died and returned to life so that he might be the Lord of
both the dead and the living. 10You, then, why
do you judge your brother? Or why do you look
down on your brother? For we will all stand
before God's judgment seat. 11It is written:

" 'As surely as I live,' says the Lord,
'every knee will bow before me;
every tongue will confess to God.' "[a]

12So then, each of us will give an account of
himself to God.

13Therefore let us stop passing judgment on
one another. Instead, make up your mind not
to put any stumbling block or obstacle in your
brother's way. 14As one who is in the Lord Jesus,
I am fully convinced that no food[b] is unclean
in itself. But if anyone regards something as
unclean, then for him it is unclean. 15If your
brother is distressed because of what you eat,
you are no longer acting in love. Do not by your
eating destroy your brother for whom Christ
died. 16Do not allow what you consider good to
be spoken of as evil. 17For the kingdom of God
is not a matter of eating and drinking, but of
righteousness, peace and joy in the Holy Spirit,
18because anyone who serves Christ in this way
is pleasing to God and approved by men.

19Let us therefore make every effort to do
what leads to peace and to mutual edification.
20Do not destroy the work of God for the sake
of food. All food is clean, but it is wrong for a
man to eat anything that causes someone else to
stumble. 21It is better not to eat meat or drink
wine or to do anything else that will cause your
brother to fall.

22So whatever you believe about these things
keep between yourself and God. Blessed is the
man who does not condemn himself by what
he approves. 23But the man who has doubts is
condemned if he eats, because his eating is not
from faith; and everything that does not come
from faith is sin.

15 We who are strong ought to bear with
the failings of the weak and not to
please ourselves. 2Each of us should please his
neighbor for his good, to build him up. 3For
even Christ did not please himself but, as it is
written: "The insults of those who insult you
have fallen on me."[c] 4For everything that was
written in the past was written to teach us, so
that through endurance and the encouragement
of the Scriptures we might have hope.

5May the God who gives endurance and encouragement give you a spirit of unity among
yourselves as you follow Christ Jesus, 6so that
with one heart and mouth you may glorify the
God and Father of our Lord Jesus Christ.

7Accept one another, then, just as Christ
accepted you, in order to bring praise to God.
8For I tell you that Christ has become a servant
of the Jews[d] on behalf of God's truth, to confirm the promises made to the patriarchs 9so
that the Gentiles may glorify God for his
mercy, as it is written:

"Therefore I will praise you among the
Gentiles;
I will sing hymns to your name."[e]

10Again, it says,

"Rejoice, O Gentiles, with his people."[f]

11And again,

"Praise the Lord, all you Gentiles,
and sing praises to him, all you
peoples."[g]

12And again, Isaiah says,

"The Root of Jesse will spring up,
one who will arise to rule over the
nations;
the Gentiles will hope in him."[h]

13May the God of hope fill you with all joy
and peace as you trust in him, so that you may
overflow with hope by the power of the Holy
Spirit.

a11 Isaiah 45:23 b14 Or *that nothing*
c3 Psalm 69:9 d8 Greek *circumcision*
e9 2 Samuel 22:50; Psalm 18:49 f10 Deut. 32:43
g11 Psalm 117:1 h12 Isaiah 11:10

14:10–12 At times we may be tempted to point out the failures of others instead of looking critically at our own lives. Our primary responsibility isn't to straighten out other people's lives. The job of keeping our own lives straight is more than enough to keep us busy. If we spend our time pointing out the failures of others, we will never make progress ourselves.

14:22–23 At times, we may be tempted to do things that are not necessarily wrong but will lead us toward a fall. Such activities are dangerous, but it is hard to turn away, especially if our friends are involved. We must learn that when we *feel* something is wrong for us to do, it *is* wrong for us. It may not be wrong for someone else, but that is not our concern. We are responsible for our own lives. We must accept this responsibility and keep our own consciences clean, avoiding sin as well as the path that leads toward sin. The people who know us can help us and hold us accountable to stay away from the paths that have led us to sin in the past.

15:1–6 God wants us to show consideration for others. Our spiritual pursuits should never cause us to be selfish. Rather, true spiritual growth will be characterized by our willingness to take others into account and show our concern for them. Christ, who is our highest spiritual example, came to serve others. We must also learn to be patient with one another. This does not come naturally for us. Therefore, we must seek God and ask him to help us develop the attitude of Christ when dealing with others. Then, as we nurture our personal relationships we can show consideration and deference toward others.

Paul the Minister to the Gentiles

[14]I myself am convinced, my brothers, that
you yourselves are full of goodness, complete in
knowledge and competent to instruct one another. [15]I have written you quite boldly on
some points, as if to remind you of them again,
because of the grace God gave me [16]to be a
minister of Christ Jesus to the Gentiles with the
priestly duty of proclaiming the gospel of God,
so that the Gentiles might become an offering
acceptable to God, sanctified by the Holy Spirit.
[17]Therefore I glory in Christ Jesus in my service to God. [18]I will not venture to speak of
anything except what Christ has accomplished
through me in leading the Gentiles to obey God
by what I have said and done— [19]by the power
of signs and miracles, through the power of the
Spirit. So from Jerusalem all the way around to
Illyricum, I have fully proclaimed the gospel of
Christ. [20]It has always been my ambition to
preach the gospel where Christ was not known,
so that I would not be building on someone
else's foundation. [21]Rather, as it is written:

"Those who were not told about him will
see,
and those who have not heard will
understand."[a]

[22]This is why I have often been hindered from
coming to you.

Paul's Plan to Visit Rome

[23]But now that there is no more place for me
to work in these regions, and since I have been
longing for many years to see you, [24]I plan to do
so when I go to Spain. I hope to visit you while
passing through and to have you assist me on
my journey there, after I have enjoyed your
company for a while. [25]Now, however, I am on
my way to Jerusalem in the service of the saints
there. [26]For Macedonia and Achaia were pleased
to make a contribution for the poor among the
saints in Jerusalem. [27]They were pleased to do
it, and indeed they owe it to them. For if the
Gentiles have shared in the Jews' spiritual blessings, they owe it to the Jews to share with them
their material blessings. [28]So after I have completed this task and have made sure that they
have received this fruit, I will go to Spain and
visit you on the way. [29]I know that when I come
to you, I will come in the full measure of the
blessing of Christ.
[30]I urge you, brothers, by our Lord Jesus
Christ and by the love of the Spirit, to join me
in my struggle by praying to God for me. [31]Pray
that I may be rescued from the unbelievers in
Judea and that my service in Jerusalem may be
acceptable to the saints there, [32]so that by God's
will I may come to you with joy and together
with you be refreshed. [33]The God of peace be
with you all. Amen.

Personal Greetings

16 I commend to you our sister Phoebe, a
servant[b] of the church in Cenchrea. [2]I
ask you to receive her in the Lord in a way
worthy of the saints and to give her any help she
may need from you, for she has been a great
help to many people, including me.

[3]Greet Priscilla[c] and Aquila, my fellow workers in Christ Jesus. [4]They risked their lives
for me. Not only I but all the churches of
the Gentiles are grateful to them.
[5]Greet also the church that meets at their
house.
Greet my dear friend Epenetus, who was the
first convert to Christ in the province of
Asia.
[6]Greet Mary, who worked very hard for you.
[7]Greet Andronicus and Junias, my relatives
who have been in prison with me. They are
outstanding among the apostles, and they
were in Christ before I was.
[8]Greet Ampliatus, whom I love in the Lord.
[9]Greet Urbanus, our fellow worker in Christ,
and my dear friend Stachys.
[10]Greet Apelles, tested and approved in Christ.
Greet those who belong to the household of
Aristobulus.
[11]Greet Herodion, my relative.
Greet those in the household of Narcissus
who are in the Lord.
[12]Greet Tryphena and Tryphosa, those women
who work hard in the Lord.
Greet my dear friend Persis, another woman
who has worked very hard in the Lord.
[13]Greet Rufus, chosen in the Lord, and his
mother, who has been a mother to me,
too.
[14]Greet Asyncritus, Phlegon, Hermes, Patrobas,
Hermas and the brothers with them.
[15]Greet Philologus, Julia, Nereus and his sister,
and Olympas and all the saints with them.
[16]Greet one another with a holy kiss.
All the churches of Christ send greetings.

[17]I urge you, brothers, to watch out for those
who cause divisions and put obstacles in your
way that are contrary to the teaching you have
learned. Keep away from them. [18]For such people are not serving our Lord Christ, but their
own appetites. By smooth talk and flattery they
deceive the minds of naive people. [19]Everyone
has heard about your obedience, so I am full of
joy over you; but I want you to be wise about
what is good, and innocent about what is evil.
[20]The God of peace will soon crush Satan
under your feet.
The grace of our Lord Jesus be with you.
[21]Timothy, my fellow worker, sends his
greetings to you, as do Lucius, Jason and Sosipa-
ter, my relatives.

[a] 21 Isaiah 52:15 [b] 1 Or *deaconess* [c] 3 Greek *Prisca,* a variant of *Priscilla*

[22]I, Tertius, who wrote down this letter, greet you in the Lord.

[23]Gaius, whose hospitality I and the whole church here enjoy, sends you his greetings.

Erastus, who is the city's director of public works, and our brother Quartus send you their greetings.[a]

[25]Now to him who is able to establish you by my gospel and the proclamation of Jesus Christ, according to the revelation of the mystery hidden for long ages past, [26]but now revealed and made known through the prophetic writings by the command of the eternal God, so that all nations might believe and obey him— [27]to the only wise God be glory forever through Jesus Christ! Amen.

[a]23 Some manuscripts *their greetings. [24]May the grace of our Lord Jesus Christ be with all of you. Amen.*

1 CORINTHIANS

The Big Picture

A. THE CHURCH IN SPIRITUAL DECLINE (1:1–6:20)

1. Divisions: Infighting Among the Believers (1:1–4:21)
2. Disorders: Serving Self Before God (5:1–6:20)

B. THE CHURCH'S ROLE IN SPIRITUAL RENEWAL (7:1–16:24)

1. Contentment: Being Happy Where We Are (7:1-40)
2. Instruction: Personal Worship (8:1–10:33)
3. Instruction: Public Worship (11:1–14:40)
4. Encouragement: Christ Is With Us (15:1–16:24)

The Greek city of Corinth was noted for its corruption, immorality and pagan religions. Following Christ in that setting meant leaving behind many of the practices accepted by the larger society. This presented the new believers with all kinds of temptations and problems.

Though the Corinthian believers had received new life in Christ, they still had much to learn. It would take time for them to mature. These believers needed further instructions about following Christ and understanding God's perspectives about right and wrong. Paul wrote this letter to help them make progress—to give them advice about how to change.

Our spiritual renewal often involves a similar struggle with the surrounding environment. Though we determine to change, the world in which we live stays much the same. We live and work with the same people, go to many of the same places and do many of the same things—all while trying to make significant changes in our lives. The feelings of loneliness that result can make us as vulnerable as the Corinthian believers once were.

Despite the difficulties we face, God understands our struggle. That is why he has given us his Word, his power and his people; they are all available to help us. This letter alone contains numerous insights for ongoing spiritual renewal. Through the book of 1 Corinthians we can learn how to separate ourselves from our old ways of life, begin living lives surrendered to God's righteous rule and follow new standards. Our spiritual renewal may be slow, maybe even painful, but by God's grace and our commitment, God will transform us.

Spiritual Renewal Themes

JESUS IS THE CENTER OF OUR SPIRITUAL RENEWAL

The Corinthian believers' lives illustrate what happens when we take our eyes off Jesus Christ. Though these people were followers of Christ, they identified themselves primarily with their various teachers. This caused unnecessary divisions among them and kept them from making progress in their spiritual growth. While the support and advice of others are important, our Savior is Jesus Christ. He must be the center of all our efforts; we

must focus on him and honor him above any person or plan for spiritual growth.

FREEDOM WITH LOVING RESTRAINT

The new believers in Corinth had to make a clean break with their past. Some of these believers were mature and no longer bothered by the temptations that had plagued them as new Christians. But others were not so secure in their faith. Paul instructed the more mature believers not to flaunt their freedom around those who still struggled. Our successful spiritual growth doesn't give us license to be inconsiderate or insensitive to others. We can show support for one another by being careful about how we use our freedom. We will always have this responsibility to care for one another.

LIFE IS TO BE ENJOYED RESPONSIBLY

The believers at Corinth lived in a very immoral, pleasure-seeking society. The standards of conduct that God set for them were quite different from the standards of their culture. But if the believers thought God's standards seemed too restrictive, they were mistaken. Longing for "freedom" apart from God's laws is like a train longing for freedom from the railroad track. The sinful behaviors that seem so tempting will only leave us stuck if we give in, and derailed from the good life God intends for us. God challenges us to live uncompromising lives because he knows that only then will we enjoy life at its deepest level and progress smoothly in our spiritual lives. What may appear to be narrow limitations in God's standards are actually guidelines designed to help us experience life as it was meant to be!

THE INVITATION TO LOVE

One of the most beautiful passages on love ever written is found in chapter 13 of this letter to the Corinthians. It describes love in terms of selfless action, not merely as an emotion. If we love, then we will act in selfless ways. When we don't feel loving or don't feel loved, 1 Corinthians 13 is a wonderful reminder of how God loves us and how we can show love to others.

Essential Facts

PURPOSE:
To encourage the Corinthian believers to resolve their problems and honor God.

AUTHOR:
The apostle Paul.

AUDIENCE:
The church at Corinth, a city in Greece.

DATE WRITTEN:
Around A.D. 55, near the end of Paul's three-year stay in Ephesus.

SETTING:
Corinth was a large, cosmopolitan city that teemed with idolatry and immorality. The church in Corinth was fairly new and was made up of many non-Jewish (Gentile) believers.

KEY VERSE:
"But by the grace of God I am what I am, and his grace to me was not without effect. No, I worked harder than all of them—yet not I, but the grace of God that was with me" (15:10).

KEY PEOPLE AND RELATIONSHIPS:
Paul with Timothy, Chloe's household and the Corinthian believers.

1 Paul, called to be an apostle of Christ Jesus by the will of God, and our brother Sosthenes,

2 To the church of God in Corinth, to those sanctified in Christ Jesus and called to be holy, together with all those everywhere who call on the name of our Lord Jesus Christ—their Lord and ours:

3 Grace and peace to you from God our Father and the Lord Jesus Christ.

Thanksgiving

4 I always thank God for you because of his grace given you in Christ Jesus. 5 For in him you have been enriched in every way—in all your speaking and in all your knowledge— 6 because our testimony about Christ was confirmed in you. 7 Therefore you do not lack any spiritual gift as you eagerly wait for our Lord Jesus Christ to be revealed. 8 He will keep you strong to the end, so that you will be blameless on the day of our Lord Jesus Christ. 9 God, who has called you into fellowship with his Son Jesus Christ our Lord, is faithful.

Divisions in the Church

10 I appeal to you, brothers, in the name of our Lord Jesus Christ, that all of you agree with one another so that there may be no divisions among you and that you may be perfectly united in mind and thought. 11 My brothers, some from Chloe's household have informed me that there are quarrels among you. 12 What I mean is this: One of you says, "I follow Paul"; another, "I follow Apollos"; another, "I follow Cephas[a]"; still another, "I follow Christ."

13 Is Christ divided? Was Paul crucified for you? Were you baptized into[b] the name of Paul? 14 I am thankful that I did not baptize any of you except Crispus and Gaius, 15 so no one can say that you were baptized into my name. 16 (Yes, I also baptized the household of Stephanas; beyond that, I don't remember if I baptized anyone else.) 17 For Christ did not send me to baptize, but to preach the gospel—not with words of human wisdom, lest the cross of Christ be emptied of its power.

Christ the Wisdom and Power of God

18 For the message of the cross is foolishness to those who are perishing, but to us who are being saved it is the power of God. 19 For it is written:

> "I will destroy the wisdom of the wise;
> the intelligence of the intelligent I will frustrate."[c]

20 Where is the wise man? Where is the scholar? Where is the philosopher of this age? Has not God made foolish the wisdom of the world? 21 For since in the wisdom of God the world through its wisdom did not know him, God was pleased through the foolishness of what was preached to save those who believe. 22 Jews demand miraculous signs and Greeks look for wisdom, 23 but we preach Christ crucified: a stumbling block to Jews and foolishness to Gentiles, 24 but to those whom God has called, both Jews and Greeks, Christ the power of God and the wisdom of God. 25 For the foolishness of God is wiser than man's wisdom, and the weakness of God is stronger than man's strength.

26 Brothers, think of what you were when you were called. Not many of you were wise by human standards; not many were influential; not many were of noble birth. 27 But God chose the foolish things of the world to shame the wise; God chose the weak things of the world to shame the strong. 28 He chose the lowly things of this world and the despised things—and the things that are not—to nullify the things that are, 29 so that no one may boast before him. 30 It is because of him that you are in Christ Jesus, who has become for us wisdom from God—that is, our righteousness, holiness and redemption.

[a] *12* That is, Peter [b] *13* Or *in;* also in verse 15
[c] *19* Isaiah 29:14

1:2 Corinth was a giant, cultural melting pot with a diversity of ethnic groups, religions, intellectual perspectives and moral standards. The city had a reputation for being fiercely independent and was as decadent as any city in the known world. Idolatry flourished, and there were more than a dozen pagan temples that at one time employed at least a thousand religious prostitutes. The new believers in this city had to deal with many deep-rooted habits and attitudes as they sought to nurture their new life in Christ. The world of Corinth was not unlike much of the world today.

1:4–9 Although there were problems among the Corinthian believers, Paul began his letter to them on a positive note. He understood that confronting others about their failures is more effective when we approach them diplomatically. By recognizing the good things in the lives of those we need to confront, we show that we are concerned about them and value them as people.

1:18–19 Some of the Corinthian believers followed the human wisdom of the day, which questioned the idea of salvation in Christ. It seemed too simple! How could God forgive us freely through Christ's death on the cross? Some of the Corinthians believed they needed to do or know something special to be saved. Paul clearly stated that we only need willing, repentant hearts to receive God's power and forgiveness. We cannot overcome the power of sin in our lives by our own power or ability. In fact, a life of self-sufficiency can ultimately be self-destructive. When we surrender our lives to God, we accept his way—the way of the cross. Only then can we experience his power in our lives.

1:26–31 Paul illustrated that God's plan for our redemption doesn't utilize our human wisdom, strength or skill. We don't have to be famous or rich to receive God's forgiveness and power. Self-sufficient people may have a hard time accepting this. We want to feel in control and worthy of our salvation. But until we admit that we need God's help to change, we will not be able to redirect the course of our lives.

31Therefore, as it is written: "Let him who boasts boast in the Lord."[a]

2 When I came to you, brothers, I did not come with eloquence or superior wisdom as I proclaimed to you the testimony about God.[b] 2For I resolved to know nothing while I was with you except Jesus Christ and him crucified. 3I came to you in weakness and fear, and with much trembling. 4My message and my preaching were not with wise and persuasive words, but with a demonstration of the Spirit's power, 5so that your faith might not rest on men's wisdom, but on God's power.

Wisdom From the Spirit

6We do, however, speak a message of wisdom among the mature, but not the wisdom of this age or of the rulers of this age, who are coming to nothing. 7No, we speak of God's secret wisdom, a wisdom that has been hidden and that God destined for our glory before time began. 8None of the rulers of this age understood it, for if they had, they would not have crucified the Lord of glory. 9However, as it is written:

"No eye has seen,
  no ear has heard,
no mind has conceived
  what God has prepared for those who
    love him"[c]—

10but God has revealed it to us by his Spirit.

The Spirit searches all things, even the deep things of God. 11For who among men knows the thoughts of a man except the man's spirit within him? In the same way no one knows the thoughts of God except the Spirit of God. 12We have not received the spirit of the world but the Spirit who is from God, that we may understand what God has freely given us. 13This is what we speak, not in words taught us by human wisdom but in words taught by the Spirit, expressing spiritual truths in spiritual words.[d] 14The man without the Spirit does not accept the things that come from the Spirit of God, for they are foolishness to him, and he cannot understand them, because they are spiritually discerned. 15The spiritual man makes judgments about all things, but he himself is not subject to any man's judgment:

16"For who has known the mind of the Lord
  that he may instruct him?"[e]

But we have the mind of Christ.

On Divisions in the Church

3 Brothers, I could not address you as spiritual but as worldly—mere infants in Christ. 2I gave you milk, not solid food, for you were not yet ready for it. Indeed, you are still not ready. 3You are still worldly. For since there is jealousy and quarreling among you, are you not worldly? Are you not acting like mere men? 4For when one says, "I follow Paul," and another, "I follow Apollos," are you not mere men?

5What, after all, is Apollos? And what is Paul? Only servants, through whom you came to believe—as the Lord has assigned to each his task. 6I planted the seed, Apollos watered it, but God made it grow. 7So neither he who plants nor he who waters is anything, but only God, who makes things grow. 8The man who plants and the man who waters have one purpose, and each will be rewarded according to his own la-

[a]31 Jer. 9:24 [b]1 Some manuscripts *as I proclaimed to you God's mystery* [c]9 Isaiah 64:4 [d]13 Or *Spirit, interpreting spiritual truths to spiritual men* [e]16 Isaiah 40:13

2:1–5 Many times when we seek to help others, we overwhelm them with a series of complicated instructions. Paul realized that complex explanations and mandates would only confuse the Corinthians, making them think that salvation was only for intellectuals or dependent on special wisdom or knowledge. So Paul brought them the plain message of the gospel, sharing simply that there is nothing we can do to save ourselves; God has done everything necessary for our deliverance. As we share God's message with others, we need to remember to speak clearly and simply, trusting the power of the Holy Spirit to work in their lives.

2:7 God has always had a good plan for us from the beginning of time. If we ask him to work in our lives, no matter how many mistakes we have made, God can still turn things around so that they work out according to his plan. Our part is to surrender our lives to him and seek to follow his will as he reveals it to us.

2:9–10 When we feel our lives are heading in the wrong direction, we may blame God or feel that somehow he had made things worse. Paul reminded the Corinthians that God had planned wonderful things for them, much better than they could have imagined. Paul's message applies to us, too. If we surrender our lives to God, he can build new lives for us that are beyond our wildest dreams.

2:11–12 Some of us may wonder how we could ever know God's will for our lives. Paul tells us that we can know God's mind and heart because he has placed his Holy Spirit within us to communicate these things to us. God's presence in our lives will guide us in the way he wants us to go. Often the Holy Spirit uses God's Word, the Bible, to communicate with us. What a privilege!

2:14–15 Our ability to see the truth is a gift from God. We must begin our quest for spiritual renewal by seeking God and surrendering to him. When we do this, we receive God's forgiveness and the gift of the Holy Spirit. In turn, it is the Holy Spirit who reveals God's truth and helps us understand God's Word (see John 16:13). The person who does not surrender to God will have no access to the understanding that only the Holy Spirit can give.

3:1–4 Part of becoming spiritually mature involves the realization that following our own desires leads down a dead-end street. As long as we demand our own way and are divisive, we are infants in our faith. We should examine our lives to see if this infantile attitude characterizes our relationships as well. If so, we need to confess our sin and ask God to help us grow up.

3:5–6 Each person has a part to play in accomplishing God's work on earth. No one person is all-important, and no one is unimportant. We must beware of elevating some individuals and tearing down others, for we all should work together to do God's will. Our focus should be to elevate God and show respect for all who do his work. We should all do our part—planting, watering or harvesting—to accomplish God's plan.

bor. 9For we are God's fellow workers; you are God's field, God's building.

10By the grace God has given me, I laid a foundation as an expert builder, and someone else is building on it. But each one should be careful how he builds. 11For no one can lay any foundation other than the one already laid, which is Jesus Christ. 12If any man builds on this foundation using gold, silver, costly stones, wood, hay or straw, 13his work will be shown for what it is, because the Day will bring it to light. It will be revealed with fire, and the fire will test the quality of each man's work. 14If what he has built survives, he will receive his reward. 15If it is burned up, he will suffer loss; he himself will be saved, but only as one escaping through the flames.

16Don't you know that you yourselves are God's temple and that God's Spirit lives in you? 17If anyone destroys God's temple, God will destroy him; for God's temple is sacred, and you are that temple.

18Do not deceive yourselves. If any one of you thinks he is wise by the standards of this age, he should become a "fool" so that he may become wise. 19For the wisdom of this world is foolishness in God's sight. As it is written: "He catches the wise in their craftiness"[a]; 20and again, "The Lord knows that the thoughts of the wise are futile."[b] 21So then, no more boasting about men! All things are yours, 22whether Paul or Apollos or Cephas[c] or the world or life or death or the present or the future—all are yours, 23and you are of Christ, and Christ is of God.

Apostles of Christ

4 So then, men ought to regard us as servants of Christ and as those entrusted with the secret things of God. 2Now it is required that those who have been given a trust must prove faithful. 3I care very little if I am judged by you or by any human court; indeed, I do not even judge myself. 4My conscience is clear, but that does not make me innocent. It is the Lord who judges me. 5Therefore judge nothing before the appointed time; wait till the Lord comes. He will bring to light what is hidden in darkness and will expose the motives of men's hearts. At that time each will receive his praise from God.

6Now, brothers, I have applied these things to myself and Apollos for your benefit, so that you may learn from us the meaning of the saying, "Do not go beyond what is written." Then you will not take pride in one man over against another. 7For who makes you different from anyone else? What do you have that you did not receive? And if you did receive it, why do you boast as though you did not?

8Already you have all you want! Already you have become rich! You have become kings—and that without us! How I wish that you really had become kings so that we might be kings with you! 9For it seems to me that God has put us apostles on display at the end of the procession, like men condemned to die in the arena. We have been made a spectacle to the whole universe, to angels as well as to men. 10We are fools for Christ, but you are so wise in Christ! We are weak, but you are strong! You are honored, we are dishonored! 11To this very hour we go hungry and thirsty, we are in rags, we are brutally treated, we are homeless. 12We work hard with our own hands. When we are cursed, we bless; when we are persecuted, we endure it; 13when we are slandered, we answer kindly. Up to this moment we have become the scum of the earth, the refuse of the world.

14I am not writing this to shame you, but to warn you, as my dear children. 15Even though you have ten thousand guardians in Christ, you do not have many fathers, for in Christ Jesus I became your father through the gospel. 16Therefore I urge you to imitate me. 17For this reason I am sending to you Timothy, my son whom I love, who is faithful in the Lord. He will remind you of my way of life in Christ Jesus, which agrees with what I teach everywhere in every church.

18Some of you have become arrogant, as if I were not coming to you. 19But I will come to you very soon, if the Lord is willing, and then I will find out not only how these arrogant people are talking, but what power they have. 20For the kingdom of God is not a matter of talk but of power. 21What do you prefer? Shall I come to you with a whip, or in love and with a gentle spirit?

Expel the Immoral Brother!

5 It is actually reported that there is sexual immorality among you, and of a kind that

a19 Job 5:13 *b20* Psalm 94:11 *c22* That is, Peter

3:18–20 Sometimes our intelligence gets in the way of our spiritual progress. Following God's plan will not always make perfect sense to us. As we analyze what God calls us to do, we may find it somewhat foolish, demeaning or even embarrassing at times. Regardless of how comfortable we feel with God's plan, God's way is best. Analyzing and seeking understanding are valuable pursuits, but we must ultimately follow God's will even if it doesn't make perfect sense to us.

4:17 Paul sent Timothy to remind the Corinthian believers of what Paul had taught them. The apostle realized that the Corinthians needed someone to hold them accountable to the truth they had been taught. He wanted Timothy to encourage them to persevere in their faith. One of the best ways to protect ourselves from sinful behavior is to be accountable to someone else. Through mentors and those who hold us accountable to obey God's Word, we develop the kind of faithfulness that is essential to spiritual growth.

5:1–5 We face many of the temptations that the Corinthians faced. Like the people of Corinth, we tend to put on a blindfold and tell ourselves that everything is all right. Ignoring the problems of illicit sexual activity can build barriers between ourselves and others. In time, we even grow distant from God. Refusal to admit the truth lets such problems in our churches and communities fes-

does not occur even among pagans: A man has his father's wife. 2And you are proud! Shouldn't you rather have been filled with grief and have put out of your fellowship the man who did this? 3Even though I am not physically present, I am with you in spirit. And I have already passed judgment on the one who did this, just as if I were present. 4When you are assembled in the name of our Lord Jesus and I am with you in spirit, and the power of our Lord Jesus is present, 5hand this man over to Satan, so that the sinful nature[a] may be destroyed and his spirit saved on the day of the Lord.

6Your boasting is not good. Don't you know that a little yeast works through the whole batch of dough? 7Get rid of the old yeast that you may be a new batch without yeast—as you really are. For Christ, our Passover lamb, has been sacrificed. 8Therefore let us keep the Festival, not with the old yeast, the yeast of malice and wickedness, but with bread without yeast, the bread of sincerity and truth.

9I have written you in my letter not to associate with sexually immoral people— 10not at all meaning the people of this world who are immoral, or the greedy and swindlers, or idolaters. In that case you would have to leave this world. 11But now I am writing you that you must not associate with anyone who calls himself a brother but is sexually immoral or greedy, an idolater or a slanderer, a drunkard or a swindler. With such a man do not even eat.

12What business is it of mine to judge those outside the church? Are you not to judge those inside? 13God will judge those outside. "Expel the wicked man from among you."[b]

Lawsuits Among Believers

6 If any of you has a dispute with another, dare he take it before the ungodly for judgment instead of before the saints? 2Do you not know that the saints will judge the world? And if you are to judge the world, are you not competent to judge trivial cases? 3Do you not know that we will judge angels? How much more the things of this life! 4Therefore, if you have disputes about such matters, appoint as judges even men of little account in the church![c] 5I say this to shame you. Is it possible that there is nobody among you wise enough to judge a dispute between believers? 6But instead, one brother goes to law against another—and this in front of unbelievers!

7The very fact that you have lawsuits among you means you have been completely defeated already. Why not rather be wronged? Why not rather be cheated? 8Instead, you yourselves cheat and do wrong, and you do this to your brothers.

9Do you not know that the wicked will not inherit the kingdom of God? Do not be deceived: Neither the sexually immoral nor idolaters nor adulterers nor male prostitutes nor homosexual offenders 10nor thieves nor the greedy nor drunkards nor slanderers nor swindlers will inherit the kingdom of God. 11And that is what some of you were. But you were washed, you were sanctified, you were justified in the name of the Lord Jesus Christ and by the Spirit of our God.

Sexual Immorality

12"Everything is permissible for me"—but not everything is beneficial. "Everything is permissible for me"—but I will not be mastered by anything. 13"Food for the stomach and the stomach for food"—but God will destroy them both. The body is not meant for sexual immorality, but for the Lord, and the Lord for the body. 14By his power God raised the Lord from the dead, and he will raise us also. 15Do you not know that your bodies are members of Christ himself? Shall I then take the members of Christ and unite them with a prostitute? Never! 16Do you not know that he who unites himself with a prostitute is one with her in body? For it is

[a]5 Or *that his body;* or *that the flesh* [b]13 Deut. 17:7; 19:19; 21:21; 22:21,24; 24:7 [c]4 Or *matters, do you appoint as judges men of little account in the church?*

---

ter until individuals and families are torn apart. We need to open our eyes to the sins around us and confront them as a community, just as Paul advised the Corinthians to do.

5:6–8 Paul urged the Corinthian believers to remove the unrepentant sinner from their fellowship; otherwise his destructive activities would destroy the church. Notice that when Paul told the Corinthians to remove this unrepentant sinner, he also reminded them to involve themselves in wholesome activities. We must also disassociate with believers who refuse to repent of sin and pull away from our own destructive activities and relationships. We need to involve ourselves in wholesome activities and build relationships with people who will encourage us with sincerity and truth.

5:9–13 Paul warned his people to avoid close relationships with people who refused to see the truth about their sin. Yet Paul didn't want the believers to isolate themselves from unbelievers. He wanted the Christians to share the Good News with people who needed to hear the message. We, too, need to reach out to unbelievers so that they can see Christ in us and repent of their sins.

6:1–6 Taking someone to court is often the world's way out of a conflict. Instead of working out their problems, people prefer to take them to an impartial judge. Though this can be helpful at times, dealing with conflict in such an indirect way usually leads to separation rather than reconciliation. Paul cautioned the Corinthian believers not to settle their disputes in front of unbelieving judges. If we claim to follow Christ, we need to resolve our conflicts with other believers through the help of the Holy Spirit and within the church whenever possible. In this way we testify to the world that true harmony can be found in Christ.

6:12 Paul wanted the Corinthian believers to avoid involvement in activities that would seduce them back into their old ways of life. Many of our old activities and relationships are not wrong in themselves. However, staying involved in these things may tempt us to sin. In that case, these activities are not good for us. We need to avoid anything that might stop or slow our spiritual growth.

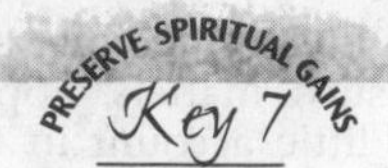

Beware of Spiritual Losses

1 Corinthians 6:9–13 Preserving our spiritual gains requires that we be careful about our physical and sexual appetites. Overindulging the appetites of the flesh with food, drink, sex or anything else can derail our spiritual lives. We must keep our appetites satisfied in ways that God desires. If we don't, our appetites can rule us and ruin us.

The Old Testament tells us that one day Esau came home so hungry that he promised his birthright to his younger brother in exchange for a bowl of stew (see Genesis 25:29–34). We are warned, "See that no one is sexually immoral, or is godless like Esau, who for a single meal sold his inheritance rights as the oldest son. Afterward, as you know, when he wanted to inherit this blessing, he was rejected. He could bring about no change of mind, though he sought the blessing with tears" (Hebrews 12:16–17). The apostle Paul wrote, " 'Everything is permissible for me'—but I will not be mastered by anything" (1 Corinthians 6:12).

We need to satisfy our appetites in appropriate ways so we don't become starved and susceptible to temptation. Some things may not qualify directly as sin, but they may exert such control over us that it's best to avoid them altogether—like taking a second look at something that might stir up lust or going to a candy store if we tend to overeat. If we let the demands of our appetites overpower us, we risk great spiritual losses.

Turn to 1 Timothy 4.

said, "The two will become one flesh."[a] 17But
he who unites himself with the Lord is one with
him in spirit.
18Flee from sexual immorality. All other sins
a man commits are outside his body, but he
who sins sexually sins against his own body.
19Do you not know that your body is a temple
of the Holy Spirit, who is in you, whom you
have received from God? You are not your own;
20you were bought at a price. Therefore honor
God with your body.

Marriage

7 Now for the matters you wrote about: It is
good for a man not to marry.[b] 2But since
there is so much immorality, each man should
have his own wife, and each woman her own
husband. 3The husband should fulfill his marital duty to his wife, and likewise the wife to her
husband. 4The wife's body does not belong to
her alone but also to her husband. In the same
way, the husband's body does not belong to
him alone but also to his wife. 5Do not deprive
each other except by mutual consent and for
a time, so that you may devote yourselves to
prayer. Then come together again so that Satan
will not tempt you because of your lack of self-
control. 6I say this as a concession, not as a
command. 7I wish that all men were as I am.
But each man has his own gift from God; one
has this gift, another has that.
8Now to the unmarried and the widows I say:
It is good for them to stay unmarried, as I am.
9But if they cannot control themselves, they
should marry, for it is better to marry than to
burn with passion.

[a]16 Gen. 2:24 [b]1 Or *"It is good for a man not to have sexual relations with a woman."*

6:18–20 The effects of sexual sins are broad and devastating. Sexual sin affects us like no other sin. When we sin sexually, we sin not only against ourselves but also against other people and against God. Our body is the dwelling place of God's Holy Spirit; our bodies belong to God. What better reason for taking care of them and seeking new life in Christ?

7:2–5 Marriage is the appropriate place for sexual expression and fulfillment. Our bodies don't belong to us; they belong to God. But Paul also says that our bodies belong to our spouses as well. If we seek sexual fulfillment outside of marriage, we will find ourselves in the trap of selfish pleasure seeking. Since we belong to God and our spouses, we should act in ways that bring them great joy. When we keep our sexuality within the bounds of marriage, we will discover the joy that comes from living faithfully with another person and before God.

7:8–9 If we are single, we may feel that our spiritual growth would be easier if we had the help of a spouse. If we are married, we may think we could focus more on spiritual growth if we were unmarried. Whether we are single or married, we will all have difficulties to deal with. When we find ourselves wishing we were in a different state, we are often attempting to avoid the responsibilities of our present situation. We should seek ways to improve our current situation rather than abandon it for something else. Abandoning a relationship or desperately grasping at a new one will never solve our problems.

THE SPIRITUAL DISCIPLINES

Fasting

Saying a Special Yes to God

1 Corinthians 7:5 We are body-and-soul people, united both in our physical and our spiritual lives. What affects the spirit affects the body, and what affects the body affects the spirit. When we fast, we affirm this relationship between body and soul. Fasting seeks to cultivate spiritual growth through a physical discipline.

Fasting is most frequently associated with food, but it is also mentioned in this passage with respect to marital relations. Paul mentions that a husband and wife may refrain from sexual intimacy for a limited time so that they can give themselves more completely to prayer. Note that this is a mutual decision, taken to pursue renewal in prayer. This form of fasting from something honorable helps check our appetites by interrupting the normal physical routines that motivate and direct so many of our activities. By saying no in this way, we prepare ourselves to say a special yes to God. Paul indirectly spoke of gaining this freedom *to do* things by overtly speaking of freeing ourselves *from* things: " 'Everything is permissible for me'—but not everything is beneficial. 'Everything is permissible for me'—but I will not be mastered by anything" (6:12). When we fast from food, sexual relations or anything else, we are not merely giving up something; we are taking back control over our lives and giving ourselves more fully to the Lord.

It is important to emphasize that fasting does not devalue the physical world. "Everything God created is good" (1 Timothy 4:4). Paul's counsel in no way diminishes the value of marital intimacy. Instead, he reminds us that we may abstain from something good for a time in order to do something special for our spiritual lives.

Putting It Into Practice

Are there good things from which you could fast in order to draw closer to God? Are there appetites that control your spiritual welfare more than they should? Choose one activity that dominates your time and interests, and fast from it for a set period of time. Ask God to make your fast a time of spiritual renewal.

For more on fasting, turn to 2 Chronicles 20.

10To the married I give this command (not I, but the Lord): A wife must not separate from her husband. 11But if she does, she must remain unmarried or else be reconciled to her husband. And a husband must not divorce his wife.

12To the rest I say this (I, not the Lord): If any brother has a wife who is not a believer and she is willing to live with him, he must not divorce her. 13And if a woman has a husband who is not a believer and he is willing to live with her, she must not divorce him. 14For the unbelieving husband has been sanctified through his wife, and the unbelieving wife has been sanctified through her believing husband. Otherwise your children would be unclean, but as it is, they are holy.

15But if the unbeliever leaves, let him do so. A believing man or woman is not bound in such circumstances; God has called us to live in peace. 16How do you know, wife, whether you will save your husband? Or, how do you know, husband, whether you will save your wife?

17Nevertheless, each one should retain the place in life that the Lord assigned to him and to which God has called him. This is the rule I lay down in all the churches. 18Was a man already circumcised when he was called? He should not become uncircumcised. Was a man uncircumcised when he was called? He should not be circumcised. 19Circumcision is nothing and uncircumcision is nothing. Keeping God's commands is what counts. 20Each one should remain in the situation which he was in when God called him. 21Were you a slave when you were called? Don't let it trouble you—although if you can gain your freedom, do so. 22For he who was a slave when he was called by the Lord is the Lord's freedman; similarly, he who was a free man when he was called is Christ's slave. 23You were bought at a price; do not become slaves of men. 24Brothers, each man, as responsible to God, should remain in the situation God called him to.

25Now about virgins: I have no command from the Lord, but I give a judgment as one who by the Lord's mercy is trustworthy. 26Because of the present crisis, I think that it is good for you to remain as you are. 27Are you married? Do not seek a divorce. Are you unmarried? Do not look for a wife. 28But if you do marry, you have not sinned; and if a virgin marries, she has not sinned. But those who marry will face many troubles in this life, and I want to spare you this.

29What I mean, brothers, is that the time is short. From now on those who have wives should live as if they had none; 30those who mourn, as if they did not; those who are happy, as if they were not; those who buy something, as if it were not theirs to keep; 31those who use the things of the world, as if not engrossed in them. For this world in its present form is passing away.

32I would like you to be free from concern. An unmarried man is concerned about the Lord's affairs—how he can please the Lord. 33But a married man is concerned about the affairs of this world—how he can please his wife— 34and his interests are divided. An unmarried woman or virgin is concerned about the Lord's affairs: Her aim is to be devoted to the Lord in both body and spirit. But a married woman is concerned about the affairs of this world—how she can please her husband. 35I am saying this for your own good, not to restrict you, but that you may live in a right way in undivided devotion to the Lord.

36If anyone thinks he is acting improperly toward the virgin he is engaged to, and if she is getting along in years and he feels he ought to marry, he should do as he wants. He is not sinning. They should get married. 37But the man who has settled the matter in his own mind, who is under no compulsion but has control over his own will, and who has made up his mind not to marry the virgin—this man also does the right thing. 38So then, he who marries the virgin does right, but he who does not marry her does even better.[a]

39A woman is bound to her husband as long as he lives. But if her husband dies, she is free to marry anyone she wishes, but he must belong to the Lord. 40In my judgment, she is happier if she stays as she is—and I think that I too have the Spirit of God.

[a]36-38 Or *36If anyone thinks he is not treating his daughter properly, and if she is getting along in years, and he feels she ought to marry, he should do as he wants. He is not sinning. He should let her get married. 37But the man who has settled the matter in his own mind, who is under no compulsion but has control over his own will, and who has made up his mind to keep the virgin unmarried—this man also does the right thing. 38So then, he who gives his virgin in marriage does right, but he who does not give her in marriage does even better.*

7:10–15 Divorce has painfully touched many of our lives, either as participants or as family and friends of divorced couples. Paul began his words on this subject with a firm reminder of God's command not to divorce. Yet Paul recognized that there are situations in which divorce is a legitimate option (7:15). The underlying principle of marriage and the command not to divorce are found here: God wants us to live in harmony with one another. When we do not experience harmony in our relationship with our spouse, we both need to examine our lives to see where we need to change. Often a marriage counselor is needed to facilitate this process. Divorce is an option only when one of the partners refuses to remain faithful to his or her marriage commitment.

7:20–24 The Roman world was filled with oppressed people, many of whom had been taken into slavery as children. Some of these slaves came to believe in Christ. Naturally, they yearned for their freedom and were tempted to believe that they could be better Christians if only they were free. We sometimes fall into the same trap. We may look at others and think that our lives would be easier if we only had their circumstances or situation. Instead of seeking new situations, we should seek a new relationship with God just as we are. Once we surrender our lives to God, we will have a new power at work within us—regardless of our outward circumstances.

Food Sacrificed to Idols

8 Now about food sacrificed to idols: We know that we all possess knowledge.[a] Knowledge puffs up, but love builds up. 2The man who thinks he knows something does not yet know as he ought to know. 3But the man who loves God is known by God.

4So then, about eating food sacrificed to idols: We know that an idol is nothing at all in the world and that there is no God but one. 5For even if there are so-called gods, whether in heaven or on earth (as indeed there are many "gods" and many "lords"), 6yet for us there is but one God, the Father, from whom all things came and for whom we live; and there is but one Lord, Jesus Christ, through whom all things came and through whom we live.

7But not everyone knows this. Some people are still so accustomed to idols that when they eat such food they think of it as having been sacrificed to an idol, and since their conscience is weak, it is defiled. 8But food does not bring us near to God; we are no worse if we do not eat, and no better if we do.

9Be careful, however, that the exercise of your freedom does not become a stumbling block to the weak. 10For if anyone with a weak conscience sees you who have this knowledge eating in an idol's temple, won't he be emboldened to eat what has been sacrificed to idols? 11So this weak brother, for whom Christ died, is destroyed by your knowledge. 12When you sin against your brothers in this way and wound their weak conscience, you sin against Christ. 13Therefore, if what I eat causes my brother to fall into sin, I will never eat meat again, so that I will not cause him to fall.

The Rights of an Apostle

9 Am I not free? Am I not an apostle? Have I not seen Jesus our Lord? Are you not the result of my work in the Lord? 2Even though I may not be an apostle to others, surely I am to you! For you are the seal of my apostleship in the Lord.

3This is my defense to those who sit in judgment on me. 4Don't we have the right to food and drink? 5Don't we have the right to take a believing wife along with us, as do the other apostles and the Lord's brothers and Cephas[b]? 6Or is it only I and Barnabas who must work for a living?

7Who serves as a soldier at his own expense? Who plants a vineyard and does not eat of its grapes? Who tends a flock and does not drink of the milk? 8Do I say this merely from a human point of view? Doesn't the Law say the same thing? 9For it is written in the Law of Moses: "Do not muzzle an ox while it is treading out the grain."[c] Is it about oxen that God is concerned? 10Surely he says this for us, doesn't he? Yes, this was written for us, because when the plowman plows and the thresher threshes, they ought to do so in the hope of sharing in the harvest. 11If we have sown spiritual seed among you, is it too much if we reap a material harvest from you? 12If others have this right of support from you, shouldn't we have it all the more?

But we did not use this right. On the contrary, we put up with anything rather than hinder the gospel of Christ. 13Don't you know that those who work in the temple get their food from the temple, and those who serve at the altar share in what is offered on the altar? 14In the same way, the Lord has commanded that those who preach the gospel should receive their living from the gospel.

15But I have not used any of these rights. And I am not writing this in the hope that you will do such things for me. I would rather die than have anyone deprive me of this boast. 16Yet when I preach the gospel, I cannot boast, for I am compelled to preach. Woe to me if I do not preach the gospel! 17If I preach voluntarily, I have a reward; if not voluntarily, I am simply discharging the trust committed to me. 18What then is my reward? Just this: that in preaching the gospel I may offer it free of charge, and so not make use of my rights in preaching it.

19Though I am free and belong to no man,

[a] 1 Or *"We all possess knowledge," as you say* [b] 5 That is, Peter [c] 9 Deut. 25:4

8:1–3 True spirituality is not evidenced by how much we know but by how well we love others. Therefore, we should not reflect on our lives to see how much we know as compared to others. Rather, our personal reflection should consider how we are demonstrating love in our everyday lives.

8:10–13 We may exercise our personal freedom until it causes others to stumble in their faith. We may justify our actions, but love is the only principle that will guide our lives properly. When we love, our freedom to do certain things will not be as important as our relationships with others. We will learn to put their needs before our own desires. Love should be the measuring stick for our behavior.

9:4–12 Paul modeled releasing personal freedom in order to show love toward others. He had all the rights we have, but Paul willingly gave them up because of his relationship with Jesus Christ and his desire to help others. We, too, have certain freedoms and rights, but if we desire to build up the church, we may have to give up some of those rights in order to help our brothers and sisters in Christ.

9:15–18 Paul gave up his right to be paid for his work in the ministry, choosing instead to support himself. At issue was not whether he should have been paid. Paul wanted to illustrate that when something is important, we may have to give up some of our rights and freedoms to accomplish it. To make spiritual progress, our relationship with Jesus Christ must take a central place in our lives. We may need to give up some of our possessions, activities and sinful relationships in order to achieve the freedom that we long for.

9:19–23 Paul gave us some helpful hints about sharing God's message with others. If we want to communicate, Paul knew that we must first take time to understand the other person. Paul listened to his audience and found common ground with them before he confronted them with their need to change. As we seek to help others, we

I make myself a slave to everyone, to win as many as possible. 20To the Jews I became like a Jew, to win the Jews. To those under the law I became like one under the law (though I myself am not under the law), so as to win those under the law. 21To those not having the law I became like one not having the law (though I am not free from God's law but am under Christ's law), so as to win those not having the law. 22To the weak I became weak, to win the weak. I have become all things to all men so that by all possible means I might save some. 23I do all this for the sake of the gospel, that I may share in its blessings.

24Do you not know that in a race all the runners run, but only one gets the prize? Run in such a way as to get the prize. 25Everyone who competes in the games goes into strict training. They do it to get a crown that will not last; but we do it to get a crown that will last forever. 26Therefore I do not run like a man running aimlessly; I do not fight like a man beating the air. 27No, I beat my body and make it my slave so that after I have preached to others, I myself will not be disqualified for the prize.

Warnings From Israel's History

10 For I do not want you to be ignorant of the fact, brothers, that our forefathers were all under the cloud and that they all passed through the sea. 2They were all baptized into Moses in the cloud and in the sea. 3They all ate the same spiritual food 4and drank the same spiritual drink; for they drank from the spiritual rock that accompanied them, and that rock was Christ. 5Nevertheless, God was not pleased with most of them; their bodies were scattered over the desert.

6Now these things occurred as examples[a] to keep us from setting our hearts on evil things as they did. 7Do not be idolaters, as some of them were; as it is written: "The people sat down to eat and drink and got up to indulge in pagan revelry."[b] 8We should not commit sexual immorality, as some of them did—and in one day twenty-three thousand of them died. 9We should not test the Lord, as some of them did—and were killed by snakes. 10And do not grumble, as some of them did—and were killed by the destroying angel.

11These things happened to them as examples and were written down as warnings for us, on whom the fulfillment of the ages has come. 12So, if you think you are standing firm, be careful that you don't fall! 13No temptation has seized you except what is common to man. And God is faithful; he will not let you be tempted beyond what you can bear. But when you are tempted, he will also provide a way out so that you can stand up under it.

Idol Feasts and the Lord's Supper

14Therefore, my dear friends, flee from idolatry. 15I speak to sensible people; judge for yourselves what I say. 16Is not the cup of thanksgiving for which we give thanks a participation in the blood of Christ? And is not the bread that we break a participation in the body of Christ? 17Because there is one loaf, we, who are many, are one body, for we all partake of the one loaf.

18Consider the people of Israel: Do not those who eat the sacrifices participate in the altar? 19Do I mean then that a sacrifice offered to an idol is anything, or that an idol is anything? 20No, but the sacrifices of pagans are offered to demons, not to God, and I do not want you to be participants with demons. 21You cannot drink the cup of the Lord and the cup of demons too; you cannot have a part in both the Lord's table and the table of demons. 22Are we trying to arouse the Lord's jealousy? Are we stronger than he?

The Believer's Freedom

23"Everything is permissible"—but not everything is beneficial. "Everything is permissible"—but not everything is constructive. 24Nobody should seek his own good, but the good of others.

25Eat anything sold in the meat market without raising questions of conscience, 26for, "The earth is the Lord's, and everything in it."[c]

27If some unbeliever invites you to a meal and you want to go, eat whatever is put before you without raising questions of conscience. 28But if anyone says to you, "This has been offered in sacrifice," then do not eat it, both for the sake of the man who told you and for con-

[a]6 Or *types;* also in verse 11 [b]7 Exodus 32:6
[c]26 Psalm 24:1

must begin by listening and showing that we care. Paul listened to the needs of people and then presented his message in a way that met their specific needs. We can do the same as we carry the message of hope to hurting people.

9:24–27 Growing in our spiritual life is like training for a sporting event or getting ready for a marathon. These activities require a great deal of endurance and strict discipline for those who want to win. Paul makes it clear that growing in our relationship with God requires discipline and perseverance too. We need to give up sinful activities that can hold us back and press on to follow God's will for us.

10:1–13 Paul used himself as an example of the disciplined, vigilant athlete. In this passage he used Israel's history as an example of what not to be like. Israel's lack of self-discipline against temptation led them into sin. Their overconfidence led to a self-destructive pride that we must avoid. Notice that Paul used Israel's failures as a warning to us. If we follow their example, we will suffer the same painful consequences that they did.

10:23–33 Paul sought to balance his argument here, for it is easy to become legalistic when pursuing spiritual growth. We can find the balance by exercising our freedom in Christ while willingly releasing any of our rights that might cause another to fall. If our actions are governed by our love for God and for those around us, we are on the right track.

science' sake[a]— 29the other man's conscience, I
mean, not yours. For why should my freedom
be judged by another's conscience? 30If I take
part in the meal with thankfulness, why am I
denounced because of something I thank God
for?
31So whether you eat or drink or whatever
you do, do it all for the glory of God. 32Do not
cause anyone to stumble, whether Jews, Greeks
or the church of God— 33even as I try to please
everybody in every way. For I am not seeking
my own good but the good of many, so that
11 they may be saved. 1Follow my example, as I follow the example of Christ.

Propriety in Worship

2I praise you for remembering me in everything and for holding to the teachings,[b] just as
I passed them on to you.
3Now I want you to realize that the head of
every man is Christ, and the head of the woman
is man, and the head of Christ is God. 4Every
man who prays or prophesies with his head
covered dishonors his head. 5And every woman
who prays or prophesies with her head uncovered dishonors her head—it is just as though her
head were shaved. 6If a woman does not cover
her head, she should have her hair cut off; and
if it is a disgrace for a woman to have her hair
cut or shaved off, she should cover her head. 7A
man ought not to cover his head,[c] since he is
the image and glory of God; but the woman is
the glory of man. 8For man did not come from
woman, but woman from man; 9neither was
man created for woman, but woman for man.
10For this reason, and because of the angels, the
woman ought to have a sign of authority on her
head.
11In the Lord, however, woman is not independent of man, nor is man independent of
woman. 12For as woman came from man, so
also man is born of woman. But everything
comes from God. 13Judge for yourselves: Is it
proper for a woman to pray to God with her
head uncovered? 14Does not the very nature of
things teach you that if a man has long hair, it
is a disgrace to him, 15but that if a woman has
long hair, it is her glory? For long hair is given
to her as a covering. 16If anyone wants to be
contentious about this, we have no other practice—nor do the churches of God.

The Lord's Supper

17In the following directives I have no praise
for you, for your meetings do more harm than

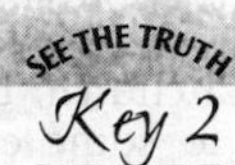

Temptation Is a Part of Life

1 Corinthians 10:12–13 It is essential that we see the reality of temptation in our lives and stop denying its existence. Temptation is part of the human condition. If we think we're beyond its reach, we are not seeing the truth.

The Bible affirms that everyone experiences temptation: "No temptation has seized you except what is common to man" (10:13). Yet even if we could rid ourselves of all external temptations, we would still have to live with the destructive desires hidden within us. "Each one is tempted when, by his own evil desire, he is dragged away and enticed" (James 1:14).

When we receive Christ as our Savior, God gives us a new nature. However, we still possess our human weaknesses—they will never completely disappear in this life. When we acknowledge that we will always be susceptible to temptation, especially in our own personal areas of weakness, we finally face reality. Seeing this truth clearly can help us avoid falling under temptation's power and enable us to approach life with our eyes wide open to what lies ahead.

Turn to Ephesians 4.

[a]28 Some manuscripts *conscience' sake, for "the earth is the Lord's and everything in it"* [b]2 Or *traditions* [c]4-7 Or *4Every man who prays or prophesies with long hair dishonors his head. 5And every woman who prays or prophesies with no covering ⌊of hair⌋ on her head dishonors her head—she is just like one of the "shorn women." 6If a woman has no covering, let her be for now with short hair, but since it is a disgrace for a woman to have her hair shorn or shaved, she should grow it again. 7A man ought not to have long hair*

good. 18In the first place, I hear that when you come together as a church, there are divisions among you, and to some extent I believe it. 19No doubt there have to be differences among you to show which of you have God's approval. 20When you come together, it is not the Lord's Supper you eat, 21for as you eat, each of you goes ahead without waiting for anybody else. One remains hungry, another gets drunk. 22Don't you have homes to eat and drink in? Or do you despise the church of God and humiliate those who have nothing? What shall I say to you? Shall I praise you for this? Certainly not!

23For I received from the Lord what I also passed on to you: The Lord Jesus, on the night he was betrayed, took bread, 24and when he had given thanks, he broke it and said, "This is my body, which is for you; do this in remembrance of me." 25In the same way, after supper he took the cup, saying, "This cup is the new covenant in my blood; do this, whenever you drink it, in remembrance of me." 26For whenever you eat this bread and drink this cup, you proclaim the Lord's death until he comes.

27Therefore, whoever eats the bread or drinks the cup of the Lord in an unworthy manner will be guilty of sinning against the body and blood of the Lord. 28A man ought to examine himself before he eats of the bread and drinks of the cup. 29For anyone who eats and drinks without recognizing the body of the Lord eats and drinks judgment on himself. 30That is why many among you are weak and sick, and a number of you have fallen asleep. 31But if we judged ourselves, we would not come under judgment. 32When we are judged by the Lord, we are being disciplined so that we will not be condemned with the world.

33So then, my brothers, when you come together to eat, wait for each other. 34If anyone is hungry, he should eat at home, so that when you meet together it may not result in judgment.

And when I come I will give further directions.

Spiritual Gifts

12 Now about spiritual gifts, brothers, I do not want you to be ignorant. 2You know that when you were pagans, somehow or other you were influenced and led astray to mute idols. 3Therefore I tell you that no one who is speaking by the Spirit of God says, "Jesus be cursed," and no one can say, "Jesus is Lord," except by the Holy Spirit.

4There are different kinds of gifts, but the same Spirit. 5There are different kinds of service, but the same Lord. 6There are different kinds of working, but the same God works all of them in all men.

7Now to each one the manifestation of the Spirit is given for the common good. 8To one there is given through the Spirit the message of wisdom, to another the message of knowledge by means of the same Spirit, 9to another faith by the same Spirit, to another gifts of healing by that one Spirit, 10to another miraculous powers, to another prophecy, to another distinguishing between spirits, to another speaking in different kinds of tongues,[a] and to still another the interpretation of tongues.[a] 11All these are the work of one and the same Spirit, and he gives them to each one, just as he determines.

One Body, Many Parts

12The body is a unit, though it is made up of many parts; and though all its parts are many, they form one body. So it is with Christ. 13For we were all baptized by[b] one Spirit into one body—whether Jews or Greeks, slave or free—and we were all given the one Spirit to drink.

14Now the body is not made up of one part but of many. 15If the foot should say, "Because I am not a hand, I do not belong to the body," it would not for that reason cease to be part of the body. 16And if the ear should say, "Because I am not an eye, I do not belong to the body," it would not for that reason cease to be part of the body. 17If the whole body were an eye, where would the sense of hearing be? If the whole body were an ear, where would the sense of smell be? 18But in fact God has arranged the parts in the body, every one of them, just as he wanted them to be. 19If they were all one part, where would the body be? 20As it is, there are many parts, but one body.

21The eye cannot say to the hand, "I don't need you!" And the head cannot say to the feet, "I don't need you!" 22On the contrary, those parts of the body that seem to be weaker are indispensable, 23and the parts that we think are

[a]10 Or *languages;* also in verse 28 [b]13 Or *with;* or *in*

11:17–22 Paul spent some time here trying to solve a problem in the Corinthian church. Apparently some of the wealthier believers looked down on the poorer members and refused to share from their abundance at the Communion meal. Paul stated that attitudes of superiority—feeling we are better than someone else—are extremely destructive and sinful. In God's eyes, no one person is better than another. We are all broken by sin and need God's transforming power. Our material possessions or educational levels do not make us better people. When we recognize this and humbly share with others, we will be able to make spiritual progress.

12:4–11 God has given each of us a special gift for the purpose of building up the church. When we don't make use of our gifts, we are rejecting what God has given us. A vital aspect of our spiritual growth and development is to discover and use our spiritual gifts. We each have a part to play in the body of Christ so that God's people can be blessed and can bless others.

12:12–26 When we become proud of our gifts and accomplishments, we invariably end up hurting ourselves and others. All of us are gifted in one way or another, and our gifts ultimately come from God. If we do not recognize this truth, we may take credit for our successes and flaunt them before others. When we possess an accurate view of ourselves, we will give God the credit for the gifts he has given us and be thankful.

THE SPIRITUAL DISCIPLINES

Service

Do What You Love to Show God's Love

1 Corinthians 12:7 Too often many of us have viewed the spiritual gifts primarily as talents God has given us for our own benefit. When considered in this way, spiritual gifts become "options" or "luxuries" that can be neglected or used according to our own whims instead of expressed through the discipline of service. But the Bible teaches us that God gives us spiritual gifts for the benefit of others and to continue Christ's work on earth. Paul asserted that "to each one the manifestation of the Spirit is given for the common good" (12:7). The gifts God has entrusted to us belong to the community of believers.

You can begin to discover your gift by prayerfully considering when you have felt the greatest energy and satisfaction in serving the Lord. Also consider these words from Psalms: "Delight yourself in the LORD and he will give you the desires of your heart" (Psalm 37:4). The good desires we have can be clues to finding our spiritual gifts. Paul lists a variety of spiritual gifts in Romans 12, 1 Corinthians 12 and Ephesians 4.

God has woven a unique design into each of our hearts. Our gifts form a part of this fabric. As we do what we love to show others God's love, we find spiritual fulfillment and renewal.

Putting It Into Practice

When have you felt the greatest energy and satisfaction in serving the Lord? Read the lists of spiritual gifts in Romans 12:6–8, 1 Corinthians 12:28 and Ephesians 4:11. Which gifts are evidenced in your most enjoyable experiences? How are you using your spiritual gifts to serve others? What could you do to further develop your gifts in service?

For more on service, turn to 1 Corinthians 13.

Responsible to Love

1 Corinthians 13:1–7 True love is not something we "fall into" or "fall out of." The kind of love God tells us to show for others is not an event we simply wait for, nor is it an experience that happens to us. Love is what God commands us to *do.* Love is a responsibility. And we cannot truly love as God commands apart from a relationship with God, who is love.

If we do not have love, nothing else matters (see 13:1–4). Love is a fruit of the Holy Spirit, produced in our lives as we yield ourselves to God (see Galatians 5:22). In fact, the Bible has its own definition for love:

> Love is patient, love is kind. It does not envy, it does not boast, it is not proud. It is not rude, it is not self-seeking, it is not easily angered, it keeps no record of wrongs. Love does not delight in evil but rejoices with the truth. It always protects, always trusts, always hopes, always perseveres. Love never fails (13:4–8).

This passage describes how God loves us. As we begin to absorb this love, we will find ourselves reaching out to love others in the same way. No one loves perfectly, but we must not give up trying. We cannot expect to be good at loving right away; we must be patient as God's love grows within us. As we accept the responsibility to love others, we can stop waiting for them to love us. When we choose to act in loving ways, the emotions will follow. Love will grow in our lives as we accept our responsibility to love and ask God to let his love flow through us.

Turn to Galatians 5.

less honorable we treat with special honor. And the parts that are unpresentable are treated with special modesty,
24while our presentable parts need no special treatment. But God has combined the members of the body and has given greater honor to the parts that lacked it,
25so that there should be no division in the body, but that its parts should have equal concern for each other.
26If one part suffers, every part suffers with it; if one part is honored, every part rejoices with it.

27Now you are the body of Christ, and each one of you is a part of it.
28And in the church God has appointed first of all apostles, second prophets, third teachers, then workers of miracles, also those having gifts of healing, those able to help others, those with gifts of administration, and those speaking in different kinds of tongues.
29Are all apostles? Are all prophets? Are all teachers? Do all work miracles?
30Do all have gifts of healing? Do all speak in tongues[a]? Do all interpret?
31But eagerly desire[b] the greater gifts.

Love

And now I will show you the most excellent way.

13 If I speak in the tongues[c] of men and of angels, but have not love, I am only a resounding gong or a clanging cymbal.
2If I have the gift of prophecy and can fathom all mysteries and all knowledge, and if I have a faith that can move mountains, but have not love, I am nothing.
3If I give all I possess to the poor and surrender my body to the flames,[d] but have not love, I gain nothing.

4Love is patient, love is kind. It does not envy, it does not boast, it is not proud.
5It is not rude, it is not self-seeking, it is not easily angered, it keeps no record of wrongs.
6Love does not delight in evil but rejoices with the truth.
7It always protects, always trusts, always hopes, always perseveres.

8Love never fails. But where there are prophecies, they will cease; where there are tongues, they will be stilled; where there is knowledge, it will pass away.
9For we know in part and we prophesy in part,
10but when perfection comes, the imperfect disappears.
11When I was a child,

[a]30 Or *other languages* [b]31 Or *But you are eagerly desiring* [c]1 Or *languages* [d]3 Some early manuscripts *body that I may boast*

12:31—13:3 Paul reminded the Corinthians that all their deeds, talents and spiritual gifts amounted to nothing if they didn't love one another. Selfless love is necessary to make all our spiritual exercises worthwhile.
13:4–7 Many people define love as only an emotion. But Paul defined love as a commitment to act in a certain way toward others. We may not always be able to feel loving, but we can certainly practice the behaviors Paul listed in these verses. The apostle knew that when we behave in loving ways, feelings of love soon follow.
13:11–13 Spiritual growth is never complete in this life. We are still like children, needing to grow and mature.

THE SPIRITUAL DISCIPLINES

Service

Caring About How We Do What We Do

1 Corinthians 13:1–13 Relationships form a key element in the discipline of service because actions—even charitable, selfless deeds—can never substitute for love. Paul attested that even if he sacrificed his body and yet didn't love others, he would "gain nothing" (13:3). Since relationships develop along the way in life, we need to be mindful of how we do what we do.

Jesus understood this. When Mary anointed his feet with expensive perfume, Judas protested the seemingly wasteful use of the perfume, arguing that it could have been sold and the proceeds given to the poor. But Jesus knew Mary's heart. He praised her for preparing him for burial in this beautiful way (see John 12:1–8). Mary's act was performed out of love for her Lord. Merely giving the money from the perfume to the poor would have been a meaningless act if she had no true concern for them.

Too often we pass right by *people* in our effort to get *things* done. Often we are more concerned with producing visible results than with caring for people. But even the most "spiritual" activities are pointless without love.

Putting It Into Practice

Rewrite 1 Corinthians 13 in your own words, using specific references to your own situation. For example, a teacher may write, "Though my students obtain all the knowledge I can communicate to their minds, unless I reach their hearts with love, it is of little value." A parent may write, "Though my family has all the food they can eat, if I don't give them love, they will starve." Then, determine specific ways to express such love as you go about your work and life.

For more on service, turn to Galatians 6.

I talked like a child, I thought like a child, I reasoned like a child. When I became a man, I put childish ways behind me. [12]Now we see but a poor reflection as in a mirror; then we shall see face to face. Now I know in part; then I shall know fully, even as I am fully known.

[13]And now these three remain: faith, hope and love. But the greatest of these is love.

Gifts of Prophecy and Tongues

14 Follow the way of love and eagerly desire spiritual gifts, especially the gift of prophecy. [2]For anyone who speaks in a tongue[a] does not speak to men but to God. Indeed, no one understands him; he utters mysteries with his spirit.[b] [3]But everyone who prophesies speaks to men for their strengthening, encouragement and comfort. [4]He who speaks in a tongue edifies himself, but he who prophesies edifies the church. [5]I would like every one of you to speak in tongues,[c] but I would rather have you prophesy. He who prophesies is greater than one who speaks in tongues,[c] unless he interprets, so that the church may be edified.

[6]Now, brothers, if I come to you and speak in tongues, what good will I be to you, unless I bring you some revelation or knowledge or prophecy or word of instruction? [7]Even in the case of lifeless things that make sounds, such as the flute or harp, how will anyone know what tune is being played unless there is a distinction in the notes? [8]Again, if the trumpet does not sound a clear call, who will get ready for battle? [9]So it is with you. Unless you speak intelligible words with your tongue, how will anyone know what you are saying? You will just be speaking into the air. [10]Undoubtedly there are all sorts of languages in the world, yet none of them is without meaning. [11]If then I do not grasp the meaning of what someone is saying, I am a foreigner to the speaker, and he is a foreigner to me. [12]So it is with you. Since you are eager to have spiritual gifts, try to excel in gifts that build up the church.

[13]For this reason anyone who speaks in a tongue should pray that he may interpret what he says. [14]For if I pray in a tongue, my spirit prays, but my mind is unfruitful. [15]So what shall I do? I will pray with my spirit, but I will also pray with my mind; I will sing with my spirit, but I will also sing with my mind. [16]If you are praising God with your spirit, how can one who finds himself among those who do not understand[d] say "Amen" to your thanksgiving, since he does not know what you are saying? [17]You may be giving thanks well enough, but the other man is not edified.

[18]I thank God that I speak in tongues more than all of you. [19]But in the church I would rather speak five intelligible words to instruct others than ten thousand words in a tongue.

[20]Brothers, stop thinking like children. In regard to evil be infants, but in your thinking be adults. [21]In the Law it is written:

"Through men of strange tongues
  and through the lips of foreigners
I will speak to this people,
  but even then they will not listen to
    me,"[e]
says the Lord.

[22]Tongues, then, are a sign, not for believers but for unbelievers; prophecy, however, is for believers, not for unbelievers. [23]So if the whole church comes together and everyone speaks in tongues, and some who do not understand[f] or some unbelievers come in, will they not say that you are out of your mind? [24]But if an unbeliever or someone who does not understand[g] comes in while everybody is prophesying, he will be convinced by all that he is a sinner and will be judged by all, [25]and the secrets of his heart will be laid bare. So he will fall down and worship God, exclaiming, "God is really among you!"

Orderly Worship

[26]What then shall we say, brothers? When you come together, everyone has a hymn, or a word of instruction, a revelation, a tongue or an interpretation. All of these must be done for the strengthening of the church. [27]If anyone speaks in a tongue, two—or at the most three—should speak, one at a time, and someone must interpret. [28]If there is no interpreter, the speaker should keep quiet in the church and speak to himself and God.

[29]Two or three prophets should speak, and the others should weigh carefully what is said. [30]And if a revelation comes to someone who is sitting down, the first speaker should stop. [31]For you can all prophesy in turn so that everyone may be instructed and encouraged. [32]The spirits of prophets are subject to the control of prophets. [33]For God is not a God of disorder but of peace.

As in all the congregations of the saints, [34]women should remain silent in the churches. They are not allowed to speak, but must be in submission, as the Law says. [35]If they want to inquire about something, they should ask their

[a]2 Or *another language;* also in verses 4, 13, 14, 19, 26 and 27 [b]2 Or *by the Spirit* [c]5 Or *other languages;* also in verses 6, 18, 22, 23 and 39 [d]16 Or *among the inquirers* [e]21 Isaiah 28:11,12 [f]23 Or *some inquirers* [g]24 Or *or some inquirer*

Only when we see God face to face will we be complete and whole. Paul shared this truth, not to discourage us, but to give us hope that someday we will be made perfect.

14:1–12 In these verses, Paul returned to the subject of spiritual gifts. He warned us not to use our gifts to build ourselves up. All spiritual gifts are given to us by God to build up others and encourage them in their spiritual growth. Using our gifts for our own purpose means that we have forgotten the one who gave the gifts in the first place—God.

THE SPIRITUAL DISCIPLINES

Worship

Worship Is More Than Attendance

1 Corinthians 14:26–33 Worship isn't a spectator sport. True worship always involves participation. In many formal church situations, it may seem as though we have a limited part to play. But in reality we are called to be more active in worship than many of us realize. While the pastor and worship leaders may have selected the songs and Scripture, all of us sing, pray and study God's Word together. We are active contributors, not passive receptors.

We find instructions for such participation in worship in 1 Corinthians 14:26–33. While this passage contains some specific guidelines for speaking in tongues and prophesying (about which there are numerous interpretations), these verses are mostly concerned with the larger scope of worship. All of us can draw a number of important principles about worship from this passage.

First, we learn that we all have something to give in worship (see 12:7). The early church worshiped in a more open, participatory way than we commonly do today. Nevertheless, we can still contribute something to worship—anything from musical ability to teaching ability to even a worshipful attitude.

Note also from this passage that everything that is done must build up the body of believers. True worship honors God *and* strengthens the church. We may find that some actions in our worship are actually counterproductive to building up God's church and need to be reevaluated. Other practices may require some explanation if they are to have meaning for the participants.

Paul also reminds us to respect and celebrate each other's contributions in worship. A holy courtesy should pervade our fellowship. We should not intrude ourselves into worship by disregarding what others have to contribute and imposing our own agenda on them. Our contributions should be available for the church, yet we must recognize that we have a responsibility to exercise proper restraint. We should monitor our worship practices, cultivating a sense of openness to the thoughts and actions of others and confronting situations that hinder such appreciation of each other's contributions.

Putting It Into Practice

Take time to consider what you can contribute to your church's worship. Possibilities could include praying, reading Scripture, giving a testimony, presenting a message, singing or playing music, performing a worshipful dance or drama, or countless other contributions to the service. You may want to suggest having an open, participatory service, or possibly you could even do this with only a few friends in a small group setting. Your pastor could help you plan such a time. Invite people to study this passage ahead of time and consider how they might contribute to the service as well.

For more on worship, turn to Revelation 4.

own husbands at home; for it is disgraceful for
a woman to speak in the church.
36Did the word of God originate with you?
Or are you the only people it has reached? 37If
anybody thinks he is a prophet or spiritually
gifted, let him acknowledge that what I am writing to you is the Lord's command. 38If he ignores this, he himself will be ignored.[a]
39Therefore, my brothers, be eager to prophesy, and do not forbid speaking in tongues. 40But
everything should be done in a fitting and orderly way.

The Resurrection of Christ

15 Now, brothers, I want to remind you of
the gospel I preached to you, which you
received and on which you have taken your
stand. 2By this gospel you are saved, if you hold
firmly to the word I preached to you. Otherwise, you have believed in vain.
3For what I received I passed on to you as of
first importance[b]: that Christ died for our sins
according to the Scriptures, 4that he was buried,
that he was raised on the third day according to
the Scriptures, 5and that he appeared to Peter,[c]
and then to the Twelve. 6After that, he appeared
to more than five hundred of the brothers at
the same time, most of whom are still living,
though some have fallen asleep. 7Then he appeared to James, then to all the apostles, 8and
last of all he appeared to me also, as to one
abnormally born.
9For I am the least of the apostles and do not
even deserve to be called an apostle, because
I persecuted the church of God. 10But by the
grace of God I am what I am, and his grace to
me was not without effect. No, I worked harder
than all of them—yet not I, but the grace of God
that was with me. 11Whether, then, it was I or
they, this is what we preach, and this is what
you believed.

The Resurrection of the Dead

12But if it is preached that Christ has been
raised from the dead, how can some of you say
that there is no resurrection of the dead? 13If
there is no resurrection of the dead, then not
even Christ has been raised. 14And if Christ has
not been raised, our preaching is useless and so
is your faith. 15More than that, we are then
found to be false witnesses about God, for we
have testified about God that he raised Christ
from the dead. But he did not raise him if in fact
the dead are not raised. 16For if the dead are not
raised, then Christ has not been raised either.
17And if Christ has not been raised, your faith is
futile; you are still in your sins. 18Then those
also who have fallen asleep in Christ are lost.
19If only for this life we have hope in Christ, we
are to be pitied more than all men.
20But Christ has indeed been raised from the
dead, the firstfruits of those who have fallen
asleep. 21For since death came through a man,
the resurrection of the dead comes also through
a man. 22For as in Adam all die, so in Christ all
will be made alive. 23But each in his own turn:
Christ, the firstfruits; then, when he comes,
those who belong to him. 24Then the end will
come, when he hands over the kingdom to God
the Father after he has destroyed all dominion,
authority and power. 25For he must reign until
he has put all his enemies under his feet. 26The
last enemy to be destroyed is death. 27For he
"has put everything under his feet."[d] Now
when it says that "everything" has been put under him, it is clear that this does not include
God himself, who put everything under Christ.
28When he has done this, then the Son himself
will be made subject to him who put everything
under him, so that God may be all in all.
29Now if there is no resurrection, what will
those do who are baptized for the dead? If the
dead are not raised at all, why are people baptized for them? 30And as for us, why do we
endanger ourselves every hour? 31I die every
day—I mean that, brothers—just as surely as I
glory over you in Christ Jesus our Lord. 32If I
fought wild beasts in Ephesus for merely human reasons, what have I gained? If the dead
are not raised,

"Let us eat and drink,
for tomorrow we die."[e]

33Do not be misled: "Bad company corrupts
good character." 34Come back to your senses as
you ought, and stop sinning; for there are some

[a]38 Some manuscripts *If he is ignorant of this, let him be ignorant* [b]3 Or *you at the first* [c]5 Greek *Cephas* [d]27 Psalm 8:6 [e]32 Isaiah 22:13

15:10 Paul recognized that without God's grace, he would never have accomplished the things he did. Our spiritual progress must be accompanied by our recognition of God's help. When we fail to give God the credit for what he has done in our lives, we deny the truth of God's grace. Notice, however, that Paul also participated in the process of his spiritual transformation. Our spiritual growth is based on God's grace and his desire to help us, but we still play a part in the equation: We have to work hard! Spiritual growth takes a combination of God's gracious power and our faithful participation.

15:12–20 Some of the Corinthian believers questioned the hope of being resurrected at Christ's return. Paul reemphasized the importance of the resurrection and the hope it offers to all of us, even to those who are already dead. The greatest expression of God's power was raising Jesus from the grave. Since God can do that, he has the power to do anything! However, if God had not raised Jesus from the grave, then he would be powerless and we would be lost. Paul also affirmed the truth that since Jesus did rise from the dead we have access to the greatest power in the universe—God himself.

15:29–34 If death is the end of everything, then a selfish, pleasure-seeking lifestyle may be a justifiable alternative. But Paul reminds us that our hope leads to an existence beyond the grave. This truth about the resurrection motivates us to make right choices and leave behind our old way of life. If we do things God's way, we can look forward to an eternity of joy and peace. If we decide to do things our own way, we face an eternity of suffering.

who are ignorant of God—I say this to your shame.

The Resurrection Body

35But someone may ask, "How are the dead raised? With what kind of body will they come?" 36How foolish! What you sow does not come to life unless it dies. 37When you sow, you do not plant the body that will be, but just a seed, perhaps of wheat or of something else. 38But God gives it a body as he has determined, and to each kind of seed he gives its own body. 39All flesh is not the same: Men have one kind of flesh, animals have another, birds another and fish another. 40There are also heavenly bodies and there are earthly bodies; but the splendor of the heavenly bodies is one kind, and the splendor of the earthly bodies is another. 41The sun has one kind of splendor, the moon another and the stars another; and star differs from star in splendor.

42So will it be with the resurrection of the dead. The body that is sown is perishable, it is raised imperishable; 43it is sown in dishonor, it is raised in glory; it is sown in weakness, it is raised in power; 44it is sown a natural body, it is raised a spiritual body.

If there is a natural body, there is also a spiritual body. 45So it is written: "The first man Adam became a living being"[a]; the last Adam, a life-giving spirit. 46The spiritual did not come first, but the natural, and after that the spiritual. 47The first man was of the dust of the earth, the second man from heaven. 48As was the earthly man, so are those who are of the earth; and as is the man from heaven, so also are those who are of heaven. 49And just as we have borne the likeness of the earthly man, so shall we[b] bear the likeness of the man from heaven.

50I declare to you, brothers, that flesh and blood cannot inherit the kingdom of God, nor does the perishable inherit the imperishable. 51Listen, I tell you a mystery: We will not all sleep, but we will all be changed— 52in a flash, in the twinkling of an eye, at the last trumpet. For the trumpet will sound, the dead will be raised imperishable, and we will be changed. 53For the perishable must clothe itself with the imperishable, and the mortal with immortality. 54When the perishable has been clothed with the imperishable, and the mortal with immortality, then the saying that is written will come true: "Death has been swallowed up in victory."[c]

55"Where, O death, is your victory?
Where, O death, is your sting?"[d]

56The sting of death is sin, and the power of sin is the law. 57But thanks be to God! He gives us the victory through our Lord Jesus Christ.

58Therefore, my dear brothers, stand firm. Let nothing move you. Always give yourselves fully to the work of the Lord, because you know that your labor in the Lord is not in vain.

The Collection for God's People

16 Now about the collection for God's people: Do what I told the Galatian churches to do. 2On the first day of every week, each one of you should set aside a sum of money in keeping with his income, saving it up, so that when I come no collections will have to be made. 3Then, when I arrive, I will give letters of introduction to the men you approve and send them with your gift to Jerusalem. 4If it seems advisable for me to go also, they will accompany me.

Personal Requests

5After I go through Macedonia, I will come to you—for I will be going through Macedonia. 6Perhaps I will stay with you awhile, or even spend the winter, so that you can help me on my journey, wherever I go. 7I do not want to see you now and make only a passing visit; I hope to spend some time with you, if the Lord permits. 8But I will stay on at Ephesus until Pentecost, 9because a great door for effective work has opened to me, and there are many who oppose me.

10If Timothy comes, see to it that he has nothing to fear while he is with you, for he is carrying on the work of the Lord, just as I am. 11No one, then, should refuse to accept him. Send him on his way in peace so that he may return to me. I am expecting him along with the brothers.

12Now about our brother Apollos: I strongly urged him to go to you with the brothers. He was quite unwilling to go now, but he will go when he has the opportunity.

13Be on your guard; stand firm in the faith; be men of courage; be strong. 14Do everything in love.

15You know that the household of Stephanas were the first converts in Achaia, and they have devoted themselves to the service of the saints. I urge you, brothers, 16to submit to such as these

[a]45 Gen. 2:7 [b]49 Some early manuscripts *so let us*
[c]54 Isaiah 25:8 [d]55 Hosea 13:14

15:35–58 Sometimes our fear of death can motivate us to seek God and surrender to him. Yet our fear of death can also lead us to despair. A fear of death can bring out the best and the worst in us. Paul reminds us that Jesus' resurrection has conquered death and sin. When we have the resurrection power of Jesus Christ at work within us, we can be confident that we will live even after we die.

16:5–18 Throughout this letter, Paul encouraged the Corinthians in their spiritual growth. In his closing remarks, Paul revealed his love for the Corinthians and his trust in them by making several personal requests. We must maintain a balance between caring for the hurts and needs of others and being able to ask for what we need as well. Healthy relationships are characterized by a balanced give-and-take.

THE SPIRITUAL DISCIPLINES

Stewardship

Giving As We Have Received

1 Corinthians 16:2 "*Before or after taxes?*" How many of us have said or heard those words in response to the exhortation to give a portion of our income back to God? Our concern with such legalities illustrates our need to remind ourselves of the true purpose of giving.

The Old Testament standard for giving was the tithe, or ten percent of any property or produce: "A tithe of everything from the land, whether grain from the soil or fruit from the trees, belongs to the LORD; it is holy to the LORD" (Leviticus 27:30). This gift was a response of thanksgiving and an expression of allegiance to God. Failure to observe the tithe was viewed as robbing God, for it belonged to him: " 'Will a man rob God? Yet you rob me.' But you ask, 'How do we rob you?' 'In tithes and offerings. You are under a curse—the whole nation of you—because you are robbing me' " (Malachi 3:8–9).

The New Testament assumed that God's people would give proportionally from their income. Paul urged the Corinthian Christians to set aside a certain amount of money on the Lord's Day, depending on how much they had earned. This would then be given to other Christians enduring hardship in Jerusalem. Paul's instructions provide us with a good model for giving today. We should give as God has blessed us. We should set aside money regularly and purposefully. This habit of regular, proportional giving will remind us of several things: (1) that God graciously provides for us; (2) that we are responsible to support others; (3) that we need to use our material treasure to secure spiritual gains.

God's grace is such that when we give him what is his, he gives generously to us. " 'Bring the whole tithe into the storehouse, that there may be food in my house. Test me in this,' says the LORD Almighty, 'and see if I will not throw open the floodgates of heaven and pour out so much blessing that you will not have room enough for it' " (Malachi 3:10). While this is not an automatic guarantee that we will receive material blessings every time we give to God, this verse does show us that God will bless us and provide for our needs.

Putting It Into Practice

Consider the way you give to the Lord. Are you regularly giving a portion of your income? What specific steps can you take to improve the way you give? Also consider how much you should give in proportion to the amount God has given to you. You may not be able to jump from your current level to your desired level, but you could increase your giving by a smaller amount now and then add one percent more each year as you are able.

For more on stewardship, turn to 2 Corinthians 8.

and to everyone who joins in the work, and
labors at it. 17I was glad when Stephanas, Fortu-
natus and Achaicus arrived, because they have
supplied what was lacking from you. 18For they
refreshed my spirit and yours also. Such men
deserve recognition.

Final Greetings

19The churches in the province of Asia send
you greetings. Aquila and Priscilla[a] greet you
warmly in the Lord, and so does the church that
meets at their house. 20All the brothers here
send you greetings. Greet one another with a
holy kiss.
21I, Paul, write this greeting in my own hand.
22If anyone does not love the Lord—a curse
be on him. Come, O Lord[b]!
23The grace of the Lord Jesus be with you.
24My love to all of you in Christ Jesus.
Amen.[c]

[a]19 Greek *Prisca,* a variant of *Priscilla* [b]22 In Aramaic the expression *Come, O Lord* is *Marana tha.* [c]24 Some manuscripts do not have *Amen.*

2 CORINTHIANS

The Big Picture

A. PAUL DISCUSSES HIS MOTIVES AND ACTIONS (1:1–2:13)

B. PAUL RELATES HIS MINISTRY TO THE NEW COVENANT (2:14–7:16)

C. PAUL APPEALS TO HIS READERS FOR SUPPORT (8:1–9:15)

D. PAUL DEFENDS HIS APOSTOLIC AUTHORITY (10:1–13:14)

Paul wrote this letter mainly to defend the authority of his teachings about Christ. The church at Corinth was struggling, and one of its problems was the presence of members who openly challenged Paul's authority. These challengers slandered Paul's character and questioned the message he preached. They also introduced a number of dangerous false teachings. Since the believers in Corinth had come to faith through Paul's ministry, these false teachers and their message put the entire church at risk.

The false teachers claimed that following the Jewish laws was a requirement for salvation. To counteract this false teaching, Paul emphasized the truth that God changes us from the inside out. We cannot change ourselves merely by changing our external behavior. As we are reconciled to God, he transforms us into entirely new people; our old selves are changed in a fundamental sense.

Change is never easy, especially when it involves our lifestyles. Old habits die hard; positive habits often fall prey to neglect. Typically the habits that die hardest are our unhealthy thoughts and behavior patterns. "Out with the old, in with the new!" sounds simple, but even as we long for an end to our bad habits, we often cling to them.

Fortunately, God's power can make a significant change in our lives. Through Christ's death and resurrection, God made it possible for us to die to our old ways of life and be reborn to a new life. These are not superficial changes in behavior; they are spiritual changes of heart that bring about the outward changes in lifestyle that we long for. By being reconciled to God, we put to death our old lives, receive new lives in Christ and are transformed from the inside out.

Spiritual Renewal Themes

GOD'S POWER FOR OUR SPIRITUAL RENEWAL

All of us have made resolutions about things in our life that we are going to change. The results are usually the same—we end up falling back into the same old bad habits we promised to abandon. The Corinthians tried to do the same thing, with the same results. What they failed to understand as they listened to the false teachers was that only God's power could change their

lives. Our own efforts always fall short. Instead of merely making resolutions to change, we need to recognize our need for God's power and surrender our lives to God. Then the Holy Spirit within us will give us the power we need for our spiritual renewal.

LEARNING TO ACCEPT CRITICISM

One of Paul's purposes in writing this letter was to discipline those who needed to be corrected. Criticism usually hurts. Yet it also reveals what we need to change. Confrontation and criticism force us to face our problems, accept responsibility for them and ask God to redirect our course. If we hope to preserve spiritual gains, we must confront and solve problems, not ignore them; that means being open to criticism.

CONFLICT CAN INSPIRE GROWTH

Interpersonal conflicts are an inevitable part of being human. How conflicts affect us depends on how we handle them. If we view conflicts as opportunities for growth as Paul urged the Corinthians to do, we can turn our struggles into something productive. If we are willing to face our problems and try to solve them in loving ways, we will make spiritual progress as we recommit ourselves to hold each other accountable. But if we ignore the problems that divide us, they can eat away at us like a cancer, destroying the work of God, not only within us, but also in others around us. Conflicts are opportunities for growth if we will use them as such.

GOD'S STRENGTH IN OUR WEAKNESS

In this letter, Paul told about a particular "thorn" in his flesh (see 12:7). We don't know what this problem was because Paul didn't describe it. Some have suggested that his problem was a physical ailment, perhaps a disease affecting his eyes. Whatever it was, this problem was debilitating and chronic, and at times it interfered with his work. It also kept Paul humble because it forced him to depend on God. Through this hardship, Paul learned to thank God for this weakness. Each of us will always have weaknesses that can hold us back. But our weaknesses also have a purpose—to bring us to God.

Essential Facts

PURPOSE:
To explain new life in Christ while also defending Paul's authority as an apostle.

AUTHOR:
The apostle Paul.

AUDIENCE:
The church at Corinth, a city in Greece.

DATE WRITTEN:
About A.D. 55, from Macedonia.

SETTING:
Paul wrote to the Corinthian believers to correct their misunderstandings about him and his message and to help them with other problems.

KEY VERSE:
"Therefore, if anyone is in Christ, he is a new creation; the old has gone, the new has come!" (5:17).

KEY PLACES:
Corinth, Macedonia, Troas and Jerusalem.

KEY PEOPLE AND RELATIONSHIPS:
Paul with Timothy, Titus, the Corinthian believers and some false teachers.

1 Paul, an apostle of Christ Jesus by the will of God, and Timothy our brother,

To the church of God in Corinth, together with all the saints throughout Achaia:

2Grace and peace to you from God our Father and the Lord Jesus Christ.

The God of All Comfort

3Praise be to the God and Father of our Lord Jesus Christ, the Father of compassion and the God of all comfort, 4who comforts us in all our troubles, so that we can comfort those in any trouble with the comfort we ourselves have received from God. 5For just as the sufferings of Christ flow over into our lives, so also through Christ our comfort overflows. 6If we are distressed, it is for your comfort and salvation; if we are comforted, it is for your comfort, which produces in you patient endurance of the same sufferings we suffer. 7And our hope for you is firm, because we know that just as you share in our sufferings, so also you share in our comfort.

8We do not want you to be uninformed, brothers, about the hardships we suffered in the province of Asia. We were under great pressure, far beyond our ability to endure, so that we despaired even of life. 9Indeed, in our hearts we felt the sentence of death. But this happened that we might not rely on ourselves but on God, who raises the dead. 10He has delivered us from such a deadly peril, and he will deliver us. On him we have set our hope that he will continue to deliver us, 11as you help us by your prayers. Then many will give thanks on our[a] behalf for the gracious favor granted us in answer to the prayers of many.

Paul's Change of Plans

12Now this is our boast: Our conscience testifies that we have conducted ourselves in the world, and especially in our relations with you, in the holiness and sincerity that are from God. We have done so not according to worldly wisdom but according to God's grace. 13For we do not write you anything you cannot read or understand. And I hope that, 14as you have understood us in part, you will come to understand fully that you can boast of us just as we will boast of you in the day of the Lord Jesus.

15Because I was confident of this, I planned to visit you first so that you might benefit twice. 16I planned to visit you on my way to Macedonia and to come back to you from Macedonia, and then to have you send me on my way to Judea. 17When I planned this, did I do it lightly? Or do I make my plans in a worldly manner so that in the same breath I say, "Yes, yes" and "No, no"?

18But as surely as God is faithful, our message to you is not "Yes" and "No." 19For the Son of God, Jesus Christ, who was preached among you by me and Silas[b] and Timothy, was not "Yes" and "No," but in him it has always been "Yes." 20For no matter how many promises God has made, they are "Yes" in Christ. And so through him the "Amen" is spoken by us to the glory of God. 21Now it is God who makes both us and you stand firm in Christ. He anointed us, 22set his seal of ownership on us, and put his Spirit in our hearts as a deposit, guaranteeing what is to come.

23I call God as my witness that it was in order to spare you that I did not return to Corinth. 24Not that we lord it over your faith, but we work with you for your joy, because it is by faith

2 you stand firm. 1So I made up my mind that I would not make another painful visit to you. 2For if I grieve you, who is left to make me glad but you whom I have grieved? 3I wrote as I did so that when I came I should not be distressed by those who ought to make me rejoice. I had confidence in all of you, that you would all share my joy. 4For I wrote you out of great distress and anguish of heart and with many tears, not to grieve you but to let you know the depth of my love for you.

[a]11 Many manuscripts *your* [b]19 Greek *Silvanus*, a variant of *Silas*

1:1–7 Not only is God the God of peace, but he is also the God of comfort. Jesus Christ suffered greatly and unjustly when he went to the cross. He fully understands and identifies with our suffering, and he knows the kind of comfort we need. Jesus is worthy of our trust and will help us through our struggles.

1:8–10 Paul wrote of his own recent need for comfort from God (see 1:3–7). Apparently, Paul and his missionary group had been near death as they ministered in the Roman province of Asia, now southwestern Turkey. Yet even though Paul and his companions faced death, God delivered them. Many of us have experienced God's delivering power in our own lives too. When everything seems to be coming apart, God can save us from what appears to be sure destruction.

1:11 We should learn to encourage others. Sometimes we can provide encouragement by praying for others. When Paul asked the Corinthian believers to intercede in prayer for the needs of the apostle and his companions, he knew the believers would be helping and strengthening him and his companions from a distance. We may be unable to personally help some of the people we care about. If they are involved in lifestyles that can lead us back into sin, we need to keep our distance. But this does not mean that we should forget about them. We can help them by praying that they will turn from their sin and seek God. He has the power to do for them what we may not be able to do through direct contact.

1:23—2:4 For all of his strength of personality Paul was not insensitive to the pain of his readers. In this case, the apostle knew that the strong rebuke he gave them would be devastating. Paul wanted to be positive, but he concluded that there was no way to avoid confronting the believers about their responsibilities before God and others. Sometimes we need to be comforted; other times we need to be confronted. The apostle Paul recognized that this was a time for honest confrontation. When we confront others about their failures, we must make sure that we are seeking their best, just as Paul did.

Forgiveness for the Sinner

[5]If anyone has caused grief, he has not so
much grieved me as he has grieved all of you,
to some extent—not to put it too severely. [6]The
punishment inflicted on him by the majority is
sufficient for him. [7]Now instead, you ought to
forgive and comfort him, so that he will not be
overwhelmed by excessive sorrow. [8]I urge you,
therefore, to reaffirm your love for him. [9]The
reason I wrote you was to see if you would
stand the test and be obedient in everything. [10]If
you forgive anyone, I also forgive him. And
what I have forgiven—if there was anything to
forgive—I have forgiven in the sight of Christ for
your sake, [11]in order that Satan might not out-
wit us. For we are not unaware of his schemes.

Ministers of the New Covenant

[12]Now when I went to Troas to preach the
gospel of Christ and found that the Lord had
opened a door for me, [13]I still had no peace of
mind, because I did not find my brother Titus
there. So I said good-by to them and went on
to Macedonia.
[14]But thanks be to God, who always leads us
in triumphal procession in Christ and through
us spreads everywhere the fragrance of the
knowledge of him. [15]For we are to God the
aroma of Christ among those who are being
saved and those who are perishing. [16]To the one
we are the smell of death; to the other, the
fragrance of life. And who is equal to such a
task? [17]Unlike so many, we do not peddle the
word of God for profit. On the contrary, in
Christ we speak before God with sincerity, like
men sent from God.

3 Are we beginning to commend ourselves
again? Or do we need, like some people,
letters of recommendation to you or from you?
[2]You yourselves are our letter, written on our
hearts, known and read by everybody. [3]You
show that you are a letter from Christ, the result

GRIEVE, FORGIVE, AND LET GO
Key 5

Letting Go of Condemnation

2 Corinthians 2:5–8 As we develop relationships with other believers and hold each other accountable, there will be times when we must confront those who continue in sin without repentance. However, while God calls us to hold each other accountable, he does not want us to frustrate those who are sincerely seeking him and trying to obey him.

In the young Corinthian church, a man was confronted and punished by the entire community because of his sin. After he repented and God turned his life around, some people refused to welcome him back into the church. But the apostle Paul told the Corinthians, "Now instead, you ought to forgive and comfort him, so that he will not be overwhelmed by excessive sorrow. I urge you, therefore, to reaffirm your love for him" (2:7–8).

Whenever others genuinely repent of their sin, regardless of how heinous we consider that sin to have been or how much trouble it caused, we are commanded to offer forgiveness and comfort. If we hold on to condemnation after a believer has repented, we are out of God's will. We must release our feelings of condemnation. Otherwise, our spiritual lives will be hindered, and we will do untold damage to others' lives as well.

Turn to 2 Corinthians 7.

2:5–11 A problem in the Corinthian church (probably the one described in 1 Corinthians 5:1–11) was the basis for this Pauline rebuke. Even though the troublemaker in question had repented of his sin and honestly faced the consequences of his behavior, the Corinthian believers refused to forgive him. Paul pointed out how cruel it was to withhold forgiveness. The apostle explained that lack of forgiveness played right into Satan's hands by discouraging the repentant party. After admitting our mistakes and trying to change, we may also have experienced the pain of rejection. We should avoid causing someone else the same kind of pain. We need to make sure that when others repent of their sin, we do our part to encourage their restoration and healing.

2:14–17 Paul shows us in these verses that sharing our faith should be a natural outworking of God's grace in our lives. As God transforms us and gives us victory over our sins, we reflect his grace in our lives. The fragrance of God's transforming work will be evident to others. We don't have to be a wonderful speaker to share the Good News. Our humble message passed along by word and deed may be all the encouragement someone needs to turn to God.

of our ministry, written not with ink but with the Spirit of the living God, not on tablets of stone but on tablets of human hearts.

4Such confidence as this is ours through Christ before God. 5Not that we are competent in ourselves to claim anything for ourselves, but our competence comes from God. 6He has made us competent as ministers of a new covenant—not of the letter but of the Spirit; for the letter kills, but the Spirit gives life.

The Glory of the New Covenant

7Now if the ministry that brought death, which was engraved in letters on stone, came with glory, so that the Israelites could not look steadily at the face of Moses because of its glory, fading though it was, 8will not the ministry of the Spirit be even more glorious? 9If the ministry that condemns men is glorious, how much more glorious is the ministry that brings righteousness! 10For what was glorious has no glory now in comparison with the surpassing glory. 11And if what was fading away came with glory, how much greater is the glory of that which lasts!

12Therefore, since we have such a hope, we are very bold. 13We are not like Moses, who would put a veil over his face to keep the Israelites from gazing at it while the radiance was fading away. 14But their minds were made dull, for to this day the same veil remains when the old covenant is read. It has not been removed, because only in Christ is it taken away. 15Even to this day when Moses is read, a veil covers their hearts. 16But whenever anyone turns to the Lord, the veil is taken away. 17Now the Lord is the Spirit, and where the Spirit of the Lord is, there is freedom. 18And we, who with unveiled faces all reflect[a] the Lord's glory, are being transformed into his likeness with ever-increasing glory, which comes from the Lord, who is the Spirit.

Treasures in Jars of Clay

4 Therefore, since through God's mercy we have this ministry, we do not lose heart. 2Rather, we have renounced secret and shameful ways; we do not use deception, nor do we distort the word of God. On the contrary, by setting forth the truth plainly we commend ourselves to every man's conscience in the sight of God. 3And even if our gospel is veiled, it is veiled to those who are perishing. 4The god of this age has blinded the minds of unbelievers, so that they cannot see the light of the gospel of the glory of Christ, who is the image of God. 5For we do not preach ourselves, but Jesus Christ as Lord, and ourselves as your servants for Jesus' sake. 6For God, who said, "Let light shine out of darkness,"[b] made his light shine in our hearts to give us the light of the knowledge of the glory of God in the face of Christ.

7But we have this treasure in jars of clay to show that this all-surpassing power is from God and not from us. 8We are hard pressed on every side, but not crushed; perplexed, but not in despair; 9persecuted, but not abandoned; struck down, but not destroyed. 10We always carry around in our body the death of Jesus, so that the life of Jesus may also be revealed in our body. 11For we who are alive are always being given over to death for Jesus' sake, so that his life may be revealed in our mortal body. 12So then, death is at work in us, but life is at work in you.

13It is written: "I believed; therefore I have spoken."[c] With that same spirit of faith we also believe and therefore speak, 14because we know that the one who raised the Lord Jesus from the dead will also raise us with Jesus and present us with you in his presence. 15All this is for your benefit, so that the grace that is reaching more and more people may cause thanksgiving to overflow to the glory of God.

[a]*18* Or *contemplate* [b]*6* Gen. 1:3 [c]*13* Psalm 116:10

3:4–5 In his letters, Paul appears to be a very confident person. However, Paul's confidence is not so much a self-confidence as it is a "God-inspired" confidence. If we trust God to work in and through us, we can be confident that resources are available to overcome any problem we might face. The most healthy foundation for self-esteem is knowing that we are made in God's image (see Genesis 1:26–27) and that we are competent because of Christ's work on our behalf.

3:6–16 Paul's contrast between the old covenant (the Law of Moses) and the new covenant (salvation through Jesus Christ) is instructive. The glory of the law and the glow on Moses' face from his encounter with God on Mount Sinai were substantial. But those elements of glory faded. Each time Moses met with God, the glory of God was refreshed in his life. Our experience of meeting God is not a once-in-a-lifetime experience. We must continually go back to God's Word and seek God's face. Then his glory will be refreshed in our lives as well.

3:17–18 The glory of God is revealed in the new covenant as well as the old. But rather than being reflected only on the outside, the glory of the new covenant is revealed from the inside out. This glory shines through the lives of all who trust Jesus Christ and are filled with the Holy Spirit. And while this glory may not be a physical manifestation in our lives as was the glow on Moses' face, God will change us from glory to glory by his grace. The further we progress in our relationship with God, the more visible God's glory will become in our lives.

4:3–4 If we do not acknowledge the sin in our lives, we refuse to see the truth and cannot accept the gift of forgiveness that God offers us through a relationship with Jesus Christ. As we reflect honestly on our lives, God will help us see where we need to change. Then we can confess our sin and trust Jesus to forgive us and empower us to make the needed changes in our lives.

4:8–11 Hard times may either crush and disillusion us or challenge and stimulate us. It is hard for us to keep going when the going gets tough. But knowing that God is with us in the midst of the trials we face and that he can also use our weaknesses for his glory can encourage us to persevere. In fact, as others see God's work in our lives, they may gain the courage to face and conquer their own sins and areas of weakness with God's powerful help.

[16]Therefore we do not lose heart. Though
outwardly we are wasting away, yet inwardly we
are being renewed day by day. [17]For our light
and momentary troubles are achieving for us an
eternal glory that far outweighs them all. [18]So
we fix our eyes not on what is seen, but on what
is unseen. For what is seen is temporary, but
what is unseen is eternal.

Our Heavenly Dwelling

5 Now we know that if the earthly tent we
live in is destroyed, we have a building
from God, an eternal house in heaven, not built
by human hands. [2]Meanwhile we groan, longing to be clothed with our heavenly dwelling,
[3]because when we are clothed, we will not be
found naked. [4]For while we are in this tent, we
groan and are burdened, because we do not
wish to be unclothed but to be clothed with our
heavenly dwelling, so that what is mortal may
be swallowed up by life. [5]Now it is God who
has made us for this very purpose and has given
us the Spirit as a deposit, guaranteeing what is
to come.

[6]Therefore we are always confident and
know that as long as we are at home in the body
we are away from the Lord. [7]We live by faith,
not by sight. [8]We are confident, I say, and
would prefer to be away from the body and at
home with the Lord. [9]So we make it our goal to
please him, whether we are at home in the body
or away from it. [10]For we must all appear before

4:16–18 When we surrender our lives to God, two opposite and somewhat confusing processes are simultaneously at work. On the one hand, physical deterioration, the distressing trials that accompany life on this earth and eventual death arc inevitable. However, our glorious inner growth prepares us daily for the glory and blessing we will experience in God's presence throughout eternity. We may have to wait awhile for these eternal blessings. But if we trust God to help us in this earthly life, we can be sure of his blessings in the future.

5:1–5 Paul reminded his readers that glorious new bodies would someday replace their weak ones. Many people pay great sums of money for cosmetic surgery, hair coloring and the like to avoid the depressing reality of the aging process. But there is a comforting side to aging if we trust Jesus Christ for our salvation. Before long, we will exchange our present physical bodies and receive glorified eternal bodies. The Holy Spirit's presence in our lives is the guarantee that we are drawing ever closer to that eternal exchange.

5:6–9 The fact that God is preparing better bodies and a better place of residence for us beyond this life cannot be proven scientifically. There is strong, unseen spiritual evidence, but it must be accepted by faith (see Hebrews 11:1). Such faith always pleases God (see Hebrews 11:6). Faith also helps us overcome our great fear of death, which is the doorway to our eternal life with God (see John 14:2–3). It is important that we surrender our lives to God and seek to do his will. Knowing that God wants to give us something special after this life can motivate us to put our lives in God's hands right now.

5:10–11 Consequences and motives are both major issues. Consequences for selfish and destructive behavior reach even beyond the boundaries of this life. All of us will have to stand before God's judgment seat and receive his piercing evaluation. For those of us who have believed

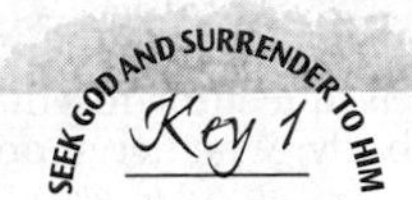

In Pursuit of Power

2 Corinthians 4:7–10 Some of us began seeking God because we realized that we were weak and in need of a greater power in our lives. Often we find ourselves in situations where we are hindered by weakness, exhaustion and the fragile nature of our mortal lives. We yearn for power because we truly need it, but we must realize that God is the proper source of that power.

The apostle Paul tells us, "We have this treasure in jars of clay to show that this all-surpassing power is from God and not from us" (4:7). Paul contrasts a precious treasure and the simple clay pot in which the treasure is stored. God's power is our treasure. Our human lives, with all their frailties and weaknesses, are the perishable clay jars. We are not born with the power of God within us. His power is poured into our lives when we repent and surrender to him. There is a paradox to this power, however, because we must surrender our human strength to God in order to receive his power.

What a relief! We don't have to be strong or pretend to be perfect. We possess human bodies beset with weakness, yet we can still find power from God to persevere. When others see God's power in our lives, they will be encouraged to seek God and surrender to him too.

Turn to Philippians 2.

the judgment seat of Christ, that each one may
receive what is due him for the things done
while in the body, whether good or bad.

The Ministry of Reconciliation

11Since, then, we know what it is to fear the
Lord, we try to persuade men. What we are is
plain to God, and I hope it is also plain to your
conscience. 12We are not trying to commend
ourselves to you again, but are giving you an
opportunity to take pride in us, so that you can
answer those who take pride in what is seen
rather than in what is in the heart. 13If we are
out of our mind, it is for the sake of God; if we
are in our right mind, it is for you. 14For Christ's
love compels us, because we are convinced that
one died for all, and therefore all died. 15And he
died for all, that those who live should no longer live for themselves but for him who died for
them and was raised again.
16So from now on we regard no one from a
worldly point of view. Though we once regarded Christ in this way, we do so no longer.
17Therefore, if anyone is in Christ, he is a new
creation; the old has gone, the new has come!
18All this is from God, who reconciled us to
himself through Christ and gave us the ministry
of reconciliation: 19that God was reconciling
the world to himself in Christ, not counting
men's sins against them. And he has committed
to us the message of reconciliation. 20We are
therefore Christ's ambassadors, as though God
were making his appeal through us. We implore
you on Christ's behalf: Be reconciled to God.
21God made him who had no sin to be sin[a] for
us, so that in him we might become the righteousness of God.

6 As God's fellow workers we urge you not to
receive God's grace in vain. 2For he says,

"In the time of my favor I heard you,
and in the day of salvation I helped
you."[b]

I tell you, now is the time of God's favor, now
is the day of salvation.

Paul's Hardships

3We put no stumbling block in anyone's
path, so that our ministry will not be discredited. 4Rather, as servants of God we commend
ourselves in every way: in great endurance; in
troubles, hardships and distresses; 5in beatings,
imprisonments and riots; in hard work, sleepless nights and hunger; 6in purity, understanding, patience and kindness; in the Holy Spirit
and in sincere love; 7in truthful speech and in
the power of God; with weapons of righteousness in the right hand and in the left; 8through
glory and dishonor, bad report and good report; genuine, yet regarded as impostors;
9known, yet regarded as unknown; dying, and
yet we live on; beaten, and yet not killed; 10sor-
rowful, yet always rejoicing; poor, yet making
many rich; having nothing, and yet possessing
everything.
11We have spoken freely to you, Corinthians,
and opened wide our hearts to you. 12We are
not withholding our affection from you, but
you are withholding yours from us. 13As a fair
exchange—I speak as to my children—open
wide your hearts also.

[a]21 Or *be a sin offering* [b]2 Isaiah 49:8

---

in Jesus Christ for salvation, this judgment will also include the giving of rewards. Understanding that our actions and commitments have eternal consequences can help us think twice before we act and motivate us to do things according to God's plan.

5:17 The new life we experience in Jesus Christ is far-reaching and complete. Though we become brand-new people through him, our old thought patterns and bad habits may not automatically vanish. But from God's point of view we have been forgiven—we are new creatures in his sight. Through the power of God's Holy Spirit, we can be completely transformed in every area of our lives.

5:18–21 We all want to reconcile our fractured relationships. At the human level, this is very difficult for us to do. On a spiritual level, God has offered to restore our broken relationship with him (though he committed none of the wrongs) through the work of Jesus Christ. By accepting the forgiveness he offers, we can have our relationship with God restored. We can then follow God and offer the gift of forgiveness to others. If someone else offers us the gift of forgiveness, we can humbly accept it as well. This process will rebuild our relationships with the people we have wronged.

6:3–4 Paul sought to live in such a way that no one would be offended or kept away from God because of Paul's behavior. Paul was a model for other believers to follow. Some of us who have been walking in faith for a while may have found it exhausting to be a model for others. We may have become so burdened by numerous expectations that we have quit trying to help others. If we find ourselves in this situation, it may be because somewhere along the line we stopped letting God work *through* us and started working *for* God. As we grow spiritually, we will always be responsible to help others, but the power to do so must always come from God. The apostle Paul took his responsibilities seriously and acted out of concern for the welfare of others, but Paul also confessed his personal weakness and his reliance on God's strength.

6:8–10 When we live for God and follow his plan for our lives, others will typically react to us in one of two ways. Some may genuinely honor us and support what we are trying to do; others will malign and dishonor us. If we are trying to impress others to bolster our self-esteem, we will be devastated when people react negatively to us. Paul found his self-esteem in his relationship with God. He did not need the honor of others; our lives should reflect the same attitude.

6:11–13 Paul wanted to reconcile his relationship with the Corinthians. Having defended his sincerity toward them (see 1:12–23), in these verses Paul again pledged his honest affection to his readers, challenging them to do the same for him. In strained relationships, often one person withholds affection in an attempt to punish another. This attitude only leads to deeper alienation and loss. We may not be able to control how another person acts in a broken relationship, but we can control how we act. We should never withhold forgiveness. We should be like Paul, extending the invitation of restoration to others, humbly and without reservation.

Do Not Be Yoked With Unbelievers

14 Do not be yoked together with unbelievers. For what do righteousness and wickedness have in common? Or what fellowship can light have with darkness? 15 What harmony is there between Christ and Belial[a]? What does a believer have in common with an unbeliever? 16 What agreement is there between the temple of God and idols? For we are the temple of the living God. As God has said: "I will live with them and walk among them, and I will be their God, and they will be my people."[b]

17 "Therefore come out from them
and be separate,
says the Lord.
Touch no unclean thing,
and I will receive you."[c]
18 "I will be a Father to you,
and you will be my sons and daughters,
says the Lord Almighty."[d]

7 Since we have these promises, dear friends, let us purify ourselves from everything that contaminates body and spirit, perfecting holiness out of reverence for God.

Paul's Joy

2 Make room for us in your hearts. We have wronged no one, we have corrupted no one, we have exploited no one. 3 I do not say this to condemn you; I have said before that you have such a place in our hearts that we would live or die with you. 4 I have great confidence in you; I take great pride in you. I am greatly encouraged; in all our troubles my joy knows no bounds.

5 For when we came into Macedonia, this body of ours had no rest, but we were harassed at every turn—conflicts on the outside, fears within. 6 But God, who comforts the downcast, comforted us by the coming of Titus, 7 and not only by his coming but also by the comfort you had given him. He told us about your longing for me, your deep sorrow, your ardent concern for me, so that my joy was greater than ever.

8 Even if I caused you sorrow by my letter, I do not regret it. Though I did regret it—I see that my letter hurt you, but only for a little while— 9 yet now I am happy, not because you were made sorry, but because your sorrow led you to repentance. For you became sorrowful as God intended and so were not harmed in any way by us. 10 Godly sorrow brings repentance that leads to salvation and leaves no regret, but worldly sorrow brings death. 11 See what this godly sorrow has produced in you: what earnestness, what eagerness to clear yourselves, what indignation, what alarm, what longing, what concern, what readiness to see justice done. At every point you have proved yourselves to be innocent in this matter. 12 So even though I wrote to you, it was not on account of the one who did the wrong or of the injured party, but rather that before God you could see for yourselves how devoted to us you are. 13 By all this we are encouraged.

In addition to our own encouragement, we were especially delighted to see how happy Titus was, because his spirit has been refreshed by all of you. 14 I had boasted to him about you, and you have not embarrassed me. But just as everything we said to you was true, so our boasting about you to Titus has proved to be true as well. 15 And his affection for you is all the greater when he remembers that you were all obedient, receiving him with fear and trembling. 16 I am glad I can have complete confidence in you.

Generosity Encouraged

8 And now, brothers, we want you to know about the grace that God has given the Macedonian churches. 2 Out of the most severe trial, their overflowing joy and their extreme poverty welled up in rich generosity. 3 For I testify that they gave as much as they were able, and even beyond their ability. Entirely on their own, 4 they urgently pleaded with us for the privilege

[a] 15 Greek *Beliar,* a variant of *Belial* [b] 16 Lev. 26:12; Jer. 32:38; Ezek. 37:27 [c] 17 Isaiah 52:11; Ezek. 20:34,41 [d] 18 2 Samuel 7:14; 7:8

6:14–18 Sometimes the spiritual changes we make can upset some of our previous friendships. Some of our old friends may be uncomfortable with us because they feel guilty about their own sins. Others may feel threatened by the spiritual changes in our lives. If a friend or an associate undermines or demeans our relationship with God, we need to be careful. We should still reach out to unbelievers, but we should not become too close to people who will lead us away from obedience to God. Our primary relationships should be with unselfish, godly people who will support our spiritual growth.

7:8–10 Paul had apparently written a short letter to the Corinthians that was sent between 1 and 2 Corinthians and was not included among the New Testament books. From his mention of the letter in these verses, it must have had quite a sharp tone. Paul admits that he had mixed feelings about sending that letter. But because of the Corinthians' positive response to the letter's discipline, all his regrets had vanished. Whenever we confront others, we take a calculated risk that can lead either to healing or to alienation. When we confront people about their problems, we must do so under God's guidance and with humility and love. As we entrust the situation to God, he will work things out according to his perfect will.

7:11–13 When we admit our failures to God and follow God's will, wonderful changes take place in our lives. In these verses, we see that repentance produces fruit in three ways: it purifies and revitalizes our lives and emotions (7:11); it renews our relationship with God (7:12) and it refreshes our relationships with others, both those we have wronged and onlookers who are encouraged by the changes that have taken place in our lives (7:12–13).

7:15 Despite all the mistakes the Corinthians made in their relationship with Paul, they did do one thing right. They listened when Titus presented Paul's version of some earlier events that they had misinterpreted. This teachability and lack of defensiveness drew great admiration and love from both Titus and Paul. A willingness to listen and be teachable is necessary for spiritual growth.

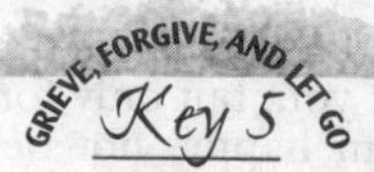

Sorrow Can Be Good for Us

2 Corinthians 7:8–11 Sometimes forgiving others or ourselves involves pain. When we confront people about their betrayal, abandonment, abuse, deception or other offenses, we face deep sorrow. True forgiveness may not always completely remove the pain we feel. We need to accept this pain as part of the consequences of sin and learn to freely express it to God. He can use the pain associated with wrongdoing to bring about good in our lives.

Not all sorrow is bad for us either. The apostle Paul wrote a letter to the Corinthians and made them very sad because he confronted them about something they were doing wrong. At first Paul was sorry that he had hurt them, but later he realized the benefit of sending the letter:

> Now I am happy, not because you were made sorry, but because your sorrow led you to repentance. For you became sorrowful as God intended and so were not harmed in any way by us. Godly sorrow brings repentance that leads to salvation and leaves no regret, but worldly sorrow brings death (7:9–10).

The grief Paul described was good, for it came from honest self-evaluation, not morbid self-condemnation. We can accept our sorrow for sin as a positive part of our spiritual growth. Whenever we encounter sorrow, we should ask God to use it to help redirect the course of our lives.

Turn to Colossians 3.

of sharing in this service to the saints. 5And they
did not do as we expected, but they gave themselves first to the Lord and then to us in keeping
with God's will. 6So we urged Titus, since he
had earlier made a beginning, to bring also to
completion this act of grace on your part. 7But
just as you excel in everything—in faith, in
speech, in knowledge, in complete earnestness
and in your love for us[a]—see that you also
excel in this grace of giving.

8I am not commanding you, but I want to
test the sincerity of your love by comparing it
with the earnestness of others. 9For you know
the grace of our Lord Jesus Christ, that though
he was rich, yet for your sakes he became poor,
so that you through his poverty might become
rich.

10And here is my advice about what is best
for you in this matter: Last year you were the
first not only to give but also to have the desire
to do so. 11Now finish the work, so that your
eager willingness to do it may be matched by
your completion of it, according to your means.
12For if the willingness is there, the gift is acceptable according to what one has, not according
to what he does not have.

13Our desire is not that others might be relieved while you are hard pressed, but that there
might be equality. 14At the present time your
plenty will supply what they need, so that in
turn their plenty will supply what you need.
Then there will be equality, 15as it is written:
"He who gathered much did not have too
much, and he who gathered little did not have
too little."[b]

Titus Sent to Corinth

16I thank God, who put into the heart of
Titus the same concern I have for you. 17For
Titus not only welcomed our appeal, but he is
coming to you with much enthusiasm and on
his own initiative. 18And we are sending along
with him the brother who is praised by all the
churches for his service to the gospel. 19What
is more, he was chosen by the churches to

[a] 7 Some manuscripts *in our love for you*
[b] 15 Exodus 16:18

8:9 The perfect model for a gracious servant is Jesus Christ. He became a lowly human being and died the death of a criminal on the cross to conquer sin and death. Jesus gave up his heavenly glory and willingly suffered on our behalf (see Philippians 2:6–8). Christ can also strongly identify with the pain and temptation we have suffered (see Hebrews 4:15). He is available and able to help us. As we receive his help, we can then reach out a helping hand to others in need.

8:10–12 The principle of perseverance is crucial for our ongoing spiritual development since it is much easier to start something than to finish it. In this case, the Corinthians had enthusiastically started a relief fund for the Jerusalem church, but then the believers had failed to follow through on their commitment. Paul confronted them and encouraged them to persevere in this worthy task. Once we have committed ourselves to spiritual growth, we need to persevere and follow through.

THE SPIRITUAL DISCIPLINES

Stewardship

Another Way to Say "I Love You"

2 Corinthians 8:1–9 Giving begins with the heart, not the checkbook. As Paul described the joy of the Macedonian Christians' giving he rejoiced in their motivation, because "they did not do as we expected, but they gave themselves first to the Lord and then to us in keeping with God's will" (8:5). Their commitment led to their sacrifice.

Sacrifice means giving up something we value for something we value more. The Macedonian Christians sacrificed because they valued the work of sharing with sisters and brothers in Christ. The greatest sacrifice of all was made when Jesus Christ sacrificed his life because he valued our redemption. "For you know the grace of our Lord Jesus Christ, that though he was rich, yet for your sakes he became poor, so that you through his poverty might become rich" (8:9).

Money can never substitute for words, but money can support our words. Our giving is one way to prove that love is real. A generous gift makes love visible in a practical way. That's why Paul speaks of the "grace of giving" (8:7). Our giving touches not only the physical needs of others but their hearts and souls as well.

For more on stewardship, turn to 2 Corinthians 9.

Putting It Into Practice

How do you use your financial and material resources to say "I love you"? Have you used them in ways that communicate a lack of care and love? Consider some specific ways you can communicate love by giving to the Lord's work and to others.

accompany us as we carry the offering, which we administer in order to honor the Lord himself and to show our eagerness to help. [20]We want to avoid any criticism of the way we administer this liberal gift. [21]For we are taking pains to do what is right, not only in the eyes of the Lord but also in the eyes of men.

[22]In addition, we are sending with them our brother who has often proved to us in many ways that he is zealous, and now even more so because of his great confidence in you. [23]As for Titus, he is my partner and fellow worker among you; as for our brothers, they are representatives of the churches and an honor to Christ. [24]Therefore show these men the proof of your love and the reason for our pride in you, so that the churches can see it.

9 There is no need for me to write to you about this service to the saints. [2]For I know your eagerness to help, and I have been boasting about it to the Macedonians, telling them that since last year you in Achaia were ready to give; and your enthusiasm has stirred most of them to action. [3]But I am sending the brothers in order that our boasting about you in this matter should not prove hollow, but that you may be ready, as I said you would be. [4]For if any Macedonians come with me and find you unprepared, we—not to say anything about you—would be ashamed of having been so confident. [5]So I thought it necessary to urge the brothers to visit you in advance and finish the arrangements for the generous gift you had promised. Then it will be ready as a generous gift, not as one grudgingly given.

Sowing Generously

[6]Remember this: Whoever sows sparingly will also reap sparingly, and whoever sows generously will also reap generously. [7]Each man should give what he has decided in his heart to give, not reluctantly or under compulsion, for God loves a cheerful giver. [8]And God is able to make all grace abound to you, so that in all things at all times, having all that you need, you will abound in every good work. [9]As it is written:

> "He has scattered abroad his gifts to the poor;
> his righteousness endures forever."[a]

[10]Now he who supplies seed to the sower and bread for food will also supply and increase your store of seed and will enlarge the harvest of your righteousness. [11]You will be made rich in every way so that you can be generous on every occasion, and through us your generosity will result in thanksgiving to God.

[12]This service that you perform is not only supplying the needs of God's people but is also overflowing in many expressions of thanks to God. [13]Because of the service by which you have proved yourselves, men will praise God for the obedience that accompanies your confession of the gospel of Christ, and for your generosity in sharing with them and with everyone else. [14]And in their prayers for you their hearts will go out to you, because of the surpassing grace God has given you. [15]Thanks be to God for his indescribable gift!

Paul's Defense of His Ministry

10 By the meekness and gentleness of Christ, I appeal to you—I, Paul, who am "timid" when face to face with you, but "bold" when away! [2]I beg you that when I come I may not have to be as bold as I expect to be toward some people who think that we live by the standards of this world. [3]For though we live in the world, we do not wage war as the world does. [4]The weapons we fight with are not the weapons of the world. On the contrary, they have divine power to demolish strongholds. [5]We demolish arguments and every pretension that sets itself up against the knowledge of God, and we take captive every thought to make it obedient to Christ. [6]And we will be ready to punish every act of disobedience, once your obedience is complete.

[7]You are looking only on the surface of things.[b] If anyone is confident that he belongs to Christ, he should consider again that we belong to Christ just as much as he. [8]For even if I boast somewhat freely about the authority the Lord gave us for building you up rather than pulling you down, I will not be ashamed of it. [9]I do not want to seem to be trying to frighten you with my letters. [10]For some say, "His letters are weighty and forceful, but in person he is unimpressive and his speaking amounts to nothing." [11]Such people should realize that what we are in our letters when we are absent, we will be in our actions when we are present.

[12]We do not dare to classify or compare ourselves with some who commend themselves. When they measure themselves by themselves and compare themselves with themselves, they are not wise. [13]We, however, will not boast

[a]9 Psalm 112:9 [b]7 Or *Look at the obvious facts*

9:6–9 The more spiritual seeds we plant by generously helping others, the greater will be our harvest of spiritual fruit. God never forces us to give; he wants us to give with willing hearts. God is not only interested in what we do; he is also interested in the attitudes and motives behind our actions. Everyone has something to give: time, talents, finances or just a listening ear. The way we give and the amount we give will show our true spiritual condition and also determine how much comes back to us from God.

10:13–15 Paul set limits on his ministry based on his understanding of God's will for him. He was confident that his leadership over the Corinthian church was a part of God's plan. Yet Paul understood that no one is called to do everything. When we know what God has called us to do, we must concentrate our limited energy on focused priorities that reflect God's will. We must discover what activities God wants us to be involved in on a daily basis too. Insight concerning God's will for us comes through

THE SPIRITUAL DISCIPLINES

Stewardship

The Harvest of Giving

2 Corinthians 9:6–10 These verses have often been interpreted as Scriptural promises that if we give to God, God will automatically give back to us wealth and health and many other blessings. Such teaching encourages us to *give to* God in order to *get from* God.

Experience teaches us, however, that many generous people live with ongoing financial pressures. As they continue to give sacrificially, God provides for their daily needs, but he doesn't always give them abundant wealth. Note also that the Bible doesn't teach us to give in order to get. The Bible says that we *get* in order to *give*. This reverse perspective makes all the difference. God blesses us so that we can give to others.

Instead of trying to manipulate God to nurture our selfish expectations, our giving should come as a response to God's blessing upon us.

For more on stewardship, turn to 1 Timothy 6.

Putting It Into Practice

How has God blessed you? Think of financial resources but also of other blessings and talents he has given you. How could you "plant" these blessings and cultivate a greater harvest for the Lord?

beyond proper limits, but will confine our
boasting to the field God has assigned to us, a
field that reaches even to you. 14We are not
going too far in our boasting, as would be the
case if we had not come to you, for we did get
as far as you with the gospel of Christ. 15Neither
do we go beyond our limits by boasting of work
done by others.[a] Our hope is that, as your faith
continues to grow, our area of activity among
you will greatly expand, 16so that we can preach
the gospel in the regions beyond you. For we do
not want to boast about work already done in
another man's territory. 17But, "Let him who
boasts boast in the Lord."[b] 18For it is not the
one who commends himself who is approved,
but the one whom the Lord commends.

Paul and the False Apostles

11 I hope you will put up with a little of
my foolishness; but you are already doing that. 2I am jealous for you with a godly
jealousy. I promised you to one husband, to
Christ, so that I might present you as a pure
virgin to him. 3But I am afraid that just as Eve
was deceived by the serpent's cunning, your
minds may somehow be led astray from your
sincere and pure devotion to Christ. 4For if
someone comes to you and preaches a Jesus
other than the Jesus we preached, or if you receive a different spirit from the one you received, or a different gospel from the one you
accepted, you put up with it easily enough. 5But
I do not think I am in the least inferior to those
"super-apostles." 6I may not be a trained speaker, but I do have knowledge. We have made this
perfectly clear to you in every way.

7Was it a sin for me to lower myself in order
to elevate you by preaching the gospel of God
to you free of charge? 8I robbed other churches
by receiving support from them so as to serve
you. 9And when I was with you and needed
something, I was not a burden to anyone, for
the brothers who came from Macedonia supplied what I needed. I have kept myself from
being a burden to you in any way, and will
continue to do so. 10As surely as the truth of
Christ is in me, nobody in the regions of Achaia
will stop this boasting of mine. 11Why? Because
I do not love you? God knows I do! 12And I will
keep on doing what I am doing in order to cut
the ground from under those who want an opportunity to be considered equal with us in the
things they boast about.

13For such men are false apostles, deceitful
workmen, masquerading as apostles of Christ.
14And no wonder, for Satan himself masquer-
ades as an angel of light. 15It is not surprising,
then, if his servants masquerade as servants of
righteousness. Their end will be what their actions deserve.

Paul Boasts About His Sufferings

16I repeat: Let no one take me for a fool. But
if you do, then receive me just as you would a
fool, so that I may do a little boasting. 17In this
self-confident boasting I am not talking as the
Lord would, but as a fool. 18Since many are
boasting in the way the world does, I too will
boast. 19You gladly put up with fools since you
are so wise! 20In fact, you even put up with
anyone who enslaves you or exploits you or
takes advantage of you or pushes himself forward or slaps you in the face. 21To my shame I
admit that we were too weak for that!

What anyone else dares to boast about—I am
speaking as a fool—I also dare to boast about.
22Are they Hebrews? So am I. Are they Israelites?
So am I. Are they Abraham's descendants? So
am I. 23Are they servants of Christ? (I am out of
my mind to talk like this.) I am more. I have
worked much harder, been in prison more frequently, been flogged more severely, and been
exposed to death again and again. 24Five times
I received from the Jews the forty lashes minus
one. 25Three times I was beaten with rods, once
I was stoned, three times I was shipwrecked, I
spent a night and a day in the open sea, 26I have
been constantly on the move. I have been in
danger from rivers, in danger from bandits, in
danger from my own countrymen, in danger

[a] *13-15* Or *13We, however, will not boast about things that cannot be measured, but we will boast according to the standard of measurement that the God of measure has assigned us—a measurement that relates even to you. 14 . . . . 15Neither do we boast about things that cannot be measured in regard to the work done by others.* [b] *17* Jer. 9:24

---

our study of the Scriptures, the help of godly friends and the guidance we receive from the Holy Spirit.

11:2–3 Paul was worried that the Corinthian believers would replace their faith in Jesus with a false faith. He was concerned for good reason. Corinth was a cosmopolitan city. Many religions and cults were practiced there. Paul also knew that if the Corinthians rejected Christ they would suffer painful consequences. Rejecting the abundant life offered by Jesus Christ would mean settling for a life of ultimate disaster. We also live in a world of multiple religions and beliefs. Only Jesus Christ paid the price for our sins and rose from the dead to prove it. Surrendering our lives to God excludes our surrendering to other gods or philosophies that oppose Jesus Christ.

11:13–15 The Corinthian believers had apparently rejected Paul's teachings and followed some false teachers who had twisted the Christian message. These false leaders were probably Judaizers who taught that salvation was only available through a combination of faith in Christ and adherence to the Jewish law (see 11:22). Paul made it clear in all of his letters that salvation is a free gift, paid for by the sacrificial work of Jesus Christ (see 1 Corinthians 2:12). Sometimes we want to prove our worthiness and earn our salvation by working hard. Most of us who have tried this approach, however, have had to admit that without God we are powerless over our sinful natures. But with his help, no problem is too great to overcome.

11:23–29 Paul demonstrated his commitment to Jesus Christ by listing a number of the hardships he had suffered. If nothing else, such ongoing mistreatment and deprivation revealed Paul's perseverance. Paul was definitely no fair-weather Christian or friend. Let us seek to imitate Paul and his faithful commitment to Christ.

from Gentiles; in danger in the city, in danger in the country, in danger at sea; and in danger from false brothers. [27]I have labored and toiled and have often gone without sleep; I have known hunger and thirst and have often gone without food; I have been cold and naked. [28]Besides everything else, I face daily the pressure of my concern for all the churches. [29]Who is weak, and I do not feel weak? Who is led into sin, and I do not inwardly burn?

[30]If I must boast, I will boast of the things that show my weakness. [31]The God and Father of the Lord Jesus, who is to be praised forever, knows that I am not lying. [32]In Damascus the governor under King Aretas had the city of the Damascenes guarded in order to arrest me. [33]But I was lowered in a basket from a window in the wall and slipped through his hands.

Paul's Vision and His Thorn

12 I must go on boasting. Although there is nothing to be gained, I will go on to visions and revelations from the Lord. [2]I know a man in Christ who fourteen years ago was caught up to the third heaven. Whether it was in the body or out of the body I do not know—God knows. [3]And I know that this man—whether in the body or apart from the body I do not know, but God knows— [4]was caught up to paradise. He heard inexpressible things, things that man is not permitted to tell. [5]I will boast about a man like that, but I will not boast about myself, except about my weaknesses. [6]Even if I should choose to boast, I would not be a fool, because I would be speaking the truth. But I refrain, so no one will think more of me than is warranted by what I do or say.

[7]To keep me from becoming conceited because of these surpassingly great revelations, there was given me a thorn in my flesh, a messenger of Satan, to torment me. [8]Three times I pleaded with the Lord to take it away from me. [9]But he said to me, "My grace is sufficient for you, for my power is made perfect in weakness." Therefore I will boast all the more gladly about my weaknesses, so that Christ's power may rest on me. [10]That is why, for Christ's sake, I delight in weaknesses, in insults, in hardships, in persecutions, in difficulties. For when I am weak, then I am strong.

Paul's Concern for the Corinthians

[11]I have made a fool of myself, but you drove me to it. I ought to have been commended by you, for I am not in the least inferior to the "super-apostles," even though I am nothing. [12]The things that mark an apostle—signs, wonders and miracles—were done among you with great perseverance. [13]How were you inferior to the other churches, except that I was never a burden to you? Forgive me this wrong!

[14]Now I am ready to visit you for the third time, and I will not be a burden to you, because what I want is not your possessions but you. After all, children should not have to save up for their parents, but parents for their children. [15]So I will very gladly spend for you everything I have and expend myself as well. If I love you more, will you love me less? [16]Be that as it may, I have not been a burden to you. Yet, crafty fellow that I am, I caught you by trickery! [17]Did I exploit you through any of the men I sent you? [18]I urged Titus to go to you and I sent our brother with him. Titus did not exploit you, did he? Did we not act in the same spirit and follow the same course?

[19]Have you been thinking all along that we have been defending ourselves to you? We have been speaking in the sight of God as those in Christ; and everything we do, dear friends, is for your strengthening. [20]For I am afraid that when I come I may not find you as I want you to be, and you may not find me as you want me to be. I fear that there may be quarreling, jealousy, outbursts of anger, factions, slander, gossip, arrogance and disorder. [21]I am afraid that when I come again my God will humble me before you, and I will be grieved over many who have sinned earlier and have not repented of the impurity, sexual sin and debauchery in which they have indulged.

Final Warnings

13 This will be my third visit to you. "Every matter must be established by the testimony of two or three witnesses."[a] [2]I already gave you a warning when I was with you the second time. I now repeat it while absent: On my return I will not spare those who sinned

[a]1 Deut. 19:15

11:30; 12:1–10 Paul's "boasting" was not intended to make him look better than he really was. Paul wanted to establish the truth about his person and apostolic authority. Even though he told about his incredible visit to heaven, Paul quickly balanced the scales by admitting his own weaknesses (11:30; 12:1–5). He also recounted God's grace at work in his life even through his chronic physical suffering and spiritual warfare (12:9–10). Paul made an honest assessment of his life, recognizing both his strengths and weaknesses. Then he accepted and received the powerful help that God offers to all who look to him. Paul is a good model for us to follow. As we make an honest assessment of our lives and learn to depend upon God's resources, we will make significant spiritual progress.

12:19–21 Everything that Paul said to the Corinthians, both negative and positive, was intended for their good. Paul was concerned that they mature in their faith. He did what he could to encourage their spiritual growth. Paul's love and concern for the Corinthians motivated the demands he made on them. Many of us realize that we often communicate with others for selfish reasons. When we compliment people, sometimes we are looking for a compliment in return. When we criticize others, we may be seeking to destroy rather than correct. As we reflect honestly on our lives, we need to see if we are using others for our own reasons. As we seek to restore our damaged relationships, the apostle Paul is an excellent model to follow.

13:2–3 Paul had warned the Corinthians that he would discipline them if they did not face their sins. In this pas-

earlier or any of the others, 3since you are demanding proof that Christ is speaking through
me. He is not weak in dealing with you, but is
powerful among you. 4For to be sure, he was
crucified in weakness, yet he lives by God's
power. Likewise, we are weak in him, yet by
God's power we will live with him to serve you.
5Examine yourselves to see whether you are
in the faith; test yourselves. Do you not realize
that Christ Jesus is in you—unless, of course,
you fail the test? 6And I trust that you will discover that we have not failed the test. 7Now we
pray to God that you will not do anything
wrong. Not that people will see that we have
stood the test but that you will do what is right
even though we may seem to have failed. 8For
we cannot do anything against the truth, but
only for the truth. 9We are glad whenever we are
weak but you are strong; and our prayer is for
your perfection. 10This is why I write these
things when I am absent, that when I come I
may not have to be harsh in my use of authority—the authority the Lord gave me for building
you up, not for tearing you down.

Final Greetings

11Finally, brothers, good-by. Aim for perfection, listen to my appeal, be of one mind, live
in peace. And the God of love and peace will be
with you.
12Greet one another with a holy kiss. 13All
the saints send their greetings.
14May the grace of the Lord Jesus Christ, and
the love of God, and the fellowship of the Holy
Spirit be with you all.

---

sage Paul gave them an additional warning. He had been away from Corinth for longer than he had intended, and Paul wanted to make sure that the people knew his warning was not hollow. Paul would indeed follow through forcefully and hold the Corinthian believers accountable to their commitments to God. We all need someone like Paul in our lives: a godly person who holds us accountable to follow God's will.

13:5–6 Paul urged the Corinthian believers to engage in serious self-examination. He wanted them to assess the nature of their commitment to God by looking closely at their own lives. If we hope to uncover the problems that tear down our relationships with others, we must admit our failures to God and trust him to help us make spiritual progress and restore our broken relationships.

13:11 As Paul closed this letter to the Corinthians, he left them with some worthy goals to pursue. He admonished the people to open their minds and hearts to personal change and the healing of their relationships. Such spiritual growth and interpersonal harmony can be fueled by faith in God, the ultimate source of healing, love and peace. As modern readers of this letter, we can benefit by acting on Paul's wise advice too.

GALATIANS

The Big Picture

Paul planted the churches in Galatia during his first missionary journey through Asia Minor. But within months of Paul's ministry there, certain people began to contradict the Good News Paul had preached. These teachers claimed that non-Jewish converts to Christ had to keep the Jewish law in order to be Christians. This meant that all Gentile believers who sought membership in the church would have to be circumcised.

This alternative gospel was very appealing to the Galatian believers. For one thing, its proponents claimed to have the direct blessing of the apostles back in Jerusalem. Their arguments from the Old Testament seemed to be flawless and irrefutable. But because Paul knew how destructive this teaching could be, he wrote this letter to correct it.

Paul made it clear to the Galatians that in Christ they were truly free: free from the demands of the Jewish law, free from the power of sin, free to live under God's grace. We may wonder why the Galatians would ever want to give up the freedom they had in Christ. But bondage is subtle. No one enters into sin with the intention of becoming a slave to it. We may slowly become dependent on behaviors, substances and attitudes that are outside God's will for us. If we are not spiritually aware, these sinful patterns may become so comfortable and familiar that they give us a false sense of security.

This letter to the Galatian believers challenges us to hold on to our freedom. Being controlled by anything or anyone other than God means living a life of slavery. Trying to attain spiritual growth by our own ability and strength is also impossible. We cannot escape the grip of sin alone, but as we seek God and continually surrender to his will, he will graciously give us the power we need to break free.

A. GREETINGS (1:1-5)

B. THE PEOPLE'S REJECTION OF GOD'S GRACE (1:6-10)

C. PAUL'S DEFENSE OF THE GOSPEL OF GRACE (1:11–6:10)

1. Confirmed by the Apostles (1:11–2:21)
2. Confirmed by the People's Membership in God's Family (3:1–4:31)
3. Confirmed by the People's Deliverance From Sin's Power (5:1–6:10)

D. CONCLUSION (6:11-18)

Spiritual Renewal Themes

THE SEDUCTION OF THE LAW

For some of us, following a set of rules may seem easier than reflecting on our spiritual condition, praying, meditating on the Bible or engaging in some other activity that leads to a deeper relationship with God. Perhaps this was the Galatians' mistake. They may have reasoned that if they had some rules to follow, they would become spiritually mature. However, merely follow-

Essential Facts

PURPOSE:
To encourage readers to depend on Christ alone for salvation and daily strength.

AUTHOR:
The apostle Paul.

AUDIENCE:
Several churches in southern Galatia.

DATE WRITTEN:
Probably between A.D. 48 and 53.

SETTING:
The most pressing controversy in the early church was whether new, Gentile converts needed to accept Jewish laws in order to be a part of the church. Paul wrote this letter to answer that question.

KEY VERSE:
"It is for freedom that Christ has set us free. Stand firm, then, and do not let yourselves be burdened again by a yoke of slavery" (5:1).

KEY PEOPLE AND RELATIONSHIPS:
Paul with the Galatian believers and with the Jerusalem apostles, as well as with the false teachers.

ing a set of rules is not a key to spiritual renewal and transformation. Not only is it impossible for us to follow such laws faithfully, but such an attitude also leads us away from dependence on God, the source of true spiritual renewal.

SPIRITUAL RENEWAL LEADS TO TRUE FREEDOM

This letter shows us how to find true spiritual freedom. Paul's advice to the Galatians applies to us as we search for freedom from our own imprisonments. True freedom is found only as we surrender our lives to God, depending not on our self-sufficiency but on his power to free us. Believing in Christ is the only way we can find true freedom from our bondage to sin.

THE POWER OF THE HOLY SPIRIT

We become believers as the Holy Spirit draws us back to God. We also are empowered in our spiritual growth by this same Holy Spirit. The faith to believe and the courage to admit our lack of power are gifts from him. The Holy Spirit instructs, guides, leads and gives us God's power. It is he who ends our bondage to self-sufficiency, pride and evil desires, breaking the cycles of sin that dominate us. And it is God's gracious Holy Spirit that bears the fruit of love, joy, peace and self-control in our lives.

THE NECESSITY OF FAITH

Some of us have been frustrated, even discouraged to the point of giving up, by our inadequate efforts to change. Freedom from sin and its destructive effects is only possible through faith in Jesus Christ. Surrendering our wills and our lives to God will bring new life. By repenting from our sins and placing our trust and confidence in Jesus Christ, we experience forgiveness and unconditional acceptance from God. His power then works within us to inspire our continued growth and dependence on him.

1 Paul, an apostle—sent not from men nor by man, but by Jesus Christ and God the Father, who raised him from the dead— 2and all the brothers with me,

To the churches in Galatia:

3Grace and peace to you from God our Father and the Lord Jesus Christ, 4who gave himself for our sins to rescue us from the present evil age, according to the will of our God and Father, 5to whom be glory for ever and ever. Amen.

No Other Gospel

6I am astonished that you are so quickly deserting the one who called you by the grace of Christ and are turning to a different gospel— 7which is really no gospel at all. Evidently some people are throwing you into confusion and are trying to pervert the gospel of Christ. 8But even if we or an angel from heaven should preach a gospel other than the one we preached to you, let him be eternally condemned! 9As we have already said, so now I say again: If anybody is preaching to you a gospel other than what you accepted, let him be eternally condemned!

10Am I now trying to win the approval of men, or of God? Or am I trying to please men? If I were still trying to please men, I would not be a servant of Christ.

Paul Called by God

11I want you to know, brothers, that the gospel I preached is not something that man made up. 12I did not receive it from any man, nor was I taught it; rather, I received it by revelation from Jesus Christ.

13For you have heard of my previous way of life in Judaism, how intensely I persecuted the church of God and tried to destroy it. 14I was advancing in Judaism beyond many Jews of my own age and was extremely zealous for the traditions of my fathers. 15But when God, who set me apart from birth[a] and called me by his grace, was pleased 16to reveal his Son in me so that I might preach him among the Gentiles, I did not consult any man, 17nor did I go up to Jerusalem to see those who were apostles before I was, but I went immediately into Arabia and later returned to Damascus.

18Then after three years, I went up to Jerusalem to get acquainted with Peter[b] and stayed with him fifteen days. 19I saw none of the other apostles—only James, the Lord's brother. 20I assure you before God that what I am writing you is no lie. 21Later I went to Syria and Cilicia. 22I was personally unknown to the churches of Judea that are in Christ. 23They only heard the report: "The man who formerly persecuted us is now preaching the faith he once tried to destroy." 24And they praised God because of me.

Paul Accepted by the Apostles

2 Fourteen years later I went up again to Jerusalem, this time with Barnabas. I took Titus along also. 2I went in response to a revelation and set before them the gospel that I preach among the Gentiles. But I did this privately to those who seemed to be leaders, for fear that I was running or had run my race in vain. 3Yet not even Titus, who was with me, was compelled to be circumcised, even though he was a Greek. 4⌊This matter arose⌋ because some false brothers had infiltrated our ranks to spy on the freedom we have in Christ Jesus and to make us slaves. 5We did not give in to them for a moment, so that the truth of the gospel might remain with you.

6As for those who seemed to be important—whatever they were makes no difference to me; God does not judge by external appearance—those men added nothing to my message. 7On the contrary, they saw that I had been entrusted

[a]15 Or *from my mother's womb* [b]18 Greek *Cephas*

1:1–5 In his greeting, Paul introduced the main themes of his letter: his God-given apostolic authority and clear teachings about the fatherhood of God and the saving power of Jesus Christ. God is our loving Father. When we surrender our lives to him, he will help us overcome our sinfulness through his Son, Jesus.

1:7–10 The Galatians were confused. Paul quickly pointed out that they had to choose between the true gospel he preached and the false gospel preached by his opponents. As we look for a way to deal with our past sins and failures, we face some choices too. Some say we can ignore our sins; why deal with them at all? Others offer us a legalistic system to effect our own salvation by adhering to a set of rules or rituals. Both of these methods represent false gospels. True spiritual renewal comes when we repent of our sins and receive God's forgiveness through the death and resurrection of Jesus Christ. Our surrender opens the way to a relationship with God in which the Holy Spirit empowers us to triumph over sin as God transforms our lives.

1:11–24 As Paul looked back on his conversion experience, he recalled that he had once been a zealous Jew. He had actively worked to defend his faith against the threat of Christianity. But then, God in Jesus Christ graciously reached out and radically transformed him. Paul recognized that all his religious activities were ultimately fruitless; through them, he could never be delivered from the sin in his life. Only God could forgive his sin and give him the power to start over again. If we have tried to overcome our sinful natures through religious activity, hard work or some ritual, we already know what it means to fail. But if we have surrendered our lives to God and learned to live by his power, we know the secret of victory. God's power through Jesus Christ is the only means to true change.

2:1–10 In this letter, Paul wanted to present a clear argument against the teachings of the Judaizers. These people recognized that God's work through Jesus Christ was important, but they also believed that people were required to follow the Jewish laws to obtain salvation. For them, salvation was based on actions as well as on God's gracious gift. Paul wanted the Galatians to realize that none of us can follow God's laws adequately on our own. Christ alone has the power to release us from sin and its destructive consequences. Most of us know that we need God's power to overcome our sinful nature. Paul's message of grace is a source of hope for us as we look to God to help us overcome sin in our lives.

with the task of preaching the gospel to the
Gentiles,[a] just as Peter had been to the Jews.[b]
8For God, who was at work in the ministry of
Peter as an apostle to the Jews, was also at work
in my ministry as an apostle to the Gentiles.
9James, Peter[c] and John, those reputed to be
pillars, gave me and Barnabas the right hand of
fellowship when they recognized the grace giv-
en to me. They agreed that we should go to the
Gentiles, and they to the Jews. 10All they asked
was that we should continue to remember the
poor, the very thing I was eager to do.

Paul Opposes Peter

11When Peter came to Antioch, I opposed
him to his face, because he was clearly in the
wrong. 12Before certain men came from James,
he used to eat with the Gentiles. But when they
arrived, he began to draw back and separate
himself from the Gentiles because he was afraid
of those who belonged to the circumcision
group. 13The other Jews joined him in his hypocrisy, so that by their hypocrisy even Barnabas was led astray.

14When I saw that they were not acting in
line with the truth of the gospel, I said to Peter
in front of them all, "You are a Jew, yet you live
like a Gentile and not like a Jew. How is it, then,
that you force Gentiles to follow Jewish customs?

15"We who are Jews by birth and not 'Gentile sinners' 16know that a man is not justified
by observing the law, but by faith in Jesus
Christ. So we, too, have put our faith in Christ
Jesus that we may be justified by faith in Christ
and not by observing the law, because by observing the law no one will be justified.

17"If, while we seek to be justified in Christ,
it becomes evident that we ourselves are sinners, does that mean that Christ promotes sin?
Absolutely not! 18If I rebuild what I destroyed,
I prove that I am a lawbreaker. 19For through
the law I died to the law so that I might live for
God. 20I have been crucified with Christ and I
no longer live, but Christ lives in me. The life I
live in the body, I live by faith in the Son of
God, who loved me and gave himself for me. 21I
do not set aside the grace of God, for if righteousness could be gained through the law,
Christ died for nothing!"[d]

Faith or Observance of the Law

3 You foolish Galatians! Who has bewitched
you? Before your very eyes Jesus Christ was
clearly portrayed as crucified. 2I would like to
learn just one thing from you: Did you receive
the Spirit by observing the law, or by believing
what you heard? 3Are you so foolish? After beginning with the Spirit, are you now trying to
attain your goal by human effort? 4Have you
suffered so much for nothing—if it really was for
nothing? 5Does God give you his Spirit and
work miracles among you because you observe
the law, or because you believe what you heard?

6Consider Abraham: "He believed God, and
it was credited to him as righteousness."[e] 7Un-
derstand, then, that those who believe are children of Abraham. 8The Scripture foresaw that
God would justify the Gentiles by faith, and
announced the gospel in advance to Abraham:
"All nations will be blessed through you."[f] 9So
those who have faith are blessed along with
Abraham, the man of faith.

10All who rely on observing the law are under
a curse, for it is written: "Cursed is everyone
who does not continue to do everything written
in the Book of the Law."[g] 11Clearly no one is
justified before God by the law, because, "The
righteous will live by faith."[h] 12The law is not
based on faith; on the contrary, "The man who
does these things will live by them."[i] 13Christ
redeemed us from the curse of the law by becoming a curse for us, for it is written: "Cursed
is everyone who is hung on a tree."[j] 14He redeemed us in order that the blessing given to
Abraham might come to the Gentiles through
Christ Jesus, so that by faith we might receive
the promise of the Spirit.

[a]7 Greek *uncircumcised* [b]7 Greek *circumcised;* also in verses 8 and 9 [c]9 Greek *Cephas;* also in verses 11 and 14 [d]21 Some interpreters end the quotation after verse 14. [e]6 Gen. 15:6 [f]8 Gen. 12:3; 18:18; 22:18 [g]10 Deut. 27:26 [h]11 Hab. 2:4 [i]12 Lev. 18:5 [j]13 Deut. 21:23

2:11–14 The apostle Peter, a Jewish Christian, recognized that salvation is a free gift of grace. He freely associated with the Gentile Christians in Antioch despite the fact that they had not fulfilled the Jewish law of circumcision. When other Jewish Christian leaders arrived in Antioch, however, Peter felt the influence of his Jewish peers. He pulled back from his relationships with the Gentile believers and began to act as if obeying the Jewish law was necessary for salvation. Paul confronted Peter about his prejudice, and the problem was resolved. Like Peter, we need to listen to others when they point out our wrong behavior. Then we can ask God to help us change.

2:20–21 What a wonderful assurance! Christ himself lives in us! Yet life is a paradox: We are crucified with him; nevertheless, we still live in the flesh. In the spiritual realm, our old natures died with Christ, and we have new natures. And yet, in the natural realm, we still struggle with our body of flesh that craves sin. We cannot make our flesh change, but by faith in Christ we can operate above the level of our sinful flesh. We can allow Jesus Christ himself to live in us and through us, empowering us to live a holy life by the power of the Holy Spirit. By faith we can live according to our new natures.

3:1–14 We become true sons of Abraham, as spoken of here in the Bible, when we receive the redemption available to us through the sacrifice of Jesus Christ. The evidence of becoming Abraham's sons and daughters is not circumcision but the presence of the Holy Spirit in our lives (3:14). We can be sure of the Holy Spirit's presence when we begin to see changes in our lives. Knowing God and being in a right relationship with him enable us to know his will and to follow it. Trying to follow God's laws in our human strength will never bring us into a right relationship with God.

The Law and the Promise

15 Brothers, let me take an example from everyday life. Just as no one can set aside or add
to a human covenant that has been duly established, so it is in this case. 16 The promises were
spoken to Abraham and to his seed. The Scripture does not say "and to seeds," meaning many
people, but "and to your seed,"[a] meaning one
person, who is Christ. 17 What I mean is this:
The law, introduced 430 years later, does not set
aside the covenant previously established by
God and thus do away with the promise. 18 For
if the inheritance depends on the law, then it no
longer depends on a promise; but God in his
grace gave it to Abraham through a promise.
19 What, then, was the purpose of the law? It
was added because of transgressions until the
Seed to whom the promise referred had come.
The law was put into effect through angels by a
mediator. 20 A mediator, however, does not represent just one party; but God is one.
21 Is the law, therefore, opposed to the promises of God? Absolutely not! For if a law had
been given that could impart life, then righteousness would certainly have come by the
law. 22 But the Scripture declares that the whole
world is a prisoner of sin, so that what was
promised, being given through faith in Jesus
Christ, might be given to those who believe.
23 Before this faith came, we were held prisoners by the law, locked up until faith should
be revealed. 24 So the law was put in charge to
lead us to Christ[b] that we might be justified by
faith. 25 Now that faith has come, we are no
longer under the supervision of the law.

Sons of God

26 You are all sons of God through faith in
Christ Jesus, 27 for all of you who were baptized
into Christ have clothed yourselves with Christ.
28 There is neither Jew nor Greek, slave nor free,
male nor female, for you are all one in Christ
Jesus. 29 If you belong to Christ, then you are
Abraham's seed, and heirs according to the
promise.

4 What I am saying is that as long as the heir
is a child, he is no different from a slave,
although he owns the whole estate. 2 He is subject to guardians and trustees until the time set
by his father. 3 So also, when we were children,
we were in slavery under the basic principles of
the world. 4 But when the time had fully come,
God sent his Son, born of a woman, born under
law, 5 to redeem those under law, that we might
receive the full rights of sons. 6 Because you are
sons, God sent the Spirit of his Son into our
hearts, the Spirit who calls out, "*Abba*,[c] Father."
7 So you are no longer a slave, but a son; and
since you are a son, God has made you also an
heir.

Paul's Concern for the Galatians

8 Formerly, when you did not know God, you
were slaves to those who by nature are not gods.
9 But now that you know God—or rather are
known by God—how is it that you are turning
back to those weak and miserable principles?
Do you wish to be enslaved by them all over
again? 10 You are observing special days and
months and seasons and years! 11 I fear for you,
that somehow I have wasted my efforts on you.
12 I plead with you, brothers, become like me,
for I became like you. You have done me no
wrong. 13 As you know, it was because of an
illness that I first preached the gospel to you.
14 Even though my illness was a trial to you, you
did not treat me with contempt or scorn. Instead, you welcomed me as if I were an angel of
God, as if I were Christ Jesus himself. 15 What
has happened to all your joy? I can testify that,
if you could have done so, you would have torn
out your eyes and given them to me. 16 Have I
now become your enemy by telling you the
truth?
17 Those people are zealous to win you over,

[a] *16* Gen. 12:7; 13:15; 24:7 [b] *24* Or *charge until Christ came* [c] *6* Aramaic for *Father*

3:15–29 God's relationship with us is not based on our ability to keep the law but on the promises made to Abraham to bless all humanity through his offspring Jesus Christ. The law demonstrates that we are sinners deserving punishment. Through the law we see that we need a Savior. The law is only a measuring stick that reveals our sin problem. None of us is capable of true and complete obedience. Though we are helpless, God desires to bless us, not curse us. His blessings come when we trust in his promises, not when we perform according to his perfect standards. Knowing that God loves us enough to pay for our sins gives us courage to honestly reflect on our lives. Jesus Christ has paid for our sins; therefore, we have nothing to fear. We can openly confess our sins to God and trust in his forgiveness. When we do, he will set us free from sin's destructive power.
3:26–29 When we surrender our lives to God in Jesus Christ, we become God's children. What an amazing truth! We are given a place in God's family! He has a plan for us, and, like any parent, he wants to help us succeed. Each of us is important to God, and he is concerned enough to help us overcome our sins and fulfill his plan for our lives. Faith in Christ is all we need to enter into this privileged status.
4:8–11 If we are not willing to trust and obey God in Jesus Christ, we soon become enslaved to something else: drugs, alcohol, sexual activity, work or even religious rituals. But these solutions can never take care of our problems. In fact, depending on anything other than God himself leads to deeper problems. Only God offers us the power to be delivered from bondage to build a new life. Turning to him for help is really the only valid option we have if we want to live freely.
4:17–20 Paul wanted the Galatians to experience the new life that God offers in Jesus Christ without asking anything in return. The false teachers were trying to lead the people back into bondage under Jewish law and demanded a position of authority in return. There is a distinct contrast between Paul's attitudes and actions and those of the false teachers. We need to know the source of the spiritual teachings to which we subscribe. Every teaching must be tested to see if it agrees with God's Word. If it

but for no good. What they want is to alienate you ⌞from us⌟, so that you may be zealous for them. 18It is fine to be zealous, provided the purpose is good, and to be so always and not just when I am with you. 19My dear children, for whom I am again in the pains of childbirth until Christ is formed in you, 20how I wish I could be with you now and change my tone, because I am perplexed about you!

Hagar and Sarah

21Tell me, you who want to be under the law, are you not aware of what the law says? 22For it is written that Abraham had two sons, one by the slave woman and the other by the free woman. 23His son by the slave woman was born in the ordinary way; but his son by the free woman was born as the result of a promise.

24These things may be taken figuratively, for the women represent two covenants. One covenant is from Mount Sinai and bears children who are to be slaves: This is Hagar. 25Now Hagar stands for Mount Sinai in Arabia and corresponds to the present city of Jerusalem, because she is in slavery with her children. 26But the Jerusalem that is above is free, and she is our mother. 27For it is written:

"Be glad, O barren woman,
who bears no children;
break forth and cry aloud,
you who have no labor pains;
because more are the children of the
desolate woman
than of her who has a husband."[a]

28Now you, brothers, like Isaac, are children of promise. 29At that time the son born in the ordinary way persecuted the son born by the power of the Spirit. It is the same now. 30But what does the Scripture say? "Get rid of the slave woman and her son, for the slave woman's son will never share in the inheritance with the free woman's son."[b] 31Therefore, brothers, we are not children of the slave woman, but of the free woman.

Freedom in Christ

5 It is for freedom that Christ has set us free. Stand firm, then, and do not let yourselves be burdened again by a yoke of slavery.

2Mark my words! I, Paul, tell you that if you let yourselves be circumcised, Christ will be of no value to you at all. 3Again I declare to every man who lets himself be circumcised that he is obligated to obey the whole law. 4You who are trying to be justified by law have been alienated from Christ; you have fallen away from grace. 5But by faith we eagerly await through the Spirit the righteousness for which we hope. 6For in Christ Jesus neither circumcision nor uncircumcision has any value. The only thing that counts is faith expressing itself through love.

7You were running a good race. Who cut in on you and kept you from obeying the truth? 8That kind of persuasion does not come from the one who calls you. 9"A little yeast works through the whole batch of dough." 10I am confident in the Lord that you will take no other view. The one who is throwing you into confusion will pay the penalty, whoever he may be. 11Brothers, if I am still preaching circumcision, why am I still being persecuted? In that case the offense of the cross has been abolished. 12As for those agitators, I wish they would go the whole way and emasculate themselves!

13You, my brothers, were called to be free. But do not use your freedom to indulge the sinful nature[c]; rather, serve one another in love. 14The entire law is summed up in a single command: "Love your neighbor as yourself."[d] 15If you keep on biting and devouring each other, watch out or you will be destroyed by each other.

Life by the Spirit

16So I say, live by the Spirit, and you will not gratify the desires of the sinful nature. 17For the sinful nature desires what is contrary to the Spirit, and the Spirit what is contrary to the sinful nature. They are in conflict with each other, so that you do not do what you want. 18But if you are led by the Spirit, you are not under law.

19The acts of the sinful nature are obvious: sexual immorality, impurity and debauchery; 20idolatry and witchcraft; hatred, discord, jealousy, fits of rage, selfish ambition, dissensions, factions 21and envy; drunkenness, orgies, and the like. I warn you, as I did before, that those who live like this will not inherit the kingdom of God.

22But the fruit of the Spirit is love, joy, peace,

[a]*27* Isaiah 54:1 [b]*30* Gen. 21:10 [c]*13* Or *the flesh;* also in verses 16, 17, 19 and 24 [d]*14* Lev. 19:18

---

does not agree with God's Word, the teaching must be rejected.

5:1–12 The Galatians faced a choice we also must make: *Should we choose a life of power and freedom in Christ or a life of slavery through useless solutions?* If we make the wrong choice, we will be cut off from the deliverance available to God's people. There is no deliverance from the power of sin except through Christ and his powerful presence in our lives.

5:16–21 God's will for us may stand directly opposed to our natural desires. We must see this truth, willingly turn away from our own selfish desires and allow God to redirect our course back to following his will. This passages lists destructive behaviors that flow out of a self-centered life. When we turn our lives over to God, we let his Spirit help us control the desires that lead us to sin. God's desires become our own desires. Considering the facts, submitting our lives to God's plan will be the best choice we can ever make.

5:22–24 These characteristics are a product of the Holy Spirit's work in a life submitted to God and his plan. Just as a tree bears fruit by means of God's silent work behind

THE SPIRITUAL DISCIPLINES

Service

Bearing Each Other's Burdens

Galatians 6:1 – 10 Supporting one another is a vital part of the spiritual discipline of service. We must walk alongside each other on the journey of discipleship, serving others by helping them stay on, or return to, the path of faithfulness. But we also need to serve them by making sure *we* continue in faithfulness. Self-neglect and irresponsibility impose an unfair burden on our sisters and brothers in Christ, for they are responsible to help us as well.

The body of Christ is not a place of self-sufficiency, but rather a place of interdependency. When we share each other's troubles and problems, we are fulfilling the law of love. Our burdens should bring us together. As we allow others to help bear our burdens, we find our love and appreciation for them growing. Our weaknesses call forth others' strengths. As we serve others, we sow the seeds of support that will bear fruit when we most need it.

Putting It Into Practice

Do you know someone who is under a heavy burden at this time? What practical way can you come alongside that person and help bear that heavy load? Prayerfully consider what God may be calling you to do, and then make yourself available to do it.

For more on service, turn to Philippians 2.

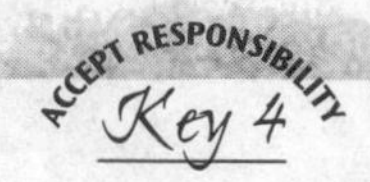

Obeying the Holy Spirit

Galatians 5:16–23 As we take responsibility for our lives, we must also take responsibility for obeying the Holy Spirit's instructions. As we continue the process of spiritual renewal, God's Spirit will begin to produce fruit in our lives.

The apostle Paul explained it in this way:

> So I say, live by the Spirit, and you will not gratify the desires of the sinful nature. For the sinful nature desires what is contrary to the Spirit, and the Spirit what is contrary to the sinful nature. They are in conflict with each other, so that you do not do what you want . . . But the fruit of the Spirit is love, joy, peace, patience, kindness, goodness, faithfulness, gentleness and self-control. Against such things there is no law (5:16–17, 22–23).

Fruit doesn't instantly appear on trees. As trees grow and seasons pass, fruit slowly develops. In a similar way, as we continue to accept our responsibility to obey the Holy Spirit, good spiritual fruit will begin to appear in our lives. Our primary responsibility is to stay connected to God. It is the Holy Spirit's responsibility to produce good fruit in us.

Turn to 2 Thessalonians 3.

patience, kindness, goodness, faithfulness,
23gentleness and self-control. Against such
things there is no law. 24Those who belong to
Christ Jesus have crucified the sinful nature
with its passions and desires. 25Since we live by
the Spirit, let us keep in step with the Spirit.
26Let us not become conceited, provoking and
envying each other.

Doing Good to All

6 Brothers, if someone is caught in a sin, you
who are spiritual should restore him gently. But watch yourself, or you also may be
tempted. 2Carry each other's burdens, and in
this way you will fulfill the law of Christ. 3If
anyone thinks he is something when he is nothing, he deceives himself. 4Each one should
test his own actions. Then he can take pride in
himself, without comparing himself to somebody else, 5for each one should carry his own
load.
6Anyone who receives instruction in the
word must share all good things with his instructor.
7Do not be deceived: God cannot be
mocked. A man reaps what he sows. 8The one
who sows to please his sinful nature, from that
nature[a] will reap destruction; the one who
sows to please the Spirit, from the Spirit will
reap eternal life. 9Let us not become weary in
doing good, for at the proper time we will reap
a harvest if we do not give up. 10Therefore, as we
have opportunity, let us do good to all people,
especially to those who belong to the family of
believers.

[a]8 Or *his flesh, from the flesh*

---

the scenes, we produce this fruit of the Spirit by means of God's power alone. Our part is to surrender our lives to him. When the Holy Spirit begins to bear this fruit in our lives, sin loses its power. With *joy* and *peace* we overcome the pain of our broken past. With *love, kindness, goodness, faithfulness,* and *gentleness* we restore our relationships and make restitution. With *patience* we persevere through the difficult times. With *self-control* we stand against temptation. God's Spirit can supply everything we need for fruitful lives.

6:1–3 Paul urged the Galatians to share their troubles with one another. He knew that this would bring healing to hurting people and provide opportunities for the believers to help one another. Since Paul knew that some would be too proud to admit their problems, he jotted a special note to encourage everyone's participation. We all need to admit our problems. With such mutual encouragement and accountability, we will all be able to lighten the burdens of our sins and the burdens of others as together we move on toward a productive future.

6:7–10 We will always reap what we have sown. Sin brings painful consequences. We might be able to fool ourselves for a while into thinking that certain activities and relationships are all right. But when the consequences catch up with us, there will be no denying the facts of sin's devastation. We need to take Paul's warning seriously and take steps to change now. Using God's Word as a measuring stick, we can reflect honestly on our lives and make the necessary adjustments, repenting of our sin and asking God to redirect our course before it's too late.

Not Circumcision but a New Creation

11See what large letters I use as I write to you
with my own hand!

12Those who want to make a good impression outwardly are trying to compel you to be
circumcised. The only reason they do this is to
avoid being persecuted for the cross of Christ.
13Not even those who are circumcised obey the
law, yet they want you to be circumcised that
they may boast about your flesh. 14May I never
boast except in the cross of our Lord Jesus
Christ, through which[a] the world has been
crucified to me, and I to the world. 15Neither
circumcision nor uncircumcision means anything; what counts is a new creation. 16Peace
and mercy to all who follow this rule, even to
the Israel of God.

17Finally, let no one cause me trouble, for I
bear on my body the marks of Jesus.

18The grace of our Lord Jesus Christ be with
your spirit, brothers. Amen.

[a]14 Or *whom*

6:11–18 In these concluding verses, Paul recapped his major arguments. He appealed to the Galatians to stand firm against the false teachers who were trying to attract people away from the liberating message of the gospel. Admitting that we are helpless to overcome our sins and accepting God's help are responsible decisions we must make in order to achieve spiritual renewal. Rather than humiliate us, God bestows dignity and healing on us when we stand firm in our faith.

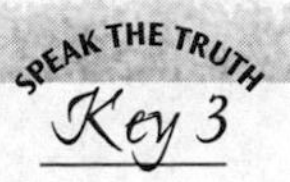

Exposing Our Buried Sins

Galatians 6:7–10 Instead of confessing our faults to another person and to God, we may fool ourselves into believing that we can simply bury our wrongs deep in our hearts and move on. In time, however, we will discover that those deeds we thought were buried once and for all were actually seeds. They will grow and bear fruit, and eventually we will have to harvest the consequences of our sin.

The apostle Paul made it clear that "A man reaps what he sows. The one who sows to please his sinful nature, from that nature will reap destruction; the one who sows to please the Spirit, from the Spirit will reap eternal life" (6:7–8). John further instructs us, "If we claim to be without sin, we deceive ourselves and the truth is not in us. If we confess our sins, he is faithful and just and will forgive us our sins and purify us from all unrighteousness" (1 John 1:8–9).

Confessing our sins includes giving an exact account in specific terms. When we get specific about our sin, we can no longer fool ourselves about the nature of our wrongs. Since we cannot ignore God and get away with it, we should tell the truth at the beginning. Then we can rid ourselves of self-deception and receive healing and cleansing.

Turn to Colossians 1.

EPHESIANS

The Big Picture

A. GREETINGS (1:1-2)

B. ASSURANCE OF GOD'S PLAN FOR SPIRITUAL RENEWAL (1:3–3:21)

C. ACCEPTANCE OF OUR SPIRITUAL RESPONSIBILITY (4:1–6:9)

D. AWARENESS OF OUR ROLE IN SPIRITUAL WARFARE (6:10-20)

E. CLOSING REMARKS (6:21-24)

Paul planted the Ephesian church (see Acts 18:19–21) and ministered there for a few years (see Acts 19:8–10; 20:31). This church thrived in a city renowned as a center for the worship of the goddess Artemis (also known as Diana). While Paul was ministering there, the Ephesian believers maintained a strong attachment to him. And when Paul moved on, the believers openly expressed their sorrow.

How could the Ephesian church survive in its hostile environment? They could not depend on Paul's presence forever; they would have to learn to stand on their own, with God's help. Paul wrote this letter to remind the Ephesian believers to place their faith in the only solid foundation for healthy living—God in Jesus Christ.

How can we maintain our spiritual growth in a hostile environment? Not one of us has the resources or strength to initiate and sustain our spiritual growth alone. But Paul understood one important fact: Our transformation is possible only on God's terms. We must break with our former ways of life and depend on God's power to help us change. While our own efforts and those of supportive people are helpful, lasting spiritual growth will only happen when we recognize our need for God—the God who created us and sustains our lives.

Belief in God, repentance from sin and continuing obedience to God's will are keys to genuine, stable spiritual growth. If our attitudes and actions reflect God's truth and we adopt a new attitude of submission to God's authority and care, we will indeed make progress. If we ignore God, as he has revealed himself in the Bible, or choose to create a "god" to our liking, our spiritual renewal is doomed to failure. True and lasting spiritual renewal comes only as we submit ourselves to the righteous rule of the true and living God.

Spiritual Renewal Themes

GOD'S DESIRE FOR OUR SPIRITUAL RENEWAL

God's plan for us doesn't include our bondage to sin or the past. God wants us to have a relationship with him so we can enjoy his love and presence. He wants this even more than we do! Some of us have distorted images of God based on painful images of authority figures from our past. The book of Eph-

esians shows us that God is a Father who has loved us from the beginning of time. He will continue to love us, no matter what we do.

THE IMPORTANCE OF JESUS CHRIST

In the New Testament, and especially in Ephesians, Jesus Christ is exalted as the focus of all history and as the only means for experiencing a meaningful life. Only through God in Jesus Christ can the power of sin be overcome. This letter urges us to keep Jesus Christ at the center of all we do, maintaining a love relationship with him on a daily basis.

TRUE SPIRITUAL RENEWAL LEADS TO WISE CONDUCT

We sometimes think of spiritual renewal only in terms of stopping destructive habits or breaking cycles of sin. But often the best way to stop destructive habits is to build constructive ones with which to replace them. When we repent, seek God, and surrender our lives to him each day, the Holy Spirit empowers us to lay aside destructive habits and break the cycle of sin. As we begin to live out God's will for our lives, we will find our old ways of life passing away and every aspect of our lives being renewed.

ADOPTION INTO GOD'S FAMILY

Some of us retain painful memories from the past, particularly if we experienced unpleasant family situations. The letter to the Ephesians reminds us that God adopts us into a new family when we surrender our lives to him. In this family, God is our perfect and loving Father. On this earth God's family, the church, has its limitations and imperfections. But our Father in heaven is perfect. Becoming a part of his family initiates the process of spiritual growth.

Essential Facts

PURPOSE:
To strengthen the believers in Ephesus in their relationship with God and with each other.

AUTHOR:
The apostle Paul.

AUDIENCE:
The believers in Ephesus, a city in western Asia Minor, and all believers everywhere.

DATE WRITTEN:
Around A.D. 60, during Paul's imprisonment in Rome.

SETTING:
This letter was a somewhat personal message from Paul to some close and dear friends in the main church of Asia. Paul probably intended this to be a circular letter passed from church to church for the believers' encouragement.

KEY VERSE:
"Finally, be strong in the Lord and in his mighty power" (6:10).

KEY PEOPLE AND RELATIONSHIPS:
Paul with Tychicus and with his close friends in the Ephesian church.

1 Paul, an apostle of Christ Jesus by the will of God,

To the saints in Ephesus,[a] the faithful[b] in Christ Jesus:

2Grace and peace to you from God our Father and the Lord Jesus Christ.

Spiritual Blessings in Christ

3Praise be to the God and Father of our Lord Jesus Christ, who has blessed us in the heavenly realms with every spiritual blessing in Christ. 4For he chose us in him before the creation of the world to be holy and blameless in his sight. In love 5he[c] predestined us to be adopted as his sons through Jesus Christ, in accordance with his pleasure and will— 6to the praise of his glorious grace, which he has freely given us in the One he loves. 7In him we have redemption through his blood, the forgiveness of sins, in accordance with the riches of God's grace 8that he lavished on us with all wisdom and understanding. 9And he[d] made known to us the mystery of his will according to his good pleasure, which he purposed in Christ, 10to be put into effect when the times will have reached their fulfillment—to bring all things in heaven and on earth together under one head, even Christ.

11In him we were also chosen,[e] having been predestined according to the plan of him who works out everything in conformity with the purpose of his will, 12in order that we, who were the first to hope in Christ, might be for the praise of his glory. 13And you also were included in Christ when you heard the word of truth, the gospel of your salvation. Having believed, you were marked in him with a seal, the promised Holy Spirit, 14who is a deposit guaranteeing our inheritance until the redemption of those who are God's possession—to the praise of his glory.

Thanksgiving and Prayer

15For this reason, ever since I heard about your faith in the Lord Jesus and your love for all the saints, 16I have not stopped giving thanks for you, remembering you in my prayers. 17I keep asking that the God of our Lord Jesus Christ, the glorious Father, may give you the Spirit[f] of wisdom and revelation, so that you may know him better. 18I pray also that the eyes of your heart may be enlightened in order that you may know the hope to which he has called you, the riches of his glorious inheritance in the saints, 19and his incomparably great power for us who believe. That power is like the working of his mighty strength, 20which he exerted in Christ when he raised him from the dead and seated him at his right hand in the heavenly realms, 21far above all rule and authority, power and dominion, and every title that can be given, not only in the present age but also in the one to come. 22And God placed all things under his feet and appointed him to be head over everything for the church, 23which is his body, the fullness of him who fills everything in every way.

Made Alive in Christ

2 As for you, you were dead in your transgressions and sins, 2in which you used to live when you followed the ways of this world and of the ruler of the kingdom of the air, the spirit who is now at work in those who are disobedient. 3All of us also lived among them at one time, gratifying the cravings of our sinful nature[g] and following its desires and thoughts. Like the rest, we were by nature objects of wrath. 4But because of his great love for us, God, who is rich in mercy, 5made us alive with Christ even when we were dead in transgressions—it is by grace you have been saved. 6And God raised us up with Christ and seated us with him in the heavenly realms in Christ Jesus, 7in

[a] 1 Some early manuscripts do not have *in Ephesus.*
[b] 1 Or *believers who are* [c] 4,5 Or *sight in love. 5He*
[d] 8,9 Or *us. With all wisdom and understanding, 9he*
[e] 11 Or *were made heirs* [f] 17 Or *a spirit* [g] 3 Or *our flesh*

1:3–6 God is sovereign over all the details of our lives. Paul reminds us that God has a special plan for us, and God's plan includes adopting us into his family. Doing things our way leads to painful consequences. With this in mind, we can be motivated to submit to God's perfect will for our lives. God wants only what is best for us. It is his will for us to find new life in him.

1:11–12 God's Word points us in the right direction to find God's will for our lives. While there are details we may never know in advance, there are many things God desires for all of us, and these are revealed in the Bible. These verses tell us that God wants us to experience an intimate relationship with him in Christ. God will delight in us in this relationship, and we will praise him in return. This is an amazing truth. No matter who we are or what we have done, because of what God has done for us in Jesus Christ, we can live lives of praise and share the Good News with others in need.

1:13–14 The Holy Spirit dwelling within us guarantees us as being spiritually genuine. Just as an official marks a document as being genuine, so the Holy Spirit's work within us guarantees our identity as one of God's adopted children. Jesus Christ and his saving work make all this possible on our behalf. As we place our faith in him, our knowledge of God's concern for us and the help he offers gives us a reason for hope as we seek to overcome our sins. When we trust God, we become part of the powerful solution he has provided to deal with the sin problem in our world.

2:1–10 In these verses Paul affirms two essential truths. He recognizes that we are fallen creatures, lacking the necessary power to stand against our tendency toward sin and failure. Paul then recognizes God's wealth of mercy and love, reminding us that even though we are far from God and enslaved by sin, God graciously reaches out to us. God wants to forgive us and give us the power we need to rebuild our lives. Through the work of Jesus Christ, God has already conquered the power of sin and death. When we admit our sin and our helplessness, asking God to act on our behalf, God makes his power available to us and helps us overcome our problems and sins.

order that in the coming ages he might show
the incomparable riches of his grace, expressed
in his kindness to us in Christ Jesus. 8For it is by
grace you have been saved, through faith—and
this not from yourselves, it is the gift of God—
9not by works, so that no one can boast. 10For
we are God's workmanship, created in Christ
Jesus to do good works, which God prepared in
advance for us to do.

One in Christ

11Therefore, remember that formerly you
who are Gentiles by birth and called "uncircumcised" by those who call themselves "the
circumcision" (that done in the body by the
hands of men)— 12remember that at that time
you were separate from Christ, excluded from
citizenship in Israel and foreigners to the covenants of the promise, without hope and without God in the world. 13But now in Christ Jesus
you who once were far away have been brought
near through the blood of Christ.

14For he himself is our peace, who has made
the two one and has destroyed the barrier, the
dividing wall of hostility, 15by abolishing in his
flesh the law with its commandments and regulations. His purpose was to create in himself
one new man out of the two, thus making
peace, 16and in this one body to reconcile both
of them to God through the cross, by which
he put to death their hostility. 17He came and
preached peace to you who were far away and
peace to those who were near. 18For through
him we both have access to the Father by one
Spirit.

19Consequently, you are no longer foreigners
and aliens, but fellow citizens with God's people and members of God's household, 20built
on the foundation of the apostles and prophets,
with Christ Jesus himself as the chief cornerstone. 21In him the whole building is joined
together and rises to become a holy temple in
the Lord. 22And in him you too are being built
together to become a dwelling in which God
lives by his Spirit.

Paul the Preacher to the Gentiles

3 For this reason I, Paul, the prisoner of
Christ Jesus for the sake of you Gentiles—

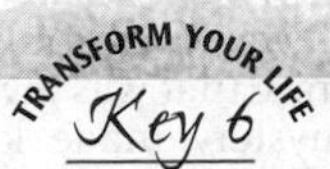

Fulfilling Our God-Given Purpose

Ephesians 2:1–13 Once we ask God to transform our lives, we are able to discover the vital role he intends for us to fulfill in his master plan. When God created us, he gave us gifts and abilities that fit with his purpose for our lives. As he transforms our lives, we are able to use our gifts in keeping with the purpose for which God created us.

Paul attested that God has a grand design for all of us, declaring "we are God's workmanship, created in Christ Jesus to do good works, which God prepared in advance for us to do" (2:10). Paul also said, "Just as each of us has one body with many members, and these members do not all have the same function, so in Christ we who are many form one body, and each member belongs to all the others" (Romans 12:4–5).

As members of Christ's body, the church, God has given each of us certain gifts and abilities. If we separate any members from their proper places within the body, they may seem odd and useless. It is only when the members are connected to the body in their appointed place and fulfilling their appointed functions that their usefulness is realized. In light of this truth, we must seek to discover our spiritual gifts and find a place where our talents and abilities can be used to help others. Then the entire church can experience spiritual growth.

Turn to 2 Timothy 4.

2:14–19 Through Jesus Christ, the barrier between God and his sinful creatures has been removed. But Christ's work of reconciliation does not stop there. He can also remove the obstacles that alienate us from other people. In Christ, we can have peace both with God and with others. Some of us may feel that our relationships with others could never be salvaged. But realizing that Christ can give us the power to live at peace with others can bring us new hope. While reconciliation with others is never guaranteed, we can be open to this possibility and free ourselves from bitterness toward them.

3:1–13 In these verses one truth stands out: God accepts all of us through faith. Our race, reputation and position have no bearing on God's forgiveness. Paul wrote these words to convince the believers of their oneness in Christ. Apparently some of the Jewish believers claimed superiori-

2Surely you have heard about the administration of God's grace that was given to me for you, 3that is, the mystery made known to me by revelation, as I have already written briefly. 4In reading this, then, you will be able to understand my insight into the mystery of Christ, 5which was not made known to men in other generations as it has now been revealed by the Spirit to God's holy apostles and prophets. 6This mystery is that through the gospel the Gentiles are heirs together with Israel, members together of one body, and sharers together in the promise in Christ Jesus.

7I became a servant of this gospel by the gift of God's grace given me through the working of his power. 8Although I am less than the least of all God's people, this grace was given me: to preach to the Gentiles the unsearchable riches of Christ, 9and to make plain to everyone the administration of this mystery, which for ages past was kept hidden in God, who created all things. 10His intent was that now, through the church, the manifold wisdom of God should be made known to the rulers and authorities in the heavenly realms, 11according to his eternal purpose which he accomplished in Christ Jesus our Lord. 12In him and through faith in him we may approach God with freedom and confidence. 13I ask you, therefore, not to be discouraged because of my sufferings for you, which are your glory.

A Prayer for the Ephesians

14For this reason I kneel before the Father, 15from whom his whole family[a] in heaven and on earth derives its name. 16I pray that out of his glorious riches he may strengthen you with power through his Spirit in your inner being, 17so that Christ may dwell in your hearts through faith. And I pray that you, being rooted and established in love, 18may have power, together with all the saints, to grasp how wide and long and high and deep is the love of Christ, 19and to know this love that surpasses knowledge—that you may be filled to the measure of all the fullness of God.

20Now to him who is able to do immeasurably more than all we ask or imagine, according to his power that is at work within us, 21to him be glory in the church and in Christ Jesus throughout all generations, for ever and ever! Amen.

Unity in the Body of Christ

4 As a prisoner for the Lord, then, I urge you to live a life worthy of the calling you have received. 2Be completely humble and gentle; be patient, bearing with one another in love. 3Make every effort to keep the unity of the Spirit through the bond of peace. 4There is one body and one Spirit—just as you were called to one hope when you were called— 5one Lord, one faith, one baptism; 6one God and Father of all, who is over all and through all and in all.

7But to each one of us grace has been given as Christ apportioned it. 8This is why it[b] says:

"When he ascended on high,
he led captives in his train
and gave gifts to men."[c]

9(What does "he ascended" mean except that he also descended to the lower, earthly regions[d]? 10He who descended is the very one who ascended higher than all the heavens, in order to fill the whole universe.) 11It was he who gave some to be apostles, some to be prophets, some to be evangelists, and some to be pastors and teachers, 12to prepare God's people for works of service, so that the body of Christ may be built up 13until we all reach unity in the faith and in the knowledge of the Son of God and become mature, attaining to the whole measure of the fullness of Christ.

14Then we will no longer be infants, tossed back and forth by the waves, and blown here and there by every wind of teaching and by the cunning and craftiness of men in their deceitful scheming. 15Instead, speaking the truth in love, we will in all things grow up into him who is

[a] 15 Or *whom all fatherhood* [b] 8 Or *God* [c] 8 Psalm 68:18 [d] 9 Or *the depths of the earth*

---

ty over the Gentile believers because of their relationship to God in the Old Testament Scriptures. Paul refuted this view by reminding them that our relationship with God is based on our trust in Jesus Christ, not on our personal history or position in society. If we seek God's forgiveness, he will accept us and help us make a new start. When we come into his family, we are all equal in God's eyes and should treat each other as such.

3:14–21 For the church to function effectively, God's dynamic and unlimited love must be its driving force. Paul prayed that his friends might be deeply anchored in and strengthened by God's love. As we begin to discover how much God loves us, we will realize that anything is possible with God. In fact, God is able to do far more in and through us than we could ever imagine! If we trust God and are grounded in his love, we will discover his restoration and healing in our lives and relationships.

4:1–6 Even though God's plan for us centers on his sovereign purposes and power, we have important responsibilities to fulfill as well. What we believe about God is crucial, but so is the manner in which we live our lives. Our spiritual growth will be hindered if we let our pride prevent us from honestly reflecting on our lives and admitting our sins. However, if we humble ourselves and trust God to help us, his Holy Spirit will transform our lives with love and patience. When God asks us to live a certain way, he provides the power we need to succeed.

4:7–16 We have been gifted in ways that make us necessary to others. Others have been gifted in ways that make them necessary to us. Some of us have special gifts for teaching others about God. Others of us may have a gift for caring for hurting people. Whatever gifts we might have, they are important for the emotional and spiritual growth of others. Since God has a purpose for each of us, it is important that we strive to know him better through prayer and meditation on his Word. As we seek God, he will show us what our gifts are and how we can use them to help others. And as we share our gifts and receive the benefits of other people's gifts, we will find the body of Christ growing stronger and healthier.

the Head, that is, Christ. 16From him the whole
body, joined and held together by every supporting ligament, grows and builds itself up in
love, as each part does its work.

Living as Children of Light

17So I tell you this, and insist on it in the
Lord, that you must no longer live as the Gentiles do, in the futility of their thinking. 18They
are darkened in their understanding and separated from the life of God because of the ignorance that is in them due to the hardening of
their hearts. 19Having lost all sensitivity, they
have given themselves over to sensuality so as
to indulge in every kind of impurity, with a
continual lust for more.

20You, however, did not come to know
Christ that way. 21Surely you heard of him and
were taught in him in accordance with the truth
that is in Jesus. 22You were taught, with regard
to your former way of life, to put off your old
self, which is being corrupted by its deceitful
desires; 23to be made new in the attitude of your
minds; 24and to put on the new self, created to
be like God in true righteousness and holiness.

25Therefore each of you must put off falsehood and speak truthfully to his neighbor, for
we are all members of one body. 26"In your
anger do not sin"[a]: Do not let the sun go down
while you are still angry, 27and do not give the
devil a foothold. 28He who has been stealing
must steal no longer, but must work, doing
something useful with his own hands, that he
may have something to share with those in
need.

29Do not let any unwholesome talk come out
of your mouths, but only what is helpful for
building others up according to their needs,
that it may benefit those who listen. 30And do
not grieve the Holy Spirit of God, with whom
you were sealed for the day of redemption.
31Get rid of all bitterness, rage and anger, brawl-
ing and slander, along with every form of malice. 32Be kind and compassionate to one another, forgiving each other, just as in Christ God
forgave you.

5 Be imitators of God, therefore, as dearly
loved children 2and live a life of love, just

[a]26 Psalm 4:4

4:31–32 Spiritual renewal involves a commitment to know God better through prayer and meditation on his Word. In examining our lives, we realize just how exacting God's standards for righteous living are. But we need not despair since it is God's grace that helps us conform to his will. As we obey him, he will teach us humility and help us forgive the people who have hurt us. God wants to heal our relationships. When we do things God's way, we can begin to reconcile with our alienated friends and build a solid foundation for further spiritual growth.

5:1–7 God wants us to follow his will for our lives and be like Jesus Christ. As we look at Jesus' life, we can see how God would like us to think and act. We must love our enemies, just as Jesus did. We should also avoid sexual impurity, greed and obscene speech since they stand

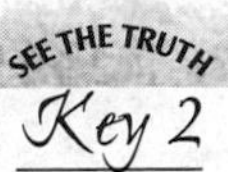

Growing Up in Truth

Ephesians 4:12–27 When the truth about ourselves makes us feel guilty, we often simply rationalize it away. But if we are to experience spiritual renewal, we must see the whole truth about ourselves. In order to see the truth we must grow in our knowledge of Jesus Christ and measure our lives by his standard for truth.

The apostle Paul instructed the church that those who believed in Christ were to function like a single body, with each member contributing in a special way to help God's people grow and mature in their understanding of the Lord (see 4:11–13). Once we reach maturity in our knowledge of Christ "we will no longer be infants, tossed back and forth by the waves, and blown here and there by every wind of teaching and by the cunning and craftiness of men in their deceitful scheming. Instead, speaking the truth in love, we will in all things grow up into him who is the Head, that is, Christ" (4:14–15).

God wants us to grow spiritually. That means growing to understand what is true. In the past we may have measured truth against whatever sounded right to us at the time. But now we must look to Jesus Christ, who is the truth. We must reevaluate our beliefs to conform them to his image.

Turn to Philippians 4.

Marriage: A Most Intimate Friendship

Ephesians 5:21–33 Marriage can be one of the most fulfilling spiritual friendships in life if it is continually cultivated. Many couples have never taken the time to nurture the spiritual life of their marriage by praying, studying God's Word and sharing together. This passage weaves the relationship of marriage and the church into a moving testimony of love and presents a number of specific principles for developing spiritual vitality.

Note that Paul urges husbands and wives to submit to one another out of reverence for Christ. They should value each other and serve each other, not only because of their devotion to each other, but also because of their devotion to Christ. Some have defined submission as "getting under and lifting up." This image of submission is not a picture of domination or subjugation. Instead, it is an image of gracious, sacrificial service. Both husband and wife support each other so that both people become all that God created them to be.

It is also important that the Lord becomes the model for the entire marriage relationship. Husbands and wives cannot look only to human models, which so often fail in one way or another. Instead, they should follow Jesus' model and lay down their lives for their spouses. When they find their security in Christ, marriage partners will also find the freedom to risk loving sacrificially as he loves.

The goal of a married couple should be to have a relationship that is without spot, wrinkle or blemish. Their marriage relationship should be an ongoing experience of grace and forgiveness. While no marriage will be perfect, the couple learns to face failure with confession and forgiveness, uprooting the weeds of bitterness and contention before they take firm root. Their marriage relationship establishes an environment in which it is safe to take risks for God, safe to fail, safe to dream and safe to rest.

A marriage relationship will always have an element of mystery. Spiritual growth brings a sense of wonder at the unsearchable riches of life in Christ. No one can fully fathom the depths of God's wisdom and grace.

Putting It Into Practice

If you are married, how has your marriage contributed to your spiritual growth? In what ways would you like your marriage to be a means of spiritual renewal? Do you see spiritual friendship as an element of your marriage? Consider how you can take steps to make this a reality.

For more on spiritual friendship, turn to Genesis 2.

as Christ loved us and gave himself up for us as a fragrant offering and sacrifice to God.

3But among you there must not be even a hint of sexual immorality, or of any kind of impurity, or of greed, because these are improper for God's holy people. 4Nor should there be obscenity, foolish talk or coarse joking, which are out of place, but rather thanksgiving. 5For of this you can be sure: No immoral, impure or greedy person—such a man is an idolater—has any inheritance in the kingdom of Christ and of God.[a] 6Let no one deceive you with empty words, for because of such things God's wrath comes on those who are disobedient. 7Therefore do not be partners with them.

8For you were once darkness, but now you are light in the Lord. Live as children of light 9(for the fruit of the light consists in all goodness, righteousness and truth) 10and find out what pleases the Lord. 11Have nothing to do with the fruitless deeds of darkness, but rather expose them. 12For it is shameful even to mention what the disobedient do in secret. 13But everything exposed by the light becomes visible, 14for it is light that makes everything visible. This is why it is said:

"Wake up, O sleeper,
  rise from the dead,
and Christ will shine on you."

15Be very careful, then, how you live—not as unwise but as wise, 16making the most of every opportunity, because the days are evil. 17Therefore do not be foolish, but understand what the Lord's will is. 18Do not get drunk on wine, which leads to debauchery. Instead, be filled with the Spirit. 19Speak to one another with psalms, hymns and spiritual songs. Sing and make music in your heart to the Lord, 20always giving thanks to God the Father for everything, in the name of our Lord Jesus Christ.

21Submit to one another out of reverence for Christ.

Wives and Husbands

22Wives, submit to your husbands as to the Lord. 23For the husband is the head of the wife as Christ is the head of the church, his body, of which he is the Savior. 24Now as the church submits to Christ, so also wives should submit to their husbands in everything.

25Husbands, love your wives, just as Christ loved the church and gave himself up for her 26to make her holy, cleansing[b] her by the washing with water through the word, 27and to present her to himself as a radiant church, without stain or wrinkle or any other blemish, but holy and blameless. 28In this same way, husbands ought to love their wives as their own bodies. He who loves his wife loves himself. 29After all, no one ever hated his own body, but he feeds and cares for it, just as Christ does the church— 30for we are members of his body. 31"For this reason a man will leave his father and mother and be united to his wife, and the two will become one flesh."[c] 32This is a profound mystery—but I am talking about Christ and the church. 33However, each one of you also must love his wife as he loves himself, and the wife must respect her husband.

Children and Parents

6 Children, obey your parents in the Lord, for this is right. 2"Honor your father and mother"—which is the first commandment with a promise— 3"that it may go well with you and that you may enjoy long life on the earth."[d]

4Fathers, do not exasperate your children; instead, bring them up in the training and instruction of the Lord.

Slaves and Masters

5Slaves, obey your earthly masters with respect and fear, and with sincerity of heart, just as you would obey Christ. 6Obey them not only to win their favor when their eye is on you, but like slaves of Christ, doing the will of God from your heart. 7Serve wholeheartedly, as if you were serving the Lord, not men, 8because you know that the Lord will reward everyone for whatever good he does, whether he is slave or free.

9And masters, treat your slaves in the same way. Do not threaten them, since you know that he who is both their Master and yours is in heaven, and there is no favoritism with him.

[a] 5 Or *kingdom of the Christ and God* [b] 26 Or *having cleansed* [c] 31 Gen. 2:24 [d] 3 Deut. 5:16

---

counter to the character of God. As difficult as following Christ's example might sound, anything is possible with God's powerful help.

5:21–33 Paul tells us that our homes should be places where love and mutual submission are exhibited. Husbands and wives need to show love to each other and be sensitive to each other's needs. By exhibiting such love, spouses reflect the loving relationship that God has established between Christ and the Christian community. The painful consequences of our sinful patterns are most deeply felt by our close family members. Any time we selfishly seek to meet our own needs, we neglect or hurt the people we are responsible to love and support. Rebuilding damaged family relationships may be one of the most important tasks we face with God's help. As we admit our sins and seek restitution with our loved ones, we can reestablish a family atmosphere characterized by love and mutual submission.

6:1–4 In these verses, Paul urged parents to show love to their children and children to show due respect to their parents. The widespread disrespect shown toward parents today leads to deep emotional scars both in parents and children. Paul also warned parents to treat their children with love and respect. Parents' ridicule and neglect can create resentment that may stay with children for life. Whether we are a parent or a child who has failed, we need to admit our sin and failures and seek to make restitution wherever possible.

Warfare Prayer

Ephesians 6:10–18 Troubles and spiritual battles are a way of life for Jesus' followers (see John 16:33). Far from excluding us from temptation, spiritual growth often stirs spiritual opposition. When we commit our lives to Christ, we enter the arena of spiritual warfare for our own souls.

Paul uses the analogy of armor and warfare to teach us about the essential equipment needed for standing against temptation and spiritual attacks. His words remind us that we are not simply fighting a physical battle but rather a spiritual one. We must rely on God's power rather than our own to fight these battles. This dependence on God is strengthened through prayer.

As we look at the armor we notice that we first must put on the belt of truth. Satan is "a liar and the father of lies" (John 8:44). He is constantly trying to deceive and trap us. In contrast, our armor is held together by truth, which comes from the Father of all truth.

Next, we put on the breastplate of God's righteousness. Though there are many levels of meaning to this phrase, the primary one is that we are not protected by our own righteousness; we need the righteousness of God. Our forgiveness and acceptance through faith in Jesus Christ shield us against Satan's accusations that we are guilty and unworthy.

We are called to put on the shoes of the gospel of peace. This peace carries us along to spread the Good News to people everywhere.

We are also given the shield of faith to protect us against Satan's accusations and persecutions. We cling to our hope in Christ and refuse to believe Satan's lies. Prayer leads us to this faith, keeping our vision clear when circumstances cloud our way.

Paul urges us to put on salvation as our helmet. In addition to protecting the wearer, a helmet identified a soldier's allegiance. We belong to the company of Christ. We have been saved from destruction and restored to new life. As our helmet of salvation protects us, we also acknowledge that we belong to the God who has made us whole again.

Finally, we are armed with the sword of the Spirit, the Word of God. The sword is our only offensive weapon. The Holy Spirit communicates God's message to others, exposing their sin and opening their hearts to God (see Hebrews 4:12–13).

Warfare prayer is a matter of claiming our authority in Christ. Because we are secure in Christ, we are to stand our ground against Satan's attacks, and we will overcome him (see 1 Corinthians 10:12–13; James 4:7).

Putting It Into Practice

Are you facing a spiritual battle right now? Are there strong temptations, interpersonal conflicts or difficult circumstances disrupting your spiritual progress? Think about the various pieces of God's armor. What piece do you need to remember to hold onto and use? Pray for God to help you take up this armor so that he can give you the victory over your struggle.

For more on prayer, turn to Philippians 1.

The Armor of God

10Finally, be strong in the Lord and in his
mighty power. 11Put on the full armor of God
so that you can take your stand against the devil's schemes. 12For our struggle is not against
flesh and blood, but against the rulers, against
the authorities, against the powers of this dark
world and against the spiritual forces of evil in
the heavenly realms. 13Therefore put on the full
armor of God, so that when the day of evil
comes, you may be able to stand your ground,
and after you have done everything, to stand.
14Stand firm then, with the belt of truth buckled
around your waist, with the breastplate of righteousness in place, 15and with your feet fitted
with the readiness that comes from the gospel
of peace. 16In addition to all this, take up the
shield of faith, with which you can extinguish
all the flaming arrows of the evil one. 17Take the
helmet of salvation and the sword of the Spirit,
which is the word of God. 18And pray in the
Spirit on all occasions with all kinds of prayers
and requests. With this in mind, be alert and
always keep on praying for all the saints.
19Pray also for me, that whenever I open my
mouth, words may be given me so that I will
fearlessly make known the mystery of the gospel, 20for which I am an ambassador in chains.
Pray that I may declare it fearlessly, as I should.

Final Greetings

21Tychicus, the dear brother and faithful servant in the Lord, will tell you everything, so that
you also may know how I am and what I am
doing. 22I am sending him to you for this very
purpose, that you may know how we are, and
that he may encourage you.
23Peace to the brothers, and love with faith
from God the Father and the Lord Jesus Christ.
24Grace to all who love our Lord Jesus Christ
with an undying love.

6:10–13 While we may be firmly grounded in sound doctrine and accept our responsibility to live godly lives, we also need to be aware of the fierce, invisible warfare being waged against us. Sometimes our spiritual struggles are the result of a direct attack by a spiritual enemy. As we surrender our lives to God, he will stand with us in the battle. When we understand that our battle is not of this world, we will realize our need to depend on God's power instead of our own.

6:13–20 Notice that each piece of our spiritual armor (except the sword) is defensive in nature. We need to make sure that each piece of the armor of God is operative in our lives. Truth, righteousness, faith and prayer protect us against the assault of hostile spiritual forces. These ungodly forces arrayed against us are powerful, but the weapons God gives us are adequate for our defense. In fact, a part of our armor—the shoes—enables us to share the Good News as we move forward in our spiritual lives.

PHILIPPIANS

The Big Picture

A. *JOY IN THE MIDST OF DIFFICULT CIRCUMSTANCES (1:1-30)*

B. *THE SECRET OF VICTORIOUS LIVING (2:1-30)*

C. *HAVING A VICTORIOUS FOCUS (3:1–4:1)*

D. *FINDING A JOYFUL FELLOWSHIP (4:2-23)*

As a missionary and traveling pastor, Paul depended on others for financial support. Paul had planted the Philippian church during his second missionary journey. The believers in Philippi had supported him ever since—for almost ten years. They were compassionate people, and their commitment to Christ and support of Christ's work were well known.

Paul wrote this letter to thank the Philippians for their continued support. He also wanted to challenge them to remain true to Christ and to be joyful in their circumstances. Contentment in life, Paul reminded them, does not come from material things or pleasant circumstances. Genuine joy, meaning and satisfaction come as we follow Christ and help others grow spiritually.

Paul knew what he was talking about. He penned this encouraging letter while imprisoned in Rome, facing a trial that might lead to his execution. Throughout his life, Paul had been rich and poor, comfortable and in pain, healthy and sick, popular and the target of mobs. Yet in spite of everything, Paul had learned to be content, even joyful, no matter what the surrounding circumstances.

The letter to the Philippians has much to say to us about joy in the midst of our everyday life too. Though we may be pursuing spiritual renewal, seeking God and obeying him, we will still face frustration, anger and conflict daily. Yet when we encounter these painful occurrences, Christ can be our joy. Trials are rarely pleasant, but we need to remember that God is with us. Because of his presence, we can have joy. The secret of maintaining this joy centers on increasing our knowledge of Christ and making him a priority in our lives each day.

Spiritual Renewal Themes

THE IMPORTANCE OF HUMILITY

When we surrender our lives to God, we will experience his power at work within us. God changes us and conforms us to his image. But beware! Continued spiritual development may cause pride to surface in our lives. We may forget our source of power and view ourselves as self-sufficient. The letter to the Philippians reminds us to be humble, to adopt the attitude of Christ, "who, being in very nature God, did not consider equal-

ity with God something to be grasped" (2:6). Our spiritual growth must always involve a spirit of humility.

SPIRITUAL RENEWAL LEADS TO TRUE JOY

When we recognize our need for God and surrender our lives to him, we embark on a journey that will lead to true joy. We can possess deep-down joy even during the tough times, because joy does not come from outward circumstances. Joy radiates from the inward strength of knowing Christ personally and depending on his strength and power on a daily basis.

SPIRITUAL RENEWAL REQUIRES SACRIFICE

A sure sign of progress in our own spiritual growth involves our increased concern for those around us who have not yet surrendered their lives to God. As Christ suffered and died so that we might have life, we must make it our goal to sacrifice for others if we would see growth in our own spiritual life. Spiritual maturity will look past our own interests and share the hope of spiritual renewal with others. If our spiritual growth is merely a selfish pursuit, we will be prone to pride and the eventual downfall it brings. When our spiritual growth is genuine, it causes us to care for others as God cares for them.

Essential Facts

PURPOSE:
To thank the Philippian believers for their support of Paul's ministry and to encourage them in their faith.

AUTHOR:
The apostle Paul.

AUDIENCE:
The believers in Philippi, a city in Macedonia.

DATE WRITTEN:
Around A.D. 61–62.

SETTING:
Paul, a prisoner in Rome, wrote this warm letter to the believers at Philippi after they had sent him a generous gift.

KEY VERSE:
"Whatever you have learned or received or heard from me, or seen in me—put it into practice. And the God of peace will be with you" (4:9).

KEY PEOPLE AND RELATIONSHIPS:
Paul with Timothy, Epaphroditus and the Philippian believers.

1

Paul and Timothy, servants of Christ Jesus,

To all the saints in Christ Jesus at Philippi, together with the overseers[a] and deacons:

[2]Grace and peace to you from God our Father and the Lord Jesus Christ.

Thanksgiving and Prayer

[3]I thank my God every time I remember you. [4]In all my prayers for all of you, I always pray with joy [5]because of your partnership in the gospel from the first day until now, [6]being confident of this, that he who began a good work in you will carry it on to completion until the day of Christ Jesus.

[7]It is right for me to feel this way about all of you, since I have you in my heart; for whether I am in chains or defending and confirming the gospel, all of you share in God's grace with me. [8]God can testify how I long for all of you with the affection of Christ Jesus.

[9]And this is my prayer: that your love may abound more and more in knowledge and depth of insight, [10]so that you may be able to discern what is best and may be pure and blameless until the day of Christ, [11]filled with the fruit of righteousness that comes through Jesus Christ—to the glory and praise of God.

Paul's Chains Advance the Gospel

[12]Now I want you to know, brothers, that what has happened to me has really served to advance the gospel. [13]As a result, it has become clear throughout the whole palace guard[b] and to everyone else that I am in chains for Christ. [14]Because of my chains, most of the brothers in the Lord have been encouraged to speak the word of God more courageously and fearlessly.

[15]It is true that some preach Christ out of envy and rivalry, but others out of goodwill. [16]The latter do so in love, knowing that I am put here for the defense of the gospel. [17]The former preach Christ out of selfish ambition, not sincerely, supposing that they can stir up trouble for me while I am in chains.[c] [18]But what does it matter? The important thing is that in every way, whether from false motives or true, Christ is preached. And because of this I rejoice.

Yes, and I will continue to rejoice, [19]for I know that through your prayers and the help given by the Spirit of Jesus Christ, what has happened to me will turn out for my deliverance.[d] [20]I eagerly expect and hope that I will in no way be ashamed, but will have sufficient courage so that now as always Christ will be exalted in my body, whether by life or by death. [21]For to me, to live is Christ and to die is gain. [22]If I am to go on living in the body, this will mean fruitful labor for me. Yet what shall I choose? I do not know! [23]I am torn between the two: I desire to depart and be with Christ, which is better by far; [24]but it is more necessary for you that I remain in the body. [25]Convinced of this, I know that I will remain, and I will continue with all of you for your progress and joy in the faith, [26]so that through my being with you again your joy in Christ Jesus will overflow on account of me.

[27]Whatever happens, conduct yourselves in a manner worthy of the gospel of Christ. Then, whether I come and see you or only hear about you in my absence, I will know that you stand firm in one spirit, contending as one man for the faith of the gospel [28]without being frightened in any way by those who oppose you. This is a sign to them that they will be destroyed, but that you will be saved—and that by God. [29]For it has been granted to you on behalf of Christ not only to believe on him, but also to suffer for him, [30]since you are going through the same struggle you saw I had, and now hear that I still have.

Imitating Christ's Humility

2

If you have any encouragement from being united with Christ, if any comfort from his love, if any fellowship with the Spirit, if any

[a] 1 Traditionally *bishops* [b] 13 Or *whole palace* [c] 16,17 Some late manuscripts have verses 16 and 17 in reverse order. [d] 19 Or *salvation*

1:3–11 Paul told the Philippians that he had been praying for them. This would have been a great encouragement to those early believers. Our spiritual awakening will cause us to feel a growing concern for people in need. As we share the message of hope with others, we can make our prayers for their progress a part of our service to them. Our commitment to pray for people struggling with sin will significantly impact their spiritual growth. When we let them know we are supporting them with our prayers, not only will they grow in their faith, but we will also experience the encouragement we need to persevere.
1:12–14 In retrospect, Paul could see that God allowed the events of his life, both positive and negative, to help spread the Good News. If we take an honest look at our lives, we will probably find the same thing to be true. Through our pain we gain the perspective needed to share the message of hope with others. As with Paul, our painful past and God's power to redeem our lives open doors to serve God and others in new ways.
1:19–24 If we belong to God, we cannot lose. Whether we live or die, we know we will win in the end. But while we live on this earth, we need to persevere in our faith so that we can make spiritual gains. Paul's primary motivation for persevering in his faith was his deep concern for others who still needed to hear about God's loving power. We will have to face death one day. However, if we persevere in our faith, we can be useful to God until the day he takes us to be with him. There is always a reason to live. God still wants to use us to minister to the lives of others.
2:1–4 The English poet and clergyman John Donne might have had these words of the apostle Paul in mind when he penned, "No man is an island, entire of itself." In these verses Paul reminds us that we are a part of a whole, a member of Christ's body. If we are part of a loving community, when others hurt, we hurt; when we hurt, they hurt too. As we grow in our faith, we will move beyond a self-centered focus and learn to be available to others. By learning to love others, they will learn to love us. As we connect with others, we will develop mutually

Praying for Others

Philippians 1:2–11 There is a blessing that comes from giving (see Acts 20:35). Nowhere is this more evident than in the area of prayer. God renews our spirits as we pray for others. Our love and compassion grow along with our faith when we come before God on behalf of others. As we pray, God often brings to mind specific ideas of ways we can support and help them as well. To paraphrase a great principle of prayer: We can do a great deal for people *after* we pray for them but little of lasting value *until* we pray for them.

We can pray specifically for others if we know their needs. But we can also request commonplace things for all people, regardless of whether we know them or not. A good example of a general request is found at the beginning of Paul's letters, including this letter to the Philippians.

Paul's letters often begin with a blessing of grace and peace. Grace is the reason for our salvation; peace is the result of it. God's grace in Jesus Christ brings us new life and peace, both with ourselves and with others. Paul never tired of reminding people of the root and fruit of their faith in Christ.

Paul then gave thanks to God for the Philippian believers. The evidence of changed lives never ceased to stir gratitude and awe in Paul's heart. He cherished God's work in and through others. Paul affirmed their partnership in Christ and consistently emphasized mutuality rather than condescension in his relationships.

Paul also expressed his confidence that God would complete the work of spiritual transformation he had begun in the Philippians. This inspiring promise encourages us to press on in our journey of faith as well. Paul exhorted the Philippians to keep their eyes on the goal in spite of the fluctuations and discouragements in their walk with Christ.

Paul's prayer for the Philippians included a blessing for grace and peace and a recognition of thanksgiving and affirmation. These qualities are the essential elements of the great keys to the spiritual life—faith, hope and love. Paul then prayed for additional requests that would aid the spiritual growth of his friends. He prayed that their love would grow within the community. He also prayed for them to grow in knowledge and understanding of Christ. And Paul also prayed that they would behave in a manner that honored God in light of the coming judgment. This is not a fear or guilt tactic. Rather it was Paul's reminder to live for the ultimate goal of heaven, not the short-term rewards of comfort or pleasure.

Paul had a lot to say to his friends, and he rooted those thoughts in loving prayer. What an ideal way to open people's hearts to teaching and ministry.

Putting It Into Practice

Select one person that God has placed on your heart. Write a prayer for them that includes the elements of Paul's prayer for the Philippians. Though not all of Paul's comments will be appropriate (such as having shared in ministry together), be as specific as possible for each element.

Also study Paul's opening prayers in his other letters. What are his consistent requests? What are his different requests? How do these apply to the particular people to whom Paul is writing? Use these reflections to help you pray for others as well.

For more on prayer, turn to Genesis 18.

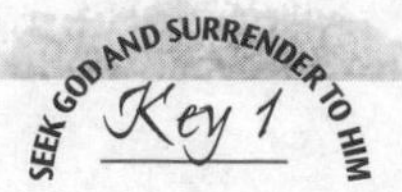

Our Prime Example of Humility

Philippians 2:5–9 Our prime example for surrender to God is Jesus Christ. Christ's humility can be seen as he continually sought his heavenly Father in prayer and relinquished his will to him.

The apostle Paul wrote,

> Your attitude should be the same as that of Christ Jesus: Who, being in very nature God, did not consider equality with God something to be grasped, but made himself nothing, taking the very nature of a servant, being made in human likeness. And being found in appearance as a man, he humbled himself and became obedient to death—even death on a cross! Therefore God exalted him to the highest place and gave him the name that is above every name (2:5–9).

In a similar vein, the author of Hebrews wrote, "Let us fix our eyes on Jesus, the author and perfecter of our faith, who for the joy set before him endured the cross, scorning its shame, and sat down at the right hand of the throne of God" (Hebrews 12:2).

Note the progression in these verses: Jesus humbled himself, yet it was because of this that God raised him up to the heights of heaven. Humility was a key element in Jesus' life as he accomplished God's plan for fallen humanity. When we surrender to God and his will for us, we need to be humble as well. Jesus did not pray solely for his own will. He humbly prayed for his Father's will to be done. We, too, ought to pray, "Father, I want your will, not mine." This is the mark of true humility and the beginning of spiritual renewal.

Turn to Titus 2.

tenderness and compassion, 2then make my joy
complete by being like-minded, having the
same love, being one in spirit and purpose. 3Do
nothing out of selfish ambition or vain conceit,
but in humility consider others better than
yourselves. 4Each of you should look not only
to your own interests, but also to the interests
of others.

5Your attitude should be the same as that of Christ Jesus:

6Who, being in very nature[a] God,
did not consider equality with God
something to be grasped,
7but made himself nothing,
taking the very nature[b] of a servant,
being made in human likeness.
8And being found in appearance as a man,
he humbled himself
and became obedient to death—
even death on a cross!
9Therefore God exalted him to the highest
place
and gave him the name that is above
every name,
10that at the name of Jesus every knee should
bow,
in heaven and on earth and under the
earth,
11and every tongue confess that Jesus Christ
is Lord,
to the glory of God the Father.

Shining as Stars

12Therefore, my dear friends, as you have always obeyed—not only in my presence, but now
much more in my absence—continue to work
out your salvation with fear and trembling,
13for it is God who works in you to will and to
act according to his good purpose.
14Do everything without complaining or arguing, 15so that you may become blameless and
pure, children of God without fault in a crook-

[a]6 Or *in the form of* [b]7 Or *the form*

accountable relationships that will help the entire body of Christ.

2:5–11 Jesus Christ is an ideal model for our humility in service. His willingness to humble himself is a great example for us. Our thoughts, attitudes and actions are to become more and more like those exhibited by Christ during his earthly life. As we reflect honestly on our lives, we can admit our faults and begin to change our sinful habits. If we can follow Jesus Christ in humility and learn to admit our failures without hesitation, we can look forward to spiritual growth.

2:12–18 Obedience to God's plan is one of the requirements for spiritual growth. Some of us may wonder how we are supposed to succeed at doing what God wants us to do, for we realize that we can never be perfect. We have already admitted that we are powerless over our sinful nature. But God not only asks us to live a godly life; he also provides us with the power to do it (2:13). He is working in our lives, helping us to obey him. As we get to know God by reading the Bible and spending time with him in prayer, he can begin to transform us from the inside out.

Being a Doorway, Not a Doormat

Philippians 2:1–11 Service grows out of the soil of humility. Too often, however, humility has been misunderstood as a negative character trait. Biblical humility does not consist in thinking less of yourself, but rather in thinking more of God and of others. In other words, humility is not about putting ourselves down; humility involves glorifying God and affirming others.

Jesus Christ is the greatest example of humility. He left his place of honor in heaven in order to become God's servant on earth. In the process, however, he didn't tear himself down or deny his value. He lifted others up through his humility and showed them how valuable they were. Jonathan's attitude toward David also provides a vivid example of humility (see 1 Samuel 23). Jonathan counted David better than himself without thinking less of himself in the process.

With these thoughts in mind, we can see that Biblical humility doesn't call us to be a doormat. Humility calls us to be a doorway, through which others enter into the presence and the power of God. By focusing on building others up and helping them along the way, we show them the love of God, who desires the best for them.

Putting It Into Practice

Reflect on the ways you can strive to put others' interests ahead of your own. In what ways can you show others how much you (and God) value them? How would Christ make himself "nothing" if he were in your place (2:7)?

For more on service, turn to Mark 10.

ed and depraved generation, in which you shine
like stars in the universe 16as you hold out[a] the
word of life—in order that I may boast on the
day of Christ that I did not run or labor for
nothing. 17But even if I am being poured out
like a drink offering on the sacrifice and service
coming from your faith, I am glad and rejoice
with all of you. 18So you too should be glad and
rejoice with me.

Timothy and Epaphroditus

19I hope in the Lord Jesus to send Timothy to
you soon, that I also may be cheered when I
receive news about you. 20I have no one else
like him, who takes a genuine interest in your
welfare. 21For everyone looks out for his own
interests, not those of Jesus Christ. 22But you
know that Timothy has proved himself, because
as a son with his father he has served with me
in the work of the gospel. 23I hope, therefore, to
send him as soon as I see how things go with
me. 24And I am confident in the Lord that I
myself will come soon.

25But I think it is necessary to send back to
you Epaphroditus, my brother, fellow worker
and fellow soldier, who is also your messenger,
whom you sent to take care of my needs. 26For
he longs for all of you and is distressed because
you heard he was ill. 27Indeed he was ill, and
almost died. But God had mercy on him, and
not on him only but also on me, to spare me
sorrow upon sorrow. 28Therefore I am all the
more eager to send him, so that when you see
him again you may be glad and I may have less
anxiety. 29Welcome him in the Lord with great
joy, and honor men like him, 30because he almost died for the work of Christ, risking his life
to make up for the help you could not give me.

No Confidence in the Flesh

3 Finally, my brothers, rejoice in the Lord!
It is no trouble for me to write the same
things to you again, and it is a safeguard for
you.

2Watch out for those dogs, those men who
do evil, those mutilators of the flesh. 3For it is
we who are the circumcision, we who worship
by the Spirit of God, who glory in Christ Jesus,
and who put no confidence in the flesh—
4though I myself have reasons for such confidence.

If anyone else thinks he has reasons to put
confidence in the flesh, I have more: 5circum-
cised on the eighth day, of the people of Israel,
of the tribe of Benjamin, a Hebrew of Hebrews;
in regard to the law, a Pharisee; 6as for zeal,
persecuting the church; as for legalistic righteousness, faultless.

7But whatever was to my profit I now consider loss for the sake of Christ. 8What is more, I
consider everything a loss compared to the surpassing greatness of knowing Christ Jesus my
Lord, for whose sake I have lost all things. I
consider them rubbish, that I may gain Christ
9and be found in him, not having a righteousness of my own that comes from the law, but
that which is through faith in Christ—the righteousness that comes from God and is by faith.
10I want to know Christ and the power of his
resurrection and the fellowship of sharing in his
sufferings, becoming like him in his death,
11and so, somehow, to attain to the resurrection
from the dead.

Pressing on Toward the Goal

12Not that I have already obtained all this, or
have already been made perfect, but I press on
to take hold of that for which Christ Jesus took
hold of me. 13Brothers, I do not consider myself
yet to have taken hold of it. But one thing I do:
Forgetting what is behind and straining toward
what is ahead, 14I press on toward the goal to
win the prize for which God has called me heavenward in Christ Jesus.

15All of us who are mature should take such
a view of things. And if on some point you
think differently, that too God will make clear
to you. 16Only let us live up to what we have
already attained.

17Join with others in following my example,
brothers, and take note of those who live ac-

[a]16 Or *hold on to*

2:25–28 Living as a believer in Christ is not always easy. As Epaphroditus clearly demonstrated, we need stamina to do the work and a servant's attitude to succeed in the spiritual battles we face. We must be willing to give ourselves to the cause of Christ, choosing to put the needs of others before our personal comforts. As we serve others, we will build meaningful relationships and a strong foundation for continued spiritual growth. By helping others, we will help ourselves and the cause of Christ.

3:2–3 The world is filled with deceivers. The false teachers of Paul's day demanded that the Gentile Christians obey the Jewish law of circumcision in order to be saved. Paul stood against this claim, reminding the Philippians that only God through Jesus Christ could bring them the deliverance they sought. While few people today would say that circumcision is necessary for salvation, many religions and spiritual beliefs do require various works to appease God. Yet this belief in salvation by works is no more correct today than it was in Paul's time. Our salvation is completely paid for in Christ; it is by his grace that we are saved.

3:4–11 In these verses Paul carefully reflected on his life. Reviewing all his credentials—including his religious activities—Paul found nothing that earned him favor with God. It was only his faith in Jesus Christ that made him right with God. By means of Paul's personal illustration, we should reflect honestly on our heritage and accomplishments. But we should not trust in them to save us. Trying hard to live a good life will not pay for our sins. Only Jesus will!

3:17–21 We must be careful to choose godly role models. On the human level, we need to pattern our lives after those who have been successful in living their entire lives for Christ regardless of their circumstances. Many people spend all their energies living only for themselves, enslaved by destructive habits and sins. We should not follow the example of such people, but rather follow the example of those who live today in the light of eternity. To-

cording to the pattern we gave you. 18For, as I
have often told you before and now say again
even with tears, many live as enemies of the
cross of Christ. 19Their destiny is destruction,
their god is their stomach, and their glory is in
their shame. Their mind is on earthly things.
20But our citizenship is in heaven. And we eagerly await a Savior from there, the Lord Jesus
Christ, 21who, by the power that enables him to
bring everything under his control, will transform our lowly bodies so that they will be like
his glorious body.

4 Therefore, my brothers, you whom I love
and long for, my joy and crown, that is
how you should stand firm in the Lord, dear
friends!

Exhortations

2I plead with Euodia and I plead with Synty-
che to agree with each other in the Lord. 3Yes,
and I ask you, loyal yokefellow,[a] help these
women who have contended at my side in the
cause of the gospel, along with Clement and the
rest of my fellow workers, whose names are in
the book of life.
4Rejoice in the Lord always. I will say it again:
Rejoice! 5Let your gentleness be evident to all.
The Lord is near. 6Do not be anxious about
anything, but in everything, by prayer and petition, with thanksgiving, present your requests
to God. 7And the peace of God, which transcends all understanding, will guard your hearts
and your minds in Christ Jesus.
8Finally, brothers, whatever is true, whatever
is noble, whatever is right, whatever is pure,
whatever is lovely, whatever is admirable—if
anything is excellent or praiseworthy—think
about such things. 9Whatever you have learned
or received or heard from me, or seen in me—
put it into practice. And the God of peace will
be with you.

[a]3 Or *loyal Syzygus*

---

gether we can look forward with great expectation to the return of Christ.

4:1–3 Since we know with certainty what our ultimate destiny will be, we can confidently face the hardships of life. Paul set a good example to help us grow spiritually and encourage others in their growth. These two Christian women had once had a harmonious relationship. Paul wanted them to reestablish this friendship, so he complimented them on their previous service to God. He assumed that they were humble enough to take criticism and change for the better. If we are truly concerned about our brothers and sisters in the church, we will hold them accountable and encourage them to continue following God's way.

4:4–9 True happiness can be found in any situation when we recognize that God is working. Because Christ is with us and his return is certain, we can act calmly in the face of painful and difficult situations. Peace comes only when we focus on those things that provide lasting value for our lives. The more we commit ourselves to knowing God's will through prayer and the study of his Word, the better prepared we will be to help ourselves and others grow spiritually.

SEE THE TRUTH

Key 2

Life's Ups and Downs

Philippians 4:10–14 To see the truth, we must accept reality as it is and still trust God. Reality isn't always kind, even when we are seeking God sincerely. Some of us are open to God's leading as long as life remains comfortable, but we close ourselves off to him when life becomes difficult.

The apostle Paul wrote, "I have learned to be content whatever the circumstances. I know what it is to be in need, and I know what it is to have plenty. I have learned the secret of being content in any and every situation, whether well fed or hungry, whether living in plenty or in want" (4:11–12). When Paul wrote these words, he was in a Roman prison, waiting to hear if he would be executed. But instead of complaining, Paul accepted the reality of life's ups and downs without closing himself off from God.

Life always has its good times and its bad times. God uses both for his good purposes. God's plan to transform our lives, purify our faith and strengthen our character continues to unfold in both good times and in bad. We must maintain an openness toward God so that we will be able to accept our true spiritual condition.

Turn to James 1.

Thanks for Their Gifts

[10]I rejoice greatly in the Lord that at last you have renewed your concern for me. Indeed, you have been concerned, but you had no opportunity to show it. [11]I am not saying this because I am in need, for I have learned to be content whatever the circumstances. [12]I know what it is to be in need, and I know what it is to have plenty. I have learned the secret of being content in any and every situation, whether well fed or hungry, whether living in plenty or in want. [13]I can do everything through him who gives me strength.

[14]Yet it was good of you to share in my troubles. [15]Moreover, as you Philippians know, in the early days of your acquaintance with the gospel, when I set out from Macedonia, not one church shared with me in the matter of giving and receiving, except you only; [16]for even when I was in Thessalonica, you sent me aid again and again when I was in need. [17]Not that I am looking for a gift, but I am looking for what may be credited to your account. [18]I have received full payment and even more; I am amply supplied, now that I have received from Epaphroditus the gifts you sent. They are a fragrant offering, an acceptable sacrifice, pleasing to God. [19]And my God will meet all your needs according to his glorious riches in Christ Jesus.

[20]To our God and Father be glory for ever and ever. Amen.

Final Greetings

[21]Greet all the saints in Christ Jesus. The brothers who are with me send greetings. [22]All the saints send you greetings, especially those who belong to Caesar's household.

[23]The grace of the Lord Jesus Christ be with your spirit. Amen.[a]

[a]23 Some manuscripts do not have *Amen.*

4:12–13 Life has its seasons of plenty and want, even for those who are totally devoted to God. In all situations, God wants us to be content. The secret to contentment, Paul found, was living his life and facing every situation through the strength of Christ. We would do well to look past the demands or needs of our circumstances to the abundant strength of Christ.

4:15–20 Paul's relationship with the Philippian believers was characterized by mutual respect and sharing. These qualities should characterize our relationships too. Paul was a great Christian leader, respected by thousands of believers in the early church. Many people in his position would have had a hard time accepting the help that the Philippians offered. It is sometimes even difficult for us to accept the help offered by others. Perhaps we feel they really don't understand us or are just doing things that make them feel good about themselves. We need to follow Paul's example. He joyfully received the help offered by the Philippian believers and, as a result, was able to stand firm through some tough, lonely times.

COLOSSIANS

The Big Picture

Colossians is a letter about the greatness of Christ. Since their initial conversion, the believers in Colosse had heard many theories about salvation. All of these false doctrines diminished Christ in some way. Some people had placed their faith in angels, some in rituals and others in various religious philosophies or practices. Paul wrote this letter to correct them all. His words ring with the message that Christ is God in the flesh and the only one sufficient to save us from sin and its destructive power.

In this letter, Paul included some practical advice about the kind of lives that the believers were supposed to live. Paul urged them to adhere to the truth, to live sexually pure lives, to live in peace with their friends and neighbors and to live in dependence on God. Paul did not expect the Colossians to accomplish these things by themselves. He emphasized the fact that when we seek to do God's will, we can depend on God's help. Our actions can be energized by the greatest power in the universe—the power of God in Jesus Christ.

Spiritual growth is easier when we lean on others, but ultimately God is the only one who can transform our sinful natures completely. We need God's power to begin the process of renewing our lives. The power that makes salvation possible is the same power that makes our transformation possible as well. We can trust Christ to save us, and in Christ we have the power to live each day as it comes.

A. THE POWER OF JESUS CHRIST (1:1–2:23)

B. CHRIST'S POWER WITHIN US (3:1–4:18)

Spiritual Renewal Themes

SPIRITUAL RENEWAL IS A LIFELONG PROCESS

We all long for a day when we will be totally free from the bondage of our sin—a day when our transformation will be complete. But our spiritual growth is a lifelong process. We face daily challenges to stay in close relationship with our powerful and loving God. This letter to the Colossian believers reminds us that our relationship with Christ is not just a one-time rescue operation but a lifelong commitment.

TRUE SPIRITUAL RENEWAL INVOLVES FAITH IN GOD

After a period of spiritual growth we sometimes forget how much we need God. We try to live in our own strength and go it

Essential Facts

PURPOSE:
To show us that Christ is fully God and that he is able to give us new life.

AUTHOR:
The apostle Paul.

AUDIENCE:
The believers at Colosse, a city in Asia Minor.

DATE WRITTEN:
Around A.D. 60–62, while Paul was in prison in Rome.

SETTING:
Paul wrote to a church that he had never visited but that had been started by some of his converts. One of these converts was a man named Epaphras.

KEY VERSES:
"For in Christ all the fullness of the Deity lives in bodily form, and you have been given fullness in Christ, who is the head over every power and authority" (2:9–10).

KEY PEOPLE AND RELATIONSHIPS:
Paul with Timothy, Tychicus, Onesimus, John Mark and Epaphras.

alone, depending on rules or formulas for "success." Paul warned the Colossians about this danger and urged them to live in daily contact and communication with God. Strength of character comes with maturity, but that does not mean we will reach a point where we will no longer need faith in God. We will always need his strength to help us follow his plan for our lives.

JESUS IS LORD OF THE UNIVERSE

Jesus Christ holds the entire universe together by his power. He is the supreme ruler of all creation and the reflection of the invisible God. Jesus Christ is eternal, preexistent, omnipotent and equal with the Father. How incredible that he invites us to have a personal relationship with him!

1 Paul, an apostle of Christ Jesus by the will of God, and Timothy our brother,

[2]To the holy and faithful[a] brothers in Christ at Colosse:

Grace and peace to you from God our Father.[b]

Thanksgiving and Prayer

[3]We always thank God, the Father of our Lord Jesus Christ, when we pray for you, [4]because we have heard of your faith in Christ Jesus and of the love you have for all the saints— [5]the faith and love that spring from the hope that is stored up for you in heaven and that you have already heard about in the word of truth, the gospel [6]that has come to you. All over the world this gospel is bearing fruit and growing, just as it has been doing among you since the day you heard it and understood God's grace in all its truth. [7]You learned it from Epaphras, our dear fellow servant, who is a faithful minister of Christ on our[c] behalf, [8]and who also told us of your love in the Spirit.

[9]For this reason, since the day we heard about you, we have not stopped praying for you and asking God to fill you with the knowledge of his will through all spiritual wisdom and understanding. [10]And we pray this in order that you may live a life worthy of the Lord and may please him in every way: bearing fruit in every good work, growing in the knowledge of God, [11]being strengthened with all power according to his glorious might so that you may have great endurance and patience, and joyfully [12]giving thanks to the Father, who has qualified you[d] to share in the inheritance of the saints in the kingdom of light. [13]For he has rescued us from the dominion of darkness and brought us into the kingdom of the Son he loves, [14]in whom we have redemption,[e] the forgiveness of sins.

The Supremacy of Christ

[15]He is the image of the invisible God, the firstborn over all creation. [16]For by him all things were created: things in heaven and on earth, visible and invisible, whether thrones or powers or rulers or authorities; all things were created by him and for him. [17]He is before all things, and in him all things hold together. [18]And he is the head of the body, the church; he is the beginning and the firstborn from among the dead, so that in everything he might have the supremacy. [19]For God was pleased to have all his fullness dwell in him, [20]and through him to reconcile to himself all things, whether things on earth or things in heaven, by making peace through his blood, shed on the cross.

[21]Once you were alienated from God and were enemies in your minds because of[f] your evil behavior. [22]But now he has reconciled you by Christ's physical body through death to present you holy in his sight, without blemish and free from accusation— [23]if you continue in your faith, established and firm, not moved from the hope held out in the gospel. This is the gospel that you heard and that has been proclaimed to every creature under heaven, and of which I, Paul, have become a servant.

Paul's Labor for the Church

[24]Now I rejoice in what was suffered for you, and I fill up in my flesh what is still lacking in regard to Christ's afflictions, for the sake of his body, which is the church. [25]I have become its servant by the commission God gave me to present to you the word of God in its fullness— [26]the mystery that has been kept hidden for ages and generations, but is now disclosed to the saints. [27]To them God has chosen to make known among the Gentiles the glorious riches of this mystery, which is Christ in you, the hope of glory.

[28]We proclaim him, admonishing and teaching everyone with all wisdom, so that we may present everyone perfect in Christ. [29]To this end I labor, struggling with all his energy, which so powerfully works in me.

2 I want you to know how much I am struggling for you and for those at Laodicea, and for all who have not met me personally. [2]My purpose is that they may be encouraged in heart and united in love, so that they may have the full riches of complete understanding, in order that they may know the mystery of God, namely, Christ, [3]in whom are hidden all the treasures of wisdom and knowledge. [4]I tell you this so that no one may deceive you by fine-sounding arguments. [5]For though I am absent from you in body, I am present with you in spirit and delight to see how orderly you are and how firm your faith in Christ is.

[a]2 Or *believing* [b]2 Some manuscripts *Father and the Lord Jesus Christ* [c]7 Some manuscripts *your* [d]12 Some manuscripts *us* [e]14 A few late manuscripts *redemption through his blood* [f]21 Or *minds, as shown by*

1:11–14 Paul was careful to point out that our strength and power come from God, not from ourselves. Only God's power at work in our lives can give us the ability to make spiritual progress.

1:15–17 These verses describe God in Jesus Christ. As the Creator of our world, God has the means to rebuild our lives no matter how broken they are. In fact, the entire universe would dissolve if he stopped holding it together. Even people who seem to have things under control could not exist a moment longer if it weren't for the power of God expended on their behalf. We all need God's power and depend on it, whether or not we realize it. God is our infinite power source. He provides all the power we need to transform our lives.

1:28–29 An essential part of rebuilding our lives involves sharing the message of Jesus Christ with others. We were far away from God because of sin, yet God provided the solution to our sin problem as well as the power to change. That is news worth sharing! We may be afraid to do this at first, but the Holy Spirit can give us the courage we need to share this news with others.

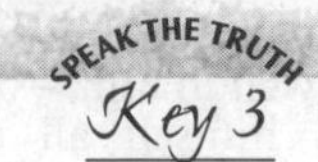

Our Need for God's Wisdom

Colossians 1:2–14 If we want to mature spiritually, we must continually confess our sins to God. We must also confess our need for God's wisdom as we seek spiritual renewal. We may not even know how to tap into God's wisdom. As we admit this to ourselves, to others and to God, we can actually open ourselves to receive his wisdom.

Some guidelines may help us identify God's wisdom in our thoughts and choices of action. According to the Bible, there are two aspects of wisdom: the spiritual and the practical. Spiritual wisdom gives insight into God's character and into the true nature of things. It is the wisdom that helps us live as God desires. Paul prayed for this sort of wisdom for both the Ephesians and the Colossians (see 1:9–10; Ephesians 1:17). We will recognize such wisdom by its qualities: "The wisdom that comes from heaven is first of all pure; then peace-loving, considerate, submissive, full of mercy and good fruit, impartial and sincere" (James 3:17).

Practical wisdom can be judged by whether or not our actions conform to God's instructions. The instructions God gives us naturally lead to healthy living and our spiritual transformation. We need this practical wisdom. James tells us, "If any of you lacks wisdom, he should ask God, who gives generously to all without finding fault, and it will be given to him" (James 1:5).

Turn to 1 Peter 3.

Freedom From Human Regulations Through Life With Christ

6So then, just as you received Christ Jesus as
Lord, continue to live in him, 7rooted and built
up in him, strengthened in the faith as you were
taught, and overflowing with thankfulness.
8See to it that no one takes you captive
through hollow and deceptive philosophy,
which depends on human tradition and the basic principles of this world rather than on
Christ.
9For in Christ all the fullness of the Deity
lives in bodily form, 10and you have been given
fullness in Christ, who is the head over every
power and authority. 11In him you were also
circumcised, in the putting off of the sinful nature,[a] not with a circumcision done by the
hands of men but with the circumcision done
by Christ, 12having been buried with him in
baptism and raised with him through your faith
in the power of God, who raised him from the
dead.
13When you were dead in your sins and in
the uncircumcision of your sinful nature,[b]
God made you[c] alive with Christ. He forgave
us all our sins, 14having canceled the written
code, with its regulations, that was against us
and that stood opposed to us; he took it away,
nailing it to the cross. 15And having disarmed
the powers and authorities, he made a public
spectacle of them, triumphing over them by the
cross.[d]
16Therefore do not let anyone judge you by
what you eat or drink, or with regard to a religious festival, a New Moon celebration or a Sabbath day. 17These are a shadow of the things
that were to come; the reality, however, is found
in Christ. 18Do not let anyone who delights in
false humility and the worship of angels disqualify you for the prize. Such a person goes
into great detail about what he has seen, and his
unspiritual mind puffs him up with idle notions. 19He has lost connection with the Head,
from whom the whole body, supported and
held together by its ligaments and sinews,
grows as God causes it to grow.
20Since you died with Christ to the basic

[a]11 Or *the flesh* [b]13 Or *your flesh* [c]13 Some manuscripts *us* [d]15 Or *them in him*

2:6–7 The same faith that we exercised when we surrendered our lives to God should be used daily to continue our spiritual growth. It is not enough to be planted; we must be rooted deeply in Christ. We must find our strength in him so that we will grow and mature in our faith.
2:11–15 The same power that raised Christ from the dead is available to help us overcome our sinfulness. Since Jesus has authority over every other power, including the power of evil, he can set us free. Yet this freedom is not just freedom from the bondage of the past but also from the spiritual bondage to our sinful natures. In Christ, we can experience the life of peace and joy that God intends for us.
2:20–23 Legalism will not remove the problem of sin.

principles of this world, why, as though you
still belonged to it, do you submit to its rules:
21"Do not handle! Do not taste! Do not
touch!"? 22These are all destined to perish with
use, because they are based on human commands and teachings. 23Such regulations indeed have an appearance of wisdom, with their
self-imposed worship, their false humility and
their harsh treatment of the body, but they lack
any value in restraining sensual indulgence.

Rules for Holy Living

3 Since, then, you have been raised with
Christ, set your hearts on things above,
where Christ is seated at the right hand of God.
2Set your minds on things above, not on earthly
things. 3For you died, and your life is now hidden with Christ in God. 4When Christ, who is
your[a] life, appears, then you also will appear
with him in glory.
5Put to death, therefore, whatever belongs to
your earthly nature: sexual immorality, impurity, lust, evil desires and greed, which is idolatry.
6Because of these, the wrath of God is coming.[b] 7You used to walk in these ways, in the
life you once lived. 8But now you must rid yourselves of all such things as these: anger, rage,
malice, slander, and filthy language from your
lips. 9Do not lie to each other, since you have
taken off your old self with its practices 10and
have put on the new self, which is being renewed in knowledge in the image of its Creator.
11Here there is no Greek or Jew, circumcised or
uncircumcised, barbarian, Scythian, slave or
free, but Christ is all, and is in all.
12Therefore, as God's chosen people, holy
and dearly loved, clothe yourselves with compassion, kindness, humility, gentleness and
patience. 13Bear with each other and forgive
whatever grievances you may have against one

[a]4 Some manuscripts *our* [b]6 Some early manuscripts *coming on those who are disobedient*

Creating rules for ourselves in order to break free from our bondage or trying harder to live good lives will never free us from sin. Paul tells us that looking to our own strength to solve our sin problem will only lead us away from the only adequate power source—God in Jesus Christ. He is the only one with the power to transform us and help us rebuild our lives.

3:1–3 Paul doesn't deny the harsh realities of life in this passage; he is simply reminding us of where our focus should be. When our eyes are on Christ, we can view life from a different perspective. There is hope, even when everything seems dark and hopeless. When we learn to see with an eternal perspective, the struggles of life won't disappear, but they will be seen in the proper light. Our struggles will not longer terrify us. When we keep our eyes on Christ and his promises, no obstacle is too great for us to overcome.

3:12–13 Paul urges us to cultivate our relationships with love, forgiveness and peace. We need to seek forgiveness from those we have hurt and to forgive those who have hurt us. Paul tells us to be gentle and not to hold grudges. As we seek to make peace, our actions are to be governed by the principle of selfless love.

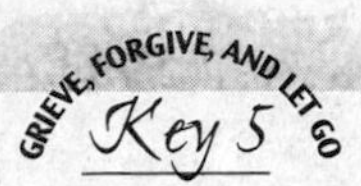

Letting Go of Our Anxiety

Colossians 3:1–4 Forgiving those who commit wrongs against us doesn't necessarily guarantee we will live easy lives. We will always have to deal with difficult people and face the stresses of life. Life involves pressures beyond our control that will wear us down if we aren't careful to release them to God.

The apostle Paul gave us a strategy to help us deal with the troubles of daily life: "Set your minds on things above, not on earthly things. For you died, and your life is now hidden with Christ in God" (3:2–3). Paul also wrote, "Do not be anxious about anything, but in everything, by prayer and petition, with thanksgiving, present your requests to God. And the peace of God, which transcends all understanding, will guard your hearts and your minds in Christ Jesus" (Philippians 4:6–7). This last verse paints a picture of a guard patrolling our hearts and minds to keep out the pressing anxieties of life.

Just as we should continually forgive others, we should also continually release our worries and specific needs to God. He will, in turn, care for us and give us his peace that passes all understanding.

Turn to 1 John 4.

God's Word As Our Counselor

Colossians 3:16 Wisdom and knowledge are vastly different. Knowledge refers to the accumulation of facts and information. Wisdom describes why things work the way they do and evaluates what things are most important. Knowledge is quantitative; wisdom is qualitative. We can possess knowledge about any number of things that have little bearing on daily life. Wisdom is primarily concerned with the key issues of life.

The Bible, God's Word, can make us wise. While it contains much knowledgeable information about creation, its primary emphasis is on wisdom—understanding life and knowing our Creator. While the Bible gives us some insights into life in the ancient world, its main purpose is to prepare us for life today. "These things happened to them as examples and were written down as warnings for us, on whom the fulfillment of the ages has come. So, if you think you are standing firm, be careful that you don't fall!" (1 Corinthians 10:11–12).

Paul exhorts us to do more than master the facts of the Bible. God's Word must make itself at home in our hearts. It is to become a part of all we think, say and do. When God's Word is woven into the fabric of our lives, we will never unravel regardless of the circumstances.

Putting It Into Practice

What one area concerns you most today? It could be a problem at work, a difficulty at school, a conflict in a relationship, a question concerning God's will, a guilty conscience or any number of things. Consider what God's Word has to say about it. If no particular verses come to mind, use a topical Bible or a concordance to discover verses that speak to your concern. What wise counsel is God giving you through these verses?

For more on Bible study and meditation, turn to 2 Timothy 3.

another. Forgive as the Lord forgave you. [14]And over all these virtues put on love, which binds them all together in perfect unity.

[15]Let the peace of Christ rule in your hearts, since as members of one body you were called to peace. And be thankful. [16]Let the word of Christ dwell in you richly as you teach and admonish one another with all wisdom, and as you sing psalms, hymns and spiritual songs with gratitude in your hearts to God. [17]And whatever you do, whether in word or deed, do it all in the name of the Lord Jesus, giving thanks to God the Father through him.

Rules for Christian Households

[18]Wives, submit to your husbands, as is fitting in the Lord.

[19]Husbands, love your wives and do not be harsh with them.

[20]Children, obey your parents in everything, for this pleases the Lord.

[21]Fathers, do not embitter your children, or they will become discouraged.

[22]Slaves, obey your earthly masters in everything; and do it, not only when their eye is on you and to win their favor, but with sincerity of heart and reverence for the Lord. [23]Whatever you do, work at it with all your heart, as working for the Lord, not for men, [24]since you know that you will receive an inheritance from the Lord as a reward. It is the Lord Christ you are serving. [25]Anyone who does wrong will be repaid for his wrong, and there is no favoritism.

4 Masters, provide your slaves with what is right and fair, because you know that you also have a Master in heaven.

Further Instructions

[2]Devote yourselves to prayer, being watchful and thankful. [3]And pray for us, too, that God may open a door for our message, so that we may proclaim the mystery of Christ, for which I am in chains. [4]Pray that I may proclaim it clearly, as I should. [5]Be wise in the way you act toward outsiders; make the most of every opportunity. [6]Let your conversation be always full of grace, seasoned with salt, so that you may know how to answer everyone.

Final Greetings

[7]Tychicus will tell you all the news about me. He is a dear brother, a faithful minister and fellow servant in the Lord. [8]I am sending him to you for the express purpose that you may know about our[a] circumstances and that he may encourage your hearts. [9]He is coming with Onesimus, our faithful and dear brother, who is one of you. They will tell you everything that is happening here.

[10]My fellow prisoner Aristarchus sends you his greetings, as does Mark, the cousin of Barnabas. (You have received instructions about him; if he comes to you, welcome him.) [11]Jesus, who is called Justus, also sends greetings. These are the only Jews among my fellow workers for the kingdom of God, and they have proved a comfort to me. [12]Epaphras, who is one of you and a servant of Christ Jesus, sends greetings. He is always wrestling in prayer for you, that you may stand firm in all the will of God, mature and fully assured. [13]I vouch for him that he is working hard for you and for those at Laodicea and Hierapolis. [14]Our dear friend Luke, the doctor, and Demas send greetings. [15]Give my greetings to the brothers at Laodicea, and to Nympha and the church in her house.

[16]After this letter has been read to you, see that it is also read in the church of the Laodiceans and that you in turn read the letter from Laodicea.

[17]Tell Archippus: "See to it that you complete the work you have received in the Lord."

[18]I, Paul, write this greeting in my own hand. Remember my chains. Grace be with you.

[a]8 Some manuscripts *that he may know about your*

4:2–3 Paul encouraged the Colossian believers to persevere in prayer. This is good advice for us too. As we pray, we are reminded to keep our eyes on God. Making prayer a daily priority reminds us to thank God for his help. We then become increasingly aware of his activity in our lives. When we are discouraged, we can still come to God in prayer. He will then empower us to persevere. As we turn to God in prayer, we will embrace the power sufficient to meet our needs and preserve our spiritual gains.

1 THESSALONIANS

The Big Picture

A. GREETINGS (1:1)

B. CONGRATULATIONS (1:2–3:13)

1. Paul's Commendation for Their Progress (1:2-10)
2. Paul's Conduct While With Them (2:1-12)
3. Paul's Concern for Their Continued Spiritual Growth (2:13–3:13)

C. CONSULTATIONS (4:1–5:22)

1. Concerning Morality (4:1-8)
2. Concerning Mutual Love (4:9-12)
3. Concerning Deceased Christians (4:13-18)
4. Concerning Accountability Before God (5:1-11)
5. Concerning Our Conduct in Relationships (5:12-22)

D. BENEDICTION AND CLOSING THOUGHTS (5:23-28)

Paul and his companions Silas and Timothy first traveled to Thessalonica on Paul's second missionary journey (see Acts 15:40—16:4; 17:1). Many people in Thessalonica who had worshiped idols turned their lives over to God. These believers gave up their empty rituals and lives of dependence upon material things to serve the living and true God. And Paul commended them for this.

Their new lives of faith were not easy, though. Despite the positive changes God had made in the believers' lives, some people harassed and teased them. Many of their friends and relatives opposed them. This persecution forced Paul and his companions to leave Thessalonica. But Paul was concerned about the new believers he had left behind. Were they strong enough in their faith in God? Would they slip back into old patterns of sin and idolatry? Paul sent Timothy to check on the Thessalonians. Encouraged by Timothy's report, Paul sent them this letter.

When we meet with opposition, we can identify with Paul and the believers at Thessalonica. Friends and family members may not understand our faith; old habits may pressure us to return to our old ways. But we can be encouraged by the progress we have already made. God's power is at work within us. We don't have to quit our spiritual journey just because we face opposition.

Spiritual Renewal Themes

GOD IS OUR SOURCE OF HOPE

If we place our trust in Christ to save us from sin, we will live with him forever; we will have eternal life. But we can have hope for more than just life beyond the grave; we can also have hope for what God can bring to our lives in the present. The power that raised Jesus Christ from the dead is the power of God—the God to whom we have entrusted our lives. With this kind of power available to us, there is always hope for a renewed life!

SPIRITUAL GROWTH IS A WAY OF LIFE

Paul challenged the Thessalonians to always live in humble anticipation of Christ's coming, realizing that each day is impor-

tant. We also need to live one day at a time, recognizing that our spiritual growth will never be complete in this life. We need to live responsibly, depending on God at all times. God is always transforming us. When we become complacent, drift away from continued dependence on God and forsake accountability to others, we endanger whatever spiritual gains we have made.

COMMITMENT THAT OVERCOMES OBSTACLES

We are all flawed human beings with many limitations and problems. Living in this world means that we will always face obstacles to our continued spiritual growth. We must stand firm in our commitment to God, knowing that the Holy Spirit empowers us with his strength. God's power is available to all of us; to make spiritual progress we must commit ourselves to actively obeying God's will.

Essential Facts

PURPOSE:
To commend the believers in Thessalonica for their trust in God, to encourage them to continue trusting him and to reassure them that Christ would return.

AUTHOR:
The apostle Paul.

AUDIENCE:
The believers in Thessalonica, a city in Macedonia.

DATE WRITTEN:
About A.D. 50–51, during Paul's second missionary journey.

SETTING:
The church in Thessalonica was only two or three years old when Paul wrote this letter. The believers needed to mature spiritually, and they needed some help in understanding the return of Christ.

KEY VERSE:
"You are all sons of the light and sons of the day. We do not belong to the night or to the darkness" (5:5).

KEY PEOPLE AND RELATIONSHIPS:
Paul with the believers at Thessalonica and with Timothy.

1

Paul, Silas[a] and Timothy,

To the church of the Thessalonians in God the Father and the Lord Jesus Christ:

Grace and peace to you.[b]

Thanksgiving for the Thessalonians' Faith

2We always thank God for all of you, mentioning you in our prayers. 3We continually remember before our God and Father your work produced by faith, your labor prompted by love, and your endurance inspired by hope in our Lord Jesus Christ.

4For we know, brothers loved by God, that he has chosen you, 5because our gospel came to you not simply with words, but also with power, with the Holy Spirit and with deep conviction. You know how we lived among you for your sake. 6You became imitators of us and of the Lord; in spite of severe suffering, you welcomed the message with the joy given by the Holy Spirit. 7And so you became a model to all the believers in Macedonia and Achaia. 8The Lord's message rang out from you not only in Macedonia and Achaia—your faith in God has become known everywhere. Therefore we do not need to say anything about it, 9for they themselves report what kind of reception you gave us. They tell how you turned to God from idols to serve the living and true God, 10and to wait for his Son from heaven, whom he raised from the dead—Jesus, who rescues us from the coming wrath.

Paul's Ministry in Thessalonica

2

You know, brothers, that our visit to you was not a failure. 2We had previously suffered and been insulted in Philippi, as you know, but with the help of our God we dared to tell you his gospel in spite of strong opposition. 3For the appeal we make does not spring from error or impure motives, nor are we trying to trick you. 4On the contrary, we speak as men approved by God to be entrusted with the gospel. We are not trying to please men but God, who tests our hearts. 5You know we never used flattery, nor did we put on a mask to cover up greed—God is our witness. 6We were not looking for praise from men, not from you or anyone else.

As apostles of Christ we could have been a burden to you, 7but we were gentle among you, like a mother caring for her little children. 8We loved you so much that we were delighted to share with you not only the gospel of God but our lives as well, because you had become so dear to us. 9Surely you remember, brothers, our toil and hardship; we worked night and day in order not to be a burden to anyone while we preached the gospel of God to you.

10You are witnesses, and so is God, of how holy, righteous and blameless we were among you who believed. 11For you know that we dealt with each of you as a father deals with his own children, 12encouraging, comforting and urging you to live lives worthy of God, who calls you into his kingdom and glory.

13And we also thank God continually because, when you received the word of God, which you heard from us, you accepted it not as the word of men, but as it actually is, the word of God, which is at work in you who believe. 14For you, brothers, became imitators of God's churches in Judea, which are in Christ Jesus: You suffered from your own countrymen the same things those churches suffered from the Jews, 15who killed the Lord Jesus and the prophets and also drove us out. They displease God and are hostile to all men 16in their effort to keep us from speaking to the Gentiles so that they may be saved. In this way they always heap up their sins to the limit. The wrath of God has come upon them at last.[c]

Paul's Longing to See the Thessalonians

17But, brothers, when we were torn away from you for a short time (in person, not in thought), out of our intense longing we made

[a] 1 Greek *Silvanus,* a variant of *Silas* [b] 1 Some early manuscripts *you from God our Father and the Lord Jesus Christ* [c] 16 Or *them fully*

1:2–3 Paul was thankful for the Thessalonian believers and for their love for each other, their faith in God and their hope in Christ's return. This triad of faith, love and hope is a summary of the Christian life (see 1 Corinthians 13:13). Faith in an all-powerful God is demonstrated by living one day at a time. Love is demonstrated through sacrificial service to others. Hope carries us through the hard times as we depend upon God.

1:4–6 The Thessalonians were examples of faithful citizens of God's kingdom. They gained freedom from idolatry because they believed in Jesus Christ and experienced his transforming power in their lives. His power makes all the difference! When we surrender our lives to God, he can redeem us and make us shining examples of his love and grace.

1:7–9 The Thessalonian believers had experienced a spiritual awakening because of their belief in Jesus Christ. They imitated his ways, despite the persecution it brought them. By doing so, their example led many in the surrounding area to experience the healing offered by God in Jesus Christ. We, too, should be changed in ways that others can see. We should share our faith in Christ as a natural outflow of our experience of salvation. By sharing our story we will not only inspire hope in others but also experience personal encouragement as we recall all the great things God has done in our lives.

2:3–12 Paul did not minister in Thessalonica to secure personal gain. Yet to discredit Paul and his message, Paul's enemies charged him with that very offense. The apostle reminded the Thessalonians that he had gained nothing materially from his ministry with them. The apostle's sincere love and empathy had motivated his work among the Thessalonians. We are called to share the message of hope to others. But before getting involved in others' lives, we need to examine our motives. Are we helping others for reasons of personal gain or because we are sincerely concerned about them?

every effort to see you. 18For we wanted to come to you—certainly I, Paul, did, again and again—but Satan stopped us. 19For what is our hope, our joy, or the crown in which we will glory in the presence of our Lord Jesus when he comes? Is it not you? 20Indeed, you are our glory and joy.

3 So when we could stand it no longer, we thought it best to be left by ourselves in Athens. 2We sent Timothy, who is our brother and God's fellow worker[a] in spreading the gospel of Christ, to strengthen and encourage you in your faith, 3so that no one would be unsettled by these trials. You know quite well that we were destined for them. 4In fact, when we were with you, we kept telling you that we would be persecuted. And it turned out that way, as you well know. 5For this reason, when I could stand it no longer, I sent to find out about your faith. I was afraid that in some way the tempter might have tempted you and our efforts might have been useless.

Timothy's Encouraging Report

6But Timothy has just now come to us from you and has brought good news about your faith and love. He has told us that you always have pleasant memories of us and that you long to see us, just as we also long to see you. 7Therefore, brothers, in all our distress and persecution we were encouraged about you because of your faith. 8For now we really live, since you are standing firm in the Lord. 9How can we thank God enough for you in return for all the joy we have in the presence of our God because of you? 10Night and day we pray most earnestly that we may see you again and supply what is lacking in your faith.

11Now may our God and Father himself and our Lord Jesus clear the way for us to come to you. 12May the Lord make your love increase and overflow for each other and for everyone else, just as ours does for you. 13May he strengthen your hearts so that you will be blameless and holy in the presence of our God and Father when our Lord Jesus comes with all his holy ones.

Living to Please God

4 Finally, brothers, we instructed you how to live in order to please God, as in fact you are living. Now we ask you and urge you in the Lord Jesus to do this more and more. 2For you know what instructions we gave you by the authority of the Lord Jesus.

3It is God's will that you should be sanctified: that you should avoid sexual immorality; 4that each of you should learn to control his own body[b] in a way that is holy and honorable, 5not in passionate lust like the heathen, who do not know God; 6and that in this matter no one should wrong his brother or take advantage of him. The Lord will punish men for all such sins, as we have already told you and warned you. 7For God did not call us to be impure, but to live a holy life. 8Therefore, he who rejects this instruction does not reject man but God, who gives you his Holy Spirit.

9Now about brotherly love we do not need to write to you, for you yourselves have been taught by God to love each other. 10And in fact, you do love all the brothers throughout Macedonia. Yet we urge you, brothers, to do so more and more.

11Make it your ambition to lead a quiet life, to mind your own business and to work with your hands, just as we told you, 12so that your daily life may win the respect of outsiders and so that you will not be dependent on anybody.

a2 Some manuscripts *brother and fellow worker;* other manuscripts *brother and God's servant* b4 Or *learn to live with his own wife;* or *learn to acquire a wife*

2:19–20 Paul discovered the message of hope in the gospel of Jesus Christ. As he grew in his faith, he joyfully began to share it with others. Notice that Paul's ministry not only helped the Thessalonians, but it also helped Paul. As Paul watched the Thessalonians grow spiritually, he experienced incredible joy in his own life. Just as their sorrow had been his sorrow, their victory became his victory. The Thessalonians became Paul's "glory and joy" (2:20). The common bond that we share with others in Christ can be a source of great encouragement when we see how they are inspired and changed by what we share with them.

3:1–4 Paul made it clear that we are to expect trouble. When we surrender our lives to God, we cannot expect everything to go smoothly. God never promised to miraculously remove all of our problems (see John 16:33). But God says he will be with us as we face our problems, giving us strength to confront each new challenge as it arises. Realizing that we will always face difficulties in this life can help us to survive the hard times. As we face reality in a fallen world, we can count on God's presence with us.

3:6–8 Timothy returned with good news from Thessalonica. The spiritual growth of the Thessalonians was a great encouragement to Paul. Timothy's glowing report helped Paul make it through his own tough times. Our relationships with others in the faith provide an essential source of shared mutual help. When we are discouraged, the successes of others can lift us up. When we are blessed, our joy can lift others out of their despair. As we share our lives with one another, we will build each other up and provide the needed encouragement to preserve spiritual gains in our lives and theirs.

3:11–13 Paul concluded this portion of his letter with a short prayer for the Thessalonian believers. Paul prayed that these spiritually transformed people would continue to mature before God. He requested that their love for God would flow out to others. Paul's prayer for these believers can be a model for us as we seek to encourage others in their spiritual growth. We can continually lift others to God in prayer and rejoice as we see God working his transformation in their lives.

4:3–8 This passage paints a clear picture of the characteristics we will exemplify if we are following God's will. This positive list is then followed by a list of things we should not be involved in. Passages like this can serve as measuring sticks for us as we reflect honestly on our lives. If we don't measure up to God's ideals, we can admit our failures to him and ask him to redirect the course of our lives. As we surrender our lives to him and let him change us, we will see these positive characteristics growing in us.

The Coming of the Lord

[13]Brothers, we do not want you to be ignorant about those who fall asleep, or to grieve like the rest of men, who have no hope. [14]We believe that Jesus died and rose again and so we believe that God will bring with Jesus those who have fallen asleep in him. [15]According to the Lord's own word, we tell you that we who are still alive, who are left till the coming of the Lord, will certainly not precede those who have fallen asleep. [16]For the Lord himself will come down from heaven, with a loud command, with the voice of the archangel and with the trumpet call of God, and the dead in Christ will rise first. [17]After that, we who are still alive and are left will be caught up together with them in the clouds to meet the Lord in the air. And so we will be with the Lord forever. [18]Therefore encourage each other with these words.

5 Now, brothers, about times and dates we do not need to write to you, [2]for you know very well that the day of the Lord will come like a thief in the night. [3]While people are saying, "Peace and safety," destruction will come on them suddenly, as labor pains on a pregnant woman, and they will not escape.

[4]But you, brothers, are not in darkness so that this day should surprise you like a thief. [5]You are all sons of the light and sons of the day. We do not belong to the night or to the darkness. [6]So then, let us not be like others, who are asleep, but let us be alert and self-controlled. [7]For those who sleep, sleep at night, and those who get drunk, get drunk at night. [8]But since we belong to the day, let us be self-controlled, putting on faith and love as a breastplate, and the hope of salvation as a helmet. [9]For God did not appoint us to suffer wrath but to receive salvation through our Lord Jesus Christ. [10]He died for us so that, whether we are awake or asleep, we may live together with him. [11]Therefore encourage one another and build each other up, just as in fact you are doing.

Final Instructions

[12]Now we ask you, brothers, to respect those who work hard among you, who are over you in the Lord and who admonish you. [13]Hold them in the highest regard in love because of their work. Live in peace with each other. [14]And we urge you, brothers, warn those who are idle, encourage the timid, help the weak, be patient with everyone. [15]Make sure that nobody pays back wrong for wrong, but always try to be kind to each other and to everyone else.

[16]Be joyful always; [17]pray continually; [18]give thanks in all circumstances, for this is God's will for you in Christ Jesus.

[19]Do not put out the Spirit's fire; [20]do not treat prophecies with contempt. [21]Test everything. Hold on to the good. [22]Avoid every kind of evil.

[23]May God himself, the God of peace, sanctify you through and through. May your whole spirit, soul and body be kept blameless at the coming of our Lord Jesus Christ. [24]The one who calls you is faithful and he will do it.

[25]Brothers, pray for us. [26]Greet all the brothers with a holy kiss. [27]I charge you before the Lord to have this letter read to all the brothers.

[28]The grace of our Lord Jesus Christ be with you.

4:13–18 Apparently the Thessalonian believers wondered what would happen to the Christians who had already died. They were afraid that believers who died before Jesus returned would lose the opportunity of sharing in Christ's glorious reign. Paul explained that Christians who had died would be raised and would share in the fellowship and reign of Jesus in God's kingdom. All believers have this hope in the future as well. When Christ returns, it won't matter whether we are dead or alive; God has a plan that includes us.

5:1–11 Paul warns us of a day when God will hold all people accountable for their attitudes and actions. This time will come unexpectedly, so we need to stay alert and ready at all times. This is especially important for those of us who tend to procrastinate. God wants us to act immediately whenever we see sin in our lives. He doesn't want us to delay confessing our sins or forgiving others. When God shows us where we have sinned, he also offers us the power to change immediately. There is no acceptable reason to put off doing what God calls us to do. The time to obey God is always now.

5:14–28 In these verses, Paul leaves us with a collection of good teachings. Following these instructions with God's help will put us well on our way to spiritual renewal. We should minister to others and actively participate in God's ongoing work on earth. Doing so will bring others hope and will preserve our own spiritual gains as well. Paul also urges us to rebuild relationships by repaying the sins of others with kindness. He calls us to live joyful lives, to be always prayerful, to continually seek God's will and to remember that God's continual helping presence is with us in the gift of the Holy Spirit. God gives us what we need to fulfill his plan for our lives. Our part is to participate in the good plan he has set out for us.

2 THESSALONIANS

The Big Picture

The message we receive is not always the message that was sent. Paul's first letter to the Thessalonians had made an impact on its readers. But it wasn't the impact Paul had intended. Paul had affirmed that Jesus would return soon. In response, some of the Thessalonian believers assumed that they should stop everything and wait for Christ's return. Some even stopped working, expecting that they would no longer need food and other supplies.

Not every believer in Thessalonica thought that way; many continued to act responsibly even as they anticipated Christ's return. But this only added to the tension between church members. The diligent believers felt pressured to pick up the slack left by the others. The idle believers claimed that they were living lives of true faith. After hearing about this problem, Paul sent this second letter to the Thessalonians.

Though Paul wanted to correct his audience's misunderstanding, he made sure to commend them for their faithfulness to God and their commitment to doing God's will. Paul was confident that God would help them resolve this issue, so his message to them was simple. He urged them to be content with their situation and disciplined about fulfilling their responsibilities.

Second Thessalonians contains good reminders for us. Though we surrender our lives to God in this life and look forward to the day when all our problems will be behind us, we still have to live in the here and now. Developing a relationship with God and pursuing spiritual growth does not mean we can neglect our families, work or friends. Accepting the responsibilities God has given us is a key to our spiritual growth.

A. GREETINGS (1:1-2)

B. COMMENDATIONS IN THE MIDST OF PERSECUTION (1:3-12)

C. CORRECTION CONCERNING THE DAY OF THE LORD (2:1-17)

D. ENCOURAGEMENT FOR PRAYER AND A DISCIPLINED LIFE (3:1-15)

E. CONCLUDING REMARKS (3:16-18)

Spiritual Renewal Themes

GOD IS THE SOURCE OF OUR HOPE

Sometimes in our spiritual growth we take our eyes off God and focus on ourselves. We tell ourselves that if we only keep up our resolve, all will be well. But placing our hope in anything other than God sets us up for a fall. Our realization that we needed God's help was what led us to desire spiritual renewal in the first place. If after depending on God and beginning the process of spiritual renewal we revert to depending on ourselves again,

Essential Facts

PURPOSE:
To encourage the Thessalonian believers to fulfill their daily responsibilities while awaiting Christ's return.

AUTHOR:
The apostle Paul.

AUDIENCE:
The church at Thessalonica, a city in Macedonia.

DATE WRITTEN:
About A.D. 51–52, during Paul's second missionary journey, shortly after he had written 1 Thessalonians.

SETTING:
Some of these believers had misunderstood Paul's first letter and believed Christ's return was imminent. They used that assumption as an excuse for being lazy while awaiting Christ's return.

KEY VERSE:
"May the Lord direct your hearts into God's love and Christ's perseverance" (3:5).

KEY PEOPLE AND RELATIONSHIPS:
Paul with Silas, Timothy and the believers at Thessalonica.

we will only face failure and frustration. We will want to quit our spiritual journey. But if we depend on God, he will provide us with the hope and joy we need to persevere in our faith.

THE IMPORTANCE OF PERSEVERANCE

Some of the believers in Thessalonica were idly waiting for the return of Christ. Their lazy, indifferent attitudes toward the concerns of everyday life kept them from living responsible lives. These believers soon became a burden to others. Entrusting our lives to God does not mean we can just sit around. We must continue to follow God's plan, trusting God to sustain us and bring about the transformation we desire. Our dependence on God is a partnership with him; he doesn't become our slave or a genie in a bottle. We must cooperate with God in both spiritual and practical ways, or we will miss God's best and alienate those who have to pick up the slack because of our lack of perseverance.

GOD'S REASSURING POWER AND PRESENCE

Evil seems to be on the increase in our society much as it was in Thessalonica. The Bible tells us that until Christ returns evil will continue to increase. But we don't need to be surprised or afraid of these changes; God is sovereign over the earth, no matter how evil our world becomes. As we continue to seek God and surrender to him, he promises to give us victory over the evil in our lives. We only need to remain faithful to God.

1 Paul, Silas[a] and Timothy,

To the church of the Thessalonians in God
our Father and the Lord Jesus Christ:

2Grace and peace to you from God the Father
and the Lord Jesus Christ.

Thanksgiving and Prayer

3We ought always to thank God for you,
brothers, and rightly so, because your faith is
growing more and more, and the love every one
of you has for each other is increasing. 4There-
fore, among God's churches we boast about
your perseverance and faith in all the persecutions and trials you are enduring.
5All this is evidence that God's judgment is
right, and as a result you will be counted worthy
of the kingdom of God, for which you are suffering. 6God is just: He will pay back trouble to
those who trouble you 7and give relief to you
who are troubled, and to us as well. This will
happen when the Lord Jesus is revealed from
heaven in blazing fire with his powerful angels.
8He will punish those who do not know God
and do not obey the gospel of our Lord Jesus.
9They will be punished with everlasting destruction and shut out from the presence of the Lord
and from the majesty of his power 10on the day
he comes to be glorified in his holy people and
to be marveled at among all those who have
believed. This includes you, because you believed our testimony to you.
11With this in mind, we constantly pray for
you, that our God may count you worthy of his
calling, and that by his power he may fulfill
every good purpose of yours and every act
prompted by your faith. 12We pray this so that
the name of our Lord Jesus may be glorified in
you, and you in him, according to the grace of
our God and the Lord Jesus Christ.[b]

The Man of Lawlessness

2 Concerning the coming of our Lord Jesus
Christ and our being gathered to him, we
ask you, brothers, 2not to become easily unsettled or alarmed by some prophecy, report or
letter supposed to have come from us, saying
that the day of the Lord has already come.
3Don't let anyone deceive you in any way, for
⌊that day will not come⌋ until the rebellion occurs and the man of lawlessness[c] is revealed,
the man doomed to destruction. 4He will oppose and will exalt himself over everything that
is called God or is worshiped, so that he sets
himself up in God's temple, proclaiming himself to be God.
5Don't you remember that when I was with
you I used to tell you these things? 6And now
you know what is holding him back, so that he
may be revealed at the proper time. 7For the
secret power of lawlessness is already at work;
but the one who now holds it back will continue to do so till he is taken out of the way. 8And
then the lawless one will be revealed, whom the
Lord Jesus will overthrow with the breath of his
mouth and destroy by the splendor of his coming. 9The coming of the lawless one will be in
accordance with the work of Satan displayed in
all kinds of counterfeit miracles, signs and wonders, 10and in every sort of evil that deceives
those who are perishing. They perish because
they refused to love the truth and so be saved.
11For this reason God sends them a powerful
delusion so that they will believe the lie 12and
so that all will be condemned who have not
believed the truth but have delighted in wickedness.

Stand Firm

13But we ought always to thank God for
you, brothers loved by the Lord, because from
the beginning God chose you[d] to be saved
through the sanctifying work of the Spirit and
through belief in the truth. 14He called you to
this through our gospel, that you might share in
the glory of our Lord Jesus Christ. 15So then,

[a]1 Greek *Silvanus,* a variant of *Silas* [b]12 Or *God and Lord, Jesus Christ* [c]3 Some manuscripts *sin* [d]13 Some manuscripts *because God chose you as his firstfruits*

1:3–4 Paul rejoiced that the Thessalonians were maturing in their faith. Their hardships had served as an important impetus to their spiritual growth. We can learn from our hardships too. Just as God used hardships to inspire growth among the Thessalonians, he can do the same with us. Painful situations force us to admit that we cannot succeed without God. When we admit our powerlessness, we can begin to rebuild our lives on the only sure foundation—Jesus Christ.
1:5–8 We often look upon difficulties as something to avoid at all cost. But we may run from painful situations only to be trapped by other serious problems. Sometimes we turn to sinful pursuits in an attempt to escape pain but only find that our sins entangle us. We need to face painful circumstances squarely with God's help. When we turn to God and ask him to help us accept reality instead of turning to sin and allowing it to distract us from reality, God can free us from the sinful habits we have used as an escape. Our hardships need not be a cause for failure and further bondage to sin; hardships can become an impetus for our spiritual growth.
1:9–10 People in hell will be eternally separated from God's healing presence. The Thessalonians escaped such a terrible fate by surrendering their lives to God. We have an opportunity to do the same. But spiritual renewal is more than a way to escape hell. True spiritual renewal involves making the most of our union with God and living in his presence each day.
2:3–10 Paul warned the Thessalonians of an evil power at work in our world. These new believers had experienced the work of this oppressor during their years as idol worshipers. We experience this same evil power at work in our lives at times, especially when we give ourselves over to the desires of our sinful natures. We can rejoice that when Jesus Christ returns, he will completely overcome the evil powers in this world. If we surrender our lives to him now, he will begin this work in our lives right away.
2:15–17 Paul praised the Thessalonians for their exemplary faith. He then went on to encourage them to continue to seek God, his will and his power. Paul also remind-

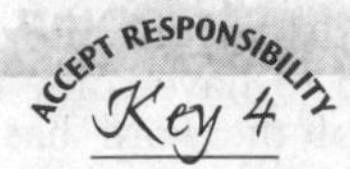

Providing for Ourselves

2 Thessalonians 3:1–8 Part of our spiritual growth involves accepting financial responsibility for ourselves. Adults have a basic responsibility to work and provide for themselves, and if they are parents, to provide for their children. Accepting this responsibility is practical advice that will help us grow in spiritual maturity too.

The apostle Paul taught us by example what it means to be responsible: "We were not idle when we were with you, nor did we eat anyone's food without paying for it. On the contrary, we worked night and day, laboring and toiling so that we would not be a burden to any of you" (3:7–8). He also instructed believers "in the Lord Jesus Christ to settle down and earn the bread they eat" (3:12).

If we have not accepted such financial responsibility, we must consider how our refusal to do so may have affected others. We may have caused others much pain if we have failed to provide for ourselves or our family's needs. If our honest reflection on our lives shows patterns of irresponsibility, we may feel shame and discouragement. However, once we face our failure and willingly change our ways, we will gain self-respect. Accepting responsibility for our finances by working hard and clearing up any financial problems will reduce daily stress and free us to focus on our spiritual growth.

Turn to Philemon.

brothers, stand firm and hold to the teachings[a]
we passed on to you, whether by word of
mouth or by letter.
16May our Lord Jesus Christ himself and God
our Father, who loved us and by his grace gave
us eternal encouragement and good hope, 17encourage
your hearts and strengthen you in every
good deed and word.

Request for Prayer

3 Finally, brothers, pray for us that the message
of the Lord may spread rapidly and be
honored, just as it was with you. 2And pray that
we may be delivered from wicked and evil men,
for not everyone has faith. 3But the Lord is faithful,
and he will strengthen and protect you from
the evil one. 4We have confidence in the Lord
that you are doing and will continue to do the
things we command. 5May the Lord direct your
hearts into God's love and Christ's perseverance.

Warning Against Idleness

6In the name of the Lord Jesus Christ, we
command you, brothers, to keep away from every
brother who is idle and does not live according
to the teaching[b] you received from us. 7For
you yourselves know how you ought to follow
our example. We were not idle when we were
with you, 8nor did we eat anyone's food without
paying for it. On the contrary, we worked
night and day, laboring and toiling so that we

[a]15 Or *traditions* [b]6 Or *tradition*

ed the believers to hold on to the truth they had been taught. We must do the same if we hope to make spiritual progress. If we cannot face the truth about our own lives, we cannot even begin the process of spiritual renewal. We must depend on God's help to survive and grow spiritually. Recognizing this truth is foundational to our spiritual growth.

3:1–2 Paul drew his readers into his life and ministry by asking them to pray for him. He didn't set himself above them as an exalted mentor, but rather shared how he needed their prayers just as he needed the power of God for continued safety. By requesting the Thessalonians' prayers Paul illustrated that his own survival was tied to the spiritual growth of others. As the Thessalonians prayed for Paul, they shared in his life. And as Paul experienced deliverance, the believers rejoiced and were strengthened by God's clear answers to their prayers. By involving the Thessalonians in his struggles, Paul also involved them in his victories. Our relationships with others in the faith can provide mutual encouragement in similar ways.

3:6–10 Apparently many of the Thessalonian believers, in anticipation of Christ's return, had stopped working. Their false understanding of Christ's return led them to live irresponsibly. Paul set things straight by urging these believers to get back to work. If they refused to work, they would have to face the consequences—they wouldn't be allowed to eat! Since God has promised to help us grow spiritually, we might be tempted to think we can sit idly by and watch it happen. This is not the case. Though the work of our salvation was accomplished by Jesus Christ, we still need to participate in the plan God has for us—seeking God and surrendering to him, seeing and speaking the truth, accepting responsibility for our lives and persevering in our spiritual renewal.

would not be a burden to any of you. 9We did
this, not because we do not have the right to
such help, but in order to make ourselves a
model for you to follow. 10For even when we
were with you, we gave you this rule: "If a man
will not work, he shall not eat."
11We hear that some among you are idle.
They are not busy; they are busybodies. 12Such
people we command and urge in the Lord Jesus
Christ to settle down and earn the bread they
eat. 13And as for you, brothers, never tire of
doing what is right.
14If anyone does not obey our instruction in
this letter, take special note of him. Do not
associate with him, in order that he may feel
ashamed. 15Yet do not regard him as an enemy,
but warn him as a brother.

Final Greetings

16Now may the Lord of peace himself give
you peace at all times and in every way. The
Lord be with all of you.
17I, Paul, write this greeting in my own hand,
which is the distinguishing mark in all my letters. This is how I write.
18The grace of our Lord Jesus Christ be with
you all.

3:11–13 Some of the Thessalonians who had stopped working had also begun to gossip about other people. This practice is extremely destructive. Not only does gossip breed discouragement among the people being talked about, but it also keeps us from examining our own lives as we should. Instead of focusing honestly on our own lives, gossip focuses our attention on the lives of others. Paul exhorted the Thessalonians to set things straight and live in the power of God; otherwise their gossiping would discourage others and undermine their own spiritual growth.

1 TIMOTHY

The Big Picture

Paul and Timothy enjoyed a special relationship. Timothy probably came to faith in Christ as a result of Paul's ministry. He quickly joined the apostle's traveling team (see Acts 16:1–4). The two became as close as a father and son as they traveled and ministered together. Timothy matured in his faith, and Paul sent him to lead the church in Ephesus. As a young minister, Timothy faced many challenges. Paul wrote this letter to counsel and encourage his young protégé.

Although this letter is personal in nature, Paul included in it a wealth of advice about dealing with problems in the church. He also painted a clear picture of the characteristics of a strong Christian church. Every church, for example, should have sound spiritual teaching, faithful worship, strong leadership, dedication to God's Word and caring ministries. These characteristics make church communities places of redemption and healing.

Spiritual renewal is a long-term process. In our search for fulfillment we need a safe, nurturing environment that allows us to surrender bad habits and build new lives. A friend or accountability group is limited in this respect. We need to find a more permanent context for long-term care and mutual accountability.

The ideal context for mutual accountability is a healthy church community. A healthy church can provide a context for loving accountability, like the ideal church described in this letter. A good church is a hospital for the hurting, a place where our old wounds can heal and our lives can be rebuilt and encouraged. God's Word is taught and upheld in a healthy church as the standard of conduct for all, and God's grace is employed to protect all from shame. We all need a healthy church family to help us in the long-term process of spiritual growth.

Spiritual Renewal Themes

THE TRUTH BRINGS HEALING AND SPIRITUAL RENEWAL

Paul urged Timothy to preserve the Christian faith and to speak only the truth. Timothy opposed false teachers who were trying to undermine his work. The only weapons Timothy possessed were the truth about Christ and his own godly lifestyle that supported everything he taught. Paul realized that only the truth

about God in Jesus Christ could bring healing and spiritual renewal to broken people. He wanted Timothy to be convinced of that as well. Only Jesus Christ can offer us the freedom we also seek. We can share this message of God's healing power through belief in Christ by speaking the truth about God's power and by backing up our words with transformed lives.

THE IMPORTANCE OF DISCIPLINE

Paul urged Timothy to discipline himself. Self-discipline does not negate our need for God's power, nor does God's gracious help negate our need for self-discipline. Both are necessary. We must reflect honestly on our lives, confessing the wrongs we uncover, accepting responsibility and trusting God to redeem our lives and redirect our course. We can preserve our spiritual gains through prayer, meditation on God's Word and ongoing accountability to others who practice these keys to spiritual renewal too. These disciplines will encourage our spiritual growth and keep us on track.

GOD WORKS THROUGH PEOPLE

An important part of spiritual renewal involves our relationships with other people. Paul instructed Timothy about his relationships with the people in his church. Paul's advice relates to our relationships as well, especially as we carry the message of hope to others. Caring for each other will demonstrate God's power at work within us and will remind us of how far God has brought us in our quest for spiritual renewal.

TAKING INVENTORY LEADS TO WISE CONDUCT

Spiritual renewal always takes place in the context of relationships. Seeing the truth about our lives in the spiritual renewal process leads us to improve the way we relate to others. We may not be in positions of leadership, but we are examples to our coworkers, friends and family. When we honestly reflect on our spiritual condition on a regular basis, everyone wins: We grow and others are encouraged.

Essential Facts

PURPOSE:
To encourage Timothy, a young pastor, during some difficult circumstances.

AUTHOR:
The apostle Paul.

AUDIENCE:
Timothy, a young pastor.

DATE WRITTEN:
Around A.D. 64, just before Paul was imprisoned in Rome.

SETTING:
Timothy was one of Paul's closest friends. Paul had sent him to help the church at Ephesus and was now writing to offer Timothy practical advice on handling some difficult problems in the church.

KEY VERSES:
"Fight the good fight, holding on to faith and a good conscience. Some have rejected these and so have shipwrecked their faith" (1:18–19).

KEY PEOPLE AND RELATIONSHIPS:
Paul with Timothy.

1 Paul, an apostle of Christ Jesus by the command of God our Savior and of Christ Jesus
our hope,

2To Timothy my true son in the faith:

Grace, mercy and peace from God the Father
and Christ Jesus our Lord.

Warning Against False Teachers of the Law

3As I urged you when I went into Macedonia,
stay there in Ephesus so that you may command certain men not to teach false doctrines
any longer 4nor to devote themselves to myths
and endless genealogies. These promote controversies rather than God's work—which is by
faith. 5The goal of this command is love, which
comes from a pure heart and a good conscience
and a sincere faith. 6Some have wandered away
from these and turned to meaningless talk.
7They want to be teachers of the law, but they
do not know what they are talking about or
what they so confidently affirm.

8We know that the law is good if one uses it
properly. 9We also know that law[a] is made not
for the righteous but for lawbreakers and rebels,
the ungodly and sinful, the unholy and irreligious; for those who kill their fathers or mothers, for murderers, 10for adulterers and perverts,
for slave traders and liars and perjurers—and for
whatever else is contrary to the sound doctrine
11that conforms to the glorious gospel of the
blessed God, which he entrusted to me.

The Lord's Grace to Paul

12I thank Christ Jesus our Lord, who has giv-
en me strength, that he considered me faithful,
appointing me to his service. 13Even though I
was once a blasphemer and a persecutor and a
violent man, I was shown mercy because I acted
in ignorance and unbelief. 14The grace of our
Lord was poured out on me abundantly, along
with the faith and love that are in Christ Jesus.

15Here is a trustworthy saying that deserves
full acceptance: Christ Jesus came into the
world to save sinners—of whom I am the worst.
16But for that very reason I was shown mercy so
that in me, the worst of sinners, Christ Jesus
might display his unlimited patience as an example for those who would believe on him and
receive eternal life. 17Now to the King eternal,
immortal, invisible, the only God, be honor
and glory for ever and ever. Amen.

18Timothy, my son, I give you this instruction in keeping with the prophecies once made
about you, so that by following them you may
fight the good fight, 19holding on to faith and
a good conscience. Some have rejected these
and so have shipwrecked their faith. 20Among
them are Hymenaeus and Alexander, whom I
have handed over to Satan to be taught not to
blaspheme.

Instructions on Worship

2 I urge, then, first of all, that requests,
prayers, intercession and thanksgiving be
made for everyone— 2for kings and all those in
authority, that we may live peaceful and quiet
lives in all godliness and holiness. 3This is

[a] 9 Or *that the law*

1:3–7 The false teachers in Ephesus claimed that certain knowledge and background were necessary for salvation. Their teachings caused division among the believers since some of them claimed to have this special knowledge. These false doctrines led the believers away from the only source of salvation—Jesus Christ. Today many people claim to have solutions for our sin problem. Many of their programs infer that we can redeem and change our lives without God's help. Paul exhorts us to steer clear of people who teach such things. Only God in Jesus Christ has the power to deliver us and transform our lives.

1:8–11 God's law is intended to convict us of our sins, lead us to admit our helplessness and receive his forgiveness. If we wish to be spiritually renewed, we will need to set some healthy boundaries for our actions. God's law contains such a set of rules for us to live by. But our spiritual growth will never be helped merely by an attempt to observe the Old Testament law. We are unable to keep this law in our own strength (see Acts 15:10). Attempting to find favor with God in this way will only lead to frustration and guilt, stifling our spiritual growth. We need to utilize the law as a means for discovering our need for Christ and allow the Holy Spirit to empower us to live as God desires.

1:12–17 Paul acknowledged his past and his persecution of the Christian community. But God mercifully intervened in Paul's life, transforming him from a persecutor to a pastor—one of the most dynamic leaders of the Christian church. As Paul shared his story, his previous status as an enemy made his message all the more powerful. The amazing changes in his life testified to God's transforming power. Some of us may feel that we will never impact the lives of others. We may feel that our sins are so bad we are beyond God's redemption. But this is not true. God can change us, no matter who we are or what we have done. And as we share our story of deliverance, others will receive hope as they glimpse what God has done in our lives.

1:18–20 Paul commanded Timothy to fight God's battles well. In one sense this command continued Paul's earlier thoughts about upholding God's truth against the false teachers. Yet our real battles are not just in the realm of sound teaching; we must also obey God and follow his plan for our lives. Paul told Timothy to cling to his faith and to keep his conscience clear. Paul wanted Timothy's life to reflect God's power. Our beliefs are important, but we must go beyond *thinking* the right things to *doing* the right things too.

2:1–2 Paul illustrated why prayer is essential for establishing a peaceful context for spiritual growth. Through both public and private prayer, order and peace are strengthened and promoted. Prayer involves thanksgiving for God's blessings as well as intercession for others. But we can easily become so focused on our own activities that we forget to turn to God for help, overlooking one of the major assets of our faith. Prayer should be our primary means for seeing the truth and developing a relationship with God.

2:3–5 God wants everyone to be saved! That is encouraging news. No matter how sinful we have been or how righteous, no matter how badly others have treated us or how badly we have treated others, God wants everyone to come to him. Sin separates all of us from God. When we surrender our lives to Christ, he bridges the gulf between

TIMOTHY

When we have found a good friend, we have found a treasure. We need people who are faithful and willing to persevere with us through the hard times. We need the love and acceptance that only a true friend can offer. The friendship between young Timothy and the apostle Paul brought significant support and encouragement to both men.

Paul described Timothy as a faithful brother with a solid reputation. Timothy was devoted to Paul and shared many of his triumphant victories in the ministry. But Timothy also persevered with Paul during the difficult times of imprisonment, torture and mockery. Their years of shared ministry grew into a lifelong friendship.

Paul referred to Timothy with admiration in many of his letters. He called him "my son whom I love, who is faithful in the Lord" (1 Corinthians 4:17) and "my fellow worker" (Romans 16:21). In his letter to the Philippians, Paul referred to Timothy with the highest praise and then added that Timothy had acted "as a son with his father" as he helped Paul preach the Good News (Philippians 2:22). In his letters to Timothy, Paul expressed great affection for him. Paul's personal involvement in Timothy's ministry was shown when Paul reminded him "to fan into flame the gift of God, which is in you through the laying on of my hands" (2 Timothy 1:6).

Timothy does not appear to have been a charismatic or strong leader. He might have even been somewhat timid and afraid to confront his people, especially the older men. But Timothy was faithful and persevered in his ministry despite his fears and trials. Paul also supported Timothy in his ministry, realizing that God had called this young man into special service for Christ. Despite his weaknesses, God used Timothy to build the church and encourage his coworker Paul.

Our continued spiritual growth requires that we have relationships with people for both support and accountability. We need to ask God for a "Timothy"—someone with integrity, who can be trusted and who will support us in both the good and bad times.

STRENGTHS AND ACCOMPLISHMENTS:

Timothy possessed an excellent reputation for his faithfulness.

He was a special friend to the apostle Paul.

Even in the most difficult circumstance, Timothy supported Paul.

Timothy was a faithful minister of the Good News.

WEAKNESSES AND MISTAKES:

Timothy sometimes allowed his youth and timidity to cause difficulty in his ministry.

LESSONS FROM HIS LIFE:

Our fears and inadequacies need not stop us from serving God.

Good friendships are extremely valuable, especially for continued spiritual growth.

KEY VERSES:

"So when we could stand it no longer, we thought it best to be left by ourselves in Athens. We sent Timothy, who is our brother and God's fellow worker in spreading the gospel of Christ, to strengthen and encourage you in your faith, so that no one would be unsettled by these trials" (1 Thessalonians 3:1–3).

Timothy is first named in Acts 16:1–5 and is mentioned at various other points in the book. He is the recipient of Paul's letters 1 and 2 Timothy. He is also mentioned in Romans 16:21; 1 Corinthians 4:17; 16:10–11; 2 Corinthians 1:1, 19; Philippians 1:1; 2:19–23; Colossians 1:1; 1 Thessalonians 1:1–10; 3:2–6; 2 Thessalonians 1:1; Philemon 1 and Hebrews 13:23.

good, and pleases God our Savior, 4who wants
all men to be saved and to come to a knowledge
of the truth. 5For there is one God and one
mediator between God and men, the man
Christ Jesus, 6who gave himself as a ransom for
all men—the testimony given in its proper time.
7And for this purpose I was appointed a herald
and an apostle—I am telling the truth, I am not
lying—and a teacher of the true faith to the Gentiles.

8I want men everywhere to lift up holy hands
in prayer, without anger or disputing.

9I also want women to dress modestly, with
decency and propriety, not with braided hair or
gold or pearls or expensive clothes, 10but with
good deeds, appropriate for women who profess to worship God.

11A woman should learn in quietness and
full submission. 12I do not permit a woman to
teach or to have authority over a man; she must
be silent. 13For Adam was formed first, then
Eve. 14And Adam was not the one deceived;
it was the woman who was deceived and became a sinner. 15But women[a] will be saved[b]
through childbearing—if they continue in faith,
love and holiness with propriety.

Overseers and Deacons

3 Here is a trustworthy saying: If anyone sets
his heart on being an overseer,[c] he desires
a noble task. 2Now the overseer must be above
reproach, the husband of but one wife, temperate, self-controlled, respectable, hospitable,
able to teach, 3not given to drunkenness, not
violent but gentle, not quarrelsome, not a lover
of money. 4He must manage his own family
well and see that his children obey him with
proper respect. 5(If anyone does not know how
to manage his own family, how can he take care
of God's church?) 6He must not be a recent
convert, or he may become conceited and fall
under the same judgment as the devil. 7He must
also have a good reputation with outsiders, so
that he will not fall into disgrace and into the
devil's trap.

8Deacons, likewise, are to be men worthy of
respect, sincere, not indulging in much wine,
and not pursuing dishonest gain. 9They must
keep hold of the deep truths of the faith with a
clear conscience. 10They must first be tested;
and then if there is nothing against them, let
them serve as deacons.

11In the same way, their wives[d] are to be
women worthy of respect, not malicious talkers
but temperate and trustworthy in everything.

12A deacon must be the husband of but one
wife and must manage his children and his
household well. 13Those who have served well
gain an excellent standing and great assurance
in their faith in Christ Jesus.

14Although I hope to come to you soon, I am
writing you these instructions so that, 15if I am
delayed, you will know how people ought to
conduct themselves in God's household, which
is the church of the living God, the pillar and
foundation of the truth. 16Beyond all question,
the mystery of godliness is great:

He[e] appeared in a body,[f]
  was vindicated by the Spirit,
was seen by angels,
  was preached among the nations,
was believed on in the world,
  was taken up in glory.

Instructions to Timothy

4 The Spirit clearly says that in later times
some will abandon the faith and follow
deceiving spirits and things taught by demons.
2Such teachings come through hypocritical liars, whose consciences have been seared as with
a hot iron. 3They forbid people to marry and
order them to abstain from certain foods, which
God created to be received with thanksgiving by
those who believe and who know the truth.
4For everything God created is good, and nothing is to be rejected if it is received with thanksgiving, 5because it is consecrated by the word of
God and prayer.

6If you point these things out to the brothers,
you will be a good minister of Christ Jesus,
brought up in the truths of the faith and of the
good teaching that you have followed. 7Have

[a]15 Greek *she* [b]15 Or *restored* [c]1 Traditionally *bishop;* also in verse 2 [d]11 Or *way, deaconesses* [e]16 Some manuscripts *God* [f]16 Or *in the flesh*

---

sinful people and God, instituting true spiritual renewal for everyone who longs to come to God. Many plans and programs promise to bring spiritual renewal, but there is no bridge other than Jesus that can span the gulf caused by sin.

3:1–7 Paul described a prospective church leader as someone who possessed self-control and spiritual maturity. Notice Paul's emphasis upon a prospective overseer's strong record of leadership within his own family. The home is the most reliable proving ground for potential leaders because it demonstrates evidence of our spiritual progress. Our true spiritual condition will be reflected by how we treat our family and relate to them. God can also use those closest to us to hold us accountable and help redirect our course in accordance with God's Word.

4:1–5 Self-indulgence breeds trouble. Some spiritual leaders and religious groups urge their followers to give up all forms of pleasure so that they will not be tempted by self-indulgence. Yet Paul warned Timothy against a religiously motivated self-denial. Such deprivation will only lead to a deeper hunger. Rigorous self-denial can sometimes lead to sin as we try to fill the need we created by depriving ourselves unnecessarily. Paul points out that the good pleasures offered by God should be enjoyed with thanksgiving and not rejected in the name of spirituality. God has given us these legitimate pleasures in this life; we are free to enjoy them as he has ordained.

4:7–10 Paul warned young Timothy to steer clear of arguments about insignificant issues. He wanted Timothy to focus on taking the necessary steps to grow spiritually. Spiritual growth cannot be achieved by arguing about meaningless details of the faith. We can keep spiritually fit only by staying close to God in prayer and by obediently following what we learn from his Word.

nothing to do with godless myths and old
wives' tales; rather, train yourself to be godly.
8For physical training is of some value, but godliness has value for all things, holding promise
for both the present life and the life to come.
9This is a trustworthy saying that deserves
full acceptance 10(and for this we labor and
strive), that we have put our hope in the living
God, who is the Savior of all men, and especially of those who believe.
11Command and teach these things. 12Don't
let anyone look down on you because you are
young, but set an example for the believers in
speech, in life, in love, in faith and in purity.
13Until I come, devote yourself to the public
reading of Scripture, to preaching and to teaching. 14Do not neglect your gift, which was given
you through a prophetic message when the
body of elders laid their hands on you.
15Be diligent in these matters; give yourself
wholly to them, so that everyone may see your
progress. 16Watch your life and doctrine closely.
Persevere in them, because if you do, you will
save both yourself and your hearers.

Advice About Widows, Elders and Slaves

5 Do not rebuke an older man harshly, but
exhort him as if he were your father. Treat
younger men as brothers, 2older women as
mothers, and younger women as sisters, with
absolute purity.
3Give proper recognition to those widows
who are really in need. 4But if a widow has
children or grandchildren, these should learn
first of all to put their religion into practice by
caring for their own family and so repaying
their parents and grandparents, for this is pleas-

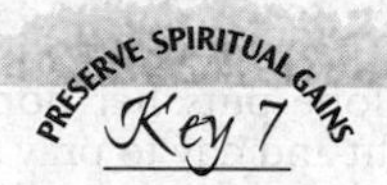

A Living Testimony

1 Timothy 4:14–16 As we seek to preserve the spiritual gains we have made, we will find it helpful to share God's life-changing message with others. Yet it's not enough to simply talk about God if our lives do not bear testimony to God's life-changing power. Only as we demonstrate our new way of life will people notice our spiritual progress. That will open the door for us to share verbally what God has done to change us.

The apostle Paul taught Timothy that in order to share his message of transformation, Timothy needed to put his beliefs into practice as well as tell others about them. Paul said, "Be diligent in these matters; give yourself wholly to them, so that everyone may see your progress. Watch your life and doctrine closely. Persevere in them, because if you do, you will save both yourself and your hearers" (4:15–16).

God wants to rescue everyone. We can participate in sharing God's message—a message that can save souls. Our lives can be used to reach those who have never surrendered to God and to draw back those who have strayed. We should continue our spiritual progress and preserve our spiritual gains so that others might have hope, repent and believe.

Turn to 2 Timothy 2.

4:11–16 Timothy was admonished to share the Good News of life in Christ in both word and deed. We sometimes forget that the most effective way we can share our faith is to live it out in front of other people. Our words can never witness as forcefully to God's power as the changes that people see in our lives. Some people will always question the legitimacy of our words, but no one can question the fact of a transformed life. When we surrender our lives to God, we can experience the new life promised in Jesus Christ. And the best way to share the news of God's transforming power is to live it—in both word and deed.

5:1–2 Paul advised Timothy to treat all people with respect. By respecting others, we remind ourselves of the importance of healthy relationships in the Christian community. Sound doctrine, proper worship and godly leadership are all important. Yet we need to undergird these principles with love and respect for each other. The godly courtesy and affection that Paul requested can make the Christian community a place where healing takes place and lives are renewed.

5:3–10 Paul made it clear that the Christian community should show special attention to its widows. Paul's directions here reflect God's Biblical concern for the helpless and rejected in society. God wants us to be concerned for all of his people; there is a place for everyone in his church. No matter who we are, what we have done or our position in society, God accepts us only on the basis of our faith in Jesus Christ. God reaches out to us all and calls us to be a part of his family.

ing to God. 5The widow who is really in need and left all alone puts her hope in God and continues night and day to pray and to ask God for help. 6But the widow who lives for pleasure is dead even while she lives. 7Give the people these instructions, too, so that no one may be open to blame. 8If anyone does not provide for his relatives, and especially for his immediate family, he has denied the faith and is worse than an unbeliever.

9No widow may be put on the list of widows unless she is over sixty, has been faithful to her husband,[a] 10and is well known for her good deeds, such as bringing up children, showing hospitality, washing the feet of the saints, helping those in trouble and devoting herself to all kinds of good deeds.

11As for younger widows, do not put them on such a list. For when their sensual desires overcome their dedication to Christ, they want to marry. 12Thus they bring judgment on themselves, because they have broken their first pledge. 13Besides, they get into the habit of being idle and going about from house to house. And not only do they become idlers, but also gossips and busybodies, saying things they ought not to. 14So I counsel younger widows to marry, to have children, to manage their homes and to give the enemy no opportunity for slander. 15Some have in fact already turned away to follow Satan.

16If any woman who is a believer has widows in her family, she should help them and not let the church be burdened with them, so that the church can help those widows who are really in need.

17The elders who direct the affairs of the church well are worthy of double honor, especially those whose work is preaching and teaching. 18For the Scripture says, "Do not muzzle the ox while it is treading out the grain,"[b] and "The worker deserves his wages."[c] 19Do not entertain an accusation against an elder unless it is brought by two or three witnesses. 20Those who sin are to be rebuked publicly, so that the others may take warning.

21I charge you, in the sight of God and Christ Jesus and the elect angels, to keep these instructions without partiality, and to do nothing out of favoritism.

22Do not be hasty in the laying on of hands, and do not share in the sins of others. Keep yourself pure.

23Stop drinking only water, and use a little wine because of your stomach and your frequent illnesses.

24The sins of some men are obvious, reaching the place of judgment ahead of them; the sins of others trail behind them. 25In the same way, good deeds are obvious, and even those that are not cannot be hidden.

6 All who are under the yoke of slavery should consider their masters worthy of full respect, so that God's name and our teaching may not be slandered. 2Those who have believing masters are not to show less respect for them because they are brothers. Instead, they are to serve them even better, because those who benefit from their service are believers, and dear to them. These are the things you are to teach and urge on them.

Love of Money

3If anyone teaches false doctrines and does not agree to the sound instruction of our Lord Jesus Christ and to godly teaching, 4he is conceited and understands nothing. He has an unhealthy interest in controversies and quarrels about words that result in envy, strife, malicious talk, evil suspicions 5and constant friction between men of corrupt mind, who have been robbed of the truth and who think that godliness is a means to financial gain.

6But godliness with contentment is great gain. 7For we brought nothing into the world, and we can take nothing out of it. 8But if we have food and clothing, we will be content with that. 9People who want to get rich fall into temptation and a trap and into many foolish and harmful desires that plunge men into ruin and destruction. 10For the love of money is a root of all kinds of evil. Some people, eager for money, have wandered from the faith and pierced themselves with many griefs.

Paul's Charge to Timothy

11But you, man of God, flee from all this, and pursue righteousness, godliness, faith, love, endurance and gentleness. 12Fight the good fight

[a]9 Or *has had but one husband* [b]18 Deut. 25:4
[c]18 Luke 10:7

5:24–25 Paul urged Timothy to confront some fellow church leaders who were living sinful lives. By confronting them about their failures, Timothy would save them from the consequences that their continued disobedience would bring them. Sometimes we must do the same for the people we love. By holding each other accountable to God's guidelines for living, we can help each other preserve our spiritual gains and experience the life God has planned for us.

6:3–10 Paul warned Timothy about those who spread false teachings among the believers. The apostle wanted to protect the true gospel from the lies of money-hungry charlatans. Anyone who promised spiritual renewal and salvation through any power other than God in Jesus Christ was not to be listened to. The same message applies to us today. Only God can free us from sin and transform our lives. And the power he offers is free of charge.

6:6–10 Paul warned Timothy about the pitfall of trusting in money. Some of us may already have experienced the emptiness of such misplaced trust. We may have believed that wealth could provide a solution to all of our problems. But no amount of money can deliver us from the power of our sins. Whether we are rich or poor, the pull of our sinful natures can be overcome only when we repent, surrender to God and seek his help.

Stewardship

Turning Wealth Into a Good Thing

1 Timothy 6:6–10, 17–19 Spiritual growth comes when we turn our attention from our own desires and invest our resources in God's priorities. The Bible consistently reminds us that the human heart is wicked and constantly tempted to replace the worship of God with idolatry or the worship of things (see Jeremiah 17:9). The Bible also warns us that "the love of money is a root of all kinds of evil" (6:10). One of the ways to guard against this temptation and loosen the world's grip on us is to consistently set aside a portion of our wealth for God's use. In this way we help turn a potential source of evil into a means for spiritual growth and renewal.

When we set aside money for God's use, we

- Demonstrate our loyalty to and dependence on God. Our use of money is one of the most tangible evidences of our priorities. We may be able to impress others with our words, but the sincerity of our faith is truly tested when our finances are challenged. When we give to God's work, we remind ourselves that our goal is to give glory to God and advance his kingdom. It also reminds us that all we possess comes from him.
- Participate in God's work here on earth. Whether we are able to give small or large amounts, our money can be used to reach out to others directly and through those who serve in ways and places that we cannot.
- Prepare for greater responsibilities. The faithful servants who were each entrusted with a portion of money were rewarded according to their stewardship (see Luke 19:11–27). The way we handle our money reveals much about how we handle our lives, preparing us for greater service to God.

Above all, we need to remind ourselves that the use of money is limited. Money will have no place in the world to come. Contentment is a sure defense against the love of money and the corrosive power of greed.

Putting It Into Practice

Review the various ways money can be used for good—both for you and for others. Which of these seem most significant to you at this time? How content are you? Do you own your wealth, or does your wealth own you?

For more on stewardship, turn to Deuteronomy 8.

of the faith. Take hold of the eternal life to
which you were called when you made your
good confession in the presence of many witnesses. **13**In the sight of God, who gives life to
everything, and of Christ Jesus, who while testifying before Pontius Pilate made the good confession, I charge you **14**to keep this command
without spot or blame until the appearing of
our Lord Jesus Christ, **15**which God will bring
about in his own time—God, the blessed and
only Ruler, the King of kings and Lord of lords,
16who alone is immortal and who lives in unap-
proachable light, whom no one has seen or can
see. To him be honor and might forever. Amen.

17Command those who are rich in this
present world not to be arrogant nor to put their
hope in wealth, which is so uncertain, but to
put their hope in God, who richly provides us
with everything for our enjoyment. **18**Command them to do good, to be rich in good
deeds, and to be generous and willing to share.
19In this way they will lay up treasure for themselves as a firm foundation for the coming age,
so that they may take hold of the life that is
truly life.

20Timothy, guard what has been entrusted to
your care. Turn away from godless chatter and
the opposing ideas of what is falsely called
knowledge, **21**which some have professed and
in so doing have wandered from the faith.

Grace be with you.

2 TIMOTHY

The Big Picture

When a loved one is about to die, we strain to hear any whispered words of blessing or advice, knowing these may be the last words we will ever hear from this person. In this letter, Paul shared his deathbed communication to Timothy, his son in the faith, passing along his final words of blessing, advice and comfort.

As he wrote this letter, Paul was awaiting his execution in a Roman prison. Paul expected death to come soon, so he penned these words of guidance and encouragement to his young protégé in Ephesus. Paul wanted to give Timothy all the tools he needed to be an effective minister of the gospel.

Paul urged Timothy to develop his relationship with God and to serve God faithfully. Paul knew that Timothy would face many problems as a church leader, so he encouraged Timothy to persevere in his faith. Challenging the young pastor to be faithful to his duties, Paul reminded Timothy to use the gifts God had given him, to hold on to the truth of God's Word, to teach others and to be willing to suffer for the sake of Christ.

Paul had made mistakes in his past, but that didn't disqualify him from helping Timothy. He had much he wanted to share with Timothy. Our mistakes don't disqualify us from reaching out to others either. Rather, God wants each of us to share something from our experiences in life. Through our spiritual renewal, God has given us important insights from which others can benefit. And sharing those insights with others is an important part of our own spiritual journey.

A. GREETINGS (1:1-2)

B. ENCOURAGEMENT TO PERSEVERE (1:3–2:26)

1. The Need to Be Faithful (1:3-18)
2. The Reality of Hardships (2:1-13)
3. The Need to Behave Responsibly (2:14-26)

C. EXHORTATIONS CONCERNING THE LAST DAYS (3:1–4:8)

D. PAUL SHARES HIS OWN PERSONAL NEEDS (4:9-22)

Spiritual Renewal Themes

GOD'S WAY CAN BE DIFFICULT

Change is always a challenge, especially when we are trying to give up old habits we have relied on for some time. The changes required for spiritual growth are sometimes uncomfortable or even painful. Some of us would rather suffer in a known situation rather than risk moving into the unknown. Though our spiritual growth may involve some pain, we can be assured that the sacrifices we make will be worthwhile in the end.

THE IMPORTANCE OF FAITHFULNESS

We will face opposition as we pursue spiritual renewal, but that

Essential Facts

PURPOSE:
To encourage a faithful but discouraged Timothy in continuing to do God's work.

AUTHOR:
The apostle Paul.

AUDIENCE:
Timothy, a young pastor.

DATE WRITTEN:
Sometime between A.D. 66–67, shortly before Paul's death during the reign of Emperor Nero.

SETTING:
When Paul wrote this letter, he was virtually alone in prison; only his friend Luke was with him. This is a very personal letter, showing Paul's vulnerability and loneliness. It also reveals his inner strength as he continued, even in his desperate situation, to encourage young Timothy.

KEY VERSE:
"Flee the evil desires of youth, and pursue righteousness, faith, love and peace, along with those who call on the Lord out of a pure heart" (2:22).

KEY PEOPLE AND RELATIONSHIPS:
Paul with Timothy, Luke and Mark.

is not all bad. Opposition often signals that important changes are taking place in our lives. Not everyone likes to see us change, even if those changes are good and healthy for us. Some may be afraid that they will lose an old friend because of these changes. Others may begin to feel guilty about their own way of life and try to stop our progress. We don't have to understand why people oppose our spiritual growth; our part is to faithfully seek God and surrender to his will. Paul was faithful to God, and he urged Timothy to follow his example. God wants each of us to do the same.

THE POWER OF GOD'S WORD

One of the primary sources of strength and guidance for us is God's Word. Paul challenged Timothy to understand God's Word and know how to apply its teachings to his life (see 2:15). God's Word teaches us what is true, makes us realize what is wrong in our lives, points us in the right direction and helps us do what is right (see 3:16). Our prayers and thoughts should be focused on God's Word, for it instructs us in the way that God wants us to live.

1 Paul, an apostle of Christ Jesus by the will
of God, according to the promise of life
that is in Christ Jesus,

2To Timothy, my dear son:

Grace, mercy and peace from God the Father
and Christ Jesus our Lord.

Encouragement to Be Faithful

3I thank God, whom I serve, as my forefathers did, with a clear conscience, as night and
day I constantly remember you in my prayers.
4Recalling your tears, I long to see you, so that
I may be filled with joy. 5I have been reminded
of your sincere faith, which first lived in your
grandmother Lois and in your mother Eunice
and, I am persuaded, now lives in you also. 6For
this reason I remind you to fan into flame the
gift of God, which is in you through the laying
on of my hands. 7For God did not give us a
spirit of timidity, but a spirit of power, of love
and of self-discipline.

8So do not be ashamed to testify about our
Lord, or ashamed of me his prisoner. But join
with me in suffering for the gospel, by the power of God, 9who has saved us and called us to
a holy life—not because of anything we have
done but because of his own purpose and grace.
This grace was given us in Christ Jesus before
the beginning of time, 10but it has now been
revealed through the appearing of our Savior,
Christ Jesus, who has destroyed death and has
brought life and immortality to light through
the gospel. 11And of this gospel I was appointed
a herald and an apostle and a teacher. 12That
is why I am suffering as I am. Yet I am not
ashamed, because I know whom I have believed, and am convinced that he is able to
guard what I have entrusted to him for that day.

13What you heard from me, keep as the pattern of sound teaching, with faith and love in
Christ Jesus. 14Guard the good deposit that was
entrusted to you—guard it with the help of the
Holy Spirit who lives in us.

15You know that everyone in the province of
Asia has deserted me, including Phygelus and
Hermogenes.

16May the Lord show mercy to the household
of Onesiphorus, because he often refreshed me
and was not ashamed of my chains. 17On the
contrary, when he was in Rome, he searched
hard for me until he found me. 18May the Lord
grant that he will find mercy from the Lord on
that day! You know very well in how many
ways he helped me in Ephesus.

2 You then, my son, be strong in the grace
that is in Christ Jesus. 2And the things you
have heard me say in the presence of many
witnesses entrust to reliable men who will also
be qualified to teach others. 3Endure hardship
with us like a good soldier of Christ Jesus. 4No
one serving as a soldier gets involved in civilian
affairs—he wants to please his commanding officer. 5Similarly, if anyone competes as an athlete, he does not receive the victor's crown unless he competes according to the rules. 6The
hardworking farmer should be the first to receive a share of the crops. 7Reflect on what I am
saying, for the Lord will give you insight into all
this.

8Remember Jesus Christ, raised from the
dead, descended from David. This is my gospel,
9for which I am suffering even to the point of
being chained like a criminal. But God's word
is not chained. 10Therefore I endure everything
for the sake of the elect, that they too may obtain the salvation that is in Christ Jesus, with
eternal glory.

1:5 Whether or not we like it, we all learn from our parents. Sometimes the instructions we learn and pass on to others are good; at other times, however, these lessons can be destructive. Notice that Timothy's mother and grandmother had modeled faith in Christ for him. As we seek to live according to God's plan, we can model transformed lives to those around us too. As our family and friends see the power of our vibrant faith in God, they may choose to follow in our steps. Like Timothy's mother and grandmother, we will rejoice when others follow our example.

1:7–14 Paul urged Timothy not to let his weaknesses stop him from ministering to others. Timothy's success was not based on his ability, skill or courage; it was based on the Holy Spirit's power working in him. Likewise, we don't possess the inherent strength, courage and self-discipline we need to live the kinds of lives God calls us to live. But we do have the Holy Spirit living in us! It is his power that enables us to enjoy the spiritual growth God wants us to experience.

1:15–18 Paul was in prison when he wrote this letter, deserted by most of his friends and followers. But Onesiphorus stood with Paul even though it was a risky thing to do. Onesiphorus's example teaches us what it means to show loyalty and love to someone in need. Like Paul, we may have been abandoned by many of our friends as we surrendered our lives to God. But we may have a loyal friend like Onesiphorus in our lives too. Realizing how essential this kind of person is to our spiritual growth should encourage us to be loyal friends to others too. By supporting our friends in need we can help them preserve their spiritual gains.

2:1–2 Notice that Paul told Timothy to be strong *in Christ Jesus*. The apostle knew that Timothy could never succeed in his ministry by depending on his *own* strength. He needed power that was sufficient for successful living. Such power comes only from God. That God empowers us to live transformed lives is good news! Paul reminded Timothy that the message of God's transforming power should be passed from one person to the next. As each of us hears about and experiences God's power, we should pass on the word to someone else. In this way we can help others receive God's gracious power and find joy as we grow in our faith too.

2:3–7 Spiritual growth brings its share of suffering. Progress requires that we follow principles of disciplined faith on a daily basis. Like a soldier, we need to set aside the obstacles to our spiritual growth and see the truth. Like the athlete, we need to follow the rules—God's will for our lives. Like the farmer, we need to work hard and persevere through the dry times as well as the storms. If we follow these principles, we will sense God at work in our lives. He will help us win life's battles; he will reward us with a prize at the end of the race (see 4:8). And we will harvest a rich crop of blessings.

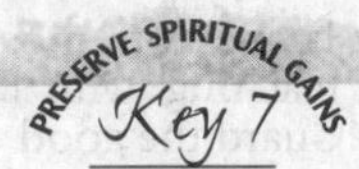

Perseverance Throughout Life

2 Timothy 2:1–8 Spiritual renewal and growth are a lifelong process. There will be times when we will grow weary, times when we will want to quit. We will experience pain, fear and many other negative emotions. We will win some battles but lose others. We may get discouraged when we can't seem to see any progress even though we have been working hard. But if we persevere in our faith through all these times, we will preserve our spiritual gains.

The apostle Paul used three illustrations to teach about perseverance. He wrote to Timothy:

> Endure hardship with us like a good soldier of Christ Jesus. No one serving as a soldier gets involved in civilian affairs—he wants to please his commanding officer. Similarly, if anyone competes as an athlete, he does not receive the victor's crown unless he competes according to the rules. The hardworking farmer should be the first to receive a share of the crops (2:3–6).

Like soldiers, we are in a war that we can win only if we fight to the end. Like athletes running a marathon, we must follow God all the way to the finish line. Like farmers, we must do our work in every season and then wait patiently to reap the benefits of our labor. If we stop before reaching our goal, we may lose our spiritual gains and everything else for which we have fought, trained and worked hard.

Turn to Hebrews 10.

11 Here is a trustworthy saying:

If we died with him,
  we will also live with him;
12 if we endure,
  we will also reign with him.
If we disown him,
  he will also disown us;
13 if we are faithless,
  he will remain faithful,
  for he cannot disown himself.

A Workman Approved by God

14 Keep reminding them of these things.
Warn them before God against quarreling
about words; it is of no value, and only ruins
those who listen. 15 Do your best to present
yourself to God as one approved, a workman
who does not need to be ashamed and who
correctly handles the word of truth. 16 Avoid
godless chatter, because those who indulge in it
will become more and more ungodly. 17 Their
teaching will spread like gangrene. Among
them are Hymenaeus and Philetus, 18 who have
wandered away from the truth. They say that
the resurrection has already taken place, and
they destroy the faith of some. 19 Nevertheless,
God's solid foundation stands firm, sealed with
this inscription: "The Lord knows those who
are his,"[a] and, "Everyone who confesses the
name of the Lord must turn away from wickedness."

20 In a large house there are articles not only
of gold and silver, but also of wood and clay;
some are for noble purposes and some for ignoble.
21 If a man cleanses himself from the latter,
he will be an instrument for noble purposes,
made holy, useful to the Master and prepared to
do any good work.

22 Flee the evil desires of youth, and pursue
righteousness, faith, love and peace, along with
those who call on the Lord out of a pure heart.
23 Don't have anything to do with foolish and
stupid arguments, because you know they produce
quarrels. 24 And the Lord's servant must
not quarrel; instead, he must be kind to everyone,
able to teach, not resentful. 25 Those who

[a] *19* Num. 16:5 (see Septuagint)

2:15 Paul urged Timothy to work hard to receive God's approval of his work. Timothy's assigned task was to study God's Word to discover God's will for him in both attitude and action. Since our spiritual growth depends on following God's will, we need to discover how God wants us to live. By seeking God's will through diligent study of his Word, we can better follow his instructions and will ultimately hear God's commendation of our lives.

2:22 Paul's advice to Timothy is appropriate for us too. We should run away from the people and situations that are likely to lead us into temptation and a fall. Instead, we should spend time with people who will support our spiritual growth. This simple advice, though at times difficult to follow, can help support our spiritual progress. If we don't have godly friends or activities that reinforce our spiritual growth, we must become involved in a community of godly and supportive people.

oppose him he must gently instruct, in the hope that God will grant them repentance leading them to a knowledge of the truth, 26and that they will come to their senses and escape from the trap of the devil, who has taken them captive to do his will.

Godlessness in the Last Days

3 But mark this: There will be terrible times in the last days. 2People will be lovers of themselves, lovers of money, boastful, proud, abusive, disobedient to their parents, ungrateful, unholy, 3without love, unforgiving, slanderous, without self-control, brutal, not lovers of the good, 4treacherous, rash, conceited, lovers of pleasure rather than lovers of God— 5having a form of godliness but denying its power. Have nothing to do with them.

6They are the kind who worm their way into homes and gain control over weak-willed women, who are loaded down with sins and are swayed by all kinds of evil desires, 7always learning but never able to acknowledge the truth. 8Just as Jannes and Jambres opposed Moses, so also these men oppose the truth—men of depraved minds, who, as far as the faith is concerned, are rejected. 9But they will not get very far because, as in the case of those men, their folly will be clear to everyone.

Paul's Charge to Timothy

10You, however, know all about my teaching, my way of life, my purpose, faith, patience, love, endurance, 11persecutions, sufferings—what kinds of things happened to me in Antioch, Iconium and Lystra, the persecutions I endured. Yet the Lord rescued me from all of them. 12In fact, everyone who wants to live a godly life in Christ Jesus will be persecuted, 13while evil men and impostors will go from bad to worse, deceiving and being deceived. 14But as for you, continue in what you have learned and have become convinced of, because you know those from whom you learned it, 15and how from infancy you have known the holy Scriptures, which are able to make you wise for salvation through faith in Christ Jesus. 16All Scripture is God-breathed and is useful for teaching, rebuking, correcting and training in righteousness, 17so that the man of God may be thoroughly equipped for every good work.

4 In the presence of God and of Christ Jesus, who will judge the living and the dead, and in view of his appearing and his kingdom, I give you this charge: 2Preach the Word; be prepared in season and out of season; correct, rebuke and encourage—with great patience and careful instruction. 3For the time will come when men will not put up with sound doctrine. Instead, to suit their own desires, they will gather around them a great number of teachers to say what their itching ears want to hear. 4They will turn their ears away from the truth and turn aside to myths. 5But you, keep your head in all situations, endure hardship, do the work of an evangelist, discharge all the duties of your ministry.

6For I am already being poured out like a drink offering, and the time has come for my departure. 7I have fought the good fight, I have finished the race, I have kept the faith. 8Now there is in store for me the crown of righteousness, which the Lord, the righteous Judge, will award to me on that day—and not only to me, but also to all who have longed for his appearing.

Personal Remarks

9Do your best to come to me quickly, 10for Demas, because he loved this world, has deserted me and has gone to Thessalonica. Crescens has gone to Galatia, and Titus to Dalmatia. 11Only Luke is with me. Get Mark and bring

---

3:1–9 This passage describes people who talk about spiritual things and may even attend church but whose lives demonstrate a refusal to surrender to God. We should not be tricked by or imitate such people. Paul made it clear that these attitudes and actions bring severe consequences. As we honestly reflect on our lives, we can use this list as a guide for what should not be evidenced in our lives. If we find any of these characteristics in our lives, we would do well to confess them and turn away from them. God will forgive them all. If we surrender our lives to God, we must be willing to let God wipe away these sinful characteristics we find in ourselves.

3:14–17 Paul reminded Timothy of the wonderful resource that God has provided for us—the Bible. The Bible is our measuring stick, helping us evaluate what is wrong in our lives. Through the power of the Holy Spirit, the Bible reveals God's will for us and shows us how to relate properly and unselfishly to God and other people. God's Word also promises God's powerful help to all who turn to him with humble hearts. God has given us a wonderful resource in his Word. Spiritual growth can only occur when we take the time to understand it and seek to obey what it says.

4:1–5 Paul strongly encouraged Timothy to share the Good News of Jesus Christ with others. Sharing our witness is an integral part of Christian living because it helps us preserve our spiritual gains. By sharing our stories of how God has changed our lives, we offer hope and new life to many needy people. As we remember God's wonderful work on our behalf, we will also be encouraged to persevere in our faith. And we will build strong relationships with others as we share our lives with them. Sharing our witness with others leads to the healthy community life necessary to support our spiritual growth on a permanent basis.

4:6–8 Paul left his young protégé these reflections to encourage him as he faced the struggle to live a godly life. Paul had fought hard to live for God and had suffered for the sake of others. Now he looked forward to the blessings he would receive in God's presence. Sharing this eternal perspective with Timothy would help the young man approach the tough times in his own life with the hope of future blessings. This same hope is available to us. We may experience rejection as we seek to share with others the hope we have experienced. Such painful times will help us recognize our need for God's help. And God will reward our perseverance with eternal peace and joy. It all will be worth it in the end.

4:11 Mark had forsaken Paul and Barnabas during their first missionary journey (see Acts 12:25—13:13). Because

Being Molded by God's Word

2 Timothy 3:16 Our outlook on life depends very much on our "in-look." If worldly assumptions, fears and pressures shape our perspective, we will fall prey to anxiety, anger and depression. But if we meditate on the Bible and allow it to take root in our hearts, we will experience the peace and goodness that God's Word brings.

In 2 Timothy 3:16, Paul outlines four ways that God's Word moves us toward spiritual maturity. Each of these ways transforms our thinking.

- God's Word teaches us what is true. We live in a world of uncertainty and contradiction. Principles based on opinions rather than on spiritual truth often govern our lives. The Bible, however, proclaims the truth about God, nature, humanity, evil, salvation, justice, love, judgment, eternity and many other things.
- God's Word rebukes our sinfulness. A good coach will tell athletes what they're doing wrong so that they can improve their performance. In the same way, God's Word shows us where we have sinned. What the world calls normal is often not what God calls moral. God's Word defines morality and rebukes sin.
- God's Word corrects us. Rebuke points out that we have left God's path. Correction shows us how to get back on it. The Bible not only points out our mistakes, but it also points the way to restoration. We learn how to confess our sins and make restitution, how to forgive and guard against bitterness, and how to break sinful habits and develop godly ones.
- God's Word teaches us to do what is right. Christ calls us to *do* certain things in his name as much as he calls us *not* to do other things. God's Word reminds us that we should perform acts of love and compassion, reaching out to the poor and seeking justice for the oppressed.

Putting It Into Practice

Review the four ways God's Word can change you. How have you experienced each of these? Consider which one God may be emphasizing in your life right now. What verses can help shape your life in this area?

For more on Bible study and meditation, turn to Hebrews 4.

him with you, because he is helpful to me in my
ministry. 12I sent Tychicus to Ephesus. 13When
you come, bring the cloak that I left with Car-
pus at Troas, and my scrolls, especially the
parchments.
14Alexander the metalworker did me a great
deal of harm. The Lord will repay him for what
he has done. 15You too should be on your guard
against him, because he strongly opposed our
message.
16At my first defense, no one came to my
support, but everyone deserted me. May it not
be held against them. 17But the Lord stood at
my side and gave me strength, so that through
me the message might be fully proclaimed and
all the Gentiles might hear it. And I was delivered from the lion's mouth. 18The Lord will
rescue me from every evil attack and will bring
me safely to his heavenly kingdom. To him be
glory for ever and ever. Amen.

Final Greetings

19Greet Priscilla[a] and Aquila and the household of Onesiphorus. 20Erastus stayed in Corinth, and I left Trophimus sick in Miletus. 21Do
your best to get here before winter. Eubulus
greets you, and so do Pudens, Linus, Claudia
and all the brothers.
22The Lord be with your spirit. Grace be with
you.

[a] 19 Greek *Prisca,* a variant of *Priscilla*

of Mark's failure, Paul had refused to allow Mark's participation in the second journey, resulting in the separation of Paul and Barnabas (see Acts 15:36–41). Though Mark had failed Paul at an earlier time, it is clear in this passage that his relationship with Paul had been restored. Mark's restoration can bring hope to all who have failed or broken a commitment. Mark went on to touch the lives of millions through his message in the Gospel of Mark. Restoration is possible for us too. No matter how great our sin or our failures in the past or what commitments we've broken, God can use us in amazing ways if we are willing to repent and surrender our lives to him.

4:16–18 Paul recalled the loneliness he felt during his first Roman imprisonment. He remembered the Lord's presence with him even after all his human companions had forsaken him. Only God could bring him comfort when he was a prisoner. As we grow in our faith, God may provide healthy relationships to support our spiritual progress. However, God may also remove those who were once our friends. During such times, we should follow Paul's example and draw closer to God himself. In time God will help us restore broken relationships and build new ones. But the experience of being alone can teach us that God is with us even in the lonely times.

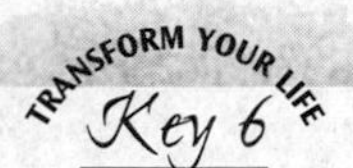

From the Past to the Future

2 Timothy 4:5–15 God wants to move us out of our sinful past and into a better future. As we cooperate with God's process of redeeming our past, we must honestly evaluate our lives and repent of our sin so that our course will be transformed according to his design.

Jesus said, "You will know the truth, and the truth will set you free" (John 8:32). The path to freedom always leads through the truth, including the truth about our past. Paul examined his past, honestly reviewing his earthly accomplishments, his wrongs, his mistakes, his gains and his losses. It was from this broad perspective that Paul wrote: "Not that I have already obtained all this, or have already been made perfect, but I press on to take hold of that for which Christ Jesus took hold of me" (Philippians 3:12).

Freedom from the past also involves facing up to the instances when others have harmed us and turning these situations over to God. The apostle Paul once wrote to young Timothy: "Alexander the metalworker did me a great deal of harm. The Lord will repay him for what he has done" (4:14). Paul readily admitted the truth about someone who had hurt him, but he left the matter in God's hands.

When we hand over our past to God and ask him to work it out for the best according to his will, we can let go of both the past and the resolution of its problems. Then God can transform us and move us toward a brighter future—a future of helping others find God's transforming power through the lessons we have learned.

Turn to Titus 3.

TITUS

The Big Picture

A. THREATS TO THE TRUTH ABOUT GOD'S GRACE (1:1-16)

B. SOUND TEACHINGS WITH RESPECT TO GOD'S GRACE (2:1–3:11)

1. Applying God's Truth to People of All Ages (2:1-10)
2. God's Grace As a Motivation for Godly Living (2:11–3:8)
3. Applying God's Truth to the Problem of Legalism (3:9-11)

C. FINAL PERSONAL REMARKS (3:12-15)

Paul wrote this letter to Titus, a young pastor on the island of Crete. Titus faced two primary problems in his church. Some of the people claimed that immoral living was all right because God's grace was sufficient for forgiveness. Another group insisted that acceptance by God came through obeying the Law of Moses. Paul encouraged Titus to confront both groups for undermining God's gracious gift of forgiveness in Christ.

Paul solved Titus's dual problem by reminding him of the importance of God's grace. When we realize the amazing grace that God has given us, we feel an incredible sense of gratitude. God's grace will motivate us to obey God's will for our lives, not to live a life of immorality because our forgiveness is guaranteed. God is not a harsh taskmaster whose favor depends on our slavish obedience to his rules. He is a gracious Father who offers us a relationship with himself, both now and throughout eternity. We can live godly lives out of gratitude to God because he loves and forgives us.

The fact that God is gracious and forgiving is essential to our spiritual renewal. We have probably tried to overcome sin and transform our lives but have failed because we don't possess the power to make those changes on our own. But God is gracious. We don't need to be afraid to admit our failures to him. He will forgive us and give us a chance to start over again. We can continue our honest self-examination without fear, daring to see the truth and confess it. God will never reject us for our failures and mistakes. God accepts us just as we are.

Spiritual Renewal Themes

THE BLESSINGS OF GOD'S GRACE

Salvation in Jesus Christ is good news! God offers salvation to us freely even though we do not deserve it. Yet salvation is more than just God's offer to pay for our sins; God also seeks to transform our lives so that we can live each day with the reality of his power inside us. We don't need to be afraid as we come before God, regardless of our sins. Our relationship with God is not based on our success at following his laws, but rather on his gracious provision for the forgiveness of our sin—Jesus Christ. As we entrust our lives to God, he forgives us and empowers us to live according to his perfect plan.

THE IMPORTANCE OF ACCOUNTABILITY

We can never make progress spiritually if we are isolated from others. Developing healthy relationships accompanies surrendering our lives to God. He commands us to love each other and live in harmony. God never designed life or spiritual growth to be undertaken alone. God often uses other people to encourage us to persevere in our faith. Paul urged Titus to be accountable to others. By depending on others, Titus could stand firm and reflect God's love and power in his life. Relationships that hold us accountable can give us the courage to do as Titus did. Relationships also help us to continually seek God for the help we need to live in harmony with other fallible people.

SPIRITUAL RENEWAL REQUIRES SACRIFICE

When we enter God's kingdom, we also enter new relationships that are subject to his commands. As we see in this letter, there should be an order to all our relationships. Everyone's role is important. If we are going to be faithful to our role, we must make sacrifices for others. Seeking spiritual renewal sometimes begins as a selfish pursuit. We tend to focus on our own problems and needs. But healthy spiritual growth moves beyond this self-focus and considers the needs of others. Each of us has something to share. We should make the sacrifices necessary to help others in need of spiritual renewal.

Essential Facts

PURPOSE:
To encourage Titus to be faithful in applying the grace of God to various circumstances.

AUTHOR:
The apostle Paul.

AUDIENCE:
Titus, a pastor on the island of Crete.

DATE WRITTEN:
Between Paul's first and second Roman imprisonments (A.D. 63 and 66).

SETTING:
Titus pastored the church on the island of Crete, a place well known for its immorality. A group of legalists had also made inroads into the church, so Titus had to deal with both immorality and legalism.

KEY VERSES:
"For the grace of God that brings salvation has appeared to all men. It teaches us to say 'No' to ungodliness and worldly passions, and to live self-controlled, upright and godly lives in this present age" (2:11–12).

KEY PEOPLE AND RELATIONSHIPS:
Paul with Titus.

1 Paul, a servant of God and an apostle of Jesus Christ for the faith of God's elect and the knowledge of the truth that leads to godliness— 2a faith and knowledge resting on the hope of eternal life, which God, who does not lie, promised before the beginning of time, 3and at his appointed season he brought his word to light through the preaching entrusted to me by the command of God our Savior,

4To Titus, my true son in our common faith:

Grace and peace from God the Father and Christ Jesus our Savior.

Titus's Task on Crete

5The reason I left you in Crete was that you might straighten out what was left unfinished and appoint[a] elders in every town, as I directed you. 6An elder must be blameless, the husband of but one wife, a man whose children believe and are not open to the charge of being wild and disobedient. 7Since an overseer[b] is entrusted with God's work, he must be blameless—not overbearing, not quick-tempered, not given to drunkenness, not violent, not pursuing dishonest gain. 8Rather he must be hospitable, one who loves what is good, who is self-controlled, upright, holy and disciplined. 9He must hold firmly to the trustworthy message as it has been taught, so that he can encourage others by sound doctrine and refute those who oppose it.

10For there are many rebellious people, mere talkers and deceivers, especially those of the circumcision group. 11They must be silenced, because they are ruining whole households by teaching things they ought not to teach—and that for the sake of dishonest gain. 12Even one of their own prophets has said, "Cretans are always liars, evil brutes, lazy gluttons." 13This testimony is true. Therefore, rebuke them sharply, so that they will be sound in the faith 14and will pay no attention to Jewish myths or to the commands of those who reject the truth. 15To the pure, all things are pure, but to those who are corrupted and do not believe, nothing is pure. In fact, both their minds and consciences are corrupted. 16They claim to know God, but by their actions they deny him. They are detestable, disobedient and unfit for doing anything good.

What Must Be Taught to Various Groups

2 You must teach what is in accord with sound doctrine. 2Teach the older men to be temperate, worthy of respect, self-controlled, and sound in faith, in love and in endurance.

3Likewise, teach the older women to be reverent in the way they live, not to be slanderers or addicted to much wine, but to teach what is good. 4Then they can train the younger women to love their husbands and children, 5to be self-controlled and pure, to be busy at home, to be kind, and to be subject to their husbands, so that no one will malign the word of God.

6Similarly, encourage the young men to be self-controlled. 7In everything set them an example by doing what is good. In your teaching show integrity, seriousness 8and soundness of speech that cannot be condemned, so that those who oppose you may be ashamed because they have nothing bad to say about us.

9Teach slaves to be subject to their masters in everything, to try to please them, not to talk back to them, 10and not to steal from them, but to show that they can be fully trusted, so that in every way they will make the teaching about God our Savior attractive.

11For the grace of God that brings salvation

[a]5 Or *ordain* [b]7 Traditionally *bishop*

1:4–5 These verses imply that Paul and Titus had ministered on the island of Crete, a ministry not mentioned in the book of Acts. Paul called upon Titus to finish organizing the churches, strengthen the believers and appoint leaders to serve them. Paul recognized that having a single leader is never ideal. A church leader who attempts to control everything by refusing to share responsibilities and power with others will severely limit that church's potential to help others. And organizations that revolve around one leader are likely to reproduce the flaws of that leader. The work of ministry should be shared by several spiritual leaders. A leadership group will balance the weaknesses of each individual. Leaders who refuse to do so are not obeying God's design.

1:6–9 This list of qualifications for church leadership makes no mention of social standing, financial resources or professional accomplishments. It is merely a simple list of character traits. Church leaders must be good spouses and parents; they need to have good reputations; they need to be humble, patient, self-controlled, hospitable, sensible and fair. These character traits have nothing to do with whether we are wealthy or poor, famous or unknown, powerful or lowly. No one can buy these character traits; no one can demand them. We can only obtain them by surrendering our lives to God and making his will our own.

1:10–14 Paul encouraged Titus to confront a group of legalists who were denying God's grace by requiring believers to earn their salvation with good works (1:10, 14). Legalism makes our obedience to rules and traditions more important than a personal and transforming relationship with God. Incorrectly assuming that we can be good under our own power, legalism takes us off course. But indulgence to sin also takes us off course. Anytime we see ourselves veering toward legalism or sinful indulgence, we need to confess these sins and allow God to redirect our course back to grace and obedience.

2:1–5 Paul urged older men and women to take special roles in the Christian community. Paul wanted them to be role models for others, teaching by the way that they lived. Many of us have experienced the benefits of an encouraging, godly mentor. As we grow spiritually, we can become healthy role models to others too. Having and being a godly mentor will enhance our spiritual growth.

2:6 Paul told Titus to urge the young people in his church to think before acting. Young people often are blind to the consequences of certain activities. They often act first and think about it later. Paul here urges young Christians to "be self-controlled." If we think before we act and conform our activities to God's plan, we will build our lives on a solid foundation.

2:11–15 The proper response to God's grace is right liv-

has appeared to all men. 12It teaches us to say
"No" to ungodliness and worldly passions, and
to live self-controlled, upright and godly lives
in this present age, 13while we wait for the
blessed hope—the glorious appearing of our
great God and Savior, Jesus Christ, 14who gave
himself for us to redeem us from all wickedness
and to purify for himself a people that are his
very own, eager to do what is good.
15These, then, are the things you should
teach. Encourage and rebuke with all authority.
Do not let anyone despise you.

Doing What Is Good

3 Remind the people to be subject to rulers
and authorities, to be obedient, to be ready
to do whatever is good, 2to slander no one, to
be peaceable and considerate, and to show true
humility toward all men.
3At one time we too were foolish, disobedient, deceived and enslaved by all kinds of passions and pleasures. We lived in malice and
envy, being hated and hating one another. 4But
when the kindness and love of God our Savior
appeared, 5he saved us, not because of righteous things we had done, but because of his
mercy. He saved us through the washing of rebirth and renewal by the Holy Spirit, 6whom he
poured out on us generously through Jesus
Christ our Savior, 7so that, having been justified
by his grace, we might become heirs having the
hope of eternal life. 8This is a trustworthy saying. And I want you to stress these things, so
that those who have trusted in God may be

ing. In the Bible, guilt and fear are never considered appropriate motivations for righteousness. When we realize that God loves us and provides the power for us to live godly lives, we should surrender to him and seek out his will. We should obey God because he loves us and has called us to live righteously. We don't need to fear God because of the mistakes we have made. He still loves us and will help us renew our spiritual lives when we confess our sins to him. Knowing that God wants us to make spiritual progress even more than we do can give us hope as we work through the process.

3:3 This verse forms the dark backdrop that magnifies the beauty of God's freedom through Jesus Christ. When we are enslaved by sin, we are filled with resentment, envy and hate. These attitudes need to be released to God. Our broken lives can be like black velvet against which God can display the bright diamond of his gracious salvation. Not one of us deserves God's gracious help. He loves us simply because he chooses to, more in spite of us than because we deserve it. No matter how dark our past or the attitudes that we have hidden within our hearts, God is willing to forgive and transform us if only we will repent.

3:4–8 Notice the terms used to describe God's grace: "kindness and love" (3:4) and "mercy" (3:5). We are justified by God's grace; that is, we are declared good in God's eyes by virtue of belonging to Christ. Recognizing this fact takes us off the performance treadmill, relieving us of the need to measure up to God's standards. Some of us have spent our lives trying to measure up and have carried a load of guilt for failing to live up to a list of rules. But when we surrender ourselves to God, he accepts us as we are, calls us to holy living and provides us with the Holy Spirit, who will help us.

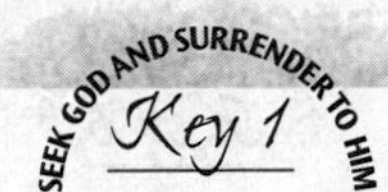

The Promise of Positive Change

Titus 2:11–14 When we seek God and surrender to him, we receive renewed hope for positive change in our lives. Of course, we may have doubts about our ability to change. These are reasonable doubts if we have failed in the past to make the changes we needed to make. But, through surrender to God, we can be assured that real change will be possible because God himself promises to help us.

Paul recognized that God can and will help us change. He encouraged Titus with the words,

> The grace of God that brings salvation has appeared to all men. It teaches us to say "No" to ungodliness and worldly passions, and to live self-controlled, upright and godly lives in this present age, while we wait for the blessed hope—the glorious appearing of our great God and Savior, Jesus Christ, who gave himself for us to redeem us from all wickedness and to purify for himself a people that are his very own, eager to do what is good (2:11–14).

God has promised to save us and make us his people! Throughout that process, God rescues us from our bondage to sin. Let us cooperate with God's plans for our salvation by surrendering to him and turning from sinful pleasures.

Turn to Hebrews 11.

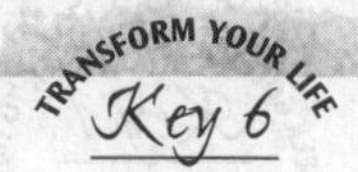

Always Remember

Titus 3:1–5 As we begin to enjoy the benefits of our transformed lives, the memories of our previous lifestyles may begin to fade. Do we vividly remember what we once were before we surrendered to God? Can we recall the dark emotions that filled our souls? Do we have true compassion and humble sympathy for those enslaved to sin and in need of God's message of salvation?

When we take God's message to others, it is vital that we never forget where we came from and how we got where we are now. Paul told Titus:

At one time we too were foolish, disobedient, deceived and enslaved by all kinds of passions and pleasures. We lived in malice and envy, being hated and hating one another. But when the kindness and love of God our Savior appeared, he saved us, not because of righteous things we had done, but because of his mercy. He saved us through the washing of rebirth and renewal by the Holy Spirit (3:3–5).

As we share our story of God's transformation of our lives, let us never forget where we came from. We, too, were slaves, just as others are today. Our hearts were filled with the confusion and painful emotions that others still feel. We were saved because of the love and kindness of God, not because we were good or wise. As we reach out to other hurting people, we must also remember that we are still free because God is with us, continually helping us and transforming our lives.

Turn to Hebrews 12.

careful to devote themselves to doing what is
good. These things are excellent and profitable
for everyone.
9But avoid foolish controversies and genealogies and arguments and quarrels about the
law, because these are unprofitable and useless.
10Warn a divisive person once, and then warn
him a second time. After that, have nothing to
do with him. 11You may be sure that such a man
is warped and sinful; he is self-condemned.

Final Remarks

12As soon as I send Artemas or Tychicus to
you, do your best to come to me at Nicopolis,
because I have decided to winter there. 13Do
everything you can to help Zenas the lawyer and
Apollos on their way and see that they have
everything they need. 14Our people must learn
to devote themselves to doing what is good, in
order that they may provide for daily necessities
and not live unproductive lives.
15Everyone with me sends you greetings.
Greet those who love us in the faith.

Grace be with you all.

PHILEMON

The Big Picture

There were millions of slaves in the Roman Empire; Onesimus was one of them. A kind Christian leader named Philemon, who happened to be one of the many people Paul had led to Christ, owned Onesimus. It appears that, out of desperation, Onesimus stole from his master and ran away. But as so often happens, Onesimus's attempt to run from his wrongdoing only added to his problem. According to the law, a runaway slave could be branded on the forehead or even executed.

Onesimus hid in Rome, and while there he met Paul. Through the apostle's influence, Onesimus came to believe in Jesus Christ. Paul, himself a prisoner at the time, wrote to his friend Philemon to tell him of Onesimus's conversion. The apostle begged Philemon to forgive Onesimus and welcome him home as a "dear brother" (v. 16). We do not know the final outcome of the story, but it seems likely that Philemon responded positively to Paul's suggestion to forgive Onesimus.

We have all been slaves at one time or another, although we may not have thought of it in those terms. Some of us have been slaves to our own sinful desires, to a false image we have created, to a set of human rules and regulations, to a job or possessions or even to the injuries of the past. Slavery of any kind diminishes our humanity, driving us to behave in ways that God never intended. God is the only one who can truly free us from slavery.

Paul's letter to Philemon reminds us that God always loves us. God cares for us, just as he cared for Onesimus. God can step into the middle of our unmanageable lives and offer us real hope for the future. As long as we see the truth of our condition, surrender our lives to God and confess our sins, we can count on God to lead us to lives of true freedom.

A. GREETINGS (1-3)

B. PAUL COMMENDS PHILEMON (4-7)

C. PAUL REQUESTS CONSIDERATION FOR ONESIMUS (8-21)

D. CONCLUDING REMARKS (22-25)

Spiritual Renewal Themes

GOD CARES FOR THE OUTCAST

In Roman society, a slave possessed no personal value. Onesimus was no different from any other slave. He had little worth apart from what he was able to do for his master. But in God's eyes Onesimus was highly valuable because no one is ever worthless to God. God's values are different from ours. He cares deeply about all people, regardless of their status in society.

Essential Facts

PURPOSE:
To convince Philemon, a Christian and a slave owner, to forgive a slave for running away.

AUTHOR:
The apostle Paul.

AUDIENCE:
Philemon, a believer in the early church.

DATE WRITTEN:
About A.D. 60, during Paul's imprisonment in Rome.

SETTING:
Slavery was common in the Roman Empire, even among new believers. Paul did not speak directly against slavery, but he did take a radical step by calling the slave Onesimus "a dear brother" (v. 16).

KEY VERSES:
"I appeal to you for my son Onesimus, who became my son while I was in chains. Formerly he was useless to you, but now he has become useful both to you and to me" (vv. 10–11).

KEY PEOPLE AND RELATIONSHIPS:
Paul with Onesimus and Philemon.

And God calls us to himself, offering us lives of spiritual renewal and hope.

THE NECESSITY OF FORGIVENESS

According to the laws of the Roman Empire, Onesimus deserved death for what he had done. But God forgave him, and Paul asked Philemon to do the same. The forgiveness granted by God and by others truly releases us. We can rejoice that when we surrender our lives to God, from whom we have run away into sin, he forgives us and transforms our lives, even though we deserve death for our sinfulness. Then God helps us to make restitution to the people we have harmed, paving the way for our forgiveness and restoration with them as well.

THE IMPORTANCE OF RESTITUTION

Onesimus had been reconciled to God; he had experienced God's forgiveness in his life. But although God had forgiven him, Onesimus was not exempt from the consequences of his earlier actions. He still had to return to Philemon to make restitution for his wrongs. Our actions can bring painful consequences; they can hurt other people. Even after we have been reconciled to God, we still need to accept responsibility for our previous actions and make restitution with those we have wronged. As hard as this may be, we can be sure that God is with us in the process. Onesimus returned to his master bearing this letter from Paul. And though there is no record of the outcome of Onesimus's return, it is unlikely that this letter would have survived had Philemon not taken Paul's advice and forgiven Onesimus.

[1]Paul, a prisoner of Christ Jesus, and Timothy our brother,

To Philemon our dear friend and fellow worker, [2]to Apphia our sister, to Archippus our fellow soldier and to the church that meets in your home:

[3]Grace to you and peace from God our Father and the Lord Jesus Christ.

Thanksgiving and Prayer

[4]I always thank my God as I remember you
in my prayers, [5]because I hear about your faith
in the Lord Jesus and your love for all the saints.
[6]I pray that you may be active in sharing your
faith, so that you will have a full understanding
of every good thing we have in Christ. [7]Your
love has given me great joy and encouragement,
because you, brother, have refreshed the hearts
of the saints.

Paul's Plea for Onesimus

[8]Therefore, although in Christ I could be
bold and order you to do what you ought to do,
[9]yet I appeal to you on the basis of love. I then,
as Paul—an old man and now also a prisoner
of Christ Jesus— [10]I appeal to you for my son
Onesimus,[a] who became my son while I was
in chains. [11]Formerly he was useless to you, but
now he has become useful both to you and
to me.
[12]I am sending him—who is my very heart—
back to you. [13]I would have liked to keep him
with me so that he could take your place in
helping me while I am in chains for the gospel.
[14]But I did not want to do anything without
your consent, so that any favor you do will be
spontaneous and not forced. [15]Perhaps the reason he was separated from you for a little while
was that you might have him back for good—

[a]10 *Onesimus* means *useful.*

3–9 Paul took some time to establish his lines of communication with Philemon. The apostle showed an appreciation for Philemon and a true concern for his family. There may be times when we will be called upon to confront others about their sins or deal with some other sensitive problem. In such situations, we must value the people involved and take the time to establish strong lines of communication. If we step in too soon with a confrontational attitude, others may feel we are just trying to hurt them. If, however, we prove our love beforehand, they will be more likely to listen to what we have to say.
14–17 Onesimus and Philemon each had a responsibility. Both men had to release their old resentments. Onesimus needed to do what he could to make restitution to Philemon; Philemon was responsible to accept Onesimus's repentant overtures. If we have wronged someone else, we need to accept responsibility for that sin and take steps toward making restitution. It is equally important, however, that we respond with forgiveness when others harm us. Bearing a grudge against someone is destructive not only to the person we turn away but also to us. A har-

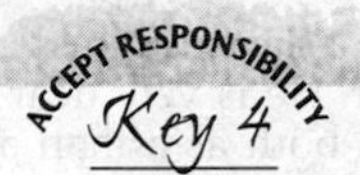

Paying Our Debts

Philemon 13–16 Sometimes taking responsibility for our lives means completing unfinished business. Some of us may have left a trail of broken relationships—things we need to address before moving on with our spiritual renewal. Others may be burdened by debts that distract us from spiritual pursuits. Tying up loose ends is something we must do before we can move forward in our spiritual growth.

A new life will never excuse us from our past obligations. While the apostle Paul was in prison, he led a runaway slave named Onesimus to Christ and a new life. But then Paul sent him back to his master even though Onesimus faced a possible death penalty for his offense. Since his previous master was a Christian brother and a friend of Paul's, Paul hoped that Onesimus would be forgiven.

Onesimus carried a letter to his master written by Paul, which read, "I would have liked to keep him with me so that he could take your place in helping me while I am in chains for the gospel. But I did not want to do anything without your consent . . . Perhaps the reason he was separated from you for a little while was that you might have him back for good—no longer as a slave, but better than a slave, as a dear brother . . . Welcome him as you would welcome me. If he has done you any wrong or owes you anything, charge it to me" (vv.13–18). Paul recognized that even though Onesimus was a forgiven Christian, he needed to address the wrongs he had committed in his past.

Before we can move ahead, we must face the unfinished business of the past. This may include facing up to our cowardly behavior, our crooked schemes or our quick-fix solutions to our problems. While God will meet us where we are—just as he met Onesimus—he won't allow us to move forward until we have taken full responsibility for the sins that brought us to our present circumstances. Once we accept full ownership of our past, God will guide us to confront our fears and tie up our loose ends. But he will do it his way, not ours.

Turn to Jude.

16no longer as a slave, but better than a slave, as
a dear brother. He is very dear to me but even
dearer to you, both as a man and as a brother
in the Lord.
17So if you consider me a partner, welcome
him as you would welcome me. 18If he has
done you any wrong or owes you anything,
charge it to me. 19I, Paul, am writing this with
my own hand. I will pay it back—not to mention that you owe me your very self. 20I do wish,
brother, that I may have some benefit from you
in the Lord; refresh my heart in Christ. 21Confi-
dent of your obedience, I write to you, knowing
that you will do even more than I ask.
22And one thing more: Prepare a guest room
for me, because I hope to be restored to you in
answer to your prayers.

23Epaphras, my fellow prisoner in Christ
Jesus, sends you greetings. 24And so do Mark,
Aristarchus, Demas and Luke, my fellow work-
ers.

25The grace of the Lord Jesus Christ be with
your spirit.

---

bored grudge will only fill us with unresolved bitterness, hindering our spiritual progress.

18–21 With the phrase "charge it to me" (v. 18), Paul was asking Philemon to reckon Onesimus's debt against Paul's account. Paul wanted Philemon to welcome Onesimus back into his household as warmly as if Paul were the one returning. Paul intervened in this situation to help these brothers resolve the resentment between them and repair this broken relationship. God has done the same thing for us through Jesus Christ. God reckons all our sins and failures to the account of Jesus Christ, who has paid the price through his death on the cross. Then God joyfully receives us into his family, just as if he were welcoming his own Son (see 2 Corinthians 5:21).

HEBREWS

The Big Picture

All of us have felt the tug back to an old habit or a former way of life. We often long for the familiar, even though it may be destructive or lead us outside of God's will. At times, the challenge to remain strong in our faith may seem too hard for us. Our old lives beckon, tempting us with familiar sources of comfort.

Many of the Jewish Christians in the first century thought about returning to their Jewish faith. Some of Jesus' teachings didn't line up with the teachings of the Jewish rabbis. Was Jesus really the Messiah? Did following him mean they had to give up their old, familiar forms of worship? Would it be wrong to go back to their old beliefs and traditions? Did it make sense to follow this new way when it would only lead to harsh persecution?

The writer of Hebrews dealt with the doubts of the Jewish believers by demonstrating that salvation in Jesus Christ is clearly superior to the way of the Jewish law. The author urged Jewish Christian readers to hold on to their new faith, to encourage one another and to look forward to the return of Jesus the Messiah. These believers were further warned of the consequences of rejecting the salvation offered by God in Christ and were reminded of the blessings promised to those who would entrust their lives to Christ.

Spiritual renewal requires that we seek God, surrender our lives to Jesus Christ and follow his ways. From time to time we will almost certainly feel a temptation to return to our former ways of life. But God is more than able to help us and to empower us to grow.

A. THE SUPERIORITY OF JESUS (1:1–10:18)

1. He Is More Powerful Than the Angels (1:1–2:18)
2. He Is Greater Than Moses and Joshua (3:1–4:13)
3. He Surpasses Everything in the Old Covenant Priesthood (4:14–7:28)
4. His New Covenant Is Superior (8:1–10:18)

B. THE FREEING POWER OF FAITH AND HUMILITY (10:19–13:25)

1. Faith Needed in Hard Times (10:19-39)
2. Faith Seen in Old Testament Times (11:1-40)
3. Faithfulness and the Loving Discipline of God (12:1-29)
4. Faithfulness and the Trustworthy Foundation of Christ (13:1-25)

Spiritual Renewal Themes

THE PRIMACY OF JESUS CHRIST

The book of Hebrews describes Jesus as God, explaining that Jesus is the ultimate power and authority in the universe, superior to any and every other leader in history. He is the full and complete revelation of God to us. And Jesus is the one who can forgive us our sins. Christ is the center of our hope and trust. For that reason he is our only real hope for spiritual renewal.

Essential Facts

PURPOSE:
To demonstrate the wisdom of following Christ and the foolishness of looking elsewhere for salvation.

AUTHOR:
The writer of this letter is uncertain, but Paul, Luke, Barnabas, Apollos, Silas, Philip, Priscilla and others have been suggested as possible authors.

AUDIENCE:
Jewish believers.

DATE WRITTEN:
Probably shortly before the destruction of the Jerusalem temple in A.D. 70.

SETTING:
Hebrews was written to Jewish believers who were being persecuted, encouraging and reassuring them that Jesus was who he claimed to be—the Son of God and the promised Messiah.

KEY VERSE:
"The Son is the radiance of God's glory and the exact representation of his being, sustaining all things by his powerful word" (1:3).

KEY PEOPLE AND RELATIONSHIPS:
Jesus Christ, along with many men and women of faith.

JESUS FULFILLS WHAT IS REQUIRED OF US

Because Jesus was the perfect sacrifice, he fulfilled all that the Old Testament sacrifices represented—he was the means of God's complete forgiveness of our sins. That means every sin—past, present and future—can be forgiven completely. Through Christ, God did for us what we could not do ourselves. Jesus removed the barrier of sin between us and God so that we could have access to God's very presence. Christ's complete sacrifice removed the guilt that accompanied our sin. Through his sacrificial death and resurrection, Jesus Christ has fulfilled all that God requires of us.

THE NECESSITY OF FAITH

Faith is "being sure of what we hope for and certain of what we do not see" (11:1). Our spiritual renewal is based on faith—our confident trust that God will help us do what we are powerless to do alone. As we place our trust in God, he will transform us with his power. He has promised this to all who believe in him.

THE IMPORTANCE OF PERSEVERANCE

Our spiritual renewal is a lifelong process. We need to learn to persevere when obstacles and problems block our way. The first readers of the book of Hebrews experienced incredible persecution for their faith. But the writer of Hebrews assured them that they could endure if they kept their eyes fixed on Jesus Christ. We also need to pray for the strength to endure because perseverance is essential to our ongoing spiritual growth.

The Son Superior to Angels

1 In the past God spoke to our forefathers
through the prophets at many times and in
various ways, 2but in these last days he has spoken to us by his Son, whom he appointed heir
of all things, and through whom he made the
universe. 3The Son is the radiance of God's glory and the exact representation of his being,
sustaining all things by his powerful word. After
he had provided purification for sins, he sat
down at the right hand of the Majesty in heav-
en. 4So he became as much superior to the angels as the name he has inherited is superior to
theirs.

5For to which of the angels did God ever say,

"You are my Son;
today I have become your Father[a]"[b]?

Or again,

"I will be his Father,
and he will be my Son"[c]?

6And again, when God brings his firstborn into
the world, he says,

"Let all God's angels worship him."[d]

7In speaking of the angels he says,

"He makes his angels winds,
his servants flames of fire."[e]

8But about the Son he says,

"Your throne, O God, will last for ever and ever,
and righteousness will be the scepter of your kingdom.
9You have loved righteousness and hated wickedness;
therefore God, your God, has set you above your companions
by anointing you with the oil of joy."[f]

10He also says,

"In the beginning, O Lord, you laid the foundations of the earth,
and the heavens are the work of your hands.
11They will perish, but you remain;
they will all wear out like a garment.
12You will roll them up like a robe;
like a garment they will be changed.
But you remain the same,
and your years will never end."[g]

13To which of the angels did God ever say,

"Sit at my right hand
until I make your enemies
a footstool for your feet"[h]?

14Are not all angels ministering spirits sent to
serve those who will inherit salvation?

Warning to Pay Attention

2 We must pay more careful attention, therefore, to what we have heard, so that we do
not drift away. 2For if the message spoken by
angels was binding, and every violation and disobedience received its just punishment, 3how
shall we escape if we ignore such a great salvation? This salvation, which was first announced
by the Lord, was confirmed to us by those who
heard him. 4God also testified to it by signs,
wonders and various miracles, and gifts of the
Holy Spirit distributed according to his will.

Jesus Made Like His Brothers

5It is not to angels that he has subjected the

[a] 5 Or *have begotten you* [b] 5 Psalm 2:7 [c] 5 2 Samuel 7:14; 1 Chron. 17:13 [d] 6 Deut. 32:43 (see Dead Sea Scrolls and Septuagint) [e] 7 Psalm 104:4 [f] 9 Psalm 45:6,7 [g] 12 Psalm 102:25-27 [h] 13 Psalm 110:1

1:1–2 Jesus Christ, the Son of God, is God's final and most perfect revelation. Yet God the Son shaped the original creation as well. As "the Alpha and the Omega" (Revelation 1:8), he is the only power capable of recreating and transforming us. As the heir of all the treasures of heaven and earth, Jesus Christ stands ready and able to help those who come to him with empty hands, acknowledging their sins and needs.

1:3 There is a vast difference between the divine infinite being (God) and limited human beings (ourselves). The only way we can understand something of God's glory and power is to get to know Jesus Christ. Jesus is simultaneously both an incredibly powerful expression of God's person and the one who lovingly entered sinful human existence to redeem and renew fallen souls. When we acknowledge our inability to save ourselves, we can confess the truth that only God has the power to accomplish what we cannot. God's power for our lives is found in a relationship with Jesus Christ.

1:4–6 The Jews greatly esteemed angels because of their role in the Old Testament as God's servants. However, as glorious as angels are, there is still no comparison between the angels and Jesus Christ. He is clearly superior in his person and in the purposes he accomplished. He is the Son of the heavenly Father (see Matthew 3:17). It is into this wonderful Father-child relationship that he draws us (see 2:11). Through Jesus, we have access to a Father who loves us and cares for our every need tenderly and with infinite wisdom (see Galatians 4:6; Ephesians 2:18). This is good news indeed!

1:7–13 This cascade of quotations from several Messianic psalms gives angels their due as powerful spirits but then contrasts them with the greater glory of Christ. He alone has the clear right to rule as Messianic King. His alone is the power over the original creation and the final re-creation when it occurs. And he alone is held in honor beside the Father.

2:1–3 This is the first of many cautionary passages in Hebrews. By it, the author sought to alert the Jewish believers to the subtle danger of drifting back into their former lifestyle in Judaism, of falling back into old ways. We must be careful not to drift away too. We should become involved in a church where God's Word is proclaimed and in a network of relationships where we are held accountable.

2:5–8 The writer of Hebrews applied a well-known psalm to Christ, possibly because of the reference to the "son of man" (see Psalm 8:4–6). Psalm 8's references are not obviously Messianic (i.e., referring to Christ). Rather, they seem to refer to humanity's status: lower than the angels yet ruler of the earth. However, in applying these verses to Christ, the writer of Hebrews put a new twist on this psalm. As the Son of Man, Christ was made lower than the

world to come, about which we are speaking.
6 But there is a place where someone has testified:

"What is man that you are mindful of him,
the son of man that you care for him?
7 You made him a little[a] lower than the
angels;
you crowned him with glory and honor
8 and put everything under his feet."[b]

In putting everything under him, God left nothing that is not subject to him. Yet at present we
do not see everything subject to him. 9 But we
see Jesus, who was made a little lower than the
angels, now crowned with glory and honor because he suffered death, so that by the grace of
God he might taste death for everyone.
10 In bringing many sons to glory, it was fitting that God, for whom and through whom
everything exists, should make the author of
their salvation perfect through suffering. 11 Both
the one who makes men holy and those who
are made holy are of the same family. So Jesus
is not ashamed to call them brothers. 12 He says,

"I will declare your name to my brothers;
in the presence of the congregation I will
sing your praises."[c]

13 And again,

"I will put my trust in him."[d]

And again he says,

"Here am I, and the children God has
given me."[e]

14 Since the children have flesh and blood, he
too shared in their humanity so that by his
death he might destroy him who holds the
power of death—that is, the devil— 15 and free
those who all their lives were held in slavery by
their fear of death. 16 For surely it is not angels
he helps, but Abraham's descendants. 17 For this
reason he had to be made like his brothers in
every way, in order that he might become a
merciful and faithful high priest in service to
God, and that he might make atonement for[f]
the sins of the people. 18 Because he himself
suffered when he was tempted, he is able to
help those who are being tempted.

Jesus Greater Than Moses

3 Therefore, holy brothers, who share in the
heavenly calling, fix your thoughts on
Jesus, the apostle and high priest whom we confess. 2 He was faithful to the one who appointed
him, just as Moses was faithful in all God's
house. 3 Jesus has been found worthy of greater
honor than Moses, just as the builder of a house
has greater honor than the house itself. 4 For
every house is built by someone, but God is the
builder of everything. 5 Moses was faithful as a
servant in all God's house, testifying to what
would be said in the future. 6 But Christ is faithful as a son over God's house. And we are his
house, if we hold on to our courage and the
hope of which we boast.

Warning Against Unbelief

7 So, as the Holy Spirit says:

[a] 7 Or *him for a little while;* also in verse 9
[b] 8 Psalm 8:4-6 [c] 12 Psalm 22:22 [d] 13 Isaiah 8:17
[e] 13 Isaiah 8:18 [f] 17 Or *and that he might turn aside God's wrath, taking away*

---

angels for a time but now is exalted to a position of authority over all things. He went before us and gives us hope as we look ahead to our ultimate future. No matter how difficult things are for us on this earth, our eventual destiny will be to rule in heaven with Christ.

2:8–14 Believers are traveling to an eternity with God, moving through a difficult territory where Christ has already been. It was God's kindness that led Jesus to his death—because by his death he purchased our salvation. It is also God's kindness that leads us through our own suffering. Through the refining fire of suffering we achieve balance and true holiness. But when we suffer, we can be sure that Jesus is with us, that he went before us and that God will use our pain for his purposes.

2:17–18 When we are depressed or struggling, we may feel that nobody cares about us or understands what we are going through. No person has ever gone to greater lengths to identify with us than Jesus Christ. Though he was limitless God, he subjected himself to all our limitations. He lived in our world as a human being, and he suffered as we do. He understands our pain and suffering from personal experience, and he is both eager and able to help us.

3:1 The writer of Hebrews reminded his readers that they were God's special people, set apart, chosen for heaven. Periodically we need to be reminded of who we are and where we are headed. Formerly, our past may have controlled our present. Now, because we have surrendered to Jesus Christ, our future sets the direction and tone for our lives. As often as we can, we should affirm who we are in Christ and remember the glorious destiny he holds for us.

3:2–6 The author of Hebrews underlined Christ's superiority to Moses by comparing the positions held by each. Christ was like a builder—the Creator. Moses was like a house that the builder constructed. We can be encouraged by remembering that God himself is in loving control of the reconstruction of our lives. In that knowledge we can find comfort, confidence and joy.

3:7–13 Most of this passage is a paraphrase of Psalm 95:7–11. The writer reminded his Jewish audience of the mistakes their ancestors had made. He recalled their unfaithfulness to God and the painful consequences they had suffered. The writer used past events to illustrate that his readers would be held accountable to live out their faith in whatever context God placed them. These verses emphasize the importance of holding each other accountable to faithfully live out our commitments to God and each other.

3:7—4:13 In this second and more extended warning section (see 2:1–4), the readers are cautioned to avoid the mistakes made by the Israelites who received the law at Mount Sinai. In spite of their spiritual privileges and visual awareness of God's awesome power, the Israelites had refused to exercise faith and enter the promised land that God had graciously offered them. Many of us make similar mistakes in our spiritual journeys. Either we don't persevere, or we don't anchor our spiritual growth in Christ. The book of Hebrews helps us put our full trust in God as he is revealed in Jesus Christ.

"Today, if you hear his voice,
8 do not harden your hearts
as you did in the rebellion,
during the time of testing in the desert,
9where your fathers tested and tried me
and for forty years saw what I did.
10That is why I was angry with that
generation,
and I said, 'Their hearts are always going
astray,
and they have not known my ways.'
11So I declared on oath in my anger,
'They shall never enter my rest.' "[a]

12See to it, brothers, that none of you has a sinful, unbelieving heart that turns away from the living God. 13But encourage one another daily, as long as it is called Today, so that none of you may be hardened by sin's deceitfulness. 14We have come to share in Christ if we hold firmly till the end the confidence we had at first. 15As has just been said:

"Today, if you hear his voice,
do not harden your hearts
as you did in the rebellion."[b]

16Who were they who heard and rebelled? Were they not all those Moses led out of Egypt? 17And with whom was he angry for forty years? Was it not with those who sinned, whose bodies fell in the desert? 18And to whom did God swear that they would never enter his rest if not to those who disobeyed[c]? 19So we see that they were not able to enter, because of their unbelief.

A Sabbath-Rest for the People of God

4 Therefore, since the promise of entering his rest still stands, let us be careful that none of you be found to have fallen short of it. 2For we also have had the gospel preached to us, just as they did; but the message they heard was of no value to them, because those who heard did not combine it with faith.[d] 3Now we who have believed enter that rest, just as God has said,

"So I declared on oath in my anger,
'They shall never enter my rest.' "[e]

And yet his work has been finished since the creation of the world. 4For somewhere he has spoken about the seventh day in these words: "And on the seventh day God rested from all his work."[f] 5And again in the passage above he says, "They shall never enter my rest."

6It still remains that some will enter that rest, and those who formerly had the gospel preached to them did not go in, because of their disobedience. 7Therefore God again set a certain day, calling it Today, when a long time later he spoke through David, as was said before:

"Today, if you hear his voice,
do not harden your hearts."[b]

8For if Joshua had given them rest, God would not have spoken later about another day. 9There remains, then, a Sabbath-rest for the people of God; 10for anyone who enters God's rest also rests from his own work, just as God did from his. 11Let us, therefore, make every effort to enter that rest, so that no one will fall by following their example of disobedience.

12For the word of God is living and active. Sharper than any double-edged sword, it penetrates even to dividing soul and spirit, joints and marrow; it judges the thoughts and attitudes of the heart. 13Nothing in all creation is hidden from God's sight. Everything is uncovered and laid bare before the eyes of him to whom we must give account.

Jesus the Great High Priest

14Therefore, since we have a great high priest

[a]*11* Psalm 95:7-11 [b]*15,7* Psalm 95:7,8 [c]*18* Or *disbelieved* [d]*2* Many manuscripts *because they did not share in the faith of those who obeyed* [e]*3* Psalm 95:11; also in verse 5 [f]*4* Gen. 2:2

3:14–19 The writer of Hebrews confirmed the need to act immediately. His readers needed to accept full responsibility for their wrong actions. This urgency to act immediately is underlined here by the emphasis on "today" (see 3:15; Psalm 95:7). Acting immediately and taking responsibility for our lives are both crucial aspects of the spiritual growth process.

4:1–3 God is always ready and willing to fulfill his promises of freedom and rest. But our unbelief and lack of faith will stop him from blessing us. God's blessings and freedom can be received only by faith. Just as the Jews of Moses' day turned back from entering the promised land, sometimes we let our difficulties cloud our thoughts and make us doubt God's ability to keep his promises. When the going seems the hardest we must consciously fix our minds on God's promises. Faith in Christ, not in our own efforts, is the only way to true spiritual growth.

4:4–11 God rested at the end of creation (see Genesis 2:1–3). And rest is promised for us too. The writer understood David's renewed offer of rest in Psalm 95 to mean that the final rest was not secured when Joshua and Israel entered the promised land. Our true rest is fulfilled in Jesus Christ.

4:12–13 During difficult times our faith may dwindle. We may grow angry and harden our hearts to the truth about ourselves. There is an antidote to this problem: the Word of God, which has the power to penetrate to the depths of our hearts. God knows everything about us, even the things we try to hide from ourselves. We can count on him, through his Word, to uncover the problems in our lives, show us the truth we need to see and help us respond to the truth that he shows us.

4:14—5:3 If Jesus weren't our high priest, it would be terrifying to admit our failures to a perfect God. But Jesus became a man and is able to deal gently with our weaknesses because he understands our problems. Unlike human priests, Jesus Christ, the ultimate high priest, has already been glorified in heaven. He suffered the same temptations we do, but he did not sin. He offered a sacrifice, but his sacrifice atoned for the sins of the world, not his own. That combination of glory and understanding beckons us to pray confidently for God's grace and mercy on an ongoing basis. Hebrews 4:14–16 reminds us that God is always willing and able to shower us with the mercy and grace we need. Our part is to continually seek God and surrender to him.

THE SPIRITUAL DISCIPLINES

Bible Study and Meditation

Letting God's Word Do Its Work

Hebrews 4:12–14 Not only do we search God's Word, but God's Word also searches us. When we seek to understand God's Word, we also seek to stand under its authority.

As we read the Bible, we may be tempted to draw back from its soul-searching power. We may argue with its teaching, resent its discipline or question its assertions. But these reactions simply alert us to the fact that God *is* searching our hearts. Spiritual renewal will come as we examine not only God's Word but also our response to it. Why do we feel upset or challenged? Why does the Bible affect us in a particular way? What specific attitudes or behaviors are suggested that differ from our way of living? Questions such as these can move us beyond impulsive reactions to spiritually productive reflection. The psalmist wrote, "Search me, O God, and know my heart; test me and know my anxious thoughts. See if there is any offensive way in me, and lead me in the way everlasting" (Psalm 139:23–24).

When we surrender our resistance to the soul-searching power of the Bible, we find the grace of Jesus Christ will sustain us. The writer of Hebrews recognized that God's Word not only exposes our sin but also reveals the remedy for that sin—Jesus, our great high priest. Through him we find his mercy that removes our sin and his power that works through our weaknesses.

Putting It Into Practice

God's Word is a mirror in which we often see things that are hidden during the ordinary course of life. It causes us to reflect on our motives, our inner thoughts and the unspoken assumptions and expectations that drive us. In what way does God's Word make you uncomfortable? Is God's Word exposing an area of your life that needs attention? Ask God to show you specific ways that you can change. Record these thoughts in your journal and refer to them from time to time to check on your progress. You may want to make the prayer of Psalm 139:23–24 your prayer as you regularly read your Bible.

For more on Bible study and meditation, turn to Deuteronomy 17.

who has gone through the heavens,[a] Jesus the Son of God, let us hold firmly to the faith we profess. [15]For we do not have a high priest who is unable to sympathize with our weaknesses, but we have one who has been tempted in every way, just as we are—yet was without sin. [16]Let us then approach the throne of grace with confidence, so that we may receive mercy and find grace to help us in our time of need.

5 Every high priest is selected from among men and is appointed to represent them in matters related to God, to offer gifts and sacrifices for sins. [2]He is able to deal gently with those who are ignorant and are going astray, since he himself is subject to weakness. [3]This is why he has to offer sacrifices for his own sins, as well as for the sins of the people.

[4]No one takes this honor upon himself; he must be called by God, just as Aaron was. [5]So Christ also did not take upon himself the glory of becoming a high priest. But God said to him,

"You are my Son;
today I have become your Father.[b]"[c]

[6]And he says in another place,

"You are a priest forever,
in the order of Melchizedek."[d]

[7]During the days of Jesus' life on earth, he offered up prayers and petitions with loud cries and tears to the one who could save him from death, and he was heard because of his reverent submission. [8]Although he was a son, he learned obedience from what he suffered [9]and, once made perfect, he became the source of eternal salvation for all who obey him [10]and was designated by God to be high priest in the order of Melchizedek.

Warning Against Falling Away

[11]We have much to say about this, but it is hard to explain because you are slow to learn. [12]In fact, though by this time you ought to be teachers, you need someone to teach you the elementary truths of God's word all over again. You need milk, not solid food! [13]Anyone who lives on milk, being still an infant, is not acquainted with the teaching about righteousness. [14]But solid food is for the mature, who by constant use have trained themselves to distinguish good from evil.

6 Therefore let us leave the elementary teachings about Christ and go on to maturity, not laying again the foundation of repentance from acts that lead to death,[e] and of faith in God, [2]instruction about baptisms, the laying on of hands, the resurrection of the dead, and eternal judgment. [3]And God permitting, we will do so.

[4]It is impossible for those who have once been enlightened, who have tasted the heavenly gift, who have shared in the Holy Spirit, [5]who have tasted the goodness of the word of God and the powers of the coming age, [6]if they fall away, to be brought back to repentance, because[f] to their loss they are crucifying the Son of God all over again and subjecting him to public disgrace.

[7]Land that drinks in the rain often falling on it and that produces a crop useful to those for whom it is farmed receives the blessing of God. [8]But land that produces thorns and thistles is worthless and is in danger of being cursed. In the end it will be burned.

[9]Even though we speak like this, dear friends, we are confident of better things in your case—things that accompany salvation. [10]God is not unjust; he will not forget your work and the love you have shown him as you have helped his people and continue to help them. [11]We want each of you to show this same diligence to the very end, in order to make your hope sure. [12]We do not want you to become lazy, but to imitate those who through faith and patience inherit what has been promised.

[a]14 Or *gone into heaven* [b]5 Or *have begotten you* [c]5 Psalm 2:7 [d]6 Psalm 110:4 [e]1 Or *from useless rituals* [f]6 Or *repentance while*

5:4–10 Like any high priest, Jesus Christ had to be chosen for his role. But Christ's was a different priesthood than the Jewish priesthood descended from Aaron. Jesus is the final and eternal high priest in the order of Melchizedek (see 7:1–21; Psalm 110:4). To prepare for that unique calling, Jesus, who was and is perfect as God, had to go through a process that culminated in his death on the cross (see 4:15; Luke 2:52). He is the one who goes before us and has prepared the way; he is with us in every step we take.

5:11–13 The writer interrupted his discussion of Melchizedek to give a lengthy warning about the spiritual dynamics underlying the readers' stalled growth in Christ (see 5:11—6:12). Having adequate time to grow and change was not their problem. But the readers, like many of us today, manifested childish behavior instead of growing to spiritual adulthood. Progress takes time, but growth is taking place, even if it comes about slowly.

5:14 Spiritual growth, eventual maturity and balance can happen only when we act on what we know to be true. We need to continue to do the right things. The more we do them, the more they become second nature to us. Like the athlete training for a sporting event, our spiritual renewal involves moral conditioning by making right choices. And right choices lead to spiritual and emotional maturity.

6:4–8 The agricultural analogy in this passage brings out the truth that if there is real spiritual life, there will be some evidence of it. Let us look for and cherish any and all signs of growth, even if they are only tiny green shoots where before there was dry, barren ground. If we are seeking to grow through faith in Christ, we can be assured that there will, in good time, be fruit.

6:9–12 In confronting his readers about their spiritual lethargy, the writer's words were strong and direct (see 5:11–14). Yet the author still chose to be positive and believe the best about his readers. He knew that in spite of their immaturity these believers were capable of much faith. His words challenged them to persevere in spiritual growth with a patient faith. We sometimes need to hear hard words of correction and challenge as well. This passage clearly illustrates how we should confront others when it is necessary and how to be open to correction from the people who love us.

The Certainty of God's Promise

[13]When God made his promise to Abraham, since there was no one greater for him to swear by, he swore by himself, [14]saying, "I will surely bless you and give you many descendants."[a] [15]And so after waiting patiently, Abraham received what was promised.

[16]Men swear by someone greater than themselves, and the oath confirms what is said and puts an end to all argument. [17]Because God wanted to make the unchanging nature of his purpose very clear to the heirs of what was promised, he confirmed it with an oath. [18]God did this so that, by two unchangeable things in which it is impossible for God to lie, we who have fled to take hold of the hope offered to us may be greatly encouraged. [19]We have this hope as an anchor for the soul, firm and secure. It enters the inner sanctuary behind the curtain, [20]where Jesus, who went before us, has entered on our behalf. He has become a high priest forever, in the order of Melchizedek.

Melchizedek the Priest

7 This Melchizedek was king of Salem and priest of God Most High. He met Abraham returning from the defeat of the kings and blessed him, [2]and Abraham gave him a tenth of everything. First, his name means "king of righteousness"; then also, "king of Salem" means "king of peace." [3]Without father or mother, without genealogy, without beginning of days or end of life, like the Son of God he remains a priest forever.

[4]Just think how great he was: Even the patriarch Abraham gave him a tenth of the plunder! [5]Now the law requires the descendants of Levi who become priests to collect a tenth from the people—that is, their brothers—even though their brothers are descended from Abraham. [6]This man, however, did not trace his descent from Levi, yet he collected a tenth from Abraham and blessed him who had the promises. [7]And without doubt the lesser person is blessed by the greater. [8]In the one case, the tenth is collected by men who die; but in the other case, by him who is declared to be living. [9]One might even say that Levi, who collects the tenth, paid the tenth through Abraham, [10]because when Melchizedek met Abraham, Levi was still in the body of his ancestor.

Jesus Like Melchizedek

[11]If perfection could have been attained through the Levitical priesthood (for on the basis of it the law was given to the people), why was there still need for another priest to come—one in the order of Melchizedek, not in the order of Aaron? [12]For when there is a change of the priesthood, there must also be a change of the law. [13]He of whom these things are said belonged to a different tribe, and no one from that tribe has ever served at the altar. [14]For it is clear that our Lord descended from Judah, and in regard to that tribe Moses said nothing about priests. [15]And what we have said is even more clear if another priest like Melchizedek appears, [16]one who has become a priest not on the basis of a regulation as to his ancestry but on the basis of the power of an indestructible life. [17]For it is declared:

"You are a priest forever,
  in the order of Melchizedek."[b]

[18]The former regulation is set aside because it was weak and useless [19](for the law made nothing perfect), and a better hope is introduced, by which we draw near to God.

[20]And it was not without an oath! Others became priests without any oath, [21]but he became a priest with an oath when God said to him:

"The Lord has sworn
  and will not change his mind:
'You are a priest forever.' "[b]

[a]*14* Gen. 22:17 [b]*17,21* Psalm 110:4

6:13–20 Abraham, the father of the Jewish nation, is a classic example of patient faith. After waiting for many years, he received his promised son Isaac, the first of many descendants (see Genesis 12:1–3; 22:16–18). Abraham's persevering faith was anchored in God's promises and based on God's unchanging nature (see 11:8–19). Like Abraham, we can trust God's promises and find absolute security in the resurrected Christ, our high priest.

7:1–3 The discussion here returned to the consideration of Melchizedek (see 5:6–10). These ideas may have been too deep for the original readers to fully understand in their state of spiritual lethargy, but the writer believed it was crucial that they hear this message and try to understand it. Aspects of Melchizedek's life paralleled events in the life of Christ (see Genesis 14:18–20). These references demonstrated that Christ truly did qualify as a priest in Melchizedek's order (see 6:20) and as our mediator for salvation and reconciliation.

7:4–10 This entire section argues that Abraham recognized Melchizedek as greater than himself and, thus, greater than any of Abraham's descendants, including Levi and the priesthood that descended from him. This discussion also established that the priesthood of Christ, according to the order of Melchizedek, is actually older (implying more stability) than that of Aaron. Such stability can be a great comfort to us. We may face circumstances that are constantly changing, but Christ will never change.

7:11–19 The new priesthood of Christ was desperately needed because the Levitical priesthood and the Law of Moses were incapable of producing true spiritual renewal. A better priesthood, a better law and a better hope for living in a growing relationship with God were necessary. Christ's qualification as high priest came not through his tribal descent but because of his resurrection to new life. The Law of Moses could not make people right with God. Only Christ could do that. We need to look to Jesus for lasting change in our lives.

7:20–28 The unchangeable oath of God regarding Christ's priesthood, stated prophetically in Psalm 110:4, meant that Christ's ministry was related to a better and final covenant. This sense of permanence means, among other things, that Christ will see us through to the end, that he is always available to help and that he is always our perfect model for right living.

[22]Because of this oath, Jesus has become the guarantee of a better covenant.

[23]Now there have been many of those priests, since death prevented them from continuing in office; [24]but because Jesus lives forever, he has a permanent priesthood. [25]Therefore he is able to save completely[a] those who come to God through him, because he always lives to intercede for them.

[26]Such a high priest meets our need—one who is holy, blameless, pure, set apart from sinners, exalted above the heavens. [27]Unlike the other high priests, he does not need to offer sacrifices day after day, first for his own sins, and then for the sins of the people. He sacrificed for their sins once for all when he offered himself. [28]For the law appoints as high priests men who are weak; but the oath, which came after the law, appointed the Son, who has been made perfect forever.

The High Priest of a New Covenant

8 The point of what we are saying is this: We do have such a high priest, who sat down at the right hand of the throne of the Majesty in heaven, [2]and who serves in the sanctuary, the true tabernacle set up by the Lord, not by man.

[3]Every high priest is appointed to offer both gifts and sacrifices, and so it was necessary for this one also to have something to offer. [4]If he were on earth, he would not be a priest, for there are already men who offer the gifts prescribed by the law. [5]They serve at a sanctuary that is a copy and shadow of what is in heaven. This is why Moses was warned when he was about to build the tabernacle: "See to it that you make everything according to the pattern shown you on the mountain."[b] [6]But the ministry Jesus has received is as superior to theirs as the covenant of which he is mediator is superior to the old one, and it is founded on better promises.

[7]For if there had been nothing wrong with that first covenant, no place would have been sought for another. [8]But God found fault with the people and said[c]:

"The time is coming, declares the Lord,
when I will make a new covenant
with the house of Israel
and with the house of Judah.
[9]It will not be like the covenant
I made with their forefathers
when I took them by the hand
to lead them out of Egypt,
because they did not remain faithful to my covenant,
and I turned away from them,
declares the Lord.
[10]This is the covenant I will make with the house of Israel
after that time, declares the Lord.
I will put my laws in their minds
and write them on their hearts.
I will be their God,
and they will be my people.
[11]No longer will a man teach his neighbor,
or a man his brother, saying, 'Know the Lord,'
because they will all know me,
from the least of them to the greatest.
[12]For I will forgive their wickedness
and will remember their sins no more."[d]

[13]By calling this covenant "new," he has made the first one obsolete; and what is obsolete and aging will soon disappear.

Worship in the Earthly Tabernacle

9 Now the first covenant had regulations for worship and also an earthly sanctuary. [2]A tabernacle was set up. In its first room were the lampstand, the table and the consecrated bread; this was called the Holy Place. [3]Behind the second curtain was a room called the Most Holy Place, [4]which had the golden altar of incense and the gold-covered ark of the covenant. This ark contained the gold jar of manna, Aaron's staff that had budded, and the stone tablets of the covenant. [5]Above the ark were the cherubim

[a]25 Or *forever* [b]5 Exodus 25:40 [c]8 Some manuscripts may be translated *fault and said to the people.* [d]12 Jer. 31:31-34

8:1–6 Christ is not only a superior high priest; he also serves in a superior sanctuary. In fact, the earthly tabernacle was never intended as anything but a limited copy of the ultimate heavenly sanctuary. It doesn't matter that Christ was never recognized as a priest during his time on earth. Through the death and resurrection of Christ, the limited earthly priesthood gave way to the perfect heavenly priesthood. It is the heavenly priesthood that provides the needed resources for salvation; any other means is inadequate.

8:7–13 Six centuries before Christ died on the cross to provide a new way for us to relate to God (see Luke 22:20), the prophet Jeremiah predicted the need for a "new covenant" to breach the separation between God and people (see Jeremiah 31:31–34). Jesus came and fulfilled this new covenant, making the old covenant obsolete. The recipients of this letter had been looking for redemption through the law instead of through the living Savior. There is only one way to experience redemption and reconciliation with God—through faith in Jesus Christ.

8:10–13 The new plan to establish our relationship with God through Jesus Christ is exciting indeed. In Christ we receive the spiritual and emotional healing we seek. Christ provides us: moral codes written in the heart, rather than imposed from without; a new desire and ability to obey God; a special, close relationship with God; a new fellowship with other believers; mercy from God, with full forgiveness of past sins and character defects. In Christ, we have all the help necessary for redemption and spiritual growth.

9:1–10 The regulations and order of the Old Testament priesthood were striking in their beauty. They powerfully symbolized the painful consequences of sin. But even though these sacrifices were effective on a short-term basis, they were not a permanent solution to the sin problem. The Old Testament sacrifices and rituals could not cleanse the consciences of the people. Their role was simply to provide ritual cleanness. Only the work of Christ and the Holy Spirit can clear our consciences and transform our hearts.

of the Glory, overshadowing the atonement
cover.[a] But we cannot discuss these things in
detail now.
6When everything had been arranged like
this, the priests entered regularly into the outer
room to carry on their ministry. 7But only the
high priest entered the inner room, and that
only once a year, and never without blood,
which he offered for himself and for the sins the
people had committed in ignorance. 8The Holy
Spirit was showing by this that the way into the
Most Holy Place had not yet been disclosed as
long as the first tabernacle was still standing.
9This is an illustration for the present time, indicating that the gifts and sacrifices being offered were not able to clear the conscience of
the worshiper. 10They are only a matter of food
and drink and various ceremonial washings—
external regulations applying until the time of
the new order.

The Blood of Christ

11When Christ came as high priest of the
good things that are already here,[b] he went
through the greater and more perfect tabernacle
that is not man-made, that is to say, not a part
of this creation. 12He did not enter by means of
the blood of goats and calves; but he entered
the Most Holy Place once for all by his own
blood, having obtained eternal redemption.
13The blood of goats and bulls and the ashes of
a heifer sprinkled on those who are ceremonially unclean sanctify them so that they are outwardly clean. 14How much more, then, will the
blood of Christ, who through the eternal Spirit
offered himself unblemished to God, cleanse
our consciences from acts that lead to death,[c]
so that we may serve the living God!
15For this reason Christ is the mediator of a
new covenant, that those who are called may
receive the promised eternal inheritance—now
that he has died as a ransom to set them free
from the sins committed under the first covenant.
16In the case of a will,[d] it is necessary to
prove the death of the one who made it, 17be-
cause a will is in force only when somebody has
died; it never takes effect while the one who
made it is living. 18This is why even the first
covenant was not put into effect without blood.
19When Moses had proclaimed every commandment of the law to all the people, he took
the blood of calves, together with water, scarlet
wool and branches of hyssop, and sprinkled the
scroll and all the people. 20He said, "This is the
blood of the covenant, which God has commanded you to keep."[e] 21In the same way, he
sprinkled with the blood both the tabernacle
and everything used in its ceremonies. 22In fact,
the law requires that nearly everything be
cleansed with blood, and without the shedding
of blood there is no forgiveness.
23It was necessary, then, for the copies of the
heavenly things to be purified with these sacrifices, but the heavenly things themselves with
better sacrifices than these. 24For Christ did not
enter a man-made sanctuary that was only a
copy of the true one; he entered heaven itself,
now to appear for us in God's presence. 25Nor
did he enter heaven to offer himself again and
again, the way the high priest enters the Most
Holy Place every year with blood that is not his
own. 26Then Christ would have had to suffer
many times since the creation of the world. But
now he has appeared once for all at the end of
the ages to do away with sin by the sacrifice of
himself. 27Just as man is destined to die once,
and after that to face judgment, 28so Christ was
sacrificed once to take away the sins of many
people; and he will appear a second time, not
to bear sin, but to bring salvation to those who
are waiting for him.

Christ's Sacrifice Once for All

10 The law is only a shadow of the good
things that are coming—not the realities
themselves. For this reason it can never, by the
same sacrifices repeated endlessly year after
year, make perfect those who draw near to worship. 2If it could, would they not have stopped
being offered? For the worshipers would have
been cleansed once for all, and would no longer
have felt guilty for their sins. 3But those sacrifices are an annual reminder of sins, 4because it
is impossible for the blood of bulls and goats to
take away sins.
5Therefore, when Christ came into the world,
he said:

"Sacrifice and offering you did not desire,

[a]5 Traditionally *the mercy seat* [b]11 Some early manuscripts *are to come* [c]14 Or *from useless rituals* [d]16 Same Greek word as *covenant*; also in verse 17 [e]20 Exodus 24:8

9:11–15 There was absolutely no comparison between the ongoing sacrifices of the earthly temple in Jerusalem and the sacrifice provided by Christ, our great high priest and mediator. Christ accomplished what the Old Testament sacrificial system never could—a once-for-all, completed redemption. Trusting in Christ's work is the only way to secure a clear conscience, complete forgiveness and eternal life. When we put our faith in Christ, we are free to joyfully know and serve God.

9:27–28 Hope for the future must be based on the reality of the past and present. Death and the coming judgment are the ultimate realities of this life. Even Jesus died! Yet Jesus was also resurrected and brought redemption and freedom from judgment for those who place their trust in him. This blend of reality and hope through faith can calm our fearful hearts. We can face any sin, any hurt—even death—knowing that Christ's sacrifice is completely sufficient to provide cleansing and new life.

10:3–10 As this section on the superiority of the new covenant draws to a close, the writer crowns his argument by asserting that the frustrating repetition of old-covenant sacrifices has now been replaced by Christ's offer of himself in accordance with the will of God (10:7, 9–10). When we reject God's offer of salvation and transformation in Jesus Christ, we reject the only means available for true spiritual renewal.

but a body you prepared for me;
6with burnt offerings and sin offerings
you were not pleased.
7Then I said, 'Here I am—it is written about
me in the scroll—
I have come to do your will, O God.'"[a]

8First he said, "Sacrifices and offerings, burnt
offerings and sin offerings you did not desire,
nor were you pleased with them" (although the
law required them to be made). 9Then he said,
"Here I am, I have come to do your will." He sets
aside the first to establish the second. 10And by
that will, we have been made holy through the
sacrifice of the body of Jesus Christ once for all.
11Day after day every priest stands and performs his religious duties; again and again he
offers the same sacrifices, which can never take
away sins. 12But when this priest had offered for
all time one sacrifice for sins, he sat down at the
right hand of God. 13Since that time he waits for
his enemies to be made his footstool, 14because
by one sacrifice he has made perfect forever
those who are being made holy.
15The Holy Spirit also testifies to us about
this. First he says:

16"This is the covenant I will make with
them
after that time, says the Lord.
I will put my laws in their hearts,
and I will write them on their minds."[b]

17Then he adds:
"Their sins and lawless acts
I will remember no more."[c]

18And where these have been forgiven, there is
no longer any sacrifice for sin.

A Call to Persevere

19Therefore, brothers, since we have confidence to enter the Most Holy Place by the blood
of Jesus, 20by a new and living way opened for
us through the curtain, that is, his body, 21and
since we have a great priest over the house of
God, 22let us draw near to God with a sincere
heart in full assurance of faith, having our
hearts sprinkled to cleanse us from a guilty conscience and having our bodies washed with
pure water. 23Let us hold unswervingly to the
hope we profess, for he who promised is faith-

[a]7 Psalm 40:6-8 (see Septuagint) [b]16 Jer. 31:33
[c]17 Jer. 31:34

10:19–25 This climactic instructional section of Hebrews begins with a summary of the argument for Christ's superiority, then shifts to the transformed attitudes that are necessary as a result. Since Christ is the final redemptive sacrifice and great high priest, we can enjoy the full privileges he has secured: personal access to God through Christ without an elaborate system, full assurance of our faith and salvation, hope for what the future holds and encouragement from other people of faith. Through Christ and a community of believers we receive everything we need for our spiritual growth.

Our Shield of Togetherness

Hebrews 10:23–34 Preserving our spiritual gains often involves spiritual warfare. God does not expect us to win our spiritual battles alone. God wants us to grow spiritually within a network of mutual commitment and accountability, helping each other to think and live in new ways. Alone we are vulnerable to temptation. Together we form a shield of protection for one another.

The apostle Paul wrote, "Take up the shield of faith, with which you can extinguish all the flaming arrows of the evil one" (Ephesians 6:16). A believer's faith means trust in Christ for salvation. Faith also means, in general terms, staying true to our convictions. Paul's analogy of the shield of faith paints a picture of the shields carried by Roman soldiers. These shields covered the entire body. To advance in battle, a group of soldiers would assemble together, making a wall of shields for protection as they moved forward.

In like manner, believers in the faith are told to stick together. The writer of Hebrews wrote, "Let us not give up meeting together, as some are in the habit of doing, but let us encourage one another—and all the more as you see the Day approaching" (10:25). We are to meet together with other believers so that we can stand firm in times of spiritual battle. Our mutual encouragement and shared faith in God and his Word will serve as a strong shield to preserve our spiritual gains.

Turn to 2 Peter 1.

ful. [24]And let us consider how we may spur one
another on toward love and good deeds. [25]Let
us not give up meeting together, as some are in
the habit of doing, but let us encourage one
another—and all the more as you see the Day
approaching.
[26]If we deliberately keep on sinning after we
have received the knowledge of the truth, no
sacrifice for sins is left, [27]but only a fearful expectation of judgment and of raging fire that
will consume the enemies of God. [28]Anyone
who rejected the law of Moses died without
mercy on the testimony of two or three witnesses. [29]How much more severely do you
think a man deserves to be punished who has
trampled the Son of God under foot, who has
treated as an unholy thing the blood of the
covenant that sanctified him, and who has insulted the Spirit of grace? [30]For we know him
who said, "It is mine to avenge; I will repay,"[a]
and again, "The Lord will judge his people."[b]
[31]It is a dreadful thing to fall into the hands of
the living God.
[32]Remember those earlier days after you had
received the light, when you stood your ground
in a great contest in the face of suffering.
[33]Sometimes you were publicly exposed to insult and persecution; at other times you stood
side by side with those who were so treated.
[34]You sympathized with those in prison and
joyfully accepted the confiscation of your property, because you knew that you yourselves had
better and lasting possessions.
[35]So do not throw away your confidence; it
will be richly rewarded. [36]You need to persevere
so that when you have done the will of God,
you will receive what he has promised. [37]For in
just a very little while,

> "He who is coming will come and will not
> delay.
> 38 But my righteous one[c] will live by faith.
> And if he shrinks back,
> I will not be pleased with him."[d]

[39]But we are not of those who shrink back and
are destroyed, but of those who believe and are
saved.

By Faith

11 Now faith is being sure of what we
hope for and certain of what we do not
see. [2]This is what the ancients were commended for.
[3]By faith we understand that the universe
was formed at God's command, so that what is
seen was not made out of what was visible.
[4]By faith Abel offered God a better sacrifice
than Cain did. By faith he was commended as
a righteous man, when God spoke well of his
offerings. And by faith he still speaks, even
though he is dead.
[5]By faith Enoch was taken from this life, so
that he did not experience death; he could not
be found, because God had taken him away.
For before he was taken, he was commended as
one who pleased God. [6]And without faith it is
impossible to please God, because anyone who
comes to him must believe that he exists and
that he rewards those who earnestly seek him.
[7]By faith Noah, when warned about things
not yet seen, in holy fear built an ark to save his
family. By his faith he condemned the world
and became heir of the righteousness that
comes by faith.
[8]By faith Abraham, when called to go to a
place he would later receive as his inheritance,
obeyed and went, even though he did not know
where he was going. [9]By faith he made his
home in the promised land like a stranger in a
foreign country; he lived in tents, as did Isaac
and Jacob, who were heirs with him of the same
promise. [10]For he was looking forward to the
city with foundations, whose architect and
builder is God.

a30 Deut. 32:35 *b30* Deut. 32:36; Psalm 135:14
c38 One early manuscript *But the righteous*
d38 Hab. 2:3,4

10:24–25 Sometimes we may pull away from healthy relationships and fall into unhealthy ones or negative situations that undermine our spiritual momentum. These verses remind us that encouraging relationships with other believers are crucial to our spiritual growth. No one can stand alone for long. Without the benefit of being held accountable by healthy relationships, we may veer off course spiritually.

10:26–39 This passage summarizes the only way to a wholehearted pursuit of emotional and spiritual healing. We can find release only by repenting of sinful patterns and receiving forgiveness. Then we must take positive steps by strengthening our right behavior and attitudes, particularly our faith in God.

11:1–3, 39–40 Faith involves trust that since God has worked in the past he is still working in the unseen spiritual realm. Those who want a vibrant spiritual life have always had to live by such faith (11:2). Seeking approval from other people is a constant battle for some of us. We need to remember that we cannot please everyone. We will make progress only when we stop trying to please others and put our trust in God, obediently following his will and striving to please him.

11:5–7 Enoch and Elijah were unique in that they did not die (11:5; see Genesis 5:21–24; 2 Kings 2:1–12). Noah also played a unique role with the ark, the flood and a new beginning (see Genesis 6—9). These characters illustrate the utter necessity of faith and earnest perseverance (11:6). As we trust and depend on God for each aspect of our lives, we can be confident that such trust pleases God and will be rewarded with his powerful help.

11:8–19 In the Hebrews 11 "Hall of Faith," a great number of the verses refer to Abraham and Sarah because they were the parents of the Jewish nation. Abraham's life repeatedly demonstrated faith as he faced circumstances that seemed to undermine the fulfillment of God's promises. Sometimes it seems that our struggles drag on forever too. At such times we can remind ourselves that even the Biblical characters who are most famous for their faith often had to persevere without seeing visible results. Abraham had to wait most of a lifetime to see God's promises partially fulfilled. God will come through for us in his timing too. We only need to wait in faith.

[11]By faith Abraham, even though he was past
age—and Sarah herself was barren—was enabled
to become a father because he[a] considered
him faithful who had made the promise. [12]And
so from this one man, and he as good as dead,
came descendants as numerous as the stars in
the sky and as countless as the sand on the
seashore.

[13]All these people were still living by faith
when they died. They did not receive the things
promised; they only saw them and welcomed
them from a distance. And they admitted that
they were aliens and strangers on earth. [14]People
who say such things show that they are
looking for a country of their own. [15]If they had
been thinking of the country they had left, they
would have had opportunity to return. [16]Instead,
they were longing for a better country—a
heavenly one. Therefore God is not ashamed to
be called their God, for he has prepared a city
for them.

[17]By faith Abraham, when God tested him,
offered Isaac as a sacrifice. He who had received
the promises was about to sacrifice his one and
only son, [18]even though God had said to him,
"It is through Isaac that your offspring[b] will
be reckoned."[c] [19]Abraham reasoned that God
could raise the dead, and figuratively speaking,
he did receive Isaac back from death.

[20]By faith Isaac blessed Jacob and Esau in
regard to their future.

[21]By faith Jacob, when he was dying, blessed
each of Joseph's sons, and worshiped as he
leaned on the top of his staff.

[22]By faith Joseph, when his end was near,
spoke about the exodus of the Israelites from
Egypt and gave instructions about his bones.

[23]By faith Moses' parents hid him for three
months after he was born, because they saw he
was no ordinary child, and they were not afraid
of the king's edict.

[24]By faith Moses, when he had grown up,
refused to be known as the son of Pharaoh's
daughter. [25]He chose to be mistreated along
with the people of God rather than to enjoy the
pleasures of sin for a short time. [26]He regarded
disgrace for the sake of Christ as of greater value
than the treasures of Egypt, because he was
looking ahead to his reward. [27]By faith he left
Egypt, not fearing the king's anger; he persevered
because he saw him who is invisible. [28]By
faith he kept the Passover and the sprinkling of
blood, so that the destroyer of the firstborn
would not touch the firstborn of Israel.

[a]*11* Or *By faith even Sarah, who was past age, was enabled to bear children because she* [b]*18* Greek *seed*
[c]*18* Gen. 21:12

11:20–31 Every key event between the life of Abraham and Israel's entrance into the promised land involved someone with exemplary faith (see 11:1, 6). God accomplishes his purposes, great and small, through the faith of his people. As we trust him with every aspect of our lives, he will accomplish his will for us. If we trust in God, nothing is impossible!

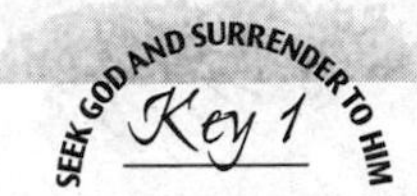

A God Worthy of Faith

Hebrews 11:1–10 If we desire spiritual renewal, we must have faith that our spiritual pursuit will be rewarded. But what is faith? The Bible says, "Faith is being sure of what we hope for and certain of what we do not see" (11:1). Faith is a certainty that what we desire will come about. The Bible also tells us that our faith is grounded in our very understanding of God: "Without faith it is impossible to please God, because anyone who comes to him must believe that he exists and that he rewards those who earnestly seek him" (11:6). If we truly believe that our search will lead somewhere—that God will indeed grant us spiritual renewal—then we will be willing to actually seek God.

If our faith has not matured to that point yet, we can start by asking God for the faith we need. This may seem like putting the cart before the horse, but God is the only one who can give us faith. In a sense, we must come to him with empty hands and ask him to fill us with faith. Learning about God through the Bible and seeing his provision for us reinforces the faith God has given us. With this reinforced faith we are renewed in our spiritual walk.

Turn to James 4.

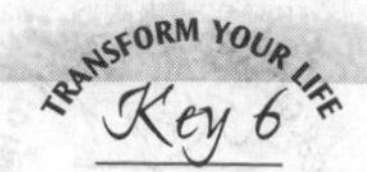

Faith to Stay on Course

Hebrews 12:1–4 God wants to transform our lives and redirect our course to follow his paths. The author of Hebrews understood this and likened the Christian life to a race. Our faith in Christ motivates us to run the race. And in spite of the number of times we stumble along the way, God's power will ultimately gives us the strength to finish the race of faith.

Hebrews 11 has been called the "Hall of Faith." This chapter contains a long list of people who accomplished great things for God because of their faith. Chapter 12 then sums up the point of this list by reflecting "since we are surrounded by such a great cloud of witnesses, let us throw off everything that hinders and the sin that so easily entangles, and let us run with perseverance the race marked out for us" (12:1). This illustration refers to the races of ancient Greece. Athletes would strip off their tunics and robes so that they could run without difficulty. If someone tried to run in his robes, that person would get tangled up, losing both the race and the prize.

It is God's will for us to finish the race of life. The entangling robes of our recurrent sins need to be laid aside. Running to win the race of faith will call for exertion on our part. Yet we are told to pace ourselves and run with endurance, remembering that "great cloud of witnesses" who have run the same race, finished the same course—despite their many mistakes—and are cheering us on. We can finish our race of faith if we continually look to God to help us. And we will be able to give this same encouragement and help to others who need it too.

Turn to 1 Peter 4.

29By faith the people passed through the Red
Sea[a] as on dry land; but when the Egyptians
tried to do so, they were drowned.
30By faith the walls of Jericho fell, after the
people had marched around them for seven
days.
31By faith the prostitute Rahab, because she
welcomed the spies, was not killed with those
who were disobedient.[b]
32And what more shall I say? I do not have
time to tell about Gideon, Barak, Samson, Jephthah, David, Samuel and the prophets, 33who
through faith conquered kingdoms, administered justice, and gained what was promised;
who shut the mouths of lions, 34quenched the
fury of the flames, and escaped the edge of the
sword; whose weakness was turned to strength;
and who became powerful in battle and routed
foreign armies. 35Women received back their
dead, raised to life again. Others were tortured
and refused to be released, so that they might
gain a better resurrection. 36Some faced jeers
and flogging, while still others were chained
and put in prison. 37They were stoned[c]; they
were sawed in two; they were put to death by
the sword. They went about in sheepskins and
goatskins, destitute, persecuted and mistreated— 38the world was not worthy of them. They
wandered in deserts and mountains, and in
caves and holes in the ground.
39These were all commended for their faith,
yet none of them received what had been promised. 40God had planned something better for
us so that only together with us would they be
made perfect.

God Disciplines His Sons

12 Therefore, since we are surrounded by such a great cloud of witnesses, let us throw off everything that hinders and the sin that so easily entangles, and let us run with perseverance the race marked out for us.
2Let us fix our eyes on Jesus, the author and perfecter of our faith, who for the joy set before him en-

[a]29 That is, Sea of Reeds [b]31 Or *unbelieving*
[c]37 Some early manuscripts *stoned; they were put to the test;*

11:32–38 Despite the brevity of this overview of people from Old Testament history who demonstrated powerful faith, it is clear that even in Old Testament times faith was not just a strict obedience to the law. Faith was a heartfelt trust in a personal God. The writer of Hebrews showed his readers that many before them had faced difficult times and had persevered by faith (11:33–38; see 10:32–36). When we feel our faith faltering, we must remember others who have gone before us. We should turn to the Bible and other Christians for real-life testimonies of how God works through faith.

12:1–3 Many have won the race of faith, including some very unlikely candidates. The author of Hebrews advises readers to forcefully cut loose from sin and focus on Christ every step of the way, knowing that Jesus has been where we are and has emerged victorious (see 4:14–15). Such focused perseverance will allow us to finish the race God has given us to run and bring him glory as well.

dured the cross, scorning its shame, and sat down at the right hand of the throne of God. 3Consider him who endured such opposition from sinful men, so that you will not grow weary and lose heart.

4In your struggle against sin, you have not yet resisted to the point of shedding your blood. 5And you have forgotten that word of encouragement that addresses you as sons:

"My son, do not make light of the Lord's
discipline,
and do not lose heart when he rebukes
you,
6because the Lord disciplines those he loves,
and he punishes everyone he accepts as a
son."[a]

7Endure hardship as discipline; God is treating you as sons. For what son is not disciplined by his father? 8If you are not disciplined (and everyone undergoes discipline), then you are illegitimate children and not true sons. 9Moreover, we have all had human fathers who disciplined us and we respected them for it. How much more should we submit to the Father of our spirits and live! 10Our fathers disciplined us for a little while as they thought best; but God disciplines us for our good, that we may share in his holiness. 11No discipline seems pleasant at the time, but painful. Later on, however, it produces a harvest of righteousness and peace for those who have been trained by it.

12Therefore, strengthen your feeble arms and weak knees. 13"Make level paths for your feet,"[b] so that the lame may not be disabled, but rather healed.

Warning Against Refusing God

14Make every effort to live in peace with all men and to be holy; without holiness no one will see the Lord. 15See to it that no one misses the grace of God and that no bitter root grows up to cause trouble and defile many. 16See that no one is sexually immoral, or is godless like Esau, who for a single meal sold his inheritance rights as the oldest son. 17Afterward, as you know, when he wanted to inherit this blessing, he was rejected. He could bring about no change of mind, though he sought the blessing with tears.

18You have not come to a mountain that can be touched and that is burning with fire; to darkness, gloom and storm; 19to a trumpet blast or to such a voice speaking words that those who heard it begged that no further word be spoken to them, 20because they could not bear what was commanded: "If even an animal touches the mountain, it must be stoned."[c] 21The sight was so terrifying that Moses said, "I am trembling with fear."[d]

22But you have come to Mount Zion, to the heavenly Jerusalem, the city of the living God. You have come to thousands upon thousands of angels in joyful assembly, 23to the church of the firstborn, whose names are written in heaven. You have come to God, the judge of all men, to the spirits of righteous men made perfect, 24to Jesus the mediator of a new covenant, and to the sprinkled blood that speaks a better word than the blood of Abel.

25See to it that you do not refuse him who speaks. If they did not escape when they refused him who warned them on earth, how much less will we, if we turn away from him who warns us from heaven? 26At that time his voice shook the earth, but now he has promised, "Once more I will shake not only the earth but also the heavens."[e] 27The words "once more" indicate the removing of what can be shaken—that is, created things—so that what cannot be shaken may remain.

28Therefore, since we are receiving a kingdom that cannot be shaken, let us be thankful, and so worship God acceptably with reverence and awe, 29for our "God is a consuming fire."[f]

[a]6 Prov. 3:11,12 [b]13 Prov. 4:26
[c]20 Exodus 19:12,13 [d]21 Deut. 9:19
[e]26 Haggai 2:6 [f]29 Deut. 4:24

12:5–10 True discipline is a form of loving correction, not hateful destruction. Many of us have suffered painful consequences for our sins. We may have become angry and wondered why God allowed us to suffer so deeply. God does not allow us to suffer because he wants revenge or because he wants to destroy us. He allows us to suffer because he loves us. Sometimes painful discipline is the only way to break through our spiritual blindness and get us back on track. As we look back over our lives, we can see that our most painful days led us to seek God and surrender to him. By allowing us to suffer, God led us into a vital relationship with himself.

12:14–29 This is the last of the warning passages spaced purposefully throughout Hebrews (see 2:1–4; 3:7—4:13; 5:11—6:12; 10:26–39). This passage served as the climactic confrontation between the author and his readers over their apparent shift from Christ back to Judaism and the law. After exhorting his readers not to miss God's grace, the writer shifted to a discussion about the consequences of rejecting faith in Christ and the redemption he offers. If we reject Christ, we also reject the only means for eternal salvation.

12:15 We need to recognize our hurts and deal with them as they occur. We must release our hurts to God. We may even need to confront those who have hurt or angered us. If we do not, we can grow angry, resentful, vengeful or bitter. Sometimes we do not recognize our own bitterness as it begins to grow. Sometimes we need others to point it out to us. Allowing ourselves to express our bitterness out loud, recognize our feelings and release them to God will begin the process of renewal. But we also need to forgive and release the injustices and hurts so that we can experience God's overwhelming forgiveness (see Matthew 18:21–35). When we hang on to our bitterness, we not only stall our own healing but also hurt others along the way.

12:22–24 A wonderful reward awaits those whose faith endures (see 11:1, 6). The clustered references to Mount Zion, Jerusalem, angels, the firstborn children, God, mediation and blood were intended to show that the new covenant and Christ offer the very things that the readers mistakenly sought by returning to Judaism. Spiritual renewal and its rewards are available only through faith in Jesus Christ.

Concluding Exhortations

13 Keep on loving each other as brothers.
2Do not forget to entertain strangers,
for by so doing some people have entertained
angels without knowing it. 3Remember those in
prison as if you were their fellow prisoners, and
those who are mistreated as if you yourselves
were suffering.
4Marriage should be honored by all, and the
marriage bed kept pure, for God will judge the
adulterer and all the sexually immoral. 5Keep
your lives free from the love of money and be
content with what you have, because God has
said,

"Never will I leave you;
never will I forsake you."[a]

6So we say with confidence,

"The Lord is my helper; I will not be
afraid.
What can man do to me?"[b]

7Remember your leaders, who spoke the
word of God to you. Consider the outcome of
their way of life and imitate their faith. 8Jesus
Christ is the same yesterday and today and forever.
9Do not be carried away by all kinds of
strange teachings. It is good for our hearts to be
strengthened by grace, not by ceremonial foods,
which are of no value to those who eat them.
10We have an altar from which those who minister at the tabernacle have no right to eat.
11The high priest carries the blood of animals
into the Most Holy Place as a sin offering, but
the bodies are burned outside the camp. 12And
so Jesus also suffered outside the city gate to
make the people holy through his own blood.
13Let us, then, go to him outside the camp, bearing the disgrace he bore. 14For here we do not
have an enduring city, but we are looking for
the city that is to come.
15Through Jesus, therefore, let us continually
offer to God a sacrifice of praise—the fruit of lips
that confess his name. 16And do not forget to do
good and to share with others, for with such
sacrifices God is pleased.
17Obey your leaders and submit to their authority. They keep watch over you as men who
must give an account. Obey them so that their
work will be a joy, not a burden, for that would
be of no advantage to you.
18Pray for us. We are sure that we have a clear
conscience and desire to live honorably in every
way. 19I particularly urge you to pray so that I
may be restored to you soon.
20May the God of peace, who through the
blood of the eternal covenant brought back
from the dead our Lord Jesus, that great Shepherd of the sheep, 21equip you with everything
good for doing his will, and may he work in us
what is pleasing to him, through Jesus Christ, to
whom be glory for ever and ever. Amen.

22Brothers, I urge you to bear with my word
of exhortation, for I have written you only a
short letter.
23I want you to know that our brother Timothy has been released. If he arrives soon, I will
come with him to see you.
24Greet all your leaders and all God's people.
Those from Italy send you their greetings.
25Grace be with you all.

[a]5 Deut. 31:6 [b]6 Psalm 118:6,7

13:1–6 This section lists a series of practical commands for faithfulness—in service to others, in the marriage relationship and in attitudes toward possessions. This faithfulness is based on God's empowerment and protection. Many professing believers waver in these areas of faithfulness today. If we are uncertain which behaviors and attitudes are acceptable, God's clear standards can be a great help. As we practice right living, God's presence and power are available to help us live in accordance with his Word.

13:7, 17 At times we may have difficulty dealing with authority figures. Apparently the readers of Hebrews, in turning back to their former Judaic lifestyle, ignored the proper authorities in their Jewish-Christian setting. The writer admonished his readers to imitate the faith and lifestyle of their former leaders and cooperate with their present leaders for the good of all involved. We must also remember the importance of other people, especially those who model spiritual growth for us.

13:8, 15–16 Though our human leaders fail in many ways, Jesus Christ is totally consistent and trustworthy. He will always be there for us, no matter what. Christ also deserves to receive the new covenant equivalent of old covenant sacrifices: praise for who he is and what he has done, good works of service and sharing with others in need (see 13:2–3). Telling others what God has done in our lives and reaching out to people in need are essential activities to our ongoing spiritual growth.

13:20–25 The writer concluded his letter to the Hebrews with a double benediction. The first benediction was a summary prayer, requesting the power of Christ's resurrection to enable the readers to do God's will and to please him. Unlike some human fathers, God the Father readily helps his children. The final concept of the letter was grace. These last lines speak volumes to those of us seeking spiritual renewal: God will give us what we need to overcome, and he will relate to us according to the principles of grace and mercy.

The Big Picture

Often we label as hypocrites those who live lives that are overtly inconsistent with their words. Yet in one way or another we are all hypocrites, whether in the church community or in the community at large. We have all said we believe in something, only to prove by our actions that we really don't!

James—the half brother of Jesus and one of the leaders of the Jerusalem church—wrote bluntly about this kind of hypocrisy. He recognized that as humans we often hear God's Word without putting it into practice. James's goal was simple: to get his audience, and all believers, to recognize that their confession of faith and conduct did not agree and to motivate them to start acting on what they claimed they believed.

James challenged his readers to be full of wisdom, faith, forgiveness, self-control and generosity to others. He encouraged them to simply do what they knew they needed to do. Their spiritual progress would only start if they admitted their responsibility to obey God. Only then could James's readers conquer hypocrisy and forge ahead with the activities and attitudes that reflected God's will for them.

A spiritual growth plan may sound good in principle, but we may never take those steps necessary for progress. James reminds us that our words are not enough. We need to do more than just say we believe God can help us. We need to show our faith and commitment by taking real steps of obedience toward spiritual growth, or we will never move forward toward lives that agree with God's will for us.

Spiritual Renewal Themes

THE IMPORTANCE OF ACTION

If faith can be alive, it can also be dead. Dead faith is a belief that does not prove itself in action. Dead faith claims to be something when it is nothing. Seeking God and surrendering to him always involve action. If we simply say that we have surrendered our lives to God but do not confess our sins, accept responsibility for our lives, repent and make restitution to those we have hurt and follow God's will, then we are only fooling ourselves. Effective spiritual growth involves following through on our professions of faith. We must also preserve whatever spiritual gains we do make by remaining in relationships with

Essential Facts

PURPOSE:
To show God's people how to live.

AUTHOR:
James, the half brother of Jesus.

AUDIENCE:
Primarily the Jewish believers living in Gentile communities outside of Palestine.

DATE WRITTEN:
This short letter was probably written between A.D. 44 and 49, before the Jerusalem council held in A.D. 50 (see Acts 15:1–35).

SETTING:
James wrote to encourage the persecuted believers who were once a part of the church in Jerusalem to live out their faith in everyday life.

KEY VERSE:
"Therefore confess your sins to each other and pray for each other so that you may be healed. The prayer of a righteous man is powerful and effective" (5:16).

KEY PEOPLE AND RELATIONSHIPS:
James with his audience.

others who are also subjects of God's kingdom and who hold us accountable to live according to his plan.

GAINING STRENGTH FROM DIFFICULT TRIALS

As we patiently face life's problems we will find our character strengthened. We can welcome trials and problems as opportunities to pray for wisdom, to ask God to give us patience and to learn to depend on God. When we turn to God in times of trial, he will teach us the lessons necessary for us to persevere and grow.

TRUE SPIRITUAL RENEWAL LEADS TO WISE SPEECH

One of the hardest things for us to control is our tongue—the words we say (1:26). James gives us very practical advice about handling our tongues. We should ask God for wisdom, be slow to speak in anger and listen more than we talk. Since our speech is a reflection of what is going on inside us, we can check our speech for clues to our strengths and weaknesses. As we reflect honestly on our lives and confess our wrongs to God, he will begin to change us on the inside. These inner changes will be reflected in our words.

1 James, a servant of God and of the Lord Jesus Christ,

To the twelve tribes scattered among the nations:

Greetings.

Trials and Temptations

2Consider it pure joy, my brothers, whenever you face trials of many kinds, 3because you know that the testing of your faith develops perseverance. 4Perseverance must finish its work so that you may be mature and complete, not lacking anything. 5If any of you lacks wisdom, he should ask God, who gives generously to all without finding fault, and it will be given to him. 6But when he asks, he must believe and not doubt, because he who doubts is like a wave of the sea, blown and tossed by the wind. 7That man should not think he will receive anything from the Lord; 8he is a double-minded man, unstable in all he does.

9The brother in humble circumstances ought to take pride in his high position. 10But the one who is rich should take pride in his low position, because he will pass away like a wild flower. 11For the sun rises with scorching heat and withers the plant; its blossom falls and its beauty is destroyed. In the same way, the rich man will fade away even while he goes about his business.

12Blessed is the man who perseveres under trial, because when he has stood the test, he will receive the crown of life that God has promised to those who love him.

13When tempted, no one should say, "God is tempting me." For God cannot be tempted by evil, nor does he tempt anyone; 14but each one is tempted when, by his own evil desire, he is dragged away and enticed. 15Then, after desire has conceived, it gives birth to sin; and sin, when it is full-grown, gives birth to death.

16Don't be deceived, my dear brothers. 17Every good and perfect gift is from above, coming down from the Father of the heavenly lights, who does not change like shifting shadows. 18He chose to give us birth through the word of truth, that we might be a kind of firstfruits of all he created.

Listening and Doing

19My dear brothers, take note of this: Everyone should be quick to listen, slow to speak and slow to become angry, 20for man's anger does not bring about the righteous life that God desires. 21Therefore, get rid of all moral filth and the evil that is so prevalent and humbly accept the word planted in you, which can save you.

22Do not merely listen to the word, and so deceive yourselves. Do what it says. 23Anyone who listens to the word but does not do what it says is like a man who looks at his face in a mirror 24and, after looking at himself, goes away and immediately forgets what he looks like. 25But the man who looks intently into the perfect law that gives freedom, and continues to do this, not forgetting what he has heard, but doing it—he will be blessed in what he does.

26If anyone considers himself religious and yet does not keep a tight rein on his tongue, he deceives himself and his religion is worthless. 27Religion that God our Father accepts as pure and faultless is this: to look after orphans and widows in their distress and to keep oneself from being polluted by the world.

Favoritism Forbidden

2 My brothers, as believers in our glorious Lord Jesus Christ, don't show favoritism.

1:2–4 Difficulties and temptations are facts of life for everyone. Yet our attitudes when we face such difficulties can make all the difference to our lives. James urges us to be joyful as we face difficulties and temptations. Joy is hardly our natural reaction to painful situations. Viewing our trials as building blocks to God's work in our lives, however, may help us change our negative attitudes toward tough times. We can maintain joy during these trials because through them we learn patience, an essential ingredient for spiritual growth.

1:5 All of us have made wrong decisions that have led to frustration and depression, ultimately affecting our relationships with God and others. James reminds us that when we ask God for wisdom, he is more than willing to give it. Since God is the source of all wisdom, turning to him for guidance can drastically reduce our unwise decisions. We find his guidance by studying his Word, being taught by those who are gifted within the body of Christ and pursuing regular times of prayer.

1:6–8 All truly wise decisions are rooted in a vital faith in God. Faith "is being sure of what we hope for and certain of what we do not see" (Hebrews 11:1). God wants us to make progress in spiritual growth. When we ask God to help us make a wise decision, we can make the request without a trace of doubt, fully believing that whatever we ask for in faith will be granted. God will supply the wisdom we need to make the right decisions.

1:19–20 The issue of who or what controls our lives is vital to our spiritual growth. For some of us, the emotion of anger overpowers us and controls us. James advises us to listen, to have self-control and to be patient, not letting anger control our actions in any situation. Everyone feels anger; God wants us to release our anger in appropriate ways. Even when we feel out of control, he can help us to maintain our composure. He can give us the strength and wisdom to think and listen before we speak or act.

1:22–25 As we honestly evaluate our lives, we need to have a godly standard, something we can measure our attitudes or actions against. Though we may not have had good role models to follow, James reminds us that God's Word can function like a mirror in our lives. God's Word presents a clear picture of what God wants us to be like. When we read God's Word we can easily see where we don't measure up to God's intended plan. But James also warns us not to walk away from God's Word and forget what we saw there. God doesn't want us just to see the truth; he wants us to change our lives in obedience to his commands.

2:1–9 Rejection is always a painful experience. All of us want to be accepted. James reminds us that Jesus wants the Christian community to graciously accept and love all people—whether they are wealthy and influential or poor and weak. Christian communities need to welcome all

SEE THE TRUTH

Key 2

Looking in the Mirror

James 1:21–25 How many times do we look into a mirror each day? Some of us check our appearance quite frequently. If we notice, for example, that we have somehow smeared something on ourselves, we will immediately wipe ourselves off and clear up the problem. In the same way, we need to routinely look at ourselves in a spiritual mirror, reflecting honestly on our spiritual condition as compared to God's Word. Then we need to make any necessary changes as God directs us to.

James says that God's Word is like a spiritual mirror. He writes,

> Anyone who listens to the word but does not do what it says is like a man who looks at his face in a mirror and, after looking at himself, goes away and immediately forgets what he looks like. But the man who looks intently into the perfect law that gives freedom, and continues to do this, not forgetting what he has heard, but doing it—he will be blessed in what he does (1:23–25).

We need to regularly examine our lives by looking into God's Word. If we see that we have fallen short of something God requires, we need to take responsibility for it and take immediate action to correct it. Recognizing the truth about our behavior is necessary for our spiritual renewal and transformation.

Turn to Revelation 3.

2Suppose a man comes into your meeting wearing a gold ring and fine clothes, and a poor man
in shabby clothes also comes in. 3If you show
special attention to the man wearing fine
clothes and say, "Here's a good seat for you," but
say to the poor man, "You stand there" or "Sit
on the floor by my feet," 4have you not discriminated among yourselves and become judges
with evil thoughts?
5Listen, my dear brothers: Has not God chosen those who are poor in the eyes of the world
to be rich in faith and to inherit the kingdom he
promised those who love him? 6But you have
insulted the poor. Is it not the rich who are
exploiting you? Are they not the ones who are
dragging you into court? 7Are they not the ones
who are slandering the noble name of him to
whom you belong?
8If you really keep the royal law found in
Scripture, "Love your neighbor as yourself,"[a]
you are doing right. 9But if you show favoritism,
you sin and are convicted by the law as lawbreakers. 10For whoever keeps the whole law
and yet stumbles at just one point is guilty of
breaking all of it. 11For he who said, "Do not
commit adultery,"[b] also said, "Do not murder."[c] If you do not commit adultery but do
commit murder, you have become a lawbreaker.
12Speak and act as those who are going to be
judged by the law that gives freedom, 13because
judgment without mercy will be shown to anyone who has not been merciful. Mercy triumphs over judgment!

Faith and Deeds

14What good is it, my brothers, if a man
claims to have faith but has no deeds? Can such
faith save him? 15Suppose a brother or sister is
without clothes and daily food. 16If one of you
says to him, "Go, I wish you well; keep warm
and well fed," but does nothing about his physical needs, what good is it? 17In the same way,
faith by itself, if it is not accompanied by action,
is dead.
18But someone will say, "You have faith; I
have deeds."
Show me your faith without deeds, and I will
show you my faith by what I do. 19You believe

[a]8 Lev. 19:18 [b]11 Exodus 20:14; Deut. 5:18
[c]11 Exodus 20:13; Deut. 5:17

who seek God. The essential truth here is that Jesus urges us to treat others just as we want them to treat us (see Matthew 7:12).

2:14–26 Faith must be accompanied by action. Some of us may find it easy to seek God's help, but when called to obey what he has said to do, we have refused. We all have made commitments that we failed to back up with our actions. James left us this powerful reminder: "Faith by itself, if it is not accompanied by action, is dead" (2:17). If we believe God can help us but refuse to obey his will, we prove that our faith is dead. True faith in God expresses itself in committed action; our actions need to back up our words.

that there is one God. Good! Even the demons believe that—and shudder.

20You foolish man, do you want evidence that faith without deeds is useless[a]? 21Was not our ancestor Abraham considered righteous for what he did when he offered his son Isaac on the altar? 22You see that his faith and his actions were working together, and his faith was made complete by what he did. 23And the scripture was fulfilled that says, "Abraham believed God, and it was credited to him as righteousness,"[b] and he was called God's friend. 24You see that a person is justified by what he does and not by faith alone.

25In the same way, was not even Rahab the prostitute considered righteous for what she did when she gave lodging to the spies and sent them off in a different direction? 26As the body without the spirit is dead, so faith without deeds is dead.

Taming the Tongue

3 Not many of you should presume to be teachers, my brothers, because you know that we who teach will be judged more strictly. 2We all stumble in many ways. If anyone is never at fault in what he says, he is a perfect man, able to keep his whole body in check.

3When we put bits into the mouths of horses to make them obey us, we can turn the whole animal. 4Or take ships as an example. Although they are so large and are driven by strong winds, they are steered by a very small rudder wherever the pilot wants to go. 5Likewise the tongue is a small part of the body, but it makes great boasts. Consider what a great forest is set on fire by a small spark. 6The tongue also is a fire, a world of evil among the parts of the body. It corrupts the whole person, sets the whole course of his life on fire, and is itself set on fire by hell.

7All kinds of animals, birds, reptiles and creatures of the sea are being tamed and have been tamed by man, 8but no man can tame the tongue. It is a restless evil, full of deadly poison.

9With the tongue we praise our Lord and Father, and with it we curse men, who have been made in God's likeness. 10Out of the same mouth come praise and cursing. My brothers, this should not be. 11Can both fresh water and salt[c] water flow from the same spring? 12My brothers, can a fig tree bear olives, or a grapevine bear figs? Neither can a salt spring produce fresh water.

Two Kinds of Wisdom

13Who is wise and understanding among you? Let him show it by his good life, by deeds done in the humility that comes from wisdom. 14But if you harbor bitter envy and selfish ambition in your hearts, do not boast about it or deny the truth. 15Such "wisdom" does not come down from heaven but is earthly, unspiritual, of the devil. 16For where you have envy and selfish ambition, there you find disorder and every evil practice.

17But the wisdom that comes from heaven is first of all pure; then peace-loving, considerate, submissive, full of mercy and good fruit, impartial and sincere. 18Peacemakers who sow in peace raise a harvest of righteousness.

Submit Yourselves to God

4 What causes fights and quarrels among you? Don't they come from your desires that battle within you? 2You want something but don't get it. You kill and covet, but you cannot have what you want. You quarrel and fight. You do not have, because you do not ask God. 3When you ask, you do not receive, because you ask with wrong motives, that you may spend what you get on your pleasures.

4You adulterous people, don't you know that friendship with the world is hatred toward God? Anyone who chooses to be a friend of the world becomes an enemy of God. 5Or do you think Scripture says without reason that the spirit he caused to live in us envies intensely?[d] 6But he gives us more grace. That is why Scripture says:

[a]20 Some early manuscripts *dead* [b]23 Gen. 15:6
[c]11 Greek *bitter* (see also verse 14) [d]5 Or *that God jealously longs for the spirit that he made to live in us;* or *that the Spirit he caused to live in us longs jealously*

3:1–2 We have all offended others either by our words or actions. When we have wrongfully offended someone, we need to ask forgiveness and make restitution for the wrongs we have committed. Sometimes a quiet change of behavior can be the most effective way to make restitution for our previous failures. By treating others with respect, we can slowly rebuild the trust we have destroyed and give back some of what we have taken. As we follow God's plan and obey his Word, we will avoid offending others but rather encourage them with our words and deeds.

3:3–12 The tongue is a difficult thing to control, but the tongue is extremely important. Like rudders that steer ships or bits that direct horses, our tongues do much to control and shape our lives. Our speech may also be instrumental in destroying our relationships, causing a painful downward spiral in our lives. We need to yield our tongues to God's control. When we alone are unable to control our destructive words, God can tame our tongues. As he transforms us from the inside out, the words we speak will soon begin to reflect the changes in our hearts. God will ultimately be able to use our words to heal our relationships and encourage others.

4:1–4 A right relationship with God is essential to spiritual growth. We should not ask for God's blessings just to satisfy our cravings for personal comfort. Seeking our own selfish pleasure allies us with God's enemies. God wants to give us an abundant life so we can pass it on to others. He blesses us so we can live according to his plan. We can experience the freedom God offers by drawing close to him and asking for his guidance and help.

4:6–10 Most of us have a hard time modeling the attitudes of submission and humility. Yet these attitudes are essential to spiritual growth because they illustrate our willingness to be guided by God. Satan's pride—and our adoption of it—opposes God's plan for right living. And

Tongue-tied

James 3:1 – 12 The discipline of silence applies not only to our relationship with God but also to our interaction with others. Paul asserted that the love of money was at the root of all evil. But James was convinced that the tongue is every bit as lethal as the love of money. When we think about the damage caused by our careless words, sarcasm, hurtful comments and bitter arguments, we will heartily agree with James. While the schoolyard quip "sticks and stones may break my bones but names will never hurt me" is often recited as a quick retort against name-callers, the reality of the injury inflicted by harsh words cannot be avoided. Bones heal, but wounded spirits can feel the pain for years.

Paul exhorted his readers, "Do not let any unwholesome talk come out of your mouths, but only what is helpful for building others up according to their needs, that it may benefit those who listen" (Ephesians 4:29). In light of this command and because of the immense power of words both to hurt and heal, we ought to guard our tongues carefully. From refusing to answer back when baited into an argument, to resisting the temptation to spread gossip, to foregoing a sarcastic remark that would have resulted in a laugh at someone else's expense, we can practice the discipline of silence in our relationships and conversations. This discipline is not intended to silence our conversation, but rather to help us fulfill Paul's exhortation to encourage each other with our words.

Putting It Into Practice

Reflect for a moment upon your most recent conversations. Was your tongue under the Holy Spirit's control? How might silence have been an asset? Even a few moments of silence can prevent us from saying something we might regret later. Use your next conversation as an opportunity to practice the discipline of silence through verbal self-control.

For more on silence, turn to Job 42.

"God opposes the proud
but gives grace to the humble."[a]

7Submit yourselves, then, to God. Resist the
devil, and he will flee from you. 8Come near to
God and he will come near to you. Wash your
hands, you sinners, and purify your hearts, you
double-minded. 9Grieve, mourn and wail.
Change your laughter to mourning and your
joy to gloom. 10Humble yourselves before the
Lord, and he will lift you up.

11Brothers, do not slander one another. Anyone who speaks against his brother or judges
him speaks against the law and judges it. When
you judge the law, you are not keeping it, but
sitting in judgment on it. 12There is only one
Lawgiver and Judge, the one who is able to save
and destroy. But you—who are you to judge
your neighbor?

Boasting About Tomorrow

13Now listen, you who say, "Today or tomorrow we will go to this or that city, spend a
year there, carry on business and make money."
14Why, you do not even know what will happen
tomorrow. What is your life? You are a mist that
appears for a little while and then vanishes.
15Instead, you ought to say, "If it is the Lord's
will, we will live and do this or that." 16As it is,
you boast and brag. All such boasting is evil.
17Anyone, then, who knows the good he ought
to do and doesn't do it, sins.

Warning to Rich Oppressors

5 Now listen, you rich people, weep and wail
because of the misery that is coming upon
you. 2Your wealth has rotted, and moths have
eaten your clothes. 3Your gold and silver are
corroded. Their corrosion will testify against
you and eat your flesh like fire. You have hoarded wealth in the last days. 4Look! The wages you

[a]6 Prov. 3:34

the way of pride and selfishness leads only to confusion and strife. True contentment comes only when we submit our lives to God and follow his plan. As we admit our failures and humbly seek to do God's will, we will find ourselves drawing close to God. As we draw close to God, he will renew our spiritual lives.

4:11–12 Many Christian communities are rendered ineffective by an attitude of self-righteous criticism. Believers become critical of those who don't measure up to their ideals of perfection. Some of us may have experienced this kind of destructive criticism firsthand. Some of us are also guilty of criticizing others. We need to behave with healthy humility. No one is perfect except God; only he is able to judge others (see Romans 14:10–12). We need to focus on our own faults, including our tendency to criticize others, and repent.

5:1–5 A selfish lifestyle inevitably leads to painful consequences. Some of us may have experienced the pain and emptiness brought on by the selfish pursuit of pleasure. A selfish lifestyle will never yield lasting joy and peace; pursuing our own way always leads to one kind of bondage or another. When we make God's will our own and follow his plan, we will experience true freedom and become a blessing to the people around us.

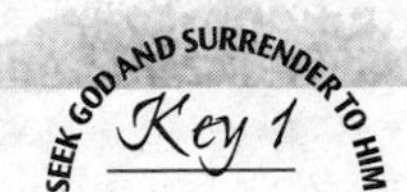

Single-minded Devotion

James 4:7–10 We may already have chosen to seek God and surrender to him, following his path for our lives. Even so, many of us still choose to take the occasional detour. We keep options open to do certain things that are contrary to God's will. But living such double lives fills us with guilt, shame and instability and only squelches our attempts at spiritual renewal.

In order to help believers guard against this kind of behavior, James wrote, "Submit yourselves, then, to God. Resist the devil, and he will flee from you. Come near to God and he will come near to you. Wash your hands, you sinners, and purify your hearts, you double-minded. Grieve, mourn and wail. Change your laughter to mourning and your joy to gloom" (4:7–9).

Even those who are mature in the faith face new moments of decision every day. We must ask God to help us follow him with single-minded devotion, for "he who doubts is like a wave of the sea, blown and tossed by the wind" (1:6). As we surrender to God and follow him faithfully, he will draw near to us and grant us the spiritual renewal we desire.

Move on to Key 2 and turn to Mark 14.

THE SPIRITUAL DISCIPLINES

Repentance and Confession

Confessing to One Another

James 5:16 Sin hides in darkness and silence, gathering energy for its work. Confession brings sin into the open where its power is broken. James, the half brother of Jesus and a leader in the early church, recognized this and exhorted his readers to practice the discipline of confession.

What are we supposed to confess? We are to confess to one another when we have sinned against each other. Unconfessed sin erects barriers in relationships. Confession and forgiveness break down these walls and allow God's love and power to flow freely among us.

There are also times when we should confess to one another sins from which we are struggling to break free. However, we do not confess to one another as a condition for forgiveness. We are forgiven solely by the grace that comes through faith in Jesus Christ. But others can provide the support, accountability, assurance and perspective that can help us move forward. Opening our hearts to a pastor, counselor or wise spiritual friend can be a step toward experiencing the freedom of forgiveness.

Putting It Into Practice

Are you harboring any sins that need to be confessed to someone? Are there areas of sin that could be overcome by having someone share your struggle and support you? As you choose such a person, carefully consider this person's own spiritual maturity and commitment to you. Ask whether the person understands the goals of the process of confession. Obtain their agreement to confidentiality and support before you share your heart.

For more on repentance and confession, turn to 1 John 1.

failed to pay the workmen who mowed your
fields are crying out against you. The cries of the
harvesters have reached the ears of the Lord
Almighty. 5You have lived on earth in luxury
and self-indulgence. You have fattened yourselves in the day of slaughter.[a] 6You have condemned and murdered innocent men, who
were not opposing you.

Patience in Suffering

7Be patient, then, brothers, until the Lord's
coming. See how the farmer waits for the land
to yield its valuable crop and how patient he is
for the autumn and spring rains. 8You too, be
patient and stand firm, because the Lord's coming is near. 9Don't grumble against each other,
brothers, or you will be judged. The Judge is
standing at the door!

10Brothers, as an example of patience in the
face of suffering, take the prophets who spoke
in the name of the Lord. 11As you know, we
consider blessed those who have persevered.
You have heard of Job's perseverance and have
seen what the Lord finally brought about. The
Lord is full of compassion and mercy.

12Above all, my brothers, do not swear—not
by heaven or by earth or by anything else. Let
your "Yes" be yes, and your "No," no, or you will
be condemned.

The Prayer of Faith

13Is any one of you in trouble? He should
pray. Is anyone happy? Let him sing songs of
praise. 14Is any one of you sick? He should call
the elders of the church to pray over him and
anoint him with oil in the name of the Lord.
15And the prayer offered in faith will make the
sick person well; the Lord will raise him up. If
he has sinned, he will be forgiven. 16Therefore
confess your sins to each other and pray for
each other so that you may be healed. The
prayer of a righteous man is powerful and effective.

17Elijah was a man just like us. He prayed
earnestly that it would not rain, and it did not
rain on the land for three and a half years.
18Again he prayed, and the heavens gave rain,
and the earth produced its crops.

19My brothers, if one of you should wander
from the truth and someone should bring him
back, 20remember this: Whoever turns a sinner
from the error of his way will save him from
death and cover over a multitude of sins.

[a]5 Or *yourselves as in a day of feasting*

5:7–11 Even though we have surrendered our lives to God, there will be times and circumstances that test our patience. We must never forget that there will come a day when we will no longer have to wait for Christ to return; he will have arrived. In the meantime, we must bear our suffering patiently and be patient with each other too.

5:13–15 Since God has the power to heal us spiritually, emotionally and physically, prayer is one of the most powerful tools available to us. When we pray to God, we display our faith in his ability to help us. Prayer is an essential part of the process of surrendering our lives to God. As we share our needs with one another and pray for one another, God displays his active presence and power in our lives.

5:16–20 Admitting our faults to God and to a trustworthy person are essential keys to our spiritual growth. When we share our faults with others, we give them the opportunity to uphold us in prayer. James reminds us that confession is an important part of our personal prayer lives. God invites us to admit our faults and failures to him through prayer. When we bring our sins and shortcomings before God, he can start the healing process in our lives. Prayer is never a waste of time; it yields wonderful results! God responds powerfully when we display our faith by sharing our problems with him.

1 PETER

The Big Picture

Peter's audience was composed of hurting people, suffering persecution from unbelievers in the form of rejection, torture, imprisonment and the threat of physical death. The price these believers paid for their faith included everything from broken relationships and loss of employment to physical pain and martyrdom.

Peter wrote this letter to encourage them. The wonderful part of his message lay in the perspective he offered his audience. In response to their cries of anguish he did not brush them off or flippantly promise them an easy road ahead. Instead, Peter gave them this hope: They belonged to God. Peter's words offer this same hope to us.

Suffering is one of the most difficult aspects of life to accept, much less understand. Though we wish we were exempt or cushioned from life's harsh blows, pain is a reality. All of us suffer; suffering is part of life (see John 16:33). We must accept the fact that we will hurt from time to time.

Yet God has equipped us with the means to live at peace in the midst of tough times. We obtain God's powerful help when we hold fast to Christ and live according to his will. This does not mean that our troubles will vanish because we believe in God. Instead, God offers to surround us with his love when problems seem overwhelming. The way out of the storm is to take comfort in God's presence and persevere through the hard times. As we do, God will use the trials to inspire our growth.

Spiritual Renewal Themes

GOD'S WAY CAN BE PAINFUL

We may be afraid of spiritual growth because the changes God asks of us may be painful. Each key to spiritual renewal holds the potential for pain on some level. Yet pain is always a part of life in a fallen world, whether we are changing for the better or for the worse. Our old way of life involved pain too, but we tried to find ways to escape it. When we decide to seek spiritual renewal, we willingly see the truth as God reveals it and release whatever we have been holding onto, including our pain. God's plan will lead to a life of joy, freedom and transformation, making all the pain worthwhile.

NOTHING IS HOPELESS WITH GOD

When we struggle spiritually, we may feel helpless and tempted to give up. But *feeling* helpless is different from *being* helpless. We are never really helpless, because with God, help is close at hand. We are not hopeless, for God is the source of all hope. When we struggle with feelings of despair, this letter reminds us to surrender our lives to God and to depend on his power. God will never leave us to face our trials alone.

THE IMPORTANCE OF RELATIONSHIPS

Surrendering our lives in repentance to Jesus Christ makes us part of God's family. We enter into a community with Jesus Christ as its founder and leader. Everyone in this community is related; no one stands alone. All healing and spiritual renewal take place in the context of relationships with others. Peter taught us how to manage those relationships: with loyalty, care and humility and prayer that we will become what God wants us to be.

Essential Facts

PURPOSE:
To show us how to live well in a shattered and hopeless world.

AUTHOR:
The apostle Peter.

AUDIENCE:
Christians who were suffering persecution for their faith.

DATE WRITTEN:
Around A.D. 64, just prior to Nero's persecutions of the early Christians.

SETTING:
This letter was written during a period in which Peter and other Christians were being tortured and martyred for their faith by both Jewish and secular authorities.

KEY VERSE:
"Live as free men, but do not use your freedom as a cover-up for evil; live as servants of God" (2:16).

KEY PEOPLE AND RELATIONSHIPS:
Peter with Silas and with John Mark.

1

Peter, an apostle of Jesus Christ,
To God's elect, strangers in the world, scattered throughout Pontus, Galatia, Cappadocia,
Asia and Bithynia, 2who have been chosen according to the foreknowledge of God the Father, through the sanctifying work of the Spirit,
for obedience to Jesus Christ and sprinkling by
his blood:

Grace and peace be yours in abundance.

Praise to God for a Living Hope

3Praise be to the God and Father of our Lord
Jesus Christ! In his great mercy he has given us
new birth into a living hope through the resurrection of Jesus Christ from the dead, 4and into
an inheritance that can never perish, spoil or
fade—kept in heaven for you, 5who through
faith are shielded by God's power until the
coming of the salvation that is ready to be revealed in the last time. 6In this you greatly rejoice, though now for a little while you may
have had to suffer grief in all kinds of trials.
7These have come so that your faith—of greater
worth than gold, which perishes even though
refined by fire—may be proved genuine and
may result in praise, glory and honor when
Jesus Christ is revealed. 8Though you have not
seen him, you love him; and even though you
do not see him now, you believe in him and are
filled with an inexpressible and glorious joy,
9for you are receiving the goal of your faith, the
salvation of your souls.
10Concerning this salvation, the prophets,
who spoke of the grace that was to come to you,
searched intently and with the greatest care,
11trying to find out the time and circumstances
to which the Spirit of Christ in them was pointing when he predicted the sufferings of Christ
and the glories that would follow. 12It was revealed to them that they were not serving themselves but you, when they spoke of the things
that have now been told you by those who have
preached the gospel to you by the Holy Spirit
sent from heaven. Even angels long to look into
these things.

Be Holy

13Therefore, prepare your minds for action;
be self-controlled; set your hope fully on the
grace to be given you when Jesus Christ is revealed. 14As obedient children, do not conform
to the evil desires you had when you lived in
ignorance. 15But just as he who called you is
holy, so be holy in all you do; 16for it is written:
"Be holy, because I am holy."[a]
17Since you call on a Father who judges each
man's work impartially, live your lives as strangers here in reverent fear. 18For you know that it
was not with perishable things such as silver or
gold that you were redeemed from the empty
way of life handed down to you from your forefathers, 19but with the precious blood of Christ,
a lamb without blemish or defect. 20He was
chosen before the creation of the world, but
was revealed in these last times for your sake.
21Through him you believe in God, who raised
him from the dead and glorified him, and so
your faith and hope are in God.
22Now that you have purified yourselves by
obeying the truth so that you have sincere love
for your brothers, love one another deeply,
from the heart.[b] 23For you have been born
again, not of perishable seed, but of imperishable, through the living and enduring word of
God. 24For,

"All men are like grass,

[a]*16* Lev. 11:44,45; 19:2; 20:7 [b]*22* Some early manuscripts *from a pure heart*

1:1–2 As the apostle greeted his friends, he reminded them of their standing with the triune God: They were chosen by God the Father, cleansed by the blood of Jesus Christ and renewed by the working of the Holy Spirit in their hearts. We, too, enjoy these privileges if we have surrendered our lives to God.

1:3–6 Peter praised God for the free gift of his loving grace. All who receive God's gift become his children and belong together in his family. All who trust in him share the hope of eternal life with God. This hope gives us the strength to joyfully persevere in our spiritual growth, despite the difficult and painful circumstances we may face.

1:7 A refiner would put a crucible of gold he had mined into a heated furnace in order to separate the worthless and impure dross from the precious and beautiful gold. The dross would rise to the top of the container and be skimmed off until the refiner could look into the crucible at the liquid gold and see his image. In like manner, God uses the fiery trials and tribulations in our lives to purify and beautify our faith so that one day he will see clearly his image reflected in us.

1:8–9 Surrendering our wills and lives to God is often difficult when we face trials. In the midst of our most painful trials, we may fail to sense God's presence with us. Yet Peter suggests that surrendering to God in difficult times can be a joyful experience. If we trust that God will use our trials to complete the process of purification in our lives, even the tough times can become times of celebration.

1:10–13 The news of God's forgiveness in Christ flows from a plan that took centuries to complete. Now that it is complete, we can count on God's continuing kindness as we trust in him. We don't have to wonder whether we are tricking ourselves into believing something that isn't true: Centuries of history and numerous promises stand behind the revelation of God in Jesus.

1:14–17 Peter warned his readers about the temptation to give up on their faith. Peter knew what it felt like to slip back into old habits. Once he had boldly proclaimed that he was willing to die in Jesus' defense, but only a few hours later he denied knowing Jesus to save his life (see Matthew 26:31–35, 69–75). The only way to keep from slipping back into sinful ways is to maintain awareness of our true identities: We are children of a holy God. Like children, we are weak and dependent. But the Father we depend on is strong, loving, just and perfect.

1:23–25 Peter contrasted the new life we have in Christ with the natural life our parents gave us. Even the most positive legacy from our natural parents will fade and decay. But the life God gives us increases in beauty and lasts forever. God's promises to save us will never fail.

and all their glory is like the flowers of
the field;
the grass withers and the flowers fall,
25 but the word of the Lord stands
forever."[a]
And this is the word that was preached to you.

2 Therefore, rid yourselves of all malice and
all deceit, hypocrisy, envy, and slander of
every kind. [2]Like newborn babies, crave pure
spiritual milk, so that by it you may grow up in
your salvation, [3]now that you have tasted that
the Lord is good.

The Living Stone and a Chosen People

[4]As you come to him, the living Stone—rejected by men but chosen by God and precious
to him— [5]you also, like living stones, are being
built into a spiritual house to be a holy priesthood, offering spiritual sacrifices acceptable to
God through Jesus Christ. [6]For in Scripture it
says:

"See, I lay a stone in Zion,
a chosen and precious cornerstone,
and the one who trusts in him
will never be put to shame."[b]

[7]Now to you who believe, this stone is precious.
But to those who do not believe,

"The stone the builders rejected
has become the capstone,[c]"[d]

[8]and,

"A stone that causes men to stumble
and a rock that makes them fall."[e]

They stumble because they disobey the message—which is also what they were destined for.
[9]But you are a chosen people, a royal priesthood, a holy nation, a people belonging to
God, that you may declare the praises of him
who called you out of darkness into his wonderful light. [10]Once you were not a people, but
now you are the people of God; once you had
not received mercy, but now you have received
mercy.
[11]Dear friends, I urge you, as aliens and
strangers in the world, to abstain from sinful
desires, which war against your soul. [12]Live such
good lives among the pagans that, though they
accuse you of doing wrong, they may see your
good deeds and glorify God on the day he visits us.

Submission to Rulers and Masters

[13]Submit yourselves for the Lord's sake to
every authority instituted among men: whether
to the king, as the supreme authority, [14]or to
governors, who are sent by him to punish those
who do wrong and to commend those who do
right. [15]For it is God's will that by doing good
you should silence the ignorant talk of foolish
men. [16]Live as free men, but do not use your
freedom as a cover-up for evil; live as servants
of God. [17]Show proper respect to everyone:
Love the brotherhood of believers, fear God,
honor the king.
[18]Slaves, submit yourselves to your masters
with all respect, not only to those who are good
and considerate, but also to those who are
harsh. [19]For it is commendable if a man bears
up under the pain of unjust suffering because
he is conscious of God. [20]But how is it to your
credit if you receive a beating for doing wrong
and endure it? But if you suffer for doing good
and you endure it, this is commendable before
God. [21]To this you were called, because Christ
suffered for you, leaving you an example, that
you should follow in his steps.

[a]25 Isaiah 40:6-8 [b]6 Isaiah 28:16 [c]7 Or *cornerstone* [d]7 Psalm 118:22 [e]8 Isaiah 8:14

2:1 Peter urges us to avoid several sinful behaviors, including hanging on to feelings of hatred, pretending to be good while there is unacknowledged sin in our hearts, harboring jealousy instead of accepting our own situations and gossiping about people instead of talking directly with them. These verses spur us to examine our hearts and continue to work toward the goals of forgiveness, honesty, contentment and openness.

2:2–3 Peter pinpointed an insight for helping us resist sin. We can live godly lives because we have tasted of God's kindness. God's love helps us resist sin. When we experience God's love (which often comes through our relationships with other people), we recognize that sin isn't good for us and doesn't satisfy our longings. This takes our focus off improving our outward behavior and puts it on seeking to experience more of God's kindness. We can come to him with all our needs, and he will fill our hearts with the love we crave.

2:4–6 These verses leave us with two wonderful promises upon which we can build our lives and our spiritual growth: We are acceptable to God because of Jesus, and God will never disappoint us if we trust in him. With these truths as the foundation for our faith, we can build lives that please God.

2:9–10 The Christian's true identity is no longer that of a sinner but that of a holy saint. Priests were given the privilege of appearing before the Lord with requests. Because of Christ's ultimate sacrifice on the cross, we are free to come before God and no longer need to offer sacrifices for sin.

2:11 Sin is alluring because there is some pleasure in it. Many of us have struggled to escape the painful realities of life by turning to the pleasures of sinful behavior. Yet sooner or later we realize that these pleasures fight against the welfare of our souls. By viewing ourselves as visitors on earth, with our real homes in heaven, we can seek God to redirect our lives away from sinful pursuits.

2:15 The testimony of a changed life is a wonderful witness of God's grace. When hurting people see how God has brought us through difficult times and transformed our lives, they will want to know how God can change them too.

2:21–23 Peter made it clear that persevering through difficulty and pain can be the God-ordained path to maturity. God does not ask us to endure anything that he did not endure himself in Christ. Like us, Jesus was tempted to give in to sinful pleasures, to lie his way out of a dilemma, to return insult for insult and to seek revenge, but he chose not to do so. Like Jesus, we can respond to injustice with a faith that entrusts all matters into God's hands and simply seeks to obey him.

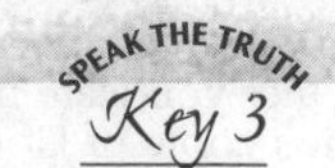

Refusing to Lie

1 Peter 3:10–17 If we truly desire renewal in our spiritual walk, we must learn to be truthful and turn away from lying. Lying can easily become a way of life. We can even lie to ourselves, covering up our problems and pretending they don't exist. But someday we must face reality. And when we do, we will see the pain caused by our lies—pain that has hurt us and our loved ones.

Think about these verses: "Whoever would love life and see good days must keep his tongue from evil and his lips from deceitful speech" (3:10). "Do not lie to each other, since you have taken off your old self with its practices and have put on the new self, which is being renewed in knowledge in the image of its Creator" (Colossians 3:9–10).

If lying is second nature to us, it may be difficult for us to change. But change we must. Lies will only hurt us and others. We must learn to guard our lips and our thoughts from lies. Then we can persevere in our spiritual growth.

Turn to 1 John 5.

22"He committed no sin,
and no deceit was found in his mouth."[a]

23When they hurled their insults at him, he did
not retaliate; when he suffered, he made no
threats. Instead, he entrusted himself to him
who judges justly. 24He himself bore our sins in
his body on the tree, so that we might die to sins
and live for righteousness; by his wounds you
have been healed. 25For you were like sheep
going astray, but now you have returned to the
Shepherd and Overseer of your souls.

Wives and Husbands

3 Wives, in the same way be submissive to
your husbands so that, if any of them do
not believe the word, they may be won over
without words by the behavior of their wives,
2when they see the purity and reverence of your
lives. 3Your beauty should not come from outward adornment, such as braided hair and the
wearing of gold jewelry and fine clothes. 4In-
stead, it should be that of your inner self, the
unfading beauty of a gentle and quiet spirit,
which is of great worth in God's sight. 5For this
is the way the holy women of the past who put
their hope in God used to make themselves
beautiful. They were submissive to their own
husbands, 6like Sarah, who obeyed Abraham
and called him her master. You are her daughters if you do what is right and do not give way
to fear.

7Husbands, in the same way be considerate
as you live with your wives, and treat them with
respect as the weaker partner and as heirs with
you of the gracious gift of life, so that nothing
will hinder your prayers.

Suffering for Doing Good

8Finally, all of you, live in harmony with one

[a]22 Isaiah 53:9

2:24 Jesus not only serves as our example for how to deal with suffering; he also suffered for us. He received the punishment for our sin so we wouldn't have to. Instead of facing terrible punishment, we can receive Christ's mercy. He desires to set us free from our bondage and heal us from the devastating effects of sin in our lives.

3:1–7 God's design for marriage involves mutual respect. A wife should respect her husband and a husband should be sensitive and loving toward his wife. Husband and wife are to receive through each other the blessings of God's loving grace and guiding truth. This sounds wonderful, but it is often hard to carry out! Mutual respect requires each spouse to be vulnerable, resolving conflicts and being confronted with the truth even when it hurts. Working through such difficulties is part of God's plan for helping marriages grow to full maturity.

3:8–11 The Christian community should be a healthy and happy family where people share their hurts and find sympathy. Within the Christian community believers can humbly express their needs and receive loving care. They can forgive one another, pray for each other and be careful not to say things that will unnecessarily hurt others. Being honest about who they are, believers seek to do good for one another and try to live in peace by resolving

another; be sympathetic, love as brothers, be
compassionate and humble. 9Do not repay evil
with evil or insult with insult, but with blessing,
because to this you were called so that you may
inherit a blessing. 10For,

"Whoever would love life
and see good days
must keep his tongue from evil
and his lips from deceitful speech.
11He must turn from evil and do good;
he must seek peace and pursue it.
12For the eyes of the Lord are on the
righteous
and his ears are attentive to their prayer,
but the face of the Lord is against those
who do evil."[a]

13Who is going to harm you if you are eager
to do good? 14But even if you should suffer for
what is right, you are blessed. "Do not fear
what they fear[b]; do not be frightened."[c] 15But
in your hearts set apart Christ as Lord. Always
be prepared to give an answer to everyone who
asks you to give the reason for the hope that you
have. But do this with gentleness and respect,
16keeping a clear conscience, so that those who
speak maliciously against your good behavior
in Christ may be ashamed of their slander. 17It
is better, if it is God's will, to suffer for doing
good than for doing evil. 18For Christ died for
sins once for all, the righteous for the unrighteous, to bring you to God. He was put to death
in the body but made alive by the Spirit,
19through whom[d] also he went and preached
to the spirits in prison 20who disobeyed long
ago when God waited patiently in the days of
Noah while the ark was being built. In it only
a few people, eight in all, were saved through
water, 21and this water symbolizes baptism that
now saves you also—not the removal of dirt
from the body but the pledge[e] of a good conscience toward God. It saves you by the resurrection of Jesus Christ, 22who has gone into
heaven and is at God's right hand—with angels,
authorities and powers in submission to him.

Living for God

4 Therefore, since Christ suffered in his
body, arm yourselves also with the same

[a]12 Psalm 34:12-16 [b]14 Or *not fear their threats*
[c]14 Isaiah 8:12 [d]18,19 Or *alive in the spirit, 19through which* [e]21 Or *response*

conflicts with each other. The community Peter described is ideal for helping us grow spiritually.

3:13–17 We may know what it feels like to be falsely accused of wrongdoing or be hurt by someone that we tried to help. People may misunderstand us and resist the changes we try to make. The challenge in such situations is to patiently maintain a quiet trust in God's promises. If we persevere, God will reward us with a mature faith and a deep experience of his love.

4:1–5 Peter urges us to follow Christ's example of self-control, resisting the sinful pleasures that come our way. We should focus our energy instead on living according to

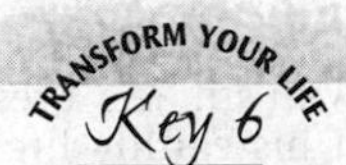

The Narrow Road

1 Peter 4:1–4 Spiritual growth takes place when we turn from our sins and selfishness that characterized our past and turn toward the new life God has for us. When we have had enough of going our own selfish way and have finally asked God to redeem our lives, we begin our journey of faith. But the path Christ calls us to follow is narrow and difficult.

Jesus said, "Wide is the gate and broad is the road that leads to destruction, and many enter through it. But small is the gate and narrow the road that leads to life, and only a few find it" (Matthew 7:13–14). Peter further pointed out, "You have spent enough time in the past doing what pagans choose to do . . . They think it strange that you do not plunge with them into the same flood of dissipation, and they heap abuse on you" (4:3–4).

People on the "road that leads to destruction" won't restrict themselves to the moral boundaries God calls us to maintain. However, when we realize the possibilities of the wonderful life here and in eternity that God has called us to, we will eagerly ask him to transform our lives and make us living testimonies to his grace.

Move on to Key 7 and turn to Matthew 26.

attitude, because he who has suffered in his body is done with sin. [2]As a result, he does not live the rest of his earthly life for evil human desires, but rather for the will of God. [3]For you have spent enough time in the past doing what pagans choose to do—living in debauchery, lust, drunkenness, orgies, carousing and detestable idolatry. [4]They think it strange that you do not plunge with them into the same flood of dissipation, and they heap abuse on you. [5]But they will have to give account to him who is ready to judge the living and the dead. [6]For this is the reason the gospel was preached even to those who are now dead, so that they might be judged according to men in regard to the body, but live according to God in regard to the spirit.

[7]The end of all things is near. Therefore be clear minded and self-controlled so that you can pray. [8]Above all, love each other deeply, because love covers over a multitude of sins. [9]Offer hospitality to one another without grumbling. [10]Each one should use whatever gift he has received to serve others, faithfully administering God's grace in its various forms. [11]If anyone speaks, he should do it as one speaking the very words of God. If anyone serves, he should do it with the strength God provides, so that in all things God may be praised through Jesus Christ. To him be the glory and the power for ever and ever. Amen.

Suffering for Being a Christian

[12]Dear friends, do not be surprised at the painful trial you are suffering, as though something strange were happening to you. [13]But rejoice that you participate in the sufferings of Christ, so that you may be overjoyed when his glory is revealed. [14]If you are insulted because of the name of Christ, you are blessed, for the Spirit of glory and of God rests on you. [15]If you suffer, it should not be as a murderer or thief or any other kind of criminal, or even as a meddler. [16]However, if you suffer as a Christian, do not be ashamed, but praise God that you bear that name. [17]For it is time for judgment to begin with the family of God; and if it begins with us, what will the outcome be for those who do not obey the gospel of God? [18]And,

"If it is hard for the righteous to be saved,
 what will become of the ungodly and
 the sinner?"[a]

[19]So then, those who suffer according to God's will should commit themselves to their faithful Creator and continue to do good.

To Elders and Young Men

5 To the elders among you, I appeal as a fellow elder, a witness of Christ's sufferings and one who also will share in the glory to be revealed: [2]Be shepherds of God's flock that is under your care, serving as overseers—not because you must, but because you are willing, as God wants you to be; not greedy for money, but eager to serve; [3]not lording it over those entrusted to you, but being examples to the flock. [4]And when the Chief Shepherd appears, you will receive the crown of glory that will never fade away.

[5]Young men, in the same way be submissive to those who are older. All of you, clothe yourselves with humility toward one another, because,

"God opposes the proud
 but gives grace to the humble."[b]

[6]Humble yourselves, therefore, under God's mighty hand, that he may lift you up in due time. [7]Cast all your anxiety on him because he cares for you.

[a]18 Prov. 11:31 [b]5 Prov. 3:34

God's will. The sins Peter lists here can exert incredible power over us. To break free of a sinful lifestyle, we have to cut ourselves off from past practices and may need to adjust our relationships. But merely to refuse a sinful lifestyle won't set us free. We also need to surrender to God and let him redirect our course to spiritual growth.

4:10–11 God has given all of us special and unique abilities. Sometimes we don't use our gifts because we feel inadequate. Some of us feel that using our gifts signals a problem with pride. But these feeling are not right. We are called to use these God-given gifts for God's glory, allowing his generosity to flow through us. If we carefully focus on God's glory and not our own, we will make proper use of our gifts and abilities.

4:12–13 Peter returned to a central theme of his letter reminding his readers not only to expect trials but also to rejoice in them. Through our difficult circumstances we receive an opportunity to share in Christ's sufferings as well as in his glory. Peter's theme offers great hope because it affirms that our suffering has a purpose. Through suffering, God will draw us close and transform us into the people he intended us to be.

4:14–16 We need God's wisdom to know the difference between suffering because of our own sin and suffering for doing what is right. When we suffer because of our own sin, we feel ashamed and recognize our need to change. But when we suffer because of our Christian conduct or godly character, we can rejoice in those sufferings because we will share Christ's glory one day.

4:19 Peter encourages us to rejoice in the persecution we face. Old friends who want us to return to our old ways of life probably have opposed us in some way. Perhaps family members are afraid of the changes we have made in our lives and put obstacles in our way. As we face these trials, we must remember that God will be faithful to us and use even our painful experiences for our good. If we suffer for our faith, we need to keep on doing what we know to be right. No matter what obstacles may be placed in our way, God will never desert us once we have entrusted our lives to him.

5:1–4 Several qualities are necessary for a Christian leader: the willingness to care for others, a desire to serve others for their benefit and the ability to lead by example rather than by intimidation. Jesus has provided the best example for us to follow. To become the type of leader God wants, we can submit to Christ's leadership and allow his grace, peace and wisdom to flow through us.

5:7 God cares about whatever troubles us. He watches over us and is continually concerned for our welfare! If we truly believe this about God we should release our

[8]Be self-controlled and alert. Your enemy the
devil prowls around like a roaring lion looking
for someone to devour. [9]Resist him, standing
firm in the faith, because you know that your
brothers throughout the world are undergoing
the same kind of sufferings.
[10]And the God of all grace, who called you
to his eternal glory in Christ, after you have
suffered a little while, will himself restore
you and make you strong, firm and steadfast.
[11]To him be the power for ever and ever.
Amen.

Final Greetings

[12]With the help of Silas,[a] whom I regard as
a faithful brother, I have written to you briefly,
encouraging you and testifying that this is the
true grace of God. Stand fast in it.
[13]She who is in Babylon, chosen together
with you, sends you her greetings, and so does
my son Mark. [14]Greet one another with a kiss of
love.

Peace to all of you who are in Christ.

[a]12 Greek *Silvanus*, a variant of *Silas*

worries to him. However, because of our background many of us find it hard to fully trust that God is truly concerned about us. We may feel that if *we* don't worry about our problems, no one else will either. One way to increase our level of trust in God is to find a mature Christian with whom we can begin to share and learn to trust. As we share our concerns with a caring person, we can consciously remind ourselves that God's concern is like our friend's, only much wider and deeper.

5:8–9 Satan lurks and prowls about in this world, seeking to devour us. We are commanded to stand firm and fight the battle, knowing that the war is already won. As we develop Christian friends and a community of support, we will see that we are not alone in the battle; others are fighting alongside us.

5:10–11 God's promise to us when we fall down or are pushed down is that he will pick us up, set us in a good and secure place and use the difficulty we have been through to make us stronger than ever! This hope gives us the courage to persevere in our spiritual journeys.

2 Peter

The Big Picture

Peter's audience had a problem. False teachers had moved into church fellowships and promoted wrong ideas about God. In many of these early churches a majority of the people were uneducated. They were easily swayed by the eloquence of traveling false teachers who intentionally deceived the people, using lies and half-truths to manipulate the believers for their own ends.

The apostle Peter sent a series of warnings to his readers: Watch out for false teachers; remember that God will hold them accountable for their errors; recognize false teachers by their deeds; remember the price they will pay for misleading people. Peter wanted his readers to experience the life-changing power of God in their lives. To do this, the believers needed to avoid manmade substitutes and the false teachings about Christ.

The challenge to Peter's audience went beyond a mere warning, however. Peter included a plan for the church's growth: "His divine power has given us everything we need for life and godliness through our knowledge of him who called us by his own glory and goodness" (1:3).

Why do the pains, disappointments and sins of life bring us down? Why do we hurt those we love the most? Perhaps we will never learn the answers to those questions. But 2 Peter does tell us how to change: Get to know God. The God of the universe has made himself available to us on a personal level. As we get to know him, he will help us overcome our shortcomings and replace them with self-control, kindness, love, forgiveness, perseverance, patience and peace.

Spiritual Renewal Themes

SPIRITUAL RENEWAL REQUIRES SURRENDER TO GOD

Some people say that we have the power to heal ourselves. That false idea is fed by our own wishful thinking, believing we have the power within ourselves to overcome all of our problems and find fulfillment in our lives. Or maybe we would rather ignore reality and enhance our spiritual lives without ever really dealing with our problems and difficult relationships. But true spiritual renewal never divorces spiritual life from the rest of life. Spiritual renewal must involve the entire person—heart, mind, spirit and will—surrendering one's whole life and being

to God's rule. It is not an easy or painless process. Surrender demands complete devotion of our lives to God. But if we are willing to repent and entrust our lives to God, we will discover the joy and peace that God intends for us.

GOD IS OUR HELP AND HOPE

Peter wrote to people who were facing severe opposition. The Roman emperor Nero had begun his persecution of Christians, and many would soon face death at his hands. At the same time, false ideas about God threatened the believers' new faith. Peter reminded these new believers to keep their eyes on God, the only reliable source of help and hope. As we also focus on God, we will find new hope no matter what circumstances we face. Then, as we persevere through tough times, our behavior will reflect that God is working powerfully in our lives.

THE IMPORTANCE OF PERSEVERANCE

Since we have been freed from our slavery to sin, we must persevere in our faith so that we do not become tangled up in sin once again. Falling back into sin makes our spiritual growth difficult, but the secret to making progress is perseverance. With God's help we can get up quickly and get back on track as soon as possible, no matter what the circumstances. When we accept God's free gift of forgiveness, we will grow closer to God, who loves us and promises to be with us. In this way, God will help us persevere through the tough times and experience his joy in the process.

Essential Facts

PURPOSE:
To help his readers keep their focus on God's grace and truth.

AUTHOR:
The apostle Peter.

AUDIENCE:
All believers everywhere.

DATE WRITTEN:
Around A.D. 66–67, a few years after 1 Peter was written.

SETTING:
Peter was probably writing from Rome, sending words of encouragement and warning to people he did not expect to see again. He wanted them to watch out for false teachings and to be faithful to God and one another.

KEY VERSE:
"His divine power has given us everything we need for life and godliness through our knowledge of him who called us by his own glory and goodness" (1:3).

KEY PEOPLE AND RELATIONSHIPS:
Peter with Paul and with the church at large.

1 Simon Peter, a servant and apostle of Jesus Christ,

To those who through the righteousness of our God and Savior Jesus Christ have received a faith as precious as ours:

2Grace and peace be yours in abundance through the knowledge of God and of Jesus our Lord.

Making One's Calling and Election Sure

3His divine power has given us everything we need for life and godliness through our knowledge of him who called us by his own glory and goodness. 4Through these he has given us his very great and precious promises, so that through them you may participate in the divine nature and escape the corruption in the world caused by evil desires.

5For this very reason, make every effort to add to your faith goodness; and to goodness, knowledge; 6and to knowledge, self-control; and to self-control, perseverance; and to perseverance, godliness; 7and to godliness, brotherly kindness; and to brotherly kindness, love. 8For if you possess these qualities in increasing measure, they will keep you from being ineffective and unproductive in your knowledge of our Lord Jesus Christ. 9But if anyone does not have them, he is nearsighted and blind, and has forgotten that he has been cleansed from his past sins.

10Therefore, my brothers, be all the more eager to make your calling and election sure. For if you do these things, you will never fall, 11and you will receive a rich welcome into the eternal kingdom of our Lord and Savior Jesus Christ.

Prophecy of Scripture

12So I will always remind you of these things, even though you know them and are firmly established in the truth you now have. 13I think it is right to refresh your memory as long as I live in the tent of this body, 14because I know that I will soon put it aside, as our Lord Jesus Christ has made clear to me. 15And I will make every effort to see that after my departure you will always be able to remember these things.

16We did not follow cleverly invented stories when we told you about the power and coming of our Lord Jesus Christ, but we were eyewitnesses of his majesty. 17For he received honor and glory from God the Father when the voice came to him from the Majestic Glory, saying, "This is my Son, whom I love; with him I am well pleased."[a] 18We ourselves heard this voice that came from heaven when we were with him on the sacred mountain.

19And we have the word of the prophets made more certain, and you will do well to pay attention to it, as to a light shining in a dark place, until the day dawns and the morning star rises in your hearts. 20Above all, you must understand that no prophecy of Scripture came about by the prophet's own interpretation. 21For prophecy never had its origin in the will of man, but men spoke from God as they were carried along by the Holy Spirit.

False Teachers and Their Destruction

2 But there were also false prophets among the people, just as there will be false teachers among you. They will secretly introduce destructive heresies, even denying the sovereign Lord who bought them—bringing swift destruc-

[a] *17* Matt. 17:5; Mark 9:7; Luke 9:35

1:1–2 Peter greeted his readers by reminding them of the gift of forgiveness and new life they had received through faith in Jesus Christ. Salvation is a gift that no one deserves; no one can claim to be worthy of the salvation God offers in Christ (see Ephesians 2:8–9). Truly God is good! Experiencing God's kindness and peace depends on how well we know him. Peter reminds us that grace and peace come when we concentrate on getting to know God better.

1:3–4 One of the most comforting by-products of faith is the simple awareness that we possess everything we need to live full and meaningful lives. We experience this provision by participating in God's nature through faith and by growing through practice into all that he has designed us to be. God redeems our past, holds our future securely in his hands and fills today with the opportunity to grow in our understanding of love, forgiveness, truth and grace! God supplies all that we need, including the ability to rise above our circumstances and temptations.

1:5–11 The apostle reminds us that when we entrust our lives to God, he expects us to follow his will and do our part in the spiritual growth process. As we seek change in our lives, we will share in God's nature and receive the ability to think new thoughts and formulate new behavior patterns.

1:12–18 We often remember the painful moments of life—the disappointments and the people who disappointed us—but find it harder to remember the many blessings we receive in small ways each day. Peter wanted his readers to overcome the pain of past trials by focusing on the good things in life, etching the truth of God's amazing love and faithfulness into their minds. We may also have painful memories that we need to release to God. As we relinquish these past hurts and the painful memories begin to fade, we can reflect on the amazing love of God, recalling the good things God has done in our lives.

1:19–21 God's truth is dependable; our human perspective often is not. God's truth is not weak or questionable; it is not a theory waiting to be disproved. God's truth is certain and can be counted on. But are we ready to believe what God says? Or do we prefer the perspectives of fallible people, the messages ingrained in our minds from past events or the doubts instilled by friends who have not yet surrendered their lives to God? As we take God's Word to heart, we come to understand more of the truth—about ourselves, about God and about our future in Christ.

2:1–12 The consequences of a self-centered pursuit of pleasure and power are terrifying. Rejecting God's plan and leading others away from the truth will result in terrible consequences. God has given us the help we need to renew our lives according to his will. It is good to be reminded every so often that we have been delivered from "swift destruction" (2:1).

tion on themselves. [2]Many will follow their
shameful ways and will bring the way of truth
into disrepute. [3]In their greed these teachers
will exploit you with stories they have made up.
Their condemnation has long been hanging
over them, and their destruction has not been
sleeping.
[4]For if God did not spare angels when they
sinned, but sent them to hell,[a] putting them
into gloomy dungeons[b] to be held for judgment; [5]if he did not spare the ancient world
when he brought the flood on its ungodly people, but protected Noah, a preacher of righteousness, and seven others; [6]if he condemned
the cities of Sodom and Gomorrah by burning
them to ashes, and made them an example of
what is going to happen to the ungodly; [7]and if
he rescued Lot, a righteous man, who was distressed by the filthy lives of lawless men [8](for
that righteous man, living among them day after day, was tormented in his righteous soul by
the lawless deeds he saw and heard)— [9]if this is
so, then the Lord knows how to rescue godly
men from trials and to hold the unrighteous for
the day of judgment, while continuing their
punishment.[c] [10]This is especially true of those
who follow the corrupt desire of the sinful nature[d] and despise authority.

Bold and arrogant, these men are not afraid
to slander celestial beings; [11]yet even angels,
although they are stronger and more powerful,
do not bring slanderous accusations against
such beings in the presence of the Lord. [12]But
these men blaspheme in matters they do not
understand. They are like brute beasts, creatures
of instinct, born only to be caught and destroyed, and like beasts they too will perish.
[13]They will be paid back with harm for the
harm they have done. Their idea of pleasure is
to carouse in broad daylight. They are blots and
blemishes, reveling in their pleasures while they
feast with you.[e] [14]With eyes full of adultery,
they never stop sinning; they seduce the unstable; they are experts in greed—an accursed
brood! [15]They have left the straight way and
wandered off to follow the way of Balaam son
of Beor, who loved the wages of wickedness.
[16]But he was rebuked for his wrongdoing by

[a]4 Greek *Tartarus* [b]4 Some manuscripts *into chains of darkness* [c]9 Or *unrighteous for punishment until the day of judgment* [d]10 Or *the flesh* [e]13 Some manuscripts *in their love feasts*

2:13–22 Peter emphasized the need for discernment and setting appropriate boundaries to help protect our spiritual health. People who do not have our best interests at heart are present even in the Christian community. Apparently in Peter's day those who once professed faith in Christ began adding to the simple truth of the gospel. These false teachers plagued the church and advocated freedom, but the freedom they espoused was only a license for immorality and slavery to sin. Setting healthy boundaries for our behavior involves knowing God's truth and allowing neither the false teachings of others nor our own sinful inclinations to lead us astray.

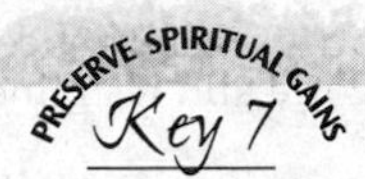

Developing Self-control

2 Peter 1:2–9 Developing self-control will help us tremendously as we seek to preserve our spiritual gains. And according to Peter, who had learned some difficult lessons about self-control himself, such self-restraint is part of a larger progression of spiritual growth. He wrote, "Make every effort to add to your faith goodness; and to goodness, knowledge; and to knowledge, self-control; and to self-control, perseverance; and to perseverance, godliness; and to godliness, brotherly kindness; and to brotherly kindness, love" (1:5–7).

Self-control is a fruit of the Holy Spirit (see Galatians 5:22–23). Self-control grows in our lives when we cling closely to God, allowing his Spirit to flow through us. As we persevere day by day, God will develop his own character in us, including the character trait of self-control.

This is the end of the New Testament reading plan.

a donkey—a beast without speech—who spoke with a man's voice and restrained the prophet's madness.

[17]These men are springs without water and mists driven by a storm. Blackest darkness is reserved for them. [18]For they mouth empty, boastful words and, by appealing to the lustful desires of sinful human nature, they entice people who are just escaping from those who live in error. [19]They promise them freedom, while they themselves are slaves of depravity—for a man is a slave to whatever has mastered him. [20]If they have escaped the corruption of the world by knowing our Lord and Savior Jesus Christ and are again entangled in it and overcome, they are worse off at the end than they were at the beginning. [21]It would have been better for them not to have known the way of righteousness, than to have known it and then to turn their backs on the sacred command that was passed on to them. [22]Of them the proverbs are true: "A dog returns to its vomit,"[a] and, "A sow that is washed goes back to her wallowing in the mud."

The Day of the Lord

3 Dear friends, this is now my second letter to you. I have written both of them as reminders to stimulate you to wholesome thinking. [2]I want you to recall the words spoken in the past by the holy prophets and the command given by our Lord and Savior through your apostles.

[3]First of all, you must understand that in the last days scoffers will come, scoffing and following their own evil desires. [4]They will say, "Where is this 'coming' he promised? Ever since our fathers died, everything goes on as it has since the beginning of creation." [5]But they deliberately forget that long ago by God's word the heavens existed and the earth was formed out of water and by water. [6]By these waters also the world of that time was deluged and destroyed. [7]By the same word the present heavens and earth are reserved for fire, being kept for the day of judgment and destruction of ungodly men.

[8]But do not forget this one thing, dear friends: With the Lord a day is like a thousand years, and a thousand years are like a day. [9]The Lord is not slow in keeping his promise, as some understand slowness. He is patient with you, not wanting anyone to perish, but everyone to come to repentance.

[10]But the day of the Lord will come like a thief. The heavens will disappear with a roar; the elements will be destroyed by fire, and the earth and everything in it will be laid bare.[b]

[11]Since everything will be destroyed in this way, what kind of people ought you to be? You ought to live holy and godly lives [12]as you look forward to the day of God and speed its coming.[c] That day will bring about the destruction of the heavens by fire, and the elements will melt in the heat. [13]But in keeping with his promise we are looking forward to a new heaven and a new earth, the home of righteousness.

[14]So then, dear friends, since you are looking forward to this, make every effort to be found spotless, blameless and at peace with him. [15]Bear in mind that our Lord's patience means salvation, just as our dear brother Paul also wrote you with the wisdom that God gave him. [16]He writes the same way in all his letters, speaking in them of these matters. His letters contain some things that are hard to understand, which ignorant and unstable people distort, as they do the other Scriptures, to their own destruction.

[17]Therefore, dear friends, since you already know this, be on your guard so that you may not be carried away by the error of lawless men and fall from your secure position. [18]But grow in the grace and knowledge of our Lord and Savior Jesus Christ. To him be glory both now and forever! Amen.

[a]22 Prov. 26:11 [b]10 Some manuscripts *be burned up*
[c]12 Or *as you wait eagerly for the day of God to come*

3:3–9 Waiting for Christ's return is difficult, particularly during trying times. We may wonder why God allows this suffering and does not intervene and return. But the answer is simple yet profoundly full of love: God is patient! He wants all to come to him and discover the only true way of life. As we wait, we can trust that God will work out our suffering for a good purpose.

1 JOHN

The Big Picture

- *A. INTRODUCTION (1:1–2:2)*
- *B. FREEDOM FROM FALSE THINKING: OBEDIENCE (2:3-27)*
- *C. FREEDOM FROM FALSE THINKING: THE WORK OF CHRIST (2:28–4:6)*
- *D. FREEDOM FROM FALSE THINKING: THE GIFTS OF GOD (4:7–5:5)*
- *E. CONCLUSION: ASSURANCE OF SPIRITUAL RENEWAL (5:6–21)*

False religious teachers were a major problem in the early church. Because the complete New Testament was not available for believers to refer to, many churches fell prey to pretenders who taught their own ideas about the gospel and advanced themselves as spiritual leaders. John wrote this letter to set the record straight on some important issues, particularly concerning the identity of Jesus Christ.

Because John's letter concerned the basics of faith in Christ, it helped his readers reflect honestly on their beliefs. It helped them determine if they were true believers. John told them that true believers could be recognized by their actions: If they loved one another, that was evidence of God's presence in their lives. But if they bickered and fought all the time or were selfish and did not care for one another, they did not know God.

Yet John acknowledged that a true believer wasn't always perfect. Believing in Christ did not remove temptation from the believers' lives. John recognized that the believers would slip and fall. But John also told his readers that a key part of true faith in Christ involves admitting our sins and seeking God's forgiveness. Depending on God for cleansing from guilt, admitting our wrongs against others and making amends are also important keys for getting to know God.

John's letter challenges us to treat others with respect and dignity as we grow spiritually. This is essential to true spiritual growth. A person transformed by Christ will reflect that transformation in their treatment of others. The keys for spiritual renewal also involve making restitution whenever we can to those we may have hurt along the way. Our spiritual growth will progress only as far as we right the wrongs we have committed against others. It takes humility and commitment to live at peace with others, but it is a price worth paying as we seek God's blessing.

Spiritual Renewal Themes

GOD'S DESIRE FOR OUR SPIRITUAL RENEWAL

One of the ways God cares for us is by listening to us. When Satan (called "the accuser" in Revelation 12:10) plants accusations in our minds, telling us that we have sinned too much for God to forgive us, John urges us not to give up hope. Jesus

Essential Facts

PURPOSE:
To set boundaries on the content of faith and to give believers assurance of their salvation.

AUTHOR:
The apostle John.

AUDIENCE:
An unnamed group of early churches.

DATE WRITTEN:
Probably between A.D. 85–96.

SETTING:
John was possibly the only surviving apostle when he wrote this letter, which circulated among the churches of Asia Minor. He lived in Ephesus at the time, supervising the churches of Asia Minor.

KEY VERSE:
"I write these things to you who believe in the name of the Son of God so that you may know that you have eternal life" (5:13).

KEY PEOPLE AND RELATIONSHIPS:
John with the believers to whom he wrote.

Christ, our advocate, has already paid the penalty for any and every wrong we have done or could do. We do not need to shy away from asking him to plead our case; he has already won it.

THE INVITATION TO LOVE

One of the evidences of salvation in a person's life is their love for others that is shown in their actions, not just their words. We must be willing to love others as God has showed his love toward us. He loved us while we were living in disobedience to his commands—we did not have to clean ourselves up to get him to love us. God also wants to love others who are disobedient to him by using us to share his love and forgiveness with them. God loves us enough to free us from bondage. And he loves us enough to use us to show his love toward others in need of spiritual renewal.

THE IMPORTANCE OF BOUNDARIES

Apparently the false teachers whom John corrected believed that they could throw off all moral restraints because their physical actions did not violate their faith (see 3:8–10). Those who believed this message became indifferent to sin and lived immorally, thinking it was all right. John pointed out that there must be boundaries for our behavior and that we are called to imitate Jesus Christ. Anything that leads us away from Christ is outside the boundaries of proper behavior. Staying focused on Christ is an essential part of our ongoing spiritual growth.

The Word of Life

1 That which was from the beginning, which we have heard, which we have seen with our eyes, which we have looked at and our hands have touched—this we proclaim concerning the Word of life. 2The life appeared; we have seen it and testify to it, and we proclaim to you the eternal life, which was with the Father and has appeared to us. 3We proclaim to you what we have seen and heard, so that you also may have fellowship with us. And our fellowship is with the Father and with his Son, Jesus Christ. 4We write this to make our[a] joy complete.

Walking in the Light

5This is the message we have heard from him and declare to you: God is light; in him there is no darkness at all. 6If we claim to have fellowship with him yet walk in the darkness, we lie and do not live by the truth. 7But if we walk in the light, as he is in the light, we have fellowship with one another, and the blood of Jesus, his Son, purifies us from all[b] sin.

8If we claim to be without sin, we deceive ourselves and the truth is not in us. 9If we confess our sins, he is faithful and just and will forgive us our sins and purify us from all unrighteousness. 10If we claim we have not sinned, we make him out to be a liar and his word has no place in our lives.

2 My dear children, I write this to you so that you will not sin. But if anybody does sin, we have one who speaks to the Father in our defense—Jesus Christ, the Righteous One. 2He is the atoning sacrifice for our sins, and not only for ours but also for[c] the sins of the whole world.

3We know that we have come to know him if we obey his commands. 4The man who says, "I know him," but does not do what he commands is a liar, and the truth is not in him. 5But if anyone obeys his word, God's love[d] is truly made complete in him. This is how we know we are in him: 6Whoever claims to live in him must walk as Jesus did.

7Dear friends, I am not writing you a new command but an old one, which you have had since the beginning. This old command is the message you have heard. 8Yet I am writing you a new command; its truth is seen in him and you, because the darkness is passing and the true light is already shining.

9Anyone who claims to be in the light but hates his brother is still in the darkness. 10Whoever loves his brother lives in the light, and there is nothing in him[e] to make him stumble. 11But whoever hates his brother is in the darkness and walks around in the darkness; he does not know where he is going, because the darkness has blinded him.

12I write to you, dear children,
  because your sins have been forgiven on
    account of his name.
13I write to you, fathers,
  because you have known him who is
    from the beginning.
I write to you, young men,
  because you have overcome the evil one.
I write to you, dear children,
  because you have known the Father.
14I write to you, fathers,
  because you have known him who is
    from the beginning.
I write to you, young men,
  because you are strong,
  and the word of God lives in you,
  and you have overcome the evil one.

Do Not Love the World

15Do not love the world or anything in the world. If anyone loves the world, the love of the Father is not in him. 16For everything in the

[a]4 Some manuscripts *your* [b]7 Or *every* [c]2 Or *He is the one who turns aside God's wrath, taking away our sins, and not only ours but also* [d]5 Or *word, love for God* [e]10 Or *it*

1:5–7 There is a strong contrast between the light in the Christian life and the darkness in a life given to sin. If we live in sin while claiming to be Christians, we deceive ourselves. Honest and accurate self-examination of our spiritual lives requires us to live in God's light. As we continually acknowledge our flaws as the light reveals them, our consciences will be cleansed and our relationships with other believers will be strengthened.
1:8–10 Careful and honest reflection on God's Word and our lives often leads us to a consciousness of sin. In these verses we are assured that if we confess our sins, we will experience the forgiveness and cleansing God has provided through the shed blood of his Son, Jesus Christ. The lesson is simple: Confession must come before cleansing.
2:1–2 In every situation, whatever our need, we can turn to the greatest resource and advocate of all: Jesus Christ. Because he received the full force of God's anger against sin, we need not live in fear of God's displeasure for our transgressions. Believing that Christ suffered for our sin, we can come to the Father freely, with complete trust that we will be accepted unconditionally.
2:3–6 How can we be sure that we belong to Christ? Our assurance is validated by our continuing desire to obey God's will for us. Those who claim to be saved but continually disobey God's will are liars. We cannot make spiritual progress unless we are willing to submit to God and obey his Word. That means we must continually reflect on our lives, promptly admit our wrongs and confess our sins to God. As we learn to love God more, this process will become more of a joy than a burden.
2:7–11 A distinctive mark of our faith is love. Love is never weak or compromising; it is a sign of emotional strength. But hatred toward other Christians is a sure sign that we need God to change our hearts. Light and darkness cannot exist in the same heart. Notice that the absence of love will keep us in the dark and prove a severe hindrance to spiritual progress.
2:15–17 The more we are wrapped up in this world and its attractions, the harder it will be to follow God. The best way to avoid entanglement with worldly values is to seek God through prayer and meditation on his Word. Then we will discover his will and his help in redirecting our lives.

Repentance and Confession

More Than Forgiveness—Acceptance

1 John 1:9 *"I just can't forgive myself . . ."* How often have we heard or spoken these words? Many of us struggle with a lingering sense of guilt in our hearts even after we have repented of our sin and know in our minds that we are forgiven.

What we need to learn in this situation is that acceptance is also a part of the discipline of repentance and confession. We must say to ourselves by faith, "In Jesus Christ, I am forgiven." As feelings arise that contradict this statement, we must affirm it again and again.

Another key to acceptance is understanding that absolute moral perfection will only be attained in heaven. We are fallible people. Scripture reminds us that "as a father has compassion on his children, so the LORD has compassion on those who fear him; for he knows how we are formed, he remembers that we are dust" (Psalm 103:13–14). We are people of dust, and often we are covered with the grit and grime of sin. But no physical body is in perfect health at all times. A body's vitality can be seen even in sickness as it fights to overcome infection or heal wounds. This self-repair is itself a sign of life and health. In the same way, our sensitivity to sin and our willingness to repent signals that our spirituality is alive and well.

Human limitations need not only be sources of shame; they can also be avenues for grace. In Jesus Christ, God loves us, and he is constantly transforming us into his image. When we are tempted to despair, we should remind ourselves at that very moment that Christ came for situations just like this!

As human beings, we have potential and limitations. Both are to be managed by the Holy Spirit. We should not let weaknesses or failures disqualify us nor discourage us from making an effort in the first place. Our attitude should say, "Though I may fail in the attempt, I will go forward." And as we take steps of faith, we can trust that God will use each failure to bring us new growth, with his grace and acceptance undergirding us.

Putting It Into Practice

When do you find it most difficult to accept God's forgiveness? Review what the Bible says about forgiveness and then write a letter in your journal of what you would to say to a person who does not feel forgiven. When you finish, read that letter aloud to yourself.

For more on repentance and confession, turn to Exodus 20.

world—the cravings of sinful man, the lust of his eyes and the boasting of what he has and does—comes not from the Father but from the world. [17]The world and its desires pass away, but the man who does the will of God lives forever.

Warning Against Antichrists

[18]Dear children, this is the last hour; and as you have heard that the antichrist is coming, even now many antichrists have come. This is how we know it is the last hour. [19]They went out from us, but they did not really belong to us. For if they had belonged to us, they would have remained with us; but their going showed that none of them belonged to us.

[20]But you have an anointing from the Holy One, and all of you know the truth.[a] [21]I do not write to you because you do not know the truth, but because you do know it and because no lie comes from the truth. [22]Who is the liar? It is the man who denies that Jesus is the Christ. Such a man is the antichrist—he denies the Father and the Son. [23]No one who denies the Son has the Father; whoever acknowledges the Son has the Father also.

[24]See that what you have heard from the beginning remains in you. If it does, you also will remain in the Son and in the Father. [25]And this is what he promised us—even eternal life.

[26]I am writing these things to you about those who are trying to lead you astray. [27]As for you, the anointing you received from him remains in you, and you do not need anyone to teach you. But as his anointing teaches you about all things and as that anointing is real, not counterfeit—just as it has taught you, remain in him.

Children of God

[28]And now, dear children, continue in him, so that when he appears we may be confident and unashamed before him at his coming.

[29]If you know that he is righteous, you know that everyone who does what is right has been born of him.

3 How great is the love the Father has lavished on us, that we should be called children of God! And that is what we are! The reason the world does not know us is that it did not know him. [2]Dear friends, now we are children of God, and what we will be has not yet been made known. But we know that when he appears,[b] we shall be like him, for we shall see him as he is. [3]Everyone who has this hope in him purifies himself, just as he is pure.

[4]Everyone who sins breaks the law; in fact, sin is lawlessness. [5]But you know that he appeared so that he might take away our sins. And in him is no sin. [6]No one who lives in him keeps on sinning. No one who continues to sin has either seen him or known him.

[7]Dear children, do not let anyone lead you astray. He who does what is right is righteous, just as he is righteous. [8]He who does what is sinful is of the devil, because the devil has been sinning from the beginning. The reason the Son of God appeared was to destroy the devil's work. [9]No one who is born of God will continue to sin, because God's seed remains in him; he cannot go on sinning, because he has been born of God. [10]This is how we know who the children of God are and who the children of the devil are: Anyone who does not do what is right is not a child of God; nor is anyone who does not love his brother.

Love One Another

[11]This is the message you heard from the beginning: We should love one another. [12]Do not be like Cain, who belonged to the evil one and murdered his brother. And why did he murder him? Because his own actions were evil and his brother's were righteous. [13]Do not be surprised, my brothers, if the world hates you.

[a]20 Some manuscripts *and you know all things* [b]2 Or *when it is made known*

2:18–23 An important secret to spiritual growth is a commitment to right beliefs. As we rely on the Holy Spirit, we can recognize the spirit of antichrist. The critical doctrinal issue for John was that of the deity of Jesus Christ. One cannot genuinely profess belief in God while denying his Son. True spiritual renewal cannot take place unless we recognize Jesus as both God and man.

2:24–27 Belief in Jesus as the Son of God and reliance on the Holy Spirit will guard us against being deceived by false doctrines. The quest for new, sophisticated solutions to the consequences of sin and despair only leads to new kinds of enslavement. Following Christ gives us the only perspective of ourselves and our world that can lead to true freedom from sin. Only the Christian faith asserts that Jesus took upon himself the penalty for our sin and gives us the power to break free from its bondage.

2:28—3:3 Many of us struggle with the issue of shame. John tells us that if we live in Christ, trusting him for forgiveness and walking with him consistently, we will have no reason to be ashamed at his return. We can rest assured that we are loved and acceptable because God himself has made us his children. As God's children, we long to be with him and to be like him. In the meantime, knowing that God is coming again will motivate us to live godly lives and to seek to know God better through prayer and meditation on his Word.

3:4–9 As we honestly reflect on our lives, we must face the essence of sin honestly: Sin is breaking God's law—doing things our own way rather than God's way. Once we surrender our lives to God, he himself gives us a new nature that is no longer comfortable with sin. We still slip into sin (see 1:8), but we no longer make it a practice. We know that our sin was the reason Jesus gave his life on the cross. Our new desire is to please him, in accordance with our new nature. When we were slaves to sin we continued with little sense of wrongdoing; now we know better. This new perspective on sin illustrates that God is truly at work in our lives.

3:10–20 Using Cain and Abel as examples, John underscored the importance of love. Having true love means we will willingly make sacrifices for the ones we love. The best way to express our love for God is to show love to others. Our actions toward others, as well as our words, matter a great deal to our spiritual growth.

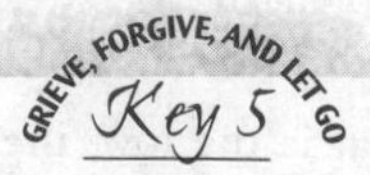

Letting Go of Hatred

1 John 4:14–21 Sometimes we find it easy to love God, but have difficulty loving other people. Yet true spiritual renewal means that we must grow to love God *and* others. God has so intertwined our love for him with our love for others that when we seek God and surrender to him, he requires us to give up our hatred and prejudice. We must love others with his love. And we can only do this through forgiveness.

The apostle John wrote, "God is love. Whoever lives in love lives in God, and God in him . . . If anyone says, 'I love God,' yet hates his brother, he is a liar. For anyone who does not love his brother, whom he has seen, cannot love God, whom he has not seen. And he has given us this command: Whoever loves God must also love his brother" (4:16, 20–21).

If we love God, God doesn't give us the option of hating our brothers and sisters. He doesn't even give us the option of hating our enemies. Jesus said, "I tell you who hear me: Love your enemies, do good to those who hate you, bless those who curse you, pray for those who mistreat you" (Luke 6:27–28). When we surrender to God, we must release our hatred, our prejudice and our bitterness to him. Surrender to God means forgiving and living a life of love.

Turn to Revelation 22.

[14]We know that we have passed from death to
life, because we love our brothers. Anyone who
does not love remains in death. [15]Anyone who
hates his brother is a murderer, and you know
that no murderer has eternal life in him.
[16]This is how we know what love is: Jesus
Christ laid down his life for us. And we ought
to lay down our lives for our brothers. [17]If anyone has material possessions and sees his
brother in need but has no pity on him, how
can the love of God be in him? [18]Dear children,
let us not love with words or tongue but with
actions and in truth. [19]This then is how we
know that we belong to the truth, and how we
set our hearts at rest in his presence [20]whenever
our hearts condemn us. For God is greater than
our hearts, and he knows everything.
[21]Dear friends, if our hearts do not condemn
us, we have confidence before God [22]and receive from him anything we ask, because we
obey his commands and do what pleases him.
[23]And this is his command: to believe in the
name of his Son, Jesus Christ, and to love one
another as he commanded us. [24]Those who
obey his commands live in him, and he in
them. And this is how we know that he lives in
us: We know it by the Spirit he gave us.

Test the Spirits

4 Dear friends, do not believe every spirit,
but test the spirits to see whether they are
from God, because many false prophets have
gone out into the world. [2]This is how you can
recognize the Spirit of God: Every spirit that
acknowledges that Jesus Christ has come in the
flesh is from God, [3]but every spirit that does not
acknowledge Jesus is not from God. This is the
spirit of the antichrist, which you have heard is
coming and even now is already in the world.
[4]You, dear children, are from God and have
overcome them, because the one who is in you
is greater than the one who is in the world.
[5]They are from the world and therefore speak
from the viewpoint of the world, and the world
listens to them. [6]We are from God, and whoever
knows God listens to us; but whoever is not
from God does not listen to us. This is how we
recognize the Spirit[a] of truth and the spirit of
falsehood.

God's Love and Ours

[7]Dear friends, let us love one another, for

[a]6 Or *spirit*

4:1–6 Anyone who denies that Jesus was God in human form is spreading false teaching and does not have the indwelling of the Holy Spirit. Such people will never achieve true transformation in their lives, for only the Holy Spirit can perform this. But those who acknowledge both Christ's humanity and deity and have surrendered their lives to him have a power that is stronger than their struggles with sin.

4:7–12 Our heavenly Father loves us so much that he sent his Son to save us. As we grow to be more like him,

love comes from God. Everyone who loves has
been born of God and knows God. [8]Whoever
does not love does not know God, because God
is love. [9]This is how God showed his love
among us: He sent his one and only Son[a] into
the world that we might live through him.
[10]This is love: not that we loved God, but that
he loved us and sent his Son as an atoning
sacrifice for[b] our sins. [11]Dear friends, since
God so loved us, we also ought to love one
another. [12]No one has ever seen God; but if we
love one another, God lives in us and his love
is made complete in us.

[13]We know that we live in him and he in us,
because he has given us of his Spirit. [14]And we
have seen and testify that the Father has sent his
Son to be the Savior of the world. [15]If anyone
acknowledges that Jesus is the Son of God, God
lives in him and he in God. [16]And so we know
and rely on the love God has for us.

God is love. Whoever lives in love lives in
God, and God in him. [17]In this way, love is
made complete among us so that we will have
confidence on the day of judgment, because in
this world we are like him. [18]There is no fear in
love. But perfect love drives out fear, because
fear has to do with punishment. The one who
fears is not made perfect in love.

[19]We love because he first loved us. [20]If anyone says, "I love God," yet hates his brother, he
is a liar. For anyone who does not love his
brother, whom he has seen, cannot love God,
whom he has not seen. [21]And he has given us

[a]9 Or *his only begotten Son* [b]10 Or *as the one who would turn aside his wrath, taking away*

we also grow in our ability to love one another with God's sacrificial love. Many of us feel our spiritual renewal would be greatly expedited if only we could see God. But no one has seen God the Father; and no one will see him until we reach heaven. But we can glimpse God's character through his people when they love one another. That is why it is so important for us to restore relationships with the people we have harmed and why we need the fellowship of believers—because we need the love they have to offer.

4:13–15 Assurance comes from believing that Jesus is the Son of God. The ability to believe is proof that God himself, through the Holy Spirit, is living in us. Confession of Christ is both the evidence and the expression of a genuine faith. More than an intellectual belief, our confession of Christ leads us to a confession of sin and a commitment to live for God, taking responsibility for our lives and dealing with our past failures and broken relationships.

4:16—5:3 John spoke again about the importance of love. True Christianity is characterized by loving relationships in which there is no fear. Experiencing such relationships—first with God, then with other believers—is at the heart of spiritual renewal. We can trust God wholly, without fear, because our punishment for sin has already taken place in Christ. When love reigns, we can be transparent with fellow believers, trusting that our honesty will not be used to hurt us. Mature Christian love delights in helping others, and it creates an environment in which we can develop accountability and a new sense of responsibility toward ourselves and toward others.

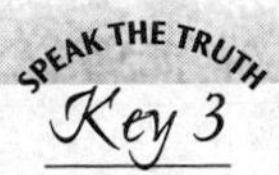

Calling for Transformation

1 John 5:11–15 Spiritual renewal involves being transformed into the person God planned each one of us to be. Confessing our sins and shortcomings is part of this process of transformation. Whenever we confess our sins, we can be confident that God will forgive us, grant us power to change and transform our lives.

The apostle Paul wrote, "He chose us in him before the creation of the world to be holy and blameless in his sight" (Ephesians 1:4). God wants to make us holy—that is, to form his character in us. Looking through the eyes of love, God already sees us as we will look when his work is done. Spiritual renewal is God's process of correcting our lives to match what he has planned them to be. Paul also tells us: "He who began a good work in you will carry it on to completion until the day of Christ Jesus" (Philippians 1:6). It is God's will for us to be made holy, and he will make sure it happens. We need only to repent and surrender to him.

And when we ask God to develop holiness in us, he will eagerly respond to our request: "This is the confidence we have in approaching God: that if we ask anything according to his will, he hears us. And if we know that he hears us—whatever we ask—we know that we have what we asked of him" (5:14–15).

Move on to Key 4 and turn to Luke 19.

this command: Whoever loves God must also love his brother.

Faith in the Son of God

5 Everyone who believes that Jesus is the Christ is born of God, and everyone who loves the father loves his child as well. 2This is how we know that we love the children of God: by loving God and carrying out his commands. 3This is love for God: to obey his commands. And his commands are not burdensome, 4for everyone born of God overcomes the world. This is the victory that has overcome the world, even our faith. 5Who is it that overcomes the world? Only he who believes that Jesus is the Son of God.

6This is the one who came by water and blood—Jesus Christ. He did not come by water only, but by water and blood. And it is the Spirit who testifies, because the Spirit is the truth. 7For there are three that testify: 8the[a] Spirit, the water and the blood; and the three are in agreement. 9We accept man's testimony, but God's testimony is greater because it is the testimony of God, which he has given about his Son. 10Anyone who believes in the Son of God has this testimony in his heart. Anyone who does not believe God has made him out to be a liar, because he has not believed the testimony God has given about his Son. 11And this is the testimony: God has given us eternal life, and this life is in his Son. 12He who has the Son has life; he who does not have the Son of God does not have life.

Concluding Remarks

13I write these things to you who believe in the name of the Son of God so that you may know that you have eternal life. 14This is the confidence we have in approaching God: that if we ask anything according to his will, he hears us. 15And if we know that he hears us—whatever we ask—we know that we have what we asked of him.

16If anyone sees his brother commit a sin that does not lead to death, he should pray and God will give him life. I refer to those whose sin does not lead to death. There is a sin that leads to death. I am not saying that he should pray about that. 17All wrongdoing is sin, and there is sin that does not lead to death.

18We know that anyone born of God does not continue to sin; the one who was born of God keeps him safe, and the evil one cannot harm him. 19We know that we are children of God, and that the whole world is under the control of the evil one. 20We know also that the Son of God has come and has given us understanding, so that we may know him who is true. And we are in him who is true—even in his Son Jesus Christ. He is the true God and eternal life.

21Dear children, keep yourselves from idols.

[a] 7,8 Late manuscripts of the Vulgate *testify in heaven: the Father, the Word and the Holy Spirit, and these three are one. 8And there are three that testify on earth: the* (not found in any Greek manuscript before the sixteenth century)

5:4–5 Believing in Jesus and living by faith equip us to triumph over the negative influences of our hostile world. For those of us who trust Christ with our lives, spiritual renewal is not only possible but also certain. Nothing can dominate us when God has promised us the power to overcome.

5:6–13 The Bible tells us that we must look for certain evidence in our lives to know whether or not we are living in a way that pleases God. Believing that Jesus is the Son of God and committing our lives to obeying him are two assurances of our spiritual growth. The Holy Spirit also will bear witness in our lives and point us to Christ. And God will give us a sense of rightness as we continue to maintain contact with him through prayer, the study of his Word and obedience to his will.

5:20–21 John ends this letter by reminding us who the true God is and warning us not to let anything take God's place in our hearts. He cautions us against entertaining any false ideas about God, which are at the root of all false religious systems. Spiritual renewal reminds us to rid ourselves of wrong ideas about God as well as any substitutes for him. God must be enthroned in his rightful place as the absolute Lord of our lives.

2 JOHN

The Big Picture

Spiritual growth is a fragile process. Without vigilance and encouragement from others, we can easily slip back into sin. Knowing this, we need help from others who possess courage and sensitivity about our situation. Harsh condemnation will not help us, but neither will friends who flatter us with falsely positive words. Diligence, together with faithful support, is what we need to maintain our spiritual growth.

John's letter is a highly personal one, dealing with the kinds of issues that are addressed in a broader way in 1 John. The tone is warm and pastoral, and John even called himself "the elder" (v. 1). He wrote this letter to commend and encourage "the chosen lady and her children" (v.1). Whether this designation refers to an actual believer and her Christian children or to a church and its members is not certain. These believers had already demonstrated their faithfulness to God; there was no need for correction. But John did not want them to trip over the obstacles ahead that might threaten their continued service to God.

In balancing commendation and encouragement, John proved himself to be a wise counselor and a splendid example to all of us. We need to recognize each other's past successes, affirming one another. At the same time, we must be willing to point out the hazards ahead when we see them, sharing our hard-won wisdom as a warning for the unwary. Pointing out the obstacles ahead and encouraging one another to be careful are the loving things to do. Thus, this letter underscores the critical importance of sharing the hope of spiritual renewal with others.

A. SALUTATION (1-3)

B. LOVE AND OBEDIENCE (4-6)

C. TRUTH AND VIGILANCE (7-11)

D. FINAL GREETINGS (12-13)

Spiritual Renewal Themes

THE IMPORTANCE OF GUARDING AGAINST HERESY

John urged his readers to be careful about those they invited into their homes for participation in the church's worship. John's words resemble the caution of David, who in Psalm 101 vowed not to allow deceitful people in his house. John instructed his readers not to encourage these false teachers in any way. Sometimes we believe that in order to be fair we need to listen to everyone's point of view, but there are dangers in

Essential Facts

PURPOSE:
To commend some faithful believers and to encourage them to continue teaching others about Christ.

AUTHOR:
The apostle John.

AUDIENCE:
"The chosen lady and her children" (v. 1), possibly referring to a church and its members.

DATE WRITTEN:
Probably before 1 John, sometime near A.D. 90.

SETTING:
As with his first letter, John was possibly the only surviving apostle when he wrote this letter, which circulated among the churches of Asia Minor. He lived in Ephesus at the time, supervising the churches of Asia Minor.

KEY VERSES:
"Anyone who runs ahead and does not continue in the teaching of Christ does not have God; whoever continues in the teaching has both the Father and the Son. If anyone comes to you and does not bring this teaching, do not take him into your house or welcome him" (vv. 9–10).

KEY PEOPLE AND RELATIONSHIPS:
John with his Christian readers, a "chosen sister" (v. 13) and "the chosen lady" (v. 1).

such an attitude. We must set limits on what we listen to if we are to protect our own spiritual growth.

THE CHALLENGE TO LOVE

Loving one another is the most basic act of obedience to God and an important element of our spiritual growth. At times, we may focus inward or become self-centered. Remembering to love others will not only please God; it will also help us to think of others and build good relationships.

1 The elder,

To the chosen lady and her children, whom
I love in the truth—and not I only, but also all
who know the truth— 2 because of the truth,
which lives in us and will be with us forever:

3 Grace, mercy and peace from God the Father and from Jesus Christ, the Father's Son, will
be with us in truth and love.

4 It has given me great joy to find some of
your children walking in the truth, just as the
Father commanded us. 5 And now, dear lady, I
am not writing you a new command but one we
have had from the beginning. I ask that we love
one another. 6 And this is love: that we walk in
obedience to his commands. As you have heard
from the beginning, his command is that you
walk in love.
7 Many deceivers, who do not acknowledge
Jesus Christ as coming in the flesh, have gone
out into the world. Any such person is the deceiver and the antichrist. 8 Watch out that you
do not lose what you have worked for, but that
you may be rewarded fully. 9 Anyone who runs
ahead and does not continue in the teaching of
Christ does not have God; whoever continues
in the teaching has both the Father and the Son.
10 If anyone comes to you and does not bring
this teaching, do not take him into your house
or welcome him. 11 Anyone who welcomes him
shares in his wicked work.
12 I have much to write to you, but I do not
want to use paper and ink. Instead, I hope to
visit you and talk with you face to face, so that
our joy may be complete.

13 The children of your chosen sister send
their greetings.

4–6 Note the wise approach John used here, commending "the chosen lady and her children" (v. 1) for their faithfulness, exhorting them to act according to Christian love and then explaining the reason for his letter. There is a pattern here for helping others: first encouragement, then exhortation and finally explanation. Even though we may communicate truths established by the authority of God's Word, sharing the Good News with others must still be accomplished in a way that will communicate effectively with people. An initial commendation will edify and build rapport; the exhortation will communicate the truth or confront a problem; an explanation will establish the truth and build the relationship.

7–9 Clear boundaries for belief and practice are essential. Many of us have been deceived and pulled into unhealthy relationships, damaging habits or false religions. We need to be aware of the subtle lies and distortions of truth used by people who would like to deceive us. The best way to avoid being deceived is to anchor our faith in God's Word and to seek his will for us through prayer. Faith in God through Jesus Christ is the only viable means for true spiritual renewal.

10–11 With heresy on the rise, John warned believers against allowing those with suspect doctrinal views to infiltrate the Christian community. He did not want new believers who had made a good beginning in the Christian faith to be led astray. We also need godly people in our lives—people like John—who can warn us away from false teachings and dangerous activities. If we don't have friends that hold us accountable, we need to take steps to develop such friendships. All of us are susceptible to deception. Fostering healthy relationships with wise and godly people is necessary to help us preserve our spiritual gains.

3 JOHN

The Big Picture

A. SALUTATION (1)

B. GAIUS: A CASE FOR COMMENDATION (2-8)

C. DIOTREPHES: A CASE FOR CONFRONTATION (9-10)

D. DEMETRIUS: A CASE FOR CONGRATULATION (11-12)

E. CONCLUDING REMARKS (13-15)

We know little about Gaius except that he was generous, hospitable and highly regarded by the apostle John. Apparently, Gaius took it upon himself to provide free room and board for traveling preachers and missionaries. In a day when most preachers had to travel from town to town with no regular means of support, this service was greatly needed. John wrote this letter to commend Gaius and to warn him to watch out for a self-important, spiritual teacher named Diotrephes. John challenged Gaius to warn others about him too and urged them not to be influenced by Diotrephes' bad example.

Aside from this warning about Diotrephes, John was primarily concerned with encouraging his friend Gaius. The simple act of including others in our lives and sharing ourselves with them is pleasing to God. One of the reasons God places people in our lives is so that we can support and encourage them. As we reach out to help others, we will also discover that we are blessed and strengthened in a special way.

Hospitality doesn't have to be complicated. It can be a simple act—setting an extra place at the table or offering someone a ride. Yet hospitality is a potent way to show love, appreciation and support. We all need a little affirmation sometimes. That affirmation can come through a simple invitation to enter someone else's life. Hospitality is a part of the process of spiritual renewal, a time to open up and support one another along the way.

Spiritual Renewal Themes

PRIDE LEADS TO A FALL

Diotrephes refused to humble himself before others and decided that he alone would be the boss. His arrogant attitude disqualified him from the very leadership role he coveted. One of the vices we face in our spiritual growth is pride. As we experience success in our spiritual growth, we can easily feel spiritually superior. We begin to think we are better than others and self-sufficient at last. A word to the wise: Pride and self-sufficiency often lead to a fall.

THE IMPORTANCE OF HELPING OTHERS

In contrast to Diotrephes, Gaius and Demetrius were commended for their service. They had generously shared with others without complaining, both in hospitality and in their teaching of the truth. In their own way, Gaius and Demetrius carried the message of God's transforming power to people who were still in bondage. John did not take these men for granted; instead, he commended them for their service, and today they live on as examples for each of us.

Essential Facts

PURPOSE:
To commend Gaius for his hospitality and encourage him in his faithfulness.

AUTHOR:
The apostle John.

AUDIENCE:
Gaius, a prominent believer, perhaps from Derbe in Asia Minor.

DATE WRITTEN:
Around A.D. 90.

SETTING:
Like 1 and 2 John, 3 John was probably written from Ephesus and circulated among the churches in Asia Minor.

KEY VERSE:
"Dear friend, do not imitate what is evil but what is good. Anyone who does what is good is from God. Anyone who does what is evil has not seen God" (v. 11).

KEY PEOPLE AND RELATIONSHIPS:
John with Gaius, with Diotrephes and with Demetrius.

[1]The elder,

To my dear friend Gaius, whom I love in the
truth.

[2]Dear friend, I pray that you may enjoy good
health and that all may go well with you, even
as your soul is getting along well. [3]It gave me
great joy to have some brothers come and tell
about your faithfulness to the truth and how
you continue to walk in the truth. [4]I have no
greater joy than to hear that my children are
walking in the truth.

[5]Dear friend, you are faithful in what you are
doing for the brothers, even though they are
strangers to you. [6]They have told the church
about your love. You will do well to send them
on their way in a manner worthy of God. [7]It was
for the sake of the Name that they went out,
receiving no help from the pagans. [8]We ought
therefore to show hospitality to such men so
that we may work together for the truth.

[9]I wrote to the church, but Diotrephes, who
loves to be first, will have nothing to do with us.
[10]So if I come, I will call attention to what he is
doing, gossiping maliciously about us. Not satisfied with that, he refuses to welcome the
brothers. He also stops those who want to do so
and puts them out of the church.

[11]Dear friend, do not imitate what is evil but
what is good. Anyone who does what is good is
from God. Anyone who does what is evil has
not seen God. [12]Demetrius is well spoken of by
everyone—and even by the truth itself. We also
speak well of him, and you know that our testimony is true.

[13]I have much to write you, but I do not want
to do so with pen and ink. [14]I hope to see you
soon, and we will talk face to face.

Peace to you. The friends here send their greetings. Greet the friends there by name.

5–8 Hospitality is a special gift that is often overlooked. John commended Gaius for the hospitality he had shown to the Christian teachers who periodically passed through town. Some of us may feel that we aren't good at sharing our faith. But hospitality may be one way we can encourage others and show them what God has done in our lives. By quietly serving others, we will illustrate the changes that have taken place in our lives, and others will wonder how it happened. This may open the way for us to share our faith in God in a more natural way. Opening our homes to others may also give people a context in which to relax and explore the truth about their own lives.

9–10 Confrontation is a necessary part of spiritual growth. But confrontation scares many of us. John dealt with an individual who had hurt many people in the Christian community. He warned Gaius and his fellow believers about this man and gave them the tools they needed to stand against him. There may be people actively opposing God's plans for us too. We may need to confront them about what they are doing. This can be difficult and can cause some pain, but it is necessary. God wants us to make spiritual progress; he will help us deal wisely with the people who stand in our way.

11–12 Good role models are important to our spiritual growth. John urged Gaius to follow good examples and to avoid imitating evil people. We need to develop relationships with people who will encourage us spiritually. This may mean that we will have to put relationships that lead us back into sin on hold for a time while we take concrete steps toward building relationships with people who model godly lifestyles. God will help us as we seek to build these healthy relationships.

JUDE

The Big Picture

Jude wrote this letter to young believers who had left their old lives behind to follow Christ. They had made a spiritual and moral commitment to do what God wanted them to do. But it was not long before false teachers claimed that believers could live however they wanted to because God had paid for their sins and would forgive them. Consequently, many new believers were tempted to go back to their old ways of life.

Jude urged his readers to stand up for the truth and not fall back into their old ways as the false teachers wrongly counseled. Jude explained that it did matter how believers lived their lives; their actions did have consequences. Returning to their old, sinful ways would cost a terrible price.

Pressures to fall back into sinful ways surround us too. There will always be people who want us to give up in our spiritual walk. Some suggest we bend or give in just a little. Others discourage us by their contempt for our beliefs or lack of hope that we will ever change completely.

Recognizing and standing up for God's truth, however, will pay off, for it is the truth that sets us free. God has given us his truth in the Bible. We must study God's Word to know this truth, then stand up for it and live it out in our lives.

A. A CAUTION TO BELIEVERS (1-16)

B. A CHALLENGE TO BELIEVERS (17-25)

Spiritual Renewal Themes

THE IMPORTANCE OF ACTION

This letter is a call to action, a call to "contend for the faith that was once for all entrusted to the saints" (v. 3). Spiritual growth is an active process, not a passive one. When things are going well in our lives, we can be tempted to sit back and relax. But spiritual growth is an ongoing process of honestly reflecting on our lives, confessing our sins, accepting responsibility, making restitution, grieving, forgiving, letting go and allowing God to redirect our course back into line with his will. We need to persevere in this process to preserve the spiritual gains we have made.

SHARING THE MESSAGE WITH OTHERS

Following Jesus is not a solitary activity. Jude urged his readers to help one another. He told them to be merciful and help each other by gently confronting one another, keeping others

Essential Facts

PURPOSE:
To warn believers of the dangers of false teachings about God.

AUTHOR:
Jude, the brother of James and half brother of Jesus.

AUDIENCE:
All believers everywhere.

DATE WRITTEN:
Probably around A.D. 65–70.

SETTING:
From the beginning, the early church had been threatened by false teachers. Jude wrote this letter warning all believers not to accept just any teaching about God but to defend the truth that they had received from the apostles.

KEY VERSES:
"But you, dear friends, build yourselves up in your most holy faith and pray in the Holy Spirit. Keep yourselves in God's love as you wait for the mercy of our Lord Jesus Christ to bring you to eternal life" (vv. 20–21).

KEY PEOPLE AND RELATIONSHIPS:
Jude with his audience.

from falling prey to destructive beliefs and activities (vv. 22–23). Spiritual renewal always gets us involved with other people. Our spiritual growth will not continue as God intends unless we make sharing the message of hope with others an integral part of our lives. As we share what God has done for us, we will gain new strength to persevere.

1Jude, a servant of Jesus Christ and a brother
of James,

To those who have been called, who are
loved by God the Father and kept by[a] Jesus
Christ:

2Mercy, peace and love be yours in abundance.

The Sin and Doom of Godless Men

3Dear friends, although I was very eager to
write to you about the salvation we share, I felt
I had to write and urge you to contend for the
faith that was once for all entrusted to the
saints. 4For certain men whose condemnation
was written about[b] long ago have secretly
slipped in among you. They are godless men,
who change the grace of our God into a license
for immorality and deny Jesus Christ our only
Sovereign and Lord.
5Though you already know all this, I want to
remind you that the Lord[c] delivered his people out of Egypt, but later destroyed those who
did not believe. 6And the angels who did not
keep their positions of authority but abandoned their own home—these he has kept in
darkness, bound with everlasting chains for
judgment on the great Day. 7In a similar way,
Sodom and Gomorrah and the surrounding
towns gave themselves up to sexual immorality
and perversion. They serve as an example of
those who suffer the punishment of eternal fire.
8In the very same way, these dreamers pollute their own bodies, reject authority and slander celestial beings. 9But even the archangel Michael, when he was disputing with the devil
about the body of Moses, did not dare to bring
a slanderous accusation against him, but said,
"The Lord rebuke you!" 10Yet these men speak
abusively against whatever they do not understand; and what things they do understand by

[a]1 Or *for;* or *in condemnation*
[b]4 Or *men who were marked out for condemnation*
[c]5 Some early manuscripts *Jesus*

3–7 Our problems don't usually attack us head-on; they often come when we least expect them. Sometimes we are completely unaware of the dangers that certain people, ideas or activities pose to us. Jude warned his readers about people who would try to lead them away from a true faith in Jesus Christ. These false teachers claimed that God's grace set them free to do whatever they wanted. Our society often presents us with a similar message, claiming that boundaries to behavior are limiting and destructive. Most of us have discovered firsthand, however, that the acceptance of this teaching leads to painful bondage. We should take Jude's warning seriously. We may need to avoid people and activities that are likely to lead us back into slavery to sin.

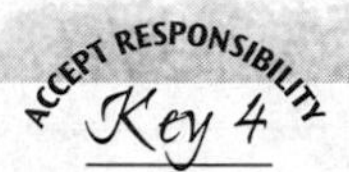

Confronting Those Who Do Wrong

Jude 20–23 God gives us the responsibility of honestly confronting those who do wrong. For some, such confrontation is a difficult task; for others, it is all too easy. We should not delight in finding fault in others, nor should we be so busy looking for sin in others' lives that we avoid facing our own problems. However, God may choose to use us to help others recognize the sin in their lives.

Jude the brother of Jesus reminded his readers that they were to deal honestly and mercifully with those who were doing wrong: "Be merciful to those who doubt; snatch others from the fire and save them; to others show mercy, mixed with fear—hating even the clothing stained by corrupted flesh" (vv. 22–23). Paul instructed his readers to do the same: "If someone is caught in a sin, you who are spiritual should restore him gently. But watch yourself, or you also may be tempted" (Galatians 6:1).

Jesus gave specific instructions for dealing with people who have sinned but refuse to see the truth and confess their sin:

> If your brother sins against you, go and show him his fault, just between the two of you. If he listens to you, you have won your brother over. But if he will not listen, take one or two others along, so that "every matter may be established by the testimony of two or three witnesses." If he refuses to listen to them, tell it to the church; and if he refuses to listen even to the church, treat him as you would a pagan or a tax collector (Matthew 18:15–17).

Responsible relationships with others are essential to our spiritual growth. As we humbly help others see their faults, we practice obedience to God and his ways. We are not responsible for their behavior, but we are responsible to tactfully point out areas that may cause them to stumble, to fall or to lose their way.

Move on to Key 5 and turn to Matthew 18.

James & Jude

Older brothers and sisters sometimes set high standards that are difficult to live up to. It can be equally difficult, and sometimes more painful, to live down the reputation of a notorious or embarrassing older sibling. James and Jude dealt with both challenges. Their older brother Jesus was perfect but, in their minds, his perfection was embarrassing.

It is probable that Mary, their mother, had always told James and Jude that Jesus was unique. But probably James and Jude had no idea just how special Jesus was. One thing is certain: Jesus would have been a hard act to follow. It may have been difficult for James, Jude and the rest of their siblings to feel close to their wonderful, different, older brother. The situation probably escalated after the death of their father, Joseph. As the oldest child, Jesus probably had to take on the role of a substitute father too.

After Jesus' public ministry began, James and Jude seemed to take a stand-back-and-watch attitude. One day Jesus would perform great miracles and receive acclamation as a hero. Yet the very next day he might present a convicting message that offended the powerful religious and political authorities. Jesus even claimed to be not only the promised Messiah but also God himself! Ultimately, he angered too many people and was sentenced to death. Without a doubt, James and Jude probably suspected that their brother was crazy (see Mark 3:21).

Yet Jesus' resurrection from the dead overcame the doubts of his younger brothers. Both James and Jude later became leaders in the early church. Their confidence in their big brother had been restored. James became one of the great leaders of the Christian community in Jerusalem. And both brothers are remembered for the books they wrote.

The transforming power of Christ's resurrection is still available for us today. The same power that transformed James and Jude can transform us and turn us from unbelieving cynics to faithful followers of Christ.

STRENGTHS AND ACCOMPLISHMENTS:

James and Jude both apparently wanted to understand and know Jesus.

Both grew beyond their misunderstandings about Jesus and became effective leaders and writers in the early church.

WEAKNESSES AND MISTAKES:

James and Jude did not really understand Jesus until after his resurrection.

They became disillusioned with Jesus' claims when he faced opposition.

LESSONS FROM THEIR LIVES:

Even those who are confused and disillusioned about Christ can regain trust and hope in him.

KEY VERSE:

"For whoever does the will of my Father in heaven is my brother and sister and mother" (Matthew 12:50).

James and Jude are named or alluded to in the Gospels and Acts 1:14. James is mentioned in Acts 15; 21; Galatians 1:19; 2; the book of James and Jude 1. Jude's name is found in Jude 1.

instinct, like unreasoning animals—these are the very things that destroy them.

[11]Woe to them! They have taken the way of Cain; they have rushed for profit into Balaam's error; they have been destroyed in Korah's rebellion.

[12]These men are blemishes at your love feasts, eating with you without the slightest qualm—shepherds who feed only themselves. They are clouds without rain, blown along by the wind; autumn trees, without fruit and uprooted—twice dead.
[13]They are wild waves of the sea, foaming up their shame; wandering stars, for whom blackest darkness has been reserved forever.

[14]Enoch, the seventh from Adam, prophesied about these men: "See, the Lord is coming with thousands upon thousands of his holy ones
[15]to judge everyone, and to convict all the ungodly of all the ungodly acts they have done in the ungodly way, and of all the harsh words ungodly sinners have spoken against him."
[16]These men are grumblers and faultfinders; they follow their own evil desires; they boast about themselves and flatter others for their own advantage.

A Call to Persevere

[17]But, dear friends, remember what the apostles of our Lord Jesus Christ foretold.
[18]They said to you, "In the last times there will be scoffers who will follow their own ungodly desires."
[19]These are the men who divide you, who follow mere natural instincts and do not have the Spirit.

[20]But you, dear friends, build yourselves up in your most holy faith and pray in the Holy Spirit.
[21]Keep yourselves in God's love as you wait for the mercy of our Lord Jesus Christ to bring you to eternal life.

[22]Be merciful to those who doubt;
[23]snatch others from the fire and save them; to others show mercy, mixed with fear—hating even the clothing stained by corrupted flesh.

Doxology

[24]To him who is able to keep you from falling and to present you before his glorious presence without fault and with great joy—
[25]to the only God our Savior be glory, majesty, power and authority, through Jesus Christ our Lord, before all ages, now and forevermore! Amen.

14–16 Jude reminded his readers that the false teachers among them would suffer terrible consequences for their selfish and sinful lifestyles. We may be tempted to follow our old friends back into our old destructive habits. Jude's warning can help us to turn away from such temptations. If we take part in sinful activities, they will enslave us. If we plant seeds of righteousness by following God's will, we will receive God's blessings and help. True freedom can be found only through a vibrant relationship with God.

17–23 Jude warns us about people who might try to hinder our spiritual growth. When we meet such people, we should be prepared to stand up against the temptations they put before us. By learning to recognize our weaknesses and by humbly following the Holy Spirit's guidance, we will be able to shun the things that could tear us down. When we seek to encourage others, our testimony of God's work in our lives must be clear and consistent with our way of life. Then we can share God's message of hope by showing others the kind of selfless love that God has already shown to us. We cannot live this kind of life under our own power, however; we can do it only by receiving the power God offers through his Holy Spirit.

Revelation

The Big Picture

A. JOHN'S PAIN AND GOD'S GLORY (1:1-20)

B. THE NEED FOR SPIRITUAL RENEWAL AMONG THE CHURCHES (2:1–3:22)

C. GOD'S GLORIOUS POWER—HOPE FOR SPIRITUAL RENEWAL (4:1–5:14)

D. GOD'S WRATH TOWARD UNBELIEF AND A REFUSAL TO SEE THE TRUTH (6:1–16:21)

E. BABYLON'S GRAND APPEARANCE AND FIERCE JUDGMENT (17:1–18:24)

F. CHRIST'S VICTORY, RULE AND FINAL JUDGMENT (19:1–20:15)

G. THE NEW HEAVENS AND NEW EARTH (21:1–22:21)

From beginning to end, the book of Revelation is about struggle. In its opening chapters, John dictated seven letters from the resurrected Christ to seven churches. Each church faced its own set of struggles, but some had deeper problems than others. In each letter, Jesus urged his people to cling to him and do what they knew to be right.

The rest of the book contains the story of another dramatic struggle: God's plan to rid the world of sin and its destructive consequences. We are told of a time when Jesus will return in glory to restore his broken world and conquer Satan, vindicating God's people and judging the wicked. On that day believers will receive eternal joy; unbelievers will receive unending separation from God. Ultimately, God will rebuild what has been broken by sin: He will create a new heaven and a new earth.

The book of Revelation ends with Christ as the victor. All that he said will come true; all that he taught will be proven right; all who followed him will be vindicated; all who rejected him will be judged. God will have his way. And he wants nothing more than to have us stand beside him as victors! Spiritual growth is often a struggle; God knows that. Throughout this book he urges us not to give up but to believe in him and to overcome. As God renews our broken world, he will make our broken lives new and perfect as well.

Spiritual Renewal Themes

GOD RULES OVER ALL

God is sovereign. He is greater than any other power in the universe. Nothing and no one can compare to him. When we look at the turmoil in the world today, the problems we face, the pain we have suffered or the pain we have caused others, we may wonder whether God will really be able to right all the wrongs. But John wrote this book to assure us that though evil may seem to win today's battles, God is all-powerful and will assert himself for his people. In the end, all things will be made new in Christ.

GOD IS THE SOURCE OF HOPE

The book of Revelation reveals to us the ultimate source of hope—Jesus Christ. He is coming again and will deal with the

problems of our sin-scarred world, restoring what is broken and dealing with the injustices around us. Life is never hopeless, regardless of what has happened to us or what we have done. We can focus on God's love, grace and forgiveness. He has made our restoration possible in Christ, and Christ will return to complete his task of renewal throughout all creation. If we are looking to Christ, we can hang on to our hope despite the difficult circumstances that we may face.

THE PAIN OF CONSEQUENCES

Every one of us cries out for justice. When evil and injustice prosper, we begin to feel angry. It often appears that people get away with their selfish and wicked deeds. But in reality God will judge all wicked actions. Those who openly defy him will ultimately face the awful consequences of their sin. Those who turn to God in repentance for forgiveness need not fear the future day of judgment. Judgment is an awful thing, and the pain of sin's consequences should motivate us to turn our lives over to God and obediently follow his plan.

Essential Facts

PURPOSE:
To give hope to believers and warn them not to compromise their loyalty to God.

AUTHOR:
The apostle John.

AUDIENCE:
Seven churches in Asia Minor.

DATE WRITTEN:
Probably about A.D. 95, during the Roman emperor Domitian's persecution of Christians.

SETTING:
John, who was in exile on the island of Patmos, wrote to the seven churches to urge them to devote themselves to Christ.

KEY VERSE:
"Here I am! I stand at the door and knock. If anyone hears my voice and opens the door, I will come in and eat with him, and he with me" (3:20).

KEY PLACES:
Patmos, seven cities in Asia Minor, Babylon and the new Jerusalem.

KEY PEOPLE:
John, the risen Christ and members of the churches of Asia Minor.

Prologue

1 The revelation of Jesus Christ, which God
gave him to show his servants what must
soon take place. He made it known by sending
his angel to his servant John, 2who testifies to
everything he saw—that is, the word of God and
the testimony of Jesus Christ. 3Blessed is the
one who reads the words of this prophecy, and
blessed are those who hear it and take to heart
what is written in it, because the time is near.

Greetings and Doxology

4John,

To the seven churches in the province of Asia:

Grace and peace to you from him who is, and
who was, and who is to come, and from the
seven spirits[a] before his throne, 5and from
Jesus Christ, who is the faithful witness, the
firstborn from the dead, and the ruler of the
kings of the earth.

To him who loves us and has freed us from
our sins by his blood, 6and has made us to be
a kingdom and priests to serve his God and
Father—to him be glory and power for ever and
ever! Amen.

7Look, he is coming with the clouds,
and every eye will see him,
even those who pierced him;
and all the peoples of the earth will
mourn because of him.
So shall it be! Amen.

8"I am the Alpha and the Omega," says the
Lord God, "who is, and who was, and who is
to come, the Almighty."

One Like a Son of Man

9I, John, your brother and companion in the
suffering and kingdom and patient endurance
that are ours in Jesus, was on the island of Patmos because of the word of God and the testimony of Jesus. 10On the Lord's Day I was in the
Spirit, and I heard behind me a loud voice like
a trumpet, 11which said: "Write on a scroll what
you see and send it to the seven churches: to
Ephesus, Smyrna, Pergamum, Thyatira, Sardis,
Philadelphia and Laodicea."

12I turned around to see the voice that was
speaking to me. And when I turned I saw seven
golden lampstands, 13and among the lampstands was someone "like a son of man,"[b]
dressed in a robe reaching down to his feet and
with a golden sash around his chest. 14His head
and hair were white like wool, as white as snow,
and his eyes were like blazing fire. 15His feet
were like bronze glowing in a furnace, and his
voice was like the sound of rushing waters. 16In
his right hand he held seven stars, and out of his
mouth came a sharp double-edged sword. His
face was like the sun shining in all its brilliance.

17When I saw him, I fell at his feet as though
dead. Then he placed his right hand on me and
said: "Do not be afraid. I am the First and the
Last. 18I am the Living One; I was dead, and
behold I am alive for ever and ever! And I hold
the keys of death and Hades.

19"Write, therefore, what you have seen,
what is now and what will take place later.
20The mystery of the seven stars that you saw in
my right hand and of the seven golden lampstands is this: The seven stars are the angels[c] of
the seven churches, and the seven lampstands
are the seven churches.

To the Church in Ephesus

2 "To the angel[d] of the church in Ephesus
write:

[a]4 Or *the sevenfold Spirit* [b]13 Daniel 7:13 [c]20 Or *messengers* [d]1 Or *messenger;* also in verses 8, 12 and 18

1:1–2 The book of Revelation tells us about things that will happen in the future. It looks forward to the time of Christ's return, when our new life in Christ will be perfected. Revelation also tells about the hard battle that God will fight to restore our world from the destructive consequences of sin. Many of the symbols in this book are difficult to interpret, but one message comes through loud and clear: No matter how bad things are right now, God has a solution! Jesus Christ will return to re-create our broken and polluted world. He will give us new bodies and healed hearts. God has already started this healing process in our lives through a relationship with Christ; he will complete this task when Christ returns.

1:4–6 Christ shed his redemptive blood on the cross in order to free us from our bondage to sin and to give us eternal life. God loved us enough to send his Son to die on our behalf. When Jesus rose from the dead, he conquered death forever! Through him, we also can rise to new life. No matter who we are or what we have done, in Christ, God has a solution for our problems. Even death has been overcome! Through Christ, we have been made citizens of God's eternal kingdom (see Philippians 3:20). We have a glorious eternity to look forward to.

1:7–8 The future coming of Jesus Christ will be a desperately painful moment for those who have refused to believe and follow him. The terrifying consequence will be eternal judgment (see 20:11–15). However, if we have put our faith in Christ, we can rejoice in the new life his return will bring. God is "the Beginning and the End" (21:6). We can have hope because God is in control of our past, present and future.

1:9–11 John had suffered a great deal for Christ and had persevered through it all. All the pain and exile had not embittered him toward God; in fact, the apostle still worshiped God faithfully. We are told that John was worshiping God when he received the visions recorded in this book. John's example gives us encouragement to persevere despite the difficulties we face. As we persevere in our spiritual growth, God can use us greatly too.

2:1–7 The Lord, through John, addressed the church in Ephesus first. During the time of Paul, the gospel messages delivered to and by the believers in Ephesus were probably the catalysts for the planting of the other churches mentioned in Revelation (see Acts 19:1–10). John began his communication to the church at Ephesus on a positive note, commending them for their perseverance through hardship. But John moved beyond these encouraging words to challenge his readers to repent and rekindle their love, which had waned. Confrontations are best made in the context of love. We need to begin our con-

These are the words of him who holds the seven stars in his right hand and walks among the seven golden lampstands: [2]I know your deeds, your hard work and your perseverance. I know that you cannot tolerate wicked men, that you have tested those who claim to be apostles but are not, and have found them false. [3]You have persevered and have endured hardships for my name, and have not grown weary.

[4]Yet I hold this against you: You have forsaken your first love. [5]Remember the height from which you have fallen! Repent and do the things you did at first. If you do not repent, I will come to you and remove your lampstand from its place. [6]But you have this in your favor: You hate the practices of the Nicolaitans, which I also hate.

[7]He who has an ear, let him hear what the Spirit says to the churches. To him who overcomes, I will give the right to eat from the tree of life, which is in the paradise of God.

To the Church in Smyrna

[8]"To the angel of the church in Smyrna write:

These are the words of him who is the First and the Last, who died and came to life again. [9]I know your afflictions and your poverty—yet you are rich! I know the slander of those who say they are Jews and are not, but are a synagogue of Satan. [10]Do not be afraid of what you are about to suffer. I tell you, the devil will put some of you in prison to test you, and you will suffer persecution for ten days. Be faithful, even to the point of death, and I will give you the crown of life.

[11]He who has an ear, let him hear what the Spirit says to the churches. He who overcomes will not be hurt at all by the second death.

To the Church in Pergamum

[12]"To the angel of the church in Pergamum write:

These are the words of him who has the sharp, double-edged sword. [13]I know where you live—where Satan has his throne. Yet you remain true to my name. You did not renounce your faith in me, even in the days of Antipas, my faithful witness, who was put to death in your city—where Satan lives.

[14]Nevertheless, I have a few things against you: You have people there who hold to the teaching of Balaam, who taught Balak to entice the Israelites to sin by eating food sacrificed to idols and by committing sexual immorality. [15]Likewise you also have those who hold to the teaching of the Nicolaitans. [16]Repent therefore! Otherwise, I will soon come to you and will fight against them with the sword of my mouth.

[17]He who has an ear, let him hear what the Spirit says to the churches. To him who overcomes, I will give some of the hidden manna. I will also give him a white stone with a new name written on it, known only to him who receives it.

To the Church in Thyatira

[18]"To the angel of the church in Thyatira write:

These are the words of the Son of God, whose eyes are like blazing fire and whose feet are like burnished bronze. [19]I know your deeds, your love and faith, your service and perseverance, and that you are now doing more than you did at first.

[20]Nevertheless, I have this against you: You tolerate that woman Jezebel, who calls herself a prophetess. By her teaching she misleads my servants into sexual immorality and the eating of food sacrificed to idols. [21]I have given her time to repent of her immorality, but she is unwilling.

---

versations by building others up and showing them that we care. After laying the groundwork, we will be better able to communicate the more painful message of confrontation.

2:8–11 Of the remaining six churches, the church in Smyrna was the closest geographically to Ephesus, and it experienced similar hardships. This small Christian community suffered from unrelenting oppression by Satan and his evil spiritual forces. John's vision reminded the believers that God would reward their perseverance through dangerous times with new life in Jesus Christ. We also are called to persevere through the tough times. As we surrender our lives to God and follow his will, he will transform us. At Christ's return, we will receive new bodies and cleansed hearts—completely new lives!

2:12–17 The church at Pergamum also had been intensely loyal to Jesus Christ through a satanic onslaught. Yet some in the church had fallen prey to sexual misconduct. Such relational and spiritual misconduct threatened to undermine, or at least neutralize, the testimony of this Christian community. Sometimes great victories can be undone by seemingly small sins. We need to be consistent in our walk with God, making sure that all areas of our lives are yielded to him. Even the smallest sin or bad habit can lead us off course over time. We consistently need to see the truth of where we are spiritually and ask God to redirect our course back in line with his will.

2:18–29 The church in Thyatira was commended for its acts of love, faith, patience and service. The church was also encouraged to persevere in doing them. However, a serious spiritual cancer was growing in the church at Thyatira. A self-styled prophetess whom John labeled Jezebel encouraged a profligate lifestyle. God's harsh punishment of this woman shows us that he wanted to protect his people from her destructive influence. It is also dangerous for us to have relationships with people who might try to lead us astray. We must carefully choose the people with whom we spend our time. A sinful relationship may lead us away from God and undermine our spiritual progress.

22 So I will cast her on a bed of suffering,
and I will make those who commit adultery with her suffer intensely, unless they
repent of her ways. 23 I will strike her children dead. Then all the churches will
know that I am he who searches hearts
and minds, and I will repay each of you
according to your deeds. 24 Now I say to
the rest of you in Thyatira, to you who do
not hold to her teaching and have not
learned Satan's so-called deep secrets (I
will not impose any other burden on
you): 25 Only hold on to what you have
until I come.
26 To him who overcomes and does my
will to the end, I will give authority over
the nations—

27 'He will rule them with an iron
scepter;
he will dash them to pieces like
pottery'[a]—

just as I have received authority from my
Father. 28 I will also give him the morning
star. 29 He who has an ear, let him hear
what the Spirit says to the churches.

To the Church in Sardis

3 "To the angel[b] of the church in Sardis
write:

These are the words of him who holds
the seven spirits[c] of God and the seven
stars. I know your deeds; you have a reputation of being alive, but you are dead.
2 Wake up! Strengthen what remains and
is about to die, for I have not found your
deeds complete in the sight of my God.
3 Remember, therefore, what you have received and heard; obey it, and repent. But
if you do not wake up, I will come like a
thief, and you will not know at what time
I will come to you.
4 Yet you have a few people in Sardis
who have not soiled their clothes. They
will walk with me, dressed in white, for
they are worthy. 5 He who overcomes will,
like them, be dressed in white. I will never
blot out his name from the book of life,
but will acknowledge his name before my
Father and his angels. 6 He who has an ear,
let him hear what the Spirit says to the
churches.

To the Church in Philadelphia

7 "To the angel of the church in Philadelphia
write:

These are the words of him who is holy
and true, who holds the key of David.
What he opens no one can shut, and what
he shuts no one can open. 8 I know your
deeds. See, I have placed before you an
open door that no one can shut. I know
that you have little strength, yet you have
kept my word and have not denied my
name. 9 I will make those who are of the
synagogue of Satan, who claim to be Jews
though they are not, but are liars—I will
make them come and fall down at your
feet and acknowledge that I have loved
you. 10 Since you have kept my command
to endure patiently, I will also keep you
from the hour of trial that is going to come
upon the whole world to test those who
live on the earth.
11 I am coming soon. Hold on to what
you have, so that no one will take your
crown. 12 Him who overcomes I will make
a pillar in the temple of my God. Never
again will he leave it. I will write on him
the name of my God and the name of the
city of my God, the new Jerusalem, which
is coming down out of heaven from my
God; and I will also write on him my new
name. 13 He who has an ear, let him hear
what the Spirit says to the churches.

To the Church in Laodicea

14 "To the angel of the church in Laodicea write:

These are the words of the Amen, the
faithful and true witness, the ruler of
God's creation. 15 I know your deeds, that
you are neither cold nor hot. I wish you
were either one or the other! 16 So, because
you are lukewarm—neither hot nor cold—
I am about to spit you out of my mouth.

[a] *27* Psalm 2:9 [b] *1* Or *messenger;* also in verses 7 and 14 [c] *1* Or *the sevenfold Spirit*

3:1–6 Most of the believers in Sardis were only following the rituals of their faith. John warned them that if they didn't make some immediate changes, they would suffer painful consequences. Some of the believers in Sardis stood firm in their faith. John promised that they would be rewarded accordingly. With God's help we can stand firm even when everyone around us is falling away. We don't have to follow the crowd; we can follow God instead. As we do, he will bless us and write our names in the book of life.

3:7–13 The church in Philadelphia was not strong, but it had remained obedient to God and had stood firm against satanic oppression. As a result, Christ promised this church protection from the greatest time of tribulation that would ever come upon the whole world. He encouraged them to persevere, promising that they would live forever with him in his new Jerusalem. This promise has been greatly delayed, but that doesn't make it any less secure (see 21:1—22:21). We still have this same hope if we entrust our lives to God through faith in Jesus Christ.

3:14–22 The believers in Laodicea thought of themselves as self-sustaining, having no needs. Christ saw their situation quite differently. To him the Laodicean believers were spiritually blind and destitute. But worst of all, they were spiritually indifferent—lukewarm. If we cannot see the truth, we cannot move back in line with the life that God wants us to live. Therefore, we must continually pray for God to heal our spiritual blindness so that we can see the truth as he reveals it to us.

17You say, 'I am rich; I have acquired
wealth and do not need a thing.' But you
do not realize that you are wretched, piti-
ful, poor, blind and naked. 18I counsel you
to buy from me gold refined in the fire, so
you can become rich; and white clothes to
wear, so you can cover your shameful nakedness; and salve to put on your eyes, so
you can see.
19Those whom I love I rebuke and discipline. So be earnest, and repent. 20Here
I am! I stand at the door and knock. If
anyone hears my voice and opens the
door, I will come in and eat with him, and
he with me.
21To him who overcomes, I will give
the right to sit with me on my throne, just
as I overcame and sat down with my Father on his throne. 22He who has an ear,
let him hear what the Spirit says to the
churches."

The Throne in Heaven

4 After this I looked, and there before me was
a door standing open in heaven. And the
voice I had first heard speaking to me like a
trumpet said, "Come up here, and I will show
you what must take place after this." 2At once I
was in the Spirit, and there before me was a
throne in heaven with someone sitting on it.
3And the one who sat there had the appearance
of jasper and carnelian. A rainbow, resembling
an emerald, encircled the throne. 4Surrounding
the throne were twenty-four other thrones, and
seated on them were twenty-four elders. They
were dressed in white and had crowns of gold
on their heads. 5From the throne came flashes
of lightning, rumblings and peals of thunder.
Before the throne, seven lamps were blazing.
These are the seven spirits[a] of God. 6Also before the throne there was what looked like a sea
of glass, clear as crystal.
In the center, around the throne, were four
living creatures, and they were covered with
eyes, in front and in back. 7The first living creature was like a lion, the second was like an ox,
the third had a face like a man, the fourth was
like a flying eagle. 8Each of the four living crea-

[a]5 Or *the sevenfold Spirit*

4:1–3 The apostle John was allowed to view this spectacular scene in God's heavenly throne room, but he was still a prisoner on the island of Patmos. We also may feel hopelessly entrapped and distant from any kind of help or deliverance. But we, like John, can draw close to God even when the world around us is dark and foreboding. John's vision of heaven gave him the hope he needed to face many lonely days ahead. And the record the apostle left us can give us hope during hard times too. Even when we are alone and helpless, God is still with us. The circumstances or situations we face will never limit God's grace and power.

4:8–11 God is worthy of our continual praise. Even the great spiritual beings in heaven praise God as their primary occupation. God is greater and more powerful than

God's Love Expels Our Fear

Revelation 3:14–22 Relationships can be difficult to maintain. When we feel threatened, we tend to become defensive and guarded. But when we feel safe in a relationship, we will be open and vulnerable. These principles are true in our relationships with people and with God.

The apostle John wrote, "There is no fear in love. But perfect love drives out fear, because fear has to do with punishment. The one who fears is not made perfect in love. We love because he first loved us" (1 John 4:18–19). If our sins were not paid for, we would have good reason to be afraid and remain defensive toward God. However, since God loves us and has paid for our sins through Jesus Christ, we can safely open ourselves to God and seek his truth.

Jesus is waiting for us to repent, receive his love and open our hearts to him. He said, "Here I am! I stand at the door and knock. If anyone hears my voice and opens the door, I will come in and eat with him, and he with me" (3:20). Love is waiting. When we open ourselves fully to God's love, we will be able to see the truth because we will no longer be afraid of God's punishment.

Move on to Key 3 and turn to Luke 11.

THE SPIRITUAL DISCIPLINES

Worship

A Glimpse of Glory

Revelation 4:1—7:17 In one way or another, we have all witnessed the effect of praise. Praise completes the joy of an experience. Have you ever been to a sporting event where the crowd was very quiet? The silence was almost unbearable. The best part of a sporting event is cheering for the home team's victorious accomplishments. The most enthusiastic fans often repeat those great moments to one another over and over again! We also will find energy coursing through our spiritual lives when we repeat—over and over—the mighty acts of God in history and his acts in our own lives. It is good to celebrate the joy and wonder of our relationship with the Lord.

Praise not only completes our joy in fellowship with the Lord; it also gives us a foretaste of heaven. Worship through praise is the chief activity of eternity. Paul admonishes us, "Since, then, you have been raised with Christ, set your hearts on things above, where Christ is seated at the right hand of God. Set your minds on things above, not on earthly things" (Colossians 3:1–2). We learn something of what Paul means by this from the book of Revelation. Though many people have pigeonholed Revelation as a book solely about prophecy, this book is one of the most profound worship manuals in the Bible. While the Psalms are our Biblical hymnbook, the book of Revelation reveals heavenly scenes of worship.

John's words in Revelation 4:1 shed new light on praise by giving us an amazing description of worship: "After this I looked, and there before me was a door standing open in heaven." It is exciting to think that worship is an open door to God's presence. Notice that John was ushered right to the throne! There is no waiting room or foyer for preparation. Why? Because the way has been completely opened through Jesus Christ! The writer of Hebrews expressed it this way: "Let us then approach the throne of grace with confidence, so that we may receive mercy and find grace to help us in our time of need" (Hebrews 4:16).

As we meditate on the realities of heaven that John colorfully describes, we find sights of glory that thrill the imagination, sounds of power, songs of praise and fragrances of incense in the prayers of the saints. As we ponder John's words, we understand that worship is much more than an exercise of the mind. It is an experience of the whole person caught up in glory.

Few activities strengthen our faith more than cultivating a richer, fuller understanding of God through worship. Praise calls us to consider the nature and character of God. In Revelation 7:12, the multitude worships and adores God by calling for seven blessings upon him: "Praise and glory and wisdom and thanks and honor and power and strength be to our God for ever and ever. Amen!" The worshipers affirm and celebrate the matchless glory of the Lord.

Reflection upon God's character is a powerful means for enriching our prayer lives. As we seek to grasp God's greatness and ascribe to him all the honor that is due him, our faith is strengthened, our hearts are encouraged and our vision of God grows. Many of us would do well to focus less on in-depth analyses of our problems and to meditate more time on the character of God, who is the answer to our problems.

Putting It Into Practice

As we honor God, we also receive a deeper sense of God's presence. When have you sensed God's presence? What was it like? How did this change your thoughts or actions? When you worship this week, quiet your heart and remind yourself that God is always present with you.

For more on worship, turn to Exodus 20.

tures had six wings and was covered with eyes
all around, even under his wings. Day and night
they never stop saying:

"Holy, holy, holy
is the Lord God Almighty,
who was, and is, and is to come."

9Whenever the living creatures give glory, honor
and thanks to him who sits on the throne and
who lives for ever and ever, 10the twenty-four
elders fall down before him who sits on the
throne, and worship him who lives for ever and
ever. They lay their crowns before the throne
and say:

11"You are worthy, our Lord and God,
to receive glory and honor and power,
for you created all things,
and by your will they were created
and have their being."

The Scroll and the Lamb

5 Then I saw in the right hand of him who
sat on the throne a scroll with writing on
both sides and sealed with seven seals. 2And I
saw a mighty angel proclaiming in a loud voice,
"Who is worthy to break the seals and open the
scroll?" 3But no one in heaven or on earth or
under the earth could open the scroll or even
look inside it. 4I wept and wept because no one
was found who was worthy to open the scroll or
look inside. 5Then one of the elders said to me,
"Do not weep! See, the Lion of the tribe of
Judah, the Root of David, has triumphed. He is
able to open the scroll and its seven seals."
6Then I saw a Lamb, looking as if it had been
slain, standing in the center of the throne, encircled by the four living creatures and the elders.
He had seven horns and seven eyes, which are
the seven spirits[a] of God sent out into all the
earth. 7He came and took the scroll from the
right hand of him who sat on the throne. 8And
when he had taken it, the four living creatures
and the twenty-four elders fell down before the
Lamb. Each one had a harp and they were holding golden bowls full of incense, which are the
prayers of the saints. 9And they sang a new
song:

"You are worthy to take the scroll
and to open its seals,
because you were slain,
and with your blood you purchased men
for God
from every tribe and language and
people and nation.
10You have made them to be a kingdom and
priests to serve our God,
and they will reign on the earth."

11Then I looked and heard the voice of many
angels, numbering thousands upon thousands,
and ten thousand times ten thousand. They encircled the throne and the living creatures and
the elders. 12In a loud voice they sang:

"Worthy is the Lamb, who was slain,
to receive power and wealth and wisdom
and strength
and honor and glory and praise!"

13Then I heard every creature in heaven and
on earth and under the earth and on the sea,
and all that is in them, singing:

"To him who sits on the throne and to the
Lamb
be praise and honor and glory and power,
for ever and ever!"

14The four living creatures said, "Amen," and the
elders fell down and worshiped.

The Seals

6 I watched as the Lamb opened the first of
the seven seals. Then I heard one of the

[a]6 Or *the sevenfold Spirit*

any difficulty we have to face. As we surrender our lives to God, let us also praise him for the amazing transformation he is working in us.

5:1–7 In heaven there was no one worthy to open the scroll of revelation and judgment except the Lamb—Jesus Christ. He is perfect and has conquered sin and death through his death and resurrection. There are many religions and paths that claim to lead to spiritual renewal, but no leader of any of these religions or other paths is worthy to open this scroll. There is no one other than Jesus Christ who is able to give us the true spiritual renewal we seek.

5:9–10 By shedding his blood on the cross, Jesus Christ, the Lamb, purchased our salvation (see John 1:29). But God does far more than just deliver us from our destructive sins. He promises to use us to restore and maintain his world. We will be members of a kingdom of priests to our God. As soon as we entrust our lives to God and seek to follow his will, we can begin our priestly duties by sharing our story of deliverance and calling others to entrust their lives to God's care. We can play an important role in the restoration of people's lives by introducing them to Jesus Christ—the only one who is able to give us true spiritual renewal.

5:11–14 In these final verses of John's description of the heavenly throne room, praise for the divine Lamb spills over from heaven to the rest of the created realm. No matter how much unbelief and rebellion dominate the earthly scene today, there will come a time when all will bow before God. We don't have to wait until Christ returns to acknowledge his lordship in our lives. We can repent and surrender to him today and begin to enjoy the immediate benefits of a vital relationship with God through Jesus Christ.

6:1–8 Jesus Christ, the Lamb, begins the process of opening the scroll (see 5:1). This sets in motion the events leading to God's victory over sin and death. War, famine and disease will be rampant during the period of the first four seals. Notice that the first steps toward God's cosmic restoration lead through painful times. Millions of people will die as God begins to deal with those who have rejected him. God often lets us wander through a period of pain as we suffer the consequences for our behavior. But God does this for our ultimate good. Even though he allows us to suffer for a time, he has plans for our restoration. God can use our suffering to teach us how helpless

four living creatures say in a voice like thunder, "Come!" 2I looked, and there before me was a white horse! Its rider held a bow, and he was given a crown, and he rode out as a conqueror bent on conquest.

3When the Lamb opened the second seal, I heard the second living creature say, "Come!" 4Then another horse came out, a fiery red one. Its rider was given power to take peace from the earth and to make men slay each other. To him was given a large sword.

5When the Lamb opened the third seal, I heard the third living creature say, "Come!" I looked, and there before me was a black horse! Its rider was holding a pair of scales in his hand. 6Then I heard what sounded like a voice among the four living creatures, saying, "A quart[a] of wheat for a day's wages,[b] and three quarts of barley for a day's wages,[b] and do not damage the oil and the wine!"

7When the Lamb opened the fourth seal, I heard the voice of the fourth living creature say, "Come!" 8I looked, and there before me was a pale horse! Its rider was named Death, and Hades was following close behind him. They were given power over a fourth of the earth to kill by sword, famine and plague, and by the wild beasts of the earth.

9When he opened the fifth seal, I saw under the altar the souls of those who had been slain because of the word of God and the testimony they had maintained. 10They called out in a loud voice, "How long, Sovereign Lord, holy and true, until you judge the inhabitants of the earth and avenge our blood?" 11Then each of them was given a white robe, and they were told to wait a little longer, until the number of their fellow servants and brothers who were to be killed as they had been was completed.

12I watched as he opened the sixth seal. There was a great earthquake. The sun turned black like sackcloth made of goat hair, the whole moon turned blood red, 13and the stars in the sky fell to earth, as late figs drop from a fig tree when shaken by a strong wind. 14The sky receded like a scroll, rolling up, and every mountain and island was removed from its place.

15Then the kings of the earth, the princes, the generals, the rich, the mighty, and every slave and every free man hid in caves and among the rocks of the mountains. 16They called to the mountains and the rocks, "Fall on us and hide us from the face of him who sits on the throne and from the wrath of the Lamb! 17For the great day of their wrath has come, and who can stand?"

144,000 Sealed

7 After this I saw four angels standing at the four corners of the earth, holding back the four winds of the earth to prevent any wind from blowing on the land or on the sea or on any tree. 2Then I saw another angel coming up from the east, having the seal of the living God. He called out in a loud voice to the four angels who had been given power to harm the land and the sea: 3"Do not harm the land or the sea or the trees until we put a seal on the foreheads of the servants of our God." 4Then I heard the number of those who were sealed: 144,000 from all the tribes of Israel.

5From the tribe of Judah 12,000 were sealed,
from the tribe of Reuben 12,000,
from the tribe of Gad 12,000,
6from the tribe of Asher 12,000,
from the tribe of Naphtali 12,000,
from the tribe of Manasseh 12,000,
7from the tribe of Simeon 12,000,
from the tribe of Levi 12,000,
from the tribe of Issachar 12,000,
8from the tribe of Zebulun 12,000,
from the tribe of Joseph 12,000,
from the tribe of Benjamin 12,000.

The Great Multitude in White Robes

9After this I looked and there before me was a great multitude that no one could count, from

[a]6 Greek *a choinix* (probably about a liter) [b]6 Greek *a denarius*

---

we are and show us how much we need him.

6:9–11 The opening of the fifth seal reveals those who have been martyred for their service to God, those waiting for God to avenge their unjust deaths. God tells them that they will have to wait because other martyrs must join their numbers. Remembering these verses we can learn to trust God with any injustices that are leveled against us.

6:12–17 The opening of the sixth seal is followed by a huge earthquake and amazing phenomena in the sky. Leaders and military commanders will want to die, mistakenly thinking that through death they can escape God's terrible judgment. Sadly, their hearts will be so hardened that even though they recognize God, they will not repent and turn to him in faith (see 9:20–21). Their continued refusal to surrender to God will lead to their eventual destruction. God wants to give us meaningful and joyful lives, but there will be wrath and judgment for those who rebel against him.

7:1–3 As difficult as things will be during the period of the seals, God's protection will also be present for those who belong to him. They will be marked with a "seal" (7:3) of God's ownership. Perhaps this seal is similar to the seal of the Holy Spirit, who is now present in the lives of all who believe in Jesus Christ (see Ephesians 1:13–14; 4:30). In either case the seal signifies an eternal relationship with God. We can begin an eternal relationship with God right now by repenting and accepting God's forgiveness through Jesus Christ and submitting our lives to his good plan.

7:9–14 This vast multitude from all races and nations is the harvest Christ envisioned from his great commission (see Matthew 28:19; Luke 10:2). This multitude is truly thankful, worshiping God to show their appreciation for his great salvation. The white garments worn by this crowd speak of their purity through the blood of Christ. By surrendering our lives to God and accepting God's forgiveness in Jesus Christ, we can join this joyful throng of people who have been saved by God's wonderful grace.

every nation, tribe, people and language, standing before the throne and in front of the Lamb.
They were wearing white robes and were holding palm branches in their hands. 10And they
cried out in a loud voice:

"Salvation belongs to our God,
who sits on the throne,
and to the Lamb."

11All the angels were standing around the
throne and around the elders and the four living creatures. They fell down on their faces before the throne and worshiped God, 12saying:

"Amen!
Praise and glory
and wisdom and thanks and honor
and power and strength
be to our God for ever and ever.
Amen!"

13Then one of the elders asked me, "These in
white robes—who are they, and where did they
come from?"
14I answered, "Sir, you know."
And he said, "These are they who have come
out of the great tribulation; they have washed
their robes and made them white in the blood
of the Lamb. 15Therefore,

"they are before the throne of God
and serve him day and night in his
temple;
and he who sits on the throne will spread
his tent over them.
16Never again will they hunger;
never again will they thirst.
The sun will not beat upon them,
nor any scorching heat.
17For the Lamb at the center of the throne
will be their shepherd;
he will lead them to springs of living
water.
And God will wipe away every tear from
their eyes."

The Seventh Seal and the Golden Censer

8 When he opened the seventh seal, there
was silence in heaven for about half an
hour.
2And I saw the seven angels who stand before
God, and to them were given seven trumpets.
3Another angel, who had a golden censer,
came and stood at the altar. He was given much
incense to offer, with the prayers of all the
saints, on the golden altar before the throne.
4The smoke of the incense, together with the
prayers of the saints, went up before God from
the angel's hand. 5Then the angel took the censer, filled it with fire from the altar, and hurled
it on the earth; and there came peals of thunder,
rumblings, flashes of lightning and an earthquake.

The Trumpets

6Then the seven angels who had the seven
trumpets prepared to sound them.
7The first angel sounded his trumpet, and
there came hail and fire mixed with blood, and
it was hurled down upon the earth. A third of
the earth was burned up, a third of the trees
were burned up, and all the green grass was
burned up.
8The second angel sounded his trumpet, and
something like a huge mountain, all ablaze,
was thrown into the sea. A third of the sea
turned into blood, 9a third of the living creatures in the sea died, and a third of the ships
were destroyed.
10The third angel sounded his trumpet, and
a great star, blazing like a torch, fell from the sky
on a third of the rivers and on the springs of
water— 11the name of the star is Wormwood.[a]
A third of the waters turned bitter, and many
people died from the waters that had become
bitter.
12The fourth angel sounded his trumpet, and
a third of the sun was struck, a third of the
moon, and a third of the stars, so that a third of
them turned dark. A third of the day was without light, and also a third of the night.
13As I watched, I heard an eagle that was
flying in midair call out in a loud voice: "Woe!
Woe! Woe to the inhabitants of the earth, because of the trumpet blasts about to be sounded
by the other three angels!"

9 The fifth angel sounded his trumpet, and I
saw a star that had fallen from the sky to
the earth. The star was given the key to the shaft
of the Abyss. 2When he opened the Abyss,
smoke rose from it like the smoke from a gigan-

[a]11 That is, Bitterness

7:15–17 This majestic passage describes the heavenly relationship between Christ and his people. They will serve him constantly, and he will always protect them. Christ, the Lamb who is also the shepherd, will meet all their needs. In such a close and secure relationship, all the tears of painful oppression, loss and misunderstanding will be done away with. What wonderful hope these verses offer us! By trusting in Jesus Christ, we can hope for a future filled with joy and peace.

8:1–2 The opening of the seventh seal on the scroll of judgment brings a short period of silence before the sounding of the seven trumpets and their horrible judgments. With such cataclysmic events foretold for the future of the earth, our spiritual inheritance takes on far greater importance. Since the earth will bear God's wrath, we will do well to invest in God's indestructible kingdom.

8:6–13 At the blowing of the trumpets, the people of our sinful world will suffer the terrible consequences of their sin. There is a day of reckoning for all who reject God's salvation; realizing this should cause us to share our faith with urgency.

9:1–4 As the fifth trumpet blows, a locust plague will be unleashed. Unlike regular locusts, however, these creatures will attack people, not plants. Notice that God will not allow these creatures to harm everyone. Those protected by God's seal will be unharmed. We can be secure in the fact that God is able and willing to care for us when we seek him.

tic furnace. The sun and sky were darkened by the smoke from the Abyss. 3And out of the smoke locusts came down upon the earth and were given power like that of scorpions of the earth. 4They were told not to harm the grass of the earth or any plant or tree, but only those people who did not have the seal of God on their foreheads. 5They were not given power to kill them, but only to torture them for five months. And the agony they suffered was like that of the sting of a scorpion when it strikes a man. 6During those days men will seek death, but will not find it; they will long to die, but death will elude them.

7The locusts looked like horses prepared for battle. On their heads they wore something like crowns of gold, and their faces resembled human faces. 8Their hair was like women's hair, and their teeth were like lions' teeth. 9They had breastplates like breastplates of iron, and the sound of their wings was like the thundering of many horses and chariots rushing into battle. 10They had tails and stings like scorpions, and in their tails they had power to torment people for five months. 11They had as king over them the angel of the Abyss, whose name in Hebrew is Abaddon, and in Greek, Apollyon.[a]

12The first woe is past; two other woes are yet to come.

13The sixth angel sounded his trumpet, and I heard a voice coming from the horns[b] of the golden altar that is before God. 14It said to the sixth angel who had the trumpet, "Release the four angels who are bound at the great river Euphrates." 15And the four angels who had been kept ready for this very hour and day and month and year were released to kill a third of mankind. 16The number of the mounted troops was two hundred million. I heard their number.

17The horses and riders I saw in my vision looked like this: Their breastplates were fiery red, dark blue, and yellow as sulfur. The heads of the horses resembled the heads of lions, and out of their mouths came fire, smoke and sulfur. 18A third of mankind was killed by the three plagues of fire, smoke and sulfur that came out of their mouths. 19The power of the horses was in their mouths and in their tails; for their tails were like snakes, having heads with which they inflict injury.

20The rest of mankind that were not killed by these plagues still did not repent of the work of their hands; they did not stop worshiping demons, and idols of gold, silver, bronze, stone and wood—idols that cannot see or hear or walk. 21Nor did they repent of their murders, their magic arts, their sexual immorality or their thefts.

The Angel and the Little Scroll

10 Then I saw another mighty angel coming down from heaven. He was robed in a cloud, with a rainbow above his head; his face was like the sun, and his legs were like fiery pillars. 2He was holding a little scroll, which lay open in his hand. He planted his right foot on the sea and his left foot on the land, 3and he gave a loud shout like the roar of a lion. When he shouted, the voices of the seven thunders spoke. 4And when the seven thunders spoke, I was about to write; but I heard a voice from heaven say, "Seal up what the seven thunders have said and do not write it down."

5Then the angel I had seen standing on the sea and on the land raised his right hand to heaven. 6And he swore by him who lives for ever and ever, who created the heavens and all that is in them, the earth and all that is in it, and the sea and all that is in it, and said, "There will be no more delay! 7But in the days when the seventh angel is about to sound his trumpet, the mystery of God will be accomplished, just as he announced to his servants the prophets."

8Then the voice that I had heard from heaven spoke to me once more: "Go, take the scroll that lies open in the hand of the angel who is standing on the sea and on the land."

9So I went to the angel and asked him to give me the little scroll. He said to me, "Take it and eat it. It will turn your stomach sour, but in your mouth it will be as sweet as honey." 10I took the little scroll from the angel's hand and ate it. It tasted as sweet as honey in my mouth, but when I had eaten it, my stomach turned sour. 11Then I was told, "You must prophesy again about many peoples, nations, languages and kings."

The Two Witnesses

11 I was given a reed like a measuring rod and was told, "Go and measure the

[a] 11 *Abaddon* and *Apollyon* mean *Destroyer.* [b] 13 That is, projections

9:12–21 As the sixth trumpet blows, an army will rise up and slaughter one-third of the remaining population of the world. Certainly, circumstances will seem hopeless to most inhabitants of the earth at this point. They can either humble themselves and surrender their lives to God or continue to rebel against the only one who could save them. Sadly, we see that only a few will accept God's gracious offer of forgiveness at this late stage in history. Spiritual blindness grows progressively worse the longer people resist God. When we see spiritual blindness occurring in ourselves or others, we should pray earnestly for eyes that can see the truth.

10:8–10 The apostle John was told to eat the scroll, much as the prophet Ezekiel had been instructed to do (see Ezekiel 2:8—3:3). The scroll would be sweet in his mouth but bitter in his stomach. God's Word to us can sometimes work the same way, containing a sweet message of deliverance for all who repent, but also a bitter account for our selfish actions. If we are willing to abide by the wise boundaries that God has set out for us, his Word is filled with promises of joy and peace.

11:1–13 The two witnesses described here will serve as God's prophets. During their 1,260-day ministry, God will protect them. But then God will remove his hand of protection and the beast from the Abyss will kill these two witnesses. Notice that God's two prophets will be treated

temple of God and the altar, and count the worshipers there. 2But exclude the outer court; do not measure it, because it has been given to the Gentiles. They will trample on the holy city for 42 months. 3And I will give power to my two witnesses, and they will prophesy for 1,260 days, clothed in sackcloth." 4These are the two olive trees and the two lampstands that stand before the Lord of the earth. 5If anyone tries to harm them, fire comes from their mouths and devours their enemies. This is how anyone who wants to harm them must die. 6These men have power to shut up the sky so that it will not rain during the time they are prophesying; and they have power to turn the waters into blood and to strike the earth with every kind of plague as often as they want.

7Now when they have finished their testimony, the beast that comes up from the Abyss will attack them, and overpower and kill them. 8Their bodies will lie in the street of the great city, which is figuratively called Sodom and Egypt, where also their Lord was crucified. 9For three and a half days men from every people, tribe, language and nation will gaze on their bodies and refuse them burial. 10The inhabitants of the earth will gloat over them and will celebrate by sending each other gifts, because these two prophets had tormented those who live on the earth.

11But after the three and a half days a breath of life from God entered them, and they stood on their feet, and terror struck those who saw them. 12Then they heard a loud voice from heaven saying to them, "Come up here." And they went up to heaven in a cloud, while their enemies looked on.

13At that very hour there was a severe earthquake and a tenth of the city collapsed. Seven thousand people were killed in the earthquake, and the survivors were terrified and gave glory to the God of heaven.

14The second woe has passed; the third woe is coming soon.

The Seventh Trumpet

15The seventh angel sounded his trumpet, and there were loud voices in heaven, which said:

"The kingdom of the world has become
the kingdom of our Lord and of his Christ,
and he will reign for ever and ever."

16And the twenty-four elders, who were seated on their thrones before God, fell on their faces and worshiped God, 17saying:

"We give thanks to you, Lord God Almighty,
the One who is and who was,
because you have taken your great power
and have begun to reign.
18The nations were angry;
and your wrath has come.
The time has come for judging the dead,
and for rewarding your servants the prophets
and your saints and those who reverence your name,
both small and great—
and for destroying those who destroy the earth."

19Then God's temple in heaven was opened, and within his temple was seen the ark of his covenant. And there came flashes of lightning, rumblings, peals of thunder, an earthquake and a great hailstorm.

The Woman and the Dragon

12 A great and wondrous sign appeared in heaven: a woman clothed with the sun, with the moon under her feet and a crown of twelve stars on her head. 2She was pregnant and cried out in pain as she was about to give birth. 3Then another sign appeared in heaven: an enormous red dragon with seven heads and ten horns and seven crowns on his heads. 4His tail swept a third of the stars out of the sky and flung them to the earth. The dragon stood in front of the woman who was about to give birth, so that he might devour her child the moment it was born. 5She gave birth to a son, a male child, who will rule all the nations with an iron scepter. And her child was snatched up

---

more despicably than Christ, who, in similar circumstances, was at least given a decent burial (see Matthew 27:57–61). In three and one-half days, however, God would ultimately raise them from the dead, showing that even death cannot thwart his plans. No obstacle is so great that God has to abandon the plan he has laid out for the world and its people.

11:15–18 The sounding of the seventh trumpet accompanies a proclamation of God's control over his kingdom. Many among the nations of the earth were angry with God without just cause. Now God's righteous anger will be released. Those who have surrendered themselves to God will be rewarded, while those who have rejected him will be judged. The same principle holds true for us. Those who reject God and his offer of salvation will have to face his terrible anger. However, we can look forward to a sure salvation by putting our faith in Christ. Jesus Christ endured the wrath of God against sin for all those who put their faith in him.

12:1–17 The birth of Christ and Satan's opposition to the event are graphically depicted in this scene. Jesus the Messiah was born into this world to implement God's plan for the world's restoration. Satan planted the destructive effects of sin into God's good creation by tempting Adam and Eve to sin. Jesus was born to reverse the effects of that sin, so Satan did all he could to destroy the infant Savior. Yet Satan was unsuccessful, and the future ruler of the world was able to complete his earthly mission. As much as Satan desires to thwart God's plan for the world's restoration, he will not be able to do it (see Job 42:2). Satan cannot thwart God's plan of salvation for us either if we surrender our lives to God by trusting Christ to pay for our sins. As we grow spiritually, we can experience the restoration that God will complete at the end of the age.

to God and to his throne. 6The woman fled into
the desert to a place prepared for her by God,
where she might be taken care of for 1,260
days.
7And there was war in heaven. Michael and
his angels fought against the dragon, and the
dragon and his angels fought back. 8But he was
not strong enough, and they lost their place in
heaven. 9The great dragon was hurled down—
that ancient serpent called the devil, or Satan,
who leads the whole world astray. He was
hurled to the earth, and his angels with him.
10Then I heard a loud voice in heaven say:

"Now have come the salvation and the
power and the kingdom of our
God,
and the authority of his Christ.
For the accuser of our brothers,
who accuses them before our God day
and night,
has been hurled down.
11They overcame him
by the blood of the Lamb
and by the word of their testimony;
they did not love their lives so much
as to shrink from death.
12Therefore rejoice, you heavens
and you who dwell in them!
But woe to the earth and the sea,
because the devil has gone down to you!
He is filled with fury,
because he knows that his time is short."

13When the dragon saw that he had been
hurled to the earth, he pursued the woman who
had given birth to the male child. 14The woman
was given the two wings of a great eagle, so that
she might fly to the place prepared for her in the
desert, where she would be taken care of for a
time, times and half a time, out of the serpent's
reach. 15Then from his mouth the serpent
spewed water like a river, to overtake the woman and sweep her away with the torrent. 16But
the earth helped the woman by opening its
mouth and swallowing the river that the dragon
had spewed out of his mouth. 17Then the dragon was enraged at the woman and went off
to make war against the rest of her offspring—
those who obey God's commandments and
13 hold to the testimony of Jesus. 1And the
dragon[a] stood on the shore of the sea.

The Beast out of the Sea

And I saw a beast coming out of the sea. He
had ten horns and seven heads, with ten crowns
on his horns, and on each head a blasphemous
name. 2The beast I saw resembled a leopard,
but had feet like those of a bear and a mouth
like that of a lion. The dragon gave the beast his
power and his throne and great authority. 3One
of the heads of the beast seemed to have had
a fatal wound, but the fatal wound had been
healed. The whole world was astonished and
followed the beast. 4Men worshiped the dragon
because he had given authority to the beast, and
they also worshiped the beast and asked, "Who
is like the beast? Who can make war against
him?"
5The beast was given a mouth to utter proud
words and blasphemies and to exercise his authority for forty-two months. 6He opened his
mouth to blaspheme God, and to slander his
name and his dwelling place and those who live
in heaven. 7He was given power to make war
against the saints and to conquer them. And he
was given authority over every tribe, people,
language and nation. 8All inhabitants of the
earth will worship the beast—all whose names
have not been written in the book of life belonging to the Lamb that was slain from the
creation of the world.[b]
9He who has an ear, let him hear.

10If anyone is to go into captivity,
into captivity he will go.
If anyone is to be killed[c] with the sword,
with the sword he will be killed.

This calls for patient endurance and faithfulness
on the part of the saints.

The Beast out of the Earth

11Then I saw another beast, coming out of
the earth. He had two horns like a lamb, but he
spoke like a dragon. 12He exercised all the authority of the first beast on his behalf, and made
the earth and its inhabitants worship the first
beast, whose fatal wound had been healed.
13And he performed great and miraculous signs,
even causing fire to come down from heaven to
earth in full view of men. 14Because of the signs
he was given power to do on behalf of the first

[a]1 Some late manuscripts *And I* [b]8 Or *written from the creation of the world in the book of life belonging to the Lamb that was slain* [c]10 Some manuscripts *anyone kills*

13:1–10 Some of Satan's primary representatives are described in these verses. For a time, God will allow them free reign in the world, making life difficult for all who trust Christ for salvation. Ever since the days when Jesus Christ walked this earth, Satan has sought to lead people away from the deliverance God offers. The creatures mentioned here are an intensified form of the spirit of antichrist already active in our world. Satan wants to destroy us. Despite the power Satan wields, he cannot remove us from God's loving care (see Romans 8:38–39). We should encourage each other with this truth when we encounter spiritual warfare.

13:11–18 Another creature representing Satan rises from the earth. Notice that it looks like a lamb, Satan's attempt to copy the appearance of Christ, the Lamb (see 5:6). Notice also that this creature's miracles copy the amazing deeds that were performed by God's two witnesses (see 11:5–6). Satan clearly attempts to deceive people into thinking this lamb represents the true God. He tries to sell a counterfeit in order to lead people away from the true deliverer—Jesus Christ. We need to be on guard against the counterfeit solutions that Satan puts before us by testing every word and every action against God's Word.

beast, he deceived the inhabitants of the earth.
He ordered them to set up an image in honor
of the beast who was wounded by the sword
and yet lived. 15He was given power to give
breath to the image of the first beast, so that it
could speak and cause all who refused to worship the image to be killed. 16He also forced
everyone, small and great, rich and poor, free
and slave, to receive a mark on his right hand
or on his forehead, 17so that no one could buy
or sell unless he had the mark, which is the
name of the beast or the number of his name.

18This calls for wisdom. If anyone has insight, let him calculate the number of the beast,
for it is man's number. His number is 666.

The Lamb and the 144,000

14 Then I looked, and there before me was
the Lamb, standing on Mount Zion,
and with him 144,000 who had his name and
his Father's name written on their foreheads.
2And I heard a sound from heaven like the roar
of rushing waters and like a loud peal of thunder. The sound I heard was like that of harpists
playing their harps. 3And they sang a new song
before the throne and before the four living
creatures and the elders. No one could learn the
song except the 144,000 who had been redeemed from the earth. 4These are those who
did not defile themselves with women, for they
kept themselves pure. They follow the Lamb
wherever he goes. They were purchased from
among men and offered as firstfruits to God
and the Lamb. 5No lie was found in their
mouths; they are blameless.

The Three Angels

6Then I saw another angel flying in midair,
and he had the eternal gospel to proclaim to
those who live on the earth—to every nation,
tribe, language and people. 7He said in a loud
voice, "Fear God and give him glory, because
the hour of his judgment has come. Worship
him who made the heavens, the earth, the sea
and the springs of water."

8A second angel followed and said, "Fallen!
Fallen is Babylon the Great, which made all the
nations drink the maddening wine of her adulteries."

9A third angel followed them and said in a
loud voice: "If anyone worships the beast and
his image and receives his mark on the forehead
or on the hand, 10he, too, will drink of the wine
of God's fury, which has been poured full
strength into the cup of his wrath. He will be
tormented with burning sulfur in the presence
of the holy angels and of the Lamb. 11And the
smoke of their torment rises for ever and ever.
There is no rest day or night for those who
worship the beast and his image, or for anyone
who receives the mark of his name." 12This calls
for patient endurance on the part of the saints
who obey God's commandments and remain
faithful to Jesus.

13Then I heard a voice from heaven say,
"Write: Blessed are the dead who die in the
Lord from now on."

"Yes," says the Spirit, "they will rest from
their labor, for their deeds will follow them."

The Harvest of the Earth

14I looked, and there before me was a white
cloud, and seated on the cloud was one "like a
son of man"[a] with a crown of gold on his head
and a sharp sickle in his hand. 15Then another
angel came out of the temple and called in a
loud voice to him who was sitting on the cloud,
"Take your sickle and reap, because the time to
reap has come, for the harvest of the earth is
ripe." 16So he who was seated on the cloud
swung his sickle over the earth, and the earth
was harvested.

17Another angel came out of the temple in
heaven, and he too had a sharp sickle. 18Still
another angel, who had charge of the fire, came
from the altar and called in a loud voice to him
who had the sharp sickle, "Take your sharp
sickle and gather the clusters of grapes from the
earth's vine, because its grapes are ripe." 19The
angel swung his sickle on the earth, gathered its
grapes and threw them into the great winepress
of God's wrath. 20They were trampled in the
winepress outside the city, and blood flowed
out of the press, rising as high as the horses'
bridles for a distance of 1,600 stadia.[b]

Seven Angels With Seven Plagues

15 I saw in heaven another great and marvelous sign: seven angels with the seven
last plagues—last, because with them God's
wrath is completed. 2And I saw what looked
like a sea of glass mixed with fire and, standing
beside the sea, those who had been victorious
over the beast and his image and over the number of his name. They held harps given them by
God 3and sang the song of Moses the servant of
God and the song of the Lamb:

[a] *14* Daniel 7:13 [b] *20* That is, about 180 miles (about 300 kilometers)

14:1–20 In these verses we see some of the blessings enjoyed by those who trust in Christ as well as the terrible consequences of rejecting him. The deliverance that God offers us through Jesus Christ is good news. We are called to receive eternal rest, to rejoice in God's infinite rule, praising him for his greatness (see Hebrews 4:3–11). If we refuse to acknowledge God's rule and insist on doing things our own way, we are headed toward complete destruction. But when we persevere in our faith in Jesus Christ, God will reward us.

15:1—16:21 These chapters portray the seven angels with the flasks of God's judgment. After their actions, the wrath of God directed against the unbelieving world will be complete (see 6:17; 11:18). As sure as the coming of the dawn, the day of reckoning will arrive. There will be a day when we have to face the truth about our lives. If we see the truth now, confess our sin and ask God to redeem us, we will not have to fear seeing the truth later.

"Great and marvelous are your deeds,
 Lord God Almighty.
Just and true are your ways,
 King of the ages.
4Who will not fear you, O Lord,
 and bring glory to your name?
For you alone are holy.
All nations will come
 and worship before you,
for your righteous acts have been revealed."

5After this I looked and in heaven the temple, that is, the tabernacle of the Testimony, was opened. 6Out of the temple came the seven angels with the seven plagues. They were dressed in clean, shining linen and wore golden sashes around their chests. 7Then one of the four living creatures gave to the seven angels seven golden bowls filled with the wrath of God, who lives for ever and ever. 8And the temple was filled with smoke from the glory of God and from his power, and no one could enter the temple until the seven plagues of the seven angels were completed.

The Seven Bowls of God's Wrath

16 Then I heard a loud voice from the temple saying to the seven angels, "Go, pour out the seven bowls of God's wrath on the earth."

2The first angel went and poured out his bowl on the land, and ugly and painful sores broke out on the people who had the mark of the beast and worshiped his image.

3The second angel poured out his bowl on the sea, and it turned into blood like that of a dead man, and every living thing in the sea died.

4The third angel poured out his bowl on the rivers and springs of water, and they became blood. 5Then I heard the angel in charge of the waters say:

"You are just in these judgments,
 you who are and who were, the Holy
 One,
 because you have so judged;
6for they have shed the blood of your saints
 and prophets,
 and you have given them blood to drink
 as they deserve."

7And I heard the altar respond:

"Yes, Lord God Almighty,
 true and just are your judgments."

8The fourth angel poured out his bowl on the sun, and the sun was given power to scorch people with fire. 9They were seared by the intense heat and they cursed the name of God, who had control over these plagues, but they refused to repent and glorify him.

10The fifth angel poured out his bowl on the throne of the beast, and his kingdom was plunged into darkness. Men gnawed their tongues in agony 11and cursed the God of heaven because of their pains and their sores, but they refused to repent of what they had done.

12The sixth angel poured out his bowl on the great river Euphrates, and its water was dried up to prepare the way for the kings from the East. 13Then I saw three evil[a] spirits that looked like frogs; they came out of the mouth of the dragon, out of the mouth of the beast and out of the mouth of the false prophet. 14They are spirits of demons performing miraculous signs, and they go out to the kings of the whole world, to gather them for the battle on the great day of God Almighty.

15"Behold, I come like a thief! Blessed is he who stays awake and keeps his clothes with him, so that he may not go naked and be shamefully exposed."

16Then they gathered the kings together to the place that in Hebrew is called Armageddon.

17The seventh angel poured out his bowl into the air, and out of the temple came a loud voice from the throne, saying, "It is done!" 18Then there came flashes of lightning, rumblings, peals of thunder and a severe earthquake. No earthquake like it has ever occurred since man has been on earth, so tremendous was the quake. 19The great city split into three parts, and the cities of the nations collapsed. God remembered Babylon the Great and gave her the cup filled with the wine of the fury of his wrath. 20Every island fled away and the mountains could not be found. 21From the sky huge hailstones of about a hundred pounds each fell upon men. And they cursed God on account of the plague of hail, because the plague was so terrible.

The Woman on the Beast

17 One of the seven angels who had the seven bowls came and said to me, "Come, I will show you the punishment of the great prostitute, who sits on many waters. 2With her the kings of the earth committed adultery and the inhabitants of the earth were intoxicated with the wine of her adulteries."

3Then the angel carried me away in the Spirit into a desert. There I saw a woman sitting on

a13 Greek *unclean*

17:1—19:5 These chapters foretell God's conquest over Satan's henchmen. God will overthrow the power of Satan when the time is right. Satan's representatives will be called to account for the suffering they have imposed on God's people. God's people will win out in the end. To become one of God's people, we need to admit our sin and need for God and trust him to deliver us from the power of sin. Then we will not weep when the evil powers in this world are destroyed; we will rejoice.

a scarlet beast that was covered with blasphemous names and had seven heads and ten
horns. 4The woman was dressed in purple and
scarlet, and was glittering with gold, precious
stones and pearls. She held a golden cup in her
hand, filled with abominable things and the
filth of her adulteries. 5This title was written on
her forehead:

MYSTERY
BABYLON THE GREAT
THE MOTHER OF PROSTITUTES
AND OF THE ABOMINATIONS OF THE EARTH.

6I saw that the woman was drunk with the
blood of the saints, the blood of those who
bore testimony to Jesus.

When I saw her, I was greatly astonished.
7Then the angel said to me: "Why are you astonished? I will explain to you the mystery of
the woman and of the beast she rides, which
has the seven heads and ten horns. 8The beast,
which you saw, once was, now is not, and will
come up out of the Abyss and go to his destruction. The inhabitants of the earth whose names
have not been written in the book of life from
the creation of the world will be astonished
when they see the beast, because he once was,
now is not, and yet will come.

9"This calls for a mind with wisdom. The
seven heads are seven hills on which the woman sits. 10They are also seven kings. Five have
fallen, one is, the other has not yet come; but
when he does come, he must remain for a little
while. 11The beast who once was, and now is
not, is an eighth king. He belongs to the seven
and is going to his destruction.

12"The ten horns you saw are ten kings who
have not yet received a kingdom, but who for
one hour will receive authority as kings along
with the beast. 13They have one purpose and
will give their power and authority to the beast.
14They will make war against the Lamb, but the
Lamb will overcome them because he is Lord of
lords and King of kings—and with him will be
his called, chosen and faithful followers."

15Then the angel said to me, "The waters you
saw, where the prostitute sits, are peoples, multitudes, nations and languages. 16The beast and
the ten horns you saw will hate the prostitute.
They will bring her to ruin and leave her naked;
they will eat her flesh and burn her with fire.
17For God has put it into their hearts to accomplish his purpose by agreeing to give the beast
their power to rule, until God's words are fulfilled. 18The woman you saw is the great city
that rules over the kings of the earth."

The Fall of Babylon

18 After this I saw another angel coming
down from heaven. He had great authority, and the earth was illuminated by his
splendor. 2With a mighty voice he shouted:

"Fallen! Fallen is Babylon the Great!
She has become a home for demons
and a haunt for every evil[a] spirit,
a haunt for every unclean and detestable
bird.
3For all the nations have drunk
the maddening wine of her adulteries.
The kings of the earth committed adultery
with her,
and the merchants of the earth grew rich
from her excessive luxuries."

4Then I heard another voice from heaven say:

"Come out of her, my people,
so that you will not share in her sins,
so that you will not receive any of her
plagues;
5for her sins are piled up to heaven,
and God has remembered her crimes.
6Give back to her as she has given;
pay her back double for what she has
done.
Mix her a double portion from her own
cup.
7Give her as much torture and grief
as the glory and luxury she gave herself.
In her heart she boasts,
'I sit as queen; I am not a widow,
and I will never mourn.'
8Therefore in one day her plagues will
overtake her:
death, mourning and famine.
She will be consumed by fire,
for mighty is the Lord God who judges
her.

9"When the kings of the earth who committed adultery with her and shared her luxury see
the smoke of her burning, they will weep and
mourn over her. 10Terrified at her torment, they
will stand far off and cry:

" 'Woe! Woe, O great city,
O Babylon, city of power!
In one hour your doom has come!'

11"The merchants of the earth will weep and
mourn over her because no one buys their cargoes any more— 12cargoes of gold, silver, precious stones and pearls; fine linen, purple, silk
and scarlet cloth; every sort of citron wood, and
articles of every kind made of ivory, costly
wood, bronze, iron and marble; 13cargoes of
cinnamon and spice, of incense, myrrh and
frankincense, of wine and olive oil, of fine flour
and wheat; cattle and sheep; horses and car-
riages; and bodies and souls of men.

14"They will say, 'The fruit you longed for is
gone from you. All your riches and splendor
have vanished, never to be recovered.' 15The
merchants who sold these things and gained
their wealth from her will stand far off, terrified

[a]2 Greek *unclean*

at her torment. They will weep and mourn
16and cry out:

" 'Woe! Woe, O great city,
dressed in fine linen, purple and scarlet,
and glittering with gold, precious stones
and pearls!
17In one hour such great wealth has been
brought to ruin!'

"Every sea captain, and all who travel by
ship, the sailors, and all who earn their living
from the sea, will stand far off. 18When they see
the smoke of her burning, they will exclaim,
'Was there ever a city like this great city?' 19They
will throw dust on their heads, and with weeping and mourning cry out:

" 'Woe! Woe, O great city,
where all who had ships on the sea
became rich through her wealth!
In one hour she has been brought to ruin!
20Rejoice over her, O heaven!
Rejoice, saints and apostles and
prophets!
God has judged her for the way she treated
you.' "

21Then a mighty angel picked up a boulder
the size of a large millstone and threw it into the
sea, and said:

"With such violence
the great city of Babylon will be thrown
down,
never to be found again.
22The music of harpists and musicians, flute
players and trumpeters,
will never be heard in you again.
No workman of any trade
will ever be found in you again.
The sound of a millstone
will never be heard in you again.
23The light of a lamp
will never shine in you again.
The voice of bridegroom and bride
will never be heard in you again.
Your merchants were the world's great
men.
By your magic spell all the nations
were led astray.
24In her was found the blood of prophets
and of the saints,
and of all who have been killed on the
earth."

Hallelujah!

19 After this I heard what sounded like the
roar of a great multitude in heaven
shouting:

"Hallelujah!
Salvation and glory and power belong to
our God,
2 for true and just are his judgments.
He has condemned the great prostitute
who corrupted the earth by her
adulteries.
He has avenged on her the blood of his
servants."

3And again they shouted:

"Hallelujah!
The smoke from her goes up for ever and
ever."

4The twenty-four elders and the four living
creatures fell down and worshiped God, who
was seated on the throne. And they cried:

"Amen, Hallelujah!"

5Then a voice came from the throne, saying:

"Praise our God,
all you his servants,
you who fear him,
both small and great!"

6Then I heard what sounded like a great multitude, like the roar of rushing waters and like
loud peals of thunder, shouting:

"Hallelujah!
For our Lord God Almighty reigns.
7Let us rejoice and be glad
and give him glory!
For the wedding of the Lamb has come,
and his bride has made herself ready.
8Fine linen, bright and clean,
was given her to wear."
(Fine linen stands for the righteous acts of the
saints.)

9Then the angel said to me, "Write: 'Blessed
are those who are invited to the wedding supper
of the Lamb!' " And he added, "These are the
true words of God."
10At this I fell at his feet to worship him. But
he said to me, "Do not do it! I am a fellow
servant with you and with your brothers who
hold to the testimony of Jesus. Worship God!
For the testimony of Jesus is the spirit of prophecy."

The Rider on the White Horse

11I saw heaven standing open and there before me was a white horse, whose rider is called
Faithful and True. With justice he judges and
makes war. 12His eyes are like blazing fire, and
on his head are many crowns. He has a name
written on him that no one knows but he himself. 13He is dressed in a robe dipped in blood,
and his name is the Word of God. 14The armies
of heaven were following him, riding on white
horses and dressed in fine linen, white and
clean. 15Out of his mouth comes a sharp sword
with which to strike down the nations. "He will

rule them with an iron scepter."[a] He treads the
winepress of the fury of the wrath of God Almighty. 16 On his robe and on his thigh he has
this name written:

KING OF KINGS AND LORD OF LORDS.

17 And I saw an angel standing in the sun,
who cried in a loud voice to all the birds flying
in midair, "Come, gather together for the great
supper of God, 18 so that you may eat the flesh
of kings, generals, and mighty men, of horses
and their riders, and the flesh of all people, free
and slave, small and great."
19 Then I saw the beast and the kings of the
earth and their armies gathered together to
make war against the rider on the horse and his
army. 20 But the beast was captured, and with
him the false prophet who had performed the
miraculous signs on his behalf. With these signs
he had deluded those who had received the
mark of the beast and worshiped his image. The
two of them were thrown alive into the fiery
lake of burning sulfur. 21 The rest of them were
killed with the sword that came out of the
mouth of the rider on the horse, and all the
birds gorged themselves on their flesh.

The Thousand Years

20 And I saw an angel coming down out of
heaven, having the key to the Abyss and
holding in his hand a great chain. 2 He seized
the dragon, that ancient serpent, who is the devil, or Satan, and bound him for a thousand
years. 3 He threw him into the Abyss, and locked
and sealed it over him, to keep him from deceiving the nations anymore until the thousand
years were ended. After that, he must be set free
for a short time.
4 I saw thrones on which were seated those
who had been given authority to judge. And I
saw the souls of those who had been beheaded
because of their testimony for Jesus and because
of the word of God. They had not worshiped
the beast or his image and had not received his
mark on their foreheads or their hands. They
came to life and reigned with Christ a thousand
years. 5 (The rest of the dead did not come to life
until the thousand years were ended.) This is
the first resurrection. 6 Blessed and holy are
those who have part in the first resurrection.
The second death has no power over them, but
they will be priests of God and of Christ and
will reign with him for a thousand years.

Satan's Doom

7 When the thousand years are over, Satan
will be released from his prison 8 and will go out
to deceive the nations in the four corners of the
earth—Gog and Magog—to gather them for battle. In number they are like the sand on the
seashore. 9 They marched across the breadth of
the earth and surrounded the camp of God's
people, the city he loves. But fire came down
from heaven and devoured them. 10 And the
devil, who deceived them, was thrown into the
lake of burning sulfur, where the beast and
the false prophet had been thrown. They will be
tormented day and night for ever and ever.

The Dead Are Judged

11 Then I saw a great white throne and him
who was seated on it. Earth and sky fled from
his presence, and there was no place for them.
12 And I saw the dead, great and small, standing
before the throne, and books were opened. Another book was opened, which is the book of
life. The dead were judged according to what
they had done as recorded in the books. 13 The
sea gave up the dead that were in it, and death
and Hades gave up the dead that were in them,
and each person was judged according to what
he had done. 14 Then death and Hades were
thrown into the lake of fire. The lake of fire is
the second death. 15 If anyone's name was not
found written in the book of life, he was thrown
into the lake of fire.

The New Jerusalem

21 Then I saw a new heaven and a new
earth, for the first heaven and the first

[a] 15 Psalm 2:9

19:6—20:10 In these verses we glimpse Christ, the conquering King. He will return to deliver all those who believe in him. Though great human armies led by Satan and his followers will gather to resist God, there will be no contest. Jesus Christ will ride to an overwhelming victory. Those of us who have already surrendered to God by following Jesus Christ will ride to victory with him. We will finally see the spiritual forces of evil, who opposed our spiritual renewal, utterly destroyed. What a glorious day that will be!

20:11–15 At the climactic, white throne judgment, those who have rejected God and his ways will have to face eternal consequences. All those who have believed in Christ, however, will be shown amazing grace. At this judgment, though, everyone is guilty. The people who believe in Christ will be forgiven; the people who choose to go their own way will be punished. No matter who we are or how terrible our sins, we can have our names written in the book of life by surrendering our lives to God in Jesus Christ and trusting him completely for our salvation. We cannot earn a place in that book; we can only receive it as a gift. If our names are not in the book of life, all our attempts at so-called spiritual renewal here on earth will make no difference at all.

21:1–7 What hope this scene gives us! Ever since the first sin in the Garden of Eden, God has been working to restore his earth to its original perfection. He even sent his Son to suffer and die to overcome the power of sin and death in our lives and to begin the process of healing. It is God's plan to make old things new! By following his will for our lives, we become part of God's plan of restoration. When Christ returns, God will restore the earth and satisfy everyone who belongs to him. The water of life will spring forth, healing our souls from their bondage to sin. By believing in Christ today, we can receive him into our lives and begin this restoration process without delay.

earth had passed away, and there was no longer any sea. [2]I saw the Holy City, the new Jerusalem, coming down out of heaven from God, prepared as a bride beautifully dressed for her husband. [3]And I heard a loud voice from the throne saying, "Now the dwelling of God is with men, and he will live with them. They will be his people, and God himself will be with them and be their God. [4]He will wipe every tear from their eyes. There will be no more death or mourning or crying or pain, for the old order of things has passed away."

[5]He who was seated on the throne said, "I am making everything new!" Then he said, "Write this down, for these words are trustworthy and true."

[6]He said to me: "It is done. I am the Alpha and the Omega, the Beginning and the End. To him who is thirsty I will give to drink without cost from the spring of the water of life. [7]He who overcomes will inherit all this, and I will be his God and he will be my son. [8]But the cowardly, the unbelieving, the vile, the murderers, the sexually immoral, those who practice magic arts, the idolaters and all liars—their place will be in the fiery lake of burning sulfur. This is the second death."

[9]One of the seven angels who had the seven bowls full of the seven last plagues came and said to me, "Come, I will show you the bride, the wife of the Lamb." [10]And he carried me away in the Spirit to a mountain great and high, and showed me the Holy City, Jerusalem, coming down out of heaven from God. [11]It shone with the glory of God, and its brilliance was like that of a very precious jewel, like a jasper, clear as crystal. [12]It had a great, high wall with twelve gates, and with twelve angels at the gates. On the gates were written the names of the twelve tribes of Israel. [13]There were three gates on the east, three on the north, three on the south and three on the west. [14]The wall of the city had twelve foundations, and on them were the names of the twelve apostles of the Lamb.

[15]The angel who talked with me had a measuring rod of gold to measure the city, its gates and its walls. [16]The city was laid out like a square, as long as it was wide. He measured the city with the rod and found it to be 12,000 stadia[a] in length, and as wide and high as it is long. [17]He measured its wall and it was 144 cubits[b] thick,[c] by man's measurement, which the angel was using. [18]The wall was made of jasper, and the city of pure gold, as pure as glass. [19]The foundations of the city walls were decorated with every kind of precious stone. The first foundation was jasper, the second sapphire, the third chalcedony, the fourth emerald, [20]the fifth sardonyx, the sixth carnelian, the seventh chrysolite, the eighth beryl, the ninth topaz, the tenth chrysoprase, the eleventh jacinth, and the twelfth amethyst.[d] [21]The twelve gates were twelve pearls, each gate made of a single pearl. The great street of the city was of pure gold, like transparent glass.

[22]I did not see a temple in the city, because the Lord God Almighty and the Lamb are its temple. [23]The city does not need the sun or the moon to shine on it, for the glory of God gives it light, and the Lamb is its lamp. [24]The nations will walk by its light, and the kings of the earth will bring their splendor into it. [25]On no day will its gates ever be shut, for there will be no night there. [26]The glory and honor of the nations will be brought into it. [27]Nothing impure will ever enter it, nor will anyone who does what is shameful or deceitful, but only those whose names are written in the Lamb's book of life.

The River of Life

22 Then the angel showed me the river of the water of life, as clear as crystal, flowing from the throne of God and of the Lamb [2]down the middle of the great street of the city. On each side of the river stood the tree of life, bearing twelve crops of fruit, yielding its fruit every month. And the leaves of the tree are for

[a]16 That is, about 1,400 miles (about 2,200 kilometers)
[b]17 That is, about 200 feet (about 65 meters)
[c]17 Or *high*
[d]20 The precise identification of some of these precious stones is uncertain.

21:7–8 In the final judgment, one group will inherit great eternal blessings. The other group will suffer the second death. The judgment described here for unrepentant people is unspeakable. However, those of us who have truly surrendered our lives to God, trusting Jesus Christ for salvation and faithfully following him, will be called children of God. Therefore, we should not glibly pursue spiritual growth as if it were just some way to enhance our lives. Those of us who look forward to eternal blessings must be compassionate enough to earnestly pray for those heading for destruction. Recognizing the reality of the final judgment should encourage us to share our faith with sincere urgency.

21:10–27 The new Jerusalem is portrayed here as a radiant bride (see 21:2). Notice that the eternal city has twelve gates, representing the twelve tribes of Israel (see 7:4–8), and twelve foundation stones, representing the twelve apostles of Christ. Thus, the city—the bride—represents the people of God. We as believers are members of the church, the bride of Christ. What a wonderful picture of grace! No matter how many mistakes we have made in the past, God forgives us through Christ and brings us into an intimate relationship with himself.

22:1–5 These verses are a climax to the book of Revelation, portraying eternity as a new and better Garden of Eden (see Genesis 2—3). God will have accomplished his desire to re-create his broken creation. God's healing power will be easily accessible. An intimate, face-to-face relationship with God will be the norm. His presence will lighten every dark corner, making cruelty and deception impossible in his new world. What we can only dream about now in our present sinful world will one day be reality. What a source of hope this picture can be for us! No matter how bad our lives are now, there is hope for the future. If we accept the wonderful offer of salvation that God holds out to us in Jesus Christ, we will someday be a part of that blessed world.

the healing of the nations. [3]No longer will there
be any curse. The throne of God and of the
Lamb will be in the city, and his servants will
serve him. [4]They will see his face, and his name
will be on their foreheads. [5]There will be no
more night. They will not need the light of a
lamp or the light of the sun, for the Lord God
will give them light. And they will reign for ever
and ever.
[6]The angel said to me, "These words are
trustworthy and true. The Lord, the God of the
spirits of the prophets, sent his angel to show
his servants the things that must soon take
place."

Jesus Is Coming

[7]"Behold, I am coming soon! Blessed is he
who keeps the words of the prophecy in this
book."

[8]I, John, am the one who heard and saw
these things. And when I had heard and seen
them, I fell down to worship at the feet of the
angel who had been showing them to me. [9]But
he said to me, "Do not do it! I am a fellow
servant with you and with your brothers the
prophets and of all who keep the words of this
book. Worship God!"
[10]Then he told me, "Do not seal up the
words of the prophecy of this book, because the
time is near. [11]Let him who does wrong continue to do wrong; let him who is vile continue to
be vile; let him who does right continue to do
right; and let him who is holy continue to be
holy."

[12]"Behold, I am coming soon! My reward is
with me, and I will give to everyone according
to what he has done. [13]I am the Alpha and the
Omega, the First and the Last, the Beginning
and the End.
[14]"Blessed are those who wash their robes,
that they may have the right to the tree of life
and may go through the gates into the city.
[15]Outside are the dogs, those who practice magic arts, the sexually immoral, the murderers, the
idolaters and everyone who loves and practices
falsehood.
[16]"I, Jesus, have sent my angel to give you[a]
this testimony for the churches. I am the Root
and the Offspring of David, and the bright
Morning Star."

[17]The Spirit and the bride say, "Come!" And
let him who hears say, "Come!" Whoever is
thirsty, let him come; and whoever wishes, let
him take the free gift of the water of life.

[18]I warn everyone who hears the words of the
prophecy of this book: If anyone adds anything
to them, God will add to him the plagues de-

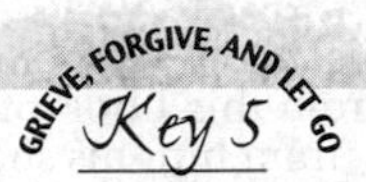

Restoring Broken Relationships

Revelation 22:1–5 We all suffer from brokenness in our lives, in our relationship with God and in our relationships with others. Brokenness weighs us down spiritually and slows our progress in spiritual renewal. God wants to heal the brokenness in our lives and in our relationships with others. We must cooperate with him by forgiving and by seeking forgiveness.

God's ultimate plan for us and our world involves our complete healing. In Revelation, the apostle John saw a vision of a new heaven and a new earth—places in which this healing would be complete: "Then the angel showed me the river of the water of life, as clear as crystal, flowing from the throne of God and of the Lamb . . . On each side of the river stood the tree of life . . . And the leaves of the tree are for the healing of the nations" (22:1–2).

Although God will heal all things when he returns to rule, we need to follow his plan for mending the brokenness right now. Jesus taught, "If you are offering your gift at the altar and there remember that your brother has something against you, leave your gift there in front of the altar. First go and be reconciled to your brother; then come and offer your gift" (Matthew 5:23–24). Giving and receiving forgiveness is an essential part of our spiritual growth. Spiritual healing requires that we make peace with God, with ourselves and with others we may have alienated. God can bring those people to mind to whom we owe an apology. When he does, we should stop everything and go to those we have offended, seeking to restore the relationship. Our willingness to ask their forgiveness will help them release whatever they are holding against us and bring about true healing.

Move on to Key 6 and turn to Matthew 14.

[a]16 The Greek is plural.

scribed in this book. 19And if anyone takes words away from this book of prophecy, God will take away from him his share in the tree of life and in the holy city, which are described in this book.

20He who testifies to these things says, "Yes, I am coming soon."

Amen. Come, Lord Jesus.

21The grace of the Lord Jesus be with God's people. Amen.

22:20–21 We can anchor our new lives in the certainty that Christ is coming again. By trusting him with our future, we can deal with our past and live a more productive present. We, like the apostle John, can pray for Christ to return soon because we know for certain that his coming will be a blessing for us. This will not only give us hope to persevere during tough times; it will also enhance the growth of our personal relationship with him. As we trust in God and have the hope of seeing him one day, we can seek to prepare ourselves to come into full union with him by growing in holiness.

STUDY HELPS

TABLE OF WEIGHTS AND MEASURES

INDEXES

TABLE OF WEIGHTS AND MEASURES

	BIBLICAL UNIT		APPROXIMATE AMERICAN EQUIVALENT	APPROXIMATE METRIC EQUIVALENT
WEIGHTS	talent	(60 minas)	75 pounds	34 kilograms
	mina	(50 shekels)	1¼ pounds	0.6 kilogram
	shekel	(2 bekas)	⅖ ounce	11.5 grams
	pim	(⅔ shekel)	⅓ ounce	7.6 grams
	beka	(10 gerahs)	⅕ ounce	5.5 grams
	gerah		1/50 ounce	0.6 gram
LENGTH	cubit		18 inches	0.5 meter
	span		9 inches	23 centimeters
	handbreadth		3 inches	8 centimeters
CAPACITY				
Dry Measure	cor [homer]	(10 ephahs)	6 bushels	220 liters
	lethek	(5 ephahs)	3 bushels	110 liters
	ephah	(10 omers)	⅗ bushel	22 liters
	seah	(⅓ ephah)	7 quarts	7.3 liters
	omer	(1/10 ephah)	2 quarts	2 liters
	cab	(1/18 ephah)	1 quart	1 liter
Liquid Measure	bath	(1 ephah)	6 gallons	22 liters
	hin	(⅙ bath)	4 quarts	4 liters
	log	(1/72 bath)	⅓ quart	0.3 liter

The figures of the table are calculated on the basis of a shekel equaling 11.5 grams, a cubit equaling 18 inches and an ephah equaling 22 liters. The quart referred to is either a dry quart (slightly larger than a liter) or a liquid quart (slightly smaller than a liter), whichever is applicable. The ton referred to in the footnotes is the American ton of 2,000 pounds.

This table is based upon the best available information, but it is not intended to be mathematically precise; like the measurement equivalents in the footnotes, it merely gives the approximate amounts and distances. Weights and measures differed somewhat at various times and places in the ancient world. There is uncertainty particularly about the ephah and the bath; further discoveries may give more light on these units of capacity.

INDEX TO TEXT NOTES

This index locates the text notes related to key issues in spiritual renewal. Related issues are named in parentheses to make an expanded study on any topic a simple task. For additional information, see the other specialized indices that follow this topical index: Index to Character Profiles, Index to Spiritual Keys Devotionals, and Index to Spiritual Disciplines Devotionals and Profiles.

DECEPTION

IDOLATRY

JEALOUSY

SADNESS

INDEX TO CHARACTER PROFILES

INDEX TO SPIRITUAL KEYS DEVOTIONALS

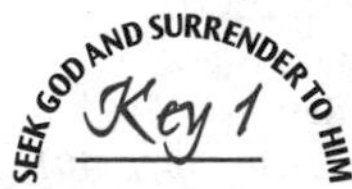

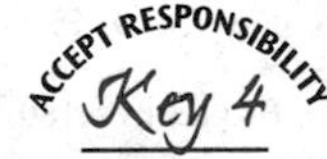

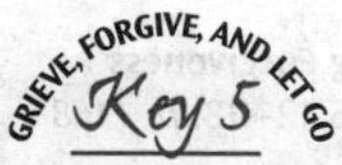
GRIEVE, FORGIVE, AND LET GO
Key 5

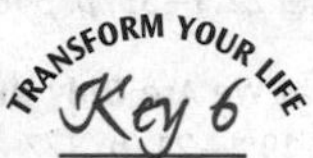
TRANSFORM YOUR LIFE
Key 6

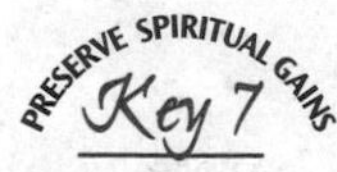
PRESERVE SPIRITUAL GAINS
Key 7

INDEX TO SPIRITUAL DISCIPLINES DEVOTIONALS AND PROFILES

NOTES

Notes

NOTES

NOTES

NOTES

NOTES

NOTES

Notes

NOTES

NOTES

NOTES

NOTES

Notes

SPIRITUAL RENEWAL BIBLE, NIV

Literary agency by
Alive Communications, Colorado Springs, CO

Interior proofreading by
Peachtree Editorial and Proofreading Service,
Peachtree City, GA

Interior typesetting by
Auto-Graphics, Pomona, CA

Printing and binding by
R.R. Donnelley, Crawfordsville, IN

Guarantee

Zondervan Publishing House guarantees leather Bibles unconditionally against manufacturing defects for six years and hardcover and softcover Bibles for four years. This guarantee does not apply to normal wear. Contact Zondervan Customer Service, 800-727-1309, for replacement instructions.

Care

We suggest loosening the binding of your new Bible by gently pressing on a small section of pages at a time from the center. To ensure against breakage of the spine, it is best not to bend the cover backward around the spine or to carry study notes, church bulletins, pens, etc., inside the cover.

Because a felt-tipped marker will "bleed" through the pages, we recommend use of a ball-point pen or pencil to underline favorite passages. Your Bible should not be exposed to excessive heat, cold, or humidity. Protecting the gold or silver edges of the paper from moisture will avoid spotting, streaking, or fading.

Definitions

Bonded leather: no less than 90% leather fibers with latex base.
Top-Grain leather: 100% pigskin
Cowhide: 100% cowhide

Map 1: WORLD OF THE PATRIARCHS

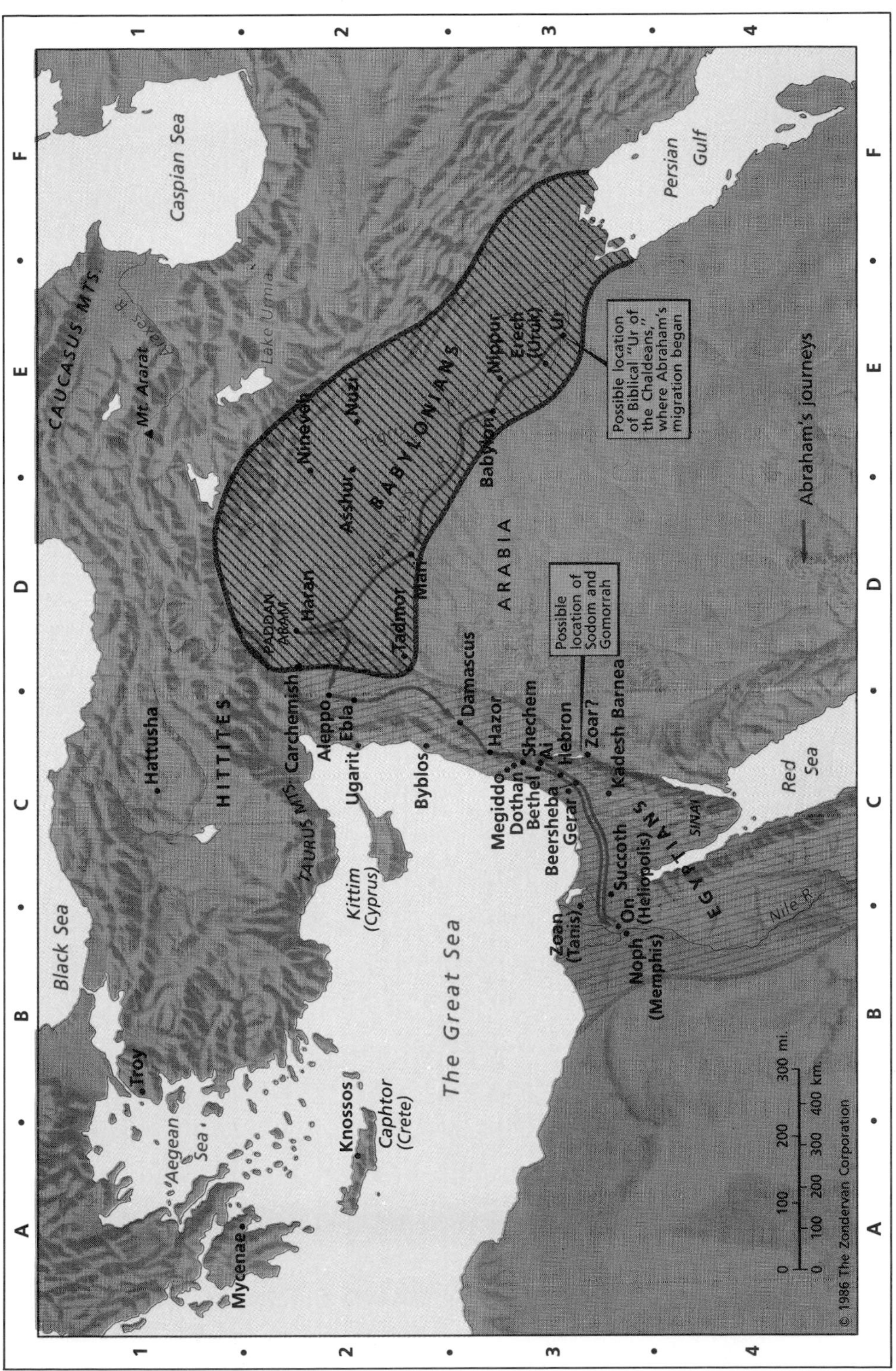

Black Sea
Caspian Sea
CAUCASUS MTS.
Mt. Ararat
Araxes R.
Lake Urmia
Persian Gulf
Aegean Sea
Troy
Mycenae
Knossos
Caphtor (Crete)
The Great Sea
Kittim (Cyprus)
Hattusha
HITTITES
TAURUS MTS.
Carchemish
Aleppo
Ebla
Ugarit
Byblos
PADDAN ARAM
Haran
Tadmor
Mari
Asshur
Nineveh
Nuzi
BABYLONIANS
Babylon
Nippur
Erech (Uruk)
Ur
Possible location of Biblical "Ur of the Chaldeans," where Abraham's migration began
ARABIA
Damascus
Hazor
Megiddo
Dothan
Shechem
Bethel
Ai
Hebron
Beersheba
Gerar
Zoar?
Possible location of Sodom and Gomorrah
Kadesh Barnea
Succoth
On (Heliopolis)
Zoan (Tanis)
Noph (Memphis)
EGYPTIANS
SINAI
Nile R.
Red Sea
Abraham's journeys
0 100 200 300 mi.
0 100 200 300 400 km.
© 1986 The Zondervan Corporation

Map 2: PALESTINE AND SINAI

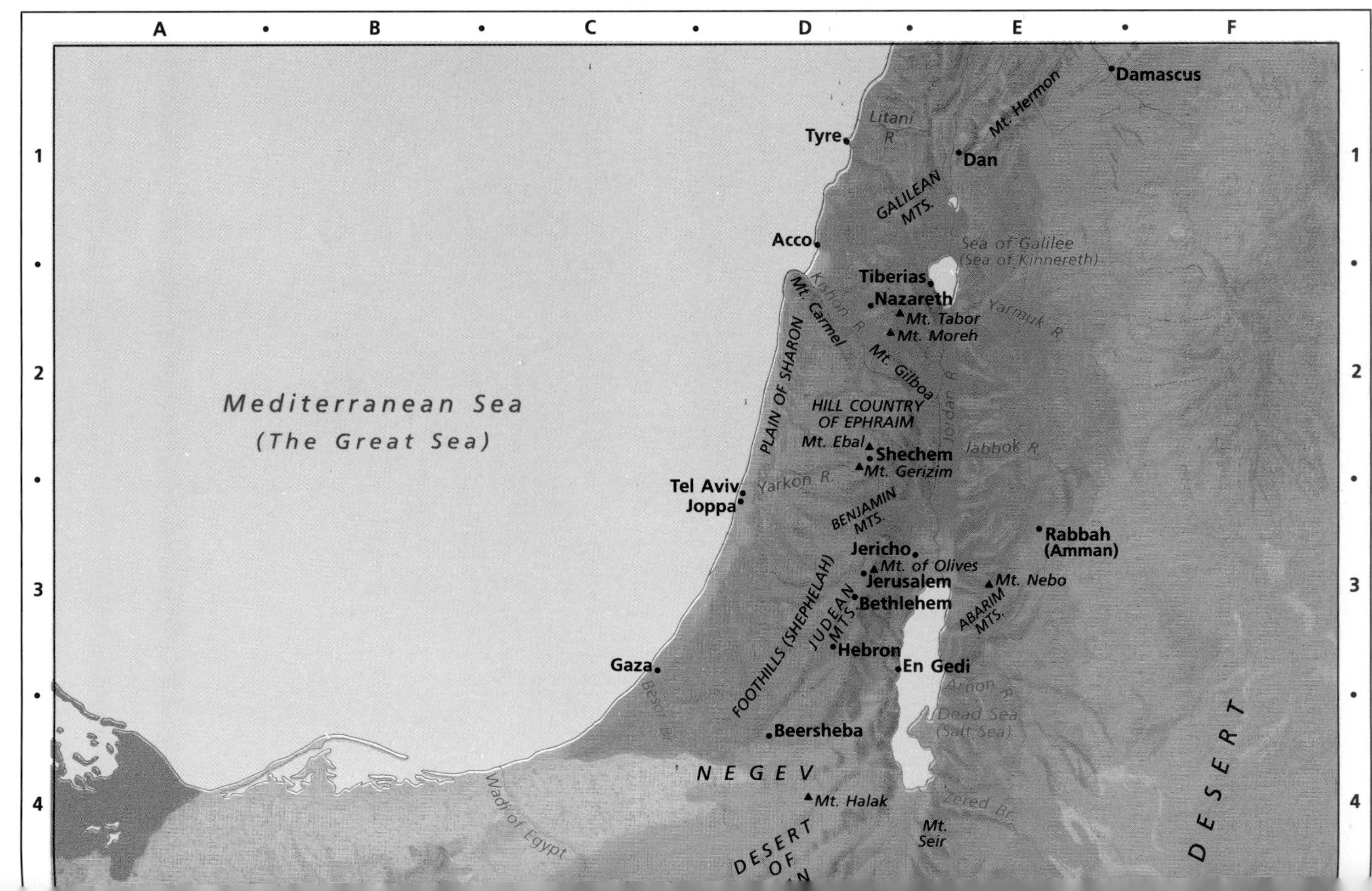

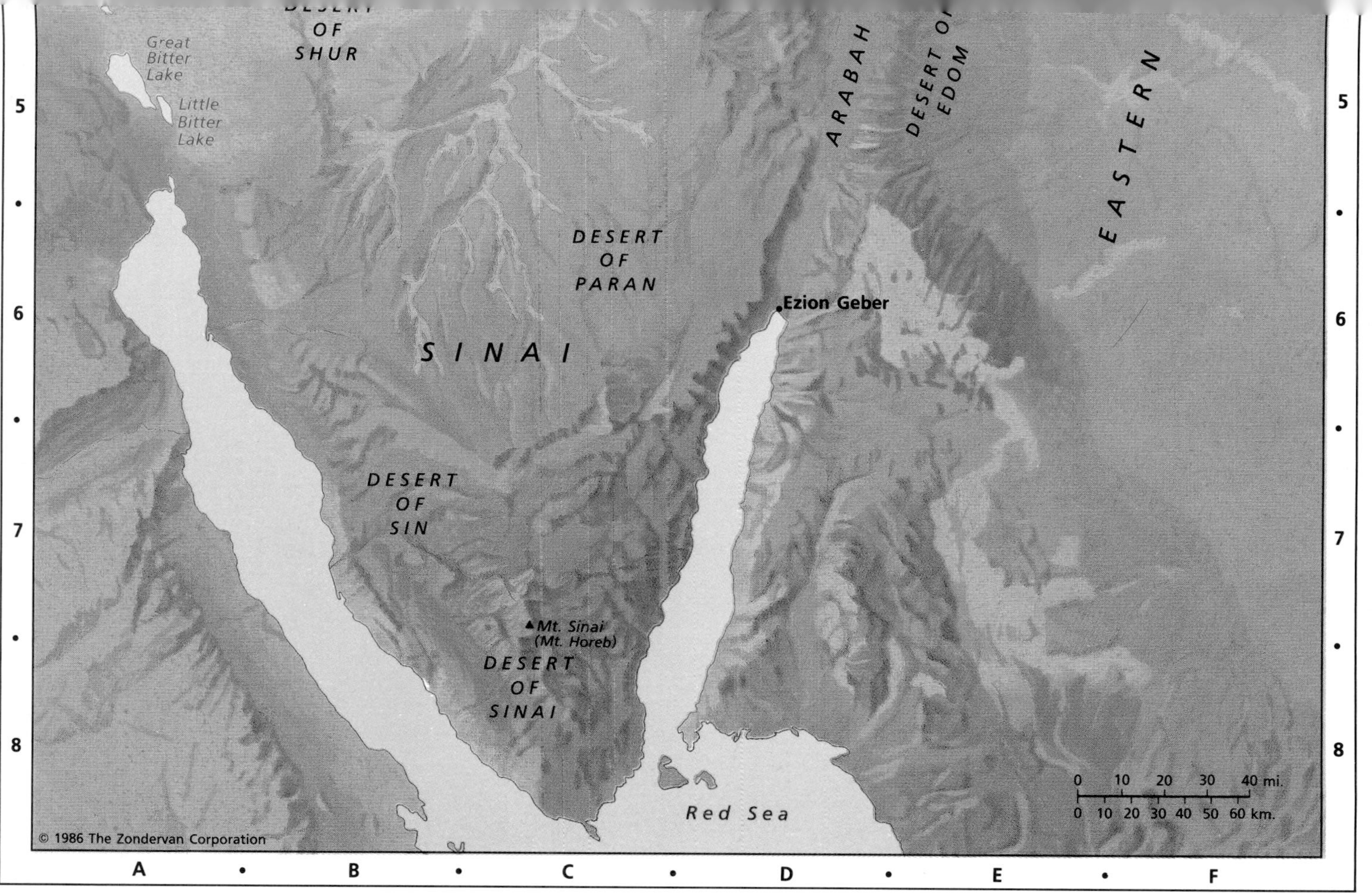
OF
SHUR
Great
Bitter
Lake
Little
Bitter
Lake
ARABAH
DESERT OF
EDOM
EASTERN
DESERT
OF
PARAN
Ezion Geber
SINAI
DESERT
OF
SIN
Mt. Sinai
(Mt. Horeb)
DESERT
OF
SINAI
Red Sea
0 10 20 30 40 mi.
0 10 20 30 40 50 60 km.
A B C D E F
5 6 7 8
5 6 7 8

Map 3: KINGDOM OF DAVID AND SOLOMON

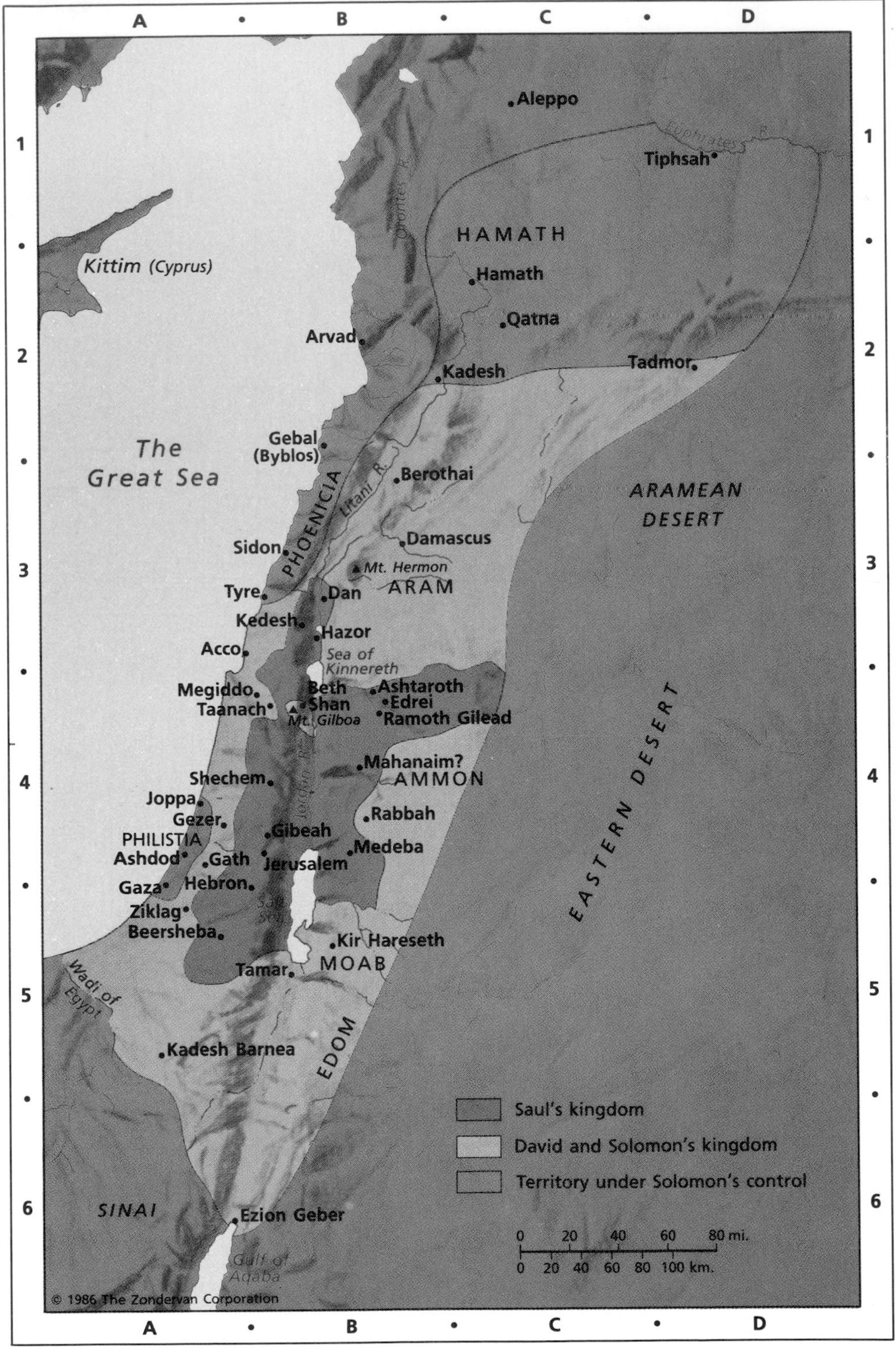

Map 4: JESUS' MINISTRY

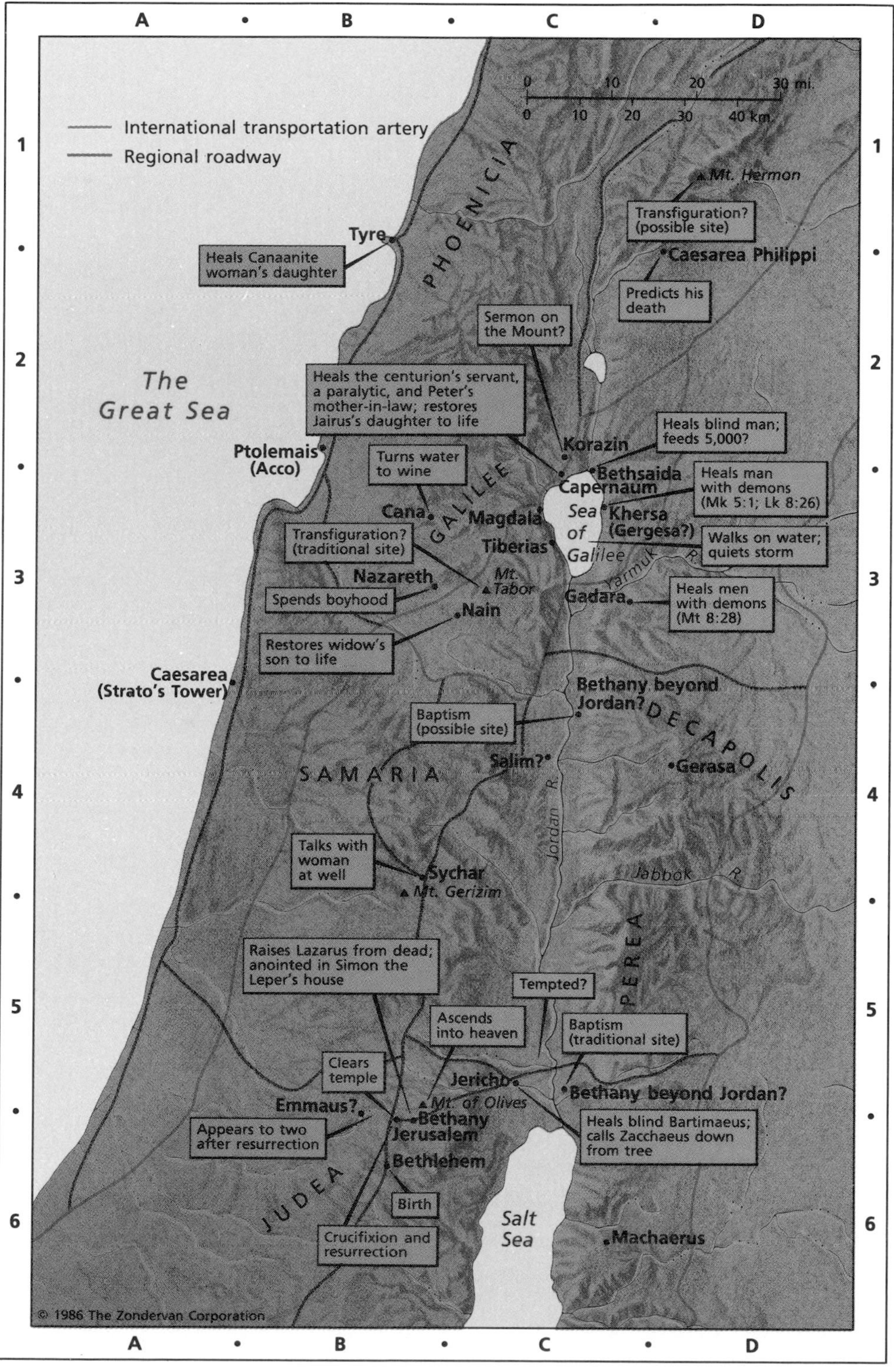

A • B • C • D
1
2
3
4
5
6
0 10 20 30 mi.
0 10 20 30 40 km.
International transportation artery
Regional roadway
PHOENICIA
Mt. Hermon
Transfiguration? (possible site)
Caesarea Philippi
Predicts his death
Tyre
Heals Canaanite woman's daughter
Sermon on the Mount?
The Great Sea
Heals the centurion's servant, a paralytic, and Peter's mother-in-law; restores Jairus's daughter to life
Heals blind man; feeds 5,000?
Korazin
Ptolemais (Acco)
Turns water to wine
Bethsaida
Capernaum
Heals man with demons (Mk 5:1; Lk 8:26)
GALILEE
Cana
Magdala
Sea of Galilee
Khersa (Gergesa?)
Transfiguration? (traditional site)
Tiberias
Walks on water; quiets storm
Yarmuk R.
Nazareth
Mt. Tabor
Spends boyhood
Gadara
Heals men with demons (Mt 8:28)
Nain
Restores widow's son to life
Caesarea (Strato's Tower)
Bethany beyond Jordan?
DECAPOLIS
Baptism (possible site)
Salim?
Gerasa
SAMARIA
Jordan R.
Talks with woman at well
Sychar
Jabbok R.
Mt. Gerizim
PEREA
Raises Lazarus from dead; anointed in Simon the Leper's house
Tempted?
Ascends into heaven
Baptism (traditional site)
Clears temple
Jericho
Bethany beyond Jordan?
Emmaus?
Mt. of Olives
Bethany
Appears to two after resurrection
Jerusalem
Heals blind Bartimaeus; calls Zacchaeus down from tree
Bethlehem
JUDEA
Birth
Salt Sea
Crucifixion and resurrection
Machaerus

Map 5: PAUL'S MISSIONARY JOURNEYS

A
B
C
D
1
2
3
4
5
6
GALLIA
GERMANIA
DALMATIA
Adriatic Sea
ITALY
Corsica
Sardinia
Rome
Forum of Appius
Three Taverns
Puteoli
Tyrrhenian Sea
EPIRUS
Rhegium
Ionian Sea
Sicily
Syracuse
NUMIDIA
Malta
AFRICA
TRIPOLITANIA
First Missionary Journey (A.D. 46–48)
Second Missionary Journey (A.D. 49–52)
Third Missionary Journey (A.D. 53–57)
Trip to Rome (A.D. 59–60)
© 1986 The Zondervan Corporation

E
F
G
H
1
2
3
4
5
6
DACIA
MOESIA
THRACE
Black Sea
BITHYNIA AND PONTUS
GALATIA
CAPPADOCIA
COMMAGENE
LYCAONIA
CILICIA
Philippi
Neapolis
phipolis
Apollonia
Samothrace
Thessalonica
Olympus
Troas
Assos
Mitylene
Aegean Sea
MYSIA
Pergamum
ASIA
Thyatira
Sardis
Philadelphia
Kios
Smyrna
LYDIA
PHRYGIA
Pisidian Antioch
Iconium
Lystra
Derbe
Tarsus
Issus
Euphrates R.
Delphi
inth
Athens
Samos
Ephesus
Laodicea
Colosse
PISIDIA
chrea
Sparta
Miletus
Patmos
Attalia
PAMPHYLIA
Perga
Antioch
Aleppo
Cos
Cnidus
LYCIA
Patara
Seleucia
Myra
Rhodes
SYRIA
Cyprus
Salamis
Paphos
Phoenix
Crete
Salmone
Lasea
Fair Havens
PHOENICIA
ABILENE
Sidon
Damascus
Tyre
Ptolemais
Caesarea
Great Sea
JUDEA
Jordan R.
Jerusalem
Salt Sea
ARABIA
CYRENAICA
EGYPT
Nile R.
Red Sea
0 100 200 mi.
0 100 200 300 km.

Map 6: JERUSALEM IN JESUS' TIME

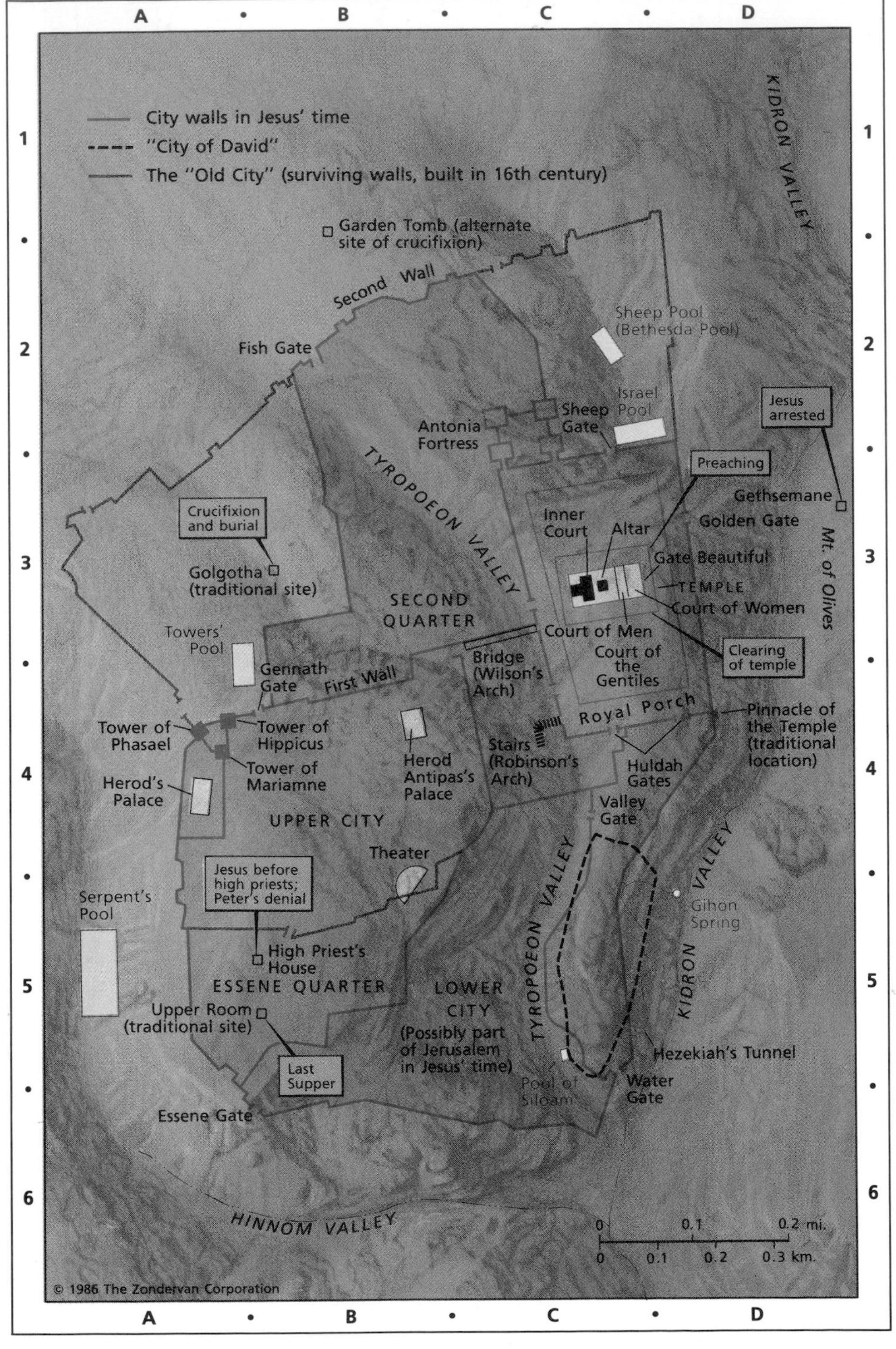

A • B • C • D
1
2
3
4
5
6
City walls in Jesus' time
"City of David"
The "Old City" (surviving walls, built in 16th century)
KIDRON VALLEY
Garden Tomb (alternate site of crucifixion)
Second Wall
Sheep Pool (Bethesda Pool)
Fish Gate
Israel Pool
Jesus arrested
Antonia Fortress
Sheep Gate
TYROPOEON VALLEY
Preaching
Gethsemane
Crucifixion and burial
Inner Court
Altar
Golden Gate
Mt. of Olives
Gate Beautiful
Golgotha (traditional site)
TEMPLE
Court of Women
SECOND QUARTER
Court of Men
Towers' Pool
Court of the Gentiles
Clearing of temple
Gennath Gate
First Wall
Bridge (Wilson's Arch)
Royal Porch
Pinnacle of the Temple (traditional location)
Tower of Phasael
Tower of Hippicus
Tower of Mariamne
Stairs (Robinson's Arch)
Herod's Palace
Herod Antipas's Palace
Huldah Gates
Valley Gate
UPPER CITY
Theater
Jesus before high priests; Peter's denial
Serpent's Pool
Gihon Spring
TYROPOEON VALLEY
KIDRON VALLEY
High Priest's House
ESSENE QUARTER
LOWER CITY (Possibly part of Jerusalem in Jesus' time)
Upper Room (traditional site)
Hezekiah's Tunnel
Last Supper
Pool of Siloam
Water Gate
Essene Gate
HINNOM VALLEY
0 0.1 0.2 mi.
0 0.1 0.2 0.3 km.
© 1986 The Zondervan Corporation